Comparative Company Law

CARSTEN GERNER-BEUERLE
and
MICHAEL SCHILLIG

OXFORD
UNIVERSITY PRESS

OXFORD
UNIVERSITY PRESS

Great Clarendon Street, Oxford, OX2 6DP,
United Kingdom

Oxford University Press is a department of the University of Oxford. It furthers the University's objective of excellence in research, scholarship, and education by publishing worldwide. Oxford is a registered trade mark of Oxford University Press in the UK and in certain other countries

First published 2019
First published in paperback 2025

Published in the United States of America by Oxford University Press
198 Madison Avenue, New York, NY 10016, United States of America

British Library Cataloguing in Publication Data
Data available

Library of Congress Cataloging in Publication Data
Data available

ISBN 978-0-19-957220-5 (Hbk.)
ISBN 978-0-19-896033-1 (Pbk.)

Printed and bound by CPI Group (UK) Ltd, Croydon, CR0 4YY

COMPARATIVE COMPANY LAW

For E. SBHA.
C.G.B.
For K. CPFE.
M.A.S.

Preface

Inspired by a postgraduate module on comparative company law that we taught together at King's College London, the initial idea for this book was conceived at a time that was still steeped in the optimism of the new millennium. The Enron crisis had been successfully overcome; regulatory competition had taken off in Europe following the CJEU's freedom of establishment case law; and new corporate governance legislation on both sides of the Atlantic had been enacted with a view to addressing the shortcomings of the prevalent contractarian model of corporate law with its emphasis on shareholder value and deregulation. Then the global financial crisis struck. Although corporate law and corporate governance failures were of limited significance as contributing factors, the belief in efficient capital markets and neo-classical economics was severely shaken. In the same way as economic theory has been looking for alternatives to traditional models ever since the crisis, corporate (law) theory is still awaiting its reconceptualization. This book seeks to contribute to this ongoing discussion by examining trends and comparing regulatory philosophies in representative jurisdictions.

Following a functional approach, we provide a detailed comparative analysis of key areas of the company laws of the United Kingdom, the United States, France, and Germany, including relevant legislative measures adopted by the EU. We present edited and, where necessary, translated versions of seminal case law, sketch the evolution of the law, and offer a view on its operation in the corporate economy. Corporate law, of course, is shaped by economic, financial, and political conditions, and shapes these conditions. We seek to understand whether differences in the corporate economy in the countries that we analyse are reflected in the law, and whether different regulatory approaches, techniques, and styles distinguish corporate law systems at a more fundamental level, be it in the tradition of 'legal families', three of which are represented in our sample of jurisdictions, or of 'varieties of capitalism'. The translation, reprint, and analysis of actual cases will enable the reader to gain a deeper understanding of the different styles adopted by legal systems and assess to what extent EU harmonization measures have achieved the desired results. Where appropriate, the discussion of the cases will be accompanied by questions that will encourage the reader to think further and relate the decisions to the economic and theoretical underpinnings of the area of law in question. These features make the book also suitable for classroom use.

Although a joint effort, Michael has assumed responsibility for Chapters 1 to 3 and 9 to 11, and Carsten for Chapters 4 to 8 (and the Appendix). We aim to state the law as of 1 December 2018.

We would like to thank Luca Enriques, Martin Gelter, Christian Hoffmann, Andrew Johnston, John Lowry, Gerry McCormack, Marc Moore, Wolf-Georg Ringe, Jessica Schmidt, and Edmund Schuster for reading draft chapters of the book and providing us with valuable feedback and suggestions. Needless to say, any remaining mistakes are our own. Further, our thanks to the editorial team at OUP who, whilst constantly encouraging completion of the project, have been very patient throughout the process and competently oversaw the book's production from start to finish. We owe a special debt to our wives, Esin and Kathryn, who have supported us throughout this laborious process with extraordinary patience.

Contents

Table of Cases

EUROPEAN COURT OF JUSTICE

AUSTRALIA

CANADA

FRANCE

GERMANY

NEW ZEALAND

UNITED KINGDOM

UNITED STATES

Hollinger v. Titan Capital Corp., 914 F.2d 1564, 1569 (9th Cir. 1990) 416–17
Hollinger, Inc. v. Hollinger International, Inc., 858 A.2d 342 (Del. Ch. 2004) 654–55
Houle v. Low, 556 N.E.2d 51:(Mass. 1990) 707–8

Table of Legislation

EUROPEAN UNION

Directives

Recommendations

Regulations

FRANCE

Codes

Other Legislation and Regulations (chronological order)

GERMANY

ITALY

NETHERLANDS

PORTUGAL

SPAIN

UNITED KINGDOM

Statutory Instruments

UNITED STATES

Uniform Laws and Model Acts

Table of Treaties and International Instruments

List of Abbreviations

ABI	American Bankruptcy Institute
AC	Appeal Cases
AFEP	Association Française des Enterprises Privées
AG	Aktiengesellschaft
AktG	Aktiengesetz
BaFin	Bundesanstalt für Finanzdienstleistungsaufsicht
BCC	British Company Law Cases
BCLC	Butterworths Company Law Cases
BEIS	Department for Business Energy and Industrial Strategy
BGB	Bürgerliches Gesetzbuch
BGBl.	Bundesgesetzblatt
BGH	Bundesgerichtshof
BGHZ	Sammlung der Entscheidungen des BGH in Zivilsachen
BODACC	Bulletin officiel des annonces civiles et commerciales
BörsG	Börsengesetz
BRIS	Business Registers Interconnection System
BT-Drucks.	Deutscher Bundestag Drucksache
CA	Cour d'Appel
CalPERS	California Public Employees' Retirement System
Cass	Cour de Cassation
CCC	California Corporations Code
CEO	Chief Executive Officer
Civ	Code civil
C.mon.fin.	Code monétaire et financier
Com	Code de commerce
COMI	Centre of Main Interests
CVA	Company Voluntary Arrangement
DGCL	Delaware General Corporation Law
DrittelbG	Drittelbeteiligungsgesetz
EEA	European Economic Area
EFTA	European Free Trade Area
EU	European Union
EUIR	European Insolvency Regulation
EURL	Entreprise unipersonnelle à responsabilité limitée
EWCA	England and Wales Court of Appeal
EWHC	England and Wales High Court
EWSC	England and Wales Supreme Court
FamFG	Gesetz über das Verfahren in Familiensachen und in den Angelegenheiten der freiwilligen Gerichtsbarkeit
FCA	Financial Conduct Authority
FMStG	Finanzmarktstabilisierungsgesetz
FRC	Financial Reporting Council
GbR	Gesellschaft bürgerlichen Rechts
GmbH	Gesellschaft mit beschränkter Haftung
GmbHG	Gesetz betreffend die Gesellschaften mit beschränkter Haftung
GVG	Gerichtsverfassungsgesetz
HGB	Handelsgesetzbuch
HMRC	Her Majesty's Revenue and Customs
InsO	Insolvenzordnung
JORF	Journal officiel de la République française
KG	Kommanditgesellschaft
KGaA	Kommanditgesellschaft auf Aktien

KWG	Kreditwesengesetz
LLC	Limited Liability Company
LLLP	Limited Liability Limited Partnership
LLP	Limited Liability Partnership
LR	Listing Rules
MBCA	Model Business Corporation Act
MEDEF	Mouvement des Entreprises de France
MitbestG	Gesetz über die Mitbestimmung der Arbeitnehmer (Mitbestimmungsgesetz)
MontanMitbestG	Gesetz über die Mitbestimmung der Arbeitnehmer in den Aufsichtsräten und Vorständen der Unternehmen des Bergbaus und der Eisen und Stahl erzeugenden Industrie
NJW	Neue Juristische Wochenschrift
NJW-RR	Neue Juristische Wochenschrift – Rechtsprechungsreport
NZG	Neue Zeitschrift für Gesellschaftsrecht
OECD	Organisation for Economic Co-operation and Development
OHG	Offene Handelsgesellschaft
OLG	Oberlandesgericht
QB	Queen's Bench
PartG	Partnerschaftsgesellschaft
PartGG	Gesetz über Partnerschaftsgesellschaften Angehöriger freier Berufe (Partner schaftsgesellschaftsgesetz)
RGAM	Règlement Général de L'Autorité des Marchés Financier
SA	société anonyme
SAS	société par actiones simplifiée
SARL	société à responsabilité limitée
SCA	société en commandite par actiones
SCS	société en commandite simple
SE	Societas Europaea
SEC	Securities and Exchange Commission
SNB	Special Negotiating Body
SNC	société en nom collectif
T com	Tribunal de commerce
TEU	Treaty on European Union
TFEU	Treaty on the Functioning of the European Union
TIAA-CREF	Teachers Insurance and Annuity Association – College Retirement Equities Fund
Trav	Code du travail
UmwG	Umwandlungsgesetz
UNCITRAL	United Nations Commission on International Trade
USC	United States Code
WLR	The Weekly Law Reports
WpHG	Gesetz über den Wertpapierhandel
WpÜG	Wertpapiererwerbs- und Übernahmegesetz

PART 1

THE BUSINESS CORPORATION AS A LEGAL INSTITUTION

In Part 1, we analyse on a comparative basis the company laws of the three largest economies in Europe—France, Germany, and the United Kingdom—as well as corporate law in the United States. Our analysis also includes the legislative measures adopted by the EU and the relevant case law of the Court of Justice of the European Union. All these legal systems have to a greater or lesser extent shaped company law reforms around the world, with US corporate law often taking an approach materially different to that of continental Europe and the UK. Part I sets the scene by defining the business corporation as *tertium comparationis*, by providing an overview of the relevant legal material, and by exploring the coming into existence at law of companies and corporations in the jurisdictions under consideration.

Consequently, in accordance with comparative law methodology, Chapter 1 delineates the focal point of our analysis in purely functional terms as the problem of 'horizontal pooling of resources' for the attainment of a specific economic purpose by more than one participant. The ensuing problems of shirking and opportunism have to be addressed through adequate institutional frameworks of which corporations and partnerships are institutional archetypes. The internal governance structures and external liability structures for these types of organizations differ. The defining properties of corporate-type entities are the principles of separate legal personality and limited liability, which greatly facilitate the emergence of delegated and centralized management as essential corporate governance features. Historically, separate legal personality and limited liability have developed separately and emerged at different times. However, in combination these principles account for the economic success and prevalence of the modern corporation as a vehicle for doing business. Contrary to 'nexus-of-contract' theories of corporate law, separate legal personality and limited liability are not trivial or 'natural' market phenomena; rather, their emergence is based on conscious policy decisions and legislative interventions in the form of organizational law. As a legal phenomenon, the modern business corporation is still predominantly a creation of domestic law in its various forms.

Whereas an international or transnational framework of corporate law has reached at best an infant stage, at regional level the European Union has issued an ever more extensive body of company and capital markets law related measures—the so-called acquis unionaire. Chapter 2 explores this Europeanization of corporate law. EU law-making in this area is informed by the internal market rationale: the breaking down of barriers to cross-border commercial activity and the enhancement of intra-Union trade. In a first wave of legislative interventions, the EU harmonized important aspects of a company's external liability structure with a view to providing counterparties with a more reliable contractual partner, thereby facilitating cross-border economic interaction. Following a paradigm shift towards a more efficiency-oriented and enabling approach, a second wave of activity largely focused on securities regulation and corporate mobility. The third wave was inspired by the global financial crisis and is still unfolding with a focus on corporate governance in listed companies. Whether and to what extent the United Kingdom's departure from the European Union will impact on the future development of EU company law remains to be seen. The CJEU's case law on the right to freedom of establishment has not only had a major impact on corporate mobility within the internal market, but to some extent has also shaped domestic company law. The impact of the Court's free movement of capital case law on core company law has been more limited.

Chapter 3 focuses on incorporation and corporate representation. Whereas the incorporation process and substantive requirements of incorporation are matters to be regulated by national law, the disclosure of company documents, the issue of a company being non-existent, the liability of promoters for contracts entered into on behalf of the company prior to registration, and the representation of the company vis-à-vis third parties through its main management body are pre-determined by EU secondary legislation. Although a very technical subject, looking at the incorporation processes across our jurisdictions shows different corporate law philosophies at work, ranging from rigid models that are liable to impede market access for newcomers to very flexible and informal models that facilitate a more dynamic economy. Naturally, the impact of EU harmonization in this area (and others) depends to a large extent on the form and shape of domestic law. For example, a quick and easy incorporation process has little need for provisions on nullity and pre-incorporation contracts. Overall, the harmonization effect in this area has been limited. Moreover, when comparing with the development of US law we can perhaps identify a form of 'natural' convergence that to some extent removes the justification for intervention at EU level.

1

Legal and Theoretical Foundations of the Business Corporation

The modern business corporation (or company)[1] is a comparatively recent phenomenon. Despite ancient and medieval ancestors, the business corporation, as we know it, is essentially a child of the nineteenth and twentieth centuries.[2] Its rise is inseparably linked with the development of the modern nation state and capitalism. Historically, as a legal concept the business corporation is first and foremost a phenomenon of domestic law, despite the fact that its earliest forms, such as the Dutch or English East India Companies, were already of global outreach and importance. Today, multi-national corporations are the drivers and main beneficiaries of globalization. They operate in a multitude of countries across the globe and can easily escape the reach of any national regulator. The problems that these organizations cause in terms of environmental damage or the exploitation of the poorest countries may be tackled eventually only on the basis of 'global laws for a global economy'.[3] However, such a truly global or transnational approach to the regulation

[1] On the different terminology see 'Concepts and Terminology in Common Law and Civil Law' (pp 4–22) below. Suffice it here to say that in the UK the term 'company' refers to the separate legal entity incorporated under the successive Companies Acts. In the United States, the equivalent term is 'corporation' whereas 'company' is sometimes used to refer to the firm as a whole, thus the 'company' General Motors consists of parent and various subsidiary 'corporations', such as General Motors Corporation, General Motors Financial Company, Inc., General Motors Holden, etc. By contrast, in the UK the technical term 'corporation' is used to refer to municipalities, eg the City of London Corporation. However, 'company' and 'corporation' may also be used interchangeably, as in 'corporate governance' or in the Corporation Tax Act 2009.

[2] See 'The Modern Corporation in Historic Perspective' (pp 50–6) below.

[3] JE Stiglitz, *Making Globalization Work* (Penguin 2006) 207.

of business associations has, for the moment, reached at best an infant stage,[4] and may even go into reverse. Even regional approaches, such as EU company law, take as a point of departure the types of business organizations that can be found in the Member States.[5] Despite a growing interest in comparative company law scholarship especially since the fall of the Berlin Wall,[6] most lawyers still approach the subject with preconceptions formed by their own domestic corporate law experience. This can be problematic as despite a certain commonality and overlap in the forms of business associations in the major Western economies as well as harmonization efforts at European level, major differences in typology, historical development, regulatory framework, and legal characteristics remain. Thus, when engaging in corporate law scholarship, domestic preconceptions may lead to abstractions and conclusions claiming universal validity, which may not hold true if viewed from a wider, comparative perspective.

A book on 'Comparative Company Law' needs to define and delineate its subject matter. It has to provide a workable conception of 'business corporation' and 'company law' that transcends national boundaries and makes sense to readers with backgrounds in different legal cultures and traditions. This is the aim and objective of the current chapter.

A. Concepts and Terminology in Common Law and Civil Law

The reader with a common law background may have a clear idea as to what a company or corporation is and what company or corporate law deals, or ought to deal, with. In an American textbook we read that 'a corporation is a particular set of rules for the organization of economic entities' with the 'core rules' being found 'in the statutes—the corporation codes—of the various states'.[7] Pursuant to the leading English textbook, the term 'company' normally refers to an 'association of a number of people' for 'economic purposes, i.e. to carry on a business for gain'. The problem of defining the scope of the subject matter is then solved by 'concentrating on those companies created by registration under the Companies Acts'.[8] In France we find a definition of 'company' (*société*) in *Code civil*, article 1832: a company is formed by two or more persons[9] who agree by contract to commit property or their business to a common venture with a view to share in the benefits or profits resulting therefrom as well as the losses.[10] Similarly, pursuant to a classic German textbook, companies (*Gesellschaften*) are private law associations formed on the basis of an agreement between the participants in order to achieve a certain common purpose. Consequently, company law encompasses all principles and rules relating to these entities.[11] Interestingly, whereas the US approach seems to be very positivistic—'corporation as a set of rules', the European legal systems seem to put greater emphasis on the social fact of a company as an association (or community) of

[4] PT Muchlinski, *Multinational Enterprises and the Law* (2nd edn, OUP 2007).

[5] See eg Directive (EU) 2017/1132 of the European Parliament and of the Council of 14 June 2017 relating to certain aspects of company law (codification), OJ EU 30.6.2017 L169/46. Annex I and II list the types of companies in the Member States to which the Directive applies. We discuss the Europeanization of corporate law in Chapter 2 below.

[6] See eg AM Fleckner and KJ Hopt (eds), *Comparative Corporate Governance* (CUP 2013); LC Backer, *Comparative Corporate Law: United States, European Union, China and Japan* (Carolina Academic Press 2002); F Dornseifer (ed), *Corporate Business Forms in Europe* (Sellier European Law Publishers 2005); R Kraakman and others, *The Anatomy of Corporate Law* (3rd edn, OUP 2017).

[7] William Klein, John Coffee Jr, and Frank Partnoy, *Business Organization and Finance* (11th edn, Foundation Press 2010) 106.

[8] P Davies and S Worthington, *Gower and Davies' Principles of Modern Company Law* (10th edn, Sweet & Maxwell 2016) para 1-1.

[9] Since 1985 a company may, where the law permits, also be formed by a single person.

[10] See M Cozian, A Viandier, and F Deboissy, *Droit de sociétés* (31st edn, LexisNexis 2018) para 3.

[11] H Wiedemann, *Gesellschaftsrecht: ein Lehrbuch des Unternehmens- und Verbandsrechts, Band I* (CH Beck 1980) 1.

persons. 'Corporate law' or 'company law' as a subject in the legal curriculum in the United States and the UK refers to a more or less well defined corpus of legal rules and principles—the relevant corporate codes or Companies Acts and the related case law. By contrast, our two civil law jurisdictions use a much broader concept of 'company' and 'company law' (*droit des sociétés, Gesellschaftsrecht*), which encompasses a multitude of different types of association on the basis of a multitude of different statutes and legal sources. Thus, in order to obtain a clearer idea and delineation of our subject matter it seems necessary to leave these domestic law definitions behind and, in accordance with the received wisdom of comparative law methodology, define the underlying socio-economic problem, as far as possible, in purely functional terms without any reference to the concepts of any legal system.[12]

The functional starting point for our comparative analysis may be described as the 'horizontal pooling of resources problem'. It consists of the following elements: (i) several types of resources are pooled for the attainment of a specific economic purpose; (ii) the resources belong to more than one person; (iii) all resources are essential to the venture; (iv) the proceeds of the venture are not the sum of separable outputs attributable to each contributing resource.[13] In short, the essence of 'horizontal pooling' is coordination, cooperation, and merging of resources by two or more persons in order to achieve something more, bigger or different than they would be able to achieve on their own.[14] Since Ronald Coase's seminal piece on 'The Nature of the Firm', published in 1937, a rich economic literature seeks to explain the integration of resources and the organization of production within firms. In Coase's own words:

> Outside the firm, price movements direct production, which is co-ordinated through a series of exchange transactions on the market. Within a firm, these market transactions are eliminated and in place of the complicated market structure with exchange transactions is substituted the entrepreneurial co-ordinator, who directs production. It is clear that these are alternative methods of co-ordinating production. Yet, having regard to the fact that if production is regulated by price movements, production could be carried on without any organisation at all, well might we ask, why is there any organisation?[15]

Coase's answer is strikingly simple. The market mechanism is costly. Each exchange transaction generates costs for obtaining the relevant price and product information and for negotiating and concluding the contract. These costs can be reduced if the multitude of different contracts is substituted with a single contract under which the seller of a resource, in exchange for certain remuneration, agrees to obey the directions of an entrepreneur, the buyer, within certain limits. A 'firm' consist of the system of relationships which comes into existence when the direction of resources is dependent on the buyer-entrepreneur in this way.[16] However, organizing production within the firm is not costless either. As a firm gets larger, the costs of organizing additional transactions within the firm rise. A firm will tend to expand only up to the point where the costs of organizing an extra transaction within the firm become equal to the costs of carrying out the same transaction by means of an exchange on the open market.[17]

[12] K Zweigert and H Kötz, *An Introduction to Comparative Law* (3rd edn, Oxford University Press 1998) 34.

[13] This is a modification of the 'team production problem' as defined by A Alchian and H Demsetz, 'Production, Information Costs, and Economic Organization' (1972) 62 American Economic Review 777, 779. The 'team production problem' is mainly concerned with 'vertical integration' in the firm. What is of interest here, however, is the horizontal pooling of resources.

[14] MM Blair and LA Stout, 'A Team Production Theory of Corporate Law' (1999) 85 Virginia Law Review 248, 260–71; Wiedemann (n 11) 9.

[15] R Coase, 'The Nature of the Firm' in O Williamson and S Winter (eds), *The Nature of the Firm: Origins, Evolution, and Development* (1993) 18, 19, first published in (1937) *Economica, New Series IV* (1937) 386.

[16] ibid 21–2. [17] ibid 23–4.

Subsequent literature has elaborated on the nature of the transaction costs that induce the rise of firms,[18] as well as the essence of the entrepreneur's authority to direct inputs.[19]

Coase tried to explain why market transactions are sometimes replaced by organization and authority. He did not directly explain, however, why actors sometimes pool resources in a non-hierarchical, horizontal way. In other words, why is it that an individual, with an interest in engaging in an economic activity, sometimes, instead of buying the physical and human resources by way of exchange transactions on the market, puts together the needed resources by pooling his own resources with those of one or more other individuals and all participants equally or proportionately share in the profits and losses of, as well as the exercise of control over, the pool of assets.[20] The key seems to be the Coasian insight of the costliness of market transactions. The price of resources increases with the risk that their owners take when contracting with the entrepreneur. An increase in risk is most easily spotted where resources (capital, physical assets, or human skills and knowledge) are bought on credit. Because of the increase in the size of fixed obligations and the increase in the price demanded by contractors, the more resources are bought on credit the higher the risk of default for the contracting parties.[21] Where no credit is at play, a contractor's risk still increases to the extent that the resource he sells to the entrepreneur becomes firm-specific, that is, once invested cannot be readily recovered and redeployed to other uses, at least not without significant costs.[22] The higher the degree of firm-specificity, the higher the risk for the contractor and the higher the price of the resource. Or viewed from a different angle, under-compensation of the contractor will result in sub-optimal firm-specific investment, a cost the entrepreneur will have to bear. There comes a point where the entrepreneur will no longer be able, or willing, to afford the price of the resource. The only solution is to 'buy' the resource in exchange for a share in the profits of the venture and/or a certain degree of control over the assets. Control on the part of the contractor reduces his risk and to the extent that the net present value of the share in profits is positive it would be rational to participate by pooling the resource with those of the entrepreneur. What ensues is the horizontal pooling of resources with the elements described above.

Horizontal pooling of resources is not costless. Individuals will only commit to participate if by doing so they can share in the economic surplus generated by pooling resources.[23] This is uncertain due to the distorting incentives that participants face. As, by definition, the output of the venture is not readily attributable to individual inputs, every participant has an incentive to shirk, that is, make a less than optimal contribution, as she will bear only a fraction of the cost of her own shirking. Moreover, participants may have an incentive to indulge in opportunistic behaviour by using their control rights, to the point of threatening to withdraw from the enterprise, for wasteful rent-seeking in order to gain a greater share of the total output (holdup problem).[24] This may potentially result in the destruction of valuable business opportunities and/or the value of any enterprise specific investments already committed.[25] A decrease in the value of the firm, in turn, increases the risk for contractors so that contracting on the market becomes more expensive. The opportunistic utilization of

[18] In particular OE Williamson, *The Economic Institutions of Capitalism* (Free Press 1985) 86–90 and passim.

[19] Alchian and Demsetz (n 13) 777 (In order to reduce shirking, a monitor is appointed to observe input behaviour. The monitor is the residual claimant and can alter the membership of the firm); SJ Grossman and OD Hart, 'The Costs and Benefits of Ownership: A Theory of Vertical and Lateral Integration' (1986) 94 Journal of Political Economy 691; O Hart and J Moore, 'Property Rights and the Nature of the Firm' (1990) 98 Journal of Political Economy 1119; O Hart, 'An Economist's Perspective on the Theory of the Firm' (1989) 89 Columbia Law Review 1757 (ownership of nun-human assets as residual right of control).

[20] Klein, Coffee, and Partnoy (n 7) 54. [21] ibid 59.

[22] MM Blair, 'Locking in Capital: What Corporate Law Achieved for Business Organizers in the Nineteenth Century' (2003) 51 UCLA Law Review 387, 401.

[23] Blair and Stout (n 14) 274. [24] ibid 266. [25] Blair (n 22) 402.

participants' control rights as well as their incentive to shirk may be harnessed by collectively delegating parts of their control rights to a central authority in order to monitor and to address shirking and opportunistic behaviour and to mediate disputes about allocation of duties and rewards. This in turn may generate costs arising from conflicting interests and information asymmetries between participants and central authority. These costs may be reduced, and pooling of resources optimized, by developing adequate institutional[26] structures for the organization of firms.

These institutional structures must provide incentives to induce participants to make the requisite investments and discourage holdups.[27] Risks and rewards as well as control rights must be allocated among the participants. Moreover, every cooperation of individuals that goes beyond a random and passive 'being-together' must adopt decision making procedures,[28] as a conduit for participants' control rights, in order to generate, and voice, an intent of the participants as a group. Thus, efficient pooling of resources on a horizontal basis requires, first, an institutional structure that internally—among participants—defines their individual contributions, their access to benefits and profits, powers of control over inputs and the pool of assets, and the process of forming an intent as a group. We may call this the 'internal governance structure'.[29]

This must be complemented by an 'external liability structure'[30] for the asset pool's interaction with other firms and individuals via the market. The pool of assets must be delineated and control rights over it must be defined in relation to third parties. Internally formed group intent has to be implemented externally in order to bind the pool of asset vis-à-vis third parties, contractually or otherwise.[31] Actions carried out on behalf of the firm must be attributed to it in one way or another.[32] Third parties' access to pool assets must be defined. In all these respects, the institutional structure should try to facilitate market transactions by reducing their costliness. Moreover, institutions must be structured so as to attract potential new participants, induce them to make the necessary firm-specific investments and to commit to the firm to a greater or lesser extent.

'Internal governance structure' and 'external liability structure' do not operate in isolation. Rather, they interact and overlap to a greater or lesser extent. This is obvious, for instance, in the internal formation and external implementation of group intent, and even more so, in the interaction of the firm with potentially new participants. However, the distinction is useful as a certain internal governance structure does not necessarily predetermine a certain external liability structure and vice versa. However, as we will see, a certain external liability structure is a quasi-precondition for some forms of internal governance structure.

All mature legal systems provide a multitude of legal institutions for the organization of business via pooling of resources. These institutions exhibit different features in respect of internal governance structure and external liability structure.

[26] For present purposes an institution may be defined as a set of formal and informal rules, including their enforcement arrangements. Institutions steer individual behaviour in a particular direction, provide structure to everyday activity and thus reduce uncertainty in human relations; EGG Furubotn and R Richter, *Institutions and Economic Theory* (2nd edn, The University of Michigan Press 2005) 7.

[27] Blair (n 22) 402.

[28] Wiedemann (n 11) 14. This author uses the example of two prisoners chained together on the run. They have to reach an agreement on where to go and act upon this decision.

[29] Governance is usually associated with the process of decision-making and the allocation of decision-making powers. In team production the allocation of control of, and access to, resources directly impacts on the allocation of decision-making rights and thus the decision-making process.

[30] The term liability in this context tries to capture the notion of responsibility, in the broadest sense, of the group or pool of assets as a whole or certain participants for acts and omissions carried out on behalf of the group/pool of assets in the course of interaction with the outside world.

[31] Wiedemann (n 11) 17.

[32] O Gierke, *Political Theories of the Middle Age* (F Maitland tr, CUP 1900) Translator's Introduction, ix.

I. Corporation and partnership as institutional archetypes

Corporation and partnership—*universitas* and *societas*, *société de capitaux*, and *société de personnes*, *Körperschaft*, and *Personengesellschaft*—signify institutional structures that can be found in all Western legal systems and may be traced back to Roman law.[33] The term 'corporation', etymologically, refers to the process of turning a collectivity into a *corpus*, a word used in Roman law to signify a legally recognized collectivity. Thus, 'corporation' connotes the separation and emancipation of a body corporate from its individual members; it emphasizes the paradox of unity arising out of plurality.[34] By contrast, 'partnership' (and also company) emphasizes the human membership of a group and the personal relationships among the individual group members.[35] The essential criterion of differentiation is the degree of independence of the group as such from its individual members. The significance of the distinction differs in our legal systems and plays out in respect of both the internal governance structure and the external liability structure to varying degrees.

1. *England and Wales*

English law distinguishes sharply between incorporated entities, on the one hand, and unincorporated entities, in particular partnerships, on the other, with a modern hybrid form bridging the gap. When registration became available as a form of incorporation under the Companies Act 1844, it merely supplemented other techniques of incorporating an entity but did not replace them.[36] These traditional techniques are incorporation by special Act of Parliament[37] or by charter granted by the Crown, either under the Royal Prerogative[38] or under powers conferred upon the Crown by statute to grant charters of incorporation.[39] In the past, incorporation by Act of Parliament was common for public utility undertakings (railway, gas, water, electricity) which usually required powers for the compulsory purchase of land. Many of these have now been privatized and registered under successive Companies Acts. Incorporation by Royal charter is still used today for organizations with a charitable or quasi-charitable purpose such as professional societies, schools or colleges.[40] The vast majority of incorporated organizations, and almost all ordinary trading concerns, are today incorporated by registration under the Companies Acts.[41]

The Companies Act 2006 offers a range of different types of companies. A first distinction is that between 'limited and unlimited companies'.[42] In an 'unlimited company' the liability

[33] Wiedemann (n 11) 89. [34] AF Conard, *Corporations in Perspective* (Foundation Press 1976) 134.

[35] ibid 137. [36] Davies and Worthington (n 8) para 1-31.

[37] This may be either a (General) Public Act under which corporate entities can be formed for special purposes, eg Industrial and Provident Societies Acts 1965-1978; Friendly Societies Act 1992, Building Societies Act 1986; or a Private Act referring specifically to an individual body. Unless explicitly excluded, statutory companies will be governed by the Companies Clauses Consolidation Act 1845.

[38] The concept of 'royal prerogative' may be defined, in accordance with Dicey, as the 'residue of discretionary or arbitrary authority, which at any given time is legally left in the hands of the Crown residual'. Today the government exercise the bulk of the prerogative powers, either in their own right or via the advice given to the queen, which she is constitutionally bound to follow. Ministry of Justice, *The Governance of Britain: Review of the Executive Royal Prerogative Powers: Final Report* (2009) http://www.peerage.org/genealogy/royal-prerogative.pdf.

[39] See eg Chartered Companies Acts 1837 and 1884, repealed in 1993.

[40] See eg the Law Society for England and Wales, the Institute of Chartered Accountants in England and Wales, the British Broadcasting Corporation (BBC), or King's College London.

[41] Building societies whose principle purpose is to make loans secured on residential property, friendly societies to provide insurance on a mutual basis against loss of income; and cooperative societies, are important for specific but limited commercial purposes. These constitute 'statutory companies' formed under the Acts cited in note 37. The open-ended investment company also has a limited commercial purpose: collective investment by pooling together small investments for better returns typically by purchasing corporate securities. Open-ended investment companies are incorporated by an authorization order made by the Financial Conduct Authority under the Open-ended Investment Companies Regulations 2001 (SI 2001/1228), as amended by SI 2005/923, SI 2009/553, and SI 2011/3049.

[42] Companies Act 2006 (CA 2006), s 3.

of the company's members to contribute, upon liquidation, to any losses sustained by the company is unlimited. Conversely, in case of a limited company the members' liability upon liquidation of the company is limited either by the amount, if any, unpaid on the shares held by them ('company limited by shares') or by the amount they promised to contribute in the event of the company being wound up ('company limited by guarantee'). The latter does not have a share capital.[43] A second important distinction is that between 'private and public companies'.[44] Public companies are permitted (not obliged) to offer their securities (equity and debt) to the public at large.[45] Where they have done so, they may seek to have their securities admitted to the 'Official List' of securities[46] to be traded on a public exchange, like the London Stock Exchange. Private companies are, *per definitionem*, companies that are not public companies and thus not permitted to conduct a public offering. In order to do that, they must reregister as a public company. In the UK, both public and private companies are governed by a single Act, with public companies being subject to more onerous regulation.[47] The vast majority of business entities are organized as public or private companies limited by shares.[48]

In terms of internal governance structure companies with a share capital provide for a clear definition of the members' contributions and their participation in profit and losses of the undertaking. The denomination of shares held by members determines the amount they have to pay the company in exchange for the shares. At the same time this amount puts a limit on the loss each member may sustain.[49] Conversely, if the enterprise is profitable the number and denomination of shares held by each member determines the proportionate participation in any dividends that may be paid and in any distributions of the company's assets upon winding up.[50] A member cannot unilaterally withdraw his contribution once rendered. The only way of exit is a transfer of his shares to a third party or, under limited circumstances, to the company. In principle, a transfer of shares does require neither the consent of the other shareholders nor of the company.[51] As for the formation of group intent, the Companies Act 2006 provides for two separate decision-making bodies: the shareholders' general meeting and the board of directors. A private company must have at least one; a public company at least two directors.[52] The Act itself provides little on the allocation of powers between general meeting and board as well as on the internal workings of the board. Much is left to the articles of association. Often the general meeting will decide on who sits on the board with the board then deciding on the day-to-day management of the company.[53] As for the external liability structure, case law provides that the internally formed group intent is implemented by the directors; only through its directors may the company interact with the outside world.[54] The acts of individual members have no effect on the company as a whole.[55] Usually, the articles of association will provide that the board of directors has

[43] CA 2006, s 5(1). The apparently contradictory provisions in s 4(2) and s 6(1)(b) relate to companies limited by guarantee with a share capital formed prior to 22 December 1980.

[44] ibid s 4. [45] ibid s 755. [46] Financial Services and Markets Act 2000, Pt VI.

[47] Davies and Worthington (n 8) para 1-19.

[48] To summarize, under the CA 2006 five different types of company may be registered: (i) public company limited by shares; (ii) private company limited by shares; (iii) private company limited by guarantee; (iv) private unlimited company with share capital; (v) private unlimited company without share capital. Very view unlimited companies are registered every year. Companies limited by guarantee are used mainly for non-profit purposes. The London School of Economics and Political Science is a company limited by guarantee.

[49] Davies and Worthington (n 8) para 1-11.

[50] See eg the Companies (Model Articles) Regulations 2008 (SI 2008/3229) Sch 1: Model Articles for Private Companies para 30; Sch 3: Model Articles for Public Companies para 71.

[51] CA 2006, s 544. [52] ibid s 154.

[53] See eg Companies (Model Articles) Regulations 2008 (SI 2008/3229) Sch 1: Model Articles for Private Companies para 3-20; Sch 3: Model Articles for Public Companies para 3-24.

[54] *Ferguson v Wilson* (1866) LR 2 Ch App 77, [89]–[90] (Cairns LJ).

[55] *Ernest v Nicholls* (1875) 6 HL Cas 401, [419] (Lord Wensleydale).

general authority to exercise the powers of the company and to authorize others to do so.[56] Third parties may rely on the power of the board of directors to bind the company.[57] With registration the members of the company are a 'body corporate' and 'capable of exercising all the functions of an incorporated company'.[58] Acts and omissions attributable to the company are the acts and omissions of the company, not acts or omissions of the individual members. The company itself is a 'legal person' and, as such, it is completely independent from the continued participation or even existence of particular members.[59] It has rights and obligations of its own, may sue, and be sued under its name. Only upon liquidation may members be asked, by the company's liquidator, to contribute to the company's liabilities, either limited to the amount, if any, outstanding on their shares, or, unlimited.[60]

By contrast, partnership law is essentially contract law and based on the law of agency. Today the law of general partnerships is largely codified in the Partnership Act 1890. A partnership is, *per definitionem*, 'the relation that subsists between persons carrying on a business in common with a view of profit'.[61] A general partnership is created by contractual agreement, formal or informal, between the partners and the carrying on of business in accordance with the agreement. No formal act of registration is required. The Partnership Act 1890 provides default rules for the internal governance structure that may be changed by the partnership agreement. The internal structure is thus even more flexible than that for companies. All the partners are entitled to share equally in the capital and profits of the business and must contribute equally towards the losses sustained by the firm.[62] A partner may assign his right to a share of profits to a third party, but may not assign his share in the partnership as such.[63] Rather, a person may be introduced as a new partner only with the consent of all existing partners.[64] However, a partner may terminate the partnership at any time where no fixed term for the duration of the partnership has been agreed.[65] The partnership also comes to an end with the death or bankruptcy of any of the partners.[66] As for the formation of the group will, every partner may take part in the management of the partnership business. Decisions concerning the ordinary course of business require support by a majority of the partners, fundamental changes require unanimity.[67] Externally, every partner is an agent for the other partners and can, when acting in the ordinary course of business of the partnership, bind all partners.[68] Although the partnership may sue and be sued under its firm name,[69] acts and omissions carried out on behalf of the partnership are binding on the partners. Even wrongful acts carried out in the ordinary course of business are attributed to every partner.[70] Consequently, every partner is liable jointly[71] with the other partners for all debts and obligations of the firm incurred while he is a partner and also severally with the partnership for wrongs committed in the ordinary course of business.[72] This liability continues even after a partner has left the firm, except where the respective creditor agrees that the retiring partner will be discharged.[73] As the partnership under English law is not a legal person,[74] the rights and obligations of the partnership are essentially the rights and obligations of the partners. Thus, English law adopts an aggregate

[56] See eg Companies (Model Articles) Regulations 2008 (SI 2008/3229) Sch 1: Model Articles for Private Companies para 3; Sch 3: Model Articles for Public Companies para 3.

[57] CA 2006, s 40. [58] ibid s 16(2)(3).

[59] See the Australian case *Re Noel Tedman Holding Pty Ltd* (1967) Qd R 561 (Queensland SC). The only two members of a company were killed in a road accident, the company survived.

[60] Insolvency Act 1986, s 74. [61] Partnership Act 1890, s 1(1). [62] ibid s 24(1).

[63] ibid s 31. [64] ibid s 24(7). [65] ibid s 26. [66] ibid s 32.

[67] ibid s 24(5), (8) and s 19. [68] ibid s 5. [69] ibid s 4. [70] ibid ss 6, 12.

[71] Under 'joint liability' an action should, in principle, be brought against all joint debtors because the cause of action is deemed to be single and indivisible; judgment against only one debtor would bar a subsequent action against another even if the first judgment remained unsatisfied; where liability is 'joint and several' an action can be brought against one individual debtor for the full amount or jointly against all debtors together.

[72] Partnership Act 1890, s 9. [73] ibid s 17.

[74] Unlike Scots law, see Partnership Act 1890, s 4(2).

approach to partnership law.[75] The problems associated with this are reflected in the difficult concept of 'partnership property'. The aggregate theory makes it necessary to distinguish between property held by partners in their individual capacity and property held for the partnership. This latter 'partnership property' is defined as all property and rights and interests in property originally brought into the partnership stock or subsequently acquired on account of the partnership or acquired for the purposes and in the course of the partnership business or on account of the partnership or with partnership money.[76] Partnership property must be held and applied by the partners exclusively for the purpose of the partnership and in accordance with the partnership agreement. However, that a certain asset is 'partnership property' does not determine the allocation of proprietary rights over the asset. Thus, a partnership asset may be held by all or some of the partners as tenants in common with each of them having an undivided share in the partnership asset; or the asset may be held by a single partner.[77] The partnership agreement as a contract only binds the partners. Their property rights are contractually subjected to the partnership agreement and they are not entitled individually to exercise proprietary rights over any of the partnership assets contrary to their agreement. As regards the outside world, however, the partnership agreement is irrelevant and the partners may exercise their respective property rights in the partnership assets at will.[78] Somewhat at odds with this is the fact that a judgment obtained by a personal creditor against a partner cannot be executed against partnership property, but can be executed against the partner's share in the partnership by means of a charging order. A charging order does not give the judgment creditor any greater right than that enjoyed by an assignee and the partners may at any time redeem the judgment debtor's share.[79]

Since 1907 the law provides for a special form of partnership under the Limited Partnership Act 1907. A limited partnership is a partnership subject to the Partnership Act 1890 and the common law of partnerships, except in so far as this would be inconsistent with the special characteristics of the limited partnership.[80] A limited partnership consists, *per definitionem*, of two classes of partners: at least one general partner whose status is identical to that of a partner in a general partnership, and at least one 'limited partner' whose liability for the partnership's debts is limited to the amount contributed when entering the partnership.[81] A limited partner must not take part in the management of the partnership and does not have authority to bind the firm. If a limited partner takes part in the management, he forgoes the privilege of limited liability for debts incurred during his participation in the management.[82] Death and bankruptcy of a limited partner do not result in dissolution; neither can a limited partner dissolve the partnership by notice.[83] However, transfer of the share of a limited partner to another person requires consent of the general partners but not the limited partners.[84] A limited partnership must be registered with the Registrar of Companies. Initially, the limited partnership has not been very popular. In recent years, however, it has been discovered as a useful vehicle for venture capital, private equity, or property investment funds.[85]

With the introduction of the limited liability partnership (LLP) pursuant to the Limited Liability Partnership Act 2000, Parliament has introduced a modern hybrid form. This vehicle is mainly interesting for professional firms, in particular audit firms, whose partners were increasingly confronted with negligence claims exceeding their professional indemnity insurance cover.[86] The internal governance structure is largely similar to that in a general

[75] The Law Commission and Scottish Law Commission, Partnership Law (Law Com No 283) (Scot Law Com No 192) (2003) para 2.5. In this Report the Law Commission suggested to confer legal person status to partnership. This was subsequently not taken up by the government.

[76] Partnership Act 1890, ss 20, 21.

[77] Law Commission Report (n 75) para 9.10.

[78] *IRC v Gray* [1994] STC 360, [377c]–[377e] (Hoffmann LJ).

[79] Partnership Act 1890, s 23(2).

[80] Limited Partnership Act 1907, s 7.

[81] ibid s 4(2).

[82] ibid s 6(1).

[83] ibid s 6(2).

[84] ibid s 6(5).

[85] Davies and Worthington (n 8) para 1-5.

[86] J Lowry and A Reisberg, *Pettet's Company Law* (4th edn, Pearson Longman 2012) 22.

partnership. However, upon registration with the Registrar of Companies the LLP constitutes a body corporate with separate legal personality.[87] The liability of members for the debts and obligations of the LLP upon liquidation will be limited to the amount that the respective member has agreed to contribute.[88] Thus, in terms of external liability structure the LLP is much more akin to a company. Consequently, company law applies, often with modifications tailored towards the special needs of the LLP.[89]

2. *United States*

State laws display a vast array of different types of associations that can be used for pooling resources to conduct a business. These are commonly classified as either 'incorporated' or 'unincorporated' associations.[90] Until the middle of the nineteenth century corporations, chartered by the state legislatures, were mainly used for organizations with political or administrative purposes, such as cities, towns, villages or parishes, or enterprises with a public interest function, such as banks, insurance companies, water companies, or companies to build and run canals, bridges, and turnpikes.[91] General commercial enterprises were run in the form of partnerships on the basis of the common law of partnerships derived from English law.[92] This changed when the states started to enact general incorporation laws making the corporate form available for all businesses. The stark dichotomy of incorporated entities (corporations) and unincorporated associations (partnerships) was significantly eased by successive reforms of partnership law. An interesting development over the past three decades has been the proliferation of hybrid entities that combine different features of corporation and partnership to varying degrees.

Incorporation is effectuated under the different state corporation laws which may differ significantly in detail but are very similar in terms of the defining features of the corporation.[93] The (Revised) Model Business Corporation Act (MBCA) as promulgated by the American Bar Association has been implemented in one form or another in the majority of US jurisdictions.[94] However, for the large publicly traded corporation the Delaware General Corporation Law (DGCL) is the most important codification: about 60 per cent of all nonfinancial publicly traded companies which had both their headquarters and their incorporation in the United States are incorporated under the law of the State of Delaware.[95] US corporate law commonly distinguishes between public (or publicly held) corporations and close (or closely held) corporations.[96] Originally, all corporations were subject to the same statutory provisions designed primarily for publicly held corporations with large numbers of equity investors who had no inclination to actively participate in the enterprise.[97] However, the special needs of small partnership-like corporations were gradually

[87] Limited Liability Partnership Act 2000, s 1(2).

[88] ibid s 1(4); Limited Liability Partnership Regulations 2001 (SI 2001/1090) reg 5 with Sch 3. This Schedule modifies the Insolvency Act 1986, in particular s 74, so as to limit the liability of partners upon liquidation of the LLP. See further the Limited Liability Partnership (Application of Companies Act 2006) Regulations 2009/1804, and various other statutory instruments (SIs 2009/1833, 2008/1911, 2008/1912, and 2008/1913).

[89] Davies and Worthington (n 8) para 1-4.

[90] WM Fletcher, 'Fletcher Cyclopedia of the Law of Corporations' §§17 (September 2018 update). For the different types of corporations, cf ibid §§49–80.

[91] These corporations are sometimes called 'public' or 'quasi-public' corporations: ibid §57. A better term seems to be 'municipal corporations', as modern terminology uses 'public corporation' as a synonym for 'publicly-held corporation' (see below).

[92] LM Friedman, *A History of American Law* (2nd edn, Simon & Schuster 1985) 188.

[93] Klein, Coffee, and Partnoy (n 7) 106.

[94] American Bar Association, *2005 Model Business Corporation Act* (2005) xix.

[95] L Bebchuk, A Cohen, and A Ferrell, 'Does the Evidence Favor State Competition in Corporate Law?' (2002) 90 California Law Review 1775, 1808.

[96] Fletcher (n 90) §56.

[97] Jesse H Choper, John C Coffee, and Ronald J Gilson, *Cases and Materials on Corporations* (8th edn, Wolters Kluwer 2013) 724.

recognized, first by the courts and subsequently by state legislatures.[98] However, there is no universally accepted definition of 'close corporation' and state approaches differ. Under New York law, for instance, special rules for close corporations apply only 'so long as no shares of the corporation are listed on a national securities exchange or regularly quoted in an over-the-counter market'.[99] A similar approach can be found under MBCA.[100] Delaware law is more specific. A close corporation is defined by reference to three cumulative elements: (i) all of the corporation's issued shares must be held by no more than 30 persons; (ii) all of the issued shares must be subject to one or more authorized restrictions on transfer; (iii) the corporation cannot make any 'public offering' of its shares within the meaning of the Securities Act 1933.[101] Other states require that the number of shareholders is fixed by the articles of association and does not exceed a certain maximum,[102] or apply close corporation benefits only to those corporations having statutorily detailed stock transfer restrictions that effectively eliminate general trading of shares.[103]

The interests of individual shareholders are reflected in 'shares of common stock' issued by the corporation and held by the shareholders usually through an intermediary. The number of shares held determines the shareholders' respective participation in the profits or losses of the corporation and in the appreciation or depreciation of its assets. Shares are generally freely transferable and, in the case of public corporations, actively traded. In close corporations, transferability of shares may be restricted. In terms of the formation of group intent, US corporate law provides, in contrast with English law, a structure consisting of three distinct elements: (i) shareholders;[104] (ii) board of directors;[105] and (iii) corporate officers.[106] By voting their shares at annual or specially called meetings, at least in theory, common shareholders select the members of the board of directors. A shareholder vote may also be required for certain fundamental issues, such as a merger of the corporation, amendments to the certificate of incorporation, sale of substantially all of the corporations' assets or liquidation. Apart from that, however, shareholders can neither act on behalf of the corporation nor give orders to directors, officers, or other employees.[107] Rather, as MBCA §8.01(b) provides, 'all corporate powers shall be exercised by or under the authority of, and the business and affairs of the corporation managed by or under the direction of, its board of directors'. The board, collectively, has the authority to bind the corporation or to delegate that authority to others. In the large public corporation envisaged by state corporation statutes, the board's authority to manage the day-to-day business of the corporation will be delegated to the corporate officers who act as agents of the corporation. The officers' authority will be detailed in the corporation's by-laws, supplemented by specific board resolutions.[108] Thus, the principal responsibility of the board of directors is to appoint and monitor the officers, rather than to manage the business.[109] The latter task is reserved for the corporate officers, and in particular the chief executive officer (CEO) as the person primarily in charge of front-line operations. The CEO will usually be a member of the board and act as its chairman. This governance structure is particularly conducive to the development of strong centralized management and the separation of ownership of cash flow rights from control of the business assets. For large publicly traded corporations with numerous passive shareholders such a structure is vital for effective governance; however, it is unsuitable for close corporations where directors/managers and controlling

98 *Galler v Galler*, 32 Ill. 2d 16, 28, 203 N.E.2d 577 (1965) with a review of the applicable case law.
99 New York Business Corporation Law, §620(c). 100 MBCA, §7.32(d). 101 DGCL, §342(a).
102 See eg California General Corporation Law, §158(a): 35 as the maximum number of shareholders.
103 eg Maryland General Corporations Law, §4-501.
104 MBCA, Chapter 7; DGCL, Subchapter VII.
105 MBCA, Chapter 8, Subchapters A-C, E, F; DGCL, §141.
106 MBCA, Chapter 8, Subchapter D; DGCL, §142. 107 Klein, Coffee, and Partnoy (n 7) 124.
108 American Bar Association, *2005 Model Business Corporation Act* (2005) 8–80 (Official Comment §8.40).
109 Klein, Coffee, and Partnoy (n 7) 132.

shareholders will often be the same persons.[110] Thus, some modern corporation laws provide that close corporations may be managed by the shareholders rather than by a board of directors.[111] Moreover, shareholders' agreements limiting the board of directors' powers and discretion may be valid,[112] contrary to the general law on public corporations. In terms of the external liability structure, public and close corporations are essentially treated in the same way as separate legal entities. Unless otherwise provided in its articles of incorporation, a corporation has perpetual existence irrespective of changing membership and has the same powers as an individual to do all things necessary or convenient to carry out its business. In particular, a corporation may sue and be sued under its name, may acquire, own, and dispose of real or personal property, incur liabilities, and participate as a member in any other entity. Acts carried out by directors or officers on behalf of the corporation are the acts of the corporation.[113] Shareholders' liability for the obligations and debts of the corporation is limited to the amount, if any, unpaid on their shares.[114]

Historically, partnership law developed out of the English common law concept of partnership on the basis of contract and agency. In 1914 the Commissioners on Uniform State Law adopted the Uniform Partnership Act, codifying much of the common law, as a model statute that was subsequently enacted in every state with the exception of the civil law jurisdiction of Louisiana.[115] In 1994 a revised Uniform Partnership Act was adopted which, after various revisions, became the Uniform Partnership Act 1997. This model statute was enacted by a majority of states,[116] but often with significant variations. Thus, a substantial core commonality aside, partnership law is not really uniform.[117] The Uniform Partnership Act 1997 reflects both the common core and modern tendencies. 'Partnership' is defined as 'an association of two or more persons to carry on as co-owners a business for profit', irrespective of whether the persons intend to form a partnership.[118] The 'co-ownership' element distinguishes a partnership from mere agency. It denotes that each partner has the power of ultimate control over the business, whereas passive co-ownership of property does not establish a partnership.[119] Subject to the partnership agreement, each partner is entitled to an equal share of the partnership profits; and losses are shared in proportion to each partner's share in the profits.[120] Similar to English law, each partner has equal rights to participate in the management and conduct of the partnership business,[121] and may assign only his share in the profits and losses to a third party but not his membership as such.[122] Entry of a new partner requires consent of all the

[110] Choper, Coffee, and Gilson (n 97) 8. [111] eg DGCL, §351. [112] eg DGCL, §350.

[113] MBCA, §3.02; DGCL, §§121, 122.

[114] MBCA, §6.22; DGCL, §162. Since 2010, a number of states, including California, New York and Delaware, have created a new form of business corporation, the so-called 'benefit corporation' or 'B corporation'. A 'benefit corporation' has three distinguishing features: (i) its corporate purpose goes beyond returning a profit for its shareholders and encompasses the creation of a positive impact on society or the environment, even at the expense of a lower profit; (ii) the fiduciary duties owed by directors and managers extend to considerations of societal and environmental interest, providing immunity from liability on purely financial grounds; and (iii) its overall social and environmental performance is to be assessed against a transparent standard determined independently by a third party. The emergence of the 'B corporation' concept has to be understood as an antidote to the prevalent shareholder wealth maximization principle. Through a B corporation, entrepreneurs may utilize their profit making activity in order to pursue wider societal goals without having to fear a derivative shareholder action for loss of profit; see W Clark and E Babson, 'How Benefit Corporations Are Redefining the Purpose of Business Corporations' (2012) 38 William Mitchell Law Review 817; Fletcher (n 90) §70.50.

[115] National Conference of Commissioners on Uniform State Laws *Uniform Partnership Act (1997) (last amended 2013) with Prefatory Note and Comments* (2014) 2.

[116] Cf https://my.uniformlaws.org/committees/community-home?CommunityKey=52456941-7883-47a5-91b6-d2f086d0bb44.

[117] Klein, Coffee, and Partnoy (n 7) 62. [118] Uniform Partnership Act (1997), §§101(6) 202.

[119] National Conference of Commissioners on Uniform State Laws (n 115) 62–3 (Comment §202).

[120] Uniform Partnership Act (1997), §401(b). [121] ibid §401(f). [122] ibid §502.

other partners.[123] And each partner may withdraw from the partnership at will.[124] Under the Uniform Partnership Act, withdrawal of a partner does not normally result in dissolution and winding up of the partnership, which continues with the remaining partners.[125] However, in a partnership at will a single partner may still force dissolution by withdrawing.[126] Decisions in the ordinary course of business require a majority of the partners; extraordinary decisions require unanimity.[127] These decisions may be implemented by each partner acting as an agent of the partnership.[128] However, each partner's authority to act as an agent on behalf of the partnership may be limited by filing a 'statement of partnership authority'.[129] Under the Uniform Partnership Act it is the partnership that is bound by an act of a partner and the partnership is also liable for loss or injury caused to a person by wrongful act or omission of a partner in the ordinary course of business.[130] This is a consequence of the Uniform Partnership Act 1997 embracing the entity theory of the partnership. The partnership is treated as a legal entity distinct from the partners.[131] Changes in membership leave the identity of the partnership intact.[132] Under the entity theory, property acquired in the name or on behalf of the partnership is the property of the partnership, not of the partners individually.[133] The partners are not co-owners of partnership property; they have no transferrable interest in partnership property whatsoever.[134] The partnership may sue and be sued in its own name.[135] From the beginnings of American partnership law, the now prevalent entity theory (or mercantile theory) has struggled against the aggregate (or common-law) theory for domination.[136] The Uniform Partnership Act 1914 left the issue largely unresolved.[137] This could have serious consequences. Under previous law, withdrawal or death of a partner meant that the partnership, as defined by its original membership, no longer existed and, where the remaining partners continued the business, they did so in a new and distinct partnership. This could mean that contracts entered into by the 'old' partnership were not enforceable by the 'new' partnership.[138] The adoption of the entity theory avoids these problems. However, in line with traditional partnership law, all partners are in principle liable jointly and severally for all obligations of the partnership.[139] Nevertheless, partnership creditors must exhaust the partnership's assets before levying on a partner's individual property where the partner is personally liable for the partnership's obligation.[140] Thus, in comparison to English law, there are two significant differences in the partnership's external liability structure: the partnership is treated as a separate legal entity and the partners' liability for the partnership's debts is 'joint and several' with the other partners but only secondary to the liability of the partnership. Thus, under the Uniform Partnership Act 1997 we see a greater degree of independence of the partnership as group from its individual members than we see under English law.

American law recognizes three variations on the partnership theme, one goes back to the beginning of the nineteenth century, the other two are of more recent origin. The limited partnership made its first appearance in the United States in a New York statute of 1822.[141] In 1916 the Commissioners on Uniform State Laws adopted the Uniform Limited Partnership Act. Following revision in 1976 and amendments in 1985, the Uniform Limited Partnership Act 2001 is the latest codification and has been adopted by almost half of the

[123] ibid §401(i). [124] ibid§601(1). [125] ibid §603(a). [126] ibid §801. [127] ibid §401(j).
[128] ibid §301. [129] ibid §303. [130] ibid §§301, 305. [131] ibid §201(a).
[132] National Conference of Commissioners on Uniform State Laws (n 115) 60 (Comment §201).
[133] Uniform Partnership Act (1997), §203. [134] ibid §501. [135] ibid§307(a).
[136] Instructive J Crane, 'The Uniform Partnership Act: A Criticism' (1915) 28 Harvard Law Review 762.
[137] National Conference of Commissioners on Uniform State Laws (n 115) 60 (Comment §201).
[138] Cf *Fairway Development Co. v Title Insurance Co.*, 621 F.Supp 120 (N.D. Ohio, 1985).
[139] Uniform Partnership Act (1997), §306(a). [140] ibid §307(d).
[141] Choper, Coffee, and Gilson (n 97) 796.

states.[142] A limited partnership has one or more general partners and one or more limited partners. Its formation requires the filing of a 'certificate of limited partnership' with the secretary of state.[143] The limited partnership is an entity distinct from its partners.[144] The status of general partners in a limited partnership is similar to that of the partners in the general partnership.[145] Limited partners, however, are neither directly nor indirectly liable for any obligations of the limited partnership.[146] At the same time, limited partners have no right to participate in the management of the business or power, as limited partners, to act for, or bind, the limited partnership.[147] Under previous law, a limited partner taking 'part in the control of the business' risked being treated as a general partner with unlimited liability for the partnership's debts. This was very ambiguous and caused considerable uncertainty. The rule was, therefore, gradually forced out.[148] Under §303 of the Uniform Limited Partnership Act 2001, a limited partner will not be liable for the limited partnership's obligations 'even if the limited partner participates in the management and control of the limited partnership'. The limited partnership has proved to be considerably more attractive in the United States than it used to be in England. This attraction to a large extent has been tax-driven. The pass-through taxation of partners is particularly advantageous for investments that – like real estate – may generate tax (but not cash) losses reducing other income for tax purposes. Also, with the top corporate tax rate approaching or exceeding the top individual tax rate avoiding the corporate double tax disadvantage may become an important factor.[149] At the same time, the limited partnership allows for effective separation of cash flow rights from control rights which makes it particularly attractive as a venture capital vehicle.[150] Limited partnerships may have large numbers of limited partners with their interests being publicly traded.

The limited liability partnership (LLP) appeared first in Texas in 1991[151] and is now available in all fifty states with some states limiting its use to professionals.[152] Under UPA 1997 the limited liability partnership is in principle a general partnership that has filed a 'statement of qualification' as a limited liability partnership.[153] A partner will not be personally liable for any obligation of the partnership, whether in contract, tort, or otherwise, incurred while the partnership was a limited liability partnership.[154] Partners remain liable for their own misconduct. However, where the partner's liability has been incurred in the ordinary course of the partnership's business the partnership is under an obligation to indemnify them.[155] The LLP is the form of choice for many law, accounting and other professional services firms as the corporate form was traditionally unavailable for professions the reputation of which relied to a great extent on personal expertise and responsibility.[156] The latest variation is the limited liability limited partnership (LLLP). General partners of a LLLP enjoy the limited liability of partners in a LLP and can thus manage the LLLP comprehensively without any fear of liability, whereas limited partners as passive investors enjoy the limited liability of the limited partnership.[157] With the rise of the limited liability company (LLC) the LLLP may be superfluous.

[142] Cf https://my.uniformlaws.org/committees/community-home?CommunityKey=d9036976-6c90-4951-ba81-1046c90da035.

[143] Uniform Limited Partnership Act 2001, §201.
[144] ibid §104(a).
[145] Fletcher (n 90) §19.

[146] Uniform Limited Partnership Act 2001, §303.
[147] ibid §302.

[148] Choper, Coffee, and Gilson (n 97) 798–800; National Conference of Commissioners on Uniform State Laws *Uniform Limited Partnership Act (2011) (last amended 2013) with Prefatory Note and Comments* (2014) 91 (Comment on §303).

[149] Klein, Coffee, and Partnoy (n 7) 100–102.
[150] Choper, Coffee, and Gilson (n 97) 797.

[151] ibid 822.
[152] Fletcher (n 90) §21.

[153] Uniform Partnership Act 1997, §101(5).

[154] ibid §306(c).

[155] National Conference of Commissioners on Uniform State Laws (n 115) 84 (Comment on §306).

[156] Choper, Coffee, and Gilson (n 97) 822. In many jurisdictions professionals may now organize in so-called 'professional corporations'. The choice between these and the LLP-form will often be tax driven; Fletcher (n 90) §70.30.

[157] Choper, Coffee, and Gilson (n 97) 823.

The LLC is a true hybrid between corporation and partnership. The first LLC statutes were enacted in 1977 in Wyoming and in 1982 in Florida, in both cases in order to attract foreign investment. Treatment as a partnership for federal income tax purposes pursuant to a ruling by the Inland Revenue Service in 1988 resulted in the enactment of LLC statutes in all fifty states.[158] Today the LLC has become the dominant form of organization for new closely held businesses. As the Uniform Limited Liability Company Act of 2006 has been enacted only by a limited number of states,[159] the Delaware Limited Liability Company Act may serve as a more or less representative example.[160] A LLC may be formed by one or more persons by executing a 'certificate of formation' to be filed with the secretary of state.[161] The internal workings of the LLC are to be regulated in a 'limited liability company agreement'.[162] This makes the LLC an extremely flexible device that can be structured in an optimal way to fit the particular purposes of entrepreneurs.[163] Subject to the LLC agreement, the following principles apply: profits and losses will be allocated on the basis of the agreed value of the contributions made by each member to the extent they have been received by the LLC and have not been returned.[164] In the same way as a partner in a partnership, a member may assign only his right to participate in the profits and losses, not his membership as such.[165] In order to admit a new member, all other members must consent.[166] This characteristic is a considerable impediment for ventures with large numbers of investors to organize as LLC.[167] Like in a corporation, withdrawal, death or bankruptcy of one member does not result in the dissolution of the LLC.[168] As a default rule, the management of a LLC will be vested in its members in proportion to the then current percentage or other interest of members in the profits of the limited liability company owned by all of the members. However, the LLC agreement may provide that management, wholly or in part, must be vested in one or more managers chosen in the manner provided in the agreement. Subject to the LLC agreement, each member and manager has the authority to bind the LLC.[169] Thus, partnership-like 'member-managed' LLCs may be distinguished from 'manager-managed' LLCs with a centralized management and separation of cash-flow rights and control. Externally, the LLC constitutes a separate legal entity distinct from its members. Neither members nor manager will be liable for any of the LLC's debts, obligations, or liabilities.[170]

It could be argued that with the prevalence of the entity theory for general partnerships and, more importantly, with the emergence of the LLP, LLLP, and LLC the distinction of incorporated and unincorporated entities has largely lost its significance.[171] In terms of formation (by filing a public document) and external liability structure these forms are very similar to corporations. The main difference is the (somewhat greater) strictures of the corporate form in terms of internal governance structure and the (even greater) flexibility in this respect of the other forms. For close corporations these corporate strictures are either significantly reduced (e.g. shareholder managed close corporations) or have no tangible purpose (e.g. corporate formalities where controlling shareholders, board members and officers are identical); and LLP, LLLP, and LLC are subject to private ordering so that any sizable business can and will adopt corporation-like centralized management structures.

[158] BJ Sklar and T Carlisle, 'The Alabama Limited Liability Company Act' (1993) 45 Alabama Law Review 145, 149–50.

[159] Cf https://my.uniformlaws.org/committees/community-home?CommunityKey=bbea059c-6853-4f45-b69b-7ca2e49cf740.

[160] LLC statutes vary widely from state to state, Fletcher (n 90) §20.

[161] Delaware Limited Liability Company Act, §18-201(a). [162] ibid §18-101(7).

[163] Fletcher (n 90) §20. [164] Delaware Limited Liability Company Act, §18-503.

[165] ibid §18-702. [166] ibid §18-301(b)(1). [167] Klein, Coffee, and Partnoy (n 7) 104.

[168] Delaware Limited Liability Company Act, §18-801(b). [169] ibid §18-401.

[170] ibid §18-303.

[171] TE Rutledge 'External Entities and Internal Aggregates: A Deconstructionist Conundrum' (2009) 42 Suffolk University Law Review 655.

3. *Germany*

Under German law, an organized plurality of persons at private law[172] (or 'company in a wider sense') may be either a form of corporation (*Körperschaft*) or a form of partnership (*Personengesellschaft*, or 'company in the narrow sense'). This distinction is clearly set out in the Civil Code of 1900 (BGB).[173] The basic type of corporation is the 'private law association' that comes into existence, as a legal person, with registration and is formed for the pursuit of a non-economic purpose.[174] The civil law partnership (*Gesellschaft des bürgerlichen Rechts*, GbR), on the other hand, is contractual in nature and comes into existence with the partners' agreement to contribute to the attainment of a certain, not necessarily economic, purpose.[175] All available forms of business associations may be allocated to either one of these categories. This is of some practical significance as lacunae in the special Acts regulating the different forms may be filled by reference to the law applicable to these basic categories.[176] Under German law, the distinction between 'corporation' and 'partnership' mainly concerns, in general terms,[177] the internal governance structure.[178] The corporation is independent from the personality of its members and will continue to exist undisturbed even where the membership changes due to withdrawal, death, or insolvency of a member or transfer of the membership. Members decide issues on the basis of majority voting (majority principle). These decisions are then implemented by special 'organs' of the corporation. These organs may be manned by third persons who are not themselves members (third party representation).[179] By contrast, the existence of a partnership depends, in principle, on the continued participation of all of its partners. Death or withdrawal of a partner terminates the partnership and results in dissolution. Entry of a new partner requires consent of all the others. Issues are decided on the basis of unanimity (unanimity principle). Special organs are unnecessary as the partners themselves implement these decisions (member representation).[180] As far as business organizations are concerned, the distinction of 'corporation and partnership' is mirrored and supplemented by the distinction of 'company with a share capital' (*Kapitalgesellschaft*) and 'personalised company' (*Personal gesellschaft*).[181] 'Companies with a share capital' are those corporations where the contribution of a certain amount of capital constitutes the essence of the membership. A common feature is the stipulation of a certain amount of share capital in the articles of association. Capital is impersonal so that the shares may be freely transferred. The majority principle is based on the proportion of capital contributed and held by each member, not on a head count. In 'personalised companies' the identity of the members matters. Members' main contribution is their skills and knowledge and their active participation in the running of the business. The success and reputation of the business depend on the personality of its members; a change in membership, thus, must have consequences for the continuation of the business.[182]

[172] German law distinguishes sharply between private law and public law. Roughly speaking, the former deals with the relations among the citizens interacting at a level playing field, the latter is concerned with the relationship between citizens and the state as well as different state institutions among each other. Public law corporations – towns, villages, professional organizations for lawyers, doctors, dentists, craftsmen etc., universities – are formed by way of a state act, be it a statute, an administrative act on the basis of a statute or state recognition. These organizations pursue their interests with the powers of the state. At the same time, they are subject to extensive state supervision. Wiedemann (n 11) 12.

[173] F Kübler and H-D Assmann, *Gesellschaftsrecht* (6th edn, C F Muller 2006) 22.

[174] BGB, §21.

[175] ibid §705.

[176] C Windbichler, *Gesellschaftsrecht* (24th edn, CH Beck 2017) 23 (§2 para 9).

[177] It is also relevant for the implementation of the group intent in the outside world, an issue that we have categorized above as part of the external liability structure.

[178] Kübler and Assmann (n 173) 22.

[179] ibid 24–5; Windbichler (n 176) 23–5 (§2 para 9-12).

[180] Kübler and Assmann (n 173) 23–4.

[181] Windbichler (n 176) 26 (§2 para 16). This distinction was originally not present in German law but is now well established owing to French and European influences.

[182] ibid §2 para 17-18; Wiedemann (n 11) 101–102.

The categorization as either a 'corporation' or a 'partnership' does not necessarily predetermine the external liability structure of an organization (although it does so in case of most business associations).[183] The law provides three options for the attribution of ownership rights and obligations to a plurality of individuals: the legal person, co-ownership, and collective ownership. The legal person constitutes a legal entity completely separate from any natural persons who may utilize it (principle of separation). The legal person alone owns its property and, through its organs, may transfer, alter, or extinguish its property rights. It is liable for its own debts and obligations and may sue and be sued under its name. 'Corporations' are, in principle, afforded legal personality.[184] However, the foundation[185] and the single-person company are legal persons but not 'corporations'; and the 'association without legal personality'[186] may possess a corporate (internal governance) structure.[187] Co-ownership[188] provides every co-owner with an undivided share in an asset or assets. A co-owner may freely transfer its share in any particular asset to third parties[189] and may force dissolution of the co-ownership by dividing the assets *in natura*, where possible, or by selling them with a subsequent distribution of the proceeds.[190] These features render co-ownership too unstable as a basis for conducting a business. Thus, the default rule for partnership type business organizations is 'collective ownership'.[191] 'Collective ownership' is a concept derived from Germanic law.[192] Unless provided otherwise in the partnership agreement, partnership property, as a pool of assets, is owned collectively by the partners as a group (*Gesamthandsge-meinschaft*).[193] Collective ownership provides a strong proprietary enclosure of partnership assets. The partners cannot dispose of their respective 'share'[194] in any particular partnership asset;[195] a partnership asset can be transferred only by all partners acting together (*mit gesamter Hand*).[196] Each partner owns, however, a share in the pool of assets that constitutes the partnership property. Subject to the partnership agreement, a partner cannot dispose of his share in the partnership property.[197] Where the partnership agreement allows for the transfer of this share, the share in partnership property may be transferred only together with the entire membership right. No partner can demand to dissolve the pool of assets.[198] In order to realize his share, a partner can terminate the partnership;[199] thereby forcing the distribution of partnership property.[200] Similarly, a partner's personal creditor may levy execution only on the partner's share in the partnership property and can then terminate the partnership in order to access partnership property.[201] Where the partnership agreement contains a continuation clause the share of a withdrawing partner automatically accrues to the remaining partners in proportion of their existing shares.[202] Where a new partner enters, he automatically acquires a share in the partnership property as collective owner.[203]

[183] Kübler and Assmann (n 173) 22, 28.

[184] T Raiser, 'Der Begriff der juristischen Person. Eine Neubesinnung' (1999) 199 Archiv für die civilistische Praxis 104, 15.

[185] BGB, §80. [186] ibid §54. [187] Kübler and Assmann (n 173) 28.

[188] BGB, §§741–758, §§1008–1011. [189] ibid §747. [190] ibid §§749, 752–4.

[191] Windbichler (n 176) 35 (§3 para 2). If partners want to conduct their business as co-owners, they can do so but must explicitly provide for it in their partnership agreement.

[192] Wiedemann (n 11) 243, claims that the concept is unique to legal systems of Germanic origin. However, it is known in France as well, cf M Germain and V Magnier, *Les sociétés commerciales* (21st edn, LGDJ 2014) para 1514.

[193] Collective ownership also occurs outside the partnership context. A community of heirs (BGB, §2033) and spouses who have agreed to pool their assets in matrimonial property (BGB, §1419) also hold their assets as collective owners. The characteristics of these collective ownership regimes are, in parts, different from each other and from collective ownership in the partnership context.

[194] It is in dispute whether shares in a single partnership asset exist at all. [195] BGB, §719(1).

[196] Windbichler (n 176) 36 (§3 para 4). [197] BGB, §719(1). [198] ibid §719(1).

[199] ibid §723. [200] ibid §730–735. [201] ibid §725.

[202] In the person of the withdrawing partner, a claim for compensation replaces his share in the partnership property, ibid §738.

[203] Windbichler (n 176) 37 (§3 para 7).

The nature of 'collective ownership' in the partnership context was the subject matter of a long-running and fierce academic debate. Pursuant to the aggregate theory, the rights and obligations of the partnership are attributable to the partners individually. Only the partners (as natural or legal persons) are entities and as such capable of having rights and obligations. Conversely, according to the entity theory the partners in their collective unity constitute an entity separate from the individual partners which, albeit not a legal person, can hold property and be subject to obligations. However, entity status was somehow limited in the sense that it lacked behind the comprehensive entity status of natural and legal persons.[204] As commercial partnerships have entity status according to statutory prescription,[205] this controversy was most relevant in practical terms and played out largely in respect of the civil law partnership.[206] In a landmark decision of 2001 the Federal Court of Justice (*Bundesgerichtshof*, BGH) adopted the entity theory:

> According to the more recent jurisprudence of the Federal Court of Justice, the civil law partnership as collectively owned by its partners may, in the course of business, in principle, that is so long as no specific factors suggest otherwise, engage in any legal relations. To the extent that it creates within this framework its own rights and obligations, it will be a legal entity (without being a legal person).[207]

Thus, the partnership as such can own property, will be liable for its own obligations, and may sue and be sued in its own name. The partners, jointly and severally, will be personally liable for the partnerships debts in analogy to the law of commercial partnerships.[208] The reasons for adopting the entity approach are mainly pragmatic: the entity theory allows for a clear distinction of the partnership's obligations and the partners' liability for these, can better explain why a civil law partnership may be transformed into other types of entity without losing its identity and avoids problems in respect of privacy of contract and changes in membership. However, not all civil law partnerships will have entity status; rather, only those which 'engage in legal relations in the course of business'. Thus, the debate shifted towards the criteria which must be met in order to afford entity status to a civil law partnership and to what extent this (limited) entity status will be afforded.[209]

We can now categorize the types of business associations available under German law. The public company (*Aktiengesellschaft*, AG), the private company (*Gesellschaft mit beschränkter Haftung*, GmbH) and the limited partnership with a share capital (*Kommanditgesellschaft auf Aktien*, KGaA) are corporations and legal persons.[210] The AG is the business form for large publicly traded enterprises. Its share capital is divided into freely transferable shares[211] that may be offered to the public and admitted to trading at a regulated exchange.[212] The governance structure relies on three distinct bodies: (i) the shareholders' general meeting; (ii) a supervisory board; and (iii) the management board.[213] The general meeting of shareholders elects the members of the supervisory board and votes on certain fundamental issues. The supervisory board appoints and dismisses the members of the management board and supervises the management board's compliance with the law and the articles of association, as well as the business strategy. Generally, it will not be involved in the day-to-day management of the company. The management board is responsible for running the business, for representing the company vis-à-vis third parties, and for establishing business policy. Its

[204] Wiedemann (n 11) 246–8; P Ulmer, 'Die Gesamthandsgesellschaft: ein noch immer unbekanntes Wesen?' (1998) 198 Archiv für die civilistische Praxis 113.

[205] HGB, §124. [206] Windbichler (n 176) 20 (§2 para 4).

[207] BGH, 29 Januar 2001, II ZR 331/00, BGHZ 146, 341, 343.

[208] BGH, 29 Januar 2001, II ZR 331/00, BGHZ 146, 341, 358.

[209] C Gerner-Beuerle, *Die Haftung von Emissionskonsortien* (Walter de Gruyter 2009) 166–88.

[210] The registered cooperative (*eingetragene Genossenschaft*) is also corporation and legal person. Its purpose is however limited to facilitating the business of its members. Kübler and Assmann (n 173) 145.

[211] AktG, §1(2). [212] BörsG, §32. [213] AktG, §§118–149; §§95–117; §§76–94.

power to bind the company vis-à-vis third parties cannot be restricted. This two-tier board structure is one of the characteristics of German corporate law. It insulates the management of the company from any direct influence of the shareholders. And it also allows for a more direct involvement of employees in the running of the company via employee representatives on the supervisory board. The AG is strictly regulated by mostly mandatory provisions that leave only limited room for private ordering.[214] The KGaA is, contrary to what its name may suggest, not a partnership but a corporation with at least one shareholder being personally liable for the company's debts.[215] In principle, the KGaA is governed by the law applicable to AGs with the exception that the relationship of the personally liable shareholders among each other and vis-à-vis the other shareholders as a group is governed by the law on limited partnerships. In particular, it is the personally liable shareholders who have the power to manage the business and to bind the company vis-à-vis third parties. KGaA-shares may be admitted to trading on a regulated market.[216] The GmbH is much more flexible than the AG as the applicable law, to a much larger extent, is based on default provisions. Each shareholder's (initial) share is determined by his contribution.[217] The shares are freely transferable; however, transfer is subject to strict formalities (notarization)[218] which decreases liquidity of shares in GmbHs significantly. A public market does not exist. The GmbH is not subject to a compulsory two-tier board structure. The shareholders, in the articles of association or by resolution, appoint (and dismiss) one or more directors who manage the company and bind it vis-à-vis third parties.[219] Exceptionally, a supervisory board will be mandatory where the GmbH is subject to the legislation on employee co-determination.

In addition to the civil law partnership (*Gesellschaft des bürgerlichen Rechts*, GbR), partnership-type entities are the commercial partnership (*Offene Handelsgesellschaft*, OHG), the limited partnership (*Kommanditgesellschaft*, KG) and the limited liability partnership (*Partnerschaftsgesellschaft*, PartG).[220] The GbR has an immensely wide scope of application. It ranges from the very smallest ad hoc enterprises to large professional partnerships and consortia of underwriters.[221] Where the partners' enterprise is of a commercial nature, the entity will be a GbR where the extent of the activity is so limited that it does not require a commercially organized business.[222] If, however, the commercial activity increases beyond this threshold the GbR becomes an OHG by operation of law. The OHG is a partnership with the purpose of operating a commercial enterprise under a common name (*Firma*), where the partners' liability for the partnership's debts is unlimited.[223] The OHG must be registered. Internally, it has the typical features of a partnership. All partners participate actively in the management of the business and can bind the partnership vis-à-vis third parties.[224] However, death, insolvency, or withdrawal of a partner does not normally result in dissolution.[225] Where a partner withdraws, he obtains a compensation claim against the partnership for his share, but cannot force dissolution. The OHG has entity status with its own rights and obligations, it can own property in its name and can sue and be sued under its name.[226] The partners are jointly and severally liable for the OHG's debts.[227] By contrast, a KG has, in addition to one or more personally liable partners, at least one partner whose liability for the partnership's debts is limited by the amount unpaid on his promised contribution.[228] Limited partners may not participate in the management of the business and cannot bind the partnership.[229] The KG is similar to the OHG in all other respects. A very

[214] ibid §23(5). [215] ibid §278.

[216] Pursuant to BörsG, §32, only negotiable instruments may be admitted to trading on a regulated exchange.

[217] GmbHG, §14. [218] ibid §15. [219] ibid §35.

[220] HGB, §§230–236 regulates also the silent (commercial) partnership: a silent partner participates in the commercial business of another person by making a capital contribution to that business in exchange for a share in the profits. Only the non-silent partner owns the business assets and is liable for business debts.

[221] On the latter cf Gerner-Beuerle (n 209) §5. [222] HGB, §1(2). [223] ibid §105(1).

[224] ibid §§114, 125. [225] ibid §131(3). [226] ibid §124. [227] ibid §128.

[228] ibid §§161, 171. [229] ibid §§164, 170.

popular variation on the KG theme is the so-called GmbH & Co KG. The only personally liable partner is a GmbH. The directors (and shareholders) of the GmbH enjoy limited liability while managing the business of the KG. This form arguably combines the advantages of corporation and partnership and was 'invented' mainly for tax purposes.[230] The 'liberal' professions of lawyers, doctors, dentists, accountants, etc were traditionally not perceived as commercial activities that would trigger applicability of the Commercial Code (HGB). These professionals could organize only as a GbR. The PartG now provides an alternative, and natural persons who conduct one of the liberal professions may organize in the form of a limited liability partnership.[231] Much of the law that applies to the OHG is applicable to the PartG as well. However, the personal liability of partners for the partnership's debts is modified. For obligations of the partnership that arise from a partner's erroneous conduct during the completion of a mandate only the partnership and the acting partner will be liable, not the other partners.[232] For all other obligations of the partnership the partners remain jointly and severally liable.[233]

German law shows great conceptual clarity by distinguishing between the internal governance structure (corporation/partnership) and the question of attribution of rights and obligations as (part of) the external liability structure. This distinction seems indeed to hold the key for a proper understanding of the 'nature of the business corporation'. As we will see, it is only now that similar ideas seem to gain momentum in Anglo-American legal academia as well.[234] By contrast, the distinction between 'legal person', on the one hand, and 'limited legal entity status', on the other, seems to be redundant. It is not clear where any practical differences may lie; in particular, in respect of the extent that the legal entity status is limited as compared to a legal person. The latter's legal status is also limited in the sense that many rights and obligations that a natural person may have are not available for legal persons. Consider only personal rights and obligations under family law or the limited protection of legal persons by human rights under the German constitution.[235] Thus, in practical and conceptual terms it seems to be preferable to forgo the distinction and accept collectively owned partnerships as legal persons, a move that has been made by French law early on.

4. *France*

The organizational forms available under French law may be categorized in a number of different ways.[236] A classic distinction of companies (*sociétés*)[237] pertains, first, between civil law companies (*sociétés civiles*) and commercial companies (*sociétés commerciales*). The former are regulated in the Civil Code (*Code civil*, Civ), Articles 1832–1873; the latter in the Second Book of the Commercial Code (*Code de commerce*, Com). The status as a civil law company is of a subsidiary nature: a company will be a civil law company only if it is not a

[230] Windbichler (n 176) 483–95 (§37). [231] Part GG, §1. [232] ibid §8(2). [233] ibid §8(1).

[234] See below. [235] Gerner-Beuerle (n 209) 519.

[236] PL Cannu and B Dondero, *Droit de société* (6th edn, LGDJ 2015) para 2; Germain and Magnier (n 192) paras 1677–82; P Merle, *Droit commerciale sociétés commerciales* (22nd edn, Dalloz 2018/2019) para 10-21.

[237] Companies are to be distinguished from associations (*associations*). Whereas companies are formed with a view to generate a profit to be shared among its members, associations are formed for a purpose other than making a profit, that is, in principle, for a non-economic purpose. Thus, associations are the organizational form for sports clubs and for religious, political or charitable organizations. Traditionally, the state was suspicious of associations with non-economic and often political purposes. The creation of associations was, therefore, more difficult than those of companies whose economic strive for prosperity the state readily accepted. Today, the situation is reversed: associations may be formed with a minimum of formalities, whereas commercial companies are subject to a significant amount of regulation and supervision. However, associations are also being used for commercial purposes, thus straying into the territory traditionally reserved for companies. For instance, clinics, travel agencies, or sports clubs may be organized as associations with a view to generate a profit for the promoters. As a result, the law applicable to companies and associations seems to be converging in the sense that legal obligations attached to the company form are increasingly extended to associations as well. Cf Germain and Magnier (n 192) paras 1524–6; Cozian, Viandier, and Deboissy (n 10) paras 85–95.

commercial company on the basis of its form, its nature or its object.[238] Since 1966, commercial companies on the basis of their form are the commercial partnership (*société en nom collectif*, SNC), the limited partnership (*société en commandite simple*, SCS), all companies that provide limited liability for their members and all companies with a share capital.[239] In principle, therefore, a company will be a civil law company only if organized in a form other than those just mentioned and conducting a business that is not 'commercial' in nature: the liberal professions, agriculture, education, or the construction industry.[240] From the time of the great codifications until today, there was significant mutual influence between the legal regimes of civil law companies and commercial companies and the law applicable to commercial companies has ventured further and further into the domain of civil law companies.[241] Today the importance of the distinction is very limited. It is still significant for the application of the general rules on merchants to commercial companies only and for the jurisdiction of the commercial courts (*tribunaux de commerce*).[242] As such, the distinction has little bearing on internal governance structure or external liability structure. As for the latter, the main reason is that under French law, in principle, all companies, with the exception of the 'undisclosed company' (*société en participation*),[243] have legal entity status and are legal persons separate from their members (*personnalité morale*).[244] Originally, there were merely two statutory hints for this assumption: Civ Article 529 provides that the interest of a member in a commercial company is movable property even where the company owns real estate; and the former Article 69 of the Code of civil procedure provided that a commercial company was to be summoned at the home of the company (*maison sociale*).[245] However, jurisprudence did not hesitate to afford commercial companies legal personality on the basis of the mere fact of their formation. In respect of a public company (*société anonyme*, SA), legal personality was, until 1867, deemed to depend on administrative authorization or concession. In respect of civil law companies, the courts were more hesitant at first, mainly because there was no requirement of publicity or a statutory prescribed legal form. However, in the light of a continuous entanglement of the ideas of 'company' and 'legal personality', the entity status of civil law companies was recognized in 1891.[246] Since 1978, this solution can be found in Civ article 1842: civil law companies acquire separate legal personality upon registration.[247]

Legal personality of companies tries to mimic, as far as possible, the legal personality of natural persons.[248] The main difference is the 'principle of speciality' in respect of the legal personality of companies. This principle has two different aspects. It concerns, first, the definition of the company's object by its members, and, secondly, the delineation of powers among the company's different organs.[249] However, similar to natural persons, a company is designated a name, has a domicile and nationality and, most importantly, has its own patrimony.[250] The company is the owner of the assets contributed by the members upon formation and of those acquired subsequently. The members have no proprietary rights in respect

[238] Civ art 1845. [239] Germain and Magnier (n 192) para 1679; Merle (n 236) para 13.

[240] Merle (n 236) para 12. [241] Germain and Magnier (n 192) paras 1677, 1678.

[242] ibid para 1678; Merle (n 236) para 17.

[243] An undisclosed company may be either civil or commercial in nature. Traditionally, its distinguishing feature was the fact that its existence was not revealed to third parties. Each partner contracted in his own name and he alone was bound vis-à-vis third parties. Today, however, its main characteristic is merely the fact of non-registration. The existence of the company may be revealed to some or all third parties are may remain hidden. Property attributed to the partnership business may be held by a single partner or as co-ownership of the partners. Cannu and Dondero (n 236) para 17.

[244] Germain and Magnier (n 192) para 1649. [245] ibid para 1650. [246] ibid.

[247] Until registration the relationship between the members will be governed by their contract and the general law of obligations. Vis-à-vis third parties, however, the company is non-existent as a legal person. The issues arising during this formation stage are discussed in Chapter 3A.IV below.

[248] Germain and Magnier (n 192) para 1652. [249] ibid para 1653.

[250] Cannu and Dondero (n 236) paras 407–44; Germain and Magnier (n 192) paras 1659–66.

of any assets belonging to the company. Moreover, the company's patrimony is pledged exclusively to the company's creditors who thus have priority vis-à-vis the members' personal creditors as far as the company's assets are concerned. The members' personal creditors have access only to the respective member's interest in the company. There can be no set-off of company debts with a member's personal claims and vice versa. The company will be liable with its patrimony on any contracts entered into by its representatives; wrongful acts committed by its organs will be attributed to it.[251]

The 'corporation/partnership' distinction familiar from the other jurisdictions finds its equivalent in the categories of 'companies with a share capital' (*sociétés de capitaux*) and personalized companies (*sociétés de personnes*). In the latter, the personality of the members is vital. The members know each other personally and contract on the basis of mutual trust and confidence. In principle, members cannot transfer their membership rights without the consent of all other members and death or incapacity of a member, in principle, brings the company to an end. Personalized companies are the commercial partnership (SNC), the limited partnership (SCS) and all civil law companies.[252] The defining feature of the SNC is the joint and several liability of all partners for the company's debts.[253] All partners are merchants and the state of their personal finances is essential for the company's creditworthiness. The joint and several liability of the partners is, however, of a subsidiary nature: a creditor of the company may pursue a partner only after his extra-judicial attempts to gain satisfaction from the company have failed. This is a manifestation of the legal personality of the company and may be contrasted with English law where the partnership's debts are essentially the debts of the partners in the sense that their liability for the partnership's debts is a primary one, essentially liability for their own debts. Subject to the articles of association, all partners have the power to manage and represent the SNC. Under the articles, the company may have one or more directors who may or may not be partners.[254] Collective decisions require unanimity unless provided otherwise.[255] General partners in the SCS have the same status as the partners in the commercial partnership. Limited partners, however, will be liable for the company's debts only up to the amount unpaid on their promised contribution.[256] Limited partners are excluded from the management of the company. If they act in contravention of this prohibition they risk personal unlimited liability for the company's debts.[257] An amendment of the articles of association requires consent of all general partners and a majority in number and capital contribution of limited partners.[258] Subject to the articles, a limited partner may transfer his interest in the partnership only with consent of all the other partners.[259] The civil law company largely resembles the SNC; however, the partners' personal liability for the company's debts is joint (not joint and several) with the other partners.[260] That is, each partner is liable in proportion to his share in the company. The general law on civil law companies is supplemented by a number of special regulations for the different non-commercial sectors.[261] Thus, one can distinguish agricultural civil law companies, real estate civil law companies and civil law companies for the liberal professions.[262]

[251] Cannu and Dondero (n 236) para 439–44; Germain and Magnier (n 192) para 1656.
[252] Merle (n 236) paras 18, 19; Germain and Magnier (n 192) para 1684. [253] Com art L221-1.
[254] Com art L221-3. [255] Com art L221-6. [256] Com art L222-1. [257] Com art L222-6.
[258] Com art L222-9. [259] Com art L222-8.
[260] Civ art 1857. This liability is also of a subsidiary nature, Civ art 1858.
[261] Cannu and Dondero (n 236) para 6.
[262] Traditionally, members of the liberal professions were prevented from organizing in companies with a share capital. Thus, and for lack of pursuing a commercial activity, the civil law company was the only organizational form available for these professions. Today, however, the liberal professions may use the limited liability company (*société de exercise liberal à responsabilité limitée*) the public company (*société de exercise liberal à forme anonyme*) the limited partnership with a share capital (*société de exercise liberal en commandite par actiones*) and also the simplified public company (*société de exercise liberal par actiones simplifiée*). Germain and Magnier (n 192) para 1682.

In 'companies with a share capital' the personality of the members is irrelevant. Each member's contribution essentially consists of capital to be paid into the company's patrimony. In exchange, the member obtains a freely transferable share in the company. Death or incapacity of a member is immaterial for the continued existence of the company. The prime example of a company with a share capital is the public company (*société anonyme*, SA).[263] This is the company form for the large enterprise that issues shares to the public which may be listed and traded at a regulated market. The shareholders have no personal connection with each other and only a financial interest in the company. Their liability for the company's losses is limited by the amount of their contribution.[264] In terms of governance, a SA may have either a one-tier[265] or a two-tier board structure.[266] Under the one-tier board structure, the general meeting of shareholders appoints, on the basis of a majority vote, the members of the administrative board[267] who, in turn, appoint a chairman of the board[268] and may appoint a general director. The chairman or general director may take responsibility for the day-to-day running of the business.[269] The administrative board assumes a supervisory function and determines the general direction of business policy and ensures its implementation.[270] The general director and the chairman of the administrative board must not be the same person. Under the German style two-tier board system, the general meeting elects the members of the supervisory board[271] who, in turn, appoint the members of the administrative board.[272] The administrative board has general powers of management with its chairman representing the company vis-à-vis third parties.[273] The supervisory board has a purely supervisory function and must not interfere in the management of the company.[274] The simplified company limited by shares (*société par actiones simplifiée*, SAS), available since 1994, is a variation on the public company theme with much of the latter's law applicable.[275] However, the SAS leaves great contractual freedom in terms of governance structure. The only mandatory organ of the company is the president to be appointed in accordance with the articles of association and with the powers conferred therein.[276] Shares of the SAS may not be offered to the public and/or traded on a regulated market.[277]

Two hybrid forms defy easy categorization.[278] The limited partnership with a share capital (*société en commandite par actiones*, SCA) adopts a personalized structure in respect of the general partners who are personally liable for the company's debts.[279] The limited partners, however, hold freely transferable shares which may be offered to the public and traded on a regulated market. In this respect this form exhibits all the features of a company with a share capital.[280] A German import of 1925, the limited liability company (*société à responsabilité limitée*, SARL) provides its members with limited liability up to the amount of their contributions.[281] It is managed by one or more directors appointed in the statutes or by majority vote of the members.[282] The number of members is limited (1 up to 100).[283] The members' interests in the company are not negotiable instruments.[284] They are transferable, but the other members may control the transfer to third parties as a majority in number of members representing at least half of the shares of the company must consent, unless the articles of associations provide for a higher majority.[285] The SARL combines limited liability as a feature

[263] Merle (n 236) para 18. [264] Com art L225-1. [265] Com art L225-17.
[266] Com art L225-57. [267] Com art L225-18. [268] Com art L225-47.
[269] Com art L225-51-1. [270] Com art L225-35. [271] Com art L225-75.
[272] Com art L225-59. [273] Com arts L225-64; L.225-66. [274] Com art L225-58.
[275] Com art L227-1. [276] Com art L227-6. [277] Com art L227-2.
[278] Another form is the cooperative society (*société cooperative*). It is formed in order to satisfy some specific needs of its members. Their involvement goes beyond the mere capital contribution. It extends also to contracting with the cooperative as seller, buyer, service provider etc. Merle (n 236) para 15.
[279] Com art L226-1. [280] Merle (n 236) para 19. [281] Com art L223-1.
[282] Com art L223-18. [283] Com art L223-3. [284] Com art L223-12.
[285] Com art L223-14. The members' interests are freely transferable to other members of the company, Com art L223-16.

of the public company with simplicity and a personalized relationship among its limited number of members.[286]

In addition to these classic categorizations (civil law companies/commercial companies; companies with a share capital/personalized companies), modern literature sometimes distinguishes, arguably in a more adequate fashion,[287] between companies with limited liability and companies were the liability of members is unlimited. SA, SARL, and SAS belong to the former group; SNC and civil law companies to the latter,[288] with SCS and SCA constituting hybrid forms.[289] Another important distinction pertains between listed companies and non-listed companies. Listed companies are subject to significant additional regulation in respect of disclosure requirements and functioning and allocation of powers between the company's organs.[290] Only SAs and SCAs may offer their shares to the public and/or have them listed to be traded on a regulated market.

The greatest achievement of French law seems to have been its early recognition of separate legal personality for all companies. This avoided the exhausting battles between the aggregate and entity theory camps that we have seen in the United States and Germany; it also avoids the practical and conceptual problems of treating the partnership as an aggregate, as is still the case in England.

II. The essential properties of the business corporation

Corporation and partnership as institutional archetypes for addressing the horizontal pooling problem cater for different types of organizations and deal with the costs of shirking and opportunism in different ways.

In partnership-type organizations the personal contributions of each participant in terms of skills, knowledge and wealth provide the *raison d'être* for the horizontal pooling of resources and for the existence of the partnership. The identity and personality of each partner matters. At the same time, each partner's investment is likely to be firm-specific to a significant degree as otherwise there would be no reason to participate as general partner. This is reflected in the internal governance structure as well as the external liability structure. Partners' extensive control rights, culminating in termination of the partnership by withdrawal, may result in significant 'holdups': by vetoing management decisions or threatening to withdraw, 'difficult' partners have great leverage to extract unjustified personal benefits at the expense of the enterprise as a whole. This is kept in check, however, by the close personal relationships between the partners, based on mutual trust and confidence, sometimes enhanced by family ties. Where these relationships break down the partnership comes to an end. As a consequence, the partnership, even if granted legal entity status, can be inherently unstable and dissolution may destroy the value of any firm-specific investment. This inherent risk of a decrease in value of partnership property renders contracting on market terms more expensive. At the same time, the personal liability of the partners for the partnership's obligations reduces the risk of default for partnership creditors by making accessible, in addition to partnership assets, the personal assets of the partners. Certainly, the inherent flexibility of the partnership form allows for significant modifications. This accounts for the varied nature of businesses organized as partnerships and allowed the rise of the multi-national professional partnerships with thousands of partners, today often organized as LLP. The fact remains, however, that the archetypical partnership is a small or medium-sized venture with

[286] Cannu and Dondero (n 236) para 9. [287] ibid para 3.

[288] In the economic interest grouping (*groupement d'intérêt économique*, GIE) members are also jointly and severally liable for the grouping's debts. The purpose of the GIE is to facilitate or develop the economic activity of its members. It was the blueprint for the European Economic Interest Grouping which, so far, has been of little practical relevance.

[289] Cannu and Dondero (n 236) paras 15, 16. [290] ibid para 21–3.

a limited number of partners who all significantly contribute to the day to day running of the business and who are personally liable for the partnership's debts.

By contrast, corporations cater for a large and fluctuating membership with little in terms of personal relationships between contributors of capital whose identity is largely irrelevant. If we look at the corporate law literature in different jurisdictions, we often find listed a number of core features that aim to define the corporate form and try to account for its success as a vehicle for large-scale business: (i) the corporation is a separate legal entity distinct from its members and hence capable of enjoying rights and of being subject to duties which are not the same as those enjoyed or borne by its members; (ii) contractual obligations and debts of the corporation are strictly the corporation's, the shareholders (or directors or employees) are not liable for the corporation's debts and risk only the amount they paid for their shares; (iii) assets of the corporation are held by the corporation and are separated from the shareholders; (iv) the corporation can take action to enforce its rights and can be sued for breach of its legal duties; (v) there is, in principle, no limit on the duration of the corporation, it remains legally unaffected by the death or withdrawal of any shareholder; (vi) investors' interests are reflected in shares of common stock as items of property which are freely transferable and which may be bought or sold on established markets; (vii) management and control of the business is delegated to a smaller group of experts who partly constitute and who are partly supervised by a board of directors.[291]

Occasionally, these lists are extended. In the UK, for instance, only companies incorporated under the Companies Acts can, in order to provide security for their debts, grant floating charges over the fluctuating pool of all the assets owned by the company from time to time,[292] whilst the company remains able to dispose of these assets in the ordinary course of business. This is, however, a national peculiarity[293] and in other legal systems the functional equivalent of this type of security is available to other forms of business organization as well. Both, German law and French law put great emphasis on the corporation's share capital as a defining feature of AG[294] and SA,[295] respectively. The rules on capital adequacy and capital maintenance are seen as the price that the latter have to pay for the privilege of limited liability.[296] However, in the United States the concept of legal capital lost its significance a long time ago.[297]

Sometimes 'investor ownership of the firm' is added as a further defining element.[298] 'Investor ownership of the firm' signifies the combination of the right to participate in control and the right to receive the firm's net earnings in proportion to the amount of capital contributed to the firm.[299] This is essentially a specification of element (vi), the free transferability of shares, as it defines the content of the bundle of rights conferred by holding a share in the corporation. Speak of 'ownership of the firm' is seriously misleading. Shareholders own shares in the company and in respect of the shares as items of property shareholders have all the powers and responsibilities normally associated with 'ownership'.[300] In respect of

[291] Klein, Coffee, and Partnoy (n 7) 108–10; Davies and Worthington (n 8) paras 2-1–2-33.

[292] CA 2006, Pt 25.

[293] A charge over chattels granted by individuals would be a bill of sale under the Bill of Sale Acts 1878 and 1882. The strict formalities imposed by these Acts, in particular the detailed specification of the covered chattels, render a floating charge impossible.

[294] AktG, §1(2). [295] Com art L225-1.

[296] Kübler and Assmann (n 173) 157–60; Germain and Magnier (n 192) para 1787.

[297] Klein, Coffee, and Partnoy (n 7) 230.

[298] Kraakman and others (n 6) 13–14; A Cahn and DC Donald, *Comparative Company Law* (CUP 2010) 9.

[299] Kraakman and others (n 6) 13.

[300] 'Ownership' is a difficult concept as it has significantly different meanings in civil law and common law jurisdictions. Without being too philosophical, it can probably be defined as the comprehensive right to deal with an asset within the limits set by law and prior rights of third parties. At the same time the owner is responsible for any harm caused by using the asset; cf BGB, §903; Article 544 Civ; E McKendrick (ed), *Goode on Commercial Law* (5th edn, Penguin 2017) 34–6.

the 'firm', the shareholder has a financial right to participate proportionally in dividends and distributions and to elect directors and vote on certain major transactions. Shareholders do not have a direct claim on any of the tangible or intangible assets of the corporation, nor do they generally have a right to control directly the decision-making by managers. Thus, in respect of the firm shareholders' rights are very limited and do not justify the label 'ownership' as commonly understood.[301] Moreover, 'investor ownership' has ideological connotations. It seeks to lend moral force to the claim that the company should be run, exclusively, in the best interest of its shareholder-owners.[302] Whether such a claim is justified requires careful analysis[303] and should not be obscured by a concept of 'investor ownership' that has little substantive content.

Instead, looking again at the list provided above, it seems possible to narrow it down. The ability to hold property (iii), to sue and be sued (iv) as well as unlimited duration irrespective of death or withdrawal of a member (v) follow directly from the corporation having separate legal personality (i). By contrast, the limitation of liability of the members of an organization for the latter's debts does not follow logically or by necessity from legal entity status.[304] Even if the legal order awards separate legal personality to a group it may still provide that some or all of its members will be liable, in full or partially, in addition to the group for any obligations incurred by the latter. We have seen that this is the case in respect of the SNC and managing partners of the SCS under French law[305] as well as for partnerships under UPA 1997 in the United States.[306] The Companies Act 2006 allows for the formation of 'unlimited companies' in the UK. And even German law, where the status of legal personality is traditionally reserved for companies with a share capital and registered associations with limited liability, grants GbR and OHG a status on all important accounts similar to that of legal persons.

This leaves us with four essential features: (i) separate legal personality (or legal entity status); (ii) limited liability; (iii) free transferability of shares; and (iv) centralized management and control.[307] As we will see, limited liability and entity status in combination, if not a necessary precondition, at least greatly facilitate the transferability of shares and the centralization of management and control. Separate legal personality and limited liability define the external liability structure of the corporate form and provide the necessary bedrock for a corporate internal governance structure. These two principles are distinct concepts.[308] They have developed separately and have entered the corporate stage at different times. Nonetheless, they are interrelated in that they, in combination, account for the defining features of modern corporate law. This makes it necessary to have a closer look at the precise meaning of the concepts of 'separate legal personality' and 'limited liability' and their economic rationale.

Questions and comments:

1. Two entrepreneurs, Mark and Eduardo, would like to form a start-up business for operating a social networking site. Their own contributions consist mainly of human capital: experience, technical know-how and expertise, and an implicit promise to provide future services to the enterprise. They also contribute intellectual property in the form of a software code for a social networking website and US$25,000 in cash. In future, they would like to locate investors—venture capitalists—to finance the business. They look for an initial investment of

[301] MM Blair, 'Corporate "Ownership": A Misleading Word Muddies the Corporate Governance Debate' (1995) 13 The Brookings Review 16, 17.
[302] ibid 18. For further details see Chapter 4A.II.
[303] Cf Chapter 4A.II.
[304] Wiedemann (n 11) 202.
[305] Com Arts L210-6; L221-1; L222-1.
[306] UPA 1997, s 201(a); s 306(a).
[307] Choper, Coffee, and Gilson (n 97) 1–3.
[308] A Diamond, 'Corporate Personality and Limited Liability' in T Orhnial (ed), *Limited Liability and the Corporation* (Croom Helm 1982) 22, 34.

US$5million in exchange for certain 'cash flow and/or control rights'. Mark and Eduardo also hope to obtain non-monetary contributions from the venture capitalist in the form of management advice and mentorship, and possibly a commitment to contribute in future rounds of financing.[309] Mark and Eduardo ask for your advice as to the most appropriate legal structure for their new business.

2. What potential shirking and hold-up problems can you foresee in this example?
3. What are the advantages and disadvantages of forming a company/corporation as compared to any of the other types of business organization we discussed in the preceding paragraphs? What type of vehicle should Mark and Eduardo choose for their business and why?[310] Does your answer depend on the jurisdiction they would like to operate under?
4. The choice of business vehicle is often driven by tax considerations. Companies/corporations are, in principle, treated as separate legal entities for income tax purposes. By contrast, partnership-like vehicles are usually taxed on the basis of a 'look through' approach. Profits and losses of the partnership are attributed directly to the partners on a pro rata basis. In terms of tax planning, what are the advantages and disadvantages of the different forms?[311] In case of a company/corporation, where are profits taxed, at company level or at shareholder level? By what means can the resulting problems be alleviated? Explain the significance of losses for tax purposes as a great advantage of partnership-type forms.

B. Separate Legal Personality

I. Meaning

In French and German legislation, we find clear statements on the separate legal personality of companies and corporations. Under French law, any commercial company attains legal personality with registration in the commercial and company register.[312] Also, under German law, the AG is a 'company with separate legal personality',[313] and the GmbH 'as such' may have its own rights and obligations.[314] In the United States, DGCL, §106 provides that, upon filing the certificate of incorporation with the Secretary of State, the incorporator or incorporators shall 'be and constitute a body corporate'. Pursuant to MBCA, §3.02, a corporation has 'the same powers as an individual to do all things necessary or convenient to carry out its business and affairs'. It is generally accepted that a corporation validly incorporated under state law is an 'entity separate and distinct from its stockholders'.[315] Frequently, courts speak of the separate corporate entity as a 'legal fiction'[316] designed to serve practical convenience by reducing complexity.[317] Similarly, under the Companies Act 2006, upon registration, the subscribers to the memorandum of association, together with subsequent members of the company, are a 'body corporate' capable of exercising all the functions of an incorporated company.[318] The meaning of this phrase was elucidated in the seminal case *of Salomon v A Salomon and Co Ltd* [1897] AC 22.

***Salomon v A Salomon & Co Ltd* [1897] AC 22**

The appellant, Aron Salomon, had been carrying on business as a leather merchant and wholesale boot manufacturer in the form of a sole proprietorship very successfully for many years. In 1892 he decided to carry on trading in form of a joint stock company, mainly in order to expand

[309] V Fleischer, 'Taxing Founders' Stock' (2011) 59 UCLA Law Review 60,70-1; *The Social Network* (Columbia Pictures 2010).
[310] V Fleischer, 'The Rational Exuberance of Structuring Venture Capital Startups' (2003) 57 Tax Law Review 137.
[311] ibid. [312] Com art L210-6. [313] AktG, §1(1). [314] GmbHG, §13(1).
[315] See eg *Illinois Central Railroad Company v Mississippi Cotton Seed Products Company*, 166 Miss. 579, 148 So. 371 (1933). Cf Fletcher (n 90) §25.
[316] For instance: *DeWitt Truck Brokers, Inc. v W. Ray Flemming Fruit Co.*, 540 F.2d 681 (CASC, 1976) ('corporate fiction'); *Zaist v Olson*, 227 A.2d 552 (Conn, 1967) ('fiction of separate legal entity').
[317] Fletcher (n 90) §25. [318] CA 2006, s 16(2), (3).

and to make provision for his family. A memorandum of association was executed by the appellant, his wife, a daughter, and four sons, each of them subscribing for one share. All the requirements of the Companies Act 1862 were duly observed and upon registration the company was incorporated under the name of 'Aron Salomon and Company, Limited' with liability limited by shares, and a nominal capital of £40,000, divided into 40,000 shares of £1 each. Subsequently, the appellant's business was transferred to the company. The price fixed by the contract, more than £39,000, exceeded the market value considerably. It was paid for in the following way: out of cash flows £30,000 were paid to Mr Salomon, and then immediately returned to the company in exchange for 20,000 fully-paid shares and promissory notes secured on the company's property (debentures) over the amount of £10,000. The balance of £9,000 was used to discharge the debts and liabilities of the business at the time of the transfer. As a result, Mr Salomon was debt free and holding 20,001 shares in the company and a preferential claim, because of the debentures, on all its assets; 6 shares were held by his wife and children.

Shortly after formation the company fell on hard times. Mr Salomon obtained a loan from a Mr Broderip over £5000 which were immediately handed over to the company. The loan was secured on the debentures held by Mr Salomon which were later cancelled and reissued to Mr. Broderip. After the company defaulted on its obligations, Mr. Broderip instituted an action in order to enforce his security against the assets of the company and the company went into liquidation. The amount realised from the assets of the company was sufficient to discharge Mr Broderip's claim. The remaining balance of about £1055 was claimed by Mr Salomon as beneficial owner of the debentures. Nothing was left for payment of the unsecured creditors, whose claims amounted to about £8000.

The liquidator lodged a counter claim against the appellant, Mr. Salomon, essentially for rescission of the original transfer agreements and repayment of all sums paid by the company to the appellant under these agreements. This claim did not succeed. However, after amendment of the counter claim, Vaughan Williams J. at first instance held that the company was a mere agent to Mr Salomon and was thus entitled to be indemnified by the appellant against the whole of the company's unsecured debts. The Court of Appeal did not follow the judge's reasoning. It held instead that the company was trustee and the appellant *cestui que* trust. This did not change the outcome of the appellant being obliged to indemnify the company.

Both the company and Mr Salomon appealed to the House of Lords.

Lord Halsbury LC

My Lords, the important question in this case, I am not certain it is not the only question, is whether the respondent company was a company at all - whether in truth that artificial creation of the Legislature had been validly constituted in this instance; and in order to determine that question it is necessary to look at what the statute itself has determined in that respect. I have no right to add to the requirements of the statute, nor to take from the requirements thus enacted. The sole guide must be the statute itself.

Now, that there were seven actual living persons who held shares in the company has not been doubted. As to the proportionate amounts held by each I will deal presently; but it is important to observe that this first condition of the statute is satisfied, and it follows as a consequence that it would not be competent to any one - and certainly not to these persons themselves - to deny that they were shareholders.

I must pause here to point out that the statute enacts nothing as to the extent or degree of interest which may be held by each of the seven, or as to the proportion of interest or influence possessed by one or the majority of the share-holders over the others. One share is enough. Still less is it possible to contend that the motive of becoming shareholders or of making them shareholders is a field of inquiry which the statute itself recognises as legitimate. If they are shareholders, they are shareholders for all purposes; ...

I am simply here dealing with the provisions of the statute, and it seems to me to be essential to the artificial creation that the law should recognise only that artificial existence—quite apart from the motives or conduct of individual corporators ... [S]hort of [proof of fraud] it seems to me impossible to dispute that once the company is legally incorporated it must be treated like any other independent person with its rights and liabilities appropriate to itself, and that the motives of those who took part in the promotion of the company are absolutely irrelevant in discussing what those rights and liabilities are.

I will for the sake of argument assume the proposition that the Court of Appeal lays down - that the formation of the company was a mere scheme to enable Aron Salomon to carry on business in the name of the company. I am wholly unable to follow the proposition that this was contrary to the true intent and meaning of the Companies Act. I can only find the true intent and meaning of the Act from the Act itself; and the Act appears to me to give a company a legal existence with, as I have said, rights and liabilities of its own, whatever may have been the ideas or schemes of those who brought it into existence ...

If the Legislature intended to prohibit something, you ought to know what that something is. All it has said is that one share is sufficient to constitute a shareholder, though the shares may be 100,000 in number. Where am I to get from the statute itself a limitation of that provision that that shareholder must be an independent and beneficially interested person?

My Lords, I find all through the judgment of the Court of Appeal a repetition of the same proposition to which I have already adverted - that the business was the business of Aron Salomon, and that the company is variously described as a myth and a fiction ...

My Lords, the learned judges appear to me not to have been absolutely certain in their own minds whether to treat the company as a real thing or not. If it was a real thing; if it had a legal existence, and if consequently the law attributed to it certain rights and liabilities in its constitution as a company, it appears to me to follow as a consequence that it is impossible to deny the validity of the transactions into which it has entered ...

My Lords, the truth is that the learned judges have never allowed in their own minds the proposition that the company has a real existence. Then have been struck by what they have considered the inexpediency of permitting one man to be in influence and authority the whole company; and, assuming that such a thing could not have been intended by the Legislature, they have sought various grounds upon which they might insert into the Act some prohibition of such a result. Whether such a result be right or wrong, politic or impolitic, I say, with the utmost deference to the learned judges, that we have nothing to do with that question if this company has been duly constituted by law; and, whatever may be the motives of those who constitute it, I must decline to insert into that Act of Parliament limitations which are not to be found there.

I have dealt with this matter upon the narrow hypothesis propounded by the learned judges below; but it is, I think, only justice to the appellant to say that I see nothing whatever to justify the imputations which are implied in some of the observations made by more than one of the learned judges. The appellant, in my opinion, is not shewn to have done or to have intended to do anything dishonest or unworthy, but to have suffered a great misfortune without any fault of his own.

Lord Macnaghten

When the memorandum is duly signed and registered, though there be only seven shares taken, the subscribers are a body corporate 'capable forthwith', to use the words of the enactment, 'of exercising all the functions of an incorporated company'. Those are strong words. The company attains maturity on its birth. There is no period of minority - no interval of incapacity. I cannot understand how a body corporate thus made 'capable' by statute can lose its individuality by issuing the bulk of its capital to one person, whether he be a subscriber to the memorandum or not. The company is at law a different person altogether from the subscribers to the memorandum; and, though it may be that after incorporation the business is precisely the same as it was before, and the same persons are managers, and the same hands receive the profits, the company is not in law the agent of the subscribers or trustee for them. Nor are the subscribers as members liable, in any shape or form, except to the extent and in the manner provided by the Act. That is, I think, the declared intention of the enactment. If the view of the learned judge were sound, it would follow that no common law partnership could register as a company limited by shares without remaining subject to unlimited liability ...

Among the principal reasons which induce persons to form private companies, as is stated very clearly by Mr. Palmer in his treatise on the subject, are the desire to avoid the risk of bankruptcy, and the increased facility afforded for borrowing money. By means of a private company, as Mr. Palmer observes, a trade can be carried on with limited liability, and without exposing the persons interested in it in the event of failure to the harsh provisions of the bankruptcy law. A company, too, can raise money on debentures, which an ordinary trader cannot do. Any member of a company, acting in good faith, is as much entitled to take and hold the company's debentures as any outside creditor. Every creditor is entitled to get and to hold the best security the law allows him to take …

The unsecured creditors of A. Salomon and Company, Limited, may be entitled to sympathy, but they have only themselves to blame for their misfortunes. They trusted the company, I suppose, because they had long dealt with Mr. Salomon, and he had always paid his way; but they had full notice that they were no longer dealing with an individual, and they must be taken to have been cognizant of the memorandum and of the articles of association. For such a catastrophe as has occurred in this case some would blame the law that allows the creation of a floating charge. But a floating charge is too convenient a form of security to be lightly abolished. I have long thought, and I believe some of your Lordships also think, that the ordinary trade creditors of a trading company ought to have a preferential claim on the assets in liquidation in respect of debts incurred within a certain limited time before the winding-up. But that is not the law at present. Everybody knows that when there is a winding-up debenture-holders generally step in and sweep off everything; and a great scandal it is.

LORD WATSON, LORD HERSHELL, LORD MORRIS and LORD DAVEY concurred.

Questions and comments:

1. The case is often referred to as the cornerstone or bedrock of English company law and credited with establishing that a company incorporated under the Companies Acts has a legal personality separate from those of its members. However, the idea that incorporated entities can be the subject of rights and obligations had, by 1897, long been accepted in English law. The case nevertheless represents a major paradigm shift in the understanding of the corporate form. The nineteenth-century Companies Acts did not purport to introduce a new form of business organization. Rather, it allowed joint stock companies organized in partnership form to obtain the advantages of separate legal existence. In the eyes of the law the company remained a kind of partnership and the shareholders its collective owners. It meant that the existence of a genuine partnership, consisting, first, of at least twenty-five, later of seven members, was a prerequisite for incorporation. *Salomon* did away with this. The idea of an association of individuals, governed by partnership principles, was replaced by an entity concept which completely separated the company and its members.[319] This concept has never been questioned since.
2. In addition, the case made the corporate form with separate legal personality and limited liability widely available for small private partnerships and sole traders.
3. Further, the case elucidates vividly the distributive consequences of incorporation and of the entity concept. By holding effectively 100 per cent of the outstanding shares Mr. Salomon could take full benefit of any upside gains. At the same time, not only was his liability limited by his initial contribution; as a secured creditor he obtained a preferential claim on this contribution and on any proceeds and profits derived from it, in priority to unsecured creditors. As a sole trader he could not have achieved this result.[320] How can we justify, in policy terms, this preferential treatment of incorporated businesses as compared to sole traders? Remember, the construction in *Salomon* only worked because at no point during the transaction did Mr Salomon act fraudulently, neither vis-à-vis the other shareholders nor the pre- and post-incorporation creditors. In the absence of fraud, can you think of any legal devices that could

[319] R Grantham, 'The Doctrinal Basis of the Rights of Company Shareholders' (1998) 57 CLJ 554, 561.

[320] Under French law, it is possible for a sole trader to separate its personal wealth from the property allocated to the business in a separate patrimony with only the latter being liable for the obligations incurred in the course of conducting the business; on this concept of 'individual entrepreneur with limited liability' (*entrepreneur individuel à responsabilité limitée*) see Merle (n 236) para 9.

be used in order to avoid the result of a shareholder as secured creditor having exclusive access to the company's assets (for a possible answer see text below)?

4. In Lord Macnaghten's view, the unsecured creditors 'have only themselves to blame for their misfortunes'. Do you agree with this assessment? Under what circumstances and in respect of what types of creditors does this argument (only) work?

The core of separate legal personality or entity status seems to be universally accepted. With incorporation, the law recognizes the company or corporation as a separate allocative end-point for the attribution of rights and obligations. These rights and obligations are solely the rights and obligations of the legal entity and are not attributed to any other person. The assets of the legal entity are reserved for the legal entity's creditors and are committed, exclusively, for discharging the obligations entered into in the entity's name. The pool of assets (and obligations) attributed to the legal person is completely separated from the members and other participants.[321] Thus, at least in Europe, members do not have any (proprietary) interest in the assets attributed to the company. In the words of Lord Buckmaster:

> [no] shareholder has any right to any item of property owned by the company, for he has no legal or equitable interest therein. He is entitled to a share in the profits while the company continues to carry on business and a share in the distribution of the surplus assets when the company is wound up.[322]

Thus, even where all shares in a company are held by a single person this person does not have an insurable interest as regards the company's property.[323] Member's rights are limited to participation rights in cash flows generated during the lifetime of the company paid out via dividends and a share in the distribution of assets upon liquidation. Personal creditors of members do not have access to the assets of the entity. These creditors can only look to, and levy assessment on, the membership rights of their respective debtors.[324] In the United States, members' interests in the corporation's property are treated somewhat differently. It has been held that shareholders do have an equitable interest in the corporation's property. This seems to mean nothing more than that, if the corporation is liquidated, the shareholders will become the legal owners of the corporate property.[325] However:

> A stockholder in a private corporation for profit is not in any proper sense the owner of the property of the corporation as such. He has, however, a direct interest in the corporation ... A stockholder has an insurable interest in the property of the corporation.[326]

Here a less far-reaching reification of the corporation under US law generates concrete practical differences.

As a consequence of the separation of entity and members, a member of a company cannot claim compensation for damage done to the company's property or business or bring legal proceedings to obtain redress for injury done to the company.[327] The company alone has standing to enforce its rights and to seek redress for the wrongs it has suffered.[328] Also, as a separate legal person, the company interacts with its members in the same way as it does with any other third parties. With its members it can, in principle, enter into any contracts be it for the transfer of property, for services, or for employment. Thus, in a single person company, one and the same natural person may act in a threefold capacity as the only shareholder, director, and employee of the company.[329]

321 Wiedemann (n 11) 196–9.
322 *Macaura v Northern Assurance Company* [1925] AC 619 (Privy Council). 323 ibid.
324 Wiedemann (n 11) 197. 325 *Fowler v Shadel*, 400 F.3d 1016 C.A.7 (Wis.) 2005.
326 *Richter v Blasingame*, 110 Cal. 530, 42 P. 1077 (Cal. 1895) (references omitted).
327 D French, *Mayson, French and Ryan on Company Law* (35th edn, OUP 2018-2019) 106; Wiedemann (n 11) 199.
328 The exception is so-called derivative actions or claims; cf Chapter 8C.II.
329 *Lee v Lee's Air Farming Ltd* [1961] AC 12; Fletcher (n 90) §29; Wiedemann (n 11) 214.

The law, in general, is geared towards individual human actors. The concept of separate legal personality attempts to treat, as far as possible, legal persons in the same way as natural persons.[330] Legal entities are assigned a name, a seat or domicile, and nationality.[331] In principle, a legal entity may enjoy all the economic rights that a natural person can hold: contractual rights, property rights, claims arising from torts or restitution, choses in action and in possession, real property, intellectual property rights, and membership rights. A legal entity will be (vicariously) liable for torts committed by its employees or its organs in the course of acting on behalf of the entity.[332] In the common law jurisdictions,[333] and since 1994 also in France,[334] a legal entity may even be criminally liable for offences committed on its behalf.

However, there are insurmountable differences between natural and legal persons that prevent a complete alignment of the legal treatment of both concepts. A legal entity can only have rights and incur liabilities that do not, by their very nature, require a natural person as allocative end-point. This is first and foremost the case with personal rights that relate to some human capacity. The most prominent examples are certain constitutional guarantees and fundamental rights. The following extract from *Browning-Ferris Industries of Vermont, Inc. v Kelco Disposal, Inc.*, (Justice O'Connor) captures the US position:

***Browning-Ferris Industries of Vermont, Inc. v Kelco Disposal, Inc.*, 492 US 257 (1989)**

In the words of Chief Justice Marshall, a corporation is 'an artificial being, invisible, intangible, and existing only in contemplation of law' ... As such, it is not entitled to 'purely personal' guarantees whose 'historic function'... has been limited to the protection of individuals' ... Thus, a corporation has no Fifth Amendment privilege against self-incrimination ... On the other hand, a corporation has a First Amendment right to freedom of speech ... and cannot have its property taken without just compensation ... A corporation is also protected from unreasonable searches and seizures ... and can plead former jeopardy as a bar to a prosecution ... Furthermore, a corporation is entitled to due process ... and equal protection ... of law.

Whether a particular constitutional guarantee applies to corporations 'depends on the nature, history, and purpose' of the guarantee ... The payment of monetary penalties, unlike the ability to remain silent, is something that a corporation can do as an entity, and the Court has reviewed fines and monetary penalties imposed on corporations under the Fourteenth Amendment at a time when the Eighth Amendment did not apply to the States ... If a corporation is protected by the Due Process Clause from overbearing and oppressive monetary sanctions, it is also protected from such penalties by the Excessive Fines Clause.[335]

The German constitution (*Grundgesetz*) provides in Article 19(3) that the constitutional rights and guarantees generally applicable to individuals may protect domestic legal persons established under private law 'to the extent that the respective rights, as to their nature, are applicable to these legal persons'. Thus, the rights relevant to, and protective of, the conduct of an economic activity can generally be relied upon by legal persons. These rights include the rights to free enjoyment of property, the right to freedom of occupation, and rights to freedom of association and assembly. By contrast, constitutional rights that relate to natural properties of human beings are unavailable to legal persons. These are, in particular, the rights to human dignity, the right to life and bodily integrity, rights to non-discrimination

[330] Germain and Magnier (n 192) para 1659. In that sense, the corporation as a legal person amounts to a 'legal fiction' in that the law extends the application of legal rules to an additional set of situations for which the rules as initially conceived were not intended; T Lawson, 'The nature of the firm and peculiarities of the corporation' (2015) 39 Cambridge Journal of Economics 1, 18–19.

[331] Germain and Magnier (n 192) paras 1660–6; Wiedemann (n 11) 211.

[332] Wiedemann (n 11) 213; Germain and Magnier (n 192) para 1673; Fletcher (n 90) §33; Davies and Worthington (n 8) paras 7-31–7.37.

[333] Fletcher (n 90) §34; Davies and Worthington (n 8) paras 7-38–7-46.

[334] Germain and Magnier (n 192) para 1674. In Germany, legal persons may be fined for misdemeanours pursuant to §30 *Gesetz über Ordnungswidrigkeiten*. Criminal liability, however, is not generally recognized.

[335] *Browning-Ferris Industries of Vermont, Inc. v Kelco Disposal, Inc.*, 492 US 257 (1989) 284–5 (references omitted).

on the basis of personal attributes such as sex, race, health etc, the right to family life, and the right not to be subjected to forced labour.[336] However, legal persons may enjoy certain aspects of the general right to freedom of personality, such as the right to one's own spoken word, as the following extract demonstrates.

BVerfGE 106, 28 (2002)

2. The right to one's own spoken word is applicable to legal persons formed under private law. The applicant as GmbH is such a legal person.

The question whether the general right to personality is applicable to legal persons formed under private law has as yet not been decided constitutionally and is in dispute among legal scholars ... By contrast, the civil courts have recognised that, in principle, legal persons may enjoy protection of their personality... The current constitutional complaint procedure does not give occasion to decide the issue comprehensively, as the right at issue here is merely the right to one's own spoken word.

a) Pursuant to Art. 19(3) GG, it is decisive whether the right to one's own spoken word is, as to its nature, applicable to legal persons. According to the jurisprudence of the *Bundesverfassungsgericht*, a fundamental right cannot be extended to legal persons, created by the legal order merely for a certain purpose, where the protection relates to properties, ways of communication or relationships that are unique to natural persons ... By contrast, protection may be extended to legal persons, where the fundamental right may be exercised also in corporate form. For instance, a limited partnership [KG] may enjoy the right to respect for its home (Art. 13(1) GG), because, in the same way as individuals, it may lawfully have a home ... Art. 13(1) GG's origin as a personal and individual right that guarantees, in light of human dignity and free evolvement, the individual person a fundamental living space ... does not prevent the extension of protection to legal persons. The same applies to the right to secrecy of telecommunications pursuant to Art. 10(1) GG ... Legal persons may use the transfer medium of telecommunication facilities and are, therefore, in a situation similar to natural persons as regards the typical dangers for an infringement of fundamental rights. In addition, the right to secrecy of telecommunications relates to the use of a specific transfer medium and does not require a content relating to a certain personal sphere.

b) The application to legal persons of the right to one's own spoken word is not prevented by the fact that the general right to personality originated as an individual right protecting the free evolvement of the personality also on the basis of the right to human dignity. Currently, only the right to one's own spoken word as one element of the general right to personality is at issue. The protection of this right is independent from any specific personal content of the communication. It guarantees that all participants in the communication process may conduct their behaviour self-determined and in accordance with the situation. In this context, a legal person, communicating via natural persons, may find itself in a situation characterised by the typical dangers for an infringement of fundamental rights.[337]

Similar principles apply under French law in respect of rights protecting reputation and honour.[338]

Differences between legal and natural persons also persist in many other areas. Many of these are subject to the randomness of positive law and not necessarily intrinsic to the 'nature' of the legal person.[339] In two areas, however, we may be able to discern at least

[336] T Kingreen and R Poscher, *Grundrechte Staatsrecht II* (32nd edn, CF Müller 2016) paras 163–86.

[337] BVerfGE 106, 28, 42 (2002).

[338] Cannu and Dondero (n 236) para 434.

[339] For instance, under German law, only natural persons may be members of administrative or supervisory boards of an AG (AktG, §§76(3) 100(1)) or directors of a GmbH (GmbHG, §6(2)). Similarly, under Delaware law only natural persons may be members of the board of directors (DGCL, §141(b)). By contrast, in the UK, prior to the Small Business, Enterprise and Employment Act 2015 (s 87) a company could serve as director of another company if at least one director was a natural person. Under French law, a legal person may be a director of an SA with a single-tier board structure (article L.225-20 Com.) or a member of the supervisory board, but not the management board, in case of a two-tier board structure (articles L.225-76, L.225-59 Com.). Director of a SARL may only be a natural person (article L.223-18 Com.).

general tendencies. Since legal persons are formed for a particular purpose it would seem natural that this purpose also limits the legal personality, and in particular the legal capacity, of the entity so formed.[340] This is indeed the gist of the classic common law doctrine of *ultra vires*. If a company acted beyond the scope of its objects as stated in its articles or memorandum of association such acts were void as beyond the company's capacity even if ratified by all members.[341] In France, the principle of speciality (*principe de spécialité*) was to the same effect.[342] However, it was abolished for SARLs and SAs as early as 1966. In the UK, the *ultra vires* doctrine, already substantially modified and limited by case law,[343] lost much of its significance with the implementation of the First Company Law Directive, abolishing the doctrine as far as third parties are concerned.[344] A similar tendency is apparent in the United States since the 1960s[345] with modern corporation statutes expressly authorizing the broadest of all-purpose clauses: 'to engage in any lawful act or activity'.[346] German law never recognized a similar doctrine for legal persons formed under private law and always put great emphasis on the protection of legitimate expectations of third parties.[347]

Above we said that a company may contract with its members in the same way as it contracts with third parties. This statement requires some qualification. There are situations where members as contractors will be treated differently. Under German law, the contractual claims of a shareholder holding at least 10 per cent of the share capital who has advanced a loan to his company will be automatically assigned deferred claim status in the company's insolvency and will be subordinated to the claims of general unsecured creditors.[348] Under US federal bankruptcy law, the court has the power of equitable subordination:[349] the claim against the corporation of a corporate insider be it a shareholder, director, or officer, may be subordinated to claims of general unsecured creditors to the extent that the transaction does not carry the earmarks of a genuine arm's length bargain, resulting in injury to other creditors or an unfair advantage for the subordinated creditor.[350] No such doctrines exist in the UK and France. However, pursuant to section 215(4) of the Insolvency Act 1986, the court may declare that a debt owed by the company to a director or shadow director liable for fraudulent or wrongful trading must be subordinated to all other debts owed by the company.[351] In France, it may amount to a management error, triggering liability under Article L651-2 of the Code de commerce, if a manager who is at the same time a shareholder grants a loan rather than injects equity capital.[352] These rules and principles reflect that, as insiders, shareholders may have an informational advantage over other creditors. This may

[340] Wiedemann (n 11) 209.

[341] *Ashbury Railway Carriage and Iron Co Ltd v Riche* [1875] LR 7 HL 653; Choper, Coffee, and Gilson (n 97) 65.

[342] Germain and Magnier (n 192) para 1653.

[343] Davies and Worthington (n 8) para 7-29.

[344] First Council Directive 68/151/EEC of 9 March 1968, [1968] OJ L65/08; as amended by Directive 2003/58/EC of 15 July 2003, amending Council Directive 68/151/EEC, as regards disclosure requirements in respect of certain types of companies [2003] OJ L 221/13, article 9(1); now Directive (EU) 2017/1132 of the European Parliament and of the Council of 14 June 2017 relating to certain aspects of company law (codification) OJ EU 30.6.2017 L169/46, Art 9(1). The implementing provision is now CA 2006, s 39.

[345] Choper, Coffee, and Gilson (n 97) 65.

[346] MBCA, §3.01(a).

[347] Wiedemann (n 11) 209.

[348] InsO, §39(1) No 5, (5). This is subject to the so-called 'corporate rescue privilege' where the shareholder has acquired the shares at a time when the company was in financial distress and with a view to effectuating a sustainable corporate rescue attempt.

[349] 11 U.S.C., §510(c).

[350] *Pepper v Litton*, 308 US 295 (Supreme Court of the United States, 1939).

[351] According to R Goode, *Principles of Corporate Insolvency Law* (4th edn, Sweet & Maxwell 2011) para 8-27, this provision gives the court all the powers it needs so that there was no need to develop a doctrine similar to the US concept of equitable subordination. Section 74(2)(f) of the Insolvency Act 1986 defers sums owed to members of the company by way of dividends, profits, or otherwise. However, the section subordinates to the claims of unsecured creditors only sums due to the member 'in his character as a member'. Sums due to a member independently of his membership will not be automatically subordinated. Cf *Soden v British & Commonwealth Holdings plc (in administration)* [1997] BCC 952.

[352] M Jeantin and P Le Cannu, *Droit commercial Entreprises en difficulté* (7th edn, Dalloz 2006) para 1293.

allow them to enforce their claims against the company before anybody else can. Also, to finance a company by debt capital rather than equity capital might create the false impression of the company being 'healthy' when in fact it is not.

Overall, therefore, the concept of separate legal personality is a device that allows the application of legal rules and principles fashioned for individual human actors to a community acting together to control a pool of assets. A complete alignment is prevented by specific traits that only persist in natural persons and the specific relationships that members have with 'their' legal person.

II. Economic rationale

The most significant aspect of separate legal personality is that the law attributes assets and liabilities exclusively to the company or corporation. Any connection between the company's property and its members has been severed. What ensues is an organized pool of assets attributed to no-one other than the entity. At the same time, the assets of the legal entity are reserved primarily for the legal entity's creditors and are committed, exclusively, for discharging the obligations entered into in the entity's name as long as there are any such obligations outstanding. This concept of separate legal personality has some obvious transaction cost implications: being able to sue and being sued significantly reduces litigation costs and was necessary, historically, to grant the joint stock company access to the common law courts at all.[353] Also, the entity concept avoids problems of privity of contract in case of a fluctuating membership.[354] Both aspects allow the company to make a firmer and more reliable commitment to its creditors. The entity concept, moreover, allows for a smooth 'transfer' of business assets when new participants are admitted and existing participants depart. And the business as a whole may be transferred more easily by transferring the shares rather than all its assets separately.[355]

However, whereas the principle of limited liability has been the focus of attention of the law and economics literature for a long time, it is only recently that scholars have tried to develop a more sophisticated economic analysis of the principle of separate legal personality (affirmative asset partitioning or entity shielding).[356] This analysis boils down to the claim that separate legal personality can reduce the costs of debt capital in various ways and that under certain circumstances this reduction is not neutralized by cost increases in other respects. Separate legal personality reduces, first and foremost, creditors' monitoring costs by protecting creditors from risks they cannot easily evaluate.[357] As the pool of assets attributed to the company is essentially pledged to the company's creditors for their preferential satisfaction, the creditors can focus their monitoring efforts exclusively on this pool of assets. If diverse activities of a firm are carried out by separate entities (within a group of companies), the creditors only need to monitor the single entity they advanced credit to. They do not have to be concerned about the other business activities they may not be familiar with. These cost savings are likely to result in more favourable credit terms.[358] At the same time concentration of similar assets and business operation in one entity increases the risk of bankruptcy as the available pool of assets will be smaller and less diversified and thus more susceptible to shocks affecting the particular industry. This may increase the costs of credit.[359] However,

[353] DL Perrott, 'Changes in Attitude to Limited Liability: the European Experience' in Tony Orhnial (ed), *Limited Liability and the Corporation* (Croom Helm 1982) 81, 96.

[354] Cf *Fairway Development Co. v Title Insurance Co.* (n 138) 120.

[355] D Goddard, 'Corporate Personality: Limited Recourse and its Limits' in RB Grantham and CEF Rickett (eds), *Corporate Personality in the 20th Century* (Hart 1998) 11, 18.

[356] H Hansmann and R Kraakman, 'The Essential Role of Organizational Law' (2000) 110 Yale Law Journal 387; H Hansmann, R Kraakman, and R Squire, 'Law and the Rise of the Firm' (2006) Harvard Law Review 1335, 1343.

[357] Hansmann, Kraakman, and Squire (n 356) 1344.

[358] Hansmann and Kraakman (n 356) 399–400.

[359] ibid 400.

creditors can still diversify by extending credit to multiple firms. Thus, the relevant cost of separate legal personality is (only) the additional cost necessary to achieve an efficient level of diversification at creditor level.[360]

More importantly, in the absence of a complete separation of entity and members, creditors of an individual member would have the right to proceed against the member's share in the firm's assets in case of the member's insolvency. Consequently, potential creditors of the firm itself would have difficulty determining the appropriate terms on which to extend credit. Familiarity with the firm's own assets and business affairs would be insufficient to assess its creditworthiness; rather the personal creditworthiness of each of the individual members including new members would have to be monitored over time.[361] Without separate legal personality, a creditor of a firm would be vulnerable to the fortunes of all business affairs and personal affairs of all members, regardless of his capacity to monitor those affairs.[362] By dedicating an entity's assets primarily to the entity's creditors, all creditors enjoy a reduction in the cost of appraising the security of their claims, permitting in turn a decrease in each firm's cost of credit. Separate legal personality, thus, promotes specialization, permitting creditors to limit the risks they face to those businesses that they know particularly well or that they can monitor with particular ease.[363] On the other hand, separate legal personality may increase debtor opportunism: by moving assets across entity boundaries a firm may be able to expand its debt by pledging the same assets more than once in order to attract new creditors. Put differently, the claims of current creditors may be subordinated to new creditors by shifting assets to a new entity which then issues new debt. Creditors may anticipate debtor opportunism and increase the interest that they charge accordingly, thus increasing the costs of credit. Moreover, as the mechanisms to address opportunism (doctrines of veil piercing, equitable subordination, and fraudulent transfer law) are standard based rather than rule based, enforcement costs will also be high.[364]

Further, separate legal personality reduces the administrative costs of bankruptcy. In bankruptcy an entity's assets are usually distributed among its general creditors on a pro rata basis. In order to establish the pay-out on each claim the value of the entity's assets are divided by the nominal value of the aggregate of all general creditors' claims, multiplied by the nominal value of an individual claim. Under the entity concept the entity's assets are pledged to the entity's creditors. Although in large corporate enterprises there may be thousands of general creditors, their number as well as the assets to be distributed will generally be manageable. However, if members' personal creditors would directly participate in entity property the individual creditors of each member would also take part in the entity's insolvency. With a multitude of members there could be an almost infinite number of creditors whose claims would have to be taken into consideration in order to ascertain the proper pay-out. And this pay-out would also depend on the personal assets of each individual member, not just the assets of the entity. This would be an almost impossible task and would be very costly in terms of time, judicial resources, and the potential for error. The less costly bankruptcy system under the entity concept may thus result in lower borrowing costs.[365]

Separate legal personality also protects a firm's going concern surplus. This is the difference by which the value of the firm as an operating unit exceeds the value of its assets on a break up basis. If members or their creditors or heirs could withdraw a member's contribution at will and thus force a partial or complete liquidation of the firm's assets some or all of the firm's going concern value could be destroyed with the consequence that the net value of

360 Hansmann, Kraakman, and Squire (n 356) 1353.
361 Hansmann and Kraakman (n 356) 402.
362 Hansmann, Kraakman, and Squire (n 356) 1344.
363 ibid 1345.
364 ibid 1351–2.
365 ibid 1346–8.

the firm available as security for its creditors might be reduced.[366] Members and their creditors may have an incentive to exercise, or threaten to exercise, withdrawal and liquidation rights in order to extract a share of the firm's profits larger than that actually owed to them on the basis of their existing claims. This is the hold-up problem we encountered earlier. Separate legal personality reduces the holdup problem[367] and protects the going concern surplus.[368] However, by extinguishing withdrawal and liquidation rights separate legal personality may increase managerial agency problems. The credible threat of withdrawal and partial liquidation can have a disciplining effect on management and co-members to contribute their fair share to the business enterprise and to prevent opportunism and shirking. Thus, whereas the entity concept reduces the hold-up problem, the shirking problem may be exacerbated.[369]

At the same time separate legal personality provides for a substitute control mechanism in that it promotes the free transferability of shares. Increased costs of borrowing in the absence of the entity concept would be borne by the members collectively in proportion to their respective shares. Thus, members would have an incentive to monitor each other's financial situation in order to reduce the risk for creditors and the costs of credit. Because of these monitoring costs, members would be reluctant to bring in new members or to allow a transfer of membership rights. By contrast, under the concept of separate legal personality the individual situation of members is irrelevant and the need to monitor other members is significantly reduced. Separate legal personality thus makes it easier for individuals to make equity investments and allows for investment in multiple firms and thus diversification of risk. Also, if new members had a right to withdraw and partially liquidate the firm, free transferability of shares would be too risky from the point of view of the firm and its members.[370] However, in order for transferability of shares to be effective as an (external) control mechanism deep and liquid stock markets are necessary with all the costly regulatory systems that come with it.[371]

Overall, therefore, the concept of separate legal personality appears to be a trade-off.[372] It reduces the costs of debt capital and allows for the establishment of large and stable asset pools. At the same time, it may increase managerial agency costs and the costs of shirking by extinguishing withdrawal and liquidation rights. In order to capture the benefits of separate legal personality and to minimize its adverse effects several mechanisms may be in operation. In small closely held firms, agency costs arising from opportunism and shirking may be kept in check by a close relationship between members on the basis of mutual trust and confidence, sometimes enhanced by family ties. This is similar to the situation in a partnership. Consequently, in small and closely held private companies we will often see governance structures functionally similar to partnerships combined with restrictions on the free transferability of shares. By contrast, where membership is widely dispersed the problems of shirking and opportunism must be addressed by a complex internal governance structure that designates a group of human persons with the authority to make decisions and to act on behalf of the entity, while at the same time ensuring that these persons may be held accountable for their activities by the participants in the business.[373] Free transferability of shares

[366] Hansmann and Kraakman (n 356) 403.

[367] LE Ribstein, 'Should History Lock in Lock-In?' (2005) 41 Tulsa Law Review 523, 527.

[368] Hansmann, Kraakman, and Squire (n 356) 1348–50.

[369] ibid 1353–5; Ribstein (n 367) 527. The entity concept itself may also reduce managerial agency costs. If diverse activities are carried out through different entities, the respective managers of these entities can only offer entity assets as security for entity debts, but not the assets of the other entities within the same firm. Creditors will have access only to the assets they have advanced credit for. This may have a disciplining effect on managers as creditors are likely to be more conservative when extending credit. This may prevent excessive borrowing on the part of single entities and their managers and may result in better management decision-making; see Hansmann, Kraakman, and Squire (n 356) 1346.

[370] Hansmann, Kraakman, and Squire (n 356) 1350.

[371] ibid 1354.

[372] Hansmann, Kraakman, and Squire (n 356) 1354; Ribstein (n 367) 529–30.

[373] Blair (n 22) 434.

may act as an additional lever for reducing agency costs via a market for corporate control. It seems, however, that the concept of separate legal personality will be able to unfold its full potential only if it is combined with the second essential feature of the corporate form, the principle of limited liability.

C. Limited Liability

I. Meaning

Despite the common usage of the term 'limited liability company'[374] or, in the words of section 3(1) of the CA 2006, 'limited company', it is not the liability of the company that is limited. Companies and corporations are liable in full, subject to a possible debt restructuring inside or outside formal insolvency proceedings, for the debts and obligations incurred in their name and on their behalf, just as any natural person is.[375] Rather, it is the company's members who may benefit from limited liability. This immediately raises two fundamental questions. First, for what obligations is the member's liability limited and to what extent is it limited? A further consideration has to be whether the privilege of limited liability encompasses other actors on the corporate stage as well.

Consider first the member's liability for obligations of the company. This liability can either be direct vis-à-vis the company's creditors, or indirect, that is, mediated by liability of members vis-à-vis the company to provide the latter with the funds required for the payment of its obligations.[376] Direct liability vis-à-vis the company's creditors as a matter of principle is, exceptions discussed below aside, largely absent in modern corporate law. This is most clearly expressed for the US in MBCA §6.22 (2): 'Unless otherwise provided in the articles of incorporation, a shareholder of a corporation is not personally liable for the acts or debts of the corporation accept that he may become personally liable by reason of his own acts or conduct'. For GmbHs and AGs, GmbHG §13(2) and AktG §1(1) sentence 2, respectively, provide in a similar vein that the company's creditors have, in respect of the debts owed by the company, access only to the company's assets. This is the so-called 'principle of separation' according to which the assets of the company, on the one hand, and the assets of the shareholders, on the other, are strictly separated. French law and UK law are somewhat less clear in this respect. That a shareholder will not be directly liable vis-à-vis the company's creditors can be inferred from Article L.223-1 and Article L.225-1 of the Code de commerce; section 3(2) of the CA 2006; and section 74(2)(d) of the IA 1986, respectively. These provisions restrict shareholders' liability to the amount promised to pay to the company for its shares.

Direct shareholder liability for (some of) the company's debts, however, does still exist under New York Business Corporation Law §630. The ten largest shareholders of a closely held corporation will be jointly and severally liable for all debts, wages, and salaries owed by the corporation to its employees. After being given notice in writing, the shareholder can be sued directly by the employee.[377] Also, the members of a SARL will be jointly liable vis-à-vis the company's creditors up to the value attributed to a contribution in kind in the articles of association if the contribution has either not been valued independently by an external auditor or the value stated in the articles is higher than the value suggested by independent valuation.[378]

[374] That is the exact translation of the French *société à responsabilité limité*, as well as of the German *Gesellschaft mit beschränkter Haftung*.

[375] FH Easterbrook and DR Fischel, *The Economic Structure of Corporate Law* (HUP 1991) 40.

[376] PI Blumberg, *The Law of Corporate Groups: Tort, Contract, and Other Common Law Problems in the Substantive Law of Parent and Subsidiary Corporations* (Little Brown 1987) 7 note 1.

[377] ibid 48. [378] Com art L223-9.

Indirect shareholder liability for the company's debts as a general principle has also largely disappeared. In case of a 'company limited by guarantee' pursuant CA 2006 s 3(3) the shareholders undertake to contribute a specified amount to the company's assets in the event of the company being wound up. Shareholder liability is limited to the amount they promised to contribute, IA 1986 s 74(3). Usually, this will be no more than £1. It could be said that the contributions to the company's assets are made for the payment of the debts and liabilities of the company, CA 2006 s 11(3)(a).[379] That would be in line with the concept of 'guarantee' as an undertaking to meet the monetary liability of the principal debtor in case of his default.[380] However, since the 'guarantee' is given to the other members rather than (future) creditors, the shareholder's liability could also be conceptualized as liability for the shareholder's own debt, rather than for those of the company.

This is the case in respect of the shareholders' liability to pay up their shares.[381] As a matter of principle, shareholders' liability is limited to the amount unpaid on the shares held by them. This is the case in respect of the SARL and SA in France (Code de commerce Article L223-1 and Article L225-1); the private and public companies limited by shares under UK law (CA 2006 s 3(2), IA 1986 s 74(2)(d)); the US corporation (MBCA §6.22 (a); DGCL, §162) as well as the German AG (AktG §54 (1)). The situation is somewhat different, however, in respect of the GmbH. In addition to the amount unpaid on their own shares, members will, pursuant to GmbHG §24, be liable on a pro rata basis for the contributions that cannot be realized either by collecting from defaulting members or by sale of the latter's shares. This liability—which only applies as a measure of 'last resort' to obtain the promised contribution—can result in one shareholder being liable for an amount equal to the entire share capital of the company.[382]

The principle of 'limited liability' is usually associated with the liability of shareholders. However, Easterbrook and Fischel have pointed out that none of the corporate constituencies contributes more to cover the company's losses than it has promised to invest.[383] This applies to creditors who will suffer a loss only up to the nominal amount of their claims; but also to managers and other workers who risk only the value of the services they have rendered as their contribution to the firm's enterprise. In particular, the directors' and managers' personal assets will, absent any breach of duty on their part, not be available to satisfy the company's obligations.[384] In this respect, it makes sense to extend the principle of 'limited liability' to encompass directors and managers as well.

II. Economic rationale

The economic rationale for limited liability has often been described. It boils down to the assumption that limited liability maximizes social wealth by enabling firms to raise the funds needed to carry out projects with positive net present value and to set incentives for the management to run the firm efficiently. In the literature influenced by law and economics scholarship, the emergence of limited liability as a default rule of corporate law is thus often portrayed as an economic necessity crucial for the development of industrial production and modern capitalism. However, there are also critical voices that challenge the traditional narrative. These voices have gathered some strength as a result of the global financial crisis of 2007–2009.

379 Davies and Worthington (n 8) para 1-9. 380 McKendrick (n 300) 828.

381 Conard (n 34) 424, therefore, wants to refer to the principle of 'non-liability' of members for corporate debts' rather than to that of 'limited liability'.

382 L Fastrich, '§§24' in A Baumbach and A Hueck (eds), *GmbH-Gesetz* (21st edn, CH Beck 2017) paras 1, 3.

383 Easterbrook and Fischel (n 375) 40.

384 Hansmann and Kraakman (n 356) 398. On the problem of promoters' and managers' liability for corporate debts incurred before registration see Chapter 3A.IV.

In order to explain the tenets of the prevalent traditional school of thought we can look at limited liability as a general rule of corporate law from three different angles. Consider first the point of view of the company. The company can raise capital by either issuing shares (equity finance), or by taking out loans or issuing debt securities such as bonds or notes (debt finance).[385] Neither will be without cost. Debt investors will charge interest on their loans; equity investors, too, expect a return on their investment, in particular the payment of dividends or an increase in the share price that can be turned into cash by selling the share on the market. The essential difference is that creditors have a fixed claim, that is, a claim for a predetermined (or determinable) amount of interest and for repayment of the loan principal; whereas shareholders as residual claimants have a right to whatever is left after the claims of creditors have been discharged.[386] As a consequence, whereas interest must be paid and loans must be discharged when repayment is due no matter whether the company is doing well or not, the return on equity depends on the economic success of the company. If the company is going through tough times, only a reduced or no dividends may be declared. Equity finance, therefore, reduces the financial burden on the company.[387] This is particularly interesting for start-ups in new industries that require huge amounts of capital. Indeed, it was the emergence of railway companies which were far larger in terms of membership than their predecessors and raised vast amounts of capital by issuing 'transferable rights to profit' which led to the development of the modern concept of the share,[388] and also to the acceptance of limited liability as a general principle.

Consider now the position of the (potential) equity investor. Under a regime of unlimited liability the shareholder would, in the event of the company's insolvency, put his entire personal wealth at risk. As a consequence, only a limited number of individuals would be willing to invest at all. It would be those with an intimate knowledge of the business in question and who are willing to participate in the day-to-day running of the firm in order to manage their risk.[389] The capital of the firm would be limited by what the proprietors could put up and by what they could borrow, which would in turn depend on what they could offer as security, essentially their personal wealth.[390] Limited liability, on the other hand, allows individuals to use a small fraction of their personal wealth to generate a possibly high return without risking a disastrous loss if the company goes bust.[391] At the same time, limited liability reduces the need for shareholders to monitor the management and their fellow shareholders. Under a regime of limited liability it is perfectly rational for equity investors to take a passive role and leave the day-to-day business of the company to the management.[392] This 'separation of ownership and control' allows for specialization of corporate functions and for more efficient corporate decision-making.[393] Under unlimited liability the likelihood for a shareholder of having to discharge the company's debts would depend on the personal wealth of the other shareholders; a creditor would pick the most suitable target. Therefore, monitoring wealth shifting on the part of the other shareholders would be a worthwhile strategy.[394] Limited liability thus reduces the costs for monitoring management and shareholders alike, thereby reducing the overall costs of equity finance. The risk for shareholders and the costs of equity finance can be reduced even further by diversification. Only under a regime of limited liability is it rational to hold small equity interests in a number of firms

385 Klein, Coffee, and Partnoy (n 7) 7–12. A third source of finance are internally generated retained profits. D Watson and A Head, *Corporate Finance: principles and practice* (7th edn, Pearson 2015) 356.

386 Klein, Coffee, and Partnoy (n 7) 8; Watson and Head (n 385) 113.

387 J Hicks, 'Limited Liability: the Pros and Cons' in T Orhnial (ed), *Limited Liability and the Corporation* (Croom Helm 1982) 11, 14. On the other hand, companies normally receive tax relief on debt interest; Watson and Head (n 385) 209.

388 P Ireland, 'Property and Contract in Contemporary Corporate Theory' (2003) 23 LS 453, 462.

389 Hicks (n 387) 11.

390 ibid.

391 HG Manne, 'Our Two Corporation Systems: Law and Economics' (1967) 53 Virginia Law Review 259, 263.

392 Easterbrook and Fischel (n 375) 41.

393 ibid.

394 ibid 42; Hansmann and Kraakman (n 356) 424.

because the risk of the shareholder's personal wealth being wiped out in case of insolvency of one of the companies does not increase.[395] This, in turn, facilitates optimal investment decisions by management.[396] They can engage in any project with a positive net present value, even if risky, because shareholders are protected by limited liability and can set-off potential losses arising from high variance undertakings by way of diversification.[397] Furthermore, free transferability of shares and functioning capital markets mean that shares can be turned into money quickly, thereby reducing the risk further still.[398] It is not entirely clear whether limited liability is a necessary prerequisite for the transferability of shares as such – historically shares seem to have been traded freely under unlimited liability –;[399] however, only under a regime of limited liability will the share price truly reflect the value of the firm and will it be independent from the identity and personal wealth of the shareholders.[400] Efficient securities markets, in turn, create an incentive for the management to do well and to keep share prices high. Otherwise, they risk being replaced after a successful control transaction when a buyer has acquired a large block of shares. This is, of course, more likely under a regime of limited liability since the buyer will not carry the risk of being liable for the target company's debts.[401] From the point of view of shareholders, therefore, limited liability provides a cap on their downside risk, whereas the chance of upside gains is unlimited.[402]

This disparity in the risks and rewards allocated to shareholders[403] can be increased by a higher debt/equity ratio. The greater the leverage, the greater the potential gains and losses for equity investors, whereas the potential gains of debt investors remain, despite increasing potential losses, the same.[404] Limited liability therefore allows shifting part of the risk of a business venture from shareholders to creditors.[405] From the point of view of creditors, therefore, limited liability of the borrower's shareholders seems to be detrimental. The risk that claims against the borrower cannot be realized is greater if the creditor has access only to the assets of the company and not also to the personal assets of its shareholders. As far as voluntary creditors are concerned, however, externalities will under normal circumstances not arise. As long as the creditor is able to assess the risk, and its potential future development, correctly he will charge a higher interest rate on his investment as full ex ante compensation for his additional risk bearing.[406] From the point of view of the shareholders, the increase in interest rate is an insurance premium paid by the residual claimants to cover the risk of loss on default.[407] Against this background it has been argued that limited liability is in fact trivial. Since bargaining in capital markets is typically conducted in the form of negotiated transactions so that transaction costs do not seem to be high, the liability regime will have no impact on the costs of capital.[408] Under unlimited liability, the decrease

[395] Easterbrook and Fischel (n 375) 43; RA Posner, *Economic Analysis of Law* (9th edn, Wolters Kluwer 2014) 540.

[396] Hansmann and Kraakman (n 356) 424.

[397] Easterbrook and Fischel (n 375) 43–4.

[398] Manne (n 391) 263; Posner (n 395) 540.

[399] Posner (n 395) 540; Ireland (n 388) 459 (arguing that limited liability is a necessary prerequisite of free transferability); Hansmann and Kraakman (n 356) 426; Henry Hansmann and Reinier Kraakman, 'Toward Unlimited Shareholder Liability for Corporate Torts' (1991) 100 Yale Law Journal 1879, 1924; PZ Grossman, 'The Market for Shares of Companies with Unlimited Liability: The Case of American Express' (1995) 24 Journal of LS 63, 72ff (showing that there can be a market for shares under a system of pro rata liability).

[400] Easterbrook and Fischel (n 375) 42–4; PJ Halpern, MJ Trebilcock, and S Turnbull, 'An Economic Analysis of Limited Liability in Corporation Law' (1980) 30 University of Toronto Law Journal 117, 126.

[401] Easterbrook and Fischel (n 375) 42.

[402] Davies and Worthington (n 8) para 8-1.

[403] ibid.

[404] Klein, Coffee, and Partnoy (n 7) 8.

[405] Posner (n 395) 540.

[406] RA Posner, 'The Rights of Creditors of Affiliated Corporations' (1975) 43 University of Chicago Law Review 499, 501.

[407] Halpern, Trebilcock, and Turnbull (n 400) 129.

[408] RE Meiners, JS Mofsky, and RD Tollison, 'Piercing the Veil of Limited Liability' (1979) 4 Delaware Journal of Corporate Law 351; RB Ekelund and RD Tollison, 'Mercantilist Origins of the Corporation' (1980) 11 Bell Journal of Economics 715, 719. The argument rests on the so called 'Coase Theorem': in a world without (or low) transaction costs, the initial allocation of property rights is immaterial because the most efficient allocation as the ultimate result will be achieved by bargaining; cf R Coase, 'The Problem of Social Cost' (1960) 3 Journal of Law and Economics 1.

in interest rate charged by creditors will be offset by an increase in the return demanded by equity investors.[409] In fact, no matter what the liability regime is, it is argued, parties will contract so as to shift the risk to the actor who is most suitable to bear the risk, that is, who is the cheapest cost avoider in respect of monitoring costs. This view seems to derive some empirical support from the fact that for a decade prior to 1830 the New England states had very different regimes in terms of limited liability without any discernible effect on economic development in these states.[410] Massachusetts and Rhode Island had unlimited liability, whereas New Hampshire, Connecticut, and Maine had limited liability. The latter states continued to lag behind in terms of economic activity.[411] There was also no significant increase in the number of incorporations when Massachusetts introduced limited liability in 1830;[412] and despite being the only state in New England between 1830 and 1847 operating under unlimited liability, Rhode Island retained its position as one of the leading states for the textile industry.[413] Others have argued that the creditors are usually in a better position to monitor the activities of the company than the shareholders.[414] Owing to specialization, debt investors, in particular banks, will often be better able to appraise the risk of a venture and to monitor it than shareholders who will often know nothing about the business at all. Moreover, the incentive to monitor on the part of creditors and shareholders is different.[415] Under a regime of unlimited liability, shareholders would have a strong incentive to monitor management and their fellow shareholders no matter what their stake in the company is. Creditors, on the other hand, can limit their exposure by the amount of credit they advance.[416] Reduced exposure means reduced incentive to monitor. Secured creditors can concentrate monitoring on the state of their collateral.[417] And suppliers often have a 'very short term horizon': they want cash and they want it promptly.[418] They have no need for monitoring the firm in the long run. Therefore, limited liability reflects the normal desires of transacting parties, avoiding the costs of parties contracting around an unlimited liability rule.[419] If in a particular case the shareholders are, by way of exception, cheapest cost avoiders, the parties may contract for unlimited liability. This view is supported by the 'immediate and startling increase' in the number of incorporations after limited liability became a general rule under British company law in 1855.[420] In fact, the American experience in New England is somewhat inconclusive. The textile industry in these states did not have the need for the same huge amounts of capital and were far less susceptible to excessive tort liability as later the railway companies.[421] And Forbes attributes to the introduction of limited liability the fact that after 1830, despite a massive slowdown in the overall number of incorporations in the textile industry, the number of incorporations in Massachusetts did not decrease.[422]

This economic rationality of limited liability makes most sense in respect of large publicly traded companies where shareholders are separated from the running of the company and where their role is reduced to that of passive holders of shares as financial property rights. Limited liability can be less easily defended in respect of small private companies

[409] Meiners, Mofsky, and Tollison (n 408) 361; Ekelund and Tollison (n 408) 719.
[410] Blumberg (n 375) 35. [411] ibid.
[412] Meiners, Mofsky, and Tollison (n 408) 362; Blumberg (n 375) 35.
[413] Blumberg (n 375) 36.
[414] Posner (n 395) 541, Hansmann and Kraakman (n 356) 426, 425.
[415] Easterbrook and Fischel (n 375) 45. [416] Posner (n 395) 541.
[417] Easterbrook and Fischel (n 375) 45.
[418] L Enriques and JR Macey, 'Creditors Versus Capital Formation: The Case Against the European Legal Capital Rules' (2001) 86 Cornell Law Review 1165, 1189.
[419] Posner n 406) 506; (n 395) 541.
[420] PL Davies, *Gower's Principles of Modern Company Law* (6th edn, Sweet & Maxwell 1997) 46.
[421] Blumberg (n 375) 36.
[422] KF Forbes, 'Limited Liability and the Development of the Business Corporation' (1986) 2 Journal of Law, Economics, and Organization 163, 166.

or closely held corporations.[423] Here the members will often have intimate knowledge of the business and will take a direct interest in its running. Transferability of shares is often restricted and a market for shares will usually not exist. The problem is exacerbated in case of single member companies and corporate groups. The one-man-company, it has been argued, is an invitation to defraud creditors.[424] Corporate concentration increases the potential for risk shifting by sacrificing undercapitalized subsidiaries to the detriment of their creditors for the benefit of the group as a whole.[425] Also, because they would still be protected by limited liability, imposing unlimited liability on a parent company would not set a disincentive for individual investors. On the other hand, the formation of corporate groups may also benefit creditors. If diverse activities are carried out by different entities within a group the creditors only need to monitor the management of the business venture they advanced credit to, but not the management of the other business activities they may not be familiar with; and neither do they have to monitor the lenders who advanced credit for these other activities as they would have to if the companies within the group were not protected by limited liability. Limited liability therefore reduces the overall costs of credit for the group. Indeed, it is the notion that limited liability does not merely shift the risk from shareholders to creditors, but reduces the total costs of risk borne by shareholders and creditors that is used to justify limited liability for private companies and closely held corporations as well.[426] Demands to make the formation of companies more difficult and expensive in order to reduce the number of cases in which the corporate form is abused[427] seem unrealistic; for many years, the trend has gone the opposite way.[428] In addition to the entrenchment of the one-man private company in Europe, major European jurisdiction, France and Germany among them, have, in the wake of the CJEU's jurisprudence on freedom of establishment, introduced corporate forms with either no minimum capital or a minimum capital of €1 or less. With the rise of the LLC, the LLP, and the LLLP in the United States, we have seen a proliferation of unincorporated business entities that afford limited liability to their members.[429] In any case, for these entities limited liability will often be illusory; members and managers of small companies will often be required to provide personal guarantees in order to obtain credit, and so will the parent companies of undercapitalized subsidiaries.[430]

Not all creditors are equally capable of obtaining ex ante compensation for their additional risk bearing or of protecting their interest via personal guarantees or debt covenants. Large institutional lenders are surely in the best position to appraise the risk of the venture and to negotiate adequate compensation and protection. Suppliers, on the other hand, will often advance credit only against the provision of some sort of security—retention of title, non-possessory pledges etc. The group of contractual creditors most likely to be unable to

[423] Halpern, Trebilcock, and Turnbull (n 400) 148; D Millon, 'Piercing the Corporate Veil, Financial Responsibility, and the Limits of Limited Liability' (2007) 56 Emory L J 1305, 1314–15.

[424] O Kahn-Freund, 'Some Reflections on Company Law Reform' (1944) 7 Modern Law Review 54, 56.

[425] JM Landers, 'A Unified Approach to Parent, Subsidiary, and Affiliate Questions in Bankruptcy' (1975) 42 University of Chicago Law Review 589, 624.

[426] LE Ribstein, 'Limited Liability and Theories of the Corporation' (1991) 50 Maryland Law Review 80, 101.

[427] Kahn-Freund (n 426) 57.

[428] See M Neville and K Engsig Sørensen, 'Promoting Entrepreneurship: The New Company Law Agenda' (2014) 15 EBOR 545.

[429] JW Callison, 'Rationalizing Limited Liability and Veil Piercing' (2003) 58 Business Lawyer 1063; DJ Morrissey, 'Piercing All the Veils: Applying an Established Doctrine to a New Business Order' (2007) 32 J Corporation Law 529.

[430] Davies and Worthington (n 8) para 8-4. *In Re Mader's Store for Men, Inc.* 77 Wis.2d 578, 609 (Wis. 1977): 'Where a small corporation is involved, lending institutions will commonly require a personal guaranty as a condition to granting a loan to even a healthy enterprise, and their willingness to lend may depend as much upon their perception of the solvency and reliability of the guarantor as upon the corporation's financial condition'. These contracting practices suggest that limited liability may in fact not be the efficient rule in these contexts. Millon (n 423) 1315.

secure ex ante compensation will be employees. Although there will be employees who are in a strong bargaining position vis-à-vis the company—high profile corporate managers and other highly skilled professionals—the average worker will neither be able to appraise the risk of the corporate venture nor to adjust his compensation accordingly.[431] Furthermore, in a dense labour market it will be this class of workers who may suffer an existential loss if the company becomes insolvent. This is recognized by New York Business Corporation Law, §630, providing for unlimited liability of the ten largest shareholders for wage claims. Some form of relief might be achieved by trade unions negotiating specific working conditions including wages, taking into account the risk of default associated with a specific industry or employer. Other protective devices would be to grant certain employee claims priorities in the company's insolvency,[432] or to pay certain employee claims out of public social security funds.[433]

Whereas employees have at least a theoretical chance of negotiating full ex ante compensation, this is not the case in respect of involuntary creditors, in particular tort victims. Involuntary creditors cannot be said to have consensually assumed the risk of limited liability. Therefore, the costs of doing business are shifted, partially, to potential tort victims and to the general public.[434] It could, however, be asked whether there is a need for a specific regime to protect involuntary creditors at all against corporate behaviour. After all, in fact everyone's liability is limited to the assets they have at their disposal, and a discharge of debts in bankruptcy allows for a fresh start.[435] Whether one is run over by a van that belongs to an insolvent individual or an insolvent company does not seem to justify different treatment.[436] In both cases it would just be bad luck. However, limited liability allows for the deliberate externalization of risks and their associated costs, without the moral and ethical constraints to which a natural person would be subject.[437] The corporation as separate legal entity insulates managers and shareholders from the real world consequences of their decisions. Corporate managers and shareholders, when pursuing (short-term) maximization of share prices, can disregard the costs of environmental pollution, injuries caused by dangerous and poorly manufactured products or the destruction of the financial system as a whole. If all goes well they will reap the profits with no upward limits. If it fails, somebody else will pick up the bill, in the last resort the taxpayer. Thus, limited liability results in an incentive to engage in excessively risky activities for the benefit of corporate managers and shareholders. The benefits thus generated for those behind the company may be far lower than the costs imposed on tort victims, and society as a whole.[438] Limited liability may still be justified based on the notion that the overall benefits it generates for society—increased entrepreneurial activity with financial returns for investors, jobs for employees, and desirable products and services for consumers—outweigh the costs for (potential) tort victims and society.[439] This is essentially an efficiency argument based on the Kaldor/Hicks criterion. Decisions based on this criterion lack moral justification and legitimacy vis-à-vis the losers. Limited liability could still be defended based on the argument that consistent

[431] Halpern, Trebilcock, and Turnbull (n 400) 149.

[432] 11 U.S.C. §§§503(b)(1)(A) 507(a)(4); Insolvency Act 1986, Sch 6.

[433] Directive 2008/94/EC of the European Parliament and of the Council of 22 October 2008 on the protection of employees in the event of the insolvency of their employer, OJ EU 28.10.2008 L283/36, provides a general framework for the protection of employee claims in the event of the employer's insolvency in the European Union. As for implementing legislation: Germany: SGB III §§165–172; France: Code du travail, art. L3253-1. In the UK, employees have a right to make a claim on the National Insurance Fund. Goode (n 353) para 8-21. Very critical on French law: Jeantin and Le Cannu (n 353) 389.

[434] Meiners, Mofsky, and Tollison (n 408) 365.

[435] Halpern, Trebilcock, and Turnbull (n 400) 127.

[436] Hansmann and Kraakman (n 399) 1886 n 16, in fact discuss whether tort claims should survive personal bankruptcy.

[437] LE Mitchell, *Corporate Irresponsibility: America's Newest Export* (Yale UP 2001) 54–5.

[438] Hansmann and Kraakman (n 399) 1917; Posner n 406) 520; Millon (n 423) 1316; RB Thompson, 'Piercing the Veil: Is the Common Law the Problem?' (2005) 37 Connecticut Law Review 619, 621.

[439] Millon (n 423) 1317.

application of the principle will, in the medium or long term, result in a general compensation for all members of society,[440] if not via the market mechanism, so at least by way of redistribution of wealth via the income tax system.[441] Thus, even the losers may be able to consent implicitly or explicitly.[442] However, the assumption that the social benefits of limited liability outweigh the social costs generated by the incentives it sets for corporate opportunism and moral hazard have come under greater scrutiny in recent years, in particular in light of the rise of global financial capitalism, the 'financialization' of corporate law[443] and the global dominance of shareholder value maximization as the unitary objective of all corporate activity.[444]

Modern critics of limited liability have famous forebears. Adam Smith, the father of modern economics, famously did not look favourably on limited liability joint stock corporations:

> The directors of such companies, being the managers rather of other people's money than of their own, it cannot well be expected, that they should watch over it with the same anxious vigilance with which the partners in a private copartnery frequently watch over their own ... Negligence and profusion, therefore, must always prevail, more or less, in the management of the affairs of such a company.[445]

It has been argued that, historically, the 'industrial revolution' in England in the late eighteenth and early nineteenth centuries did not require general incorporation under limited liability. Ordinary partnerships were largely adequate for that purpose and in fact dominated the cotton and iron industries. Where the required amount of capital was very high—as with railways—chartered companies were available to accommodate these needs. Entrepreneurs did not lobby for general incorporation combined with limited liability, but were generally content with ordinary partnerships.[446] Only with the rise of the railway companies and the rapid growth of a new class of passive investors in search for new investment opportunities did it become necessary to make the share 'safe', not in the interest of industry and productivity, but in the interest of financial investment.[447] Limited liability as a general principle was, accordingly, not a predetermined and natural reaction of the legal system to economic reality and the needs of entrepreneurs; rather it was a conscientious political decision in the interest of passive finance that purported to profit from entrepreneurial activity without being itself part of it. Pursuant to this narrative, limited liability is not the result of market forces; rather, it is a top down intervention partly replacing the market mechanism.[448] Despite a de facto freedom from liability in large unincorporated joint stock corporations and exclusion of liability by contract, without legislative intervention, Davies writes, 'limited liability could never have been attained in a satisfactory and clear cut fashion, and it was this intervention which finally established companies as the

440 H-B Schafer and C Ott, *Lehrbuch der ökonomischen Analyse des Zivilrechts* (4th edn, Springer 2005) 35, 45.

441 ibid 53.

442 M Erlei, M Leschke, and D Sauerland, *Neue Institutionenökonomik* (Schäffer Poeschel 1999) 20.

443 P Ireland, 'Financialization and Corporate Governance' (2009) 60 NILQ 1; R Romano, 'After the Revolution in Corporate Law' (2005) 55 Journal of Legal Education 342.

444 H Hansmann and R Kraakman, 'The End of History for Corporate Law' (2001) 89 Georgetown Law Journal 439.

445 A Smith, *An Inquiry into the Nature and Causes of the Wealth of Nations* (RH Campbell and AS Skinner (eds), Liberty Press 1976) 741, 757–8. The formation of a joint stock company was, according to Adam Smith, reasonable only under three cumulative conditions: the business was reducible to strict rule and method, the undertaking was of greater and more general utility than common trades, and it required a capital greater than can easily be raised by a private copartnery. This was the case essentially only in respect of banking and insurance business, and maintaining a canal and water supply to a big city.

446 P Ireland, 'Limited Liability, Rights of Control and the Problem of Corporate Irresponsibility' (2010) 34 Cambridge Journal of Economics 837, 840–1.

447 ibid 842–7.

448 D Campbell and S Griffin, 'Enron and the End of Corporate Governance' in Sorcha Macleod (ed), *Global Governance and the Quest for Justice, Volume II: Corporate Governance* (Hart Publishing 2006) 47, 59–63.

major instrument in economic development'.[449] If the market were given free rein, shareholders and the executives acting in their interest would be personally responsible for their actions. Those who share the profits of an enterprise ought also to be subject to its losses.[450] The entrepreneur in a competitive economy must be careful in the disposition of his resources, and in investing and producing. If unsuccessful, unlimited liability, as part of the competitive system, would automatically remove him from the market.[451] By contrast, limited liability permits a man to avail himself of acts if advantageous to him, and not to be responsible for them if they should be disadvantageous.[452] Thus, shareholders and their executives are insulated from the competitive pressures of the market.[453] The result is corporate irresponsibility.[454] Shareholders and managers enjoy income rights without having to worry about how these income streams are generated. Shareholders have little incentive to ensure that their executives behave legally, ethically, or decently; in a world of remuneration by stock options, managers have every incentive to maximize share prices at all cost.[455] Owing to limited liability, the corporation becomes the 'perfect externalizing machine'.[456] The result is, so runs the argument, a massive increase in speculative financial exchanges, regular financial crises, numerous corporate scandals, falling growth rates, a reduction in the rates of productivity growth and soaring executive remuneration.[457] In order to remedy the situation, a number of commentators have argued for a system of unlimited liability, or pro rata liability, of shareholders and/or managers for tort claims.[458] Others are in favour of a presumption of liability of a parent company for the debts of its subsidiary[459] or for 'entity liability' of a corporate group as a whole.[460] The most radical approach argues for the reinstitution of unlimited liability as a general principle as the return to the competitive market.[461] More limited is the suggestion to decouple limited liability and control rights; in other words, limited liability can be retained only in exchange for renouncing control of the company.[462]

Given that since the beginning of the nineteenth century the quality of life of the largest part of the population in the developed world has improved exponentially, the question is whether this improvement is due to sustainable and fully costed economic growth generated or at least facilitated by the corporate revolution and limited liability, or whether this growth occurred despite limited liability. In other words, is the rate of investment and growth produced by limited liability superior to that which would be produced under a system of unlimited liability? This is obviously an empirical question and if the answer was clear the respective policy choice could be easily implemented. However, it is much more likely that we will never know the answer for certain. Therefore, we can only rely on the analytical framework.

The general assumption that the benefits of limited liability outweigh its costs is plausible only to the extent that on the whole shareholders, managers, and creditors have an economic interest in the overall success of the company and in the maximization of its value. In light of the development, over the last twenty years, of global financial capitalism this general assumption seems to have lost some of its plausibility. The 'derivatives revolution' and, hand in hand with technological innovation, the development of share trading techniques allows equity and debt investors as well as executives to decouple cash flow rights

[449] Davies (n 420) 46.
[450] EW Cox, *New Law and Practice of Joint Stock Companies* (4th edn, Law Times Office 1857) 38.
[451] W Eucken, *The Foundations of Economics* (John Wiley and Sons, 1992) 316.
[452] Cox (n 450) 38.
[453] Campbell and Griffin (n 448) 59.
[454] Mitchell (n 437) 55–60.
[455] Ireland (n 446) 846–7.
[456] Mitchell (n 437) 53.
[457] Ireland (n 446) 853.
[458] For instance Halpern, Trebilcock, and Turnbull (n 400) 149; CD Stone, 'The Place of Enterprise Liability in the Control of Corporate Conduct' (1980) 90 Yale Law Journal 1, 68; Hansmann and Kraakman, (n 399) 1879 ff.
[459] Muchlinski (n 4) 321–6.
[460] PI Blumberg, 'The Transformation of Modern Corporate Law: The Law of Corporate Groups' (2005) 37 Connecticut Law Review 605; AA Berle, 'The Theory of Enterprise Entity' (1947) 47 Columbia Law Review 343.
[461] Campbell and Griffin (n 448) 68–71.
[462] Ireland (n 446) 854–5.

from control rights.[463] This can be achieved through 'record date capture' in the context of stock lending,[464] or by taking the short side of an 'equity swap' (or 'contract for difference', CfD).[465] Executives can hedge their exposure through so-called collars, buying a put and simultaneously selling a call option in the stock of their companies.[466] A debt investor may hedge its exposure by holding a 'credit default swap' (CDS).[467] Securitization, via 'collateralised debt obligations' (CDOs), is another common technique.[468] The widespread use of these decoupling techniques may result in shareholders, managers, and creditors having a significantly reduced (potentially to zero) or even a negative economic interest in the company. Owing to (distressed) debt trading and fragmentation of debt via CDOs, the traditional house bank of the debtor will no longer necessarily have an economic interest in the debtor company and therefore no longer have an incentive to monitor its performance. Traders in distressed debt and CDO investors as holders of the economic interest or, more likely, a fraction thereof, will have neither the knowledge nor the infrastructure for effective monitoring. Moreover, due to the use of credit derivatives the monitor's economic interest may be negative and she may profit from and even encourage irresponsible corporate behaviour.[469]

The possibility of a negative economic interest in a company for shareholders and creditors alike makes corporate opportunism more likely, increases moral hazard, and thus the probability that negative externalities will exceed the benefits for the corporation. On the other hand, the benefits of limited liability are still real and important. Moreover, decoupling techniques are not necessarily always bad. They allow for risk spreading and efficient risk bearing, greater diversification and enhanced access to capital and liquidity. Hence, the return to unlimited liability or the prohibition of decoupling techniques are neither desirable nor, given market realities, feasible options. However, what is required and what can be

[463] HTC Hu and B Black, 'The New Vote Buying: Empty Voting and Hidden Ownership' (2006) 79 Southern California Law Review 811; 'Equity and Debt Decoupling and Empty Voting II: Importance and Extensions' (2008) 156 University of Pennsylvania Law Review 635; 'Debt, Equity, and Hybrid Decoupling: Governance and Systemic Risk Implications' (2008) 14 European Financial Management 663.

[464] Before a shareholder meeting, the company establishes a 'record date'. Those who are members on that date are entitled to vote, even if at the date of the meeting they no longer hold the shares. Under a typical stock lending agreement, the shares are transferred from the lender to the borrower on the basis that the borrower retransfers the shares to the lender at any time at the election of either side and pays to the lender an amount equal to any dividends or distributions the borrower receives on the shares. Where stock lending takes place prior to and around the 'record date' the borrower as shareholder obtains the right to vote; whereas the long-term economic interest remains with the lender. Hu and Black (2006) (n 463) 832.

[465] Under a CfD the party who takes the 'long' side of the swap receives from the other party, holding the 'short' side, an economic return equivalent to the return on the underlying shares. The short side will usually hedge against exposure under the swap by acquiring the equivalent number of underlying shares; or conversely, a shareholder may hedge by taking the short side of an equity swap. This party has formal voting rights but has no economic interest in the company. ibid 828.

[466] See J Sasseen, 'Some CEOs are Selling their Companies Short' *Bloomberg Business Week* (25 February 2010); E Dash, 'Stock Hedging Lets Banks Skirt Efforts to Overhaul Pay' *New York Times* (5 February 2011).

[467] Under a simple CDS, if a credit event occurs the protection seller will compensate the protection buyer based on the difference between the nominal value of the credit instrument and its market value shortly after the credit event. "Credit event" may be the opening of formal insolvency proceedings, payment default or an informal workout. During the swap term the protection buyer typically pays the seller a fixed periodic amount. Although fully hedged through the CDS, the protection buyer retains all contractual rights under the credit instrument and may exercise, waive or renegotiate these rights and vote on a plan for reorganization in corporate insolvency; M Schillig, 'Corporate Insolvency in the Twenty-First Century: State Imposed or Market Based?' (2014) 14 JCLS 1, 10.

[468] In a 'cash' CDO a pool of debt contracts is transferred by the originator to a special purpose vehicle (SPV). The returns from the pool are repackaged into separate tranches based on difference in credit quality. The SPV issues financial instruments backed by the underlying debt contracts or swaps to be sold off to investors. Under these structures the contractual control rights may remain with the originator or may lie with the SPV. The holders of the tranches will be exposed to the economic interest, but only partially since the SPV's portfolio will usually be highly diversified; ibid 11.

[469] Hu and Black, 'Debt, Equity, and Hybrid Decoupling: Governance and Systemic Risk Implications' (n 463) 693–4.

achieved is a recalibration of limited liability so as to ensure that its benefits for technological innovation and production are not jeopardized by a misguided focus on share prices and speculative temptations.[470]

Corporate law and corporate insolvency provide a number of mechanisms that could form the basis for such a recalibration. We will discuss some of these in the following chapters.

Questions:

1. In what respects does the legal personality of natural persons and of companies/corporations differ?
2. Legal entity status and limited liability in combination allow and greatly facilitate the free transferability of shares, the centralization of management and control, and the development of well-functioning capital markets. Summarize the economic rationality of the principles of separate legal personality and limited liability, and explain in what way they are essential for these features of the modern business corporation.
3. The success of the corporation as a business vehicle is usually attributed to the features mentioned in Question 2. Can you explain why?

D. The Modern Corporation in Historic Perspective

Historically, separate legal personality and limited liability have developed separately and in different contexts. It is, however, the combination of both principles in a unified concept that accounts for the success of the modern business corporation.[471]

The notion of an association having rights and obligations different and separate from its members was well established under Roman law. It is not entirely clear whether the Romans had accepted the concept of a 'legal person' separate from its members; it is, however, generally recognized that the notion of the aggregate of members being able to have rights and duties different from their individual rights and duties was present in Roman law.[472] These corporations (*universitas*) were established primarily as municipal or religious bodies. In the sphere of commerce, they occurred in form of the guilds of artisans. Although being capable of owning property, members did not pool their resources; each individual worked on their own account.[473] The members of Roman law corporations do not seem to have been able to rely on limited liability. Von Savigny writes that, although 'the Credits and Debts of Juristical Persons concern them solely as an artificial Whole', corporations could 'compel their own members to contribute towards the payment of the Corporate Debts'.[474] The Roman law partnership (*societas*) as the early ancestor of our modern business associations seems to have been purely contractual in nature.[475] Where partnership property existed it was owned

[470] D Harvey, *A Brief History of Neoliberalism* (OUP 2005) 32.

[471] Perrott (n 353) 85.

[472] Cf Wiedemann (n 11) 191; Perrott (n 353) 85; Conard (n 34) 127; FK von Savigny, 'System des heutigen Römischen Rechts' in WH Rattigan, *Jural Relations; or, The Roman Law of Persons as Subjects of Jural Relations: Being a Translation of The Second Book of Savigny's System of Modern Roman Law* (Hyperion 1884 (1979)) §92.

[473] See von Savigny (n 472) §88.

[474] ibid §92; S Williston, 'History of the Law of Business Corporations before 1800, II' (1888) 2 Harvard Law Reports 149, 160. According to Conard (n 34) 424, however, 'there is no doubt that as a general principle the members are not liable for a corporation's debts'. A form of limited liability in business transactions could, however, be achieved under the concept of *peculium*. A *pater familias*, as single owner of all family assets, could provide his son or slave with a set of assets for a business venture. These assets as well as all profits generated in trading belonged to the *pater familias*. He was also liable for any debts so incurred, however, only to the extent of the *peculium* and not with his remaining assets. Perrott (n 353) 86, who comes to the conclusion: 'the Romans had a well developed concept of limited liability and also of corporate personality, but they took no special pains to relate the two together'.

[475] von Savigny (n 472) §§88. According to von Savigny, some partnerships maintained the right of corporations in particular for working of mines and salt-pans and for the farming of tolls.

by the partners as co-owners.[476] Partners in a Roman law partnership (*societas*) were liable to third parties with their individual assets.[477]

Roman ideas on corporations (*universitas*) were revived by canonists in the thirteenth and fourteenth centuries and applied to municipalities, churches, parishes, and other ecclesiastical bodies and religious orders. These bodies were of perpetual existence, independent from their members, could own property, and sue and be sued; in short, they showed many of the indicia of separate legal personality. In general, however, they were distinctly non-commercial in nature.[478] However, commercial ingenuity experienced a leap in Renaissance Italy. City states began to finance their wars and colonial adventures by public loans which were open for subscription to the citizens. Sometimes the debtor city was unable to pay interest or redeem the loan. In that case it farmed out the collection of taxes or the administration of colonies to the creditors, essentially as a form of security. Where the interest rate proved to be too high it was replaced with a sum varying according to the yield of the revenue. Creditors' rights were divided into freely tradable units later to be known as *actiones* in French or *Aktien* in German. The combination of loan and farming grant required some kind of permanent administration for the collection of the yield which gave the scheme the semblance of a body corporate. These schemes were, however, not corporations but essentially secured loans. There seems to be no evidence that the concept has spread northwards and has had any impact on the development of the modern business corporation.[479]

In late medieval times, incorporation was effectuated largely in order to exercise sovereign power and privileges and, thus, required a concession from the sovereign: a Royal charter, concession, or *octroi*.[480] In the sphere of commerce, guilds of merchants and merchant companies founded for colonial undertakings began to seek incorporation in the fifteenth and sixteenth centuries.[481] The (English) East India Company was first chartered in 1600, the Dutch East India Company was formed in 1602. Companies chartered by other European sovereigns followed, France and some German states among them.[482] The main reason of incorporation for these entities was to acquire a monopoly of trade for their members and governmental power over the colonial territory for the company itself.[483] Incorporation as a convenient method of distinguishing the rights and liabilities of the association from those of its members was hardly needed since each member traded on his own account subject only to obedience to the regulation of the guild or company.[484] However, in the vaults of these so-called 'regulated companies'[485] a different type of sub-organization developed: some of the members, often on a local basis, began to trade on a joint account, first for a single voyage, then for a period of years and finally on a more permanent basis. Gradually, the joint stock so formed encompassed all members and trading on private account was outlawed.[486] Thus, by the second half of the seventeenth century the incorporated joint stock company had developed as the organizational platform for doing large-scale overseas business. Incorporation by Royal charter created a separate legal entity and afforded most of the advantages usually associated with corporate personality. A corporation was capable of existing in perpetuity, it could sue outsiders as well as its own members, it had a common seal in order to distinguish its own acts from those of its members and shares were freely transferable.[487] At first, however, there was no complete

476 M Kaser, *Das Römische Privatrecht* (CH Beck 1971) 573.

477 Perrott (n 353) 87.

478 Conard (n 34) 128.

479 CM Schmitthoff, 'The Origin of the Joint-Stock Company' (1939) 3 Toronto Law Journal 74, 76–9.

480 Davies (n 420) 18; K Macharzina, 'Corporate Forms and Limited Liability in German Company Law' in T Orhnial (ed), *Limited Liability and The Corporation* (Croom Helm 1982) 44, 47; Conard (n 34) 180.

481 Davies (n 420) 19; Conard (n 34) 181.

482 Schmitthoff (n 479) 93; Germain and Magnier (n 192) para 1881.

483 Davies (n 420) 20; Perrott (n 353) 89.

484 Davies (n 420) 19.

485 Regulated by their charters.

486 Davies (n 420) 20; Schmitthoff (n 479) 88–92.

487 Davies (n 420) 21.

separation of corporation and members. The corporation was still thought of as a collection of individuals. This would change only towards the middle of the nineteenth century when the share emerged as a free-standing item of property in its own right.[488] Founders started to seek charters in order to obtain limited liability only in the second half of the eighteenth century.[489] Although direct liability of members for the corporation's debts ceased by the end of the seventeenth century at the latest,[490] absent specific provision in the charter, the corporation could still levy assessment on shareholders, that is, demand a contribution, in order to cover the corporation's debts, a remedy enforceable by the corporation's creditors.[491] Despite surviving as a matter of legal principle, indirect liability came to an end in practical terms when more and more charters were granted with clauses prohibiting assessment beyond the basic capital subscription.[492]

The process of obtaining a Royal charter or concession was long and expensive[493] and only worth the trouble if the benefits outweighed the costs. That was not the case for the overwhelming majority of business associations both in England and on the continent. Consequently, most businesses operated in unincorporated form. On the continent an organizational structure has been available for centuries which allowed limiting the liability of most partners to the amount of their investment. In the late medieval *commenda*, as developed in northern Italy, one partner (*comendator*) would supply capital to finance overseas trade or other risky enterprises to be carried out by the other partner (*tractator*) who supplied commercial skill and management presence. Originally dissolved after every voyage, in the fifteenth century more permanent limited partnerships developed. At least one partner with unlimited liability would carry out the business venture and manage the enterprise and a number of limited partners contributed a specified amount of money and received a share in the profits.[494] Where the limited partnership was equipped with a share capital, shares of limited partners became freely tradable. These forms survive more or less unchanged in the present-day forms of the *société en commandite simple* (or *par actiones*) in France and the *Kommanditgesellschaft* (*auf Aktien*) in Germany.

The concept has never been very popular in England[495] where commercial enterprise was increasingly being carried out by unincorporated joint stock companies. The unincorporated joint stock company was formed by a 'deed of settlement'. The company's property would be vested in trustees holding the legal title for the benefit of the members as *cestuis que* trust, who in turn held transferrable shares as equitable interests in the company's property.[496] Although legally a partnership and, thus, without corporate legal status, by skilful drafting of deeds of settlement promoters sought to mimic the advantages of incorporation. Usually, deeds of settlement would provide that the trustees could sue or be sued on behalf of the company. Whereas in the court of equity suits by trustees seem to have been generally permitted, actions at common law had to be brought by or against all the partners, essentially barring unincorporated joint stock companies from common law courts.[497] An attempt to achieve limited liability similar to that of chartered companies was made by including clauses in the deed of settlement limiting direct and indirect liability of members to the amount of their stock interest. In addition, contracts with third parties contained clauses stipulating that liability will be limited to the assets of the company.[498] The efficacy

[488] P Ireland, 'Capitalism without the Capitalist: The Joint Stock Company Share and the Emergence of the Modern Doctrine of Separate Corporate Personality' (1996) 17 Legal History 41.

[489] Blumberg (n 375) 11 n 9.

[490] *Edmunds v Brown and Tillard* [1669] 1 Lev 237; where it was held that the members of the chartered Company of Woodmongers could not be sued on a bond for £500 given by the company. Cf Blumberg (n 375) 10.

[491] *Salmon v The Hamborough Company* (1671) 1 Ch Cas 204; Williston (n 474) 161.

[492] Blumberg (n 375) 12. [493] ibid 13. [494] Perrott (n 353) 92.

[495] Introduced by the Limited Partnership Act 1907, the number of limited partnership has been growing in recent years. This largely due to limited partnerships being used as a vehicle for venture capital and private equity investment funds and for tax purposes. cf Davies and Worthington (n 8) para 1-5 note 21.

[496] Davies (n 420) 28. [497] ibid 29–31; Perrott (n 353) 96. [498] Blumberg (n 375) 15.

of these clauses was far from clear. It was only by the middle of the nineteenth century that their validity was finally confirmed by the courts in respect of express clauses in insurance policies,[499] whereas a clause in the deed of settlement was deemed to be insufficient, even if the creditor had notice thereof.[500] In practice, however, it was almost impossible to obtain judgment against the fluctuating body of shareholders, never mind to enforce it against the members whose identities would often be concealed.[501] Unlimited liability, therefore, was, in the words of Davies, 'a delusion rather than a protection to the public and no handicap at all for the dishonest promoter'.[502]

The first two decades of the eighteenth century saw a significant increase in the formation and flotation of joint stock companies, both incorporated and unincorporated, mainly with a view to increase overseas trade and to exploit colonial territories. The form of the joint stock company proved to be particularly suitable for unscrupulous promoters and managers to exploit the gullibility of the general public. Fraud and corruption were widespread and resulted in major financial scandals and collapses in France (*Compagnie des Indes* initiated by the Scotsman John Laws) and in England (South Sea Company and South Sea Bubble).[503] In 1720, England introduced the Bubble Act which made it illegal for an unincorporated company to act as corporate body and to raise transferable stock or transfer any shares therein without legal authority granted by Act of Parliament or Crown charter.[504] The effects were initially an increase in the number of petitions for charters and later the number of attempts to introduce private bills in Parliament. However, corporate charters were granted only sparingly and subject to restrictive conditions.[505] Many entrepreneurs had no choice but to rely on unincorporated companies which started to reappear after the initial shock subsided. In order to avoid prosecution under the Act, share transfers were initially severely restricted. In the second half of the century however things had reverted back to normal and free transferability was assumed to be permissible.[506] The Bubble Act was finally repealed in 1825.

The nineteenth century was to become the century of the modern business corporation. Increasing industrialization resulted in heightened demand for the privileges of incorporation. On the continent, France was first to react. In its *Code de commerce* of 1807 it granted free incorporation to limited partnerships with a share capital (*sociétés en commandite par actiones*). This was deemed to be acceptable since at least one member remained personally liable for the partnership's obligations. The Code also introduced the *société anonyme* as a form for large-scale companies with a share capital. Pursuant to Article 33, 'the members [of a *société anonyme*] are liable only for the loss of the amount of their interest in the company', thus introducing limited liability as a general principle of incorporation for the first time. For the *société anonyme* the *octroi* system was retained. Incorporation remained dependent upon authorization by the government and government approval of the company's constitution.[507] Thus, the limited partnership with a share capital became the prime vehicle for corporate enterprise in nineteenth-century France; with fraudulent speculation triggering a reform of the law in 1838.[508] Jurisprudence early on accepted separate legal personality for all commercial partnerships and companies on the basis of the mere fact of their formation, in respect of *sociétés anonymes* still depended on administrative authorization. The company was not regarded as being liable for the personal debts of its members, nor for obligations undertaken by the manager under his private signature.[509] It took, however, sixty years

499 *Halket v Merchant Traders' Ship, Loan & Insurance Association* (1849) 13 QB 960.

500 *Re Sea, Fire & Life Insurance Co* (1854) 3 De GM & G 459.

501 RR Formoy, *The Historical Foundations of Modern Company Law* (Sweet & Maxwell 1923) 35 ff.

502 Davies (n 420) 32.

503 Windbichler (n 176) 288 (§25 para 26); Germain and Magnier (n 192) para 1881; Davies (n 420) 24–8.

504 Davies (n 420) 25. 505 ibid 27. 506 ibid 28–9.

507 Germain and Magner (n 192) paras 1883–4.

508 M Lobban, 'Corporate Identity and Limited Liability in France and England 1825-67' (1996) 25 Anglo-American Law Review 397, 412–13.

509 ibid 407.

before the principle of general incorporation, subject only to compliance with certain formalities, was finally adopted in 1867.[510] As a result the number of incorporations increased rapidly.[511] The private company introduced in 1863 did not find much favour in the eyes of promoters, largely owing to certain obligations imposed on directors.[512] The limited liability (private) company (*société en responsabilité limité*) was finally introduced in 1925 following the German model of the GmbH.[513]

The sphere of application of the Napoleonic *Code de commerce* was extended by force of arms to a number of German states who came under French rule during Napoleon's military campaigns.[514] Some of these states retained the Code even after the fall of Napoleon until its replacement by German legislation.[515] The influence exerted by the *Code de commerce* on subsequent German legislation was immense. The *Aktiengesellschaft* provided for in the *Allgemeines Deutsches Handelsgesetzbuch* (ADHGB) which was adopted in 1861 as a uniform model law to be implemented by the German states closely followed the model of the *société anonyme.*[516] The *Aktiengesellschaft* 'as such' may have its own rights and obligations, may own real property, and sue and be sued under its own name.[517] The liability of shareholders was limited by the amount of their contributions without being personally liable for the company's debts.[518] Thus, corporate personality and limited liability became the defining features of the *Aktiengesellschaft*. The ADHGB, too, followed the *octroi* system, making incorporation subject to government concession.[519] However, before the Act was adopted as a Federal statute of the German Empire in 1871, the *octroi* system was replaced by a system of general incorporation subject to compliance with certain legal formalities.[520] In 1892 with the passing of the *GmbH-Gesetz*, legal personality and limited liability became available for small private companies with a personalized partnership-type structure.

In England the charter system was finally[521] replaced by general incorporation under the Joint Stock Companies Registration and Regulation Act of 1844. As mentioned above, this Act was not seen as creating a new form of trading institution. Rather, it conferred on the unincorporated joint stock company, organized in partnership form, some of the advantages of corporate personality. The company registered under the Act was to have a common seal, be able to sue and be sued, enter into contracts, and hold land in its corporate name.[522] However, in the eyes of the law the company remained a kind of partnerships and the shareholders its collective owners. It was the members who were incorporated, rather than a new legal person being created. It also meant that only a genuine partnership, consisting of at least twenty-five, later seven, members could incorporate.[523] Moreover, in line with partnership principles, the 1844 Act retained unlimited liability of members for unsatisfied corporate debts.[524] However, creditors had to proceed against the assets of the company first and its bankruptcy did not necessarily involve bankruptcy of its members.[525] But things were about to change with the rapid development of railways after 1844.[526] The railway industry required huge amounts of capital that could only be raised by large numbers of shares with small denominations held by a multitude of shareholders. This in turn required developed capital markets where these shares could be traded freely. The share emerged as a free-standing item of property in its own right severed from the property owned by the company. Shareholders were externalized from the companies in which they were members. Gradually, the company emerged as a reified entity completely separate from its members.[527]

510 AK Kuhn, *A Comparative Study of the Law of Corporations* (Columbia University Press 1912) 57.
511 Cf for empirical material Blumberg (n 375) 39; Germain and Magnier (n 192) para 1887.
512 Germain and Magnier (n 192) para 1885. 513 ibid para 1775. 514 Kuhn (n 510) 65.
515 ibid. 516 ibid 66. 517 ADHGB, §213. 518 ibid §207. 519 ibid §208.
520 Macharzina (n 480) 48.
521 Under the Trading Companies Act 1934, later re-enacted as Chartered Companies Act 1937, the Crown could confer, by letters patent, any of the privileges of incorporation without actually granting a charter.
522 Lobban (n 508) 416. 523 Grantham (n 319) 561. 524 Davies (n 420) 38.
525 ibid 38–9. 526 Blumberg (n 375) 18–20. 527 Ireland (n 488) 67–9.

At the same time railways were exposed to heavy tort liability which could not be eliminated by contractual limitations and public notice. However, limited liability remained a highly contentious political issue.[528] Only after a long and heated debate[529] was limited liability finally welcomed as a general feature of company law. This was achieved in 1855 with the Limited Liability Act 1855 and the subsequent Joint Stock Companies Act 1856.[530] After consolidation of various amendments, the Companies Act 1862 emerged as the first modern company law statute in England. These developments culminated in the famous decision in *Salomon & A Salomon & Co Ltd*,[531] decided by the House of Lords in 1897, which consolidated the entity concept and opened the corporate form for all entrepreneurs, including small partnerships and sole traders. The Companies Acts 1900 and 1907 legitimized the private company by exempting it from certain publicity requirements.[532]

Early American settlers would have been familiar with the joint stock company in both its incorporated and unincorporated form.[533] The American experience departed from the English experience with the revolution in 1776. The power to grant corporate charters moved to the then thirteen states. In contrast to England, charters were granted more readily; at first only to corporations with public functions, financial institutions, and insurance companies, subsequently, with growing industrialization, also to manufacturing businesses.[534] Before the passing of general incorporation statutes after about 1810, unincorporated joint stock companies on the basis of partnership law and with increasingly elaborate articles of association were used in order to emulate the advantages of the corporate form.[535] There was considerable uncertainty about whether US courts would regard unincorporated joint stock companies as separate entities,[536] and the notion that shares in unincorporated joint stock companies could be freely traded was clearly affirmed only in 1827.[537] By contrast, a corporate charter would create a separate legal entity which could hold business property separate from the personal property of individual promoters and protect the business property from subdivision and seizure. This was necessary in light of the public interest nature and capital intensity of the businesses that obtained charters at that time.[538] Massachusetts adopted the first general incorporation act for manufacturing companies in 1809, New York followed in 1811. Over time, more and more states enacted general incorporation statutes with an ever broader scope of application.[539] Early case law emphasized that the resources invested in a corporation no longer belonged to the shareholders, but rather, remained the property of the corporation unless and until paid out in the form of dividends.[540] Direct and indirect shareholder liability typically was limited to a greater or lesser extent in the charters of 'public function' companies and financial companies. By contrast, the members of manufacturing companies at first remained directly liable for the company's debts.[541] Early in the nineteenth century, courts in Massachusetts[542] and

[528] Davies (n 420) 40–6.

[529] Forbes (n 420) 171, advances an interesting theory for the comparatively late development of limited liability in highly industrialized England: Whereas limited liability is most useful for new firms which require the pooling of savings from a large number of individuals, England had well established industries and wealth was concentrated in viewer hands. These established industrialists did not need the additional funds generated by limited liability in order to expand. Indeed, limited liability as a general principle meant enhanced competition and potentially loss of market shares. Hence the resistance to the introduction of limited liability by British industrialists.

[530] Blumberg (n 375) 19; Davies (n 420) 44–6. [531] [1897] AC 22. [532] Davies (n 420) 48.

[533] Blair (n 22) 415.

[534] Blumberg (n 375) 24, 28; S Livermore, 'Unlimited Liability in Early American Corporations' (1935) 43 Journal of Political Economy 674.

[535] Blair (n 22) 419. [536] ibid 422.

[537] HL Sowards and JS Mofsky, 'Factors Affecting the Development of Corporation Law' (1969) 23 University of Miami Law Review 476, 482.

[538] Blair (n 22) 424. [539] ibid 426.

[540] *Brightwell v Mallory*, 18 Tenn (1 Yer) 196, 197–98 (1836). [541] Blumberg (n 375) 26, 30.

[542] *Wood v Dummer* 30 F. Cas. 435, 436 (C.C. Me. 1824) (Story J): 'The individual stockholders are not liable for the debts of the bank in their private capacities. The charter relieves them from personal responsibility, and substitutes the capital stock in its stead'.

Pennsylvania[543] decided that, absent an express provision to the contrary in the corporate charter, shareholders were not liable directly or indirectly for the company's debts. The legislatures followed suit. New York's general incorporation statute of 1811 provided for double liability, that is, liability for corporate obligations up to an amount equal to the par value of the shares held, to be later replaced by limited liability.[544] Rhode Island came last in 1847.[545] A number of states maintained some form of qualified limited liability well into the twentieth century.[546] The US experience is particularly interesting because of the existence, for a period of time, of very different liability regimes side by side.[547]

By the beginning if the twentieth century the business corporation with separate legal personality, limited liability and freely transferable shares had become the predominant form of business organization in all jurisdictions here under consideration. Despite many reforms of corporate and company law during the course of the last century,[548] often triggered by excessive speculation, economic crises, and corporate scandals, the basic features of the business corporation remain remarkably stable and still define the modern business corporation of today.

E. Corporate (Law) Theory: The Nature of the Corporation

The development of the modern business corporation was largely driven by economic developments, the needs of a burgeoning industrial revolution and/or the demands of a new class of financial capitalists. Law was often reactive when it pragmatically tried to accommodate these new economic realities. The question may, therefore, be asked whether thinking about corporate (law) theory is a worthwhile endeavour at all.[549] In other words, can knowledge and understanding of corporate theory at least contribute to our better understanding of the modern business corporation and corporate law?

Corporate (law) theories, as any theory about law, usually have both a positive and a normative dimension. In their positive dimension corporate theories purport to describe and analyse the positive law—statutes and cases—and legal practice in a coherent fashion. Legal and extra-legal material is ordered so as to reconcile disparate and, on the surface, conflicting rules, decisions, and practices. In order to achieve this, corporate theories aim to unearth a deeper meaning, sense, principle, or justification underlying different and seemingly unconnected rules and cases, linking them up so that they form a coherent body of law. A particular corporate theory cannot as such be 'right' or 'wrong'. Rather, its 'validity' depends on its force of persuasion within the relevant reference community. This in turn is a function of how well the theory can accommodate the legal material and practice of the time and how attractive its ideological underpinnings are for the participants in the relevant discourse. The principles (allegedly) underlying the positive law, giving them sense and meaning, form the basis for the normative dimension of corporate theory. As the inner justification for law and regulation, they may provide ammunition for critiquing the law as it stands, reasons and guidelines for law reform, as well as arguments in actual litigation. Coherence and normative saturation enhance predictability and even allow for the anticipation of future legal developments.

When we now look at the theories that have been developed over time we will see certain recurring patterns. Theories that have emerged at certain times and in certain places may

[543] *Myers v Irwin*, 1816 WL 1539, 1541 (Pa. 1816) (Tilghman CJ): 'personal responsibility of the stockholder is inconsistent with the nature of a body corporate'.

[544] Blumberg (n 375) 34. [545] ibid. [546] ibid 42–52. [547] ibid 35.

[548] For Germany: Windbichler (n 176) 291–6 (§25 para 30-34); for France: Germain and Magnier (n 192) paras 1883–99; for England: Davies (n 420) 48–50.

[549] LE Mitchell, 'The Relevance of Corporate Theory to Corporate and Economic Development: Comment on the Transplantation of the Legal Discourse on Corporate Personality Theories' (2006) 63 Washington & Lee Law Review 1489.

reappear in a different guise, in a different place and context. Depending on the respective socio-economic and political circumstances, the issues addressed by these theories may differ; their emphasis shifts in accordance with the pressing legal and economic problems of the day. Thus, the great theory debates in Germany and France in the nineteenth century focused on the role of the state in the process of company formation and freedom of association. The reception of these theories in the United States in the early twentieth century was largely owed to the questions associated with the protection of corporations through rights granted by the Constitution. In the 1930s and 1940s the emphasis shifted towards what is now called 'corporate governance': in whose interest should corporations be run and how should the law react to the immense power these organizations could wield? With the advent of neoliberalism in the 1960 and 1970s the emphasis changed again towards free markets and deregulation, and a different attitude to corporate governance took hold. Most theories are ideology driven. There is as such nothing wrong with that, as long as we are aware of the fact and realize that none of these theories is capable of providing the only and immutable truth.

We begin our survey with nineteenth-century Germany. This was the battleground for the two great theories on the nature of the legal person that have influenced in one way or another all future discourse: the 'fiction theory', associated with the name of Friedrich Carl von Savigny (and his pupils); and the 'real entity theory', formulated in its most prominent form by Otto Gierke. Von Savigny's 'fiction theory', derived from Roman and Canon law,[550] rests on the assumption that only the individual human being can have legal personality. Positive law may extend this natural concept of the person by conferring legal personality on entities that are not human beings, that is, by creating a legal person.[551] Legal persons are artificial entities, assumed only for legal purposes as a mere fiction. The essence of the legal person is the capacity to hold property.[552] Legal persons are generally formed, not by the mere will of their members, but by a concession of the highest power within the state, either explicitly by actual recognition, or impliedly through toleration. For von Savigny, the necessity of state authority to form a legal person had a compelling legal reason: unlike individual human beings, legal persons lack actual physical appearance; in order to make third parties aware of their rights, natural affirmation had to be substituted by an act of state authority. Otherwise, uncertainty of the highest order would result.[553] In order to acquire property legal persons must be represented by their agents. Agency as an artificial construct is effectuated by a legal person's constitution.[554] As a mere property-owning entity without a will of its own, a legal person is outside the scope of criminal law.[555] The same applies in respect of torts.[556]

The core of Gierke's real entity theory was the idea of the 'real aggregate person' (*reale Gesamtperson*). In its essence the legal person is a real collective unit, different from the aggregate of its constituting individual members, recognized by law in its legal personality.[557] Although the theory was committed to the principle of freedom of association,[558] it did not deny that a legal person may exist only by the legitimizing force of the law and that the state can stipulate the preconditions for the recognition of a legal person.[559] But it cannot create the real world substratum of this legal personality. Rather, law selects the entities on which it will confer legal personality among the entities it finds in the real world.[560] In this respect, Gierke's approach is not yet very different from von Savigny's, who also recognized

550 The fiction theory is often attributed to Pope Innocent IV; see WS Holdsworth, *A History of English Law, Vol III* (Methuen 1927) 470.

551 See von Savigny (n 472) §60.
552 ibid §85.
553 ibid §89.
554 ibid §90.
555 ibid §94.
556 ibid §95.
557 O Gierke, *Deutsches Privatrecht Band I: Allgemeiner Teil und Personenrecht* (Nachdruck 1895) 469.
558 O Gierke, *Genossenschaftstheorie und die deutsche Rechtsprechung* (Nachdruck 1887) 16.
559 ibid 19–20; Gierke (n 557) 471.
560 Gierke (n 558) 22.

the extra-legal and social reality of certain collective entities.[561] The main difference in terms of legal reasoning is that, according to Gierke, it was inherent to the 'concept of law' (*Rechtsidee*) that it cannot arbitrarily grant legal personality to, or withhold legal personality from, any particular thing. Only entities capable of forming a human will are suitable to have legal personality. Thus, the law can only recognize human beings and human collectives as 'persons'; and the 'concept of law' demands the recognition of legal personality of collective units that can form a collective will.[562] Through its organs, the collective person is capable of willing and acting. What an organ wills and does within the boundaries of its competence is the will and action of the legal person itself. Agency is inapplicable.[563] The legal person is responsible for its own faults and may be liable in crime and in tort. Its legal personality does not just relate to the ability to hold property, it also encompasses personal rights (name, seat, honour).[564]

It is important to realize that both theories, when they were developed, did not have the modern business corporation in mind. When von Savigny wrote, in the first half of the nineteenth century, the ascent of this organizational form was only just beginning and it certainly had not reached the dominance we have seen from the early twentieth century to the present day. Rather, what both theories were concerned with are any organizations—in the public interest, for business, or any other purpose—in which human beings could come together and pool resources in order to pursue a common objective. Von Savigny was suspicious of these 'intermediate powers' (intermediate between the individual and the state). With the concentration of economic power and a potentially democratic internal structure they posed a challenge to the traditional power centres of state and aristocracy.[565] They had to be kept in check und subjected to close scrutiny. By contrast, Gierke adhered to the liberal ideal of freedom of association that could facilitate the organization of progressive forces in society and a movement to more democratic structures. With the great codifications in Germany at the end of the nineteenth century and a consequent move towards legal positivism, the debate subsided. The legislator refrained from endorsing any particular theory. However, with the introduction of general incorporation, tort liability of corporations for the acts of their organs[566] and unlimited authority to represent the company vis-à-vis third parties, important elements of the real entity theory made it into law. However, von Savigny's legacy is the realization that in order to allow legal persons to participate in business and public life the state has to make sure by some act of publicity that the legal person actually exists.[567]

In France, the discussion proceeded along slightly different lines. One debate concerned the nature of the legal person (*personnalité morale*). Here we find essentially the familiar 'fiction' and 'real entity' theories with frequent reference to the writings of von Savigny and Gierke.[568] As in Germany, this debate was not limited to the business corporation, but encompassed all legal persons, including those of public law. It also has lost much of its significance today. A second and different discourse related to the nature of the company (*société*) as such. Remember that in France this term encompasses both corporate as well as partnership type entities, and all have, in principle, legal personality separate from their members. On the basis of Roman law ideas, the first half of the nineteenth century was dominated by the contractual theory. As defined in the *Code civil* of 1804, the company is a contract between two or more persons.[569] With the conclusion of this contract, an act of free will of

[561] von Savigny (n 472) §§86. [562] Gierke (n 558) 471. [563] ibid 472.

[564] ibid 472. Inapplicable are the rights that relate to individual existence.

[565] von Savigny (n 472) §89. He thought that corporations and foundations may be used to promote immoral and dangerous ideas and that there was also a danger of concentration of wealth and property in the 'dead hand'.

[566] BGB, §31. [567] K Schmidt, *Gesellschaftsrecht* (4th edn, Heymann 2002) 191.

[568] cf L Michoud, *La Théorie De La Personnalité Morale: Son Application Au Droit Français, Tome Premier* (LGDJ 1924) 16, 67.

[569] Civ art 1832; amendments had to be made to accommodate the single-person company where the existence of the company depends on an act of will of the single promoter.

the participating persons, the company comes into existence as between the shareholders or partners, but also vis-à-vis third parties. This is because the contract objectively changes the legal situation.[570] This theory resonated well with the general notions of free will and freedom of contract that were prevalent in nineteenth-century France. It advocated the free formation of business entities and culminated in the availability of general incorporation in form of the *société anonyme* in 1867.[571] At the same time the rise of the *société anonyme* highlighted the considerable conceptual difficulties of the contractual theory. The registration requirement, the majority principle, the increase of mandatory regulation, a *numerus clausus* of possible company forms, the idea that the company has an interest of its own different from those of its members, its (potentially) indefinite life span, legal personality, and patrimony all suggested that a company cannot simply emanate from the free will of the participants and goes far beyond a mere contract between the parties.[572]

At a time when civilian doctrine tried to safeguard the classic conception of freedom of contract and the idea of private autonomy against ever-increasing mandatory regulation, commercial doctrine turned to the notion of the institution, derived from public law theory.[573] 'Institution' in this context means a social organization accepted by the majority of the members of a group of people in view of the pursuit of a common objective. The institution goes beyond the human person and pursues aims to which the individual wills must be subordinated. In that way it balances the conflicting interests of the participants and unites them in a durable state of social peace.[574] This means that the rights and obligations of the participants are not fixed in a definitive manner by the contract of formation; rather they are subject to modification by majority decisions if the interest of the company so requires. Also, the directors of the company are not simply the agents of the shareholders; rather they have the authority to assure the realization of the common goal.[575] The theory provides a neat metaphor without precisely defining any particular legal regime. Normatively, it may provide a justification for mandatory regulation of corporate activity and state intervention into the market and the economy, possibly in the interest of stakeholders and the wider society. It has dominated the larger part of the twentieth century. In fact, depending on the density of regulation and its retreat at any particular time, corporate theory in France has oscillated between 'institutionalisation' and 'contractualisation' of corporate law.[576]

Since in France all companies have legal personality, both contractual and institutional theory mainly concerned the internal governance structure of the company. Whereas contractual theory seems to fit for personalized companies; the institutional theory can better accommodate companies with a share capital where individual membership does not matter. However, both theories have in mind a group of people as substratum of the company and have difficulty in accommodating phenomena where the emphasis is on a pool of assets rather than on the people that the assets are attributed to. In the second half of the twentieth century a new theory emerged. This new functional theory criticizes the traditional approach for ignoring the essential difference between the 'enterprise' and the 'company'. The enterprise is an economic organization for the production, transformation, or commercialization of goods and services. It is not a legal concept, but a social phenomenon. The existence of the enterprise and its activity give rise to a multitude of different interests with the enterprise as their centre and focus. The company as a legal concept facilitates the activity of the enterprise. It is a device for organizing the enterprise and for protecting and balancing the various interests involved, and for enforcing that balance. The company thus emerges

570 Germain and Magnier (n 192) para 1517.

571 ibid.

572 J-P Bertrel, 'Liberté contractuelle et sociétés' (1996) 49 RTD com 595, 611–12; Cozian, Viandier, and Deboissy (n 10) paras 9–12.

573 Cozian, Viandier, and Deboissy (n 10) para 10.

574 Bertrel (n 572) 613.

575 Germain and Magnier (n 192) para 1518.

576 Cozian, Viandier, and Deboissy (n 10) para 10; Cannu and Dondero (n 236) paras 274, 280–281.

as a technique for organizing an enterprise. This functional definition of the company does not in any way prejudge the legal nature of that organization which can be institutional (a mandatory organization imposed by the legislator), contractual (an organization designed by the participants), or both. Mandatory law and/or contract, as the case may be, determine the nature of the organization and its author.[577] In this vain, legal personality emerges as a response to the economic need of granting an enterprise legal autonomy for the conduct of economic activity.[578] Under this theory, the substratum of the company is the enterprise as an assemblage of assets, manpower, organizational structures, goodwill etc. brought together in order to achieve a certain purpose. People, as groups or individually, are no longer the focal point of the company. What matters is the organization. The functional theory has become widely accepted by commentators and even the legislator, and is prevalent today. Its great strength is its flexibility. Contract and institution do no longer appear as irreconcilable opposites. Mandatory regulation is a fact, as is the contractual nature of much of what is going on within the company.[579] However, the theory is normatively indeterminate and neutral in ideological terms. Any normativity must be imported from other sources, be they freedom of contract, economic efficiency or protection of stakeholder interests.

English lawyers are generally not interested in high-level theory, but in practical solutions on the basis of the facts of the case. This is particularly true for company law which, in the mind of company lawyers, exists for the very down-to-earth reason of generating a profit for investors. It is therefore no surprise that in England corporate theory has never been of similar importance as in our two civil law jurisdictions.[580] In fact, corporate theory was seen not even as part of company law, but as the domain of jurisprudence. In England freedom of association has never been much of an issue. The availability of the trust made it possible to grant a multitude of persons economic rights in trust property. These organizations could function sufficiently well without having obtained legal personality.[581] Despite this apparent lack of interest, it is still possible to identify the ideas on the emerging business corporation that were prevalent at the time of its inception. There is first the fiction theory, combined with the concession theory.[582] It was received into English law from Roman and Canon law sources, mainly in order to explain the property holding capacity of ecclesiastical and municipal bodies.[583] As early as 1765, Blackstone wrote: 'it has been found necessary, when it is for the advantage of the public to have any particular rights kept on foot and continued, to constitute artificial persons, who may maintain a perpetual succession, and enjoy a kind of legal immortality. These artificial persons are called bodies politic, bodies corporate, or corporations'.[584] He goes on to explain that '[t]he king's consent is absolutely necessary to the erection of any corporation; either impliedly or expressly given'.[585] The fiction/concession theory treats the (incorporated) company as an artificial person whose separate legal personality is granted as a privilege by the state. The idea of a grant or concession by the crown was originally necessary to legitimize the exercise of state and monopoly power by the great colonial companies of the seventeenth century. It was later used in order to justify the

[577] J Paillusseau, *Les fondements du droit moderne des société* (JCP 1984) 3148.

[578] J Paillusseau, *La droit moderne et la personalité morale* (RTD 1993) 705.

[579] Cozian, Viandier, and Deboissy (n 10) para 10.

[580] NHD Foster, 'Company Law Theory in Comparative Perspective: England and France' (2000) 48 American Journal of Comparative Law 573, 587.

[581] Maitland (n 32) xxix; Holdsworth (n 550) Volume IX 47.

[582] M Stokes, 'Company Law and Legal Theory' in W Twining (ed), *Legal Theory and Common Law* (Blackwell's 1986) 155, 162. Fiction theory and concession theory are sometimes treated separately; cf RWM Dias, *Jurisprudence* (Butterworths 1964) 297–8. According to this writer, the identification of 'law' with 'state' is necessary for the concession theory, but not for the older 'fiction theory'. The latter first appeared at a time when there was no nation state in the modern sense. In the nineteenth and early twentieth century both theories collapse into one.

[583] Holdsworth (n 550) Volume III 471.

[584] W Blackstone, *Commentaries on the Laws and Constitution of England* (ABA Publishing 2009) 71.

[585] ibid 72.

control and subordination to the state of 'large associations of men' as the only way they 'can be safely allowed to lead an active life'.[586] The theory is also well in accordance with practice in the early nineteenth century when corporate charters were granted sparingly and mainly for undertakings that operated in the public interest. It found its doctrinal expression in the *ultra vires* principle that keeps corporate entities within the narrow confines of the powers granted to them by the statute or charter conferring corporate identity upon them.[587] It is sometimes said that it also shines through in Lord Macnaughten's famous statement in the *Salomon case* that at law the company 'is a different person altogether from the subscribers to the memorandum'.[588]

Unincorporated joint stock companies were a form of partnership and even the successive Companies Acts of the 1840s and 1850s were not perceived as changing the partnership status of these businesses after incorporation. A natural conclusion was, thus, to analyse the company as a form created by free agreement amongst the shareholders, and thus as a contract.[589] As in France, the prevalence of general ideas of freedom of contract and free enterprise during the development of *laissez-faire* capitalism in the nineteenth century rendered this theory very attractive to the legal community.[590] The failure of the Bubble Act of 1720 to suppress joint stock companies and to destroy the trade in their shares proved that modern capitalistic forms could flourish without the open support of sovereign power.[591] English lawyers maintained that only natural persons occupied the legal world. Trustees held the corporate property on trust for the aggregate of shareholders as beneficiaries and acted as their human agents.[592] When general incorporation became available the contractarian theory could fruitfully be combined with the fiction theory in that the fluctuating body of a multitude of shareholders could now be perceived as a fictional entity. In *Canada National Fire Insurance Co v Hutchings*[593] Sir Walter Phillimore remarked that UK companies 'are formed by contract, whether it be under deed of settlement or under memorandum and articles of association to which the Registrar of Joint-Stock Companies necessarily assents if the documents are regular in form'. The contractarian theory faces similar conceptual difficulties as in France: majority principle, extensive mandatory regulation, the need of state intervention in order to grant legal personality and limited liability.[594] Regardless, the great importance of contractual principles for the internal relationships in the company is recognized by what is now section 33(1) of the Companies Act 2006: 'The provisions of a company's constitution bind the company and its members to the same extent as if they were covenants on the part of the company and of each member to observe those provisions'.[595]

Gierke's real entity theory also gained some foothold in England. It was popularized by Frederic William Maitland's translation into English of part of Gierke's work, first published in 1900.[596] As in Germany, the company was seen as a natural or real entity which exists separately and is distinct from the shareholders. Dicey wrote 'whenever man act in concert for a common purpose they tend to create a body, which from no fiction of law but from the very nature of things, differs from the individuals of whom it is constituted'.[597] This body is, in Maitland's words, 'no fiction, no symbol, no piece of the state's machinery, no collective name

[586] Holdsworth (n 550) Volume IX 47.

[587] *Ashbury Railway Carriage and Iron Company v Riche* [1874-80] All ER Rep Ext 2219.

[588] Foster (n 580) 582. [589] Stokes (n 582) 162. [590] ibid.

[591] AJ Jacobson, 'The Private Use of Public Authority: Sovereignty and Association in the Common Law' (1980) 29 Buffalo Law Review 599, 662.

[592] ibid 663. [593] [1918] AC 451, 456 (PC). [594] Foster (n 580) 586.

[595] But see M Moore, 'Private Ordering and Public Policy: The Paradoxical Foundations of Corporate Contractarianism' (2014) 34 Oxford Journal of Legal Studies 693, 719: 'the very formal status of the corporate constitution as a supposedly 'private' contractual document rests paradoxically on a *public* statutory basis' (emphasis in original).

[596] Maitland (n 32).

[597] AV Dicey, *Lectures on the Relationship between Law and Public Opinion in England during the Nineteenth Century* (Macmillan 1905) 153.

for individuals, but a living organism and a real person, with body and members and a will of its own. Itself can will, itself can act; it wills and acts by the men who are its organs as a man wills and acts by brain, mouth and hand'.[598] It found favour mainly with academic writers,[599] rather than the legal professions, but also had some impact on legal doctrine. In *Lennard's Carrying Co. v Asiatic Petroleum Co Ltd*[600] Viscount Haldane LC said that a corporation 'has no mind of its own any more than it has a body of its own; its active and directing will must consequently be sought in the person of somebody who for some purposes may be called an agent, but who is really the directing mind and will of the corporation, the very ego and centre of the personality of the corporation ... [H]is action is the very action of the company itself'. This was taken further by Denning LJ (as he then was) in *Bolton (Engineering) Co Ltd v Graham & Sons*:[601] 'A company may in many ways be likened to a human body. It has a brain and nerve centre which controls what it does. It also has hands which hold the tools and act in accordance with directions from the centre. Some of the people in the company are mere servants and agents ... Others are directors and managers who represent the directing mind and will of the company'. This is still the basis for holding incorporated bodies themselves liable for wrongs committed by their agents in the course of their employment.[602]

This state of affairs neatly reflects the English attitude towards corporate theory.[603] The different theories appear as a set of ideas developed at different times and for various purposes. They are available for use if necessary and the English lawyer has no problem in relying soon on one, soon on the other theory as long as this furthers a reasonable outcome in the case at hand.[604] Thus, for long stretches of the twentieth-century fiction/concession, contract and real entity theory existed side-by-side in peaceful harmony, without much academic interest in the debate. Only in the 1990s do we see a revived interest in corporate theory, mainly triggered by the law and economics movement.[605] But this is a global phenomenon that started in the United States, which is where we turn to now.

American corporate law and theory in the first half of the nineteenth century was dominated by fiction/concession theories.[606] This is captured by the often-cited statement of Chief Justice Marshall in the *Dartmouth College* case: 'a corporation is an artificial being, invisible, intangible, and existing only in contemplation of law'.[607] This was the phase where incorporation depended on the grant of a charter by the state legislature. The idea persisted that a charter was granted not merely for private profit-making purposes but at least partly also in the public interest. Corporations were conceptualized as artificial or fictitious entities with an existence separate from the persons who formed it. This separate existence was owed to the state.[608]

When, in the second half of the nineteenth century, general incorporation became widely available, guaranteeing equal access to the corporate from, incorporation was no longer regarded as a special privilege granted by the state, but as a normal way of doing business.[609] Individuals could come together voluntarily to form a corporation by following a simple procedure with little in the way in terms of substantive requirements. The fiction/concession theories were no longer tenable. One way of reconceptualizing the corporation was to draw

[598] Maitland (n 32) xxvi.
[599] Holdsworth (n 550) Volume IX 47; F Pollock, 'Has the Common Law Received the Fiction Theory' (1911) 27 LQR 219, 235.
[600] [1915] AC 705, 713 (HL).
[601] [1957] 1 QB 159, 172 (CA).
[602] Davies and Worthington (n 8) paras 7-30–7-46.
[603] For a modern take on this see French (n 327) 139–40.
[604] Foster (n 580) 590.
[605] BR Cheffins, 'Using Theory to Study Law: A Company Law Perspective' (1999) 58 CLJ 197.
[606] MJ Phillips, 'Reappraising the Real Entity Theory of the Corporation' (1994) 21 Florida State University Law Review 1061, 1065.
[607] *Trustees of Dartmouth College v Woodward* 17 US (14 Wheat) 518, 636 (1819).
[608] WW Bratton, 'The New Economic Theory of the Firm: Critical Perspectives from History' (1989) 41 Stanford Law Review 1471, 1484.
[609] D Millon, 'Theories of the Corporation' (1990) Duke Law Journal 201, 208.

an analogy to the partnership and view it as a creature of free contracting among individual shareholders.[610] Contractarian or aggregate theories have in common that the corporation as an entity separate from its members does not exist; it is nothing more than, and not different from, the sum, or aggregate, of its constituent parts.[611] Aggregate theories could take many different forms and support different and conflicting normative claims. Some were hostile to the corporation as a device of concentrating economic power and inhibiting free competition. These theories advocated a return to the partnership concept, reserving the corporate form for natural monopolies.[612] On the other hand, aggregate theories could be used to defend the corporation against state regulation. In the *Railroad Tax Cases* Justice Field held that although private corporations are artificial persons, 'they consist of aggregations of individuals united for some legitimate business ... It would be a most singular result if a constitutional provision intended for the protection of every person against partial and discriminating legislation by the states, should cease to exert such protection the moment the person becomes a member of a corporation'.[613] Moreover, 'the property of a corporation is in fact the property of the corporators. To deprive the corporation of its property, or to burden it, is, in fact, to deprive the corporators of their property or to lessen its value'.[614] Thus, by 'disaggregating' the corporation and focusing on the shareholders, courts were able to extend the application of constitutional rights, notably the fourteenth amendment equal protection clause, to corporations.[615]

However, the partnership analogy did not fit the large management-oriented corporation that emerged at the turn of the nineteenth century to the twentieth century. With thousands of shareholders who, as passive investors, did not know and had never met each other, the conceptualization as mere contracts was difficult to maintain.[616] Even before the writings of Gierke and Maitland became widely known, American writers had already started to conceptualize corporations as 'autonomous, self-sufficient and self-renewing bodies' that 'may determine and enforce their common will'.[617] Modifying Gierke's theory significantly, Ernst Freund wrote in 1897 that: '[t]he association becomes visible and active through individuals only, but the common purpose, the concerted action, and the combined resources, produce upon our mind the impression that the association itself enjoys something like the power of individual personal agency'.[618] Arthur Machen later wrote: 'A corporation exists as an objectively real entity, which any well-developed child or normal man must perceive: the law merely recognizes and gives legal effect to the existence of this entity ... [A]n entity—not imaginary or fictitious, but real, not artificial but natural. Its existence is as real as that of an army or of the Church'.[619] As an entity that was created 'naturally' through the free initiative of its members, the corporation was seen as less deserving of state intervention and interference.[620] Thus, real entity theories had a deregulatory bias. In contrast to many aggregate theories, corporations were not seen as a threat to free markets and free competition. Concentration of economic powers was perceived to be natural,[621] and the real entity of the corporation could partake in market and competition in the same way an individual could.[622] Within this historical context, real entity theories, thus, could be seen as

[610] V Morawetz, *A Treatise on the Law of Private Corporations* (Little Brown 1886) iii, 24.
[611] Phillips (n 606) 1066.
[612] MJ Horwitz, 'Santa Clara Revisited: The Development of Corporate Theory' (1985) 88 West Virginia Law Review 173, 205.
[613] *The Railroad Tax Cases: County of San Mateo v Southern Pacific R Co*, 13 F 722, 743 (C.C. Cal, 1882).
[614] ibid 747.
[615] *County of Santa Clara v Southern Pacific R Co*, 118 US 394 (US 1886); see Horwitz (n 612) 176–8.
[616] Phillips (n 606) 1067.
[617] JP Davis, 'The Nature of Corporations' (1887) 12 Political Science Quarterly 273, 294.
[618] E Freund, *The Legal Nature of Corporations* (Batoche 1897) 59.
[619] AW Machen, 'Corporate Personality' (1911) 24 Harvard Law Review 253, 261–2.
[620] Millon (n 609) 213. [621] Horwitz (n 612) 190. [622] Bratton (n 608) 1490.

legitimizing the large management-oriented corporations just when they came to dominate American business.[623]

The real entity theory dominated the first two decades of the twentieth century, until the prolific corporate theory debate came to an end during the late 1920s, when legal realism took hold of academia and practice.[624] In an important paper, published in 1926, philosopher John Dewey asserted the pointlessness of any inquiry into the true nature or essence of the legal person including the corporation. In Dewey's view, corporate theories were irredeemably indeterminate: 'Each theory has been used to serve the same ends, and each has been used to serve opposing ends'.[625] All that mattered were the social consequences that flowed from attributing legal rights and duties to an entity be it an individual or a body corporate. This paper marked the end of the traditional essentialist discourse in corporate theory. Thereafter, the emphasis shifted.

At the end of the nineteenth century the typical business corporation was still a single-purpose enterprise engaged in only one specific industry and was controlled by a single owner or a small group of people, often with family ties. Over the first two decades of the twentieth century corporations proved to be exceptionally effective units of production, and capital and economic power became ever more concentrated in the hands of the major corporations. In the course of vertical integration, corporations started to acquire their sources of supply and their retail distributors, mainly in order to obtain greater security in terms of access to resources and retail markets. Internal coordination and governance arrangements became ever more complex. A multi-level management infrastructure developed with increasing specialization along functional lines (production, sales, finance) and top executives directing overall business strategy.[626] At the same time, share ownership became more widely dispersed with a growing middle class starting to invest in railway and other companies. Against this backdrop, in 1932 Adolf Berle and Gardiner Means published their famous book *The Modern Corporation and Private Property*,[627] which would set the agenda for the next fifty years and beyond.

Berle and Means' central thesis is that the rise of the modern business corporation has revolutionized the way in which private property is held and productive activity is carried out. Under the traditional conception of private enterprise the self-interested property owner who was in control of the means of production would seek to maximize his profit for the benefit of society as a whole, subject only to the forces of free competition and the laws of supply and demand.[628] In the context of the modern business corporation with widely dispersed share ownership this has changed. The security holders as the 'owners' of the means of production are no longer in control of use and deployment of productive assets. Control has been surrendered to a management hierarchy that may become a self-perpetuating body where ownership is sufficiently widely dispersed.[629] The stockholders exchange their position as independent owners to become 'merely the recipients of the wages of capital'.[630] This 'Separation of ownership and control' raises fundamental questions as to the relation between ownership and control groups and the effect on the conduct of production. Berle

[623] Horwitz (n 612) 224. [624] Bratton (n 608) 1491.

[625] J Dewey, 'The Historic Background of Corporate Legal Personality' (1926) 35 Yale Law Journal 655, 669.

[626] Bratton (n 608) 1487–9.

[627] AA Berle and GC Means, *The Modern Corporation & Private Property* (Transaction 2009) first published in 1922.

[628] ibid 9.

[629] The authors distinguish five major types of control: (1) control by almost complete ownership, as in small closely held corporations; (2) majority control, where the 'separation of ownership from control' concerns only the minority; (3) control through legal devices without majority ownership, through pyramid structures, non-voting stocks, and voting trusts; (4) minority control through the ability to attract from scattered owners proxies sufficient to control a majority of votes; (5) management control where ownership is so widely dispersed that no shareholders can dominate the votes of the company. ibid 66–111.

[630] ibid 5.

and Means conclude that the interests of ownership and control are radically different and often opposed. The shareholders are interested in the company earning the maximum profit, and in their shares remaining freely marketable at a fair price. The control group are interested in their own personal profit; 'they can serve their own pockets better by profiting at the expense of the company than by making a profit for it'.[631] The separation of ownership and control, and the strengthening of the powers of control, call for a decision as to whether the law should ensure that corporations are operated primarily in the interests of the 'owners' or also in the interests of some other or wider group.[632] Berle and Means do not commit explicitly to any of the traditional corporate theories.[633] These were largely unimportant for their inquiry, which redefined the theoretical discourse in corporate law.

Following the publication of their book, corporate law scholarship, to the present day, has focused on the factual accuracy of their central claim of 'separation of ownership from control',[634] the conflict of interest between shareholders and management, how it could be alleviated, and whether corporations should be run in the interest of shareholders only, or whether the interest of other constituencies—employees, creditors, the community—should be taken into account.[635] This latter aspect, in particular, formed the basis for the social responsibility movement that became dominant during the two decades after the Second World War. Adherents sought to reconceptualize the public corporation as a social institution and subordinated the interests of shareholders to those of other groups or society as a whole. The idea of (corporate) social responsibility resurfaced at the start of the millennium, albeit in modified form, in the wake of the enormous corporate scandals of Enron, WorldCom, Global Crossing etc.[636] In the meantime, however, a new paradigm had taken hold of corporate theory. The rise of neoliberalism in combination with the law and economics movement would have a profound impact on corporate theory.

The two decades after the Second World War were dominated by a Keynesian approach to fiscal and monetary policy. State intervention in industries and markets was seen as legitimate and widely deployed in order to promote full employment, economic growth, and the welfare of the population. By the end of the 1960s, however, the post war period of high-level rates of economic growth in the industrialized world came to an end. Rising unemployment and inflation ushered in a period of 'stagflation' that would last throughout the 1970s. Keynesianism was unable to cope with fiscal crises of various states including Britain, the implications of the OPEC oil embargo and the breakdown of the Bretton Woods agreement of fixed exchange rates.[637] A new paradigm was necessary and in the struggle

[631] ibid 114.

[632] ibid 293. Interestingly, Berle and Means discuss whether the shareholders, 'by surrendering control and responsibility over the active property, have surrendered the right that the corporation should operate in their sole interest'. This would not necessarily mean that the new powers should be used exclusively in the interest of the controlling groups. Rather, the control groups have 'cleared the way for the claims of a group far wider than either the owners or the control. They have placed the community in a position to demand that the modern corporation serve not alone the owners or control but all society. Neither the claims of ownership nor those of control can stand against the paramount interest of the community'. ibid 312.

[633] Their focus on the relationship between shareholder 'owners' and management in control has led some to believe that implicitly their work is based on an aggregate theory of the corporation; Millon (n 609) 222–3. However, certain formulations may suggest otherwise: 'Since the corporation is a distinct legal identity, separate and apart from stockholders, it may become necessary to determine whether a director can be honest and faithful with regard to the whole corporation at the same time that he is taking a hostile position towards an individual shareholder'. (Berle and Means (n 627) 197); 'For the tens and even hundreds of thousands of workers and of owners in a single enterprise, individual initiative no longer exists. Their activity is group activity on a scale so large that the individual, except he be in a position of control, has dropped into relative insignificance'. (ibid 116).

[634] BR Cheffins and SA Bank, 'Is Berle and Means a Myth' (2009) 83 Business History Review 443.

[635] JL Weiner, 'The Berle-Dodd Dialogue on the Concept of the Corporation' (1964) 64 Columbia Law Review 1458.

[636] P Ireland and R Pillay, 'Corporate Social Responsibility and the New Constitutionalism' in P Utting and JC Marques (eds), *Corporate Social Responsibility and Regulatory Governance: Towards Inclusive Development?* (UNRISD/Palgrave-Macmillan 2008).

[637] Harvey (n 470) 10–12.

of ideas neoliberalism would emerge successful.[638] Promoted by figures such as the philosopher Friedrich von Hayek and the economist Milton Friedman, neoliberalism adhered to the free market principles of neoclassical economics. The role of the state is limited to providing a framework of strong private property rights, including their enforcement and defence, free markets, and free trade. Within that framework human well-being can best be advanced by giving free rein to individual entrepreneurial activity, keeping state intervention to the absolute minimum.[639] When Margaret Thatcher became Prime Minister of the United Kingdom in 1979 and Ronald Reagan was elected President of the United States a year later, neoliberalism and its radical deregulatory agenda finally occupied key political positions of power und subsequently came to dominate international institutions such as the IMF and the World Bank.[640] This intellectual and ideological climate proved to be a fertile ground also for a paradigm change in corporate theory.

Economists in the 1970s started to look inside the 'black box', as the firm was characterized in neoclassical terms, and tried to analyse how the conflicting objectives of the participants involved could yield the profit maximizing behaviour attributed to firms as market actors in the neoclassical model.[641] Given the increasing prominence of 'law and economics' as a method of legal inquiry, the economists' insights were enthusiastically taken up by legal scholars and 'nexus of contract' theories, in one form or another, have dominated corporate theory for the last thirty years.[642]

Building on Coase's earlier insights,[643] economists began to characterize the firm as a system of exchange contracts, albeit with particular features.[644] Under such a view it makes little sense to distinguish contracts 'inside' the firm from those 'outside' the firm. The logical consequence was to conceptualize the firm as a nexus for a set of contracting relationships among individuals. The corporation as a 'nexus of contracts' mediates the complex relationships of those who associate voluntarily with the corporation, in particular the multitude of different classes of creditors—debt investors, employees, suppliers, consumers—and equity investors.[645] Whereas the different classes of creditors, in principle, all have fixed interests in the firm, the equity investors (or shareholders), by contrast, have a right to the firm's residual income and receive what is left over after all fixed-interest claims have been discharged.[646] The shareholders are the corporation's residual risk bearers: the risk of failure and the rewards of success will impact most heavily on the shareholders, because the value of their equity in the company will directly reflect the profits earned or losses incurred in the project.

638 The reasons for neoliberalism's triumph are complex. However, the backing by wealthy and politically powerful elites seems to have played a significant role, ibid 21.

639 ibid 2. 640 ibid 22–6, 29.

641 MC Jensen and WH Meckling, 'Theory of the Firm: Managerial Behavior, Agency Costs, and Ownership Structure' in MC Jensen, *A Theory of the Firm: Governance, Residual Claims, and Organizational Forms* (HUP 2003) 83, 84.

642 The classical legal treatise is Easterbrook and Fischel (n 375); see also R Romano, *The Genius of American Corporate Law* (AEI Studies in Regulation and Federalism 1993). The literature is immense. Early proponents are HG Manne, 'Mergers and the Market for Corporate Control' (1965) 73 Journal of Political Economy 110; RK Winter, 'State Law, Shareholder Protection, and the Theory of the Corporation' (1977) 6 Journal of LS 251. For a critique see for instance WW Bratton, 'The "Nexus of Contracts" Corporation: A Critical Appraisal' (1989) 74 Cornell Law Review 407; MA Eisenberg, 'The Conception that the Corporation is a Nexus of Contracts and the Dual Nature of the Firm' (1998) 24 Journal of Corporation Law 819. For an overview of proponents and opponents see G Kelly and J Parkinson, 'The Conceptual Foundations of the Company: A Pluralist Approach' (1998) 2 Company Financial and Insolvency Law Review 174.

643 See text accompanying notes 15–17. 644 Alchian and Demsetz (n 13) 777.

645 See Jensen and Meckling (n 641) 88 ('The private corporation or firm is simply one form of legal fiction which serves as a nexus for contracting relationships and which is also characterized by the existence of divisible residual claims on the assets and cash flows of the organization which can generally be sold without permission of the other contracting individuals'); Easterbrook and Fischel (n 375) 12 ('corporation as a "nexus of contracts"); and, slightly differently, J Armour, HB Hansmann, R Kraakman, and M Pargendler, 'What is Corporate Law? in R Kraakman and others (eds), *The Anatomy of Corporate Law* (3nd edn, OUP 2017) 5 (the firm as a 'nexus *for* contracts', emphasis in the original).

646 Easterbrook and Fischel (n 375) 67.

Consequently, it is argued, shareholders have optimal incentives to monitor the management and to ensure that the management pursues optimal investment strategies.[647] As summarized by Kelly and Parkinson: '[w]here there is one residual claimant and the other parties receive fixed returns, maximising the residual is the same as maximising the total value received by all the parties and hence maximises social wealth'.[648] Consequently, the maximization of shareholders' returns on their investments as observable in share prices becomes the overriding objective of corporate activity. Shareholders and management find themselves in a principal–agent relationship. The divergence of interest between management and shareholders is the source of agency costs that arise from efforts to commit the agent to act in the best interest of the principal (bonding cost), from monitoring the agent (monitoring costs), and from the 'residual loss' resulting from remaining divergences.[649] However, under the condition of functioning capital markets, the firm will internalize these costs, as the share price will correctly reflect the divergence of interests.[650] Moreover, the 'market for corporate control' sets an incentive to focus on share prices and to keep them high. Otherwise, management risks a hostile takeover and subsequent replacement with a more efficient management team.[651] The consequence is a deregulatory agenda.[652] The role of the state is limited to providing the framework for functioning capital markets. All else can be left to the free negotiation of the participants. Corporate law in this conception is limited to the shareholder/director/management relationship and is essentially an 'off-the-shelf' standard form contract of a default nature.[653] It exists only in order to save the costs of negotiating every contract term anew whenever a new corporation is formed.

Thus, 'nexus of contract' theories have strong normative implications: shareholder wealth maximization as (more or less) the only objective of corporate activity, deregulation of (mandatory) corporate law in order to allow the parties to structure their enterprise in the most efficient way, and a strong capital markets orientation.[654] The theory originated in the United States and is most influential there, not least because it has strong predictive force, at least if one focuses purely on the shareholder/director/management relationship, in particular with the strong focus on shareholder wealth maximization ever since the Michigan Supreme Court famously opined that: '[a] business corporation is organized and carried on primarily for the profit of the stockholders'.[655] The theory has also gained some popularity in European academic circles.[656] Its impact on legal doctrine in our European jurisdictions is not as dominant as in the United States, but very significant. In the UK, 'nexus of contract' arguments have had a marked impact on company law reform[657] leading up to the Companies Act 2006, in particular in respect of the codification of directors' duties and the 'enlightened shareholder value approach'.[658] The underlying ideology is also visible in the Report of the High-level Group of Company Law Experts when they write that '[c]ompany law should first of all facilitate the running of efficient and competitive business enterprises'.[659] In line with

647 ibid 68. 648 Kelly and Parkinson (n 642) 179. 649 Jensen and Meckling (n 641) 86.
650 ibid 90. 651 Easterbrook and Fischel (n 375) 171. 652 ibid 286–300.
653 ibid 15; Posner (n 395) 540 ('The Corporation as a Standard Contract').
654 Hansmann and Kraakman (n 444) 439.
655 *Dodge v Ford Motor Co.*, 170 N.W. 668, 684 (Mich. 1919); for voices that doubt the significance of the case for the principle of shareholder wealth maximization see Clark and Babson (n 114) 825–6. The principle has been reaffirmed, however, in *eBay Domestic Holdings, Inc v Newark*, 16 A.3d 1 (Del Ch 2010). For details see Chapter 4C. II.
656 BR Cheffins, *Company Law: Theory, Structure, and Operation* (OUP 1997); P Didier, 'La théorie contractualiste de la société' (2000) Revue des sociétés 95.
657 A Consultation Document from The Company Law Review Steering Group, Modern Company Law for a Competitive Economy: The Strategic Framework (February 1999) paras 5.1.5; 5.1.12.
658 Now embodied in CA 2006, s 172(a). In this approach, shareholder value maximization is the predominant objective of corporate activity. However, the interests of other constituencies, notably employees, suppliers, customers, and the environment, are to be taken into account to the extent that doing so increases (long term) shareholder value.
659 Report of the High-level Group of Company Law Experts, A Modern Regulatory Framework for Company Law in Europe (Brussels 2002) 29.

the deregulatory agenda, the Companies Act 2006 has relaxed the regulatory burden in respect of small and medium-sized companies.[660] With the introduction of the '€1 SARL'[661] in France and the *Unternehmergesellschaft* (entrepreneur GmbH)[662] in Germany, going hand in hand with a reduction of formalities on formation and the running of these company forms, continental legal systems seemed to move in a similar direction.

Indeed, 'nexus of contract' theories appear to be most appropriate in respect of small partnership-like companies, where all members maintain personal relationships and potentially contribute actively in the business. It also captures much of what is going on during formation and growth of start-up companies.[663] However, 'nexus of contract' theories may be criticized both at a positive and at a normative level.

At the positive level, these theories cannot account for the two most important legal features of corporations: separate legal personality and limited liability.[664] According to Hansmann, Kraakman, and Squire, the reservation of the company's assets for the company's creditors under exclusion of the shareholders' personal creditors—'affirmative asset partitioning' or 'entity shielding'—cannot be achieved by contract[665] because transaction costs would be prohibitively high.[666] In order to grant a firm's creditors priority on the firm's assets by contract, every 'owner' of the firm would have to obtain from all of their personal creditors, both past and future, agreements subordinating their claims on the respective owner's assets to those of the firm's creditors. The costs of negotiating and obtaining these subordination agreements would be extremely high in most cases and would increase with the number of 'owners' of the firm.[667] In addition, it would be impossible to credibly promise the firm's creditors priority on the firm's assets because compliance with the subordination requirements could not easily be monitored or bonded. Moreover, every owner of the firm has an incentive to opportunistically omit the subordination clause in agreements with his own personal creditors, as this would reduce his personal costs of credit.[668] The problem can be overcome only by a special rule of property law committing assets to the firm and granting priority to firm creditors. In this respect, 'organizational law' as a 'form of property law' fulfils a necessary and indispensable function.[669]

[660] Davies and Worthington (n 8) para 1-28.

[661] Germain and Magnier (n 192) para 1779. The change was introduced by Loi 2003-721 of 1 August 2003. Previously, the minimum capital requirement was €7,500.

[662] GmbHG §§5a. This provision was introduced by *Gesetz zur Reform des GmbH-Rechts und zur Bekämpfung von Missbrächen (MoMiG)* of 23 October 2008 and entered into force on 1 November 2008. It allows for the formation of a GmbH with a minimum capital as low as €1. However, as a general principle, the minimum capital remained at €25,000 (GmbHG §§5).

[663] The founders with their initial business idea and some initial capital come together and form a corporation; subsequently they enlist the help of business angels and venture capitalists in exchange for preferred stock; at some point the corporation may offer its shares to the public or may be acquired by another firm; the founders may exit by cashing in on the common stock that they hold. Most of these transactions are contractual in nature.

[664] This deficiency invalidates 'nexus of contract' also for small privately held corporations.

[665] When economists speak of 'contracting relationships among individuals' they do not have in mind the legal meaning that is attributed to the term contract, that is, a promise that is legally enforceable between the parties. Rather, what they have in mind is 'relationships characterized by reciprocal expectations and behavior'. See Hart (n 19) 1764 note 30; Eisenberg (n 642) 822–3.

[666] Hansmann and Kraakman (n 356) 406–22; Hansmann, Kraakman, and Squire (n 356) 1340–3.

[667] Hansmann, Kraakman, and Squire (n 356) 1340.

[668] ibid. According to these authors, 'liquidation protection' against a personal creditor seizing a member's share and forcing liquidation also cannot be achieved by contract alone. The respective clause preventing liquidation in the members' agreement would bind each member but not a member's personal creditor, ibid 1342. However, it is at least conceivable that the personal creditor could be bound by the respective non-liquidation clause. After all, the personal creditor steps into the shoes of the member, why should he have greater rights than the member had himself. This is confirmed by BGB, §725(1) which allows the personal creditor of the member of a German civil law partnership to liquidate the partnership if he has levied assessment on the share of the member. Without this mandatory provision, liquidation would be prevented by the members' agreement, Windbichler (n 176) 92 (§10 para 6). Thus, here the situation is the reverse of what Hansmann, Kraakman, and Squire postulate. Contract is sufficient to provide liquidation protection; a mandatory provision of law is necessary in order to allow the creditor to liquidate.

[669] Hansmann and Kraakman (n 356) 422.

Limited liability, under 'nexus of contract', is perceived as a default rule provided by corporate law as 'off the shelf' standard contract terms between the company's owners and its creditors.[670] If limited liability were not a feature of corporate law, firms would create it by contract.[671] If the firm's owners were more risk averse than the creditors or if the latter were in a better position to monitor the firm's activities shareholders would be willing to buy insurance from the creditors for the risk of default. 'The legal rule of limited liability is a shortcut to this position, avoiding the costs of separate transactions'.[672] If limited liability is unsuitable in a particular case the parties may contract around it by granting guarantees or other personal security. However, 'nexus of contract' cannot explain limited liability in respect of tort creditors. Tort victims do not consent to forgo the chance to go against the company's shareholders and managers in exchange for ex ante compensation. To create in these situations limited liability by contract seems conceptually impossible. Adherents to nexus-of-contract theories justify limited liability in respect of tort victims with the argument that the efficiency gains of limited liability offset the costs imposed on tort creditors; however, without being able to give a satisfactory conceptual explanation.[673] In order to overcome the problem of tort creditors, a complete separation of company and shareholders is necessary. Thus, limited liability is as essential as 'affirmative asset partitioning' because only under a rule of limited liability can the share emerge as a completely free-standing form of financial property.[674] Again, a rule of law is necessary in order to afford the corporation one of its most characteristic features.[675]

At the normative level, 'nexus of contract' is disingenuous and unworkable. It is disingenuous in respect of its deregulatory claim. The large body of mandatory regulation that is imposed on corporations, be it through accounting rules, securities regulation, or insolvency law, can be reconciled with 'nexus of contract' on the basis that these rules are necessary in order to provide a framework for a functioning market.[676] This is particularly true for rules on disclosure of corporate information and rules against insider trading and market manipulation. However, the property rights, to be freely allocated by the market mechanism, are themselves the product of state intervention and regulation. The share as a bundle of economic and control rights could not have emerged as a freely transferable form of intangible property without legally separating the corporation completely from its shareholders.[677] Moreover, the share as a form of intangible property is particularly vulnerable. The income stream it confers depends on a large number of actors—management, employees, government bodies, but also competitors, consumers and the general public—acting so as to increase or at least maintain its value. Consequently, the share's financial integrity requires an extraordinarily wide range of legal and other interventions aimed at securing the continuous flow of returns: in addition to securities regulation and insolvency law, also individual and collective labour law, competition/antitrust law, general contract and property law, tort law, environmental law, and more.[678] The point is that the property rights of shareholders do not reflect a natural or God-given order brought about by the market only to be given free rein. Rather, they are themselves the product of conscious regulatory policy choices at certain points in time and depend, for their future viability, on continued protection by the law.[679]

[670] Posner (n 395) 425. [671] Easterbrook and Fischel (n 375) 41. [672] ibid 48.

[673] Ribstein (n 428) 127; Easterbrook and Fischel (n 375) 52–4; Callison (n 431) 1065 note 12.

[674] Ireland (n 388) 462 note 34 and 485–500.

[675] Moreover, many predictions made on the basis of 'nexus-of-contract' theories do not withstand empirical scrutiny, see M Klausner, 'Fact and Fiction in Corporate Law and Governance' (2013) 65 Stanford Law Review 1325. On the tension between the US Supreme Court's decision in *Citizen United v FEC*, 558 US 310 (2010), and 'conservative' corporate law theory. See L Strine and N Walter, 'Conservative Collision Course? The Tension between Conservative Corporate Law Theory and Citizen United' (2015) 100 Cornell Law Review 334.

[676] Eisenberg (n 642) 823–5; see further Moore (n 597). [677] Ireland (n 388) 486–91.

[678] ibid 493–4. [679] ibid 491.

In light of the corporate and financial crises of the last decade, 'nexus of contract' theorists' deregulatory agenda has softened somewhat.[680] By contrast, shareholder wealth maximization is still going strong.[681] However, it is both implausible and unworkable. The underlying idea for the shareholder value rationale is that by maximizing the return for shareholders as residual claimants, the return for all corporate constituencies and for society as a whole will be maximized also. However, we have seen above, that by using modern financial techniques shareholders may have no economic interest or even a negative financial interest in the company. If, for instance, a shareholder S in the bidder company X takes the short side of an equity swap with X as reference entity, and S also holds shares in the target company Y, this shareholder may benefit if X overpays for Y in a takeover. The share price for Y is likely to increase as a consequence of the takeover, whereas the share price of X is likely to decline, against which event S is hedged. S's economic interest in X is negative. His wealth will be maximized by a management decision that decreases the value of X.[682] The use of derivatives and other techniques which allow to decouple the economic interest from the formal holding of shares suggest that the interests of shareholders are no longer as homogeneous as they used to be. If the objective is shareholder wealth maximization, then the question is which shareholders' wealth is to be maximized?

Shareholder wealth maximization also falls down at the practical level. It is simply not workable as a guideline for management to base their decisions on, other than for short-term share price movements mainly in the takeover context. Producing and marketing all but the simplest of products requires a myriad of different decisions at different stages during research and development, production, and marketing. In respect of almost all of these decisions it will not be clear at all, at the time when they are taken, whether they will increase shareholder value or not. For example, the British manufacturer ICI's expansion into pharmaceuticals after the Second World War was very slow to generate returns. For years the pharmaceutical division was a drain on ICI's resources, until the discovery of beta-blockers in the 1960s. More discoveries followed, and the pharmaceutical division became the growth engine of the company.[683] The development, production, and marketing processes, and the process of generating revenue, entail so many steps that require the setting and achievement of so many intermediate goals. Many of these intermediate goals will be arrived at only by trial and error. So many people are involved on whose judgment management must rely: researchers, designers, engineers, marketing people, and many more. Success depends on the knowledge, skills, and initiative of these people and this cannot be effectively monitored and supervised. 'Shareholder wealth maximization' is, therefore, far too abstract as a guideline as that it could inform in any meaningful way any of the decisions during this process. What can inform decisions from development to the finished product at every stage of the process is, however, the desire to make the best product possible, given certain social, economic, and natural constraints. 'Boing created the commercially most successful aircraft company, not by love of profits, but through love of planes'.[684] Empirical research shows that firms that focus on their products do much better in the long run, also in terms of shareholder value, than firms that actively, aggressively, and directly try to pursue shareholder wealth.[685]

[680] See eg R La Porta, F Lopez-de-Silanes, A Shleifer, and R Vishny, 'Investor Protection and Corporate Governance' (2000) 58 Journal of Financial Economics 3 ('The legal approach to corporate governance holds that the key mechanism is the protection of outside investors—whether shareholders or creditors—through the legal system, meaning both laws and their enforcement').

[681] HTC Hu and JL Westbrook, 'Abolition of the Corporate Duty to Creditors' (2007) 107 Columbia Law Review 1321, 1360–2.

[682] HTC Hu and B Black, 'Equity and Debt Decoupling and Empty Voting II: Importance and Extensions' (2008) 156 University of Pennsylvania Law Review 625, 633–4, with an example.

[683] J Kay, *Obliquity: Why Our Goals Are Best Achieved Indirectly* (Profile 2011) 19–20.

[684] ibid 21.

[685] ibid 23–5.

Out of 'nexus of contract', 'proprietary theories' of corporate law are slowly emerging. These theories build on the 'property rights theory of the firm' that identifies a firm with all the nonhuman assets that belong to it.[686] The firm appears as a collection of assets, tangible and intangible. The owner of the firm has the residual right of control over the assets the firm consists of; he has the right to use the assets in any way not inconsistent with prior contracts or legal rules. Thus, in a world of transaction costs and incomplete contracts, residual rights of control affect ex ante incentives to invest in the relationship as well as ex post bargaining power in respect of the distribution of surplus.[687] These ideas have already had an impact on legal scholarship. According to Hansmann, Kraakman, and Squire the reservation of the company's assets for the company's creditors under exclusion of the shareholders' personal creditors—'affirmative asset partitioning'—cannot be achieved by contract alone because transaction costs would be prohibitively high.[688] In this respect, 'organizational law' as a 'form of property law' fulfils a necessary and indispensable function.[689] Similarly, for Blair the unique contribution of the corporation to economic development lies in its entity status and separate governance which helped to attract and to keep capital, once invested, in the enterprise and thereby helped the firm to draw in other valuable resources and in particular firm specific investment.[690] The most elaborate exposition has been developed by Armour and Whincop.[691] Building on contractarian theories and the 'property rights theory' they distinguish between the 'proprietary foundation' and the contractual superstructure of corporate law. The authors' starting point is the definition of 'ownership' as the 'entitlement to exercise "residual rights of control"'. The firm necessarily requires a conception of shared entitlements to control as part of a theory of governance between the different participants. The structure of the allocation of control rights is a mechanism for reducing the agency costs between participants.[692] Entitlements to control are shared among participants through 'sharing agreements' specifying which entitlement in relation to the assets is exercisable by whom, and under what circumstances. The typical sharing arrangements in a public company consist of: (i) 'joint sharing' among the shareholders; (ii) 'delegation' by the shareholders of day-to-day management to an agent subject to removal in case of unsatisfactory performance; (iii) 'sequential sharing' between shareholders and creditors in the sense that entitlements will remain with the shareholders as long as the firm continues to make repayments.[693] 'In the property rights framework, the firm is therefore characterized as a collection of people and assets, with ownership of the latter carefully allocated amongst the former'.[694] The importance of organizational law in this context consist of making the 'sharing arrangements' enforceable against third parties, thus giving these arrangements a proprietary nature.[695] For instance, a shareholder or agent may alienate an asset of the firm in order to maximize his own private benefit. If the sharing arrangement has proprietary effect, the shareholder or agent simply cannot alienate the asset without the co-owner's consent. In other words, the asset can be reclaimed from third parties. This greatly reduces internal monitoring costs.[696] At the same time, third parties may suffer a reliance loss. In order to reduce the total costs, the legal system employs a mix of 'balancing strategies' in order to keep the costs for third parties in check, for instance, the doctrines of apparent authority and bona fide purchaser protection.[697] In short, the law assists participants in delineating the contents of their voluntary contractual entitlement-sharing agreements by providing default 'standard forms' that participants may use. In addition, the law grants certain aspects

[686] Grossman and Hart (n 19) 693; Hart and Moore (n 19) 1120; Hart (n 19) 1766.
[687] Hart (n 19) 1766.
[688] Hansmann, Kraakman, and Squire (n 356); Hansmann and Kraakman (n 356).
[689] Hansmann and Kraakman (n 356) 422.
[690] Blair (n 22); Ribstein (n 367).
[691] J Armour and MJ Whincop, 'The Proprietary Foundations of Corporate Law' (2007) 27 OJLS 429.
[692] ibid 438.
[693] ibid 441.
[694] ibid.
[695] ibid 444.
[696] ibid.
[697] ibid 445–6.

of these sharing agreements proprietary effect by making them enforceable against third parties. The latter constitutes the 'proprietary foundations' of corporate law; the former are the 'contractarian superstructure'.[698]

Proprietary theories recognize the importance, and are capable of explaining 'affirmative asset partitioning' or separate legal personality. The identification of the firm with the pool of assets that belong to it is of course not new. As early as the nineteenth century the German scholar Brinz developed a theory of the corporation that identified it as a pool of assets for a certain purpose, eliminating any anthropomorphic element.[699] To the extent that 'proprietary theory' rests upon and tries to improve contractarian theories, it shares the same flaws. This is true in particular of the commitment to shareholder wealth maximization.[700] Also, the picture that Armour and Whincop draw only fits the small partnership-like company or start-up. An investor who buys and sells shares in the stock market is not interested at all in the assets of a particular company; some would say he is not even interested in the future cash flows of the securities. The only thing that matters to him is what, in his view, other market participants will be willing to pay for the securities in the future. The idea that these investors negotiate 'sharing agreements' with their fellow shareholders and management has no relation to reality. Moreover, limited liability is still largely referred to the realm of contract.[701] These approaches suffer from the same explanatory difficulties in respect of tort creditors as contractarian theories do.[702] Only Ireland's approach of complete separation of corporation and shareholder by conceptualizing the share as a 'fully autonomous' form of financial property[703] overcomes the problem of tort creditors.

A proper understanding of the corporation requires first to distinguish between the corporation as a social phenomenon and as a legal concept.[704] Even in a world where the costs of transacting via the market mechanism are ever decreasing, largely on the basis of developments in information technology and transport, corporations as social phenomena appear to be something more tangible than an amorphous web of contracts. People experience, to a greater or lesser extent, the boundaries of corporations in terms of their physical assets and manpower, but also in respect of intangible assets such as internal coordination and control systems, structured approaches to research and development, and specialized marketing and training programmes, as well as brand identities and other reputational capital.[705] Corporations are independent in their existence from the people who at any particular time occupy the roles assigned to them within the organizational structure. Knowledge and skills are preserved by the implementation of sets of formal and informal norms even if the personnel changes. The corporation as a social phenomenon is therefore more than just the people it 'consists' of. The people are only part of a social structure that has a certain solidity and consistency within space and time.[706] Here we come full circle and arrive at our

[698] ibid 448–9.

[699] A Brinz, *Lehrbuch der Pandekten, Band I* (3rd edn, Deichert 1884) §§60, 61; Wiedemann (n 11) 195–6.

[700] Blair and Stout conceptualize the corporation as a 'mediating hierarchy' with the board of directors as 'mediating hierarchs' whose task it is to balance the conflicting interests of all participants in the corporate enterprise. This is a pluralistic approach to corporate governance and overcomes the shareholder value paradigm. Blair and Stout (n 14); Blair (n 22).

[701] According to Hansmann, Kraakman, and Squire, limited liability would be quite possible to create by contract without the need for organizational law; see Hansmann, Kraakman, and Squire (n 356) 1341; Hansmann and Kraakman (n 356) 430. Similarly, Armour and Whincop analyse the principle of limited liability and some of its exceptions under English law, such as 'wrongful trading', as part of the contractual superstructure. Only the rules on transactions at an undervalue and preferences could be understood as part of the proprietary foundations, Armour and Whincop (n 693) 453–4.

[702] Since they advocate unlimited liability for tort creditors this obviously does not apply to Hansmann and Kraakman's concept; see Hansmann and Kraakman (n 356) 431.

[703] Ireland (n 388).

[704] This notion was of course already present in the works of both von Savigny and Gierke; see also Lawson (n 331) 15: the firm as a real community that is legally positioned.

[705] Blair (n 22) 395.

[706] Eisenberg (n 642) 829.

comparative starting point: the corporation as one form of social institution for the horizontal pooling of resources.

The corporation as a legal concept consists of two different regulatory spheres: the external liability structure and the internal governance structure. The law must decide in what way and to what extent the corporation interacts with other market participants, bearing in mind that the market is itself a product of the law. For that purpose, the law may fashion the corporation as a pool of assets and liabilities that can be used to bind the corporation to the contracts it enters into with market participants, at the same time determining their order of priority. The corporation interacts with the market also by creating and assigning to market participants financial claims against its future cash flows, secured with the company's current assets with a particular order of priority. The law may thus create and determine the corporation's external liability structure on the basis of the principles of separate legal personality and limited liability. At the same time, the law may regulate to a greater or lesser extent the corporation's internal information and control processes and mechanisms. It may determine control entitlements in respect of the assets attributed to the corporation as well as the decision-making processes in this respect. However, to the extent that these internal governance questions have no external effect on other market participants, the law may leave these questions to private ordering or contract, with one exception and this is the clear assignment of authority as to how the corporation may commit its assets vis-à-vis third parties.

This conceptualization of the corporation gives great leeway to the legislature. It may structure and fashion the legal attributes of corporations (as social phenomena) in the way it sees fit, subject only to natural constraints. Where corporations are to be available as a capital accumulation device they must be afforded separate legal personality and limited liability. In terms of the internal structure, however, law is not essential. Consequently, the general incorporation laws in the United States are largely of a default nature. Shareholders under this conception may appear on both sides of the divide. They are first and foremost market participants. As such their dealings with the company are subject to mandatory regulation concerning accounting, disclosure of information, and securities fraud. To the extent that they are afforded actual control over the corporation's assets, by law or by contract, they are also 'insiders' and, thus, subject to the internal governance structure. This conception of the company or corporation is probably closest to the French functional theory.[707] Like this theory it is normatively indeterminate. In other words, the 'nature of the corporation' does not allow for the deduction of any statement as to what the law should be in respect of corporations. Instead, we must decide what kind of society we want and must set the goals to get there. We can then determine in what form corporations may contribute to the attainment of these goals. Maybe they can best be achieved by focusing on shareholder value or maybe not. What is essential is that the respective goals and objectives are determined through the political and democratic process.[708] Corporate law can then be structured accordingly. In order to find the most efficient way economics has an important role to play. It is, however, wrong to think that by unearthing the nature of the corporation in some pseudo-scientific sense any valuable insights into what corporate law should be can be obtained.

Questions and comments:

1. Fiction/concession, 'nexus of contract'/contractarian, and real-entity theories, in one form or another, have had an impact in all four jurisdictions. Why do you think that is?
2. Whereas it will be difficult to demonstrate that a particular legal rule or development is owed to the influence of one particular theory, it is the case that certain trends or problems can be better explained with a particular theory in mind. For instance, the First Company Law

[707] Paillusseau (n 579) 3148; (n 580) 705.

[708] Moore (n 597) 728.

Directive[709] (now Directive (EU) 2017/1132[710]) installed a system of company representation under which the authority of company representatives to represent the company vis-à-vis third parties is, in principle, limited only by law and cannot be fettered by decisions of another organ of that company. Although adapted to meet the concerns of the other initial Member States, this approach essentially followed German law which alone adhered to an 'organ theory' of company representation which in turn rests on the assumption that the company exists as a social reality outside the law. As a living social organism, it wills and acts through its organs. The organ acting for the company is not acting as the company's agent; rather it is acting as the company itself. Consequently, any internal restrictions on the organ's authority are meaningless vis-à-vis third parties. By contrast, English law, following the concession theory, perceived the company as acting through its agents. Under general principles of agency law, the agent's actual authority may be limited by the principal with third party effect, subject to the doctrine of apparent authority. The implementation of the First Company Law Directive in the UK proved to be particularly difficult.[711] These difficulties can at least be partly explained by the different conceptual frameworks.[712]

3. In *Cartesio*, the Court of Justice elaborated on its case law on the right to freedom of establishment of companies. The Court's starting point was its reasoning in *Daily Mail*: '[C]ompanies are creatures of national law and exist only by virtue of the national legislation which determines [their] incorporation and functioning'.[713] The Court then held that 'in the absence of a uniform Community law definition of the companies which may enjoy the right of establishment on the basis of a single connecting factor determining the national law applicable to a company', the question of whether a company actually has the right to freedom of establishment is 'a preliminary matter which, as Community law now stands, can only be resolved by the applicable national law'.[714] Thus, a Member State has the power, first, to define the connecting factor required of a company if it is to be regarded as incorporated under the law of that Member State. In this respect, freedom of establishment does not apply.[715] Secondly, according to the Court, the Member State also has the power to prevent a company governed by its law from retaining that status if the company intends to move its seat to the territory of another Member State, 'thereby breaking the connecting factor required under the law of incorporation'.[716] In what way could the theories discussed above be used to either support or criticize the Court's reasoning in *Cartesio*?[717] In this context, would you say that these theories are indeterminate in the sense that they could be used to support either outcome?
4. Contractarian corporate theories are still dominant and underpin much of the important contemporary discussions on corporate governance. Can you summarize the line of reasoning that supports these theories? How can it be criticized?

F. Sources of Domestic Corporate Law

We can now map the sets of legal rules in our four jurisdictions that define and regulate the corporation as market actor (external liability structure) and internally (internal governance structure). Obviously, the entire body of law may have an impact on

[709] First Council Directive of 9 March 1968 on coordination of safeguards which, for the protection of the interests of members and others, are required by Member States of companies within the meaning of the second paragraph of Article 58 of the Treaty, with a view to making such safeguards equivalent throughout the Community (68/151/EEC), OJ 1968 L65/8. Directive 2009/101/EC of the European Parliament and of the Council of 16 September 2009 on coordination of safeguards which, for the protection of the interests of members and others, are required by Member States of companies within the meaning of the second paragraph of Article 48 of the Treaty, with a view to making such safeguards equivalent (codified version), OJ 2009 L258/11.

[710] Directive (EU) 2017/1132 of the European Parliament and of the Council of 14 June 2017 relating to certain aspects of company law (codification), OJ EU 30.6.2017 L169/46.

[711] See Chapter 3B.II.

[712] V Edwards, *European Company Law* (OUP 1999) 35, 42.

[713] Case C-210/06 *Cartesio* [2008] ECLI:EU:C:2008:723 para 104.

[714] ibid para 109.

[715] ibid para 110.

[716] ibid para 110.

[717] For a comprehensive discussion of the case cf C Gerner-Beuerle and M Schillig, 'The Mysteries of Freedom of Establishment after *Cartesio*' (2010) 59 ICLQ 323.

the corporation. Even traffic rules may influence the way the corporation deploys its resources. Competition/anti-trust law, environmental law, and administrative law, but also general contract law, tort law, property law, and criminal law set important parameters for a corporation's interaction with others. This may also filter through and influence its internal structures. For instance, competition law may require the installation of independent boards and chairmen in group companies in order to guarantee some degree of independence. However, most of the rules that these laws contain are not specific to corporations. They apply equally to a sole trader or commercial partnership. Corporate law is therefore narrower and what will concern us here is the law specific to corporations. This is obviously the core corporate or company law to be found in company law statutes. It is also the law of securities regulation or capital markets law that determines the issuing of financial assets by the company. Corporate insolvency law has an impact on both the external liability structure of the corporation as well as the governance structure, at least when the company enters formal proceedings. Where do we find the respective sets of rules in our four legal systems?

I. United Kingdom

Statutory law, common law, and 'soft law' may be distinguished. Statutory law may itself be subdivided into primary legislation, secondary legislation and rules issued by independent bodies which have been granted the power of delegated rule-making.[718] The most significant piece of primary legislation in the area of company law is the Companies Act 2006. It replaced the earlier Companies Act 1985 and is the result of a comprehensive review of company law starting in 1998 and culminating in the Companies Bill which obtained Royal Assent in 2006. With more than 1,300 sections, the Companies Act 2006 is arguably the longest Act ever produced by Parliament.[719] It covers both public and private companies limited by share, as well as companies limited by guarantee and unlimited companies. The Act contains detailed provisions for a company's entire life span from formation to its striking off from the register, including transformation from one company type into another, accounting and audit, company charges, scheme of arrangements, and takeovers. The Act restated the extensive case law—grown over 150 years—on directors' duties,[720] and introduced a statutory derivative claim,[721] partly replacing earlier case law.[722] Despite its length and detail, the Act leaves large parts of the internal governance structure to be regulated by the company's articles of association. For instance, section 154 lays down the minimum number of directors,[723] but neither this section nor the rest of the Act define the function of directors or prescribe structure and form of corporate management generally.[724] The significance of the articles of association under this system is reflected in section 19 granting the Secretary of State the power to prescribe, through regulations, model articles of associations for companies. In contrast to earlier versions, the current statutory instrument[725] creates a different set of model articles for private companies limited by shares and public companies. These model articles are of a default nature. They apply and form part of a company's articles only where either no articles of association have been registered, or to the extent that they have not been excluded or modified by the company's registered articles of association.[726] The version of the model articles that forms part of a company's articles is the version current when the company is formed.[727] Thus, the subsequent promulgation of a revised version will not affect

718 Davies and Worthington (n 8) para 3-1.
719 ibid para 3-3.
720 CA 2006, ss 170–177.
721 ibid ss 260–269.
722 The so-called rule in *Foss v Harbottle* (1843) 2 Hare 461.
723 At least two directors for public companies; one for private companies.
724 Davies and Worthington (n 8) para 14-2.
725 Companies (Model Articles) Regulations 2008 (SI 2008/3229).
726 CA 2006, s 20(1).
727 ibid s 20(2).

the companies already registered. As a consequence, many companies are still governed by model articles promulgated under the 1985 or even the 1948 legislation.[728] Other important primary legislation is contained in the Insolvency Act 1986, providing a framework for company liquidation and rescue. This Act further contains the important 'wrongful trading' provision for the protection of creditors in the vicinity of insolvency.[729] The Company Directors Disqualification Act 1986 is, as the name suggests, essentially a device to discipline company directors and to encourage appropriate behaviour when managing their companies. The prohibition on insider trading can be found in the Criminal Justice Act 1993.[730] The Financial Services and Markets Act 2000 provides the basis for much of the capital markets law relating to public offerings and listing of shares. It is in this area that the legislator extensively enlists the help of professional experts by delegating law-making powers to the Financial Conduct Authority (FCA). The FCA is a private company limited by guarantee financed by fees levied on those who engage in the financial services industry. It promulgates the Listing Rules for companies whose securities have been entered into the 'official list'. The FCA has also introduced Prospectus, Disclosure, and Transparency Rules, largely driven by EU requirements, as well as a Code of Market Conduct to specify the meaning of the statutory prohibition on market abuse.[731] A further area of extensive delegated rule-making is accounting and auditing of company accounts. The Financial Reporting Council (FRC) and its subsidiaries were, by the secretary of state, assigned powers to make rules in relation to accounting standards, accuracy of accounts, auditing standards, and regulation of auditors and accountants. The FRC and its subsidiaries are companies limited by guarantee, with its directors being appointed by the secretary of state.[732]

Despite this wealth of primary, secondary, and delegated legislation, the common law—here to be understood as the rules and principles developed by case law—remains of utmost importance. Neither the Companies Act 2006, nor any other of the Acts mentioned above, amounts to a codification of company law in the sense of a comprehensive and systematic reformulation of the law. Rather, in line with statutory law in England in general, it builds on concepts and terminology elaborated by the body of existing case law, constantly interacts with the case law and can only be properly comprehended against the background of the case law. The newly 'codified' law on directors' duties is instructive. The general duties in sections 170 to 177 are all derived from case law which they replace as far as they go.[733] The case law remains important, however, for the interpretation of the open textured statutory provisions,[734] which leave room for further development and organic growth of the case law under the headings they provide. Moreover, the legislature has refrained from codifying the remedies of a breach of directors' duties.[735] Here, the case law remains preeminent. Without these remedies directors' duties would be pointless. Only statute and case law together provide a complete picture of the law and workable solutions.

Self-regulation and 'soft law' also play an important role. Originally, the regulation of takeovers was accomplished without any statutory framework at all. The City Code on Takeovers and Mergers was a self-regulatory measure adopted by the City of London in 1968. It was administered and enforced by the Panel on Takeovers and Mergers, an independent body consisting of appointees representing those routinely involved in takeovers, such as banks, investment funds, insurance companies, but also trade unions.[736] In the course of the implementation of the EU Directive on Takeover-bids,[737] Panel and Code had to be granted a statutory footing. Section 942 of the Companies Act 2006 now confers certain statutory powers on the Panel without, however, regulating its constitution. Pursuant to section 943,

[728] Davies and Worthington (n 8) para 3-14.
[729] Insolvency Act 1986, s 214.
[730] Criminal Justice Act 1993, ss 52–64.
[731] Davies and Worthington (n 8) para 3-7.
[732] ibid para 3-9.
[733] CA 2006, s 170(3).
[734] ibid s 170(4).
[735] ibid s 178.
[736] Davies and Worthington (n 8) paras 28-3–28-4.
[737] Directive 2004/25/EC of 21 April 2004 on takeover bids (Text with EEA relevance) [2004] OJ L142/12.

the Panel has both the obligation and the authority to promulgate rules governing the conduct of takeovers. The obligation relates only to those rules that Member States are required to introduce under the Directive. Since the early 1990s, many countries all over the world as well as international organizations have issued codes, guidelines, principles, and statements on good corporate governance. They were initiated by a number of different actors, such as the OECD, top executives, investment funds, expert groups, and certain companies. These codes are usually not formally endorsed by the national legislator and do not have the force of law; they constitute a form of self-regulation within the respective industry.[738] In the UK, the corporate governance movement started with the Cadbury Committee in 1992.[739] A number of different expert committees followed,[740] resulting in the Combined Code on Corporate Governance, now the UK Corporate Governance Code, published by the Financial Reporting Council.[741] It only applies to listed companies and derives its normative force from the Listing Rules which require companies with a premium listing in the UK to disclose in their annual report the extent to which they have complied with the Code during the previous twelve months and to give reasons for areas of non-compliance ('comply or explain' approach).[742] Consequently, companies are free to deviate from any or all recommendations of the Code as long as they explain the reasons for doing so.

II. Germany

The sources of corporate law in Germany can be divided into statutory law, case law, and soft law. The law relating to public corporations and limited liability companies is divided between two different Acts. The *Aktiengesetz* (AktG) contains a detailed and comprehensive codification of the law relating to public companies. It deals with formation; the rights and obligations of shareholders vis-à-vis the company; corporate governance, in particular the internal workings of, and allocation of authority between, management board, supervisory board, and general meeting; the raising and maintenance of capital; amendments to the articles of association; changes in the capital structure of the company by way of increase or decrease of capital; annulment of shareholder resolutions; company liquidation for reasons other than insolvency; and the law on corporate groups. The provisions of the AktG are in principle mandatory. A company's articles of association may deviate from the statute only where this is explicitly permitted.[743] The rationale is investor protection. Investors can be confident that the bundle of rights that they obtain with their shares is standardized in accordance with the AktG. Some flexibility is achieved through the validity of shareholders' agreements.[744] By contrast, the law relating to limited liability companies, contained in the *Gesetz betreffend die Gesellschaften mit beschränkter Haftung* (GmbHG), leaves room for contractual autonomy of the members. They may determine their rights and obligations in the articles of association, unless the GmbHG provides otherwise.[745] For accounting purposes, the AktG is

[738] H-M Ringleb, T Kremer, M Lutter, and A Werder, *Kommentar zum Deutschen Corporate Governance Kodex* (6th edn, CH Beck 2016) paras 5, 80.

[739] Report of the Committee on the Financial Aspects of Corporate Governance, 1992, http://www.ecgi.org/codes/all_codes.php.

[740] Directors' Remuneration: Report of a Study Group chaired by Sir Richard Greenbury, 1995; Committee on Corporate Governance: Final Report 1998 (Hampel Report); The Institute of Chartered Accountants in England and Wales, Internal Control: Guidance for Directors on the Combined Code, 1999 (Turnbull Report); D Higgs, Review of the Role and Effectiveness of Non-executive Directors, 2003 (Higgs Review); Financial Reporting Council, Audit Committees Combined Code Guidance, 2003 (Smith Report); all http://www.ecgi.org/codes/all_codes.php.

[741] Financial Reporting Council, UK Corporate Governance Code, July 2018;, https://www.frc.org.uk/getattachment/88bd8c45-50ea-4841-95b0-d2f4f48069a2/2018-UK-Corporate-Governance-Code-FINAL.PDF.

[742] LR 9.8.6. (5) and (6). [743] AktG, §23(5).

[744] M Henssler and H Wiedemann, 'Die Aktiengesellschaft im System des deutschen Gesellschaftsrechts' in W Bayer and M Habersack (eds), *Aktienrecht im Wandel, Band II: Grundsatzfragen des Aktienrechts* (Auflage 2007) 9.

[745] GmbHG, §45(1).

supplemented by the Third Book of the *Handelsgesetzbuch* (HGB) or Commercial Code.[746] Moreover, for the famous German co-determination, the AktG relies on three further Acts which, depending on the size of the company and the industry in which it operates, determine the number and process of appointing employee representatives as members of the supervisory board.[747] These are the *Montan-Mitbestimmungsgesetz* (MontanMitgbestG) for the mining (coal), iron, and steel industry; the *Mitbestimmungsgesetz* (MitbestG) for companies with more than 2,000 employees and the *Drittelbeteiligungsgesetz* for companies with more than 500 employees. The AktG does not regulate mergers of two or more companies, or the separation and spin-off of part of a company into a separate entity. This is dealt with by the *Umwandlungsgesetz* (UmwG) which also provides for the transformation of a corporation into another form of business association and vice versa. The *Börsengesetz* (BörsG) regulates the admission of shares to trading on a regulated market. For listed companies the *Wertpapierhandelsgesetz* (WpHG) stipulates a prohibition of insider trading and market manipulation. It imposes duties to disclose dealings of directors in the shares of their company, material information, and an increase or decrease of shareholdings beyond certain thresholds. The statute also installs the *Bundesaufsicht für Finanzdienstleistungen* (BAFin) as supervisory authority for the financial services industry. The *Wertpapiererwerbs- und Übernahmegesetz* (WpÜG) provides a regulatory framework for tender offers in respect of listed companies. Finally, the *Insolvenzordnung* (InsO), or Insolvency Act, imposes duties on management to file for insolvency proceedings when the company is insolvent on either a balance sheet or cash flow basis, and changes the governance structure of the company during insolvency proceedings which may result in reorganization or liquidation.

Despite the detailed and often mandatory regulation in statutes, the case law of the Federal Court of Justice (BGH) has proved to be of immense importance for the development and consolidation of corporate law.[748] The BGH, and in particular its Second Senat, has issued over the years many leading cases that established concepts and doctrines of great practical significance.[749] The Court has developed a doctrine of the 'pre-company' for the time between the completion of the founding documents and registration.[750] The concept of the 'hidden contribution in kind' was developed by case law, for both GmbH and AG.[751] The Court has extended the authority of the general meeting to have a say on structural changes that come close to an amendment of the articles of association.[752] It also introduced substantive requirements for exclusion and limitation of shareholders' pre-emptive rights when new shares are being issued.[753] Both controlling and minority shareholders may be subject to fiduciary duties, requiring them to exercise their voting rights in good faith and for the benefit of the company.[754] Overall, the German court has often been very proactive in interpreting and shaping corporate law.

In Germany the idea of a code of corporate governance took hold only in 2000/2001 with the appointment, by the Federal Ministry of Justice, of the Codex Commission to elaborate a uniform code of corporate governance. The Commission consists of prominent executives of important German corporations, academics, and others representing all social groups affected by the project. The Commission presented the German Code of Corporate Governance in 2002. It was published on the homepage of the Federal Ministry

[746] AktG, §150. [747] AktG, §§95, 96.

[748] P Ulmer, 'Aktienrecht und richterliche Rechtsfortbildung' in W Bayer and M Habersack (eds), *Aktienrecht im Wandel, Band II: Grundsatzfragen des Aktienrechts* (Auflage 2007) 114.

[749] ibid 120.

[750] First developed in respect of the GmbH, BGHZ 80, 129, but extendable to the AG by way of analogy, Ulmer (n 753) 121.

[751] BGHZ 110, 47 (IBH/Lemmertz); BGHZ 118, 83 (BuM); BGHZ 132, 133.

[752] BGHZ 83, 122 (Holzmüller); BGHZ 159, 30 (Gelatine).

[753] BGHZ 71, 40 (Kali und Salz); BGHZ 83, 319 (Holzmann); BGHZ 136, 133 (Siemens/Nold).

[754] BGHZ 103, 183 (Linotype); BGHZ 129, 136 (Girmes).

of Justice and in the *Federal Gazette*. The objective of the Code is to make the German corporate governance system transparent and comprehensible so that national and international investors can be confident that listed companies in Germany are managed properly.[755] For that purpose it contains 'recommendations' and 'suggestions' for good management practice. Because the corporate governance system of the AktG is already very detailed and mandatory, the role that these recommendations can play in practice is somewhat limited.[756] Pursuant to AktG, §161, management board and supervisory board of listed companies must declare annually either that they adhere to the recommendations of the Code, or name the recommendations that they have not implemented and explain why not ('comply or explain' approach). This declaration must be made available to the shareholders on a continuous basis. Owing to its non-binding nature the Code is usually referred to as 'soft law'. However, in light of the statutory duty to declare its application or justify non-application in combination with the Code's elaboration, doubts have been raised as to whether it is compatible with the constitutional principles of democracy and the rule of law.[757]

Rules promulgated by highly specialized professional organizations are of great importance (also) in the area of accounting law. The accounting principles stipulated by way of statute are very abstract, and require specification by case law, customary principles as well as detailed standards developed by professional organizations such as the German Accounting Standards Committee.[758] For listed companies there are further the listing rules of the Frankfurt stock exchange. Again, because of the detailed and mandatory character of the AktG, these rules are less detailed and of less significance than their New York and London counterparts.[759]

III. France

France comes closest to a comprehensive codification of company law. Since 2000, the law on commercial companies can be found in the 2nd Book of the Code de Commerce.[760] Title II deals with the particularities of the different commercial companies. Chapter III is dedicated to the private company, or limited liability company (*société à responsabilité limitée*). Chapter IV contains the provisions common to all companies with a share capital. Public companies (*sociétés anonymes*) are regulated in Chapter V. Nine sections deal with their constitution, their different organs under the one-tier or two-tier board structures, the general meeting of shareholders, modifications of share capital, employee share schemes, company audit, transformation, dissolution, and civil liability of promoters and directors, as well as, on a voluntary basis, employee participation. The provisions are detailed and to a large extent mandatory. The limited partnership with a share capital is regulated in Chapter VI, and the simplified public company (*société par actionnes simplifiée*) in Chapter VII. Chapter VIII contains the provisions on equity and debt securities, in particular on the relationship between the company, on the one hand, and the shareholders and bondholders, on the other. This chapter does not contain a comprehensive codification of securities regulation, however. On the contrary, it is incomplete and often refers to the Monetary and Financial Code (*Code monétaire and financier*).[761] The latter also contains the prohibition of insider trading,[762] whereas other provisions of the Market Abuse

[755] Government Commission, German Corporate Governance Code, as amended in February 2017 Foreword https://www.dcgk.de//files/dcgk/usercontent/en/download/code/170214_Code.pdf.

[756] Kübler and Assmann (n 173) 174.

[757] Ringleb, Kremer, Lutter, and Werder (n 740) paras 82–4.

[758] Windbichler (n 176) 406-7 (§31 para 4).

[759] Cahn and Donald (n 299) 16.

[760] Here, the Code reproduces the provisions that could previously be found in a separate statute, the Law of 24 July 1966. See also Germain and Magnier (n 192) para 1894.

[761] ibid.

[762] C.mon.fin art L465-1.

Directive (now Regulation) were implemented in the General Regulation of the Financial Markets Authority (*Règlement Général de L'Autorité des Marchés Financier*).[763] The latter is an independent public body with the task of overseeing and regulating the financial markets.[764] It has the power to issue general regulations on the rules for public offerings and admission to trading on a regulated market, as well as standards of good professional conduct for market participants and financial services providers.[765] Title III of the 2nd Book of the Commercial Code contains the provisions common to all types of commercial companies, in particular company accounts, nullity, merger and separation, and liquidation. It also contains the provisions on the early warning procedure for companies in financial difficulties.[766] Insolvency law is regulated in the 6th Book of the Commercial Code. Title V Chapter I contains the practically very important action against company directors for an insufficiency of the company's assets (*action de la responsabilité pour insuffisance d'actifs*). The Regulatory Parts of the Codes add a second level of regulation, usually issued in the form of decree laws as secondary legislation that provide guidance on the application of the provisions in the Codes.[767]

Despite this detailed multi-layered legislation case law still plays a very significant role. It was the courts that first established the separate legal personality of all commercial companies in the middle of the nineteenth century.[768] In order to protect minority shareholders against the power of the majority, but also to protect the shareholders against abusive minority behaviour, the courts developed, outside the framework of the Codes, the doctrines of *abus de majorité* and *abus de minorité*.[769] Another example is the doctrine of *confusion the patrimoine*. If there is no clear separation of assets and liabilities of the company, on the one hand, and its shareholders and managers, on the other, all natural and legal persons involved may be treated as a single economic unit.[770] Case law is not just important for the development of new doctrines outside and in addition to the Codes. It obviously plays a significant role when it comes to the interpretation of open textured norms. For example, the substantive ground for a director's personal liability pursuant to Com Article L651-1 (*action de la responsabilité pour insuffisance d'actifs*) is a fault in management that was causal for the excess of liabilities over assets. A statutory definition of management fault does not exist. The term is fact sensitive and has been applied flexibly by the courts in order to accommodate the circumstances in each case at hand.[771]

The French 'Corporate Governance Code of Listed Corporations' is the result of a consolidation of the Viénot reports of July 1995 and July 1999, the Bouton report of September 2002 and the January 2007 and October 2008 recommendations concerning the compensation of executive directors of listed companies, as well as the April 2010 recommendation on the presence of women on the board. This collection of reports and recommendations was prepared and regularly updated by working groups of the *Association Française des Entreprises Privées* (AFEP) and the *Mouvement des Entreprises de France* (MEDEF).[772] Thus, the business community itself initiated these projects with a view to improve management practices and to enhance investor confidence. The 2018 version of the Code takes into account the public consultations of 2013 and 2016.[773] The Code applies to listed companies only and also follows the 'comply or explain' approach, which is enshrined in Com Articles 225-37 and 225-68.[774]

[763] RGAM arts 622-1, 622-2, 633-1, 633-4. [764] C.mon.fin art L621-1.
[765] C.mon.fin art L621-6, L621-7. [766] Cozian, Viandier, and Deboissy (n 10) para 1199.
[767] Germain and Magnier (n 192) para 1899. [768] ibid para 1650.
[769] Cozian, Viandier, and Deboissy (n 10) paras 575–84. [770] Cf Chapter 10E.III. [771] ibid.
[772] AFEP and MEDEF, Corporate Governance Code of Listed Corporations, 2013, 1 http://www.ecgi.org/codes/documents/afep_medef_code_revision_jun2013_en.pdf.
[773] AFEP and MEDEF, Code de gouvernement d'entreprise des sociétés cotées, juin 2018 file:///Users/zfzz6786/Downloads/8aa47dca7788a4a9b02c74c6d9da4bb9ad90f450.pdf.
[774] Germain and Magnier (n 192) para 2776.

IV. United States

Corporate law in the United States consists of a complex mix of legislation at state and federal level, statute, and case law. The general incorporation statutes that provide for the formation of a corporation are state laws, for instance the Delaware General Corporation Law (DGCL), or the California Corporations Code (CCC).[775] The idea of having federally chartered corporations on the basis of a federal incorporation statute has never caught on.[776] In 1950, the Committee on Corporate Law of the American Bar Association issued a Model Business Corporation Act (MBCA) that has since undergone major revisions. A large number of states have based their corporation statutes on the (Revised) MBCA; however, important states such as Delaware, California, and New York have not.[777] Under the 'internal affairs doctrine', the internal affairs of a corporation will be governed by the corporation statute of the state where the company is incorporated, regardless of where it does business, or where its assets or personnel are located.[778] 'Internal affairs' refers, by and large, to the allocation of powers between management and shareholders and the rights and obligations of management and shareholders vis-à-vis, and amongst, each other.[779] This largely coincides with the content of the general incorporation statutes. These statutes are, for the most part, enabling in nature, providing merely default provisions.[780] Thus, corporate promoters have not only fifty different sets of default rules to choose from but they may also adapt the chosen set to their specific needs. When newly formed, incorporation will usually occur under the law of the state where the incorporators actually plan to do business, simply in order to save the fees and taxes imposed by states on 'foreign' corporations (those incorporated in another state). However, more than 50 per cent of the corporations listed on the New York Stock Exchange and more than 60 per cent of the Fortune 500 have reincorporated[781] in Delaware under the DGCL.[782] Since the early twentieth century, Delaware has been a leader in the development of corporate law among the different states. The success of Delaware in attracting large publicly held corporations has helped to establish the notion of regulatory competition in corporate law between states. However, recent research suggests that no other state actively seeks to attract incorporations.[783] However, Delaware's innovations are often subsequently adopted by other states.[784] Whether this results in a 'race to the bottom' to the laxest standard, or a 'race to the top' to the most efficient corporate statute is an open question and empirically difficult to verify.[785] Some states, notably California, seek to apply their own corporation statutes to 'foreign' corporations doing business within their territory, subject to certain activity thresholds.[786] As a result the internal affairs of a corporation may be governed partly by the corporate law of the state of incorporation and partly by the host state.[787] It is unclear whether this is in line with the US Constitution.[788]

Securities regulation largely takes place at federal level. The Securities Act 1933 was enacted as part of the 'New Deal' to cope with the Great Depression. It basically requires the registration of securities before their issuance. Registration entails the preparation and filing

[775] *CTS Corp v Dynamics Corp of America*, 481 US 69 (1987): 'It ... is an accepted part of the business landscape in this country for States to create corporations, to prescribe their powers, and to define the rights that are acquired by purchasing their shares'.

[776] FA Gevurtz, *Gevurtz's Corporation Law* (2nd edn, West Academic 2010) 38.

[777] ibid.

[778] *VantagePoint Venture Partners 1996 v Examen, Inc.*, 871 A.2d 1108 (Delaware Supreme Court 2005).

[779] ibid ('The internal affairs doctrine applies to those matters that pertain to the relationships among or between the corporation and its officers, directors, and shareholders').

[780] H Hansmann, 'Corporation and Contract' (2006) 8 American Law and Economics Review 1.

[781] Reincorporation is effectuated by incorporating a new corporation in the state of destination and then merging the existing company into the new company.

[782] Cf https://corp.delaware.gov/stats/.

[783] M Kahan and E Kamar, 'The Myth of State Competition in Corporate Law' (2002-2003) 55 Stanford Law Review 679.

[784] Choper, Coffee, and Gilson (n 97) 230.

[785] Bebchuk, Cohen, and Ferrell (n 96).

[786] CCC, §2115(a).

[787] ibid §2115(b).

[788] Gevurtz (n 778) 36–8.

with the Securities and Exchange Commission (SEC) of an extensive disclosure document consisting of a 'prospectus' and additional information. The prospectus is to be disseminated to investors.[789] Whereas the 1933 Act deals with the initial public issuance of securities (primary market), the Securities Exchange Act 1934 is concerned with securities when they are traded in the market (secondary market). The Act regulates a wide range of matters such as proxy solicitation, securities fraud, and tender offers, but also periodic disclosure of important information in quarterly and annual reports and reports for certain significant events.[790] The 1934 Act was significantly amended by the Sarbanes-Oxley Act (or Public Company Accounting Reform and Investor Protection Act) 2002 as a reaction to the accounting scandals involving Enron, WorldCom, and other major companies. Its main objective is to ensure greater accuracy of financial statements by tackling conflicts-of-interest between issuer and auditors, requiring an audit committee of the board of directors composed of independent directors, and enhanced internal controls and record-keeping.[791] The 1934 Act established the SEC as the regulator to oversee the securities industry. The SEC has broad authority over all aspects of securities regulation including extensive rule-making powers in order to properly implement the open textured provisions of the Acts.[792] One of its most prominent rules is Rule 10b-5 which became the legal basis for private action in case of insider trading.[793] In addition to this federal regulation, there are state securities laws, or so-called 'blue sky' laws.[794] These statutes are very diverse, but typically contain criminal sanctions for securities fraud; registration and regulation of persons who trade in securities; registration of any securities to be sold within the state, occasionally subject to an assessment of the security's merit.[795] Today, securities listed, or to be listed, at the New York or American Stock Exchanges or NASDAQ are no longer required to go through the occasionally onerous registration under state securities laws.[796]

Corporate insolvency law is also largely federal in nature.[797] The Bankruptcy Code of 1978 contains provisions on company liquidation (Chapter 7) and reorganization (Chapter 11). As filing under the Code does not require the corporation to be insolvent,[798] Chapter 11 is an important device to reorganize a corporation's capital structure. In this context, filing, and the reorganization plan process have significant corporate governance implications. Creditor protection is largely achieved through bankruptcy law doctrines such as the 'strong arm powers'[799] and 'equitable subordination'.[800] Fraudulent transfer law is an important device in this respect.[801] Fraudulent transfer statutes are state laws[802] addressing the issue of corporate insiders siphoning away assets of the corporation to the detriment of its creditors. The Bankruptcy Code contains similar provisions that only apply in case of transactions involving two or more states.[803]

789 ibid 568. 790 ibid 570–2. 791 ibid 573.

792 M Eisenberg, Corporations and other Business Organizations: Cases and Materials (9th edn, Foundation Press 2005) 209.

793 Choper, Coffee, and Gilson (n 97) 323–4.

794 Enacted first by Kansas in 1911 to tackle the sale of investments which had no more substance than buying 'so many square feet of blue sky'; Gevurtz (n 778) 559.

795 ibid 559–61. 796 Securities Act 1933, §18.

797 State corporation laws may contain provisions on corporate insolvency, in particular on the appointment of a receiver over the corporation's assets, for instance DGCL, §§291–303.

798 However, pursuant to §1112(b) of the Bankruptcy Code (11 U.S.C.) on motion of 'a party in interest', a case may be converted to a case under Chapter 7 or may be dismissed for 'cause'. A case will be subject to dismissal unless filed in 'good faith'. Cf *In re SGL Carbon Corporation*, 200 F.3d 154 (3d Cir. 1999) 160 and 166 ('Courts ... have consistently dismissed Chapter 11 petitions filed by financially healthy companies with no need to reorganize under the protection of Chapter 11').

799 11 U.S.C., §544. The provision ensures that the trustee can assert the rights that creditors could assert against the debtor's property outside of bankruptcy, in particular assets subject to an non-perfected security interest.

800 11 U.S.C., §510(c). The court may subordinate the claim of a creditor for distribution purposes to the claims of other creditors.

801 RC Clark, *Corporate Law* (2nd edn, Wolters Kluwer 1986) 38.

802 Most states have adopted the Uniform Fraudulent Transfer Act. 803 11 U.S.C., §548.

As far as 'soft law' is concerned, many different instruments have been issued by a number of different organizations.[804] The American Law Institute has promulgated 'Principles of Corporate Governance: Analysis and Recommendation'. There are 'Principles of Corporate Governance' by the Business Roundtable, composed of corporate counsel and chief executive officers. The National Association of Corporate Directors' has published 'Key Agreed Principles to Strengthen Corporate Governance in US Publicly Traded Companies'. The Council of Institutional Investors has issued 'Core Policies, General Principles, Positions & Explanatory Notes' as well as 'Corporate Governance Policies'. Powerful institutional investors, such as TIAA-CREF (Teachers Insurance and Annuity Association-College Retirement Equities Fund) and CalPERS (California Public Employees' Retirement System) have come out with their own policies and principles on corporate governance that they expect the companies they invest in to adhere to. There is further the 'Report of the New York Stock Exchange Commission on Corporate Governance'. These codes and principles all rely on self-regulation. The scope of the 'comply-or-explain' approach that can be found in the Sarbanes-Oxley Act and the implementing SEC Rule[805] is somewhat limited. It only relates to whether the principal executive officer, principal financial officer, principal accounting officer or controller, or persons performing similar functions are subject to a 'code of ethics' adopted by the issuer. However, much of what corporate governance codes usually recommend is compulsory for listed companies under the Sarbanes-Oxley Act, the amendments introduced in the wake of the global financial crisis by the Dodd-Franck Wall Street Reform and Consumer Protection Act of 2010, and the Listing Rules of the New York Stock Exchange and NASDAQ, in particular the introduction of board committees on audit, nomination, and compensation, manned by independent directors.[806]

Given the huge number of state and federal courts that may have to deal, in one way or another, with corporate law issues it is not surprising that corporate law and securities regulation also consist of an extensive body of case law. The rulings of the Delaware Court of Chancery and the Delaware Supreme Court are, however, of particular and nationwide importance. These courts deal almost exclusively with corporate cases.[807] Their judges do not face the political pressures of the state legislature and enjoy a high degree of political independence.[808] At the same time, the judges have achieved great expertise in business and financial matters. They have also demonstrated their ability to quickly respond to business litigation by granting expedited hearings and speedy decisions.[809] Delaware case law is also very flexible. Courts are willing to revise previously announced legal doctrine on the basis that a different approach may generate a sounder outcome.[810] The criteria of the business judgment rule, the transactions that may trigger the duty of loyalty, the standard for assessing management's response to a hostile takeover bid, all are based on case law.[811] Indeed, in the absence of statutory provisions in DGCL, the entire machinery of fiduciary duties was developed by the courts. Delaware case law has great persuasive authority. Courts in many states have decided to follow it.[812]

Question:

- Comparative law traditionally distinguishes between civil law (Germany, France) and common law (England, United States) legal systems. What are the main characteristics of these legal systems in terms of sources of law, methodology and style? Do you recognize these characteristics when you look at the sources of corporate law in our four jurisdictions? Does the traditional distinction still make sense, in general and in corporate law?

[804] Downloadable from the European Corporate Governance Institute's website at https://ecgi.global/content/codes.

[805] Sarbanes-Oxley Act, §406, SEC Rule 33-8177, §229.406.

[806] Gevurtz (n 778) 242; Kraakman and others (n 6) 68.

[807] Choper, Coffee, and Gilson (n 97) 231.

[808] JE Fisch, 'The Peculiar Role of Delaware Courts in the Competition for Corporate Charters' (2000) 68 University of Cincinnati Law Review 1061, 1075.

[809] ibid 1077.

[810] ibid.

[811] ibid 1074.

[812] ibid 1078.

2

The Europeanization of Corporate Law

In the previous chapter, we saw that the business corporation as a legal phenomenon was, and still is, predominantly shaped by domestic law. However, over the years, European Union law has had a significant impact on corporate law. On the basis of a robust legislative competence, the EU has harmonized by way of directives a number of areas of substantive company law, with varying importance for domestic corporate law and practice. In respect of securities market regulation, the Union has emerged as the primary legislator. In addition, the case law of the Court of Justice of the European Union on the Treaty right to freedom of establishment has had a transformative impact on intra-Union cross-border corporate mobility. Whereas the impact of the right to free movement of capital on core company law seems to have been limited, the Member States' options in retaining control following the privatization of formerly state-owned undertakings has been severely curtailed. Following the global financial crisis and the eurozone crisis, new measures venture further into the realm of corporate governance. With the United Kingdom's decision to leave the EU, the future of EU company law has become more unpredictable.

This chapter provides, first, an overview of the nature and effects of EU law and the EU law-making process, with particular focus on the internal market. This is followed by an analysis of the *acquis unionaire*—the EU law with company law relevance at both Treaty level and the level of secondary legislation (regulations and directives). Many of these instruments will be discussed more thoroughly in the following chapters. The emphasis here is on the trajectory of EU company law and its development in distinguishable 'waves'. We then turn to the issue of corporate mobility within the Union, on the basis of the Court's case law on freedom of establishment as well as the emerging EU law infrastructure for corporate mobility transactions. In respect of the free movement of capital, the Court has developed an elaborate doctrine dealing with so-called 'golden shares' by virtue of which Member States seek to retain a certain influence in privatized firms. Although these 'golden shares' have almost invariably been struck down by the Court, overall the impact on general corporate law seems to have been limited. The chapter concludes with some speculation about the future of EU company law in the light of the UK's decision to withdraw from the Union (Brexit).

A. Laws and Law-making in the EU

The European Union is a supranational organization.[1] According to the Court of Justice in its famous decision in *Van Gend en Loos*,[2] it

> constitutes a new legal order of international law for the benefit of which the states have limited their sovereign rights, albeit within limited fields, and the subjects of which comprise not only Member States but also their nationals. Independently of the legislation of Member States, Community law therefore not only imposes obligations on individuals but is also intended to confer upon them rights which become part of their legal heritage. These rights arise not only where they are expressly granted by the Treaty, but also by reason of obligations which the Treaty imposes in a clearly defined way upon individuals as well as upon the Member States and upon the institutions of the Community.

Unlike other international organizations, through its institutions,[3] which are 'endowed with sovereign rights', the EU can issue legal instruments that are not only binding on its Member Sates but also within the Member States in the sense that citizens can rely on these enactments in front of national courts. Depending on the nature and content of the legal instrument, there is no need for implementation into national law: the EU legal instrument may be 'directly effective'. Moreover, in *Costa v ENEL*[4] the Court of Justice has endowed the EU legal order with precedence or primacy (i.e. supremacy) over national law:

> The integration into the laws of each Member State of provisions which derive from the Community, and more generally the terms and the spirit of the Treaty, make it impossible for the states, as a corollary, to accord precedence to a unilateral and subsequent measure over a

[1] Formed as the European Economic Community by the Treaty of Rome in 1957, the European Union in its current form emerged as a result of the Lisbon Treaty, which entered into force in 2009, following several Treaty amendments the most important of which are the Single European Act (in force 1987), the Maastricht Treaty (in force 1994), the Treaty of Amsterdam (in force 1999), and the Nice Treaty (in force 2003). For details see P Craig and G de Búrca, *EU Law* (5th edn, OUP 2011) 1–29. Following several waves of enlargement, the EU currently encompasses 28 Member States: the founding members Belgium, France, Germany, Italy, Luxembourg, and the Netherlands; Denmark, Ireland, and the United Kingdom joined in 1973; followed by Greece in 1981; Portugal and Spain in 1986; Austria, Finland, and Sweden in 1995; Cyprus, the Czech Republic, Estonia, Hungary, Latvia, Lithuania, Malta, Poland, Slovakia, and Slovenia in 2004; Bulgaria and Rumania in 2007; and Croatia in 2013. In 2016, the United Kingdom decided in a referendum to exit from the European Union. The exit clause (Art 50 TEU) was triggered on 19 March 2017, setting in motion a two-year period for negotiating and concluding a withdrawal agreement.

[2] Case 26/62 *NV Algemene Transport- en Expeditie Onderneming van Gend en Loos v Netherlands Inland Revenue Administration* ECLI:EU:C:1963:1.

[3] These are the European Parliament (directly elected by the citizens of Member States), the Council (consisting of representatives of Member States at ministerial level), the European Council (consisting of the heads of state or government of the Member States), the European Commission (the members of which are appointed on the basis of equal rotation between the Member States), the Court of Justice of the European Union, the European Central Bank, and the Court of Auditors; Art 13 (1) TEU. The European Parliament and the Council jointly exercise the Union's legislative functions (Art 14(1) and 16(1) TEU), whereas the Commission as the Union's executive has the power to propose legislation (Art 17 TEU).

[4] Case 6/64 *Flaminio Costa v ENEL* ECLI:EU:C:1964:66.

> legal system accepted by them on a basis of reciprocity. Such a measure cannot therefore be inconsistent with that legal system'.

On this view, any (directly effective) provision of EU law, of whatever level within the hierarchy of norms of EU law, will prevail over a conflicting provision of national law of whatever level within the hierarchy of norms of national law. Thus, an obscure provision in an EU implementing act may prevail over national constitutional law. According to the Court, the primacy of EU law derives its normative force from the founding Treaties themselves: by creating a Community having

> real powers stemming from a limitation of sovereignty or a transfer of powers from the states to the Community, the Member States have limited their sovereign rights, albeit within limited fields, and have thus created a body of law which binds both their nationals and themselves ... The executive force of Community law cannot vary from one state to another in deference to subsequent domestic laws, without jeopardizing the attainment of the objectives of the Treaty'.

However, national constitutional courts do not universally accept this view.[5]

It is clear from these statements of the Court that only 'within limited fields' can the Union exercise the sovereign powers conferred on it by the Member States and within which the latter have limited their own sovereignty. This is the principle of conferral of powers: the EU may act only within the limits of the competences conferred upon it by the Member States and in order to achieve the objectives set out in the Treaties.[6] Competences not conferred on the Union remain with the Member States.[7] The competences conferred on the Union fall into three principal categories: exclusive competence, shared competence, and the competence to support, coordinate, or supplement the actions of the Member States.[8] Where the Union has exclusive competence in a specific area, only the Union may legislate and adopt legally binding acts; the Member States are precluded from doing so except where they are specifically empowered by the Union.[9] Areas of exclusive competence include the customs union, competition law, monetary policy for the eurozone, the common fisheries policy and the common commercial policy.[10] Where the Union shares competence with the Member States, both Union and Member States may legislate; however, Member States may do so only to the extent that the Union has not exercised its competence or has decided to cease exercising its competence.[11] Areas of shared competence include the internal market, social policy, the environment, consumer protection, energy, and the area of freedom, security, and justice.[12] A competence to support, coordinate, or supplement entitles the Union to pass legally binding acts short of harmonization which, to the extent set out in the act, constrain the Member States' powers in areas[13] such as the protection and improvement of human health, industry, culture, tourism, and education.[14] The Union competence for company law harmonization aims to attain the right to freedom of establishment as one of the fundamental internal market freedoms;[15] securities regulation may be based, in addition or alternatively, on the general competence for the approximation of laws with a view to establishing or enhancing the functioning of the internal market.[16] Given their internal market focus,[17] the EU competences for company law and securities regulation are shared competences. The same is true where the 'flexibility clause'[18] is used for the creation of new types of business entities under EU law. The exercise of a Union competence, other than an

[5] For an overview of the approach taken by national (constitutional) courts D Chalmers, G Davies, and G Monti, *European Union Law* (3rd edn, CUP 2014) 222–45.

[6] Article 5(1) and (2) TEU. [7] ibid Art 4(1). [8] Article 2 TFEU. [9] ibid Art 2(1).

[10] ibid Art 3. [11] ibid Art 2(2). [12] ibid Art 4. [13] ibid Art 2(5). [14] ibid Art 6.

[15] ibid Art 50(2)g. [16] ibid Art 114. [17] For a definition see ibid Art 26(2).

[18] ibid Art 352. The 'flexibility clause' allows the Union, subject to unanimity in the Council, to adopt those legal acts that are necessary to attain one of the objectives set out in the Treaties where the Treaties do not provide the necessary powers.

exclusive competence, is subject to the principle of subsidiarity.[19] Accordingly, the Union may only act to the extent that the objectives of the proposed action cannot be sufficiently achieved by the Member States; but rather, owing to the scale and effects of the proposed action, can be better achieved at Union level. National parliaments have been granted an important monitoring function in terms of subsidiarity.[20] Moreover, according to the principle of proportionality, which applies to all Union competences, including exclusive competences, the content and form of a Union action must not exceed what is necessary to achieve the objectives of the Treaties.[21] Whether and to what extent the principles of subsidiarity and proportionality are actually capable of limiting the exercise of a Union competence the prerequisites of which have been met remains doubtful.[22]

The applicable Union competence determines the relevant legislative process and may restrict the available instruments. Both the EU competence for the harmonization of core company law and the general internal market competence refer to the ordinary legislative procedure. Under the former, the Union can only act by way of a directive, whereas the latter is not restricted in this way.[23] The 'flexibility clause' is also not limited to any particular EU instrument, but relies on a special legislative procedure that requires unanimity in the Council and the consent of the European Parliament, following a proposal from the Commission.[24] Given the internal market focus of the Union's competences in company law and securities regulation, it is important to have a clear idea of the functioning of the internal market before we look more closely at the different EU law instruments, their effects, and the legislative process.

I. The operation of the internal market

The internal market remains the Union's principal economic rationale.[25] Going beyond the 'Ricardian model' of comparative advantage, according to which trade between nations can be beneficial also for lower productivity countries,[26] the internal market seeks to merge the markets of the Member States into a single much larger market with a certain degree of uniformity of market conditions, thereby acting as a catalyst also for social and political integration.[27] As a form of economic integration, the internal market can be distinguished, in terms of the level and intensity of involvement, from a free trade area, a customs union, and an economic union.[28] A free trade area consists of the removal of all customs duties and quotas on trade passing between the participating states, with each of them remaining free to determine unilaterally the level of customs duties on imports from outside the free trade area. A customs union is essentially a free trade area combined with an agreed common level of tariff on imports from outside the union. The internal market consists of an area without internal frontiers in which the free movement of goods is combined with the free movement of persons, services, and capital.[29] The key elements of the internal market are thus the four market freedoms: free movement of goods,[30] free movement of persons, including workers and self-employed natural and legal persons,[31] the freedom to provide services,[32] and free movement of capital.[33] To this may be added the principle of undistorted competition.[34] An

[19] Art 5(3) TEU; Protocol (No 2) on the Application of the Principles of Subsidiarity and Proportionality.
[20] Articles 6–8 of Protocol (No 2).
[21] Article 5(4) TEU.
[22] M Schillig, *Konkretisierungskompetenz und Konkretisierungsmethoden im Europäischen Privatrecht* (de Gruyter 2009) 41–6.
[23] Article 50(1), 114(1) TFEU with Art 294 TFEU.
[24] Article 352 TFEU with Art 289(2) TFEU.
[25] Craig and de Búrca (n 1) 581.
[26] D Ricardo, *On the Principles of Political Economy and Taxation* (1817) Chapter 7 (https://www.marxists.org/reference/subject/economics/ricardo/tax/index.htm).
[27] Chalmers, Davies, and Monti (n 5) 669.
[28] Craig and de Búrca (n 1) 581 (reprinting an extract from D Swann, *The Economics of the Common Market* (7th edn, Penguin 1992) 11–12).
[29] Article 26(2) TFEU.
[30] ibid Arts 28–37.
[31] ibid Arts 45–55.
[32] ibid Arts 56–62.
[33] ibid Arts 63–66.
[34] Schillig (n 22) 23.

internal market combined with a complete unification of monetary and fiscal policy on the basis of a centrally controlled common currency constitutes an economic union.

Despite differences in their scope and subject matters of protection as well as the available defences provided for in the TFEU, the general structure of the four market freedoms has converged over the years.[35] In respect of the free movement of goods, the focus quickly shifted from 'quantitative restrictions on imports' to 'measures having equivalent effect',[36] which were interpreted very widely by the Court of Justice[37] and extended so as also to encompass measures that apply without distinction to domestic and foreign suppliers.[38] Thus, free movement of goods evolved from a provision that was geared towards tackling the discrimination of foreign goods to a general prohibition of all restrictions, a development that was subsequently extended to the other market freedoms as well.[39] Hand in hand with the extension of the protective ambit of the market freedoms, the Court provided new grounds on the basis of which national restrictions could be justified, going beyond the defences already stipulated in the Treaties. Thus, whereas directly discriminatory measures can only be justified on the basis of the exceptions provided for in the Treaties on grounds of public morality, public policy, public security, public health etc,[40] and subject to a strict application of proportionality considerations, indistinctly applicable measures may also be justified on the basis of 'mandatory requirements' necessary to protect the effectiveness of fiscal supervision, the fairness of commercial transactions, the interests of consumers, and the environment etc.[41] Moreover, in *Keck* the Court of Justice introduced a distinction between product-related requirements (designation, form, size, weight, composition, presentation, labelling, packaging, etc), and 'certain selling arrangements' (opening hours, working time, or types of business premises). The former are subject to the full force of free movement review; the latter will be subject to free movement review only where the national measure discriminates, in law or in fact, against foreign products.[42] The distinction between product requirements and selling arrangements seems to be somewhat formalistic and is not always clear in practice. Therefore, in the search of *Keck*'s underlying rationale the idea of unrestricted market access has gained significant ground.[43] Under this approach, the issue is whether a national measure specifically and substantially restricts market access for foreign products and suppliers, by, for example, preventing a Union-wide marketing strategy and, thus, the realization of economies of scale.[44] If this is the case, the measure is subject to unqualified free movement review; otherwise, free movement does not apply. If *Keck* is to be understood in this way, its rationale can be extended beyond the free movement of goods and applied with equal force in the context of the other market freedoms.[45]

The four market freedoms are directly effective:[46] free movement of goods, persons, and services since the expiry of the 'transitional period' on 31 December 1969,[47] and free movement of capital only since 1 January 1994.[48] Because of the primacy of EU law, national

[35] ibid 287. [36] Article 34 TFEU.

[37] Case 8/74 *Procureur du Roi v Dassonville* ECLI:EU:C:1974:82 para 5: 'All trading rules enacted by Member States which are capable of hindering, directly or indirectly, actually or potentially, intra-Community trade are to be considered as measures having an effect equivalent to quantitative restrictions'.

[38] Case 120/78 *Rewe-Zentral AG v Bundesmonopolverwaltung für Branntwein* ECLI:EU:C:1979:42 para 8 (*Cassis de Dijon*).

[39] Schillig (n 22) 287. [40] Articles 36, 45(3) and (4), 51, 52, 62, and 65 TFEU.

[41] Case 120/78 *Cassis de Dijon* (n 38) para 8; Case C-55/94 *Gebhard v Consiglio dell'Ordine degli Avvocati e Procuratori di Milano* ECLI:EU:C:1995:411 para 37.

[42] Joined Cases C-267 and 268/91 *Criminal Proceedings against Keck and Mithouard* ECLI:EU:C:1993:905 paras 15–18.

[43] Craig and de Búrca (n 1) 662–7. [44] Schillig (n 22) 289. [45] ibid 289–90.

[46] Case 26/62 *NV Algemene Transport- en Expeditie Onderneming van Gend & Loos v Netherlands Inland Revenue Administration* (n 2).

[47] W Schön, 'Free Movement of Capital and Freedom of Establishment' Max Planck Institute for Tax Law and Public Finance Working Paper 2015-03 (June 2015) 2.

[48] What is now Art 63 TFEU became directly effective only with the entering into force of the Maastricht Treaty on 1 January 1994.

legislation in breach of the market freedoms is *ipso iure* inapplicable. The effect of the market freedoms is, therefore, deregulatory: restrictive national provisions are cut back as far as cross-border cases are concerned, resulting in an approximation of laws in a 'negative' sense. However, based on the grounds of 'mandatory requirements' or the defences provided for in the TFEU, the Member States may seek to retain, or introduce, obstacles to free movement that are justified and therefore cannot be torn down by direct application of the four freedoms. 'Positive' harmonization through Union legislation is required in order to remove these remaining barriers, whilst at the same time preventing a regulatory vacuum and adequately protecting the public interests that provided the justification for the national measures in the first place.[49] Positive harmonization may take different forms according to the room for manoeuvre left for the Member States. Minimum harmonization allows the Member States to go beyond the level of protection determined by a common Union-wide standard. When implementing the relevant EU benchmark, usually set out in a directive, into national law, Member States must take the Union standard as a base line and are free to determine the level of protection up to a ceiling that is marked by the four market freedoms and the principle of proportionality. Minimum harmonization has been criticized for not actually removing hindrances to free movement: by leaving room for national deviations, Member States may retain or introduce new obstacles contrary to the idea of the internal market. This is one reason for the Union to increasingly rely on maximum harmonization where possible. Maximum harmonization leaves, in principle, no room for the Member States when implementing a Union standard. Member States can go neither below nor beyond the common benchmark. A maximum harmonization directive may still leave room for deviations in clearly delineated areas and allow Member States to provide tailored rules for certain specifically defined fact patterns.[50] Depending on the applicable Union competence, the Union may opt for setting uniform rules that are directly applicable across the Member States. Here, the latter will be bound and cannot deviate from the regulatory regime at Union level. Such a unification of national laws can be achieved through the legal instrument of a regulation.[51]

II. Nature and effect of EU law and EU legal instruments

The sources of EU law are commonly divided into primary sources and secondary sources. The former consist of written sources in the form of the Treaty provisions, together with the protocols annexed to the Treaties and the EU Charter of Fundamental Rights. Unwritten sources of primary law are the general principles of EU law developed by the Court of Justice on the basis of the constitutional traditions of the Member States and international human rights treaties,[52] such as the principle of proportionality, fundamental rights, legal certainty, legitimate expectations, or procedural justice.[53] Written and unwritten sources of primary EU law share the same level within the hierarchy of norms.[54] They take precedence over the secondary sources of EU law and provide the standard for judicial review[55] and guidance

[49] M Schillig, 'The Interpretation of European Private Law in the Light of Market Freedoms and EU Fundamental Rights' (2008) 15 Maastricht Journal of European and Comparative Law 285, 288.

[50] Schillig (n 22) 46–50. [51] ibid 23.

[52] Case 29/69 *Stauder v City of Ulm* ECLI:EU:C:1969:57; Case 11/70 *Internationale Handelsgesellschaft v Einfuhr und Vorrahtsstelle für Getriede und Futtermittel* ECLI:EU:C:1970:114; Case 4/73 *Nold v Commission* ECLI:EU:C:1974:51.

[53] Craig and de Búrca (n 1) 109.

[54] H Hofmann, G Rowe, and A Türk, *Administrative Law and Policy of the European Union* (OUP 2011) 68. In fact, the interaction between written and unwritten sources of primary law is more complex. On the one hand, general principles may play a gap filling and subsidiary role; on the other, they may guide the interpretation, and restrict the ambit, of Treaty provisions, thus operating as meta-rules; ibid 71.

[55] See Art 263(2) TFEU: The Court of Justice shall have jurisdiction to review legal acts issued by EU institutions 'on grounds of lack of competence, infringement of essential procedural requirement, infringement of the Treaties or of any rule of law relating to their application, or misuse of powers'.

for the interpretation of the latter.[56] Secondary sources of EU law consist of the legal instruments adopted by the EU institutions on the basis of the Treaties,[57] either directly or indirectly. Within secondary law, the TFEU establishes a further hierarchy, in descending order, of legislative acts, delegated acts and implementing acts. Legislative acts are those legal acts adopted through the ordinary or special legislative procedures by the European Parliament and the Council acting jointly.[58] Delegated acts are adopted by the Commission on the basis of a power delegated to it in a legislative act that specifies the objectives, content, scope, and duration of the delegation of power. Delegated acts are of general application, supplementing or amending certain non-essential elements of the legislative act; the essential elements of an area are reserved for the legislative act and are not subject to a delegation of power.[59] Finally, implementing acts are adopted by the Commission, on the basis of implementing powers conferred on it by either legislative or delegated acts where uniform conditions for implementing legally binding Union acts are needed.[60] Implementing acts execute legislative or delegated acts without amending or supplementing them, although in practice it may be difficult to determine whether this is the case or not.[61] Secondary law at any level within the hierarchy of norms may take the form of a regulation, a directive, or a decision. It is important to realize that these legal instruments do not vary in their respective characteristics depending on whether they are adopted as legislative acts, delegated acts or implementing acts; however their normative force within the hierarchy of secondary legislation depends on their attribution to any of these categories.[62] In addition, the Union may issue recommendations and opinions, which have no binding force. As soft law, they may have legal effect as interpretative guidelines and by directing the exercise of discretion.[63]

A regulation has general application, is binding in its entirety and directly applicable in all Member States.[64] In general, regulations do not require implementation and upon their entering into force create rights and obligations not just for the Member States and their authorities, but also for individual market participants. Regulations are the instrument for enacting uniform law. However, this does not prevent the Union from adopting regulations that may require supplementation through national implementing measures. One example is the Council Regulation (EC) No 2157/2001 on the Statute for a European company (*Societas Europaea* or SE),[65] which only contains core provisions on the formation of an SE, its governance structure, and the transfer of its seat. Otherwise, an SE will be governed by its constitutional documents to the extent that this is expressly authorized by the Regulation, the national laws implementing the Regulation, and finally the national laws on public limited liability companies in the Member State where the SE has its seat.[66] In addition to the creation of new Union-level types of business entities,[67] regulations are increasingly being used in the area of securities regulation[68] and are relevant for insolvency law.[69]

[56] Schillig (n 49) 288. [57] Article 288 TFEU. [58] ibid Art 289(3). [59] ibid Art 290.
[60] ibid Art 291. [61] Craig and de Búrca (n 1) 116–17. [62] ibid 104. [63] ibid 107–108.
[64] Article 288(2) TFEU.
[65] Council Regulation (EC) 2157/2001 of 8 October 2001 on the Statute for a European company (SE), OJ 2001 L294/1.
[66] ibid Art 9(1).
[67] In addition to the SE, see Council Regulation (EEC) 2137/85 of 25 July 1985 on the European Economic Interest Grouping (EEIG) [1985] OJ L199/1; Regulation (EC) No 1435/2003 of 22 July 2003 on the statute for a European co-operative society (SCE) [2003] OJ L207/1, supplemented by Directive 2003/72/EC of 22 July 2003 on employee participation [2003] OJ L207/25.
[68] Regulation (EU) No 600/2014 of the European Parliament and of the Council of 15 May 2014 on markets in financial instruments and amending Regulation (EU) No 648/2012, OJ EU L173/84 12.6.2014 (MiFIR); Regulation (EU) No 596/2014 of the European Parliament and of the Council of 16 April 2014 on market abuse (market abuse regulation) and repealing Directive 2003/6/EC of the European Parliament and of the Council and Commission Directives 2003/124/EC, 2003/125/EC and 2004/72/EC, OJ EU L173/1 12.6.2014; Regulation (EU) 2017/1129 of the European Parliament and of the Council of 14 June 2017 on the prospectus to be published when securities are offered to the public or admitted to trading on a regulated market, and repealing Directive 2003/71/EC, OJ EU 30.6.2017 L168/12.
[69] Regulation (EU) 2015/848 of the European Parliament and of the Council of 20 May 2015 on insolvency proceedings (recast) OJ EU 5.6.2015 L141/19.

A directive is binding upon each Member State to which it is addressed as to the result to be achieved, however it leaves to the national authorities the choice of form and methods.[70] Consequently, the concept of a directive envisages a two-level legislative process. In a first step, the Union adopts a directive, which obliges the Member States to achieve a certain result within a certain time limit by amending and adapting their domestic laws. A directive is binding on the Member States, but in principle not within the Member States. In a second step, the Member States must implement the directive into national law with a view to achieving the intended result, but are free to select the form and method that best suits their national particularities. The directive embodies a compromise between the effective realization of Union aims and objectives, on the one hand, and the protection of national sovereignty to the greatest possible extent, on the other, with a view to enhancing the acceptance of Union measures and benefiting from local expertise.[71] In case of correct and timely implementation, market participants are affected by a directive's intended regulatory objectives through the medium of national implementing legislation. However, as a consequence of Member States' reluctance when it comes to timely implementation, the Court of Justice has significantly extended the effect of directives within the Member States in the absence of correct implementation.[72] According to the Court's well established case law,[73] following the expiration of the deadline for implementation, market participants may invoke and rely on directives directly before the national courts (direct effect), provided the directive has not been implemented (correctly) and the provisions that the individual seeks to rely on are 'sufficiently clear and precise' and 'unconditional'.[74] The underlying question for establishing these preconditions is not whether the provision at issue is vague or open-textured, but whether it is complete in the sense that it can be applied and is operable without the need for national implementing measures. It is also well established that directives have 'direct effect' only vertically; that is, they may be invoked by an individual against emanations of a Member State[75] (but not vice versa).[76] Moreover, the Court has continuously held that directives do not have 'horizontal direct effect'; their provisions cannot be invoked by private individuals or firms against each other.[77] Consequently, the concept of direct effect seems to be of limited significance within the area of company law.[78] The so-called indirect effect or harmonious interpretation of national law is the most significant concept developed by the CJEU in this context. It is the conveyer belt through which the key concepts of a directive, as interpreted by the Court of Justice, are translated into, and to be given effect in, national law by national authorities.

[70] Article 288(3) TFEU. [71] Schillig (n 22) 73. [72] ibid 77.

[73] Case 9/70 *Grad v Finanzamt Traunstein* ECLI:EU:C:1970:78 para 5; Case 33/70 *SACE v Italian Ministry of Finance* ECLI:EU:C:1970:118; Case 41/74 *Van Duyn v Home Office* ECLI:EU:C:1974:133; Case 8/81 *Becker v Finanzamt Münster* ECLI:EU:C:1982:7 para 25.

[74] Case 41/74 *Van Duyn v Home Office* (n 73) paras 13–14; Joined Cases C-397/01 and C-403/01 *Pfeiffer v Deutsches Rotes Kreuz* ECLI:EU:C:2004:584 para 5; Case 152/84 *Marshall v Southampton and South-West Hampshire Area Health Authority* ECLI:EU:C:1986:84 para 52; Case 50/88 *Kühne v Finanzamt München III* ECLI:EU:C:1989:262 para 26.

[75] Case C-188/89 *Foster v British Gas plc* ECLI:EU:C:1990:313.

[76] Joined Cases C-387/02, C-391/02, and C-403/02 *Berlusconi and Others* ECLI:EU:C:2005:270.

[77] Case 152/84 *Marshall v Southampton and South-West Hampshire Area Health Authority* (n 74) para 48; Joined Cases C-397/01 and C-C-403/01 *Pfeiffer* (n 74) paras 108–109.

[78] However, directives frequently have a direct impact, even in disputes amongst private individuals and firms; Case C-194/94 *CIA Security International SA v Signalson and Securitel SPRL* ECLI:EU:C:1996:172; Case C-443/98 *Unilever Italia SpA v Central Food SpA* ECLI:EU:C:2000:496. The Court seems to work on the basis that whereas a directive may have the effect of excluding the application of national provisions in horizontal relationships; it may not directly define the rights and obligations of the parties. Accordingly, in horizontal disputes directives may have an 'exclusionary' or negative effect; not however a positive or 'replacement' effect. However, this distinction seems to be very formal and artificial. It seems preferable to conceptualize this phenomenon as an emanation of the principle of indirect effect or harmonious interpretation of national law so as to give effect to the aims and objectives of the directive. Subject to national methods of legal reasoning, this may result in a reduction of the scope of a national provision to 'zero', that is, to the extent that a provision is incompatible with a directive it is disapplied; Schillig (n 22) 79.

According to the long-standing case law of the Court of Justice, all national authorities, including the national courts within their jurisdiction, must interpret all national law as far as possible in accordance with, and in the light of, the wording and purpose of the directive in order to achieve the desired result.[79] One of the leading cases concerning indirect effect is the Court's decision in *Marleasing* concerning the interpretation of the First Company Law Directive[80] (now Directive (EU) 2017/1132)[81] and its interaction with Spanish law.[82] The Directive limits the grounds on which a company may be found to be a nullity and had, at the time, not been implemented into Spanish law. Following a narrow interpretation of the grounds for nullity under the Directive, the issue was whether this narrow interpretation could be given effect under Spanish law, which at the time allowed a finding of nullity on a much broader scale:

> 6 With regard to the question whether an individual may rely on the directive against a national law, it should be observed that, as the Court has consistently held, a directive may not of itself impose obligations on an individual and, consequently, a provision of a directive may not be relied upon as such against such a person (judgment in Case 152/84 Marshall v Southampton and South-West Hampshire Area Health Authority [1986] ECR 723).
>
> 7 However, it is apparent from the documents before the Court that the national court seeks in substance to ascertain whether a national court hearing a case which falls within the scope of [the First Company Law Directive] is required to interpret its national law in the light of the wording and the purpose of that directive in order to preclude a declaration of nullity of a public limited company on a ground other than those listed in Article [12] of the directive.
>
> 8 In order to reply to that question, it should be observed that, as the Court pointed out in its judgment in Case 14/83 Von Colson and Kamann v Land Nordrhein-Westfalen [1984] ECR 1891, paragraph 26, the Member States' obligation arising from a directive to achieve the result envisaged by the directive and their duty under Article [4(3) TEU] to take all appropriate measures, whether general or particular, to ensure the fulfilment of that obligation, is binding on all the authorities of Member States including, for matters within their jurisdiction, the courts. It follows that, in applying national law, whether the provisions in question were adopted before or after the directive, the national court called upon to interpret it is required to do so, as far as possible, in the light of the wording and the purpose of the directive in order to achieve the result pursued by the latter and thereby comply with the third paragraph of Article [289 TFEU].

In *Pfeiffer*, the Court held that the national court must consider national law as a whole in order to assess to what extent it may be applied so as not to produce a result contrary to that pursued by the directive. If the application of interpretative methods recognized by national law enables, in certain circumstances, a provision of domestic law to be construed in such a way as to avoid conflict with another rule of domestic law or the scope of that provision to be restricted to that end by applying it only in so far as it is compatible with the rule concerned, the national court is bound to use those methods in order to achieve the result sought by the directive. Consequently, in a dispute between private individuals

[79] Case 14/83 *Von Colson and Kamann v Land Nordrhein-Westfalen* ECLI:EU:C:1984:153 para 26; Case C-106/89 *Marleasing SA v La Comercial Internacionale de Alimentacion SA* ECLI:EU:C:1990:395 para 8; Case C-91/92 *Faccini Dori* ECLI:EU:C:1994:292 para 26; Joined Cases C-240 to C-244/98 *Océano Grupo Editorial SA v Murciano Quintero and Salvat Editores SA v Sánchez Alcón Prades and Others* ECLI:EU:C:2000:346 para 30.

[80] First Council Directive 68/151/EEC of 9 March 1968, on co-ordination of safeguards which, for the protection of the interests of members and others, are required by Member States of companies within the meaning of the second paragraph of Article 58 of the Treaty, with a view to making such safeguards equivalent throughout the Community [1968] OJ L65/08; 'codified' as Directive 2009/101/EC of the European Parliament and of the Council of 16 September 2009 on coordination of safeguards which, for the protection of the interests of members and others, are required by Member States of companies within the meaning of the second paragraph of Article 48 of the Treaty, with a view to making such safeguards equivalent (codified version) OJ 2009 L258/11.

[81] Directive (EU) 2017/1132 of the European Parliament and of the Council of 14 June 2017 relating to certain aspects of company law (codification) OJ EU 30.6.2017 L169/46.

[82] Case C-106/89 *Marleasing SA v La Comercial Internacionale de Alimentacion SA* (n 79).

the national court must 'do whatever lies within its jurisdiction, having regard to the whole body of rules of national law', in order to ensure that a directive is fully effective.[83] This would suggest that even an interpretation contrary to the clear wording of the national provisions may be required under EU law. A harmonious interpretation would find its limits only where the national legislator clearly intended to deviate from the directive's provisions. However, in *Adelener* the Court somewhat qualified this extensive obligation by subjecting it to the general principles of law, in particular the principles of legal certainty and non-retroactivity.[84] Harmonious interpretation cannot serve as a basis for an interpretation of national law *contra legem*. However, the wording of the national provisions still does not seem to constitute an absolute boundary. A national court would overstep its jurisdiction and decide *contra legem* only where an interpretation of national law in accordance with the directive would be unacceptable on the basis of national legal methods. Thus, scope and constraints of the principle of harmonious interpretation are determined by national methods of legal reasoning in the sense that within this framework an interpretation in conformity with the directive must be an acceptable option. This is the main difference as compared to a rejected horizontal direct effect, although the boundaries are becoming increasingly blurred.[85] The bulk of core company law provisions at Union level have been issued in the form of directives.

Decisions are binding in their entirety, and may be either of general application or binding only on those to whom they are addressed.[86] Decisions are usually issued in the latter form, and are of particular relevance in the context of competition law and state aid.[87] In company law and securities regulation they are of limited significance. This is different for recommendations and opinions. Recommendations have gained in importance since the 2002 Report of the High-level Group of Company Law Experts.[88] One of the elements of the Commission's then new approach was a greater reliance on non-binding soft-law measures, in particular two recommendations on remuneration of directors[89] and the role of non-executive directors in listed companies,[90] respectively; and more recently on corporate governance reporting.[91] To this may be added the Recommendation on a new approach to business failure and insolvency.[92] In addition to their function as interpretative guidelines and instruction for the exercise of discretion, recommendations may inspire and act as a catalyst for law reform in the Member States.

III. Overview of the law-making process

The legal competences in the areas of company law and securities regulation[93] refer to the ordinary legislative procedure[94] for the passing of legislative acts in these areas. For securities

[83] Joined Cases C-397/01 and Case C-403/01 *Pfeiffer* (n 74) paras 115–18.

[84] Case C-212/04 *Adeneler v Ellinikos Organismos Galaktos* ECLI:EU:C:2006:443 para 110.

[85] Schillig (n 22) 80–1. [86] Article 288(4) TFEU. [87] Craig and de Búrca (n 1) 107.

[88] Report of the High-level Group of Company Law Experts on a Modern Regulatory Framework for Company Law in Europe (Brussels 2002).

[89] Commission Recommendation 2004/913/EC of 14 December 2004 fostering an appropriate regime for the remuneration of directors of listed companies (Text with EEA relevance), OJ EU L385/55 29.12.2004; Commission Recommendation 2009/384/EC of 30 April 2009 on remuneration policies in the financial services sector (Text with EEA relevance) OJ EU L120/22 15.5.2009; Commission Recommendation 2009/385/EC of 30 April 2009 complementing Recommendations 2004/913/EC and 2005/162/EC as regards the regime for the remuneration of directors of listed companies (Text with EEA relevance) OJ EU L120/28 15.5.2009.

[90] Commission Recommendation 2005/162/EC of 15 February 2005 on the role of non-executive or supervisory directors of listed companies and on the committees of the (supervisory) board; OJ EU L52/51 25.2.2005.

[91] Commission Recommendation 2014/208/EU of 9 April 2014 on the quality of corporate governance reporting ('comply or explain') (Text with EEA relevance) OJ EU L109/43 12.4.2014.

[92] Commission Recommendation of 12.3.2014 on a new approach to business failure and insolvency C(2014) 1500 final.

[93] Articles 50(2)g, 114 TFEU. [94] ibid Art 294.

regulation and capital markets law, delegated and implementing acts are particularly relevant. Their adoption is embedded into a multi-level law-making process, which until 2009 was governed by the so-called Lamfalussy process[95] as a special form of comitology.[96] It has been significantly amended under the Lisbon Treaty[97] and following the installation of a new architecture for financial regulation and supervision at Union level.[98]

Formally, the ordinary legislative procedure begins with the Commission submitting a proposal to the European Parliament and the Council. A legislative act will be adapted if both the European Parliament and the Council agree on a text, possibly following an intervention of a Conciliation Committee. In a process of 'back-and-forth', Council and European Parliament may repeatedly exchange possibly amended proposals. The process comes to end when both institutions approve of a text upon which the legislative act is adopted; or when, after a third reading and following an intervention of the Conciliation Committee, one of the institutions finally rejects the proposal upon which it will have failed. Throughout the process, strict time limits apply which may, however, be extended.[99] The Council acts by qualified majority, which, in principle, requires a majority of at least 55 per cent of the members of the Council, comprising at least fifteen of them and representing Member States comprising at least 65 per cent of the population of the Union. A blocking minority must include at least four Council members; otherwise, the qualified majority will be deemed attained.[100] The process is based on the idea of institutional cooperation between the Commission, the European Parliament, and the Council, with an emphasis on dialogue and compromise so as to facilitate the successful passing of an act. In practical terms, Union law-making seeks to combine external expertise with political authority, taking into account the different interests of various groups and of the public in general.[101] Consequently, before the Commission publishes a formal proposal, Union policies for a particular area will be introduced to the public through so-called 'green papers'[102] and 'action plans',[103] giving affected stakeholders an opportunity to comment and voice their opinion. An actual proposal will then be drafted in close collaboration and consultation with national experts, civil servants, and representatives of interest groups.[104] Following the publication of the proposal in the *Official Journal*, stakeholders have another opportunity to comment on it within certain time limits. Even before the proposal reaches the Council it will have been thoroughly discussed by working groups composed of national officials and experts from the Member States. In the European Parliament, the main legislative work will be carried out by standing committees with particular subject-matter expertise.[105] The participation and input of interest groups is institutionalized in the

[95] See Final Report of the Committee of Wise Men on the Regulation of European Securities Markets (Brussels 2001) (*Lamfalussy* Report).

[96] Hofmann, Rowe, and Türk (n 54) 273–6; F Walla, '§4 Process and Strategies of Capital Markets Regulation in Europe' in R Veil (ed), *European Capital Markets Law* (2nd edn, Hart Publishing 2017) 39, 43.

[97] The Treaty of Lisbon emerged from the failure of the Constitutional Treaty with a focus on institutional reform, notably greater parliamentary involvement and citizen engagement; see Chalmers, Davies, and Monti (n 5) 38–46.

[98] Following the proposals of the de Larosière Report the regulatory framework for financial services has been completely reconstructed in an attempt to address some of the shortcomings that contributed to the financial crisis. Macro-prudential supervision has been assigned to the newly established European Systemic Risk Board (ESRB) and micro-prudential supervision to a new European System of Financial Supervisors (ESFS). This is a network of national supervisors coordinated by the new European Supervisory Authorities (ESAs). This seeks to enhance effective cooperation between national authorities, while leaving day-to-day supervision in their hands; M Schillig, *Resolution and Insolvency of Banks and Financial Institutions* (OUP 2016) 21 (para 2.08).

[99] Article 294 TFEU. [100] Article 16(4) TEU. [101] Schillig (n 22) 66–7.

[102] See eg Green Paper: 'The EU corporate governance framework' COM(2011) 164 final.

[103] See eg Communication from the Commission to the European Parliament, the Council, the European Economic and Social Committee and the Committee of the Regions, 'Action Plan: European company law and corporate governance—a modern legal framework for more engaged shareholders and sustainable companies' COM(2012) 740 final.

[104] Craig and de Búrca (n 1) 147. [105] ibid 148–9.

Economic and Social Committee; informally these groups contribute at every stage of the law-making process. Moreover, so-called trilogues featuring representatives of the Council, the European Parliament, and the Commission seek to facilitate compromise at all stages of the ordinary legislative procedure.[106] A minimum of democratic legitimacy is achieved through the direct representation of Union citizens in the European Parliament and the accountability of Council members vis-à-vis their national parliaments. The comprehensive collaboration and coordination between Union institutions, Member States, interest groups, and other stakeholders seeks to ensure optimum information gathering and processing, maximum acceptance, and compatibility of legislative acts with national law. On the other hand, the need for compromise and the balancing of conflicting interests may result in the watering down of legislative measures to mere 'regulatory torsos', as happened with Council Regulation (EC) No 2157/2001 on the Statute for a European company (SE), which started out as a proposal for a comprehensive European company law statute and, in the course of thirty years of negotiations, was reduced to a limited number of provisions heavily reliant on national law.[107] Sometimes a project has to be abandoned altogether when compromise cannot be reached, as was the case, for example, with the failed Fifth Company Law Directive on board structures.[108]

In accordance with the Lamfalussy Report and the changes introduced by the Lisbon Treaty and as a reaction to the global financial crisis of 2007–2009, Union law-making in the area of securities regulation and capital markets (as well as in banking and insurance law) is a four-level process.[109] This is particularly relevant in the context of market abuse and securities prospectuses,[110] and under the so-called MiFID II package.[111] At Level 1, following a Commission proposal, the European Parliament and the Council adopt a legislative act in the form of a framework directive or regulation by going through the ordinary legislative procedure. Examples are MiFID II, the Market Abuse Regulation, and the Prospectus Regulation. The Level 1 legislative act contains a delegation of power to the Commission for issuing delegated acts, implementing acts and/or regulatory technical standards, or implementing technical standards. At Level 2, the Commission may exercise this power by adopting delegated acts that supplement or amend certain non-essential elements of the Level 1 act, or by adopting implementing acts in order to ensure the uniform implementation across the Union of the Level 1 act.[112] The Commission may further issue regulatory technical standards and implementing technical standards. The former are delegated acts that are

[106] ibid 127–8. [107] Schillig (n 22) 68. [108] ibid.

[109] S Kalss, '§20 Kapitalmarktrecht' in K Riesenhuber (ed), *Europäische Methodenlehre* (3rd edn, de Gruyter 2015) 453, 456 (§20 paras 6–7); Walla (n 96) 45–51.

[110] Regulation (EU) No 596/2014 of the European Parliament and of the Council of 16 April 2014 on market abuse (market abuse regulation) and repealing Directive 2003/6/EC of the European Parliament and of the Council and Commission Directives 2003/124/EC, 2003/125/EC and 2004/72/EC, OJ EU L173/1 12.6.2014; Regulation (EU) 2017/1129 of the European Parliament and of the Council of 14 June 2017 on the prospectus to be published when securities are offered to the public or admitted to trading on a regulated market, and repealing Directive 2003/71/EC, OJ EU 30.6.2017 L168/12.

[111] Directive 2014/65/EU of the European Parliament and of the Council of 15 May 2014 on markets in financial instruments and amending Directive 2002/92/EC and Directive 2011/61/EU, OJ EU L173/349 12.6.2014; Regulation (EU) No 600/2014 of the European Parliament and of the Council of 15 May 2014 on markets in financial instruments and amending Regulation (EU) No 648/2012, OJ EU L173/84 12.6.2014.

[112] In respect of implementing acts, the Commission can rely on the support of the European Securities Committee (ESC), consisting of high-level representatives from the Member States. The ESC's influence depends on the applicable procedure. Under the 'advisory procedure', which constitutes the default option, the Commission merely takes the utmost account of the conclusions of the ESC; however, the final decision-making power rests with the Commission. By contrast, under the 'examination procedure', in principle, the ESC's approval is required in order for an implementing act to pass. It only applies where the implementing act is of general scope and in other limited circumstances; Regulation (EU) No 182/2011 of the European Parliament and of the Council of 16 February 2011 laying down the rules and general principles concerning mechanisms for control by Member States of the Commission's exercise of implementing powers OJ EU L55/13 28.2.2011.

technical in nature and do not imply any strategic decisions or policy choices;[113] the latter are implementing acts that are also technical in nature and merely determine the conditions for the application of the Level 1 act.[114] Regulatory technical standards and implementing technical standards are drafted by the relevant European Supervisory Authority (ESA)—for securities regulation and capital markets law, this is the European Securities and Markets Authority (ESMA)—following public consultation and a cost-benefit analysis. The standards are then subject to endorsement by the Commission.[115] Level 3 concerns the consistent implementation and application of Level 1 and Level 2 acts in the Member States coordinated through the relevant ESA. For this purpose, the ESMA (and the other ESAs) may issue non-binding guidelines and recommendations, which may carry significant persuasive authority.[116] Level 4 concerns the enforcement in respect of Member States' compliance with Union law.[117]

Questions and comments:

1. EU law and law-making is a complex affair. This is largely attributable to the nature of the EU as a supranational organization that has no parallel in international law or at the level of the nation state. A broad range of national, individual, and group interests have to be balanced and weighed against each other, which necessitates a law-making process that facilitates compromise. As a consequence, the ordinary legislative procedure is rather lengthy and is often perceived as being inefficient. To some extent, this problem is alleviated by the possibility of issuing broad framework legislative acts that are then supplemented by delegated or implementing acts. However, the distinction between these latter categories is not always clear, and the categorization is also incomplete with regulatory technical standards and implementing standards further complicating the picture. This hotchpotch of regulatory acts seems to be unnecessary in this complexity and is not conducive to furthering the legitimacy of EU law.
2. It is often said that EU law-making suffers from a democratic deficit. Looking at the ordinary legislative procedure, wherein lies the democratic deficit? Compare your findings with the legislative process at national level and at international level, with particular focus on corporate law-making and securities market regulation.

B. The *acquis unionaire*—An Overview

The *acquis unionaire*—the existing body of Union law—consists of a considerable number of directives, some regulations, and a few recommendations, and includes legislative, delegated, and implementing acts. To this may be added the constitutional or Treaty foundations of EU company law and securities regulation, which provide the Union competences and rationale for the secondary Union law instruments in this area. Since the inception of the First Company Law Directive of 1968,[118] Union law-making seems to exhibit a cyclical trajectory: periods of high activity with ambitious proposals and adopted acts have been followed by periods of failure and stagnation, until some internal or external development

[113] Regulation (EU) No 1095/2010 of the European Parliament and of the Council of 24 November 2010 establishing a European Supervisory Authority (European Securities and Markets Authority), amending Decision No 716/2009/EC and repealing Commission Decision 2009/77/EC, OJ EU L331/84 15.12.2010, Art 10(1).

[114] Regulation (EU) No 1095/2010, Art 15(1).

[115] Regulation (EU) No 1095/2010, Arts 10–15.

[116] Regulation (EU) No 1095/2010, Art 16.

[117] Kalss (n 109) 457–9 (§20 para 8-15); Walla (n 96) 50.

[118] First Council Directive of 9 March 1968 on co-ordination of safeguards which, for the protection of the interests of members and others, are required by Member States of companies within the meaning of the second paragraph of Article 58 of the Treaty, with a view to making such safeguards equivalent throughout the Community (68/151/EEC), OJ 1968 L65/8.

may trigger a reorientation resulting in renewed interest, initiatives, and legislative action with a new focus and direction. Accordingly, up until today we can perhaps distinguish three 'waves' of Union corporate law-making, each of these characterized by its specific regulatory themes, techniques, and strategies, often determined by the needs of the day.[119] Given the UK's vote to leave the European Union, we may have reached the next crossroads for EU company law-making and the focus may shift again, at least in the medium and long term.

I. Constitutional foundations

In combination with the free movement of goods, services, and workers, the rights to freedom of establishment and free movement of capital form the bedrock of the internal market. These freedoms seek to break down national barriers to market entry (and exit). Consequently, restrictions on the freedom of establishment of nationals of a Member State in the territory of another Member State are prohibited. Freedom of establishment entails the right to set up and manage undertakings, in particular companies and firms, under the same conditions that the host Member State imposes on its own nationals (primary establishment). It also encompasses the setting-up of agencies, branches, or subsidiaries by nationals of any Member State in the territory of any other Member State (secondary establishment).[120] For these purposes, companies or firms formed in accordance with the law of a Member State and having their registered office, central administration, or principal place of business within the Union are to be treated in the same way as natural persons who are nationals of a Member State.[121] Freedom of establishment was already present in its current form in the Treaty of Rome, and has been directly effective since the expiry of the transitional period,[122] although its content had to be fleshed out by the Court of Justice. By contrast, free movement of capital became fully operational only with the adoption of Council Directive 88/361/EEC,[123] requiring the removal of restrictions of all capital movements between residents of most Member States from 1 July 1990.[124] Since 1 January 1994, the Treaty provisions on free movement of capital have direct effect and prohibit all restrictions on the movement of capital between Member States and between Member States and third countries.[125] Thus, whereas freedom of establishment can only be relied on in cross-border scenarios between Member States, free movement of capital also applies in relations to third countries.[126]

Commentators have speculated that one of the likely main reasons for including a Union competence for the harmonization of company law in the Treaty was as an antidote to the liberal right of establishment. A number of delegations were concerned that the Netherlands, famous at the time for its enabling company law without minimum capital requirements, would become a 'European Delaware'.[127] Companies could be established there with a low burden of legal rules and subject to low tax rates, and then set up agencies and branches in other Member States, with limited protection for local creditors and (minority) shareholders. Freedom of establishment thus seemed acceptable only if combined with a harmonization programme in order to provide a minimum level of protection for stakeholders and

[119] J Wouters, 'European Company Law: Quo Vadis?' (2000) 37 Common Market Law Review 257, 268; J Armour and W-G Ringe, 'European Company Law 1999-2010: Renaissance and Crisis' (2011) 48 Common Market Law Review 125; S Grundmann, 'The Structure of European Company Law: From Crisis to Boom' (2004) 5 European Business Organization Law Review 601.

[120] Article 49 TFEU.

[121] ibid Art 54: 'companies or firms' are defined as companies or firms constituted under civil or commercial law, including cooperative societies, and other legal persons governed by public or private law, excluding non-profit-making entities.

[122] Case 2/74 *Reyners v Belgium* ECLI:EU:C:1974:68 para 25.

[123] Council Directive 88/361/EEC of 24 June 1988 for the implementation of Art 67 of the Treaty, OJ 1988 L178/5.

[124] For Greece, Ireland, Portugal, and Spain, there was a temporary postponement until 31 December 1992.

[125] Article 63 TFEU. [126] Schön (n 47) 4.

[127] On regulatory competition and the so-called 'Delaware effect' see below pp 112–16.

to prevent a 'race to the bottom'.[128] Consequently, in order to attain freedom of establishment, the Union has the competence to coordinate 'to the necessary extent the safeguards which, for the protection of the interests of members and others, are required by Member States of companies or firms within the meaning of the second paragraph of Article 54 with a view to making such safeguards equivalent throughout the Union'. The provision received a broad interpretation by the Court of Justice in *Daihatsu*:[129]

> 18 It must be pointed out that [Article 50(2)(g)] must be read in the light not only of [Articles 49 and 50] of the [Treaty], which clearly show that the coordination of systems of company law forms part of the general programme for the abolition of restrictions on freedom of establishment, but also of [former Article 3(1)(h) TEC], which [provided] that the activities of the Community are to include the approximation of national laws to the extent required for the functioning of the common market.
>
> 19 Furthermore, the very wording of [Article 50(2)(g)] of the Treaty refers to the need to protect the interests of 'others' generally, without distinguishing or excluding any categories falling within the ambit of that term.
>
> 20 Consequently, the term 'others', as contemplated in [Article 50(2)(g)] of the Treaty, cannot be limited merely to creditors of the company.

On that basis, the Union could harmonize by way of directives practically all aspects of company law, not just the relations of shareholders, board members, corporate officers and the company itself, but also interactions with creditors and third parties, notably employees and their representatives.[130]

Article 114 of the TFEU, the internal market competence, has been used for the harmonization of national laws on securities regulation. It is equally broad, if not broader. The Union may 'adopt the measures for the approximation of the provisions laid down by law, regulation or administrative action in Member States which have as their objective the establishment and functioning of the internal market'. The Court held that the internal market competence does not grant the Union legislator a general competence to regulate the internal market. Such an interpretation would be incompatible with the wording of the Treaty and with the principle of conferral of powers. A mere finding of disparities between national legal provisions does, without more, not trigger the applicability of Article 114 of the TFEU as a legal basis for a harmonization measure. Otherwise, the Court could not discharge its task of monitoring compliance with the Treaty. Rather, the measure at issue must genuinely have as its objective the overcoming of actual obstacles to the exercise of fundamental market freedoms, or the elimination of distortions of competition arsing therefrom. Otherwise, the competence of the Union legislator would be practically limitless, contrary to the principle of conferral of powers.[131] These prerequisites are still rather vague. Consequently, the degree of scrutiny that the Court is willing to apply when assessing a measure against these criteria is critical. In this respect, the Court has adopted a rather lenient approach.[132]

On the basis of these broad competence titles, the Union has enacted an extensive body of Union company law and securities regulation, relying mainly on directives but occasionally also on regulations and recommendations. The impact that individual measures have had on

[128] Wouters (n 119) 269; A Conard, 'The European Alternative to Uniformity in Corporation Laws' (1991) 89 Michigan Law Review 2150, 2152–6; S Grundmann, 'The Structure of European Company Law: From Crisis to Boom' (2004) 5 European Business Organization Law Review 601, 605.

[129] Case C-97/96 *Daihatsu* ECLI:EU:C:1997:581.

[130] Schillig (n 22) 36.

[131] Case C-376/98 *Germany v European Parliament and Council* ECLI:EU:C:2000:544 paras 83–107.

[132] See eg Case C-66/04 *United Kingdom v European Parliament and Council* ECLI:EU:C:2005:743 paras 42–43; Case C-217/04 *United Kingdom v European Parliament and Council* ECLI:EU:C:2006:279; in particular Case C-380/03 *Germany v European Parliament and Council* ECLI:EU:C:2006:772. In its Second Tobacco Advertising judgment on Directive 2003/33/EC, the Court formally relied on the criteria established above, but then came to the conclusion that these prerequisites had been met merely on the basis of a disparity of national laws, without ascertaining whether there were in fact any actual obstacles, or a concrete risk of such obstacles, for the exercise of market freedoms.

Member States' laws has varied greatly over time, depending on subject matter and the stage of development of the respective national legal system.

II. First wave—external liability structure

Over a period of about twenty years, beginning in 1968, the Union used its legislative competence for the coordination of safeguards for the protection of 'members and others' to harmonize core aspects of company law by way of directives. The First Company Law Directive of 9 March 1968,[133] applicable to public and private limited companies, deals with disclosure requirements of company documents; corporate representation, and restrictions on the grounds of finding the company to be non-existent (nullity). The Second Company Law Directive of 13 December 1976[134] was more ambitious. Applicable to public companies only, it installed a mandatory system of legal capital, including a minimum capital requirement, and detailed provisions on the raising and maintenance of capital, as well as the increase and reduction of capital. The Third Company Law Directive of 9 October 1978[135] and the Sixth Company Law Directive of 17 December 1982,[136] respectively, dealt with domestic mergers and divisions of public companies. A package of three accounting directives forms another key element of this period:[137] the Fourth Company Law Directive of 9 October 1978 on annual accounts,[138] the Seventh Company Law Directive of 13 June 1983 on consolidated accounts for corporate groups,[139] and the Eighth Company Law Directive on statutory audits of accounting documents.[140] The Union also created the first EU level type of business

[133] First Council Directive of 9 March 1968 on co-ordination of safeguards which, for the protection of the interests of members and others, are required by Member States of companies within the meaning of the second paragraph of Article 58 of the Treaty, with a view to making such safeguards equivalent throughout the Community (68/151/EEC), OJ 1968 L65/8; later 'codified' as Directive 2009/101/EC of the European Parliament and of the Council of 16 September 2009 on coordination of safeguards which, for the protection of the interests of members and others, are required by Member States of companies within the meaning of the second paragraph of Article 48 of the Treaty, with a view to making such safeguards equivalent (codified version), OJ 2009 L258/11.

[134] Second Council Directive of 13 December 1976 on coordination of safeguards which, for the protection of the interests of members and others, are required by Member States of companies within the meaning of the second paragraph of Article 58 of the Treaty, in respect of the formation of public limited liability companies and the maintenance and alteration of their capital, with a view to making such safeguards equivalent (77/91/EEC), OJ 1977 L26/1; recast as Directive 2012/30/EU of the European Parliament and of the Council of 25 October 2012 on coordination of safeguards which, for the protection of the interests of members and others, are required by Member States of companies within the meaning of the second paragraph of Article 54 of the Treaty on the Functioning of the European Union, in respect of the formation of public limited liability companies and the maintenance and alteration of their capital, with a view to making such safeguards equivalent (Recast), OJ EU 14.11.2012 L315/74.

[135] Third Council Directive 78/855/EEC of 9 October 1978, based on Article 54(3)(g) of the Treaty concerning mergers of public limited liability companies, OJ 20.10.1978 L295/36; recast as Directive 2011/35/EU of the European Parliament and of the Council of 5 April 2011 concerning mergers of public limited liability companies (Text with EEA relevance), OJ EU 29.4.2011 L110/1.

[136] Sixth Council Directive 82/891/EEC of 17 December 1982, based on Article 54(3)(g) of the Treaty concerning the division of public limited liability companies, OJ 31.12.1982 L378/47.

[137] See also the much later Regulation (EC) No 1606/2002 of the European Parliament and of the Council of 19 July 2002 on the application of international accounting standards, OJ 11.9.2002 L243/1.

[138] Fourth Council Directive 78/660/EEC of 25 July 1978, based on Article 54(3)(g) of the Treaty on the annual accounts of certain types of companies, OJ 14.8.1978 L222/11.

[139] Seventh Council Directive 83/349/EEC of 13 June 1983, based on the Article 54(3)(g) of the Treaty on consolidated accounts, OJ 18.7.1983 L193/1. The Fourth and Seventh Directives are now consolidated in Directive 2013/34/EU of the European Parliament and of the Council of 26 June 2013 on the annual financial statements, consolidated financial statements and related reports of certain types of undertakings, amending Directive 2006/43/EC of the European Parliament and of the Council and repealing Council Directives 78/660/EEC and 83/349/EEC (Text with EEA relevance), OJ 29.6.2013 L182/19.

[140] Eighth Council Directive 84/253/EEC of 10 April 1984, based on Article 54(3)(g) of the Treaty on the approval of persons responsible for carrying out the statutory audits of accounting documents, OJ 12.5.1984 L126/20; repealed by Directive 2006/43/EC of the European Parliament and of the Council of 17 May 2006 on statutory audits of annual accounts and consolidated accounts, amending Council Directives 78/660/EEC and 83/349/EEC and repealing Council Directive 84/253/EEC (Text with EEA relevance), OJ EU 9.6.2006 L157/87.

association with Council Regulation (EEC) No 2137/85 of 25 July 1985 on the European Economic Interest Grouping (EEIG),[141] which has not found much popularity in business circles. This period of activity and successful adoption of EU level measures fizzled out with the Eleventh Company Law Directive,[142] concerning disclosure requirements in respect of branches opened by companies in Member States other than their own, and the Twelfth Company Law Directive[143] on single-member private limited liability companies, both of 21 December 1989.[144]

Looking at the content of these directives from a bird's eye view, it is perhaps possible to identify a certain pattern: the focus seems to be on the external liability structure of a company, putting in place minimum safeguards for creditors and (minority) shareholders.[145] Prior to making an investment decision, equity and debt investors can more easily obtain corporate information through disclosure of corporate documents, including the company's capital structure and accounts. Creditors, including customers and suppliers, are protected by robust rules on corporate representation, restrictions on nullity, and, arguably,[146] also by the rules on the raising and maintenance of capital. Moreover, the rules on the payment for shares protect equity investors against a watering down of their holdings; measures that would increase or reduce the company's legal capital figure are generally reserved for the authority of the general meeting of shareholders. Domestic mergers and divisions also require shareholder approval, on the basis of detailed information concerning the legal and economic consequences of the respective transactions. In internal market terms, there seems to be a certain logic behind the harmonization programme: debt and equity investors, but also customers, suppliers, and employees, can interact with companies from across the EU with greater confidence. Knowing who and what they are dealing with, they are better able to assess the risks that they are taking and can prize their investments accordingly.[147] To what extent the harmonization programme actually made a difference for the better, in national law and for entrepreneurs and their business partners, is difficult to assess and much depends on the state of the national law prior to implementation, as well as local practices and traditions.[148] For example, it has been said that the First Company Law Directive's provisions on pre-incorporation contracts had a positive impact on English law,[149] whereas the Third and Sixth Company Law Directives remained more or less a dead letter in the United Kingdom. It is perhaps fair to say that some of the measures were innovative at the time and resulted in considerable improvement of some national company law systems;[150] other measures were of little significance in some or even most Member States and have been described as 'trivial'.[151]

[141] Council Regulation (EEC) No 2137/85 of 25 July 1985 on the European Economic Interest Grouping (EEIG), OJ 31.7.1985 L199/1.

[142] Eleventh Council Directive 89/666/EEC of 21 December 1989 concerning disclosure requirements in respect of branches opened in a Member State by certain types of company governed by the law of another State, OJ 30.12.1989 L395/36.

[143] Twelfth Council Directive 89/667/EEC of 21 December 1989, on single-member private limited-liability companies, OJ 30.12.1989 L395/40; recast as Directive 2009/102/EC of the European Parliament and of the Council of 16 September 2009 in the area of company law on single-member private limited liability companies (Text with EEA relevance), OJ 1.10.2009 L258/20.

[144] Without changing their content, Directives 82/891/EEC (domestic divisions), 89/666/EEC (foreign branches), 2005/56/EC (cross-border mergers), 2009/101/EC (disclosure), 2011/35/EU (domestic mergers), and 2012/30/EU (legal capital) have now been codified in a single instrument: Directive (EU) 2017/1132 of the European Parliament and of the Council of 14 June 2017 relating to certain aspects of company law (codification), OJ EU 30.6.2017 L169/46.

[145] Grundmann (n 128) 621.

[146] The efficacy in terms of creditor protection of legal capital regimes is very doubtful; for details see Chapter 9.

[147] S Grundmann, *European Company Law* (2nd edn, Intersentia 2012) 23–4.

[148] Wouters (n 119) 264.

[149] P Davies and S Worthington, *Gower and Davies' Principles of Modern Company Law* (10th edn, Sweet & Maxwell 2016) 111–14 (paras 5-24–5-28).

[150] Wouters (n 119) 265.

[151] L Enriques, 'EC Company Law Directives and Regulations: How Trivial Are They?' (2006) 27 University of Pennsylvania International Journal of International Economic Law 1.

The need to compromise often means that agreement can be reached only on the lowest common denominator, for example, harmonizing rules on corporate representation at board level when most contracts are concluded by corporate agents below the level of the board,[152] or the granting of various options to the Member States, as with the Fourth Company Law Directive,[153] which means that the harmonizing effect may only be very limited. In addition, there may be significant deviations in the interpretation of implementing legislation by national courts; the First Company Law Directive's (now Directive (EU) 2017/1132's) provisions on pre-incorporation contracts provide an illustrative example.[154]

The first wave of company law harmonization came to a grinding hold at the beginning of the 1990s, vividly symbolized by the failure of two ambitious and controversial projects. The Draft Fifth Directive[155] dealt with board structure and employee representation, seeking to install a German style two-tier board structure, initially on a mandatory basis, later only optionally, together with some form of employee representation. The Draft Ninth Directive on corporate groups[156] was heavily influenced by German group law. Political consensus could not be reached because national differences were simply too great. National rules on corporate governance, employee representation, and parent company liability in corporate groups may be deeply rooted in national legal traditions, which in turn are closely linked to the organization of the national economy in terms of the role of labour and unions, as well as the prevalent mode of corporate finance through bank lending, capital markets, or otherwise.[157] Many of these rules have strong redistributive effects. For example, rules on employee participation may protect workers against the expropriation of firm specific investment; or, where group law removes the parent's limited liability, creditors of a parent company may suddenly find themselves in competition with the creditors of the subsidiary for the parent's assets. The enlargement from six to fifteen members during this period added further complexity to the harmonization process, and the introduction of the principle of subsidiarity through the Maastricht Treaty in 1994 had an important signalling effect in the sense that action at Union level had to be better justified.[158] In addition, there is the wider political and socio-economic context. By the end of the 1980s, the replacement of Keynesianism with neoliberalism as the prevalent paradigm for fiscal and economic policy was complete. At the same time, the 'financialization' of corporate law on the basis of 'nexus-of contract' theories promoted a strong deregulatory agenda, with the role of the state being reduced to providing the framework for functioning capital markets. In this model, corporate law is nothing more than an 'off-the-shelf' standard form contract of a default nature, leaving maximum room for the free negotiation of the parties.[159] In such a political and ideological climate, it was difficult to justify further EU intervention of a mandatory nature into core company law. Moreover, with the fall of the Berlin Wall and the end of communism the 'end of history' seemed to have been reached.[160] At the same time, largely attributable to the immense costs of reunification the German 'social-democratic' model appeared to be unable to cope with the challenges of the approaching new millennium. Many viewed the financial-markets oriented Anglo-Saxon model as a much more attractive option and commentators predicted a convergence towards this model also for corporate law and theory: the 'end of history' for corporate law.[161]

[152] See Chapter 3B below. [153] Grundmann (n 128) 607. [154] Chapter 3A.IV below.

[155] European Commission, Proposal for a Fifth Directive on the Structure of public limited companies and the powers and obligations of their organs, COM(83) 85 final.

[156] European Commission, Amended draft proposal for a ninth Directive based on Art 54(3)(g) of the EEC Treaty on links between undertakings, and in particular on groups (1983—unpublished).

[157] Wouters (n 119) 280; Armour and Ringe (n 119) 125, 129. [158] Wouters (n 119) 276–9.

[159] See Chapter 1E.

[160] F Fukuyama, *The End of History and the Last Man* (Penguin Books 2012; first published 1992).

[161] H Hansmann and R Kraakman, 'The End of History for Corporate Law' (2001) 89 Georgetown Law Journal 439.

III. Second wave—securities regulation and corporate mobility

The 'financialization of corporate law' carried the ideological seed for a strong capital markets orientation. This was further highlighted by political developments and technological advances. Capital markets (securities) regulation had been on the European agenda since the late 1970s.[162] Following the Commission's White Paper on the Internal Market of 1985, in which it called for the development of a European securities market system, regulatory regimes on public offer prospectuses, the information to be published on acquisition of major holdings, on insider dealing, and on investment services were adopted, based on minimum harmonization combined with mutual recognition and home Member State control. By 1997, the harmonized structure contained the basic elements of securities regulation and a common core of basic rules applied in most Member States. However, large areas of regulation remained unharmonized, the implementation of directives was inconsistent and often delayed; supervisory cooperation remained underdeveloped. Overall, the regime seemed ill-equipped to cope with the enormous demands which would be placed on it by the arrival of the monetary union, the internet explosion, and the increase in cross-border activity triggered by these developments in combination with the technological progress in securities trading.[163] EC securities regulation entered a new phase with the Commission's Financial Services Action Plan of 1999,[164] setting out a framework for the reform of existing legislation and the enactment of new legislation in areas, which had not been included in the preceding harmonization attempts. Without fully embracing maximum harmonization, EU legislation following the FSAP created self-standing pan-European regulatory regimes in a number of areas where the EU emerged as the primary regulator for the EU's financial markets.[165] The implementation of FSAP legislation was inextricably linked with the adoption of the *Lamfalussy* process[166] for financial market law-making as a form of comitology, which has undergone significant change on the basis of the Lisbon Treaty and the post-financial crisis reforms.[167] Replacing the older Investment Services Directive,[168] the Markets in Financial Instruments Directive (MiFID)[169] contains a set of rules for the authorization and operation of investment firms and alternative providers of trading services in financial instruments, facilitating market access through a single 'European passport'[170] and seeking to ensure

[162] The history of EC securities regulation goes back to the *Segré* Report of 1966 on the Development of a European Capital Market. This was followed by a first phase of legislative efforts, which were directed towards the construction of a single deep, and liquid securities market that issuers across the EC could access for their financing needs. During this phase directives on the admission to the official listing process and on the disclosure required when an issuer makes a public offer or officially lists securities were adopted between 1979 and 1982; N Moloney, *EU Securities and Financial Markets Regulation* (2nd edn, OUP 2014) 22.

[163] Moloney (n 162) 23–4.

[164] Communication of the Commission, 'Financial Services: Implementing the Framework for Financial Markets: Action Plan', COM(1999) 232 (Financial Services Action Plan; FSAP).

[165] Moloney (n 162) 27–8.

[166] Final Report of the Committee of Wise Men on the Regulation of European Securities Markets (Brussels 2001) (*Lamfalussy* Report).

[167] See above pp 96–7.

[168] Council Directive 93/22/EEC of 10 May 1993 on investment services in the securities field, OJ 11.6.1993 L141/27.

[169] Directive 2004/39/EC of the European Parliament and of the Council of 21 April 2004 on markets in financial instruments amending Council Directives 85/611/EEC and 93/6/EEC and Directive 2000/12/EC of the European Parliament and of the Council and repealing Council Directive 93/22/EEC, (MiFID) OJ 30.4.2004 L145/1; now Directive 2014/65/EU of the European Parliament and of the Council of 15 May 2014 on markets in financial instruments and amending Directive 2002/92/EC and Directive 2011/61/EU (MiFID II), OJ EU L173/349 12.6.2014; and Regulation (EU) No 600/2014 of the European Parliament and of the Council of 15 May 2014 on markets in financial instruments and amending Regulation (EU) No 648/2012 (MiFIR), OJ EU L173/84 12.6.2014.

[170] The concept of the 'European passport' entails the idea that a firm authorized by the authorities in one Member State is entitled to provide services in any other Member State (without the need to obtain a further authorization in the host Member State).

investor protection. The Prospectus Directive (now Regulation)[171] provides a unified regime for the drawing up, and the scrutiny of, the disclosure documents that are used for the public offer of equity and non-equity securities, or the admission of such securities to trading on regulated markets in the European Union; a prospectus approved by the home Member State is valid for the public offer or the admission to trading in any number of host Member States, thus creating a single 'European passport'. The Transparency Directive[172] imposes a continuing obligation on all issuers whose securities are already admitted to trading on a regulated market to disclose financial information and new developments. It covers in particular annual and semi-annual financial reporting and the publication of interim statements. The principal objective of the Market Abuse Directive (now Regulation)[173] is to ensure the integrity of EU financial markets and to enhance investor confidence in those markets. For that purpose, it provides an EU-wide prohibition of insider dealing and market manipulation. In the aftermath of the global financial crisis and the eurozone crisis, these measures have been comprehensively overhauled with a view to enhancing resilience, transparency, and efficiency of financial markets.[174] All of these instruments have been supplemented by various delegated and implementing acts.

Around the beginning of the new Millennium, core company law experienced a paradigm shift and a reorientation. One major catalyst was the corporate scandals involving the bursting of the 'dot com' bubble and later the insolvencies of large multi-national corporations such as Enron, WorldCom, Global Crossing, and Parmalat.[175] The Court's case law on freedom of establishment and free movement of capital constituted a further important factor.[176] In a string of decisions at around the turn of the Millennium, the Court defined scope and force of the right to freedom of establishment for companies.[177] Accordingly, freedom of establishment requires each and every Member State to recognize, as such, companies incorporated in another Member State, no matter where their central place of administration is located within the Union. Company promoters can choose the law of incorporation freely within the Union and then establish the real seat or centre of administration of their company anywhere within the Union. The law of the host state is applicable only to the extent that the law of the state of incorporation does not, or cannot, provide adequate protection for a particular legitimate interest. As a result, company promoters are able to overcome obstacles to freedom of establishment emanating from differences in national company laws through their own free choice by selecting their preferred law of incorporation and then operating under this company law freely within the Union.[178] On that basis, the concept of mandatory harmonization gave way to the idea of regulatory competition as the potential way forward for EU company law.[179] Regulatory competition can only work if there is a real and not only a theoretical possibility to choose

[171] Directive 2003/71/EC of the European Parliament and of the Council of 4 November 2003 on the prospectus to be published when securities are offered to the public or admitted to trading and amending Directive 2001/34/EC, OJ 31.12.2003 L345/64; now Regulation (EU) 2017/1129 of the European Parliament and of the Council of 14 June 2017 on the prospectus to be published when securities are offered to the public or admitted to trading on a regulated market, and repealing Directive 2003/71/EC, OJ EU 30.6.2017 L168/12.

[172] Directive 2004/109/EC of the European Parliament and of the Council of 15 December 2004 on the harmonisation of transparency requirements in relation to information about issuers whose securities are admitted to trading on a regulated market and amending Directive 2001/34/EC, OJ 31.12.2004 L390/38.

[173] Directive 2003/6/EC of the European Parliament and of the Council of 28 January 2003 on insider dealing and market manipulation (market abuse), OJ 12.4.2003 L96/16; now Regulation (EU) No 596/2014 of the European Parliament and of the Council of 16 April 2014 on market abuse (market abuse regulation) and repealing Directive 2003/6/EC of the European Parliament and of the Council and Commission Directives 2003/124/EC, 2003/125/EC and 2004/72/EC (Text with EEA relevance), OJ 12.6.2014 L173/1.

[174] Moloney (n 162) 35. [175] Armour and Ringe (n 119) 150. [176] ibid 149–50.

[177] Case C-212/97 *Centros Ltd v Erhvervs-og Selskabsstyrelsen* ECLI:EU:C:1999:126; Case C-208/00 *Überseering* ECLI:EU:C:2002:632; Case C-167/01 *Inspire Art* ECLI:EU:C:2003:512.

[178] Schillig (n 22) 37.

[179] Wouters (n 119) 281–9.

the applicable corporate law, not just at the formation stage by choosing the place of incorporation, but also subsequently through reincorporation.[180] Consequently, legislative intervention at EU level with a view to facilitating cross-border mobility would still seem a legitimate pursuit.[181]

The legal characteristics of a share—the rights and protections that come with it—determine, in combination with the share's economic and financial features, the share as a financial product; and are part of the package that the investor buys into. The same is true, albeit to a lesser extent, for debt. In line with the regulatory competition paradigm and to the extent that investors are fully informed, there seems to be no need for a top-down harmonization of the rights and protections of shareholders (and creditors). The value of the share's legal make-up is factored into the investment decision. However, on that basis, a case can be made for harmonized information rules at both the stage where securities are issued and admitted to trading for the first time (primary market), and later on when the securities are being actively traded (secondary market). The trade in shares must be safe and secure; investors must be able to invest across borders and be able to effectively exercise the rights that the share conveys.[182] In this respect, the Court of Justice has made another important contribution by exploring the boundaries of the right to free movement of capital in the context of the so-called 'golden shares' cases. In the course of the privatization of previously state-owned companies, Member States often wish to retain a certain amount of control and influence over these companies. This is achieved by conferring on the Member State special rights such as rights to oppose or veto certain transactions, appointment rights, or voting caps. In the course of a number of proceedings, the Court found in all but one of the cases[183] that the use of the golden shares at issue formed unjustified restrictions of the right to free movement of capital.[184] The essence of this case law is the liberalization of market access: financial products of formerly state-owned companies become available to foreign investors, which can then exercise their shareholder rights undisturbed by state privileges.

In September 2001, the Commission set up a High-level Group of Company Law Experts to prepare a report on future priorities for European company law in general.[185] The Report of the High-level Group was followed by a Communication from the Commission on 'Modernising Company Law and Enhancing Corporate Governance in the European Union—A Plan to Move Forward'.[186] Therein the Commission adopted a new approach to company law-making. This new approach had as its main objective 'to provide a legal framework for those who wish to undertake business activities efficiently, in a way they consider to be best suited to attain success'. It focused on cross-border mobility and the strengthening of

[180] E Kieninger, 'The Legal Framework of Regulatory Competition Based on Company Mobility: EU and US Compared' (2004) 6 German Law Journal 741.

[181] Schillig (n 22) 37–3. [182] Grundmann (n 128) 614.

[183] Case C-503/99 *Commission v Belgium* ECLI:EU:C:2002:328.

[184] Case C-58/99 *Commission v Italy* ECLI:EU:C:2000:280; Case C-174/04 *Commission v Italy* ECLI:EU:C:2005:350; Case C-326/07 *Commission v Italy* ECLI:EU:C:2009:193; Case C-367/98 *Commission v Portugal* ECLI:EU:C:2002:326; Case C-171/08 *Commission v Portugal* ECLI:EU:C:2010:412; Case C-543/08 *Commission v Portugal* ECLI:EU:C:2010:669; Case C-483/99 *Commission v France* ECLI:EU:C:2002:327; Case C-463/00 *Commission v Spain* ECLI:EU:C:2003:272; Case C-274/06 *Commission v Spain* ECLI:EU:C:2008:86; Case C-207/07 *Commission v Spain* ECLI:EU:C:2008:428; Case C-98/01 *Commission v United Kingdom* ECLI:EU:C:2003:273; Joined Cases C-282 & 283/04 *Commission v Netherlands* ECLI:EU:C:2006:608; Case C-112/05 *Commission v Germany* ECLI:EU:C:2007:623; Joined Cases C-463/04 & C-464/04 *Federconsumatori v Commune di Milano* ECLI:EU:C:2007:752; Case C-196/07 *Commission v Spain* ECLI:EU:C:2008:146; Case C-95/12 *Commission v Germany* ECLI:EU:C:2013:676.

[185] Report of the High-level Group of Company Law Experts on a Modern Regulatory Framework for Company Law in Europe (n 88).

[186] Communication from the Commission to the Council and the European Parliament, 'Modernising Company Law and Enhancing Corporate Governance in the European Union—A Plan to Move Forward' COM(2003) 284 final.

shareholder and third party rights in particular as regards investment in listed companies.[187] Directive 2004/24/EC on Takeover Bids addresses the exercise of voting rights in the case of a takeover bid (for a listed company): the breakthrough rule neutralizes pre-bid defences; the board is subject to an obligation of neutrality during the bid; the mandatory bid rule and sell out rights protect minority shareholders.[188] Directive 2005/56/EC on cross-border mergers of limited liability companies allows the merger of a company with a foreign shell company thereby effectively transferring the registered office without moving the central administration of the company.[189] Directive 2006/46/EC required listed companies to provide information on their corporate governance practices, in particular by reference to the compliance with the applicable corporate governance codes; it also modified the accounting directives and imposed disclosure requirements with a view to preventing conflicts of interest, notably disclosure of related party transactions and off-balance sheet arrangements.[190] Directive 2007/36/EC on shareholder rights in listed companies introduced minimum standards ensuring timely access to complete information on general meetings, thereby facilitating access to the general meeting and putting at the disposal of shareholders simple and effective means to exercise their voting rights.[191] The Recommendations on non-executive supervisory directors[192] and on remuneration of directors of listed companies[193] also belong in this context. These recommendations highlight a further aspect of the Commission's new approach: the reliance on soft law. One may further add Regulation (EC) No 1346/2000 on insolvency proceedings,[194] which also has a distinct cross-border focus.

The formation of a European Company (*Societas Europaea*) constitutes an alternative for a cross-border corporate restructuring.[195] More than forty years in the making, the SE statute was finally adopted by the EU in 2001 and came into force in 2004.[196] The SE has been reasonably successful, at least in some Member States, and some major international concerns have converted to SE status.[197]

[187] ibid paras 2.1 and 2.2.

[188] Directive 2004/25/EC of 21 April 2004 on takeover bids (Text with EEA relevance), OJ 30.4.2004 L142/12.

[189] Directive 2005/56/EC of the European Parliament and of the Council of 26 October 2005 on cross-border mergers of limited liability companies, OJ 25.11.2005 L310/1; now part of Directive (EU) 2017/1132 of the European Parliament and of the Council of 14 June 2017 relating to certain aspects of company law (codification), OJ EU 30.6.2017 L169/46.

[190] Directive 2006/46/EC of the European Parliament and of the Council of 14 June 2006 amending Council Directives 78/660/EEC on the annual accounts of certain types of companies, 83/349/EEC on consolidated accounts, 86/635/EEC on the annual accounts and consolidated accounts of banks and other financial institutions and 91/674/EEC on the annual accounts and consolidated accounts of insurance undertakings (Text with EEA relevance), OJ 16.8.2006 L224/1.

[191] Directive 2007/36/EC of the European Parliament and of the Council of 11 July 2007, on the exercise of certain rights of shareholders in listed companies, OJ 14.7.2007 L184/17; amended by Directive (EU) 2017/828 of the European Parliament and of the Council of 17 May 2017 amending Directive 2007/36/EC as regards the encouragement of long-term shareholder, OJ EU 20.5.2017 L132/1.

[192] Commission Recommendation 2005/162/EC of 15 February 2005 on the role of non-executive or supervisory directors of listed companies and on the committees of the (supervisory) board, OJ EU L52/51 25.2.2005.

[193] Commission Recommendation 2004/913/EC of 14 December 2004 fostering an appropriate regime for the remuneration of directors of listed companies (Text with EEA relevance), OJ EU L385/55 29.12.2004; Commission Recommendation 2009/384/EC of 30 April 2009 on remuneration policies in the financial services sector (Text with EEA relevance), OJ EU L120/22 15.5.2009; Commission Recommendation 2009/385/EC of 30 April 2009 complementing Recommendations 2004/913/EC and 2005/162/EC as regards the regime for the remuneration of directors of listed companies (Text with EEA relevance), OJ EU L120/28 15.5.2009.

[194] Council Regulation (EC) No 1346/2000 of 29 May 2000 on insolvency proceedings, OJ 30.06.2000 L160/1; now Regulation (EU) 2015/848 of the European Parliament and of the Council of 20 May 2015 on insolvency proceedings (recast), OJ EU 5.6.2015 L141/19.

[195] See below.

[196] Council Regulation (EC) No 2157/2001 of 8 October 2001 on the Statute for a European Company (SE), OJ 10.11.2001 L294/1; Council Directive 2001/86/EC of 8 October 2001 supplementing the Statute for a European Company with regard to the involvement of employees, OJ 10.11.2001 L294/22.

[197] For example Allianz, AVIVA, BASF, Bombardier, Elcoteq, Fresenius, Porsche, and SCOR. There is further the European cooperative society, which is of less significance; Regulation (EC) No 1435/2003 of 22 July 2003 on the statute for a European co-operative society (SCE), OJ 18.8.2003 L207/1, supplemented by Directive 2003/72/EC of 22 July 2003 on employee participation, OJ 18.8.2003 L207/25.

IV. Third wave—corporate governance in listed companies

This was the state of play when, first, the global financial crisis and, shortly thereafter, the eurozone crisis hit. It is generally accepted that the global financial crisis was caused by the coinciding of certain macro-economic developments, combined with regulatory and policy failures and general human fallibility;[198] and that the eurozone crisis was largely attributable to a negative feedback loop between the banking sector, sovereign debt, and the wider economy.[199] In the aftermath of these crises, the EU has embarked on a comprehensive and far-reaching reform of the financial sector,[200] including the reconstruction of the architecture for financial regulation and supervision.[201] Throughout, it has been less clear whether and to what extent failures in company law and corporate governance have been a contributing factor. Following the *de Larosière* report,[202] the Commission announced that it would examine corporate governance rules and practices within financial institutions and make recommendations in order to address weaknesses in corporate governance systems in this sector.[203] In the following Green Paper on corporate governance in financial institutions and remuneration policies, the Commission pointed out that 'strengthening corporate governance [was] at the heart of the Commission's programme of financial market reform and crisis prevention'.[204] It identified three core issues of corporate governance that needed addressing: The financial crisis had clearly shown that boards were unable to exercise effective control over senior management; financial institutions often neglected the basic rules of risk management and control; and shareholders sometimes seemed to have little interest in the long term viability of a company and may have been responsible for excessive risk taking in view of their short term investment horizons. The Commission focused on financial institutions first because of their systemic importance.[205] However, some points were of more

[198] E Avgouleas, *Governance of Global Financial Markets* (CUP 2012) Chapter 3; R Lastra and G Wood, 'The Crisis of 2007-09: Nature, Causes, and Reactions' (2010) 13 Journal of International Economic Law 531, 537–45.

[199] European Commission, 'Commission Staff Working Document—Economic Review of the Financial Regulation Agenda' SWD(2014) 158 final, 35–6; see further Schillig (n 98) 16–20 (paras 2.02–2.06).

[200] Communication for the Spring European Council: Driving European Recovery, COM(2009) 114 final; Communication from the Commission, European Financial Supervision, COM(2009) 252 final; Communication from the Commission to the European Parliament, the Council, the European Economic and Social Committee and the European Central Bank: Regulating financial services for sustainable growth, COM(2010) 301 final; Communication from the Commission to the European Parliament, the Council, the European Economic and Social Committee and the Committee of the Regions: A reformed financial sector for Europe, COM(2014) 279 final.

[201] Schillig (n 98) 21–3 (paras 2.07–2.11).

[202] The High-level Group on Financial Supervision in the EU, chaired by Jacques de Larosière, Report (Brussels 25 February 2009) (*de Larosière* Report).

[203] Communication for the Spring European Council: Driving European Recovery, COM(2009) 114 final.

[204] European Commission, Green Paper: Corporate Governance in financial institutions and remuneration policies, COM(2010) 284 final, 2.

[205] ibid 4. Most of the proposals for financial institutions have been enacted as part of the so-called CRD IV-package (Regulation (EU) No 575/2013 of the European Parliament and of the Council of 26 June 2013 on prudential requirements for credit institutions and investment firms and amending Regulation (EU) No 648/2012, OJ EU 27.6.2013 L176/1; Directive 2013/36/EU of the European Parliament and of the Council of 26 June 2013 on access to the activity of credit institutions and the prudential supervision of credit institutions and investment firms, amending Directive 2002/87/EC and repealing Directives 2006/48/EC and 2006/49/EC; OJ EU 27.6.2013 L176/338). In particular, the management body as a whole should at all times commit sufficient time and possess adequate knowledge, skills, and experience fully to understand the business and the risk exposure. To avoid groupthink and to facilitate critical exchange, management boards should be sufficiently diverse as regards age, gender, geographical provenance, educational, and professional background so as to present a variety of views and experiences. The management body should be accountable for the overall risk strategy and for the adequacy of the risk management system. A separate risk committee should be set up and there should be an independent risk management function to form an effective and holistic view of the whole range of risk. Moreover, credit institutions are required to establish and maintain for staff whose professional services have a material impact on their risk profile (senior managers, risk takers) remuneration policies and practices that are consistent with effective risk management, in particular a remuneration structure that does not encourage excessive risk taking or moral hazard and that is aligned with the long-term interests of the firm.

general relevance, and the Commission launched a review and discussion covering all listed companies with a Green Paper: EU corporate governance framework of 5 April 2011.[206] Therein the Commission addressed three principal issues: the role and composition of the board of directors; shareholder activism and short-termism; and the effectiveness of the so-called 'comply or explain' approach in respect of corporate governance codes. On the basis of extensive consultation and stakeholder feedback, the Commission launched its Action Plan: European company and corporate governance—a modern legal framework for more engaged shareholders and sustainable companies in 2012.[207] According to the Commission, 'European company law is a cornerstone of the internal market' and facilitates freedom of establishment of companies while enhancing transparency and legal certainty.[208] Building on the issues highlighted in the Green Paper, the Commission identified three main lines of further legislative action: (i) Transparency should be enhanced by, on the one hand, companies providing better information about their corporate governance arrangements; and on the other, companies being allowed to know who their shareholders are and how institutional investors intend to exercise their voting rights. (ii) Shareholders should be encouraged to engage more in corporate governance through being better able to oversee remuneration policy and related party transactions, which necessitates better shareholder cooperation; in addition, institutional investors, asset managers, and proxy advisers will face a number of obligations to encourage their effective engagement. (iii) Finally, conducting cross-border operations of European business needs to be simplified, in particular for small and medium-sized companies.[209] The 2012 Action Plan is a continuation of the 2003 Action Plan: there is a focus on listed companies, in particular for corporate governance measures, and on cross-border mobility.[210] There is also the reliance on soft law measures that are applied in addition to legally binding acts. Disclosure remains the predominant theme. However, there is much greater emphasis on the substance of corporate governance than before. Some of the measures discussed in the Action Plan have already found their way into legislation.

Specifically, Directive 2013/34/EU on financial reporting requires listed companies to include a corporate governance statement in their management report.[211] Therein, they have to point out the corporate governance code that they are subject to or apply voluntarily, and have to explain and justify any departure from the relevant provisions of the code. A Commission recommendation on the quality of corporate governance reporting provides further guidance on this 'comply or explain' approach.[212] In their corporate governance statements, listed companies are further required to set out their internal control and risk management systems in relation to financial reporting, information on significant shareholdings, special control rights, and voting restrictions in accordance with Directive 2004/25/EC on takeover bids, as well as a description of the workings of the shareholder meeting, its powers, and the shareholders' rights and how they can be exercised. Moreover, listed companies have to describe the composition and operation of their administrative, management, and supervisory boards and their committees. According to the Commission, increased transparency of board diversity will encourage companies to reflect more on the issue and increase board diversity in the long term, with a view to avoiding groupthink and enable boards to more effectively scrutinize and challenge management decisions.[213]

[206] European Commission, Green Paper: The EU corporate governance framework, COM(2011) 164 final.

[207] Communication from the Commission to the European Parliament, the Council, the European Economic and Social Committee and the Committee of the Regions, Action Plan: European company law and corporate governance—a modern legal framework for more engaged shareholders and sustainable companies, COM(2012) 740 final.

[208] ibid 4. [209] ibid 4–5. [210] ibid 5. [211] Directive 2013/34/EU, Art 20.

[212] Commission Recommendation of 9 April 2014 on the quality of corporate governance reporting ('comply or explain'), OJ 12.4.2014 L109/43.

[213] Communication from the Commission to the European Parliament, the Council, the European Economic and Social Committee and the Committee of the Regions, Action Plan: European company law and corporate governance—a modern legal framework for more engaged shareholders and sustainable companies, COM(2012) 740 final, 6.

In this context, the Commission has issued a separate proposal with a view to improving the gender balance among non-executive directors of listed companies, with a target of 40 per cent female non-executive directors.[214] Directive 2013/50/EU[215] introduced important amendments to the Transparency Directive by seeking to prevent investors from secretly building up a controlling stake in a listed company through financial instruments that mimic the economic effects of holding shares ('hidden ownership'; 'empty voting'). Directive (EU) 2017/828 amending the Shareholder Rights Directive seeks to contribute to the long-term sustainability of EU companies by improving the efficiency of the equity investment chain.[216] For that purpose, the Directive aims, first, to enhance the transparency of institutional investors and asset managers by requiring them to develop a policy on shareholder engagement with a view to managing actual or potential conflicts of interests.[217] Further, in an attempt to strengthen the link between pay and performance of directors, the Directive seeks to improve shareholder oversight of directors' remuneration. Detailed and user-friendly information on remuneration policy and on individual remuneration of directors has to be disclosed and shareholders have a right to approve the remuneration policy and to vote on the remuneration report, which explains how the remuneration policy has been applied in the previous year. However, the decision on the actual remuneration to be paid remains with the board.[218] Moreover, 'material' related party transactions are subject to transparency and shareholder approval. The definition of what constitutes a 'material transaction' is delegated to individual Member States.[219] In addition, proxy advisers—providing advisory and other services to institutional investors with diversified portfolios on how they should vote in general meetings—are required to disclose certain key information related to the preparation of their voting recommendations; clients and listed companies must be informed about any actual or potential conflicts of interests that may influence the voting recommendations.[220] This seeks to guarantee that voting recommendations are adequate and reliable, based on the best information available and not tainted by ulterior motives. Lastly, in order to improve visibility of shareholders and the exercise of shareholder rights, listed companies are offered the possibility of having their shareholders identified.[221] Throughout, the Commission has been granted powers to adopt implementing acts.

[214] European Commission, Proposal for a Directive of the European Parliament and of the Council on improving the gender balance among non-executive directors of companies listed on stock exchanges and related measures, COM(2012) 614 final.

[215] Directive 2013/50/EU of the European Parliament and of the Council of 22 October 2013 amending Directive 2004/109/EC of the European Parliament and of the Council on the harmonisation of transparency requirements in relation to information about issuers whose securities are admitted to trading on a regulated market, Directive 2003/71/EC of the European Parliament and of the Council on the prospectus to be published when securities are offered to the public or admitted to trading and Commission Directive 2007/14/EC laying down detailed rules for the implementation of certain provisions of Directive 2004/109/EC (Text with EEA relevance), OJ 6.11.2013 L294/6.

[216] European Commission, Proposal for a Directive of the European Parliament and of the Council amending Directive 2007/36/EC as regards the encouragement of long-term shareholder engagement and Directive 2013/34/EU as regards certain elements of the corporate governance statement, COM(2014) 213 final, 2.

[217] Directive 2007/36/EC (as amended), Art 3g–3i. Institutional investors will be required to disclose to the public how their equity investment strategy is aligned with the structure of their liabilities and contributes to the medium to long-term performance of their assets. Asset managers will be required to disclose to institutional investors how their investment strategy is in accordance with the underlying arrangements between institutional investor and asset manager, the main elements of which must also be disclosed to the public.

[218] Directive 2007/36/EC (as amended), Art 9a, 9b.

[219] ibid Art 9c.

[220] Directive 2007/36/EC (as amended), Art 3j.

[221] ibid Art 3a–3c. On the request of a company, intermediaries should transmit shareholder details to the company without undue delay. Where shares are held through a chain of intermediaries, the information is to be passed on through the chain without undue delay. Intermediaries are further required to facilitate the exercise of shareholder rights, in particular voting rights, either by making the necessary arrangements for allowing the shareholder or a nominee to cast the vote themselves, or by voting on the shareholder's behalf on the basis of an explicit authorization or instruction.

In addition to these corporate governance initiatives, the Commission's Company Law Package of proposals focuses on cross-border mobility measures,[222] and digitalization.[223] Further, the Commission's Action Plan on Building a Capital Markets Union also has implications for EU company law and securities regulation.[224] Most of the measures envisaged therein concern financial regulation. However, three initiatives have a more direct relevance for core company law. The envisaged modernization of the Prospectus Directive has now become a reality with the Prospectus Regulation, streamlining the approval process and providing a more proportionate regime for small and medium-sized enterprises so as to make it easier for them to access capital markets.[225] In order to encourage cross-border investing, the Commission will broaden and enhance existing measures that seek to improve the determination with legal certainty of securities ownership where issuer and investor are located in different Member States and/or securities are held by financial institutions in different Member States.[226] Finally, and from the point of view of core company law perhaps most importantly, the Commission has proposed a Directive on business insolvency, focusing on early restructuring and second chance measures, with a view to addressing the most important barriers to the free flow of capital.[227]

The third wave of EU company law-making is still unfolding. The currently proposed or envisaged measures may or may not become law in the future. Overall, the reasons for the relative success of the second wave, as pointed out by Armour and Ringe,[228] remain valid today. Market-based finance is still unevenly distributed across Europe and the absolute number of companies that will be affected—listed companies—is small in relation to the overall universe of corporate entities. With its focus on listed companies and cross-border mobility, the proposals remain close to the heart of the internal market and can plausibly contribute to market integration.[229] Reliance on delegated and implementing acts are likely to facilitate the reaching of consensus on framework directives and regulation, leaving the technical details to technocrats less susceptible to political interference. Technical issues such as the determination of securities ownership are unlikely to face significant opposition.

[222] A study on the application of the Cross-border Merger Directive (Bech-Bruun and Lexidale, 'Study on the Application of the Cross-Border Mergers Directive' (September 2013) has recommended certain improvements for the existing cross-border merger regime and the need for an instrument on cross-border divisions. Consequently, the Commission's mobility proposal seeks to comprehensively reform the legal framework for cross-border mergers and to introduce a legal regime for cross-border divisions. Moreover, in light of the *Cartesio*, *VALE*, and *Polbud* decisions on freedom of establishment, the proposal provides for the cross-border conversion of companies; Commission Proposal for a Directive of the European Parliament and of the Council amending Directive (EU) 2017/1132 as regards cross-border conversions, mergers, and divisions COM(2018) 241 final (Mobility Proposal). Whereas the Proposal for a European Private Company Statute has been shelved, the Commission has published a Proposal for a Directive on single-member private limited liability companies, which would replace Directive 2009/102/EC. Under the Proposal, Member States would provide in their legal systems a national company law form that would follow the same rules in all Member States, with a harmonized (on-line) registration procedure, a uniform template of articles and low capital requirements; registered office and central administration would not have to be in the same Member State; European Commission, Proposal for a Directive of the European Parliament and of the Council on single-member private limited liability companies, COM(2014) 212 final. This is part of a strategy that aims to improve the business environment for small and medium sized enterprises by allowing them to benefit fully from the internal market.

[223] The Commission's Digitalization Proposal mandates the introduction of an (almost pure) online incorporation process and envisages the possibility for exclusive online disclosure and communication with the companies register throughout a company's entire life-cycle; Commission Proposal for a Directive of the European Parliament and of the Council amending Directive (EU) 2017/1132 as regards the use of digital tools and processes in company law, COM(2018) 239 final.

[224] Communication form the Commission to the European Parliament, the Council, the European Economic and Social Committee and the Committee of the Regions: Action Plan on Building a Capital Markets Union COM(2015) 468 final.

[225] ibid 12. [226] ibid 23–4.

[227] ibid 25; Proposal for a Directive of the European Parliament and of the Council on preventive restructuring frameworks, second chance and measures to increase the efficiency of restructuring, insolvency and discharge procedures and amending Directive 2012/30/EU COM(2016) 723 final.

[228] Armour and Ringe (n 119) 154–7. [229] ibid 156.

The prospect of the Commission's initiative on insolvency law is perhaps the most uncertain element within this strategy.

With the UK's vote to leave the EU, the long-term future of EU company law and securities regulation has become somewhat unpredictable. In the more recent past, the UK has often been an innovator and driving force for company and capital markets law reform.[230] Its departure could mean the removal of opposition to ambitious projects and an acceleration of the EU company law agenda, or it could mean a change in direction, prolonged reorientation, and stalemate between the remaining EU Member States. We will return to the implications of this development for both EU and UK company law further below.

Question:

- According to Grundmann, a 'distinction has to be made between the rules on the trade in shares and the rules about the rights conferred by these shares, that is to say, the content of the "product" marketed. The rules on the trade in shares are largely harmonized, although they are mainly information rules.... Conversely, the content of the 'product' marketed is determined largely by national law rules'.[231] Does this quote correctly reflect the regulatory strategy that informed European company law-making over the years? If so, how can this strategy be justified?

C. Free Movement of Companies

As we have seen, the internal market constitutes an area without internal frontiers in which not only goods, services, and capital can circulate freely, but which also guarantees the free movement of natural and legal persons. Freedom of establishment gives companies formed in accordance with the law of a Member State and having their registered office, central administration, or principal place of business within the Union the right to set up and manage undertakings (primary establishment) as well as agencies, branches, or subsidiaries (secondary establishment) in the territory of any other Member State.[232] Both company promoters and companies (with the stated attributes) may rely on freedom of establishment.[233] The exercise of the right to freedom of establishment through corporate mobility may take various forms, depending largely on the underlying motivation for the transaction. In accordance with what we said in Chapter 1, it is important to distinguish between the company as a legal concept, on the one hand, and its business as a social phenomenon, on the other, with the latter including its central administration or head office and its principal place of business as determined by major production sites or business premises from which it operates. Corporate mobility for tax planning or insolvency purposes usually requires (at least) a transfer of the company's central administration as the connecting factor for tax residency or of its centre of main interests (COMI) determining insolvency jurisdiction. In the aftermath of the CJEU's decisions on freedom of establishment, notably *Centros*,[234] *Uberseering*,[235] and *Inspire Art*,[236] the paradigm of regulatory competition emerged as an alternative, or complementary, to the harmonization of European company law. Where corporate mobility is motivated by legal or regulatory arbitrage—lower minimum capital requirements, eligibility for listing on particular exchanges, opting in or out of a specific accounting framework—the legal entity itself will usually have to be incorporated in the Member State that provides the desired legal framework and then conduct business, through a branch or otherwise, in the Member State of destination. Companies validly formed under the law of a Member State may need to change their legal outfit and, by way of reincorporation, may slip into a

[230] ibid 155. [231] Grundmann (n 128) 614. [232] Article 49 TFEU. [233] ibid Art 54.
[234] Case C-212/97 *Centros* (n 177). [235] Case C-208/00 *Überseering* (n 177).
[236] Case C-167/01 *Inspire Art* (n 177).

corporate form provided by the Member State that offers more beneficial rules.[237] In the absence of a comprehensive EU framework for corporate mobility transactions, company promoters and companies have to rely on national law mechanisms.[238] Although the right to freedom of establishment is directly applicable, its content had to be fleshed out by the Court of Justice over the years, gradually filling the gap left by the failed Convention on the Mutual Recognition of Companies and Bodies Corporate.[239]

I. Regulatory competition

Regulatory competition is based on the idea that law is a product offered by the state on a market for different legal orders where states actively compete in order to attract users. The paradigm of regulatory competition in corporate law emerged in the United States, where, since the turn of the nineteenth century to the twentieth century, Delaware has become the state of choice for (re)incorporation for large publicly traded corporations, the so-called 'Delaware effect'.[240] Similar to competition in other fields, regulatory competition has a supply and a demand side. On the supply side, there must be incentives for corporate law-makers to design their products in accordance with the needs of those who decide on the place of incorporation or reincorporation. On the demand side, there must be a real and not only a theoretical possibility to select the applicable corporate law by selecting the place of incorporation or reincorporation.[241] The framework of US constitutional and private international law is uniquely conducive to meeting these prerequisites.

Substantive company law is essentially a matter for state legislation. The commerce clause of Article 1 Section 8 of the US Constitution confers substantial powers on Congress to regulate in the area of company law, which has been used mainly in the aftermath of corporate crises or scandals.[242] The traditional role of the states in the regulation of corporate law is succinctly expressed by the majority opinion of Justice Powell in *CTS Corp v Dynamics Corp of America*:[243]

***CTS Corp v Dynamics Corp of America*, 481 US 69 (1987)**

Every State in this country has enacted laws regulating corporate governance. By prohibiting certain transactions, and regulating others, such laws necessarily affect certain aspects of interstate commerce. This necessarily is true with respect to corporations with shareholders in States other than the State of incorporation. Large corporations that are listed on national exchanges, or even regional exchanges, will have shareholders in many States and shares that are traded frequently. The markets that facilitate this national and international participation in ownership of corporations are essential for providing capital not only for new enterprises but also for established companies that need to expand their businesses. This beneficial free market system depends at its core upon the fact that a corporation--except in the rarest situations--is organized

[237] E Ferran, 'Corporate Mobility and Company Law' (2016) 79 Modern Law Review 813, 813–14.

[238] ibid 814.

[239] EC Convention on the Mutual Recognition of Companies and Bodies Corporate of 29 February 1968, OJ EC Supplement 2/69, 7–18.

[240] W Cary, 'Federalism and Corporate Law: Reflections Upon Delaware', (1974) 83 Yale Law Journal 663; R Romano, 'Law as a Product: Some Pieces of the Incorporation Puzzle' (1985) 1 Journal of Law, Economics & Organization 225; M Kahan and E Kamar, 'The Myth of State Competition in Corporate Law' (2003) 55 Stanford Law Review 679; L Bebchuk and A Hamadi, 'Vigorous Race or Leisurely Walk: Reconsidering the Competition over Corporate Charters' (2002–2003) 112 Yale Law Journal 553.

[241] Kieninger (n 180) 741.

[242] The Securities Act 1933 and the Securities Exchange Act 1934 were enacted after the Great Depression. In 2002, after the high profile bankruptcies of Enron, WorldCom, and Global Crossing, Congress issued the Sarbanes-Oxley Act. The Dodd-Frank Act of 2010 seeks to address the shortcomings that contributed to the global financial crisis of 2007–2009.

[243] 481 US 69 (1987).

under, and governed by, the law of a single jurisdiction, traditionally the corporate law of the State of its incorporation ...

It thus is an accepted part of the business landscape in this country for States to create corporations, to prescribe their powers, and to define the rights that are acquired by purchasing their shares. A State has an interest in promoting stable relationships among parties involved in the corporations it charters, as well as in ensuring that investors in such corporations have an effective voice in corporate affairs.

Whereas the corporate laws of the various states are very similar on many issues, significant variations exist. Some of these reflect important state policies, for example the scope of permissible takeover defensive tactics, the ability of the board of directors to terminate derivative litigation, or the majority requirements for a mergers or sale of the corporation's assets.[244] Pursuant to the 'internal affairs rule', regardless of where the corporation operates or where its shareholders or assets are located, it will be the state of incorporation that controls issues of internal corporate governance.[245] The 'internal affairs rule' is summarized by Holland J in *VantagePoint Venture Partners 1996 v Examen, Inc.*:[246]

***VantagePoint Venture Partners 1996 v. Examen, Inc.*, 871 A.2d 1108 (Delaware Supreme Court 2005)**

...

Internal Affairs Doctrine

[2] ... The internal affairs doctrine is a long-standing choice of law principle which recognizes that only one state should have the authority to regulate a corporation's internal affairs--the state of incorporation.

[3] The internal affairs doctrine developed on the premise that, in order to prevent corporations from being subjected to inconsistent legal standards, the authority to regulate a corporation's internal affairs should not rest with multiple jurisdictions. It is now well established that only the law of the state of incorporation governs and determines issues relating to a corporation's internal affairs. By providing certainty and predictability, the internal affairs doctrine protects the justified expectations of the parties with interests in the corporation.

[4] [5] The internal affairs doctrine applies to those matters that pertain to the relationships among or between the corporation and its officers, directors, and shareholders. The Restatement (Second) of Conflict of Laws § 301 provides: 'application of the local law of the state of incorporation will usually be supported by those choice-of-law factors favoring the need of the interstate and international systems, certainty, predictability and uniformity of result, protection of the justified expectations of the parties and ease in the application of the law to be applied.' Accordingly, the conflicts practice of both state and federal courts has consistently been to apply the law of the state of incorporation to 'the entire gamut of internal corporate affairs.'[247]

The 'internal affairs doctrine' also applies in respect of shareholders' and managers' liability vis-à-vis third parties.[248] It is, however, not without exceptions. Where another state has a more significant relationship to the parties and the transaction, courts will apply this state's law even when contrary to the law of the state of incorporation, the law of the shareholders' domicile, and the law of the forum.[249] This is re-emphasized by the fact that some states, notably New York and California, have 'pseudo-foreign' corporation statutes that require

[244] W Klein, J Coffee, and F Partnoy, *Business Organizations and Finance* (11th edn, Foundation Press 2010) 151.

[245] ibid. [246] 871 A.2d 1108 (Delaware Supreme Court 2005).

[247] The court goes on to say that the 'internal affairs doctrine' is not just a conflicts of law principle, but is mandated by constitutional principles, notably by the Fourteenth Amendment Due Process Clause and the Commerce Clause. Pursuant to the former, directors and officers have a right to know what law will apply to their actions; shareholders have a right to know by which standards corporate management may be held accountable. Under the latter, a state has no interest in regulating the internal affairs of foreign corporations.

[248] Restatement (Second) Conflict of Laws, §§307–309.

[249] P Blumberg, *The Law of Corporate Groups: Substantive Law* (Little Brown & Co 1987) 624.

foreign corporations whose activities are mainly located within their territory to comply with the essential provisions of their incorporation statutes.[250]

Owing to these rules of private international law and the constitutional framework, the founders of a company are free to choose the state of incorporation regardless of where the actual centre of administration will be situated or the main business activity will be carried out. Moreover, corporations are free to reincorporate, that is to transfer their statutory seat without changing the real seat. This is usually done by incorporating a new (shell) company in the state of destination and merging the reincorporating company into the new one. By the end of 1999, nearly 60 per cent of all non-financial publicly traded companies, which had both their headquarters and their incorporations in the United States, were incorporated in Delaware.[251] No other state attracted more than 3 per cent of out-of-state incorporations. The overwhelming majority of these incorporations are reincorporations. At the start, many companies are incorporated under the laws of their real seat in order to spare the extra costs of franchise tax in Delaware. Re-incorporations take place only later when, owing to the success of the business, the benefits of reincorporation outweigh its costs. In an influential paper, Roberta Romano sought to explain the reasons for the migration to Delaware of publicly held companies.[252] In undertaking her study, Romano worked under the hypothesis that reincorporation was motivated by the anticipation of transactions that could be carried out more cheaply in the state of destination. Given that reincorporation is not costless, migration is likely to be associated with specific transactions that the law of the state of destination treats more favourably. This is particularly relevant for transactions that are more likely to bring the corporation into contact with the legal system, that is, activities that tend to generate minority shareholder litigation. Romano was able empirically to confirm this hypothesis: She

> found that most reincorporations preceded or coincided with a series of distinct and identifiable transactions, the most frequent being a public offering (for the most part, the firm's first public offering), the initiation or expansion of an active mergers and acquisitions program, and antitakeover defensive measures. Of the reincorporations whose associated transaction type could be identified, these three categories comprise 72%. All of these transactions increase the likelihood that a firm will be taken to court.

In these situations, a corporate code and well-developed case law can directly reduce the cost of certain transactions and decrease the cost of litigation.

As for supply, initially the premise was that states vigorously compete for incorporations.[253] It was believed that states derive considerable benefits from attracting incorporations, in the form of both monetary and non-monetary benefits. The former may be generated either directly via taxation, or indirectly via the revenue generated by the corporate bar in a certain state. The latter are much harder to grasp. In respect of monetary benefits, the traditional position is summarized by Romano:[254]

> Commentators assume that solving the state's problem of maximizing the number of incorporations will solve the revenue maximization problem, although the formal equivalence of the problems is not demonstrated. The legislative desire to maximize revenues thus functions as an invisible hand guiding the decentralized system of state corporation laws to codify the most efficient arrangements, the laws that maximize firm value. The explanation is in effect one of survivorship—only states offering efficient laws can sustain a healthy chartering business. As a corollary of the process's efficient (optimal) outcome uniform statutes are predicted.

250 Klein, Coffee, and Partnoy (n 244) 152.

251 L Bebchuk, A Cohen, and A Ferrell, 'Does the Evidence Favor State Competition in Corporate Law?' (2002) 90 California Law Review 1775, 1808.

252 Romano (n 240). 253 Bebchuk and Hamadi (n 240) 561. 254 Romano (n 240) 229.

Recent analysis suggests, however, a more cautious approach. It is still undisputed that Delaware is the state, which is most responsive to new ideas. Although not always the leader in corporate law innovation, Delaware seems to introduce rules, tailored to modern needs developed elsewhere, rapidly into its corporate code. Apart from that, empirical evidence on whether other states compete is rather inconclusive. Romano's study suggests that although states are to a larger or lesser extent[255] responsive to corporate law innovation, they do not compete to attract new incorporations; rather, they adapt a 'defensive strategy of maintaining rather than expanding revenues'.[256] More recent studies have pointed out that states have even lesser (monetary) incentives to join in a defensive competition.[257] Based on an analysis of the annual franchise tax regimes and initial incorporation tax regimes in varies states, these authors maintain that, apart from Delaware, no state actively competes for attracting or maintaining incorporations under its laws.[258]

Traditionally much debated was the question of whether regulatory competition results in desirable outcomes. The two competing views are generally referred to as the 'race to the bottom' and the 'race to the top' approach. According to the former, regulatory competition contributes to the deterioration of corporation standards, a movement toward the least common denominator in both legislation and case law. In order to generate a climate that is favourable for corporate management, shareholder rights vis-à-vis management have been watered down and fiduciary standards and standards of fairness have been relaxed so as to minimize directors' responsibility to both the corporation and its shareholders, all with a view to foster incorporation in Delaware. The normative consequence of this approach is the propagation of federal minimum standards that could prevent the downward spiral.[259] By contrast, adherents of the 'race to the top' approach argue that regulatory competition results in 'better', more efficient corporate regulation. This is essentially attributable to management's self-interest and the market's 'invisible hand'. Managers that seek to attract investment have to promise a governance structure that is most beneficial to the investors; if they do not, management pay through lower prices for the corporate securities they issue. Consequently,

> [t]he managers who pick the state of incorporation that is most desirable from the perspective of investors will attract the most money. The states that select the best combination of rules will attract the most corporate investment (and therefore increase tax collections). So states compete to offer, and managers compete to use, beneficial sets of rules.[260]

The next stage in this debate is marked by attempts to prove one or the other approach empirically. If the 'race to the bottom' approach were correct, corporations that reincorporate in Delaware would do poorly for investors and share prices would decrease; conversely, under the 'race to the top' approach, reincorporating firms could expect increasing share prices following the move.[261] Accordingly, scholars have carried out various reincorporation event studies measuring share price reaction to a corporation's reincorporation from one state to another in the search for positive or negative abnormal returns.[262] Overall, the picture that emerges seems to be one of modest share price increases in the 1 per cent region. However, it is far from clear whether these gains are attributable to the superiority of Delaware corporate law. This is because reincorporation is not a random event, but motivated by specific corporate transactions—an initial public offering, an extensive mergers and acquisition strategy, anti-takeover defences. It

255 Depending on the percentage of a state's total tax collections coming from franchise tax.
256 Romano (n 240) 238. 257 Kahan and Kamar (n 240) 699.
258 ibid; Bebchuk and Hamadi (n 240). 259 Cary (n 240).
260 F Easterbrook, 'Managers' Discretion and Investors' Welfare: Theories and Evidence' (1984) 9 Delaware Journal of Corporate Law 540, 545.
261 ibid 549. 262 These studies are reviewed in Bebchuk, Cohen, and Ferrell (n 251).

could well be, and is indeed more likely, that any gains are attributable to these events in the life of the corporation, rather than to a superior corporate law regime.[263] Given the varied and uncertain motivations and effects of reincorporation decisions, and their relatively minor consequences for shareholder value, the available empirical material appears to be inconclusive.[264] However, the idea that regulatory competition may be beneficial in some areas of corporate law, in particular areas where managers' and shareholders' interests are aligned, and may be detrimental in other areas where managers' and shareholders' interests collide, as for example in the takeover context,[265] has a certain plausibility to it.

Despite the presence of the right to freedom of establishment in the Treaty, the situation within the European Union was initially radically different. Companies and entrepreneurs that sought to rely on the freedom of establishment faced a formidable obstacle in the conflicting legal traditions in the Member States as regards the conflict of laws rules that determine the applicable company law. Traditionally, there are two principal alternatives for the corporate law conflicts rule—the real seat theory and the incorporation theory—that both occur in many variations.[266] Prevalent in the continental European jurisdictions, the real seat theory stipulates that the applicable company law is the law of the state where the company's central administration is situated, that is, where the principal management decisions are being made and implemented on a day-to-day basis. Thus, the law of the state of the company's central administration determines incorporation, separate legal personality and limited liability status, governance structures, representation, and liquidation and dissolution. The real seat theory seeks to protect local creditors, shareholders, and employees.[267] For example, where a company wishes to relocate its central administration for tax purposes from a Member State that follows the real seat theory to another Member State, the relocation would trigger liquidation of the company under the law of the Member State of origin with the consequence that creditors, including tax authorities and local employees, would have to be paid first, before any remaining assets could be used to reincorporate in the Member State of destination. If the Member State of destination adheres to the real seat theory, following the mere relocation of the central administration, the company would not be in existence as a corporate body under the law of that Member State so that the shareholders may be personally liable for debt incurred on behalf of the company in that Member State.

The incorporation theory is particularly popular with states that have a history of colonial empire building, notably the UK, or are keen on a liberal approach to trade, such as Switzerland or the Netherlands.[268] The applicable company law is the company law of the State where the company has been incorporated, although the criteria for identifying the state of incorporation are not always entirely clear.[269] English law relies on the company's 'domicile' as the country under whose law the company was created.[270] The location of the company's central administration or principal place of business is irrelevant for determining the applicable law. The law of incorporation governs the existence and dissolution of a company,[271] as well as its capacity and internal management, the composition and powers of

[263] ibid 1790. [264] Klein, Coffee, and Partnoy (n 244) 154.

[265] Bebchuk, Cohen, and Ferrell (n 251) 1800–20.

[266] For example, either theory or conflicts rule may occur in form of a reference to the substantive law only of the state of the real seat or incorporation; or may include the conflicts rules of that state also (renvoi); C Behme, *Rechtsformwahrende Sitzverlegung und Formwechsel von Gesellschaften über die Grenze* (Mohr Siebeck 2015) 11.

[267] C Panayi, 'Corporate Mobility in Private International Law and European Community Law: Debunking Some Myths' (2009) Yearbook of European Law 123, 128–30.

[268] ibid 125. The US 'internal affairs doctrine' is of course an emanation of the incorporation theory.

[269] Behme (n 266) 14–15. It is possible to have recourse to the company's registered office as stipulated in its articles of association; or one could rely on the promoters' will and intentions regarding the applicable law.

[270] L Collins and others (eds), *Dicey, Morris & Collins on the Conflict of Laws* (15th edn, Sweet & Maxwell 2016) Rule 173 with Comment 30-002.

[271] ibid Rule 177.

corporate organs, the validity of the appointment of their members, the nature and extent of director's duties as well as the members' personal liability for corporate debts.[272] This approach has the advantage of greater clarity—the law of incorporation is easier identifiable than the fact-sensitive location of the central management or principal place of business. It caters for the needs and party autonomy of sophisticated investors who can more freely choose, and rely on, the applicable law, whereas local non-adjusting creditors may be faced with an alien legal structure that potentially curtails their rights. It also potentially facilitates abuse in form of so-called 'letterbox' companies with little or no presence in the state of incorporation.[273] The incorporation theory enhances corporate mobility in the sense that the location and transfer of the company's central administration or principal place of business are irrelevant for the status of the company under its law of incorporation, both from the point of view of the Member State of origin and from the Member State of destination. However, a change of the applicable company law for legal arbitrage purposes usually requires reincorporation in the Member State of destination.

These principles of domestic private international law underwent a significant modification as a consequence of the Court of Justice's interpretation of the right to freedom of establishment. The Court's decisions in *Centros*,[274] *Überseering*,[275] and *Inspire Art*[276] seemed to mandate the incorporation theory as a binding standard for Member States, at least for 'inbound mobility' where a foreign company moves its principal place of business or central administration to the territory of another Member State. In the aftermath of these decisions, the English private company limited by shares became for a while the vehicle of choice for incorporations from across the EU, largely with a view to avoiding minimum capital requirements and burdensome rules on company formation.[277] In turn, several European jurisdictions, including France, Germany and the UK, have reformed their law on small and medium-sized entities.[278] In France and Germany, reforms were not introduced to attract incorporations from abroad but to support local small and medium-sized start-up enterprises.[279] In the UK, on the other hand, company law reform, which led to the new Companies Act 2006 and reduced burdens on small and medium-sized forms, was carried out with a clear view to make the UK more attractive as a state of incorporation.[280] It should be noted that this form of regulatory competition in the EU is rather different from its US counterpart: it largely concerns small, start-up companies at the incorporation stage. In the EU the free choice of the applicable law for existing companies remains incomplete. Although underpinned by the right to freedom of establishment, the legal framework for a transfer of seat in national law as well as for the reception of incoming foreign companies intent on converting to a corporate form of the host state contains serious gaps and uncertainties. A self-standing EU legal infrastructure is only slowly emerging. Both the Cross-border Merger Directive and the Regulation on the European Company (SE) allow a company to change the substantive company law regime that is applicable to it. A legal instrument that would deal more comprehensively with a cross-border conversion from one type of company into a company type of another Member State has recently received new impetus.

[272] ibid Rule 175 with Comment 30-028; see further *Konamaneni v Rolls-Royce Industrial Power (India) Ltd* [2003] BCC 790, 801–803.

[273] Panayi (n 267) 126–7.

[274] Case C-212/97 *Centros* (n 177).

[275] Case C-208/00 *Überseering BV v Nordic Construction Baumanagement GmbH* (n 177).

[276] Case C-167/01 *Inspire Art* (n 177).

[277] Armour and Ringe (n 119) 142–3.

[278] In France it is now possible to found a SARL with a minimum capital of €1 and with a minimum of formalities of incorporation. Similarly, Spain has reduced the minimum capital to €3,012 in respect of its *Sociedad Limitada Nueva Empresa*. Germany allows the formation of a GmbH-type company with a legal capital as low as €1.

[279] Kieninger (n 180) 768.

[280] Department of Trade and Industry, 'White Paper: Company Law Reform' (March 2005) 9.

II. Freedom of establishment

In a string of key decisions over the last 30 years, the Court of Justice has developed an elaborate freedom of establishment doctrine. Oscillating between a conservative approach—notably in *Daily Mail*[281] and *Cartesio*[282]—and a more liberal attitude—most famously in *Centros*,[283] *Überseering*,[284] *Inspire Art*,[285] *VALE*,[286]and, more recently, in *Polbud*[287]—this doctrine is based on subtle distinctions and complexities, a 'rules jungle', that is often difficult to navigate.[288] Significant gaps and uncertainties remain, and are perhaps best resolved through legislative intervention at the EU level.

1. *Scope of application*

Following *Centros*,[289] *Überseering*,[290] and *Inspire Art*,[291] the treatment of 'incorporation and recognition' for the purpose of primary or secondary establishment is relatively clear. In this scenario, company promoters incorporate a company[292] under the law of a Member State with a view to operating the company's business, either through a branch or a primary establishment, in a different Member State. Freedom of establishment can be invoked by 'a company that was formed in one Member State only for the purpose of establishing itself in a second Member State where its main or indeed entire business is to be conducted'.[293]

Case C-212/97 *Centros* ECLI:EU:C:1999:126

Two Danish nationals had bought an off-the shelf private company limited by shares in the UK and wanted to register a branch in Denmark (secondary establishment). Registration of the branch was denied for the reason that by registering a branch of an English company the stricter Danish regulations could be avoided.

19 As to the question whether, as Mr and Mrs Bryde claim, the refusal to register in Denmark a branch of their company formed in accordance with the law of another Member State in which its has its registered office constitutes an obstacle to freedom of establishment, it must be borne in mind that that freedom, conferred by [Article 49 TFEU on Union] nationals, includes the right for them to take up and pursue activities as self-employed persons and to set up and manage undertakings under the same conditions as are laid down by the law of the Member State of establishment for its own nationals. Furthermore, under [Article 54 TFEU] companies or firms formed in accordance with the law of a Member State and having their registered office, central administration or principal place of business within the Community are to be treated in the same way as natural persons who are nationals of Member States.

20 The immediate consequence of this is that those companies are entitled to carry on their business in another Member State through an agency, branch or subsidiary. The location of their registered office, central administration or principal place of business serves as the connecting

[281] Case 81/87 *Daily Mail* ECLI:EU:C:1988:456. [282] Case C-210/06 *Cartesio* ECLI:EU:C:2008:723.

[283] Case C-212/97 *Centros* (n 177).

[284] Case C-208/00 *Überseering BV v Nordic Construction Baumanagement GmbH* (n 177).

[285] Case C-167/01 *Inspire Art* (n 177). [286] Case C-378/10 *VALE Építési kft* ECLI:EU:C:2012:440.

[287] Case C-106/16 *Polbud* ECLI:EU:C:2017:804.

[288] T Biermeyer, 'Shaping the space of cross-border conversions in the EU. Between right and autonomy: VALE: Case C-378/10, *VALE Építési kft*, Judgment of the Court of Justice (Third Chamber) of 12 July 2012, nyr (2013) 50 Common Market Law Review 571.

[289] Case C-212/97 *Centros* (n 177).

[290] Case C-208/00 *Überseering BV v Nordic Construction Baumanagement GmbH* (n 177).

[291] Case C-167/01 *Inspire Art* (n 177).

[292] Cf Art 54(2) EC: the wording of this provision is misleading ('and other legal persons'); it covers entities that enjoy separate legal personality as well as civil or commercial partnerships that under the applicable law are not afforded separate legal personality.

[293] Case C-167/01 *Inspire Art* (n 177) para 95; referring to Case C-212/97 *Centros* (n 177) para 17, and Case 79/85 *Segers* ECLI:EU:C:1986:308 para 16.

factor with the legal system of a particular State in the same way as does nationality in the case of a natural person ...

21 Where it is the practice of a Member State, in certain circumstances, to refuse to register a branch of a company having its registered office in another Member State, the result is that companies formed in accordance with the law of that other Member State are prevented from exercising the freedom of establishment conferred on them by [Articles 49 and 54 TFEU].

Moreover, where a company validly formed and with its registered office in Member State A is, according to the law of Member State B, treated as having transferred its central administration or principal place of business to Member State B, the rules that Member State B imposes on and applies to the company will be subject to the right to freedom of establishment.[294]

Case C-208/00 *Überseering* ECLI:EU:C:2002:632

Two German nationals living in Germany had acquired all the shares of a company incorporated and registered in the Netherlands. When the Dutch company sought to sue one of its contractors in Germany it was denied standing before the German courts. Applying the real seat theory, according to the German courts, the company was governed by German law. Because it had not complied with the German provisions on company formation it did not exist as a company under German law.

80. Überseering, which is validly incorporated in the Netherlands and has its registered office there, is entitled under Articles [49 and 54 TFEU] to exercise its freedom of establishment in Germany as a company incorporated under Netherlands law. It is of little significance in that regard that, after the company was formed, all its shares were acquired by German nationals residing in Germany, since that has not caused Überseering to cease to be a legal person under Netherlands law.

81. Indeed, its very existence is inseparable from its status as a company incorporated under Netherlands law since, as the Court has observed, a company exists only by virtue of the national legislation which determines its incorporation and functioning (see, to that effect, Daily Mail and General Trust, paragraph 19). The requirement of reincorporation of the same company in Germany is therefore tantamount to outright negation of freedom of establishment.

82. In those circumstances, the refusal by a host Member State (B) to recognise the legal capacity of a company formed in accordance with the law of another Member State (A) in which it has its registered office on the ground, in particular, that the company moved its actual centre of administration to Member State B following the acquisition of all its shares by nationals of that State residing there, with the result that the company cannot, in Member State B, bring legal proceedings to defend rights under a contract unless it is reincorporated under the law of Member State B, constitutes a restriction on freedom of establishment which is, in principle, incompatible with Articles [49 and 54 TFEU].

In both *Centros* and *Inspire Art*,[295] the company's business in the host Member State was conducted via a registered branch (in a strictly formal sense).[296] However, given the decision in *Überseering* and the inclusive language in *Inspire Art*,[297] freedom of establishment

[294] Case C-208/00 *Überseering BV v Nordic Construction Baumanagement GmbH* (n 177) para 52.

[295] Case C-167/01 *Inspire Art* (n 177). A company incorporated in England had a branch registered in the Netherlands. The Dutch authorities tried to impose its rules on formally foreign companies (WFBV) on the company including rules on minimum capital and unlimited liability of directors in case of non-compliance: '105. It must ... be concluded that Articles [49 and 54 TFEU] preclude national legislation such as the WFBV which imposes on the exercise of freedom of secondary establishment in that State by a company formed in accordance with the law of another Member State certain conditions provided for in domestic law in respect of company formation relating to minimum capital and directors' liability. The reasons for which the company was formed in that other Member State, and the fact that it carries on its activities exclusively or almost exclusively in the Member State of establishment, do not deprive it of the right to invoke the freedom of establishment guaranteed by the Treaty, save where abuse is established on a case-by-case basis'.

[296] Case C-212/97 *Centros* (n 177), para 17; Case C-167/01 *Inspire Art* (n 177) para 97.

[297] Case C-167/01 *Inspire Art* (n 177) paras 95–6.

also seems to apply where the company's establishment in the Member State of destination is the company's only establishment. Registration of a branch in the Member State of destination,[298] therefore, does not seem to be a necessary prerequisite for enjoying the protection of freedom of establishment.[299] Moreover, disclosure requirements are harmonized by Directive (EU) 2017/1132, and are applicable to both private and public limited liability companies, giving local creditors the opportunity to inform themselves in the foreign, and prospectively an integrated EU-wide, register. In this 'incorporation and recognition' scenario it is clear that the host Member State is obliged to recognize a company incorporated abroad as a company under its law of incorporation; the Member State may apply its own law only to the extent that this is justified in order to protect imperative requirements in the public interest. As a consequence, company promoters can select the company law regime that they deem to be most suitable for their purposes and utilize this corporate vehicle to set up shop and operate in, and out of, any of the Member States. In the aftermath of *Centros*, *Überseering*, and *Inspire Art*, the UK became the predominant destination for incorporations,[300] a development which peaked in the latter half of the 2000s but has subsided.[301]

By contrast, it is less clear whether and to what extent provisions of the home Member State that render a company's departure, in one form or another, impossible or more burdensome are also subject to freedom of establishment.[302] In *Daily Mail*, a UK-company wanted to transfer its central management and control to the Netherlands for tax purposes. The company was prevented from doing so by HM Treasury, refusing to grant the necessary approval. The Court held that 'in the present state of Community law', Articles 49 and 54 of the TFEU 'cannot be interpreted as conferring on companies incorporated under the law of a Member State a right to transfer their central management and control and their central administration to another Member State while retaining their status as companies incorporated under the legislation of the first Member State'.[303] Neither in *Überseering* nor in *Inspire Art* did the Court in any way depart from *Daily Mail* in respect of the 'relations between a company and the Member State under the laws of which it had been incorporated' and whose laws restricted the company's mobility. The Court seemed to differentiate between the question of applicability of freedom of establishment and the preliminary question of whether the company was validly formed, and remained in existence, under the law of a Member State. This is because 'unlike natural persons, companies are creatures of the law and, in the present state of Community law, creatures of national law. They exist only by virtue of the varying national legislation which determines their incorporation and functioning'.[304] In *Lasteyrie du Sallaint*, the Court held that Article 49 of the TFEU 'prohibits the Member State of origin from hindering the establishment in another Member State of one of its own nationals' and consequently precludes a Member State from establishing, in order to prevent a risk of tax avoidance, a mechanism for taxing as yet unrealized increases in value, where a taxpayer transfers his tax residence outside that state.[305] However, given that the case had a natural person at its centre whose existence clearly does not depend on the legal system of its home Member State, the decision could be distinguished from *Daily Mail*. In *Marks & Spencer* the Court held that the provisions concerning freedom of establishment also 'prohibit the

[298] Pursuant to the Eleventh Council Directive 89/666/EEC of 21 December 1989 concerning disclosure requirements in respect of branches opened in a Member State by certain types of company governed by the law of another State, OJ 30.12.1989 L395/36; and implementing legislation.

[299] C Gerner-Beuerle and M Schillig, 'The Mysteries of Freedom of Establishment after *Cartesio*' (2010) 59 International and Comparative Law Quarterly 303, 305.

[300] M Becht, C Mayer, and H Wagner, 'Where Do Firms Incorporate? Deregulation and the Cost of Entry' (2008) 14 Journal of Corporate Finance 241.

[301] W-G Ringe, 'Corporate Mobility in the European Union: a Flash in the Pan? An empirical study on the success of lawmaking and regulatory competition' (2013) 10 European Company and Financial Law Review 230.

[302] Gerner-Beuerle and Schillig (n 299) 305–306.

[303] Case 81/87 *Daily Mail* (n 281) para 24.

[304] ibid para 19.

[305] Case C-9/02 *Lasteyrie du Saillant* ECLI:EU:C:2004:138.

Member State of origin from hindering the establishment in another Member State … of a company incorporated under its legislation'.[306] A national rule, which allows a parent company to set-off losses incurred by resident subsidiaries, but not the losses incurred by subsidiaries incorporated in another Member State, was liable to deter the parent company 'from setting up subsidiaries in other Member States'[307] and, thus, constituted a restriction[308] to freedom of establishment. Again, *Daily Mail* could be distinguished because the setting up by a company incorporated in one Member State of a subsidiary in another Member State (secondary establishment) does not affect the parent company's existence as a 'creature of the law' of the Member State of incorporation. In *Cartesio*, the Court had to address directly the question of whether and to what extent the home Member State can prevent a company's relocation to another Member State.

Case C-210/06 *Cartesio* ECLI:EU:C:2008:723

A limited partnership sought to transfer its operational headquarters from Hungary to Italy, but wished to remain registered in Hungary, so that its legal status would continue to be governed by Hungarian law. The Hungarian commercial court refused to enter the new address in the local register on the ground that the transfer was not possible under Hungarian law. On appeal the Court of Justice was asked whether Articles 49 and 54 TFEU preclude national rules, which make it impossible for a company constituted under national law to transfer its operational headquarters to another Member State.

109.… [I]n accordance with Article [49 TFEU], in the absence of a uniform Community law definition of the companies which may enjoy the right of establishment on the basis of a single connecting factor determining the national law applicable to a company, the question whether Article [49 TFEU] applies to a company which seeks to rely on the fundamental freedom enshrined in that article—like the question whether a natural person is a national of a Member State, hence entitled to enjoy that freedom—is a preliminary matter which, as Community law now stands, can only be resolved by the applicable national law. In consequence, the question whether the company is faced with a restriction on the freedom of establishment, within the meaning of Article [49 TFEU], can arise only if it has been established, in the light of the conditions laid down in Article [54 TFEU], that the company actually has a right to that freedom.

110. Thus a Member State has the power to define both the connecting factor required of a company if it is to be regarded as incorporated under the law of that Member State and, as such, capable of enjoying the right of establishment, and that required if the company is to be able subsequently to maintain that status. That power includes the possibility for that Member State not to permit a company governed by its law to retain that status if the company intends to reorganize itself in another Member State by moving its seat to the territory of the latter, thereby breaking the connecting factor required under the national law of the Member State of incorporation.

111. Nevertheless, the situation where the seat of a company incorporated under the law of one Member State is transferred to another Member State with no change as regards the law which governs that company falls to be distinguished from the situation where a company governed by the law of one Member State moves to another Member State with an attendant change as regards the national law applicable, since in the latter situation the company is converted into a form of company which is governed by the law of the Member State to which it has moved.

112. In fact, in that latter case, the power referred to in paragraph 110 above, far from implying that national legislation on the incorporation and winding-up of companies enjoys any form of immunity from the rules of the [TFEU] on freedom of establishment, cannot, in particular, justify the Member State of incorporation, by requiring the winding-up or liquidation of the

306 Case C-446/03 *Marks & Spencer plc v HM's Inspector of Taxes* ECLI:EU:C:2005:763 para 31.

307 ibid para 33.

308 The Court held that the restriction was justified to the extent that the losses incurred by the non-resident subsidiary could be taken into account in the subsidiary's state of residence.

company, in preventing that company from converting itself into a company governed by the law of the other Member State, to the extent that it is permitted under that law to do so.

113. Such a barrier to the actual conversion of such a company, without prior winding-up or liquidation, into a company governed by the law of the Member State to which it wishes to relocate constitutes a restriction on the freedom of establishment of the company concerned which, unless it serves overriding requirements in the public interest, is prohibited under Article [49 TFEU] …

Accordingly, a Member State has the power, first, to define the connecting factor required of a company if it is to be regarded as incorporated under the law of that Member State—be it on the basis of incorporation or having its registered office, central administration or principal place of business, or a combination of these factors, in that Member States. In this respect, freedom of establishment does not apply. This seems to follow logically from the Court's premise in the *Daily Mail* case that 'companies are creatures of national law and exist only by virtue of the national legislation which determines [their] incorporation and functioning'.[309] Secondly, according to the Court, the Member State also has the power to prevent a company governed by its law from retaining that status if the company intends to move its seat to the territory of another Member State, 'thereby breaking the connecting factor required under the law of incorporation'. This does not seem to be a logical consequence of the reasoning in *Daily Mail*. The company has been validly formed in accordance with the law of a Member State and retains its registered office, central administration or principle place of business within the Union. It is, therefore, hard to see why the company's mobility should be outside the protective ambit of the right to freedom of establishment. The Court's reasoning has the consequence that Member States are unconstrained by the right to freedom of establishment, not only in respect of the connecting factor for incorporation and formation, but also in respect of decisions taken by lawfully established companies if they intend to remain subject to the law of incorporation.[310] The Court distinguishes this situation (of a company moving its seat to another Member State whilst retaining its status as company under the law of the Member State of origin) from the situation where a company moves to another Member State in order to convert into a company form provided under the law of that Member State (reincorporation). Provisions of the law of the Member State of incorporation that may prevent a company from converting into a company governed by the law of the host Member State are subject to freedom of establishment, however, according to *Cartesio* only 'to the extent that [the company] is permitted under [the law of the host Member State] to do so'.

This latter passage raises the question of whether and to what extent freedom of establishment has a bearing on the domestic legal infrastructure provided by Member States that may be utilized to carry out corporate mobility transactions. In *SEVIC*, the Court has held that cross-border merger operations 'constitute particular methods of exercise of the freedom of establishment, important for the proper functioning of the internal market'.[311] Thus, a receiving Member State is prevented from treating a merger between a foreign and a domestic company differently from the merger of purely domestic companies.[312] In that sense, *SEVIC* merely dealt with a discrimination against foreign companies from the point of view of the state of destination. It remained unclear whether freedom of establishment required from the Member States to provide a specific regime that allows for cross-border mergers. This issue has been addressed by Directive 2005/56/EC of the European Parliament and of the Council of 26 October 2005 on cross-border mergers of limited liability companies (now part of Directive (EU) 2017/1132). For cross-border company conversions, the issue has been clarified in *VALE*.

[309] Case C-210/06 *Cartesio* (n 282) para 104.
[310] Gerner-Beuerle and Schillig (n 299) 311.
[311] Case C-411/03 *SEVIC Systems AG* ECLI:EU:C:2005:762 para 19.
[312] ibid para 31.

Case C-378/10 *VALE Építési kft* ECLI:EU:C:2012:440

VALE Costruzioni Srl, a limited liability company incorporated under Italian law and registered in the Rome commercial register asked to be removed from the Italian register with a view of transferring its seat and its business to Hungary and to discontinue business in Italy. This request was granted by the register in Rome. Subsequently, the director of VALE Costruzioni and another natural person adopted the articles of association of VALE Építési and paid up the share capital in accordance with Hungarian law in order to have this company registered as a Hungarian limited liability company. The representative of VALE Építési applied for registration to the Hungarian commercial register, seeking an entry to the effect that VALE Costruzioni was the predecessor in law of VALE Építési. Application for registration was rejected by the commercial court and on appeal because a company, which was incorporated and registered in Italy, cannot, by virtue of Hungarian company law, transfer its seat to Hungary and cannot obtain registration there with the requested predecessor statement. On further appeal, the Supreme Court stated that the transaction in question could not be regarded as a conversion under Hungarian law, since national law on conversions applies only to domestic situations. However, the Supreme Court had doubts whether this was compatible with the right to freedom of establishment and referred a number of questions to the Court of Justice, essentially asking whether Articles 49, 54 TFEU precluded national legislation that allowed the conversion from one company form to another of domestic companies but not the conversion of a foreign company into a domestic company form; and to what extent Articles 49, 54 TFEU had a bearing on the procedural requirements under national law for the carrying out of domestic and cross-border conversions.

The scope of Articles 49 TFEU and 54 TFEU

29.... a Member State ... has the power to define both the connecting factor required of a company if it is to be regarded as incorporated under its national law and as such capable of enjoying the right of establishment, and the connecting factor required if the company is to be able subsequently to maintain that status (Cartesio, paragraph 110, and National Grid Indus, paragraph 27).

30. In the light of the settled case-law ... the Court notes that any obligation, under Articles 49 TFEU and 54 TFEU, to permit a cross-border conversion neither infringes the power, referred to in the preceding paragraph, of the host Member State nor that State's determination of the rules governing the incorporation and functioning of the company resulting from a cross-border conversion.

31. As is apparent from the case-law ... such a company is necessarily governed solely by the national law of the host Member State, which determines the connecting factor required and the rules governing its incorporation and functioning.

32. It is thus apparent that the expression 'to the extent that it is permitted under that law to do so', in paragraph 112 of Cartesio, cannot be understood as seeking to remove, from the outset, the legislation of the host Member State on company conversions from the scope of the provisions of the Treaty on the Functioning of the European Union governing the freedom of establishment, but as reflecting the mere consideration that a company established in accordance with national law exists only on the basis of the national legislation which 'permits' the incorporation of the company, provided the conditions laid down to that effect are satisfied.

33. In the light of the foregoing, the Court concludes that national legislation which enables national companies to convert, but does not allow companies governed by the law of another Member State to do so, falls within the scope of Articles 49 TFEU and 54 TFEU.

...

42. [Further,] the referring court asks, in essence, whether Articles 49 TFEU and 54 TFEU must be interpreted, in the context of a cross-border conversion, as meaning that the host Member State is entitled to determine the national law applicable to such an operation and thus to apply the national law provisions on domestic conversions governing the incorporation and functioning of a company ...

43. In that regard, the Court notes, first, that, since secondary law of the European Union, as it currently stands, does not provide specific rules governing cross-border conversions, the provisions which enable such an operation to be carried out can be found only in national law, namely the law of the Member State of origin of the company seeking to convert and the law of the host Member State in accordance with which the company resulting from that conversion will be governed.

44. The implementation of a cross-border conversion requires ... the consecutive application of two national laws to that legal operation.

45. Second, although specific rules capable of substituting national provisions cannot be inferred from Articles 49 TFEU and 54 TFEU, the application of such national provisions cannot escape all review in the light of those Treaty provisions.

46. As is apparent from the answer given to the first two questions referred, Articles 49 TFEU and 54 TFEU require Member States which make provision for the conversion of companies governed by national law to grant that same possibility to companies governed by the law of another Member State which are seeking to convert to companies governed by the law of the first Member State.

47. Consequently, provisions of national law must be applied consistently with that requirement, in accordance with Articles 49 TFEU and 54 TFEU.

48. In that regard, the Court notes that, in many areas, it is settled case-law that, in the absence of relevant European Union rules, the detailed procedural rules designed to ensure the protection of the rights which individuals acquire under European Union law are a matter for the domestic legal order of each Member State, provided that they are not less favourable than those governing similar domestic situations (principle of equivalence) and that they do not render impossible in practice or excessively difficult the exercise of rights conferred by the European Union legal order (principle of effectiveness) ...

49. The Court notes that the logic underlying that case-law is also valid in the legal context of the case in the main proceedings. As in that case-law, the company concerned enjoys a right granted by the European Union legal order, in this instance, the right to carry out a cross-border conversion, the implementation of which depends, in the absence of European Union rules, on the application of national law.

50. In that regard, the Court notes that the determination, by the host Member State, of the applicable national law enabling the implementation of a cross-border conversion is not, in itself, capable of calling into question its compliance with the obligations resulting from Articles 49 TFEU and 54 TFEU.

It follows from *VALE* that the host Member State's legislation dealing with company conversions is subject to assessment on the basis of freedom of establishment in the cross-border context. However, given that such a conversion can be carried out only on the basis of national law, which provides the necessary infrastructure, the standard of assessment is reduced to the principles of equivalence and effectiveness. This provides the Member States with greater regulatory autonomy and accounts for the fact that a workable conversion regime cannot be deduced from the right to freedom of establishment. We will return to the principles of equivalence and effectiveness further below.

In *VALE*, the Court also noted 'that the concept of establishment within the meaning of the Treaty provisions ... involves the actual pursuit of an economic activity through a fixed establishment in the host Member State for an indefinite period'. On that basis, and from the point of view of both home and host Member State, the Court seemed to be in favour of physical relocations—as necessary for tax or insolvency/restructuring purposes—but reluctant to allow mobility for pure legal arbitrage purposes. Incorporation would have been treated significantly different from reincorporation: based on *Centros*, *Überseering*, and *Inspire Art*, company promoters can select the law of any of the Member States as the governing law for their company regardless of where the central administration or principal place of business will be situated; however, once established, a company could change its applicable law only if accompanied by pursuing an economic activity in the Member State of destination. It is difficult to see how this unequal treatment could have been justified.

Perhaps, once established, a company's stakeholders—notably creditors, minority shareholders, and employees—have acquired certain legitimate expectations as regards the applicable law and their rights thereunder which may require protection; however, such protection would hardly be achived by requiring some form of economic activity in the host Member State. In its latest instalment in the freedom of establishment saga, the Court addressed the question of whether a company may rely on freedom of establishment in respect of a reincorporation—or cross-border conversion—carried out for pure legal arbitrage purposes.

Case C-106/16 *Polbud* ECLI:EU:C:2017:804

A Polish limited liability company resolved to transfer its registered office to Luxembourg in order to convert into a company governed by Luxembourg law. Under Polish law, a transfer of the registered office abroad triggers the liquidation of the company, although a transfer within the EU/EEA does not result in the loss of legal personality. Following registration in Luxembourg, Polbud applied to the Polish registry court to have its registration as a Polish company removed. The application was refused when Polbud failed upon request to provide the necessary documentation attesting to the liquidation of the company. The lower courts dismissed Polbud's appeals and the Supreme Court of Poland referred to the Court of Justice. The Court's decision is premised on the assumption that Polbud did not intend to also transfer its real head office to Luxembourg or to carry out any business activity there.

35 … [F]reedom of establishment confers on Polbud, a company incorporated under Polish law, the right to convert itself into a company incorporated under Luxembourg law, provided that the conditions laid down by Luxembourg legislation are satisfied and, in particular, that the test adopted by Luxembourg to determine the connection of a company or firm to its national legal order is satisfied.

36 That conclusion is not called into question by the arguments made by the Polish and Austrian governments.

37 First, the argument of the Austrian government that no business is actually being conducted by Polbud in the host Member State cannot be accepted.

38 The Court has held that freedom of establishment extends to a situation in which a company formed in accordance with the legislation of one Member State, where it has its registered office, wants to set up a branch in another Member State, even where that company was formed, in the first Member State, solely for the purpose of establishing itself in the second, where its main, or indeed entire, business is to be conducted …. Equally, a situation in which a company formed in accordance with the legislation of one Member State wants to convert itself into a company under the law of another Member State, with due regard to the test applied by the second Member State in order to determine the connection of a company to its national legal order, falls within the scope of freedom of establishment, even though that company conducts its main, if not entire, business in the first Member State.

39 …

40 … [I]t must be observed that, as the Court has previously held, the fact that either the registered office or real head office of a company was established in accordance with the legislation of a Member State for the purpose of enjoying the benefit of more favourable legislation does not, in itself, constitute abuse …

41 It follows that, in the main proceedings, the fact that it was decided to transfer to Luxembourg the registered office alone of Polbud, that transfer not affecting the real head office of that company, cannot, in itself, mean that such a transfer does not fall within the scope of Articles 49 and 54 TFEU.

42 Second, as regards the judgments of 27 September 1988, *Daily Mail and General Trust* (81/87, EU:C:1988:456), and of 16 December 2008, *Cartesio* (C-210/06, EU:C:2008:723), it does not follow, contrary to the submissions of the Polish Government, that the transfer of the registered office of a company should necessarily be accompanied by the transfer of its real head office in order to fall within the scope of freedom of establishment.

43 On the contrary, it follows from those judgments, and from the judgment of 12 July 2012, *VALE* (C-378/10, EU:C:2012:440), that, as EU law currently stands, each Member State has the

power to define the connecting factor required of a company if that company is to be regarded as incorporated in accordance with its national legislation. In the event that a company governed by the law of one Member State converts itself into a company under the law of another Member State while satisfying the conditions imposed by the legislation of the latter if it is to exist within its legal order, that power, far from implying that the legislation of the Member State of origin on the incorporation or winding-up of companies enjoys any immunity from the rules relating to freedom of establishment, cannot provide justification for that Member State preventing or deterring the company concerned from undertaking a cross-border conversion by means of, in particular, the imposition, with respect to such a cross-border conversion, of conditions that are more restrictive than those that apply to the conversion of a company within that Member State itself…

44 In the light of the foregoing, the answer to the third question is that Articles 49 and 54 TFEU must be interpreted as meaning that freedom of establishment is applicable to the transfer of the registered office of a company formed in accordance with the law of one Member State to the territory of another Member State, for the purposes of its conversion, in accordance with the conditions imposed by the legislation of the other Member State, into a company incorporated under the law of the latter Member State, when there is no change in the location of the real head office of that company.

In *Polbud* the Court does away with the poorly defined requirement for an economic activity in the host Member State, and treats the 'incorporation and recognition' and 'reincorporation' scenarios in essentially the same way. Accordingly, EU law generally accepts that a company's registered office and its head office or real seat may be situated in different Member States.[313] This improves the coherence of the freedom of establishment doctrine significantly. Following *VALE* and *Polbud*, it remains unclear whether companies have an (absolute) right in EU law to carry out cross-border conversions with a corresponding obligation on the Member States to introduce provisions on company conversions (if they have not already done so for purely domestic conversions). The Court speaks of 'the right to carry out a cross-border conversion' 'granted by the European Union legal order' that the company enjoys, and the implementation of which depends on the application of national law.[314] This seems to suggest that Member States cannot avoid freedom or establishment assessment by refraining from providing national legislation for company conversions.[315] However, this right for companies and the corresponding obligation for Member States seems to be conditional and dependent on the respective Member State having made 'provision for the conversion of companies governed by national law'.[316] This is supported by the Court's further statement that Member States are 'not required to treat cross-border operations more favourably than domestic operations',[317] which they would if they had to provide for cross-border conversions, even though no provisions for domestic conversions have been made. This uncertainty is reflective of the inherent tension between company incorporation, and reincorporation, being a matter solely governed and defined by national law, on the one hand, and the equal treatment of natural and legal persons for freedom of establishment purposes, on the other: natural persons as company promoters are free to select the applicable company law regardless of where they intend to do business across the EU; established companies need to rely on domestic law in order to be able to change their governing law. In the end, this tension can only be resolved by the EU legislator, providing for an EU legal framework that comprehensively deals with the cross-border conversion of companies.[318]

[313] W Bayer and J Schmidt, 'Grenzüberschreitende Mobilität von Gesellschaften: Formwechsel durch isolierte Satzungssitzverlegung' (2017) ZIP Zeitschrift für Wirtschaftsrecht 2225, 2230.

[314] Case C-378/10 *VALE Építési kft* (n 286) para 49; Case C-106/16 *Polbud* (n 287) paras 33, 35.

[315] Biermeyer (n 288) 580.

[316] Case C-378/10 *VALE Építési kft* (n 286) para 46; Case C-106/16 *Polbud* (n 287) paras 33, 35.

[317] Case C-378/10 *VALE Építési kft* (n 286) para 48.

[318] Bayer and Schmidt (n 313) 2231.

For now the following gaps remain within the scope of freedom of establishment:[319] Member States are free to prevent a company from removing its central administration and/or principal place of business (and/or its registered office) from a Member State's jurisdiction to the extent that the company seeks to retain that Member State's law as the applicable company law. The question of whether and to what extent Member States are free (not) to provide for company conversions—domestic and cross-border—in national law also remains shrouded in uncertainty. However, where the necessary regulatory infrastructure is in place, neither home Member State nor host Member State are able to prevent a cross-border conversion, regardless of whether it is accompanied by the company carrying out a minimum of economic activity in the host Member State, or not. For example, an English private company limited by shares doing business exclusively in the Netherlands (the *Inspire Art* scenario) may be able to convert into a private company limited by shares under Irish law, perhaps motivated by Brexit, without carrying out any economic activity in Ireland.

2. *Restrictions and justification*

Article 49 TFEU confers the right to freedom of establishment only under the conditions laid down by the host Member State for its own nationals. However, in line with the Court's case law on the market freedoms in general,[320] the Court has, in principle, extended the scope of freedom of establishment so as to encompass not just discriminatory measures but also national measures which are 'liable to hinder or make less attractive' the exercise of freedom of establishment.[321] The Court has found that the host Member State's refusal to register a branch of a company having its registered office in another Member State amounted to a restriction of freedom of establishment.[322] The refusal by a host Member State to recognize the legal capacity of a company formed in accordance with the law of another Member State was deemed to be an outright negation of freedom of establishment.[323] The imposition by the host Member State on a company formed in accordance with the law of another Member State of certain conditions provided for in domestic law in respect of company formation amounts to a restriction,[324] as does requiring the winding-up or liquidation of a company by the Member State of incorporation in order to prevent the company from converting itself into a company governed by the law of another Member State.[325] These national measures have in common that they directly prevent a company

[319] The question of the scope of application of freedom of establishment has to be distinguished from the question whether market participants are prevented from relying on their EU rights in exceptional cases because they seek to improperly or fraudulently take advantage of provisions of EU law. It is clear, however, that 'the fact that a national of a Member State who wishes to set up a company chooses to form it in the Member State whose rules of company law seem to him the least restrictive and to set up branches in other Member States cannot, in itself, constitute an abuse of the right of establishment'; Case C-212/97 *Centros* (n 177) para 27; see also Case C-106/16 *Polbud* (n 287) para 39. In other words, 'the fact that the company was formed in a particular Member State for the sole purpose of enjoying the benefit of more favourable legislation does not constitute abuse even if that company conducts its activities entirely or mainly in that second State'; Case C-167/01 *Inspire Art* (n 177) paras 96, 138. This is because the 'right to form a company in accordance with the law of a Member State and to set up branches in other Member States is inherent in the exercise, in a single market, of the freedom of establishment guaranteed by the Treaty'; Case C-212/97 *Centros* (n 177) para 27. It remains unclear what circumstances would amount to an abuse of right. What matters seems to be the abuse of a right under EU law—here freedom of establishment—not, however, the abuse of the corporate form itself. Generally, the hurdle for assuming an abuse of right seems to be a high one. Presumably, intentionally using a formally foreign company to deceive or cause loss to other market participants would amount to an abuse of freedom of establishment; in particular where company promoters are 'attempting, by means of the formation of the company, to evade their obligations towards private or public creditors established on the territory of a Member State concerned'; Case C-212/97 *Centros* (n 177) para 38.

[320] Case 8/74 *Dassonville* (n 37) (free movement of goods); Case C-76/90 *Säger* ECLI:EU:C:1991:331 (freedom to provide services); Case C-415/93 *Bosman* ECLI:EU:C:1995:463 (free movement of workers).

[321] Case 55/94 *Gebhard* (n 41) para 37.

[322] Case C-212/97 *Centros* (n 177) para 21.

[323] Case C-208/00 *Überseering BV v Nordic Construction Baumanagement GmbH* (n 177) para 82.

[324] Case C-167/01 *Inspire Art* (n 177) para 105.

[325] Case C-210/06 *Cartesio* (n 282) para 112; Case C-106/16 *Polbud* (n 287) paras 46–51.

from exercising its Treaty rights in form of primary or secondary establishment, or have a direct impact on the company's existence. Where the exercise of the right to freedom of establishment is dependent on the infrastructure provided for by national law, the Court has been more cautious. In *SEVIC*, the receiving Member State was prevented from treating a merger between a foreign and a domestic company differently from the merger of purely domestic companies.[326] Similarly, in *VALE* national legislation that provided only for the conversion of companies which already had their seat in the Member State concerned, and thus treated companies differently according to whether the conversion is domestic or of a cross-border nature was found to be liable to deter companies from exercising their right to freedom of establishment and thus amounting to a restriction.[327] This seems to suggest that in these latter two cases the Court is applying a discrimination standard, which on closer inspection may not be very useful. For example, where national law provides for the conversion of one specific company form into another—say from a domestic private company into a domestic public company, and vice versa—the assumption that this set up is discriminatory of a foreign private company that seeks to convert into a domestic private company is not immediately obvious and requires some argumentative effort,[328] perhaps along the lines that the foreign private company actually intends to convert, first, into a domestic public company followed by a further conversion into a domestic private company, which may not be easy to argue if the necessary documentation has not been prepared and the minimum capital requirements have not been complied with. In the interest of consistency, not just across the market freedoms but also for different scenarios within the context of freedom of establishment—'incorporation and recognition' and 'reincorporation' from both the inbound and outbound perspective—it would have been preferable if the Court had adopted more explicitly a general test of market access, which does have some footing in *VALE* ('is likely to deter . . .').[329] In accordance with the rationale in *Keck*,[330] domestic conflict of laws and substantive company law rules that 'apply to all relevant traders operating within the national territory' and 'affect in the same manner, in law and in fact' domestic entrepreneurs and those from other Member States should be deemed as not amounting to restrictions to freedom of establishment. Such provisions do not specifically impede market access by foreign companies and incorporators more than they impede domestic companies and company formation by domestic promoters.[331] In *VALE* the idea of market access has found a new manifestation in the form of the principles of equivalence and effectiveness applied in the freedom of establishment context.

Case C-378/10 *VALE Építési kft* ECLI:EU:C:2012:440

[Facts as above.]

54. As regards the principle of equivalence, the Court notes that, pursuant to that principle, a Member State is not required to treat cross-border operations more favourably than domestic operations. That principle merely implies that the detailed rules of national law aimed at safeguarding the rights which individuals derive from European Union law cannot be less favourable than those governing similar situations under national law.

55. Thus, in the context of a domestic conversion, if the legislation of a Member State requires strict legal and economic continuity between the predecessor company which applied to be converted and the converted successor company, such a requirement may also be imposed in the context of a cross-border conversion.

56. However, the refusal by the authorities of a Member State, in relation to a cross-border conversion, to record in the commercial register the company of the Member State of origin as the 'predecessor in law' to the converted company is not compatible with the principle of

[326] Case C-411/03 *SEVIC Systems AG* (n 311) para 31.

[327] Case C-378/10 *VALE Építési kft* (n 286) para 36.

[328] Biermeyer (n 288) 580.

[329] A Khan, 'Corporate mobility, market access and the internal market' (2015) 40 European Law Review 371.

[330] Joined Cases C-267 and 268/91 *Keck and Mithouard* (n 42).

[331] cf Case C-384/93 *Alpine Investment BV v Minister van Financiën* ECLI:EU:C:1995:126 para 37.

> equivalence if, in relation to the registration of domestic conversions, such a record is made of the predecessor company...
>
> ...
>
> 58. Next, so far as concerns the principle of effectiveness, the question arises in this instance as to the account which the host Member State must take, in the context of an application for registration, of documents obtained from the authorities of the Member State of origin. In the context of the dispute in the main proceedings, that question relates to the examination, to be made by the Hungarian authorities, of the issue whether VALE Costruzioni dissociated itself from Italian law, in accordance with the conditions laid down thereunder, while retaining its legal personality, thereby enabling it to convert into a company governed by Hungarian law.
>
> 59. Since that examination constitutes the indispensable link between the registration procedure in the Member State of origin and that in the host Member State, the fact remains that, in the absence of rules under European Union law, the registration procedure in the host Member State is governed by the law of that State, which thus also determines, in principle, the evidence which must be furnished by the company seeking to be converted, certifying that conditions compatible with European Union law and required by the Member State of origin have been satisfied in that regard.
>
> 60. However, a practice on the part of the authorities of the host Member State to refuse, in a general manner, to take account of documents obtained from the authorities of the Member State of origin during the registration procedure is liable to make it impossible for the company requesting to be converted to show that it actually complied with the requirements of the Member State of origin, thereby jeopardising the implementation of the cross-border conversion to which it has committed itself.

Normally, the principles of equivalence and effectiveness are used to provide Member States with a certain degree of procedural autonomy where, in the absence of harmonization, the exercise of Treaty rights depends on domestic law.[332] In the context of freedom of establishment, equivalence and effectiveness ensure market access by removing hindrances that would uniquely affect foreign companies. The principles are essentially a compromise aimed at resolving the tension apparent in the judgment and highlighted above between the substantive conditions and procedural requirements of incorporation and reincorporation being a matter for national law and the equal treatment of natural and legal persons, once established, for freedom of establishment purposes. On the one hand, the Court preserves national autonomy for substantive company law and related conflicts rules; on the other hand, national company law does not escape freedom of establishment completely, but is subject to a less intrusive test that seeks to facilitate corporate mobility in the absence of harmonization.[333]

According to the Court's case law,

> national measures liable to hinder or make less attractive the exercise of fundamental freedoms guaranteed by the Treaty must, if they are to be justified, fulfil four conditions: they must be applied in a non-discriminatory manner; they must be justified by imperative requirements in the public interest; they must be suitable for securing the attainment of the objective which they pursue, and they must not go beyond what is necessary in order to attain it.[334]

As imperative requirements in the public interest the Court has explicitly recognized the protection of the interests of creditors, minority shareholders, employees, the preservation of the effectiveness of fiscal supervision and the fairness of commercial transactions.[335] Although the Court seems to be generous when it comes to the acceptance of imperative requirements or overriding reasons in the public interest, in its assessment of the suitability

[332] Khan (n 329) 376. [333] ibid 377; Biermeyer (n 288) 582.

[334] Case C-167/01 *Inspire Art* (n 177) para 133; Case C-212/97 *Centros* (n 177) para 34; Case C-55/94 *Gebhard* (n 41) para 37.

[335] Case C-378/10 *VALE Építési kft* (n 286) para 39; Case C-106/16 *Polbud* (n 287) para 54.

and necessity of a national measure for attaining the objective pursued the Court generally adopts a rather strict approach. In both *Centros* and *Inspire Art*, the Court held that by holding itself out as a company governed by foreign law, creditors would be on sufficient notice that the company is governed by legislation other than domestic law, in particular in terms of the rules on minimum capital and directors' liability.[336] In addition, EU company law, notably on disclosure, minimum capital and legal capital requirements, foreign branches, and financial reporting provides a certain level of protection. The Court relied on these considerations in situations where the host Member State refused to register a branch of a company incorporated in a different Member State or sought to apply its own company law provision to such a branch (incorporation and recognition). An argument based on creditors being on notice does not work in the *VALE* and *Polbud* types of cases where an existing company seeks to convert into a company governed by the law of a different Member State (reincorporation). The home Member State could justify provisions that adequately seek to protect the interests of creditors, minority shareholders, and employees. However, the mandatory liquidation of a company that seeks to transfer its registered office would seem to be largely unsuitable for the attainment of these objectives and disproportionate.[337] Mandatory liquidation may actually be detrimental to the interests of creditors who lose their contractual partner, employees who lose their employer, and minority shareholders who are referred to the proceeds in liquidation. Moreover, less restrictive measures are feasible: creditors could be adequately protected through bank guarantees or other security; employees through a regime similar to that applicable in the context of cross-border mergers; and minority shareholders through a sell out right on the basis of fair market value.[338] Perhaps more generally, where domestic provisions aimed at protecting creditors and employees would mimic the EU regime on cross-border mergers and national law implementing the EU domestic mergers regime as part of Directive (EU) 2017/1132, they should not fall foul of the requirements of freedom of establishment.

III. EU legal infrastructure

Given the remaining gaps within the freedom of establishment doctrine, the EU legal infrastructure for cross-border mobility transactions is of great relevance, but remains underdeveloped. Prior to the enactment and implementation of the Cross-border Merger Directive[339] (now part of Directive (EU) 2017/1132) the European Company (SE) provided the only safe vehicle for a reincorporation and/or the (subsequent) cross-border transfer of the registered and head offices, albeit subject to significant restrictions and onerous procedural requirements. The Cross-border Merger Directive has ushered in a new era of cross-border merger activity, which since the Directive's inception has increased significantly.[340] Following the CJEU's decisions in *Cartesio* and *VALE* and the ensuing uncertainty, a legal instrument that would allow the transfer of a company's seat or cross-border conversion—the so-called Fourteenth Company Law Directive—is back on the EU's legislative agenda.[341]

[336] Case C-212/97 *Centros* (n 177) para 36; Case C-167/01 *Inspire Art* (n 177) para 135.

[337] Case C-106/16 *Polbud* (n 287) paras 52–65.

[338] AG Kokott, Opinion Case C-106/16 *Polbud* ECLI:EU:C:2017:351 paras 56–65.

[339] Directive 2005/56/EC of the European Parliament and of the Council of 26 October 2005 on cross-border mergers of limited liability companies, OJ 25.11.2005 L310/1.

[340] Bech-Bruun and Lexidale (n 222) 5; T Biermeyer and M Meyer, *Cross-border Corporate Mobility in the EU: Empirical Findings 2018* (ETUI 2018).

[341] Communication from the Commission to the European Parliament, the Council, the European Economic and Social Committee and the Committee of the Regions, Action Plan: European company law and corporate governance—a modern legal framework for more engaged shareholders and sustainable companies COM(2012) 740 final, para 41; Mobility Proposal (n 222); J Borg-Barthet, *The Governing Law of Companies in EU Law* (Hart Publishing 2012) 142–70.

1. Statute for a European company (SE)

Council Regulation (EC) No 2157/2001 on the Statute for a European company (SE)[342] and the supplementing Council Directive 2001/86/EC on the involvement of employees[343] provide the regulatory framework for the European Company as a new type of business organization that co-exists side by side with corporate-type entities provided for under the laws of the Member States. The SE has separate legal personality and a capital divided into shares. Shareholders' liability is limited by the amount they have subscribed.[344] Moreover, an SE will be treated in every Member State as if it were a public limited liability company formed in accordance with the law of the Member State in which it has its registered office.[345] The idea to provide businesses with the option of creating and managing companies with a European dimension free from the obstacles arising from the disparity and the limited territorial application of national law[346] was first floated in 1957.[347] The Commission's first proposal of 1970[348] contained a complete Code for a European public company including rules on employee representation, corporate groups, insolvency, and taxation. Whereas the contentious issues of corporate groups and taxation were dropped in subsequent proposals,[349] employee representation proved to be an insurmountable stumbling block for thirty years until agreement was finally reached in 2001.[350] The result of this long and protracted legislative process is not a self-standing EU law entity that completely transcends domestic corporate law regimes; but a mere torso of a company law regime leaving many important issues to be regulated by national company law.[351]

Article 9(1) of the SE Regulation establishes the hierarchy of legal sources that govern any particular SE. This is first and foremost the SE Regulation itself as directly applicable law within the Member States. However, only four areas are dealt with at EU level in any detail: (i) the formation of an SE;[352] (ii) the transfer of an SE's seat within the European Union;[353] (iii) its board structure under either a two-tier or single-board system;[354] and (vi) the involvement of employees outsourced into the accompanying Directive.[355] Secondly, where expressly authorized by the SE Regulation,[356] an SE is governed by its statutes consisting of the SE's instrument of incorporation and, where separate, its articles of association. The third level of legal sources is the provisions adopted by Member States in implementation of the SE Regulation and Directive. Fourthly, on legal matters where no specific rules on the SE exist, the provisions generally applicable to a public limited liability company of the Member State where the SE has its registered office will apply to the SE as well. Finally, it is the SE's articles of association again, now in the same way as they would apply to a public limited liability company formed in accordance with the law of the Member States where the SE has

[342] Council Regulation (EC) 2157/2001 of 8 October 2001 on the Statute for a European Company (SE), OJ 2001 L294/1.

[343] Council Directive 2001/86/EC of 8 October 2001 supplementing the Statute for a European company with regard to the involvement of employees, OJ 2001 L294/22.

[344] Regulation (EC) 2157/2001, Art 1(1)–(3). [345] ibid Art 10. [346] ibid recital 7.

[347] In the Council of Europe and in 1959 by the Congress of French Notaries and later in the inaugural lectures of Professors Sanders and Ulmer; for details see V Edwards, 'The European Company: Essential Tool or Eviscerated Dream?' (2003) 40 Common Market Law Review 443, 443–50; Grundmann (n 147) 811–14.

[348] Proposal for a Council regulation embodying a Statute for the European Company of 30 June 1970, COM(70) 600 final; and further Amended proposal for a Council Regulation on the Statute for European Companies of 30 April 1975, COM(75) 150 final.

[349] Proposal for a Council Regulation on the Statute for a European Company of 25 August 1989, COM(89) 268 final.

[350] See also Davignon Report, Group of Experts: 'European Systems of Worker Involvement' (with regard to the European Company Statute and the other pending proposals), May 1997 http://ec.europa.eu/internal_market/company/otherdocs/index_en.htm.

[351] The following draws on M Schillig, 'Chapter 9: European Company Statute' in C Gerner-Beuerle and C Fleet (eds), *Gore-Browne on EU Company Law* (Jordan 2017 update) para 9[3].

[352] Regulation (EC) 2157/2001, Arts 17–37. [353] ibid Arts 7, 8. [354] ibid Arts 38–51.

[355] Council Directive 2001/86/EC of 8 October 2001 supplementing the Statute for a European company with regard to the involvement of employees, OJ 2001 L294/22.

[356] The prime example of such authorization is the choice between a two-tier or single-tier board structure.

its registered office. As a consequence, any particular SE is still firmly rooted in the national company law of the Member State where it has its registered office; in particular legal capital and capital maintenance, corporate finance and the issuance of debt and equity securities, the rights and obligations of (minority) shareholders, multiple voting rights and takeover defences, directors' duties, derivative actions, corporate accounting and audit, winding-up, and liquidation on insolvency are almost completely regulated by national law.[357]

(a) Formation

The SE Regulation provides for a *numerus clausus* of five different and more or less tightly regulated ways of creating an SE, all entailing structural changes of existing companies or other entities, with a certain cross-border dimension, depending on the mode of formation.[358] The main drivers for setting up an SE seem to be the possibility to consummate a cross-border merger and to transfer the registered office for tax purposes.[359] As a consequence, formation of an SE by merger and transformation of an existing public company into an SE are particularly relevant for present purposes.[360]

Formation by merger is only available for public limited liability companies.[361] The formation procedure is regulated by reference to the Third Council Directive 78/855/EEC (later Directive 2011/35/EU, and now part of Directive (EU) 2017/1132) concerning mergers of public limited liability companies. At least two of the participating public companies must be governed by the law of different Member States; in this respect, there are no time constraints. The merger may be carried out in accordance with either of two procedures laid down by Directive (EU) 2017/1132.[362] In case of a merger by acquisition one or more of the participating companies transfer their assets to an existing company which issues shares, or makes a cash payment not exceeding 10 per cent of the nominal value of the shares so issued, to the shareholders of the transferring entities which are than dissolved.[363] In case of a merger by formation of a new company the participating companies transfer their assets to a newly formed SE, which issues shares, or makes a cash payment not exceeding 10 per cent of the nominal value of the shares so issued, to the shareholders of the participating companies which are than dissolved.[364] To the extent that the respective procedure is not, or only partly, covered by the SE Regulation, each participating company will be subject to

[357] Schillig (n 351) para 9[3].

[358] ibid paras 9[5]–9[10]; Regulation (EC) 2157/2001, Art 2: (i) An SE may be created by the merger of at least two public limited liability companies formed under the law of a Member State with registered offices and head offices within the EU, provided that at least two of these companies are governed by the law of different Member States. (ii) Secondly, an SE may be formed as a holding SE by public and private limited liability companies formed under the law of a Member State, with registered offices and head offices within the EU, provided that each of at least two of them is governed by the law of a different Member State, or has for at least two years had a subsidiary governed by the law of another Member State or a branch in a another Member State. (iii) A subsidiary SE may be formed by companies or firms within the meaning of Art 54 TFEU and other legal bodies governed by public or private law formed under the law of a Member State, with registered offices and head offices within the EU, by subscribing for the SE's shares, provided that at least two of the participating entities are governed by the law of a different Member State or have for at least two years had a subsidiary governed by the law of another Member State or a branch situated in another Member State. (iv) A public limited liability company formed under the law of a Member State which has its registered office and head office within the Community may be transformed into an SE, if for at least two years it has had a subsidiary governed by the law of another Member State. (v) A derivative mode of formation is the setting up of a subsidiary in the form of an SE by an existing SE.

[359] In addition to the possibility to choose between a one-tier and two-tier board structure and/or to reduce the number of the members of the supervisory board (as compared to national law) as well as to freeze the level of mandatory employee participation.

[360] Empirical material is provided by H Eidenmüller, A Engert, and L Hornuf, 'Incorporating under European Law: The Societas Europaea as a Vehicle for Legal Arbitrage' (2009) 10 European Business Organization Law Review (EBOR) 1, 1–33; European Commission, Report from the Commission to the European Parliament and the Council: The application of Council Regulation 2157/2001 of 8 October 2001 on the Statute for a European Company (SE), COM(2010) 676 final.

[361] As a consequence, private companies intent on participating in a merger would have to convert into public companies under the applicable national law first.

[362] Regulation (EC) 2157/2001, Art 17(2).

[363] Directive (EU) 2017/1132, Art 89(1).

[364] ibid Art 90(1).

the provisions of the law of its Member State regulating mergers of public limited liability companies in accordance with Directive (EU) 2017/1132.[365] Overall, these processes allow for the cross-border reincorporation of existing companies: by incorporating a shell public limited liability company in another Member State, a company can establish itself through a merger by acquisition as an SE in that Member State (reverse vertical merger) or even in a third Member State when a merger by formation is utilized. Importantly, however, the emerging SE's operational head office must be situated in the host Member State,[366] which reduces cross-border mobility in the form of reincorporation significantly.

The procedure is rather onerous and costly and would seem to reserve these transactions for sufficiently large companies where the potential benefits outweigh the costs. The boards of the participating companies must draw up and publish written draft terms of the merger setting out specific information, including the share-exchange ratio and the amount of any compensation; the terms for the allotment of shares in the SE; the relevant dates for dividend and accounting purposes and information as regards employee involvement.[367] The boards of each participating company must then draw up a detailed written report explaining the draft terms and setting out prescribed information including the legal and economic grounds for the terms and in particular the share-exchange ratio.[368] One or more experts, acting on behalf of each of the merging companies but independent of them, will examine the draft terms and draw up a written report to the shareholders stating whether in the expert's opinion the share-exchange ratio is fair and reasonable.[369] The merger requires approval of the general meeting of each of the participating companies.[370] For each participating company, the legality of the merger is to be scrutinized in accordance with the law on mergers of public limited liability companies of the Member State to which the merging company is subject. In each Member State concerned the court, notary, or other competent authority issues a certificate conclusively attesting that the pre-merger acts and formalities have been complied with.[371] The legality of the completion of the merger and the formation of the SE is to be scrutinized by the competent authority in the Member State of the proposed registered office of the SE.[372] The merger and the simultaneous formation of an SE take effect on the date on which the SE is registered in the Member State in which it has its registered office.[373] Once the SE has been registered, a merger may no longer be declared null and void.[374]

365 Council Regulation (EC) 2157/2001, Art 18. 366 ibid Art 7.

367 ibid Art 20; Directive (EU) 2017/1132, Arts 91 and 109(1).

368 Directive (EU) 2017/1132, Arts 95 and 109(1).

369 ibid Arts 96 and 109(1). As an alternative to experts operating on behalf of each of the merging companies, one or more independent experts may be appointed at the joint request of the participating companies by a judicial or administrative authority in the Member State of one of the merging companies or of the proposed SE and may draw up a single report to all the shareholders; Council Regulation (EC) 2157/2001, Art 22. In the case of a merger by acquisition these procedures may be simplified where the acquiring company holds 90% or more or even all of the voting securities of the transferring company; ibid Art 25.

370 ibid Art 23(1). Member States may provide that the decision requires either: (i) a majority of not less than two-thirds of the votes attaching either to the shares or to the subscribed capital represented; or (ii) a simple majority of such votes when at least half of the subscribed capital is represented; ibid Art 7(1).

371 ibid Art 25.

372 ibid Art 26. For that purpose, the participating companies shall submit to the competent authority the certificate of completion within six months of the issue together with a copy of the draft terms of merger approved by the company.

373 ibid Arts 27 and 12. In case of a merger by acquisition, with registration all the assets and liabilities of each company being acquired are transferred to the acquiring company; the shareholders of the company being acquired become shareholders of the acquiring company; the company being acquired ceases to exist; and the acquiring company adopts the form of an SE. In case of a merger by formation of a new company, all the assets and liabilities of the merging companies are transferred to the SE; the shareholders of the merging companies become shareholders of the SE; and the merging companies cease to exist; ibid Art 29. In any case, these effects occur *ipso jure* and simultaneously: the assets and liabilities are transferred, the shareholders are substituted, the companies being acquired or the merging companies cease to exist and the acquiring company adopts the form of an SE.

374 ibid Art 30. The SE Regulation allows Member States to introduce into their laws a procedure which enables a Member State's competent authorities to oppose the participation of a company incorporated under the law of that Member State in a merger on grounds of public interest. Such opposition will be subject to judicial review; ibid Art 24.

Using the formation of an SE by transformation (conversion) of an existing public limited liability company for corporate mobility transactions involves a two-step-process: the conversion into an SE is to be followed by a transfer of the SE's registered office.[375] This option would therefore seem to be more cumbersome and costly than formation by merger. Moreover, only a public limited liability company formed under the law of a Member State may be converted into an SE, provided it has had for at least two years a subsidiary company governed by the law of another Member State.[376] The procedure follows a pattern similar to that in case of a merger.[377] The management of the company in question draw up draft terms of conversion and a report explaining and justifying the legal and economic aspects of the conversion and indicating the implications for the shareholders and for the employees. Prior to the general meeting, one or more experts appointed or approved by judicial or administrative authority in the Member State to which laws the converting company is subject will certify that the company has net assets at least equivalent to its capital plus non-distributable reserves. The general meeting must approve the draft terms of conversion together with the articles of the new SE.[378]

(b) Transfer of the registered office

A major advantage of the SE is the possibility to transfer an SE's registered office from one Member State to another without a winding up of the SE and without the creation of a new legal entity.[379] In this context, it has to be kept in mind however, that the registered office of an SE has to be located within the EU, and in the same Member State in which its head office is situated.[380] Where an SE no longer complies with this requirement, the Member State in which the SE's registered office is situated will take appropriate measures to oblige the SE to regularize its position within a specified period either by re-establishing its head office in the Member State in which its registered office is situated or by transferring the registered office to the Member State where the head office is located. The Member State of the registered office must ensure that an SE which does not regularize its situation within the given time limit will be liquidated.[381]

In order to effectuate a transfer of the registered office, the management or administrative board of the SE has to draw up a transfer proposal and publicize it in accordance with the provisions implementing Article 16 of Directive (EU) 2017/1132 in the Member State where the SE's registered office is situated. This proposal must cover, in addition to such obvious information as the proposed registered office, the implications the transfer may have on employees' involvement and any rights provided for the protection of shareholders and/or creditors. In addition, the board draws up a report explaining and justifying the legal and economic aspects of the transfer and explaining its implications for shareholders, creditors, and employees. Shareholders and creditors are entitled to examine the transfer proposal and the report at the SE's registered office at least one month prior to the general meeting called upon to decide on the transfer.[382]

[375] The registered office may not be transferred from one Member State to another at the same time as the conversion is effected; ibid Art 37(3).

[376] ibid Art 2(4).

[377] ibid Art 37(4)-37(9).

[378] The required majorities are taken from ibid Art 93, either: (i) a majority of not less than two-thirds of the votes attaching either to the shares or to the subscribed capital represented; or (ii) a simple majority of such votes when at least half of the subscribed capital is represented. Member States may also condition a conversion to a favourable vote of a qualified majority or even unanimity in the organ of the company in which employee participation is organized.

[379] ibid Art 8(2)–(13). A transfer of the registered office is prohibited for SEs subject to insolvency and similar proceedings. Moreover, Member States may provide that competent authorities of the Member State of the (old) registered office may, within the two-month period, oppose a transfer entailing a change in the applicable law on grounds of public interest. Where a competent authority opposes a transfer, this will be subject to judicial review; ibid Art 8(14) and (15).

[380] ibid Art 7.

[381] ibid Art 64.

[382] They may also request copies of these documents free of charge.

Member States may put in place appropriate provisions for the protection of opposing minority shareholders. The SE's general meeting decides on the transfer no sooner than two months after publication of the proposal. A majority of not less than two-thirds of the votes cast is required, unless the law applicable to public limited liability companies in the Member State where the SE's registered office is situated requires or permits a larger majority.[383] In the Member State in which the SE has its registered office, the competent authority will issue a certificate attesting the completion of the acts and formalities to be accomplished before the transfer.[384] The new registration may only be effectuated on the basis of this certificate and further evidence that the formalities for registration in the Member State of the new registered office have been completed. The transfer and the consequent amendment of the articles take effect on the date on which the SE is registered in the register of the new registered office.[385] The new registration must then be publicized in all the Member States involved in accordance with Directive (EU) 2017/1132 and the implementing legislation.

(c) Employee involvement

The concept of employee involvement laid down by the SE-Directive is central to the formation and functioning of an SE.[386] An SE may only come into existence if the issue of employee involvement has been addressed.[387] The issue of employee involvement, and in particular employee participation,[388] was one of the main obstacles for the adoption of the SE Statute. Agreement could only be reached on the basis of a compromise that may be summarized as 'primacy of negotiation' combined with the 'before-and-after principle' in the sense that employee rights in existence before the formation of the SE will form the basis for employee rights within the SE.[389] The aim is not enhancing employee rights but preservation, subject to party agreement.[390]

As soon as possible after publishing the draft terms of merger or after agreeing a plan to transform into an SE, the management or administrative organs of the participating companies must take the necessary steps to start negotiations with the representatives of the companies' employees on arrangements for the involvement of employees in the SE.[391] The employees of the participating companies, their subsidiaries, and establishments will

[383] Council Regulation (EC) 2157/2001, Arts 8(6) and 59. A Member State may also provide that where at least half of an SE's subscribed capital is represented, a simple majority of the votes cast shall suffice.

[384] This certificate may only be issued where the competent authority is satisfied that in respect of any liabilities arising prior to the publication of the transfer, or, at the Member States' option, prior to the transfer, the interests of creditors and holders of other rights have been adequately protected.

[385] The registry of the new registration notifies the registry of the old registration, which may then delete the old registration on the basis of the notification.

[386] Schillig (n 351) paras 9[17]–9[20].

[387] Council Regulation (EC) 2157/2001, Art 12(2). An SE may be registered only where either (i) management and employee representatives have reached an agreement on employee involvement; or (ii) the employee representatives have decided that they do not wish to negotiate special involvement arrangements for the SE; or (iii) the period for negotiations has expired without agreement having been reached, in which case the standard rules set out in the Annex of the SE-Directive may apply.

[388] 'Employee involvement' is an umbrella term that encompasses any mechanism, including information, consultation and participation, through which employees' representatives may exercise an influence on decisions to be taken within the company; Council Directive 2001/86/EC, Art 2(h). Information simply means that the competent organ of the SE informs the body representative of the employees and/or employees' representatives on questions, which concern the SE and its subsidiaries; ibid Art 2(i). Consultation means the establishment of dialogue and exchange of views between the body representative of the employees and/or employees' representatives and the competent organ of the SE; ibid Art 2(j). 'Participation' is the most contentious and means the influence of the body representative of the employees and/or the employees' representatives by way of a right to select or appoint some of the members of the company's supervisory or administrative organ, or the right to recommend and/or oppose the appointment of some or all of the members of the company's supervisory or management organ; ibid Art 2(k).

[389] ibid recitals 3 and 18. [390] Edwards (n 347) 459.

[391] Council Directive 2001/86/EC, Art 3(1).

be represented by a special negotiating body (SNB).[392] The SNB and the competent organs of the participating companies seek to agree on arrangements for the involvement of employees within the SE. In the case of an SE established by transformation, the agreement must provide for at least the same level of all elements of employee involvement as the ones existing within the company to be transformed into an SE, thus ensuring that the level of employee representation is to be maintained.[393] Normally, the SNB takes decisions with an absolute majority of its members provided that they also represent an absolute majority of the employees, each member having one vote.[394] With a majority of two-thirds of the members representing at least two-thirds of the employees, including the votes of members representing employees employed in at least two Member States, the SNB may decide not to open negotiations or to terminate negotiations.[395] In that case, the national provisions on employee information and consultation in the Member States where the SE has employees will apply.[396] No such decision may be taken where an SE is established by transformation and the company to be transformed is subject to employee participation. A two-thirds majority in the SNB is further required for a reduction of participation rights, if in case of an SE established by merger at least 25 per cent of all employees are covered by participation.[397] The SE Directive envisages the negotiations to take six months from the establishment of the SNB.[398] If within that period no agreement has been reached, the standard rules in the Annex to the SE Directive may come into play.

The standard rules on information and consultation[399] only apply: where (i) the negotiating parties so agree; or (ii) where no agreement has been reached within the given timeframe and the SNB has not decided to terminate negotiations and the competent organ of each participating company accepts the application of the standard rules.[400] Whether and under what circumstances the standard rules on employee participation[401] apply depends, in addition to (i) and (ii) above, on the mode of formation of the SE. Where an SE is established by transformation, the standard rules apply if the transformed company was subject to employee participation under national law.[402] Here the standard rules require that all aspects of employee participation applicable before transformation continue to apply to the emerging SE. In the case of transformation, the level of employee participation cannot be reduced by agreement and the SNB cannot decide to not open or terminate negotiations. Therefore, the level of employee participation in the SE will be at least the same as it was for the transformed company. Establishment of a higher level by agreement is possible. Where an SE is established by merger, the standard rules will

[392] ibid Art 3(2). Member States must ensure that the members of the SNB are elected or appointed in proportion to the number of employees employed in each Member State by the participating companies and relevant subsidiaries and establishments.

[393] ibid Art 4. [394] ibid Art 3(4). [395] ibid Art 3(6).

[396] P Davies, 'Workers on the Board of the European Company?' (2003) 23 Industrial Law Journal 75.

[397] Reduction of participation rights means a proportion of employee representatives on the SE's relevant board which is lower than the highest proportion existing within the participating companies; Council Directive 2001/86/EC, Art 3(4). It appears that what matters is solely the proportion of board members subject to employee input. The quality of that input is irrelevant; Davies (n 396) 75.

[398] Council Directive 2001/86/EC, Art 5. By agreement this period may be extended up to one year.

[399] The standard rules must contain provisions on the composition of the body representative of the employees in accordance with Pt 1 of the Annex, as well as provisions on the competence and powers of the representative body as regards information and consultation in accordance with Pt 2 of the Annex.

[400] Council Directive 2001/86/EC, Art 7(1).

[401] Except where the SE is formed by transformation, the standard rules must provide that the employees of the SE, its subsidiaries and establishments, and/or their representative body shall have the right to elect, appoint, recommend, or oppose the appointment of a number of members of the administrative or supervisory body of the SE equal to the highest proportion in force in the participating companies concerned before registration of the SE. As for the 'highest proportion', again, only the proportion of board members subject to employee influence matters. Whether the regime is based on recommendation or opposition or direct election or appointment is irrelevant.

[402] Council Directive 2001/86/EC, Art 7(2)(a).

apply only where either (1) at least 25 per cent of the total number of employees in all participating companies are covered by employee participation in one form or another; or (2) if the SNB unilaterally opts for the application of the standard rules.[403] However, in that case Member States may provide that the standard rules on representation will not apply at all.[404]

Consequently, if there was no participation in the management of the participating companies there will be none in the management of the SE. In case of formation by transformation, the employee participation in the SE will be at least equal to the level of employee representation in the transforming company. Where the SE is formed by merger and participation covered at least 25 per cent of the total number of employees, participation rights may only be reduced on the basis of a two-thirds majority in the SNB representing at least two-thirds of all employees. Where negotiations fail, the standard rules will apply, provided that the competent organs of the participating companies so decide and either the respective percentage of all employees is covered by participation rights, or the SNB opts for the standard rules. In that case the highest proportion of employee participation in force in the participating companies will prevail in the SE. These rules leave considerable room for manoeuvre, despite their complexity, uncertainty, and bias towards the status quo. Even in the case of a formation by transformation employee representation regimes can be streamlined, which makes the SE an attractive option in Member States with strong employee representation, notably in Germany and the Czech Republic.[405]

2. *Cross-border Merger Directive*

The Cross-border Merger Directive of 2005 (now part of Directive (EU) 2017/1132) has significantly enhanced the EU legal framework for cross-border mobility transactions. The relevant provisions apply to both public and private limited liability companies, which makes the incorporation of a shell company in the Member State of destination with a view to executing a reverse vertical merger easier and cheaper. The rules on employee participation are more flexible and the emerging company is governed by the law of the Member State of destination, with which the market may be more familiar than with the complex hierarchy of legal sources to which an SE is subject.[406] The 2013 Study on the Application of the Cross-border Merger Directive has found that the Directive provides a clear and predictable framework for carrying out cross-border mergers within the EU/EEA in a way that is quick and cost-effective. Remaining weaknesses concern underharmonization in respect of inter-agency cooperation, safeguards for creditors, employees and minority shareholders, and the lack of a fast-track procedure.[407] Moreover, the freedom to select the governing law through reincorporation remains limited, because the Member State of destination may continue to require the company, in addition to registration under its law, to have some permanent presence and possibly also its operational headquarters within its territory.[408]

(a) Scope of application

The provisions on cross-border mergers apply to mergers of limited liability companies formed in accordance with the law of a Member State and having their registered office, central administration or principal place of business within the Union. Moreover, at least two of the

[403] ibid Art 7(2)(b). [404] ibid Art 7(3). [405] Schillig (n 351) para 9[20].

[406] M Andenas and F Wooldridge, *European Comparative Company Law* (CUP 2009) 493.

[407] Bech-Bruun and Lexidale (n 222). Some of these weaknesses are addressed in the Commission's Mobility Proposal (n 222). The latest report is Biermeyer and Meyer (n 340).

[408] Borg-Barthet (n 341) 88.

participating companies must be governed by the laws of different Member States.[409] 'Limited liability company' encompasses the public and private limited liability companies referred to in Annex II of Directive (EU) 2017/1132, and, in addition, any company with a share capital that has a separate legal personality and assets, which alone serve to cover its debts, and is further subject to corporate law publicity requirements.[410] This seems to include limited liability partnership-type entities, which are formally not companies but share most of their traits. Moreover, cross-border mergers are only possible between the types of companies, which may merge under the national law of the relevant Member States.[411]

The Directive applies to mergers by acquisition and mergers by formation of a new company, where one or more of the participating companies transfer their assets to an existing company or a newly formed company, which issues shares, or makes a cash payment not exceeding 10 per cent of the nominal value of the shares so issued, to the shareholders of the transferring entities which are than dissolved.[412] However, the Directive also applies where the law of at least one of the Member States concerned allows the cash payment to exceed 10 per cent of the nominal value of the shares representing the capital of the emerging company.[413] And further, the Directive covers a situation where a 100 per cent subsidiary transfers all its assets and liabilities to its parent company before the subsidiary is being dissolved without going into liquidation.[414]

(b) Cross-border merger procedure

The cross-border merger procedure closely resembles the procedure for domestic mergers pursuant to Directive 2011/35/EU and consequently the formation of an SE by merger. Each participating company has to comply with the provisions and formalities of the national law to which it is subject, in particular as regards the decision-making process relating to the merger, and the protection of creditors, debenture holders, holders of securities and shares, and employees of the merging companies.[415] The applicable procedure follows the familiar pattern:[416] the boards of the participating companies draw up and publish written draft terms of the merger setting out specific information, including the share-exchange ratio and the amount of any compensation; and information as regards employee involvement.[417] The boards of each participating company must then draw up a detailed written report explaining and justifying the legal and economic aspects of the cross-border merger and explaining the implications of the cross-border merger for members, creditors, and employees.[418] One or more experts, acting on behalf of each of the merging companies but independent of them, will examine the draft terms and draw up a written report to the shareholders stating whether in their opinion the share-exchange ratio is fair and reasonable.[419] The cross-border merger requires approval of the general meeting of each of the participating companies.[420] The necessary majorities are governed by the applicable national law. For each participating company, the legality of the cross-border merger is to be scrutinized as regards the part of the procedure that is subject to this Member State's

[409] Directive (EU) 2017/1132, Art 118. [410] ibid Art 119(1).

[411] ibid Art 121(1)(a). Collective investment funds are excluded, and Member States may exclude cooperative societies from the Directive's scope; ibid Art 120(2) and (3).

[412] ibid Art 119(2)(a) and (b). [413] ibid Art 120(1). [414] ibid Art 119(2)(c).

[415] ibid Art 121(1)(b).

[416] In the case of a merger by acquisition these procedures may be simplified where the acquiring company holds 90% or more or even all of the voting securities of the transferring company; ibid Art 132.

[417] ibid Art 122, 123.

[418] ibid Art 124. Under the Mobility Proposal (n 222), a separate report would have to be drawn up for the employees; new Art 124a.

[419] ibid Art 125. As an alternative, one or more independent experts may be appointed at the joint request of the participating companies by a judicial or administrative authority in the Member State of one of the merging companies and may draw up a single report to all the shareholders.

[420] ibid Art 126.

law by the competent authority in the Member State the law of which governs the respective participating company.[421] Following such scrutiny, the competent authorities in the Member States concerned issue a certificate conclusively attesting that the pre-merger acts and formalities have been complied with. The legality of the part of the procedure concerning the completion of the cross-border merger and, where applicable, the formation of a new company, is to be scrutinized by the competent authority in the Member State the law of which governs the company resulting from the cross-border merger.[422] The law of the Member State to whose jurisdiction the resulting company is subject determines the date on which the cross-border merger takes effect.[423] The registry of the resulting company notifies the registries of the participating companies so that the necessary adjustments can be made.[424] A cross-border merger which has taken effect may no longer be declared null and void.[425]

(c) Employee participation

The Directive adopts the regime on employee participation applicable to the formation of an SE with certain modifications that render the framework for the resulting company even more flexible.[426] The Directive does not contain any provisions on employee information or consultation. The provisions on employee participation closely resemble the SE regime,[427] however, with three important adjustments: The boards of the participating companies may choose to apply the standard rules for employee participation in accordance with the law applicable to the resulting company without any prior negotiation.[428] This saves time and facilitates a swift completion of the cross-border merger. Member States may limit the proportion of employee representatives in the administrative organ of the resulting company to one-third,[429] thus restricting the 'before-and-after' principle.[430] Provided the law of the resulting company does not impose employee participation or imposes it only in weaker form, the resulting company is obliged to retain the employee participation regime determined in accordance with the Directive only for a period of three years after the cross-border merger has taken effect. Thereafter, employee participation may be reduced in the course of domestic mergers.[431]

3. *Fourteenth Company Law Directive on Transfer of the Registered Office (Cross-border Conversions)*

A Fourteenth Company Law Directive on the transfer of a company's registered office appeared as a short-term priority of the Commission's 2003 Action Plan on Modernising

[421] ibid Art 127. Under the Mobility Proposal (n 222), outvoted minority shareholders and those holding non-voting shares would be granted a sell-out right; new Art 126a. Creditor protection under the Proposal may take the form of a declaration of solvency issued by management, and creditors have a right to apply to the competent authority for adequate safeguards; a merger will be deemed to not be prejudicial where an independent expert report comes to this conclusion and where creditors are offered a right to payment of similar credit quality and equivalent value as their original claim either against a third party guarantor or the company resulting from the merger; new Art 126b.

[422] ibid Art 128. For that purpose, the participating companies shall submit to the competent authority the certificate of completion within six months of the issue together with a copy of the draft terms of merger approved by the company. The competent authority shall in particular ensure that the participating companies have approved draft terms of merger on the same terms and that arrangements for employee involvement have been determined.

[423] ibid Art 129.

[424] ibid Art 130. With registration all the assets and liabilities of the participating companies are transferred to the resulting company; the shareholders of the participating companies become shareholders of the resulting company; the participating companies cease to exist, except the resulting company in case of a cross-border merger by acquisition; ibid Art 131.

[425] ibid Art 134.
[426] Grundmann (n 147) 707.
[427] Directive (EU) 2017/1132, Art 133.
[428] ibid Art 133(4)(a).
[429] ibid Art 133(4)(c).
[430] Grundmann (n 147) 707.
[431] Directive (EU) 2017/1132, Art 133(7).

Company Law.[432] After three consultations between 2003 and 2006 and an impact assessment on a prospective directive of 2007, the Commission surprisingly decided in October 2007 not to pursue the project of a Fourteenth Directive any further.[433] However, following the Court's decisions in *Cartesio*, *VALE*, and *Polbud* there has been renewed interest in legislative intervention at European level in respect of a transfer of a company's registered office.[434] In a 2012 resolution, the European Parliament urged the Commission to adopt a legislative proposal on the matter,[435] and the Commission has carried out a further consultation in 2013[436] and mandated a study on the law applicable to companies.[437] The European Parliament's 2012 resolution made some recommendations for the content of a prospective Fourteenth Directive. A new comprehensive proposal has recently been published as part of the EU Company Law Package.[438]

The Proposal applies to both public and private limited liability companies;[439] co-operative societies may be excluded. Each Member State should recognize the right of a company governed by its national law to transfer its registered office to another Member State in order to acquire a new legal personality. The host Member State should not be allowed to refuse registering a company, which satisfies the essential substantive and formal requirements for the registration of national companies.[440] One of the key issues has been whether a company's registered office and operational head office must coincide and can only be transferred together. In its 2004 consultation, the Commission contemplated that Member States may be granted the option of introducing this as a substantive requirement, which would have been in line with the Court's reasoning in *Cartesio* and the provisions on a transfer of the seat of an SE.[441] Following *Polbud*, it would seem that such a requirement would be incompatible with the right to freedom of establishment.[442] Consequently, the Proposal does not contain a requirement along these lines. However, it does respect a Member State's competence to define the connecting factor that determines the applicability of national company law. In other words, under the Proposal the Member State of destination may require the transfer of the registered office only or of both registered office and central administration or principal place of business for a conversion into its law to take effect.[443] In any case, a transfer of the registered office and/or head office should be tax-neutral and should not affect the rights of third parties.[444]

[432] Communication from the Commission to the Council and the European Parliament, 'Modernising Company Law and Enhancing Corporate Governance in the European Union—A Plan to Move Forward', COM(2003) 284 final, 20.

[433] G-J Vossestein, 'Transfer of the registered office: The European Commission's decision not to submit a proposal for a Directive' (2008) 4 Utrecht Law Review 53.

[434] Communication from the Commission to the European Parliament, the Council, the European Economic and Social Committee and the Committee of the Regions, Action Plan: European company law and corporate governance—a modern legal framework for more engaged shareholders and sustainable companies, COM(2012) 740 final, para 41.

[435] European Parliament resolution of 2 February 2012 with recommendations to the Commission on a 14th company law directive on the cross-border transfer of company seats (2011/2046(INI)) (Regner Report).

[436] See European Commission, Feedback Statement Summary of Responses to the Public Consultation on Cross-border Transfers of registered offices of companies (September 2013).

[437] C Gerner-Beuerle, F Mucciarelli, E-P Schuster, and M Siems, 'Study on the Law Applicable to Companies, Final Report' (June 2016) https://publications.europa.eu/en/publication-detail/-/publication/259a1dae-1a8c-11e7-808e-01aa75ed71a1.

[438] Commission Proposal for a Directive of the European Parliament and of the Council amending Directive (EU) 2017/1132 as regards cross-border conversions, mergers and divisions COM(2018) 241 final (Mobility Proposal). On the earlier (1997) proposals see Grundmann (n 147) 642–65.

[439] Mobility Proposal, new Art 86a; Regner Report, Recommendation 1.

[440] Mobility Proposal, recital (2); Regner Report, Recommendation 2.

[441] Gerner-Beuerle and Schillig (n 299) 303, 313; the link in fn 62 to the Commission 2004 online consultation is no longer available.

[442] Bayer and Schmidt (n 313) 2233.

[443] Mobility Proposal, recitals (3) and (8).

[444] Regner Report, Recommendation 2.

In terms of procedure, the Proposal follows the pattern familiar from the transfer of the seat of an SE with certain modifications: draft terms of conversion drawn up by the company's management, accompanied by two management reports that explain the legal and economic implications and the rationale of the transfer to the shareholders and to the employees, combined with an assessment of the draft terms and reports by an independent expert.[445] Shareholders will have to approve the draft terms with the necessary majority of between two-thirds and 90 per cent.[446] The competent authority of the company's home Member State would verify whether the conversion procedure has been carried out in accordance with its law and issue a pre-conversion certificate attesting compliance. The competent authority of the home Member State should refuse authorization of the conversion where following an examination of all relevant facts and circumstances of the case it comes to the conclusion that the transaction constitutes an artificial arrangement aimed at obtaining undue tax advantages or at unduly and prejudicially infringing the rights of employees, creditors, or minority shareholders.[447] Outvoted minority shareholders and those holding non-voting shares are protected by a sell-out right.[448] Creditor protection may take the form of a declaration of solvency issued by management, and creditors have a right to apply to the competent authority for adequate safeguards; a conversion will be deemed not to be prejudicial where an independent expert report finds accordingly and where creditors are offered a right to payment of similar credit quality and equivalent value as their original claim either against a third party guarantor or the company after conversion.[449] The thorny issue of employee participation is likely to be dealt with in accordance with the regime applicable to the formation of an SE.[450] Following receipt of the pre-conversion certificate, the competent authority of the Member State of destination would verify that the conversion procedure as well as the requirements for the formation of a company under its law have been complied with.[451] Upon registration of the company in the host Member State (the new home Member State) the former home Member State authorities will be informed so that the company can be removed from the register there. Conversion takes effect, and may not be declared null and void, with registration in the Member State of destination.[452] As a consequence, all contracts, credits, rights, and obligations automatically vest in the converted company; shareholders become shareholders in the converted company, subject to the exercise of any sell-out right; employment contracts are transferred to the converted company by operation of law.[453]

Questions:

1. In Chapter 1 we discussed varies corporate theories that seek to explain the 'nature' of the business corporation—real entity theory, fiction theory, concession theory, nexus-of-contract theories, and proprietary theories. Which of these theories, if any, provides the best justification for the Court's case law on freedom of establishment?
2. ABC Ltd, a private company limited by shares, is incorporated in Utopia, a Member State of the European Union. ABC Ltd has its head office and principal place of business in Utopia. ABC Ltd develops and markets chocolate bars for the local market in Utopia. However, ABC considers expanding its business into Ruritania, a neighbouring EU Member State. There, DEF Plc, a public company limited by shares incorporated and headquartered in Ruritania, is in the same line of business and serves the local market. Ruritania is very protective of its domestic companies and seeks to prevent foreign companies from entering its market to the greatest

[445] Mobility Proposal, new Arts 86d, 86e, 86f, and 86g.
[446] ibid new Art 86i.
[447] ibid new Arts 86c(3), 86m, and 86n.
[448] ibid new Art 86j.
[449] ibid new Art 86k.
[450] ibid new Art 86l.
[451] ibid new Art 86p.
[452] ibid new Arts 86r and 86u.
[453] ibid new Art 86s.

possible extent. From a company law perspective, what are ABC Ltd's options for accessing the market in Ruritania with a view to selling its products there? To what extent and through what measures may Ruritania try lawfully to discourage foreign companies from entering its market?

3. Although an SE may transfer its registered office from one Member State to another, the registered office has to be located in the same Member State as the head office. In the light of the Court's case law, notably *Polbud*, are these provisions compatible with the right to freedom of establishment?

D. Free Movement of Capital

The right to free movement of capital has been a late bloomer amongst the internal market freedoms. Council Directive 88/361/EEC,[454] requiring the removal of restrictions of all capital movements between residents of most Member States from 1 July 1990,[455] rendered it fully operational. However, only under the Maastricht Treaty, did free movement of capital obtain direct effect. The freedom prohibits all restrictions on the movement of capital between Member States and between Member States and third countries.[456] The significance of the right to free movement of capital for company law came to the fore in a long line of cases since 2000 dealing with so-called 'golden shares':[457] in the course of a wave of privatizations of formerly state-owned companies carried out by various Member States throughout the 1990s, Member States frequently sought to retain some form of control over the now often publicly traded limited liability companies, in particular in respect of companies active in the electricity, oil and gas or defence sectors, but also in telecommunication, banking, insurance, airports and even tobacco industries. The control retained in the form of 'special rights' could range from purely administrative regimes to standard company law solutions. In the chronology of cases decided by the Court of Justice we can observe a development from the former towards the latter, with increasing relevance for general company law. Although the free movement of capital doctrine is now fairly settled pursuant to the Court's jurisprudence, many Member States have demonstrated significant reluctance in implementing judgments that invalidate their retained 'special rights'.[458]

I. Golden shares

A 'golden share' may be defined in a broad sense as a special right of the state, or its emanations, to exert control and influence, directly or indirectly, in the management of a company. Golden shares vary widely both in terms of form and substance. On the basis of the Court's case law, it is possible to discern the following formal typology:

[454] Council Directive 88/361/EEC of 24 June 1988 for the implementation of Art 67 of the Treaty, OJ 1988 L178/5.

[455] For Greece, Ireland, Portugal, and Spain, there was a temporary postponement until 31 December 1992.

[456] Art 63(1) TFEU.

[457] Case C-58/99 *Commission v Italy* (n 184); Case C-174/04 *Commission v Italy* (n 184); Case C-326/07 *Commission v Italy* (n 184); Case C-503/99 *Commission v Belgium* (n 183); Case C-367/98 *Commission v Portugal* (n 184); Case C-171/08 *Commission v Portugal* (n 184); Case C-543/08 *Commission v Portugal* (n 184); Case C-483/99 *Commission v France* (n 184); Case C-463/00 *Commission v Spain* (n 184); Case C-274/06 *Commission v Spain* (n 184); Case C-207/07 *Commission v Spain* (n 184); Case C-98/01 *Commission v United Kingdom* (n 184); Joined Cases C-282 & 283/04 *Commission v Netherlands* (n 184); Case C-112/05 *Commission v Germany* (n 184); Joined Cases C-463/04 & C-464/04 *Federconsumatori v Commune di Milano* (n 184); Case C-196/07 *Commission v Spain* (n 184); Case C-95/12 *Commission v Germany* (n 184).

[458] J Ganza, 'Obstructionist National Protectionism in the EU: Qualitative Analysis of Member States' Compliance with the CJEU's Judgments in "Golden Shares" Cases (September 2014, unpublished PhD Thesis, on file with the authors).

(i) In its early case law, the Court was asked to ascertain the compatibility with free movement of capital of purely administrative regimes. These may take the form of a system of prior administrative approval by a competent public authority of certain corporate transactions, notably a reduction of the state's shareholding below a specified threshold; the acquisition by a third party of a shareholding above a certain threshold; the carrying out of structural changes (voluntary winding-up, demerger, merger, disposal of major assets, change of the company's objects).[459] Another version is the outright limitation, by administrative decree or statutory instrument, of the participation of foreign entities in the share capital of a domestic company; combined with a forced sale of any shares exceeding the specified limits and loss of the voting rights attached.[460] It is perhaps fair to say that the cases concerning these purely administrative regimes are of limited significance for general company law.

(ii) This is also true, albeit to a lesser extent, for 'golden shares' created for the state, or its emanations, by a special statute or statutory instruments that derogate from the otherwise applicable company law. In these cases, a special statute or statutory instrument creates, upon privatization of the company at issue, a 'golden share' to be vested in the state and to which special rights are attached.[461] These may include the right to oppose the disposal of certain strategic assets (prior to the transaction or subsequently within a certain time limit), the right to appoint a certain number of government representatives to the board of directors (in a voting or non-voting capacity), who may apply, within a certain period of time, to the competent authority to have certain management decisions annulled. The government's opposition to a transfer or the annulment of a certain management decision may be subject to more or less strictly prescribed substantive requirements.[462]

(iii) We move closer to core company law with 'golden shares' created by, and contained in, the respective company's articles of association. The 'golden shares' in the articles may be authorized by the respective statutes that govern the privatization of state-owned undertakings; in addition, statutory instruments may require the insertion of 'golden shares' in the articles prior to privatization and may also define the prerequisites for the exercise of the special rights attached to the 'golden shares'.[463] These special rights may include a power to oppose the acquisition by investors of significant shareholdings exceeding a certain threshold (e.g. 5%); a power to oppose the conclusion of contracts between the company and shareholders representing a certain threshold of voting rights (e.g. 5%); a power to veto shareholder resolutions on structural changes (dissolution of the company, transfer of its business or its headquarters abroad, mergers, amendment of the articles or objects); and/or a power to appoint a voting or non-voting director.[464] Another technique is that certain decisions require approval by (a majority of) the holders of the 'golden shares';[465] these decisions may include the appointment of a certain number of directors, the appropriation of the net income for a year, the amendment of the articles, an increase in share capital, the issues of bonds and other securities, relocation of the registered office. The exercise of these special rights may be subject to specific restrictions: a real and serious risk to the public interest or service that the 'golden share' seeks to protect such as a minimum national

[459] Case C-463/00 *Commission v Spain* (n 184).

[460] Case C-367/98 *Commission v Portugal* (n 184).

[461] Case C-483/99 *Commission v France* (n 184); Case C-503/99 *Commission v Belgium* (n 183); Case C-174/04 *Commission v Italy* (n 184).

[462] Case C-503/99 *Commission v Belgium* (n 183).

[463] Case C-58/99 *Commission v Italy* (n 184); Case C-326/07 *Commission v Italy* (n 184); Case C-171/08 *Commission v Portugal* (n 184); Case C-543/08 *Commission v Portugal* (n 184).

[464] Case C-326/07 *Commission v Italy* (n 184).

[465] Case C-171/08 *Commission v Portugal* (n 184). A similar result may be achieved by capping the voting rights of ordinary shares at, say, 5% and exempting the 'golden shares' from such voting cap; Case C-543/08 *Commission v Portugal* (n 184).

supply of energy, oil and gas, telecommunication services, transportation, national defence, or public health.[466]

(iv) The final category concerns 'golden shares' created by the company's articles of association in accordance with general company law.[467] These 'golden shares' may require the consent of their holders for article amendments, in particular in respect of the special rights attached to the 'golden share' itself, but also for a ceasing of the company of exercising control in any of its strategic subsidiaries, their winding-up or dissolution, or disposition of strategic assets. This may be combined with a right to attend and speak at any general meeting, a right to redeem the 'golden share' at par, and a general voting cap of ordinary shareholders of a certain threshold (say 15%).[468] The 'golden shares' may give their holders special rights of prior approval of a wide range of transactions including the issuing of shares, the acquisition by the company of its own shares, structural changes such as mergers, dissolutions, and article amendments, or the distribution of dividends.[469] In addition to rights of appointment of members of the management or supervisory boards, voting caps (of say 20%) may be combined with a supermajority for certain structural changes and significant transactions that goes beyond the supermajority already required under general corporate law (say, a 75% supermajority may be increased to 80%).[470] Although in these cases, the 'golden share' in the articles of association is in accordance with general company law, it will have been created at a time when the state was the sole shareholder of the respective company,[471] and/or the articles will subsequently have been approved by the competent public authority[472] or the 'golden share' may even have been endorsed and replicated by statute.[473] The 'golden share' may name the state (or its emanations) explicitly as the only permitted holder of the special rights attached to it;[474] but it may also benefit and/or disadvantage all shareholders equally regardless of their identity—such as a voting cap combined with a supermajority.[475] In these latter cases the 'golden share' derives its specific significance indirectly from the fact that the state happens to hold a blocking minority of votes, which allows it to prevent certain structural changes. It is the extension of free movement of capital into the realm of general non-state specific company law arrangements where its potential impact on domestic company law is deemed to be greatest.[476]

II. Capital movements

Art 63(1) of the TFEU prohibits all restrictions on the movement of capital between Member States as well as between Member States and third countries. Although 'movement of capital' is not defined in the Treaty, it is the well-established case law of the Court of Justice that the 'nomenclature of movements of capital' set out in Annex I to Council Directive 88/361/EEC and the explanatory note thereto is of 'indicative value'. Consequently, movements of capital include in particular 'direct investments' as well as 'portfolio investments'.[477] The former

[466] Case C-326/07 *Commission v Italy* (n 184).

[467] 'General' company law may also provide that 'golden shares' may be created for the benefit of the state; Joined Cases C-463/04 & C-464/04 *Federconsumatori v Commune di Milano* (n 184).

[468] Case C-98/01 *Commission v United Kingdom* (n 184).

[469] Joined Cases Case C-282 & 283/04 *Commission v Netherlands* (n 184).

[470] Case C-112/05 *Commission v Germany* (n 184); see further Case C-95/12 *Commission v Germany* (n 184).

[471] Joined Cases C-282 & 283/04 *Commission v Netherlands* (n 184).

[472] Case C-98/01 *Commission v United Kingdom* (n 184).

[473] Case C-112/05 *Commission v Germany* (n 184).

[474] Case C-98/01 *Commission v United Kingdom* (n 184); Joined Cases Case C-282 & 283/04 *Commission v Netherlands* (n 184).

[475] Case C-112/05 *Commission v Germany* (n 184).

[476] Armour and Ringe (n 119) 148.

[477] See eg Joined Cases C-282 and 283/04 *Commission v Netherlands* (n 184) para 19; Case C-171/08 *Commission v Portugal* (n 184) para 49.

constitute 'investments of any kind undertaken by natural or legal persons which serve to establish or maintain lasting and direct links between the person providing the capital and the undertaking to which that capital is made available in order to carry on an economic activity'. Where the investment consists in shareholdings, 'the objective of establishing or maintain lasting economic links presupposes that the shares held by the shareholder enable him, either pursuant to the provisions of the national laws relating to companies limited by shares or in some other way, to participate effectively in the management of that company or in its control'.[478] The possibility of 'effectively participating' in the company's management and control falls short of being a controlling shareholder; however, the Court does not provide any specific thresholds. It is a subjective concept: any shareholder with an intention to invest in a company long term and with a view to exercising voting rights—even if in the minority—would come under the heading of 'direct investment'. By contrast, 'portfolio investments' constitute investments in the form of the acquisition of shares on the capital markets solely with an intention of making financial investments and without intention to influence the management and control of the undertaking.[479] Again, the emphasis is on the investor's intention as the decisive criterion for distinguishing 'direct' and 'portfolio' investments.

There is a significant overlap in terms of scope of free movement of capital and freedom of establishment. According to the Court's well-established case law, 'provisions of national law which apply to the possession by nationals of one Member State of holdings in the capital of a company established in another Member State allowing them to exert a definite influence on the company's decisions and to determine its activities fall within the ambit *ratione materiae* of the provisions' on freedom of establishment.[480] The decisive criterion as to whether one or the other or both freedoms provide the appropriate standard of assessment is the rationale of the national legislation to be assessed. Consequently, 'national legislation intended to apply only to those shareholdings which enable the holder to exert a definite influence on a company's decisions and to determine its activities falls within the provisions of the Treaty on freedom of establishment'; whereas 'national provisions which apply to shareholdings acquired solely with the intention of making a financial investment without any intention to influence the management and control of the undertaking must be examined exclusively in light of the free movement of capital'.[481] It is clear that in the latter scenario only free movement of capital applies; freedom of establishment simply has not been triggered.[482] The former scenario, however, seems to fall within the ambit of both freedoms and the fact that the Court relies 'exclusively' on one of the freedoms only in the latter scenario seems to suggest that in the former free movement of capital is not totally superseded, and rendered inapplicable, by freedom of establishment.[483] The first scenario thus seems to be more akin to the situation of 'national legislation not intended to apply only to those shareholdings which enable the holder to have definite influence on a company's decisions and to determine its

[478] Case C-112/05 *Commission v Germany* (n 184) para 18.

[479] See eg Joined Cases C-282 and 283/04 *Commission v Netherlands* (n 184) para 19; Case C-171/08 *Commission v Portugal* (n 184) para 49.

[480] Case C-112/05 *Commission v Germany* (n 184) para 13; Case C-326/07 *Commission v Italy* (n 184) para 34; Case C-543/08 *Commission v Portugal* (n 184) para 41.

[481] Joined Cases C-436/08 & C-437/08 *Haribo Lakritzen Hans Riegel BetriebsgmbH v Finanzamt Linz* ECLI:EU:C:2011:61 para 35.

[482] Schön (n 47) 20.

[483] ibid; see also Case C-326/07 *Commission v Italy* (n 184) para 39: 'Although, measures that only concern shareholders capable of exerting a definite influence must be examined "solely" from the point of view of freedom of establishment; any effects of these measures on free movement of capital 'would be the unavoidable consequence of any restriction on freedom of establishment and would not merit independent examination in the light of [Art 63 TFEU]'.

activities but which applies irrespective of the size of the holding which the shareholder has in a company', which may be assessed in accordance with both freedoms.[484] In these cases the Court normally starts with the freedom that appears to be closer to the issue that informs the underlying dispute. The outcome of that assessment then normally also determines the outcome of the assessment under the freedom that is secondary to the issues at hand.[485] For example, in many of the 'golden shares' cases, the Court concluded that to the extent that the relevant national measures entail restrictions to freedom of establishment, these are a direct consequence of the obstacles to free movement of capital to which they are inextricably linked. Thus, where an infringement of free movement of capital has been established, the Court feels that there is no need for a separate assessment of the national measure under freedom of establishment.[486]

Whereas for capital movements between Member States the delineation of free movement of capital and freedom of establishment is of secondary importance, the interaction of both freedoms is of great significance in relation to third countries. Vis-à-vis third countries free movement of capital applies, whereas freedom of establishment does not.[487] In its recent case law, the Court again has recourse to the 'purpose of national legislation'. Whereas national rules, which do not apply exclusively to situations in which the shareholder situated in a third country exercises decisive influence over the company, can be assessed in light of free movement of capital; national legislation that purports to only apply to those shareholdings which enable the third-country holder to exert a definite influence on the decisions of the company and to determine its activities, can be assessed neither under Article 49 of the TFEU nor Article 63 of the TFEU.[488] Thus, although freedom of establishment does not apply at all in these latter circumstances owing to its lack of territorial scope, it still excludes free movement of capital, the scope of which would otherwise cover the factual circumstances in the scenario at issue.[489] The Court has justified this approach on the basis that third country economic operators that cannot rely on freedom of establishment owing to that freedom's territorial limitations have to be prevented from accessing, and freely setting up shop in, the internal market on the back of free movement of capital quasi 'through the backdoor'.[490]

III. Restrictions

It is clear from its wording that Article 63(1) of the TFEU seeks to eliminate all restrictions to the free movement of capital, and not just the unequal treatment of investors and issuers on grounds of nationality.[491] According to the Court, a national measure amounts to a restriction in respect of 'direct investments' and/or 'portfolio investments' if it is liable to prevent or limit the acquisition of shares in the undertaking concerned or to deter investors of other Member States from investing in its capital.[492] In this respect, both the form and

484 Case C-326/07 *Commission v Italy* (n 184) para 36; Case C-543/08 *Commission v Portugal* (n 184) para 43.

485 Schön (n 47) 21.

486 Case C-98/01 *Commission v United Kingdom* (n 184) para 52; Case C-367/98 *Commission v Portugal* (n 184) para 56; Case C-463/00 *Commission v Spain* (n 184) para 86; Case C-483/99 *Commission v France* (n 184) para 56; Joined Cases C-282 & 283/04 *Commission v Netherlands* (n 184) para 43; Case C-171/08 *Commission v Portugal* (n 184) para 80.

487 Schön (n 47) 21–2.

488 Case C-35/11 *Test Claimants in the FII Group Litigation v Commissioners of Inland Revenue* ECLI:EU:C:2012:707 paras 96–100.

489 Schön (n 47) 22.

490 Case C-35/11 *Test Claimants in the FII Group Litigation v Commissioners of Inland Revenue* ECLI:EU:C:2012:707 para 100; Schön (n 47) 23.

491 Case C-483/99 *Commission v France* (n 184) para 40; Case C-367/98 *Commission v Portugal* (n 184) para 44.

492 Case C-463/00 *Commission v Spain* (n 184) para 61; Case C-367/98 *Commission v Portugal* (n 184) para 45; Case C-171/08 *Commission v Portugal* (n 184) para 50; Case C-543/08 *Commission v Portugal* (n 184) para 47.

the substance of 'golden shares' become relevant. In terms of form, purely administrative regimes (our category (i) above) as well as 'golden shares' created by special statutes or statutory instruments (our category (ii)) are clearly national measures that are capable, in principle, to restrict free movement of capital.[493] In terms of substance, any right to veto, oppose, or have subsequently annulled corporate transactions, including structural changes and disposals of strategic assets, are, to the extent that these rights confer on the state an influence on the management and control of the company that goes beyond the size of the state's shareholding, liable to discourage direct investments because (foreign) investors could not be involved in the management and control of the company in proportion to the value of their shareholdings.[494] Moreover, these rights may also have a deterrent effect on portfolio investment. This is because the state's blocking of important decisions and transactions that the corporate organs deem to be in the best interest of the company may result in a reduction of share prices and thus reduce the attraction of an investment in these shares.[495] Limitations on the acquisition of shareholdings beyond a certain threshold, in the form of an outright ban or subject to prior approval, are liable to impede the acquisition of shares in the companies concerned and to deter 'direct investment' as well as 'portfolio investment', rendering the free movement of capital 'illusory'.[496] Rights conferred on the state (or its emanations) to appoint directors or members of the supervisory board that provide the respective state authorities with a level of influence that exceeds their level of investment result in a diminished influence of the other shareholders below a level commensurate with their level of investment, and thus has a deterrent effect on 'direct investment'.[497] Given that voting rights are the principal way by which investors can actively participate in the management and control of a company, any measure that is designed to prevent those rights from being exercised or subjects them to qualifications is liable to deter investors from acquiring stakes in the company concerned. As a consequence, voting caps and suspension of voting rights that only apply to ordinary shareholders, and not the holder of the 'golden share', amount to a restriction on capital movement in the form of 'direct investment'.[498] The same is true where a voting cap is combined with a supermajority in a way that allows state authorities to block important resolutions and transactions.[499] In all these incidents it is not a valid defence for the Member State to invoke empirical evidence demonstrating that the shares of the company are in fact widely and actively traded[500] or that a certain number of foreign 'direct investors' fill the ranks of the company's shareholders.[501] What matters is whether 'direct investors from other Member States, whether actual or potential, may have been deterred from acquiring a stake in the capital of the company'.[502] Although decided explicitly only for restrictions on 'direct investment', one suspects that restrictions to 'portfolio investments' will be treated in the same way.

The situation is somewhat more complicated where the 'golden shares' are created and conferred on the state by the company's articles of association, either on the basis of a special statute and/or statutory instrument (our category (iii)), or on the basis of general company law albeit with state approval or endorsement (our category (iv)). These measures do not fall

[493] Case C-463/00 *Commission v Spain* (n 184) para 61; Case C-367/98 *Commission v Portugal* (n 184) para 44; Case C-483/99 *Commission v France* (n 184) para 41; Case C-503/99 *Commission v Belgium* (n 183) para 39; Case C-174/04 *Commission v Italy* (n 184) paras 29–31.

[494] Case C-171/08 *Commission v Portugal* (n 184) para 60; Case C-543/08 *Commission v Portugal* (n 184) para 56, 58.

[495] Case C-171/08 *Commission v Portugal* (n 184) para 61; Case C-543/08 *Commission v Portugal* (n 184) para 57.

[496] Case C-367/98 *Commission v Portugal* (n 184) para 45; Case C-483/99 *Commission v France* (n 184) para 41.

[497] Case C-112/05 *Commission v Germany* (n 184) para 64; Case C-543/08 *Commission v Portugal* (n 184) para 64.

[498] Case C-543/08 *Commission v Portugal* (n 184) para 58.

[499] Case C-112/05 *Commission v Germany* (n 184) para 54.

[500] ibid para 53.

[501] Case C-543/08 *Commission v Portugal* (n 184) para 71.

[502] ibid.

outside the scope of the right to free movement of capital on the basis of the logic underlying the *Keck* judgment.[503] According to *Keck*, certain selling arrangements do not fall within the scope of the right to free movement of goods provided the respective provisions apply to all relevant traders operating within a Member State and affect in the same manner, in law and in fact, domestic and foreign products.[504] Whereas certain selling arrangements concern the circumstances of marketing and distribution of a product such as opening hours or the nature of the distributor; product-related rules deal with the form, size, weight, composition, presentation, labelling, and packaging of a product.[505] State-imposed 'golden shares' within a company's capital structure regulate the attributes, in terms of control and/or cash flow rights, of the ordinary shares as a financial product much the same way that product-related, and therefore non-exempt, provisions regulate the attributes of goods. Moreover, for 'golden shares' of the category (iii) variety it is quite clear that they are not the result of the application of general company law. Rather, it is the respective Member State which in its capacity as legislature authorized the creation of 'golden shares', then, in its capacity as public authority, decided to introduce 'golden shares' in the articles of the respective company, defined the special rights attached to them and allocated them to itself. The creation of the 'golden shares' is thus attributable to the state, in particular where the 'golden shares' are non-transferable.[506] Attribution to the state also poses little difficulty for category (iv) 'golden shares' where the company's articles were approved by the Member State in its capacity as a public authority,[507] or where the 'golden shares' are the result of decisions taken by the Member State in the course of the privatization of the company with a view to reserving certain special rights for the respective Member State.[508]

The situation in *Commission v Germany* posed a specific problem. The articles of Volkswagen, later endorsed by statute, provided for a 20 per cent voting cap combined with an 80 per cent supermajority for structural changes,[509] thus increasing the normally applicable 75 per cent supermajority.[510] Both measures were perfectly valid under general company law and applied to the benefit or detriment, as the case may be, of all shareholders and were not reserved for the state or its emanations.[511] Shortly after privatization of Volkswagen when the 'golden shares' were endorsed by statute the Federal Republic and the Region of Lower Saxony were the two main shareholders, holding 20 per cent each. Whereas the Federal Republic had subsequently parted with its interest, Lower Saxony retained a shareholding in the region of 20 per cent. According to the Court, the voting cap in combination with the supermajority enabled the federal and regional authorities to obtain a blocking minority allowing them to oppose important resolutions. Public authorities were thus able to exercise a degree of influence not commensurate with the level of their investment, resulting in a deterrent for direct investment from other Member States.[512] Irrespective of the statutory endorsement of the 'golden shares' created by the articles,[513] they were attributable to the state and its emanations because they created a de facto veto right for state authorities owing to the company's ownership structure.[514] The decision has sparked some speculation

[503] Case C-171/08 *Commission v Portugal* (n 184) paras 65–7; Case C-367/98 *Commission v Portugal* (n 184) paras 65–8.

[504] Joined Cases C-267 and C-268/91 *Keck and Mithouard* (n 42) paras 15–18.

[505] See text accompanying n 42 above.

[506] Case C-171/08 *Commission v Portugal* (n 184) paras 54, 55; Case C-367/98 *Commission v Portugal* (n 184) para 51.

[507] Case C-98/01 *Commission v United Kingdom* (n 184) para 48.

[508] Joined Cases C-282 & 283/04 *Commission v Netherlands* (n 184) para 22.

[509] Case C-112/05 *Commission v Germany* (n 184).

[510] AktG, §§179(2), 179a(1), and 182(2).

[511] Case C-112/05 *Commission v Germany* (n 184) para 47.

[512] ibid paras 48–52.

[513] ibid para 26: this alone would bring the measure within the ambit of free movement of capital.

[514] Armour and Ringe (n 119) 148.

as to whether free movement of capital may be used to assess, and put to a proportionality test, any provision in a company's articles that in accordance with general company law deviates from the 'one-share, one vote' principle.[515] For example, if in the Volkswagen case Lower Saxony had also parted with its 20 per cent shareholding, would the voting cap combined with the supermajority still have amounted to a restriction of free movement of capital? In a German case, it has been argued before the Federal Supreme Court, in a complaint against a rejection of a right to appeal, that a provision in the articles granting certain shareholders appointment rights to the supervisory board constituted an infringement of the right to free movement of capital.[516] It could be argued that a potential investor would be equally deterred by voting caps or appointment rights if a private shareholder were to benefit from the respective provisions in the company's articles, rather than the state.[517] However, it seems to be quite clear from the Court's reasoning that state involvement is crucial. According to the Court, 'there is a difference between a power made available to shareholders, who are free to decide whether or not they wish to use it, and a specific obligation imposed on shareholders by way of legislation, without the possibility to derogate from it'.[518] Moreover, where a 'facility can be conferred by legislation as a right of a qualified minority, it is clear that it must, in such a case, be accessible to all shareholders and must not be reserved exclusively to the State'.[519] Normatively, this outcome can be justified by the consideration that the articles of association freely negotiated by the company promoters and the rights allocated to the shares therein are attributes of the shares as a financial product similar to the (non-regulatory) attributes of other products. Product attributes—like taste, style, or quality—determine demand for the product and are subject to market forces and competition; they are irrelevant for the market freedoms (as long as they remain unregulated). In the same way, investors may purchase a stake in a company on the basis of the control and cash flow rights that they are being promised. Unless these are determined by the state, directly or indirectly, there is no room for free movement of capital to intervene. Moreover, only where the state is involved as the holder of a 'golden share' is there a unique danger that special rights may be exploited out of political opportunism in a way that is detrimental to the other shareholders' interests.[520]

IV. Justification

A restriction to free movement of capital may be justified on the basis of the reasons referred to in Article 65 of the TFEU—public policy, public security, or public health—or by overriding requirements of the general interest provided these interests are not already adequately protected by harmonising measures at EU level. In either case, in order to be justified, the national measure must observe the principle of proportionality, which requires that the national legislation must be appropriate for securing the attainment of the objective, which it pursues and must not go beyond what is necessary for attaining it.[521]

Safeguarding the supplies of energy resources, in particular of petroleum products, natural gas, and electricity, as well as of telecommunication services in case of crisis, war, or

[515] ibid; W-G Ringe, 'Case C-112/05, *Commission v. Germany* ("VW law"), Judgment of the Grand Chamber of 23 October 2007, nyr' (2008) 45 Common Market Law Review 537, 543.

[516] BGH, 8 June 2009, II ZR 111/08. The Federal Supreme Court held without further reasoning that an infringement of free movement of capital may only lie in special rights granted to Federal or regional authorities to the extent that this constitutes a deviation from generally applicable company law. A reference for a preliminary ruling to the CJEU was deemed to be unnecessary, presumably on the basis of the *acte clair* doctrine.

[517] Ringe (n 515) 543.

[518] Case C-112/05 *Commission v Germany* (n 184) para 40.

[519] Case C-543/08 *Commission v Portugal* (n 184) para 62.

[520] Ringe (n 515) 543.

[521] Case C-112/05 *Commission v Germany* (n 184) paras 72, 73; Case C-171/08 *Commission v Portugal* (n 184) para 69; Case C-367/98 *Commission v Portugal* (n 184) para 83.

terrorism may constitute a ground of public security and possibly justify a restriction to free movement of capital.[522] As derogation from the fundamental principle of free movement of capital, the requirements of public security must be interpreted narrowly. According to the Court, only a genuine and sufficiently serious threat to a fundamental interest of society may allow a Member State to invoke public security concerns,[523] although this threat does not have to be immediate. However, it is for the Member State to demonstrate that the 'golden share' at issue would enable the public authorities to prevent such threat from materializing. In particular, the acquisition of a major shareholding by foreign or domestic private investors, in principle, cannot be regarded as a real and serious threat to public security.[524] Moreover, powers of opposition to corporate transactions and/or the acquisition of stakes in a company are likely to be unsuitable for attaining the public security objective if the exercise of these powers is not linked to a genuine and sufficiently serious threat.[525] The principle of proportionality requires further that the Member State's rights of intervention are defined as precisely as possible with reference to the specific objective circumstances in which the special powers may be exercised. A lack of precision increases the uncertainty for market participants and gives national authorities an amount of discretion that makes the exercise of these special rights in accordance with EU law difficult.[526] Also, because it respects the decision-making autonomy of the company to a greater extent, a system of opposition *ex post facto* is less intrusive than a regime of prior authorization;[527] the latter will go beyond what is necessary for attaining the objective pursued if the former would be sufficient. In any case, the exercise of powers must be subject to a strict timetable; the Member State should be obliged to give reasons for any particular interference, allowing for effective judicial review, which must be available for the company concerned. Thus far, only in *Commission v Belgium* did the 'golden shares' meet these requirements to the effect that the infringement of free movement of capital was justified.[528]

As for the overriding reasons in the general interest capable of justifying a restriction to the free movement of capital, the Court has recognized the guarantee of a universal postal service, the protection of workers' interests, as well as the protection of minority shareholders.[529] By contrast, economic grounds such as the general financial interest of the Member States or competition concerns can never provide adequate justification.[530] Consequently, 'golden shares' in the tobacco industry and in the traditional banking sector cannot be justified.[531] As for the protection of workers and minority shareholders, in *Commission v Germany* the Member State failed to demonstrate why the presence of a large dominant shareholder would endanger workers' rights and why the 'golden share' in form of appointment rights and a voting cap combined with a supermajority benefiting federal and regional authorities was suitable and necessary for protecting Volkswagen's workers. Similarly, the Member State was unable to show that the level of influence reserved for federal and state authorities was appropriate and necessary to protect the interests of minority shareholders.[532]

522 Case C-503/99 *Commission v Belgium* (n 183) para 46; Case C-483/99 *Commission v France* (n 184) para 47, Case C-174/04 *Commission v Italy* (n 184) para 40; Case C-171/08 *Commission v Portugal* (n 184) para 72; Case C-543/08 *Commission v Portugal* (n 184) para 84.

523 Case C-326/07 *Commission v Italy* (n 184) para 48; Case C-171/08 *Commission v Portugal* (n 184) para 73; Case C-543/08 *Commission v Portugal* (n 184) para 85.

524 Case C-326/07 *Commission v Italy* (n 184) para 48.

525 Case C-171/08 *Commission v Portugal* (n 184) para 74; Case C-543/08 *Commission v Portugal* (n 184) para 87.

526 Case C-483/99 *Commission v France* (n 184) para 51; Case C-326/07 *Commission v Italy* (n 184) paras 51–3; Case C-171/08 *Commission v Portugal* (n 184) paras 75–7; Case C-543/08 *Commission v Portugal* (n 184) paras 90–2.

527 Case C-503/99 *Commission v Belgium* (n 183) para 49; Case C-483/99 *Commission v France* (n 184) para 52.

528 Case C-503/99 *Commission v Belgium* (n 183) paras 50–2.

529 Case C-112/05 *Commission v Germany* (n 184) paras 74, 77.

530 Case C-367/98 *Commission v Portugal* (n 184) para 52; Case C-171/08 *Commission v Portugal* (n 184) para 71.

531 Case C-463/00 *Commission v Spain* (n 184) para 70.

532 Case C-112/05 *Commission v Germany* (n 184) paras 74, 78.

Question:

- Utopia, an EU Member State, imposes a tax on dividend payments to shareholders resident in Utopia. Under Utopia's tax regime, for shares of companies incorporated in Utopia, a tariff of 10 per cent applies for shareholdings of up to 50 per cent; for shareholdings of more than 50 per cent, a 20 per cent tariff applies. For shares of companies incorporated abroad, the respective tariffs are 20 per cent and 30 per cent. Martin is resident in Utopia and holds 49 per cent of the voting capital of a company incorporated in Member State Ruritania. Bernhard, also resident in Utopia, holds 51 per cent of the voting capital in a company incorporated in Geldania, a third country. Both Martin and Bernhard apply for the reduced tax rate in Utopia. In both cases, the tax authorities of Utopia reject the application and apply the higher rate for companies incorporated abroad. Advice Martin and Bernhard on their rights under the EU Treaties.

E. The Future of EU Company Law Post-Brexit

On 23 June 2016, the voting public in the UK decided in a non-binding referendum by a narrow majority to leave the European Union. Whether and to what extent the UK's departure will affect company law in the UK as well as EU company law will depend on the precise mode of exit and, more importantly, the model of interaction that is established between the UK and the EU thereafter. This may range from EEA and EFTA membership, at one end of the spectrum, to a so-called 'hard Brexit' in form of a falling back on WTO rules with, at least initially, no softening trade agreement in place, on the other. Between these two 'extremes' sits the more fluid option of a bespoke framework of bilateral agreements that would cover various areas to a greater or lesser extent. Under the EEA option, the UK would stay in the single market; EU company law and securities regulation would remain in place in the UK and the UK would be bound by any future EU measures.[533] The UK would no longer have any formal say in the EU law-making process; however, given the size of its economy the UK may still be able to wield considerable informal power. The EEA option entails the continuation of the free movement of persons, the curtailment of which was one of the key motivating factors underlying the Brexit vote. Therefore, politically this option seems unlikely. A 'hard Brexit' would be the default option in the absence of a timely withdrawal agreement. Given the potentially catastrophic economic disruption that might ensue in this case, possibly exceeding the fallout of the Lehman bankruptcy, it is perhaps fair to assume that both the EU and the UK would seek to prevent this outcome at all cost, by for example agreeing a generous transition period. A bespoke solution is the UK government's preferred option. However, the probability and eventual content of such a deal remain uncertain for the time being. In any case, negotiation takes place in the shadow of a 'hard Brexit' which will therefore provide the basis for the following analysis.[534]

A hard Brexit entails the repeal of the European Communities Act 1972 in its current form.[535] As a consequence, the right to freedom of establishment would no longer apply to companies incorporated under UK law and companies incorporated elsewhere seeking to do business or establish themselves in the UK.[536] Empirical studies have shown that the UK became the predominant destination for incorporations following the handing down of the *Centros*-line of judgments.[537] Although incorporation in the UK for businesses situated elsewhere in the EU has lost some of its attraction,[538] a significant number of English

[533] Agreement on the European Economic Area, OJ L1, 3.1.1994, Arts 31 and 34, 77, and Annex XXII.

[534] See further M Schillig, 'Corporate Law after Brexit' (2016) 27 King's Law Journal 431.

[535] European Union (Withdrawal) Act 2018, s 1.

[536] The repeal would only have declaratory effect because the application of the Treaties and any laws derived therefrom will come to an end automatically with the UK's withdrawal from the EU taking effect.

[537] Becht, Mayer, and Wagner (n 300). [538] Ringe (n 299).

private companies limited by shares with a minimal link to the UK still operate in various EU Member States. If a hard Brexit takes effect, the shareholders and directors of these companies may find themselves in a difficult position. UK incorporated companies will no longer be able to rely on the right to freedom of establishment and the UK obtains third country status. In relation to a public company incorporated in Switzerland, but with its central administration in Germany, the German Federal Supreme Court has applied the real seat theory.[539] The Court's reasoning is of great relevance for the UK's relationship with the EU after Brexit. Although a member of EFTA, Switzerland is not an EEA Member State so that freedom of establishment does not apply. There is no bilateral treaty that would mandate applying the incorporation theory to a Swiss company with its central administration in Germany. Also, the fact that Swiss law is very much harmonized in accordance with EU law does not justify the application of the incorporation theory. Rather, the rejection of EU and EEA membership is a conscious decision that prevents making an exception to the principle that in relation to third countries the real seat theory applies. As a consequence, companies incorporated in third countries with their central administration in Germany will be treated as partnership-type entities under Germany law, resulting in the personal liability of their members for corporate debt. The safest option for UK incorporated companies that have their central administration in real seat countries is to convert into a company form of another Member State prior to Brexit taking effect.[540]

Similar to the Treaty provisions, EU regulations would cease to apply. Under the European Union (Withdrawal) Act 2018, the existing body of direct EU legislation, including regulations, in force on the day of Brexit will remain operative as part of English domestic law.[541] In respect of these instruments, the principle of supremacy of EU law will continue to apply.[542] This would be particularly relevant for the small number of European Companies with their registered office in the UK.[543] Much of the substantive EU company law is contained in EU directives that have been implemented through the Companies Act 2006. The repeal of the European Communities Act 1972 would have no direct impact on implementing legislation stemming from an Act of Parliament. These provisions would remain in place until Parliament, or the UK Government under so-called Henry VIII clauses,[544] decides to repeal, amend or replace them. Given that UK company law only very recently underwent the most comprehensive review and revision process in its history, culminating in the Companies Act 2006, it is very unlikely that there will be much appetite for significant repeals or amendments, at least in the short and medium term.[545] Moreover, the Review of the Balance of Competences between the United Kingdom and the European Union[546] did not identify any significant concerns in this area. Future EU law instruments and amendments will not have to be implemented in the UK, and the Court of Justice's future case law on interpreting EU

[539] BGH, 8.10.2009–IX ZR 227/06, NJW 2009, 289.

[540] Through a cross-border merger on the basis of the national legislation implementing the Cross-Border Merger Directive or through a cross-border conversion on the basis of the *Cartesio*, *VALE*, and *Polbud* line of cases. Following Brexit, neither of these options may be available any longer. The German government has introduced a proposal for legislation that would facilitate the conversion of English companies limited by shares into domestic forms of business organization; Gesetzentwurf der Bundesregierung, Entwurf eines Vierten Gesetzes zur Änderung des Umwandlungsgesetzes (10 October 2018) https://www.bmjv.de/SharedDocs/Gesetzgebungsverfahren/DE/Umwandlungsgesetz_viertes.html.

[541] European Union (Withdrawal) Act 2018, s 3.

[542] ibid s 5(2).

[543] Transitional provisions will have to ensure that these entities are not automatically liquidated on Brexit, and get the option to convert into a domestic public company limited by shares (or transfer their registered and head office to an EU Member State prior to Brexit).

[544] European Union (Withdrawal) Act 2018, s 8.

[545] But see Department for Business, Energy & Industrial Strategy, Insolvency and Corporate Governance: Government response (26 August 2018) para 1.48, considering a comprehensive review of the UK's dividend regime.

[546] HM Government, 'Review of the Balance of Competences between the United Kingdom and the European Union. The Single Market: Free Movement of Services' (Summer 2014).

company law would no longer be binding in the UK.[547] Over time, there is likely to be some divergence as regards the harmonized areas between the UK and the rest-EU. It is worth noting that when she launched her bid for the leadership of the Conservative Party, the Prime Minister Theresa May not only went beyond current EU law by advocating a binding shareholder vote on directors' remuneration; she also argued for German-style employee representation on corporate boards,[548] an issue that has been a major obstacle for agreement at EU level in the past.

The impact of Brexit on the future trajectory of EU company law is more difficult to predict. For the EU it would make sense to push ahead and intensify work on corporate governance and capital market related reforms. For now, London remains the dominant financial centre in Europe. As such it benefits from the 'passport mechanism' provided for by the Prospectus Directive (now Regulation). Once the prospectus has been approved by the competent authority of the home Member State it is valid, under the 'passport regime', for the public offer and admission to trading in any number of host Member States.[549] Thus, a prospectus of a German company approved by BAFin is sufficient to fulfil the prospectus requirement for admission to the 'official list' and to trading on the London Stock Exchange's Main Market.[550] Vice versa, a prospectus approved by the FCA may be used to seek admission to the Frankfurt Stock Exchange or any of the stock exchanges in Stockholm, Paris, Madrid, Milan, or Warsaw. Perhaps more importantly, third-country issuers may currently use London as the gateway to the EU securities markets. A third-country issuer that intends to offer securities to the public, or to seek their admission to trading, for the first time in the UK, can have the respective prospectus approved by the FCA. This prospectus can then be used to meet publication requirements for public offers or admission to trading on any of the stock exchanges within the EU.[551] Even if, following a hard Brexit, the UK would leave the current implementing legislation in place, London may still forgo some of its appeal. National legislation implementing the 'passporting regime' (as well as the new Regulation) requires approval through the competent authorities of EEA Member States. As a consequence, although a BAFin-approved prospectus could still be used in the UK;[552] the FCA-approved prospectus of, say, a US or Chinese company could no longer be used to obtain admission to trading in Frankfurt.[553] To what extent this effect would damage London as a financial centre in the long term is hard to predict. However, it should be an incentive for the rest-EU to catch up and seek to provide better integrated and deeper securities markets from which other financial centres and exchanges may emerge as the new gateway to Europe.

[547] European Union (Withdrawal) Act 2018, s 6. However, for domesticated EU law the retained case law of the CJEU remains relevant: a question on the validity or interpretation of retained EU law is to be decided 'in accordance with any retained case law' of the CJEU.

[548] Theresa May—2016 Speech to Launch Leadership Campaign, 11 July 2016 (http://www.ukpol.co.uk/2016/07/11/theresa-may-2016-speech-to-launch-leadership-campaign/). The Prime Minister has now softened her approach and will not impose employee representatives on UK companies.

[549] Directive 2003/71/EC, Arts 17–19 (Regulation (EU) 2017/1129, Arts 24–27).

[550] Financial Services and Markets Act 2000, ss 87H, 87I; FCA Listing Rules 2.2.10.

[551] Directive 2003/71/EC, Art 20 (Regulation (EU) 2017/1129, Art 28).

[552] Pursuant to the European Union (Withdrawal) Act 2018, s 8(2)(c), the UK government could repeal the respective domesticated provisions in order to address the lack of reciprocity.

[553] See eg the German WpPG, §17(3). The equivalence regime under the new Prospectus Regulation (Arts 29–30) would not provide any relief in this respect. The prospectus of a third country issuer drawn up in accordance with the law of the third country that meets the equivalence and cooperation requirements still requires approval by the competent authority of the issuer's home Member State (the Member State where the issuer intends to offer the securities to the public for the first time).

3

Incorporation and Corporate Representation

In Chapter 1, we saw that in the course of the nineteenth century, partly driven by the economic needs of the industrial revolution, the traditional charter, concession, or *octroi* systems of incorporation were gradually replaced with systems of general incorporation. Under these, the privileges of separate legal personality and limited liability can be obtained simply by complying with a set of formalities and disclosure requirements. Transparency at varying degrees is the price to pay for the privileges that come with incorporation.[1] Depending on the legal system, the process of incorporation may be a matter of hours or may take several weeks, although technological advancement has generally resulted in speeding it up. The longer it takes to complete the incorporation process, the more likely it is during the formation process that the business corporation will already be interacting with other market participants, entering into contracts, and incurring obligations etc. Depending on the outcome of the formation process, these pre-incorporation transactions have to be dealt with either by attributing them to the eventually established corporation or by assigning them to other actors involved should the incorporation process fail. Disclosure and transparency

[1] D French, *Mayson, French & Ryan on Company Law* (35th edn, OUP 2018–2019) 39.

remain relevant throughout the corporation's existence, also, and particularly, in the context of corporate representation. As a legal construct, a corporation can only act through humans whose conduct on behalf of the corporation must then be attributed to it in such a way that third parties seeking to contract with the corporation can rely on it. In this respect, the 'organ theory' and 'agency theory' of corporate representation provide alternative models that legal systems may rely on to a greater or lesser extent.

For our EU jurisdictions, certain aspects of incorporation and of corporate representation have been harmonized by the First Company Law Directive,[2] providing, in the interest of third parties, a disclosure regime for company documents and particulars, restricting the grounds that may render invalid transactions entered into on behalf of the company and limiting the grounds on which a company may be found to be non-existent (a 'nullity'). Its scope extended to all limited liability companies, private and public, and included limited partnerships with a share capital, where available.[3] For public companies, the disclosure regime was supplemented by the Second Company Law Directive.[4] A further EU instrument in this area was Directive 2012/17/EU on the interconnection of central, commercial, and company registers.[5] All these measures have now been codified in Directive (EU) 2017/1132.[6] The underlying rationale is to provide market participants with the necessary information so that they can be confident when contracting with companies across Europe, thus enhancing cross-border economic activity for the benefit of the internal market.[7] Given their internal market rationale, a comparative analysis of the national laws within the wider context of the scope of application of these measures allows us to assess whether and to what extent the underlying objectives have been achieved. This may then be contrasted with the situation in the United States, where differences between state corporation laws on the matters covered by these measures seem to have caused little difficulties for interstate trade.[8]

[2] First Council Directive of 9 March 1968 on coordination of safeguards which, for the protection of the interests of members and others, are required by Member States of companies within the meaning of the second paragraph of Article 58 of the Treaty, with a view to making such safeguards equivalent throughout the Community (68/151/EEC), OJ 1968 L65/8; 'codified' as Directive 2009/101/EC of the European Parliament and of the Council of 16 September 2009 on coordination of safeguards which, for the protection of the interests of members and others, are required by Member States of companies within the meaning of the second paragraph of Article 48 of the Treaty, with a view to making such safeguards equivalent (codified version), OJ 2009 L258/11.

[3] Directive (EU) 2017/1132, Arts 7, 13, and Annex II (previously Directive 2009/101/EC, Art 1).

[4] Second Council Directive of 13 December 1976 on coordination of safeguards which, for the protection of the interests of members and others, are required by Member States of companies within the meaning of the second paragraph of Article 58 of the Treaty, in respect of the formation of public limited liability companies and the maintenance and alteration of their capital, with a view to making such safeguards equivalent (77/91/EEC), OJ 1977 L26/1; recast as Directive 2012/30/EU of the European Parliament and of the Council of 25 October 2012 on coordination of safeguards which, for the protection of the interests of members and others, are required by Member States of companies within the meaning of the second paragraph of Article 54 of the Treaty on the Functioning of the European Union, in respect of the formation of public limited liability companies and the maintenance and alteration of their capital, with a view to making such safeguards equivalent (Recast), OJ EU 14.11.2012 L315/74.

[5] Directive 2012/17/EU of the European Parliament and of the Council of 13 June 2012 amending Council Directive 89/666/EEC, and Directives 2005/56/EC and 2009/101/EC of the European Parliament and of the Council as regards the interconnection of central, commercial and companies registers, OJ EU 16.6.2012 L156/1; with Commission Implementing Regulation (EU) 2015/884 of 8 June 2015 establishing technical specifications and procedures required for the system of interconnection of registers established by Directive 2009/101/EC of the European Parliament and of the Council (Text with EEA relevance) OJ EU 10.6.2015 L144/1.

[6] Directive (EU) 2017/1132 of the European Parliament and of the Council of 14 June 2017 relating to certain aspects of company law (codification) OJ EU 30.6.2017 L169/46. As part of the EU Company Law Package, the Commission has proposed significant changes with a view to the complete digitalization of the incorporation and disclosure process; European Commission, Proposal for a Directive of the European Parliament and of the Council amending Directive (EU) 2017/1132 as regards the use of digital tools and processes in company law COM(2018) 239 final (Digitalisation Proposal).

[7] S Grundmann, *European Company Law* (2nd edn, Intersentia 2012) 146–7.

[8] P Leleux, 'Corporation Law in the United States and in the EEC' (1968) 5 Common Market Law Review 133, 147, 153.

A. Incorporation

As a remnant of the old idea that incorporation is a privilege conferred by the state, general incorporation requires a formal process that company promoters[9] have to go through and at the end of which the company or corporation emerges as a separate legal entity. Since investors will have access only to the corporate property, a certain degree of publicity is required in order to facilitate a clear attribution of assets and liabilities to a specific corporate entity. Disclosure is therefore an important element of the incorporation process, and remains significant throughout a company's entire lifecycle. Traditionally, there have been significant differences as regards the incorporation procedures in our common law and civil law jurisdictions.[10] The former rely on fast and easy processes involving merely the filing of the right documents with a state official upon which a certificate of incorporation will be issued and the company comes into being. The civil law procedures are generally more onerous, involving greater scrutiny of the documentation submitted and are much more concerned with the concept of legal capital and the raising of capital contributions.[11] Directive (EU) 2017/1132 harmonizes incorporation only in respect of disclosure requirements (and the raising of the initial capital).[12] The substantive requirements of incorporation remain, by and large, regulated by national laws.[13] The more complex and onerous the incorporation process in any particular jurisdiction, the greater the propensity for defects that may affect the validity of incorporation. This is a further aspect of the incorporation process harmonized by Directive (EU) 2017/1132. Third parties must be able to rely on the information disclosed and should not be faced with a situation where their contractual counterparty is subsequently held to be non-existent. This is meant to strengthen the stability of cross-border transactions with a view to enhancing the internal market. Finally, the longer the incorporation process takes until completion, the more likely that the company promoters may enter into pre-incorporation contracts on behalf of the company in formation. In this respect, Directive (EU) 2017/1132 seeks to provide a third party contracting with a company during the pre-incorporation phase with an identifiable debtor, regardless of the outcome of the incorporation process.

I. Incorporation processes

Whereas in the United States and, to a lesser extent, in the UK the processes for the incorporation of publicly held corporations/public companies and closely held corporations/private companies are essentially the same, German law and French law exhibit some differences as regards the formation processes for public and private companies, which are perceived as different types of entity in these jurisdictions.[14] In practice, almost all companies are formed as private companies, necessitating a conversion where the company subsequently contemplates issuing securities to the public. In respect of public and private

[9] The concept of 'promoter' encompasses a wide range of persons that are involved in the formation and organization of a company, including the initial shareholders and directors of a company, but also professional incorporation agents who cease to participate in the company after its formation; P Davis and S Worthington, *Gower and Davies' Principles of Modern Company Law* (10th edn, Sweet & Maxwell 2016) 102–104 (paras 5-2–5-5); J Choper, J Coffee, and R Gilson, *Cases and Materials on Corporations* (8th edn, Aspen Publishers 2013) 282. In civil law countries, the emphasis seems to be more on the initial shareholders.

[10] A Cahn and D Donald, *Comparative Company Law* (CUP 2010) 131.

[11] See Chapter 9 for details.

[12] But see the Commission's Digitalisation Proposal (n 6), providing that Member States must provide rules that allow the registration of companies to be effectuated fully online. The raising of capital is discussed in Chapter 9B.

[13] See further M Schillig, 'Chapter 2: General Company Law Provisions: Establishment and Functioning of Limited Liability Companies' in C Gerner-Beuerle (ed), *Gore-Browne on EU Company Law* (Jordan Publishing 2017).

[14] M Andenas and F Wooldridge, *European Comparative Company Law* (CUP 2009) 52; French (n 1) 58.

limited companies the impact upon the incorporation process of Directive (EU) 2017/1132 is limited to requiring the Member States to provide for either preventive administrative or judicial control at the time of formation of a company or certification in due legal form of the instruments of constitution, the company statutes, and any amendments to these documents.[15] National law must further provide that the respective control or certification bodies can examine the company documents and can refuse registration if there are grounds for nullity as defined in the Directive.[16] National law may impose additional restrictions on registration, but does not have to do so.[17] For the formation of public companies, Directive (EU) 2017/1132 postulates further requirements.[18] We begin our survey of national incorporation procedures with our European jurisdictions, in descending order of complexity, reflecting the modern trend towards reducing the burden of incorporation, followed by the laws of the United States.

1. Germany

Despite a largely similar trajectory, the incorporation processes and formalities for private companies and public companies differ significantly. Conceptualized for large business enterprises with capital market access, the incorporation process for public companies has traditionally been particularly complex and rigid.[19] This is attributable, not least, to the extensively regulated initial legal capital requirements, which also apply on a subsequent capital increase.[20] From its inception, the formation of the private company (GmbH) for small and medium-sized businesses has been more flexible and cheaper, although in international comparison it can still be rather complex and lengthy. Faced with stiff regulatory competition, in particular through incorporations in the UK enabled by the CJEU's case law on freedom of establishment,[21] reform legislation of 2008[22] introduced a simplified incorporation procedure available for companies with three members or less and also the entrepreneur company (with limited liability) as a variation on the GmbH theme, with a much reduced minimum capital.[23] In absolute terms, incorporations of private companies are much more frequent, although ever since the liberalization of the law for small public companies and the introduction of the single member public company in 1994[24] incorporations of public companies have become more relevant.[25] The provisions on public company formation also apply where a private company or partnership is converted into a public company,[26] usually with a view to gaining access to capital markets. Despite the differences in the incorporation processes, the principles relating to the different stages of formation ('pre-formation company', 'pre-company'), developed by

[15] Directive (EU) 2017/1132, Art 10. The Commission's Digitalisation Proposal (n 6) requires Member States to lay down detailed rules for the online registration of companies with a view to ensuring that all the benefits of incorporation can be achieved by following a pure online process without any involvement of public authorities and officials. This would be compulsory only for private companies; for public companies, Member States would be able to opt out of the requirement (Art 13f).

[16] Directive (EU) 2017/1132, Art 11.

[17] Grundmann (n 7) 153.

[18] Directive (EU) 2017/1132, Art 3: The statutes or the instrument of incorporation must contain at least the following information: (i) the type and name of the company; (ii) its objects; (iii) the amount of the subscribed capital; and if it has an authorized capital, also the amount thereof; (iv) the rules governing the number and the procedure for appointing members to the bodies responsible for managing and representing the company and the allocation of powers among these bodies, albeit only to the extent that these issues are not determined by national law; and (v) the duration of the company if it is not indefinite. Article 4 of Directive (EU) 2017/1132 provides for further information to be given upon formation and throughout the life of the company and qualifies the general disclosure regime in respect of public companies.

[19] C Windbichler, *Gesellschaftsrecht* (24th edn, Beck 2017) 286 (§25 para 21).

[20] See Chapter 9B and D for details.

[21] See Chapter 2C.II for details.

[22] *Gesetz zur Reform des GmbH-Rechts und zur Bekämpfung von Missbrächen (MoMiG)* of 23 October 2008.

[23] GmbHG §5a.

[24] *Gesetz für kleine Aktiengesellschaften und zur Deregulierung des Aktienrechts* of 2 August 1994.

[25] Windbichler (n 19) 286 (§25 para 21).

[26] UmwG §197.

case law, apply, by and large, to both types of company, with much greater relevance for GmbHs, which are more frequent and usually more thinly capitalized, making them more prone to failure.[27]

(a) Private company (GmbH)

A private company may be incorporated by one or more persons for any lawful purpose,[28] including, but not limited to, the conduct of a business or a trading activity. With the signing of the articles of association by all promoters in notarized form, the company emerges[29] in form of the pre-GmbH. The pre-GmbH is not (yet) a legal person but a form of collective ownership with its own organizational structure.[30] On the basis of the articles of association in the prescribed form, the members are committed to contribute to the company's legal capital and to establish the governance structure of the pre-GmbH.[31] The GmbH with separate legal personality (and limited liability) comes into existence (only) with its registration in the commercial register,[32] which marks the end of the incorporation process. Prior to the execution of the articles of association in notarized form, the future promoters may constitute a 'pre-formation company', with the purpose of pursuing the incorporation of the GmbH.[33] Unless such an agreement is also notarized, its participants are not obliged to participate in the subsequent incorporation process.

The articles of association are an organizational contract and require notarization,[34] that is, the entire document has to be read by a notary in front of the promoters who then have to sign it in front of the notary before the latter confirms the signatures. One of the innovations of the 2008 reforms was the introduction of a simplified incorporation procedure, which may only be used where the envisaged company will have no more than three members and only one director. In this case, the model articles, attached as an annex to the GmbHG, may form the articles of association; additional provisions that deviate from the statutory outline may not be included.[35] The model articles still require notarization, and seem to be suitable mainly for single member GmbHs and entrepreneur companies (with limited liability).[36] The articles of association must contain[37] the name of the company (Firma) with an indication of its legal nature (GmbH),[38] and further the 'seat' of the company. This is the 'registered office', which must be situated in Germany.[39] By contrast, the company's head office or principal place of business may be situated abroad. This seeks to facilitate corporate mobility within the EU, in accordance with the CJEU's case law on freedom of establishment. The articles must also determine the company's objects, which must be sufficiently specific.[40] The articles must further contain the amount of the company's share capital as well as the quantity and nominal value of the shares that each member takes in return for a contribution to the share capital. Individual members may take more than one share. The nominal value of each share must be in full euros; individual shares may have different nominal values. However, the aggregate of the nominal values of all shares must be equal to the amount of the share capital, which must be at least €25,000[41] (unless the company is formed as an

[27] Windbichler (n 19) 215–16 (§21 para 16); F Kübler and H-D Assmann, *Gesellschaftsrecht* (6th edn, CF Müller Verlag 2006) 377; C Kersting, *Die Vorgesellschaft im europäischen Gesellschaftsrecht* (Carl Heymanns Verlag 2000) 9–10.

[28] GmbHG §1. [29] AktG §29 by way of analogy. [30] BGHZ 80, 129, 135 (1981).

[31] Windbichler (n 19) 216–17 (§21 para 18); Kübler and Assmann (n 27) 377. [32] GmbHG §11(1).

[33] BGHZ 91, 148, 151 (1984).

[34] GmbHG §2(1). In its current form, the Commission's Digitalisation Proposal (n 6) allows for the retention of the notarization requirement: when laying down detailed rules for the online registration of companies, Member States may provide for the involvement of notaries (Art 13f(4)(e)).

[35] GmbHG §2(2). [36] Windbichler (n 19) 210 (§21 para 3).

[37] See GmbHG §3(1) for a list of the minimum requirements. [38] ibid §4. [39] ibid §4a.

[40] 'The conduct of a trading activity of any kind' would be insufficient in this respect; by contrast, 'the management of the company's own assets' is frequently used where companies are incorporated as shelf companies for subsequent usage; Windbichler (n 19) 211 (§21 para 4).

[41] GmbHG §5.

entrepreneur company with limited liability). Where shares are taken in return for non-cash contributions, the articles have to specify the non-cash assets and the nominal value of the shares in return for which the non-cash contribution is to be made. Moreover, the members have to draw up a report that explains the basis for the valuation of the non-cash assets and their adequacy as a non-cash contribution.[42] Where the valuation of the non-cash asset in the articles significantly exceeds the actual value, the register court must decline registration.[43] In addition to these mandatory items, the articles may include further provisions in particular on ancillary obligations of the members, governance structures that deviate from the statutory scheme, pre-emptive rights, restrictions on the transferability of shares, etc.

The entrepreneur company (with limited liability) is an innovation introduced by the 2008 reform package. The key feature is that the share capital is below the statutory minimum of €25,000.[44] Given that the company needs at least one member with at least one share with a nominal value in full euros, the company may be formed with a share capital of as little as €1. Non-cash contributions are ruled out. The company may be formed through the simplified procedure (relying on the model articles) or through the normal process. The entrepreneur company may become a normal GmbH (without a conversion) by increasing the share capital to or beyond the statutory minimum.[45] This is facilitated by the fact that the statutory reserve into which a quarter of annual profits have to be channelled may only be used, in addition to a compensation for annual losses or losses carried forward from previous years, to effectuate a (nominal) increase of share capital by capitalization of accumulated reserves.[46]

The GmbH must have at least one director.[47] The directors are appointed either in the articles of association or in a subsequent shareholders' resolution.[48] During the formation process, the directors receive the member's contributions and apply for the company's registration in the commercial register to the court in the district of which the company has its registered office.[49] The application for registration may only be made where cash contributions of at least one-quarter of the nominal value of each share has been paid in. Non-cash considerations have to be transferred in full and in a way so that they are at the free disposal of the directors. Overall, prior to the application for registration the paid in cash and transferred non-cash considerations together must at least reach the amount of €12,500.[50] For the entrepreneur company (with limited liability) all cash contributions must have been paid in full.[51] The application for registration must be accompanied by the articles of association; proof of the appointment of the directors (if not contained in the articles); a list of the members, signed by the applicant, containing name, date of birth, and address, as well as nominal values, the consecutive numbers of each of the shares to which the shareholders have subscribed and the relevant percentage interest in the share capital conferred by the nominal value of each respective share; in case of non-cash contributions, the contracts that have been concluded in order to effectuate them as well as the report concerning their adequacy; and further documentation confirming that the value of the non-cash consideration is at least equal to the nominal value of the respective shares. The application must contain a statement of compliance that the contributions required to be made prior to application have been received and the directors have to give assurance that there are no legal reasons that would prevent their lawful appointment. The application must further contain a domestic business address of the company, as well as the nature and extent of the directors' authority

42 ibid §5(4). Where, at the time of the application for registration, the value of the non-cash contribution is lower than the nominal value of the relevant shares, the respective member has to pay the difference in cash; ibid §9.

43 ibid §9c(1).

44 ibid §5a. The amount of the share capital can be freely determined in the articles, but must be below the €25,000 minimum. Otherwise, the company will be a regular GmbH.

45 ibid §5a(5). 46 ibid §5a(3). 47 ibid §6(1). 48 ibid §6(3). 49 ibid §7(1).

50 ibid §7(2). 51 ibid §5a(2).

to represent the company.[52] The register court ascertains whether the incorporation process and the application for registration are free from defects. The standard of assessment for the substantive incorporation requirements is limited to the mandatory content of the articles of association, a breach of provisions that aim to protect the company's creditors or the public interest, or the breach of which renders the articles void. If the articles fall short on any of these grounds, the register court has to reject the application for registration, in particular where the actual value of non-cash contributions is lower than the value stated in the articles.[53] With registration the GmbH comes into existence;[54] and most formation defects will be cured.

The notary and court fees for a GmbH with the minimum share capital will amount to approximately €1,250. The registration process may take from a few days up to several weeks if the register court has to perform extensive examinations of documents in respect of non-cash contributions.[55] As an alternative, company promoters may acquire a shelf company or reactivate a defunct company. Upon registration of the required changes in terms of company name and/or directors, the provisions on incorporation apply by way of analogy, in particular the provisions on share capital and cash and non-cash contributions.[56]

(b) Public company (AG)

The incorporation of a public company is more complex and more tightly regulated; the overall trajectory is, however, quite similar. The AktG distinguishes between the standard incorporation procedure and the qualified incorporation procedure,[57] which applies, in particular, where non-cash considerations are involved.[58] Similar to the law on the GmbH, the company emerges as pre-AG with the completion of the articles of association in the prescribed form and the AG comes into existence as a separate legal person with registration.[59] The different steps on the way are somewhat more onerous, in particular for a qualified incorporation.

An AG may be formed by one or more persons.[60] The articles of association (constitution) have to be established through a notarial document consisting of the actual articles and the so-called statement of subscription.[61] The latter identifies the promoters, the par value (or for accountable par value shares:[62] the quantity and issue price), and, where applicable, the classes of shares that each promoter subscribes to take, as well as the amount of the paid in share capital.[63] The articles must determine[64] the company's name with a specification of the legal form (AG)[65] and its registered office, which must be within Germany,[66] whereas its head office or principal place of business may be abroad. The articles must further contain an objects clause, which in case of a manufacturing and trading company has to specify sufficiently the products to be manufactured and goods to be traded.[67] The articles also stipulate the amount of the share capital which must be at least €50,000[68] and the way the share capital is divided into shares.[69] The articles have to contain provisions on the number of the

[52] ibid §8. [53] ibid §9c. [54] ibid §11(1).

[55] F Dornseifer, 'Germany' in F Dornseifer (ed), *Corporate Business Forms in Europe* (Sellier 2005) 211, 269 (paras 120–1).

[56] BGHZ 153, 158 (2002).

[57] Windbichler (n 19) 304 (§26 para 1); Kübler and Assmann (n 27) 187.

[58] AktG §27. This provision applies to two slightly different situations: (i) subscribers pay for shares in consideration other than cash, notably by transferring to the company assets such as IP rights, real property or (part of) a business; (ii) the company acquires from subscribers or third parties existing or future assets, notably equipment or facilities, in exchange for a purchase price. Both situations are treated in the same way. In the following, the term 'non-cash contribution' will be used as shorthand to refer to both situations.

[59] Windbichler (n 19) 306 (§26 para 4); Kübler and Assmann (n 27) 189. [60] AktG §2.

[61] ibid §23(1). [62] On this terminology see Chapter 9A. [63] AktG §23(2).

[64] ibid §23(3). [65] ibid §4. [66] ibid §5. [67] ibid §23(3) No 2. [68] ibid §7.

[69] The shares may be either par value shares, in which case the articles have to determine the different par values (if any) and the quantity of shares for each par value; or, alternatively, accountable par value shares where their quantity has to be specified. If there is more than one class of shares, the articles have to specify the different classes and the quantity of shares of each class; and, further, whether the shares are to bearer or to order; ibid §23(3) No 4 and No 5.

members of the management board or the rules on how to determine that number, as well as in what form the company effectuates its announcements.[70] The provisions of the AktG are mandatory and the articles can deviate therefrom only to the extent that this is explicitly permitted; additional and supplementary provisions are possible except where the statutory rules are exclusive.[71] In case of a qualified incorporation involving non-cash contributions, the articles have to specify the non-cash assets to be contributed; the person who contributes the asset; and the par value (or quantity) of the shares for which the non-cash contribution is to be made.[72] If the non-cash contribution is not specified in the articles the member remains liable for a contribution in cash, which may be reduced, however, by the actual value of the non-cash asset that the company has received.[73]

The company emerges, as pre-AG, with the subscription of all its shares.[74] This occurs upon the completion of the articles of association and statement of subscription in notarial form. The subscribers become the incorporators[75] and have to appoint a first supervisory board and initial auditor. The appointment requires notarization; the provisions on employee representation do generally not apply to the first supervisory board, which will remain in office only until the end of the (first) general meeting, which decides on their discharge for the first financial year. The first supervisory board appoints the first management board.[76] Where, in case of a qualified incorporation, an operational business is to be contributed by way of a non-cash contribution, the promoters only appoint the members of the supervisory board that, under the applicable employee participation statute, are appointable by the general meeting. Immediately following the contribution or acquisition of the business, the management board announces the applicable provisions that determine the composition of the supervisory board and the existing members are supplemented (or partially replaced) by employee representatives,[77] ensuring their future input.

The promoters have to draw up a written report on the formation process, describing the essential underlying facts, which account for the adequacy of the value attributed to non-cash contributions. The report must further explain whether and to what extent shares have been subscribed on behalf of members of the management or supervisory boards and whether and to what extent board members have obtained special benefits.[78] The incorporation process then has to be audited by the members of the management board and supervisory board. Where a board member has participated as promoter, obtained shares or other benefits, or where the incorporation involves non-cash contributions, the incorporation process has to be examined by specific incorporation auditors. In the first two cases (shares or other benefits), the audit may be carried out by the notary who notarized the articles of association; otherwise, an audit by a qualified accountant is required.[79] The audit has to cover in particular whether the promoters' statements relating to the subscription of shares, the contributions to the share capital, and on non-cash contributions are correct and complete, and whether the value of non-cash contributions is at least equal to the nominal value of the shares plus any premium. Every audit requires a written report, describing the relevant non-cash assets and the valuation methods that have been applied. The reports are submitted to the supervisory board and the court, and are available to the public.[80] Prior to the application for registration, at least one-quarter of the par value (or accountable par) plus any premium must have been paid in for each share; non-cash contributions have to be made in full or, where it involves the transfer of an asset to the company such transfer must be due to be carried out within five years of the company's registration. Any contribution received must be at the free disposal of the management board.[81]

[70] ibid §23(3) No 6. [71] ibid §23(5).

[72] Relevant non-cash assets may only be assets with an ascertainable commercial value; not, however, an undertaking to provide services.

[73] AktG §27. [74] ibid §29. [75] ibid §28. [76] ibid §30. [77] ibid §31.

[78] ibid §32. [79] ibid §33. [80] ibid §34. [81] ibid §§36(2), 36a.

All the promoters, the members of the management board, and the members of the supervisory board together have to file the application for registration.[82] The application must contain a statement that the required contributions prior to the application for registration have been made. The members of the management board must give assurance that there are no legal impediments to their appointment. The application has to specify in what way the members of the management board have authority to represent the company. It must be accompanied by the notarial documents containing the articles of association and the statement of subscription; the contracts relating to non-cash contributions as well as a calculation of the cost of incorporation; the documents concerning the appointment of the members of the supervisory board and the management board; the promoters' incorporation report and the incorporation audit reports of management board, supervisory board, and incorporation auditors.[83] The register court has to ascertain whether the incorporation process and the application for registration are in order. The court may reject the application where it transpires that the promoters' incorporation report or the board members' incorporation audit reports are incomplete, incorrect, or do not comply with the statutory provisions. The same applies where the actual value of non-cash considerations is significantly lower than the par value (or accountable par) plus any premium of the relevant shares. Other than that, the court may reject the application only where the articles do not comply with mandatory prerequisites prescribing their content, are in breach of provisions that are aimed at the protection of the company's creditors or the public interest, or suffer from a defect which renders the articles void.[84] The AG comes into existence as a separate legal person with its registration;[85] most defects of the incorporation process will then be cured. Only on registration do the actual shares come into being and may be issued and sold to the public.[86] The cost for forming an AG with the minimum share capital of €50,000 are approximately €2,000. The incorporation process can take from a few weeks up to several months if the register court has to perform extensive examinations.[87]

The provisions on incorporation apply, and are perhaps more important, where a partnership type entity or GmbH is converted into an AG.[88] Such conversion requires a resolution of the members,[89] based on a conversion report, which explains in legal and economic terms the conversion and the future participation of the members under the new organizational form.[90] The resolution for conversion has to be notarized and requires a 75per cent majority of voting members where a private company is being converted or unanimity in case of a partnership type entity.[91] It must specify in particular the share capital and its division into shares, as well as the allocation of shares to the members.[92] The resolution has to be filed and the conversion takes effect upon registration.[93] The entity as the holder of legal rights and obligations continues;[94] only its organizational form changes from whatever it was before into an AG.

2. *France*

Although different entity types, the processes and formalities for the incorporation of a private company (SARL), and of a public company (SA) are fairly similar under French law. However, the different functions of these entity types necessitate a number of substantive deviations. In particular, an SA may be incorporated either as a publicly held SA with an initial public offering during the formation phase,[95] or as a privately held SA without a public

[82] ibid §36(1). [83] ibid §37. [84] ibid §38. [85] ibid §41(1).
[86] ibid §41(4). [87] Dornseifer (n 55) 226 (para 25).
[88] UmwG §197; also Kübler and Assmann (n 27) 187. [89] UmwG §193. [90] ibid §192.
[91] ibid §§217, 240. [92] ibid §194. [93] ibid §§198, 202. [94] ibid §202(1) No 1.
[95] Com Art L225-2–L225-11.

offering.[96] Other notable differences are largely attributable to different minimum capital requirements and governance structures. Since 2003, and as a reaction to the CJEU's case law on freedom of establishment,[97] the SARL is no longer subject to a minimum capital requirement,[98] or rather the minimum capital may be as low as €1, where previously it was €7,500. Both SARL and SA (in either form) obtain separate legal personality with their registration in the commercial and company register.[99] Prior to that, a 'company in formation' may ensue upon the completion of the articles of association in the prescribed form,[100] or perhaps earlier, depending on the applicable incorporation process. Although the 'company in formation' cannot itself be the holder of company property or be subject to obligations, it is nevertheless important for the allocation of liabilities incurred during the formation phase.[101] The comprehensive reform project Loi PACTE (Project de loi relative à la croissance et la transformation des entrepries) envisages changes to the incorporation process, notably the creation of a single online platform for corporate formalities and online registration.

(a) Private company (SARL)

A SARL may be formed by one or more persons, but cannot have more than 100 shareholders.[102] In accordance with general principles, incorporation requires a contract[103] between the parties by which they commit to pursue a common purpose, make contributions to its attainment, and share in the profits and losses.[104] The company is established at the time when all promoters have signed the articles of association, which creates the promoters' obligations to contribute to the company's share capital. However, only with registration will the company obtain its separate legal personality. The articles as the company's constitution may take the form of a notarial deed or may simply be signed by the promoters. They must identify[105] the entity type and its business name, which must be accompanied by an indication of the type of company (SARL).[106] The articles must further stipulate the company's duration, which must not exceed ninety-nine years; and the company's registered office, which must be located in France in order for French law to apply.[107] The objects of the company must be sufficiently specified.[108] The articles must further determine the amount of the company's registered capital, which is divided into equal shares.[109] All the shares must be subscribed by the promoters and the articles must contain a list of all subscribers and their respective shareholdings.[110] For non-cash contributions, the articles must contain the valuation of each contribution, based on the valuation report of an independent expert, which must be attached to the articles.[111] In addition to these mandatory provisions, the articles should contain rules on the appointment and the powers of the managers, on the transfer of shares, the decision-making of the shareholders, and all other provisions that are necessary for the effective running of the company.[112] The initial managers as the representatives of the company may be appointed in the articles or, following the signing of the articles, through a shareholder resolution.[113] The founders and initial managers are responsible for applying for the company's registration, either with the Centre for Enterprise Formalities (*centre de*

[96] Com Art L225-12–L226-16-1. [97] See Chapter 2C.II. [98] Com Art L223-2.
[99] Com Art L210-6.
[100] M Germain and V Magnier, *Les sociétés commerciales* (21st edn, LGDJ 2014) paras 1563–70; P Merle, *Droit commerciale: sociétés commerciales* (22nd edn, Dalloz 2018/2019) para 97.
[101] Kersting (n 27) 88–91.
[102] Com Art L223-1. If, over the course of the company's lifecycle, its membership increases beyond the 100 member mark, it shall be dissolved at the end of a one-year period, unless during the year the membership falls back to 100 or lower; Com Art L223-3.
[103] Or a unitary act of will in case of a company formed by a single person; on the *entreprise unipersonnelle à responsabilité limitée (EURL)* see Germain and Magnier (n 100) paras 1868–76; Merle (n 100) paras 275–90.
[104] Civ Art 1832. [105] Com Art L210-2. [106] Com Art L223-1. [107] Com Art L210-3.
[108] Germain and Magnier (n 100) paras 1558. [109] Com Art L223-2. [110] Com Art L223-7.
[111] Com Art L223-9.
[112] C Della Berta, 'France' in F Dornseifer (ed), *Corporate Business Forms in Europe* (Sellier 2005) 169, 198 (para 182).
[113] Andenas and Wooldridge (n 14) 63.

formalités des entreprises) or with the secretariat of the commercial court. Either way, application can be made electronically.

Prior to registration, non-cash considerations must have been provided in full; of contributions in cash at least 20 per cent of the nominal value of each share must have been paid up, with the remainder being payable within five years of registration.[114] The money paid up under these provisions cannot be withdrawn until the company has been registered and the incorporation process is complete.[115] The application for registration must be accompanied by copies of the articles of association (the original if not in a notarial deed) and the documents appointing the managers (where not included in the articles), photocopies of the passports of the managers, documentary evidence that the company either owns or rents the premises where the registered office is situated, a statement by the managers that they have not been found guilty of any criminal offence, and documentation of the subscription of shares and the required pre-registration contributions. A statement of compliance with the necessary procedural requirements must also be submitted. Following the public announcement of the fact of the company's formation and of its articles of association in a newspaper designated as competent to publish legal announcements, the competent official verifies whether the company has been formed in accordance with the prerequisites of the incorporation process and the formalities of the Commercial and Companies Register.[116] Where this is the case, the company will be registered, upon which it emerges as a separate legal person.[117] Registration will then be publicly announced in the *Official Bulletin for Civil and Commercial Announcements* (*BODACC*).[118] Overall, the process may be completed within a few days.

(b) Public company (SA)

Under the Commercial Code, the incorporation of an SA with an initial public offering (publicly held SA) is conceptually the standard case, although in practice an initial public offering during the formation phase is rare. In any case, an SA cannot be set up with less than seven shareholders.[119] The formation process of a publicly held SA is by necessity a multi-step process.[120] One or more promoters draw up and sign the draft articles of association and deposit them with the Commercial and Companies Register of the district where the company's registered office is situated. Subsequently, the articles are publicly announced.[121] Having complied with these formalities an initial public offering may be made, as a result of which the company's share capital of at least €225,000 must be fully subscribed.[122] Subscription is effectuated through a subscription form in which the future shareholder subscribes to a certain quantity of shares in exchange for a specified contribution.[123] Non-cash contributions must be provided immediately and in full; the provision of services is not suitable as a contribution. Cash contributions must be paid up to at least 50 per cent of the par value of the respective shares, with the balance payable within five years of the company's registration.[124] The funds so raised, together with a list of the subscribers specifying the amounts paid by each of them, are deposited with an appointed depository, which evidences the subscriptions and contributions through a certificate.[125] When the certificate has been issued, the promoters call an initial general meeting of the subscribers, which determines that the capital has been fully subscribed and that the required contributions have been made. It further decides on the approval of the articles of association and appoints the first directors where the company is formed with a one-tier board structure, or the members of the supervisory board under a two-tier board structure, who then appoint the members of the management

[114] Com Art L223-7. [115] Com Art L223-8.
[116] Com Art L210-7; Germain and Magnier (n 100) para 1577. [117] Com Art L210-6.
[118] Germain and Magnier (n 100) para 1807. [119] Com Art L225-1.
[120] Germain and Magnier (n 100) para 1929. [121] Com Art L225-2. [122] Com Art L225-3.
[123] Com Art L225-4. [124] Com Art L225-3. [125] Com Art L225-5; L225-6.

board.[126] The initial general meeting decides further on the valuation of non-cash contributions and the granting of special benefits to members or third parties. For that purpose, one or more experts have to be appointed by the promoters. The experts have to assess the value of the non-cash contributions and any special benefits and file a report with the Register.[127] Two copies of the articles of association have to be deposited with the Register, as well as a statement of compliance with the statutory formalities, the documents appointing the directors or members of the supervisory and management boards, the certificate of deposit, a list of the subscribers, and the valuation report for non-cash contributions. Following the public announcement of the articles, the company will be registered on the basis of a specific administrative form for the purposes of registration to which birth certificates of all board members have to be attached. The SA emerges as a separate legal entity with registration.[128]

The incorporation process of an SA without an initial public offering (closely held SA) is much simpler and the formation is instantaneous.[129] The draft articles of association are deposited with the Register and publicly announced. Thereafter, all the shares are subscribed, forming the share capital which must reach at least the statutory minimum of €37,000. The provisions dealing with the necessary pre-registration contributions, non-cash contributions, and special benefits, including valuation requirements are essentially the same as in the case of the formation of a publicly held SA.[130] All subscribers sign the articles of association, which have to be in notarial form only where any non-cash contributions include real property. Following the deposit of the articles accompanied by the usual documentation with the Register and the obligatory public announcement, the SA will be registered and obtain separate legal personality. Completion of the incorporation process normally takes around one or two weeks, but may be accomplished within three days in case of urgency. The total cost of incorporation is about €500.[131]

3. *United Kingdom*

The overwhelming majority of business corporations or companies are formed by registration under the Companies Act 2006.[132] The formation process pursuant to Part 2 of the Act is essentially the same for both public and private companies (limited by shares). The minimum capital requirement for public companies necessitates certain additional prerequisites before a public company may start trading. However, most companies start out as private companies;[133] in order to be able to issue securities to the public, a subsequent conversion into a public company will be necessary. The public authority in charge of the registration process is the Registrar of Companies, exercising its powers through Companies House as an executive agency of the Department for Business, Energy and Industrial Strategy (BEIS).[134]

One or more persons may form a company by subscribing their names to a memorandum of association and complying with the registration requirements pursuant to Part 2 of the Companies Act 2006.[135] The memorandum of association is a simple document stating that the subscribers wish to form a company under the Act, that they agree to become members of the company, and to take at least one share each. The memorandum must be in the prescribed form and authenticated by each subscriber.[136] Very simple templates are available through the Companies House website.[137] The memorandum of association must then be delivered to the Registrar of Companies, together with an application for registration

126 Com Art L225-7. 127 Com Art L225-8. 128 Germain and Magnier (n 100) paras 2005–9.
129 ibid para 2011. 130 Com Art L225-12–L225-15.
131 Germain and Magnier (n 100) paras 2011–17; A Garnier and V Buseine, 'VIII. France' in K van Hulle and H Gesell (eds), *European Corporate Law* (Nomos 2006) 141, 142 (para 9).
132 On companies formed by Royal Charter or Act of Parliament see Chapter 1A.I.1.
133 Davis and Worthington (n 9) 82 (para 4-11); French (n 1) 4.
134 Davis and Worthington (n 9) 77 (para 4-4); French (n 1) 40–1; see also the Contracting Out (Functions in Relation to the Registration of Companies) Order 1995 (SI 1995/1013).
135 Companies Act 2006, s 7. 136 ibid s 8.
137 https://www.gov.uk/limited-company-formation/memorandum-and-articles-of-association.

containing the required information and documentation and a 'statement of compliance'.[138] The application must state the proposed name of the company; whether its registered office is to be in England and Wales, in Scotland, or Northern Ireland;[139] whether the liability of the members of the company is to be limited and, if so, whether it is limited by shares or by guarantee; and whether the company is to be a private company or a public company.[140] Following the Small Business, Enterprise and Employment Act 2015, the application must contain a statement of the type of company it is to be and its intended principal business activities, both defined by reference to predetermined classification schemes.[141] For companies with a share capital, in particular private and public companies limited by shares, the application must contain a statement of capital and initial shareholdings.[142] It must further contain the prescribed information for identifying the subscribers to the memorandum, and must state the number, nominal value, and classes of shares taken by each subscriber upon formation and the amount paid up and outstanding on each share, including the share premium (if any).[143] The application for registration must also contain a statement of the company's proposed officers, including the required particulars of the person or persons who are to be the first director or directors[144] of the company and the first secretary (if any)[145] of the company.[146] Under the Small Business, Enterprise and Employment Act 2015, the application must also contain a statement of initial significant control;[147] and for private companies the subscribers may give notice of election if they opt to have any registers,[148] including of people with significant control (PSC register), held at Companies House.[149] Finally, the application for registration must state the intended address of the company's registered office, and must contain a copy of the proposed articles of association to the extent that they deviate from the applicable model articles of association.[150] Consequently, where

[138] Companies Act 2006, s 9(1).

[139] Determining the relevant Registrar of Companies the application is to be delivered to.

[140] Companies Act 2006, s 9(2).

[141] ibid s 9(5)(c), (5A), and (5B), as amended by the Small Business, Enterprise and Employment Act 2015, s 93.

[142] Companies Act, s 10; stating the total number of shares to be taken on formation by the subscribers to the memorandum; the aggregate nominal value of these shares; the aggregate amount unpaid on those shares (including a share premium if any); for each class of shares, the prescribed particulars of the rights attached to the shares, the total number of shares of each class and the aggregate nominal value of shares of that class.

[143] Companies Act 2006, ss 9(4)(a) and 10.

[144] Private companies must have at least one director; public companies at least two; Companies Act 2006, s 154.

[145] Having a company secretary is compulsory for public companies only; Companies Act 2006, ss 270, 271.

[146] Companies Act 2006, ss 9(4)(c) and 12. The required particulars are the name, service address, country of residence, nationality, occupation, date of birth, and residential address of directors, and name and address of secretaries; Companies Act 2006, ss 163, 277.

[147] Significant control is defined as holding more than 25% of the shares, or more than 25% of the voting rights in a company, or holding the right to appoint or remove a majority of the board of directors, or holding the right to exercise significant influence or control over the company; Companies Act 2006, Sch 1A Pt 1.

[148] The following registers may be held centrally at Companies House: register of members, of directors and/or directors' residential addresses, of secretaries, and the PSC register; see further French (n 1) 244, 352, 422, 517.

[149] Companies Act 2006, ss 128B(1), 167A(2), 279A(1), and 790X(1).

[150] ibid s 9(5). The information required by Art 3 of Directive (EU) 2017/1132 is contained, not in the memorandum or the articles of association, but in the application for registration, which includes the statement of capital and initial shareholdings and statement of proposed officers. Under the Companies Act 2006, a company no longer needs to stipulate its objects in its constitutional documents. A company's objects will be unrestricted unless specifically limited in its articles; Companies Act 2006, s 31. This would seem to be compatible with Directive (EU) 2017/1132. Art 3(b) merely requires the objects to be stated in the company's constitutional documents if it has an objects clause at all; it does not require the company to have an objects clause in any case; Davis and Worthington (n 9) 173 (para 7-29 n 89). This is also in line with Directive (EU) 2017/1132's rationale of limiting the impact of the *ultra vires* doctrine. There is some uncertainty as to whether Directive (EU) 2017/1132, Art 2(e) has been adequately implemented in the UK. The provision requires that the instrument of incorporation contains information on the allocation of powers among the bodies managing and representing the company. The 'bodies' referred to are the management board and supervisory board under a two-tier board structure as is compulsory for public companies in Germany and optional in France; V Edwards, *EC Company Law* (OUP 1999) 58. It is unclear whether 'bodies' also includes executive and non-executive members of the board of directors under a one-tier board structure or the chief executive officer and the board. If these latter situations were covered, which is perhaps not the most straightforward reading of the provision, it could be argued that implementation is inadequate in the UK because the allocation of powers between executive and non-executive directors is not determined by national law, but is subject to private ordering; see F Wooldridge, *The Harmonisation of Company Law* (Acta Juridica 1978) 327, 335.

the promoters do not register any articles of association the model articles for private or public companies,[151] as the case may be, will apply by default.[152] Conversely, promoters may register a complete set of articles specifically devised for their company and thus explicitly or impliedly exclude the applicable model articles. In practice, promoters will usually rely on the model articles subject to specific amendments tailor made for their needs.[153] The model articles assume a gap-filling role by governing the matters not dealt with in specifically devised articles of association.[154] The application for registration must be accompanied by a statement of compliance stating that the requirements of the Companies Act 2006 as to registration have been complied with; the Registrar may accept this statement as sufficient evidence of compliance.[155]

If the Registrar of Companies is satisfied that the registration requirements are complied with he must register the documents delivered to him[156] and issue a certificate of incorporation stating the name and number of the company, the date of incorporation, the type of company, and whether its registered office is in England and Wales, Scotland, or Northern Ireland.[157] The certificate of incorporation is conclusive evidence that the requirements of the Companies Act 2006 as to registration have been complied with and that the company is duly registered under the Act. From the stated date of incorporation the subscribers to the memorandum of association and any subsequent members form a body corporate capable of exercising all the functions of an incorporated company. The subscribers become shareholders of the shares specified in the statement of capital and initial shareholdings. The persons named in the statement of proposed officers are deemed to have been appointed as directors or officers, as the case may be.[158] The functions of the Registrar of Companies are administrative, rather than judicial.[159] The registration requirements under the Act to be assessed by the Registrar include that a company may only be formed for a lawful purpose,[160] which excludes formation for purposes, which are criminalized, and/or, which are regarded as being contrary to public policy.[161] A refusal to register can be challenged through judicial review.[162]

The vast majority of registrations are effectuated electronically, for which Companies House provides two electronic services. The web incorporation service can be used by anyone for the registration of private companies limited by shares with model articles. The software incorporation service is available to accredited company formation agents only, and can be used for the registration of any type of company and with tailor-made articles of association.[163] Registering a private company limited by shares using the model articles costs £15 and takes 24 hours; same day registration is available for £30.[164] The possibility of electronic registration has reduced the need for incorporation agents to incorporate large numbers of dormant shelf companies the shares of which promoters can buy and vote in order to appoint new directors, change company name and registered office, and then report all of these changes to Companies House.[165] The purchase of a shelf company remains an alternative to incorporation and is available for as little as £45. Pursuant to the Small Business, Enterprise and Employment Act 2015, Companies House and HMRC were tasked with establishing a 'streamlined company registration' process consisting of a system that

[151] Companies (Model Articles) Regulations 2008 (SI 2008/3229), Sch 1: Model Articles for private companies limited by shares; Sch 3: Model Articles for public companies.

[152] Companies Act 2006, s 20.

[153] Davis and Worthington (n 9) 60 (para 3-15).

[154] ibid. There is some tension here with the rule that the articles of association must be contained in a single document; Companies Act 2006, s 18(3)(a).

[155] Companies Act 2006, s 13.

[156] ibid s 14.

[157] ibid s 15.

[158] ibid s 16.

[159] Davis and Worthington (n 9) 92 (para 4-34).

[160] Companies Act 2006, s 7(2).

[161] Davis and Worthington (n 9) 78 (para 4-5 n 10); French (n 1) 47.

[162] French (n 1) 47.

[163] ibid 41, 43.

[164] The Registrar of Companies (Fees) (Companies, Overseas Companies and Limited Liability Partnerships) Regulations 2009 (SI 2009/2101).

[165] Davis and Worthington (n 9) 81 (para 4-9).

allows for the electronic registration of company incorporation documents, as well as the documents for VAT, corporation tax, and PAYE purposes.[166]

In accordance with Directive (EU) 2017/1132, public companies are subject to a minimum capital requirement of £50,000, referring to the nominal value of the company's allotted share capital (the authorized minimum).[167] A newly formed public company, although a body corporate from the date of incorporation, must not do business or exercise any borrowing powers unless it has obtained a trading certificate from the Registrar of Companies.[168] The application for such certificate must state that the nominal value of the company's allotted share capital is not less than the authorized minimum, and specify the amount of the company's preliminary expenses and of any benefits that the promoters have received. It must be accompanied by a statement of compliance, which the Registrar may accept as sufficient evidence that the requirements as regards the authorized minimum have been met.[169] If, on that basis, the Registrar is satisfied that the nominal value of the company's allotted share capital is not less than the authorized minimum he must issue a trading certificate, which is conclusive evidence that the company is entitled to do business and exercise any borrowing powers from the date of issue.[170]

As mentioned above, most public companies are not formed as such but emerge from a conversion (or reregistration) of a private company into a public company. Such a reregistration requires a special resolution (75% majority) that the company should be so reregistered; the company must meet certain preconditions relating to capital requirements; and an application for reregistration, supported by the necessary documentation, has to be made to the Registrar of Companies.[171] In accordance with the provisions on the raising of capital,[172] at the time of the special resolution the nominal value of the company's allotted share capital must not be less than the authorized minimum; and each allotted share must be paid up at least as to one-quarter of the nominal value of the share and the whole of any premium.[173] In line with the provisions on capital maintenance,[174] the company must obtain a balance sheet as at a date not more than seven months before the date of the application, accompanied by an unqualified report on that balance sheet by the company's auditors and a written statement by the auditors that, in their opinion at the balance sheet date, the amount of the company's net assets was not less than the aggregate of its called-up share capital and non-distributable reserves. No negative change must have occurred during the time between the balance sheet date and the application date in this respect.[175] Finally, where the company has allotted shares for consideration otherwise than in cash during the period between the balance sheet date and the special resolution, the relevant provisions on non-cash considerations have to be complied with, requiring an independent valuation of the consideration and a valuer's report as of a date not more than six months before the allotment.[176] In addition to the documentation relating to these capital requirements, the application for reregistration must be accompanied by the special resolution and a copy of the company's articles with the necessary amendments for becoming a public company. The application must further contain a statement of the company's proposed name on reregistration (plc instead of ltd), and a

[166] Small Business, Enterprise and Employment Act 2015, s 15.

[167] Companies Act 2006, s 763(1). The authorized minimum must have been allotted; the amount to be paid up may be as low as 25% of the nominal value of each share allotted. Thus, the actual amount of capital paid in may be only £12,500, accompanied by a right to call on members to pay in the outstanding amount.

[168] ibid s 761(1). [169] ibid s 762. [170] ibid s 761(2) and (4). [171] ibid s 90.

[172] For details see Chapter 9B.

[173] Companies Act 2006, s 91. Where shares have been allotted as fully or partly paid up for a consideration otherwise than in cash consisting of, or including, an undertaking to the company, such undertaking must have been performed or otherwise discharged; alternatively, and provided the undertaking does not consist in doing work or performing services, a contract must stipulate that the undertaking is to be performed within five years from the time of the special resolution.

[174] For details see Chapter 9C. [175] Companies Act 2006, s 92.

[176] ibid s 93; for details on the relevant provisions see Chapter 9B.I.

statement of the company's proposed secretary if it does not already have one. Finally, there is the statement of compliance that the requirements of reregistration have been met.[177] Where the Registrar is satisfied that the company is entitled to be reregistered, for which he may treat the statement of compliance as sufficient evidence, he reregisters the company accordingly and issues an amended certificate of incorporation. By virtue of the issue of the certificate, the company becomes a public company and the changes in the company's name and articles take effect. The certificate is conclusive evidence that the requirements as to reregistration have been complied with.[178]

4. *United States*

In the United States, the general incorporation statutes that allow persons to form a corporation are a matter of state law.[179] Consequently, 'a corporation … is organized under, and governed by, the law of a single jurisdiction, traditionally the corporate law of the State of its incorporation'.[180] A corporation owes its existence solely to a privilege granted by the state in which it is incorporated.[181] It follows that a state may restrict the business activity that a 'foreign' corporation undertakes within its territory and may subject it to authorization requirements (intrastate commerce).[182] On the other hand, pursuant to the Commerce Clause,[183] states are prevented from unduly impeding interstate commerce. Moreover, the 'full faith and credit clause'[184] requires each state to recognize the public acts of every other state, including the act of incorporation under a state general incorporation statute. Consequently, promoters may select the general incorporation law of any of the fifty states for setting up their corporation and may subsequently use it as the vehicle for conducting business across the entire United States. The internal affairs of the corporation—notably the relationships among or between the corporation and its officers, directors, and shareholders—will be governed by the law of the state of incorporation.[185] States in which the corporation's activity reaches a certain threshold may impose further conditions, in particular authorization and taxation requirements. Small local businesses whose activities are in principle confined to a single state will normally incorporate there in order to prevent the additional costs ensuing from having to comply with the regulatory prerequisites of both the state of incorporation and the state of the business activity.[186] For promoters with a view to engaging in multi-state business it makes sense to select an incorporation law that best suits their particular business needs.[187] However, such considerations are much more relevant for mature corporations that seek to reincorporate, often in preparation for a significant corporate transaction such as a merger, takeover, or initial public offering.

With minor differences in substance and terminology across the states, the incorporation process is a simple and straightforward procedure that involves the filing by one or more persons of the articles of incorporation with the competent state official (usually the Secretary of State) upon which the latter issues a certificate of incorporation as conclusive evidence that the corporation has been formed.[188] The minimum content of the articles of incorporation includes the name of the corporation with an appropriate denotation of the corporate entity; the address of the corporation's registered office in the state of incorporation and the name of its registered agent at this address; the nature of the business or purposes to be conducted or promoted, which may be any lawful act or activity for which corporations may be organized; the various

177 Companies Act 2006, s 94. 178 ibid s 96. 179 Chapter 1F.IV.
180 *CTS Corp v Dynamics Corp of America*, 481 U.S. 69, 89 (1987).
181 *Bank of Augusta v Earle*, 38 U.S. 519 (1839). 182 Leleux (n 8) 137–8.
183 US Constitution, Art I §8. 184 ibid Art IV §1.
185 *VantagePoint Venture Partners 1996 v Examen, Inc.*, 871 A.2d 1108, 1113 (Del. 2005).
186 Choper, Coffee, and Gilson (n 9) 229.
187 On the concept of regulatory competition see Chapter 2C.I.
188 W Klein, J Coffee, and F Partnoy, *Business Organization and Finance* (11th edn, Foundation Press 2010) 139.

classes of stock and the respective total number of shares in each class that the corporation is authorized to issue; whether these shares are at par value or no par value, and, if the former, the par value of the shares; the name and mailing address of the promoters ('incorporators'), and/or the names and mailing address of the persons to serve as initial directors.[189] The articles may also contain provisions that define the powers of the corporation, its directors, officers and various classes of shareholders, grant pre-emptive rights to all or certain shareholders, or limit the corporation's duration.[190] However, most matters concerning the corporation's internal governance structure will normally be regulated in its by-laws.[191] The articles of association are signed by the incorporators and delivered to the office of the Secretary of State accompanied by the payment of the required fees and taxes.[192] If everything is in order, which it normally is, the articles will be filed in the designated state office and the certificate of incorporation will be issued as a matter of course.[193] Following the issue of the certificate of incorporation the incorporators or initial directors if named in the articles hold a first meeting where they issue the shares to the corporation's shareholders, adopt the by-laws, appoint the officers, and deal with certain routine matters such as the opening of bank accounts etc.[194]

In practice, filing is done online either through an attorney or an online incorporation firm. These service providers will also deal with the preparation of the by-laws, the calling for, and minuting of, the initial board meeting, and will ensure that the shares are properly issued. Incorporation is relatively cheap and can be a matter of hours. For example, for a Delaware corporation the following fees apply: US$89.00 state tax and filing fee; US$50.00 for a certified copy, US$50.00 for twenty-four-hour filing, US$100.00 for same day filing, US$500.00 for two-hour-filing, and US$1000.00 for one-hour-filing.[195]

Questions and comments:

(1) The incorporation process is a very technical subject that on its surface seems to leave very little room for interesting policy considerations. However, it has been said that '[i]ncorporation procedures ... exemplify the workings of corporate law models ranging from the most formalistic to the most informal, as well as how courts may react differently to problems thrown out by different statutory configurations'.[196] If we look at our survey of different incorporation processes, it is perhaps fair to say that Germany has the most rigid and cumbersome process and state incorporation statutes in the United States have adopted the most *laissez-faire* approach, with France and the UK being situated somewhere in between. Different models of incorporation tell us something about the prevalent variety of capitalism within a society and the general attitude to business activity. A lengthy and cumbersome incorporation process seems to inhibit market access for newcomers who want to do business in corporate form, thus protecting existing firms from competition. Market participants can rely to a greater extent on a vetting process carried out by the state in terms of the respectability of potential contractual counterparties. Where incorporation is fast and easy, firms in corporate form may quickly emerge and disappear. Contractual counterparties have an incentive to protect themselves by looking carefully on who and what they are dealing with. Fast and easy incorporations seem to suggest a more dynamic economy and, over recent decades, the trend has certainly been towards a more flexible model of incorporation. However, it also has its inherent dangers and whether any particular model is inherently superior is perhaps impossible to say. Quick and easy incorporation can easily be used for hiding assets from creditors, for laundering money, and for financing crime and terrorism. These downsides may be addressed by robust laws on fraudulent transfers, directors' and shareholders' liability, or white-collar crime. Whether this is sufficient in any particular case depends on many factors, not

[189] MBCA, §2.02.(a); DGCL, §102(a).
[190] ibid §102(b).
[191] Klein, Coffee, and Partnoy (n 188) 140.
[192] MBCA, §2.01; DGCL, §103.
[193] Choper, Coffee, and Gilson (n 9) 237.
[194] Klein, Coffee, and Partnoy (n 188) 140.
[195] https://corp.delaware.gov/Julyfee.pdf.
[196] Cahn and Donald (n 10) 131.

least the efficiency and efficacy of the relevant court and legal system as a whole. In that sense, the incorporation process raises important policy questions and choices.

(2) In the EU, firms obtain significantly more (debt) funding through bank lending, than from directly accessing capital markets. In the United States, capital market-based financing plays a much greater role than in the EU.[197] To what extent, if at all, can the differences in incorporation processes be linked to these differences in funding practices? The Commission's Action Plan on building a Capital Markets Union seeks to address the imbalance between bank lending and capital market funding, with a view to increasing the latter within the EU.[198] Should this have an impact on incorporation procedures in EU Member States?

II. Disclosure, in particular upon formation

At EU level, only the disclosure aspect of incorporation has been harmonized. Directive (EU) 2017/1132 mandates a disclosure regime for company documents and particulars applicable to public and private companies, albeit enhanced for public companies by the accounting directives.[199] The EU disclosure regime deals with three principal issues: the media of disclosure, the items to be disclosed, and the effects of (non-)disclosure. The regimes applicable under state incorporation laws in the United States appear to be less tightly regulated.

1. Media of disclosure

The Directive's key provision requires each Member State to provide for a file to be opened in a central commercial or companies register for each of the companies registered. All documents and particulars subject to disclosure must be kept in the file or entered in the register and the subject matter of any entry in the register must appear in the file.[200] Since 1 January 2007, Member States must provide for registration in electronic form as an alternative to registration in paper form, and all information on the register must also be kept in electronic form.[201] For now, the documents and particulars subject to disclosure must also be published or announced in the national gazette or through equally effective means; either way, publication may be done electronically.[202] Until recently, the national registers

[197] ECB, Banking Structures Report 2013 (November 2013) https://www.ecb.europa.eu/pub/pdf/other/bankingstructuresreport201311en.pdf.

[198] Communication from the Commission to the European Parliament, the Council, the European Economic and Social Committee and the Committee of the Regions: Action plan on building a Capital Markets Union, COM(2015) 468 final.

[199] Fourth Council Directive 78/660/EEC of 25 July 1978, based on Article 54(3)(g) of the Treaty on the annual accounts of certain types of companies, OJ 1978 L222/11; Seventh Council Directive 83/349/EEC of 13 June 1983, based on Article 54(3)(g) of the Treaty on consolidated accounts, OJ 1983 L193/1; now consolidated in Directive 2013/34/EU of the European Parliament and of the Council of 26 June 2013 on the annual financial statements, consolidated financial statements and related reports of certain types of undertakings, amending Directive 2006/43/EC of the European Parliament and of the Council and repealing Council Directives 78/660/EEC and 83/349/EEC (Text with EEA relevance), OJ 29.6.2013 L182/19.

[200] Directive (EU) 2017/1132, Art 16(1) and (3).

[201] Article 1(3) of Directive 2003/58/EC of the European Parliament and of the Council of 15 July 2003 amending Council Directive 68/151/EEC, as regards disclosure requirements in respect of certain types of companies, OJ 2003 L221/13.

[202] Directive (EU) 2017/1132, Art 16(5). Member States must implement the necessary measures to avoid any discrepancy between what is disclosed in the national gazette and what appears on the register; Directive (EU) 2017/1132, Art 16(7). Documents and particulars shall be filed in one of the official languages of the Member State where the register is kept. In addition, Member States may provide for voluntary disclosure in any of the official languages of the European Union or any other language. In case of a discrepancy between disclosure in the official language of the register and translations from voluntary disclosure in another language, the company cannot rely, vis-à-vis third parties, on the latter. By contrast, third parties may rely on it unless the company can prove that they had knowledge of the official language version; Directive (EU) 2017/1132, Art 21. Under the Commission's Digitalisation Proposal (n 6) publication in the Gazette would no longer be compulsory; Member States may retain the requirement under the proviso that the information to be published in the national gazette is to be sent by the register (rather than the company).

have been operating on a country-by-country basis. In order to optimize the functioning of the internal market the integration of national registers into an electronic network was felt to be necessary, in particular in the context of cross-border mergers, seat transfers, and the setting up of foreign branches.[203] The issue was initially dealt with in Directive 2012/17/EU regarding the interconnection of central, commercial, and companies registers.[204] By amending Directive 2009/101/EC, it introduced a system of interconnection of registers consisting of the registers of Member States, a European central platform, and a portal serving as the European electronic access point;[205] the relevant provisions are now contained in Articles 22–25 of Directive (EU) 2017/1132. Member States are required to provide companies with a 'unique identifier' so as to allow their unequivocal identification within the EU and the EEA.[206] Moreover, Member States should make sure that the documents and information filed with their registers are available through the system of interconnection of registers in a standard message format and accessible by electronic means.[207] The Commission is responsible for operating the European central platform, and may do so either directly or through a third party.[208] The technical details of the operation of the system are laid down in the Commission's Implementing Regulation (EU) 2015/884 of 8 June 2015.[209] Directive 2012/17/EU was to be implemented by Member States by 7 July 2014, and Member States had two years following the Commission's implementing acts to render the system operational.[210] Consequently, the Business Registers Interconnection System (BRIS) went live in June 2017.[211] In order to benefit from disclosure, third parties must have access to the information on the register. Consequently, Article 16(4) of Directive (EU) 2017/1132 provides that a copy of the whole or any part of the documents or particulars subject to disclosure under the Directive must be obtainable on application to the register, for a fee not exceeding the administrative costs involved. According to the Court of Justice's judgment in *Daihatsu*, access to the register is not confined to members, creditors, or employees of a company; rather, any interested persons must be able to inform themselves of the matters contained in the documents and particulars to be disclosed.[212]

In the UK, the relevant provision on the company register is section 1080 of the Companies Act 2006, providing that the Registrar shall continue to keep records of the information contained in documents delivered to him. The records of information contained in documents delivered to the Registrar constitute 'the register'. Registration of a document that has been delivered occurs when the Registrar has checked its acceptability and has completed the administrative process of registering it.[213] Pursuant to section 1077, the Registrar must cause to be published in the *Gazette* or by alternative means notice of the receipt of any documents that are subject to the Directive's disclosure requirements.[214] In the UK, any person may

[203] The following draws on Schillig (n 13).

[204] Directive 2012/17/EU of the European Parliament and of the Council of 13 June 2012 amending Council Directive 89/666/EEC, and Directives 2005/56/EC and 2009/101/EC of the European Parliament and of the Council as regards the interconnection of central, commercial and companies registers, OJ EU 16.6.2012 L156/1.

[205] Directive (EU) 2017/1132, Art 22(2).

[206] ibid Art 16(1).

[207] ibid Art 18(2).

[208] ibid Art 23.

[209] Commission Implementing Regulation (EU) 2015/884 of 8 June 2015 establishing technical specifications and procedures required for the system of interconnection of registers established by Directive 2009/101/EC of the European Parliament and of the Council (Text with EEA relevance) OJ EU 10.6.2015 L144/1.

[210] Directive 2012/17/EU, Art 5.

[211] https://e-justice.europa.eu/content_business_registers_at_european_level-105-en.do.

[212] Case C-97/96 *Daihatsu* ECLI:EU:C:1997:581 para 22.

[213] French (n 1) 45.

[214] The official language of the register is English: Companies Act 2006, s 1103. A Welsh company may deliver its documents in Welsh, together with a certified translation into English; Companies Act 2006, s 1104. Certain documents may also be delivered in any other language but must be accompanied by a certified translation into English; Companies Act 2006, s 1105.

inspect the register and may obtain a copy of any material on the register for a fee not exceeding the administrative costs.[215] However, certain sensitive material has been excluded from public inspection, for instance directors' residential addresses.[216]

In Germany, the commercial register is to be maintained in electronic form;[217] responsible are the county courts (*Amtsgerichte*),[218] with jurisdiction being determined by a company's registered office.[219] As a consequence, the (various) commercial registers are decentralized at the state level. However, their content is universally accessible through the common portal maintained by the states and the (federal) business register. The latter provides a 'one-stop-shop' for business-related information, including the information contained in the commercial registers, as well as additional company law, insolvency law and capital markets law-related announcements and annual financial statements.[220] The business register is a mere access portal; it does not generate the legal consequences of registration in the commercial registers. Everybody has access to the commercial register and the business register;[221] there is no need for demonstrating a legitimate interest or the like. Following registration in the commercial register, the entry is to be publicly announced in electronic form through a website for commercial register announcements.[222] This website is maintained as a common project of the German states.[223]

In France, following the signing of the company's articles of association, notice of the company formation is to be given in a newspaper designated for legal announcement in the district of the company's seat. Proof that public announcement has been requested is sufficient to then apply for registration.[224] The commercial and companies register is maintained by each local commercial court, in the hands of the Registrar and overseen by the presiding judge.[225] The National Institute of Industrial Property maintains a national commercial register that centralizes the various local registers. All register entries are publicly announced through the *Official Bulletin for Announcements in Civil and Commercial Matters (BOACC)*.[226]

Questions and comments:

1. An integrated EU-wide platform for retrieving company information is a great enhancement of the legal and business infrastructure in Europe. Investors and their legal and financial advisers, in principle, should be able to retrieve—often free of charge—the items of disclosure (discussed below) for any company registered anywhere within the EU (and the EEA). The information on a company's financial situation, its capital and governance structure will allow a much more seamless cross-border interaction of entrepreneurs, financiers but also potential customers and suppliers. BRIS went live only fairly recently. There are currently issues in terms of the retrievability of certain items from certain Member States. Hopefully, over time these issues will be addressed so that BRIS can reach its full potential as an indispensable tool for doing business within the internal market.
2. Through BRIS, try to obtain the most recent annual accounts of APCOA Parking AG, APCOA Parking (UK) Ltd, and of Renault SA. How would you summarize your experience?

[215] ibid ss 1085–1087.
[216] ibid s 1087(1), but see The Companies (Disclosure of Address) Regulations 2009, SI 2009/214, last amended by the Companies (Disclosure of Address) (Amendment) Regulations 2018, SI 2018/528.
[217] HGB §8. [218] GVG §§23a(1) No 2, (2) No 3; FamFG §376. [219] FamFG §377.
[220] HGB §8b. [221] ibid §9. [222] ibid §10.
[223] The official language of the register is German. In addition, the relevant documents and content of entries may be submitted in any of the EU's official languages; HGB §11.
[224] Germain and Magnier (n 100) para 1576. [225] Com Art L123-6.
[226] Germain and Magnier (n 100) paras 1577–8.

2. *Items to be disclosed*

Pursuant to Article 14 of Directive (EU) 2017/1132, at least the following documents and particulars are subject to compulsory disclosure: (i) the instrument of constitution (memorandum) and the statutes (articles), any amendments thereto and the complete text after every amendment; (ii) the appointment, termination of office and particulars of the persons who are either as a body or members of such a body, alone or jointly, authorized to represent the company vis-à-vis third parties and take part in the administration, supervision, or control of the company; (iii) where the instrument or statutes mention an authorized capital, at least once a year the amount of the subscribed capital; (vi) the accounting documents for each financial year in accordance with the accounting directives; (v) any change of the registered office; (vi) winding up of the company, declaration of nullity, and appointment of liquidators, including their particulars and powers if not derived from law or the company's constitution; and (vii) termination of liquidation. This applies to both public and private companies. For public companies, Article 4 of Directive (EU) 2017/1132 requires further information to be disclosed, either as part of the instrument of incorporation or the articles, or in a separate document to be published in accordance with Article 16 of Directive (EU) 2017/1132.[227] In addition, for private and public companies alike, letters, order forms, and websites must include the information necessary to identify the relevant register, the legal form of the company, the location of its registered office and, where applicable, the fact that it is being wound up. Any reference to the capital of the company, is to be a reference to the capital subscribed and paid up.

In the UK, Articles 14 and 4 of Directive (EU) 2017/1132 are implemented by section 1078 of the Companies Act 2006 and the various provisions referred to therein.[228] Article 14(d)(i) of Directive (EU) 2017/1132 requires disclosure of 'whether the persons who are authorised to represent the company may do so alone or act jointly'. This may be contrasted with sections 162–167 of the Companies Act 2006, which merely require the names of company directors and their particulars to be kept on a register at the company's registered office and notice of any changes in the persons of directors and/or their particulars to be given to the Registrar. According to the Court of Justice in *Haaga*, it is important that any person wishing to establish and develop trading relations with companies situated in other Member States should be able to easily obtain essential information related to the powers of persons authorized to represent a company. All the relevant information should be expressly stated

[227] Thus disclosure of the following information is required: (i) the registered office; (ii) the nominal value of the shares subscribed and at least once a year their number, or only the number of shares if issued as accountable par; (iii) limitations on transferability of shares if any; (iv) the information under (ii) and (iii) for each class of shares, if there is more than one class, and the rights attaching to the shares of each class; (v) whether shares are registered or issued to bearer and the procedure for their conversion if not provided by law; (vi) the amount of the subscribed capital paid up at the time of incorporation or when the company is authorized to commence business; (vii) the nominal value of shares, or their number for accountable par, issued for a consideration other than cash, the nature of the consideration and the name of the person providing this consideration; (viii) the identity of the promoters of the company; (ix) the total amount of costs payable by the company by reason of its formation; (x) any special advantage granted at the time of formation or authorization to commence business to anyone who was involved in the formation of the company.

[228] The registration of the company's initial memorandum and articles of association follows from Companies Act 2006, s 9. The articles of association are to be registered only to the extent that they are not supplied by the default application of the model articles for public or private companies as promulgated by the Secretary of State. Articles as amended are to be registered pursuant to Companies Act 2006, s 26. A change in the company's name is to be registered pursuant to Companies Act 2006, s 79. The duty to file annual accounts and reports with the registrar follows from Companies Act 2006, ss 441–7, and for the company's annual confirmation statement from Companies Act 2006, ss 853A–L. Pursuant to Companies Act 2006, ss 853B–I, the confirmation statement contains detailed information on the company's share capital structure. The information on the company's capital is further supplemented by the items listed in Companies Act 2006, s 1078(3) and the transactions and provisions referred to therein. Registration of a winding up order and related issues is governed by the Insolvency Act 1986, in particular its ss 109, 201, and 202; see Schillig (n 13).

in official registers or records, even if certain information follows automatically from national legislation or may appear self-evident. Third parties cannot be expected to have full knowledge of the legislation or current commercial practice in another Member State. It is thus necessary to require, as far as the power of representation of directors is concerned, that an entry in the register should convey information as to whether the members of the board of directors may represent the company alone or must act jointly.[229] Under common law and the Model Articles, directors represent the company jointly, subject to the articles of association providing otherwise. There is no specific disclosure requirement as to the ability to act alone under UK law. It could thus be argued that the standards of disclosure required by the Directive have not been fully met,[230] although the articles deviating from the Model Articles will be on file with the Registrar of Companies and accessible by interested parties.

In Germany, the actual entry in the register is limited to the company's name, registered seat, objects, amount of share capital, date of completion of the articles, identity of the directors, and the way in which they may represent the company; where relevant also the duration of the company and any provisions on authorized capital.[231] For public companies, the items to be publicly announced go further and encompass additional information on the division of the share capital, type and classes of shares, and non-cash contributions.[232] This is compatible with Articles 14 and 4 of Directive (EU) 2017/1132 because the relevant information is contained in the articles of association, which are kept at the Register and are publicly accessible.[233] In France, the entry in the register includes the name of the company, its start date and end date, its legal form and corporate objectives, the address of its registered office, and its unique identification number.[234] Moreover, the register provides a depot for the storage of the constitutive corporate documents and annual accounts.[235] Similar to Germany, the public announcement goes further and includes also the relevant information on shares and share capital, as well as on corporate representation.[236]

3. *Effects of (non-)disclosure*

The effects of disclosure and of inadequate or non-disclosure are regulated in Article 16(6) and (7) of Directive (EU) 2017/1132. Accordingly, third parties can always rely on the actual legal situation, even where a legal change should have been disclosed and disclosure has not been completed.[237] The company can invoke the actual legal situation only if a legal change has been duly disclosed or where the company proves that, despite non-disclosure, the third party had knowledge of the legal change. Even where the legal change was fully disclosed, third parties have a grace period of fifteen days following disclosure, during which they may prove that it was impossible for them to have knowledge.[238] In the event of a discrepancy between register and publication, the company may not invoke the text as published in the *Gazette* against third parties. However, third parties can rely on the text published in the *Gazette*, unless the company proves that they had knowledge of the text in the register.[239] It

[229] Case 32/74 *Haaga* ECLI:EU:C:1974:116; Written Question No 23/77 of 16 March 1977, OJ 1977 C289/1.
[230] Written Question No 23/77 of 16 March 1977, OJ 1977 C289/1; Edwards (n 150) 25.
[231] AktG §39; GmbHG §10. [232] AktG §40.
[233] National law shall provide 'appropriate penalties' at least in case of a failure to disclose accounting documents and omission of compulsory information on commercial documents and websites; Directive (EU) 2017/1132, Art 28. In both *Daihatsu* and *Commission v Germany*, the Court of Justice found German legislation to be inadequate in this respect; Case C-97/96 *Daihatsu* ECLI:EU:C:1997:581 paras 22–25; Case C-191/95 *Commission v Germany* ECLI:EU:C:1998:441 para 69. See further Joined Cases C-387/02, C-391/02, and C-403/02 *Berlusconi and Others* ECLI:EU:C:2005:270; Joined Cases C-23/03, C-52/03, C-133/03, C-337/03, and C-473/03 *Mulliez and Others* ECLI:EU:C:2006:285; Case C-418/11 *Texdata Software GmbH* ECLI:EU:C:2013:588 paras 43–61.
[234] Com Art R123-86. [235] Com Art R123-103. [236] Com Art R123-157.
[237] Directive (EU) 2017/1132, Art 16(7). This is only relevant where the legal change takes effect without registration or publication; in other words where registration and publication is not constitutive; Grundmann (n 7) 182.
[238] Directive (EU) 2017/1132, Art 16(6). [239] ibid Art 16(7).

seems to be immaterial, whether only the register or only the *Gazette* or both are wrong. It is, however, unclear whether an incorrect extract from the register or incorrect information on business correspondence can be the basis for third party protection.[240]

German and French law closely follow the structure of the Directive:

German Commercial Code (HGB)

§ 15[241]

(1) As long as a fact that is subject to registration in the commercial register has not be registered and disclosed, the person in whose business affairs the fact ought to be registered cannot invoke this fact against a third party unless the third party knew of the fact.
(2) If the fact has been registered and disclosed, a third party cannot deny its occurrence. This does not apply in respect of transactions carried out within 15 days of disclosure, provided the third party can prove that they neither knew nor ought to have known of the fact.
(3) If a fact subject to registration has been disclosed erroneously a third party can invoke the fact as disclosed against the person in whose business affairs the fact ought to be registered unless the third party knew that the disclosure was erroneous.
(4) ...

French Commercial Code[242]

Article L.123-9

In carrying out their activity, persons subject to registration duties may not invoke the facts and actions subject to registration against third parties or public authorities unless these facts and actions have been disclosed in the register. However, third parties and public authorities may rely on such facts and actions.

...

Article L.210-5

In the course of the operations of a société à responsabilité limitée and société par actiones, acts and notifications subject to disclosure occurring prior to the sixteenth day from publication in the Bulletin Officiel des Annonces Civiles et Commerciales shall not be effective against third parties provided that they can prove that it had been impossible for them to have become acquainted therewith.

...

Should there be any discrepancy in the publication of acts and notifications relating to sociétés à responsabilité limitée and sociétés par actiones between the text filed with the commercial and companies register and the text published in the Bulletin Officiel des Annonces Civiles et Commerciales, the version in the said Bulletin shall not be effective against third parties, who may, however, rely on it for legal purposes unless the company is able to prove that they have been acquainted with the text filed with the commercial and companies register.

These provisions deal with three situations: (i) Where an event or fact that is subject to registration has not been registered and/or publicly announced, the company can invoke this event or fact against a third party only where the third party had knowledge of the event or fact. Thus, where registration is declaratory and not constitutive (that is, registration is not a requirement of legal validity) a third party can rely on the silence of the register (and/or lack of public announcement). For example, a director authorized to represent the company individually may be removed from office and prior to the removal being registered and announced may agree with a third party that the company's claim against the third party is waived. Here, the waiver of claim will be effective for the benefit of the third party, provided

[240] Grundmann (n 7) 184.
[241] This and the following translations of German statutory material in this Chapter are our own.
[242] https://www.legifrance.gouv.fr/Traductions/en-English/Legifrance-translations.

that they were unaware of the removal from office of the director. Moreover, the third party can always rely on the actual legal situation—i.e. the valid removal of the director—if this is advantageous to them, for example where they entered into a contract with the company represented by the same director that turns out to be disadvantageous to the third party. In fact, in respect of the same event—removal of the director from office—a third party may in one context rely on the silence of the register (waiver of claim) and invoke the actual legal situation in another (disadvantageous contract). (ii) Where an event or fact has been duly registered and announced the company can rely on that event or fact vis-à-vis third parties, regardless of whether the third party knew of the event or consulted the register. There is, however, a fifteen-day grace period, during which the third party may demonstrate that they neither knew nor ought to have known about the event or fact. (iii) Whereas a third party can rely on the silence of the register, the protection of reliance on the truthfulness of a register entry and/or the related announcement is more limited. Where an event or fact has been duly registered, but the subsequent public announcement has been incorrect, a third party can invoke the legal situation ensuing on the basis of the incorrect public announcement, unless they had knowledge of the actual legal situation. The same applies in the more common situation where both registration and announcement are incorrect and also where only the registration is incorrect. Thus, where a company is represented by its directors jointly and an incorrect registration and/or announcement is made to the effect that a single director can represent the company individually, a third party can rely on the faulty registration/announcement and a contract entered into by the director acting singly on behalf of the company will be valid, provided the third party was unaware of the true situation. In any case, the third party may invoke the actual legal situation (where, for example, the contract turns out to be detrimental to it).

In the UK, the implementing provision is section 1079 of the Companies Act 2006:

Companies Act 2006

Section 1079 - Effect of failure to give public notice

(1) A company is not entitled to rely against other persons on the happening of any event to which this section applies unless—
   (a) the event has been officially notified at the material time, or
   (b) the company shows that the person concerned knew of the event at the material time.
(2) The events to which this section applies are—
   (a) an amendment of the company's articles,
   (b) a change among the company's directors,
   (c) (as regards service of any document on the company) a change of the company's registered office,
   (d) the making of a winding-up order in respect of the company, or
   (e) the appointment of a liquidator in a voluntary winding up of the company.
(3) If the material time falls—
   (a) on or before the 15th day after the date of official notification, or
   (b) where the 15th day was not a working day, on or before the next day that was, the company is not entitled to rely on the happening of the event as against a person who shows that he was unavoidably prevented from knowing of the event at that time.

The provisions on discrepancy between registration and notice appear not to have been specifically implemented. The latter would appear to be of little significance, given that publication is effectuated by Companies House causing the publication of a mere notice in the *London Gazette* of receipt of any documents subject to the disclosure regime.[243] Moreover, section 1079 is aimed at protecting third parties dealing with companies, rather than protecting companies themselves.[244] As a consequence, an official notification

[243] Companies Act 2006, s 1077.
[244] *Official Custodian for Charities v Parway Estates Developments Ltd* [1985] Ch 151.

of any of the events listed in section 1079(2) does not amount to constructive notice to third parties that the event has occurred.[245]

4. *The situation in the United States*

This tightly regulated disclosure regime is not fully replicated under US state incorporation laws. As part of the incorporation process, the articles of incorporation have to be filed with the secretary of state or some other designated state official.[246] In addition, by-laws may be required to be filed for public inspection at designated offices. Incorporation statutes may further impose a duty to file with the secretary of state an annual report containing information on the corporation's name, its registered office and head office, its directors and principal officers, and the nature of its business, as well as on its authorized and issued shares.[247] In Delaware, this information is publicly available to anyone for a small fee.[248] Corporations are further subject to a duty to keep books and records at their registered or principal office in which they collect and record permanently (in written form or electronically) the articles and by-laws, in their original and amended forms, as well as other information on important events throughout the life of the corporation.[249] Corporate books and records are not public records in a strict sense.[250] In most states, inspection rights are restricted and only current shareholders and directors have access to corporate books and records.[251] Where the statutory provisions are not limited in this way and keep, in principal, inspection open for the general public, a specific pecuniary interest in the corporation may still be required in order to grant an inspection request. This may be relevant in particular for current corporate creditors.[252] Corporations having securities registered on a national securities exchange are subject to extensive filing and reporting duties with the Securities and Exchange Commission under the Securities Exchange Act 1934.

III. Nullity

Articles 11 and 12 of Directive (EU) 2017/1132 restrict the events in which a company may be declared to be non-existent (that is, a nullity). The idea is that third parties must be able to rely on the information disclosed in the register and through publication and should not be faced with a situation where their contractual counterparty is subsequently found to be non-existent.[253] These provisions catch any national rule, which, on the basis of a reason existing at the time of formation, generally withdraws from the limited liability company the capacity to have rights and obligations or renders enforcement of such rights or obligations more difficult.[254] Third parties may legitimately rely on the information concerning a company only when that information has been disclosed in accordance with the Directive. Consequently, the rules on nullity do not apply where the existence of the company involved had not been confirmed through the public register, because the formalities for incorporation required by national law had not been completed.[255] Nullity can only be declared by the decision of

[245] French (n 1) 91.
[246] WM Fletcher, *Cyclopedia of the Law of Corporations* (Thomson Reuters, Update 2018) §2195.
[247] MBCA, §16.21. [248] https://icis.corp.delaware.gov/Ecorp/EntitySearch/NameSearch.aspx.
[249] Including the minutes of shareholders' and directors' meetings, all actions taken by the shareholders, directors, or board committees without a meeting, as well as share transfers and a list of shareholders and the classes and numbers of shares held by each of them, the names and business addresses of current directors and officers, a copy of the annual report filed with the secretary of state, annual financial statements and accounts, and possibly further information; MBCA, §16.01; Fletcher (n 246) §2186.
[250] Fletcher (n 246) §2186.10. [251] MBCA, §§16.02, 16.05. [252] Fletcher (n 246) §2236.
[253] This section draws on Schillig (n 13).
[254] Directive (EU) 2017/1132, Art 11 sentence 2; Grundmann (n 7) 152.
[255] Case 136/87 *Ubbink* ECLI:EU:C:1988:423. Moreover, Arts 11 and 12 are inapplicable to a regime under which companies are liable for a breach of capital markets law; for these circumstances, the national regime may entail a cancellation of the contract for the purchase of shares; Case C-174/12 *Hirmann v Immofinanz AG* ECLI:EU:C:2013:856, paras 49–63.

a court of law,[256] which can be relied on against third parties only if duly disclosed. With declaration of nullity the company goes into liquidation, which itself is governed by national law. Nullity has effect only *ex nunc*; it does not affect the validity of transactions entered into by or with the company prior to the declaration of nullity. The effect of nullity on the relationship between members of the company is generally determined by national law with the exception that shareholders remain liable to pay up any contribution unpaid on their shares to the extent that the company's liability vis-à-vis its creditors so requires.[257]

The grounds for nullity listed in Article 11(b) are exclusive; any other grounds for nullity in national law are prohibited. Nullity may be declared on the grounds: (i) that no instrument of constitution was executed or the requisite legal formalities were not complied with; (ii) that the objects of the company are unlawful or contrary to public policy; (iii) that the constituting documents do not show the name of the company, the amount of the individual subscription of capital, the total amount of capital or the objects of the company; (iv) of a failure to pay up the minimum amount of capital required by national law; (v) of incapacity of all the founding members; or (vi) that contrary to national law the number of founding members is less than two. According to the Court of Justice in *Marleasing*, in order to provide legal certainty for third parties, it is necessary to interpret the grounds for nullity as narrowly as possible. In respect of 'unlawful objects of the company' this means only the objects of the company as stated in its articles are relevant. The provision does not apply where the company is merely used for unlawful purposes.[258]

Judgment of the Court of 13 November 1990, Case C-106/98 *Marleasing SA v La Comercial Internacional de Alimentacion SA*, ECLI:EU:C:1990:395

1 By order of 13 March 1989, which was received at the Court on 3 April 1989, the Juzgado de Primera Instancia e Instrucción No 1, Oviedo, referred a question to the Court pursuant to Article [234 of the TFEU] for a preliminary ruling on the interpretation of Article [11 of Directive (EU) 2017/1132].

2 Those questions arose in a dispute between Marleasing SA, the plaintiff in the main proceedings, and a number of defendants including La Comercial Internacional de Alimentación SA (hereinafter referred to as 'La Comercial'). The latter was established in the form of a public limited company by three persons, including Barviesa SA, which contributed its own assets.

3 It is apparent from the grounds set out in the order for reference that Marleasing's primary claim, based on Articles 1261 and 1275 of the Spanish Civil Code, according to which contracts without cause or whose cause is unlawful have no legal effect, is for a declaration that the founders' contract establishing La Comercial is void on the ground that the establishment of the company lacked cause, was a sham transaction and was carried out in order to defraud the creditors of Barviesa SA, a co-founder of the defendant company. La Comercial contended that the action should be dismissed in its entirety on the ground, in particular, that Article [11 of Directive (EU) 2017/1132], which lists exhaustively the cases in which the nullity of a company may be ordered, does not include lack of cause amongst them.

...

10 With regard to the interpretation to be given to [Article 11] of the directive, in particular [Article 11(2)(b)], it should be observed that that provision prohibits the laws of the Member States from providing for a judicial declaration of nullity on grounds other than those exhaustively listed in the directive, amongst which is the ground that the objects of the company are unlawful or contrary to public policy.

11 According to the Commission, the expression 'objects of the company' must be interpreted as referring exclusively to the objects of the company as described in the instrument of incorporation or the articles of association. It follows, in the Commission' s view, that a declaration of

[256] Directive (EU) 2017/1132, Art 11(a). Where national law allows the decision to be challenged this will be possible only within six months of public notice of the decision.

[257] ibid Art 12. [258] Case C-106/89 *Marleasing* ECLI:EU:C:1990:395.

nullity of a company cannot be made on the basis of the activity actually pursued by it, for instance defrauding the founders' creditors.

12 That argument must be upheld. As is clear from the preamble to [Directive (EU) 2017/1132], its purpose was to limit the cases in which nullity can arise and the retroactive effect of a declaration of nullity in order to ensure 'certainty in the law as regards relations between the company and third parties, and also between members' … Furthermore, the protection of third parties 'must be ensured by provisions which restrict to the greatest possible extent the grounds on which obligations entered into in the name of the company are not valid'. It follows, therefore, that each ground of nullity provided for in Article 11 of the directive must be interpreted strictly. In those circumstances the words 'objects of the company' must be understood as referring to the objects of the company as described in the instrument of incorporation or the articles of association.

13 The answer to the question submitted must therefore be that a national court hearing a case which falls within the scope of [Directive (EU) 2017/1132] is required to interpret its national law in the light of the wording and the purpose of that directive in order to preclude a declaration of nullity of a public limited company on a ground other than those listed in [Article 11] of the directive.

Questions and comments:

1. It is interesting to reflect on the consequences of the Court's decision in *Marleasing*. Marleasing was an important creditor of Barviesa. The latter (allegedly) incorporated La Comercial for the sole purpose of putting Barviesa's assets beyond the reach of its creditors. By making the formation of La Comercial and Barviesa's contribution to its capital unassailable, Marleasing was prevented from reaching these assets.
2. Whereas Directive (EU) 2017/1132 aims at protecting third parties, the Court's interpretation of Article 11 means that the third party, Marleasing, is actually worse off than it would have been without the Directive. How can this outcome be justified? What is the underlying trade-off?
3. In what other context is *Marleasing* important?

The provisions on nullity are of particular relevance where incorporation processes and formalities are elaborate and cumbersome, rendering incorporation much more susceptible to being defective. Accordingly, under German law in the course of an action for nullity brought by a shareholder or a member of the management or supervisory board the court may determine that the articles of association are subject to defects that result in their nullity only where the articles do not show the total amount of legal capital or the objects of the company; or the objects of the company are unlawful.[259] Other defects[260] require the register court to request the company to cure the defect by amending its articles within a certain period of time; failure to do so results in the register court's determination that the articles are defective and the company is dissolved.[261] The determination of the nullity (or defectiveness) of the articles of association does not have retroactive effect; the company is to be liquidated in accordance with the general liquidation procedure.[262] In France, the grounds for nullity of private limited companies and public companies limited by shares have been restricted to the incapacity of all founding members and to the illegality of the company's objects.[263] These grounds have to be invoked through an action for nullity, which, if successful,

[259] AktG, §275; GmbHG, §75. Defects concerning the company's objects may be cured by amending its articles; Windbichler (n 19) 318 (§26 para 37).

[260] The articles do not show the name of the company; the amount of the individual subscriptions of capital, their number, par value, or class; the number of the members of the supervisory board; or the amount of legal capital specified in the articles is unlawful.

[261] AktG, §262(1) No 5; GmbHG, §60(1) No 6; FamFG, §399.

[262] Windbichler (n 19) 318 (§26 para 37).

[263] Com Art L235-1.

results in the company's dissolution.[264] The provisions on nullity are of little significance in the UK and have not been specifically implemented. The certificate of incorporation, issued by the Registrar of Companies, is conclusive evidence that the requirements of the Act have in fact been complied with. This makes English companies very robust and renders them virtually immune from any problems arising from defective incorporation.[265] The Attorney-General may, however, apply to the court and obtain *certiorari* to quash the registration. This was successfully done in *R v Registrar of Companies, ex parte HM's Attorney-General* in respect of a company whose stated objects were unlawful as contrary to public policy ('to carry on the business of prostitution').[266]

In the United States, incorporation under modern statutes can be so fast, easy and cheap that the problems addressed by the provisions on nullity do not normally arise. Similar to the United Kingdom (UK), the certificate of incorporation duly issued by the Secretary of State is conclusive evidence that the preconditions for incorporation have been complied with, subject to the state's power to cancel or revoke the incorporation. Delaware law goes even further by providing that 'no corporation of this state and no person sued by any such corporation shall be permitted to assert the want of legal organization as a defense to any claim', thus ensuring that third parties will never be denied a proper defendant. As in *Marleasing*, this may not necessarily be in the third party's interest because it also (presumably) means that shareholders benefit from the privilege of limited liability. Prior to electronic filings becoming widespread, defective incorporation remained an issue and a complex case law had developed, distinguishing between de jure corporations, de facto corporations, and corporations by estoppel. This case law has now lost much of its relevance. The different concepts and the trajectory are explained in the following extract:

***Robertson v Levy*, 197 A2d 443 (Court of Appeals, District of Columbia, 1964)**

Hood, Chief Judge:

The case presents the following issues on appeal: Whether the president of an 'association' which filed its articles of incorporation, which were first rejected but later accepted, can be held personally liable on an obligation entered into by the 'association' before the certificate of incorporation has been issued, or whether the creditor is 'estopped' from denying the existence of the 'corporation' because, after the certificate of incorporation was issued, he accepted the first installment payment on the note.

...

For a full understanding of the problems raised, some historical grounding is not only illuminative but necessary. In early common law times private corporations were looked upon with distrust and disfavor. This distrust of the corporate form for private enterprise was eventually overcome by the enactment of statutes which set forth certain prerequisites before the status was achieved, and by court decisions which eliminated other stumbling blocks. Problems soon arose, however, where there was substantial compliance with the prerequisites of the statute, but not complete formal compliance. Thus the concepts of de jure corporations, de facto corporations, and of 'corporations by estoppel' came into being.

...

Taking each of these in turn, a de jure corporation results when there has been conformity with the mandatory conditions precedent (as opposed to merely directive conditions) established by the statute. A de jure corporation is not subject to direct or collateral attack either by the state in a quo warranto proceeding or by any other person. A de facto corporation is one

[264] Germain and Magnier (n 100) paras 1582–3.

[265] Davies and Worthington (n 9) 92–94 (paras 4-34–4-37); French (n 1) 48.

[266] [1991] BCLC 476. Given that prostitution can be carried out without committing any criminal offence it is questionable whether today, almost thirty years later, a similar objects clause would still be found to infringe public policy; Davies and Worthington (n 9) 93 (paras 4–35) n 137.

which has been defectively incorporated and thus is not de jure. The Supreme Court has stated that the requisites for a corporation de facto are: (1) A valid law under which such a corporation can be lawfully organized; (2) An attempt to organize thereunder; (3) Actual user of the corporate franchise. Good faith in claiming to be and in doing business as a corporation is often added as a further condition. A de facto corporation is recognized for all purposes except where there is a direct attack by the state in a quo warranto proceeding. The concept of de facto corporation has been roundly criticized.

...

Cases continued to arise, however, where the corporation was not de jure, where it was not de facto because of failure to comply with one of the four requirements above, but where the courts, lacking some clear standard or guideline, were willing to decide on the equities of the case. Thus another concept arose, the so-called 'corporation by estoppel'. This term was a complete misnomer. There was no corporation, the acts of the associates having failed even to colorably fulfill the statutory requirements; there was no estoppel in the pure sense of the word because generally there was no holding out followed by reliance on the part of the other party. Apparently estoppel can arise whether or not a de facto corporation has come into existence. Estoppel problems arose where the certificate of incorporation had been issued as well as where it had not been issued,

...

One of the reasons for enacting modern corporation statutes was to eliminate problems inherent in the de jure, de facto and estoppel concepts. Thus sections 29-921c and 950 were enacted as follows: '§ 29-921c. Effect of issuance of incorporation. 'Upon the issuance of the certificate of incorporation, the corporate existence shall begin, and such certificate of incorporation shall be conclusive evidence that all conditions precedent required to be performed by the incorporators have been complied with and that the corporation has been incorporated under this chapter, except as against the District of Columbia in a proceeding to cancel or revoke the certificate of incorporation'. '§ 29-950. Unauthorized assumption of corporate powers. 'All persons who assume to act as a corporation without authority so to do shall be jointly and severally liable for all debts and liabilities incurred or arising as a result there-of'.

...

The authorities which have considered the problem are unanimous in their belief that section 29-921c (similar to [MBCA §2.03(b)]) and section 29-950 (similar to [MBCA §2.04]), have put to rest de facto corporations and corporations by estoppel.

...

The portion of § 29-921c which states that the certificate of incorporation will be 'conclusive evidence' that all conditions precedent have been performed eliminates the problems of estoppel and de facto corporations once the certificate has been issued. The existence of the corporation is conclusive evidence against all who deal with it. Under § 29-950, if an individual or group of individuals assumes to act as a corporation before the certificate of incorporation has been issued, joint and several liability attaches. We hold, therefore, that the impact of these sections, when considered together, is to eliminate the concepts of estoppel and de facto corporateness under the Business Corporation Act of the District of Columbia. It is immaterial whether the third person believed he was dealing with a corporation or whether he intended to deal with a corporation. The certificate of incorporation provides the cut off point; before it is issued, the individuals, and not the corporation, are liable.

Questions and comments:

1. Provisions such as MBCA §§2.03 and 2.04 as well as DGCL §329(1) have largely eliminated the need for the common law concepts of de facto corporations and corporations by estoppel. Only full compliance with the prerequisites of incorporation will confer the privilege of limited liability. However, certain exceptions are still being discussed: (i) if a corporate organizer enters into a transaction in the name of the corporation when he reasonably and honestly believes that articles have been filed but they have not been due to attorney neglect or other cause; (ii) if a transaction is entered into after the articles have been mailed or delivered to the

filing office but have not been received in the filing office through no fault of the filer; (iii) if a person knows that no corporation has been formed, but insists that his contract be immediately entered into in the name of the corporation.[267]

2. What is the common denominator of exceptions (i) and (ii)? Are these exceptions acceptable from the point of view of the contracting parties? What about (iii)?

IV. Pre-incorporation contracts

The longer the incorporation process takes, the more likely the company promoters (or incorporators) will enter into contracts and carry out transactions on behalf of the company in formation, be it the hiring of office staff, the renting or buying of business premises, or the appointment of legal and financial advisers to deal with the incorporation process. Even where online incorporations are fast and easy, such pre-incorporation contracting may still occur prior to the articles of association being finalized and submitted to the registrar, in particular where an existing business is to be continued in corporate form which involves trading during the formation phase. For these situations, Directive (EU) 2017/1132 aims to provide a third party purporting to contract with a company in formation with an identifiable debtor. Consequently, Article 7(2) stipulates the joint and several liability of persons, acting in the name of a company being formed and before it has acquired legal personality, for any obligations arising from such action if the company, upon formation, does not assume these obligations.[268] This liability is subject to party agreement. The regime applies to actions carried out in the name and on behalf of the future legal person ('acting for company X'). However, it is less clear whether it also covers actions in the name of the company prior to registration whatever its legal nature at this stage ('acting for company X in formation'). According to the Court of Justice in *Ubbink*, where acts performed in the name of a company not yet incorporated are regarded by national law as having been performed in the name of the 'company being formed', as provided for by Article 7(2), joint and several liability will be incurred by the persons who acted.[269] The Court's reference to national law leaves room for some uncertainty. Where the person clearly acts in the name of a company not yet incorporated (company X in formation), the parties may spell out in their contract that only the company will be bound following its incorporation, in which case there would be an agreement excluding liability under Article 7(2) (if it were applicable).[270] Alternatively, the parties may explicitly provide for a contract that is enforceable on both sides immediately, which requires the promoter to be bound. In the absence of a clear contractual stipulation there will be room for interpretation. In these cases, and where it is not made clear that a person is acting on behalf of 'company X in formation', Article 7(2) should apply. Otherwise,

[267] American Bar Association, Model Business Corporation Act Annotated (American Bar Association 2005) Official Comment to §2.04 (2-18–2-20).

[268] Article 5 of Directive (EU) 2017/1132 also belongs here. It provides that, where the laws of a Member State prescribe that a company may not commence business without authorization, they shall make provisions for responsibility for liabilities incurred by or on behalf of the company during the period before authorization is granted or refused. Pursuant to the Companies Act 2006, s 761, a public company must not do business or exercise any borrowing powers unless the Registrar has issued it with a trading certificate. A trading certificate will only be issued where the registrar is satisfied that the nominal value of the company's allotted share capital is not less than the authorized minimum of £50,000 or euro equivalent. Article 5 of Directive (EU) 2017/1132 is implemented by Companies Act 2006, s 767(3). Transactions entered into prior to a trading certificate being issued remain valid. However, if a company enters into a transaction prior to a trading certificate being issued and fails to comply with its obligations under that transaction within 21 days from being called on to do so the directors of the company will jointly and severally be liable to indemnify the other party to the transaction in respect of any loss or damage suffered due to the company's failure to comply with its obligations.

[269] Case 136/87 *Ubbink* ECLI:EU:C:1988:423.

[270] Agreements on liability that deviate from Art 7 require the consent of the third party; a clause in the statutes of the company will be insufficient. See Grundmann (n 7) 157.

the provision's efficacy in protecting third parties and providing them with a debtor would be rather limited.[271] Personal liability of the acting persons will come to an end as soon as the company upon formation assumes the respective obligations. 'Assumption' of obligations does not require actual consent of the company or of the third party; assumption by operation of law is sufficient.[272]

The Directive's provisions on pre-incorporation transactions were inspired by German and Italian law and were largely uncontroversial at the time;[273] arguably, their implementation had a significant impact on the common law jurisdictions. It is interesting to note that in Germany the significance of the implementing legislation is limited owing to the doctrine on the 'pre-GmbH/AG'. Despite the fast and easy incorporation process in the United States, jurisdictions still have to wrestle with the issue of pre-formation transactions and an elaborate body of case law has emerged.

1. *United Kingdom*

A private company limited by shares is not subject to minimum capital requirements and can be formed without elaborate provisions that seek to ensure the adequacy of capital contributions. As a consequence, there is limited scope for the problems that Article 7(2) of Directive (EU) 2017/1132 seeks to address.[274] However, a number of issues have occupied the courts over the years, notably whether promoters may be liable for contracts that they concluded on behalf of an as yet non-existent company and whether such liability may be extended to other promoters not involved in the actual contracting; whether and in what way the company, following incorporation, may assume such contracts and release promoters from liability. The case law addressing these issues prior to the implementation of the First Company Law Directive has widely been perceived as unsatisfactory. It remains relevant for filling the gaps left by the implementing legislation.[275]

In *Kelner v Baxter*,[276] the promoters sought to set up a company to run a hotel. Prior to incorporation, they ordered wine for the company and signed the contract 'on behalf of the Gravesend Royal Alexandra Hotel Company Limited'. Both parties to the contract were aware that at that time the company did not (yet) exist. Following incorporation, the company approved the contract, but became insolvent shortly thereafter. The promoters were held to be personally liable under the contract. If the company had been in existence at the time of the agreement, the persons who signed it would have signed as agents of the company. However, since there was no company at the time, the contract would be wholly inoperative unless it was held to be binding on the persons who signed it. In this case, both parties expected the company to be formed and the plaintiff parted with the goods in reliance on the defendants' undertaking that the price should be paid when due. It was a contract to buy and in no way contingent on the company being formed.[277] Thus, the contract could only be operative and meaningful if the defendants were themselves bound. This case may be contrasted with *Newborne v Sensolid (Great Britain) Ltd*.[278] During the formation of a company, the plaintiff sold goods to the defendants, signing the contractual documents as 'Yours faithfully, Company X Ltd', with the plaintiff's name underneath. When subsequently the market price in the goods fell, the defendants refused to take delivery and tried to wriggle out of the contract. During proceedings to enforce the contract, the parties discovered that, at the time of the agreement, the company had in fact not been registered. It was held that the contract purported to be a contract by the company; the only person who had any contract was the company and the plaintiff's signature merely confirmed the company's signature. As

[271] ibid 156. [272] ibid 157. [273] Edwards (n 150) 31. [274] Kersting (n 27) 147.
[275] Davis and Worthington (n 9) 111–14 (paras 5-23–5-28).
[276] *Kelner v Baxter* (1866) LR 2 CP 174. [277] ibid 183 (Earle CJ).
[278] *Newborne v Sensolid* [1954] 1 QB 45.

the company was not in existence when the contract was signed, there never was a contract that the plaintiff could rely on.[279] One way of reconciling both decisions would be to distinguish between the different ways a contract on behalf of a company in formation has been signed: a signature 'on behalf of the company' results in a binding contract with the person signing; a signature as 'the company' would not result in a contract at all.[280] Alternatively, and preferably, one could rely on the contracting parties' intentions. In *Kelner*, both parties knew that there was no company but still wanted an enforceable contract. This was possible only if the promoters were bound themselves. In *Newborne*, both parties wanted to contract only for and with the company; a contract between the plaintiff and the defendants was never on anyone's mind. Thus, what matters under common law is the intention of the parties, objectively ascertained on the basis of the facts of the case.[281]

Pursuant to section 51(1) of the Companies Act 2006, a contract that purports to be made by or on behalf of a company at a time when the company has not been formed has effect as one made with the person purporting to act for the company or as agent for it, and this person will be personally liable under the contract. This is subject to any agreement to the contrary. Thus, whereas the common law has recourse to the parties' intentions without any presumption either way, the implementing legislation creates a presumption for a contract between the third party and the promoter,[282] unless the parties specifically agree that the promoter will not be personally liable under the contract; merely signing as an agent of the company would be insufficient.[283] Where section 51 applies, the effects of the envisaged contract will ensue between the promoter and the third party. It follows that the promoter may assume the contract and enforce it against the third party in its own name.[284] The provision leaves a number of issues unresolved. Where an acting promoter is liable under a pre-incorporation contract, the question arises whether a co-promoter who was not involved in the actual contracting may also be liable. Such liability may arise where a promoter has actual authority to bind the co-promoters; apparent authority requires the holding out of the acting promoter as having authority by the co-promoters vis-à-vis the third party. This will be a rare occasion in the context of pre-incorporation contracts.[285] Co-promoters may further be liable on the basis of partnership principles. However, activities in preparation of opening a business upon incorporation, such as pre-ordering goods or opening a bank account in the company's name, are insufficient to create a partnership of the promoters.[286] This may be different where the promoters operate a pre-existing business, which is to be continued in corporate form. In this latter case, partnership law may apply prior to incorporation.[287] A further question concerns the assumption of pre-incorporation contracts by the company following registration and, closely linked, the release of the promoters from personal liability. When the company comes into existence 'it is a totally new creature, having rights and obligations from that time, but no rights or obligations by reason of anything which might have been done before'.[288] Consequently, there is no automatic assumption of pre-incorporation contracts by the company, even though the business operated before including its personnel may be exactly the same. There is no continuity between pre-incorporation phase and the company following incorporation. Also, the company cannot unilaterally assume a contract concluded between the promoters and third parties.

[279] ibid 51 (Lord Goddard CJ).
[280] *Phonogram Ltd v Lane* [1982] 1 QB 938, 943–4 (Lord Denning).
[281] ibid 945–6 (Oliver LJ); *Cotronic (UK) Ltd v Dezonie* [1991] BCC 200, 205 (Dillon LJ).
[282] Davis and Worthington (n 9) 113 (para 5-27).
[283] *Phonogram Ltd v Lane* (n 280) 944 (Lord Denning).
[284] *Braymist Ltd v Wise Finance Co Ltd* [2002] 1 BCLC 415.
[285] T Reith, 'The Effect of Pre-incorporation Contracts in German and English Company Law' (1988) 37 ICLQ 109, 115.
[286] *Keith Spicer Ltd v Mansell* [1970] 1 WLR 333 (CA).
[287] Reith (n 285) 116–17.
[288] *Kelner v Baxter* (1866) LR 2 CP 174, 183 (Earle CJ).

The only way in which the company can assume the contract is by entering into a post-incorporation agreement with the third party on the same terms (novation). In order to release the promoters from personal liability, they have to be parties to the new agreement under which they are expressly released.[289] The situation can be relieved by contractual stipulations in the pre-incorporation agreement between promoters and third party to the effect that the third party agrees in advance to the novation following incorporation and that the promoters' personal liability comes to an end when the company is incorporated and enters into an agreement on similar terms.[290]

Common law principles remain relevant where section 51 does not apply. In *Oshkosh B'Gosh Inc v Dan Marbell Inc Ltd*,[291] the section was held to be inapplicable where the company was undergoing a change of name rather than being registered for the first time. In *Cotronic (UK) Ltd v Dezonie*[292] the parties thought that the company existed, although it had been struck from the register. The Court of Appeal held that the contract did not 'purport' to be made on behalf of a similarly named company, which had been incorporated only after the parties had discovered their mistake. The third party defendant was not liable because the contracts concluded by the plaintiff on behalf of a non-existent company were a nullity under common law in line with the reasoning in *Newborne*.

2. *Germany*

With a complex and lengthy incorporation process, the issue of pre-incorporation transactions has particular significance in Germany. The German provisions on the liability of persons acting on behalf of the company in formation served as a model for the Directive's pre-incorporation regime.[293] For both public and private companies, those acting in the name of the company prior to its registration are personally liable, jointly and severally, for the obligations so created.[294] However, these provisions received a narrow interpretation by the courts. At the same time, the courts developed an elaborate doctrine on the 'pre-company' which has emerged as the predominate mechanism for dealing with pre-incorporation transactions. Although relevant mainly in the context of the incorporation of private companies (GmbHs), the 'pre-company' doctrine applies in much the same way to public companies (AGs).[295]

Generally, the formation of a company may be characterized as a process in three stages. First, people come together with a view to pursue the incorporation of a company; they privately negotiate their future roles and contributions and instruct a notary with the drafting of the articles of association and the further documents required for registration. Even during this earliest phase, contracts may be entered into on behalf of the future company; in particular where an existing business is to be continued in corporate form. Where the promoters are contractually committed to pursuing the incorporation of a company they may constitute a 'pre-formation company', which is either a civil law partnership or, where the pre-formation company already runs a business, may be a commercial partnership.[296] Importantly, there is no continuation between the 'pre-formation company', the subsequent 'pre-company', and the (eventual) company. The 'pre-formation company' is governed exclusively by partnership law; company/corporate law does not apply. If the assets acquired by the 'pre-formation company' are to be available to the 'pre-company' or company, they have to be transferred individually. Similarly, the 'pre-company' or company may contractually and individually accede to the obligations incurred by the 'pre-formation company' as a co-debtor; a release of the 'pre-formation company' requires the consent of the third party

[289] Davis and Worthington (n 9) 114 (para 5-28).
[290] ibid 111 (para 5-23); French (n 1) 632.
[291] [1989] BCLC 507.
[292] [1991] BCC 200.
[293] Edwards (n 150) 31.
[294] GmbHG §11(2); AktG §41(1) sentence 2.
[295] Windbichler (n 19) 216 (§21 para 16); Kübler and Assmann (n 27) 377.
[296] Kersting (n 27) 10.

creditor. The promoters as the members of the pre-formation company will be jointly and severally liable for the 'pre-formation company's' debts under partnership law principles.[297] The statutory liability for persons acting on behalf of the company in formation does not apply at this stage. The 'pre-formation company' comes to an end normally with the realization of the objectives for which it has been formed.[298] Depending on the promoters' agreement, this may be either the signing of the articles of association in notarial form or the registration of the company. If the latter, 'pre-formation company' and 'pre-company' may exist in parallel for a certain period of time, and must be distinguished in terms of the assets and obligations attributable to each.[299]

The incorporation process moves into its second phase with the signing of the articles of association in notarial form and, for public companies, the subscription of shares.[300] This is the moment when the 'pre-company' emerges. The 'pre-company' (pre-GmbH or pre-AG) is a necessary intermediate step towards obtaining separate legal personality through registration. It is generally perceived as an entity *sui generis* without legal personality that may nevertheless own property and be subject to its own obligations. Corporate law (GmbHG, AktG) is applicable to the extent that the respective provision does not require registration and is not incompatible with the situation prior to obtaining separate legal personality.[301] The 'pre-company operates under an internal corporate governance structure: its directors or members of the management board may represent it externally vis-à-vis third parties. It owns a dedicated and enclosed asset fund consisting of paid up contributions and claims for the contributions that remain unpaid.[302] The pre-company may sue and be sued under its own name, and may appear in the land register as the owner of real property.[303] A key issue of the incorporation process, resulting from the strict legal capital doctrine,[304] is that a legal person may only come into existence where the amount of legal capital stipulated in its articles is intact so that it can serve as a fund to which its creditors have preferential access. This fund must not be reduced prior to registration by incurring liabilities that are not predetermined by, and necessary under, either the applicable statute or the articles of association.[305] Prior to 1981, the courts sought to ensure this by limiting the directors' or board's authority to represent the pre-company to those transactions that were legally or economically necessary in order to facilitate the registration of the company. Any liabilities that were incurred as a result of transactions that went beyond these limitations could not be assumed by the company upon registration.[306] In 1981, the Federal Supreme Court abandoned this line of reasoning. The Court made clear that all assets and liabilities of the pre-company would be assumed automatically by the company with registration, establishing the principle of continuity.[307] The directors' power to represent the 'pre-company', in principle, remains limited to the transactions necessary to facilitate incorporation; however, the members may unanimously extend that power and even grant a comprehensive power to represent the 'pre-company', which may also be done implicitly. This will normally be the case where the pre-company continues to run a business that has been received as a contribution in kind. Other than that, however, the commencement of a business activity requires unanimous authorization by the members.[308] The rationale of having the share capital contributions intact as a fund for the preferential satisfaction of the creditors is achieved through the concept of 'loss compensation liability' (*Verlustdeckungshaftung*) of the members/promoters

[297] ibid 10–11; Kübler and Assmann (n 27) 378.

[298] BGB §726.

[299] Windbichler (n 19) 216 (§21 para 17); Kübler and Assmann (n 27) 378.

[300] AktG §29.

[301] Windbichler (n 19) 217 (§21 para 19): for example, the articles of association may only be amended unanimously because the statutory provisions on article amendment do not (yet) apply. The same applies to changes in the membership; an outright share transfer is not (yet) possible. See further BGH, 27.01.1997—II ZR 123/94 (BGHZ 134, 333) I.1.

[302] BGH, 09.03.1981—II ZR 54/80 (BGHZ 80, 129) 1.

[303] Kersting (n 27) 13.

[304] See Chapter 9 for details.

[305] BGH, 09.03.1981—II ZR 54/80 (BGHZ 80, 129) 2.b).

[306] Kersting (n 27) 21.

[307] BGH, 09.03.1981—II ZR 54/80 (BGHZ 80, 129) 2.b).

[308] ibid.

prior to registration,[309] which will be transformed into and continue as a 'deficit liability' (*Unterbilanzhaftung*) upon registration.[310] In addition, there is the statutory 'liability of those acting on behalf of the company prior to registration'. The 'loss compensation liability' (*Verlustdeckungshaftung*) and the 'liability of those acting on behalf of the company' are relevant prior to registration. Pursuant to the doctrine of 'loss compensation liability', the pre-company's members/promoters who consented to the commencement of business prior to registration will be liable pro rata, in accordance with their participation in the share capital, for any losses incurred that exceed the 'pre-company's' property. This 'loss compensation liability' is unlimited (i.e. not limited to any amounts unpaid on the shares) and conceptually an internal liability between the pre-company and its members. In principle, creditors cannot sue the members directly. Rather, they must obtain judgment against the 'pre-company' on the basis of which they may then seize the pre-company's claims against its members. In exceptional circumstances, creditors may sue members/promoters directly. This will be the case where there is only one member/promoter, and also where the pre-company has no or only insignificant property, in particular where an insufficiency of assets prevents the opening or continuation of insolvency proceedings.[311] Practically, these latter situations are likely to be the more common scenarios where a pre-company cannot, or refuses to, pay its creditors. In any case, it is unclear whether liability only arises where the incorporation process has ultimately failed, in which case the 'pre-company' will be dissolved and must be liquidated[312] without ever having been transformed into the company through registration; or whether liability ensues and can be enforced whenever losses have been incurred prior to registration.

Whereas the 'loss compensation liability' targets the members/promoters in a 'pre-company', the statutory 'liability of those acting on behalf of the company in formation' is limited to the directors of a pre-GmbH and the members of the management board in a pre-AG. Only the corporate body with statutory power to represent the company may be liable under this heading; not the members/promoters nor any person authorized by such body. Liability is triggered by acting in the name of either the company (to be incorporated) or the company in formation (that is, the 'pre-company'). The liability of those acting on behalf of the company in formation has the same content as the liability of the 'pre-company' itself under the respective transaction (specific performance); however, those acting on behalf of the company in formation cannot enforce the counterclaim which is owned by the 'pre-company'. Liability may be excluded on the basis of a clear and unambiguous agreement between the person acting on behalf of the company and the counterparty. The liability of those acting on behalf of the company comes to an end as soon as the pre-company becomes the company with registration.[313]

This is the third and final stage of the incorporation process. With registration, the company emerges as a legal person.[314] By way of continuity, it assumes all the assets and the liabilities of the pre-company; the liability of those acting on its behalf comes to an end. However, the members/promoters may be liable under the concept of 'deficit liability' (*Unterbilanzhaftung*). This is the continuation of the 'loss compensation liability' (*Verlustdeckungshaftung*) following registration.[315] Where, at the time of registration, the company's net asset value is lower than the amount of the share capital stated in the articles of association the members will be liable on a pro rata basis and unlimited up to the amount

[309] ibid 2.c). [310] BGH, 27.01.1997—II ZR 123/94 (BGHZ 134, 333) II.2.

[311] BGH, 27.01.1997—II ZR 123/94 (BGHZ 134, 333) II and III. Prominent commentators advocate an unlimited direct liability of members/promoters vis-à-vis the creditors along the lines of HGB, §128 (applied by way of analogy); W Bayer in M Lutter and P Hommelhoff (eds), *GmbH-Gesetz* (19th edn, Dr Otto Schmidt 2016) §11 para 18-22.

[312] Kersting (n 27) 11. [313] ibid 14–20. [314] GmbHG §11(1); AktG §41(1).

[315] BGH, 27.01.1997—II ZR 123/94 (BGHZ 134, 333) II.2.c).

of the deficit. Again, this liability is conceptualized as internal between the company and its members.[316]

3. *France*

Similar to the situation under German law, incorporation can be a lengthy and highly formalized process. A company obtains legal personality with registration in the commercial and companies register. For the time prior to registration, the Code de commerce explicitly recognizes the company in formation (*société en formation*).[317] This French concept of the 'company in formation' is, however, radically different from the German 'pre-company'. It is essential for the applicability of the liability regime for pre-incorporation contracts implementing the Directive, as well as for the assumption by the company of these contracts following registration.[318]

It is not entirely clear at what point the 'company in formation' emerges. A common intention to form a company, as evidenced by the signing of the articles of association or the depositing of the draft articles with the Register in case of a publicly held SA, seems to be essential. Occasionally it may be sufficient that, prior to the signing of the articles, the intention to form a company becomes obvious through, for example, negotiations with third parties, the opening of bank accounts, or application for licences, etc.[319] The 'company in formation' does not have legal personality; it cannot own property or incur liabilities in its name and can neither sue nor be sued. Contributions that have to be made prior to registration remain the property of the contributor until the company is registered and obtains legal personality. The same applies where a non-cash contribution consists of an existing business. Until registration, the contributor remains the owner of the business assets and liable for any obligations incurred in the course of running the business. These liabilities may, however, be assumed by the company following registration, resulting in the contributor's release.[320] The relationships between the members of the company in formation are governed by the articles of association and by the general law governing contracts and obligations.[321] Given that the company in formation cannot incur liabilities in its name, there cannot be any liability of its members for such liabilities either. The only recourse for third parties contracting with the company in the process of formation is provided through the statutory liability of the persons acting in the name of the company in formation before registration.[322] The persons who may act in the name of the company in formation include the promoters and members as well as the directors and members of the management board (in an SA with a two-tier board structure). The ensuing liability relates to a specific act and the resulting obligations; it may be incurred by those who directly contract with third parties, but also by those who granted the authority to act, and even those who approved the acts of others who contracted directly or granted authority. This latter point is relevant for members who signed the articles of association, including an annex listing the pre-incorporation transactions with a view to effectuating the assumption of these transactions by the company upon registration (*reprise*).[323] Liability is triggered by acting in the name of the company in formation. This requires that the company in formation is still in existence (and has not been replaced by a *société créée de fait*)[324] and that it has been made clear to the third party that it is contracting with a company in formation. Where a person acts in the name of the as yet non-existent company, there will be no contract; however, the person acting and failing to make it sufficiently clear to the third party that he is acting for the 'company in formation' will himself be

[316] BGH, 09.03.1981—II ZR 54/80 (BGHZ 80, 129) 2.c). [317] Com Art L210-6.
[318] Kersting (n 27) 88. [319] ibid 88–91. [320] ibid 96–102.
[321] Civ Art 1842; Germain and Magnier (n 100) para 1565.
[322] Com Art L210-6; Germain and Magnier (n 100) para 1566. [323] Kersting (n 27) 102–108.
[324] See below.

bound.[325] Where liability under this heading is triggered it will be unlimited and joint and several. Liability may be subject to a condition subsequent to the effect that liability comes to an end upon the occurrence of a specified event. According to law, it is by necessity subject to the condition subsequent that the company following registration assumes the respective obligations.[326] There are a number of ways for such assumption; however, the company is under no obligation to assume any pre-incorporation contracts.

The 'company in formation' comes to an end with registration when the company emerges with separate legal personality. It also ends if the company has not been registered within six months of the initial contributions being deposited and the contributors request the court for permission to withdraw their contributions.[327] Moreover, the company in formation comes to an end when it is transformed into a 'company created de facto' (*société créée de fait*).[328] Generally, a 'company created de facto' ensues where two or more persons act like shareholders in a company without having the intention to incorporate a company.[329] This will be deemed to be the case where the company in formation has begun to operate its (newly established) business permanently and to an extent that goes beyond a mere preparatory activity that is necessary for incorporation.[330] It will further be the case where the promoters no longer have, or never had, an intention to register the company. Much remains unclear and each case is to be judged on its own merits.[331] A 'company created de facto' is governed by the law on 'undeclared partnerships';[332] a form of partnership that only exists internally as between the partners. It does not have separate legal personality and does not require registration.[333] If the undeclared partnership operates a business the provisions of the commercial partnership apply.[334] This means that its members will be jointly and severally liable vis-à-vis third parties for any obligations incurred in the course of the business activity pursued by the 'company created de facto'.[335] Even where a 'company in formation' has become a 'company created de facto' registration remains possible. However, it is unclear whether a 'company created de facto' may revert back to a 'company in formation,' for example where the business activity is reduced to what is necessary for incorporation and the promoters pursue registration once more. The alternative is that the company remains a 'company created de facto' until registration with the effect that the law on the 'company in formation' remains inapplicable.[336] This has consequences for the assumption of pre-incorporation contracts by the company following registration.

When the company emerges upon registration it has the option to assume certain pre-incorporation contracts and the related liabilities. Such assumption will trigger the release from liability of those who acted in the name of the company in formation. The company may assume only those obligations that were entered into in the name of the company in formation;[337] those entered into in the name of the company are void and cannot be assumed. Moreover, at the time when the obligation is created the 'company in formation' must have been in existence. If at that time the company had become a 'company created de facto' the obligations incurred through the operation of a newly established business cannot be assumed by the company. This situation is to be distinguished from the continuation of a pre-existing business that has been contributed to a company in formation as a non-cash contribution. Generally, the company may assume any obligation incurred in the name of the 'company in formation' that has any bearing on, and is relevant for,

[325] Kersting (n 27) 106. [326] ibid 107–108. [327] Com Art L223-8; L225-11.

[328] This is to be distinguished from the concept of the de facto company (*société de fait*), which denotes the situation where the promoters had the intention of forming a corporation that turned out to be a nullity or has been declared to be a nullity by the courts after it has been operating for a while; see Germain and Magnier (n 100) para 1537.

[329] ibid para 1538. [330] ibid para 1564. [331] Kersting (n 27) 94–5. [332] Civ Art 1873.

[333] Civ Art 1871. [334] Civ Art 1871-1. [335] Civ Art 1872-1. [336] Kersting (n 27) 95.

[337] Germain and Magnier (n 100) para 1568.

achieving the company's objects; unless the promoters have begun to operate a newly established business permanently and to a significant extent in which case the 'company in formation' will become a 'company created de facto'.[338] Eligible pre-incorporation liabilities will be assumed automatically by the company with registration if they are listed in an annex attached to the articles of association prior to the articles being signed by the initial members. For each transaction, the annex must state the commitments and obligations assumed by the company. The signing of the articles by the initial members then results in the automatic assumption of the respective liabilities by the company upon registration.[339] The liability of those who acted in the name of the company in formation will come to an end. Eligible liabilities to be incurred in the period between the signing of the articles and the company's registration will be assumed automatically by the company where the underlying transactions have been authorized in an annex to the articles or in a separate shareholder resolution.[340] Such an authorization must be sufficiently specific in terms of both the kind of the transaction to be carried out as well as its content. In order for the ensuing liability to be assumed automatically, the person so authorized must further act in exercise of the specific authorization and not on the basis of a general power to represent the company in formation as, for instance, its director. Finally, those liabilities that for one reason or another are not assumed by the company automatically may be assumed following registration on the basis of a shareholder resolution to that effect; a simple majority suffices.[341] As a result of an assumption, the company will be deemed to have been subject to the respective obligations from the time of their creation (*ex tunc* effect).[342] The company assumes the role of the contractual counterparty in its entirety; in addition to the liability side of the bargain, acquired rights and assets will vest in the company. Those who acted in the name of the company in formation will be released from liability; but also forgo acquired rights to the benefit of the company.[343]

4. *United States*

Despite incorporation being particularly fast and straightforward in the United States, the issue of pre-incorporation contracts may still arise. In preparation for incorporation, the promoters may hire lawyers and financial advisers for the drafting of the necessary documents, they may purchase or rent the business premises and may sign contracts for goods and services, perhaps taking advantage of particularly favourable market movements at the time.[344] Similar to our European legal systems, such pre-incorporation contracts raise the issue of whether and to what extent the promoters and their co-promoters are bound and liable for performance or non-performance; and further whether and how the corporation, following completion of the incorporation process, may assume these contracts and the ensuing liabilities, perhaps resulting in the release of the promoters from liability. Normally, these issues should be addressed and dealt with explicitly in the pre-incorporation contract, avoiding any problems through careful drafting. Litigation may ensue in the absence thereof and the courts have to fall back on general principles of contractual interpretation and agency, unless the issue is governed by statute.[345]

As a general rule under common law, promoters will be personally liable on their pre-incorporation contracts even though the contract was made on behalf of the corporation to be formed, unless there was an express or implied agreement that the other party should

[338] Kersting (n 27) 109-12.

[339] Com Art R210-5(1) and (2) (SARL); Art 210-6(1) and (2) (closely held SA); Art R210-7(1) and (2) (publicly held SA); Germain and Magnier (n 100) para 1568.

[340] Com Art R210-5(3) (SARL); Art 210-6(3) (closely held SA); Art R210-7(3) (publicly held SA).

[341] Germain and Magnier (n 100) para 1568.

[342] Com Art L210-6.

[343] Kersting (n 27) 116.

[344] Choper, Coffee, and Gilson (n 9) 282.

[345] ibid 283-4.

look to the corporation only.[346] The promoters' personal liability on pre-incorporation contracts ensues because at the time the contract was concluded there was no principal for which the promoters could have acted as agents. In order to escape personal liability, the promoters must demonstrate that the parties intended to hold only the corporation liable; what matters are the terms of the contract and the intention of the parties.[347] The possible interpretations of an agreement made on behalf of a corporation to be formed—the plaintiff had performed certain architectural services based on a contract that was signed by the defendant as 'Edwin A. Boss, agent for a Minnesota corporation to be formed who will be the obligor'—are explained in the following extract:

***Stanley J. How & Assoc., Inc. v Boss*, 222 F. Supp. 936 (United States District Court, Southern District of Iowa, 1963)**

Hanson, District Judge:

...

Comment b under Section 326 of the R.S. of Agency sets out the three possible understandings that the parties may have when the agreement is made on behalf of a corporation to be formed by one of the parties. These are as follows: [First] An offer or option to the corporation to be formed which will result in a contract if it is accepted when the corporation is formed. The correlative promise for the continuing offer or option is the promoter's promise to organize the corporation and give it the opportunity to pay the debt.

...

The second type of situation is where the parties agree to a present contract by which the promoter is bound, but with an agreement that his liability terminates if the corporation is formed and manifests its willingness to become a party. This is an agreement for a future novation.... This second possible interpretation is not very important in this case because a novation was not pleaded or argued.

...

The third type of understanding is where the parties have agreed to a present contract upon which, even though the corporation later becomes a party, the promoter remains liable either primarily or as surety for the performance of the corporation's obligation.

...

In the present case, the contract was signed: 'Edwin A. Boss, agent for a Minnesota corporation to be formed who will be the obligor'. The defendant argues that this is an agreement that the new corporation is solely liable. The problem here is what is the import of the words 'who will be the obligor'. It says nothing about the present obligor. The words 'will be' connote something which will take place in the future.... [T]his is a situation where the parties used ambiguous words to describe their intentions. To resolve this ambiguity, it is helpful to resort to the usual rules of interpretation of ambiguous contracts. One rule of interpretation is to give meaning to all parts of the contract unless there are parts of the writing so inconsistent that it is impossible. The contract states that three-fourths of the contract price was to have been paid by the time the drawings and specifications were completed, and that this was to have been paid in monthly payments. If this part of the contract is given effect, it clearly tends to show that the parties intended that there was to be a present obligor on the contract. The plaintiff's interpretation of the way the contract was signed is consistent with all parts of the contract. The defendant's interpretation is inconsistent with the payment provisions of the contract.... Another rule is that the writing must be strictly construed against the party who drafted the writing in question.... In this case, it was the defendant who wrote the ambiguous words and they must be construed in favor of the plaintiff. Also, and perhaps most important, there are a number of cases which say that in the promoter contract cases where the contract called for performance, at least in part, before the corporation is organized, this indicates that the promoter is intended to be personally liable on the contract.

...

[346] *Sherwood & Roberts-Oregon, Inc v Alexander*, Or., 525 P.2d 135, 139 (1974).
[347] Fletcher (n 246) §215.

> In this case, the defendant was the principal promoter, acting for himself personally and as President of Boss Hotels, Inc. The promoters abandoned their purpose of forming the corporation. This would make the promoter liable to the plaintiff unless the contract be construed to mean: (1) that the plaintiff agreed to look solely to the new corporation for payment, and (2) that the promoter did not have any duty toward the plaintiff to form the corporation and give the corporation the opportunity to assume and pay the liability.
>
> ...
>
> Applying this law to the present case, the court would have to hold that even if the plaintiff had agreed to look to the credit of the new corporation, the defendant would be liable. The defendant was the key promoter and as such would be a primary factor in abandoning the project. This would make the defendant liable.

As the case demonstrates, courts will look carefully at the specific fact patterns of each case. An implicit agreement to look to the corporation only may be inferred where the third party insists that only the corporation is named in the contract and declines to do business otherwise although they knew that the corporation did not exist at the time.[348] The same may apply where the promoter expressly declines to be named individually in the contract, does not make any promises or receive any benefits individually under the provisions of the contract, all the while the other party knows of the corporation's non-existence.[349] Co-promoters not directly involved in the contracting may be liable under partnership principles.[350] The coming into existence of the corporation and its adoption, acceptance, or ratification of any pre-incorporation contracts does not automatically and in itself release the promoters from liability. These are merely necessary pre-conditions for such a release. In addition, it must have been the intention of the parties that the promoters' liability should come to an end, which may be achieved through an express or implied condition subsequent to that effect. Other than that, promoters may be released through novation where all parties agree that henceforth only the corporation will be liable, which may also be implied from the conduct of the parties.[351]

Following completion of the formation process, the corporation may become a party to a pre-incorporation contract and assume liability under it only through an affirmative corporate act by which the corporation adopts the contract, ratifies it, accepts a continuing offer or executes a novation agreement. Absent a statutory or charter provision, there is no automatic assumption of liability (or release of the promoters from liability). Whether the corporation assumes the pre-incorporation contract through ratification, adoption, acceptance of a continuing offer or through novation may not be entirely clear, unless the contract explicitly provides that it may be assumed only in a specific form, say through ratification by the board of directors. Ratification results in the corporation assuming liability from the date the contract had initially been made; whereas adoption leads to liability from the date of the corporation's affirmative act. These distinctions may have implications for the application of statutes of limitations.[352] In general, a corporation may only assume those contracts which it could have concluded itself; it cannot assume *ultra vires* contracts or illegal contracts. Assumption requires some affirmative and unequivocal act by the corporation (following its incorporation) in full knowledge of all the material facts. Such affirmative action may be express or implied; the latter may be the case where the corporation, with full knowledge of the contract, receives and accepts benefits and services under the contract and offers performance of its side of the bargain.[353] A novation requires the creditors' consent to the substitution of the company as a new obligor, which may be inferred from a creditor's acceptance of performance by the corporation, provided this is understood as an offer for novation.[354] Ratification, adoption, acceptance, or novation is to be made in the same manner as the

[348] *Sherwood & Roberts-Oregon, Inc v Alexander* (n 346).
[349] *Stewart Realty Co. v Keller*, 193 N.E.2d 179 (1962). [350] Fletcher (n 246) §215.
[351] ibid §216. [352] ibid §§205, 207. [353] ibid §§208, 209. [354] ibid §209.

corporation would have concluded the contract. Thus, where the original contract would have required a shareholder resolution or a resolution by the board of directors the affirmative act of assumption requires similar board or shareholder action. An effective assumption results in the corporation incurring full contractual liability under the contract, combined with a right to enforce the terms of the contract.[355]

Questions and comments:

1. It is probably fair to say that the harmonization achieved as regards pre-incorporation contracts is rather limited. The domestic provisions implementing Article 7(2) of Directive (EU) 2017/1132 have been interpreted very differently by national courts. In Germany, these provisions only apply to those statutorily charged with representing the company—directors and members of the management board; whereas the respective provisions in the UK and France are not limited in this way. In the UK, the issue of assumption by the company of pre-incorporation contracts and the promoters' release from liability has not been addressed by the implementing legislation; whereas German and French law also remain very different in this respect. It is perhaps one of the great ironies of EU company law that the German provisions that served as the model for the European regime have lost much of their relevance in their country of origin.
2. Within the overall framework of what used to be the First Company Law Directive this lack of harmonization is perhaps no major tragedy. The cross-border relevance of pre-incorporation issues and their significance for the internal market seems to be rather limited. Even where a pre-existing business is to be continued in corporate form, these issues will normally arise at an early stage in the firm's development where its involvement in cross-border trading activities is likely to be modest at best. What might be the reason for nonetheless regulating these issues in the First Company Law Directive with its clear internal market rationale?
3. Comparing the (continental) European regimes and United States law, we can again observe different corporate law philosophies at work. Whereas the former seek to impose statutory (or case law) solutions, under the latter, party autonomy rules supreme. It is up to the parties to negotiate and agree whether the promoter and/or the corporation will be bound and whether and at what point promoters may be released from liability. The principles of contractual interpretation may be used to fill any gaps. What are the advantages and disadvantages, in policy terms, of the continental European approach, on the one hand, and the US approach, on the other?

B. Corporate Representation

Once incorporated, the company or corporation conducts its business by contracting and transacting with other market participants. This requires the attribution of the acts of natural persons—the making or accepting of offers, the terminating of contracts, the accepting or rejecting of the delivery of goods, the making of payments through company accounts, etc—to the corporation, causing the corporate property to be subject to, or released from, liability, or to be increased or decreased by the receipt or disposal of assets.[356] In Chapter 1 we discussed the two great theories on the nature of the legal person—the 'fiction theory' and the 'real entity theory'.[357] Two corresponding theories seek to conceptualize the representation

[355] ibid §§210–14.

[356] *Meridian Funds Management Asia Ltd v Securities Commission* [1995] 2 AC 500, 506 (Lord Hoffmann): 'It is therefore a necessary part of corporate personality that there should be rules by which acts are attributed to the company. These may be called 'the rules of attribution'.

[357] See Chapter 1E.

of the legal person through natural persons acting on its behalf—the 'mandate theory' and the 'organ theory'.[358]

The 'fiction theory' is based on the idea that legal persons are created by law as artificial entities. Their formation requires a formal act of concession by the state. In order to acquire and dispose of property, legal persons must be represented by their agents, with agency being an artificial construct is effectuated by a legal person's constitution.[359] A number of consequences follow, albeit perhaps not by logical necessity. Given that the legal person derives its existence from a formal act of concession, this act determines conclusively the powers of the legal person so created. Thus, where the corporation's constitution limits corporate activity to certain objects the act of concession transforms these limitations into legal boundaries of corporate powers and capacity.[360] This is the origin of the *ultra vires*—doctrine: the corporation does not have the capacity to act outside its objects as adopted in its constitution; *ultra vires* acts are not legally binding on the corporation.[361] Moreover, since the legal person as principal acts through its agents, the agents' authority to represent the corporation may be limited in accordance with general agency principles by the corporation's constitutions and other acts established in accordance with it. This is the 'mandate theory'. Prior to the implementation of the First Company Law Directive it was prevalent, albeit not in pure form, in the common law systems[362] and in continental Europe, with the exception of Germany.[363]

The latter followed by and large the 'organ theory' corresponding to the 'real entity theory'. In its essence the legal person is a real collective unit, different from the aggregate of its constituting individual members, recognized by law in its legal personality. The law can only recognize human beings and human collectives as 'persons'; and the 'concept of law' demands the recognition of the legal personality of collective units that can form a collective will. Through its organs, the collective person is capable of willing and acting. What an organ wills and does within the boundaries of its competence is the will and action of the legal person itself. Agency is inapplicable. Conceptually, there is no difference between the legal personality of individuals and of collective units. In the same way that an individual's capacity is not limited by an objects clause, the powers and capacity of a collective unit with legal personality is by necessity unlimited (vis-à-vis third parties).[364] *Ultra vires* does not apply (at least not externally). The acts of a corporate organ are the acts of the corporation itself. It follows that an organ's power to act cannot be restricted by an act of another corporate organ. The boundaries of an organ's competence can only be established by law, not by private ordering.[365] Consequently, vis-à-vis third parties an organ's power to act on behalf of the corporation is, in principle, unlimited.

In more modern parlance, these theories may be couched in terms of economic theory. At issue is the allocation of the risk that management enters into a transaction in breach of constitutional restrictions to the detriment of the company. Under the 'organ theory', this risk is to be borne by the company and its shareholders; whereas the 'mandate theory' allocates the risk to the company's contractual counterparty. Pursuant to the concept of the 'cheapest cost avoider', the risk should be allocated to the party that is in the best position to control

[358] Edwards (n 150) 35.

[359] FK von Savigny, 'System des heutigen Römischen Rechts § 92' in WH Rattigan, *Jural Relations; or, The Roman Law of Persons as Subjects of Jural Relations: Being a Translation of The Second Book of Savigny's System of Modern Roman Law* (Hyperion 1884) §§85–90.

[360] Choper, Coffee, and Gilson (n 9) 64.

[361] Klein, Coffee, and Partnoy (n 188) 155.

[362] *Ferguson v Wilson* (1866) LR 2 Ch App 77, 89: 'The company ... can only act through directors, and the case is, as regards those directors, merely the ordinary case of principal and agent'.

[363] Edwards (n 150) 35; H Ault, 'Harmonization of Company Law in the European Economic Community' (1968) 20 Hastings Law Journal 77, 101–106 (on German and French law prior to the implementation of the First Company Law Directive).

[364] O Gierke, *Deutsches Privatrecht Band I: Allgemeiner Teil und Personenrecht* (1895) 469–72.

[365] Edwards (n 150) 35.

and limit its materialization at the least cost.[366] Whether the shareholders or the contractual counterparty is the 'cheapest cost avoider' seems to depend on a number of considerations: where the shareholders are closely involved in the company's management they seem to be in the best position to make sure that constitutional restrictions are complied with; by contrast, the passive and widely diversified shareholders in a listed company may not be able to control management in any meaningful sense. In this latter case, it may be easy for sophisticated third parties to ascertain any constitutional restrictions by inspecting the company register enabling them to making sure that any restrictions are observed. However, this very much depends on the type of restriction and whether it is ascertainable from the register. To cut a long story short, it is difficult to determine definitively the person of the cheapest cost avoider in a way that would allow standardization in corporate legislation. In practice, the differences between 'mandate theory' and 'organ theory' may be marginal. However, it is probably fair to say that at least conceptually the 'organ theory' tends to render corporate transactions with third parties more stable. A third party contracting with a corporation does not have to worry about whether the transaction is covered by the corporation's objects clause or *ultra vires*, and they can rely on the fact that the corporate organ they deal with has the powers conferred upon them by law. These features are particularly useful in a cross-border context when third parties deal with corporate entities that are different from those under their domestic law. Given the internal market focus of Directive (EU) 2017/1132 it is perhaps no surprise that it largely adopts the 'organ theory', albeit with certain modifications.[367] It does not regulate the bodies or persons who may represent the company or their respective powers to do so. These questions are relegated to national law. Protection of third parties is nevertheless achieved to some extent by insulating the general power to represent the company in its dealings with outsiders from internal irregularities and restrictions that are not easily ascertainable by third parties.[368] The Directive addresses the issue of *ultra vires*, and focuses on the primary rules of attribution,[369] that is, the rules that deal with the attribution to the corporation of acts done by its primary decision-making bodies (board of directors).[370] Its impact on the general rules of attribution—those applicable to all principals regardless of whether they are a corporate entity or not, essentially the law of agency[371]—is limited.

I. Ultra vires

The *ultra vires* doctrine is neatly summarized by Lord Cairns LC's speech in

> ***Ashbury Railway Carriage and Iron Co Ltd v Riche*** **(1875) LR 7 HL 653**
>
> Lord Cairns, LC:
>
> ...
>
> With regard to the articles of association, those articles play a part subsidiary to the memorandum of association. They accept the memorandum of association as the charter of

[366] M Schillig, *Konkretisierungskompetenz und Konkretisierungsmethoden im Europäischen Privatrecht* (de Gryuter 2009) 466–7.

[367] Directive (EU) 2017/1132, recital (7).

[368] Grundmann (n 7) 158–9.

[369] Directive (EU) 2017/1132, Arts 8 and 9.

[370] *Meridian Funds Management Asia Ltd v Securities Commission* [1995] 2 AC 500, 506 (Lord Hoffmann): 'The company's primary rules of attribution will generally be found in its constitution, typically the articles of association, and will say things such as "for the purpose of appointing members of the board, a majority vote of the shareholders shall be a decision of the company" or "the decisions of the board in managing the company's business shall be the decisions of the company" '.

[371] ibid: 'These primary rules of attribution are obviously not enough to enable a company to go out into the world and do business. Not every act on behalf of the company could be expected to be the subject of a resolution of the board or a unanimous decision of the shareholders. The company therefore builds upon the primary rules of attribution by using general rules of attribution which are equally available to natural persons, namely, the principles of agency'.

> incorporation of the company, and so accepting it, the articles proceed to define the duties, the rights and the powers of the governing body as between themselves and the company at large, and the mode and form in which the business of the company is to be carried on, and the mode and form in which changes in the internal regulations of the company may from time to time be made. With regard, therefore, to the memorandum of association, if you find anything which goes beyond that memorandum, or is not warranted by it, the question will arise whether that which is so done is *ultra vires*, not only of the directors of the company, but of the company itself. With regard to the articles of association, if you find anything which, still keeping within the memorandum of association, is a violation of the articles of association, or in excess of them, the question will arise whether that is anything more than an act *extra vires* the directors, but *intra vires* the company.
>
> ...
>
> The question is not as to the legality of the contract; the question is as to the competency and power of the company to make the contract. Now, I am clearly of opinion that this contract was entirely, as I have said, beyond the objects in the memorandum of association. If so, it was thereby placed beyond the powers of the company to make the contract. If so, my Lords, it is not a question whether the contract ever was ratified or was not ratified. If it was a contract void at its beginning, it was void because the company could not make the contract. If every shareholder of the company had been in the room, and every shareholder of the company had said, 'That is a contract which we desire to make, which we authorize the directors to make, to which we sanction the placing the seal of the company', the case would not have stood in any different position from that in which it stands now.
>
> ...

The *ultra vires* doctrine is a shareholder protection device. Corporate management are prevented from investing in potentially risky projects that are not covered by the objects clause and that, therefore, the shareholders could not have envisaged when they acquired their shares. This comes at the expense of contractual counterparties who arguably could have protected themselves by inspecting the register and realizing that the envisaged transaction was *ultra vires*.[372] Even prior to the First Company Law Directive and its implementation, the effects of the *ultra vires* doctrine had been significantly watered down through legal practice and case law. In order to not unduly restrict the future activities of the company, incorporators started to insert long and extensive lists of potential activities into the objects clause of the memorandum. The effectiveness of this practice was rendered ever more robust over the years.[373] A watershed moment was the Court of Appeal's decision in *Rolled Steel Products (Holding) Ltd v British Steel Corporation*,[374] where it was held that:

> [w]hile due regard must be paid to any express conditions attached to or limitations on powers contained in a company's memorandum (e.g., a power to borrow only up to a specified amount), the court will not ordinarily construe a statement in a memorandum that a particular power is exercisable 'for the purposes of the company' as a condition limiting the company's corporate capacity to exercise the power; it will regard it as simply imposing a limit on the authority of the directors ...[375]

It follows that for most practical purposes, *ultra vires* was abolished as a limit on the company's capacity and transformed into a restriction on the authority of its directors.[376] It remains relevant in this context, subject, however, to the statutory interventions in the course of the implementation of the First Company Law Directive.[377] Directive (EU) 2017/1132 takes as a baseline the principle that *ultra vires* does not apply vis-à-vis third parties: 'Acts done by the organs of the company shall be binding upon it even if those acts are not within the objects of the company, unless such acts exceed the powers that the law

[372] A Reisberg and A Donovan, *Pettet, Lowry and Reisberg's Company Law: Company Law & Corporate Finance* (5th edn, Pearson 2018) 124; Klein, Coffee, and Partnoy (n 188) 155; French (n 1) 608–609.

[373] Reisberg and Donovan (n 372) 124–30; French (n 1) 608–9.

[374] [1986] Ch 246.

[375] ibid 295E.

[376] Reisberg and Donovan (n 372) 128.

[377] See further below.

confers or allows to be conferred on those organs'.[378] By way of compromise between the German position and those in other Member States,[379] the general principle is modified by allowing Member States to provide that the company may not be bound by *ultra vires* acts if it proves that the third party knew or ought to have known that the act was *ultra vires*, whereby the mere disclosure of the company's founding documents is insufficient for providing such proof.[380]

In the UK, successive legislative interventions have essentially 'codified' the common law position on *ultra vires* in accordance with the *Rolled Steel* case.[381] Implementing the First Company Law Directive, section 39(1) of the Companies Act 2006 provides that the validity of an act done by the company may not be called into question on the ground of a lack of capacity by reason of anything in the company's constitution. The UK does not allow the company to get out of *ultra vires* contracts by proving the third party's knowledge of the *ultra vires* nature of the transaction. However, section 39 has to be read in conjunction with section 171(a) pursuant to which a director must act in accordance with the company's constitution. As a consequence, when acting *ultra vires*, a director may be liable for a breach of directors' duties and shareholders may seek an injunction in order to prevent the company and/or its directors for engaging in *ultra vires* transactions.[382] Moreover, any restrictions in terms of the company's objects limit directors' authority to represent the company—similar to the situation following *Rolled Steel*, although this issue has also been addressed by statute.[383] Companies incorporated under the Companies Act 2006 are unrestricted in their objects, unless the articles specifically contain restrictions in this respect.[384] Thus, objects clauses as restrictions on directors' authority remain relevant for companies incorporated under previous acts, and for those that maintain an objects clause although incorporated under the 2006 legislation.[385]

French company law adheres to the principle of speciality (*spécialité*) comprising two subprinciples: legal speciality (*spécialité légale*) and statutory speciality (*spécialité statutaire*). The former requires the sufficient specification of the company's objects in its constitutional documents; the latter traditionally restricted the authority of the company organs to represent the company, not the capacity of the company itself. The doctrine is therefore different from the common law *ultra vires* doctrine in its original form,[386] albeit quite similar to the doctrine's mode of operation following the *Rolled Steel* case. And similar to *ultra vires* the practical relevance of the doctrine has been in decline. French law implemented the provisions of the First Company Law Directive more or less verbatim: vis-à-vis third parties, a company will be bound by the acts of its board of directors or managers even if these acts do not come within the purview of the company's objects, unless the company can prove that the third party knew or ought to have known under the circumstances that the specific act was outside the company's objects. The mere publication of the company's constitution does not amount to such proof.[387] Vis-à-vis the company and the shareholders, the board of directors or managers are bound by the objects of the company. Where they act outside the company's objects, they may be personally liable vis-à-vis the company.

Under German law, *ultra vires* as a restriction on the company's capacity did not have any relevance when the First Company Law Directive came into force.[388] As a general principle, vis-à-vis third parties the management board's or the directors' power to represent the company is unlimited and cannot be restricted by the articles of association, a resolution of the

[378] Directive (EU) 2017/1132, Art 9(1) sub-para 1.
[379] Edwards (n 150) 33.
[380] Directive (EU) 2017/1132, Art 9(1) sub-para 2.
[381] Reisberg and Donovan (n 372) 130.
[382] ibid 130, 132; French (n 1) 609, 633.
[383] Companies Act 2006, s 40(4) and (5).
[384] ibid s 31(1).
[385] Reisberg and Donovan (n 372) 132. The objects clauses of companies registered under previous Companies Acts have become a provision in its articles, from which they may be removed by special resolution unless they are subject to entrenchment; Companies Act 2006, ss 28, 21, and French (n 1) 633.
[386] Germain and Magnier (n 100) para 1653.
[387] Com Arts L223-18, L225-35, L225-56.
[388] Ault (n 363) 101–103.

shareholders, or in any other way.[389] Irrespective of the company's objects clause, the management board or the directors can bind it to any contract that the respective type of company can enter into under the general law. Internally, however, the management board or the directors are bound by any restrictions in the articles of association, or imposed by resolution of the shareholders or the supervisory board.[390] By acting in breach of the articles, members of the management board and directors may trigger personal liability vis-à-vis their company for breach of duty.[391] In this respect, German law is very similar to English law and French law and we can observe a significant conversion. Whether, in order to achieve this conversion, an intervention in form of a directive was necessary seems doubtful given that corporate law in the United States largely follows a similar trajectory.

In the United States, at common law, contracts *ultra vires* the corporation were void and unenforceable.[392] However, a contract that had been fully executed on both sides could not be challenged on *ultra vires* grounds. The *ultra vires* defence was available for contracts that were wholly executory. Moreover, by unanimous action, the shareholders could authorize or ratify *ultra vires* transactions. In the absence thereof, shareholders can enjoin corporate action that is *ultra vires* and sue for damages by way of a derivative action the directors or officers responsible for *ultra vires* transactions.[393] Today, virtually every state has enacted legislation that largely eliminates the effects of the *ultra vires* doctrine vis-à-vis third parties.[394] Incorporation statutes allow corporations to be organized for the broadest of objects: to conduct or promote any lawful business or purpose except as provided otherwise by the law of the respective state.[395] By statute, corporations are equipped with long lists of powers that legitimize virtually any act that is conceivable in conducting a business, rounded off with a general and incidental power to do what is necessary or convenient to the conduct, promotion, or attainment of the business or purposes set forth in the certificate of incorporation.[396] The *ultra vires* defence is usually explicitly excluded by statute: no corporate act can be challenged on the basis of a lack of corporate capacity or powers; although shareholders may still enjoin the corporation from engaging in *ultra vires* acts, and may sue officers and directors for damages caused by *ultra vires* acts. Moreover, the Attorney General's power to dissolve a corporation is being preserved,[397] without addressing the issue whether the corporation acting *ultra vires* justifies dissolution. Importantly, these statutory provisions do not deal with the issue of directors or officers overstepping the scope of their actual or apparent authority, which is governed by the law of agency.[398]

II. Primary rules of attribution

Article 9 of Directive (EU) 2017/1132 addresses issue of the primary rules of attribution, that is, the extent of the power to represent the company on the basis of membership of a company's organ of representation.[399] Adopting the German 'organ theory' model, the underlying idea is that the power of the (members of the) board to represent the company is unrestricted vis-à-vis third parties. Therefore, a third party who contracted with the board (or a board member) that was formally appointed and duly disclosed can always be sure that the company will be bound.[400] Moreover, a company cannot invoke any irregularities in the appointment of persons to the board if particulars of these persons have been duly disclosed, unless the company proves that the third party had knowledge of

[389] GmbHG, §37(2); AktG, §82(1). [390] GmbHG, §37(1); AktG, §82(2).
[391] GmbHG, §43; AktG, §93. [392] Klein, Coffee, and Partnoy (n 188) 155.
[393] Choper, Coffee, and Gilson (n 9) 67–68. [394] ibid 68; Klein, Coffee, and Partnoy (n 188) 155.
[395] MBCA, §3.01; DGCL, §101(b). [396] DGCL, §§121, 122. [397] ibid §124.
[398] American Bar Association, *Model Business Corporation Act Annotated* (American Bar Association, 2005) Official Comment to §3.04 (3-12–3-14).
[399] The section draws on Schillig (n 13). [400] Grundmann (n 7) 159.

these irregularities.[401] Restrictions on the powers of the organ of representation arising from the company's constitution or from a decision of the company's organs cannot be invoked against third parties, even where the restrictions have been disclosed.[402]

This general principle of unrestricted and unrestrictable power to represent the company is subject to exceptions. First, a company will not be bound by acts that 'exceed the powers that the law confers or allows to be conferred'[403] on the particular company organ. What matters, and what a third party is required to examine, is the powers that a company organ *may* have under national law, irrespective of whether it actually has been granted these powers in any particular case.[404] Secondly, as for restrictions on the basis of the company's constitution or shareholders' or directors' resolutions three different scenarios may be distinguished:[405] (i) As discussed above, Member States may provide that where the organ acts outside the confines of an objects clause, and therefore *ultra vires*, the company will not be bound, provided it can prove that the third party knew or ought to have known that the act was *ultra vires*. Disclosure of the articles is insufficient proof of the third party's knowledge.[406] (ii) Where national law provides that the power to represent the company rests with the board acting jointly, it may allow conferral of this power to a single board member. Such a conferral of power in the articles would be an enhancement of the power to represent the company, not a restriction. Hence Article 9(2) would not apply and the company can invoke the respective clause against third parties.[407] In the reverse scenario, national law provides for representation by single board members as the standard mode of operation, but the company's articles stipulate representation by the board acting jointly, the respective clause is a restriction and within the ambit of Article 9. However, Article 9(3) allows the company to rely on the clause if duly disclosed in accordance with the Directive. (iii) Any restrictions on the basis of a company's constitution and board or shareholder resolutions will be effective against third parties only where the third party acted fraudulently or in collusion with the organ overstepping its powers.[408] Some commentators let mere knowledge on the part of the third party suffice.[409]

The third, and most problematic, exception relates to particular fact patterns of conflicts of interest in a concrete case, which, under national law, may restrict an organ's power of representation.[410] In *Rabobank*, the holding company acted as the sole director of a newly established subsidiary within the group.[411] Both, holding and subsidiary, were party to a netting agreement with a third party bank. Pursuant to the agreement, the credit and debit balances held by the bank for any group members could be netted out. When the subsidiary entered insolvency proceedings, the receiver tried to seize the amount standing to the credit of the subsidiary. However, the bank offered only a reduced amount, having set off various debits standing to other members of the group. The receiver argued that the netting agreement with the bank was invalid, because under national law the holding company as director had no authority to represent the subsidiary company in case of a conflict of interest between a director (holding) and the company (subsidiary). The Court held that Article 9(1) was concerned only with the limits on the powers granted by law to the various organs of a company, and was not meant to harmonize the domestic laws on a conflict of interest between a member of an organ and the company. Consequently, rules governing the enforceability as against third parties of acts done by board members in these circumstances fell outside the normative framework of the Directive and were matters for national law. The decision reduces the protective ambit of the Directive considerably. It requires third parties to ascertain whether a fact pattern exists that may result in a conflict of interest on the part of the acting

[401] Directive (EU) 2017/1132, Art 8. [402] ibid Art 9(2). [403] ibid Art 9(1).
[404] Grundmann (n 7) 160; Advocate General Mayras in Case 32/74 *Haaga* ECLI:EU:C:1974:107.
[405] Grundmann (n 7) 160–1. [406] Directive (EU) 2017/1132, Art 9(1) sub-para 2.
[407] Edwards (n 150) 45. [408] ibid 39–40. [409] Grundmann (n 7) 161. [410] ibid 161–4.
[411] Case C-104/96 *Rabobank* ECLI:EU:C:1997:610.

organ with the result of preventing it from representing the company. This may be very difficult in practice, certainly more so than detecting restrictions in the company's constitutions from the company's disclosed documents, and in this instance even the third party's actual knowledge may be insufficient to render these restrictions effective.[412]

1. United Kingdom

The Companies Act 2006 provides for two principal company organs: the board of directors[413] and the shareholders in general meeting.[414] The statute does not, in principle, determine the allocation of the powers to manage the company between these principal company institutions. This is largely left to the articles of association.[415] The Model Articles for public and for private companies provide that the 'directors are responsible for the management of the company's business, for which purpose they may exercise all the powers of the company'.[416] The shareholders may, however, by a special (75%) resolution direct the directors to take, or refrain from taking, any particular action.[417] The directors may also delegate any of their powers to other persons or committees to such an extent as they see fit, and may authorize further delegation of their powers by the persons to whom powers were delegated.[418] The directors have authority to represent the company only if they act jointly as a board (unless provided otherwise in the articles);[419] delegation to a third person or one of the directors also requires the board of directors to act jointly.[420] Third parties are protected by (what is now) section 161 of the Companies Act 2006, providing that the acts of a person acting as a director are valid notwithstanding that it is afterwards discovered that the appointment was defective, that he was disqualified from holding office, that he had ceased to hold office or that he was not entitled to vote on the matter in question. The provision only applies to a defective appointment, not to a situation where there has been no appointment at all.[421] A third party relying on this provision must have been in good faith, that is, must not have known of the defect at the time of appointment.[422]

Since the nineteenth century, the common law had been dominated by the doctrine of constructive notice: a person dealing with a company registered under successive Companies Acts was deemed to have notice of the company documents required to be filed at Companies House, including its articles and memorandum of association. As a consequence, the company could defeat the claim of a third party with a defence based on any restrictions on the board's authority within the articles (or memorandum), such as requirements for shareholder approval, a certain quorum or majority for board resolutions, or the outright prohibition of certain transactions. Where under these circumstances a contract was not binding on the company, the latter could still opt for ratifying it but didn't have to.[423] This position was somewhat softened by the 'rule in *Turquand*'s case' or 'indoor management rule'. Under this rule, a third party can, absent any circumstances giving

[412] Grundmann (n 7) 163–4. [413] Companies Act 2006, Pt 10. [414] ibid Pts 8, 9, 11, 13.

[415] Reisberg and Donovan (n 372) 121–2.

[416] The Companies (Model Articles) Regulations 2008, Schedule 1 (Model Articles for private companies limited by shares) para 3; Schedule 3 (Model Articles for public companies) para 3.

[417] Model Articles for private companies limited by shares, para 4; Model Articles for public companies, para 4.

[418] Model Articles for private companies limited by shares, para 5; Model Articles for public companies, para 5.

[419] *Heiton v Waverley Hydropathic Co Ltd* (1877) 4 R 830, 843; *Re Marseilles Extension Railway Co, ex parte Crédit Foncier and Mobilier of England* (1871) LR 7 Ch App 161, 168 (Mellish LJ): 'a director is simply a person appointed to act as one of a board, with power to bind the company when acting as a board, but having otherwise no power to bind them'.

[420] Model Articles for private companies limited by shares, paras 7, 8, and 11; Model Articles for public companies, paras 7, 10, and 11.

[421] *Morris v Kanssen* [1946] AC 459.

[422] *Channel Collieries Trust Ltd v Dover, St Margaret's and Martin Mill Light Railway Co* [1914] 2 Ch 506.

[423] Davis and Worthington (n 9) 154–5 (para 7-6).

rise to suspicion, assume that all formal or procedural requirements necessary to establish the board's authority for a particular transaction, like a shareholder resolution approving the transaction or quora in board meetings, have been complied with.[424] The rule cannot overcome outright bans on certain types of contracts, for example loans exceeding a specified amount, and does not apply where the third party has been put on (actual) notice of the restriction on the board's authority (or has been given reason for making further enquiries).[425]

The legislation implementing Article 9 of Directive (EU) 2017/1132 had a significant impact on this common law position.

Companies Act 2006

Section 40—Power of directors to bind the company

(1) In favour of a person dealing with a company in good faith, the power of the directors to bind the company, or authorise others to do so, is deemed to be free of any limitation under the company's constitution.
(2) For this purpose—
  (a) a person 'deals with' a company if he is a party to any transaction or other act to which the company is a party,
  (b) a person dealing with a company—
    (i) is not bound to enquire as to any limitation on the powers of the directors to bind the company or authorise others to do so,
    (ii) is presumed to have acted in good faith unless the contrary is proved, and
    (iii) is not to be regarded as acting in bad faith by reason only of his knowing that an act is beyond the powers of the directors under the company's constitution.
(3) The references above to limitations on the directors' powers under the company's constitution include limitations deriving—
  (a) from a resolution of the company or of any class of shareholders, or
  (b) from any agreement between the members of the company or of any class of shareholders.
(4) This section does not affect any right of a member of the company to bring proceedings to restrain the doing of an action that is beyond the powers of the directors. But no such proceedings lie in respect of an act to be done in fulfilment of a legal obligation arising from a previous act of the company.
(5) This section does not affect any liability incurred by the directors, or any other person, by reason of the directors' exceeding their powers.
(6) This section has effect subject to—
section 41 (transactions with directors or their associates), and
section 42 (companies that are charities).

Section 40(1) of the Companies Act 2006 provides that: '[i]n favour of a person dealing with a company in good faith the power of the directors to bind the company, or authorise others to do so, shall be deemed to be free of any limitations under the company's constitution'. The provision applies to limitations on the directors' powers stemming from the company's constitution as defined in sections 17 and 29 of the Companies Act 2006—the articles of association and special resolutions or unanimous agreements that would otherwise require a special resolution; however, its ambit goes further and includes limitations deriving from any resolutions of the company or of any class of its shareholders or from any agreement between the members or any class of shareholders.[426] In principle, any 'person

[424] *Royal British Bank v Turquand* (1856) 6 El & Bl 327, 332: '[O]n reading the [articles of association] [the third party] would find not a prohibition from borrowing, but a permission to do so on certain conditions. Finding that the authority might be made complete by a resolution, [the third party] would have a right to infer the fact of a resolution authorising that which on the face of the document appeared to be legitimately done'.

[425] Davis and Worthington (n 9) 156–7 (para 7-8).

[426] Companies Act 2006, s 40(3).

dealing with a company' may be protected. However, the protection of corporate insiders is much reduced.[427] A transaction that is valid only because of the application of section 40(1) is voidable[428] at the instance of the company where the parties include a director of the company[429] or of its holding company or a person connected with a director.[430] Regardless of whether the transaction is avoided or not, the contracting director (or connected person) and any director authorizing the transaction is liable to account for any profits they have made resulting from the transaction and to indemnify the company for any losses or damages incurred as a consequence of the transaction.[431] A person 'deals with' a company if he is a party to any transaction or other act to which the company is a party.[432] This definition is distinctly unhelpful and circular: whether the third party and the company are parties to a transaction is precisely the issue that section 40 seeks to address. What is meant seems to be an intention to contract with the company, rather than with any other person such as a director or shareholder in their personal capacity.[433] A person dealing with the company is presumed to have acted in good faith unless the contrary is proved.[434] Thus, the burden of proof is on the company. Moreover, a third party is not bound to enquire as to any limitations on the powers of the directors to bind the company or to authorize others to do so.[435] What was left of the constructive notice doctrine after *Turquand* is thus further undermined.[436] And further, not even actual knowledge that an act is beyond the powers of the directors results, without more, in bad faith of a third party dealing with the company.[437] Despite these far reaching protections, the provision may still leave certain gaps. In the context of the primary rules of attribution it deals with the limitations in the company's constitution on the powers of directors to bind the company. At common law, the directors have authority to represent the company only if they act jointly as the board. This limitation is imposed by law, not by the company's constitution, and cannot be overcome by section 40. Thus, the question arises whether section 40 can apply at all where a third party seeks to contract with a company not through the board properly constituted, but only through one or more of the directors or through an inquorate board.[438] The issue was discussed *obiter* by Robert Walker and Carnwath LJJ in *Smith v Henniker-Major and Co.*[439] One of the two directors of a company sued a firm of solicitors for breach of a contract the firm had with the company. The plaintiff argued that the company had assigned to him its cause of action. He had convened a meeting of the board, but the other director could not attend. The plaintiff proceeded to hold the meeting himself. At a board meeting, convened by the plaintiff that the other director was unable to attend, the plaintiff intended to act

427 Davis and Worthington (n 9) 159–61 (para 7-12). A member of the company cannot rely on s 40 when contracting with the company: *EIC Services Ltd v Phipps* [2004] EWCA Civ 1069 para [37].

428 Companies Act, s 41(2). The transaction is no longer voidable if (i) restitution of the asset subject to the transaction is no longer possible, (ii) the company has been indemnified for any losses incurred, (iii) rights acquired bona fide for value and without actual notice of the directors overstepping their authority by a person who is not a party to the transaction would be affected by the avoidance, or (iv) the transaction is affirmed by the company: Companies Act 2006, s 41(4).

429 In *Smith v Henniker-Major and Co* [2003] Ch 182 the Court of Appeal held that a director who was also the Chairman of the board could not rely on s 40 at all with the consequence that the transaction was void, and not merely voidable as s 41 provides (Robert Walker LJ dissenting); for a critical assessment, see Davis and Worthington (n 9) 160–1 (para 7-12).

430 Companies Act 2006, ss 252–6.

431 ibid s 41(3). Persons other than a director of the company (i.e. connected persons and directors of the holding company) are not liable if they can show that at the time the transaction was entered into they did not know that the directors were exceeding their powers; Companies Act 2006, s 41(5). Moreover, the rights of parties who are not themselves insiders remain unaffected even if the transaction is voidable. However, on the application of the company or any such party, the court may make an order affirming, severing or setting aside the transaction on such terms as the court deems to be fair: Companies Act 2006, s 41(6).

432 ibid s 40(2)(a).

433 Reisberg and Donovan (n 372) 144; French (n 1) 624.

434 Companies Act 2006, s 40(2)(b)(ii).

435 ibid s 40(2)(b)(i).

436 Reisberg and Donovan (n 372) 144.

437 Companies Act 2006, s 40(2)(b)(iii).

438 Davis and Worthington (n 9) 161 (para 7-13).

439 [2003] Ch 182.

as the board and minuted that the board was authorizing him to execute an assignment from the company to himself of the company's claim for damages against the defendant. The articles of association required a quorum of two. The written assignment was signed by the plaintiff. The issue was whether the plaintiff could rely on the predecessor of section 40. According to Robert Walker LJ (as he then was), this provision may only apply if there was a genuine decision taken by a person or persons who can on substantial grounds claim to be the board of directors acting as such, even if the proceedings of the board are tainted with procedural irregularities of a more or less serious nature. This was the 'irreducible minimum,' that distinguished a non-event from a procedural irregularity.[440] By contrast, Carnwath LJ favoured a lower threshold. If a document is put forward as a decision of the board by someone appearing to act on behalf of the company, in circumstances where there is no reason to doubt its authenticity, a person dealing with the company in good faith should be able to take it at face value.[441] This latter approach seems to be more in line with Directive (EU) 2017/1132's underlying rationale.[442] In the end, the question as to the 'irreducible minimum' necessary to invoke section 40 was not decisive in the case since the assignee as a director was a corporate insider that, according to the majority of the Court of Appeal, could not benefit from section 40 at all. Internally, section 40 does not prevent a member from restraining a director who purports to act beyond his powers or to hold him liable for having done so.[443]

2. *Germany*

German public companies are subject to a mandatory two-tier board structure. Consequently, in addition to the general meeting of shareholders,[444] a public company has a management board[445] and a supervisory board[446] as principal governance organs. The management board runs the business of the company.[447] It represents the company vis-à-vis third parties and determines business policy.[448] The supervisory board appoints and dismisses the members of the management board and supervises the management board's compliance with the general law and the company's articles as well as business strategy.[449] The supervisory board may not be involved in the day-to-day management of the company. Depending on company size and number of employees, the members of the supervisory board are appointed partly by the shareholders and partly in accordance with the rules on employee representation.[450]

German Stock Corporation Akt

§78—Representation

(1) The management board represents the company in all matters, both in court and extra-judicially. If there is no management board (absence of management), the company will be represented by the supervisory board in the case that the company is the recipient of legal notices or is being served with documents.

(2) If the management board consists of more than one person, only all the members of the management board acting jointly can represent the company, unless the articles of association provide otherwise. If the company is the recipient of a legal notice, receipt of the notice by a single member of the management board, or in the case of paragraph 1 sentence 2, by a single member of the supervisory board is sufficient....

(3) The articles of association may also provide that individual members of the management board may represent the company, either individually or jointly with a *prokurist*. The

[440] ibid 198. [441] ibid 212–14. [442] French (n 1) 624.
[443] Companies Act 2006, s 40(4) and (5). [444] AktG, §§118–277. [445] ibid §§76–94.
[446] ibid §§95–116. [447] ibid §76. [448] ibid §§77, 78. [449] ibid §§101, 111.
[450] ibid §96. For details see Chapter 5D.III.

supervisory board may make an order to the same effect, if authorized to do so in the articles of association. Paragraph 2 sentence 2 applies by way of analogy.

(4) The members of the management board who can represent the company only jointly may authorize individual members to represent the company individually in respect of certain predetermined transactions or types of transactions. The same applies where an individual member is authorized to represent the company jointly with a *prokurist*.

§82

(1) The management board's authority to represent the company cannot be restricted.

(2) Internally as between the members of the management board and the company, the members of the management board are obliged to adhere to the restrictions on their management powers stipulated, in accordance with the provisions on public companies, in the articles of association, by the supervisory board, the general meeting and in the bylaws of management board and supervisory board.

The power to represent the company in all matters vis-à-vis third parties rests with the management board.[451] Where the management board consists of more than one member, the power to represent the company can only be exercised jointly, unless the articles provide otherwise.[452] Joint representation may take the form of board members actually acting together by, for example, all of them signing a contract; alternatively board members may consent to the actions of one of them or approve individual actions subsequently. The board may also authorize one of its members to represent the company for certain transactions or certain types of transactions. The articles may provide, or empower the supervisory board to provide, for a different mode of representation. In this respect, it is reasonably common that two members of the management board may represent the company by acting jointly, or one member of the management board acting jointly with a *prokurist*, that is, an agent with comprehensive authority to represent the company in all business matters.[453] Representation by a single member of the management board is also frequent.[454] The move from joint representation to representation by a single board member or some board members acting jointly or together with a *prokurist* constitutes an extension of the board's power to represent the company and is therefore not subject to the constraints of Article 9 of Directive (EU) 2017/1132.

The management board's power to represent the company vis-à-vis third parties is unlimited and cannot be restricted by the company's articles, by resolutions of the supervisory board, or by the shareholders.[455] Interestingly, however, in all those instances where under any form of joint representation the board members (perhaps together with a *prokurist*) do not actually act together, the contractual counterparty carries the risk that the action of a single board member has been validly approved by the board, or authority to act alone has been validly granted and the board member has acted within the confines of this authority. The 'irreducible minimum' is therefore the valid exercise of the authority of the board with no room for any procedural irregularities. Some limited protection for third parties may be available on the basis of the general rules of attribution (apparent authority). The management board's power to represent the company is subject to certain statutory restrictions. The board cannot represent the company vis-à-vis a member of the management board, in which case the supervisory board steps in.[456] For settlements or waivers of the company's claims for breach of duty against promoters, and members of the management or supervisory board,

451 ibid §78.

452 Individual members do, however, have the power of acting singly to receive notice on behalf of the company.

453 On *prokura* see below pp 214-5.

454 Windbichler (n 19) 331 (§27 para 19); Kübler and Assmann (n 27) 204.

455 AktG, §82(1).

456 ibid §112.

the management board requires approval of the general meeting of shareholders.[457] For loans granted by the company to persons connected to the members of the management board a resolution of the supervisory board is necessary; the same applies to loans granted to certain corporate officers that exceed their monthly salary.[458] Important transactions that affect the foundations of the company require approval by the general meeting of shareholders with a qualified majority, in particular contracts by which the company submits to the control of another firm or undertakes to transfer its profits to another firm, contracts of merger, and contracts concerning the transfer of (virtually) all of the company's assets and liabilities.[459] These statutory restrictions may be invoked against third parties. Internally, the management board remains bound by any restrictions imposed by the articles of association, the by-laws of management board and the supervisory board, by decisions of the latter, and, where possible, by resolutions of the general meeting.[460] These restrictions do not affect the management board's power to represent the company (externally), but only its power to manage the company (internally).[461] Exceptionally, however, such restrictions may have an effect vis-à-vis third parties. This is the case where the management board and the third party act collusively together—knowingly and with intent to cause loss to the company. The same applies where the third party knows (or is recklessly unaware) that the management board has consciously exceeded its powers to the detriment of the company.[462] These exceptions to the general rule seem to be in line with the Court of Justice's decision in *Rabobank*.

German private companies have two principal organs: the board of directors[463] and the general meeting of shareholders.[464] The installation of a supervisory board is possible; it is mandatory only where, owing to its size and number of employees, the company is subject to the regimes on employee representation.[465] Vis-à-vis third parties, a company will be represented by its board of directors, normally acting jointly but subject to provisions for single or other forms of representation provided by the articles of association,[466] similar to the law on public companies. The board's power to represent the company is unrestricted and unrestrictable by the articles or by shareholder resolutions. Internally, however, the board is bound by such restrictions, and also by management guidelines contained in shareholder resolutions.[467] In respect of the power to represent the company vis-à-vis third parties, similar principles apply as for public companies.[468]

3. *France*

Traditionally, French law on public companies closely adhered to the mandate theory. Public companies were managed and represented by agents, and in accordance with the general law on agency, any limitations on the agents' power to represent the company were effective against third parties. By contrast, the French private company took German law as a model. The comprehensive power to represent the company was conferred onto one or more directors and restrictions on this power were rendered ineffective vis-à-vis third parties.[469] Successive reforms have resulted in significant changes.

Depending on a choice made in the articles of association, a public company may be managed either, under an English style one-tier board system, by a board of directors appointed, in principle, by the general meeting of shareholders; or under a German style two-tier board structure, by a management board appointed, and supervised by a supervisory board.[470] Under a one-tier board structure, the board of directors determines the company's business

[457] ibid §§50, 93(4), 116. [458] ibid §89(2) and (3). [459] ibid §§293, 179a; UmwG, §§4, 13, 65.
[460] AktG, §82(2). [461] Windbichler (n 19) 331 (§27 para 20).
[462] ibid 143 (§14 para 13); Kübler and Assmann (n 27) 204, 82–3. [463] GmbHG, §§35–51b.
[464] ibid §§53–58e. [465] ibid §52. [466] ibid §35. [467] ibid §37.
[468] Windbichler (n 19) 233–4 (§22 paras 10, 11).
[469] Ault (n 363) 103–106; Germain and Magnier (n 100) para 1670.
[470] Germain and Magnier (n 100) paras 2177–9.

strategy and ensures its implementation. The board has comprehensive management powers, subject, however, to the company's objects and those powers expressly reserved for the general meeting of shareholders. The board, acting jointly, can bind the company vis-à-vis third parties even with acts that fall outside the company's objects, unless the company can show that the third party knew or ought to have known under the circumstances that the company was acting *ultras vires*.[471] The board of directors elect from its members a president[472] and, in addition, may appoint a general manager.[473] The president is tasked with organizing and overseeing the work of the board and reporting to the general meeting. He further supervises the company's management structures and ensures their proper functioning.[474] The general management of the company is to be carried out either by the president or by the general manager if the board decides to appoint a person to this office.[475] In addition, on the proposal of the general manager (or the president, where no general manager is appointed), the board may appoint one or more deputy general managers.[476] The general manager (or president where no general manager is appointed) is invested with the most extensive powers to act on behalf of the company, subject to the company's objects and those powers specifically allocated to the board of directors and the general meeting. The general manager (or president) represents the company vis-à-vis third parties. The company will be bound even by acts that fall outside the company's objects, unless the company can prove that the third party knew or ought to have known that the act was *ultra vires*. Restrictions on the powers of the general manager (or president) to represent the company in the company's constitution or decisions of the board are ineffective against third parties.[477] Although the board of directors determines the scope of the powers of the deputy general managers, vis-à-vis third parties, deputy general managers have the same unrestricted powers as the general manager.[478] For non-financial companies, the furnishing of guarantees requires the authorization of the board of directors.[479] This is a restriction by statute that can be invoked against third parties. A guarantee agreement without authorization by the board is unenforceable against the company.[480] A problem may arise where the board authorizes the general manager (or president) to furnish guarantees up to a certain maximum amount, or authorizes maximum amounts for a series of individual guarantees. Any guarantee granted in excess of the authorized amount requires a new authorization by the board. However, where a guarantee that exceeds the maximum amount authorized by the board has been granted, the limit cannot be invoked against third parties, unless they knew that the amount of the guarantee exceeded the authorized limit.[481]

Where the company adopts a two-tier board structure, it will be managed by a management board, appointed and supervised by a supervisory board. The functions of the management board may be carried out by a single person—the sole managing director.[482] The management board has comprehensive powers to manage the company, subject to the company's objects and the powers expressly attributed to the supervisory board and the general meeting. The management board binds the company vis-à-vis third parties even when acting *ultra vires*, unless the company can show that the third party knew or ought to have known about the *ultra vires* nature of the transaction. Restrictions in the company's constitution that limit the power of the management board to represent the company are ineffective against third parties.[483] Normally, the company will be represented vis-à-vis third parties by the president of the management board (or the sole managing director). However, the company's constitution may allow the supervisory board to assign the same power of

[471] Com Art L225-35. [472] Com Art L225-47. [473] Com Art L225-51-1.
[474] Com Art L225-51. [475] Com Art L225-51-1. [476] Com Art 225-53.
[477] Com Art L225-56(I). [478] Com Art L225-56(II).
[479] Com Art L225-35 with Com Art R225-28. [480] Germain and Magnier (n 100) para 2221.
[481] Com Art R225-28; Germain and Magnier (n 100) para 2221. [482] Com Art L225-58, L225-59.
[483] Com Art L225-64.

representation to one or more other members of the management board—the managing directors. Any limitations in the company's constitution on these powers to represent the company will be ineffective vis-à-vis third parties.[484] However, the transfer of real property, the total or partial transfer of equity holdings, the granting of security and the furnishing of guarantees requires the approval of the supervisory board.[485] This is a legal restriction and as such is effective against third parties.[486] Where the company's articles limit the management board's powers of representation by subjecting certain transaction to a requirement of prior approval by the supervisory board,[487] an interpretation in conformity with Directive (EU) 2017/1132 would seem to suggest that such restrictions cannot be invoked against third parties, unless the third party was aware of the restriction.

In respect of private companies, the law has not changed substantively. A private company will be managed by one or two directors. Vis-à-vis third parties, the director or directors are vested with comprehensive powers to act on behalf of the company, subject only to the powers reserved for the shareholders by law. Even *ultra vires* acts are binding on the company, unless the company can show that the other party knew or ought to have known about the *ultra vires* nature of the transaction. Restrictions in the company's constitution on the directors' powers to represent the company are ineffective vis-à-vis third parties. Importantly, and contrary to German law, where a company has more than one directors, each single director has the power to represent the company vis-à-vis third parties. Where one director objects to the acts of another, this will have no effect against third parties, unless the company can show that the third party had knowledge of the objection.[488] This is not precisely what Article 9(3) of Directive (EU) 2017/1132 deals with. It could perhaps be argued that a third party is less worthy of protection where it actually knows of the objection, compared to a scenario where the directors may only act jointly and, despite disclosure, the third party has no actual knowledge of this. On this interpretation, French law would seem to be in line with the Directive.

4. *United States*

The internal governance structures of corporations incorporated under the different state laws may vary significantly. This is attributable to the flexibility that state incorporation statutes provide for private ordering and the allocation of powers and responsibilities between the three principal participants: the board of directors, corporate officers, and shareholders. The members of the board of directors are appointed by shareholder vote. The board of directors, in turn, normally appoint the corporate officers.[489] Incorporation statutes confer on the board of directors the authority to exercise all corporate powers and to manage the business and affairs of the corporation, either directly or through corporate officers under the direction and subject to the oversight of the board.[490] Much of the board's management authority will normally be delegated to a chief executive officer and other corporate officers on the basis of the corporation's by-laws and board resolutions, so that corporate officers will normally carry out the day-to-day management. There will usually be some overlap in personnel between the board and the officers. The chief executive officer may or may not serve as the chairman of the board; and the chief financial and chief operating officers are also usually board members.[491] The shareholders vote on structural changes, normally proposed by the board of directors, but other than that have no input into the management of the corporation's business.[492]

[484] Com Art L225-66. [485] Com Art L225-68. [486] Germain and Magnier (n 100) para 2271.
[487] Com Art L225-68. [488] Com Art L223-18. [489] Choper, Coffee, and Gilson (n 9) 53.
[490] MBCA, §8.01(b); DGCL, §141(a). [491] Choper, Coffee, and Gilson (n 9) 5–18.
[492] ibid 53.

The board of directors has comprehensive powers to manage the corporation and to represent it vis-à-vis third parties. These powers are specified in corporation statutes, the articles of incorporation and the by-laws. The board of directors has the power to do whatever is necessary to manage the business of the corporation, subject, however, to any express restrictions in the articles, by-laws, or general law. The power rests with the board as a whole, not with individual directors. Any action taken by an individual director on behalf of the corporation requires board approval.[493] The powers of the board of directors are received from the state through the act of incorporation:

> The board of directors of a corporation do not stand in the same relation to the corporate body which a private agent holds toward his principal. In the strict relation of principal and agent, all the authority of the latter is derived by delegation from the former, and if the power of substitution is not conferred in the appointment, it cannot exist at all. But in corporate bodies the powers of the board of directors are, in a very important sense, original and undelegated. The stockholders do not confer, nor can they revoke those powers. They are derivative only in the sense of being received from the State in the act of incorporation. The directors convened as a board are the primary possessors of all the powers which the charter confers, and like private principals they may delegate to agents of their own appointment the performance of any acts which they themselves can perform. The recognition of this principle is absolutely necessary in the affairs of every corporation whose powers are vested in a board of directors.[494]

As a consequence, the board's power to represent the corporation cannot be revoked by the shareholders.[495] The directors' powers are, however, limited by the corporate charter and may be restricted by corporate by-laws; under some state laws for closely held corporations also by shareholders' agreements.[496] The effect that these restrictions, and generally a failure to comply with formalities, may have on transactions with third parties seems to depend on the particular infringement in the case at hand. In *Hurley v Ornstein*, two out of three directors of a corporation agreed to waive a claim that the corporation had against the defendant. The trustee in bankruptcy of the corporation sued the defendant for the outstanding claim:

***Hurley v Ornsteen*, 311 Mass. 477, 480-481 (1942)**

Dolan, Justice

...

> We are of opinion, however, that it cannot be said properly that the evidence would support a finding in the present case of an accord satisfaction that was binding upon the corporation. It is true as argued by the defendant that the corporation through its board of directors had authority to compromise claims in its favor or against it under the terms of the agreement of association whereby 'the entire control and management of the corporation, its property and business' was confided to the directors.... It is also true that where a majority of a board of directors of a corporation participate in the doing of a corporate act within their powers and the other directors have knowledge of and adopt it by acquiescence or otherwise the corporation is bound by their action, and this without a formal meeting and vote of the board..., but this does not mean that a majority may bind the corporation by an act required to be performed by the directors where the other members of the board have no knowledge of the transaction at the time it is entered into, and do not subsequently adopt it either expressly or impliedly, except in some rare and unusual circumstances not shown to have been present in the case at bar.
>
> ...
>
> [The court goes on to discuss whether the acting director had apparent authority for a waiver of claim as a corporate officer, which was rejected on the evidence.]

This may be contrasted with *Colcord v Granzow*.[497] The corporation had issued debt beyond its subscribed capital stock, contrary to statute. This was based on decisions taken at special

[493] Fletcher (n 246) §505.
[494] *Hoyt v Thomspon's Executor*, 19 N.Y. 207, 216 (1859).
[495] Fletcher (n 246) §507.
[496] ibid §510.
[497] 278 P. 654 (Okla. 1928).

board meetings, none of which was 'held upon the regular meeting day as fixed by the by-laws, nor was any special meeting called in writing by the president or vice president, nor was written notice of any meeting given to the directors as provided by said by-laws'. Upon an action brought by the creditors against the directors, the court held that:

> the function of a by-law is to prescribe the rights and duties of the members with reference to internal government of the corporation, the management of its affairs, and the rights or duties existing between the members inter se. ... The same rule does not apply to third persons or strangers, especially in the absence of a showing that such third persons had knowledge of the by-law.... It would be inequitable and unjust to place upon third persons, dealing with a corporation, the duty of first ascertaining whether the directing officers had complied with its own regulations adopted for its own convenience and safety.[498]

In terms of the underlying policies, both cases are somewhat difficult to reconcile. Whereas *Colcord* seems to be in line with the English rule in *Turquand*'s case, *Hurley* is not. To justify the difference in outcome on the basis that *Colcord* concerned a breach of the by-laws, whereas in *Hurley* a breach of the articles was at issue seems to be too formalistic. Depending on state law, the articles and/or by-laws may or may not be publicly available, but nothing in the cases seems to draw on this. Perhaps, at the heart of the matter is the concept of the 'irreducible minimum' discussed by the English Court of Appeal in *Smith v Henniker-Major & Co*.[499] On that analysis, the involvement of all board members in an act, or at least their knowledge thereof, is part of the 'irreducible minimum' necessary for the board members to act as the board. By contrast, formal irregularities cannot be invoked against third parties, at least if they had no knowledge thereof. Moreover, a decision of the board that suffers from such irregularities can be ratified by the board, in which case any such irregularities will be cured.[500]

Whereas the directors' authority to represent the corporation is original and non-delegated, the officers' power as agents is derived from a delegation of authority from the corporation, either directly through the articles or by-laws, or indirectly through the board of directors. The officers' powers are governed by the general rules of agency, subject to the articles of incorporation and by-laws. The officers only have such authority to represent the corporation as was conferred upon them by the principal; any contracts concluded in excess of that authority will not be binding on the corporation (unless there is apparent authority).[501] These are the general rules of attribution which we turn to in the next section.

III. General rules of attribution

The vast majority of contracts entered into by a company or corporation will not be signed by the board of directors or even the CEO or general manager. Rather, most everyday contracts, and even some of the more significant ones, will be concluded on behalf of the company by a single director, by middle or lower management, by branch managers, or other employees.[502] These people derive their power to represent the company through a chain of authorizations leading up to the company's primary organ of representation. The delegation of authority and its exercise by people in the hierarchy below the board of directors is generally governed by the law of agency—the 'general rules of attribution' that apply to any principal regardless of its corporate nature.[503] The law of agency conceptually differs significantly between the continental European legal systems and the common law.[504] Directive

498 ibid 662. 499 [2003] Ch 182.
500 *Meyers v El Tejon Oil & Refining Co.*, 29 Cal.2d 184, 186–7 (1946). 501 Fletcher (n 246) §434.
502 Davis and Worthington (n 9) 163 (para 7-16). 503 ibid 178 (para 7-16).
504 See K Zweigert and H Kötz, *An Introduction to Comparative Law* (Tony Weir tr, 3rd edn, OUP 1998) 431–41.

(EU) 2017/1132 has no impact on the law of agency. A number of company specific particularities merit further discussion.

1. *United Kingdom*

Under the common law, agency arises where a principal appoints an agent to create, modify, or terminate legal relations between the principal and a third party. To the extent that the agent acts within the authority conferred on him by the principal, the contractual rights and obligations brought about by the agent vest in the person of the principal so that the latter may be sued by, and can sue, the third party. When contracting with a third party the agent may or may not disclose that he is acting for the principal; which is conceptually different from civil law jurisdictions where only disclosed agency (direct representation) generates effects similar to that of agency.[505] Where the principal remains undisclosed, the third party is protected by being able to invoke against the principal any defences they would have had against the agent, and by having a choice as to whether to enforce the contract against the principal or the agent.[506] In any case, the principal will only be bound by the agent's actions to the extent that the agent acts within the scope of his authority, which may be actual or apparent.[507] It is in the context of the latter that the rule in *Turquand's* case and section 40 of the Companies Act 2006 modify the general rules of agency.

An agent acts with actual authority when he does exactly what he has been authorized to do. Actual authority can be express or implied. Usually, actual authority derives from an express conferral of authority by way of agreement between the principal and the agent.[508] In the corporate context, it is express

> when a board of directors pass a resolution which authorises two of their number to sign cheques. It is implied when it is inferred from the conduct of the parties and the circumstances of the case, such as when the board of directors appoint one of their number to be managing director. They thereby impliedly authorise him to do all such things as fall within the usual scope of that office.[509]

The managing director may then further delegate authority to other managers and employees. Actual authority requires that all formalities and restrictions imposed by the company's constitution have been complied with. If this is not the case, the agent may have apparent authority.

Apparent authority is the authority of the agent as it appears to the third party. It may coincide with actual authority, but is most relevant where it goes beyond the agent's actual authority, in particular where the latter has been expressly limited. Where this appearance of authority, wider than the actual authority, is somehow attributable to the principal, he will be estopped from denying that appearance.[510] In *Freeman & Lockyer*, Diplock LJ summarized the prerequisites of apparent authority as follows:

***Freeman & Lockyer (a firm) v Buckhurst Park Properties (Mangal) Ltd* [1964] 2 QB 480, 506**

Diplock LJ:

> ...
>
> It must be shown:
>
> (1) that a representation that the agent had authority to enter on behalf of the company into a contract of the kind sought to be enforced was made to the contractor;

[505] E McKendrick, *Goode on Commercial Law* (5th edn, Penguin 2017) 181–4.
[506] ibid 195.
[507] ibid 197–8; Reisberg and Donovan (n 372) 137; French (n 1) 609.
[508] Reisberg and Donovan (n 372) 137–8; French (n 1) 610.
[509] *Hely-Hutchinson v Brayhead Ltd* [1968] QB 549, 583 (Lord Denning).
[510] Reisberg and Donovan (n 372) 138; French (n 1) 611.

(2) that such representation was made by a person or persons who had 'actual' authority to manage the business of the company either generally or in respect of those matters to which the contract relates;
(3) that he (the contractor) was induced by such representation to enter into the contract, that is, that he in fact relied upon it; and
(4) that under its memorandum or articles of association the company was not deprived of the capacity either to enter into a contract of the kind sought to be enforced or to delegate authority to enter into a contract of that kind to the agent.

As for (1):

> The commonest form of representation by a principal creating an 'apparent' authority of an agent is by conduct, namely, by permitting the agent to act in the management or conduct of the principal's business. Thus, if in the case of a company the board of directors who have 'actual' authority under the memorandum and articles of association to manage the company's business permit the agent to act in the management or conduct of the company's business, they thereby represent to all persons dealing with such agent that he has authority to enter on behalf of the corporation into contracts of a kind which an agent authorized to do acts of the kind which he is in fact permitted to do usually enters into in the ordinary course of such business.[511]

As for (2) and (4):

> [T]he representation as to the authority of the agent which creates his 'apparent' authority must be made by some person or persons who have 'actual' authority from the corporation to make the representation. Such 'actual' authority may be conferred by the constitution of the corporation itself, as, for example, in the case of a company, upon the board of directors, or it may be conferred by those who under its constitution have the powers of management upon some other person to whom the constitution permits them to delegate authority to make representations of this kind. It follows that where the agent upon whose 'apparent' authority the contractor relies has no 'actual' authority from the corporation to enter into a particular kind of contract with the contractor on behalf of the corporation, the contractor cannot rely upon the agent's own representation as to his actual authority. Moreover, [p]rima facie it falls within the 'actual' authority of the board of directors, and unless the memorandum or articles of the company either make such a contract ultra vires the company or prohibit the delegation of such authority to the agent, the company is estopped from denying to anyone who has entered into a contract with the agent in reliance upon such 'apparent' authority that the agent had authority to contract on behalf of the company.[512]

It is here that section 40 of the Companies Act 2006 may be of relevance again.[513] Any limitations under the company's constitution on the director's powers to 'authorise others' to bind the company will be deemed to be non-existent vis-à-vis third parties dealing with the company in good faith. Where the articles directly or indirectly[514] prevent the board from either entering or authorizing others to enter into certain types of contracts on behalf of the company—say contracts worth more than £1 million—the effect of section 40 is that this restriction is deemed to be non-existent so that the board can make the representation of authority necessary for the agent having apparent authority. However, section 40 only applies to limitations on the directors' powers contained in the company's constitution as defined; thus, limitations arising from by-laws and other internal arrangements of the board are not

[511] *Freeman & Lockyer (a firm) v Buckhurst Park Properties (Mangal) Ltd* [1964] 2 QB 480, 505.

[512] ibid. [513] But see French (n 1) 611: because of s 40, point (4) is no longer relevant at all.

[514] It is not entirely clear whether s 40 applies in situations where the articles do not explicitly limit the directors' power to authorize others to represent the company ('The board of directors cannot authorize the managing director to enter into contracts with a nominal value exceeding £1 million'), but directly and immediately provide for a limitation on the managing director's powers ('The managing director cannot enter into contracts with a nominal value exceeding £1 million'). Strictly speaking, this is not a limitation on the powers of the board of directors, although it could be said that indirectly and de facto it contains such a limitation: not only is the managing director prevented from entering into such contracts, implicitly the board cannot confer the required authority. On this issue see Reisberg and Donovan (n 372) 145.

within the section's remit.[515] Further, it is not entirely clear whether section 40 only applies in cases where authorization has been obtained directly from the board, as opposed to situations where authority has been delegated further down the chain of management (indirect authorization). If the latter type of situation would not be covered, the scope of application of section 40 would be rather limited. However, even if the scope of section 40 can be extended so as to cover indirect authorization it would still only deem away restrictions on the power of the directors contained in the company's constitution; not restrictions that were inserted into the delegation of authority from one level of management to the next.[516] For limitations that are outside the remit of section 40, the rule in *Turquand's* case may still provide some relief for third parties.[517]

As for (3), a third party can be said to have relied on the principal's representation only where the third party neither knew nor ought to have known that the agent had no actual authority.[518] Within the scope of application of section 40, the doctrine of constructive notice is stripped of much of its bite by section 40(2)(b): the third party is not bound to enquire into any constitutional limitations on the directors' power to delegate authority, the burden of proof for bad faith is on the company, and not even the third party's knowledge that an act goes beyond the constitutional restrictions is enough to destroy good faith. However, section 40 protects a third party only in its reliance on the belief that the directors' power to authorize others to represent the company is free from any constitutional restrictions. A third party is still required to ascertain whether the directors did in fact authorize the person purporting to act on behalf of the company where the circumstances suggest that such enquiry should be made.[519] Outside the scope of section 40, *Turquand* may again provide some relief.

2. *France and Germany*

French and German literature on corporate law have in common that the general rules of attribution are normally not discussed therein. The reason may be that the authorization of corporate agents below board level follows the general rules on agency without any corporate law-specific modifications, unlike the situation in the UK. The French and German laws on agency have many features in common: the principal will only be bound where the agent acts in the name of the principal and within the authority granted by the principal (direct representation).[520] Where the principal remains undisclosed (indirect representation) agency principles do not apply. German law clearly distinguishes between the agent's authority to act on behalf of the principal and the underlying reason for granting that authority, which may be a contract of employment or mandate or other contract. In principle, the validity of the agent's authority is independent from the validity of the underlying contract.[521] Both legal systems know a functional equivalent to apparent authority. Under French law, apparent authority is particularly relevant where a corporate employee below board level seeks to contract on behalf of the company. A third party may rely on apparent authority where they have been subject to a 'legitimate error', that is, under the circumstances the third party was justified in assuming that the agent had the alleged authority and there were no obvious reasons to doubt the agent's authority. This normally requires that the relevant corporate organ has made a representation regarding the authority of the agent

515 Davis and Worthington (n 9)164 (para 7-16).
516 ibid 169–70 (para 7-25).
517 But see French (n 1) 615: the rule in *Turquand's* case replaced completely by s 40, except for charitable companies.
518 Davis and Worthington (n 9) 168 (para 7-24).
519 *Wrexham Association Football Club Ltd v Crucialmove Ltd* [2006] EWCA Civ 237, para [47].
520 Civ Art 1984; BGB, §164.
521 BGB, §§167, 168.

on which the third party relied.[522] Under German law, apparent authority arises where the principal knows and tolerates that the agent acts in such a way that a third party may reasonably conclude that the agent has the respective authority. Further, the third party must have been in good faith, that is, they neither knew nor ought to have known about the agent's lack of authority.[523] Under both French and German law, apparent authority results in the principal being bound as if the agent had actual authority. This situation may be distinguished from a concept which may be termed 'authority by negligence'. Here, the principal does not know that the agent has been acting continuously on the principal's behalf in such a way that third parties could reasonably assume that the agent had been granted authority. Where the principal could have known about the agent's activities if the principal had taken the necessary care and the third party is in good faith, under German law the principal will again be bound as if the agent had actual authority.[524] French law is slightly different. Where apparent authority fails for some reason, the principal may be liable in tort vis-à-vis a third party in good faith for negligently projecting the appearance of the authority of the agent.[525]

As merchants by law,[526] German private and public companies may grant authority in form of *prokura* and may appoint a *prokurist*.[527] There is no French equivalent to this concept. However, the German primary rules of attribution rely on the concept in the sense that in deviation from the general joint representation by all board members, the articles may provide for representation by a single board member acting jointly with a *prokurist*.[528] *Prokura* can only be conferred by way of an express declaration. Its characteristic feature is the extent of authority it confers on the *prokurist*: he is authorized to enter into all transactions and carry out any legal acts that may occur in the course of conducting a business, not just the business for which *prokura* has been granted.[529] Vis-à-vis third parties, the *prokura* is unrestricted and unrestrictable; it cannot be limited to certain transactions or certain types of transactions.[530] The granting of *prokura* is to be registered and disclosed in the commercial register, as is the withdrawal of *prokura*.[531] Registration of either event has only declaratory effect. However, third parties are protected: where the withdrawal of *prokura* has not been registered, the lack of authority cannot be invoked against third parties unless they knew of the withdrawal.[532]

3. *United States*

The officers' powers to represent the corporation are governed by the general rules of agency, which are very similar to English law. In principle, any officer has only such powers and authority as has been delegated to him by the corporation, either in its articles of association or by-laws, or by the board of directors. As long as an officer as an agent of the corporation acts within the authority so conferred the corporation will be bound; otherwise it will be bound only where the act or transaction is subsequently ratified or the corporation is estopped from invoking lack of authority because the agent had apparent authority.[533] Ratification of an act outside the officer's authority by the corporation requires that the principal, in full knowledge of the facts, expresses a clear and absolute intent to ratify the act, in which case the act binds the corporation as if it had been originally authorized.[534]

[522] C Frey, 'Frankreich' in W Hadding an U Schneider (eds), *Die Vertretung verselbständigter Rechtsträger in europäischen Ländern* (Ducker & Humboldt 2003) 187–93.
[523] BGH, (2007) Neue Juristische Wochenschrift 312, 314.
[524] BGHZ 5, 111, 116 (1952).
[525] Frey (n 522) 187.
[526] GmbHG, §13(3); §AktG, §3(1).
[527] HGB, §48.
[528] AktG, §78(3).
[529] HGB, §49. The *prokurist* may dispose of real property only if specifically authorized to do so.
[530] HGB, §50.
[531] ibid §53.
[532] ibid §15(1).
[533] Fletcher (n 246) §434.
[534] ibid §437.100.

Actual authority is the authority intentionally conferred on the agent by the principal, either expressly and through specific instructions, or impliedly. Depending on the nature of the business and the position of the agent within the hierarchy of the firm, the agent will be deemed to have incidental powers to carry out those acts that are reasonable and necessary for the agent to effectively exercise his express authority. Implied authority may thus be characterized as 'actual authority circumstantially proved'.[535] The principal intends the agent to have these incidental powers and they are proper, usual, and necessary for the exercise of the authority actually granted.[536] Apparent authority arises where a principal voluntarily places an agent in a position where an ordinary business person is justified in believing that the agent is acting in accordance with actual authority.[537] In other words, the principal must have caused a third party's believe that the agent 'is clothed with apparent authority' by either holding the agent out as possessing sufficient authority for the act at issue, or by knowingly permitting the agent to act as having such authority.[538] Importantly, and similar to English law, apparent authority does not arise from the agent's own acts; it is the principal's direct or indirect representation to a third party which brings about apparent authority. A single transaction may be sufficient.[539] In addition, the third party contracting with the agent must have been acting in good faith and reasonably believed that the agent had the necessary authority to bind the principal. There is no absolute duty to inquire about a corporate officer's authority. A third party can rely on the apparent authority until something occurs that would cause a reasonable person to make further inquiries, such as a contract or transaction that is unusual or extraordinary for the corporation at issue.[540]

Ascertaining whether a corporate officer had apparent authority is a fact-sensitive affair; what matters are the nature and size of the corporation's business and all the surrounding circumstances.[541] A specific form of apparent authority is inherent authority or inherent powers (contrary to implied authority which is a form of actual authority). Inherent authority is based on the idea of the 'customary authority' of a person in a specific agency relationship so that no further representation is required than the existence of the agency relationship as such. In a situation where the principal has restricted an agent's authority, a third party may reasonably believe that the agent has the powers that are usual or incidental to the transactions that the agent is authorized to conduct unless the third party has notice that the agent's authority is restricted in this way. These inherent powers may be inferred from the status of the agent's office relieving a third party from inquiring whether the officer's authority has possibly been limited. The appointment of a person as CEO and chairman of the board may be sufficient to create the apparent authority of a general agent for the corporation.[542]

Questions and comments:

1. When the First Company Law Directive was enacted, the *ultra vires* doctrine was already on its way out as far as transactions with third parties were concerned. Having accelerated this process was a positive aspect of the Directive and it may be argued that it contributed to removing uncertainty in cross-border contracting. Whether at the time of the Directive's enactment the national rules constituted an actual impediment to cross-border trade is perhaps impossible to verify empirically. The fact, however, that corporate laws in the United States largely followed a similar

[535] ibid §438. [536] ibid §440. [537] ibid §442. [538] ibid §451. [539] ibid §449.
[540] ibid §451. [541] ibid.
[542] Normally, however, the inherent powers of officers to represent the company are rather limited; generally, titles of office may only in combination with other circumstances suggesting authority justify the reliance by third parties on the outward appearance; ibid §441.

trajectory would seem to suggest that convergence occurred 'naturally' over time and would have continued with similar results even without a Directive. What may be the reasons for this 'natural' convergence?

2. By insulating the board's authority to represent the company from constitutional restrictions, the Directive assigns the risk of detrimental transactions resulting from a breach of constitutional restrictions on corporate capacity and representation to the company and its shareholders as the deemed 'cheapest cost avoiders'. The primary rules of attribution in accordance with the Directive seem to provide greater certainty for third parties aiming to contract with the company. Third parties generally do not have to study the articles of association when they deal with a company through the board; this may save time and transaction costs. However, the protection for third parties is not complete. The 'irreducible minimum' that is necessary in order to invoke the national provisions implementing the Directive remains an unresolved issue. Take the factual setting in *Hurley*. If the case would have to be decided in application of the principles enshrined in Directive (EU) 2017/1132 would the outcome be any different?
3. Moreover, the vast majority of contracts are not concluded through the board, but through lower level management acting on the basis of delegated authority. The law of agency applies. Directive (EU) 2017/1132 has no impact on these general rules of attribution. In the UK, the national legislation implementing the Directive is extended, by way of 'gold plating', so as to modify certain aspects of agency law. Given that the rules on agency seem to be much more important for corporate representation, what might be the reason for the lack of harmonization in this area?

C. Concluding Remarks

In this chapter, we have looked at the incorporation process and corporate representation, largely following the regulatory pattern set out by the First Company Law Directive, now Directive (EU) 2017/1132. A strict, onerous, and lengthy incorporation process that involves detailed assessment of incorporation documents by a designated authority favours market integrity and respectability of market participants over dynamism and easy market access. By contrast, fast and easy incorporation processes create an entrepreneurial environment in which anyone can easily commence business in corporate form; it also makes it easier to abuse the legal entity form—by hiding assets from creditors, manipulating financial statements, moving assets around within a group of companies, etc.—and this needs to be tackled with strong complementary regulation. The configuration of the incorporation process is, in the end, a political decision shaped by prevalent attitudes in the business, legal and financial communities within a jurisdiction. These attitudes are historically conditioned, at least partially, and influenced by current competitive pressures and recent events such as corporate scandals and financial crisis. Despite the latter, over the last two decades we have experienced a shift towards more flexible approaches to incorporation; not, however, without some strong resistance in particular in Germany .

The First Company Law Directive provides an interesting case study on the political feasibility and practical significance of early company law harmonization. The First Company Law Directive was aimed at protecting the interests of third parties contracting with companies with a view to establishing and enhancing the internal market. This is to be achieved through harmonizing four themes: disclosure of company information; limiting the grounds for nullity; pre-incorporation contracts; and corporate representation. In all four areas the Directive's success in achieving its objectives seems to be limited. The disclosure of standardized corporate information in a public register allows third parties to ascertain who and what they are dealing with. Given the often confusing structures of corporate groups with a multitude of subsidiaries with similarly sounding names, this may be essential for being able to allocate assets and liabilities reliably amongst different group entities. As long as registers remain fragmented along national lines, the internal market effect will be limited. An EU-wide register went live only in June 2017, and it is at the time of writing still not fully operational. Although the Directive aims to protect third parties, a narrow interpretation of the grounds for nullity may actually be detrimental to third parties by depriving them of access to corporate assets, as was the outcome in the famous *Marleasing* case. The case demonstrates the inherent tension between the abstract protection of third parties linked to the internal market and their substantive protection in a concrete case. In the view of the Court of Justice, the former seems to outweigh the latter; although in *Rabobank* the Court's decision resulted in the substantive protection of the company contrary to the internal market rationale. In policy terms, both cases are hard to reconcile. The interpretation of the implementing provisions on pre-incorporation contracts by the national courts of the Member States under consideration varies considerably, and sometimes the respective provisions are surrounded and supplemented by a complex national doctrine. For the establishment of the internal market, these rules seem to matter little because the entities in respect of which these issues typically arise are unlikely to trade much across borders. The removal of (the external effect of) the *ultra vires* doctrine and the insulation from constitutional restrictions of the primary rules of attribution render transactions concluded through the board more stable. However, many loopholes remain and the practically more important secondary rules of attribution have not been addressed at all. On that basis, although often hailed as a cornerstone of EU company law,[543] the First Company Law Directive's symbolic significance as the EC's first venture into the heartland of commercial/corporate law seems to be more important than its practical impact.

[543] Grundmann (n 7) 146–7.

PART 2

STRATEGIES TO REDUCE AGENCY COSTS BETWEEN DIRECTORS AND SHAREHOLDERS

In the next five chapters, we will analyse the distribution of decision-making power within the corporation and strategies to supervise those in control in order to ensure that they do not use their powers to engage in activities imposing costs on other corporate insiders. This fundamental problem of corporate law is often said to be the domain of corporate governance. Corporate governance has seen a remarkable growth in scholarship over the last decades and a proliferation of regulatory initiatives dealing with questions of board structure, shareholder engagement, and the compensation of officers and directors, to name but a few topics. In the wake of the global financial crisis of 2007–2009, compensation practices and opaque corporate structures attracted significant criticism for facilitating excessive risk-taking, failing to promote a sustainable development of the enterprise, and preventing the board and shareholders from effectively monitoring management.[1] As a result of the financial crisis and other corporate scandals, in most legal systems, a detailed body of rules exists today that governs the internal structure of the company and the role and position of the corporate insiders.

Thus, corporate governance can claim to be a field of research and policy-making in its own right, not merely a subfield of corporate law that is confined to some questions of detail. It transcends corporate law in that governance structures are a function of the multifaceted activities that a corporation pursues. Corporate law proper regulates the relationship of the corporate organs to each other and, to some extent, the protection of the company's creditors. But the business corporation is more than a nexus of legal relationships between the shareholders, managers, and creditors. It is an employer of persons that rely on the successful operation of the company for their subsistence. It is an actor in product markets, and as such subject to the forces of competition and the legal rules that govern its transactions with other market participants. It may raise capital by issuing shares and bonds to the public. It must, therefore, abide by the regulatory regime that shapes the financial markets, is supervised by a public regulator, and makes use of the services of financial intermediaries, so-called gatekeepers. The level of its debt may exert a disciplining effect on management.[2] Lastly, and not least importantly, the corporation is based in a community and is subject to

[1] See, for example, Basel Committee on Banking Supervision, Principles for enhancing corporate governance (March 2010); European Commission Green Paper on corporate governance in financial institutions and remuneration policies, COM(2010) 284 final; OECD Steering Group on Corporate Governance, The Corporate Governance Lessons from the Financial Crisis (February 2009); Walker Review of Corporate Governance in UK Banks and Other Financial Industry Entities (November 2009).

[2] SJ Grossman and OD Hart, 'Corporate Financial Structure and Managerial Incentives' in JJ McCall (ed), *The Economics of Information and Uncertainty* (University of Chicago Press 1982) 107–37 (arguing that the issuing of debt is a bonding device that allows the managers to convince the market that they will act in the shareholders' interest).

social and political pressures and the various legal rules that order society, for example tax law and environmental regulation.

While we will concentrate in the following chapters on the legal mechanisms that are commonly seen as a part of corporate law, we should not lose sight of the social dimension of the business corporation, the interconnectedness of corporate governance and regulatory strategies from other areas of law, and the extra-legal factors that impose constraints on managerial discretion. As we will see, it is the role of corporate governance to determine to what extent the managers are expected to take the corporation's social dimension into account when they make business decisions and, thus, which social conflicts are addressed by corporate law and which are left to be regulated by other mechanisms. As we assess the efficiency of corporate governance institutions from a comparative perspective, it is important to understand that regulatory regimes may pursue different goals. Even where the goal is the same, for example the protection of investors, it may be achieved by means of different legal tools or indeed non-legal substitutes, such as the company's debt-equity ratio or the concentration of equity in the hands of a controlling shareholder.[3] Therefore, the comparison of corporate governance systems from different jurisdictions has to involve a comprehensive assessment of legal, economic, and other social factors that together determine regulatory outcomes.

Chapter 4 introduces the concept of agency costs, which is the central element of much of modern corporate governance theory. It has informed the orthodox view of the regulatory objectives of corporate governance since Michael Jensen and William Meckling built a new theory of the firm around agency costs in a seminal article from 1976.[4] Chapter 4 also presents the main corporate actors and examines the body of rules that lies at the heart of corporate governance: board structure regulation, consisting of both statutory rules and non-binding best practice standards laid down in corporate governance codes. In this context, we will analyse the main feature that distinguishes corporate governance systems, the design of the board of directors as a one-tier or two-tier board. The former combines full-time managers (executive directors) and corporate outsiders, who have a largely supervisory role (non-executive directors), on one board of directors. The latter differentiates more formally between executive directors, who sit on the management or executive board, and non-executive directors, who sit on the supervisory board. In addition, we will discuss how boards—in both one-tier and two-tier systems—should be structured to ensure that they function well. For example, should they be composed of a majority of independent directors, should the board form committees that are entrusted with particularly sensitive decisions, such as succession planning, and what should be the role of the chairman of the board?

Chapter 5 takes the analysis of the nature of the company and the objectives of corporate governance regulation a step further by asking who holds ultimate decision-making power in the corporation, the shareholders or the board of directors. This question can only be understood historically, since the allocation of corporate power is influenced by the legal principles that were used to conceptualise the business corporation when it emerged in its modern form in the nineteenth century. It has ramifications for modern-day corporate governance regulation, because it determines the law's understanding of what kind of creature the business corporation is: an entity that should be run in the interests of the shareholders, who are seen as synonymous with the company, or one that has a more inclusive purpose, since the shareholders are only one of several constituencies that are affected by, and

[3] Ownership structure is interpreted as a substitute for minority shareholder protection by R La Porta, F Lopez-de-Silanes, A Shleifer, and RW Vishny, 'Law and Finance' (1998) 106 Journal of Political Economy 1113.

[4] MC Jensen and WH Meckling, 'Theory of the Firm: Managerial Behaviour, Agency Costs, and Ownership Structure' (1976) 3 Journal of Financial Economics 305; reproduced in MC Jensen, *A Theory of the Firm: Governance, Residual Claims, and Organizational Forms* (Harvard University Press 2000) 83–135. See also the brief discussion in Chapter 1E above.

participate in, the exercise of corporate power. Notwithstanding the answer to this question, it is clear that decision-making power cannot be exercised in an unconstrained fashion to the detriment of other corporate actors whose legal or economic position is affected by the decision. In Chapter 5, we will therefore also discuss a first type of constraint on corporate power, the distribution of decision-making power among different corporate actors, and the safeguarding of this allocation, either by explicit statutory determination of the competences of the corporate organs or implicitly by drawing on general conceptions of the corporation. Furthermore, we will review the main element that constitutes what could be called shareholder democracy: the right of the shareholders to vote, in particular in elections to the board of directors.

Chapters 6 and 7 address the second important type of standards that the law has developed to limit power and make corporate actors responsive to the consequences of their actions: fiduciary duties. Directors' duties, notably the duties of care and loyalty, which are the focus of Chapter 6, are well developed in most legal systems. They constrain the discretion of directors and seek to ensure that management decisions are taken in the best interest of the company and the shareholders. In addition, most legal systems, albeit to differing degrees, use duties more generally to impose constraints on corporate actors who are in a position to affect the well-being of others. Therefore, in Chapter 7, we will examine the duty-based constraints imposed on majority (and, in some cases, minority) shareholders who adopt resolutions in general meeting or take other actions that have an effect on individual shareholders.

Finally, Chapter 8 deals with a second dimension of what has been discussed in the previous chapters: enforcement. A legal system may provide for detailed and well-formulated rules to protect investors and other stakeholders in the corporation, but if these rules are not effectively enforced, the actual level of protection may be low. Lack of enforcement may have different reasons. The procedural rules that define by whom and under which conditions an action can be brought may not be conducive to litigation; potential claimants may lack the incentive to bring an action, in particular because they bear the litigation risk and must share the proceeds of a successful lawsuit; or private parties may prefer alternatives to litigation because of certain deficiencies in the workings of judicial institutions.[5] Again, we need to be mindful that regulatory outcomes may be achieved through different channels. A substitute for weak private enforcement, for example because of the ineffective design of minority shareholder lawsuits, is public enforcement, which may consist in liability under criminal law or administrative sanctions. We will focus on private enforcement, particularly the minority shareholder lawsuit, but also refer to substitute mechanisms where appropriate.

[5] For example, the long duration of lawsuits can be a factor that deters investors from bringing litigation. See M Ventoruzzo, 'Experiments in Comparative Corporate Law: The Recent Italian Reform and the Dubious Virtues of a Market for Rules in the Absence of Effective Regulatory Competition' (2004) 40 Texas International Law Journal 113, 142.

4

Corporate Governance Regulation

A. Power and Legitimacy in Business Corporations

Power requires legitimation.[1] It is evident that corporations wield significant power over the economy, the community, and the lives of individuals. Their business decisions influence the labour market and the capital markets, the financial position of suppliers, consumers, creditors, and investors. What is more, not only those who enter into contracts with a company are affected by its operations, but often the wider community feels the reverberations of corporate success or failure. The consequences may be local, for example, when a company decides to relocate its head office, production plants, or research facilities, with a corresponding negative effect on the demand for labour, economic development, and possibly

[1] To be more precise, in order to translate into acceptable authority, power must be legitimate. For a classic treatment of both concepts, power and authority, see M Weber, *Economy and Society* (1922, G Roth and C Wittich (eds), University of California Press 1978) 53, 212–301, 941–55 and *passim*. Economic power, exercised by 'large-scale capitalistic enterprise[s]' (ibid 941) is addressed at 941–8, and the problem of legitimation (understood as an empirical, not a normative concept) at 212–16, 954.

social cohesion in the municipality or region where they are situated. Notably, the well-being of a company's employees depends to a large extent on the business decisions of the company. This begins with the decision to hire an applicant, continues throughout the employment relationship, since an employer is generally able to give directions within the terms of the employment contract,[2] and may culminate in the restructuring of the corporation and ensuing redundancies. Furthermore, resource-intensive industries may put a significant strain on the environment through their use of energy and raw materials and the creation of emissions, even if they operate within legal limits.

However, the consequences of business decisions may go far beyond a region or even a nation. We have seen throughout history that the failure of a firm may have ripple effects felt also by those who do not stand in a legal relationship with the failing corporation. An example is the bankruptcy of Lehman Brothers in 2008, which brought the global financial system to the brink of collapse. These ripple effects are a result of the interconnectedness of businesses in the global economy. Interconnectedness is particularly pronounced in the financial sector, where the failure of a large, systemically important financial institution may have severe effects on the financial condition of other institutions.[3] An example of the transmission of a financial shock that initially only affects individual institutions in a systemic fashion is the forced fire sale of assets. Assume that the market has doubts about the solvency of a financial institution. As a consequence, the institution's refinancing costs will increase, up to the point where the institution might have to sell its long-term assets to repay its debt. If the sale is of sufficient magnitude, it will depress the price of the assets in the market. Other institutions that hold the same assets and that mark to market, i.e. that value assets in their books at the current market price, will have to recognize the decline in the assets' value as losses and may, accordingly, experience financial distress themselves.[4] Because of this fragility of the financial system, an important part of recent initiatives to reform corporate governance has focused on the financial sector. In many jurisdictions, we are now dealing with two fairly distinct sets of corporate governance rules: one for financial institutions, which is characterized by a high degree of detail and the binding nature of the rules,[5] and one for other corporations that is more permissive and follows in part the so-called 'comply or explain' principle.[6]

[2] In firms, the allocation of factors of production (labour and capital) between different uses is not achieved by means of the price mechanism, but by direction through the entrepreneur, see RH Coase, 'The Nature of the Firm' (1937) Economica 386, 388. The reason is that, at least up to a certain point, market transactions involve higher transaction costs than the establishment and maintenance of a hierarchical organization. See ibid 390–5 and Chapter 1A above. For a more detailed discussion of transaction costs and the implications of using the market mechanism as opposed to hierarchical structures, see O Williamson, *The Economic Institutions of Capitalism* (Free Press 1985) 18–22, 90–5, 131–62 (arguing that market-mediated transactions rely more on high-powered incentives than hierarchical organizations). The discretion of the entrepreneur in allocating factors of production is, of course, qualified by legal constraints, mainly stemming from employment law. For the UK, see eg *Malik v Bank of Credit and Commerce International SA* [1998] AC 20 (HL) (holding that employment contracts contain an implied term of mutual trust and confidence requiring employers not to act in a manner that is likely to destroy or seriously damage that relationship without reasonable and proper cause); *Eastwood v Magnox Electric Plc* [2004] UKHL 35 (emphasizing that employers must treat their employees fairly, responsibly, and in good faith); *Jones v Associated Tunnelling Co Ltd* [1981] IRLR 477 (EAT) (employer had power to assign employee to a different workplace, but only a place that was 'within reasonable daily reach' of the employee's home); but see also *Lesney Products & Co v Nolan* [1976] EWCA Civ 8 (CA) (reorganization that reduced the amount of overtime did not of itself create a redundancy situation). A detailed coverage of the employment-related issues is beyond the scope of our inquiry.

[3] For a good overview of the role of systemic risk during the global financial crisis, see MF Hellwig, 'Systemic Risk in the Financial Sector: An Analysis of the Subprime-Mortgage Financial Crisis' (2009) 157 De Economist 129, 167–97.

[4] ibid 170–2.

[5] For example, the Capital Requirements Directive of 2013 (CRD IV), Directive 2013/36/EU on access to the activity of credit institutions and the prudential supervision of credit institutions and investment firms, [2013] OJ L176/338, contains detailed rules on board structure and remuneration policy, Arts 88–96. See also the European Commission Green Paper 'Corporate governance in financial institutions and remuneration policies', COM(2010) 284 final.

[6] More on 'comply or explain' in section C.III below.

Thus, we can see that the exercise of corporate power has various implications, both for corporate insiders and outsiders. In this chapter, we will first analyse whether the corporation is merely a profit-maximizing entity or whether it performs a more inclusive, social function (this section). We will then discuss some basic economic concepts that are important in order to understand the underlying conflicts that corporate governance regulation seeks to address, such as efficiency, incomplete contracts, and agency costs (section B). Section C will examine the goals that corporate governance regulation in the United States, the UK, Germany, and France pursues and will give an overview of the evolution of the corporate governance movement, which started in the United States in the 1970s. Section D will introduce the most important corporate actors—officers, directors, and shareholders—and explore whether patterns of ownership of public stock corporations have changed over time and continue to differ between our four countries. Finally, in section E, we will ask how corporate boards should be structured, for example as far as their size or composition is concerned, in order to ensure that they work well. We will analyse how one-tier and two-tier boards are designed and how best practice standards promulgated by corporate governance codes shape the composition of boards.

I. The corporation as a public institution

The fact that corporations wield significant power has led some commentators to argue that they are *social* or *public* institutions.[7] This claim goes to the heart of much that this and the following chapters are about: the legitimacy of corporate power, the goal of corporate governance, the composition of the governing organs of a corporation, and the duties of directors. However, the debate is complicated by the absence of an established definition of a 'social' or 'public' institution. In order to get a clearer sense of these terms, and hence the social dimension of corporations, the economic concept of 'externalities' may be a useful starting point. An externality is commonly defined as the effects of the actions of an agent in the economy on the well-being of another which are not mediated by the price mechanism.[8] For example, if the emissions produced by a firm in the process of manufacturing a good affect the health of people living in the vicinity of the factory *and* the people have not agreed with the firm to tolerate the emissions and be compensated for them, they are a negative externality. Externalities, therefore, do not arise if actions are performed within a contract, because then the effects on both parties are priced in according to the agreement between them. If the contract is incomplete, default rules may apply that fill the gaps or the law may grant the aggrieved party a remedy. Furthermore, externalities can be internalized by operation of law, for example tort law, if a legal rule exists that allows the affected party to claim compensation.

In light of these considerations, one way to distinguish social from private acts is to ask whether the acts create externalities by affecting members of society outside of a legal relationship. We have mentioned an example of such social consequences above: the systemic effects of the financial distress of a credit institution on the financial system as a whole. Arguably, however, the social dimension of the corporation, as understood in parts of the literature, goes beyond externalities.[9] Owing to their financial and economic power, large corporations can influence the political processes that produce the laws and regulations applicable to them, they enjoy strong bargaining power, which may give them an advantage in the negotiation of contracts with smaller firms or individuals, for example their employees,

[7] See eg JE Parkinson, *Corporate Power and Responsibility* (Oxford University Press 1993) 23; RA Dahl, *After the Revolution? Authority in a Good Society* (Yale University Press 1970) 119–21.

[8] A Mas-Colell, MD Whinston, and JR Green, *Microeconomic Theory* (Oxford University Press 1995) 352.

[9] See Parkinson's discussion of corporate power (n 7) 8–21. Parkinson distinguishes between social decision-making power and political power, ie the power of corporations to influence government policy and law-making.

and, at least in imperfectly competitive markets, they set prices and have some discretion over the quality of their goods or services.[10] In a more subtle way, they can shape markets and consumer demand through the decision to pursue or discontinue particular product lines and even influence social values by setting consumption trends or promoting certain business policies, for example workforce diversity or the support of local suppliers.[11]

The qualification of business enterprises as public or private institutions is important for several reasons. First, the allocation of corporations to the public realm would remove a constraint from regulatory intervention. Inspired by ideas of natural rights, the distinction between the public and the private sphere emerged in England in the seventeenth century as a means to protect the individual against the powers of the monarch or parliament.[12] Individual freedoms of an economic or non-economic nature are now enshrined in the constitutions of most states.[13] Protection of property, freedom of contract, and freedom of occupation are regarded as defining distinctly private spheres. The state is not entitled to encroach upon them without justification.[14] The market as the social space where freedom of contract and occupation are pursued is seen as a means to allocate resources in an apolitical and efficient way.[15] Of course, the institutions of property and contract require the existence of a regulatory framework and the enforcement of that framework. Both the provision of legal rules and their enforcement are commonly undertaken by the state. For this reason, the legal realist movement, which was particularly influential in the United States in the early twentieth century, challenged the distinction between public and private law. The legal realists submitted that no legal doctrine was completely devoid of public interest considerations, even those that originated from an individualistic understanding of natural law principles, such as freedom of contract. They argued that the freedom of private parties to order their affairs according to their individual preferences was never accepted without limitations.[16] To

[10] A market is perfectly competitive if all economic agents are price-takers, ie their actions do not influence prices. This, in turn, requires that: (1) there are many sellers and buyers in an industry, each with a small market share; (2) the products are homogenous, ie the goods produced by firm 1 are a perfect substitute for those produced by firm 2; (3) buyers have perfect information about the quality of the goods; and (4) entry and exit are free. It is easy to see why these conditions are important. Generally speaking, a firm maximizes profit (revenue minus cost) if marginal cost (the cost of producing one additional unit of a good) equals marginal revenue (the revenue from producing the additional unit of the good). As long as marginal cost is below marginal revenue, the firm could do better by increasing production, whereas it is loss-making as soon as marginal cost exceeds marginal revenue. If a firm has market power, the decision how much to produce has an effect on prices. If the firm increases production, the price falls (the demand curve is downward-sloping: given no change in demand, the price must fall if quantity increases). This means that marginal revenue for a monopolist is less than the price that would prevail in a competitive market. One additional unit of output can only be sold at a price that is slightly lower than the price at which the previous unit was sold. In more technical terms, the monopolist's marginal revenue curve is below the demand curve, while both are identical in the case of perfect competition. Consequently, the monopolist will produce less than the competitive firm and sell at a higher price. However, if other firms can easily enter the market or consumers can switch to comparable goods offered by other producers, these other firms will undercut the price of the former monopolist, thus reducing price and monopoly profits in the long run. In reality, most markets do not meet the conditions of perfect competition. See eg VJ Tremblay, CH Tremblay, *New Perspectives on Industrial Organization* (Springer 2012) 177–210.

[11] Parkinson (n 7) 19.

[12] MJ Horowitz, 'The History of the Public/Private Distinction' (1982) 130 University of Pennsylvania Law Review 1423; R Pound, 'Liberty of Contract' (1909) 18 Yale Law Journal 454, 455–62.

[13] See for example Arts 12, 14 of the German Basic Law (Grundgesetz), protecting property rights and the right to choose one's occupation and place of work.

[14] FA Hayek, *The Constitution of Liberty* (1960, Routledge Classics 2006) 123–5, is one of the most prominent advocates of a system of property rights and freedom of contract as devices to protect individual liberties against coercion by the state. For an early exposition of the limits of the state and the protected private sphere of the individual as mediated, for example, by property rights see JS Mill, *On Liberty* (1859, Penguin Classics 1985) Chapter IV, in particular 155–6 (arguing that property, income, and other aspects of work relations belong to the private realm). See also Pound (n 12) 457–62, who explains how the individualistic conception of justice prevalent in common law increased (in his view: exaggerated) the importance of property and contract.

[15] Horowitz (n 12) 1425–6.

[16] Pound (n 12) 470–87, gives examples and traces the development of contract law during the end of the nineteenth and beginning of the twentieth century to illustrate how public policy considerations became increasingly important in a field of law initially dominated by libertarian ideas.

the extent that it was accepted, the decision to uphold and enforce private agreements rested on a public interest rationale itself.[17]

Nevertheless, the public/private distinction, even if it cannot be maintained with perfect conceptual clarity, carries some weight because it determines the 'burden of proof' regarding the suitability and necessity of regulatory intervention. If corporations are public institutions that pursue a social purpose, it is natural to hold that the state can exercise regulatory control over them and has the authority to intervene in their operations whenever this is deemed expedient.[18] If they are private institutions, the public discourse that precedes regulatory intervention will presumably expect some justification on the part of the policy-maker of why private ordering is inadequate to achieve an efficient allocation of resources, or why it is not appropriate to use economic efficiency as a benchmark. Prima facie, in the private realm, unimpeded activity by private actors following the abstract and general rules of contracts and property initially set by the legislator is deemed the more suitable and morally defensible way to order social affairs.[19]

Secondly, the question has implications for the structure and composition of the corporation's governance organs. If it is accepted that corporations are public institutions akin to bodies that perform state functions, a strong case can be made that the legitimacy of corporations should be decided according to the same principles that legitimize government authorities. For the pluralistic state of Western European provenance, this would mean: power must derive 'from fully democratic processes'.[20] Thus, it has been suggested that all affected interests should be reflected in the governance structure of the corporation, either through self-management by the workers and possibly other constituencies or representation of interested groups on the board of directors.[21]

Finally, the public or private qualification of business enterprises may tell us something about how corporate power can be legitimized, which, in turn, influences the purposes for which it can be exercised. As far as the legitimate objectives of corporate activity are concerned, we can read in the literature that the corporation, understood as a social enterprise, must serve 'public or social purposes'[22] or that corporate power is to be exercised 'in the public interest'.[23] In economic terms, this means that corporate activity transcends the narrow objective of shareholder value maximization. In order to assess whether the production plan of a corporation is optimal, we would not only consider the corporation's costs of production and expected revenue, but also the costs to any other member of society. If the production of a particular good imposes a cost on society that is not internalized, for example because the company is not required to compensate neighbours for emissions that reduce the value of their property, it is intuitive that the company will produce more than is socially optimal.[24] Managers who were required to act in the

[17] MR Cohen, 'The Basis of Contract' (1933) 46 Harvard Law Review 553, 558–62, 585–92.

[18] For such an argument see eg Parkinson (n 7) 23.

[19] For an analysis of the suitability of regulatory intervention from an economic point of view see RH Coase, *The Firm, the Market, and the Law* (University of Chicago Press 1988) 24–6.

[20] Dahl (n 7) 7.

[21] ibid 130–9. See also our discussion in the text to nn 167–172 below. Some successful examples of self-management exist. The most famous is probably the Mondragón Corporation, an association of cooperatives that was founded in the Basque region of Spain in 1956 and has grown from relatively humble beginnings to one of Spain's largest business enterprises. The association is based on ten basic cooperative principles that provide, inter alia, that all workers are members of the cooperatives, have one vote per person, and that the organization follows democratic principles. The members do not only have the right, but the obligation to vote in the central governing body, the General Assembly. The General Assembly elects the Governing Council, which in turn appoints (and can remove) the managers. For a description of the governance structure and organizational charts see RAG Monks and N Minow, *Corporate Governance* (5th edn, Wiley 2011) 403–9.

[22] RA Dahl, 'A Prelude to Corporate Reform' (1972) 1 Business and Society Review 17; Parkinson (n 7) 23.

[23] Parkinson (n 7). The terms 'social purposes' and 'public interest' are usually not clearly defined in the literature. See section II below.

[24] The reason is the following: We said above (n 10) that the firm maximizes profit if it expands production until marginal cost equals marginal revenue. In the case of negative externalities, the company's marginal cost function is below the society's cost function. If we take only the company's private cost into account (and we assume that the marginal cost function is increasing), the marginal condition (marginal cost equals marginal revenue) is satisfied by a larger quantity of output than would be the case if we considered also social cost.

public interest would therefore have to choose a different production plan: one that maximized the aggregate welfare of shareholders and all other parties that were affected by the company's operations. In other words, managers would be required to maximize social welfare.[25]

We can pursue this thought further. If it is correct, as we said above, that the social dimension of the corporation goes beyond the notion of externalities, it will not be sufficient to choose a production plan that maximizes revenue minus *social* cost.[26] It could be argued that managers should not only be guided by considerations of efficiency (including by adopting the perspective of society at large), but that they should take the wider social implications of their business decisions into account. To give a specific example, the decision of a corporation to close a plant may be efficient in that it maximizes profit and does not create externalities, because the workers are relocated to a different plant and the local economy was not dependent on the business generated by the plant. Alternatively, it is conceivable that changed market conditions have led to an excess of supply and the plant operates at a loss. In that case, potential negative externalities may be outweighed by the increased profitability of the firm after closure of the plant. However, in both cases, the closure may nevertheless be in conflict with the public interest, which may be defined as encompassing, in addition to considerations of revenue maximization or cost minimization, values such as the legitimate expectations of the workers to continue to work at that particular plant or the notion of autonomy, which may be impaired if persons lose their means of subsistence or are relocated to other parts of the country.[27]

In legal terms, this question is concerned with the definition of directors' duties. Most legal systems impose the explicit or implicit duty on directors to act in the best interest of the company.[28] However, directors' duties are often phrased in an open-ended way and do not specify what is the 'best interest' of the company. The two alternative conceptions of the corporation, as an institution that operates in the public interest or pursues private, economic goals, give us some guidance how we should understand ambivalent terms such as 'corporate interest'. Several approaches to interpreting directors' duties have been developed over time, which incorporate different variants of the public or private interest conception of the corporation. It may be helpful to divide these approaches into three groups, which we may call 'the strict economic view', 'the strict public interest perspective', and 'the qualified economic view'.

The strict economic view requires directors to achieve a clearly specified economic goal, for example the maximization of profits. The other extreme is the strict public interest perspective, which also specifies clear objectives. However, in contrast to the first view, it does not (or does not exclusively) define them with respect to some notion of economic efficiency, but establishes other standards that directors are required to meet, for example the protection of the rights of affected constituencies. Both views have in common that they restrict managerial discretion. In any given situation, only a limited number of actions will be duty-compliant. The third approach, the qualified economic view, defines the interest of the corporation in economic terms but grants directors discretion not to implement the optimal

[25] In practice, it would of course be difficult to identify the welfare-maximizing production plan, given that social welfare is a deeply ambiguous term and the measurement of welfare is highly problematic. For a good overview of the discussion see L Kaplow and S Shavell, 'Fairness versus Welfare' (2001) 114 Harvard Law Review 961, 977–98. For problems of measurement and interpersonal comparisons of welfare, see A Sen, *Choice, Welfare and Measurement* (Harvard University Press 1982) 203–81 and *passim*.

[26] See n 24 above.

[27] For another example, see Monks and Minow (n 21) 55–6: The CEO of Control Data Corporation, one of the leading computer manufacturers in the US in the 1960s, decided to move factories into the inner cities and provide jobs and training to persons from disadvantaged communities. These decisions were probably not in the financial interest of the company; the CEO was eventually ousted when CDC experienced financial difficulties. However, from a public purpose perspective, the CEO's actions might have been optimal.

[28] See section C.II below.

business decision (optimal in terms of maximizing or minimizing a single-valued function, for example the firm's profit or cost function) if they deem another, possibly social, goal to be more important or seek to balance several competing values.[29] This view, also known as the theory of managerial autonomy, was for some time seen as the preferred approach to designing directors' duties. Managers were trusted to be neutral arbiters of the conflicting interests of different stakeholders.[30] However, it has fallen out of favour since the 1980s because of the concern that managers and directors may use the broad discretion accorded to them to engage in self-serving behaviour.[31]

The three views are closely related to current debates in corporate governance. We will discuss them in more detail in section C.II below. For now, it is important to note that the discussion about the public or private nature of corporations has an obvious bearing on how directors' duties are to be interpreted. The view that corporate power is not legitimate unless it is exercised in the public interest leads to the second of the above approaches to directors' duties. It presupposes that the public interest can be identified with sufficient certainty, which may be difficult in practice, notably because it would need to be possible to assign weights to the interests of the different affected groups. However, at least in theory, this approach would require directors to act in a specified manner, namely in the public interest, which would be reviewable in court and might involve the restriction of shareholder rights and the reduction of e corporate profits.[32]

If the corporation is seen as a private, economic institution, the outcome is more open-ended. It would be necessary to rationalize the objectives of the corporation in economic terms.[33] The most prominent branch of normative economics, welfare economics, which uses efficiency criteria to assess the desirability of social states, may well lead to the result that the sole duty of directors is the maximization of shareholder value.[34] However, not all accounts of normative economics are based on a utilitarian calculus that entails the maximization of the welfare of some section of society (or, for that matter, the aggregate welfare of society).[35] Economic concepts are sufficiently elastic to support more inclusive approaches that encompass, for example, autonomy- or equality-based considerations.[36]

In addition, qualifying the corporation as a private, economic institution places individual action at the centre of analysis, rather than subordinating corporate activity to a particular understanding of the public interest. While normative discourse in economics, as in other disciplines, requires the postulation of criteria that function as terms of reference

[29] For a famous example see *Dodge v Ford Motor Co.*, 204 Mich. 459 (Mich. 1919), discussed in section C.I below.

[30] AA Berle and GC Means, *The Modern Corporation and Private Property* (1932, Transaction Publishers 1991), considered management by neutral technocrats who balance 'a variety of claims by various groups in the community' (ibid 312) as a solution to the problem of legitimacy and a third way between subordinating management to the exclusive interests of 'inactive and irresponsible security owners' and granting 'the controlling group free rein, with the corresponding danger of a corporate oligarchy coupled with the probability of an era of corporate plundering' (ibid 311).

[31] In particular, agency theory and transaction cost economics argue that management should be effectively controlled by the board of directors and that the board's primary function is to safeguard the interests of the stockholders, see FH Easterbrook and DR Fischel, *The Economic Structure of Corporate Law* (Harvard University Press 1991) 38; Williamson (n 2) 316–18.

[32] Parkinson (n 7) 23–5.

[33] Or in terms of property rights or freedom of contract, depending on whether the emphasis is placed on the *economic* or, more generally, the *private* nature of corporations.

[34] This is not necessarily always the result implied by efficiency criteria, because social welfare takes externalities into account. For a discussion of welfare and utility maximization in normative and positive economics, see DM Hausman and MS McPherson, *Economic Analysis, Moral Philosophy, and Public Policy* (2nd edn, Cambridge University Press 2006) 64–72, and for a discussion in the present context see section B.I below.

[35] See eg A Sen, 'The Moral Standing of the Market' (1985) 2 Social Philosophy and Policy 1, who distinguishes between 'welfarism', defined as 'judging states of affairs only by utility information', and 'consequentialism', ie 'judging actions, rules, etc, ultimately by the goodness of the state of affairs resulting from them' (ibid 8). For a further discussion see A Sen, 'Utilitarianism and Welfarism' (1979) 76 Journal of Philosophy 463; A Sen, *The Idea of Justice* (Penguin 2009) 277–8.

[36] Hausman and McPherson (n 34) 167–8; Sen (n 25) 25–31.

for the evaluation of social action, it does not determine a priori the range of acceptable individual actions. Rather, it allows variation (for example, in the form of the doctrine of freedom of contract) and subjects the consequences to scrutiny in order to assess empirically whether the regulatory framework is adequate in light of the postulated criteria and the criteria themselves are appropriate as a normative foundation.[37] Thus, the private and economic view of the corporation implies that there is not necessarily one optimal corporate governance structure or definition of directors' duties, and what is optimal may be contingent and subject to change. Depending on the consequences of different corporate governance arrangements, and having regard to other areas of regulation and the realities of market conditions, any one of the approaches to construing directors' duties outlined above may be adequate.

II. Limits to the public-interest conception of corporate power

Should the corporation be seen as a public or a private, economic institution? We will first discuss two arguments that are often advanced by those who consider that the corporation is a public institution. They submit that private ordering does not always lead to mutually beneficial results, because the parties do not enjoy equal bargaining power, and that it is not justified to qualify the shareholders as owners of the corporation. Corporate power, accordingly, should not only be exercised in the interests of the shareholders, but also in the interest of other parties that have a stake in the corporation.[38] We will then consider a number of arguments against the qualification of the corporation as a public institution and identify questions that are not resolved by either view. These questions will concern us throughout this chapter and the following chapters.

Unequal bargaining power. It has been said that the absence of the government from dealings between private parties, who can exercise their authority to form business associations and enter into contracts, increases individual freedom.[39] However, it is questionable whether this is always the case. For example, to say that an employer has no more or less power to manage and assign workers to various tasks than a consumer with respect to her vendor because both can switch to a different contracting party if they find the terms offered unacceptable, ignores the social realities of the employment relationship.[40] Typically, the bargaining power between employer and employee is unevenly distributed,

[37] In the literature, this process has been described as the 'two concepts of rationality' in economics, namely constructivist rationality and ecological rationality, see VL Smith, *Rationality in Economics* (Cambridge University Press 2008) 2. The former refers to the 'deliberate design of rule systems to achieve desirable performance' (ibid 2) and the latter to a social system that is 'adapted to the structure of its environment' (ibid 36). Smith explains that '[e]very business decision is someone's constructivist idea of a best or appropriate action, but whether that decision is ecologically fit is up to socioeconomic forces far beyond the originator'. He continues to point out that where the 'specific abstract propositions [of constructivist rationality] lead to some form of implementation, it must survive tests of acceptability, fitness, and/or modification'. ibid 25. See also ibid 38 for the evolutionary connotations of constructivist and ecological rationality. Variations in institutional design (possibly, but not only, as a consequence of variations in the normative foundations that are postulated) allow mechanisms of selection to apply that operate on the basis of goodness-of-fit and acceptability (adaptation to the structure of the system's environment).

[38] See eg Parkinson (n 7) 16-17 and 33–41.

[39] See Pound (n 12) 454, 463; Weber (n 1) 729–31.

[40] AA Alchian and H Demsetz, 'Production, Information Costs, and Economic Organization' (1972) 62 American Economic Review 777, interpret the employment relationship as a process of constant renegotiation as the employer directs or assigns the employee to new tasks and the employee does not terminate the employment relationship. In their view, the difference between a contract to buy, say, groceries and the relationship between an entrepreneur and her employees is that the latter is characterized by 'a team use of inputs and a centralized position of some party in the contractual arrangements of all other inputs'. This 'centralized contractual agent in a team productive process' is missing in other contractual arrangements and distinguishes the firm from those arrangements, not 'some superior authoritarian directive or disciplinary power': ibid 778.

because the transaction costs of the employee to find a new job are higher than those of the employer to find a new employee. The same can be said about many other contractual relationships with the corporation as one of the contracting parties. Suppliers may be economically dependent on the corporation because they have made firm-specific investments to develop products specifically suited to the needs of the corporation. Switching to a different purchaser would mean losing this investment. Likewise, customers may not be able to threaten credibly that they will purchase the goods or services elsewhere because the seller is a regional monopolist and contracting with another producer or service provider would involve high transaction costs. In these cases, it may not be easy to find a moral justification for private institutions that operate largely free from state intervention.[41]

Shareholders as owners. It is also not self-evident why shareholders should be regarded as the sole owners of the enterprise, in whose interests the corporation should be managed. The political scientist Robert Dahl called shareholder ownership 'the great myth of the nineteenth century'[42] and Adolf Berle and Gardiner Means maintained that a corporation belonged to its shareholders only '[b]y tradition'.[43] In the small owner-managed firm with a limited number of employees that was typical of most of the nineteenth century, the identification of those whose interests were at stake did not pose any difficulties. However, in the beginning of the twentieth century, and particularly in the decades after the First World War, the corporate economy experienced a profound transformation.[44] It came to be characterized by high concentration and large, integrated combines with complex, multidivisional structures and a workforce numbering in the thousands or, in some cases, tens or even hundreds of thousands.[45] The organizational tasks could no longer be fulfilled by the classical owner-entrepreneur of the nineteenth century. Instead, the professional, technically skilled manager evolved who was entrusted with decision-making.[46] In many capital-intensive corporations, the founders relinquished control by selling part or all of their shares to the public.[47] Often, the public shareholders were not interested in the details of the business operations or the long-term prospects of the firm. They saw their holdings merely as an investment that would generate a rate of return and was to be divested when a more attractive investment opportunity arose. Thus, the roles of the corporate actors and the nature of the relationship between the 'owners' and the enterprise changed fundamentally. The two developments sketched here, the transformation of family-run enterprises into multidivisional firms with full-time, salaried, managers recruited from outside the founders' families, and the offering of shares to the public at large and the ensuing dispersion of the shareholder

[41] Weber (n 1) 729–31.

[42] Dahl (n 7) 131. See also P Ireland, 'Company Law and the Myth of Shareholder Ownership' (1999) 62 Modern Law Review 32.

[43] Berle and Means (n 30) 310.

[44] The classic treatment of this topic is AD Chandler, *Scale and Scope: The Dynamics of Industrial Capitalism* (Harvard University Press 1990) (analyzing the economies of the US, UK, and Germany). For an in-depth historical assessment of the British industry and corporate economy, see also B Cheffins, *Corporate Ownership and Control* (Oxford University Press 2008); and L Hannah, *The Rise of the Corporate Economy* (2nd edn, Methuen 1983).

[45] For organization charts of multidivisional firms of the early years of managerial capitalism, see Chandler (n 44) 44, 86–88. For a concise account of the transformation from the centralized, functionally departmentalized or unitary (U-form) structure to the multidivisional (M-form) structure, see Williamson (n 2) 279–85. The main structural innovation of the M-form is 'the creation of semiautonomous operating divisions ... organized along product, brand, or geographic lines', which were managed separately (ibid 281). Oversight is exercised by a general office that is responsible for the monitoring of divisional performance, resource allocation, and long-term planning. Thus, the M-form separates strategic from operational decision-making (ibid 281, 283–4).

[46] Hannah (n 44) 3–4, 70–89.

[47] For the reasons of this development in the UK, see Cheffins (n 44) 252–67. For example, the bullish stock market during some of that time gave proprietors an opportunity to cash out at a premium, ibid 263.

structure, led to the widely discussed 'separation of ownership from control'.[48] Its legal implications are far-reaching and remain a matter of debate. For present purposes, it should be clear that the owner-manager of the small nineteenth-century manufacturing enterprise and the shareholder of the modern large business corporation are two very different persons, as far as the social dimension of the firm-shareholder relationship is concerned. It is, therefore, somewhat surprising that the legal treatment of both is the same.

At law, ownership rights, notably the right to use, transfer, and exclude others from an asset, exist with respect to the shares of the corporation. Shares themselves are an elusive legal concept that differs between legal systems. Without going into details, shares, as understood by most legal systems, can be described as a bundle of rights.[49] They comprise participatory rights, in particular the right to vote at general meetings, financial rights, for example the right to dividend payments and to a share of the surplus that remains after all other debts have been paid in the company's winding-up, and the interest in the share certificate if the shares are issued in certificated form.[50] However, they do not comprise any legal or equitable interest in the corporation's assets. Thus, the shareholders enjoy ownership rights over their shares, but only indirect and limited rights over the corporation and its assets, as defined in the articles of association and in legislation.

In principle, this position is not fundamentally different from that of debt holders or the corporation's employees. The debtholders' rights are *choses in action*, i.e. the legal qualification is similar to that of shares.[51] Standard loan agreements contain provisions that are intended to give the lender some control over the company's operations.[52] These rights do not

[48] Berle and Means (n 30) 3–10, 112–16 and *passim*. The concept was succinctly described ibid 5: The investor 'in a modern corporation so far surrenders his wealth to those in control of the corporation that he has exchanged the position of independent owner for one in which he may become merely recipient of the wages of capital'. See also H Hansmann, *The Ownership of Enterprise* (Harvard University Press 1996) 11, 299, who points out that it is more precise to speak of the separation of 'ownership from *effective* control', since the definition of ownership implied control. This is, of course, exactly the question: Whether it is justified to continue to call the shareholders 'owners' of the enterprise. We will discuss changes in ownership structure further in section D.IV below.

[49] In UK law, the most famous definition stems from Farwell J in *Borland's Trustee v Steel Brothers & Co* [1901] 1 Ch 279, 288: 'A share ... is an interest measured by a sum of money and made up of various rights contained in the contract [i.e., the articles of association], including the right to a sum of money of a more or less amount'.

[50] The nature of the interest in certificated and uncertificated shares is complex. Under UK law, shares are commonly classified as choses in action (for an early authority see *Colonial Bank v Whinney* (1886) 11 App Cas 426). However, it has been pointed out in the literature that a share is much more than a mere right *in personam*. It is an object of personal property that affords legal and equitable ownership. See PL Davies and S Worthington, *Gower's Principles of Modern Company Law* (10th edn, Sweet & Maxwell 2016) para 23-2. For example, in the case of certificated shares, legal title to the shares, and with it the bundle of membership rights, is transferred when the transfer form and the share certificate are delivered to the transferee and the corporation enters the name of the transferee in the register of members; ibid para 27-5. Beneficial interest, on the other hand, may pass at an earlier time, notably when the transfer documents are delivered; ibid 27-8. In the case of uncertificated shares, the shares are transferred electronically by means of book entry. The UK's electronic transfer system, CREST, also maintains a register of members for the participating companies (see the Uncertificated Securities Regulations 2001, SI No 3755, Art 20). The transferee acquires legal title when the shares are credited to his or her account with CREST and the register of members is updated. If a broker acts as nominee for the investor, which will be the case if the investor does not have an account with CREST, the broker acquires legal title and the investor beneficial ownership. For more details, see ibid 27-12. US laws qualifies the share (the bundle of membership rights) as intangible personal property and the share certificate as evidence of the shareholder's property interest (*Jellenik v Huron Copper-Mining Co.*, 177 U.S. 1, 11 (1900); *Kaiser v Moulton*, 631 S.W.2d 44, 48 (Mo. App. E.D. 1981)). In modern securities markets, the shares are generally intermediated and the shareholders do not hold legal title. According to the Uniform Commercial Code (UCC) §8-501(b)(1), they only acquire a so-called *security entitlement* if they transact with a securities intermediary. The security entitlement is seen as a 'sui generis form of property interest' (JS Rogers, 'Policy Perspectives on Revised U.C.C. Article 8' (1996) 43 UCLA Law Review 1431, 1496) that stands between claims *in personam* and claims *in rem* and gives the acquirer the position of a beneficial owner. The entitlement holder's property interest is specified in UCC, §8-503. For a summary of the operation of UCC Art 8 see C Bamford, *Principles of International Financial Law* (2nd edn, OUP 2015) 5.101–5.107.

[51] See Bamford (n 50) 5.18. For a classification of shares, see the previous footnote.

[52] For example, the standard form agreement of the Loan Market Association has space for financial covenants that typically include provisions concerning the borrower's debt-equity ratio, minimum working capital, liability/asset ratio, and dividend payments. Other undertakings may restrict the borrower's discretion how to run the business, for example, by prohibiting mergers and substantial changes of business or by requiring authorization for specified transactions. For a comprehensive treatment of loan agreements see J Benjamin, *Financial Law* (OUP 2007) 8.27–8.47.

derive from a statutory grant of authority, as in many legal systems the powers of the shareholders,[53] but the effect of the contractual provisions is the same. They mitigate investment risk by limiting the decision-making authority of the company's organs and reallocate the statutory distribution of corporate power.[54] We can go even further in our reinterpretation of the ownership position of shareholders. Some commentators regard corporate law as a set of default terms that the incorporators would have chosen had they been able to consider all possible problems ex ante and transaction costs had not been prohibitive.[55] On this view, corporate law is a shortcut that reduces the costs of bargaining and incorporation by supplying rules that are generally efficient, because they are in the parties' mutual interest. The parties are free to deviate from the default position and adopt rules tailored to their situation and preferences if a default term is not appropriate in a given case.[56] Through this lens, the safeguards contained in a loan agreement are merely contractual alterations of the default allocation of power, which is itself an expression of the implicit bargain underlying much of corporate law.[57]

Similar considerations apply to employees. With respect to their remuneration claims, they are creditors of the corporation and hold *choses in action*. Furthermore, depending on their position in the company, they may have significant influence on the company's operations. High-level employees, for example the senior managers, are recipients of delegated corporate power.[58] If they are also members of the board of directors, some corporation laws entrust them with original decision-making power.[59] Just as shareholders, employees (and also lenders if the loan agreement contains provisions to that effect) have qualified control over the corporation's assets to the extent that they are authorized to make corporate decisions. The exact demarcation between the shareholders' decision-making power and the powers of other constituencies is a matter for corporate law, the articles, and other contractual instruments.

The identification of the shareholders as the sole owners of the corporation is even less convincing from an economic point of view. Shareholders provide one factor of production, equity capital. Other factors of production include the financial capital supplied by lenders and buyers of debt securities, the capital stock (land, buildings, machinery) and materials that the firm acquires, and labour, i.e. the human effort used in the production process. Providers of financial capital are risk bearers who expect a return on their investment and suffer a loss if the firm's operations are not profitable. It is important to note that the risk-bearing function is not only borne by the shareholders, but by all providers of financial capital.[60] Financial capital differs in the expected return and the risk borne by investors. Shares are riskier than bonds because bondholders are paid first out of the firm's income, but the shareholders' return is potentially higher.[61] As far as labour input is concerned, some economists distinguish between the labour provided by the firm's workers and the coordinating

[53] See our discussion of the origins of corporate power in Chapter 5A. [54] Benjamin (n 52) 8.47.

[55] Easterbrook and Fischel (n 31) 34–5. [56] ibid.

[57] In some legal systems, the contractual nature of the corporation features prominently in court decisions as an interpretive device. See eg the judgment of the UK Court of Appeal in *Imperial Mercantile Credit Association v Coleman* (1870–71) LR 6 Ch App 558. Referring to the articles of association of companies, the court held: 'It must be left to [adult] persons to form their own contracts and engagements, and this Court has only to sit here and construe them'. ibid 568. We will discuss this and other related cases in Chapter 5A.

[58] Corporate power is generally delegated from the board of directors by means of a provision in the articles, bylaws, or a resolution of the board, see eg UK Model Articles for Public Companies, Art 5; Del. Gen. Corp. Law, §142; MBCA, §8.01(b).

[59] This is the case in Delaware (see Del. Gen. Corp. Law, §141(a)) and Germany (AktG, §76(1)), but not in the UK, where decision-making power is only vested in the directors by virtue of a default rule in the Model Articles (Model Articles for Public Companies, Art 3). The Companies Act 2006 does not contain any binding rules on the allocation of corporate power.

[60] EF Fama, 'Agency Problems and the Theory of the Firm' (1980) 88 Journal of Political Economy 288, 290.

[61] For a brief overview of the differences of debt and equity, see J Tirole, *The Theory of Corporate Finance* (Princeton University Press 2006) 75–7.

efforts of management. Management activities are a specific factor of production responsible for arranging and carrying out the contracts with the other input factors and directing the production process. If the risk-bearing and management functions are combined in one person, it may be justified to speak of this person (the entrepreneur) as the owner of the firm. But in many large modern corporations, risk-bearing and management are separated.[62] The production process depends on the coordinated interaction of many factors of production.[63] There is no economic reason why the shareholders should be singled out and their interest in the enterprise accorded a special position.[64] Once we recognize that '[e]ach factor in a firm is owned by somebody',[65] the focus shifts from the interests of 'the owner' of the firm to the owners of the various factors of production.

Thus, both points—unequal bargaining power and the fallacy of shareholder ownership—call into question the case for unregulated private ordering and a system of corporate governance oriented towards shareholder primacy.[66] However, convincing as this view may be, it does not show why corporations should be qualified as public, as opposed to private, institutions. We mentioned above that most instances of private ordering require a regulatory framework within which they unfold.[67] The fact that contractarian or other supposedly private mechanisms fail to provide for an appropriate balancing of conflicting interests does not mean that these legal or economic institutions should be reinterpreted from a public purpose perspective. In many cases, targeted regulatory intervention in private affairs may be all that is necessary, and such regulatory intervention is, of course, commonplace in the business world. Therefore, we need to enquire further into the divide between the public and the private realm to understand the role of the business corporation.

The concept of the public sphere. Public action is usually associated with the political sphere and the concept of the state. The Weberian definition of the state, which continues to command widespread support in the literature,[68] asserts that one of the key elements of the state, and indeed of political action in general, is the actual or potential application of physical force.[69] An organization belongs to the 'state' if it advances and 'upholds the claim to the *monopoly* of the *legitimate* use of physical force in the enforcement of [the state's] order'.[70] In opposition to this narrow definition, some political scientists assign any relationship of influence or domination to the public (political) sphere, such as the business enterprise, trade union, or family.[71] However, this view creates two problems. First, it marginalizes an important qualitative difference between the latter organizations and the state,

[62] Text to n 48 above. [63] Fama (n 60) 291, speaks of 'teams of cooperating factors of production'.

[64] It is frequently pointed out that the shareholders have most at stake because they are the residual risk-bearers: their claims are satisfied after those of all other providers of input factors. Consequently, it is claimed that they are more interested than other constituencies in the long-run profit-maximization of the corporation, which in turn benefits all parties that have a stake in the firm: Easterbrook and Fischel (n 31) 36. However, this view does not account for the fact that shareholders are often well diversified and can shift their investments with relatively low transaction costs in capital markets. Other constituencies, notably the employees, cannot diversify and may not be able to devote their human capital easily to other uses in the labour market. Therefore, it is not obvious that the residual risk-bearers have the greatest interest in the long-run viability of the firm. See Fama (n 60) 291–2.

[65] Fama (n 60) 290.

[66] We will discuss the case for private ordering and different models of corporate governance in more detail in sections B and C.II below.

[67] See text to nn 12–19.

[68] See C Hay, M Lister, and D Marsh (eds), *The State: Theories and Issues* (Palgrave Macmillan 2006) 5–6.

[69] Weber (n 1) 54. Weber defines a political organization as an organization whose 'existence and order is continuously safeguarded within a given territorial area by the threat and application of physical force'. On the distinction between political and economic action, see ibid 64–5.

[70] ibid 54.

[71] For example, Dahl (n 7) 6–7; reiterated in RA Dahl and B Stinebrickner, *Modern Political Analysis* (6th edn, Prentice Hall 2003) 22–6.

namely that they do not partake in the state's monopoly to use force.[72] Secondly, most social relationships are characterized by *some* exercise of influence or domination. Accordingly, the public or political sphere as defined by the second view would be very broad[73] and leave a large grey zone, where it would be unclear whether interaction amounted to 'exercise of influence or domination'.[74]

The problem of defining the public interest. This brings us to the next point. If business corporations were held to be part of the public sphere (however defined), it would be necessary to give concrete meaning to the concept of 'public interest'. Only a precise understanding of its content and limits could inform policy choices regarding the allocation of decision rights, composition of the company's governance organs, and definition of directors' duties.[75] However, the notion of 'public interest' or 'public good' is inherently difficult to state precisely, and no commonly accepted definition has yet emerged. Indeed, it is telling that even those who advocate most ardently that corporations should be managed in the public interest readily admit that they are concerned less 'with what the public interest actually is … than with appropriate mechanisms for securing it'.[76] A first possibility is to understand 'public interest' in the sense of welfare economics, that is, as the maximization of a social welfare function that aggregates the utilities of all members of society.[77] This view, of course, disregards a number of important questions, notably distributive issues and the relevance of non-utility information in the assessment of policy choices, such as equal treatment or autonomy. It would also not suggest a normative view of company law fundamentally different from the prevailing view in most capitalist economies. Regulatory intervention is widely accepted to correct externalities (and, as we will discuss, other market failures), and regulation is often informed by utility as well as non-utility considerations.[78] The question is usually only whether the most suitable regulatory tool to pursue the relevant policy goal is to be found in company law or in other legal areas, such as tax law or anti-discrimination law. Re-conceptualizing the business corporation as a public institution does not seem to be helpful in answering this question.

More widely understood, the notion of public interest may encompass social preferences and prevailing societal values.[79] As mentioned above, this view is concerned with the power of corporations to influence the political process or social values without

[72] J Hoffman, *Beyond the State* (Polity Press 1995) 45.

[73] See the examples in Dahl and Stinebrickner (n 71) 24, ascribing political aspects, inter alia, to private clubs and even romantic couples.

[74] For this reason, Weber suggests defining political organizations purely with a view to the means peculiar to them, namely the potential or actual use of force, and not the ends to which their actions are devoted or their consequences; see n 1 at 55.

[75] See our discussion in section I above.

[76] Parkinson (n 7) 22. The author continues to explain that 'referring to the "public interest" is [not] necessarily intended to suggest that there is an interest that should be served that transcends the interests of the individuals who are affected by corporate activity. Rather the term is meant to refer to some defensible balancing of the interests of affected groups, be they for example employees, customers, suppliers, the local community, or the community at large on the one hand, with on the other hand those of the shareholders and creditors that are the more traditional concern of company law', ibid.

[77] Sen (n 25) 18–19.

[78] On externalities, see text to nn 7–8 above, and on market failures more generally section B.I below.

[79] Parkinson (n 7) 317, gives the following examples of such preferences and values: safeguarding the environment 'for its own sake' (ie irrespective of the existence of negative externalities), ensuring the non-exploitative treatment of Third-World trading partners, and preserving the vitality of city centres by curtailing out of town shopping malls. As mentioned, economic concepts such as 'utility' are flexible enough to incorporate the attitudes of social actors towards these questions in the assessment of policy choices (although classical welfare economics rarely does so), see the references in n 36 above. The more important argument of those who advocate a re-conceptualization of companies as public institutions, it seems, is that companies may interfere with the public discourse that defines the relevant policy goals and regulation is not always capable of altering or constraining corporate behaviour so that it reflects existing social preferences, Parkinson (n 7) 324–9.

proper democratic legitimation.[80] These are, of course, valid concerns. However, it is also clear that they only apply to a small subset of companies: those with significant economic power, the 'giant corporations'[81] that started to be the target of criticism from the so-called corporate social responsibility movement in the United States in the 1970s.[82] The public interest conception that is intended to rein in such corporations, therefore, faces two definitional challenges. It has to distinguish between 'public' and 'private' companies, which would presumably not map neatly onto the demarcation between the different types of company that already exists under company law, since many public companies in the traditional sense do not have sufficient economic or political influence to mould societal expectations.[83] In addition, it has to identify the relevant social preferences or values that companies are expected to take into consideration and promote. It is suggested that they can be identified by giving those who are 'affected' by the activities of the company a role in shaping corporate conduct.[84] However, this simply replaces one ill-defined concept—public interest—with another: the group of people 'affected' by the company. In many cases, business decisions, for example the closure of a factory, will have numerous effects not only on those with whom the company stands in direct contact, but indirectly on members of their social networks, communities, and possibly society at large. It seems impossible to determine the relevant persons and interests with any certainty in practice.[85]

Thus, it is difficult to translate the public interest conception of the corporation into clear precepts that could inform the design and interpretation of corporate law. Irrespective of the conception of the corporation, we will see that externalities, unequal bargaining power, and other considerations not normally part of a utilitarian calculus are concerns of policy-makers in all legal systems. This is not different in our four jurisdictions, even though they all conceptualize the corporation as a private economic institution. However, this does not imply that they embrace shareholder value to the same degree, and their attitude towards the corporate economy has fluctuated over the course of history. In section C, we will examine how the interests of the corporation and the goal of corporate governance regulation are defined in our four legal systems, but first we will need to clarify some economic concepts in more detail, since much of modern corporate governance theory revolves around these concepts.

B. Corporate Governance as an Economic Problem

The basic social conflict that corporate governance addresses is very simple and was described succinctly by Adam Smith in words already quoted in Chapter 1. Given that the directors of a corporation are 'the managers rather of other people's money than of their own, it cannot well be expected, that they should watch over it with the same anxious vigilance with which the partners in a private copartnery frequently watch over their own.'[86] Thus, the conflict arises because in virtually all but the smallest business enterprises,

[80] These concerns go beyond the economic concept of externalities, see text to nn 9–11.

[81] R Nader, M Green, and J Seligman, *Taming the Giant Corporation* (Norton 1976).

[82] We will discuss corporate social responsibility and competing corporate governance theories in section C.II.

[83] Many legal systems, including Delaware, France, and Germany, have created several types of company with different attributes. Some are traditionally used by smaller businesses, while others, such as the French *société anonyme* or the German *Aktiengesellschaft*, are used by larger ones, but this is not necessarily always the case. In the UK, the main difference between public and private companies is that only the former can offer shares to the public: Companies Act 2006, s 755.

[84] Parkinson (n 7) 345–6, 365–6.

[85] If this assessment is correct, it will also not be feasible to impose a duty on directors to balance the affected interests in line with what we called the 'strict public interest perspective', see text to n 32 above.

[86] Adam Smith, *An Inquiry into the Nature and Causes of the Wealth of Nations* (1776, Edwin Cannan (ed), Methuen & Co. 1905) Book V, Chapter 1.107.

those who manage the corporation, and hence all its assets, are not the same as those who provide the assets. In other words, we observe a 'separation of ownership and control'.[87] It should be emphasized that the separation of ownership and control as such does not necessarily require regulatory intervention. However, it becomes problematic if the owners of the firm—the shareholders—act under incomplete information, because then they cannot discount the price they pay for their shares in light of the costs that arise as a consequence of the managers not watching over their investment with the necessary 'anxious vigilance'. It is clear that informational asymmetries exist between managers and shareholders. The owners cannot monitor those in control, at least not perfectly, in order to ensure that the latter exercise their control rights exclusively in the interest of the owners. They will not be in a position to review every decision that the managers take and assess the effort level they employ. They do not know whether the managers work as hard as they could, refrain from acting opportunistically, and consider carefully all available information before taking decisions. Thus, the separation of ownership and control *in combination with* informational asymmetries create what economists call a *principal-agent problem*: The welfare of the principal (in our context the owners of the corporation) depends on the acts of the agent (the corporation's managers). In the following sections, we will discuss the implications of this, and other, agency problems created by the use of the corporate form in more detail. We will first introduce some basic economic concepts that are necessary to understand the claims made by, and the consequences of, different theories of corporate governance fully. We will then give an overview of the strategies employed by legal systems to address the managerial and other agency problems. Finally, we will ask whether different perceptions of the corporation and approaches to corporate governance can be explained in light of different models of the market economy that countries have adopted. As we will see, countries can be distinguished by how they regulate the market economy. It would not be surprising if the regulatory response to agency problems in corporations reflected the general model of market capitalism that characterized an economy.

I. Efficiency and social welfare

Many scholars of corporate governance believe that the problems that corporate law deals with—notably managers serving their own interests instead of the interests of the shareholders and majority shareholders expropriating the minority—will be solved generally by the operation of the market.[88] Investors will not be willing to part with their money if managers are likely to appropriate the firm's profits and pay less than a competitive rate of return. Managers who take advantage of investors will face an increased cost of capital because investors will discount the securities offered by the corporation. Eventually, the corporation will be driven out of the market. At the same time, corporations are not entities with a predetermined organizational structure that investors have to accept. Rather, the governance structure of a company is designed by the incorporators, equity investors, and potentially the creditors in a way that best serves the needs of the different constituencies. The corporation is the product of a continuous negotiation process—it is a nexus of contracts. Optimal results will be achieved if the law allows for uninhibited contracting; the parties will opt for the organizational structure that is most appropriate for their purposes.[89]

This view goes back to Adam Smith's famous 'invisible hand'[90] and the first theorem of welfare economics: In a competitive marketplace, all mutually beneficial trades will be executed,

[87] Berle and Means (n 30) 84–111.
[88] For this view, see eg B Cheffins, *Company Law* (Clarendon Press 1997); Easterbrook and Fischel (n 31) 15–22.
[89] Easterbrook and Fischel (n 31) 17.
[90] Smith (n 86) Book IV, Chapter 2.9.

thus leading to an equilibrium allocation of resources that is economically efficient.[91] Economic efficiency in this context refers to the notion of *Pareto efficiency*. An allocation of goods is Pareto efficient if no one can be made better off without making someone else worse off.[92] To take a simple example: A values a certain good at £100. According to the theorem, if B values the same good at £120, the parties will enter into an agreement for the sale of the good from A to B for any price between £100 and £120 (depending on the bargaining skills of both parties). Once the sale is concluded, both parties will be better off (or one of the parties will be better off without leaving the other party worse off if the sale is executed at either £100 or £120). The transaction will lead to an increase in aggregate social welfare. Further transactions may ensue; A and B (and possibly other participants in the market) may continue to exchange goods as long as the exchange increases the utility of at least one of the participating persons and does not decrease the utility of the other(s).[93] Because no further trades will occur once the parties have maximized their utility, the resulting allocation is in equilibrium.

The same rationale can be applied to the formation and operation of corporations. If a corporation is understood as a nexus of contracts—contracts between the incorporators that deal with the internal structure of the corporation, between the shareholders (acting through the medium of the corporation) and the managers, other employees and creditors of the corporation, and contracts between existing shareholders and investors that subscribe for newly issued securities—and if all of these contracts are qualified as exchange relations, it follows that the parties, in bargaining and executing the contracts, will arrive at efficient outcomes. For instance, let us take the act of formation of the corporation—the filing of the memorandum of association and the drafting of the articles. This is not an exchange transaction in legal terms; the interests of the parties are not antagonistic but aligned. However, for purposes of economic analysis, the process of formation is comparable in that it serves to attain an optimal allocation of factors of production. Outside of the firm, factors of production (and other resources) are allocated according to the price mechanism. A series of transactions such as the ones described above direct the economic system. An entrepreneur who wishes to manufacture a good will buy the necessary materials, rent machinery to process the materials, and hire workers to operate the machinery and assemble the good. Each step might be implemented as an independent transaction, the entrepreneur entering into a contract only if it increases his or her utility. The defining characteristic of the firm is that this market-based mechanism of allocation is superseded by one that relies on coordination within an organized structure. Following a predetermined decision-making process, the factors of production are assigned in a way that is independent of the price mechanism.[94] The founders of the firm (the incorporators or the partners in a partnership) relinquish control—the possibility to make use of the price mechanism to achieve efficient results.[95]

[91] The notion of equilibrium (literally 'equal balance'), that is, the realization that 'a social system moved by independent actions in pursuit of different values is consistent with a final coherent state of balance' has been called 'the most important intellectual contribution that economic thought has made to the general understanding of social processes'. See KJ Arrow and FH Hahn, *General Competitive Analysis* (North-Holland 1971) 1. For a formal treatment of general equilibrium and the first theorem of welfare economics see eg DM Kreps, *A Course in Microeconomic Theory* (Prentice Hall 1990) 199–200.

[92] Kreps (n 91) 153–6.

[93] The economist will ask whether the marginal rates of substitution between the market participants, ie the amount of a good that a person is willing to give up in order to obtain one additional unit of another good, are identical. If A was willing to give up two units of good 1 in order to obtain one additional unit of good 2, whereas B was willing to give up one unit of good 2 in order to obtain an additional unit of good 1, both parties could be better off by trading, e.g. by A exchanging one and a half units of good 1 for one unit of good 2.

[94] Coase (n 2) 388–9.

[95] How much control the founders relinquish depends on the organizational structure of the firm. In small, closely held enterprises the owners may manage the firm, thus retaining a great degree of influence over business operations . In large, public corporations they will often not have more than a modicum of control in the form of the right to appoint the directors or approve fundamental transactions in general meeting. However, even in small partnerships or closely held corporations, the price mechanism is supplanted by central planning: The partners or incorporators agree on certain procedures to adopt decisions, for example majority voting, or the transfer of management powers to one partner or incorporator, thus restricting their autonomy.

In return, they expect that certain costs are reduced that are associated with the use of the price mechanism: costs of information, negotiating and concluding separate contracts, and enforcing the contracts (so-called *transaction costs*).[96] The act of formation of a business organization, therefore, constitutes an exchange of autonomy for a reduction in transaction costs.[97]

On the other hand, organizing transactions within a firm entails costs: the costs of coordination, for example of setting up decision-making processes and enforcing them, distributing competences and responsibilities, communicating between different geographical locations and different technical departments of the firm, monitoring agents that are entrusted with management tasks, and costs that result from the organizers not placing the factors of production in their best use, for example when a manager invests in a product line that turns out to be unprofitable. Both types of costs tend to increase with the size of the firm. As the firm decides to produce dissimilar goods, production and marketing costs rise; as it decides to build additional factories, the task of allocating resources between the factories becomes more complex. As the business expands, management is prone to make more mistakes in allocating factor inputs. As the firm hires more employees, supervision requires the deployment of more resources. The complexity of the firm will, therefore, eventually reach a level where the cost of internalizing one additional transaction equals the cost of carrying out the transaction on the open market. Firms will come into existence if coordination is cheaper than making use of the market mechanisms, and they will continue to expand until the marginal cost of production within the firm is identical to the cost of a market transaction.[98]

Coordination costs depend on the internal structure of the firm. Furthermore, not all organizational settings are equally suitable for all businesses. For instance, a family owned business might not see the need to set up structures to control management, for example by appointing outside directors, because all owners have a seat on the board and an equal say in the management of the firm. Similarly, a business that does not wish to attract outside investors but relies on the retention of earnings to finance operations may not wish to publish its financial statements or disclose other inside information. Consequently, the detailed organizational structure of a firm will be decided on a case-by-case basis by the founders. In line with the first theorem of welfare economics, in a competitive marketplace, the organizational setting that is most beneficial to all parties will emerge. Accordingly, proponents of this school of thought advocate flexibility and contractual freedom in corporate law.[99] Regulatory intervention, for example the provision of a limited number of business forms with mandatory governance features, will, at best, produce little additional benefit and, at worst, impede private ordering and prevent an efficient allocation of resources. The market, not the law, will protect the interests of the participating parties. If a role remains for the law, then it is that of making available standby terms that may be relied upon by the market participants if high transaction costs prevent them from arriving at comprehensive agreements. The standby terms, therefore, should contain the rules that rational parties would

[96] Coase (n 2) 390–2.

[97] The Coasian view of the firm has been further developed, inter alia, by Alchian and Demsetz (n 40) (claiming that the internal workings of the firm take on some characteristics of an efficient market in that the firm's owner—the employer—allocates resources by continuously negotiating and renegotiating the input contracts instead of using authoritarian control, as Coase could be understood to imply); O Williamson, *Markets and Hierarchies: Analysis and Antitrust Implications. A Study in the Economics of Internal Organisation* (Free Press 1975); O Williamson, 'Corporate Governance' (1984) 93 Yale Law Journal 1197 (distinguishing between *ex ante* and *ex post* transaction costs and analysing the impact that different governance structures have on these costs).

[98] Coase (n 2) 395.

[99] Frequently, this approach is referred to as *private ordering*: Production and consumption decisions are decentralized and private parties are allowed to transact in accordance with their individual preferences and incentives, see Cheffins (n 88) 6.

have negotiated had they been in a position to address all relevant issues (the so-called *hypothetical bargaining model*).[100]

However, the first theorem of welfare economics relies on certain assumptions that are not necessarily representative of the workings of the real economy. Most importantly, the theorem presupposes the existence of a competitive marketplace. In practice, markets are not perfectly competitive. Four basic reasons can be identified why markets fail: market power (e.g. monopoly power), incomplete information, externalities (the indirect effect of a consumption or production activity that is not reflected in the market price), and public goods (goods that are non-excludable and non-rivalrous, i.e. others cannot be prevented from consuming the goods and consumption by one party does not render the goods unavailable to others).[101] State intervention through regulation of market operations is justified to the extent that it addresses these market imperfections. Indeed, many legal rules are a response to the economic problems posed by market failures. Competition law seeks to prevent firms from obtaining monopoly power, tort law internalizes externalities by requiring, for example, polluters to pay damages, copyright and patent laws provide means to exclude non-paying persons from duplicating artistic works and inventions and thus incentivize artists and scientists to create art or undertake research.

For purposes of company law, the second type market failure is of particular significance: incomplete information. Informational asymmetries may exist ex ante—before the parties enter into a transaction—or *ex post*—after the contract has been concluded. The former problem is referred to as *adverse selection*: If a purchaser cannot verify that the object of the trade possesses the agreed features he may refrain from trading or insist on a lower price than the seller is willing to accept. As a consequence, sellers have an incentive to reduce the quality of their products.[102] The latter problem is known as *moral hazard*: How can a party to a contract be motivated to act in the best interest of the other party if informational asymmetries prevent the other person from evaluating whether the contract terms are honoured? Moral hazard problems frequently arise in so-called principal-agent relationships. The costs associated with such relationships, for instance the costs of supervising the agent or receiving low-quality services by the agent, are called *agency costs*. The concept of agency costs is central to corporate governance and, in fact, the whole field of company law. Many rules of corporate law can best be understood if they are interpreted as addressing the agency problems that business associations are confronted with. Therefore, we will analyse agency costs in more detail in the next section.

II. Agency cost theory

A principal-agent relationship is an arrangement between two parties in which the welfare of one party (the principal) depends on the acts of the other party (the agent). The informational asymmetry characterizing the principal-agent relationship is due to the fact that the principal, in general, is not as well informed about the acts of the agent as the agent himself. As a consequence, he has to monitor the agent. Often, he will not be able to ascertain the quality of the agent's work with certainty. In light of sub-optimal supervision, the agent has an incentive to act in furtherance of his own interests rather than the interests of the principal. Efficiency losses are the result. Furthermore, in the market for managerial services managers face costs to show that they provide services of a high quality (so-called signalling

[100] Cheffins (n 88) 264–307; Easterbrook and Fischel (n 31) 15.

[101] Mas-Colell, Whinston, and Green (n 8) 308–309, 350.

[102] A market in which variation in product quality compels high quality producers to reduce the quality of their products or ultimately be driven out of the market is called a 'market for lemons'. The expression goes back to G Akerlof, 'The Market for "Lemons": Quality Uncertainty and the Market Mechanism' (1970) 84 Quarterly Journal of Economics 488. Legal bonding, signalling, and other strategies can be used to prevent the market from deteriorating, but these strategies are costly.

or legal bonding costs). They will try to communicate that the costs of monitoring and efficiency losses will be lower than average if they are entrusted with the management of the company. If they fail to do so, the owners will not be willing to offer a level of remuneration higher than one that is commensurate with the (average) agency costs they expect. This, in turn, will favour managers who provide lower-than-average services (that is, services that entail higher-than-average agency costs). They will receive benefits that exceed the marginal revenue product of their labour,[103] thus decreasing the firm's total profits, while managers that provide higher-than-average services will have an incentive to reduce their productivity in order to meet average levels. The quality of managerial services will decrease; ultimately, the whole market might unravel.

In the context of corporate governance, agency problems can be observed in different relationships. First, management acts as an agent of the shareholders (the principals). Secondly, majority shareholders assume the role of agents in relation to minority shareholders (principals) in voting on shareholder resolutions that are binding on the minority. Thirdly, the company, when entering into contracts with other constituencies (employees, customers, or creditors), affects the welfare of the other party. Therefore, it can be seen as the agent of the other party. Fourthly, at the same time, the other constituencies are agents of the company in so far as their performance of the contract has a bearing on the welfare of the company. For instance, the firm's revenue and thus profit depends on the productivity of its employees. Company law tackles the first two agency conflicts and contains some rules that are of relevance to the third, notably provisions that protect the company's creditors, such as capital maintenance requirements, or third parties relying in good faith on the authority of those held out as directors or managers by the company. The fourth agency problem is predominantly dealt with by contract and employment law.

Legal systems pursue different strategies to address the managerial and majority-minority shareholder agency problems. In either case, the goal is to ensure that the agent (managers or majority shareholders) act to maximize firm value (and hence the wealth of all shareholders) instead of their own utility by seeking to obtain private benefits of control. An obvious avenue of influence for shareholders is the right to elect directors and replace inefficient or self-serving members of the board. However, in general, shareholders have no means of controlling management directly. The managers (the officers) of the corporation are appointed by the board,[104] and shareholders may only interfere with the appointment decisions of the directors by changing the composition of the board, which can be a lengthy process. Furthermore, dispersed shareholders may face problems in collecting a sufficient number of votes to mount a concerted attack on individual directors. Additionally, staggered boards may help directors to remain in office for a prolonged time.[105] Alternatively, the law may require certain actions to be approved by the general meeting. Most company law statutes provide for shareholder ratification of fundamental changes such as mergers and divisions. This strategy comes with its own problems, though. Again, dispersed and small shareholders might lack the incentive to inform themselves of the benefits and risks of a transaction or attend the general meeting in order to vote. Governance problems can be reduced if the interests of shareholders and directors are aligned, for instance by requiring directors to take a stake in the company or awarding performance-based remuneration, such as stock options or a cash bonus.[106] However, stock options can have the effect of inducing management to focus on short-term profit maximization, whereas investors—at least certain types of investors—might prefer the adoption of a less myopic view.[107]

[103] The marginal revenue product of labour is the additional revenue from one additional unit of labour.

[104] See section D.I below.

[105] Appointment and removal rights are discussed in Chapter 5D.

[106] These strategies are described in detail in R Kraakman and others, *The Anatomy of Corporate Law* (3rd edn, Oxford University Press 2017) 31–7. Kraakman and others distinguish between governance strategies—the three strategies mentioned in the text above—and regulatory strategies; see the following paragraph.

[107] We will discuss the problem of short-termism in capital markets in Chapter 5C.I.1.

The mechanisms mentioned so far may be characterized as ex ante strategies.[108] They can be distinguished from *ex post* strategies that are invoked once it becomes apparent that the agent performs sub-standard. *Ex post* strategies are, for example, directors' duties such as the duty of care or the duty of loyalty that give rise to a claim for damages if the director acts without due care or in violation of certain fiduciary principles. Finally, as an *ultima ratio*, a shareholder may decide to exit the company. Company law statutes frequently provide for exit rights after a fundamental change that has been opposed by some shareholders in the general meeting. In such a case, the shareholders will focus on obtaining a fair value for the shares they tender rather than restraining the managers from acting opportunistically and implementing the change. However, the exit of many (or a few large) shareholders from the company may send a powerful signal about the quality of management to the market. Beyond protecting dissenting shareholders, exit (or the threat of exit) can therefore function as an effective strategy constraining managerial discretion and reducing agency costs.

The second central agency conflict in companies, between majority and minority shareholders, often receives less attention than the agency relationship between the shareholders and managers. Company law statutes, while setting out the powers, competences, and duties of directors in detail, usually do not define the relationship between majority and minority shareholders comprehensively. In some countries, the courts have developed mechanisms resembling directors' duties to prevent the majority from expropriating the minority. However, the case law is, at best, ambiguous and fragmentary. Possible strategies to address the issue mirror the mechanisms used to alleviate the managerial agency conflict.[109] A principle of formal equality might require all shareholders to be accorded the same rights, weighted by the number of shares held, that is, the same voting rights and financial claims on the balance sheet profits. Supermajority voting requirements protect large minority shareholders (the so-called blocking minority, which is typically one-quarter or one-third). Minority shareholders may be entitled to call a general meeting or instigate legal proceedings on behalf of the company.[110] Finally, minority interests might seek representation on the board, for example through cumulative voting or, more indirectly, by ensuring that the directors are independent from the majority shareholders.[111]

III. Models of the market economy and the corporation

Considerations of efficiency and the minimization of agency costs reflect one side of the economics underlying corporate governance regulation. They allow us (or the policy-maker) to assess the desirability of different regulatory choices, given particular social goals that the policy-maker seeks to achieve. However, regulatory mechanisms will rarely affect only one constituency, and comparisons of welfare implications between individuals or groups of persons are difficult to make.[112] For example, a legal rule that requires directors to act exclusively in the interest of the shareholders may have negative effects on the company's employees. Whether the rule is nevertheless desirable from a social-welfare perspective depends on the *relative* effect on both shareholders and employees. Most people would admit that utility levels are not quantifiable in a sense that would allow for meaningful interpersonal comparisons. Therefore, policy-makers may rationally disagree on the most appropriate ranking and weighting of utility levels in a particular situation as a precondition of choosing between regulatory strategies.

[108] With the exception of the dismissal of a director after he has held office for a certain period of time. Kraakman and others (n 106) 37–8, identify ex ante and ex post elements in all of the analysed strategies.

[109] ibid 79–88.

[110] The minority shareholder lawsuit is discussed in Chapter 8C.II.

[111] We will discuss different voting procedures in Chapter 5C.I.2.

[112] Kreps (n 91) 157. See also the references in n 25 above.

An influential school of thought in institutional economics, the so-called 'varieties of capitalism' literature, has argued that legal systems vary systematically in how they make these choices.[113] They classify countries according to the role that market competition and non-market coordination play in governing the economy. All market economies use a combination of both competition and coordination to allocate factors of production and determine the relationship between market actors. An economic system that places greater emphasis on competitive markets, a liberal market economy, relies predominantly on arm's length exchange and the price mechanism to solve these problems, whereas a coordinated economy makes use of non-market institutions, such as business or employers' associations, cross-shareholdings, or information-sharing systems to facilitate coordination and the adoption of strategies that would not have been supported by the price mechanism alone.[114] Importantly, the varieties-of-capitalism literature does not make any claims about the superiority of either regulatory approach in terms of macroeconomic outcomes, notably economic growth. Both liberal and coordinated market economies are capable of producing satisfactory levels of economic performance over extended periods.[115] Empirical evidence indicates that the general regulatory philosophy adopted by a country is less important than the awareness of 'institutional complementarities': regulatory approaches in different spheres of the political economy need to be coordinated in order to unlock the full potential of productive activity.[116] For example, a legal system that encourages employees to develop firm-specific skills by providing for a high degree of job security and facilitating industry-wide wage negotiations is more effective if it also adopts a corporate governance regime that insulates managers to some extent from short-term fluctuations in the company's profitability. Managers are then able to pursue investment strategies that rely on skills acquired by working in the same company for a longer period and that, therefore, may only generate a return after several years.[117] We will return to this point repeatedly in this and the following chapter as we analyse the role and competences of shareholders, directors, and managers in different corporate law systems. However, we should note that the empirical findings of the varieties of capitalism literature, intuitive as they might be, rest on a limited number of variables capturing aspects of a country's company law.[118] Therefore, generalizations should be treated with caution. We will endeavour to analyse our subset of liberal market economies (the UK and the United States) and coordinated economies (France and Germany) at a more granular level, which should enable us to assess to what extent the market/non-market dichotomy maps onto the reality of corporate governance regulation in these countries.

It is clear that the prevalence of market or non-market institutions may influence the design of a country's preferred corporate governance model. As defined above, we would expect the corporate governance system of a liberal market economy to make use of the

[113] Foundational works of the 'varieties of capitalism' literature include PA Hall and D Soskice (eds), *Varieties of Capitalism: The Institutional Foundations of Comparative Advantage* (Oxford University Press 2001); B Hancké, M Rhodes, and M Thatcher (eds), *Beyond Varieties of Capitalism: Conflict, Contradictions, and Complementarities in the European Economy* (Oxford University Press 2007); and B Hancké (ed), *Debating Varieties of Capitalism* (Oxford University Press 2009).

[114] The defining features of liberal versus coordinated market economies are summarized by PA Hall and D Soskice, 'An Introduction to Varieties of Capitalism' in PA Hall and D Soskice (eds), *Varieties of Capitalism: The Institutional Foundations of Comparative Advantage* (Oxford University Press 2001) 8–12. Of our four jurisdictions, the US and the UK are classified as liberal market economies, Germany as a coordinated market economy, and France as an economy that displays traits of both types: ibid 19–21.

[115] ibid 21.

[116] PA Hall and DW Gingerich, 'Varieties of Capitalism and Institutional Complementarities in the Political Economy: An Empirical Analysis' (2009) 39 British Journal of Political Science 449, 467–73.

[117] Hall and Soskice (n 114) 27, 39–44 (arguing that coordinated market economies are better at supporting incremental innovation consisting in the improvement of existing product lines, whereas liberal market economies have a comparative advantage in promoting radical innovation, which requires access to new technologies through the acquisition of other companies and the possibility to adjust the workforce quickly in response to the introduction of new or the suspension of existing product lines).

[118] See eg the description of the variables used by Hall and Gingerich (n 116) 455.

price mechanism in competitive markets to coordinate between different corporate stakeholders. For example, the relationship between the firm and the employees would be determined by supply and demand in the labour market and the relationship between the firm and external providers of finance by the capital and credit markets. Coordination within firms by means of hierarchical structures is, of course, important in all economies, coordinated systems as well as more market-oriented ones.[119] In all models of corporate governance, exchange transactions on the market are partly suppressed by the hierarchical organization of the firm. However, market-based corporate governance models will place a greater emphasis on private ordering (usually in the form of contracting) to align interests, and coordinated market economies on the mandatory establishment of inclusive governance mechanisms that facilitate communication and consensus building among stakeholders.

If correct, the market/non-market dichotomy should be reflected in the structure of a country's corporate governance system along several dimensions: the degree of contractual freedom that is permitted in company law, especially in order to modify the default allocation of corporate power and channels of decision-making in the company, the structure of corporate boards, including the involvement of stakeholders in corporate governance, for example the company's employees, the definition of directors' duties, and more fundamentally the conception of what a corporation is and in whose interest the company should be managed.[120] Thus, there are certain parallels between what we have called the economic and public interest conceptions of the corporation[121] and the implications of different models of the corporate economy identified by the varieties of capitalism literature. We said that a conceptualization of the company based on economic precepts stemming from optimization theory and welfare economics implied that directors should generally (but not necessarily always[122]) act to maximize shareholder value, and private ordering should be facilitated to allow for experimentation and the adaptability of the rule system that structures corporate activity.[123] These features characterize, in the view of the varieties of capitalism literature, liberal market economies. A public interest conception of the corporation, on the other hand, involves an authoritative determination of the relevant public interest, which by definition entails a restriction of private ordering and often a more inclusive view of the goals of corporate activity than pure shareholder value maximization.[124] This conception resonates with the description of a corporate governance system typically found in coordinated market economies, using the terminology of the varieties of capitalism literature. Thus, the debates about the private or public character of the corporation and the model of the market economy essentially deal with the same questions. They differ only in the perspective that they adopt. The varieties of capitalism literature is mainly concerned with the macroeconomic consequences of different economic institutions, while corporate governance theory draws on microeconomic concepts to consider the reduction of agency costs, maximization of social welfare, or similar issues.

[119] Hall and Soskice (n 114) 8–9. On hierarchies as an efficient organizational device, see Williamson (n 2) 16–17, 206–39.

[120] See also S Vitols, 'Varieties of Corporate Governance: Comparing Germany and the UK' in PA Hall and D Soskice (eds), *Varieties of Capitalism: The Institutional Foundations of Comparative Advantage* (Oxford University Press 2001) 337, who identifies several corporate governance institutions that distinguish liberal from coordinated market economies: single/dual board structure, weak/strong employee participation rules, shareholder/stakeholder model of corporate governance, and ownership structures (small, dispersed shareholdings by portfolio investors in liberal market economies, large shareholdings by strategic investors in coordinated economies); ibid 339; K Pistor, 'Legal Ground Rules in Coordinated and Liberal Market Economies' in KJ Hopt and others (eds), *Corporate Governance in Context: Corporations, States and Markets in Europe, Japan, and the US* (Oxford University Press 2005) 249 (arguing that liberal and coordinated market economies can be distinguished by certain procedural and substantive 'ground rules' that concern in particular the extent of contractibility, the primacy of individual as opposed to social preferences, and the possibility of individuals to enforce rights judicially: ibid 258).

[121] Section A.I. [122] See text to nn 33–36 above. [123] See text to n 37 above.

[124] See text to n 32 above.

For our purposes, the comparative study of corporate governance regimes, the relevance of economic theory is accordingly twofold. On the one hand, we want to assess whether regulatory techniques that we find in different legal systems are effective, and our definition of effectiveness may be informed by concepts of microeconomic theory. On the other hand, the varieties of capitalism literature reminds us that corporate governance institutions influence in various ways, and are influenced by, the wider macroeconomic environment. While the identification of causal relationships is not possible without controlling for a large number of legal and non-legal variables, which is not our ambition here, a detailed comparative analysis of corporate governance institutions against the backdrop of the predictions of the varieties of capitalism literature may contribute to a better understanding of their role in a country's economic system.

C. Corporate Governance as a Regulatory Technique

I. Domain of corporate governance regulation

In Chapter 1, we distinguished between the internal governance structure and the external liability structure of the corporation. Corporate governance deals, first and foremost, with the internal aspects: the allocation of control rights, decision-making procedures, monitoring of those that exercise control rights, and sanctions that apply in case of deviation from the agreed allocation and procedures. Accordingly, corporate governance has been defined as 'the system by which companies are directed and controlled',[125] 'a complex system of checks and balances' to ensure 'the creation of long-term, sustainable, renewable value',[126] and, from an economic point of view, as 'the ways in which suppliers of finance to corporations assure themselves of getting a return on their investments'.[127]

However, questions of direction and control of the company's management and protection of the suppliers of finance clearly do not only involve internal governance arrangements, for example the determination of the role and competences of different corporate organs, the process of appointing directors and other office holders, or fiduciary constraints on the discretion of corporate decision-makers. Various constraints external to the company influence directors and officers. They may consist of mechanisms that monitor the actions of the corporate insiders or incentivize them to act in the interest of the investors. The first such mechanism is the so-called market for corporate control. The term refers to transactions entered into with a view to acquiring control of a company, for example by offering to buy the shares of the target company's shareholders or merging the acquirer and the target. The market for corporate control was first interpreted as a mechanism to promote managerial efficiency by the US-American legal scholar Henry Manne in a seminal article of 1965.[128] The argument is simple. If it is correct that a high positive correlation exists between a company's share price and managerial efficiency, companies that are badly managed will be undervalued relative to competitors that are better managed, everything else being

[125] Cadbury Committee Report on the Financial Aspects of Corporate Governance, para 2.5 (1992). More recent UK corporate governance codes reproduce this definition, see Financial Reporting Council (FRC), UK Corporate Governance Code (2018) p 1. The Code is available for download from the website of the FRC http://www.frc.org.uk/. For an overview of the definitions of corporate governance in the corporate governance codes of several EU Member States and international organizations, see Weil, Gotshal & Manges, *Comparative Study of Corporate Governance Codes Relevant to the European Union and Its Member States*, study on behalf of the European Commission (January 2002) 289.

[126] Monks and Minow (n 21) xxii–xxiii.

[127] A Shleifer and RW Vishny, 'A Survey of Corporate Governance' (1997) 52 Journal of Finance 737; J Tirole, *The Theory of Corporate Finance* (Princeton University Press 2006) 16.

[128] HG Manne, 'Mergers and the Market for Corporate Control' (1965) 73 Journal of Political Economy 110.

equal.[129] They will therefore constitute an attractive takeover target, provided the acquirer is able to replace the existing management team. Managers, knowing that this is the case, will seek to maximize the value of the firm. In this way, the market for corporate control operates as a mechanism that protects dispersed, non-controlling shareholders.[130] From a normative point of view, if a policy-maker is of the opinion that the benefits of enhanced control of management outweigh the potentially detrimental effects of a highly active market for corporate control,[131] the law should facilitate mergers and acquisitions. This may involve adopting strict duties that prevent directors from taking defensive actions,[132] the absence of a rule of equal treatment that would require the bidder to pay the control premium to all shareholders, including the minority,[133] and keeping the cost of proxy fights to a minimum, notably by not requiring extensive disclosure of information when a bidder solicits proxies.[134]

Secondly, providers of financial services, lawyers, and other so-called reputational intermediaries may ensure that an issuer complies with the applicable regulations. Such intermediaries are sometimes called gatekeepers, because issuers have to rely on their services to access a particular market.[135] For example, in order to offer shares to the public, issuers have to produce audited financial statements and generally rely on investment banks to underwrite their securities and market the offering to the public. The involvement of reputational intermediaries constitutes a potentially powerful enforcement mechanism that supplements public enforcement by the market regulator. Theoretically, gatekeepers should be sufficiently incentivized to monitor compliance with the applicable laws by an issuer without any further regulatory intervention. Their business model relies on their reputation: auditors, lawyers, and investment banks are able to attract clients if they have built a reputation for providing services of a high quality.[136] In order to safeguard their reputational capital, they have an incentive to verify carefully that the issuer's financial accounts are correct, contracts are legally binding, and investors do not lose money when they invest in securities underwritten by them. In addition, they receive a smaller payoff from the transaction than the issuer in the form of fees for their services, rather than the proceeds, for example, of a public offering. They are, therefore, easier to deter. They have less to gain and more to lose from engaging in misrepresentations, corporate fraud, or other violations of the law.[137] Nevertheless, various corporate scandals, of course, show that gatekeepers fail in preventing misconduct or collude with the issuer in defrauding investors. The reasons for gatekeeper failure have been discussed widely after a string of financial scandals in the United States and Europe in the

[129] ibid 112. [130] ibid 113.

[131] Acquisition strategies can also be driven by ulterior motives that do not necessarily increase the combined value of the target and the bidder, for example the desire of the bidder's CEO to build an empire, the target CEO's expectation to receive a large severance payment, or simply hubris on the part of bidders, who overestimate their ability to manage the combined enterprise more efficiently, E Berkovitch and MP Narayanan, 'Motives for Takeovers: An Empirical Investigation' (1993) 28 Journal of Financial and Quantitative Analysis 347; R Morck, A Shleifer, and RW Vishny, 'Do Managerial Objectives Drive Bad Acquisitions?' (1990) 45 Journal of Finance 31. Whether takeovers are on balance value-enhancing is an empirical question. Research shows that bidders tend to underperform after a takeover and target shareholders realize positive abnormal returns; see M Martynova and L Renneboog, 'A century of corporate takeovers: What have we learned and where do we stand?' (2008) 32 Journal of Banking and Finance 2148.

[132] FH Easterbrook and DR Fischel, 'The Proper Role of a Target's Management in Responding to a Tender Offer' (1981) 94 Harvard Law Review 1161.

[133] Easterbrook and Fischel (n 31) 118–19, 126–9. See also our discussion in Chapter 7C.I.

[134] When we analyse proxy voting in Chapter 5C.II, we will see that the US proxy rules do not conform to this precept, but rather make waging a proxy fight a difficult and costly affair.

[135] The concept of the gatekeeper was developed by Reinier Kraakman in two seminal articles: 'Corporate Liability Strategies and the Costs of Legal Controls' (1984) 93 Yale Law Journal 857; and 'Gatekeepers: The Anatomy of a Third-Party Enforcement Strategy' (1986) 2 Journal of Law, Economics & Organization 53. Kraakman defines gatekeepers as 'private parties who are able to disrupt misconduct by withholding their cooperation from wrongdoers' (1986) 2 Journal of Law, Economics & Organization 53.

[136] J Coffee, 'Gatekeeper Failure and Reform: The Challenge of Fashioning Relevant Reforms' (2004) 84 Boston University Law Review 301, 308.

[137] ibid.

late 1990s and the first years of the new Millennium, including the notorious bankruptcies of Enron and WorldCom in 2001 and 2002, respectively.[138] Explanations include agency problems within the gatekeeper firm that induce the firm's partners or employees not to act in the best interest of the firm, the structure of the market for gatekeeper services, which often exhibits oligopolistic tendencies that attenuate competitive pressures and hence reduce the value of the gatekeeper's reputational capital, and other reasons for a decline in the cost of wrongdoing, for example because of the low likelihood of detection and litigation.[139] The regulator has responded to these problems, among other measures, by adopting more stringent liability provisions[140] and strengthening the independence of certain gatekeepers, in particular auditors.[141] While the design of gatekeeper regulation remains a controversial topic, for our purposes, it is important to note that the presence of gatekeepers in a market exerts pressures on the issuer's management that may help to alleviate the managerial agency problem.

Thirdly, a transparent, efficient capital market that ensures that all material information is reflected in the share price can play an important role in corporate governance. Agency cost theory as formulated by Jensen and Meckling posits that the value of a firm equals the firm's discounted future cash flows minus the private benefits extracted by the controller and the cost of monitoring (agency costs).[142] If investors are able to make unbiased estimates of this function, they will discount the securities offered to them accordingly. The controller will therefore bear the difference between the value of the firm with and without agency costs.[143] Alternatively, the controller may voluntarily limit the opportunity to exploit private benefits of control, for example by giving an undertaking limiting discretion or appointing independent monitors, such as auditors or non-executive directors.[144] In both cases, the level of rent extraction and monitoring or bonding will only be optimal if the market can correctly assess the amount of private benefits to be extracted and the effectiveness of any monitoring or bonding activity.[145] In theory, the controller should have an interest in disclosing the firm's governance structure voluntarily, since investors

[138] The most comprehensive treatment is by J Coffee, *Gatekeepers: The Professions and Corporate Governance* (Oxford University Press 2006). See also J Coffee, 'Understanding Enron: It's About the Gatekeepers, Stupid' (2002) 57 Business Law 1403. For more information on the Enron and WorldCom scandals see text to nn 329–330 below.

[139] Coffee (n 136) 310.

[140] The quintessential gatekeeper liability provision is probably s 11(a)(5) of the US Securities Act 1933, which imposes liability for misleading statements in a registration statement or public offering prospectus on the underwriters. The standard of liability is the same as for corporate insiders (directors and officers who sign the registration statement). Notably, the underwriters are responsible for the accuracy of the whole registration statement. They are liable to investors for mistakes or omissions unless they can exculpate themselves pursuant to s 11(b) Securities Act 1933.

[141] See eg the reforms introduced by the Sarbanes-Oxley Act in the US after the Enron and WorldCom scandals. An overview of the reforms is given in the text to nn 331–342 below.

[142] MC Jensen and WH Meckling, 'Theory of the Firm: Managerial Behavior, Agency Costs and Ownership Structure' (1976) 3 Journal of Financial Economics 305, 317–8, 323–5.

[143] ibid 319, 325. [144] ibid 325–6.

[145] That this is true can be illustrated with the help of a simple example (following Jensen and Meckling (n 142) 313–19). Assume that the value of a company is V, which equals the present value of future cash flows generated by the firm (ie no private benefits of control are consumed and no monitoring or bonding costs are incurred). Whether a controller will decide to extract private benefits depends on the amount of equity held by the controller and the utility the controller derives from the rent extraction. In the most basic case, where the controller is the sole owner and all benefits are of a pecuniary nature, there is no incentive to extract rents. Since the consumption of benefits worth US$1 reduces firm value by US$1, the wealth of the controller/sole owner is not affected by the rent extraction. This changes if the benefits are of a non-pecuniary nature and the controller values wealth (owning cash flows generated by the firm) and non-pecuniary benefits differently (the original model by Jensen and Meckling (n 142) 316, is based on this assumption). Now the controller will extract benefits at a level B^* that depends on the utility that the controller derives from different combinations of pecuniary and non-pecuniary payoffs. The consumption of the benefits reduces firm value to V^*. Next, assume that the controller sells a fraction $1 - \alpha$ of the firm's equity (with $0 < \alpha < 1$). The extraction of US$1 of private benefits now leads to a reduction in the controller's wealth of $\alpha \times$ US$1. The remaining reduction in the value of the firm ($(1 - \alpha) \times$ US$1) is borne by the outside investor. Thus, the optimal level of rent extraction from the perspective of the controller (who can determine that level) is higher than in the case of a wholly owned firm, and it increases as α decreases. This means that

will otherwise assume that private benefits can be extracted without restriction and price the firm's equity lower.[146] Once disclosed, investors will adjust the price they are willing to pay in light of the effect that the governance structure has on firm value and benefit consumption. In reality, however, voluntary disclosure may not occur for various reasons, for example because the managers are hesitant to divulge information that may be beneficial to competitors.[147] In addition, it is doubtful whether equity markets are able to assess the effects of monitoring accurately. Therefore, we find both mandatory disclosure rules and mandatory corporate governance provisions in all legal systems. However, we observe considerable variation between jurisdictions and within jurisdictions across time in the prescriptiveness and extent of the required disclosures. Corporate governance codes have required the disclosure of essential features of a company's corporate governance architecture on a voluntary ('comply-or-explain') basis for many decades.[148] These include, among other things, information on the structure of the board of directors and its committees, for example the balance between executive and non-executive directors and any circumstances that may impair the independence of the non-executive directors, arrangements made to ensure the integrity of the financial statements, and the processes used to determine the remuneration of the executives. More recently, policy-makers impose increasingly extensive mandatory disclosure obligations on listed companies. Such companies have to describe the composition and operation of the board of directors, the powers of the general meeting, shareholder rights,[149] and the measures taken to regulate issues particularly susceptible to conflicts of interest, notably internal control and risk management[150] and executive remuneration.[151] Thus, nowadays, investors have relatively comprehensive information at their disposal to evaluate the quality of the corporate governance architecture of firms before they make an investment decision. Whether this information is indeed used by investors to penalize firms with poor governance is, of course, a different question that can only be answered empirically.[152]

the value of the firm $V^0 = V - B^0 < V^* = V - B^*$, where V^0 is the value of a firm with outside investors and B^0 and B^* are the private benefits consumed in the presence and absence of outside investors, respectively. Well informed outside investors will therefore only pay a price equalling $1 - \alpha$ times a (reduced) value of the firm V' that reflects the rent-seeking behaviour of the controller. Alternatively, the investors may request, or the controller may decide to implement voluntarily, governance mechanisms that limit the possibility to consume private benefits. These monitoring or bonding mechanisms come at a cost M, so that the value of the firm is now $V'' = V - B - M$. If we assume that increases in monitoring (or bonding) will reduce private benefits at a decreasing rate, the controller will agree to such activity up to the point where the marginal benefits of monitoring equal the marginal costs for the controller, ie where the increase in the controller's share of firm value equals the marginal private benefits given up because of monitoring. Firm value increases as a consequence, so that $V'' > V'$. If the investors are fully informed (and the equity market is competitive), they will be indifferent between paying $(1 - \alpha) \times V'$ without monitoring and $(1 - \alpha) \times V''$ with monitoring. The important point is that the parties will not agree on the optimal level of monitoring and private benefits (note that firm value is not necessarily maximized at a level of monitoring where $B = 0$, since perfect monitoring may be too expensive or simply impossible) if the investors underestimate the level of rent extraction or overestimate the effectiveness of monitoring or bonding. It is the function of disclosure regulation to furnish investors with the information necessary to minimize this risk.

146 See the previous footnote.

147 Easterbrook and Fischel (n 31) 25–6.

148 We will discuss the corporate governance movement and the technique of 'comply-or-explain' in more detail in section C.III below.

149 In the EU, disclosure requirements can be found, inter alia, in Directive 2013/34/EU on the annual financial statements, consolidated financial statements and related reports of certain types of undertakings, [2013] OJ L182/19, Art 20(1)(e), (f). In the US, extensive disclosure obligations pertaining to corporate governance are laid down in Item 407 of SEC Regulation S-K, 17 CFR 229.407. Regulation S-K sets out information that has to be filed by companies governed by the Securities Act 1933 and the Securities Exchange Act 1934, for example as part of their annual report.

150 Directive 2013/34/EU, Art 20(1)(c).

151 See eg the detailed disclosures required by Item 402 of SEC Regulation S-K, 17 CFR 229.402 in the US and the Large and Medium-sized Companies and Groups (Accounts and Reports) (Amendment) Regulations, Statutory Instrument 2013 No 1981, in the UK.

152 Some empirical studies confirm that information on governance arrangements is incorporated into share prices, for example P Gompers, J Ishii, and A Metrick, 'Corporate Governance and Equity Prices' (2003) 118 Quarterly Journal of Economics 107 (finding that firms with stronger shareholder rights had higher firm value, higher profits, higher sales growth, and lower capital expenditures).

To conclude, we may distinguish between *internal* governance, which is concerned with the internal organization of the corporation and the balance of power between the corporate organs, and *external* corporate governance, which relies on market forces and market participants that are external to the corporation. The dichotomy of internal and external corporate governance mirrors, at least to some extent, the distinction between corporate law on the one hand and takeover and securities regulation on the other. With the rapid development of the capital markets—in the United States in the beginning of the twentieth century,[153] in the United Kingdom with so-called Big Bang in 1986,[154] and in continental Europe starting in the 1990s[155]—the conflicts of interest that impede an efficient functioning of the corporation and an adequate protection of investors are now tackled from two angles, through traditional channels of corporate governance and by legal institutions that belong to takeover law and securities regulation. In this and the following chapters, we will focus largely on the traditional tools of corporate governance, but we will also make references to takeover law and securities regulation where appropriate. The interdependencies of internal and external governance mechanisms are evident. For example, whether the market for corporate control is effective in addressing the managerial agency problem depends not only on the regulation of the bidding process, but also the design of directors' duties, which may or may not allow directors to adopt defensive strategies against hostile takeover bids, and more generally on the ease with which shareholders can remove managers. We will come back to these points in the relevant contexts. In addition, we can observe a general development—at least with respect to the public company—away from traditional concepts of corporate governance towards a market-based approach centred on transparency and market integrity. The goals of transparency and market integrity are implemented through increasingly comprehensive and detailed disclosure obligations and an elaborate enforcement system consisting of both sanctions imposed by the public regulator and litigation brought by investors. Thus, we have effectively two systems of corporate governance: one for the unlisted (private or public) company and a more stringent, densely structured regime for the listed company.

II. Goal of corporate governance regulation

Any attempt to assess the composition, role, and duties of the corporate organs has to start with the question: For whom do corporate organs exercise their powers? Or, in other words: Whose interests does the corporation embody? These questions are closely related to the debate about the nature of the corporation as such, which we covered in detail in Chapter 1.[156] We traced the evolution of the debate from its beginnings in the nineteenth century, when the discussion centred on the description of the company as a 'legal fiction' or a 'real entity', to what is today known as corporate governance theory: the conceptualization of the company as a 'nexus of contracts', consisting of utility-maximizing individuals that negotiate the optimal arrangements to allocate resources and minimize agency costs, or a social phenomenon that cannot be captured fully by limiting the enquiry to contractual relationships. We distinguished between the positive and normative dimensions of the

[153] JM Landis, 'The Legislative History of the Securities Act of 1933' 28 George Washington Law Review (1959) 29.

[154] See R Michie, *The London Stock Exchange: A History* (Oxford University Press 2001) 543–95.

[155] For an assessment of the evolution of capital markets reform in continental Europe, largely driven by initiatives of the European policy-maker, see T Tridimas, 'EU Financial Regulation: Federalization, Crisis Management, and Law Reform' in P Craig and G de Búrca (eds), *The Evolution of EU Law* (2nd edn, Oxford University Press 2011) 783. For an empirical study of the financial consequences of stock market liberalization, see PB Henry, 'Stock Market Liberalization, Economic Reform, and Emerging Market Equity Prices' (2000) 55 Journal of Finance 529 (finding that the announcement by a government to open the domestic stock market to foreign investment leads to abnormal returns of 3.3 per cent, thus reducing the cost of equity capital for companies issuing shares in the liberalizing economy).

[156] Chapter 1E.

debate and noted the 'deregulatory agenda' and goal of shareholder wealth maximization that the nexus of contracts theory may give rise to, but we did not elaborate on the normative implications of alternative conceptualizations of the firm, and we did not discuss the choices made by policy makers in Europe and the United States. This is the topic of this chapter.

In corporate governance theory, as in corporate theory more generally, we can distinguish between a positive and a normative dimension. The positive dimension presents models that seek to explain why particular governance structures have emerged and become predominant, legal systems follow different models of corporate governance, corporations grow in scale and complexity, use different combinations of equity and debt financing, and how governance structures affect the behaviour of corporate actors and firm performance. We have come across several building blocks of positive corporate governance theory. Coase's work on 'the nature of the firm' uses transaction costs to explain why we find 'islands of conscious power [firms] in [an] ocean of unconscious co-operation [the market] like lumps of butter coagulating in a pail of buttermilk',[157] and why it is efficient for firms to expand up to a certain point, but no further.[158] Agency cost theory explains how the presence of informational asymmetries between principal and agent and costs of monitoring and bonding alter managerial incentives, investment decisions, and capital structure.[159] While the conceptualization of the firm as a 'nexus for a set of contracting relationships among individuals' can be traced back to agency cost theory,[160] it was not initially proposed with a specific policy objective in mind. Rather, the aim was to improve on neoclassical economics, which treated the firm as a 'black box',[161] an actor in markets just like an individual that chose from a set of technologically feasible production plans the one that maximized profits. Thus, neoclassical economics modelled production decisions of a firm by analysing markets for factors of production and product markets, and not by examining how those within the firm decided on the use of resources. Both transaction cost theory and agency cost theory enriched this picture. A number of seminal contributions that date mostly from the 1970s and 1980s developed the tools necessary to understand how the internal structure of a firm influenced the transformation of factors of production into outputs. These contributions made use of well-established economic concepts, such as optimization, equilibrium allocation[162] and Pareto efficiency,[163] to compare the effects of different governance arrangements.[164] However, importantly, the authors did not perceive these terms as embodying policy recommendations. In their writings, they did not take sides in the debate about the social responsibility of companies,[165] which attracted increasing attention in the United States at about the same

[157] Coase (n 2) 388 (quoting DH Robertson, *Control of Industry* (Nisbet and Co. 1923) 85).

[158] See the discussion in n 2 above. Jensen and Meckling (n 142) 319–23, 326, analyse the same question, allowing for agency costs.

[159] ibid 312–51. [160] ibid 310.

[161] ibid 306; H Demsetz, 'The Firm in Economic Theory: A Quiet Revolution' (1997) 87 American Economic Review 426.

[162] See text to n 91 above. [163] See text to nn 92–93 above.

[164] See eg Jensen and Meckling (n 142) 327–8, analysing which level of private benefit consumption and monitoring expenditure was 'optimal' and 'efficient'.

[165] For example, Jensen and Meckling (n 142) 311 explicitly point out that it is the role of the legal system to set 'bounds on the kinds of contracts into which individuals and organizations may enter' and thus shape the contracts that represent, according to their view, the corporation. Moreover, they acknowledge that by intervening in contractual relations, the law may 'serve as a vehicle for redistribution of wealth', ibid. Fama (n 60) 290, explains that 'ownership of capital should not be confused with ownership of the firm. Each factor in a firm is owned by somebody. The firm is just the set of contracts covering the way inputs are joined to create outputs and the way receipts from outputs are shared among inputs … Dispelling the tenacious notion that a firm is owned by its security holders is important because it is a first step toward understanding that control over a firm's decisions is not necessarily the province of security holders'. However, in other, less scientific writings some of these scholars advanced unabashedly political statements; see eg MC Jensen and WH Meckling, 'Can the Corporation Survive?' (1978) 34 Financial Analysts Journal 31 (offering the rather bold prediction that the 'corporate form of organization … is likely to disappear completely' because of government interference with the rights of shareholders and creditors, leading to lower rates of return and a drying up of available capital, ibid 32, 36–7).

time when agency cost theory was first proposed (although there were exceptions, as we shall see[166]).

This debate between what has become known as shareholder and stakeholder theory was galvanized by the publication of two books in the mid-1970s: Christopher Stone's *Where the Law Ends*[167] and *Taming the Giant Corporation* by Ralph Nader, Mark Green, and Joel Seligman.[168] A central thesis of these publications was the claim that neither the market nor additional, targeted regulation was a substitute for requiring directors to act socially responsibly. The market mechanism did not guarantee that corporations would pursue socially desirable goals because those who interacted with the corporation often lacked the necessary information to assess the consequences of the corporation's actions and price them correctly, or they were not in a position to penalize companies that imposed a cost on them.[169] In addition, importantly, they argued that even if it was theoretically possible to identify the instances when corporate activity imposed a cost on society that could not be internalized by the market mechanism (i.e. when externalities arose), it was unlikely that regulatory intervention by the policy-maker, for example environmental legislation, was more effective than relying on corporate directors to avoid externalities. One reason is that the law is inherently reactive. Policy-makers will often only intervene in response to a problem once it has arisen, but have difficulties to foresee potentially harmful behaviour and prohibit such behaviour ex ante.[170] In addition, political economy problems call into question the effectiveness of regulation. Regulation may fail to further social welfare because policy-makers lack the resources or relevant information to take adequate regulatory action, or companies have sufficient lobbying power to influence the rule-making process in their favour.[171] In order to address these problems, the authors suggest structural and procedural changes to the governance architecture of corporations exceeding a certain size, including, famously, the appointment of 'general public directors'.[172]

The shift from positive to normative agency cost theory was an explicit response to the rise of stakeholder theory. Interestingly, it did not come from the economists who had pioneered agency cost theory, but from a number of legal scholars who embraced the nexus-of-contracts view of the corporation and the concept of agency costs (in combination with some other economic concepts developed at the time[173]) to propose a tightly argued,

[166] In particular, Milton Friedman was an outspoken proponent of shareholder wealth maximization as a normative goal; see the quote in the text to n 197 below.

[167] CD Stone, *Where the Law Ends: The Social Control of Corporate Behavior* (Harper & Row 1975).

[168] Nader, Green, and Seligman (n 81). For a critical discussion of both books, see DL Engel, 'An Approach to Corporate Social Responsibility' (1979) 32 Stanford Law Review 1. For additional references to the contemporary legal literature and policy initiatives, see DR Fischel, 'The Corporate Governance Movement' (1982) 35 Vanderbilt Law Review 1259, 1260, nn 1–6.

[169] Stone (n 167) 89. This is essentially a criticism of the assumption of informational efficiency underlying Jensen and Meckling's model.

[170] Stone (n 167) 94.

[171] ibid 94–6.

[172] Nader, Green, and Seligman (n 81) 123–31 (suggesting that general public directors be elected by the social groups that are substantially affected by a company's activities and giving as an example a company with nine directors responsible for (1) employee welfare, (2) consumer protection, (3) environmental protection, (4) shareholder rights, (5) legal compliance, (6) finances, (7) purchasing and marketing, (8) management efficiency, and (9) planning and research; each of the directors is given separate responsibility to promote the public concern that this director represents, which supplements the general duties of directors); Stone (n 167) 152–73 (proposing that the number of general public directors depend on the size of the corporation and that they be nominated by a federal commission such as the SEC, appointed by a majority, and removed by a unanimous vote of the board of the company concerned).

[173] Important economic building blocks of the emerging normative (legal) agency theory were the efficient market hypothesis, which posits (in its semi-strong form) that in efficient capital markets all publicly available information is incorporated quickly into securities prices (EF Fama, 'Efficient Capital Markets: A Review of Theory and Empirical Work' (1970) 25 Journal of Finance 383), the so-called Coase theorem, which holds that, in the absence of transaction costs, the initial allocation of rights is irrelevant because private parties will negotiate to bring about Pareto-efficient outcomes (RH Coase, 'The Problem of Social Cost' (1960) 3 Journal of Law and Economics 1, 2–8), and modern portfolio theory, which present a framework to design an optimal portfolio of assets given a particular level of risk (or variance) (H Markowitz, 'Portfolio Selection' (1952) 7 Journal of Finance 77). Thus, less than a quarter of a century of research in economics and finance (1952-1976, when Jensen and Meckling's theory of the firm was published) prepared the ground for a fundamental shift in corporate theory.

internally consistent theory of the corporation and the objectives of corporate governance. The most influential representatives of this emerging school of thought were Frank Easterbrook and Daniel Fischel of Chicago Law School.[174] They were blunt in their rejection of stakeholder theory, claiming that 'the arguments of those who advocate the need for a change in corporate governance are based on a failure to understand the economics of the corporate form'.[175] Their criticism was not only directed at the main tenets of stakeholder theory, but more generally at constraining entrepreneurial activity through regulatory intervention. The approach to corporate governance advocated by Easterbrook and Fischel, and those following them, was characterized by a clear deregulatory agenda. This agenda was based on the following line of reasoning. Pursuant to Jensen and Meckling, a governance structure is optimal if the cost of additional monitoring and bonding is equal to the reduction in rent-seeking behaviour by the controller brought about by the improvement in monitoring.[176] They posited that if equity markets were well informed and made unbiased estimates of the controller's incentives to engage in rent seeking, the investors and the controller would voluntarily implement a governance arrangement that was efficient and allocated the residual loss to the controller.[177] Easterbrook and Fischel, consequently, cautioned against corporate governance reform that might result in imposing additional regulatory costs on companies without a commensurate reduction in agency costs. In their view, it was doubtful that regulatory intervention would be efficient, since adequate constraints on managerial authority were already in place. The labour, product, and capital markets, they explained, gave managers strong incentives to agree to governance arrangements that ensured the maximization of shareholder value. In a competitive market for managerial talent, managers who created wealth for shareholders could charge a higher fee for their services. Firms that were efficiently managed could sell their products at a lower price than their inefficiently managed competitors. Finally, and most directly related to Jensen and Meckling's model, badly managed companies faced a higher cost of capital.[178] Given the existence of these market-based constraints, Easterbrook and Fischel argued that proposals to reform corporate governance, ranging from strengthening shareholder engagement to increasing the number of independent directors on corporate boards or improving the enforcement of the duty of care, were misguided.[179] Excluding shareholders from the management of the company was based on a division-of-labour rationale, and there was no reason to grant shareholders, among all those who provided factors of production, the right to influence the company's decision-making processes. The most effective mechanism to protect equity investors who disagreed with management was their right to exit the company and sell their shares in the market.[180] Independent directors, or board committees composed of independent directors, created costs since they were often not sufficiently familiar with the firm or lacked the expertise to contribute meaningfully to decision-making.[181] Similarly, the benefits of stringently formulated directors' duties and mechanisms that facilitated the enforcement of duties by minority shareholders would in all likelihood be outweighed by their detrimental effects. Managers would become more bureaucratic and risk-averse, litigation would prove disruptive, and the courts, in any case, were not well equipped to assess business decisions.[182] In all of these cases, market incentives could be expected to give rise to more finely nuanced governance structures that were responsive to the particular situation

[174] Easterbrook and Fischel laid the foundations for their theory in a series of articles published in the 1980s, culminating in their book *The Economic Structure of Corporate Law* (n 31), which is partly based on these articles.

[175] Fischel (n 168) 1260.

[176] Hence, agency costs, consisting of the cost of monitoring and bonding as well as the so-called residual loss (the remaining private benefits consumed by the controller), are minimized; see Jensen and Meckling (n 142) 308 and the text to nn 143–146.

[177] See the summary of Jensen and Meckling's model in n 145 above.

[178] Fischel (n 168) 1263–4.

[179] ibid 1274–91.

[180] ibid 1276–8.

[181] ibid 1282–4.

[182] ibid 1286–91.

of the company and the preferences of investors. Thus, this view of corporate governance is characterized by the primacy of private ordering. Legal rules, if they exist at all, should be formulated as default rules, similar to standard form contracts that are made available by the policy-maker to reduce the cost of contracting.[183]

The agency-cost approach to corporate governance has become extraordinarily influential, as both an intellectual framework and a policy programme.[184] Major reforms of corporate governance have of course been undertaken since Easterbrook and Fischel presented their theory, in the United States notably the adoption of the Sarbanes-Oxley and Dodd-Frank Acts in 2002 and 2010, respectively, and in Europe the promulgation of corporate governance codes by virtually all EU Member States since the 1990s.[185] Nevertheless, agency cost theory and the attempt to balance carefully the costs and benefits of regulatory intervention are still very much concerns of policy-makers, even if different countries solve the optimization problem differently. It is telling that the US reforms of 2002 and 2010 stem from federal laws, while many state legislators, including Delaware, continue to regulate corporate governance lightly and protect the wide managerial discretion that is the default of most state company laws.[186] In Europe, the main goals of the corporate governance movement that started in the 1990s, strengthening the independence of the board of directors and encouraging shareholder engagement, are embedded in codes of best practice, not in binding laws. Increased regulatory competition within the EU prompted some Member States to facilitate incorporations, reduce mandatory regulatory requirements and strengthen private ordering.[187] After the global financial crisis, some regulators and policy-makers take a more interventionist stance, but for most purposes, normative agency cost theory continues to provide the relevant frame of reference.

Some criticisms that can be levelled at the pure welfare-maximizing calculus underlying agency cost theory were discussed above.[188] Here, we want to focus on two additional points. First, without addressing the point explicitly, legal agency cost theory imported a number of assumptions of economic (positive) agency cost theory into their normative framework. Most importantly, as mentioned, Jensen and Meckling's model assumes that investors act rationally and with sufficient information to assess an issuer's governance structure.[189] The informational efficiency of markets has indeed been corroborated by empirical studies, but we can also find many studies that have called various aspects of the efficient market hypothesis into question.[190] It seems now reasonably well established that capital markets are at least not *always* informationally efficient. The market, accordingly, does not necessarily give the right incentives to issuers to adopt efficient governance mechanisms in all cases. As some commentators have pointed out, the purchase of a share represents 'a lump choice, one in which the many components of firm success—or expected success—are combined in the single bundle to be bought or sold. The choice to buy or sell thus represents a complex mixture of satisfactions and dissatisfactions with components of the bundle;

[183] Easterbrook and Fischel (n 31) 34–5; R Romano, *The Genius of American Corporate Law* (AEI Press 1993) 85. This approach gives clear guidance to policy makers and the courts on how to design and interpret corporate law. Corporate law 'fills in the blanks and oversights with the terms that people would have bargained for had they anticipated the problems and been able to transact costlessly in advance': Easterbrook and Fischel (n 31) 34.

[184] Kraakman and others' *Anatomy* (n 106) for example, is structured around the main agency problems in the corporation. For a collection of representative writings, see R Romano (ed), *Foundations of Corporate Law* (Oxford University Press 1993). Referring to the use of economics and finance to reinterpret the objectives of corporate law, Romano speaks of the 'revolution' that corporate law underwent 'over the past decade' (ie the 1980s): ibid v.

[185] We will discuss these reforms in section C.III below.

[186] This is particularly evident in the interpretation of the duty of care by Delaware courts, which refrain from intervening in business decisions, provided that directors acted on an informed basis, in good faith and without any conflict of interest. We will analyse the leading Delaware duty of care case law in Chapter 6B.I.2.

[187] See Chapter 1E. [188] Section A.I, text to nn 22–27. [189] See n 145 above.

[190] A good overview of the debate is given by A Shleifer, *Inefficient Markets: An Introduction to Behavioral Finance* (Oxford University Press 1999) 1–27. For a comprehensive criticism of market efficiency see also RJ Shiller, *Irrational Exuberance* (3rd edn, Princeton University Press 2015).

but significantly, the choice does not permit separation of the treatment, which a rational owner would effect, of the quality of management or the terms of its retention from other factors'.[191] In addition, there is a risk that inefficient governance structures may become 'traditionalised' in the market.[192] If a sufficiently large number of managers have adopted a particular governance model, the market may reach a stable, but inefficient equilibrium where managers do not have any incentive to improve on the standard model and curtail their private benefit consumption, because they know that other managers are in the same position. It should be noted that Easterbrook and Fischel did not claim that these market failures did not exist and markets were able to price governance terms perfectly. Rather, their deregulatory policy agenda rests on the less ambitious assumption that markets can assess a firm's governance *better* than policy-makers.[193] However, whether this is the case is still an empirical question, and Easterbrook and Fischel offer only limited evidence in support of their claim.[194]

Secondly, agency cost theory is usually associated with shareholder wealth maximization, both by critics[195] and those who embrace the normative dimension of agency cost theory. Easterbrook and Fischel argued that the corporation, as a legal fiction and a nexus of contracts, 'is incapable of having social or moral obligations'. Only people, they observed, could have such obligations.[196] This statement reiterates a point made, famously, by Milton Friedman in an article in the *New York Times Magazine* in 1970:[197]

> When I hear businessmen speak eloquently about the 'social responsibilities of business in a free-enterprise system,' I am reminded of the wonderful line about the Frenchman who discovered at the age of 70 that he had been speaking prose all his life. The businessmen believe that they are defending free enterprise when they declaim that business is not concerned 'merely' with profit but also with promoting desirable 'social' ends; that business has a 'social conscience' and takes seriously its responsibilities for providing employment, eliminating discrimination, avoiding pollution and whatever else may be the catchwords of the contemporary crop of reformers. In fact they are—or would be if they or anyone else took them seriously—preaching pure and unadulterated socialism. Businessmen who talk this way are unwitting puppets of the intellectual forces that have been undermining the basis of a free society these past decades.
>
> The discussions of the 'social responsibilities of business' are notable for their analytical looseness and lack of rigor. What does it mean to say that 'business' has responsibilities? Only people can have responsibilities. A corporation is an artificial person and in this sense may have artificial responsibilities, but 'business' as a whole cannot be said to have responsibilities, even in this vague sense.... The whole justification for permitting the corporate executive to be selected by the stockholders is that the executive is an agent serving in the interests of his principal ... which generally will be to make as much money as possible.

[191] V Brudney, 'Corporate Governance, Agency Costs, and the Rhetoric of Contract' (1985) 85 Columbia Law Review 1403, 1424. This argument is also discussed in Parkinson (n 7) 185. Arguably, to give a real-world example, this is precisely the reason why the listing of the Chinese e-commerce company Alibaba on the New York Stock Exchange in 2014 was highly successful, in spite of a corporate governance structure that entrenched the control of the corporate insiders over the board of directors. On this case, see also Chapter 5C.I.1.

[192] LL Dallas, 'Two Models of Corporate Governance: Beyond Berle and Means' (1988) 22 *University of Michigan Journal of Law Reform* 19, 46 (critically reflecting on the argument that efficient governance structures will prevail in the market through a process similar to natural selection).

[193] Easterbrook and Fischel (n 31) 19.

[194] ibid 20–2, who refer to several studies that show how stock market prices react to governance terms. This, of course, does not prove the claim that a governance system provided by a regulator or policy-maker is less efficient than the market solution.

[195] See eg Parkinson (n 7) 46–8.

[196] Quote from Fischel (n 168) 1273. A similar statement can be found in FH Easterbrook and DR Fischel, 'Antitrust Suits by Targets of Tender Offers' (1982) 80 Michigan Law Review 1155, 1177.

[197] M Friedman, 'The Social Responsibility of Business Is to Increase Its Profits' *The New York Times Magazine* (13 September 1970), reprinted in WC Zimmerli, M Holzinger, and K Richter (eds), *Corporate Ethics and Corporate Governance* (Springer 2007) 173.

It is easy to see how the private-ordering focus of normative agency cost theory supports the shareholder wealth maximization rationale and militates against stakeholder theory. Since shareholders are the residual risk bearers, they are regarded as having contracted 'for a promise to maximize long-run profits of the firm'.[198] Creditors (including suppliers, customers, and the firm's employees), on the other hand, have contracted for a fixed return and do not require the managers to act in their interest or balance the interests of the shareholders and creditors. This arrangement, which is of course not set out explicitly in any contract between the shareholders and the company, but imputed by law (assuming that directors' duties are interpreted in light of shareholder value maximization), is economically sensible. By acting exclusively in the interest of the residual risk bearers, managers automatically benefit other constituencies. Since the claims of the creditors are first in line, maximizing profits ensures that the creditors are paid, and whatever remains can be distributed to the shareholders.[199]

Again, these considerations are not part of, and do not follow directly from, positive agency cost theory. As developed by economists, agency cost theory does not suggest that control over the firm should be vested exclusively in the stockholders, or their interests should be paramount.[200] Rather, economists model the consequences of different control arrangements and ownership structures. If externalities do not exist and a policy-maker decides that social objectives going beyond considerations of utility maximization are irrelevant, acting solely in the interest of the shareholders may be the preferred policy choice, but as we have discussed above, other approaches are equally defensible within the conceptual framework of positive agency cost theory.[201] Nevertheless, the Anglo-American model of corporate governance is firmly based on a normative understanding of the insights of agency cost theory.

Is shareholder wealth maximization an accurate description of the law as it stands? This depends, first of all, on the legal system in question. Not surprisingly, given our discussion so far, common law and civil law countries follow somewhat different approaches in how they define the role of shareholder wealth maximization. However, it is important to recognize that the choice between different systems of corporate governance is not a binary one. No country, including the United States, which is most clearly associated with agency cost theory and shareholder wealth maximization, embraces one approach to the exclusion of the other. Rather, in all legal systems, we find elements of both shareholder and stakeholder theory. The question, therefore, is not whether a country's corporate governance system is based on shareholder wealth maximization *or* stakeholder theory, but how the interests of shareholders *and* stakeholders are balanced. We begin our more detailed analysis of the law with a famous case from the United States, *Dodge v Ford*, which seems to represent a rather one-sided view on the right balance between shareholder and stakeholder interests.

***Dodge v. Ford Motor Co.*, 204 Mich. 459 (Supreme Court of Michigan 1919)**

[T]he plaintiffs, who together own 2,000 shares, or one-tenth of the entire capital stock of the Ford Motor Company, on the 2d of November, 1916, filed in the circuit court for the county of Wayne, in chancery, their bill of complaint, which bill was later, upon leave granted, on April 26, 1917, amended, in which bill they charge that since 1914 they have not been represented on the board of directors of the Ford Motor Company, and that since that time the policy of the board of directors has been dominated and controlled absolutely by Henry Ford, the president of the company, who owns and for several years has owned 58 per cent. of the entire capital stock of the company ... Setting up that on the 31st of July, 1916, the end of its last fiscal year, the said Henry Ford gave out for publication a statement of the financial condition of the company ... that for a number of years a regular dividend, payable quarterly, equal to 5

[198] Easterbrook and Fischel (n 31) 36. [199] ibid 38. [200] See the reference in n 165 above.
[201] See section A.

per cent. monthly upon the authorized capital stock, and the special dividends hereinbefore referred to, had been paid, it is charged that notwithstanding the earnings for the fiscal year ending July 31, 1916, the Ford Motor Company has not since that date declared any special dividends: 'And the said Henry Ford, president of the company, has declared it to be the settled policy of the company not to pay in the future any special dividends, but to put back into the business for the future all of the earnings of the company, other than the regular dividend of five per cent. (5%) monthly upon the authorized capital stock of the company-two million dollars ($2,000,000)' ...

Ostrander, CJ

The rule which will govern courts in deciding these questions is not in dispute. It is, of course, differently phrased by judges and by authors, and, as the phrasing in a particular instance may seem to lean for or against the exercise of the right of judicial interference with the actions of corporate directors, the context, or the facts before the court, must be considered. This court, in Hunter v. Roberts, Throp & Co., 83 Mich. 63, 71, 47 N. W. 131, 134, recognized the rule in the following language:

'It is a well-recognized principle of law that the directors of a corporation, and they alone, have the power to declare a dividend of the earnings of the corporation, and to determine its amount. Courts of equity will not interfere in the management of the directors unless it is clearly made to appear that they are guilty of fraud or misappropriation of the corporate funds, or refuse to declare a dividend when the corporation has a surplus of net profits which it can, without detriment to its business, divide among its stockholders, and when a refusal to do so would amount to such an abuse of discretion as would constitute a fraud, or breach of that good faith which they are bound to exercise towards the stockholders' ...

When plaintiffs made their complaint and demand for further dividends, the Ford Motor Company had concluded its most prosperous year of business. The demand for its cars at the price of the preceding year continued. It could make and could market in the year beginning August 1, 1916, more than 500,000 cars. Sales of parts and repairs would necessarily increase. The cost of materials was likely to advance, and perhaps the price of labor; but it reasonably might have expected a profit for the year of upwards of $60,000,000. It had assets of more than $132,000,000, a surplus of almost $112,000,000, and its cash on hand and municipal bonds were nearly $54,000,000. Its total liabilities, including capital stock, was a little over $20,000,000. It had declared no special dividend during the business year except the October, 1915, dividend. It had been the practice, under similar circumstances, to declare larger dividends. Considering only these facts, a refusal to declare and pay further dividends appears to be not an exercise of discretion on the part of the directors, but an arbitrary refusal to do what the circumstances required to be done. These facts and others call upon the directors to justify their action, or failure or refusal to act. In justification, the defendants have offered testimony tending to prove, and which does prove, the following facts: It had been the policy of the corporation for a considerable time to annually reduce the selling price of cars, while keeping up, or improving, their quality. As early as in June, 1915, a general plan for the expansion of the productive capacity of the concern by a practical duplication of its plant had been talked over by the executive officers and directors and agreed upon; not all of the details having been settled, and no formal action of directors having been taken. The erection of a smelter was considered, and engineering and other data in connection therewith secured. In consequence, it was determined not to reduce the selling price of cars for the year beginning August 1, 1915, but to maintain the price and to accumulate a large surplus to pay for the proposed expansion of plant and equipment, and perhaps to build a plant for smelting ore. It is hoped, by Mr. Ford, that eventually 1,000,000 cars will be annually produced. The contemplated changes will permit the increased output ...

Mr. Henry Ford is the dominant force in the business of the Ford Motor Company. 'My ambition,' said Mr. Ford, 'is to employ still more men, to spread the benefits of this industrial system to the greatest possible number, to help them build up their lives and their homes. To do this we are putting the greatest share of our profits back in the business' ...

The record, and especially the testimony of Mr. Ford, convinces that he has to some extent the attitude towards shareholders of one who has dispensed and distributed to them large gains and that they should be content to take what he chooses to give. His testimony creates the impression, also, that he thinks the Ford Motor Company has made too much money, has had too large profits, and that, although large profits might be still earned, a sharing of them with the public, by reducing the price of the output of the company, ought to be undertaken. We have no doubt that certain sentiments, philanthropic and altruistic, creditable to Mr. Ford, had large influence in determining the policy to be pursued by the Ford Motor Company—the policy which has been herein referred to.

It is said by his counsel that—'Although a manufacturing corporation cannot engage in humanitarian works as its principal business, the fact that it is organized for profit does not prevent the existence of implied powers to carry on with humanitarian motives such charitable works as are incidental to the main business of the corporation' ...

We do not draw in question, nor do counsel for the plaintiffs do so, the validity of the general proposition stated by counsel nor the soundness of the opinions delivered in the cases cited [by counsel]. The case presented here is not like any of them. The difference between an incidental humanitarian expenditure of corporate funds for the benefit of the employés, like the building of a hospital for their use and the employment of agencies for the betterment of their condition, and a general purpose and plan to benefit mankind at the expense of others, is obvious. There should be no confusion ... of the duties which Mr. Ford conceives that he and the stockholders owe to the general public and the duties which in law he and his codirectors owe to protesting, minority stockholders. A business corporation is organized and carried on primarily for the profit of the stockholders. The powers of the directors are to be employed for that end. The discretion of directors is to be exercised in the choice of means to attain that end, and does not extend to a change in the end itself, to the reduction of profits, or to the nondistribution of profits among stockholders in order to devote them to other purposes.

There is committed to the discretion of directors, a discretion to be exercised in good faith, the infinite details of business, including the wages which shall be paid to employés, the number of hours they shall work, the conditions under which labor shall be carried on, and the price for which products shall be offered to the public.

It is said by appellants that the motives of the board members are not material and will not be inquired into by the court so long as their acts are within their lawful powers. As we have pointed out, and the proposition does not require argument to sustain it, it is not within the lawful powers of a board of directors to shape and conduct the affairs of a corporation for the merely incidental benefit of shareholders and for the primary purpose of benefiting others, and no one will contend that, if the avowed purpose of the defendant directors was to sacrifice the interests of shareholders, it would not be the duty of the courts to interfere.

We are not, however, persuaded that we should interfere with the proposed expansion of the business of the Ford Motor Company. In view of the fact that the selling price of products may be increased at any time, the ultimate results of the larger business cannot be certainly estimated. The judges are not business experts. It is recognized that plans must often be made for a long future, for expected competition, for a continuing as well as an immediately profitable venture ...

[A]ssuming that the plans required an expenditure sooner or later of $9,895,000 for duplication of the plant, and for land and other expenditures $3,000,000, the total is $24,220,000. The company was continuing business, at a profit—a cash business. If the total cost of proposed expenditures had been immediately withdrawn in cash from the cash surplus (money and bonds) on hand August 1, 1916, there would have remained nearly $30,000,000.

Defendants say, and it is true, that a considerable cash balance must be at all times carried by such a concern. But, as has been stated, there was a large daily, weekly, monthly, receipt of cash. The output was practically continuous and was continuously, and within a few days, turned into cash. Moreover, the contemplated expenditures were not to be immediately made. The large sum appropriated for the smelter plant was payable over a considerable period of time. So that, without going further, it would appear that, accepting and approving the plan of the directors, it was their duty to distribute on or near the 1st of August, 1916, a very large sum of money to stockholders.

Comments and questions:

1. *Dodge v. Ford Motor Co.* is commonly referred to as a case epitomizing the shareholder-value-maximization approach to corporate governance, notably in light of the court's seemingly unambiguous statement that '[a] business corporation is organized and carried on primarily for the profit of the stockholders' and directors were required to exercise their discretion to that end, rather than in a manner that mounted 'to a change in the end itself, to the reduction of profits, or to the non-distribution of profits among stockholders in order to devote them to other purposes'. Do you agree? What remains of the directors' discretion after *Dodge v. Ford*?
2. There is a sub-context to the judgment that may partly explain the uncompromising language of the court. In their bill, the claimants argued that 'there are many other corporations engaged in the business of manufacturing cars in competition with the only car manufactured by the Ford Motor Company, to wit, the class recognized in the trade as "low-priced cars". That the annual production of such other companies of such class of cars runs into the hundreds of thousands of cars per annum. That if the said Henry Ford is permitted to continue the policy that he has inaugurated and announced he is determined to carry out, of increasing production, reducing the price of cars, and increasing the capital investments in the conduct of such business by withholding the dividends from stockholders to which they are entitled, the necessary result will be the destruction of competition on the sale of the class of cars manufactured by such corporation and the creation of a complete monopoly in the manufacture and sale of such cars in violation of the state, federal and common law'.[202] The claimants, the Dodge brothers, were founders of a company initially building engines for Ford Motor Co and had acquired a combined stake of 10 per cent of Ford's capital stock. Shortly before Henry Ford decided to suspend the payment of a special dividend, the Dodge brothers had decided to begin producing their own cars. In referring in the bill to 'the destruction of competition', they were clearly concerned about their own market position and their prospects of competing with a company that was producing cars at low prices. While the court did not address Ford's allegedly anti-competitive behaviour explicitly, it can be assumed that it influenced the judges' decision. Ostrander CJ acknowledged that it was within the powers of the managers 'to carry on with humanitarian motives ... charitable works' and that there was 'committed to the discretion of directors, a discretion to be exercised in good faith, the infinite details of business'. However, any humanitarian motives must be incidental to the business, rather than the main purpose of the director's actions. Courts will not interfere with business decisions, such as the expansion of production proposed by Henry Ford, since 'the judges are not business experts',[203] but they will hold directors liable if their 'avowed purpose ... was to sacrifice the interests of shareholders'.
3. Almost a century after *Dodge v. Ford*, the US courts were confronted with another case where explicit non-profit motives clashed with the profit orientation of investors. In *eBay Domestic Holdings, Inc. v. Newmark*,[204] the Delaware Court of Chancery had to decide on the legality of a number of board actions diluting the rights of eBay, a minority shareholder in the company craigslist, with a blocking minority of about 28 per cent and one seat on the board of directors. craigslist is an online portal operating a classified advertisements site in the United States and other countries. In addition to eBay, its other two shareholders at the time of the litigation were its founder Craig Newmark and its CEO, James Buckmaster, who together owned 71.6 per cent of the company. craigslist has a unique corporate culture; it is organized as a for-profit company under Delaware law, but its majority shareholders conceive it as a 'community service'. As a consequence, most of the ads are placed free of charge, the

[202] *Dodge v Ford Motor Co.*, 204 Mich. 473.

[203] This approach closely mirrors the law as it stands today, which is commonly conceptualized as the so-called 'business judgment rule'. We will discuss the business judgment rule in detail in Chapter 6B.I.2.

[204] 16 A.3d 1 (Del. Ch. 2010).

company does not sell advertising space on its website, and generally does not seek to monetize the website and maximize profits.[205] eBay attempted for a while to introduce a more profit-oriented focus. When these attempts failed it launched its own online classifieds website to compete with craigslist. In response, the board of craigslist took three measures to dilute eBay's shareholding and keep eBay out of the boardroom. First, they introduced a staggered board with three classes of directors, one director per class, and each class serving a three-year term. The staggered board effectively rendered the cumulative voting provision in craigslist's articles obsolete, since only one director was elected each year. Secondly, the directors adopted a shareholder rights plan. Pursuant to the plan, all shareholders received one right per share to purchase two shares in craigslist at US$0.00005 per share if any of the existing shareholders acquired 0.01 per cent of additional craigslist stock or an outside investor became the beneficial owner of at least 15 per cent of the company's outstanding shares. Thirdly, the two majority shareholders and the company entered into an agreement providing that all shareholders would receive one newly issued share for every five shares over which they granted the company a right of first refusal.[206] Craig Newmark and James Buckmaster made use of the possibility to grant a right of first refusal over their shares, but eBay refused to do so. New shares were duly issued to Newmark and Buckmaster, and eBay's ownership was diluted to below 25 per cent as a result.

The Court of Chancery held that the three actions were subject to three different standards of review: the staggered board amendments were reviewed under the regular business judgment rule standard, the rights plan had to be a reasonable and proportional response to a takeover threat, and the right of first refusal was subject to an entire fairness test, because the directors who executed the agreement on behalf of the company were also parties to the agreement in their capacity as shareholders. The three standards all derive from the fiduciary position of directors.[207] The court, accordingly, discussed whether directors of a Delaware for-profit company could legally pursue 'a corporate policy that specifically, clearly, and admittedly seeks *not* to maximize the economic value of [the company] for the benefit of its stockholders'.[208] The answer was unequivocal: 'Promoting, protecting, or pursuing nonstockholder considerations must lead at some point to value for stockholders'.[209] In other words, the interests of non-stockholder constituencies can be taken into consideration by directors, but there must be a 'rational' or 'plausible' connection between protecting these interests and promoting shareholder value.[210] The court accordingly invalidated the shareholder rights plan and the right of first refusal. However, it upheld the introduction of the staggered board. Here, the less exacting standard of review of the business judgment rule made a difference. Directors, of course, are still required to promote the interests of the shareholders, but the courts will not question the directors' actions if they can rationally argue that pursuing stakeholder interests will ultimately benefit the shareholders. In *eBay v. Newmark*, Newmark and Buckmaster's intention to prevent eBay from using confidential information discussed in board meetings to advance the interests of its competing business represented a rational business purpose, which justified the introduction of a staggered board and thus preventing a representation of the minority shareholder on the board of directors.[211]

4. The decision in *eBay v. Newmark* can be seen as both a confirmation and a qualification of *Dodge v. Ford*. It is a confirmation because the Delaware Court of Chancery reaffirmed that shareholder interests are paramount. Any action of the directors must be linked in some form, at least indirectly, to the interests of the shareholders. On the other hand, provided this link

[205] ibid 8. [206] ibid 22–4.

[207] For details, see Chapter 6B.I.2 and C.I.2. In short, as a default, the business judgment rule grants directors wide discretion, provided that they act in good faith, with sufficient information, and without a personal interest in the transaction. If the company is the target of a hostile takeover, the test under the business judgment rule is 'enhanced' and the courts require that the defensive action was reasonable and proportional in light of the threat posed by the takeover. Finally, if the directors are conflicted, for example because they stand on both sides of the transaction, the courts scrutinize whether the transaction is entirely fair to the company.

[208] See *eBay v Newmark*, 16 A.3d 34. [209] ibid 33.

[210] J Macey, 'A Close Read of an Excellent Commentary on Dodge v. Ford' (2008) 3 Virginia Law & Business Review 177, 179.

[211] See *eBay v Newmark*, 16 A.3d, 38–40.

exists, directors have wide discretion in managing the company. The Court of Chancery in *eBay v. Newmark* explicitly acknowledged that the directors were entitled to give up shareholder value in the short run, for example in order to make a charitable contribution or pay employees higher salaries, as long as the long-run nexus between their actions and shareholder value was preserved.[212] In this respect, the decision echoes prior Delaware case law. In particular, in an influential takeover case, *Paramount Communications, Inc. v. Time Inc.*,[213] the Delaware Supreme Court distinguished between maximizing shareholder value within a time frame as determined by the board of directors, and realizing an immediate benefit for the shareholders. While the former is part of the duties that directors owe to the company, the latter is not. In *Paramount*, Time had agreed on a business combination with the entertainment company Warner Communications, Inc. after extensive negotiations. Shortly before the merger was intended to be implemented, Time's shareholders received an all-cash tender offer by Paramount to purchase the outstanding shares of Time at a substantial premium. Time's directors were concerned that the shareholders 'would not comprehend the long-term benefits of the Warner merger'.[214] In order to safeguard the deal with Warner, they restructured the transaction so that Time's shareholders were prevented from voting on the deal. The court rejected Paramount's legal challenge, explaining that

> it [is] unwise to place undue emphasis upon long-term versus short-term corporate strategy. Two key predicates underpin our analysis. First, Delaware law imposes on a board of directors the duty to manage the business and affairs of the corporation. This broad mandate includes a conferred authority to set a corporate course of action, including time frame, designed to enhance corporate profitability. Thus, the question of 'long-term' versus 'short-term' values is largely irrelevant because directors, generally, are obliged to chart a course for a corporation which is in its best interests without regard to a fixed investment horizon. Second, absent a limited set of circumstances ... a board of directors, while always required to act in an informed manner, is not under any *per se* duty to maximize shareholder value in the short term, even in the context of a takeover.[215]

5. The plaintiffs in *eBay v. Newmark* largely succeeded because craigslist had been incorporated as a for-profit company, with the consequence that the general shareholder-value focus of directors' duties applied as in any other company, in spite of the allegedly non-profit-driven corporate philosophy of craigslist. The founders of craigslist could have avoided these consequences, while still taking advantage of Delaware corporate law, by forming a so-called public benefit corporation, which was introduced into Delaware law in 2013.[216] The Delaware General Corporation Law defines a 'public benefit corporation' as 'a for-profit corporation ... that is intended to produce a public benefit or public benefits and to operate in a responsible and sustainable manner'.[217] The directors of such a company are required to manage the corporation 'in a manner that balances the pecuniary interests of the stockholders, the best interests of those materially affected by the corporation's conduct, and the specific public benefit or public benefits identified in its certificate of incorporation'.[218] Thus, while the financial interests of the shareholders still feature in the relevant calculus,

[212] ibid 33. [213] 571 A.2d 1140 (Del. 1989). [214] ibid 1148.

[215] ibid 1150. The standard of review was that of the 'enhanced' business judgment rule (see n 207 above). The directors were required to show that they had reasonable grounds for believing that Paramount's tender offer constituted a threat to corporate policy and that their defensive measures were reasonable and proportional in relation to that threat. The court held that they had met this burden, emphasizing that 'precepts underlying the business judgment rule militate against a court's engaging in the process of attempting to appraise and evaluate the relative merits of a long-term versus a short-term investment goal for shareholders'. ibid 1153.

[216] Over the last few years, more than 30 US states have introduced benefit corporation statutes, often based on a model statute drafted by pro bono attorneys and promoted by B Lab, a non-profit organization that certifies companies meeting high standards of social and environmental performance and accountability. The model law can be accessed at http://benefitcorp.net/attorneys/model-legislation. For a discussion of benefit corporations, see JH Murray, 'Social Enterprise Innovation: Delaware's Public Benefit Corporation Law' (2014) 4 Harvard Business Law Review 345.

[217] Del. Gen. Corp. Law, §362(a). [218] ibid §365(1).

the directors are entitled to pursue a corporate policy that is not designed to maximize either short-term or long-term profits.

Being required to balance a variety of interests, of course, raises the question to whom directors are accountable and who can enforce breaches of duty. Granting all interested constituencies standing to sue the directors on the ground that they did not balance the interests of shareholders and other affected parties correctly would open the door to frequent litigation and pose substantial liability risks, since courts could easily disagree with the directors about an inherently ill-defined notion such as the 'right' balance of shareholder and stakeholder interests.[219] On the other hand, allowing directors wide discretion without effective control mechanisms would also raise concerns. A criticism directed at stakeholder theory generally is that 'a manager told to serve two masters (a little for the equity holders, a little for the community) has been freed of both and is answerable to neither. Faced with a demand from either group, the manager can appeal to the interests of the other. Agency costs rise and social wealth falls'.[220] The Delaware legislator was evidently more concerned about the former problem than the latter. The law on the public benefit corporation maintains the general rule of corporate law that fiduciary duties are only owed to the company and the stockholders and not to other stakeholders. In addition, the law provides for a safe harbour for directors in balancing competing interests and the public benefit. Directors are deemed to have satisfied this duty if their decision 'is both informed and disinterested and not such that no person of ordinary, sound judgment would approve'.[221] This standard of review, which is at least as protective of directors as the business judgment rule, combined with the lack of standing of non-shareholder constituencies to bring a claim, makes it unlikely that directors will be found liable for violating the balancing requirement.[222] On the other hand, it can be expected that directors of public benefit corporations will be subject to more stringent financing or reputational constraints than directors of for-profit corporations. A public benefit corporation will be quickly out of business if it cannot convince its customers or investors that it pursues its goals in an appropriate manner. The wide discretion that the Delaware law grants directors, therefore, functions less as an accountability mechanism, and more as a shield against situations where directors are challenged for promoting societal goals too ardently, as in *eBay v. Newmark*.

The case law discussed above shows that it would be misleading to equate the Delaware approach to corporate governance with a simplistic formula requiring the maximization of shareholder value. If this were the case, it would be difficult to argue that directors were justified in preventing the shareholders from realizing an immediate, large control premium, as the Delaware Supreme Court held in *Paramount v Time*. Because of the uncertain long-run effects of the Time-Warner merger and the potentially long time horizon, the net present value of any future value increase would need to be discounted substantially, thus biasing any such calculation towards the short term. The Delaware Supreme Court came to a different conclusion because Delaware law is infused with a heavy dose of managerial autonomy. If the directors have conceived a well-informed corporate plan in good faith and without being motivated by self-interest, the courts will not require the directors to abandon this plan for a short-term profit.[223] Nevertheless, on a continuum ranging from a pure shareholder focus to a more pluralistic view encompassing a variety of stakeholder interests, Delaware law is clearly located close to the former end. Can the same be said about other common law jurisdictions, notably the UK and other states of the United States? Consider the following two provisions from the UK Companies Act 2006 and the New York Business Corporation Law.

219 Murray (n 216) 355, points out that 'balancing' seems to require more than simply considering the interests of stakeholders (which is the requirement pursuant to the model statute (n 216) §301(a)), but he also refers to Delaware law-makers who suggested that prioritizing some interests and giving others only negligible weight would still comply with the duty to 'balance'.

220 Easterbrook and Fischel (n 31) 38.

221 Del. Gen. Corp. Law, §365(b).

222 Murray (n 216) 363.

223 *Paramount Communications, Inc. v Time Inc.* 571 A.2d 1154.

UK Companies ACT 2006

Section 172—Duty to promote the success of the company

(1) A director of a company must act in the way he considers, in good faith, would be most likely to promote the success of the company for the benefit of its members as a whole, and in doing so have regard (amongst other matters) to—
   (a) the likely consequences of any decision in the long term,
   (b) the interests of the company's employees,
   (c) the need to foster the company's business relationships with suppliers, customers and others,
   (d) the impact of the company's operations on the community and the environment,
   (e) the desirability of the company maintaining a reputation for high standards of business conduct, and
   (f) the need to act fairly as between members of the company.
(2) Where or to the extent that the purposes of the company consist of or include purposes other than the benefit of its members, subsection (1) has effect as if the reference to promoting the success of the company for the benefit of its members were to achieving those purposes.
(3) The duty imposed by this section has effect subject to any enactment or rule of law requiring directors, in certain circumstances, to consider or act in the interests of creditors of the company.

New York Business Corporation Law

§ 717—Duty of directors

(a) A director shall perform his duties as a director, including his duties as a member of any committee of the board upon which he may serve, in good faith and with that degree of care which an ordinarily prudent person in a like position would use under similar circumstances....
(b) In taking action, including, without limitation, action which may involve or relate to a change or potential change in the control of the corporation, a director shall be entitled to consider, without limitation, (1) both the long-term and the short-term interests of the corporation and its shareholders and (2) the effects that the corporation's actions may have in the short-term or in the long-term upon any of the following:
   (i) the prospects for potential growth, development, productivity and profitability of the corporation;
   (ii) the corporation's current employees;
   (iii) the corporation's retired employees and other beneficiaries receiving or entitled to receive retirement, welfare or similar benefits from or pursuant to any plan sponsored, or agreement entered into, by the corporation;
   (iv) the corporation's customers and creditors; and
   (v) the ability of the corporation to provide, as a going concern, goods, services, employment opportunities and employment benefits and otherwise to contribute to the communities in which it does business.

   Nothing in this paragraph shall create any duties owed by any director to any person or entity to consider or afford any particular weight to any of the foregoing or abrogate any duty of the directors, either statutory or recognized by common law or court decisions.

These two provisions can be called 'constituency statutes'.[224] They enable directors to take a broader array of interests than shareholder value into account. However, do they represent

[224] SM Bainbridge, 'Interpreting Nonshareholder Constituency Statutes' (1992) 19 Pepperdine Law Review 971. For a list of US states that have adopted such statutes, see ES Adams and JH Matheson, 'A Statutory Model for Corporate Constituency Concerns' (2000) 49 Emory Law Journal 1085, 1086–7, and for a classification of constituency statutes as 'permissive' (the majority of states), permissive without dominance of shareholder interests (Indiana, Iowa, and Pennsylvania), and 'mandatory' (Connecticut), see C Hansen, 'Other Constituency Statutes: A Search for Perspective' (1991) 46 Business Law 1355, 1376.

a shift towards stakeholder theory? Note how section 172 of the UK Companies Act 2006 is formulated. Directors are required to 'promote the success of the company for the benefit of its members' (the shareholders). *In doing so*, they must have regard to the interests of other stakeholders. Thus, the relevant point of reference of the duty to promote the success of the company is exclusively the benefit of the shareholders (unless the company's constitutional documents define the success of the company differently[225]). Taking a decision that balanced the interests of the employees, customers etc, without benefiting the shareholders would constitute a breach of directors' duties. In this respect, the provision is in line with pre-2006 case law, which was based on the principle that constituency interests could be taken into account if this advanced the interests of the shareholders. As the Court of Appeal of England and Wales famously observed in the nineteenth century: 'The law does not say that there are to be no cakes and ale, but there are to be no cakes and ale except such as are required for the benefit of the company'.[226] Differently formulated, directors had to act in good faith in the best interest of the company,[227] and the interests of the company were defined as 'the interests of both present and future members', but not of other stakeholder groups.[228]

The Company Law Review Steering Group that prepared the 2006 reform of company law made it clear that the codification of the duty to act in the best interest of the company in section 172 of the Companies Act 2006 was not intended to shift the law towards a pluralistic model involving duties owed to stakeholders. This, the Steering Group explained

> would impose a distributive economic role on directors in allocating the benefits and burdens of management of the company's resources; ... this role would be uncontrolled if left to directors in the form of a power or discretion; and ... a similarly broad role would be imposed on the judges if the new arrangement took the form of an enforceable obligation conferring rights on all the interested parties to argue for their interests in court.[229]

Instead, the Company Law Review favoured what has been called an *enlightened shareholder value approach*.[230] Directors would not be turned 'from business decision makers into moral, political or economic arbiters', but they should be encouraged to adopt an 'inclusive' view that took 'due account of wider interests'.[231] In practice, this is close to the 'present

[225] This is permissible pursuant to s 172(2). See also Companies Act 2006, Explanatory Notes, para 330 (confirming that 'it is possible for any company to have "unselfish" objectives which prevail over the "selfish" interests of members' or for a company to be set up 'partially for the benefit of its members and partly for other purposes').

[226] *Hutton v West Cork Railway Co* (1883) 23 Ch D 654, 673. In this case, the company had resolved to make a severance payment to some of its employees, even though they had no legal claim to such payment. The court held that making gifts to employees was not impermissible per se, provided it was 'reasonably incidental to the carrying on of the company's business for the company's benefit' (ibid 672). However, in the case at hand, the company was being wound up. Accordingly, there was no business that could have been promoted by the severance payment.

[227] *Re Smith & Fawcett Ltd* [1942] Ch 304.

[228] *Gaiman v National Association for Mental Health* [1971] Ch 317. The case dealt with the expulsion of a large number of members that had recently joined the National Association for Mental Health (NAMH) on the grounds that they were affiliated with the Church of Scientology. The Council of NAMH made use of a provision of the articles of association authorizing it to request members to resign in order to expel the Scientology members who, it was argued, posed a threat to the association. Some of the Scientology members brought an action for breach of the council's duties. The court discussed, inter alia, whether the council had exercised its power under the articles to expel members in good faith in the best interests of the association. In the following excerpt, the court refers to 'the association' (NAMH), which was a charity in the form of a company limited by guarantee, but the dictum is equally applicable to business corporations: '[I]t is not very easy to determine what is in the best interests of the association without paying due regard to the members of the association. The interests of some particular section or sections of the association cannot be equated with those of the association, and I would accept the interests of both present and future members of the association, as a whole, as being a helpful expression of a human equivalent': ibid 330. The court concluded that the decision was taken by the council 'in good faith and in what were believed to be the best interests of the association and the members as a whole': ibid 331.

[229] Company Law Review Steering Group, *Modern Company Law for a Competitive Economy: Developing the Framework* (2000) para 2.12.

[230] ibid para 2.21.

[231] ibid paras 2.21–2.22.

and future members' formula of the common law. The directors have to ensure that the company is a viable, profitable business in the long run, which involves paying due regard to the company's employees, suppliers, customers, and other constituencies affected by the company's operations. The actions of employees and those who enter into transactions with the company are directly linked to the company's financial position. Even without explicitly mentioning these stakeholders in section 172, directors would be required to consider the effect that operational decisions have on them and their likely reaction.[232] Similarly, wider societal interests may affect the company at least indirectly. A business that pays no regard to environmental matters may damage its reputation, which in turn has financial consequences for the company.

The standard of review applicable pursuant to section 172 is also equivalent to that under common law. Directors must act in a way they believe, in good faith, promotes the success of the company. The test, therefore, is largely subjective. If the director actually believed that the decision was in the best interest of the company and its members, there is no liability. Similarly, under common law, the courts inquired into the director's state of mind and sought to assess what the director 'honestly believed'.[233] However, since such an assessment generally needs to rely on circumstantial evidence, certain objective elements creep into the test. The courts will not accept the director's contentions if 'no reasonable director ... could have believed the transaction was in the best interests of the company'.[234] It has been argued that this standard must be distinguished from an objective 'reasonable director' standard, which applies, for example, in duty of care cases.[235] The question is not how a reasonable director in the same position would act, but whether *any* director could reasonably be expected to have such a belief.[236] Therefore, it may be more accurate to speak of a rationality standard. As an objective lower bound of the otherwise subjective test, the courts will ask whether the arguments advanced by the director are rational.[237] The same considerations apply in the interpretation of the codified version of the duty to act in the best interest of the company.

The addition of a list of stakeholder interests in section 172 is unlikely to increase the liability risk of directors substantially. Whether directors had regard to the interests of these stakeholders is assessed according to the duty of care.[238] Hence, an objective standard applies, but 'having regard' to stakeholder interests can be documented easily and does not mean that the directors have to act on their considerations. In addition, the notes to the Companies Act 2006 explain that directors will not be held liable for procedural failures in considering stakeholder-regarding interests if their decision how best to promote the success of the company would not have been different.[239] Thus, it would not be accurate to conclude that the enlightened shareholder value approach protected stakeholder interests by extending the fiduciary duties of directors. Instead, the goal of the reform was to raise awareness of the interdependence between shareholder interests and wider societal interests and strengthen transparency, so that the public could assess how companies dealt with these wider interests.[240] To this effect, the law now requires large companies[241] to prepare a strategic report

[232] It may be argued that this follows directly from the duty to act in good faith in the best interest of the company. Alternatively, the duty of care, which requires directors to make informed, well-considered decisions, would impose the same obligations; D Kershaw, *Company Law in Context* (2nd edn, OUP 2012) 384.

[233] *Regentcrest plc v Cohen* [2001] BBCC 494, 513.

[234] *Fraser v Oystertec plc* [2004] BBCC 233, 265.

[235] Companies Act 2006, s 174(2)(a).

[236] Kershaw (n 232) 344.

[237] See eg *Regentcrest* (n 233) 519 (holding that the waiver of a clawback claim of the company against two of its directors did not amount to a violation of the duty to act bona fide in the interests of the company because the directors believed that the waiver was necessary 'to maintain a united board, and not to create a situation in which two of the directors were being sued by Regentcrest' at a critical time when the company was financially distressed). For a further discussion of this case and the standard of review pursuant to s 172, see Chapter 5B.I.

[238] Companies Act 2006, Explanatory Notes, para 328.

[239] ibid.

[240] Company Law Review Steering Group (n 229) para 2.22.

[241] Large companies are companies not entitled to the small companies' exemption pursuant to ss 381–384 of the Companies Act 2006.

for each financial year that must contain, inter alia, an analysis of the company's business in light of environmental and employee matters.[242] If the company is quoted, the strategic report must also set out information regarding the impact of the company's business on the environment, as well as social, community and human rights issues that are necessary to understand the performance or position of the company.[243]

Section 717 of the New York Business Corporation Law reproduced above is structurally comparable to the UK provision, albeit with certain differences. Subsection (a) codifies the general standard of conduct expected of directors of New York business corporations. Subsection (b) contains a list of stakeholder interests similar to section 172 of the UK Companies Act. However, in contrast to the latter, directors are not required to have regard to these non-shareholder interests. Rather, they are merely 'entitled' to consider them, and the law does not specify any particular relationship or hierarchy between shareholder and non-shareholder interests.[244] Section 717(b) was amended in response to the seminal Delaware duty of care case *Smith v Van Gorkom*,[245] which increased the liability risk for directors who adopted decisions (in that case the sale of a company) without comprehensive information. The goal of the amendment was to grant directors the flexibility, in appropriate cases, not to choose a course of action that maximized shareholder value in the short-term, and instead consider broader corporate as well as societal interests.[246] In addition, adoption of the provision was motivated by certain protectionist sentiments. Section 717(b) allows directors to take measures to frustrate a hostile takeover bid. Even if the bid offers the best short-term value to the shareholders, directors can argue that long-term considerations of shareholder value and the effects of the corporation's actions on the listed non-shareholder constituencies militate against the bid.[247] For example, directors may decide that the bidder's strategic vision is not compatible with the community orientation of their business and is too much focused on revenue generation and service expansion.[248] Thus, compared with Delaware law, directors of New York corporations enjoy a greater degree of discretion in takeover cases. They are protected by the general business judgment rule, while Delaware law requires that any defensive action constitute a reasonable and proportional response to the threat posed by the takeover.[249] Offering this protection makes it easier for the target to resist a takeover offer and thus shields domestic corporations from foreign hostile bidders.[250]

Nevertheless, the wide-ranging list of non-shareholder interests that directors can take into account under New York law does not mean that they could ignore shareholder value. As in the UK, the relevant point of reference in assessing the directors' actions is the success of the company.[251] The common law principles determining what is and what is not a valid exercise of business judgment continue to apply, as explicitly stated in the last sentence of Section 717(b). Similarly, according to these principles, directors' duties may be owed

[242] Companies Act 2006, s 414C(4).

[243] ibid s 414C(7). For an assessment of the effectiveness of such extended reporting obligations, see S Schaltegger and RL Burritt, 'Sustainability accounting for companies: Catchphrase or decision support for business leaders?' (2010) 45 Journal of World Business 375.

[244] This permissive, rather than obligatory nature is typical of US constituency statutes; see n 224 above and E Brodsky and MP Adamski, *Law of Corporate Officers and Directors: Rights, Duties, and Liabilities* (Thomson Reuters 2018–2019) §2:8.

[245] 488 A.2d 858 (Del. 1985). We will discuss this decision in Chapter 6B.I.2(b).

[246] RL Haig (ed), *Commercial Litigation in New York State Courts* (4th edn, Thomson Reuters 2015–2018) §89:14.

[247] ibid. See also the reference to change of control transactions in §717(b) New York Business Corporation Law.

[248] *Minzer v Keegan* (E.D.N.Y. 1997) 1997 WL 34842191, 12.

[249] See n 207 above (the so-called enhanced business judgment rule).

[250] Haig (n 246) §89:14.

[251] See eg *Auerbach v Bennett*, 47 N.Y.2d 619, 629 (N.Y. 1979), defining the New York business judgment rule as a doctrine that 'bars judicial inquiry into actions of corporate directors taken in good faith and in the exercise of honest judgment in the lawful and legitimate furtherance of corporate purposes'. See also *Minzer v Keegan* (n 248) 12, discussing whether the directors were entitled to believe that their business would benefit from preferring one bidder to another.

directly to the shareholders,[252] but they are not owed to any other constituency by virtue of section 717(b).[253]

On the shareholder/stakeholder continuum, we move further in the direction of a pluralistic view of directors' duties as we come to continental European jurisdictions. The markedly different emphasis (which, however, does not necessarily translate into a substantially different application of directors' duties in the courts) is exemplified well by the following quote by Ferdinand Piech, long-time CEO and chairman of the German car manufacturer Volkswagen AG, and grandson of Ferdinand Porsche, the automotive engineer and founder of the car company bearing his name: 'Yes, we have heard of shareholder value. But we put customers first, then workers, business partners, suppliers and dealers, and then shareholders'.[254] While Volkswagen is, arguably, an unusual company in that the business had, from its inception, a clear social dimension and is partly owned by the state,[255] the comment should probably not be taken literally. Currently close to 90 per cent of Volkswagen's capital stock are held by private and foreign institutional and retail investors, who clearly expect a return on their investment.[256] Nevertheless, the quote shows that stakeholder considerations may feature prominently in corporate decision-making.

This pluralistic view is in line with German company law. The German Stock Corporation Act does not specify in whose interest the directors of a company have to perform their duties.[257] However, the official explanatory statement to the current Stock Corporation Act (dating from 1965) refers to an older version of the law stemming from 1937 that stipulated that directors were bound to exercise their powers 'for the benefit of the enterprise and its workforce, as well as the general benefit of society and state'.[258] One group is conspicuous by its absence from the provision: the shareholders. This omission can be explained with the historical context of the Act of 1937. First attempts to reform stock corporation law began in the 1920s. They were influenced by the economic and financial conditions of the time, which shook public confidence in the free-market rationale that had underpinned the German corporate economy until then, even though the legal framework governing companies, arguably, did not play any role in the financial crises of the 1920s and 1930s.[259] The hyperinflation of 1922–1923 was caused by a combination of lack of access to external credit, large foreign payment obligations, and the willingness of the government to accept inflation in order to bring about a renegotiation of reparation payments.[260] High inflation, in turn, led to a 'flight into shares', which were better insulated from inflationary pressures than fixed interest securities, and thus increased volatility and speculation on German stock exchanges.[261] The capital markets remained volatile after the currency was stabilized in late 1923. A major

[252] *Bernheim v 136 East 64th Street Corp.*, 128 A.D.2d 434, 435 (N.Y. App. Div. 1987).

[253] New York Business Corporation Law, §717(b) last sentence.

[254] Quoted by C Mayer and J Franks, 'Different votes for different folks' *Financial Times* (19 October 2006).

[255] For a brief description of the history of the company, see the opinion of Advocate General Colomer in Case C-112/05 *Commission v Germany* [2007] ECR I-8995 paras 17–29 (explaining that the company was formed with the aim 'to build a simple car which most Germans would be able to afford without imposing an excessive burden on their finances'; ibid para 18).

[256] The remaining 12% are held by the state of Lower Saxony, where Volkswagen's main factories are located.

[257] See §76(1) AktG, which simply provides that '[t]he management board shall manage the company under its own responsibility'.

[258] See §70(1) AktG 1937 [Gesetz über Aktiengesellschaften und Kommanditgesellschaften auf Aktien], RGBl I 1937, 107 (in the original: '… wie das Wohl des Betriebs und seiner Gefolgschaft und der gemeine Nutzen von Volk und Reich es fordern').

[259] We will discuss different aspects of German stock corporation law reflecting its generally permissive nature until the reforms of 1937 in section E.I.3 below (board structure regulation) and Chapter 5A.III (origin of corporate power).

[260] V Hentschel and W Stern, 'German economic and social policy, 1815–1939' in P Mathias and S Pollard (eds), *The Cambridge Economic History of Europe from the Decline of the Roman Empire, vol 8* (Cambridge University Press 1989) 752, 784; DE Moggridge, 'The gold standard and national financial policies, 1919-39' in P Mathias and S Pollard (eds), *The Cambridge Economic History of Europe from the Decline of the Roman Empire, vol 8* (Cambridge University Press 1989) 250, 275–6.

[261] FW Henning, 'Börsenkrisen und Börsengesetzgebung von 1914 bis 1945 in Deutschland' in H Pohl (ed), *Deutsche Börsengeschichte* (Fritz Knapp 1992) 226, 227, 235.

stock market crash occurred in 1927 and stock prices declined steadily thereafter, culminating in the global financial and economic crisis of 1929–1933.[262] Against this backdrop, it is maybe unsurprising that the government commission preparing the reform of stock corporation law emphasized in 1930 that the understanding of what a stock corporation is had shifted over the last decades from a largely individualistic conceptualization to a more holistic one. The corporation had to be seen as more than an aggregation of the interests of its founders. It had interests of its own, which might conflict with those of the shareholders and were equally deserving of protection by the legislator.[263] Interestingly, the commission used words to describe this potential conflict, and the way to resolve it, that are reminiscent of modern-day enlightened shareholder value theory: 'Assuming proper management of the company and the right attitude of the individual shareholders, there is in reality no conflict of interest between the enterprise and its stockholders'.[264] Presumably, by referring to the shareholders' 'right attitude', the commission implied that speculative behaviour and short-term maximization of shareholder value were not in line with the legislative conception of the corporation. On the other hand, the commission believed that ensuring that the company prospered in the long run would promote both the societal goal of sustainable corporate management and the shareholders' financial interests.[265] To this effect, the commission argued that the management board had to be able to manage the company independently 'of changing shareholder majorities'.[266] First steps to implement the strengthened position of the board in a proposal of 1930 were, arguably, timid,[267] and the proposal did not suggest a reformulation of the duties of directors that would exclude shareholder interests.[268] However, it can be argued that the seeds of a shift from an individualistic to a more collectivist understanding of the corporation can be found in the reform discussions of the 1920s. This shift was undoubtedly supported by the political climate of the day and gathered speed after the ascent of the National Socialists to power in 1933.

The reform act of 1937 was largely based on the 1930 proposal, but it also went beyond the proposal in important ways. In particular, it restricted the rights of the shareholders to influence the management of the company[269] and identified the interests of 'society and state' as points of reference for managerial action. The National Socialist ideology, with its distrust of the capitalist system and the belief in the importance of strong leadership, is discernible in these changes.[270] Nevertheless, the amendments did not intend to render shareholder interests irrelevant. It was clear to the drafters of the law that shareholders as providers of equity capital were central to corporate activity, and the new law preserved important powers for the general meeting.[271] For the same reason, it was not disputed that directors could and should take shareholder interests into account, which were considered to be part of the interests of the enterprise.[272] On the other hand, the provision clearly went further than, for

[262] For a discussion of the reasons why Germany was more affected by the Wall Street Crash of 1929 and the Great Depression than other European countries, see Pohl (n 261) 262–3.

[263] Reichsjustizministerium, Entwurf eines Gesetzes über Aktiengesellschaften und Kommanditgesellschaften auf Aktien, including explanatory comments (1930), reprinted in W Schubert (ed), *Quellen zur Aktienrechtsreform der Weimarer Republik (1926-1931)* (Peter Lang 1999) 845, 936. This approach is sometimes called the theory of the 'enterprise as such', a phrase that goes back to a monograph by W Rathenau, *Vom Aktienwesen* (S Fischer 1917). For a more recent discussion, see C Windbichler, 'The Public Spirit of the Corporation' (2001) 2 EBOR 795, 808–809.

[264] Schubert (n 263) 936–7 (translation by authors).

[265] However, other statements of the reform commission indicate that the commission was not quite sure how to define the relationship between shareholder interests and societal interests. For example, the commission stressed that 'the modern stock corporation is not only a vehicle for the pursuit of individual profit, but it also has to serve, to different degrees, the general interests of society': ibid 937.

[266] ibid 936.

[267] For an assessment of the proposal, see W Schubert, 'Einleitung' in Schubert (ed) (n 263) 28–9.

[268] The proposal did not include a provision comparable to §70(1) AktG 1937.

[269] These changes are examined in Chapter 5A.III.

[270] Schubert (n 263) 31.

[271] See Chapter 5A.III.

[272] F Schlegelberger and others (eds), *Aktiengesetz vom 30. Januar 1937* (3rd edn, F Vahlen 1939) §70, no 5.

example, section 172 of the UK Companies Act 2006, because the pluralistic description of the duties of the management board gave directors wide discretion and the provision did not provide for any hierarchical relationship between the interests of the different constituencies.

In the decades after the Second World War, the law remained initially unchanged. Its pluralistic approach was seen as reflecting the spirit of the 'social market economy', the model of market capitalism underpinning the post-war reconstruction of West Germany.[273] On this view, directors of public stock corporations have a socio-political function in addition to their managerial duties.[274] In principle, this function still exists today. The reference to society and state was omitted when the Stock Corporation Act was reformed in 1965.[275] However, this change was only intended to remove terminology that had connotations of National Socialist ideology. The legislator did not want to bring about substantive changes and, in fact, believed that the reference was unnecessary, because in a social market economy it was self-evident that directors had to consider the public good.[276] Today, therefore, directors have to balance the interests of the shareholders, workers, creditors, and society at large. In doing so, they probably enjoy a wider discretion than their American or British counterparts. They are not required to choose the profit-maximizing course of action, not even in the long run, provided they act within the confines of the general duty of care and there is a link between the directors' decision and the interests of the enterprise.[277] In spite of this continuity in the law, the changing times— notably the rise of agency cost theory and the increased presence of foreign institutional investors in German capital markets—can be expected to have some influence on the interpretation of the objectives of corporate management. This influence, arguably, can be discerned in a certain shift of emphasis. In the 1960s, before the reference to society and state was removed, the common good, as the overarching goal of all corporate activity, was central to an analysis of the role of directors.[278] Today, the director is first and foremost seen as the guarantor of the success of the enterprise. It is still widely acknowledged that 'success' should be defined in a pluralistic sense, and the focus is now on the question of how directors should balance the relevant interests to promote the success of the enterprise in a sustainable manner.[279]

The view of the stock corporation espoused by the reform proposals of 1930 and codified by the Act of 1937 was by no means novel in the history of German legal thought, although it constituted a break with the free-market orientation that had characterized the German corporate economy before the First World War. The pluralistic view can be traced back to the writings of the German legal historian Gierke, who regarded the corporation as a social entity, a real person that was not to be equated with its members, but had interests of its own.[280] The intellectual legacy of Gierke's theory is clearly visible in the pluralistic approach that informs German law.[281] Indeed, it could be argued that modern-day

[273] W Schmidt and J Meyer-Landrut in W Gadow and others (eds), *Großkommentar zum Aktiengesetz* (2nd edn, de Gruyter 1961) §70, no 11.

[274] ibid. [275] For the current formulation, see n 257 above.

[276] G Spindler in W Goette and M Habersack (eds), *Münchener Kommentar zum Aktiengesetz, vol 2* (5th edn, CH Beck 2019) §76, para 4. For a comparison of the 1937 and 1965 versions of the provision see also H Fleischer, 'Unternehmensinteresse und intérêt social: Schlüsselfiguren aktienrechtlichen Denkens in Deutschland und Frankreich' (2018) 47 ZGR 703, 714-5.

[277] ibid paras 64–80, 105–14. [278] See eg Schmidt and Meyer-Landrut (n 273) §70, no 11.

[279] See eg Spindler (n 276) paras 72-3, 113.

[280] O Gierke, *Das Deutsche Genossenschaftsrecht, vols 1-4* (Weidmannsche Buchhandlung 1868-1913), partly translated by FW Maitland in *Political Theories of the Middle Age* (1938, Lawbook Exchange Ltd 2002). See in particular the introduction to the translation at pp xviii–xliii. For a more extensive discussion of the 'real entity' theory and other nineteenth-century theories of the corporation, in particular the so-called fiction and aggregate theories, see Chapter 1E.

[281] The authors of the 1930 proposal were familiar with the idea of the corporations as a 'real person' and consciously argued in that tradition, see eg F Schlegelberger, *Juristische Wochenschrift* (1930) 3712.

stakeholder theory and corporate social responsibility are natural extensions of Gierke's conception of the corporation as a real entity. If the corporation is abstracted from the shareholders and seen as a person that interacts in multiple ways with its social environment, it is intuitive to argue that it also assumes responsibilities in this context—*social* responsibilities, as suggested by stakeholder theory. A second intellectual link may be said to exist between the German pluralistic model of corporate governance and the concept of a coordinated market economy, as developed by the varieties of capitalism literature.[282] Since the German approach ascribes a certain distributive function to directors, who are to be guided by the general notion of the 'common good' in their actions, the price mechanism plays a less important role in the allocation of resources. For this reason, some commentators have concluded that stakeholder theory is typical of coordinated market economies and shareholder theory of liberal market economies.[283] With the caveat that the dichotomy of shareholder/stakeholder theories, as explained, overstates the actual differences between legal systems, this observation may be an accurate representation of economic and legal realities in Germany. However, it should be noted that the distributive function of directors, in and of itself, does not say much about the character of the capitalist economy. The wide discretion enjoyed by American or British CEOs leaves them in at least as powerful a position as CEOs of German public companies.[284] In all three legal systems, CEOs are able to decide, and they do decide in practice, not to rely exclusively on marginal calculations and competitive markets to structure the relationship between the firm, factors of production, and third parties. The difference is not so much the choice of non-market as opposed to market institutions by the policy-maker to determine how these relationships are structured,[285] but the political and cultural factors that influence how the directors' discretion is constrained.[286] Furthermore, there is no reason to assume that the pluralistic model is linked to the civil-law nature of the German legal system, as is sometimes alleged in the literature.[287] As mentioned, before the 1920s corporate governance in German stock corporations had a strong shareholder-focus. The conceptual changes considered by the legal reforms of the 1920s and implemented in the Stock Corporation Act of 1937 were not a function of particularities of German civil law, but of the economic and political conditions of the time.

French corporate governance has revolved around two distinct conceptions of the corporation: an institutional and a contractual view.[288] On the one hand, it is commonly accepted that companies, including stock corporations, are based on a contract between the shareholders.[289] This conception finds its origins in Roman law and the theories developed by

[282] See section B.III above. [283] Vitols (n 120) 337--8.

[284] ibid 339, 344—5. Vitols identifies institutions structuring top management as a main difference in corporate governance between the UK and Germany, with the single board of UK companies being dominated by a powerful CEO, whereas German companies are characterized by 'multiple power centers'. The more distributed power structure in German companies is seen as an example of the widespread use of non-market institutions, whereas market relationships play a more prominent role in the UK. However, this interpretation does not seem to take sufficient account of the limited influence that other corporate organs have over the decisions of the management board of German public companies (see in particular the discussion in Chapter 5A.III).

[285] This is a central contention of the varieties of capitalism literature; see eg Vitols (n 120) 338.

[286] As the discussion above has shown, one important constraint is the formulation of the goals of corporate governance. Other constraints, which we will discuss later in this and the following chapters, are the ease with which shareholders can influence business operations and the procedures to appoint and remove managers (where, importantly, the workforce has a say under German co-determination rules, see Chapter 5D.III). In all three respects, US, UK, and German law differ substantially, but it seems misplaced to explain these differences with the choice between market and non-market institutions.

[287] R La Porta, F Lopez-de-Silanes, and A Shleifer, 'The Economic Consequences of Legal Origins' (2008) 46 Journal of Economic Literature 285, 300 (with further references).

[288] See Chapter 1E above.

[289] See eg D Schmidt, 'Gestaltungsfreiheit im französischen Gesellschaftsrecht' in M Lutter and H Wiedemann (eds), *Gestaltungsfreiheit im Gesellschaftsrecht: Deutschland, Europa und USA* (de Gruyter 1997) 291.

Jean Domat (1625–1696) and Robert Joseph Pothier (1699–1772),[290] whose writings were instrumental in the codification of French civil law. The contractual conception can still be seen in the structure of the French Civil Code, which treats the company's articles as a special contract alongside rental agreements and loan agreements.[291] Accordingly, it is widely accepted that the general provisions on contracts in the Civil Code apply to companies. Furthermore, the chapter of the French Civil Code dealing with firms and companies serves a gap-filling function if the Commercial Code does not address a question.[292] It is a common theme underpinning these provisions that companies must 'be formed in the common interest of the members'.[293]

On the other hand, from the nineteenth century onwards, the growth of capitalism prompted a more institutional perception of the company. Under the impression of the spread of listed companies, whose shares were increasingly easy to trade, companies came to be seen as structures that institutionalized a complex web of relationships between changing shareholders—or, as one author put it, as a 'wonderful instrument of capitalism'[294]—rather than as a purely contractual arrangement. At the end of the nineteenth century, the law had evolved sufficiently for the *Cour de Cassation* to note that the corporate contract led to the emergence of an entity with a legal personality separate from that of its shareholders.[295] This decision, which was handed down after the Companies Act 1867 had made incorporation by registration possible,[296] reinforced a conception of the company that went beyond a contractual lens. The Court explained that the relevant provisions of the Civil Code[297] personified the company by avoiding any reference to the relationship among the shareholders, and instead linking the shareholders to the company. In particular, the Court explained that the company was, for so long as it was in existence, a moral person and the rightful owner of the corporate assets.

With the emergence of legislative instruments outside of the Civil Code, the technical influence of contract law diminished. The Law of 22 November 1913[298] was a first blow to the application of the general principle of the binding force of contracts enshrined in Article 1134 of the 1804 Civil Code,[299] which subjects the variation and revocation of agreements to the mutual consent of all parties.[300] It gave the power to modify any provision contained in a company's articles to the general meeting of shareholders based on the will of only a majority of shareholders.[301] In a similar vein, the Law of 4 January 1978 allowed for the free removability of managers by a majority of the members in the absence of any provision to the contrary in the articles.[302] This resulted in the articles of association becoming increasingly subject to change, since any change to the composition of the board of directors had to be reflected in the articles.[303] The 1978 law also inserted Article 1842 into the Civil

[290] RJ Pothier, *Oeuvres de Pothier, tome troisième* (Bechet Ainé 1823–1825) 445 (emphasizing that companies emerge from the *droit naturel des contrats*). Parts of this publication dealing with companies have been translated as *A Treatise on the Contract of Partnership* (OD Tudor trans., Butterworths 1845). For a discussion of the contribution of Domat and Pothier to the drafting of the Code civil, see J Ghestin and G Goubeaux, *Traité de droit civil: Introduction générale* (4th edn, LGDJ 1994) 89–99, nos 118–38.

[291] Title IX of Book III of the French Civil Code on the *contrat de société* (which is inserted between the provisions on the *contrat de louage* and *contrat de prêt*).

[292] Civ, Arts 1832–1873. [293] Civ, Art 1833.

[294] G Ripert, *Aspects juridiques du capitalisme moderne* (2nd edn, LGDJ 1951, reprint 1998) no 46 s.

[295] Cass req, 23 February 1891 (*Banque Générale des Alpes Maritimes c/ Rigal*), S 1892. 1. 73, note E Meynial.

[296] Act of 24 July 1867 (Loi sur les Sociétés), *Bull. des Lois* 1867 no 1513, 94.

[297] Notably, Arts 1845–1848, 1850, 1852, 1855, 1859, 1867.

[298] Law of 22 November 1913, JORF of 23 November 1913, 10178.

[299] Now Art 1103 Code civil as amended by Ordinance no 2016-131 of 10 February 2016 (Ordonnance portant réforme du droit des contrats, du régime général et de la preuve des obligations), JORF no 35 of 11 February 2016.

[300] J Julien, 'Observations jurisprudentielles du sort des associés dans la société civile' (2001) RTD Com 841.

[301] T Favario, 'Regards civilistes sur le contrat de société' (2008) Revue des sociétés 53.

[302] Civ, Art 1851, as amended by Law no 78-9 of 4 January 1978, JORF of 5 January 1978, 179.

[303] See Julien (n 300) 841.

Code, pursuant to which companies were only endowed with moral personality once they were registered with the *Registre de Commerce et des Sociétés*. Thus, it became clear that the conclusion of a contract between private parties was not sufficient for a company to come into legal existence. However, even as the contractual link became more tenuous, the provisions of the Civil Code continued to leave considerable freedom to contracting parties to decide on the terms of the company's articles, and this remains today an important feature of French law.

Yet, despite the evolution of company law as a separate body of law and the emphasis that courts placed on the separate legal identity of the company, the question in whose interests the company should be operated remained largely unanswered. Jurisprudential developments offer only limited guidance in this respect. On the one hand, the landmark case of *Fruehauf* from 1965[304] appeared to mark a victory for the development of a distinct *intérêt social* that was to be distinguished from the goal of shareholder value maximization. This case concerned the French subsidiary of an American financial group, Fruehauf International Inc. The French subsidiary had entered into a contract for the delivery of trailers to the People's Republic of China. At the time, the hostile relations between the United States and China led the parent company to order the termination of the contract, a decision that threatened the economic viability of the French subsidiary. To substantiate its decision to appoint an administrator in charge of the subsidiary and thereby avert bankruptcy, the French court specifically noted the consequences that the parent company's decision would have on the subsidiary's employees.[305] On the other hand, this case remains an isolated and context-specific instance of judicial activism. In a decision of 21 January 1970,[306] concerning the takeover of a company experiencing financial difficulties with the goal of recapitalizing the company, the Cour de Cassation reasserted the paramount importance of shareholder interests. The court noted that the company was a going concern and it was therefore only necessary to consider whether the interests of the shareholders had been safeguarded and, in particular, the interests of particular shareholders had not been promoted at the expense of others. Furthermore, just a year after *Fruehauf*, in 1966, the introduction of the two-tier board system[307] provoked a wave of disappointment amongst those who had nourished the hope of seeing employee representatives sitting on supervisory boards.[308] Authors commented that the reforms of 1966 could hardly be regarded as pursuing the protection of other interests than those of the shareholders.[309]

Many of those who argue that the protection of stakeholder interests is an integral part of French company law rely on the Viénot Report of 1995, the first report on corporate governance in listed companies in France. This report explained that 'the company [should be] considered as a separate economic agent, pursuing its own objectives which are distinct from those of shareholders, employees, creditors including the internal revenue authorities,

[304] CA Paris, 22 May 1965 (*Fruehauf*), *JCP* 1965, II, no 14274 bis, *Recueil Dalloz* 1968, 147, note R Contin.

[305] The provisions of the Code de commerce concerning the appointment of an administrator (*procédure de sauvegarde*—safeguarding procedure) refer to the company's employees as a relevant factor in the decision on the opening of the proceedings. The purpose of the safeguarding procedure is 'the reorganisation of the business in order to allow the continuation of the economic activity, the maintenance of employment and the settlement of liabilities', Art L620-1. The judge decides on the commencement of the proceedings after having heard 'the debtor, representatives of the works council or, in the absence of a works council, the employee delegates' and after having considered the 'financial, economic and employment situation' of the company, Art L621-1. However, the *Fruehauf* decision, arguably, goes further than what the Code de commerce requires. The Court of Appeal held that the employees' interests were part of the *intérêt social*, which was different from, and in fact prevailed over, the interests of shareholders considered in isolation.

[306] Cass com, 21 January 1970 (*Saupiquet-Cassegrain*) *JCP* 1970, II, no 16541, note B Oppetit.

[307] See n 538 below and accompanying text.

[308] A Pirovano, 'La "boussole" de la société. Intérêt commun, intérêt social, intérêt d'entreprise?' (1997) Recueil Dalloz 1997 189.

[309] ibid.

suppliers and customers. It nonetheless represents the common interest of all of these persons, which is for the company to remain in business and prosper'.[310] Yet, it is also a fundamental principle underpinning the Viénot Report that the board of directors represents the shareholders, rather than a multitude of stakeholders with possibly conflicting interests.[311] Thus, while the position of the Viénot Report regarding the corporate interest is ambivalent, the report stands firmly on the ground of shareholder theory when it comes to the more concrete guidance it gives on how directors should exercise their powers. This approach highlights the difference between the French and German conceptions of the role of the board of directors. Similarly, more recent corporate governance reports, notably the Hellebuyck Commission Recommendations of June 1998[312] and the Viénot II Report of July 1999,[313] which inform the current French corporate governance code,[314] cannot be relied on to promote a more pluralistic view of French corporate governance regulation. The two reports do not elaborate on the notion of 'common interest' (*intérêt social commun*); nor do they address the shareholder-stakeholder debate.

Thus, the picture in French law can best be described as a blurry one, with some relatively isolated examples of a push for a greater protection of stakeholder interests. For example, the notion of the 'interests of the corporation' has recently been rephrased as 'the interests of the group' in some legislative instruments.[315] A good example is Article L225-231 of the Commercial Code, which specifies that any written question issued by a shareholder about the management of the company must be evaluated in light of the 'interests of the group'.[316] It can only be presumed that the term 'interests of the group' has the same meaning as in the *Rozenblum* decision, where the Court of Appeal of Paris explained that it refers to 'an economic, social or financial common interest in light of the policy established for the group as a whole'.[317]

Perhaps the solution offered by French law in order to strike a balance between the different interests at play in companies is embodied by the possibility for public companies[318] to issue free shares to their employees.[319] This includes executive directors, members of the board of directors and other managers, but also all employees of the company in the broader sense. This option enables companies to align the interests of one particular stakeholder group with those of the shareholders, with maximized returns becoming a shared goal. Besides creating a right to dividends, it also enables employees to exercise the shareholders' participatory rights. In this way, the voice of employees in the company is strengthened and

[310] Conseil National du Patronat Français (CNPF) and Association Française des Entreprises Privées (AFEP), *The Boards of Directors of Listed Companies in France* (Viénot I) (1995) 7.

[311] ibid 12 (in the original: 'le conseil d'administration représente collectivement l'ensemble des actionnaires; il n'est pas un agrégat disparate de représentants d'intérêts contradictoires; sa mission doit s'exercer dans l'intérêt social commun').

[312] Association Française de la Gestion Financière—Associations des Sociétés et Fonds Français d'Investissement (AFG-ASFI), Recommendations on Corporate Governance (1998).

[313] Conseil National du Patronat Français (CNPF) and Association Française des Entreprises Privées (AFEP), The Boards of Directors of Listed Companies in France (Viénot II) (1999).

[314] See text to nn 400–407 below.

[315] A shift in emphasis would also be brought about by a recent legislative reform proposal, Projet de loi relatif à la croissance et la transformation des entreprises (Loi PACTE). The reform act proposes to change Art 1833 Code civil (n 293) by stipulating that a company must be managed in the interest of its members, 'taking into consideration the social and environmental dimensions of the company's activities'. Thus, the reform act introduces a hierarchy similar to s 172(1) of the UK Companies Act 2006. The provision does not require the managers to prioritize social interests or balance such interests and the interests of the members, but they must *have regard* to them in managing the company.

[316] Com, Art L225-231, para 1, as amended by Art 114 Law no 2001-420 of 15 May 2001 (Loi relative aux nouvelles régulations économiques (NRE)), JORF no 113 of 16 May 2001, 7776.

[317] CA Paris, Crim, 4 February 1985, no 84-91581 (*Rozenblum*).

[318] The companies concerned are the *société anonyme*, the *société en commandite par actions*, and the *société par actions simplifiée*.

[319] Com, Art L225-197-1 (and, by way of cross-reference, Arts L226, para 2 and M227-1, para 3).

their interests may be reflected in corporate decisions. Some limitations, however, exist, particularly since the issuance of free shares is merely an option for companies, often linked to a form of financial reward system for employees. In addition, more formal employee participation arrangements at board level are a recent innovation from 2013, and they remain more limited in scope than the German system of co-determination.[320]

III. The corporate governance movement

In many legal systems, we can observe a trend towards supplementing the statutory regime regulating a company's governance architecture with a set of non-binding rules, or best practice standard, that are designed to address the conflicts of interest prevalent in corporations in a flexible, yet increasingly detailed manner. Statutory regulation has been seen as too rigid and not able to respond to the idiosyncrasies and regulatory needs of different companies adequately. As a consequence, over the last few decades, governments, regulators and private sector associations have set up committees of experts that have promulgated corporate governance codes containing standards of good governance that operate on a voluntary, comply-or-explain, basis. Today, virtually all European countries and many countries worldwide have corporate governance codes in place that apply to listed companies, or a subset of such companies (typically companies with securities trading on the prime market of a stock exchange).

This trend began in the United States in the early 1970s. Organisations such as the Business Roundtable, composed of the chief executive officers of the 200 largest companies in the United States, the National Association of Corporate Directors, and the Council of Institutional Investors all produced declarations that dealt with the role and responsibilities of directors and discussed how the corporate governance structure of American companies could be improved.[321] The first comprehensive project to analyse and advance the US corporate governance regime was undertaken by the American Law Institute (ALI). Preparatory work, including the organization of conferences and the issuance of guidebooks, led to the adoption of 'Principles of Corporate Governance: Analysis & Recommendations', completed in 1992 and published in 1994, albeit amid much controversy and criticism from lobbying organizations that represented corporate managers.[322] The efforts of the ALI were largely met with disregard by the business community and legal practitioners. The Principles were rarely cited in court and did not attain much practical significance. The codes of some large institutional investors and self-regulatory organizations came to be of greater relevance. For example, the Teachers Insurance and Annuity Association-College Retirement Equities Fund (TIAA-CREF) and the California Public Employees' Retirement System (CalPERS), the largest US pension fund, have issued, and regularly update, influential principles of corporate governance.[323] The funds expect that the companies they invest in be governed in accordance with their principles, and they execute their proxy voting responsibilities in furtherance of the standards laid down in the codes. In addition, national stock exchanges have included corporate governance rules in their listing manuals and require most listed companies to comply with the rules (exceptions exist for foreign issuers).[324] The manuals contain

[320] The German co-determination regime and the French reforms of 2013 (again revised in 2015) are discussed in Chapter 5D.III.

[321] See eg Business Roundtable, 'The Role and Composition of the Board of Directors of the Large Publicly Owned Corporation' (1978) 33 Business Law 2083.

[322] An overview of the activities of the ALI is given by MA Eisenberg, 'The Modernization of Corporate law: An Essay for Bill Cary' (1983) 37 University of Miami Law Review 187, 209.

[323] TIAA-CREF Policy Statement on Corporate Governance (6th edn 2011) ; CalPERS Global Governance Principles (2015); CalPERS Governance and Sustainability Principles (2018). The Global Principles are based on the standards adopted by the International Corporate Governance Network (ICGN).

[324] See eg s 303A of the Listed Company Manual of the New York Stock Exchange (NYSE).

provisions on board composition,[325] independence requirements for outside directors,[326] committees of the board,[327] and powers of the shareholders.[328]

The relatively disimpassioned movement towards a modern corporate governance system took a dramatic turn in the United States in the beginning of the new Millennium with a number of high-profile corporate scandals that exposed widespread mismanagement, insider dealing, and accounting fraud. The probably most infamous of these scandals was Enron, which filed for bankruptcy in 2001.[329] Enron was followed, within a few years, by a number of major US corporations—WorldCom, Adelphia, Global Crossing, and Tyco, to name just the largest cases—which announced restatements of their financial results in the range of billions of dollars, filed for bankruptcy protection and destroyed hundreds of billions of dollars in shareholder value in the process. The damage to investors caused by WorldCom alone is estimated to be close to US$180 billion. The scandals provoked a dramatic loss of confidence in the stock market and in the American business model in general. The Dow Jones Industrial Average dropped from a high of more than 11,000 to approximately 4,000 in the wake of the corporate scandals. These events changed the political climate, which had been dominated by a generally non-interventionist, liberal economic approach in the decades before the 2000s. The federal government decided to step in and carry out a comprehensive overhaul of the regulatory system. A legislative proposal that had largely been ignored by the leading political class and corporate scholars suddenly came to the fore: the Public Company Accounting Reform and Investor Protection Act. It is better known under its short title, which refers to its draftsmen, Senator Paul Sarbanes of Maryland and Congressman Michael Oxley of Ohio: the Sarbanes-Oxley Act of 2002.[330] The act is structurally different from the private sector initiatives to improve corporate governance that had been promoted until then. It amends, inter alia, the Securities Exchange Act of 1934 and constitutes, therefore, binding law that has to be observed by all corporations within its scope of application. Owing to its importance and the significant changes that it has brought for the US corporate governance system, it is useful to present its main features briefly.

The act establishes a Public Company Accounting Oversight Board (PCAOB) that regulates the accounting profession by promulgating auditing, quality control, ethics, and independence rules, conducting inspections of registered public accounting firms, and imposing sanctions in case of violations of the rules.[331] The act also increases auditor independence by requiring the unbundling of contemporaneous audit and non-audit services (with narrow exceptions for certain pre-approved non-audit services) and the rotation of the lead audit partner every five years.[332] In addition, it prohibits an accounting firm from performing audit services for an issuer if a senior financial executive of the issuer was an employee of the accounting firm and participated in the audit of the issuer during the 1-year period preceding the audit.[333]

The Sarbanes-Oxley Act also lays down rules for the internal governance structure of companies. It mandates that the audit committee of public companies, rather than management

[325] For example, pursuant to §303A.01 NYSE Listed Company Manual, listed companies must have a majority of independent directors.

[326] See eg §303A.02 NYSE Listed Company Manual.

[327] See eg §§303A.04-07 NYSE Listed Company Manual: Listed companies must have a nominating/corporate governance committee, a compensation committee and an audit committee.

[328] See eg §303A.08 NYSE Listed Company Manual: Shareholders must be given the opportunity to vote on all equity-compensation plans.

[329] For a chilling account of the corporate governance failures that led ultimately also to the dissolution of Arthur Andersen, Enron's auditors, see *In re Enron Corp. Securities, Derivative & ERISA Litigation*, 235 F. Supp. 2d 549 (S.D. Tex. 2002).

[330] Pub.L. 107-204 of 30 July, 2002, 116 Stat. 745.

[331] Sarbanes-Oxley Act, §§101–109.

[332] ibid §§201–209, amending Securities Exchange Act 1934, s 10A. The unbundling of audit services and non-audit services is laid down in s 10A(g)–(i) and audit partner rotation in s 10A(j).

[333] Sarbanes-Oxley Act, §206, amending Securities Exchange Act 1934, s 10(A)(l).

or inside directors, be directly responsible for the appointment, compensation, and oversight of the work of the external auditor.[334] Furthermore, it stipulates that the audit committee must consist exclusively of independent directors. An independent director is defined by the act as a person who does not, 'other than in his or her capacity as a member of the audit committee, the board of directors, or any other board committee (i) accept any consulting, advisory, or other compensatory fee from the issuer; or (ii) be an affiliated person of the issuer or any subsidiary thereof'.[335] In order to improve the reliability of financial statements further, the act requires the chief executive officer and the chief financial officer to review the annual and quarterly reports and certify that they do not contain any untrue statements. The signing officers have to set up internal control mechanisms that ensure that material information is made known to them,[336] and the auditor has to attest to the effectiveness of the internal control mechanisms as assessed by management.[337] In addition to the existing administrative and criminal sanctions in the case of accounting misstatements, the CEO and CFO forfeit any bonus or other incentive-based compensation or any profits realized from the sale of securities of the issuer during the twelve-month period following the filing of a financial document that overstated the company's earnings.[338] Thus, the Sarbanes-Oxley Act penalizes the two highest-ranking officers in the company irrespective of any personal misconduct and, at the same time, addresses the problem that the payments received by executives are often perceived to be disproportionate in the wake of a financial scandal, when it becomes known that the company's financial position is worse than thought.

Finally, the Sarbanes-Oxley Act enhances transparency, inter alia, by mandating that financial reports disclose all off-balance sheet transactions and other relationships of the issuer with unconsolidated entities that may have a material effect on the financial condition of the issuer.[339] Directors, officers, and substantial shareholders (those with a shareholding of more than 10%) are required to disclose their holdings in equity securities of the issuer in a timely manner.[340] Loans of an issuer to its directors and officers and comparable transactions are barred, subject to certain exceptions.[341] Issuers must disclose whether they have adopted a code of ethics for senior financial officers, defined as standards that are 'reasonably necessary to promote honest and ethical conduct, including the ethical handling of actual or apparent conflicts of interest between personal and professional relationships'.[342] If they decide not to adopt such a code, issuers have to give reasons for their non-compliance.

Some of the corporate governance provisions of the Sarbanes-Oxley Act were further amplified when the next major financial crisis, the subprime mortgage crisis of 2007-2009, triggered another major intervention by the federal legislator. The sprawling Dodd-Frank Act of 2010,[343] which brought about mainly changes to the US system of financial regulation, also included a number of provisions changing board structure regulation and executive remuneration. Most importantly, the Dodd-Frank Act requires companies to provide reasons if they decide not to separate the roles of chairman of the board of directors and chief executive officer[344] (which is common in US companies[345]), establish a compensation committee

[334] Sarbanes-Oxley Act, §301, amending Securities Exchange Act 1934, s 10(A)(m).

[335] Securities Exchange Act 1934, s 10(A)(m)(3)(B).

[336] Sarbanes-Oxley Act, §302.

[337] ibid §404. Most of the criticism levelled at the Sarbanes-Oxley Act focuses on §404 and the cost implications that this provision—as initially interpreted by the PCAOB, which required a full audit—entails. In order to relieve in particular smaller and mid-size companies of the cost burden, the PCAOB and the SEC modified their rules a few years after the entry into force of the Sarbanes-Oxley Act, SEC Press Release 2007-101 of 23 May 2007.

[338] Sarbanes-Oxley Act, §304.

[339] ibid §401, amending Securities Exchange Act 1934, s 13(j).

[340] Sarbanes-Oxley Act, §403, amending Securities Exchange Act 1934, s 16(a).

[341] Sarbanes-Oxley Act, §402, amending Securities Exchange Act 1934, s 13(k).

[342] Sarbanes-Oxley Act, §406.

[343] Dodd-Frank Wall Street Reform and Consumer Protection Act, Pub.L. 111–203 of 21 July 2010, 124 Stat. 1376.

[344] Dodd-Frank Act, §972, inserting s 14B into the Securities Exchange Act 1934.

[345] We will discuss this and other questions of board structure regulation in sections E.I and III below.

composed exclusively of independent directors,[346] disclose additional information about the compensation received by the executives,[347] and submit the remuneration of the most highly compensated executive officers to an advisory shareholder vote at least every three years.[348] Both Sarbanes-Oxley and Dodd-Frank exemplify a 'federalisation' of US corporate governance. As a part of corporate law, corporate governance falls within the domain of the US states, unless the federal legislator can assume legislative authority under the interstate commerce clause of the US constitution.[349] This shift of corporate governance legislation from the state level to the federal level has been criticized in the academic literature,[350] notably because it forecloses room for experimentation and does not offer the same incentives as a competitive environment to develop optimal regulatory solutions.[351] On the other hand, it may be argued that the corporate governance interventions of the federal legislator show a certain uneasiness with the professed beneficial consequences of regulatory competition and the level of investor protection that exists under state law.[352]

In Europe, the path of corporate governance reform was different. While the national or European legislator stepped in occasionally to supplement the soft-law initiatives of corporate governance committees, for example by regulating—similar to Sarbanes-Oxley—the composition and remit of the audit committee in a binding manner,[353] most European countries continue to rely on codes of best practice promulgated by a designated private or semi-public body to regulate the more detailed questions of corporate governance that would not normally be addressed in legislation. The main innovation in Europe was the introduction of a disclosure obligation that requires companies to declare in the annual report whether they comply with the main corporate governance code in force in their home country, or explain which best practice provisions they depart from, and why they depart from them. This comply-or-explain principle is now a harmonized rule laid down in European legislation and applies to all companies whose shares are admitted to trading on a regulated market of any EU Member State.[354] It stems from the UK Cadbury Code, the first corporate governance code adopted in Europe. The Cadbury Code was published in 1992 by the so-called Cadbury Committee, named after its chairman Sir Adrian Cadbury. The Committee was set up by the Financial Reporting Council, the London Stock Exchange (LSE), and the accounting profession in response to a series of financial scandals and the collapse of several large UK companies. In December 1992, the Committee published its report on 'the Financial Aspects of Corporate Governance',[355] which contained a Code of Best Practice addressed to listed

[346] Dodd-Frank Act, §952, inserting s 10C into the Securities Exchange Act 1934.

[347] Dodd-Frank Act, §953, amending Securities Exchange Act 1934, s 14. The new rules require, inter alia, the disclosure of information showing 'the relationship between executive compensation actually paid and the financial performance of the issuer', for example in the form of a graph comparing total shareholder return and the compensation paid over several years, see SEC Release No 34-74835 (April 29, 2015), 'Pay versus performance'.

[348] Dodd-Frank Act, §951, inserting s 14A into the Securities Exchange Act 1934.

[349] The interstate commerce clause, Art 1, s 8, cl 3 of the US Constitution, was the legislative basis for the adoption of the federal securities laws.

[350] Particularly forceful has been the criticism by R Romano, 'The Sarbanes-Oxley Act and the Making of Quack Corporate Governance' (2005) 114 Yale Law Journal 1521.

[351] ibid 1597–9.

[352] Regulatory competition in company law is discussed in more detail in Chapter 2C.

[353] Statutory Audit Directive, Directive 2006/43/EC, Art 36 stipulates that 'public interest entities' shall have an audit committee composed of a majority of independent members and that at least one member shall have competence in accounting or auditing. Public interest entities are defined as companies whose securities are admitted to trading on a regulated market of an EU Member State, certain credit institutions and insurance undertakings, and other legal entities designated as public-interest entities by Member States (Statutory Audit Directive, Art 2(13)).

[354] Directive 2013/34/EU on the annual financial statements, consolidated financial statements and related reports of certain types of undertakings, Art 20.

[355] The report is available on the website of the European Corporate Governance Institute (ECGI): https://ecgi.global/content/codes. The ECGI is an international scientific non-profit association that was founded in 2002. It is committed to improving corporate governance and draws on the research and activities of its members, who range from academics to practitioners and regulators.

companies.[356] The Committee believed that regulating by means of a non-binding code of best practice would be effective if the best practice rules were combined with a reporting requirement to identify and give reasons for any areas of non-compliance.[357] In this way, investors would be able to assess whether the internal governance arrangements of a company were adequate and, if not, penalize the company by selling their shares or requiring a better price for newly issued equity. Thus, the Cadbury Code, and following it all other corporate governance codes of EU Member States, co-opt the market mechanism to enforce best practice standards.

The principles of the Cadbury Code followed a threefold objective: They intended to increase company-related information, strengthen the integrity of financial reporting, and improve the accountability of boards of directors to shareholders.[358] In order to meet these objectives, the Code required, inter alia, a clearly accepted division of responsibilities at the helm of the company, that is, the posts of chief executive and chairman of the board should generally not be combined. If they were combined, a strong independent element should exist on the board able to ensure a balance of power and preventing any one individual from exercising unfettered powers of decision.[359] Furthermore, the board should include a sufficient number of non-executive directors for their views to carry significant weight in the board's decisions.[360] Matters of importance for the direction and control of the company had to be reserved for decision by the full board as opposed to the executive officers alone.[361] Finally, the Code set out standards of independence for non-executive (outside) directors on the board,[362] required disclosure of the directors' total emoluments, including pension contributions, stock options and separate figures for salary, and performance-related elements,[363] and envisaged a system of sub-committees of the board to propose the appointment of new executive and non-executive directors (nomination committee, which had to have a majority of non-executive directors on it),[364] oversee the determination of the executive directors' pay (remuneration committee, which was to be made up wholly or mainly of non-executive directors),[365] and review the company's financial statements and the work of the external auditor (audit committee, which had to be comprised of at least three non-executive directors and no executive director).[366] The LSE appended the Code of Best Practice to its Listing Rules and required all companies within its regulatory ambit to report on their compliance with the Code.

The Cadbury report left some questions unanswered. First, the standards of independence for non-executive directors were ambiguous. The Report stipulated that '[a]part from their directors' fees and shareholdings, [the non-executive directors] should be independent of management and free from any business or other relationship which could materially interfere with the exercise of their independent judgement'.[367] However, the

356 Cadbury Committee Report, para 3.1.
357 ibid para 3.7.
358 ibid paras 3.2–3.4.
359 Cadbury Code of Best Practice, s 1.2.
360 ibid s 1.3. The dominance of executive directors on the board had been, for a long time, a cause for concern in the UK. For example, J Dahya, JJ McConnell, and NG Travlos, 'The Cadbury Committee, Corporate Performance, and Top Management Turnover' (2002) 57 Journal of Finance 461, 462, reported that 'during 1988, for only 21 companies of the *Financial Times* (FT) 500 did outside directors comprise a majority of the board and, when boards are ranked according to the fraction of outside board members, outsiders comprised only 27 percent of the median board's membership … In comparison, outsiders comprised a majority of the board for 387 of the Fortune 500 [US] companies. Furthermore, for the median board of the Fortune 500 companies, outside directors comprised 81 percent of the membership …'.
361 Cadbury Code of Best Practice, s 1.4. Paragraph 4.24 of the Cadbury Committee Report defines such matters as transactions that include: (a) acquisition and disposal of assets of the company or its subsidiaries that are material to the company; and (b) investments, capital projects, authority levels, treasury policies, and risk management policies.
362 Cadbury Code of Best Practice, s 2.2; Cadbury Committee Report, paras 4.12–4.13.
363 Cadbury Code of Best Practice, s 3.2.
364 Cadbury Committee Report, para 4.30.
365 Cadbury Code of Best Practice, s 3.3.
366 ibid s 4.3; Cadbury Committee Report, paras 4.33–4.37.
367 Cadbury Committee Report, para 4.12.

Report also acknowledged that it was 'for the board to decide in particular cases whether this definition is met'.[368] Secondly, the Report did not specify the composition of the board. Most importantly, it did not require boards to be made up of a majority of outside directors.[369] The report merely provided that 'the calibre and number of non-executive directors on a board should be such that their views will carry significant weight in the board's decisions' and that 'all boards will require a minimum of three non-executive directors'.[370]

Spiralling executive pay in the early 1990s, in particular in the privatized utilities industry, led to the establishment of a second committee on the initiative of the Confederation of British Industry (CBI). The Greenbury Study Group, chaired by Sir Richard Greenbury and comprising leading British investors and industrialists, focussed on directors' remuneration. In its report, published in July 1995, it recommended the establishment of a remuneration committee, consisting entirely of non-executive directors,[371] enhanced disclosure of remuneration levels, broken down into the remuneration received by each individual director and type of remuneration (basic salary, benefits in kind, bonus, and long-term incentive schemes),[372] the approval of long-term incentive schemes, including share option schemes, by shareholders,[373] the prohibition of stock options exercisable after less than three years,[374] and the limitation of the notice period in the director's service contract to one year or less in order to avoid excessive compensation payments for unsatisfactory performance upon dismissal.[375] The LSE incorporated the recommendations into its Listing Rules, as it had done before with the recommendations of the Cadbury Code. However, the rules were not widely accepted and failed to halt the continuing rise in directors' pay.

A third committee, the Hampel Committee, undertook to review the progress achieved by the Cadbury and Greenbury Reports. The final report, published in January 1998, reiterated many of the principles of the Cadbury and Greenbury Codes of Best Practice. It suggested careful alterations, for example the requirement that at least one-third of the membership of the board should be made up of non-executive directors[376] or that a senior non-executive director should be identified in the annual report to whom concerns could be conveyed.[377] The report also sought to enhance shareholder involvement in the governance of the company by encouraging institutional investors to vote the shares under their control, enable shareholders to vote separately on each substantially separate issue (i.e. disallow the bundling of unrelated proposals in a single resolution) and increase the transparency of the proxy voting process.[378] Key issues such as the level of directors' remuneration, however, remained largely unchanged. In general, the report was less innovative than its predecessors.[379] A further point of criticism directed not only at the Hampel Report, but also the Cadbury and Greenbury Reports, was that they adopted a shareholder-centric view and, accordingly, saw the directors as the agents of the company and its members, ignoring the interests of other constituencies.[380]

The recommendations of the Cadbury and Greenbury Codes, as amended by the Hampel Report, were incorporated into one comprehensive Code on Corporate Governance, since 2010 simply called UK Corporate Governance Code,[381] which is published by the

[368] ibid.

[369] See ibid para 4.1: '[The] board [should be] made up of a combination of executive directors, with their intimate knowledge of the business, and of outside, non-executive directors'.

[370] ibid para 4.11. [371] Greenbury Code of Best Practice, A4. [372] ibid B4.

[373] ibid B12, C7. [374] ibid C6. [375] ibid D2. [376] Hampel Committee Report, 3.14.

[377] ibid 3.18. [378] ibid 5.6-5.9, 5.17.

[379] See the assessment by A Dignam, 'A principled approach to self-regulation? The report of the Hampel Committee on Corporate Governance' (1998) 19 Company Lawyer 140.

[380] See B Cheffins, 'Current trends in corporate governance: Going from London to Milan via Toronto' (1999) 10 Duke Journal of Comparative & International Law 5, for an analysis of all three reports.

[381] Before 2010, the code was called the Combined Code on Corporate Governance.

Financial Reporting Council and updated approximately every two years. The main tenets of the Cadbury and Greenbury Codes are generally revised incrementally, but in 2018 the FRC ushered in a change of tone by stressing, for the first time, that companies generate not only value for shareholders, but contribute 'to wider society' and have responsibilities to 'shareholders and stakeholders'.[382] In addition, the 2018 Code accords a (limited) corporate governance role to the workforce. Companies have to use one of three methods to facilitate engagement with its workforce: the appointment of a director from the workforce, a formal workforce advisory panel, or a designated non-executive director.[383] The workforce 'should be able to raise any matters of concern' with the board.[384] The board, in turn, is required to ensure that 'workforce policies and practices are consistent with the company's values'[385] and explain how the company invests in and rewards its workforce.[386] Thus, the 2018 Code has taken the first steps towards qualifying the traditional shareholder focus of the UK corporate governance codes,[387] although it has been criticized for seemingly giving precedence to the interests of the workforce and ignoring other stakeholder interests.[388]

The UK Corporate Governance Code applies to all companies with a premium listing of equity shares in the United Kingdom, irrespective of where they are incorporated.[389] The comply-or-explain principle, on the other hand, only applies to companies incorporated in the UK. It is set out in the listing rules promulgated by the UK Listing Authority, which is part of the Financial Conduct Authority (FCA), the UK's main market regulator. The corporate governance code and the listing rules distinguish between 'principles' and 'provisions'. The principles are general statements of best practice, for example that '[t]he board and its committees should have a combination of skills, experience and knowledge[;] [c]onsideration should be given to the length of service of the board as a whole and membership regularly refreshed'.[390] Owing to their generality, the principles allow for a wide margin of discretion in how they are translated into concrete governance arrangements. On the other hand, they are binding and have to be implemented by the company in one form or another.[391] The comply-or-explain principle only applies to the code's 'provisions', more specific prescriptions of best practice in corporate governance that may not be suitable for all companies.[392] Therefore, companies can deviate from the provisions, but they need to identify the specific provision(s) they do not comply with in the annual report and give reasons for their non-compliance.[393]

UK listing rules

LR 9.8.6R—Annual financial report: additional information

In the case of a listed company incorporated in the United Kingdom, the following additional items must be included in its annual financial report: ...

(5) a statement of how the listed company has applied the Main Principles set out in the UK Corporate Governance Code, in a manner that would enable shareholders to evaluate how the principles have been applied;

[382] UK Corporate Governance Code 2018, Principles A and D. [383] ibid Provision 5.

[384] ibid Principle E and Provision 6. [385] ibid. [386] ibid Provision 2.

[387] See text to n 380 above.

[388] IM Esser, I MacNeil, and K Chalaczkiewicz-Ladna, 'Proposed revisions to the UK Corporate Governance Code: a step forward in recognising a company's responsibilities towards wider stakeholders?' (2018) 39 Company Lawyer 254, 255.

[389] UK Corporate Governance Code 2018, 3. Issuers with a premium listing are required to comply with extended listing requirements that go beyond those applicable to listings on the standard main market and under EU regulations. These requirements are laid down in particular in Listing Rules LR 6, LR 7.2, and LR 10–13.

[390] UK Corporate Governance Code 2018, Principle K. [391] Listing Rules LR 9.8.6(5).

[392] We will discuss the most important provisions of the current corporate governance code pertaining to board structure regulation in section E.III below.

[393] Listing Rules LR 9.8.6(6)(b).

(6) a statement as to whether the listed company has:
  (a) complied throughout the accounting period with all relevant provisions set out in the UK Corporate Governance Code; or
  (b) not complied throughout the accounting period with all relevant provisions set out in the UK Corporate Governance Code and if so, setting out:
    (i) those provisions, if any it has not complied with;
    (ii) in the case of provisions whose requirements are of a continuing nature, the period within which, if any, it did not comply with some or all of those provisions; and
    (iii) the company's reasons for non-compliance …

In other European countries, codes comparable to those developed in the United Kingdom have emerged since the second half of the 1990s.[394] In France, two major codes exist: The 'Recommandations sur le gouvernement d'entreprise' (Recommendations on Corporate Governance) issued by the *Association Française de la Gestion Financière* (AFG),[395] the French Asset Management Association, and the 'Code de gouvernement d'entreprise des sociétés cotées' (Corporate Governance Code of Listed Corporations), developed by the Association Française des Entreprises Privées (AFEP) and the Mouvement des Entreprises de France (MEDEF),[396] two associations representing corporate issuers. The latter code consolidates the recommendations of the committee on corporate governance chaired by Marc Viénot, former chairman of the bank Société Générale, who published two pioneering reports on corporate governance in France, the Viénot I Report of 1995[397] and the Viénot II Report of 1999.[398] These two reports were products of initiatives of the business community itself, which felt that an overhaul of French corporate governance was necessary in light of the expectations of foreign investors, who were increasingly present in the French capital markets and who might have 'little knowledge of the rules and practices applied by the boards of directors of listed companies in France'.[399] The recommendations, accordingly, sought to reinforce the confidence of investors and the public by improving transparency and good management practices.

The comply-or-explain principle is implemented in the French Commercial Code, which requires companies to provide an explanation if they depart from a code of corporate governance.[400] However, the statute does not refer to a specific applicable code, but leaves it to the companies to identify the code they intend to be governed by, or indeed declare that they do not apply any code (provided they offer an explanation for their general non-compliance). Thus, neither the AFEP-MEDEF code nor the AFG code are designated as the 'official' French corporate governance code, although the former stipulates that listed companies 'should report' on the implementation of the AFEP-MEDEF recommendations,[401] whereas the AFG code is intended mainly as a guide to the exercise of the voting rights of institutional investors.[402]

[394] A comprehensive, worldwide compilation of codes, many of them in English, has been made available online by the ECGI (n 355). On the spread of corporate governance codes, see also C Gerner-Beuerle, 'Diffusion of regulatory innovations: the case of corporate governance codes' (2017) 13 Journal of Institutional Economics 271.

[395] Available on the website of the AFG http://www.afg.asso.fr; earlier versions are also available on the website of the ECGI (n 355).

[396] Available on the website of AFEP http://www.afep.com/contenu/mediatheque/bibliotheque; earlier versions are also available on the website of the ECGI (n 355).

[397] See Viénot I Report (n 310).

[398] See Viénot II Report (n 313).

[399] Viénot I Report (n 310) 3.

[400] Com, Art L225-37.

[401] AFEP-MEDEF Corporate Governance Code of Listed Corporations 2018, s 27.1. The code is also specific in determining the information that companies should provide when they depart from the recommendations. 'The explanation … must be comprehensible, relevant and detailed. It must be substantiated and adapted to the company's particular situation and must convincingly indicate why this specific aspect justifies an exemption. It must state the alternative measures that have been taken, if applicable, and must describe the actions that allow the company to comply with the aims of the relevant provision of the code', ibid.

[402] AFG Recommendations on Corporate Governance 2017, 1.

In Germany, several corporate governance codes for quoted companies have been issued since 2000.[403] The most comprehensive preparatory work was undertaken by a commission initiated by the federal government in 2001. The *Regierungskommission Deutscher Corporate Governance Kodex* (Government Commission on the German Corporate Governance Code), chaired by Gerhard Cromme, then chairman of the supervisory board of ThyssenKrupp AG, and comprising several high-ranking representatives of the industry and academia, presented its recommendations, the German Corporate Governance Code (sometimes called the Cromme Code after the commission's chairman), in February 2002.[404] The Code seeks to specify the duties and obligations of the management board and improve the control of management by the supervisory board. The method it employs is similar to that found in the corporate governance codes of the United Kingdom and France: to remove conflicts of interest and increase transparency. However, it is often less specific than its counterparts in other countries and makes use of more open-ended, general formulations.[405] Another difference is its approach to self-regulation. As opposed to the solution found in the UK or the United States, where we find references to the codes in the rules of self-regulatory organizations—stock exchanges—or the regulations promulgated by the public regulator, and as opposed to France, where the Commercial Code does not specify the applicable corporate governance code, the German legislator amended the Stock Corporation Act to determine in a binding manner which code will apply and which companies it applies to.

German Stock Corporation Act

§ 161—Declaration regarding the corporate governance code

(1) The management board and supervisory board of listed companies shall declare annually that they have complied and continue to comply with the recommendations of the 'German Corporate Governance Code' published by the Federal Ministry of Justice and Consumer Protection in the official section of the Federal Gazette or which recommendations are not being applied and why they are not applied. The same shall apply to the management board and supervisory board of a company which has issued exclusively other securities than shares for trading on an organised market within the meaning of § 2(5) Securities Trading Act [Wertpapierhandelsgesetz] and whose issued shares are, on the company's own initiative, only traded via a multilateral trading facility within the meaning of § 2(3) Sentence 1, no. 8 Securities Trading Act.

(2) The declaration shall be made permanently accessible to the public on the company's website.

French Commercial Code[406]

Art. L225-37

...

In companies whose financial securities are admitted to trading on a regulated market, the president of the board of directors must report on the composition of the board in a report appended to the [annual] report ... concerning the application of the principle of gender-balanced representation on the board, the conditions for preparing and organising the work of the board, as well as on the internal control and risk management procedures put in place by the company, and in particular giving the details of those procedures concerning the preparation and

[403] For example, the German Code of Corporate Governance of June 2000, drafted by the Berlin Initiative Group German Code of Corporate Governance, available on the website of the ECGI (n 355).

[404] The current and former versions of the code are published on the website of the Government Commission on the German Corporate Governance Code www.dcgk.de/en/code.html.

[405] For example, compare the enumeration of criteria indicating independence in the UK Corporate Governance Code 2018, Provision 10, with the definition of independence of the German Corporate Governance Code 2017, s 5.4.2: 'Supervisory Board members are to be considered non-independent in particular if they have a personal or business relationship with the corporation, its governing bodies, a controlling shareholder or a company affiliated with the controlling shareholder that may cause a substantial and not merely temporary conflict of interest.'

[406] Translation by Legifrance, https://www.legifrance.gouv.fr/Traductions/en-English/Legifrance-translations.

treatment of accounting and financial information for the corporate financial statements and, if relevant, for the consolidated financial statements . . .

When a company refers voluntarily to a code of corporate governance drawn up by organisations representing companies, the report specified in this article shall also set out the provisions that have been ruled out and the reason for this decision.

The report shall also specify the place where this code may be consulted.

If a company does not refer to such a code of corporate governance, this report shall indicate the rules used in addition to the legal requirements and state the reasons why the company has decided not to apply any provision of this code of corporate governance.

Comments and questions:

1. Note that §161 German Stock Corporation Act does not stipulate that the provisions of the Corporate Governance Code have to be complied with, i.e. that the *content* of the Code is binding. The function of §161 is merely to ensure that all listed companies issue a corporate governance declaration pursuant to the provision. The declaration of compliance does not need to be published in the Federal Gazette or included in the annual report of the company.[407] It is sufficient that it is made accessible to shareholders by other means, for example by publication on the website of the company.[408]
2. The nature of the rules of the German Corporate Governance Code is controversial. Are they comparable to statutory law or do they constitute commercial customs? In light of their general applicability, their incorporation into the Stock Corporation Act via §161, and their claim to validity (albeit with the possibility of firms to depart from them), they are commonly qualified as legal norms.[409] This has given rise to an additional controversially debated issue: The Code has been drafted by a government commission and approved by the Ministry of Justice. It has not been issued following the constitutional procedure for adopting laws, that is, with the participation of the legislature. This has prompted a number of commentators to conclude that the Code is unconstitutional and §161 Stock Corporation Act, as a consequence, not effective.[410]
3. The legal nature of corporate governance codes is related to another question: whether a decision not to comply with the code, or an incorrect declaration of compliance, may give rise to a claim for damages by the company against the directors or by the shareholders against the company or the company's directors responsible for the declaration of conformity. In both Germany and France, these liability issues have been discussed in the literature.

   The members of the board of directors (or in two-tier systems the members of the management and supervisory boards) may be liable for failure to comply either with the provision mandating the comply-or-explain declaration[411] or the best practice standards laid down in the code. The former—the members have not published any declaration of conformity or an incorrect one—constitutes a violation of their duties and thus gives rise to a claim for damages by the company.[412] However, in general, the company will not have suffered a loss as a result of the breach of duty. Therefore, it seems unlikely that the directors will be held liable for an incorrect declaration of compliance in practice.

[407] But see §§285 no 16, 314(1) no 8 HGB [Commercial Code], which require a statement in the annual accounts that the declaration pursuant to §161 AktG has been made. Note that the declaration itself does not have to be included in the accounts. Accordingly, the accuracy of the declaration, ie compliance with the Code as declared, is not audited.

[408] See §161(2) AktG. Most companies opt for online publication. Links to the declarations of most German blue chip companies (companies that are part of the DAX30 index) and other large (mid-cap) companies (companies that are part of the MDAX index) are compiled by the Government Commission on the German Corporate Governance Code, see https://www.dcgk.de/en/declarations-of-compliance.html.

[409] The discussion is summarized in U Hüffer and J Koch, *Aktiengesetz* (13th edn, CH Beck 2018) §161, para 3.

[410] ibid §161, paras 4–5a.

[411] In Germany, §161 AktG, and in France, Art L225-37 Code de commerce.

[412] We will discuss the relevant provisions in detail in Chapter 6B.

As explained, the recommendations of corporate governance codes themselves are not binding. The managers may deviate from the recommendations if they explain why they do so in the corporate governance statement. In spite of the non-binding character of the code, some commentators argue that non-compliance indicates a violation of the fiduciary duties of directors. The provisions of the code determine what constitutes good governance, and any deviation, it is argued, establishes a prima facie case of violation of the duty to employ due diligence and care.[413] It is correct that any decision of the directors, and hence also the decision to depart from non-binding best practice rules, may give rise to liability if the directors act negligently and the company suffers a loss as a consequence of the directors' actions. On the other hand, it is difficult to see why one corporate governance arrangement is prima facie in line with the directors' fiduciary duties, whereas another is not, especially if rational reasons are given for the latter. In light of the wide discretion that directors commonly enjoy in determining which actions are in the best interest of the company,[414] it is, arguably, unlikely that they would be found liable if they decided to depart from the provisions of the applicable corporate governance code.

The liability of the company or members of the management or supervisory board directly to the shareholders is equally problematic. It is possible that the share price of a company declines if the company either declares that it does not apply the code (or parts of the code) or because members of the management or supervisory board act in contravention of principles of the code that were part of the declaration of conformity.[415] Although the details are disputed, in such a case, the shareholders will generally only be able to challenge the actions of the company on the basis of tort law.[416] In Germany, the relevant provisions, to be found in the Civil Code, are formulated in a restrictive way and cannot easily be interpreted to fit the particularities of corporate law. The most likely basis for a damages claim requires intentional behaviour and the violation of public policy or the good morals.[417] Shareholders, therefore, face an almost insurmountable burden of proof. In France, the general tort law provision of the Civil Code is more open-ended,[418] and it is easier to argue that the violation of a code provision by a company that has declared to comply with the code constitutes a tortious act.[419] Nevertheless, the shareholder bears the burden of proving a causal relationship between the violation of the code and a personal loss suffered by the shareholder,[420] which can probably only be shown in exceptional cases.

4. The degree of compliance with corporate governance codes and the quality of companies' corporate governance statements varies in the EU. In some countries, such as the UK, compliance is high, with commonly more than 90 per cent of FTSE 350 companies complying with all,

[413] An overview of the literature advancing such arguments is given by Hüffer and Koch (n 409) §161, para 26.

[414] See section C.II above and Chapter 6A.I.

[415] A number of studies examine the correlation between compliance with corporate governance codes and firm performance, eg C Andres and E Theissen, 'Setting a fox to keep the geese: Does the comply-or-explain principle work?' (2008) 14 Journal of Corporate Finance 289 (examining the characteristics of firms complying with the requirement to disclose the remuneration of the members of the executive board pursuant to the German Corporate Governance Code and finding that firms with higher Tobin's Q and firms with more dispersed ownership were more likely to comply); A Knyazeva, D Knyazeva, and RW Masulis, 'The Supply of Corporate Directors and Board Independence' (2013) 26 Review of Financial Studies 1561 (showing that board independence has a positive effect on firm value and operating performance).

[416] Duties under company law are generally not owed directly to the shareholders. Shareholders, therefore, are required to take recourse to general principles of law, in particular tort law. We will discuss this issue in Chapter 6A.II.

[417] Legal basis of a cause of action is §826 BGB, which provides: 'A person who, in a manner contrary to public policy, intentionally inflicts damage on another person is liable to the other person to make compensation for the damage'.

[418] Civ, Art 1240 provides: 'Any act whatever of man, which causes damage to another, obliges the one by whose fault it occurred, to compensate it'. Translation by Legifrance, https://www.legifrance.gouv.fr/Traductions/en-English/Legifrance-translations.

[419] D Martin and OT Tieu, 'La responsabilité civile des administrateurs de sociétés; Évolutions jurisprudentielles' (2010) JCP no 26–740.

[420] As we shall see in Chapter 6A.II, in order to succeed in a direct claim for damages, shareholders have to show that the loss they suffered is distinct from any loss incurred by the company due to the tortious acts of the directors and not simply a reflection of the reduction in the company's share price (so-called reflective loss principle, see also Chapter 8C.II).

or all but one or two, of the code's provisions.[421] If UK companies depart from the code, they do so most frequently with regard to the requirement that at least half of the board should be independent, followed by best practice rules on chair independence and the composition of board committees.[422] In Germany and France, compliance is also relatively high, in the case of Germany between 80 and 90 per cent,[423] and in the case of France around 70 per cent.[424] An analysis of the quality of the explanations given by companies that depart from best practice recommendations gives a more mixed picture. A broad comparative study (based, however, on a limited sample of 270 companies EU-wide) has found that companies give specific reasons for their non-compliance relating to the particular situation of the company only in 34 per cent of the cases.[425] Again, we can see considerable variation between countries. In the UK, Sweden, the Netherlands, and France, the explanations are generally good, whereas they are phrased in general terms without referring to a company-specific situation in other countries, such as Portugal, Denmark, and also Germany.[426]

Faced with this unsatisfactory situation, the European Commission has produced a recommendation that seeks to improve the quality of comply-or-explain reporting.[427] Notably, the recommendation stipulates that companies should state clearly which specific best practice rules they have departed from and for each departure, '(a) explain in what manner the company has departed from a recommendation; (b) describe the reasons for the departure; (c) describe how the decision to depart from the recommendation was taken within the company; (d) where the departure is limited in time, explain when the company envisages complying with a particular recommendation; (e) where applicable, describe the measure taken instead of compliance and explain how that measure achieves the underlying objective of the specific recommendation or of the code as a whole, or clarify how it contributes to good corporate governance of the company'.[428] In addition, companies are reminded that the explanations 'should be sufficiently clear, accurate and comprehensive to enable shareholders, investors and other stakeholders to assess the consequences arising from the departure from a particular recommendation' and that they should 'refer to the specific characteristics and situation of the company, such as size, company structure or ownership or any other relevant features'.[429]

D. Corporate Actors and Patterns of Corporate Ownership

In this and the next sections, we will examine in more detail how corporate governance regulation structures the relationship between the main corporate actors. In particular, we will discuss how legal systems regulate corporate boards, which are, in all jurisdictions, at the heart of the corporate governance regime. To begin with, and in order to clarify some

[421] FRC, *Proposed Revisions to the UK Corporate Governance Code* (December 2017) 3. For compliance data going back to the late 1990s, see S Arcot, B Valentina, and A Faure-Grimaud, 'Corporate governance in the UK: Is the comply or explain approach working?' (2010) 30 International Review of Law and Economics 193.

[422] FRC (n 421) 4.

[423] MS Rapp, CRG Kohl, C Strenger, and M Wolff, 'Akzeptanz des Deutschen Corporate Governance Kodex: Ergebnisse einer Langzeitbetrachtung über die ersten zehn Kodexfassungen' (2014) Zeitschrift für Corporate Governance 197, 199 (using a broad sample of all companies with a prime standard listing on the Frankfurt Stock Exchange).

[424] AMF (Autorité des Marchés Financiers), *Rapport 2015 sur le gouvernement d'entreprise et la rémunération des dirigeants de sociétés cotées*, 52 (figures refer to the constituent companies of the CAC 40, an index comprising the most important companies among the 100 issuers with the highest market capitalization listed on the Paris Stock Exchange).

[425] RiskMetrics Group, *Study on Monitoring and Enforcement Practices in Corporate Governance in the Member States* (2009) 84.

[426] ibid. A more detailed assessment of the quality of the explanations given by UK companies can be found in the FRC report on Developments in Corporate Governance and Stewardship 2015 (January 2016) 6–9 (observing that 'almost 70 per cent of the relevant FTSE 350 companies [set] out their reasons fully', but also that 'explanations were better where companies depart from the Code due to force of circumstances—such as directors leaving the board at short notice': ibid 6).

[427] Commission Recommendation of 9 April 2014 on the quality of corporate governance reporting ('comply or explain') [2014] OJ L109/43.

[428] ibid Art 8. [429] ibid Art 9.

commonly used terminology, it is useful to give an overview of the main players in the arena of (internal) corporate governance: the officers (managers), directors, and shareholders.[430] In this context, we will also discuss how ownership of corporations differs between countries and offer some tentative explanation of these differences.[431]

I. Officers

The officers are employees of the company, who are appointed by the board of directors (or the supervisory board in legal systems that provide for a dual or two-tier board[432]) and who devote their full time to managing the company's affairs. The most important corporate officers are the chief executive officer (CEO), the chief financial officer (CFO), the chief operating officer (COO), and the chief accounting officer (CAO). Sometimes the title of president is used interchangeably for the CEO, sometimes for the COO. In some countries, the CEO is known as the general manager (France: *directeur général*; Germany: chairman of the management board—*Vorstandsvorsitzender*). In the United States, usually only the CEO, the COO, and the CFO sit on the board of directors. In contrast, in European legal systems that follow the one-tier board structure, most top-level managers have seats on the board. In companies with a two-tier board structure, the officers are synonymous with the members of the management organ, which, in turn, is sometimes identified as the board of directors. Therefore, the term 'director' may denote different responsibilities and roles, depending on the corporate governance system prevalent in the respective jurisdiction.

The treatment of officers in company law often belies their dominant role in the managerial hierarchy of the corporation. The UK Companies Act 2006 mentions officers only in passing[433] and directors' duties do not apply to officers who are not members of the board of directors.[434] The Delaware General Corporation Law devotes one section to officers, which leaves the determination of their position, term of office, and manner of appointment to the by-laws.[435] The French Commercial Code envisages that the board of directors 'deals with all matters relating to the conduct of the company's business'.[436] The board has to have a chairman (*président*), who must be one of the directors.[437] Traditionally, the chairman was also general manager of the company,[438] but a reform of 2001 now allows companies to distinguish between executive and non-executive functions on the board by appointing different individuals as chairman and general manager.[439] On a proposal by the general manager, the

[430] In some legal systems, the company's workforce is also entrusted with important governance functions. We will discuss the role of employees in Chapter 5D.III.

[431] One aspect of the changing patterns of corporate ownership, the rise of institutional investors since the 1970s and 1980s, will be taken up in Chapter 5C.I.3.

[432] For more on one-tier and two-tier board systems, see section E.I below.

[433] For example, ss 9(4)(c), 12 of the Companies Act 2006 requires the incorporators to disclose the company's proposed officers in the application for registration of the company. Note that the term 'officer', as used in the Companies Act 2006, is broader than how it is used here (referring to the top-level executives in the company, which corresponds to the meaning of the term, for example, in §8.40 MBCA and §§142 Del. Gen. Corp. Law). For purposes of the Companies Act 2006, 'officer' includes a director, manager or secretary, s 1173(1).

[434] Directors' duties, however, apply to directors if they act in their capacity as officer, Davies and Worthington (n 50) para 16-11.

[435] Del. Gen. Corp. Law, §142.

[436] Com, Art L225-35. Translation by Legifrance, https://www.legifrance.gouv.fr/Traductions/en-English/Legifrance-translations.

[437] ibid Art L225-47.

[438] The first modern French company legislation, the Companies Act 1867 (n 296) stipulated that the directors could either entrust the chairman or an external person with the management of the company (Art 22). Amendments from 1940 consolidated the role of chairman and general manager in one person: Art 2 Act of 16 November, JORF no 305 of 26 November 1940, 5828.

[439] Com, Art L225-51-1, introduced by Law no 2001-420 of 15 May 2001 (Loi relative aux nouvelles régulations économiques (NRE)), JORF no 113 of 16 May 2001, 7776. For a more detailed discussion, see section E.I.4 below.

board may appoint further officers (assistant general managers).[440] The Commercial Code sets out how the general manager and assistant general managers can be removed and which powers they have,[441] but the law contains otherwise only a fragmentary description of their rights and duties.[442] Only German stock corporation law provides for a detailed and comprehensive regulation of officers (i.e. members of the management board), including their election and removal, qualifications, competences and duties, and relationship with other corporate organs.[443] This, of course, is simply a function of the formalized separation between management and control in a two-tier board system.

The legislative terseness of most legal systems can probably be explained with the fact that much of corporate law predates the rise of the modern business enterprise led by salaried managers, who were distinct from the company's owners and their representatives on the board of directors. The emergence of modern professional management structures, so-called managerial capitalism, occurred first in the United States and Germany in the beginning of the twentieth century.[444] In Britain, large sections of the corporate economy were managed in a way that has been described as 'personal capitalism' until well after the Second World War. Companies were administered without an extensive managerial hierarchy, often by members of the family who had founded the enterprise.[445] Similarly, in France, rationalization and professionalization of the management of industrial enterprises took place on a large scale only in the post-war period.[446]

II. Directors

The board of directors is in all legal systems the central governance organ in public stock corporations (although, as we will see, this was not necessarily always the case in historical perspective[447]). We have already mentioned that certain executive officers may sit on the board of directors and that some legal systems require companies to establish a board composed exclusively of executive directors, which is supervised by a second board composed of non-executive directors. We can therefore distinguish between executive directors, who are salaried employees of the company performing management functions, and non-executive directors, who are separate from management. The non-executive directors may represent important investors or creditors or they have no prior relationship with the company, for example, because they come from a different sector of the economy or from academia and are appointed to the board because of their expertise or independence. They meet regularly to ensure that the executives discharge their duties carefully and in line with legal requirements and take part in deciding matters of particular strategic importance for the company. Sometimes the executive directors are referred to as inside directors and the non-executives as outside directors, given that they are commonly external to the company (although some

440 Com, Art L225-53.

441 ibid Arts L225-55, L225-56.

442 For example, the provisions of the Code de Commerce regulating related party transactions apply to both directors and officers (the general manager and assistant general managers) Arts L225-38 to L225-43.

443 Sock Corporation Act, §§76–94.

444 Chandler (n 44) 85–9 (United States) 497–502 (Germany) (pointing also out, however, that the development in Germany and the US differed in important respects, particularly in that the founding families of the large industrial German corporations 'continued to have a powerful, even a decisive, say in management', whereas this was not the case in the US: ibid 501).

445 ibid 235–42. This fact has been seen as a major reason why British entrepreneurs failed to make use of the economies of scale and scope made possible by the second industrial revolution. They did not make the necessary investments in professional managerial structures and hence lacked the organizational capabilities to compete effectively with American or German enterprises, ibid 236–7, 390.

446 P Fridenson, 'France: The relatively slow development of big business in the twentieth century' in AD Chandler, F Amatori, and T Hikino, *Big Business and the Wealth of Nations* (CUP 1997) 207, 215–21; DS Landes, *The Unbound Prometheus: Technological Change and Industrial Development in Western Europe from 1750 to the Present* (CUP 1969) 528–9.

447 Section E.I below.

may have worked for the company for many years before they become non-executive directors, and some may represent the company's workforce). We will use both terms—executive and inside director, as well as non-executive and outside director—interchangeably.

Ideally, in order to be able to fulfil their control functions effectively, the non-executive directors should not only be external to, but also independent from, the company's management, although this is not a defining criterion of an outside director. In this case, they are often called independent non-executive directors (INEDs). How independence is defined depends on the legal system in question. Often the definition will include the requirement that the director has not worked for the company for a specified number of years before becoming a member of the board, has no material business relationships with the company and no close family ties with any of the company's insiders.[448] Whether a director who represents a large shareholder can be qualified as independent is controversial. The UK Corporate Governance Code is comparatively strict, stipulating that directors who represent 'a significant shareholder' should generally not be regarded as independent.[449] In economies with a traditionally more concentrated ownership structure than the UK, such as France and Spain, policy-makers have been more hesitant. They are mindful that a definition of independence that is too broad may reduce the pool of suitable candidates for board positions and run counter to established business practices.[450] However, under the impression of Anglo-American conceptions of best practice in corporate governance, we can observe more recently some convergence in how independence is understood.[451]

In spite of the prominent role that the concepts of the non-executive and independent director play in modern corporate governance,[452] corporation statutes generally do not distinguish between them.[453] The reason is that these concepts are fairly recent regulatory innovations that have only been discussed in policy-making circles, at least in Europe, since about the 1990s. A consequence of the inherent inertia of law is its difficulty to keep pace with the realities of the business world and the activities of standard setters that are not subject to the checks and balances of democratic processes. With time, it can be expected that the binding legislative environment will reflect regulatory innovations such as the independent director.[454] For now, however, it is necessary to keep in mind that company law, in particular in one-tier board systems, when it refers to the 'director', deals with individuals with very different responsibilities and tasks in the corporation. We will consider the implications of this observation in one of the following chapters when we analyse directors' duties.[455] The duty of care, for example, requires all directors

[448] For a particularly detailed definition, see UK Corporate Governance Code 2018, Provision 10.

[449] ibid.

[450] See eg the Special Commission to Consider a Code of Ethics for Companies' Boards of Directors, *The Governance of Listed Companies* (1998) (Olivencia Report) s 2.1: '[T]he Commission is aware that the process of including the figure of the independent director in corporate practice should be managed with prudence. On the one hand, it is impossible to ignore the highly concentrated ownership structure of our stock market. On the other hand, the process should be implemented gradually while avoiding sharp changes in the composition of the boards of our listed companies and in step with the development of what has been referred to as the "market in independents". If we really aspire to independence being more than just a label, it will be necessary to build a tradition (as yet only incipient in Spain) that highly qualified professionals serve and acquire responsibilities in companies to which their sole link may be share ownership'.

[451] For example, the French corporate governance code now refers to 'significant shareholders' when defining independence, which is held to mean that the director 'has no relationship of any kind whatsoever with the corporation', AFEP-MEDEF Corporate Governance Code of Listed Corporations 2018, Art 8.2.

[452] See section C.III above.

[453] An exception is §11(f)(2) of the US Securities Act of 1933, which deals with the liability of company insiders and outsiders for false or misleading statements in the registration statement that has to be filed in order to be able to offer securities to the public.

[454] In fact, in some legal systems, this has already happened; see for example the Spanish Companies Law, Art 529-duodecies, as amended by Law 31/2014, which provides for a definition of independence. The German AktG also contains rules on the eligibility supervisory board members in §100(2) that can be interpreted as requiring a certain level of independence, but these requirements fall short of international best practice standards.

[455] Chapter 6B.I.

to act with the knowledge, skill, and experience that can reasonably be expected of a director.[456] Outside directors will generally know less about the company than the inside directors and may not have as much experience in the relevant business segment. Thus, their informational disadvantage and different background may necessitate a differentiated interpretation and application of the duty of care in order to develop an adequate standard of liability.

A further terminological distinction often used by company law is that between de jure and de facto directors. The former are persons who have been validly appointed as directors pursuant to the relevant rules in the companies act and the company's constitution.[457] The appointment of the latter is marred by procedural or substantive defects, for example because the appointee does not satisfy the eligibility requirements of a director, but he or she is being held out as a director by the company. Generally, all provisions addressed at 'directors' apply to both de jure and de facto directors. For example, the UK Companies Act determines that 'director' includes any person occupying the position of director, by whatever name called.[458] This implies that a valid appointment is not a precondition for being regarded as a director, and the courts have indeed defined de facto directors as persons 'who assume to act as directors without having been appointed validly or at all'.[459] They ask whether the de facto director was part of the central governance structure of the company and undertook functions 'which could properly be discharged only by a director'.[460] Similarly, United States, German, and French law all recognize the legal position of persons whose election as director was irregular.[461] Such de facto directors have generally the same authority and obligations as de jure directors.[462]

The UK legislator has introduced a third type of director that does not exist, in this form, in most other legal systems, the so-called shadow director. Shadow directors are persons 'in accordance with whose directions or instructions the directors of the company are accustomed to act'.[463] As colourfully explained by Millett J in *Re Hydrodan (Corby) Ltd*, a shadow director 'claims not to be a director. He lurks in the shadows, sheltering behind others who, he claims, are the only directors of the company to the exclusion of himself'.[464] An indication of a person being a shadow director is 'a pattern of behaviour in which the board did not exercise any discretion or judgment of its own, but acted in accordance with the directions of

[456] This formulation of the duty of care paraphrases the UK Companies Act 2006, s 174(2)(a).

[457] We will discuss these rules in Chapter 5D.

[458] Companies Act 2006, s 250.

[459] *Re Hydrodan (Corby) Ltd* [1994] BCC 161, 162 (Chancery Division). See also *Revenue and Customs Commissioners v Holland* [2010] UKSC 51 (holding that the de jure director of a company that was the corporate director of several operating companies was not a de facto director of the operating companies solely because of acts done in the capacity as director of the corporate director, see in particular paras 94–6).

[460] *Re Hydrodan (Corby) Ltd* (n 459) 163.

[461] The Delaware courts define a de facto director as 'one who is in possession of and exercising the powers of that office under claim and color of an election, although he is not a director de jure and may be removed by proper proceedings', *Prickett v American Steel & Pump Corp.*, 253 A.2d 86, 88 (Del. Ch. 1969). The German courts speak of the 'factual exercise of the functions of a corporate organ' by someone who has not been appointed at all or not been appointed validly, BGHZ 148, 167, 169. In France, the term de facto director is used more broadly, as we will discuss below; see text to nn 472–475.

[462] Delaware: EP Welch and others, *Folk on the Delaware General Corporation Law: Fundamentals* (Wolters Kluwer 2016) §141.05[C]; France: M Cozian, A Viandier, and F Deboissy, *Droit des sociétés* (31st edn, LexisNexis 2018) paras 362–72; Germany: Spindler (n 276) §84, paras 241–53. In the EU Member States, the (formerly First) Company Law Directive protects the good faith of third parties who deal with de facto directors; see Art 8 Directive (EU) 2017/1132 and our discussion in Chapter 3B.

[463] Companies Act 2006, s 251(1). Identical definitions are contained in s 22(5) of the Company Directors Disqualification Act 1986, s 251 of the Insolvency Act 1986, and s 417 of the Financial Services and Markets Act 2000. Lawyers, consultants, and others who give advice in a professional capacity are excluded from the definition, and a holding company is not to be regarded as a shadow director of its subsidiary by virtue of the fact that the directors of the subsidiary are accustomed to act in accordance with the directions of the holding company: s 251(2), (3).

[464] *Re Hydrodan (Corby) Ltd* (n 459) 163.

[the alleged shadow director]'.[465] The law extends the scope of some provisions expressly to shadow directors.[466] In other cases, it may depend on the facts of the case whether shadow directors are treated in the same way as de jure directors. In particular, the general duties of directors apply to shadow directors only 'where and to the extent that they are capable of so applying'.[467] It has been suggested that shadow directors owe fiduciary duties at least in relation to the part of a company's affairs that they have influenced through their directions or instructions.[468]

The concept of shadow director can become important in corporate groups, where it may, under appropriate circumstances, give rise to remedies of the subsidiary against the parent for a breach of duties that the parent, as shadow director, owed to the subsidiary.[469] It is maybe not surprising, therefore, that shadow directors have not become as relevant in other legal systems that use different strategies in order to protect creditors in corporate groups, such as substantive consolidation in the United States[470] or corporate group law in Germany.[471] However, we find a notion similar to the UK shadow director in French law, which effectively combines what we have called de facto and shadow directors under the term *dirigeants de fait*. A *dirigeant de fait* is a person who 'interferes in the central governance functions of the company in a sustained manner and by exercising effective and continuous control'.[472] This definition has been held to be satisfied in the case of majority shareholders, notably the parent company[473] and major creditors.[474] However, as under English law, the mere exercise of control rights, for example the parent's voting rights, is not sufficient to qualify a person as a *dirigeant de fait*. Rather, the company and its organs must have been deprived of all autonomy and fundamental decisions taken solely by the *dirigeant de fait*.[475] If this is the case, the legal consequences are far-reaching. The Commercial Code extends a number of criminal sanctions to *dirigeants de fait*, including the important offence of abuse of corporate assets.[476] Furthermore, if the de facto director's actions amount to mismanagement and have

[465] ibid. It should be noted that the abrogation of discretion or the assumption of 'a subservient role' by the properly appointed directors is a sufficient, but not a necessary condition: 'The purpose of the legislation is to identify those, other than professional advisers, with real influence in the corporate affairs of the company ... It will, no doubt, be sufficient to show that in the face of "directions or instructions" from the alleged shadow director the properly appointed directors or some of them cast themselves in a subservient role or surrendered their respective discretions. But I do not consider that it is necessary to do so in all cases. Such a requirement would be to put a gloss on the statutory requirement that the board are "accustomed to act" "in accordance with" such directions or instructions'. See *Secretary of State for Trade and Industry v Deverell* [2001] Ch 340, 354.

[466] For example, ss 4(2), 6(3C) of the Company Directors Disqualification Act 1986 (disqualification for fraud and unfitness).

[467] Companies Act 2006, s 170(5), as amended by the Small Business, Enterprise and Employment Act 2015, s 89(1).

[468] *Vivendi SA v Richards* [2013] EWHC 3006 (Ch) paras 142–3. In practice, this means that directors would, for example, need to act in the company's best interest when giving instructions, but they would not necessarily be bound by the duty not to exploit corporate opportunities, Davies and Worthington (n 50) 16-10 (fn 52).

[469] When the company has gone into insolvent liquidation, the liquidator may also claim that the parent should contribute to the insolvent company's assets pursuant to s 214 Insolvency Act 1986 because it should have known that the company would not avoid going into insolvent liquidation and did not use its influence to cause the company to cease trading (wrongful trading). This provision is addressed to directors as well as shadow directors, s 214(7). However, the mere fact that the subsidiary is wholly owned by the parent does not mean that the parent is a shadow director of the subsidiary. Rather, the criteria outlined above, text to nn 463–465, apply. For an analysis of this question, see also V Finch and D Milman, *Corporate Insolvency Law* (3rd edn, CUP 2017) 504–505.

[470] Substantive consolidation leads to the pooling of the assets and liabilities of group companies. It may be ordered by the bankruptcy court if the companies are 'inextricably linked'; Finch and Milman (n 469) 503.

[471] AktG, §§291–318.

[472] Cour d'Appel de Paris, 11 June 1987, *Bull. Joly Sociétés* 1987, 719.

[473] Cass com, 6 June 2000, *Revue de jurisprudence de droit des affaires* 2000, no 868.

[474] Cass com, 27 June 2006, *Recueil Dalloz* 2006, 1892, note A Lienhard.

[475] ibid.

[476] Com, Arts L241-9, L245-16, L246-2 (providing that the respective sanctions shall apply to anyone 'who, directly or through an intermediary, has effectively managed, administered or run' the company. Translation by Legifrance, https://www.legifrance.gouv.fr/Traductions/en-English/Legifrance-translations). Abuse of corporate assets (*abus de biens sociaux*) is discussed in Chapter 6B.I.4(b). See also Cass crim, 20 September 2000, *Revue de jurisprudence de droit des affaires* 2001, no 38.

contributed to the insolvency of the company, the bankruptcy court may determine that the de facto director is liable for all or part of the company's debts.[477] Finally, *dirigeants de fait* are liable for a breach of duty on the same grounds as de jure directors, for example if they are negligent in managing the company.[478]

III. Shareholders

The shareholders are commonly regarded as the owners of the corporation, although, as we have seen, this view can be debated.[479] In all legal systems, shareholders enjoy important rights in relation to the corporation by virtue of their ownership position. Most importantly, they are entitled to the balance sheet profit, provided the competent organ does not decide to withhold the profit and, for example, transfer it to revenue reserves. Further rights are the right to attend the general meeting, receive information about the company's affairs, and vote at general meetings. We will discuss these rights at different points in this and the next chapter.[480] In many legal systems, companies are required to treat all shareholders equally in the same circumstances. In Europe, this duty is laid down in two directives, Directive (EU) 2017/1132 codifying certain aspects of EU company law and the Transparency Directive (the latter for corporations whose equity or debt securities are admitted to trading on a regulated market).[481] In the United States, the requirement of equal treatment of all shareholders in the same position is not expressly stated in the corporation acts. With respect to some issues, for example the payment of dividends, minority shareholders may be able to invoke a duty requiring the company to treat them equally.[482] In other respects, however, the matter is contested. Generally, US corporations seem to have more leeway in implementing fundamental changes without strict observance of a principle of formal equality.[483] These questions are

[477] Com, Art L651-2 (*action de la responsabilité pour insuffisance d'actif*) (referring expressly to 'dirigeants de droit ou de fait'); Cass com, 6 June 2000 (n 473); Cass com, 2 November 2005, no 02-15895. We will discuss *responsabilité pour insuffisance d'actif* in Chapter 10E.II.

[478] However, in this case, liability is not based on the respective provisions of the Code de commerce (see our discussion in Chapter 6B.I.4(a)), but the general liability provision of the Code civil, Art 1240. See Cass com, 20 November 2007, no 06-16933, and Cozian, Viandier, and Deboissy (n 462) para 370.

[479] See text to nn 42–67 above.

[480] Information rights are examined in section E.IV below, decision rights in Chapter 5A and appointment rights in Chapter 5D.

[481] Article 85 Directive (EU) 2017/1132 (formerly Art 46 Directive 2012/30/EU (Second Company Law Directive)) provides that 'the laws of the Member States shall ensure equal treatment to all shareholders who are in the same position'. Similar rules can be found in Arts 17(1), 18(1) of Directive 2004/109/EC (Transparency Directive). In national law, the equal treatment requirement can be found, for example, in the UK FCA Disclosure and Transparency Rules 6.1.3, §53a of the German AktG, and Arts L225-204, L225-209-2, L823-11 of the French Code de commerce. From the literature, see E Ferran and LC Ho, *Principles of Corporate Finance Law* (2nd edn, OUP 2014) 122–3; P Merle, *Droit commercial: Sociétés commerciales* (22nd edn, Dalloz 2018) para 576; T Raiser and R Veil, *Recht der Kapitalgesellschaften* (6th edn, Vahlen 2015) §11/58–65. However, the Court of Justice of the EU in Case C-101/08 *Audiolux SA v Groupe Bruxelles Lambert SA (GBL)* [2009] ECR I-9823 clarified that the above provisions of EU law could not be interpreted as giving rise to a general principle of equality of shareholders and only required equal treatment in specific contexts. For example, the reference to equal treatment in Directive (EU) 2017/1132 concerns the increase or reduction of capital, and even in this context, it is subject to exceptions, such as the possibility to exclude the pre-emption rights of some shareholders (Art 72 of the Directive). See Case C-101/08 *Audiolux* paras 37–40.

[482] Companies, of course, can issue several classes of shares with different dividend rights, eg §151(c) Del. Gen. Corp. Law. However, in appropriate circumstances, payment of a dividend on one class of shares, but not another may be a violation of fiduciary duties. The Supreme Court of Delaware in *Sinclair Oil Corp. v Levien*, 280 A.2d 717, 721 (Del. 1971) gives the following example: '[S]uppose a parent dominates a subsidiary and its board of directors. The subsidiary has outstanding two classes of stock, X and Y. Class X is owned by the parent and Class Y is owned by minority stockholders of the subsidiary. If the subsidiary, at the direction of the parent, declares a dividend on its Class X stock only, this might well be self-dealing by the parent. It would be receiving something from the subsidiary to the exclusion of and detrimental to its minority stockholders. This self-dealing, coupled with the parent's fiduciary duty, would make intrinsic fairness the proper standard by which to evaluate the dividend payments'.

[483] JD Cox, 'Equal Treatment for Shareholders: An Essay' (1997) 19 Cardozo Law Review 615. Easterbrook and Fischel (n 31) 110–11, 117–24, argue that a principle of strict equality can have a welfare-decreasing effect.

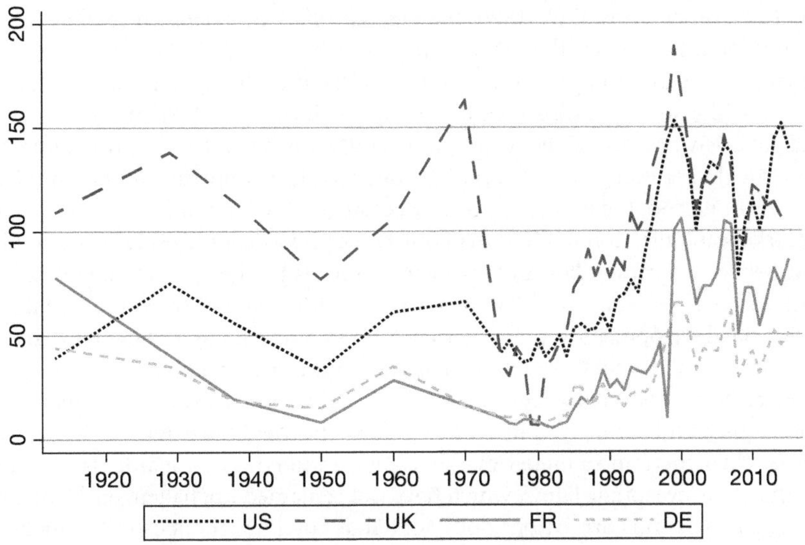

Figure 1 Evolution of stock market capitalization as a percentage of GDP

Sources: Data until 1970 is from RG Rajan and L Zingales, 'The great reversals: the politics of financial development in the twentieth century' (2003) 69 Journal of Financial Economics 5, 15. More recent data is from the World Bank, World Development Indicators, and the Federal Reserve Bank of St Louis, FRED Economic Data. Since 1975, data is annual; before 1975, we have data for 1913, 1929, 1938, 1950, 1960, and 1970. We have used linear extrapolation for the years between observations; the graph should therefore not be taken as representing actual values for other years than those mentioned.

ultimately concerned with the problem of how to protect minority shareholder(s) against expropriation by the majority. Even though an equal treatment principle is not universally acknowledged, all legal systems provide for mechanisms to ensure that majority shareholders do not abuse their voting rights to the detriment of the minority. We will examine the most important such strategies in a later chapter.[484]

IV. Patterns of ownership

In the legal systems that we investigate in this book, the type of person who invests in companies and the shareholder structure of companies in general have changed fundamentally since the nineteenth century, when incorporation by registration became available in all four countries. In addition, there have always been, and there still are to a significant degree, differences in shareholder structure between the United States, the UK, Germany, and France. As a first indication of how differently the corporate economy is organized in these countries, we may compare the market capitalization of domestic firms as a fraction of the country's GDP. This does not tell us who owns stock corporations, but to what extent companies raise equity in public markets and, hence, whether we can expect a comparatively greater or smaller proportion of a company's shareholders to be outside investors who are not affiliated with the founders. Figure 1 gives an overview of the development of stock market capitalization in our four countries since the early twentieth century.[485]

[484] Chapter 7.

[485] Data from the nineteenth century is fragmentary and comparisons are difficult. For a good overview of the available nineteenth-century data, see M Becht and FB DeLong, 'Why Has There Been So Little Block Holding in America?' in RK Morck (ed), *A History of Corporate Governance around the World* (University of Chicago Press 2005) 613; C Fohlin, 'The History of Corporate Ownership and Control in Germany' in ibid 223; J Franks, C Mayer, and S Rossi, 'Spending Less Time with the Family: The Decline of Family Ownership in the United Kingdom' in ibid 581; AE Murphy, 'Corporate Ownership in France: The Importance of History' in ibid 185.

Particularly for the time since 1970, the data is sufficiently detailed to allow us to identify major economic events: the stock market crash of 1973–1974, which was triggered by the break-up of the Bretton Woods system of fixed exchange rates and a sharp rise in energy prices (the so-called oil shock of 1973), the dot-com bubble of the late 1990s, and the financial crisis of 2007–2008. More importantly, for our purposes, the figure seems to indicate a divide between the common law and civil law countries in our sample. For almost the whole period, the two common law countries, the United States and the UK, had a higher market capitalization to GDP than our two civil law countries, France and Germany. This split between common law and civil law countries has been confirmed by researchers for a larger sample of countries.[486] Controversially, it prompted them to attribute the different financial development to differences between common law and civil law. Investors in common law countries, they argued, benefitted from more stringent disclosure regulation and better minority shareholder protection laws. Therefore, outside investors were willing to acquire equity, and companies in common law countries, consequently, had smaller and more dispersed owners and a higher market capitalization than companies in civil law countries.[487] These are sweeping claims, which have not remained unchallenged.[488] In particular, identifying patterns and correlations does not tell us anything about causal influences. Legal families may exhibit preferences for different types of regulatory strategy, as we will indeed see in the next chapters. However, it is not clear whether these differences have a causal effect on financial development, or conversely, different stages of financial development change political dynamics and regulatory expectations of market actors, which in turn leads to the adoption of novel regulatory mechanisms.[489] We will analyse a variety of legal strategies to control both the management and major shareholders in the following chapters, which should enable us to assess, at least for our sample of four countries, whether common law is indeed superior to civil law in protecting (minority) shareholders.

As a second method to analyse differences in ownership structure, we may wish to investigate whether control is widely distributed or concentrated in listed companies. We mentioned the changes that occurred in the corporate economy in many industrialized as well as industrializing countries at the end of the nineteenth century and beginning of the twentieth century above.[490] The transition from an owner-managed enterprise to one that was controlled by a class of professional managers and owned by outside investors, who were often widely dispersed and owned only a small stake in the company, was analysed for the first time in detail by Adolf Berle and Gardiner Means in their influential treatise *The Modern Corporation and Private Property*. Their observation that a 'separation of ownership and control' had taken place in US corporations during the first decades of the twentieth century[491]

[486] R La Porta, F Lopez-de-Silanes, A Shleifer, and RW Vishny, 'Legal Determinants of External Finance' (1997) 52 Journal of Finance 1131, 1138–9; R La Porta, F Lopez-de-Silanes, and A Shleifer, 'What Works in Securities Laws?' (2006) 61 Journal of Finance 1, 14–23.

[487] La Porta, Lopez-de-Silanes, and Shleifer (n 486) 1139–49; La Porta, Lopez-de-Silanes and Shleifer (n 287) 291–8, 315–23; R La Porta, F Lopez-de-Silanes, A Shleifer, and RW Vishny, 'Law and Finance' (1998) 106 Journal of Political Economy 1113, 1145–51; R La Porta, F Lopez-de-Silanes, A Shleifer, and RW Vishny, 'Investor Protection and Corporate Governance' (2000) 58 Journal of Financial Economics 3, 13–17; R Sylla and GD Smith, 'Information and Capital Market Regulation in Anglo-American Finance' in MD Bordo and R Sylla (eds), *Anglo-American Financial Systems: Institutions and Markets in the Twentieth Century* (Irwin 1995) 179.

[488] For a few contributions from the voluminous literature, see J Armour and others, 'How do legal rules evolve? Evidence from a cross-country comparison of shareholder, creditor, and worker protection' (2009) American Journal of Comparative Law 579; JC Coffee, 'The Rise of Dispersed Ownership: The Roles of Law and the State in the Separation of Ownership and Control' (2001) 111 Yale Law Journal 1; BR Cheffins, 'Does Law Matter? The Separation of Ownership and Control in the United Kingdom' (2001) 30 Journal of Legal Studies 459; M Siems, 'What does not work in comparing securities laws: A critique on La Porta and others' methodology' (2005) 16 International Company and Commercial Law Review 300; H Spamann, 'The "Antidirector Rights Index" Revisited' (2009) 23 Review of Financial Studies 467.

[489] See Coffee (n 488) 80 (arguing that La Porta and others 'may in effect read history backwards').

[490] See text to nn 42–48.

[491] Berle and Means (n 30) 84–111.

became a much-repeated dictum that contributed to the rise of agency cost theory and influenced policy reform.[492] It is commonly pointed out that the United States, and to a lesser extent the UK, are paradigmatic examples of economies with widely dispersed ownership, whereas continental European economies are often characterized by a more concentrated ownership structure. Many companies in continental Europe are still family owned; they are controlled a number of large shareholders and only a minority of the shares are in free floatation and actively traded.[493] In an important study from 2001, Fabrizio Barca and Marco Becht, together with researchers from a number of European countries, sought to quantify this claim by identifying the ultimate owners of listed companies in Europe and the United States and the size of their voting blocks.[494] Their findings confirmed that companies listed on the New York Stock Exchange, NASDAQ, and the London Stock Exchange are only rarely controlled by a single shareholder or a group of shareholders. In more than half of all listed companies in the United States and the UK, the largest voting block was less than 10 per cent, compared with more than 50 per cent in non-financial listed companies in Austria, Belgium, Germany, and Italy, and between 20 per cent and 40 per cent in other continental European countries, including France.[495]

Has this situation changed since 2001? Following the Barca and Becht study, we can visualize ownership concentration in an intuitive way by plotting the cumulative distribution of the largest voting bloc in listed companies, with the size of the largest stake expressed in percentage terms on the vertical axis and the fraction of companies whose largest shareholder owns a smaller stake on the horizontal axis.[496] For ease of comparison, we add a 45° reference line. Observations comparatively close to or above the reference line indicate a more concentrated ownership structure. The figures below are not based on a full sample of all listed companies, but only the largest companies in the economy: the constituent companies of the S&P 500 in the United States, the FTSE 100 in the UK, the CAC 40 and CAC Next 20 in France, and the DAX and MDAX in Germany.[497] In comparing the four figures, we note that ownership structure is relatively widely dispersed in all four countries, at least as far as the largest companies in the economy are concerned. As in the study by Barca and Becht, the median largest ownership block is smallest in the United States and UK, with 9.34 per cent and 8.97 per cent, respectively. However, we now find a distribution that is only slightly more concentrated in France, where the median largest shareholder owns 11.44 per cent of the voting rights. In Germany, ownership is significantly less concentrated than what Barca and Becht found, with a median largest voting block of 18.64 per cent. Our results are not comparable with those by Barca and Becht, because our sample of German companies is much smaller.[498] However, they are comparable across countries, since the indices represent

[492] Jensen and Meckling (n 142) 327, describe agency costs as 'the costs of the "separation of ownership and control" . . . which Berle and Means . . . popularized'.

[493] R La Porta, F Lopez-de-Silanes, and A Shleifer, 'Corporate Ownership Around the World' (1999) 54 Journal of Finance 471.

[494] F Barca and M Becht (eds), *The Control of Corporate Europe* (OUP 2001).

[495] M Becht and C Mayer, 'Introduction' in F Barca and M Becht (eds), *The Control of Corporate Europe* (OUP 2001) 1, 19. In France, the median largest voting block controlled 20% of the votes, significantly less than in Germany (56%) and other continental European countries, for example Spain (34.5%). However, the French sample was based only on the CAC 40, the 40 listed companies with the highest market capitalization on the Paris Stock Exchange, while the German and Spanish samples were much larger. The results, therefore, are not comparable, since we would expect ownership structure in large companies to be more widely dispersed, everything else being equal.

[496] Ownership data is from Capital IQ.

[497] The S&P 500 comprises the 500 largest US-domiciled companies by market capitalization with a primary listing on one of the main US stock exchanges; the FTSE 100 is an index of the 100 companies with the highest market capitalization listed on the London Stock Exchange; for the CAC 40, see n 424 above; the CAC Next 20 comprises the 20 companies ranked after the CAC 40 constituents by market capitalization and listed on Euronext Paris; finally, DAX and MDAX track the performance of the 30 and 50 largest companies in terms of market capitalization and trading volume, respectively, listed in the Prime Standard segment of the Frankfurt Stock Exchange.

[498] Becht and Mayer (n 495) 19, used a sample of 372 German companies.

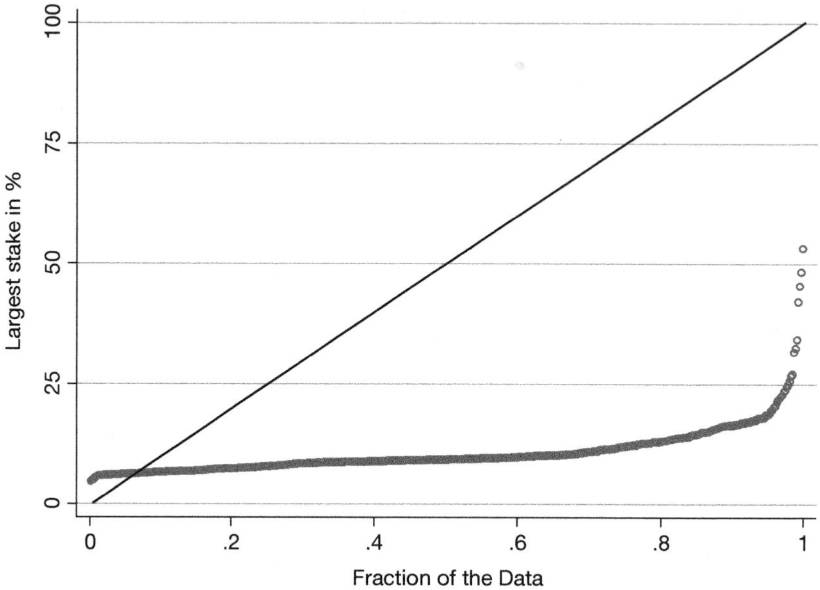

Figure 2 Percentile plot of largest equity stake in US listed companies

a roughly equal proportion of all shares listed on the respective markets.[499] Thus, the analysis confirms what we found when we compared the evolution of stock market capitalization in the four countries. Companies in the two common law countries (see Figure 2 for the United States and Figure 3 for the UK) tend to rely to a greater extent on outside equity than companies in the two civil law countries, and the ownership of French companies (Figure 4) is more dispersed than that of German companies (Figure 5). It is also interesting to note that, in many companies, investors seem to target important voting thresholds.[500] In the UK, we can see a clustering of firms around the 25 per cent threshold, and in Germany around the 25 per cent, 50 per cent, and 75 per cent thresholds, which represent the blocking minority, simple majority and supermajority voting levels pursuant to the UK Companies Act 2006[501] and the German Stock Corporation Act.[502] In France, in contrast, extraordinary resolutions require a majority of two-thirds of the votes.[503] Not surprisingly, the 25 per cent and 50 per cent thresholds, accordingly, do not stand out in Figure 4, but instead we observe a certain clustering around 33 per cent.

The disparity in ownership concentration that (still) exists between economies has historical reasons. In the last decades of the nineteenth century, the capital markets in the United States and in Europe began to develop similarly. They were initially relatively concentrated in all four jurisdictions. The industrialization and the rapid growth of the economy, first in England, then on the continent and in the United States, led to an increase in the demand of capital. However, in each country, different factors determined

[499] The index companies represent about 80% of total market capitalization. Key data on the indices can be obtained from http://us.spindices.com/indices/equity/sp-500 (S&P 500), www.ftse.com/analytics/factsheets (FTSE 100), www.enternext.biz/indices/index-factsheets (CAC 40 and CAC 60), and https://www.dax-indices.com/indices (follow hyperlinks 'Resources' and 'Guides & Factsheets') (DAX and MDAX).

[500] Becht and Mayer (n 495) 26, made a similar observation.

[501] In the UK, special resolutions require a majority of not less than 75% of the votes cast: Companies Act 2006, s 283(1).

[502] AktG, §133(1) (simple majority). A supermajority of 75% of the legal capital represented at the general meeting is required, for example, for amendments of the articles (§179) and changes to the capital structure (§§182, 193, 202, 222).

[503] Com, Art L225-96.

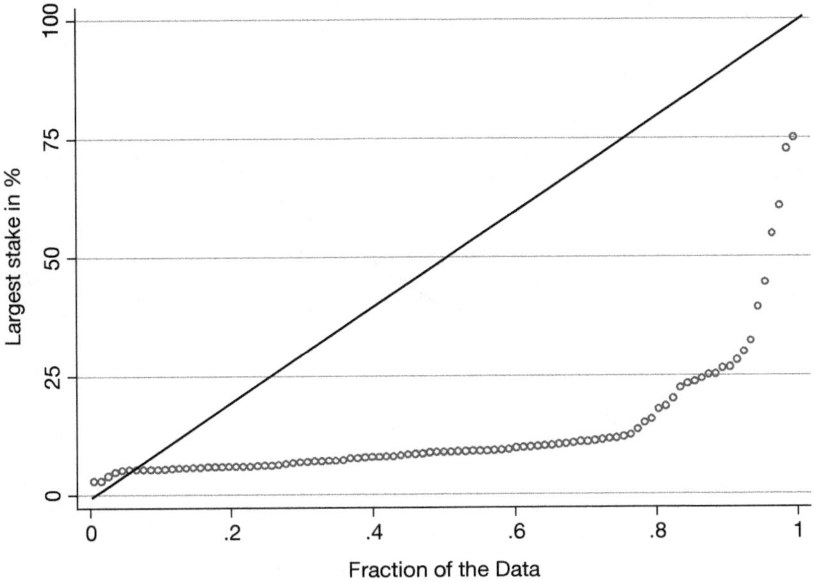

Figure 3 Percentile plot of largest equity stakes in UK listed companies

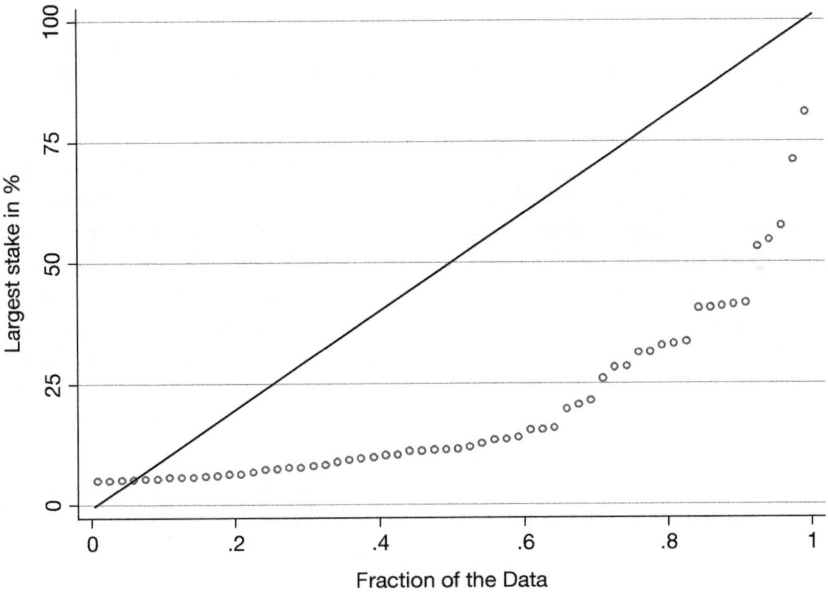

Figure 4 Percentile plot of largest equity stake in French listed companies

the path of financial development. In the United States, private banks and their customers searched for ways to utilize new financial resources. The trading companies, formerly established as partnerships or closely held corporations, reorganized as public corporations and offered their shares and bonds to the public. Investment banks expanded nationwide and established a network of brokers and dealers in order to facilitate the distribution of the securities they had underwritten.[504] In addition, it has been argued that the merger wave

[504] Coffee (n 488) 25–32.

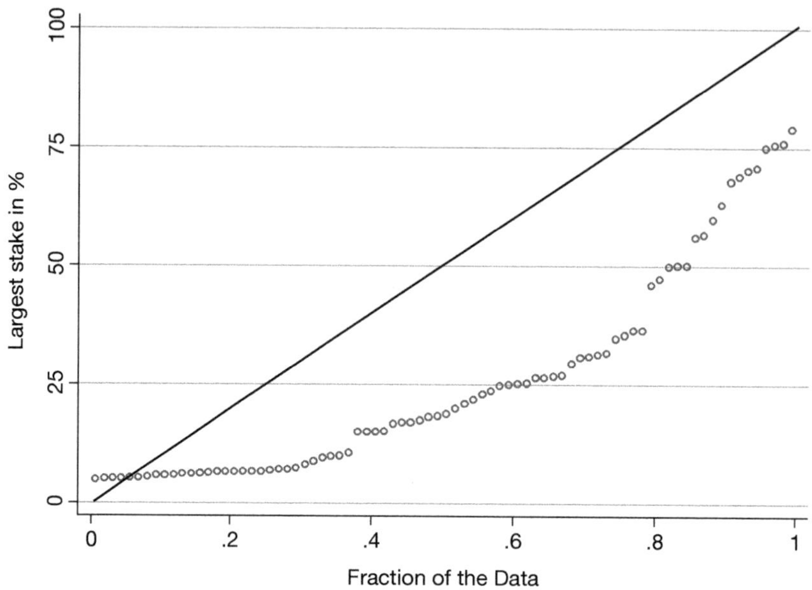

Figure 5 Percentile plot of largest equity stake in German listed companies

of 1895–1903, which was a reaction to the adoption of the Sherman Antitrust Act of 1890, diluted existing blockholders and led to the emergence of large-scale businesses with dispersed ownership.[505]

In the UK, industrials started to offer shares to the public and obtain a stock exchange listing in notable numbers towards the end of the nineteenth century.[506] However, as opposed to the United States, widely dispersed ownership did not yet arise. The proprietors of most corporations, except railways and banks, retained large block holdings.[507] The probably most widely accepted explanatory account holds that British industrial corporations did not have the same need for capital as United States and German enterprises, because they failed to make the necessary investments in manufacturing, marketing, and management and hence did not expand as rapidly.[508] Other possible reasons include the reluctance of English merchant banks of the nineteenth and early twentieth centuries to underwrite domestic securities offerings and market them to institutional and retail investors,[509] the existence of attractive foreign investment opportunities,[510] and weak legal protection of outside investors.[511] Between the two world wars, public offerings became increasingly popular as a means of financing.[512] The shift to an outsider/arm's-length system of ownership and

[505] ibid 33.

[506] For data, see Franks, Mayer, and Rossi (n 485) 588. The number of companies listed on the London Stock Exchange rose from 70 to 571 between 1880 and 1907 and to 1,700 by 1913.

[507] Cheffins (n 44) 225–51.

[508] Chandler (n 44) 235. See also n 445 above and accompanying text. For a critical assessment of Chandler's view and further references, see Cheffins (n 44) 223–4.

[509] It is hotly debated why the English merchant banks neglected the domestic industry. Some commentators argue that the banks focused on foreign business ventures, which promised higher profit margins; see B Elbaum and W Lazonick, 'The Decline of the British Economy: An Institutional Perspective' (1984) 44 Journal of Economic History 567, 570. Others have pointed out that English banks were comparatively small and traditionally followed a more conservative business model, which did not include high-risk transactions, such as the underwriting of corporate securities; see Coffee (n 488) 32.

[510] Cheffins (n 44) 192–4.

[511] ibid 194–7.

[512] For the reasons, see ibid 252–67. For example, the upbeat stock market during some of that time gave proprietors an opportunity to cash out at a premium: ibid 263.

control, however, was not complete until the 1960s or 1970s.[513] In the decades following the Second World War, increased competition and the need for expensive new investment reduced the profit margins of UK family businesses and forced the proprietors to look for new ways of financing. According to one commentator, these market conditions made exit by way of a public offering an attractive option for blockholders.[514] In addition, high income tax rates, a tax bias against dividends, and changes to stock exchange regulation that made the extraction of private benefits of control more difficult reduced the opportunities for insiders to profit from block holdings.[515] On the buy side, the rise of institutional investors, in particular pension funds and insurance companies, contributed to the ultimate divorce of ownership from control in the UK.[516]

While ownership concentration began to fall in the UK towards the end of the nineteenth century, it remained high in Germany.[517] As in the UK, founders divested parts of their holdings during the first half of the twentieth century.[518] However, their stakes were replaced by equally (or even more) concentrated holdings by banks and other corporations.[519] Thus, as opposed to the development in the UK, the fact that the founding families decided to disinvest did not lead to a decrease in ownership concentration, but rather to the much-discussed phenomenon of horizontal integration and inter-corporate holdings that should characterize the German corporate economy for decades to come.[520] The Nazi regime and the Second World War, however, represented probably the most significant breaks with the development since the introduction of incorporation by registration in 1870. During the Nazi era, the number of public stock corporations dropped significantly, because the government encouraged entrepreneurs to take their companies private[521] and intervened widely in economic activity to rationalize enterprises, promote cartelization and suppress industries that were seen as 'parasitical'.[522] The Second World War left much of the financial infrastructure, including the banking industry and the stock exchanges, in ruins.[523] In order to stabilize the economy after the war, the German government regulated the issuance and trading of securities restrictively and granted tax subsidies to certain fixed-interest investments. These measures made investing in the capital markets unattractive for private individuals and set a trend in motion that led to the widespread disregard of equity capital as a

[513] ibid 303–307. [514] ibid 319–21. [515] ibid 321–33.

[516] ibid 344–9. For the factors that triggered the rise of institutional investors, see ibid 350–70.

[517] See eg the time series plots in J Franks, C Mayer, and HF Wagner, 'The Origins of the German Corporation: Finance, Ownership and Control' (2006) 10 Review of Finance 537, 566.

[518] It is difficult to assess how extensive the initial ownership by founders was. Franks, Mayer and Wagner (n 517) note that the holdings of founding families fluctuated considerably. They classify 13 out of 55 firms as founding-family owned and observe that family ownership was decreasing over time, ibid 579–81. Of course, it did not disappear completely from the German corporate landscape. A study analysing large quoted companies found that family groups accounted for more than one-fifth of dominant shareholdings in 1990, defined as block holdings of at least 25 per cent, see J Franks and C Mayer, 'Ownership and Control of German Corporations' (2001) 14 Review of Financial Studies 943, 947.

[519] Franks, Mayer, and Wagner (n 517) 568–73, 581. It should be noted that bank ownership is often overstated in the data because of the high proportion of proxy votes exercised by banks; on this see ibid 575–6. In fact, Franks and Mayer (n 518) 947–8, find that banks were less common as large blockholders than other corporations, institutional investors, and family groups. For further data see Fohlin (n 485) 237–46 (rejecting the notion that the large equity holdings of the German universal banks were the reason why the German capital markets developed comparatively less well than in other countries).

[520] Fohlin (n 485) 229–30, 233–7; Franks, Mayer, and Wagner (n 517) 582–3; Franks and Mayer (n 518) 946–52.

[521] Fohlin (n 485) 230.

[522] The government's powers over the economy can be traced back to the interwar years. They started to be exercised extensively during the great depression, but the scale of government intervention and its goals changed with the accession of the National Socialists to power, Landes (n 446) 401–405. The regime viewed in particular those industries as 'parasitical' where Jewish entrepreneurs were prominent, such as banking, brokerage and retail trade, ibid 403.

[523] B Rudolph, 'Effekten- und Wertpapierbörsen, Finanztermin- und Devisenbörsen seit 1945' in H Pohl (ed), *Deutsche Börsengeschichte* (Fritz Knapp 1992) 291, 293.

means of corporate finance.[524] The situation began to change only with several reform acts adopted since the 1990s.[525] Companies now rely more on equity finance raised in capital markets, and the shareholder body of the largest companies has become more dispersed and international.[526]

France followed yet another path to modern finance capitalism. Traditionally, French industrial corporations relied to a greater extent on self-financing than their counterparts in Germany, the UK or the United States, and family ownership of companies was more prominent than in other countries.[527] These features of the French corporate economy have been attributed to structural weaknesses in the banking system and the capital markets, which in turn were a legacy of several 'financial traumas' of the eighteenth and nineteenth centuries: the failure of John Law's system of fiat money following the establishment of the Banque Générale and the Company of the West (the Mississippi Company) in 1716, the hyperinflation of the years after the French revolution, and the collapse of the two large banking companies Crédit Mobilier in 1867 and Union Générale in 1878.[528] As a consequence of these experiences, entrepreneurs and the public exhibited a deep-seated mistrust of the banking system, financial innovation, and capital markets. It has been observed that until well into the twentieth century, bank credit was not widely available and France was heavily underbanked in comparison with other European countries and the United States.[529] French corporations started to modernize, adopt management structures resembling those of American firms, and replace family chairmen by salaried managers in the 1950s and 1960s.[530] The improvement of organizational capabilities went hand in hand with a greater reliance on bank credit and the stock market to finance operations, rather than on retained earnings.[531] The retreat of the state as a major borrower in financial markets, the privatizations of the 1980s and 1990s, and a raft of legislative reforms adopted since the late 1970s further contributed to the growth in size and trading volume of French markets.[532] Nevertheless, as in Germany, financial development has been slow and vibrant capital markets are a relatively recent phenomenon.

[524] ibid 297–9. The differential tax treatment of debt and equity ended in 1954, but continued to influence financing patterns thereafter. Fohlin (n 485) 232, points out that the shareholding of private households fell from 48.6 per cent in 1950 to 17 per cent in 1996. Over the same time, the proportion of shares held by nonfinancial firms increased from 18 per cent to more than 41 per cent.

[525] The most important of these reforms were the four Financial Market Development Acts (*Finanzmarktförder ungsgesetze*) of 1989 (BGBl I, 1412), 1994 (BGBl I, 1749), 1998 (BGBl I, 529), and 2002 (BGBl I, 2010).

[526] IPO activity was further stimulated by tax reforms that discontinued double taxation of dividends and an improvement in the general economic climate in the 1980s and 1990s, Rudolph (n 523) 322–5. For a detailed study of recent changes, see also WG Ringe, 'Changing Law and Ownership Patterns in Germany: Corporate Governance and the Erosion of Deutschland AG' (2015) 63 American Journal of Comparative Law 493.

[527] Murphy (n 485) 187–9. By the 1990s, the picture had changed somewhat. J Franks and C Mayer, 'Corporate Ownership and Control in the U.K., Germany, and France' (1997) 9 Journal of Applied Corporate Finance 30, 33–5, compare the owners of large stakes in German and French listed companies and note that families owned only 7.5% of stakes in excess of 25% in France, compared with 20.5% in Germany. The most common block holders were other French companies (46.8%, compared with 27.3% in Germany).

[528] Murphy (n 485) 191–205.

[529] A Gueslin, 'Banks and state in France from the 1880s to the 1930s: The impossible advance of the banks' in Y Cassis (ed), *Finance and Financiers in European History 1880-1960* (CUP 1992) 63. See also M Lévy-Leboyer, 'The Large Corporation in France' in A Chandler and H Daems (eds), *Managerial Hierarchies: Comparative Perspectives on the Rise of the Modern Industrial Enterprise* (Harvard University Press 1980) 122, 127 (pointing out that the first noteworthy stock market boom in France took place more than a quarter of a century later than in other leading industrial nations, namely from 1926 to the start of the Second World War).

[530] Fridenson (n 446) 216. [531] ibid 226–8.

[532] Important legislation includes Law no 78-741 of 13 July 1978 (Loi d'orientation de l'épargne), JORF of 14 July 1978, 2799; Law no 83-1 of 3 January 1983 (Loi sur le développement des investissements et la protection de l'épargne), JORF of 4 January 1983, 162; and Law no 2003-706 of 1 August 2003 (Loi de sécurité financière), JORF no 177 of 2 August 2003, 13220. The first two laws were largely deregulatory in nature and used tax incentives to promote financial development (for a discussion, see G Hawawini, 'Financial Innovation and Recent Developments in the French Capital Markets' (1987) 9 University of Pennsylvania Journal of International Law 145, 155–62); the third sought to strengthen corporate governance and overhauled the institutional regulatory architecture, establishing the market regulator AMF (Autorité des marchés financiers).

E. Board Structure Regulation

US MBCA

§ 8.01—Requirements for and functions of board of directors

(a) …
(b) All corporate powers shall be exercised by or under the authority of the board of directors of the corporation, and the business and affairs of the corporation shall be managed by or under the direction, and subject to the oversight, of its board of directors, subject to any limitation set forth in the articles of incorporation …

§ 8.40—Officers

(a) A corporation has the officers described in its bylaws or appointed by the board of directors in accordance with the bylaws.
(b) The board of directors may elect individuals to fill one or more offices of the corporation. An officer may appoint one or more officers if authorized by the bylaws or the board of directors.
(c) The bylaws or the board of directors shall assign to one of the officers responsibility for preparing the minutes of the directors' and shareholders' meetings and for maintaining and authenticating the records of the corporation required to be kept under sections 16.01(a) and 16.01(e).
(d) The same individual may simultaneously hold more than one office in a corporation.

§ 8.43—Resignation and Removal of Officers

(a) An officer may resign at any time by delivering notice to the corporation …
(b) An officer may be removed at any time with or without cause by: (i) the board of directors; (ii) the officer who appointed such officer, unless the bylaws or the board of directors provide otherwise; or (iii) any other officer if authorized by the bylaws or the board of directors.
(c) In this section, 'appointing officer' means the officer (including any successor to that officer) who appointed the officer resigning or being removed.

Delaware General Corporation Law

§ 141—Board of directors …

(a) The business and affairs of every corporation organized under this chapter shall be managed by or under the direction of a board of directors, except as may be otherwise provided in this chapter or in its certificate of incorporation. If any such provision is made in the certificate of incorporation, the powers and duties conferred or imposed upon the board of directors by this chapter shall be exercised or performed to such extent and by such person or persons as shall be provided in the certificate of incorporation.
(b) The board of directors of a corporation shall consist of 1 or more members, each of whom shall be a natural person. The number of directors shall be fixed by, or in the manner provided in, the bylaws, unless the certificate of incorporation fixes the number of directors, in which case a change in the number of directors shall be made only by amendment of the certificate. Directors need not be stockholders unless so required by the certificate of incorporation or the bylaws. The certificate of incorporation or bylaws may prescribe other qualifications for directors …
(c)(1) …
(2) The board of directors may designate 1 or more committees, each committee to consist of 1 or more of the directors of the corporation … Any such committee, to the extent provided in the resolution of the board of directors, or in the bylaws of the corporation, shall have and may exercise all the powers and authority of the board of directors in the management of the business and affairs of the corporation, and may authorize the seal of the corporation to be affixed to all papers which may require it; but no such committee shall have the power or authority in reference to the following matter: (i) approving or adopting, or recommending to the stockholders, any action or matter (other than the election or removal of directors) expressly required by this chapter to be submitted

to stockholders for approval or (ii) adopting, amending or repealing any bylaw of the corporation.

§ 142 Officers; titles, duties, selection, term ...

(a) Every corporation organized under this chapter shall have such officers with such titles and duties as shall be stated in the bylaws or in a resolution of the board of directors which is not inconsistent with the bylaws and as may be necessary to enable it to sign instruments and stock certificates which comply with §§ 103(a)(2) and 158 of this title. One of the officers shall have the duty to record the proceedings of the meetings of the stockholders and directors in a book to be kept for that purpose. Any number of offices may be held by the same person unless the certificate of incorporation or bylaws otherwise provide.
(b)Officers shall be chosen in such manner and shall hold their offices for such terms as are prescribed by the bylaws or determined by the board of directors or other governing body. Each officer shall hold office until such officer's successor is elected and qualified or until such officer's earlier resignation or removal. Any officer may resign at any time upon written notice to the corporation ...

UK Companies Act 2006

Section 154—Companies required to have directors

(1) A private company must have at least one director.
(2) A public company must have at least two directors.

Section 156A—Each director to be a natural person

(1) A person may not be appointed a director of a company unless the person is a natural person.
(2) Subsection (1) does not prohibit the holding of the office of director by a natural person as a corporation sole or otherwise by virtue of an office.
(3) An appointment made in contravention of this section is void.
(4) ...

Section 157—Minimum age for appointment as director

(1) A person may not be appointed a director of a company unless he has attained the age of 16 years.
(2) ...

UK Model Articles for Public Companies

3. Directors' general authority
Subject to the articles, the directors are responsible for the management of the company's business, for which purpose they may exercise all the powers of the company.
4. Members' reserve power
(1) The members may, by special resolution, direct the directors to take, or refrain from taking, specified action ...

German Stock Corporation Act

§ 76—Management of the stock corporation

(1) The management board shall manage the company under its own responsibility.
(2) The management board may consist of one or more persons. In companies with a share capital of more than 3 million euros the management board shall consist of at least two persons, unless the articles provide that it shall consist of one person. The provisions regarding the appointment of worker directors shall be unaffected.
(3) Only a natural person with full legal capacity may be a member of the management board ...

§ 78—Representation

(1) The management board represents the company in court and out of court ...

§ 95—Number of the supervisory board members

The supervisory board shall consist of three members. The articles of association may provide for a greater number. This number must be divisible by three. The maximum number of supervisory board members shall be in companies with a legal capital of

up to	1,500,000	Euros nine,
more than	1,500,000	Euros fifteen,
more than	10,000,000	Euros twenty-one.

The foregoing provisions shall not affect provisions to the contrary of the Co-Determination Act of 4 May 1976 (Federal Gazette I, p. 1153), the Coal and Steel Co-Determination Act, and the Act Supplementing the Coal and Steel Co-Determination Act of 7 August 1956 (Federal Gazette I, p. 707) – Co-Determination Supplementary Act.

§ 100—Personal qualifications of supervisory board members

(1) Only a natural person with full legal capacity may be a member of the supervisory board . . .
(2) A person may not be a member of the supervisory board if this person:

1. is a member of the supervisory board of ten commercial companies that are required by law to set up a supervisory board,
2. is the legal representative of a dependent enterprise of the company,
3. is the legal representative of another capital company, on whose supervisory a member of the management board of the company serves,
4. was in the last two years a member of the management board of the same stock exchange listed company, unless the director was appointed on a proposal by shareholders holding more than 25% of the voting rights in the company.

   In determining the maximum number pursuant to Sentence 1, no. 1, no account shall be taken of up to five supervisory board seats which a legal representative (or, in the case of a sole proprietorship, the owner) of the controlling enterprise of a group has on supervisory boards of commercial companies which are members of such a group and which are required by law to form a supervisory board. Supervisory board seats within the meaning of no. 1 shall be counted twice for purposes of calculating the maximum number pursuant to Sentence 1, no. 1 if the member was elected as chairman.

(3) The further personal qualifications of supervisory board members representing the employees and additional members of the supervisory board shall be determined in accordance with the Co-determination Act, the Coal and Steel Co-determination Act, the Co-Determination Supplementary Act, the One-Third Participation Act, and the Act on the Co-Determination of Employees in Cross-Border Mergers.
(4) The articles may stipulate personal qualifications only for those members of the supervisory board who are elected by the general meeting otherwise than according to binding nominations or who are appointed to the supervisory board pursuant to the articles.
(5) In companies within the meaning of § 264d of the Commercial Code [companies with securities admitted to trading on a regulated market] at least one independent member of the supervisory board must have expertise in the areas of accounting or auditing. . . .

§ 105—Incompatibility of Membership of both the Management Board and the Supervisory Board

(1) A member of the supervisory board may not be at the same time a member of the management board, a permanent deputy member of the management board, an officer of the company with statutory authority or a person with general commercial power of representation.
(2). . .

§ 111—Duties and Rights of the Supervisory Board

(1) The supervisory board shall supervise the management of the company.
(2) The supervisory board may inspect and examine the books and records of the company as well as the corporate assets, in particular cash and inventories of securities and merchandise. It may also instruct individual members of the board or, with respect to specific assignments, external experts to conduct the investigation. It shall appoint the auditor of the annual and consolidated financial accounts pursuant to § 290 of the Commercial Code.
(3) The supervisory board shall call a general meeting whenever the interests of the company so require. The resolution requires a simple majority.

(4) Management responsibilities may not be conferred on the supervisory board. However, the articles or the supervisory board shall determine that specific types of transaction may be entered into only with its consent. If the supervisory board refuses to grant consent, the management board may request that a general meeting shall resolve whether to grant consent. The resolution of the general meeting granting consent requires a majority of at least three-quarters of the votes cast. The articles may neither require a different majority nor provide for additional requirements.
(5) Members of the supervisory board may not entrust their responsibilities to other persons.

French Commercial Code[533]

Art. L225-17

A limited company is administered by a board of directors composed of at least three members. The memorandum and articles of association stipulate the maximum permissible number of board members, which shall not exceed eighteen.

The appointment of the board of directors must seek to achieve a balanced representation of men and women …

Art. L225-21

No natural person shall concurrently hold more than five directorships of limited companies having their registered office on French soil.

Contrary to the provisions of the first paragraph, this shall not apply to directorships or supervisory board membership of companies that are controlled, within the meaning of Article L233-16, by the company of which that natural person is a director …

Art. L225-35

The board of directors determines the broad lines of the company's business activities and ensures their implementation. Without prejudice to the powers expressly invested in meetings of the shareholders, and in so far as the memorandum and articles of association permit, it deals with all matters relating to the conduct of the company's business and decides all pertinent issues through its deliberations …

Art. L225-47

The board of directors shall elect a chairman from among its members who, in order for the appointment to be valid, must be a natural person. It shall determine his remuneration.

The chairman shall be appointed for a term which may not exceed his term of office as a director. He shall be eligible for re-election.

The board of directors may dismiss him at any time. Any provision to the contrary shall be deemed null and void.

Art. L225-51

The chairman of the board of directors organises and oversees its work and reports to the General Meeting thereon. He sees to it that the company's management structures function well and ensures, in particular, that the directors are able to accomplish their task.

Art. L225-51-1

The general management of the company shall be assumed under their responsibility by either the chairman of the board of directors or by another natural person appointed by the board of directors and bearing the title of general manager.

In accordance with the conditions defined by its memorandum and articles of association, the board of directors shall choose between the two forms of performance of the general management referred to in subparagraph one. The shareholders and third parties shall be informed of this choice in accordance with the conditions laid down by a decree of the Conseil d'Etat.

If the general management of the company is assumed by the chairman of the board of directors, the provisions of this sub-section relating to the general manager shall apply to him.

[533] Translation by Legifrance, https://www.legifrance.gouv.fr/Traductions/en-English/Legifrance-translations.

Art. L225-53

On the proposal of the general manager, the board of directors may appoint one or more natural persons charged with assisting the general manager, with the title of assistant general manager.

The memorandum and articles of association shall determine the maximum number of assistant general managers, which may not exceed five.

The board of directors shall determine the remuneration of the general manager and the assistant general managers.

Art. L225-55

The general manager may be dismissed at any time by the board of directors. The same shall apply, on the proposal of the general manager, to the assistant general managers. Should the dismissal be decided without good cause, it may give rise to damages, except when the general manager assumes the office of chairman of the board of directors.

Should the general manager cease to or be unable to perform their office, the assistant general managers shall retain their office and remuneration, unless decided otherwise by the board, until the appointment of the new general manager.

Art. L225-56

I. - The general manager shall be invested with the most extensive powers to act on behalf of the company in all circumstances. They shall exercise their powers subject to those that the Law allocates explicitly to shareholders' meetings and to the board of directors.

They shall represent the company in its dealings with third parties ...

II. - In agreement with the general manager, the board of directors shall determine the scope and the term of the powers conferred upon the assistant general managers.

The assistant general managers shall have the same powers as the general manager with respect to third parties.

I. One-tier and two-tier board paradigm

The board of directors constitutes the link between the shareholders and the full-time managers. It oversees the operation of the company, supervises the executive management, and takes decisions of strategic importance. That much is undisputed, but there is considerable variation between legal systems in how the board of directors achieves these functions. At the most basic level, legal systems distinguish between a one-tier and a two-tier board. In the former case, both management and supervisory functions are exercised by a unitary board of directors. In legal systems following the two-tier board model, on the other hand, management and supervisory functions are allocated to two separate organs, a management or executive board and a supervisory board. In addition, as we will see, jurisdictions have developed various intermediate or hybrid organizational forms that modify elements of the one-tier or two-tier board model.

The unitary board is prevalent in Anglo-American jurisdictions (although it is not necessarily always mandated by law, for example in the UK), and the dual board in countries belonging to the German legal tradition. In Germany and Austria, it is mandatory for public companies,[534] which are governed by a management board (*Vorstand*) and a supervisory board (*Aufsichtsrat*). The supervisory board enjoys various information and inspection rights to fulfil its supervisory functions[535] and has certain limited decision rights that reach into the sphere of managerial decision-making.[536] Other legal systems that provide for this

[534] It is, in general, not mandatory for the closely held company (*Gesellschaft mit beschränkter Haftung—GmbH*), but see n 600 below.

[535] Pursuant to §90 AktG, the management board must give regularly reports to the supervisory board, and the supervisory board can request additional information about the company's affairs at any time. Furthermore, the supervisory board may inspect the corporate books and records, inventories, and any other data files of relevance, §111(2). For a more detailed discussion of the supervisory board's information rights, see section IV below.

[536] See section I.3 below. For a more general discussion of the allocation of powers between the management board, supervisory board and shareholders, see also Chapter 5A.III.

organizational structure include Slovakia and the Czech Republic, as well as the Netherlands (even though it is not a country belonging to the German legal tradition), where the two-tier board model is mandatory for certain large companies (so-called 'structure regime', applicable to *structuurvennootschappen*, i.e. structure regime companies).[537]

In an increasing number of legal systems, we observe hybrid organizational forms that allow either the incorporators to choose between the unitary and dual board models or combine elements of both paradigmatic models. Prominent examples are France, Italy, Portugal, and the European company (SE). In France, since a company law reform of 1966,[538] the public limited company (*société anonyme*) may elect to be governed under the two-tier board system modelled on the German regime with a management board (*directoire*) and a supervisory board (*conseil de surveillance*),[539] instead of the traditional one-tier system with a unitary board of directors (*conseil d'administration*).[540] The Regulation on the statute for the European Company (SE) allows the same choice, with a unitary governance structure consisting of an 'administrative organ' and a dual structure consisting of a 'management organ' and a 'supervisory organ'.[541] The SE Regulation defines the basic structure of the two board systems, but does not deal with all relevant questions in detail.[542] Thus, national laws remain relevant to regulate matters not expressly addressed by the SE Regulation, and some Member States were required to amend their national laws to make allowance for the choice of board structure in the SE.[543] For example, Germany introduced a set of rules for the SE with a unitary board, which emulates, as far as possible, the respective provisions on board structure in the German Stock Corporation Act.[544] Interestingly, the UK did not implement corresponding changes to accommodate SEs with a two-tier board structure, because it was felt that English law was sufficiently flexible and permitted companies to structure their boards as they wished.[545] As we will see, English law indeed stands out among the legal systems we analyse, because the UK Companies Act contains few binding rules on corporate governance. It is left largely to the shareholders to design the company's governance architecture in the articles of association.[546]

Italy and Portugal offer three alternative management structures. In Italy, the default model provides for a board of directors (*consiglio di amministrazione*) and a board of statutory auditors (*collegio sindacale*). Alternatively, the shareholders may opt for the two-tier model, consisting of a management board (*consiglio di gestione*) and supervisory board (*consiglio di sorveglianza*), or a one-tier board (*consiglio di amministrazione*) with executive

[537] *Structuurvennootschappen* are companies with a subscribed capital of at least €16 million and at least 100 employees in the Netherlands. The regime applies to the large NV (*naamloze vennootschap* or public company) and the large BV (*besloten vennootschap* or private limited company). For a discussion of the Dutch regime, see J van Bekkum and others, 'Corporate Governance in the Netherlands' (2010) 14 Electronic Journal of Comparative Law 1.

[538] Law no 66-537 of 24 July 1966 (Loi sur les sociétés commerciales), JORF of 26 July 1966, 6402.

[539] Com, Arts L225-57 to L225-93.

[540] ibid Arts L225-17 to L225-56. The majority of large French companies continue to be established under the unitary board system, see n 653 below.

[541] Regulation (EC) No 2157/2001 of 8 October 2001 on the Statute for a European company (SE) [2001] OJ L294/1, Art 38.

[542] For example, Art 43(3) of the Regulation provides that '[t]he member or members of the administrative organ [in the one-tier system] shall be appointed by the general meeting', but it does not contain any provisions about the removal of directors or details of the appointment and removal process, for example the required majority for a removal of directors.

[543] Article 9(1)(c) of the SE Regulation provides that the laws of the Member States shall apply where the Regulation does not address a matter, and Arts 39(5) and 43(4) explicitly empower Member States to 'adopt the appropriate measures in relation to SEs' where their laws do not make any provision for a one-tier or two-tier system.

[544] SE Implementation Act (Gesetz zur Ausführung der Verordnung (EG) Nr. 2157/2001 des Rates vom 8. Oktober 2001 über das Statut der Europäischen Gesellschaft (SE)) §§20–49.

[545] Implementing legislation exists in the UK that deals with other questions, see European Public Limited-Liability Company Regulations 2004 (SI 2004/2326).

[546] We will discuss contractual freedom in UK company law further in Chapter 5A.I.

and independent non-executive directors.[547] Portuguese law contains similar options.[548] Swiss law, while formally based on the unitary board model, is so flexible that some companies effectively establish a two-tier board by delegating competences to managers who are not members of the board.[549] The traditional Scandinavian model is another example of a hybrid system. Formally, the governance structure consists of two boards, a board of directors and an executive board. However, it is closer to the Anglo-American than the German model,[550] because both boards enjoy executive powers and they are composed of executive as well as non-executive directors. The executive board is entrusted with the day-to-day management, while the board of directors is responsible for the overall strategic direction of the company and the supervision of the executive board.[551]

In both one-tier and two-tier systems, a division of functions between supervisory competences (exercised through the board of directors or the supervisory board) and executive competences (exercised through the officers or the management board) exists. In one-tier systems, corporate powers are formally vested in the directors, but in practice usually delegated to the officers. That this delegation is permissible can be concluded, for instance, from the formulation of the Delaware General Corporation Law that the powers of the corporation may be exercised 'under the direction of a board of directors'.[552] However, the division between supervisory and executive functions is less institutionalized and, in practice, less strictly observed than in legal systems that have adopted the two-tier board model. In fact, the officers often hold important positions on the board of directors. For example, in the United States, the chief executive officer is generally also chairman of the board of directors.[553] In France, the positions of chairman of the board (*président du conseil d'administration*) and general manager (*directeur general*) may be combined, creating the powerful position of *président directeur general*.[554] In the UK, following the recommendations of the Cadbury report and subsequent corporate governance codes, the roles of CEO—often called managing director—and chairman of the board are commonly separated, but many members of the board hold executive positions. However, even in two-tier systems, the supervisory board is not always as independent from management as the legislative concept envisages. In Germany, suitable candidates for positions on the supervisory board are in practice identified by the management board, even though they are formally appointed by the general meeting. In addition, management board members frequently receive positions on the supervisory board upon retirement.[555] Therefore, they may be associated with the managers at a personal level and may not always act as independent supervisors.

[547] Italian Civil Code, Art 2380(1).

[548] Portuguese Code of Commercial Companies, Art 278.

[549] P Forstmoser, 'Monistische oder dualistische Unternehmensverfassung? Das Schweizer Konzept' (2003) 32 ZGR 688, 698–9, 705–706.

[550] For this reason, it is called 'dual executive system'; see eg JL Hansen, 'The New Danish Companies Act of 2009' (2010) 11 EBOR 87, 89.

[551] See eg JL Hansen, 'The Danish Green Paper on Company Law Reform: Modernising Company Law in the 21st Century' (2009) 10 EBOR 73, 87; Danish Recommendations on Corporate Governance of 2017, 6. The Danish Companies Act, §111(1)(a) requires a majority of the members of the board of directors to be non-executive directors.

[552] Del. Gen. Corp. Law, §141(a). Similar formulations are contained in §8.01 of the MBCA and Art L225-51-1 of the French Code de commerce. In the UK, the permissibility of delegation is a function of the contractual nature of the allocation of decision-making power (on this point, see Chapter 5A.I). The authority to act on behalf of the company originates with the shareholders. As a default, it is delegated to the directors in the articles, who can (and usually do) delegate it further to the full-time managers; see Model Articles for Public and Private Companies, Arts 3–5.

[553] For an overview of changes to the composition of boards of Delaware corporations since the 1970s, see B Cheffins, 'Delaware and the Transformation of Corporate Governance' (2015) 40 Delaware Journal of Corporate Law 1.

[554] See section III.4 below.

[555] C Jungmann, 'The Effectiveness of Corporate Governance in One-Tier and Two-Tier Board Systems: Evidence from the UK and Germany' (2006) 3 ECFR 426, 450.

Another important feature distinguishing one-tier and two-tier board systems is the degree of integration of management into the corporate governance architecture of the firm. According to US economist Oliver Williamson, two models define the relationship between the managers and directors, the 'monitoring model' and the 'participatory board'.[556] The first approach holds that the function of the board of directors is primarily to control the executives and safeguard the interests of the stockholders. It would be counterproductive, therefore, to involve managers at board level. Instead, this approach implies a clear hierarchy, with the non-executive directors at the apex of the firm and the executives in a subordinated role. The participatory board model, on the other hand, suggests that the participation of managers on the board has a number of important advantages. First, it enables the board to evaluate the quality and outcome of managerial decisions and management performance more accurately. Consequently, if necessary, the board can correct appointment errors more quickly. Secondly, because of the significant informational advantages enjoyed by the managers, the board is in a better position to assess the merits of competing investment proposals. Thirdly, board membership gives management a forum to voice grievances or concerns and, hence, safeguards the employment relationship between management and the firm.[557] Williamson acknowledges these advantages, but for him it is important to strike the right balance. The principal function of the board, he argues, remains the monitoring of management. Managers should participate on the board so that the directors can avail themselves of the above advantages, but their participation should be limited and not compromise the basic purpose of the board.[558]

Arguably, in all four countries that we discuss, regulation seeks to strike this balance, albeit in different ways. In one-tier board systems, typically, several managers participate on the board of directors, while best practice rules or binding company law seek to ensure that a majority of the board are composed of non-executive directors. Two-tier board systems are closer to Williamson's 'monitoring model', and the built-in informational disadvantages of the supervisory directors need to be counterbalanced by information rights and reporting obligations that guarantee the flow of information between the two boards. The simple choice between the one-tier and two-tier board model, without more, is unlikely to produce effective results in either case. Both board models have certain advantages, but also disadvantages that need to be addressed by regulation. On the other hand, this also implies that it is difficult to argue that one board model is inherently superior to the other. Indeed, empirical studies show that both board systems are, in principle, capable of responding quickly to inadequate performance by directors.[559]

Whether boards function well in individual cases is often determined by subtle factors that promote an independent and outspoken attitude of the non-executive directors and provide the right environment for balanced, critical, and constructive discussions in the boardroom. It is a valid question whether intervention by a legislator (or, for that matter, a standard setter promulgating best practice rules contained in corporate governance codes) is able to influence such interpersonal factors. After all, independence in judgment and 'a culture of openness and debate' among directors, as the UK Corporate Governance Code puts it,[560] cannot simply be prescribed by regulation, but depend crucially on personal characteristics and the dynamics in the boardroom. In the following sections, we will pursue

[556] Williamson (n 2) 316. [557] ibid 317. [558] ibid.

[559] Jungmann (n 555) 446–8 (comparing board turnover in British and German companies as a response to poor financial performance); SN Kaplan, 'Corporate governance and corporate performance: A comparison of Germany, Japan, and the US' (1997) 9 Journal of Applied Corporate Finance 86 (arguing that there is no clear difference between German, Japanese and US-American systems of corporate governance in responding to poor stock and earnings performance; however, also finding that the US system is more effective in discouraging overinvesting, because the directors of US companies hold greater equity positions and dividend distributions are less stringently regulated than in the other two countries).

[560] UK Corporate Governance Code 2018, Principle F.

these questions. We will examine board structure regulation in our four main jurisdictions in more detail and discuss how boards should be composed in order to support the policy goals of corporate governance, as expressed, for example, in the UK Corporate Governance Code.[561] In this context, we will introduce some concepts from social psychology, which explores when decision-making in small groups can be expected to produce rational, well-founded outcomes.[562]

1. UK

The Companies Act 2006 contains surprisingly few provisions dealing with the governance structure of a company and the role of the company's organs. In fact, the Act does not specify how many and which organs public or private companies must have, but leaves these questions to the contractual autonomy of the incorporators. The incorporators enjoy largely unfettered freedom to structure the company's internal affairs, shape the composition of the board, and allocate decision-making competences between the different organs in the articles of association as they deem expedient.[563] The Companies Act 2006 only requires that a private company must have at least one director and a public company two.[564] At least one of the directors must be a natural person.[565] The board of directors as a corporate organ is mentioned for the first time in Part 15 of the Companies Act on accounts and reports, laying down the obligation of the board to approve the accounts and the directors' reports.[566] Where the Companies Act allocates decision-making power, the power is usually vested in individual directors or shareholders (members), not in an abstract *organ* of the company that has some legal existence beyond that of the members of the organ.[567]

This focus on individuals, rather than corporate organs, and the wide scope left for private ordering distinguishes UK company law from that of many continental European jurisdictions, but also from the United States. The reason for these differences may be found in the strong influence that English partnership law exerted on the development of corporate law and in a general legal environment during the formative years of modern UK company law that was characterized by the belief in freedom of contract.[568] As a consequence of the Bubble Act of 1720,[569] which restricted the use of the corporate form, and the difficulties experienced by some industrial enterprises in obtaining an Act of Parliament or Royal Charter for incorporation, a growing number of entrepreneurs resolved to trade as so-called 'deed of settlement companies'.[570] These 'companies' were technically partnerships that were formed

[561] Section III below. [562] Section II below.

[563] The Companies Act does not regulate the content of articles of association (see s 18). The registration documents must include a statement of the company's proposed officers (s 9(4)(c)) containing personal information about the directors (as set out in ss 163–164), but the provisions do not restrict the incorporators' freedom to determine the company's governance structure.

[564] Companies Act 2006, s 154. [565] ibid s 155.

[566] ibid ss 414, 419, 422. The only other place in the Companies Act where reference is made to the board (as opposed to the individual directors) is as part of the definitions of 'subsidiary', and 'parent undertaking' (ss 1159, 1162).

[567] See, for example, the transactions between the company and a director listed in ss 188–225 of the Companies Act 2006 or the ratification of conduct giving rise to liability pursuant to s 239. The transactions must be approved, and the conduct ratified, by a resolution of the *members*, which may or may not be adopted in general meeting.

[568] PS Atiyah, *The Rise and Fall of Freedom of Contract* (Clarendon Press 1979) 562–8. The formative years of UK company law were probably the decades between the adoption of the Joint Stock Companies Registration and Regulation Act of 1844 and the Companies Act 1862, which consolidated several acts regulating different types of company and introduced model articles annexed to the Act.

[569] The Bubble Act was adopted as a reaction to the speculation in the stock of the South Sea Company, which enjoyed a monopoly of the trade to South America. The investment frenzy was fuelled by extravagant rumours about the prospects of the company and left many investors ruined after the bubble burst in 1720. For a brief description of the boom of 1719–1720 and the Bubble Act, see WS Holdsworth, *A History of English Law, vol VIII* (Methuen 1925) 212–13, 218–21.

[570] See the account by BC Hunt, *The development of the business corporation in England, 1800-1867* (Harvard University Press 1936) 9–13.

by means of a deed of settlement executed between the shareholders and one or several trustees. In regulations governing the association, set out in the deed, they approximated the features of an incorporated body. Shares were made transferrable, the management of the enterprise was vested in directors, and the directors held business assets as trustees.[571] The Joint Stock Companies Registration and Regulation Act of 1844, the first modern corporation law of the UK, recognized the need to increase legal certainty by giving the unincorporated enterprises the recognition of the law. The regulatory philosophy of the Act of 1844 was not to supplant the pre-existing legal forms of business association by a comprehensive and binding new legal framework for corporations. Rather, the law sought to protect the public by improving publicity. It allowed incorporation by registration, requiring, inter alia, the filing of the deed of settlement and the production of audited accounts.[572]

The *laissez-faire* approach of UK company law is now exemplified by the interaction between the binding company legislation and the company's articles of association. The Companies Act 2006 does not decide between the one-tier or two-tier board structure, but the Model Articles for Public and Private Companies, which can, of course, be altered by the members, are based on the one-tier model. Pursuant to the Model Articles, executive power is vested in the board of directors.[573] The directors may delegate their powers to individual managers or committees.[574] The Model Articles contain detailed rules on directors' decision-making.[575] However, they, or the Companies Act, do not provide for any mechanism to control the (executive) directors, either through a separate corporate organ or the imposition of requirements regarding the composition of the board of directors. The reason is that English company law expects the shareholders to perform the function of controlling the executives. This intention is expressed in provisions that furnish the shareholders with the right to intervene in the directors' decision-making[576] or remove the directors at any time with or without cause.[577]

At least in widely held corporations it is questionable whether shareholder control rights alone are sufficient to prevent self-serving behaviour of managers. Therefore, a third level of regulation (in addition to binding company legislation and the articles of association) can be found in the UK Corporate Governance Code, which has introduced mechanisms designed to address conflicts of interest at the board level. The Code seeks to ensure a balance of power on the board so that no one individual or group of persons can abuse their decision-making authority.[578] To that effect, the Code employs in particular three strategies. First, it stipulates that the roles of chief executive and chairman of the board must be separated.[579] Secondly, it requires an 'appropriate' number of directors to be independent.[580] Finally, decisions that

[571] G Morse (ed), *Palmer's Company Law* (Sweet & Maxwell 2018) 1.103. For a more detailed description see AB DuBois, *The English Business Company after the Bubble Act, 1720-1800* (The Commonwealth Fund 1938) 215–42; FW Maitland, 'Trust and Corporation' in FW Maitland (ed), *Selected Essays* (CUP 1936) 208–13.

[572] Hunt (n 570) 94–7. For a comprehensive review of the 1844 Act, see RR Formoy, *The Historical Foundations of Modern Company Law* (Sweet & Maxwell 1923) 67–83.

[573] Model Articles for Public Companies, Art 3; Model Articles for Private Companies, Art 3.

[574] Model Articles for Public Companies, Art 5; Model Articles for Private Companies, Art 5.

[575] The directors decide either at a meeting or in the form of written resolutions (Model Articles for Public Companies, Art 7; Model Articles for Private Companies, Art 7). Meetings may be called by any director by giving notice to the directors (Model Articles for Public Companies, Art 8; Model Articles for Private Companies, Art 9). Decisions are generally taken by majority vote (Model Articles for Public Companies, Art 13; Model Articles for Private Companies, Art 7(1)) at a meeting where a quorum is present (Model Articles for Public Companies, Art 10(1); Model Articles for Private Companies, Art 11(1)). The quorum is two, unless otherwise determined by a decision of the directors (Model Articles for Public Companies, Art 10(2); Model Articles for Private Companies, Art 11(2)).

[576] Model Articles for Public Companies, Art 4(1); Model Articles for Private Companies, Art 4.

[577] Companies Act 2006, s 168.

[578] See UK Corporate Governance Code 2018, Principle G: 'The board should include an appropriate combination of executive and non-executive directors (and, in particular, independent non-executive) directors, such that no individual or small group of individuals dominates the board's decision-making'.

[579] ibid Principle G, Provision 9.

[580] ibid Principle G. See section III.1 below.

are particularly prone to conflicts of interest, namely succession planning, determination of the executive directors' remuneration, monitoring the company's financial position, and appointing the external auditor, are allocated to board committees composed of a majority of, or exclusively of, independent non-executive directors.[581] In this way, the UK system approximates a separation of management and control functions, albeit in a less rigid way than two-tier models.

2. *US*

In contrast to UK law, the company laws of the United States, for example the General Corporation Law of Delaware, contain several provisions regarding the corporate governance organization of companies, the role and competences of the board of directors, and the rights of shareholders. The laws are based on the one-tier model and they provide that corporations must be managed by or under the direction of a board of directors.[582] However, in most corporations, it is not the board that determines day-to-day business operations, but the senior executives, to whom power is delegated in the certificate of incorporation or, more commonly, the by-laws. The board retains the power to suspend or remove officers at any time with or without cause. Given that traditionally only the highest-ranking officers are members of the boards of US corporations, and the majority of board members are company outsiders,[583] we can speak of a separation between operational decision-making and supervision of management that is similar to the division of functions in UK companies. On the other hand, the possibilities of US shareholders to shape the corporate governance structure of the company or influence the decision-making of directors and managers are more limited than in UK companies. While the incorporators are free to alter the governance arrangements in the articles or in shareholder agreements,[584] the prominent position of the default rules in the corporation statute, rather than in the model articles, is an indication of the more rigid design of US corporate governance. In addition, we will see in the next chapter that contractual freedom to provide for non-traditional forms of corporate governance in shareholder agreements is restricted in the United States, certainly if compared with English law.[585]

Once the governance arrangements have been put in place, they can generally not be changed unilaterally by the shareholders. The certificate of incorporation can only be amended if the board of directors first adopts a resolution setting out the proposed amendment.[586] The shareholders have the power to amend or repeal the by-laws without prior board resolution, but they have to call a special meeting in order to do so (or wait for the annual general meeting) and comply with the SEC's proxy rules, which may involve substantial costs.[587] Apart from their right to elect the directors and amend the articles or by-laws, the competences of the shareholders are confined to voting on structural changes. A precondition for shareholder action is generally a resolution of the board of directors approving the proposed change. The allocation of competences and the lack of a shareholder right of initiative are laid down as default or mandatory rules in the corporation laws.[588] The picture

[581] Section III.1. [582] Del. Gen. Corp. Law, §141(a); MBCA, §8.01(b).

[583] This is now also enshrined in regulation, see for example NYSE Listed Company Manual, Rule 303A.02, requiring listed companies to have a majority of independent directors.

[584] See eg Del. Gen. Corp. Law, §141(a): '... except as may be otherwise provided in ... [the company's] certificate of incorporation'; MBCA, §8.01(b): '... subject to any limitation set forth in the articles of incorporation or in an agreement authorized under section 7.32 [shareholder agreements]'.

[585] See Chapter 5A.II.

[586] Del. Gen. Corp. Law, §242(b); MBCA, §10.03. For a more detailed discussion, see Chapter 5A.II.

[587] MBCA, §10.20. The SEC's proxy rules are contained in Exchange Act Regulation 14A. We will discuss the proxy rules in Chapter 5C.II.2.

[588] Del. Gen. Corp. Law, §§251 (mergers), 271 (sale of assets), 275 (dissolution); MBCA, §§11.04 (mergers), 12.02 (sale of assets), 14.02 (dissolution). Under Delaware law, the shareholders may dissolve the company without board resolution if all shareholders entitled to vote consent in writing, Del. Gen. Corp. Law, §275(c).

is completed by the absence of an important device that exists under UK law to empower shareholders: the right to give instructions to the directors, both with regard to day-to-day operational decisions and strategic policy-making.[589]

Why does private ordering play a less prominent role in US than UK corporate governance? The identification of causal factors determining the trajectory of legal evolution poses significant challenges, given the large number of potential explanatory variables, but we may offer some conjectures. Large-scale industrial activity began in the United States only in the second half of the nineteenth century, after the development of the railroad and telegraph system made nation-wide trade possible.[590] Until about 1850, most enterprises were sufficiently small to be operated in the form of partnerships. Equity investors did not require the protection of limited liability because they had full control over business operations: 'Owners managed and managers owned'.[591] The railways and other capital-intensive businesses such as mines or enterprises for the construction of bridges and canals were among the first to make use of the corporate form. In the manufacturing sector, corporations became widespread only towards the end of the nineteenth century.[592] Consequently, entrepreneurs in the United States never operated in an environment that was shaped by the Bubble Act's hostility to incorporations, and the legislator was not confronted with the social fact of contractually designed corporate governance arrangements that were used widely to circumvent restrictive legislation.[593] When increases in the size and scale of businesses created a greater demand for incorporation by registration, the state legislatures responded fast and enacted general corporation laws.[594] These laws were modelled after the charters of publicly held corporations,[595] which arguably predetermined the development of US corporate law in two important respects. First, the laws established the main features of the US corporate governance system that we are familiar with today: a strong centralized authority of the board of directors and relatively limited competences of the shareholders, who were already fairly dispersed in some industries at that time.[596] Secondly, the rules were mandatory.[597] Arguably, these two features set US corporate law on a different path from UK law.[598]

[589] See n 576 above for the position in the UK. [590] Chandler (n 44) 53. [591] ibid.

[592] Berle and Means (n 30) 11–17.

[593] Some scholars have argued that the uncertain and time-consuming process of incorporation by charter or special act before the adoption of the general corporation laws prompted entrepreneurs to form so-called 'joint stock associations'. These associations were comparable to deed of settlement companies. They were technically partnerships, but the partners sought to replace a number of particularly cumbersome features of partnership law (eg the lack of free transferability of shares, limited existence of the association that ended with the death of a partner, or the requirement to sue in the names of all partners) by employing concepts of trust law. However, in contrast to the situation in the UK, the use of non-chartered associations did not seem to have been common, but was restricted to the land merchandising industry. For a more comprehensive analysis of the joint stock association in the US, see HL Sowards and JS Mofsky, 'Factors Affecting the Development of Corporation Law' (1968–1969) 23 University of Miami Law Review 476, 481–91.

[594] New Jersey is commonly credited with the adoption of the first modern corporation law in 1875 (Rev. Stat. 1875, 175). The state became attractive to incorporations especially with an amendment in 1891 that allowed corporations to hold stock in other corporations and issue its own stock as payment, and with further liberalizing reforms in 1896. For an annotated version of the N.J. Gen. Corp. Law of 1896, see JB Dill, *The Statutory and Case Law Applicable to Private Companies under the General Corporation Act of New Jersey and Corporation Precedents* (3rd edn, Baker, Voorhis & Co 1901). New Jersey maintained its leading position until about 1910, when amendments to its own laws and the recent adoption of a liberal corporation statute in Delaware (Act of 9 March 1899, 21 Del. Laws ch 273) meant that incorporations shifted to the latter state, see C Grandy, 'New Jersey Corporate Chartermongering, 1875-1929' (1989) 49 Journal of Economic History 677, 687–9; J Seligman, 'A Brief History of Delaware's General Corporation Law of 1899' (1976) 1 Delaware Journal of Corporate Law 249, 270. For data on the state of incorporation of industrial companies listed on the New York Stock Exchange and Curb Exchange (which later became the American Stock Exchange) from 1850–1931, see RC Larcom, *The Delaware Corporation* (Johns Hopkins Press 1937) 175–6.

[595] HG Manne, 'Our Two Corporation Systems: Law and Economics' (1967) 53 Virginia Law Review 259, 276–7.

[596] Berle and Means (n 30) 11–13.

[597] Mandatory rules designed with the public corporation in mind made the new general corporation laws ill-suited to smaller corporations that would have benefited from more flexible governance arrangements and led to the later adoption of closed corporation statutes; see Manne (n 595) 277.

[598] We will discuss these questions in detail in Chapter 5A.

3. Germany

The German Stock Corporation Act regulates the corporate governance structure of the public company in considerable detail.[599] According to the relevant rules, which can only be altered in the articles of association if explicitly provided for in the Act,[600] public companies must have a management board and a supervisory board. The Stock Corporation Act distinguishes between the overall direction of the affairs of the company[601] and the responsibility for the day-to-day business operations.[602] Both tasks are assigned to the management board. The management board discharges its functions under its own responsibility. It represents the company in and out of court.[603] In relation to third parties, the board's authority cannot be restricted, although the articles, the supervisory board, or the general meeting may limit the authority internally, provided this is permitted by law.[604] Accordingly, transactions entered into in disregard of the internal limitations are generally valid, but the directors may be liable to the company for breach of their duties. These rules are an expression of the board's independence from the general meeting. Since a sweeping corporate law reform of 1937, the directors' powers are perceived to derive from the statute.[605] They are not delegated by the shareholders and, consequently, cannot be restricted by them at will, nor can the shareholders give the directors instructions.[606] The general meeting decides only on matters expressly provided for by the Stock Corporation Act,[607] or if requested to do so by the management board.[608]

The supervisory board is largely a control organ that participates in the management of the company only in limited circumstances. It meets at least two times per half-year.[609] Its main tasks are the appointment and removal of the members of the management board and the supervision of the company's management.[610] In order to be able to perform its

[599] In Book I, Part IV (§§76–147).

[600] For a discussion of this principle see Chapter 5A.III. The shareholders of the private limited company (GmbH) have more flexibility in devising the corporate governance structure of their corporation. The law only requires that the corporation shall have one or more managing directors (GmbHG [Limited Liability Companies Act], §6) and it defines the competences, rights and duties of the directors (§§35–44) and the general meeting (§§45–51b). The limited company may, but does not need to, have a supervisory board (§52), unless the company has generally more than 2,000 employees. In that case, the MitbestG [Co-Determination Act], §§1(1), 6, requires the establishment of a supervisory board responsible for the appointment and removal of the managing directors. Additional evidence of the increased contractual freedom in the limited liability company is the flexibility that the shareholders enjoy in determining the composition and competences of the supervisory board, if the articles of association provide for such an organ. While some limits exist (eg the Higher Regional Court Frankfurt invalidated the appointment of the same person as managing director and member of the supervisory board, arguing that it was 'a binding organisational principle that these two roles were incompatible': see OLG Frankfurt, GmbHR 1982, 159), the shareholders are generally free to deviate from the default rules in the act (GmbHG, §52).

[601] 'Leitung der Aktiengesellschaft', AktG, §76(1).

[602] 'Geschäftsführung', AktG, §77.

[603] ibid §78(1).

[604] ibid §82. Because of the binding nature of most provisions of German stock corporation law, the scope for a limitation of the management board's authority is narrow. The acts of the directors must fall within the objects of the company as prescribed by the articles of association (§23(3), no 2). However, the shareholders cannot formulate the objects in a way that would effectively remove all managerial discretion. The general meeting and the supervisory board are bound by the allocation of competences between the different corporate organs as laid down in the Stock Corporation Act. As a consequence, they can only impose restrictions within the meaning of §82(2) if the Act grants these organs the authority to make decisions in the first place (see the discussion in the text). The management board can also establish internal limitations by adopting by-laws that determine individual portfolios of the members of the board.

[605] Gesetz über Aktiengesellschaften und Kommanditgesellschaften auf Aktien (Aktiengesetz) of 30 January 1937, RGBl I, 107. For an analysis of the reform, see FA Mann, 'The New German Company Law and Its Background' (1937) 19 Journal of Comparative Legislation and International Law 220.

[606] This is derived from §§76(1), 119(2) AktG. For a discussion, see K Schmidt, *Gesellschaftsrecht* (4th edn, Carl Heymanns 2002) §28 II 1 a.

[607] The most important shareholder decision rights are enumerated in §119(1) AktG, which we will examine in Chapter 5A.III.

[608] ibid §119(2).

[609] ibid §110(3).

[610] ibid §§84, 111(1). A violation of the duties by the members of the supervisory board leads to liability comparable to that of the members of the management board, §§116, 93. We will discuss liability questions in Chapter 6B.I.3 and the appointment and removal of directors in Chapter 5D.

supervisory duties effectively, the supervisory board may, inter alia, inspect and examine the books and records of the company,[611] call a general meeting whenever the interests of the company so require,[612] require a report from the management board on the affairs of the company,[613] and issue by-laws for the conduct of business by the management board.[614]

In certain situations, the supervisory board enjoys powers going beyond its control function. In particular, the supervisory board concludes the contract with the external auditor on behalf of the company[615] and acts when conflicts of interest call into question the ability of the members of the management board to adopt disinterested decisions. Most importantly, the supervisory board determines the remuneration of the management board members[616] and assumes the power to represent the company in transactions with the managers or enforce the company's claims against them.[617] In addition, the Stock Corporation Act envisages that certain types of transaction, as specified in the articles of association or determined by the supervisory board, require the authorization of the supervisory board.[618] Whether the management board should be required to obtain the supervisory board's consent was initially at the discretion of the drafters of the articles and the supervisory board itself. Since 2002, the Stock Corporation Act provides that some transactions *must* be authorized by the supervisory board.[619] The act does not specify what types of transaction are caught by the provision, but the aims that the legislator pursued with the reform can give some guidance. The amendment intends to strengthen the preventative aspects of the supervisory board's control function and ensure that the board is involved in decisions that are particularly important for the company, for example determining the company's business strategy or deciding on significant investment projects.[620] The German Corporate Governance Code now states that approval of the supervisory board will be required for decisions 'that fundamentally change the company's net assets, financial status or results of operations'.[621] It is part of the duties of the members of the supervisory board to identify the transactions that satisfy these criteria and to make sure that they are involved in the decision-making process. On the other hand, the approval requirement must not be used to change the governance structure of the stock corporation and divest the management board of its statutory powers to manage the company.[622] The supervisory board would exceed its competences if it formulated the consent requirement in an overly broad way, for example by stipulating that 'all important transactions' required the board's approval. The description of the relevant transactions in general terms, such as 'all property or credit transactions that exceed a specified limit', however, is permissible.[623] If the supervisory board refuses to grant its consent, the management board may refer the matter to the general meeting. The general meeting can overrule the supervisory board by adopting a resolution with qualified majority of three-quarters of the votes cast.[624]

This fairly clear separation between the management and supervisory boards, both functionally and personally, goes back to the legal reforms of 1937. Initially, the internal governance structure of the corporation was a matter for the shareholders to decide in the company's

611 AktG, §111(2). 612 ibid §111(3). 613 ibid §90(3). 614 ibid §77(2).

615 ibid §111(2) third sentence. Contracting with the auditor needs to be distinguished from the act of appointing the auditor for purposes of company law, which falls within the powers of the general meeting pursuant to §119(1), no 4. Generally, the authority to enter into contracts on behalf of the company is part of the powers of the management board, which traditionally included hiring an auditor. A legal reform of 1998 (Gesetz zur Kontrolle und Transparenz im Unternehmensbereich (KonTraG) [Control and Transparency in the Corporate Sector Act] of 1 May 1998, BGBl I, 786, Art 1, no 12) transferred this power to the supervisory board in order to strengthen the independence of the auditor.

616 AktG, §87. 617 ibid §112. We will analyse this provision in Chapter 6C.I.3.

618 ibid §111(4) sentence 2.

619 The provision was amended by Transparenz- und Publizitätsgesetz (TransPuG) [Transparency and Publicity Act] of 19 July 2002, BGBl I, 2010.

620 BT-Drs [Journal of the Federal Parliament] 14/8769, 17.

621 Corporate Governance Code 2017, s 3.3. 622 See text to nn 601–602 above.

623 Hüffer and Koch (n 409) §111, paras 41, 43. 624 AktG, §111(4) sentences 3–4.

statutes.[625] The law only prescribed that the corporation had to have a management board[626] and sketched the composition, rights, and duties of the board mostly by way of default rules.[627] The founders were not required to provide for a supervisory board; if they did so, they had wide discretion in shaping the powers of that board and the relationship between the supervisory board and the other corporate organs.[628] The two-tier governance structure was made mandatory in 1870, but without specifying the rights and duties of the supervisory board.[629] The main function of the supervisory board, as envisaged by the law, was, of course, the supervision of the corporation's management.[630] However, because of the largely unfettered contractual freedom of the founders, the majority shareholders were able to confer broad management powers on the supervisory board, place their nominees on that board and arrange for inexperienced or acquiescent individuals to be appointed to the management board.[631] In this way, the supervisory board often became the real centre of power in the corporation. It was often authorized to direct the management board in operational matters, implemented the wishes of the majority shareholders, and was not subject to control by any other organ.[632] This development was seen as problematic, because it allowed the majority shareholders to acquire a dominant position and ensure that the business was run exclusively in their interest. It explains the abrupt shift away from contractual freedom to a mandatory governance structure with a binding delineation of the competences of the management board, supervisory board, and general meeting in the Stock Corporation Act of 1937.[633]

4. *France*

The organizational structure of the public stock corporation (*société anonyme*) is determined in a binding and fairly detailed way in the Commercial Code.[634] Historically, all stock corporations had to have a board of directors (*conseil d'administration*), whose members were

[625] This was the situation under the Allgemeines Deutsches Handelsgesetzbuch (ADHGB) [General German Commercial Code] of 1861. See L Pahlow, 'Aktienrecht und Aktiengesellschaft zwischen Revolution und Reichsgründung. Das Allgemeine Deutsche Handelsgesetzbuch von 1861' in W Bayer and M Habersack (eds), *Aktienrecht im Wandel, vol 1: Entwicklungen des Aktienrechts* (Mohr Siebeck 2007) 8/59.

[626] ADHGB 1861, Art 227.

[627] ibid Arts 227–241. For example, Art 227 provided that: '[t]he management board shall consist of one or more members; the members may be paid or unpaid, shareholders or non-shareholders. Their appointment can be revoked at any time, notwithstanding claims arising out of existing contracts'.

[628] The only provision that contained more than a brief reference to the supervisory board was Art 225 ADHGB 1861, which provided, inter alia, that the board shall supervise the management, examine the annual accounts and call a general meeting if the interests of the company so require.

[629] Gesetz betreffend die Kommanditgesellschaften auf Aktien und die Aktiengesellschaften of 11 June 1870 (Erste Aktiennovelle), RGBl, 375, Art 209(6).

[630] See n 628 above and Act of 1870, Art 225a.

[631] KJ Hopt, 'Zur Funktion des Aufsichtsrats im Verhältnis von Industrie und Bankensystem' in N Horn and J Kocka (eds), *Law and the Formation of the Big Enterprises in the 19th and Early 20th Centuries* (Vandenhoeck & Ruprecht 1979) 228–30, 232–3; J Lieder, 'Die 1. Aktienrechtsnovelle vom 11. Juni 1870' in W Bayer and M Habersack (eds), *Aktienrecht im Wandel, vol 1: Entwicklungen des Aktienrechts* (Mohr Siebeck 2007) 10/76–7. Until the reforms of 1937, the law did not entrust any particular organ with the appointment of the members of the management board. This was a matter for the company's articles, which could theoretically provide that both boards were to be elected by the general meeting. However, in practice, it was often the supervisory board that appointed the managers; see A Pinner, *Das Deutsche Aktienrecht* (HW Müller 1899) 129.

[632] The management board was indispensable because it was the organ with authority to represent the corporation with respect to third parties: ADHGB 1861, Art 230. However, by requiring the management board in the articles to carry out all instructions by the supervisory board it could be divested of all management powers and discretion, see Lieder (n 631) 10/77.

[633] For a more detailed discussion of the reforms (including their consequences for the powers of the general meeting, which were mainly restricted to electing the supervisory board and voting on the most important structural changes), see Chapter 5A.III.

[634] This has been the case since the important corporate law reform of 1867 (n 296), which replaced the fragmentary old regime that had left considerable scope for private ordering in the company's statutes (see Code de commerce of 1807, Arts 31, 32). The Law of 1867 remained largely unchanged until the reforms of 1966; see n 538 above.

chosen from among the shareholders and who were entrusted with the management of the company.[635] However, the large, complex business associations that emerged in France at the end of the nineteenth century increasingly required a specialized, professional management. For this reason, in practice, the board became an organ that was generally not concerned with the day-to-day business operations, but assumed the role of setting the general business strategy and taking fundamental corporate decisions. The day-to-day operational business was either carried out by the chairman of the board or a committee of board members, or, more commonly, by a third person (*directeur général*) to whom the board delegated management functions.[636] In this way, a separation of management and control evolved, which is still reflected in the Commercial Code, for example when the Code stipulates that the board 'determines the broad lines of the company's business activities and ensures their implementation',[637] whereas '[t]he general management of the company shall be assumed under [the board's] responsibility by either the chairman of the board of directors or by another natural person appointed by the board of directors and bearing the title of general manager'.[638]

Since 1966, incorporators have been able to choose whether to retain the traditional one-tier board structure or to adopt a governance model that separates the management and control functions of the board of directors formally. In the latter case, the company operates with two boards that have powers similar to the two boards of German public companies, which may accordingly be translated as management (or executive) board (*directoire*) and supervisory board (*conseil de surveillance*).[639] As in the German dual system, which was the model for the 1966 reforms, the supervisory board appoints the members of the management board and determines their remuneration,[640] and the general meeting appoints the members of the supervisory board.[641] The latter exercises its supervisory powers by carrying out the inspections it considers appropriate and may request any relevant documents.[642] In addition, the management board is required to furnish the supervisory board with a quarterly report on the activities of the company and present the accounts to the supervisory board for verification.[643] The supervisory board, in turn, presents a report on the governance of the company and its comments on the directors' report to the general meeting.[644] Finally, again similar to German law, some management powers can be transferred to the supervisory board by providing in the articles of association that certain transactions require the authorization of the supervisory board.[645] If a member of the management board is interested in a transaction with the company, either directly or indirectly (for example because the director owns or participates in the management of another company that transacts with the director's company), a complex authorization procedure is set in motion that involves obtaining the prior consent of the supervisory board.[646]

[635] Code de commerce of 1867, Art 22.

[636] N Horn, 'Aktienrechtliche Unternehmensorganisation in der Hochindustrialisierung (1860-1920): Deutschland, England, Frankreich und die USA im Vergleich' in N Horn and J Kocka (eds), *Law and the Formation of the Big Enterprises in the 19th and Early 20th Centuries* (Vandenhoeck & Ruprecht 1979) 123, 146. However, as we noted above, the transition from 'personal' to 'managerial capitalism' (to use the taxonomy of Chandler (n 44) 12) was probably slower in France than in the US, UK, or Germany, and the largest French businesses of the late nineteenth and early twentieth centuries were neither as large, nor did they have organizational structures that were as sophisticated as the leading enterprises in the other three countries; see Fridenson (n 446) 213–17, and text to n 530.

[637] Com, Art L225-35. Translation by Legifrance, https://www.legifrance.gouv.fr/Traductions/en-English/Legifrance-translations.

[638] ibid Art L225-51-1. Translation by Legifrance, https://www.legifrance.gouv.fr/Traductions/en-English/Legifrance-translations.

[639] The organization of the stock corporation under the one-tier model is laid down in Arts L225-17 to L225-56 of the Code de commerce and the two-tier model in Arts L225-57 to L225-93.

[640] Com, Arts L225-59. [641] ibid Art L225-75. [642] ibid Art L225-68, para 3.

[643] ibid Art L225-68, paras 4, 5. [644] ibid Art L225-68, para 6. [645] ibid Art L225-68, para 2.

[646] ibid Art L225-86. The consent requirement does not apply if the agreement can be qualified as an 'ordinary transaction' entered into under normal conditions, Art L225-87. The law requires, further, that the auditors

In spite of the influence that the German dual board model had on the French reforms of 1966, an important difference exists. The position of the French supervisory board can be defined to large extent contractually. If the drafters of the articles so desire, the supervisory board can be vested with far-reaching managerial powers, for example the power to appoint the officers (*directeurs généraux*) or intervene in management decisions.[647] Therefore, the distinction between the management board and the supervisory board may become rather blurred. This illustrates the prominent role that the principle of contractual freedom continues to play in French company law,[648] in stark contrast to German law on the public stock corporation.[649] The greater involvement of the members of the supervisory board in management matters may have consequences for their responsibility, but it is not illegal per se.[650]

In 2001, the law introduced a further differentiation and now requires companies with a one-tier board to either combine the roles of chairman and general manager in the person of the *président directeur général* (in short *PDG*) or divide the functions by appointing another person as general manager.[651] Thus, French law effectively offers three distinct governance models for public companies: the unitary board structure characterized by a centralization of power at the helm of the company, the unitary board with decentralized power in the form of a separation of the positions of chairman and CEO (general director), and the dual board model. The most common is the first model, but large listed companies increasingly appoint a non-executive chairman of the board or, if the roles are not separated, a senior independent director in response to international best practice standards and the expectations of international investors.[652] The two-tier board model, on the other hand, has not become popular in France. Only a small number of the largest listed companies have opted for it.[653] Even where the roles of chairman of the board and general manager in companies with a unitary board are not exercised by the same person, the separation of functions may suffer from similar defects to those in the German two-tier system.[654] In a number of large listed companies, the *président directeur général*, upon reaching the statutory age limit for the office of general manager,[655] has remained on the board as a non-executive chairman. In

prepare a special report on the transaction and the transaction is submitted to the general meeting for approval, Art L225-88. We will discuss these requirements and the approval process generally in Chapter 6C.I.4.

647 Merle (n 481) para 511. 648 See text to nn 288–320 above. 649 See Chapter 5A.III.

650 Members of the supervisory board are not subject to the general liability provisions applying to directors in the one-tier system and to members of the management board in the two-tier system (Arts L225-249 to L225-255, L225-256). Thus, they are generally not liable for management mistakes, but only 'for negligent or tortious acts committed by them in a personal capacity in the performance of their duties' pursuant to Art L225-257, Cass com, 13 February 1996, *Bull. civ.* IV, no 50, 38. However, depending on the extent of their involvement in the management of the company, they may be qualified as de facto directors (*dirigeants de fait*), Cass com, 12 July 2005, *Rev. sociétés* 2006, 162, note FX Lucas. In this case, they are liable for mismanagement; see n 478 above and accompanying text.

651 Com, Art L225-51-1. This choice was introduced by Law no 2001-420 of 15 May 2001 (n 439), which brought substantial changes in particular for stock-exchange listed companies. Before 2001, it was mandatory to combine the two roles, which had been criticized increasingly with the rise of the corporate governance movement, see Merle (n 481) para 476. The non-executive functions of the chairman of the board are set out in Art L225-51.

652 The French corporate governance code does not require companies to separate the roles of chairman and CEO. It states that '[t]he law does not favour either formula [separation or no separation] and allows the Board of Directors to choose between the two forms of exercise of executive management. It is up to the Board to decide and explain its decision.... The chosen formula and the reasons for this decision are communicated to shareholders and third parties'. See AFEP-MEDEF Corporate Governance Code of Listed Corporations 2018, Arts 3.2, 3.4. The AMF reports that 67% of public companies with a unitary board have not separated the roles of chairman and general manager, but that 56% of these companies have appointed a senior independent directors), AMF Report 2015 (n 424) 53. The figures are based on a sample of listed companies.

653 AMF Report 2015 (n 424) 53 (reporting that 85% of public companies have a unitary board and only 15% a dual board). For an academic discussion of the French board models, see also PL Davies and KJ Hopt, 'Corporate Boards in Europe: Accountability and Convergence' (2013) 61 American Journal of Comparative Law 301, 316.

654 See text to n 555 above.

655 In the absence of a provision to the contrary in the articles, the general manager has to retire at the age of 65, Com, Art L225-54.

addition, it is not uncommon that companies combine the two positions again after a transition period.[656]

If the company choses the unitary board model and the functions of chairman and CEO are divided, the general manager may or may not be a member of the board of directors. The general manager may be assisted by one or more, but not more than five, assistant general managers (*directeurs généraux délégués*).[657] The assistant general managers are appointed by the board of directors upon the proposal of the general manager.[658] They too can, but do not have to be members of the board. Irrespective of their membership of the board, they have the status of an organ of the company and exercise corporate functions.[659] In particular, they are empowered by law to represent the company as against third parties.[660] Often, managerial functions are further delegated to so-called technical directors (*directeurs techniques*). While these may also have the title of director (for example, 'finance director', 'director of production', etc.), they are not directors or general managers in the legal sense and accordingly do not partake in the respective statutory powers.[661]

II. Boards as small groups

In 1951, the social psychologist Salomon Asch published the findings of an experiment designed to study when individuals make independent judgments and when they submit to group pressure.[662] He believed that, if faced with a clearly correct answer, people could be expected to rise above group prejudices and resist external pressure. In the experiment, a group of eight male college students were asked to perform a 'vision test' and compare the length of lines. They were shown two cards, one with a single vertical line and the other with three comparison lines. One of the comparison lines was of the same length as the original line and the other two were substantially different. The subjects had to announce their answers publicly in the order in which they were seated in the room. Unbeknown to one of the participants, the other seven individuals were confederates of the experimenter. They were instructed by the experimenter to give correct answers in the first two rounds of the experiment and then answer incorrectly in unanimity. The participant who was not privy to the arrangement was seated towards the end of the row. He therefore found himself in a position of unanimous opposition when it was his turn to answer. Even though the correct answer was unambiguous, Asch found that participants were increasingly uncomfortable and hesitant in disagreeing with the majority. Some hesitated, were apologetic, or answered in a low voice. Even more astonishingly, while less than 1 per cent of participants made mistakes in matching the lines when they were alone with the experimenter or together with one other participant, the error rates rose dramatically when the subjects were confronted with the wrong judgment of a unanimous group of two or more persons. The experiment also showed that the size of the majority was important. A unanimous majority of two swayed 13.6 per cent of participants. If the majority was increased to three, the percentage of subjects submitting to the majority jumped to 31.8 per cent, and it levelled off at around 37 per cent as the majority was increased further. Disturbing the unanimous majority had

[656] See Merle (n 481) para 470. [657] Com, Art L225-53. [658] ibid.

[659] They are *mandataires sociaux*; see Cozian, Viandier, and Deboissy (n 462) paras 839, 849.

[660] Com, Art L225-56. Internally, the powers of the assistant general managers may be restricted by the board of directors in agreement with the general manager; see Art L225-56, II. Note that the assistant general managers, as opposed to the general manager, are not captured by the provisions establishing civil liability for management mistakes (Art L225-251). See Chapter 6B.I.4(a).

[661] Cozian, Viandier, and Deboissy (n 462) para 839.

[662] SE Asch, 'Effects of group pressure upon the modification and distortion of judgments' in H Guetzkow (ed), *Groups, Leadership and Men* (Carnegie Press 1951) 177. The experiment is also described in SE Asch, 'Opinions and Social Pressure' (1955) 193 Scientific American 31.

an equally striking effect. Even if only one other person dissented together with the naïve subject, the rate of agreement dropped to one-quarter of what it had been with a unanimous majority. These findings are powerful testimony to the tendency of people to conform to widely accepted norms and opinions. We seek to avoid being regarded as different or deviant and behave in a way that we think will meet with the approval of others. Other studies found that the pressure to conform depended on a variety of factors, including cultural background,[663] membership of a group that competed with other groups,[664] and status and expertise of those who expressed their opinion first.[665] For our purposes, this means that assertive leadership and the forceful expression of an opinion by a small group of persons with expert knowledge, such as the executives on a board of directors, may prevent other members of the board from voicing criticism or refusing to support decisions they disagree with.

Research in social psychology has identified a second behavioural pattern that may arise in small groups and hold lessons for our topic, the question of how to structure the deliberations of corporate boards in ways that avoid poor decision-making. It is widely acknowledged that deliberating groups perform a useful function by facilitating the exchange of ideas and competing views, which will often lead to better outcomes and indeed underpins the political ideal of a 'deliberative democracy'. However, groups can also succumb to dynamics that result in polarization and the convergence on extreme viewpoints not held by the individual group members before the deliberations began.[666] This phenomenon is often called 'groupthink', after an influential book by the psychologist Irving Janis, who analysed why certain foreign policy decisions ended in disaster.[667] He argued that groupthink is likely to arise when the following structural and procedural factors are present in the deliberating group: a high degree of cohesiveness; insulation of the group from expert opinions and information that calls into question the assumptions of the group members; a leader who uses his or her power and status to influence decision-making, instead of encouraging open inquiry and critical evaluation in an impartial manner; lack of established procedures to deal with the decision-making tasks; and pressure to reach a decision quickly.[668] If these conditions are present, the group members tend to overestimate the power and inherent morality of the group, experience pressures towards uniformity, which involve self-censorship of deviations from the apparent group consensus, an illusion of unanimity and appeals to loyalty and shared commitments to suppress dissent, and the failure to examine risks and alternatives properly.[669] Of course, the insights of groupthink derive from an analysis of decision-making in the political sphere, and they should be applied to management decisions with caution. Indeed, later research found that management success was positively correlated with some symptoms of groupthink, notably cohesiveness of the management team and strong, opinionated leadership.[670] Nevertheless, other

[663] R Bond and PB Smith, 'Culture and conformity: A meta-analysis of studies using Asch's (1952b, 1956) line judgment task' (1996) 119 Psychological Bulletin 111 (finding that collectivist countries tend to show higher levels of conformity than individualist countries).

[664] M Deutsch and HB Gerard, 'A study of normative and informational social influences upon individual judgment' (1955) 51 Journal of Abnormal and Social Psychology 629.

[665] CA Kiesler and SB Kiesler, *Conformity* (Addison-Wesley 1969) 24–39.

[666] CR Sunstein, 'Deliberating trouble? Why groups go to extremes' (2000) 110 Yale Law Journal 71, 73–5.

[667] IL Janis, *Groupthink: Psychological Studies of Policy Decisions and Fiascoes* (2nd edn, Wadsworth 1982). Janis presented four case studies of US foreign policy fiascos, on which his analysis of groupthink was based: the Bay of Pigs invasion of 1961 by a brigade of Cuban exiles, who were aided by the US navy, air force, and the CIA, the attempt to occupy North Korea in 1950, the failure to respond to warnings that a Japanese attack on Pearl Harbour was imminent, and the decision to escalate the Vietnam War.

[668] ibid 176–7. [669] ibid 174–5.

[670] RS Peterson and others, 'Group Dynamics in Top Management Teams: Groupthink, Vigilance, and Alternative Models of Organizational Failure and Success' (1998) 73 Organizational Behavior and Human Decision Processes 272, 291–2. See also M Harris and A Raviv, 'A Theory of Board Control and Size' (2008) 21 Review of Financial Studies 1797 (developing a model showing that an insider-controlled board can be value-increasing compared with a less cohesive board controlled by outsiders).

research attributed some high-profile corporate failures, for example the Enron scandal, to the groupthink phenomenon.[671] They pointed out that many scandal-ridden companies, including Enron, were exemplary in complying with corporate governance best practice standards, but corporate boards still failed to detect and prevent egregious misconduct.[672] The reason, they argued, was that corporate governance reform at the time was not sufficiently responsive to the cognitive biases that compromised the performance of boards. For example, instead of simply focussing on the independence of non-executive directors, they suggested that it was important to institutionalize processes that could be expected to reduce cohesiveness, introduce a variety of opinions, and change the self-perception of directors as having to promote consensus and avoid behaviour that others may interpret as disloyal. A powerful mechanism to achieve some of these goals is the designation of one director as devil's advocate, ideally with a different director performing the role at each board meeting.[673] It has also been argued that more diversity on boards—notably racial and gender diversity—would broaden the values, experiences, and temperaments represented in the boardroom and thus address one of the main causes of groupthink, the highly cohesive nature of traditional corporate boards.[674]

In the next section, we will revisit these questions and consider whether the current regulatory framework is sufficiently well designed to encourage open debate and avoid the pitfalls of conformity and groupthink.

III. Board composition

The composition of the board of directors is typically regulated in a fragmentary way in binding company legislation. In some cases, the legislation simply lays down the minimum number of directors on the board.[675] Legislation that is more elaborate also sets out eligibility requirements that directors have to satisfy, but even such legislation will leave many questions of board composition open, ranging from the overall size of the board to the requirement to appoint independent directors, form board committees, or separate the positions of chairman and CEO. These questions may be addressed in the company's articles of association, and they are increasingly also regulated by best practice rules laid down in corporate governance codes. In addition to basic rules on board structure, notably the size of the board and the qualifications of directors, we will focus on four areas that have received much attention in policy circles in recent years: the split between executive and non-executive directors, attempts to safeguard the independence of the non-executive directors who are entrusted with supervising the executives, the delegation of certain issues to board committees and the composition of these committees, and increased gender diversity on corporate boards. Some of these reform initiatives, arguably, are of central importance if we consider the high cohesiveness of corporate boards as a problem and seek to promote open, critical discussions in the boardroom that are not dominated by the CEO or the executive directors.

[671] MA O'Connor, 'The Enron Board: The Perils of Groupthink' (2002–2003) 71 University of Cincinnati Law Review 1233, 1261–93; NF Sharpe, 'Process Over Structure: An Organizational Behavior Approach to Improving Corporate Boards' (2012) 85 Southern California Law Review 261, 286–8. See also MB Dorff, 'The Group Dynamics Theory of Executive Compensation' (2007) 28 Cardozo Law Review 2025, 2035–242 (explaining the failure of boards to rein in executive compensation partly with groupthink).

[672] Sharpe (n 671) 263–4.

[673] O'Connor (n 671) 1304–306. This suggestion was initially made by Janis (n 667) 267–8. However, Janis also points out that the use of devil's advocate can become 'ritualised' and merely serve the purpose of proving for the record that decisions were taken after a thorough debate.

[674] O'Connor (n 671) 1306–14.

[675] Of our four jurisdictions, this is the case in the UK, as we will discuss presently.

1. UK

One of the most parsimonious company law statutes with regard to corporate governance is the UK Companies Act 2006, which only provides that a private company must have at least one director and a public company two directors.[676] The act does not prescribe any qualifications for directors, except for the requirement that at least one director must be a natural person and directors must have attained a certain minimum age.[677] Virtually all rules on board composition are to be found in the UK Corporate Governance Code, thus emphasizing the contractual freedom that still permeates UK company law[678] and reinforcing the belief of the policy-maker in a corporate governance regime with 'in-built flexibility for companies to adapt their practices to take into account their particular circumstances'.[679] The best practice standards pioneered by the Cadbury Code—the division of responsibilities at the helm of the company, a 'sufficient' number of non-executive directors on the board, independence of some directors, and the establishment of board committees[680]—have been maintained and formulated more stringently by successive editions of the UK Corporate Governance Code. The Code now requires the roles of chairman and chief executive officer to be separated[681] and, in addition, prohibits the CEO from becoming chairman of the same company.[682] These best practice standards intend to minimize the risk that a pre-existing relationship between the chairman and the executive directors compromises the chairman's ability to lead an open-ended discussion in the boardroom and mediate, if necessary, in a constructive and objective manner between different views. In order to facilitate the expression of dissenting opinions, the Code also envisages that companies designate a 'senior independent director' who acts as an intermediary if concerns exist that cannot be resolved through communications with the chairman, CEO, or other executive directors.[683] The non-executive directors are also expected to meet regularly without the executives, both with the chairman and, led by the senior independent director, without the chairman to appraise the chairman's performance.[684] These requirements go some way towards incorporating the insights from social psychology and the theory of small groups that we discussed in the previous section.[685] In order to prevent group dynamics and opinionated leadership from stifling debate, it is important to break up cohesive groups and provide for an environment that encourages those who disagree with the opinion leaders to speak up. Ultimately, the success of this strategy, of course, still depends on the individuals involved, but regulation can play a meaningful role in ensuring that an appropriate institutional setting is in place.

Furthermore, the Corporate Governance Code provides that the board of directors should have a 'combination of skills, experience and knowledge' and should consist of 'an appropriate combination of executive and non-executive (and, in particular, independent non-executive) directors'.[686] These rather vague statements are part of the code's principles. They are binding on companies incorporated in the UK and with a premium listing of equity shares. The general statements are rendered more precise, and the company's compliance with them more easily verifiable, by 'code provisions'[687] stipulating that at least half

[676] Companies Act 2006, s 154.

[677] ibid ss 155, 157(1). Changes introduced by the Small Business, Enterprise and Employment Act 2015 s 87 will require all directors to be natural persons: Companies Act 2006, s 156A(1). These changes have not yet entered into force.

[678] See section E.I.1 above.

[679] Corporate Governance Code 2016, 2.

[680] See text to nn 359–366.

[681] Corporate Governance Code 2018, Provision 9.

[682] ibid. The Code further stipulates that if 'exceptionally, this [a chief executive becoming chairman] is proposed by the board, major shareholders should be consulted ahead of appointment. The board should set out its reasons to all shareholders at the time of the appointment and also publish these on the company website': ibid. The role of the chairman is described in Principle F.

[683] ibid Provision 12.

[684] ibid Provisions 12, 13.

[685] See section E.II.

[686] Corporate Governance Code 2018, Principles G, K.

[687] See the text to nn 390–393 above for a discussion of the difference between 'principles' and 'code provisions'.

the board, excluding the chairman, should be non-executive directors.[688] In addition, these directors (and the chairman of the board) are required to be independent. Independence is defined somewhat ambivalently in the Code.[689] On the one hand, the corporate governance code provides for a list of clearly defined circumstances that are regarded as likely to impair independence, including the absence of family ties and material business relationships with the company, no receipt of performance-based remuneration, and no cross-directorships.[690] Further, the code stipulates that an independent director must not have been an employee of the company within the last five years, represent a significant shareholder, or have served on the board for more than nine years.[691]

On the other hand, even where one or more of these circumstances apply, the board may determine that the non-executive director is independent, provided the board provides 'a clear explanation'.[692] How should the requirement to provide 'a clear explanation' be understood? Technically, a board that gives reasons why a director is seen as independent, although one or more of the criteria laid down in the Code are not satisfied, is in compliance with the code provision, since the board is allowed to deviate from the list of independence criteria within the provision (and not only by virtue of the comply-or-explain principle).[693] Consequently, on this reading, the board is not required to identify the provision as one it has not complied with, and give reasons for the non-compliance, in the annual report. Giving an explanation in a different form, for example by circulating a statement to the existing shareholders, is sufficient, although presumably such a statement does not result in the same level of transparency as disclosure in the annual report.

Finally, as we mentioned above, the Corporate Governance Code recommends that companies establish three committees: a nomination committee, an audit committee, and a remuneration committee.[694] These three committees were already identified as particularly important in the Cadbury Report.[695] However, the Code of Best Practice that was appended to the Report only referred to the remuneration and audit committees and did not make use of the concept of 'independent' director to insulate the committees from management influence.[696] This was changed with the Combined Code on Corporate Governance of 2003, which required the nomination committee to be composed of a majority, and the remuneration and audit committees entirely, of independent non-executive directors.[697] In addition, at least one member of the audit committee must have relevant financial experience.[698] Thus, we can again observe a strengthening of the requirements in successive corporate governance codes. Over time, the UK codes have become both more detailed and more prescriptive. We will see that a similar development has occurred in other countries.

[688] Corporate Governance Code 2018, Provision 11.

[689] This was already the case in the Cadbury Code; see text to nn 367–368 above.

[690] Corporate Governance Code 2018, Provision 10.

[691] ibid. The Corporate Governance Code does not define the term 'significant shareholder', but the definition in the Listing Rules, LR 11.1.4A, may be used as guidance; see Kershaw (n 232) 259. The Listing Rules stipulate that 'related party' for purposes of the regulation of related party transactions includes a 'substantial shareholder', which is 'any person who is entitled to exercise, or to control the exercise of, 10% or more of the votes able to be cast on all or substantially all matters at general meetings of the company'.

[692] Corporate Governance Code 2018, Provision 10.

[693] Kershaw (n 232) 258.

[694] Corporate Governance Code 2018, Provisions 17, 24, 32.

[695] Notes 364–366 above.

[696] Cadbury Code of Best Practice, ss 3.3, 4.3. The Report explained that sub-committees of the board should be composed of 'a minimum of three non-executive directors' and 'two of the three should be independent in the terms set out in the [report]', para 4.11. The independence requirement was not carried over to the Code of Best Practice, which only required the remuneration and audit committees to consist of non-executive directors.

[697] Combined Code, A.4.1, B.2.1, C.3.1.

[698] ibid C.3.1.

2. US

Board structure regulation in the United States is largely a product of the regulatory activities of the stock exchanges and the federal legislator, whereas state corporate law is similarly permissive to UK law. For example, the Delaware General Corporation Law simply provides that the board of directors is to consist of one or more members and that all of the directors must be natural persons.[699] The Act allows, but does not require, the board to create committees.[700] Other provisions concern the division of the board into several classes,[701] quorum and majority requirements, and procedural questions regarding board meetings.[702] Thus, the directors and shareholders enjoy wide contractual freedom to structure the board as they wish.[703]

However, for certain types of company, the level of regulation is higher. Since the beginning of the 2000s, the New York Stock Exchange and other US securities exchanges have adopted demanding corporate governance regulation applicable to most companies with common equity securities listed on the exchange.[704] As discussed above, these stringent requirements were largely a reaction to Enron and other scandals of the early 2000s.[705] Listed companies are now subject to requirements very similar to the UK Corporate Governance Code. They must have a majority of independent directors.[706] Independence is generally defined as the absence of any 'material relationship[s] with the listed company ([which the director has] either directly or as a partner, shareholder or officer of an organization that has a relationship with the company)'.[707] As in the UK Code, the general definition is supplemented by a list of factors that disqualify a director from being considered independent, including an employment relationship of the director (or an immediate family member, as defined in the corporate governance standards) with the company during the last three years, the receipt of substantial direct compensation from the company other than director fees, and being a partner or employee of the company's auditors.[708] However, two differences to the UK Code are noteworthy. First, if the director does not satisfy any of the criteria enumerated in the listed company manual, he is not independent. The ultimate decision, therefore, does not fall within the discretion of the board. Secondly, being a significant shareholder of the company (and, by extension, representing a significant shareholder) does not bar a finding of independence. The manual explains that the test is concerned with independence from management, not from major shareholders.[709] The difference to the UK is somewhat surprising, because the ownership structure of large listed companies is comparable in the two countries.[710] Arguably, the US approach is more convincing. In block-holder economies where family-owned companies are prevalent, such as many continental European countries, independence from major shareholders is an essential mechanism to protect outside investors. In the United States (and the UK), even significant shareholders tend to be too small to have a dominating influence on the company. A strong voice of the institutional investors on the board can be an important check on management power, which—as we

[699] Del. Gen. Corp. Law, §141(b). [700] ibid §141(c).

[701] ibid §141(d). Boards with several classes of directors (staggered boards) will be discussed in Chapter 5D.

[702] The Act provides that a majority of the total number of directors shall constitute a quorum for the transaction of business and the vote of the majority of the directors present at a meeting shall be the act of the board of directors, unless the certificate of incorporation or the by-laws provide differently, §141(b) Del. Gen. Corp. Law.

[703] Indirectly, state fiduciary law exerts pressure on companies to include independent directors on corporate boards. For example, a committee composed of independent directors may be able to discontinue derivative litigation instigated by shareholders: *Zapata Corp. v Maldonado*, 430 A.2d 779 (Del. 1981). We will discuss this case in Chapter 8C.II.3.

[704] NYSE Listed Company Manual, §303A.00.

[705] Text to n 329 above. Stock exchange regulation had been more permissive before the 2000s; for an overview of the historical evolution, see JN Gordon, 'The Rise of Independent Directors in the United States, 1950-2005: Of Shareholder Value and Stock Market Prices' (2007) 59 Stanford Law Review 1465, 1478–83.

[706] NYSE Listed Company Manual, §303A.01. [707] ibid §303A.02(a)(i).

[708] ibid §303A.02(b). [709] ibid §303A.02(a), Commentary. [710] See section D.IV above.

will see—is considerable in the United States,[711] and can therefore be beneficial to all outside shareholders. In addition, if the threshold of 'significant' or 'substantial shareholder' is set too low, this may reduce the pool of suitable candidates to fill the positions reserved for independent directors.[712]

Another important difference to the UK is the position of the CEO in US companies. The listing manuals of the stock exchanges do not prohibit the combination of the roles of CEO and chairman, thus reflecting common practice in the United States. Accordingly, the listing manuals do not contain any statement regarding the independence of the chairman. They also do not recommend the appointment of a lead independent director as a counterweight to the power of the combined chairman/CEO. The initiatives of institutional investors are more ambitious. The governance principles promulgated by the California Public Employees' Retirement System (CalPERS), for example, provide for a separation of chairman and CEO in all but 'very limited circumstances' and the designation of a lead independent director if the company does not follow the recommendations.[713]

The NYSE Listed Company Manual further requires the creation of three committees of the board similar to those envisaged by the Cadbury Code: a nominating/corporate governance committee, a compensation committee, and an audit committee.[714] As the name indicates, the remit of the nominating/corporate governance committee is broader than that of a Cadbury-style nomination committee. It is not only responsible for the identification of candidates for board positions, who it may nominate or recommend to the board, but also for the development of a set of corporate governance guidelines.[715] All three committees must be composed entirely of independent directors, thus going beyond the requirements of the UK Corporate Governance Code or the recommendations of the European Commission.[716]

Since the adoption of the Sarbanes-Oxley and Dodd-Frank Acts, the committee structure is now partly enshrined in binding federal law for companies falling within the scope of the Securities Exchange Act 1934. Such companies must have an audit committee and a compensation committee, each consisting of independent directors.[717] In order to qualify as independent, committee members must not be employees of the issuer, control 5 per cent or more of the voting shares, or receive directly or indirectly (e.g. through a close family member[718]) any consulting, advisory, or other fees from the issuer.[719] The provisions of the Securities Exchange Act have been implemented by rules promulgated by the SEC, which direct national securities exchanges (as well as NASDAQ) to prohibit the listing of any security of issuers that do not comply with the act. The SEC rules replicate the definition of the Securities Exchange Act closely,[720] but both the New York Stock Exchanges and NASDAQ, interestingly, have adopted considerably more demanding independence requirements.[721]

711 Chapter 5A.II.

712 For the meaning of the term 'significant shareholder' in the UK, see n 691 above.

713 CalPERS Governance and Sustainability Principles, B.5.

714 NYSE Listed Company Manual, §§303A.04–07.

715 ibid §303A.04(b)(i).

716 Commission Recommendation 2005/162/EC of 15 February 2005 on the role of non-executive or supervisory directors of listed companies and on the committees of the (supervisory) board, [2005] OJ L52/51, Art 5.

717 Securities Exchange Act 1934, as amended by Dodd-Frank, §§10A(m)(3), 10C(a)(2). See also text to nn 334–335 and 346 above.

718 HS Bloomenthal and S Wolff, *Securities Law Handbook* (Thomson Reuters 2018) §15:7. The relevant family relationships are defined in Securities Act Rule 10A-3(e)(8).

719 Securities Exchange Act 1934, §§10A(m)(3)(B), 10C(a)(3). The requirement not to be an employee or significant shareholder of the issuer is part of the definition of 'affiliated person' referred to in the section. The definition itself comes from the Investment Company Act of 1940, §2(a)(3), and is incorporated into the Securities Exchange Act by reference, §3(a)(19) of the 1934 Act.

720 See Securities Act Rules 10A-3(b) (independence standards of audit committee members), 10C-1(b) (independence standards of compensation committee members). The rationale for the SEC's actions is set out in Securities Act Release No 8220 of 9 April 2003 and Release No 33-9330 of 20 June 2012.

721 Bloomenthal and Wolff (n 718) §15:7.

Finally, the listing standards also incorporate certain elements that can be interpreted as embracing the insights developed by group theory, although in a more rudimentary fashion than the UK Corporate Governance Code. The NYSE Listed Company Manual expects the non-executive directors to meet regularly for sessions without the management in order to 'promote open discussion among the non-management directors'.[722] However, UK innovations such as the independent chairman or senior independent director have not been emulated.[723] The manual leaves it to the companies to decide how to organize the executive sessions. They do not necessarily need to be chaired by an independent director or indeed the same non-executive director.[724]

3. *Germany*

Not surprisingly, the German Stock Corporation Act is more specific and prescriptive than both English law and state corporation law in the United States. Both the size of the management and supervisory boards and the general qualifications of board members are laid down in the Act. The management board must consist of one or more persons, and of at least two persons in the case of companies with a share capital of more than three million Euros, unless the articles provide otherwise.[725] The supervisory board must have between three and, depending on the legal capital of the company, twenty-one members,[726] or in companies with employee co-determination an even number of board position with a maximum of twenty supervisory directors in large companies (ten shareholder representatives and ten employee representatives).[727] Evidently, a member of the management board cannot be, at the same time, a member of the supervisory board in the same company.[728] The Stock Corporation Act also prohibits persons who have been convicted of certain economic offences from serving on the management board, but otherwise does not require any particular qualifications.[729] On the other hand, the Act provides for detailed eligibility requirements of supervisory directors, which we find in the United States and UK only in corporate governance codes or the listing rules of stock exchanges. Supervisory board members are not permitted to serve on the supervisory board of more than ten commercial companies (unless the companies belong to the same corporate group).[730] They must not be legal representatives of a dependent undertaking or members of the management board of a corporation if a member of the management board of the supervisory director's corporation serves on the supervisory board of that company (i.e. cross-directorships are prohibited).[731] If the company is stock exchange listed, they also cannot have been members of the same company's management board for the last two years before their appointment. However, this requirement can be disregarded if the candidate is appointed upon a motion by shareholders holding more than 25 per cent of the voting rights in the

[722] NYSE Listed Company Manual, §§303A.03.

[723] However, both the independent chairman and the lead independent director are recommended by the CalPERS Governance and Sustainability Principles, B.5; see text to n 713 above.

[724] NYSE Listed Company Manual, §§303A.03. [725] AktG, §76. [726] ibid §95.

[727] Co-determination will be discussed in Chapter 5D.III; at this point, we will therefore only examine the general rules pursuant to the German Stock Corporation Act.

[728] AktG, §105(1). [729] ibid §76(3).

[730] ibid §100(2), no 1. The provision does not address the combination of supervisory and management board positions in unrelated companies (apart from the prohibition of cross-directorships, §100(2), no 3), but the German Corporate Governance Code recommends that supervisory directors do not accept more than three supervisory board mandates if they are also members of the management board of a listed company, s 5.4.5. For banking institutions that are significant in terms of size and nature, scope and complexity of their activities, the corporate governance provisions contained in the CRD IV legislative package (n 5) are more restrictive. Executive and non-executive directors are prohibited from combining either one executive directorship with two non-executive directorships or four non-executive directorships, Directive 2013/36/EU, Art 91(3).

[731] AktG, §100(2), nos 2, 3.

company.[732] Clearly, these requirements pursue the same goal as the concept of the independent director in many corporate governance codes: to ensure that no relevant relationship exists between the supervisory board members and the members of the management board that may compromise the supervisory board's effectiveness as a control organ. The prohibition of being the legal representative of a dependent undertaking and the prohibition of cross-directorships were introduced in 1965 and thus predate the emergence of the independent director as a corporate governance device in the United States in the 1970s and in Europe in the 1990s.[733] The required cooling-off period, on the other hand, is of a more recent pedigree, dating from 2009.[734] The legislator expected a non-binding best practice standard to be ineffective, given that it was often 'a matter of prestige for former management board members to switch to the supervisory board'.[735] The right of the 25 per cent minority to disapply the prohibition was not seen as running counter to the legislative goal. The law sought to prevent the appointment of supervisory board members effectively by co-optation by the management board in cases where the shareholders were too dispersed to put forward their own nominees. On the other hand, if large shareholders existed and regarded the appointment of a former management board member as beneficial, the legislator believed that it was not the role of the law to bar such a person from moving to the supervisory board.[736]

The eligibility requirements laid down in the Stock Corporation Act, while more prescriptive than those of many other companies acts, are less comprehensive than the definition of independence in the UK Corporate Governance Code or the NYSE Listed Company Manual. For this reason, the German Corporate Governance Code provides for additional independence requirements. However, in comparison with the UK and US requirements, the German norms are strikingly open-ended and vague. The supervisory board 'shall include what it considers to be an appropriate number of independent members', and independence is defined as the absence of a 'personal or business relationship with the corporation, its governing bodies, a controlling shareholder or a company affiliated with the controlling shareholder that may cause a substantial and not merely temporary conflict of interest'.[737] The chairman of the supervisory board does not need to be independent.[738] Furthermore, the Code requires only the establishment of an audit and a nomination committee,[739] while the compensation of the management board members is a matter for the full supervisory board to determine.[740] Neither the audit committee nor the nomination committee needs to be composed of a majority (or exclusively) of independent directors, only the chairman of the audit committee is required to be independent.[741]

The indeterminate nature of the best practice standards is surprising, given that binding German company law is characterized by a diametrically opposed regulatory style: the frequent use of detailed rules, rather than broad standards. An explanation may be the perceived reduced need for strict independence requirements and a system of board committees, since a certain degree of insulation of the supervisory board members from the management is inherent in the two-tier board structure and, as discussed, the Stock Corporation Act imposes several specific independence requirements. On the other hand, the vague formulation may also be a function of path-dependence and a different political economy of standard setting in Germany. As we have seen, the notion of independence has been an integral feature of the

[732] ibid §100(2), no 4, as amended by Gesetz zur Angemessenheit der Vorstandsvergütung (VorstAG) [Act regarding the Adequacy of Executive Compensation] of 31 July 2009, BGBl I, 2509. A similar provision is contained in the German Corporate Governance Code 2017, s 5.4.4.
[733] Gordon (n 705) 1478–80.
[734] Act regarding the Adequacy of Executive Compensation (n 732) Art 1, no 3c).
[735] BT-Drs [Journal of the Federal Parliament] 16/13433, 11.
[736] ibid.
[737] German Corporate Governance Code, s 5.4.2. More specifically, the Code also requires that the supervisory board shall not include more than two former members of the management board, ibid.
[738] ibid s 5.2.
[739] ibid s 5.3.
[740] ibid s 4.2.2.
[741] ibid ss 5.3.2, 5.3.3.

corporate governance movement in the UK since the Cadbury Report. Its wide international diffusion is largely a result of the influence of the Cadbury Code, which has shaped the expectations of international investors, rather than of the endogenous evolution of independence within different legal systems.[742] The composition of the German and UK committees that draft the codes is also markedly different. The clear majority of members of the UK drafting committee come from the audit profession or the institutional investor community, whereas the majority of members of the German corporate governance committee have served, or still serve, on the boards of large listed corporations.[743] It is maybe natural that the best practice standards developed by standard setters with such different biographies differ in style and content.

4. France

The governance structure of French public companies that opt for the unitary board model consists of an administrative board that must be composed of at least three, and not more than 18, directors, who can be natural or legal persons.[744] The Commercial Code does not require any particular professional qualifications.[745] Since 2008, it is also no longer necessary for the directors to be shareholders of the company. However, the articles of association may continue to impose this requirement,[746] and the French corporate governance code stipulates that directors should hold a 'significant' number of shares in the company.[747] Furthermore, in order to ensure that directors have sufficient time to exercise their duties adequately, the Commercial Code restricts the number of board positions that can be held concurrently by the same individual. In general, the number of appointments is limited to five (positions on boards of subsidiaries are disregarded).[748] If a director is general manager or member of the executive board in a company that has adopted the two-tier board system, this position cannot be combined with another position as general manager or member of the executive board, unless neither of the companies involved is listed on a regulated market.[749] Notwithstanding the aforementioned prohibitions, the combination of executive and non-executive positions, for example as managing director in one company and non-executive director (or supervisory board member) in other companies, must not exceed five posts.[750]

[742] The German Corporate Governance Code does not contain an explicit reference to the Cadbury Code, but other codes do. See, for example, the Belgian Corporate Governance Recommendations, published by the Federation of Belgian Enterprises (1998) 3: 'The VBO/FEB has used, as the basis for its activities, the "Code of best practice" which has been recommended by the Cadbury Committee in the United Kingdom. These recommendations are very authoritative on an international level, and they are the result of activities which have been carried out at the initiative of Europe's leading stock exchange'. Similar references can be found in the early codes of other countries, e.g. Norwegian Code of Practice for Corporate Governance (2004) 6; Swiss Code of Best Practice for Corporate Governance (2008) 6.

[743] The composition of the members of the FRC Codes and Standards Committee, which drafts the UK Corporate Governance Code, including their affiliation and a brief biography, is disclosed at www.frc.org.uk (follow hyperlinks 'About the FRC', 'Codes & Standards Committee'), and the composition of the German drafting commission at www.dcgk.de/en (follow hyperlinks 'Commission' and 'Members').

[744] Com, Art L225-17. The boards of the largest French companies, the constituent companies of the CAC 40, have on average 14 directors, Merle (n 481) para 421. If a legal entity is appointed as director, the legal entity must designate a 'permanent representative', a natural person who is subject to the same duties as all de jure directors, Com, Art L225-20.

[745] However, the law contains mechanisms that provide for the ineligibility of persons to serve as directors in certain situations, notably in the case of a disqualification order pursuant to Arts L653-2 to L635-8 Code de commerce. These provisions will be discussed in Chapter 8D.

[746] Com, Art L225-25.

[747] AFEP-MEDEF Corporate Governance Code of Listed Corporations 2018, s 19.

[748] Com, Art L225-21. The same applies to supervisory board positions in the two-tier system, Art L225-77.

[749] ibid Arts L225-54-1, L225-67. Note that, somewhat counterintuitively, the law does not prohibit the combination of the positions of general manager (or member of the executive board) and assistant general manager.

[750] ibid Art L225-94-1.

As we have seen above, in the unitary board system, executive functions are exercised either by the chairman of the board (as *président directeur general*) or delegated to another person called general manager (*directeur général*), who may be assisted by up to five assistant general managers.[751] The general manager and the assistant general managers may or may not be members of the board of directors. Thus, the Commercial Code leaves a wide margin of discretion to companies in organizing the composition of the board and the board's internal operations. Nevertheless, implicitly, the law provides for a certain binding structure that involves a split between executive and non-executive functions on the unitary board. The general manager and the assistant general managers are entrusted with the day-to-day business operations of the company, while the board as a whole is responsible for strategic decisions and for overseeing their implementation. Importantly, while the law does not explicitly refer to the role of non-executive directors, limits on the number of executive directors can be derived from the requirement that a company must not have more than five assistant general managers and not more than one-third of the directors may have an employment contract with the company.[752]

Influenced by the corporate governance debate in Britain, the Viénot Report discussed the introduction of the concept of independent directors in France and initially suggested that at least two board members should be independent.[753] This requirement was extended in subsequent codes. The French AFEP-MEDEF Code now stipulates that half of the board members in listed companies must be independent if the company is widely held and one-third if the company is controlled by a major shareholder.[754] The committee structure pioneered by the UK codes has also been largely emulated by the AFEP-MEDEF Code. Companies have to establish audit, remuneration and nomination committees. The committees must be composed exclusively of non-executive directors and a majority, or in the case of the audit committee two-thirds, of independent directors.[755] The majority of listed companies comply with these recommendations.[756]

We observe a similar convergence of French and UK standards with respect to the definition of independence. As a general rule, a director is considered independent if 'he or she has no relationship of any kind whatsoever with the corporation, its group or its management that may interfere with his or her freedom of judgment'.[757] This general definition is amplified by a list of criteria ranging from the absence of an employment relationship with the company in the last five years to not being a material customer, supplier, or banker of the company or having family ties with an executive director.[758] The criteria inform the review of the classification of directors as independent that has to be carried out annually by the nomination committee and the board of directors.[759] In addition, even though the ownership structure of French corporations is still comparatively concentrated, the concept includes independence from significant shareholders (without, however, defining who is a significant shareholder).[760] Best practice standards pursuant to the

751 See section E.I.4.

752 Com, Art L225-22. If the company adopts the two-tier board structure, the members of the executive board can have (but are not required to have) an employment contract with the company. Similar to the German Stock Corporation Act, the law prohibits members of the supervisory board to serve on the executive board and thus ensures a clear separation between executive and supervisory functions, Com, Art L225-74.

753 Viénot I Report (n 310) 13.

754 AFEP-MEDEF Corporate Governance Code of Listed Corporations 2018, s 8.3

755 ibid ss 15.1, 16.1, 17.1.

756 For data, see AMF Report 2015 (n 424) 64 (reporting that on average 65% of directors are independent in CAC 40 companies and 58% in a sample of other listed companies).

757 AFEP-MEDEF Corporate Governance Code of Listed Corporations 2018, s 8.2.

758 ibid s 8.5.

759 ibid s 8.4. The criteria are not conclusive. The board may decide that a director cannot be regarded as independent 'owing to the specific circumstances of the person or the company, due to its shareholding structure or for any other reason', even though all independence criteria are met, and conversely, that a director who does not meet the criteria is nevertheless independent: ibid.

760 ibid s 8.2. See also s 8.7.

French code, therefore, are generally closer to what we find in the UK than in Germany. However, in one important respect, the AFEP-MEDEF Code falls short of the benchmark set by the UK Corporate Governance Code. It does not require a separation of the offices of chairman and CEO, and most listed companies with a unitary board indeed combine the two roles.[761]

5. *Gender diversity*

Another aspect of board diversity that has received increasing attention in both policy circles and the academic literature in recent years is gender diversity. The promotion of gender equality on corporate boards is, first, a matter of social justice, but it also addresses concerns of groupthink. Boards may take ill-conceived decisions because of their high cohesiveness and lack of diversity. Therefore, we may expect greater gender equality to have a positive effect on the quality of decision-making and firm performance. We will discuss some studies below that have assessed whether this is indeed the case. While the empirical evidence is not unambiguous, it is clear that, at least from a social justice perspective, regulatory initiatives promoting gender equality are to be welcomed. Currently, in most EU Member States, the gap between men and women on the boards of large listed companies is significant (although a trend towards greater equality can be identified, which is largely attributable to an increasing number of Member States adopting binding quotas or requiring companies to disclose their policy on gender diversity). On average, in the EU, women hold around 23 per cent of board positions, defined as positions on the highest decision-making body in the company (the board of directors or supervisory board), up from 11.9 per cent in 2010.[762] Between countries, the differences continue to be marked. The highest percentage of women on boards can be found in France (37.1%), where, as we will see, the legislator has introduced a quota, and the lowest in Malta (5.0%). Germany and the UK belong to the top third of countries in terms of gender balance, with 27.2 per cent and 27.1 per cent of board positions, respectively, being held by women. The share of companies with a woman as CEO or board chair is much lower, although it has also risen since 2010. EU-wide, 5.1 per cent of the largest listed companies have appointed a woman CEO and 7.0 per cent a female board chair.[763] These figures are similar to the United States, where (on the basis of a sample of different size, the S&P 500) about 20 per cent of board members are women and about 5 per cent CEOs.[764]

In most countries, soft law mechanisms, notably corporate governance codes, have encouraged companies to improve the gender balance on the board of directors for some time. For example, the UK Corporate Governance Code stipulates, rather generally, that appointments and succession plans 'should promote diversity of gender, social and ethnic backgrounds'[765] and the annual report should include a description of the board's 'policy on diversity and inclusion, its objectives and linkage to company strategy, how it has been implemented and progress on achieving the objectives'.[766] The German Corporate Governance

[761] See n 652 above.

[762] European Commission, Gender balance on corporate boards: Europe is cracking the glass ceiling (July 2016) 1. For recent data, see the EU's database on women and men in decision-making (http://ec.europa.eu/justice/gender-equality/gender-decision-making; follow hyperlinks 'Gender balance in decision-making positions', 'Database on women and men in decision-making'). See also C Seierstad, P Gabaldon, and H Mensi-Klarbach (eds), *Gender Diversity in the Boardroom, vol 1: The Use of Different Quota Regulations* (Palgrave Macmillan 2017), and for a broad cross-section of 67 countries, based on data from 2013, see S Terjesen, RV Aguilera, and R Lorenz, 'Legislating a Woman's Seat on the Board: Institutional Factors Driving Gender Quotas for Boards of Directors' (2015) 128 Journal of Business Ethics 233, 234.

[763] European Commission (n 762) 4.

[764] 2016 Catalyst Census: Women Board Directors; Catalyst, Women in S&P 500 Companies (both documents are available at http://www.catalyst.org; follow hyperlink 'Top Stats').

[765] UK Corporate Governance Code 2018, Principle J. [766] ibid Provision 23.

Code provides that the management and supervisory boards 'shall take diversity into account' when appointing the company's executives and 'in particular endeavour to achieve the appropriate consideration of women for such positions'.[767] The supervisory board is required to determine targets for the share of women on the management board, and the management board for the share of women on the two management levels below the board.[768] The French AFEP-MEDEF Code requires boards to 'consider what the desirable balance of its membership and that of the Board committees should be, particularly in terms of diversity (gender representation, nationalities, age, qualifications, professional experience, etc.)'.[769] The publications of the New York Stock Exchange on corporate governance mention the value of diversity in general terms, which 'should be broadly defined, to include experience as well as other criteria', but they do not explicitly refer to gender diversity,[770] and the NYSE Listed Company Manual does not address it at all. Some other US corporate governance codes are more explicit, stating, for example, that '[b]oard diversity should be thought of in terms of skill sets, gender, age, nationality, race, sexual orientation, gender identity, and historically under-represented groups'.[771] However, apart from the requirement to consider board diversity as one of several relevant factors in the process of director nominations,[772] they do not recommend any specific steps to promote the representation of women on boards.

In several countries, the legislator decided to rely not solely on voluntary compliance by companies, but impose quotas that will become, or have become, binding after a transition period.[773] For example, this is the case in Germany, where the Stock Corporation Act requires that at least 30 per cent of supervisory board positions in large listed companies must be allocated to members of the underrepresented sex.[774] Similarly, in France, the Commercial Code was amended in 2011 to provide that board appointments must 'seek to achieve a balanced representation of men and women'.[775] This still open-ended provision was amplified in 2014. Certain large listed companies were given until 2017 to ensure that the representation of neither sex on the board of directors or, in the two-tier system, on the supervisory board was less than 40 per cent and the difference in the number of board positions held by women and men was not more than two.[776] The European Commission also works on a legislative measure to improve gender balance and eliminate the discrepancies

[767] German Corporate Governance Code 2017, ss 4.1.5, 5.1.2.

[768] ibid.

[769] AFEP-MEDEF Corporate Governance Code of Listed Corporations 2018, s 6.2. Earlier versions of the code required companies to reach the threshold of 40 per cent of women directors within a specified number of years, see eg AFEP-MEDEF Corporate Governance Code of Listed Corporations 2015, s 6.4. These thresholds have become obsolete since French companies are now required by law to comply with gender quotas, see our discussion in the text below.

[770] NYSE, Report of the New York Stock Exchange Commission on Corporate Governance (2010) 26.

[771] CalPERS Governance and Sustainability Principles, B.9.

[772] ibid B.9.c.

[773] For an overview of legislation in the EU Member States, see European Commission (n 762) 6–7.

[774] See AktG, §96(2) which provides: 'In the case of stock exchange listed companies that are subject to the Co-Determination Act, the Coal and Steel Co-Determination Act, or the Co-Determination Supplementary Act, at least 30 percent of the supervisory board shall be composed of women and at least 30 percent shall be composed of men. The minimum percentage requirement applies to the supervisory board as a whole. If the shareholder representatives or the employee representatives adopt a resolution by majority vote before the election notifying the chairman of the supervisory board of their objection to applying the minimum percentage with regard to the supervisory board as a whole, the shareholder representatives and the employee representatives shall comply with the minimum percentage requirement separately'. This provision was inserted by Art 3, no 4 of the Act on Equal Participation of Women and Men in Leadership Positions in the Private Sector and the Public Sector [Gesetz für die gleichberechtigte Teilhabe von Frauen und Männern an Führungspositionen in der Privatwirtschaft und im öffentlichen Dienst] of 24 April 2015, BGBl I, 642.

[775] Com, Art L225-17.

[776] Com, Arts L225-18-1 (unitary boards), L225-69-1 (dual boards) as adopted by Law no 2014-873 of 4 August 2014 (Loi pour l'égalité réelle entre les femmes et les hommes), JORF no 179 of 5 August 2014, 12949. As of 2017, the 140 largest listed French companies had close to 40 per cent of women on their boards; see E Zenou, I Allemand, and B Brullebaut, 'Gender Diversity on French Boards: Example of a Success from a Hard Law' in C Seierstad, P Gabaldon, and H Mensi-Klarbach (eds), *Gender Diversity in the Boardroom, vol 1: The Use of Different Quota Regulations* (Palgrave Macmillan 2017) 103.

that exist between the EU Member States.[777] The directive, if adopted, would apply to companies with securities admitted to trading on a regulated market, with the exception of small and medium-sized enterprises.[778] It would require these companies to appoint members of the under-represented sex to at least 40 per cent of the non-executive director positions, or alternatively, if permitted by the Member State, to one-third of all director positions, executive and non-executive, over a specified number of years.[779]

Several studies have examined the effect of gender diversity on corporate governance and firm performance.[780] They have found, for example, that CEO turnover is more sensitive to stock price performance in companies with a greater proportion of women on the board, female directors have better attendance records than male directors, and—interestingly—the attendance of male directors improves if the board is more gender-diverse.[781] The composition of the CEO's remuneration also changes with the proportion of women on boards. In companies with more gender-diverse boards, a higher fraction of CEO compensation tends to consist of stock options and deferred shares.[782] These findings have been interpreted as suggesting that female directors monitor the executives more strictly and place greater emphasis on an alignment with shareholder interests than male directors.[783] On the other hand, the empirical evidence of the relationship between gender diversity and firm performance, measured for example as return on assets or Tobin's q (the ratio of total market value of the company and total book value of assets plus liabilities), is inconsistent. Some studies have found a positive association,[784] others a negative one,[785] and yet others no association.[786] Arguments from corporate governance theory can be found in support of either direction. Diversity on boards can improve decision-making by adding different skill-sets, experiences, and expertise. On the other hand, especially the introduction of hard quotas may result in less experienced boards, because the pool of female candidates with top-level management experience is small.[787] This problem can be expected to disappear over time, as more women are appointed to board positions. In fact, regulatory intervention can be seen as breaking a vicious circle, since a gender gap will be self-reinforcing if directors adopt an appointment policy that focuses on experience.[788] More fundamentally, however, it has also been argued that a diverse board may reduce firm value even as it improves corporate governance.[789] As we have seen, some evidence suggests that more diversity on boards leads

[777] Proposal for a Directive on improving the gender balance among non-executive directors of companies listed on stock exchanges and related measures, COM/2012/0614 final.

[778] ibid Arts 1, 3. [779] ibid Art 4.

[780] For an overview of the literature, see D Ferreira, 'Board diversity' in HK Baker and R Anderson (eds), *Corporate Governance: A Synthesis of Theory, Research, and Practice* (Wiley 2010) 225; DL Rhode and AK Packel, 'Diversity on Corporate Boards: How Much Difference Does Difference Make?' (2014) 39 Delaware Journal of Corporate Law 377, 382–90.

[781] RB Adams and D Ferreira, 'Women in the boardroom and their impact on governance and performance' (2009) 94 Journal of Financial Economics 291, 296–301.

[782] ibid 301–304. [783] ibid 301, 303.

[784] D Carter, B Simkins, and W Simpson, 'Corporate governance, board diversity, and firm value' (2003) 38 Financial Review 33; Credit Suisse Research Institute, Gender diversity and corporate performance (2012). For further references, see RB Adams, 'Women on boards: The superheroes of tomorrow?' (2016) 27 The Leadership Quarterly 371, 383–4; Rhode and Packel (n 780) 384–7.

[785] Adams and Ferreira (n 781) 304–307; KR Ahern and AK Dittmar, 'The Changing of the Boards: The Impact on Firm Valuation of Mandated Female Board Representation' (2012) 127 Quarterly Journal of Economics 137. For further references, see Rhode and Packel (n 780) 387–90.

[786] I Gregory-Smith, BGM Main, and CA O'Reilly III, 'Appointments, Pay and Performance in UK Boardrooms by Gender' (2014) 124 Economic Journal F109; JL Pletzer, R Nikolova, KK Kedzior, and SC Voelpel, 'Does Gender Matter? Female Representation on Corporate Boards and Firm Financial Performance: A Meta-Analysis' (2015) PLoS ONE 10(6).

[787] Adams (n 784) 384 (giving an overview of the arguments); Ahern and Dittmar (n 785) 169–74 (analysing the case of Norway, where a 40% quota was introduced in 2003, at a time when only 9% of directors were women).

[788] Ahern and Dittmar (n 785) 173 show that the gender gap cannot be explained with a lower level of education of female candidates. They find that female board appointees are more likely to be higher educated than incumbent male directors.

[789] Adams and Ferreira (n 781) 304–307.

to more stringent monitoring. This, in turn, may result in more interference in operational decision-making and thus decrease shareholder value. If this is correct, greater gender diversity may be valuable to some firms with otherwise weak governance structures and harmful to others.[790] Thus, we may conclude that the moral case for gender equality on corporate boards is probably stronger than the economic case. Nevertheless, policy-makers generally (also) base their proposals on economic evidence. More problematically, sometimes they seem to do so selectively[791] or without distinguishing between correlation and causation in the date,[792] arguably undermining their case for regulatory intervention.[793]

IV. Information rights

In order to discharge its control function effectively, the board must have comprehensive information about the company's operations at its disposal. This consideration applies, in principle, to companies with a one-tier board and two-tier board alike. In one-tier boards the problem may be less pronounced if a substantial number of directors perform executive functions. As we have seen, this is the case in some, but not all legal systems employing the one-tier board model. In the United States, for example, the board is predominantly composed of non-executive directors that are not involved full-time in the company's management. In companies with a two-tier board structure, the formalized separation between management and control functions, the fact that the shareholder representatives and some of the employee representatives on the supervisory board are outside directors,[794] and that the supervisory board is only required by law to meet two times per year (four times in listed companies),[795] mean that it is particularly important to ensure that the members of the supervisory board receive comprehensive and accurate information about the business.

All legal systems, notwithstanding the board model they follow, provide for rules that seek to ensure that outside director are apprised of all relevant information and that they can inspect corporate books and records when deemed necessary. The following are the most import four jurisdictions.

US MBCA

§ 16.05—Inspection of Records by Directors

(a) A director of a corporation is entitled to inspect and copy the books, records and documents of the corporation at any reasonable time to the extent reasonably related to the performance of the director's duties as a director, including duties as a member of a committee, but not for any other purpose or in any manner that would violate any duty to the corporation …

Delaware General Corporation Law

§ 220—Inspection of books and records

(d) Any director shall have the right to examine the corporation's stock ledger, a list of its stockholders and its other books and records for a purpose reasonably related to the director's position as a director … The burden of proof shall be upon the corporation to establish that the inspection such director seeks is for an improper purpose …

[790] This is precisely what Adams and Ferreira (n 781) 307 found for a sample of US firms.

[791] See eg European Commission, Impact assessment on costs and benefits of improving the gender balance in the boards of companies listed on stock exchanges, accompanying the Proposal for a Directive on improving the gender balance among non-executive directors of companies listed on stock exchanges and related measures, SWD(2012) 348 final (reviewing the empirical evidence on pp 13–16 and concluding that 'the overwhelming majority of studies find a positive correlation between increased female presence on boards and better performance', 15).

[792] Adams (n 784) 383–4.

[793] This point is also made by Gregory-Smith, Main, and O'Reilly III (n 786) F125.

[794] The German Co-Determination Act stipulates that, depending on the size of the supervisory board, four to seven members should come from the company's workforce and two to three should be representatives of workers' unions; see MitbestG, §7(2).

[795] AktG, §110(3). In practice it is common that the supervisory board meets three to four times a year.

UK Companies Act 2006

Section 388—Where and for how long records to be kept

(1) A company's accounting records—

(a) must be kept at its registered office or such other place as the directors think fit, and
(b) must at all times be open to inspection by the company's officers ...

UK Corporate Governance Code 2018

Principle F

[T]he chair facilitates constructive board relations and the effective contribution of all non-executive directors, and ensures that directors receive accurate, timely and clear information.

Principle I

The board, supported by the company secretary, should ensure that it has the policies, processes, information, time and resources it needs in order to function effectively and efficiently.

German Stock Corporation Act

§ 90—Reports to the supervisory board

(1) The management board shall report to the supervisory board on:

1. The intended business policy and other fundamental matters of corporate policy (in particular, financial, investment, and human resources planning); it shall comment on deviations of the actual development from reported goals and give reasons for such deviations;
2. The profitability of the company and in particular the return on equity;
3. Business operations, in particular turnover and the situation of the company;
4. Transactions that are actually or potentially of material importance for the profitability or liquidity of the company ...

In addition, the management board is required to report to the chairman of the supervisory board on important developments; an important development shall include a transaction of an affiliated enterprise[796] that has come to the attention of the management board and that is actually or potentially of material importance for the situation of the company.

(2) The reports pursuant to Subsection 1, sentence 1, no. 1-4 shall be submitted in the following form:

1. Reports pursuant to no. 1 at least once a year, unless new developments or newly arising issues require immediate reporting;
2. Reports pursuant to no. 2 in the supervisory board meeting dealing with the annual accounts;
3. Reports pursuant to no. 3 periodically, but at least quarterly;
4. Reports pursuant to no. 4, if possible, in time to enable the supervisory board to give comments before the transactions are carried out.

(3) The supervisory board can request from the management board a report concerning the company's affairs, its legal and business relationships with affiliated enterprises, and the business operations of these enterprises that are actually or potentially of material importance for the situation of the company. Individual members of the supervisory board can request a report, but only to the board.

(4) The reports shall conform to the principles of diligent and true accounting. ...

(5) Each member of the supervisory board has the right to be informed of the reports ... The chairman has to apprise the members of the supervisory board of reports pursuant to Subsection 1, sentence 3 at the next meeting of the supervisory board at the latest.

[796] [Footnote by authors.] Affiliated enterprises are defined by the AktG, §15, as enterprises that are majority-owned by, or hold a majority of the shares, or own cross-shareholdings of more than 25% of the legal capital of another enterprise, or are otherwise controlled by or control another enterprise, are parties to a domination agreement, or have been integrated into each other.

§ 111—Duties and Rights of the Supervisory Board

(1) …
(2) The supervisory board may inspect and examine the books and records of the company as well as the corporate assets, in particular cash and inventories of securities and merchandise. …

French Commercial Code[797]

Article L225-35

…

The board of directors shall carry out the inspections and verifications which it considers appropriate. The company's chairman or general manager is required to send all the documents and information necessary to perform this task to each director.

Comparing these provisions, it is apparent that the most detailed regulation of information rights exists in German law, which is arguably a necessary legislative response to the informational asymmetry between the two boards of a German public stock corporation. The relevant provisions of US and French law can be more succinct, since information flows in one-tier boards are largely a matter of how the board is structured and tasks are allocated (we omit here the French rules pertaining to the two-tier board option). Thus, legislation simply stipulates that the directors shall have the right to inspect the company's books and records. In some US jurisdictions, this right is absolute and unqualified. Directors can demand inspection at all reasonable times during their tenure.[798] In other jurisdictions, for example Delaware, and pursuant to the MBCA, the right is subject to the condition that the inspection is 'reasonably related to the performance of the director's duties'[799] or 'to the director's position as a director'.[800] This qualification has been said to stem from the fiduciary position of directors, which obliges them not to act detrimentally to the interests of the corporation whenever they make use of their powers.[801] In assessing whether the director's request to examine corporate records is made properly, the court will enquire into the motives of the director and what use the director intends to make of the information.[802] For example, if the director seeks to obtain trade secrets for personal gain or in order to assist a competitor, the company can refuse disclosure, and a director who takes steps to gain access to the information nonetheless acts wrongfully.[803]

Under French law, a right to information of the members of the *conseil d'administration* was initially developed by the courts.[804] The Cour de Cassation derived this right from the general powers of the board of directors to '[deal] with all matters relating to the conduct of the company's business and [decide] all pertinent issues'.[805] The court argued that if the board was to be able to fulfil its role, it had to be furnished with all relevant information. The chairman of the board (the *président* of the company) was required to make the necessary information available to each director, and a corresponding obligation is now laid down in the Commercial Code.[806] Resolutions of the board adopted on the basis of insufficient

[797] Translation by Legifrance, https://www.legifrance.gouv.fr/Traductions/en-English/Legifrance-translations.

[798] *Fletcher Cyclopedia of the Law of Corporations* (perm edn, Thomson Reuters 2018) §2235. From the case law, see eg *Halperin v Air King Products Co.*, 59 N.Y.S. 2d 672 (N.Y. 1945). In such a jurisdiction, if the director uses the inspection right to pursue a goal inimical to the interests of the corporation, the only remedy is removal of the director, *Wilkins v M. Ascher Silk Corporation*, 201 N.Y.S. 739 (N.Y. App. Div. 1923). The inspection right of stockholders, on the other hand, is a qualified right in all jurisdictions. They must show a 'proper purpose', which is defined, for example by the Delaware General Corporation Law, as 'a purpose reasonably related to [the stockholder's] interest as a stockholder', §220(b).

[799] MBCA, §16.05(a). [800] Del. Gen. Corp. Law, §220(d).

[801] *State v Seiberling Rubber Co.*, 3 Storey 295, 298 (Del. 1961). This case was decided under common law, which also recognized an inspection right, but the same considerations apply to the information right codified in the Delaware General Corporation Law.

[802] ibid. [803] *Morton v Rogers*, 514 P.2d 752, 757 (Ariz. Ct. App. 1973).

[804] Cass com, 2 July 1985 (*Cointreau*), *JCP E* 1985, 14758, note A Viandier.

[805] Com, Art L225-35(1).

[806] ibid Art L225-35(3) second sentence. For a decision interpreting this duty, see Cass com, 8 October 2002 (*Mme Tassel c/Sté Nordatec*), *JCP E* 2003, no 317, note A Viandier (holding that the president is required to provide the directors with all information necessary for informed deliberations in advance of a board meeting, even if the directors have not requested the information).

information in violation of this duty are null and void.[807] The duty is complemented by a right of the directors to inspect records and request information.[808] However, as under Delaware law, this right is not absolute. It has to be exercised in the interest of the company, and the requested records must be related to the responsibilities of the directors.[809]

In the tradition of a minimalist regulation of board processes, the UK Companies Act 2006 does not codify a general right of the directors to information. The Companies Act provides for a right of the 'officers' to inspect the company's accounting records at all times,[810] which includes the directors.[811] As in the other two legal systems that we have discussed, this provision is an expression of a more fundamental right of directors to inspect not only the company's books and records, but also any other documents that they require in order to carry out their duties as directors.[812] This right exists at common law and— again as in the other jurisdictions—it is subject to certain qualifications. Directors generally do not need to give reasons to exercise their right, but the court may enjoin them from accessing corporate information if evidence is presented that it was a director's 'intention ... to abuse the confidence reposed in him as director and materially to injure the company'.[813] More detailed rules on information flows within the company, in particular from the executives to the non-executives, cannot be found in the Companies Act or in English common law. For listed companies, the UK Corporate Governance Code makes it clear that the chairman of the board plays an important role in this regard. The chair oversees the establishment of processes that facilitate the flow of information and ensures that directors receive relevant, accurate and clear information in a timely manner.[814]

In contrast to these fairly general principles, the German Stock Corporation Act establishes an elaborate system of information rights of the supervisory board and disclosure duties of the management board. The management board has to report to the supervisory board on various aspects of the company's business at regular intervals.[815] This duty is not only intended to enable the supervisory board to exercise its main function of supervising the management,[816] but also to involve the supervisory board in important business decisions and allow the utilization of a broader range of expertise and experience.[817] The scope of the reporting duty was extended by several statutory amendments; it now comprises forward-looking information concerning business strategy (particularly financial, investment, and human resources planning); information regarding the return on the company's capital; a quarterly report on the company's business and financial position; and the duty to inform the supervisory board of transactions that may have a substantial effect on the company's profits and current assets before the transaction is carried out.[818] In addition, the management board has to inform the chairman of the supervisory board of any other important developments of material importance without delay.[819] The provision refers to the chairman of the supervisory board, rather than the full board, because the matter may require immediate attention. The chairman, accordingly, may take action without convening

[807] Cass com, 24 April 1990 (*Cointreau*), *Bull. Joly* 1990, 511 no 134, note P Le Cannu.

[808] Com, Art L225-35(3) first sentence.

[809] Cozian, Viandier, and Deboissy (n 462) para 792.

[810] Companies Act 2006, s 388(1).

[811] ibid s 1173(1). In other legal systems, the term usually has a narrower meaning; see text to nn 433–443 above.

[812] *Conway v Petronius Clothing Co* [1978] 1 WLR 72, 89–90 (following *Burn v London and South Wales Coal Co* (1890) 7 TLR 118); *Oxford Legal Group Ltd v Sibbasbridge Services Plc* [2008] BCC 558, 567.

[813] *Conway v Petronius Clothing Co* (n 812) 90 (quoting *Edman v Ross* (1922) 22 SR (NSW) 351, 361). However, the court also pointed out that different principles apply if the director is charged with misconduct and a general meeting has been convened to remove the director. In such a case, the court will generally not intervene before the company had had a chance to consider the matter at the general meeting, unless it was 'essential for the protection of the company or indeed for the personal protection of the director that he be allowed to inspect the company's books': ibid 91. In the case at hand, the plaintiffs were refused access to corporate information because it was alleged that they sought to obtain the information as competitors of the company.

[814] UK Corporate Governance Code 2018, Principles F, I.

[815] AktG, §90(1), (2).

[816] ibid §111(1).

[817] Spindler (n 276) §90, para 1.

[818] AktG, §90(1) sentence 1, nos 1–4.

[819] ibid §90(1) sentence 3. Such developments might be a disruption of operations, the default of a debtor, or a judgment in an important lawsuit, Spindler (n 276) §90, para 31.

the board, but he or she is required to make the management board's report available to all members of the supervisory board in due course.[820]

Reporting duties alone cannot ensure that the supervisory board is always informed of relevant developments and is in a position to intervene when necessary, since the management board ultimately decides how to present information and whether certain matters are of sufficient importance to trigger one of the reporting duties.[821] For this reason, the Stock Corporation Act stipulates that the supervisory board as an organ and individual board members have a right to request information from the management board concerning any aspect of the company's affairs, and the supervisory board (but not an individual director) has a right to inspect corporate books and records.[822] The management board is generally not entitled to refuse the supervisory board's request, including requests that concern confidential information.[823] The only limitation results from the general unwritten requirement not to abuse legal rights, for example by exercising the right to information so frequently that it disrupts the work of the management board,[824] or if a supervisory board member intends to exploit information for personal gain.[825]

[820] AktG, §90(5) sentence 3.

[821] In making this assessment, the members of the management board are of course subject to their fiduciary duties. However, as we will see in Chapter 7B.I.3, the duties are broadly formulated and allow for a margin of discretion, which may make it difficult to argue in individual cases that information was not presented in an adequate format or reports were incomplete.

[822] AktG, §§90(3), 111(2).

[823] BGHZ 20, 239, 246. As a corollary of the right to access confidential information, the members of the supervisory board are bound by a duty of confidentiality, which is part of their general fiduciary duties.

[824] BT-Drs [Journal of the Federal Parliament] 14/8769, 14.

[825] OLG Karlsruhe, OLGZ 1985, 41, 44 (regarding the private limited company).

5
Elements of Shareholder Democracy

A. Origins of Corporate Power

We saw in Chapter 4 that the shareholders are commonly considered the owners of the corporation. This is questionable in an economic and social, if not a legal, sense.[1] Even if it is true in a legal sense, it does not tell us much about the power of the shareholders to direct the operations of the business that comes with their legal ownership, because ownership rights, as all legal rights, are in various ways restricted by the rights of others and the regulatory framework in general.[2] Indeed, as the following discussion will show, the position of shareholders in many legal systems is confined to that of mere investor who acquires cash flow rights, but has minimal (and only indirect) influence on business operations through the election of directors. If the characterization of shareholders as owners is correct, we would expect them to have at least a residual right of control that comes to the fore when decisions have to be made that affect the shareholders' rights substantially, such as fundamental changes to the corporation's charter, when all or a qualified majority of the shareholders

[1] See Chapter 4A.

[2] This holds at the level of civil and commercial law as much as the constitutional level. For an example, see the German constitution, Art 14 Grundgesetz [Basic Law]:

> (1) Property and the right of inheritance shall be guaranteed. Their content and limits shall be defined by the laws.
> (2) Property entails obligations. Its use shall also serve the public good.

agree that the directors should act, or refrain from acting, in a certain way, or when the other corporate organs are incapacitated, for example because of a conflict of interest. On the other hand, where shareholders (or, for that matter, directors) have the power to decide, the law needs to ensure that they do not abuse their position of power to the detriment of corporate actors that are bound by the decision without being able to influence it. Legal systems differ in the answers that they give to these questions. However, all legal systems have in common that they seek to achieve some balance of power and interests in the corporation, which may resemble, at least at a basic level, a system of governance informed by democratic procedures.[3]

I. UK

In order to assess the rights and competences of the directors and shareholders and identify the limits on their discretion, it is necessary to understand the conceptual foundation of the corporation and the origin of corporate power. These questions became relevant in the nineteenth century, when the modern corporate form emerged. While the conception of the corporation may have evolved since then and responded to subsequent changes in the regulatory environment, the basic tenets determining the position of the directors and shareholders continue to be informed by the views prevalent during the formative decades of the modern corporation. We will focus on two leading cases from this period, which have been particularly influential in the development of English company law. Many current rules on the relationship between the general meeting and the board of directors can only be fully appreciated in light of these cases. The first is *Isle of Wight Railway Company v Tahourdin*.[4] In this case, shareholders of the claimant railway company requisitioned the directors to call an extraordinary general meeting for the following purposes:[5]

1. To appoint a committee to inquire into the working and general management of the company, and the means of reducing the working expenses. To empower such committee to consolidate all or any of the duties of secretary, general manager, accountant, and cashier, and to concentrate the offices in the Island, and to remove any of the officers or servants of the company and appoint others, and to authorize and require the directors to carry out the recommendations of the committee.
2. To remove (if deemed necessary or expedient) any of the present directors, and to elect directors to fill any vacancy in the board.

The directors, understandably, were not enthusiastic to comply with the requisition. They did call a meeting; however, they restricted the objects of that meeting to discuss 'the appointment of a committee to inquire into the working and general management of the company and the means of reducing the working expenses'.[6] The defendants and other discontented shareholders refused to attend the meeting and issued a notice of their own

[3] See eg PY Gomez and H Korine, 'Democracy and the Evolution of Corporate Governance' (2005) 13 Corporate Governance 739 (identifying three procedures of democracy—enfranchisement, separation of powers, and representation with (public debate)—and claiming that corporate governance systems become more responsive to these ideas, and incorporate them to a greater extent, as they evolve). Democratic concepts are most often invoked by the proponents of stakeholder theory who argue that the legitimation of corporate power requires the democratic representation of all affected constituencies, see the references in Chapter 4A, or C Driver and G Thompson, 'Corporate Governance and Democracy: The Stakeholder Debate Revisited' (2002) 6 Journal of Management and Governance 111; E Engelen, 'Corporate governance, property and democracy: a conceptual critique of shareholder ideology' (2002) 31 Economy and Society 391. The comparison is also emphasized by K Schmidt, *Gesellschaftsrecht* (4th edn, Carl Heymanns 2002) §28 V (with respect to the checks and balances in German corporate governance).

[4] [1884] LR 25 Ch D 320 (Court of Appeal).

[5] ibid 321–2. The Companies Clauses Consolidation Act 1845, s 70, which applied to the company, entitled 'twenty or more shareholders holding in the aggregate not less than one tenth of the capital of the company' to require the directors to call an extraordinary meeting.

[6] ibid 322.

calling a meeting for the original purposes. The issue was whether the shareholders were entitled to do so, which depended on the question of whether the directors had failed 'to call such meeting' as requested by the shareholders.[7] At first instance, Justice Kay granted an injunction enjoining the meeting from being held. He interpreted the law as meaning that the directors were only required to call a 'proper' meeting, that is, a meeting not only called legally, but also pursuing legal objects. The legality of the objects was contested in so far as the shareholders sought to *empower* the committee to alter the management structure of the company and remove any of the directors (as opposed to merely mandating an inquiry). Justice Kay held:[8]

> The simple question is, would it or would it not be within the right of a general meeting to empower a committee to do all these things? In my opinion it clearly would not be. It would be to displace the directors, and to transfer to a committee to be appointed the functions of the directors to a very considerable extent. It seems to me that a general meeting has no power whatever to give any authority of that kind to a committee ... The meeting is not, according to the requisition, summoned for the purpose of determining whether the offices shall be consolidated, which might or might not be perfectly legal, and upon which I give no opinion, but is summoned for the purpose of appointing a committee, to which committee the power of doing that is thereupon and at once to be given. Clearly to my mind it would be entirely illegal to attempt to give such a power to a committee so appointed ... There is another, and to my mind a completely fatal, objection to that part of the requisition [empowering the committee to remove directors] ... [H]ow were the shareholders to know what director it would be proposed to remove. It is not said to remove all of them. That would have been quite a different thing. It is to remove any of them, and it does not say which. It is as vague and indefinite as it can possibly be, and therefore it seems to me that the directors were quite right in saying that they had no power to summon a meeting for any such vague purpose as that ...

The Court of Appeal disagreed. The following excerpt contains the main arguments of the Court.

***Isle of Wight Railway Company v Tahourdin* [1884] LR 25 Ch D 320**

Cotton LJ:

It is a very strong thing indeed to prevent shareholders from holding a meeting of the company, when such a meeting is the only way in which they can interfere, if the majority of them think that the course taken by the directors, in a matter which is *intra vires* of the directors, is not for the benefit of the company ...

I am of opinion that if the object for which it is proposed to call a meeting is one which can be carried out in a legal way, then, although the notice may be so expressed that resolutions following its precise terms would be illegal, it is not right for the directors to limit the notice so as to prevent the meeting from entering into the question simply because the terms of the notice would justify a resolution which would be *ultra vires*. Directors have great powers, and the Court refuses to interfere with their management of the company's affairs if they keep within their powers, and if a shareholder complains of the conduct of the directors while they keep within their powers, the Court says to him, 'If you want to alter the management of the affairs of the company go to a general meeting, and if they agree with you they will pass a resolution obliging the directors to alter their course of proceeding'.

In my opinion much of the criticism on the first part of this notice proceeds upon a misconstruction of the notice itself ... I do not mean to give any opinion upon the question whether it would be legal to give to a committee power to do the things mentioned in the notice, it is unnecessary in my opinion to decide that question, as I am clear that such is not the object of the notice, for a scheme which the committee were intended to carry into effect of their own authority would not have been spoken of as "recommendations of the committee'.

[7] Companies Clauses Consolidation Act 1845, s 70.

[8] [1884] LR 25 Ch D 320, 326–7.

Now would it be right to pass a resolution requiring the directors to carry into effect the recommendations of the committee without their being submitted to a general meeting? I am inclined to think that it would not. It seems to me that the proper course would be to appoint a committee, and to require them to report to an adjourned meeting, which can consider the remaining point mentioned in the notice, viz., whether the directors shall not only be authorized, (which perhaps is unnecessary,) but be required, to carry out the recommendation of the committee. I think the right plan would be to appoint the committee, without giving any direction to the directors as to what they have to do until the report of the committee is before the general meeting. The adjourned special meeting, having undoubtedly a power to direct and control the board in the management of the affairs of the company, when they see what the committee recommend will say whether they will or will not require their board to carry those recommendations into effect…

Then there is a second object, 'To remove (if deemed necessary or expedient) any of the present directors, and to elect directors to fill any vacancy in the board' … I think that a notice in that form is quite sufficient for all practical purposes. If when the recommendations of the committee were known, or when the committee had been appointed, the directors or some of them were to say, 'We will not act any longer if you insist upon this. We will not follow out the recommendations whatever they may be', then very likely the general meeting would say, 'If that be so we do not wish to have you as directors any longer, and we will remove you'. That shews why the words 'any of' were put in. If the committee make recommendations which are accepted by the company, some of the directors, though disapproving of them, may say, 'We think this unadvisable, but as the company wishes it we submit to their wishes', and then very likely the meeting will say, 'We will not remove those gentlemen, but we will remove those who at the meeting refuse to take the course which we consider conducive to the interests of the company'. I am of opinion that under sect. 91[9] a general meeting of shareholders has power to remove directors, and that the notice was sufficiently distinct, and if so, the notice issued by the directors was insufficient in this respect also.

…

The second seminal UK decision concerning the division of corporate powers between the shareholders and directors was issued about two decades later. In *Automatic Self-Cleansing Filter Syndicate Co Ltd v Cuninghame*,[10] the company's articles vested 'the management of the business and the control of the company' in the directors, but provided that the directors' authority was subject 'to such regulations … as may from time to time be made by extraordinary resolution'.[11] In order to sell the undertaking of the company, the majority shareholder prepared a resolution specifying the particulars of the sale and requesting the directors to carry out the sale. The resolution was adopted by a simple majority (1,502 out of 2,700 voting shares) at a general meeting with the votes of the majority shareholder and his friends. The directors were of the opinion that the transaction was not in the best interest of the company and refused to comply with the resolution. The following excerpt is from the decision of the Court of Appeal, after the majority shareholder's motion asking the court to compel the directors to effect the sale had been rejected at first instance.

***Automatic Self-Cleansing Filter Syndicate Co Ltd v Cuninghame* [1906] 2 Ch 34**

Collins MR:

[T]he question is whether under the memorandum and articles of association here the directors are bound to accept, in substitution of their own view, the views contained in the resolution of the company. Warrington J. [the judge of first instance] held that the majority could not impose that obligation upon the directors, and that on the true construction of the articles the directors were the persons authorized by the articles to effect this sale, and that unless the other powers given by the memorandum were invoked by a special resolution, it was impossible for a

[9] [Footnote by authors.] Companies Clauses Consolidation Act 1845, s 91, provides in relevant part: '[T]he choice and removal of the directors … shall be exercised only at a general meeting of the company'.

[10] [1906] 2 Ch 34 (Court of Appeal).

[11] Article 96 of the company's articles.

mere majority at a meeting to override the views of the directors. That depends, as Warrington J. put it, upon the construction of the articles.

... [B]y article 96 [the directors] are given in express terms the full powers which the company has, except so far as they 'are not hereby or by statute expressly directed or required to be exercised or done by the company', so that the directors have absolute power to do all things other than those that are expressly required to be done by the company; and then comes the limitation on their general authority—'subject to such regulations as may from time to time be made by extraordinary resolution'. Therefore, if it is desired to alter the powers of the directors that must be done, not by a resolution carried by a majority at an ordinary meeting of the company, but by an extraordinary resolution. In these circumstances it seems to me that it is not competent for the majority of the shareholders at an ordinary meeting to affect or alter the mandate originally given to the directors, by the articles of association. It has been suggested that this is a mere question of principal and agent, and that it would be an absurd thing if a principal in appointing an agent should in effect appoint a dictator who is to manage him instead of his managing the agent. I think that that analogy does not strictly apply to this case. No doubt for some purposes directors are agents. For whom are they agents? You have, no doubt, in theory and law one entity, the company, which might be a principal, but you have to go behind that when you look to the particular position of directors. It is by the consensus of all the individuals in the company that these directors become agents and hold their rights as agents. It is not fair to say that a majority at a meeting is for the purposes of this case the principal so as to alter the mandate of the agent. The minority also must be taken into account. There are provisions by which the minority may be over-borne, but that can only be done by special machinery in the shape of special resolutions. Short of that the mandate which must be obeyed is not that of the majority--it is that of the whole entity made up of all the shareholders. If the mandate of the directors is to be altered, it can only be under the machinery of the memorandum and articles themselves ...

Cozens-Hardy, LJ:

It is somewhat remarkable that in the year 1906 this interesting and important question of company law should for the first time arise for decision, and it is perhaps necessary to go back to the root principle which governs these cases under the Companies Act, 1862. It has been decided that the articles of association are a contract between the members of the company inter se. That was settled finally by the case of *Browne v. La Trinidad*, 37 Ch. D. 1, if it was not settled before. We must therefore consider what is the relevant contract which these shareholders have entered into, and that contract, of course, is to be found in the memorandum and articles ... [I]t seems to me that the shareholders have by their express contract mutually stipulated that their common affairs should be managed by certain directors to be appointed by the shareholders in the manner described by other articles, such directors being liable to be removed only by special resolution. If you once get a stipulation of that kind in a contract made between the parties, what right is there to interfere with the contract, apart, of course, from any misconduct on the part of the directors? ... [I]t is a fallacy to say that the relation [between shareholders and directors] is that of simple principal and agent. The person who is managing is managing for himself as well as for the others. It is not in the least a case where you have a master on the one side and a mere servant on the other. You are dealing here, as in the case of a partnership, with parties having individual rights as to which there are mutual stipulations for their common benefit, and when you once get that, it seems to me that there is no ground for saying that the mere majority can put an end to the express stipulations contained in the bargain which they have made ...

Questions and comments:

1. In *Tahourdin*'s case, do Justice Kay and Lord Justice Cotton disagree about the division of powers between the general meeting and the board of directors? If not, what does their disagreement centre on?
2. It is sometimes said that the law changed between the time of *Tahourdin*'s case and *Cuninghame*'s case. For example, *Davies* and *Worthington* interpret the two decisions as being

instances of two different conceptions of the corporation.[12] The first conception, underlying *Tahourdin*'s case, characterizes the relationship between the shareholders (or the company) and the directors as that of principal and agent (in the legal sense). The principal authorizes the agent to act on the principal's behalf. Within the scope of (actual or ostensible) authority, the agent can bind the principal through his acts, but the agent, of course, remains subject to the principal's control and the principal is generally able to alter or revoke the authorization unilaterally and at any time.[13] The consequence of this view is that it should be possible for the shareholders, as principals, acting by ordinary resolution at a general meeting, to bypass the directors or instruct them to take specified action.[14] This result should also hold in cases where the articles require a special resolution[15] to remove the directors or give instructions to them, as in *Cuninghame*'s case, because the principal who revokes the agent's authority may be in breach of contract, but the termination of authority is nonetheless effective.

The second conception attributes greater significance to the articles. The allocation of competences as provided for in the articles is seen as authoritative, as 'something in the nature of a constitutional division of powers'.[16] If the articles require a special resolution, the shareholders cannot issue binding instructions by ordinary resolution, based on the argument that they are, in law, the principals and the directors their agents. The Court of Appeal in *Cuninghame*'s case clearly adopted this second interpretation. This is convincing from a dogmatic point of view. As opposed to conventional agent-principal relationships, we are here concerned with three actors. The company is interposed between the shareholders and directors. The company, not the shareholders, creates the agency relationship and acts as principal in the eyes of the law. The question of how the company can modify or revoke the directors' authority has to be distinguished from how the company acts. With respect to the latter point, the articles come into play. If they require a qualified majority to restrict the directors' general authority to manage the company's business, for example in the form of a resolution as in *Cuninghame*'s case, the shareholders are bound by this requirement.

Given these considerations, is it correct to say that the law has been altered by *Cuninghame*'s case? Is it helpful to distinguish between a conception of the company based on agency principles (understood in the legal sense) and one based on a constitutional division of powers? Note that the Court in *Cuninghame* did not overrule *Isle of Wight v Tahourdin*, but distinguished the earlier case on the basis 'that the resolution which [the defendants and other shareholders in *Tahourdin*'s case] proposed to submit to the meeting, and upon which the question arose, was one which could be carried by a simple majority of the company'.[17]

3. The Model Articles for Public and Private Companies contain provisions similar to the one in *Cuninghame*'s case, vesting an instruction right in the members that can be exercised by special resolution.[18] Therefore, if the company follows the Model Articles, it is clear that the

[12] PL Davies and S Worthington, *Gower's Principles of Modern Company Law* (10th edn, Sweet & Maxwell 2016) para 14-3.

[13] In some instances, the authority may become irrevocable, see for example *Gaussen v Morton* (1830) 10 B & C 731 (authority coupled with an interest); *Seymour v Bridge* (1885) 14 QBD 460 (the agent would become liable to personal loss).

[14] This was precisely what was argued in the two cases excerpted above, see [1884] LR 25 Ch D 320, 324; [1906] 2 Ch 34, 37.

[15] Now s 283 Companies Act 2006.

[16] Davies and Worthington (n 12) para 14-3.

[17] [1906] 2 Ch 34, 39 (Warrington J). See also the Court of Appeal (Collins MR): 'Isle of Wight Ry. Co. v Tahourdin ... rests upon a different statute, a statute differing in the most essential point, namely, in the limitation of the directors' authority'.

[18] Model Articles for Public Companies, Art 4(1); Model Articles for Private Companies, Art 4(1). Note that the provision of the articles in *Cuninghame*'s case spoke of '*regulations* ... as may from time to time be made by extraordinary resolution' (emphasis by authors). It caused some confusion whether this provision should be interpreted as an instruction right, i.e. the term 'regulation' was synonymous with 'shareholder resolution', or whether it referred to an amendment of the articles, see *Quin & Axtens Ltd v Salmon* [1909] AC 442 (doubting that 'regulations' included any directions given to the directors). The 1985 Table A articles, Art 70, and following them the current model articles, clarified the legal situation by providing that the directors' management powers shall be subject to '*directions* given by special resolution' (emphasis by authors).

shareholders cannot limit the directors' authority by ordinary resolution.[19] Could the general meeting, acting with the required majority, change the articles, provide for an instruction right to be exercised by ordinary resolution, and henceforth interfere in the management of the company whenever the majority of the shareholders disagreed with the course of action chosen by the directors? What could be the unwelcome consequences of such a broad instruction right? Alternatively, if the articles do not contain an instruction right, can the shareholders still adopt resolutions (possibly by qualified majority) to issue binding directions specifying how the directors should run the business of the company? Can they do so if they act unanimously?[20] Finally, assume that the articles provide for a shareholder instruction right (to be exercised by special resolution), but also contain a provision that requires the approval by a director for specific transactions. Can the shareholders circumvent the approval requirement by adopting a special resolution directing the director to approve the transaction?

4. With regard to the last point (requirement of director approval), the decision of the House of Lords in *Quin & Axtens Ltd v Salmon* [1909] AC 442, is instructive, although the facts were slightly different from the hypothetical in the preceding comment. The company's articles provided that the directors' powers were 'subject to such regulations ... as may be prescribed by the company in general meeting'. Furthermore, the articles stipulated that resolutions of the board of directors (not the general meeting) concerning the acquisition or letting of premises were only valid if neither of the managing directors Axtens and Salmon dissented. When the directors adopted a resolution falling within the ambit of this provision and Salmon dissented, the shareholders called an extraordinary general meeting and passed a resolution to the same effect. The House of Lords, according to Lord Loreburn LC, stressed that the courts would enforce the bargain made between the shareholders, as laid down in the articles of association: The bargain

> amounts for the purpose in hand to this, that the directors should manage the business; and the company, therefore, are not to manage the business unless there is provision to that effect. Further the directors cannot manage it in a particular way—that is to say, they cannot do certain things if Mr. Salmon or Mr. Axtens objects. Now I cannot agree ... that the failure of the directors upon the objection of Mr. Salmon to grant these leases of itself remitted the matter to the discretion of the company in general meeting. They could still manage the business, but not altogether in the way they desired ... [I]t seems to me that the regulations or resolutions which have been passed are of themselves inconsistent with the provisions of these articles ...

5. According to section 168 of the Companies Act 2006, the shareholders may remove a director before the expiration of his period of office by ordinary resolution. Is it sensible to provide for an instruction right to be exercised by special resolution, but allow the removal of directors by ordinary resolution?

[19] For a more recent case, see *Breckland Group Holdings v London & Suffolk Properties* (1988) 4 BCC 542, where the company's articles contained a provision almost identical to the one at issue in *Cuninghame*'s case. London & Suffolk had two shareholders, a company called Crompton Enterprises, which held 51% of the share capital, and the claimant Breckland Group, holding 49%. The issue was whether the majority shareholder Crompton could adopt a resolution in general meeting against the wishes of the minority shareholder and bring proceedings against, among others, the principal shareholder in Breckland Group, who was at the same time managing director of London & Suffolk. The court held that, where the model articles applied, the institution of legal proceedings fell within the remit of the board. In such a case, 'it is not for the general meeting to interfere': ibid 547, even though one of the directors was clearly conflicted.

[20] Consider in this context *In Re Duomatic Ltd* [1969] 2 Ch 365 (Buckley J): '[W]here it can be shown that all shareholders who have a right to attend and vote at a general meeting of the company assent to some matter which a general meeting of the company could carry into effect, that assent is as binding as a resolution in general meeting would be'. This is called 'the *Duomatic* principle'. See also *Cane v Jones* [1980] 1 WLR 1451: The company's share capital was equally divided between two families. The articles provided that the chairman of the board should have a casting vote both at board meetings and at general meetings of the company. Two decades after the company was formed, all of the shareholders entered into a written agreement depriving the chairman of the casting vote. The Court, referring to the *Duomatic* principle, held that a special resolution, adopted pursuant to the statutory procedure, was not the only way in which the articles of association could be altered. An agreement between all the shareholders may be 'as effective as a special or extraordinary resolution' and override the articles, ibid 1460–1. This result is supported by s 29(1) Companies Act 2006, which lists shareholder agreements as one of several 'resolutions and agreements' that may 'affect ... a company's constitution' and that must, accordingly, be filed with the registrar.

II. US

In the United States, our journey also starts in the nineteenth century. Similar to the UK, early US decisions emphasized that the corporate charter was akin to a contract between the shareholders, and the corporation to a partnership, with the consequence that the shareholders had ultimate control over the corporation, but could not alter the charter unless all of the shareholders consented.[21] This stringent view was soon found to lead to 'tyranny by the minority' and hinder economic progress, because important transaction could be blocked by one dissenting shareholder.[22] The general corporation acts of the late nineteenth century strengthened majority decision-making[23] and provided for clearly defined responsibilities of the directors in the management of the corporation.[24] The courts amplified the statutory provisions. While they stressed that the directors were 'trustees for the stockholders'[25] and their powers could not go beyond the limitations laid down in the certificate of incorporation and by-laws,[26] they also held that the shareholders were not entitled to interfere in the company's management by the directors, provided the directors acted within the scope of the authority conferred on them and 'without fraud, or by action ultra vires, or in gross abuse of trust'.[27]

A good example of this early approach of the US courts is the decision of the New Jersey Court of Chancery in *Loewenthal v Rubber Reclaiming Co.*,[28] a case somewhat similar to *Automatic Self-Cleansing Filter Syndicate*. The defendant company's by-laws provided for six directors, who were distributed among the constituent organizations that had formed the corporation and elected by cumulative voting to ensure that all of the constituent

[21] See, for example, *Kean v Johnson*, 9 N.J. Eq. 401 (N.J. Ch. 1853). The plaintiffs were minority shareholders in a railroad corporation. They challenged the sale of the corporation's assets (the railroad) to another railroad company. The sale was effected by the individual defendants, who were majority shareholders and directors in the two companies. The Court held: 'I cannot divert my mind from the conclusion that a sale of their road, and the employment of the capital they invested in it to other uses, does affect the right of every stockholder in a railroad company. As stockholders, they own the road in common, to be employed in specified uses ... The directors are their trustees to employ the joint capital in the management of the road, and the road only, to the end that from the investment the stockholders have chosen they may reap the contemplated profits. And this is the agreement of the stockholders among themselves. They each contract with the other that their money shall be so employed. What the majority determine *within the scope* of this mutual contract, they each agree to abide by, but there their mutual contract ends, and no majority, however large, has a right to divert one cent of the joint capital to any purpose not consistent with, and growing out of this original fundamental joint intention'. *Kean v Johnson* was followed by *Zabriskie v Hackensack & N.Y.R. Co.*, 18 N.J. Eq. 178 (N.J. Ch. 1867); *Black v Delaware & R. Canal Co.*, 24 N.J. Eq. 455 (N.J. Err. & App. 1873). The doctrine established in *Kean v Johnson* draws on an English case from 1824, *Natusch v Irving* (not reported), dealing with partnership law.

[22] EJ Weiss, 'The Law of Take Out Mergers: A Historical Perspective' (1981) 56 New York University Law Review 624, 629, giving examples of 'strike suits' that were brought by minority shareholders primarily with a view to delaying commercial transactions and extract a settlement value.

[23] See, for example, New Jersey Gen. Corp. Act 1896, which was the most influential US corporation law until approximately 1910 (see Chapter 4E.I.2 above). The Act allowed for fundamental changes to be implemented by qualified (two-thirds) majority, see §27 (amendments of the certificate of incorporation, such as a change of business or an increase of capital), §31 (voluntary dissolution), §105 (merger).

[24] For example N.J. Gen. Corp. Act 1896, §12: 'The business of every corporation shall be managed by its directors'.

[25] See JB Dill, *The Statutory and Case Law Applicable to Private Companies under the General Corporation Act of New Jersey and Corporation Precedents* (3rd edn, Voorhis & Co. 1901) 26, for references.

[26] *Ellerman v Chicago Junction Railways & Union Stock-Yards Co.*, 49 N.J. Eq. 217, 232 (N.J. Ch. 1891).

[27] *Benedict v Columbus Construction Co.*, 49 N.J. Eq. 23, 36 (N.J. Ch. 1892). The Court pointed out that '[i]f stockholders in a corporation disapprove of the company's management, [but there is no case of fraud etc.], their remedy is to elect new officers, or sell their shares, and withdraw': ibid. See also *Ellerman v Chicago Junction Railways* (n 26): 'Individual stockholders cannot question in judicial proceedings the corporate acts of directors, if the same are within the powers of the corporation and in furtherance of its purposes, are not unlawful or against good morals, and are done in good faith and in the exercise of an honest judgment. Questions of policy of management, of expediency of contracts or action, of adequacy of consideration not grossly disproportionate, of lawful appropriation of corporate funds to advance corporate interests, are left solely to the honest decision of the directors, if their powers are without limitation and free from restraint'.

[28] 52 N.J. Eq. 440 (N.J. Ch. 1894).

organizations were represented on the board. The by-laws further provided that any amendment or alteration should require the affirmative vote of stockholders representing at least two-thirds of the capital stock. A simple majority of the shareholders sought to amend the certificate of incorporation and by-laws to discontinue cumulative voting. The shareholders relied on a supplement to the general corporation act that allowed such changes to be adopted 'with the assent of a majority in interest of [the corporation's] stockholders'.[29] The Court held:[30]

> If the certificate of incorporation and the by-laws of a corporation form a contract between the stockholders, then the legislature has no power to authorize a mere majority to alter it, except in the manner provided by the contract itself. That the ordinary certificate of organization does form such contract seems too plain for argument. It takes the place of the special charter under which our corporations were usually organized before the constitutional amendments of 1875. Whether any particular by-law also forms a part of such contract depends upon the time when, and circumstances under which, it was adopted. If it was adopted as a part of the original organization of the company, so that the subscriptions of stock were made, and money paid thereon, upon the strength of it, then it becomes a part of the fundamental contract between the stockholders.... [The Court analysed the by-laws and concluded that they had become part of the contract between the stockholders.] [T]herefore ... [they] cannot be altered, except in the manner therein provided, or by the consent of all the stockholders ... In this connection, it is worthy of remark that the stockholders, as such, have no power to make any contract or execute any work. Their power is confined to electing directors, and advising them in their conduct of the business of the company.

Thus, the Court of Chancery, as the English Court of Appeal in *Automatic Self-Cleansing Filter Syndicate*, qualifies the certificate of incorporation and by-laws as a contract. The incorporators enjoy broad discretion in shaping the governance structure of the corporation in this contract. However, once the rules have been laid down in the constitutional documents, the shareholders are bound by them and the court will enforce the corporate contract. Accordingly, corporations could provide for a shareholder instruction right in the certificate or by-laws and the courts would accept the limitation on the directors' authority. In this respect, US law is no different from English law. But the default rule is that an instruction right does not exist.[31] The last part of the excerpt from *Loewenthal v Rubber Reclaiming Co.* reproduced above indicates that if the corporation's charter does not deviate from the default rule and the general corporation law does not authorize the shareholders to act, the New Jersey courts would consider a shareholder resolution directing the directors to perform a specified act as merely 'advisory'.[32]

This was the situation at the turn of the century, when Delaware began its rise to become the pre-eminent US jurisdiction for incorporations. Delaware corporation law was modelled after the law of New Jersey.[33] Over the course of the first half of the twentieth century a number of statutory amendments shifted the default allocation of power further from the shareholders to the directors. They were authorized to issue shares,[34] determine the

[29] ibid 441. [30] ibid 441–6.

[31] See n 24 above for New Jersey law and Del. Gen. Corp. Law, §141(a).

[32] 52 N.J. Eq. 446, relying on *Plaquemines Tropical Fruit Co. v Buck*, 52 N.J. Eq. 219 (N.J. Ch. 1893). In the latter case, the court explained: 'It may sometimes become necessary in the transaction of some kind of business of a corporation to have the consent of all the stockholders, or of a certain proportion of them; and resolutions giving such consent or advice have the effect of empowering the directors to act. But the board of directors is the legal executive, recognized as such, not only in practice and on principle, but by the statute. The sixteenth section of the corporation act provides that the business of every such company shall be managed and conducted by the directors thereof. I regard the passage of this resolution by the stockholders [ordering the directors to carry into effect a purchase] as simply advisory': ibid 238–9.

[33] RC Larcom, *The Delaware Corporation* (Johns Hopkins Press 1937) 15.

[34] Now Del. Gen. Corp. Law, §161 (provided the shares of capital stock authorized by the certificate of incorporation have not yet all been issued).

consideration for stock to be issued,[35] allocate the consideration received to the capital or surplus account,[36] and decide on the utilization of surplus funds and the time and manner of dividend payments.[37] Furthermore, the certificate of incorporation could vest authority in the directors to define the characteristics, voting power, and other rights of classes of stock,[38] and make, alter, or repeal by-laws.[39] As a contemporary commentator observed, these changes were adopted because they were 'considered to be desirable for the efficient management of the corporation'.[40] Apart from the appointment and removal of directors, an involvement of the shareholders is now only mandatory for an amendment of the certificate of incorporation[41] or fundamental corporate changes, such as mergers[42] or a sale of assets.[43] Even in these cases, the shareholders cannot act of their own accord, but only upon a resolution adopted by the board of directors setting out the proposed action.[44]

Given this clear bias of default rules in favour of director autonomy, how can shareholders restrict director discretion and assert influence over the company's management and business operations? One possibility is to structure the certificate of incorporation in a way that reverses the default allocation of power and transfers responsibilities back to the shareholders. Alternatively, can the shareholders by agreement among themselves (but without changing the articles, which may not be feasible because of lack of director participation[45]) divert management powers from the directors, establish a veto right over board decisions, or give directions to the directors regarding the management of the business? And do they have to act unanimously in doing so or does less than unanimity suffice? The following decision of the New York Court of Appeals shows the generally hostile attitude of the US courts towards agreements that alter the statutory allocation of managerial authority.

***McQuade v. Stoneham*, 263 N.Y. 323 (N.Y. 1934)**

Pound Ch J:

The action is brought to compel specific performance of an agreement between the parties, entered into to secure the control of National Exhibition Company, also called the Baseball Club (New York Nationals or 'Giants'). This was one of Stoneham's enterprises which used the New York polo grounds for its home games. McGraw was manager of the Giants. McQuade was at the time the contract was entered into a City Magistrate. He resigned December 8, 1930.

Defendant Stoneham became the owner of 1,306 shares, or a majority of the stock of National Exhibition Company. Plaintiff and defendant McGraw each purchased seventy shares of his stock. Plaintiff paid Stoneham $50,338.10 for the stock he purchased. As a part of the transaction the agreement in question was entered into. It was dated May 21, 1919. Some of its pertinent provisions are

'VIII. The parties hereto will use their best endeavors for the purpose of continuing as directors of said Company and as officers thereof the following:

Directors:

Charles A. Stoneham,

John J. McGraw,

Francis X. McQuade,

with the right to the party of the first part [Stoneham] to name all additional directors as he sees fit.

Officers:

Charles A. Stoneham, President,

John J. McGraw, Vice-President,

Francis X. McQuade, Treasurer.

'IX. No salaries are to be paid to any of the above officers or directors, except as follows ...

[35] Now ibid §152. [36] Now ibid §154. [37] Now ibid §§170, 173. [38] Now ibid §151.
[39] Now ibid §109. [40] Larcom (n 33) 145. [41] Del. Gen. Corp. Law, §242. [42] ibid §251.
[43] ibid §271 (shareholder authorization is required if the corporation intends to 'sell, lease or exchange all or substantially all of its property and assets').
[44] ibid §242(b) (amendments of the certificate of incorporation), §251(b), (c) (mergers).
[45] ibid §242(b).

'X. There shall be no change in said salaries, no change in the amount of capital, or the number of shares, no change or amendment of the by-laws of the corporation or any matters regarding the policy of the business of the corporation or any matters which may in anywise affect, endanger or interfere with the rights of minority stockholders, excepting upon the mutual and unanimous consent of all of the parties hereto …

In pursuance of this contract Stoneham became president and McGraw vice-president of the corporation. McQuade became treasurer … He continued to act until May 2, 1928, when Leo J. Bondy was elected to succeed him. The board of directors consisted of seven men. The four outside of the parties hereto were selected by Stoneham and he had complete control over them. At the meeting of May 2, 1928, Stoneham and McGraw refrained from voting, McQuade voted for himself and the other four voted for Bondy. Defendants did not to keep their agreement with McQuade to use their best efforts to continue him as treasurer. On the contrary, he was dropped with their entire acquiescence. At the next stockholders' meeting he was dropped as a director although they might have elected him …

The cause for dropping McQuade was due to the falling out of friends. McQuade and Stoneham had disagreed. The trial court has found in substance that their numerous quarrels and disputes did not affect the orderly and efficient administration of the business of the corporation; that plaintiff was removed because he had antagonized the dominant Stoneham by persisting in challenging his power over the corporate treasury and for no misconduct on his part. The court also finds that plaintiff was removed by Stoneham for protecting the corporation and its minority stockholders. We will assume that Stoneham put him out when he might have retained him, merely in order to get rid of him.

Defendants say that the contract in suit was void because the directors held their office charged with the duty to act for the corporation according to their best judgment and that any contract which compels a director to vote to keep any particular person in office and at a stated salary is illegal. Directors are the exclusive executive representatives of the corporation, charged with administration of its internal affairs and the management and use of its assets. They manage the business of the corporation. (Gen. Corp. Law; Cons. Laws, ch. 23, § 27.) 'An agreement to continue a man as president is dependent upon his continued loyalty to the interests of the corporation' …

Plaintiff contends that the converse of this proposition is true and that an agreement among directors to continue a man as an officer of a corporation is not to be broken so long as such officer is loyal to the interests of the corporation and that, as plaintiff has been found loyal to the corporation, the agreement of defendants is enforceable.

[I]t has been held that an agreement among stockholders whereby it is attempted to divest the directors of their power to discharge an unfaithful employee of the corporation is illegal as against public policy … it must be equally true that the stockholders may not, by agreement among themselves, control the directors in the exercise of the judgment vested in them by virtue of their office to elect officers and fix salaries. Their motives may not be questioned so long as their acts are legal. The bad faith or the improper motives of the parties does not change the rule … Directors may not by agreements entered into as stockholders abrogate their independent judgment …

Stockholders may, of course, combine to elect directors. That rule is well settled … The power to unite is, however, limited to the election of directors and is not extended to contracts whereby limitations are placed on the power of directors to manage the business of the corporation by the selection of agents at defined salaries.

The minority shareholders whose interests McQuade says he has been punished for protecting, are not, aside from himself, complaining about his discharge. He is not acting for the corporation or for them in this action. It is impossible to see how the corporation has been injured by the substitution of Bondy as treasurer in place of McQuade …

It is urged that we should pay heed to the morals and manners of the market place to sustain this agreement and that we should hold that its violation gives rise to a cause of action for damages rather than base our decision on any outworn notions of public policy. Public policy is a dangerous guide in determining the validity of a contract and courts should not interfere lightly with the freedom of competent parties to make their own contracts. We do not close our eyes to the fact that such agreements, tacitly or openly arrived at, are not uncommon, especially in close corporations where the stockholders are doing business for convenience under a corporate organization. We know that majority stockholders, united in voting trusts, effectively manage the business of a corporation by choosing trustworthy directors to reflect their policies in the corporate management. Nor are we unmindful that McQuade has, so the court has found, been shabbily treated as a purchaser of stock from Stoneham. We have said: 'A trustee is held to something stricter than the morals of the market place' ... but Stoneham and McGraw were not trustees for McQuade as an individual. Their duty was to the corporation and its stockholders, to be exercised according to their unrestricted lawful judgment. They were under no legal obligation to deal righteously with McQuade if it was against public policy to do so.

The courts do not enforce mere moral obligations, nor legal ones either, unless someone seeks to establish rights which may be waived by custom and for convenience. We are constrained by authority to hold that a contract is illegal and void so far as it precludes the board of directors, at the risk of incurring legal liability, from changing officers, salaries or policies or retaining individuals in office, except by consent of the contracting parties. On the whole, such a holding is probably preferable to one which would open the courts to pass on the motives of directors in the lawful exercise of their trust ...

Questions and comments:

1. According to *McQuade* (and, possibly, also *Automatic Self-Cleansing*?), are the directors agents of the shareholders? If not, what are they? Could we say that they are 'Platonic guardians of a sui generis entity in which shareholders are but one of many contracting inputs'?[46] Is an interpretation that qualifies them as independent or *sui generis* actors/fiduciaries consistent with economic theory, that is, does such an interpretation achieve economically efficient results, given what we discussed in Chapter 4?
2. US law acknowledges the existence of certain exceptions to the principle established in *McQuade*. In *Clark v Dodge*,[47] the New York Court of Appeals held that: '[w]here the directors are the sole stockholders, there seems to be no objection to enforcing an agreement among them to vote for certain people as officers'.[48] The decision was based on two considerations. First, in the opinion of the court, the relevant public policy concern that led to the invalidation of the shareholder agreement in *McQuade* was the protection of creditors and minority shareholders. If the corporation does not have any minority shareholders that are external to the agreement and the terms of the agreement do not pose any risk to creditors (no externalities), the public has no interest in holding it illegal.[49] Secondly, in *Clark v Dodge* the agreement impinged only 'slightly' upon the powers of the directors. As the court put it: 'There was no attempt to sterilize the board of directors'.[50]

   For some time, it was not clear whether the two conditions mentioned in *Clark v Dodge* had to be satisfied cumulatively, that is, shareholder agreements had to be adopted

[46] SM Bainbridge, 'The Business Judgment Rule As Abstention Doctrine' (2004) 57 Vanderbilt Law Review 83, 102–103.

[47] 199 N.E. 641 (N.Y. 1936).

[48] ibid 642.

[49] ibid. See also *Triggs v Triggs*, 46 N.Y.2d 305 (N.Y. 1978), where the court elaborated on the role of the board in protecting minority shareholders: '[T]he effect of such an agreement [entered into between some, but not all, of the shareholders] is to deprive the other shareholders of the benefits and protections which the law perceives to exist when the corporation is managed by an independent board of directors, free to use its own business judgment in the best interest of the corporation'.

[50] *Clark v Dodge*, 199 N.E. 643: 'The only restrictions on Dodge [one of the directors] were (a) that as a stockholder he should vote for Clark as a director—a perfectly legal contract; (b) that as director he should continue Clark as general manager, so long as he proved faithful, efficient, and competent—an agreement which could harm nobody; (c) that Clark should always receive as salary or dividends one-fourth of the 'net income'. For the purposes of this motion, it is only just to construe that phrase as meaning whatever was left for distribution after the directors had in good faith set aside whatever they deemed wise; (d) that no salaries to other officers should be paid, unreasonable in amount or incommensurate with services rendered—a beneficial and not a harmful agreement. If there was any invasion of the powers of the directorate under that agreement, it is so slight as to be negligible; and certainly there is no damage suffered by or threatened to anybody'.

unanimously and were not permitted to impinge more than slightly on the directors' authority, or either of them was sufficient to validate a shareholder agreement. In New York and Delaware, the former seems to have been the case.[51] New York courts outlawed agreements that were concluded by all shareholders where the board was deprived of most management powers.[52] In *Galler v Galler*,[53] on the other hand, a case decided under the law of Illinois, the Illinois Supreme Court allowed a shareholder agreement that was adopted by the majority shareholders without participation of a minority shareholder owning 5 per cent of the company's capital. The court argued that in spite of a lack of unanimity, the agreement was enforceable because the minority shareholder did not object, the agreement was limited in scope, and its terms (salary continuation after the death of one of the founding directors to support dependent family members) were a common feature of corporate executive employment.[54]

The fact that the corporation in *Galler v Galler* was a close corporation (a corporation with a limited number of shareholders and shares that were not publicly traded) was another reason why the court was prepared to uphold the shareholder agreement. The court explained that minority shareholders in close corporations may have committed a significant proportion of their wealth. However, in contrast to public corporations with an active market for their shares, they do not have the possibility to exit the company if they disagree with management policies. Consequently, they often require an enforceable shareholder agreement to safeguard their position. The court identified a substantive difference between a shareholder in a public and a private (close) corporation. The latter is 'more than a mere investor'; while he may not have a sufficiently large shareholding to influence the composition of the board, he feels 'that his voice should be heard concerning all corporate activity'.[55] Accordingly, the court argued in favour of a distinct legal treatment of public and private corporations.[56]

Following this and similar cases, most states have amended their business corporation laws or adopted special close corporation statutes in order to lay down the requirements for valid shareholder agreements.[57] The respective provisions of the Model Business Corporation Act[58] may serve as an example of the content of such a statute. According to the MBCA, shareholders may enter into an agreement that is inconsistent with the general corporation law if it is approved by all shareholders and a number of additional requirements are satisfied; notably, the shares of the corporation must not be listed on a national securities exchange. Under these conditions, the shareholders may provide for a far-reaching appropriation of the powers of the board. For example, they may establish 'who shall be directors or officers of the corporation, or their terms of office or manner of selection or removal',[59] transfer 'to one or more shareholders or other persons all or part of the authority to exercise the corporate powers or to manage the business and affairs of the corporation',[60] or eliminate the board of directors altogether.[61] However, if the shareholders restrict the discretion or powers of the board in this way they incur liability 'for acts or omissions imposed by law on directors'.[62] In other words,

[51] See *Triggs v Triggs* (n 49) 314: 'In those cases in which the agreement is made by less than all the shareholders, almost any attempt to reduce the authority granted to the board by law will create a significant potential for harm to other shareholders'; see also *Zion v Kurtz*, 50 N.Y.2d 92 (N.Y. 1980) (holding that under Delaware law a shareholder agreement providing that 'no "business or activities" of the corporation shall be conducted without the consent of a minority stockholder' was enforceable if all of the shareholders had agreed to it).

[52] *Long Park, Inc. v Trenton-New Brunswick Theatres Co.*, 297 N.Y. 174 (N.Y. 1948). The shareholder agreement provided that one of the shareholders, who was called 'the manager' in the agreement, was 'given full authority and power to supervise and direct the operation and management' of the company's business (the operation of theatres). The board was not authorized to change this delegation of management powers to the shareholder: ibid 177–8. The court held that 'the powers of the directors over the management of its theatres, the principal business of the corporation, were completely sterilized. Such restrictions and limitations upon the powers of the directors are clearly in violation of section 27 of the General Corporation Law [stipulating that "[t]he business of a corporation shall be managed by its board of directors"]': ibid 179.

[53] 32 Ill. 2d 16 (Ill. 1964). [54] ibid 586–7. [55] ibid 584. [56] ibid 585.

[57] In Delaware: Gen. Corp. Law, §§341–356. [58] MBCA, §7.32. [59] ibid §7.32(a)(3).

[60] ibid §7.32(a)(6). [61] ibid §7.32(a)(1).

[62] ibid §7.32(e).

the shareholders who exercise the board's powers become subject to the directors' fiduciary and legal duties.

These provisions show that US law effectively provides for two distinct sets of rules: one for the public and one for the closely held corporation. Where a separate close corporation statute exists, companies may opt into the regime for close corporations if the number of their shareholders does not exceed a certain limit.[63] The latter set of rules is characterized by a great degree of flexibility, which can be used by shareholders to strengthen their rights and influence on business operations. On the other hand, in public corporations, US courts are likely to enforce the statutory division of powers strictly, following the rationale of *McQuade*. Why do US courts adopt this strict stance when they deal with public corporations? Would it be advisable to introduce the degree of flexibility that is available under the close corporation statutes also for the public corporation in order to enhance shareholder democracy?

3. In comparison with the United States, UK courts are more lenient in allowing shareholder agreements that alter the allocation of power. See, for example, *Breckland Group Holdings v London & Suffolk Properties*,[64] where the two shareholders of London & Suffolk had entered into an agreement that restricted the powers of the board in several ways. In particular, the agreement determined the constitution of the board, provided that the two shareholders should have a representative on the board at all times, and specified decisions of the board required the approval of the shareholder representatives on the board.[65] Such provisions are common in investment agreements used by venture capital or private equity firms that inject a substantial amount of equity capital into a business.[66] The court accepted that shareholders enjoy the power to set out corporate governance arrangements in a shareholder agreement and relied on the agreement to delineate the competences of the general meeting and the board.[67]

   In general, English courts will enforce shareholder agreements and impose only the requirement that they do not limit the company's statutory powers.[68] Of course, where a shareholder agreement contradicts the articles a problem will arise as to which provision shall apply. But in contrast to the legal situation in the United States, this is a problem of the interpretation and reconcilement of two conflicting (essentially contractual) documents, not of the violation of public policy by one of the documents because of the transfer of management powers. For example, it is common for a shareholder agreement to bestow the power to make specified decisions on individual shareholders or on the general meeting. Such an arrangement is in conflict with the default allocation of powers pursuant to the model articles, which provide that the directors shall be responsible for managing the company.[69] The law is not entirely clear on how to resolve this conflict. The safest practice is to draft the shareholder agreement and the articles together and exclude the conflicting model article.[70] If this does not happen, we may distinguish between two cases. If the shareholders act unanimously, it can be argued that the *Duomatic* principle applies.[71] The agreement simultaneously alters the articles that accord the directors unfettered decision-making power. Consequently, it is enforceable against the shareholders and the company. If the agreement is not concluded between all shareholders, but the company and/or directors are parties to it, enforceability is more difficult to assess. Following the decision in *Russell v Northern Bank*,[72] courts may hold that the agreement is not

[63] In Delaware, the maximum number of shareholders is 30; see Del. Gen. Corp. Law, §342(a)(1).

[64] (1988) 4 BCC 542. The facts are summarized in n 19 above.

[65] ibid 544.

[66] K Reece Thomas and C Ryan, *The Law and Practice of Shareholders' Agreements* (4th edn, LexisNexis 2014) para 4.158 and Appendix, Precedents 5 and 6.

[67] *Breckland Group* (n 19) 545.

[68] For example, it was decided that a company cannot contract out of its right to alter its articles of incorporation. See *Punt v Symons & Co Ltd* [1903] 2 Ch 506; *Russell v Northern Bank Development Corpn Ltd* [1992] 1 WLR 588. However, in the latter case the House of Lords held that the shareholders were still bound by the agreement, even though the company was not, and had to exercise their voting rights accordingly.

[69] Article 3 of the Model Articles for Public or Private Companies.

[70] See Reece Thomas and Ryan (n 66) paras 1.34, 4.19; and the examples given in the Appendix, Precedent 3, cl 1.2; Precedent 6, cl 1.2.

[71] Note 20 above.

[72] Note 68 above.

enforceable against the company and the directors because it fetters the board's constitutional powers, but the company's and the directors' undertaking is separable from that of the shareholders. As a consequence, the shareholders would be bound by the agreement and required to take all necessary steps (within the law) to achieve the aims of the agreement.[73]

Further difficult questions, to be distinguished from the effect that private ordering has on the default allocation of powers, concern the relationship between shareholder agreements and directors' fiduciary duties. Section 173(2) of the Companies Act 2006 clarifies that shareholder agreements can, in principle, constrain the directors' independent judgment. This provision is in line with pre-Companies Act 2006 case law, but the courts emphasize that each case has to be judged on its own merits. Directors are required to act in good faith in the best interest of the company.[74] Where they bind themselves for the future, such a restriction of their discretion, accordingly, must be in the best interest of the company, for example because the company obtains important benefits under the agreement, and may cease to have effect when the circumstances change.[75]

4. In both private and public US companies, shareholders retain the right to alter the by-laws or articles and remove directors for cause or fill vacancies on the board, even if this power is vested in the directors by the certificate of incorporation. In addition, they have the right to be heard and express an opinion on all relevant matters, including those that fall within the purview of the board of directors. The common law considers such powers to be inherent in the position of a shareholder.[76] However, most corporation statutes in the United States have now curtailed the shareholders' authority significantly by requiring both director and shareholder action for an amendment of the articles. The board adopts the proposed amendment and then submits it to the shareholders for their approval.[77]

   As far as adopting and amending the company's by-laws are concerned, the shareholders have retained greater powers, at least in the states that follow the Model Business Corporation Act. Bylaws are typically more detailed than the articles and govern the internal affairs of the corporation. They deal with matters such as the qualifications of directors, quorum and notice requirements, and other procedural rules for calling and voting at board and shareholder meetings. They may also determine how the board is structured, for example how many and which committees are to be established, and fix the number and duties of the corporate officers. As opposed to the articles, by-laws can be changed unilaterally by the general meeting or the board of directors.[78] Furthermore, in most states, the law stipulates that the directors do not have the power to amend the by-laws if 'the shareholders in amending, repealing, or adopting a bylaw expressly provide that the board of directors may not amend, repeal, or reinstate that bylaw'.[79] This qualification is intended to prevent the shareholders and directors from repealing the other side's by-laws and reinstating their own version in a perpetual cycle.

[73] For a comprehensive discussion of these issues, including an analysis of Canadian and US law, see Reece Thomas and Ryan (n 66) 4.112–4.146; CA Riley, 'Vetoes and Voting Agreements: Some Problems of Consent and Knowledge' (1993) 44 Northern Ireland Legal Quarterly 34.

[74] Companies Act 2006, s 172.

[75] *Fulham Football Club Ltd v Cabra Estates plc* [1992] BCC 863, relying on the High Court of Australia in *Thorby v Goldberg* (1964) 112 CLR 597; *Boulting v Association of Cinematograph, Television and Allied Technicians* [1963] 2 QB 606 (stressing that 'no one, who has duties of a fiduciary nature to discharge, can be allowed to enter into an engagement by which he binds himself to disregard those duties or to act inconsistently with them' and an agreement suffering from such a conflict is unlawful: ibid 626 (Lord Denning MR)).

[76] *Auer v Dressel*, 118 N.E. 2d 590 (N.Y. 1954). In the words of the US Supreme Court in *Rogers v Hill*, 289 U.S. 582 (US 1933) (applying the law of New Jersey): '[A] charter provision or by-law adopted by incorporators or shareholders delegating power to directors may not reasonably be held to take from the stockholders any of the power conferred upon them by the statute ... It would be preposterous to leave the real owners of the corporate property at the mercy of their agents, and the law has not done so'. ibid 589. Note that this holding refers only to private ordering, i.e. the attempt to divest the shareholders of their power to alter the articles or by-laws by delegating this power *in the articles* to the directors. If legislation restricts the power of the shareholders to amend the articles, for example by requiring a resolution by the board of directors in addition to a shareholder resolution (see the references in the next footnote), then this statutory allocation of power is, of course, binding. *Auer v Dressel* is discussed further in section C.II.2 below.

[77] Del. Gen. Corp. Law, §242(b)(1); MBCA, §10.03.

[78] MBCA, §10.20.

[79] ibid §10.20(b)(2).

Notably, this power is only given to the shareholders, not the directors, and thus reflects the common law rule that sees the shareholders as the source of the power to promulgate and change by-laws.

An important qualification to this approach can be found in the Delaware General Corporation Law. In Delaware, shareholders have the power to adopt, amend or repeal by-laws, unless this power is conferred on the directors in the certificate of incorporation.[80] Such a conferral does not divest the shareholders of their power, but since by-laws have to be consistent with the articles,[81] the question arises whether the shareholders can make the bylaw immune from repeal or amendment by limiting the board's authority to that effect. A second problem is whether the shareholders can circumvent the allocation of managerial authority in §141(a) Del. Gen. Corp. Law by deciding business matters in the by-laws. There is no bright-line answer to these questions under Delaware law,[82] but the courts generally prohibit an encroachment upon the board's powers to manage the company's business by the shareholders. The Delaware Supreme Court emphasizes that 'stockholders of a corporation subject to the DGCL may not directly manage the business and affairs of the corporation, at least without specific authorization in either the statute or the certificate of incorporation. Therefore, the shareholders' statutory power to adopt, amend or repeal by-laws is not coextensive with the board's concurrent power and is limited by the board's management prerogatives under Section 141(a)'.[83] The question, according to the Supreme Court, is whether the shareholders determine in the by-laws 'how the board should decide specific substantive business decisions', or they simply intend to 'define the process and procedures by which those decisions are made'.[84] In the latter case, the bylaw is valid; in the former case, it is in violation of the 'cardinal precept of the General Corporation Law of the State of Delaware ... that directors, rather than shareholders, manage the business and affairs of the corporation'.[85] This legal situation has led one commentator to conclude that '[t]he shareholder power to initiate bylaw amendments without prior board action is unique. It is also an historical anachronism states unthinkingly codified from old common law principles lacking either rhyme or reason'.[86] Is this the right conclusion to be drawn from the above case law and the process to be followed in order to amend the articles of association, as laid down, for example, in §242(b)(1) Del. Gen. Corp. Law?

5. While the courts have not objected to, and are prepared to carry into effect, the director bias of the modern corporation laws in the United States (and in particular Delaware), they take any encroachment upon the remaining (narrow) shareholder franchise seriously. We will discuss some of the most important cases in the next section.[87] These cases generally involve fundamental changes to the corporate structure, that is, the directors seek to exclude the shareholders from deciding on fundamental aspects of their involvement in the corporation and the corporation's future. Short of such fundamental changes, the courts are reluctant to interfere with the broad discretion and management powers that the corporation statutes confer on directors.
6. Is it correct to say that while UK and US law started from the same point, they have evolved in opposite directions as far as the position of the shareholders and the allocation of corporate power between the board of directors and the general meeting are concerned? If yes, how do you explain this divergence? Is this observation in line with the path dependence thesis[88] and legal origins (LLSV), which claim that corporate rules and structures depend to a large extent on the rules and structures that existed in the legal and economic system at earlier times?

[80] Del. Gen. Corp. Law, §109(a).

[81] ibid §109(b).

[82] The first question is considered by *General DataComm Industries, Inc. v State of Wis. Inv. Bd.*, 731 A.2d 818, 821, fn. 1 (Del. Ch. 1999) (suggesting *in obiter* that the board can repeal a stockholder-approved bylaw if it has shared authority to adopt, amend or repeal by-laws pursuant to §109(a) Del. Gen. Corp. Law).

[83] *CA, Inc. v AFSCME Employees Pension Plan*, 953 A.2d 227, 232 (Del. 2008).

[84] ibid 235.

[85] ibid 232, fn 6 (quoting *Aronson v Lewis*, 473 A.2d 805, 811 (Del. 1984)).

[86] SM Bainbridge, *Corporate Law* (2nd edn, Foundation Press 2009) 19.

[87] Section B.II.

[88] See, for example, Lucian A Bebchuk and Mark J Roe, 'A Theory of Path Dependence in Corporate Ownership and Governance' (1999) 52 Stanford Law Review 127.

III. Germany

Initially, shareholders in German stock corporations were in a position that was very similar to shareholders of UK companies. Until the law on stock corporations was codified in the Stock Corporation Act of 1937,[89] the general meeting was seen as the supreme organ of the corporation.[90] Corporate power originated from the shareholders, who exercised it 'in particular with respect to the management of the company'[91] in general meeting or delegated management powers to the management and/or supervisory board. As discussed above, the Act of 1937 divested the supervisory board of virtually all management powers, restricted the decision-making powers of the general meeting to cases explicitly provided for in the act and the articles of incorporation, and established the management board as the central governance organ within the corporation.[92]

One of the reasons for the overhaul of the law was that in the eyes of the public the financial crises of the time were associated with the rise of the anonymous, capitalist corporation. Many perceived capital as dominating, rather than serving, the real economy and shareholders as pursuing their profit interest in an 'irresponsible' way, instead of acting constructively for the benefit of the company as a whole.[93] The reform, which had begun in the 1920s before the National Socialists came to power and was, therefore, initially not influenced by national socialist ideology, intended to curtail the power of large blockholders and strengthen the authority and responsibilities of the management board. After 1933, the reorganization of the internal governance structure of the stock corporation was reinterpreted in light of the *Führerprinzip* (leader principle). Elevating the management board to the corporation's central governance organ that was furnished with broad powers and had to exercise these powers in the general interest, not the financial interests of the shareholders,[94] and at the same time restricting the competences of the general meeting, was in line with the Nazi's general distrust of the capitalist system and disregard for majority rule.[95] However, in spite of this rhetoric, most of the amendments can be seen as the continuation of the earlier reform programme and logical reaction to the perceived deficiencies of the old law and the criticism already voiced in the 1920s.[96] Indeed, the reform was heavily criticized by authors who were sympathetic to the national socialist regime.[97] The central capitalist tenets of the corporation—general incorporation and, within limits, contractual freedom to draft and alter the articles, financing of the corporation through the issue of fungible shares, and managing the enterprise without state intervention—were never seriously called into question.[98] The now predominant view is that the 1937 Act was a largely apolitical, technically sound piece of legislation.[99] After the fall of the Nazi regime, the legislature, accordingly, decided not to initiate yet another comprehensive overhaul of the law. The parameters of

[89] See Chapter 4E.I.3.

[90] U Hüffer, 'Der Vorstand als Leitungsorgan und die Mandats- sowie Haftungsbeziehungen seiner Mitglieder' in W Bayer and M Habersack (eds), *Aktienrecht im Wandel, vol 2: Grundsatzfragen des Aktienrechts* (Mohr Siebeck 2007) 7/10.

[91] HGB [Commercial Code] 1897, §250.

[92] Chapter 4E.I.3.

[93] See W Bayer and S Engelke, 'Die Revision des Aktienrechts durch das Aktiengesetz von 1937' in W Bayer and M Habersack (eds), *Aktienrecht im Wandel, vol 1: Entwicklungen des Aktienrechts* (Mohr Siebeck 2007) 15/2, 5, with references.

[94] The provision of the AktG of 1937 defining the powers of the management board, §70(1), did not mention shareholder interests, but only the interests of 'the enterprise and its workforce, as well as the general benefit of society and state'. This provision is discussed in Chapter 4C.II above.

[95] Bayer and Engelke (n 93) 15/16.

[96] See our discussion in Chapter 4C.II. For a careful analysis of this issue, see also FA Mann, 'The New German Company Law and Its Background' (1937) 19 Journal of Comparative Legislation and International Law 220. According to Mann, the most significant change to the balance of power within the corporation was the deprivation of the shareholders' right to dispose of the annual accounts, if the supervisory board approved the accounts as prepared by the management board; ibid 229–30 and AktG 1937, §125(4) (now AktG 1965, BGBl I, 1089, §173(1)).

[97] Bayer and Engelke (n 93) 15/28.

[98] ibid 15/41–52.

[99] ibid 15/122.

the internal organization of the stock corporation, as they were laid down in the 1937 Act, remain applicable today.[100]

The main innovations of the 1937 Act with respect to the allocation of power were the following. The statutory power to manage the corporation was transferred from the general meeting to the management board.[101] The general meeting was prohibited from deciding on matters of management, unless requested to do so by the management board.[102] Furthermore, the law now explicitly stipulated that management powers could not be vested in the supervisory board.[103] The supervisory board was only authorized to 'supervise' the management.[104] In doing so, it was empowered to request a report on the operations of the corporation from the management board and inspect the books and records of the company.[105] It was entitled and required to call a general meeting when this was necessary to safeguard the interests of the company.[106] The general meeting elected the members of the supervisory board and could remove them at any time with or without cause with qualified majority.[107] The supervisory board, in turn, appointed and removed the members of the management board. Removal before the end of a member's tenure required serious cause, for example a gross breach of duty.[108] Thus, the management board became somewhat insulated from the demands of the shareholders. However, the shareholders retained at least indirect influence on the conduct of the business through the appointment of the supervisory board. It was commonly accepted that an expression of no confidence by the general meeting entitled the supervisory board to remove the respective member of the management board.[109] The actual decision was at the discretion of the supervisory board, but since the right of the general meeting to remove supervisory board members was not subject to further requirements, it was unlikely that the supervisory board would go against the clear wishes of the shareholders. In addition, other competences of the general meeting, such as the requirement that the general meeting vote annually on the discharge of the members of the management and supervisory boards[110] or its control of the enforcement of the corporation's claims against the members of both boards,[111] ensured that a modicum of oversight remained with the shareholders.

The current Stock Corporation Act, which was adopted in 1965,[112] brought about a selective strengthening of the rights of the general meeting and minority shareholders to make

[100] The law was reformed in 1965, when the current Stock Corporation Act was adopted, but the reforms had no implications for the allocation of power in the corporation.

[101] AktG 1937, §70(1). [102] ibid §103(2) (now AktG 1965, §119(2)).

[103] AktG 1937, §95(5) (now AktG 1965, §111(4)). The only exception that the Act allowed was the provision that particular types of transaction required the approval by the supervisory board. The AktG 1965 has retained this exception.

[104] AktG 1937, §95(1) (now AktG 1965, §111(1)).

[105] AktG 1937, §95(2), (3) (now AktG 1965, §111(2)).

[106] AktG 1937, §95(4) (now AktG 1965, §111(3)).

[107] AktG 1937, §87(1), (2) (now AktG 1965, §§101(1), 103(1)).

[108] AktG 1937, §75(1), (3) (now AktG 1965, §84 (1), (3)).

[109] Bayer and Engelke (n 93) 15/81. The current law is more restrictive. The AktG 1965, §83(4) provides that serious cause does not exist if the vote of no confidence was made for arbitrary reasons. The more restrictive interpretation was initiated by BGHZ 13, 188 (*Gerling*), a decision that concerned the pre-1965 law. The interpretation offered by the court was codified in the 1965 amendments. The court pointed out: 'Generally, the withdrawal of confidence in a member of the management board by the general meeting constitutes serious cause justifying the removal of that member. It is not necessary to verify that the removal is warranted in the individual case because the position of the management board is based on trust, and the authority of the board is legitimised by this relationship of trust … According to §231(3) HGB 1897 it was possible to revoke the appointment of the members of the management board arbitrarily. This was changed by [AktG 1937,] §75(3), to preclude the management board from becoming heavily dependent on the supervisory board. The members of the management board should be relieved of the risk of removal without reason in order to provide them with security in their work': ibid.

[110] AktG 1937, §104 (now AktG 1965, §120).

[111] AktG 1937, §122 (now AktG 1965, §147). Enforcement required a resolution adopted by simple majority or a motion of minority shareholders holding at least 10% of the capital.

[112] See n 96 above.

the stock corporation more attractive to small investors and encourage the development of a more liquid capital market, but left the basic allocation of power as formulated in the Act of 1937 in place.[113] The separation of competences between the general meeting and the management board is now mainly determined by two provisions of the Stock Corporation Act: §76(1), which vests unfettered management powers in the management board, and §119.[114]

German Stock Corporation Act

§ 119—Competences of the general meeting

(1) The general meeting decides in the cases expressly provided for by law or in the articles of association, namely:
   1. the appointment of the members of the supervisory board [. . .];
   2. the appropriation of the balance sheet profit;
   3. the discharge of the members of the management board and supervisory board;
   4. the appointment of the statutory auditors;
   5. amendments of the articles;
   6. capital increases and reductions of capital;
   7. the appointment of auditors for the examination of matters in relation to the formation or management of the company;
   8. the liquidation of the company.

(2) The general meeting shall decide on matters of the company's management only if the management board requests such a decision.

§119 shows that, in the opinion of the 1965 legislator, the sphere of shareholder competences should relate in particular to two areas: fundamental corporate changes, such as an amendment of the articles or liquidation of the company, which affect the position of the shareholders in the company substantially,[115] and matters where both the management and supervisory board can be said to be conflicted, notably the appointment of the supervisory board members, discharge of the members of both boards, and appointment of the external auditor who examines the company's accounts.[116] The allocation of powers as laid

[113] For a discussion of the reform, see B Kropff, 'Reformbestrebungen im Nachkriegsdeutschland und die Aktienrechtsreform von 1965' in Bayer and Habersack (n 90) ch 16. The 1965 legislator decided that the allocation of responsibilities as laid down in the Act of 1937 was, in principle, appropriate: ibid 16/60. The changes included the prohibition of multiple voting shares (AktG 1965, §12(2)), greater involvement of the general meeting in the decision on the appropriation of the balance sheet profit (AktG 1965, §§58, 174; generally, the management board and supervisory board approve the annual accounts and determine the allocation of the company's surplus, see §172, but the law prescribes that not more than half of the annual surplus shall be transferred to retained earnings, and the general meeting decides on the use of the remainder, §58(2), (3)), a strengthened right of shareholders to demand information (compare AktG 1937, §112, with AktG 1965, §131), and an extension of the reporting requirements of the management board to the supervisory board (compare AktG 1937, §81, with AktG 1965, §90). Later amendments further strengthened shareholder and minority rights as well as the right to information of the supervisory board, but again did not alter the basic allocation of power. The most important of these later reforms were Gesetz zur Kontrolle und Transparenz im Unternehmensbereich (KonTraG) [Control and Transparency in the Corporate Sector Act] of 1 May 1998, BGBl I, 786; and Transparenz- und Publizitätsgesetz (TransPuG) [Transparency and Publicity Act] of 19 July 2002, BGBl I, 2010.

[114] The instances of shareholder decision-making listed in §119(1) are amplified elsewhere in the Stock Corporation Act and other laws; for example, for the appropriation of the balance sheet profit see §§58, 174 AktG, discharge of the members of the management and supervisory board §120 AktG, appointment of the auditors §318(1) HGB [Commercial Code], amendment of the articles §179 AktG, increase of capital in return for contributions §182 AktG, and liquidation §262(1) no 2 AktG.

[115] §119(1) does not provide for an exhaustive list of instances where the general meeting has exclusive decision-making power; other fundamental corporate changes that fall within the domain of the general meeting include the sale of the company's entire assets (AktG, §179a), enterprise agreements (AktG, §293), and mergers (UmwG [Transformation Act], §65).

[116] Again, §119(1) is not exhaustive. Examples of other matters falling within the competences of the shareholders, typically concerning conflicts of interest of the generally competent organ, include a waiver of the company's damages claims against members of the management or supervisory board (§§93(4), 116), enforcement of such claims (§147), determination of the compensation of supervisory board members (§113), or the removal of members of the supervisory board (§103(1)).

down in §119 is not subject to private ordering. The incorporators are not permitted to encroach upon the protected areas of shareholder competences by drafting the articles in a director-friendly way. Conversely, it is also impermissible to extend the competences of the general meeting to replace the management board, grant the shareholders an instruction right, or make certain management decisions dependent upon shareholder approval.[117] The general meeting is only authorized to decide on matters of business operations if the management board requests the shareholders to do so.[118] The managers may find this course of action advisable when they decide on high-risk investment projects to limit their potential liability.[119]

The rigid delineation of the organs' competences is a function of the principle of limited contractual freedom (*Grundsatz der Satzungsstrenge*) that characterizes the German law on the public stock corporation.[120] However, the following decision of the Bundesgerichtshof shows that the division of powers, as codified in the Stock Corporation Act, may not always be able to provide for an adequate balancing of the interests of the corporate organs. In some cases, it may be necessary, and courts are prepared, to go beyond the letter of the law.

BGH Judgment of 25 February 1982, BGHZ 83, 122 (*Holzmüller*)

The plaintiff is acting as executor of the deceased merchant R, who was a shareholder of the defendant company with an equitable interest of 250,000 DM in the company's 3.2 million DM capital. According to § 2 of the company's articles of association, the nature and purpose of its business was the trading with wood and other commodities as well as the procurement, carrying out and financing of transactions involving wood. The original version of § 2(1) no. 3 of the articles provided that the objects also included 'the acquisition of interests in other companies trading with wood and in companies engaged in similar industries as well as the buy-out or acquisition of such companies, as the case may be'. An amendment to the articles adopted by the general meeting held on 14 July 1972 reformulated this provision. The plaintiff agreed to the revised form of the provision.

§ 2(2) of the articles as amended read as follows: 'The stock corporation is further authorized to establish, purchase and hold shares in other companies. It may transfer some or all of its business to such other companies'.

A board member explained at the general meeting that the purpose of this change was 'to enable the spinning off of the seaport business and allow it to be transferred to a KGaA [limited partnership with a share capital] that was to be newly established. The defendant stock corporation would function as a holding company and receive shares in the KGaA in exchange for the seaport business'.

[117] Schmidt (n 3) §28 V 2 a. Therefore, the contractual freedom of the incorporators is limited. If a matter is allocated to the management board pursuant to the Stock Corporation Act, the articles cannot alter this statutory distribution of powers (see AktG, §23(5)). As a consequence, the reference in §119(1) to the articles of association is largely irrelevant (for a discussion of this point, see J Koch in U Hüffer and J Koch, *Aktiengesetz* (13th edn, CH Beck 2018) §119, para 10, giving mainly §68(2) sentence 3 AktG as an example of a case where the articles may vest decision-making power in the general meeting).

[118] AktG, §119(2).

[119] See AktG, §93(4) sentence 1: The members of the management board are not liable if the decision was based on a lawful resolution by the general meeting. If the management board decides to procure a shareholder resolution, it is bound by that resolution; see §84(2).

[120] This principle is laid down in §23(5) AktG. The articles may only deviate from the provisions of the Stock Corporation Act if this is expressly permitted in the Act. The rationale behind this approach is the desire to protect creditors and future shareholders. For a detailed and comparative discussion of the principle of limited contractual freedom, and the more unfettered contractual freedom existing under UK law and, with some qualifications, also US and French law, see M Lutter and H Wiedemann (eds), *Gestaltungsfreiheit im Gesellschaftsrecht: Deutschland, Europa und USA* (de Gruyter, 1997); and for a short exposition in English see P Mäntysaari, *Comparative corporate governance: shareholders as a rule-maker* (Springer 2005) 246–7. If the incorporators wish to design the governance structure differently, for example by granting particular shareholders a veto right, they need to take resort to the private limited company (GmbH), which is not subject to the principle of limited contractual freedom. Rather, comparable to the conception of the company under UK law, the shareholders of the private limited company are seen as possessing ultimate authority. They enjoy largely unfettered freedom in structuring the corporate contract (GmbHG [Limited Liability Companies Act], §45) and can give the managers directions in all matters of management (GmbHG, §37).

The spokesman referred to the fact that the seaport business had evolved into an independent business that no longer relied on timber trade. Following the defendant's acquisition of all transshipment rights in 1967, it had become largely a detached company division.

The H. Hafenbetriebs-Beteiligungs GmbH was founded on 22 June 1972. On 13 November 1972, the GmbH, the defendant company and three other founders formed the H. Seehafenbetrieb Kommanditgesellschaft auf Aktien (H. KGaA) with an authorized share capital of 4.8 million DM and the GmbH as general partner with unlimited liability. In accordance with the articles of association, the defendant company contributed the seaport business with all assets and liabilities and subscribed to 95,997 shares with a nominal capital of 50 DM per share. The H. KGaA was registered in the commercial register on 27 December 1972. As of today, the defendant company holds all shares and the whole registered capital of the general partner GmbH.

The plaintiff is of the opinion that the transfer of the seaport business without the approval of the general meeting is void due to a violation of §[179a] AktG, an unauthorized change of the company's objects and a contravention of §138 BGB [German Civil Code].[121] He claims that the seaport business constituted the defendant company's core business and that the remaining assets, in particular the timber trade, were insignificant in comparison. The purpose of the outsourcing was to enable the defendant company to conduct a capital increase for the promising seaport business without participation of the minority shareholders, thus excluding their pre-emptive rights.

The plaintiff moves for a declaration

1. that the transfer of the seaport business as a contribution in kind from the defendant company to the KGaA and all transactions in connection with the transfer are invalid; ...

alternatively

3. that the defendant ... is required

a) to obtain approval of the general meeting of the defendant company, acting with commensurate majority, for all measures required under law to be adopted by the general meeting of the KGaA with a three-fourths majority;

b) in particular for any increase in capital of the H. KGaA, including those capital increases that are provided for in the articles of association, to obtain approval of the general meeting of the defendant company, acting with the majority required by law for the respective measure ...

Both courts of lower instance have dismissed the claim....

Reasons for the decision

I.

The plaintiff's main claim, the declaration of invalidity of all transactions in relation to the outsourcing of the seaport business, is unfounded, as held by the Court of Appeal ...

The transfer of the seaport business is not void pursuant to §[179a] AktG due to the lack of shareholder approval in general meeting. The defendant company has not, as required by the provision, transferred its entire corporate undertaking to the H. KGaA. The case would have had to be assessed differently if the transfer had left the company with no more than insignificant assets ... However, this is not the case ...

[It is questionable whether] the management board had the competence to decide on the spinning off of the seaport business without laying the question before the general meeting ... If the law provides that the general meeting shall decide on a certain matter, as in §293 or §[179a] AktG, the mandatory nature of such rules shows that the articles may not deviate from them (§23(5) AktG). However, even if a case does not fall within the scope of these sections but is closely related to the respective requirements, the management board may, by way of exception, be under a duty to lay the matter before the general meeting. While it is, in general, in the discretion of the management board whether to procure a decision of the general meeting pursuant

[121] [Footnote by authors.] §138 BGB provides: '(1) A legal transaction which is contrary to public policy is void. (2) In particular, a legal transaction is void by which a person, by exploiting the predicament, inexperience, lack of sound judgement or considerable weakness of will of another, causes himself or a third party, in exchange for an act of performance, to be promised or granted pecuniary advantages which are clearly disproportionate to the performance.'

to §119(2) AktG and thus limit its exposure to liability (§93(4) sentence 1 AktG), certain fundamental transactions ... interfere so substantially with the rights of the members and their financial interests that the board cannot reasonably assume that it may decide on them in its own right and without participation of the general meeting. In such cases the board violates its duty of care if it does not proceed according to §119(2) AktG ...

The outsourcing of the seaport business and its transfer to the newly formed subsidiary was a measure of such importance for the company and its members that the management board was not entitled to circumvent the general meeting when deciding on it. The transaction was part of the core activities of the company; according to the Court of Appeal, it affected the most valuable branch of the company's business and entailed a fundamental change in the structure of the company. Consequently, it exceeded management authority, which generally also comprises the setting up or the acquisition of subsidiaries and their financing. For the legal position of the shareholders the outsourcing was of vital significance, as will be shown below. The management board, therefore, was not entitled to execute the transaction without the approval of the general meeting of the defendant company.

d) However, the violation of this (internal) obligation does not affect the validity of the transactions challenged by the plaintiff. Pursuant to §82(1) AktG the authority of the management board to represent the company may only be restricted by law.

[The court argued that once the subsidiary had become a company in its own right, general legal relationships and the public had become affected. Both the reassignment of the seaport business to the defendant company and a liquidation of the subsidiary would be illegal pursuant to §§57(1), 278(3) AktG.]

Therefore, the transfer of the seaport business may not be invalidated on the basis that the management board made use of its power to represent the company in relation to third parties in contravention of (internal) duties or because it acted contrary to public policy ...

III.

The plaintiff's second subsidiary motion [3] is unfounded insofar as the plaintiff moves for a declaration that the defendant company is required to obtain approval of its general meeting for all measures required under law to be adopted with a three-fourths majority of the general meeting of the H. KGaA.

1.... A fundamental transaction by means of which a company transfers significant parts of its assets to a subsidiary impairs the position of its shareholders even if the subsidiary is wholly-owned by the holding company. Most notably, the shareholders lose the possibility to influence, within the scope of §119(2) AktG, the use of the transferred assets, the risk of their loss, and the distribution of the profits. All shareholder rights in the subsidiary are exercised by the management board of the parent company. Notwithstanding potential liability under §93 AktG, neither the articles of association of the subsidiary nor qualified majority voting requirements can serve as an effective check on the board's discretion. Furthermore, the board is subject to virtually no restrictions in deciding on the appropriation of the balance sheet profit.

In this way, important decisions are transferred together with the assets from the parent to the subsidiary. In addition, the management board may, by entering into control or profit transfer agreements with a third party or by admitting new members, for example in the course of a capital increase, further dilute the rights of the parent's shareholders. This can lead to an actual financial loss for the parent company's shareholders (e.g. if new shares are issued at a low price) ...

The Stock Corporation Act offers inadequate protection to the shareholders of parent companies against such interventions. Its explicit rules are predominantly designed to protect the outside shareholders of dependant companies....

In order to ameliorate this unsatisfactory situation, parts of the literature propose to grant the general meeting of the parent company 'unwritten participatory rights' ... if the shareholders are affected in their legal position by fundamental changes in the dependant company ... Accordingly, the parent's shareholders have the right to be involved in the decision-making process in the subsidiary in the same way and in application of the same majority requirements that would govern the adoption of the respective decisions in the parent before the subsidiary may implement the actions ...

[The court acknowledged that the right to participate in the adoption of certain fundamental decisions in the subsidiary might be a necessary and adequate mechanism to protect the interests of shareholders of a holding company in situations comparable to the one at issue. However, it continued:]

4. In light of the facts of the case it is ... not necessary to discuss which decisions should be subject to approval by the general meeting internally. As the Court of Appeal has correctly emphasised, the plaintiff's claim that all resolutions that have to be adopted by qualified majority in the subsidiary should be subject to this requirement is, in this general form, too extensive. True, such resolutions will commonly concern issues of particular importance for the shareholders and will frequently have a bearing on the holding company. One might think of the aforementioned enterprise agreements and capital increases, but also of the transfer of substantially all of the assets of the undertaking pursuant to §[179a] AktG or the voluntary dissolution of the company (§262(1) no. 2, §289(4) AktG). However, this might not always be the case. Some amendments of the articles do not or do not significantly affect the legal and economic relationships of the holding company and its shareholders, for example the change of the subsidiary's seat, the change of its name or possibly the requirement that management needs to procure the consent of the supervisory board for certain types of action (§111(4) Sentence 2 AktG ...), which do not significantly alter the balance of power at least in the case of a wholly owned subsidiary. To this extent, it would not be justified to interfere with the authority of the management board to manage the company under its own responsibility (§76(1) AktG).

For this reason, the claim of the plaintiff at 3a ... has to fail.

IV.

However, the second part of the subsidiary motion (at 3b), which refers to capital increases in the H. KGaA, is to be treated differently ...

2. Capital increases in a subsidiary that has been formed for the purpose of spinning off substantial parts of the company's assets come with particular risks for the shareholders of the holding company. The increases can indirectly result in an impediment of the interests of the members of the parent company, a dilution of their shareholdings and a restriction of their pre-emptive rights, notwithstanding the fact that the parent company might effectively manage the subsidiary by means of the subsidiary's personally liable partner, which it controls. Accordingly, the literature characterises the capital increase as the paradigm of a transaction that requires the approval of the holding company in general meeting.

Indeed, such a participation of the primary decision-making organ of the parent company is indispensable in the present circumstances. The fact that the management board intends to fully exercise the pre-emptive rights of the holding company, which is the sole shareholder of the subsidiary, does not justify a different assessment ... In such a case, the shareholders are deprived of the opportunity to increase their holdings by investing in 'their' business. Instead, the parent company uses funds for investments in the subsidiary that stem from the contributions of the shareholders. This process causes the competence to decide on the employment of capital and the associated risks to shift from the parent to the subsidiary. Furthermore ... there is no guarantee that the management board may not abstain from exercising some or all of the pre-emptive rights of the parent company for the benefit of third parties....

Therefore, it must be left to the defendant company in general meeting to decide whether the share capital of the H. KGaA should be increased under these conditions or the pre-emptive rights of the defendant excluded and instead its shareholders vested with the right to subscribe to the newly issued shares in analogy to §186(1), (2) and (5) AktG.[122] ... The resolutions that are required according to these principles have to be adopted in compliance with the same rules and voting requirements that would be applicable to comparable resolutions to raise capital for the holding company pursuant to §§182 et seq. AktG ...

[122] [Footnote by authors.] §186(1) AktG, which is, for present purposes, the most relevant of the three subsections quoted by the court, provides: 'Each shareholder shall be entitled, upon demand, to new shares in proportion to his holding in the existing share capital. A period of not less than two weeks shall be provided for the exercise of such subscription rights'.

Questions and comments:

1. *Holzmüller* is arguably the most famous and, even thirty-five years on, one of the most important decisions in German corporate law. However, a number of questions remained open for some time after *Holzmüller*. First, the dogmatic foundations of the decision were unclear. In *Holzmüller*, the court had held that the discretion of the management board to lay a matter before the general meeting pursuant to §119(2) was transformed into a duty under the appropriate circumstances. This was criticized in the literature. §119(2), it was argued, dealt with a different case than the *Holzmüller*-scenario. The latter was concerned with an encroachment upon shareholder rights, the former with the authority of the management board to request a decision of the general meeting regarding matters that fell formally within the board's remit.[123] In two more recent decisions, *Gelatine I and II*,[124] the Court of Justice modified its position. It now relies on the provisions of the Stock Corporation Act that provide for an explicit shareholder decision right, rather than §119(2), and emphasizes that the *Holzmüller*-doctrine applies if the case at issue is comparable to, but does not fall directly within the scope of, one of the express competences. However, as we could see in the *Holzmüller* judgment, the management board's failure to procure a shareholder resolution does not entail the invalidity of the transaction in relation to third parties, which would generally be the consequence if the board disregarded one of the express competence provisions of the Stock Corporation Act.[125] The effects are internal to the corporation: The managers violate their duties pursuant to §93(1) Akt. In addition, the shareholders can bring proceedings against the company in their own name, claiming that the board violated their membership rights, and seek restoration of the position prior to the breach, if possible.[126]

   Secondly, the precise thresholds triggering the *Holzmüller*-obligations were contested. Some courts held that the sale of assets representing as little as 30 per cent of the company's revenue gave rise to the requirement to procure a decision of the general meeting,[127] while others required a higher percentage.[128] Furthermore, it was problematic whether any sale of assets of sufficient volume was subject to the *Holzmüller*-requirements or only a transaction that interfered with shareholder rights in a more direct way, for example by removing an asset from the reach of the shareholders, but leaving it under the control of the management board, as in *Holzmüller*. Again, the *Gelatine* decisions brought clarity on these issues. The decisions concerned the restructuring of Deutsche Gelatine-Fabriken Stoess AG. The management board decided to transfer the corporation's holdings in two subsidiaries to another, wholly owned, subsidiary without obtaining a resolution by the general meeting. The two first-tier subsidiaries were, therefore, converted into second-tier subsidiaries. The Court of Justice held that the *Holzmüller* doctrine rested on two legs, a quantitative and a qualitative one. As far as the quantitative part of the test is concerned, the transaction must interfere 'fundamentally' or 'severely' with shareholder rights,[129] which is usually understood to mean that the assets in question must amount to 75–80 per cent of total assets or revenue.[130] As regards the qualitative leg of the test, the court focussed on the 'intermediating effect' of the transaction that was at issue in *Gelatine* (and also in *Holzmüller*).[131] It was important that the cases did not deal with a sale of assets to a third party, but a reorganization that frustrated participation rights and the possibility of the shareholders to exert direct control over the assets. This was, in the eyes of the court, the decisive factor that warranted the qualification

[123] Schmidt (n 3) §28 V 2 b.

[124] BGHZ 159, 30; BGH ZIP 2004, 1001.

[125] G Spindler in W Goette and M Habersack (eds), *Münchener Kommentar zum Aktiengesetz, vol 2* (5th edn, CH Beck 2019) §82, para 26. In other words, the authority of the management board to represent the company pursuant to §82(1) AktG is unaffected by the failure to obtain a shareholder resolution.

[126] BGHZ 83, 122, 125–127, 133–136.

[127] Regional Court (LG) Frankfurt, ZIP 1997, 1698, and Higher Regional Court (OLG) Frankfurt, ZIP 1999, 842 (*Altana/Milupa*).

[128] Higher Regional Court (OLG) Stuttgart, ZIP 2003, 1981.

[129] BGHZ 159, 30, 36, 41.

[130] See the references in C Gerner-Beuerle, D Kershaw, and M Solinas, 'Is the Board Neutrality Rule Trivial? Amnesia about Corporate Law in European Takeover Regulation' (2011) 22 EBLR 559, 600; and generally on the nature of the bifurcated *Holzmüller/Gelatine*-test: ibid 601.

[131] BGHZ 159, 30, 41.

of the transaction as a 'structural measure', that is, a measure comparable to the transactions that gave rise to explicit shareholder decision rights under the Stock Corporation Act.[132] Thus, following *Gelatine*, reorganizations that transfer direct holdings to second-tier subsidiaries are candidates for an application of the *Holzmüller*-doctrine, but not simple sales of assets.[133]

2. The US scholars Henry Hansmann and Rainier Kraakman argued in their influential article *The End of History for Corporate Law*[134] that *Holzmüller*, in showing the use of judicial discretion in extending shareholder decision-making rights and generally resolving disputes among corporate actors, was an example for the increasing convergence of common law and civil law corporate governance systems.[135] Do you agree?

IV. France

We have seen above that corporate power in France was historically contractual in nature. Certain remnants of this contractual conception are still discernible in French company law, notably in the form of the general provisions on companies in the Civil Code that apply to all forms of business association, unless more specific legislative acts provide for different rules.[136] The first legislation regulating incorporated and unincorporated business enterprises, the Commercial Code of 1807, dealt with the *société anonyme* only in a fragmentary way. In particular, the Commercial Code of 1807 did not provide for any particular, binding governance structure.[137] This changed with a reform act of 24 July 1867, which contained detailed rules on the function and powers of the board of directors and general meeting. The Act of 1867 thus constituted a first step towards a more institutionalized view of the corporation, with regulation playing a comparatively greater, and private ordering a diminished role in defining the internal organisation of the *société anonyme*. However, the collective will of the shareholders, as expressed in general meeting, continued to be paramount. The Act of 1867 conceptualized the general meeting as the highest organ of the company and conferred specific powers on it that were regarded as being of particular importance to shareholders, for example the right to amend the articles or elect the members of the board of directors. The general meeting was also entitled to decide on or instruct the managers in matters of management and business strategy. This right was a logical consequence of the characterization of directors as mandatories (*mandataires*), comparable to agents in common law terminology.[138] It permeates all types of company recognized under French law and has the consequence that the general rules of the Code civil on agency (Articles 1984–2010) inform the relationship between the company and the directors where the Code de commerce does not regulate a question, thus importing further contractual elements into company law.

Today, for the stock corporation, *société anonyme*, and the limited liability company, *société à responsabilité limitée*, the contractual origins of companies are to a large part overlaid with a detailed system of binding rules. In these corporate forms, contractual freedom is restricted to the areas not explicitly addressed by the Commercial Code. As far as the corporate governance structure of public and private companies is concerned, little scope

[132] ibid 36–41.
[133] See T Raiser and R Veil, *Recht der Kapitalgesellschaften* (6th edn, Vahlen 2015) §16/14, for further references.
[134] (2000–2001) 89 Georgetown LJ 439. [135] ibid 458–9.
[136] See our discussion above in Chapter 4C.II and Civ, Art 1832, which describes the company as founded on contract.
[137] See Code de commerce of 1807, Arts 29–37.
[138] For example, Art 22 of the Act of 1867 referred to the persons in charge of the administration of the *société anonyme* as 'mandataires'. See also N Horn, 'Aktienrechtliche Unternehmensorganisation in der Hochindustrialisierung (1860-1920): Deutschland, England, Frankreich und die USA im Vergleich' in N Horn and J Kocka (eds), *Law and the Formation of the Big Enterprises in the 19th and Early 20th Centuries* (Vandenhoeck & Ruprecht 1979) 123, 156–7.

remains for private ordering.[139] In particular, it is generally not permissible to alter the allocation of powers to the different corporate organs in the articles.[140] On the other hand, the corporate governance architecture of the French public company as established in the Commercial Code is less rigid than under German law, where the limitation of contractual freedom has been elevated to a principle of the law on the stock corporation (but not the limited liability company).[141] Whether an alteration in the articles is possible depends on the function and rationale of the statutory rules. Notably, rules that confer decision-making power on the general meeting in order to protect the shareholder franchise and facilitate the control of management cannot be reassigned to the board. These powers include (in the *société anonyme*) the right to amend the articles of association,[142] appoint or remove the directors,[143] vote on the total amount of the directors' compensation,[144] approve related-party transactions, such as agreements between the company and the general managers,[145] appoint the company's auditors,[146] and determine the dividends to be paid out to the shareholders.[147] Other competences, for example the power to decide on a capital increase and a disapplication of pre-emption rights, can be delegated to the board of directors, but ultimate authority remains with the shareholders, which is illustrated by provisions of the Commercial Code that establish time limits for the delegation or allow the shareholders to delimit the scope of the delegated authority.[148]

Commercial Code[149]

Art. L225-96

Only an extraordinary General Meeting is authorized to amend any provision of the articles of association. Any clause to the contrary is deemed unwritten. It may nevertheless not increase the shareholders' commitments, without prejudice to transactions resulting from a properly executed share consolidation.

It may validly deliberate when first convened only if the shareholders present or represented hold at least one quarter of the voting shares and, if reconvened, one fifth of the voting shares. Failing this, the second meeting may be postponed to a date not later than two months after the date originally scheduled. In companies which do not make public offerings, the memorandum and articles of association may require higher quorums.

It rules on a majority of two thirds of the votes held by the shareholders present or represented.

Art. L225-98

The ordinary general meeting makes all decisions other than those referred to in Articles L225-96 and L225-97.[150]

[139] This has been the case especially since the reforms of French company law of 24 July 1966, Law no 66-537 (Loi sur les sociétés commerciales), JORF of 26 July 1966, 6402, already mentioned in Chapter 4E.I. For examples where private ordering may become relevant, see Y Guyon, 'Zur Gestaltungsfreiheit im französischen Gesellschaftsrecht' in M Lutter and H Wiedemann (eds), *Gestaltungsfreiheit im Gesellschaftsrecht: Deutschland, Europa und USA* (de Gruyter, 1997) 297, 300–1.

[140] The 1966 reforms and the lack of flexibility of the French system, as well as the increased use of civil and criminal sanctions in company law after the reforms, were widely criticized; see for example JP Bertrel 'Liberté contractuelle et sociétés: Essai d'une théorie du "juste milieu" en droit des sociétés' (1996) RTD Com 595; P Bissara, 'L'inadaption du droit français aux besoins des entreprises et les aléas des solutions' (1990) Revue des sociétés 553; J Paillusseau, 'La modernisation du droit des sociétés commerciales: "Une reconception du droit des sociétés commerciales"' (1996) Recueil Dalloz 287 (Chronique); E du Pontavice, 'Le droit des sociétés commerciales en question' (1989) RJC 241. As a reaction, in 1994 the legislator introduced a form of stock corporation allowing for more contractual freedom, including in corporate governance matters: the so-called simplified joint-stock company (*société par actions simplifiée*). For a brief discussion, see Chapter 1.

[141] See n 120 above. [142] Com, Art L225-96. [143] ibid Art L225-18.

[144] ibid Art L225-45.

[145] ibid Art L225-40. Related-party transactions are discussed in detail in Chapter 6C.I.

[146] ibid Art L225-228. [147] ibid Art L232-12.

[148] The competences of the general meeting to decide on capital increases and the disapplication of pre-emption rights are laid down in Arts L225-129, 135 of the Code de commerce.

[149] Translation by Legifrance, https://www.legifrance.gouv.fr/Traductions/en-English/Legifrance-translations.

[150] [Footnote by authors.] Art L225-96 is reproduced above and Art L225-97 refers to the power of the special shareholders' meeting to change the nationality of the company.

It may validly deliberate when first convened only if the shareholders present or represented hold at least one fifth of the voting shares. In companies which do not make public offerings, the memorandum and articles of association may require a higher quorum. If it is reconvened, no quorum is required.

It rules on a majority of the votes held by the shareholders present or represented.

Conversely, matters that are normally within the authority of the board can be bestowed on the general meeting even if they involve decisions of an operational nature.[151] Here, accordingly, the traditional contractual view and the understanding of directors as agents whose powers devolve from the general meeting are still noticeable. Nevertheless, we can observe a clear, albeit gradual, shift from a contractual to an institutional approach since the early days of French company law, in particular with a decision of the Cour de Cassation from 1946.[152] In this case, the court annulled a resolution of the general meeting that attributed all powers of the board of directors to the *président directeur général*. The court held that the organs of the *société anonyme* stand in a 'hierarchical relationship' and the company's business activities are to be carried out by a board of directors elected by the general meeting. Therefore, 'it is not for the general meeting to encroach upon the powers of the board of directors in management matters'.[153] This does not mean that the articles cannot reserve the authority to decide on particular issues pertaining to the conduct of the company's business for the general meeting. However, the board must not be divested completely of the management powers conferred on it by virtue of the Commercial Code.[154]

Some scope for private ordering also remains where the law does not contain specific rules. For example, the incorporators of a *société anonyme* are entitled to establish the position of vice-president of the board of directors or a board of statutory auditors, provided that competences that are vested in other organs by law are not transferred to the newly created positions.[155] The Supreme Court also held, and the Commercial Code now explicitly provides for companies that do not offer shares to the public, that the shareholders can increase the quorum requirements for general meetings in the articles.[156] Similarly, the rule that the ordinary general meeting adopts resolutions by simple majority of the votes present is subject to contractual freedom, provided, however, that the necessary majority

[151] Guyon (n 139) 304.

[152] Cass civ, 4 June 1946 (*Sté de teinturerie c/ Motte*), *JCP* 1947, II, 3518, note D Bastian.

[153] ibid.

[154] Com, Art L225-35. The article is reproduced above in Chapter 4E. See also Cass com, 11 June 1965, no 63-10240. In this case, the majority shareholder of a *société anonyme* agreed with the *président directeur général* of the company to provide financial assistance to the company and required in exchange that his consent be obtained before any expenditure in relation to the employees, suppliers or production process of the company was incurred. The court held that this arrangement conferred on the shareholder comprehensive corporate power, which was not to be exercised concurrently with that of the general manager, but effectively 'eliminated' or 'neutralised' it ('les pouvoirs directoriaux d'X ... [the majority shareholder] ... auraient pu tout au plus être égaux à ceux de Y ... [the general manaer] et s'exercer concurremment mais n'auraient certes pu les annihiler ou, tout au moins, les neutraliser'). The delegation of powers was consequently held to be void. The Court of Appeal in the same case had relied on a line of reasoning resembling *McQuade* (see section A.II above), arguing that the delegation was in conflict with public policy ('ordre public') by limiting the powers conferred on the general manager by statute (see also text to nn 165–169 below). Another example for how the contractual understanding has been supplanted by an institutional conception is Art L225-253, para 2. This article provides that the discharge (*quitus*) of the directors by the general meeting does not have the effect of extinguishing any claims of the company against the directors for a breach of duty. An agency-based conception would not be in line with this provision, since the principal would be free to waive any claims.

[155] Guyon (n 139) 301.

[156] Cass com, 20 February 1978, *Revue des sociétés* 1978, 746, note B Bouloc. The Code de commerce distinguishes between ordinary general meetings, extraordinary meetings, and special meetings of shareholders of particular classes. Ordinary general meetings can deliberate if a quorum of one fifth of the voting shares is present (Art L225-98, as amended by Law of 26 July 2005 (Loi pour la confiance et la modernisation de l'économie, so-called 'loi Breton')), extraordinary meetings require a quorum of one-quarter of the voting shares (Art L225-96, as amended), and special meetings a quorum of one-third of the relevant class (Art L225-99). If the general meeting is reconvened, the quorum requirements are lower (no quorum if an ordinary general meeting is reconvened and one fifth of the voting shares in the other two cases).

for the removal of directors is not increased.[157] The requirement that the extraordinary general meeting shall rule on a two-thirds majority, on the other hand, is considered to be binding.[158] One commentator has called the fact that the articles of association can be changed by the extraordinary general meeting with a two-thirds majority 'the triumph of the institutional conception of the company' over the contractual conception.[159] If the articles were truly a contract between the incorporators, it should not be possible to modify them with less than unanimity, or, if we assume that the incorporators agreed on a procedure for the amendment of the articles based on majority voting, they should be free to change the majority requirements. As we have seen, this used to be the approach under English law, and still today English law is in many respects closer to the contractual conception than French law or the other jurisdictions that we have analysed.[160]

Questions and comments:

1. In all four jurisdictions discussed above the right to amend the articles of association is vested in the general meeting. However, we can observe significant differences in how this right is designed. The Delaware General Corporation Law provides for a two-step process. First, the board of directors must adopt a resolution setting out the proposed amendment. The board then calls a special shareholder meeting or includes the proposal in the agenda for the next annual general meeting. The proposed amendment is adopted if a majority of the outstanding stock entitled to vote is voted in favour of the proposal.[161] Thus, any amendment of the certificate of incorporation requires the consent of both the shareholders and the board.[162] In France, Germany, and the United Kingdom, on the other hand, the general meeting can amend the articles without participation of the board.[163] Why is Delaware law reluctant to grant the shareholders the right to initiate structural changes? Are there advantages to giving the board a veto right over changes to the articles, and what are the consequences of such a veto power for investor protection?
2. In France, as in the other jurisdictions, shareholder agreements play an important role in supplementing the articles and achieving an additional degree of minority investor protection. They are often used in corporate groups where a subsidiary is owned by more than one parent. Typical provisions include pre-emption rights, the right to inspect the corporate books and records, voting agreements, or the obligation to pay compensation if the majority shareholder sells its stake.[164] While contractual freedom principally applies to these agreements, they are subject to the *ordre public* of French corporate law. The French courts refer to the notion of *ordre public* to ensure that shareholder agreements do not contravene the company's interests, the essential rights of the shareholders, and the binding rules of corporate law regarding the organization of the company.[165] For example, the shareholders' power to replace the directors at any time is considered to be part of the *ordre public* of corporate law. Accordingly, the undertaking of an investor who had just acquired majority control not to dismiss certain directors was found to be invalid.[166] In the same vein, agreements that impede the removal

[157] P Merle, *Droit commercial: Sociétés commerciales* (22nd edn, Dalloz 2018) para 544. For an early decision confirming the existence of contractual freedom in altering majority requirements, see Cass com, 4 June 1966, *Bull. civ.* III, no 284. However, removal of directors must be possible at any time by simple majority of the ordinary general meeting, see Art L225-18 Code de commerce.

[158] Art L225-96. For an analysis of the provision, see Merle (n 157) para 555.

[159] ibid.

[160] For example, the articles may contain 'entrenched' provisions that can only be amended if conditions are satisfied that are more restrictive than a special resolution (Companies Act 2006, s 22), and the shareholders may always act unanimously, even if they do not follow the procedures in the act (see n 20 above). For a discussion of the interaction of the institutional and contractual notion of the company in English law see also H Rajak, 'Gestaltungsfreiheit im Gesellschaftsrecht des Vereinigten Königreichs' in M Lutter and H Wiedemann (eds), *Gestaltungsfreiheit im Gesellschaftsrecht: Deutschland, Europa und USA* (de Gruyter, 1997) 187, 208–10.

[161] Del. Gen. Corp. Law, §242(b). The MBCA is similar; see §10.03.

[162] This is different for by-laws; see our discussion above in section A.II, comment 4.

[163] See French Code de commerce, Art L225-96; German AktG, §179; UK Companies Act 2006, s 21(1).

[164] Guyon (n 139) 305.

[165] ibid 306.

[166] Cass com, 17 January 1984, *Bull. civ.* IV, no 21.

of directors by providing for significant compensation payments triggered by the removal are seen with suspicion by the courts.[167] However, since the *ordre public* is largely undefined, it is in many cases difficult to determine whether a particular provision of company law is of such importance that it cannot be altered or circumvented by a shareholder agreement. The situation is, therefore, characterized by a considerable degree of legal uncertainty.[168] Comparing the French approach with that of US law, we can see that the two legal systems operate with similar concepts. When we discussed *McQuade v Stoneham* above, we saw that the US courts hold that the public policy considerations underlying corporate law trump conflicting shareholder agreements.[169]

3. How would you position Germany and France, as far as the rights and competences of the general meeting and the management board are concerned, in relation to UK and US law? Are German and French law more similar to US law in that the directors enjoy relatively far-reaching autonomy, or to UK law in that the rights of the shareholders are more extensive than under US law? Would it be an accurate summary of the law to say that in the United States and Germany, director power is original and not delegated, whereas in the UK (and France?) corporate power originates from the shareholders and is delegated to the board of directors?[170] Why have these differences evolved?

B. Limits of Corporate Power

Corporate law acknowledges that positions of power come with responsibilities. These responsibilities take different forms. We have seen some instances of constraints on managerial power in the previous section. The directors cannot divest the shareholders of their inherent right to amend the by-laws or remove the directors,[171] or they have to procure a shareholder resolution for particularly important transactions.[172] In this section, we will address the problem of legal constraints on corporate power in a more structured way. In economic terms, these limitations are all responses to agency problems in the firm. As the previous sections have illustrated, most corporate power is concentrated in the hands of the directors. Accordingly, corporate governance is primarily concerned with regulating the discretion of the directors (agents) in order to protect the shareholders (principals). However, the shareholders retain important competences, which they commonly exercise by majority voting in general meeting. Thus, the majority shareholders (now as agents) are in a position to influence the welfare of the minority (principal).[173] The law has developed additional mechanisms, or adapted some of the mechanisms that constrain the discretion of the directors, to ensure that the majority does not exercise their powers to the detriment of the minority.

[167] Cass com, 2 June 1992, *Revue des sociétés* 1992, 750, note Y Guyon. [168] Guyon (n 139) 309.

[169] See the section on US law, A.II above. Contrast this approach with English law, A.II comment 3.

[170] With respect to US law, compare, on the one hand, SM Bainbridge, 'Director Primacy: The Means and Ends of Corporate Governance' (2003) 97 Northwestern University Law Review 547, 605 (arguing that the term 'director primacy' is an accurate description of the board's sovereignty under US law), and *Manson v Curtis*, 223 N.Y. 313 (N.Y. 1918) (holding: 'In corporate bodies, the powers of the board of directors are, in a very important sense, original and undelegated. The stockholders do not confer, nor can they revoke, those powers'. ibid 322), and on the other hand, *Blasius Industries, Inc. v Atlas Corp.*, 564 A.2d 651 (Del. Ch. 1988) (emphasizing: 'The theory of our corporation law confers power upon directors as the agents of the shareholders; it does not create Platonic masters': ibid 663). With respect to UK law, see D Kershaw, *Company Law in Context* (2nd edn, OUP 2012) 230 (arguing that the United Kingdom is a 'shareholder primacy' jurisdiction).

[171] US law: section A.II, comment 4 above. [172] German law: *Holzmüller* decision, section A.III.

[173] To be more precise, an agency problem arises whenever an individual or a plurality of shareholders can take decisions that affect the whole class. This may be less than an absolute majority, for example the blocking minority of 25% for the disapplication of preemption rights pursuant to s 571 Companies Act 2006 or §186(3) German AktG, minority shareholders that enjoy veto rights, or individual shareholders that can challenge resolutions of the general meeting (e.g., §§241–249 AktG); see R Kraakman and others, *The Anatomy of Corporate Law* (3rd edn, Oxford University Press 2017) 30. For a detailed discussion of agency cost theory see also Chapter 4B. II above.

The literature has proposed a taxonomy of strategies that may be used to address the managerial and other agency problems.[174] We will not replicate the full taxonomy here, but suggest that most of the case law and statutory measures can be understood by distinguishing between two approaches to the problem of constraining corporate power. The first approach seeks to provide for an adequate determination of the boundaries of discretion, the second seeks to define *how* the agents should act within the margin of discretion that the law accords to them.[175] Or, to put it differently, the first strategy determines the balance of power and the relationship between the different corporate actors ex ante, the second allows for intervention ex post if the ex ante determination of the agent's authority is not sufficient to minimize agency costs.[176] A determination of the boundaries of discretion is achieved primarily by allocating decision-making power, either by statutory definition of the competences of the corporate organs or by drawing on the general conception of the corporation, as discussed in the previous section. The most important mechanism to conduct an ex post review of the agents' actions are fiduciary duties.[177]

The dividing line between the two strategies is not that between rules, that is, the advance determination of the boundaries of permissible conduct, and standards, which leave the specification to the adjudicator.[178] Both specific rules in the form of decision rights or the prohibition of particular types of action[179] and broad standards, such as the freedom of the incorporators to draft the constitutional documents according to their preferences or the duty of directors under UK law to exercise their powers only for the purposes for which they are conferred,[180] help to establish the distribution of power in the company. This

[174] Kraakman and others (n 173) 31–8. They distinguish between 'regulatory strategies' that provide for substantive terms governing the content of the principal-agent relationship, and 'governance strategies' that strengthen the principal's control over the agent or align the incentives of agent and principal. Both groups are further divided and virtually all provisions of corporate law assigned to one of the groups and interpreted in light of the different agency problems. Regulatory strategies are said to be advantageous where coordination costs between shareholders are high: Rules or standards (for an analysis of the difference see L Kaplow, 'Rules versus Standards: An Economic Analysis' (1992) 42 Duke LJ 557) that regulate the agent's behaviour do not have to be exercised or implemented, but only enforced in case of noncompliance. Governance strategies, on the other hand, often require the consultation and interaction of a multitude of individuals; see Kraakman and others, ibid 31–2.

[175] In Kraakman and others' taxonomy, the first approach corresponds mainly (but not exclusively, as the following discussion will show) to two types of governance strategy (appointment and decision rights), the second to what they term 'open standards', a type of regulatory strategy, ibid 33.

[176] This definition requires two specifications. First, both strategies have ex ante and ex post elements. The determination of the balance of power has ex post-effects in that noncompliance with the regulatory structure entails questions of whether transactions are valid and the principal has remedies against the noncompliant agent (see the *Holzmüller* case, s 171 Companies Act 2006, and the case law discussed in this section). The ex post correction of the agent's behaviour has ex ante elements in that the law formulates expectations with respect to how the agent should discharge his or her duties. The difference is one of emphasis: Since the business environment is too complex to account ex ante for all eventualities by way of specific rules, agents need to be granted discretion. The boundaries of their discretion are drawn in a way that is believed to be generally adequate or efficient. In individual cases, however, it will be more efficient to allow for an examination of the agent's behaviour ex post, rather than uphold the unfettered discretion of the agent (this calculation involves, on the one hand, the minimization of costs created by allowing the ex post evaluation and possibly reversal of the agent's actions, i.e. costs created by the increased uncertainty in the system, which may lead to risk-averse behaviour on the part of the agent, and the costs of maintaining and using enforcement mechanisms, notably the judicial system, and, on the other hand, the costs of unfettered discretion, i.e. self-serving actions by the agent). The second caveat is that an efficient solution may not involve the minimization of agency costs, but the minimization of the sum of agency costs and the costs of externalities (see Chapter 4B.I, II).

[177] Note that according to UK law, the duty of care (s 174 Companies Act 2006) is not a fiduciary duty (see s 178(2) Companies Act 2006). This is a function of the existence of two different sources of directors' duties: Fiduciary principles, which give rise to the duty of loyalty, and the law of negligence, which informs the duty of care. See Davies and Worthington (n 12) paras 16-15, 16-21. In other jurisdiction (including, in spite of its English law origin, the United States) this distinction is not normally made. Accordingly, we will refer indiscriminately to fiduciary duties when we mean any of the duties that directors are subject to.

[178] Kaplow (n 174) 560.

[179] For example, the prohibition of transactions with directors without shareholder approval pursuant to ss 188–225 Companies Act 2006.

[180] Companies Act 2006, s 171(b). See the discussion in the next section.

also means that it is not useful to emphasize the distinction between the shareholders' individual (decision-making) rights and the duties that the directors owe to the company[181] when discussing the remedies open to the company and the shareholders in the case of non-compliance by the directors. Noncompliance by directors with the allocation of powers, even in the form of a broad standard or duty, constitutes an encroachment upon shareholder rights and can be enforced by an action brought by the shareholders individually. The exercise of an existing discretion that does not comply with behavioural standards or expectations constitutes a breach of duty towards the company, with the consequence that the proper plaintiff in an action enforcing directors' duties is generally the company.[182] If the company does not act through its proper organ(s) to initiate legal proceedings, which is typically the board of directors or the general meeting, minority shareholders are required to take recourse to a derivative action. In many legal systems, derivative actions are severely restricted.[183] Therefore, the question of how to distinguish between the distribution of power and requirements regarding the exercise of an existing discretion has important implications for shareholder protection. The classification suggested here may capture the relevant social conflicts more accurately than the rather formalistic distinction between directors' duties and shareholder decision rights.[184]

These are difficult questions that we will revisit at a later point. The discussion that follows is structured according to the distinction proposed above. The next sections analysing our four jurisdictions can be seen as an extension of our assessment of the origin of corporate power. They will help us to understand how the boundaries of discretion are adjusted in particular situations, for example when a company is the target of a takeover bid. The second approach to the problem of limiting corporate power, the imposition of (fiduciary) duties that constrain existing discretion, will be addressed in the following two chapters.

I. UK

The distribution of power in UK companies, as shaped by cases such as *Automatic Self-Cleansing*, has been refined by the courts to deal with interference by the directors with the shareholder franchise. The response of UK law to this problem was developed mainly in two decisions where the directors made use of their power to issue and allot shares in order to frustrate a takeover bid: the High Court case *Hogg v Cramphorn Ltd*[185] and the

[181] Under most legal systems, directors owe their duties to the company, not the individual shareholders, see Chapter 6A.II.

[182] For the UK, see *Foss v Harbottle* (1843) 2 Hare 461 (establishing the so-called 'proper plaintiff rule'); United States: *Zapata Corp. v Maldonado*, 430 A.2d 779 (Del. 1981) (holding that the decision whether to initiate, or refrain from initiating, litigation to enforce potential claims of the corporation falls within the ambit of managerial decision-making power pursuant to Del. Gen. Corp. Law, §141(a), ibid 782); Germany: pursuant to §§112, 147 AktG, the corporation acts through the supervisory board and at the instigation of the general meeting to enforce directors' duties; France: the general managerial powers pursuant to Art. L225-35 Code de commerce include the decision to enforce a claim of the company in the form of an *action sociale ut universi*.

[183] We will discuss the derivative action in Chapter 8C.II.

[184] See for example *Re a Company (No 005136 of 1986)* [1987] BCLC 82 (allowing a shareholder's personal action where it was claimed that the issue of shares was an improper use by the directors of their fiduciary powers—however, note also that this decision predates the codification of this principle, the so-called proper purpose doctrine, as a duty in s 171(b) of the Companies Act 2006); Kershaw (n 170) 404 (submitting that the proper purpose doctrine may be seen 'as a default constitutional rule distributing power between the board and the shareholder body rather than [only] a director's duty', with the consequence that shareholders would be entitled to enforce their personal rights, in addition to bringing a derivative action). The *Holzmüller* decision gives rise to similar ambivalence in qualifying the nature of the directors' obligations as duty-based or competence/authority-based. For a discussion of this point see Gerner-Beuerle, Kershaw, and Solinas (n 130) 603–4. In the *Holzmüller* case, the plaintiffs enforced their personal rights and did not bring a derivative action. However, note that they sued for declaratory relief and not for damages. Damages could only be recovered in a personal lawsuit if the plaintiffs were able to argue that they had suffered a personal loss that was not simply a reflection of the company's loss (so-called reflective loss principle; see Chapter 8C.II), which may be difficult to show in the present context.

[185] [1967] Ch 254.

Privy Council case *Howard Smith Ltd v Ampol Petroleum Ltd*.[186] The decisions gave rise to what has become known as the 'proper purpose doctrine'. A fiduciary power, such as that of a company director, must be 'exercised for the purpose for which it was conferred'.[187] The doctrine is now codified in section 171(b) of the Companies Act 2006. It can be understood as a restriction on the statutory grant of power in the Companies Act and an adjustment of the contractual demarcation of the corporate organs' competences in the articles of association by means of a flexible standard. Shareholders can take recourse to this standard where actions of the directors are within the letter of the statutory or contractual grant of power, but not in line with the spirit of the provision or the nature of the relationship between the directors and shareholders.

In *Hogg v Cramphorn*, the claimant, Mr Hogg, was a minority shareholder in Cramphorn Ltd, a company carrying on the business of corn and seed merchant. An outside investor, Mr Baxter, proposed to the managing director to buy the whole of the company's issued share capital. The managing director was concerned that Mr Baxter, who had no experience of the corn and seed merchant business, would substantially change the nature of the company's trading and that this would 'unsettle the company's staff'.[188] As a reaction to Mr Baxter's offer, the board devised a scheme under which the company entered into a trust deed established for the benefit of the employees. The trustees were three shareholders affiliated with the directors. Relying on an authorization in the articles, the board allotted a large number of unissued shares to the trust and provided that they should carry ten votes per share. These votes, together with the shares already held by the directors, enabled them to control more than half of the voting capital of the company and repel the hostile bid. Mr Hogg sought a declaration that the share issue was *ultra vires* and void.

***Hogg v Cramphorn Ltd* [1967] Ch 254**

Buckley J:

I now turn to what has been the main matter of debate in this case, which is whether the allotment of the 5,707 shares was an improper use by the directors of their discretionary and fiduciary power under article 10, to decide to whom these unissued shares should be allotted . . .

It is common ground that the scheme of which this allotment formed part was formulated to meet the threat, as the directors regarded it, of Mr. Baxter's offer. The trust deed would not have come into existence, nor would the 5,707 shares have been issued as they were, but for Mr. Baxter's bid and the threat that it constituted to the established management of the company. It is also common ground that the directors were not actuated by any unworthy motives of personal advantage, but acted as they did in an honest belief that they were doing what was for the good of the company. Their honour is not in the least impugned, but it is said that the means which they adopted to attain their end were such as they could not properly adopt.

I am satisfied that Mr. Baxter's offer, when it became known to the company's staff, had an unsettling effect upon them. I am also satisfied that the directors and the trustees of the trust deed genuinely considered that to give the staff through the trustees a sizeable, though indirect, voice in the affairs of the company would benefit both the staff and the company. I am sure that Colonel Cramphorn [the managing director] and also probably his fellow directors firmly believed that to keep the management of the company's affairs in the hands of the existing board would be more advantageous to the shareholders, the company's staff and its customers than if it were committed to a board selected by Mr. Baxter. The steps which the board took were intended not only to ensure that if Mr. Baxter succeeded in obtaining a shareholding which, as matters stood, would have been a controlling shareholding, he should not secure control of the company, but also, and perhaps primarily, to discourage Mr. Baxter from proceeding with his bid at all . . .

Accepting as I do that the board acted in good faith and that they believed that the establishment of a trust would benefit the company, and that avoidance of the acquisition of control by Mr. Baxter would also benefit the company, I must still remember that an essential element of

[186] [1974] AC 821. [187] ibid 834. [188] [1967] Ch 254, 258.

the scheme, and indeed its primary purpose, was to ensure control of the company by the directors and those whom they could confidently regard as their supporters. Was such a manipulation of the voting position a legitimate act on the part of the directors?

... Unless a majority in a company is acting oppressively towards the minority, this court should not and will not itself interfere with the exercise by the majority of its constitutional rights or embark upon an inquiry into the respective merits of the views held or policies favoured by the majority and the minority. Nor will this court permit directors to exercise powers, which have been delegated to them by the company in circumstances which put the directors in a fiduciary position when exercising those powers, in such a way as to interfere with the exercise by the majority of its constitutional rights; and in a case of this kind also, in my judgment, the court should not investigate the rival merits of the views or policies of the parties ... It is not, in my judgment, open to the directors in such a case to say, 'We genuinely believe that what we seek to prevent the majority from doing will harm the company and therefore our act in arming ourselves or our party with sufficient shares to outvote the majority is a conscientious exercise of our powers under the articles, which should not be interfered with'.

Such a belief, even if well founded, would be irrelevant. A majority of shareholders in general meeting is entitled to pursue what course it chooses within the company's powers, however wrong-headed it may appear to others, provided the majority do not unfairly oppress other members of the company. These considerations lead me to the conclusion that the issue of the 5,707 shares, with the special voting rights which the directors purported to attach to them, could not be justified by the view that the directors genuinely believed that it would benefit the company if they could command a majority of the votes in general meetings. The fact that, as I have held, the directors were mistaken in thinking that they could attach to these shares more than one vote each is irrelevant. The power to issue shares was a fiduciary power and if, as I think, it was exercised for an improper motive, the issue of these shares is liable to be set aside.

... Had the majority of the company in general meeting approved the issue of the 5,707 shares before it was made, even with the purported special voting rights attached ... I do not think that any member could have complained of the issue being made, for in these circumstances, the criticism that the directors were by the issue of the shares attempting to deprive the majority of their constitutional rights would have ceased to have any force. It follows that a majority in a general meeting of the company at which no votes were cast in respect of the 5,707 shares could ratify the issue of those shares. Before setting the allotment and issue of the 5,707 shares aside, therefore, I propose to allow the company an opportunity to decide in general meeting whether it approves or disapproves of the issue of these shares to the trustees ...

[The Court then analysed the execution of the trust deed and an interest-free loan made by the board to the trustees to finance the share acquisition. It concluded that these transactions were 'integral part[s] of a scheme for securing for the directors the support of a controlling body of voters'.[189] They were effected with 'the primary objective of ... depriv[ing] those who were not supporters of the board of their controlling position'.[190] The court concluded that the share issue and the other transactions were ultra vires the directors and invalid unless ratified by the company in general meeting.]

...

The second important case in this context, *Howard Smith v Ampol*, dealt with a comparable situation: The Australian oil company Ampol Petroleum Ltd and another company, Bulkships Ltd, which was associated with Ampol, had acquired together about 55 per cent of the issued share capital of Millers. Ampol made an offer for the remaining shares in Millers, which was rejected as too low. Millers' directors were unsure about the intentions of Ampol and believed that they could achieve a higher price from an outside investor, Howard Smith Ltd, who had been in negotiations with Millers and was willing to make a tender offer. Ampol and Bulkships reacted to the competing offer by announcing that they 'intended to act jointly in relation to the future operation of Millers' and to reject any offer for their shares.[191] Millers' board then resolved to make a large issue of shares to Howard Smith.

[189] ibid 270. [190] ibid 271. [191] [1974] AC 821, 830.

The issue was justified on the grounds that Millers required a capital increase to finance the construction of two tankers. The court accepted that Millers was in need of capital, but it concluded that the primary purpose of the share issue was 'to reduce the proportionate combined shareholding of Ampol and Bulkships in order to induce Howard Smith to proceed with its takeover offer'.[192]

***Howard Smith Ltd v Ampol Petroleum Ltd* [1974] AC 821**

Lord Wilberforce:

[T]he directors' power [to issue and allot shares] is a fiduciary power: and it remains the case that an exercise of such a power though formally valid, may be attacked on the ground that it was not exercised for the purpose for which it was granted. It is at this point that the contentions of the parties diverge. The extreme argument on one side is that, for validity, what is required is bona fide exercise of the power in the interests of the company: that once it is found that the directors were not motivated by self-interest—i.e. by a desire to retain their control of the company or their positions on the board—the matter is concluded in their favour and that the court will not inquire into the validity of their reasons for making the issue. All decided cases, it was submitted, where an exercise of such a power as this has been found invalid, are cases where directors are found to have acted through self-interest of this kind.

On the other side, the main argument is that the purpose for which the power is conferred is to enable capital to be raised for the company, and that once it is found that the issue was not made for that purpose, invalidity follows ...

In their Lordships' opinion neither of the extreme positions can be maintained. It can be accepted, as one would only expect, that the majority of cases in which issues of shares are challenged in the courts are cases in which the vitiating element is the self-interest of the directors, or at least the purpose of the directors to preserve their own control of the management ...

But it does not follow from this, as the appellants assert, that the absence of any element of self-interest is enough to make an issue valid. Self-interest is only one, though no doubt the commonest, instance of improper motive ...

[I]t is, in their Lordships' opinion, too narrow an approach to say that the only valid purpose for which shares may be issued is to raise capital for the company. The discretion is not in terms limited in this way: the law should not impose such a limitation on directors' powers. To define in advance exact limits beyond which directors must not pass is, in their Lordships' view, impossible. This clearly cannot be done by enumeration, since the variety of situations facing directors of different types of company in different situations cannot be anticipated....

In their Lordships' opinion it is necessary to start with a consideration of the power whose exercise is in question, in this case a power to issue shares. Having ascertained, on a fair view, the nature of this power, and having defined as can best be done in the light of modern conditions the, or some, limits within which it may be exercised, it is then necessary for the court, if a particular exercise of it is challenged, to examine the substantial purpose for which it was exercised, and to reach a conclusion whether that purpose was proper or not. In doing so it will necessarily give credit to the bona fide opinion of the directors, if such is found to exist, and will respect their judgment as to matters of management; having done this, the ultimate conclusion has to be as to the side of a fairly broad line on which the case falls ...

The constitution of a limited company normally provides for directors, with powers of management, and shareholders, with defined voting powers having power to appoint the directors, and to take, in general meeting, by majority vote, decisions on matters not reserved for management. Just as it is established that directors, within their management powers, may take decisions against the wishes of the majority of shareholders, and indeed that the majority of shareholders cannot control them in the exercise of these powers while they remain in office (*Automatic Self-Cleansing Filter Syndicate Co. Ltd v Cuninghame* [1906] 2 Ch. 34), so it must be unconstitutional for directors to use their fiduciary powers over the shares in the company purely for the purpose of destroying an existing majority, or creating a new majority which did not previously exist. To do so is to interfere with that element of the company's constitution which is separate from and set against their powers. If there is added, moreover, to this immediate purpose, an ulterior

[192] ibid 833.

purpose to enable an offer for shares to proceed which the existing majority was in a position to block, the departure from the legitimate use of the fiduciary power becomes not less, but all the greater. The right to dispose of shares at a given price is essentially an individual right to be exercised on individual decision and on which a majority, in the absence of oppression or similar impropriety, is entitled to prevail. Directors are of course entitled to offer advice, and bound to supply information, relevant to the making of such a decision, but to use their fiduciary power solely for the purpose of shifting the power to decide to whom and at what price shares are to be sold cannot be related to any purpose for which the power over the share capital was conferred upon them . . .

Questions and comments:

1. The Privy Council in *Howard Smith v Ampol* made several important observations that elaborated on the holding in *Hogg v Cramphorn.* First, it discussed what is required of directors when they exercise the powers formally vested in them under the articles. The court emphasized that the motive of the directors to protect the company against the risk of harm, or the fact that the directors believed in good faith that they were acting in the interests of the company, was irrelevant for the question of whether the exercise of the directors' powers was 'improper'. The impropriety derives from the transgression of the limits of the directors' discretion.[193] How can these limits be determined? According to the Privy Council, the first step is to ascertain the nature of the power in question and the limits within which it may be exercised. The courts then examine the 'substantial purpose' (or, as the High Court in *Hogg v Cramphorn* put it, the 'primary purpose') for which the power was exercised in the particular case and ask whether it was within the limits thus defined.[194]

   Is this an objective or a subjective test? The determination of the 'substantial purpose' for which the directors' power was exercised involves an inquiry into the directors' motives and state of mind. On the other hand, the courts refer to the constitutional division of powers within the corporation, which does not depend on any particular motivation of the directors.[195] The directors in *Howard Smith v Ampol* were adamant that the primary purpose for the share issue was 'to meet an urgent capital need of Millers',[196] which was corroborated by the minutes of the board meeting that decided on the allotment to Howard Smith.[197] Nevertheless, the court stated: 'It is unreal and unconvincing to hear [the directors] assert in the witness box that their dominant purpose was to obtain capital rather than to promote the Howard Smith takeover offer, and I do not believe these assertions'.[198] Is this really an assessment of the intentions and motives of the directors, based on the available evidence and giving 'credit to the bona fide opinion of the directors'?[199] Or does the court simply rely on the objective circumstances of the case: that the directors carried out a share issue of sufficient size to convert an existing majority position into a minority position and thus frustrate a pending takeover offer that the board had rejected?[200] Furthermore, is the test developed in *Howard Smith v Ampol*

193 *Howard Smith Ltd v Ampol Petroleum Ltd* [1974] AC 821, 835.

194 See ibid and the sixth paragraph in the excerpt above.

195 See ibid 837 and the last paragraph in the excerpt above. 196 ibid 833. 197 ibid 832.

198 ibid 833. 199 See ibid 835 and the sixth paragraph in the excerpt above.

200 See ibid 832, where the court describes its approach: '[W]hen a dispute arises whether directors of a company made a particular decision for one purpose or for another, or whether, there being more than one purpose, one or another purpose was the substantial or primary purpose, the court, in their Lordships' opinion, is entitled to look at the situation objectively in order to estimate how critical or pressing, or substantial or, per contra, insubstantial an alleged requirement may have been. If it finds that a particular requirement, though real, was not urgent, or critical, at the relevant time, it may have reason to doubt, or discount, the assertions of individuals that they acted solely in order to deal with it, particularly when the action they took was unusual or even extreme'. See also *Eclairs Group Ltd v JKX Oil & Gas Plc* [2016] B.C.C. 79, 89–90: Where the directors are concurrently motivated by several purposes, some proper and some improper, the primary purpose is 'the purpose which caused the decision to be made as it was. . . . One has to focus on the improper purpose and ask whether the decision would have been made if the directors had not been moved by it. If the answer is that without the improper purpose(s) the decision impugned would never have been made, then it would be irrational to allow it to stand simply because the directors had other, proper considerations in mind as well, to which perhaps they attached greater importance. . . . Correspondingly, if there were proper reasons for exercising the power and it would still have been exercised for those reasons even in the absence of improper ones, it is difficult to see why justice should require the decision to be set aside'.

workable? The Privy Council itself acknowledges that it is not possible to define the exact limits of discretion. What does it mean to ascertain the limits 'as can best be done in the light of modern conditions'?[201]

2. Part of the ambivalence of *Howard Smith v Ampol* may be attributable to the attempt of the court to reconcile two legal concepts that apply to distinct situations, but that were not always clearly separated in the case law: the exercise of corporate powers for proper purposes, as developed in *Hogg v Cramphorn* and *Howard Smith v Ampol* and now codified in section 171(b) of the Companies Act 2006, and the common law duty to act in good faith in the best interests of the company, codified in section 172 of the Companies Act 2006. The latter duty is largely subjective and characterized by judicial deference to the management decisions of the board of directors. The Privy Council in *Howard Smith v Ampol* expressed this approach in the following words: '[I]t would be wrong for the court to substitute its opinion for that of the management, or indeed to question the correctness of the management's decision, on [matters involving the management of the company, such as the raising of finance'], if bona fide arrived at'.[202]

   The content of the duty to act in good faith in the best interests of the company is well developed in the case law. A good early statement of the duty is the decision of the Court of Appeal in *Re Smith & Fawcett*.[203] Smith & Fawcett was a private company with two shareholder-directors that both held half of the company's ordinary share capital. Article 10 of the company's articles of association provided: 'The directors may at any time in their absolute and uncontrolled discretion refuse to register any transfer of shares'.[204] When one of the directors, Fawcett, died, the executors of his will applied to the other director, Smith, to be registered as members. Smith refused to consent to the registration and instead offered to buy half of the testator's shares and register the other half. The court first assessed the permissibility of Article 10 conferring wide discretion on the directors to restrict the transferability of the shares:

   > There is nothing, in my opinion, in principle or in authority to make it impossible to draft such a wide and comprehensive power to directors to refuse to transfer as to enable them to take into account any matter which they conceive to be in the interests of the company ... such matters, for instance, as whether by their passing a particular transfer the transferee would obtain too great a weight in the councils of the company or might even perhaps obtain control. The question, therefore, simply is whether on the true construction of the particular article the directors are limited by anything except their bona fide view as to the interests of the company. In the present case the article is drafted in the widest possible terms, and I decline to write into that clear language any limitation other than a limitation, which is implicit by law, that a fiduciary power of this kind must be exercised bona fide in the interests of the company.[205]

   The remaining issue was whether the evidence supported the view that Smith did not act bona fide in the best interests of the company, but rather for some collateral purpose, namely in order to preserve his dominating position. The court was hesitant to infer this conclusion from circumstantial evidence:

   > [I]t is [not] illegitimate in a proper case to draw inferences as to bona fides or mala fides in cases where there is on the face of the affidavit sufficient justification for doing so, but where the oath of the deponent is before the court, as it is here, and the only grounds on which the court is asked to disbelieve it are matters of inference, many of them of a doubtful character, I decline to give to those suggestions the weight which is desired. In the present case the principal director has sworn an affidavit which, if accepted, makes it clear that, whether rightly or wrongly, the directors have bona fide considered the interests of the

[201] *Howard Smith Ltd v Ampol Petroleum Ltd* [1974] AC 821, 832. For a critical assessment of the workability of the test in *Howard Smith v Ampol* see D Kershaw, 'The Illusion of Importance: Reconsidering the UK's Takeover Defence Prohibition' (2007) 56 ICLQ 267, 282–6 (arguing that the proper purpose doctrine is not a rule of construction regarding the extent and limits of an individual power or discretion, but a constitutional rule determining the balance of power between the board and the shareholders).

[202] [1974] AC 821, 832.

[203] [1942] Ch 304. For the question of how to define the interests of the company, see Chapter 4C.II above.

[204] [1942] Ch 304, 305. [205] ibid 308.

company and come to the conclusion that it would be undesirable to register the transfer of the totality of these shares. Accordingly, on the evidence I am satisfied ... that there is no ground shown here for saying that the directors' refusal has been due to anything but a bona fide consideration of the interests of the company as the directors see them.[206]

Was *Howard Smith v Ampol*, where the Privy Council referred to the limited judicial review of management decisions, in line with this holding? Did the Privy Council *rely* on the principle expounded in *Re Smith & Fawcett*?[207]

3. Does *Re Smith & Fawcett* mean that the courts will not intervene so long as the director honestly believed that the decision was in the best interests of the company, no matter how unreasonable the belief? In general, this question has to be answered in the affirmative, but the case law shows that the courts take recourse to an objective lower threshold when evaluating the credibility of the directors' assertion that they acted bona fide. In most cases, the assessment of the director's state of mind will depend on circumstantial evidence. The courts will ask whether, in light of the evidence, it is *plausible* that the directors honestly believed, as they will usually claim, that the challenged action was in the interests of the company.[208]
4. The holdings in *Hogg v Cramphorn* and *Howard Smith v Ampol* were to some extent qualified in a more recent decision of the High Court, *Criterion Properties plc v Stratford UK Properties LLC*.[209] Criterion and Stratford UK Properties ('Oaktree') had formed a joint venture with a

[206] ibid 308–9.

[207] In this context, see also *Regentcrest plc v Cohen* [2001] 2 BCLC 80. In this case, one of the directors of Regentcrest was alleged to have breached his duty to act in good faith in the best interest of the company by waiving a (contested) clawback claim that entitled the company to reclaim parts of the purchase price paid for a piece of development land from two of its directors. As regards the applicable standard of review, the court explained: 'The duty imposed on directors to act bona fide in the interests of the company is a subjective one ... The question is not whether, viewed objectively by the court, the particular act or omission which is challenged was in fact in the interests of the company; still less is the question of whether the court, had it been in the position of the director at the relevant time, might have acted differently. Rather, the question is whether the director honestly believed that his act or omission was in the interests of the company. The issue is as to the director's state of mind. No doubt, where it is clear that the act or omission under challenge resulted in substantial detriment to the company, the director will have a harder task persuading the court that he honestly believed it to be in the company's interest; but that does not detract from the subjective nature of the test ... The position is different where a power conferred on a director is used for a collateral purpose. In such circumstances it matters not whether the director honestly believed that in exercising the power as he did he was acting in the interests of the company; the power having been exercised for an improper purpose, its exercise will be liable to be set aside (see eg *Hogg v Cramphorn Ltd* [1967] Ch 254). However, it has not been contended that that principle applies in the instant case'. ibid 513–14.

[208] For example, in *Regentcrest plc v Cohen* (see the previous footnote for the facts), the court accepted the contention of the defendant that the waiver of the clawback claim was justified on commercial grounds, in particular to maintain a united board and avoid a situation where two of the company's directors would be sued in financially difficult times for Regentcrest: 'In my judgment ... the circumstantial evidence to which I have referred does not, when considered in context, suggest that ... the [defendant and his brother, also director of Regentcrest (the Richardson brothers)] did not honestly believe that the waiver of the clawback claim was in the interests of Regentcrest, and that their only reason for agreeing to the waiver was to protect [the debtors of the claim] against a liquidator seeking to pursue the claim against them. On the contrary, in my judgment the evidence as a whole supports the conclusion that ... the Richardson brothers were still prepared to support Regentcrest [when they decided on the waiver] and were genuinely seeking to achieve its survival. Had that not been the case, it is impossible satisfactorily to explain Mr Roy Richardson's conduct in continuing thereafter to negotiate with the banks and in procuring the delisting of Regentcrest's shares. The notion that in so doing he was acting out some kind of charade in order to mask his true motives is simply not credible'. [2001] 2 BCLC 520. In *Gaiman v National Association for Mental Health* [1971] Ch 317, the court accepted that the decision to expel a large number of the defendant's members was taken in good faith in the best interests of the association because the evidence provided 'ample grounds for saying that at the very lowest [the concern that the members posed a threat to the association] is a possible view to hold'. See [1971] Ch 331. For a discussion of this issue see also Kershaw (n 170) 343–5.

[209] [2002] EWHC 496 (Ch); *reversed* [2002] EWCA Civ 1783 (Court of Appeal). The test becomes more demanding if the directors fail to give actual consideration to the best interests of the company, for example because the company is part of a corporate group and the directors seek to benefit the group as a whole, *Charterbridge Corp v Lloyds Bank Ltd* [1970] Ch. 62, or if they do not consider the interests of the creditors at a time when the company is in financial difficulties and they are required to act in the creditors' interests (s 172(3) Companies Act 2006), *Re HLC Environmental Projects Ltd* [2014] B.C.C. 337. In these cases, the proper test is objective: 'whether an intelligent and honest man in the position of a director of the company concerned could in the circumstances have reasonably believed that the transaction was for the benefit of the company [or the creditors]', ibid 339.

view to investing in real estate. In order to protect Criterion against a potential hostile take-over bid, the parties entered into a supplementary agreement providing that in the event of a change in control of Criterion or removal of Criterion's executive directors Oaktree would be entitled to require Criterion to buy out Oaktree's interest in the joint venture at a price very favourable to Oaktree. Criterion later sought rescission of the supplementary agreement and brought an action for the agreement to be set aside. The issue was whether the board of Criterion had used its powers to contract for an improper purpose when it entered into the supplementary agreement on behalf of Criterion. The directors argued that they acted in the best interest of the company because the individuals behind the potential bidder were 'disreputable people' who intended 'to wind up Criterion's business and to liquidate the company'.[210] The trial judge referred approvingly to a number of authorities that seemingly qualified the strict stance adopted in *Hogg v Cramphorn* and *Howard Smith v Ampol*. The court argued that 'the principle [in *Hogg v Cramphorn*] must not be carried too far' and directors acted within the fiduciary limits of their discretion if they used their powers, for example to issue shares, in order to maintain their control and prevent the company 'from being reduced to impotence and beggary' at the hands of a hostile bidder.[211] However, the judge held that the buy-out provision in the agreement was too wide and interference with the constitutional rights of the shareholders to remove the directors could therefore not be justified.[212] While the outcome in this case is, accordingly, in line with *Hogg v Cramphorn* and *Howard Smith v Ampol*, can the same be said about the reasoning of the trial judge? In light of the decisions discussed in this section, which mechanisms do directors of a UK company have at their disposal to defend against a bid that may cause serious economic harm to the target company?

5. At least one decision has held that a violation of the proper purpose doctrine constitutes an infringement of the shareholders' individual rights, as opposed to the rights of the company. This distinction is important because it determines how shareholders can enforce a breach of duty. Hoffmann J, as he then was, argued that the action, dealing with an allegedly unlawful allotment of shares, was not a derivative action. Rather, '[t]he true basis of the action [was] an alleged infringement of the petitioner's individual rights as a shareholder. The allotment [was] alleged to be an improper and unlawful exercise of the powers granted to the board by the articles of association, which constitute a contract between the company and its members'.[213] Accordingly, the court dealt with 'an infringement of a member's contractual rights under the articles'[214] and the member could bring a personal action to set aside the challenged transaction.

   It should be noted that the two principal cases presented above, *Hogg v Cramphorn* and *Howard Smith v Ampol*, also involved actions brought by shareholders individually and on behalf of other shareholders, rather than actions on behalf of the company. In spite of these judgments, the nature and consequences of a breach of the proper purpose doctrine remain ambivalent. On the one hand, the exercise of the directors' powers for an improper purpose constitutes an infringement of the contract between the members *and the company*. On the other hand, if the duty is also owed to the company, as is now expressly stipulated in the Companies Act 2006,[215] the shareholders should have a choice between a personal action against the company and a derivative action on behalf of the company against the directors.

[210] [2002] EWHC 496, para 16.

[211] ibid para 17. The judgments referred to were, inter alia, *Cayne v Global Natural Resources plc* (unreported) (12 August 1982) and *Teck Corpn Ltd v Millar* (1972) 33 DLR (3d) 288.

[212] [2002] EWHC 496, paras 20–3. The Court of Appeal agreed with the trial judge. It argued that the agreement 'went far beyond anything which could be justified for the purpose of deterring an unwelcome predator. The buy-back provision could be triggered by any take-over, not only by a hostile predator, but even by one regarded as wholly beneficial (or even by Oaktree itself). Furthermore, it could be triggered by the departure of [the executive directors], even in circumstances which had nothing to do with a change of control, for example death or dismissal due to misconduct ... Had the agreement been so drafted as to be confined to the purpose of seeing off the particular predator, the present dispute would not have arisen. It is therefore unnecessary to decide to what extent "poison pills", limited to that purpose, are permissible in English law. However, ... the agreement went far beyond that limited purpose. Even if one accepts the lawfulness of the purpose, and the power of the directors to use the mechanism of a "contingent transfer" of assets to achieve it, it is very difficult to see how this particular agreement could be justified as a reasonable exercise of that power in the interests of the company'.

[213] *Re Sherborne Park Residents Co Ltd* (1986) 2 BCC 99528, 99530–1 (Ch).

[214] ibid 99531.

[215] See s 170(1): 'The general duties specified in sections 171 to 177 are owed by a director of a company to the company'. Thus, this clearly includes the duty to exercise powers for proper purposes (s 171(b)).

However, the availability of a personal action is a factor that the courts must take into account in considering whether to grant permission to continue a derivative claim.[216] It is an open question whether one or the other action takes precedence as a general rule, or the courts will decide on a case-by-case basis.[217]

II. US

We mentioned above that US courts take encroachments upon the shareholder franchise by the directors seriously. A good example is the decision of the US District Court of Nevada in *Hilton Hotels Corporation v ITT Corp.*,[218] a takeover case that was decided in reliance on Delaware law as persuasive authority. In order to defend against a tender offer by Hilton, ITT announced a comprehensive plan to restructure the corporation. The plan proposed to split ITT into three new entities, the largest of which (ITT Destinations) would account for approximately 93 per cent of ITT's assets. The board of ITT Destinations was to be comprised of the members of ITT's current board, with the following difference:

> The new board would be a 'classified' or 'staggered' board divided into three classes with each class of directors serving for a term of three years, and with one class to be elected each year. Moreover, a shareholder vote of 80% would be required to remove directors without cause, and 80% shareholder vote would also be required to repeal the classified board provision or the 80% requirement to remove directors without cause.[219]

ITT intended to implement the restructuring without shareholder approval. Hilton sought an injunction enjoining ITT from proceeding with the plan. In the context of analysing Delaware case law on the permissibility of takeover defences, the court made important statements concerning the relationship between the shareholders and the board. The following excerpt focuses on these aspects of the case.

***Hilton Hotels Corporation v ITT Corp.*, 978 F. Supp. 1342 (D. Nev. 1997)**

Pro, District Judge:

These cases [from Delaware] have drawn a distinction between the exercise of two types of corporate power: 1) power over the assets of the corporation and 2) the power relationship between the board (management) and the shareholders. Actions involving the first type of power invoke the business judgment rule, or *Unocal* if an action is in response to a reasonably perceived threat to the corporation.[220] Actions involving the second power invoke a *Blasius* analysis [and thus requiring a 'compelling justification'].[221] The issues raised in this case require the Court to focus

[216] Companies Act 2006, s 263(3)(f).

[217] For a discussion of this point see Kershaw (n 170) 565–7 (referring to *Franbar Holdings Ltd v Patel* [2008] EWHC 1534 (Ch), where the court did not grant permission to continue a derivative claim because the shareholder had already brought an unfair prejudice petition (Companies Act 2006, s 994), and arguing that the holding could not be generalized since different cost rules applied to the s 994 petition and the derivative action).

[218] 978 F. Supp. 1342 (D. Nev. 1997).

[219] ibid 1344.

[220] [Footnote by authors.] The District Court refers to *Unocal Corp. v Mesa Petroleum Co.*, 493 A.2d 946 (Del. 1985), which introduced an enhanced business judgment rule for defensive board action, mainly requiring that the defensive measure must be proportionate in relation to the threat posed by the tender offer.

[221] [Footnote by authors.] See *Blasius Industries v Atlas Corp.*, 564 A.2d 651 (Del. 1988): 'The shareholder franchise is the ideological underpinning upon which the legitimacy of directorial power rests. Generally, shareholders have only two protections against perceived inadequate business performance. They may sell their stock (which, if done in sufficient numbers, may so affect security prices as to create an incentive for altered managerial performance), or they may vote to replace incumbent board members ... [A] decision by the board to act for the primary purpose of preventing the effectiveness of a shareholder vote inevitably involves the question who, as between the principal and the agent, has authority with respect to a matter of internal corporate governance ... A board's decision to act to prevent the shareholders from creating a majority of new board positions and filling them does not involve the exercise of *the corporation's power* over its property, or with respect to *its* rights or obligations; rather, it involves allocation, between shareholders as a class and the board, of effective power with respect to governance of the corporation ... Judicial review of such action involves a determination of the legal and equitable obligations of an agent towards his principal. This is not, in my opinion, a question that a court may leave to the agent finally to decide so long as he does so honestly and competently; that is, it may not be left to the agent's business judgment'. ibid 659–60.

on the power relationship between ITT's board and ITT shareholders, not on the ITT board's actions relating to corporate assets …

ITT's response to Hilton's tender offer touches upon issues of control, and this Court must determine whether the response purposefully disenfranchises ITT's shareholders. If so … it is not a reasonable response unless a 'compelling justification' exists. It is important to note that in *Blasius,* the board did something that normally would be entirely permissible under Delaware law and its own by-laws: it expanded the board from seven to nine individuals. It did this in the face of a hostile takeover by a company financed through 'junk bonds' and two individuals who sought to substantially 'cash out' many of the target corporation's assets … Still, while the board in *Blasius* had a good faith reason to act as it did, and it acted with appropriate care, the board could not lawfully prevent the shareholders from electing a majority of new directors.

Blasius' factual scenario is strikingly similar to the circumstances surrounding ITT's actions. Normally, a corporation is free to adopt a classified board structure. In fact many companies, including Hilton, have classified boards. As long as the classified board is adopted in the proper manner, whether through charter amendment, changes in the by-laws of a company or through shareholder vote, it is permissible. However, *Blasius* illustrates that even if an action is normally permissible, and the board adopts it in good faith and with proper care, a board cannot undertake such action if the primary purpose is to disenfranchise the shareholders in light of a proxy contest … Thus, while ITT could normally adopt a classified board or issue a dividend of shares creating ITT Destinations, it cannot undertake these actions if the primary purpose is to disenfranchise ITT shareholders …

[The court then analysed the circumstances of ITT's restructuring plan, inter alia the timing, the plan's effect on the directors' tenure, and the arguments advanced by ITT to justify the plan. The court pointed out that the plan was developed as a response to Hilton's tender offer, that it was to be implemented in a short period of time (a little over two months), and designed to take effect shortly before the annual general meeting at which the shareholders would have had an opportunity to vote on the annually elected board. The effect of the plan would have been to appoint the current members of the board to more insulated positions. Furthermore, the majority of board members would have avoided standing for reelection at the upcoming annual general meeting. Finally, ITT did not advance any credible justification for not seeking shareholder approval of the plan. It merely claimed that it wanted to 'avoid market risks and other business problems'.[222] The Court concluded:]

Shareholders do not exercise day-to-day business judgments regarding the operation of a corporation—those are matters left to the reasonable discretion of directors, officers and the corporation's management team. Corporate boards have great latitude in exercising their business judgments as they should … For this reason, interference with the shareholder franchise is especially serious. It is not to be left to the board's business judgment, precisely because it undercuts a primary justification for allowing directors to rely on their business judgment in almost every other context. Indeed, as the court in *Shoen* noted, 'one of the justifications for the business judgment rule's insulation of directors from liability for almost all of their decisions is that unhappy shareholders can always vote the directors out of office'.[223] …

ITT strongly argues that its Comprehensive Plan is superior to Hilton's alternative tender offer. This argument should be directed to ITT's shareholders, not this Court. ITT also claims that it has properly considered other constituencies in responding to Hilton's offer, as it is expressly allowed to do under N.R.S. § 78.138.[224] ITT is correct. Other constituencies may be considered under that provision, but nothing in that statute suggests that the interests of third

[222] *Hilton Hotels Corporation v ITT Corp.*, 978 F. Supp. 1342, 1349 (D. Nev. 1997).

[223] [Footnote by authors.] The full reference of the quote is *Shoen v AMERCO*, 885 F. Supp. 1332, 1340 (D. Nev. 1994).

[224] [Footnote by authors.] N.R.S. [Nevada Revised Statutes] §78.138 provides that directors, in exercising their powers, 'may consider:

(a) The interests of the corporation's employees, suppliers, creditors and customers;
(b) The economy of the State and Nation;
(c) The interests of the community and of society; and
(d) The long-term as well as short-term interests of the corporation and its stockholders'.

parties are as important as the right of shareholder franchise. While the two interests are not exclusive, neither are they equal. The right of shareholders to vote on directors at an annual meeting is a fundamental principle of corporate law, and it is not outweighed by the interests listed in N.R.S. § 78.138.

Likewise, the good faith of the ITT board in implementing the Comprehensive Plan does not change this Court's analysis. Shoen relying on Blasius, recognized a good faith breach of duty under Nevada law. Simply put, there is no compelling justification for infringement of the shareholder franchise as proposed by the implementation of ITT's Comprehensive Plan before the 1997 annual meeting.

The ultimate outcome of the election of directors at ITT's 1997 annual meeting is not a relevant inquiry for this Court. That is something for the shareholders who own ITT to decide when they select the board who will lead the corporation. If a majority of the incumbent ITT board is re-elected after a fully-informed and fair shareholder vote, that board will be free to implement any business plan it chooses so long as that plan is consistent with ITT's charter and by-laws, and governing law.

This Court concludes that the structure and timing of ITT's Comprehensive Plan with its classified board provision for ITT Destinations, is preclusive and leaves no doubt that the primary purpose for ITT's proposed implementation of the Comprehensive Plan before the 1997 annual meeting is to impermissibly impede the exercise of the shareholder franchise by depriving shareholders of the opportunity to vote to re-elect or to oust all or as many of the incumbent ITT directors as they may choose at the upcoming annual meeting. It has as its primary purpose the entrenchment of the incumbent ITT board. As a result, the Court concludes that Hilton has prevailed on the merits of its claim for permanent injunctive relief.

Questions and comments:

1. *Hilton Hotels* illustrates that Delaware courts (and courts from other states as well) will apply two different standards of review when a shareholder challenges the actions of directors. If the board decides on matters of management, the directors are protected by the so-called 'business judgment rule', which means that courts will generally refrain from reviewing the business decision on its merits, provided that the directors acted on an informed basis, in good faith, and without a conflict of interest.[225] In a takeover situation, the test under the business judgment rule is enhanced, following *Unocal* (the defensive measure must be a proportionate response to the perceived threat of the takeover), but the issue does not concern the constitutional allocation of corporate power between the board of directors and the shareholder body. In the words of the District Court in *Hilton Hotels*, the board is vested with 'power over the assets of the corporation'. The question is not whether the board has authority to take a particular decision, but how it should make use of its authority to comply with the fiduciary duties of directors.

   The standard of review changes radically if a decision relates to 'the power relationship between the board (management) and the shareholders'. Now the directors must advance a 'compelling justification' for their interference with the shareholder franchise. *Hilton Hotels* shows that it is not always easy to distinguish between this second case and management decisions that fall within the ambit of the board's general authority. The court acknowledges that the board may have the power to restructure the corporation and, in doing so, adopt a classified board.[226] Whether the board's action encroaches upon the shareholder franchise depends on the purpose of the action. If 'the primary purpose is to disenfranchise the shareholders in light of a proxy contest', it is no longer sufficient that the board acts in good faith and with proper

[225] We will discuss the business judgment rule in Chapter 6B.I.2.

[226] See *Hilton Hotels* (n 222) 1348, and the third paragraph in the excerpt above. Pursuant to Del. Gen. Corp. Law, §141(d), a classified board may be established by the certificate of incorporation, the initial by-laws, or by a bylaw adopted by a vote of the stockholders. Thus, the introduction of a staggered board after formation requires shareholder approval. In *Hilton Hotels*, the directors hoped to be able to avoid a shareholder vote by forming a new corporation and providing for a staggered board *ab initio*.

care.[227] The action is outside the scope of the business judgment rule and requires a compelling justification.

Is this test comparable to the one formulated in *Hogg v Cramphorn* and *Howard Smith v Ampol*, where the courts also used the concept of 'primary purpose'? And is the enhanced business judgment rule that reviews the proportionality of a target board's response to a takeover comparable with the approach taken in *Criterion Properties*?

2. The 'primary purpose' and 'improper purpose' terminology can be found in other Delaware cases. *Condec Corp. v Lunkenheimer Co.*[228] dealt with a factual pattern very similar to *Howard Smith v Ampol*. In order to dilute an existing majority shareholding by Condec and frustrate Condec's takeover attempt, Lunkenheimer issued a large number of treasury shares to an affiliated corporation. The Delaware Court of Chancery observed that 'the primary purpose of the issuance of [the] shares was to prevent control of Lunkenheimer from passing to Condec'.[229] Quoting another Delaware case,[230] the court held that it constituted a breach of duty 'for directors to make use of the issuance of shares to accomplish an improper purpose, such as to enable a particular person or group to maintain or obtain voting control'.[231] The issue of Lunkenheimer's treasury shares to the third party, the court continued, 'was clearly unwarranted because it unjustifiably strikes at the very heart of corporate representation by causing a stockholder with an equitable right to a majority of corporate stock to have his right to a proportionate voice and influence in corporate affairs to be diminished by the simple act of an exchange of stock'.[232] Note that the decision does not establish a general prohibition of issuing shares to a preferred party to defend against a takeover offer. The important point was that Condec had already acquired 'a contractual right to assert voting control' and was deprived of such control 'by what is virtually a corporate legerdemain'.[233] In *Schnell v Chris-Craft Industries, Inc.*,[234] the management of the defendant corporation advanced the date of the annual general meeting to give dissident shareholders less time to prepare for a proxy contest against management. The Delaware Supreme Court held that this was an inequitable purpose, 'contrary to established principles of corporate democracy'.[235]

   In spite of these cases, the concept of 'improper purpose' plays a less important role in the United States than the UK. First, in the UK, the doctrine is listed as one of the duties of directors in the Companies Act 2006, whereas it is unwritten and its boundaries are somewhat indeterminate in the United States. Secondly, it is formulated broadly in the Companies Act 2006. It applies to any powers of the directors and requires them to use these powers only for purposes for which they were conferred (by the shareholders expressly or through the Companies Act). The doctrines developed in *Unocal*, *Blasius*, and their progeny,[236] on the other hand, operate along different lines. They help to determine the dividing line between management decisions and structural decisions that disenfranchise the shareholders, notably by eroding the shareholders' rights to replace incumbent board members and sell their shares to the highest bidder.

3. Two further examples from US law where the courts are prepared to intervene because the directors have encroached upon the shareholder franchise are the manipulation of *blank check preferred shares* and the so-called *de facto merger doctrine*. The case *Unilever Acquisition Corp. v Richardson-Vicks, Inc.*[237] illustrates how blank check preferred shares can be used as a takeover defence: The board of Richardson-Vicks sought to refute an unsolicited tender offer by Unilever by issuing a new class of preferred stock as a stock dividend to common stockholders. The preferred shares entitled the holders to cast twenty-five votes on all issues on which the common shares could vote. However, if the preferred shares were transferred, the voting rights would fall to five votes per share for the first thirty-six months the stock was held. This enabled a minority shareholder who opposed the tender offer (the Richardson family) to prevent Unilever from gaining control of the company even if Unilever succeeded

[227] ibid 1348–9, and the third paragraph in the excerpt above.
[228] 230 A.2d 769 (Del. Ch. 1967).
[229] ibid 775.
[230] *Yasik v Wachtel*, 17 A.2d 309 (Del. Ch. 1941).
[231] *Condec*, 230 A.2d 775.
[232] ibid 777.
[233] ibid.
[234] *Schnell v Chris-Craft Industries, Inc.*, 285 A.2d 437 (Del. 1971).
[235] ibid 439.
[236] See nn 220–221 above and *Hilton Hotels* (n 222) for references.
[237] 618 F. Supp. 407 (S.D.N.Y. 1985).

in acquiring all remaining shares. Under Delaware law, which was applicable to the case, the rights of stockholders and any qualifications or limitations of the rights are generally to be spelled out in the certificate of incorporation. In order to change shareholder rights, the board has to submit a proposed amendment to the general meeting. However, the certificate of incorporation may authorize the board to issue stock with the terms to be set by the board.[238] This authorization is widely used for the issuance of preferred stock. Preferred stock competes with debt securities, and in order to set a dividend rate on the preferred that is competitive with the prevailing interest rate on debt it is necessary for the board to be able to act at short notice. In *Unilever*, the court held that the board had misused its discretion in making use of the authority granted by the certificate of incorporation: '[A] change in corporate structure of this magnitude, reducing the transferability of a shareholder's ability to vote and the value of his or her asset to this degree, requires stockholder approval which has not been obtained'.[239]

De facto mergers have arisen as a response to the general requirement to procure a shareholder vote on a plan of merger or a sale of substantially all of the corporation's assets.[240] In many jurisdictions, dissenting shareholders have the right to obtain payment of the fair value of their shares if they do not vote in favour of the transaction (appraisal right).[241] In some cases, boards have sought to avoid voting and appraisal rights of shareholders by structuring transactions in a way that does not conform to the definition of a merger or sale of assets under the applicable company law statute while achieving the same economic result (hence the term 'de facto merger'). For instance, in *Farris v Glen Alden Corp.*,[242] a Delaware holding company, List Industries, owning interests in a variety of companies from motion picture theatres to warehouses and oil and gas operations, bought 38.5 per cent of the outstanding stock of the defendant, a Pennsylvania mining corporation. The acquisition enabled List to place three of its directors on the board of Glen Alden. The two corporations then entered into a 'reorganisation agreement', according to which Glen Alden was to acquire all of the assets of List in consideration for shares equal to about three times Glen Alden's outstanding shares of stock. List was to be dissolved and Glen Alden adopt its name. Effectively, owing to the large amount of newly issued shares, control of Glen Alden would have passed to the shareholders of List without Glen Alden being required to adhere to the merger provisions of the Pennsylvania business corporation law. The court considered the transaction to be a de facto merger and invalidated it.[243]

Not all US jurisdictions are willing to follow the approach adopted by the Pennsylvania Supreme Court in *Glen Alden*. Notably, the Delaware courts point out that an action that has been based lawfully on one provision of the corporation code will not be invalidated because the same result can be achieved pursuant to a different provision only under additional requirements (so-called *doctrine of independent legal significance*): '[It constitutes a] general theory of the Delaware Corporation Law that action taken pursuant to the authority of the various sections of that law constitute acts of independent legal significance and their validity is not dependent on other sections of the Act'.[244]

[238] Del. Gen. Corp. Law, §151(a).

[239] *Unilever*, 618 F. Supp. 410.

[240] MBCA, §§11.04, 12.02; Del. Gen. Corp. Law, §§251(c), 271(a).

[241] MBCA, §§13.01–13.31; Del. Gen. Corp. Law, §262. Note that in Delaware appraisal rights only exist for dissenting shareholders in a merger or consolidation. In the jurisdictions following the MBCA, appraisal rights are available in the event of a number of corporate actions, including (in addition to mergers) sale of assets, amendment of the articles, domestication, and conversion of the corporation to an unincorporated entity, see MBCA, §13.02(a) and Chapter 7C.II.

[242] 393 Pa. 427 (Pa. 1958).

[243] *Glen Alden*, 393 Pa. 438: '[W]e will not blind our eyes to the realities of the transaction. Despite the designation of the parties and the form employed, Glen Alden does not in fact acquire List, rather, List acquires Glen Alden'.

[244] *Hariton v Arco Electronics, Inc.*, 41 Del. Ch. 74, 77 (Del. 1963). In the case, the Delaware Supreme Court was asked to address the validity of a transaction similar to that in *Glen Alden*. The transaction was valid under the sale-of-assets statute of the Delaware General Corporation Law, but would have given rise to appraisal rights under the merger statute.

III. Civil law jurisdictions

Civil law countries generally do not possess a well-developed, freestanding proper purpose doctrine. The closest equivalent may be the duty to act in good faith, which derives from the general obligation to perform obligations according to the requirements of good faith. This duty underlies the law of obligations and is applied by analogy to the position of company directors.[245] In France, constraints on the directors' decision-making authority can also be derived from the general rules of Book III, Title IX of the Code civil that apply to all types of company. In particular, Article 1833 Code civil requires directors to act in the corporate interest. However, this duty bears more similarity to the duty of UK directors to act 'in good faith in the best interests of the company' (s 172 Companies Act 2006) than the proper purpose doctrine. A proper purpose constraint on managerial decision-making power that otherwise safeguards the allocation of powers between the directors and shareholders has not been developed by the French courts or policy makers. Rather, the French legal system relies on the legislative provisions of the Code de commerce that confer relatively broad decision-making power on the general meeting in order to protect the shareholder franchise and facilitate the control of management.

Both the duty to act in good faith and the duty to act in the corporate interest, as they are formulated in civil law countries, are too broad and ambivalent to impose clearly defined constraints on the behaviour of directors, at least until the courts develop criteria that apply specifically to the allocation of corporate authority between the directors and shareholders. Such a body of case-law-driven rules has not yet emerged in civil law jurisdictions. However, a civil law country where the courts have displayed some willingness to go beyond the codified rules allocating decision-making power and draw on general principles of corporate law to delimit the spheres of authority of the board and the shareholders is Germany. Above we discussed the *Holzmüller* decision of the Federal Court of Justice, which can be interpreted as a first step in the direction of an unwritten duty-based constraint on managerial authority when board action compromises the membership rights of the shareholders.[246] However, we also recognized that the *Holzmüller* doctrine must be interpreted narrowly, in particular after the court's clarifications in *Gelatine I* and *II*.[247] It is not (yet) a comprehensive doctrine that applies flexibly to all situations where the directors use their powers to achieve ends that are not covered by the purpose of the statutory conferral of powers, or where their actions affect the position of shareholders in a significant way. Rather, as we have seen, the *Holzmüller* doctrine requires that the effect of the challenged transaction is both quantitatively significant and qualitatively of an 'intermediating' nature.[248] A situation such as in *Hilton Hotels v ITT*, where the directors evaded the requirement to obtain shareholder approval by structuring the transaction so that it did not qualify as a fundamental change requiring a vote of the general meeting may well be comparable to the *Holzmüller* scenario. Similarly, it could be argued that contractual devices intended to insulate the board against removal, for example shareholder rights plans (so-called 'poison pills') used to deter hostile takeover bidders, reach the required level of interference with the shareholders' membership rights to trigger the *Holzmüller* doctrine.[249] In the end, however, the application of *Holzmüller* involves a highly fact-specific inquiry, and the implications

[245] See, for example, German BGB, §242; Italian Codice civile [Civil Code], Arts 1175, 1375.

[246] For a discussion of the ambivalent nature of *Holzmüller*, on the one hand, as a duty-based constraint that requires the directors to procure a shareholder resolution under certain circumstances and, on the other hand, a doctrine that allocates competences, with the consequence that a violation of the *Holzmüller* requirements is tantamount to interfering with the shareholders' individual rights; see Gerner-Beuerle, Kershaw, and Solinas (n 130) 603–4.

[247] See above text to nn 124–133.

[248] See above text to nn 129–131.

[249] Gerner-Beuerle, Kershaw, and Solinas (n 130) 598–602.

of the doctrine in situations that do not fall exactly within the ambit of the decided cases remain uncertain.[250]

In a number of decisions, the German Federal Court of Justice addressed another instance of managerial decision-making that potentially impinges on the position of the shareholders without being a structural change that would trigger *Holzmüller*: delisting from the regulated market of a stock exchange. In the first decision dealing with this question, *Macrotron*,[251] minority shareholders challenged a resolution of the general meeting authorizing the delisting of a company. They claimed that the delisting, which was intended to save the company the expenses associated with a stock exchange listing, lacked a proper business reason and affected their rights disproportionately. The court held that the decision to delist did not fall within the exclusive competences of the board and, consequently, required the approval of the general meeting. However, the case was not comparable to a scenario triggering the *Holzmüller* doctrine or requiring justification on grounds of business necessity,[252] since the delisting did not change the internal structure of the company or dilute the shareholders' membership rights through intermediation.[253] Nevertheless, the court was of the opinion that delisting from the regulated market affected the economic interests of the shareholders, because it removed the market for their shares and limited the shares' fungibility.[254] In order to ensure that minority shareholders were fully protected, the company or the majority shareholder were required to make an offer to buy out the minority at a fair price. In addition, the minority had to have the right to apply to the court for an appraisal of the fairness of the price.[255] Thus, drawing on general considerations regarding the nature of the position of shareholders and their interest in the company, the court constructed a shareholder protection regime consisting of a refined allocation of competences, as well as exit and appraisal rights.[256]

About a decade later, in 2013, the court, however, dismantled most of this shareholder protection regime. In a case were the management board and supervisory board of a company decided to delist from the regulated market of the Berlin stock exchange and list instead on the open market of the Frankfurt stock exchange, a market segment not qualifying as a regulated market (hence, this was not a case of complete delisting, but rather 'downlisting'),

[250] There is limited authority that has applied *Holzmüller* to takeover defenses deployed by the board, see Landgericht [Regional Court] Düsseldorf, WM 2000, 528 (*Mannesmann*). The court discussed the permissibility of the target board's advertising campaign advocating the rejection of a hostile takeover bid. It held that defensive measures, in principle, might be subject to the requirements of *Holzmüller*, but the required level of intensity of interference with shareholder rights was not reached in the present case, where the board actively campaigned against accepting the offer by means of newspaper advertisements and Internet announcements. Since 2001, the Securities Acquisition and Takeover Act (WpÜG) explicitly allows board action to defend against takeovers, provided 'a prudent and conscientious manager of a company not affected by a takeover bid' would have taken such an action, the supervisory board gives its consent, or the action consists in the search for a competing offer (WpÜG, §33(1)).

[251] BGH BKR 2003, 253.

[252] We will see in Chapter 9D.I.2 that the German courts require that certain transactions, for example the exclusion of the shareholders' preemption rights, be necessary to protect overriding interests of the company.

[253] As discussed above, in *Gelatine I* and *II* the Federal Court of Justice held that the *Holzmüller* doctrine applied to situations that were functionally equivalent to one of the express competence provisions of the Stock Corporation Act requiring a shareholder resolution adopted by a qualified majority of 75% (see text to n 124).

[254] BGH BKR 2003, 253, 255. This argument goes back to a number of decisions of the Federal Constitutional Court extending the protection of property pursuant to Art 14 of the German Constitution to the fungibility of shares (for the text of Art 14, see n 2 above), BVerfGE 100, 289 (*DAT/Altana*); BVerfG ZIP 2000, 1670 (*Moto Meter*). However, more recently, the Constitutional Court modified its approach, holding that only the *legal* transferability of shares was protected by the constitution, not their actual fungibility. Whether shares could be sold easily was a commercial question that did not impact on the substance of the shareholders' property rights. BVerfG, judgment of 11 July 2012, BVerfGE 132, 99.

[255] BGH BKR 2003, 253, 256.

[256] In *Macrotron*, the plaintiffs lost the case because the defendant company had complied with the above conditions. The board had obtained a resolution of the general meeting and the majority shareholder had offered to buy out the minority.

the Court of Justice declined to follow *Macrotron*.[257] The court argued that downlisting and delisting were management decisions. Therefore, the management board was under no obligation to obtain a resolution of the general meeting approving the transaction. Moreover, the transaction did not give rise to an appraisal right by minority shareholders, because it affected neither the organizational structure of the company nor the participatory rights of shareholders, and only indirectly the shareholders' economic interests.[258] In the court's view, the fact that the regulatory environment changed with a delisting, which might result in reduced transparency and less comprehensive protection against insider dealing and market manipulation, was not a matter for corporate law, but securities regulation. Indeed, German capital markets law provides that the admission of securities to listing on a regulated market shall not be revoked if this is detrimental to the interests of investors.[259] For this reason, the listing rules of some stock exchanges require, for example, that securities remain listed for several months after the decision to delist has been taken, unless the company or a major shareholder offers to buy the minority out, so that shareholders are able to sell their shares in the regulated market if they decide to divest. Any risk that delisting poses for minority shareholders, the court concluded, needed to be addressed by such mechanisms, rather than changes to the allocation of power within the corporation.[260]

The court was probably influenced in its decision by the fact that the open market of the Frankfurt stock exchange is not less liquid than the regulated market of the Berlin stock exchange, which is one of the smaller exchanges in Germany. In the case before the court, it was therefore difficult to argue that the position of the minority shareholders was negatively affected by the downlisting. However, the decision goes further than this. It effectively overrules *Macrotron* and reduces the role of the shareholders in cases where decision-making power is not allocated explicitly to the general meeting pursuant to the Stock Corporation Act. The somewhat wavering stance of the German courts underlines the difficulties that they have in defining the relative position of shareholders and directors by drawing on general considerations. While the rights of shareholders in Delaware corporations are certainly not more extensive than those in German public stock corporations, the Delaware Court of Chancery's 'power over the corporate assets' and 'power relationship between the board and the shareholders' dichotomy[261] constitutes a flexible backstop that can be invoked whenever actions of the management disenfranchise the shareholders. The real difference between the common law and civil law, then, is maybe the greater flexibility that the common law offers in dealing with novel problems not explicitly addressed by the statute, rather than any inherent difference in the level of investor protection.[262]

C. Shareholder Decision-making

In this section, we are concerned with four questions: First, why should shareholders (and *only* shareholders) be given decision rights? Secondly, how should their rights be fashioned? In other words: should shares be designed in a way that ensures strict proportionality between financial rights and control rights, especially by providing for 'one share, one vote' and disallowing so-called control enhancing mechanisms, or should contractual freedom prevail and shareholders be entitled to structure control rights according to their preferences? Furthermore, how should voting in the general meeting be regulated? Notably, when directors are elected to the board, can shareholders cumulate their votes, are board elections

[257] BGH NJW 2014, 146. [258] ibid 147–8.
[259] BörsG [Stock Exchange Act], §39(2) sentence 2. [260] BGH NJW 2014, 146, 148–9.
[261] *Hilton Hotels* (n 222), discussed in section B.II above.
[262] This is not a novel argument. It has been expressed probably most forcefully by FA Hayek, *Law, Legislation and Liberty, vol 1: Rules and Order* (University of Chicago Press 1973) 86–7.

governed by principles of proportionate representation, or are directors simply appointed by a majority of the votes? Thirdly, can we be sure that shareholders will exercise their voting rights? If not, what can the law do to facilitate shareholder voting? Finally, in the case of procedural irregularities or if the minority shareholders are overborne by the majority, how can outside investors be protected?

The answer to the first question seems obvious. Shareholders are the owners of the corporation; as residual claimants, they 'have the appropriate incentives ... to make discretionary choices'[263] and maximize firm value. Debt investors have negotiated their return ex ante. Provided the firm does not default on its obligations, they do not have anything to gain from spending time and money influencing the management of the corporation. The same applies, with qualifications, to employees. Performance-based compensation may give employees an incentive to urge management to adopt profit-maximising policies, but performance-based components will only constitute a fraction of total compensation.[264] Therefore, only the shareholders' returns are perfectly aligned with firm performance.[265] If it is accepted that one of the objectives of corporate law is the provision of a regulatory environment that supports the maximization of corporate profits, it is sensible to give shareholders voting rights, and not creditors or other stakeholders. Of course, this goes right to the heart of the shareholder-stakeholder debate, and a different approach to the objectives of the corporation and corporate law may provoke a different response to the question of who should receive voting rights. Indeed, some legal systems, for example France, encourage companies to vest voting rights not only in shareholders, but also in employees. French public companies can opt into a system of worker participation by issuing employee shares, which are owed collectively by the employees in the form of a workers' cooperative (*société à participation ouvrière*).[266] The employees are represented at general meetings by elected members of the cooperative who exercise the workers' voting rights, which correspond to the proportion of employee shares to the total number of shares outstanding.[267] Even without governance structures intended to facilitate the participation of employees in corporate decision-making, companies in many legal systems set up employee share plans, which may allow the employees to subscribe for shares at preferential conditions or enjoy tax advantages.[268] Legal systems may also allow voting rights to be conferred on bondholders, either in addition to or instead of shareholders. Under Delaware law, for example, the certificate of incorporation may stipulate that the holders of bonds and debentures shall be treated as stockholders, enjoy all rights that stockholders have pursuant to the law, and even provide that the stockholders shall be divested of their right to vote on certain corporate matters.[269] Thus, while the statement that shareholders, as owners of the company, enjoy far-reaching control rights is correct at a general level, on closer inspection the picture is more nuanced. Most legal systems, including those that are commonly perceived to be modelled on a shareholder-oriented view of the company, envisage a governance structure where control is shared, in some form and usually not evenly, between the shareholders and certain other stakeholder groups.

[263] FH Easterbrook and DR Fischel, *The Economic Structure of Corporate Law* (Harvard University Press 1991) 68.

[264] This fraction will be significant in the case of senior management, but comparatively smaller if the employee does not belong to top-level management.

[265] However, note that this statement is no longer true if the company is in financial distress. Because shareholders enjoy downside protection in the form of limited liability, they do not partake in the losses in the same way as in the profits. As a consequence, the shareholders have an incentive to pursue inefficiently risky projects in the vicinity of insolvency. This problem is discussed in more detail in Chapter 11B.

[266] Com, Arts L225-259 to L225-261. See also section D.III below.

[267] Com, Art L225-263.

[268] For example, pursuant to the German Stock Corporation Act, the management board of public companies may be authorized to issue bonus shares to employees out of distributable profits, §204(3).

[269] Del. Gen. Corp. Law, §221. However, the stockholders cannot be divested of their right to amend the articles of association.

The second question is more controversial. In many economies, control-enhancing mechanisms such as multiple voting rights are fairly common.[270] They are criticized frequently for leading to distorted investment decisions[271] or tunnelling—the transfer of assets out of the firm for the benefit of the controlling shareholder, for example in a related-party transaction.[272] To see why, assume that the controlling shareholder is presented with two investment opportunities, one of which has a higher expected value than the other. If the less valuable investment project generates private benefits of control that exceed the private benefits of the first project, the controlling shareholder may decide to forgo the higher-value project to take advantage of the larger private benefits that come with the second project. The reason is clear: The return on investment needs to be shared with all shareholders, whereas the controller retains all of the private benefits. Importantly, the incentive to choose the less valuable investment opportunity will be higher, the smaller the financial stake of the controller in the company.[273] On the other hand, it has also been pointed out that mechanisms that preserve control may function as substitutes for underdeveloped economic or legal institutions, for example incomplete capital markets that make it necessary to rely on internal sources of capital[274] or insufficient shareholder rights.[275] In addition, if the position of some shareholders, for example the founders of a family owned business, is secured by control-enhancing mechanisms, they may have a greater opportunity to pursue a long-term strategy and act in the interests of different stakeholders, rather than exclusively in the interests of investors hoping for a return in the short run.[276] Thus, the welfare implications of multiple voting rights and other control enhancing mechanisms depend on various factors, such as the wider economic and legal environment in which the company operates, the extent of the decoupling of cash-flow rights from control rights, and the intentions of those who benefit from the control enhancing mechanisms.[277]

The question is, of course, also political. A strict enforcement of the one share, one vote principle strengthens the hand of outside investors who want to be sure that their influence on business operations is commensurate with their stake in the company and the risk of the controller extracting private benefits is limited. Allowing control-enhancing mechanisms, on the other hand, may be an indication that the policy maker places greater emphasis on the stability of business relations between founders, managers, and companies holding cross-shareholdings. We therefore see again that the precise contours of legal institutions depend on underlying basic policy choices, in particular the reliance on competitive market

[270] Firms typically issue two classes of stock, one with multiple voting rights and the other with single or no voting rights. Other commonly used control enhancing mechanisms are stock pyramids, voting right ceilings, and cross-shareholdings. For an analysis of the situation in 16 EU Member States, as well as Australia, Japan, and the United States, see ISS Europe, ECGI, Shearman & Sterling, *Report on the proportionality principle in the European Union* (2007).

[271] LA Bebchuk, R Kraakman, and G Triantis, 'Stock Pyramids, Cross-Ownership, and Dual Class Equity: The Mechanisms and Agency Costs of Separating Control from Cash-Flow Right' in RK Morck, *Concentrated Corporate Ownership* (University of Chicago Press 2000) 295, 301–3.

[272] S Johnson, R La Porta, F Lopez-de-Silanes, and A Shleifer, 'Tunneling' (2000) 90 American Economic Review 22.

[273] The calculation is straightforward. Bebchuk, Kraakman, and Triantis (n 271) 301–2, propose the following formula to illustrate the conflicting incentives. Controllers will choose Project X with expected value V_X and private benefits B_X, instead of Project Y with V_Y and B_Y, if and only if: $\alpha(V_X - B_X) + B_X > \alpha(V_Y - B_Y) + B_Y$, where α is the fraction of the firm's equity cash-flow rights held by the controller. To take an example, if we assume that the controlling shareholder holds 10% of the cash-flow rights and Project X's expected value is 10% higher than that of Project Y, the above inequality means that the controller will only choose the more valuable project if the private benefits of control generated by the other project (Y) do not exceed those of Project X by more than approximately 11%.

[274] T Khanna and Y Yishay, 'Business Groups in Emerging Markets: Paragons or Parasites?' (2007) 45 Journal of Economic Literature 331, 336.

[275] This is, of course, the argument advanced by La Porta and others that we discussed in Chapter 4D.IV.

[276] M Pagano and PF Volpin, 'Managers, workers, and corporate control' (2005) 60 Journal of Finance 841.

[277] For an overview of the literature and empirical evidence see R Adams and D Ferreira, 'One Share-One Vote: The Empirical Evidence' (2008) 12 Review of Finance 51.

institutions or collaboration and strategic interaction between firms and stakeholders.[278] However, the dichotomy between competitive and collaborative institutions is not unambiguous. A free market system implies that parties can contract freely to provide for arrangements that best suit their aims, including by designing control-enhancing mechanisms. Through this lens, requiring adherence to the one share, one vote principle presents itself as an intervention in the market economy to protect the interests of a particular stakeholder group, outside investors.

Thirdly, it has long been a concern that shareholders are largely passive and do not make use of their voting rights, or allow financial intermediaries to exercise the rights on their behalf without giving voting instructions. In economies characterized by widely dispersed shareholders, this behaviour may be perfectly rational. It is, accordingly, often referred to as 'rational apathy'.[279] The costs to shareholders of informing themselves, coordinating with others, and exercising their voting rights will often exceed the benefits expected from voting.[280] This may explain the relatively low turnout at general meetings that has been observed in some countries, for example in continental Europe,[281] and the low level of opposition to resolutions proposed by management.[282] As a consequence, the general meeting's effectiveness as an organ to correct misconduct and monitor conflicts of interest is impaired. Policy makers are, therefore, grappling with the question of how to foster shareholder engagement.[283]

On the other hand, after the financial crisis of 2007–2008, it has been recognized that shareholder engagement is not a panacea, but can lead to problems of its own. Different types of shareholder may pursue very different objectives as they exercise their appointment and decision rights or seek to influence business operations informally in discussions with management. In a family owned company, we can expect shareholders to be interested in a long-term, profitable development of the business and in mutually beneficial, stable relationships with other stakeholders, whereas other investors may seek to realize a short-term return on their investment. This problem is particularly acute in the case of investment funds, because asset managers owe fiduciary duties to the investors in the fund to maximize their financial returns,[284] and their performance is often measured against a benchmark index, thus creating incentives to divest as soon as a portfolio company underperforms the benchmark.[285]

[278] See our discussion of 'varieties of capitalism' in Chapter 4B.III.

[279] For an early discussion of rational apathy see RC Clark, 'Vote Buying and Corporate Law' (1979) 29 Case Western Reserve Law Review 776, 779–83.

[280] The same collective action problem exists with respect to elections for parliament, a fact that is often not appreciated, see K Binmore, *Playing for Real* (OUP 2007) 9–10.

[281] P Hewitt, 'The Exercise of Shareholder Rights: Country Comparison of Turnout and Dissent' (2011) *OECD Corporate Governance Working Papers* 3, 15–16. The lowest average attendance at annual general meetings in the sample, covering general meetings held in 32 countries over the last two financial years before publication of the study, was recorded in Denmark, with 38.10% of voting rights in attendance. Switzerland and Belgium also stand out as countries where average attendance was below 50%. Of our four jurisdictions, the United States saw the highest average turnout with 81.78%, followed by the UK with 67.62%, France with 66.84%, and Germany with 64.86%.

[282] ibid 20. Over the full sample, dissent (defined as votes cast against the recommendation of company management on a resolution) was a mere 3.48% on average. It was even lower in Germany (2.70%) and the UK (2.93%), and somewhat higher in the United States (5.49%) and France (5.92%).

[283] Communication from the Commission, Action Plan: European company law and corporate governance—a modern legal framework for more engaged shareholders and sustainable companies, COM(2012) 740 final, 8–11; Directive (EU) 2017/828 of 17 May 2017 amending Directive 2007/36/EC as regards the encouragement of long-term shareholder engagement, [2017] OJ L132/1.

[284] It is controversial how much leeway fiduciary law grants asset managers to forgo a short-term return in favour of considerations of long-term performance. For a brief discussion of this point, see J Kay, *Kay Review of UK Equity Markets and Long-Term Decision Making*, Final Report July 2012, para 9.20 (referring to *Cowan v Scargill* [1985] Ch 270 and *Buttle v Saunders* [1950] 2 All ER 193).

[285] Impact Assessment accompanying the Proposal for a Directive amending Directive 2007/36/EC as regards the encouragement of long-term shareholder engagement and Directive 2013/34/EU as regards certain elements of the corporate governance statement and Commission Recommendation on the quality of corporate governance reporting ('comply or explain'), SWD(2014) 127 final, 17–25.

Fourthly, small shareholders who cannot effectively influence the decision-making of the majority (outside investors) have to rely on the law to ensure that their interests are protected and the majority does not use its voting power to divert corporate assets away from a use that would benefit the company as a whole. Thus, even in the absence of control-enhancing mechanisms, the law needs to be concerned with legal tools that protect outside investors against overreaching decisions by the majority. For obvious reasons, this problem is particularly salient in economies dominated by large blockholders. Accordingly, we may expect to find more developed legal institutions allowing minority investors to challenge majority decision-making in such economies, whereas corporate economies characterized by comparatively widely dispersed shareholders, such as the United States and UK, may focus on facilitating the enforcement of shareholder rights in general against an otherwise largely unconstrained management.

In the next sections, we will come back to these problems as we discuss shareholder decision-making in our four jurisdictions. The first two sections (I and II below) examine the process of shareholder voting, both by shareholders who attend the general meeting and by those who vote by proxy, and the question of how rational apathy can be overcome and shareholder voting facilitated. The third section (III) deals with the last problem we raised above, mechanisms to challenge decision-making in the general meeting in order to protect outside investors.

I. Shareholder voting rights

1. *One share, one vote?*

In the spirit of contractual freedom, common law systems often grant firms great latitude in structuring voting rights. The Delaware General Corporation Law could not be clearer. It provides that shares 'may have such voting powers, full or limited, or no voting powers, and such designations, preferences and relative, participating, optional or other special rights, and qualifications, limitations or restrictions thereof, as shall be stated and expressed in the certificate of incorporation or of any amendment thereto, or in the resolution or resolutions providing for the issue of such stock adopted by the board of directors pursuant to authority expressly vested in it by the provisions of its certificate of incorporation'.[286] Companies must have at least one class of shares with voting rights. In practice, it is not unusual for companies to issue several classes of shares, one class of common stock with one vote per share and one or more additional classes with no or multiple voting rights. For example, Alphabet Inc., the holding company of Google, has issued three classes of stock. Class A common stock carries one vote per share, Class B common stock ten votes, and Class C capital stock has no voting rights.[287] Classes A and C are traded, whereas Class B is neither listed nor traded. More than 90 per cent of the Class B shares are held by the two founders of Google and by the CEO of the company, representing almost 60 per cent of the voting power of all outstanding capital stock.[288] Since the voting rights of holders of Classes A and C shares are different, we may expect the two classes to trade at different prices. This is indeed the case, although the price differential is rather small at around 2–3 per cent. The small premium of voting shares over non-voting shares may be surprising at first sight, but as we have seen, the capital structure of Alphabet Inc. is designed to keep control firmly in the hands of the corporate insiders. Consequently, neither Class A nor Class C shareholders can effectively influence

[286] Del. Gen. Corp. Law, §151(a). The Model Business Corporation Act is similar; see §7.21 (providing for one vote, one share as a default rule, which can be modified in the articles of association). Shares of its own capital stock held by the company or by controlled undertakings are not entitled to vote and also do not count for quorum purposes (a company is a controlled undertaking if a majority of the shares entitled to vote in the election of directors of that company are owned by the controlling undertaking), Del. Gen. Corp. Law, §160(c), MBCA, §7.21(b).

[287] Alphabet Inc., Form 10-K for fiscal year 2017, 18.

[288] ibid.

the composition of the board of directors or corporate matters on which shareholders vote, including important control transactions.[289]

The permissiveness of state company law is here, as elsewhere,[290] somewhat curtailed by the federal securities laws and stock exchange regulations, but the general principle that companies can deviate from the one share, one vote principle (and still obtain a stock exchange listing) is preserved. The New York Stock Exchange (NYSE) listing rules only prohibit a reclassification of shares that has the effect of disparately reducing or restricting voting rights of 'existing shareholders of publicly traded common stock', for example through the issuance of stock with multiple voting rights.[291] However, the exchange generally permits the listing of companies with an existing dual class capital structure or outstanding non-voting common stock, as well as the issuance of additional shares of an existing class of super voting stock.[292] Because of this flexibility, NYSE has attracted high-value IPOs of some foreign issuers that had failed to obtain a listing on other exchanges.[293]

The rationale of the prohibition by the NYSE and other stock exchanges[294] is clear: changes that affect the rights of the *existing* shareholders adversely amount to a disenfranchisement of the shareholders. The shareholders of the affected class, of course, have the right to vote on the amendment,[295] and the law affords minority shareholders protection against coercion by the majority or by a large shareholder.[296] However, as we will discuss later, in the US, major shareholders owe no general fiduciary duty to act in the interest of the shareholders as a whole or ensure that all shareholders are treated equally. A shareholder vote that is 'fully informed and devoid of any fraud, waste, manipulative or other inequitable conduct' (such as coercion) is valid, even if the votes of a controlling stockholder who benefits from the

[289] Note that even fundamental corporate changes such as mergers usually only require approval by a majority of the outstanding voting stock of the company, Del. Gen. Corp. Law, §251(c), or by a majority of the votes cast at a meeting at which a quorum consisting of a majority of the shares entitled to vote is present, MBCA, §11.04(e).

[290] See for example the regulation of proxy voting discussed in section C.II.2 below.

[291] NYSE Listed Company Manual, §313. [292] ibid.

[293] A famous example is the IPO of Alibaba Group, the Chinese e-commerce company. Alibaba does not provide for dual-class shares, but the corporate insiders have put a corporate governance structure in place that ensures that they will always command a majority on the board of directors (the governance structure is explained in detail in their public offering registration statement, Form F-1, as filed with the SEC on 6 May 2014, pp. 206–21). For this reason, the company was not allowed to list on the Hong Kong Stock Exchange, but it was able to listed on the NYSE in September 2014 in what was the largest IPO of all times, raising US$25 billion. For a critical assessment of the decision of the Hong Kong regulator, see S Wei and A Young, 'Dual Share Plan in Context: Making Sense of Hong Kong's Decision Not to Embrace Alibaba's Listing' (2015) 26 International Company and Commercial Law Review 4.

[294] NASDAQ has adopted identical rules, NASDAQ Listing Rule 5640: Voting Rights.

[295] Del. Gen. Corp. Law, §242(b)(2).

[296] Wrongful coercion has been defined as an action that has 'the effect of causing the stockholders to vote in favor of the proposed transaction for some reason other than the merits of that transaction', *Williams v Geier*, 671 A.2d 1368 (Del. 1996). For an example, see *Lacos Land Co. v Arden Group*, 517 A.2d 271 (Del. Ch. 1986). In this case, the shareholders of the defendant Arden Group had authorized a recapitalization that created a new Class B common stock possessing ten votes per share and being entitled to elect 75% of the members of the board of directors. The new stock was available to all Class A shareholders on the basis of a share-for-share exchange offer, but it was designed to be attractive mainly to Arden's principal shareholder and CEO because of its reduced dividend rights and restrictions on the stock's transfer. The creation of the Class B stock was approved by the required majority of shareholders, who resolved to amend the certificate of incorporation accordingly. The court pointed out that all of the characteristics of the Class B stock were in principle permissible under §§151(a), 202 Del. Gen. Corp. Law. However, it held that the amendments to Arden's certificate were voidable because the main shareholder and CEO had threatened to use his power to block transactions that may be in the best interest of the company if the amendments were not approved. It should be noted that the threat was considered to constitute coercion by the principal shareholder acting *qua* director and officer (rather than *qua* shareholder): ibid 276–8. He was therefore subject to more stringent fiduciary duties than a shareholder, notably the duty to act with undivided loyalty solely in the interests of the company and its shareholders: ibid 278. However, in principle, the actions of the majority shareholder can also constitute coercion of the minority where the majority shareholder is not a director, *Williams v Geier*: ibid 1382–3 (but the facts in this case did not support a finding of coercion).

amendment to a greater extent than the minority carry the resolution.[297] The creation of a new class of super-voting stock or the reclassification of shares into two classes with differential voting rights could, therefore, in appropriate circumstances legally disenfranchise certain shareholder groups if the listing rules did not prohibit such practices. On the other hand, if a company issues a new class of *lower* or non-voting stock, the same risk does not exist. Shareholders acquiring the lower voting stock are, of course, still at a disadvantage compared with other shareholders, especially if preferential financial rights do not compensate for the lower voting rights.[298] However, if the investors are fully informed of the company's capital structure, as they will be if the company is subject to the disclosure regime of the federal securities laws, they are able to set the price for the shares so that it reflects the voting rights differential. The market, therefore, functions as a substitute for legal mechanisms that protect minority shareholders in these cases.[299]

The UK Companies Act 2006 is less explicit than the Delaware General Corporation Law. It merely acknowledges that companies have the power to issue more than one class of shares,[300] without specifying how the voting rights of shares shall be fashioned or prohibiting, for example, shares with multiple voting rights. It is therefore uncontroversial that companies can adopt a dual class structure composed of voting and non-voting shares,[301] and many large companies in fact issue non-voting preference shares.[302] The permissibility of shares with multiple voting rights is more difficult to assess, but there is some judicial authority sanctioning such shares, at least in small, family owned companies.[303] Nevertheless, multiple voting rights are very rare among listed companies.[304] They are strongly opposed by institutional investors,[305] which are by far the most important owners of shares in UK quoted companies.[306] In addition, the Listing Rules promulgated by the Financial Conduct Authority (FCA), the UK market regulator, impose some constraints on the listing of companies with capital structures that are designed to entrench control. The Listing Rules require issuers that seek a premium listing (the market segment of the London Stock Exchange with highest standards of regulation and corporate governance) to demonstrate that they 'will be carrying on an independent business'.[307] Whether this requirement is satisfied will be assessed on a case-by-case basis, considering a number of factors including whether the issuer is economically dependent on a controlling shareholder, or the controlling shareholder

[297] *Williams v Geier* (n 296) 1380–1 (quoting *Stroud II*, 606 A.2d 75). Delaware law does not require that the 'majority of the minority', i.e. a majority of the disinterested shareholders, approve the transaction (unless the resolution concerns the approval of an interested director transaction, *Fliegler v Lawrence*, 361 A.2d 218 (Del. 1976), discussed in Chapter 6C.I.2. However, the Delaware courts apply a more stringent test requiring entire fairness if the board lacks independence (or the presumptions of the business judgment rule are rebutted for other reasons): ibid 1384. The entire fairness test has become relevant in particular in the case of freeze-out mergers, see the text to nn 692–696 below for a brief overview and Chapter 7C.II for more details. For an analysis of the business judgment rule, see Chapter 6B.I.2.

[298] In the example of Alphabet/Google from above, dividend rights and all other rights of Class A and Class C shares are identical. The company has never paid dividends on either class of shares, and the management emphasizes that they 'intend to retain any future earnings and do not expect to pay any cash dividends in the foreseeable future', Alphabet Inc., Form 10-K for fiscal year 2017, 21.

[299] RJ Gilson, 'Evaluating Dual Class Common Stock: The Relevance of Substitutes' (1987) 73 Virginia Law Review 807, 808–9.

[300] See, for example, Companies Act 2006, s 550.

[301] For example, in *Re Bradford Investments plc* [1991] BCLC 224, the company had issued preference shares that were not entitled to vote unless the dividend that the preference shareholders were entitled to was in arrears.

[302] ISS Europe, ECGI, Shearman & Sterling (n 270) 78.

[303] *Bushell v Faith* [1970] AC 1099 (House of Lords), discussed in detail below in section D.II. The use of multiple voting rights was particularly problematic in this case because they were designed specifically to prevent the directors from being removed against their will.

[304] ISS Europe, ECGI, Shearman & Sterling (n 270) 78.

[305] Kay (n 284) para 8.34.

[306] As of 2016, UK individuals owned about 19% of quoted UK shares, a decline of 35 percentage points compared with 1963. International investors, most of them financial institutions, owned 49%, and domestic institutional investors (unit trusts, other financial institutions, insurance companies, and pension funds) 27%. See Office for National Statistics, Statistical Bulletin: Ownership of UK Quoted Shares (2016) 5, 12–13, 22–3.

[307] Listing Rules LR 6.1.4.

has influence over the operations of the issuer going beyond the influence exerted by shareholders through normal governance channels.[308] A controlling shareholder is defined as 'any person who exercises or controls ... 30% or more of the votes able to be cast on all or substantially all matters at general meetings of the company'.[309] The listing of companies with a controlling shareholder is not prohibited (provided they carry on an independent business), but the Listing Rules put additional safeguards in place to ensure that outside investors are protected, for example by requiring the appointment of independent directors to be approved by the non-controlling shareholders[310] and the controlling shareholder to give a legally binding undertaking that related-party transactions will be conducted at arm's length and on normal commercial terms.[311] In addition, equity shares[312] of the same class must carry an equal number of votes if that class has been admitted to premium listing.[313] If the company's equity share capital is divided into more than one class admitted to premium listing, the Listing Rules provide that 'the aggregate voting rights of the shares in each class should be broadly proportionate to the relative interests of those classes in the equity of the listed company'.[314] This does not exclude all deviations from the one share, one vote principle, but the FCA has explained that multiple classes of shares 'that differ only in their voting power and have been deliberately structured to maintain control within a small group of shareholders' will be in conflict with the Premium Listing Principles.[315] Thus, the flexibility that companies commonly have under the Companies Act 2006 to design their capital structure is limited if the company seeks admission to the premium segment of the stock market. Outside of the premium segment, however, it remains largely unconstrained.

In continental Europe, we frequently see less scope for contractual freedom to deviate from the one share, one vote principle. In Germany, the Stock Corporation Act has prohibited the issuance of shares with multiple voting rights since 1998.[316] On the other hand, companies can still adopt a dual-class capital structure consisting of ordinary shares with voting rights and preference shares without voting rights.[317] In addition, it is possible to provide for maximum voting rights or a voting cap in the articles, for example by stipulating that no shareholder may have more than 10 or 20 per cent of the voting rights, even if the shares represent more than one-tenth or one-fifth of the share capital.[318] However,

[308] ibid LR 6.1.4AG. [309] ibid LR 6.1.2A.

[310] ibid LR 6.1.4B(2), 9.2.2.E. However, if a candidate was rejected by the independent shareholders, the company can propose the person again for election as an independent director 90 days after the original vote. The appointment then no longer requires a separate approval by the independent shareholders: LR 9.2.2F.

[311] ibid LR 6.1.4B(1), 6.1.4D(1).

[312] Equity shares, as defined in the Companies Act 2006, s 548, exclude preference shares with fixed distribution rights.

[313] Listing Rules LR 7.2.1A, Premium Listing Principle 3.

[314] ibid LR 7.2.1A, Premium Listing Principle 4.

[315] Financial Services Authority, Enhancing the effectiveness of the Listing Regime and feedback on CP 12/2 (October 2012) para 7.148. The FCA has further elaborated that the goal of the prohibition is only 'to prevent artificial structures' that aim to entrench control and that the FCA will focus on 'flagrant examples' of such entrenchment mechanisms, rather than on 'borderline cases', FCA, Feedback on CP12/25: Enhancing the effectiveness of the Listing Regime and further consultation (November 2013) paras 10.12–10.13. LR 7.2.4G provides guidance as to the factors that the FCA will take into account in assessing whether the voting rights attaching to different classes of premium-listed shares are proportionate.

[316] AktG, §12(2), as amended by KonTraG 1998 (n 113) Art 1 no 3. Since 1937, the adoption of a capital structure with a class of shares carrying multiple voting rights had already been severely restricted and required ministerial authorization.

[317] AktG, §12(1) sentence 2.

[318] ibid §134(1) sentence 2. A famous example was the voting cap of Volkswagen Group, albeit not provided for in Volkswagen's articles of association, but in a separate act of parliament, the so-called VW Law (Gesetz über die Überführung der Anteilsrechte an der Volkswagenwerk Gesellschaft mit beschränkter Haftung—VWGmbHÜG), BGBl 1960 I, 585, and BGBl 1960 III, 641-1-1. The voting cap, together with two other provisions of the VW Law impeding a takeover of the company, were challenged before the Court of Justice of the EU at a time when Porsche AG attempted to acquire VW; see Case C-112/05 *Commission v Germany* [2007] ECR I-8995. The Court of Justice decided partially in Porsche's favour and held that the voting cap was in violation of the free movement of capital (Art 63 TFEU), but it crucially did not invalidate another provision of the VW Law, providing for a supermajority requirement of 80% for major corporate changes. As a result of the partial repeal of the VW Law, Porsche's takeover attempt failed.

in a further sign that the German legislator has increasingly embraced the idea that deviations from proportionality between ownership and voting rights may lead to inefficiencies and entrenchment problems,[319] maximum voting rights can only be introduced if the company is not listed on a regulated market.[320] The permissibility of voting caps (unless the company is listed) and the prohibition of shares with multiple voting rights create certain tensions. If the voting cap applies only to some shareholders, but not to others, the economic effects of super-voting shares could be mimicked by excluding certain shareholders from the voting cap. Consequently, the voting rights of the excluded shareholders would increase disproportionately. In order to prevent an evasion of the prohibition on issuing super-voting shares, the Stock Corporation Act requires that limitations on voting rights shall not be imposed on individual shareholders.[321] This leaves open the question whether it is permissible to provide for such restrictions in respect of individual classes of shares. Doing so may allow companies to use voting caps for purposes that are in conflict with the policy goal of not outlawing voting caps, namely limiting the influence of blockholders, and potentially exacerbates agency problems between different shareholder groups. Nevertheless, the prevailing view in the German literature favours a restrictive interpretation of the provision that does not exclude the differential treatment of two or more classes of shares, because the legislator considered the issue and decided against prohibiting a limitation of the voting rights of individual classes.[322]

The French Commercial Code stipulates that 'voting rights ... shall be in proportion to the share of the capital they represent and each share shall entitle the holder to at least one vote'.[323] This is an expression of a basic principle of French company law, the requirement to treat all shareholders equally. As a consequence of the equality principle, French law initially prohibited the issuance of any shares without voting rights.[324] The first step towards a liberalization of the regime was taken in 1978 with the introduction of non-voting preference stock (*action de préférence sans droit de vote*), which could be issued for up to 25 per cent of the legal capital, provided that the preference shares carried increased dividend rights.[325] However, the new regime was subject to mandatory, complex rules that made the issuance of non-voting preference stock unattractive in practice.[326] In 2004, the law was reformed to ease the adoption of dual-class structures.[327] The Commercial Code now allows the issuance of preference shares with or without voting rights and only requires that non-voting preference shares shall not represent more than one half of the share capital, or more than one quarter if the company's shares are admitted to trading on a regulated market.[328] The company enjoys broad freedom in defining the further characteristics of the preference shares in the articles of association in line with general principles of French company law.[329] Furthermore, the articles may determine the maximum number of votes that each shareholder can exercise at general meetings, provided the voting cap applies to all shares of all voting classes.[330] However,

[319] For an overview of the literature analysing these inefficiencies, see R Adams and D Ferreira, 'One Share-One Vote: The Empirical Evidence' (2008) 12 Review of Finance 51.

[320] AktG, §134(1) sentence 2, as amended by KonTraG 1998 (n 113) Art 1 no 20.

[321] ibid §134(1) sentence 5.

[322] Koch (n 117) §134, para 14. However, Koch also suggests that a capital structure is in conflict with §134(1) sentence 5 AktG if the only difference between two classes of shares is the limitation of voting rights imposed on one of the classes.

[323] Com, Art L225-122(1). Translation by Legifrance, https://www.legifrance.gouv.fr/Traductions/en-English/Legifrance-translations. An important exception to this principle are double-voting rights for long-term shareholders pursuant to Art L225-123. We will discuss these rights below; see text to nn 332–337.

[324] PH Conac, 'The New French Preferred Shares: Moving towards a More Liberal Approach' (2005) 2 ECFR 487, 489.

[325] Law no 78-741 of 13 July 1978, introducing former Arts L228-11 to L228-20 of the Code de commerce.

[326] Conac (n 324) 492. [327] Ordinance no 2004-604 of 24 June 2004. [328] Com, Art L228-11.

[329] For an overview of possible features of preference shares, see Conac (n 324) 494–501.

[330] Com, Art L225-125.

similar to German law, contractual freedom does not extend to the issuance of shares with multiple voting rights, at least in public companies.[331] The general principle mentioned above, mandating proportionality between voting rights and the share of the capital they represent, prevents public companies (with one exception, to be discussed presently) from issuing super-voting shares.

More recently, we can observe a trend in some countries in continental Europe to move away from a comparatively strict implementation of the one share, one vote principle. In light of increasing concerns of short-termism in the capitals markets,[332] policy makers have adopted regulatory initiatives that make it easier for companies to make use of 'tenured' or 'time-phased' voting rights (sometimes also called 'loyalty shares'). Tenure voting is based on the idea that the number of voting rights per share increases in proportion to the duration of the shareholder's ownership.[333] Thus, investors are incentivized to hold their shares for longer periods and focus on long-term value creation. At the same time, tenure voting is seen as a less blatant deviation from the proportionality principle than dual-class capital structures that concentrate control in the hands of a few owners of super-voting shares.

The most striking example of tenured voting rights was introduced by the so-called 'Loi Florange' in France in 2014.[334] Pursuant to the French Commercial Code, public companies can include a provision in their articles of association granting shareholders of record double voting rights if they have held their shares for at least two years.[335] Many French companies have made use of this possibility,[336] but the Florange law went a step further and changed the authorization into a default rule for listed companies. Shareholders of record in such companies therefore now receive double voting rights automatically once they have owned their shares for the required period of time. The rule can of course be disapplied or modified, but this requires—as all amendments of the articles of French public companies—a resolution adopted by a two-thirds majority. Because of its character as a default rule and the relatively high threshold for its disapplication, the act has been widely criticized by institutional investors and proxy voting firms, who have adopted voting strategies in reaction to the law aimed at amending the articles to prohibit double voting rights.[337]

[331] The simplified joint stock company (*société par actions simplifiée*) is regulated more liberally. In particular, Art L225-122 (see n 323 above) does not apply, Com, Art L227-1. However, the simplified joint stock company cannot issue shares to the public or apply for admission of its shares to trading on a regulated market, Art L227-2. It will therefore often not be a suitable form of business association, including for start-ups that may at one point wish to go public.

[332] See text to nn 284–285 above.

[333] For an in-depth analysis of tenure voting, see DJ Berger, SD Davidoff and AJ Benjamin, 'Tenure Voting and the U.S. Public Company' (2016) SSRN: http://ssrn.com/abstract=2740538; LL Dallas and JM Barry, 'Long-Term Shareholders and Time-Phased Voting' (2015) 40 Delaware Journal of Corporate Law 541.

[334] Law no 2014-384 of 29 March 2014 (Loi visant à reconquérir l'économie réelle), JORF no 77 of 1 April 2014, 6227. The act is called 'Loi Florange' because its adoption was partly a response to the closure of blast furnaces in Florange, France, by ArcelorMittal, several years after Mittal Steel had taken over and merged with the French-Luxembourgish-Spanish steel making group Arcelor.

[335] Com, Art L225-123.

[336] M Ventoruzzo, 'The Disappearing Taboo of Multiple Voting Shares: Regulatory Responses to the Migration of Chrysler-Fiat' (2015) ECGI Working Paper no 288/2015, 8.

[337] See, for example, ISS Continental Europe Proxy Voting Guidelines, 2018 Benchmark Policy Recommendations, 14–15 (recommending, on a case-by-case basis, a vote against the reelection of directors or supervisory board members, the approval of the discharge of directors, or the approval of the annual report and accounts if the company does not currently have a bylaw prohibiting double voting rights). Most companies with a one-share one-vote structure before the introduction of the Florange law indeed opted out of the loyalty share system shortly after the introduction of the law, with the notable exception of companies where the state owned a sufficiently large stake to block the resolution necessary to reinstate the old voting structure, see M Becht, Y Kamisarenka, and A Pajuste, 'Loyalty Shares with Tenure Voting - A Coasian Bargain? Evidence from the Loi Florange Experiment' (2018) ECGI Law Working Paper No 398/2018.

Loyalty shares rewarding shareholders who hold their shares for a specified period of time also exist in other continental European countries, albeit not as default rules. In the Netherlands, companies can issue shares with multiple voting rights. The Italian car manufacturer Chrysler-Fiat reincorporated in the Netherlands in 2014 to take advantage of this flexibility and issued 'special voting shares' to shareholders whose common shares were registered in a 'loyalty register' for an uninterrupted period of three years on the basis of one special voting share for each registered common share.[338] The Italian legislator, probably at least partly in order to prevent further companies from migrating to legal systems offering such flexibility, introduced a form of loyalty share in 2014 in a regulatory initiative that did not go as far as the Florange law, but still attracted considerable criticism from international investors. Italian company law, similar to German law, used to follow a strict one share, one vote principle. With the 2014 reforms, the legislator amended the law to allow non-listed companies to issue shares carrying a maximum of three votes per share[339] and listed companies to adopt a provision in their articles stipulating that double voting rights should be attributed to shares being held by the same shareholder for at least two years (thus, technically, the additional voting rights are not loyalty shares, but conditional features of the relevant class of shares).[340] The legislative amendments were criticized because the double voting rights could initially (for a limited period of time) be introduced by simple majority, in deviation from general Italian company law, which requires a resolution adopted by a two-thirds majority at an extraordinary general meeting to amend the articles.[341] In light of the criticism, the government decided not to make the reduced majority requirement permanent, and the introduction of loyalty shares now requires the regular supermajority.

While these reforms are a recent development in continental Europe, loyalty shares are by no means a novel phenomenon that sets continental European jurisdictions apart from other legal systems. In the United States, loyalty shares or tenure voting plans have been used by companies for decades, although they are less common than other forms of dual class structures.[342] As we have seen, firms have wide discretion in how to structure the company's capital under US law. Tenured voting rights have accordingly been held to be permissible under state corporate law.[343] However, it is currently unclear whether mid-stream recapitalizations to provide for tenured rights are in line with the listing rules of US stock exchanges, which refer to time-phased voting plans as an example of impermissible voting rights restrictions.[344] This lack of legal certainty may explain why they are used rarely.[345] In the UK as well, companies are in principle free to introduce dual class structures and issue shares with differential or weighted voting rights. That such deviations from the one vote, one share principle remain rare in practice is less a function of legal constraints,

[338] Fiat Chrysler Automobiles, Special Voting Shares—Terms and Conditions, available at www.fcagroup.com (follow hyperlinks 'Investors', 'Stock Info & Shareholder Corner' and 'Special Voting Shares').

[339] Codice civile, Art 2351(4), as amended by Law No 116/2014.

[340] Decreto Legislativo no 58—Testo Unico della Finanza [Consolidated Law on Finance, Legislative Decree no 58] of 24 February 1998, Art 127-*quinquies*, as amended. Other types of super-voting share cannot be issued by listed companies, ibid Art 127-*sexies*. For a more detailed discussion of the double voting rights, see Ventoruzzo (n 336) 14.

[341] Codice civile, Arts 2368, 2369.

[342] An example is *Williams v Geier* (n 296), which involved the introduction of a recapitalization plan granting all stockholders multiple voting rights, which would revert to one share, one vote upon transfer until the share was held for three years by the transferee. For comprehensive data see Dallas and Barry (n 333) 578–80 (descriptive statistics about dual class firms in general) and 592–9 (time-phased voting plans).

[343] See *Williams v Geier* (n 296).

[344] NYSE Listed Company Manual, §313; NASDAQ Listing Rule 5640.

[345] Berger, Davidoff, and Benjamin (n 333) argue convincingly that tenure voting plans should be held to be consistent with the listing rules, since they do not 'disparately reduce' voting rights of existing shareholders within the meaning of the rules. Rather, they grant '*all* stockholders *equal* per share voting rights and *equal* opportunity to gain additional voting rights by holding their shares over time': ibid 35 (emphasis in the original).

at least outside of the premium segment of the stock market, and more of the opposition of UK institutional investors.[346]

These observations pose something of a puzzle. As mentioned, loyalty shares and tenured voting rights are an effective mechanism to combat short-termism and allow managers to pursue business strategies with a longer time horizon. On the other hand, it may be argued that they benefit primarily the corporate insiders, for example a founding family or the directors, by allowing them to consolidate and preserve their control while decreasing their economic stake in the company.[347] Thus, allowing loyalty shares and tenured voting rights gives rise to a trade-off. Whether the beneficial effects of reducing harmful short-termism outweigh the potential detrimental effect of increasing agency costs for outside investors is, of course, not an empirical question that can be studied in isolation. Rather, the net effects will differ depending, on the one hand, on the short term pressures that investors can exert over managers, and on the other hand, on other legal mechanisms that minority shareholders have at their disposal to prevent value destruction by corporate insiders. We have seen above that the starting point of legal systems concerning the determination of the position and powers of the shareholders in relation to the directors is markedly different in the countries that we have analysed, with the UK standing out as a legal system where corporate power is ultimately vested in the shareholders, who have strong control rights.[348] In addition, investors in large listed companies can rely on a liquid market to make use of their exit right if they are concerned that corporate insiders divert corporate assets. In such a system, the risk that managers will be focused on short-term share prize maximization is evidently higher than in many continental European economies, where structural features of company law[349] and the presence of blockholders insulate the managers from outside investor pressure, but also potentially increase agency costs. Therefore, assuming that policy makers seek to approximate an optimal balance between reducing externalities and agency costs, we would expect loyalty shares to be pervasive in economies such as the UK, and we would expect their adoption to be prohibited or at least not facilitated in economies where managers already enjoy a certain degree of insulation. However, the brief overview above seems to indicate that the opposite is true.[350]

2. *Calling a general meeting and voting at meetings*

Not only the design of the shareholder's voting rights as such determines how easy or difficult it is for shareholders to exercise their voice, but also the rules that specify who can call a meeting and who can put items on the agenda, the regulation of the mechanics of general meetings, and how decisions are taken and majorities are computed. We will discuss these three points in turn.

In all legal systems, the board of directors (in Germany both the management board and the supervisory board) is the organ primarily responsible for calling general meetings, drawing up the agenda and tabling resolutions.[351] In addition, shareholders owning a specified proportion of the legal capital may have a right to request that the directors call a meeting and that particular items are included in the agenda, or they may apply to a court to order a meeting to be convened. These rights have been strengthened continuously over the last

[346] Text to nn 302–304 above. [347] Dallas and Barry (n 333) 565–8.

[348] Section A.I above. See also our discussion of removal rights in section D.II below, which confirms that shareholders in UK companies are in a strong position to ensure that directors act in their interest.

[349] See section A.III above on the allocation of corporate power under the German Stock Corporation Act.

[350] For the above reasons, the restrictions on deviations from the one share, one vote principle imposed by the UK Listing Rules and the Premium Listing Principles have been criticized by commentators as 'a regressive and thus lamentable development', MT Moore and E Walker-Arnott, 'A Fresh Look at Stock Market Short-termism' (2014) 41 Journal of Law and Society 416, 444.

[351] See the Appendix for an overview and references to the relevant statutory provisions.

decades in Europe, partly as a result of initiatives of the European legislator to increase participation in general meetings and protect minority investors. Pursuant to the Shareholder Rights Directive, which was adopted in 2007 and applies to companies incorporated in the EU and listed on a regulated market operating within a Member State,[352] shareholders representing a share capital that shall not be set at a higher threshold than 5 per cent must have the right to put items on the agenda of the general meeting and table resolutions.[353] Member States may provide that the right to put items on the agenda shall be restricted to the annual general meeting, but the shareholders must then be able to call an extraordinary general meeting, as long as they satisfy the threshold requirement.[354] In several Member States, including France, Germany, and the UK, the same threshold, while not required by the Directive, is now used to determine when shareholders of public companies in general, and not only shareholders of listed companies, can request that a meeting be called at the expense of the company.[355]

However, in the finer details, the laws of the Member States continue to display considerable variation. In the UK, the directors are only required to call a meeting if the members who request them to do so represent 5 per cent of the paid-up capital carrying the right to vote at general meetings.[356] Pursuant to the German Stock Corporation Act, it is irrelevant whether the shares have been fully paid and whether or not they carry voting rights, provided they give shareholders the right to attend the meeting.[357] French law grants the same right to shareholders holding at least 5 per cent of the share capital of public companies generally,[358] and in addition to associations of shareholders, which can be formed by shareholders of listed companies representing 1–5 per cent of the voting rights, depending on the size of the company's capital.[359] In comparison, in Delaware, shareholders have no right to call a special meeting, unless the certificate of incorporation provides for such a right,[360] and in states having implemented the Model Business Companies Act, the threshold is set at 10 per cent of all votes entitled to be cast on an issue to be considered at the special meeting.[361]

Legal systems differ further in how they regulate the manner of calling a meeting and the conduct of meetings. Again, for the EU Member States, the Shareholder Rights Directive constitutes the lowest common denominator. The Directive requires that ordinary general meetings shall be called by notice of at least 21 days and special meetings by notice of at least 14 days.[362] The notice needs to contain the minimum information set out in the Directive, including a description of the procedures that shareholders must comply with in order to be able to participate in the meeting or vote by proxy, a statement of the record date, if applicable, and a reference to the draft resolutions and other relevant documents.[363] Since one of the goals of the Directive is the facilitation of the cross-border exercise of shareholder rights,[364] the Directive requires the notice to be disseminated in a manner that ensures 'fast access to it on a non-discriminatory basis',[365] irrespective of where the investor is located in

[352] Directive 2007/36/EC on the exercise of certain rights of shareholders in listed companies, [2007] OJ L184/17, Art 1(1).

[353] ibid Art 6(1), (2). [354] ibid.

[355] Some Member States continue to draw a distinction between listed and unlisted companies, see e.g. the Italian Codice civile, Art 2367(1) (providing for a threshold of 10% in the case of companies not listed on a regulated market).

[356] Companies Act 2006, s 303(2).

[357] AktG, §122(1). Generally, all shareholders have the right to attend the general meeting, irrespective of their voting rights (see, in particular, §140(1) for non-voting preference shares).

[358] Com, Art L225-103-II.

[359] ibid Art L225-120. The lowest threshold, 1%, applies to companies with a share capital exceeding 15 million euros, and the highest threshold, 5%, to companies with a share capital of not more than 750,000 euros.

[360] Del. Gen. Corp. Law, §211(d).

[361] MBCA, §7.02(a)(2). The articles may provide for a lower or a higher threshold, which however shall not exceed 25%.

[362] Directive 2007/36/EC, Art 5(1). [363] ibid Art 5(3). [364] ibid recital 2.

[365] ibid Art 5(2).

the EU. In addition, the notice, the total number of shares and voting rights, draft resolutions and proxy forms must generally be made available on the website of the company.[366] However, the Directive does not require the translation of any information into the language of Member States where the company has issued shares or where investors reside.

Another point of great practical importance is the question of how shareholders who wish to add an item to the agenda or propose a resolution can communicate the necessary information to the other shareholders. As we will see when we discuss proxy voting, if shareholders cannot rely on the corporate machinery to reach out to the other shareholders, they are severely hampered in challenging management resolutions by tabling a counter-proposal.[367] The Shareholder Rights Directive has brought an important—albeit incomplete—innovation in this respect. If shareholders make use of their right to add items to the agenda, the company is required to circulate the revised agenda in the same manner as the original agenda.[368] However, the Directive does not specify whether the shareholder has to pay the expenses of the company. Also, those who propose a resolution will generally seek to furnish the shareholders with additional information in support of their proposal. Whether the shareholders can request the company to circulate such a statement, and whether the company has to do so at its own expense, is left to the national laws of the Member States, which—unsurprisingly—differ considerably. UK law is comparatively restrictive. Shareholders representing at least 5 per cent of the total voting rights or at least 100 members who have a right to vote at the meeting may request that the company include additional items in the agenda of the meeting and circulate them, as well as a copy of any resolution proposed by the shareholders, to all members of the company. However, the company is only required to comply with the request if it is received no later than six weeks before the annual general meeting or before the time at which the company gives notice of the meeting.[369] The shareholders bear the cost of circulating the matters, unless the request was made before the end of the financial year preceding the meeting.[370] Similarly, the shareholders can issue statements with respect to any business to be dealt with at the meeting and request the company to circulate the statement if it does not exceed 1,000 words and is received at least one week before the meeting, but they have to pay the company's expenses unless the request is made before the end of the financial year.[371]

The German Stock Corporation Act is more facilitative of shareholder engagement. The company has to give notice of items added to the agenda upon the request of shareholders, even if these are received after notice of the meeting has been given.[372] It also has to make counter-proposals of the shareholders concerning any item on the agenda available if they are submitted at least 14 days before the meeting.[373] In order to reduce the regulatory burden on companies, they do not have to forward the proposal, or any accompanying statement, to the shareholders. Publication on the website of the company is sufficient and, if the company is listed on a stock exchange, required by the statute.[374] French law pursues a similar strategy. Five per cent shareholders (or holders of smaller stakes if the share capital of the company exceeds certain thresholds[375]) can request inclusion of items in the agenda if they do so at least twenty-five days before the meeting.[376] The company has to make the draft resolutions and added items available on its website.[377] Thus, in both countries, the law adopts a

[366] ibid Art 5(4). [367] Section C.II below. [368] Directive 2007/36/EC, Art 6(4).
[369] UK Companies Act 2006, ss 338–339, 340A. [370] ibid ss 340(1), 340B(1).
[371] ibid ss 314–316.
[372] AktG, §124(1). However, shareholders only have the right to request items to be included in the agenda if the request is received at least 24 days, or in the case of listed companies 30 days, before the general meeting: AktG, §122(2).
[373] ibid §126(1). [374] ibid §126(1) sentence 3.
[375] Com, Art R225-71(2) (eg, for companies with a share capital of more than €15 million, the threshold is as low as 0.5%).
[376] ibid Art R 225-72(2) (all public companies) Art R225-73-II (listed companies).
[377] ibid Art R225-73-1(3).

pragmatic solution that reduces the costs for the company, while ensuring that shareholders are informed about all proposals and counter-proposals before the meeting.

Again, in comparison, US law is both less prescriptive and less accommodating to shareholder activism. The company laws of the US states generally do not specify the information that needs to be made available to shareholders ahead of a meeting, and often they do not even require the notice of the annual general meeting to include a description of the purposes for which the meeting is called.[378] The laws also do not provide for an express right of the minority to submit counter-proposals or add items to the agenda. These are matters left to the articles or by-laws, which typically require that proposed resolutions be submitted in writing to the company a prescribed number of days in advance of the meeting.[379] In addition, if the company is subject to the Securities Exchange Act of 1934, shareholders are, under certain conditions, able to request that the company include their proposal in the management's proxy statement. This right is evidently of great importance. Shareholders in widely held public companies will have very little chance of success if they have not communicated the proposal to the other shareholders in advance of the meeting and solicited proxies in favour of it. They can, of course, sent out their own proxy materials, but this will generally involve significant costs. In practice, it is therefore often a crucial question whether or not the company has to include a shareholder proposal. We will return to this question below.[380]

We now turn to the last—and arguably most important—point mentioned above: When is the general meeting quorate to conduct business and how are majorities computed? Most legal systems establish different quorum and majority requirements depending on the type of corporate action at issue. Typically, both quorum and majority requirements will be more demanding if the resolution deals with important corporate changes, for example an amendment of the articles, the approval of a merger, or the voluntary winding up of the company. In these cases, the position of minority shareholders may be severely affected. The law therefore grants large minority shareholders a veto right. In Europe, the law typically distinguishes between ordinary and extraordinary or special resolutions. Corporate actions that can only be adopted by a special resolution are set out in the relevant legislation, which also specifies the minimum majority required for such a resolution to pass.[381] In all countries analysed here, an ordinary resolution is passed by a simple majority of the votes, unless the articles require a higher majority.[382] In the case of a special resolution, the quorum ranges from one shareholder (Germany and the UK[383]) to one-fourth or one-third (France[384]), and the majority from two-thirds (France[385]) to three-fourths of the votes (UK[386]) or of the legal

[378] MBCA, §7.05(b). By contrast, notice of a special meeting must include the purpose for which the meeting is called, ibid §7.05(c).

[379] American Bar Association, *Model Business Corporation Act* (ABA 2010) 7–23.

[380] Section C.II.2.

[381] For an overview of important corporate actions and the respective quorum and majority requirements, see the Appendix.

[382] French Code de commerce, Art L225-98; German AktG, §133(1); UK Companies Act 2006, s 282(1). The quorum is one-fifth in France (Com, Art L225-98) and one shareholder in Germany and the UK (discussed in more detail in the next footnote).

[383] The German Stock Corporation Act does not contain any provision on the required quorum; therefore, even attendance of only one shareholder is sufficient, Imperial Court, RGZ 82, 386, 388 (with one exception, approval of the acquisition of an asset for a consideration exceeding one-tenth of the legal capital by the company from a major shareholder within one year of the formation of the company, AktG, §52(5), in which case one-fourth of the company's legal capital constitutes a quorum). In the UK, one person constitutes a quorum if the company is a one-member company; in all other cases, two persons are necessary, Companies Act 2006, s 318.

[384] The Code de commerce provides for a quorum of one-fourth for decisions of the extraordinary general meeting, which is competent, inter alia, to pass resolutions on an amendment of the articles (Art L225-96), a transfer of the registered office (Art L225-97) and the voluntary winding-up of the company (Art L225-246). If a special resolution of a class of shareholders is required, which is the case if class rights are varied, the quorum for resolutions of the affected class is one-third (Art L225-99). See also n 156 on quorum requirements.

[385] Com, Arts L225-96 (extraordinary general meetings), L225-99 (special meetings).

[386] UK Companies Act 2006, s 283(1).

capital represented at the meeting (Germany[387]). Delaware law and the laws of others US states do not lay down special majorities for extraordinary resolutions, but a greater quorum or majority than the default can be provided for in the articles of incorporation.[388] If no such provision is included in the articles, the number of shares that constitute a quorum for business to be transacted at the general meeting is generally a majority of the shares entitled to vote,[389] and a resolution is adopted if the majority of shares present at the meeting are voted in favour of the resolution.[390] For fundamental changes, the laws of some states require not a simple majority of the shares present, but an absolute majority of the outstanding stock of the company entitled to vote on the matter.[391]

If the shareholder resolution concerns the election of members to the board of directors (or to the supervisory board in two-tier board systems), more complex considerations inform the regulatory design. The shareholder vote could be compared to the election of candidates to political positions. It is therefore not surprising that different voting mechanisms stemming from the political sphere have been discussed and, in some legal systems, used as a template for the election of directors. The first possibility is election by a plurality of the votes. Somewhat counterintuitively, in plurality voting, shareholders do not vote for or against individual directors, but either support a list of candidates or withhold their support for individual candidates (or for all of them). The candidates with the most votes are elected as directors. This is the default rule in the United States.[392] However, it is viewed critically by some activist shareholders because plurality voting allows directors to be elected by comparatively few votes, especially if there are exactly as many candidates as board vacancies and a large number of shares are withheld.

Majority voting, which is common in France (if the one-tier board system is chosen)[393] and the UK,[394] avoids this problem, since shareholders can vote for or against a candidate and directors are elected if they receive a simple majority of the votes cast. However, under both majority and plurality voting, a shareholder or a group of shareholders owning a majority of the voting shares is able to dominate the election and appoint all members of the board. Minority shareholders will only be guaranteed representation on the board if they are able to negotiate the right to nominate one or more directors with the majority. Such a right may be laid down in a shareholder agreement or in the company's articles.

[387] This is the case, for example, for an amendment of the articles (AktG, §179(2)) and an increase of capital (§182(1)). To be more precise, in order to be adopted, the resolution must be passed by a simple majority of the votes (pursuant to §133(1), see n 382 above) *and* three-fourths of the legal capital voting either in favour of or against the resolution, disregarding abstentions. This double-majority requirement is intended to preserve the blocking minority of shareholders even if proportionality between ownership and voting rights is not observed, for example because of a voting cap (see text to nn 318–322 above). Assume, for example, that a company has five shareholders. One of these shareholders owns 30% of the legal capital, three others 20%, and the remaining shareholder 10%. If all shares carry one vote, the first shareholder can of course block any resolution requiring a supermajority of 75%. Now assume that the company limits the votes of each shareholder to 20%. The share of the first shareholder's votes decreases from 30% to 22% (20 votes out of a total of 90). The shareholder would consequently lose the blocking minority if the double-majority requirement did not exist.

[388] MBCA, §7.27.

[389] For example, Del. Gen. Corp. Law, §216(1). The articles can provide for a different quorum, provided that the quorum does not consist of less than one third of the shares entitled to vote, §216, first sentence.

[390] Del. Gen. Corp. Law, §216(2). Special rules apply to the election of directors, which we will discuss presently.

[391] For example, Del. Gen. Corp. Law, §251(c) (mergers).

[392] Del. Gen. Corp. Law, §216(3); MBCA, §7.28(a). If the stockholders adopt a bylaw amendment changing the default rule, the amendment cannot be amended further or repealed by the directors, Del. Gen. Corp. Law, §216, last sentence.

[393] Com, Art L225-18.

[394] The Companies Act 2006 is silent on the question of how directors are elected, except for requiring that the appointment of directors in a public company shall be made individually, rather than by a single resolution, s 160. The Model Articles for Public and Private Companies stipulate that directors may be appointed by ordinary resolution or by a decision of the directors (Art 20 Model Articles for Public Companies, Art 17(1) Model Articles for Private Companies). These rules, of course, can be changed, and there is nothing in the Companies Act requiring that directors have to be appointed by the general meeting or indeed by any of the shareholders.

As a different method to increase minority representation, companies may include a provision in the articles of incorporation permitting the shareholders to cumulate their votes, which is possible under both Delaware law and the MBCA.[395] In this case, the shareholders' votes are multiplied by the number of directors to be elected and the shareholders may distribute their votes among the candidates as they wish. For example, if three shareholders owning twenty, twenty, and sixty shares, respectively, are asked to fill five vacancies on the board, the first shareholder could cast 100 votes for a candidate for one of the board positions and none for the others. If all three shareholders distributed their votes accordingly, the largest shareholder would be able to elect three persons to the board and the other two shareholders one director each, thus resulting in a composition of the board reflecting the shareholders' relative stakes in the company. In Delaware and most US states, cumulative voting is designed as an opt-in mechanism. If it is not provided for in the original articles of incorporation, shareholders will therefore require the consent of the directors to change the articles and introduce cumulative voting.[396] This may explain why cumulative voting is used rarely in public companies.

A fourth possibility, which has been used by the German legislator in the election of the employee representatives to the supervisory board (but, importantly, not in the election of the shareholder representatives, which follows general rules for resolutions of the general meeting[397]), is proportionate representation.[398] Proportionate representation, which is common in political elections, requires the submission of at least two competing lists of candidates for two or more vacancies on the board. Board positions are allocated according to the number of votes received by each list. The first board position is allocated to the list with the highest number of votes; for the second position, the numbers of votes of that list are divided by two (or by another divisor), and the board seat is again allocated to the list with the highest (remaining) number of votes. This process is repeated, with successively higher divisors, until all board positions are allocated.[399] The effect of proportionate representation is therefore similar to cumulative voting. Under both systems, at least some minority representation on the board is ensured (however, not necessarily resulting in perfectly proportionate representation as in the example above), without the need to negotiate appointment rights with the majority shareholder.

The decision between majority or plurality voting on the one hand and cumulative voting and proportionate representation on the other is, arguably, one of the most significant policy decisions in corporate governance. We will discuss the appointment of directors in more detail below,[400] but we can note at this point that, apart from the specific case of the election of employee representatives to the supervisory board under German law, legal systems, as a default, do not provide for voting systems that can be expected to result in a composition of the board that reflects the composition of the constituencies electing the directors. There are good policy reasons for this choice of the legislator. Cohesion on the board of directors is important to facilitate decision-making and an efficient management of the company. In addition, directors are bound to act in the interest of the shareholders as a group, which may require, in some situations, to

[395] Del. Gen. Corp. Law, §214; MBCA, §7.28(b).

[396] See text to n 77 above.

[397] Pursuant to §133(1) AktG, a simple majority of the votes is sufficient, unless the articles of association provide for a different majority.

[398] We will discuss the appointment of directors to the supervisory board under co-determination rules in section D.III below.

[399] For example, assume that three competing lists of candidates are submitted for three board positions. The first list receives 100 votes, the second 60, and the third 40. Under a system of proportionate representation, the votes are divided by a series of divisors, for example 1, 2, 3, etc, and the board positions allocated successively to the lists with the highest numbers. In our example, the first two candidates on the first list and the top candidate on the second list are appointed as directors, since the highest votes after division are 100 (list 1) 60 (list 2), and 50 (again list 1). No candidate on the third list receives a position on the board of directors.

[400] Section D.I.

take actions that run counter to the interests of individual shareholders. A fragmented board may lead to deadlock and prevent commercially important, but contentious decisions from being implemented. On the other hand, this also means that shareholder democracy (as indeed any democratic system) cannot rely on elections alone to function properly.[401]

3. *Shareholder engagement and incentives*

In this section, we go beyond the legal analysis of the structure of voting rights and the mechanics of general meetings. We will explore whether shareholders have sufficient incentives to make use of their voting rights, and if so, whether we can be sure that they will always act in a way that maximizes their expected return on investment, which means—at least in the absence of private benefits of control and market imperfections—that they will require the company to be run profitably. As we said above,[402] dispersed shareholders face a collective action problem. If it is not possible for them to coordinate and exercise their rights at low cost, a rationally acting shareholder will abstain from participating in shareholder decision-making, and as a consequence shareholders may fail to take actions that would be in their common interest.[403] In order to address this problem, legal systems have introduced reforms designed to facilitate the exercise of voting rights, notably by requiring companies to allow shareholders to appoint a proxy who can vote on their behalf. We will discuss these reforms in the next section. Here, we will analyse what could be called an endogenous response to the shareholders' collective action problem: the pooling of assets in the hands of professional intermediaries, who invest on behalf of individual savers, the ultimate beneficiaries, in stock corporations. We will see that institutional investors, such as pension funds, mutual funds, or hedge funds have succeeded in mobilizing increasingly large amounts of capital and hence play an important role as shareholders in today's capital markets, but they do not necessarily overcome the problem of shareholder passivity and may indeed give rise to problems of their own. We will then discuss another recent phenomenon that may further distort incentives of shareholders to vote in the economic interest of the company: the use of financial derivatives to 'decouple' voting rights from economic exposure. For example, investor may enter into a swap agreement entitling them to claim the difference in the stock price from the counterparty if the company's stock declines in value. Accordingly, they are hedged against a downturn in the company's fortunes and may not be interested in voting at all or pursue ulterior motives with their vote. Policy makers in several countries have contemplated this and related problems, but a coherent regulatory response to the decoupling of voting rights and economic control has not yet emerged.

The ownership share of institutional investors in large, publicly traded companies has steadily increased since the 1970s and 1980s. In the United States, institutional investors, including domestic private and public pension funds, mutual funds, closed-end funds, and exchange-traded funds, owned a combined 14 per cent of corporate equities in 1965, and households and non-profits 84 per cent.[404] Six decades later, the picture is markedly different. Domestic institutional investors own about 44.4 per cent and households only 39

[401] We have already seen that all legal systems have developed mechanisms going beyond the allocation of decision rights to protect the interests of the relevant corporate actors (see section B above). In Chapter 7, we will discuss additional legal constraints imposed on shareholders to avoid a 'tyranny of the majority'.

[402] Text to nn 279–283.

[403] For a succinct and critically review of shareholder passivity, see BS Black, 'Shareholder Passivity Reexamined' (1990) 89 Michigan Law Review 520. More recently see also SM Bainbridge, 'The Case for Limited Shareholder Voting Rights' (2005–2006) 53 UCLA Law Review 601.

[404] M Kahan and E Rock, 'Embattled CEOs' (2010) 88 Texas Law Review 987, 996. For historical data from 1945 to the present day, see Board of Governors of the Federal Reserve System, *Financial Accounts of the United States*, available from the website of the Federal Reserve, https://www.federalreserve.gov/releases/z1/.

per cent of equities.[405] Considering that foreign investors, who comprise 15.6 per cent of owners,[406] are also mostly institutions, the extent of the shift away from households to institutions becomes even more pronounced. Similarly, in the UK, individuals and households were the largest shareholder group in the 1960s. Now institutional investors, including to a significant extent international investors, own more than 75 per cent of the value of the UK stock market, and the share of individuals has decreased to around 19 per cent.[407] This development has been attributed to two main factors: the post-World War II policy decision to focus on privately funded pensions to provide for retirement security and the rise of portfolio theory, which presents a theoretical framework suggesting that securities should be held in large, well-diversified portfolios.[408]

The changing ownership structure of companies has implications for regulatory design for two reasons. First, institutional investors, and in particular investment funds,[409] may have a different time horizon than households. They may be prepared to make use of their exit right earlier than other investors and hence increase the pressure for managers to focus on share price movements to the detriment of long-term indicators of business success. Secondly, the concentration of ownership in the hands of institutional investors, who function as intermediaries for the ultimate beneficiaries, for example individuals who pay into a pension fund, creates additional agency costs—or, as they have been called in the literature, 'the agency costs of agency capitalism'.[410] As opposed to the traditional managerial agency problem, we can observe diverging interests not only between investors and managers, but also between record owners (the institutional investors) and their beneficiaries or shareholders. Competitive pressures force institutional investors to minimize costs, while trying not to underperform (and ideally outperform) their closest competitors. For this reason, many institutional investors will not have the resources to engage in active monitoring of the portfolio company's management, scrutinize the company's governance structure and performance, and make use of their voting rights to force the management to implement changes where appropriate. This lack of activism is an agency cost borne by the beneficiary, who would benefit from better performance and more stringent governance structures. It could be said that the benefits of diversification are inversely related to this type of agency cost. The larger the investor's portfolio, the less likely it is that the investor will be able to use its governance rights effectively, since this requires firm-specific investigations.[411]

Policy makers grapple with the question of how to react to these challenges. One strategy, chosen by the European legislator in the 2017 revisions of the Shareholder Rights Directive, is the imposition of mandatory disclosure obligations on asset managers and institutional investors that force them to reflect on their medium to long-term orientation. The amended Directive requires institutional investors and asset managers to develop and publicly disclose an engagement policy that describes how they monitor investee companies on a variety of matters, including financial and non-financial performance, social and environmental impact, and corporate governance. In addition, they must publish a description of their voting behaviour and explain how their investment strategy contributes to the medium to long-term performance of the investee companies.[412] Another strategy to address short-termism that we discussed above is a regulatory environment that allows the issuing of loyalty shares rewarding long-term shareholders. However, we said that this strategy might not be equally effective in all legal systems. In addition, it does not overcome the problem that both small retail investors and large institutional investors may be rationally passive. A more optimistic

405 Federal Reserve Statistical Release, Flow of Funds, Balance Sheets, and Integrated Macroeconomic Accounts, Historical Annual Tables 2005-2015 (June 2016) 123.

406 ibid.

407 See n 306 above.

408 RJ Gilson and JN Gordon, 'The Agency Costs of Agency Capitalism Activist Investors and the Revaluation of Governance Rights' (2013) 113 Columbia Law Review 863, 878–86.

409 See nn 284–285 above and accompanying text.

410 Gilson and Gordon (n 408).

411 ibid 889–91.

412 Directive 2007/36/EC, Arts 3g–3i.

view, held by some commentators, argues that institutional investors, rather than being simply passive, are 'rationally reticent'.[413] While pension funds or mutual funds may not make the necessary investment to acquire firm-specific information that would allow them to expose underperformance and act on that information, they are willing to exercise their voting rights according to the recommendations of specialized actors, 'governance intermediaries', that have made this investment. These specialist investors may be proxy advisors such as Institutional Shareholder Services (ISS) or Glass Lewis, hedge funds, or engagement funds that invest in a relatively small portfolio of companies and seek to generate a superior return by bringing about corporate change in the portfolio companies. If this view is correct, regulatory intervention should focus less on addressing investor apathy or reticence as such, and more on ensuring that activist investors can recoup the costs incurred by investigating portfolio companies, running activist campaigns, and holding an undiversified portfolio.[414] The return they are able to secure will be higher the later they are required to disclose that they have acquired a stake in the target company, since their return depends on the size of their equity position and disclosure will drive up the share price of the target. Thus, reform proposals include suggestions to set comparatively high ownership thresholds triggering disclosure obligations, extend the period until when disclosure has to be made after the ownership threshold has been reached, and facilitate the use of equity derivatives by not including them in the disclosure regime.[415]

This brings us to the second problem. An issue that has received much attention in recent years and potentially calls the central role of shareholder voting as a part of shareholder democracy into question is the separation of control rights and economic exposure. Granting shareholders the right to vote on the most important corporate decisions rests on the assumption that shareholders will make use of their voting rights in a manner that is conducive to the profitable operation of the company, since their financial rights are proportionate to (or, in the case of control-enhancing mechanisms, at least positively associated with) their voting rights. However, if we assume a situation where the investors' economic exposure is decoupled from their voting rights, this basic assumption no longer holds. Investors may now use their voting rights to pursue an ulterior goal that is actually detrimental to the economic interests of the company, such as favouring a competitor, or they may fail to exercise their voting rights altogether. This phenomenon—the investors own voting rights but have hedged against a downturn in the company's share price, so that they are presumably indifferent to the economic success of the company—has been called 'empty voting'. The reverse problem—the investor gains economic exposure to the company, but holds no voting rights—is known as 'hidden ownership'.[416] The latter situation can also give rise to problems, because investors can be seen as owners for economic purposes, but they may not be subject to any legal duties that normally come with ownership, notably disclosure obligations.

The decoupling of economic exposure and voting rights can result from the use of equity derivatives, such as cash-settled equity swaps and contracts for differences. In an equity swap transaction, the parties promise to exchange two cash flows that are determined by

[413] Gilson and Gordon (n 408), 867.

[414] Studies have shown that campaigns involving a proxy contest cost close to US$11 million on average; see NM Gantchev, 'The Costs of Shareholder Activism: Evidence from a Sequential Decision Model' (2013) 107 Journal of Financial Economics 610, 623.

[415] Gilson and Gordon (n 408), 902–16.

[416] The first comprehensive studies of empty voting and hidden ownership were presented by HTC Hu and B Black, 'The new vote buying: empty voting and hidden ownership' (2006) 79 Southern California Law Review 811; HTC Hu and B Black, 'Hedge funds, insiders, and the decoupling of economic and voting ownership: empty voting and hidden (morphable) ownership' (2007) 13 Journal of Corporate Finance 343; HTC Hu and B Black, 'Equity and debt decoupling and empty voting II: importance and extensions' (2008) 156 University of Pennsylvania Law Review 625 ('Empty voting II'). More recently see also WG Ringe, *The Deconstruction of Equity: Activist Shareholders, Decoupled Risk, and Corporate Governance* (OUP 2016).

reference to underlying assets or index values. For example, one reference value may be the London Interbank Offered Rate (LIBOR) and the other the return of a corporate stock (comprising of dividend payments and changes in the stock price). If the stock appreciates in value, the so-called long party has a claim against the counterparty, the short party, for the difference. The swap agreement may provide that the transaction has to be settled in cash or through physical delivery of the stock, or the short party may be able to choose either cash or physical settlement. By contrast, the long party is required to make up the difference if the stock decreases in value (hence the names 'long party' and 'short party'). The short party can in any case claim interest based on the interbank lending rate or another reference value and will possibly charge a fee for running the swap, especially if it is an investment bank.[417]

Thus, it is easy to see that the long party is in an economic position identical to that of a shareholder. The long party bears the risk of the stock price decreasing and has a claim to the same returns on investment as a shareholder. At the same time, the long party is not an actual owner of stock and, of course, cannot exercise any shareholder rights that come with ownership. The long party, therefore, is a 'hidden owner'. Hidden ownership has given rise to litigation and enforcement actions by the public regulator in several countries, because it was claimed that the hidden owner, in the same way as the actual shareholders, should have disclosed its economic exposure to the company pursuant to the relevant disclosure rules. In the EU, these rules are laid down in the Transparency Directive, which provides that shareholders and certain other parties who acquire or dispose of shares of an issuer whose shares are admitted to trading on a regulated market shall notify the issuer of the voting rights held by them if thresholds beginning at 5 per cent are reached or crossed.[418] Among others, the disclosure requirements initially also applied to persons holding 'financial instruments that result in an entitlement to acquire, on such holder's own initiative alone, under a formal agreement, shares to which voting rights are attached, already issued, of an issuer whose shares are admitted to trading on a regulated market'.[419] This definition captures the long party to a physically settled equity swap, since the swap agreement gives that party a legally enforceable entitlement to acquire securities upon settlement of the swap. However, it does not capture the long party to a cash-settled equity swap, even if the short party can elect to settle the swap physically, because in this case the long party does not have any 'entitlement' to the securities.

From an economic point of view, both transactions may have similar effects. This can be illustrated by the (ultimately successful) takeover attempt of the German automotive parts manufacturer Continental AG by the much smaller, privately held ball-bearing-maker Schaeffler.[420] Schaeffler succeeded in building up a stake of about 36 per cent in Continental without disclosing its position by entering into three different types of transaction: an outright acquisition of shares just below the threshold of 3 per cent triggering disclosure obligations under German law, physically settled equity swaps representing slightly less than 5 per cent of the voting rights in Continental, again just below the relevant disclosure threshold, and cash-settled equity swaps representing about 28 per cent of the voting rights.[421] The investment banks that were counterparties to the cash-settled equity swaps had hedged their position by either buying the underlying shares or entering into offsetting derivative transactions. According to the swap agreement, they were able to close

[417] Contracts for differences are comparable to cash-settled equity swaps. The seller pays to the buyer the difference between the current value of an asset and its value at contract time, see the definition in Financial Services and Markets Act 2000 (Regulated Activities) Order 2001, s 85 (see in particular s 85(2), which emphasizes that the concept excludes arrangements that are settled by physical delivery of the assets).

[418] Directive 2004/109/EC, Art 9(1).

[419] ibid Art 13(1), as originally promulgated.

[420] The case is described in detail by D Zetzsche, 'Hidden Ownership in Europe: BAFin's Decision in Schaeffler v. Continental' (2009) 10 EBOR 115.

[421] ibid 118–19.

out the positions in Continental shares upon termination of the swap agreement 'in a commercially reasonable manner', including by accepting Schaeffler's tender offer.[422] Under the circumstances, it was commercially advantageous for the investment banks to accept the tender offer, rather than sell their securities in the market. Consequently, Schaeffler had taken a large equity stake in Continental out of the market before any other market participants realized that a takeover attempt was in progress and before Schaeffler had to announce its public offer.

The German market regulator BaFin cleared Schaeffler of any violations of disclosure obligations, holding that Schaeffler did not have an 'unconditional right to acquire the underlying shares', only an economic expectation.[423] This regulatory loophole was seen as problematic. The eventual disclosure of the long party's equity position can provoke erratic market reactions.[424] It may also be argued that the use of derivative transactions to acquire a stake of more than 30 per cent of voting rights in Continental, which is the proportion that triggers a mandatory bid under German takeover law,[425] deprived shareholders who sold before the disclosure of Schaeffler's acquisition of the opportunity to obtain a takeover premium. The European legislator reacted to the perceived loophole by amending the Transparency Directive in 2013 and extending the disclosure obligations to holders of financial instruments that 'are referenced to shares ... and with economic effect similar to that of the financial instruments [that grant the holder the unconditional right to acquire the underlying securities], whether or not they confer a right to a physical settlement'.[426] Thus, the amendment targets precisely situations such Schaeffler and Continental. The structure of the swap agreement at issue in that case, in particular the right of the counterparty to close out the swap positions 'in a commercially reasonable manner', created economic effects

[422] ibid 124.

[423] Directive 2007/14/EC implementing the Transparency Directive, Art 11(1). This question was also litigated in other countries. See, for example, *CSX v The Children's Investment Fund (TCI)*, F. Supp. 2d 511 (S.D.N.Y. 2008), affirmed in part, vacated in part, *CSX v The Children's Investment Fund Management (UK) LLP*, 654 F.3d 276 (2d Cir. 2011). The two decisions interpreted s. 13(d) of the Securities Exchange Act 1934 and Exchange Act Rule 13d, which require investors to disclose their position when they own, or beneficially own, 5% or more of a company's stock. A beneficial owner is defined by Rule 13d-3(a) as a person who exercises voting or investment power over the security. Voting power is 'the power to vote, or to direct the voting of, [the] security', and investment power 'the power to dispose, or to direct the disposition of, [the] security', Rule 13d-3(a)(1), (2). It is clear that the long party to a cash-settled total return swap has neither the power to direct the voting of the security, nor the power to dispose of the security. The case, therefore, turned on the question of whether TCI had engaged in 'a plan or scheme to evade the reporting requirements', Rule 13d-3(b). The Court of Appeal rejected this claim. It argued that '[i]f the transaction under scrutiny does not have substantially the characteristics or expected benefits that are intended to be regulated, then an evasion provision simply does not apply. Evasion of Section 13(d) [Securities Exchange Act 1934] is not present in cash-settled total-return equity swaps because the swaps themselves provide no means of exercising control. As explained in the discussion of Rule 13d-3(a), an owner of such swaps cannot seek to exercise control without buying the actual shares in an open competitive market. In the present case, when the Funds could not persuade CSX to change its policies, they had to make actual purchases of CSX stock, a step that would have been unnecessary if the swaps they held were the substantial equivalent of beneficial ownership. It is also critical to note that the swaps here were not sham transactions creating a false appearance while lacking economic substance. Long counterparties to such swaps have legitimate economic purposes. As the district court found with regard to TCI, the swaps would enable TCI to reap a leverage-amplified profit if CSX's management, faced with the Funds' potential challenge, instituted new policies that increased the value of the company ... If that occurred, a successful insurgent proxy fight or other control transaction would have been precluded, but TCI would share in the increased value resulting from its efforts. Similarly, if competing bidders appeared with a higher price for the company, TCI would share in the increased share price'. *CSX*, 654 F.3d at 306–7.

[424] For example, in 2008, the undisclosed use of derivatives by Porsche to acquire a large stake in Volkswagen reduced the free-float of VW shares in the market to such an extent that short sellers scrambled to exit their positions and Volkswagen's stock rose by close to 350% within two days, making VW briefly the largest company in the world by market capitalization; see MW Palombo, 'Short-Changing of Investors: Why a Short Sale Price Test Rule is Necessary in Today's Markets' (2009–2010) 75 Brooklyn Law Review 1447, 1454.

[425] Securities Acquisition and Takeover Act [Wertpapiererwerbs- und Übernahmegesetz (WpÜG)], §§35, 29(2).

[426] Transparency Directive, Art 13(1), as amended by Directive 2013/50/EU. The calculation of the number of voting rights related to cash-settled financial instruments (which is not necessarily equal to the number of voting rights of the underlying shares) is set out in Commission Delegated Regulation (EU) No 2015/761 supplementing Directive 2004/109/EC.

similar to a physically settled swap agreement. Under current EU law, only the long party has to disclose such positions, not the short party,[427] and all financial instruments relating to the same underlying issuer, as well as shares of the issuer that the party acquires, are aggregated to calculate whether the applicable disclosure thresholds are reached.[428]

The use of derivative transactions may also give rise to the second phenomenon mentioned above, empty voting. A person who seeks to obtain additional votes without increasing its economic exposure to the issuer may adopt a two-step strategy that involves acquiring the shares and then hedging the economic return on the shares by entering into an equity swap agreement.[429] The effect of the scheme is similar to vote buying, which is restrictively regulated in many jurisdictions.[430] However, it does not satisfy the legal definition of vote buying, the transfer of voting rights without the transfer of economic risk, because the empty voter obtains the voting rights by acquiring the shares, as in any regular share transaction.[431] Similarly, a person may borrow shares in the share loan market shortly before the record date, the date when a company determines who is eligible to vote at a general meeting, in order to be in control of additional voting rights at the meeting (so-called 'record date capture'). It is not clear whether share borrowing actually influences voting outcomes in practice.[432] However, at least in theory it may distort voting results because, without economic exposure, investors may exercise their voting rights in a way that is not in the best interest of the company and the other shareholders.

As a response to these practices, EU law now requires both stock lenders and borrowers to disclose their holdings.[433] More interventionist proposals to combat the use of stock lending were discussed, but not adopted. For example, the European Commission considered introducing more stringent disclosure obligations regarding the transfer of voting rights independently of the underlying shares between the record date and the general meeting that would be triggered at lower thresholds than the general transparency obligations, or prohibiting borrowers from voting borrowed shares. However, market participants expressed concern that the reform proposals would interfere disproportionately with contractual freedom and it was not sufficiently well understood whether, and in which situations, empty voting posed problems.[434]

Thus, in summary, the regulatory responses to the related phenomena of passive investors, hidden ownership and empty voting discussed in this section remain fragmentary and somewhat inconsistent. In spite of an in-depth treatment of rational apathy, misaligned incentives between management, institutional investors, and their beneficiaries, and the decoupling of economic and voting ownership in the academic literature, regulators do not (yet) seem to be prepared to reinterpret the concept of equity ownership more fundamentally in light of changing ownership structures and market practices.

[427] Transparency Directive, Art 13(1a).

[428] ibid Art 13a. The regime of the Transparency Directive is modelled on the UK disclosure rules, where the requirement to disclose (gross) long positions on cash settled derivatives had already been introduced in 2009, see Disclosure Rules and Transparency Rules DTR 5.3.1.

[429] Hu and Black, 'Empty voting II' (n 416) 640–1.

[430] For Delaware, see *Schreiber v Carney*, 447 A.2d 17 (Del. Ch. 1982) (requiring that vote buying passes an intrinsic fairness test).

[431] Hu and Black, 'Empty voting II' (n 416) 641.

[432] ESMA, Feedback Statement: Call for Evidence on Empty Voting, ESMA/2012/415, 9–10.

[433] Stock borrowers become owners of the shares and therefore need to disclose their position pursuant to Art 9 of the Transparency Directive. Lenders have a right to reacquire the shares. ESMA has clarified that financial instruments within in the meaning of Art 13(1b) of the Transparency Directive that are subject to notification requirements under that article include rights to recall lent shares, see ESMA, Indicative list of financial instruments that are subject to notification requirements according to Article 13(1b) of the revised Transparency Directive, ESMA/2015/1598.

[434] Commission Staff Working Paper, Impact assessment accompanying the proposal for a Directive amending Directive 2004/109/EC on the harmonisation of transparency requirements in relation to information about issuers whose securities are admitted to trading on a regulated market, SEC/2011/1279 final, 124–5.

II. Proxies

EU Directive 2007/36/EC

Article 10—Proxy voting

(1) Every shareholder shall have the right to appoint any other natural or legal person as a proxy holder to attend and vote at a general meeting in his name. The proxy holder shall enjoy the same rights to speak and ask questions in the general meeting as those to which the shareholder thus represented would be entitled.

Apart from the requirement that the proxy holder possess legal capacity, Member States shall abolish any legal rule which restricts, or allows companies to restrict, the eligibility of persons to be appointed as proxy holders.

(2) ...

(3) Apart from the limitations expressly permitted in paragraphs 1 and 2, Member States shall not restrict or allow companies to restrict the exercise of shareholder rights through proxy holders for any purpose other than to address potential conflicts of interest between the proxy holder and the shareholder, in whose interest the proxy holder is bound to act, and in doing so Member States shall not impose any requirements other than the following:

(a) Member States may prescribe that the proxy holder disclose certain specified facts which may be relevant for the shareholders in assessing any risk that the proxy holder might pursue any interest other than the interest of the shareholder;

(b) Member States may restrict or exclude the exercise of shareholder rights through proxy holders without specific voting instructions for each resolution in respect of which the proxy holder is to vote on behalf of the shareholder;

(c) Member States may restrict or exclude the transfer of the proxy to another person, but this shall not prevent a proxy holder who is a legal person from exercising the powers conferred upon it through any member of its administrative or management body or any of its employees.

A conflict of interest within the meaning of this paragraph may in particular arise where the proxy holder:

(i) is a controlling shareholder of the company, or is another entity controlled by such shareholder;

(ii) is a member of the administrative, management or supervisory body of the company, or of a controlling shareholder or controlled entity referred to in point (i);

(iii) is an employee or an auditor of the company, or of a controlling shareholder or controlled entity referred to in (i);

(iv) has a family relationship with a natural person referred to in points (i) to (iii).

(4) The proxy holder shall cast votes in accordance with the instructions issued by the appointing shareholder.

Member States may require proxy holders to keep a record of the voting instructions for a defined minimum period and to confirm on request that the voting instructions have been carried out.

(5) A person acting as a proxy holder may hold a proxy from more than one shareholder without limitation as to the number of shareholders so represented. Where a proxy holder holds proxies from several shareholders, the applicable law shall enable him to cast votes for a certain shareholder differently from votes cast for another shareholder.

Article 11—Formalities for proxy holder appointment and notification

(1) Member States shall permit shareholders to appoint a proxy holder by electronic means. Moreover, Member States shall permit companies to accept the notification of the appointment by electronic means, and shall ensure that every company offers to its shareholders at least one effective method of notification by electronic means.

(2) Member States shall ensure that proxy holders may be appointed, and that such appointment be notified to the company, only in writing. Beyond this basic formal requirement, the appointment of a proxy holder, the notification of the appointment to the company and the issuance of voting instructions, if any, to the proxy holder may be made subject only to

such formal requirements as are necessary to ensure the identification of the shareholder and of the proxy holder, or to ensure the possibility of verifying the content of voting instructions, respectively, and only to the extent that they are proportionate to achieving those objectives.
(3) The provisions of this Article shall apply mutatis mutandis for the revocation of the appointment of a proxy holder.

US Securities Exchange Act 1934

§ 14—Proxies

(a) Solicitation of proxies in violation of rules and regulations

(1) It shall be unlawful for any person, by the use of the mails or by any means or instrumentality of interstate commerce or of any facility of a national securities exchange or otherwise, in contravention of such rules and regulations as the Commission may prescribe as necessary or appropriate in the public interest or for the protection of investors, to solicit or to permit the use of his name to solicit any proxy or consent or authorization in respect of any security (other than an exempted security) registered pursuant to section 12 of this title....

SEC Exchange Act Rules

Rule 14a-8—Shareholder proposals

This section addresses when a company must include a shareholder's proposal in its proxy statement and identify the proposal in its form of proxy when the company holds an annual or special meeting of shareholders. In summary, in order to have your shareholder proposal included on a company's proxy card, and included along with any supporting statement in its proxy statement, you must be eligible and follow certain procedures. Under a few specific circumstances, the company is permitted to exclude your proposal, but only after submitting its reasons to the Commission. We structured this section in a question-and-answer format so that it is easier to understand. The references to 'you' are to a shareholder seeking to submit the proposal.

(a) Question 1: What is a proposal? A shareholder proposal is your recommendation or requirement that the company and/or its board of directors take action, which you intend to present at a meeting of the company's shareholders. Your proposal should state as clearly as possible the course of action that you believe the company should follow. If your proposal is placed on the company's proxy card, the company must also provide in the form of proxy means for shareholders to specify by boxes a choice between approval or disapproval, or abstention. Unless otherwise indicated, the word 'proposal' as used in this section refers both to your proposal, and to your corresponding statement in support of your proposal (if any).

(b) Question 2: Who is eligible to submit a proposal, and how do I demonstrate to the company that I am eligible? (1) In order to be eligible to submit a proposal, you must have continuously held at least $2,000 in market value, or 1%, of the company's securities entitled to be voted on the proposal at the meeting for at least one year by the date you submit the proposal. You must continue to hold those securities through the date of the meeting...

(c)–(h) ...

(i) Question 9: If I have complied with the procedural requirements, on what other bases may a company rely to exclude my proposal?

  (1) *Improper under state law*: If the proposal is not a proper subject for action by shareholders under the laws of the jurisdiction of the company's organization;

  (2) *Violation of law*: If the proposal would, if implemented, cause the company to violate any state, federal, or foreign law to which it is subject;

  (3) *Violation of proxy rules*: If the proposal or supporting statement is contrary to any of the Commission's proxy rules, including Rule 14a-9, which prohibits materially false or misleading statements in proxy soliciting materials;

  (4) *Personal grievance; special interest*: If the proposal relates to the redress of a personal claim or grievance against the company or any other person, or if it is designed to result

in a benefit to you, or to further a personal interest, which is not shared by the other shareholders at large;

(5) *Relevance*: If the proposal relates to operations which account for less than 5 percent of the company's total assets at the end of its most recent fiscal year, and for less than 5 percent of its net earnings and gross sales for its most recent fiscal year, and is not otherwise significantly related to the company's business;

(6) *Absence of power/authority*: If the company would lack the power or authority to implement the proposal;

(7) *Management functions*: If the proposal deals with a matter relating to the company's ordinary business operations;

(8) *Director elections*: If the proposal:
  (i) Would disqualify a nominee who is standing for election;
  (ii) Would remove a director from office before his or her term expired;
  (iii) Questions the competence, business judgment, or character of one or more nominees or directors;
  (iv) Seeks to include a specific individual in the company's proxy materials for election to the board of directors; or
  (v) Otherwise could affect the outcome of the upcoming election of directors.

(9) *Conflicts with company's proposal*: If the proposal directly conflicts with one of the company's own proposals to be submitted to shareholders at the same meeting;

(10) *Substantially implemented*: If the company has already substantially implemented the proposal;

(11) *Duplication*: If the proposal substantially duplicates another proposal previously submitted to the company by another proponent that will be included in the company's proxy materials for the same meeting;

(12) *Resubmissions*: If the proposal deals with substantially the same subject matter as another proposal or proposals that has or have been previously included in the company's proxy materials within the preceding 5 calendar years, a company may exclude it from its proxy materials for any meeting held within 3 calendar years of the last time it was included if the proposal received:
  (i) Less than 3% of the vote if proposed once within the preceding 5 calendar years;
  (ii) Less than 6% of the vote on its last submission to shareholders if proposed twice previously within the preceding 5 calendar years; or
  (iii) Less than 10% of the vote on its last submission to shareholders if proposed three times or more previously within the preceding 5 calendar years; and

(13) *Specific amount of dividends*: If the proposal relates to specific amounts of cash or stock dividends....

Rule 14a-9—False or misleading statements

(a) No solicitation subject to this regulation shall be made by means of any proxy statement, form of proxy, notice of meeting or other communication, written or oral, containing any statement which, at the time and in the light of the circumstances under which it is made, is false or misleading with respect to any material fact, or which omits to state any material fact necessary in order to make the statements therein not false or misleading or necessary to correct any statement in any earlier communication with respect to the solicitation of a proxy for the same meeting or subject matter which has become false or misleading....

UK Companies Act 2006

Section 324—Rights to appoint proxies

(1) A member of a company is entitled to appoint another person as his proxy to exercise all or any of his rights to attend and to speak and vote at a meeting of the company.
(2) In the case of a company having a share capital, a member may appoint more than one proxy in relation to a meeting, provided that each proxy is appointed to exercise the rights attached to a different share or shares held by him, or (as the case may be) to a different £10, or multiple of £10, of stock held by him.

Section 324A—Obligation of proxy to vote in accordance with instructions

A proxy must vote in accordance with any instructions given by the member by whom the proxy is appointed.

Section 325—Notice of meeting to contain statement of rights

(1) In every notice calling a meeting of a company there must appear, with reasonable prominence, a statement informing the member of—
 (a) his rights under section 324, and
 (b) any more extensive rights conferred by the company's articles to appoint more than one proxy.
(2) Failure to comply with this section does not affect the validity of the meeting or of anything done at the meeting.
(3) If this section is not complied with as respects any meeting, an offence is committed by every officer of the company who is in default.
(4) A person guilty of an offence under this section is liable on summary conviction to a fine not exceeding level 3 on the standard scale.

Section 326—Company-sponsored invitations to appoint proxies

(1) If for the purposes of a meeting there are issued at the company's expense invitations to members to appoint as proxy a specified person or a number of specified persons, the invitations must be issued to all members entitled to vote at the meeting.
...

UK Listing Ruleshowe

LR 9.3.6R—Proxy forms

A listed company must ensure that, in addition to its obligations under the Companies Act 2006, a proxy form:
 (1) [deleted]
 (2) provides for at least 3three3-way voting on all resolutions intended to be proposed (except that it is not necessary to provide proxy forms with 3three3-way voting on procedural resolutions); and3
 (3) [deleted]
 (4) states that if it is returned without an indication as to how the proxy shall vote on any particular matter, the proxy will exercise his discretion as to whether, and if so how, he votes.

UK Model Articles for Public Companies

38—Content of proxy notices

(1), (2) ...
(3) Proxy notices may specify how the proxy appointed under them is to vote (or that the proxy is to abstain from voting) on one or more resolutions.
(4) Unless a proxy notice indicates otherwise, it must be treated as—
 (a) allowing the person appointed under it as a proxy discretion as to how to vote on any ancillary or procedural resolutions put to the meeting...

German Stock Corporation Act

§ 134—Voting right

(1), (2) ...
(3) The voting right can be exercised by an agent. If the shareholder authorizes more than one agent, the company may reject one or more of them. The granting of the proxy, its revocation, and proof of the authorization given to the company must be in text form,[435] unless the articles

[435] [Footnote by authors.] See §126(b) BGB: 'If text form is prescribed by statute, a readable declaration, in which the person making the declaration is named, must be made on a durable medium. A durable medium is any medium that 1. enables the recipient to retain or store a declaration included on the medium that is addressed to him personally such that it is accessible to him for a period of time adequate to its purpose, and 2. that allows the unchanged reproduction of such declaration'.

of association or the notice, if so authorized under the articles, provide otherwise, or the requirements are relaxed in the case of listed companies. Listed companies are at least required to make provision for the electronic submission of the proof of authorization. If proxy holders are appointed by the company, the company is required to retain the proxy for review for three years; § 135(5) shall apply accordingly…

§ 135—Exercise of voting rights by credit institutions and professional agents

(1) A credit institution is only entitled to exercise voting rights attached to shares not owned by the credit institution and not registered under its name in the shareholder register if it has been authorized to do so. The proxy must be granted to a specific credit institution and kept for review by that institution. The proxy form must be completed in full and contain only statements concerning the exercise of voting rights. If the shareholder does not give an express instruction, a general proxy may not authorize the credit institution to exercise voting rights except

1. in accordance with its own voting proposals (subsections (2) and (3)) or
2. in accordance with the proposals of the management board or supervisory board or, in case of deviating proposals, the proposals of the supervisory board (subsection (4)).

If the credit institution offers the exercise of voting rights pursuant to sentence 4 no. 1 or no. 2, it shall also offer until further notice, so far as is reasonable, to furnish a shareholders' association or another representative at the election of the shareholder with the documents necessary for an exercise of voting rights. The credit institution shall annually advise the shareholder of, and emphasise, the possibility of revoking the proxy or changing the proxy holder at any time. The issuing of instructions concerning individual items on the agenda, the granting and revocation of a general proxy pursuant to sentence 4 and a request pursuant to sentence 5 by the shareholder, as well as any changes of such a request, shall be facilitated by making available a form or an online form.

(2) A credit institution that intends to exercise voting rights on the basis of a proxy pursuant to subsection 1, sentence 4, no. 1 is required to furnish the shareholder in a timely manner with its own proposals for the exercise of voting rights regarding each agenda item. In making these proposals, the credit institution shall act in the interest of the shareholder and have organisational arrangements in place to ensure that the institution's own interest from other operational divisions does not influence the proposals; the institution shall designate a member of the management responsible for supervising compliance with these duties as well as the proper exercise of the voting rights and its documentation. Together with its proposals, the credit institution is required to indicate that it will exercise the voting rights in line with these proposals unless the shareholder gives different instructions in due time. The credit institution shall specify if a member of the management board or an employee of the credit institution is a member of the supervisory board of the company, or a member of the management board or an employee of the company is a member of the supervisory board of the credit institution. The same obligation applies if the credit institution holds an interest in the company that has to be notified pursuant to § 21 of the Securities Trading Act or it is a member of an underwriting syndicate that has underwritten the last securities offering of the company in the past five years.

(3) If the shareholder has not given the credit institution any instructions on how to exercise the voting rights, the credit institution shall exercise such voting rights in the case of subsection 1, sentence 4, no. 1 in accordance with its own proposals, unless it is entitled to assume, in light of the circumstances, that the shareholder would approve the different exercise of the voting rights with full knowledge of the facts. If the credit institution deviates from a shareholder instruction or, in the absence of any shareholder instruction, from its own proposal in exercising the voting rights, it shall notify the shareholder and give reasons. In its own general meeting the authorized credit institution shall only exercise voting rights under the proxy if the shareholder has given an express instruction in respect of the individual items on the agenda. The same applies in the general meeting of a company if the credit institution holds directly or indirectly more than 20 percent of the legal capital of that company.

(4) A credit institution that intends to exercise voting rights in the general meeting on the basis of a proxy pursuant to subsection 1, sentence 4, no. 2 is required to furnish the

shareholders with the proposals of the management and supervisory boards, unless this is accomplished otherwise. Subsection 2, sentence 3 and subsection 3 sentences 1-3 shall apply accordingly.
(5) If the proxy permits, the credit institution may delegate authority to persons not employed by the credit institution. If the proxy does not provide otherwise, the credit institution exercises the voting rights in the name of the interested person.[436] If postal voting is permitted at the company, the authorized credit institution may make use of it. Notwithstanding further requirements for the exercise of voting rights provided for in the articles of association, proof of the authority to vote can be given in the form of a certificate pursuant to § 123(3) if the company is stock exchange listed.
(6) Without authorization, a credit institution shall not exercise voting rights of registered shares not owned by the credit institution but registered under its name in the share register. Subsections 1-5 shall apply to the authorization accordingly.
(7) The validity of votes cast shall not be affected by noncompliance with subsection 1, sentences 2-7 and subsections 2-6.
(8) Subsections 1-7 shall apply analogously to shareholders' associations and persons who professionally offer the exercise of voting rights in the general meeting as a service to shareholders; however, the foregoing shall not apply if the person intending to exercise voting rights is the legal representative, spouse, or unmarried partner of the shareholder or is related to the shareholder by birth or marriage up to the fourth degree.
(9) The liability of the credit institution to pay damages for the loss caused by a violation of subsections 1-6 cannot be excluded or limited in advance....

French Commercial Code[437]

Article L225-106

I. Shareholders may elect to be represented by another shareholder, their spouse or the partner with whom they are in a civil union.

They may also elect to be represented by any other natural or legal person of their choosing:

1 When the company's shares are admitted to trading on a regulated market;

2 When the company's shares are admitted to trading in a multilateral trading system subject to paragraph II of Article 433-3 of the Monetary and Financial Code under the conditions specified by the General Regulations of the Financial Markets Authority, shown on a list prepared by the authority in accordance with the conditions established by its General Regulations, and when the company's constitution so provides.

II. The proxy and, where appropriate, its revocation shall be in writing and sent to the company. The rules governing the application of this paragraph shall be specified by a Conseil d'Etat decree.

III. Before each general meeting, the president of the board of directors or the executive board, as the case may be, may organise a consultation with the shareholders mentioned in Article L. 225-102 to enable them to appoint one or more representatives to represent them at the meeting in accordance with the provisions of this Article.

This consultation is mandatory where, following the amendment of the constitution pursuant to Article L. 225-23 or Article L. 225-71, the ordinary general meeting is required to appoint to the board of directors or the supervisory board, as the case may be, one or more shareholder employees or members of the supervisory boards of the collective funds that hold the company's shares.

This consultation is also mandatory where an extraordinary general meeting is required to decide on an amendment to the constitution pursuant to Article L. 225-23 or Article L. 225-71.

Any clauses that conflict with the provisions of the preceding paragraphs shall be deemed unwritten.

For every recorded proxy of a shareholder without a pre-indicated proxy vote, the president of the general meeting shall vote in favour of adopting the draft resolutions submitted or approved by the board of directors or the executive board, as the case may be, and vote against the

436 [Footnote by authors.] Interested person is the beneficial owner.
437 Translation by Legifrance, https://www.legifrance.gouv.fr/Traductions/en-English/Legifrance-translations.

adoption of all other draft resolutions. To make any other vote, the shareholder must appoint a proxy who agrees to vote in the manner indicated by the principal.

Article L225-106-1

Where, in the cases set out in the third and fourth paragraphs of I of Article L. 225-106, shareholders elect to be represented by a person other than their spouse or partner with whom they are in a civil union, their proxy-holder shall inform them of any fact that allows them to assess the risk that the proxy-holder would pursue an interest other than their own. . . .

Article L225-106-2

Anyone who actively solicits proxies, by proposing directly or indirectly to one or more shareholders, in any form and by any means whatsoever, to receive proxy to represent them at the meeting of a company mentioned in the third and fourth paragraphs of Article L. 225-106, shall announce their voting policy.

That person can also announce their voting intentions on the draft resolutions presented to the shareholders. In that case, for any proxy received without voting instructions, the person shall vote consistently with the voting intentions announced.

The implementing provisions of this article shall be specified by a Conseil d'Etat decree.

1. *Proxy voting and proxy regulation*

Many shareholders, especially retail investors, will rarely attend a general meeting of the companies they invest in. They may either have a diverse investment portfolio so that it is impossible for them to attend all meetings of the companies in their portfolio, or their shareholding is so small that the difference that their presence might make will not compensate for the time and cost involved in attending the meeting. In order to ensure that even such shareholders can be represented at general meetings, legal systems may allow shareholders to appoint an agent to exercise their voting rights. This mechanism is called proxy voting. The instrument instructing the agent to vote on behalf of the shareholder is referred to as 'proxy' and the agent as 'proxy holder', or sometimes simply as 'proxy'. Proxy voting has for a long time been a common practice in many legal systems. However, in the past, the mechanism was often designed in a way that would effectively limit the shareholders' control over the proxy machinery and give the board of directors or credit institutions that held the issuer's shares in custody more influence over the company. For example, in the UK, the regulation of proxy voting was left to the articles until the Companies Act 1948, and in practice many companies did not allow the appointment of a proxy who was not a member of the company. The 1948 amendments provided for a statutory right to appoint another person as proxy, including someone who was not a member, and prohibited provisions in the articles that required the lodging of proxy forms more than forty-eight hours before a meeting.[438] However, the 1948 Act did not regulate the *process* of soliciting proxies by the management. It only imposed the requirement that proxy solicitations had to be sent to all members if they were issued at the company's expense.[439] Thus, the directors could set out their views on resolutions to be adopted by the general meeting in the proxy form, invite members to appoint a person affiliated with them as proxy, and incentivize the shareholders to return the proxy form by providing them with a prepaid and addressed envelope. This prompted commentators to observe that proxy voting, rather than encouraging shareholder democracy, 'helped to enhance the dictatorship of the board'.[440]

These tensions existed in many countries.[441] Legal systems employed different methods to limit the risk of abuse. Before adoption of the Shareholder Rights Directive, which we will

[438] 11 & 12 Geo. 6, c. 38, s 136. [439] ibid s 136(4).

[440] Davies and Worthington (n 12) para 15-67.

[441] The situation was different in Germany, as we will discuss below; see section C.II.3.

analyse in more detail in the next paragraphs, they often consisted in restricting the group of persons who were entitled to serve as proxy holders. For example, in France, only shareholders and spouses could be appointed as proxies (this restriction still exists for companies not listed on a regulated market[442]), and in Italy proxy holders could not represent more than ten shareholders (this rule also continues to be in force for non-listed companies, but since 2004 with an increased limit of twenty persons[443]).

Such rules met with criticism at the European level. It was felt that direct communication between shareholders and the company was difficult and the exercise of voting rights by shareholders cumbersome and costly, especially if the shareholders held shares in companies established in other jurisdictions. The High-level Group of Company Law Experts in their report of 2002, therefore, focussed on two issues: the statutory provision of the right to vote by proxy in all Member States, and the existence of facilities that allowed electronic access to meeting materials and proxy forms, for example on the company's website, and the electronic submission of proxies.[444] The recommendations of the High-level Group were implemented by the Shareholder Rights Directive.[445] The Directive requires Member States to ensure that shareholders of companies incorporated in a Member State and with shares admitted to trading on a regulated market within the EU have the right to appoint any natural or legal person as proxy holder.[446] This right can only be limited in order to address conflicts of interest between the proxy holder and the shareholder that may exist, for example, where the proxy holder is a director, controlling shareholder, or auditor of the company.[447] The Directive sets out the mechanisms that the Member States may employ to alleviate such conflicts of interest. The national legislator can impose disclosure obligations on the proxy holder, prohibit the proxy holder from acting without specific voting instructions by the shareholder, or restrict the transfer of the proxy.[448] Restrictions going beyond this list of permitted measures are prohibited, as are any limitations on the number of shareholders that a proxy holder may represent.[449]

As far as the second point is concerned that the High-level Group identified as requiring reform, electronic access to meeting materials and proxy forms, the Directive also brought a number of important innovations. For at least three weeks before the general meeting, companies have to make the agenda and all draft resolutions, including those proposed by shareholders, available on the company's website.[450] Proxy forms must be sent either directly to the shareholders or made available on the website, and the shareholders must be able to appoint proxy holders by electronic means.[451] In practice, many companies provide for facilities that allow shareholders to issue proxy and voting instructions directly on the company's website or download and email the proxy form. Nevertheless, the exercise of shareholder rights in a cross-border context continues to meet with obstacles. First of all, companies may have difficulties to identify who their shareholders are. This may be the case because the beneficial owner holds the shares through a chain of intermediaries and only the last link in this chain, the custodian company, appears on the company's share register.[452] In

[442] Com, Art L225-106-I(1). The old rules could be maintained for such companies because the Shareholder Rights Directive applies only to listed companies.

[443] Codice civile, Art 2372.

[444] Final Report of the High-level Group of Company Law Experts on a Modern Regulatory Framework for Company Law in Europe (November 2002) 49–53.

[445] See n 352 above.

[446] Directive 2007/36/EC, Art 10(1).

[447] The Directive also allows the imposition of certain requirements of a more formal nature, notably the limitation of the appointment of the proxy holder to a single meeting, ibid Art 10(2).

[448] ibid Art 10(3).

[449] ibid Art 10(5).

[450] ibid Art 5(4).

[451] ibid Art 13(1).

[452] This is the situation under English law. The custodian is the shareholder for purposes of company law, but the company's articles can provide that the beneficial owner shall be entitled to exercise all or certain rights of the members, Companies Act 2006, s 145(1). Furthermore, the position of the custodian is generally regarded as that of a trustee who holds the shares on trust for the beneficiary. The beneficiary, therefore, has the power under trust law to instruct the custodian how to exercise the rights. On the other hand, in the absence of an instruction, the

other legal systems, the shareholder may be seen as the legal owner even if the shareholding is intermediated, but the company may not have to maintain a register of shareholders, for example because it issues only bearer shares.[453] These problems are aggravated in an international setting where the holding chain crosses jurisdictional boundaries and the relationships between the parties in the chain are governed by different legal systems.[454] Secondly, even if the company was able to identify its shareholders, it was until recently uncertain whether information about meetings and resolutions would be passed on through the chain to the ultimate owner in a timely manner. While some legal systems required companies to inform intermediaries or the ultimate owner upon request, there was no general rule in the EU imposing the obligation on companies to ensure that their shareholders received relevant communications.[455] Thus, whether shareholders could effectively exercise their voting rights depended, in many cases, on the arrangements between the shareholder and the intermediary and on shareholders taking the initiative in order to obtain the necessary information.[456]

In 2017, the Shareholder Rights Directive was amended to address the fragmented legal situation in Europe.[457] The amended Directive requires all Member States to establish a legal mechanism enabling companies to request information including the name and contact details of their shareholders from intermediaries, irrespective of the type of share—registered or bearer—that they issue. In custody chains the request will be passed up the chain and all intermediaries are under an obligation to transmit the relevant information back to the company.[458] However, Member States may restrict the identification obligation to shareholders holding more than a certain percentage of shares or voting rights (not exceeding 0.5 per cent), thus calling into question the effectiveness of the amendments where the exercise of shareholder rights is most problematic, namely in companies with small, dispersed shareholders. Furthermore, companies are free to decide not to engage in direct communication with their shareholders. In this case, the amended Directive provides that the intermediary is responsible for delivering the information necessary to exercise voting rights to the shareholders.[459] Finally, the third building block facilitating the participation of investors in the governance of the company deals with the actual exercise of the shareholder's voting rights. Again, the intermediary plays a central role. It must either make

trustee is under no obligation to consult the beneficiary. The trustee can exercise the rights in his or her discretion in the best interests of the beneficiary; see *Kirby v Wilkins* [1929] 2 Ch 444.

[453] This is the case in Germany, where stock corporations are only required to maintain a shareholder register if they issue registered shares, AktG, §67. Registered shares have become more popular among large listed companies over the last 10–15 years, because it was felt that the share register facilitated communication with the shareholders.

[454] For an example of a case where the shareholders themselves seem to have been mistaken about who was entitled to exercise shareholder rights, see *Eckerle v Wickeder Westfalenstahl GmbH* [2013] EWHC 68 (Ch). This decision is discussed by E Micheler, 'Intermediated Securities and Legal Certainty', *LSE Law, Society and Economy Working Papers* 3/2014, 4–7.

[455] The legal situation is currently still different from country to country until implementation of the revisions to the Shareholder Rights Directive (to be discussed presently). In the UK, registered members who hold shares in listed companies on behalf of another person may nominate that person to enjoy the information rights of members (Companies Act 2006, ss 146–151). In Germany, companies are required to send the notice of a general meeting to all shareholders on the share register, as well as credit institutions and shareholder associations that exercised voting rights on behalf of shareholders in the last general meeting (AktG, §125). Credit institutions, in turn, have to forward the communications to their clients who are the ultimate owners if the clients are not known to the company, for example because the credit institution is the registered shareholder (AktG, §128). In France, companies have the right to request the central custodian (if bearer shares have been issued) or the registered intermediary (in the case of registered shares) to provide them with the names, nationality, and addresses of their shareholders (Com, Arts L228-1 to L228-3). The board of directors must then make all documents available to the shareholders that are necessary to enable them to make an informed decision at the general meeting (Com, Art L225-108). For a broad comparative overview of the rules in other countries, see T2S Taskforce on Shareholder Transparency, Market Analysis of Shareholder Transparency Regimes in Europe (2011).

[456] Impact Assessment accompanying the Proposal for a Directive amending the Shareholder Rights Directive, SWD(2014) 127 final, 34–6.

[457] Directive (EU) 2017/828 (n 283). [458] Directive 2007/36/EC, Art 3a. [459] ibid Art 3b.

the necessary arrangements for shareholders to exercise their voting rights, or exercise them on behalf of the shareholders. The shareholders must be given, at least upon request, confirmation that their votes have been recorded and counted by the company.[460] The Directive leaves some discretion to the Member States in how these requirements are to be implemented, but it is clear that intermediaries will have to take responsibility for the receipt and submission of proxy forms and shareholder instructions.

A second potential shortcoming of the Shareholder Rights Directive, not addressed by the amendments, is the fact that management retains a certain preponderance in the proxy voting process in many countries despite the prescriptive rules of the Directive. In France, shareholders are able to grant a general proxy (so-called *pouvoir en blanc*) that does not designate a nominee or set out voting instructions. If they make use of this possibility, the Commercial Code provides that the chairman of the general meeting shall cast the votes in favour of resolutions submitted or approved by the management, and against resolutions submitted by anyone else.[461] In the UK, the managers are still allowed to solicit proxies at the company's expense. As under the Act of 1948, the Companies Act 2006 does not regulate the form of the solicitation or the content of proxy statements. The only safeguard provided by the law, which is in this regard identical to the 1948 Act, is the requirement that the invitation must be issued to all members entitled to vote if the company pays for it.[462] The strategic disadvantages of shareholders are somewhat ameliorated—although not eliminated—by two mechanisms. First, shareholders representing at least 5 per cent of the voting rights, or at least 100 members, can request that the company circulate statements relating to matters to be dealt with at the general meeting at the company's expense, unless the request constitutes an abuse of rights.[463] Minority shareholders holding a sufficient number of voting shares can, therefore, react to the management's proxy solicitation and present their views on resolutions proposed by the directors.[464] Secondly, the FCA's listing rules require proxy forms of listed companies to provide for three-way voting (for, against, and abstain) and to state explicitly that the proxy holder will exercise voting rights in his or her discretion if the proxy form is returned without indicating the shareholder's preferences.[465]

In the two jurisdictions not yet discussed in detail, the United States and Germany, the basic problems of proxy voting are similar. However, for different reasons, proxy voting arrangements prevalent in practice and approaches to regulating them are distinct and have triggered a considerable amount of debate and litigation. We will therefore examine both jurisdictions in more detail, beginning with the United States.

2. *The US model: managers as proxy holders*

Regulating the voting rights of shareholders, as an integral feature of corporate governance, is a matter of state law. State corporation laws, however, are often somewhat perfunctory in their regulation of proxy voting. They commonly only stipulate that shareholders shall be authorized to appoint another person as proxy holder, and maybe prescribe the manner in which such authorization can be effected.[466] The vast majority of proxy regulation in the United States is federal law, enacted by the SEC under Section 14 of the Securities Exchange Act 1934. During the deliberations that led to the adoption of the 1934 Act, the legislator noted that the extant rules of company law offered shareholders little protection against the 'promiscuous solicitation of their proxies, on the one hand by irresponsible outsiders seeking to wrest control of the corporation away from honest and conscientious officials; on the other hand by unscrupulous corporate officials seeking to retain control of the management by concealing

[460] ibid Art 3c.
[461] Com, Art L225-106-III(5). [462] Companies Act, s 326. [463] ibid ss 314–317.
[464] Minority shareholders of public companies can, of course, also request the company to circulate their own resolutions (and if the company is listed other matters) pursuant to ss 338–340B Companies Act 2006.
[465] LR 9.3.6R. [466] See eg Del. Gen. Corp. Law, §212(b), (c).

or distorting facts'.[467] Both the provisions in the 1934 Act and the rules and regulations promulgated subsequently by the SEC, therefore, pursue a twofold objective: They seek to protect the integrity of the voting process from outside interference and prohibit false or misleading statements or other fraudulent acts in connection with the solicitation of proxies.[468]

Proxy regulation in the United States now constitutes a veritable body of rules, known as Regulation 14A and Schedule 14A, which implement and amplify Section 14(a) of the Securities Exchange Act.[469] The rules can best be understood by distinguishing between three issues that arise when proxies are solicited. First, whenever the management or shareholders engage in a proxy solicitation, they are required to disclose comprehensive information on the matters to be voted on. The proxy rules set out what has to be disclosed. Secondly, if the disclosures contain incorrect information or omit material facts, shareholders have, under certain conditions, a private cause of action against those who are responsible for the misinformation. Thirdly, in many cases, shareholders will not want to mount a proxy contest using their own proxy materials, for example in order to elect a competing slate of directors, but seek to be included in the company's annual proxy solicitation. The question is then whether the company is required to include the shareholder's proposals in its proxy materials and circulate them at the company's expense to all shareholders. We will deal with the three issues in turn.

(1) The proxy rules apply to every solicitation of a proxy registered pursuant to the Securities Exchange Act of 1934.[470] The SEC's rules define 'solicitation' broadly as '[a]ny request for a proxy' and '[t]he furnishing of a form of proxy or other communication to security holders under circumstances reasonably calculated to result in the procurement, withholding or revocation of a proxy'.[471] This wide formulation, especially the reference to any 'other communication', creates legal uncertainty, and the boundaries between permissible communications among and with shareholders and impermissible statements intended to condition the shareholders with a view to a future solicitation are not always clear. It has been held that communications not involving any authorization to exercise voting rights nevertheless fall within the scope of the proxy rules if they are 'part of "a continuous plan" intended to end in solicitation'[472] or they are designed, and can reasonably be expected, to influence the voting decisions of shareholders.[473] On the other hand, the SEC is mindful that the effective exercise of shareholder rights requires communication and coordination among shareholders without incurring undue regulatory costs. Therefore, the unilateral announcement by shareholders of how they intend to vote is not subject to the information and filing requirements of the proxy rules.[474] Furthermore, the proxy rules provide for an exemption for communications by shareholders (not the issuer or an officer or director of the issuer, if the communication is financed by the issuer), provided they do not seek, directly

[467] S. Rep. No. 1455, 73d Cong., 2d Sess. 77 (1934).

[468] See, in particular, Exchange Act Rule 14a-9.

[469] 17 CFR §240.14a-1 to §240.14b-2 and 17 CFR 240.14a-101. Further regulations implement the other subsections of s 14(a) Securities Exchange Act, notably Regulations 14D and 14E the rules governing tender offers.

[470] Securities Exchange Act 1934, s 12.

[471] Exchange Act Rule 14a-1(l)(1).

[472] *Studebaker Corp. v Gittlin*, 360 F.2d 692, 696 (2d Cir. 1966) (dealing with the solicitation of authorizations sufficient to meet the 5% threshold required under New York company law for an inspection of the stockholders list).

[473] *Long Island Lighting Co. v Barbash*, 779 F.2d 793, 796 (2d Cir. 1985) (holding that '[t]he question in every case is whether the challenged communication, seen in the totality of circumstances, is "reasonably calculated" to influence the shareholders' votes'); *Shoen v AMERCO* (n 223) 1345 (holding that a two-page notice contained in the monthly company newsletter constituted a 'solicitation' within the meaning of the proxy rules because it forcefully encouraged the shareholders to support the recommendations of the incumbent directors).

[474] *Regulation of Communications among Shareholders*, SEC Exchange Act Release No. 34-31326 (16 October 1992) 52 S.E.C. Docket 2028, 14–15. Exchange Act Rule 14a-1(l)(2)(iv) now provides for a safe harbour, inter alia, for voting announcements that are published, broadcast or otherwise disseminated to the media. For an analysis of the 1992 reforms, see JC Coffee, Jr, 'The SEC and the Institutional Investor: A Half-Time Report' (1994) 15 Cardozo Law Review 837 (reporting estimates of a shareholder association that the costs of targeting the 1,000 largest shareholders of a corporation fell from US$1 million for a full scale proxy statement to US$5,000–US$10,000 after the 1992 reforms: ibid at 841).

or indirectly, the power to act as proxy.[475] This exemption is of particular importance in encouraging discussion among institutional investors and, thus, facilitating shareholder engagement.[476]

If the communication falls within the scope of the proxy rules, each person solicited must be furnished with a proxy statement drawn up in the prescribed form and containing the information set out in Schedule 14A.[477] The proxy rules also specify the form of the proxy itself, which has to provide for a three-way choice between approval, disapproval, or abstention with respect to each separate matter to be voted upon.[478] In most cases, the proxy statement and form of proxy must be filed with the SEC at least ten days prior to their delivery to the shareholders.[479] The proxy rules seek to ensure that shareholders are comprehensively informed about all facts that may be of relevance to their decision how to vote. Thus, Schedule 14A requires not only disclosure of the particulars of the general meeting, the persons making the solicitation, and the mechanisms of granting proxy, but also of any circumstances that may give rise to a conflict of interest on the part of those who solicit the proxy. For example, any direct or indirect interest of the directors or officers of the issuer, or any other person who sponsors or finances the solicitation, in the matters to be acted upon must be described in the statement.[480] Management's proxy statements must also disclose the compensation of the directors and executive officers if the general meeting is to decide on the election of directors or compensation-related matters[481] and contain information on the issuer's auditors.[482] Other required information includes a description of significant transactions that shareholders will vote upon, for example mergers, consolidations, issues of securities, or property transactions, in each case accompanied by financial statements,[483] reasons for any amendment to the articles,[484] and an explanation of applicable voting procedures.[485]

(2) Given the scope and level of detail of the disclosure obligations, it is not surprising that legal disagreements have arisen about the compliance of proxy solicitations with the disclosure rules. The SEC has used its wide authority under Section 14(a) Securities Exchange Act to adopt a broad prohibition, Rule 14a-9, which outlaws the use of proxy statements that contain false or misleading information concerning material facts or fail to state any material fact. If a management or shareholder solicitation is incorrect or incomplete, the SEC can bring a claim for injunctive relief and request the court to order that corrective disclosures are made, a new meeting is held, or, if possible, the *status quo* prior to the tainted shareholder vote is restored.[486]

On a literal reading, Rule 14a-9 provides for no express private cause of action. However, the courts were prepared to imply a private cause of action to facilitate enforcement of the prohibition and protect stockholders who suffered an injury resulting from a violation of the proxy rules. In *J.I. Case Co. v Borak*,[487] the US Supreme Court explained:

> Private enforcement of the proxy rules provides a necessary supplement to Commission action. As in anti-trust treble damage litigation, the possibility of civil damages or injunctive relief serves as a most effective weapon in the enforcement of the proxy requirements. The Commission advises that it examines over 2,000 proxy statements annually and each of them must necessarily be expedited. Time does not permit an independent examination of the facts set out in the proxy material and this results in the Commission's acceptance of the representations contained

[475] Exchange Act Rule 14a-2(b)(1).

[476] However, if shareholders avail themselves of the exemption they are precluded from soliciting proxies regarding a matter that was the subject of the exempt solicitation throughout the soliciting period, SEC Exchange Act Release No 34-31326 (n 474) 12.

[477] Exchange Act Rule 14a-3. [478] ibid Rule 14a-4. [479] ibid Rule 14a-6.

[480] Schedule 14A, item 5. [481] ibid item 8. [482] ibid item 9. [483] ibid items 11–15.

[484] ibid item 19. [485] ibid item 21.

[486] An example of the latter type of relief is *Crouch v Prior*, 905 F. Supp. 248 (D. Vi. 1995) (reinstating a former board member and officers ousted from the corporation following a proxy solicitation containing material misstatements).

[487] 377 U.S. 426 (1964).

> therein at their face value, unless contrary to other material on file with it … We, therefore, believe that … it is the duty of the courts to be alert to provide such remedies as are necessary to make effective the congressional purpose.[488]

A plaintiff wo seeks recovery under Rule 14a-9 must (1) have standing to bring a claim; (2) show that the proxy materials contained a material misstatement or omission of a material fact; (3) the defendant acted with negligence; and (4) the plaintiff suffered a loss as a result of the misstatement. In the following leading case on the interpretation of Rule 14a-9, the Supreme Court addressed several of these requirements.

***Mills v. Electric Auto-Lite Co.*, 396 U.S. 375 (1970)**

Harlan, Justice:

Petitioners were shareholders of the Electric Auto-Lite Company until 1963, when it was merged into Mergenthaler Linotype Company. They brought suit on the day before the shareholders' meeting at which the vote was to take place on the merger against Auto-Lite, Mergenthaler, and a third company, American Manufacturing Company, Inc. The complaint sought an injunction against the voting by Auto-Lite's management of all proxies obtained by means of an allegedly misleading proxy solicitation; however, it did not seek a temporary restraining order, and the voting went ahead as scheduled the following day. Several months later petitioners filed an amended complaint, seeking to have the merger set aside and to obtain such other relief as might be proper.

In Count II of the amended complaint, which is the only count before us, petitioners predicated jurisdiction on s 27 of the 1934 Act. They alleged that the proxy statement sent out by the Auto-Lite management to solicit shareholders' votes in favor of the merger was misleading, in violation of s 14(a) of the Act and SEC Rule 14a-9 thereunder. Petitioners recited that before the merger Mergenthaler owned over 50% of the outstanding shares of Auto-Lite common stock, and had been in control of Auto-Lite for two years. American Manufacturing in turn owned about one-third of the outstanding shares of Mergenthaler, and for two years had been in voting control of Mergenthaler and, through it, of Auto-Lite. Petitioners charged that in light of these circumstances the proxy statement was misleading in that it told Auto-Lite shareholders that their board of directors recommended approval of the merger without also informing them that all 11 of Auto-Lite's directors were nominees of Mergenthaler and were under the 'control and domination of Mergenthaler'. Petitioners asserted the right to complain of this alleged violation both derivatively on behalf of Auto-Lite and as representatives of the class of all its minority shareholders …

Where the misstatement or omission in a proxy statement has been shown to be 'material,' as it was found to be here, that determination itself indubitably embodies a conclusion that the defect was of such a character that it might have been considered important by a reasonable shareholder who was in the process of deciding how to vote. This requirement that the defect have a significant propensity to affect the voting process is found in the express terms of Rule 14a-9, and it adequately serves the purpose of ensuring that a cause of action cannot be established by proof of a defect so trivial, or so unrelated to the transaction for which approval is sought, that correction of the defect or imposition of liability would not further the interests protected by s 14(a).

There is no need to supplement this requirement, as did the Court of Appeals, with a requirement of proof of whether the defect actually had a decisive effect on the voting. Where there has been a finding of materiality, a shareholder has made a sufficient showing of causal relationship between the violation and the injury for which he seeks redress if, as here, he proves that the proxy solicitation itself, rather than the particular defect in the solicitation materials, was an essential link in the accomplishment of the transaction. This objective test will avoid the impracticalities of determining how many votes were affected, and, by resolving doubts in favor of those the statute is designed to protect, will effectuate the congressional policy of ensuring that the shareholders are able to make an informed choice when they are consulted on corporate transactions …

Our conclusion that petitioners have established their case by showing that proxies necessary to approval of the merger were obtained by means of a materially misleading solicitation

[488] ibid 432–3.

implies nothing about the form of relief to which they may be entitled. We held in *Borak* that upon finding a violation the courts were 'to be alert to provide such remedies as are necessary to make effective the congressional purpose,' noting specifically that such remedies are not to be limited to prospective relief. 377 U.S., at 433, 434, 84 S.Ct. at 1560. In devising retrospective relief for violation of the proxy rules, the federal courts should consider the same factors that would govern the relief granted for any similar illegality or fraud. One important factor may be the fairness of the terms of the merger. Possible forms of relief will include setting aside the merger or granting other equitable relief, but, as the Court of Appeals below noted, nothing in the statutory policy 'requires the court to unscramble a corporate transaction merely because a violation occurred'. 403 F.2d, at 436. In selecting a remedy the lower courts should exercise 'the sound discretion which guides the determinations of courts of equity', keeping in mind the role of equity as 'the instrument for nice adjustment and reconciliation between the public interest and private needs as well as between competing private claims'. *Hecht Co. v. Bowles*, 321 U.S. 321, 329—330, 64 S.Ct. 587, 591—592, 88 L.Ed. 754 (1944), quoting from *Meredith v. Winter Haven*, 320 U.S. 228, 235, 64 S.Ct. 7, 11, 88 L.Ed. 9 (1943) ...

Questions and comments:

1. The holding in *Mills v. Electric Auto-Lite* is remarkable in that the Supreme Court establishes relatively lenient requirements to bring an action under Rule 14a-9, especially if compared with another famous implied right of action, Exchange Act Rule 10b-5. Rule 10b-5, adopted under Section 10(b) of the Securities Act of 1933, prohibits the use of 'any device, scheme, or artifice to defraud, ... [making] any untrue statement of a material fact ... [or engaging] in any act, practice, or course of business which operates or would operate as a fraud or deceit upon any person'. The provision has been interpreted as a 'catch-all clause to prevent manipulative devices'[489] that can be used as a private cause of action to claim damages, for example, from those who make misrepresentations to the public in connection with a securities transaction or trade on the basis of inside information.[490] The cause of action requires that the defendant acted knowingly or recklessly (scienter) and there was a causal link between the prohibited conduct and the purchase or sale of a security by the plaintiff.[491] An action for proxy fraud, on the other hand, can be brought by any shareholder whose votes were solicited by means of the allegedly incorrect proxy statement. It is not necessary that the shareholder actually did provide the proxy, and certainly not that the shareholder was prompted by the misrepresentation to purchase or sell shares, as in Rule 10b-5 cases. Further, the plaintiff is not required to show scienter on the part of the defendant. In contrast to an action under Rule 10b-5, it is sufficient that those who made the misstatement or failed to disclose a material fact were negligent. While Rules 10b-5 and 14a-9 are phrased similarly, the reason for the different interpretation can be seen in the more limited

[489] *Ernst & Ernst v Hochfelder*, 425 U.S. 185 (US 1976), quoting Hearings on H.R. 7852 and H.R. 8720 before the House Committee on Interstate and Foreign Commerce, 73d Cong., 2d Sess., 115 (1934).

[490] Rule 10b-5 was first recognized as a private cause of action in *Kardon v National Gypsum Co.*, 69 F. Supp. 512 (D.C. Pa. 1946).

[491] *Ernst & Ernst v Hochfelder* (n 489) 197: 'Section 10(b) makes unlawful the use or employment of "any manipulative or deceptive device or contrivance" in contravention of Commission rules. The words "manipulative or deceptive" used in conjunction with "device or contrivance" strongly suggest that s 10(b) was intended to proscribe knowing or intentional misconduct.' Later cases held that recklessness was a form of intentional conduct satisfying the standard of *Ernst & Ernst v Hochfelder*. Recklessness has been defined as conduct involving 'not merely simple or even inexcusable negligence, but an extreme departure from the standards of ordinary care ... that present[s] a danger of misleading buyers or sellers which is either known to the defendant or is so obvious that the defendant must have been aware of it', *Broad v Rockwell Intern. Corp.*, 642 F.2d 929, 961-962 (5th Cir. 1981). Similar *Hollinger v Titan Capital Corp.*, 914 F.2d 1564, 1569 (9th Cir. 1990); *Sundstrand Corp. v Sun Chem. Corp.*, 553 F.2d 1033, 1045 (7th Cir. 1977). The causality requirement is modified in actions for damages against a defendant trading on inside information. Section 20A(a) of the Securities Exchange Act 1934 provides that a person engaging in insider trading shall be liable 'to any person who, contemporaneously with the purchase or sale of securities that is the subject of [a violation of the insider trading rules], has purchased (where such violation is based on a sale of securities) or sold (where such violation is based on a purchase of securities) securities of the same class'.

rulemaking authority granted to the SEC under §10(b) Securities Exchange Act. The reference in Section10(b) to a 'manipulative or deceptive' device has been interpreted as implying an element of fraud,[492] whereas §14(a) simply speaks of the 'contravention of such rules and regulations as the Commission may prescribe as necessary or appropriate in the public interest or for the protection of investors'.[493]

2. Another difference to Rule 10b-5 is the approach to causation taken by the court in *Mills*. In traditional common law fraud cases, the misrepresentation must have caused another party to act in reliance on a material incorrect statement. Rule 10b-5 is no different in this respect. The plaintiff is required to show that he relied on the incorrect disclosure in deciding to purchase or sell securities.[494] In *Mills*, however, the court seems to conflate the two elements of materiality and reliance. The Court of Appeals in the proceedings had held that liability under Rule 14a-9 required that the misleading statement had caused the submission of sufficient proxies for the proposal to pass. Since it would be close to impossible for plaintiffs in companies with a large number of shareholders to provide evidence that the misstatement had influenced enough shareholders to vote in favour of the proposal, the Court of Appeals introduced a presumption of reliance. The presumption could be rebutted by the defendants if they showed that the transaction was fair to the minority shareholders. In this case, courts were 'justified in concluding that a sufficient number of shareholders would have approved the [transaction] had there been no deficiency in the proxy statement'.[495] The Supreme Court considered this approach to be too restrictive. The court was concerned that shareholders could easily be bypassed, since a 'judicial appraisal of the merger's merits could be substituted for the actual and informed vote of the stockholders'.[496] As a consequence of the Court of Appeals' approach, an entire category of proxy violations would be insulated from private redress, namely misrepresentations that did not relate to the terms of a transaction.[497]

   However, the test proposed by the Supreme Court in place of the traditional reliance requirement is by no means clear. The court holds that 'where there has been a finding of materiality, a shareholder has made a sufficient showing of causal relationship between the violation and the injury for which he seeks redress if, as here, he proves that the proxy solicitation itself, rather than the particular defect in the solicitation materials, was an essential

[492] *Chiarella v United States*, 445 U.S. 222, 235 (1980): 'Section 10(b) is aptly described as a catch-all provision, but what it catches must be fraud.' See also the quote from *Ernst & Ernst v Hochfelder* (n 489).

[493] *Gerstle v Gamble-Skogmo, Inc.*, 478 F.2d 1281, 1299 (2d Cir. 1973).

[494] Case law has developed a presumption of reliance, known as the 'fraud on the market' theory, which allows plaintiffs to argue that they relied on the integrity of the market price of a security without having acted on, or been aware of, the misstatement, for example incorrect information contained in an offering prospectus. The market price of a security is assumed to reflect all publicly available information in an efficient market and hence also the defendant's misrepresentation. The consequence is that the burden of proof shifts to the defendant to show that the plaintiff would have traded irrespective of the market price, for example because of antitrust problems or political pressure to divest from shares of certain businesses, or the misrepresentation did not actually affect the market price of the stock, *Basic Inc. v Levinson*, 485 U.S. 224 (US 1988). The assumptions underlying the fraud-on-the-market theory, in particular the question whether and when markets are sufficiently informationally efficient to price in (mis-)statements, has remained controversial since *Basic*. The Supreme Court assessed recent empirical evidence from behavioural finance and reaffirmed the fraud-on-the-market theory in *Halliburton Co. v Erica P. John Fund, Inc.*, 573 U.S. 258 (US 2014). The court distinguished between two types of market efficiency: fundamental efficiency, which requires that information is *correctly* and *completely* reflected in securities prices, that is, market prices do not underreact or overreact to news, and informational efficiency, which simply holds that public disclosures have *some* effect on securities prices. Whether markets are efficient in the former sense of the term has been called into question by research in finance, see, for example, RJ Shiller, 'Do stock prices move too much to be justified by subsequent changes in dividends?' (1981) 71 American Economic Review 421. However, the presumption in *Basic*, the Supreme Court explained, was based on the latter type of efficiency: 'Halliburton's criticisms fail to take *Basic* on its own terms. Halliburton focuses on the debate among economists about the degree to which the market price of a company's stock reflects public information about the company—and thus the degree to which an investor can earn an abnormal, above-market return by trading on such information.... The academic debates discussed by Halliburton have not refuted the modest premise underlying the presumption of reliance. Even the foremost critics of the efficient-capital-markets hypothesis acknowledge that public information generally affects stock prices.... Debates about the precise *degree* to which stock prices accurately reflect public information are thus largely beside the point. "That the ... price [of a stock] may be inaccurate does not detract from the fact that false statements affect it, and cause loss," which is "all that *Basic* requires." *Schleicher v. Wendt*, 618 F.3d 679, 685 (C.A.7 2010)': ibid 271–2.

[495] *Mills*, 396 U.S. at 380. [496] ibid 381. [497] ibid 382.

link in the accomplishment of the transaction'.[498] The crucial question here is what constitutes an 'essential link' between the proxy solicitation and the transaction. This question was addressed two decades after *Mills* in *Virginia Bankshares, Inc. v Sandberg*.[499] The case dealt with the freeze-out merger of a subsidiary of Virginia Bankshares, Inc. into the parent company. Virginia law required only the circulation of a statement of information to the shareholders, but the directors solicited proxies, stating in the proxy materials that 'they had approved the plan because of its opportunity for the minority shareholders to achieve a "high" value'.[500] This statement was found to be misleading on the ground that Virginia Bankshare's stock had not been valued correctly and the directors had not recommended the merger because of the high value to be received by the minority shareholders, but because they sought to retain their seats on the board.

Ultimately, the Supreme Court rejected the claims because it did not find an essential link between the solicitation of the proxies and the implementation of the transaction. As opposed to *Mills*, the votes of the minority shareholders were not needed to authorize the merger, since the parent company held the majority of voting rights required under state corporate law. However, this did not end the enquiry. The plaintiffs argued that the proxy solicitation was 'essential' because the vote of the minority shareholders foreclosed remedies they had under state law. The Supreme Court agreed in principle with this line of reasoning. It suggested in obiter that an essential link existed if the proxy solicitation was 'a step in the process of barring a class of shareholders from resort to a state remedy otherwise available'.[501] This would be the case, for example, if minority shareholders were induced by the misleading proxy statement to approve a merger and, as a consequence, forfeited the right to seek appraisal of their shares, or they were enjoined from challenging the validity of a transaction that was tainted by a conflict of interest. In the present case, the approval of the merger, however, did not lead to the forfeiture of any minority rights under state law. The applicable Virginia merger statute did not provide for an appraisal right of dissenting shareholders. Moreover, state law prevented shareholders from challenging a conflicted transaction only if they had ratified the transaction after full disclosure of all material facts.[502] Later decisions of federal courts relied on the Supreme Court's obiter dictum in holding that the loss of a state law remedy was sufficient to establish the required essential link.[503]

3. The standard definition of materiality was formulated by the Supreme Court in the landmark case *TSC Industries, Inc. v. Northway, Inc.*[504] The court established a so-called 'total mix of information test', which is relevant in different contexts when US securities regulation speaks of 'material facts', including in Rule 14a-9 and Rule 10b-5 cases. Following *TSC Industries*, the courts ask whether there is 'a substantial likelihood that a reasonable shareholder would consider [the incorrect or omitted fact] important in deciding how to vote ... [and] the omitted fact would have assumed actual significance in the deliberations of the reasonable shareholder'. In other words, 'there must be a substantial likelihood that the disclosure of the omitted fact would have been viewed by the reasonable investor as having significantly altered the "total mix" of information made available'.[505]
4. Often, plaintiffs in Rule 14a-9 cases seek prospective relief in the form of an injunction enjoining the use of the misleading proxy statement and any proxies thus far solicited. If necessary, the court may also order that the general meeting be postponed in order to allow sufficient time to resolicit proxies.[506] In other cases (as in *Mills v. Electric Auto-Lite*), it may be too late for an injunction. Plaintiffs will then either seek to have the transaction that was the subject of the challenged vote set aside or claim damages. Courts are understandably reluctant to reverse a transaction that has already been implemented, although they have done so in some cases. The Supreme Court in *Mills v. Electric Auto-Lite* explains the factors that courts will take into consideration:

[498] ibid 385. [499] 501 U.S. 1083 (1991). [500] ibid 1088. [501] ibid 1106.
[502] ibid 1107–8.
[503] For example, *Howing Co. v Nationwide Corp.*, 972 F.2d 700 (6th Cir. 1992); *Wilson v Great American Industries, Inc.*, 979 F.2d 924 (2d Cir. 1992).
[504] 426 U.S. 438 (1976). [505] ibid 449. [506] *SEC v May*, 229 F.2d 123 (2d Cir. 1956).

> [A] determination of what relief should be granted in Auto-Lite's name must hinge on whether setting aside the merger would be in the best interests of the shareholders as a whole. In short … the merger should be set aside only if a court of equity concludes, from all the circumstances, that it would be equitable to do so.[507]
>
> It is potentially more promising for plaintiffs to seek monetary relief, provided they are able to show that they suffered a loss: Where the defect in the proxy solicitation relates to the specific terms of the merger, the district court might appropriately order an accounting to ensure that the shareholders receive the value that was represented as coming to them. On the other hand, where, as here, the misleading aspect of the solicitation did not relate to terms of the merger, monetary relief might be afforded to the shareholders only if the merger resulted in a reduction of the earnings or earnings potential of their holdings. In short, damages should be recoverable only to the extent that they can be shown. If commingling of the assets and operations of the merged companies makes it impossible to establish direct injury from the merger, relief might be predicated on a determination of the fairness of the terms of the merger at the time it was approved.[508]

(3) The third question, whether the company is required to include shareholder proposals in its proxy materials, thus saving the shareholders the costs of printing and mailing their own proxy statements, is addressed by Rule 14a-8, the so-called 'town meeting rule'. Shareholder proposals are often used to advance corporate social responsibility and corporate governance issues. Typical corporate social responsibility issues include climate change, product safety, disclosure of corporate lobbying and political spending, and employment discrimination.[509] Although these resolutions receive rarely more than 5 per cent of the votes, they heighten awareness of social issues, and it is not uncommon that they lead to negotiations with management and concrete steps to change corporate policy. Corporate governance proposals generally garner more interest and support from shareholders. Topics that regularly receive substantial support deal with proxy access, board declassification, majority voting in director elections, and the elimination of supermajority vote requirements.[510] Especially the first type of proposal, seeking to amend the company's constitution to allow shareholders access to the company's proxy statement in order to nominate their own candidates for the board of directors, has become more important in recent years. This development was triggered by a rule adopted by the SEC in 2010, Rule 14a-11. This rule required companies to include shareholder nominees for director elections in their proxy materials if candidates were put forward by shareholders holding at least 3 per cent of the voting rights for a minimum of three years.[511] Only one year later, Rule 14a-11 was invalidated by the US Court of Appeals for the DC Circuit because the SEC had failed 'adequately to assess the economic effects' of the rule.[512] In reaction to the decision, shareholders began to submit proposals under the town meeting rule, Rule 14a-8, requesting that companies amend their governing documents to provide for proxy access. Proxy advisory firms often look favourably at these proposals. For example, ISS recommends a vote in favour of mechanisms granting proxy access

[507] *Mills*, 396 U.S. at 388. [508] ibid 388–9.

[509] A good overview of shareholder activism in the field of corporate social responsibility is given by the Interfaith Center on Corporate Responsibility (ICCR), 2018 Proxy Resolutions and Voting Guide, available at http://www.iccr.org(follow hyperlink 'Corporate Engagements'). The ICCR is an umbrella organization that brings together faith-based institutions, socially responsible asset management companies, unions, pension funds, and universities seeking to engage with corporations on environmental and social issues. Each year, ICCR members file several hundred shareholder resolutions, representing more than 80% of all social issue shareholder resolutions submitted to American companies.

[510] Data is collected by Institutional Shareholder Services (ISS). For an overview of recent trends, see the ISS Market Reviews, http://www.issgovernance.com (follow hyperlink 'Governance Exchange: Market Reviews').

[511] *Facilitating Shareholder Director Nominations*, SEC Exchange Act Release Nos 33-9136; 34-62764 (25 August 2010), 99 S.E.C. Docket 694, 99 S.E.C. Docket 439. For a discussion of the rule see LA Bebchuk and S Hirst, 'Private Ordering and the Proxy Access Debate' (2010) 65 Business Law 329.

[512] *Business Roundtable v SEC*, 647 F.3d 1144, 1148 (D.C. Cir. 2011).

if the proposal mirrors Rule 14a-11, that is, if it contains the same ownership threshold and ownership duration requirements and caps the number of shareholder nominees at 25 per cent of all board positions.[513] Because of the support from proxy advisory firms, these proposals are comparatively successful and passed frequently.

Shareholders are eligible to submit proposals under Rule 14a-8 if they have continuously held at least US$2,000 or 1 per cent of the company's securities for at least one year.[514] Proposals can relate, in principle, to any issue that the company can lawfully act on,[515] not only actions falling within the powers of the general meeting.[516] The rationale for this interpretation of the proxy rules can be found in an old decision of the Court of Appeals of New York, *Auer v. Dressel*.[517] In this decision, the court held that shareholders had the right to issue advisory resolutions requesting the directors to take specified actions.[518] Thus, even if shareholders do not have the power to adopt the desired change directly, the company cannot exclude a proposal if it is formulated as a recommendation or request.[519] Typically, proposals therefore start with a phrase such as: 'RESOLVED, that the shareholders of XYZ Company hereby request that the company/the board of directors ... '. Of course, such a proposal, if adopted, is not binding on the board, and the directors may decide that the company's interests are better served by not implementing the requested action. If they do so, their decision is subject to review pursuant to general fiduciary standards. In most cases, this means that shareholders will only be able to challenge the decision if it falls outside the bounds of the business judgment rule.[520]

If the directors disagree with the shareholder proposal, they may decide that it is in the company's best interest to refuse the inclusion of the proposal in the company's proxy statement. Rule 14a-8(i) lists the situations in which the company is entitled to exclude a shareholder proposal, even though it is submitted following the proper procedural steps. In practice, a company that intends to omit a shareholder proposal will request a 'no-action' letter from the SEC confirming that the SEC will take no legal action against the corporation. The shareholders, in turn, are able to challenge the no-action letter by filing a lawsuit against the corporation and seeking an injunction compelling the corporation to include the proposal.[521] The company's management sustains the burden of proving that the proposal could properly be omitted. We will discuss the three most important (and controversial) grounds for omission in more detail, the exclusion of a proposal because it is not significantly related to the company's business,[522] it deals with a matter relating to ordinary business operations,[523] or concerns director elections.[524]

A proposal can be excluded because it lacks relevance if it relates to operations accounting for less than 5 per cent of the company's total assets, net earnings and sales, and is not otherwise significantly related to the company's business. Whether the quantitative threshold is met can be ascertained relatively easily, but the qualitative threshold, the requirement that the proposal must not be otherwise significantly related to the company's business, is more difficult to

[513] ISS, 2015 Benchmark U.S. Proxy Voting Policies: Frequently Asked Questions on Selected Topics (19 February 2015) 3–4.

[514] Rule 14a-8(b).

[515] Exceptions, which we will discuss in the next paragraphs, are laid down in Rule 14a-8(i).

[516] Matters falling solely within the powers of the general meeting are very few, since shareholders lack the right of initiative for most purposes, see our discussion in section A.II above.

[517] 118 N.E. 2d 590 (N.Y. 1954). We already examined some aspects of this decision in the text to n 76 above.

[518] *Auer v Dressel* (n 76) 593.

[519] If the proposal was phrased differently, it could be excluded pursuant to Rule 14a-8(i)(1) on the ground that it was 'not a proper subject for action by shareholders'. In its explanatory note to Rule 14a-8(i)(1), the SEC elaborates that '[d]epending on the subject matter, some proposals are not considered proper under state law if they would be binding on the company if approved by shareholders. In our experience, most proposals that are cast as recommendations or requests that the board of directors take specified action are proper under state law'.

[520] See Chapter 6B.I.2.

[521] Shareholders, accordingly, have an implied cause of action under s 14(a) Securities Exchange Act and Rule 14a-8 to enforce the corporation's obligation to include shareholder proposals in annual meeting proxy materials, *Roosevelt v E.I. Du Pont de Nemours & Co.*, 958 F.2d 416 (D.C. Cir. 1992).

[522] Rule 14a-8(i)(5). [523] Rule 14a-8(i)(7). [524] Rule 14a-8(i)(8).

define. The leading case is *Lovenheim v. Iroquois Brands, Ltd.*[525] In this case, the plaintiff's proposal called upon the directors of Iroquois Brands to form a committee to investigate whether the production methods of the company's French suppliers involved cruelty towards animals. The proposal related to less than 0.05 per cent of the assets of Iroquois Brands, and the case therefore turned on the interpretation of the 'not otherwise significant' exception. The court was of the opinion that significance should not only be understood in economic terms, but could also be a function of the ethical and social implications of the proposal.[526] In *Iroquois Brands*, the proposal was held to be of ethical and social significance, given the history of animal protection legislation in the United States going back to the seventeenth century and the attention that activist groups campaigning for the prevention of animal cruelty received.[527]

The ordinary business operations exclusion has a long and rather tumultuous history. Initially, the SEC argued that the exception applied only to 'routine, day-to-day matter[s] relating to the conduct' of the company's business, because it believed that such matters were 'of little interest or importance to most security holders'[528] and it would be 'manifestly impracticable in most cases for stockholders to decide management problems at corporate meetings'.[529] On the other hand, proposals regarding 'matters which have significant policy, economic or other implications inherent in them' were not excludable.[530] These are, of course, ambivalent standards. We can think of various matters that are routinely encountered by companies as part of their day-to-day operations, but that are also of general political, social or economic relevance. For example, can a chemical company, some of whose products have a military use, exclude a shareholder proposal requesting an amendment to the articles that would require the company's sales personnel to ensure that the products were not used against human beings?[531] The SEC used to decide such questions on a case-by-case basis. However, in 1992, the SEC revised its interpretation of Rule 14a-8. In a no-action letter requested by the restaurant and gift store chain Cracker Barrel Old Country Store, it adopted a bright-line approach and qualified any proposals related to employment matters concerning the company's non-executive workforce as falling within the scope of ordinary business operations.[532] The case concerned the announcement of a discriminatory employment policy by Cracker Barrel in a press release, stating that '[i]t is inconsistent with our concept and values, and is perceived to be inconsistent with those of our customer base, to continue to employ individuals ... whose sexual preferences fail to demonstrate normal heterosexual values which have been the foundation of families in our society'.[533] The SEC determined that the company could omit a shareholder proposal aimed at changing the

[525] 618 F. Supp. 554 (D.D.C. 1985). [526] ibid 561. [527] ibid 559.

[528] *Proposals by Security Holders: Notice of Proposed Amendments to Rule*, SEC Exchange Act Release No. 34-12598 (20 July 1976), 41 Fed. Reg. 29982, 8.

[529] Hearings on SEC Enforcement Problems before a Subcom. of the Senate Comm. on Banking and Currency, 85th Cong., 1st Sess., pt 1 (1957), quoted in *Medical Committee for Human Rights v SEC*, 432 F.2d 659, 678 (D.C. Cir. 1970).

[530] *Adoption of Amendments Relating to Proposals by Security Holders*, SEC Exchange Act Release No. 34-12999 (22 November 1976), 41 Fed. Reg. 52994.

[531] The case, *Medical Committee for Human Rights*, quoted in the previous footnote, dealt with a proposal of shareholders of the Dow Chemical Company requesting 'that napalm shall not be sold to any buyer unless that buyer gives reasonable assurance that the substance will not be used on or against human beings': ibid 662. The court held that the proposal could not properly be excluded. Referring to the management's statement that the decision to manufacture and market napalm was made because it was considered to be 'morally and politically desirable', the court argued 'that there is a clear and compelling distinction between management's legitimate need for freedom to apply its expertise in matters of day-to-day business judgment, and management's patently illegitimate claim of power to treat modern corporations with their vast resources as personal satrapies implementing personal political or moral predilections': ibid 681.

[532] *Cracker Barrel Old Country Store, Inc.*, SEC No-Action Letter, 1992 WL 289095 (13 October 1992). The no-action letter was the subject of a lawsuit in *New York City Employees' Retirement System v SEC*, 45 F.3d 7 (2d Cir. 1995) (dismissing the claim as not reviewable because the plaintiffs had an effective alternative to suing the SEC at their disposal, namely bringing a lawsuit against Cracker Barrel).

[533] Quoted in *New York City Employees' Retirement System*: ibid 9.

company's policy to expressly prohibit discrimination on the basis of sexual orientation. The Commission argued that 'the fact that a shareholder proposal concerning a company's employment policies and practices for the general workforce is tied to a social issue will no longer be viewed as removing the proposal from the realm of ordinary business operations', because 'the line between includable and excludable employment-related proposals ... [is] tenuous, without substance and effectively nullifying the application of the ordinary business exclusion to employment related proposals'.[534]

The SEC's bright-line rule was effectively overturned a year later by a federal district court in *Amalgamated Clothing and Textile Workers Union v. Wal-Mart Stores, Inc.*,[535] which dealt with a shareholder proposal seeking to require Wal-Mart to report on equal employment opportunity and affirmative action policies. The court held that no-action letters did not constitute expressions of agency interpretation to which courts had to defer.[536] Furthermore, the court was not impressed by the SEC's reasoning in *Cracker Barrel*, noting that it contravened the Commission's own release interpreting Rule 14a-8, which permitted the omission of proposals as relating to ordinary business operations if they were 'mundane in nature *and* [did] not involve any substantial policy or other considerations'.[537] The SEC subsequently reverted to its old case-by-case approach and now (again) draws a distinction between issues 'fundamental to management's ability to run a company on a day-to-day basis', for example 'the hiring, promotion, and termination of employees, decisions on production quality and quantity, and the retention of suppliers', and 'proposals relating to such matters but focusing on sufficiently significant social policy issues (e.g., significant discrimination matters)'.[538] The former are excludable, the latter are not, because they 'transcend the day-to-day business matters'.[539]

Rule 14a-8 also stipulates that shareholder proposals disqualifying a nomine standing for election to the board of directors, removing an incumbent director, seeking to include a specific individual as nominee in the company's proxy materials, or otherwise affecting the outcome of an election can be omitted by the company.[540] This exclusion is based on the Commission's view that contested elections to the board are adversarial in nature.[541] Shareholders who oppose the management's nominees are therefore required to wage a proxy contest and file their own materials in an attempt to convince the other shareholders to elect their slate of nominees. While it is thus clear that proposals relating to the election or removal of specific individuals can be properly omitted from the company's proxy statement, the question whether proposals aimed at amending the corporate by-laws to change the *process* or *manner* of elections fall within the scope of the exclusion is more difficult to answer. For example, can shareholders use the company's proxy statement to propose a bylaw amendment establishing a procedure by which shareholder-nominated candidates may be included on the corporate ballot, without identifying individual nominees? Case law indicates that such proposals are not excludable.[542] The SEC, after first adopting a restrictive position,[543] has now codified an approach that could be found in older no-action letters, distinguishing between proposals related to the election procedure and proposals 'that could affect the outcome of the upcoming election of directors'.[544] This interpretation is also in line with Delaware law,

[534] *Cracker Barrel*, SEC No-Action Letter (n 532) 1. [535] 821 F. Supp. 877 (S.D.N.Y. 1993).
[536] ibid 884.
[537] ibid 890, quoting SEC Exchange Act Release No. 34-12999 (3 December 1976), 41 Fed. Reg. 52994 (emphasis added).
[538] *Amendments to Rules on Shareholder Proposals*, SEC Exchange Act Release No. 34-40018 (21 May 1998), 67 S.E.C. Docket 373, 4.
[539] ibid. [540] Rule 14a-8(i)(8).
[541] TL Hazen, *Principles of Securities Regulation* (4th edn, West 2017) §71.
[542] *American Federation of State, County & Municipal Employees v American International Group, Inc.*, 462 F.3d 121 (2d Cir. 2006) (relying on SEC Exchange Act Release No. 34-12598 (n 528) in finding that 'the election exclusion is limited to shareholder proposals used to oppose solicitations dealing with an identified board seat in an upcoming election': ibid 128).
[543] *Shareholder Proposal Relating to the Election of Directors*, SEC Exchange Act Release No. 34-56914 (6 December 2007), 92 S.E.C. Docket 256.
[544] Rule 14a-8(i)(8)(v).

which allows the adoption of bylaw provisions granting shareholders access to the company's proxy statement for the purpose of including one or more shareholder director nominees.[545] While some legal uncertainty remains, it can be concluded, therefore, that proposals calling for cumulative voting,[546] setting out qualifications that directors must meet in subsequent elections (but not in the upcoming election),[547] or requiring that at least two-thirds of the board be composed of independent directors[548] can generally not be omitted.

3. *The German model: banks as proxy holders*

The general legal framework governing proxy voting in Germany is remarkably parsimonious, especially in comparison with US proxy rules. Following the requirements of the Shareholder Rights Directive, German law provides that voting rights may be exercised by the shareholders or a proxy authorized by them.[549] In principle, any person is eligible to act as proxy holder. Until a reform of 2001,[550] it was controversial whether a nominee of the issuer could be appointed as proxy holder. The courts tended to adopt a restrictive approach and allowed the authorization of a nominee of the issuer only if the shareholder gave specific instructions on how to exercise the voting rights.[551] Since 2001, it is clear that the proxy holder can be freely chosen, also from the issuer's employees and persons affiliated with the company's management.[552] Other rules regulate the form of the proxy, modalities of its submission, and an obligation of the company to retain proxies for three years.[553] Thus, on a literal interpretation, the law does not prohibit shareholders from granting a general proxy to issuer nominees or impose restrictions on the use of a proxy by the proxy holder. However, commentators debate whether restrictive conditions that apply to credit institutions as proxy holders, in particular the requirement that banks exercise proxy voting rights in their own general meeting only according to express instructions given by the shareholders,[554] should also apply to nominees of the issuer. Arguably, in both cases the same conflict of interest exists. The shareholders as owners of the business have to rely on individuals affiliated with the issuer, and in many cases more specifically the issuer's management, to exercise the control functions of the general meeting objectively.[555] The expansive interpretation would also be in line with the Shareholder Rights Directive,[556] but the legal situation remains unclear. In any case, the German Corporate Governance Code now recommends that management board representatives shall exercise the shareholders' voting rights 'in accordance with their instructions'.[557]

While the general regulation of proxies in the Stock Corporation Act is, therefore, fragmentary, the law contains detailed rules on the exercise of proxy voting rights by credit institutions.[558] This somewhat skewed regulatory focus can be explained historically. German credit institutions have traditionally obtained a proxy from their customers to vote the shares they hold in custody. This practice has received considerable attention from economic historians who argue that it played an important role in shaping Germany's financial development. It allowed the large universal banks that were established in the second half of the nineteenth century, among them Deutsche Bank and Commerzbank, still two of the

[545] Del. Gen. Corp. Law, §112.

[546] *Boeing Co.*, SEC No-Action Letter, 2000 WL 286281 (6 March 2000).

[547] *Adams Express Co.*, SEC No-Action Letter, 2000 WL 1877569 (28 December 2000).

[548] *Peabody Energy Corp.*, SEC No-Action Letter, 2004 WL 334474 (19 February 2004).

[549] AktG, §134(3).

[550] Gesetz zur Namensaktie und zur Erleichterung der Stimmrechtsausübung [Act on Registered Shares and for the Simplification of the Exercise of Voting Rights] (NaStraG) of 18 January 2001, BGBl I, 123.

[551] LG Baden-Baden, AG 1998, 534.

[552] See the wording of AktG, §134(3).

[553] ibid §134(3) sentences 3–5.

[554] ibid §135(3) sentence 3. We will discuss the proxy voting power of banks in more detail in the next paragraphs.

[555] For an overview of this debate see M Arnold in W Goette and M Habersack (eds), *Münchener Kommentar zum Aktiengesetz, vol 3* (4th edn, CH Beck 2018) §134, paras 38–44.

[556] See Directive 2007/36/EC, Art 10(3)(b).

[557] German Corporate Governance Code 2017, s 2.3.2.

[558] AktG, §135.

leading financial institutions in Germany, to gain significant influence over industrial corporations. The banks were able to establish formal, long-term relationships that involved placing their representatives on corporate boards and taking an active part in the governance of companies.[559] This, in turn, reduced informational asymmetries and facilitated the monitoring of debt. Thus, so the argument goes, the banks' influence, mediated by their proxy voting rights and the voting rights they had acquired for their own account, determined financing patterns and contributed to the emergence of a system of concentrated ownership.[560]

We cannot address all facets of this discussion here, especially the question whether a financial system dominated by large universal banks has a positive or negative impact on the efficiency of corporate finance and, more generally, on economic growth.[561] This question goes back to the fundamental debate about financial system design and the merits of bank-based compared with market-based systems that we discussed above.[562] Here, the analysis will be confined to sketching the evolution of proxy regulation in Germany in order to show that banks indeed had far-reaching leeway to exercise the voting rights attached to shares they held in custody until well into the twentieth century.[563]

The Stock Corporation Reform Act of 1884 was the first law to regulate proxy voting. It allowed the exercise of voting rights by an agent, provided the proxy was given in writing.[564] The banks made use of this provision as a matter of course, often simply by providing in their terms and conditions that they were authorized to exercise the voting rights of shares held in custody at their discretion, unless otherwise instructed. This practice was considered to be, in principle, in line with the legal requirements, unless the shareholders' acceptance of the terms and conditions was part of a separate statement.[565] However, the lenient regulation was widely criticized for giving banks too much power over industrial corporations and emasculating the general meeting. The Reform Act of 1937, accordingly, introduced some careful alterations designed to restrict the banks' control over the company's proxy

[559] Seminal works studying the relationship between the large universal banks and industrial corporations in Germany in the late nineteenth and early twentieth centuries include J Riesser, *Die deutschen Großbanken und ihre Konzentration im Zusammenhang mit der Entwicklung der Gesamtwirtschaft in Deutschland* (4th edn, G Fischer 1912), translated as *The German Great Banks and their Concentration in Connection with the Economic Development of Germany* (National Monetary Commission 1911); R Hilferding, *Das Finanzkapital* (Wiener Volksbuchhandlung 1927), translated as *Finance Capital: A Study of the Latest Phase of Capitalist Development* (Routledge & Kegan Paul 1981); O Jeidels, *Das Verhältnis der deutschen Großbanken zur Industrie* (Duncker & Humblot 1905).

[560] Jeidels (n 559) 99–162, gives a detailed description of the different types of business relationships that the universal banks established. For an accessible, succinct overview see AD Chandler, *Scale and Scope: The Dynamics of Industrial Capitalism* (Harvard University Press 1990) 416–19. The view that universal banks exerted a domineering influence over firms' operations has been challenged by parts of the more recent literature, for example C Fohlin, *Finance Capitalism and Germany's Rise to Industrial Power* (Cambridge University Press 2007) (Fohlin, 'Finance Capitalism') 169–97; C Fohlin, 'The rise of interlocking directorates in imperial Germany' (1999) 52 *Economic History Review* 307.

[561] Fohlin, 'Finance Capitalism' (n 560) 30–37, 52–63, and C Fohlin, *Mobilizing Money* (Cambridge University Press 2012) (Fohlin, 'Mobilizing Money') 3–7, give a good overview of the debate.

[562] See the varieties of capitalism literature presented in Chapter 4B.III and Fohlin, 'Mobilizing Money' (n 561) 7–9.

[563] For data on the extent of the banks' control through own shares and proxies, see T Baums, 'The German Banking System and its Impact on Corporate Finance and Governance' in M Aoki and H Patrick (eds), *The Japanese Main Bank System: Its Relevance for Developing and Transforming Economies* (OUP 1995) 409, 426–9 (reporting that banks controlled on average more than 80% of the shares present at 1986 general meetings of the largest non-family owned German corporations).

[564] Gesetz, betreffend die Kommanditgesellschaften auf Aktien und die Aktiengesellschaften [Act concerning limited partnerships by shares and joint stock corporations], RGBl 1884, 123, inserting Arts 190, 221 into the ADHGB [General German Commercial Code].

[565] In this case, the shareholder's acceptance was held not to be in the required written form because the document did not contain the bank's terms and conditions, see Imperial Court, decision of 24 October 1922, RGZ 105, 289, 292–3.

machinery. It required proxies to be granted separately and limited itheirts validity to fifteen months.[566] The reforms, however, did not address one issue that had given cause for concern. Save any instructions by the shareholders, the banks were able to exercise the shareholders' voting rights in their discretion. They were under no obligation to disclose their voting policies or vote in a particular manner, for example in line with management recommendations. Banks, therefore, continued to enjoy a position of considerable influence. They were able to pursue their own interests as major shareholders or lenders to the company through proxy voting, leaving especially small investors without effective representation. Importantly, since the banks' influence was augmented by shareholder proxies, their control rights did not match their economic exposure, thus potentially creating incentives not to act in the best interest of the company. This situation is similar to the problem of empty voting that we discussed above.[567]

The reform discussions have continued and the rules on proxy voting have been amended several times over the course of the last decades.[568] The legal situation fluctuated for a number of years, because additional organizational obligations imposed on credit institutions to eliminate conflicts of interest created administrative costs, and banks became reluctant to function as proxy holders. This, in turn, led to a decline in attendance rates at general meetings.[569] The current law constitutes a compromise between protecting shareholders effectively, and as a corollary restricting the discretion of banks and their control over the proxy machinery, and ensuring that proxy voting is not overregulated.

In order to protect investors, the Stock Corporation Act provides for several safeguards. First, banks that hold directly or indirectly 20 per cent of the legal capital of a company have to choose whether they wish to exercise their own voting rights or their customers' proxy rights in the general meeting.[570] They cannot exercise both, unless the customer has given express instructions regarding individual items on the agenda of the meeting.[571] The rationale behind the rule is clear. The law presumes that banks are conflicted if they also hold proprietary shares. However, given what we said above about the mismatch between control rights and economic exposure, it may be argued that the opposite is true. The smaller the banks' own equity stake in the company, the more likely are they to vote in their own interest, even if this affects the return on the shareholders' investment negatively.[572] The bank's exposure as a lender, on the other hand, is not addressed by the rule at all. In addition, it seems rather counterproductive to prescribe a remedy against the abuse of proxy voting that consists in shareholders potentially forfeiting their voting rights at the election of the bank.

Secondly, credit institutions are generally only allowed to exercise proxy voting rights according to an express instruction by the shareholder, or in the absence of specific instructions in accordance with their own voting proposals or the proposals of the management or

566 Gesetz über Aktiengesellschaften und Kommanditgesellschaften auf Aktien [Act concerning stock corporations and limited partnerships by shares], RGBl I 1937, 107, §114(4).

567 See section C.I.3.

568 Important changes came with the AktG 1965, BGBl I, 1089, and the reforms of the KonTraG 1998 (n 113) and the Gesetz zur Umsetzung der Aktionärsrechterichtlinie [Act Implementing the Shareholder Rights Directive] (ARUG) of 30 July 2009, BGBl I, 2479.

569 BT-Drs [Journal of the Federal Parliament] 16/11642, 33.

570 AktG, §135(3) sentence 4.

571 If a shareholder gives instructions concerning some, but not all items on the agenda, the bank's voting rights are, accordingly, split. The bank is authorized to vote both its own and its customers' shares on resolutions where it has received instructions, and it must make a choice when voting on the other resolutions.

572 Interestingly, the provision initially applied if a bank held more than 5% of the legal capital of a company (§135(1) sentence 3, as amended by KonTraG 1998 (n 113) Art 1, no 19b). The stake was increased in 2009 (see ARUG (n 568), Art 1, no 21), because it was thought that regulatory intervention was not warranted below the threshold of 20%.

supervisory board of the issuer.[573] If a shareholder grants a general proxy without further instructions, the bank is subject to certain organizational and notification obligations. It is required to make either its own voting proposals or the issuer's recommendations available to the shareholder, for example on its website, and then vote according to them, unless doing so would evidently be in conflict with the shareholder's interests because of a material change of circumstances.[574] This may be the case if it becomes clear in the general meeting that only the management's proposal for a reorganization of the company has chances of being adopted, and the proxy holder's opposition to the plan would force the company to file for the opening of insolvency proceedings.[575] If the credit institution decides to deviate from existing proposals or instructions because of such a change of circumstances, it has to notify the shareholder and give reasons for its decision. In addition, the bank has to put organizational arrangements in place that address conflicts of interest. Such arrangements typically involve a separation of managers responsible for proxy voting from other divisions of the bank, most importantly the lending, underwriting, and investment management divisions.[576]

Thirdly, a credit institution is required to disclose if members of its management board or other employees hold positions on an issuer's supervisory board and vice versa, it owns 3 per cent or more of the voting rights of the issuer, or underwrote the last securities offering of the company.[577] The first requirement, disclosure of supervisory board positions, relates to the longstanding debate about the influence of German banks over industrial corporations that we mentioned above.[578] Commentators have pointed out that the banks' influence stemmed not primarily, or at least not directly, from their equity holdings or proxy voting rights, but from board positions held by bankers.[579] The practice of banks to secure the appointment of representatives to corporate boards was not only widespread during the early decades of industrial capitalism in Germany, when policy makers and academics started to discuss the issue critically,[580] but continued to be common until well into the second half of the twentieth century.[581] Since the 1990s, the interconnections between banks and industrial corporations, however, have become much less pronounced.[582] It is, therefore, not surprising that the regulatory response of policy makers is cautious and the preferred approach is based on disclosure, rather than a more interventionist strategy.

In spite of changes in the 'German model' of bank-firm relationships and the role of banks in corporate governance that have occurred since the 1990s,[583] proxy voting by banks is still important, and the question of how to regulate it remains controversial. On the one hand, proxy voting is an important mechanism to address the problem of rational apathy of small shareholders. Furthermore, it has been pointed out that the banks' involvement in German industrial corporations has contributed to the stability and growth of the German

573 AktG, §135(1) sentence 4. 574 ibid §135(2)–(4). 575 LG Düsseldorf, AG 1991, 409.

576 AktG, §135(2) sentence 2. 577 ibid §135(2) sentences 4–5.

578 See the references in nn 559–560.

579 C Harm, 'The relationship between German banks and large German firms' (1992) *World Bank Policy Research Working Papers* 900, 17.

580 Jeidels (n 559) 143–62; Riesser (n 559) 303–4, 651–72.

581 See Harm (n 579) 18–19; Baums (n 563) 430–3, for data from the 1970s and 1980s (reporting, inter alia, that of the 92 largest firms with a supervisory board in 1986, banks held more than 10% of all seats and more than 20% of the seats reserved for the shareholder representatives under co-determination).

582 I Dittmann, E Maug, and C Schneider, 'Bankers on the Boards of German Firms: What They Do, What They Are Worth, and Why They Are (Still) There' (2010) 14 Review of Finance 35, 45–7 (finding that the percentage of bankers on corporate boards fell from 9.6% to 5.6% between 1994 and 2005 and average equity ownership by banks from 4% to 0.4% during the same time); P Windolf, 'The Corporate Network in Germany, 1896-2010' in T David and G Westerhuis (eds), *The Power of Corporate Networks: A Comparative and Historical Perspective* (Routledge 2014), 66, 75–78.

583 A good overview of the debate surrounding the transformation or, as some scholars put it, decline of the German model of capitalism is given by A Busch, 'Globalisation and National Varieties of Capitalism: The Contested Viability of the "German Model"' in K Dyson and S Padgett (eds), *The Politics of Economic Reform in Germany: Global, Rhineland or Hybrid Capitalism?* (Routledge 2006) 11–25.

economy.[584] On the other hand, it is reasonable to assume that banks, especially if they are also lenders to the company, tend to prefer profits to be reinvested in the business, rather than distributed as dividends to shareholders. This means that companies are less attractive to equity investors and have higher costs of raising equity capital in the market. It is well known that German capital markets have been, for a long time, considerably smaller and less liquid than financial markets in the United States, UK, and certain other countries. The extent of bank shareholdings in German industrial corporations, coupled with their proxy voting rights and board positions, is seen by some academics as an important factor explaining this situation.[585]

Given the pervasiveness of proxy voting by banks in Germany, it may be expected that this practice is also prevalent in other countries. However, in most advanced economies, it is of no practical importance and has not received much regulatory attention. How can we explain this striking difference in the organization of the corporate economy? It is beyond the scope of this book to explore the question in detail, but a few points may be made. During the formative stages of industrial capitalism, in the late nineteenth and early twentieth centuries, when proxy-voting rights of banks became a common phenomenon in Germany, the banking industries of other industralizing economies were markedly different (and, to some extent, they are still today). As mentioned, in Germany, universal banks were important financiers of the industry. Their close connection with industrial corporations has given rise to what has been called a 'relationship banking system'.[586] In contrast, an arms-length banking system is characterized by the limited corporate governance role that banks play in non-financial corporations. In such a system, banks are commonly only providers of debt financing or facilitate the issuing of equity capital, for example by underwriting a public offering. The United States are a paradigmatic example of an arms-length system. This structure of the US financial system can be traced back to particular regulatory interventions. In the United States, the public has traditionally been deeply suspicious of the accumulation of power, both politically and economically. In the financial sphere, this suspicion led to public inquiries,[587] litigation,[588] and highly restrictive regulation of the banking industry. Well known is the Glass-Stegall Act of 1933,[589] which required the separation of investment banking and commercial banking and was only repealed in 1999.[590] However, restrictive regulation is much older. In the nineteenth century, state and federal laws established often crippling regulatory requirements, including demanding capital adequacy ratios, restrictions on the types of collateral that banks could accept, and, probably most importantly, prohibitions on branching.[591] For these reasons, banks remained relatively small and specialized.

[584] Monopolkommission, *Hauptgutachten II: Fortschreitende Konzentration bei Großunternehmen* (1978).

[585] It is not easy to disentangle the effect of proxy voting (or in general the involvement of banks in industrial corporations) from that of other variables potentially influencing the development of stock markets. For an overview of the discussion and references see C Fohlin, 'Universal Banking in Pre-World War I Germany: Model or Myth?' (1999) 36 Explorations in Economic History 305.

[586] Fohlin, 'Mobilizing Money' (n 561) 143 (identifying three main characteristics of relationship banking, which were all present in late nineteenth-century Germany: proxy-voting, equity shares held by banks and bank representation on boards of directors).

[587] The most influential inquiries were the Pujo investigation, Hearings before a Subcommittee of the House Committee on Banking and Currency, H.Res. 429 and 504, 62d Cong., 2d Sess. (1912), and the Gray-Pecora investigation, Hearings before Senate Committee on Banking and Currency, S.Res. 84, as amended, 72d Cong., 1st Sess. (1932) and S.Res. 56 and S.Res. 97, as amended, 73rd Cong., 1st Sess. (1933). The Pujo committee investigated an alleged conspiracy by the so-called 'money trust', a cartel of investment bankers, to control sectors of the US economy. The Gray-Pecora hearings dealt with investment banking practices in the years before the great crash of 1929.

[588] For example, *U.S. v Morgan*, 118 F. Supp. 621 (S.D.N.Y. 1953).

[589] Banking Act of 1933, Pub.L. 73-66, 48 Stat. 162, ss 16, 20–21, 32.

[590] Gramm-Leach-Bliley Act (Financial Services Modernization Act of 1999), Pub.L. 106-102, 113 Stat. 1338.

[591] EN White, 'The Political Economy of Banking Regulation, 1864-1933' (1982) 42 Journal of Economic History 33, 34–40 (explaining that branch banking was prohibited or severely limited until well into the 20th century because of the lobbying power of unit bankers, which were well established especially in southern and western states).

They did not evolve into the universal banks that could be found in Germany and that engaged in relationship banking.

In the United Kingdom, a comparable prohibition on branching did not exist and regulation was generally less concerned with tendencies of concentration in the financial sector than in the United States. Consequently, by the early 1900s, a number of large, financially powerful joint stock banks had appeared that were operating nationwide.[592] Nonetheless, most historians agree that they did not provide finance to the domestic industry to the same extent as their German counterparts.[593] It has been suggested that they focused instead on colonial enterprises, which promised higher returns,[594] preferred to invest in liquid assets, or grew more conservative in reaction to financial crises.[595] Alternatively, it was also pointed out that the British economy simply did not require the same amounts of fixed capital as continental European countries, which were relative industrial latecomers with rapidly growing, capital-intensive industries in the late nineteenth century.[596] The exact reasons for the apparent (and contested[597]) failure of banks to provide the necessary finance to industry remain controversial, but they all imply that British banks were not in a position to develop the same close relationships with industrial corporations as German universal banks. Finally, in France, as in Britain, regulation was relatively conducive to the emergence of large credit institutions, and they did in fact emerge earlier than in most other countries, but industrial corporations had a strong preference to finance expansion out of profits.[598] In addition, in the last decades of the nineteenth century, political and social tensions and economic depression resulted in French banks becoming increasingly reluctant to be involved in industrial finance.[599] This brief historical sketch shows that no case is alike. At the end of a complex developmental path, we may find surprising similarities and differences between countries: here, the absence of bank proxy voting in the United States, the UK, and France, and its prevalence in Germany. However, the factors that have shaped each country's path are very different and range from regulatory intervention to the lack of demand for, or supply of, bank finance. The regulation of proxy voting, on the other hand, clearly reflects the economic relevance that this legal institution has in different countries. In Germany, the policy maker has grappled with the question of how best to regulate proxy voting by credit institutions for more than a century, whereas it has not attracted much controversy in the other three countries.

III. Challenging shareholder decision-making

Majority rule is a necessity especially in larger companies, where it is unrealistic to expect all shareholders to meet and agree on matters falling within the remit of the general meeting. However, it gives rise to the risk that the majority will exercise their voting rights for self-serving ends and the minority or other stakeholders are overborne. Legal systems, therefore, need to develop strategies that address these potential conflicts, which are simply further

[592] PL Cottrell, *Industrial Finance 1830-1914* (Methuen 1980), 195.

[593] For an overview of the literature and some critical observations, see PL Cottrell, 'Domestic finance, 1860-1914' in R Floud and P Johnson (eds), *The Cambridge Economic History of Modern Britain, Vol II: Economic Maturity, 1860-1939* (CUP 2004), 253, 255–6.

[594] For a critical discussion of this point, see S Pollard, 'Capital Exports, 1870-1914: Harmful or Beneficial?' 38 Economic History Review 495.

[595] Cottrell (n 593) 255.

[596] Cottrell (n 592) 244.

[597] See F Capie, 'Prudent and Stable (but Inefficient?): Commercial Banks in Britain, 1890-1940' in MD Bordo and R Sylla (eds), *Anglo-American Financial Systems: Institutions and Markets in the Twentieth Century* (Irwin 1995) 41.

[598] DS Landes, *The Unbound Prometheus: Technological Change and Industrial Development in Western Europe from 1750 to the Present* (CUP 1969) 210.

[599] H Bonin, 'The Case of the French Banks' in R Cameron and VI Bovykin (eds), *International Banking 1870-1914* (OUP 1991) 72, 73.

manifestations of the ubiquitous agency problems that we discussed above.[600] Similar to the managerial agency problem, we can distinguish between two legal strategies to eliminate or attenuate majority-minority and shareholder-stakeholder agency conflicts: rules that enumerate fairly precisely what the majority can decide and how the minority, and possibly other persons, can challenge the majority's decisions, and typically broadly phrased standards that prescribe how the majority shall exercise their voting power. We are here interested in the former strategy, which is part of the regulatory framework governing decision-making by the general meeting. In Chapter 7, we will ask whether the law imposes further constraints on the majority, similar to directors' duties, when shareholders make use of their decision-making power within the applicable regulatory framework.

Our four legal systems pursue markedly different approaches to regulating resolutions adopted by the general meeting. As the following provisions show, German law provides for a detailed set of rules laying down nullity grounds and the procedure to be followed in order to challenge shareholder decision-making. The French Commercial Code is much more parsimonious, and we do not find any provisions explicitly addressing these questions in the UK Companies Act 2006 or the Delaware General Corporation Law.

Delaware General Corporation Law

§ 225—Contested election of directors; proceedings to determine validity

(a) Upon application of any stockholder or director, or any officer whose title to office is contested, the Court of Chancery may hear and determine the validity of any election, appointment, removal or resignation of any director or officer of any corporation, and the right of any person to hold or continue to hold such office, and, in case any such office is claimed by more than 1 person, may determine the person entitled thereto; and to that end make such order or decree in any such case as may be just and proper, with power to enforce the production of any books, papers and records of the corporation relating to the issue ...
(b) Upon application of any stockholder or upon application of the corporation itself, the Court of Chancery may hear and determine the result of any vote of stockholders upon matters other than the election of directors or officers ...

German Stock Corporation Act

§ 241—Grounds for nullity

Apart from the cases specified in §192(4), §§212, 217(2), §228(2), §234(3), and §235(2), a resolution of the general meeting is only null and void if it:

1. has been adopted by a general meeting convened in violation of §121, Subsections (2) and (3), Sentence 1, or Subsection (4);
2. has not been documented pursuant to §130, Subsections (1) and (2), Sentence 1, and Subsection (4);
3. is incompatible with the nature of the stock corporation or, by virtue of its contents, is in violation of provisions adopted with a view to protecting exclusively or primarily the company's creditors, or which are otherwise adopted in the public interest;
4. is, by virtue of its contents, contrary to public policy;
5. has been declared null and void by a final judgment on an action for annulment; ...

§ 242—Curing of nullity

(1) It shall no longer be possible to plead nullity of a resolution of the general meeting, which has not, or not properly, been documented in contravention of §130, Subsections (1) and (2), Sentence 1, and Subsection (4) if the resolution has been entered into the commercial register.
(2) In case of a resolution of the general meeting that is null and void pursuant to §241, nos. 1, 3 or 4, it shall no longer be possible to plead nullity if the resolution has been entered into the commercial register and three years have elapsed since then ...

[600] Chapter 4B.II.

§ 243—Grounds for annulment

(1) A resolution of the general meeting may be challenged by an action for annulment on the grounds that it is in violation of the law or the articles.
(2) The action may also be based on the ground that a shareholder sought to obtain a special advantage for himself or another person through the exercise of voting rights to the detriment of the company and the resolution is suitable for such purpose, unless the resolution provides for adequate compensation to the other shareholders.
(3) ...
(4) The provision of incorrect or incomplete information, or the refusal to provide information, may only be a ground for annulment if a reasonable shareholder would have regarded the information as material for the proper exercise of participation or membership rights. An action for annulment may not be based on incorrect, incomplete, or insufficient information given in the general meeting concerning the determination, amount, or adequacy of compensation payments if the law provides for an appraisal proceeding for such complaints.

§ 245—Standing

The following persons shall have standing to bring a lawsuit challenging a resolution:

1. any shareholder present at the general meeting, provided that he acquired the shares prior to the publication of the agenda and raised an objection to the resolution for the record;
2. any shareholder not present at the general meeting, provided that he was wrongfully not admitted to the general meeting or the general meeting was not duly called or the subject matter of the resolution not properly announced;
3. in the case of §243(2) every shareholder, provided that he acquired the shares prior to the publication of the agenda;
4. the management board;
5. any member of the management board or supervisory board if they would commit a criminal or administrative offence by implementing the resolution or be liable for compensation.

§ 246—Action for annulment

(1) Any action for annulment must be brought within one month after adoption of the resolution.
(2) The action shall be brought against the company. The company is represented by the management board and supervisory board. In case the action is brought by the management board or a member of the management board, the company is represented by the supervisory board, and in case the action is brought by a member of the supervisory board, the company is represented by the management board ...

§ 246a—Release procedure

(1) If the action for annulment is directed against a resolution of the general meeting concerning a capital increase, capital reduction (§§182–240), or an enterprise agreement (§§291–307), the court can decide upon a motion by the company that the action does not constitute a bar to registration and defects of the general meeting's resolution do not affect the legal consequences of registration....
(2) A decision pursuant to subsection (1) is adopted if:
    1. the action for annulment is inadmissible or evidently unfounded,
    2. the plaintiff does not provide documentary evidence within one week after the motion was served that he has held shares to the amount of at least EUR 1,000 since the notice of the general meeting was published,
    3. the immediate effectiveness of the resolution seems to be in the overriding interest of the company, because the material disadvantages to the company and its shareholders as set forth by the applicant outweigh in the opinion of the court the disadvantages to the respondent, unless the infringement is particularly severe.
(3) ... The decision is binding on the court of the commercial register; the determination of the validity of the registration has effects *erga omnes*....

(4) If the action for annulment is well founded, the company that has obtained the release decision shall be required to compensate the respondent for the loss suffered as a result of the registration of the general meeting's resolution in reliance on the release decision. After entry into the commercial register, defects of the resolution shall not affect the resolution's implementation; the elimination of this effect of the registration cannot be demanded as damages.

French Commercial Code[601]

Article L235-1

The invalidity of a company or the annulment of an instrument amending the constitution may result only from an express provision in this book or from the acts governing the rescission of contracts. With regard to sociétés à responsabilité limitée and joint-stock companies, the dissolution of the company may result neither from a defect in consent nor from incapacity or prohibition from acting, unless this affects all the founding members....

The annulment of acts or deliberations other than those specified in the above paragraph may result only from the breach of a mandatory provision in this book or in the laws governing contracts.

Article L235-2-1

Decisions made in breach of the provisions that govern the voting rights attached to shares may be annulled.

Article L235-3

The action for a declaration of invalidity or for annulment shall lapse when the reason for this ceases to exist on the day when the court rules on the merits at first instance, except where this action for invalidity or annulment is based on the unlawfulness of the company's object.

Article L235-6

In the event of the invalidity of a company (including partnerships) or of annulment of acts and deliberations subsequent to its formation, based on a defect in consent or the disqualification of a member, and where the situation may be rectified, any person with a vested interest may send formal notice to the appropriate person to either rectify the situation or bring an action for a declaration of invalidity or for annulment within six months, under pain of forfeiture. This formal notice shall be reported to the company ...

Article L235-9

Actions for a declaration of invalidity of a company or annulment of acts and deliberations subsequent to its formation shall be time-barred three years after the date on which the invalidity came to pass, without prejudice to the period of limitation referred to in Article L235-6.

However, actions for the annulment of a merger or demerger of companies are time-barred six months after the date of the last entry in the commercial and companies register made necessary by the operation.

An action for annulment based on Article L225-149-3 is time-barred three months after the date of the general meeting following the decision to increase the capital.

Article L235-12

Neither the company nor the members may rely on a nullity (company invalidity or ground for annulment) with regard to third parties acting in good faith. However, the nullity resulting from disqualification or a defect in consent shall be binding even on third parties in respect of the person disqualified and their legal agents or the member whose consent has not been obtained due to error, fraud or duress.

The undoubtedly most sophisticated and far-reaching regime to scrutinize and challenge resolutions of the general meeting has emerged in Germany, where such a right of minority shareholders was acknowledged by the courts as early as the mid-nineteenth century.[602]

[601] Translation by Legifrance, https://www.legifrance.gouv.fr/Traductions/en-English/Legifrance-translations.

[602] See eg Reichsoberhandelsgericht [Higher Commercial Court of the Reich], decision of 20 October 1877, ROHGE 23, 273, 275.

It was codified for the first time by the Stock Corporation Reform Act of 1884[603] and can now be found in §§241–257 Stock Corporation Act. Most other jurisdictions do not provide for a specific, codified review procedure, and the courts draw on general legal principles, for example tort law, to determine whether a shareholder resolution is valid and binding. We will present the German position in some detail and then give an overview of the mechanisms that apply in the other legal systems in place of a codified review procedure where resolutions of the general meeting intrude on the interests of the minority.

1. *Germany: legality review*

German law distinguishes between void and voidable resolutions. Certain types of defects, listed in §241 Stock Corporation Act, result in a resolution being null and void *ab initio*,[604] whereas other resolutions adopted in violation of the law or the articles are voidable upon an action filed by shareholders or members of the management or supervisory board (§§243–246 Stock Corporation Act). Void resolutions do not need to be challenged pursuant to specified legal proceedings, although shareholders and members of the management and supervisory boards may bring a lawsuit to seek declaratory relief (*Nichtigkeitsklage*).[605] Voidable resolutions are valid and binding unless challenged within a month after adoption; void resolutions generally do not entail legal effects and must not be implemented by the management board or supervisory board.

The Stock Corporation Act provides for three types of nullity grounds: violations of formalities regarding the general meeting,[606] certain essential shareholder rights and organizational requirements,[607] and public policy considerations.[608] An example of a formal defect leading to nullity is a general meeting that has been called by an unauthorized person.[609] Organizational requirements rendering a resolution null and void in case of non-compliance include rules on employee participation,[610] the maximum number of members of the supervisory board,[611] and personal eligibility requirements for board members.[612] The most elusive group of nullity grounds is the third. Public interest and public policy are notoriously difficult to define, and the courts have not yet answered all questions conclusively.

The Stock Corporation Act refers, first, to resolutions incompatible with the nature of the stock corporation, in violation of provisions adopted with a view to protecting the company's creditors, or contrary to provisions otherwise adopted in the public interest.[613] It is fairly well established that capital maintenance provisions are of such importance for the protection of creditors that their violation results in the nullity of an offending shareholder resolution. For example, the Federal Court of Justice held that a resolution increasing the capital of a company (a private limited liability company in the case decided by the court) and providing that the company should subscribe for the new shares was void because it violated the requirement that only fully paid-up shares could be purchased by the company, provided the company had sufficient distributable reserves.[614]

[603] Act concerning limited partnerships by shares and joint stock corporations (n 564) inserting Arts 190a, 190b, 222 into the ADHGB.

[604] But see AktG, §242 (reproduced above). It should be noted that the formulation of the law is somewhat inaccurate. §242 speaks of impossibility 'to plead nullity', but the provision is commonly interpreted as meaning that the defect is cured *ex tunc* and all corporate organs are required to treat the resolution as valid and binding; see Raiser and Veil (n 133) §16/120.

[605] ibid §249.

[606] ibid §241, nos 1, 2.

[607] ibid §§212 (rights of shareholders to receive shares from a capital increase out of the company's reserves), 250 (composition of the supervisory board), and 256 (certain mistakes in the annual financial accounts).

[608] ibid §241, nos 3, 4.

[609] ibid §121(2).

[610] ibid §§250(1) no 1, 96(2).

[611] ibid §§250(1) no 3, 95.

[612] ibid §§250(1) no 4, 100(1), (2).

[613] ibid §241, no 3.

[614] BGH NJW 1955, 222. The relevant requirements are laid down in §33 GmbHG.

This holding can be generalized, and commentators argue that analogous provisions from the law of the public stock corporation, for example the prohibition of an acquisition of the company's own shares if the transaction is not covered by one of the narrowly defined cases set out in the Stock Corporation Act[615] or the repayment of contributions to the shareholders,[616] including in the form of disguised distributions,[617] have an equivalent standing. Similarly, the requirement to provide security to creditors before certain fundamental changes are implemented, such as capital reductions,[618] termination of control or profit transfer agreements,[619] and mergers,[620] is qualified as 'protecting exclusively or primarily the company's creditors' and hence falling within the scope of §241 Stock Corporation Act.[621]

It is more controversial how provisions 'otherwise adopted in the public interest' are to be interpreted. For example, it is unclear whether all resolutions changing the articles in contradiction to binding law are null and void because they violate the fundamental principle of limited contractual freedom,[622] or only resolutions that contravene core elements of the regulatory framework, such as the statutory allocation of competences between the general meeting, management board, and supervisory board.[623] The Federal Court of Justice has so far left the question open.[624] It could be argued that the distinction drawn by the Stock Corporation Act between void and voidable resolutions militates in favour of the second, narrower interpretation. If all contraventions of binding provisions were void, the relevance of the right to challenge resolutions pursuant to §243 Stock Corporation Act would be significantly curtailed.[625] Notwithstanding this question, courts have held that resolutions affecting essential features of the shareholders' franchise constitute provisions adopted in the public interest. For example, a resolution changing the articles in order to require a transfer of shares to be notarized were found to be in violation of 'the principle of free transferability of the membership right' and thus null and void.[626] Similarly, the squeeze-out of a minority shareholder not in compliance with the statutory requirements[627] was seen as 'a most fundamental interference with membership rights' and thus infringing public interests.[628]

The third type of defect referred to in §241, no 3, incompatibility with the nature of the stock corporation, is of limited relevance compared with the other two grounds for nullity. Since significant violations of the law will generally either encroach upon creditor interests or on a position protected in the public interest, the phrase 'nature of the stock corporation'

[615] AktG, §71(1). [616] ibid §57. [617] See Chapter 9B.I.5. [618] AktG, §§225, 233.
[619] ibid §303. [620] UmwG, §22. [621] Raiser and Veil (n 133) §16/113.
[622] See n 120 above.
[623] For a summary of the discussion, see U Hüffer and C Schäfer in W Goette and M Habersack (eds), *Münchener Kommentar zum Aktiengesetz, vol 4* (4th edn, CH Beck 2016) §241, paras 60–1.
[624] BGH NJW 1987, 902. The case dealt with the appointment of members of the supervisory board. The challenged changes to the articles provided that reserve candidates that had acceded to the board upon early retirement of an incumbent director would lose their position when the general meeting appointed a new director to replace the retired member. The court held that this provision effectively allowed the general meeting to remove some board members with simple majority and without cause, thus contravening §103(1) AktG and the (unwritten) principle of equality of all members of the supervisory board. However, the court did not decide whether the contravention resulted in nullity or only contestability, since the defect had been cured pursuant to §242(2) AktG; see ibid 903.
[625] See eg Raiser and Veil (n 133) §16/115.
[626] BGH NJW 2004, 3561. The court pointed out that registered shares could be transferred by written or oral contract without further formalities pursuant to §§398, 413 BGB, and that modifications to this basic rule in amendments to the articles required the consent of all affected shareholders (§180(2) AktG).
[627] Pursuant to §327a AktG, a shareholder holding at least 95% of the legal capital can request the general meeting to resolve that the shares of the minority shall be transferred to the majority shareholder.
[628] OLG München, AG 2007, 173. In this case, a majority shareholder had reached the 95% threshold necessary for a squeeze-out by borrowing securities from other shareholders, who retained the cash-flow rights attached to their shares. The court held that legal title without beneficial ownership did not satisfy the requirement to 'own' 95% of the share capital within the meaning of §327a AktG.

is restricted to exceptional situations that do not come under any of the issues explicitly addressed by the Stock Corporation Act.[629]

Finally, resolutions are null and void if they are contrary to public policy by virtue of their content.[630] This is the case if the resolution as such is against public policy, not the circumstances under which it was adopted, for example by abusing majority power, or the goal pursued with the resolution.[631] Again, there is a clear overlap with the other grounds for nullity, in particular a violation of provisions protecting creditors. An example of a resolution that is contrary to public policy from the case law is the appropriation of private benefits by a majority shareholder who enters into a related party transaction with the company.[632]

Other violations of the law or the company's articles of association do not result in the nullity of a resolution *ab initio*, but the resolution can be challenged pursuant to a procedure set out in §§243–246 of the Stock Corporation Act, the so-called action for annulment (*Anfechtungsklage*). This action can be brought within one month after adoption of the resolution[633] by any shareholder who attended the meeting and raised an objection to the resolution,[634] as well as the management board and individual members of the management or supervisory board if they would commit an offence by implementing the resolution.[635] For retail investors, these requirements are not easy to satisfy. While it is sufficient that they are represented by someone else in the general meeting, the voting rights of many smaller investors are exercised by their banks, which are unlikely to object to a resolution unless explicitly instructed to do so. Attendance at the general meeting and raising an objection are dispensed with if the general meeting was not properly convened or a shareholder was wrongfully excluded,[636] or if the resolution served to confer a special advantage on a shareholder or another person to the detriment of the company and the remaining shareholders.[637]

The Stock Corporation Act does not specify whether a violation of the law or the articles must have been a causal factor in the adoption of the challenged resolution, in the sense of a 'but for' relationship between the contravention and the decision of the general meeting. The relevant sections of the Act simply stipulate that an action for annulment can be brought if the resolution is in violation of the law or the articles. If the violation consists in the provision of incorrect information, a reasonable shareholder must have regarded the information 'as material' when voting.[638] Not surprisingly, the ambivalent rules have given rise to a considerable amount of case law discussing the required link between the violation and the voting decision of the shareholders. However, the courts have not developed uniform criteria, but apply different tests depending on the type of illegality at issue. We will discuss the different situations in turn.

First, as far as procedural defects are concerned, for example non-compliance with the rules on calling a general meeting and the conduct of meetings,[639] the courts do not require (potential) causality, that is, a showing that the resolution would not have been adopted but

[629] Case law invoking the nature of the company is rare. An example is a decision of the Imperial Court from 1901, reported in RGZ 49, 77. In this case, the articles of association provided that shareholders had to be members of a professional organization. When the claimant resigned from the organization, the general meeting adopted a resolution excluding him from the company. The court held that the company's articles, and hence also the resolution of the general meeting, were invalid and in conflict with the nature of the stock corporation as a (potentially anonymous) association of persons who were primarily expected to make a financial contribution. If personal qualifications or other personal attributes of the members were at the heart of the venture, other forms of business association than the public stock corporation would be more appropriate

[630] AktG, §241, no 4. The German term (*die guten Sitten*) is also occasionally translated as 'good morals' instead of 'public policy'.

[631] BGHZ 101, 113.

[632] BGHZ 15, 382.

[633] AktG, §246(1).

[634] ibid §245, no 1.

[635] ibid §245, nos 4, 5.

[636] ibid §245, no 2.

[637] ibid §245, no 3.

[638] ibid §243(1), (4).

[639] ibid §§121–137. Examples for noncompliance with such procedural rules are the failure to give notice at least 30 days prior to the date of the meeting (§124(1)), include all requested items in the agenda (§124), or record the resolution correctly in the minutes (§130), for example because the votes of shareholders not entitled to vote were counted (BGHZ 104, 66).

for the violation. It is sufficient that the violation was 'relevant' to a proper exercise of the individual shareholder's membership rights.[640] An example may illustrate what is meant by this. The Stock Corporation Act provides that the management board and supervisory board shall give recommendations concerning each agenda item.[641] In a case decided by the Federal Court of Justice, the required recommendation was given by one of the members of a two-member management board while the other board position was vacant.[642] The court held that the agenda had not been published in accordance with the legal requirements because the recommendation had to be given by the board as an organ and not by an individual director, and the management board was not constituted correctly at the time.[643] This procedural defect was 'relevant' because the law prohibited the adoption of resolutions concerning agenda items not published duly, thus emphasising the importance of full information for the shareholders' participation rights.[644] In general, when the shareholders are not fully and correctly informed, the courts ask whether a reasonable shareholder would have deemed the information to be material in order to exercise membership rights properly.[645] Thus, the relevant information must be of such importance that a reasonable shareholder would have requested correct disclosure before deciding how to vote. On the other hand, it is not necessary to show that the shareholder would have actually voted differently.[646] Furthermore, in some situations, the breach may routinely be assumed to be relevant. For example, if shareholders are unlawfully excluded from a general meeting and thus deprived of their voting rights, they are generally entitled to challenge resolutions adopted in their absence.[647]

Secondly, a resolution may be voidable because it is in conflict with substantive requirements of corporate law. Relevant substantive provisions include the requirement to treat the shareholders equally,[648] which may be violated if shares are issued at par value to some shareholders under exclusion of the other shareholders' pre-emption rights in a situation where the shares could have been sold at a much higher price,[649] and the (unwritten) fiduciary duty of shareholders to exercise their voting rights with due regard for the interests of the other shareholders.[650] The Federal Court of Justice also requires a substantive review of resolutions adopting certain structural changes, for example a capital increase that excludes pre-emption rights[651] or transactions that result in a company becoming a dependent undertaking.[652] Such resolutions must be justified in the interest of the company.[653] Given the rather open-ended nature of the term 'interest of the company', it is easy to see that shareholders who challenge a resolution on the ground that the potentially conflicting interests of majority and minority shareholders were not balanced appropriately have considerable leverage over the company's operations. We will come back to this problem and the legislator's response to it below. In any case, an action for annulment is not available if the law provides for a special procedure to challenge structural changes, as, for example, pursuant to the Transformation Act for valuation questions in mergers, divisions, and changes of the corporate form.[654] If an action for annulment can be based on a violation of fiduciary duties

[640] BGHZ 160, 253, 255–6. [641] AktG, §124(3). [642] BGHZ 149, 158.

[643] Pursuant to §76(2) AktG, the management board of a company with a legal capital of more than three million euro shall consist of two or more persons. See also Chapter 4E.III.3.

[644] BGHZ 149, 158. The court relied on §124(4) sentence 1 AktG, which provides that a resolution shall not be adopted unless the respective agenda item was duly published.

[645] AktG, §243(4) sentence 1. This provision was amended by Gesetz zur Unternehmensintegrität und Modernisierung des Anfechtungsrechts [Act on Corporate Integrity and Modernisation of the Law of Avoidance] (UMAG) of 22 September 2005, BGBl I, 2802, in order to consolidate recent decisions of the courts (starting with the judgment referred to in n 642 above) that no longer required a showing that a reasonable shareholder would have voted differently without the breach. Such a requirement had been imposed by older case law, eg BGHZ 36, 121, 140.

[646] BR-Drs [Journal of the Federal Council] 3/05, 53. [647] Raiser and Veil (n 133) §16/147.

[648] AktG, §53a. [649] BGHZ 21, 354. [650] We will discuss this duty in detail in Chapter 7B.III.

[651] BGHZ 71, 40 (*Kali & Salz*). [652] BGHZ 80, 68 (*Süssen*).

[653] We will discuss the precise contours of the substantive review in Chapter 9D.I.2.

[654] AktG, §243(4); UmwG, §§14(2), 15 (merger), 125 (division), 195(2), 196 (change of form).

of shareholders, or a substantive review of a resolution leads to the conclusion that it was not adopted in the best interest of the company, questions of causality do not arise. The resolution is illegal because of its content, since it encroaches upon the minority shareholders' rights, and will be set aside for this reason.

Thirdly, different rules apply if a resolution confers a special advantage on a shareholder. A special advantage has been defined as any benefit amounting to an improper preference of a shareholder or third person incompatible with the interests of the company or the shareholders as a whole.[655] The provision's importance has remained limited, because §243(1) covers most relevant cases and offers advantages to objecting shareholders, who do not have to show that the defendant *intended* to obtain an advantage to the exclusion of the other shareholders. An example of a case where the demarcation between the first two subsections of §243—violation of the law and conferring a special advantage—was unclear concerned the dissolution of a company. The Federal Court of Justice held that a resolution liquidating a company was not subject to any unwritten substantive requirements, because the right to divest was part of the shareholders' ownership rights. The shareholders, accordingly, were entitled to dissolve the company with the required majority at any time and free up the invested capital.[656] It follows that minority shareholders generally cannot challenge the resolution of the general meeting on substantive grounds. However, if a majority shareholder liquidates the company in order to acquire core corporate assets and minority shareholders are effectively excluded from bidding for these assets because the majority has already (informally) agreed on an acquisition with the company's management, the majority shareholder obtains an improper benefit to the detriment of the minority and, at the same time, violates fiduciary duties owed to the minority. According to the Federal Court of Justice, this is ostensibly a case of §243(2), where the expeditious acquisition of assets at what is probably a favourable price constitutes a special advantage.[657] On the other hand, given that minority shareholders can challenge a winding-up resolution only if they can show that the majority breached its (unwritten) fiduciary duties, a challenge can also be brought under §243(1) for a violation of the law. Hence, an objecting minority shareholder has a choice to bring a lawsuit either under subsection 1 or 2.[658]

As mentioned before, the fact that the action for annulment can be used to challenge resolutions by invoking broadly formulated and inherently ambivalent terms entails the risk of strike suits that are brought solely for their settlement value. Before legal reforms introduced a so-called release procedure in 2005,[659] it was questionable whether a challenged resolution could be entered into the commercial register before the action for annulment was resolved.[660] A number of shareholders gained notoriety for filing lawsuits only in order to settle with their companies, which would typically face market pressures to bring about legal certainty and implement the challenged resolution in a timely fashion.[661] The reforms of 2005 now allow companies to petition the Court of Appeal for a declaration that the action for annulment does not preclude the transaction from being entered into the commercial register. The court will grant the motion if the action is inadmissible or evidently unfounded,

[655] BGHZ 138, 71, 80–81.

[656] BGHZ 103, 184 (*Linotype*). Excerpts of this case are reproduced in Chapter 7B.III.

[657] See the excerpt from *Linotype* in Chapter 7B.III.

[658] U Hüffer and C Schäfer in Goette and Habersack (n 623) §243, para 73.

[659] AktG, §246a, inserted by UMAG (n 645) and amended by ARUG (n 568).

[660] In some cases, the law precludes a transaction from being entered into the commercial register while an action for annulment is pending, see eg §16(2) UmwG for mergers. In other cases, the court of the commercial register has discretion whether or not to enter the transaction. It will assess the prospects of success of the action and generally refuse to register the transaction unless the action is inadmissible or fails to state a claim, see Hüffer and Schäfer (n 658) para 135.

[661] For data on the number of annulment actions filed in the years before and after the introduction of §246a AktG, the identity of repeat plaintiffs, and the settlement values extracted, see T Baums, A Keinath, and D Gajek, 'Fortschritte bei Klagen gegen Hauptversammlungsbeschlüsse? Eine empirische Studie' (2007) 28 ZIP 1629.

the plaintiff does not hold shares to the amount of at least 1,000 euro, or the court finds that the economic interests of the company in registering the transaction outweigh the disadvantages for the plaintiff.[662] These rules are designed to limit the risk of strike suits, without depriving minority shareholders of a mechanism offering effective protection against encroachment upon their rights by the majority. Especially the last of the aforementioned conditions illustrates how the legislator sought to balance the different interests at play. The financial consequences of a bar to registration for the company will often be of critical importance to the court's assessment.[663] On the other hand, economic factors are not decisive if an infringement of minority rights is particularly serious, for example in the case of an intentional breach that affects minority shareholders more severely than other shareholders, or if it is not possible to compensate the plaintiff for the detrimental effects of the transaction by awarding damages.[664] If the motion is granted, but the action for annulment later proves to be well founded, the transaction remains valid and binding. However, the plaintiff can claim compensation from the company for the loss suffered as a result of the implementation of the transaction, for example if the plaintiff's stake is diluted by a capital increase without pre-emption rights.[665]

2. *Other jurisdictions*

The French Commercial Code, while being less prescriptive than the German Stock Corporation Act, contains some rules on the nullity of acts of corporate organs (together with rules on the nullity of company formations and structural changes such as mergers and divisions) in Articles L235-1 to L235-14. For present purposes most important, Article L235-1, subsection 1 Code de commerce deals with challenges to resolutions modifying the constitution, and subsection 2 with other acts of corporate organs. As far as the former are concerned, the law provides that acts amending the corporate constitution shall only be null and void if they are in violation of 'express provisions' of the law on commercial companies to be found in Book II of the Commercial Code or of provisions of contract law that entail the invalidity of a contract. 'Express provisions' of company law refer to articles of the Commercial Code explicitly stipulating that non-compliance shall result in the nullity of the challenged act, for example where the general meeting is not convened lawfully[666] or quorum and majority requirements are violated.[667] A corporate decision is invalid pursuant to general principles of contract law if it pursues an unlawful object or lacks the necessary consent.[668] A relevant example is an act that amounts to fraud on the company's creditors or minority shareholders, for instance where minority shareholders were illegally refused access to the general meeting in order to prevent them from exercising their blocking minority.[669]

Acts that do not amend the company's constitutions are null and void if they are in violation of 'mandatory provisions' of company or contract law. Article L235-1 applies to both resolutions of the general meeting, for example regarding the appointment of a director or the approval of the company's accounts, and decisions of other corporate organs, notably the board of directors. This much is clear, but the remainder of the provision is fraught with legal uncertainty. It is unclear whether the breach of a provision not laid down in Book II of the Commercial Code, but for example in a decree-law (a statutory instrument in British parlance) or in the articles of association, entails nullity as a sanction, and when a provision is 'mandatory' within the meaning of Article L235-1. The courts are hesitant to declare

[662] AktG, §246a(2). [663] See eg LG München I BB 2006, 459, 460. [664] BT-Drs 16/11642, 41.
[665] BT-Drs 15/5092, 28. [666] Com, Art L225-104(2).
[667] Com, Art L225-121 lists several provisions that resolutions of the general meeting must comply with, including quorum and majority requirements at ordinary general meetings (Art L225-98) and extraordinary meetings (Art L225-96).
[668] M Cozian, A Viandier, and F Deboissy, *Droit des sociétés* (31st edn, LexisNexis 2018) para 627.
[669] Cass com, 6 July 1983, no 82-12910, *Bull. civ.* IV, no 206.

decisions null and void for the sole reason that they breach secondary legislation or the company's articles, without contravening a binding provision of Book II.[670]

Of course, in many cases, the challenged act of a corporate organ will concern both a mandatory provision of company law and rules or regulations that are laid down by the company for the internal governance of its affairs. Therefore, it will often be a matter of interpretation whether a breach flows primarily (or exclusively) from the company's statutes or from mandatory law. In a leading case, the Cour de Cassation had to decide whether the deliberations of the board of directors of a simplified joint-stock company (SAS)[671] whose articles required the board to be composed of at least four members, one half each to be appointed by the two shareholder groups holding the company's capital, were null and void after one director resigned and the board met with only three members.[672] The claimant, the underrepresented party on the board of directors after the resignation, argued that the board had breached the company's articles because it had refused to appoint an additional director by co-optation, as proposed by the underrepresented side. Further, this breach amounted to a violation of mandatory provisions of the law governing contracts, since the Civil Code provided that contracts lawfully entered into should 'have the force of law for those who have made them'.[673] The Cour de Cassation disagreed. It held that non-compliance with the articles or internal by-laws did not render the decision of a corporate organ null and void, unless the rule in question was adopted 'by making use of an authorization granted by a mandatory provision' of company or contract law. Accordingly, it can be concluded that non-compliance with a provision of the company's articles resulting in a situation that could not be provided for lawfully under the applicable rules of mandatory company law gives rise to nullity, but not non-compliance with provisions such as those at issue in the case decided by the Cour de Cassation, since the Commercial Code does not prevent a board from meeting after the resignation of one director or require the board to fill the vacancy immediately by co-optation. However, commentators have pointed out that it is also possible to interpret the case differently. The board, it has been said, was only able to exercise its powers if it was composed of an equal number of representatives of the two shareholder factions, as required by the articles of association. In the case of the simplified joint-stock company, the powers of the board are conferred by the articles.[674] Thus, by not complying with the articles, the board acted *ultra vires* and hence also in violation of binding company law.[675] This example shows that the rules of the Commercial Code on the potential nullity of corporate acts are deceptively simple, but give rise to uncertainty in their application in practice. The courts have not yet succeeded in eliminating this uncertainty by offering a clear and consistent interpretation of Article L235-1.

While the Commercial Code does not explicitly distinguish between void and voidable acts and does not provide for two different routes to challenging such acts, in contrast to the German Stock Corporation Act, a comparable distinction is nevertheless not unknown to French company law. An act may either be null and void by operation of the law, or the nullity may be 'facultative'. In the latter case, it is in the discretion of the judge whether or not to annul the act. Nullity is generally facultative where a decision suffers from a procedural defect, for example if the general meeting has not been convened correctly.[676] An action for annulment can be brought by any interested party[677] within the period of limitation prescribed

[670] For a discussion and references see Cozian, Viandier, and Deboissy (n 668) paras 630–4.

[671] The rules governing the simplified joint-stock company are laid down in Com, Arts L227-1 to L227-20.

[672] Cass com, 18 May 2010, no 09-14855, *Bull. Joly Sociétés* 2010, 651, note H Le Nabasque.

[673] Civ, Art 1103.

[674] Com, Art L227-5.

[675] M Cozian, A Viandier, and F Deboissy, *Droit des sociétés* (28th edn, LexisNexis 2015), para 464.

[676] Com, Arts L223-27(9) (SARL), L225-104(2) (SA).

[677] In order to determine the group of persons having standing to sue, it is therefore necessary to interpret the provision that has been violated and identify the interests it intends to protect. Thus, if a general meeting has been convened unlawfully, only the shareholders have standing to bring an action for annulment, not a manager who does not hold any shares, Cass com, 17 December 2002 (*SARL Marquette Hellige c/ Brousse*), *Bull. Joly Sociétés* 2003, 307, note P Le Cannu.

by the Commercial Code, which is generally three years from the time when the reason for the nullity arose.[678] If the judge invalidates the act, it is null and void *ex tunc*. However, neither the company nor the shareholders can rely on the nullity in relation to third parties acting in good faith, unless the nullity results from a failure to obtain a required consent or from lack of capacity of the person acting.[679] After expiration of the period of limitation, the decision of the corporate organ can no longer be challenged, but nullity can still be used as a defence in an action seeking to enforce a claim based on the void decision.[680]

Common law jurisdiction agree that a shareholder vote is only valid if the statutory requirements regarding notice periods, quorum and, of course, majority requirements are complied with. Furthermore, a violation of other provisions regulating the conduct of meetings may also invalidate shareholder resolutions. For example, English law requires that an ordinary resolution to be proposed at a general meeting may only be amended if notice of the proposed amendment is given at least forty-eight hours before the meeting and the amendment does not 'materially alter the scope of the resolution'.[681] A special resolution may only be amended if 'the amendment does not go beyond what is necessary to correct a grammatical or other non-substantive error in the resolution'.[682] These principles were initially introduced by case law.[683] They are now part of the model articles for public companies and invalidate resolutions adopted in breach of the articles.[684]

In the United States, we have seen that federal legislation has added a layer of regulation setting out in considerable detail the process of soliciting proxies in public corporations.[685] In the case of violations of the proxy rules, the Commission has the power to issue cease-and-desist orders, impose monetary sanctions,[686] or void all proxies and require solicitations to recommence for a rescheduled meeting of shareholders.[687] In addition, Exchange Act Rule 14a-9 allows shareholders to claim damages if a proxy statement contains false or misleading information. Besides damages, investors (or the SEC) can bring, in principle, a claim for injunctive relief, and a court may order that the *status quo* existing before the proxy solicitation shall be restored.[688] However, where a decision has already been implemented and third party rights would be affected by a return to the *status quo ante*, courts are reluctant to invalidate a transaction.

On the other hand, neither Delaware nor the UK provide for any specific rules setting out when resolutions of the general meeting are void or voidable, although shareholders are, of course, able to file a lawsuit to contest the validity of resolutions adopted by the general meeting.[689] Note the difference especially to German law, which specifies not only the consequences of procedural defects in the conduct of meetings, but also lays down standards of review that enable shareholders (and courts) to scrutinize the content of resolutions,

[678] Com, Art L235-9(1). For example, if the challenge concerns a resolution of the general meeting deciding on the acquisition by a company of an asset from a shareholder within two years of formation without an auditor having been appointed as required by Art L225-101, the statute of limitation commences when the general meeting adopted the resolution, Cour d'Appel de Paris, 6 December 2000, *Bull. Joly Sociétés* 2001, 417. On the other hand, it has also been held that an action for annulment is not time-barred if the reason for the nullity does not consist in an irregularity affecting the decision-making of the corporate organ, but 'a defect that affects the act itself', Cass com, 20 March 2012, no 11-13534 (in this case, dealing with a redemption of shares, the claimant's consent had been obtained under duress).

[679] Com, Art L235-12.

[680] For example, a debtor can invoke the nullity of a lease entered into without the required authorization by the board of directors in an action seeking to enforce the lease even after expiration of the three-year limitation period, Cass 3e civ, 2 December 1998, *Rev. sociétés* 1999, 359, note Y Chartier.

[681] Model Articles for Public Companies, Art 40(1). [682] ibid Art 40(2).

[683] *In re Moorgate Mercantile Holdings Ltd* [1980] 1 WLR 227, 242–3. [684] ibid.

[685] See above section C.II. [686] Securities Exchange Act 1934, ss 21B, 21C.

[687] *Kaufman v Cooper Companies, Inc.*, 719 F. Supp. 174 (S.D.N.Y. 1989).

[688] *Crouch v Prior*, 905 F. Supp. 248 (D.Vi. 1995) (granting relief to preserve the composition of the board of directors).

[689] For Delaware, see Del. Gen. Corp. Law, §225.

for example with a view to assessing whether resolutions are 'incompatible with the nature of the stock corporation' or with provisions intended to protect creditors or certain other public interests. Of course, the conflicts that the German Stock Corporation Act seeks to address also exist in other jurisdictions whenever the allocation of decision-making power and the structure of voting rules allow the majority to adopt decisions that affect the position of the minority or other stakeholders. In all jurisdictions analysed here, the courts have developed answers to the problem of an abuse of majority voting power, which display, at least at first sight, a certain degree of resemblance. The UK courts hold that the voting power of shareholders, 'like all other powers, [must] be exercised subject to those general principles of law and equity which are applicable to all powers conferred on majorities and enabling them to bind minorities'.[690] It follows that shareholders must act 'bona fide for the benefit of the company as a whole'.[691] US courts acknowledge that majority power entails in certain situations the obligation to act in good faith and in the interest of all shareholders,[692] or they require the transaction to be intrinsically or entirely fair to the company, including the minority shareholders.[693] Such duties were held to exist where the controlling shareholders used their control over the board to make large dividend payments,[694] entered into a freeze-out merger,[695] or control was sold at a premium to a customer of the company who wanted to gain access to an important corporate asset.[696] But the reach of these cases is not always clear and considerable differences exist between US jurisdictions. Finally, French courts have developed the doctrine of *abus de majorité*, which supplements the rules of the Commercial Code presented above. The doctrine allows the courts to invalidate resolutions that are contrary to the best interests of the company and have been adopted for the sole purpose of conferring a benefit upon the majority to the detriment of the minority. We will discuss all of these approaches in more detail in chapter 7, where we deal with duty-based constraints on shareholder decision-making power.

Why do we observe these distinct differences between UK and Delaware law on the one hand, and French and especially German law on the other hand? One possible explanation is that ownership structure plays a role. In countries with large blockholders, a formalized procedure allowing aggrieved minority shareholders to challenge decisions of the majority is evidently more important than in economies where most companies do not have dominant stockholders. A somewhat more subtle explanation may refer to the far-reaching powers of directors in Delaware corporations. If stockholders have only a limited say in corporate decision-making, it is sensible for the law to focus on constraining the discretion of directors. This may be achieved by imposing fiduciary duties on directors, which can be enforced by minority shareholders in a derivative action. Thus, through this lens, the action for annulment under German and French law presents itself as a functional substitute for (possibly) less developed or less vigorously enforced duties of directors.[697]

D. Appointment and Removal of Directors

US MBCA

§ 8.03—Number and Election of Directors

(a) A board of directors must consist of one or more individuals, with the number specified in or fixed in accordance with the articles of incorporation or by-laws.

[690] *Allen v Gold Reefs of West Africa Ltd* [1900] 1 Ch 656, 671. [691] ibid.
[692] *Zahn v Transamerica Corp.*, 162 F.2d 36, 42 (3d Cir. 1947) (applying Kentucky law).
[693] *Sinclair Oil Corp. v Levien*, 280 A.2d 717, 720 (Del. 1971). [694] ibid.
[695] *Weinberger v UOP, Inc.*, 457 A.2d 701 (Del. 1983).
[696] *Perlman v Feldmann*, 219 F.2d 173 (2d Cir. 1955).
[697] On this point see M Gelter, 'Why Do Shareholder Derivative Suits Remain Rare in Continental Europe' (2011–2012) 37 Brookings Journal of International Law 843, 881–7.

(b) The number of directors may be increased or decreased from time to time by amendment to, or in the manner provided in, the articles of incorporation or the by-laws.
(c) Directors are elected at the first annual shareholders' meeting and at each annual meeting thereafter unless their terms are staggered under section 8.06.

§ 8.05—Terms of Directors Generally

(a) The terms of the initial directors of a corporation expire at the first shareholders' meeting at which directors are elected.
(b) The terms of all other directors expire at the next, or if their terms are staggered in accordance with section 8.06, at the applicable second or third, annual shareholders' meeting following their election …

§ 8.06—Staggered Terms for Directors

The articles of incorporation may provide for staggering the terms of directors by dividing the total number of directors into two or three groups, with each group containing one-half or one-third of the total, as near as may be practicable. In that event, the terms of directors in the first group expire at the first annual shareholders' meeting after their election, the terms of the second group expire at the second annual shareholders' meeting after their election, and the terms of the third group, if any, expire at the third annual shareholders' meeting after their election. At each annual shareholders' meeting held thereafter, directors shall be chosen for a term of two years or three years, as the case may be, to succeed those whose terms expire.

§ 8.08—Removal of Directors by Shareholders

(a) The shareholders may remove one or more directors with or without cause unless the articles of incorporation provide that directors may be removed only for cause.
(b) If a director is elected by a voting group of shareholders, only the shareholders of that voting group may participate in the vote to remove that director.
(c) If cumulative voting is authorized, a director may not be removed if the number of votes sufficient to elect the director under cumulative voting is voted against removal. If cumulative voting is not authorized, a director may be removed only if the number of votes cast to remove exceeds the number of votes cast not to remove the director.
(d) A director may be removed by the shareholders only at a meeting called for the purpose of removing the director and the meeting notice must state that the purpose, or one of the purposes, of the meeting is removal of the director.

Delaware General Corporation Law

§ 141—Board of directors …

(a)-(c) …
(d) The directors of any corporation organized under this chapter may, by the certificate of incorporation or by an initial bylaw, or by a bylaw adopted by a vote of the stockholders, be divided into 1, 2 or 3 classes; the term of office of those of the first class to expire at the first annual meeting held after such classification becomes effective; of the second class 1 year thereafter; of the third class 2 years thereafter; and at each annual election held after such classification becomes effective, directors shall be chosen for a full term, as the case may be, to succeed those whose terms expire. The certificate of incorporation or bylaw provision dividing the directors into classes may authorize the board of directors to assign members of the board already in office to such classes at the time such classification becomes effective. The certificate of incorporation may confer upon holders of any class or series of stock the right to elect 1 or more directors who shall serve for such term, and have such voting powers as shall be stated in the certificate of incorporation. The terms of office and voting powers of the directors elected separately by the holders of any class or series of stock may be greater than or less than those of any other director or class of directors. In addition, the certificate of incorporation may confer upon 1 or more directors, whether or not elected separately by the holders of any class or series of stock, voting powers greater than or less than those of other directors. Any such provision conferring greater or lesser voting power shall apply to voting in any committee or subcommittee, unless otherwise provided in the certificate of incorporation or by-laws. If the certificate of incorporation provides that 1 or more directors shall

have more or less than 1 vote per director on any matter, every reference in this chapter to a majority or other proportion of the directors shall refer to a majority or other proportion of the votes of the directors.

(e)-(j) ...

(k) Any director or the entire board of directors may be removed, with or without cause, by the holders of a majority of the shares then entitled to vote at an election of directors, except as follows:

(1) Unless the certificate of incorporation otherwise provides, in the case of a corporation whose board is classified as provided in subsection (d) of this section, stockholders may effect such removal only for cause; or

(2) In the case of a corporation having cumulative voting, if less than the entire board is to be removed, no director may be removed without cause if the votes cast against such director's removal would be sufficient to elect such director if then cumulatively voted at an election of the entire board of directors, or, if there be classes of directors, at an election of the class of directors of which such director is a part.

Whenever the holders of any class or series are entitled to elect 1 or more directors by the certificate of incorporation, this subsection shall apply, in respect to the removal without cause of a director or directors so elected, to the vote of the holders of the outstanding shares of that class or series and not to the vote of the outstanding shares as a whole.

UK Companies Act 2006

Section 168—Resolution to remove director

(1) A company may by ordinary resolution at a meeting remove a director before the expiration of his period of office, notwithstanding anything in any agreement between it and him.

(2) Special notice is required of a resolution to remove a director under this section or to appoint somebody instead of a director so removed at the meeting at which he is removed ...

(5) This section is not to be taken—

(a) as depriving a person removed under it of compensation or damages payable to him in respect of the termination of his appointment as director or of any appointment terminating with that as director, or

(b) as derogating from any power to remove a director that may exist apart from this section.

UK Model Articles for Public Companies

20. Methods of appointing directors

Any person who is willing to act as a director, and is permitted by law to do so, may be appointed to be a director—

(a) by ordinary resolution, or

(b) by a decision of the directors.

21. Retirement of directors by rotation

(1) At the first annual general meeting all the directors must retire from office.

(2) At every subsequent annual general meeting any directors—

(a) who have been appointed by the directors since the last annual general meeting, or

(b) who were not appointed or reappointed at one of the preceding two annual general meetings, must retire from office and may offer themselves for reappointment by the members.

German Stock Corporation Act

§ 84—Appointment and removal of the members of the management board

(1) Members of the management board are appointed by the supervisory board for a maximum of five years. The appointment may be renewed or the term of office extended, in each case for a maximum of five years. The renewal or extension requires a new resolution by the supervisory board, which may not be given earlier than one year before expiration

of the term of office. A new resolution is not necessary if the appointment was for less than five years, provided that the total term of office does not exceed five years after extension. This shall apply mutatis mutandis to the employment contract; the contract may, however, provide that it shall remain in force in the event of an extension of the term of office until the expiration of such extended term.

(2) If several persons are appointed as members of the management board, the supervisory board may designate one of them as chairman of the management board.

(3) The supervisory board may revoke the appointment as member of the management board or chairman for an important cause. Such a cause shall be in particular a gross breach of duty, incapacity to manage the company properly, or withdrawal of confidence by the general meeting, unless the withdrawal was made for manifestly arbitrary grounds. This also applies to the management board appointed by the first supervisory board. The revocation is valid until its invalidity has been determined by final court decision. Claims arising under the employment contract are governed by general law.

(4) The provisions of the Act on employee participation in the supervisory boards and management boards of companies in the mining and coal and steel industries of 21 May 1951 (Federal Gazette I, p. 347)—Coal and Steel Co-Determination Act—regarding the special majority requirements for resolutions of the supervisory board and the appointment of a worker director or the revocation of such appointment shall be unaffected.

§ 101—Appointment of the members of the supervisory board

(1) The members of the supervisory board shall be elected by the general meeting, unless they are appointed to the supervisory board or they are elected as representatives of the employees pursuant to the Co-Determination Act, the Co-Determination Supplementary Act, the One-Third Participation Act, or the Act on the Co-Determination of Employees in Cross-Border Mergers....

§ 103—Removal of the members of the supervisory board

(1) Members of the supervisory board who have been elected by the general meeting without a binding nomination may be removed before the expiration of their term of office. The resolution requires a majority of at least three-fourths of the votes cast. The articles may provide for a different majority and further requirements.

(2) A member of the supervisory board who has been appointed to the board pursuant to the articles may be removed at any time by the person who has the appointment right and replaced by another person. If the preconditions for the existence of the appointment right pursuant to the articles are no longer met, the general meeting may remove the appointed member by simple majority.

(3) Upon a motion by the supervisory board, the court shall remove a member of the supervisory board if an important reason exists concerning that member personally. The supervisory board shall resolve to file the motion by simple majority. If the member of the supervisory board has been appointed to the board pursuant to the articles, shareholders holding at least ten percent of the legal capital, or a fraction of the legal capital representing at least one million Euros, shall have the right to file the motion. The decision is subject to appeal.

(4) Notwithstanding Subsection 3, the Co-Determination Act, Coal and Steel Co-Determination Act, Co-Determination Supplementary Act, One-Third Participation Act, SE Co-Determination Act, and the Act on the Co-Determination of Employees in Cross-Border Mergers shall apply to the removal of members of the supervisory board who have neither been elected by the general meeting without a binding nomination nor appointed to the board pursuant to the articles.

French Commercial Code[698]

Article L225-18

The directors shall be appointed by the constitutive shareholders' meeting or by the routine shareholders' meeting. In the circumstances specified by Article L225-16, they shall be designated in

[698] Translation by Legifrance (26 November 2018) https://www.legifrance.gouv.fr/Traductions/en-English/Legifrance-translations.

> the articles of association. The term of their office shall be determined by the memorandum and articles of association but may not exceed six years. However, in the event of merger or division, the appointment may be made by the special shareholders' meeting.
>
> The directors shall be eligible for re-election unless otherwise specified in the memorandum and articles of association. They may be dismissed at any time by the routine shareholders' meeting.

A central tenet of shareholder democracy that all legal systems agree about is the election of the directors by the shareholders. In the finer details, however, legal systems differ considerably in how they regulate board appointments. These differences do not only relate to the question whether the company shall have a one-tier or two-tier board (in the latter case, the shareholder franchise will typically only encompass elections to the supervisory board), but also the process of appointment and, crucially, the ease with which shareholders can remove directors before the end of their tenure. We will first deal with the general rules on appointment and removal. In this context, we will also discuss strategies that make it more difficult for shareholders to remove the directors, either as a general matter or more specifically after a change of control, and the response of the law to such strategies. Finally, we will examine how the rules on appointment and removal are modified if the company operates under a regime of co-determination and some of the members of the (supervisory) board are appointed by the company's workforce.

I. Appointment

We are already familiar with the parsimonious character of the UK Companies Act 2006 in corporate governance matters. It is, therefore, not surprising that the act does not set out any procedure for the appointment of directors, with the exception of the requirement that the application for registration of a company must indicate the persons who will be the first directors of the company.[699] Case law has established the rule that the shareholders have an inherent power to appoint directors, which may be exercised by ordinary resolution in general meeting.[700] However, the articles may provide for a different system, for example the appointment by co-optation through the incumbent directors. The model articles for private or public companies allow both avenues: A person may be appointed a director by ordinary resolution or by a decision of the directors.[701] In the case of public companies, the model articles require that a director who was appointed by the decision of the incumbent directors retire at the next annual general meeting and offer himself for reappointment by the members.[702] If the general meeting votes on the appointment of directors, motions for the appointment of two or more directors may not be combined in a single resolution, unless the general meeting unanimously adopts a corresponding resolution.[703]

Appointment rights are regulated in more detail in the United States. The Model Business Corporation Act and the Delaware General Corporation Law, as well as the laws of other US states, envisage either a staggered (classified) or a non-staggered board. In the former case, the board is divided into up to three classes, each class containing an equal number of directors who are required to step down every two or three years, corresponding to the division of the board into two or three classes, and stand for re-election at the annual general meeting.[704] In the latter case, the whole board is generally elected at each annual general meeting.[705]

[699] Companies Act 2006, s 12(1)(a). The articles often require the first directors to retire at the first annual general meeting, see s 21(1) Model Articles for Public Companies.

[700] *Worcester Corsetry Ltd v Witting* [1936] Ch 640; *Link Agricultural Pty Ltd v Shanahan* (1998) 28 ACSR 498.

[701] Model Articles for Private Companies, s 17(1); Model Articles for Public Companies, s 20.

[702] Model Articles for Public Companies, s 21(2)(a).

[703] Companies Act 2006, s 160.

[704] Del. Gen. Corp. Law, §141(d); MBCA, §8.06.

[705] Del. Gen. Corp. Law, §141(d); MBCA, §§8.03(c), 8.05.

As we have discussed above, shareholders who seek to contest a board election and file their own slate of candidates are generally required to draw up and mail their own proxy statements.[706] A new proxy rule adopted in 2010 that would have granted shareholders owning at least 3 per cent of the voting rights access to the company's proxy materials in order to nominate candidates was invalidated by the Court of Appeals for the DC Circuit.[707] This holding has been criticized for stifling shareholder democracy and usurping the SEC's rule-making authority.[708] However, it should be noted that the court was concerned with a problem that all legal systems face when they regulate the appointment and removal of directors. On the one hand, it is important to protect the shareholder franchise, mitigate the collective action problem that exists in large companies, and support an open competition for board positions to ensure that well qualified directors are elected. On the other hand, contested elections can be disruptive and costly. In addition, intense shareholder pressure may lead to a focus on short-term objectives and impede the ability of directors to manage the company for the benefit of a broader set of interests.[709] When the SEC makes use of its rulemaking authority under the Securities Acts, it is required to consider not only the goal of investor protection, but also the wider economic effects of its actions.[710] This was, in the view of the Court of Appeals, the SEC's shortcoming in adopting the rule on shareholder proxy access: The SEC had failed to perform a convincing cost-benefit analysis that was based on all relevant facts and free of contradictions.[711] While the federal proxy rules, therefore, continue to regulate proxy access restrictively, some state laws are more accommodating.[712] The Delaware General Corporation Law provides that the by-laws may grant shareholders the right to include one or more director nominees in the company's proxy statement.[713] This right may or may not be subject to additional requirements, such as a minimum ownership of shares by the nominating stockholder or a minimum duration of ownership.[714] Thus, the question is relegated to private ordering. This falls short of the unequivocal shareholder right that the SEC had sought to adopt, given that both the board and the shareholders have control over the by-laws in Delaware, but it has the advantage of leaving the difficult quantification of the costs and benefits of shareholder proxy access—a question that the SEC evidently struggled with—to those who are best placed to judge the individual circumstances of the company: the company's directors and shareholders.

Germany is another example of a country where the policy maker, in balancing the interests of shareholders in retaining direct control over the board and wider societal interests in insulating managers against short-term pressures of the market, sided (eventually) with the latter. In public stock corporations, the members of the management board are appointed by the supervisory board for a renewable period of not more than five years.[715] The supervisory board members, in turn, are elected by the general meeting,[716] unless the company is subject

[706] Exchange Act Rule 14a-8(i)(8) allows the company to omit shareholder proposals seeking to include specific individuals in the company's proxy materials for election to the board, see text to nn 540–541 above.

[707] *Business Roundtable v SEC* (n 512) 1144. See nn 511–512 above for further references.

[708] JD Cox and JC Baucom, 'The Emperor Has No Clothes: Confronting the D.C. Circuit's Usurpation of SEC Rulemaking Authority' (2012) 90 Texas Law Review 1811; GM Hayden and MT Bodie, 'The Bizarre Law and Economics of Business Roundtable v. SEC' (2012) 38 Journal of Corporate Law 101.

[709] For a critical assessment of these consequences of shareholder power, see WW Bratton and ML Wachter, 'The Case against Shareholder Empowerment' (2010) 158 University of Pennsylvania Law Review 653.

[710] When determining whether an action is necessary in the public interest, the Commission has to consider 'in addition to the protection of investors, whether the action will promote efficiency, competition, and capital formation', s 3(f) Securities Exchange Act of 1933.

[711] *Business Roundtable* (n 512) 1148–9.

[712] See text to nn 542–548 above for a discussion of the relationship between bylaw amendments allowing shareholder-nominated candidates to be included on the corporate ballot and the federal proxy rules.

[713] Del. Gen. Corp. Law, §112. See also text to n 545 above.

[714] ibid §112(1).

[715] AktG, §84(1). If the management board consists of more than one member, the supervisory board may appoint one of the members as chairman, ibid §84(2).

[716] ibid §101(1).

to one of the employee participation regimes provided for by German legislation.[717] This division of appointment rights between the general meeting and the supervisory board may seem intuitive, since it reflects the hierarchical structure of the two-tier board, and it can be found in most other legal systems that allow for dual boards, including France.[718] However, it is important to recognize that the layering of appointment (and removal) rights embodies a political decision and is not a feature inherent in the two-tier board model. In fact, as we saw above, until 1937, the supervisory board was not vested with the right to appoint the members of the management board, but the German Commercial Code (which contained the law on public stock corporations) left it to the articles of association to determine how the members of both boards should be appointed.[719] Thus, the shareholders could retain full and direct control over both boards. The law was changed because the policy maker intended to curb the rights of shareholders, who had been criticized for having exercised their powers in a manner that had given rise to allegedly unbridled and harmful capitalism in the years before the Great Depression. Coupled with limited removal rights, which were introduced at the same time, the reform shielded the managers, at least to some extent, from the pressures of investors and capital markets. This legal model has remained in force since the 1937 reforms. In line with the principle of limited contractual freedom,[720] it cannot be modified in the articles of association. Therefore, the general meeting cannot contractually be granted greater control rights than provided for in the Stock Corporation Act. The articles can also not do so indirectly, for example by vesting the power to appoint the members of the management board in a committee of the supervisory board or in an individual supervisory director who is the shareholders' nominee. The supervisory board has to decide as the full board by majority vote.[721]

Appointment procedures in continental European jurisdictions that follow predominantly the one-tier board model resemble the UK rules. In France, if the company opts for the one-tier board, the directors are appointed by the ordinary general meeting for a term of office not exceeding six years.[722] A vacancy that arises in the time between two ordinary general meetings can be filled by co-optation, subject to confirmation by the next ordinary general meeting (unless the number of directors falls below the legal minimum of three, in which case the board must immediately convene a general meeting).[723] If the company decides to set up a two-tier board (which, as we have seen, only a minority of French companies do), the executive directors are appointed by the supervisory board and the supervisory board members by the ordinary general meeting.[724] The supervisory board is also responsible for appointing one of the members of the executive board as president, who has the power to represent the company in transactions with third parties, unless the articles provide for a different arrangement.[725] However, the power to manage the company is not vested in the

[717] Employee participation regimes are laid down in three acts, Gesetz über die Mitbestimmung der Arbeitnehmer (MitbestG) [Co-Determination Act 1976], Gesetz über die Mitbestimmung der Arbeitnehmer in den Aufsichtsräten und Vorständen der Unternehmen des Bergbaus und der Eisen und Stahl erzeugenden Industrie (MontanMitbestG) [Coal and Steel Co-Determination Act 1951], Gesetz zur Ergänzung des Gesetzes über die Mitbestimmung der Arbeitnehmer in den Aufsichtsräten und Vorständen der Unternehmen des Bergbaus und der Eisen und Stahl erzeugenden Industrie (MontanMitbestGErgG) [Coal and Steel Co-Determination Act 1956], and Gesetz über die Drittelbeteiligung der Arbeitnehmer im Aufsichtsrat (DrittelbG) [Co-Determination Act 2004]. We will discuss the appointment and removal of members of the supervisory board under these regimes below in section D.III.

[718] Com, Art L225-59 (appointment of the members of the executive board), Art L225-75 (appointment of members of the supervisory board).

[719] See section D.III below.

[720] See text to n 120 above.

[721] AktG, §§107(3) sentence 3, 108(1).

[722] Com, Art L225-18.

[723] ibid Art L225-24. The board is required to fill the vacancy by co-optation if the number of directors falls below the minimum number determined in the articles, without falling below the legal minimum pursuant to Art L225-17.

[724] See n 718 above.

[725] Com, Art L225-66.

president alone, but in the executive board as a whole, which acts collectively and performs the same functions as the general manager in the one-tier company.[726] Therefore, in this respect, the president is comparable to the chairman of the management board of German companies,[727] but not to the CEO in Anglo-American corporate governance systems.

II. Removal

The right of shareholders to remove directors is representative of the general character of the relationship between the shareholders and directors propagated by a legal system. We can imagine a continuum of removal rights of differing strengths, with an unconditional right to remove directors at any time, with or without cause, by a simple majority of the votes cast in the general meeting at one extreme, and the lack of any direct right of the shareholders to dismiss directors, and this right instead being vested in the board of directors itself, at the other extreme. In most legal systems, we may expect to find gradual variations that are located in between these two extremes and tend towards either the paradigm of an absolute removal right or that of no removal right. Such variations may consist, for example, in a default unconditional right to dismiss directors that can be modified in the articles by providing that dismissal shall only be possible for cause, or in the vesting of the removal right in a third corporate organ, such as the German supervisory board. Asking where the actual removal right is located on the hypothetical continuum is useful because it tells us something about an important policy decision of the legislator. Should directors be insulated from shareholder pressure, or should shareholders have full control over the board to ensure that the directors and managers pursue a business strategy that is completely aligned with their preferences? We have touched upon this question repeatedly, especially in our analysis of the origins and limits of corporate power.[728] In our discussion below, we will see that the design of removal rights does not follow traditional boundaries of legal origins, competitive market economies versus coordinated economies, or shareholder versus stakeholder theory.[729] Rather, it reflects an understanding of the corporation as either predominantly a contractual institution or an institution created and structured by statute, which has implications for the question of who is regarded as the ultimate source of corporate power: the shareholders or the legislator who allocates decision-making power in a binding manner. Consequently, we will see that the UK and France congregate at one end of the spectrum, and the United States and Germany at the other.

Before we come to the operation of removal rights under UK, US, German, and French law, it may be useful to clarify one additional preliminary point. The dismissal of a director does not affect the contract of employment or the service contract that a director concludes with the company. Appointment and removal of directors are acts with significance for corporate law. They assign the legal status as a member of a corporate organ (the board of directors or the management board) to a particular individual. The employment or service contract, on the other hand, is governed by general principles of contract law. It obliges the director to render services to the company and gives an entitlement to remuneration. Even if a director has been removed for serious cause, this does not necessarily constitute a ground for dismissal without notice, i.e., the instant termination of the service contract. Therefore, in many cases, the company may be obliged under contract law to continue to remunerate directors even after they have been removed from office. In practice, in order to terminate

[726] ibid Art L225-64. With the consent of the supervisory board, management tasks can be delegated to individual board members, see Merle (n 157) para 502.

[727] As in France, the default rule in Germany is that management powers are exercised by the management board as a whole, AktG, §77(1).

[728] Above sections A and B.

[729] On competitive market economies and coordinated economies, see Chapter 4B.III.

a service contract amicably, a director will often receive a substantial severance payment, a so-called golden handshake.

UK law provides for a—seemingly—unambiguous bright line rule. The model articles envisage that a director retires at every third annual general meeting and may offer himself or herself for reappointment by the members.[730] Before the expiration of the director's term of office, the shareholders may remove the director by ordinary resolution with or without cause.[731] As explicitly stated in the Companies Act, this right cannot be waived in the articles or in any agreement between the director and the company.[732] It may be argued that there is a certain tension between the regulatory design of the removal right and the default rule to require a special resolution for shareholder instructions.[733] Arguably, if the directors can be removed by an ordinary resolution, they will be inclined to follow shareholder instructions even if these have not been adopted with the required supermajority. In any case, the Companies Act does not qualify the removal right and only provides for certain procedural steps to protect directors. The shareholders have to notify the director of the intended resolution. The director has the right to respond in writing and orally at the next general meeting.[734]

The rules in the United States are principally similar, with one important difference. Pursuant to the Model Business Corporation Act, a director can be removed with or without cause by a simple majority of the votes cast.[735] However, as opposed to UK law, the articles can provide that removal shall only be possible for cause or, by introducing cumulative voting,[736] that a minority of shareholders can prevent the removal of a director.[737] Delaware law goes a step further. If the board is classified, the default rule is that removal shall only be possible for cause.[738] Cause may consist, for example, in the director's lack of loyalty to the interests of the shareholders or lack of due care.[739] However, the courts also emphasize that if cause for the director's removal exists, certain procedural steps must be followed by those who intend to dismiss the director. It has been said that 'there must be the giving of specific charges, adequate notice, and full opportunity of meeting the accusation'.[740] If the shareholders fail to observe these due process requirements, the removal is void.

The rationale of the Delaware default rule is clear: The purpose of a classified board is to allow directors to serve a longer term of office without having to stand down and offer themselves for re-election at each annual general meeting. This purpose could be defeated easily if the shareholders could remove directors at any time. On the other hand, for the same reason, the introduction of a staggered board is of considerable importance. It implies not only that the directors' term of office is extended, but also that their removal is made more difficult. Thus, it can be seen as a mechanism to insulate directors against shareholder pressure, and it is indeed used by companies as a defensive strategy against hostile takeover bids.

In spite of the bright line rule that exists under UK law (and the default bright line rule under the MBCA and in Delaware in the absence of a classified board), directors may be able to mitigate or effectively abrogate the statutory removal right through appropriate contractual arrangements. This problem, the use of private ordering to entrench the directors in office, can appear in different guises and has arisen in most legal systems. The following two

[730] Model Articles for Public Companies, s 21(2)(b). The UK Corporate Governance Code 2018 is more stringent and requires in Provision 18 that '[a]ll directors should be subject to annual re-election. The board should set out in the papers accompanying the resolutions to elect each director the specific reasons why their contribution is, and continues to be, important to the company's long-term sustainable success.'

[731] Companies Act 2006, s 168. [732] ibid s 168(1).

[733] Davies and Worthington (n 12) para 14-49. [734] Companies Act 2006, s 169.

[735] MBCA, §8.08. [736] For a discussion of cumulative voting, see text to nn 395–396 above.

[737] A director cannot be removed if a number of votes sufficient to elect the director (which, as will be recalled, is not necessarily a majority of the votes cast in the case of cumulative voting) is voted against the director's removal, MBCA, §8.08(c).

[738] Del. Gen. Corp. Law, §141(k)(1). [739] *Bossier v Connell*, 1986 WL 12785 (Del. Ch.).

[740] ibid, following *Campbell v Loews, Inc.*, 134 A.2d 852 (Del. Ch. 1957).

cases, the first from the UK and the second from Delaware, present two examples of contractual devices that render it more difficult for shareholders to replace the incumbent directors. The courts, therefore, had to deal with the same underlying conflict, albeit in different contexts, and they resolved the conflict by relying on different legal principles.

***Bushell v Faith* [1970] AC 1099 (House of Lords)**

The plaintiff was a director of and shareholder in the company, which had been incorporated on September 19, 1960, by herself and her mother, Mrs. Agnes Sophia Mary Faith. Mrs. Agnes Faith was, prior to the incorporation of the company, the owner of a block of 17 flats situate at and known as Bush Court, Southgate, N.14, in the County of Greater London. She transferred that block of flats to the company in consideration of which the company issued 299 of its 300 shares to her and one share to her nominee. The company was incorporated with the object of acquiring, owning, leasing and managing Bush Court. It had an issued capital of £300 in £1 shares. It was a private company and adopted Table A of the Companies Act, 1948, as its articles of association with certain modifications, of which one was contained in article 9 of its articles and read as follows:

In the event of a resolution being proposed at any general meeting of the company for the removal from office of any director, any shares held by that director shall on a poll in respect of such resolution carry the right to three votes per share and regulation 62 of Part 1 of Table A shall be construed accordingly.

In November 1968, the company had three shareholders: the plaintiff, the defendant, Geoffrey Leopold Faith, who was her brother and the only other director, and their sister, Dr. Kathleen Bayne. Each of them held 100 shares. The plaintiff and her sister, being dissatisfied with the conduct of the defendant as a director, requisitioned a general meeting of the company to be held on November 22, 1968, to consider and, if thought fit, to pass a resolution for the removal of the defendant from office as a director. On a poll at the meeting, the plaintiff and her sister voted for the resolution, and the defendant voted against it. A dispute then arose as to whether the resolution had been passed or defeated. The plaintiff contended that it had been passed by 200 votes, being those of herself and her sister, to 100, being those of the defendant. He, however, contended that in accordance with article 9 his 100 shares carried 300 votes and that, therefore, the resolution was defeated by 300 votes to 200. The plaintiff issued a writ on behalf of herself and all the other shareholders in the company other than the defendant, claiming a declaration that the defendant had been validly removed from office as a director and an injunction restraining him from acting or purporting to act as a director. The company was joined as a defendant formally for the purpose of being bound by the decision of the court. On an application by motion for an interlocutory injunction Ungoed-Thomas J. held that article 9 was invalid because it infringed section 184(1) of the Companies Act, 1948,[741] and that, therefore, the resolution had been validly passed, so that the defendant had been removed from office as a director....

Lord Donovan [for the majority]

My Lords, the issue here is the true construction of section 184 of the Companies Act, 1948: and I approach it with no conception of what the legislature wanted to achieve by the section other than such as can reasonably be deduced from its language.

Clearly it was intended to alter the method by which a director of a company could be removed while still in office. It enacts that this can be done by the company by ordinary resolution. Furthermore, it may be achieved notwithstanding anything in the company's articles, or in any agreement between the company and the director.

Accordingly any case (and one knows there were many) where the articles prescribed that a director should be removable during his period of office only by a special resolution or an extraordinary resolution, each of which necessitated inter alia a three to one majority of those present and voting at the meeting, is overridden by section 184. A simple majority of the votes will now suffice; an ordinary resolution being, in my opinion, a resolution capable of being carried by such a majority. Similarly any agreement, whether evidenced by the articles or otherwise, that a director shall be a director for life or for some fixed period is now also overreached.

[741] [Footnote by authors.] Comparable to s 168 Companies Act 2006.

The field over which section 184 operates is thus extensive for it includes, admittedly, all companies with a quotation on the Stock Exchange.

It is now contended, however, that it does something more; namely, that it provides in effect that when the ordinary resolution proposing the removal of the director is put to the meeting each shareholder present shall have one vote per share and no more: and that any provision in the articles providing that any shareholder shall, in relation to *this* resolution, have 'weighted' votes attached to his shares, is also nullified by section 184. A provision for such 'weighting' of votes which applies generally, that is as part of the normal pattern of voting, is accepted by the appellant as unobjectionable: but an article such as the one here under consideration which is special to a resolution seeking the removal of a director falls foul of section 184 and is overridden by it.

Why should this be? The section does not say so, as it easily could. And those who drafted it and enacted it certainly would have included among their numbers many who were familiar with the phenomenon of articles of association carrying 'weighted votes'. It must therefore have been plain at the outset that unless some special provision were made, the mere direction that an ordinary resolution would do in order to remove a director would leave the section at risk of being made inoperative in the way that has been done here. Yet no such provision was made, and in this Parliament followed its practice of leaving to companies and their shareholders liberty to allocate voting rights as they pleased.

When, therefore, it is said that a decision in favour of the respondent in this case would defeat the purpose of the section and make a mockery of it, it is being assumed that Parliament *intended* to cover every possible case and block up every loophole. I see no warrant for any such assumption. A very large part of the relevant field is in fact covered and covered effectively, and there may be good reasons why Parliament should leave some companies with freedom of maneuver in this particular matter. There are many small companies which are conducted in practice as though they were little more than partnerships, particularly family companies running a family business; and it is, unfortunately, sometimes necessary to provide some safeguard against family quarrels having their repercussions in the boardroom. I am not, of course, saying that this is such a case: I merely seek to repel the argument that unless the section is construed in the way the appellant wants, it has become 'inept' and 'frustrated'.

I would dismiss the appeal.

Lord Morris of Borth-Y-Gest [dissenting]

My Lords, it is provided by section 184(1) that a company may by ordinary resolution remove a director before the expiration of his period of office. The company may do so notwithstanding anything to the contrary in its articles. So if an article provided that a director was irremovable he could nevertheless be removed if an ordinary resolution to that effect was passed. So also if an article provided that a director could only be removed by a resolution carried by a majority greater than a simple majority he would nevertheless be removed if a resolution was passed by a simple majority.

Some shares may, however, carry a greater voting power than others. On a resolution to remove a director shares will therefore carry the voting power that they possess. But this does not, in my view, warrant a device such as article 9 introduces. Its unconcealed effect is to make a director irremovable. If the question is posed whether the shares of the respondent possess any added voting weight the answer must be that they possess none whatsoever beyond, if valid, an ad hoc weight for the special purpose of circumventing section 184. If article 9 were writ large it would set out that a director is not to be removed against his will and that in order to achieve this and to thwart the express provision of section 184 the voting power of any director threatened with removal is to be deemed to be greater than it actually is. The learned judge thought that to sanction this would be to make a mockery of the law. I think so also.

I would allow the appeal.

An entrenchment problem essentially similar to that addressed by the House of Lords in *Bushell v Faith* was faced by the Delaware courts in the following case, which deals with the permissibility of defensive measures, here a so-called 'dead hand' poison pill, adopted by the board of directors to frustrate a hostile takeover bid.

***Carmody v Toll Bros.*, 723 A.2d 1180 (Del. Ch. 1998)**

Jacobs, Vice Chancellor:

[T]he complaint states a claim that the 'dead hand' provision would impermissibly interfere with the directors' statutory power to manage the business and affairs of the corporation. That power is conferred by 8 Del. C. § 141(a) ... The 'dead hand' poison pill is intended to thwart hostile bids by vesting shareholders with preclusive rights that cannot be redeemed except by the Continuing Directors. Thus, the one action that could make it practically possible to redeem the pill-replacing the entire board-could make that pill redemption legally impossible to achieve. The 'dead hand' provision would jeopardize a newly-elected future board's ability to achieve a business combination by depriving that board of the power to redeem the pill without obtaining the consent of the 'Continuing Directors', who (it may be assumed) would constitute a minority of the board. In this manner, it is claimed, the 'dead hand' provision would interfere with the board's power to protect fully the corporation's (and its shareholders') interests in a transaction that is one of the most fundamental and important in the life of a business enterprise.

The statutory analysis employed, and the result reached here, are consistent with and supported by *Bank of New York Co. v Irving Bank Corp.* There, the New York Supreme Court invalidated a 'continuing director' provision that the target company board had adopted as an amendment to a preexisting rights plan, as a defense against a tender offer/proxy contest initiated by a hostile bidder. The New York court observed that the continuing director provision at issue there created several different classes of directors having different powers, and that it also effectively limits the powers of the future board which is not a continuation of the present board or which is not approved by it, while still leaving those powers to a board which is approved. For example, the present board, or one approved by it, may redeem the rights. A future board, properly elected by a fifty-one percent majority, but not approved by the present board, may not redeem the shares. Those observations apply equally here.

In Bank of New York, the court found that the continuing director provision violated the New York Business Corporation Law requirement that restrictions upon the board's powers are invalid, unless all the incorporators or all shareholders of record authorize the inclusion of the limitations or restrictions in the certificate of incorporation. Although the relevant language of the Delaware and New York statutes is not identical, their underlying intent is the same: both statutes require that limitations upon the directors' power be expressed in the corporation's charter.... [T]he Toll Brothers 'dead hand' provision, if legally valid, would embed structural power-related distinctions between groups of directors that no successor board could abolish ....'

Questions and comments:

1. The court in *Carmody* refers to a 'dead hand' poison pill. A poison pill is a takeover defence that usually consists in the distribution of a dividend in the form of a new class of convertible preferred stock by the company to its shareholders. The new security is convertible into a large number of common shares at least equal to the number of outstanding shares. The shareholder rights plan under which the convertible stock is distributed typically provides that if an acquirer purchases in excess of a specified percentage of the target's stock (for example, 20%) and thereafter acquires the target in a business combination (merger, sale of assets etc.), the preferred stock becomes convertible into the common stock of the acquirer at a conversion ratio that permits the holder of the preferred to purchase the acquirer's common stock at a substantial discount (so-called flip-over provision). Thus, the poison pill forces the bidder to tender for all or a high percentage of the target's shares in order to minimize the dilutive effect of the flip over on its own stock.

   Poison pill plans are vulnerable if the target's board has the power to redeem the pill. This used to be a common feature of poison pill plans. The board could redeem the preferred security at a modest price for a limited period after the triggering event occurred in order to force the bidder to negotiate with the target's board. The bidder can then combine a tender offer with a proxy fight for the appointment of new directors, conditioning the tender offer on the redemption of the target's poison pill by the bidder's nominees if the proxy fight is successful. The effect of this strategy is to make the proxy fight a referendum on the offer and to put the decision whether or not to redeem the pill in the hands of the shareholders. The 'dead hand' pill is a variant of the poison pill designed to close this loophole. It includes a prohibition of its redemption by directors other than those in office at the time of the pill's adoption, or their nominees. In other words, the pill is frozen in place until the expiration of its typically 10-year term.

2. What is the underlying rationale of section 168 of the Companies Act 2006 and why was the House of Lords in *Bushell v Faith* prepared to accept an arrangement that rendered section 168 ineffective? Can we generalize *Bushell v Faith* and apply the ruling to any type of company?
3. Comparing *Bushell v Faith* and *Carmody*, which legal principles were determinative of the permissibility of the multiple voting rights and the 'dead hand' poison pill, respectively? Are the two cases examples of a more fundamental difference in the approach of Delaware and English law to the position of directors and shareholders in the company?

In legal systems providing for a two-tier board system, the design of removal rights is, unsurprisingly, more complex. In Germany, it is—broadly speaking—a mirror imagine of the appointment process. The members of the management board are removed by a resolution of the supervisory board[742] and the members of the supervisory board by the general meeting (or, in the case of employee representatives on the supervisory board, by the constituency that has appointed the member).[743] However, the Stock Corporation Act draws an important distinction between the removal of management board members and supervisory board members. The latter can be removed at any time, with or without cause. As far as shareholder-appointed members of the supervisory board are concerned, all that is required is a qualified majority of three-fourths of the votes cast.[744] The members of the management board, on the other hand, can only be removed for serious cause.[745] Again, we can see that the Stock Corporation Act insulates the managers, at least to a certain extent, from external pressures. The law seeks to ensure that they can act in the best interest of the company, understood as a broader coalition of interests than short-term shareholder value maximization, and without having to be concerned about interference by the supervisory board (or the shareholders) in day-to-day business operations.[746]

The Stock Corporation Act provides for a non-exhaustive list of grounds to remove members of the management board: gross breach of duty, incapacity to manage the company properly, and withdrawal of confidence by the general meeting.[747] More generally, the courts define 'serious cause' as a situation where it is unreasonable to expect the company to wait until the end of the director's term of office to replace the director.[748] Examples of a gross breach of duty include investments in speculative ventures that damage the reputation of the company,[749] commission of a crime,[750] or misappropriation of corporate assets.[751] Examples of the second type of serious cause, inability to manage the company properly, include long-lasting illness, lack of the necessary knowledge, or personal animosity towards other members of the management board that make it impossible for the managers to work together and manage the company effectively.[752] On the other hand, simple disagreements about business strategy between the management board and the supervisory board (or the shareholders)

[742] AktG, §84(3). [743] ibid §103. [744] ibid §103(1) sentence 2. [745] ibid §84(3).

[746] See also §76(1) AktG, which emphasizes that the company shall be managed by the management board under its own responsibility.

[747] AktG, §84(3) sentence 2. [748] BGH AG 2007, 125. [749] BGH WM 1956, 865.

[750] BGH NJW 1956, 1513. The criminal act does not need to be related to the performance of the manager's duties as a member of the management board.

[751] BGH WM 1984, 29. [752] ibid.

generally do not justify the removal of the managers.[753] The statutory restriction of removal rights is intended to address precisely this type of conflict. It is the prerogative of the management board to decide on matters of corporate policy, and the supervisory board is generally required to wait until the management board members stand for re-election if it disagrees.

Finally, a withdrawal of confidence by the general meeting constitutes sufficient cause to remove a member of the management board, even if the manager has not neglected his duties and is able to manage the company properly. In general, a withdrawal of confidence requires a resolution by the general meeting. It is unclear whether shareholders implicitly withdraw their confidence if they refuse to ratify the acts of the managers at the annual general meeting,[754] A number of commentators argue that this is the case, but at least one court of appeal has held that shareholders may decide for different reasons not to ratify the acts of the management, which may or may not amount to a withdrawal of confidence.[755] Furthermore, it should be noted that the power of the general meeting to remove a management board member by withdrawing its confidence is limited in two important respects. First, the supervisory board is not entitled to remove a director if the withdrawal was made for manifestly arbitrary reasons. Reasons are manifestly arbitrary if they are clearly untenable and the shareholders pursue ulterior motives with the no-confidence resolution; for example, where they seek to remove a manager because the manager refused to act according to instructions of the shareholders that could not be given legally[756] or they pursue an illegal objective, such as replacing the director with another person who is more amenable to colluding with the shareholder in an illicit activity.[757] Secondly, the supervisory board is free to follow the resolution of the general meeting and remove the director or disregard the resolution. In deciding on the removal, the members of the supervisory board are bound by the general duties of directors and required to act in the best interest of the company.[758]

Turning to France, we find again that the rules largely resemble UK law. The general meeting has the right to remove directors at any time with or without cause by ordinary resolution.[759] The general meeting is not required to give any reasons for the dismissal,[760] but the exercise of the right to remove a director is subject to the same legal constraints as any other action by the shareholders. In particular, the requirement not to act in a manner that constitutes an abuse of law generally makes it necessary to notify the directors of the intention to remove them and give them the opportunity to be heard before the general meeting votes on the matter.[761] However, this does not change the fact that the shareholders' right to dismiss directors is absolute and limitations in the articles or otherwise, for example in a shareholder agreement, are generally invalid. For example, a provision in a shareholder agreement stipulating that no director shall be dismissed without prior approval by the board of directors is unenforceable and does not give rise to damages for breach of contract if the shareholders remove the director in violation of the agreement.[762] Courts are also prepared to invalidate agreements that do not directly impede the shareholders' removal right, but dissuade shareholders from exercising their right because of the financial implications of

[753] Koch (n 117) §84, para 36. [754] AktG, §120. [755] Kammergericht Berlin, AG 2007, 745.

[756] Kammergericht Berlin, ZIP 2003, 1042. As we have seen, shareholders do not have an instruction right under German stock corporation law, section A.III above.

[757] BGHZ 13, 188.

[758] If a question arises about the legality of the removal, the director can file a lawsuit against the company, alleging that the supervisory board did not act in the best interest of the company or incorrectly assumed that there was serious cause for a removal of the director. If the court determines in a final and binding manner (i.e. no appeal is permissible) that serious cause did not exist, the director will be reinstated. However, until the court decision becomes final, the director has lost the position on the board and cannot exercise any powers that come with that position, see §84(3) sentence 4 AktG.

[759] Com, Art L225-18. [760] Cass com, 3 January 1985, *Bull. civ.* IV, no 6.

[761] Cass com, 14 May 2013, *Bull. civ.* IV, no 80.

[762] ibid. The director cannot claim to be reinstated if these requirements are violated, but can only claim damages. The burden of proving that the shareholders acted in bad faith or with the intent to harm is borne by the director, Merle (n 157) para 435.

the dismissal, for example if the agreement provides for a large termination payment to be made to the director.[763]

It is noteworthy that the same principles apply to companies with a two-tier board. In such companies, the general meeting has the right to remove the members of both the executive board[764] and the supervisory board.[765] In addition, the members of the executive board may be dismissed by the supervisory board if the articles of association provide for this power.[766] Furthermore, the Commercial Code provides that the general meeting has the authority to remove the directors even if this is not on the agenda of the meeting.[767] Thus, in contrast to the German version of the two-tier system, the French legislator sought to ensure that the general meeting retains full control over the managers. The law requires neither serious cause for removal, nor a resolution adopted by a supermajority, nor indeed that the supervisory board is involved in the decision. As we have seen, this strong position of the general meeting, potentially with direct control over both boards, was also a feature of the German law on the public stock corporation when the German rules were initially drafted in the nineteenth century.[768] However, the development of German company law reached a critical juncture in the 1920s and 1930s not experienced by French law, when extraordinary economic and political conditions created the momentum for a fundamental reorientation of company law legislation that resulted in the partial disempowerment of German shareholders.[769]

III. Appointment and removal under co-determination

German Co-determination Act

§ 7—Composition of the supervisory board

(1) The supervisory board of an enterprise
   1. with in general not more than 10,000 employees is composed of six members representing the owners and six members representing the employees;
   2. with in general more than 10,000, but not more than 20,000, employees is composed of eight members representing the owners and eight members representing the employees;
   3. with in general more than 20,000 employees is composed of ten members representing the owners and ten members representing the employees.

   In the case of the enterprises mentioned in Sentence 1, no. 1, the articles of association may provide that Sentence 1, no. 2 or no. 3 shall apply. In the case of the enterprises mentioned in Sentence 1, no. 2, the articles of association may provide that Sentence 1, no. 3 shall apply.

(2) The members of the supervisory board representing the employees shall include
   1. in a supervisory board with six members representing the employees, four employees of the enterprise and two representatives of labour unions;
   2. in a supervisory board with eight members representing the employees, six employees of the enterprise and two representatives of labour unions;
   3. in a supervisory board with ten members representing the employees, seven employees of the enterprise and three representatives of labour unions.

[763] Cass com, 5 February 1974, *Bull. civ.* IV, no 51 (dealing with an agreement that granted the general manager the right to receive a termination payment equivalent to his gross salary for 30 months, unless the dismissal was for gross negligence). But see also Cass com, 15 November 2011, case no 10-20544 (holding that a provision in the articles of association requiring serious cause was valid). For listed companies, severance pay is now regulated in Art L225-42-1 Code de commerce, inserted by Law no 2007-1223 of 21 August 2007 (Loi en faveur du travail, de l'emploi et du pouvoir d'achat—TEPA), JORF no 193 of 22 August 2007, 13945, and amended by Law no 2015-990 of 6 August 2015 (Loi pour la croissance, l'activité et l'égalité des chances économiques), JORF no 181 of 7 August 2015, 13537. In addition, the AFEP-MEDEF Corporate Governance Code of Listed Corporations of 2018 recommends that termination payments should not exceed two years' salary, s 24.5.1.

[764] ibid Art L225-61. [765] ibid Art L225-75. [766] ibid Art L225-61.

[767] ibid Art L225-105, para 3. [768] Chapter 4E.I.3. [769] Text to nn 93–111 above.

(3) Of the supervisory board members representing the employees of a stock exchange listed enterprise within the meaning of § 1(1) [public stock corporations, limited partnerships by shares, private limited liability companies and cooperatives with in general more than 2,000 employees], in the case of § 96(2), Sentence 3 of the Stock Corporation Act,[770] at least 30% shall be women and at least 30% shall be men.

(4) The employees of the enterprise referred to in Subsection 2 shall be of the age of 18 or above and shall have been employed by the company for at least one year. Periods of employment in another enterprise whose employees have the right to participate in the election of the supervisory board members of the enterprise pursuant to this Act shall be taken into account in calculating the one-year threshold.[771] These periods must immediately precede the date from which the employees are entitled to elect supervisory board members of the enterprise. The further eligibility requirements pursuant to § 8(1) of the Works Council Constitution Act must be met.[772]

(5) The labour unions referred to in Subsection 2 must be represented in the enterprise itself or in another enterprise whose employees have the right to participate in the election of the supervisory board members of the enterprise pursuant to this Act.

§ 27—Chairman of the supervisory board

(1) The supervisory board elects a chairman and a vice-chairman from among its members by a majority of two-thirds of the statutory members of the supervisory board.

(2) If the required majority pursuant to Subsection 1 has not been reached in the election of the chairman or the vice-chairman, a second vote shall be held to elect the chairman and the vice-chairman. In the second round of voting, the supervisory board members representing the owners elect the chairman and the supervisory board members representing the employees elect the vice-chairman by a simple majority of the votes cast.

(3) Immediately after the election of the chairman and the vice-chairman, the supervisory board shall set up a committee composed of the chairman, the vice-chairman, and one member elected by a majority of the votes cast by the supervisory board members representing the employees and the supervisory board members representing the owners, respectively, to perform the duties pursuant to § 31(3), Sentence 1.

§ 28—Quorum

The supervisory board is only quorate if at least half of the statutory members of the board participate in the decision-making. . . .

§ 29—Voting

(1) Notwithstanding Subsection 2 and §§27, 31 and 32, resolutions of the supervisory board require a majority of the votes cast.

(2) In the case that a vote in the supervisory board results in a tie, the chairman of the supervisory board shall have a second vote in a new vote on the same matter, if this vote also results in a tie . . . The vice-chairman shall not have such a second vote.

[770] [Footnote by authors.] The text of §96(2) AktG is reproduced in Chapter 4E.III.5.

[771] [Footnote by authors.] Pursuant to §5(1) MitbestG, the employees of companies that are part of a corporate group within the meaning of §18 AktG have the right to participate in elections of employee representatives to the supervisory board of the controlling enterprise. 'Control' for purposes of forming a corporate group is defined in §§17–18 AktG. For example, a company is controlled by another undertaking if the latter holds a majority of the voting rights in the former, §17(2) AktG.

[772] [Footnote by authors.] §8(1) Betriebsverfassungsgesetz [Works Council Constitution Act] provides that '[a]ll employees who are entitled to vote and who have been employed in the establishment, or principally worked for the establishment from home, for six months shall be eligible for election to the works council . . . Persons who have been disqualified from holding public office pursuant to a conviction of a criminal offence shall not be eligible for election to the works council'.

§ 31—Appointment and removal

(1) Notwithstanding Subsections 2-5, the appointment of the members of the organ authorized to represent the enterprise and the removal of such members shall be governed by §§84 and 85 of the Stock Corporation Act. This shall not apply to limited partnerships by shares.
(2) The supervisory board shall appoint the members of the organ authorized to represent the enterprise by a majority of at least two-thirds of the votes of the board's members.
(3) Failing an appointment pursuant to Subsection 2, the committee of the supervisory board referred to in § 27(3) is required to submit a nomination for the appointment to the supervisory board within one month after the vote was held in which the required majority pursuant to Subsection 2 was not obtained; this nomination does not exclude other nominations. The supervisory board appoints the members of the organ authorized to represent the enterprise by a majority of the votes of its members.
(4) Failing an appointment pursuant to Subsection 3, the chairman of the supervisory board shall have a second vote in a new vote; Subsection 3, Sentence 2 shall apply ... The vice-chairman shall not have such a second vote.
(5) Subsections 2-4 shall apply mutatis mutandis to the removal of a member of the organ authorized to represent the enterprise.

French Commercial Code[773]

Article L225-23

In companies whose securities are admitted to trading on a regulated market, if the report presented to the general meeting by the board of directors pursuant to Article L225-102 establishes that the shares held by the companies' staff and by the staff of affiliated companies within the meaning of Article L225-180 represent more than 3% of the company's share capital, one or more directors shall be elected by the general meeting of shareholders on a proposal from the shareholders as provided for in Article L225-102. The shareholders shall vote on these appointments under the conditions determined in the constitution. These directors shall be elected from among the employee-shareholders or, if appropriate, from among the employee-shareholders who are members of the supervisory board of a company investment trust that holds shares in the company. Such directors are not counted when the minimum and maximum numbers of directors are determined pursuant to Article L225-17 ...

Article L225-27

The constitution may specify that, in addition to the directors whose number and method of appointment are specified in Articles L225-17 and L225-18, the board of directors shall contain directors elected either by the company's employees or by the employees of the company and those of its direct or indirect subsidiaries which have their registered office located on French territory. The number of these directors may not exceed four, or five in companies whose shares are admitted to trading on a regulated market, nor may they exceed one third of the number of the other directors. If the number of directors elected by the employees is equal to or in excess of two, professional technical staff, executives and similar employees shall have at least one seat.

The directors elected by the employees shall not be taken into account for the determination of the minimum number and the maximum number of directors specified in Article L225-17, nor for the application of the first paragraph of Article L225-18-1.

Article L225-27-1

I. In companies that employ, at the end of two consecutive financial years, at least one thousand permanent employees in the company and its direct or indirect subsidiaries, where these companies have their registered office in France, or that employ at least five thousand permanent employees in the company and its direct or indirect subsidiaries, where the companies have their registered office in France and abroad, it must be provided in the constitution that the board of directors comprise, in addition to the directors to be appointed pursuant to Articles L225-17 and L225-18 of this code, directors representing the employees ...

[773] Translation by Legifrance, https://www.legifrance.gouv.fr/Traductions/en-English/Legifrance-translations.

II. There shall be at least two directors representing employees in companies with more than twelve directors, as set out in Articles L225-17 and L225-18, and at least one director if the number of directors is equal to or less than twelve.

Directors representing employees are not taken into account when determining the minimum and maximum number of directors specified in Article L225-17, or for the purposes of the first paragraph of Article L225-18-1. The election of directors representing employees pursuant to the first paragraph of section III of this article must respect parity in accordance with Article L225-28. Where two directors are appointed pursuant to the second paragraph of section III of this article, the group works council, the central works council of the enterprise, or the works council shall appoint a woman and a man.

III. Within six months after the end of the second of the two financial years mentioned in I, having considered the opinion of the group works council, the central works council of the enterprise or the works council, as applicable, the extraordinary general meeting shall amend the constitution to determine the conditions under which the directors representing the employees are appointed, based on one of the following methods:

1 Organization of an election by employees of the company and its direct or indirect subsidiaries, whose registered office is located in France, under the conditions set out in Article L225-28;
2 Appointment by the group works council specified in Article L2331-1 of the Labour Code, the central works council or the works council of the company mentioned in I of this article, as the case may be;
3 Appointment by the trade union organization that obtained the most votes during the first round of the elections mentioned in Articles L2122-1 and L2122-4 of the Labour Code in the company and its direct or indirect subsidiaries, whose registered office is located in France, when only one director is to be appointed, or by each of the two trade union organizations having obtained the most votes in the first round of these elections when two directors are to be appointed;
4 When at least two directors are to be appointed, the appointment of one of the directors according to one of the methods set out in points 1 to 3, and the other by the European works council, if there is one, or for European companies as defined by Article L2351-1 of the Labour Code by the employee representative body mentioned in Article L2352-16 of the same code or, failing that, by the works council of the European company mentioned in Article L2353-1 of the said code.

The election or appointment of directors representing employees shall take place within six months of the amendment of the constitution provided for in the first paragraph of this section III.

IV.-V. . . .

One of the politically most charged issues in corporate law is the participation of workers in the management of companies. Certain information and consultation rights of employees are now fairly widespread, especially in the European Union, where companies with at least 1,000 employees have to establish so-called works councils if requested to do so by at least 100 employees.[774] The idea of employee participation in the management of companies, also called co-determination, goes beyond such consultation models. It involves the appointment of employee representatives to the board of directors (or the supervisory board in two-tier board systems), where they perform the same functions, and have the same duties, as all other directors. Models of employee participation have been discussed in some European countries since the nineteenth century,[775] and the first legislative steps towards board level

[774] Directive 2009/38/EC on the establishment of a European Works Council or a procedure in Community-scale undertakings and Community-scale groups of undertakings for the purposes of informing and consulting employees, [2009] OJ L122/28.

[775] HJ Teuteberg, *Geschichte der industriellen Mitbestimmung in Deutschland: Ursprung und Entwicklung ihrer Vorläufer im Denken und in der Wirklichkeit des 19. Jahrhunderts* (Mohr 1961).

representation were taken in Germany in the interwar years.[776] More comprehensive regulation was adopted after World War II, again especially in Germany, which became the country with the most extensive employee participation regime in capitalist economies.[777] However, it has been pointed out that this strengthening of employee participation rights 'has not followed any logical sequence ... [and] has not occurred as a result of rational decision, but rather through a process of political assertion and compromise'.[778] This statement underlines the political nature of codetermination, which is not an intrinsic feature of corporate governance systems, but an outcome of a bargaining process between institutional actors, in the case of Germany employers, employees, and trade unions.[779] Under different conditions, this bargaining process produces different outcomes, as can be seen in the United States and UK, where co-determination was discussed at different points in time, but never embraced by the legislator.[780]

Another widely discussed dimension of codetermination is its impact on firm performance and firm behaviour. A large number of empirical studies seek to identify whether the participation of employees in the management of companies is conducive or detrimental to financial outcomes such as profitability, productivity, and innovative activity. However, in spite of decades of research, the empirical evidence is not conclusive and the matter continues to be controversial.[781] To give an example, some studies that investigate the effect of the German rules on co-determination find that more extensive employee representation requirements[782] are statistically significantly and negatively associated with the company's market-to-book ratio of equity and Tobin's q (the market value of the firm divided by the replacement cost of assets) and positively associated with the ratio of employees to sales and the wage bill to sales.[783] Thus, these findings indicate that codetermination results in the diversion of resources from the shareholders to the employees. Companies employ more workers and pay their workers more, and shareholder value is destroyed. While the results do not allow us to make any claims regarding the overall efficiency of a particular corporate governance arrangement, namely its impact on social welfare, they are in line with a narrative that views corporate actors as rent-seeking agents. As power is redistributed within the firm, different stakeholders succeed in appropriating a greater share of corporate wealth. However, the findings have been called into question by other studies that have found a positive effect of co-determination on the value of German firms, at least in complex industries requiring

[776] See Betriebsrätegesetz [German Works Council Act] of 4 February 1920, RGBl I, 147, and the implementing Gesetz über die Entsendung von Betriebsratsmitgliedern in den Aufsichtsrat [Act on the Appointment of Members of the Works Council to the Supervisory Board] of 15 February 1922, RGBl I, 209, requiring the appointment of one or two employee representatives to the supervisory board.

[777] For a historical account of post-Second World War regulation of co-determination in Germany, see W Streeck, *Social Institutions and Economic Performance* (Sage 1992) 137–68.

[778] KJ Hopt, 'New Ways in Corporate Governance: European Experiments with Labor Representation on Corporate Boards' (1984) 82 Michigan Law Review 1338, 1348.

[779] CW Summers, 'Worker Participation in the U.S. and West Germany: A Comparative Study from an American Perspective' (1980) 28 American Journal of Comparative Law 367, 374–5.

[780] ibid 375–7; Lord Wedderburn, 'The Legal Development of Corporate Responsibility' in KJ Hopt and G Teubner, *Corporate Governance and Directors' Liability* (de Gruyter 1985) 3, 32–40.

[781] For a summary of the empirical evidence, see JT Addison and C Schnabel, 'Worker Directors: A German Product that Didn't Export?' (2009) IZA Discussion Paper No 3918. Similar studies have sought to identify the effect of works councils on firm performance and found conflicting evidence of a negative or positive association, or no statistically significant association, depending on the sample of firms and the economic outcomes investigated. A good survey of the literature is given by JT Addison, *The Economics of Codetermination: Lessons from the German Experience* (Palgrave Macmillan 2009); JT Addison, C Schnabel, and J Wagner, 'The Course of Research into the Economic Consequences of German Works Councils' (2004) 42 British Journal of Industrial Relations 255.

[782] German law provides for two main types of codetermination: the requirement that employee representatives receive one-third or one-half of supervisory board positions, see n 787 below.

[783] G Gorton, and FA Schmid, 'Capital, Labor, and the Firm: A Study of German Codetermination' (2004) JEEA 863.

high levels of coordination with workers and in more concentrated industries where firms have greater free cash flow.[784] Thus, in appropriate circumstances, employee representatives seem to facilitate coordination within the firm, provide an improved channel of communication, and reduce the ability of management to extract private benefits of control.[785]

Given the prominence of co-determination in German corporate governance, we will start our legal analysis with that country and present the relevant rules in some detail. The general German corporate law that we discussed above[786] is complemented by several statutes laying down participation rights of employees. The most important of these statutes, providing for the most extensive rights of employees, is the Co-Determination Act 1976. Enterprises are subject to the provisions of the act if they are established, inter alia, in the form of a German private or public limited company (GmbH or AG) or a limited partnership with shares (KGaA) and have on average more than 2,000 employees.[787] In determining whether the parent company has reached the statutory threshold, the employees of subsidiaries are aggregated.[788] However, the Act does not explicitly state whether the same applies to employees working abroad for a branch or a subsidiary of the company, or employees only count towards the threshold if they are employed in Germany. Given that the German co-determination rules implement policy goals that reflect a specific social equilibrium, and that they are part of a broader legislative framework regulating the German corporate economy in light of this equilibrium, it is convincing to argue that only employees working in Germany should be taken into account in calculating the total number of the company's employees. Indeed, this is the view of most commentators, who argue that the scope of the employee participation laws should be determined according to the principle of territoriality.[789] As a further consequence of the application of the territoriality principle, workers of the company or a subsidiary located outside of Germany do not have the right to vote or stand as candidates in elections of employee representatives to the supervisory board, and employees on the supervisory board are required to resign when they take up a position in another country. Some workers of German corporate groups based in other Member States of the EU challenged this interpretation of the Co-Determination Act, arguing that it infringed the prohibition of discrimination on grounds of nationality and freedom of movement for workers under the EU Treaties.[790] These arguments initially met with success in several German courts. The courts held that disregarding employees working in establishments of a company in other Member States would lead to distortions of competition and discriminate against these employees, who could be assumed to be generally not German citizens. Furthermore, the risk of losing their seat on the supervisory board might dissuade workers

[784] L Fauver and ME Fuerst, 'Does good corporate governance include employee representation? Evidence from German corporate boards' (2006) 82 Journal of Financial Economics 673.

[785] ibid 677. However, the authors also claim that the optimal level of employee representation is likely below 50%, i.e. below the level mandated by the most demanding German co-determination regime: ibid 703.

[786] Sections D.I and D.II.

[787] MitbestG, §1. Special rules exist for companies in the mining and iron and steel producing industries with more than 1,000 employees on average (Coal and Steel Co-Determination Act 1951 or 1956) and for companies with less than 2,000 but on average more than 500 employees (Co-Determination Act 2004 (One-Third Participation Act), which provides for an appointment of one-third of the members of the supervisory board by the employees). Currently, 651 enterprises are subject to the Co-Determination Act 1976, including 253 public companies and 343 private limited companies. Regularly updated information on employee participation in Germany and Europe is provided by the Hans Böckler Stiftung http://www.boeckler.de/index_mitbestimmung.htm.

[788] MitbestG, §5.

[789] W Däubler, 'Mitbestimmung und Betriebsverfassung im Internationalen Privatrecht' *RabelsZ* 1975, 444. This was also the opinion of the drafters of the Co-Determination Act 1976; see BT-Drs [Journal of the Federal Parliament] 7/4845, 4. Employees working abroad may count for purposes of calculating the thresholds under the employment participation laws if their work placement is temporary and the employment contract is governed by German law, G Annuß in Goette and Habersack (125), §3 MitbestG, para 18.

[790] Treaty on the Functioning of the EU (TFEU) Arts 18, 45.

from moving to another Member State, thus restricting their free movement rights.[791] Since the question turned on the interpretation of the Treaty on the Functioning of the EU, it was referred to the Court of Justice of the EU (CJEU).[792] The CJEU compared rules on employee representation with social security legislation, since they determined conditions of employment, and held that Member States were free to define the scope of application of such legislation.[793] In principle, Germany would therefore be entitled to adopt a more inclusive approach to defining the territorial scope of the Co-Determination Act 1976. However, since the restrictive view is supported by the legislative materials,[794] it is likely to remain the authoritative interpretation of the Act.[795]

The Co-Determination Act 1976 envisages a procedure for the appointment and removal of directors that differs in several respects from the Stock Corporation Act, both as regards the members of the supervisory board and the management board.[796] If the company falls within the ambit of the Co-Determination Act, half of the members of the supervisory board must be composed of employee representative and half of shareholder representatives. The shareholder representatives are elected by the general meeting, and the employee representatives by the company's workforce. The employee representatives are drawn from the companies' employees and from workers unions with members among the company's workforce. Depending on the total number of employees, the supervisory board consists of twelve, sixteen, or twenty members.[797] Two or three of the positions reserved for the employee representatives are held by members of the workers unions, the others are allocated to employees representing different segments of the company's workforce (managers, manual, and non-manual workers).[798] The Co-Determination Act does not require the employee representative to have any particular experience in matters of corporate governance or the management of companies (of course, neither does the Stock Corporation Act with regard to the shareholder representatives). All individuals who are of age and who have been employees of the company for at least one year are eligible to stand for election.[799]

[791] LG Frankfurt am Main, decision of 16 February 2015, 3-16 O 1/14; Kammergericht Berlin, decision of 16 October 2015, 14 W 89/15; OLG Munich, decision of 20 February 2017, 31 Wx 321/15. The case decided by the District Court Frankfurt concerned the Frankfurt Stock Exchange, which employs fewer than 2,000 employees in Germany and several thousand additional employees in other EU countries. The supervisory board of the Stock Exchange, accordingly, is not composed of an equal number of employee and shareholder representatives, but of employee representatives amounting to one-third pursuant to the Co-Determination Act 2004; see n 787 above. The litigation before the Berlin Higher Regional Court was brought by a shareholder of the travel company TUI, Mr Erzberger. TUI employed more than 10,000 workers in Germany and, hence, fell within the scope of the Co-Determination Act 1976. Mr Erzberger claimed that the Co-Determination Act did not apply because it was in violation of EU law and TUI's supervisory board, accordingly, should be composed exclusively of shareholder representatives. A similar argument was made in the case before the Munich Higher Regional Court.

[792] Case C-566/15 *Erzberger v TUI AG* ECLI:EU:C:2017:562.

[793] ibid para 37.

[794] See n 789 above.

[795] The implications of the *Erzberger* decision of the CJEU are more ambivalent than this discussion may imply. It is clear that a Member State has the authority to determine the territorial scope of the rules that determine the involvement of the workers in the management of companies governed by their corporate law. This was the case in all three proceedings referred to in n 791 above. It is a different question whether a Member State may provide that its employee participation regime shall apply to a foreign company that has a connection to the Member State's territory, for example because an establishment, its real seat, or indeed all of its operations are located there. Some German commentators suggest that the German co-determination regime, because of its societal dimension, should apply to foreign companies with their real seat in Germany, see P Kindler, 'Internationales Handels- und Gesellschaftsrecht' in *Münchener Kommentar zum BGB, vol 12* (7th edn, CH Beck 2018) paras 570–4 for an overview of the debate. This question hinges on the classification of rules on employee representation as part of company law for purposes of private international law. If the German co-determination regime, for example, is classified as company law, it will not apply to companies that are incorporated in another EU Member State, unless the rules on co-determination can be interpreted as overriding mandatory provision, see Chapter 2C. II.2. The *Erzberger* decision of the CJEU is ambiguous in this regard. On the one hand, the Court seems to treat co-determination rules as part of social security legislation, which implies that they may be governed by the territoriality principle (*Erzberger* (n 792), para 34). On the other hand, the Court stressed that the participation mechanism in the case at hand was governed by both German company law and German labour relations law (*Erzberger* (n 792), para 38), which implies that the question of determining the international scope of the co-determination regime becomes only relevant if the *lex societatis* is German law.

[796] MitbestG, §31.

[797] ibid §7(1).

[798] ibid §§7(2), 15.

[799] ibid §7(4).

The election process is as rigidly regulated as the composition of the supervisory board. Candidates can be nominated by one-fifth of the workforce or by 100 employees,[800] with the exception of the representatives of the workers unions, which are nominated by the unions themselves.[801] Nominations are submitted as lists of candidates, which may contain more or fewer nominees than the number of board positions to be filled. In large companies with more than 8,000 employees, the employees elect delegates,[802] who then elect both the representatives of the company's workforce and the representatives of the workers unions by secret ballot and pursuant to the principle of proportionate representation.[803] Once the supervisory directors have been chosen, the board is required to appoint a chairman and vice-chairman. As we shall see, the role of chairman is important to break a potential deadlock between the shareholder and employee representatives. For this reason, the Co-Determination Act sets out a specific procedure for the election of the chairman and vice-chairman. In the first round of voting, the board has to appoint both directors by a two-thirds majority. In case a candidate does not receive the necessary majority, the Act provides that the shareholder representatives shall elect the chairman and the employee representatives the vice-chairman with simple majority.[804]

The Co-Determination Act 1976 also modifies the decision-making process of the supervisory board. Decisions are generally adopted by simple majority, as under the general law.[805] However, the fact that the supervisory board of a company with co-determination consists of an even number of directors, in contrast to boards of companies without co-determination, which have to be divisible by three,[806] gives rise to a risk of deadlock, especially when the board debates contentious issues that set the employees against the shareholders. In order to mitigate this risk, the law stipulates that the chairman (but not the vice-chairman in the absence of the chairman) has a second vote if a resolution does not receive the necessary simple majority in the first two rounds of voting.[807] Thus, while the law seeks to ensure a relatively even representation of shareholder and employee interests on the supervisory board, it provides for a built-in safeguard against disagreements rendering the board incapable of performing its functions. In addition, it can be seen that employee co-determination, far-reaching as it is, does not amount to a rejection of the orthodox conception of the shareholders as owners of the company. The right of the shareholder representatives to appoint the chairman of the board, in combination with the second vote of the chairman in the case of an impasse, results in a slight preponderance of the equity ownership side on the supervisory board. On the other hand, the fact that this preponderance only becomes operational when the shareholder and employee representatives are unable to agree in two rounds of voting underlines the main strategy that the law pursues with employee co-determination: to facilitate constructive dialogue on the board leading to decisions that are in the mutual interest of both shareholders and employees.

Turning to the appointment of the members of the management board, we find a similar multi-tiered process of decision-making on the part of the supervisory directors. The resolution of the supervisory board appointing the members of the management board generally has to be adopted by a two-thirds majority. If the supervisory board fails to elect a member of the management board with the required majority, a simple majority is sufficient in the second round of voting. Finally, if a simple majority cannot be obtained either, for example because the vote is evenly split between the shareholder and employee representatives, the chairman of the supervisory board has two votes in the third round of voting.[808] In addition, the Co-Determination Act 1976 and the Coal and Steel Co-Determination Act 1951 require that a works director be appointed to the management board who is responsible for human

[800] ibid §15(2). [801] ibid §16(2). [802] ibid §§10–14.
[803] ibid §§15(1), 16(1). On the principle of proportionate representation see text to n 399 above.
[804] MitbestG, §27. [805] ibid §29(1). [806] AktG, §95. [807] MitbestG, §29(2).
[808] ibid §31. Again, only the chairman receives a second vote, not the vice-chairman.

resources on the board.[809] The appointment procedure is the same as outlined above, with one important difference if the company falls within the scope of the Coal and Steel Co-Determination Act 1951. In this case, the works director must not be appointed against the majority of the employee representatives on the supervisory board.[810]

In spite of the detailed regulation of employee participation under German law, the extent of the employees' rights may be open to contestation. The problems are exemplified by a decision of the Federal Court of Justice dealing with a stock corporation that fell within the scope of the Co-Determination Act 1976.[811] At the constituent meeting of the newly elected supervisory board, its chairman said he believed there was common consent that the committee responsible for the selection of candidates for the management board (the so-called management board committee) should consist of three members, the chairman and two further members of the supervisory board, as had been the case in previous years. He then suggested, in addition to himself, the appointment of two individuals who were both shareholder representatives. He and the other two candidates were elected with the votes of the shareholder representatives and against the votes of the employee representatives on the board. The Co-Determination Act does not address the issue,[812] and the Stock Corporation Act simply provides that the board may set up committees and appoint the committee members from among the supervisory directors.[813]

The Court of Justice, while not establishing a general rule that committees of the supervisory board had to reflect the shareholder-employee split of the whole board, underlined the special role of the management board committee.[814] It emphasized that, at least in the case at hand, it would be contrary to the goal of the Co-Determination Act if the employees were not able to influence the decisions of the committee. The court discussed several approaches to determining the composition of the management board committee made in the literature, ranging from parity if the board itself was composed of an equal number of employee and shareholder representatives to a general prohibition of discrimination, without specifying a minimum number of employee representatives to be appointed to committee positions. The court acknowledged that there were no general rules and what constituted an adequate level of participation depended on the function of the committee in question. However, in the case of a committee dealing with personnel matters, such as the management board committee, the requirement not to act in a discriminatory manner towards the employee representatives prohibited their complete exclusion from the committee. Thus, the employee side of the supervisory board had to be represented by at least one member with full voting rights on the committee.

In a number of other countries that provide for a two-tier board structure, the employees have the right to elect representatives to the supervisory board. These are mostly countries of Central and Eastern Europe that are part of the German legal tradition, for example Austria, the Czech Republic, and Slovakia. However, participation rights are less extensive than in Germany, and the positions of employee representatives on the supervisory

[809] ibid §33; MontanMitbestG, §13. [810] MontanMitbestG, §13.

[811] BGH Judgement of 17 May 1993, BGHZ 122, 342.

[812] §27(3) MitbestG prescribes the composition of the committee set up to resolve a potential deadlock in the appointment of candidates to the management board who fail to obtain the necessary majority pursuant to §31(2). The committee must be composed of an even number of employee and shareholder representatives: the chairman, vice-chairman, and one additional member appointed by each side. These requirements do not apply to other supervisory board committees.

[813] AktG, §107(3).

[814] Note that the management board committee does not have the power to make actual appointments to the management board (this falls within the authority of the supervisory board as a whole and cannot be delegated to a committee, see §107(3) AktG). However, the committee determines the criteria that a prospective member of the management board must meet, undertakes a pre-selection of the candidates and prepares the employment contract. Often, it does not present more than one candidate to the supervisory board. Therefore, it has considerable influence over the appointment process and ultimately the composition of the management board.

board are usually limited to one-third. In the Netherlands, certain large companies[815] are subject to a set of special corporate governance rules, the so-called structure regime. As we have seen, these companies are generally required to establish a supervisory board. The structure regime regulates the composition of the supervisory board, including rules on employee representation. The supervisory board, which generally has the right to nominate candidates, must select candidates recommended by the works council for one-third of the positions on the board.[816] As opposed to the German co-determination regime, the actual appointment of the persons recommended by the works council is not made by the workforce, but by the general meeting or the supervisory board itself. According to the structure regime, the general meeting has the right to reject nominations by absolute majority of the votes cast. If the general meeting neither appoints nor rejects a nominated person, the supervisory board is entitled to appoint the person as supervisory director.[817] In addition, the supervisory directors, including those nominated by the works council, cannot be employed by the company or by a labour union.[818] Thus, in spite of the one-third-representation rule, the employees of Dutch large companies play a less active role in the governance of their companies than the employees of German public stock corporations.

In France, organized labour has been an important factor in economic life since the nineteenth century.[819] However, employee representation on the board of directors has been minimal until recently, especially if compared with the German co-determination regime, and it is still weaker than in many other continental European countries. This may again be explained with the comparative strength and different agenda of the political actors that were in a position to influence the structure of the French corporate governance system.[820] Alternatively, it may simply be a function of the absence of the two-tier board system in France before the reforms of 1966.[821] Indeed, comparing more generally European legal systems, we can see that codetermination correlates highly with the availability of the two-tier board structure.[822] This is not surprising, since employee representatives, who will generally not be trained managers, can more easily be incorporated into the company's governance system if an organ exists that is not primarily entrusted with management functions. On the other hand, as the French reforms of 2013 show, which we will discuss presently, the presence of a small number of employee representatives on a one-tier board may not be incompatible with the managerial functions of that board.

The mandatory French regime on employee representation is limited to a maximum of two employee representatives on the board of directors. The Labour Code requires the appointment of two members of the social and economic committee to the board of directors.[823] While these members can participate in board discussions and enjoy information rights, they are not formally directors and cannot vote. In 2013, as part of a fundamental

[815] See Chapter 4E.I. [816] Dutch Civil Code, Art 2:158(6). [817] ibid Art 2:158(9).

[818] ibid Art 2:160.

[819] S Laulom, 'System of Employee Representation in Enterprises in France' in R Blanpain, H Nakakubo, and T Araki (eds), *Systems of Employee Representation at the Enterprise* (Kluwer Law International) 33.

[820] For an interesting cross-sectional study exploring whether different corporate governance factors and political factors can explain the emergence of codetermination, see G Jackson, 'Employee Representation in the Board Compared: A Fuzzy Sets Analysis of Corporate Governance, Unionism, and Political Institutions' (2005) 12 Industrielle Beziehungen 252 (arguing that employee representation was set up by the governing Socialist party without the support of the unions or corporate owners and therefore remained weak and lacked legitimacy, ibid 275).

[821] F Wooldridge, 'Employee Participation in France and Germany' (2002) 43 Amicus Curiae 25, 32.

[822] C Gerner-Beuerle, P Paech, and E Schuster, *Study on Directors' Duties and Liability, prepared for the European Commission* (April 2013) 4–12. The only exception to the rule that countries that require some form of employee representation at board level also provide for a mandatory or at least optional two-tier board is Sweden; see ibid 12.

[823] Labour Code, Art L2312-72. The social and economic committee, established by Ordinance no 2017-1386 of 22 September 2017, JORF no 223 of 23 September 2017, will replace the existing employee representation bodies and assume their functions. It must be established in companies with 50 or more employees by January 2020.

reform of the labour market,[824] the position of the employee representatives was strengthened. In companies with at least 1,000 employees in France or 5,000 employees worldwide, one or two directors, depending on the size of the board, must be elected by the workforce or appointed by the works council or the trade unions that are involved in the company.[825] The persons must have been employees of the company for at least two years.[826] Once appointed, they are board members with all rights and responsibilities, including, importantly, the right to vote in board meetings. Finally, if the company is listed on a regulated market and the company's employees hold more than 3 per cent of the share capital, one or more of the directors must be elected by the general meeting from among the employee-shareholders.[827] Employee representation going beyond these minimum requirements can be provided for in the articles, but must not exceed four directors (or five in listed companies), and one-third of the number of the other directors.[828] These directors are full members of the board who have the right to vote and are subject to directors' duties. Furthermore, public companies can elect to be companies with worker participation (*société anonyme à participation ouvrière*). The company is then governed by a set of additional rules,[829] which involve issuing employee shares that are collectively owned by the workers forming a cooperative.[830] Boards of directors of such companies must include one or more representatives of the workers' cooperative according to the ratio of employee shares to capital shares, who are elected by the general meeting from among the employees who represent the cooperative at the general meeting.[831]

[824] Law no 2013-504 of 14 June 2013 (Loi de sécurisation de l'emploi), JORF no 138 of 16 June 2013, 9958, further amended by Law no 2015-994 of 17 August 2015 (Loi relative au dialogue social et à l'emploi), JORF no 189 of 18 August 2015, 14346. The initial version of the law provided for thresholds of at least 5,000 employees in companies, including subsidiaries with their registered seat in France, or at least 10,000 employees in group companies with their registered seat either in France or abroad. These thresholds were reduced to 1,000 and 5,000 employees, respectively, in 2015.

[825] Com, Art L225-27-1 (Art L225-79-2 if the company has a two-tier board).

[826] ibid Art L225-28.

[827] ibid Art L225-23 (Art L225-71 if the company has a two-tier board).

[828] ibid Art L225-27. The same applies if the company elects the two-tier board model, in which case the employee representatives are appointed to the supervisory board, Art L225-79.

[829] ibid Arts L225-258 to L225-270.

[830] ibid Art L225-261.

[831] ibid Art L225-268.

6

Constraints on Discretion: Part 1—Directors

A. Introduction

I. Managerial decision-making and legal constraints

How do we want directors and managers to make business decisions? Speaking in financial terms, we want them to pursue business projects with a positive net present value. This is a basic rule of making investment decisions: the company should invest in a business project if the present value of future income streams generated by the investment is greater than its costs (net present value rule).[1] However, even under a fairly clear-cut rule such as net present value, it is evident that directors and managers are required to make business decision under conditions of uncertainty. In applying the net present value rule, they must assess the expected payoff of the business project under consideration, identify alternative investment

[1] Present value is calculated by discounting the future cash flows, using a discount rate that reflects the opportunity cost incurred by not being able to invest the money in the next best alternative investment project and earn a return on that investment. In practice, it may be difficult to identify the 'correct' discount rate. Since investors want to be compensated for taking on risk, the 'next best' alternative investment should have a similar risk profile as the actual investment project in order to be useful as a benchmark. However, the riskiness of an investment project can be difficult to quantify, both conceptually (how can we measure risk?) and because of data constraints (consider, for example, a start-up without a track record of doing business and no quoted securities). For a more detailed discussion of these questions, see WA Klein, JC Coffee, Jr, and F Partnoy, *Business Organization and Finance: Legal and Economic Principles* (11th edn, Foundation Press 2010), Ch 5 I.

opportunities with a similar risk profile, and calculate the expected return on these investments in order to estimate the opportunity cost of pursuing the project.[2] This requires that they rely on historical data, for example past securities prices and their variance, probabilities of what the future will be like, and their subjective assessment of how risky the business project is. They must make difficult judgments and may sometimes invest in projects that do not pay off.

What is the role of law in this? It is clear that directors and managers must be granted a margin of discretion in assessing whether a business project is worth pursuing. Because business decisions depend on a multitude of factors and each case is different, it is impossible for the law to determine in advance how directors and managers should run their business and what they should decide in specific situations. Rather, company law is confined to imposing broad standards that describe in abstract terms how directors are expected to arrive at their decisions and how they should discharge their duties. In other words, the law generally has to look at the *process* of decision-making, rather than the content of the directors' decisions.

Jurisdictions differ in how they design these standards. Some legal systems may combine the behavioural expectations into one or two broadly phrased standards, whereas others break them down into more specific duties.[3] Legal systems also differ in the precise formulation of the behavioural expectations, for example the level of care with which directors have to analyse the available information before making a business decision or the form of disclosure and approval requirements that they have to observe when they transact with the company. Notwithstanding these differences, we can distinguish between two general types of behavioural expectation that can be found, in one form or another, in most legal systems. Using common law terminology, these are the duties of care and loyalty. The former deals with the care, skill, and diligence that a director is expected to employ in managing the company and the latter with situations where a director's interest conflicts with the interests of the company, notably where the director is a shareholder or otherwise involved in a business partner of the company or takes advantage of a business opportunity that could also be of commercial interest to the company. We will discuss both duties in the next sections.

II. The fiduciary basis of directors' duties

Before we will analyse the duties in detail, it is useful to review how the courts and the law conceptualize the position of directors in a corporation and the consequences that this may have for determining the scope of their duties.[4] In common law jurisdictions, directors are often 'referred to as 'trustees',[5] 'fiduciaries',[6] or 'agents' of the shareholders.[7] A fiduciary has been defined as 'someone who has undertaken to act for or on behalf of another in a particular matter in circumstances which give rise to a relationship of trust and confidence'.[8] More specifically, in the corporate context, it has been said that in exercising their powers of management and control 'directors are charged with an unyielding fiduciary duty to protect

[2] ibid Ch 5 I D.

[3] An example of the former regulatory technique is Dutch law, which provides that directors shall be responsible 'for a proper performance of the tasks assigned to [them]', Dutch Civil Code, s 2:9(1), examples of the latter are the Spanish Corporate Enterprises Act, ss 225–232, and the UK Companies Act 2006, ss 171–177. For a comparative analysis of all EU Member States, see C Gerner-Beuerle and E Schuster, 'Mapping Directors' Duties: The European Landscape' in H Birkmose, M Neville, and K Engsig Sørensen (eds), *Boards of Directors in European Companies* (Kluwer Law International 2013) 13–55.

[4] For a general discussion of the position of directors, see Chapter 4D.II above.

[5] *Percival v Wright* [1902] 2 Ch 421, 425 (referring to *Great Eastern Ry Co v Turner* (1872) LR.8 Ch 149, 152; *Re Forest of Dean Coal Mining Co* (1878) 10 Ch D 450, 453; *Re Lands Allotment Company* [1894] 1 Ch 616, 631). See also LS Sealy, 'The Director as Trustee' (1967) 25 Cambridge Law Journal 83.

[6] *Aberdeen Railway Company v Blaikie Bros* [1854] 1 Macq 461.

[7] ibid.

[8] *Bristol and West Building Society v Mothew* [1998] Ch 1, 18.

the interests of the corporation and to act in the best interests of its shareholders'.[9] This fiduciary dimension of the directors' position in common-law countries may be a consequence of the use of English partnership and trust law by deed of settlement companies before incorporation by registration was made possible in the 19th century.[10] However, it has also been pointed out that the directors of deed of settlement companies were generally not trustees in the technical sense and the analogy of directors as trustees in case law predated the emergence of such companies.[11] An alternative explanation posits that company law cases were naturally brought before the courts of Chancery, which had traditionally exercised jurisdiction over partnership matters. They applied the legal concepts familiar to them that seemed to be the most suitable to address the issues at hand, namely those of trust law.[12] In any case, the importance of partnership and trust law for the development of company law and especially directors' duties is still apparent in the terminology used by common law courts today.

Given that the influence of fiduciary principles was mediated by the English courts of equity and was, therefore, a function of the distinction between law and equity, which is peculiar to common law, it is not surprising that the fiduciary nature of the position of company directors is less pronounced in civil law countries. Nevertheless, many civil law jurisdictions acknowledge that directors are subject to a general duty to act in good faith and in the best interest of the company and to avoid conflicts of interest, even if the codified law does not expressly provide for such behavioural constraints.[13] The origin and legal basis of these constraints are not always clear. It has been said that they arise under the employment or service contract with the director,[14] lie in the nature of the position of director,[15] or stem from the fact that the director is entrusted with advancing the financial interests of other persons.[16] Whatever the precise dogmatic foundation, it is evident that civil law countries have developed legal instruments that perform a function similar to common law fiduciary principles in shaping the role and duties of directors. It is a different question whether these similarities are the result of a conscious adoption of the common law understanding of directors' duties by civil law judges, or the judges simply utilize legal principles that have always been an integral part of their legal systems to address problems that arise both in common law and civil law countries if the economic conditions are comparable. If the first explanation is correct, we could speak of convergence between common law and civil law. This is a popular claim in parts of the literature, who argue that because of certain perceived advantages of common law governance mechanisms, corporate governance regimes converge towards a standard model largely informed by Anglo-American law.[17] On the other hand, the second explanation, if correct, would attest to the fact that legal systems, no matter what their legal tradition, are in principle elastic enough to allow courts to provide for appropriate solutions to social conflicts, if necessary by drawing on related legal areas and general principles of law.[18]

[9] *Cede & Co. v Technicolor, Inc.*, 634 A.2d 345, 360 (Del. 1993). [10] See Chapter 4E.I.1.

[11] Sealy (n 5) 84–5. [12] ibid 85–6.

[13] For France, see for example Cass com, 24 February 1998, *Bull. Joly Sociétés* 1998, 813; for Germany, see BGH WM 1967, 679.

[14] Germany: BGHZ 10, 187, 192–3; 20, 239, 248.

[15] France: H Hovasse, 'Devoir de loyauté du dirigeant et cession de droits sociaux' (2008) Droit des sociétés 156.

[16] Germany: BGHZ 129, 30, 34.

[17] RH Kraakman and HB Hansmann, 'The End of History for Corporate Law' (2001) 89 Georgetown Law Journal 439, 449–51. See also H Fleischer, 'Legal Transplants in European Company Law: The Case of Fiduciary Duties' (2005) 2 European Company and Financial Law Review 378 (arguing that common law fiduciary duties can be interpreted as legal transplants introduced into civil law jurisdictions by judges influenced by the Anglo-American corporate governance movement: ibid 382–5).

[18] The second explanation is favoured, for example, by C Windbichler, *Gesellschaftsrecht* (24th edn, CH Beck 2017) §27/9, in particular fn 20 (arguing that a fiduciary understanding of the directors' position under German law was inherent in the concept of a 'corporate organ' and did not need to be imported from common law jurisdictions as a legal transplant). Courts are notoriously reluctant to make explicit references to foreign legal concepts.

We can conclude that not only the common law, but also many civil law jurisdictions qualify directors as fiduciaries who are required to act in good faith for the benefit of another person and exercise a high standard of care and loyalty in managing the other person's financial interests. If we accept this conceptualization of a director, the next question is who the beneficiary of the duties is and in whose interest the director is expected to act. This question resonates with considerations of shareholder primacy and stakeholder theory that we discussed above.[19] However, it has an additional dimension to it. Directors may be required to act in the interest of the shareholders, but owe their duties to the company. On this view, the company would represent the interests of the ultimate beneficiaries (shareholders or, following a pluralistic approach, also other stakeholders), who would not stand in a direct legal relationship with the director. The issue is by no means trivial or only of academic interest. If the duties are owed to the company, the company is the proper plaintiff in the case of a breach of duty. In deciding whether to bring a lawsuit, the company is represented by the authorized organ, often the board of directors. If the authorized organ decides not to bring a lawsuit, shareholders that disagree with the decision must take recourse to a derivative action, that is, an action allowing minority shareholders to enforce a claim of the company, provided such a mechanism exists.[20] Depending on the legal system, the derivative action mechanism, in turn, may only be accessible under restrictive conditions.[21]

English law follows the approach outlined in the preceding paragraph. Directors owe their duties to the company, not to shareholders individually,[22] even though they have to discharge their duties for the benefit of the company's shareholders.[23] For example, in the early case *Percival v Wright*,[24] the shareholders had approached the directors and offered to sell their shares at a specified price, which the directors accepted. Subsequently, they discovered that the directors had been in negotiations to sell the company's business to an outside investor at a price considerably above that paid to the shareholders. The negotiations ultimately provided abortive. The shareholders brought a lawsuit in their own name to set aside the sale of their shares to the directors, claiming that the directors had breached their duties by not disclosing the negotiations with the outside investor. The court held that directors were not fiduciaries for the individual shareholders. A different view, the court explained, 'would place directors in a most invidious position, as they could not buy or sell shares without disclosing negotiations, a premature disclosure of which might well be against the best interests of the company'.[25] It was important that the shareholders had approached the directors and had named the price at which they were willing to sell. Thus, there was, in the words of the court, 'no question of unfair dealing in this case'.[26] This means that if the facts are altered and the directors approach the shareholders and persuade them to sell their shares to the directors or a third party controlled by the directors, a direct fiduciary relationship may arise between the directors and the shareholders.[27] In particular, this may be the case in

This holds particularly true for French decisions, which are traditionally very brief and devoid of dogmatic deliberations, but it is also the case in Germany. See e.g. BGH, judgment of 21 April 1997, BGHZ 135, 244 (*ARAG/Garmenbeck*), discussed in section B.I.3 below, where the court seemed to be inspired by the US business judgment rule, but did not mention the concept or refer to any US case law. For this reason, it is difficult to draw any conclusions from the fact that civil law courts arrive at solutions resembling concepts developed at an earlier time by common law courts.

[19] Chapter 4C.II.

[20] All of our four jurisdictions provide for a minority shareholder lawsuit, but a derivative action does not exist in some other countries, for example the Netherlands, see Chapter 8D.

[21] The most famous example for a highly restrictive minority shareholder action is the so-called rule in *Foss v Harbottle* (1843) 2 Hare 461, which required that the directors had committed a wrong that benefitted them personally, i.e. they committed a fraud, and they had de jure or de facto control of the general meeting. The rule has now been superseded by ss 260–264 of the Companies Act 2006, but it continues to apply, for example, in Ireland. Questions of enforcement of breaches of directors' duties by corporate litigation will be discussed in more detail in Chapter 8C.

[22] Companies Act 2006, s 170(1). [23] ibid s 172(1). [24] [1902] 2 Ch 421. [25] ibid 426.

[26] ibid. [27] See *Coleman v Myers* [1977] 2 NZLR 225 (New Zealand).

small, family-owned companies or when the directors have material inside knowledge that the shareholders do not possess.[28] More generally, it has been held that directors may owe fiduciary duties to shareholders where a 'special factual relationship' exists between them, that is, where they are in 'direct and close contact with the shareholders in a manner capable of generating fiduciary obligations'.[29] Thus, directors may be subject to two sets of duties, one arising out of their appointment as director, which is owed to the company, and the other out of a 'special factual relationship' with the shareholders. The former are now comprehensively regulated in the Companies Act 2006, the latter continue to follow common law principles.[30] It should be noted that these considerations do not apply to other stakeholders. Directors do not owe any duties to individual employees or creditors, even if they are in 'direct and close contact' with them, unless the interaction gives rise to an established fiduciary legal relationship such as agency or the law provides for such duties.[31]

US courts adopt a more open-ended approach. While directors, of course, owe fiduciary duties to the company, it is commonly accepted that they also stand in a fiduciary relationship to the shareholders, who, accordingly, are entitled to bring an individual claim for breach of duty under appropriate circumstances.[32] However, it is not entirely clear what these circumstances are and what form the duties take. The question usually arises in the context of the dissemination of incorrect information by the directors. In *Malone v Brincat*,[33] the Delaware Supreme Court distinguished between three scenarios: 'public statements made to the market, including shareholders; statements informing shareholders about the affairs of the corporation without a request for shareholder action; and statements to shareholders in conjunction with a request for shareholder action'.[34] How the third case should be treated is well established. Delaware courts have held that directors are required to disclose fully and fairly all material information when they seek shareholder action.[35] For example, when the directors recommend amendments to the articles and knowingly include false statements in the notice of annual meeting, the shareholders have a cause of action for breach of the duty of disclosure, which has been said to be a specific application of the directors' general fiduciary duties.[36] In *Malone v Brincat*, the issue was more complicated. The directors did not provide information in the context of a transaction for which they sought shareholder approval, but knowingly overstated the company's earnings in their reports to the shareholders. Extending the scope of previous decisions, the Supreme Court held that 'directors who knowingly disseminate false information that results in corporate injury or damage to

[28] ibid.

[29] *Peskin v Anderson* [2001] BCC 874 (Court of Appeal). The court explained that such 'duties are, in general, attracted by and attached to a person who undertakes, or who, depending on all the circumstances, is treated as having assumed, responsibility to act on behalf of, or for the benefit of, another person. That other person may have entrusted or, depending on all the circumstances, may be treated as having entrusted, the care of his property, affairs, transactions or interests to him. There are, for example, instances of the directors of a company making direct approaches to, and dealing with, the shareholders in relation to a specific transaction and holding themselves out as agents for them in connection with the acquisition or disposal of shares; or making material representations to them; or failing to make material disclosure to them of insider information in the context of negotiations for a take-over of the company's business; or supplying to them specific information and advice on which they have relied. These events are capable of constituting special circumstances and of generating fiduciary obligations, especially in those cases in which the directors, for their own benefit, seek to use their position and special inside knowledge acquired by them to take improper or unfair advantage of the shareholders': ibid 880.

[30] PL Davies and S Worthington, *Gower's Principles of Modern Company Law* (10th edn, Sweet & Maxwell 2016) 16-5.

[31] ibid 16-10. In the vicinity of insolvency directors are required to act in the interest of the creditors as a whole, that is, creditors, rather than shareholders, are the primary point of reference of the duty to promote the success of the company, see Companies Act 2006, s 172(3), and from the case law, for example, *Liquidators of West Mercia Safetywear Ltd v Dodd* [1988] BCLC 250; *Colin Gwyer and Associates Ltd v London Wharf [Limehouse] Ltd* [2003] 2 BCLC 153.

[32] *Malone v Brincat*, 722 A.2d 5 (Del. 1998). [33] ibid. [34] ibid 11.

[35] *Stroud v Grace*, 606 A.2d 75, 84–5 (Del. 1992). [36] *Malone v Brincat* (n 32).

an individual stockholder violate their fiduciary duty',[37] even if the miscommunication occurs publicly and without a request for shareholder action.[38]

This holding raises a number of issues. First, in the quote from the preceding sentence, the court seems to suggest that liability requires dishonesty, but at a later point the court explains: 'When the directors disseminate information to stockholders when no stockholder action is sought, the fiduciary duties of care, loyalty and good faith apply. Dissemination of false information could violate one or more of those duties'.[39] The two statements are ambivalent because it is clear that the duty of care may also be violated by unintentional actions in good faith.[40] Secondly, in the case at hand, the false disclosures had damaged the company, which had lost most of its equity. The plaintiffs did not substantiate why they asserted an individual cause of action, rather than a derivative claim. An individual claim requires that the misinformation caused a personal injury, which is difficult to show when the directors make general misstatements about the company.[41] Finally, the distinction between this case and the first scenario mentioned above, public statements to the market, is problematic. Disclosure in the capital markets is comprehensively regulated by the federal securities laws, which provide for several private causes of action if the issuer disseminates incorrect information.[42] The Delaware courts have consistently held that shareholders cannot bring a claim under state corporate law if the effect would be to replicate the liability provisions of the federal securities laws.[43] Furthermore, common law tort claims such as negligent misrepresentation, while in principle not pre-empted by the federal securities laws, cannot be based on concepts developed in the context of the federal laws.[44] Where the federal liability provisions do not apply, however, misinformation of the shareholders, also by means of a public statement, implicates the directors' fiduciary duties.[45]

Our two civil law countries have developed responses to the issues at hand that are distinct from the common law, but also from each other. The German Stock Corporation Act provides explicitly that directors' duties are owed to the company and not to individual shareholders.[46] While fiduciary elements are not alien to the German understanding of the position of directors,[47] the management board and supervisory board are primarily conceptualized as *organs* of the company and the directors as members of these organs rather than as fiduciaries.[48] For this reason, and because the Stock Corporation Act aspires to regulate

[37] ibid 9. [38] ibid 10. [39] ibid 12.

[40] For a discussion of when directors are under an affirmative obligation to disclose in the absence of a request for stockholder action, see HM Barbera, 'Fiduciary Duties and Disclosure Obligations: Resolving Questions after *Malone v. Brincat*' (2001) 26 Delaware Journal of Corporate Law 563, 574–81, and for a discussion of whether allegations of negligence or recklessness are sufficient: ibid 580.

[41] On this question, see ibid 571–4.

[42] The most important such causes of action exist under s 14(a) of the Securities Exchange Act of 1934 in connection with Exchange Act Rule 14a-9 (imposing liability for materially misleading information in a proxy statement), s 14(e) of the Act of 1934 (liability for untrue statements in connection with a tender offer), s 10(b) of the Act of 1934 in connection with Exchange Act Rule 10b-5 (securities fraud), and s 18(a) of the Act of 1934 (right of action in favour of persons who purchase or sell securities at a price that was affected by false or misleading statements in documents filed with the SEC). Pursuant to these provisions, liability can be imposed on the corporation that issues the statement and under certain conditions the corporation's directors. Rules 14a-9 and 10b-5 are discussed in Chapter 5C.II.2.

[43] *Arnold v Society for Sav. Bancorp, Inc.*, 678 A.2d 533, 539 (Del. 1996); *Malone v Brincat* (n 32) 13.

[44] *Gaffin v Teledyne, Inc.*, 611 A.2d 467, 472 (Del. 1992); *Deutschman v Beneficial Corp.*, 132 F.R.D. 359 (D. Del. 1990) (holding that the so-called fraud-on-the-market theory, which can be invoked in a s 10(b)/Rule 10b-5 claim to establish a presumption of reliance, does not apply in cases involving common law negligent misrepresentation). The fraud-on-the-market theory is briefly discussed in Chapter 5C.II.2.

[45] In *Malone*, it was held that remedies under the federal securities laws were not available because the plaintiffs were not purchasers or sellers of securities; see *Malone v Brincat* (n 32) 13. Whether a violation of directors' duties gives rise to a derivative claim on behalf of the corporation or an individual shareholder action depends on who suffered an injury: ibid 14.

[46] AktG, §93(2) sentence 1 (liability of the members of the management board); §116 (liability of the members of the supervisory board).

[47] See our discussion above, text to nn 13–16.

[48] See Chapter 1E on the concept of 'corporate organ'.

the affairs of corporations exhaustively, the German statutory provisions are less susceptible to being supplemented by fiduciary principles than the common law rules.

Rights and obligations exist directly between the members of the management board or supervisory board and the shareholders only within the confines of established legal relationships. These legal relationships may be contractual in nature, for example when the directors are entrusted with carrying out a transaction for the shareholders,[49] quasi-contractual,[50] or tortious. The latter are the most problematic, and it is necessary to be familiar with the particularities of German tort law in order to appreciate the scope of the directors' tortious responsibility. As opposed to French law, German tort law does not provide for a general provision establishing liability for any wrongful act that causes damage.[51] In particular, pure economic loss can generally only be recovered if it is the result of the breach of a statutory provision that is intended to protect the party who suffered the loss[52] or an intentional act that is contrary to public policy.[53] Importantly, the courts have held that the provisions of the Stock Corporation Act laying down the general duties of directors[54] are not intended to protect the shareholders or other individual persons.[55] The old Imperial Court that was the first to address the question explained that the statutory rules were designed to structure the legal relationship between the company and the natural persons who act on the company's behalf. All rights and obligations develop within this relationship and can generally not be extended to third parties by virtue of tort law.[56] Subsequent decisions, however, accepted limited exceptions to the general rule, in particular with respect to criminal statutes that have the aim of protecting identifiable individuals against being defrauded, such as the subscribers for newly issued shares.[57]

The second tort law provision that is potentially applicable, liability for intentional acts against public policy, has also been interpreted restrictively by the courts. The courts define 'public policy' as 'the moral sentiments of all those who think equitably and fairly'.[58] The provision was utilized to protect creditors against looting of the company by the corporate insiders.[59] For shareholders it became relevant in the context of incorrect ad-hoc disclosures in the capital markets.[60] The Federal Court of Justice held that the disclosure of fictitious transactions with the intention to manipulate the stock price and mislead the public about the financial

[49] Bürgerliches Gesetzbuch (BGB) [Civil Code], §662 (agency).

[50] For example, the persons (directors and others) who disseminate incorrect information in order to induce investors to invest in a mutual fund or another investment vehicle may be held liable for breach of pre-contractual duties (*culpa in contrahendo*), see, e.g., BGHZ 71, 284; 72, 382.

[51] For the respective French provisions, see Code civil, Arts 1240, 1241.

[52] BGB, §823(2) (violation of a so-called protective law or *Schutzgesetz*).

[53] BGB, §826. [54] See n 46 above.

[55] Reichsgericht (Imperial Court), RGZ 63, 324.

[56] ibid 328. In this case, the founder and sole executive director had intentionally misstated the financial position of the company and falsified the books and accounts. The plaintiff had purchased shares in the company in reliance on the misstatements. Later, the manager's fraudulent activities were discovered and the company became insolvent. The plaintiff brought a lawsuit against the supervisory directors, claiming that they had breached their duty to supervise the executive director and review carefully the company's accounts. The court held that the plaintiff did not belong to the protected group of persons within the meaning of §823(2) BGB and, accordingly, rejected the claim.

[57] See, e.g., BGHZ 105, 121 (holding that §399(1) no 4 AktG, which establishes a criminal offence for members of the management or supervisory board who make incorrect statements in connection with a capital increase, was intended to protect the subscribers for new shares). Other provisions that have been held to constitute 'protective laws' within the meaning of §823(2) BGB include the criminal offences of making false or misleading statements laid down in the other subsections of §399 as well as in §400 AktG, investment fraud pursuant to §264a Strafgesetzbuch (StGB) [Criminal Code], and embezzlement and abuse of trust pursuant to §266 StGB. See, for example, BGHZ 160, 134, 138–42 (*Infomatec I*), and for further references J Koch in U Hüffer and J Koch, *Aktiengesetz* (13th edn, CH Beck 2018) §93 paras 65–6.

[58] RGZ 48, 114, 124. [59] See Chapter 10C.

[60] Ad hoc disclosures are required by issuers of financial instruments admitted to trading on a regulated market pursuant to the EU Market Abuse Regulation (Regulation (EU) No 596/2014, [2014] OJ L173/1). Article 17(1) of the Regulation provides that issuers must 'inform the public as soon as possible of inside information which directly concerns' them.

position of the issuer constituted a tortious act in violation of public policy.[61] Investors who bought shares in reliance on the false announcements were entitled to claim damages from those responsible for the disclosures.[62] These examples show that under specific circumstances the directors of German stock corporations owe duties directly to the shareholders. However, such duties are not a function of the directors' fiduciary position or an extension of their duties under corporate law, but derive from general principles of tort and contract law.

French law is unique among our four jurisdictions in that the duties of directors are not understood as flowing from, and being constrained by, the director's legal relationship with the company. Rather, according to the statutory formulation, the directors are responsible for management mistakes and violations of the law and the articles of association 'towards the company and third parties'.[63] Thus, the protected group potentially includes shareholders as well as employees, creditors, and other market participants. All of these stakeholders may be claimants in an action for damages against the directors. In order to understand how the law apportions responsibility, it is necessary to distinguish between liability towards the company and the shareholders on the one hand and liability towards third parties on the other hand. As regards the former, French law is not concerned with the scope of the duties or possible fiduciary relationships in order to identify the proper claimant, but sees the allocation of responsibility as an aspect of enforcement. If the company has suffered a loss, the claim is brought either by the directors (*action sociale ut universi*) or by one or more shareholders in the name of the company (*action sociale ut singuli*).[64] If a shareholder claims damages for a loss suffered personally, the claim is brought in the form of an *action individuelle* in the shareholder's name. Thus, the responsibility of the directors to the shareholders depends on the distinction between the shareholder's personal loss and the harm caused to the company.

The French courts have held that a loss suffered by the shareholders as a consequence of a reduction of the company's share price, for example because of mismanagement, does not qualify as a personal loss distinct from that of the company.[65] On the other hand, the Cour de Cassation decided that the loss of a controlling interest in the company[66] or the overvaluation of a contribution in kind, leading to the devaluation of the existing shareholders' interests, can constitute a harm inflicted directly on the shareholders.[67] Shareholders can also bring an action in their own name if the directors acquire shares from them without disclosing information material to the shareholders' decision to sell. For example, in a case somewhat resembling *Percival v Wright*, the plaintiff had asked the company's president to assist her in the sale of her shares.[68] The president arranged the sale, not disclosing to

[61] BGHZ 160, 149, 154–8 (*Infomatec II*).

[62] Since the burden of proof is on the plaintiffs, reliance is often a significant practical obstacle to recovery; see BGHZ 160, 134, 144–7 (*Infomatec I*).

[63] Com, Art L225-251 (stock corporation); Code civil, Art 1850 (civil law partnership).

[64] The *action ut singuli* is laid down in Art 1843-5 Code civil and applies to all types of company. It is subsidiary to the *action ut universi* and can only be brought if the authorized representatives of the company fail to initiate proceedings; see Cass crim, 12 December 2000 (*Sté Testut*), *Rev. sociétés* 2001, 323.

[65] Cass com, 1 April 1997, *Bull. Joly Sociétés* 1997, 650, note JF Barbièri; Cass crim, 13 December 2000, *Bull. Joly Sociétés* 2001, 497. This is comparable to the so-called reflective loss principle under English law; see *Prudential Assurance Co Ltd v Newman Industries Ltd (No 2)* [1982] Ch 204 and Chapter 8C.II.1.

[66] Cass com, 18 February 1997 (*Sté Dassault*), *Bull. Joly Sociétés* 1997, 408, note JJ Daigre. In this case, Sogitec, a company that developed flight simulators, was economically dependent on its only customer Dassault, a manufacturer of civil and military aircraft. When Sogitec was in financial distress, Dassault proposed a capital increase, as a consequence of which it acquired 90% of the shares in Sogitec. The founders of Sogitec, now minority shareholders, claimed that Sogitec's financial problems had been caused by Dassault abusing its dominant economic position and, in this way, forcing Sogitec to sell a majority interest in the company. They filed an individual lawsuit to have the capital increase set aside. The Cour de Cassation agreed with the plaintiffs that the loss of control was distinct from the harm allegedly inflicted on the company through the exploitative behaviour of Dassault, and the shareholders were entitled to seek recovery individually. However, the claim eventually failed on remand because it could not be established that Dassault's actions had caused Sogitec's financial difficulties.

[67] Cass com, 28 June 2005 (*Sté Total Fina Elf c/ Sté KPMG*), *JCP E* 2005, 1325, note H Hovasse. Similarly Cass com, 26 April 2017, no 15-28104, *Bull. Joly Sociétés* 2017, 513, note JF Barbiéri.

[68] Cass com, 27 February 1996 (*Vilgrain*), *JCP E* 1996, II, 838, note D Schmidt and N Dion.

the seller that he was in negotiations with a potential buyer who was prepared to pay a substantially higher price than that offered to the plaintiff. The Cour de Cassation held that directors owe a duty of loyalty to all shareholders individually. In the case at hand, the president had breached this duty by concealing the negotiations.

Another opportunity to refine the personal loss rule arose in the wake of the collapse of the dot-com bubble in the early 2000s. The French courts faced the question of how to treat claims of shareholders who had bought or sold shares in the financial markets in reliance on incorrect market disclosures that had affected the price of the securities. Similar to the solution found in Germany, the courts decided that the investors could bring an individual action against the directors claiming compensation for the loss suffered as a result of transactions entered into because of false information.[69]

As regards the directors' liability towards third parties, French law is more restrictive, at least as long as the company is solvent. While the statutory rules, in principle, do not distinguish between the company, shareholders, and third parties for purposes of determining the directors' liability,[70] the courts have established heightened requirements for a breach of duty if other parties than the shareholders or the company claim damages. The directors must have committed a breach that is separable from their functions (*faute séparable des fonctions*), which is in particular the case if they engage in fraudulent activities.[71]

In conclusion, the statutory framework in France is phrased in a broad way, which makes it suitable to protect all constituencies that are potentially adversely affected by the acts of company directors and respond flexibly to developments that may not have been addressed expressly or comprehensively by the legislator, such as securities fraud. As a consequence of the wide formulation of the statutory rules, the courts are vested with a considerable degree of discretion. They have used this discretion to differentiate between different groups of claimants and shape the duties of directors in light of typical cases of misconduct.

B. Duty of Care

I. Structure of the duty of care

1. *UK*

Companies Act 2006

Section 174—Duty to exercise reasonable care, skill and diligence

(1) A director of a company must exercise reasonable care, skill and diligence.
(2) This means the care, skill and diligence that would be exercised by a reasonably diligent person with—
  (a) the general knowledge, skill and experience that may reasonably be expected of a person carrying out the functions carried out by the director in relation to the company, and
  (b) the general knowledge, skill and experience that the director has.

The UK duty of care, now embodied as the duty of 'care, skill and diligence' in section 174 of the Companies Act 2006, has undergone major changes since the late 19th century. The duty of care has its origins in the law of negligence, which applies a largely objective test to

[69] Cass com, 22 November 2005 (*Sté Eurodirect marketing c/ Pfeiffer*), *RTD com.* 2006, 445. As under German law, it is necessary to prove specific reliance, i.e. the fraud on the market theory (see Chapter 5C.II.2) was not adopted by the French courts. *Eurodirect marketing* was confirmed in Cass com, 9 March 2010 (*Gaudriot*), *Revue des sociétés* 2010, 230.

[70] See text to n 63 above.

[71] We will discuss the concept of 'separable fault' in more detail in section B.I.4(a) below.

determine the required standard of care.[72] However, early English decisions focused on the qualifications and knowledge of the individual director, thus emphasizing the subjective elements of the standard of care. For example, in *Re Brazilian Rubber Plantations*,[73] a corporation had been incorporated to purchase estates in North Brazil and cultivate rubber, coffee, and other produce thereon. The liquidator of the corporation, Brazilian Rubber Plantations and Estates, Ltd., brought a claim for damages against the corporation's directors alleging that, in signing and carrying out the contract, the directors had relied on a report greatly overstating the size of the estate and the estimated amount of rubber that could be produced without verifying the facts. As a consequence, the corporation was bound to purchase the property for £150,000, while the original vendors in Brazil had sold it for £15,000 to middlemen in England. It was undisputed that the fraudulent acts were committed by some of the middlemen. They had formed a syndicate to sell the property to Brazilian Rubber Plantations, Ltd., and one of the intermittent vendors 'had made up the report in London from some correct but scanty data supplied by [the Brazilian vendors] and his own imagination'.[74] The issue was whether the directors had exercised 'reasonable care', as required by precedent, in relying on the accuracy of the report and executing the contract, although they were aware of the fact that the price of the property had increased substantially between the original sale by the Brazilian vendors and the acquisition by Rubber Plantations, Ltd., and that the author of the report was a vendor in one of the intermittent sales. The court described some of the director-defendants as follows:[75]

> Sir Arthur Aylmer was absolutely ignorant of business. He only consented to act because he was told the office would give him a little pleasant employment without his incurring any responsibility. H.W. Tugwell was partner in a firm of bankers in a good position in Bath; he was seventy-five years of age and very deaf; he was induced to join the board by representations made to him in January, 1906. Barber was a rubber broker and was told that all he would have to do would be to give an opinion as to the value of rubber when it arrived in England. Hancock was a man of business who said he was induced to join by seeing the names of Tugwell and Barber, whom he considered good men.

The court summarized the required standard of care as what 'is reasonably to be expected from [a director], having regard to his knowledge and experience'.[76] On closer inspection, this is an ambivalent standard. On the one hand, the court does not expect a minimum level of knowledge or expertise or, in fact, any participation in the corporation's affairs. A director is

> not bound to bring any special qualifications to his office. He may undertake the management of a rubber company in complete ignorance of everything connected with rubber, without incurring responsibility for the mistakes which may result from such ignorance; while if he is acquainted with the rubber business he must give the company the advantage of his knowledge when transacting the company's business. He is not ... bound to take any definite part in the conduct of the company's business ....[77]

On the other hand, so far as the director does concern himself with the company's business, he is required to display reasonable care, which is 'the care an ordinary man might be expected to take in the same circumstances on his own behalf'.[78] Thus, the court develops what are effectively two distinct standards: the first one, arguably, of a subjective nature and the second one of an objective nature. However, the court does not explain how the two standards relate to each other. How is a director to be judged who has minimal or no knowledge

[72] See, for example, *Blyth v The Company of Proprietors of the Birmingham Waterworks* (1856) 11 Ex 781, 784: 'Negligence is the omission to do something which a reasonable man, guided upon those considerations which ordinarily regulate the conduct of human affairs, would do, or doing something which a prudent and reasonable man would not do'.

[73] [1911] 1 Ch 425. [74] ibid 428. [75] ibid 427. [76] ibid 437. [77] ibid.

[78] ibid.

of the relevant business area but takes an active part in the company's operations? *Brazilian Rubber Plantations* provides that this director shall not be responsible 'for the mistakes which may result from [his] ignorance', but at the same time requires that he shall display the care that an 'ordinary' man would take on his own behalf. Surely, an ordinary man in the same circumstances would obtain expert advice before making decisions concerning matters in which he was not knowledgeable.

On the basis of these principles, the court in *Brazilian Rubber Plantations* denied any negligence on the part of the directors, holding that

> [b]usiness men have very frequently to act on information derived from interested persons. In so doing the wise men amongst them no doubt make an allowance for exaggeration, but exaggeration and fraud are not the same thing. If the report had been merely exaggerated, there was no fear of the company making a bad bargain; there was ample margin to allow for exaggeration.[79]

This seems to be an application of the second (objective) standard, since the court did not pay much heed to the qualifications of the individual directors (or, rather, the lack thereof). If the objective test is passed, the first, more lenient standard is naturally also satisfied. Therefore, the court did not have to address, and for that reason possibly did not pursue, the problematic issue of how to reconcile the two standards in conflicting cases. If this interpretation is correct, and the court did not (implicitly) reduce the standard of care that 'is reasonably to be expected' in light of the lack of experience of the defendant directors, the objective standard does not seem to be very demanding. The benchmark is the care that an ordinary man would display in his own affairs, for which it is sufficient, in the court's opinion, to verify information stemming from third parties in a cursory way. This holds even in circumstances that should give rise to suspicion (notably the fact that the author of the report was interested).

These issues were addressed more comprehensively in *Re City Equitable Fire Insurance Company Ltd*,[80] which was the leading case on the duty of care until the 1990s. The case is important both for the general comments that the court of first instance made concerning the care and skill to be displayed by directors and the more specific question of whether and to what extent directors are entitled to rely on the information provided by the corporation's officers or other employees who intend to defraud the company.[81] We will focus here on the first question and revisit the case later to discuss the second aspect of the judgment.[82] City Equitable Fire Insurance was a financially sound company when a certain Gerrard Lee Bevan was appointed managing director in 1916. Within six years, the company was insolvent. While the company's reinsurance business had continued to be profitable after the appointment of Bevan, an investigation revealed that various industrial investments and property acquisitions of the company had generated significant losses and that Bevan had arranged for large sums of money to be paid to himself and the company's broker, a partnership of which he was the senior partner. Bevan, who the court later described as an 'unprincipled scoundrel',[83] was tried and convicted of fraud. The official receiver brought an action against the directors for negligence in respect of the transactions and payments of dividends out of capital.

The claim ultimately failed against all directors except Bevan because the company's articles included a provision stipulating that the directors should only be answerable for 'their own wilful neglect or default',[84] which, according to the court, required an intentional breach of duty or recklessness,[85] while the directors (other than Bevan) had acted in good faith

[79] ibid 438. [80] [1925] Ch 407.

[81] The claimant (the official receiver of the corporation) appealed from the decision of the court of first instance, but the appeal concerned only the liability of the auditors. The excerpts quoted below are from the judgment of the High Court, Chancery Division.

[82] Section B.II. [83] [1925] Ch 474. [84] ibid 430. [85] ibid 434.

throughout. However, the court also set out the applicable negligence standard in general terms and discussed in the excerpt below whether the directors had met this standard. The court concluded that they had failed to do so because, among other things, they had not maintained control over current assets and should not have relied on the unverified assurances of Bevan.

***Re City Equitable Fire Insurance Co Ltd* [1925] Ch 407 (Chancery Division)**

Romer J:

It has sometimes been said that directors are trustees. If this means no more than that directors in the performance of their duties stand in a fiduciary relationship to the company, the statement is true enough. But if the statement is meant to be an indication by way of analogy of what those duties are, it appears to me to be wholly misleading. I can see but little resemblance between the duties of a director and the duties of a trustee of a will or of a marriage settlement. It is indeed impossible to describe the duty of directors in general terms, whether by way of analogy or otherwise. The position of a director of a company carrying on a small retail business is very different from that of a director of a railway company. The duties of a bank director may differ widely from those of an insurance director, and the duties of a director of one insurance company may differ from those of a director of another …

In discharging the duties of his position thus ascertained a director must, of course, act honestly; but he must also exercise some degree of both skill and diligence. To the question of what is the particular degree of skill and diligence required of him, the authorities do not, I think, give any very clear answer. It has been laid down that so long as a director acts honestly he cannot be made responsible in damages unless guilty of gross or culpable negligence in a business sense. But as pointed out by Neville J. in *In re Brazilian Rubber Plantations and Estates, Ld.*,[86] one cannot say whether a man has been guilty of negligence, gross or otherwise, unless one can determine what is the extent of the duty which he is alleged to have neglected. For myself, I confess to feeling some difficulty in understanding the difference between negligence and gross negligence, except in so far as the expressions are used for the purpose of drawing a distinction between the duty that is owed in one case and the duty that is owed in another. If two men owe the same duty to a third person, and neglect to perform that duty, they are both guilty of negligence, and it is not altogether easy to understand how one can be guilty of gross negligence and the other of negligence only. But if it be said that of two men one is only liable to a third person for gross negligence, and the other is liable for mere negligence, this, I think, means no more than that the duties of the two men are different. The one owes a duty to take a greater degree of care than does the other … If, therefore, a director is only liable for gross or culpable negligence, this means that he does not owe a duty to his company, to take all possible care. It is some degree of care less than that. The care that he is bound to take has been described by Neville J. in the case referred to above as 'reasonable care' to be measured by the care an ordinary man might be expected to take in the circumstances on his own behalf. In saying this Neville J. was only following what was laid down in *Overend & Gurney Co.* v. *Gibb*[87] as being the proper test to apply, namely: 'Whether or not the directors exceeded the powers entrusted to them, or whether if they did not so exceed their powers they were cognisant of circumstances of such a character, so plain, so manifest, and so simple of appreciation, that no men with any ordinary degree of prudence, acting on their own behalf, would have entered into such a transaction as they entered into?'

There are, in addition, one or two other general propositions that seem to be warranted by the reported cases: (1.) A director need not exhibit in the performance of his duties a greater degree of skill than may reasonably be expected from a person of his knowledge and experience. A director of a life insurance company, for instance, does not guarantee that he has the skill of an actuary or of a physician. In the words of Lindley M.R.: 'If directors act within their powers, if they act with such care as is reasonably to be expected from them, having regard to their knowledge and experience, and if they act honestly for the benefit of the company they represent, they

[86] [Footnote by authors.] See n 73 above.

[87] [Footnote in the original.] LR 5 HL 480, 486.

discharge both their equitable as well as their legal duty to the company': see *Lagunas Nitrate Co. v. Lagunas Syndicate.*[88] It is perhaps only another way of stating the same proposition to say that directors are not liable for mere errors of judgment. (2.) A director is not bound to give continuous attention to the affairs of his company. His duties are of an intermittent nature to be performed at periodical board meetings, and at meetings of any committee of the board upon which he happens to be placed. He is not, however, bound to attend all such meetings, though he ought to attend whenever, in the circumstances, he is reasonably able to do so ...

Questions and comments:

1. Romer J in *City Equitable Fire Insurance* refers to *Brazilian Rubber Plantations* as authority and builds on the 'reasonable care' standard expounded there. However, he does not fully subscribe to the objective standard that can be read into *Brazilian Rubber Plantations* as one of two possible constructions of the directors' duty of care. Rather, in the last paragraph of the above excerpt Romer J holds that a director is required to display the care that 'may reasonable be expected from a person of *his* knowledge and experience'. How should this sentence be understood and reconciled with the reference in the preceding paragraph to the care that the 'ordinary man' of *Brazilian Rubber Plantations*, acting on his own behalf, is expected to take? In the second statement, Romer J does not seem to have the 'ordinary man' or 'ordinary director' benchmark in mind, but the individual director and his or her actual knowledge and experience. The director's knowledge and experience have to be applied in a 'reasonable' way, which introduces some objectivity into the test, but, focusing on Romer J's second statement, the minimum threshold would be determined by subjective attributes. Does this set a higher or lower threshold than in *Brazilian Rubber Plantations* (or an identical threshold)? Is such a standard useful to constrain the directors' discretion and protect shareholders?
2. The interpretation in the preceding paragraph has been called the 'amiable lunatic' standard.[89] A director who has very little experience and knowledge of the company's business will not be held accountable for mistakes that could have been avoided by a director with average experience, but that may reasonably be made by persons of the director's level of knowledge and experience. This interpretation of *City Equitable Fire Insurance* was criticized for overemphasizing the relevance of Romer J's second statement (the subjective standard) and neglecting the rest of the judgment, where Romer J concentrated on what could, in the circumstances, reasonably be expected of an ordinary or average person, rather than the individual defendant.[90] Therefore, it was suggested in the literature that the correct reading of *City Equitable Fire Insurance* was to take Romer J's first statement (the reference to *Brazilian Rubber Plantations*, that is, the reasonable care of an ordinary man in his own affairs) as promoting a 'minimum and irreducible objective standard'.[91] Individual expertise and specialist knowledge would

[88] [Footnote in the original.] [1899] 2 Ch 392, 435.

[89] A Hicks, 'Directors' Liability for Management Errors' (1994) 110 Law Quarterly Review 390, 392.

[90] After setting out the relevant legal principles, Romer J observed: 'Cases have not been unknown in which a director has lent his name to a company for what may be called window dressing purposes, and has treated himself as having thereby given ample consideration for his remuneration and as being absolved from any further effort towards promoting the welfare of the company. This cannot be said of any one of the respondent directors ... I am satisfied from the evidence adduced before me that each one of the respondent directors was willing and anxious to give of his best to the company and at all times took as active a part in the work of the board as circumstances would reasonably permit'. [1925] Ch 444. Having passed this initial threshold of being an active director, as opposed to a mere figurehead, Romer J seems to assume that the directors, accordingly, and notwithstanding possible differences in their knowledge and experience, have to conform to reasonable expectations of the business world concerning their skill and care. See, for example, the following passage from the judgment: '[T]o keep a list of all cheques that he [the director] signed would have been quite impracticable and far outside any duty that a director owes his company. Nor can I think that a director fails in his duty by reason of lapses of memory that are in the circumstances reasonably excusable. He only undertakes to bring to the service of the company a memory of the normally imperfect nature, and [the defendant's] memory would appear to have been of this order ... Most assuredly [Mr. Bevan's] colleagues were deceived, and I can find nothing to suggest that they were more gullible than the majority of mankind': ibid 458–9.

[91] Hicks (n 89) 392.

have the effect of holding the director to a higher standard, but lack of expertise would not reduce the standard of care 'below that of the reasonably ordinary businessman'.[92]

3. The uncertainty concerning the right construction of the standard of care pursuant to *Brazilian Rubber Plantations* and *City Equitable Fire Insurance* was resolved by two High Court judgments, both delivered by Lord Hoffmann. The first, *Norman v Theodore Goddard*,[93] was another case where the defendant director acted in good faith but was induced to authorize a transaction harmful to the corporation because of the fraudulent acts of another person. Without discussing the controversy surrounding the case law regarding the duty of care, Lord Hoffmann summarized the applicable standard as follows: '[A] director performing active duties on behalf of the company need not exhibit a greater degree of skill than may reasonably be expected from a person undertaking those duties ... It may be that in considering what a director ought reasonably to have known or inferred, one should also take into account the knowledge, skill and experience which he actually had in addition to that which a person carrying out his functions should be expected to have'.[94] Note that Lord Hoffmann does not adopt Romer J's formulation of the standard of care depending on the director's knowledge and experience. Rather, the starting point of the analysis is the degree of skill that may reasonably be expected from a person *in the position* of the director. Subjective characteristics may be taken into account, but only *in addition to* this binding standard, not by way of substituting it.

   Counsel for Theodore Goddard, a law firm that was one of the defendants, submitted, and Lord Hoffmann accepted, that the test was accurately stated in s 214(4) of the Insolvency Act 1986, which provides that directors will be held accountable to the standard of 'a reasonably diligent person having both—(a) the general knowledge, skill and experience that may reasonably be expected of a person carrying out the same functions as are carried out by that director in relation to the company, and (b) the general knowledge, skill and experience that that director has'. Thus, *Theodore Goddard* advocates a dual standard, consisting of an objective lower benchmark, which may be increased, but not lowered, by specialized knowledge that the individual director has.

   This test was confirmed in the second case, *Re D'Jan of London Ltd.*,[95] where Lord Hoffman simply reiterated: 'In my view, the duty of care owed by a director at common law is accurately stated in sec. 214(4) of the Insolvency Act 1986'.[96] Is this succinct treatment of the issue justified in light of the contradictory case law?

4. Lord Hoffmann's approach is now codified in section 174 of the Companies Act 2006, which reproduces section 214(4) of the Insolvency Act almost word by word. Accordingly, it promulgates an objective/subjective standard, subsection (a) embodying the objective, irreducible part and subsection (b) the potentially duty-increasing subjective part.[97] Note that in spite of its wording, section 174 is commonly regarded as codifying one integrated duty of care and not three separate duties of care, skill, and diligence. This is in line with the overwhelming majority of pre-2006 case law, which applied one uniform standard.[98]

   A second point to note is that section 174(a) qualifies the objective standard in one important respect. The benchmark director is a person who carries out the *functions* of the director whose conduct is under review *in relation to the company*. In most corporations, the duties of the members of the board are divided along functional lines. First, in companies with a unitary board system we can distinguish between executive and non-executive directors, that is, between those who take business decisions and those who monitor the executives.[99] Furthermore, the responsibilities of the executive directors are often divided to reflect the organizational structure of the corporation. For example, in a large, globally

[92] ibid. [93] [1992] BCC 14. [94] ibid 15. [95] [1993] BCC 646. [96] ibid 648.

[97] See the Explanatory Notes to the Companies Act 2006 para 337.

[98] A rare exception is *Dorchester Finance Co v Stebbing* [1989] BCLC 498.

[99] See, for example, UK Corporate Governance Code, Principle H: 'Non-executive directors ... should provide constructive challenge, strategic guidance, offer specialist advice and hold management to account'. This distinction between executive and supervisory functions is mirrored at the head of the company by the division of powers between the chairman of the board and the chief executive. See UK Corporate Governance Code, Principle G: 'There should be a clear division of responsibilities between the leadership of the board and the executive leadership of the company's business'.

operating car manufacturer, the board may contain, in addition to the CEO and CFO, directors with executive responsibility for different regions (e.g., North America, Europe, Asia) or different product lines (e.g., commercial vehicles, passenger cars, and sports cars), for global manufacturing, global purchasing, labour affairs, human resources, marketing, or sustainability and corporate social responsibility.[100] A banking corporation may have, in addition to the CEO and CFO, a chief risk officer on the board and directors who are responsible for the corporation's investment, retail, and private wealth management.

Does this mean that directors will only be held accountable for the knowledge and experience that is necessary to discharge the *particular* functions carried out by the individual director? And, importantly, does it mean that less is expected of non-executive than executive directors, given that the former naturally have less knowledge of the corporation and possibly less experience in the respective line of business? The UK corporate governance framework is based on the principle of 'collective responsibility'.[101] The board as an organ is responsible for promoting 'the long-term sustainable success of the company',[102] not groups of individual directors, and, in doing so, the board decides about important transactions such as mergers or changes to the capital structure. This indicates that, in spite of the division of responsibilities on the board, the law expects all directors to have sufficient knowledge of all aspects of the corporation's affairs to make an informed decision and act with ordinary competence and care within the general scope of the board's authority. The reference in section 174 of the Companies Act to the functions carried out by a director allows for some differentiation in the standard of care, but having responsibility for, say, production or marketing, as opposed to finance or the company's internal audit function, does not exempt the director from the requirement to act with ordinary care and have average knowledge in finance matters, which he or she has to deploy when reviewing and approving the annual accounts.[103]

5. Some judicial guidance concerning the individual amplification of the objective standard of care is provided by the Supreme Court of New South Wales, which has sharpened the Australian duty of care in a line of cases since the early 2000s. In *Australian Securities & Investments Commission (ASIC) v Rich*,[104] ASIC brought an action against the three executive directors and the non-executive chairman of the board of an Australian telecommunications group that had been placed into liquidation after the deterioration of its financial position. ASIC alleged that the chairman of the board, an experienced chartered accountant who was also chairman of the finance and audit committee, was subject to a higher standard of care than the other non-executive directors. The chairman, ASIC claimed, 'had special responsibilities beyond those of the other non-executive directors, by reason of his positions as chairman of the board and the finance and audit committee, and also by reason of his high qualifications, experience and expertise relative to the other directors'.[105] The court was receptive to ASIC's arguments and rejected the chairman's motion to dismiss the claim. The section of the Australian Corporations Act that codifies the duty of care provides for a determination of the applicable degree of care and diligence in light of 'the corporation's circumstances', the 'office held by' and the 'responsibilities' of the defendant director.[106] The main issue was whether these terms permitted or required an individuation of the standard of care.

[100] In practice, the distribution of responsibilities varies greatly and depends on the business operations of the individual corporation and the regulatory environment where it is incorporated. See, for example, the board and senior officers of Ford Motor Company, http://corporate.ford.com (follow hyperlinks 'Company' and 'Corporate Governance'): only two of the officers are members of the board of directors (the CEO and executive chairman), which consists of ten persons. Compare this with the management and supervisory boards of Volkswagen AG, www.volkswagenag.com (follow hyperlinks 'Investor Relations', 'Corporate Governance', 'Executive Bodies'), consisting of nine executive members with different, clearly defined functional responsibilities, and twenty non-executive directors, some of whom held executive positions in the Volkswagen group before being appointed to the supervisory board.

[101] UK Corporate Governance Code 2018, p 1. [102] ibid Principle A.

[103] See Companies Act 2006, s 414(1). [104] 174 FLR 128 (2003). [105] ibid 130.

[106] Corporations Act, s 180(1). The exact wording of the section is: 'A director or other officer of a corporation must exercise their powers and discharge their duties with the degree of care and diligence that a reasonable person would exercise if they: (a) were a director or officer of a corporation in the corporation's circumstances; and (b) occupied the office held by, and had the same responsibilities within the corporation as, the director or officer'.

According to the Supreme Court, the legislative history of the Corporations Act suggested

> that the word 'responsibilities' was intended to direct attention to the factual arrangements operating within the company and affecting the director in question ... The content of [the] specific duties would be affected by the factual matters specified by the section, relating to the corporation's circumstances, the nature of the director's office, and the director's responsibilities. The director's responsibilities would include arrangements flowing from the experience and skills that the director brought to his or her office, and also any arrangements within the board or between the director and executive management affecting the work that the director would be expected to carry out. The precise duty of care flowing from these arrangements would be subject, of course, to a minimum standard of care and diligence set by the statute in reflection of the common law position. Therefore, it is in my opinion incorrect to say ... that the word 'responsibilities' refers only to specific tasks delegated to the relevant director, through the articles or by resolution or otherwise. It is a wider concept, referring to the acquisition of responsibilities not only through specific delegation but also through the way in which work is distributed within the corporation in fact, and the expectations placed by those arrangements on the shoulders of the individual director ... Mr Greaves' [the chairman's] qualifications, experience and expertise, and his occupation of the position of 'foundation' director, chairman and chairman of the finance and audit committee, are all matters that may make up or contribute to the responsibilities within the corporation that Mr Greaves had ... [107]

6. A second influential decision by the Federal Court of Australia brought further guidance. *ASIC v Healey*[108] concerned a major accounting scandal surrounding the Centro group, a large Australian real estate investment trust. Eight directors, most of them without any accounting background, were sued for damages because they had signed off financial accounts that contained material misstatements. In setting out what was expected of directors with regard to the review of the company's accounts, the court explained that

> a director, whatever his or her background, has a duty greater than that of simply representing a particular field of experience or expertise. A director is not relieved of the duty to pay attention to the company's affairs which might reasonably be expected to attract inquiry, even outside the area of the director's expertise ... What each director is expected to do is to take a diligent and intelligent interest in the information available to him or her, to understand that information, and apply an enquiring mind to the responsibilities placed upon him or her. Such a responsibility arises in this proceeding in adopting and approving the financial statements. Because of their nature and importance, the directors must understand and focus upon the content of financial statements, and if necessary, make further enquiries if matters revealed in these financial statements call for such enquiries.

In the case at hand, all eight directors were found liable because they did not make such further enquiries, even though the inaccuracies in the financial statements

> were matters that could have been seen as apparent without difficulty upon a focussing by each director, and upon a careful and diligent consideration of the financial statements. As I have said, the directors were intelligent and experienced men in the corporate world. Despite the efforts of the legal representatives for the directors in contending otherwise, the basic concepts and financial literacy required by the directors to be in a position to properly question the apparent errors in the financial statements were not complicated.[109]

2. US

The US duty of care is peculiar in that the law imposes on directors the obligation to act with the care that can be expected of a reasonably prudent person in a like position,

[107] 174 FLR 140. [108] [2011] FCA 717.

[109] On the other hand, some reliance on the expertise of others is of course unavoidable and the fact that a director has sought professional advice may indeed be seen as an important factor in determining whether the director has breached the duty to exercise reasonable care, *Re Pro4Sport Ltd (in liq.)* [2015] EWHC 2540 (Ch).

but allows the courts to adopt a more deferential approach when they review the acts of directors. In other words, US law is based on two diverging standards: a standard of conduct, which represents the substantive legal principle intended to direct the behaviour of autonomous agents, and a standard of review, which reflects the test actually applied in court.[110] This dichotomy is expressed in the Model Business Corporation Act and also in Delaware case law. The MBCA provides for standards regulating how directors should discharge their duties[111] and for 'standards of liability' that set out the elements necessary to establish the liability of directors.[112] The Delaware General Corporation Law does not specify the applicable standard of care (or review), but the courts are explicit in distinguishing between these two standards. For example, in *Re Walt Disney Co. Derivative Litigation*,[113] the Delaware Court of Chancery held, on the one hand, that '[t]he fiduciary duty of due care requires that directors of a Delaware corporation "use that amount of care which ordinarily careful and prudent men would use in similar circumstances", and "consider all material information reasonably available" in making business decisions',[114] but, on the other hand, it stressed that courts will not review business decisions if the directors acted 'on an informed basis' and 'in the honest belief that the action taken was in the best interests of the company'.[115]

MBCA

§ 8.30—Standard of Conduct for Directors

(a) Each member of the board of directors, when discharging the duties of a director, shall act: (1) in good faith, and (2) in a manner the director reasonably believes to be in the best interests of the corporation.
(b) The members of the board of directors or a committee of the board, when becoming informed in connection with their decision-making function or devoting attention to their oversight function, shall discharge their duties with the care that a person in a like position would reasonably believe appropriate under similar circumstances.
(c) In discharging board or committee duties a director, who does not have knowledge that makes reliance unwarranted, is entitled to rely on the performance by any of the persons specified in subsection (e)(1) or subsection (e)(3) to whom the board may have delegated, formally or informally by course of conduct, the authority or duty to perform one or more of the board's functions that are delegable under applicable law.
(d) In discharging board or committee duties a director, who does not have knowledge that makes reliance unwarranted, is entitled to rely on information, opinions, reports or statements, including financial statements and other financial data, prepared or presented by any of the persons specified in subsection (e).
(e) A director is entitled to rely, in accordance with subsection (c) or (d), on:
    (1) one or more officers or employees of the corporation whom the director reasonably believes to be reliable and competent in the functions performed or the information, opinions, reports or statements provided;
    (2) legal counsel, public accountants, or other persons retained by the corporation as to matters involving skills or expertise the director reasonably believes are matters (i) within the particular person's professional or expert competence or (ii) as to which the particular person merits confidence;

    or

    (3) a committee of the board of directors of which the director is not a member if the director reasonably believes the committee merits confidence.

[110] For a discussion, see WT Allen, JB Jacobs, and LE Strine, 'Realigning the Standard of Review of Director Due Care with Delaware Public Policy: A Critique of Van Gorkom and its Progeny as a Standard of Review Problem' (2002) 96 Northwestern University Law Review 449; MA Eisenberg, 'The Divergence of Standards of Conduct and Standards of Review in Corporate Law' (1993) 62 Fordham Law Review 437.

[111] MBCA, §8.30(b). [112] MBCA, §8.31(a)(2). See the excerpts of the MBCA in the text.

[113] 907 A.2d 693 (Del. Ch. 2005). [114] ibid 749.

[115] ibid 747 (quoting *Aronson v Lewis*, 473 A.2d 805, 812 (Del. 1984)).

§ 8.31—Standards of Liability for Directors

(a) A director shall not be liable to the corporation or its shareholders for any decision to take or not to take action, or any failure to take any action, as a director, unless the party asserting liability in a proceeding establishes that:
   (1) ...
   (2) the challenged conduct consisted or was the result of:
      (i) action not in good faith; or
      (ii) a decision
         (A) which the director did not reasonably believe to be in the best interests of the corporation, or
         (B) as to which the director was not informed to an extent the director reasonably believed appropriate in the circumstances; or
      (iii) a lack of objectivity due to the director's familial, financial or business relationship with, or a lack of independence due to the director's domination or control by, another person having a material interest in the challenged conduct ... ; or
      (iv) a sustained failure of the director to devote attention to ongoing oversight of the business and affairs of the corporation, or a failure to devote timely attention, by making (or causing to be made) appropriate inquiry, when particular facts and circumstances of significant concern materialize that would alert a reasonably attentive director to the need therefore; or
      (v) receipt of a financial benefit to which the director was not entitled or any other breach of the director's duties to deal fairly with the corporation and its shareholders that is actionable under applicable law.
(b) The party seeking to hold the director liable:
   (1) for money damages, shall also have the burden of establishing that:
      (i) harm to the corporation or its shareholders has been suffered, and
      (ii) the harm suffered was proximately caused by the director's challenged conduct...

Section 8.30(b) MBCA speaks of the care that a *person in a like position* would reasonably believe appropriate, while §8.31(a)(2)(ii)(B) MBCA refers to the *director's* reasonable belief as to what information was appropriate in the circumstances. The first provision, determining the standard of conduct (as opposed to the standard of review or liability), builds on the 'ordinarily prudent person' standard that is generally the benchmark applicable in tort law.[116] Thus, §8.30(b) establishes an objective standard that refers to the 'common sense, practical wisdom and informed judgment'[117] of a person in the position of the director, not the individual director's attributes.[118] It is also important to note that the objective standard of §8.30(b) applies to directors when they are 'becoming informed'. This phrase emphasizes that the duty of care is primarily concerned with the process of decision-making, not the content of the decision.[119] The directors are required to inform themselves appropriately before taking a decision. Depending on the circumstances, the duty to be informed may involve not only a review of the materials provided at board meetings, but also a consultation of experts, such as legal counsel and public accountants, the use of industry studies, or discussions with management and other employees.[120] Finally, §8.30(b) distinguishes between

[116] The MBCA used to reproduce the 'ordinarily prudent person' standard of the law of negligence verbatim, but in order to avoid creating the impression that §8.30(b) defined the relevant criterion for measuring *actionable* conduct, which is the function of the 'ordinarily prudent person' standard in tort law, the formulation was changed. See Official Comment to §8.30 s 2.

[117] ibid.

[118] The further qualifications 'in a like position' and 'under similar circumstances' are not only intended to permit taking account of the size of the corporation, type of business, and other factors not related to the subjective attributes of the individual director, but also the defendant director's 'special background, qualifications, and management responsibilities'. See ibid. Thus, §8.30(b) functions in a similar way to s 174 UK Companies Act 2006. Directors are always required to exercise the common sense etc. of an ordinary director, but special qualifications may lead to a higher standard.

[119] See text to n 148 below.

[120] Official Comment to §8.30 s 2.

two main functions of directors: the decision-making function and the oversight function. This distinction is reflected in the case law of many states, including Delaware. When the courts review management decisions, they will pay attention to the requirement that the directors were well informed. However, they have to apply a different test when the issue is not about positive action, but the failure to act, notably the failure to ensure that an effective information and reporting system is in place that relays all important information to the board.[121] From the 'standard of conduct' perspective of §8.30(b), the law requires directors to obtain assurances from management that appropriate control systems have been established and to monitor these systems on an ongoing basis.[122]

Section 8.31(a)(2), on the other hand, shows that the courts will not apply the negligence-based test that underlies §8.30(b) when they review the conduct of directors. A director is not liable unless the plaintiff can show either that the director acted in bad faith, not in the best interest of the corporation, or without being appropriately informed.[123] If the plaintiff fails to establish any of these alternatives, the courts will not review the director's decision further. In particular, the courts will not apply the objective standard of §8.30(b). Conversely, if the plaintiff succeeds in showing bad faith, acting not in the best interest of the corporation, or lack of information, the director will not automatically be held liable. We will discuss this issue, and the standard that applies if the threshold requirements of §8.31(a)(2) (or the corresponding threshold conditions under Delaware law) are overcome, more fully below.[124] As far as the requirement is concerned that the director must have acted on an informed basis, the test applicable pursuant to §8.31(a)(2) is individualized. It has been said that so long as the director's belief that the decision is based on appropriate information is 'rational' and 'within the bounds of reason',[125] the director is protected by §8.31(a)(2). Therefore, the standard of review combines objective and subjective elements. Depending on the director's subjective belief, the 'ordinary person' standard of §8.30(b) may be reduced, but rationality as an objective concept establishes an irreducible lower benchmark.[126]

We now turn to the case law that has developed the above rules and refines them. We will concentrate on the law of Delaware, where the MBCA has not been adopted, but the considerations apply, *mutatis mutandis*, in most states. It will become clear that directors are accorded considerable protection under the relevant principles, provided they have not acted disloyally.

(a) Abstention doctrine

The operation of the rules outlined above is well illustrated by the case *Shlensky v Wrigley*.[127] The plaintiff in this case was a minority shareholder of the Chicago National League Ball Club, which operates the Major League Baseball team 'Chicago Cubs'. The plaintiff claimed that the directors of the corporation had acted negligently in failing to install lights in Wrigley Field, the Cubs' ballpark, and schedule night baseball games. More specifically, the plaintiff alleged:[128]

> ... that since night baseball was first played in 1935 nineteen of the twenty major league teams have scheduled night games ... Plaintiff alleges that every member of the major leagues, other

[121] We will discuss the applicable standard of review in section B.II below.

[122] Official Comment to §8.30 s 2.

[123] This is essentially a codification of the business judgment rule, see the discussion in the next section, and *Aronson v Lewis* (n 115) 812. Additional grounds for liability are contained in §8.31(a)(2)(iii)–(v).

[124] The standard of review that applies in this case is not necessarily that of §8.30(b); see section 2(d) below.

[125] Official Comment to §8.31, 'Note on the Business Judgment Rule'. An example of behaviour outside the bounds of reason is corporate waste, see, e.g., *In re Walt Disney Co. Derivative Litigation*, 906 A.2d 27, 73–5 (Del. 2006), discussed below, text to nn 194–196.

[126] Official Comment to §8.31, 'Note on the Business Judgment Rule'.

[127] 237 N.E.2d 776 (Ill. App. 1968). [128] ibid 777–8.

than the Cubs, scheduled substantially all of its home games in 1966 at night, exclusive of opening days, Saturdays, Sundays, holidays and days prohibited by league rules. Allegedly this has been done for the specific purpose of maximizing attendance and thereby maximizing revenue and income.

The Cubs, in the years 1961–65, sustained operating losses from its direct baseball operations. Plaintiff attributes those losses to inadequate attendance at Cubs' home games. He concludes that if the directors continue to refuse to install lights at Wrigley Field and schedule night baseball games, the Cubs will continue to sustain comparable losses and its financial condition will continue to deteriorate …

Plaintiff compares attendance at Cubs' games with that of the Chicago White Sox, an American League club, whose weekday games were generally played at night. The weekend attendance figures for the two teams was similar; however, the White Sox week-night games drew many more patrons than did the Cubs' weekday games.

The president of the corporation, Philip K. Wrigley, refused to install lights 'because of his personal opinions that baseball is a "daytime sport" and that the installation of lights and night baseball games will have a deteriorating effect upon the surrounding neighborhood'.[129] It was alleged that Mr Wrigley had admitted that he was 'not interested in whether the Cubs would benefit financially from such action because of his concern for the neighborhood'.[130] The plaintiff relied on *Dodge v Ford Motor Co.*, which we discussed above,[131] in arguing that the directors were under an obligation to act in the best *financial* interest of the corporation. The Appellate Court of Illinois, analysing Delaware and Illinois case law, held:[132]

[W]e are not satisfied that the motives assigned to Philip K. Wrigley, and through him to the other directors, are contrary to the best interests of the corporation and the stockholders. For example, it appears to us that the effect on the surrounding neighborhood might well be considered by a director who was considering the patrons who would or would not attend the games if the park were in a poor neighborhood. Furthermore, the long run interest of the corporation in its property value at Wrigley Field might demand all efforts to keep the neighborhood from deteriorating. By these thoughts we do not mean to say that we have decided that the decision of the directors was a correct one. That is beyond our jurisdiction and ability. We are merely saying that the decision is one properly before directors and the motives alleged in the amended complaint showed no fraud, illegality or conflict of interest in their making of that decision.

While the Appellate Court made some suggestions why the business decision of the president might not have been a bad one, it explained that this question was, ultimately, irrelevant. Quoting from *Ford Motor Co.*, the court emphasized: 'The judges are not business experts'.[133] Accordingly, it refused to review the reasons for Mr Wrigley's business decision. This, the court argued, was a matter for the board, not the judges. *Shlensky* is an example of an approach of the US courts that has been labelled the 'abstention doctrine'.[134] The courts adopt a deferential attitude to, and abstain from reviewing, good faith business decisions of directors. They will generally only intervene if the directors' behaviour amounts to, as the Appellate Court in *Shlensky* put it, 'fraud, illegality, or conflict of interest'. The legal mechanism or standard of review applied to achieve the protection of the directors' good faith decisions is the well-known *business judgment rule*.[135]

Several reasons exist for this deferential approach. Courts often lack the competence to judge complex business decisions of a financial or other technical nature. In addition, they do not want to set the wrong incentives and discourage directors from pursuing projects that

[129] ibid 778. [130] ibid. [131] Chapter 4C.II. [132] 237 N.E.2d 180–1. [133] ibid 780.

[134] SM Bainbridge, 'The Business Judgment Rule as Abstention Doctrine' (2004) 57 Vanderbilt Law Review 83.

[135] The Delaware formulation of the business judgment rule will be discussed in the next paragraphs. In the MBCA, the business judgment rule is codified in §8.31(a)(2), not in §8.30(b), in contrast to what some courts have held. For a discussion and references, see Official Comment to §8.31, Note on Directors' Liability.

make economic sense because the directors are risk-averse. Finally, the courts are mindful that directors have to make decisions under uncertainty and with imperfect information.[136] In hindsight, the risks and probabilities that business decisions turn out successfully are often judged differently than at the time when the decision was made. This phenomenon is called 'hindsight bias' in psychology. People tend to overestimate their ability to predict the outcome of an event after the event has occurred.[137] Judges may be as much prone to this bias as other people.

The *Shlensky* rule is, in principle, also the law in Delaware, although Delaware courts formulate the test somewhat differently. They qualify the business judgment rule as a 'presumption' that in making business decisions, directors 'acted on an informed basis, in good faith, and in the honest belief that the action taken was in the best interests of the company'.[138] In order to rebut the presumption, the claimant must present evidence of 'fraud, bad faith, or self-dealing'.[139] How the presumption and the required evidence for a rebuttal interrelate is not always expressed clearly in the case law. Some judgments refer to good faith and the absence of self-dealing as threshold requirements. If the director has not acted in good faith or was interested, the business judgment rule does not apply and the burden shifts to the defendant director to prove the 'entire fairness' of the transaction.[140] In other decisions, the courts treat the question of whether the directors exercised an informed business judgment as the threshold issue and refuse to enquire into the good faith of the directors if they fail to inform themselves adequately.[141] The differences are probably of a terminological, not a substantive nature. In *Walt Disney*,[142] on appeal, the plaintiff-appellants claimed that the Court of Chancery had 'failed to make a "threshold determination" of gross negligence' with respect to the process of acting on an informed basis.[143] The Supreme Court was not particularly troubled by this claim. After giving the familiar definition of the business judgment rule's presumptions, the court summarized the onus that is on the plaintiff as follows: 'Those presumptions [under the business judgment standard] can be rebutted if the plaintiff shows that the directors breached their fiduciary duty of care or of loyalty or acted in bad faith'.[144] Both lack of due care (i.e., gross negligence) and bad faith are threshold requirements that may be invoked to rebut the business judgment rule presumptions.[145]

What exactly does the plaintiff have to show under the three headings 'duty of care', 'duty of loyalty' and 'bad faith'? That the presumptions of the business judgment rule can be rebutted by a showing that the defendant director breached the duty of care seems to be, at first sight, circular, given that the business judgment rule restricts the enforceability of potential duty of care violations in the first place.[146] When the courts speak of the duty of care in this context, they mean that the directors must act on an informed basis.[147] Thus, in this respect, the formulation in *Walt Disney* is identical to the first definition given above (the standard of

[136] See section A.I above.

[137] Hindsight bias as a rationale for the business judgment rule is discussed in *Re Citigroup Inc. Shareholder Derivative Litigation*, 964 A.2d 106, 124 (Del. Ch. 2009).

[138] *Aronson v Lewis* (n 115) 812. This definition has been reiterated consistently by the Delaware courts, see, e.g., *Citigroup* (n 137) 124; *In re Walt Disney Co. Derivative Litigation* (n 125) 52; *Smith v Van Gorkom*, 488 A.2d 858, 872 (Del. 1985).

[139] *Cede & Co. v Technicolor, Inc.*, 634 A.2d 345 (Del. 1993) (Cede II), quoting *Grobow v Perot*, 539 A.2d 180, 187 (Del. 1988).

[140] ibid. See also *Aronson* (n 115) 814.

[141] *Van Gorkom* (n 138) 889: '[C]onsiderations of good faith, including the presumption that the directors acted in good faith, are irrelevant in determining the threshold issue of whether the directors as a Board exercised an informed business judgment'. See also *Cede II* (n 139) 367–8.

[142] See n 125 above. [143] *In re Walt Disney Co. Derivative Litigation* (n 125) 52. [144] ibid.

[145] ibid 53.

[146] For a critical discussion of the case law, in particular *Cede II* (n 139), from this perspective see SM Bainbridge, *Corporate Law* (2nd edn, Foundation Press 2009) 101–102.

[147] See, e.g., *Cede II* (n 139) 367: 'The duty of the directors of a company to act on an informed basis, as that term has been defined by this Court numerous times, forms the duty of care element of the business judgment rule'.

Aronson v Lewis). The function of the business judgment rule is that the *content* of a business decision will not be evaluated, provided that the decision-making *process* is free from defects. For this reason, the business judgment rule has been called 'process oriented'.[148] The directors are protected if they have informed themselves, 'prior to making a business decision, of all material information reasonably available to them'.[149] In collecting the required information and making business decisions, the directors must 'use that amount of care which ordinarily careful and prudent men would use in similar circumstances'.[150] Consequently, the duty of care element of the business judgment rule is assessed objectively, with the 'ordinarily careful and prudent man' as a benchmark. Of course, this standard still leaves room for interpretation, and the Delaware courts are careful not to impose overly burdensome requirements on directors. They commonly hold that the test of reasonableness and the ordinary person standard are based on the concept of gross negligence. Deficiencies in the decision-making process must amount to this heightened level of negligence in order to be actionable.[151]

The duty of loyalty is implicated if directors are interested in a transaction, engage in self-dealing, or lack independence.[152] The Supreme Court of Delaware in *Aronson v Lewis* described the duty of loyalty element of the business judgment rule as follows: '[D]irectors can neither appear on both sides of a transaction nor expect to derive any personal financial benefit from it in the sense of self-dealing, as opposed to a benefit which devolves upon the corporation or all stockholders generally'.[153] Examples include transactions between a parent and a subsidiary where the directors of the subsidiary are nominated by the parent and are officers or directors of the parent,[154] or transactions between a corporation and a business enterprise in which the director holds a controlling interest.[155] We will discuss the duty of loyalty in more detail at a later point.[156]

The third category that may be used to rebut the business judgment rule presumptions, bad faith, is the most elusive. It is elusive because, for a long time, it was unclear what good faith involved and whether the duty to act in good faith was a separate duty, complementing the other two fiduciary duties of Delaware corporate law and serving as an independent basis for an action against the directors, or merely an element of the duties of care and loyalty giving rise to liability under one of these rubrics if the directors lacked good faith.[157] The Delaware General Corporation Law refers to good faith repeatedly, but not as a freestanding legal concept. Rather, it is, inter alia, a precondition for the exculpation of directors in the articles of association,[158] the approval of a transaction between the director and the corporation by the disinterested directors,[159] and the indemnification of directors against legal expenses by the corporation.[160] The most comprehensive analysis of the concept was offered

[148] *In re Caremark Intern. Inc. Derivative Litigation*, 698 A.2d 959, 968 (Del. Ch. 1996) (see also the first paragraph of the excerpt of *Caremark* reproduced below, section B.II).

[149] *Aronson* (n 115) 812.

[150] *Graham v Allis-Chalmers Mfg. Co.*, 188 A.2d 125, 130 (Del. 1963); *In re Walt Disney Co. Derivative Litigation* (n 113) 749.

[151] *Aronson* (n 115) 812; *Van Gorkom* (n 138) 873; *Brehm v Eisner*, 746 A.2d 244, 259 (Del. 2000); *Walt Disney* (n 113) 749. We will analyse below what gross negligence involves; see section 2(b).

[152] *Aronson* (n 115) 812; *Brehm* (n 151) 264; *Walt Disney* (n 113) 747.

[153] *Aronson* (n 115) 812.

[154] *Sinclair Oil Corp. v Levien*, 280 A.2d 717 (Del. 1971).

[155] *Fliegler v Lawrence*, 361 A.2d 218 (Del. 1976).

[156] See section C below.

[157] MA Eisenberg, 'The Duty of Good Faith in Corporate Law' (2005) 31 Delaware Journal of Corporate Law 1; SJ Griffith, 'Good Faith Business Judgment: A Theory of Rhetoric in Corporate Law Jurisprudence' (2005) 55 Duke Law Journal 1; MJ Loewenstein, 'The Diverging Meaning of Good Faith' (2009) 34 Delaware Journal of Corporate Law 433; HA Sale, 'Delaware's Good Faith' (2004) 89 Cornell Law Review 456.

[158] Del. Gen. Corp. Law, §102(b)(7): The articles of association may include: 'A provision eliminating or limiting the personal liability of a director to the corporation or its stockholders for monetary damages for breach of fiduciary duty as a director, provided that such provision shall not eliminate or limit the liability of a director: (i) For any breach of the director's duty of loyalty to the corporation or its stockholders; (ii) for acts or omissions not in good faith or which involve intentional misconduct or a knowing violation of law . . .'.

[159] Del. Gen. Corp. Law, §144(a).

[160] Del. Gen. Corp. Law, §145(a), (b). For an overview of the role of good faith in state corporation laws and case law, see Eisenberg (n 157) 6–12.

by the Supreme Court of Delaware in obiter in *Walt Disney*.[161] The case dealt with the question whether the directors of Disney had breached their fiduciary duties in agreeing on a large severance payment for Michael Ovitz, who had been hired just one year earlier as CEO and whose employment was terminated because of his failure to adapt to Disney's corporate culture.[162] The following excerpt sets out the Supreme Court's understanding of the concept of good faith.[163]

***In re Walt Disney Co. Derivative Litigation*, 906 A.2d 27 (Del. 2006)**

Jacobs, Justice:

[A]s a matter of simple logic, at least three different categories of fiduciary behavior are candidates for the 'bad faith' pejorative label.

The first category involves so-called 'subjective bad faith', that is, fiduciary conduct motivated by an actual intent to do harm. That such conduct constitutes classic, quintessential bad faith is a proposition so well accepted in the liturgy of fiduciary law that it borders on axiomatic. We need not dwell further on this category, because no such conduct is claimed to have occurred, or did occur, in this case.

The second category of conduct, which is at the opposite end of the spectrum, involves lack of due care-that is, fiduciary action taken solely by reason of gross negligence and without any malevolent intent. In this case, appellants assert claims of gross negligence to establish breaches not only of director due care but also of the directors' duty to act in good faith. Although the Chancellor found, and we agree, that the appellants failed to establish gross negligence, to afford guidance we address the issue of whether gross negligence (including a failure to inform one's self of available material facts), without more, can also constitute bad faith. The answer is clearly no.

From a broad philosophical standpoint, that question is more complex than would appear, if only because (as the Chancellor and others have observed) 'issues of good faith are (to a certain degree) inseparably and necessarily intertwined with the duties of care and loyalty . . .'. But, in the pragmatic, conduct-regulating legal realm which calls for more precise conceptual line drawing, the answer is that grossly negligent conduct, without more, does not and cannot constitute a breach of the fiduciary duty to act in good faith. The conduct that is the subject of due care may overlap with the conduct that comes within the rubric of good faith in a psychological sense, but from a legal standpoint those duties are and must remain quite distinct. Both our legislative history and our common law jurisprudence distinguish sharply between the duties to exercise due care and to act in good faith, and highly significant consequences flow from that distinction.

The Delaware General Assembly has addressed the distinction between bad faith and a failure to exercise due care (i.e., gross negligence) in two separate contexts. The first is Section 102(b)(7) of the DGCL, which authorizes Delaware corporations, by a provision in the certificate of incorporation, to exculpate their directors from monetary damage liability for a breach of the duty of care. That exculpatory provision affords significant protection to directors of Delaware corporations. The statute carves out several exceptions, however, including most relevantly, 'for acts or omissions not in good faith . . .'. Thus, a corporation can exculpate its directors from monetary liability for a breach of the duty of care, but not for conduct that is not in good faith. To adopt a definition of bad faith that would cause a violation of the duty of care automatically to become an act or omission 'not in good faith', would eviscerate the protections accorded to directors by the General Assembly's adoption of Section 102(b)(7).

A second legislative recognition of the distinction between fiduciary conduct that is grossly negligent and conduct that is not in good faith, is Delaware's indemnification statute, found at 8 *Del. C.* § 145. To oversimplify, subsections (a) and (b) of that statute permit a corporation to indemnify (inter alia) any person who is or was a director, officer, employee or agent of the corporation against expenses (including attorneys' fees), judgments, fines and amounts paid in

[161] *In re Walt Disney Co. Derivative Litigation* (n 125).

[162] See the account given by the Court of Chancery, *Walt Disney* (n 113) 713–14.

[163] References of the Supreme Court to the 'Chancellor' refer to Chancellor Chandler's holding in *Walt Disney* (n 113).

settlement of specified actions, suits or proceedings, where (among other things): (i) that person is, was, or is threatened to be made a party to that action, suit or proceeding, and (ii) that person 'acted in good faith and in a manner the person reasonably believed to be in or not opposed to the best interests of the corporation . . .'. Thus, under Delaware statutory law a director or officer of a corporation can be indemnified for liability (and litigation expenses) incurred by reason of a violation of the duty of care, but not for a violation of the duty to act in good faith.

Section 145, like Section 102(b)(7), evidences the intent of the Delaware General Assembly to afford significant protections to directors (and, in the case of Section 145, other fiduciaries) of Delaware corporations. To adopt a definition that conflates the duty of care with the duty to act in good faith by making a violation of the former an automatic violation of the latter, would nullify those legislative protections and defeat the General Assembly's intent. There is no basis in policy, precedent or common sense that would justify dismantling the distinction between gross negligence and bad faith.[164]

That leaves the third category of fiduciary conduct, which falls in between the first two categories of (1) conduct motivated by subjective bad intent and (2) conduct resulting from gross negligence. This third category is what the Chancellor's definition of bad faith-intentional dereliction of duty, a conscious disregard for one's responsibilities-is intended to capture. The question is whether such misconduct is properly treated as a non-exculpable, nonindemnifiable violation of the fiduciary duty to act in good faith. In our view it must be, for at least two reasons.

First, the universe of fiduciary misconduct is not limited to either disloyalty in the classic sense (i.e., preferring the adverse self-interest of the fiduciary or of a related person to the interest of the corporation) or gross negligence. Cases have arisen where corporate directors have no conflicting self-interest in a decision, yet engage in misconduct that is more culpable than simple inattention or failure to be informed of all facts material to the decision. To protect the interests of the corporation and its shareholders, fiduciary conduct of this kind, which does not involve disloyalty (as traditionally defined) but is qualitatively more culpable than gross negligence, should be proscribed. A vehicle is needed to address such violations doctrinally, and that doctrinal vehicle is the duty to act in good faith. The Chancellor implicitly so recognized in his Opinion, where he identified different examples of bad faith as follows:

The good faith required of a corporate fiduciary includes not simply the duties of care and loyalty, in the narrow sense that I have discussed them above, but all actions required by a true faithfulness and devotion to the interests of the corporation and its shareholders. A failure to act in good faith may be shown, for instance, where the fiduciary intentionally acts with a purpose other than that of advancing the best interests of the corporation, where the fiduciary acts with the intent to violate applicable positive law, or where the fiduciary intentionally fails to act in the face of a known duty to act, demonstrating a conscious disregard for his duties. There may be other examples of bad faith yet to be proven or alleged, but these three are the most salient.

Those articulated examples of bad faith are not new to our jurisprudence. Indeed, they echo pronouncements our courts have made throughout the decades.[165]

Second, the legislature has also recognized this intermediate category of fiduciary misconduct, which ranks between conduct involving subjective bad faith and gross negligence. [The

[164] [Footnote in the original.] Basic to the common law of torts is the distinction between conduct that is negligent (or grossly negligent) and conduct that is intentional. And in the narrower area of corporation law, our jurisprudence has recognized the distinction between the fiduciary duties to act with due care, with loyalty, and in good faith, as well as the consequences that flow from that distinction. Recent Delaware case law precludes a recovery of rescissory (as distinguished from out-of-pocket) damages for a breach of the duty of care, but permits such a recovery for a breach of the duty of loyalty. *See Cinerama, Inc. v Technicolor, Inc.*, 663 A.2d 1134, 1147–50 (Del. Ch. 1994), *aff'd*, 663 A.2d 1156 (Del. 1995).

[165] [Footnote in the original.] See, e.g., *Allaun v Consol. Oil Co.*, 147 A.257, 261 (Del. Ch. 1929) (further judicial scrutiny is warranted if the transaction results from the directors' 'reckless indifference to or a deliberate disregard of the interests of the whole body of stockholders'); *Gimbel v Signal Cos., Inc.*, 316 A.2d 599, 604 (Del. Ch. 1974), *aff'd*, 316 A.2d 619 (Del. 1974) (injunction denied because, inter alia, there was '[n]othing in the record [that] would justify a finding . . . that the directors acted for any personal advantage or out of improper motive or intentional disregard of shareholder interests'); *In re Caremark Int'l Derivative Litig.* 698 A.2d 959, 971 (Del. Ch. 1996) ('only a sustained or systematic failure of the board to exercise oversight-such as an utter failure to attempt to assure a reasonable information and reporting system exists-will establish the lack of good faith that is a necessary condition to liability') . . .

> Court refers to the Del. Gen. Corp. Law, § 102(b)(7), discussed above, and concludes:] Because the statute exculpates directors only for conduct amounting to gross negligence, the statutory denial of exculpation for 'acts ... not in good faith' must encompass the intermediate category of misconduct captured by the Chancellor's definition of bad faith.

The definition of good faith developed by the Court of Chancery and adopted by the Supreme Court in *Walt Disney* restricts bad faith to intentional conduct. According to Chancellor Chandler, bad faith consists in the '*intentional dereliction of duty*, a *conscious disregard for one's responsibilities* ... [d]eliberate indifference and inaction *in the face of a duty to act*',[166] or intentional acts 'with a purpose other than that of advancing the best interests of the corporation'.[167] This approach was reiterated by the Supreme Court of Delaware in *Wood v Baum*.[168] When the plaintiffs need to show bad faith because the directors are exculpated from liability for mere negligence, they must 'plead particularized facts that demonstrate that the directors acted with scienter, *i.e.*, that they had "actual or constructive knowledge" that their conduct was legally improper'.[169]

The Supreme Court in *Walt Disney* did not decide whether the duty to act in good faith constituted a full-fledged fiduciary duty that could be invoked by plaintiffs as an independent cause of action, or it became only relevant in the context of one of the two traditional duties, the duty of care and the duty of loyalty.[170] The Court of Chancery interpreted the directors' duties as 'constituent elements of the overarching concepts of allegiance, devotion and faithfulness that must guide the conduct of every fiduciary'.[171] The court continued: 'The good faith required of a corporate fiduciary includes not simply the duties of care and loyalty, in the narrow sense ... but all actions required by a true faithfulness and devotion to the interests of the corporation and its shareholders'.[172] These statements are ambivalent and were probably not intended to settle the issue. It is clear, on the one hand, that the three duties overlap substantially,[173] but, on the other hand, the Court of Chancery also emphasized that some scope remained for the duty to act in good faith that was not captured by due care or loyalty.

The Supreme Court finally clarified the issue in *Stone v Ritter*.[174] It observed that, at least where director oversight liability was concerned,[175] lack of good faith was a 'necessary condition' of liability. In the court's opinion, this meant that a failure to act in good faith was not conduct that resulted, *ipso facto*, in the imposition of fiduciary liability.[176] Rather, good faith was a 'subsidiary element', a 'condition' of the duty of loyalty.[177] Lack of good faith could not, by itself, establish liability for breach of a fiduciary duty.[178] This interpretation has two somewhat counterintuitive consequences. First, oversight liability does not implicate the duty of care, but the duty of loyalty, even though the failure of directors to monitor employees and provide for effective control systems is closer to the type of behaviour associated with a lack of due care, rather than disloyal behaviour.[179] Secondly, and following from the first observation, the scope of the duty of loyalty is extended. It comprises not only cases involving a

[166] *Walt Disney* (n 113) 755. [167] ibid. [168] 953 A.2d 136 (Del. 2008).

[169] ibid 141. See also *In re Citigroup Inc. Shareholder Derivative Litigation* (n 137) (quoting *Walt Disney* and *Wood v Baum* and holding that bad faith requires a showing 'that a director *knowingly* violated a fiduciary duty or failed to act in violation of a *known* duty to act': ibid 125).

[170] *Walt Disney* (n 125) 67. [171] *Walt Disney* (n 113) 755. [172] ibid.

[173] See, for example, the discussion ibid 755–6: A director who deliberately disregards the interests of the corporation or the shareholders may act both in bad faith and violate the duty of loyalty. The sustained or systematic failure of the board to exercise oversight and monitor others to whom duties are delegated may constitute a breach of the duty of care and at the same time demonstrate a lack of good faith (see *In re Caremark Intern. Inc. Derivative Litigation* (n 148) 971, reproduced below, 'Internal control systems').

[174] 911 A.2d 362 (Del. 2006). [175] See the discussion in section B.II below.

[176] *Stone* (n 174) 369.

[177] ibid 370 (quoting *Guttman v Huang*, 823 A.2d 492, 506 n 34 (Del. Ch. 2003)). [178] ibid.

[179] ibid: 'It follows that because a showing of bad faith conduct, in the sense described in *Disney* and *Caremark*, is essential to establish director oversight liability, the fiduciary duty violated by that conduct is the duty of loyalty'.

conflict of interest, but also other cases where a director disregards the interests of the corporation and the shareholders to an extent that amounts to bad faith.[180]

In the following sections, we will discuss three remaining questions in more detail. First, how do courts assess whether the directors have acted on an informed basis? Secondly, if the plaintiff fails to rebut the business judgment rule presumptions (i.e. the directors acted on an informed basis, in good faith, and were not conflicted), does the enquiry of the courts end or will they verify that the directors conformed to an objective minimum standard of care regarding the content of their decision? Thirdly, if the directors fail any one or more of the above elements of the threshold test, for example, they acted with the intention to defraud the shareholders, what is the standard of review to examine the directors' actions? We will deal with each question in a separate section.

(b) Process due care

The most famous case discussing process due care, that is, the due care element of the business judgment rule in the parlance of the Delaware courts, is the 1985 judgment *Smith v Van Gorkom*[181] by the Supreme Court of Delaware. It is also one of the few cases where the plaintiffs were successful in rebutting the presumptions of the business judgment rule because the directors were not adequately informed.

***Smith v. Van Gorkom*, 488 A.2d 858 (Supreme Court of Delaware 1985)**

[Van Gorkom was the chairman and chief executive of Trans Union Corporation, a publicly-traded, diversified holding company with a cash flow of hundreds of millions of dollars annually. Because the company had difficulties in generating sufficient taxable income to offset investment tax credits, the senior management of Trans Union considered selling the company in a leveraged buy-out to a buyer with a large amount of taxable income. The shares of Trans Union were trading during the relevant period at about $38. Based on preliminary calculations considering the cash flow needed to service the debt, the management believed that a buy-out for an offer price of between $50 and $60 per share would be feasible. Van Gorkom, who was approaching 65 years of age and mandatory retirement, decided that he would be willing to sell his stake for $55 per share. He assembled a financing structure that would allow the buyer to pay off the debt portion of the purchase price within a few years. Without consulting his board, he approached a well-known corporate takeover specialist, Mr Pritzker, who eventually agreed to make a cash-out merger offer at $55 per share. However, he insisted that the board act on the proposal within the next three days and before the opening of the stock markets on Monday morning. According to the court, Van Gorkom had chosen the $55 figure based solely on the feasibility of a leveraged buy-out: 'Apart from the Company's historic stock market price, and Van Gorkom's long association with Trans Union, the record is devoid of any competent evidence that $55 represented the per share intrinsic value of the Company'. The following excerpt gives a detailed account of the decision-making process of the board.]

Horsey, Justice:

On Friday, September 19, Van Gorkom called a special meeting of the Trans Union Board for noon the following day. He also called a meeting of the Company's Senior Management to convene at 11:00 a.m., prior to the meeting of the Board. No one, except Chelberg and Peterson, was told the purpose of the meetings. Van Gorkom did not invite Trans Union's investment banker, Salomon Brothers or its Chicago-based partner, to attend.

[180] ibid. Accordingly, it could be argued that bad faith necessarily implicates the duty of loyalty, but that not all conduct that infringes the duty of loyalty constitutes acts in bad faith. For example, a director may engage in self-dealing in the belief that the transaction will be beneficial to the corporation. However, arguably, the scope of this type of behaviour (good faith breach of the duty of loyalty) is narrow. Pursuant to Delaware law, a conflicting interest transaction is valid if the board or the shareholders authorize the transaction after full disclosure or the transaction is fair to the corporation (Del. Gen. Corp. Law, §144(a)). The failure to comply with either requirement, i.e. the transaction is neither fair, nor has it been disclosed to or approved by the directors or shareholders (hence, the director does not comply with the duty of loyalty), may give rise to an inference of bad faith. See Official Comment to §8.31(a) MBCA, 'Good faith'.

[181] *Smith v Van Gorkom* (n 138).

Of those present at the Senior Management meeting on September 20, only Chelberg and Peterson had prior knowledge of Pritzker's offer. Van Gorkom disclosed the offer and described its terms, but he furnished no copies of the proposed Merger Agreement. Romans [the CFO of Trans Union] announced that his department had done a second study which showed that, for a leveraged buy-out, the price range for Trans Union stock was between $55 and $65 per share. Van Gorkom neither saw the study nor asked Romans to make it available for the Board meeting.

Senior Management's reaction to the Pritzker proposal was completely negative. No member of Management, except Chelberg and Peterson, supported the proposal. Romans objected to the price as being too low; he was critical of the timing and suggested that consideration should be given to the adverse tax consequences of an all-cash deal for low-basis shareholders; and he took the position that the agreement to sell Pritzker one million newly-issued shares at market price would inhibit other offers, as would the prohibitions against soliciting bids and furnishing inside information to other bidders. Romans argued that the Pritzker proposal was a 'lock up' and amounted to 'an agreed merger as opposed to an offer'. Nevertheless, Van Gorkom proceeded to the Board meeting as scheduled without further delay.

Ten directors served on the Trans Union Board, five inside (defendants Bonser, O'Boyle, Browder, Chelberg, and Van Gorkom) and five outside (defendants Wallis, Johnson, Lanterman, Morgan and Reneker). All directors were present at the meeting, except O'Boyle who was ill. Of the outside directors, four were corporate chief executive officers and one was the former Dean of the University of Chicago Business School. None was an investment banker or trained financial analyst. All members of the Board were well informed about the Company and its operations as a going concern. They were familiar with the current financial condition of the Company, as well as operating and earnings projections reported in the recent Five Year Forecast. The Board generally received regular and detailed reports and was kept abreast of the accumulated investment tax credit and accelerated depreciation problem.

Van Gorkom began the Special Meeting of the Board with a twenty-minute oral presentation. Copies of the proposed Merger Agreement were delivered too late for study before or during the meeting. He reviewed the Company's ITC [investment tax credits] and depreciation problems and the efforts theretofore made to solve them. He discussed his initial meeting with Pritzker and his motivation in arranging that meeting. Van Gorkom did not disclose to the Board, however, the methodology by which he alone had arrived at the $55 figure, or the fact that he first proposed the $55 price in his negotiations with Pritzker.

Van Gorkom outlined the terms of the Pritzker offer as follows: Pritzker would pay $55 in cash for all outstanding shares of Trans Union stock upon completion of which Trans Union would be merged into New T Company, a subsidiary wholly-owned by Pritzker and formed to implement the merger; for a period of 90 days, Trans Union could receive, but could not actively solicit, competing offers; the offer had to be acted on by the next evening, Sunday, September 21; Trans Union could only furnish to competing bidders published information, and not proprietary information; the offer was subject to Pritzker obtaining the necessary financing by October 10, 1980; if the financing contingency were met or waived by Pritzker, Trans Union was required to sell to Pritzker one million newly-issued shares of Trans Union at $38 per share.

Van Gorkom took the position that putting Trans Union 'up for auction' through a 90-day market test would validate a decision by the Board that $55 was a fair price. He told the Board that the 'free market will have an opportunity to judge whether $55 is a fair price'. Van Gorkom framed the decision before the Board not as whether $55 per share was the highest price that could be obtained, but as whether the $55 price was a fair price that the stockholders should be given the opportunity to accept or reject.

Attorney Brennan advised the members of the Board that they might be sued if they failed to accept the offer and that a fairness opinion was not required as a matter of law.

Romans attended the meeting as chief financial officer of the Company. He told the Board that he had not been involved in the negotiations with Pritzker and knew nothing about the merger proposal until the morning of the meeting; that his studies did not indicate either a fair price for the stock or a valuation of the Company; that he did not see his role as directly addressing the fairness issue; and that he and his people 'were trying to search for ways to justify a price in connection with such a [leveraged buy-out] transaction, rather than to say what the shares are worth'. Romans testified:

> I told the Board that the study ran the numbers at 50 and 60, and then the subsequent study at 55 and 65, and that was not the same thing as saying that I have a valuation of the company at X dollars. But it was a way—a first step towards reaching that conclusion.

Romans told the Board that, in his opinion, $55 was 'in the range of a fair price', but 'at the beginning of the range'.

Chelberg, Trans Union's President, supported Van Gorkom's presentation and representations. He testified that he 'participated to make sure that the Board members collectively were clear on the details of the agreement or offer from Pritzker'; that he 'participated in the discussion with Mr. Brennan, inquiring of him about the necessity for valuation opinions in spite of the way in which this particular offer was couched'; and that he was otherwise actively involved in supporting the positions being taken by Van Gorkom before the Board about 'the necessity to act immediately on this offer', and about 'the adequacy of the $55 and the question of how that would be tested'.

The Board meeting of September 20 lasted about two hours. Based solely upon Van Gorkom's oral presentation, Chelberg's supporting representations, Romans' oral statement, Brennan's legal advice, and their knowledge of the market history of the Company's stock, the directors approved the proposed Merger Agreement ...

[Shareholder of Trans Union commenced a class action seeking damages from the directors for breach of the duty of care. The Court of Chancery ruled that the board's approval of the merger agreement fell within the protection of the business judgment rule. The Supreme Court disagreed:]

Under Delaware law, the business judgment rule is the offspring of the fundamental principle ... that the business and affairs of a Delaware corporation are managed by or under its board of directors ... The rule itself 'is a presumption that in making a business decision, the directors of a corporation acted on an informed basis, in good faith and in the honest belief that the action taken was in the best interests of the company'.... Thus, the party attacking a board decision as uninformed must rebut the presumption that its business judgment was an informed one.

The determination of whether a business judgment is an informed one turns on whether the directors have informed themselves 'prior to making a business decision, of all material information reasonably available to them'....

We think the concept of gross negligence is ... the proper standard for determining whether a business judgment reached by a board of directors was an informed one.[182] ...

On the record before us, we must conclude that the Board of Directors did not reach an informed business judgment on September 20, 1980 in voting to 'sell' the Company for $55 per share pursuant to the Pritzker cash-out merger proposal. Our reasons, in summary, are as follows:

The directors (1) did not adequately inform themselves as to Van Gorkom's role in forcing the 'sale' of the Company and in establishing the per share purchase price; (2) were uninformed as to the intrinsic value of the Company; and (3) given these circumstances, at a minimum, were grossly negligent in approving the 'sale' of the Company upon two hours' consideration, without prior notice, and without the exigency of a crisis or emergency.

As has been noted, the Board based its September 20 decision to approve the cash-out merger primarily on Van Gorkom's representations. None of the directors, other than Van Gorkom and Chelberg, had any prior knowledge that the purpose of the meeting was to propose a cash-out merger of Trans Union. No members of Senior Management were present, other than Chelberg, Romans and Peterson; and the latter two had only learned of the proposed sale an hour earlier....

Without any documents before them concerning the proposed transaction, the members of the Board were required to rely entirely upon Van Gorkom's 20-minute oral presentation of the

[182] [Footnote in the original.] Compare *Mitchell v Highland-Western Glass* [167 A. 831 (Del. Ch. 1933)], where the Court posed the question as whether the board acted 'so far without information that they can be said to have passed an unintelligent and unadvised judgment': 167 A. at 833. Compare also *Gimbel v Signal Companies, Inc.* 316 A.2d 599, *aff'd per curiam* Del. Supr., 316 A.2d 619 (1974), where the Chancellor, after expressly reiterating the *Highland-Western Glass* standard, framed the question, 'Or to put the question in its legal context, did the Signal directors act without the bounds of reason and recklessly in approving the price offer of Burmah?' Id.

proposal. No written summary of the terms of the merger was presented; the directors were given no documentation to support the adequacy of $55 price per share for sale of the Company; and the Board had before it nothing more than Van Gorkom's statement of his understanding of the substance of an agreement which he admittedly had never read, nor which any member of the Board had ever seen …

The defendants rely on the following factors to sustain the Trial Court's finding that the Board's decision was an informed one: (1) the magnitude of the premium or spread between the $55 Pritzker offering price and Trans Union's current market price of $38 per share; (2) the amendment of the Agreement as submitted on September 20 to permit the Board to accept any better offer during the 'market test' period; (3) the collective experience and expertise of the Board's 'inside' and 'outside' directors; and (4) their reliance on Brennan's legal advice that the directors might be sued if they rejected the Pritzker proposal. We discuss each of these grounds seriatim:

(1) A substantial premium may provide one reason to recommend a merger, but in the absence of other sound valuation information, the fact of a premium alone does not provide an adequate basis upon which to assess the fairness of an offering price. Here, the judgment reached as to the adequacy of the premium was based on a comparison between the historically depressed Trans Union market price and the amount of the Pritzker offer. Using market price as a basis for concluding that the premium adequately reflected the true value of the Company was a clearly faulty, indeed fallacious, premise, as the defendants' own evidence demonstrates.

The record is clear that before September 20, Van Gorkom and other members of Trans Union's Board knew that the market had consistently undervalued the worth of Trans Union's stock, despite steady increases in the Company's operating income in the seven years preceding the merger. The Board related this occurrence in large part to Trans Union's inability to use its ITCs as previously noted. Van Gorkom testified that he did not believe the market price accurately reflected Trans Union's true worth; and several of the directors testified that, as a general rule, most chief executives think that the market undervalues their companies' stock. Yet, on September 20, Trans Union's Board apparently believed that the market stock price accurately reflected the value of the Company for the purpose of determining the adequacy of the premium for its sale.

In the Proxy Statement, however, the directors reversed their position. There, they stated that, although the earnings prospects for Trans Union were 'excellent', they found no basis for believing that this would be reflected in future stock prices. With regard to past trading, the Board stated that the prices at which the Company's common stock had traded in recent years did not reflect the 'inherent' value of the Company. But having referred to the 'inherent' value of Trans Union, the directors ascribed no number to it. Moreover, nowhere did they disclose that they had no basis on which to fix 'inherent' worth beyond an impressionistic reaction to the premium over market and an unsubstantiated belief that the value of the assets was 'significantly greater' than book value …

As of September 20, the Board had made no evaluation of the Company designed to value the entire enterprise, nor had the Board ever previously considered selling the Company or consenting to a buy-out merger. Thus, the adequacy of a premium is indeterminate unless it is assessed in terms of other competent and sound valuation information that reflects the value of the particular business …

We do not imply that an outside valuation study is essential to support an informed business judgment; nor do we state that fairness opinions by independent investment bankers are required as a matter of law. Often insiders familiar with the business of a going concern are in a better position than are outsiders to gather relevant information; and under appropriate circumstances, such directors may be fully protected in relying in good faith upon the valuation reports of their management.

Here, the record establishes that the Board did not request its Chief Financial Officer, Romans, to make any valuation study or review of the proposal to determine the adequacy of $55 per share for sale of the Company. On the record before us: The Board rested on Romans' elicited response that the $55 figure was within a 'fair price range' within the context of a leveraged buy-out. No director sought any further information from Romans. No director asked him why he put $55 at the bottom of his range. No director asked Romans for any details as to his study, the reason why it had been undertaken or its depth. No director asked to see the study; and no director asked Romans whether Trans Union's finance department could do a fairness study within the remaining 36-hour period available under the Pritzker offer.

Had the Board, or any member, made an inquiry of Romans, he presumably would have responded as he testified: that his calculations were rough and preliminary; and, that the study was not designed to determine the fair value of the Company, but rather to assess the feasibility of a leveraged buy-out financed by the Company's projected cash flow, making certain assumptions as to the purchaser's borrowing needs. Romans would have presumably also informed the Board of his view, and the widespread view of Senior Management, that the timing of the offer was wrong and the offer inadequate.

The record also establishes that the Board accepted without scrutiny Van Gorkom's representation as to the fairness of the $55 price per share for sale of the Company—a subject that the Board had never previously considered. The Board thereby failed to discover that Van Gorkom had suggested the $55 price to Pritzker and, most crucially, that Van Gorkom had arrived at the $55 figure based on calculations designed solely to determine the feasibility of a leveraged buy-out. No questions were raised either as to the tax implications of a cash-out merger or how the price for the one million share option granted Pritzker was calculated.

We do not say that the Board of Directors was not entitled to give some credence to Van Gorkom's representation that $55 was an adequate or fair price. Under § 141(e), the directors were entitled to rely upon their chairman's opinion of value and adequacy, provided that such opinion was reached on a sound basis. Here, the issue is whether the directors informed themselves as to all information that was reasonably available to them. Had they done so, they would have learned of the source and derivation of the $55 price and could not reasonably have relied thereupon in good faith …

(2) This brings us to the post-September 20 'market test' upon which the defendants ultimately rely to confirm the reasonableness of their September 20 decision to accept the Pritzker proposal. In this connection, the directors present a two-part argument: (a) that by making a 'market test' of Pritzker's $55 per share offer a condition of their September 20 decision to accept his offer, they cannot be found to have acted impulsively or in an uninformed manner on September 20; and (b) that the adequacy of the $17 premium for sale of the Company was conclusively established over the following 90 to 120 days by the most reliable evidence available—the marketplace. Thus, the defendants impliedly contend that the 'market test' eliminated the need for the Board to perform any other form of fairness test either on September 20, or thereafter.

Again, the facts of record do not support the defendants' argument. There is no evidence: (a) that the Merger Agreement was effectively amended to give the Board freedom to put Trans Union up for auction sale to the highest bidder; or (b) that a public auction was in fact permitted to occur. The minutes of the Board meeting make no reference to any of this. Indeed, the record compels the conclusion that the directors had no rational basis for expecting that a market test was attainable, given the terms of the Agreement as executed during the evening of September 20. We rely upon the following facts which are essentially uncontradicted: …

Van Gorkom states that the [Merger] Agreement as submitted incorporated the ingredients for a market test by authorizing Trans Union to receive competing offers over the next 90-day period. However, he concedes that the Agreement barred Trans Union from actively soliciting such offers and from furnishing to interested parties any information about the Company other than that already in the public domain …

(3) The directors' unfounded reliance on both the premium and the market test as the basis for accepting the Pritzker proposal undermines the defendants' remaining contention that the Board's collective experience and sophistication was a sufficient basis for finding that it reached its September 20 decision with informed, reasonable deliberation …

(4) Part of the defense is based on a claim that the directors relied on legal advice rendered at the September 20 meeting by James Brennan, Esquire, who was present at Van Gorkom's request … Several defendants testified that Brennan advised them that Delaware law did not require a fairness opinion or an outside valuation of the Company before the Board could act on the Pritzker proposal. If given, the advice was correct. However, that did not end the matter. Unless the directors had before them adequate information regarding the intrinsic value of the Company, upon which a proper exercise of business judgment could be made, mere advice

of this type is meaningless; and, given this record of the defendants' failures, it constitutes no defense here.

We conclude that Trans Union's Board was grossly negligent in that it failed to act with informed reasonable deliberation in agreeing to the Pritzker merger proposal on September 20 …

[The Court then addressed the question whether the directors of Trans Union should be treated as one or individually in terms of invoking the protection of the business judgment rule and, in particular, whether the outside directors were entitled to rely in good faith on 'reports', including legal advice, rendered by inside directors and the Board's special counsel. The Court concluded:] (1) that since all of the defendant directors, outside as well as inside, take a unified position, we are required to treat all of the directors as one as to whether they are entitled to the protection of the business judgment rule; and (2) that considerations of good faith, including the presumption that the directors acted in good faith, are irrelevant in determining the threshold issue of whether the directors as a Board exercised an informed business judgment … The business judgment rule, which was properly applied by the Chancellor, allows directors wide discretion in the matter of valuation and affords room for honest differences of opinion. In order to prevail, plaintiffs had the heavy burden of proving that the merger price was so grossly inadequate as to display itself as a badge of fraud. That is a burden which plaintiffs have not met.

However, plaintiffs have not claimed, nor did the Trial Court decide, that $55 was a grossly inadequate price per share for sale of the Company. That being so, the presumption that a board's judgment as to adequacy of price represents an honest exercise of business judgment (absent proof that the sale price was grossly inadequate) is irrelevant to the threshold question of whether an informed judgment was reached …

[The Court reversed the judgment of the Chancery Court and remanded the case.]

McNeilly, Justice, dissenting:

The majority opinion reads like an advocate's closing address to a hostile jury. And I say that not lightly. Throughout the opinion great emphasis is directed only to the negative, with nothing more than lip service granted the positive aspects of this case. In my opinion Chancellor Marvel (retired) should have been affirmed. The Chancellor's opinion was the product of well reasoned conclusions, based upon a sound deductive process, clearly supported by the evidence and entitled to deference in this appeal. Because of my diametrical opposition to all evidentiary conclusions of the majority, I respectfully dissent …

The majority has spoken and has effectively said that Trans Union's Directors have been the victims of a 'fast shuffle' by Van Gorkom and Pritzker. That is the beginning of the majority's comedy of errors. The first and most important error made is the majority's assessment of the directors' knowledge of the affairs of Trans Union and their combined ability to act in this situation under the protection of the business judgment rule.

Trans Union's Board of Directors consisted of ten men, five of whom were 'inside' directors and five of whom were 'outside' directors … At the time the merger was proposed the inside five directors had collectively been employed by the Company for 116 years and had 68 years of combined experience as directors. The 'outside' directors [with one exception] were all chief executive officers of Chicago based corporations that were at least as large as Trans Union. The five 'outside' directors had 78 years of combined experience as chief executive officers, and 53 years cumulative service as Trans Union directors.

The inside directors wear their badge of expertise in the corporate affairs of Trans Union on their sleeves. But what about the outsiders? Dr. Wallis is or was an economist and math statistician, a professor of economics at Yale University, dean of the graduate school of business at the University of Chicago, and Chancellor of the University of Rochester. Dr. Wallis had been on the Board of Trans Union since 1962. He also was on the Board of Bausch & Lomb, Kodak, Metropolitan Life Insurance Company, Standard Oil and others.

William B. Johnson is a University of Pennsylvania law graduate, President of Railway Express until 1966, Chairman and Chief Executive of I.C. Industries Holding Company, and member of Trans Union's Board since 1968. [The dissent continues to list the credentials of the outside directors.]

Directors of this caliber are not ordinarily taken in by a 'fast shuffle'. I submit they were not taken into this multi-million dollar corporate transaction without being fully informed and aware of the state of the art as it pertained to the entire corporate panorama of Trans Union.

True, even directors such as these, with their business acumen, interest and expertise, can go astray. I do not believe that to be the case here. These men knew Trans Union like the back of their hands and were more than well qualified to make on the spot informed business judgments concerning the affairs of Trans Union including a 100% sale of the corporation. Lest we forget, the corporate world of then and now operates on what is so aptly referred to as 'the fast track'. These men were at the time an integral part of that world, all professional business men, not intellectual figureheads . . .

I have no quarrel with the majority's analysis of the business judgment rule. It is the application of that rule to these facts which is wrong. An overview of the entire record, rather than the limited view of bits and pieces which the majority has exploded like popcorn, convinces me that the directors made an informed business judgment which was buttressed by their test of the market.

At the time of the September 20 meeting the 10 members of Trans Union's Board of Directors were highly qualified and well informed about the affairs and prospects of Trans Union. These directors were acutely aware of the historical problems facing Trans Union which were caused by the tax laws. They had discussed these problems ad nauseam. In fact, within two months of the September 20 meeting the board had reviewed and discussed an outside study of the company done by The Boston Consulting Group and an internal five year forecast prepared by management . . . The above facts reveal that the Board did not act in a grossly negligent manner in informing themselves of the relevant and available facts before passing on the merger . . .

Questions:

1. It has been said that the 'response of the corporate bar to *Van Gorkom* was one of shocked incredulity'[183] and that '*Van Gorkom* exploded on the world of corporate directors'.[184] The judgment garnered fierce criticism, both by practitioners and academics. For example, Prof Fischel called it 'the worst decision in the history of corporate law'.[185] Do you agree? What are the contours of the business judgment rule after *Van Gorkom*?
2. The Delaware legislator responded to *Van Gorkom* (and the criticism), possibly motivated by the concern that Delaware would lose its leading position in the US market for incorporations,[186] by inserting §102(b)(7) into the Delaware General Corporation Law. §102(b)(7) allows companies to include a provision in the certificate of incorporation eliminating the personal liability of a director for monetary damages for breach of the duty of care, provided the director did not act in bad faith and the act did not involve intentional misconduct or a knowing violation of law.[187] Most publicly traded Delaware corporations have made use of the provision.[188] Liability on the basis of facts as in *Van Gorkom* has therefore become unlikely, and the focus of inquiry in more recent cases is often on questions of bad faith.[189]
3. Did the court apply a gross negligence standard in *Van Gorkom*, or was the standard in reality an ordinary negligence standard, as was argued in the literature?[190] In other cases, the Delaware courts defined gross negligence as a 'reckless indifference to or a deliberate disregard of the whole body of stockholders', as actions 'without the bounds of reason',[191] or 'a

[183] HN Butler, '*Smith v. Van Gorkom*, Jurisdictional Competition, and the Role of Random Mutations in the Evolution of Corporate Law' (2006) 45 Washburn Law Journal 267, 273 (quoting RW Hamilton, *Cases and Materials on Corporations Including Partnerships and Limited Liability Companies* (6th edn, West 1998) 698).

[184] WT Allen, 'The Pride and the Hope of Delaware Corporate Law' (2000) 25 Delaware Journal of Corporate Law 70, 76.

[185] DR Fischel, 'The Business Judgement Rule and the Trans Union Case' (1985) 40 Business Law 1437, 1455.

[186] AR Pinto and DM Branson, *Corporate Law* (5th edn, LexisNexis 2018) §8.05[A].

[187] However, those aiding or abetting a violation of the duty of care by the board of directors may still be found liable, *RBC Capital Markets, LLC v Jervis*, 129 A.3d 816 (Del. 2015). Furthermore, §102(b)(7) does not apply to officers.

[188] Pinto and Branson (n 186).

[189] See our discussion of good faith above, section 2(a).

[190] Allen, Jacobs, and Strine (n 110) 458.

[191] *Tomczak v Morton Thiokol, Inc.*, 1990 WL 42607, at 12 (Del. Ch. 1990) (quoting *Allaun v Consolidated Oil Co.* (n 165) 261, and *Gimbel v Signal Companies, Inc.* (n 165) 615); *In re Walt Disney Co. Derivative Litigation* (n 113) 750.

wide disparity between the process the directors used ... and that which would have been rational'.[192] It has been observed that this is a definition of gross negligence different from, and establishing (from the perspective of the plaintiff) a more demanding standard than, that of regular tort law.[193] Is *Van Gorkom* in line with these definitions?

(c) Review without rebuttal of the business judgment rule

***Litwin v Allen*, 25 N.Y.S.2d 667 (Supreme Court of New York 1940)**

McGeehan, J:

This transaction involves the participation by the Trust Company or Guaranty Company or both, to the extent of $3,000,000, in a purchase of Missouri Pacific Convertible debentures on October 16, 1930, through the firm of J. P. Morgan & Co. at par, with an option to the seller, Alleghany Corporation to repurchase them at the same price at any time within six months.

In the fall of 1930, the question of putting Alleghany Corporation in funds to the extent of $10,500,000 was first broached. Alleghany had purchased certain terminal properties in Kansas City and St. Joseph, Missouri, and the balance of the purchase price, amounting to slightly in excess of $10,000,000 and interest, had to be paid by October 16. Alleghany needed money to make this payment. Because of the borrowing limitation in Alleghany's charter (which limitation had been reached or exceeded in October 1930) Alleghany was unable to borrow the money. To overcome this borrowing limitation and solely to enable Alleghany to consummate the purchase of the terminal properties, discussions were commenced concerning the means whereby the necessary money could be raised ...

Not being able to make a loan, the way that Alleghany could raise the necessary funds was by sale of some of the securities that it held. Among them was a large block of about $23,500,000 of Missouri Pacific convertible 5 1/2% debentures. These were unsecured and subordinate to other Missouri Pacific bond issues. They were convertible into common stock at the rate of ten shares for each $1,000 bond. In 1929, Guaranty Company had participated to the extent of $1,500,000 in the underwriting of these bonds at 97 1/2. At one time in 1929 the bonds had sold as high as 124 and had never gone below par except in November 1929 when they sold at 97. Between October 1 and October 10, 1930 Missouri Pacific Common stock had dropped from 53 to 44. There was a decline in the bonds from 113 in April 1930 to 107 on October 1, 1930, and thereafter a decline of about two more points to 105 1/2 by the date of the consummation of the transaction we are considering on October 16, 1930.

The Van Sweringens [owners of Alleghany] suggested that $10,000,000 of these bonds be sold to J. P. Morgan & Co. for cash at par [with the Trust Company participating in the purchase], the latter to give an option to Alleghany to buy them back within six months for the price paid. If the transaction were carried through on that basis, namely, a sale by Alleghany with an option to them to repurchase at the same price, the same purpose would be accomplished, for Alleghany at any rate, as if a loan had been made.

The defendants testified that they were informed that the Van Sweringens insisted upon the option to repurchase within six months in order that there might be no possibility of their loss of control of Missouri Pacific through Alleghany, since these bonds were convertible and the privilege to do so might be exercised by third parties in the event of a distribution of these bonds in the market; this, despite the fact that the common stock of Missouri Pacific was then quoted in the neighborhood of 44, while the conversion price was 100.

The fact is that the only purpose served by the option was to make the transaction conform as closely as possible to a loan without the usual incidents of a loan transaction ...

The decline in the market continued. On October 23, 1930, when the Executive Committee of the Trust Company approved the transaction the Missouri Pacific bonds were at 103 7/8. On November 5, 1930, when the Board of Directors of the Trust Company gave its approval, the bonds sold for 102 7/8, and on November 18, 1930, when the board of the Guaranty Company approved its commitment, the bonds had dropped to 98 5/8. At the end of the six months' period, on April 16, 1931, the bonds sold at 86 high and 81 low (the quotations being for the

[192] *Guttman v Huang* (n 177) 507 n. 39.

[193] Allen, Jacobs, and Strine (n 110) 453.

week ending April 18), and Guaranty Company took them over from the Trust Company at par and accrued interest and carried them on its books as an investment...

I shall now proceed to consider generally the rules to be applied in determining the liability of directors. It has sometimes been said that directors are trustees. If this means that directors in the performance of their duties stand in a fiduciary relationship to the company, that statement is essentially correct...

[D]irectors are liable for negligence in the performance of their duties. Not being insurers, directors are not liable for errors of judgment or for mistakes while acting with reasonable skill and prudence. It has been said that a director is required to conduct the business of the corporation with the same degree of fidelity and care as an ordinarily prudent man would exercise in the management of his own affairs of like magnitude and importance. General rules, however, are not altogether helpful. In the last analysis, whether or not a director has discharged his duty, whether or not he has been negligent, depends upon the facts and circumstances of a particular case, the kind of corporation involved, its size and financial resources, the magnitude of the transaction, and the immediacy of the problem presented. A director is called upon 'to bestow the care and skill' which the situation demands...

Undoubtedly, a director of a bank is held to stricter accountability than the director of an ordinary business corporation. A director of a bank is entrusted with the funds of depositors, and the stockholders look to him for protection from the imposition of personal liability... But clairvoyance is not required even of a bank director. The law recognizes that the most conservative director is not infallible, and that he will make mistakes, but if he uses that degree of care ordinarily exercised by prudent bankers he will be absolved from liability although his opinion may turn out to have been mistaken and his judgment faulty...

[I]t would seem that if it is against public policy for a bank, anxious to dispose of some of its securities, to agree to buy them back at the same price, it is even more so where a bank purchases securities and gives the seller the option to buy them back at the same price, thereby incurring the entire risk of loss with no possibility of gain other than the interest derived from the securities during the period that the bank holds them. Here, if the market price of the securities should rise, the holder of the repurchase option would exercise it in order to recover his securities from the bank at the lower price at which he sold them to the bank. If the market price should fall, the seller holding the option will not exercise it and the bank will sustain the loss. Thus, any benefit of a sharp rise in the price of the securities is assured the seller and any risk of heavy loss is inevitably assumed by the bank. If such an option agreement as is here involved were sustained, it would force the bank to set aside for six months whatever securities it had purchased. A bank certainly could not free itself from this obligation by engaging in a 'short sale'. In other words, while a resale option would force a bank to freeze an amount of cash equal to the selling price of the securities sold by it, a repurchase option would force a bank to freeze the securities themselves for the period of the option. In both situations the true financial condition of the bank could not be determined wholly from its books. It would depend upon the fluctuations of the market. In both cases there is a contingent liability which the balance sheet does not show.

Directors are not in the position of trustees of an express trust who, regardless of good faith, are personally liable for losses arising from an infraction of their trust deed. *Matter of Smith*, 279 N.Y. 479, 489, 18 N.E.2d 666; see Fletcher Cyc. Corp., Perm.Ed., § 847. If liability is to be imposed on these directors it should rest on a more solid foundation. I find liability in this transaction because the entire arrangement was so improvident, so risky, so unusual and unnecessary as to be contrary to fundamental conceptions of prudent banking practice. A bank director when appointed or elected takes oath that he will, so far as the duty devolves on him 'diligently and honestly administer the affairs of the bank or trust company'. Banking Law, § 117. The oath merely adds solemnity to the obligation which the law itself imposes. Honesty alone does not suffice; the honesty of the directors in this case is unquestioned. But there must be more than honesty—there must be diligence, and that means care and prudence, as well. This transaction, it has been said, was unusual; it was unique, yet there is nothing in the record to indicate that the advice of counsel was sought. It is not surprising that a precedent cannot be found dealing with such a situation.

What sound reason is there for a bank, desiring to make an investment, short term or otherwise, to buy securities under an arrangement whereby any appreciation will inure to the benefit of the seller and any loss will be borne by the bank? The five and one-half point differential is no answer. It does not meet the fundamental objection that whatever loss there is would have to be borne by the Bank and whatever gain would go to the customer. There is more here than a question of business judgment as to which men might well differ. The directors plainly failed in this instance to bestow the care which the situation demanded. Unless we are to do away entirely with the doctrine that directors of a bank are liable for negligence in administering its affairs liability should be imposed in connection with this transaction ...

The real issue as to damages is whether the directors should be liable for the total loss suffered when the bonds were ultimately sold, approximately an 81% loss, or only for that portion of the loss which accrued within the six months option period, making allowance for a period thereafter during which defendants could make reasonable and diligent efforts to sell the bonds. The record discloses that none of the bonds were sold until October 8, 1931, about six months after the Alleghany option had expired, and that they were not completely disposed of until December 28, 1937. The Missouri Pacific Railroad went into receivership in April, 1933, and between August 2 and September 25, 1933, $126,000 more of the bonds were purchased by the Company in an attempt to reduce the loss. A total loss was sustained on the bonds of approximately $2,250,000.

I believe that as to the decline of the bonds after April 16, 1931, there is no causal connection with the option which had expired on that date. A director is not liable for loss or damage other than what was proximately caused by his own acts or omissions in breach of his duty ... The portion of the present transaction which is tainted with improvidence and negligence is the repurchase option ... Once the option had expired, there was nothing to prevent the directors of the Company, which had taken over the bonds in accordance with its agreement, from selling them. Any loss on the bonds which was incurred after the option had expired on April 16, 1931, was occasioned as a result of the directors' independent business judgment in holding them thereafter ...

Questions and comments:

1. The Supreme Court of New York in *Litwin v Allen* took issue with the actions of the defendant directors because the challenged transaction 'was so improvident, so risky, so unusual and unnecessary as to be contrary to fundamental conceptions of prudent banking practice'. Does this constitute a review of the *content* of the directors' decision or the *process* of decision-making? In other words, is *Litwin v Allen* about reviewing the substance of directors' business decisions or a rebuttal of the business judgment rule?
2. *Litwin v Allen* is commonly seen as an example of the courts' willingness to intervene in business decisions in exceptional cases even if the directors acted on an informed basis and in good faith. The Delaware Court of Chancery in *Walt Disney* put it this way: 'In the absence of [fraud, bad faith, or self-dealing], the board's decision will be upheld unless it cannot be "attributed to any rational business purpose"'.[194] A variant of this standard of review based on rationality is the so-called waste claim, which was, for example, put forward by the plaintiffs in the Disney litigation. In the following excerpt, the Supreme Court of Delaware discusses the plaintiffs' claim that the severance payment of approximately US$130 million to the outgoing CEO Michael Ovitz, consisting of his remaining salary, unaccrued bonuses, and options, constituted a waste of assets. Recall that the employment of Ovitz was terminated after only one year because he failed to 'adapt' to the corporate culture at Disney. The board considered whether terminating Ovitz's employment for cause was possible, which would not have triggered the various financial obligations of Disney under the employment agreement, but decided that cause, defined as gross negligence or malfeasance, could not be established. The court held:

[194] *Walt Disney* (n 113) 747 (quoting *Sinclair Oil Corp. v Levien* (n 154) 720; *Unocal Corp. v Mesa Petroleum Co.*, 493 A.2d 946, 954 (Del. 1985)).

The appellants' final claim is that even if the approval of the OEA [Ovitz Employment Agreement] was protected by the business judgment rule presumptions, the payment of the severance amount to Ovitz constituted waste. This claim is rooted in the doctrine that a plaintiff who fails to rebut the business judgment rule presumptions is not entitled to any remedy unless the transaction constitutes waste...

To recover on a claim of corporate waste, the plaintiffs must shoulder the burden of proving that the exchange was 'so one sided that no business person of ordinary, sound judgment could conclude that the corporation has received adequate consideration'. A claim of waste will arise only in the rare, 'unconscionable case where directors irrationally squander or give away corporate assets'. This onerous standard for waste is a corollary of the proposition that where business judgment presumptions are applicable, the board's decision will be upheld unless it cannot be 'attributed to any rational business purpose'.

The claim that the payment of the NFT [Non-Fault Termination] amount to Ovitz, without more, constituted waste is meritless on its face, because at the time the NFT amounts were paid, Disney was contractually obligated to pay them. The payment of a contractually obligated amount cannot constitute waste, unless the contractual obligation is itself wasteful. Accordingly, the proper focus of a waste analysis must be whether the amounts required to be paid in the event of an NFT were wasteful ex ante...

The approval of the NFT provisions in the OEA had a rational business purpose: to induce Ovitz to leave CAA [Creative Artists Agency], at what would otherwise be a considerable cost to him, in order to join Disney.[195] ... Because the appellants have failed to show that the approval of the NFT terms of the OEA was not a rational business decision, their waste claim must fail.[196]

3. Successful waste claims are extremely rare in Delaware. In fact, then-Chancellor Allen of the Delaware Court of Chancery quipped: 'There surely are cases of fraud; of unfair self-dealing and, much more rarely negligence. But rarest of all-and indeed, like Nessie, possibly non-existent-would be the case of disinterested business people making non-fraudulent deals (non-negligently) that meet the legal standard of waste!'[197] An example of a case where the plaintiff's waste claim survived a motion to dismiss is *Telxon Corp. v Bogomolny*.[198] In this case, the founder, former CEO, and then chairman of the board of Telxon received stock options giving him the right to acquire 10 per cent of the equity of one of Telxon's subsidiaries. The award was made under an incentive programme designed to reward employees who had worked on successful corporate acquisitions. When Telxon came under new ownership, it filed a lawsuit against the directors who had approved the agreement. The complaint alleged that the option agreement 'was devoid of business purpose and constituted an extraordinarily unusual transaction for a public company', because the company gave financial assistance to the defendant for the purchase of the subsidiary's shares, which, it was alleged, had the consequence that the company assumed the risk of the investment being profitable,[199] and the defendant received pre-emptive rights allowing him to buy additional shares in order to protect his 10 per cent equity interest against dilution. The court held that it could not be ruled out that the option may constitute waste. The record is relatively scarce on the details of the allegations, but the court seems to have been moved in part by the fact that the company failed to keep minutes of the relevant board and committee meetings and that the transaction was highly unusual.[200]

The Delaware Court of Chancery also held that payments to directors for services already rendered, for example in the form of severance pay or appreciation awards not provided for in

[195] [Footnote in the original.] See *Kerbs v California Eastern Airways*, 90 A.2d 652, 656 (Del.1952) ('Sufficient consideration to the corporation may be, *inter alia*, the retention of the services of an employee, or the gaining of the services of a new employee, provided there is a reasonable relationship between the value of the services to be rendered by the employee and the value of the options granted as an inducement or compensation').

[196] *Walt Disney* (n 125) 73–5.

[197] *Steiner v Meyerson*, 1995 WL 441999 (Del. Ch. 1995) 5.

[198] 792 A.2d 964 (Del. Ch. 2001).

[199] The defendant paid the purchase price of the shares by delivering a non-recourse note to Telxon: ibid 969.

[200] Note the cautionary language of the court: 'I mean to suggest only that the terms and circumstances of the Aironet Option appear at this point sufficiently unusual to require the court to allow the claim to survive beyond the pleading stage': ibid 976.

the employment agreement, were a waste of corporate assets.[201] However, such payments are not illegal *per se*; rather, the court applies a regular waste analysis and asks whether there was a rational basis for the payments because the company received at least *some* consideration, for example in the form of a general release of claims,[202] or the amount awarded was 'not unreasonable in view of the [past] services rendered'.[203]

4. Given the definition of waste developed by the Delaware Court of Chancery in *Walt Disney* and other case law, is this claim conceptualized in a way that it can ever become relevant in practice, except in highly unusual cases? The function of the waste claim is the determination of the outer limits of the business judgment rule. If a director's behaviour lies outside of these limits, the protections of the business judgment rule do not apply and the courts will conduct a full review of the challenged conduct. However, as discussed, the business judgment rule only applies if the director acted on an informed basis and in good faith. Is it conceptually possible to find a business decision that is the product of a well-informed and good faith decision-making process, but that cannot be 'attributed to any rational business purpose'?

(d) Review after rebuttal of the business judgment rule

We mentioned above[204] that the burden of proof shifts to the directors to demonstrate that the transaction was 'entirely fair' to the corporation when the presumptions of the business judgment rule are rebutted.[205] The last piece of the business judgment rule puzzle, therefore, is a description of the entire fairness test. This test is not only relevant in the context of the duty of care, but also in duty of loyalty cases, which should not be surprising, given the integration of good faith and loyalty into the business judgment rule as threshold requirements.[206] In fact, most decisions that discuss entire fairness deal with interested transactions that implicate the duty of loyalty. One of the leading cases on entire fairness, and in particular on the question of how the fairness of a merger price should be determined, is the judgment of the Delaware Supreme Court in *Weinberger v UOP*.[207] In this case, Signal Companies, an energy and technology company, had acquired a majority of the stock of UOP in an uncontested tender offer. Three years after the tender offer, Signal decided to conduct a cash-out merger in order to obtain the remaining outstanding stock of UOP. It offered a price per share that was substantially above the market value of UOP's shares at that time (US$21 when the shares were trading at US$14.50), but at the lower end of a price range at which a feasibility study described the transaction as beneficial to Signal (US$21–US$24). The study had been prepared by two UOP directors (Arledge and Chitiea) for the use of Signal and was not disclosed to the other directors or the minority shareholders of UOP. Other irregularities referred to by the plaintiffs were the hurried way in which the merger was implemented, allowing UOP's board only four business days to consider the proposal, and the cursory nature of the fairness opinion provided by Lehman Brothers. The court held

[201] *Fidanque v American Maracaibo Co.*, 92 A.2d 311 (Del. Ch. 1952). The court examined an agreement under which the former president of American Maracaibo, in spite of his old age and poor health, would be employed as a consultant for life at the same salary that he had received as president and general manager of the company. The court was convinced 'that he larger part of the compensation provided under this contract … was in payment for past services' and held that '[i]f the value of the compensation to be paid to [the former president] is so out of all proportion to the value of the services which he would be expected to render that no reasonable person would consider that the corporation would receive a quid pro quo, then the contract would constitute a gift of corporate funds and would be illegal': ibid 320–1.

[202] See, e.g., *Zucker v Andreessen*, 2012 WL 2366448 (Del. Ch. 2012).

[203] *Freedman v Adams*, 58 A.3d 414 (Del. 2013) (bonus payments of US$130 million not wasteful); *Zupnick v Goizueta*, 698 A.2d 384, 388 (Del. Ch. 1997) (quoting *Blish v Thompson Automatic Arms Corporation*, 64 A.2d 581 (Del. 1948), where retroactive executive compensation was upheld because 'the services rendered by [the executive] were unusual in character and extraordinary, from which [the corporation] received great gains and profits').

[204] Text to n 140.

[205] See, for example, *Walt Disney* (n 113) 747.

[206] For example, Del. Gen. Corp. Law, §144(a)(3), stipulates that a related party transaction is valid if it is 'fair as to the corporation'.

[207] 457 A.2d 701.

that Signal had failed to establish the entire fairness of the transaction. The following excerpt defines entire fairness and applies the definition to the facts of the case.

***Weinberger v. UOP, Inc.*, 457 A.2d 701 (Supreme Court of Delaware 1983)**

Moore, Justice:

The concept of fairness has two basic aspects: fair dealing and fair price. The former embraces questions of when the transaction was timed, how it was initiated, structured, negotiated, disclosed to the directors, and how the approvals of the directors and the stockholders were obtained. The latter aspect of fairness relates to the economic and financial considerations of the proposed merger, including all relevant factors: assets, market value, earnings, future prospects, and any other elements that affect the intrinsic or inherent value of a company's stock ... However, the test for fairness is not a bifurcated one as between fair dealing and price. All aspects of the issue must be examined as a whole since the question is one of entire fairness. However, in a non-fraudulent transaction we recognize that price may be the preponderant consideration outweighing other features of the merger ...

Part of fair dealing is the obvious duty of candor ... Moreover, one possessing superior knowledge may not mislead any stockholder by use of corporate information to which the latter is not privy ... Delaware has long imposed this duty even upon persons who are not corporate officers or directors, but who nonetheless are privy to matters of interest or significance to their company ... With the well-established Delaware law on the subject, and the Court of Chancery's findings of fact here, it is inevitable that the obvious conflicts posed by Arledge and Chitiea's preparation of their 'feasibility study', derived from UOP information, for the sole use and benefit of Signal, cannot pass muster.

The Arledge-Chitiea report is but one aspect of the element of fair dealing. How did this merger evolve? It is clear that it was entirely initiated by Signal. The serious time constraints under which the principals acted were all set by Signal. It had not found a suitable outlet for its excess cash and considered UOP a desirable investment, particularly since it was now in a position to acquire the whole company for itself. For whatever reasons, and they were only Signal's, the entire transaction was presented to and approved by UOP's board within four business days. Standing alone, this is not necessarily indicative of any lack of fairness by a majority shareholder. It was what occurred, or more properly, what did not occur, during this brief period that makes the time constraints imposed by Signal relevant to the issue of fairness.

The structure of the transaction, again, was Signal's doing. So far as negotiations were concerned, it is clear that they were modest at best. Crawford, Signal's man at UOP, never really talked price with Signal, except to accede to its management's statements on the subject, and to convey to Signal the UOP outside directors' view that as between the $20-$21 range under consideration, it would have to be $21. The latter is not a surprising outcome, but hardly arm's length negotiations. Only the protection of benefits for UOP's key employees and the issue of Lehman Brothers' fee approached any concept of bargaining ...

There was no disclosure of the circumstances surrounding the rather cursory preparation of the Lehman Brothers' fairness opinion. Instead, the impression was given UOP's minority that a careful study had been made, when in fact speed was the hallmark, and Mr. Glanville, Lehman's partner in charge of the matter, and also a UOP director, having spent the weekend in Vermont, brought a draft of the 'fairness opinion letter' to the UOP directors' meeting on March 6, 1978 with the price left blank. We can only conclude from the record that the rush imposed on Lehman Brothers by Signal's timetable contributed to the difficulties under which this investment banking firm attempted to perform its responsibilities. Yet, none of this was disclosed to UOP's minority.

Finally, the minority stockholders were denied the critical information that Signal considered a price of $24 to be a good investment. Since this would have meant over $17,000,000 more to the minority, we cannot conclude that the shareholder vote was an informed one ...

Given these particulars and the Delaware law on the subject, the record does not establish that this transaction satisfies any reasonable concept of fair dealing ...

Turning to the matter of price, plaintiff also challenges its fairness. His evidence was that on the date the merger was approved the stock was worth at least $26 per share. In support, he offered the testimony of a chartered investment analyst who used two basic approaches to valuation: a comparative analysis of the premium paid over market in ten other tender offer-merger combinations, and a discounted cash flow analysis.

In this breach of fiduciary duty case, the Chancellor perceived that the approach to valuation was the same as that in an appraisal proceeding. Consistent with precedent, he rejected plaintiff's method of proof and accepted defendants' evidence of value as being in accord with practice under prior case law. This means that the so-called 'Delaware block' or weighted average method was employed wherein the elements of value, i.e., assets, market price, earnings, etc., were assigned a particular weight and the resulting amounts added to determine the value per share. This procedure has been in use for decades … However, to the extent it excludes other generally accepted techniques used in the financial community and the courts, it is now clearly outmoded. It is time we recognize this in appraisal and other stock valuation proceedings and bring our law current on the subject.

While the Chancellor rejected plaintiff's discounted cash flow method of valuing UOP's stock, as not corresponding with 'either logic or the existing law' (426 A.2d at 1360), it is significant that this was essentially the focus, i.e., earnings potential of UOP, of Messrs. Arledge and Chitiea in their evaluation of the merger. Accordingly, the standard 'Delaware block' or weighted average method of valuation, formerly employed in appraisal and other stock valuation cases, shall no longer exclusively control such proceedings. We believe that a more liberal approach must include proof of value by any techniques or methods which are generally considered acceptable in the financial community and otherwise admissible in court … This will obviate the very structured and mechanistic procedure that has heretofore governed such matters …

Fair price obviously requires consideration of all relevant factors involving the value of a company. This has long been the law of Delaware as stated in *Tri-Continental Corp.*, 74 A.2d at 72:

> The basic concept of value under the appraisal statute is that the stockholder is entitled to be paid for that which has been taken from him, viz., his proportionate interest in a going concern. By value of the stockholder's proportionate interest in the corporate enterprise is meant the true or intrinsic value of his stock which has been taken by the merger. In determining what figure represents this true or intrinsic value, the appraiser and the courts must take into consideration all factors and elements which reasonably might enter into the fixing of value. Thus, market value, asset value, dividends, earning prospects, the nature of the enterprise and any other facts which were known or which could be ascertained as of the date of merger and which throw any light on *future prospects* of the merged corporation are not only pertinent to an inquiry as to the value of the dissenting stockholders' interest, but *must be considered* by the agency fixing the value. (Emphasis added)

This is not only in accord with the realities of present day affairs, but it is thoroughly consonant with the purpose and intent of our statutory law. Under 8 Del.C. § 262(h), the Court of Chancery:

> shall appraise the shares, determining their *fair* value exclusive of any element of value arising from the accomplishment or expectation of the merger, together with a fair rate of interest, if any, to be paid upon the amount determined to be the *fair* value. In determining such *fair* value, the Court shall take into account *all relevant factors* … (Emphasis added) …

It is significant that section 262 now mandates the determination of 'fair' value based upon 'all relevant factors'. Only the speculative elements of value that may arise from the 'accomplishment or expectation' of the merger are excluded. We take this to be a very narrow exception to the appraisal process, designed to eliminate use of *pro forma* data and projections of a speculative variety relating to the completion of a merger. But elements of future value, including the nature of the enterprise, which are known or susceptible of proof as of the date of the merger and not the product of speculation, may be considered. When the trial court deems it appropriate, fair value also includes any damages, resulting from the taking, which the stockholders sustain as a class. If that was not the case, then the obligation to consider 'all relevant factors' in the valuation process would be eroded …

Questions and comments:

1. In *Weinberger*, the plaintiff brought a class action seeking rescissory damages, rather than appraisal. The claim was based on the argument that the defendants had breached their fiduciary duties by entering into merger terms that were unfair to the minority shareholders. Case law prior to *Weinberger* had allowed such claims and awarded equitable remedies under appropriate circumstances.[208] In *Weinberger*, the Delaware Supreme Court departed from the old case law and held that a plaintiff's monetary remedy in a freeze-out or cash-out merger (that is, a merger where the minority shareholders receive cash instead of shares in the combined business enterprise) 'ordinarily' was confined to an appraisal proceeding.[209] However, in order to preserve the rights of the current plaintiffs, who had forgone an appraisal in reliance on the old case law, the court exempted pending lawsuits from the new approach and allowed the plaintiffs to test the fairness of the merger price by the appraisal standards established in *Weinberger*. In Chapter 7, we will discuss in more detail when the appraisal remedy is available and whether it is always the exclusive remedy in a cash-out merger.[210]
2. In the excerpt above, the Delaware Supreme Court refers to the so-called 'Delaware block' approach to valuing the shares of minority shareholders. According to this approach, also called the 'weighted average method of valuation', fair value was determined by weighting, and adding up, mainly three factors that were considered relevant to the 'fair' or 'proper' price of a share: the value of the corporate assets, the market value of the stock and its earnings value.[211] For example, as far as a stock's earnings value was concerned, a court might take the earnings of a company over a period of five years prior to the merger, average them and then choose a multiplier to capitalize the earnings.[212] The resultant figure was seen as the best approximation of the present value of a company's future earnings.[213] The court would then assign a particular weighting to the earnings, as well as the other relevant factors, depending on their contribution to fair value in the individual case. For example, in an e-commerce company with few assets, earnings would receive a higher weight than assets, and in a company without a liquid market for its stock, market value would be regarded as less important than the other factors.[214]

   The limitations of the 'Delaware block' approach are readily apparent. First, choosing a capitalization rate and assigning weights to the different components of the model is a subjective exercise that creates a considerable degree of legal uncertainty.[215] In addition, the Delaware block method was based largely on backward looking indicators of firm value measured over a relatively short period of time. The firm's earnings value typically corresponded to average earnings over the past five years, and the value of corporate assets was derived from book value and hence the historical cost of an asset, rather than its market value. While a historical dimension also plays an important role in other valuation methods, for example discounted

[208] For example, *Lynch v Vickers Energy Corp.*, 429 A.2d 497 (Del. 1981) (*Lynch II*).

[209] *Weinberger v UOP, Inc.* (n 207) 714.

[210] Chapter 7C.II. The short answer is that appraisal is not exclusive in certain cases, as pointed out by the Delaware Supreme Court in *Weinberger*: Appraisal 'may not be adequate ... where fraud, misrepresentation, self-dealing, deliberate waste of corporate assets, or gross and palpable overreaching are involved' (n 207) 714.

[211] *Lynch II* (n 208) 499.

[212] Capitalization of earnings refers to the discounting of future cash flows to calculate the present value of the cash flows. For example, if a company is expected to generate annual earnings of $500,000 in perpetuity and investments with a comparable risk profile earn a return of 10%, the value of the company, based on capitalized earnings, would be $5 million (the present value *PV* of a perpetuity is calculated according to the following formula: $PV = \frac{\textit{annual cash flow}}{\textit{capitalization rate}}$, hence: $PV = \frac{500{,}000}{0.1} = 5{,}000{,}000$. The multiplier used by courts is simply the inverse of the capitalization rate.

[213] *Universal City Studios, Inc. v Francis I. duPont & Co.*, 334 A.2d 216, 218 (Del. 1975).

[214] *Piemonte v New Boston Garden Corp.*, 387 N.E.2d 1145 (Mass. 1979).

[215] The Delaware Supreme Court admitted as much when it pointed out that 'the application of a multiplier to average earnings in order to capitalize them lies within the realm of judgment ... [and] [t]here is no hard and fast rule to govern the selection', *Application of Delaware Racing Ass'n*, 213 A.2d 203, 213 (Del. 1965).

cash flow (DCF) analysis, the focus of DCF analysis is on an estimation of future cash flows, which arguably reflects investor views more accurately.[216]

Delaware law now allows valuation by any technique 'generally considered acceptable in the financial community'.[217] This may be DCF, with the discount rate being determined by the Capital Asset Pricing Model,[218] an analysis of comparative takeover premiums, stock price, deal or merger price, or a combination of several factors similar to the Delaware block method.[219] The only requirement is that elements of future value must be 'susceptible of proof … and not the product of speculation'.[220] Thus, an expected increase in value from the accomplishment of a merger will generally be labelled as speculative by the courts.[221] On the other hand, if an acquirer in a two-step cash-out transaction has already formed concrete plans to restructure the company and taken steps to implement these plans during the period between the initial acquisition of a majority stake and the second-step merger, the value added because of the planned restructuring is susceptible of proof.[222]

3. The deal or merger price will be a predominant or even the sole factor determining fair value if it results from an arm's length transaction involving 'a robust market check'.[223] While Delaware law does not provide for a legal presumption in favour of the deal price, the Supreme Court of Delaware held in *DFC Global Corporation v Muirfield Value Partners, L.P.* that the sale value resulting from a robust sale process, defined as 'an open process, informed by robust public information, and easy access to deeper, non-public information, in which many parties with an incentive to make a profit had a chance to bid', is the most reliable evidence of fair value.[224] In *DFC Global*, the Supreme Court reversed a decision of the Court of Chancery that had accorded only one-third weight to the deal price, and one-third each to a discounted cash flow valuation and a comparable companies valuation, in spite of finding 'that: i) the transaction resulted from a robust market search that lasted approximately two years in which financial and strategic buyers had an open opportunity to buy without inhibition of deal protections; ii) the company was purchased by a third party in an arm's length sale; and iii) there was no hint of self-interest that compromised the market check'.[225] Deal price will not necessarily be used as the *sole* evidence of fair value in such a case, but the Supreme Court emphasized that 'second-guessing the value arrived upon by the collective views of many sophisticated parties with a real stake in the matter is hazardous'.[226]

In a second important decision by the Delaware Court of Chancery on appraisal valuation, *Dell, Inc. v Magnetar Global Event Driven Master Fund Ltd*,[227] the Supreme Court reversed a decision of the Court of Chancery because the trial court had given no weight to either Dell's stock price or the price at which Dell's management had bought out the company, instead relying exclusively on its own DCF analysis. The Supreme Court held that the deal price had 'heavy, if not overriding, probative value'.[228] A management buyout may display structural features that call into question the suitability of the deal price as evidence of fair value,[229] but

[216] DCF analysis relies on historical data in determining the applicable discount factor, which, using for example the Capital Asset Pricing Model, is a function of the risk-free rate and the market risk premium, measured on the basis of past returns.

[217] *Weinberger* (n 207) 713.

[218] For an example, see *Global GT LP v Golden Telecom, Inc.*, 993 A.2d 497 (Del. Ch. 2010).

[219] Pinto and Branson (n 186) §6.06[A][1].

[220] *Weinberger* (n 207) 713.

[221] See also Del. Gen. Corp. Law, §262(h), which stipulates that the fair value of shares for purposes of appraisal rights of minority shareholders objecting to a merger should be determined 'exclusive of any element of value arising from the accomplishment or expectation of the merger'.

[222] *Cede & Co. v Technicolor, Inc.*, 684 A.2d 289, 296–9 (Del. 1996). This holding is in line with §262(h) of the Del. Gen. Corp. Law, quoted in the previous footnote, because the Delaware courts interpret the 'accomplishment or expectation of the merger' exception narrowly. In *Weinberger*, the Supreme Court explained that the exception was 'designed to eliminate use of *pro forma* data and projections of a speculative variety relating to the completion of a merger' (*Weinberger v UOP, Inc.* (n 207) 713), and in *Cede & Co.*, the Court added that the exclusion did 'not encompass known elements of value, including those which exist on the date of the merger because of a majority acquiror's interim action in a two-step cash-out transaction', 684 A.2d at 299. These elements of value added by the acquirer 'during the transient period of a two-step merger [accrue] to the benefit of all shareholders and must be included in the appraisal process on the date of the merger': ibid.

[223] *DFC Global Corporation v Muirfield Value Partners, L.P.*, 172 A.3d 346, 366 (Del. 2017).

[224] ibid 349.

[225] ibid.

[226] ibid 366.

[227] 177 A.3d 1 (Del. 2017).

[228] ibid 30.

[229] These features are discussed ibid 31–4.

in the present case these features were not present. Dell's sale process was characterized by 'many mechanisms designed to minimize conflict and ensure stockholders obtain the highest possible value'.[230] In particular, the Supreme Court observed that extensive information about Dell was widely available, the information had been priced into Dell's stock price since the company had a vast and diffuse base of public shareholders that traded actively in Dell's stock, and a special committee composed of independent directors oversaw a robust go-shop process (a period after receiving a firm offer during which a target company can, and did in the case of Dell, solicit competing offers) that raised 'fewer structural barriers than the norm'.[231] Competing bidders, therefore, had 'a realistic pathway to succeeding'[232] in an acquisition of Dell and 'faced minimal structural barriers to a deal'.[233] As a consequence, the Court of Chancery had erred in disregarding the deal price:

> In so holding, we are not saying that the market is always the best indicator of value, or that it should always be granted some weight. We only note that, when the evidence of market efficiency, fair play, low barriers to entry, outreach to all logical buyers, and the chance for any topping bidder to have the support of [the CEO's] own votes is so compelling, then failure to give the resulting price heavy weight . . . abuses even the wide discretion afforded the Court of Chancery in these difficult cases.[234]

4. An example of the first aspect of fairness mentioned in *Weinberger*, fair dealing (or lack thereof), is given by *Rabkin v Philip A. Hunt Chem. Corp.*,[235] decided shortly after *Weinberger*. In *Rabkin*, Olin Corp. had acquired a majority interest in Hunt Corp. for US$25 per share. At the selling shareholder's insistence, the stock purchase agreement included an undertaking to pay the minority shareholders in Hunt Corp. a price 'substantially equivalent in value to at least the net purchase price per share paid pursuant to this agreement' should Olin decide to acquire the remaining Hunt stock within one year of the initial transaction. It was clear from the evidence that Olin had always anticipated to acquire 100 per cent of Hunt, but at the time of the initial acquisition the company issued a press release stating that 'while it was "considering the acquisition of the remaining public shares of Hunt, it [had] no present intention to do so"'.[236] In order to avoid having to pay US$25 per share for the minority interest, Olin's management took the decision to merge Hunt into Olin and cash out the remaining shareholders a few weeks after the end of the one year period. The Supreme Court of Delaware held that the plaintiff's assertion that Olin had purposely timed the merger so as to 'deprive the Hunt minority of the same bargain that Olin made with Hunt's former majority shareholder' supported a claim of unfair dealing, and the Court of Chancery's decision to dismiss the actions for failure to state a claim was accordingly reversed.[237]

3. *Germany*

Stock Corporation Act

§ 93—Duty of care and responsibility of the members of the management board

(1) The members of the management board shall exercise the care of a diligent and conscientious manager in managing the company. A management decision shall be deemed not to be a violation of this duty if the member of the management board reasonably believed that he acted in the best interest of the company and the decision was based on appropriate information. Members of the management board shall not disclose confidential matters and secrets of the company, in particular trade and business secrets of which they have become aware by reason of their position on the management board . . .

[230] ibid 38. [231] ibid 31. [232] ibid. [233] ibid 35. [234] ibid.
[235] 498 A.2d 1099 (Del. 1985). [236] ibid 1101.
[237] ibid 1106–7. On remand, the plaintiffs failed to prove that Olin had made the decision to acquire the Hunt minority before the expiry of the one-year commitment and deliberately timed the merger to avoid the price commitment. Hence, the Court of Chancery ruled that Olin had not unfairly dealt with the Hunt minority; see *Rabkin v Olin Corp.*, 1990 WL 47648.

(2) Members of the management board who violate their duties shall be jointly and severally liable to the company for the resulting damage. They shall bear the burden of proving that they exercised the care of a diligent and conscientious manager. If the company takes out insurance to protect members of the management board against risks relating to their occupational activity for the company, the insurance policy shall provide for an excess of at least 10 per cent of the damage and at least one and a half times the director's fixed annual remuneration.

(3) The members of the management board shall in particular be liable where, in violation of this Act:
1. Contributions are repaid to the shareholders;
2. Interest or shares in the profits are paid to the shareholders;
3. The company's own shares or shares of another company are subscribed to, acquired, pledged, or redeemed;
4. Shares are issued before the issue price has been paid up in full;
5. Assets of the company are distributed;
6. Payments are made in violation of § 92(2);
7. Remuneration is paid to members of the supervisory board;
8. Credit is granted;
9. New shares are issued in a contingent capital increase contrary to the stated purpose of the capital increase or before the full contribution has been made.

(4) In relation to the company, the obligation to pay damages does not arise if the challenged action was based on a lawful resolution of the general meeting. The obligation to pay damages shall not be excluded by an approval of the action by the supervisory board. The company shall not waive or settle a claim earlier than three years after the claim has arisen, and then only if the general meeting approves the waiver or settlement and no objection is registered in writing by a minority representing at least 10 per cent of the legal capital. The period of limitation shall not apply if the person liable to pay damages is insolvent and enters into a settlement with the creditors to avoid insolvency proceedings or the obligation to pay damages is part of an insolvency plan.

(5) The company's claim may also be asserted by the creditors of the company to the extent that they are unable to obtain satisfaction from the company. However, in other cases than those pursuant to Subsection 3 this shall only be possible if the members of the management board have grossly breached the duty to exercise the care of a diligent and conscientious manager; Subsection 2, sentence 2 shall apply analogously. In relation to creditors, the obligation to pay damages shall neither be excluded by a waiver or settlement by the company, nor by virtue of the fact that the action was based on a resolution of the general meeting. If insolvency proceedings have been opened, the liquidator or trustee shall exercise the creditors' rights as against the members of the management board during the proceedings.

(6) No action shall be maintained to enforce any claim arising under these provisions unless brought within ten years in the case of companies that were stock-exchange listed at the time of the breach of duty, and five years in the case of other companies.

§ 116—Duty of care and responsibility of the members of the supervisory board

§ 93 concerning the duty of care and responsibility of the members of the management board shall apply analogously to the duty of care and responsibility of the members of the supervisory board, with the exception of Subsection 2, sentence 3. In particular, the members of the supervisory board are required not to disclose confidential reports they receive or confidential deliberations. They are notably liable to pay compensation if they set remuneration at an inappropriate level (§87(1)).

Civil Code

§ 826—Intentional damage contrary to public policy

A person who, in a manner contrary to public policy, intentionally inflicts damage on another person is liable to the other person to pay compensation for the damage.

The central provision of German corporate law laying down the duties of directors in public companies is §93 Stock Corporation Act.[238] The provision applies to the members of the management board and, pursuant to §116 Stock Corporation Act, also to members of the supervisory board. Reading §93 and the other sections of the chapter of the Stock Corporation Act dealing with the management board,[239] two observations are noteworthy. First, the act does not provide for an exhaustive enumeration of directors' duties, as in the UK and many other civil law countries.[240] Secondly, §93 ostensibly only regulates the duty of care. The duty of loyalty is not mentioned and provisions that can be interpreted as representing individual aspects of loyalty are scattered throughout the act.[241] This is somewhat at odds with the traditional regulatory philosophy of German law, which aspires to regulate the relevant issues expressly and comprehensively. In order to avoid regulatory gaps, §93 is commonly interpreted as performing two functions. It contains a definition of the required standard of care in subsection 1 and a broad liability rule in subsection 2. The latter applies not only to violations of the duty of care, but establishes a general cause of action entitling the company to claim damages whenever a director breaches any of the duties laid down in the Stock Corporation Act or derived from case law.[242] In addition, directors may be liable based on principles of tort law, for example §826 of the Civil Code. While liability pursuant to §93 exists only in relation to the company, tort claims may also be brought by the shareholders individually or by third parties, for example creditors.[243]

We will focus here on the duty of care and the directors' liability under §93(2) Stock Corporation Act. Pursuant to §93(2), the company can claim damages if (1) a director (2) breaches a duty owed to the company (3) with the required level of fault and (4) the company suffers a loss as a consequence of the breach. Elements (2) and (3) of the cause of action are the most problematic. We will discuss them in turn.[244]

Subsection 1 of §93 elaborates on the second element of an action for breach of the duty of care, behaviour giving rise to a breach. Directors are required to 'exercise the care of a diligent and conscientious manager'. The statute, therefore, establishes an objective definition of the standard of care. Consequently, defendants cannot plead that they lacked the necessary experience or competence.[245] On the other hand, what can be expected of a diligent and conscientious manager depends on the individual circumstances of the case, in particular the type of company and industry, the financial situation of the company, general market conditions, and the director's role within the company's governance structure.[246] More is expected of directors with respect to matters that fall within their respective fields of responsibility. For example, a management board member responsible for controlling and accounts cannot simply rely on information received from subordinates, but is required to take a proactive approach, obtain the relevant documents, and review all data carefully.[247]

[238] The duties of the managers of private limited companies can be found in §43 Gesetz betreffend die Gesellschaften mit beschränkter Haftung (GmbHG) [Limited Liability Companies Act].

[239] AktG, §§76–94.

[240] See, for example, the Italian Civil Code, Arts 2390–2393; Spanish Corporate Enterprises Act, ss 225–232.

[241] For example, see AktG, §88 (duty not to compete with the company); §89 (prohibition to grant loans to members of the management board without approval by the supervisory board); §93(1) sentence 3 (duty of confidentiality); §112 (the supervisory board represents the company as against the members of the management board, i.e. directors are not empowered to enter into self-dealing transactions).

[242] T Raiser and R Veil, *Recht der Kapitalgesellschaften* (6th edn, Vahlen 2015) §14/65.

[243] See the discussion above, text to nn 51–62.

[244] We have dealt with the first element, the addressees of the duties, in Chapter 4D.II. For the fourth element, see Koch (n 57) §93 paras 47–50.

[245] BGH WM 1981, 440; NJW 1983, 1856.

[246] Raiser and Veil (n 242) §14/89.

[247] Administrative Court Frankfurt am Main, judgment of 8 July 2004, 1 E 7363/03 (I), para 23. The court argued that these heightened expectations also applied in relation to departments that were not directly managed by the defendant director, but were closely connected to the defendant's scope of duties, ibid. This part of the holding was criticized heavily in the literature, see, e.g., M Habersack, 'Gesteigerte Überwachungspflichten des Leiters eines "sachnahen" Vorstandsressorts?' WM 2005, 2360; U Hüffer, 'Der Vorstand als Leitungsorgan und

Similarly, heightened standards apply when directors enter into transactions that are particularly risky or significant in terms of volume,[248] or companies operate in difficult market conditions, such as insurance undertakings that make investment decisions during times of financial turmoil.[249]

We can distinguish between different types of behaviour potentially amounting to a breach of duty.[250] First, directors must act in compliance with the law and the company's articles of association. The law attaches particular importance to the statutory rules on capital requirements and capital maintenance. If directors violate any of these rules, referred to in §93(3), for example by arranging for the acquisition of the company's own shares[251] or returning value to the shareholders without complying with the requirements for distributions,[252] the Stock Corporation Act establishes a presumption that the company has suffered a loss equal to the amount that was paid out[253] or not paid in.[254] Thus, a plaintiff does not have to prove loss causation, but either party may rebut the presumption by showing that the actual damage was different.[255] Other provisions that impose behavioural expectations and duties on the members of the management board stem from criminal and accounting law.[256] In addition, the management board has to ensure that the company complies with all applicable legal rules, such as environmental laws, labour law, tax, social security, health and safety obligations, and competition law. A director, therefore, is liable for the damage sustained by the company as a result of not acting in accordance with any of these rules, for example, because the company has to pay an administrative penalty or suffers reputational damage.[257]

The articles of association may restrict the powers of the management board, for example, by requiring the management board to obtain the consent of the supervisory board for specified types of transaction.[258] In this case, the members of the management board breach their duties if they enter into transactions on behalf of the company without obtaining the required authorization. Similarly, where the management board violates the written or unwritten[259] allocation of competences between the board and the general meeting and carries out a transaction without the required shareholder approval, it violates its internal duties to the company.[260] Finally, the directors must observe the limits of the company's field of operations as described in the objects clause of the articles.[261] If they wish to pursue business projects falling outside of the company's objects, they must first arrange for the articles to be amended.[262]

die Mandats- sowie Haftungsbeziehungen seiner Mitglieder' in W Bayer and M Habersack (eds), *Aktienrecht im Wandel, vol 2: Grundsatzfragen des Aktienrechts* (Mohr Siebeck 2007) 7/91.

248 Administrative Court Frankfurt am Main (n 247) para 23. 249 ibid para 27.

250 The following paragraphs are not concerned with the duty of loyalty, which we will examine separately in section C below.

251 The acquisition of the company's own shares is only permissible in the situations listed in §71 AktG.

252 See, e.g., OLG Köln, AG 1988, 349 (*Aachener Rück/BfG*), dealing with the payment of 1.5 million DM by the management board to a shareholder in order to induce the shareholder to waive his right to challenge a resolution of the general meeting increasing the share capital to finance an important acquisition. The shareholders' right to challenge resolutions of the general meeting is laid down in §§243–246 AktG and discussed in Chapter 5C.III.1.

253 AktG, §93(3) nos 1–3, 5–9. 254 ibid §93(3) no 4.

255 OLG Stuttgart, WM 2010, 120, 121.

256 Relevant accounting rules are laid down in the Handelsgesetzbuch (HGB) [Commercial Code], §§238–335b. In addition, IFRS may apply pursuant to the IAS Regulation (Regulation (EC) No 1606/2002).

257 For references see Raiser and Veil (n 242) §14/81–2.

258 AktG, §111(4) sentence 2.

259 The competences of the general meeting are enumerated in AktG, §119(2). In addition, the BGH has developed unwritten competences of the general meeting for 'structural measures' that interfere severely with shareholder rights (so-called *Holzmüller* jurisprudence), see Chapter 5A.III.

260 The transaction may, however, be valid in relation to third parties; see, e.g., BGHZ 83, 122 (*Holzmüller*).

261 The articles must contain an objects clause pursuant to AktG, §23(3) no 2.

262 For an example where the directors violated their duties because they acted outside of the company's objects, see OLG Düsseldorf, decision of 9 December 2009 (*IKB*), discussed below in this section.

Secondly, the directors are required to cultivate a collegial atmosphere and cooperate in good faith when performing their functions. They must inform their colleagues truthfully and comprehensively of all relevant matters and implement board resolutions adopted with the required majority effectively, even if they voted against them. For example, a director is liable if he does not apprise the board of suspected wrongdoing of a colleague brought to his attention and does not attempt to find a solution first through internal investigations and deliberations, but instead immediately informs the supervisory authority and thus prompts an external investigation.[263]

Thirdly, the duty of care establishes an expectation that directors have the required knowledge to discharge their functions effectively and make business decisions according to commonly accepted principles of prudent management. This means that they must be familiar with established concepts of business administration, accounting, and financial planning. For example, a director cannot insist on inspecting corporate books and records or audit reports together with an external expert. The courts have held that directors 'must possess, or acquire, the minimum level of knowledge and skills necessary to understand and assess adequately and without external help all processes and transactions that are part of a company's regular business operations'.[264] This applies to the members of the management board as well as the supervisory board members. Furthermore, directors must ensure that they are aware of new developments in fields relevant to their responsibilities and the company's activities. They must make business decisions based on appropriate information and consider carefully risk factors and the implications of the decision for the company. Risks should be minimized as far as possible, which involves providing for security and refraining from entering into excessively risky or speculative transactions.[265]

A breach of duty, established according to these precepts, leads to liability if the director acts with 'fault'. In principle, liability pursuant to §93(2) follows general tenets of fault-based responsibility.[266] Directors are, therefore, responsible for any type of negligence that inflicts a loss on the company.[267] The burden of proof is on the director to show that he exercised the care of a diligent and conscientious manager.[268] However, this general rule is modified by the second sentence of §93(1) Stock Corporation Act. A business decision is deemed to be duty-compliant if the director reasonably believed that he acted in the best interest of the company and the decision was based on appropriate information. The provision establishes

[263] BGH WM 1966, 968.

[264] BGH NJW 1983, 991 (*Hertie*). In this case, one of the employee representatives on the supervisory board of Hertie requested to be accompanied by an external expert while inspecting the report of the independent auditor. The court held that the chairman of the supervisory board was justified in refusing the plaintiff's request. However, it acknowledged *in obiter* that board members were not required to have specialized knowledge in all fields in which the supervisory board might have to take action. They were entitled to obtain expert advice on *specific questions* if the supervisory board was not able to fulfil its functions otherwise, ibid 991–2. See also AktG, §109(1) sentence 2, which allows the supervisory board to ask external experts to attend a board meeting in order to advise on 'individual matters'.

[265] See BGH 69, 207, 213–15 (holding that the members of the supervisory board of a partnership limited by shares, who were asked to give their consent to a substantial investment in another company that had not yet started operations and whose financial position was not secured, violated their duties (analogy to AktG, §§116, 93), since 'the potential advantages of the investment were disproportionate to the risk'); OLG Jena, NZG 2001, 86 (holding that the shipment of cars abroad without obtaining a guarantee payable upon first demand, as was common in the industry, constituted a violation of the directors' duties); OLG Munich, AG 2001, 723 (finding that directors who entered into an interest rate and currency swap without hedging against the foreign exchange risk breached their duties). The next two decisions reproduced in the text, *ARAG/Garmenbeck* and *IKB*, are further examples of cases where the directors entered into risky and speculative transactions without the necessary safeguards.

[266] The basic provision dealing with responsibility for breaches of legal obligations is contained in the general part of the law of obligations, §276 BGB, which provides that parties are 'responsible for intentional acts and negligence'.

[267] Negligence is generally defined as the failure 'to exercise reasonable care', §276(2) BGB. What is reasonable is determined in light of what can be expected of a diligent and conscientious manager.

[268] AktG, §93(2) sentence 2.

a non-rebuttable presumption to the effect that, if the conditions of §93(1), sentence 2 are met, the court will make no further assessment of the defects of the director's decision, and the plaintiff will not be allowed to show that the director acted negligently. Sentence 2 was adopted in 2005 in order to codify case law that was inspired by the Delaware business judgment rule.[269] The following judgment is the leading case.

Bundesgerichtshof, judgment of 21 April 1997, BGHZ 135, 244 (*ARAG/Garmenbeck*)

The plaintiffs, members of the supervisory board of the defendant, a legal expenses insurance firm in the form of a stock corporation, challenge the resolutions of the advisory board concerning item 8 b) of the agenda of 25 June 1992 and item 9 of the agenda of 15 June 1993, which rejected the enforcement of damages claims against the chairman of the management board of the defendant company, Dr. L.F.

The defendant company and its wholly owned subsidiaries, A Ltd. and AR B.V., which were founded 1984 and 1989, respectively, and whose managing director with authority to bind the company was, among others, Dr. L.F., entered into business relations with G Ltd., a company that was incorporated in London, but only had its registered office there. Managing director of G Ltd. was W.A., an electrician with a long criminal record. W.A. used G Ltd. to conduct investment business from Switzerland. G Ltd. raised capital at interest rates that were significantly above market levels and granted cheap loans at interest rates below market levels. For a limited time, it was able to compensate for the losses incurred by expanding business operations, employing a kind of 'Ponzi scheme'. In the beginning of 1990, the G-group finally collapsed.

Due to the collapse, the defendant company and its subsidiaries suffered a loss of interest payments of ca. 421,000.00 DM. In addition, according to the plaintiffs, the losses of the defendant company from related credit transactions of the AR B.V. amounted to more than 80 million DM …

The Court of Appeals accords the supervisory board a 'decision prerogative' when assessing the prospects of legal proceedings to enforce claims for damages against members of the management board. The Court of Appeals argued that the decision of the supervisory board was not fully reviewable in court because it involved an element of prognosis. In addition, the supervisory board had wide discretion in the discharge of its duties, which restricted judicial review of its decisions … Limited judicial review of supervisory board decisions was necessary in order to ensure that the work of the supervisory board, which had to supervise not only the legality, but also the usefulness and effectiveness of the management board's activities, was not overburdened with legalistic requirements and the corporate organs had sufficient leeway to take autonomous business decisions. A reduction of the discretion to zero and, accordingly, a duty to act could only be assumed in exceptional circumstances, for example when the refusal of the supervisory board to adopt the requested course of action was clearly illegal or gave rise to severe disadvantages for the company, for instance when it threatened its existence. In the opinion of the Court of Appeals, this was not the case here …

The Court of Appeals correctly assumes that the supervisory board has responsibility to assess the existence of claims for damages of the company against members of the management board that arise out of their acts as a corporate organ and to enforce these claims, provided the applicable legal requirements are satisfied … This responsibility stems from the function of the supervisory board to supervise the management of the company (§ 111(1) AktG), including where transactions have already been completed … and from the fact that the supervisory board represents the company in and out of court as against the management board (§ 112 AktG) …

However, the criteria that the supervisory board has to employ when discharging this duty have been defined incorrectly or imprecisely by the Court of Appeals.

aa) The decision of the supervisory board whether to claim damages from a member of the management board for a violation of management duties requires, first of all, a determination of the elements that give rise to the claim both in factual and legal terms, as well as an analysis of the litigation risk and the enforceability of the claim. When making this assessment, the

[269] Gesetz zur Unternehmensintegrität und Modernisierung des Anfechtungsrechts (UMAG), law of 22 September 2005, BGBl I, 2802, Art 1 no 1a.

supervisory board has to consider that the management board must be accorded a wide margin of discretion in managing the company, without which entrepreneurial activity would not be possible. This includes, in addition to the deliberate assumption of business risks, the danger of making errors in judgment, which even the most conscientious manager is exposed to. If the supervisory board obtains the impression that the management board lacks the necessary intuition to manage the business successfully, that the directors' tenure is ill-fated, they may decide to work towards replacing the managers. However, this does not mean that the managers are liable to pay damages. The duty to pay damages only arises where the boundaries have been clearly transgressed within which a responsible manager should operate who acts solely in the interests of the company and who has carefully determined the basis of his decision-making, where the willingness to engage in entrepreneurial risk-taking has been carried too far in an irresponsible manner, or the acts of the management board have to be regarded as non-compliant for other reasons.

bb) In contrast to the opinion of the Court of Appeals, a 'decision prerogative', which would result in limited judicial review, does not apply to this part of the supervisory board's decision. When examining the existence and enforceability of a claim for damages, the supervisory board does not act differently from anyone who has to assess on his own or on someone else's behalf a legal claim and the prospects of its enforcement in court. The justifiability and accuracy of the board's assessment of the prospects of success of such litigation can be fully reviewed in court, since these questions do not relate to the sphere of action, but to that of knowledge, for which at most a limited margin of discretion can be recognized. Discretion can only exist where the decision between different courses of action is to be made.

cc) Where a careful and adequate analysis of the litigation risk by the supervisory board leads to the conclusion that the company is probably—certainty cannot be expected in such cases—entitled to damages from one of the members of the management board, the question may then arise whether the supervisory board can refrain from enforcing the claim and hence from recovering the losses suffered by the company.

In contrast to the opinion of the Court of Appeals, in this question the supervisory board cannot be accorded a scope of autonomous entrepreneurial discretion either. Entrepreneurial discretion is part and necessary complement of the powers of management, which are vested in the management board and not the supervisory board. The supervisory board only partakes in managing the company where the legislator confers management powers on it, for example when appointing and removing members of the management board, or in the context of §111(4), sentence 2 AktG, i.e. whenever the supervisory board contributes to managerial activity in the sense of exercising ex ante control. However, the decision to enforce damages claims against members of the management board who are in breach of duty is part of the board's ex post supervisory function, which has the aim of ensuring that the management board acts in a duty-compliant way and preventing the company from suffering a loss ... In exercising this control function and assessing whether breaches of a managerial duty exist, the supervisory board has to consider the scope of entrepreneurial discretion that the management board is entitled to (see above aa). However, in making their own decision, the supervisory board does not benefit from a scope of entrepreneurial discretion, in contrast to what the Court of Appeals assumes. Since the supervisory board's decision has to be taken solely in the interests of the company, which will generally demand recovery, the board can refrain only exceptionally from asserting well-founded damages claims against a noncompliant member of the management board if important interests of the company militate in favour of accepting the loss without compensation. This condition will generally only be satisfied if the interests of the company that suggest that the company should refrain from claiming compensation outweigh the factors that speak in favour of enforcement or if they are at least roughly equivalent to them. In this context, the factors emphasized by the Court of Appeals, such as adverse effects on business operations and the reputation of the company in the public eye, disruption of management activities and the disturbance of the work climate, may become important. The supervisory board, however, may not make allowance for other considerations that are not related to the interests of the company, such as the desire to spare a long-serving member of the management board or the social consequences of litigation for the defendant or his family, save in exceptional cases. Such exceptional cases may exist, on the one hand, if the breach of duty is not particularly severe and the loss suffered by the company is relatively minor, and on the other hand, grave consequences are to be expected for the member of the management board who is liable to pay compensation ...

The supervisory board can only have discretion within these narrow limits and only with respect to the question of whether it is permissible, by way of exception and because of overriding reasons in the interest of the company, to refrain from enforcing a claim for damages in spite of the likely success of an action.

Questions and comments:

1. The court in *ARAG/Garmenbeck* makes several important observations that have influenced the development of the duty of care under German law. First, the court holds that the members of the management board enjoy a wide margin of discretion in making business decisions. Their decisions will not be reviewed by the courts, unless they transgress the boundaries 'within which a responsible manager should operate who acts solely in the interests of the company and who has carefully determined the basis of his decision-making' or they exhibit a 'willingness to engage in entrepreneurial risk-taking [that is being] carried too far in an irresponsible manner'. This passage has been interpreted by large parts of the literature as incorporating a Delaware-style business judgment rule into German law.[270] Do you agree? Consider also the codified business judgment rule in §93(1), sentence 2 Stock Corporation Act, which builds on *ARAG/Garmenbeck*, but refines and clarifies the elements of the rule. Does the codification replicate the Delaware version of the business judgment rule? If not, in what ways does it differ from Delaware law?

   Secondly, the court held that the supervisory board did not enjoy any margin of discretion as far as it acted in its supervisory role, for example by assessing potential claims of the company against members of the management board.[271] Whether or not a claim should be enforced was not a business decision on which people may rationally disagree, the court argued, but, in principle, a binary decision: A well-founded claim had to be enforced, save in exceptional circumstances (see also the next comment). Furthermore, whether a claim was well-founded could be fully reviewed in court, since this question related not to the 'sphere of action' (*Handlungsbereich*), but to the 'sphere of knowledge' (*Erkenntnisbereich*). Is this distinction helpful, and is it true that enforcing a claim against a director is different from taking a management decision? In Chapter 8, we will see that the Delaware courts qualify enforcement decisions differently. They fall squarely within the managerial powers of the board, and the directors, accordingly, benefit from the protections of the business judgment rule.[272]
2. Section 93(1), sentence 2 Stock Corporation Act ostensibly establishes the following threshold conditions of the German business judgment rule: In taking a business decision, directors must believe that they act in the best interest of the company and the decision is based on appropriate information. However, the explanatory memorandum for the act explains that the provision must be read as containing two additional, implicit requirements. To give a complete list of the threshold conditions, the business judgment rule presupposes that (1) the challenged act was a business decision; (2) the director acted in good faith; (3) without a conflict of interest; (4) in the best interest of the company; and (5) on the basis of appropriate information.[273] The director bears the burden of proving that these conditions are met, since the general allocation of the burden of proof pursuant to §93(2), sentence 2 also applies to the threshold conditions.[274]

   Business decisions are characterized by an element of prognosis and subjective evaluation. They necessarily imply a certain scope of discretion and are, for this reason, not fully justiciable. Conversely, where a specific course of action is required by law or the articles of

[270] See e.g. Raiser and Veil (n 242) §14/66.
[271] For an overview of the limited managerial functions of the supervisory board, see Chapter 4E.I.3.
[272] Chapter 8C.II.3. [273] BT-Drs [Documentation of the Federal Parliament] 15/5092, 11.
[274] ibid 12.

association, the protections of the business judgment rule do not apply.[275] *ARAG/Garmenbeck* illustrates the distinction between justiciable and non-justiciable decisions clearly. In deciding whether to enforce a claim of the company for damages against a member of the management board, the supervisory board does not enjoy a margin of discretion or, as the court puts it, a 'decision prerogative'. The supervisory board is not called upon to decide between two or more legally permissible courses of action. Rather, there is only one 'right' answer: The supervisory board must enforce the company's claim if an examination of the prospects of the claim and the litigation risk leads to the conclusion that the company will probably succeed in court, unless exceptional circumstances in the company's interest outweigh the interest that the company has in recovering damages. On the other hand, where management powers are vested in the supervisory board, which is the case when the supervisory board appoints or removes members of the management board or is authorized pursuant to the articles to approve specified transactions, it enjoys the same protections of the business judgment rule as the management board.[276]

The other threshold conditions, acting in good faith, without a conflict of interest, in the best interest of the company and on the basis of appropriate information, are assessed from the perspective of the defendant director. The requirements are satisfied if the director could 'reasonable assume' that his or her actions were in the best interest of the company and complied with the other conditions. Thus, the law does not establish a negligence or gross negligence standard, but asks whether the director's subjective assessment was reasonable in light of the circumstances of the case.[277] For example, the assessment is unreasonable where the director 'misjudges the risk associated with the managerial decision in an entirely irresponsible way'.[278] This approach goes in the direction of the subjective standard that applies under section 172 of the UK Companies Act 2006, but the similarities or differences depend on how the courts interpret the indefinite term 'reasonable'.[279]

Business decisions are in the best interest of the company if they 'further the long-run profitability and competitiveness of the company and its products or services'.[280] Directors are entitled to take the interests of the corporate group and subsidiaries into account,[281] but the separate legal personality of the group companies must, of course, be respected and decisions must ultimately promote the interests of the director's company. It is noteworthy that the German legislator emphasizes the 'long-run profitability' of the company. This formulation illustrates the more pluralistic approach to corporate governance prevalent in Germany. If a case can be made that the long-run profitability of the company is promoted, directors are allowed to adopt decisions that favour the employees, clients, or societal interests over those of the shareholders in the short run. In fact, given the purpose of the legislation, it can be argued that the decision to make investments that are highly profitable in the short-run but put the long-run development of the company at risk, are not protected by the business judgment rule and violate the directors' duties. We will come back to this point when we discuss the duties of directors in the context of the subprime mortgage crisis.[282]

The requirement to act in the best interest of the company implies that the directors must avoid conflicts of interest.[283] Conflicts exist where a director or a relative has an interest in the transaction or the director acts under the influence of another party. Here the perspective of the director is again decisive. The director may for example reasonably assume that the decision was taken in the best interest of the company if the conflict of interest is fully disclosed and the other directors decide that the transaction is beneficial to the company and should go ahead.[284]

[275] ibid 11. [276] AktG, §111(4). [277] BT-Drs (n 273) 11. [278] ibid.

[279] This term is expressly mentioned in §93(1) sentence 2 German AktG and was used by the English courts to establish objective outer limits of the subjective test now contained in s 172 UK Companies Act. See for example *Charterbridge Corp. Ltd v Lloyd's Bank Ltd* [1970] Ch 62, 74: 'The proper test ... must be whether an intelligent and honest man in the position of a director of the company concerned, could, in the whole of the existing circumstances, have reasonably believed that the transactions were for the benefit of the company'.

[280] BT-Drs (n 273) 11. [281] ibid.

[282] See the *IKB* decision of the OLG Düsseldorf, the next case reproduced here.

[283] BT-Drs (n 273) 11. [284] ibid.

Finally, the directors must reasonably believe to be appropriately informed. The law does not require the directors to act on the basis of complete information, and directors are not expected to obtain and analyse all objectively available information. Rather, it falls within the director's managerial discretion to decide how much information is appropriate in the individual case. On the other hand, as with the other elements of the business judgment rule, the outer limits of the director's discretion are objective and reviewable in court. What is appropriate depends on the available time, potential market pressures, the importance of the decision for the company, and generally accepted views of what constitutes good managerial practice.[285] It is not always necessary, but also not necessarily sufficient, to obtain the opinion of an outside expert. The explanatory memorandum stresses that expert advice is not a panacea and the test of appropriateness must reflect the individual circumstances of the case, rather than a hypothetical formal checklist.[286]

Our next case illustrates another mechanism that facilitates the supervision of directors and protects (minority) shareholders: the right to appoint a special auditor. Often, it is difficult for the shareholders, in particular the minority shareholders, to judge the prospects of an action for damages against the directors. The rules on special audits, which form part of the chapter on general meetings and the rights of stockholders,[287] are intended to enable the shareholders to obtain a clear picture of the factual setting that may substantiate a damages claim.[288] The special auditor is appointed by ordinary resolution of the general meeting in order to investigate any matter 'in relation to the formation or management of the company', including the conduct of the supervisory board members.[289] If the general meeting rejects the proposal to appoint a special auditor or revokes the resolution at a later point, minority shareholders holding at least 1 per cent of the share capital or the proportionate amount of €100,000 can apply to the court for the appointment of an auditor.[290] The minority right requires, however, that the petitioners 'present facts that give rise to the suspicion that the matter involved dishonesty or gross violations of the law or the articles'.[291] Once appointed, the auditor has far-reaching rights of inquiry. He can, for example, inspect the company's books and records and request information from the members of the management board and supervisory board.[292] The auditor produces a report, which has to be filed with the commercial court where the company is registered and submitted to the management board. The management board circulates the report to the supervisory board and presents it at the next general meeting.[293] The general meeting then decides whether to instigate proceedings or to take other measures. Thus, while the special auditor investigates potential violations of the law and breaches of the directors' duties, the report is not decisive of a finding of liability. On the other hand, a report that uncovers instances of wrongdoing will likely trigger further shareholder litigation. Therefore, the appointment of the auditor is often hotly contested, as the *IKB* case that is reproduced below shows.

The decision in *IKB* is important because it forms part of the judicial response to the subprime mortgage crisis in Germany. It should, therefore, be seen in the context of cases such as *Citigroup* and *Goldman Sachs*, decided by the Delaware Court of Chancery and discussed elsewhere in this chapter.[294] In *IKB*, a German bank that provided loans to medium-sized enterprises suffered heavy losses owing to its investments in collateralized debt obligations (CDOs) backed by US subprime mortgages. It had to be bailed out by the German government, which took a controlling stake in the company and appointed a special auditor by resolution of the general meeting to investigate possible wrongdoings of the members of the management and supervisory boards in connection with the CDO investments.

[285] ibid 12. [286] ibid. [287] AktG, §§142–146. [288] Koch (n 57) §142 para 1.
[289] AktG, §142(1). [290] ibid §142(2). [291] ibid. [292] ibid §145(1), (2).
[293] ibid §145(6). [294] See section B.II below.

The government later sold its stake in the bank to Lone Star Funds (LSF), a US headquartered private equity firm. LSF convened an extraordinary general meeting and repealed the resolution appointing the special auditor. Minority shareholders applied to the court, requesting the appointment of an auditor by court order. They argued that the respondent's investments in subprime CDOs, made either directly or through a special purpose vehicle incorporated in the US, had amounted at one point to 47 per cent of the bank's total business volume. This, it was claimed, violated the company's objects to provide credit to local, medium-sized enterprises and led to excessive, undiversified risk. In addition, the management board did not base its investment decisions on sufficient information, ignored warning signs, and displayed an overreliance on the ratings published by credit rating agencies. The petitioners further argued that the supervisory board failed to monitor the management board's investment strategy properly and did not address the bank's significant exposure to the subprime mortgage market. The trial court issued the requested order.[295] The respondent appealed.

Oberlandesgericht [Higher Regional Court] Düsseldorf, decision of 9 December 2009 (*IKB*)

The petitioner's motion satisfies the substantive requirements of § 142(2), sentence 1 AktG.

a) The appointment of special auditors by court order requires that facts justify the assumption that the issue at hand involved dishonesty or gross violations of the law or the articles of association (§ 142(2), sentence 1 AktG). It is, first of all, necessary that the petitioner pleads facts that substantiate, at least indirectly, this assumption. Unsubstantiated claims, mere allegations, or speculations are not sufficient ... On the other hand, whether dishonesty or gross violations of the law or the articles have really occurred is not part of the proceedings deciding on the appointment of the special auditor, nor are the possible legal consequences of such a finding. Otherwise the outcome of the special audit would be predetermined.

aa) Breaches of duty which do not violate the good morals and which are, accordingly, not dishonest, justify the appointment of a special auditor only if they constitute gross departures from expected behaviour. This requires, on the one hand, a damaging behaviour and, on the other hand, that the departure from the directors' duties was not only minor, but serious. A breach of duty may be qualified as gross if the degree of fault or the damage caused by the breach is particularly significant. Violations of the law or the articles are gross if it would be intolerable not to enforce the breach in light of the facts of the individual case.

bb) In addition to the element 'gross', the right to apply to the court is restricted by the general principle of proportionality. This test, which has to be performed by the court *ex officio*, cannot be derived from the wording of § 142(2); however, it is justified in light of the structure of the law and is expressly demanded by the explanatory memorandum to the Act. According to the memorandum, 'a proportionality test ... should also be performed in *de minimis* cases where the costs and repercussions of a special audit for the company are not proportionate to the damage caused by the wrongdoing'.

cc) On the basis of the pleaded facts, there must be probable cause for dishonesty or a gross breach of duty, that is, these must not only be possible, but probable pursuant to rules of logic.

b) In the Court's view, the facts indicate that the matters under investigation involve gross breaches of duty by the management board and the supervisory board.

aa) First of all, there are sufficient reasons to conclude that the management board and supervisory board grossly violated the company's objects clause and, thus, breached their duties of care and monitoring in a material way (§§ 93(1), sentence 1, 111(1) AktG).

§ 2 of the respondent's articles of association, in the version in force since September 2006, provides as follows:

> 'The objects of the undertaking are the promotion of trade and industry, in particular through the provision of mid- and long-term financing or equity capital, equity surrogates, and leasing,

[295] Landgericht (Regional Court) Düsseldorf, decision of 14 August 2009, 31 O 38/09.

as well as related advisory services. The financial needs of medium-sized enterprises shall receive particular consideration.

The Company may conduct any type of banking business and provide financial services of any kind.

The Company shall be entitled to undertake all transactions and actions likely to serve the objects of the undertaking. It may implement its business activities wholly or partly through subsidiaries, affiliates or joint ventures and may for this purpose form, acquire or take participating interests in other undertakings at home or abroad'.

This description of the objects of the company clearly indicates that the respondent's activities focus on the promotion and financing of trade and industry, in particular medium-sized enterprises, and all of its transactions and measures are required to further this purpose. As far as the respondent's reliance on the general authorisation of § 2(2) is concerned, which allows any type of banking business and the provision of financial services of any kind, and which is used to justify the engagement in the securitization sector, two points can be made. First, under an appropriate construction of § 2, this authorization must be seen as being subordinate to the overarching purpose of the promotion and financing of industry and trade. It must, accordingly, serve the direct or indirect attainment of this objective. Secondly, the terms 'banking business' and 'financial services' do not encompass any type of securities transaction or risky and speculative trading, especially not the betting with financial innovations and derivatives …

It is reasonable to conclude that the company's objects were violated because the respondent's own engagement in the securitization sector, investments in international credit portfolios (€7bn), and the respondent's contingent liabilities, that is, irrevocable loan commitments in favour of special purpose vehicles operating in the collateralization sector (€17.7bn), totalled ca. €24.7bn in the fiscal year 2006/2007, while the respondent's core medium-sized enterprise business, that is, receivables against clients, was only slightly larger, totalling €29.3bn. Thus, the respondent's securitization business equalled ca. 46 per cent of the total volume of its business. However, pursuant to its objects, the respondent was required not to engage in securitizations at all or at least not more than marginally.

The management board enjoys no margin of discretion if it violates the law or the articles of association. Binding provisions of acts of parliament or articles of association have the function of imposing limits on the addressee's discretion that are not subject to qualifications or modification whenever convenient. The protections of the business judgment rule (§ 93(1), sentence 2 AktG) do not apply in the case of violations of the law or the articles. The members of the management board are only accorded a margin of discretion with regard to the question of how to act within the limits drawn by legislation and the articles in order to manage the company as successfully as possible. [The court concluded that the violation of the articles was 'gross' because the management board clearly transgressed the discretionary limits imposed by the objects clause and the company suffered a loss of several billion euros. The court further held that the supervisory board was aware of the transgressions and should have intervened.]

bb) Furthermore, it is reasonable to assume that the respondent's management board violated its duties grossly because the board did not act on the basis of sufficient information and knowingly took excessive risks, in particular concentration risks.[296]

aaa) Pursuant to § 93(1), sentence 2 AktG, a management decision shall not be deemed a breach of duty if the member of the management board reasonably believed that he took the challenged decision on the basis of appropriate information and in the best interest of the company. This statutory formulation imposes a duty on directors to obtain sufficient information. Directors have to utilize all sources of information at their disposal. This means that they must do more than merely rely on the information provided by third parties. They are expected to

[296] [Footnote by authors.] Concentration risks, also called 'bulk risks', are risks that arise because investments are not well diversified or risks of different categories are correlated. For a formal definition see, for example, European Banking Authority/Committee of European Banking Supervisors, CEBS Guidelines on the management of concentration risk under the supervisory review process, 2 September 2010, 5–6.

establish information systems within the company, monitor their functioning, and make good use of them.

(1) The exceeding complexity and lack of transparency of securitizations entail the virtual impossibility of the management board to take decisions based on appropriate information. [The court discussed the operation of asset backed securities and CDOs and observed that the risks associated with multi-layered structured finance products were particularly difficult to assess. The court continued:]

(2) The external ratings of American credit rating agencies did not excuse the management board from its duty to obtain its own information.

First of all, it is evident that credit rating agencies as private for-profit organisations that issue ratings for financial products of a particular client against a fee and advise their clients on the structure of the products do not evaluate these products objectively. The rating agencies were subject to a conflict of interest, as the management board could clearly see … In addition, the rating agencies lacked experience in the evaluation of asset backed securities, which were relatively recent financial products. It would constitute a clear violation of the management board's duty to utilize all available sources of information if it took the ratings as the only source of information for its investment decisions.

(3) The respondent submitted that it did not only rely on external ratings, but also developed an internal rating system to assess the risk of an investment … However, the respondent did not elaborate on the internal rating system. Therefore, the submission is unsubstantiated and insufficient to rebut the reasonable assumption [of a breach of duty]. In any case, even according to the submission, the external ratings were the main factor on which decisions were based and, in addition, the internal system was evidently useless.

bbb) Even on the assumption that the management board was appropriately and fully informed of the risks of the securitized products, it is reasonable to conclude that it took excessive risks through the respondent's direct and indirect engagement (granting of lines of credit to the special purpose vehicles) in the CDO market. No management board acts in compliance with the duty of care if it takes risks that will render the company insolvent if they materialize. The management board … assumed the quality risk, market risk and concentration risk, i.e. the accumulation of similar risks of default, of the acquired securities totalling several billion euros. However, the sufficient diversification of the credit portfolio and thus in particular the prevention of concentration risk is part of the principles of prudent banking. The securities concerned mortgages and consumer credits of a large number of unknown debtors. Consequently, the risk of default was the same. This is precisely the problem that the requirement to avoid concentration risk is intended to address.

It is inconsistent with the care of a prudent director of a medium-sized bank to invest in foreign, largely unknown and ultimately uncontrollable securities to an extent as in the present case.

[In the next section of the judgment, the court held that the supervisory board should have been aware of the existential risks the bank was exposed to. If the supervisory board had not been informed adequately by the management board, it should have investigated and asked more critical questions. Accordingly, the court found that there were reasonable grounds to conclude that the supervisory board had also committed a gross violation of its monitoring duties.]

Questions and comments:

1. Note that the court approaches the issue of a breach of duty from three angles. First, the court argues that the management board, through the company's substantial involvement in the CDO and subprime mortgage markets, violated the objects clause contained in IKB's articles of association. The protections of the business judgment rule do not apply to a business decision that is illegal or in contradiction to the articles. However, even if the objects clause is construed more permissively and the directors' conduct, accordingly, complies with the articles, the decision to invest in CDOs is, in the court's view, in breach of duty. The business judgment rule requires that the directors are appropriately informed when they take business decisions. The court argues that, owing to the 'exceeding complexity and lack of transparency of securitizations' it was virtually impossible for the directors to act in an informed way. Finally, notwithstanding the lack of information, there were reasonable grounds to find the

directors liable because IKB's investments were excessively risky. The court points out that 'no management board acts in compliance with the duty of care if it takes risks that will render the company insolvent if they materialize'. In other words, the business judgment rule does not apply to business decisions that are so risky that they lead to the company's potential bankruptcy or breakup.

2. As far as the last two strands of the court's decision are concerned, would an investment in derivatives or, in fact, any business decision that involves risk ever be in compliance with the directors' duties? Derivatives and securitized products, of course, perform useful economic functions, for example in allowing firms to hedge against exposure, diversify, and raise funds that would otherwise not be available to them.[297] In addition, virtually all business decisions involve risk. Depending on the volume of the transaction, some highly unlikely scenario may exist that would result in the firm's bankruptcy. Therefore, does the court's approach present a realistic model of how to deal with risk and manage corporations, in particular financial institutions?[298]

4. *France*

The French Code de commerce does not spell out the duties of directors in detail. It contains one general provision addressed at the members of the board of directors (*administrateurs*) and the general director (*directeur général*[299]), but not at the deputy general directors (*directeurs généraux délégués*),[300] establishing liability for unlawful, tortious, or negligent acts, Article L225-251 Code de commerce.[301] However, it does not provide for a duty of care specifically designed for company directors and managers, determine the level of care that directors are expected to employ, or codify a business judgment rule. Furthermore, in order to obtain a complete picture of the duties of company directors and the extent of the liability risk that they face, it is necessary to analyse both civil and criminal liability, which plays a far greater role under French law than in Germany or the common law jurisdictions that we analysed above.

(a) Civil liability

Commercial Code[302]

Article L225-251

The directors and the general director shall be individually or jointly and severally liable to the company or third parties either for infringements of the laws or regulations applicable to public

[297] For a summary of the functions of securitization and how certain structural defects of securitization contributed to the subprime mortgage crisis see SL Schwarcz, 'The Future of Securitization' (2009) 41 Connecticut Law Review 1313.

[298] For a critical discussion of *IKB* that raises these issues, see H Fleischer, 'Verantwortlichkeit von Bankgeschäftsleitern und Finanzmarktkrise' (2010) NJW 1504.

[299] Also sometimes called managing director in English translations.

[300] Thus, if the deputy general directors are not members of the board of directors, Art L225-251 is not applicable; see Cour d'Appel de Versailles, 7 September 2007, *Revue des sociétés* 2007, 637, note I Urbain-Parleani. The company may, however, have a claim under general law, in particular Art 1240 Code civil. This has the consequence that the claim against the deputy general director is subject to a limitation period of five years, whereas claims against the directors and the general director are subject to the shorter period of three years pursuant to Art L225-254 Code de commerce.

[301] Article L225-251 applies to the *société anonyme* with a one-tier board. For companies with a two-tier board, Arts L225-256 and L225-257 determine the responsibility of the members of the management board and supervisory board, respectively. While Art L225-256 simply refers to the regime applicable to one-tier board companies, Art L225-257 provides that the members of the supervisory board shall be liable for negligent or tortious acts committed in the performance of their duties, but not for acts of management, unless they were aware of criminal offences committed by members of the management board and did not report these offences to the general meeting. Finally, Art L223-22 establishes a comparable liability regime for the managers of the *société à responsabilité limitée*.

[302] Translation by Legifrance, https://www.legifrance.gouv.fr/Traductions/en-English/Legifrance-translations.

limited companies, or for breaches of the memorandum and articles of association, or for management mistakes.

If more than one director, or more than one director and the general director, have participated in the same acts, the Court shall determine the share to be contributed by each of them to the compensation awarded.

Article L225-253

Any clause in the memorandum and articles of association the effect of which would be to make the exercise of any action subject to prior notice or to the consent of the general meeting, or to waive the right to any such action in advance, shall be deemed non-existent.

No decision of the general meeting shall have the effect of extinguishing an action for liability against the directors or the general director for a tortious or negligent act committed in the performance of their duties.

Article L225-254

Any action for liability against the directors or the general director, either by an individual or individuals or by the company, must be brought within three years of the act or event causing the loss or damage, or, if the same was concealed, the discovery thereof. Nevertheless, where the act is defined as a criminal offence, the said period shall be extended to ten years.

Article L225-251 is best described as a tort-law-based cause of action. French company law does not, at least not explicitly, utilize notions of fiduciary law.[303] Rather, in the tradition of the general tort law provisions of the French Code civil,[304] directors are held liable for illegal acts or management mistakes, that is, intentional or negligent acts committed in the course of managing a company that inflict a loss on the company or third parties. The elements of the cause of action, accordingly, correspond to those of tort law claims. The plaintiff must show a fault on the part of the director (*faute*), a loss suffered by the plaintiff (*préjudice*), and a causal link between the director's conduct and the loss (*causalité*).[305] In spite of the differences in the formulation and the legal concepts used, it can be seen that the structure of the cause of action is comparable to those for a breach of duty under German and common law.[306] Common law duties do not operate with the notion of 'fault', but they ask whether the director has 'breached a duty'. The breach depends on the failure to meet certain behavioural standards, for example the failure to employ the required level of care. Fault and breach of duty, consequently, perform the same function of identifying conduct that gives rise to liability if the company or, in exceptional cases, third parties have suffered a loss as a result of the director's actions.

We can derive three such types of misconduct from the first paragraph of Article L225-251: infringements of laws or regulations, breaches of the company's articles of association, and intentional or negligent acts of mismanagement (*faute de gestion*). Examples for violations of the law that may result in liability include the failure to keep corporate books and records, the refusal to disclose the company's books to the shareholders, or the distribution of unlawful dividends. Breaches of the articles include, for example, non-compliance by the directors with the requirement to obtain shareholder authorization for transactions above a certain value.[307]

303 D Martin and OT Tieu, 'La responsabilité civile des administrateurs de sociétés; Évolutions jurisprudentielles' (2010) JCP 740 para 2.

304 Code civil, Arts 1240, 1241.

305 P Merle, *Droit commercial: Sociétés commerciales* (22nd edn, Dalloz 2018) para 458.

306 The German cause of action pursuant to §93(2) AktG is commonly conceptualized as flowing from the position of the director as an organ of the company. For an overview of the discussion, see Koch (n 57) §93 para 36.

307 Cour d'Appel de Paris, 21 February 2003, *Droit des sociétés* 2004, no 5.

The third category, management mistakes, poses the greatest challenges. It is well established that directors may violate their duties both through positive action and the failure to act where the director's circumspection could have prevented the company from suffering a loss.[308] Furthermore, intentional or reckless behaviour as well as ordinary negligence may give rise to liability. However, the law does not contain any definition of mismanagement or lack of due care, and the concept of negligence is highly fact-specific, something that we have already seen in the other jurisdictions. Starting point of the analysis is generally the company's interest (*l'intérêt social*).[309] It has been said that directors can be held responsible for all acts or omissions that are contrary to the interests of the company.[310] The notion of the company's interest is an open-ended concept without clearly defined boundaries that is developed on a case-by-case basis. Its precise contours remain uncertain and change depending on the context. However, some general guidance can be derived from case law and French corporate governance initiatives. In general, French law employs a relatively wide understanding of the corporate interest that goes beyond the contractual understanding prevalent in common law jurisdictions.[311] The first French corporate governance report, the Viénot-Report of 1995,[312] explicitly distinguished the more pluralistic or institutional French approach from the shareholder value goal of Anglo-American jurisdictions. The report explained that the company should be 'considered as a separate economic agent, pursuing its own objectives which are distinct from those of shareholders, employees, creditors including the internal revenue authorities, suppliers and customers'. The interest of the company 'represents the common interest of all of these persons, which is for the company to remain in business and prosper'.[313] Thus defined, the notion is relevant to both civil and criminal liability of the directors.[314]

The courts have held that directors act in violation of the company's interest if they enter into risky transactions, such as the ill-advised expansion of business operations without proper financing,[315] accept the provision of loans on onerous terms by the parent company,[316] sell the company's business below value without attempting to find a buyer offering a better price and without conducting a proper valuation,[317] distribute extraordinary dividends financed out of reserves during a time of contracting business operations, even if the

[308] Cass com, 25 March 1997, *Bull. Joly Sociétés* 1997, 799 (*faute d'abstention*), note G Baranger.

[309] See M Cozian, A Viandier, and F Deboissy, *Droit des sociétés* (31st edn, LexisNexis 2018) para 565: 'l'intérêt social est ... un impératif de conduite, une règle déontologique, en clair la boussole qui indique la marche à suivre'.

[310] JP Valuet and A Lienhard, *Code des Sociétés* (34th edn, Dalloz 2018); Com Art L225-251, Commentaire, I Principe.

[311] However, the contractual approach is not entirely alien to French law. In fact, Art 1833 Code civil, which is in the chapter of the Civil Code containing general provisions on companies, provides that firms are 'formed in the common interest of the members'. Insofar as the company is a legal construct established by a legal act, the interests of the company are determined by those who are parties to this act, namely the members or shareholders (*associés*). But in contrast to the orthodox contractarian view, French corporate law does not stop there. Where the interests of other constituencies are concerned, for example the employees, company law does not accord preeminence to one constituency, but seeks to reconcile the different interests, see Cozian, Viandier, and Deboissy (n 309) para 566.

[312] *The Boards of Directors of Listed Companies in France (Viénot I)*, Report of the Conseil National du Patronat Français (CNPF) and the Association Française des Enterprises Privées (AFEP), June 1995. The report can be downloaded from the website of the European Corporate Governance Institute, www.ecgi.global (follow hyperlink 'Codes').

[313] ibid I.1. But see also the 2018 MEDEF Corporate Governance Code of Listed Corporations, stipulating in Art 2.1 that the board of directors is 'a collegial body mandated by all shareholders'. For a more detailed discussion of the notion of the corporate interest, see Chapter 4C.II.

[314] See the reference to the interests of the company in Art L242-6(3) Code de commerce, discussed in the next section, which lays down the criminal offence of abuse of corporate assets.

[315] Cass com, 3 January 1995 (*Nasa Electronique*), *Bull. Joly Sociétés* 1995, 432, note A Couret.

[316] ibid.

[317] Cass com, 8 March 2016, no 14-16621 (*Sté Xithe*), *Bull. Joly Sociétés* 2016, 475, note S Schiller.

reserves are distributable and the distribution is approved by the general meeting,[318] grant excessive executive compensation,[319] or do not show vigilance in supervising the activities of the *président-directeur général* and fail to require that the company ceases to trade in a state of insolvency and file for the opening of insolvency proceedings.[320] In practice, it is rare that the directors of a solvent company are found liable for management mistakes. Usually, litigation ensues once insolvency proceedings are opened. In this case, the question of whether the directors breached the duty of care, to speak in common law terms, does not become relevant in the context of a claim for damages brought by the company, but a declaration that the director is liable for all or part of the deficiency in the company's assets.[321]

Since the French courts assess the conduct of directors against the benchmark of the company's interest, judgments are generally not concerned with a specification of the required standard of care in abstract terms. The courts usually simply state that the directors are required to conduct themselves as 'prudent and diligent managers', if they address this point at all.[322] This is interpreted in the literature as establishing a standard of care similar to that of the *bonus pater familias* of Roman law or its equivalent in the commercial world, the 'good manager' (*bon administrateur de société*).[323] Thus, on this view, the standard of care is comparable to the objective leg of the English duty of care.[324] Directors must exercise the care and diligence that can reasonably be expected from them in light of the circumstances of the case, including the director's role in the company and the type of company, for example its character as a small family owned business or a large stock exchange listed corporation.[325] Incompetence, inactivity, or the fact that they are mere 'figurehead directors' does not exonerate them.[326] However, matters are not always that clear, as the following decision by the French Supreme Court and the comments below show.

318 Cass com, 25 October 2011 (*Sté Sorim*), *Bull. Joly Sociétés* 2012, 243, note D Poracchia. The dividend payments corresponded to the profits of six months and turnover of two months of Société Sorim and its controlling company Stima. They deprived the two companies of a significant proportion of their available reserves at a time when the companies' liabilities had not yet been paid back and the companies had just lost several large clients. The court, accordingly, held that the distributions were contrary to the interests of the two companies and instead benefitted their common holding company SIL Finance, of which the director of Sorim and Stima was the majority shareholder and managing director. This judgment is unusual in that an act falling within the competence of the general meeting, the decision to distribute a dividend (see Art L232-12 Code de commerce), which was furthermore adopted in compliance with the legal requirements on distributions, was held to be able to contravene the interests of the company and give rise to a management mistake.

319 Cass com, 31 May 2016, no 14-24779; CA Rennes, 13 December 1995, *Droit des sociétés* 1996, no 195, note Y Chaput.

320 Cass com, 25 March 1997, *Bull. Joly Sociétés* 1997, 799. The legal representative of the company, that is, in the public company the general manager (Art L225-56 Code de commerce), has a duty to request the opening of reorganization or liquidation proceedings within 45 days after the cessation of payments (see Art L631-4 Code de commerce for the *redressement judiciaire* and Art L640-4 for the *liquidation judiciaire*). In the above case, the court did not accept the director's argument that the individual members of the board of directors, other than the general manager or *président-directeur général*, did not have the power to file for the opening of insolvency proceedings and consequently could not be held responsible for the president's failure to file. Rather, they should have spoken up in board meetings and demanded forcefully that the president take the necessary steps.

321 In all of the aforementioned cases, the directors were held liable pursuant to Art L651-2 Code de commerce (*responsabilité pour insuffisance d'actif*). The conditions for liability are similar to those under Art L225-251, with the exception that directors will not be liable for *insuffisance d'actif* if they acted with simple negligence, introduced by Act no 2016-1691 of 9 December 2016, JORF no 0287 of 10 December 2016 (Loi Sapin 2). The plaintiff must show that the director committed a fault, defined as above, that contributed to the company's insolvency. Art L651-2 is discussed in more detail in Chapter 10E.

322 Cass com, 30 March 2010 (*Crédit Martiniquais*), *Revue des sociétés* 2010, 304, note P Le Cannu.

323 See, for example, Martin and Tieu (n 303) para 17.

324 UK Companies Act 2006, s 174(2)(a).

325 Merle (n 305) para 458.

326 Cass com, 23 June 1998, *JCP E* 1998, 29, note A Viandier and JJ Caussain. The court held that the 20-year-old daughter of the de facto manager of the business, a student with no business experience who was appointed as a de jure director by her father, was liable for *faute de gestion*, because she did not concern herself with the running of the business and simply obeyed the instructions of her father. The court did not accept the youth and inexperience of the daughter as exonerating circumstances. See also Cass com, 25 March 1997, *Bull. Joly Sociétés* 1997, 799, note G Baranger: 'That a part of the board of directors is composed of figurehead directors [*d'administrateurs de complaisance*] cannot be an argument to exonerate those who do not intend to raise their voice, express their concerns, have them recorded in the minutes, and ultimately resign'.

Cour de Cassation, Commercial Chamber, 30 March 2010, appeal no 08-17841 (*Crédit Martiniquais*)

Whereas, according to the judgments under appeal ... the Banking Commission inspected the Crédit Martiniquais and its main shareholder, Cofidom, from May to October 1996; two reports were issued on 24 October 1996, concluding that the situation of the company was severely compromised due to the serious insufficiency of provisions necessary to cover credit default risks; by a letter dated 30 September 1999, the chairman of the Banking Commission recommended that the Deposit Guarantee Fund (the Fund), which had just been established by the Law of 25 June 1999 ... should intervene for preventive purposes in the Crédit Martiniquais;[327] as part of the proposed plan, which was approved by the shareholders of the Crédit Martiniquais, the Fund paid out to the bank, now renamed Financière du Forum, the sum of 1,614,000,000 francs (246,052,713.82 euros) on 12 and 14 January 2000, of which 1,382,000,000 francs (210,684,541.82 euros) were intended to cover the shortfall in assets; with complaints served on 16, 17 and 18 May 2000, the Fund instigated legal actions for damages on the basis of Article L312-6 of the Monetary and Financial Code,[328] claiming reimbursement for the sums concerned, less those recovered, against the former directors of the Crédit Martiniquais and the persons who, according to the Fund, contributed wrongfully and deliberately to the seriously compromised situation of the company, in particular the auditors; ...

Whereas [the appellants] also criticized the judgment for having rejected the motion to dismiss the action for damages brought by the Fund in light of the statute of limitations applicable to that action, claiming, according to the ground of appeal put forward:

1°/ that the three-year limitation period pursuant to Article L225-254 of the Code de commerce runs from the time of the revelation of the harmful act, instead of the time when it was committed, only as against those persons who knowingly concealed the relevant facts; that [the appellants] emphasized in their submissions that they had never participated in any concealment of the harmful acts, so that the starting point of the limitation period of the action for damages brought against them should be the time when the harmful acts were committed; that by simply noting the existence of faults in the management of the bank, which were harmful and concealed, without investigating or determining that they were imputable to [the appellants], who would have knowingly concealed them, in order to argue that the starting point of the limitation period was the time when the harmful acts were revealed and thus reject the motion to dismiss based on the expiry of the limitation period, the Court of Appeal deprived its decision of a legal basis under the relevant provision; ...

6°/ that [one of the appellants] argued that the public had been informed by numerous press reports of the situation of the Crédit Martiniquais from the beginning of 1997; that, in addition to an article in the newspaper 'Libération' of 5 February 1997, they quoted in support of their claims an article from the newspaper 'Les Echos' dated 23 April 1997 ... ; that [one of the appellants] consequently ... concluded that the three-year limitation period had expired in the present case, given that the legal action of the Fund was brought more than three years after the public was informed of the situation, so that by confining itself to stating that the article in the newspaper 'Libération' of 5 February 1997 could not constitute a revelation within the meaning of the statute of limitations, based on the fact that the source of the information was not disclosed, in order to argue that the starting point of the limitation period was on May 20th, 1997, the date of the appointment of the temporary administrator, and that the action for damages was thus not time barred ... the Court of Appeal disregarded the requirements of Article 455 of the Code of Civil Procedure;

7°/ that the starting point of the period of limitation, being the date when the harmful act was committed, cannot be deferred unless the act was concealed, and that such concealment requires a knowing behaviour, which is necessarily assessed on an individual basis looking at each of the

[327] [Footnote by authors.] Such an intervention is based on Art L312-5 Code monétaire et financier [Monetary and Financial Code].

[328] [Footnote by authors.] Article L312-6 Code monétaire et financier provides, in relevant parts: 'The deposit guarantee fund is subrogated in the rights of the beneficiaries of its intervention in direct proportion to the sums it has paid. The guarantee fund may bring any action for damages against the de facto and de jure executives of the institutions it intervenes in to secure repayment of some or all of the sums it has paid'.

defendant directors, and that it falls on the claimant to prove such knowing concealment; that by simply noting that the alleged facts were such as to constitute extraordinarily harmful and perfectly concealed mismanagement without determining, with regard to [the individual appellants], an intent to conceal the harmful act suitable to defer the starting point of the period of limitation of the action for damages against any of the appellants, the Court of Appeal deprived its decision of a legal basis under Article L225-254 of the Code de commerce; ...

But considering, firstly, that it constitutes an individual fault of each member of the board of directors or supervisory board of a stock corporation [if the company has opted for the two-tier board structure] to participate, either through action or abstention, in a wrongful decision of this organ, unless it is demonstrated that he conducted himself as a prudent and diligent manager, in particular by opposing the decision; that the judgment states that the board of directors of the Crédit Martiniquais approved accounts not representing a true and fair view of the financial year 1996, stemming particularly from a deficiency in provisions amounting to 800,000,000 francs (€121,959,213.79), thus concealing the financial difficulties of the enterprise; that on these grounds alone, without being compelled to investigate further, since none of those who were directors at the relevant time established, or even alleged, that they personally opposed the decision adopting the financial statements, the Court of Appeal was entitled to infer the intention to conceal the harmful act on the part of each member of the board of directors and held correctly that the starting point of the three-year limitation period of the damages action against the directors should be the time when the act was revealed;

Considering, secondly, that it is by exercising its full judicial discretion regarding the assessment of the evidence submitted, that the Court of Appeal, which was not bound to explain the reasons for rejecting evidence and which has not ruled based on general reasons, determined that the harmful act could have been revealed at the earliest on May 20th, 1997, the date of the appointment of the temporary administrator by the Banking Commission;

Therefore it follows that the ground of appeal is unfounded in all its parts ...

Questions and comments:

1. In challenging the judgment of the Court of Appeal, the appellants focused on the interpretation of the statute of limitations pursuant to Article L225-254 Code de commerce, but the real importance of the decision lies in the Supreme Court's conclusions regarding the relationship between the directors' responsibilities as individuals and their collective decision-making as an organ. Liability under Article L225-251, and French tort law in general, are based on individual fault.[329] If several directors contribute to the loss inflicted upon the company, the law provides that they will be liable jointly and severally, but each director's fault continues to be assessed individually. This is the main point of the first ground of the appeal above. The appellants argued that the Court of Appeal misapplied the law in referring simply to the faulty decision of the board, which adopted the incorrect financial statements, without investigating whether the decision was attributable to the defendants, that is, whether each of the board members who were held liable had committed a management mistake. The burden of proof for showing a management mistake is generally borne by the plaintiff. This burden was not met, the appellants submitted, and the judgment lacked any determination that the individual defendants had failed to exercise the care of a prudent and diligent manager, not to mention that they had knowingly concealed the relevant facts so as to defer the start of the period of limitation. The Supreme Court did not accept this argument. It held that it was sufficient for the plaintiff to show that the board as an organ adopted a wrongful decision. Once this burden has been met, it is for the director to establish 'that he conducted himself as a prudent and diligent manager, in particular by opposing the decision'. In other words, the Supreme Court establishes the rebuttable presumption that 'it constitutes an individual fault of each member of the board' if the board adopts a wrongful decision.[330] This presumption applies not only to

[329] Martin and Tieu (n 303) para 13.

[330] On the question whether the Supreme Court's formulation should be interpreted as a rebuttable presumption, see P Le Cannu, 'La faute individuelle des membres d'un organe social collectif' (2010) *Revue des sociétés* 304

directors who participate actively in the board decision, but also to those who abstain. The latter must accordingly show that they had a good reason to abstain. Of course, in practice it may be difficult to show opposition to a wrongful board decision. The obvious source to substantiate the director's opposition are the minutes of the relevant meeting, but they may sometimes be very brief, fail to convey an accurate picture of the discussion preceding the decision, and in any case be anonymized. In addition, the possibility to articulate clearly an opposing view depends on the climate in the boardroom, the temperament of the directors, and the forcefulness with which debates are steered in a particular direction by the inside directors and in particular the president.[331] These are questions that the case law will need to address, thus refining the basic rule set out by the Cour de Cassation in *Crédit Martiniquais*.

2. Notwithstanding the special case discussed in the previous comment, French law distinguishes between so-called obligations of conduct (*obligations de moyens*) and obligations guaranteeing a certain result (*obligation de résultat*) in allocating the burden of proof in actions for damages. In the former case, the plaintiff bears the burden of proving that the obligation is violated, in the latter case it is presumed that the debtor acted in violation of the obligation if the promised result is not achieved. The duty to manage the company with due care and not to commit management mistakes is qualified as an obligation of conduct since directors generally only promise to employ their best efforts, but do not want to commit to achieving specified operational or financial results. However, the situation may be different where a director does not comply with legal requirements or violates the company's articles.
3. Another problem raised by the judgment but not answered conclusively is the different treatment, if any, of members of the board of directors with potentially very different backgrounds, for example full-time executive and part-time non-executive directors or directors with specialist knowledge and those without. If all board members are *prima facie* responsible for wrongful decisions of the board, what is the relevance of individual characteristics in rebutting the presumption that each board member is liable?[332] It has been argued in the literature that what is necessary to rebut the presumption should depend on the type of director. Independent outside directors who are inevitably less familiar with the company than the insiders can exonerate themselves by showing that they had no reason to suspect wrongdoing.[333] However, presumably no simple formula suffices to define what can be expected of outside (or inside) directors. All directors must be well informed and can be expected to make further inquiries, rather than simply rely on reports furnished by the executives, where a decision is of crucial importance to the company's future. For example, what would be the position of the independent directors in a scenario such as that in *Van Gorkom* under French law? We can also find case law, albeit predating *Crédit Martiniquais*, rejecting the liability of individual board members because they were inexperienced and played only a minor role in the management of the company.[334] Does this mean that directors who lack certain skills or experience can exonerate themselves more easily?[335] Conversely, is more required of directors with expert knowledge performing important functions on the board, for example as members of the audit committee? There are good reasons to answer at least the latter question in the positive. The courts tend to hold those to a higher standard who are entrusted with special duties, receive additional remuneration for the discharge of these duties, and possess particular expertise.[336] These three criteria are generally satisfied in the case of members of the audit

para 14. Le Cannu also argues that the rule established by the Supreme Court assumes relevance for all collegiate corporate bodies, see ibid para 5.

[331] On these points see ibid para 19.

[332] For a discussion of this point with regard to English law see text to nn 99–109 above.

[333] Le Cannu (n 330) para 22.

[334] TGI Guéret, 20 February 2007, no 06/00052 (*Abela c/ Gaudriot*) (liability for incorrect market disclosures). For a discussion see Martin and Tieu (n 303) para 17.

[335] Note that the TGI Guéret assessed the liability of the directors on the basis of the stricter standard that the fault had to be of a particular gravity and incompatible with the normal exercise of a director's corporate functions (see p 14 of the judgment), which on appeal was held not to be the correct standard (Cass com, 9 March 2010, see n 338 below). This may help to reconcile the judgment of the TGI Guéret with those discussed in n 326 above, where lack of competence was not accepted as an excuse.

[336] See P Merle, 'Les nouvelles responsabilités des comités d'audit' (2009) *Bull. Joly Sociétés* 216.

committee.[337]

4. Do we find in *Crédit Martiniquais* or other French decisions concerning management mistakes any signs of a legal institution comparable to the Delaware business judgment rule? If not, does this mean that directors face a greater risk of liability in France than, for example, the United States?

We mentioned above that the liability of directors to third parties (understood as parties other than the company *or* the shareholders[338]) is subject to narrower requirements.[339] Directors are only liable if the plaintiff can prove that they committed a fault separable from their functions (*faute séparable des fonctions*). Initially, the courts were reluctant to conclude that directors had committed a separable fault rendering them liable to third parties. Even intentional misrepresentations[340] or acting in transgression of the director's powers[341] were not held to give rise to liability. The first step towards a more assertive jurisprudence was taken in 2003. The Cour de Cassation found that the managing director of a company who assigned receivables twice, first to a bank and subsequently to a supplier as consideration for the delivery of goods, had committed a fault separable from her functions since she had intentionally misled the supplier about the solvency of the company.[342] The supplier, accordingly, had a claim for damages directly against the manager. In this decision, the Cour de Cassation also gave a definition of *faute séparable*, which the court described as 'an intentional fault of a particular gravity that is incompatible with the normal exercise of a director's corporate functions'.[343] Thus, according to this formulation, a separable fault consists of two elements: intentional misconduct and a fault of particular gravity. Following the judgment of 2003, the courts considered these two elements to be satisfied, for example, where a manager allowed an employee of a company to use a company car even though the car was no longer insured because the manager had failed to pay the insurance premium,[344] or where a manager, having received advance payment for a building project, assigned the contract to another company without informing the client and then liquidated the company in order to evade the contractual obligations to the client.[345] Incompetence, on the other hand, or inactivity of the directors generally do not qualify as separable faults.[346] In 2009, in the decision reproduced below, the Cour de Cassation developed the doctrine of *faute séparable des fonctions* further. This case is notable because the defendant directors had, arguably, merely exercised their management functions, rather than transgressing these functions and acting in a manner not connected with the company's operations.[347]

[337] Com, Art L823-19 requires the members of the audit committee to have expertise in finance or accounting and sets out the remit of the committee.

[338] Whether the shareholders were to be qualified as 'third parties', thus triggering the more stringent requirements that we will discuss presently, was a matter of some debate until the judgment in Cass com, 9 March 2010 (*Gaudriot*), *Revue des sociétés* 2010, 230, which clarified that the directors' liability to the shareholders was not subject to the same requirements as their liability towards third parties.

[339] See text to nn 70–71 above.

[340] Cass com, 28 April 1998, *Bull. Joly Sociétés* 1998, 888, note P Le Cannu.

[341] Cass com, 9 May 2001, *Droit et Patrimoine* 2002, 98, note D Poracchia (rejecting the liability of a director who granted a guarantee without the required approval by the board of directors).

[342] Cass com, 20 May 2003 (*Sté d'application de techniques de l'industrie (SATI)*), *Bull. Joly Sociétés* 2003, 786, note H Le Nabasque. This decision is discussed in Chapter 10E.I.

[343] ibid. [344] Cass com, 4 July 2006, *Recueil Dalloz* 2006, 1958, note A Lienhard.

[345] Cass 3e civ, 11 January 2012, no 10-20633.

[346] Cass com, 8 November 2017, no 16-10626, *Bull. Joly Sociétés* 2018, 84, note B Dondero; Cass com, 5 July 2017, no 15-22707, *Bull. Joly Sociétés* 2017, 678, note B Brignon; Cass com, 23 June 2009, no 08-15312, *Bull. Joly Sociétés* 2009, 1094, note B Dondero.

[347] Cass com, 10 February 2009, *JCP E* 2009, 1602, note B Dondero; *Bull. Joly Sociétés* 2009, 499, note S Messaï-Bahri; *Revue des sociétés* 2009, 328, note JF Barbièri.

Cour de Cassation, Commercial Chamber, 10 February 2009, appeal no 07-20445 (*Société de gestion Pierre Cardin c/ Société MMS International*)

Whereas, according to the judgment under appeal, the company MMS International, having terminated three license agreements concluded with the management company Pierre Cardin in March 2000 before their date of expiration, was ordered by final judgments of 19 May 2004 to pay a specified sum to the latter company; the management company Pierre Cardin, unable to obtain payment of this sum and arguing that the directors of MMS International had caused the insolvency of the company, sought to hold M. Albert Lucky, chairman of the board of directors, and M. Yves Lucky, general manager, liable; MMS International was placed under judicial receivership on April 12, 2006; …

Considering Article L225-251 of the Code de commerce;

Whereas, in order to reject the claim of the management company Pierre Cardin, after noting that it had been alleged that MM. Albert and Yves Lucky did not make provisions in the financial statements of MMS International from the financial year 2000 onwards for the amount of the license fees outstanding under the three license agreements improperly terminated and then for the amount of damages imposed on the company under the three judgments of the Commercial Court delivered in 2002 in spite of the auditor's repeated reservations, the Court of Appeal holds that the decision not to make special provisions for the years 2000 to 2003 was taken by the board of directors and approved by the general meeting of MMS International and that, even assuming that this decision constituted a breach by the company's directors, it could not be considered as separable from their functions, since such a decision fell perfectly within the scope of their functions;

Whereas, in deciding accordingly, without investigating whether the challenged actions constituted intentional breaches of a particular gravity incompatible with the normal exercise of the directors' corporate functions, even if they acted within the limits of their duties, the Court of Appeal did not provide a legal basis for its decision;

For these reasons … the decision of the Court of Appeal of Aix-en-Provence is set aside …

Questions and comments:

1. The decision of the Cour de Cassation seems to reach a paradoxical result. An action may fall within the scope of the directors' functions or duties, but nevertheless be separable from their functions. How is this possible? In addition, it is noteworthy that the decision of the Court of Appeal rejecting the directors' liability was overruled, even though the challenged action was taken by the board of directors and had been approved by the general meeting. This illustrates that the French courts seem to have adopted a more stringent approach to the responsibility of directors towards third parties since 2009.
2. Given that a fault separable from the directors' functions requires intentional misconduct, the parallels to criminal law are evident. Conversely, does every commission of a criminal offence by the director constitute a fault separable from the director's functions, without having to examine whether the fault is of a particular gravity?[348] This question was initially answered in the negative by the civil division of the Cour de Cassation,[349] but the commercial division decided in 2010 that a director who intentionally commits a criminal offence is liable to pay damages to those who were injured by the criminal act.[350] Such an act, the court held, is necessarily incompatible with the normal exercise of a director's corporate functions. In the case decided by the Cour de Cassation, the manager of a construction company had failed to take out mandatory liability insurance for construction defects, which constituted a criminal offence. When the company became insolvent, the buyers could not enforce their claims under the guarantee given by the company and instead claimed damages from the director. The court noted that

[348] The commission of a criminal offence requires, in principle, intent, see Art 121-3 para 3, Criminal Code.

[349] Cass 3e civ, 4 January 2006, *Bull. Joly Sociétés* 2006, 527, note S Messaï-Bahri.

[350] Cass com, 28 September 2010, *Droit des sociétés* 2011, no 225, note M Roussille. See also Cass com, 9 December 2014, no 13-26398, *RJDA* 3/15 no 199; Cass 3e civ, 10 March 2016, no 04-14731, *RJDA* 6/16 no 451.

the manager had negotiated with the insurance company but had not yet signed the insurance policy when the construction work commenced. Under these circumstances, the court concluded that the manager could not have been unaware of non-compliance with the insurance requirement and hence had committed an intentional fault.

3. In spite of the attempts of the courts to clarify the reach of the doctrine of *faute séparable des fonctions*, the requirements for holding directors responsible for the damage inflicted on third parties remain indeterminate and are refined by the courts on a case-by-case basis. This has led to a considerable degree of legal uncertainty, but in practice it is relatively rare that directors are found liable. Of course, third parties can sue the company if the director's misconduct is imputable to the company. In this case, the company can take recourse against the director without having to show that the harmful act was incompatible with the regular exercise of the director's functions. Internal liability follows the normal rules, so that any type of management mistake gives rise to an obligation to compensate the company.[351] Similarly, if the company has filed for insolvency and the liquidator claims that the directors' conduct contributed to the insolvency, it is not necessary to show a fault separable from the director's functions.[352]

(b) Criminal liability

Commercial Code[353]

Article L242-6—Offences relating to management and administration

The following shall be punished by a prison sentence of five years and a fine of 375,000 euros:

1° If the chairman, directors or managing directors of a public limited company distribute sham dividends between the shareholders in the absence of an inventory or using fraudulent inventories;

2° If the chairman, directors or managing directors of a public limited company publish or present to the shareholders, even in the absence of any distribution of dividends, annual accounts not providing, for each financial year, a fair representation of the results of the operations for the financial year, financial situation and assets on the expiration of this period, in order to hide the company's true situation;

3° If the chairman, directors or managing directors of a public limited company use the company's property or credit, in bad faith, in a way which they know is contrary to the interests of the company, for personal purposes or to benefit another company or undertaking in which they are directly or indirectly involved;

4° If the chairman, directors or managing directors of a public limited company use the powers which they possess or the votes which they have in this capacity, in bad faith, in a way which they know is contrary to the interests of the company, for personal purposes or to benefit another company or undertaking in which they are directly or indirectly involved.

...

The offence pursuant to subsection 3 shall be punished by a prison sentence of seven years and a fine of 500,000 euros if it has been carried out or facilitated by means of accounts opened or contracts signed with organizations established abroad, or the interposition of natural or legal persons or any organization, trust, or comparable institution established abroad.

The practically most relevant criminal offence applicable to the directors of public stock corporations and private limited companies is the abuse of corporate assets (*abus de biens sociaux*), laid down in the third paragraph of Article L242-6,[354] and, closely related to it, the abuse of the director's corporate powers or votes (*abus de pouvoirs ou de voix*) pursuant to

[351] Cass 1re civ, 15 May 2007, *Droit des sociétés* 2007, no 151, note R Mortier.

[352] Cozian, Viandier, and Deboissy (n 309) para 411.

[353] Translation by Legifrance, https://www.legifrance.gouv.fr/Traductions/en-English/Legifrance-translations.

[354] Article L242-6 applies to the *société anonyme*. For the *société à responsabilité limitée*, see Com, Art L241-3.

the fourth paragraph of the provision. Members of the board or managing (general) directors[355] commit the offence of abuse of corporate assets if they use the company's property or credit for their personal benefit or the benefit of another company in which they are directly or indirectly interested.[356] Since the provision is understood to protect not only the shareholders, but generally the company's assets and all parties who may be negatively affected by their depletion, it is irrelevant whether the general meeting or all of the shareholders unanimously approve the director's conduct or the directors compensate the company retroactively for the loss suffered.[357]

The offence has four elements, two of an objective and two of a subjective nature: Members of the board or managing directors must (1) use corporate assets (or, in the other alternatives of the provision, the company's credit, powers, or votes) (2) contrary to the interests of the company (3) in bad faith and (4) with the intention to use them for private purposes. The use of corporate assets may consist in the outright embezzlement of corporate funds, charging private expenses to the company's account, purchasing a luxury car or other items that serve no business purpose at the company's expense, extending a business trip in order to have a vacation, or exploiting a corporate opportunity.[358] It may also consist in acts of management that result in a waste of assets, in particular concluding a transaction that does not provide for any, or not for adequate, consideration for the company. This was held to be the case where a director received excessive remuneration[359] or remuneration that had not been authorized,[360] assets were transferred or services rendered at rates below market value within a corporate group,[361] or a director entered into a self-dealing transaction that was not of economic value to the company.[362] The company's credit is used if a director arranges for a company to grant a security interest over its assets or guarantee an obligation.

The use of corporate powers in paragraph four of Article L242-6 refers to conduct of the directors in exercise of the powers vested in them under the law. The offence may be committed both through action and inaction. For example, a director who does not take measures to prevent the company from suffering a loss arising from transactions with a customer who is heavily indebted may be liable, provided, of course, that the other conditions of the

[355] Managing directors include the general director (*directeur général*) and deputy general directors (*directeurs généraux délégués*), see Art L248-1 Code de commerce.

[356] Cass crim, 29 June 2016, no 15-81871, *Revue des sociétés* 2017, 104, note B Bouloc; Cass crim, 22 January 2014, no 12-87105, *Revue des sociétés* 2014, 452, note B Bouloc.

[357] Cass crim, 5 November 1963, *Bull. crim.* no 307 (not accepting the defendants' argument that they were not guilty of abuse of corporate assets because all of the shareholders had given their consent to the challenged act).

[358] For a list of examples and references, see Cozian, Viandier, and Deboissy (n 309) para 926; Merle (n 305) para 469.

[359] Cass crim, 22 September 2004, no 03-82266 (*Sté Sunn SA*), *Bull. Joly Sociétés* 2005, 45, note JF Barbièri. In this case, the president of the company received an annual fee of more than 2 million francs during a time when the company faced serious financial difficulties. He also manipulated the sales and earnings figures in order to influence the performance-based portion of his salary and caused the company to finance personal insurance contracts for him. The Court of Appeal had held that the president's activities did not constitute an abuse of corporate assets because the remuneration was determined by the board and not by the president himself, the statutory auditor and tax audit did not take issue with the amount of remuneration, the sales and earnings figures were later corrected, and the insurance contracts did not damage the company. The Cour de Cassation overruled this judgment, arguing that approval by the board, lack of objections by the auditors, and correction of the financial figures after the fact could not eliminate the criminal character of the president's conduct and that the Court of Appeal had not elaborated on the benefits that the company had allegedly derived from the insurance contracts.

[360] Cass crim, 22 March 2017, no 15-84229, *Revue des sociétés* 2017, 591, note B Bouloc (dealing with bonus payments that had not been authorized by the board of directors, as required by Art L225-53(3) Code de commerce).

[361] Cass crim, 25 October 2006, no 05-85998 (*Sté Lambda/Matra-Hachette*), *Bull. Joly Sociétés* 2007, 243, note JF Barbièri. In this case, two companies entered into an agreement requiring them to pay a fee equal to 0.2% of their consolidated revenue for management and other services provided by another company controlled by the same person who controlled the first two companies. Although the agreements were approved by the companies' general meetings, the court found that they were an abuse of corporate assets because the fees far exceeded the value of the services rendered.

[362] Cass crim, 12 September 2001, no 01-80895, *Droit des sociétés* 2002, no 6, note JJH Robert.

offence are satisfied.[363] Likewise, members of the board who approve a related-party transaction between the general manager and the company that is manifestly one-sided may abuse their powers,[364] as does the president of a company who uses his influence on the board to replace the members of the remuneration committee and obtain a more favourable remuneration package for himself.[365] On the other hand, the acquisition of shares in a competing company for the directors' own account does not qualify as an exercise of the powers that the directors possess in their capacity *as directors*, but their personal powers.[366] Finally, the last alternative of the offence, use of votes, applies to the exercise of proxy voting rights of the shareholders who entrust the directors with representing them at the general meeting.

The use of corporate assets or powers must be contrary to the corporate interest. As mentioned above, the notion of the corporate interest is elusive and must be interpreted in light of the relevant context, here the criminal offence of *abus de biens sociaux*.[367] Initially, the offence was intended to penalize the disregard of the separation between the company's assets and the directors' personal assets. Consequently, Article L242-6(3) applied in particular to the outright expropriation of corporate funds by the director and their use for private purposes.[368] However, because of the open-ended nature of the concept, the courts were able to construe the provision expansively.[369] Now any act that results in the diminution of the company's assets, the risk of such diminution, or the loss of an opportunity to realize a gain, may constitute a violation of the *intérêt social*.[370]

As far as the subjective elements of the offence are concerned, the statute imposes a double standard. The defendant must act with the general wilful intent to use corporate assets or powers contrary to the interests of the company and with the specific intent to use them for personal purposes. The director is presumed to have acted with the general intent to commit the offence if he or she must have been aware, in light of the circumstances, that the use of the assets infringed the company's interests.[371] The second subjective element, the furtherance of personal interests, is also understood broadly by the courts. Any material or immaterial, direct or indirect interest is sufficient. For example, directors act for personal purposes if they intend to maintain good relationships with political circles[372] or support a relative or friend.[373] Likewise, transactions concluded for the benefit of another company that is controlled by the directors or in which they are interested may qualify as an abuse of corporate assets.[374] In order to facilitate a proof of the furtherance of personal interests, the courts have established a rebuttable presumption that if assets are taken out of the company in a disguised manner, it will be assumed that the directors intend to use them for private purposes, unless they show that the assets were employed exclusively in the interest of the company.[375]

363 Cozian, Viandier, and Deboissy (n 309) para 926. 364 ibid.

365 Cour d'Appel de Versailles, 19 May 2011, *Bull. Joly Sociétés* 2011, 597, note B Dondero.

366 Cour d'Appel de Limoges, 21 November 1963, *Recueil Dalloz jurisprudence* 1964, 219.

367 See text to nn 309–314. 368 Merle (n 305) para 469.

369 The extensive interpretation was criticized in the literature, see for example C Mascala, 'Le dérapage de l'interprétation jurisprudentielle en droit pénal des affaires' (2004) *Recueil Dalloz* 3050 (arguing that the courts' approach violates the requirement to construe criminal offences narrowly in order to ensure predictability and legal certainty).

370 Cozian, Viandier, and Deboissy (n 309) para 927.

371 See, for example Cass crim, 26 September 2001, no 00-84368, *Bull. Joly Sociétés* 2002, 74 (holding that loans to companies formed by the directors without providing for any security in order to generate private profits constituted an abuse of corporate assets; the requirement of bad faith derived from the fact that the directors interposed legal persons and used a multiplicity of book entries to disguise the destination of the funds).

372 Cass crim, 14 November 2007, no 06-87378, *Revue des sociétés* 2008, 159, note B Bouloc.

373 Cass crim, 17 October 2007, no 07-81038, *BRDA* 2007, 3.

374 Cass crim, 26 September 2001, no 00-84368, *Bull. Joly Sociétés* 2002, 74.

375 Cass crim, 29 June 2016, no 15-84228, *Bull. Joly Sociétés* 2016, 648, note N Bargue; Cass crim, 31 January 2007, no 02-85089 (*Elf*), *Revue des sociétés* 2007, 379, note B Bouloc; Cass crim, 11 January 1996, no 95-81776, *Revue des sociétés* 1996, 586, note B Bouloc.

In some cases, the question arose whether an act that was illegal but gave the company material advantages could be contrary to the corporate interest. The following decision addresses this issue and offers general observations regarding the notion of the company's interest, as defined for purposes of the offence of abuse of corporate assets.

Cour de Cassation, Criminal Chamber, 27 October 1997, appeal no 96-83698 (*Carignon*)[376]

Whereas it follows from the judgment under appeal that at the end of 1985, Alain X [Alain Carignon], mayor of Grenoble since 1983, who intended to grant a concession for the supply of water to the city, indicated to Marc-Michel C that, if he wanted the group which he led to be considered in the tender that was about to be published, he should buy and make available to X an apartment in Paris; on 14 January 1986, the group C acquired a 280 sq. m apartment located at 286 Boulevard Saint-Germain in Paris for the sum of 5,000,000 francs and expended another 1,000,000 francs for works and furniture; the apartment was occupied from 1986 to 1988 by X, who became minister for the environment, under a lease concluded by the association 'Modernité Régionale', and by his advisor, Jean-Louis Y, leaving unpaid rent in the amount of 726,800 francs;

On September 1987, X, who had just benefited from a Mediterranean cruise with his family aboard a schooner rented for the occasion by the group C from 8 to 23 August 1987 at a price of 170,784 francs, informed C that he wanted ownership of the apartment on Boulevard Saint-Germain to be transferred to him as consideration for the award of the Grenoble water supply concession to group C;

The parties determined the main features of the concession award during a lunch on 3 October 1987 at the *conseil général* of [the county of] Isère … and the decision to grant the concession for a period of twenty-five years to the company COGESE, a joint venture of group C and Lyonnaise des Eaux, was finally signed by the mayor on November 3, 1989; …

On the fourth ground of appeal submitted by Alain X, based on its first two parts, the fifth and ninth grounds of appeal submitted by Jean-Louis Y and the grounds of appeal of the other applicants:

Whereas the applicants dispute that the expenses incurred by group C for the apartment on Boulevard Saint-Germain in Paris and the travels of X, and by the group Lyonnaise des Eaux [for other contributions made in connection with the concession] were contrary to the interests of the companies and the group interest, since the companies received as consideration the award of the water supply concession for the city of Grenoble to COGESE;

Whereas, in order to dismiss this argument, the judges point out that the costs of the benefits provided by the companies C, amounting to nearly 19 million francs, are part of a 'mad spiral of money' and that the 'considerable' amount of money allowed the companies to obtain the concession at a high price; they note that Marc-Michel C—who has not appealed against his conviction for abuse of corporate assets and bribery—acknowledged having acted in his personal interest with a view to maintaining good relations with the mayor of Grenoble and admitted that the various gifts made by the companies of his group to X and Y, whose demands were, according to him, 'verging on blackmail', were contrary to the corporate interest; …

Considering that, on the basis of these findings, the Court of Appeal established the offence of abuse of corporate assets in all its elements, including the violation of the corporate interest;

That, whatever the short-term benefits that may have been obtained, the use of corporate assets for the sole purpose of committing a crime such as bribery is in violation of the corporate interest in that it exposes the legal person to the abnormal risk of criminal or tax penalties against itself and its directors and damages its credit and reputation;

That, consequently, the grounds of appeal must be dismissed; …

For these reasons, the appeals of Alain X, Jean-Louis Y … are rejected …

[376] Discussed by JF Barbièri, *Bull. Joly Sociétés* 1998, 11; B Bouloc, *Revue des sociétés* 1997, 869.

Questions and comments:

1. The outcome in *Carignon* is not surprising, given the clearly illicit actions of the directors of the companies that were vying for the municipal water services concession. The directors, accordingly, were convicted of abuse of corporate assets and bribery, and the mayor and his adviser of receiving bribes and assets contrary to the company's interest. The case is not an outlier. In France, a large number of decisions have treated other cases of corruption and bribery similarly,[377] and other countries provide for equivalent rules imposing both criminal and civil sanctions on directors who use their company's assets to pursue illegal objectives.[378] More unusual is the court's line of reasoning. The court intimated that an illegal act *as such* was not necessarily contrary to the corporate interest, but that its disadvantageous consequences gave rise to the offence, namely exposing the company to the risk of criminal or civil liability and damaging its reputation, which would presumably outweigh the short-term benefits obtained as a result of the bribe. Could a similar argument be used in order to hold directors in such situations liable under, for example, section 172 of the UK Companies Act 2006 or §93(2) German Stock Corporation Act?
2. Criminal liability pursuant to Article L242-6 Code de commerce goes hand in hand with civil liability. A director who commits the offence of abuse of corporate assets will generally also be liable to pay damages under Article L225-251 Code de commerce for violations of the law and inflicting a loss on the company. In this case, the company or the shareholders can enforce their damages claims in the criminal courts by means of a so-called *action civile*.[379] The *action civile* has advantages for plaintiffs compared with instituting a lawsuit in the civil courts. The plaintiffs can take an active role in the criminal proceedings and benefit from the discovery conducted by the public prosecutor. For these reasons, it is an important mechanism to enforce directors' duties in practice.[380]
3. The French Code of Criminal Procedure provides that everybody who 'personally suffered damage directly caused by the offence' has standing to bring an *action civile*.[381] As we saw above, the offence of abuse of corporate assets aims to protect the company's assets for the benefit of the shareholders and all other stakeholders.[382] For this reason, damage that is 'directly caused' by the abuse within the meaning of the Code of Criminal Procedure is understood to refer only to the diminution of the company's assets, with the consequence that the *action civile* is open to the company[383] or shareholders enforcing the company's claim by way of an *action ut singuli*, but not to shareholders bringing an individual action.[384] It has also been held to be permissible for the acquiring company in a merger to enforce the claims of the acquired company or its subsidiaries where they suffered a loss as a consequence of the abuse of corporate assets.[385] On the other hand, the required direct causal link between the loss suffered and the offence does not exist if shareholders seek compensation in their own name for a depreciation in the value of the company's securities, which, in turn, resulted from an abuse of corporate assets by the chairman of the board.[386] Similarly, employees who suffer a loss because their share in the profits of the company is reduced or their employment terminated as a consequence of the abuse do not have standing to bring an *action civile*,[387] and neither

[377] For references, see Cozian, Viandier, and Deboissy (n 309) para 929.

[378] See, for example, the UK Bribery Act 2010. Pursuant to s 7 of the Bribery Act, the commercial organization is also liable if it did not have adequate procedures in place to combat bribes given with the intention to obtain or retain business for the organization. In addition, a director who uses corporate assets for personal profit is, of course, liable for a violation of the no-conflict/no-profit rule, s 175(1) Companies Act 2006.

[379] Code de procédure pénale [Code of Criminal Procedure], Arts 2, 3, 85.

[380] PH Conac, L Enriques, and M Gelter, 'Constraining Dominant Shareholders' Self-Dealing: The Legal Framework in France, Germany, and Italy' (2007) 4 European Company and Financial Law Review 491, 518–19; M Gelter, 'Why Do Shareholder Derivative Suits Remain Rare in Continental Europe' (2011–2012) 37 Brooklyn Journal of International Law 843, 887–8. See also our discussion in Chapter 8D.

[381] Code de procédure pénale, Art 2.

[382] See text to n 357 above.

[383] Cass crim, 16 February 1999, *JCP E* 1999, 1633, note JH Robert.

[384] See n 64 above.

[385] Cass crim, 2 April 2003, *Bull. Joly Sociétés* 2003, 929, note JF Barbièri.

[386] Cass crim, 12 December 2000, *Bull. Joly Sociétés* 2001, 497, note JF Barbièri.

[387] Cass crim, 7 March 2000, *Bull. Joly Sociétés* 2000, 720, note P Scholer.

do creditors who cannot obtain satisfaction of their claims because the company became insolvent.[388]

II. Internal control systems and excessive risk-taking

In large business organizations, the directors are not able to take all relevant operational decisions personally. The day-to-day management of the business is often delegated to professional managers, who may or may not be members of the board of directors.[389] The high-level managers in turn delegate functions to lower levels of management. The result is a complex system of delegated tasks and responsibilities. The directors have to rely on the information provided, and the orderly discharge of their duties, by those to whom tasks are delegated. However, most legal systems do not accept that the directors satisfy their duties simply by selecting the lower-level managers and trusting that the delegated tasks are carried out carefully unless they have reason to assume otherwise. Rather, the directors are required to be proactive, ensure that information is transmitted quickly and accurately within the organization so that they are fully informed of all relevant developments and misconduct is detected early on. The exact scope and content of this duty, which can be interpreted as an aspect of the directors' general duty of care, however, differ between jurisdictions and are not always well defined. This section deals with the answers developed by our four jurisdictions to the problems posed by complex business organizations and the impact that delegation has on the duties of company directors. First, we will discuss two English decisions that illustrate how the expectations imposed on directors to monitor and control their colleagues on the board and employees at lower levels of the business organization have changed over time, similar to the development of the general definition of due care in English law that we observed above.[390]

***Re City Equitable Fire Insurance Co Ltd* [1925] Ch 407 (Chancery Division)**

Romer, J:

The larger the business carried on by the company the more numerous, and the more important, the matters that must of necessity be left to the managers, the accountants and the rest of the staff. The manner in which the work of the company is to be distributed between the board of directors and the staff is in truth a business matter to be decided on business lines . . .

In order, therefore, to ascertain the duties that a person appointed to the board of an established company undertakes to perform, it is necessary to consider not only the nature of the company's business, but also the manner in which the work of the company is in fact distributed between the directors and the other officials of the company, provided always that this distribution is a reasonable one in the circumstances, and is not inconsistent with any express provisions of the articles of association . . .

In respect of all duties that, having regard to the exigencies of business, and the articles of association, may properly be left to some other official, a director is, in the absence of grounds for suspicion, justified in trusting that official to perform such duties honestly. In the judgment of the Court of Appeal in *In re National Bank of Wales, Ld.*[391], the following passage occurs in relation to a director who had been deceived by the manager, and managing director, as to matters within their own particular sphere of activity: 'Was it his duty to test the accuracy or completeness of what he was told by the general manager and the managing director? This is a question on which opinions may differ, but we are not prepared to say that he failed in his legal duty. Business cannot be carried on upon principles of distrust. Men in responsible positions must be trusted by those above them, as well as by those below them, until there is reason to distrust them. We agree that care and prudence do not involve distrust; but for a director acting

[388] Cass crim, 30 May 1994, *Bull. Joly Sociétés* 1994, 1205, note JJ Daigre.
[389] See Chapter 4D.I.
[390] Section B.I.1.
[391] [Footnote in the original.] [1899] 2 Ch 629, 673.

honestly himself to be held legally liable for negligence, in trusting the officers under him not to conceal from him what they ought to report to him, appears to us to be laying too heavy a burden on honest business men'. That case went to the House of Lords, and is reported there under the name of *Dovey* v. *Cory*.[392] Lord Davey, in the course of his speech to the House, made the following observations: 'I think the respondent was bound to give his attention to and exercise his judgment as a man of business on the matters which were brought before the board at the meetings which he attended, and it is not proved that he did not do so. But I think he was entitled to rely upon the judgment, information and advice, of the chairman and general manager, as to whose integrity, skill and competence he had no reason for suspicion. I agree with what was said by Sir George Jessel in *Hallmark's Case*[393], and by Chitty J. in *In re Denham & Co.*[394], that directors are not bound to examine entries in the company's books. It was the duty of the general manager and (possibly) of the chairman to go carefully through the returns from the branches, and to bring before the board any matter requiring their consideration; but the respondent was not, in my opinion, guilty of negligence in not examining them for himself, notwithstanding that they were laid on the table of the board for reference'.

Questions and comments:

1. Recall the excerpt of *City Equitable Fire Insurance* discussed in one of the previous sections of this chapter.[395] There, we said that the standard of care that directors had to employ was defined subjectively, taking into account the individual director's capabilities and experience, although we saw that the court's approach was somewhat ambivalent, including subjective as well as objective elements. This ambivalence of *City Equitable* can also be observed in the present excerpt. Romer J points out that in a large business the work of the company must necessarily be distributed between the directors and other members of staff. This distribution is a business decision, which implies that the directors enjoy a margin of discretion in how to structure the company's internal organization. In the opinion of Romer J, the distribution of responsibilities seems to have implications for the duties of the board members. He holds that we must interpret the scope of the directors' duties in light of the manner in which the work of the company is allocated. Directors, therefore, can limit their own exposure by delegating duties. However, Romer J introduces again an objective element. It is required that '[the] distribution is a reasonable one in the circumstances'. If this threshold condition is satisfied, 'a director is, in the absence of grounds for suspicion, justified in trusting [the official to whom duties were delegated] to perform such duties honestly'. Notably, directors are not required to make enquiries, verify information that they receive, and 'examine entries in the company's books', if they delegate the control of the financial or commercial operations, or some of them, such as branch operations, to other managers. Do these rules strike the right balance between the need to delegate tasks and trust officials at lower levels of the managerial hierarchy, and the overall responsibilities of the board for the company's business?
2. The next important step in the development of the directors' duties to exercise oversight and control was taken more than 70 years after *City Equitable* in the aftermath of a well-known corporate scandal that led to the downfall of Barings Bank, one of the oldest and most venerable banking institutions in Britain. We turn to this case next.

***Re Barings plc and Others (No 5)* [1999] 1 BCLC 433 (Chancery Division)**

[In 1995 the Barings Group collapsed following the unauthorised proprietary trading activities of a single trader, Nick Leeson, in Singapore. Mr Leeson was in charge of Baring Futures Singapore plc Ltd (BFS). Administration orders were made in relation to three companies in the group. The Secretary of State for Trade and Industry applied under s 6 of the Company

[392] [Footnote in the original.] [1901] AC 477.
[393] [Footnote in the original.] (1878) 9 Ch D 329.
[394] [Footnote in the original.] 25 Ch D 752.
[395] Section B.I.1.

Directors Disqualification Act 1986 for disqualification orders against three respondents, Mr Tuckey, Mr Baker, and Mr Gamby, who were executive directors of the companies and performed various functions on different committees, for example the executive committee of the Barings board that took all important management decisions or the 'asset and liability committee' that had oversight over Barings' trading books, including daily profit and loss positions reported from BFS in Singapore. The only issue before the court in relation to each of the respondents arose under s 6(1)(b) of the Act, namely whether his conduct as a director, in the specific respects complained of by the Secretary of State, was such as to make him 'unfit to be concerned in the management of a company'. The Secretary of State's general case was that each respondent was guilty of serious failures of management in relation to Mr Leeson's activities, thereby demonstrating incompetence of such a high degree as to justify a disqualification order. In particular: (i) from the time when he started trading on SIMEX in July 1992 until the collapse in February 1995, Mr Leeson was left in full control of both the front and back offices at BFS (i.e. dealing and settlement), and his roles were never segregated. This was allowed to occur despite the fact that in October 1994 an internal audit specifically recommended that his roles be segregated; (ii) from (at the latest) early 1994 until the collapse, Mr Leeson made unsubstantiated requests for funding on an increasingly massive scale, all of which requests were met and funds paid over to BFS without any proper investigation and without any attempt to reconcile the amounts requested with the underlying positions; (iii) the failures of the internal management controls within the Barings Group which allowed Mr Leeson to operate as he did, and which thus led directly to the collapse, were described as being 'crass' and 'absolute'.]

Parker, J:

[E]ach individual director owes duties to the company to inform himself about its affairs and to join with his co-directors in supervising and controlling them... It is of the greatest importance that any individual who undertakes the statutory and fiduciary obligations of being a company director should realise that these are inescapable personal responsibilities...

This does not mean, of course, that directors cannot delegate. Subject to the articles of association of the company, a board of directors may delegate specific tasks and functions. Indeed, some degree of delegation is almost always essential if the company's business is to be carried on efficiently: to that extent there is a clear public interest in delegation by those charged with the responsibility for the management of a business ...

But just as the duty of an individual director as formulated by the Court of Appeal in *Re Westmid Packing Services Ltd* does not mean that he may not delegate, neither does it mean that, having delegated a particular function, he is no longer under any duty in relation to the discharge of that function, notwithstanding that the person to whom the function has been delegated may appear both trustworthy and capable of discharging the function ...

It is not in dispute in the instant case that where delegation has taken place the board (and the individual directors) will remain responsible for the delegated function or functions and will retain a residual duty of supervision and control ... [T]he precise extent of that residual duty will depend on the facts of each particular case, as will the question whether it has been breached. These are matters which are in dispute in the instant case. It is the Secretary of State's case (denied by the respondents) that each of the respondents was incompetent in failing to discharge his individual duties as a director.

Directors' duties of skill, care and diligence have been exhaustively analysed by the Supreme Court of New South Wales in *Daniels v Anderson* (1995) 16 ACSR 607. Of particular materiality in the instant case is the following passage in the judgment (at 668):

> 'A person who accepts the office of director of a particular company undertakes the responsibility of ensuring that he or she understands the nature of the duty a director is called upon to perform. That duty will vary according to the size and business of the particular company and the experience or skills that the director held himself or herself out to have in support of appointment to the office. None of this is novel. It turns upon the natural expectations and reliance placed by shareholders on the experience and skill

> of a particular director … The duty includes that of acting collectively to manage the company'.

I respectfully adopt those observations as representing what I understand to be the law of England in this respect.

Where there is an issue as to the extent of a director's duties and responsibilities in any particular case, the level of reward which he is entitled to receive or which he may reasonably have expected to receive from the company may be a relevant factor in resolving that issue. It is not that the fitness or otherwise of a respondent depends on how much he is paid. The point is that the higher the level of reward, the greater the responsibilities which may reasonably be expected (prima facie, at least) to go with it. As Sir Richard Scott V-C said when making a disqualification order in respect of Mr Maclean (see *Re Barings plc, Secretary of State for Trade and Industry v Baker* [1998] BCC 583 at 586):

> '[Counsel for the respondent] made the point that if an efficient system is in place, or if the individual in question has good reason for believing there to be an efficient system in place, the delegation within the system of functions to be discharged in accordance with the system by others cannot be the subject of serious criticism if, in the event, the persons to whom responsibilities are delegated fail properly to discharge their duties. That may be so up to a point in theory, but the higher the office within an organisation that is held by an individual, the greater the responsibilities that fall upon him. It is right that that should be so, because status within an organisation carries with it commensurate rewards. These rewards are matched by the weight of responsibilities that the office carries with it, and those responsibilities require diligent attention from time to time to the question whether the system that has been put in place and over which the individual is presiding is operating efficiently, and whether individuals to whom duties, in accordance with the system, have been delegated are discharging those duties efficiently'.

In summary, the following general propositions can, in my judgment, be derived from the authorities to which I was referred in relation to the duties of directors:

(i) Directors have, both collectively and individually, a continuing duty to acquire and maintain a sufficient knowledge and understanding of the company's business to enable them properly to discharge their duties as directors.
(ii) Whilst directors are entitled (subject to the articles of association of the company) to delegate particular functions to those below them in the management chain, and to trust their competence and integrity to a reasonable extent, the exercise of the power of delegation does not absolve a director from the duty to supervise the discharge of the delegated functions.
(iii) No rule of universal application can be formulated as to the duty referred to in (ii) above. The extent of the duty, and the question whether it has been discharged, must depend on the facts of each particular case, including the director's role in the management of the company …

Questions and comments:

1. The court in *Barings* found that the three respondents were liable for breaches of the duty of care and, furthermore, that their breaches were serious, demonstrated 'a culpable degree of inactivity', and the directors bore 'a heavy responsibility' for Barings' insolvency. Accordingly, the court held that the directors were unfit to be concerned in the management of a company within the meaning of section 6 of the Company Directors Disqualification Act 1986 and made disqualification orders for them. In order to give a flavour of the conduct that amounted to a breach of duty, see the following excerpt of the internal report auditing the control structures of BFS:[396]

[396] [1999] 1 BCLC 606, 610–11.

In the first 7 months of 1994 BF(S)'s proprietary trading/arbitrage activities have generated an estimated $30 m in realised p&l. One focus of our audit was to seek answers to some of the questions raised by such exceptional results:

- Have the rules been broken to make these profits?
- Have exceptional risks been taken?
- Does the business have a monopoly situation?
- Are these profits going to last?

...

Back office controls

3.1 Concentration of Responsibilities in the role of General Manager

Despite the significant turnover of BF(S) it is a relatively small company with straightforward systems. Perhaps as a consequence of this both the front and back office operations are managed and controlled by the General Manager, Nick Leeson.

This represents an excessive concentration of powers; companies commonly divide responsibility for initiating, settling and recording transactions among different areas to reduce the possibility of error and fraud.

The back office has functioned efficiently under the current arrangements. The General Manager likes to be involved in the back office and does not regard it as an undue burden ...

In normal circumstances it would not be desirable for one individual to combine the roles of dealing and trading manager with those of settlements and accounting manager. Given the lack of experienced and senior staff in the back office, we recognise that the General Manager must continue to take an active role in the detailed operations of both the front and the back office.

Recommendation

BF(S)'s back office should be reorganised so that the General Manager is no longer directly responsible for the back office. Specifically the General Manager should not:

- Retain sole responsibility for the supervision of BF(S)'s back office team;
- Retain cheque-signing or journal-passing powers;
- Review and sign off SIMEX deposit, variation margin and collateral reconciliations; and
- Review and sign off bank reconciliations.

Besides the General Manager, BF(S) back office staff are relatively junior and inexperienced, it will thus be necessary for him to retain some involvement in the control areas. For example, he should continue to double-check the back office's output as often as he deems appropriate and be available to assist with reconciliation problems. He would of course continue to fulfil back office roles which do not involve the settlement and recording of transactions such as liaison with the SIMEX authorities and the arrangement of funding in conjunction with Group Treasury. We envisage the General Manager's current powers with respect to personnel matters such as recruitment and remuneration remaining unchanged.

The responsibility for performing daily bank reconciliations should be transferred to BS(S)'s accounts department.

A manager outside BF(S)'s back office should approve and sign off all journals and new account openings as well as perform a daily review of system-generated print-outs of journal entries and standing data amendments.

Other responsibilities relinquished by the General Manager should be taken on by the BS(S)'s Director of Finance and Operations. The main requirement is to ensure that the settlement and recording processes are adequately supervised ...

Mr Gamby, who was responsible for settlement in the banking, equities, and derivatives businesses, was a recipient of the audit report, but did not take any action. Mr Baker was head of a division of Barings called the Financial Products Group (FPG). The FPG had control over Barings' proprietary trading in derivatives. The actual trading was concentrated in five regional centres, one of them Singapore. The regional centres were managed independently, but FPG had global oversight.[397] Mr Baker, accordingly, was global head of the proprietary derivatives trading business, but he was not line manager of Nick Leeson, i.e. Mr Leeson did not report directly to him.[398] In his function as head of FPG, Mr Baker received the internal audit report, but did not act upon it. Mr Tuckey was a member of Barings' executive committee, the executive committee of BSL, a Barings' subsidiary operating as a broker dealer primarily in the Asia Pacific region and owning indirectly Baring Securities (Singapore) Ltd, and chairman of the management committee of a further subsidiary. He did not see the audit report. However, the court did not accept his contention that in having delegated the responsibility to supervise BSL to another committee, Mr Tuckey was divested of all supervisory responsibilities:

> 'Mr Tuckey relies on the fact that the Internal Audit Department reported to a Plc audit committee and not to [the management committee], "thereby preserving its independence from other management structures". In my judgment, however, the existence of an internal audit function reporting to a committee of which Mr Tuckey was not a member cannot have the effect of relieving Mr Tuckey of any of his management responsibilities as chairman of [the management committee] ... It is to be noted that Mr Tuckey is not saying in terms that he was aware at the time that there was an internal audit report in existence relating specifically to BFS. If he was aware of the existence of such a report, he should certainly have required a sight of it. If he was not aware of the existence of such a report, he cannot rely on the existence of the internal audit function as in some way reducing his management responsibilities in relation to BFS'.[399]

2. In light of *City Equitable Fire Insurance* and *Barings*, is the delegation of responsibilities permissible under English law? If yes, what are the remaining duties of the delegating director? In this context, what is the relationship between *City Equitable Fire Insurance* and *Barings*? Has the latter case overruled the former?[400]
3. The improvement of internal control structures continues to be high on the agenda of policy makers after the financial crisis of 2007–2008. The UK Corporate Governance Code 2018 provides that '[t]he board should ... establish a framework of prudent and effective controls, which enable risk to be assessed and managed'.[401] More specifically, the board is required to 'establish procedures to manage risk, oversee the internal control framework, and determine the nature and extent of the principal risks the company is willing to take in order to achieve its long-term strategic objectives'.[402] The principal risks, as well as the procedures adopted to identify emerging risks and manage or mitigate them, must be described in the annual report, and the board must carry out at least annually a review of the effectiveness of the company's risk management and internal control systems.[403] In addition to these soft law requirements,

[397] The structure was described by Barings as 'a federal structure centred in London': ibid 449.

[398] Barings operated two management systems, line management and the so-called matrix management. The court explained: 'Under [the matrix management system], each type of trading or business activity, or financial product, had a global head, responsible for the conduct of that activity or for that product throughout the world, and across the various companies in the Group. Matrix management is to be distinguished from "line management" (which the Group also operated). Line management involved juniors reporting to seniors in a particular geographic location or, as the case may be, within a particular company. A local manager in Barings might, therefore, fulfil the roles of both line manager in relation to his particular location or company, and matrix manager (also known as product manager) in relation to a particular trading activity or product worldwide': ibid 448. Thus, Mr. Baker performed the role of matrix manager, but not of line manager with respect to Nick Leeson.

[399] ibid 525.

[400] See for a recent case dealing with these issues *Lexi Holdings Plc (In Administration) v Luqman* [2009] EWCA Civ 117 (finding that two non-executive directors, the sisters of the executive director who had misappropriated funds, were liable because they remained inactive although they were aware of a directors' loan account and other transactions with connected parties which suggested contraventions of the law by the executive director).

[401] Principle C. [402] Principle O. [403] Provisions 28, 29.

similar (binding) monitoring and disclosure obligations are imposed on listed companies by the UK Listing Authority's Disclosure and Transparency Rules. Listed companies must describe the main features of the internal control and risk management systems in the corporate governance statement, which is part of the annual directors' report.[404] The report must be circulated to all members of the company, filed with the registrar, and (in case of a quoted company) published on the company's website.[405]

An important function in supervising the effectiveness of the company's control structures is played by the internal audit function. The Corporate Governance Code does not require companies to have an audit function, but the audit committee has to consider annually whether an internal audit function is needed and offer an explanation if it concludes that this is not the case.[406] For financial service providers (those carrying on a regulated activity within the meaning of Part IV of the Financial Services and Markets Act 2000), the FCA has promulgated detailed rules concerning the organizational structure and control systems that firms must, or should (where the rules are guidance), have in place, which include a compliance function,[407] audit function,[408] and, depending on the size, nature and complexity of the firm, a risk officer or risk committee as part of the firm's risk control arrangements.[409]

In the US, the leading Delaware case concerning the failure of directors to provide for adequate internal control structures and monitor the corporation's officers and other employees is *In re Caremark Intern. Inc. Derivative Litigation*.[410] The facts were as follows: Caremark was a provider of health care services. It had approximately 7,000 employees and ninety branch operations. In 1991–1992, several government agencies, among others the Department of Justice, commenced investigations of Caremark for violations of the Anti-Referral Payments Law, which prohibited health care providers from paying remuneration to induce the referral of Medicare or Medicaid patients, and other federal and state laws. Caremark had a practice of entering into consultation agreements and awarding research grants to physicians, some of whom prescribed or recommended Caremark services. The corporation had issued an internal guide advising its employees that no payments should be made in exchange for or to induce patient referrals. In addition, it had a board ethics committee and an internal audit plan designed to ensure compliance with business and ethics policies. However, there was some uncertainty within the corporation regarding the precise scope of the legal prohibitions.

After the commencement of the government investigations, Caremark revised its ethics manual, required employees to participate in training sessions concerning compliance with the law, and employed an outside auditor to review the corporation's internal control structures. The outside auditor did not identify any material weaknesses in the control structures. Caremark nevertheless took several additional steps to strengthen the supervision of management and branch operations. For example, it appointed a compliance officer and required branch managers to secure home office approval for specified transactions. The government investigations uncovered widespread violations of federal and state laws by Caremark's employees and a number of its officers, but no senior officers or directors were involved in the wrongdoing. Caremark entered into settlement agreements with the government agencies and private insurers that resulted in civil obligations and criminal fines totalling US$250 million. Minority stockholders brought a derivative action alleging that the directors had breached their duty of care by failing to supervise Caremark's employees adequately.

[404] Disclosure and Transparency Rules (DTR), 7.2.5R. The content of the directors' report and corporate governance statement are laid down in Companies Act 2006, ss 416–418, and DTR 7.2.

[405] Companies Act 2006, ss 423–453.

[406] UK Corporate Governance Code 2018, Provisions 25, 26.

[407] Senior Management Arrangements, Systems and Controls (SYSC), 6.1

[408] SYSC 6.2.

[409] SYSC 21.

[410] 698 A.2d 959 (Del. Ch. 1996).

The Court held:

***In re Caremark Intern. Inc. Derivative Litigation*, 698 A.2d 959 (Del. Ch. 1996)**

Allen, Chancellor:

1. Potential liability for directoral decisions:

Director liability for a breach of the duty to exercise appropriate attention may, in theory, arise in two distinct contexts. First, such liability may be said to follow from a board decision that results in a loss because that decision was ill advised or 'negligent'. Second, liability to the corporation for a loss may be said to arise from an unconsidered failure of the board to act in circumstances in which due attention would, arguably, have prevented the loss … The first class of cases will typically be subject to review under the director-protective business judgment rule, assuming the decision made was the product of a process that was either deliberately considered in good faith or was otherwise rational … What should be understood, but may not widely be understood by courts or commentators who are not often required to face such questions, is that compliance with a director's duty of care can never appropriately be judicially determined by reference to the content of the board decision that leads to a corporate loss, apart from consideration of the good faith or rationality of the process employed. That is, whether a judge or jury considering the matter after the fact, believes a decision substantively wrong, or degrees of wrong extending through 'stupid' to 'egregious' or 'irrational', provides no ground for director liability, so long as the court determines that the process employed was either rational or employed in a good faith effort to advance corporate interests. To employ a different rule-one that permitted an 'objective' evaluation of the decision-would expose directors to substantive second guessing by ill-equipped judges or juries, which would, in the long-run, be injurious to investor interests.[411] Thus, the business judgment rule is process oriented and informed by a deep respect for all good faith board decisions.

Indeed, one wonders on what moral basis might shareholders attack a good faith business decision of a director as 'unreasonable' or 'irrational'. Where a director in fact exercises a good faith effort to be informed and to exercise appropriate judgment, he or she should be deemed to satisfy fully the duty of attention. If the shareholders thought themselves entitled to some other quality of judgment than such a director produces in the good faith exercise of the powers of office, then the shareholders should have elected other directors …

2. Liability for failure to monitor:

The second class of cases in which director liability for inattention is theoretically possible entail circumstances in which a loss eventuates not from a decision but, from unconsidered inaction. Most of the decisions that a corporation, acting through its human agents, makes are, of course, not the subject of director attention. Legally, the board itself will be required only to authorize the most significant corporate acts or transactions: mergers, changes in capital structure, fundamental changes in business, appointment and compensation of the CEO, etc. As the facts of this case graphically demonstrate, ordinary business decisions that are made by officers and employees deeper in the interior of the organization can, however, vitally affect the welfare of the corporation and its ability to achieve its various strategic and financial goals … [W]hat is the board's responsibility with respect to the organization and monitoring of the enterprise to assure that the corporation functions within the law to achieve its purposes? …

[411] [Footnote in the original.] The vocabulary of negligence while often employed, e.g., *Aronson v Lewis*, Del.Supr., 473 A.2d 805 (1984) is not well-suited to judicial review of board attentiveness, see, e.g., *Joy v North*, 692 F.2d 880, 885-6 (2d Cir. 1982), especially if one attempts to look to the substance of the decision as any evidence of possible 'negligence'. Where review of board functioning is involved, courts leave behind as a relevant point of reference the decisions of the hypothetical 'reasonable person', who typically supplies the test for negligence liability. It is doubtful that we want business men and women to be encouraged to make decisions as hypothetical persons of *ordinary* judgment and prudence might. The corporate form gets its utility in large part from its ability to allow diversified investors to accept greater investment risk. If those in charge of the corporation are to be adjudged personally liable for losses on the basis of a substantive judgment based upon what persons of ordinary or average judgment and average risk assessment talent regard as 'prudent', 'sensible', or even 'rational', such persons will have a strong incentive at the margin to authorize less risky investment projects.

In 1963, the Delaware Supreme Court in *Graham v. Allis-Chalmers Mfg. Co.*,[412] addressed the question of potential liability of board members for losses experienced by the corporation as a result of the corporation having violated the anti-trust laws of the United States. There was no claim in that case that the directors knew about the behavior of subordinate employees of the corporation that had resulted in the liability. Rather, as in this case, the claim asserted was that the directors ought to have known of it and if they had known they would have been under a duty to bring the corporation into compliance with the law and thus save the corporation from the loss. The Delaware Supreme Court concluded that, under the facts as they appeared, there was no basis to find that the directors had breached a duty to be informed of the ongoing operations of the firm. In notably colorful terms, the court stated that 'absent cause for suspicion there is no duty upon the directors to install and operate a corporate system of espionage to ferret out wrongdoing which they have no reason to suspect exists'. . . .

How does one generalize this holding today? Can it be said today that, absent some ground giving rise to suspicion of violation of law, that corporate directors have no duty to assure that a corporate information gathering and reporting systems exists which represents a good faith attempt to provide senior management and the Board with information respecting material acts, events or conditions within the corporation, including compliance with applicable statutes and regulations? I certainly do not believe so. I doubt that such a broad generalization of the *Graham* holding would have been accepted by the Supreme Court in 1963. The case can be more narrowly interpreted as standing for the proposition that, absent grounds to suspect deception, neither corporate boards nor senior officers can be charged with wrongdoing simply for assuming the integrity of employees and the honesty of their dealings on the company's behalf . . .

A broader interpretation of *Graham v. Allis-Chalmers*-that it means that a corporate board has no responsibility to assure that appropriate information and reporting systems are established by management-would not, in any event, be accepted by the Delaware Supreme Court in 1996, in my opinion. In stating the basis for this view, I start with the recognition that in recent years the Delaware Supreme Court has made it clear—especially in its jurisprudence concerning takeovers, from *Smith v. Van Gorkom* through *Paramount Communications v. QVC*[413]—the seriousness with which the corporation law views the role of the corporate board. Secondly, I note the elementary fact that relevant and timely information is an essential predicate for satisfaction of the board's supervisory and monitoring role under Section 141 of the Delaware General Corporation Law . . .

In light of these developments, it would, in my opinion, be a mistake to conclude that our Supreme Court's statement in *Graham* concerning 'espionage' means that corporate boards may satisfy their obligation to be reasonably informed concerning the corporation, without assuring themselves that information and reporting systems exist in the organization that are reasonably designed to provide to senior management and to the board itself timely, accurate information sufficient to allow management and the board, each within its scope, to reach informed judgments concerning both the corporation's compliance with law and its business performance.

Obviously the level of detail that is appropriate for such an information system is a question of business judgment. And obviously too, no rationally designed information and reporting system will remove the possibility that the corporation will violate laws or regulations, or that senior officers or directors may nevertheless sometimes be misled or otherwise fail reasonably to detect acts material to the corporation's compliance with the law. But it is important that the board exercise a good faith judgment that the corporation's information and reporting system is in concept and design adequate to assure the board that appropriate information will come to its attention in a timely manner as a matter of ordinary operations, so that it may satisfy its responsibility.

Thus, I am of the view that a director's obligation includes a duty to attempt in good faith to assure that a corporate information and reporting system, which the board concludes

[412] [Footnote in the original.] Del. Supr., 41 Del. Ch. 78, 188 A.2d 125 (1963).

[413] [Footnote in the original.] *E.g., Smith v Van Gorkom*, Del. Supr., 488 A.2d 858 (1985); *Paramount Communications v QVC Network*, Del. Supr., 637 A.2d 34 (1994).

> is adequate, exists, and that failure to do so under some circumstances may, in theory at least, render a director liable for losses caused by non-compliance with applicable legal standards ...
>
> Generally where a claim of directorial liability for corporate loss is predicated upon ignorance of liability creating activities within the corporation, as in *Graham* or in this case, in my opinion only a sustained or systematic failure of the board to exercise oversight—such as an utter failure to attempt to assure a reasonable information and reporting system exists—will establish the lack of good faith that is a necessary condition to liability. Such a test of liability—lack of good faith as evidenced by sustained or systematic failure of a director to exercise reasonable oversight—is quite high. But, a demanding test of liability in the oversight context is probably beneficial to corporate shareholders as a class, as it is in the board decision context, since it makes board service by qualified persons more likely, while continuing to act as a stimulus to good faith performance of duty by such directors.
>
> Here the record supplies essentially no evidence that the director defendants were guilty of a sustained failure to exercise their oversight function. To the contrary, insofar as I am able to tell on this record, the corporation's information systems appear to have represented a good faith attempt to be informed of relevant facts. If the directors did not know the specifics of the activities that lead to the indictments, they cannot be faulted ...

The subprime crisis of 2007–2008 brought the importance of effective internal control structures and the limitations of the *Caremark* rule in protecting aggrieved shareholders into sharp focus. For example, *In re Citigroup Inc. Shareholder Derivative Litigation,*[414] decided by the Delaware Court of Chancery in 2009, dealt with a derivative action brought by shareholders of Citigroup seeking to recover for the company its losses from exposure to the subprime lending market. The plaintiffs claimed that the defendant directors and officers of Citigroup had breached their fiduciary duties by investing in collateralized debt obligations (CDOs) and accumulating an exposure of US$55 billion to the subprime mortgage market. The plaintiffs further alleged that the directors continued to invest in spite of mounting warning signs that market conditions were worsening, such as the bankruptcy of subprime lenders or the downgrade of mortgage backed securities by Moody's and Standard and Poor's.[415] The court first distinguished between the *Caremark* scenario, that is, liability for oversight failure (or board *in*action), and liability for director action:

> Plaintiffs' theory of how the director defendants will face personal liability is a bit of a twist on the traditional *Caremark* claim. In a typical *Caremark* case, plaintiffs argue that the defendants are liable for damages that arise from a failure to properly monitor or oversee employee misconduct or violations of law ... In contrast, plaintiffs' *Caremark* claims are based on defendants' alleged failure to properly monitor Citigroup's *business risk*, specifically its exposure to the subprime mortgage market ... Plaintiffs point to so-called 'red flags' that should have put defendants on notice of the problems in the subprime mortgage market ... Although these claims are framed by plaintiffs as *Caremark* claims, plaintiffs' theory essentially amounts to a claim that the director defendants should be personally liable to the Company because they failed to fully recognize the risk posed by subprime securities. When one looks past the lofty allegations of duties of oversight and red flags used to dress up these claims, what is left appears to be plaintiff shareholders attempting to hold the director defendants personally liable for making (or allowing to be made) business decisions that, in hindsight, turned out poorly for the Company.[416]

The court, accordingly, had doubts to qualify the plaintiffs' allegations as *Caremark* claims. It nevertheless engaged in a substantive analysis of the merits of the claims, applying the standard developed in *Caremark*:

[414] 964 A.2d 106 (Del. Ch. 2009). [415] ibid 113–15. [416] ibid 123–4.

To the extent the Court allows shareholder plaintiffs to succeed on a theory that a director is liable for a failure to monitor business risk, the Court risks undermining the well settled policy of Delaware law by inviting Courts to perform a hindsight evaluation of the reasonableness or prudence of directors' business decisions. Risk has been defined as the chance that a return on an investment will be different than expected. The essence of the business judgment of managers and directors is deciding how the company will evaluate the trade-off between risk and return. Businesses—and particularly financial institutions—make returns by taking on risk; a company or investor that is willing to take on more risk can earn a higher return. Thus, in almost any business transaction, the parties go into the deal with the knowledge that, even if they have evaluated the situation correctly, the return could be different than they expected. It is almost impossible for a court, in hindsight, to determine whether the directors of a company properly evaluated risk and thus made the 'right' business decision ...

It is well established that the mere fact that a company takes on business risk and suffers losses—even catastrophic losses—does not evidence misconduct, and without more, is not a basis for personal director liability. That there were signs in the market that reflected worsening conditions and suggested that conditions may deteriorate even further is not an invitation for this Court to disregard the presumptions of the business judgment rule and conclude that the directors are liable because they did not properly evaluate business risk. What plaintiffs are asking the Court to conclude from the presence of these 'red flags' is that the directors failed to see the extent of Citigroup's business risk and therefore made a 'wrong' business decision by allowing Citigroup to be exposed to the subprime mortgage market ...

Citigroup was in the business of taking on and managing investment and other business risks. To impose oversight liability on directors for failure to monitor 'excessive' risk would involve courts in conducting hindsight evaluations of decisions at the heart of the business judgment of directors. Oversight duties under Delaware law are not designed to subject directors, even expert directors, to personal liability for failure to predict the future and to properly evaluate business risk ...

[I]t is tempting in a case with such staggering losses for one to think that they could have made the 'right' decision if they had been in the directors' position. This temptation, however, is one of the reasons for the presumption against an objective review of business decisions by judges, a presumption that is no less applicable when the losses to the Company are large.[417]

Consequently, the court rejected all claims against the directors of Citigroup based on the CDO transactions. In a second high-profile case that dealt with excessive risk taking during the financial crisis, *In re Goldman Sachs Group, Inc. Shareholder Litigation*,[418] the plaintiffs advanced, again to no avail, the *Caremark* claim from a different angle. They alleged that Goldman's compensation structure, which linked compensation to the company's performance and awarded management a significant proportion of net revenue,[419] gave incentives to engage in risky trading practices and maximize short-term profits. It thus led, in the words of the plaintiffs, to 'unethical and illegal practices', and the directors 'failed to satisfy their oversight responsibilities with regard to those practices'.[420] The court examined the plaintiffs' claim under two aspects: the 'original' *Caremark* claim, which involved the failure to oversee conduct that led to violations of law, and the new version of the claim, which is in some sense a product of the subprime mortgage crisis and seeks to hold directors responsible for

[417] ibid 126–31. [418] 2011 WL 4826104 (Del. Ch. 2011).

[419] In the years 2007 to 2009, total compensation paid by Goldman to its employees ranged between 36% and 48% of total net revenue: ibid 3.

[420] ibid 2. The plaintiffs also alleged that the directors had breached their duty of care by approving the compensation structure and the compensation payments constituted corporate waste. These two claims also failed. Plaintiffs fared better in *In re American Intern. Group, Inc.*, 965 A.2d 763 (Del. Ch. 2009). However, in this case, in contrast to *Citigroup* and *Goldman Sachs*, the court found evidence of 'pervasive, diverse, and substantial financial fraud involving managers at the highest levels of AIG' (ibid 776). Thus, the court held that it was inferable that the defendant directors 'knew that AIG's internal control were broken' and the plaintiffs had successfully stated a *Caremark* claim (ibid 799).

not identifying and addressing business risks that lead to substantial losses. In the following excerpt, the court discusses both aspects.

***In re Goldman Sachs Group, Inc. Shareholder Litigation*, 2011 WL 4826104 (Del. Ch. 2011)**

Glasscock, Vice Chancellor:

1. Unlawful Conduct

[T]he Plaintiffs must plead particularized facts suggesting that the board failed to implement a monitoring and reporting system or consciously disregarded the information provided by that system. Here, the Plaintiffs assert that the Goldman employees engaged in unethical trading practices in search of short term revenues. Although the Plaintiffs' allegations fall short of the florid contentions about the corporation made elsewhere,[421] the Plaintiffs provide examples, based on the Permanent Subcommittee report, of conduct they believe was unethical and harmful to the company. The Plaintiffs argue that the Director Defendants should have been aware of purportedly unethical conduct such as securitizing high risk mortgages, shorting the mortgage market, using naked credit default swaps, and 'magnifying risk' through the creation of synthetic CDOs. The Plaintiffs also allege that Goldman's trading business often put Goldman in potential conflicts of interest with its own clients and that the Director Defendants were aware of this and have embraced this goal.

... The 'unethical' conduct the Plaintiffs allege here, however, is not the type of wrongdoing envisioned by *Caremark*. The conduct at issue here involves, for the most part, *legal* business decisions that were firmly within management's judgment to pursue. There is nothing intrinsic in using naked credit default swaps or shorting the mortgage market that makes these actions illegal or wrongful. These are actions that Goldman managers, presumably using their informed business judgment, made to hedge the Corporation's assets against risk or to earn a higher return. Legal, if risky, actions that are within management's discretion to pursue are not 'red flags' that would put a board on notice of unlawful conduct.

...

The heart of the Plaintiffs' *Caremark* claim is in the allegation that Goldman's 'trading practices have subjected the Firm to civil liability, via, inter alia, an SEC investigation and lawsuit'. Once the legal, permissible business decisions are removed, what the Plaintiffs are left with is a single transaction that Goldman settled with the SEC.

In 2007 Goldman designed a CDO, Abacus 2007–AC1, with input from the hedge fund founder John Paulson. The Plaintiffs allege that Paulson helped select a set of mortgages that would collateralize the CDO and then took a short position, betting that the same mortgages would fall in value. The Plaintiffs point out that meanwhile Goldman was selling long positions in the CDO without disclosing Paulson's role in selecting the underlying collateral or Paulson's short position. The Plaintiffs allege that 'Goldman's clients who took long positions in Abacus 2007–AC 1 lost their entire $1 billion investment'. As a result, on April 16, 2010 the SEC charged Goldman and a Goldman Vice President with fraud for their roles in creating and marketing Abacus 2007–AC 1. On July, 14, 2010, Goldman settled the case with the SEC. As part of the settlement, Goldman agreed to disgorge its profits on the Abacus transaction, pay a large civil penalty, and evaluate various compliance programs.

The Abacus transaction, with its disclosure problems, is unique. The complaint does not plead with factual particularity that the other highlighted transactions contain disclosure omissions similar to Abacus, and the Abacus transaction on its own cannot demonstrate the willful ignorance of 'red flags' on the part of the Defendants that might lead to a reasonable apprehension of liability. Though the Plaintiffs allege that the 'Abacus deals are likely just the tip of the iceberg', conclusory statements are not particularized pleadings. The single Abacus transaction without more is insufficient to provide a reasonable inference of bad faith on the part of the Director Defendants.

[421] [Footnote in the original.] Matt Taibbi, *The Great American Bubble Machine*, Rolling Stone Magazine, 9–23 July 2009, at 52 ('[Goldman] is a great vampire squid wrapped around the face of humanity, relentlessly jamming its blood funnel into anything that smells like money').

2. Business Risk

Part of the Plaintiffs' *Caremark* claim stems from the Director Defendants' oversight of Goldman's business practices. As a preliminary matter, this Court has not definitively stated whether a board's *Caremark* duties include a duty to monitor business risk. In *Citigroup*, then-Chancellor Chandler posited that 'it may be possible for a plaintiff to meet the burden under some set of facts'. Indeed, the *Caremark* court seemed to suggest the possibility of such a claim ...

As was the case in *Citigroup*, however, the facts pled here do not give rise to a claim under *Caremark*, and thus I do not need to reach the issue of whether the duty of oversight includes the duty to monitor business risk.

As the Court observed in *Citigroup*, 'imposing *Caremark*-type duties on directors to monitor business risk is fundamentally different' from imposing on directors a duty to monitor fraud and illegal activity ...

Although the Plaintiffs have molded their claims with an eye to the language of *Caremark*, the essence of their complaint is that I should hold the Director Defendants 'personally liable for making (or allowing to be made) business decisions that, in hindsight, turned out poorly for the Company'. If an actionable duty to monitor business risk exists, it cannot encompass any substantive evaluation by a court of a board's determination of the appropriate amount of risk. Such decisions plainly involve business judgment.[422]

... Goldman had an Audit Committee in place that was 'charged with assisting the Board in its oversight of the Company's management of market, credit liquidity and other financial and operational risks'. ...

Goldman's board and management made decisions to hedge exposure during the deterioration of the housing market, decisions that have been roundly criticized in Congress and elsewhere. Those decisions involved taking objectively large risks, including particularly reputational risks. The outcome of that risk-taking may prove ultimately costly to the corporation. The Plaintiffs, however, have failed to plead with particularity that the Director Defendants consciously and in bad faith disregarded these risks; to the contrary, the facts pled indicate that the board kept itself informed of the risks involved. The Plaintiffs have failed to plead facts showing a substantial likelihood of liability on the part of the Director Defendants under *Caremark*.

Questions and comments:

1. Compare *Caremark* with *Barings*. Is the English standard for holding directors responsible for a failure to establish effective control structures more stringent than the Delaware standard? Is it more appropriate?
2. The court in *Goldman* leaves the question open whether a duty to monitor business risk exists. However, *in obiter* the court also suggests a possible standard of review if such a duty is found to exist. The plaintiff must show 'that the board *consciously* failed to implement any sort of risk monitoring system or, having implemented such a system, *consciously* disregarded red flags signalling that the company's employees were taking facially improper, and not just ex-post ill-advised or even bone-headed, business risks'.[423] This definition, of course, is modelled along the lines of the *Caremark* bad faith standard. But is it really merely a *process-based* standard, i.e. a standard directed at the actions that the directors have taken to ensure that proper information systems are in place, or is it a standard that is even more difficult to satisfy by the plaintiffs, since it refers to the conscious failure to implement risk monitoring systems *and* the disregard of red flags? According to the court, the existence of red flags seems to depend on the *content* of the decision engendering business risk, not only the process of decision-making.

[422] [Footnote in the original.] While a valid claim against a board of directors in a hierarchical corporation for failure to monitor risk undertaken by corporate employees is a theoretical possibility, it would be, appropriately, a difficult cause of action on which to prevail. Assuming excessive risk-taking at some level becomes the misconduct contemplated by *Caremark*, the plaintiff would essentially have to show that the board *consciously* failed to implement any sort of risk monitoring system or, having implemented such a system, *consciously* disregarded red flags signaling that the company's employees were taking facially improper, and not just ex-post ill-advised or even bone-headed, business risks. Such bad-faith indifference would be formidably difficult to prove ...

[423] ibid.

This is an aspect of managerial conduct that the courts normally do not review under the business judgment rule. In other words, has the *Caremark* standard, under *Goldman*, been conflated with the concept of waste?[424]

3. What is the function of a duty to monitor business risk? First, it addresses the agency problem between the shareholders and directors/managers. Excessive risk-taking potentially leads to substantial losses and diminishes shareholder equity, as could be seen in both *Citigroup* and *Goldman*. However, the problem is more complex, as the subprime mortgage crisis has shown. If a company is of systemic importance because of its interconnectedness, financial distress experienced by the company may have ripple effects and lead to losses suffered by other market participants. This is an example of the well-known economic problem of externalities. Externalities lead to an inefficiently high (in the case of negative externalities[425]) or low (positive externalities[426]) activity level. Consider a competitive market where the price of a good does not change with the quantity that any given producer supplies. The producer will produce more goods up to the point where the cost of producing one additional unit of the good (marginal cost) equals the revenue that the producer obtains for that unit (marginal revenue), which is the price of the good in the market. Thus, producers supply the quantity demanded where marginal cost equals marginal revenue. This is called an efficient equilibrium because customers would not pay a higher price and suppliers would not produce a larger quantity at the same price. Now consider that some costs of the production process are externalized, for example because the producers are not liable for the environmental damage they cause. These costs are, accordingly, not part of the producers' production function; in a graph, their (private) marginal cost curve is below that of society, since society bears the costs of environmental degradation. This means that they can supply a larger quantity at the same price than producers with fully internalized costs. The result is an inefficiently high level of production.

   This intuition can be applied to the financial markets. If the costs of risk-taking are partially externalized because they are borne by other market participants or the taxpayer when the government bails out distressed institutions, companies have an incentive to engage in a socially inefficient level of risk-taking. This is not identical to the managerial agency problem. Shareholders may benefit as much from excessive risk-taking as managers (or more); they may not, therefore, demand that the managers adopt a more conservative business strategy. In fact, it was pointed out in the wake of the subprime mortgage crisis that shareholders did not oppose 'misaligned' incentive structures.[427] Rather, they 'encouraged financial institutions to act in a short-term perspective and to make as much profit as possible to the detriment of credit quality and prudence'.[428] In light of these considerations, should corporate governance mechanisms such as the duty of care apply in the regular way to constrain excessive risk-taking, for example in the form of the Delaware business judgment rule and the *Caremark* claim, or do they require modification? Alternatively, are other regulatory strategies more promising to address this problem?

4. The Delaware Court of Chancery's decisions in *Goldman* and *Citigroup* and the decision of the Higher Regional Court Düsseldorf in *IKB*, discussed above,[429] come to markedly different outcomes on the basis of similar facts. How can we explain these differences? Are they a function of differences in the legal rules? Note that both courts applied their versions of the business judgment rule. As we mentioned above,[430] the German business judgment rule (§93(1) sentence 2 Stock Corporation Act) was inspired by the Delaware rule. If the differences in outcome, accordingly, cannot be explained satisfactorily in light of legal differences, what drives them? As you read the three decisions, did you note any difference in terms of the courts'

[424] See text to nn 194–203 above.

[425] Negative externalities are costs that are not reflected in the price of a good, for example the consequences of pollution. See also Chapter 4A.I.

[426] Positive externalities are benefits not reflected in the price of a good.

[427] Communication from the European Commission of 30 April 2009, COM(2009) 211 final, 2.

[428] European Commission, Report of the High-Level Group on EU financial supervision (de Larosière report) (February 2009), 30.

[429] B.I.3. [430] ibid.

style of reasoning and approach to the business judgment rule? Could the observed differences have something to do with the fact that the Court of Chancery is a 'specialized' court dealing mainly with company law matters and its judges are experts in corporate law, whereas the Higher Regional Court Düsseldorf is a general court? Which court develops the more appropriate solution to the problem of excessive risk-taking?

In our two civil law countries, courts and policy makers of course faced the same questions of how to adapt the duty of care in the context of delegated decision-making and what to expect of directors with respect to the establishment of internal control structures. In Germany, it is undisputed that the duties to monitor and, where appropriate, establish internal control and information systems are part of the management board's general managerial responsibilities,[431] which may lead to liability pursuant to §93(2) Stock Corporation Act if the directors neglect them.[432] If duties are allocated horizontally between different members of the board or delegated to subordinates, the directors retain a residual duty to supervise and control. They are required to monitor their colleagues on the board and intervene when the circumstances indicate that a responsible director does not perform allocated tasks adequately.[433]

As far as the vertical delegation of functions is concerned, the duty to monitor can be broken down into several more specific behavioural standards. Directors are responsible for the careful selection, instruction, and supervision of those to whom duties are delegated.[434] They must, first of all, ensure that the persons possess the necessary personal and professional qualifications to be able to discharge the functions properly. Secondly, they must instruct them comprehensively and, if necessary, provide for training and continuing education. Depending on the circumstances, directors may be required to give not only general instructions, but also highlight specific legal requirements and technical hazards.[435] Thirdly, the directors are required to supervise the discharge of the delegated functions. The intensity of the duty to monitor depends on the size and organizational structure of the company, the experience and qualifications of the instructed person, the importance of the delegated tasks, and the financial situation of the enterprise. For example, while directors are generally entitled to trust those to whom they have delegated functions, they may be expected to monitor the discharge of the duties more closely and make regular checks if the company is in financial distress and the orderly fulfilment of the company's obligations does not seem to be ensured.[436]

A decision of the Federal Court of Justice from 1996 illustrates these principles.[437] A private limited company had two managing directors. The company had financial problems and did not pay national insurance contributions for its employees, which constituted a criminal offence. The directors argued that they were not personally responsible for the payments, but had delegated this task to the company's clerk. The court emphasized that the

[431] Derived from §76 AKTG.

[432] See BT-Drs [Documentation of the Federal Parliament] 13/9712, 15.

[433] BGHZ 133, 370, 378; OLG Köln, AG 2001, 363, 364. But see Administrative Court Frankfurt am Main (n 247). The Administrative Court distinguished between matters that fell within the director's scope of duties and matters for which another member of the management board was responsible. As regards the latter, the court held that it was generally sufficient to review the plausibility of reports and other information received from subordinates, unless there was reason for suspicion (para 23). Matters falling within the director's own or a closely related field, however, required more than a simple plausibility check. The director was 'under the obligation to inquire actively, procure verifiable documents, and in case the verification fails ... inform the management board and, if necessary, the supervisory board'. ibid.

[434] BGH NJW 1995, 326, 329.

[435] See, for example, KG [Higher Regional Court] Berlin, 25 July 1980, WuW/E OLG 2330 (*Revisionsabteilung*) (holding that the duty to supervise required more than the instruction not to violate applicable competition laws; generally, the directors had to advise the employees specifically and in writing of applicable legal requirements, if necessary including a list of typical examples of prohibited price-fixing agreements).

[436] BFH [Federal Fiscal Court], judgment of 26 April 1984, V R 128/79.

[437] BGHZ 133, 370.

company was required under law to pay national insurance contributions and it was part of the managing directors' duties to make sure that the company did not act illegally. This responsibility did not end with the delegation to the clerk, but was transformed into the duty to monitor and intervene if necessary. In the present case, the directors were held to have violated these duties. They were not allowed to rely on the clerk and expect the timely payment of the contributions because they knew that the company was in financial difficulties and payments had been deferred in the past in agreement with the relevant public authorities. Under such circumstances, the directors had to ensure the orderly payment personally.[438]

In addition, the Stock Corporation Act now contains an explicit duty to establish internal control and information systems. This duty is laid down in §91(2).

German Stock Corporation Act

§ 91—Organisation. Accounting

(1) The management board shall keep the necessary books and accounts.
(2) The management board shall adopt suitable measures and in particular establish an internal control system in order to ensure the early detection of developments endangering the continued existence of the company.

The provision was introduced in 1998[439] in order to amplify the directors' obligations and codify case law that had always recognized a duty to provide for control structures.[440] Similar to the delegation of specific functions to individuals, the content of the duty depends on factors including the size and structure of the company, the industry, and the existence of a public market for the company's shares.[441] According to the legislator, 'developments endangering the continued existence of the company' include risky transactions, accounting irregularities, and violations of the law that have significant implications for the financial position of the company or corporate group.[442] It has been argued in the literature that the goal of the provision is not the establishment of a system that allows the *management* of the company's risk profile.[443] Rather, more narrowly, the directors are required to implement structures that *detect* developments putting the company's continued existence at risk and enable them to adopt countermeasures before it is too late. The directors must, therefore, ensure that the internal audit and control functions work well and they are informed about critical developments without delay. This involves a clear determination of responsibilities, lines of reporting, and adequate documentation standards.[444] In a corporate group, the parent's control system must cover developments in subsidiaries that may affect the position of the parent.[445] On the other hand, §91(2) does not deal with the question of how risks that have been identified are to be managed. The directors decide in line with their general responsibilities whether and how to respond.

If a company is stock exchange listed, the external auditor has to pass an opinion on the suitability of the adopted measures and the existence of a control system that is able to perform the required functions.[446] The result of the review has to be presented in a separate

[438] ibid 378–9.

[439] Gesetz zur Kontrolle und Transparenz im Unternehmensbereich (KonTraG) [Control and Transparency in the Corporate Sector Act] of 1 May 1998, BGBl. I, 786, Art 1 no 9.

[440] See, e.g., OLG Köln, AG 2001, 363, 364.

[441] See the explanatory memorandum for the amendment in n 432 above, 15.

[442] ibid.

[443] Koch (n 57) §91, paras 8–9. More detailed regulations apply to credit institutions governed by the Kreditwesengesetz (KWG) [Banking Act], including the requirement to provide for 'an adequate and effective risk management system', see §§25a, 26a KWG.

[444] Koch (n 57) §91 para 10.

[445] Explanatory memorandum for the amendment in n 432 above, 15. See also BGH NJW 2009, 850, 852 (*MSP*).

[446] HGB, §317(4), inserted by Gesetz zur Kontrolle und Transparenz im Unternehmensbereich (n 439) Art 2 no 6.

part of the audit report, including, where necessary, suggestions for improvements of the control system.[447] In addition, the German Corporate Governance Code provides that the internal audit committee, which has to be set up as a committee of the supervisory board of listed companies, oversees the effectiveness of the internal control system.[448] Failing to establish an effective control system may lead to liability of the members of the management board as well as the supervisory board.[449] Since §91(2) is an expression of the general duties of directors, the company can claim damages pursuant to §93(2) in accordance with the principles governing the responsibility of directors discussed above.[450] In particular, the directors bear the burden of proving that the control system is adequate and the board is informed in a timely manner.[451]

In France, as in our other jurisdictions, the duties of directors do not end with the delegation of functions. First of all, the members of the board of directors are required to monitor the activities of the general director and the deputy general directors.[452] However, cases where directors have been found liable for lack of monitoring are relatively rare and generally relate to a complete failure to participate in the management of the company and take action where reasons for concern existed. For example, the Court of Appeal Paris found three directors of a board of four responsible for parts of the debts of a company in insolvency (*responsabilité pour insuffisance d'actif*) because they had failed to supervise the fourth director, who had been appointed as *président directeur général*, under circumstances where they 'had not taken any part in the management and administration of the company during the 18 months from the date of their appointment until the date of their dismissal'.[453] In another case, *Société Etablissements Victor Glorieux*, again decided in the context of an *action de la responsabilité pour insuffisance d'actif*, the question arose whether the directors should have uncovered the wrongdoings of the *président directeur general*.[454] The facts resemble in many ways *City Equitable Fire Insurance*. The company's board was composed of the general director, two of his close relatives, and a corporate director that had formed Etablissements Victor Glorieux through a division. The general director had not only managed the business poorly, but also embezzled funds and falsified the accounts in order to conceal his wrongdoings and the precarious financial situation of the company. The other directors argued that they had not been aware of the general director's misconduct and had, in hindsight, 'overestimated his abilities and character'.[455]

The court's conclusion that the directors were liable for oversight failure was based on several considerations. First, the court found it 'incomprehensible that the directors of the insolvent company had left the entire management of the business to Victor Glorieux [the general director] ... without supervising him thoroughly'.[456] Already the fact that the directors had completely abstained from taking part in the company's management, except for a few minor interventions, justified holding them responsible for the company's debts. Secondly, the directors worked in the same profession, possessed the skills to exercise

[447] HGB, §321(4).

[448] German Corporate Governance Code 2017, 5.3.2. The law does not require the establishment of an internal audit committee for all stock corporations, but provides for the possibility to set up such a committee, see AKTG, §107(3) sentence 2. This is in compliance with Directive 2006/43/EC on statutory audits of annual accounts and consolidated accounts, which permits Member States to provide that the functions of the audit committee, such as monitoring of the company's internal controls (Art 41(2)(b)), may be performed by the supervisory board as a whole or by a body having equivalent functions to an audit committee, Art 41(1), (5) Directive 2006/43/EC. See also §324 HGB, which requires the establishment of an audit committee in certain types of company without a supervisory board.

[449] BGH NJW 2009, 850, 853. [450] See section B.I.3. [451] BGH NJW 2009, 850, 853.

[452] See text to n 320 above.

[453] Cour d'Appel de Paris, 8 March 1958, *Recueil Dalloz jurisprudence* 1958, 342.

[454] T com Roubaix, 26 September 1956, *Recueil Dalloz jurisprudence* 1957, 10, note F Goré.

[455] ibid 12. [456] ibid.

active and effective supervision over the business, and were closely related to the general director. For these reasons, the court held that they had to meet higher standards than directors in many other situations. Thirdly, the accounts showed irregularities, for example, current assets were partly composed of items such as an undefined 'client account'. These irregularities should have alerted the directors and caused them to conduct an investigation, which would have revealed the falsifications by the general director. Instead, by relying on the 'incorrect explanations furnished by Victor Glorieux, without making an effort to verify them', the directors had breached their duties.[457]

The judgment falls short of imposing a duty on directors to be intimately involved in all aspects of the company's operations and question the information provided by the executives as a matter of course. On the other hand, it illustrates that directors are expected to exercise some minimum level of supervision even if they do not have any reason for suspicion. Being passive and refusing to play any role in the company's administration will make it difficult for the directors to argue that they discharged their duties adequately. More is expected of directors who are well positioned to appreciate the company's business and assess its financial situation, given their skills and experience. Finally, if specific facts, for example accounting irregularities, indicate problems, the directors are required to investigate and, importantly, verify the explanations given by the general manager or other persons.[458]

Furthermore, the executive directors cannot avoid liability by pointing out that they delegated functions to lower-level executives. For example, the *président-directeur général* of a public stock corporation selling computer hardware was held criminally liable for tax evasion even though he claimed that he had delegated the respective duties to the finance director.[459] In this case, the conviction was based partly on the fact that the director had retained effective oversight of the discharge of the company's duties towards the tax authorities. By virtue of his position, a general director bears ultimate responsibility for violations that occur in the company. However, for purposes of criminal liability, the director may exonerate himself by showing that he delegated duties to a person who was competent and authorized to discharge them independently.[460]

The Code de commerce contains few provisions dealing with the duty to monitor and the establishment of internal control and risk management systems. The Code empowers the board of directors to carry out all inspections and verifications of the business that it considers appropriate, which shows that the board is seen as the highest controlling organ in the company.[461] Among the board members, the chairman occupies a position of particular responsibility. He or she must ensure that the other directors are capable of performing their functions, in particular that they receive the relevant information from the managers, possess the necessary qualifications, and have the physical capacity to discharge their monitoring duties effectively.[462]

In companies with securities admitted to trading on a regulated market, the chairman of the board must include a description of the main features of the company's risk management and internal control systems in the corporate governance statement, which forms part of the directors' annual report.[463] The external auditors, in turn, produce a report

[457] ibid 13.

[458] For a more recent judgment along these lines, see Cour d'Appel de Paris, 4 February 1994 (*Leguay c/ FNB*), *Bull. Joly Sociétés* 1994, 402, note M Pariente (reiterating *Etablissements Victor Glorieux* in holding that the directors must exercise 'active and effective supervision' and, where necessary, particularly during a period of financial difficulties, take the initiative and question the executive directors in order to obtain a clear picture of the financial situation of the company, instead of waiting to be informed by the latter and relying on the accuracy of the executive directors' statements).

[459] Cass crim, 19 August 1997, *Bull. Joly Sociétés* 1998, 36, note C Mascala.

[460] Mascala (n 459) I.4.

[461] Com, Art L225-35 para 3.

[462] Merle (n 305) para 477.

[463] Com, Art L225-37 para 6. This requirement stems from EU law and is, accordingly, harmonized for all Member States; see Fourth Council Directive 78/660/EEC, Art 46(1)(c), inserted by Directive 2006/46/EC.

commenting on the chairman's description of the internal control systems as far as they relate to the financial reporting process.[464] In addition, listed companies must establish an audit committee that is responsible, inter alia, for monitoring the effectiveness of the risk management and internal control systems.[465] The law emphasizes that the audit committee acts under the responsibility of the board of directors,[466] which implies that all members of the board, including those who are not members of the audit committee, retain the ultimate responsibility for the financial health of the company and the soundness of the control and risk management systems.[467] It is not entirely clear how this rule can be reconciled with the decision of the Cour de Cassation in *Crédit Martiniquais*, discussed above,[468] where the court established the presumption that all board members are responsible for wrongful decisions of the board, unless they can show that they exercised the care of a prudent and diligent manager. Applied strictly, the court's presumption would place the directors who are not committee members in a difficult position. They would be required to review carefully the work of the committee, even though the law entrusts the committee with monitoring the effectiveness of the internal control systems, and some degree of reliance on the work of the committee is certainly inevitable.[469] Finally, for financial institutions the Monetary and Financial Code (*Code monétaire et financier*) contains more specific provisions regarding internal monitoring, auditing and risk-management structures.[470]

C. Duty of Loyalty

The duty of loyalty deals mainly (but not exclusively[471]) with two situations: first, transactions of a director (or a legal entity in which the director is interested) with the company (self-dealing), and second, the use of a corporate opportunity by the director, i.e. the expropriation of a business opportunity that 'belongs' (in some sense of the word) to the corporation. In many legal systems, including the US, Germany, and France, the law does not distinguish explicitly between these two instances of the duty of loyalty. In the US, the same general principle applies, namely that directors are not permitted to use their position to further their private interests.[472] The law then provides for differentiations depending on the circumstances of the individual case. In Germany and France, self-dealing, which we conceptualize here as an aspect of loyalty, is subject to specific rules allocating decision-making authority and requiring the board or the shareholders to give their consent. These rules are supplemented by a general unwritten duty of loyalty that fills gaps and can be used, in particular, to regulate corporate opportunities. The UK Companies Act 2006, in comparison, contains several specific duties that fall under the umbrella of the duty of loyalty. These are: the duty not to accept benefits from third parties,[473] the duty to declare the director's interest in a proposed transaction with the company,[474] and, as a residual provision, the general duty to avoid conflicts of interest.[475] In the following sections, we will analyse the duty of loyalty under the two rubrics of self-dealing and corporate opportunities.

[464] Com, Art L225-235.

[465] Com, Art L823-19, implementing Directive 2006/43/EC on statutory audits of annual accounts and consolidated accounts, Art 41(2)(b).

[466] ibid. [467] See on this point Le Cannu (n 330) para 7. [468] Section B.I.4(a).

[469] For a discussion, see Le Cannu (n 330) para 21; and for an analysis of the implications of the new regulation for the liability of the members of the audit committee, see Merle (n 336).

[470] See, for example, C.mon.fin., Arts L511-40 to L511-46.

[471] See, for example, text to nn 179–180 above (for US law).

[472] *Guth v Loft, Inc.*, 23 Del. Ch. 255, 270 (Del. 1939). [473] Companies Act 2006, s 176.

[474] ibid s 177. [475] ibid s 175.

I. Self-dealing

1. UK

In the UK, different facets of the duty of loyalty are codified in three sections of the Companies Act 2006, sections 175–177. Here, we will focus on the duty to declare a director's interest in a proposed transaction (section 177), which targets cases of self-dealing, i.e. transactions of a director with his or her company. The duty to avoid conflicts of interest (section 175), which captures (among other cases) transactions of a director with third parties that affect the company's interests, for example because the transaction is related to the company's activities and concerns a valuable business opportunity, will be discussed in the next section.

Companies Act 2006

Section 177—Duty to declare interest in proposed transaction or arrangement

(1) If a director of a company is in any way, directly or indirectly, interested in a proposed transaction or arrangement with the company, he must declare the nature and extent of that interest to the other directors.
(2) The declaration may (but need not) be made—
 (a) at a meeting of the directors, or
 (b) by notice to the directors in accordance with—
  (i) section 184 (notice in writing), or
  (ii) section 185 (general notice).
(3) If a declaration of interest under this section proves to be, or becomes, inaccurate or incomplete, a further declaration must be made.
(4) Any declaration required by this section must be made before the company enters into the transaction or arrangement.
(5) This section does not require a declaration of an interest of which the director is not aware or where the director is not aware of the transaction or arrangement in question.
 For this purpose a director is treated as being aware of matters of which he ought reasonably to be aware.
(6) A director need not declare an interest—
 (a) if it cannot reasonably be regarded as likely to give rise to a conflict of interest;
 (b) if, or to the extent that, the other directors are already aware of it (and for this purpose the other directors are treated as aware of anything of which they ought reasonably to be aware); or
 (c) if, or to the extent that, it concerns terms of his service contract that have been or are to be considered—
  (i) by a meeting of the directors, or
  (ii) by a committee of the directors appointed for the purpose under the company's constitution.

Pursuant to section 177, if directors transact with their company, the transaction will only be valid if they declare the nature and extent of their interest to the other directors *before* the company enters into the transaction. If the required declaration is made, the transaction is valid and does not require approval by the company's members.[476] According to section 177, when the board of directors decides on the transaction after disclosure, the interested director does not need to abstain from voting. However, the Model Articles provide that the interested director is not to be counted as participating in the meeting for quorum or voting purposes.[477] If the director fails to declare his or her interest, the civil consequences are determined by the common law in force before adoption of the Companies Act 2006.[478]

[476] The Companies Act requires approval by the members for a number of particularly important transactions, see ss 188–225.
[477] Art 16 Model Articles for Public Companies, Art 14 Model Articles for Private Companies.
[478] See Companies Act 2006, ss 178(1), 180(1).

In addition, the director continues to be subject to the duty to make full disclosure after the company has entered into the transaction.[479] Violation of the continuing disclosure obligation results in criminal liability.[480]

In order to understand the scope of the statutory duties and the civil consequences of a failure to disclose, it is necessary to be familiar with the common law on self-dealing and conflicts of interest that forms part of the genesis of the statutory rules.[481] A famous early expression of the common law rules can be found in *Aberdeen Railway Company v Blaikie Bros*, a case from 1854.[482] The respondents Blaikie Bros had agreed to manufacture iron chairs (to fix rails to the ground) for Aberdeen Railway at £8.50 per ton. Aberdeen Railway repudiated the contract and Blaikie Bros sued for specific performance. The railway company pleaded that it was not bound by the contract because the chairman of its board of directors, Mr Blaikie, was also managing partner of Blaikie Bros. The House of Lords held:

> It is a rule of universal application that no one, having [fiduciary] duties to discharge, shall be allowed to enter into engagements in which he has, or can have, a personal interest conflicting, or which possibly may conflict, with the interests of those whom he is bound to protect. So strictly is this principle adhered to that no question is allowed to be raised as to the fairness or unfairness of a contract so entered into.

Consequently, the court invalidated the contract between Blaikie Bros and the railway company, explaining:

> Mr Blaikie [while being a director of Aberdeen Railway] entered into a contract on behalf of the company with his own firm ... His duty to the company imposed on him the obligation of obtaining these iron chairs at the lowest possible price. His personal interest would lead him in an entirely opposite direction—would induce him to fix the price as high as possible. This is the very evil against which the rule in question is directed ... [It is irrelevant] that he was not the sole person trading with the company. He was one of the firm of Blaikie Brothers with whom the contract was made, and so was interested in driving as hard a bargain with the company as he could induce them to make ...

Aberdeen Railway imposes an outright prohibition on transactions in which a director is interested. Courts are not asked to examine whether the transaction is fair to the corporation, in contrast to the test that US courts apply when the business judgment rule has been rebutted (for example, because of a conflict of interest of the directors).[483] The House of Lords explained the rationale for the strict approach in *Bray v Ford*:[484] '[H]uman nature being what it is, there is danger, in such circumstances [i.e., the case of interested transactions], of the person holding a fiduciary position being swayed by interest rather than by duty, and thus prejudicing those whom he was bound to protect'.[485] However, one of the judges in this case also pointed out: 'But I am satisfied that [the rule prohibiting such transactions] might be departed from in many cases, without any breach of morality, without any wrong being inflicted, and without any consciousness of wrong-doing. Indeed, it is obvious that it might sometimes be to the advantage of the beneficiaries that their trustee should act for them professionally rather than a stranger, even though the trustee were paid for his services'.[486]

Aberdeen Railway did not establish when, and under what conditions, a departure from the strict rule of equity was permissible. In particular, it may be said that the rationale of the rule loses its force when those whom it is intended to protect, namely the shareholders (or 'beneficiaries' in the parlance of *Bray v Ford*), agree that they do not require protection and permit the directors to go ahead with a transaction. The approval by shareholders may be given either ex ante (consent or authorization[487]) or ex post after the director breached

[479] ibid s 182. [480] ibid s 183. [481] See ibid s 170(4). [482] [1854] 1 Macq 461 (n 6).
[483] Entire fairness test, see section B.I.2(d).
[484] [1896] AC 44. [485] ibid 51. [486] ibid 52 (Lord Herschell).
[487] See now Companies Act 2006, s 180(4)(a).

the duty by inducing the company to enter into the interested transaction (ratification).[488] Furthermore, the shareholders' permission may be laid down in the articles, applying to all conflicted transactions and providing for a general dispensation from the prohibition of self-dealing, or establishing a tailored disclosure and approval procedure, for example disclosure to and approval by the disinterested directors. Alternatively, the shareholders' approval may be given by a resolution of the general meeting and relate to a specific transaction. Before codification in the Companies Act 2006, it was not always clear which of these mechanisms were lawful.

The following decision shows the flexibility that the courts allowed shareholders in attenuating the rule in *Aberdeen Railway* in the articles of association.

***Imperial Mercantile Credit Association v Coleman* (1870–71) L.R. 6 Ch. App. 558 (Court of Appeal)**

[Mr Coleman was a director of the Imperial Mercantile Credit Association and also partner in a brokerage firm. The brokerage firm had agreed to place shares and debentures of a railway company. It submitted a proposal to Imperial Mercantile Credit to purchase a number of the debentures with a commission of 1½ per cent (the brokerage firm retained a further 3½ per cent as commission, i.e. the issuer received 95 per cent of the face value of the debentures). Before the board of Imperial Mercantile Credit decided on the proposal, Coleman stated that he was interested in the sale of the debentures and offered to leave the room while the proposal was discussed, but was told by the chairman that this was unnecessary. The board then passed a resolution accepting the proposal. The debentures later greatly depreciated in value, causing Imperial Mercantile Credit to be wound up. The liquidators brought an action against the brokerage firm seeking repayment of the brokerage firm's commission (3½ per cent of the face value of the debentures). The articles of association of Imperial Mercantile Credit contained the following provision (Art 83): 'The office of a director shall be vacated if he contracts with the company, or is concerned in or participate in the profits of any contract with the company, or participate in the profits of any work done for the company, without declaring his interest at the meeting of the directors at which such contract is determined on or work ordered, if his interest then exists, or in any other case, at the first meeting of the directors after the acquisition of his interest; and no director so interested shall vote at any meeting or on any committee of the directors on any question relating to such contracts or work'.]

Lord Hatherley, L.C.:

This is a case in which the official liquidator of the Imperial Mercantile Credit Association, in the name of the company, has filed a bill in order to have it declared that a certain sum of money received by the Defendants ... is a sum for which Mr. Coleman, who was a director of the company, is answerable to the company on the general principle that a person holding a fiduciary position with regard to a company cannot obtain for himself a benefit derived from the employment of the funds of the company in any matter in which he, the director, may happen to be engaged. The principle is so firmly established that I should be extremely sorry to say anything which would in the slightest decree impeach it ...

[T]he company have a right to the services of their directors, whom they remunerate by considerable payments; they have a right to their entire services, they have a right to the voice of every director, and to the advice of every director in giving his opinion upon matters which are brought before the board for consideration; and ... the general rule that no trustee can derive any benefit from dealing with those funds of which he is a trustee applies with still greater force to the state of things in which the interest of the trustee deprives the company of the benefit of his advice and assistance.

However, the question then remains, whether the company cannot stipulate that this is a benefit of which they do not desire to avail themselves, and if they are competent so to stipulate, whether they may not think that in large financial matters of this description it is better to have directors who may advance the interests of the company by their connection, and by the part

[488] See now ibid s 239.

which they themselves take in large money dealings, than to have persons who would have no share in such transactions as those in which the company is concerned.

It is not for me to say which was the wiser or better course of the two, nor do I think that this Court professes to lay down rules for the guidance of men who are adult, and can manage and deal with their own interests. It would be a violent assumption if any thing of that kind were attempted. It must be left to such persons to form their own contracts and engagements, and this Court has only to sit here and construe them, and also to lay down certain general rules for the protection of persons who may not have been aware of what the consequences would be of intrusting their property to the management of others where nothing is expressed as to the implied arrangement. In this case it does appear to me that there was a distinct contemplation of directors being interested in the concerns of the company, and acting and voting when the matter came before the board of directors, and that the shareholders took such precautions as they thought necessary:—[His Lordship then read the 83rd clause.] Is it possible to read that clause and find any mode by which it could be maintained that the company meant to exclude a director from his office in case he should have an interest in a contract, or to exclude any contract being made in which any director should be interested? It seems to me to be perfectly impossible. The whole clause would be idle. They have taken the matter into their own hands, and have said: 'We do not mind a director who has an interest, but all that we provide is this—that he shall fairly state that interest at the time when the matter is under discussion. He shall not vote on the matter himself, and if he acquires an interest after the matter has been discussed, and after he has voted upon it, or whether he has voted upon it or not, if after the matter is discussed he acquires an interest which he does not disclose he shall be forthwith disqualified'. . . .

[T]he company could not have the advantage from such large transactions of this kind being brought to them by brokers without submitting to the brokers taking an interest in the business which they brought, and the company chose to make that arrangement, if the director disclosed his interest. The fact of [Mr Coleman's] appearing before them as a broker was known to every one of them, and shewed that he would get what they call the 'usual broker's commission'. . . .

I have regarded this case with very great anxiety, because I would not be supposed for one moment to throw out a word that could tend to lead any trustee into the notion that he may deal with the persons for whom he is a trustee, or for whom he is a trustee with others, in any manner which will give him a benefit or put money into his own pocket. But that, like any other rule of the Court, is open to contract between the parties, for it is not a principle the benefit of which parties cannot waive by express and direct contract for the sake of other advantages which they suppose they derive . . .

The rules of the company seem to prescribe a mode of proceeding by which they exempted this particular case from the operation of the general rule of the Court of Equity, and it appears to me that Mr. Coleman sufficiently complied with that rule when he made it clear to all the persons (and they all admit that he made it clear) that he had an interest as a broker which placed him in exact hostility to the others. I ought not to omit noticing an argument . . . that Mr. Coleman being present, and not leaving the room, might be taken as voting in the matter as director; and that he ought to have quitted the room, otherwise his undue influence was employed in acting upon the minds of the directors. I think that that would be straining the expression, that 'no director shall vote', to the highest degree, and would not touch the point and pith of the case; because the pith of the case really is, whether the directors who were assembled were aware of Mr. Coleman being in that position. If so, any speech or any statement he could make to induce them to make the arrangement they would know to be the speech or advice of a person directly interested in the matter; and therefore the directors were by the very terms of the contract put upon their guard, and told that they were to be careful in coming to a conclusion as to the transaction before them . . .

Questions and comments:

1. Why was the court in *Imperial Mercantile* willing to deviate from the strict prohibition expounded in *Aberdeen Railway*? What are the beneficial consequences of introducing more

flexibility into the law on self-dealing, and what is the legal concept that the court uses in order to achieve this flexibility?

2. Before adoption of the Companies Act 2006, the courts were prepared to accept modifications of the rule in *Aberdeen Railway* that gave the interested directors even more freedom than the provision at issue in *Imperial Mercantile*. For example, in *Boulting v Association of Cinematograph, Television and Allied Technicians*,[489] the Court of Appeal held that the 'articles may validly permit directors to be present at board meetings and even to vote when proposed contracts in which they are interested are being discussed'.[490] Does this degree of laxity take sufficient account of the shareholders' interests, in particular those of minority shareholders? Does the answer to this question depend on the type of company at issue and its shareholder structure?

Pursuant to *Imperial Mercantile*, shareholders enjoyed a largely unfettered freedom of contract to give *ex ante* approval of related-party transactions or empower the board to exempt the interested director from the prohibition of *Aberdeen Railway*. As far as ex post ratification of the transaction was concerned, the legal situation was, in principle, also characterized by a deferential attitude of the courts to the autonomy of shareholders to treat the interested transaction as they saw fit. However, the courts also recognized the risk that the interested directors could distort the shareholder vote by voting their shares in favour of ratification. In their response to this risk, the courts sought to tread a fine line between upholding contractual freedom, and hence showing deference to the views of the majority shareholders, and intervening in corporate decision-making to protect the minority. Two exemplary judgments are *North-West Transportation Co Ltd v Beatty*[491] and *Cook v Deeks*.[492] In the first case, one of the directors of North West Transportation Co, Mr James Hughes Beatty, sold a steamer to his company. The sale was approved by the board of directors, consisting of five directors, and a few days later ratified or confirmed by a majority of the shareholders in general meeting. The defendant directors held the majority of the voting capital in the company and voted (with one exception) in favour of ratification of the contract at the meeting. The interested director's votes were decisive for the outcome in favour of ratification. One of the minority shareholders brought a lawsuit against the company and the directors to set aside the sale. The Privy Council overruled the judgment of the previous instance, the Supreme Court of Canada, and held that the shareholders had validly confirmed the contract. The Privy Council described the two relevant legal principles that were in conflict in this case as follows:

> [T]he resolution of a majority of the shareholders, duly convened, upon any question with which the company is legally competent to deal, is binding upon the minority, and consequently upon the company, and every shareholder has a perfect right to vote upon any such question, although he may have a personal interest in the subject-matter opposed to, or different from, the general or particular interests of the company.
>
> On the other hand, a director of a company is precluded from dealing, on behalf of the company, with himself, and from entering into engagements in which he has a personal interest conflicting, or which possibly may conflict, with the interests of those whom he is bound by fiduciary duty to protect … Any such dealing or engagement may, however, be affirmed or adopted by the company, provided such affirmance or adoption is not brought about by unfair or improper means, and is not illegal or fraudulent or oppressive towards those shareholders who oppose it …
>
> The only unfairness or impropriety which, consistently with the admitted and established facts, could be suggested, arises out of the fact that the defendant J. H. Beatty possessed a voting power as a shareholder which enabled him, and those who thought with him … to ratify and adopt a voidable contract, into which he, as a director, and his co-directors had entered …
>
> [T]he acquisition of the *United Empire* [the steamer] was a pure question of policy, as to which it might be expected that there would be differences of opinion, and upon which the voice of the majority ought to prevail; to reject the votes of the defendant upon the question of the adoption

[489] [1963] 2 QB 606. [490] ibid 636. [491] (1887) LR 12 App Cas 589 (Privy Council).
[492] [1916] 1 AC 554 (Privy Council).

of the bye-law would be to give effect to the views of the minority, and to disregard those of the majority.

The second case, *Cook v Deeks*, dealt with the use of a corporate opportunity by three of the four directors of the Toronto Construction Company. The directors were also shareholders of the company, each holding one fourth of the share capital. When the fourth director brought a lawsuit against the other board members because they had formed a new company to take over a contract they had negotiated as directors of the Toronto Construction Company, the defendant directors convened a shareholder meeting and ratified their actions against the votes of the plaintiff. The court held that the ratification was invalid because the defendant directors who were in breach of duty controlled the meeting with their votes.[493]

How can we reconcile the two cases? The nature of the transaction in *North-West Transportation v Beatty* was of crucial importance to the outcome of the case.[494] It was uncontested that the acquisition of the steamer was essential to the company's business, because the company had lost one of its steamers and needed a replacement for another. In addition, the steamer was well suited for the company's needs and the price was reasonable.[495] Consequently, the Privy Council in *North-West Transportation v Beatty* reasoned that the acquisition of the steamer 'was a pure question of policy'. The court in *Cook v Deeks*, the later of the two judgments, focused on this point to distinguish the decision. It identified a fundamental difference between two types of conflicted transaction: self-dealing (the scenario at issue in *North-West Transportation v Beatty*) and the use of a corporate opportunity. In the former case, a director sells property to the company that is 'in equity as well as at law his own' and that he can, in principle, dispose of as he sees fit.[496] In the second case, the courts treat the corporate opportunity as an asset that belongs in equity to the company. As a consequence, directors who make use of the business opportunity are regarded as holding the property or rights thus acquired on behalf of the company. They must account to the company for the profits made. In the court's opinion, it follows that 'a resolution that the rights of the company should be disregarded in the matter [because the acts of the directors are ratified] would amount to forfeiting the interest and property of the minority of shareholders in favour of the majority, and that by the votes of those who are interested in securing the property for themselves'.[497] Such a use of voting power is not legitimate and constitutes oppression of the minority.[498]

Cook v Deeks has been interpreted by some commentators as an expression of the common law principle that some wrongs, notably the misappropriation of company property by the directors, are non-ratifiable by the shareholders.[499] Thus, under this interpretation, the issue in *Cook v Deeks* was not so much whether the conflicted directors were permitted to vote, but rather whether the shareholders were capable of ratifying the breach. If the wrong was non-ratifiable, the ratifying resolution would be invalid, even if the conflicted shareholders abstained from voting or their votes were not required for the majority.[500]

How does this case law relate to the codified rules in the Companies Act 2006? The provisions on ratification no longer distinguish between the two main types of conduct captured by the duty of loyalty, the *Cook v Deeks* and *North-West Transportation v Beatty* scenarios. Section 239 allows the members of a company to ratify any breach of duty (both under the umbrella of the duty of care and the duty of loyalty, that is, including negligence and fiduciary

[493] ibid 563–5.

[494] See the Privy Council, (1887) LR 12 App Cas 600, criticizing the decision of the Supreme Court of Canada for not taking into consideration the nature of the transaction at issue.

[495] ibid 596. [496] [1916] 1 AC 563. [497] ibid 564. [498] ibid.

[499] Davies and Worthington (n 30) para 16-124.

[500] Presumably, this is different if the shareholders act unanimously (*Duomatic* principle), see ibid and presently in the text. The *Duomatic* principle is discussed in Chapter 5A.I.

wrongs), but the votes of the implicated director and any member connected with him must be disregarded.[501] This restriction is subject to the law on unanimous consent. Directors may vote and ratify a breach of duty if all shareholders agree (*Duomatic* principle).[502] Does section 239 supersede the doctrine of non-ratifiable wrongs, so that the distinction between *Cook v Deeks* and *North-West Transportation v Beatty* has become redundant? It would seem that this is the case. The main concern of *Cook v Deeks* was that the majority, by ratifying the appropriation of the corporate opportunity, acted oppressively towards the minority. This is no longer an issue if the interested shareholders do not vote.[503] Furthermore, section 239 does not refer to the concept of non-ratifiable wrong. On the other hand, section 239(7) stipulates that rules of law imposing limitations or restrictions on what may be ratified shall not be affected. This proviso indicates that the legislator did not intend to overrule *Cook v Deeks*, but leave the further development of the principles laid down in section 239 to the courts.

2. *US*

Initially, US law on self-dealing provided for a rule that was as strict as the one established by the English courts in *Aberdeen Railway*. In the late 19th century, the predominant view was that contracts between a director and the corporation were void. It was irrelevant whether a majority of disinterested directors approved the contract or the transaction was favourable or fair to the corporation.[504] This rule applied even to interlocking directorates where some (but not all) of the directors of the two contracting corporations were identical and to cases where one corporation held a controlling interest in the other and appointed its directors.[505]

The approach of the courts is exemplified by *Wardell v Union Pacific Railroad Co.*,[506] one of the leading cases of the time. The Union Pacific Railroad Co. entered into a contract with Mr Wardell and a business partner concerning the exploitation of coal found along its railroad passing from Omaha to Utah. The contract provided that the railroad should purchase the coal needed for its operations and provide facilities for the exploitation of the coal, for example furnish railroad cars and free passes on its roads and lease the coal lands it owned to the contractors. In January 1869, some months after the initial agreement, a corporation called the Wyoming Coal and Mining Company, was formed to develop and work the mines. A majority of the company's stock was taken by six of the directors of the railroad company. In March 1874, the officers and agents of Union Pacific took forcible possession of the mines, claiming that the initial contract was a fraud upon the company; that it was made on its part by the executive committee of its board of directors, a majority of whom were, by previous agreement, to be equally interested with the contractors in it, and for that reason its terms were made so favourable to the contractors and unfavourable to the railroad company as to enable the former to make large gains at the expense of the latter. The US Supreme Court held:

[501] Companies Act 2006, s 239(4). 'Connected person' is defined in s 252 and comprises, in particular, members of the director's immediate family (s 253) and bodies corporate in which the director and persons connected with him hold at least 20% of the share capital or where they are entitled to exercise more than 20% of the voting power (s 254).

[502] Section 239(6)(a).

[503] Davies and Worthington (n 30) para 16-124.

[504] H Marsh, Jr, 'Are Directors Trustees? Conflict of Interest and Corporate Morality' (1966) 22 Business Law 35, 37, explains that the courts adopted this strict stance because they were concerned that the interested director, even if prohibited from participating in the board decision, may exert influence over his fellow board members that would taint the approval. Marsh quotes *Cumberland Coal and Iron Co. v Parish*, 42 Md. 598, at 606 (Md. 1875): '[T]he remaining directors are placed in the embarrassing and invidious position of having to pass upon, scrutinize and check the transactions and accounts of one of their own body, with whom they are associated on terms of equality in the general management of all the affairs of the corporation'.

[505] For references see Marsh (n 504) 37–8.

[506] 103 U.S. 651 (US 1880).

[The contract] was evidently drawn more for the benefit of the contractors than for the interest of the company … [C]oal could be delivered to the company at a cost of two dollars per ton, yet the contract, which was to remain in force fifteen years, stipulated that the company should pay treble this amount per ton for the coal the first two years, two and a half times the amount for the next three years, twice the amount for the following four years, and one-half more for the balance of the time … These terms and the leasing of all the coal lands of the company for fifteen years to those parties upon a royalty of twenty-five cents a ton for the first nine years, and without any royalty afterwards if the price of the coal should be reduced to three dollars, with the stipulation to provide side-tracks to the mines, and also the furnish cars for transportation of coal for general consumption, and after charging them only what was charged to others, to allow them a drawback of twenty-five per cent on the sums paid, gave to them a contract of the value of millions of dollars. These provisions would of themselves justly excite a suspicion that the directors of the railroad company, who authorized the contract on its behalf, had been greatly deceived and imposed upon, or that they were ignorant of the cost at which the coal could be taken from the mines and delivered to the company. But the evidence shows that those directors were neither deceived nor imposed upon, nor were they without information as to the probable cost of taking out and delivering the coal. And what is of more importance, it shows, as alleged, their previous agreement with the contractors for a joint interest in the contract, and, in order that they might not appear as co-contractors, that a corporation should be formed in which they should become stockholders, and to which the contract should be assigned; and that this agreement was carried out by the subsequent formation of the Wyoming Mining and Coal Company and their taking stock in it …

It is among the rudiments of the law that the same person cannot act for himself and at the same time, with respect to the same matter, as the agent of another whose interests are conflicting. Thus a person cannot be a purchaser of property and at the same time the agent of the vendor. The two positions impose different obligations, and their union would at once raise a conflict between interest and duty; and, 'constituted as humanity is, in the majority of cases duty would be overborne in the struggle'.… Directors of corporations, and all persons who stand in a fiduciary relation to other parties, and are clothed with power to act for them, are subject to this rule; they are not permitted to occupy a position which will conflict with the interest of parties they represent and are bound to protect. They cannot, as agents or trustees, enter into or authorize contracts on behalf of those for whom they are appointed to act, and then personally participate in the benefits. Hence all arrangements by directors of a railroad company, to secure an undue advantage to themselves at its expense, by the formation of a new company as an auxiliary to the original one, with an understanding that they, or some of them, shall take stock in it, and then that valuable contracts shall be given to it, in the profits of which they, as stockholders in the new company, are to share, are so many unlawful devices to enrich themselves to the detriment of the stockholders and creditors of the original company, and will be condemned whenever properly brought before the courts for consideration …

Note how the assessment of human nature by the US Supreme Court in *Wardell v Union Pacific Railroad* resembles that by the English courts: In the case of a conflict between duty and personal interest, the steadfastness of human nature cannot be trusted. Duty will 'be overborne in the struggle';[507] 'the person holding a fiduciary position [will be] swayed by interest rather than by duty'.[508] However, in the following decades, the courts moved away from a strict prohibition on self-dealing. They realized that it was unrealistic to expect directors to work without compensation or shareholders to decide on all aspects of the directors' employment. Therefore, as early as the turn of the century, they recognized the power of the board to fix the salary of their members.[509] But in doing so, the board was subject to stringent fiduciary requirements.

[507] *Wardell v Union Pacific Railroad Co.*, 103 U.S. 658.

[508] *Bray v Ford* [1896] AC 44 (see also text to n 484 above).

[509] See, e.g., *Fitchett v Murphy*, 26 Misc. 544, 545 (N.Y. 1899): 'Directors of a corporation have no right to vote salaries to themselves as mere incidents to their offices, as was done here. They are not, however, debarred from becoming employees of the corporation, and they are entitled to a reasonable compensation for their services as such'.

The courts did not hesitate to review not only the board's decision-making process, but also the substance of the directors' decision. The contract between a director and the corporation would be void unless it was 'in all things fair and equitable' and the corporation was 'represented by a majority of its directors, each of whom [was] acting as a free agent and under no controlling influence or restraint on the part of the contracting director'.[510] The courts looked closely at the circumstances of the individual transaction and the relationship between the interested director and the other board members. If the interested director took part in the vote or there was concern that the director exercised undue influence on the other board members, the transaction would not stand.[511] The requirement that the transaction be fair and equitable involved a determination of the 'reasonableness' of the director's remuneration, and the courts were prepared to specify what they thought was reasonable in the circumstances.[512]

These principles were then applied to other instances of self-dealing. For example, in *Globe Woolen Co. v Utica Gas & Electric Co.*,[513] the director, Mr Maynard, stood on both sides of a transaction between a corporation operating two spinning mills and a utility company providing electricity to the mills. Mr Maynard was a director, president, and the majority shareholder of the textile corporation, and also a director of, but not a shareholder in, the utility company. The contract was mainly devised by Mr Maynard and adopted by the utility's board of directors, which was not fully informed of the contract's implications and did not realize that it was highly disadvantageous to the company. Mr Maynard abstained from voting. The Court of Appeals of New York based its decision to invalidate the contract on two considerations. First, although Mr Maynard did not make any incorrect disclosure and did not vote on the contract, the court held that he exerted a dominating influence on the dealings between the two companies, including the decision of the board of directors. This influence was a function of his superior knowledge of the consequences of the contract and the fact that the contract was negotiated with, and the board informed by, a manager of the utility company who, in the words of the court, 'looked up to him [Maynard] as to a superior, and was alert to serve his pleasure'.[514] Secondly, reiterating the case law on directors' remuneration, the Court of Appeals held that the contract was not 'fair and just' to the utility company, but rather one-sided and left the company at the other party's mercy.[515]

The decision is important, and not easy to interpret, because it represents US law on self-dealing at a transitory stage. The decision rests on two strands of case-law, one deciding unequivocally that an interested transaction will be set aside unless it is fair and equitable to the corporation, the conflicted director abstains from voting, *and* the other directors are under no influence from the conflicted director,[516] and the other holding that when directors vote in their own matters, or influence a board decision that is to their advantage, the *presumption* is that the transaction is improper.[517] In other words, the first approach requires *cumulatively*

[510] *Crocker v Cumberland Min. & Mill. Co.*, 139 N.W. 783, 784–5 (S.D. 1913).

[511] *Crocker* (n 510) 785 (holding that 'dummie' directors who were appointed to the board to advance the interests of the conflicted director and acted under his influence were to be disregarded for purposes of establishing a quorum for board meetings and were not entitled to vote on the interested transaction); *Adams v Burke*, 201 Ill. 395, 399 (Ill. 1903) (a resolution awarding salary 'is illegal if it is carried by [the vote of the interested director] or produced by his influence, where he has a controlling interest'); *Fitchett* (n 509) 545 (three directors awarded themselves salary payments, each abstaining from voting on the resolution concerning his own compensation; the courts invalidated the resolutions: 'That each one refrained from voting on the resolution fixing his salary does not change the case. Too much importance is attached to that formality. Wool is not so easily pulled over the eyes of the law').

[512] *Crocker* (n 509) 784. [513] 121 N.E. 378 (N.Y. 1918). [514] ibid 380. [515] ibid.

[516] *Crocker* (n 509) 783, and the cases cited there (relied on by *Globe Woolen* (n 513) 380).

[517] *Davids v Davids*, 135 A.D. 206 (N.Y. 1909); Sage v Culver, 147 N.Y. 241 (N.Y. 1895) (relied on by *Globe Woolen* (n 513) 379–80).

fairness and abstention from voting by the interested director and all other directors who are in some way conflicted. The second approach is a procedural rule. If the interested directors do not take part in the board's decision, the plaintiff bears the burden of proving that the transaction was prejudicial to the interests of the corporation. Conversely, if the directors who are implicated in self-dealing participate in the vote, they are required to show that the transaction was fair and no undue advantage was taken by them. The Court of Appeals in *Globe Woolen* quotes the latter strand of cases approvingly.[518] On the other hand, it also emphasizes that '[t]here must be candor and equity in the transaction, *and* some reasonable proportion between benefits and burdens',[519] which can be interpreted as meaning that both the decision-making process must be free from impropriety and the substance of the transaction fair.

In later decisions, the New York courts made it clear that they followed the second, less stringent, approach to self-dealing. For example, in *Bayer v Beran*[520] the Supreme Court of New York held that the fairness of the related-party transaction, without approval by a majority of the disinterested directors, was sufficient to exonerate the directors from a breach of duty. This became the rule in most states and corresponds to the law as it stands today: self-dealing is lawful *either* if the transaction has been approved by the disinterested directors *or* it is fair to the corporation. It is also the law in Delaware, which is codified in §144 Del. Gen. Corp. Law.

Delaware General Corporation Law

§ 144—Interested directors; quorum

(a) No contract or transaction between a corporation and 1 or more of its directors or officers, or between a corporation and any other corporation, partnership, association, or other organization in which 1 or more of its directors or officers, are directors or officers, or have a financial interest, shall be void or voidable solely for this reason, or solely because the director or officer is present at or participates in the meeting of the board or committee which authorizes the contract or transaction, or solely because any such director's or officer's votes are counted for such purpose, if:
  (1) The material facts as to the director's or officer's relationship or interest and as to the contract or transaction are disclosed or are known to the board of directors or the committee, and the board or committee in good faith authorizes the contract or transaction by the affirmative votes of a majority of the disinterested directors, even though the disinterested directors be less than a quorum; or
  (2) The material facts as to the director's or officer's relationship or interest and as to the contract or transaction are disclosed or are known to the stockholders entitled to vote thereon, and the contract or transaction is specifically approved in good faith by vote of the stockholders; or
  (3) The contract or transaction is fair as to the corporation as of the time it is authorized, approved or ratified, by the board of directors, a committee or the stockholders.
(b) Common or interested directors may be counted in determining the presence of a quorum at a meeting of the board of directors or of a committee which authorizes the contract or transaction.

The operation of §144 Del. Gen. Corp. Law is discussed in the following decision of the Supreme Court of Delaware.

***Fliegler v. Lawrence*, 361 A.2d 218 (Del. 1976)**

McNeilly, Justice:

In November, 1969, defendant, John C. Lawrence (then president of Agau, a publicly held corporation engaged in a dualphased gold and silver exploratory venture) in his individual capacity,

[518] See, e.g., *Globe Woolen* (n 513) 379: 'The refusal to vote has, indeed, this importance: It gives to the transaction the form and presumption of propriety, and requires one who would invalidate it to probe beneath the surface'.

[519] ibid 380 (emphasis added).

[520] 49 N.Y.S.2d 2 (N.Y. 1944).

acquired certain antimony properties under a lease-option for $60,000.[521] Lawrence offered to transfer the properties, which were then 'a raw prospect', to Agau, but after consulting with other members of Agau's board of directors, he and they agreed that the corporation's legal and financial position would not permit acquisition and development of the properties at that time. Thus, it was decided to transfer the properties to USAC (a closely held corporation formed just for this purpose and a majority of whose stock was owned by the individual defendants), where capital necessary for development of the properties could be raised without risk to Agau through the sale of USAC stock; it was also decided to grant Agau a long-term option to acquire USAC if the properties proved to be of commercial value.

In January, 1970, the option agreement was executed by Agau and USAC. Upon its exercise and approval by Agau shareholders, Agau was to deliver 800,000 shares of its restricted investment stock for all authorized and issued shares of USAC. The exchange was calculated on the basis of reimbursement to USAC and its shareholders for their costs in developing the properties to a point where it could be ascertained if they had commercial value ...

In July, 1970, the Agau board resolved to exercise the option, an action which was approved by majority vote of the shareholders in October, 1970. Subsequently, plaintiff instituted this suit on behalf of Agau to recover the 800,000 shares and for an accounting.

II

The Vice-Chancellor determined that the chance to acquire the antimony claims was a corporate opportunity which should have been (and was) offered to Agau, but because the corporation was not in a position, either financially or legally, to accept the opportunity at that time, the individual defendants were entitled to acquire it for themselves after Agau rejected it.

We agree with these conclusions ... Accordingly, Agau was not entitled to the properties without consideration ...

Nevertheless, our inquiry cannot stop here, for it is clear that the individual defendants stood on both sides of the transaction in implementing and fixing the terms of the option agreement. Accordingly, the burden is upon them to demonstrate its intrinsic fairness ... The issue is where the 800,000 restricted investment shares of Agau stock, objectively, was a fair price for Agau to pay for USAC as a wholly-owned subsidiary.[522]

A.

Preliminarily, defendants argue that they have been relieved of the burden of proving fairness by reason of shareholder ratification of the Board's decision to exercise the option. They rely on 8 Del. C. s 144(a)(2) and *Gottlieb v. Heyden Chemical Corp.*, Del.Supr., 33 Del.Ch. 177, 91 A.2d 57 (1952).

In *Gottlieb*, this Court stated that shareholder ratification of an 'interested transaction', although less than unanimous, shifts the burden of proof to an objecting shareholder to demonstrate that the terms are so unequal as to amount to a gift or waste of corporate assets ... The Court explained:

'(T)he entire atmosphere is freshened and a new set of rules invoked where formal approval has been given by a majority of independent, fully informed (share)holders'. 91 A.2d at 59.

The purported ratification by the Agau shareholders would not affect the burden of proof in this case because the majority of shares voted in favor of exercising the option were cast by defendants in their capacity as Agau shareholders. Only about one-third of the 'disinterested' shareholders voted, and we cannot assume that such non-voting shareholders either approved

[521] [Footnote in the original.] Antimony is a metallic element used in a wide variety of alloys, especially with lead in battery plates, and in the manufacture of flame-proofing compounds, paints, semiconductors and ceramic products.

[522] [Footnote in the original.] The date at which this transaction must be scrutinized for intrinsic fairness is critical to the resolution of this question. We agree with the Vice-Chancellor that as of January 28, 1970, when the option was formally executed, that the transaction was one which would have commended itself to an independent corporation in Agau's position ... However, we are not concerned so much with Agau's Acquisition of the option, but rather with the Exercise thereof and implementation of its terms. In other words, the focus must be on the actual exchange of Agau's stock for USAC's stock and the test is whether that which Agau received was a fair quid pro quo for that which it had to pay. Since that exchange did not and could not, in fact occur until shareholder approval had been given in October, 1970, we must examine the transaction as of that point in time.

or disapproved. Under these circumstances, we cannot say that 'the entire atmosphere has been freshened' and that departure from the objective fairness test is permissible …

Nor do we believe the Legislature intended a contrary policy and rule to prevail by enacting 8 Del.C. s 144 …

Defendants argue that the transaction here in question is protected by s 144(a)(2) which, they contend, does not require that ratifying shareholders be 'disinterested' or 'independent'; nor, they argue, is there warrant for reading such a requirement into the statute … We do not read the statute as providing the broad immunity for which defendants contend. It merely removes an 'interested director' cloud when its terms are met and provides against invalidation of an agreement 'solely' because such a director or officer is involved. Nothing in the statute sanctions unfairness to Agau or removes the transaction from judicial scrutiny.

B.

Turning to the transaction itself, we note at the outset that from the time the option arrangement was conceived until the time it was implemented, there occurred marked changes in several of the factors which formed the basis for the terms of the exchange. As of the critical date, the market value of Agau shares had risen and shares were being traded at about $3.00 per share; thus, while initially the maximum discounted market value of the $800,000 was considered to be $500,000, by the time in question it was $1.2 million. Development expenses, originally anticipated to range from $250,000–$500,000, but as actually incurred, were towards the lower end of that scale … USAC found itself unable to obtain sufficient capital through sale of stock; thus it was forced to borrow $300,000, the debt being secured by USAC property as well as by Agau stock purchase warrants. It also appears that only $83,000 in cash was actually received through sales of stock.

On the basis of these changed conditions and in light of the fact that the exchange price was originally calculated simply to reimburse the USAC shareholders for their costs, plaintiff argues that the issuance of 800,000 shares of Agau stock, having a market value of at least 1.2 million dollars, to acquire a corporation in which only $83,000 in cash had been invested, and whose property was subject to loans of $300,000, is patently unfair.

The difficulty with this argument for purposes of the fairness test is that it impermissibly attempts to equate and compare two different standards of value (if indeed USAC's debt/equity ratio is a standard of value) in order to demonstrate the inadequacy of the consideration Agau received … In fact, a reference to market sales of the stock involved, might support a finding of fairness. It appears that, although USAC was closely held, there was one arms-length sale of 75 USAC shares to non-affiliated investors for $160 per share. At this rate, the value of the 10,000 USAC shares would be 1.6 million, $400,000 more than the value of the shares given up by USAC. Furthermore, the market value of Agau's stock, even discounted, is an unrealistic indicator of the true value of what Agau gave up as it was clearly inflated due to Agau's possession of the option to acquire USAC whose properties were increasing in value largely as a result of the time and efforts expended by the individual defendants …

Viewing the two corporations as going concerns from the standpoint of their current and potential operational status presents a clearer and more realistic picture not only of what Agau gave up, but of what it received.

Agau was organized solely for the purpose of developing and exploring certain properties for potentially mineable gold and silver ore. The bulk of its cash, raised through a public offering, had been expended in 'Phase I' exploration of the properties which failed to establish a commercial ore body, although it did reveal 'interesting' zones of mineralization which indicated to Lawrence that 'Phase II' development and exploration might eventually be desirable. However, plans for further development had been temporarily abandoned as being economically unfeasible due to Agau's lack of sufficient funds to adequately explore the properties, as well as to the falling market price of silver. It further appears that other than a few outstanding unexercised stock purchase warrants, Agau did not have any ready sources of capital. Thus, as the Vice-Chancellor found, had the option not been exercised, Agau might well have gone out of business.

By comparison, the record shows that USAC, while still considered to be in the exploratory and development stage, could reasonably be expected to produce substantial profits. At the time in question, the corporation had established a sizeable commercial ore body, had proven markets for its product, and was in the midst of constructing a major ore separation facility expected to produce a high grade ore concentrate for market.

An admittedly 'conservative' report submitted in June, 1970, by Pennebaker, an independent geologist retained by USAC, confirmed the presence of a sizeable ore body and projected for the corporation a three-year net pre-tax profit of $660,000 after deducting all costs from ground to market including property payments, a complete return of the capitalized construction costs of the ore separation facility and $120,000 per year for further exploration and development. Without allowing for capital return and exploration and development costs, he projected a three-year profit of $1,357,500 ...

Considering all of the above factors, we conclude that defendants have proven the intrinsic fairness of the transaction ...

Questions and comments:

1. Assuming that the directors obtain approval of the conflicted interest transaction by the shareholders pursuant to §144(a)(2) Del. Gen. Corp. Law, will the courts review the transaction? If yes, what is the standard of review? Does it matter whether the majority of the shareholders voting in favour of approval is disinterested? Note in this context that §144(a)(1) speaks of the *disinterested* directors, but subsection 2 contains no such qualification with respect to the shareholders.
2. §144(a)(1) Del. Gen. Corp. Law provides that a transaction between the corporation and one or more of its directors is not void or voidable *solely for this reason* if the board is fully informed about the director's interest and a majority of the disinterested directors authorizes the transaction in good faith. The interested director can participate in the meeting and may be counted for purposes of a quorum.[523]

   How should we interpret the clause 'solely for this reason'? Does the enquiry of the courts end if the disinterested directors have acted with the necessary majority, or does the law impose additional requirements, for example that the transaction is fair to the corporation? In *Marciano v Nakash*,[524] the Supreme Court of Delaware followed an intermediate line: 'Just as the statute cannot "sanction unfairness" neither can it invalidate fairness if, upon judicial review, the transaction withstands close scrutiny of its intrinsic elements ... On the other hand, approval by fully informed disinterested directors under section 144(a)(1), or disinterested stockholders under section 144(a)(2), permits invocation of the business judgment rule and limits judicial review to issues of gift or waste with the burden of proof upon the party attacking the transaction'.[525] Thus, the rules laid down in §144(a) are not seen as exhaustive. Rather, the courts apply a 'two-tiered analysis'.[526] §144(a) plays the role of allocating the burden of proof and determining the standard of review. Generally, the directors bear the burden of proving the intrinsic fairness of transactions in which they are interested. However, compliance with §144(a)(1) or (2) has the effect of enabling the interested director to rely on the protections of the business judgment rule. Accordingly, the evidentiary burden shifts to the plaintiffs to show a waste of corporate assets.
3. The final subsection of §144(a) provides for a third method of validating conflicted interest transactions. The transaction is not void if it is fair to the corporation as of the time it is authorized, approved, or ratified by the board of directors or shareholders. The provision aims at cases where the board or the general meeting decides to enter into or confirm the transaction on behalf of the corporation, but the interested director failed to make the required disclosures under §144(a)(1) or (2) (disclosure of the material facts regarding the director's interest and the transaction) or abstain from voting pursuant to §144(a)(1). It was held that, as under prior case law, in such a case the director bears the burden of proving the intrinsic fairness of the challenged transaction.[527]

[523] Del. Gen. Corp. Law, §144(b). [524] 535 A.2d 400 (Del. 1987). [525] ibid 405 and n 3.
[526] ibid 404 (referring to *Fliegler v Lawrence* (n 155)). [527] ibid 405, n 3.

Should we interpret §144(a)(3) as stipulating that where the board or the general meeting does not approve a transaction, for example because the CEO acts without referring the matter to the board, intrinsic fairness ceases to be a defence? §144(a)(3) does not apply in such a case, given its explicit reference to fairness *as of the time* the transaction is approved. However, as mentioned, the Delaware courts do not treat §144(a) as the sole basis for validating a conflicted interest transaction. The common law principles on related party transactions continue to supplement and inform the codified rules. Outside the scope of §144(a)(3), they apply to allow the directors to avoid the transaction being set aside by showing entire fairness.[528]

Finally, how is 'intrinsic fairness' defined in this context? Does it comprise fair dealing and fair price, as stipulated in *Weinberger v UOP*, and does it also require full disclosure of all material facts? Delaware courts have held that the *Weinberger* standard applies, but lack of disclosure of the director's interest does not automatically preclude a finding of fair dealing.[529] This is convincing. §144(a)(3) would lose much of its relevance if intrinsic fairness required full disclosure, because in that case validation will often be possible pursuant to §144(a)(1) or (2). On the other hand, defendants arguably face greater practical difficulties in convincing a court that the corporation could not have obtained a better price if the negotiations had been led at arms-length and without the directors concealing their interest.[530]

3. *Germany*

Stock Corporation Act

§ 112—Representation of the company as against the members of the management board

The supervisory board represents the company as against the members of the management board in court and out of court . . .

As mentioned above, the regulation of the German duty of loyalty is fragmentary.[531] This is to some extent a function of the two-tier board structure that is mandatory for German stock corporations, at least as far as the regulation of self-dealing is concerned. The law assumes that the supervisory board is a neutral arbiter that is well positioned to judge whether a related-party transaction is beneficial to the company or tainted by the type of conflict of interest that led the UK and US courts to condemn initially all transactions between directors and their companies.[532] In theory, therefore, inserting an independent organ and vesting it with the authority to decide on conflicted transactions addresses both the concern that related-party transactions may damage the company, shareholders and creditors, and the need to provide for flexibility so that the company can make use of the expertise and business connections of the director. Of course, this presupposes that the independence and objectivity of the supervisory board is safeguarded, which may be doubted

[528] ibid 403–4.

[529] See, e.g., *HMG/Courtland Properties, Inc. v Gray*, 749 A.2d 94, 114–16 (Del. Ch. 1999).

[530] See ibid 117–18: 'The defendants have failed to persuade me that HMG would not have gotten a materially higher value . . . had Gray and Fieber [the defendant directors] come clean about Gray's interest. That is, they have not convinced me that their misconduct did not taint the price to HMG's disadvantage. I base this conclusion on several factors. First, the defendants' own expert on value . . . testified that his opinion that the prices paid in the Transactions were fair was premised on his assumption that Gray was not the leading negotiator from HMG's side . . . [In addition], a skilled and properly motivated negotiator could have done better . . . I have no confidence that Gray negotiated with the Fiebers in any vigorous or skillful way. Since he wanted to participate on the buy-side, he had less than a satisfactory incentive to do so . . . Finally, had Gray disclosed his interest, I believe that HMG would have terminated his involvement in the negotiations and have taken a much more traditional approach to selling the affected properties . . . Taken together, these factors lead me to conclude that the defendants have not demonstrated that they paid a fair price in the sense inherent in the entire fairness standard'.

[531] See text to nn 240–242 and the references in n 242.

[532] See *Aberdeen Railway Company v Blaikie Bros* (n 6) and *Wardell v Union Pacific Railroad Co.* (n 507).

in some circumstances.[533] In any case, the regulatory strategy of (re-)allocating decision-making power between different corporate organs in order to address the conflicts created by related-party transactions may explain the absence of an all-encompassing duty of loyalty familiar from common law jurisdictions.[534]

German stock corporation law implements the re-allocation strategy in §112 Stock Corporation Act. Pursuant to this provision, the supervisory board is competent to conclude a service contract with a new member of the management board and enter into connected transactions, for example in the context of the termination of the new member's previous employment agreement.[535] Beyond these cases of a clear conflict of interest, the provision applies to all transactions between a company and a *de jure* or *de facto* member of the management board, including former members, that give rise to an actual or potential conflict of interest.[536] The provision is intended to address all instances where the theoretical risk exists that the management board is not able to act independently and exclusively in the interest of the company.[537] In order to assess whether this is the case, the courts consider the 'typical consequences' of a scenario such as the one before the court.[538] For example, it has been held that a consultancy agreement of a member or former member of the management board with the company creates a potential conflict even if no claims of impropriety have been raised and the disinterested directors sanction the agreement.[539] Thus, the courts interpret the requirement of an actual or potential conflict triggering the shift of decision-making power fairly broadly.

On the other hand, occasionally the courts have pointed out that §112 does not apply if there is not even 'an abstract risk that the board lacks independence.'[540] For example, in a case concerning an action of a former director claiming payment for loss of office under terms that had been fixed at an earlier time, the court argued: 'The present lawsuit does not deal with the effectiveness of the resignation of the director, nor with questions of breach of duty or the amount of pay-scale retirement benefits, or comparable questions that could affect the current management board. The subject matter of the lawsuit is the amount of the plaintiff's compensation for loss of office. However, this has no bearing on the current management board because, as opposed to pay-scale retirement benefits, the plaintiff's claim is based on an agreement that was individually negotiated with the plaintiff. In particular, it cannot be assumed that the issue of contractual interpretation that is the subject matter of the present lawsuit will become relevant in the same or a comparable way to the relationship between the company and the current management board in the future.'[541] This holding is difficult to reconcile with the generally expansive interpretation of what constitutes a potential conflict of interest in other cases.[542] The court submitted that the case concerned the interpretation of an agreement that had been negotiated individually between the company and the plaintiff. The outcome of the case was therefore not of relevance to the position of the current directors in relation to the company. However, even if this is correct, §112 arguably addresses a wider array of considerations. For example, the board's independence may not only be affected because of the current directors' self-interest with regard to future lawsuits or transactions with the company, but also simply because they have or had a good and close relationship with the plaintiff.

Section 112 speaks of dealings with 'the members of the management board'. It is, therefore, not clear whether the provision only applies to direct conflicts, that is, transactions of a director personally with his or her company, or also indirect conflicts arising out of dealings

[533] See our discussion above Chapter 4E.I.

[534] Gerner-Beuerle and Schuster (n 3) 24–8. Most jurisdictions with a two-tier board structure (that all belong to the civil law tradition) use the re-allocation strategy to regulate self-dealing, for example Austria, Poland, and Slovenia. See ibid 26.

[535] Koch (n 57) §112 para 2.

[536] BGH AG 1991, 269 (holding that the management board does not have the authority to represent the company in an action brought by a former member of the management board).

[537] BGH AG 1991, 269, 270; BGH NJW 1997, 2324. [538] ibid. [539] BGH AG 1994, 35.

[540] OLG Köln, OLGZ 1993, 337, 338. [541] ibid 338.

[542] For example BGH AG 1994, 35; see n 539 above.

between the company and a legal person in which the director holds an interest, or between the company and a natural person who is affiliated with the director.[543] Courts have held that indirect conflicts between the director's company and another company are only caught by §112 if the director and the other company are 'economically identical'.[544] Economic identity is understood to mean complete identity of economic interest, for example where a legal person is wholly owned by the director.[545] It has been submitted in the literature that a substantial, even controlling interest in the third party was not sufficient.[546] The following case illustrates this approach. A member of a two-person management board of a public company was also a minority shareholder and one of two managing directors of a private limited company. The other managing director was his wife. The director, acting on behalf of the public company, entered into a loan agreement with the private company, which was represented by his wife in the transaction. Pursuant to the articles of the public company, the director was authorized to represent the company without participation of the other member of the management board. The court decided that §112 did not apply, in spite of the fact that the director was a minority shareholder and managing director of the private limited company.[547]

Dealings of a company with relatives of a director are generally also outside the scope of §112, unless the claim of the director's relative arises under the director's service contract or depends otherwise on the position as director.[548] For example, the management board lacks authority to represent the company in a lawsuit brought by the widow of a former director claiming pension payments that were granted to her in her husband's employment contract but not paid out because the company was in a state of financial distress.[549]

In private limited companies governed by the Limited Liability Companies Act, the re-allocation strategy is a less natural solution to the problem of related-party transactions. The two-tier board structure is not mandatory for private companies, unless the company is subject to employee participation legislation, in which case a supervisory board must be established to accommodate the co-determination system.[550] Accordingly, the Limited Liability Companies Act does not re-allocate decision-making authority for particular types of transaction to an independent organ. Maybe surprisingly, it also does not stipulate a general duty to avoid conflicts of interest. The Act only provides that the shareholders must decide on the appointment and removal of the managers,[551] which the courts construe to include the authority to conclude, amend, and terminate the managers' service contracts on behalf of the company[552] and enforce the company's damages claims against the managers.[553] Other dealings of the managers with the company are governed by general rules of civil law, notably §181 Civil Code, which provides that an agent may not 'enter into a legal transaction in the name of principal with himself in his own name or as an agent of a

[543] Recall that the UK duty of loyalty, for example, explicitly covers indirect conflicts (Companies Act 2006, s 175(1)).

[544] OLG Saarbrücken, AG 2001, 483. But see OLG München, judgment of 9 February 2009, 21 U 4853/08, expressing *in obiter* the view that even in a case of economic identity §112 did not apply, as this would contravene the basic principle that a company has a separate legal personality from its members and would be detrimental to legal certainty. In the case at hand, a director owned 40% of a company directly and was beneficial owner of the remaining 60%. The court held that a potential or abstract conflict did not exist because the subject matter of the action was not the conclusion of a transaction between the director and the company, but its termination. Similar OLG München, judgment of 10 May 2012, 14 U 2175/11. The Federal Court of Justice has not yet solved the conflict between the two state courts. See also text to n 568 below for a wider definition of indirect conflicts under the revised Shareholder Rights Directive, applicable to listed companies.

[545] OLG Saarbrücken, judgment of 11 October 2012, 8 U 22/11-6 (holding that 'at least' in the case of a one-member company it is justified to speak of economic identity). See also OLG München, judgment of 10 May 2012, 14 U 2175/11 (arguing *in obiter* that a shareholding of 24.99% by the director, with another 9.07% being held by his wife and 51.18% by his children, did not amount to economic identity).

[546] M Habersack in W Goette and M Habersack (eds), *Münchener Kommentar zum Aktiengesetz, vol 2* (5th edn, CH Beck 2019) §112 para 9.

[547] OLG Saarbrücken, AG 2001, 483.

[548] Habersack (n 546) para 16.

[549] BGH NZG 2007, 31.

[550] See in particular §1(1) no 3 Drittelbeteiligungsgesetz (DrittelbG) [One-Third Participation Act]; §1(1) Mitbestimmungsgesetz (MitbestG) [Co-Determination Act].

[551] GmbHG, §46 no 5.

[552] BGH NJW 1991, 1680.

[553] GmbHG, §46 no 8.

third party'. Thus, by virtue of general private law, managers lack the authority to represent their company in self-dealing transactions. However, non-conflicted managers may act on behalf of the company, even if the default rule of joint representation by all managers[554] has not been changed in the articles,[555] or the shareholders may suspend the application of §181 Civil Code.[556] If a supervisory board must be formed pursuant to the employee participation laws, §112 Stock Corporation Act applies.[557]

Does a broad no-conflict rule such as the one underlying the English duty of loyalty[558] protect the interests of the shareholders and third parties better than the re-allocation of decision-making power to an independent corporate organ? The preceding considerations have shown that the German rules are less expansive than the English and American versions of the duty of loyalty. While they are similar as far as their material scope of application is concerned, that is, they apply to any transaction giving rise to an actual or potential conflict of interest, their personal scope of application is narrower. Generally, the power to represent the company shifts only to the supervisory board if the company deals with a member of the management board personally. The management board retains its authority if the board member holds an interest in another legal person that deals with the company, even if the interest is substantial or controlling, or the company enters into transactions with a relative of the director. Thus, if the company's articles disapply the default rule of joint representation by all members of the management board[559] and vest the power to represent the company in one of the members acting alone or together with the company's clerk, which is permissible,[560] this director may legitimately enter into transactions with a company in which he or she holds a substantial or controlling interest without the requirement to submit the decision to the disinterested members of the management board or the supervisory board for approval.[561] The law also does not provide for an explicit duty to disclose the transaction *ex ante* to the other board members or the supervisory board. Such a duty can only be derived from the directors' general duties, for example the duty to cooperate in good faith with colleagues on the board[562] or inform the supervisory board.[563] The latter duty applies in particular to 'transactions which are, or can be, of significant importance for the profitability or solvency of the company'.[564] However, in comparison, for example, with the duty to declare an interest in a proposed transaction pursuant to the UK Companies Act 2006,[565] these duties are relatively indeterminate and open to interpretation. In addition, the general duty to cooperate in good faith with other board members does not provide for a procedure setting out how the declaration, if any, should be made.[566] Therefore, the law exhibits a certain tension between, on the one hand, the stated objective of §112 to safeguard the independence of the organ authorized to represent the company and prevent even abstract or potential threats to the company's interests, and on the other hand, the interpretation of §112 as

[554] GmbHG, §35(2). [555] BGHZ 64, 72, 75–6.

[556] BGHZ 33, 189, 190–2 (holding that the organ that is authorized to appoint the managers, i.e. generally the shareholders' meeting, is also competent to disapply §181 BGB). If a company has only one managing director, who is the sole shareholder, §181 in principle also applies, since the provision is not only intended to protect the shareholders, but also the creditors, see §35(3) GmbHG. In this case if the shareholders wish to disapply §181 BGB, they must do so in the articles, and hence the decision must be published in the commercial register, in order to achieve the goal of creditor protection, see BGHZ 87, 59, 60–61. In other cases, the shareholders may grant the dispensation by means of a resolution for individual transactions, which, according to one view (KG Berlin, GmbHR 2002, 327) is valid without a corresponding authorization of the shareholders in the articles, or, according to another view (e.g., OLG Munich NZG 2010, 795, 796; BayObLGZ 1984, 109, 111), if the articles authorize the shareholders to dispense with §181. For further references, see W Zöllner and U Noack in A Baumbach and A Hueck (eds), *GmbHG* (20th edn, CH Beck 2013) §35 para 132.

[557] See DrittelbG, §1(1) no 3; MitbestG, §25(1) no 2.

[558] See *Aberdeen Railway Company v Blaikie Bros* (n 6) and accompanying text. For a further discussion of the no-conflict rule, see also section C.II.1 below.

[559] AktG, §78(2) sentence 1. [560] ibid §78(3) sentence 1.

[561] See, for example, OLG Saarbrücken, AG 2001, 483, discussed above, text to n 547.

[562] See text to n 263 above. [563] AktG, §90(1). [564] ibid sentence 1 no 4. [565] Section 177.

[566] AktG, §90(2) no 4 requires the management board to report to the supervisory board 'early enough to give the supervisory board the opportunity to comment on the transaction before it is carried out'.

an exception to the general allocation of authority in the stock corporation that should be construed narrowly and not extended to indirect conflicts.[567]

For listed companies, some of these deficiencies will be remedied when the 2017 revisions to the Shareholder Rights Directive, set out in Directive (EU) 2017/828 (Shareholder Rights Directive II), Article 9c, are adopted. In two respects, the related party regime of the Shareholder Rights Directive II is broader than the scope of §112 German Stock Corporation Act. First, it captures transactions between a company and a controlling or significant shareholder of the company as well as close family members of the management board member. Secondly, it also captures transactions between the director's company and another company that is controlled, significantly influenced or managed by the director. Consequently, within the scope of the Shareholder Rights Directive, it is no longer permissible to restrict the involvement of the supervisory board to cases of economic identity between the management board member and third parties transacting with the company. The German legislator will implement the Directive by providing that related party transactions with the same counterparty exceeding 2.5 per cent of the company's fixed and current assets in any twelve-month period must be approved by the supervisory board. If the supervisory board refuses to give its approval, the management board can refer the matter to the general meeting for authorization by the non-related shareholders.[568]

4. *France*

Commercial Code[569]

Article L225-38

Any agreement entered into, either directly or through an intermediary, between the company and its general manager, one of its assistant general managers, one of its directors, one of its shareholders holding a fraction of the voting rights greater than 10% or, in the case of a corporate shareholder, the company which controls it within the meaning of Article L233-3, must be subject to the prior consent of the board of directors.

The same applies to agreements in which a person referred to in the previous paragraph has an indirect interest.

Agreements entered into between the company and another firm are also subject to prior consent if the company's general manager, one of its assistant general managers or one of its directors is the owner, a partner with unlimited liability, a manager, a director or a member of that firm's supervisory board or, more generally, is in any way involved in its management.

The prior authorization of the board of directors must be substantiated by giving reasons why the agreement is in the interest of the company, in particular by specifying the financial conditions attached to the agreement.

Article L225-39

The provisions of Article L225-38 are not applicable to agreements relating to current operations entered into under normal terms and conditions or to agreements entered into between

[567] For the former goal, see, e.g., BGHZ 103, 213, 214; 130, 108, 111–112, and for the latter, OLG München, judgment of 9 February 2009, 21 U 4853/08.

[568] Referentenentwurf des Bundesministeriums der Justiz und für Verbraucherschutz, Entwurf eines Gesetzes zur Umsetzung der zweiten Aktionärsrechterichtlinie [Legislative Proposal of the Federal Ministry of Justice and Consumer Protection, Draft of a Law Implementing the Second Shareholder Rights Directive] (ARUG II), 11 October 2018, inserting, inter alia, §§111a–c into the Stock Corporation Act. The disclosure obligations of the Shareholder Rights Directive II are laid down in §48a Wertpapierhandelsgesetz [Securities Trading Act]. In line with Art 9(5) and (6) of the Shareholder Rights Directive II, the approval and disclosure requirements do not apply to transactions entered into in the ordinary course of business and concluded on normal market terms and certain other transactions that are regulated elsewhere or do not put the interests of minority shareholders at risk, such as transactions concerning the remuneration of directors or transactions offered to all shareholders on the same terms, §111a(2), (3) AktG, as amended. The definition of related party is discussed in the Referentenentwurf p 75 (explaining, for example, that a 'significant influence' over a company within the meaning of the applicable accounting standards is presumed to exist if a shareholder holds directly or indirectly 20 per cent of the voting rights).

[569] Translation by Legifrance, https://www.legifrance.gouv.fr/Traductions/en-English/Legifrance-translations.

two companies, one of which holds, directly or indirectly, the entire share capital of the other, less, where applicable, the minimum number of shares required to meet the requirements of Article 1832 of the Civil Code or Articles L225-1 and L226-1 of this Code.

Article L225-40

The interested party must inform the board immediately upon becoming aware of an agreement to which Article L225-38 applies. They may not participate in the vote on the requested prior approval of the Board.

The chairman of the board of directors shall advise the auditors of all agreements authorised and entered into and shall submit them to the general meeting for approval.

The auditors shall present a special report on the agreements to the general meeting, which shall pass a resolution on this report.

The interested party may not participate in the vote and their shares shall not be taken into account for the calculation of the quorum and the majority.

Article L225-40-1

Agreements entered into and authorized in previous financial years, the execution of which was continued during the last financial year, shall be reviewed each year by the board of directors and communicated to the external auditor for the purpose of preparing the report provided for in the third paragraph of Article L225-40.

Article L225-41

Agreements approved by the meeting shall have effect with respect to third parties, as shall those which it refuses, unless they are annulled because of fraud.

Even in the absence of fraud, the prejudicial consequences to the company of agreements not approved by the general meeting may be charged to the interested party and, potentially, to the other members of the board of directors.

Article L225-42

Without prejudice to the liability of the interested party, agreements referred to in Article L225-38 and entered into without the prior authorisation of the board of directors may be cancelled if they have prejudicial consequences for the company.

Nullity proceedings shall be time-barred after three years with effect from the date of the agreement. However, should the agreement have been concealed, the starting point for the period of limitation shall be carried forward to the date on which it was revealed.

Nullity may be avoided by a vote of the general meeting taken on the special report of the auditors setting out the circumstances by virtue of which the authorisation procedure was not followed. The provisions of subparagraph four of Article L225-40 shall apply.

Article L225-43

On pain of nullity of the contract, directors, other than corporate directors, are prohibited from entering into loan agreements with the company, irrespective of their form, arranging for the company to grant an overdraft on a current account or otherwise, or to guarantee their obligations to third parties...

French law seeks to solve the tension between allowing a company to enter into potentially beneficial transactions with a director and preventing directors from taking advantage of their position for private gains by distinguishing between three types of transaction and establishing regulatory requirements of different intensity, depending on the abstract risk they pose to the company's interests: prohibited agreements (*conventions interdites*), regulated agreements (*conventions réglementées*), and non-regulated or free agreements (*conventions libres*). Prohibited agreements are those listed in Article L225-43 Code de commerce, in particular loans granted by the company to directors and their close relatives or security given for the directors' obligations towards third parties.[570] Such agreements are null and void, irrespective of any damage suffered by the company as a consequence of the transaction

[570] If the director is a legal person, the provision applies to the general manager and assistant general managers of the corporate director. Note that the discussion in the following paragraphs is limited to the *société anonyme*.

or the agreement's approval by the board or the general meeting. The consequences are far-reaching. For example, the company can rely on the nullity of a guarantee given for a loan of a director as against third parties, unless the third party was not aware, and should not have been aware, of the fact that the recipient was a director of the guarantor company (i.e. the third party acted in good faith pursuant to Article L235-12 Code de commerce). Furthermore, if a director received a loan which was secured by a guarantee given by the company, the nullity extends to the loan and can be invoked by the director as against the third-party lender, provided that the loan and the guarantee are 'indissociable'. This was held to be the case where a loan was given on the condition that a guarantee was provided.[571]

Non-regulated agreements are agreements that satisfy two conditions: they relate to the company's current operations and are entered into under normal terms and conditions, thus, they correspond to an arms-length transaction. If both conditions are satisfied, the agreement is valid without further formalities or approval by the board or the shareholders.[572] Whether a transaction is part of the company's current operations is assessed objectively in light of the company's objects, but the courts generally also require that the company enters into the transaction on a regular basis.[573] According to these criteria, the sale of a product from the company's range of products qualifies as a normal business operation, as does the transfer of a patent held by a director to a company that has as its object the exploitation of patents and trademarks.[574] Intra-group transactions are more difficult to assess. They are in principle caught by the regime on regulated transactions, since Article L225-38 applies to agreements between both a company and its directors and shareholders holding more than 10 per cent of the share capital with voting rights.[575] However, they are common in practice and performed regularly. Courts therefore hold that they do not require board approval, provided the services rendered by one of the group companies are charged at cost.[576] The latter requirement refers to the second condition of Article L225-39 Code de commerce. The transaction must be concluded under normal conditions, which means that it must be possible for the company to enter into a transaction on similar terms in the market. 'Similar terms' include not only the price, but all aspects of an agreement, for example the duration of the contract, its execution, penalties, or guarantees that are commonly required.

Finally, all agreements that are neither prohibited nor free are called regulated agreements. For them, the Commercial Code establishes an elaborate disclosure and approval procedure.[577] The procedure involves the following five steps, laid down in Article L225-40 Code

In the *société à responsabilité limitée*, the regulated agreement procedure exhibits certain differences (see Code de commerce, Arts L223-19, L233-20, L223-21).

[571] Cass com, 25 April 2006 (*Compagnie européenne d'opérations immobilières BIE c/ Le Floch, épouse Boennec*), *Revue des sociétés* 2006, 818, note R Routier (holding that the lender, a bank, should have known that the borrower was a director of the company that secured the loan, and allowing the director to rely on the nullity of the transaction as against the bank because the loan was granted conditional on the provision of security and hence inseparably connected with the mortgage).

[572] Com, Art L225-39. A second type of non-regulated agreement concerns the dealings of a parent company with its wholly owned subsidiary, Com, Art L225-39, as amended by Decree no 2014-863 of 31 July 2014, JORF no 0177 du 2 August 2014, 12820.

[573] Cozian, Viandier, and Deboissy (n 309) para 892.

[574] Cour d'Appel de Paris, 4 June 2003, *Bull. Joly Sociétés* 2003, 1315, note L Godon.

[575] Com, Art L225-38. The provision captures direct as well as indirect conflicts, for example agreements with another company controlled by a director as president, see the last paragraph of Art L225-38 and T com. Paris, 20 June 2006, *Revue des sociétés* 2006, 825, note JJ Daigre. However, transactions with wholly-owned subsidiaries are qualified as non-regulated agreements, see n 572.

[576] See, for example, Cour d'Appel de Paris, 17 October 2003, *Bull. Joly Sociétés* 2004, 224, note D Schmidt.

[577] However, the procedure does not apply to decisions that are subject to a separately codified approval mechanism, such as the determination of the remuneration of the chairman of the board (president), the general manager, and the assistant general managers by the board (Arts L225-47, L225-53) or decisions vested in the general meeting, for example the approval of a merger (Art L236-2). But see also Arts L225-22-1, 225-42-1, providing that in companies whose securities are admitted to trading on a regulated market elements of remuneration or other benefits due on occasion of the executive director's loss of office or change of functions are subject to the procedure governing regulated agreements. The approval procedure is not expected to change significantly in the process of implementation of the

de commerce. First, the interested party must inform the board of directors of the interested transaction without delay after becoming aware of it. Secondly, the interested party must request prior approval of the board and abstain from participating in the board decision on the transaction. If all board members are interested, the board cannot authorize the transaction and it is for the general meeting to decide.[578] Thirdly, the chairman of the board must notify the auditors of the authorized agreement within one month and give reasons why he or she regards the agreement as being in the interest of the company.[579] Fourthly, the auditors draw up a report describing the relevant details of the transaction in order to enable the shareholders to make an informed decision on the approval of the transaction. The report must set out the nature of the director's interest, the purpose of the transaction, any special advantages obtained by the director, for example a discount or payment deferral, and the reasons why the agreement is in the interest of the company.[580] Fifthly, the shareholders are furnished with the auditor's report, and the annual general meeting passes a resolution on the report. The interested party is again prohibited from participating in the vote.

While the approval procedure, therefore, is set out clearly in the law, the consequences of a violation of any of the above steps are less straightforward. The agreement is voidable if it is not submitted to the board for prior approval or the board refuses to give their approval *and* the agreement has prejudicial consequences for the company, notably because the company does not receive adequate compensation.[581] However, the general meeting may decide to confirm the agreement on the basis of the auditor's report explaining why prior approval of the board was not obtained.[582] If the requirement to obtain board approval is complied with but the chairman of the board does not notify the auditors, the general meeting refuses to give its consent, or the vote of the general meeting is tainted by irregularity,[583] the agreement retains its validity, except in the case of fraud.[584] Apart from potential nullity, the interested director, and possibly other board members who do not take the necessary steps to protect the company, may incur liability if the procedure governing regulated agreements is not observed and the company suffers a loss as a consequence of the transaction. The directors' responsibility follows general rules concerning the liability of directors laid down in the Commercial Code.[585] Thus, the elements of a cause of action for damages that we discussed above must be satisfied.[586]

Shareholder Rights Directive II (text to n 541 above), since the French regime already distinguishes between what the Directive calls 'material transactions' and transactions 'entered into in the ordinary course of business'. The relevant legislation, Projet de loi relatif à la croissance et la transformation des entreprises (Loi PACTE), Art 66 III-3 (and Art 66 III-5 for companies with a two-tier board structure), will insert a new Art L225-40-2 into the Code de commerce implementing the disclosure obligations of Art 9c(2) Shareholder Rights Directive II, which are applicable to listed companies. In addition, for all companies (i.e. not only listed companies), the scope of Art L225-40 paras 1 and 4 will be extended and require persons both 'directly and indirectly interested in an agreement' to inform the board of the conflict of interest and abstain from voting on the agreement (Art 66 III-2 Loi PACTE).

[578] P Le Cannu and B Dondero, *Droit des sociétés* (7th edn, LGDJ 2018) para 762.

[579] See Art R225-30 Code de commerce, as amended by Decree no 2015-545, 18 May 2015, JORF no 0115 of 20 May 2015, 8506.

[580] Com, Art R225-31, as amended by Decree no 2015-545 (n 579).

[581] ibid Art L225-42.

[582] ibid para 3.

[583] For example because the interested party participates in the vote of the general meeting in violation of Com, Art L225-40 para 4. For a discussion of this point, see B Saintourens, 'Note: Conventions réglementées: questions pratiques sur le risque de nullité de la convention et de responsabilité du dirigeant' (2010) *Bull. Joly Sociétés* 814, at I. The resolution of the general meeting is null and void if the shareholders decide without having received the special report of the auditors, Art L235-1 para 2 (for a discussion of whether this provision also applies if the report has been issued but is defective, see Merle (n 305) para 452). In the first case mentioned above—failure to obtain prior approval by the board—irregularities in the vote by the general meeting are of crucial importance. Since the general meeting can avoid nullity pursuant to Art L225-42 para 3, an invalid vote does not have the desired effect of confirming the interested agreement, which may be set aside if it is prejudicial to the company. In the second case—board approval has been obtained—the resolution of the general meeting does not affect the validity of the agreement (see Art L224-41 para 1), but the director can be held liable for the damage inflicted on the company pursuant to Art L224-41 para 2, since the agreement has not been approved by the general meeting. See Saintourens, ibid, and the discussion above in the text.

[584] Com, Art L225-41 para 1. The directors act for example fraudulently if they conceal the agreement or furnish the general meeting with incorrect information to induce its approval, see Le Cannu and Dondero (n 578) para 762 (n 260).

[585] Com, Arts L225-251 to L225-254.

[586] Section B.I.4(a). See also Saintourens (n 583) III.

Liability may arise, in principle, for defects at any stage of the procedure. First of all, a director may be liable for failure to obtain the required authorization by the board of directors.[587] It is equally clear that an agreement that inflicts a loss on the company and is not approved by the shareholders in general meeting triggers the director's liability, even if board authorization is given.[588] More problematic are intermediate cases where the general meeting approves the agreement, but the procedure is marred by other defects, for example the invalidity of the board's authorization or the failure by the director to disclose all relevant facts. This problem is illustrated by a case decided by the Cour de Cassation in 2010, *Société Maaldrift BV*.[589] In this case, the plaintiff, Maaldrift, was a minority shareholder of a public stock corporation, Comireg. Comireg, in turn, was owned by a company called Finaries, which held about 88 per cent of Comireg's share capital. The defendant was chairman of the board and general director (*président directeur général*) of Comireg and deputy executive director of Finaries. Maaldrift challenged the acquisition of 60,000 shares of another company, Tesson Informatique, by Comireg from Finaries. Initially, the plan had been for Comireg to take over Tesson Informatique, but for financial reasons the interest in Tesson Informatique was first purchased by Finaries and later sold to Comireg. The formal steps prescribed by the Commercial Code for regulated agreements were observed. The board of directors authorized the acquisition of the interest in Tesson Informatique, the auditors drew up a special report, and the general meeting approved the acquisition. However, Maaldrift submitted that the board's authorization was defective because the defendant had not abstained from participating in the decision, as required by law.[590] Furthermore, he had not informed the general meeting that Tesson Informatique had become insolvent by the time of the share transfer, and the interested parties had participated in the resolution of the general meeting.[591] Consequently, Maaldrift argued that the defendant was liable pursuant to Article L225-42 Code de commerce.[592] The Court of Appeal rejected these arguments, holding that the resolution of the general meeting had not been challenged and had consequently become binding,[593] thus foreclosing the claims of Maaldrift. The court explained that 'even under the hypothesis that the authorization of the board of directors was affected by an irregularity because, in violation of Article L225-40 Code de commerce, it had not been demonstrated that [the director] had not participated in the vote, the [defects] were rectified by the resolution of the general meeting pursuant to the last paragraph of Article L225-42 of the same Code'. The Cour de Cassation overruled the decision in part, pointing out that this reasoning did not sufficiently take account of the fact that the director had allegedly failed to disclose the imminent insolvency of Tesson Informatique to the general meeting and, accordingly,

[587] Com, Art L225-42 para 1. See, for example, Cass com, 15 June 1993, *Revue des sociétés* 1993, 806, note B Saintourens.

[588] Com, Art L225-41 para 2. The Commercial Code speaks of 'refused agreements', but it has been argued that the rejection of the agreement and the lack of a vote by the general meeting should have the same consequence of giving rise to personal liability of the interested director, see Le Cannu and Dondero (n 578) para 762. For a case concerning liability pursuant to Art L225-41 para 2, see Cass com, 8 July 2009 (*Sté Havas c/ Hérail*), *Revue des sociétés* 2009, 823, note D Poracchia. In this case, M Hérail had served, among other functions, as general director of Havas before he was dismissed. His compensation package was rejected by the general meeting and the company claimed damages. The Cour de Cassation dismissed the claim, holding that the company had not shown that M Hérail's services had been of no value to the company or that he had received 'excessive and unusual advantages' under the agreement.

[589] Cass com, 15 June 2010, *Bull. Joly Sociétés* 2010, 814, note B Saintourens. The events also led to an unsuccessful lawsuit for abuse of corporate assets, see Cass crim, 10 April 2013, no 12-81048.

[590] Com, Art L225-40 para 1.

[591] This is prohibited pursuant to Art L225-42 para 3, which refers to Art L225-40 para 4.

[592] Maaldrift also sought to have the share transfer set aside, arguing that the resolution of the general meeting approving the transaction pursuant to Art L225-42 para 3 was invalid because the special report of the auditors informing the general meeting of the interested transaction was incomplete and the interested parties did not abstain from voting on the authorization (see the second ground of the appeal, first and second part, no of the appeal: 09-10961, not reproduced in *Bull. Joly*). However, the court did not address the substance of these grounds of the appeal because Maaldrift had failed to submit them in the previous instance.

[593] See, Cozian, Viandier, and Deboissy (n 309) para 636, for an overview of the mechanisms to challenge resolutions of the general meeting or other corporate acts.

'acted knowingly in violation of the interests of the company Comireg'.[594] While this judgment does not answer all questions, it clarifies that directors may be held liable for defects in the procedure governing regulated agreements even if the general meeting resolves to avoid nullity pursuant to the last paragraph of Article L225-42 Code de commerce.[595]

The rules on regulated agreements have attracted criticism, on the one hand because the cumbersome approval procedure is not appropriate for all types of company, in particular medium-sized, family-owned enterprises where outside shareholders may not exist, and on the other hand because of their complexity, which has created legal uncertainty. The effectiveness of the rules is also questionable, given that the directors, including those who are interested, decide whether a transaction qualifies as an unregulated agreement relating to current operations and entered into under normal conditions or a regulated agreement that must be submitted for further scrutiny.[596] Even if agreements are submitted to the auditors and the general meeting for approval, it was pointed out that in practice the general meeting remains largely ignorant of the details of the transaction and, therefore, has difficulties to function as an effective controlling organ and enforce the directors' responsibility where it is engaged.[597] In order to address these deficiencies, the French securities regulator (*Autorité des marchés financiers*) produced a report suggesting changes to the regime, for example encouraging companies to establish a charter defining which agreements are submitted to the regulated agreement procedure, requiring the board of directors to give reasons for their decision authorizing a regulated agreement, and enhancing the content of the information provided in the auditors' special report.[598] Some of these changes have been implemented, notably in the form of the requirement that directors explain why, and the auditors assess in their report whether, a related party transaction is in the interest of the company (Articles R225-30 and R225-31 Code de commerce, as amended in 2015). However, it is questionable whether these changes are sufficient to overcome the informational disadvantages of the shareholders.[599]

The regime governing regulated agreements is only one aspect of the French system of rules and duties addressing situations that would fall under the common law duty of loyalty. Since the dichotomy between the duty of loyalty and the duty of care is informed by common law concepts (although it is also discernible in the German case law on directors' duties), it is not surprising that it is not reflected in the approach of the French courts to scrutinizing related-party transactions. French law is primarily concerned with specific rules determining decision and information rights, such as the regime on regulated agreements, and the consequences of a violation of these rules, which take us back to the tort-law-based general provisions concerning the responsibility of directors and managers.[600] While the existence of an unwritten duty of loyalty

[594] This part of the holding was based on the third part of the second ground of appeal. The Cour de Cassation rejected the fourth part of that ground (see n 592 above regarding the other parts), according to which the interested directors breached their duties and were liable if they participated in the resolution of the general meeting in violation of Arts L225-42 para 3, L225-40 para 4, notwithstanding the fact that the resolution had become binding.

[595] On this point see also Saintourens (n 583) III.

[596] D Schmidt, 'Conventions réglementées: commentaire du rapport du groupe de travail de l'AMF sur les assemblées générales d'actionnaires de sociétés cotées' (2012) *Revue des sociétés* 139 para 4. The first draft proposal of the Loi PACTE (n 550), as adopted by the National Assembly on 9 October 2018, would have provided in Art 66 III-6 that the directors had to make a list of agreements available to the shareholders relating to current operations and entered into under normal conditions within the meaning of Art L225-39 Code de commerce, thus enabling the shareholders to police whether the directors' classification of agreements as regulated and non-regulated was adequate. However, in the first reading of the proposal in the Senate on 12 February 2019, this provision was deleted and replaced with a provision requiring 'the board of directors to put in place a procedure to evaluate whether the agreements relating to current operations and concluded under normal conditions fulfill these conditions', Art 66 III-1*bis*.

[597] Schmidt (n 596) paras 5–10 (pointing out that the auditors' report is usually very brief, does not give sufficient information to appreciate the implications of the transaction, and the general meeting is often not even furnished with the text of the agreement at issue).

[598] AMF, Report of the Working Group on General Meetings of Shareholders of Listed Companies, 7 February 2012, Proposals 20–34.

[599] Schmidt (n 596) para 41. For further disclosure obligations imposed on listed companies in the course of implementing the Shareholder Rights Directive II, see n 577 above.

[600] See our discussion in section B.I.4(a) above.

is acknowledged in French law,[601] the courts usually do not engage in a demarcation of care and loyalty, but examine cases through the more holistic lens of managerial misconduct. Behaviour calling into question both the exercise of due care and the director's loyalty may give rise to what the French courts call a 'managerial fault', leading to liability either under the general rules on directors' duties[602] or, if the company has entered insolvent liquidation and the challenged conduct amounts to more than simple negligence, for *l'insuffisance d'actif*.[603]

An example is a decision of the Cour de Cassation of 2011, *Société Sorim*, which we already mentioned in the context of the duty of care.[604] In this case, the director of Sorim initiated the payment of a large extraordinary dividend in difficult market conditions and thus, the court argued, compromised the economic future of the company.[605] The issue was conceptualized as one of mismanagement (*faute de gestion*),[606] which is reminiscent of formulations used by the common law in connection with the duty of care, but at the heart of the case was a conflict of interest. The director was also majority shareholder and managing director of the holding company of Sorim and arranged for the distribution in order to allow the holding company to reduce its debts, without having regard to the financial needs of the subsidiary. Thus, the breach of duty consisted in giving preference to the director's own interests over the company's interests.[607]

Finally, the last piece of the French regulatory system is criminal law, notably the offence of abuse of corporate assets, also already discussed in the section of this chapter on the duty of care.[608] Self-dealing or transactions within a corporate group that are contrary to the interests of one of the group companies may constitute an abuse of corporate assets. The offence is in some sense wider than the regime governing regulated agreements because an approval by the general meeting does not affect the director's criminal responsibility.[609] On the other hand, the offence is only engaged if a director acts with the intention to use the corporation's assets for private purposes.[610] This may not always be the case with related-party transactions, for example where intra-group transactions benefit the interests of the group.[611]

II. Corporate opportunities

1. UK

Companies Act 2006

Section 175—Duty to avoid conflicts of interest

(1) A director of a company must avoid a situation in which he has, or can have, a direct or indirect interest that conflicts, or possibly may conflict, with the interests of the company.
(2) This applies in particular to the exploitation of any property, information or opportunity (and it is immaterial whether the company could take advantage of the property, information or opportunity).

[601] See, for example, Cozian, Viandier, and Deboissy (n 309) para 375, and the discussion of corporate opportunities in section C.II.4 below. In the latter context, the unwritten French duty of loyalty is of particular importance.
[602] Com, Art L225-251. [603] ibid, Art L651-2; see n 321 above.
[604] Cass com, 25 October 2011, *Bull. Joly Sociétés* 2012, 243. [605] For more details, see n 318 above.
[606] The question was whether the director had committed a management fault within the meaning of Art L651-2 Code de commerce (*action de la responsabilité pour insuffisance d'actif*) and could, accordingly, be held liable for the deficiency in the company's assets.
[607] The Cour de Cassation held that the director was liable because his action 'was directly contrary to the interest of [Sorim] and allowed him to benefit [the holding company], of which he was the majority shareholder and in which he was directly interested'.
[608] Com, Art L242-6. See section B.I.4(b) above.
[609] Cass crim, 12 December 1994, *Bull. Joly Sociétés* 1995, 427 (finding that a director who received remuneration for fictitious services that had been approved by both the board of directors and the general meeting was liable for abuse of corporate assets).
[610] See above text to nn 372–375.
[611] But see text to n 374 above for indirect personal interests that trigger the offence.

(3) This duty does not apply to a conflict of interest arising in relation to a transaction or arrangement with the company.
(4) This duty is not infringed—
  (a) if the situation cannot reasonably be regarded as likely to give rise to a conflict of interest; or
  (b) if the matter has been authorised by the directors.
(5) Authorisation may be given by the directors—
  (a) where the company is a private company and nothing in the company's constitution invalidates such authorisation, by the matter being proposed to and authorised by the directors; or
  (b) where the company is a public company and its constitution includes provision enabling the directors to authorise the matter, by the matter being proposed to and authorised by them in accordance with the constitution.
(6) The authorisation is effective only if—
  (a) any requirement as to the quorum at the meeting at which the matter is considered is met without counting the director in question or any other interested director, and
  (b) the matter was agreed to without their voting or would have been agreed to if their votes had not been counted.
(7) Any reference in this section to a conflict of interest includes a conflict of interest and duty and a conflict of duties.

Corporate opportunities concern a specific type of conflict of interest between a company and a director: the exploitation of a business opportunity that the law regards as being 'reserved' for the company. Accordingly, under UK law, corporate opportunities are regulated as part of the general duty to avoid situations that may give rise to a conflict of interest, set out in subsection 1 of section 175 Companies Act 2006. Subsection 2 of section 175 provides that the general rule will apply '*in particular* to the exploitation of any property, information or opportunity'.[612] Thus, section 175(1) formulates a broadly phrased behavioural expectation that encompasses any type of actual or potential, direct or indirect conflict between the company's interests and the director's private interests, with the exception of self-dealing transactions that we discussed above and that are governed, as we have seen, by section 177 as *lex specialis*.[613]

Section 175 codifies two common law principles: the no-conflict and no-profit rules. The no-conflict rule was expressed by the courts in uncompromising terms as early as the mid-19th century, for example in the leading case *Aberdeen Railway Company v Blaikie Bros*, where the House of Lords held: '[I]t is a rule of universal application, that no one, having [fiduciary] duties to discharge, shall be allowed to enter into engagements in which he has, or can have, a personal interest conflicting, or which possibly may conflict, with the interests of those whom he is bound to protect'.[614] Applied to corporate opportunities, the common law rule prohibited directors from taking advantage of a business opportunity that was of commercial value to the company, unless the shareholders approved the transaction. If the directors violated the no-conflict or no-profit rule, they were accountable to the company for the profit that they had made from exploiting the opportunity. Section 175(5)–(6) now provides for an additional, alternative, mechanism to validate a transaction exploiting a corporate opportunity: ex ante authorization of the transaction by the disinterested directors.[615] In public companies, the constitution must enable the directors to authorize the matter; in private companies the default rule is that authorization by the directors is permissible.[616]

[612] Emphasis added. Another case that may fall within the scope of s 175 (and not s 177) is that of competing directorships.

[613] See s 175(3).

[614] (1854) 1 Macq 461. The no-profit rule essentially deals with the same social problem and overlaps largely with the duty to avoid situations that give rise to a conflict of interest. It has been held that directors must not use their position and their knowledge as directors to obtain a profit for themselves, see *Regal (Hastings) Ltd v Gulliver* [1942] 1 All ER 378.

[615] Pursuant to s 175(6), the conflicted director may participate in the board meeting authorizing the transaction, but he and any other interested director count neither for purposes of quorum nor voting. Note that s 175(6) distinguishes between 'the director in question' (who intends to make use of the corporate opportunity) and other interested directors, who are also barred from voting. The provision does not define, however, when a director is interested in another director's business opportunity. For a discussion of this point, see Davies and Worthington (n 30) para 16-103.

[616] Section 175(5).

The corporate opportunities doctrine has created a wealth of case law. The cases mainly centre on three questions: When does a business opportunity belong to the corporation and when are the directors, accordingly, prohibited from pursuing the opportunity for their own account? Secondly, can an opportunity be taken up by the directors if the company declines it or is unable to exploit the opportunity, for example because of financial constraints? Finally, does a director who resigns from the board continue to be subject to the duty under section 175(2)? The following excerpt addresses some of these issues.

Bhullar v Bhullar **[2003] BCC 711 (Court of Appeal)**

[From the 1950s two brothers, Sohan and Mohan Singh Bhullar, ran a grocery shop in Huddersfield. The business became successful and was incorporated in 1964. Sohan and Mohan were the first shareholders and directors. The objects of the company as set out in its memorandum of association included the acquisition of property for investment. The company acquired a number of properties and an investment property which was used as a bowling hall. Other family members became directors, including Sohan's two sons (the appellants) and Mohan's son. The shares were held as to 50 per cent by Mohan and his family and as to 50 per cent by Sohan and his family. Sohan's family had a 3:2 majority on the board. By 1998 the relationship between the two families had broken down. Mohan and his son informed Sohan and the appellants at a board meeting that the time had come for the two families to go their separate ways and that in the meantime the company should not acquire any more properties. Sohan's family accepted that decision in principle. In 1999, when they were going bowling with a visitor, the two sons of Sohan discovered that a property adjacent to the company's investment property was up for sale. The appellants acquired the property in the name of another company, Silvercrest.]

Jonathan Parker, LJ:

[Counsel for the appellants], in his attractively presented submissions, submits that a director of a company is under no duty to offer to the company business opportunities which come to him privately, notwithstanding that the company may be in a position to exploit such opportunities. He submits that the judge was in error in holding that because the company might possibly have been interested in acquiring the property, ergo the appellants were in breach of their fiduciary duty in acquiring it for themselves. He submits that, applying the principles laid down in Phipps v Boardman,[617] the first step is to identify the nature and scope of the appellants' pre-existing duty as fiduciaries in relation to the purchase of the property. Until the nature and scope of that pre-existing duty has been identified, he submits, one cannot determine whether in purchasing the property the appellants breached that duty ...

[In addition, counsel] submits, on the uncontested evidence any interest on the part of the company in acquiring the property can only have been an extremely limited one. In support of this submission, he points to the evidence that the company's main business consisted of operating supermarkets; that it owned only one commercial investment property (albeit adjacent to the property); and that when the property was acquired the company had been trying unsuccessfully to sell one of its supermarkets for some two years ...

Conclusions

[T]he concept of a conflict between fiduciary duty and personal interest presupposes an existing fiduciary duty. But it does not follow that it is a prerequisite of the accountability of a fiduciary that there should have been some improper dealing with property 'belonging' to the party to whom the fiduciary duty is owed, that is to say with trust property. The relevant rule, which Lord Cranworth LC in *Aberdeen Railway Co v Blaikie Bros* described as being 'of universal application', and which Lord Herschell in *Bray v Ford [1896] AC 44* at p.51, described as 'inflexible', is that (to use Lord Cranworth's formulation) no fiduciary 'shall be allowed to enter into engagements in which he has, or can have, a personal interest conflicting, or which may possibly conflict, with the interests of those whom he is bound to protect' ...

As it seems to me, the rule is essentially a simple one, albeit that it may in some cases be difficult to apply. The only qualification which is required to Lord Cranworth's formulation of it is that which was supplied by Lord Upjohn in *Phipps v Boardman*, where he said this (at p.124):

[617] [Footnote by authors.] [1967] 2 AC 46.

'The phrase "possibly may conflict" requires consideration. In my view it means that the reasonable man looking at the relevant facts and circumstances of the particular case would think that there was a real sensible possibility of conflict; not that you could imagine some situation arising which might, in some conceivable possibility in events not contemplated as real sensible possibilities by any reasonable person, result in a conflict.'

... [T]he authority which (of those cited to us) is nearest on its facts to those of the instant case is the decision of Roskill J in *Industrial Development Consultants Ltd v Cooley*.[618] In that case, a commercial opportunity was offered to the defendant, who was at the time the managing director of the plaintiff company, in his private capacity. The defendant subsequently obtained his release by the company in order to exploit that opportunity for his own benefit. Had the company known that he had been offered that opportunity, it would not have agreed to release him. He was held accountable for the benefits he had received by exploiting the opportunity. The opportunity was not one which the company could itself have exploited.

Roskill J, after quoting extensively from Lord Upjohn's speech in *Phipps v Boardman* ... said (at p.451):

'The first matter that has to be considered is whether or not the defendant was in a fiduciary relationship with his principals, the plaintiffs. [Counsel for the defendant] argued that he was not because he received this information which was communicated to him privately. With respect, I think that argument is wrong. The defendant had one capacity and one capacity only in which he was carrying on business at that time. That capacity was as managing director of the plaintiffs. Information which came to him while he was managing director and which was of concern to the plaintiffs and was relevant for the plaintiffs to know, was information which it was his duty to pass on to the plaintiffs because between himself and the plaintiffs a fiduciary relationship existed ...'

... Like the defendant in *Industrial Development Consultants Ltd v Cooley*, the appellants in the instant case had, at the material time, one capacity and one capacity only in which they were carrying on business, namely as directors of the company. In that capacity, they were in a fiduciary relationship with the company. At the material time, the company was still trading, albeit that negotiations (ultimately unsuccessful) for a division of its assets and business were on foot. As [one of Sohan's sons] accepted in cross-examination, it would have been 'worthwhile' for the company to have acquired the property. Although the reasons why it would have been 'worthwhile' were not explored in evidence, it seems obvious that the opportunity to acquire the property would have been commercially attractive to the company, given its proximity to Springbank Works. Whether the company could or would have taken that opportunity, had it been made aware of it, is not to the point: the existence of the opportunity was information which it was relevant for the company to know, and it follows that the appellants were under a duty to communicate it to the company ...

[Accordingly, the Court of Appeal upheld the decision of High Court declaring that Silvercrest held the property on trust for Sohan and Mohan's company.]

Questions and comments:

1. *Bhullar v Bhullar* raises a number of points. First, the appellants discovered the business opportunity, an investment property, not while they were concerned with company business, but during their free time. Some precedents, while not addressing the question directly, could be understood as defining corporate opportunities only as such opportunities that came to the attention of the directors while discharging their functions *as director*. Notably, in *Regal (Hastings) Ltd v Gulliver*,[619] a case that concerned an action by Regal against its former directors to recover profits made by them upon the acquisition and sale of shares in a subsidiary of Regal, the House of Lords held, *per* Lord Russell of Killowen: '[T]he directors standing in a fiduciary relationship to Regal in regard to the exercise of their powers as directors, and having obtained these shares *by reason and only by reason* of the fact that they were directors of Regal and in the course of the execution of that office, are accountable for the profits which they have made out of them.'[620] This quote seems to place emphasis on the fact that the directors had obtained the

[618] [Footnote by authors.] [1972] 2 All ER 162.
[619] [1967] 2 AC 134.
[620] ibid 149 (emphasis by authors).

investment opportunity because of their position and while exercising their functions as directors of Regal. Thus, the judgment implies a causal relationship between the execution of their office and the acquisition of the business opportunity by the directors. However, in *Industrial Development Consultants Ltd v Cooley*,[621] followed by *Bhullar v Bhullar*, the courts took a different approach. Directors have 'one capacity and one capacity only', namely that of a director. Accordingly, they stand in a fiduciary relationship with the company whatever they do, and it does not matter whether the business opportunity was communicated to them in a private capacity or connected with the director's office. The question is only whether the opportunity is 'relevant' or 'worthwhile' for the company. We will come back to this point below in our next main case.[622] Secondly, we learn from the facts of *Bhullar v Bhullar* that the company was supposed to be divided between the two families and it had been decided that it should not acquire any more properties. This argument also did not sway the court to hold in favour of the appellants. The court stated succinctly that the likely decision of the company not to take the opportunity was 'not to the point'. Again, it is only relevant whether the opportunity is 'commercially attractive' to the company. If yes, the directors are prohibited from exploiting it.

2. *Bhullar v Bhullar* touches upon the capacity of a company to exploit an opportunity. In passing, the court mentioned that it was irrelevant '[w]hether the company could or would have taken [the] opportunity'.[623] The court also referred to *Industrial Development Consultants Ltd v Cooley*, where a director's company had unsuccessfully attempted to an then opportunity, which was then offered to the director in his private capacity. The court found that the director was in breach of the duty of loyalty, even though the company could not have exploited the opportunity itself. This raises the question when a practical impediment, for example the failure of a company to obtain a valuable contract or its financial incapacity to take advantage of an opportunity, releases the director from the prohibition to pursue the business opportunity privately.[624] The short answer is that a practical impediment never releases the director. *Regal (Hastings) v Gulliver*, mentioned above,[625] illustrates the consequences of financial incapacity. Regal did not have sufficient funds to provide the required financing for its subsidiary, which had been formed to take a lease of two cinemas. For this reason, the directors took 2,000 of the total share capital of 5,000 shares themselves. In spite of the fact that the company could not muster additional funds and possibly would have had to forgo the profitable investment without the directors' intervention, the court found that the corporate opportunities doctrine applied.[626] The court was invited to distinguish the precedents establishing a strict prohibition on the grounds 'that it was impossible for Regal to get the shares owing to lack of funds, and that the directors in taking the shares were really acting as members of the public'.[627] The court held: 'I cannot accept this argument … The suggestion that the directors were applying simply as members of the public is a travesty of the facts. They could, had they wished, have protected themselves by a resolution (either antecedent or subsequent) of the Regal shareholders in general meeting. In default of such approval, the liability to account must remain'.[628] The Companies Act 2006 confirms this strict approach. Pursuant to section 175(2), it is immaterial whether the company can take advantage of the opportunity.[629]

Bhullar v Bhullar and the decisions referred to in that case show that the business opportunities doctrine operates as a rigid constraint on the directors' discretion. The Companies Act 2006 replicates this strict prohibition, which is only subject to two exceptions. The duty arising under section 175 is not infringed if 'the situation cannot reasonably be regarded as

[621] See n 618 above. [622] *Wilkinson v West Coast Capital* [2005] EWHC 3009.

[623] [2003] BCC 711, 723.

[624] Distinguish this case from the second point discussed in the preceding comment, where the company voluntarily decides that it is not interested in the opportunity.

[625] See n 619 above.

[626] However, it must also be mentioned that the directors did not make an effort to obtain additional financing on behalf of the company and refused to provide personal guarantees that would have relieved them of the necessity to subscribe for shares personally: ibid 146.

[627] ibid 149. [628] ibid 149–50.

[629] See also *Boardman v Phipps* [1967] 2 AC 46, a trust case where the court held that '[w]hether or not the trust or the beneficiaries in their stead could have taken advantage of the information is immaterial': ibid 111.

likely to give rise to a conflict of interest' or 'the matter has been authorised by the directors'.[630] We are here concerned with the first of these exceptions, which goes to the heart of the duty of loyalty as expressed in section 175(1).[631] If the directors are required to avoid any conflict of interest, then the duty logically presupposes that the situation must be such as to give rise to the possibility of a conflict. This was also the understanding of Lord Cranworth in *Aberdeen Railway Co v Blaikie Bros* and Lord Upjohn in *Phipps v Boardman*, both quoted above in *Bhullar v Bhullar*. Lord Cranworth proposed a definition of what constitutes a possible conflict: '[T]he reasonable man looking at the relevant facts and circumstances of the particular case [must] think that there was a *real sensible possibility of conflict*'.[632] A 'real sensible possibility of conflict' may not exist for two reasons. First, the company may not be interested in the opportunity because it falls outside of the company's actual line of business or objects as defined in the articles. It is always conceivable that the shareholders amend the articles to change the objects clause or decide to diversify into different industries, but when is this possibility so remote that we can no longer speak of any 'real sensible possibility of conflict'? Secondly, as briefly discussed above in the second comment on *Bhullar v Bhullar*, a company may not be able to take advantage of an opportunity, for example because of legal restrictions or financial constraints. We have learned that financial constraints are generally irrelevant. But is the situation different if the company is prevented from exploiting the opportunity because of a legal prohibition, for example one that arises under competition law? And how should we treat the case of a provision in the articles requiring approval of a transaction by a particular director or a supermajority of the shareholders that is unlikely to be forthcoming? The following case grapples with these questions.

***Wilkinson v West Coast Capital* [2007] BCC 717 (Chancery Division)**

[NGS was incorporated as the holding company of another company called TGS (The Gadget Shop), which sold gadgets popular as gifts. NGS had four shareholders. The petitioner, Mr Wilkinson, held 40 percent of the share capital. The remaining shares were being held by West Coast Capital (WCC), a Scottish private equity firm (25 percent), and two individuals, Mr Gorman (25 percent) and Mr Elvidge (10 percent). The two directors of NGS were Mr Gorman and Mr McMahon, who was also a partner in WCC. In late 2002, NGS was in negotiations with a company called Birthdays Group Ltd, a chain of retail shops selling greetings cards, toys, and small gifts, concerning the trial of TGS products in Birthdays shops. At about the same time, one of the founding partners of WCC, Sir Tom Hunter, had become aware from other sources that the venture capital houses backing Birthdays wanted to sell their investments. A possible acquisition of Birthdays was briefly discussed at an NGS board meeting and also at later management meetings. In addition, NGS personnel carried out due diligence work with respect to Birthdays. Sir Tom Hunter and Mr Gorman considered two alternative methods of structuring the acquisition, the first through NGS and the second through WCC. Eventually they decided for the second alternative, because they could not agree with Mr Wilkinson on his stake in a combined TGS/Birthdays enterprise. The financial position of Birthdays was found to be less satisfactory than expected and the company was later sold at a loss. Mr Wilkinson challenged the acquisition, claiming that Mr Gorman, a de jure director of NGS, and Sir Tom Hunter, who was alleged to be a de facto director, had breach their fiduciary duties in expropriating a corporate opportunity belonging to NGS. The members of NGS had entered into a shareholder agreement providing that certain activities of the company, including the acquisition of any company or business, required the consent of more than 65 percent of the shareholders. Sir Tom Hunter and Mr Gorman claimed that they would have walked away from the Birthdays deal, rather than allowed NGS to acquire Birthdays with the then existing shareholder structure, if they had been advised that they could not properly acquire the company for themselves.]

[630] Companies Act 2006, s 175(4). In addition, shareholders can of course give their consent or ratify a breach of duty. The requirements for valid shareholder consent are set out, for example, in *Sharma v Sharma* [2013] EWCA Civ 1287, para 52.

[631] For the second exception, see text to n 662 below.

[632] *Boardman v Phipps* (n 629) 124 (emphasis by authors).

Warren, J:

There are two important rules which, if not qualified, generally affect directors, as they affect all fiduciaries. They can be called the 'no conflict' rule and the 'no profit' rule[633] ...

The purpose of the [no conflict] rule is to prevent the fiduciary being swayed by personal considerations of his personal interests or competing fiduciary interests in the exercise of the powers exercisable by him in a fiduciary capacity. If he has no powers to exercise, then the foundation for the rule has ... been undermined and the rule will not apply ... although he may remain liable under the 'no profit' rule if he uses for his own benefit property of the company or information which he has acquired as a director and which is of value to the company.

It is important to note that the 'no conflict' rule can apply to a fiduciary in some situations where he neither makes a profit from trust property nor from his fiduciary position. This is because he has a duty to protect those to whom his duties are owed. He cannot prefer his own interests to those of his beneficiaries. His problem arises where he enters into a transaction inconsistent with his duty of loyalty to his beneficiaries. One of the difficulties, however, for the fiduciary (and for the court) may be in identifying, in any given situation, whether the relevant element of conflict is present.

[The court examines when the director's personal interest 'possibly may conflict' with the interest of the company, in particular where the company's business is different from the business opportunity. The court explains:] A company with a wide objects clause could, in theory, diversify its business in limitless ways if the necessary funding were available. But a director of a company selling fashion clothing for women could hardly be in breach of the 'no conflict' rule if he took a stake in a company distributing farm machinery, even if the company did have such a wide objects clause. There would simply be no 'real sensible possibility' of conflict. In contrast, if the board of the fashion clothing company had been actively considering diversification into the distribution of farm machinery, there would be a real sensible possibility of conflict in a director taking a stake in such a company. He could escape the conflict only by resigning as a director (although if he had by then learnt of a relevant business opportunity, at least if that was by virtue of his directorship, the 'no profit' rule might apply).

Turning to the 'no profit' rule, this is summarised [in the literature] in this way: 'If a trustee or other fiduciary without authority makes a profit directly or indirectly from the use of property subject to the trust or other fiduciary relationship, or in the course of the fiduciary relationship and by reason of his fiduciary position, then he is not permitted to retain the profit'....

[The court first discusses the application of the no-conflict rule. It refers to the partnership case *Aas v Benham* [1891] 2 Ch. 244, dealing with a partner in a ship-broking firm, Mr Benham, who also acted as advisor of a ship-building company and made a profit for himself as a result of information given to the ship-building company that he had learned of while travelling in Spain on behalf of the ship-broking firm. In that case, the Court of Appeal had held that if a partner avails himself of information which the partnership is entitled to 'for any purpose which is within the scope of the partnership business ... he must account to the firm for any benefits which he may have derived from such information ... By 'information which the partnership is entitled to' is meant information which can be used for the purposes of the partnership'. The court interprets this holding for purposes of the present case:] [W]hat [*Aas v Benham*] does establish, or reflect as existing law, is that the scope of the duty of a partner is circumscribed by the partnership agreement; and that the mere use of information or an opportunity obtained and acquired while acting in his fiduciary capacity does not necessarily mean that the partner cannot use that information or take advantage of that opportunity on his own account. The case possibly establishes, or re-affirms, a *negative* proposition, *viz.* that there is no principle which entitles a firm to benefits derived from the use of information for purposes which are wholly outside the scope of the firm's activities.

In applying that negative principle, one must act with care because the firm's activities may not be limited by the formal partnership agreement. For instance, if Mr Benham had been mandated, with a view to a possible extension of the firm's business, by his partners to investigate, on behalf of the firm, a possible investment in ship-building opportunities while in Spain and Portugal conducting business on behalf of the firm, the relevant activities might thereby have been extended to ship-building. Whilst the partners could not, in fact, have extended the scope of the business without Mr Benham's consent as a partner, and even though he might, on his

[633] [Footnote by authors.] For a discussion of the no-conflict/no-profit dichotomy and whether it is of continuing validity after codification of the duty of loyalty in s 175 Companies Act 2006; see Davies and Worthington (n 30) para 16-87.

return to England, refuse to agree to such an extension, it does not necessarily follow that he would have been entirely outside the constraints of the 'no conflict' and 'no profit' rules …

It is clear that the fact that a company might have been practically unable to take up an opportunity does not exonerate a director who takes it for himself. That is a hard rule: but it is a clear rule. So it seems to me that one needs to approach with caution the situation where the inability arises, or is said to arise, not from a practical inability but from a structural restriction comparable to that in *Aas v Benham*. The argument, in that sort of situation, is that, since there are constitutional restrictions on what the company can do, an activity within the scope of that restriction cannot be an activity within the scope of the company's affairs; so that if the directors, personally, carry out that activity they cannot, *ex hypothesi*, [appropriate a corporate opportunity.] …

Mr McCaughran [counsel for one of the respondents] accepts that, once a conflict has arisen and a profit has been made, it is no defence for the director to allege that the company could not as a matter of fact have acquired the opportunity itself, for example because the company could not afford to pursue the opportunity (as in *Regal (Hastings) Ltd v Gulliver*) or because the third party would not have wanted to deal with the company (as in *Industrial Development Consultants Ltd v Cooley*). But he submits that none of the cases is concerned with the situation where, as in *Aas v Benham* there was a legal impediment to the company taking up the opportunity; he says that, where there is a legal impediment of this sort, there is no relevant conflict of interest. On the facts of the present case there was, he submits, a legal impediment to the acquisition of Birthdays by NGS and therefore no relevant conflict of interest in the acquisition by WCC and Mr Gorman.

By legal impediment, I understand Mr McCaughran to be focusing essentially on constitutional documents such as partnership agreements, articles of association and shareholders agreements. A contractual restraint arising under an agreement with a third party (such [as] an anti-competition covenant given on the sale of a business) would, I apprehend, more properly be regarded as a practical impediment although a statutory prohibition would certainly fall to be treated as a legal impediment. But even a legal bar (save a statutory prohibition and, perhaps, a true restriction on the powers of a company in its objects clause) in the sense used by Mr McCaughran is not conclusive as to the scope of the activities of a company or partnership.

However, what I think is important in the present case is not so much the effect of a legal impediment on the duty of directors generally; but rather the impact of the director himself being able, in a non-fiduciary capacity, to prevent the company of which he is a director from obtaining the benefit of the opportunity. I doubt very much that a legal impediment requiring shareholder consent to certain matters impacts to any great extent on the duties of a director who is not a shareholder. It does not follow from the fact that a particular acquisition requires shareholder consent that a director is freed from any duty which would otherwise arise to bring an opportunity of acquisition to the attention of the board and the shareholders. In contrast, the ability of a shareholder, who also happens to be a director, to block certain action on the part of the company may be of great importance in the context of his duties to account under the 'no conflict' and 'no profit' rules …

[T]here has, in my judgment, been no breach by Mr Gorman or Mr McMahon (or indeed by Sir Tom even if he is a de facto director) of the 'no conflicts' rule. On my findings of fact, there was no agreement that NGS should acquire Birthdays so that they were, as shareholders, able to block the acquisition. There is no question, on my findings, of the board being able to proceed with the acquisition in the face of the provisions of the shareholders agreement to which NGS itself was a party. In any event, Mr Gorman and Mr McMahon could not be criticised if, acting as board members, they had voted against NGS acquiring Birthdays in order to respect the provisions of shareholders agreement which, as between 100 per cent of the shareholders and NGS itself, were stated to take precedence over the unamended articles …

There is more difficulty with the 'no profit' rule … [A] considerable amount of work in the evaluation of the Birthdays business was carried out by NGS personnel in NGS time and, initially at least, at NGS expense. In these circumstances, WCC and Mr Gorman were able to make the successful bid only by use of the information provided to TGS and work done by NGS personnel …

Had a profit been made out of Birthdays, this would be a real issue: were NGS bringing an action to make Mr Gorman—and possibly Mr McMahon (and even Sir Tom if he was a de facto director)—account for the profit made, then there are powerful arguments that he (or they) should do so. However, the fact is that Birthdays was sold at a loss and there is no profit to account for …

[Mr Wilkinson's petition, accordingly, was dismissed.]

Questions and comments:

1. *West Coast Capital* gives important guidance on the nexus that must exist between the business opportunity and the company's line of business so that we can speak of a 'real sensible possibility of conflict'. Either the opportunity or information must be of use, that is, of some commercial value, to the company, given its *current* scope of business, as circumscribed, for example, by the articles,[634] or the company must *actively consider* diversifying into the relevant line of business.[635] On the other hand, where the opportunity is 'wholly outside the scope of the firm's activities' the corporate opportunities doctrine does not apply.[636] A few years after *West Coast Capital*, the Court of Appeal seemed to narrow the 'scope of business' exception to the corporate opportunities doctrine. In *Re Allied Business & Financial Consultants Ltd* (also known as *O'Donnell v Shanahan*),[637] a case decided by the Court of Appeal still under the common law and not the Companies Act 2006, one of the three directors of a company providing financial advice, including arranging bank loans, mortgages and insurance, challenged a property acquisition by the other two directors. The challenged transaction had initially been devised as a business transaction between two of the company's clients on which the company would have earned a commission. When the prospective buyer withdrew from the transaction, the respondents formed a joint venture with another client to purchase the property for their own account. Under the new arrangement, the company did not receive a commission, although the third director was partially compensated out of company funds for the loss of her share of the expected payment that would have been distributed among the three directors. The main issue was whether the respondents had violated the no-profit and no-conflict rules in not putting the company forward as a co-venturer, but instead acquired the property in their individual capacity.

   Similar to the High Court in *West Coast Capital*, the Court of Appeal in *O'Donnell v Shanahan* addressed the no-profit and no-conflict rules separately.[638] It rejected the application of *Aas v Benham*, discussed above in *West Coast Capital*, and hence any scope of business considerations, to the no-profit rule. Reviewing the relevant authorities, the court argued that whenever an agent made a profit, 'without the knowledge of his principal, in the course and execution of his agency', he must account for the profit to the principal.[639] Thus, whether the company itself could have obtained the profit, any loss is caused to the company, or the business opportunity falls within the company's scope of business is irrelevant.[640] In the present case, once it was found that 'the opportunity to buy [the property] came to the respondents' attention in their capacity as directors of the company acting on the company's business and using information they also obtained in the course of so acting, that was the end of the point'.[641] By taking advantage of the opportunity personally without offering it to the company and obtaining the consent of the members if the company was not interested in exploiting it, the directors breached the no-profit rule. The court distinguished *Aas v Benham* on the basis

[634] When discussing the scope of business test, the court in *Wilkinson v West Coast Capital* referred to *Aas v Benham* [1891] 2 Ch 244, which established the rule under partnership law that information obtained in the course of the transaction of partnership business must not be used by the partners 'for any purpose which is within the scope of the partnership business': ibid 255–6. In *Aas v Benham*, it was held that the ship-broking business of the defendant's partnership was sufficiently distinct from the business of ship-building. The fact that the defendant advised a ship-building company, accordingly, did not constitute a breach of duty.

[635] This point was also discussed by the court in *Aas v Benham* (n 634) and it was concluded that the partnership had not intended to enlarge the scope of its business: ibid 258–9.

[636] *Wilkinson v West Coast Capital* [2007] BCC 717, 775.

[637] [2009] BCC 822.

[638] The no-profit and no-conflict rules have not always been treated as separate rules in the case law (see the observation of the trial court in *O'Donnell v Shanahan* [2009] BCC 517, 554) and it is unclear to what extent they followed different common law concepts. Section 175 of the Companies Act 2006 no longer distinguishes between the two rules.

[639] *O'Donnell v Shanahan* (n 637) 839 (quoting *Parker v McKenna* (1874–75) LR 10 Ch App 96, 118).

[640] ibid 843.

[641] ibid 841. The respondents had used information obtained in the course of acting on the company's business because they had commissioned a valuation report and procured other information while still attempting to arrange the initial sale to one of the company's clients for the company's account: ibid 830.

that it was a partnership case and partnership agreements were special in that they usually defined a precise area of business pursued by the partnership and determining the boundaries of the partners' fiduciary obligations. Directors, on the other hand, occupied a fiduciary position that was not similarly circumscribed by contract. As a consequence, their fiduciary duties were, in principle, 'unlimited'.[642] In addition, the court held that the directors breached the no-conflict rule because they pursued a business arrangement under which the company would no longer have a claim to a commission.[643]

Several comments can be made about *O'Donnell v Shanahan* and how the decision can be reconciled with prior case law and the codified duty under section 175. First, while the court holds that *Aas v Benham* provides, as a matter of principle, 'no assistance in determining the nature and reach of the "no profit" rule' in the context of company directors,[644] it should be noted that the company had an open-ended objects clause[645] and actually ventured into the real estate business by acting as an estate agent in the first transaction that proved ultimately abortive. The court placed some emphasis on these facts,[646] and it can be assumed that the outcome would have been less unreserved had the articles circumscribed the scope of the company's business unambiguously. Secondly, the decision is not directly in conflict with *West Coast Capital*. In *West Coast Capital*, the scope of business test informed the reach of the no-conflict rule, not the no-profit rule. In *O'Donnell v Shanahan*, the conflict that gave rise to a breach of the former rule consisted in the fact that the directors abandoned any efforts to find a buyer who was prepared to pay commission and instead pursued the joint venture, knowing that the other parties were only willing to participate on terms not in the best interest of the company.[647] Through this lens, the company's scope of business was not an issue. Finally, it is questionable in how far the court's reasoning regarding the no-profit rule holds under the Companies Act 2006, given that section 175 frames the duty of loyalty exclusively in terms of the avoidance of a conflict of interest and stipulates that the duty is not infringed if the situation cannot reasonably be regarded as likely to give rise to a conflict. Arguably, such a situation exists where the opportunity has no connection with the company's business and the company has not shown any sign that it intends to move into the new area of business.[648]

2. As regards the second of the questions raised above, Warren J distinguished between a 'structural' or 'constitutional' restriction and the 'practical inability' of the company to make use of the business opportunity. What is meant by this distinction and what are the implications for purposes of section 175 of the Companies Act 2006? More specifically, Warren J indicated that if a director was able, 'in a non-fiduciary capacity, [i.e., as a shareholder,] to prevent the company of which he [was] a director from obtaining the benefit of the opportunity', then the director was free to pursue the opportunity personally. How can this holding be reconciled with section 175(2), which states that the company's inability to take advantage of the opportunity, for whatever reason, will be immaterial? Furthermore, consider a business opportunity that requires a merger of the directors' company with a competitor. Assume also that there is no structural restriction comparable to the shareholder agreement in *West Coast Capital*. However, the Companies Act stipulates that mergers must be approved by a majority of shareholders representing at least 75 per cent of the company's share capital.[649] If the directors who would like to exploit the

[642] ibid 841–3 (relying on the treatment of *Aas v Benham* (n 634) in *Boardman v Phipps* (n 629), where the former case was distinguished on the same grounds by the majority).

[643] ibid 844. [644] ibid 843.

[645] The articles of association empowered the company 'to carry on "the business of financiers, bankers, financial agents" and like activities and to carry on "any other trade or business which can, in the opinion of the Board of Directors, be advantageously carried on by the Company ..."': ibid 826.

[646] See ibid 844: 'There was no bright line marking off what it did and did not do'. [647] ibid.

[648] For a discussion of s 175 and in particular the exception laid down in subsection (4)(a) in light of *O'Donnell v Shanahan* (n 637) and related case law see E Lim, 'Directors' Fiduciary Duties: A New Analytical Framework' (2013) 129 Law Quarterly Review 242 (arguing that the scope of business test, in the sense of 'what a reasonable person thinks is relevant and of concern to the company', remains applicable under s 175(4)(a), see ibid 245, 257–9). For an analysis of *O'Donnell v Shanahan* see D Ahern, 'Guiding Principles for Directorial Conflicts of Interest: Re Allied Business & Financial Consultants Ltd; O'Donnell v Shanahan' (2011) 74 Modern Law Review 596.

[649] Companies Act 2006, s 899(1) (scheme of arrangement), s 907(1) (merger).

opportunity in their private capacity hold more than 25 per cent of the share capital, will they be exempted from the prohibition of section 175(2) because they are, 'as shareholders, able to block the acquisition', to use the words of Warren J in *West Coast Capital*?[650]

3. A particular problem is posed by directors who resign in order to pursue an opportunity or exploit information that 'belongs' to the company. Section 170(2)(a) has this case in mind when it stipulates that a director will continue to be subject to the duty not to exploit corporate opportunities after he ceases to hold office, provided 'he became aware [of the property, information or opportunity] at a time when he was a director'. Before codification in the Companies Act 2006, this issue was difficult to resolve and generated a considerable amount of highly fact-specific case law. The problem was that the common law took the position that 'a fiduciary obligation [did] not continue after the determination of the relationship which [gave] rise to it'.[651] Thus, it was necessary to show that the director had violated the duty before or at the time of resignation. Simply exploiting knowledge or information which a director had acquired while being in office did not give rise to a breach of duty. Rather, the courts distinguished between the use by the directors of their 'general fund of knowledge and expertise [that they had obtained] in the course of their work', which did not implicate the duty of loyalty,[652] and the exploitation of a *maturing business opportunity*, defined as a specific or 'ripe' opportunity that the company was 'actively pursuing' at the time of resignation.[653] The distinction between the permissible use of the director's general fund of knowledge and the impermissible exploitation of a maturing business opportunity was a function of a number of considerations,[654] but in general it could be said that a director who resigned in order to take advantage of an opportunity sought by the company was liable for breach of the duty of loyalty.[655]

   The codified rule now seems to go in the direction of a stricter application of the prohibition in line with the standard formulation of the corporate opportunities doctrine. Pursuant to section 170(2)(a), it is ostensibly sufficient to show that the opportunity falls within the definition of a corporate opportunity (as opposed to a *maturing* business opportunity) and that the director learnt of it while in office. However, this cannot be the end of the enquiry. In the case of non-resigning directors, the required link between the opportunity and the company is the actual or *potential* conflict created if the director takes advantage of the opportunity for his own benefit.[656] If the mere potentiality of a conflict was sufficient to bring a former director within the scope of section 175(2), directors would be severely restricted in the activities they could undertake after resignation.[657] For this reason, decisions applying the statutory rules hold that the pre-Companies Act 2006 precedents continue to inform the

[650] For a discussion of these issues, see also D Kershaw, *Company Law in Context* (2nd edn, OUP 2012) 551–2.

[651] *CMS Dolphin Ltd v Simonet* [2002] BCC 600, 623.

[652] *Island Export Finance Ltd v Umunna* [1986] BCLC 460: 'It would, it seems to me, be surprising to find that directors alone, because of the fiduciary nature of their relationship with the company, were restrained from exploiting after they had ceased to be such any opportunity of which they had acquired knowledge while directors. Directors, no less than employees, acquire a general fund of knowledge and expertise in the course of their work, and it is plainly in the public interest that they should be free to exploit it in a new position'.

[653] *CMS Dolphin Ltd v Simonet* (n 651) 621–2 (quoting *Canadian Aero Service Ltd v O'Malley* (1973) 40 DLR (3d) 371, 382 (Supreme Court of Canada), where the concept of maturing business opportunities was developed).

[654] ibid 622 (quoting *Canadian Aero Service* (n 653) 391): 'The general standards of loyalty, good faith and avoidance of a conflict of duty and self-interest to which the conduct of a director or senior officer must conform, must be tested in each case by many factors which it would be reckless to attempt to enumerate exhaustively. Among them are the factor of position or office held, the nature of the corporate opportunity, its ripeness, its specificness and the director's or managerial officer's relation to it, the amount of knowledge possessed, the circumstances in which it was obtained and whether it was special or, indeed, even private, the factor of time in the continuation of fiduciary duty where the alleged breach occurs after termination of the relationship with the company, and the circumstances under which the relationship was terminated, that is whether by retirement or resignation or discharge'.

[655] See, for example, *CMS Dolphin Ltd v Simonet* (n 651), where the director resigned in order to set up a competing business and then approached the company's clients.

[656] See the formulation in Companies Act 2006, s 175(1), (4)(a).

[657] See the quote in n 652 above, stressing the social utility of allowing directors to engage in commercial activity after their resignation.

application of the corporate opportunities doctrine to resigning directors. *Thermascan Ltd v Norman*,[658] for example, framed the issue in terms of a maturing business opportunity. In this case, the director of a company surveying commercial buildings resigned and started to canvass the company's clients. The High Court referred to the pre-2006 case law[659] in arguing that it was not necessary for the claimant to show that formal negotiations had been underway between the company and the client, but it had to be possible to describe the business obtained by the director as 'a business opportunity in the course of maturing' at the time of the director's resignation.[660] The court answered this question in the negative in the case at hand, because efforts to retain a client would commonly only be made as the next survey date approached, which had been more than eight months away at the relevant time. Donaldson QC explained: 'I find it hard to see how a claimant can demonstrate the existence of a "maturing business opportunity" if there had been no or no significant discussion of the potential business'.[661]

4. Consider a director who identifies a business opportunity that is of interest to the corporation. Realizing that section 175(2) prevents him from exploiting the opportunity, he decides not to pursue it. However, the director fails to communicate the opportunity to the company, which accordingly cannot take advantage of it. Has the director violated the duty of loyalty? Has he violated the duty of care?
5. Note that neither section 175 nor any other provision in the relevant chapter of the Companies Act 2006 contain rules on the mechanism of ex ante shareholder approval (authorization) of the exploitation of a corporate opportunity. Section 239, which we discussed above, is concerned with ex post ratification. Therefore, conflicted directors are, in principle, entitled to vote their shares in the general meeting that decides on the interested transaction before it is carried into effect. The *Cook v Deeks* doctrine that some conduct is not capable of being approved by the shareholders applies here as well,[662] but the protection of minority shareholders is clearly less comprehensive than under section 239 of the Companies Act. Is this apparent inconsistency justified?

2. US

The leading Delaware case on corporate opportunities is *Guth v Loft*,[663] which, despite its age, continues to be the main point of reference for the Delaware courts. Loft Inc. was engaged in the manufacturing and selling of candies, syrups, beverages, and foodstuffs. Mr Guth, a man of long experience in the soft drink business, became vice president of Loft in 1929 and its president in 1930. In 1931, he decided to discontinue the sale of Coca-Cola syrup at its stores after the Coca-Cola Company had refused to give Loft the same discount that it had granted to other users of the syrup. At the same time, the National Pepsi-Cola Company was adjudicated a bankrupt and its secret formula and trademark were up for sale. Guth was acquainted with the controlling stockholder in Pepsi, Mr Megargel, and the two men entered into an agreement under which Megargel set up a new corporation, Pepsi-Cola Co., with an authorized capital of 300,000 shares. He kept 100,000 shares for himself. Grace Co., a manufacturer of syrups for soft drinks which was owned by Guth and his family, received 100,000 shares, and the remaining shares were held as treasury stock. Later Guth and Grace Co. received a large number of treasury stock and stock owned by Megargel in settlement of Pepsi's and Megargel's indebtedness to the parties. Guth, accordingly, obtained complete control of Pepsi. He also dominated Loft's board of directors (it was claimed that Guth 'manifested some of the qualities of a dictator'[664]) and drew upon Loft's funds and assets to further the Pepsi enterprise. He used Loft's plant facilities, materials, credit, executives, and

[658] [2011] BCC 535.
[659] Inter alia, *CMS Dolphin Ltd v Simonet* (n 651) and the principles reproduced in n 654 above.
[660] *Thermascan Ltd v Norman* [2011] BCC 535, 542.
[661] ibid 541.
[662] Davies and Worthington (n 30) para 16-103.
[663] 5 A.2d 503 (Del. 1939).
[664] ibid 512.

employees to produce the syrup and advanced parts of Loft's funds to Pepsi. It was alleged that most of the advances were repaid. The Chancellor found that the Pepsi opportunity belonged in equity to Loft, but that Guth had never offered it to the company. Consequently, the Chancellor ordered Guth and Grace Co. to transfer all Pepsi shares held by them to Loft.[665]

***Guth v. Loft*, 5 A.2d 503 (Del. 1939)**

Layton, Chief Justice:

Corporate officers and directors are not permitted to use their position of trust and confidence to further their private interests. While technically not trustees, they stand in a fiduciary relation to the corporation and its stockholders. A public policy, existing through the years, and derived from a profound knowledge of human characteristics and motives, has established a rule that demands of a corporate officer or director, peremptorily and inexorably, the most scrupulous observance of his duty, not only affirmatively to protect the interests of the corporation committed to his charge, but also to refrain from doing anything that would work injury to the corporation, or to deprive it of profit or advantage which his skill and ability might properly bring to it, or to enable it to make in the reasonable and lawful exercise of its powers. The rule that requires an undivided and unselfish loyalty to the corporation demands that there shall be no conflict between duty and self-interest. The occasions for the determination of honesty, good faith and loyal conduct are many and varied, and no hard and fast rule can be formulated. The standard of loyalty is measured by no fixed scale.

If an officer or director of a corporation, in violation of his duty as such, acquires gain or advantage for himself, the law charges the interest so acquired with a trust for the benefit of the corporation, at its election, while it denies to the betrayer all benefit and profit. The rule, inveterate and uncompromising in its rigidity, does not rest upon the narrow ground of injury or damage to the corporation resulting from a betrayal of confidence, but upon a broader foundation of a wise public policy that, for the purpose of removing all temptation, extinguishes all possibility of profit flowing from a breach of the confidence imposed by the fiduciary relation. Given the relation between the parties, a certain result follows; and a constructive trust is the remedial device through which precedence of self is compelled to give way to the stern demands of loyalty ...

The rule, referred to briefly as the rule of corporate opportunity, is merely one of the manifestations of the general rule that demands of an officer or director the utmost good faith in his relation to the corporation which he represents.

It is true that when a business opportunity comes to a corporate officer or director in his individual capacity rather than in his official capacity, and the opportunity is one which, because of the nature of the enterprise, is not essential to his corporation, and is one in which it has no interest or expectancy, the officer or director is entitled to treat the opportunity as his own, and the corporation has no interest in it, if, of course, the officer or director has not wrongfully embarked the corporation's resources therein ...

On the other hand, it is equally true that, if there is presented to a corporate officer or director a business opportunity which the corporation is financially able to undertake, is, from its nature, in the line of the corporation's business and is of practical advantage to it, is one in which the corporation has an interest or a reasonable expectancy, and, by embracing the opportunity, the self-interest of the officer or director will be brought into conflict with that of his corporation, the law will not permit him to seize the opportunity for himself. And, if, in such circumstances, the interests of the corporation are betrayed, the corporation may elect to claim all of the benefits of the transaction for itself, and the law will impress a trust in favor of the corporation upon the property, interests and profits so acquired ...

It was incumbent upon Guth to show that his every act in dealing with the opportunity presented was in the exercise of the utmost good faith to Loft; and the burden was cast upon him satisfactorily to prove that the offer was made to him individually ... It is entirely reasonable to infer that Megargel approached Guth as president of Loft, operating, as it did, many soft drink

[665] Eventually, the Pepsi enterprise proved highly successful and Loft and Pepsi merged in 1941.

fountains in a most necessary and desirable territory where Pepsi-Cola was little known, he well knowing that if the drink could be established in New York and circumjacent territory, its success would be assured. Every reasonable inference points to this conclusion. What was finally agreed upon between Megargel and Guth, and what outward appearance their agreement assumed, is of small importance. It was a matter of indifference to Megargel whether his co-adventurer was Guth personally, or Loft, so long as his terms were met and his object attained.

Leaving aside the manner of the offer of the opportunity, certain other matters are to be considered in determining whether the opportunity, in the circumstances, belonged to Loft; and in this we agree that Guth's right to appropriate the Pepsi-Cola opportunity to himself depends upon the circumstances existing at the time it presented itself to him without regard to subsequent events, and that due weight should be given to character of the opportunity which Megargel envisioned and brought to Guth's door.

The real issue is whether the opportunity to secure a very substantial stock interest in a corporation to be formed for the purpose of exploiting a cola beverage on a wholesale scale was so closely associated with the existing business activities of Loft, and so essential thereto, as to bring the transaction within that class of cases where the acquisition of the property would throw the corporate officer purchasing it into competition with his company. This is a factual question to be decided by reasonable inferences from objective facts …

The appellants suggest a doubt whether Loft would have been able to finance the project along the lines contemplated by Megargel, viewing the situation as of 1931. The answer to this suggestion is two-fold. The Chancellor found that Loft's net asset position at that time was amply sufficient to finance the enterprise, and that its plant, equipment, executives, personnel and facilities, supplemented by such expansion for the necessary development of the business as it was well able to provide, were in all respects adequate. The second answer is that Loft's resources were found to be sufficient, for Guth made use of no other to any important extent.

Next it is contended that the Pepsi-Cola opportunity was not in the line of Loft's activities which essentially were of a retail nature. It is pointed out that, in 1931, the retail stores operated by Loft were largely located in the congested areas along the Middle Atlantic Seaboard, that its manufacturing operations were centered in its New York factory, and that it was a definitely localized business, and not operated on a national scale; whereas, the Megargel proposition envisaged annual sales of syrup at least a million gallons, which could be accomplished only by a wholesale distribution. Loft, however, had many wholesale activities. Its wholesale business in 1931 amounted to over $800,000. It was a large company by any standard. It had an enormous plant. It paid enormous rentals. Guth, himself, said that Loft's success depended upon the fullest utilization of its large plant facilities. Moreover, it was a manufacturer of syrups and, with the exception of cola syrup, it supplied its own extensive needs. The appellants admit that wholesale distribution of bottled beverages can best be accomplished by license agreements with bottlers. Guth, president of Loft, was an able and experienced man in that field. Loft, then, through its own personnel, possessed the technical knowledge, the practical business experience, and the resources necessary for the development of the Pepsi-Cola enterprise.

But, the appellants say that the expression, 'in the line' of a business, is a phrase so elastic as to furnish no basis for a useful inference. The phrase is not within the field of precise definition, nor is it one that can be bounded by a set formula. It has a flexible meaning, which is to be applied reasonably and sensibly to the facts and circumstances of the particular case. Where a corporation is engaged in a certain business, and an opportunity is presented to it embracing an activity as to which it has fundamental knowledge, practical experience and ability to pursue, which, logically and naturally, is adaptable to its business having regard for its financial position, and is one that is consonant with its reasonable needs and aspirations for expansion, it may be properly said that the opportunity is in the line of the corporation's business.

The manufacture of syrup was the core of the Pepsi-Cola opportunity. The manufacture of syrups was one of Loft's not unimportant activities. It had the necessary resources, facilities, equipment, technical and practical knowledge and experience. The tie was close between the business of Loft and the Pepsi-Cola enterprise … Conceding that the essential of an opportunity is reasonably within the scope of a corporation's activities, latitude should be allowed for development and expansion. To deny this would be to deny the history of industrial development.

It is urged that Loft had no interest or expectancy in the Pepsi-Cola opportunity. That it had no existing property right therein is manifest; but we cannot agree that it had no concern or expectancy in the opportunity within the protection of remedial equity. Loft had a practical and essential concern with respect to some cola syrup with an established formula and trademark. A cola beverage has come to be a business necessity for soft drink establishments; and it was essential to the success of Loft to serve at its soda fountains an acceptable five cent cola drink in order to attract into its stores the great multitude of people who have formed the habit of drinking cola beverages. When Guth determined to discontinue the sale of Coca-Cola in the Loft stores, it became, by his own act, a matter of urgent necessity for Loft to acquire a constant supply of some satisfactory cola syrup, secure against probable attack, as a replacement; and when the Pepsi-Cola opportunity presented itself, Guth having already considered the availability of the syrup, it became impressed with a Loft interest and expectancy arising out of the circumstances and the urgent and practical need created by him as the directing head of Loft …

As a general proposition it may be said that a corporate officer or director is entirely free to engage in an independent, competitive business, so long as he violates no legal or moral duty with respect to the fiduciary relation that exists between the corporation and himself. The appellants contend that no conflict of interest between Guth and Loft resulted from his acquirement and exploitation of the Pepsi-Cola opportunity … The facts and circumstances demonstrate that Guth's appropriation of the Pepsi-Cola opportunity to himself placed him in a competitive position with Loft with respect to a commodity essential to it, thereby rendering his personal interests incompatible with the superior interests of his corporation; and this situation was accomplished, not openly and with his own resources, but secretly and with the money and facilities of the corporation which was committed to his protection …

Upon a consideration of all the facts and circumstances as disclosed we are convinced that the opportunity to acquire the Pepsi-Cola trademark and formula, goodwill and business belonged to the complainant, and that Guth, as its President, had no right to appropriate the opportunity to himself.

Questions and comments:

1. The Delaware courts refer to the main principles expounded in *Guth v Loft* as the 'Guth rule' and the 'Guth corollary'. As summarized by the Supreme Court of Delaware in *Broz v Cellular Information Systems, Inc.*,[666] the Guth rule establishes that a corporate officer or director may not take a business opportunity for his own if the following four conditions are met:

   > (1) the corporation is financially able to exploit the opportunity; (2) the opportunity is within the corporation's line of business; (3) the corporation has an interest or expectancy in the opportunity; and (4) by taking the opportunity for his own, the corporate fiduciary will thereby be placed in a position [inimical] to his duties to the corporation.[667]

   The corollary is

   > that a director or officer may take a corporate opportunity if: (1) the opportunity is presented to the director or officer in his individual and not his corporate capacity; (2) the opportunity is not essential to the corporation; (3) the corporation holds no interest or expectancy in the opportunity; and (4) the director or officer has not wrongfully employed the resources of the corporation in pursuing or exploiting the opportunity.[668]

   The rule and corollary, of course, cannot account for a large number of intermediate cases. All they say is that a director violates the duty of loyalty if the four conditions of the rule are met, and he does not violate the duty if *all* of the four elements of the corollary are present. *Guth*

[666] 673 A.2d 148 (Del. 1996).
[667] ibid 155. The rule is derived from the fifth paragraph in the above excerpt.
[668] ibid. This is derived from the fourth paragraph in the above excerpt.

does not provide guidance on how to judge cases where some, but not all, of the corollary's elements hold. In *Broz*, the Supreme Court of Delaware promoted a flexible application of the tests established in *Guth*. As the court explained, they only 'provide guidelines to be considered by a reviewing court in balancing the equities of an individual case. No one factor is dispositive and all factors must be taken into account insofar as they are applicable'.[669] Arguably, this creates a rather unsatisfactory situation. Hard and fast rules do not exist, as the court in *Broz* admitted,[670] and the enquiry ultimately turns on the overall fairness of the director's actions.[671]

In *Broz*, the director of Cellular Information System (CIS), a corporation providing cell phone service, learned of the opportunity to acquire a cellular telephone licence in his individual and not his corporate capacity. He brought the opportunity informally to the attention of the board of directors, but acquired the licence eventually for another corporation that he owned, because the directors of CIS that he had sought out did not express great interest in the acquisition and CIS was not financially capable of exploiting the business opportunity at the time. CIS was, however, in the process of being acquired by yet another cell phone operator, PriCellular. The acquisition was completed a few days after the director's company had obtained the licence. PriCellular discharged and replaced the incumbent directors and caused CIS to commence the action against Mr Broz. The Court of Chancery found that Mr Broz had breached his duty of loyalty because he had failed to consider whether the opportunity was in the interest of PriCellular. The Supreme Court reversed. It considered 'the totality of the circumstances'[672] to determine whether the business opportunity properly belonged to CIS and concluded that this was not the case. More specifically, without considering any one factor to be dispositive, the Supreme Court held that: (1) Broz became aware of the opportunity in his individual capacity and did not misuse the corporation's proprietary information; (2) the corporation was in a precarious financial position; (3) PriCellular's tender offer for CIS stock had not yet closed and the acquisition of CIS was contingent and speculative; therefore, the financial position of PriCellular and its intentions with respect to the licence were immaterial; (4) CIS did not have a cognizable interest or expectancy in the opportunity;[673] and (5) there was no conflict between the director's duties to the corporation and his self-interest.

2. Under Delaware law, it is not essential that the conflicted director obtains approval by the disinterested directors before he takes the opportunity. In *Broz*, the defendant had spoken with members of the board, but had not made a formal presentation to the board of directors. The Court of Chancery criticized the lack of formal board action, but the Supreme Court held that the interested director was under no obligation to procure a resolution of the board. On the other hand, where the director presents the matter to the board and the board resolves that the corporation is not interested in pursuing the opportunity, this creates a safe harbour for the interested director.[674] Therefore, in cases where the opportunity is not clearly outside of the corporation's line of business, it is advisable to obtain formal board approval. As matters stood in *Broz*, the defendant's informal discussions with the members of

[669] ibid. [670] ibid.

[671] See also *Johnston v Greene*, 121 A.2d 919 (Del. 1956), quoted by *Broz* (n 666) 155: 'Whether or not a director has appropriated for himself something that in fairness should belong to the corporation is "a factual question to be decided by reasonable inference from objective facts"'. ibid 923 (quoting, in turn, *Guth* (n 663) 513).

[672] *Broz* (n 666) 157.

[673] This was, arguably, not a clear-cut issue, given that the cell phone licence was within CIS' line of business. The court explained: '[F]or an opportunity to be deemed to belong to the fiduciary's corporation, the corporation must have an interest or expectancy in that opportunity. As this Court stated in *Johnston*, 121 A.2d at 924 "[f]or the corporation to have an actual or expectant interest in any specific property, there must be some tie between that property and the nature of the corporate business." Despite the fact that the nature of the ... opportunity was historically close to the core operations of CIS, changes were in process. At the time the opportunity was presented, CIS was actively engaged in the process of divesting its cellular license holdings. CIS' articulated business plan did not involve any new acquisitions. Further, as indicated by the testimony of the entire CIS board, the ... license would not have been of interest to CIS even absent CIS' financial difficulties and CIS' then current desire to liquidate its cellular license holdings': ibid 156.

[674] See ibid 157: 'The teaching of *Guth* and its progeny is that the director or officer must analyze the situation ex ante to determine whether the opportunity is one rightfully belonging to the corporation. If the director or officer

the board were one of several factors that the court considered in assessing the 'totality of the circumstances'.[675]

3. In both *Guth* and *Broz*, the courts discussed whether the corporation was financially capable of pursuing the business opportunity. Does this mean that financial inability can be used as a defence by the interested director? When we discussed UK law, we saw that the courts are adamant that the *practical* inability of the corporation to take up the opportunity, for financial or other reasons, does not exonerate the directors.[676] US courts adopt a more flexible approach. In *Broz*, the financial position of the corporation was relevant to the court's investigation into the nature of the business venture as a corporate opportunity or an opportunity open to the directors in their individual capacity. But the Delaware Supreme Court did not go so far as to hold that the business venture ceased to be a corporate opportunity if the corporation was not financially able to take advantage of it. Applying the above-mentioned 'totality of the circumstances' analysis, financial capability was merely one of a number of factors to be considered.[677] Other US jurisdictions attribute greater importance to the financial position of a corporation. For example, the Superior Court of Pennsylvania allowed the defendant directors to rely on the financial inability of their corporation as a defence against a breach of duty.[678]
4. Pursuant to the Delaware General Corporation Law, a corporation has the power to renounce in its certificate of incorporation or by action of the board of directors any interest or expectancy in specified business opportunities that are presented to the corporation or its officers, directors or stockholders, with the consequence that the latter are free to pursue the opportunity for their own account.[679] This provision was added in 2000 in order to allow companies to limit the scope of the courts' multi-factor test in favour of legal certainty. Under the provision, companies can designate individual businesses or classes of businesses in which they do not have an interest.[680] If companies make use of this authority, and considering also that the board is able to approve self-dealing through the votes of the disinterested directors,[681] what remains of the Delaware duty of loyalty? Are minority shareholders still sufficiently well protected?
5. How does a flexible approach, such as Delaware's multi-factor test, compare with the UK corporate opportunities doctrine? Legal certainty militates in favour of the UK solution (although, as we have seen, section 175 UK Companies Act also gives rise to highly fact-specific inquiries, notably when directors resign in order to take up a business opportunity). On the other hand, could it be argued that Delaware law is superior in that it ensures a more efficient allocation of resources?

believes, based on one of the factors articulated above, that the corporation is not entitled to the opportunity, then he may take it for himself. Of course, presenting the opportunity to the board creates a kind of "safe harbor" for the director, which removes the specter of a *post hoc* judicial determination that the director or officer has improperly usurped a corporate opportunity. Thus, presentation avoids the possibility that an error in the fiduciary's assessment of the situation will create future liability for breach of fiduciary duty. It is not the law of Delaware that presentation to the board is a necessary prerequisite to a finding that a corporate opportunity has not been usurped'.

[675] ibid.

[676] *Regal (Hastings) Ltd v Gulliver* [1942] 1 All ER 378; *Wilkinson v West Coast Capital* (n 622).

[677] *Broz* (n 666) 155–6. But compare this decision with *Schreiber v Bryan*, 396 A.2d 512 (Del. Ch. 1978) (arguing that the financial ability of the corporation is one of three 'essential element[s] necessary to find a loss of corporate opportunity' ibid 519–20). The US courts apply a demanding standard in order to determine whether a corporation is financially able to take advantage of a business opportunity. It was held that 'financial inability must amount to insolvency to the point where the corporation is practically defunct. Mere technical insolvency, such as inability to pay current bills when due or mere inability to secure credit, will not suffice. The corporation must be actually insolvent'. *Stephanis v Yiannatsis*, 19 Delaware Journal of Corporate Law 895, 903 (Del. Ch. 1993); *CST, Inc. v Mark*, 520 A.2d 469, 472 (Pa. Super. 1987) (both decisions quoting 18B Am.Jur.2d *Corporations* §1790, at 642–3 (1985)).

[678] *CST* (n 677) 472.

[679] Del. Gen. Corp. Law, §122(17).

[680] WE Knepper and DA Bailey, *Liability of Corporate Officers and Directors* (8th edn, LexisNexis 2011) §4.11.

[681] Del. Gen. Corp. Law, §144(a)(1).

3. Germany

German Stock Corporation Act

§ 88—Prohibition of competition

(1) Without the consent of the supervisory board, the members of the management board shall not engage in any trade or enter into transactions in the company's line of business for their own account or the account of a third party. Without the supervisory board's consent, they shall also not be a member of the management board or managing director or personally liable partner of another commercial company. The consent of the supervisory board can only be granted for specific trading businesses or commercial companies or for specific types of transactions.

(2) If a member of the management board violates this prohibition, the company may claim damages. Alternatively, the company may request the member to accept transactions entered into for the member's own account as having been concluded for the account of the company, and surrender the remuneration received for transactions entered into for the account of another or assign his claim to such remuneration to the company.

(3) The company's claims shall be unenforceable three months after the other members of the management board and the members of the supervisory board have acquired knowledge of the action giving rise to the damages claim or should have acquired knowledge without gross negligence. Irrespective of such knowledge or grossly negligent lack of knowledge, the claims shall be unenforceable five years after they came into existence.

We mentioned before that the duty of loyalty is incompletely regulated under German law. This is exemplified by §88 Stock Corporation Act, the core statutory provision on loyalty-based constraints on directors.[682] §88 does not lay down a broad duty to avoid conflicts of interest, but embodies three specific prohibitions that capture aspects of the common law duty of loyalty and the corporate opportunities doctrine. Without ex ante consent of the supervisory board, members of the management board are prohibited from: (1) engaging in any trade;[683] (2) entering into transactions in the company's line of business for their own account or the account of a third person;[684] and (3) being a member of the management board or managing director or personally liable partner of another commercial company.[685] We will deal with each prohibition in turn. It should be noted that §88 does not apply to the members of the supervisory board, but only to management board members.[686]

The first prohibition seeks to ensure that directors devote their full attention and work to the company.[687] For this reason, the provision does not require that the trade pursued by a director falls within the company's scope of business or an actual or potential conflict of interest exists. It is also irrelevant whether the company could have taken advantage of the business transaction or suffered a loss because of the director's conduct. Rather, engaging in any trade, defined by the courts and the Commercial Code as any gainful occupation of a permanent nature not under the direction of another, with the exception of the liberal professions, that requires a commercial business organization is prohibited.[688] It follows from this definition that management board members are, in principle, free to perform services

[682] For other statutory expressions of the duty of loyalty see n 241 above.

[683] AktG, §88(1) sentence 1. [684] ibid. [685] ibid §88(1) sentence 2.

[686] ibid §116, which determines the responsibility of the supervisory board members, only refers to the duty of care pursuant to §93.

[687] G Spindler in Goette and Habersack (n 546) §88 para 1.

[688] BGHZ 33, 321, 324. The term 'trade' (*Handelsgewerbe*) is defined in §1(2) HGB as 'any commercial operation, unless the enterprise does not require a commercial business organisation, considering its type and scope'. §§2-5 HGB contain additional rules that qualify the basic definition. The code does not provide for a definition of 'commercial operation', which has been developed by the courts and is paraphrased above in the text.

as, for example, a lawyer, tax adviser, or accountant,[689] and also pursue minor commercial operations.[690] However, in light of the aim of the provision it can be argued that any occupation requiring time and effort comparable to a trade falls within the ambit of §88(1) sentence 1.[691]

The second alternative of §88(1) sentence 1 is both wider and narrower than the first. Members of the management board are generally prohibited from entering into transactions within the company's line of business for the purpose of realizing a profit. The provision is wider than the first alternative because transactions of any type are caught, not only business activity of a continuing nature to provide a sustained source of income. At the same time, it is narrower for two reasons. First, the transaction must be intended to generate a profit. This is not the case where it serves the director's private needs and is of a 'personal character'.[692] For example, the Bundesgerichtshof held that the acquisition by a director of two properties that belonged to the portfolio of residential properties managed by the director's company with a view to using them partly as a family home and partly as an investment was not beyond what could be qualified as a transaction for private purposes.[693] Secondly, the transaction must be within the company's line of business. Starting point for a determination of the company's scope of business are the articles, which must under German law describe the company's objects.[694] However, if the business actually pursued by the company is wider or narrower, the director is bound by the actual scope of business.[695] Thus, as opposed to the first alternative, the aim of this provision is the prevention of an *actual* conflict with the company, namely engaging in competitive behaviour.

Finally, a management board member is not allowed to be a member of the management board of another public stock corporation, managing director of a private limited company, or personally liable partner of a commercial partnership. The provision is interpreted broadly and also applies to comparable positions in foreign companies.[696] The objective of this prohibition is identical to the first alternative of §88(1) sentence 1: to prevent directors from taking on substantial additional commitments and thus potentially neglecting their duties towards the company. Consequently, the scope of business of the two enterprises is irrelevant. On the other hand, it is widely accepted that members of the management board can accept positions on the supervisory boards of other stock corporations, which is common practice and only subject to the statutory restrictions regarding the eligibility of supervisory board members.[697] In addition, they can be involved as shareholder or limited partner[698] in other commercial companies.[699] The latter point poses the problem, discussed above in the context of related-party transactions,[700] that a conflict may arise when a director is

[689] These occupations have been qualified as belonging to the liberal professions, which are not trades within the meaning of §88 AktG. For references see K Schmidt in K Schmidt (ed), *Münchener Kommentar zum Handelsgesetzbuch, vol 1* (4th edn, CH Beck 2016) §1 para 34.

[690] This would not satisfy the definition of trade in §1(2) HGB, see n 688 above.

[691] OLG Frankfurt, AG 2000, 518, 519 (holding that §88 AktG applies to the liberal professions if the occupation, given the required time and workload, jeopardizes the orderly discharge of the director's functions).

[692] BGH NJW 1997, 2055, 2056.

[693] ibid. *In obiter*, the court explained that a property investment may be caught by §88(1) sentence 1 if the director intends to realize a profit by selling the property in the near future.

[694] AktG, §23(3) no 2.

[695] See, for example, BGHZ 70, 331, 332 (dealing with the partner of a limited partnership, who is subject to the same prohibition of competitive behaviour pursuant to §112 HGB).

[696] Spindler (n 687) §88 para 20.

[697] In particular, §100(2), nos 2 and 3 AktG, providing that a person is not eligible to be a member of the supervisory board of a company if he or she is a member of the management board or the legal representative of a controlled company within the meaning of §17 AktG (but not if the person is a member of the management board of the *controlling* company) or a member of the management board of a corporation where a member of the director's management board sits on the supervisory board.

[698] A limited partner is not entitled to participate in the management of the limited partnership: HGB, §164.

[699] For references see Spindler (n 687) §88, paras 20, 21.

[700] See text to nn 544–547.

indirectly interested in another business venture that is also of interest to the company. As before, the literature is reluctant to apply §88 to such indirect conflicts, apart from the exceptional case that a director is virtually identical with the legal person, in particular where he or she is the sole shareholder,[701] or the involvement in the other company includes management duties.[702] It is unsurprising that §88(1) sentence 2 does not capture these cases, since the provision is not concerned with related-party transactions or the appropriation of a corporate opportunity, but a more subtle conflict of interest: the risk that directors who have too many other commitments cannot fulfil their duties adequately.

If a director violates any of the prohibitions, the company can claim damages or, if applicable, assume the rights under the contract with the director, who has to account for the profits made.[703] The company's claim follows the general rules applicable to claims for a breach of duty brought by a company against a director.[704] Consequently, recovery by the company requires that the director infringed the duties pursuant to §88(1) negligently or intentionally.[705] The company can recover damages for the loss sustained, including lost profits if it can show that valuable business opportunities would have been available to the company without the director's misconduct.[706]

Depending on the circumstances, it may be easier for a company to bring an action to recover the profits actually realized by the director, in particular if the damage sustained is difficult to quantify or it is unclear whether the company could have obtained the contract secured by the director in breach of §88(1). For this reason, §88(2) gives the company the choice, to be exercised through a decision of the supervisory board,[707] to treat the transaction entered into by the director as concluded for the account of the company. The company does not assume the rights and obligations under the contract in relation to the third party, but the director is liable to account for the profits.[708] Similar to damages, the company's claim requires that the director acted with 'fault' and the burden of proof is reversed.[709] An accounting for profits is available to the company not only in the case of contraventions of the second prohibition of §88(1), transactions in the company's line of business, but also the third, participation as a personally liable partner in a general or limited partnership. In the latter case, the company has a claim to the profits obtained as a result of the director's involvement in the other business enterprise.[710]

We can see that §88, which is probably the closest equivalent of section 175 UK Companies Act 2006 in the German Stock Corporation Act, is less comprehensive than its English counterpart. This is, first of all, a function of the different regulatory techniques employed. The German provision specifies the cases in which it applies relatively precisely, whereas the English law contains, in addition to a codification of the corporate opportunities doctrine, a catch-all clause for conflicts of interest not related to corporate opportunities.[711] It is also a function of the objectives of the German provision. While all three prohibitions laid down in §88 of the Stock Corporation Act address some type of conflict between the director's private interests and the interests of the company, the provision is not intended to codify a duty comparable to the common law no-profit and no-conflict rules, but prevent directors from

[701] Spindler (n 687) §88 para 21.
[702] Koch (n 57) §88 para 4.
[703] AktG, §88(2).
[704] See ibid §93(2) and text to nn 244, 266–268 above. The business judgment rule (§93(1) sentence 2) is only relevant in duty of care cases and does not apply here.
[705] The burden of proof is reversed pursuant to §93(2) sentence 2 AktG.
[706] The rules regarding recovery for lost profits are laid down in the BGB, §252.
[707] In application of AktG, §112.
[708] BGHZ 38, 306, 310–11.
[709] Spindler (n 687) §88 para 30. This has been criticized by parts of the literature; see, for example, H Fleischer in G Spindler and E Stilz (eds), *Kommentar zum Aktiengesetz, vol 1* (4th edn, CH Beck 2019) §88 para 37.
[710] BGHZ 38, 306, 308–10; 89, 162, 171.
[711] See UK Companies Act 2006, s 175(2): The duty to avoid conflicts of interest 'applies *in particular* [i.e., not only] to the exploitation of any property, information or opportunity' (emphasis by authors).

competing with the company or dividing their work between different business enterprises. As a result, the provision does not capture some situations falling under section 175 of the UK Companies Act 2006. For example, a director who enters into a transaction that is outside of the line of business actually pursued by the company, but does not amount to a trade within the meaning of the Commercial Code, does not violate the prohibitions of §88(1) Stock Corporation Act. However, the director's conduct may well fall within the scope of the English corporate opportunities doctrine, at least where the competing business venture is of commercial interest to the company and it is not inconceivable that the company may in the future reorient its business and take advantage of the opportunity.[712] Similarly, a director who competes with the company in the company's line of business through a legal person acts generally in compliance with §88(1). The first alternative of the provision does not apply because investing in a company is no trade. The second and third alternatives are also commonly regarded as inapplicable, provided the director does not control the legal entity and does not function as a member of the management board or managing director of that entity.[713] Section 175(1) UK Companies Act 2006, on the other hand, prohibits any type of direct or indirect conflict, which includes any interest in another legal entity, unless the interest is so insubstantial that it cannot reasonably be regarded as likely to give rise to a conflict of interest.[714] Finally, a director who enters into a transaction in the company's line of business not (or not predominantly) to realize a profit, but for a private, non-commercial purpose, does not infringe the second alternative of §88(1) sentence 1 Stock Corporation Act. Again, as far as the English corporate opportunities doctrine is concerned, it would be irrelevant whether the director sees the transaction as a commercial venture or a private affair or, indeed, whether he obtains any benefit at all.

Because of these regulatory gaps, the courts have acknowledged that a general, unwritten duty of loyalty exists that has been said to derive from general principles of good faith and fair dealing underlying all legal relationships or from the trust-like position of directors.[715] This duty affects all aspects of the conduct of company directors,[716] but it has become particularly relevant in the context of corporate opportunities, which are imperfectly regulated under §88 Stock Corporation Act, as we have seen. German courts have addressed some of the instances where the English no-profit and no-conflict rules and the statutory duties of directors under German law lead to different results by relying on the unwritten duty of loyalty. For example, in a decision of the Bundesgerichtshof from 1967,[717] the director of a private limited company was asked to purchase a property owned by a local authority on behalf of his company with a view to constructing factory buildings there. In order to entice the company to relocate its headquarters to the district, the local authority offered the director additional properties at the price paid by the company, which was significantly below market value. Without informing the company of the offer, the director purchased the properties and resold them two years later, realizing a substantial profit. The court held that the director had grossly breached his duties, irrespective of the fact that the company had no use for the other properties and had taken no steps to enquire whether they were for sale. It constitutes a violation of the duty of loyalty if a director takes advantage of a business opportunity that

[712] As analysed above, English case law is somewhat ambivalent as to the existence and substance of a 'scope of business' test, see in particular *Wilkinson v West Coast Capital* (n 636) and *Re Allied Business & Financial Consultants Ltd (O'Donnell v Shanahan)* (n 637) 822, text to nn 634–648 above. Notwithstanding the question of how these cases should be interpreted, after codification in the Companies Act 2006 the relevant benchmark is now whether the situation can 'reasonably be regarded as likely to give rise to a conflict of interest' (s 175(4)(a) Companies Act 2006). Arguably, this is wider than the formulation of §88(1) sentence 1 German AktG, which simply prohibits transactions in the company's line of business.

[713] Spindler (n 687) §88, paras 19, 21.

[714] UK Companies Act 2006, ss 175(4)(a), 177(6)(a).

[715] See text to nn 14–16 above.

[716] For an overview see Raiser and Veil (n 242) §14/92.

[717] BGH GmbH-Rundschau 1968, 141.

is brought to his attention in connection with the discharge of his managerial duties and that he would not have been able to exploit on the same terms but for his position.[718]

Pursuant to the unwritten duty of loyalty, as developed by the courts,[719] directors are prohibited from taking advantage of a business opportunity for their own account or the account of a related party if the opportunity falls within the company's line of business or is closely related to it[720] and must be deemed as 'belonging' to the company in light of the facts of the individual case.[721] The Bundesgerichtshof held that the latter condition is generally satisfied if the company first encounters the opportunity and the director is concerned with it in his capacity as director, in particular where he is involved in the negotiations on behalf of the company.[722] However, even if the business opportunity is offered to the director in his private capacity or he learns of it from a source unrelated to his managerial functions, he may still be required to pass it on to the company. The courts argue that the duties of directors are 'not divisible'. During their term of office, directors are required to consider the best interest of the company in all their actions, notwithstanding whether they act in a professional or private capacity.[723] It may, however, be more difficult to argue that an opportunity 'belongs' to the company, in the sense of having been 'assigned' to it, if the opportunity has not come to the director in connection with his professional duties.[724]

The necessary nexus between the opportunity and the company was held to exist where it was evident that the opportunity was important for the company's business or steps were taken to acquire it on behalf of the company. For example, in one case a director received an offer to acquire a property that was rented by the company and used as the company's main business premises.[725] Instead of informing the company of the opportunity, the director arranged for his wife to purchase the property and renew the lease at a higher rent. The Bundesgerichtshof held that

> if the opportunity arises to acquire the commercial premises that form the foundation of the business and thereby eliminate the insecurity that is part of a tenancy agreement ... the director is under the duty to take all necessary measures to realise the acquisition and refrain from anything that may jeopardise it. He is only released from the duty if the other partners [or shareholders or the supervisory board, depending on the type of company] reject the opportunity after full information.[726]

In another case decided by the Bundesgerichtshof, a director learned of an opportunity while reading a newspaper. He passed the opportunity on to the company, made enquiries in the name of the company, and discussed the acquisition with the company's

[718] ibid 142.

[719] See, for example, BGH NJW 1989, 2687 (holding that the unwritten duty of loyalty applies to limited partners of a limited partnership who are generally not subject to the codified duty not to compete with the company, see §§112, 165 HGB); BGH NJW 1986, 584 (concerning the general partnership); BGH NZG 2013, 216 (applying the corporate opportunities doctrine to the managing partner of a civil law partnership that pursued commercial objects).

[720] As in BGH GmbH-Rundschau 1968, 141.

[721] BGH NJW 1989, 2687–2688; BGH NZG 2013, 216, 218.

[722] ibid 2688. In this case, the director negotiated the acquisition of a property for the company, a limited partnership that had been formed by his father as unlimited partner and him as limited partner. When father and son fell out, the son bought the property for his own account.

[723] BGH NJW 1986, 585, 586.

[724] The requirement that the opportunity must 'belong' to the company, i.e. that it must have been assigned to it in light of the circumstances of the case, was established in a number of judgments by the Bundesgerichtshof; see n 721 for references. A somewhat wider approach seems to be favoured by the OLG Frankfurt am Main, GmbH-Rundschau 1998, 376, 378, defining a corporate opportunity as 'an opportunity falling within the company's ordinary scope of operations, or being of considerable interest to the company'. According to this view, it is not necessary that the opportunity has been 'assigned' to the company; it is sufficient that the company's interests are 'potentially threatened'. This also holds where the opportunity is not brought to the director's attention in his professional capacity, but offered to him by a personal friend: ibid.

[725] BGH NJW 1986, 584, 585.

[726] ibid.

tax advisor, before deciding to take advantage of it privately. The court concluded that the opportunity had become specific enough to 'belong' to the company.[727]

The unwritten duty of loyalty does not depend on the financial capacity of the company to exploit the opportunity. If a company lacks the necessary funds, directors must first seek to raise additional funds, for example by obtaining a bank loan or increasing the company's capital, before they are entitled to take advantage of the opportunity privately.[728] An opportunity that belongs to the company according to these principles is exclusively the company's. It is up to the competent organ, the general meeting of partners or shareholders (if the company is a general or limited partnership or a private limited company without supervisory board[729]) or the supervisory board (if the company is a public stock corporation[730]), to decide whether to pursue the opportunity or authorize the directors to do so for their own account.

The duties under §88 of the Stock Corporation Act end when the director ceases to be a member of the management board.[731] The conflicts that arise when directors resign in order to take advantage of a business opportunity are therefore left to the unwritten duty of loyalty. The courts have applied the duty not to appropriate corporate opportunities to resigning directors in a number of decisions. The duty is clearly breached if the company entered into a contract while the director was in office and the director performs the contractual obligations after resignation for his own account,[732] but also if a director opens a competing business to exploit a patentable idea that was offered to him while he served as a director and that would have allowed the company to gain a competitive advantage.[733] These holdings do not simply represent an extension of the prohibition to compete with the company pursuant to §88(1) Stock Corporation Act to events taking place after resignation. The courts acknowledge that directors are entitled to enter into transactions in the company's line of business for their own account after they resign.[734] Rather, as the two examples show, the continuing obligation is triggered by behaviour *before* resignation. In the first example, the opportunity was specific and tangible at the time of resignation, since the company had already entered into a contract. In the second example, the director was required to safeguard the company's competitive position while in office and neglected this duty by resigning. Thus, the holdings are somewhat comparable to the English maturing business opportunities doctrine that also relies on events taking place before resignation.[735] The contours of the German version of the doctrine are, however, not well developed owing to the small number of reported decisions.[736]

4. *France*

Similar to German law, a codified equivalent of the common law duty of loyalty, for example in the form of a comprehensive duty of directors to avoid any type of conflict with their company, does not exist in French law. We have seen that some situations giving rise to a conflict of interest are addressed by the rules on prohibited and regulated agreements in the

[727] BGH NZG 2013, 216, 218. [728] BGH NJW 1986, 584, 585.

[729] BGH NJW 1989, 2687, 2688. [730] In analogy to §88(1) AktG.

[731] However, the duties continue to take effect if the director is dismissed but the company does not terminate the service contract and continues to pay the director's remuneration, OLG Frankfurt, AG 2000, 518, 519.

[732] BGH GmbH-Rundschau 1977, 43.

[733] BGH NJW 1986, 585 (pointing out that it was irrelevant whether the opportunity was offered to the director in his private or professional capacity).

[734] ibid 586. [735] See text to nn 651–661 above.

[736] For a comparative analysis of these questions under German and English law, see H Fleischer, 'Gegenwartsfragen der Geschäftschancenlehre im englischen und deutschen Gesellschaftsrecht' in J Taeger and A Wiebe (eds), *Informatik—Wirtschaft—Recht. Regulierung in der Wissensgesellschaft. Festschrift für Wolfgang Kilian zum 65. Geburtstag* (Nomos 2004) 645.

Code de commerce[737] and the courts acknowledge that directors owe a duty of loyalty to shareholders, which can be enforced with the *action individuelle* by shareholders in their own name.[738] The Code de commerce also lays down an obligation of the directors not to disclose confidential information conveyed to them during board meetings.[739] More generally, the French Corporate Governance Code provides that directors are required to disclose any actual or potential conflict of interest to the board and abstain from voting on resolutions related to the conflict.[740] It is clear that these rules fail to capture all situations where the interests of the company may be compromised, notably cases where the directors engage in economic activity falling within the company's line of business. For this reason, the courts have held that directors are not only bound by a broad, unwritten duty of loyalty owed to the shareholders, but also to the company. The following is the leading case on the issue, which illustrates one application of the unwritten duty of loyalty, the establishment of a competing business by a resigning director.[741]

Cour de Cassation, Commercial Chamber, 24 February 1998, appeal no 96-12638 (*SA PIC c/ Kopcio*)

Whereas it follows from the judgment under appeal that M. Kopcio, after having worked as a regional director in the company CRPI, was appointed as the manager of one of its subsidiaries, the company PIC, on 25 January 1990, this company having as its object the distribution and maintenance of fire-fighting equipment; that the appointment was linked to a covenant not to compete with the company for a period of three years from the resignation of the director from his functions and providing for a penalty of one million francs in the case of non-compliance; that on 26 December 1990, PIC was transformed into a public stock corporation [*société anonyme*] and the appointment of M. Kopcio as manager was terminated; that on 15 March 1991, the board of directors appointed him as general director and it was stipulated in the minutes that any contract of employment existing between the company and M. Kopcio shall thereby be terminated without compensation; that on March 30th, 1992, M. Kopcio resigned from his position and soon thereafter formed a competing company, ORSI; PIC claimed damages from him before the *Tribunal de Grande Instance* for breach of the non-compete clause signed on 25 January 1990; ...

[The Cour de Cassation first held that the non-compete clause had ceased to have effect with the transformation of PIC into a public stock corporation and the attendant termination of all agreements between the parties. The court continued:]

Considering Article 1382 of the Code civil;[742]

Whereas, in order to reject the claim for damages brought by PIC, the decision [of the Court of Appeal] states that M. Kopcio, being released from the non-compete clause, had complete freedom to work and compete with PIC and that, if other employees of that company also 'resigned en masse' at the time when he resigned from the company, it was not established that this collective resignation constituted a concerted action organized by M. Kopcio; the judgment also states that some of those who were the subject of complaints or proceedings of PIC were thereafter hired by ORSI, formed by M. Kopcio, but that it is not proven that the latter had plotted or exerted pressure to entice the personnel of PIC to resign and join ORSI;

Whereas, by reaching these conclusions, while having found that M. Kopcio had served successively as manager and then, after its transformation into a public stock corporation, as general director of PIC, from which it follows that he was subject to a duty of loyalty towards the company, and after noting the mass resignations of the employees of PIC in order to join the company formed by M. Kopcio, without examining precisely, as argued by PIC in its pleadings, the circumstances under

737 See section C.I.4 above. 738 See text to nn 65–68. 739 Com, Art L225-37 para 5.

740 2018 MEDEF Corporate Governance Code of Listed Corporations, Art 19.

741 For an analysis of the decision see B Petit, *Bull. Joly Sociétés* 1998, 813.

742 [Footnote by authors.] Article1382 Code civil has been renumbered as Article 1240 and provides: 'Any act whatever of man, which causes damage to another, obliges the one by whose fault it occurred, to compensate it'.

which some of them had been released from the non-compete clause to which they had agreed, M. Kopcio still being general director of the company, the Court of Appeal did not provide a legal basis for its decision;

For these reasons, the decision of the Court of Appeal of Amiens ... is set aside ...

Questions and comments:

1. The reference to Article 1382 Code civil (now Article 1240), the general tort law basis for claiming damages, indicates that the Cour de cassation considers the unwritten duty of loyalty of directors to derive from tort law. This is somewhat surprising, given that it is commonly acknowledged that company directors are subject to stringent behavioural expectations by virtue of their position and the fact that they are entrusted with administering the financial interests of others, whereas tort law imposes general standards of due care on those who interact with other persons outside the scope of pre-existing legal relationships.[743] In fact, in a prior judgment, the Cour de Cassation assessed the duty of loyalty of a former manager of a private limited company within the context of the manager's contractual duties flowing from the contract of employment.[744] The tort law foundation of the duty of loyalty has also been questioned by the literature.[745] On the other hand, it is well established that Articles 1240 and 1241 Code civil can be used as a basis of an unfair competition claim.[746] In addition, as we have seen, qualifying liability for breach of the duty of loyalty as deriving from tort law fits well with the general conceptualization of the directors' liability under French law, also where such liability is based on Article L225-251 Code de commerce,[747] and does not prevent the courts from defining the scope of the duty in light of the notion of a director as someone akin to a fiduciary.[748]
2. As in our other jurisdictions, the treatment of cases involving competitive behaviour or the exploitation of corporate opportunities by directors depends on whether the director still holds office or has resigned. As far as the former situation is concerned, the Cour de Cassation established in two judgments from 2001 and 2002 that the executive directors of public and private companies, that is, the managers (*gérants*) of the SARL, the general director (*directeur général*), deputy general directors (*directeurs généraux délégués*), and chairman (*président du conseil d'administration*) in public companies with a one-tier board, and the members of the management board (*directoire*) in public companies with a two-tier board, are prohibited from competing with the company.[749] The court held that managers (or executive directors) are subject to a duty of loyalty and good faith by reason of their position as managers of the company, which requires them not to enter into transactions for their own account or as the manager of another company that operates within the same line of business.[750] For example, in *DL finances*,[751] decided by the Cour de Cassation in 2011, the director and one of the shareholders of a private limited liability company called Clos du Baty took over the second tranche of a property development programme that had been offered to Clos du Baty. DL finances, another shareholder of Clos du Baty, brought an action for damages against both the managing director and the shareholder that had taken advantage of the opportunity, claiming damages for breach of the duty of loyalty. The court dismissed the action against the shareholder, based on tort law,[752] arguing that shareholders, in their capacity *as shareholders* and without being *de*

[743] See our discussion above, section A.II.

[744] Cass com, 7 June 1994 (*Dallest c/ SARL PRO SI DEX*), *Bull. Joly Sociétés* 1994, 1232, note B Saintourens. In this case, the director had made preparations to set up a competing business while he was still managing director of the company, which may explain the different dogmatic treatment compared with *Kopcio*.

[745] See, for example, Petit (n 741) fn 2. [746] ibid. [747] See text to nn 303–304 above.

[748] But see also Cass com, 15 November 2011 (*DL finances*), *Bull. Joly Sociétés* 2012, 112, note H Le Nabasque, discussed in the next comment.

[749] Cass com, 6 June 2001, *Lamy soc. com.* 2002, no 144, note I Grossi; Cass com, 12 February 2002 (*Etablissements Darrès*), *Revue des sociétés* 2002, 702, note L Godon. For a discussion of the case law see Le Nabasque (n 748).

[750] Cass com, 15 November 2011 (*DL finances*), *Bull. Joly Sociétés* 2012, 112 (in the original text, this duty is called an 'obligation de loyauté et de fidélité').

[751] ibid. [752] Civ, Art 1240.

facto directors, were under no obligation to refrain from engaging in a competitive activity or indeed to inform the company of any such activity. The only limits imposed on their behaviour were those stemming from the law against unfair competition, that is, the general regulations applying to all market participants. Managers (or executive directors), on the other hand, were bound by a duty of loyalty going beyond the unfair competition rules. They breached this duty if they entered into transactions that fell within the company's field of activity. The defendant director in *DL finances* had argued (and the Court of Appeal had accepted the argument and thus dismissed the claim for damages) that the development project had changed over the course of the execution of the first tranche and that the second tranche, taken up by the defendants for their own account, had effectively been a different project not offered to, and not accepted by, Clos du Baty. In the eyes of the Cour de Cassation, this point was irrelevant. The court did not pursue the question of whether the company had, or could have, obtained the contract for the execution of the second project, if it was indeed a distinct project. It was sufficient that the project fell within the company's line of business. In that case, a director who exploits the opportunity for his own account acts contrary to the company's interests and hence violates the duty of loyalty. In *DL finances*, the director was found liable pursuant to the general provision embodying the responsibility of directors of private limited liability companies for violations of the law, the company's articles, and management mistakes.[753] Thus, the court drew a distinction between the liability of shareholders and former directors (as in *Kopcio*), which is seen as tortious, and that of current directors. Are these dogmatic differentiations convincing, and are they of practical relevance?

3. If directors pursue a competitive activity after resigning from the board, more is required to engage their responsibility. *Kopcio* was a clear case since the director resigned in order to form a competing company and enticed other employees to leave by offering attractive employment opportunities in the newly created business. A case decided by the Cour de Cassation in 2002, *Etablissements Darrès*, that falls somewhat between the situation of current and resigning directors competing with the company may illustrate how the test applied by the courts changes.[754] In this case, a director, M. Darrès, resigned and started a competing business during the last month of the notice period, thus before he had ceased to be a director. The new company was called SVIV, but the director used his last name on marketing materials and other business documents and thus, the plaintiff submitted, created the misleading impression of a connection with Etablissements Darrès. The plaintiff claimed damages and an injunction enjoining M. Darrès from using his last name on the company's documents. The court held, first, that M. Darrès was subject to a duty of loyalty and good faith owed to the company until he ceased to hold office, that is, until the end of the notice period. He was in breach of this duty since he had formed a competing company, and the company had commenced business operations, before that date. Secondly, as far as the injunction was concerned, the court decided that the use of the company's name, even though it was M. Darrès' last name, constituted an act of unfair competition. Consequently, M. Darrès was also found liable on that count. The judgment shows a distinct treatment of the periods before and after a director's resignation takes effect. Before resignation, the director is bound by a strict duty of loyalty, which prohibits any type of competitive behaviour. The courts do not examine whether the challenged conduct qualifies as an act of unfair competition. The duty is independent of any contractually agreed non-compete obligation. It is 'functional' in character, as has been suggested in the literature, since it is 'inherent in the functions of a director'.[755] If this interpretation is correct, it follows that the duty ends when the director ceases to hold office. After this point in time, and notwithstanding any contractual arrangements to the contrary, the basic principle of freedom to undertake economic activity applies. The former director is able to compete with the company and is only bound by the unfair competition rules that constrain the conduct of all market participants.[756] This, in fact, is how both *Kopcio* and *Etablissements Darrès* have been interpreted in the literature.[757]

[753] Com, Art L223-22.
[754] Cass com, 12 February 2002, *Revue des sociétés* 2002, 702.
[755] Godon (n 749) para 7.
[756] ibid para 9.
[757] Cozian, Viandier, and Deboissy (n 309) para 375.

4. In both *DL finances* and *Etablissements Darrès*, the Cour de Cassation speaks of the duty of loyalty *and* good faith (*obligation de loyauté et de fidélité*). It has been argued in the literature that the requirement to act in good faith aligns the duties existing under an employment contract and those of company directors. On this view, the contract of employment and the corporate relationship binding a director to his or her company are not fundamentally different; both give rise to the same obligations to discharge the respective duties faithfully and loyally. As a consequence, a company director is as much required to abstain from competitive activity as an employee.[758] However, the precise contours of the duty to act in good faith and the differences, if any, between loyalty and good faith remain uncertain, as these concepts await further refinement by the courts.
5. In comparison with our two common law jurisdictions, where the no profit and no conflict rules were well established by the second half of the 19th century, the French version of the duty of loyalty is of very recent origin. In this regard, French law is not alone in the civil law world. A number of other jurisdictions of French legal origin adopted duties prohibiting directors from competing with the company and exploiting corporate opportunities only in the first decade of the new millennium. The Italian corporate law reforms of 2003 introduced a codified corporate opportunities doctrine that supplements the already existing duty not to compete with the company[759] and requires directors to refrain from taking advantage of business opportunities that they obtain in connection with their appointment.[760] The Spanish Corporate Enterprises Act of 2010 also lays down, for the first time for the public stock corporation, both a duty not to compete with the company and not to exploit opportunities that a director learned of by reason of his or her position, provided that the opportunity 'is offered to the company or the company has an interest therein'.[761] This gap in the regulation of conflict of interest situations in civil law countries was noted by parts of the international finance literature and ascribed to deficiencies inherent in the civil law tradition, notably a greater reliance on statutes rather than broad principles based on notions of fairness, such as fiduciary duties, and a greater responsiveness to stakeholder interests and hence less focus on the managerial agency problem.[762] Is this claim still justified, in light of the more recent jurisprudence of the French courts? What may be a reason for the slow reaction of the legislator and judiciary to problems implicating the duty of loyalty in these jurisdictions? Consider the following observation by the economist F.A. Hayek, made in the context of a discussion of how the common law and civil law evolve through adjudication and precedent: 'It seems that the constant necessity of articulating rules in order to distinguish between the relevant and the accidental in the precedents which guide him, produces in the common law judge a capacity for discovering general principles rarely acquired by a judge who operates with a supposedly complete catalogue of applicable rules before him ... The common law judge is bound to be very much aware that words are always but an imperfect expression of what his predecessors struggled to articulate'.[763] Can this observation serve as an explanation of the delayed development of the duty of loyalty in civil law countries?
6. Comparing the scope of the unwritten French duty of loyalty and the common law corporate opportunities doctrine, we can observe several commonalities and differences. First, under both concepts, directors are not prohibited from serving on the boards of other companies.[764] However, if they accept more than one directorship, they are under the obligation to avoid

758 Godon (n 749) para 12.

759 Italian Civil Code, Art 2390 (providing that directors shall not compete with the company for their own account or the account of a third party or be appointed as director or general manager in a competing company without authorization by the general meeting).

760 Italian Civil Code, Art 2391(5), as amended by Legislative Decree No 6 of 17 January 2003, Gazz. Uff. no 17 (22 January 2003).

761 Spanish Corporate Enterprises Act, Arts 228, 230.

762 S Johnson, R La Porta, F Lopez-de-Silanes, and A Shleifer, 'Tunneling' (2000) 90 American Economic Review 22, 24 (discussing a number of French, Italian, and Belgian decisions from the late 20th century where the courts rejected challenges to related party transactions and the exploitation of corporate opportunities brought by minority shareholders, *inter alia*, Cass com, 4 October 1994, *SAICO c/ SARL Péronnet*, JCP E 1994, no 48).

763 FA Hayek, *Law, Legislation and Liberty, vol 1: Rules and Order* (University of Chicago Press 1973), 87.

764 However, the Code de commerce stipulates that directors who are natural persons shall not hold more than five positions on the board of public stock corporations having their seat in France, Art L225-21 para 1 (similarly

engaging in business dealings contrary to the interests of any of the companies, which is particularly problematic in corporate groups.[765] Secondly, French law is narrower than English law, but not necessarily narrower than the law of Delaware, in that it establishes a strict line of business test. A business opportunity is only a corporate opportunity if it falls within the sphere of economic activity pursued by the director's company. Whether a certain degree of flexibility is retained by the French test is somewhat unclear owing to the small number of decisions, but we have seen that English law is also characterized by some uncertainty after codification of the no-conflict rule in the Companies Act 2006.[766] Thirdly, apart from the line of business test, the French doctrine seems to be relatively demanding and adaptable to different situations, for example where it is unclear whether a company could have obtained an opportunity[767] or a director has resigned, but begins the competitive activity before the resignation takes effect.[768] However, again, it is dangerous to make generalizations based on only a few decisions, and it is difficult to predict, for example, how French courts will judge a situation where a company is not able to exploit an opportunity owing to a specific practical or structural impediment.[769] Fourthly, it has been noted that there is no general duty of directors under French law to disclose situations of conflict or the existence of a corporate opportunity.[770] But this is principally not different under English law—at least no explicit duty to disclose exists outside of section 177 Companies Act 2006[771]—and the French duty of loyalty seems to be wide enough to prevent the exploitation of an opportunity by the directors for their own account whenever this is contrary to the interests of the company. Fifthly, the treatment of resigning directors is distinctly different from English law. French law accords considerable importance to the freedom to undertake economic activity, with the consequence that the required balancing of the interests of the company in being protected against competitive behaviour and the interests of the resigning director in being allowed to engage in economic activity leads to a different policy outcome than under English law.

in the two-tier system Art L225-77 para 1 for members of the supervisory board). Furthermore, natural persons are not permitted to be general director or (in the two-tier system) member of the management board in more than one company, Arts L225-54-1 para 1, L225-67 para 1. Finally, Art L225-94-1 para 1 provides that natural persons shall not hold more than five positions as general director, member of the one-tier board of directors, management board, or supervisory board of public stock corporations having their seat in France.

765 Godon (n 749) para 10. The interest of the individual company is only replaced by the group interest if the requirements of the *Rozenblum* doctrine are satisfied; see Chapter 10E.II.

766 See section II.1 above.

767 See *DL finances* (n 750).

768 See *Etablissements Darrès* (n 754).

769 On the difference between practical and structural impediments in English law, see the text to nn 649–650 above.

770 M Corradi, 'Les opportunités d'affaires saisies par les administrateurs de la société en violation du devoir de loyauté' (2011) *Bull. Joly Sociétés* 157.

771 See comment 4 after *Wilkinson v West Coast Capital*, section II.1 above.

7

Constraints on Discretion: Part 2—Shareholders

A. Introduction

Unlike the powers of directors, the voting rights of shareholders do not derive from their position in relation to the company, and they do not exist in order to promote an abstract interest, such as the 'corporate interest'. They are one element of the share as a species of property; thus, it should, in principle, be permissible for shareholders to exercise them solely in their own interest. At the same time, if the property analogy is taken seriously, it could be argued that corporate changes that affect the rights and obligations attached to shares can only be implemented with the consent of the affected shareholder. This was indeed the position in the early days of corporate law, the second half of the nineteenth and beginning of the twentieth centuries, when many legal systems provided that fundamental changes such as mergers required unanimous approval by the shareholders.[1] However, as the corporate economy evolved, it became clear that unanimity requirements severely impeded business activity. Any one shareholder could hold up important changes, thus making it difficult for corporations to adapt to new economic conditions.[2] For this reason, legal systems universally moved to majority decision-making, including for transactions that changed the structure of the enterprise fundamentally.[3] This trend towards greater flexibility continued over the course of the twentieth century, in the US for example by reducing the majority required to adopt fundamental changes from two-thirds to a simple majority and permitting the disparate treatment of majority and minority shareholders, the latter receiving cash in exchange for their shares in a merger, to force the minority out of the company.[4] Thus,

[1] EF Greene, 'Corporate Freeze-out Mergers: A Proposed Analysis' (1975–1976) 28 Stanford Law Review 487; RB Thompson, 'Exit, Liquidity, and Majority Rule: Appraisal's Role in Corporate Law' (1995) 84 Georgetown Law Journal 1, 12.

[2] Thompson (n 1) 13.

[3] For an overview of this development in the United States, see Thompson (n 1) 14–15.

[4] Cash-out or squeeze-out mergers were initially regarded as illegal by US courts, see, e.g., *Colgate v United States Leather Co.*, 67 A.657, 668 (N.J. Ch. 1907). However, in the 1960s, states began to amend corporation statutes to allow the use of cash as a consideration and courts sanctioned the practice of cashing out minority shareholders in a merger with the parent company, *Coyne v Park & Tilford Distillers Corp.*, 154 A.2d 893 (Del. 1959); *Stauffer v Standard Brands Inc.*, 187 A.2d 78 (Del. 1962). For a discussion of these decisions, see Thompson (n 1) 19–20, 21–2.

while the shift to a majoritarian system was a necessary response to the growth of industrial corporations from small, localized businesses to conglomerates operating nationwide and having a large number of widely dispersed shareholders, legal systems had to develop mechanisms to restrain an abuse of majority rule. This is the topic of this chapter.

We will distinguish between constraints imposed on the majority or controlling shareholder (or indeed, in exceptional cases, on a minority shareholder) in the context of business operations that affect the minority detrimentally but do not result in a change in ownership of the business (section B), and in sale of control transactions, such as a merger, sale of all or almost all of the company's assets, or a takeover (section C).[5] In both cases, agency problems arise between majority and minority shareholders, but legal systems provide for distinct solutions that reflect the different economic importance of the two types of transaction and the fact that minority shareholders are particularly vulnerable to collective action problems when control of the company changes hands.

B. Constraints without a Sale of Control

I. UK

1. Shareholder voting and duties

It may be thought that large shareholders who have control over the composition of the board of directors and, hence, at least indirectly over business operations, or who may sit on the board themselves, are in a comparable position to directors and should consequently be subject to similar duties. We will see that this is indeed the position in many legal systems. UK law, however, is an outlier in our sample of jurisdictions in that the courts consistently reject the notion that shareholders are fiduciaries. Their powers are not unconstrained, as we will discuss below, but as a starting point of an analysis of their rights and duties, it is useful to explore why they are not bound by fiduciary duties. The following case elaborates on this fundamental distinction between directors and shareholders under UK law.

***Northern Counties Securities Ltd v Jackson & Steeple Ltd* [1974] 2 All ER 625 (Chancery Division)**

[In an action against the defendant company, the company had given an undertaking to the court to use its best endeavours to obtain a stock exchange quotation for its shares and allot a certain number of shares to the plaintiffs. Having failed to comply with the undertaking, the plaintiffs filed a motion seeking an order that the company and its directors convene an extraordinary general meeting to approve the issue and allotment of the shares, as required by stock exchange rules, notify the shareholders that the company was contractually bound to issue and allot the shares, and restrain the directors, who were also shareholders, from voting against the resolution.]

Walton JR:

Mr. Price [counsel for the plaintiffs] argued that, in effect, there are two separate sets of persons in whom authority to activate the company itself resides. Quoting the well-known passages from Viscount Haldane L.C. in *Lennard's Carrying Co. Ltd. v. Asiatic Petroleum Co. Ltd.* [1915]

[5] The literature sometimes draws a distinction between control transactions, understood to refer only to takeovers, and 'fundamental changes', encompassing mergers and the sale of the company's assets. The argument is that the legal techniques used to carry out takeovers and mergers are too disparate to lend themselves to the development of common principles. In the case of a takeover, control shifts as a consequence of a contract between an acquirer and the target's shareholders, whereas a merger or sale of assets requires a decision by the companies involved (or at least one of the companies), R Kraakman and others, *The Anatomy of Corporate Law* (3rd edn, Oxford University Press 2017) 205. However, in different economies, the transactions are used interchangeably to achieve identical economic outcomes. Therefore, unsurprisingly, the economic problems that arise are largely comparable and legal systems make use of similar concepts, for example exit rights, to achieve their regulatory goals.

A.C. 705, he submitted that the company as such was only a juristic figment of the imagination, lacking both a body to be kicked and a soul to be damned. From this it followed that there must be some one or more human persons who did, as a matter of fact, act on behalf of the company, and whose acts therefore must, for all practical purposes, be the acts of the company itself. The first of such bodies was clearly the body of directors, to whom under most forms of articles ... the management of the business of the company is expressly delegated. Therefore, their acts are the defendant company's acts; and if they do not, in the present instance, cause the defendant company to comply with the undertakings given by it to the court, they are themselves liable for contempt of court ...

But, continues Mr. Price, this is only half of the story. There are some matters in relation to which the directors are not competent to act on behalf of the company, the relevant authority being 'the company in general meeting', that is to say, a meeting of the members. Thus in respect of all matters within the competence—at any rate those within the exclusive competence—of a meeting of the members, the acts of the members are the acts of the company, in precisely the same way as the acts of the directors are the acts of the company. Ergo, for any shareholder to vote against a resolution to issue the shares here in question to the plaintiffs would be a contempt of court, as it would be a step taken by him knowingly which would prevent the defendant company from fulfilling its undertaking to the court. Mr. Price admitted that he could find no authority which directly assisted his argument, but equally confidently asserted that there was no authority which precluded it.

Mr. Instone [counsel for the directors] indicted Mr. Price's argument as being based upon 'a nominalistic fallacy'. His precise proposition was formulated as follows:

'Whilst directors have special responsibilities as executive agents of the defendant company to ensure that the company does not commit a contempt of court, a shareholder, when the position has been put before the shareholders generally, who chooses to vote against such approval will not himself be in contempt of court.' . . .

In my judgment, these submissions of Mr. Instone are correct. I think that, in a nutshell, the distinction is this: when a director votes as a director for or against any particular resolution in a director's meeting, he is voting as a person under a fiduciary duty to the company for the proposition that the company should take a certain course of action. When a shareholder is voting for or against a particular resolution he is voting as a person owing no fiduciary duty to the company and who is exercising his own right of property, to vote as he thinks fit. The fact that the result of the voting at the meeting (or at a subsequent poll) will bind the company cannot affect the position that, in voting, he is voting simply in exercise of his own property rights.

Perhaps another (and simpler) way of putting the matter is that a director is an agent, who casts his vote to decide in what manner his principal shall act through the collective agency of the board of directors; a shareholder who casts his vote in general meeting is not casting it as an agent of the company in any shape or form. His act therefore, in voting as he pleases, cannot in any way be regarded as an act of the company ...

I now come to paragraph 4 of the notice of motion, which seeks an order restraining the individual respondents and each of them from voting against the resolution. Mr. Price says that, as the executive agents of the defendant company, they are bound to recommend to its shareholders that they vote in favour of the resolution to issue the shares, and hence, at the least, they cannot themselves vote against it, for they would thereby be assisting the defendant company to do that which it is their duty to secure does not happen. If, as executive officers of the defendant company, they are bound to procure a certain result if at all possible, how can they, as individuals, seek to frustrate that result?

I regret, however, that I am unable to accede to Mr. Price's arguments in this respect. I much regret it, because I cannot see how, in common honesty, directors who have committed a company to a particular course of action can themselves seek, by their own acts as individuals, to frustrate it, more especially when they will thereby be rendering the company liable to pay damages, and possibly very heavy damages indeed. But even if that were not the case, the point on commercial honesty would remain.

However, I do not see where this is meant to lead me. Suppose, for example, that a minority of the board had been throughout strenuously opposed to the company's entering into this contract, are they nevertheless, as individuals, to lose control of their right to vote adversely thereto? Suppose that, before the question of implementation arose, there had been a complete change in the character of the composition of the board, and the existing board were all bitterly hostile to their predecessors' actions? True it is that they would still be bound to procure the defendant company to honour its undertakings, but it is far from clear to me upon what principle they would be obliged, at the least, to have their own votes as members sterilised. Suppose that the members of the present board resigned on the eve of this meeting; would they then be entitled to vote as ordinary members, or not?

These examples show, I think, that Mr. Price's proposition is far from self-evident. I think it is wrong. I think that a director who has fulfilled his duty as a director of a company, by causing it to comply with an undertaking binding upon it is nevertheless free, as an individual share-holder, to enjoy the same unfettered and unrestricted right of voting at general meetings of the members of the company as he would have if he were not also a director . . .

Questions and comments:

1. *Northern Counties Securities* is an accurate summary of the well-established rule that shareholders, in exercising their voting rights, are not in the position of a fiduciary. Hence, they are not bound by the stringent duties that the law imposes on directors, for example the duty not to make a profit out of their trust and to avoid all situations where their personal interest may conflict with the interests of the principal.[6] However, both case-law and statutory provisions have restricted the freedom of shareholders to have regard solely for their personal advantage in certain circumstances when a conflict of interest exists and the majority uses its superior voting powers to the detriment of the minority. The most important statutory exceptions are as follows:

   (1) When a company wishes to ratify conduct by a director amounting to negligence, default, breach of duty or breach of trust in relation to the company, the votes of the director and any member connected with him[7] must be disregarded.[8]

   (2) A resolution in connection with an off-market purchase of the company's own shares is not effective if members holding shares to which the resolution relates exercise voting rights carried by the shares to be purchased.[9]

   (3) A resolution of a private company authorizing the payment out of capital for redemption or purchase of the company's own shares is not effective if members holding shares to which the resolution relates exercise voting rights carried by the shares to be redeemed or repurchased.[10]

2. Apart from these clear-cut statutory limitations on the shareholders' voting rights, the courts have sought to establish general principles to curtail majority power and protect the minority from opportunistic behaviour. However, it has been pointed out that the courts have been less than successful in producing coherent legal principles and the law remains 'somewhat untidy'.[11] On the one hand, the courts have held that there is no fiduciary relationship between the shareholders and the company or between different groups

[6] *Bristol & West Building Society v Mothew* [1998] Ch 1, 18. On the differences between the duties of majority shareholders and fiduciary duties, see also PL Davies and S Worthington, *Gower's Principles of Modern Company Law* (10th edn, Sweet & Maxwell 2016) para 19-4.

[7] Definition of 'connected person' in s 252.

[8] Companies Act 2006, s 239.

[9] ibid ss 695, 698.

[10] ibid s 717.

[11] Davies and Worthington (n 6) para 19-7, quoting *Constable v Executive Connections Ltd* [2005] EWHC 3, para 30. The authors also observe that '[t]he courts have hovered uncomfortably between an unwillingness to determine how businesses should be run and an equally deeply felt unease that simple majoritarianism would leave the minority exposed to opportunistic treatment by the majority': ibid para 19-4.

of shareholders, for example the majority and the minority.[12] On the other hand, the courts have construed duties of shareholders that seem to be, at least at first sight, akin to the fiduciary duties of directors. This is particularly true of the duty to exercise voting rights 'bona fide for the benefit of the company as a whole', as expressed for the first time in *Allen v Gold Reefs of West Africa Ltd.*[13] In this case, a company had amended its articles so as to provide for a lien for all debts owed by a member to the company upon all shares (fully or not fully paid) held by that member. One shareholder had acquired shares that were not fully paid up. The company sought to assert its lien on the fully paid shares of that member, who brought an action to obtain a declaration that the company had no lien on the shares. The court held:

> The power ... conferred on companies to alter the regulations contained in their articles is limited only by the provisions contained in the statute and the conditions contained in the company's memorandum of association. Wide, however, as the language of [what is now section 21(1) CA 2006] is, the power conferred by it must, like all other powers, be exercised subject to those general principles of law and equity which are applicable to all powers conferred on majorities and enabling them to bind minorities. It must be exercised, not only in the manner required by law, but also bona fide for the benefit of the company as a whole, and it must not be exceeded. These conditions are always implied, and are seldom, if ever, expressed.[14]

This paragraph may be interpreted as establishing a broad equitable principle requiring shareholders to act in the best interest of the company when they vote on resolutions amending the articles of association, not dissimilar to the duty of directors to promote the success of the company pursuant to section 172 of the Companies Act 2006. However, the court also emphasized that if a particular matter can properly be regulated in a company's articles, such as whether the company shall have a lien on shares, then the shareholders have the power to change the articles with the requisite majority and introduce such regulations, even if they alter existing rights of the shareholders. The idea here is that the shareholders take their shares, and the concomitant rights, subject to alteration in accordance with the statutory procedure for an amendment of the articles.[15] A different view is only warranted if a shareholder has 'special rights' acquired by contract between the member and the company, which may exclude the member from the operation of an altered article.[16] However, this was not the case in *Allen v Gold Reefs of West Africa*, and the court consequently held that the company was able to amend its articles and extend the lien to the fully paid-up shares of the plaintiff.

3. Courts have struggled to develop clear contours of the duty to act bona fide for the benefit of the company ever since *Allen v Gold Reefs of West Africa*. It is clear that the Court of Appeal in *Allen v Gold Reefs* did not intend to introduce a broad fiduciary-type duty that constrained the exercise of shareholder decision-making similar to the fiduciary duties of directors whenever the majority made use of its powers under the Companies Act. However, the courts have, by and large, failed to give consistent guidance on where the limits of majority power should be drawn and when judicial interference with majority rule was justified. Early case law dealing with amendments to the articles that allowed a majority shareholder to force the minority to transfer their shares oscillated between holding that expropriating the minority was never for

[12] See the excerpt from *Northern Counties Securities* reproduced above. The same approach can be found in other common law jurisdictions, see, for example, *Brant Investments Ltd v KeepRite Inc.*, 80 DLR (4th) 161 (Ontario Court of Appeal 1991); *Peters' American Delicacy Co Ltd v Heath*, 61 CLR 457 (High Court of Australia 1939). The reasoning mirrors that of the High Court in *Northern Counties Securities*: 'The power of alteration is not fiduciary. The shareholders are not trustees for one another, and, unlike directors, they occupy no fiduciary position and are under no fiduciary duties. They vote in respect of their shares, which are property, and the right to vote is attached to the share itself as an incident of property to be enjoyed and exercised for the owner's personal advantage'. *Peters' American Delicacy Co*: ibid 504.

[13] [1900] 1 Ch 656, 671. [14] ibid. [15] ibid 672–3.

[16] The question whether the alteration of the company's articles may constitute a breach of contract between the company and its members is addressed in more detail in Chapter 5A.II (comment 3 after the excerpt from *McQuade v Stoneham*).

the benefit of the company as a whole, but merely for the benefit of the majority,[17] and examining whether the majority had a business reason for the elimination of the minority, in which case the amendment to the articles was held to be valid.[18] It was further unclear whether the 'benefit for the company' test was largely subjective and the courts would not intervene as long as the majority shareholders gave a *plausible* explanation as to why they believed that the challenged amendment was in the interest of the company,[19] or they bore the burden of establishing that the amendment *actually* benefited the company, which would be fully reviewable in court.[20] This question was resolved by the Court of Appeal in *Shuttleworth v Cox Brothers and Co (Maidenhead) Ltd* in favour of the first approach:[21]

> It is not matter of law for the Court whether or not a particular alteration is for the benefit of the company, nor is it the business of a judge to review the decision of every company in the country on these questions ... [Rather,] the question is solely for the shareholders acting in good faith. The circumstances may be such as to lead to one conclusion only, that the majority of the shareholders are acting so oppressively that they cannot be acting in good faith; or, to put it in another way, it may be that their decision must be one which could [not] be taken by persons acting in good faith with a view to the benefit of the company. But these are matters outside and apart from the question, does this or that tribunal consider, in the light of events which have happened, that the alteration was or was not for the benefit of the company?[22]

The quote illustrates that the standard of review adopted by the court is a form of rationality review. The majority shareholder's submission that they acted in good faith for the benefit of the company will be accepted unless there is evidence to the contrary or the circumstances are such that no one could have reasonably believed that the resolution was in the interest of the company.[23] While the court did not frame the issue in terms of the rationality of the decision, it could be argued that no reasonable man will consider a resolution to be for the benefit of the company if it is not supported by a rational business reason.[24]

[17] *Brown v British Abrasive Wheel Co Ltd* [1919] 1 Ch 290. In this case, the majority, representing 98% of the shares, had agreed to provide additional funds at a time when the company was in urgent need of further capital, but only if they could buy out the 2% minority. The court was not convinced by the majority's argument that the buy-out of the minority was for the benefit of the company as a whole: 'I find it very difficult to follow how it can be just and equitable that a majority, on failing to purchase the shares of a minority by agreement, can take power to do so compulsorily. The defendants contend that it is for the benefit of the company as a whole because in default of further capital the company might have to go into liquidation. The plaintiff is willing to risk that. The proposed alteration is not directly concerned with the provision of further capital, nor does it insure that it will be provided. It is merely for the benefit of the majority. If passed, the majority may acquire all the shares and provide further capital. That would be for the benefit of the company as then constituted. But the proposed alteration is not for the present benefit of this company'. ibid 295–6.

[18] *Sidebottom v Kershaw, Leese & Co Ltd* [1920] 1 Ch 154 (exclusion of members who were carrying on a competing businesses). *Brown v British Abrasive Wheel Co Ltd* (n 17) was distinguished on the ground that the majority in the latter case had not acted bona fide for the benefit of the company, but 'entirely for their own benefit, and in their own interests': ibid 167.

[19] In *Sidebottom v Kershaw*, the court implied that this was the correct approach. It stressed that the question whether the exclusion of a competing member was for the benefit of the company 'ought to be decided by the voices of the business men who understand the business and understand the nature of competition' and not by the court: ibid 166.

[20] *Dafen Tinplate Co Ltd v Llanelly Steel Co (1907) Ltd* [1920] 2 Ch 124, 140–2: 'It has been suggested that the only question in such a case as this is whether the shareholders bona fide or honestly believed that the alteration was for the benefit of the company. But this is not, in my view, the true meaning of the words of Lindley MR [in *Allen v Gold Reefs of West Africa*] ... The question is whether in fact the alteration is genuinely for the benefit of the company ... The power of compulsory acquisition by the majority of shares which the owner does not desire to sell is not lightly to be assumed whenever it pleases the majority to do so ... I am of opinion that such a power cannot be supported if it is not established that the power is bona fide or genuinely for the company's benefit'.

[21] [1927] 2 KB 9. [22] ibid 26–7.

[23] ibid 18: 'The alteration may be so oppressive as to cast suspicion on the honesty of the persons responsible for it, or so extravagant that no reasonable men could really consider it for the benefit of the company. In such cases the Court is, I think, entitled ... to say that the alteration of a company's articles shall not stand if it is such that no reasonable men could consider it for the benefit of the company'.

[24] On this view, the requirement to act in good faith for the benefit of the company resembles the duty to promote the success of the company (s 172 Companies Act 2006), which is discussed in Chapter 5B.I (comments 2 and 3 after the excerpt from *Howard Smith v Ampol Petroleum*). A similar, albeit not identical, standard of review exists in the United States when a plaintiff fails to rebut the presumptions of the business judgment rule; see Chapter 6B.I.2(c).

4. More recently, the English courts may have introduced again a more objective element into the enquiry. In *Re Charterhouse Capital Ltd*,[25] the shareholders amended the articles to provide for a drag-along right forcing the minority to sell their shares if the holders of 50 per cent or more of the share capital agreed to sell shares representing not less than 50 per cent of the voting rights in the company. The court reiterated the subjective *Shuttleworth* test, but also held that the power of the majority to amend the articles was constrained by the purpose of that power[26] and a resolution would be invalid if there was evidence of bad faith *or* improper motive.[27] It is not entirely clear whether the references to the purpose of the shareholders' power and a 'proper motive', reminiscent of the proper purpose doctrine now laid down in section 171(b) of the Companies Act 2006,[28] were intended to alter the *Shuttleworth* test.[29] Some commentators have interpreted *Re Charterhouse* in this way.[30] However, it is questionable whether the proper purpose doctrine is a helpful analogy. Unlike the powers of directors, the power to amend the articles pursuant to section 21(1) of the Companies Act is not conferred on a qualified majority of shareholders with a specific purpose in mind. Amendments must, of course, comply with binding law in order to be valid, but with this qualification, it is the purpose of section 21(1) of the Companies Act to facilitate private ordering and enable a sufficiently large number of shareholders to arrange the affairs of the company as they see fit. The court in *Charterhouse*, presumably, wanted to stress that certain types of behaviour were generally impermissible because they were pursued with an improper motive or for improper ends, such as oppressing a minority.[31] However, this begs the question of how to identify an improper motive and thus determine the limits of a proper exercise of majority power.
5. The 'benefit of the company' test is not meaningful if a resolution relates to a matter in which the company—understood as an entity separate from the shareholders—has no interest, for example the allotment of shares or the power to transfer shares. A good example of such a case is the decision of the Court of Appeal in *Greenhalgh v Ardene Cinemas Ltd*.[32] In this case, the defendant company's articles provided for pre-emption rights of existing members if a shareholder wished to transfer his shares to an outsider. One of the defendants negotiated the sale of a controlling interest in the company to a third party. In order to give effect to the agreement he procured a special resolution of the general meeting amending the articles and making it possible to disapply the plaintiff's pre-emption rights by ordinary resolution. The plaintiff claimed that the resolution had not been passed bona fide for the benefit of the company and should be set aside. The court, acknowledging that the test as enunciated in *Allen v Gold Reefs of West Africa* and *Shuttleworth* had to be modified, suggested that 'the company as a whole' should be understood as 'the corporators as a general body'. Accordingly, 'an individual hypothetical member [should be taken] and it [should] be asked whether what is proposed is, in the honest opinion of those who voted in its favour, for that person's benefit'.[33] From a logical point of view, it is convincing to focus on the individual shareholders, rather than the company as a separate entity, since the interests of the company do not provide a useful benchmark if a dispute concerns exclusively the rights and responsibilities of two groups of shareholders. However, it remains entirely unclear how the interests of the 'hypothetical member' can be identified, given that shareholders pursue a variety of goals when they invest in shares. In most companies, it will not be possible to speak of a typical or an average member whose interests can be taken to represent those of the company as a whole. Maybe for this reason, the court in *Greenhalgh* outlined a second test:

[25] [2015] EWCA Civ 536.

[26] ibid paras 90 and 95 (citing *Allen v Gold Reefs of West Africa* (n 13), as well as the High Court of Australia in *Peters' American Delicacy Co.* (n 12), where the court held that the challenged resolution must not 'imply any purpose outside the scope of the power').

[27] ibid paras 97 and 104.

[28] See Chapter 5B.I.

[29] The Australian case *Gambotto v WCP Ltd* (1995) 182 CLR 432 has more explicitly embraced a 'proper purpose test' as part of the review of shareholder voting.

[30] Davies and Worthington (n 6) paras 19-9, 19-11.

[31] See, in particular, *Re Charterhouse Capital Ltd* (n 25) para 95.

[32] [1951] Ch 286.

[33] ibid 291.

> [T]he matter can, in practice, be more accurately and precisely stated ... by saying that a special resolution of this kind would be liable to be impeached if the effect of it were to discriminate between the majority shareholders and the minority shareholders, so as to give to the former an advantage of which the latter were deprived.[34]

This formulation continues to pose serious problems of interpretation. On a narrow view, requiring direct discrimination, minority shareholders would be left largely without protection. Consider, for example, the amendments to the articles that were at issue in the expropriation cases discussed above. The amendments provided for special rights of shareholders who held a specified fraction of the share capital, but they did not overtly exclude any shareholder from an enjoyment of these rights. Indeed, in *Greenhalgh*, the court did not feel that the circumvention of the plaintiff's pre-emption rights amounted to discrimination within the meaning of the test it had proposed.[35] On a broad reading, on the other hand, all of the above cases would involve discrimination, since the majority always sought to obtain an advantage from which the minority was effectively excluded. In light of these difficulties, recent case law has tried to refine the *Greenhalgh* test by identifying 'vitiating factors' that allow a court to impeach a resolution if it involves 'oppression of the minority or is otherwise unjust or is outside the scope of the power'.[36] The refined formula, of course, relies on equally ambiguous terms as the original hypothetical member and discrimination tests, and it seems unlikely that it constitutes an endpoint in the development of the legal doctrines.

2. *Unfairly prejudicial conduct (s 994 Companies Act 2006)*

UK Companies Act 2006

Part 30 Protection of members against unfair prejudice

Section 994—Petition by company member

(1) A member of a company may apply to the court by petition for an order under this Part on the ground—
  (a) that the company's affairs are being or have been conducted in a manner that is unfairly prejudicial to the interests of members generally or of some part of its members (including at least himself), or
  (b) that an actual or proposed act or omission of the company (including an act or omission on its behalf) is or would be so prejudicial.

(1A) For the purposes of subsection (1)(a), a removal of the company's auditor from office—
  (a) on grounds of divergence of opinions on accounting treatments or audit procedures, or
  (b) on any other improper grounds, shall be treated as being unfairly prejudicial to the interests of some part of the company's members.

(2) The provisions of this Part apply to a person who is not a member of a company but to whom shares in the company have been transferred or transmitted by operation of law as they apply to a member of a company.

(3) ...

Section 996—Powers of the court under this Part

(1) If the court is satisfied that a petition under this Part is well founded, it may make such order as it thinks fit for giving relief in respect of the matters complained of.

[34] ibid

[35] ibid 292: 'I think that the answer is that when a man comes into a company, he is not entitled to assume that the articles will always remain in a particular form; and that, so long as the proposed alteration does not unfairly discriminate in the way which I have indicated, it is not an objection, provided that the resolution is passed bona fide, that the right to tender for the majority holding of shares would be lost by the lifting of the restriction. I do not think that it can be said that that is such a discrimination as falls within the scope of the principle which I have stated'.

[36] *Re Charterhouse Capital Ltd* (n 25) paras 90, 95–6, quoting the High Court of Australia case *Peters' American Delicacy Co. Ltd v Heath* (n 12).

(2) Without prejudice to the generality of subsection (1), the court's order may—
   (a) regulate the conduct of the company's affairs in the future;
   (b) require the company—
      (i) to refrain from doing or continuing an act complained of, or
      (ii) to do an act that the petitioner has complained it has omitted to do;
   (c) authorise civil proceedings to be brought in the name and on behalf of the company by such person or persons and on such terms as the court may direct;
   (d) require the company not to make any, or any specified, alterations in its articles without the leave of the court;
   (e) provide for the purchase of the shares of any members of the company by other members or by the company itself and, in the case of a purchase by the company itself, the reduction of the company's capital accordingly.

In addition to the case law-based doctrines summarized in the previous section, UK law provides for a statutory minority shareholder protection mechanism, the unfair prejudice remedy pursuant to section 994 of the Companies Act 2006.[37] The unfair prejudice remedy can be traced back to section 210 of the Companies Act 1948, which provided relief if the affairs of a company were being conducted in a manner oppressive to some part of the members. The provision was interpreted narrowly and, as a consequence, remained largely a dead letter.[38] In order to strengthen minority shareholder protection, the law was reformed by the Companies Act 1985, which replaced the term 'oppressive' with 'unfairly prejudicial' (section 459), thus opening the way for petitioners to challenge formally legal acts. Any member of a company may apply to the court by petition for an order on the ground that the company's affairs are being or have been conducted in a manner that is unfairly prejudicial to the interests of members generally or of some part of its members (including at least himself) or that an actual or proposed act or omission of the company is or would be prejudicial.[39] If the petition is successful, the court has wide discretion and may make such order as it thinks fit for giving relief in respect of the matter complained of, for example by regulating the conduct of the company's affairs for the future or requiring the company to refrain from doing an act complained of or to do an act that the petitioner has complained it has omitted.[40] The most common order, however, is to provide for the purchase of the shares of any member of the company by other members or by the company itself.[41]

The meaning of 'unfairly prejudicial conduct' is explained in the following case, *O'Neill v Phillips*, the first decision on the provision by the House of Lords. The case concerned a small private company operating in the construction industry that was initially wholly owned by the respondent, Mr Phillips. In 1983, the company hired the petitioner, Mr O'Neill, as a manual worker. In 1985, Mr Phillips appointed Mr O'Neill as a director and allowed him to acquire 25 per cent of the share capital. Around the same time, the two men 'had an informal discussion at which Mr Phillips expressed the hope that Mr O'Neill would be able to take over fully the day-to-day running of the company'.[42] Mr Phillips also indicated that in that case Mr O'Neill would be entitled to an equal share of the company's profits. Mr O'Neill subsequently assumed sole responsibility for the management of the business and was credited with half of the profits, partly in the form of salary and partly in the form of dividends, with Mr Phillips waiving a third of his 75 per cent entitlement in favour of Mr O'Neill to produce equality. During 1989 and 1990, discussions took place with a view to increasing Mr

[37] Pursuant to s 994(1) Companies Act 2006, any 'member of a company' has standing to petition for relief, not just minority shareholders. However, a majority shareholder is generally able to control the challenged conduct and therefore cannot claim that the company's affairs are conducted in an unfairly prejudicial manner; see *Re Legal Costs Negotiators Ltd* [1999] BCC 547.

[38] In *Scottish Co-Operative Wholesale Society Ltd v Meyer* [1959] AC 324, 342, the House of Lords had defined behaviour as 'oppressive' if shareholders exercised their authority in a manner 'burdensome, harsh and wrongful', which implied that the unfair prejudice remedy required illegality or the invasion of a legal right.

[39] Companies Act 2006, s 994(1). [40] ibid s 996. [41] ibid s 996(2)(e).

[42] *O'Neill v Phillips* [1999] 1 WLR 1092, 1095.

O'Neill's shareholding to 50 per cent, subject to the achievement of certain financial targets. However, before the parties concluded any formal agreement, the construction sector went into recession and the company began to struggle. Mr Phillips became concerned about Mr O'Neill's management and decided to resume personal command. Mr O'Neill henceforth received only his salary and dividends in proportion to his 25 per cent holding. He made preparations to resign from the company and filed a section 994 petition, alleging that Mr Phillips had broken his promises to pay him 50 per cent of the profits and to allot him 50 per cent of the shares.

***O'Neill v Phillips* [1999] 1 WLR 1092 (House of Lords)**

Lord Hoffmann:

My Lords, this appeal raises, for the first time in your Lordships House, a question on the scope of the remedy which [ss. 994-996 CA 2006] provides for a member of a company, typically holding a minority of the shares, who considers that the company's affairs are being conducted in a manner unfairly prejudicial to his interests . . .

5. 'Unfairly prejudicial'

In [what is now s. 994] Parliament has chosen fairness as the criterion by which the court must decide whether it has jurisdiction to grant relief. It is clear from the legislative history . . . that it chose this concept to free the court from technical considerations of legal right and to confer a wide power to do what appeared just and equitable. But this does not mean that the court can do whatever the individual judge happens to think fair. The concept of fairness must be applied judicially and the content which it is given by the courts must be based upon rational principles. As Warner J. said in *In re J.E. Cade & Son Ltd* [1992] B.C.L.C. 213, 227: 'The court . . . has a very wide discretion, but it does not sit under a palm tree' . . .

In the case of section [994], the background has the following two features. First, a company is an association of persons for an economic purpose, usually entered into with legal advice and some degree of formality. The terms of the association are contained in the articles of association and sometimes in collateral agreements between the shareholders. Thus the manner in which the affairs of the company may be conducted is closely regulated by rules to which the shareholders have agreed. Secondly, company law has developed seamlessly from the law of partnership, which was treated by equity, like the Roman societas, as a contract of good faith. One of the traditional roles of equity, as a separate jurisdiction, was to restrain the exercise of strict legal rights in certain relationships in which it considered that this would be contrary to good faith. These principles have, with appropriate modification, been carried over into company law.

The first of these two features leads to the conclusion that a member of a company will not ordinarily be entitled to complain of unfairness unless there has been some breach of the terms on which he agreed that the affairs of the company should be conducted. But the second leads to the conclusion that there will be cases in which equitable considerations make it unfair for those conducting the affairs of the company to rely upon their strict legal powers. Thus unfairness may consist in a breach of the rules or in using the rules in a manner which equity would regard as contrary to good faith . . .

6. Legitimate expectations

In *In re Saul D. Harrison & Sons Plc.* [1995] 1 B.C.L.C. 14, 19, I used the term 'legitimate expectation', borrowed from public law, as a label for the 'correlative right' to which a relationship between company members may give rise in a case when, on equitable principles, it would be regarded as unfair for a majority to exercise a power conferred upon them by the articles to the prejudice of another member. I gave as an example the standard case in which shareholders have entered into association upon the understanding that each of them who has ventured his capital will also participate in the management of the company. In such a case it will usually be considered unjust, inequitable or unfair for a majority to use their voting power to exclude a member from participation in the management without giving him the opportunity to remove his capital upon reasonable terms. The aggrieved member could be said to have had a 'legitimate expectation' that he would be able to participate in the management or withdraw from the company.

It was probably a mistake to use this term, as it usually is when one introduces a new label to describe a concept which is already sufficiently defined in other terms. In saying that it was 'correlative' to the equitable restraint, I meant that it could exist only when equitable principles of the kind I have been describing would make it unfair for a party to exercise rights under the articles. It is a consequence, not a cause, of the equitable restraint. The concept of a legitimate expectation should not be allowed to lead a life of its own, capable of giving rise to equitable restraints in circumstances to which the traditional equitable principles have no application. That is what seems to have happened in this case.

7. Was Mr. Phillips unfair?

The Court of Appeal found that by 1991 the company had the characteristics identified by Lord Wilberforce in *In re Westbourne Galleries Ltd* [1973] A.C. 360 as commonly giving rise to equitable restraints upon the exercise of powers under the articles. They were (1) an association formed or continued on the basis of a personal relationship involving mutual confidence; (2) an understanding that all, or some, of the shareholders shall participate in the conduct of the business; and (3) restrictions on the transfer of shares, so that a member cannot take out his stake and go elsewhere. I agree. It follows that it would have been unfair of Mr. Phillips to use his voting powers under the articles to remove Mr. O'Neill from participation in the conduct of the business without giving him the opportunity to sell his interest in the company at a fair price. Although it does not matter, I should say that I do not think that this was the position when Mr. O'Neill first acquired his shares in 1985. He received them as a gift and an incentive and I do not think that in making that gift Mr. Phillips could be taken to have surrendered his right to dismiss Mr. O'Neill from the management without making him an offer for the shares. Mr. O'Neill was simply an employee who happened to have been given some shares. But over the following years the relationship changed. Mr. O'Neill invested his own profits in the company by leaving some on loan account and agreeing to part being capitalised as shares. He worked to build up the company's business. He guaranteed its bank account and mortgaged his house in support. *In re H. R. Harmer Ltd* [1959] 1 W.L.R. 62 shows that shareholders who receive their shares as a gift but afterwards work in the business may become entitled to enforce equitable restraints upon the conduct of the majority shareholder.

The difficulty for Mr. O'Neill is that Mr. Phillips did not remove him from participation in the management of the business. After the meeting on 4 November 1991 [at which Mr. Phillips informed Mr. O'Neill that he would no longer receive 50% of the profits] he remained a director and continued to earn his salary as manager of the business in Germany. The Court of Appeal held that he had been constructively removed by the behaviour of Mr. Phillips in the matter of equality of profits and shareholdings. So the question then becomes whether Mr. Phillips acted unfairly in respect of these matters.

To take the shareholdings first, the Court of Appeal said that Mr. O'Neill had a legitimate expectation of being allotted more shares when the targets were met. No doubt he did have such an expectation before 4 November and no doubt it was legitimate, or reasonable, in the sense that it reasonably appeared likely to happen. Mr. Phillips had agreed in principle, subject to the execution of a suitable document. But this is where I think that the Court of Appeal may have been misled by the expression 'legitimate expectation'. The real question is whether in fairness or equity Mr. O'Neill had a right to the shares. On this point, one runs up against what seems to me the insuperable obstacle of the judge's finding that Mr. Phillips never agreed to give them. He made no promise on the point. From which it seems to me to follow that there is no basis, consistent with established principles of equity, for a court to hold that Mr. Phillips was behaving unfairly in withdrawing from the negotiation. This would not be restraining the exercise of legal rights. It would be imposing upon Mr. Phillips an obligation to which he never agreed. Where, as here, parties enter into negotiations with a view to a transfer of shares on professional advice and subject to a condition that they are not to be bound until a formal document has been executed, I do not think it is possible to say that an obligation has arisen in fairness or equity at an earlier stage.

The same reasoning applies to the sharing of profits. The judge found as a fact that Mr. Phillips made no unconditional promise about the sharing of profits. He had said informally that he would share the profits equally while Mr. O'Neill managed the company and he himself did not have to be involved in day-to-day business. He deliberately retained control of the company and with it, as the judge said, the right to redraw Mr. O'Neill's responsibilities. This he did without objection in August 1991. The consequence was that he came back to running the business and Mr. O'Neill was no longer managing director. He had made no promise to share the profits equally in such circumstances and it was therefore not inequitable or unfair for him to refuse to carry on doing so. The Court of Appeal seems to have contemplated that Mr. Phillips might have been entitled to do what he did if he had given Mr. O'Neill notice of his intentions and treated him more politely at the meeting on 4 November 1991. But these matters cannot affect the question of whether a change in the profit-sharing arrangements was a breach of faith.

It follows in my opinion that there was no basis for the Court of Appeal's finding that Mr. O'Neill had been driven out of the company . . .

8. No-fault divorce?

Mr. Hollington, who appeared for Mr. O'Neill, said that it did not matter whether Mr. Phillips had done anything unfair. The fact was that trust and confidence between the parties had broken down. In those circumstances it was obvious that there ought to be a parting of the ways and the unfairness lay in Mr. Phillips, who accepted this to be the case, not being willing to allow Mr. O'Neill to recover his stake in the company. Even if Mr. Phillips was not at fault in causing the breakdown, it would be unfair to leave Mr. O'Neill locked into the company as a minority shareholder.

Mr. Hollington's submission comes to saying that, in a 'quasi-partnership' company, one partner ought to be entitled at will to require the other partner or partners to buy his shares at a fair value. All he need do is to declare that trust and confidence has broken down. In the present case, trust and confidence broke down, first, because Mr. Phillips failed to do certain things which, on the judge's findings, he had never promised to do; secondly, because Mr. O'Neill wrongly thought that Mr. Phillips had committed various improprieties; and finally because, as the judge said . . . he was 'inclined to see base motives in everything that Mr. Phillips did'. Nevertheless it is submitted that fairness requires that Mr. [Phillips] or the company ought to raise the necessary liquid capital to pay Mr. O'Neill a fair price for his shares.

I do not think that there is any support in the authorities for such a stark right of unilateral withdrawal. There are cases, such as *In re A Company (No. 006834 of 1988), Ex parte Kremer* [1989] B.C.L.C. 365, in which it has been said that if a breakdown in relations has caused the majority to remove a shareholder from participation in the management, it is usually a waste of time to try to investigate who caused the breakdown. Such breakdowns often occur (as in this case) without either side having done anything seriously wrong or unfair. It is not fair to the excluded member, who will usually have lost his employment, to keep his assets locked in the company. But that does not mean that a member who has not been dismissed or excluded can demand that his shares be purchased simply because he feels that he has lost trust and confidence in the others. I rather doubt whether even in partnership law a liquidation would be granted on this ground in a case in which it was still possible under the articles for the business of the partnership to be continued. And as Lord Wilberforce observed in *In re Westbourne Galleries Ltd* [1973] A.C. 360, 380, one should not press the quasi-partnership analogy too far: 'A company, however small, however domestic, is a company not a partnership or even a quasi-partnership . . .' . . .

10. The offer to buy

Mr. Ralls, who appeared for Mr. Phillips, submitted that even if his conduct had been unfairly prejudicial, the petition should have been dismissed because he had made an offer to buy the shares at a fair price, which was the whole of the relief to which Mr. O'Neill would have been entitled. In view of the conclusion I have reached about the absence of unfair prejudice, with which I understand your Lordships to agree, this point does not need to be decided. Nevertheless, the effect of an offer to buy the shares as an answer to a petition under section [994] is a matter of such great practical importance that I would invite your Lordships to consider it.

The petition was presented on 22 January 1992 and points of defence were delivered on 16 March 1992. The points of defence contained no offer to buy but asked that Mr. Phillips or the company should be 'at liberty' to buy the shares 'at a fair value to be fixed by the court upon such basis as to the court shall seem just and equitable and depending upon its finding in respect of the various issues between the parties disclosed on the pleadings herein'.

This plainly contemplated that the petition would go to full hearing and be decided on the merits. There was then considerable delay and a number of interlocutory hearings. On 28 November 1994, pursuant to an undertaking given to the court, Mr. Phillips made an offer in terms scheduled to a consent order of that date. The offer was to purchase at a price to be agreed or in default fixed by a chartered accountant as valuer on the basis that the value was one-quarter of the fair value of the entire issued share capital. The offer was rejected on various grounds, one being that it made no provision for Mr. O'Neill's costs. The result was that the petition went to a full hearing.

The judge, who dismissed the petition, did not find it necessary to deal with the offer. The Court of Appeal accepted the argument that Mr. O'Neill was justified in rejecting it because it did not provide for his costs.

In my opinion the Court of Appeal was right. The offer is only material to the outcome at the trial if the court considers that the petitioner is otherwise entitled to succeed. So the fact that he was made an earlier offer of the relief to which the court has now held him entitled after trial can logically go only to the question of costs. If the petitioner was offered everything to which he has been held entitled, the respondent may . . . be entitled to say that the costs after the date of that offer should be borne by the successful petitioner, who ought to have accepted the offer and brought the litigation to an end. On the other hand, it seems to me that in the case of a petition which has been on foot for nearly three years, a petitioner who, we are assuming, has a well founded case will not obtain everything to which he is entitled unless there is an offer of costs . . .

In the present case, Mr. Phillips fought the petition to the end and your Lordships have decided that he was justified in doing so. But I think that parties ought to be encouraged, where at all possible, to avoid the expense of money and spirit inevitably involved in such litigation by making an offer to purchase at an early stage. This was a somewhat unusual case in that Mr. Phillips, despite his revised views about Mr. O'Neill's competence, was willing to go on working with him. This is a position which the majority shareholder is entitled to take, even if only because he may consider it less unattractive than having to raise the capital to buy out the minority. Usually, however, the majority shareholder will want to put an end to the association. In such a case, it will almost always be unfair for the minority shareholder to be excluded without an offer to buy his shares or make some other fair arrangement. The Law Commission Report on Shareholder Remedies . . . has recommended that in a private company limited by shares in which substantially all the members are directors, there should be a statutory presumption that the removal of a shareholder as a director, or from substantially all his functions as a director, is unfairly prejudicial conduct. This does not seem to me very different in practice from the present law. But the unfairness does not lie in the exclusion alone but in exclusion without a reasonable offer. If the respondent to a petition has plainly made a reasonable offer, then the exclusion as such will not be unfairly prejudicial and he will be entitled to have the petition struck out. It is therefore very important that participants in such companies should be able to know what counts as a reasonable offer.

In the first place, the offer must be to purchase the shares at a fair value. This will ordinarily be a value representing an equivalent proportion of the total issued share capital, that is, without a discount for its being a minority holding . . .

Secondly, the value, if not agreed, should be determined by a competent expert. The offer in this case to appoint an accountant agreed by the parties or in default nominated by the President of the Institute of Chartered Accountants satisfied this requirement. One would ordinarily expect the costs of the expert to be shared but he should have the power to decide that they should be borne in some different way.

Thirdly, the offer should be to have the value determined by the expert as an expert. I do not think that the offer should provide for the full machinery of arbitration or the half-way house of an expert who gives reasons. The objective should be economy and expedition, even if this carries the possibility of a rough edge for one side or the other (and both parties in this respect take the same risk) compared with a more elaborate procedure . . .

Fourthly, the offer should, as in this case, provide for equality of arms between the parties. Both should have the same right of access to information about the company which bears upon the value of the shares and both should have the right to make submissions to the expert, though the form (written or oral) which these submissions may take should be left to the discretion of the expert himself.

Fifthly, there is the question of costs. In the present case, when the offer was made after nearly three years of litigation, it could not serve as an independent ground for dismissing the petition, on the assumption that it was otherwise well founded, without an offer of costs. But this does not mean that payment of costs need always be offered. If there is a breakdown in relations between the parties, the majority shareholder should be given a reasonable opportunity to make an offer (which may include time to explore the question of how to raise finance) before he becomes obliged to pay costs. As I have said, the unfairness does not usually consist merely in the fact of the breakdown but in failure to make a suitable offer. And the majority shareholder should have a reasonable time to make the offer before his conduct is treated as unfair. The mere fact that the petitioner has presented his petition before the offer does not mean that the respondent must offer to pay the costs if he was not given a reasonable time.

11. Conclusion

I would allow the appeal and dismiss the petition …

Questions and comments:

1. In interpreting the meaning of 'unfair prejudice', Lord Hoffmann relied on the earlier House of Lords decision *Ebrahimi v Westbourne Galleries Ltd*.[43] This case concerned a closely related procedure to protect minority shareholders, the just and equitable winding up of a company.[44] Adopted with the aim of enabling shareholders to resolve deadlocks in corporate decision-making, 'just and equitable winding up' was held to allow the courts more generally to take account of considerations of 'a personal character between one individual [member of a company] and another, which may make it unjust, or inequitable, to insist on legal rights, or to exercise them in a particular way'.[45] This rationale implies that just and equitable winding up is only possible in small companies characterized, similar to partnerships, by a personal relationship between the members involving mutual confidence, an understanding that all, or some, of the shareholders shall participate in the conduct of the business, and restrictions on the transfer of shares, so that a shareholder cannot simply sell out if there is a breakdown in the relationship of mutual confidence.[46] The scope of section 994 of the Companies Act 2006 is not limited in the same manner, but Lord Hoffmann makes it clear that if a petition is based on equitable considerations, an informal arrangement between the parties is required, which can typically only be shown in small, partnership-like companies. Thus, the scope of application of section 994 is largely restricted to such 'quasi-partnerships'.
2. The key to understanding the House of Lord's judgment in *O'Neill v Phillips* is the suggested change in terminology from 'legitimate expectations' to 'equitable considerations'. Lord Hoffmann was concerned that the term 'legitimate expectations', borrowed from public law and used by himself in *Re Saul D. Harrison & Sons Plc*[47] and other cases, did not accurately capture the equitable nature of the constraints that the law imposes in section 994 cases on shareholders. Sketching the origin of these constraints in partnership law and equity, Lord Hoffmann explained that it was traditionally the role of equity 'to restrain the exercise of strict legal rights in certain relationships in which it considered that this would be contrary to good faith'.[48] Applied to the present context, this meant that it must be unfair 'for those conducting the affairs of the company to rely upon their strict legal powers' and exercise rights under company law or the articles.[49] A petitioner may have a legitimate expectation that a majority shareholder will refrain from exercising a right, but the concept of 'legitimate expectations' is

[43] [1973] AC 360. [44] Insolvency Act 1986, s 122(1)(g).
[45] *Ebrahimi v Westbourne Galleries Ltd* [1973] AC 360, 379. [46] ibid.
[47] [1994] BCC 475, 490.
[48] *O'Neill v Phillips* [1999] 1 WLR 1092, 1098. [49] ibid 1099.

clearly wider and also covers situations where the petitioner seeks to compel the respondent to grant an advantage that the petitioner expected to receive without being legally entitled to it. In the interest of legal certainty, Lord Hoffmann decided to restrict section 994 to the former type of situation, if a petition was based on equitable considerations and not the illegality of the challenged conduct. The petition can be used to restrain the exercise of a legal right, but it cannot be used to claim, for example, an allotment of additional shares or a greater share in the company's profits. In this, *O'Neill v Phillips* was different from the standard case of legitimate expectations, the removal of the founders of a company from the board of directors and their exclusion from the management of the company. If those who contribute capital do so based on the assumption that they will participate in the management of the company, and this assumption is shared by the other shareholders, they can use a section 994 petition to constrain the majority's right under section 168 Companies Act 2006 to remove directors by simple majority.[50] It can be argued that the removal affects them not only in their capacity as a director or manager, but, as required by section 994, also in their capacity as a member.[51] This is particularly clear if the shareholders receive a return on their investment in the form of salary rather than dividend payments. More generally, it has been held that a board position enables shareholders to monitor and protect their investment, and dismissal therefore affects their interests qua member.[52]

3. Apart from the dismissal of one of the members as director in a company that returns value to the shareholders in the form of salary rather than dividends, the unfair prejudice remedy has also been used by shareholders who were never involved in the management of the company to challenge a policy of non-payment of dividends or paying excessively high executive remuneration. In general, shareholders do not have any entitlement to dividend payments, unless the articles provide that such rights shall be attached to shares generally or to specific classes of shares (typically preference shares). Therefore, in the absence of an understanding to the contrary between the members, it cannot be assumed that shareholders have a legitimate expectation that dividends will be paid.[53] However, it has also been held that the decision to pay no dividends, or to pay dividends that are inadequate considering the profits of the company and the amount of cash in hand, is capable of amounting to unfair prejudice if the company's dividend policy is used to deny some members who do not receive directors' fees any income from the company.[54] Similarly, how much a company pays its directors and managers is a matter that falls within the discretion of the board or the competent organ designated by the articles or the board of directors.[55] Remuneration decisions are of course subject to the general fiduciary duties of directors, but these give directors considerable latitude in determining executive pay. Courts will generally not assess whether the amount of remuneration is reasonable or commercially justified. The amount, it has been said, 'whether it be mean or generous, must be a matter of management for the company to determine in accordance with its [constitution]'.[56] However, if the board does not follow the applicable procedures in determining executive remuneration, the courts will exercise greater scrutiny. In a section 994 petition, it falls on the respondents 'to justify by objective commercial criteria that [a company's] dividend policy was a reasonable one and that the remuneration the ... directors were paid by the [company] was within the bracket that executives carrying the sort of responsibility and discharging the sort of duties that they were carrying and discharging would expect to receive'.[57] Thus,

[50] *Re Saul D. Harrison & Sons Plc* [1994] BCC 475, 490.

[51] Companies Act 2006, s 994(1)(a).

[52] See Davies and Worthington (n 6) para 20–4, with references.

[53] *Irvine v Irvine* [2006] EWHC 406, paras 272–3.

[54] *In Re Sam Weller & Sons Ltd* [1990] Ch 682, 693; *Re McCarthy Surfacing Ltd* [2009] BCC 464, 491–2.

[55] Model Articles for Private Companies Limited by Shares, Art 19; Model Articles for Public Companies, Art 23.

[56] *Re Halt Garage* (1964) Ltd [1982] 3 All ER 1016, 1030. This case is discussed in more detail in Chapter 9C.I.3.

[57] *Re A Company (No 004415 of 1996)* [1997] 1 BCLC 479, 492, quoted approvingly by *Irvine v Irvine* [2006] EWHC 406, para 267. See also *Re McCarthy Surfacing Ltd* [2009] BCC 464 (award of a large proportion of the profits to the shareholder-directors without disclosure to the board or board approval and with the intention to ensure that no part of the profits of a major contract became available for distribution to the shareholders was held to amount to unfair prejudice); *Sikorski v Sikorski* [2012] EWHC 1613 (a majority shareholder's causing a company to charge its subsidiary less than the agreed rent so that no profits would be available for distribution was held to be unfairly prejudicial to the interests of the minority shareholder).

a shareholder may succeed in establishing unfair prejudice if a company has a policy of returning all or most of the divisible profits in one form or another to the shareholders and the director(s) draw inadequately high remuneration. In this case, the sums in excess of such adequate remuneration would have been available for distribution among the shareholders, and not distributing them is prejudicial to the interests of the non-director shareholders.[58]

4. As indicated by Lord Hoffmann in *O'Neill v Phillips*, the unfair prejudice remedy has resulted in a number of lengthy and expensive litigations where the costs by far exceeded the value of the assets fought over. It seems that the procedure is often used in retribution rather than to recover a financial loss. The costs of an unfair prejudice petition may even result in the procedure being employed as a means of oppression itself.[59] Lord Hoffmann was concerned about these potential inefficiencies, which he sought to address by suggesting, *in obiter*, a procedure encouraging the parties to resolve the dispute out of court. If a petitioner pursues the unfair prejudice remedy in order to be bought out at a fair price, as is often the case, and the respondent has made a 'reasonable offer' to purchase the petitioner's shares, the respondent is entitled to have the section 994 petition struck out as an abuse of process.[60] An offer is 'reasonable' if it is at fair value, as determined by an independent expert, both parties have the same right of access to relevant information about the company and the right to make submissions to the expert, and, where necessary, the respondent must offer to pay the petitioner's costs.[61] The offer must include an offer to pay the costs of the section 994 petition if the majority shareholder did not make a buy-out offer within a reasonable time after the breakdown in relations, but instead waited until the proceedings were well advanced, as, for example, in *O'Neill v Phillips*. This approach has been followed in later section 994 cases and is now widely accepted.[62]

5. Unfairly prejudicial conduct typically involves a breakdown in the relationship between the shareholders. In order to be protected against future prejudicial actions by the majority, it is therefore in the interest of minority shareholders to exit the company and receive a fair price for their shares, rather than compensation for the harm suffered. However, in the type of company where an unfair prejudice petition is most likely to succeed, small companies with the characteristics of a partnership, minority shareholders will commonly have difficulties to sell their shares at fair value, if at all, since a liquid market in the shares of such companies rarely exists. The unfair prejudice remedy provides an exit right at fair value, which is otherwise only available in UK law if an offeror has acquired 90 per cent of the total number of shares after a tender offer and the shareholder in question has not accepted the offer.[63] While the court enjoys wide discretion in an unfair prejudice petition to make such order as it thinks fit for giving relief,[64] courts most commonly use their power to order the majority shareholder to buy the petitioner's shares.[65] Exceptionally, the majority shareholder may be ordered to sell its shares to the petitioner.[66] When a buy-out order is made, the question inevitably arises how fair value is to be determined. The courts have established a presumption that shares should be valued on a pro-rata basis if the company is a 'quasi-partnership' and otherwise discounted to reflect the fact that the petitioner's shareholding is a minority holding.[67] Usually the going-concern

[58] *Irvine v Irvine* [2006] EWHC 406, paras 275, 322.

[59] Law Commission, Report on Shareholder Remedies, 24 October 1997, paras 1.5–1.7.

[60] *O'Neill v Phillips* [1999] 1 WLR 1092, 1107. [61] ibid 1107–8.

[62] See, for example, *Harborne Road Nominees Ltd v Karvaski* [2011] EWHC 2214; *North Holdings Ltd v Southern Tropics Ltd* [1999] 2 BCLC 625.

[63] Companies Act 2006, s 983. [64] ibid s 996(1). [65] ibid s 996(2)(e).

[66] *Re Brenfield Squash Racquets Club Ltd* [1996] 2 BCLC 184.

[67] *In Re Bird Precision Bellows Ltd* [1984] Ch 419, 430–1; *CVC/Opportunity Equity Partners Ltd v Demarco Almeida* [2002] BCC 684, 692–3. Since the seller (typically the minority shareholder) is an unwilling vendor in the sense that it is no longer tolerable for him to retain his interest in the company because of the unfair prejudice and a sale of the shares will usually be the only remedy short of a winding up, the court argued that 'it would not merely not be fair, but most unfair, that he should be bought out on the fictional basis applicable to a free election to sell his shares in accordance with the company's articles of association, or indeed on any other basis which involved a discounted price' (*In Re Bird Precision Bellows Ltd*, ibid 430). If the company is not a quasi-partnership, these arguments do not hold. In particular, if a minority shareholder had acquired the shares as an investment and paid a price lower than the pro rata value of the shares, courts will generally discount the shares accordingly; see *Re Elgindata Ltd* (1991) BCLC 959, 1007.

value of the company at the time of the court order[68] is used as a basis of the valuation, provided the purchaser intends to continue to carry on the business of the company as a going concern.[69]

II. US

In contrast to the UK, US courts recognized early on that there was no fundamental difference between the duties of a director and those of shareholders who were in a position to affect the rights of the minority. The US Supreme Court in *Southern Pacific Co. v. Bogert*[70] expressed this approach very clearly as early as 1919: 'The majority has the right to control; but when it does so, it occupies a fiduciary relation toward the minority, as much so as the corporation itself or its officers and directors.'[71] Interestingly, in establishing this rule, the Supreme Court relied on an old English case from 1874, *Menier v. Hooper's Telegraph Works*.[72] Thus, in spite of the fact that the UK courts do not qualify the position of a majority shareholder as that of a fiduciary, the constraints on majority shareholders in US and UK law share a common origin.

Fiduciary duties of the majority shareholder are most developed in closely held companies. As we will see in the context of share repurchases,[73] a shareholder who has the power to control the corporation may owe fiduciary duties to the minority. The leading case is *Donahue v Rodd Electrotype Co.*,[74] dealing with the repurchase of the shares of the controlling shareholder at a favourable price without offering the same opportunity to the minority shareholders. The Supreme Judicial Court of Massachusetts, in no uncertain terms, held that the shareholders of a close corporation, similar to partners in a partnership, owe stringent fiduciary duties to one another, which include the right to equal opportunity in share repurchases:

> When the corporation reacquiring its own stock is a close corporation, the purchase is subject to the additional requirement … that the stockholders, who, as directors or controlling stockholders, caused the corporation to enter into the stock purchase agreement, must have acted with the utmost good faith and loyalty to the other stockholders. To meet this test, if the stockholder whose shares were purchased was a member of the controlling group, the controlling stockholders must cause the corporation to offer each stockholder an equal opportunity to sell a ratable number of his shares to the corporation at an identical price … The controlling group may not, consistent with its strict duty to the minority, utilize its control of the corporation to obtain special advantages and disproportionate benefit from its share ownership.[75]

Subsequent case law introduced certain qualifications of the uncompromising *Donahue* principle, acknowledging that shareholders, in principle, have the right to exercise voting rights in their own interest. This right to 'selfish ownership' had to be balanced against the majority's fiduciary obligation to deal with the minority with the utmost good faith and loyalty.[76] The Supreme Judicial Court of Massachusetts suggested the following two-step

[68] *Re London School of Electronics Ltd* [1986] Ch 211, 224; *Re Elgindata Ltd* (1991) BCLC 959, 1006–7; *Re KR Hardy Estates Ltd* [2014] EWHC 4001, para 93. Alternatively, the courts may order the shares to be purchased at the value which they would have had at the date of the petition if there had been no oppression, *Scottish Co-operative Wholesale Society Ltd v Meyer* [1958] 3 All ER 66, or at another date that the court considers to be fair, for example when a company was reconstructed or its business changed significantly, so that it acquired a new economic identity, *Profinance Trust SA v Gladstone* [2002] 1 WLR 1024, para 61, *Re OC (Transport) Services Ltd* [1984] BCLC 251, 258.

[69] *CVC/Opportunity Equity Partners Ltd v Demarco Almeida* [2002] BCC 684, 692.

[70] 250 U.S. 483 (1919).

[71] ibid 487–8. The Delaware courts embrace a similar approach. In *Harris v Carter*, 582 A.2d 222, 234–5 (Del. Ch. 1990), the Court of Chancery emphasized: 'It is established American legal doctrine that, unless privileged, each person owes a duty to those who may foreseeably be harmed by her action to take such steps as a reasonably prudent person would take in similar circumstances to avoid such harm to others.'

[72] (1874) 9 Ch App 350. [73] Chapter 9C.I.4, II.4. [74] 367 Mass. 578 (Mass. 1975).

[75] ibid 598.

[76] *Wilkes v Springside Nursing Home, Inc.*, 353 N.E.2d 657, 663 (Mass. 1976). In this case, three of four shareholders 'froze out' the minority shareholder by not re-electing him as a director and officer and discontinuing his salary.

test in order to reconcile the principle of majority rule with the majority's fiduciary duties. The majority is accorded broad discretion in establishing the business policy of the corporation and deciding, for example, to withhold dividends, merge or consolidate the company, determine the salaries of corporate officers, dismiss directors, and hire and fire corporate employees. In taking these actions, the majority is required to set out a legitimate business purpose. It is then 'open to minority stockholders to demonstrate that the same legitimate objective could have been achieved through an alternative course of action less harmful to the minority's interest'.[77]

Many states of the United States have embraced the *Donahue* principle and the duty of utmost good faith and loyalty.[78] Delaware law, however, is more hesitant to accept a broad principle of equal treatment of all shareholders. The Delaware courts acknowledge that majority stockholders owe fiduciary duties to minority stockholders.[79] However, these duties, or indeed the duties of directors and officers, do not include the requirement to treat stockholders equally for all purposes. For example, in *Nixon v. Blackwell*,[80] the Supreme Court of Delaware held that providing shareholders of one class of shares with liquidity that shareholders of another class did not enjoy was permissible if it was the result of the operation of an employee stock ownership plan.[81]

Whether a majority shareholder (or indeed any shareholder) is subject to fiduciary duties in publicly held companies is more controversial. In circumstances where a holding company uses its control over the subsidiary to cause the subsidiary 'to act in such a way that the parent receives something from the subsidiary to the exclusion of, and detriment to, the minority stockholders of the subsidiary', courts will impose a fiduciary obligation on the parent to show the intrinsic fairness of the parent-subsidiary dealings.[82] A more ambitious formulation of the duties of majority stockholders is presented by the following case from California. While the company in this case, a chartered savings and loan association incorporated with stock, was closely held, the Supreme Court of California formulated the duties of stockholders broadly and ostensibly without differentiating between public and private companies.

***Jones v H.F. Ahmanson & Co.*, 1 Cal. 3d 93 (Supreme Court of California, 1969)**

Traynor, CJ:

June K. Jones, the owner of 25 shares of the capital stock of United Savings and Loan Association of California brings this action on behalf of herself individually and of all similarly situated minority stockholders of the Association. The defendants are United Financial Corporation of California, fifteen individuals, and four corporations, all of whom are present or former stockholders or officers of the Association. Plaintiff seek damages and other relief for losses allegedly suffered by the minority stockholders of the Association because of claimed breaches of fiduciary responsibility by defendants in the creation and operation of United Financial, a Delaware holding company that owns 87 percent of the outstanding Association stock ...

In 1958 investor interest in shares of savings and loan associations and holding companies increased. Savings and loan stocks that were publicly marketed enjoyed a steady increase in market price thereafter until June 1962, but the stock of United Savings and Loan Association was not among them. Defendants determined to create a mechanism by which they could participate in the profit taking by attracting investor interest in the Association. They did not, however, undertake to render the Association shares more readily marketable. Instead, the United Financial Corporation of California was incorporated in Delaware by ... the ... defendants ... On May 14, 1959, pursuant to a prior agreement, certain Association stockholders who among them

[77] ibid.

[78] For references, see AR Pinto and DM Branson, *Corporate Law* (5th edn, Carolina Academic Press 2018) §11.07[C].

[79] *Riblet Products Corp. v Nagy*, 683 A.2d 37 (Del. 1996).

[80] 626 A.2d 1366 (Del. 1993).

[81] ibid 1376–7.

[82] *Sinclair Oil Corp. v Levien*, 280 A.2d 717, 720 (Del. 1971).

owned a majority of the Association stock exchanged their shares for those of United Financial, receiving a 'derived block' of 250 United Financial shares for each Association share.

After the exchange, United Financial held 85 percent of the outstanding Association stock. More than 85 percent of United Financial's consolidated earnings and book value of its shares reflected its ownership of this Association stock. The former majority stockholders of the Association had become the majority shareholders of United Financial and continued to control the Association through the holding company. They did not offer the minority stockholders of the Association an opportunity to exchange their shares.

The first public offering of United Financial stock was made in June 1960. To attract investor interest, 60,000 units were offered, each of which comprised two shares of United Financial stock and one $100, 5 percent interest-bearing, subordinated, convertible debenture bond. The offering provided that of the $7,200,000 return from the sale of these units, $6,200,000 would be distributed immediately as a return of capital to the original shareholders of United Financial, i.e., the former majority stockholders of the Association …

A public offering of 50,000 additional shares by United Financial with a secondary offering of 600,000 shares of the derived stock by the original investors was made in February 1961 for a total price of $15,275,000. The defendants sold 568,190 shares of derived stock in this secondary offering. An underwriting syndicate of 70 brokerage firms participated. The resulting nationwide publicity stimulated trading in the stock until, in mid-1961, an average of 708.5 derived blocks were traded each month. Sales of Association shares decreased during this period from a rate of 170 shares per year before the formation of United Financial to half that number. United Financial acquired 90 percent of the Association shares that were sold …

Defendants then proposed an exchange of United Financial shares for Association stock. Under this proposal each minority stockholder would have received approximately 51 United Financial shares of a total value of $2,400 for each Association share. When the application for a permit was filed with the California Corporations Commissioner on August 28, 1961, the value of the derived blocks of United Financial shares received by defendants in the initial exchange had risen to approximately $8,800.[9] The book value of the Association stock was in excess of $1,700 per share, and the shares were earning at an annual rate of $615 per share. Each block of 51 United Financial shares had a book value of only $210 and earnings of $134 per year, 85 percent of which reflected Association earnings. At the hearings held on the application by the Commissioner, representatives of United Financial justified the higher valuation of United Financial shares on the ground that they were highly marketable, whereas Association stock was unmarketable and poor collateral for loans. Plaintiff and other minority stockholders objected to the proposed exchange, contending that the plan was not fair, just, and equitable. Defendants then asked the Commissioner to abandon the application without ruling on it.

Plaintiff contends that in following this course of conduct defendants breached the fiduciary duty owed by majority or controlling shareholders to minority shareholders. She alleges that they used their control of the Association for their own advantage to the detriment of the minority when they created United Financial, made a public market for its shares that rendered Association stock unmarketable except to United Financial, and then refused either to purchase plaintiff's Association stock at a fair price or exchange the stock on the same basis afforded to the majority. She further alleges that they also created a conflict of interest that might have been avoided had they offered all Association stockholders the opportunity to participate in the initial exchange of shares …

I

Plaintiff's Capacity to Sue

We are faced at the outset with defendants' contention that if a cause of action is stated, it is derivative in nature since any injury suffered is common to all minority stockholders of the Association. Therefore, defendants urge, plaintiff may not sue in an individual capacity or on behalf of a class made up of stockholders excluded from the United Financial exchange, and in any case may not maintain a derivative action without complying with Financial Code section 7616. Defendants invoke *Shaw v. Empire Sav. & Loan Assn.*, 186 Cal.App.2d 401 [9 Cal.Rptr. 204]. There the defendant majority stockholder, who controlled the board of directors, had the bylaws amended to delete a provision granting preemptive rights and thereafter caused the Association to issue shares to himself at less than market or book value, thus diluting plaintiff minority stockholder's interest. Plaintiff sought a declaration that he was entitled to maintain his proportionate interest in the Association either through purchase of a proportionate number of shares from the buyer or issuance of a proportionate number of additional shares to him by the Association on the same terms. The Court of Appeal concluded that inasmuch as the injury to the plaintiff was no different from that caused other minority stockholders, relief was available only in a derivative action.

Analysis of the nature and purpose of a shareholder's derivative suit will demonstrate that the test, adopted in the *Shaw* case does not properly distinguish the cases in which an individual cause of action lies. A shareholder's derivative suit seeks to recover for the benefit of the corporation and its whole body of shareholders when injury is caused to the corporation that may not otherwise be redressed because of failure of the corporation to act. Thus, 'the action is derivative, i.e., in the corporate right, if the gravamen of the complaint is injury to the corporation, or to the whole body of its stock and property without any severance or distribution among individual holders, or it seeks to recover assets for the corporation or to prevent the dissipation of its assets'.... 'A stockholder's derivative suit is brought to enforce a cause of action which the corporation itself possesses against some third party, a suit to recompense the corporation for injuries which it has suffered as a result of the acts of third parties. The management owes to the stockholders a duty to take proper steps to enforce all claims which the corporation may have. When it fails to perform this duty, the stockholders have a right to do so. Thus, although the corporation is made a defendant in a derivative suit, the corporation nevertheless is the real plaintiff and it alone benefits from the decree; the stockholders derive no benefit therefrom except the indirect benefit resulting from a realization upon the corporation's assets. The stockholder's individual suit, on the other hand, is a suit to enforce a right against the corporation which the stockholder possesses as an individual'....

It is clear from the stipulated facts and plaintiff's allegations that she does not seek to recover on behalf of the corporation for injury done to the corporation by defendants. Although she does allege that the value of her stock has been diminished by defendants' actions, she does not contend that the diminished value reflects an injury to the corporation and resultant depreciation in the value of the stock. Thus the gravamen of her cause of action is injury to herself and the other minority stockholders ...

II

Majority Shareholders' Fiduciary Responsibility

Defendants take the position that as shareholders they owe no fiduciary obligation to other shareholders, absent reliance on inside information, use of corporate assets, or fraud. This view has long been repudiated in California. The Courts of Appeal have often recognized that majority shareholders, either singly or acting in concert to accomplish a joint purpose, have a fiduciary responsibility to the minority and to the corporation to use their ability to control the corporation in a fair, just, and equitable manner. Majority shareholders may not use their power to control corporate activities to benefit themselves alone or in a manner detrimental to the minority. Any use to which they put the corporation or their power to control the corporation must benefit all shareholders proportionately and must not conflict with the proper conduct of the corporation's business ...

The extensive reach of the duty of controlling shareholders and directors to the corporation and its other shareholders was described by the Court of Appeal in *Remillard Brick Co. v. Remillard-Dandini Co., supra.*, 109 Cal.App.2d 405, where, quoting from the opinion of the United States Supreme Court in *Pepper v. Litton*, 308 U.S. 295 [84 L.Ed. 281, 60 S.Ct. 238], the court held: 'A director is a fiduciary ... So is a dominant or controlling stockholder or group of stockholders ... Their powers are powers of trust ... Their dealings with the corporation are subjected to rigorous scrutiny and where any of their contracts or engagements with the corporation is challenged the burden is on the director or stockholder not only to prove the good faith of the transaction but also to show its inherent fairness from the viewpoint of the corporation and those interested therein ... The essence of the test is whether or not under all the circumstances the transaction carries the earmarks of an arm's length bargain. If it does not, equity will set it aside' ...

Defendants assert, however, that in the use of their own shares they owed no fiduciary duty to the minority stockholders of the Association. They maintain that they made full disclosure of the circumstances surrounding the formation of United Financial, that the creation of United Financial and its share offers in no way affected the control of the Association, that plaintiff's proportionate interest in the Association was not affected, that the Association was not harmed, and that the market for Association stock was not affected. Therefore, they conclude, they have breached no fiduciary duty to plaintiff and the other minority stockholders.

Defendants would have us retreat from a position demanding equitable treatment of all shareholders by those exercising control over a corporation to a philosophy much criticized by commentators and modified by courts in other jurisdictions as well as our own. In essence defendants suggest that we reaffirm the so-called 'majority' rule reflected in our early decisions. This rule, exemplified by the decision in *Ryder v. Bamberger*, 172 Cal. 791 [158 P. 753], but since severely limited, recognized the 'perfect right [of majority shareholders] to dispose of their stock … without the slightest regard to the wishes and desires or knowledge of the minority stockholders; …' (p. 806) and held that such fiduciary duty as did exist in officers and directors was to the corporation only. The duty of shareholders as such was not recognized unless they, like officers and directors, by virtue of their position were possessed of information relative to the value of the corporation's shares that was not available to outside shareholders. In such case the existence of special facts permitted a finding that a fiduciary relationship to the corporation and other shareholders existed …

We had occasion to review these theories as well as the 'minority rule' that directors and officers have an obligation to shareholders individually not to profit from their official position at the shareholders' expense in *American Trust Co. v. California etc. Ins. Co.*, 15 Cal.2d 42 [98 P.2d 497] … The rule that has developed in California is a comprehensive rule of 'inherent fairness from the viewpoint of the corporation and those interested therein'. … The rule applies alike to officers, directors, and controlling shareholders in the exercise of powers that are theirs by virtue of their position and to transactions wherein controlling shareholders seek to gain an advantage in the sale or transfer or use of their controlling block of shares. Thus we held … that majority shareholders do not have an absolute right to dissolve a corporation, although ostensibly permitted to do so by Corporations Code section 4600, because their statutory power is subject to equitable limitations in favor of the minority. We recognized that the majority had the right to dissolve the corporation to protect their investment if no alternative means were available and no advantage was secured over other shareholders, and noted that '[t]here is nothing sacred in the life of a corporation that transcends the interests of its shareholders, but because dissolution falls with such finality on those interests, above all corporate powers it is subject to equitable limitations'. …

The increasingly complex transactions of the business and financial communities demonstrate the inadequacy of the traditional theories of fiduciary obligation as tests of majority shareholder responsibility to the minority. These theories have failed to afford adequate protection to minority shareholders and particularly to those in closely held corporations whose disadvantageous and often precarious position renders them particularly vulnerable to the vagaries of the majority. Although courts have recognized the potential for abuse or unfair advantage when a controlling shareholder sells his shares at a premium over investment value (*Perlman v. Feldmann*, 219 F.2d 173 [50 A.L.R.2d 1134] [premium paid for control over allocation of production in time of shortage]; *Gerdes v. Reynolds*, 28 N.Y.S.2d 622 [sale of control to looters or incompetents]; *Porter v. Healy*, 244 Pa. 427 [91 A. 428]; *Brown v. Halbert*, *supra.*, 271 Cal.App.2d 252 [sale of only controlling shareholder's shares to purchaser offering to buy assets of corporation or all shares]) or in a controlling shareholder's use of control to avoid equitable distribution of corporate assets (*Zahn v. Transamerica Corp.* (3rd Cir. 1946) 162 F.2d 36 [172 A.L.R. 495] [use of control to cause subsidiary to redeem stock prior to liquidation and distribution of assets]), no comprehensive rule has emerged in other jurisdictions …

The case before us, in which no sale or transfer of actual control is directly involved, demonstrates that … injury … can be inflicted with impunity under the traditional rules and supports our conclusion that the comprehensive rule of good faith and inherent fairness to the minority in any transaction where control of the corporation is material properly governs controlling shareholders in this state.

[The court held that the defendants were in breach of the majority's fiduciary obligation to the minority.]

Questions and comments:

1. The reach of the 'comprehensive rule of good faith and inherent fairness'[83] that the California Supreme Court established in *Jones v. H.F. Ahmanson* is seemingly broad. Using sweeping language, the court held that the duty applied to controlling stockholders 'in the exercise of powers that are theirs by virtue of their position and to transactions wherein [they] seek to gain an advantage in the sale or transfer or use of their controlling block of shares'.[84] However, the case could also be interpreted more narrowly as an instance of the usurpation of a corporate opportunity, namely the ability to benefit from a public market in the corporation's shares. This would explain the strict duty imposed on the controlling shareholders. On the other hand, the court's insistence that the case does not deal with an injury done to the corporation, but an injury to the minority shareholders in their personal capacity,[85] weighs against framing the issue as one of corporate opportunities. If the complaint was about misappropriation of a corporate opportunity, shareholders should be able to claim recovery only derivatively, whereas they were allowed to maintain an individual action in *Ahmanson*. In addition, it is difficult to see why the existence of a public market in shares is a *corporate* opportunity. It makes an investment in the company of course more attractive, but does not alter the *company's* portfolio of investment opportunities. Alternatively, it has been suggested that the case is an example of oppressive behaviour towards the minority.[86] The facts of *Ahmanson* fit the typical pattern of oppression of the minority in closely held corporations where the minority does not have an effective exit right. The actions of the controlling shareholders depressed the value of Association shares, and the defendants sought to take advantage of this by offering to buy out the minority at a low price. However, at least some subsequent decisions have understood the ruling more broadly and applied *Ahmanson*'s duty of good faith and inherent fairness to publicly traded companies, where the oppression rationale is less forceful because minority shareholders can exit the company easily.[87] Yet other commentators have argued that the *Ahmanson* court failed to understand the economic significance of the majority's transaction.[88] The majority shareholders wished to consolidate several businesses in one holding company. In doing so, they incurred costs and risks in the expectation that the consolidation would produce efficiency gains. The court's sharing requirement allowed the minority shareholders to freeride on these benefits, thus reducing the incentives of controlling shareholders to carry out value-enhancing consolidations.[89]
2. Not only controlling shareholders are subject to fiduciary duties. In certain circumstances, minority shareholders of closely held corporations may be liable for a breach of fiduciary obligations owed to the majority. This was held to be the case, for example, in *Smith v. Atlantic Properties, Inc.*,[90] where a company had to pay penalty taxes because one of four equal shareholders exercised his power pursuant to the articles of incorporation to veto a declaration of dividends. The Appeals Court of Massachusetts held that a minority shareholder in a close corporation who has a veto right over corporate actions and, accordingly, has an 'ad hoc controlling interest' with regard to these actions owes a duty of 'utmost good faith and loyalty' to the other shareholders.[91] In the case at hand, the objecting shareholder was found to have breached this duty by blocking dividend payments for personal tax reasons and was liable for the damage caused to the company.
3. In addition to the general imposition of fiduciary duties on shareholders under the laws of many US states, as formulated in *Donahue*, *Ahmanson* and *Smith v. Atlantic Properties*, US

[83] *Jones v H.F. Ahmanson & Co.*, 1 Cal. 3d at 112. [84] ibid 110. [85] ibid 107.
[86] Pinto and Branson (n 78) §10.04[C].
[87] For example, *Klaus v Hi-Shear Corp.*, 528 F.2d 225 (9th Cir. 1975).
[88] FH Easterbrook and DR Fischel, 'Corporate Control Transactions' (1981) 91 Yale Law Journal 698, 720–1.
[89] ibid 721. [90] 422 N.E.2d 798 (Mass. 1981).
[91] ibid 802. The formulation 'utmost good faith and loyalty' was used by the Massachusetts Supreme Judicial Court in *Donahue v Rodd Electrotype Co.*, 328 N.E.2d 505 (Mass. 1975) (see also text to nn 74–75 above). As mentioned, the Supreme Judicial Court postulated a general duty of shareholders that was 'substantially the same fiduciary duty . . . that partners [in a partnership] owe to one another', ibid 593. The Appeals Court in *Smith v Atlantic Properties* was doubtful whether this 'sweeping language' of *Donahue* could be taken literally, but it acknowledged that a duty of 'utmost good faith and loyalty' arose in appropriate circumstances, 422 N.E.2d at 801.

courts have developed an oppression remedy operating, at least at first sight, similarly to the unfair prejudice remedy under English law. The remedy is available to shareholders of closely held corporations and can be based on the ground that their 'reasonable expectations' were frustrated. For example, New York courts have held that '[a] shareholder who reasonably expected that ownership in the corporation would entitle him or her to a job, a share of corporate earnings, a place in corporate management, or some other form of security, would be oppressed in a very real sense when others in the corporation seek to defeat those expectations'.[92] If the expectations, 'objectively viewed, were both reasonable under the circumstances and were central to the petitioner's decision to join the venture' and the majority shareholders were aware, or should have been aware, of the minority's expectations, the court may order involuntary dissolution of the company or grant another form of relief, such as an injunction against a specific act of oppression or a buy-out of one party by the other.[93] Thus, the concept of 'reasonable expectations' is seemingly more elastic than that of 'legitimate expectations' as defined in the English case *O'Neill v Phillips*.[94] As we have seen, in that case, Lord Hoffmann regarded the term 'legitimate expectations' as a misnomer, since the expectations of a minority shareholder, even though legitimate or reasonable, for example the expectation to share in the company's profits, without more, did not give rise to rights enforceable through the unfair prejudice remedy. Therefore, conduct by the majority was not unfairly prejudicial or oppressive if such expectations were disappointed. UK courts instead investigate whether an informal understanding existed between the members of the company that was contravened by the exercise of the majority's legal rights arising under the Companies Act or the articles of association.[95] US law on oppression does not draw this distinction. However, it is unlikely that the outcome of litigation will differ much in the two countries. US decisions, such as the judgment of the New York Court of Appeals referred to above, generally find that the majority behaves oppressively when the minority is 'frozen out' of the company, for example by excluding minority shareholders from the management of the company, receiving a salary, or other benefits that come with holding a corporate office, the minority shareholders had committed their capital based on the understanding that they would be involved in the governance of the company, and they had indeed been so involved for some time.[96]

III. Germany

In contrast to both UK and US corporate law, German law provides for a statutory mechanism allowing any shareholder to apply to the court to declare resolutions of the general meeting null and void because they suffer from certain particularly serious defects enumerated in the Stock Corporation Act (*Nichtigkeitsklage*)[97] or challenge resolutions with an action for annulment (*Anfechtungsklage*) if they were otherwise adopted in violation of the

[92] *In Re Kemp & Beatley, Inc.*, 473 N.E.2d 1173, 1179 (N.Y. 1984) (concerning a company that awarded de facto dividends in the form of 'extra compensation bonuses' to all shareholders except two minority shareholders whose employment had been terminated).

[93] ibid 1179–80. For an overview of the remedies available in different states of the United States, see Pinto and Branson (n 78) §11.07[H].

[94] Section B.I.2 above.

[95] See, in particular, the passage of Lord Hoffmann's opinion at [1999] 1 WLR 1092, 1103.

[96] See, e.g., *Meiselman v Meiselman*, 307 S.E.2d 551 (N.C. 1983), where a minority shareholder was fired from his position, his participation in a profit-sharing trust was terminated, and his car insurance, health and life insurance policies were cancelled. But see also *Bonavita v Corbo*, 692 A.2d 119 (N.J. 1996). In this case, a company did not pay dividends, but the two shareholders drew a substantial salary. When one of the shareholders died, his salary ceased to be paid. His widow complained that the refusal of the company to pay dividends rendered her stake in the company effectively worthless, since her investment was illiquid. Even though the surviving shareholder had not taken any action to freeze out the deceased or his widow, the court argued that the widow's reasonable expectations demanded the provision of 'some alternative benefit to the holder of the [deceased's] stock … [which may] include a buy-out, a distribution of dividends, some form of salary continuation, or some other form of benefit/compensation': ibid 128.

[97] AktG, §§241–242, 249.

law or the articles.[98] We have discussed both types of lawsuit in detail in Chapter 5.[99] There, we said that nullity may be a result of, among other grounds, the violation of provisions 'adopted in the public interest',[100] which includes not only the legal framework for the protection of creditors, in particular the capital maintenance regime, but also core elements of the governance architecture of companies, such as the statutory allocation of competences between the general meeting, management board, and supervisory board or essential features of the shareholders' membership rights.[101] More generally, a resolution can be challenged if it violates the law or the articles of association or is intended and suitable to confer a special advantage on a shareholder or another person to the detriment of the company and the remaining shareholders.[102] Legal provisions relevant in the present context that render a resolution voidable in case of noncompliance include the requirement to treat the shareholders equally[103] or provide a substantive justification for certain resolutions, for example by showing that the exclusion of pre-emption rights is in the interest of the company.[104] In addition, the question has arisen whether shareholders, in exercising their voting rights, owe a fiduciary duty to each other. If so, a resolution that did not respect minority shareholder interests would be in violation of the law and, accordingly, would be open to a legal challenge by the minority.[105] Alternatively, the minority may claim that a resolution conferred a special advantage on the majority (or an affiliated person) to the detriment of the other shareholders.[106] This latter route is usually more difficult for an objecting shareholder to pursue, since it requires a showing of intent to obtain an advantage to the exclusion of the other shareholders.[107] However, overall the grounds to challenge resolutions of the general meeting are broadly formulated and capture a variety of structural changes that may affect the position of the minority. As a result, the action for annulment has become one of the most important minority shareholder protection mechanisms available under German law.

The courts have only recently recognized the existence of fiduciary duties among the shareholders. Traditionally, the only duty-type constraints imposed on shareholders in the exercise of their voting rights were the requirements under general civil law to act in good faith and without intentionally inflicting damage on another person in a manner that was contrary to public policy.[108] The following decision, *Linotype*, is the first case where the

[98] ibid §§243–246. Pursuant to general civil law (§§134, 138 BGB), legal transactions incompatible with the law or the good morals are void. Shareholder resolutions are 'legal transactions' in this sense. As a consequence, the invalidity of a resolution sanctioning, for example, a merger or an increase of capital could be challenged by anyone even after years. In order to avoid legal uncertainty, §§241–249 AktG replace the general law and limit the grounds for nullity of a resolution.

[99] Chapter 5C.III.1.

[100] AktG, §241 no 3.

[101] See, e.g., OLG München, AG 2007, 173, holding that the squeeze-out of a minority shareholder in violation of the statutory requirements (see section C.II below) amounted to 'a most fundamental interference with membership rights' and thus infringed public interests.

[102] AktG, §243(1), (2).

[103] ibid §53a. As discussed in Chapter 5C.III.1, an example of a transaction that violates the equal treatment provision is a share issue at par value to some shareholders under exclusion of the other shareholders' pre-emption rights in a situation where the shares could have been sold at a much higher price; see BGHZ 21, 354.

[104] See Chapter 9D.I.2.

[105] Such a challenge would be based on AktG, §243(1).

[106] ibid, §243(2). It is commonly acknowledged that neither subsection bars the other. A shareholder can accordingly choose whether to challenge a resolution under subsection 1 or 2, provided the requirements of both provisions are satisfied, U Hüffer and C Schäfer in W Goette and M Habersack (eds), *Münchener Kommentar zum Aktiengesetz, vol 4* (4th edn, CH Beck 2016) §243 para 73. It can be argued that this will generally be the case if §243(2) applies, because a shareholder who obtains a special advantage to the detriment of the other shareholders or the company will usually either violate a fiduciary duty owed to the company or the other shareholders or act in contravention of the general principle of equal treatment of all shareholders; see Hüffer and Schäfer, ibid.

[107] It is not necessary that the majority shareholder intended to damage the company or the other shareholders, although this will usually be the case if the majority seeks to obtain a special advantage. For a discussion of this point, see Hüffer and Schäfer (n 106) §243, paras 85–6.

[108] BGB, §§226, 242, 826. This interpretation was espoused by the Imperial Court in the nineteenth and early twentieth centuries, e.g., RGZ 107, 72; 112, 14; 119, 248. The Federal Court of Justice initially followed a similar approach, holding that shareholders owed a duty to the company, but not the other shareholders, to refrain from exercising their voting rights in order to gain private benefits not related to the corporate purpose and in a manner detrimental to the company, see BGHZ 14, 25; BGH JZ 1976, 561.

courts acknowledged that majority shareholders may in appropriate circumstances owe a duty to non-controlling shareholders to have due regard to their interests.

BGH Judgment of 1 February 1988, BGHZ 103, 184 (*Linotype*)

[The plaintiff was a minority shareholder with four votes. The majority shareholder was L-GmbH. In order to take over the company's most profitable branch of business, L-GmbH initiated a resolution to liquidate the company. This resolution was passed in the general meeting with the support of the majority shareholder's votes but against the votes of the plaintiff, who duly objected to the resolution. The plaintiff challenged the resolution, among other reasons, on the ground that the majority shareholder had abused its voting rights. The plaintiff alleged that the acquisition of the most profitable branch of the business had been systematically prepared by negotiations between L-GmbH and the company's management long before the resolution in question was passed and the parties had not agreed on a price reflecting fair market value.]

The Court of Appeal's rejection of the challenge to the resolution of the general meeting of 24 April 1985 is unfounded ...

3. The Appeal Court rightly held that the fact that the majority shareholder of the defendant company initiated the resolution with the declared and later realized aim to acquire substantial parts of the undertaking of the company is not a sufficient reason to challenge the resolution of 24 April 1985 pursuant to §243(1) and (2) AktG.

a) The resolution to dissolve the defendant company cannot be reviewed in order to assess whether it is objectively justified. In a line of cases, the Court has addressed the question whether resolutions of the general meeting of a stock corporation adopted by a majority vote and interfering with shareholders' rights may be reviewed in respect of their content. The Court has confirmed in a number of cases that it may be necessary to undertake such a review ... It appears that this case law has been largely welcomed.

However, the Court has declined to apply such a review to a resolution to liquidate a company. It has held that such a resolution required only the majority prescribed by law, provided the articles of association did not impose further requirements. No further requirements had to be satisfied for the resolution to be valid. In particular, it was not necessary to justify the resolution in the interest of the company, since it carried its justification in itself ... This approach has been criticised on the ground that the authority of the requisite majority to decide on the dissolution of the company and hence the withdrawal of the invested capital, which is enshrined in law, did not change the fact that the fiduciary duty existing among the shareholders required that the power to dissolve the company was to be exercised with due regard for the interests of the minority ... Furthermore, in order to avoid undue pressure, it has been argued that a resolution affecting the very foundations of the company should be subject to a substantive review in line with the principles of necessity and proportionality ... The Court feels unable to follow these suggestions. They would result in a heightened commitment of the invested capital going beyond the limits prescribed by law and lacking any legal foundation. Rather, the shareholders of a company are permitted to bring the corporate purpose to an end, acting with the requisite majority as laid down in the law and the articles, and thereby terminate the rights of the minority that were created as part of the agreement on the corporate purpose. Whether and under what conditions the exercise of this right may be abusive requires a case-by-case assessment, but the consequence is not that resolutions to liquidate a company are subject to a general substantive review.

b) The resolution to liquidate the company with the – stated and later realized – aim to acquire substantial parts of the undertaking that was adopted with the votes of the majority shareholder and against the votes of the minority shareholder did not amount to an abusive exercise of the right to vote and hence did not render the resolution voidable. Parts of the literature argue that the conduct of the majority was abusive in such cases, because it was the goal of the provisions on liquidation to allow the majority shareholder to liquidate and free up the invested capital, so that it could be used for other purposes (so-called divestment). A majority shareholder who did not act with this aim in mind, but instead liquidated the company in order to take over the corporate assets and remove the minority shareholder from the company circumvented the provisions on the squeeze-out of minority shareholders in an abusive manner, if an exclusion of the minority shareholder was not possible pursuant to the law or the articles ... The Court cannot accept this view either ... It is generally possible to liquidate a company at any time and without additional requirements by adopting a resolution with the requisite majority prescribed by law or the articles. Provided the minority shareholder has, in law, the same opportunity as the majority shareholder to acquire all or part of the company's assets with a view to continuing the undertaking, the situation is not comparable to the exclusion of a minority shareholder. In practice, the minority shareholder will often not be able to acquire the company's assets and continue its business due to a lack of funds and the failure to find a third party investor able to acquire the undertaking and operate the business with the minority shareholder in the form of a partnership. However, exclusion from a company pursuant to §737 BGB [Civil Code] and §140 HGB [Commercial Code][109] has the consequence that the shareholder is legally prevented from continuing the operation of the business. Furthermore, the argument that the majority shareholder uses the resolution to liquidate the company not for the purpose of divestment, but to pursue self-serving interests which are alien to the purposes envisaged by the legislator … is unpersuasive. Given that the company may be liquidated at any time by the majority shareholder, thus interfering with the rights of the minority grounded in the corporate purpose, and all shareholders are affected by the legal consequences of the liquidation in proportion to their holdings in the same manner (§§264 et seq. AktG), it cannot be argued that the majority exercised their powers abusively. The liquidation results in the invested capital being freed from any commitment to the corporate purpose. The law does not contain anything that would prevent the majority shareholder from investing the freed-up capital by acquiring all or substantial parts of the corporate assets in the course of the liquidation.

4. However, in analogy to §243(2) AktG,[110] it is possible to challenge the resolution of the general meeting if L-GmbH as majority shareholder had entered into negotiations and agreements with the defendant's management regarding the acquisition of substantial parts of the defendant's undertaking and assets in advance of the resolution of 24 April 1984. Under these circumstances, the majority shareholder would have exercised its voting rights in order to gain a special advantage to the detriment of the minority shareholders in breach of its fiduciary duty owed to the plaintiff as minority shareholder. The resolution would have also been suitable to attain the aim of gaining a special advantage.

a) According to the Court of Appeal, in order to determine whether rights of the plaintiff had been violated, it was crucial whether more than negotiations had taken place between L-GmbH and the defendant's management prior to the resolution, for example, whether the parties had already agreed on a price or entered into a binding sales contract. In this case, the majority shareholder would have had prevented the minority shareholder legally from acquiring the undertaking and continuing operations alone or together with other investors.

This starting point of the Court of Appeal can be affirmed. Had such an agreement existed between the defendant and its majority shareholder before the resolution liquidating the company was adopted on 24 April 1984, L-GmbH would indeed have prevented the plaintiff and the other minority shareholders from attempting to acquire the business and continue operations in some form. This would also be the case if no contractual and legally enforceable commitment existed, as long as other circumstances guaranteed in the same way as a contractual commitment that only L-GmbH would be able to acquire the undertaking and other shareholders would be excluded from the transaction. Such a behaviour would constitute a breach of the fiduciary duties that the majority shareholder owed to the minority shareholders, enabling the majority, as intended from the outset, to acquire substantial assets of the defendant and take on the employees necessary for their operation after the adoption of the resolution dissolving the defendant.

A fiduciary duty under company law exists also between shareholders. As far as the private limited liability company [GmbH] is concerned, the Court has recognised that not only the legal relationship between the company and the shareholders, but also the relationship among the shareholders may be defined by a fiduciary duty. The reason for this assumption was not

[109] [Footnote by authors.] §737 BGB and §140 HGB deal with the exclusion of a partner of a civil law partnership and a commercial partnership, respectively. At the time of the decision, a squeeze-out right did not exist in stock corporations (now §327a AktG, see our discussion in section C.II below).

[110] [Footnote by authors.] See text to n 106 above and Chapter 5C.III.1.

just that the organisation and economic activities of a private limited liability company are often largely subject to the direct control of the shareholders and its structure is therefore similar to that of a partnership, but also the fact that the majority shareholders have the power to interfere with the interests of the other shareholders by influencing the management of the company, which must be counterbalanced by a corporate law duty of the majority to have due regard for the minority's interests . . . In respect of public companies, the Court has recognised the existence of fiduciary duties between the company and the shareholders . . . However, for the relationship between the shareholders, it has held that fiduciary duties going beyond the general legal principles laid down in §§226, 242 and 826 BGB did not exist[111] . . . This approach overemphasized the corporate structure of public companies, which gave rise to the view that legal relations existed only between the company and the shareholders . . . In contrast, in line with the recent legal literature. . . it is to be recognised that the relationship among the members of a corporation may also be characterised as a fiduciary relationship. As in other business associations, the majority shareholder of a stock corporation has the power to interfere with the interests of the minority in the corporation by influencing the management. Therefore, it is necessary to impose a duty under stock corporation law to have due regard for the minority's interests as a counterbalance to the power of the majority. Furthermore, it should be borne in mind that a public company may have an organisational structure similar to that of a private limited liability company and hence resemble a partnership. The fact that the legal form of a company may be changed without any alteration of its internal organisation and structure shows that the recognition of fiduciary duties among shareholders cannot depend on the legal form of a business association, but generally only on its organisational structure. Indeed, it seems incomprehensible that the law would reject the existence of a fiduciary duty among the shareholders of a stock corporation, but accept that such a duty arises when the stock corporation is transformed into a partnership, even though the internal structure and organisation of the company might not change . . . It should be noted, however, that the corporate law duties of a small shareholder will usually not be determined by fiduciary principles . . .

b) [The Court went on to hold that the Court of Appeal had not sufficiently considered the factual basis for the plaintiff's claim that there had been an agreement in advance between L-GmbH and the defendant company's management. Hence, the further appeal was successful.]

Questions and comments:

1. Although the Bundesgerichtshof refuses to accept a general right to have a resolution to liquidate a company reviewed on objective grounds, the recognition that the majority's powers need to be counterbalanced by a duty to have due regard for the minority's interests opens the door for just such a general right of review. Indeed, some commentators have argued that the requirement to provide for a substantive justification of certain resolutions of the general meeting, which can be reviewed in court, is simply a special case of the general fiduciary duties that exist among shareholders and constrain any exercise of majority power.[112] Given that the attainment of a special advantage within the meaning of §243(2) AktG generally also implicates the shareholders' fiduciary duties, as *Linotype* shows, this view implies that fiduciary principles more generally guide the assessment of resolutions adopted pursuant to the express provisions of the Stock Corporation Act. Relatedly, note that the court in *Linotype* held that a resolution liquidating a company was only invalid if the majority shareholder obtained a special advantage *in breach of its fiduciary duty* owed to the minority. Without such a breach, consisting in the present case in the understanding between the majority shareholder and the company's management that the company's assets would only be sold to the majority shareholder, the resolution could not have been challenged under either §243(1) or (2). On the other hand, acting in contravention of the shareholders' fiduciary duties constitutes a violation of the law within the meaning of §243(1). The challenge in *Linotype* could therefore also have

[111] [Footnote by authors.] See n 108 above and accompanying text.
[112] J Koch in U Hüffer and J Koch, *Aktiengesetz* (13th edn, CH Beck 2018) §243, paras 24 and 27.

been brought under that provision. Thus, on this interpretation, the second subsection of §243 becomes largely redundant.[113]

2. The court in *Linotype* argued that shareholder duties have their origin in the organizational structure of public companies, which may be similar to small, closely held companies and partnerships. The actual internal structure of the business, not its legal form, was relevant in determining whether fiduciary duties existed. Commentators qualified this statement by pointing out that fiduciary duties arose in *any* association of two or more persons to pursue a common goal. The question was not whether or not they existed in a stock corporation, but how and to what extent they constrained shareholder decision-making.[114] This depended on a variety of factors: the size and type of company, the number of shareholders, the position of the defendant shareholder within the governance structure of the company, and the type of resolution at issue. For example, on this view, the intensity of shareholder duties is higher in a family-owned company with few shareholders than in a large, listed corporation.[115] Conversely, shareholders enjoy greater latitude when the resolution concerns primarily their cash flow rights, in particular when they decide on dividend payments, than when interests of the company itself are at stake, such as in a winding up or a resolution changing the capital structure.[116]

Linotype only dealt with the duties of a majority shareholder, which are a function of the majority's ability to affect, and change the constitutional parameters of, the position of non-controlling shareholders. Indeed, the court in *Linotype* intimated in the last sentence of the excerpt reproduced above that the fiduciary constraints imposed on the conduct of the majority did not extend to small minority shareholders. However, minority shareholders may also have the power to obstruct or block corporate resolutions through the exercise of minority rights, especially if a resolution requires a supermajority, and thus prevent important transactions from being implemented. In doing so, their actions may be prejudicial to the interests of the company and the other shareholders. The following case, *Girmes*, addresses the question whether, in such a situation, minority shareholders are subject to fiduciary duties similar to those of the majority established in *Linotype*. In this case, the management of a stock corporation, the Girmes-Werke AG, proposed a reorganization plan that involved a capital reduction with a 5:2 ratio in response to financial difficulties that had reduced the net assets of the company to less than half of the legal capital. The reorganization plan had already been approved by the creditors, who had promised to waive part of their claims. However, the capital reduction failed to garner the necessary supermajority of votes of the shareholders, because the defendant, himself not a shareholder, had convinced a blocking minority of shareholders to appoint him as proxy to vote against the capital reduction. He argued that the reorganization plan would disadvantage the outside shareholders and requested a more favourable reduction ratio, which, however, was rejected by the creditors. As a consequence of the failed reorganization, the company went into insolvent liquidation. The plaintiff, who held 350 shares in the company, sued the defendant for damages.

BGH Judgment of 20 March 1995, BGHZ 129, 136 (*Girmes*)

The Court of Appeal has correctly held that the defendant is not liable for breach of a fiduciary duty under corporate law [since he is not a shareholder]. However, the Court has failed to recognise that, based on the submissions of the plaintiff, the defendant may be liable in analogy to §179(1) BGB.[117] …

[113] See Hüffer and Schäfer (n 106) §243, para 73, and our discussion in Chapter 5C.III.1.
[114] K Schmidt, *Gesellschaftsrecht* (4th edn, Carl Heymanns 2002) §20 IV. [115] ibid IV.2.d).
[116] T Raiser and R Veil, *Recht der Kapitalgesellschaften* (6th edn, Vahlen 2015) §11/51.
[117] [Footnote by authors.] §179(1) BGB deals with the liability of an unauthorized agent and provides: 'A person who has entered into a contract as an agent is, if he does not furnish proof of his power of agency, obliged to the other party at the other party's choice either to perform the contract or to pay damages to him, if the principal refuses to ratify the contract'.

1. In a public stock corporation, fiduciary duties are not only owed by the majority shareholder to the minority or outside shareholder, but also by the minority or outside shareholder to the majority shareholder or other minority shareholders ...

[In *Linotype*], the question was left open whether fiduciary duties impose constraints only on the exercise of majority power or more generally on the exercise of shareholder rights, in particular a shareholder's right to influence and control managerial decision-making. In line with the nearly universal view in the literature, this question should be answered in the affirmative ...

2. The idea that a shareholder's responsibilities, including the duty to have regard for the interests of the company and the other shareholders, are proportionate to the extent of the shareholder's power is central to the notion of fiduciary duties as a general principle of corporate law ... In other words, as the courts have put it, the power to interfere with the interests of the shareholders in a corporation by influencing business operations must be counterbalanced by a duty to have regard for these interests ... This notion applies not only to the conduct of the majority shareholder, but equally to the minority shareholders. Accountability and the duty to have regard for the interests of the other shareholders in a stock corporation is typically only relevant in relation to the majority shareholder or a majority of shareholders ... especially in a stock corporation with widely dispersed ownership, because influence is usually exerted through control of the company, which requires a corresponding majority. In contrast, the minority shareholder's power to exert influence is limited. However, minority shareholders also have rights at their disposal that can be exercised in a manner detrimental to the interests of the other shareholders and that are, consequently, subject to the duty to take these interests into account. For example, the right to attend the general meeting may be abused by disrupting the meeting or the right to speak by filibustering ... In these cases, fiduciary constraints become relevant ...

These fiduciary duties apply also to the right of the shareholders to information (§131 AktG) and the right to challenge resolutions of the general meeting (§243 AktG). However, in practice, it will generally not be necessary to impose fiduciary limits on the exercise of these rights because of their content (right to challenge resolutions) or legal structure (right to information) ... By exercising his right to vote, the minority shareholder will usually not be able to exert influence, and his duty to take the interests of the other shareholders into account will therefore be irrelevant. This changes, however, if the minority shareholder's voting power reaches a threshold that allows the shareholder to pursue certain rights (see, inter alia, §122(1) and (3),[118] §142(2),[119] §147(1) AktG[120]) or block otherwise valid resolutions (see, inter alia, §179(2), §182(1), §186(3), §222(1) AktG[121] ...). If a shareholder is in a position where he can exert influence through the exercise of such minority rights, which, accordingly, requires some form of control to protect the interests of the other shareholders, the minority right can only be exercised within the limits set by the shareholder's fiduciary duties ...

3. It is questionable whether the exercise of voting rights by minority shareholders is subject to fiduciary duties if they do not reach the necessary threshold to pursue a minority right or block a resolution as individuals, but only by acting together. The literature answers this question in the affirmative if the votes are bundled in order to achieve a common goal (so-called effects-based fiduciary duty). According to the literature, this is the case, on the one hand, if the minority shareholders agree on how to vote (acting in concert), and on the other hand, if minority shareholders appoint a third party (external to the company) as proxy to exercise their voting rights, who develops an independent voting strategy or recommends to vote in a particular way and solicits proxies in order to implement the strategy or recommendation. In contrast, where voting rights are bundled in the sense that a proxy requests voting instructions from the shareholders, which results coincidentally in a minority large enough to pursue the above rights or block resolutions, fiduciary constraints do not apply ...

[118] [Footnote by authors.] Right to call a general meeting.

[119] [Footnote by authors.] Right to request a special audit.

[120] [Footnote by authors.] Right to bring a derivative action.

[121] [Footnote by authors.] These provisions require a supermajority of not less than three fourths of the share capital for amendments of the articles, capital increases, an exclusion of pre-emption rights, and capital reductions, respectively.

Whether a shareholder is bound by fiduciary duties owed to the other shareholders in the exercise of voting rights has to be determined in light of the content of the relevant duty arising in the specific situation and not the general scope of the shareholders' duties. Therefore, fiduciary constraints may exist in any of the three scenarios mentioned above, irrespective of the question whether the relevant voting threshold was exceeded by coincidence or in pursuit of a common goal. It is only relevant that the exercise of the individual shareholder's voting rights constitutes a breach of duty and all votes that were cast in breach of duty together form a blocking minority.

In the present case, the behaviour of the minority shareholders who appointed the defendant as a proxy to exercise their voting rights goes beyond the coincidental formation of a blocking minority and amounts to vote bundling in pursuit of a common goal ...

The rejection of the management proposal to reorganise the company by the defendant constitutes a breach of fiduciary duty owed by the shareholders who had appointed the proxy to the plaintiff. The shareholders are liable for this breach of duty based on the principles expressed in §§166, 278 BGB[122] ...

a) An obligation to vote for a reorganisation does not follow from a fiduciary duty owed to the company. A company is generally not protected against liquidation by its members. Rather, the shareholders have the power to dissolve the company at any time without a business reason ... Similarly, there is no obligation of shareholders to rescue a company when it approaches insolvency or insolvency proceedings have been opened and the company may therefore be wound up pursuant to §262(1), no. 3 AktG ... According to the law, the duty of shareholders to promote the interests of the company is limited to paying the par value or, if higher, the issue price of the shares (§54(1) AktG), provided the articles do not impose any additional obligations (§55 AktG).

b) However, the right to decide on the winding up of a stock corporation requires a resolution adopted by a qualified majority as laid down in the law or the articles (§262(1), no. 2 AktG). As long as no such resolution has been adopted with the requisite majority, the company continues in existence. A minority cannot force the dissolution of the company ... The minority must have due regard for the interests of the majority of shareholders, taking into account the purpose of the company. This duty is subject to the principles of proportionality and necessity ... In the case of a company that needs to be restructured, it prohibits an individual shareholder from voting against a sensible reorganisation plan endorsed by the majority for self-serving motives ...

In order to reach the necessary majority for a capital reduction (§229(3) in conjunction with §222(1) AktG), a vote by the minority in favour of the capital reduction was not required. Since abstentions are not taken into account in the calculation of the relevant percentage, it would have sufficed if the defendant had abstained from voting to ensure a majority of three fourths ...

In light of the requirements emanating from the duty to have due regard for the interests of the other shareholders, it has been pointed out correctly that shareholders are prohibited from frustrating a sensible and widely endorsed reorganisation plan for self-serving motives under the following conditions. Without the reorganisation plan, the failure of the company must be inevitable; if the company does indeed fail, the position of an individual shareholder must be worse than it would have been had the shareholder exited the company while it was a going concern—in the case of a stock corporation by selling the shares; the implementation of the reorganisation plan would have ensured the continued existence of the company in the long run; and a less intrusive reorganisation was not possible ...

[The court discussed the financial position of the company and concluded that the failure of the company had been an inevitable consequence of the rejection of the reorganisation plan. Hence, the defendant was found liable on appeal.]

Questions and comments:

1. Since the defendant was not himself a shareholder in Girmes-Werke AG and, consequently, not subject to fiduciary duties under corporate law, the court had to use a somewhat circuitous legal argument to hold the defendant accountable. It based the defendant's liability on an

[122] [Footnote by authors.] §166 BGB provides that the knowledge of an agent is attributable to the principal, and §278 BGB provides that a debtor is liable for the wrongful acts of his agent.

analogy to §179(1) BGB, which provides that an agent who acts without authority is liable to the person who relies on the validity of a contract entered into by the agent on behalf of the principal. It has been argued that the provision is based on the more general idea that parties who deal with an agent should be able to enforce their claims against the agent if enforcement against the principal fails due to the acts of the agent. This general idea applied in the present context, because the defendant refused to reveal the names of the shareholders who had authorized him to vote on their behalf. The plaintiff, therefore, could not enforce his claim for damages against the minority shareholders who had blocked the capital reduction. Such a claim did however exist. Again relying on general principles of civil law (§§166, 278 BGB[123]), the court explained that the defendant's misconduct was attributable to the minority shareholders, even though they were not present in the general meeting and possibly not fully aware of the discussions about a different reduction ratio and hence the risk that a rejection of the reorganization plan would lead to the winding up of the company.

2. In spite of the aforementioned legal technicalities, the general message of *Girmes* is easy to understand. Minority shareholders are, in principle, subject to the same fiduciary constraints as majority shareholders. These constraints are conditional on the minority being in a position to abuse their rights in a disruptive fashion or in a manner detrimental to the interests of the company and the other shareholders. This does not necessarily require a blocking minority. A shareholder who holds only one or a few shares may also abuse minority rights, for example, by requesting redundant or irrelevant information and thus obstructing the conduct of a general meeting or by bringing an action for annulment solely for its settlement value.[124] While the fiduciary duty is therefore conceptually the same for all shareholders, irrespective of the size of their shareholdings, it will in practice vary in intensity. Commensurate with their greater influence on business operations, the conduct of controlling and other large shareholders will be reviewed more stringently than those of small shareholders, especially in companies with widely dispersed owners.[125]
3. In *Girmes*, the objecting minority shareholders were not required to vote in favour of a resolution they disagreed with, but they were required to abstain from voting against it. Under appropriate circumstances, the fiduciary duty of shareholders may go further and entail the obligation to vote in a particular way. The court in *Girmes* implied as much. If a reorganization plan is indispensable to ensure the continued existence of a company and no alternatives are available that interfere less with the interests of the minority, the shareholders do not enjoy any margin of discretion. They have to vote in favour of the reorganization measure if it would otherwise not be adopted.[126] In spite of its interventionist character, this aspect of the shareholders' fiduciary duty is now widely accepted in the case law, both when a capital reduction is required in order to reorganize a company in financial difficulties and in other contexts, for example when changed conditions make an amendment of the articles necessary.[127]
4. Note that the fiduciary duty of shareholders is owed directly to the other shareholders. A breach of duty, therefore, constitutes an infringement of a shareholder's individual right, similar to the situation in *Holzmüller*,[128] and not (only) a right of the company. Consequently, shareholders have standing to bring an individual lawsuit, which is what the plaintiff did in *Girmes*. This is usually easier than enforcing a claim of the company in a derivative action, since the latter is only open to shareholders holding at least one percent of the share capital and requires that enforcement of the claim is not contrary to overriding interests of the company.[129] Relief can be obtained in the form of an annulment of the challenged resolution (if an

[123] See text to n 122.

[124] BGHZ 107, 296 (*Kochs-Adler*). We discussed this problem in Chapter 5C.III.1.

[125] Raiser and Veil (n 116) §11/51; Schmidt (n 114) §28 I.4.a).

[126] Generally, abstaining from voting will be sufficient to ensure the success of the resolution, because, as mentioned by the court in *Girmes*, abstentions do not count towards the 'share capital represented' at a meeting within the meaning of §179 AktG and other provisions that require a supermajority of three fourths of the share capital, see U Stein in Goette and Habersack (n 106) §179, para 82.

[127] For references, see Raiser and Veil (n 116) §11/54 and §28/42.

[128] See Chapter 5A.III.

[129] AktG, §148. We will discuss the advantages of an action for infringement of an individual right compared with the derivative action in Chapter 8C.II.1.

action for annulment pursuant to §243(1) AktG is brought, as in *Linotype*) or damages (as in *Girmes*). In the latter case, it is important to identify who has suffered a loss. If the challenged action has resulted in damage to the company's assets, and only indirectly in a loss suffered by the shareholder because of a decline in the value of the company, the shareholder has to claim payment to the company.[130]

5. Compare German law with US law. Could it be said that they are closer to each other than either of them is to UK law? What might be the reason?

IV. France

In Chapter 5, we discussed that challenges to a shareholder resolution or a resolution of the board of directors under French law, while possible pursuant to Article L235-1 of the Code de commerce, are restricted to violations of 'mandatory legal provisions', a requirement that has given rise to a considerable degree of legal uncertainty.[131] The statutory regime, therefore, was deemed to be insufficient to protect the minority against an overbearing majority, but also to protect shareholders against abusive minority behaviour. In response, the courts have developed two doctrines, *abus de majorité* and *abus de minorité*, which impose unwritten constraints on the exercise of the voting power of shareholders. The doctrines have been refined and applied by a rich body of case law and have become important elements of the governance architecture of French corporations.

Abus de majorité has its origin in the general doctrine of abuse of rights, which has been recognized by French courts since the early twentieth century.[132] The classic definition of an abuse of majority power is:

> A resolution by a shareholders' meeting which is contrary to the best interests of the company and has the sole purpose of conferring a benefit upon the majority to the detriment of the minority . . .[133]

Consequently, *abus de majorité* consists of two elements: (i) a violation of the company's interests, and (ii) a breach of the principle of equal treatment among the shareholders.[134] These conditions are applied in a strict manner. Without more, the doctrine may not be used to challenge an unsuitable management policy or contentious resolutions rejected by the minority shareholders.[135] Rather, as a typical example of an abuse of majority power, consider the following case, where the exercise by the majority of their constitutional rights (here the right to decide on the apportionment of the balance sheet profit) was held to confer a benefit on the majority to the detriment of the minority and contrary to the interests of the company.

Cour de Cassation, Commercial Chamber, 6 June 1990, appeals no 88-19420 and 88-19783 (*Société Huber*)

Whereas, according to the judgment under appeal . . ., the widow Mrs. Alfred Z . . . , Miss Yvette and Miss Annie Z . . . , Mr. Jean-Pierre Z . . . , Mrs. X . . . , Y . . . , A. . . and Mrs. Hardy (the joint litigants Z . . .), holders of shares in the private limited liability company Huber & Co. (the company Huber), have claimed the nullity of the resolutions of the annual general meetings of the years 1978 to 1984, as well as damages;

According to the sole ground of appeal n° 88-19420, in its two parts:

[130] Raiser and Veil (n 116) §11/50. [131] Chapter 5C.III.2.

[132] PH Conac, 'The Shareholders' Duty Not to Abuse Rights' in HS Birkmose (ed), *Shareholders' Duties* (Wolters Kluwer 2017) 363, 366.

[133] Cass com, 30 November 2004, no 01-16581, *Bull. Joly* 2005, 241, no 42.

[134] M Cozian, A Viandier, and F Deboissy, *Droit des sociétés* 31st edn, LexisNexis 2018) para 576.

[135] P Merle, *Droit commercial: Sociétés commerciales* (22edn edn, Dalloz 2018), para 664, with references.

Whereas the company Huber criticizes the judgment, confirming the first instance judgment in this regard, for having annulled the resolutions of the general meetings of June 1980 and June 1984 on the grounds that the vote of the majority shareholders that transferred the profits of the financial years 1979 and 1983 to reserves, instead of distributing them to the shareholders, constituted an abuse of rights to the detriment of the minority shareholders, while, according to the appeal, on the one hand, it does not appear from the court's reasoning that the challenged resolutions were adopted contrary to the interests of the company and with the sole intention of benefitting the majority shareholders to the detriment of the minority shareholders; in particular, the court of appeal, which has merely made the general observation that the formation of reserves appears to be a prudent policy that 'must not be systematic', has not shown how this policy was, in this case, contrary to the interests of the company, nor established the systematic character of the policy; neither has the court of appeal explained how the challenged resolutions conferred a benefit on the majority shareholders, the finding that they were granted remuneration being on its own insufficient in this regard, since it was neither determined that the amount was excessive, nor shown how remuneration was granted or increased by the challenged resolutions; in the same manner, the court of appeal has not explained how the retention of profits, which increased the value of the shares of all shareholders, harmed the minority shareholders without harming the majority, instead merely asserting the existence of a harm, which it regards as obvious but does not identify; thus, not having identified the abuse of right that it has held had been committed, the court of appeal has not provided a lawful basis for its decision under Article 1382 of the Code civil [now Article 1240 Code civil];[136] furthermore, on the other hand, an abuse of right, being exclusively sanctioned by imposing civil liability on the tortfeasor, can only justify a measure taken against that person and providing for a form of relief appropriate to the harm caused by the abuse; consequently, the court of appeal could not, while deciding on an abuse allegedly committed by certain shareholders, declare, as against the company, the challenged resolutions null and void, since this, not involving the distribution of the profits that were set aside, does not constitute an appropriate form of relief for the harm caused by the failure to distribute profits; in declaring nevertheless that the resolutions were null and void, the court of appeal violated Article 1382 Code civil;

But considering, on the one hand, that the judgment has held, substantiated by both its own reasons and reasons adopted from the first instance judgment, that since the formation of company Huber, all operating profits were transferred to reserves in their entirety, increasing their amount to twenty-two times that of capital, while the transfer to reserves did not have any effect on the investment policy of the enterprise and the two shareholders holding four fifths of the capital received substantial remuneration, whose growth was unusually fast and which, notably, enabled the manager to make personal investments replacing those that would normally have been made by the company Huber with regard to the buildings it occupied and for which it had to pay rent to the manager; that, furthermore, the fact that the reserves that were formed were never transferred to capital and the limitations imposed by the articles of association on the transferability of shares to third parties deprived the minority shareholders of any prospect of recovering the undistributed profits that might have increased the value of the shares; that the court of appeal, which has thus shown that the systematic transfer of profits to reserves was neither in line with the objects nor in the best interest of company Huber and that these decisions benefitted the majority shareholders to the detriment of the minority, has identified an abuse of right by the majority;

Considering, on the other hand, that the abuse itself, committed by exercising the right to vote at a general meeting, affects the legality of the resolutions adopted at that meeting;

It follows that the appeal is unfounded in both parts;

According to the sole ground of appeal n° 88-19783, in its two parts:

Whereas the joint litigants Z ... criticize the judgment, rejecting the first instance judgement in this regard, for having declared their damages claim inadmissible on the ground that it was

[136] [Footnote by authors.] Art 1240 Code civil provides: 'Any act whatever of man, which causes damage to another, obliges the one by whose fault it occurred, to compensate it'.

brought against the company Huber and not the majority shareholders pursuant to Article 41 of the Law of 24 July 1966,[137] while, according to the appeal, on the one hand, Article 41 of the Law of 24 July 1966 provides that an action for damages must be brought against the shareholders and first managers if the damage results from the nullity of the company, whereas this case did not concern a loss stemming from the nullity of the company but a loss resulting from abusive resolutions adopted by the general meeting of shareholders; from which it follows that the court of appeal has incorrectly applied and consequently violated the provisions of Article 41 of the Law of 24 July 1966; on the other hand, a company is liable for the wrongful acts of its organs, and given that the general meeting of shareholders, decision-making organ of the company, abused its powers, the company is liable for the harmful consequences of this abuse, from which it follows that the court of appeal has violated the provisions of Article 1382 Code civil;

But considering that apart from the redundant point just criticized by the first part of the appeal, the court of appeal, having held that the adoption of the challenged resolutions constituted an abuse of right by the majority, has decided correctly that only the majority shareholders that committed the abuse were responsible for it to the claimants and that, consequently, the cause of action brought against the company Huber was inadmissible, the appeal cannot be upheld;

For these reasons: the appeals are dismissed.

Questions and comments:

1. *Société Huber* shows that the retention of profits may be challenged by minority shareholders as an abuse of majority power. However, the minority is only likely to succeed in exceptional cases.[138] Note that the Cour de Cassation emphasized that since the formation of company Huber, *all* operating profits had been transferred to reserves *in their entirety*, while the company did not change their investment policy and did not use the funds, for example, to acquire the buildings it was renting. Secondly, the two main shareholders received unusually high, and rapidly rising, remuneration. Thirdly, one of them used the remuneration to acquire the properties occupied by the company and obtain a profit from renting them out to the company. Thus, the case involved not only oppressive behaviour towards the minority, but also the appropriation of a corporate opportunity. Both points—excessive remuneration and the exploitation of a corporate opportunity—gave rise to a conflict of interest and, consequently, implicated the duty of loyalty. Finally, the (valid) argument that the retention of profits benefitted all shareholders in proportion to their holdings by increasing the value of the company (although not to the same extent as the use of the funds to pursue positive-net-present-value projects) was not accepted by the court, because the transferability of shares was restricted and the minority, accordingly, could not realize the increase in value by selling their shares. While it is not necessary that all of these elements—failure to distribute *any* profits without a proper business reason, conflict of interest, and the lack of a market in the minority's shares—are present, recall that a claim of *abus de majorité* requires that the challenged conduct is both contrary to the best interests of the company and based *solely* on the intent to benefit the majority to the detriment of the minority. In the present context, the first condition was satisfied because the company had adopted a policy of *systematic* non-distribution of profits and at the same time did not put them to good use by investing the funds, and the second condition because the majority received a pecuniary advantage in the form of remuneration and rent income from which the minority was excluded.[139]

[137] [Footnote by authors.] Loi no 66-537 sur les sociétés commerciales, JORF of 26 July 1966, p. 6402. This provision is now laid down in Art L223-10 Code de commerce, dealing with the responsibility of the first managers and shareholders if the formation of a company is invalid.

[138] Conac (n 132) 366–7; Merle (n 135) para 664, both with references (pointing out that French courts are reluctant to second-guess business decisions and assume that the retention of profits is in the interest of the company, unless the objecting shareholder establishes a clear case of abuse).

[139] Other cases where the minority shareholders were successful in claiming that the retention of profits constituted an abuse of majority power involved similar fact patterns, see e.g. Cass com, 22 April 1976 (*Langlois et Peters*), *Revue des sociétés* 1976, 479, note D Schmidt (the two majority shareholders systematically transferred profits to an extraordinary reserve, did not distribute a dividend for 20 years, and drew a substantial salary as

2. The doctrine of *abus de majorité* has not only been invoked where the actions of the majority prevented the minority shareholders from realizing a financial return on their investment, but also in a variety of other circumstances. For example, the Cour de Cassation held that the increase of a company's capital constituted an abuse of majority rights where a minority shareholder could not subscribe for the newly issued shares for financial reasons and the majority had carried out the capital increase in order to dilute the interests of the minority before the proceeds of the sale of a valuable asset were received.[140] Likewise, organizing the management of a company in a way that favours a certain family may be regarded as an abuse of majority power.[141] Reminiscent of the German *Holzmüller* case that we discussed in Chapter 5,[142] it has also been held that the transfer of a business to a newly formed company that is majority-owned by the transferring corporation, thus leaving the objecting shareholder as a minority shareholder in a holding company, may amount to an *abus de majorité* if the restructuring is intended to benefit the majority shareholder, for example because the majority can now decide on the use of the balance sheet profit without interference by the minority shareholder.[143]
3. If behavior of the majority shareholder amounts to *abus de majorité*, the minority shareholders can bring an *action en nullité* to seek a declaration that the resolution in question is null and void. In addition, as *Société Huber* makes clear, the majority shareholder who committed the abuse of rights, rather than the company, may be liable for damages. Dogmatically, this result follows from the general tort law provisions of the French Code civil, which serve as a basis for a private course of action in various situations where corporate transactions are challenged, for example because of a conflict of interest.[144] This solution is, of course, also economically sensible, because holding the company liable would lead to a circular flow of funds, where part of the compensation payment is borne by the minority shareholders in the form of a decrease in the value of their investment.
4. Note that the definition of *abus the majorité* is almost identical to that of a special advantage pursuant to §243(2) AktG. Overall, however, German law is broader, since the unwritten fiduciary duty established in *Linotype* and *Girmes*, which, admittedly, introduces an element of legal uncertainty by requiring shareholders to have 'due regard' for the interests of the other shareholders, allows the courts to react flexibly to transactional structures that are

executive directors); Cass com, 1 July 2003, no 99-19328, *Bull. Joly Sociétés* 2003, 1137, note A Constantin (facts similar to *Langlois et Peters*: the company systematically allocated profits to reserves and paid one of two controlling shareholders 'excessive' remuneration); Cass civ, 12 November 2015, no 14-23716, *Revue des sociétés* 2016, 526, note E Schlumberger (retention of almost all of the profits of a property company (*société civile immobilière*) without a proper business reason in order to deprive one of the founders of the company of his dividend income, which had the effect of placing him in a 'precarious financial position').

[140] Cass civ, 8 July 2015, no 13-14348 (*Sté Bruxys*), *Bull. Joly Sociétés* 2015, 643, note H Hovasse. See also Cass com, 22 May 2001, no 98-19086 (*Sté Exploitation du Château Giscours*), *Bull. Joly Sociétés* 2001, 1003, note H Le Nabasque (increase of capital with the aim of diluting the minority by issuing few shares with a very high premium so that minority shareholders would not be able to subscribe for the shares for lack of financial means was, in the case at hand, held not to be abusive, because 'the premium was justified in light of the reserves, turnover and value of the company's shares').

[141] Cour d'Appel de Paris, 27 February 1997, *Bull. Joly* 1997, 573, no 227, note JP Garçon.

[142] Chapter 5A.III.

[143] Cass com, 30 November 2004, no 01-16581 (*Sté Champagnes Giesler*), *Bull. Joly* 2005, 241, no 42, note P Le Cannu. In this case, the objecting minority shareholder held approximately 28% of the share capital of Champagnes Giesler (below the blocking minority under French law) and had a seat on the board of directors of a subsidiary, which owned the main operating business of the group. The new operating company was set up in the form of a partnership limited by shares. Champagnes Giesler became a limited partner (i.e. a partner excluded from the management of the partnership) and the majority shareholder of Champagnes Giesler a general partner. It could therefore be argued that the claimant had had some influence on corporate affairs, which he lost with the restructuring. However, on remand, the Court of Appeal of Versailles rejected the claim, arguing that the claimant had never had any effective decision-making power regarding the distribution of the profits of the operating business because of the structure of the corporate group and had also not suffered any other loss as a consequence of the alleged abuse of majority power, Cour d'Appel de Versailles, 20 June 2006, *Bull. Joly* 2006, 1424, no 292, note P Le Cannu.

[144] See our discussion in Chapter 6B.I.4(a) and C.II.4. For further differences between an action for annulment and an action for damages, see Cozian, Viandier, and Deboissy (n 134) paras 579–80.

perceived to confer an unfair advantage on the majority. The UK approach, on the other hand, differs substantially from both French and German law and seems to be narrower than either solution. Can this be explained with the long tradition of fiduciary duties in English law, and hence the fact that their content and limits are well-established,[145] whereas German and French courts started from a 'clean slate' when minority shareholders began to litigate these issues, and thus were less constrained by orthodox conceptions of who a fiduciary was?[146]

Some shareholder resolutions require a qualified majority. Typical examples are an amendment of the company's articles of association, an increase of the share capital, or the prolongation of the life of the company when it approaches its end date pursuant to the articles. In these cases, minority shareholders who command a sufficient number of votes to block the resolution (one-third under French law) gain negative control over the transaction. French courts have developed the doctrine of *abus de minorité* to constrain the exercise of the minority's negative control in the same way as majority power. The doctrine accordingly mirrors *abus the majorité* and requires the claimant, the company, to show that the challenged behaviour is (i) contrary to the general interests of the company and (ii) based solely on the intent to further the minority's own interests to the detriment of the other shareholders.[147] One can distinguish between *abus positif*, where a shareholder exercises a minority right with an abusive intent, and, more importantly, *abus negative*, where the minority uses its power to block a resolution that is important to the company. A minority shareholder may, for example, commit *abus positif* if the shareholder requests information from the board of directors and petitions the court to appoint an independent expert to review the management of the company without fulfilling the relevant legal requirements.[148] *Abus negative* typically involves situations where the minority shareholder blocks a transaction that is 'essential for the future and survival of the company',[149] for example where the company requires a capital increase to avert financial distress. Whether the refusal to endorse a particular resolution amounts to *abus de minorité* is assessed on a case-by-case basis, taking into account all relevant factors.[150] Blocking a capital increase may thus be permissible if the minority shareholders seek to prevent a significant dilution of their holdings, but the result may be different if the capital increase is necessary to avoid the insolvency of the company.[151]

The consequences of an abuse of minority rights are difficult to determine, since there is no resolution that could be annulled. Majority shareholders can be awarded damages to be paid by the minority, but this may not be sufficient to protect their interests if the company does not survive.[152] Furthermore, the judges of the Cour de Cassation, concerned about the danger of a *gouvernement de juges*, are hesitant to take a decision with respect to the challenged transaction on behalf of the minority shareholders.[153] Emphasizing that 'the court

[145] See for example the clear distinction between the positions of shareholder and director drawn in *Northern Counties Securities Ltd v Jackson & Steeple Ltd* [1974] 1 WLR 1133, reproduced in part in section B.I.1 above.

[146] However, note also that the French approach has been criticized for being too restrictive and not protecting minority shareholders sufficiently well, particularly because it is difficult for the objecting shareholder to prove that the majority's conduct was based *solely* on the intent to favour themselves to the detriment of the minority; see Conac (n 132) 367.

[147] Cass com, 4 December 2012, no 11-25408 (*Sté La Compagnie du Vent*), *Revue des sociétés* 2013, 150, note A Viandier; Cass com, 15 July 1992, no 90-17216 (*Sté Tapisseries de France*), *Revue des sociétés* 1993, 400, note P Merle.

[148] Cass com, 12 January 1976, *Revue des sociétés* 1976, 330, note P Merle (dealing with minority rights now laid down in Art L225–231 Code de commerce).

[149] See, e.g., the decision in *Sté La Compagnie du Vent* (n 147).

[150] See Merle (n 135) para 665, for references.

[151] Conac (n 132) 370.

[152] For example, in Cass com, 12 January 1976 (n 148), a case where a minority shareholder had made demands on a company in contravention of the requirements laid down expressly in the law, it was held that the award of damages was appropriate and sufficient.

[153] Merle (n 135) para 665.

cannot substitute itself for the competent organ of the company',[154] they allow the appointment of an ad hoc representative for the minority shareholders who is authorized to exercise their voting rights as a compromise solution.[155] The courts will not prescribe how the representative is to exercise the right to vote, they only require the ad hoc representative to act in the best interest of the company as well as the legitimate interests of the minority shareholders.[156]

C. Constraints in Sale of Control Transactions

When we speak of control transactions, we have changes to the corporation in mind that alter the legal or shareholder structure of the corporation fundamentally, in particular because the company is party to a merger or being taken over. The sale of all or almost all of the company's assets is comparable to these changes in its economic effects, since the business of the company passes into new ownership. In these cases, the agency problem between majority and minority shareholders is often salient. Majority shareholders may have an interest in carrying out the sale of a business or the combination of two businesses at a price that does not reflect the 'true' value of the target company, for example because they also hold a controlling interest in the acquirer.[157] A similar problem arises where a bidder, having acquired a majority of shares in a target company, now seeks to squeeze or freeze out the remaining minority shareholders. Again, the majority shareholder has an interest in paying a price for the minority shares that is as low as possible, and the law has to ensure that minority shareholders have remedies at their disposal to challenge the transaction if the price is not 'fair'. Control transactions, of course, do not only give rise to agency problems between the majority and minority shareholders, but also between the shareholders as a group and the managers or directors of the corporation. For example, in a takeover, the target's managers and directors may use their powers under corporate law to frustrate the bidder's offer to purchase the target's shares, because they anticipate that they will be replaced as soon as the bidder has acquired majority ownership of the company. Many legal systems have adopted tailor-made rules to address this problem, for example by requiring directors not to take any action that may frustrate a bid when an offer has been made (Article 9 EU Takeover Directive). In addition, jurisdictions may draw on general legal mechanisms that address conflicts of interest between the directors and shareholders, notably directors' duties, in order to prevent managers from frustrating bids that are financially attractive to the shareholders. We have discussed some of these mechanisms in Chapter 5 in the context of our analysis of the limits of corporate power.[158] Here, we will examine takeovers and mergers only insofar as they risk compromising the position of minority shareholders in relation to the majority.

Legal systems have developed a variety of strategies to protect minority shareholders in change of control situations.[159] We will discuss the most important such strategies in the next sections: exit rights of dissenting (outside) shareholders, notably in the form of a requirement imposed on the acquirer to make a mandatory bid, freeze-out or squeeze-out rights of the bidder, and an application of the more general fiduciary or fiduciary-like constraints that we discussed in Part B of this chapter.

[154] Cass com, 9 March 1993, no 91-14685 (*Flandin*), *JCP E* 1993, II, 448, note A Viandier.
[155] Leading case is *Flandin* (n 154). For a discussion of the ad hoc representative, see Cozian, Viandier, and Deboissy (n 134) para 584; Merle (n 135) para 665.
[156] Cass com, 4 February 2014, no 12-29348, *Bull. Joly* 2014, 302, note D Schmidt.
[157] For an example of such a scenario, see *Global GT LP v Golden Telecom, Inc.*, 993 A.2d 497 (Del. Ch. 2010).
[158] Chapter 5B.
[159] For an overview, see Kraakman and others (n 5) 208.

I. Exit I: Mandatory bid/pro rata sharing

An investor who buys a controlling stake in a corporation will generally pay a premium over market price, the so-called control premium. The existence of a control premium is well documented empirically in many markets.[160] The reasons why acquirers may be willing to pay more than the current market price are varied and include the (perceived) ability to manage the target company more efficiently, operating synergies, and opportunities to extract private benefits of control. The latter may be pecuniary, for example in the form of asset sales and other intragroup transactions that benefit the controlling shareholder, excessive executive compensation, and an expropriation of corporate opportunities, or nonpecuniary, such as the social status derived from controlling a large corporate group.[161]

The policy question that arises in this context is whether all shareholders should be given a right to share in the control premium. One view, expressed as early as the 1930s by Adolf Berle and Gardiner Means in their influential treatise *The Modern Corporation and Private Property*, stipulates that control is a corporate asset, and thus all shareholders have a claim to the premium realized upon a sale of control.[162] They reason that the value of control can be seen in the opportunity that it affords to use corporate assets in a manner that serves the interests of the controller, for example in a related party transaction. The opposing view holds that a legal requirement to share the premium from a sale of control among all shareholders simply reduces the likelihood that there will be anything to share.[163] Their key argument is that small (outside) shareholders have an equal chance to participate or not in the gains of a control transaction by holding a diversified portfolio of shares. They will then be on the winning side of some transactions, for example as shareholders of a holding company that freezes out the minority in the subsidiary, and on the losing side of others, for example as minority shareholders in a company bought by an acquirer who pays a control premium only to the owner of the control bloc.[164] Given that such control transactions are generally value increasing and at least some transactions become too expensive if the control premium has to be shared,[165] it is argued that a rule that does not require sharing, but allows acquirers to discriminate between the target's shareholders (so-called 'market rule'[166]), maximizes investor wealth.[167]

The above reasoning of course holds if *all* control transactions are value increasing and none value destroying.[168] If control transactions produce gains in aggregate, but some destroy value (as both sides of the debate admit), a comparison of the efficiency of the sharing rule with the market rule is more complicated. It can be shown that some value-destroying transfers of control are accomplished under a market rule (but generally no value-increasing transfers are prevented), and some value-increasing transfers are prevented under a mandatory sharing rule (but no value-destroying transfers can be accomplished).[169] Hence, the question is under which rule the net efficiency costs are higher. This is difficult to estimate

[160] A Dyck and L Zingales, 'Private Benefits of Control: An International Comparison' (2004) 59 Journal of Finance 537.

[161] RJ Gilson, 'Controlling Shareholders and Corporate Governance: Complicating the Comparative Taxonomy' (2006) 119 Harvard Law Review 1641, 1663–4.

[162] AA Berle and GC Means, *The Modern Corporation and Private Property* (1932, Transaction Publishing 1991) 217–19.

[163] Easterbrook and Fischel (n 88) 703–15.

[164] ibid 712–14.

[165] For a numerical example, see ibid 709.

[166] For a formal definition of the market rule, see EP Schuster, 'The Mandatory Bid Rule: Efficient, After All? (2013) 76 Modern Law Review 529, 539.

[167] Easterbrook and Fischel (n 88) 703–704.

[168] Easterbrook and Fischel emphasize that value-destroying control transactions are generally self-deterring, and even if some are not self-deterring, they can be distinguished fairly easily from value-increasing transactions, ibid 707–708.

[169] Schuster (n 166) 548–53.

and opinions differ.[170] Furthermore, it has been pointed out that a sharing rule (at least in the form of the so-called mandatory bid rule[171]) outperforms a market rule in scenarios where more than one bidder can make a bid. Since a bidder has to pay the same price to all shareholders under a sharing rule, the maximum price a bidder is able to pay depends on the overall value the bidder expects to create. The most value-creating bidder will offer the highest price. Accordingly, the transaction will not only be guaranteed to be efficient (i.e. value-creating compared to the status quo), but it will also lead to an optimal (first-best) allocation of corporate control.[172] This is different under a market rule. Here, the price a bidder is willing to pay is not a function solely of the value of the firm after the control transaction, but will also depend on the private benefits of control the buyer expects to extract. A bidder who extracts high private benefits of control may then be able to outbid competitors even though a sale to a competitor would be efficient because it would create higher total value (calculated as the sum of cash flows and private benefits of control).[173] As this discussion shows, the choice between the two regulatory approaches involves intricate considerations and is at least partly dependant on the decision of the policy maker to prioritize the facilitation of (potentially) value-increasing transactions, in which case a policy maker will opt for the market rule, or ensure that no value-destroying transfers are accomplished, in which case the mandatory bid rule is superior. It is not surprising, therefore, that both approaches can be found in the legal systems that are the focus of our study (the market rule, however, only in the US).

Sharing rules come in two forms, as a pro rata sharing rule and a mandatory bid rule. A pro rata sharing rule allows buyers to determine the percentage of shares they intend to acquire, which may be less than 100 per cent, but they must make the offer to buy pro rata from all shareholders at the same price. A mandatory bid rule requires buyers to offer to buy *all* shares at the same price. An example of a (limited) pro rata sharing rule is Exchange Act Rule 14d-10, reproduced below. The rule requires bidders to pay the same price to all security holders in a public tender offer (which may, however, not be all security holders of the target, if a private block trade is followed by a tender offer to the remaining stockholders). Importantly, bidders do not have to offer to buy out the security holders (hence, Rule 14d-10 does not operate as a mandatory bid rule), but they have to give the security holders within the offer an equal opportunity to tender the same proportion of their securities at the same price. The rule has a limited scope of application. A statutory definition of 'tender offer' does not exist and the SEC and the courts use a multiple factor test to determine whether an offer to acquire securities amounts to a tender offer.[174] While some legal uncertainty remains, private acquisitions even of majority control will generally not qualify as a tender offer.[175]

[170] See LA Bebchuk, 'Efficient and Inefficient Sales of Corporate Control' (1994) 109 Quarterly Journal of Economics 957, 974–81 (arguing that the market rule is, under most scenarios, superior); Schuster (n 166) 553–4 (challenging some of the arguments advanced against the sharing/mandatory bid rule).

[171] More on the mandatory bid rule in the next paragraph. [172] Schuster (n 166) 556–7.

[173] ibid 554–6. The crucial difference between the two rules, therefore, is the requirement under a mandatory bid rule to share not only the cash flows created after the transaction, but also any private benefits of control, since these affect the buyer's willingness to pay and, hence, the price that must be offered to outside shareholders. A numerical example can illustrate this result (see ibid 556). The price a buyer is willing to pay for control is the net present value of the expected return on the transaction, which is composed of future cash flows (dividend payments) and private benefits of control. Thus, under a market rule, $P_{max} = \alpha CF + PB$, where α is the fraction of cash flow rights acquired by the buyer, *CF* is the net present value of future dividend payments and *PB* the net present value of private benefits of control. Let us assume that $\alpha = 30\%$. Now consider two bidders, B_1, who will create cash flows with a net present value of 150 and private benefits of control with a net present value of 30, and B_2, who will create cash flows of 100 and private benefits of control of 70. A sale to B_1 is efficient, since the transaction will create a value of 180, compared with 170 if the firm is sold to B_2. However, B_2 is able to outbid B_1, because $P_{max2} = 0.3CF_2 + PB_2 = 100$, whereas $P_{max1} = 0.3CF_1 + PB_1 = 75$. This result is avoided under a sharing rule, where $P_{max} = \alpha CF + \alpha PB$.

[174] For an overview, see TL Hazen, *Principles of Securities Regulation* (4th edn, West Academic Publishing 2017) §76.

[175] *Astronics Corp. v Protective Closures Co., Inc.*, 561 F. Supp. 329 (W.D.N.Y. 1983).

Similarly, open market purchases without the widespread solicitation of stockholders do not come within the scope of the rule.[176] The rule's equal treatment and best price requirement's apply only to shares purchased as part of a tender offer. Thus, it is possible to structure a transaction in two distinct steps, with a private acquisition of a control bloc at one price, followed by a tender offer at a different (typically lower) price.[177] Outside the scope of Rule 14d-10, US law is generally based on the market rule.[178] In contrast, the EU Takeover Directive, also reproduced in relevant part below, requires the EU Member States to ensure that a bidder who has acquired 'control' (as defined in national law) of a target company, must make a bid addressed to all of the target's security holders for all of their holdings at an 'equitable price'.[179] An 'equitable price' is defined as the highest price paid for the securities by the offeror over a period of not less than six months before the bid.[180]

Sec Exchange Act Rules

Rule 14d-10— Equal treatment of security holders

EU Directive 2004/25/EC (Takeover Directive)

Article 3—General principles

(a) No bidder shall make a tender offer unless:
  (1) The tender offer is open to all security holders of the class of securities subject to the tender offer; and
  (2) The consideration paid to any security holder for securities tendered in the tender offer is the highest consideration paid to any other security holder for securities tendered in the tender offer ...

1. For the purpose of implementing this Directive, Member States shall ensure that the following principles are complied with:
  (a) all holders of the securities of an offeree company of the same class must be afforded equivalent treatment; moreover, if a person acquires control of a company, the other holders of securities must be protected ...

Article 5—Protection of minority shareholders, the mandatory bid and the equitable price

1. Where a natural or legal person, as a result of his/her own acquisition or the acquisition by persons acting in concert with him/her, holds securities of a company as referred to in Article 1(1) which, added to any existing holdings of those securities of his/hers and the holdings of those securities of persons acting in concert with him/her, directly or indirectly give him/her a specified percentage of voting rights in that company, giving him/her control of that company, Member States shall ensure that such a person is required to make a bid as a means of protecting the minority shareholders of that company. Such a bid shall be addressed at the earliest opportunity to all the holders of those securities for all their holdings at the equitable price as defined in paragraph 4.

[176] *Brascan Ltd. v Edper Equities Ltd.*, 477 F. Supp. 773 (S.D.N.Y. 1979) (holding that if a buyer's 'purchasing was not contingent on a minimum fixed number of shares being offered, [the buyer] did not put out an offer at a fixed price and the form of the transaction did not provide for tenders by the selling shareholders to be held for some period of time by the purchaser or a depositary... [but the buyer instead acquired] a large amount of stock in open market purchases, bidding cautiously so as to avoid bidding up the price of the stock to excessive levels unless there was large volume available at such prices ... [the buyer did not make] a tender offer, even if a large volume of stock is accumulated in such fashion', ibid 789). Compare *Brascan* with *Wellman v Dickinson*, 475 F. Supp. 783 (S.D.N.Y. 1979), where the court held that an offer made to some 30 institutions which resulted in the acquisition of 34% of the target company's stock was a tender offer because it involved the active and widespread solicitation of institutional shareholders for a substantial percentage of the target's stock at a premium over market price that was conditioned on the bidder acquiring a specified proportion of the outstanding shares. In addition, importantly, the court stressed that the acquisition was 'infected with the basic evil which Congress sought to cure by enacting the [takeover] law' (ibid 822), namely the practice to force shareholders to make a decision in a short period of time (in the case at hand between half an hour and overnight) and without adequate information (ibid 821–2).

[177] Hazen (n 174) §77.

[178] This holds for the economically most important states, Delaware, New York and California, and many other states, with only a few states having adopted a version of the mandatory bid rule, see Schuster (n 166) 536.

[179] Takeover Directive, Art 5(1).

[180] ibid Art 5(4).

2. Where control has been acquired following a voluntary bid made in accordance with this Directive to all the holders of securities for all their holdings, the obligation laid down in paragraph 1 to launch a bid shall no longer apply.
3. The percentage of voting rights which confers control for the purposes of paragraph 1 and the method of its calculation shall be determined by the rules of the Member State in which the company has its registered office.
4. The highest price paid for the same securities by the offeror, or by persons acting in concert with him/her, over a period, to be determined by Member States, of not less than six months and not more than 12 before the bid referred to in paragraph 1 shall be regarded as the equitable price. If, after the bid has been made public and before the offer closes for acceptance, the offeror or any person acting in concert with him/her purchases securities at a price higher than the offer price, the offeror shall increase his/her offer so that it is not less than the highest price paid for the securities so acquired.

   Provided that the general principles laid down in Article 3(1) are respected, Member States may authorise their supervisory authorities to adjust the price referred to in the first subparagraph in circumstances and in accordance with criteria that are clearly determined. To that end, they may draw up a list of circumstances in which the highest price may be adjusted either upwards or downwards, for example where the highest price was set by agreement between the purchaser and a seller, where the market prices of the securities in question have been manipulated, where market prices in general or certain market prices in particular have been affected by exceptional occurrences, or in order to enable a firm in difficulty to be rescued. They may also determine the criteria to be applied in such cases, for example the average market value over a particular period, the break-up value of the company or other objective valuation criteria generally used in financial analysis.

   Any decision by a supervisory authority to adjust the equitable price shall be substantiated and made public.
5. By way of consideration the offeror may offer securities, cash or a combination of both.

   However, where the consideration offered by the offeror does not consist of liquid securities admitted to trading on a regulated market, it shall include a cash alternative.

   In any event, the offeror shall offer a cash consideration at least as an alternative where he/she or persons acting in concert with him/her, over a period beginning at the same time as the period determined by the Member State in accordance with paragraph 4 and ending when the offer closes for acceptance, has purchased for cash securities carrying 5% or more of the voting rights in the offeree company.

   Member States may provide that a cash consideration must be offered, at least as an alternative, in all cases.
6. In addition to the protection provided for in paragraph 1, Member States may provide for further instruments intended to protect the interests of the holders of securities in so far as those instruments do not hinder the normal course of a bid.

The market rule, which applies in most states of the United States, provides that 'absent looting of corporate assets, conversion of a corporate opportunity, fraud or other acts of bad faith, a controlling stockholder is free to sell, and a purchaser is free to buy, that controlling interest at a premium price'.[181] US courts acknowledge that the control premium reflects the added value that stems from being able to influence the corporation's affairs by voting controlling shares, which, accordingly, does not have to be shared with the non-controlling shareholders.[182] On the other hand, the quote also makes it clear

[181] *Zetlin v Hanson Holdings, Inc.*, 397 N.E.2d 387, 388 (N.Y. 1979).

[182] ibid. A rare case where a controlling shareholder was found to be accountable to minority stockholders for the control premium, thus effectively establishing a pro rata sharing rule, is *Perlman v Feldmann*, 219 F.2d 173 (2d Cir. 1955), which was decided under the law of Indiana. However, it is important not to generalize the holding. The facts were unusual in that the defendant Feldmann, the dominant shareholder of a steel corporation, sold control to a syndicate consisting of end-users of steel at a time of shortage in the steel market because of the Korean war. The buyers sought to obtain control in order to secure a source of supply. Under these circumstances, the court

that the market rule has fiduciary limits. Notably, controlling shareholders owe a duty to minority shareholders not to transfer control to a buyer who plans to deprive the company of its assets through illegal or fraudulent acts.[183] This duty is violated if the controlling shareholder sells in knowledge of a corresponding intention of the buyer. It may also be violated where the seller is ignorant of the buyer's intentions but circumstances give reason to suspect that the buyer is dishonest, for example because the purchase price is excessively high.[184] In such a case, the shareholder is required to investigate and refrain from the transaction, unless the investigation 'discloses such facts as would convince a reasonable person that no fraud is intended or likely to result'.[185] *Jones v. H.F. Ahmanson*, discussed above,[186] may be interpreted as representing a more demanding standard under California law that requires dominant shareholders to abstain from a sale of control not only in the case of looting, fraud, or bad faith, but generally when they obtain a control premium in exclusion of the minority stockholders.[187] However, as we said above, the broad language used by the Supreme Court of California must be read in context. The decision of the majority not to use the United Savings and Loan Association to go public, and instead transfer their shares to a holding company that then made a public offering, may have been interpreted by the court as a situation comparable to the usurpation of a corporate opportunity.[188] In *this* context, controlling shareholders are subject to a sharing requirement, but the decision cannot be read to impose a general pro rata sharing rule.

In the EU, a sharing requirement in the form of a mandatory bid rule is enshrined in Article 5(1) of the Takeover Directive. The requirement to make a bid arises if a person acquires, directly or indirectly, a sufficient number of voting rights to give the bidder control of the target company, unless control was acquired as a consequence of a voluntary bid to all shareholders of the target made in accordance with the Takeover Directive and aimed at acquiring all of their shares.[189] Most Member States define control formally based on the percentage of voting rights acquired, rather than by examining whether the

qualified the sale of control as the sale of a corporate asset, since it involved the power to control the allocation of the company's products in a time of short supply. This, the court argued, was comparable to the misappropriation of a corporate opportunity. The company could have used the period of short supply to improve its profits. By selling control to a customer, the defendant sacrificed this element of corporate good will for personal gain and was thus in breach of the fiduciary duties he owed both as a director and a dominant stockholder to the corporation: ibid 178.

[183] *Gerdes v Reynolds*, 28 N.Y.S.2d 622, 649–52 (N.Y. 1941): 'Inherent in the very nature of stock corporations as constituted by our law are the settled principles that the shares of stock are the property of the stockholders, that the stockholders may sell their shares when and to whom they please and for such price as they can get, that they may sell to buyers of whose identity and integrity and responsibility they are unaware ... that the purchase price paid upon such sales belongs to the sellers, and that these same rights exist even where the stockholders hold a majority of the stock and where the sellers are a group who together own and sell such a majority ... [However], it would be illegal for officers and directors to resign and elect as their successors persons [and for stockholders to sell to persons] who they knew intended to loot the corporation's treasury'.

[184] ibid 654.

[185] *Swinney v Keebler Co.*, 480 F.2d 573, 577 (4th Cir. 1973). See also *Harris v Carter*, 582 A.2d 222, 235 (Del. Ch. 1990) ('when the circumstances would alert a reasonably prudent person to a risk that his buyer is dishonest or in some material respect not truthful, a duty devolves upon the seller to make such inquiry as a reasonably prudent person would make, and generally to exercise care so that others who will be affected by his actions should not be injured by wrongful conduct').

[186] See section B.II.

[187] See, for example, the formulation in *Jones v H.F. Ahmanson & Co.*, 1 Cal.3d 93, 109–10 (Cal. 1969), where the court rejects the 'perfect right [of majority shareholders] to dispose of their stock ... without the slightest regard to the wishes and desires or knowledge of the minority stockholders' and instead applies the duty of directors not to profit from their official position at the shareholders' expense to controlling shareholders that 'seek to gain an advantage in the sale or transfer or use of their controlling block of shares'.

[188] In this regard, *Jones v H.F. Ahmanson* is comparable to *Perlman*, n 182 above, which is also cited in the judgment, 1 Cal. 3d at 111.

[189] Takeover Directive, Art 5(2). When a voluntary bid has been made 'in accordance' with the Takeover Directive is not defined in the Directive. Some Member States, for example Germany, implicitly require compliance with the rules of the Takeover Directive on the level and nature of consideration (Art 5(4), (5), see text

acquirer is able to exercise effective control, which depends on the shareholder structure of the target. In France, Germany and the United Kingdom, the threshold for control is 30 per cent of the voting rights of a company.[190] If this threshold is reached (or exceeded in the case of France), the acquirer has to extend an offer to the holders of all classes of equity shares, with or without voting rights.[191] Exceptionally, when it is clear that crossing the threshold does not afford control and the requirement to make a mandatory bid would be inappropriate, for example because an unrelated majority shareholder remains in the company, the regulator may exempt the acquirer from the mandatory bid rule.[192] Furthermore, UK and French regulations provide that holders of shares representing 30 per cent or more, but not more than 50 per cent, of the voting rights have the same obligation if they increase their stake at any time after the initial acquisition of control. In the UK, this obligation is triggered whenever controlling shareholders acquire additional shares, irrespective of the number of shares.[193] In France, it applies to persons who increase their holdings by 1 per cent or more in any twelve-month period.[194] German law does not provide for a comparable requirement. This creates the risk that acquirers may circumvent the mandatory bid rule by launching a voluntary offer, or crossing the 30 per cent threshold and making a mandatory offer, at a time when the minimum price required under law is low and the public offer, accordingly, can also be made at a low price (so-called *low-balling*). They can then acquire additional shares and obtain majority control of the company without being required to make another mandatory bid.[195] This strategy was indeed deployed a number of times in Germany, for example in the attempted takeover of VW by Porsche in 2007 and the successful takeover of Hochtief by ACS in 2010. In both cases, the mandatory bid was unattractive and, as planned, only a few shareholders tendered their shares, leaving the acquirers free to build up their stakes gradually and without having to bid for full control. As a result, minority shareholders were left vulnerable. This has led to calls for regulatory reform (which were possibly further motivated by the protectionist desire to make takeovers of domestic companies more difficult).[196] However, so far, neither the European Commission, nor the German legislator, have taken any steps to prevent lowball offers.

to nn 211–224 below). For a voluntary offer, the minimum price rules are set out in §31 Wertpapiererwerbs- und Übernahmegesetz (WpÜG) [Securities Acquisition and Takeover Act], §§ 3–7 WpÜG-Angebotsverordnung [German Takeover Act Offer Ordinance]. These price rules are in line with the requirements of Art 5(4) Takeover Directive (however, in other respects, differences exist between voluntary and mandatory bids, with voluntary bids generally allowing for more flexibility; for a comparison, see M Schlitt in W Goette and M Habersack (eds), *Münchener Kommentar zum Aktiengesetz, vol 6* (4th edn, CH Beck 2017), WpÜG §35, paras 260–6). In contrast, most other Member States do not apply the price rules of the Takeover Directive to voluntary offers, see, for example, Rules 6 and 11 of the UK Takeover Code.

[190] France: AMF [Autorité des Marchés Financiers] General Regulation, Art 234-2; Germany: WpÜG, §29(2). UK: Takeover Code, Rule 9.1. For a comprehensive overview of the definition of control in the EU Member States, see C Clerc and others, *A Legal and Economic Assessment of European Takeover Regulation* (Marccus Partners and Centre for European Policy Studies 2012), 57.

[191] AMF General Regulation, Art 234-2(1); German WpÜG, §35(2); UK Takeover Code, Rule 9.1(a).

[192] AMF General Regulation, Arts 234-7, 234-9(6), (6*bis*); German WpÜG, §37(1); UK Takeover Code, Rule 9.1, note 5 of 'Notes on dispensation' (providing that the Takeover Panel may waive the requirement for a general offer where holders of shares carrying 50% or more of the voting rights state in writing that they would not accept the offer or shares carrying 50% or more of the voting rights are already held by another person). The regulations mention other cases where a dispensation from the requirement to make a mandatory bid may be granted, for example, if a company buys back its own shares and a shareholder crosses the control threshold as a consequence, UK Takeover Code, Rule 37.1; however, the Takeover Panel will only waive the mandatory bid requirement if the independent shareholders agree and the offeror follows the 'whitewash' procedure set out in Appendix 1 to the Takeover Code. French and German law contain similar exemptions: see AMF General Regulation, Art 234-9; WpÜG-Angebotsverordnung, §9.

[193] UK Takeover Code, Rule 9.1(b).

[194] AMF General Regulation, Art 234-5.

[195] Clerc and others (n 190) 62.

[196] KJ Hopt, 'European Takeover Reform of 2012/2013 – Time to Re-examine the Mandatory Bid' (2014) 15 EBOR 143, 177–8.

The Takeover Directive provides further that the voting rights of the acquirer and 'persons acting in concert with him/her' shall be aggregated for purposes of calculating whether control has been obtained. Pursuant to the Takeover Directive, persons act in concert if they 'cooperate with the offeror or the offeree company on the basis of an agreement, either express or tacit, either oral or written, aimed either at acquiring control of the offeree company or at frustrating the successful outcome of a bid'.[197] Some Member States replicate this definition faithfully.[198] Others combine the Takeover Directive's definition with the definition laid down in the Transparency Directive, which stipulates that for purposes of the requirement to disclose major holdings, voting rights held by more than one person shall be aggregated if the parties conclude 'an agreement, which obliges them to adopt, by concerted exercise of the voting rights they hold, a lasting common policy towards the management of the issuer in question'.[199] Thus, according to the second approach, acting in concert occurs if voting rights are exercised with a view to implementing a common policy that is intended to influence the management and strategy of the target company, irrespective of the acquisition of additional shares after the coordinated strategy has been formulated.[200] In Member States where acting in concert is defined broadly, concerns have been expressed that the aggregation rules could stifle shareholder engagement and activism.[201] The UK Takeover Panel has addressed these concerns by clarifying that only an agreement in respect of 'a board control-seeking proposal' shall constitute acting in concert, but not voting together on other resolutions.[202] In addition, if a party acquires voting rights without the knowledge of other persons with whom he or she subsequently comes together to cooperate as a group to obtain control of a company, the Takeover Panel will not normally require a mandatory offer to be made, unless a member of the group subsequently acquires additional shares.[203]

The German legislator has sought to limit the reach of acting in concert in a similar, albeit ultimately narrower, way. The Securities Acquisition and Takeover Act provides that voting rights shall only be aggregated if the parties 'reach a consensus on the exercise of [these] rights or collaborate in another manner with the aim of bringing about a permanent and material change in the target company's business strategy'.[204] Thus, a coordinated acquisition of shares, without more, does not qualify as acting in concert.[205] Likewise, agreements with a view to influencing the composition of the management board, or other decisions taken by the supervisory board, do not generally lead to an aggregation of voting rights.[206] On the other hand, it is not necessary that shareholders coordinate their activities by agreeing

197 Takeover Directive, Art 2(1)(d).

198 For example, the UK, see Takeover Code, Definitions C1.

199 Transparency Directive, Art 10(b). This definition can be found in the French Code de commerce, Art L233-10, and the German WpÜG [Securities Acquisition and Takeover Act], §2(5).

200 Clerc and others (n 190) 59–60.

201 D Kershaw, *Principles of Takeover Regulation* (OUP 2016) para 8.16.

202 Takeover Code, Rule 9.1, note 2. Whether a proposal seeks control of the board is determined in light of a number of factors, including the relationship between the proposed directors and the activist shareholders proposing them (or their supporters), the number of directors to be appointed or replaced compared with the total size of the board, the board positions held by the directors being replaced, and the relationship between the proposed directors and the existing directors.

203 Takeover Code, Rule 9.1, note 1. See also ESMA, Information on shareholder cooperation and acting in concert under the Takeover Bids Directive, ESMA31-65-682, 8 February 2019, providing for a 'white list' of activities that will not, in and of themselves, qualify as acting in concert in order to facilitate shareholder engagement and good corporate governance.

204 WpÜG, §30(2) sentence 2.

205 Raiser and Veil (n 116) §75/30.

206 BGH, judgment of 18 September 2006, BGHZ 169, 98 (*WMF*), arguing that the members of the supervisory board were independent and required to act exclusively in the interest of the company. Therefore, they could not be regarded as 'agents' of the shareholders and, hence, their actions did not qualify as coordinated conduct of the offeror and other holders of voting rights. This decision was adopted before a revision of §30(2) WpÜG in 2008. The current definition mirrors the restrictive reading of the Bundesgerichtshof in *WMF*, which therefore continues to guide the interpretation of the term 'acting in concert', U Wackerbarth in Goette and Habersack (n 189) WpÜG §30, para 53.

on how to exercise their shareholder rights in the general meeting. Any form of coordination, for example by lobbying management in one-on-one meetings, potentially brings them within the scope of acting in concert.[207] In contrast, the French statutory definition is open-ended and applies to any acquisition, sale or exercise of voting rights 'to implement a common policy in relation to the [target] company'.[208] Thus, the statute only requires that the persons acting in concert pursue a common goal, but not that the coordinated conduct is intended to affect the business strategy of the target or secure control of the board.[209] Because of this wide definition, the French approach is highly fact specific and has resulted in a considerable number of administrative and judicial proceedings.[210]

The Takeover Directive implements the sharing rule by requiring that a person who acquires control shall make a mandatory bid at the 'equitable price', defined as the highest price at which the bidder, or persons acting in concert with the bidder, have acquired shares of the same class over a period of six to twelve months before the bid.[211] Consideration may be offered in cash, securities, or a combination of both. A cash alternative must be offered if the securities are not liquid and admitted to trading on a regulated market or the bidder has acquired securities for cash that represent 5 per cent or more of the voting rights in the target company.[212] The latter requirement seeks to ensure that the target's shareholders are treated equally, thus putting into effect the general equal treatment principle of Article 3(1)(a) of the Takeover Directive.[213] Member States have made use of the discretion granted under the Directive, and national law therefore displays some variation in how the equitable price is determined. In the UK and France, a twelve-month reference period applies, while German law provides for a six-month period.[214] The Directive allows Member States to authorize their supervisory authorities to adjust the highest price upwards or downwards in accordance with clearly specified criteria.[215] Some Member States, for example the UK, implement this provision by listing a number of generic criteria referring, for example, to the size and timing of the transactions used to calculate the highest price or the acquisition of shares at high prices from insiders, and empowering the regulator to determine a 'fair and reasonable' price.[216] Similarly, the French market regulator is able to request or authorize a modification of the price if the characteristics of the target company or market conditions change 'manifestly', in particular if events occur during the relevant twelve-month period that materially alter the value of the securities or the target is in financial difficulties.[217] For example, the AMF made use of its powers to accept a lower price than the normally applicable price in a case where a company suffered a significant decline in its share price during the reference period because a contraction in the credit market raised doubts about the ability of the company to refinance its debts. The AMF held that a modification of the offer price was justified because the highest price was paid by the acquirer several months before the contraction

[207] Raiser and Veil (n 116) §75/29.

[208] Com, Art L233-10(I). If the common policy consists in securing control of a company or frustrating a takeover bid, the law establishes a presumption that the parties act in concert, ibid Art 233-10-1.

[209] Cass com, 27 October 2009, *RJDA* 21/09, inf 23 no 3.

[210] For examples of behaviour that constitutes, and does not constitute, acting in concert, see A Charveriat, A Couret, and B Zabala, *Mémento Pratique Sociétés Commerciales* (Francis Lefebvre 2017), paras 64179–82; Cozian, Viandier, and Deboissy (n 134) para 1408.

[211] Takeover Directive, Art 5(4) sentence 1. If the bidder acquires securities at a higher price than the offer price after publication of the bid and before closing of the offer, the offer must be increased accordingly, Art 5(4) sentence 2.

[212] Takeover Directive, Art 5(5). Some Member States apply this requirement also to voluntary bids, see, for example, German WpÜG, §31(1), and AMF General Regulation, Art 231-8, others use different thresholds triggering the requirement to make a cash offer, for example UK Takeover Code, Rule 11.1.

[213] Raiser and Veil (n 116) §73/9.

[214] AMF General Regulation, Art 234-6(1); German WpÜG, §31(1) in conjunction with WpÜG-Angebotsverordnung, §4; UK Takeover Code, Rule 9.5(a).

[215] Takeover Directive, Art 5(4) subs 2.

[216] UK Takeover Code, Rule 9.5 note 3.

[217] AMF General Regulation, Art 234-6.

in the credit market, the transaction took place on the stock exchange, it related to a small fraction of the target's equity (0.01 per cent), and the average acquisition price was much lower than the highest price.[218] The mandatory bid price is then determined on the basis of a multi-factor test that takes account of generally accepted objective valuation criteria, the characteristics of the target company and the market for its securities.[219]

Other Member States provide for a test that always involves the cumulative application of multiple criteria. For example, German law stipulates that the consideration 'must be *at least* equal to the value of the highest consideration paid or agreed [to be paid] by the offeror' during the reference period.[220] If the shares are admitted to trading on a regulated market and the weighted average stock exchange price of the shares during the last three months prior to the publication of the offer is higher, the bidder must offer to buy the shares at this higher price.[221] If the average stock exchange price is not meaningful because of limited trading in the shares, the target's business has to be valued according to generally accepted valuation methods.[222] In another deviation from the minimum requirements of the Takeover Directive and the national laws of most Member States, including France and the UK, German law imposes an obligation on acquirers to compensate shareholders who accepted the tender offer for the difference between the offer price and a higher price paid by the acquirer in off-market purchases of the target company's shares within one year of the publication of the offer.[223] The provision seeks to prevent the circumvention of the price determination rules, but it comes at the price of making acquisitions significantly more expensive if shareholders with a stake exceeding the squeeze-out threshold remain in the target company after the mandatory bid to negotiate a high post-bid price for their shares.[224]

II. Exit II: Buy-out/freeze-out and appraisal

An appraisal right is the right of shareholders who object to certain fundamental corporate changes to demand a determination of the value of their shares by the court. Historically, appraisal rights were created as a substitute for the common law requirement of unanimous shareholder consent to fundamental corporate changes. As we discussed above (section A), legal systems replaced the unanimity rule with majority voting to address the significant holdout problems it engendered as corporations grew in size. More subtly, even without a unanimous consent requirement, shareholders have an incentive not to tender their shares if they expect a bidder to operate the company more profitably than under current management and benefit from the ensuing appreciation in the price of their shares. Thus, the bidder may not be able to recoup the costs incurred in pursuing the control transaction and, as a consequence, value-increasing transactions may not take place.[225] Given this problem,

[218] AMF, decision 209C0559 of 22 April 2009, Official Bulletin of the AMF no 49, 24 April 2009 (*Sté GECIMED*). In this case, the acquirer had bought shares of the target in several low-volume market transactions at prices between €1.78 and €2.08. The block trade that triggered the mandatory bid requirement occurred several months later at a price of €0.70 per share, and the average acquisition price over twelve months was €0.76 per share.

[219] AMF General Regulation, Art 234-6 last sentence.

[220] WpÜG-Angebotsverordnung, §4.

[221] ibid §§5, 6. The weighted average price is defined as 'the average price, weighted according to turnover', ibid §5(3). The German legislator adopted the multiple factor test in response to two decisions by the Federal Constitutional Court, BVerfGE 100, 289 (*DAT/Altana*) and BVerfG ZIP 1999, 1804 (*Hartmann & Braun*), where the court had interpreted the constitutional right to property (Art 14(1) Grundgesetz [Basic Law]) as requiring that the target's shareholders must receive at least the price they could obtain for their shares in the market at the time of the transaction, see Wackerbarth (n 206), WpÜG §31 para 37. See further BGHZ 186, 229 (*Stollwerck*) and BGH AG 2011, 590, holding that a three-month period ending with the *announcement* of the transaction should be used to calculate the weighted average stock market price (and modifying the decision of the Bundesgerichtshof in the *DAT/Altana* proceedings, BGHZ 147, 108, where the court had referred to the date when the relevant corporate organ *approved* the transaction).

[222] WpÜG-Angebotsverordnung, §5(4).

[223] WpÜG, §31(5).

[224] Clerc and others (n 190) 67–8.

[225] SJ Grossman and OD Hart, 'Takeover bids, the free-rider problem, and the theory of the corporation' (1980) 11 Bell Journal of Economics 42, 43.

Delaware law and other jurisdictions have become increasingly accommodating to the attempts of majority shareholders to eliminate the remaining minority shareholders in a control transaction. Appraisal rights provide a necessary safeguard against abuse of this power by the majority.

In an appraisal proceeding, the court will direct the company to pay the fair value of the shares to the objecting stockholders, who have to surrender their shares to the company. Thus, the appraisal remedy can also be conceptualized as an exit right, which entitles a shareholder to be bought out by the company at a price determined by a neutral arbiter.[226] The best known such appraisal remedy is §262 Delaware General Corporation Law, reproduced below.

Delaware General Corporation Law

§ 262—Appraisal rights

(a) Any stockholder of a corporation of this State who holds shares of stock on the date of the making of a demand pursuant to subsection (d) of this section with respect to such shares, who continuously holds such shares through the effective date of the merger or consolidation, who has otherwise complied with subsection (d) of this section and who has neither voted in favor of the merger or consolidation nor consented thereto in writing pursuant to § 228 of this title shall be entitled to an appraisal by the Court of Chancery of the fair value of the stockholder's shares of stock under the circumstances described in subsections (b) and (c) of this section. As used in this section, the word 'stockholder' means a holder of record of stock in a corporation; the words 'stock' and 'share' mean and include what is ordinarily meant by those words; and the words 'depository receipt' mean a receipt or other instrument issued by a depository representing an interest in 1 or more shares, or fractions thereof, solely of stock of a corporation, which stock is deposited with the depository.

(b) Appraisal rights shall be available for the shares of any class or series of stock of a constituent corporation in a merger or consolidation to be effected pursuant to § 251 (other than a merger effected pursuant to § 251(g) of this title and, subject to paragraph (b)(3) of this section, § 251(h) of this title), § 252, § 254, § 255, § 256, § 257, § 258, § 263 or § 264 of this title:

 (1) Provided, however, that, except as expressly provided in § 363(b) of this title, no appraisal rights under this section shall be available for the shares of any class or series of stock, which stock, or depository receipts in respect thereof, at the record date fixed to determine the stockholders entitled to receive notice of the meeting of stockholders to act upon the agreement of merger or consolidation, were either: (i) listed on a national securities exchange or (ii) held of record by more than 2,000 holders; and further provided that no appraisal rights shall be available for any shares of stock of the constituent corporation surviving a merger if the merger did not require for its approval the vote of the stockholders of the surviving corporation as provided in § 251(f) of this title.

 (2) Notwithstanding paragraph (b)(1) of this section, appraisal rights under this section shall be available for the shares of any class or series of stock of a constituent corporation if the holders thereof are required by the terms of an agreement of merger or consolidation pursuant to §§ 251, 252, 254, 255, 256, 257, 258, 263 and 264 of this title to accept for such stock anything except:

  a. Shares of stock of the corporation surviving or resulting from such merger or consolidation, or depository receipts in respect thereof;

  b. Shares of stock of any other corporation, or depository receipts in respect thereof, which shares of stock (or depository receipts in respect thereof) or depository receipts at the effective date of the merger or consolidation will be either listed on a national securities exchange or held of record by more than 2,000 holders;

[226] Kraakman and others (n 5) 186. How 'fair value' should be determined is, of course, the crucial question. Unsurprisingly, a large number of cases have tackled this question, and the approach to valuing shares has not always been consistent. We will analyse some of the most important decision on the next pages. See also Chapter 6B.I.2(d) for valuation questions under Delaware law and recent case law.

c. Cash in lieu of fractional shares or fractional depository receipts described in the foregoing paragraphs (b)(2)a. and b. of this section; or
d. Any combination of the shares of stock, depository receipts and cash in lieu of fractional shares or fractional depository receipts described in the foregoing paragraphs (b)(2)a., b. and c. of this section.

(3) In the event all of the stock of a subsidiary Delaware corporation party to a merger effected under § 251(h), § 253 or § 267 of this title is not owned by the parent immediately prior to the merger, appraisal rights shall be available for the shares of the subsidiary Delaware corporation.

(4) ...

(c) Any corporation may provide in its certificate of incorporation that appraisal rights under this section shall be available for the shares of any class or series of its stock as a result of an amendment to its certificate of incorporation, any merger or consolidation in which the corporation is a constituent corporation or the sale of all or substantially all of the assets of the corporation. If the certificate of incorporation contains such a provision, the provisions of this section, including those set forth in subsections (d), (e), and (g) of this section, shall apply as nearly as is practicable.

(d) Appraisal rights shall be perfected as follows:

(1) If a proposed merger or consolidation for which appraisal rights are provided under this section is to be submitted for approval at a meeting of stockholders, the corporation, not less than 20 days prior to the meeting, shall notify each of its stockholders who was such on the record date for notice of such meeting (or such members who received notice in accordance with § 255(c) of this title) with respect to shares for which appraisal rights are available pursuant to subsection (b) or (c) of this section that appraisal rights are available for any or all of the shares of the constituent corporations, and shall include in such notice a copy of this section and, if 1 of the constituent corporations is a nonstock corporation, a copy of § 114 of this title. Each stockholder electing to demand the appraisal of such stockholder's shares shall deliver to the corporation, before the taking of the vote on the merger or consolidation, a written demand for appraisal of such stockholder's shares. Such demand will be sufficient if it reasonably informs the corporation of the identity of the stockholder and that the stockholder intends thereby to demand the appraisal of such stockholder's shares. A proxy or vote against the merger or consolidation shall not constitute such a demand. A stockholder electing to take such action must do so by a separate written demand as herein provided. Within 10 days after the effective date of such merger or consolidation, the surviving or resulting corporation shall notify each stockholder of each constituent corporation who has complied with this subsection and has not voted in favor of or consented to the merger or consolidation of the date that the merger or consolidation has become effective; or

(2) If the merger or consolidation was approved pursuant to § 228, § 251(h), § 253, or § 267 of this title, then either a constituent corporation before the effective date of the merger or consolidation or the surviving or resulting corporation within 10 days thereafter shall notify each of the holders of any class or series of stock of such constituent corporation who are entitled to appraisal rights of the approval of the merger or consolidation and that appraisal rights are available for any or all shares of such class or series of stock of such constituent corporation, and shall include in such notice a copy of this section and, if 1 of the constituent corporations is a nonstock corporation, a copy of § 114 of this title. Such notice may, and, if given on or after the effective date of the merger or consolidation, shall, also notify such stockholders of the effective date of the merger or consolidation. Any stockholder entitled to appraisal rights may, within 20 days after the date of mailing of such notice or, in the case of a merger approved pursuant to § 251(h) of this title, within the later of the consummation of the offer contemplated by § 251(h) of this title and 20 days after the date of mailing of such notice, demand in writing from the surviving or resulting corporation the appraisal of such holder's shares. Such demand will be sufficient if it reasonably informs the corporation of the identity of the

stockholder and that the stockholder intends thereby to demand the appraisal of such holder's shares . . .

(e) Within 120 days after the effective date of the merger or consolidation, the surviving or resulting corporation or any stockholder who has complied with subsections (a) and (d) of this section hereof and who is otherwise entitled to appraisal rights, may commence an appraisal proceeding by filing a petition in the Court of Chancery demanding a determination of the value of the stock of all such stockholders. Notwithstanding the foregoing, at any time within 60 days after the effective date of the merger or consolidation, any stockholder who has not commenced an appraisal proceeding or joined that proceeding as a named party shall have the right to withdraw such stockholder's demand for appraisal and to accept the terms offered upon the merger or consolidation. Within 120 days after the effective date of the merger or consolidation, any stockholder who has complied with the requirements of subsections (a) and (d) of this section hereof, upon written request, shall be entitled to receive from the corporation surviving the merger or resulting from the consolidation a statement setting forth the aggregate number of shares not voted in favor of the merger or consolidation and with respect to which demands for appraisal have been received and the aggregate number of holders of such shares. Such written statement shall be mailed to the stockholder within 10 days after such stockholder's written request for such a statement is received by the surviving or resulting corporation or within 10 days after expiration of the period for delivery of demands for appraisal under subsection (d) of this section hereof, whichever is later. Notwithstanding subsection (a) of this section, a person who is the beneficial owner of shares of such stock held either in a voting trust or by a nominee on behalf of such person may, in such person's own name, file a petition or request from the corporation the statement described in this subsection.

(f) . . .

(g) At the hearing on such petition, the Court shall determine the stockholders who have complied with this section and who have become entitled to appraisal rights. The Court may require the stockholders who have demanded an appraisal for their shares and who hold stock represented by certificates to submit their certificates of stock to the Register in Chancery for notation thereon of the pendency of the appraisal proceedings; and if any stockholder fails to comply with such direction, the Court may dismiss the proceedings as to such stockholder. If immediately before the merger or consolidation the shares of the class or series of stock of the constituent corporation as to which appraisal rights are available were listed on a national securities exchange, the Court shall dismiss the proceedings as to all holders of such shares who are otherwise entitled to appraisal rights unless (1) the total number of shares entitled to appraisal exceeds 1% of the outstanding shares of the class or series eligible for appraisal, (2) the value of the consideration provided in the merger or consolidation for such total number of shares exceeds $1 million, or (3) the merger was approved pursuant to § 253 or § 267 of this title.

(h) After the Court determines the stockholders entitled to an appraisal, the appraisal proceeding shall be conducted in accordance with the rules of the Court of Chancery, including any rules specifically governing appraisal proceedings. Through such proceeding the Court shall determine the fair value of the shares exclusive of any element of value arising from the accomplishment or expectation of the merger or consolidation, together with interest, if any, to be paid upon the amount determined to be the fair value. In determining such fair value, the Court shall take into account all relevant factors. Unless the Court in its discretion determines otherwise for good cause shown, and except as provided in this subsection, interest from the effective date of the merger through the date of payment of the judgment shall be compounded quarterly and shall accrue at 5% over the Federal Reserve discount rate (including any surcharge) as established from time to time during the period between the effective date of the merger and the date of payment of the judgment. At any time before the entry of judgment in the proceedings, the surviving corporation may pay to each stockholder entitled to appraisal an amount in cash, in which case interest shall accrue thereafter as provided herein only upon the sum of (1) the difference, if any, between the amount so paid and the fair value of the shares as determined by the Court, and (2) interest theretofore accrued, unless paid at that time. Upon application by the surviving or resulting corporation or by any stockholder entitled to participate in the appraisal proceeding, the Court may, in its discretion, proceed to trial upon the appraisal prior to the final determination of the stockholders entitled to an appraisal. Any stockholder whose name appears on the list filed by the surviving or resulting corporation pursuant to subsection (f) of this section and who has submitted such stockholder's certificates of stock to the Register in Chancery, if such is required, may participate fully in all proceedings until it is finally determined that such stockholder is not entitled to appraisal rights under this section.

(i) The Court shall direct the payment of the fair value of the shares, together with interest, if any, by the surviving or resulting corporation to the stockholders entitled thereto. Payment shall be so made to each such stockholder, in the case of holders of uncertificated stock forthwith, and the case of holders of shares represented by certificates upon the surrender to the corporation of the certificates representing such stock. The Court's decree may be enforced as other decrees in the Court of Chancery may be enforced, whether such surviving or resulting corporation be a corporation of this State or of any state.

(j) The costs of the proceeding may be determined by the Court and taxed upon the parties as the Court deems equitable in the circumstances. Upon application of a stockholder, the Court may order all or a portion of the expenses incurred by any stockholder in connection with the appraisal proceeding, including, without limitation, reasonable attorney's fees and the fees and expenses of experts, to be charged pro rata against the value of all the shares entitled to an appraisal.

(k) …

(l) The shares of the surviving or resulting corporation to which the shares of such objecting stockholders would have been converted had they assented to the merger or consolidation shall have the status of authorized and unissued shares of the surviving or resulting corporation.

Under Delaware law, the appraisal remedy is available to shareholders in a merger of two (or more) corporations, both where the consideration received by the shareholders of the target company is shares or other securities of the acquiring company (or securities of another company) and where it is cash.[227] In a stock-for-stock merger, the shareholders of all merging companies have to approve the merger,[228] and those not voting in favour of the merger are entitled to an appraisal of the fair value of their shares by the Delaware Court of Chancery. However, in an important exception to the general rule, shareholders do not receive appraisal rights if the shares are either listed on a national securities exchange or held of record by more than 2,000 holders (so-called 'market out' provision).[229] In this case, the shareholders are assumed to be able to exit the company at a fair price by selling their shares on the market, thus obviating the need for an independent appraisal. Furthermore, pursuant to an amendment to the Delaware appraisal regime introduced in 2016, the court will dismiss the proceedings unless the dissenting shareholders hold more than 1 per cent of the shares eligible for appraisal or the value of the consideration for these shares provided in the merger exceeds $1 million (*de minimis* exception).[230]

In a number of situations, the shareholders of the merging companies lose their voting and appraisal rights in a stock-for-stock merger. No shareholder vote is required for a merger with a wholly-owned subsidiary, provided the merger does not result in any alteration of the rights of the shareholders of the holding company,[231] and appraisal rights are not available.[232] Furthermore, a parent company holding at least 90 per cent of the outstanding voting stock of the subsidiary can merge the subsidiary into the parent without obtaining shareholder approval from either company (so-called short-form merger).[233] Again, the shareholders of the parent company are not entitled to an appraisal of their shares.[234] However, the minority

227 Del. Gen. Corp. Law, §262(b). 228 ibid §251(c). 229 ibid §262(b)(1).
230 ibid §262(g). 231 ibid §251(g). 232 ibid §262(b).
233 ibid §253(a). If the parent is merged into the subsidiary, the parent's shareholders have to approve the merger.
234 This follows from the fact that §262(b), which lists the types of merger giving rise to appraisal rights, does not refer to §253.

shareholders of the subsidiary retain their appraisal rights in a short-form merger.[235] Finally, no vote of the shareholders of the *surviving* corporation is necessary, and they do not have any appraisal rights, if the common shares of that corporation issued under the plan of merger do not exceed 20 per cent of the shares of common stock outstanding immediately prior to the effective date of the merger.[236] The shareholders of the target company, on the other hand, have to approve the merger, and they receive appraisal rights, unless the market out exception applies.[237]

If the shareholders of the acquiring company are paid a consideration in cash, the rules are partly different. In application of the same provision as in a merger that does not increase the outstanding common stock of the surviving company by more than 20 per cent, the shareholders of the acquirer have neither voting nor appraisal rights.[238] The target's shareholders, however, can vote on the merger and request an appraisal, irrespective of whether or not their shares are listed on a national stock exchange. The reason is that appraisal rights exist in Delaware whenever the consideration does not consist in shares of the corporation surviving the merger or any other corporation with a public market for its shares.[239] A variant of this transaction is the so-called freeze-out or cash-out merger, which commonly involves the following steps. First, the acquirer makes a tender offer to the shareholders of the target to acquire their shares, typically for a cash consideration. The acquirer then sets up a wholly-owned subsidiary and uses its control of the target to merge the target into the subsidiary (triangular merger) or the subsidiary into the target (reverse triangular merger). The minority shareholders of the target receive cash (or fixed-return securities) for their shares and are thus squeezed out of the combined business. If the triangular merger is carried out as a classical merger (that is, a merger pursuant to §251(c) Delaware General Corporation Law), it requires shareholder resolutions adopted by the acquirer and target shareholders by simple majority. This technique, therefore, is comparatively more time-intensive and costly than, for example, a short-form merger.[240] It involves convening a general meeting and soliciting proxies in advance of the meeting if the companies are publicly traded.

In order to simplify the two-step transaction, the Delaware legislator amended the General Corporation Law in 2013.[241] The DGCL now allows listed companies[242] to dispense with the shareholder vote on the second-stage merger if the acquirer offers to purchase all shares that would otherwise be entitled to vote on the merger, the merger pays the same consideration as the tender offer, the acquirer owns, as a result of the tender offer, at least the percentage of shares required to approve the merger under Delaware law and the company's certificate of incorporation, and the merger is effected as soon as practicable after consummation of the

[235] ibid §262(b)(3). Note that the *automatic* retention of the subsidiary shareholders' appraisal rights applies only in mergers pursuant to §253, i.e. where the parent owns at least 90% of the shares of the subsidiary. In that case, the appraisal rights are also not subject to the *de minimis* exception of §262(g). Whether appraisal rights exist in other parent-subsidiary mergers depends on the general rules laid down in §262, in particular on the question whether the shares of the subsidiary have a public market (in which case the market out exception applies, n 229 above).

[236] ibid §§251(f), 262(b)(1). [237] ibid §251(f). [238] ibid.

[239] ibid §262(b)(2). Delaware courts have held that this exception to the market-out provision does not apply if the merger agreement offers shareholders the choice between a cash consideration, publicly traded shares of the acquirer, and a mix of cash and shares, and the agreement further provides that shareholders receive cash if they fail to make an election. The Court of Chancery argued that shareholders 'were not "required" to accept any type of consideration that would restore appraisal rights under the "exception to the exception" [i.e. §262(b)(2)]', *Krieger v Wesco Financial Corp.*, 30 A.3d 54, 58.

[240] For an empirical analysis of the effect of the speed of completion on the choice of deal structure, see D Offenberg and CA Pirinsky, 'How do acquirers choose between mergers and tender offers?' (2015) 116 Journal of Financial Economics 331.

[241] H.B. 127, 147th Gen. Assembly, 79 Del. Laws, c. 72, §6 (2013), adding §251(h).

[242] To be more precise, the companies must have shares listed on a national stock exchange or held of record by more than 2,000 holders, §251(h).

tender offer (so-called medium-form merger).[243] Unsurprisingly, after the introduction of the medium-form merger mechanism, the use of two-step tender offers for Delaware targets increased significantly.[244] Somewhat more surprisingly, in spite of the fact that an acquirer can force a substantial minority of potentially close to 50 per cent out of the target company without a shareholder vote, studies have found that the new mechanism had a positive effect on acquisition premiums and combined abnormal returns for Delaware targets, compared with target companies incorporated in other states.[245] The reason may be that the market test that the DGCL establishes by requiring the tender offer price and merger price to be identical, and general fiduciary principles that apply when the acquirer in a merger controls the target, protect a dissenting minority sufficiently well.[246] In addition, regardless of the structure of the cash-out merger, the target's shareholders retain their appraisal rights. In a merger pursuant to §251(c) DGCL, this is a consequence of the fact that they are paid in cash.[247] If the transaction is structured as a medium-form merger, the DGCL provides that appraisal rights shall always be available to the target's shareholders.[248]

As an alternative to a merger or tender offer, the acquirer may decide to purchase all of the assets, or selected valuable assets, of the target. An asset deal has the same economic effects as a merger if the target is dissolved after the sale, the consideration received from the acquirer distributed to its shareholders, and the acquirer assumes all of the liabilities of the target.[249] However, under Delaware law, the legal treatment of the transaction is different from a merger in two important respects. First, the shareholders of the acquirer do not have any vote on the transaction, which is regarded as an investment in assets that falls within the general authority of the board pursuant to §141(a) DGCL, rather than a fundamental corporate change.[250] Secondly, neither the shareholders of the target nor the acquirer have appraisal rights, because the Delaware appraisal statute is restricted to mergers.[251] On the other hand, asset sales require approval by the target's shareholders if 'all or substantially all' of the company's property and assets are sold.[252] This condition is interpreted flexibly by the courts. Rather than using a bright-line test based exclusively on quantitative thresholds, the courts combine qualitative and quantitative criteria.[253] They ask whether the sale is of assets that are 'quantitatively vital to the operation of the corporation' and the transaction 'is out of the ordinary and substantially affects the existence and purpose of the corporation'.[254]

[243] Before the 2013 amendments, companies sought to avoid the requirement to convene a general meeting by bringing the merger within the ambit of §253. In order to facilitate reaching the ownership threshold of 90% pursuant to §253(a), targets often granted a 'top-up option', which entitled the acquirer to purchase additional shares issued by the target. However, the top-up option was criticized for being complex and not eliminating all uncertainty, since the target's authorized capital might not be sufficient to get the acquirer to 90%, see M Gatti, 'Reconsidering the Merger Process: Approval Patterns, Timeline, and Shareholders' Role' (2018) 69 Hastings LJ 835.

[244] AL Boone, BJ Broughman, and AJ Macias, 'Shareholder approval thresholds in acquisitions: Evidence from tender offers' (2018) 53 Journal of Corporate Finance 225, 229–33, 237–8.

[245] ibid 238–9.

[246] We will discuss these principles in section C.III below.

[247] See n 239 above and accompanying text.

[248] Del. Gen. Corp. Law, §262(b)(3).

[249] WW Bratton, *Corporate Finance* (8th edn, Foundation Press 2016) 1137–8.

[250] This is different under the MBCA, §6.21(f), and the listing rules of US stock exchanges, e.g. NYSE Listed Company Manual, Section 312.03(c), if the acquirer issues common stock as consideration equal to or in excess of 20% of the number of shares outstanding prior to the transaction.

[251] In certain cases, this is again different under the MBCA, §13.02(a)(3).

[252] Del. Gen. Corp. Law, §271(a).

[253] In contrast to the MBCA, §12.02(a), which stipulates that a shareholder vote is required if the sale 'would leave the corporation without a significant continuing business activity'. The provision further defines 'significant business activity' as an activity that represents 'at least 25% of total assets at the end of the most recently completed fiscal year, and 25% of either income from continuing operations before taxes or revenues from continuing operations for that fiscal year'.

[254] *Gimbel v Signal Companies, Inc.*, 316 A.2d 599, 606 (Del. Ch. 1974). The Court of Chancery further elaborated that the transaction must be so unusual as to 'strike at the heart of the corporate existence and purpose'. Citing Fletcher, *Cyclopedia Corporations*, the court explained that this was the case if the transaction led to 'the destruction of the means to accomplish the purposes or objects for which the corporation was incorporated and actually performs', ibid.

Thus, a sale of assets involving less than 70 per cent of the firm's business may amount to 'substantially all of the company's property', if these assets represent the only profitable part of the business,[255] whereas a transaction in the ordinary course of business will never, and even a major restructuring will not necessarily, require a shareholder vote.[256]

If appraisal rights are available, the company is required to notify all shareholders at least twenty days prior to the general meeting of their rights. Shareholders who decide to demand an appraisal of their shares have to deliver a written request for appraisal to the corporation before the vote on the merger is taken.[257] They then have 120 days from the effective date of the merger to either reach an agreement with the company or file a petition in the Court of Chancery demanding a determination of the value of their shares.[258] In the appraisal proceeding, the court determines the 'fair value' of the shares, exclusive of the effect of the merger on the value of the business.[259] The court's valuation is binding on all shareholders who were entitled to an appraisal and made a demand on the company, including those who did not join the appraisal proceeding.[260] If the share's fair value is found to exceed the merger price, the court will direct the company to pay the requisite amount to all shareholders entitled thereto.[261] The shares of the objecting shareholders are transferred to the surviving company (or the company resulting from the merger) and are treated as authorized and unissued shares.[262] Thus, appraisal is both an exit right, providing shareholders who object to a fundamental change with liquidity if a market in their shares is not readily available,[263] and a mechanism to combat the conflicts of interest that arise when a controlling shareholder stands on both sides of a transaction that affects the position of the minority.

The appraisal remedy has a number of limitations which render it less attractive than other remedies.[264] As mentioned, relief under the appraisal remedy does not reflect any increase in the value of the stock that results from the merger.[265] Equitable remedies, on the other hand, for example rescissory damages, may be measured by the value of the shares at the time of judgment and thus capture an increase in the share price after consummation of the transaction.[266] Appraisal proceedings also involve substantial costs for the shareholders

[255] *Thorpe v CERBCO, Inc.*, 676 A.2d 436, 444 (Del. 1996).

[256] *Gimbel v Signal Companies, Inc.* (n 254) 606; *Hollinger, Inc. v Hollinger International, Inc.*, 858 A.2d 342, 378–9 (Del. Ch. 2004).

[257] Del. Gen. Corp. Law, §262(d)(1). Special rules exist if no vote is required, §262(d)(2).

[258] ibid §262(e). Both holders of record and the beneficial owners of shares have the right to file a petition in the Court of Chancery in their own name, see the last sentence of subsection (e).

[259] ibid §262(h). If the effect of the merger on the business was included in the determination of fair value, the inefficiencies created by holdout problems that cash-out mergers and other techniques to eliminate a minority were intended to address would be reintroduced, see text to n 225 above.

[260] However, the expenses of the petitioner(s) may be charged pro rata against the value of all shares entitled to an appraisal, Del. Gen. Corp. Law, §262(j).

[261] ibid §262(i). [262] ibid §262(l).

[263] In line with this rationale, the market-out rule of §262(b)(1) Del. Gen. Corp. Law excludes appraisal rights if a trading market in the shares exists, which is assumed to be the case if the shares are listed or held by more than 2,000 shareholders. It has been observed that the importance of the appraisal remedy's liquidity function has decreased over time. Today, most business combinations that trigger an appraisal are designed as cash-out mergers and thus, by definition, entail the exit of the shareholder, Thompson (n 1) 21–3.

[264] Appraisal litigation has nevertheless increased in Delaware in recent years. For data, see CR Korsmo and M Myers, 'Appraisal Arbitrage and the Future of Public Company M&A' (2015) 92 Washington University Law Review 1551, 1567–72. The authors attribute the rise in litigation to the emergence of sophisticated petitioners, such as hedge funds that specialize in pursuing appraisals, ibid 1572–6, 1582–3.

[265] Del. Gen. Corp. Law, §262(h). However, the exclusion of 'any element of value arising from the accomplishment or expectation of the merger' from the appraisal is interpreted restrictively by the Delaware courts: 'We take this to be a very narrow exception to the appraisal process, designed to eliminate use of *pro forma* data and projections of a speculative variety relating to the completion of a merger. But elements of future value, including the nature of the enterprise, which are known or susceptible of proof as of the date of the merger and not the product of speculation, may be considered.' See *Weinberger v UOP, Inc.*, 457 A.2d 701, 713 (Del. 1983). See also Chapter 6B.I.2(d).

[266] *Lynch v Vickers Energy Corp.*, 429 A.2d 497, 501 (Del. 1981) (holding that rescission was the preferable remedy if a party had been induced to contract because of materially misleading representations, and where rescission was not feasible because it would interfere with the corporate structure, the monetary equivalent of rescission was to be paid as damages).

who instigate the proceeding, because all expenses, including for the expert witness that will generally need to be produced, are initially borne by the shareholders.[267] Another disadvantage is that the dissenting shareholder does not receive any money while the proceeding is pending and thus may be inclined to accept a merger price that is, in the shareholder's estimate, less than fair value.[268] For these reasons, shareholders may seek to pursue additional or alternative remedies. The question is then whether appraisal is exclusive or can be combined with other remedies, for example where a merger involves a controlling group allegedly breaching their fiduciary duties.

The general approach, at least in Delaware, is that minority shareholders cannot normally rely on other remedies when appraisal is available. However, certain exceptions exists to the rule of appraisal exclusivity, as acknowledged in *Weinberger v UOP*,[269] the landmark decision reforming the Delaware appraisal remedy and liberalizing the valuation techniques admissible in court that we examined in Chapter 6.[270] In *Weinberger*, the Delaware Supreme Court held that '[w]hile a plaintiff's monetary remedy ordinarily should be confined to the more liberalized appraisal proceeding herein established, ... appraisal ... may not be adequate in certain cases, particularly where fraud, misrepresentation, self-dealing, deliberate waste of corporate assets, or gross and palpable overreaching are involved'.[271] Later decisions reiterated that appraisal was not the exclusive remedy if defendants were charged with bad faith going beyond issues of 'mere inadequacy of price'.[272] Thus, the complaint must relate to defects in the process followed by the defendants, such as unfair dealing within the meaning of *Weinberger*,[273] rather than issues of valuation (fairness of the merger price). If appraisal is not the exclusive remedy, plaintiffs may claim equitable relief on fairness grounds. For example, they may seek to obtain an injunction or rescissory damages, which are generally advantageous in comparison with an appraisal.[274]

EU Directive 2004/25/EC (Takeover Directive)

Article 15—The right of squeeze-out

1. Member States shall ensure that, following a bid made to all the holders of the offeree company's securities for all of their securities, paragraphs 2 to 5 apply.
2. Member States shall ensure that an offeror is able to require all the holders of the remaining securities to sell him/her those securities at a fair price. Member States shall introduce that right in one of the following situations:

    (a) where the offeror holds securities representing not less than 90% of the capital carrying voting rights and 90% of the voting rights in the offeree company,

    or

    (b) where, following acceptance of the bid, he/she has acquired or has firmly contracted to acquire securities representing not less than 90% of the offeree company's capital carrying voting rights and 90% of the voting rights comprised in the bid.

[267] Del. Gen. Corp. Law, §262(j). For this reason, minority shareholders would prefer a class action. However, a class action may not be allowed and would, in any case, result in a smaller class than other remedies because of the requirement that shareholders have demanded appraisal, Pinto and Branson (n 78) §6.06.

[268] Some jurisdictions have addressed this problem by requiring the company to pay each dissenter the amount the company regards to be fair value, plus accrued interest, e.g. MBCA, §13.24. Under Delaware law, the company *may* pay dissenting shareholders before the conclusion of the appraisal proceeding, but it is not required to do so, Del. Gen. Corp. Law, §262(h). The purpose of the provision, which was introduced in 2016, is to allow the company to stop interest from accruing on the amount paid.

[269] *Weinberger* (n 265) 701. [270] Chapter 6B.I.2(d). [271] *Weinberger* (n 265) 714.

[272] *Rabkin v Philip A. Hunt Chem. Corp.*, 498 A.2d 1099, 1107 (Del. 1985) (pointing out that if appraisal was exclusive, 'we [would] face the anomalous result that stockholders who are eliminated without appraisal rights can bring class actions, while in other cases a squeezed-out minority is limited to an appraisal, provided there was no deception, regardless of the degree of procedural unfairness employed to take their shares', ibid 1108). For a summary of the facts of *Rabkin*, see Chapter 6B.I.2(d).

[273] See Chapter 6B.I.2(d).

[274] See text to nn 265–266 above.

In the case referred to in (a), Member States may set a higher threshold that may not, however, be higher than 95% of the capital carrying voting rights and 95% of the voting rights.

3. Member States shall ensure that rules are in force that make it possible to calculate when the threshold is reached.

   Where the offeree company has issued more than one class of securities, Member States may provide that the right of squeeze-out can be exercised only in the class in which the threshold laid down in paragraph 2 has been reached.
4. If the offeror wishes to exercise the right of squeeze-out he/she shall do so within three months of the end of the time allowed for acceptance of the bid referred to in Article 7.
5. Member States shall ensure that a fair price is guaranteed. That price shall take the same form as the consideration offered in the bid or shall be in cash. Member States may provide that cash shall be offered at least as an alternative.

   Following a voluntary bid, in both of the cases referred to in paragraph 2(a) and (b), the consideration offered in the bid shall be presumed to be fair where, through acceptance of the bid, the offeror has acquired securities representing not less than 90% of the capital carrying voting rights comprised in the bid.

   Following a mandatory bid, the consideration offered in the bid shall be presumed to be fair.

Article 16—The right of sell-out

1. Member States shall ensure that, following a bid made to all the holders of the offeree company's securities for all of their securities, paragraphs 2 and 3 apply.
2. Member States shall ensure that a holder of remaining securities is able to require the offeror to buy his/her securities from him/her at a fair price under the same circumstances as provided for in Article 15(2).
3. Article 15(3) to (5) shall apply *mutatis mutandis*.

As we have seen, under the company laws of most US states a shareholder holding a simple majority of shares can freeze out all other shareholders by merging the subsidiary into the parent and compensating the minority shareholders with cash. This is far below the threshold that most European legal systems require for the majority to be able to squeeze out the minority.[275] The Takeover Directive provides that offerors shall have the right to force the minority to sell their shares at a fair price if they hold either a minimum fraction of the target's capital carrying voting rights and the target's voting rights that must be set at between 90 and 95 per cent, or the offeror has acquired at least between 90 and 95 per cent of the capital carrying voting rights and the target's voting rights *bid for*[276] (i.e. essentially excluding the shares held by the offeror[277]). The consideration offered in a voluntary or mandatory bid is

[275] However, it may be possible to choose a transactional structure that gives the majority shareholder greater flexibility than a takeover (where, as will be discussed presently, the minority cannot be frozen out unless the majority acquires at least 90–95% of the voting capital). Notably, in the UK, the same results as in a takeover can be achieved by way of a so-called scheme of arrangement (ss 895–901 Companies Act 2006), with the important difference that a majority of 75% can force a dissenting minority to transfer their shares, provided the scheme is approved by the court. Using schemes of arrangement to squeeze out minority shareholders has been held not to amount to an evasion of the stricter takeover rules. For references, see Davies and Worthington (n 6) paras 28-69, 29-3.

[276] Takeover Directive, Art 15(2).

[277] In France and Germany, partial offers are prohibited and a takeover bid (voluntary or mandatory) must be made for *all* shares of *all* shareholders, AMF General Regulation, Art 231-6 (France); §32 WpÜG (Germany) . Hence, the two alternatives set out in Art 15(2) Takeover Directive result in differences only to the extent that the offeror already holds securities in the target (note that partial offers are permitted in France in certain cases, for example if the offer is not for more than 10% of the equity securities with voting rights of the target company, including the securities already held by the offeror, i.e. the offer falls within the scope of the simplified offer procedure pursuant to Art 233-1 AMF General Regulation, and in Germany if the offer is not aimed at an acquisition of at least 30 per cent of the target's voting rights, i.e. it is not a takeover offer within the meaning of §29 WpÜG). In the UK, partial offers require the consent of the Takeover Panel under Rule 36.1 of the Takeover Code. For a discussion of this rule and the cases when consent will typically be granted, see Kershaw (n 201) paras 6.07–6.08.

presumed to represent a fair price (however, in the case of a voluntary bid, the presumption only applies if the offeror has acquired 90 per cent or more of the capital of the target through the bid).[278] This right of the offeror is mirrored by a right of the target's remaining shareholders to require the offeror to buy their shares at a fair price. Again, Member States have to provide for such a sell-out right where the offeror holds securities representing not less than 90–95 per cent of the voting rights in the target.[279]

Member States have implemented the requirements of the Directive with certain variations.[280] In the UK, a squeeze-out right exists if the offeror in a takeover has acquired at least 90 per cent of the shares of the target. The French AMF General Regulation contains a squeeze-out right of shareholders owning 95 per cent of the company's shares. German law provides for two thresholds, a 95 per cent threshold for a general squeeze-out right of majority shareholders under corporate law and a squeeze-out right following a voluntary or mandatory offer under takeover law, and a 90 per cent threshold if the target is merged into the controlling shareholder.[281] The scope of application of the squeeze-out rules also differs between the Member States. In the UK, the right arises when an offeror acquires 90 per cent in value of the shares to which a 'takeover offer' relates, defined as an offer to acquire all the shares in a company on the same terms (or, where a company has more than one class of shares, all the shares of one or more classes on terms that are the same in relation to each class).[282] It must be exercised within three months from the last day on which the offer can be accepted (or six months if the offer is not subject to the Takeover Code).[283] Similarly, in France, the offeror can require securities not tendered in a public offer to be transferred to him within three months of the close of the offer.[284] As an alternative, and without being bound by the three-month time limit, a 95 per cent shareholder may file a so-called buy-out offer (*offre publique de retrait*) for the equity securities he does not already hold.[285] If minority shareholders remain in the company following the buy-out offer, these shareholders may be squeezed out by the majority.[286] As mentioned, shareholders in German public stock corporations who own at least 95 per cent of the share capital with voting rights also have two procedures at their disposal to eliminate a minority interest. After a voluntary or mandatory bid, they may apply to the district court Frankfurt, which has exclusive jurisdiction in the matter, to transfer the remaining shares to them.[287] In addition, the general meeting of a German public corporation has the power to adopt a squeeze-out resolution at any time, irrespective of the timing or manner of acquisition of the requisite percentage of the controlled company's share capital.[288]

The price at which the shares of non-tendering minority shareholders are transferred to the majority is closely regulated in all Member States, but again we observe differences in how each of the three jurisdictions discussed here seeks to ensure that outside shareholders

[278] Takeover Directive, Art 15(5). [279] ibid Art 16.

[280] For a comparative overview of squeeze-out and sell-out rights in Europe, see C van der Elst and L van den Steen, 'Balancing the Interests of Minority and Majority Shareholders: A Comparative Analysis of Squeeze-out and Sell-out Rights' (2009) 6 ECFR 391.

[281] UK: Companies Act 2006, s 979; France: AMF General Regulation, Art 237-1; Germany: AktG, §327a(1); WpÜG, §39a(1); UmwG [Transformation Act], §62(5). The presumption of fairness pursuant to Art 15(5) Takeover Directive only applies to the squeeze-out pursuant to §39a(1) WpÜG. For a comparison of the different squeeze-out rights, see Raiser and Veil (n 116) §74/3.

[282] Companies Act 2006, ss 974, 979(2). [283] ibid s 980(2).

[284] AMF General Regulation, Art 237-14.

[285] ibid Art 236-3. This procedure predates the Takeover Directive and was introduced by Law no 89-531 of 2 August 1989, JORF of 4 August 1989, 9822 (regulating the buyout offer) and Law no 93-1444 of 31 December 1993, JORF no 3 of 5 January 1994, 231 (introducing the possibility to squeeze out the non-accepting minority following a buyout offer). Minority shareholders also have the right to apply to the AMF to require a 95% shareholder to file a buyout offer (i.e. they have a sell-out right), AMF General Regulation, Art 236-1.

[286] ibid Art 237-1. [287] WpÜG, §39a.

[288] AktG, §327a(1). The squeeze-out right pursuant to the Transformation Act (n 281 above) follows—with the exception of the threshold of 90%—the procedure set out in the Stock Corporation Act, see UmwG, §62(5) last sentence.

are protected. The UK Companies Act 2006 provides that an offeror who gives notice to the remaining outside shareholders to purchase their shares is bound to acquire the shares on the final terms of the takeover offer.[289] Thus, if the offeror gave shareholders a choice of consideration, the same choice must be given to the non-accepting shareholders, and the same level of consideration must be offered.[290] Within six weeks from the date when the squeeze-out notice was given, minority shareholders have the right to apply to the court for an order amending the terms on which the offeror is entitled and bound to acquire the shares.[291] However, the court may not raise the price to be paid for the shares, unless the petitioning shareholder can show that the offer value is unfair.[292] The provision implements the presumption of fairness of Article 15(5) of the Takeover Directive, which is triggered when 90 per cent of the shareholders have accepted the offer.[293] The non-accepting shareholders, therefore, face a heavy burden to overcome the presumption, which usually requires a showing of a flawed bid process. In practice, shareholders were successful where they could demonstrate that the decision of the board to recommend the offer was based on inadequate advice[294] or the accepting shareholders were not independent of the bidder.[295] On the other hand, the Companies Act facilitates a review of the fairness of the offer price by stipulating that no order for costs or expenses may be made against a non-accepting shareholder, unless the application was unnecessary, improper or vexatious, there was an unreasonable delay in making the application, or the conduct of the shareholder in conducting the proceedings was unreasonable.[296]

French law implements the fair price guarantee of Article 15(5) of the Takeover Directive as follows. If the squeeze-out follows a regular takeover offer, as opposed to a buy-out offer,[297] the offeror must have informed the AMF of the intention to reserve the right to implement a squeeze-out within the applicable three-month period, provided the takeover offer results in an acquisition of the required percentage of shares.[298] The offeror must provide a valuation study of the securities of the target, which must be reviewed by an independent expert,[299] unless the squeeze-out is made in the wake of a takeover offer following the 'standard procedure', i.e. an offer by a person (or persons acting in concert) holding less than half of the shares of the target, and the non-accepting shareholders receive the same cash consideration that was offered in the takeover bid.[300] Thus, in this case, the high acceptance rate implies the fairness of the squeeze-out price. If the squeeze-out follows a buy-out offer, the price to be paid to the minority must be at least equivalent to the buy-out offer. It has to be higher if subsequent events affect the valuation of the securities.[301] The AMF reviews whether the minority's compensation is fair and equitable and has been determined using relevant and sufficient valuation criteria.[302] The AMF's assessment can be challenged in court. The buy-out offer must be accompanied by a valuation study using a multi-criteria valuation method.[303] The target's securities have to be valued at the time of the filing of

[289] Companies Act 2006, s 981(2). [290] ibid s 981(3). [291] ibid s 986(1).
[292] ibid s 986(4)(a). [293] See text to n 278 above.
[294] *Re Lifecare International plc* (1989) 5 BCC 755, 757; *Re Chez Nico (Restaurants) Ltd* [1991] BCC 736, 751–3.
[295] *Re Bugle Press* [1961] Ch 270, 284–7.
[296] Companies Act 2006, s 986(5). An application has been defined as 'vexatious' 'where it is clear that there was no possible ground upon which the application could succeed'; see Kershaw (n 201) para 2.24, fn 28, citing Hoffmann J (as he then was) in the first instance judgment in *Re Britoil Plc* (unreported).
[297] See text to nn 285–286 above. [298] AMF General Regulation, Art 237-15.
[299] Valuation is based on a multi-factor approach that takes the value of the company's assets, its past earnings, market value, and business prospects into account: ibid Art 237-16(II). For the requirement to provide an assessment by an independent expert, see the Recommendations of the AMF of 28 September 2006 and 27 July 2010 and Merle (n 135) para 772.
[300] AMF General Regulation, Art 237-16(I). The standard offer procedure is laid down in Arts 232-1 to 232-13 AMF General Regulation and applies unless the offer comes within the scope of Art 233-1, in which case a simplified offer procedure may be used.
[301] ibid Art 237-8(2). [302] Cour d'Appel de Paris, 19 December 2000, *RJDA* 4/01, no 457.
[303] AMF General Regulation, Art 237-2(2). The valuation method is the same as that described above, n 299.

the draft buy-out offer with the AMF, but not (again) at the time when the squeeze-out is implemented (in contrast to valuation—if required—in a squeeze-out following a takeover offer),[304] unless valuation-relevant events intervene after that time. This approach has been criticized by commentators[305] and was challenged by the French Association for the Defence of the Interests of Minority Shareholders (*L'Association de Défense des Actionnaires Minoritaires*), but the Cour de Cassation held that it was compatible with both the relevant French legislation and the protection of property pursuant to the European Convention on Human Rights.[306]

As far as German law is concerned, we have observed that two techniques to eliminate minority shareholders are available to the majority: squeeze-out by court order after a takeover offer and by resolution of the general meeting. The two techniques display several differences, in particular with regard to the type of permissible consideration and the procedure to review the compensation of the outside shareholders. As required by the Takeover Directive, the consideration offered in a squeeze-out pursuant to the Securities Acquisition and Takeover Act must be of the same type as that offered in the takeover. In addition, cash shall always be offered as an alternative.[307] The 'fairness' of the price is assessed by the district court Frankfurt, unless the presumption of Article 15(5) of the Takeover Directive applies.[308] On the other hand, in a squeeze-out procedure according to the Stock Corporation Act, the price at which the minority's shares are transferred is determined by the majority shareholder.[309] The Stock Corporation Act provides that the consideration must be in cash, 'take into account the circumstances of the company at the time of the adoption of the resolution by the general meeting',[310] and the adequacy of the consideration must be reviewed by a court-appointed auditor.[311] The act does not prescribe a particular valuation method. Any standard method, for example discounted cash flow analysis or—more common in Germany—the capitalization of earnings[312] is generally accepted by the courts.[313] If the company is stock exchange listed, the stock market price of the shares represents a lower limit of what has to be paid to the minority shareholders.[314]

Shareholders do not have standing to bring an action for annulment of the squeeze-out resolution by the general meeting[315] on the ground that the compensation offered by the majority shareholder is inadequate.[316] The legislator was concerned that outside shareholders might otherwise use intractable valuation questions to prevent a legitimate and economically

[304] The offeror may either request that the squeeze-out be implemented once the buyout offer has closed or reserve the right to apply for a squeeze-out: ibid Art 237-2(1). In the latter case, the offeror must inform the AMF within ten trading days of the close of the offer of the intention to proceed with the squeeze-out and the price it proposes to pay for the minority shares, Art 237-8(1), (2). The AMF then reviews the terms of the squeeze-out and determines the date when it shall become effective, Art 237-8(3).

[305] For example, Merle (n 135) para 772.

[306] Cass com, 29 April 1997 (*Sogénal*), *Droit des sociétés* 1997, no 114.

[307] WpÜG, §39a(3).

[308] ibid. The presumption has been implemented by §39a(3) third sentence, stipulating that the consideration 'shall be considered to be fair where the offeror has acquired, on account of the offer, shares representing not less than 90 per cent of the share capital comprised in the bid'.

[309] AktG, §327b(1).

[310] ibid §327(1) first sentence.

[311] ibid §327c(2).

[312] The difference between the two methods is that DCF analysis discounts future free cash flows (the amount of cash that can be paid out to shareholders because it is not required for operations or investments to expand the company's asset base), whereas the earnings value method discounts future earnings.

[313] Raiser and Veil (n 116) §62/87.

[314] Constitutional law requires that the compensation received by the minority shareholders is not lower than the stock market price, see n 221 and accompanying text for an analogous interpretation of the 'equitable price' in a mandatory bid. See also Raiser and Veil (n 116) §62/83-84, §66/13. The stock market price is calculated as the average price, weighted by turnover, in the three months before the announcement of the intention to squeeze out the minority shareholders, unless the requisite resolution of the general meeting is adopted significantly later (i.e. typically more than half a year). In this case, the subsequent development of the stock market price may be taken into account, BGHZ 186, 229 (*Stollwerck*).

[315] AktG, §§243–246. The action for annulment is discussed briefly in section B.III above and in greater detail in Chapter 5C.III.1.

[316] AktG, §327f first sentence.

sensible squeeze-out resolution from being entered into the commercial register and thus becoming valid (as had indeed happened in other contexts under the law before adoption of the 1965 Stock Corporation Act).[317] However, similar to the Delaware appraisal remedy, outside shareholders can challenge the adequacy of the price in appraisal proceedings (*Spruchverfahren*).[318] Any outside shareholder (i.e. any shareholder whose shares are transferred to the majority) has standing to apply for an appraisal of their shares.[319] The court's decision is binding on all outside shareholders, including those who do not participate in the proceedings.[320] The procedure displays a number of differences to Delaware law, which redress some of the limitations of the Delaware appraisal remedy that we discussed above.[321] Importantly, as in the UK, the costs of the proceedings are generally borne by the majority shareholder.[322] In addition, the outside shareholders, including those who apply to the court for an appraisal, can continue to claim payment of the amount offered by the majority shareholder.[323] Incentive distortions as under Delaware law, where shareholders may refrain from filing a petition for appraisal even though they consider the compensation to be inadequate, since they would otherwise need to forgo any payment while the appraisal proceeding is pending, therefore do not arise.[324] This explains that appraisal proceedings are common in Germany.[325] Furthermore, the willingness of companies to settle is high, because proceedings are lengthy and cost rules, as discussed, favour the petitioners.[326] This results in frequent substantial improvements in the compensation offered to outside shareholders.[327]

III. Fiduciary constraints

Control transactions may be subject to fiduciary review going beyond an appraisal of the fairness of the price received by minority shareholders. In this section, we will address the question whether the majority owes fiduciary or fiduciary-like duties to the minority in control transactions, with the consequence that minority shareholders can bring an action—possibly a class action—seeking relief, for example rescissory damages, or challenging the legality of the merger itself if these duties have been breached.[328]

[317] The outside shareholders' shares are transferred to the majority shareholder upon registration of the resolution in the commercial register, ibid §327e(3). While an action for annulment is pending, the court of the commercial register will generally refuse to register any resolutions, unless the company successfully applies to the court to remove the block on the commercial register pursuant to §246a. For a discussion of these issues, see Chapter 5C.III.1 and Raiser and Veil (n 116) §62/92.

[318] AktG, §327f. Detailed rules are laid down in a separate act, the Spruchverfahrensgesetz (SpruchG) [Act on Appraisal Proceedings] of 12 June 2003, BGBl I, 838.

[319] SpruchG, §3 no 2. [320] ibid §13. [321] Text to nn 264–268.

[322] Gesetz über Kosten der freiwilligen Gerichtsbarkeit für Gerichte und Notare [Law Governing the Costs in Matters of Voluntary Jurisdiction] of 23 July 2013, BGBl I, 2586, §23 no 14. However, the court may order the shareholders to bear some or all of the costs, SpruchG, §15(1). In addition, the default rule does not apply to expenses incurred by shareholders out of court, unless it is fair and equitable to impose these costs on the majority shareholder, ibid §15(2). In particular, if minority shareholders decide to obtain a second valuation study (in addition to the study of the court-appointed auditor pursuant to §327c(2) AktG), they may only be able to recover the costs if the study is necessary to respond to disputed findings of the valuation study by the court-appointed auditor or to a valuation study submitted by the majority shareholder, see D Kubis in W Goette and M Habersack (eds), *Münchener Kommentar zum Aktiengesetz, vol 5* (4th edn, CH Beck 2015) SpruchG §15, para 23.

[323] Payment is due with the registration of the squeeze-out resolution in the commercial register, B Grunewald in Goette and Habersack (n 322) AktG §327e para 14. Since shareholders have standing to claim appraisal if they are shareholders at the time of registration, rather than the time when the appraisal application is filed (SpruchG, §3 sentence 1, no 2 and sentence 2), they can accept the compensation offered, relinquish their shares and file for an appraisal within three months from registration (ibid §4); see Kubis (n 322) SpruchG §3, para 11.

[324] See text to n 268 above. [325] Kubis (n 322) SpruchG Vorbemerkung, paras 6–8.

[326] According to D Lorenz, 'Das Spruchverfahren: dickes Ende oder nur viel Lärm um nichts?' (2012) Die Aktiengesellschaft 284, 287, the average length of proceedings is seven years.

[327] On average around 16%; see ibid.

[328] Claiming relief other than an assessment of the fairness of the merger price requires that appraisal is not available or not the exclusive remedy. This point has been discussed above, text to nn 269–274.

Initially, the Delaware courts held that controlling shareholders who eliminated the minority in a cash-out merger had to meet the burden of proving entire fairness and, in addition, that the merger was not accomplished solely to freeze-out the minority but served a valid business purpose.[329] An application of the entire fairness test is consistent with the structure of fiduciary duties under Delaware law (and the laws of other US states). As we saw in Chapter 6, the duty of loyalty, which Delaware law imposes not only on directors but also on controlling shareholders, demands entire fairness if a transaction gives rise to a conflict of interest.[330] In a freeze-out merger, the acquirer has gained control of the target, for example through a public offer, and then merges the target into itself, using cash as consideration. The acquirer, standing on both sides of the transaction, is evidently subject to a conflict of interest, which warrants enhanced scrutiny in the form of the entire fairness test. The business purpose test, on the other hand, is not a well-developed concept of Delaware law. The Delaware General Corporation Law is silent on the question whether a merger must have a valid business purpose, and the courts never developed a workable definition of 'business purpose'. The first decision of the Supreme Court of Delaware that espoused the business purpose test, *Singer v. Magnavox*,[331] simply stated that a merger, 'made for the sole purpose of freezing out minority stockholders, was an abuse of the corporate process'.[332] In *Tanzer v. International General Industries, Inc.*,[333] the Supreme Court was more specific. It held that a merger designed primarily for the purpose of benefiting the parent was permissible under Delaware law, provided the parent company had a business reason for the merger, for example to facilitate financing, and did not solely intend 'to rid itself of unwanted minority shareholders in the subsidiary'.[334] As interpreted in *Tanzer*, the business purpose test was largely inconsequential. It was not difficult for a controller to establish a valid business purpose, since at least efficiency gains could generally be expected to result from a freeze-out transaction. A few years after *Tanzer*, the Supreme Court therefore took a logical step in *Weinberger v. UOP* and eliminated the test, explaining: 'In view of the fairness test which has long been applicable to parent-subsidiary mergers… the expanded appraisal remedy now available to shareholders, and the broad discretion of the Chancellor to fashion such relief as the facts of a given case may dictate, we do not believe that any additional meaningful protection is afforded minority shareholders by the business purpose requirement'.[335]

The entire fairness test that we discussed in Chapter 6, of course, remains applicable.[336] As we said there, entire fairness consists of two elements, fair dealing and fair price. In a control transaction subject to entire fairness, such as a freeze-out merger,[337] 'the ultimate burden of proof is on the majority shareholder to show by a preponderance of the evidence that the transaction is fair'.[338] However, the Supreme Court of Delaware in *Weinberger* also held that the burden of proof reverts to the plaintiff 'where corporate action has been approved by an informed vote of a majority of the minority shareholders'.[339] Importantly,

[329] *Singer v Magnavox*, 380 A.2d 969 (Del. 1977).

[330] Chapter 6B.I.2(d) and C.I.2.

[331] 380 A.2d 969 (Del. 1977).

[332] ibid 980. The Supreme Court in *Singer* acknowledged that the business purpose test 'immediately leads to such questions as: "Whose purpose?" or "Whose business?" Is it that of the corporations whose shares are (or were) held by the minority? If so, it may well be that the business purpose of that company (qua company) is advanced by the merger, but that could be an academic result if the complainants (as here) are no longer shareholders because they have been cashed-out. On the other hand, if the corporation in which the complainants held shares "vanishes" in the merger, inquiry as to purpose may be unrealistic if not academic. And if the business purpose of the parent (or dominant) corporation should be examined (as defendants argue), minority shareholders of the subsidiary (or controlled corporation) may have undue difficulty in raising and maintaining the issue'. ibid 976. Because these questions were irrelevant to the resolution of the case at hand, the Supreme Court left them unanswered.

[333] 379 A.2d 1121 (Del. 1977).

[334] ibid 1124.

[335] *Weinberger v UOP, Inc.* (n 265) 715.

[336] Chapter 6B.I.2(d).

[337] Not all control transactions require entire fairness, see text to nn 350–351 below.

[338] *Weinberger* (n 265) 703.

[339] ibid.

majority of the minority approval only affects the allocation of the burden of proof. As opposed to general conflict of interest inquiries, where approval by a majority of disinterested shareholders leads to a reinstatement of the business judgment rule and hence both a reversion of the burden of proof and a shift in the standard of review from entire fairness to the waste claim,[340] the entire fairness standard is retained in the present context. This reflects the heightened risk of coercion or other forms of influence on the process of voting in the presence of a controlling shareholder. For example, controlling shareholders may implicitly or explicitly threaten to change the company's dividend policy or to vote against future transactions that are in the best interest of the company and thus influence the minority vote in their favour.[341] Furthermore, in order to be valid, the minority vote must not only be free of coercion, but also informed. This requires that all material facts relevant to the transaction are disclosed.[342] The burden of establishing full disclosure is on the defendant.[343]

A second possibility to shift the burden of proof, also mentioned in *Weinberger*, is the appointment of a negotiating committee composed of directors of the controlled company who are independent from the controlling shareholder.[344] Again, entire fairness as the applicable standard of review is retained in order to take account of the fact that a controlling shareholder, because of its dominant position in the company, may influence the conduct of outside directors, even where these directors are formally regarded as independent.[345] It should be noted that independence is used with a different meaning in most corporate governance codes today, which typically interpret business or other relationships with corporate insiders as indications of lack of independence.[346] Under Delaware law, in contrast, there is a presumption that directors are independent. In order to rebut the presumption, plaintiffs must show that the controlling shareholder dominated or controlled the directors.[347] This is the case if the directors 'are beholden to the controlling person' and act 'in such a way as to comport with the wishes or interests of the corporation (or persons) doing the controlling'.[348] In addition, 'the majority shareholder must not dictate the terms of the merger ... [and] the special [negotiating] committee

[340] See our discussion in Chapter 6C.I.2.

[341] *Citron v E.I. Du Pont de Nemours & Co.*, 584 A.2d 490, 502 (Del. Ch. 1990), holding that '[e]ven where no coercion is intended, shareholders voting on a parent subsidiary merger might perceive that their disapproval could risk retaliation of some kind by the controlling stockholder ... At the very least, the potential for that perception, and its possible impact upon a shareholder vote, could never be fully eliminated. Consequently, in a merger between the corporation and its controlling stockholder—even one negotiated by disinterested, independent directors—no court could be certain whether the transaction terms fully approximate what truly independent parties would have achieved in an arm's length negotiation. Given that uncertainty, a court might well conclude that even minority shareholders who have ratified a parent-subsidiary merger need procedural protections beyond those afforded by full disclosure of all material facts'.

[342] *Weinberger* (n 265) 703.

[343] ibid. In *Weinberger*, the cash-out merger was conditional on a majority of the minority approving the merger. However, the burden of proof did not shift to the plaintiff by reason of the minority shareholder vote, because the court found that material information (a study identifying a price range at which the merger was regarded as feasible and beneficial to the majority) had been withheld from the minority, ibid 709.

[344] ibid 709, fn 7.

[345] This is comparable to the approach of the Delaware courts to independent litigation committees that decide on the continuation of a derivative lawsuit, see *Zapata Corp v Maldonado*, 430 A.2d 779 (Del. 1981), discussed in Chapter 8C.II.3.

[346] Chapter 4C.III.

[347] *Aronson v Lewis*, 473 A.2d 805, 815–17 (Del. 1984). *Aronson* is a case dealing with demand futility in a derivative action, which we will discuss in Chapter 8C.II.3. The court's definition of independence is of general relevance and, for example, applied to going private transactions by a controlling shareholder, *In re MFW Shareholders Litigation*, 67 A.3d 496, 509 (Del. Ch. 2013).

[348] *Aronson v Lewis* (n 348) 815–16.

must have real bargaining power that it can exercise with the majority shareholder on an arm's length basis'.[349]

A controlling shareholders could try to avoid the demanding standard of entire fairness that applies in a freeze-out merger by structuring the transaction as a tender offer aimed at buying enough of the remaining minority shares to be able to implement a short-form merger, which requires the parent corporation to own at least 90 per cent of the outstanding shares of the subsidiary.[350] The advantage of structuring the transaction in this way is that the acquirer formally does not have a conflict of interest. The acquiring company does not stand on both sides of the transaction, as acquirer and controlling shareholder of the target, but deals directly with the target's minority shareholders. Consequently, Delaware law does not require the parent company to establish entire fairness in a short-form merger, provided the offer is not structurally coercive and full disclosure has been made.[351] Nevertheless, it may be argued that a heightened level of scrutiny is warranted. While minority shareholders, of course, are free not to tender if they believe the price is inadequate, they face a form of prisoner's dilemma.[352] If they do not tender, but a sufficient number of other minority shareholders sell, they could be forced out of the company in the second-step short-form merger at an even less attractive price. Even if the acquirer does not reach the necessary threshold of 90 per cent ownership, the non-tendering minority shareholders may find themselves in a thinly traded company and thus in a worse position than the shareholders who tendered. For this reason, the Delaware courts impose additional requirements on tender offers by controlling shareholders who desire to accomplish a second-step short-form merger. In order to minimize the distorting influence of the tendering process on shareholder choice, the Court of Chancery held in *In re Pure Resources, Inc., Shareholders Litigation* that a tender offer by a controlling shareholder will be considered as non-coercive (and hence not triggering entire fairness review) only when:[353]

> 1) it is subject to a non-waivable majority of the minority tender condition; 2) the controlling stockholder promises to consummate a prompt [short-form] merger at the same price if it obtains more than 90% of the shares; and 3) the controlling stockholder has made no retributive threats ... The informational and timing advantages possessed by controlling stockholders also

[349] *Kahn v Lynch Communication Systems, Inc.*, 638 A.2d 1110, 1117 (Del. 1994) (quoting *Rabkin v Olin Corp.*, 16 Del. J. Corp. L. 851, 861–2 (Del. Ch. 1990)). In other words, the independent negotiating committee must 'appropriately simulate ... a third-party transaction, where negotiations are conducted at arm's-length and there is no compulsion to reach an agreement': ibid 1121. This test was not met in *Kahn*, because the negotiating committee was coerced into accepting the acquirer's offer by the threat that the acquirer would proceed with an unfriendly tender offer at a lower price if the target did not agree to the price offered. On remand, the Delaware Court of Chancery found that despite the acquirer's coercive behaviour, the transaction was entirely fair: *Kahn v Lynch Communication Systems, Inc.*, 1995 WL 301403 (Del. Ch. 1995). The court held that 'the absence of certain elements of fair dealing does not mandate a decision that the transaction was not entirely fair': ibid 1. In the present case, the acquirer had sustained the burden of establishing entire fairness because the initiation and timing of the transaction were responsive to the target's changed business needs, the independent negotiating committee was fully informed, and the merger price was entirely fair. The plaintiff appealed again, and the Supreme Court now upheld the decision of the Court of Chancery, *Kahn v Lynch Communication Systems, Inc.*, 669 A.2d 79 (Del. 1995). In arriving at this conclusion, the court distinguished between coercion with respect to the dealings of the negotiating committee, and coercion with respect to 'the transaction as a whole': ibid 86. Only coercive conduct directed at the selling shareholders, as opposed to the committee, which had a material influence on the decision to sell prevented a finding of entire fairness. 'In this case', the court held, the acquirer 'offered cash for all the minority shares and paid cash for all shares tendered. Clearly there was no coercion exerted which was material to this aspect of the transaction, and thus no finding of *per se* liability is required'. ibid.

[350] Del. Gen. Corp. Law, §253. On short-form mergers, see text to nn 233–235 above.

[351] *Glassman v Unocal Exploration Corp.*, 777 A.2d 242 (Del. 2001). Given that the short form merger statute authorizes the elimination of minority shareholders by a summary process that dispenses with formalities such as prior notice or the requirement of a shareholder vote, the court argued that it would be meaningless to require fair dealing. Consequently, 'absent fraud or illegality, the only recourse for a minority stockholder who is dissatisfied with the merger consideration is appraisal': ibid 243.

[352] *In re Pure Resources, Inc., Shareholders Litigation*, 808 A.2d 421, 442 (Del. Ch. 2002).

[353] ibid 445.

> require some countervailing protection if the minority is to truly be afforded the opportunity to make an informed, voluntary tender decision. In this regard, the majority stockholder owes a duty to permit the independent directors on the target board both free rein and adequate time to react to the tender offer, by (at the very least) hiring their own advisors, providing the minority with a recommendation as to the advisability of the offer, and disclosing adequate information for the minority to make an informed judgment. For their part, the independent directors have a duty to undertake these tasks in good faith and diligently, and to pursue the best interests of the minority.

A further question is whether the acquiring company can implement procedural safeguards that address the conflict of interest and threat of coercion existing in freeze-out mergers and tender offers so comprehensively that the consequence is not only a reversal of the burden of proof, but also that the standard of review shifts from entire fairness and the *Pure* duties, respectively, to business judgment review. The Delaware courts answered the question in the affirmative in *In re MFW Shareholders Litigation*.[354] In this case, the acquirer, a holding company that owned 43 per cent of MFW, offered to purchase the rest of the target's equity in a going private merger and undertook 'not [to] proceed with any going private transaction that was not approved: (i) by an independent special committee; and (ii) by a vote of a majority of the stockholders unaffiliated with the controlling stockholder'.[355] The Court of Chancery held that the dual approval condition had a 'cleansing effect' under the business judgment rule. The Supreme Court agreed, describing the operation of the protection mechanism as follows:[356]

> [I]n controller buy-outs, the business judgment standard of review will be applied *if and only if*: (i) the controller conditions the procession of the transaction on the approval of both a Special Committee and a majority of the minority stockholders; (ii) the Special Committee is independent; (iii) the Special Committee is empowered to freely select its own advisors and to say no definitively; (iv) the Special Committee meets its duty of care in negotiating a fair price; (v) the vote of the minority is informed; and (vi) there is no coercion of the minority.
>
> If a plaintiff that can plead a reasonably conceivable set of facts showing that any or all of those enumerated conditions did not exist, that complaint would state a claim for relief that would entitle the plaintiff to proceed and conduct discovery. If, after discovery, triable issues of fact remain about whether either or both of the dual procedural protections were established, or if established were effective, the case will proceed to a trial in which the court will conduct an entire fairness review.

In the view of the Court of Chancery, a transactional structure that is conditioned upon both majority of the minority approval and approval by an independent negotiating committee is fundamentally different from one with only one of these procedural protections.[357] It replicates the protections of a third-party merger and improves the position of minority shareholders in several respects, compared with a going private transaction that requires *either* the establishment of a special committee *or* majority of the minority approval. First, the dual protection structure gives independent directors an incentive to negotiate effectively on behalf of the minority, because they know that their recommendation will be subject to scrutiny and disapproval by the minority shareholders.[358] Secondly, importantly, the acquirer

354 67 A.3d 496 (Del. Ch. 2013), *aff'd*, *Kahn v M & F Worldwide Corp.*, 88 A.3d 635 (Del. 2014).

355 *In re MFW Shareholders Litigation* (n 354) 499.

356 *Kahn v M & F Worldwide Corp.* (n 354) 645–6.

357 *In re MFW Shareholders Litigation* (n 354) 528.

358 ibid 528–9, observing that 'independent directors are presumed to be motivated to do their duty with fidelity, like most other people, and ... have a more self-protective interest in retaining their reputations as faithful, diligent fiduciaries. The requirement that a majority of the minority approve the special committee's recommendation enhances both motivations, because most directors will want to procure a deal that their minority stockholders think is a favorable one, and virtually all will not want to suffer the reputational embarrassment of repudiation at the ballot box. That is especially so in a market where many independent directors serve on several boards, and where institutional investors and their voting advisors, such as ISS and Glass Lewis, have computer-aided memory banks available to remind them of the past record of directors when considering whether to vote for them or withhold votes at annual meetings of companies on whose boards they serve'.

in *In re MFW Shareholders Litigation* had made it clear that it would not proceed with *any* going private transaction if it did not have the support of the special committee, including a tender offer directly to the minority shareholders.[359] Thus, the special committee had the power to simply say 'no' to an inadequate offer, and the controlling shareholder could not coerce the committee into approving a merger by threatening a tender offer at a lower price.[360] Thirdly, for the same reason, the minority shareholders are not in a prisoner's dilemma. They have a say on the going private transaction *as a whole* in the context of a merger. A merger is intrinsically less coercive than a tender offer because shareholders can vote no and still receive the merger consideration if the majority of the minority approves the transaction.[361]

While not relevant to the case, *In re MFW Shareholders Litigation* also illustrates how transaction planners can avoid an entire fairness review in a two-step tender offer/short-form merger transaction. Analogous to the dual protection mechanism in *In re MFW Shareholders Litigation*, controlling shareholders would need to combine the burden-of-proof-shifting tender offer protections enunciated in *In re Pure Resources*[362] with the establishment of an independent committee that has the right to say 'no' to the tender offer.[363] As in *In re MFW Shareholders Litigation*, the right to say 'no' means that the controller undertakes not to pursue the going private transaction if the independent negotiating committee does not approve the proposal. If the committee gives its approval and the tender offer is non-coercive in the sense of *Pure*, the business judgment rule applies and the minority shareholders are limited to appraisal. If the committee does not approve the proposal and the controller nevertheless proceeds with the tender offer, the transaction is subject to entire fairness review.[364]

General fiduciary constraints play a less prominent role in our three European jurisdictions. This is not to say that a majority shareholder does not owe fiduciary duties to the minority in control transactions. We have seen that the courts have recognized the existence of certain fiduciary-type constraints on majority power in all three jurisdictions (in the UK, these constraints are not fiduciary in nature within the meaning of English law, but they perform a similar function as in France and Germany, albeit with a more limited scope).[365] In principle, these constraints apply in control transactions as in transactions not involving a sale of control. In particular, the German duty to have due regard for the interests of the minority shareholders is sufficiently broad and flexible to lend itself to a review of transactions between a bidder and a target company already majority-owned by the bidder. The French doctrine of *abus de majorité* and the understanding of shareholder rights primarily as proprietary rights in English law, subject only to the constraint of acting bona fide for the benefit of the company, on the other hand, are less suitable if the goal is to ensure that minority shareholders receive a fair price in control transactions. As noted above, *abus de majorité* requires that the transaction is contrary to the interests of the company (here the target of the acquisition) *and* the majority shareholder acts *solely* to obtain a benefit to the detriment of the minority.[366] These two conditions, which have to be met cumulatively, are difficult to establish for an objecting minority shareholder. In particular, it will often be possible to argue that the elimination of the minority is in the interest of the target company.[367] In practice, the doctrine, accordingly, does not seem to play a role in mergers and acquisitions.

359 ibid 508. 360 This had happened in *Kahn v Lynch*; see n 349 above.

361 *In re MFW Shareholders Litigation* (n 354) 532. 362 See text to n 353 above.

363 RJ Gilson and JN Gordon, 'Controlling Controlling Shareholders' (2003) 152 University of Pennsylvania Law Review 785, 838–40.

364 ibid 839–40. 365 Section B.I, III–IV above.

366 Section B.IV and Conac (n 132) 366–7.

367 See text to n 334 above for a similar deficiency of the business purpose test established by the Supreme Court of Delaware in *Singer v Magnavox* (n 329).

Similarly, it is unlikely that the requirement under English law to act bona fide for the benefit of the company provides an effective mechanism for outside shareholders to challenge the terms of a control transaction. Case law has dealt with the question whether shareholders could amend the articles of association of a company to allow a 90 per cent majority to buy out the minority[368] or introduce a drag-along right forcing the minority to sell if the majority sold 50 per cent or more of the voting rights in the company.[369] As we have seen, the legal principles developed by the courts are permissive. While certain ambiguities exist, the *Shuttleworth* test of 1927[370] still represents the general approach of English law. According to this test, courts will not interfere with shareholder decision-making, including decisions that encroach upon the rights of the minority, if the majority can give a plausible explanation why the decision is for the benefit of the company.[371] As under French law, it therefore comes down to the question whether a business reason can be found for the elimination of the minority, which generally does not pose difficulties for a controlling shareholder. It has been suggested in the literature that oppressive behaviour may lie in the fact that a minority is squeezed out 'at an obvious undervalue'.[372] Arguably, this type of oppression is confined to exceptional cases, since the largely subjective *Shuttleworth* test would require that the price could not be substantiated by any reasonable valuation method.[373] That the common law does not regulate control transactions adequately is supported by the perceptions of unfairness and abuse of power that characterized the UK takeover market in the decades before the adoption of the Takeover Code. Transactions were criticized for favouring institutional investors to the detriment of retail investors, lacking transparency and giving rise to erratic price movements.[374] The duty to act bona fide for the benefit of the company as a whole was evidently not able to address these problems.

The German approach, in spite of its potentially greater flexibility, has not fared much better than the French and English doctrines. This is illustrated by *Audi/NSU*, a case in which the Bundesgerichtshof was asked to review the takeover of Audi/NSU by Volkswagen, the German car manufacturer.[375] Volkswagen had initially proposed an exchange ratio unfavourable to the minority shareholders of Audi/NSU. The plaintiff therefore sold his Audi/NSU shares on the stock exchange. In response to a legal challenge by another shareholder, Volkswagen later improved the exchange ratio. The plaintiff argued that Volkswagen, as majority shareholder of Audi/NSU, owed a fiduciary duty to the outside shareholders in the target company, which required Volkswagen to advise the minority shareholders against a sale of their shares in light of the pending legal challenge. The court dismissed the claim, holding that fiduciary duties did not exist among shareholders. This case predates the court's decisions in *Linotype* and *Girmes*, discussed above,[376] where the court acknowledged that shareholders were subject to a duty to have due regard for the interests of the company and the other shareholders in the exercise of their rights. Thus, we may speculate that *Audi/NSU* would be decided differently today. However, the important point is that the restrictive approach of the Bundesgerichtshof in takeovers has never been explicitly revised. This is a function of both the small size of the market for corporate control in Germany, and hence the limited opportunity of the court to refine its case law, and the adoption of the Securities Acquisition and Takeover Act that implemented the Takeover Directive and now covers this

[368] *Brown v British Abrasive Wheel Co Ltd* [1919] 1 Ch 290, discussed in n 17 above and the accompanying text. More recently, this question was also addressed by the High Court of Australia in *Gambotto v WCP Ltd* (1995) 182 CLR 432.

[369] *Re Charterhouse Capital Ltd* [2015] EWCA Civ 536, discussed in the text to n 25 above.

[370] *Shuttleworth v Cox Brothers and Co (Maidenhead) Ltd* [1927] 2 KB 9.

[371] Section B.I.1.

[372] Davies and Worthington (n 6) para 19-8, fn 30.

[373] See ibid, quoting *Shuttleworth* [1927] 2 KB 9, 18. The resolution must be such 'that no reasonable man could consider it for the benefit of the company as a whole'.

[374] Kershaw (n 201) paras 3.46–3.61, 6.46.

[375] BGH JZ 1976, 561.

[376] Section B.III.

situation. As a consequence, the company law principles are not well developed and ill-suited to function as a regulatory backstop where the takeover regime does not apply.[377]

Thus, none of the European jurisdictions has produced a set of rules comparable to the broad entire fairness standard of Delaware law and its finely tuned qualifications—majority of the minority approval and appointment of an independent negotiating committee, which shift the burden of proof and, in combination, the standard of review. It may be argued that such a fairly complex system of procedural and substantive rules is neither efficient nor necessary in the three European jurisdictions that we have analysed. It is not efficient because the rules, as shown, are continuously evolving and hence come at the price of reduced legal certainty and consequently increased transaction costs. It is not necessary because the Takeover Directive provides for broad minority protection, particularly in the form of the mandatory bid rule and a demanding definition of a fair price if the acquirer makes use of its squeeze-out right. The *Weinberger* entire fairness test and its qualifications are a functional substitute of the mechanisms promulgated by the Takeover Directive that, as a broad standard, may be criticized as being inferior to the rule-based approach that obtains in Europe.[378] On the other hand, the mandatory bid rule and ancillary mechanisms are of relatively recent provenance, especially in France and Germany, and in all three European countries the market for corporate control was underregulated before their adoption. This was not only a consequence of the much smaller size of the European markets, compared with the US, and hence less impetus for regulatory reform, but also of the reluctance or outright refusal of the courts to assess the actions of shareholders through the lens of entire fairness or a comparable standard.

Furthermore, it could be argued that the different regulatory techniques that we have described in this chapter reveal a deeper difference in the understanding of the nature of shares in the United States on the one hand, and the three European jurisdictions on the other hand. US law embraces an idea of share ownership that is informed by finance theory. Shares are seen as future income streams with a present value that is a function of the risk-free rate of return and the risk of the respective asset. The stocks of companies with a similar risk profile are perfect substitutes. Hence, an investor generally does not have a legally cognizable interest in remaining a shareholder of a particular company, provided the financial interests of the investor are safeguard. This conceptualization of share ownership explains why the default remedy in the United States is appraisal, with entire fairness as a backstop if the transaction is tainted by a conflict of interest (that is, in a freeze-out merger or a tender offer by a controlling shareholder, followed by a second-step short-form merger) that has not been 'cleansed' as set out in *In re MFW Shareholders Litigation*. In contrast, the three European jurisdictions adopt a proprietary perspective. This is particularly clear in the UK, where the proprietary understanding of the position of shareholders has predetermined the approach of the courts to reviewing control transactions that are not subject to the Takeover Code. It has also had an influence on the development of legal doctrines in France and Germany, where the courts, with mixed results, took recourse to the 'blunt' tool of protection of property as a fundamental right in order to amplify the provisions of the Takeover Directive and achieve a modicum of investor protection outside the scope of the Directive.[379]

[377] See Raiser and Veil (n 116) §11/64, pointing out that it is not clear whether a general corporate law principle exists independent of the sharing rules of takeover regulation that would require the equal treatment of all outside investors in control transactions.

[378] On the advantages and disadvantages of regulating by means of standards versus rules, see L Kaplow, 'Rules versus Standards: an Economic Analysis' (1992) 42 Duke Law Journal 557, and Chapter 5B.

[379] See, e.g., Cass com, 29 April 1997 (*Sogénal*) (n 306) and the German decisions discussed in Chapter 5B.III.

8

Enforcement

A. Introduction

It has been argued that the quality of corporate law enforcement—law in action—rather than the content of the legal rules—law on the books—determines whether investors are well protected.[1] Thus, on this view, it is of secondary importance how, say, the standard of care is defined or how related party transactions are regulated, provided the law facilitates access to the courts and the court system operates effectively and reliably. In previous chapters, we have seen that shareholder rights and directors' duties differ considerably across legal systems, but we did not identify a consistently lower level of investor protection in our two civil law countries in comparison with common law countries. This chapter explores whether the lower level of investor protection that some commentators associate with civil law jurisdictions[2] can be explained with deficiencies in the enforcement mechanisms that investors, and in particular minority shareholders, have at their disposal. We will start with a discussion of what we call the 'contractualisation of responsibility' (section B). It is common to insure directors partially or fully against the risk of liability incurred by accepting a position on the board. In some legal systems, companies go beyond simply providing for insurance. In addition, they promise to indemnify directors against liability, or the founders seek to authorize actions of the directors that would constitute a breach of duties or exclude liability for certain types of misconduct in the articles altogether. We will examine whether, and to what extent, such contractual modifications of directors' duties are possible. In this context, it is important to bear in mind that the duties that we analysed in Chapter 6 are largely conceptualized as being inherent in the position of a director and as flowing from the fiduciary nature of that position. Therefore, we would expect them not to be subject to private ordering, but be binding on all directors.

[1] R La Porta, F Lopez-de-Silanes, and A Shleifer, 'The Economic Consequences of Legal Origins' (2008) 46 *J. Econ. Lit.* 285, 293, with references.

[2] See our discussion in Chapter 4D.IV.

We will then discuss how claims that a company has against its own directors can be enforced (section C). The first possibility is to entrust the organ commonly authorized to act on behalf of the company—the board of directors—with taking the decision whether or not to bring litigation. However, except in cases where conflicts of interest result in the transfer of decision-making authority to another organ, such as the supervisory board in companies with a two-tier board structure, the directors may be reluctant to file a lawsuit against one of their fellow board members. Legal systems have developed responses to this problem, the most important being the right of minority shareholders to bring litigation on behalf of the company (derivative action). A major part of this chapter is devoted to examining how the minority shareholder lawsuit is regulated in our four jurisdictions and whether it ensures the effective enforcement of directors' duties. We will see that the derivative action suffers from design flaws in some of the jurisdictions, notably Germany and France (but also, until recently, the UK), which may explain why the view has taken hold among some commentators that investor protection is insufficient in civil law countries. However, it is not possible to come to robust conclusions on this point unless we account for the possibility that the absence of an effective derivative action is compensated for by other enforcement mechanisms. The last part of this chapter, therefore, gives an overview of substitute enforcement mechanisms that are relevant in practice in our jurisdictions (section D). In contrast to litigation by the company (acting through its authorized organ or minority shareholders), these substitute mechanisms are predominantly of a public law nature. Thus, section D will illustrate how some legal systems have a preference for public enforcement, while others rely extensively on private enforcement.

B. Contractualization of Responsibility

A violation of the behavioural standards that we discussed in Chapter 6 is not necessarily synonymous with liability on the part of directors. Directors and shareholders have various ways to limit liability, either with regard to a specific incidence, notably by adopting a resolution dealing with the director's conduct, or more generally in the articles of association. We will first discuss shareholder action to authorize a specific action ex ante or absolve the directors of liability by ratifying a breach ex post, and then examine the permissibility of provisions in the articles limiting or excluding liability.

I. Authorization and ratification

Following the terminology of the UK Companies Act 2006, we refer to shareholder authorization as the approval of the director's conduct before the act in question is carried out, and ratification as the approval after a breach of duty has occurred.[3] In all legal systems, shareholders are able to authorize or ratify actions of the directors under certain conditions. In the UK, somewhat oddly, ratification has been codified in the Companies Act,[4] while authorization continues to be governed by the common law that applied to both ratification and authorization before the 2006 Act entered into force. The common law differs from the statutory rules, with the consequence that different regimes now apply to ratification and authorization, even though it is difficult to identify a substantive reason for the difference. Most importantly, under the common law, interested directors are allowed to participate in the shareholder vote authorizing their own conduct, unless the directors' conduct constitutes a non-ratifiable breach.[5] Pursuant to the Companies Act, on the other hand, the votes

[3] Companies Act 2006, ss 180(4)(a), 239, 263(2)(b), (c), (3)(c).

[4] ibid s 239.

[5] We discuss non-ratifiable breaches in Chapter 6C.I.1.

of interested directors, as well as the votes of any connected member, are disregarded for the purpose of ratifying a breach of duty.[6]

The Delaware General Corporation Law does not contain any express rules on shareholder authorization or ratification,[7] but the common law recognizes ratification as a defence to the illegality of corporate actions. Similar to UK law, ratification is only possible if the relevant act is ratifiable, which has been held not to be the case if the act is *ultra vires*,[8] fraudulent or a waste of corporate assets.[9] The failure to reach an informed business judgment, conversely, constitutes a voidable, rather than a void act that can be ratified.[10] Ratification requires a fully informed vote of the disinterested shareholders.[11] A unique feature of the Delaware rules is the contingent effect that shareholder ratification has. In *Gantler v Stephens*,[12] the Delaware Supreme Court held that a ratifying shareholder vote generally does not extinguish any claim that the company may have against a director, but the challenged action becomes reviewable under the business judgment rule.[13] Thus, in contrast to the consequences that a rebuttal of the business judgment rule normal entails, the failure of a director to consider all relevant information (breach of the duty of care) or the presence of a conflict of interest (invoking the duty of loyalty) does not result in a shift of the burden of proof to the defendant director and an entire fairness review of the transaction if the shareholders have ratified the action. Rather, in order to succeed, an objecting shareholder has to show irrationality or a waste of corporate assets.[14]

Thus, UK and US law are characterized by a comparatively high degree of flexibility and the primacy of the decision of the shareholders, who as (indirect) beneficiaries of the directors' duties are at liberty to waive the protection afforded by the law. This stands in contrast to the approach found in our two civil law jurisdictions. In Germany, ex ante authorization of an action by the general meeting is, in principle, possible. However, the shareholders do not enjoy general authority to pass a resolution on a proposed action of the directors. Rather, they can only validly act in the limited instances where the Stock Corporation Act allocates decision-making power to them, or if the management board

[6] Companies Act, s 239(4). The term 'connected member' is defined in ss 239(5)(d), 252.

[7] With the exception of the approval of related party transactions by the shareholders pursuant to §144(a)(2) Del. Gen. Corp. Law. However, such approval should be distinguished from the common law doctrine of ratification, which does not affect the case law interpreting §144, see *Gantler v Stephens*, 965 A.2d 695, 713, fn 54 (Del. 2009). For a detailed discussion of §144, see Chapter 6C.I.2.

[8] *Ultra vires* acts have been defined as 'acts specifically prohibited by the corporation's charter, for which no implicit authority may be rationally surmised, or those acts contrary to basic principles of fiduciary law', *Solomon v Armstrong*, 747 A.2d 1098, 1114, fn 45 (Del. Ch. 1999).

[9] *Michelson v Duncan*, 407 A.2d 211, 219 (Del. 1979). However, note that Delaware law allows ratification of fraudulent, wasteful, or *ultra vires* acts by unanimous shareholder vote.

[10] *Smith v Van Gorkom*, 488 A.2d 858, 889 (Del. 1985); *In re Wheelabrator Technologies, Inc.*, 663 A.2d 1194, 1202 (Del. Ch. 1995).

[11] In addition, it has been held that common law ratification only applies to 'director action that does *not* legally require shareholder approval in order to become legally effective'; see *Gantler v Stephens*, 965 A.2d 695, 713. Thus, shareholder resolutions required by statute, for example in order to approve a merger, do not fall within the scope of the common law doctrine. The relevance of this conceptual differentiation is that such votes are generally not invalid solely because a controlling shareholder who benefits from the transaction does not abstain from voting, see e.g. *Williams v Geier*, 671 A.2d 1368, 1382 (Del. 1996) (holding that '[t]here is no requirement under the Delaware General Corporation Law that a majority of the outstanding minority shares must vote in favor of a transaction which benefits the majority'; however, note that in certain circumstances, for example in the case of a cash-out merger transaction by the controlling shareholder, approval by the majority of the minority may shift the burden of proving unfairness to the plaintiff; see *Kahn v Lynch*, 638 A.2d 1110, 1116 (Del. 1994) and Chapter 7 C.III).

[12] 965 A.2d 695 (Del. 2009).

[13] ibid 713. This constitutes a deviation from pre-*Gantler* case law, which distinguished between breaches of the duty of care and the duty of loyalty. Ratification of the former extinguished the claim, whereas ratification of the latter gave rise to the familiar business judgment standard, *In re Wheelabrator Technologies, Inc.*, 663 A.2d 1194, 1200–3.

[14] The irrationality/waste standard that applies if the presumptions of the business judgment rule are not rebutted is examined in Chapter 6B.I.2(c).

lays a matter before the general meeting.[15] If the general meeting is authorized to act and adopts a valid resolution sanctioning the proposed conduct,[16] the directors are not liable *to the company*.[17] However, the resolution does not have any effect in relation to the creditors of the company,[18] and acting on the basis of a shareholder resolution, as such, does not render the directors' actions duty-compliant.[19] If their actions constitute a breach of duty, the creditors (or the liquidator when the company files for the opening of insolvency proceedings) can enforce the company's claim for damages, even though the company cannot do so itself.[20] Furthermore, ratification, referred to as a waiver of the directors' liability to the company in the German Stock Corporation Act, is prohibited for three years after the claim came into existence. Thereafter, it requires a resolution of the general meeting, without any minority shareholder holding at least 10 per cent of the legal capital raising an objection.[21]

Even more restrictively, the French Commercial Code prohibits any waiver of liability, either ex ante in the articles of association or ex post by a resolution of the general meeting.[22] This prohibition is interpreted strictly. A resolution of the general meeting approving the actions of the directors has no effect with regard to their responsibility under the law. Even shareholders who voted in favour of the resolution can exercise their right (to be discussed below) to enforce the company's claim for damages against the director.[23]

II. Indemnification and insurance

A widely used strategy to protect directors more broadly against liability and ensure that they are incentivized to take appropriate levels of risk is the contractual or statutory provision of an indemnity or insurance coverage. In some jurisdictions, directors have a statutory right to indemnification for the costs incurred in successfully defending themselves in a lawsuit brought against them in their capacity as directors.[24] More often, the law allows companies to indemnify directors voluntarily against expenses and liability incurred by them, provided the directors' conduct satisfies certain conditions. Typically, the directors must have acted in good faith and reasonably believed that the challenged conduct was in the best

[15] AktG, §119(2). On the limited powers of the general meeting, see Chapter 5A.III.

[16] The resolution must be neither null and void pursuant to §241, nor voidable pursuant to §§243–246 AktG. These provisions are analysed in Chapter 5C.III.1.

[17] AktG, §93(4) sentence 1. [18] ibid §93(5) sentence 3.

[19] It has been argued that a valid resolution of the general meeting will generally exonerate the directors, since they are required to implement shareholder resolutions pursuant to §83(2), and liability of the managers cannot arise where they are legally obliged to act, G Spindler in W Goette and M Habersack (eds), *Münchener Kommentar zum Aktiengesetz, vol 2* (5th edn, CH Beck 2019) §93 para 266. However, the managers may be liable if they breached their duties in soliciting the resolution, for example because they did not inform the shareholders fully and correctly, or carrying out the resolution was in conflict with the interests of the company because of changed circumstances: ibid paras 274–6.

[20] The enforcement right of the creditors is subject to the following additional requirements pursuant to §93(5) sentences 1 and 2. The creditors must have a claim against the company which the company is not able to satisfy, and the claim of the company against the director must arise either from a violation of certain capital maintenance provisions listed in §93(3) or from a grossly negligent or intentional breach of duty. Section §93(3) is discussed in more detail in Chapter 6B.I.3.

[21] AktG, §93(4) sentence 3. Again, the waiver has no effect in relation to the company's creditors, §93(5) sentence 3. The same considerations as before, nn 19–20, apply.

[22] Com, Art L225-253.

[23] C Gerner-Beuerle, P Paech, and E Schuster, *Study on Directors' Duties and Liability, prepared for the European Commission* (April 2013) A304.

[24] MBCA, §8.52 (providing that '[a] corporation shall indemnify a director who was wholly successful, on the merits or otherwise, in the defense of any proceeding to which the director was a party because he or she was a director of the corporation against expenses incurred by the director in connection with the proceeding'). New York Bus. Corp. Law, §723(a) contains a similar provision. Companies may go beyond the statutory right and indemnify directors—under certain additional conditions—also if they are found liable, see the discussion presently in the text.

interest of the company.[25] Whether this is the case is assessed by the disinterested directors or shareholders, who also decide on authorizing the conduct or indemnifying the director.[26] Importantly, however, indemnification is excluded as far as actions by the company against a director or derivative actions in the right of the company are concerned.[27] In such cases, indemnification would simply give rise to circular payments from the director to the company and back to the director and in addition the obligation to pay the fees of the director's lawyers.[28] According to a third approach, among our four jurisdictions only to be found in Germany,[29] companies are generally prohibited from indemnifying the directors. Indemnity against liability to third parties is not addressed in the German Stock Corporation Act.[30] However, we noted above that the power of the shareholders to exempt directors from liability is limited and cannot be extended by private ordering. This also calls into question the legality of the provision of an indemnity. In the literature, it has been argued that indemnification by the company would be tantamount to a violation of the limitations on waivers under the Stock Corporation Act, at least if the director's liability to the third party also involved the breach of a duty owed to the company.[31]

The provision of directors' and officers' liability insurance is less restrictively regulated. Legal systems generally allow the company to take out insurance for the benefit of its directors and do not define the conduct that can be covered as narrowly as under the indemnification statutes.[32] Importantly, the coverage can—and it typically does—extend to claims of the company and derivative actions, which are commonly non-indemnifiable.[33] The reason for the different treatment is easy to see. In a reasonably well functioning market for insurance services, the insurance contract will reflect the probability of litigation against a director and the extent to which the director can control the risk of liability. Accordingly, certain types of behaviour, especially intentional conduct, will be excluded contractually from coverage, and there is less need for legislative intervention.[34] This is reflected in the regulatory approach of our common law countries. The Delaware General Corporation Law simply states that a corporation 'shall have power to purchase and maintain insurance on behalf of any person who is or was a director, officer, employee or agent of the corporation ... against any liability asserted against such person ... whether or not the corporation would have the power to indemnify such person against such liability'.[35] The Model

[25] Del. Gen. Corp. Law, §145(a); MBCA, §8.51(a); UK Companies Act 2006, s 234. The French Code de commerce does not deal with the question, and it is unclear whether indemnification against liability of the director to third parties would be permissible. In any case, indemnification against liability to the company would constitute a violation of Art L225-253 of the Code de commerce; B Black and others, 'Legal Liability of Directors and Company Officials Part 2: Court Procedures, Indemnification and Insurance, and Administrative and Criminal Liability' (2008) Columbia Business Law Review 1, 58.

[26] Del. Gen. Corp. Law, §145(d); MBCA, §8.55. The UK Companies Act 2006 adopts a different strategy. It does not exclude specified types of conduct, but certain types of sanctions from the scope of any permissible indemnity provision: fines imposed in criminal proceedings and regulatory sanctions, s 234(3)(a).

[27] Del. Gen. Corp. Law, §145(a); MBCA, §8.51(d)(1); UK Companies Act 2006, s 232(2). However, the company has the power to indemnify a director against expenses and attorney's fees in an action by the company or in a derivative action if the director has met the relevant standard of conduct, Del. Gen. Corp. Law, §145(b); MBCA, §8.51(d)(1). Similarly, the UK Companies Act 2006, s 234(3)(b)(ii) allows indemnification against costs incurred in defending civil proceedings brought by the company, unless judgment is given against the director.

[28] American Bar Association, *Model Business Corporation Act* (ABA 2010) 8–81.

[29] There is some legal uncertainty regarding the permissibility of indemnification in France; see n 25 above.

[30] This is not surprising, because German law does not conceptualize the directors as standing in a direct legal relationship with third parties, see §93(2) sentence 1 AktG. Of course, as discussed in Chapter 6A.II, in certain cases directors may be liable directly to third parties, but such liability will generally not arise under company law.

[31] W Wellhöfer, M Peltzer, and W Müller, *Die Haftung von Vorstand, Aufsichtsrat, Wirtschaftsprüfer* (CH Beck 2008) §7 para 18.

[32] Del. Gen. Corp. Law, §145(g); MBCA §8.57; UK Companies Act 2006, s 233; German AktG, §93(2) sentence 3; France: Cass civ, 1 June 2011, decision no 10-18143, *Bull. Joly Sociétés* 2011, 860, note A Constantin.

[33] There are certain exceptions. See n 27 above.

[34] PL Davies and S Worthington, *Gower's Principles of Modern Company Law* (10th edn, Sweet & Maxwell 2016) para 16-130.

[35] Del. Gen. Corp. Law, §145(g).

Business Corporation Act and the UK Companies Act 2006 contain similar provisions.[36] In contrast, French and German law are more interventionist (although they too regulate insurance more leniently than indemnification). In Germany, the insurance policy must provide for an excess of at least 10 per cent of the damage and at least one and a half times the director's fixed annual remuneration.[37] In France, it is prohibited to insure against criminal liability and liability arising from intentional or fraudulent conduct.[38] However, it seems doubtful whether these restrictions are indeed necessary. In practice, insurance coverage is often more limited than the law requires. Policies regularly provide for large deductibles, also in jurisdictions where this is not mandated by law, and contain exclusion clauses, for example with regard to intentional or reckless behaviour or violations of securities regulation.[39] Directors in small and medium-sized public companies are often not insured at all, because coverage is too expensive or simply unavailable.[40] It has also been observed that the insurance industry is responsive to changes in the legal environment. After an explosion of liability actions in the first half of the 1980s, including high profile cases such as the Delaware decision in *Van Gorkom*, which seemed to usher in a substantial increase in the risk of liability for good-faith breaches of the duty of care, directors' and officers' insurance became difficult to obtain in the United States.[41]

III. Contractual modification of directors' duties

Going beyond indemnification and insurance, we may ask whether it is possible for shareholders or those who set up a company to exempt directors from liability for certain types of conduct generally, or for breaches of whole categories of duties. In many jurisdictions of the United States, the answer is 'yes'. Within statutory limits, company law in Delaware and other US states allow the contractual modification of directors' duties in the certificate of incorporation. In response to *Van Gorkom*, the Delaware state legislature amended its corporation statute in 1988 to authorize charter amendments that eliminate a director's liability for breaches of the duty of care, provided the director acts in good faith.[42] Within a matter of a few years, most US states followed suit and adopted similar statutes.[43] In addition, as discussed elsewhere, Delaware law permits companies to define in the certificate of incorporation or by action of the board categories of business opportunities that do not qualify as corporate opportunities for purposes of the duty of loyalty, with the consequence that the directors are free to pursue these opportunities.[44] It may be said that these provisions are an expression of the normative paradigm of corporation statutes as 'standard form contracts', which can be disapplied or modified by firms if they are found to be inefficient in individual cases.[45] For example, if it is difficult to attract qualified directors in a litigious environment, it

[36] MBCA §8.57; UK Companies Act 2006, s 233.

[37] AktG, §93(2) sentence 3. The provision was introduced by Art 1, no 2 Gesetz zur Angemessenheit der Vorstandsvergütung (VorstAG) [Act regarding the Adequacy of Executive Compensation] of 31 July 2009, BGBl. I, 2509.

[38] Insurance Code, Art L113-1(2).

[39] Gerner-Beuerle, Paech, and Schuster (n 23) A308; AR Pinto and DM Branson, *Understanding Corporate Law* (5th edn, LexisNexis 2018) §14.11[H].

[40] Gerner-Beuerle, Paech, and Schuster (n 23) A308.

[41] Pinto and Branson (n 39) §14.11[H]. *Van Gorkom* is discussed in Chapter 6B.I.2(b). On the 'insurance crisis' of the 1980s, see also R Romano, 'Corporate Governance in the Aftermath of the Insurance Crisis' (1990) 39 Emory Law Journal 1155, 1157–9.

[42] Del. Gen. Corp. Law, §102(b)(7).

[43] Romano (n 41) 1160.

[44] Del. Gen. Corp. Law, §122(17). RF Balotti and JA Finkelstein, *Delaware Law of Corporations and Business Organizations, vol 2* (3rd edn, WoltersKluwer 2018), DGCL §122, explain that categories of business opportunities may be delineated 'by line or type of business, identity of the originator of the business opportunity, identity of the party or parties to or having an interest in the business opportunity, identity of the recipient of the business opportunity, periods of time or geographical location'. The provision is analysed further in Chapter 6C.II.2.

[45] H Easterbrook and DR Fischel, *The Economic Structure of Corporate Law* (Harvard University Press 1991) 34–5; R Romano, *The Genius of American Corporate Law* (AEI Press 1993) 85. See also Chapter 4C.II.

may be efficient to eliminate liability for negligence and even gross negligence, as is possible in Delaware. Similarly, we have seen that the test developed by the Delaware courts to assess whether a business opportunity 'belongs' to the corporation is fact-specific and open-ended.[46] The benefits of a broad and flexible corporate opportunities doctrine (in terms of a reduction in agency costs) may not outweigh the costs of legal uncertainty engendered by the Delaware test. Thus, granting companies the power to limit the liability of directors[47] can be value-increasing. On the other hand, some questions remain. If it is correct that the corporate contract is written with a view to providing for an efficient corporate governance framework, why does Delaware General Corporation Law establish mandatory fiduciary thresholds that cannot be reduced further (namely good faith and loyalty)?[48] Should we not expect shareholders to adopt, say, the duty of loyalty voluntarily if that duty is indeed of value to them?[49] Of course, the 'standard form contracts' analogy relies crucially on the assumption that investors make informed choices and collective investment decisions are able to separate the effect of corporate governance rules from other factors that are associated with firm value. As discussed, it is questionable whether this assumption holds.[50] The duty of loyalty, referred to by proponents of an enabling company law regime as 'a paradigmatic example of ... a rule from which no firm's shareholders would wish to deviate',[51] actually casts doubt on the responsiveness of private ordering to deficiencies in corporate governance regulation. We have said that the duty of loyalty is comparatively underdeveloped in civil law jurisdiction. French and German law employ different mechanisms to regulate related party transactions and corporate opportunities. These mechanisms are too rigid and narrow to provide for satisfactory regulatory solutions in all cases.[52] Nevertheless, there is no evidence that shareholders seek to replicate a duty of loyalty resembling US law contractually in these countries. The Delaware legislator may have shared these concerns and, for this reason, left a mandatory duty framework in place in the General Corporation Law.[53] Furthermore, it should be noted that not only shareholders, but also directors are empowered to renounce particular categories of business opportunities under §122(17) Delaware General Corporation Law. This reflects the decision-making prerogative of the directors under Delaware law. As part of their general powers, the directors decide which opportunities are of interest to the corporation. Therefore, the provision represents not so much a confirmation of the nature of corporate law as a standard form contract among shareholders, but rather an attempt to reduce the high transaction costs created by the corporate opportunities doctrine in Delaware.

We have seen that the scope of contractual freedom is greater in UK than US corporate law.[54] However, the duties codified in the Companies Act 2006 are an exception to the generally enabling nature of UK corporate governance regulation. In particular, the fiduciary

[46] Chapter 6C.II.2.

[47] Note that §102(b)(7) of the Delaware General Corporation Law does not limit the scope of fiduciary duties, but only the directors' personal liability. Thus, an injunction is still possible.

[48] Note that the duty of loyalty cannot be disapplied contractually, Del. Gen. Corp. Law, §102(b)(7). The function of §122(17) is merely to permit corporations to renounce specified types of opportunities in advance, rather than changing the level of judicial scrutiny that applies once it has been determined that a business opportunity properly belongs to the corporation; see Balotti and Finkelstein (n 44) DGCL, §122. As part of the multi-factor test used to determine whether an opportunity belongs to the company, the Delaware courts consider the company's intent to make use of the opportunity, *Broz v Cellular Information Systems, Inc.*, 673 A.2d 148, 151 (Del. 1996). In this context, §122(17) becomes relevant.

[49] It has indeed been argued that a mandatory duty of loyalty is unnecessary because investors would not be willing to pay much for a company's shares if the articles did not include such a rule, R Romano, 'Answering the Wrong Question: The Tenuous Case for Mandatory Corporate Laws' (1989) 89 Columbia Law Review 1599, 1601–2.

[50] Chapter 4C.II. [51] Romano (n 49) 1602. [52] Chapter 6C.

[53] The scope for private ordering is broader in the limited liability company, where fiduciary duties can be largely eliminated; Delaware Limited Liability Company Act, §18-1101.

[54] See our discussion in Chapter 5A.I (UK) and A.II (US).

principles that flow from the position of directors and shape their duties, for example the no-conflict rule, are principally not subject to private ordering. Nevertheless, as early as the nineteenth century, UK courts recognized that it was important to allow companies to adapt duties contractually in light of business needs.[55] The flexibility introduced by case law has been retained by the Companies Act 2006. Importantly, the act does not provide for a blanket prohibition of related party transactions. Instead, it requires disclosure of the conflict of interest and, as a default rule in the articles, abstention of the interested director from voting when the board of directors decides on the matter.[56] Similarly, a director is allowed to take advantage of a corporate opportunity, or act in any other situation that gives rise to a conflict of interest, if the articles enable the disinterested directors to authorize the matter or provide for other mechanisms by which a director may be exempted from the duty to avoid conflicts of interest.[57] More generally, directors' duties 'have effect subject to any rule of law enabling the company to give authority, specifically or generally, for anything to be done (or omitted) by the directors … that would otherwise be a breach of duty'.[58] The boundaries of these provisions are not easy to understand. On the one hand, section 232 of the Companies Act declares any provision void that exempts a director from liability, with limited exceptions for indemnification and insurance as discussed above. On the other hand, section 180(4) preserves the equitable and common law rules that permitted companies to authorize, 'specifically or generally',[59] any actions of the directors and regulate conflicts of interest in the articles of association in deviation from the Companies Act.[60] Can companies rely on these provisions to disapply directors' duties by giving broad ex ante authorization of a breach of duty in the articles? A general exemption from liability would be difficult to reconcile with section 232(1).[61] With regard to self-dealing transactions, pre-2006 case law held that the equitable principle that 'a director [must not place] himself in a position in which his duty to the company conflicts with his personal interest or his duty to another' could be modified or disapplied in the articles, provided full disclosure was made and the director did not prefer his own interests over those of the company.[62] This somewhat inconsistent statement has been interpreted in the literature as meaning that the articles can determine what shall and shall not constitute a *potential* conflict of interest (which must be avoided in the same way as an actual conflict[63]), but the articles cannot absolve a director from promoting the company's interests where the latter *actually* conflict with the director's interests.[64] However, it has also been pointed out that this interpretation is not particularly satisfying. It is clear that a company can authorize even actual conflicts of interest—presumably subject to the proviso that the authorization identifies the relevant circumstances sufficiently clearly.[65] Furthermore, it is unclear whether the scope of core duties, notably the corporate opportunities doctrine

[55] See, for example, *Imperial Mercantile Credit Association v Coleman* (1870–71) LR 6 Ch App 558, 568, raising the question 'whether the company cannot stipulate that [the no-conflict and no-profit rule] is a benefit of which they do not desire to avail themselves, and if they are competent so to stipulate, whether they may not think that … it is better to have directors who may advance the interests of the company by their connection, and by the part which they themselves take in large money dealings, than to have persons who would have no share in such transactions as those in which the company is concerned'. As we have seen in Chapter 6C.I.1, the court answered the question in the affirmative and sanctioned a provision in the articles that permitted the disinterested directors to authorize contracts between the company and one of its directors.

[56] Companies Act 2006, s 177; Model Articles for Public Companies, Art 16(1); Model Articles for Private Companies, Art 14(1).

[57] Companies Act 2006, ss 175(4)(b), (5), 180(4)(b). Section 175(5) is discussed in Chapter 6C.II.1.

[58] Companies Act 2006, s 180(4)(a).

[59] ibid.

[60] ibid s 180(4)(b). This means in particular in deviation from ss 175(5), 177 CA 2006.

[61] S Witney, 'Corporate opportunities law and the non-executive director' (2016) 16 JCLS 145, 168 (fn 116).

[62] *Movitex Ltd v Bulfield* [1988] BCLC 104, 120–1.

[63] Companies Act 2006, s 175(1).

[64] Davies and Worthington (n 34) para 16-127.

[65] ibid. As mentioned, s 180(4)(a) speaks of giving authority 'specifically or generally', which implies that whole categories of actions can be exempted from the scope of the duties, but a general exclusion of liability for disregarding the interests of the company would be in conflict with the common law.

and the duty not to compete with the company,[66] can be delimited in the articles. Thus, the question is whether the articles can define a category of business opportunities that do not fall within the company's line of business and that the company will never pursue, or determine when a director acts in the capacity as director of the company, and when in a different capacity, for example as director of another company.[67] Case law is ambivalent. Some decisions seem to indicate that such provisions would be impermissible. They draw a distinction between commercial partnerships, where the precise area of business activity can be defined contractually, and corporations, where the directors' 'fiduciary duties are not similarly circumscribed by the terms of a contract'.[68] Further, they stress that the fiduciary duties of directors do not end when they encounter a business opportunity in their 'private capacity', that is, while they were not acting on company business.[69] On the other hand, it has been acknowledged that directors can act in different capacities[70] and the corporate opportunities doctrine is only engaged if there is a 'real sensible possibility of conflict' between the director and the company, which depends on how the company's line of business is defined.[71] If this is correct, there should be a role for the articles in delineating the boundaries of the duties.[72]

In summary, neither US law nor UK law exclude the possibility of contractually modifying directors' duties completely, but both legal systems grapple with the difficulty of determining the scope of private ordering and the relationship between contractual freedom and the binding fiduciary principles that are inherent in the position of a director. The legal situation is less ambiguous in our civil law countries. The principle of limited contractual freedom underlying the German Stock Corporation Act[73] is commonly interpreted as meaning that the duties of directors cannot be modified in the articles or by contract with the effect of either extending the scope of the duties or reducing the standard of liability, for example by limiting liability to gross negligence or bad faith.[74] Likewise, the equivalent of the corporate opportunities doctrine in German stock corporation law, the prohibition to engage in competitive behaviour,[75] cannot be qualified contractually. The courts assess whether the directors' activities fall within the line of business *actually* pursued by the company, irrespective of a wider or narrower formulation in the articles.[76] We also said that a general power of the shareholders to authorize or ratify specific actions of the directors is lacking.[77] A fortiori, shareholders cannot authorize types of conduct more generally that would otherwise be in

[66] Companies Act 2006, s 175(2), (7) (competition with the company may be conceptualized as a conflict of duties within the meaning of s 175(7) if a director serves on the board of two competing corporations).

[67] Recall that a business opportunity is not a 'corporate opportunity' if it is 'wholly outside the scope of the firm's activities', *Wilkinson v West Coast Capital* [2007] BCC 717, 775. It is clear that a company can define the scope of the firm's activities in an 'objects clause': Companies Act 2006, s 31. However, the question is whether particular classes of transactions can be excluded from the firm's activities irrespective of any clause restricting the company's objects specifically for the purpose of limiting the scope of the corporate opportunities doctrine, similar to §122(17) Del. Gen. Corp. Law (see n 47 above).

[68] *Re Allied Business & Financial Consultants Ltd* (*O'Donnell v Shanahan*) [2009] BCC 822, 843. For a critical discussion of this decision, and its strength as a precedent, see Chapter 6C.II.1.

[69] *Bhullar v Bhullar* [2003] BCC 711, 722; *Industrial Development Consultants Ltd v Cooley* [1972] 1 WLR 443, 447, 451.

[70] For example, in *Bhullar v Bhullar* [2003] BCC 711, 723, the court pointed out that the directors 'had, *at the material time*, one capacity and one capacity only in which they were carrying on business, namely as directors of the company' (emphasis by authors). This implies that there are other cases when directors may act in a different capacity and consequently are not bound by fiduciary duties. See also *Wilkinson v West Coast Capital* [2007] BCC 717, 778, where the court distinguished between the capacity of the defendant acting as a director and as a shareholder, i.e. in a non-fiduciary capacity. Any interpretation that did not make allowance for directors acting in different capacities would pose problems especially for non-executive directors, who often hold more than one directorship. This point is discussed by Witney (n 61) 171–2, 176–84.

[71] *Wilkinson v West Coast Capital* (n 70) 768. For a more detailed analysis, see Chapter 6C.II.1.

[72] However, note that if *Movitex* (n 62) were interpreted as drawing a distinction between actual and potential conflicts (see text to nn 62–64 above), no such contractual provision could exempt directors from liability if they pursued their own interests in a situation of an actual conflict, Davies and Worthington (n 34) para 16-127.

[73] AktG, §23(5). See Chapter 5A.III.

[74] BGH NJW 1975, 1412; Spindler (n 19) §93 para 27.

[75] AktG, §88.

[76] For more details, see Chapter 6C.II.3.

[77] Section I above.

contravention of a duty.[78] These provisions, taken together, present a picture that conforms to the regulatory model of the German stock corporation that we have developed in previous chapters. The law assigns a clearly defined role and specific duties to the different organs in a corporation, which are not subject to private ordering. The absence of a power of the shareholders to authorize or ratify a breach of duty is the logical consequence of the position accorded to the shareholders pursuant to the Stock Corporation Act. The shareholders do not have ultimate control over a 'corporate contract' that is written with a view to promoting solely their interests. The general meeting is one of several organs. It does not occupy a position of supremacy within the corporate hierarchy and can influence the enforceability of a breach of duty only as part of its role as defined by the statute.[79]

In French company law, contractual freedom plays a more prominent role.[80] Nevertheless, similar to the position in Germany, the duties of directors and the standard of responsibility laid down in the Commercial Code are seen as not negotiable. It is impermissible to derogate in the articles of association from provisions holding directors liable for unintentional management mistakes and other breaches of the duty of care, disregarding the regime on prohibited and regulated agreements, or for violations of the unwritten duty of loyalty. While the content of the French corporate opportunities doctrine is not well established, owing to the small number of cases applying that doctrine, the case law that does exist seems to indicate that the test is largely objective and it is irrelevant whether the company was actually pursuing the opportunity, provided it falls within the company's sphere of economic activity.[81] As in the case of Germany, this relatively inflexible approach can be explained with the historical trajectory of French company law. Over the course of the nineteenth and twentieth centuries, the initially contractual view of the company was gradually replaced by a more institutional conception.[82] The relevant provisions of the Commercial Code, accordingly, are not simply an expression of a contractual or principal-agent relationship between the shareholders and directors, which would allow the principle to limit the agent's responsibility, but constitute a binding determination of the role and duties of the directors.

C. Legal Action

I. Litigation by the company

When we speak of 'the company' bringing an action to enforce its rights against a director or third parties, we think in the first instance of the organs that are authorized to act on behalf of the company pursuant to general rules of company law. In most countries, an application of general rules of company law allocating decision rights and corporate power would mean that the board of directors is competent to decide whether to bring a lawsuit and how to conduct litigation. Indeed, this is the default position in three of our four legal systems. In the UK, United States, and France, filing a lawsuit is regarded as a management decision and, hence, as falling within the general powers of the board.[83] In Germany, again

[78] Spindler (n 19) §93 para 271 (arguing that authorization, insofar as it is possible, must identify the action that is being authorized precisely).

[79] ibid paras 265–6. [80] See Chapter 4C.II and Chapter 5A.IV.

[81] See, for example, Cass com, 15 November 2011 (*DL finances*), *Bull. Joly Sociétés* 2012, 112, analysed in Chapter 6C.II.4. See also M Gelter and G Helleringer, 'Opportunity Makes a Thief: Corporate Opportunities as Legal Transplant and Convergence in Corporate Law' (2018) 15 Berkeley Business Law Journal 92, 134–8.

[82] Chapter 5A.IV.

[83] In the UK, this follows from the broad delegation of authority to the directors pursuant to Art 3 of the Model Articles for Public and Private Companies, in Delaware from s 141(a) of the Del. Gen. Corp. Law, as interpreted, for example, by *Zapata Corp v Maldonado*, 430 A.2d 779, 782 (Del. 1981), discussed in section C.II.3 below. In French public companies with a one-tier board, the decision is primarily made by the board of directors, Art L225-35 Code de commerce (providing that 'the board of directors deals with all matters relating to the conduct of the company's business', translation by Legifrance, https://www.legifrance.gouv.fr/Traductions/en-English/Legifrance-translations), in which case the litigation is referred to as *action sociale ut universi*; see Chapter 6A.II.

in application of general rules of the Stock Corporation Act, the supervisory board enforces claims of the company against members of the management board, and the management board has authority to decide on actions regarding other claims of the company, including against members of the supervisory board.[84] In all legal systems, as part of their general duties, the competent directors must carefully consider whether the company has a cause of action and it is in the interest of the company to pursue that action in court. However, we observe variation in how courts review the directors' enforcement decision. One approach is to apply the same principles as in any other business decision. Thus, in assessing the prospects of success of an action or the effect of litigation on the company, for example the risk that litigation poses to the company's reputation or the potential disruption of business operations, the directors would generally benefit from wide discretion and, where applicable, the protections of the business judgment rule. As we will see, this is the case, for example, in Delaware, where the enforcement decision of the board will only be reviewed by the courts if it can be shown that the directors were interested, lacked independence, or acted grossly negligently in obtaining the information on which they based their decision.[85] Alternatively, a policy maker may take the view that the decision to enforce a claim of the company is not comparable to other business decisions. In a typical case of managerial decision-making, the board is presented with a variety of options, for example different investment opportunities, whose ultimate outcome is uncertain.[86] In order to assess the opportunities adequately, financial expertise and business experience are paramount. Accordingly, it is sensible for courts to grant a wide margin of discretion to directors and not to intervene in matters they are often less well equipped to evaluate than professional managers. In contrast, it could be argued that the litigation decision primarily involves legal considerations. If the directors conclude that the company is most likely entitled to damages, enforcement will generally be in the interest of the company. This is the position of the German courts. They hold that supervisory board members do not enjoy a 'decision prerogative' when considering litigation, but their decision is in principle fully reviewable by the courts. If the claim is well founded, litigation must be brought, unless important reasons in the company's best interest outweigh the interests of the company in obtaining compensation in exceptional cases.[87]

Directors' duties, therefore, provide for certain safeguards against enforcement decisions by the board that are not in the best interest of the company. In particular, if directors are

[84] AktG, §§78, 112.

[85] *Aronson v Lewis*, 473 A.2d 805, 812–13 (Del. 1984). The fact that the defendant director, who is also the majority shareholder, selects the other board members, appoints them, and generally dominates decision-making on the board, without more, is not sufficient to substantiate the allegation that the other directors were conflicted and lacked independence. On the other hand, the Delaware courts also allow litigation to proceed if the plaintiff can create a reasonable doubt that the challenged transaction was the product of a valid exercise of business judgment. Both aspects of the Delaware approach, as developed in *Aronson v Lewis*, are discussed in section C.II.3 below. While a business judgment rule is not part of UK or French company law, the courts in these countries apply directors' duties in a similarly consistent manner to the board's enforcement decision.

[86] See Chapter 6A.I.

[87] BGHZ 135, 244 (*ARAG/Garmenbeck*) paras 23–5: 'When examining the existence and enforceability of a claim for damages the supervisory board does not act differently than anyone who has to assess on his own or someone else's behalf a legal claim and the prospects of its enforcement in court. The justifiability and accuracy of the board's assessment of the prospects of success of such litigation can be fully reviewed in court, since these questions do not refer to the sphere of taking action … Discretion can only exist where the decision between different courses of action is to be made … [T]he decision to enforce damages claims against members of the management board who are in breach of duty is part of the [supervisory] board's ex post supervisory function, which has the aim of ensuring that the management board acts in a duty-compliant way and to prevent the company from suffering a loss … In exercising this control function and assessing whether breaches of managerial duty exist, the supervisory board … cannot rely on a scope of entrepreneurial discretion'. The courts are only prepared to grant a limited margin of discretion to the supervisory board when the board assesses whether the negative consequences of litigation outweigh the benefits of obtaining damages, ibid. para. 26. A longer excerpt of the decision is reproduced in Chapter 6B.I.3.

conflicted, notably because they would be defendants in the lawsuit, they are required to abstain from the decision of the board.[88] However, our discussion of review standards in the previous paragraph and more generally of directors' duties in Chapter 6 has shown that duties do not necessarily capture all forms of behaviour that involve negligence or the pursuit of an ulterior motive. For example, directors may qualify as formally disinterested persons, but refrain from bringing an action against their colleagues on the board for personal reasons, or they may not pursue the lawsuit as forcefully as they could.[89] For this reason, legal systems often acknowledge that enforcing the company's claims falls not solely within the domain of the directors, but the general meeting, or individual shareholders, are also competent to bring an action. In the UK, the general meeting has this authority pursuant to the default model articles, which provide that the shareholders can give the directors instructions by special resolution.[90] However, there is also support in the case law for the proposition that the general meeting has an implied unwritten power to decide on litigation by simple majority, even if the shareholders' instruction right requires a resolution adopted by a qualified majority or the articles do not contain an instruction right at all. Whether the residual authority to bring litigation is a general power of the shareholders or a conditional power is not entirely clear. Case law has held that the majority can bring an action if the board of directors is unable to do so, for example because the company does not have any directors at the relevant time, there is a deadlock on the board, or the directors are disqualified from voting.[91] Some commentators would go further and allow the general meeting to exercise this authority whenever the directors fail to file a lawsuit.[92] Similarly, in Germany, the general meeting, acting by simple majority, can either request the management or supervisory board (as applicable) to pursue a claim or, if it doubts the impartiality of the authorized organ, appoint a special representative, for example a shareholder, a particular member of the management or supervisory board, or a lawyer, who is authorized to bring litigation on behalf of the company.[93] The potential defendant, if he or she is also a shareholder, is excluded from the vote.[94] In our other two countries, the

[88] In the UK, this follows from s 175(1) of the Companies Act 2006. For the United States, see n 85 above and accompanying text. If the decision is not taken by a majority of the disinterested directors, the protections of the business judgment rule do not apply and the court will proceed to a full fairness review. Similarly, in France, it is well established that the company must be represented by the disinterested directors if one or more current members of the board are among the defendants. See P Merle, *Droit commercial: Sociétés commerciales* (22nd edn, Dalloz 2018) para 462. In Germany, this problem, of course, does not arise, since the authority to represent the company shifts from the management board to the supervisory board: AktG, §112.

[89] For an example of such a case from France, see Cass crim, 16 December 2009, *JCP E* 2010, 1993, no 1, note F Deboissy and G Wicker.

[90] UK Model Articles for Public and Private Companies, Art 4.

[91] *Alexander Ward v Samyang* [1975] 1 WLR 673, 679 (quoting approvingly Gower, *Modern Company Law* (3rd edn, Sweet & Maxwell 1969) 136–7.

[92] Davies and Worthington (n 34) para 17-3. In obiter, some of the judges in *Alexander Ward v Samyang* seemed to imply that inaction of the board for any reason triggered the shareholders' residual power; see [1975] 1 WLR at 679. Authority referred to in *Alexander Ward* as supporting this view is critically discussed by D Kershaw, *Company Law in Context* (2nd edn, OUP 2012) 598–601, who concludes that the shareholders could only be held to retain co-decision-making authority over the litigation decision in situations of 'acute conflict' between the directors and the shareholders, i.e. where 'the directors who would be sued control the board decision-making process': ibid 599. Irrespective of how broadly the shareholders' residual power is construed, such a power is in conflict with the prevalent approach in UK law, which regards the articles as a contract that binds the shareholders. If decision-making power is delegated to the directors in the articles and the shareholders' instruction right has to be exercised by special resolution, then this, in principle, leaves no room for shareholder action by ordinary resolution, see *Automatic Self-Cleansing Filter Syndicate Co Ltd v Cunninghame* [1906] 2 Ch 34, discussed in Chapter 5A.I. The residual power of the shareholders, accordingly, must be interpreted as a limited exception to this general rule for the question of whether litigation should be initiated, Davies and Worthington, ibid.

[93] AktG, §147.

[94] ibid §136(1). Note that this is different in the UK. The Companies Act 2006 provides that the votes of interested directors will be disregarded when the general meeting ratifies the conduct of a director (n 6 above), but not in the case of other shareholder resolutions.

authority of the general meeting is defined differently. Delaware law, true to the precept of vesting broad powers in the board of directors and excluding the shareholders from management decisions,[95] does not recognize a residual power of the general meeting to bring an action. The board is the proper organ to take enforcement decisions, and this, in principle, does not change when the directors are conflicted or refuse to assert the company's claim for other reasons.[96] In France, litigation on behalf of the company may be brought either in the form of a lawsuit *ut universi* or *ut singuli*.[97] The former has to be filed by the board of directors, whereas the *action sociale ut singuli* allows individual shareholders or groups of shareholders, and hence of course also a majority of the shareholders, to initiate litigation on behalf of the company.[98]

Thus, a majority of the shareholders plays a certain, at least subsidiary, role in the litigation decision of the company in most legal systems. Nevertheless, it is clear that this, as well, will not necessarily ensure effective enforcement of claims belonging to the company in all circumstances. The general meeting may be dominated by the potential defendants or affiliated parties,[99] or its decision-making may be compromised by a collective action problem. Therefore, the power of individual shareholders, or groups of minority shareholders, to file a lawsuit is an integral part of the enforcement architecture in many jurisdictions. This is the topic we turn to now.

II. Minority shareholder lawsuit

US MBCA

§ 1.43—Qualified Director

(a) A 'qualified director' is a director who, at the time action is to be taken under:
 (1) section 7.44, does not have (i) a material interest in the outcome of the proceeding, or (ii) a material relationship with a person who has such an interest …
(b) For purposes of this section:
 (1) 'material relationship' means a familial, financial, professional, employment or other relationship that would reasonably be expected to impair the objectivity of the director's judgment when participating in the action to be taken; and
 (2) 'material interest' means an actual or potential benefit or detriment (other than one which would devolve on the corporation or the shareholders generally) that would reasonably be expected to impair the objectivity of the director's judgment when participating in the action to be taken.
(c) The presence of one or more of the following circumstances shall not automatically prevent a director from being a qualified director:
 (1) nomination or election of the director to the current board by any director who is not a qualified director with respect to the matter (or by any person that has a material relationship with that director), acting alone or participating with others;

95 Chapter 5A.II. See also *Aronson v Lewis* (n 85) 811 (holding that '[a] cardinal precept of the General Corporation Law of the State of Delaware is that directors, rather than shareholders, manage the business and affairs of the corporation'); *Mayer v Adams*, 141 A.2d 458, 461 (Del. 1958) ('gravely' doubting 'whether the majority stockholders, as such, may take over the duties of the directors in respect of litigation' in a case where the board was disqualified or non-functioning, and also emphasizing 'that in the ordinary case the stockholders in meeting could not satisfactorily determine the probable merits of a minority stockholder's suit without a reasonably complete presentation and consideration of evidentiary facts[; a] stockholders' meeting is not an appropriate forum for such a proceeding').

96 *Aronson v Lewis* (n 85) 813 (pointing out that 'in either the demand-refused or the demand-excused case [i.e. where the board is conflicted, see our analysis of the demand rule in section C.II.3 below], the board still retains its Section 141(a) managerial authority to make decisions regarding corporate litigation').

97 See n 83 above.

98 Merle (n 88) para 462.

99 Interested parties are not always required to abstain from voting on the shareholder resolution, see n 94 above.

(2) service as a director of another corporation of which a director who is not a qualified director with respect to the matter (or any individual who has a material relationship with that director), is or was also a director; or

(3) with respect to action taken under section 7.44, status as a named defendant, as a director against whom action is demanded, or as a director who approved the conduct being challenged.

§ 7.40—Subchapter Definitions

In this subchapter:

(1) 'Derivative proceedings' means a civil suit in the right of a domestic corporation or, to the extent provided in section 7.47, in the right of a foreign corporation ...

§ 7.41—Standing

A shareholder may not commence or maintain a derivative proceeding unless the shareholder:

(1) was a shareholder of the corporation at the time of the act or omission complained of or became a shareholder through transfer by operation of law from one who was a shareholder at the time; and

(2) fairly and adequately represents the interests of the corporation in enforcing the right of the corporation.

§ 7.42—Demand

No shareholder may commence a derivative proceeding until:

(1) a written demand has been made upon the corporation to take suitable action; and

(2) 90 days have expired from the date delivery of the demand was made unless the shareholder has earlier been notified that the demand has been rejected by the corporation or unless irreparable injury to the corporation would result by waiting for expiration of the 90-day period.

§ 7.44—Dismissal

(a) A derivative proceeding shall be dismissed by the court on motion by the corporation if one of the groups specified in subsection (b) or subsection (e) has determined in good faith, after conducting a reasonable inquiry upon which its conclusions are based, that the maintenance of the derivative proceeding is not in the best interests of the corporation.

(b) Unless a panel is appointed pursuant to subsection (e), the determination in subsection (a) shall be made by:

(1) a majority vote of qualified directors present at a meeting of the board of directors if the qualified directors constitute a quorum; or

(2) a majority vote of a committee consisting of two or more qualified directors appointed by majority vote of qualified directors present at a meeting of the board of directors, regardless of whether such qualified directors constitute a quorum.

...

(d) If a majority of the board of directors consisted of qualified directors at the time the determination was made, the plaintiff shall have the burden of proving that the requirements of subsection (a) have not been met; if not, the corporation shall have the burden of proving that the requirements of subsection (a) have been met.

(e) Upon motion by the corporation, the court may appoint a panel of one or more individuals to make a determination whether the maintenance of the derivative proceeding is in the best interests of the corporation. In such case, the plaintiff shall have the burden of proving that the requirements of subsection (a) have not been met.

§ 7.46—Payment of Expenses

On termination of the derivative proceeding the court may:

(1) order the corporation to pay the plaintiff's expenses incurred in the proceedings if it finds that the proceedings has resulted in a substantial benefit to the corporation;

(2) order the plaintiff to pay any defendant's expenses incurred in defending the proceeding if it finds that the proceeding was commenced or maintained without reasonable cause or for an improper purpose; or
(3) order a party to pay an opposing party's expenses incurred because of the filing of a pleading, motion or other paper, if it finds that the pleading, motion or other paper was not well grounded in fact, after reasonable inquiry, or warranted by existing law or a good faith argument for the extension, modification or reversal of existing law and was interposed for an improper purpose, such as to harass or cause unnecessary delay or needless increase in the cost of litigation.

Delaware Chancery Court Rules

Rule 23.1—Derivative actions by shareholders

(a) In a derivative action brought by one or more shareholders or members to enforce a right of a corporation or of an unincorporated association, the corporation or association having failed to enforce a right which may properly be asserted by it, the complaint shall allege that the plaintiff was a shareholder or member at the time of the transaction of which the plaintiff complains or that the plaintiff's share or membership thereafter devolved on the plaintiff by operation of law. The complaint shall also allege with particularity the efforts, if any, made by the plaintiff to obtain the action the plaintiff desires from the directors or comparable authority and the reasons for the plaintiff's failure to obtain the action or for not making the effort.

...

UK Companies Act 2006

Section 260—Derivative claims

(1) This Chapter applies to proceedings in England and Wales or Northern Ireland by a member of a company—
  (a) in respect of a cause of action vested in the company, and
  (b) seeking relief on behalf of the company.
  This is referred to in this Chapter as a 'derivative claim'.
(2) A derivative claim may only be brought—
  (a) under this Chapter, or
  (b) in pursuance of an order of the court in proceedings under section 994 (proceedings for protection of members against unfair prejudice).
(3) A derivative claim under this Chapter may be brought only in respect of a cause of action arising from an actual or proposed act or omission involving negligence, default, breach of duty or breach of trust by a director of the company.
  The cause of action may be against the director or another person (or both).
(4) It is immaterial whether the cause of action arose before or after the person seeking to bring or continue the derivative claim became a member of the company.
(5) For the purposes of this Chapter—
  (a) 'director' includes a former director;
  (b) a shadow director is treated as a director; and
  (c) references to a member of a company include a person who is not a member but to whom shares in the company have been transferred or transmitted by operation of law.

Section 261—Application for permission to continue derivative claim

(1) A member of a company who brings a derivative claim under this Chapter must apply to the court for permission (in Northern Ireland, leave) to continue it.
(2) If it appears to the court that the application and the evidence filed by the applicant in support of it do not disclose a prima facie case for giving permission (or leave), the court—
  (a) must dismiss the application, and
  (b) may make any consequential order it considers appropriate.

(3) If the application is not dismissed under subsection (2), the court—
  (a) may give directions as to the evidence to be provided by the company, and
  (b) may adjourn the proceedings to enable the evidence to be obtained.
(4) On hearing the application, the court may—
  (a) give permission (or leave) to continue the claim on such terms as it thinks fit,
  (b) refuse permission (or leave) and dismiss the claim, or
  (c) adjourn the proceedings on the application and give such directions as it thinks fit.

Section 263—Whether permission to be given

(1) The following provisions have effect where a member of a company applies for permission (in Northern Ireland, leave) under section 261 or 262.
(2) Permission (or leave) must be refused if the court is satisfied—
  (a) that a person acting in accordance with section 172 (duty to promote the success of the company) would not seek to continue the claim, or
  (b) where the cause of action arises from an act or omission that is yet to occur, that the act or omission has been authorised by the company, or
  (c) where the cause of action arises from an act or omission that has already occurred, that the act or omission—
    (i) was authorised by the company before it occurred, or
    (ii) has been ratified by the company since it occurred.
(3) In considering whether to give permission (or leave) the court must take into account, in particular—
  (a) whether the member is acting in good faith in seeking to continue the claim;
  (b) the importance that a person acting in accordance with section 172 (duty to promote the success of the company) would attach to continuing it;
  (c) where the cause of action results from an act or omission that is yet to occur, whether the act or omission could be, and in the circumstances would be likely to be—
    (i) authorised by the company before it occurs, or
    (ii) ratified by the company after it occurs;
  (d) where the cause of action arises from an act or omission that has already occurred, whether the act or omission could be, and in the circumstances would be likely to be, ratified by the company;
  (e) whether the company has decided not to pursue the claim;
  (f) whether the act or omission in respect of which the claim is brought gives rise to a cause of action that the member could pursue in his own right rather than on behalf of the company.
(4) In considering whether to give permission (or leave) the court shall have particular regard to any evidence before it as to the views of members of the company who have no personal interest, direct or indirect, in the matter.

...

German Stock Corporation Act

§ 147— Enforcement of Claims for Compensation

(1) Compensation claims of the company on grounds of ... mismanagement against members of the management or supervisory board or pursuant to § 117 must be enforced if the general meeting so resolves by simple majority. The compensation claim shall be asserted within six months since the day of the general meeting.
(2) In order to enforce the compensation claim the general meeting may appoint special representatives. On a petition of shareholders whose shares together represent one tenth of the legal capital or 1 million EUR, the court (§ 14) shall appoint other persons than those normally representing the company pursuant to §§ 78, 112 [management and supervisory board, respectively] or those pursuant to sentence 1 as representatives of the company if this is deemed to be appropriate for an orderly enforcement of the claim ...

§ 148—Claim Admission Procedure

(1) Shareholders whose shares together represent 1% of the legal capital or 100,000 EUR at the time of the petition can apply for permission to enforce the compensation claims of the

company referred to in § 147(1), sentence 1, in their own name. The court will admit the action if:

1. the shareholders prove that they held the shares before they or, in the case of universal succession, their predecessors become aware of the alleged breach of duty by way of a publication;
2. the shareholders prove that they requested the company to pursue the claim in its own name, setting a reasonable time limit, but that the company failed to do so;
3. facts justify the assumption that the company suffered a loss due to dishonesty or a gross violation of legal provisions or the articles of association; and
4. pursuing the claim is contrary to overriding considerations in the interest of the company.

(2) The regional court at the place where the company has its seat has jurisdiction to decide on the petition for admission …

(3) The company may pursue at any time the compensation claim itself; if the company commences an action, the shareholders' claim admission procedure or legal action becomes inadmissible. The company has the right to take over an action regarding its compensation claim at any stage of the proceedings …

(4) If the claim is admitted, the action may be brought before the competent court pursuant to paragraph (2) within three month after the decision has become legally binding, provided that the shareholders request the company again to pursue the claim in its own name, setting a reasonable time limit, and the company fails to do so. The action must be brought against the persons referred to in § 147(1), sentence 1, and compensation must be sought for the company. An intervention by shareholders is no longer possible after admission of the claim. Several actions shall be combined for the purpose of a joint hearing and decision.

(5) A judgment, including a dismissal, binds the company and all shareholders. The same shall apply to settlements that must be published pursuant to § 149; however, settlements shall only bind the company after admission of the claim.

(6) The costs of the claim admission procedure are borne by the petitioner if the petition is dismissed. If the dismissal is based on overriding considerations in the interest of the company, which could have been disclosed by the company before the petition for admission was filed, but which were not disclosed, the company shall reimburse the petitioner for the costs. Otherwise a decision on the costs shall be made in the final judgment. If the company brings the action or takes over a pending lawsuit brought by the shareholders, it bears the petitioner's costs accrued until the date of commencement of the company's action or assumption of the lawsuit. The company cannot withdraw the action unless the conditions pursuant to § 93(4), sentences 3 and 4, with the exception of the period of limitation, are satisfied. If the action is dismissed completely or partially, the company shall reimburse the plaintiffs for the costs borne by them, unless the plaintiffs obtained the admission through intentionally or grossly negligently incorrect submissions. Shareholders acting jointly as petitioners or as joint litigants shall only be reimbursed for the costs of one representative altogether, unless an additional representative was essential for the enforcement of the claim.

French Commercial Code[100]

Art. L225-252

Apart from actions for personal loss or damage, shareholders may either individually or in an association fulfilling the conditions laid down in Article L225-120, or acting as a group in accordance with conditions to be laid down by an Order approved by the Conseil d'Etat, bring an action for liability on behalf of the company against its directors or managing director. The plaintiffs are entitled to pursue compensation for the entire loss suffered by the company, to which the damages, if any, shall be awarded.

[100] Translation by Legifrance, https://www.legifrance.gouv.fr/Traductions/en-English/Legifrance-translations.

Art. L225-120

I. In companies whose shares are admitted to trading on a regulated stock market, shareholders whose shares have been registered for at least two years and who hold at least 5% of the voting rights may form associations to represent their interests within the company ...

II. Where, however, the company's capital exceeds 750,000 euros, the share of voting rights to be represented pursuant to the preceding paragraph is reduced according to the number of the voting rights relating to the capital, as follows:

1° 4% between 750,000 euros and 4,500,000 euros;

2° 3% between 4,500,000 euros and 7,500,000 euros;

3° 2% between 7,500,000 euros and 15,000,000 euros;

4° 1% over 15,000,000 euros.

1. *Incentive problems and the derivative action*

Given the inherent conflict of interest that exists when the board of directors (and to some extent the supervisory board in two-tier systems) decides on enforcing the company's claims against a director, it is apparent that the right of minority shareholders to commence legal proceedings on behalf of the company—the so-called derivative action—is an important element of an effective corporate governance system. Most legal systems, accordingly, provide for procedural mechanisms that allow shareholders to pursue the company's claims in court if the company, acting either through the board of directors or the general meeting, refuses to bring litigation. Nevertheless, it has been observed that minority shareholder lawsuits remain rare in many countries, with the United States being a notable exception.[101] From a theoretical point of view, the lack of shareholder lawsuits, in spite of their procedural availability, is easy to understand. Derivative lawsuits exhibit characteristics of a public good. Since they are used to enforce a claim of the company, the shareholder-litigant can only demand payment to the company. Thus, all shareholders partake in the benefits of successful litigation, without sharing the plaintiff's expenses and litigation risk.[102] A likely consequence, typical for public goods, is that the parties underinvest in the good, which will accordingly be undersupplied (in other words, less of the good is supplied than optimal, given existing demand). For minority shareholder lawsuits, this means that it is rational for shareholders to remain passive and attempt to 'free-ride' on the efforts of another shareholder to enforce the company's claim. The disincentives are greater, the more widely dispersed a company's owners are and, hence, the smaller the indirect benefit of litigation is to the individual shareholders.

The most common responses to the undersupply of a public good are the allocation of property rights that allow the rights holder to exclude others from consumption of the good (that is, 'privatising' the public good) and the supply of the good by the government. Legal systems are reluctant to use the former strategy widely in the present context. As we have seen, the law has developed rules to differentiate between cases where the company's claims are at stake, and cases where a shareholder seeks to enforce a personal claim.[103] The

[101] J Armour and others, 'Private Enforcement of Corporate Law: An Empirical Comparison of the United Kingdom and the United States' (2009) 6 Journal of Empirical Legal Studies 687; BR Cheffins and BS Black, 'Outside Director Liability across Countries' (2006) 84 Texas Law Review 1385; M Gelter, 'Why Do Shareholder Derivative Suits Remain Rare in Continental Europe?' (2012) 37 Brooklyn Journal of International Law 843; DW Puchniak, H Baum, and M Ewing-Chow (eds), *The Derivative Action in Asia* (Cambridge University Press 2012).

[102] By bringing a derivative action, the plaintiff not only incurs expenses and opportunity costs (because the time spent could be used otherwise), but also bears the risk of losing in court and having to pay the attorney's fees of the opposing party. Under general civil procedure law, a 'loser pays' system exists in France, Germany, and the UK. In the United States, on the other hand, the default rule is that each party is responsible for its own attorney's fees (although various exceptions exist in some states and in federal statutes). However, it should also be noted that the extent of reimbursement under a 'loser pays' rule may be limited, notably to court fees in France. In this case, the litigation risk is comparable to that under the American approach; Gelter (n 101) 863–4.

[103] Chapter 6A.II.

company is the proper plaintiff if a wrong has been committed against the company, which may consist in a breach of directors' duties, of other provisions of company law, or general duties falling outside of company law. A personal claim arises if the shareholder's personal rights are invaded,[104] duties are owed to the shareholder directly,[105] or the challenged act is conceptualized as a tortious act against a shareholder, a breach of contract, or quasi-contract between the shareholder and the defendant director.[106] From the shareholder's perspective, the distinction, of course, does not make any economic difference. A harm done to the company may affect the shareholder's wealth as much as the loss suffered from a wrong committed directly against the shareholder. The main rationale for denying the shareholder an action for particular types of wrong can be seen in the desire to protect the company's assets for the creditors of the company.[107] Since this is a general concern, it is not surprising that the problem of how to distinguish between the company's claims and the shareholders' personal claims has been discussed in all legal systems dealt with in this book and the distinction follows broadly similar lines. Legal systems seek to define spheres where the interests of the creditors are prioritized when the risk of managerial misconduct materializes (by allocating corresponding claims to the company), and spheres where the interests of the shareholders are prioritized (by allowing them to pursue claims in their own name and on their own account).

Where exactly the dividing line is drawn, however, differs between legal systems (and is often uncertain even within a legal system). It seems to be largely a function of the path dependent development of legal institutions and somewhat arbitrary dogmatic compartmentalization, rather than the deliberate decision of a policy-maker to determine appropriate spheres of risk for creditors and shareholders. For example, under French law, the dilution of a shareholder's equity position as a consequence of the overvaluation of a contribution in kind has been qualified as a personal loss, and the shareholder is therefore entitled to bring an action for infringement of an individual right.[108] In contrast, under

[104] Germany: BGHZ 83, 122 (*Holzmüller*); UK: *Pender v Lushington* (1877) 6 Ch D 70 (Ch). In *Pender v Lushington*, the company's articles contained a cap on voting rights that was evaded by the plaintiff, Mr Pender, by assigning some of his shares to nominees. The chairman of the general meeting refused to count the votes cast by the plaintiff and his nominees, which was challenged by the plaintiff in court. The Chancery Division held that this case concerned the enforcement of a personal right of the shareholder, not a right of the company: 'This is an action by Mr. Pender for himself. He is a member of the company, and whether he votes with the majority or the minority he is entitled to have his vote recorded—an individual right in respect of which he has a right to sue. That has nothing to do with the question like that raised in *Foss v Harbottle* and that line of cases. He has a right to say, "Whether I vote in the majority or minority, you shall record my vote, as that is a right of property belonging to my interest in this company, and if you refuse to record my vote I will institute legal proceedings against you to compel you". What is the answer to such an action? It seems to me it can be maintained as a matter of substance, and that there is no technical difficulty in maintaining it'. In Delaware, the courts have moved away from a focus on a 'special injury' suffered by shareholders, for example, as a result of the invasion of a right existing independently of any right of the company, and now ask who suffered the alleged harm; see *Tooley v Donaldson, Lufkin & Jenrette, Inc.*, 845 A.2d 1031 (Del. 2004), discussed in n 2 below and the accompanying text. For France, see the next footnote.

[105] France: Cass com, 27 February 1996 (*Vilgrain*), *JCP E* 1996, II, 838; UK: *Percival v Wright* [1902] 2 Ch 421; US: *Malone v Brincat*, 722 A.2d 5 (Del. 1998). As mentioned, in France duties are generally owed to the company and shareholders directly (as well as to third parties in particular circumstances, see Chapter 6B.I.4(a)), Com, Art L225-251. The proper plaintiff is determined by differentiating between the company's loss and the shareholder's individual loss. In the former case, the company is the proper plaintiff, which enforces claims typically arising from mismanagement by means of the so-called *action sociale*. In the latter case, that is, when shareholders have suffered a loss that is distinguishable from the loss of the company, they have standing to bring an *action individuelle* to enforce their rights in their own name. For more details, see Chapter 6A.II.

[106] In both France and Germany, certain violations of disclosure obligations are qualified as a tort, see Chapter 6A.II.

[107] See, for example, *Johnson v Gore Wood & Co* [2002] 2 AC 1, 62.

[108] Cass com, 28 June 2005 (*Sté Total Fina Elf c/ Sté KPMG*), *JCP E* 2005, 1325, note H Hovasse. The court held that 'the overvaluation of contributions in kind by a shareholder, which results in an unjustified increase in the value of that shareholder's interest in the company's capital, inflicts a loss on the other shareholders that is not the corollary of the loss suffered by the company'. Thus, the court acknowledged not only that the shareholders had a personal claim, but also held that the reflective loss principle, to be discussed presently in the text, did not apply. Compare this decision with the English case *Prudential Assurance Co Ltd v Newman Industries Ltd (No 2)* [1982] Ch 204, also to be discussed presently.

English law, overvaluation potentially gives rise to a claim of the company against the allottee and the directors who authorized the share issue below market value (against the latter for breach of the duty to promote the success of the company), but not to a claim of the individual shareholders.[109] Arguably, the different treatment of this case by the French courts is aided by the fact that a direct relationship of rights and duties among the shareholders and between the shareholders, directors and third parties is not alien to French company law.[110]

Another example is the liability of directors for not having informed the shareholders adequately. According to English law, a duty of disclosure to the shareholders arises only if 'a special factual relationship [exists] between the directors and the shareholders'.[111] Such a requirement is absent in Delaware law, where the courts hold that whenever directors 'are deliberately misinforming shareholders about the business of the corporation, either directly or by a public statement, there is a violation of fiduciary duty'.[112] The more restrictive approach of the English courts is a function of the conceptualization of directors as fiduciaries in the traditional common law sense. Fiduciary duties, which encompass the core duties of loyalty and fidelity (but not the duty of care), presuppose 'a relationship of trust and confidence'.[113] For the same reason, US courts are prepared to draw on directors' duties to fill gaps in the system of investor protection of the federal securities laws and hold directors responsible for the dissemination of incorrect information to the public, whereas English law takes recourse to tort law principles in such cases.[114] Different considerations, but nonetheless of a path-dependent nature, have led German courts to apply tort law to incorrect market disclosures.[115] As early as the beginning of the twentieth century, courts held that directors' duties are not intended to protect individual shareholders.[116] In addition, the German Stock Corporation Act states explicitly that the codified duties are owed only to the company.[117] Therefore, it is difficult for the courts to develop general unwritten disclosure duties, and using tort law was probably the more obvious choice.[118]

The reluctance of legal systems to 'privatise' the enforcement of claims against the directors is reinforced by a rule that has become known as the 'reflective loss' principle in English law. In some cases, a harmful act of the directors will constitute both a breach of directors' duties and an invasion of the shareholders' personal rights. For example, a director who distributes an incorrect circular to the shareholders in order to induce them to approve a self-dealing transaction violates both a duty owed to the company and a duty owed directly to the shareholders.[119] In such a case, the shareholder has no right to sue in a personal capacity if the shareholder's loss reflects the loss suffered by the company. The typical example is a reduction in the share price or dividend payments because of the loss inflicted on the

[109] Davies and Worthington (n 34) paras 11-5, 11-16.

[110] See the references in n 105 above and compare Art L225-251 of the French Code de commerce, which stipulates that the directors 'shall be ... liable to the company or third parties', with s. 170(1) UK Companies Act 2006 and §93(2) German AktG, which provide that directors' duties 'are owed by a director of a company to the company' and directors shall be 'liable to the company', respectively.

[111] *Peskin v Anderson* [2001] BCC 874, 880.

[112] *Malone v Brincat* (n 105).

[113] *Bristol and West Building Society v Mothew* [1998] Ch 1, 18, cited approvingly in *Peskin v Anderson* [2000] BCC 1110, 1122 (Ch), affirmed [2001] BCC 874 (CA).

[114] US: *Malone v Brincat* (n 105) 11–14; UK: *Derry v Peek* (1889) LR 14 App Cas 337; *Al-Nakib Investments v Longcroft* [1990] 3 All ER 321; *Possfund Custodian Trustees v Diamond* [1996] 2 All ER 77.

[115] For example, BGHZ 160, 134; 160, 149 (*Infomatec I and II*).

[116] Reichsgericht (Imperial Court), RGZ 63, 324. See also our discussion in Chapter 6A.II.

[117] AktG, §93(2) sentence 1.

[118] For another example of the impediment that the rigid statutory framework poses to the development of unwritten disclosure duties, see our analysis of the regulation of self-dealing transactions in Germany: Chapter 6C.I.3.

[119] *Prudential Assurance Co Ltd v Newman Industries Ltd (No 2)* [1982] Ch 204 (see also n 108 above). Similarly, a breach of the proper purpose doctrine, s 171(b) of the UK Companies Act 2006 can be interpreted as a breach of a duty owed to the company and a breach of the shareholders' constitutional rights; see Chapter 5B.I.

company.[120] The policy rationale behind the rule is clear. Allowing both the company and the shareholder to sue would lead to double recovery for the shareholder: directly as a result of the personal action and indirectly because the company could claim compensation for the diminution in the value of the company's assets.[121] A similar rule can be found in many legal systems. In Delaware, the courts ask two questions: '(1) who suffered the alleged harm (the corporation or the suing stockholders, individually); and (2) who would receive the benefit of any recovery or other remedy (the corporation or the stockholders, individually)?'[122] The first prong of the test supports a direct action if the shareholder's injury 'is not dependent on a prior injury to the corporation' or, to put it differently, if the shareholder had demonstrated 'that he or she can prevail without showing an injury to the corporation'.[123] Under the second prong, the question is to whom the remedy would flow. The answer generally follows logically from the first prong of the analysis. However, in certain cases, where both the company and shareholders individually suffered a loss, a derivative as well as a direct action may be available. The choice between the two then depends on the relief sought, and courts are prepared to allow a direct action, for example, if the shareholder sues for injunctive relief or the company has been wound up.[124] Examples of claims that can only be pursued with a derivative action include compensation for mismanagement of corporate assets, excessive issuance of stock options to managers, or overpayment for a corporate asset by the company.[125] On the other hand, share exchanges with the goal of preventing a stockholder from gaining control,[126] reorganizations that affect the shareholders' voting rights,[127] or the refusal to pay

[120] *Prudential Assurance Co Ltd v Newman Industries Ltd (No 2)* [1982] Ch 204, 222-223. An example for a loss of the shareholders that is not reflective is *Heron International Ltd v Lord Grade* [1983] BCLC 244, where the directors, through actions that were alleged to have violated their duties, had prevented the shareholders from accepting a higher takeover offer than the one that the directors preferred. The court held (ibid 262) that the loss 'of the opportunity of realising their shares to greater advantage ... is a loss suffered exclusively to the pockets of the shareholders, and is in no sense a loss to the coffers of the company, which remain totally unaffected ... [Therefore,] any one or more or all of the former shareholders in [the target company] can seek to sue [the] directors in order to recover for the benefit of their own individual pockets the difference between the takeover value per share which they are constrained to accept and the higher takeover value which they lost the chance of accepting'.

[121] *Prudential Assurance Co Ltd v Newman Industries Ltd (No 2)* [1982] Ch 204, 222–3. English law provides for an exception to the reflective loss principle if the company is unable to pursue its claim because of the actions of the wrongdoer, for example because the company does not have sufficient funds to give security for the costs of the proceedings as a result of the wrongdoing; see *Giles v Rhind* [2003] Ch 618.

[122] *Tooley v Donaldson, Lufkin & Jenrette, Inc.*, 845 A.2d 1031, 1033 (Del. 2004). The decision constitutes a departure from prior law, which was based on the so-called 'special injury' test and required for an individual action that shareholders must 'allege either "an injury which is separate and distinct from that suffered by other shareholders" ... or a wrong involving a contractual right of a shareholder, such as the right to vote, or to assert majority control, which exists independently of any right of the corporation': *Moran v Household International, Inc.*, 490 A.2d 1059, 1070 (Del. Ch. 1985) (quoting *Fletcher Cyclopedia Corporations* (perm edn, Thomson Reuters, 1984) §5921, at 451).

[123] *Agostino v Hicks*, 2004 WL 443987, 7 (Del. Ch. 2004).

[124] For example, it has been held that overpayment for a corporate asset inflicts direct and individual injury on (minority) shareholders if the controller causes the company to issue shares to the controller in consideration for overvalued assets and with the aim of diluting the minority shareholders' economic interest and voting power. In this case, in principle, both a derivative action and a direct action are available, *Gentile v Rossette*, 906 A.2d 91 (Del. 2006); *In re Tri-Star Pictures, Inc.*, 634 A.2d 319 (Del. 1993). See also *Grimes v Donald*, 673 A.2d 1207 (Del. 1996), where the plaintiff did not seek to recover damages for injury to the company, but a declaration that the employment agreement with the chief executive was invalid because it amounted to an abdication of the board's responsibilities. The court held that a direct action, rather than a derivative action, was appropriate.

[125] *Bokat v Getty Oil Co.*, 262 A.2d 246 (Del. 1970); *Kramer v Western Pacific Industries, Inc.*, 546 A.2d 348 (Del. 1988). However, see also the previous footnote for the special case of overpayment in the form of 'over-issuing' shares to the controlling stockholder.

[126] *Lipton v News Intern., Plc*, 514 A.2d 1075 (Del. 1986) (still applying the 'special injury' test, but the outcome would have been the same under the two-pronged standard established in *Tooley*).

[127] *Eisenberg v Flying Tiger Line, Inc.*, 451 F.2d 267 (2d Cir. 1971). In this case, which resembles *Holzmüller* (see Chapter 5A.III), Flying Tiger entered into a reorganization and merger that had the effect of transferring Flying Tiger's operating business to a wholly owned subsidiary of a newly established holding company, whose shareholders were the former shareholders of the original operating company. Applying New York law, the court qualified the lawsuit as a personal action, because 'the reorganization deprived [the plaintiff] and other minority stockholders of any voice in the affairs of their previously existing operating company': ibid 271.

a dividend[128] give rise to a direct action. French courts bar actions by shareholders in their own right if the loss for which they seek compensation is 'a corollary' of the company's loss. As under English law, this has been held to be the case where the shareholder's loss derives from the diminution in the value of the company.[129] In other situations, however, French courts seem to be more readily prepared to accept that a wrong affects the shareholders personally than their English counterparts, such as in the case of the overvaluation of a contribution in kind mentioned above.[130] In Germany, courts rely on the principles of capital maintenance and equal treatment of shareholders to argue that shareholders do not have standing to bring an action in their own right if their loss is 'congruent' with the company's loss.[131] The definition of 'congruent loss' is again very similar to the reflective loss principle under English law. A shareholder has suffered an indirect loss if the injury to the company is reflected in the diminution in the value of the plaintiff's shares.[132] However, in some cases, shareholders were allowed to bring a personal action where the company was unable to recover damages, for example because its claim was time-barred or it decided not to pursue the claim.[133]

We can observe elements of the second common response to the undersupply of a public good, the provision of the good by the state, more frequently in the design of enforcement mechanisms in corporate law. It is common that private enforcement is supplemented to a greater or lesser degree by public enforcement of the company's rights against corporate insiders. As we will see, in some countries, for example the Netherlands, public enforcement largely replaces private lawsuits, and in others, for example France and the UK, criminal and administrative sanctions (especially the disqualification of directors) are important substitute mechanisms.[134] As far as the minority shareholder lawsuit is concerned, some legal systems seek to incentivize shareholders by shifting the litigation risk to the company, thus effectively 'socialising' it. Others allow the shareholder-plaintiffs to enter into contingency fee agreements with their lawyers. Shareholders then only bear the court fees and similar charges (and, depending on the applicable cost rules, the lawyer's fees of the winning party[135]), but they do not have to pay their own lawyer's fees if the case is not successful. Such arrangements to shift the litigation risk to the company or the lawyers solve the 'free rider' problem that may prevent individual shareholders from bringing a lawsuit that benefits all shareholders. However, they also create incentives for lawyers to pursue derivative litigation in their own, and not their clients', interests. With the lawyer, rather than a nominee shareholder, being the real party in interest, there is a danger that litigation is initiated merely for its nuisance value and even meritorious claims are settled in a collusive way by lawyers striking a deal with the defendants.[136] Thus, legal systems need to erect procedural safeguards to differentiate between frivolous litigation with a negative net present value from the company's perspective (but not, of course, from the lawyer's or shareholder's perspective,

[128] *In re Worldcom, Inc.*, 323 B.R. 844, 850 (Bankr. S.D.N.Y. 2005) (quoting MP Dooley, *Fundamentals of Corporation Law* (Foundation Press 1995) 301–2).

[129] Chapter 6A.II.

[130] Cass com, 28 June 2005 (*Sté Total Fina Elf c/ Sté KPMG*) (n 108) (compare this case with *Gentile v Rossette* and *In re Tri-Star Pictures* (n 124), where the Supreme Court of Delaware comes to a similar result). For another example of a distinct loss, see Cass com, 18 February 1997 (*Sté Dassault*), *Bull. Joly Sociétés* 1997, 408, discussed in Chapter 6A.II.

[131] BGH NJW 1988, 413, 415; NJW 1987, 1077, 1079–80. The formulation 'congruence of loss' is used by Spindler (n 19) §93 para 352.

[132] BGH NJW 1987, 1077, 1079. [133] BGH NJW 1969, 1712. [134] Section D below.

[135] See n 102 above. Shareholder-plaintiffs, of course, can take out insurance to cover the costs awarded against them under a 'loser pays' rule.

[136] JC Coffee, 'Understanding the Plaintiff's Attorney: The Implications of Economic Theory for Private Enforcement of Law through Class and Derivative Actions' (1986) 86 Columbia Law Review 669, 714–20 (arguing that plaintiff's attorneys are biased in favour of early settlement, in particular if their fees are calculated on the basis of the so-called 'lodestar' formula, according to which fees are a function of both the amount recovered and the time spent on the case).

who bring the lawsuit for its settlement value), and non-frivolous litigation. As we shall see, all legal systems provide for such safeguards, but in different forms, and the difficult question is often whether they succeed in striking the right balance between providing for a legal environment that encourages derivative litigation and discourages nuisance suits.

In light of the above discussion, it can be argued that a well-designed derivative action mechanism is characterized by several elements that must all be present for the mechanism to be effective: first, reasonably generous standing rules providing, for example, that ownership of one share is sufficient to bring an action; secondly, cost rules ensuring that the plaintiff generally does not bear the litigation risk, even if the derivative action is ultimately unsuccessful; and thirdly, a 'screening mechanism' that filters out frivolous actions without making it excessively difficult to bring a non-frivolous lawsuit.[137] Arguably, even if only one of these conditions is not satisfied, derivative actions will be largely ineffective. As opposed to differences in the design of substantive investor protection mechanisms, for example the content of directors' duties, which typically have a gradual impact on the effectiveness of the mechanism, design flaws in the minority shareholder lawsuit are likely to have binary effects. If standing or screening requirements are too onerous, shareholders will generally not be in a position to bring an action, and if the disincentives illustrated above are not rectified, they will not be willing to do so. It has been pointed out that this is the reason why the level of private enforcement of directors' duties is low (or virtually zero) in Continental Europe. Policy-makers in European jurisdictions often do not quite 'get it right' with regard to all three dimensions: standing, screening, and cost rules.[138] In the next sections, we will examine minority shareholder lawsuits in our four jurisdictions along these three dimensions, followed by an assessment of the comparative effectiveness of the mechanisms.

2. UK

For almost two centuries, the law on minority shareholder lawsuits in England was, and to a certain extent it still is, determined by the rule in *Foss v Harbottle*,[139] which has been dubbed 'the deepest mystery of company law'.[140] In spite of its reputation for lack of clarity and consistency, the basic principles established in *Foss v Harbottle*, often said to consist of two rules, are easily summarized. First, the company, acting through its authorized organs, is the proper plaintiff in a lawsuit enforcing a claim of the company. Secondly, considerations of justice may make it necessary to allow individual shareholders to bring the lawsuit if no adequate remedy could be obtained otherwise. However, this power of minority shareholders does not exist if the general meeting could lawfully confirm (or ratify) the challenged act: 'The very fact that the governing body of proprietors assembled at the special general meeting may . . . bind even a reluctant minority is decisive to shew that the [minority shareholder] suit cannot be sustained whilst that body retains its functions'.[141] Importantly,

[137] An example of an excessively restrictive screening mechanism is the English common law rule in *Foss v Harbottle*, discussed in the next section.

[138] Gelter (n 101) 845–6 (referring to this observation as the 'Anna Karenina Principle', in adaptation of Leo Tolstoy's remark in his eponymous novel that it is possible for a family to be unhappy in many different ways, but happy only if certain universally applicable conditions are satisfied). See also C Gerner-Beuerle and EP Schuster, 'The Evolving Structure of Directors' Duties in Europe' (2014) 15 EBOR 191, 214–22 (developing an 'ease of enforcement' index based on the three dimensions above and covering all EU Member States). Gelter identifies two additional requirements that must be satisfied, in his view, for derivative litigation to be effective: plaintiffs must have sufficient access to relevant information, in particular internal documents of the company, and they must be able to bring the action against a variety of defendants, not only directors (ibid. 856). We do not discuss these additional conditions, because a right to information or inquiry is generally available at least for shareholders that would have standing to bring a derivative action (ibid. 870-875), and we are here interested particularly in the enforcement of claims for a breach of directors' duties against the company's directors.

[139] (1843) 2 Hare 461.

[140] SW Mayson, D French, and C Ryan, *Company Law* (35th edn, Oxford University Press 2018) 18.3.2.

[141] (1843) 2 Hare 461, 494.

it was not necessary that the general meeting had actually ratified the act in question. The court's considerations were based on an efficiency rationale. If the majority shareholders had implicitly approved of the directors' actions by not bringing legal proceedings on behalf of the company *and* they were legally entitled to ratify the breach of duty, allowing a minority shareholder lawsuit to go ahead would be an exercise in futility. The majority could defeat the litigation simply by 'resolving upon the confirmation of the very acts which are the subject of the suit'.[142]

Minority shareholder lawsuits, therefore, were only permissible in limited circumstances. Most importantly, they were available if the act complained of 'amount[ed] to ... a fraud on the minority and the wrongdoers [were] themselves in control of the company'[143] or the act could only be approved or ratified by a special majority of the shareholders.[144] The reasons for these two exceptions are evident. In the former case, the wrongdoers were typically not able to ratify the challenged act, but could nevertheless prevent the company from suing. In the latter case, a simple majority of shareholders could circumvent any supermajority requirement if it were able to block the minority from enforcing violations of the requirement to adopt a resolution by special majority.[145] The 'fraud on the minority' exception made derivative lawsuits virtually impossible, at least in widely held and listed companies. It was somewhat uncertain how 'fraud' should be interpreted, but it was clear that more was required than a negligent breach of duty.[146] In addition, the persons implicated in the fraud had to be 'in control' of the company, understood—also somewhat ambivalently—as majority voting control or de facto control because other shareholders could be expected not to oppose them.[147] Given these restrictive conditions, it was unsurprising that very few derivative lawsuits were filed against directors of public companies, and it was commonly acknowledged that the risk of being found liable was very low under the rule in *Foss v Harbottle*.[148]

The Law Commission, an independent body established by the UK parliament to advise on legal reform, expressed the opinion that the rule in *Foss v Harbottle* and its exceptions were 'complex and obscure'[149] and recommended the adoption of a new derivative action procedure to replace the common law in a report published in 1997.[150] Following the report, a codified derivative action mechanism was introduced by the Companies Act 2006,

[142] ibid. For a more recent summary of the rationale of this rule, see *Edwards v Halliwell* [1950] 2 All ER 1064, 1066–7.

[143] ibid 1067. [144] ibid. [145] *Cotter v National Union of Seamen* [1929] 2 Ch 58, 69–70.

[146] Some courts held that acts falling short of common law fraud, but 'having an improper tendency', sufficed: *MacDougall v Gardiner* (1875) LR 20 Eq 383, 395; others argued that it would be 'quite monstrous' if the exceptions to *Foss v Harbottle* 'were drawn so narrowly that directors could make a profit out of their negligence', and they accordingly allowed a derivative action where directors personally benefited from a breach of duty without acting fraudulently: *Daniels v Daniels* [1978] Ch 406, 413–14.

[147] *Prudential Assurance Co Ltd v Newman Industries Ltd (No 2)* [1982] 1 All ER 354, 364, held that 'control' 'embraces a broad spectrum extending from an overall absolute majority of votes at one end to a majority of votes at the other end made up of those likely to be cast by the delinquent himself plus those voting with him as a result of influence or apathy'. The exceptions to *Foss v Harbottle* were further narrowed in *Smith v Croft (No 2)* [1988] Ch 114. The court explained that the appropriate organ to decide on bringing litigation were the shareholders who were entitled to vote on the matter (that is, excluding generally the wrongdoers). If a majority of these shareholders were 'for disinterested reasons satisfied that the proceedings [would] be productive of more harm than good', the court believed that it was not justified to allow the action to go ahead, ibid 185. The holding can be interpreted as establishing an additional 'majority of the independent minority' requirement (Davies and Worthington (n 34) para 17-21), although the court only held 'that it [was] proper to have regard to the views of independent shareholders', ibid. As we will see, an almost identical formulation is now part of the statutory derivative action mechanism (s 263(4) Companies Act 2006).

[148] For data, see Armour and others (n 101) 698–700 (finding that out of 27,099 filings in the Companies Court list of the Chancery Division of the English High Court from 2004 to 2006, only one involved a claim for damages against a director of a publicly traded company, and even this filing did not seem to be a genuine claim because the claimant did not submit any supporting details). Kershaw (n 92) 605, reports that 'the last reported derivative litigation involving a listed company was in 1982' (*Prudential Assurance Co Ltd v Newman Industries Ltd (No 2)* [1982] 1 All ER 354).

[149] Law Commission, Consultation Paper No 142, para 1.6.

[150] Law Commission, Shareholder Remedies Report, para 6.15.

laid down in sections 260–264 of the Act. In analysing the procedure, we will follow the three steps set out above, which—as we argued—determine the effectiveness of the minority shareholder lawsuit: initial standing requirements, further conditions that need to be satisfied to bring a derivative action, and cost rules.[151]

Derivative claims are defined as proceedings by a member of a company in respect of a cause of action vested in the company and seeking relief on behalf of the company.[152] 'Member' is a technical term which, according to the statutory definition, refers to persons whose name has been entered in the register of members or to whom shares have been transferred by operation of law.[153] As under the common law, all members owning at least one share have standing to bring a derivative claim, irrespective of whether the cause of action arose before or after they became members of the company.[154] A first important deviation from the common law is the broader determination of the types of misconduct that can be challenged with the statutory derivative action mechanism. As mentioned, the rule in *Foss v Harbottle* required a breach of duty involving more than mere negligence. The legislator decided against maintaining this requirement and instead allowed shareholders to enforce a claim derivatively if it arises from an act or omission 'involving negligence, default, breach of duty or breach of trust' by a director or shadow director of the company.[155]

The main innovation of the statutory procedure is that it replaces the proper plaintiff rule of the common law with a claim admission procedure. Under the statutory regime, a member who intends to initiate a shareholder lawsuit must first apply to the court for permission to continue the derivative claim.[156] The court must dismiss the application if the claimant has not made out a prima facie case for granting permission or one or more of the following three grounds for dismissal are satisfied: if a person acting in accordance with the duty to promote the success of the company would not seek to continue the claim; the challenged conduct has not yet occurred and has been authorized by the company; or it was previously authorized or subsequently ratified.[157] If the application survives this stage of the admission procedure, the court has discretion whether to grant permission to continue to claim. The Companies Act sets out a non-exhaustive list of seven criteria that courts must take into account in deciding on the application, including the good faith of the member in bringing the action, the possibility and likelihood that the wrong will be ratified, any decision of the company not to pursue the claim, the existence of a cause of action regarding the challenged act or omission that the member could pursue in his own right, and the views of other disinterested members of the company.[158] Thus, the statutory derivative action mechanism seeks to balance the competing goals of avoiding frivolous litigation and facilitating access of minority shareholders to the courts by employing the courts as gatekeepers: neutral arbiters that decide based on the above criteria whether the lawsuit should proceed. The reform thus introduces a degree of flexibility that was missing in the common law, which used the 'wrongdoer control' formula as an arguably inaccurate and rigid proxy for what was in the best interest of the company.

We will discuss the criteria that inform the court's decision at the mandatory and discretionary stages of the proceedings in turn. The court will initially determine on the basis of the evidence filed by the claimant shareholder whether a prima facie case for granting permission exists. In order to minimize disruption to the company's business, the company is not a party to the proceedings at this stage, and neither the company nor the defendant directors are required to submit evidence.[159] The court will assess whether, prima facie, the company has a good cause of action arising out of negligence, default, breach of duty or

[151] Text to nn 137–138. [152] Companies Act 2006, s 260(1). [153] ibid ss 112, 260(5)(c).
[154] ibid s 260(4).
[155] ibid s 260(3), (5)(b). For a summary of the reform discussion concerning this point, see Law Commission (n 150) paras 6.38–6.41.
[156] Companies Act 2006, s 261(1). [157] ibid ss 261(2), 263(2). [158] ibid s 263(3), (4).
[159] Civil Procedure Rules, 19.9A.

breach of trust by a director.[160] If the court concludes that this is the case, the claim will proceed to the second stage. Now, all parties involved, including the company, will be heard, and the court forms a view on the strength of the claim in light of the more complete evidence before it in order to consider the statutory grounds for mandatory refusal and discretionary grant of permission.[161] It is clear that a claim has no chance of success if it has been duly authorized or ratified. In such a case, the statute accordingly requires the court to refuse permission.[162] The third ground for mandatory refusal, the decision of a hypothetical director seeking to promote the success of the company not to continue the claim, is more difficult to apply, especially since the same formulation is used as one of the discretionary factors to be taken into account by the court in deciding whether to grant permission.[163] The following case interprets this and some of the other criteria laid down in the statute.

***Iesini v Westrip Holdings Ltd* [2010] BCC 420 (Chancery Division)**

Lewison, J:

[*Mandatory refusal of permission if a person acting in accordance with section 172 would not seek to continue the claim (s. 263(2)(a))*]

As many judges have pointed out (e.g. Warren J. in *Airey v Cordell* [2007] EWHC 2728 (Ch); [2007] B.C.C. 785 , 800 and Mr William Trower QC in *Franbar Holdings Ltd v Patel* [2008] EWHC 1534 (Ch); [2008] B.C.C. 885 , 893-894) there are many cases in which some directors, acting in accordance with s. 172, would think it worthwhile to continue a claim at least for the time being, while others, also acting in accordance with s. 172, would reach the opposite conclusion. There are, of course, a number of factors that a director, acting in accordance with s. 172, would consider in reaching his decision. They include: the size of the claim; the strength of the claim; the cost of the proceedings; the company's ability to fund the proceedings; the ability of the potential defendants to satisfy a judgment; the impact on the company if it lost the claim and had to pay not only its own costs but the defendant's as well; any disruption to the company's activities while the claim is pursued; whether the prosecution of the claim would damage the company in other ways (e.g. by losing the services of a valuable employee or alienating a key supplier or customer) and so on. The weighing of all these considerations is essentially a commercial decision, which the court is ill-equipped to take, except in a clear case.

In my judgment therefore ... s. 263(2)(a) will apply only where the court is satisfied that *no* director acting in accordance with s.172 would seek to continue the claim. If some directors would, and others would not, seek to continue the claim the case is one for the application of s. 263(3)(b). Many of the same considerations would apply to that paragraph too ...

[*Whether the act or omission gives rise to a cause of action that the member could pursue in his own right rather than on behalf of the company (s. 263(3)(f))*]

The relevant alternative remedy in the present case is an unfair prejudice petition under s. 994. From the point of view of the company itself a petition under s. 994 is far preferable, principally because it will only be a nominal party and will not incur legal costs; whereas in the ordinary way if a derivative action is brought for its benefit it will be liable to indemnify the claimant against his costs, even if the claim is unsuccessful: *Wallersteiner v Moir (No.2)* ...

The justification for the indemnity is that the claimant brings his claim for the benefit of the company (and ex hypothesi under the new law the court has allowed it to proceed). Once the court has reached the conclusion that the claim ought to proceed for the benefit of the company, it ought normally to order the company to indemnify the claimant against his costs.

The potential liability of the company for costs is, in my judgment, a proper consideration for the court in deciding whether to allow a derivative claim to proceed. In the present case the combination of that potential liability and the availability of an alternative remedy under s. 994 [leads to the conclusion that it is not] appropriate to allow the derivative claim to proceed.

Views of members with no personal interest [*(s. 263(4)*]

[S]ub-section [263(4)] is not easy to understand. All the members of a company have an obvious interest in any claim brought on the company's behalf. The value of their shareholdings

[160] *Iesini v Westrip Holdings Ltd* [2010] BCC 420, 440 (Ch). [161] ibid.
[162] Companies Act 2006, s 263(2)(b), (c). [163] ibid s 263(3)(b).

may be increased or diminished depending on the outcome. Unless 'personal interest' is being used in contra-distinction to 'financial interest' it is difficult to see who would not have an interest. Another possible reading is that 'the matter' is not the question whether or not to give permission, but is the alleged default (etc.) of the directors out of which the cause of action has arisen. It may be that what the section is trying to get at is that the court must have regard to the views of members of the company who are not implicated in the alleged wrongdoing, and who do not stand to benefit otherwise than in their capacity as members of the company. If that reading is correct (as I think it probably is) it raises another question: how is the court to resolve any dispute about whether a member or the company is or is not involved in the alleged wrongdoing or stands to benefit otherwise than [in] his capacity as a member of the company?

... It seems to me that in order for the court to be in a position to have 'particular' regard to the views of certain members of the company it must be as satisfied as it can be on an interim application that they are not financially interested in the outcome (beyond their interest as shareholders in the company) ...

Questions and comments:

1. According to *Iesini v Westrip*, the 'duty to promote the success of the company' test, both as a ground for mandatory refusal in section 263(2) and part of the discretionary decision of the court in section 263(3), is a multi-faceted test. The court is expected to assess and balance a variety of factors that include legal questions—the likely success of the litigation—as well as commercial questions—for example, how disruptive the proceedings will be, whether they risk damaging the company's reputation or business relationships with important customers or suppliers. As the court in *Iesini v Westrip* admits, courts are ill-equipped to make such business judgments, except in clear cases. We have seen that this is precisely the reason why the standard of review pursuant to section 172 is subjective. Directors will not be found liable if they believe, in good faith, that they promote the success of the company.[164] When deciding whether to grant permission to continue a derivative action, the court cannot defer to the *bona fides* of the directors. The court is required to form its own view on the desirability of litigation. Can we expect courts to exercise their business judgment as independently as the statute apparently demands? As far as the mandatory-refusal alternative of the test is concerned, the formulation proposed in *Iesini v Westrip*, arguably, emulates the subjective standard used to assess whether directors have breached their duty under section 172. Requiring that 'no director' would seek to continue the claim comes close to holding that a hypothetical director's good faith in promoting the interests of the company was not plausible, which is when courts are prepared to second-guess a director's judgment. However, section 263(2) seems to establish a different standard: Permission must not only be refused if it cannot rationally be argued that litigation is in the company's best interest, but also if a hypothetical (ordinary) director would conclude that it is not in the best interest of the company.[165] Even at the discretionary stage, the reluctance of the UK courts to engage in a cost-benefit analysis is discernible in some decisions, where the courts refer to section 263(3)(b), but do not analyse the economic implications of the lawsuit in detail.[166] In other decisions, the courts have considered a multitude of non-legal factors, including the effect that the loss of experienced directors (who are made defendants in the derivative lawsuit) would have on staff morale and the trading performance of the company, the possibility to find replacement directors of similar calibre at short notice,

[164] See Chapter 5B.I.

[165] For a similar interpretation, see Kershaw (n 92) 616–17 (pointing out that the provision refers to 'a person acting in accordance with section 172 ... not seek[ing] to continue the claim', and not to 'no person').

[166] For example, in *Iesini v Westrip*, the court spent several pages analysing the merits of the claim ([2010] BCC 420, 442–5) and then simply concluded that '[t]he strength of the claim against the board is so weak that ... a person acting in accordance with s.172 would attach little weight to continuing it' (ibid 445). Similarly, in *Franbar Holdings Ltd v Patel* [2008] BCC 885, the court focused on whether 'there were obvious breaches of duty' and 'the recovery to be expected in consequence of those breaches would be substantial' (ibid 895), but it did not consider any other business-related factors. A similar analysis was conducted by the court in *Re Seven Holdings Ltd* [2011] EWHC 1893.

and the distraction that litigation would provide to the remaining managers.[167] Yet, courts still often seem to confine their analysis to simply noting that these factors are relevant, rather than forming their independent view on the strength of the factors.[168]

2. A conflict between the derivative action and an alternative claim 'that the member could pursue in his own right' may arise if the shareholder can claim that the act complained of constitutes unfair prejudice according to section 994 of the Companies Act 2006.[169] As explained in *Iesini v Westrip*, the problem is that the company will generally have to indemnify the claimant in a derivative action, whereas an unfair prejudice petition is cost-neutral for the company.[170] Thus, a shareholder who could either enforce a claim of the company derivatively or bring a petition for relief because of unfairly prejudicial conduct may decide to pursue the former primarily in order to obtain indemnification. According to *Iesini v Westrip*, this will weigh against allowing the derivative action to continue. However, the derivative action is not always subordinate to an unfair prejudice petition whenever the latter is available to the shareholder-claimant. The question is rather which cause of action is the 'appropriate' remedy in a given case. This depends primarily on the relief sought by the claimant. An unfair prejudice petition may be used to either claim damages on behalf of the company[171] or—more commonly—be bought out by the company or the major shareholder.[172] If evidence is presented to the court in a derivative action that the claimant is interested in a buy-out, the court will most likely consider the filing of the derivative action as an attempt to avoid the costs of the unfair prejudice proceedings.[173] On the other hand, if relief is sought on behalf of the company, there is no reason why the claimant should be referred to the unfair prejudice petition only because it is theoretically available.[174]
3. The third factor analysed by the court in *Iesini v Westrip*, the requirement to have particular regard to the views of members of the company who do not have a personal interest in the matter (section 263(4)), proves particularly elusive. As the court noted, the term 'not having a personal interest in the matter' is only meaningful if it is held to refer to the absence of any implication in the alleged wrongdoing. If it is interpreted in this way, the consideration resembles the test in *Smith v Croft* mentioned before.[175] Does the 'majority of the minority' criterion established in *Smith v Croft*, accordingly, continue to be of relevance? This seems to be the case, but with one important difference. Under the common law, the possibility that the majority of shareholders (other than the wrongdoers) could ratify the conduct complained of was a bar to bringing a derivative action. Now the views of the independent members are not conclusive, but one of several factors to be considered by the court (albeit an important factor, as can be

[167] *Kleanthous v Paphitis* [2012] BCC 676, 695–6.

[168] For example, in *Kleanthous v Paphitis* (n 167) 696, the court presented the arguments of a committee of the board set up to assess the derivative proceedings and composed of directors who had joined the company after the challenged conduct had occurred. Without critically reflecting on the arguments, the court concluded that 'there is much force in what [one of the directors on the committee] says'.

[169] The unfair prejudice remedy is examined in Chapter 7B.I.2.

[170] We will discuss cost rules below in the text to nn 191–198.

[171] Companies Act 2006, s 996(2)(c). [172] ibid s 996(2)(e).

[173] *Kleanthous v Paphitis* (n 167) 696–7. An unfair prejudice petition may also be the more appropriate remedy for other reasons than the desire of the claimant to be bought out, for example because the complaint is based principally on misrepresentation by the defendant to the claimant and not on a breach of duty owed to the company, *Singh v Singh* [2014] EWCA Civ 103, paras 22–4 (holding that in this case both a personal action and a section 994 petition were more appropriate).

[174] *Stainer v Lee* [2011] BCC 134, 147–8: 'In the present action, the applicant is not seeking to be bought out. He commenced these proceedings, with the support of 35 other minority shareholders, seeking financial remedies for misconduct against the two directors personally . . . Such orders could not be made on an unfair prejudice petition, albeit that the court could by way of remedy authorise the bringing of proceedings in the name of the company by the petitioner: s.996(2)(c). But that would then give rise to a subsequent and further set of proceedings. I consider that given what is at the heart of the present case, a derivative action is entirely appropriate and therefore the theoretical availability to the applicant of proceedings by way of an unfair prejudice petition is not a reason to refuse permission'. See also *Cullen Investments Ltd v Brown* [2015] BCC 539, 552 (holding that it weighed against refusing permission to continue a derivative action if there was 'a very real possibility that the losses caused by [the defendants'] alleged wrongdoing are losses which only [the company] can recover as a result of the reflective loss principle' and not the shareholder under a personal claim; see text to nn 119–133 for a discussion of the reflective loss principle).

[175] See n 147 above.

concluded from the use of the attribute 'particular' and the fact that the criterion is laid down in a separate subsection).[176]

It is also not evident how section 263(4) relates to the requirement to consider the likelihood that the challenged conduct will be authorized or ratified.[177] The latter factor brings two changes in comparison with the common law. First, pursuant to the rule in *Foss v Harbottle*, a derivative action would be struck out if the wrong was ratifiable, irrespective of how likely it was that the shareholders would actually authorize or ratify the act. Under the statutory derivative action mechanism, the court has to assess not only whether the act constitutes a non-ratifiable breach,[178] but also consider evidence of the intention of the shareholders who are entitled to vote on the act to approve it. Secondly, the likelihood of authorization or ratification is a discretionary factor, not an absolute bar to litigation. However, it is unlikely that a court will allow the derivative action to proceed if the evidence shows that a majority of shareholders is prepared to authorize or ratify the directors' conduct.[179] If the evidence is inconclusive, the court may adjourn the proceedings to give the company the opportunity to call a meeting and procure a resolution on the matter.[180] The statutory regulation of ratification and the requirement to consider the views of the members are largely equivalent (although probably not identical), because they both refer to disinterested members: the votes of the implicated director and connected persons are disregarded when the general meeting decides on ratification, and the views of members with a 'personal interest, direct or indirect, in the matter' are disregarded when the court considers the derivative action.[181] The difference, then, between the two considerations in section 263 is presumably to be found in the subject matter of the disinterested members' views: in the case of section 263(4), the court takes account of their views on the commercial reasons for pursuing the action, and in the case of section 263(3)(c) and (d) of their views on whether the directors should be released of liability.[182] Arguably, shareholders may reject the latter, while deciding that the derivative action is (currently) not in the best interest of the company.

4. Two factors listed in section 263(3) remain to be discussed: whether the member who seeks to continue the claim acts in good faith,[183] and whether the company has decided not to pursue the claim.[184] The courts have held that a claim is made in 'good faith' if 'it is made honestly and with no ulterior motive'.[185] The claimant must bring the action 'bona fide for the benefit of the company for wrongs to the company'.[186] Pursuing additional benefits does not necessarily mean that the derivative action is brought for a collateral purpose, provided the additional benefit is 'reasonably related to the provision of some form of redress for [the] grievance'[187] raised with the derivative action and the action *also* benefits the company.[188]

[176] This was also the view of the Law Commission when it proposed the inclusion of this factor (n 150) paras 6.88–6.90.

[177] Companies Act 2006, s 263(3)(c), (d).

[178] On non-ratifiable breaches, see Chapter 6C.I.1.

[179] For this reason, the Law Commission (n 150) para 6.84, considered the proposed change to constitute only 'to a small extent . . . a change from the position under the [common] law'.

[180] ibid.

[181] As far as authorization is concerned, the differences are clearer. As discussed, authorization continues to be governed by the common law, which treats shareholder votes as proprietary rights and allows all shareholders to exercise their rights freely, provided the authorized conduct does not give rise to a non-ratifiable breach, see text to nn 4–6 above.

[182] This seems to have been the opinion of the Law Commission (n 150) para 6.88.

[183] Companies Act, s 263(3)(a).

[184] ibid s 263(3)(e).

[185] *Central Estates (Belgravia) Ltd v Woolgar* [1972] 1 QB 48, 55 (cited in *Iesini v Westrip* [2010] BCC 420, 448).

[186] *Barrett v Duckett* [1995] BCC 362, 367.

[187] *Goldsmith v Sperrings Ltd* [1977] 1 WLR 478, 503. The court explained further: 'On the other hand, if it can be shown that a litigant is pursuing an ulterior purpose unrelated to the subject matter of the litigation and that, but for his ulterior purpose, he would not have commenced proceedings at all, that is an abuse of process'.

[188] For example, in *Iesini v Westrip*, the claimants had the benefit of an indemnity from a company that had entered into a joint venture with Westrip. In return, they had promised to use their best endeavours to cause Westrip to terminate the joint venture. It was argued that the claimants had brought the derivative action not for the benefit of Westrip, but the other party to the joint venture. After quoting *Goldsmith v Sperrings Ltd* (n 187), the court concluded: 'In my judgment if the claimant brings a derivative claim for the benefit of the company, he will not be disqualified from doing so if there are other benefits which he will derive from the claim . . . [T]he dominant purpose of the action was to benefit Westrip. It cannot, in my judgment, be said that but for the collateral purpose, the claim would not have been brought at all. The claim is, in my judgment, brought in good faith'. See *Iesini v Westrip* [2010] BCC 420, 448–9.

The company's decision not to pursue a claim may be taken by the shareholders or the board of directors. It is to be distinguished from a decision to authorize or ratify an alleged breach of duty. The company retains its claim against the directors, but the general meeting or the board express their view that litigation is not advisable. In both cases, the weight that the court will give to the company's view will depend crucially on whether those who take the decision were implicated in the challenged conduct and what their relationship is to the defendant directors.[189] If the board wants to make a forceful claim against continuing a derivative action, one strategy would be the formation of a committee of independent directors to assess the action.[190]

We come now to the third dimension in the assessment of the effectiveness of the derivation action: cost rules. Under common law, the courts had developed the rule that 'where a shareholder has in good faith and on reasonable grounds sued as plaintiff in a minority shareholder's action, ... which it would have been reasonable for an independent board of directors to bring in the company's name', the court would normally order the company to pay the shareholder's costs.[191] The courts were acutely aware of the disincentives that would exist if the claimant shareholders were asked to bear the full litigation risk, while any benefits of the litigation accrued to the company.[192] The common law rule applied irrespective of whether or not the litigation was ultimately successful, and the claimants were entitled, in principle, to indemnification of costs down to judgment.[193] The new statutory derivative action mechanism does not contain any cost rules; the common law therefore continues to apply.[194] It can be argued that the conditions established by the courts for an indemnification order (good faith, reasonable grounds, and the hypothetical actions of an independent board of directors) are subsumed by the discretionary criteria for granting permission in the Companies Act. Thus, if the court grants permission to continue a derivative action, the claimant can normally also expect to be indemnified against costs.[195]

A recent legal innovation may further mitigate the incentive misalignments in minority shareholder lawsuits and strengthen the enforcement of directors' duties. Since 2013, contingency fees are permissible in civil litigation in England and Wales (called 'damages-based agreements').[196] Under a damages-based agreement, the law firm and the client provide that the law firm will only be paid for the legal services rendered if the client wins the lawsuit. The lawyer's fees are calculated as a percentage of the award as agreed by the parties, but capped at 50 per cent of the award.[197] Thus, contingency fees, if used in derivative actions,[198] in combination with an indemnification order would protect the shareholder-claimants from bearing the costs of an unsuccessful lawsuit, while incentivizing shareholders (and, indeed, their lawyers) to pursue claims aggressively.

[189] *Bridge v Daley* [2015] EWHC 2121; *Cullen Investments Ltd v Brown* [2015] BCC 539, 552.
[190] This was the board's strategy in *Kleanthous v Paphitis* (n 167); see n 168 above.
[191] *Wallersteiner v Moir (No 2)* [1975] QB 373, 403–404. [192] ibid.
[193] However, the courts reviewed at each stage of the litigation whether continuation of the action was reasonable: ibid 404.
[194] See also Civil Procedure Rules, 19.9E (confirming that the court 'may order the company ... to indemnify the claimant against liability for costs incurred in the permission application or in the derivative claim or both').
[195] *Iesini v Westrip* [2010] BCC 420, 450; *Stainer v Lee* [2011] BCC 134, 148.
[196] Courts and Legal Services Act 1990, s 58AA, as amended by the Legal Aid, Sentencing and Punishment of Offenders Act 2012 (LASPO), s 45.
[197] Damages-Based Agreements Regulations 2013, Statutory Instrument 2013 No 609, s 4(3).
[198] There is some legal uncertainty whether damages-based agreements are available to claimants in a derivative action. According to the statutory definition, the recipient of legal services promises in a damages-based agreement 'to make a payment to the person providing the services if the recipient obtains a specified financial benefit in connection with the matter in relation to which the services are provided': Courts and Legal Services Act 1990, s 58AA(3). However, in a derivative action, the benefit accrues to the company and not (at least not directly) the recipient of the legal services, the shareholder. On this point, see Kershaw (n 92) 638.

3. US

In US law, similar to English law, a derivative suit is defined as a lawsuit in the right of the corporation.[199] However, in contrast to English law, anyone can be sued, whereas section 260(3) of the UK Companies Act 2006 restricts the derivative action to negligence, default, breach of duty, or breach of trust by a director. If the action is successful, the court may order the corporation to pay the plaintiff's reasonable expenses, including lawyer's fees.[200] In order to avoid collusive settlements, any settlement reached between the parties must be approved by the court.[201]

A shareholder has standing to bring a lawsuit if he or she was a shareholder at the time when the wrong was committed, the rationale being that the price of shares acquired afterwards will reflect the injury suffered by the corporation.[202] More importantly, the company laws of most US states establish two additional procedural barriers to bringing a derivative action, the so-called 'demand rule' and the use of litigation committees. According to the former, derivative litigation will only be admissible if the plaintiff first makes a demand on the board to bring the action or demand is excused. Empirical evidence indicates that boards usually reject demand. Hence, plaintiffs seldom make a demand and argue instead that demand is excused. The circumstances under which demand will be excused vary among the states. According to Delaware law, the plaintiff must allege that a majority of the board personally benefited from the challenged transaction or was otherwise subject to a legally disabling conflict of interest. The following is one of the leading cases on the demand rule. After discussing *Aronson v Lewis*, we will turn to the second procedural barrier to derivative litigation, the establishment of a litigation committee that takes over the shareholder lawsuit and may decide to discontinue the action.

***Aronson v. Lewis*, 473 A.2d 805 (Supreme Court of Delaware 1984)**

Moore, J:

This suit[, which was brought without making demand on the board of directors,] challenges certain transactions between Meyers and one of its directors, Leo Fink, who owns 47% of its outstanding stock …

[Fink had been CEO of the parent company of Meyers and chairman of the board of Meyers. Upon his retirement], the defendants approved an employment agreement between Meyers and Fink for a five year term with provision for automatic renewal each year thereafter, indefinitely. Meyers agreed to pay Fink $150,000 per year, plus a bonus of 5% of its pre-tax profits over $2,400,000. Fink could terminate the contract at any time, but Meyers could do so only upon six months' notice. At termination, Fink was to become a consultant to Meyers and be paid $150,000 per year for the first three years, $125,000 for the next three years, and $100,000 thereafter for life. Death benefits were also included. Fink agreed to devote his best efforts and substantially his entire business time to advancing Meyers' interests. The agreement also provided that Fink's compensation was not to be affected by any inability to perform services on Meyers' behalf. Fink was 75 years old when his employment agreement with Meyers was approved by the directors. There is no claim that he was, or is, in poor health …

The complaint charges that these transactions had 'no valid business purpose', and were a 'waste of corporate assets' because the amounts to be paid are 'grossly excessive', that Fink performs 'no or little services', and because of his 'advanced age' cannot be 'expected to perform any such services' …

The complaint alleged that no demand had been made on the Meyers board because:

13.… such attempt would be futile for the following reasons:

(a) All of the directors in office are named as defendants herein and they have participated in, expressly approved and/or acquiesced in, and are personally liable for, the wrongs complained of herein.

[199] MBCA, §7.40(1). [200] ibid §7.46(1). [201] ibid §7.45. [202] ibid §7.41.

(b) Defendant Fink, having selected each director, controls and dominates every member of the Board and every officer of Meyers.

(c) Institution of this action by present directors would require the defendant-directors to sue themselves, thereby placing the conduct of this action in hostile hands and preventing its effective prosecution.

...

A.

A cardinal precept of the General Corporation Law of the State of Delaware is that directors, rather than shareholders, manage the business and affairs of the corporation ... The existence and exercise of this power carries with it certain fundamental fiduciary obligations to the corporation and its shareholders ... Moreover, a stockholder is not powerless to challenge director action which results in harm to the corporation. The machinery of corporate democracy and the derivative suit are potent tools to redress the conduct of a torpid or unfaithful management. The derivative action developed in equity to enable shareholders to sue in the corporation's name where those in control of the company refused to assert a claim belonging to it. The nature of the action is two-fold. First, it is the equivalent of a suit by the shareholders to compel the corporation to sue. Second, it is a suit by the corporation, asserted by the shareholders on its behalf, against those liable to it.

By its very nature the derivative action impinges on the managerial freedom of directors. Hence, the demand requirement of Chancery Rule 23.1 exists at the threshold, first to insure that a stockholder exhausts his intracorporate remedies, and then to provide a safeguard against strike suits. Thus, by promoting this form of alternate dispute resolution, rather than immediate recourse to litigation, the demand requirement is a recognition of the fundamental precept that directors manage the business and affairs of corporations.

In our view the entire question of demand futility is inextricably bound to issues of business judgment and the standards of that doctrine's applicability. The business judgment rule is an acknowledgment of the managerial prerogatives of Delaware directors under Section 141(a) ... It is a presumption that in making a business decision the directors of a corporation acted on an informed basis, in good faith and in the honest belief that the action taken was in the best interests of the company ... Absent an abuse of discretion, that judgment will be respected by the courts. The burden is on the party challenging the decision to establish facts rebutting the presumption ...

The function of the business judgment rule is of paramount significance in the context of a derivative action. It comes into play in several ways-in addressing a demand, in the determination of demand futility, in efforts by independent disinterested directors to dismiss the action as inimical to the corporation's best interests, and generally, as a defense to the merits of the suit. However, in each of these circumstances there are certain common principles governing the application and operation of the rule.

First, its protections can only be claimed by disinterested directors whose conduct otherwise meets the tests of business judgment. From the standpoint of interest, this means that directors can neither appear on both sides of a transaction nor expect to derive any personal financial benefit from it in the sense of self-dealing, as opposed to a benefit which devolves upon the corporation or all stockholders generally ... Thus, if such director interest is present, and the transaction is not approved by a majority consisting of the disinterested directors, then the business judgment rule has no application whatever in determining demand futility. See 8 Del.C. § 144(a)(1).

Second, to invoke the rule's protection directors have a duty to inform themselves, prior to making a business decision, of all material information reasonably available to them. Having become so informed, they must then act with requisite care in the discharge of their duties. While the Delaware cases use a variety of terms to describe the applicable standard of care, our analysis satisfies us that under the business judgment rule director liability is predicated upon concepts of gross negligence ...

However, it should be noted that the business judgment rule operates only in the context of director action. Technically speaking, it has no role where directors have either abdicated their functions, or absent a conscious decision, failed to act. But it also follows that under applicable principles, a conscious decision to refrain from acting may nonetheless be a valid exercise of business judgment and enjoy the protections of the rule.

The gap in our law, which we address today, arises from this Court's decision in *Zapata Corp. v. Maldonado*. There, the Court defined the limits of a board's managerial power granted by Section 141(a) and restricted application of the business judgment rule in a factual context similar to this action . . .

By way of background, this Court's review in *Zapata* was limited to whether an independent investigation committee of disinterested directors had the power to cause the derivative action to be dismissed. Preliminarily, it was noted in *Zapata* that '[d]irectors of Delaware corporations derive their managerial decision-making power, which encompasses decisions whether to initiate, or refrain from entering, litigation, from 8 Del.C. § 141(a)'. *Zapata*, 430 A.2d at 782 (footnotes omitted). In that context, this Court observed that the business judgment rule has no relevance to corporate decision-making until after a decision has been made. *Id.* In *Zapata*, we stated that a shareholder does not possess an independent individual right to continue a derivative action. Moreover, where demand on a board has been made and refused, we apply the business judgment rule in reviewing the board's refusal to act pursuant to a stockholder's demand. *Id.* at 784 & n. 10. Unless the business judgment rule does not protect the refusal to sue, the shareholder lacks the legal managerial power to continue the derivative action, since that power is terminated by the refusal. *Id.* at 784. We also concluded that where demand is excused a shareholder possesses the ability to initiate a derivative action, but the right to prosecute it may be terminated upon the exercise of applicable standards of business judgment. *Id.* The thrust of *Zapata* is that in either the demand-refused or the demand-excused case, the board still retains its Section 141(a) managerial authority to make decisions regarding corporate litigation. Moreover, the board may delegate its managerial authority to a committee of independent disinterested directors. *Id.* at 786. See 8 Del.C. § 141(c). Thus, even in a demand-excused case, a board has the power to appoint a committee of one or more independent disinterested directors to determine whether the derivative action should be pursued or dismissal sought. *Zapata*, 430 A.2d at 786. Under *Zapata*, the Court of Chancery, in passing on a committee's motion to dismiss a derivative action in a demand excused case, must apply a two-step test. First, the court must inquire into the independence and good faith of the committee and review the reasonableness and good faith of the committee's investigation. *Id.* at 788. Second, the court must apply its own independent business judgment to decide whether the motion to dismiss should be granted. *Id.* at 789.

After *Zapata* numerous derivative suits were filed without prior demand upon boards of directors. The complaints in such actions all alleged that demand was excused because of board interest, approval or acquiescence in the wrongdoing. In any event, the *Zapata* demand-excused/demand-refused bifurcation has left a crucial issue unanswered: when is demand futile and, therefore, excused?

Delaware courts have addressed the issue of demand futility on several earlier occasions . . . The rule emerging from these decisions is that where officers and directors are under an influence which sterilizes their discretion, they cannot be considered proper persons to conduct litigation on behalf of the corporation. Thus, demand would be futile. See, e.g., *McKee v. Rogers*, Del.Ch., 156 A. 191, 192 (1931) (holding that where a defendant controlled the board of directors, '[i]t is manifest then that there can be no expectation that the corporation would sue him, and if it did, it can hardly be said that the prosecution of the suit would be entrusted to proper hands'). But see, e.g., *Fleer v. Frank H. Fleer Corp.*, Del.Ch., 125 A. 411, 415 (1924) ('[w]here the demand if made would be directed to the particular individuals who themselves are the alleged wrongdoers and who therefore would be invited to sue themselves, the rule is settled that a demand and refusal is not requisite'); *Miller v. Loft, Inc.*, Del.Ch., 153 A. 861, 862 (1931) ('if by reason of hostile interest or guilty participation in the wrongs complained of, the directors cannot be expected to institute suit, . . . no demand upon them to institute suit is requisite').

However, those cases cannot be taken to mean that any board approval of a challenged transaction automatically connotes 'hostile interest' and 'guilty participation' by directors, or some other form of sterilizing influence upon them. Were that so, the demand requirements of our law would be meaningless, leaving the clear mandate of Chancery Rule 23.1 devoid of its purpose and substance . . .

Our view is that in determining demand futility the Court of Chancery in the proper exercise of its discretion must decide whether, under the particularized facts alleged, a reasonable doubt is created that: (1) the directors are disinterested and independent and (2) the challenged transaction was otherwise the product of a valid exercise of business judgment. Hence, the Court of Chancery must make two inquiries, one into the independence and disinterestedness of the directors and the other into the substantive nature of the challenged transaction and the board's approval thereof. As to the latter inquiry the court does not assume that the transaction is a wrong to the corporation requiring corrective steps by the board. Rather, the alleged wrong is substantively reviewed against the factual background alleged in the complaint. As to the former inquiry, directorial independence and disinterestedness, the court reviews the factual allegations to decide whether they raise a reasonable doubt, as a threshold matter, that the protections of the business judgment rule are available to the board. Certainly, if this is an 'interested' director transaction, such that the business judgment rule is inapplicable to the board majority approving the transaction, then the inquiry ceases. In that event futility of demand has been established by any objective or subjective standard ...

However, the mere threat of personal liability for approving a questioned transaction, standing alone, is insufficient to challenge either the independence or disinterestedness of directors, although in rare cases a transaction may be so egregious on its face that board approval cannot meet the test of business judgment, and a substantial likelihood of director liability therefore exists ... In sum the entire review is factual in nature. The Court of Chancery in the exercise of its sound discretion must be satisfied that a plaintiff has alleged facts with particularity which, taken as true, support a reasonable doubt that the challenged transaction was the product of a valid exercise of business judgment. Only in that context is demand excused.

B.

Having outlined the legal framework within which these issues are to be determined, we consider plaintiff's claims of futility here: Fink's domination and control of the directors, board approval of the Fink-Meyers employment agreement, and board hostility to the plaintiff's derivative action due to the directors' status as defendants.

Plaintiff's claim that Fink dominates and controls the Meyers' board is based on: (1) Fink's 47% ownership of Meyers' outstanding stock, and (2) that he 'personally selected' each Meyers director. Plaintiff also alleges that mere approval of the employment agreement illustrates Fink's domination and control of the board. In addition, plaintiff argued on appeal that 47% stock ownership, though less than a majority, constituted control given the large number of shares outstanding, 1,245,745.

Such contentions do not support any claim under Delaware law that these directors lack independence ... [I]n the demand context even proof of majority ownership of a company does not strip the directors of the presumptions of independence, and that their acts have been taken in good faith and in the best interests of the corporation. There must be coupled with the allegation of control such facts as would demonstrate that through personal or other relationships the directors are beholden to the controlling person ...

The requirement of director independence inheres in the conception and rationale of the business judgment rule. The presumption of propriety that flows from an exercise of business judgment is based in part on this unyielding precept. Independence means that a director's decision is based on the corporate merits of the subject before the board rather than extraneous considerations or influences. While directors may confer, debate, and resolve their differences through compromise, or by reasonable reliance upon the expertise of their colleagues and other qualified persons, the end result, nonetheless, must be that each director has brought his or her own informed business judgment to bear with specificity upon the corporate merits of the issues without regard for or succumbing to influences which convert an otherwise valid business decision into a faithless act.

Thus, it is not enough to charge that a director was nominated by or elected at the behest of those controlling the outcome of a corporate election. That is the usual way a person becomes a corporate director. It is the care, attention and sense of individual responsibility to the performance of one's duties, not the method of election, that generally touches on independence.

We conclude that in the demand-futile context a plaintiff charging domination and control of one or more directors must allege particularized facts manifesting 'a direction of corporate conduct in such a way as to comport with the wishes or interests of the corporation (or persons) doing the controlling'. [The court concludes that the plaintiff has not met this burden in the present case.] ...

C.

Turning to the board's approval of the Meyers-Fink employment agreement, plaintiff's argument is simple: all of the Meyers directors are named defendants, because they approved the wasteful agreement; if plaintiff prevails on the merits all the directors will be jointly and severally liable; therefore, the directors' interest in avoiding personal liability automatically and absolutely disqualifies them from passing on a shareholder's demand.

Such allegations are conclusory at best. In Delaware mere directorial approval of a transaction, absent particularized facts supporting a breach of fiduciary duty claim, or otherwise establishing the lack of independence or disinterestedness of a majority of the directors, is insufficient to excuse demand. Here, plaintiff's suit is premised on the notion that the Meyers-Fink employment agreement was a waste of corporate assets. So, the argument goes, by approving such waste the directors now face potential personal liability, thereby rendering futile any demand on them to bring suit. Unfortunately, plaintiff's claim fails in its initial premise. The complaint does not allege particularized facts indicating that the agreement is a waste of corporate assets ...

In essence, the plaintiff alleged a lack of consideration flowing from Fink to Meyers, since the employment agreement provided that compensation was not contingent on Fink's ability to perform any services. The bare assertion that Fink performed 'little or no services' was plaintiff's conclusion based solely on Fink's age and the existence of the Fink-Prudential employment agreement. As for Meyers' loans to Fink, beyond the bare allegation that they were made, the complaint does not allege facts indicating the wastefulness of such arrangements. Again, the mere existence of such loans, given the broad corporate powers conferred by Delaware law, does not even state a claim ...

D.

Plaintiff's final argument is the incantation that demand is excused because the directors otherwise would have to sue themselves, thereby placing the conduct of the litigation in hostile hands and preventing its effective prosecution. This bootstrap argument has been made to and dismissed by other courts ... Its acceptance would effectively abrogate Rule 23.1 and weaken the managerial power of directors. Unless facts are alleged with particularity to overcome the presumptions of independence and a proper exercise of business judgment, in which case the directors could not be expected to sue themselves, a bare claim of this sort raises no legally cognizable issue under Delaware corporate law.

E.

In sum, we conclude that the plaintiff has failed to allege facts with particularity indicating that the Meyers directors were tainted by interest, lacked independence, or took action contrary to Meyers' best interests in order to create a reasonable doubt as to the applicability of the business judgment rule. Only in the presence of such a reasonable doubt may a demand be deemed futile ...

Questions and comments:

1. The demand test that *Aronson v Lewis* describes performs a similar function to the claim admission procedure at the heart of the statutory derivative action mechanism of the UK Companies Act 2006. In both cases, the court is seen as a neutral arbiter that screens derivative actions in order to differentiate between meritorious litigation and strike suits. Conceptually, however, the demand rule and the claim admission procedure are different. The latter results from legislative intervention to overwrite the rule in *Foss v Harbottle*, which is based on the traditional position of English company law locating ultimate corporate power in the general meeting and holding that decision-making by the members is by majority rule.[203] The demand rule, on the other hand, 'is a recognition of the fundamental precept that directors manage the

[203] Mayson, French, and Ryan (n 140) 18.3.3.2.

business and affairs of corporations',[204] 'which encompasses decisions whether to initiate, or refrain from entering, litigation'.[205] Since the derivative action encroaches upon the powers of the directors, the shareholder-plaintiffs are required to make a demand on the directors to initiate the desired action.[206] Shareholders only have the power to bring litigation if demand has been refused *and* the directors are not protected by the business judgment rule in their refusal to sue. This approach is entirely consistent from the perspective of Delaware law. If the decision whether or not to bring litigation is a management decision, falling within the general managerial powers of section 141(a) of the Delaware General Corporation Law, the business judgment rule applies to that decision. Thus, refusing demand extinguishes the shareholders' right to bring a derivative action, unless the directors were conflicted, acted in bad faith, or were not sufficiently well informed about the claim or the implications of granting and refusing demand.[207] *Aronson v Lewis* analyses in detail what amounts to a conflict of interest in the context of litigation decisions. Importantly, the court held that the mere threat of personal liability or the fact that the defendant director controlled the corporation and appointed the other members of the board was insufficient to challenge the independence or disinterestedness of directors.[208] Rather, the shareholder-plaintiffs must show 'a direction of corporate conduct in such a way as to comport with the wishes or interests of the corporation (or persons) doing the controlling'.[209]

2. A second avenue for shareholders to bring a derivative action, chosen in *Aronson v Lewis*, is to argue that making a demand on the board would be futile because the board could not be expected to exercise its independent business judgment in deciding on the demand. In such a case, demand is said to be 'excused'. Since the directors have not yet acted and hence not exercised their business judgment, it is difficult to apply the business judgment rule to a demand-excused case.[210] The Delaware Supreme Court, accordingly, applied a modified version of the business judgment rule in *Aronson v Lewis*: The plaintiffs must plead particularized facts that create 'a reasonable doubt ... that: (1) the directors are disinterested and independent and (2) the challenged transaction was otherwise the product of a valid exercise of business judgment'.[211] Thus, the court introduced a two-pronged test that requires an inquiry into the independence and disinterestedness of the directors and the substance of the challenged transaction. However, as set out in *Aronson v Lewis*, the test is not entirely clear. Are shareholders required to raise a reasonable doubt regarding both factors, or is the test disjunctive? Later decisions clarified that the latter is correct. Demand is excused when the shareholder-plaintiffs create a reasonable doubt that the protections of the business judgment rule would not have applied to the decision on the demand *or* they did not apply to the earlier approval of the challenged transaction.[212]
3. Even if demand is excused, a plaintiff may still be barred from proceeding if the corporation successfully moves to dismiss the action after a special litigation committee has decided that the action is not in the best interest of the company. Litigation committees often decide that an action should be dismissed, especially if it is against sitting, as opposed to former, directors.[213] Hence, the standard used by courts to review the committee's decision

[204] *Aronson v Lewis* (n 85) 812.
[205] ibid 813, quoting *Zapata Corp. v Maldonado*, 430 A.2d 779, 782 (Del. 1981).
[206] For example, Delaware Chancery Court Rule 23.1; MBCA, §7.42.
[207] *Zapata Corp. v Maldonado*, 430 A.2d 779, 784.
[208] *Aronson v Lewis* (n 85) 815.
[209] ibid 816, quoting *Kaplan v Centex Corp.*, 284 A.2d 119, 123 (Del. Ch. 1971). Commentators have pointed out that post Enron, the Delaware courts seem to be more readily prepared to find a lack of independence, Pinto and Branson (n 39) §14.05[D][2][d]. For example, in *In re Limited Inc. Shareholders Litigation*, 2002 WL 537692 (Del. Ch. 2002), the fact that a director's principal employment was as an officer of the company and he received an annual salary of about $1.8 million was held to be sufficient to raise a reasonable doubt as to the director's independence from the largest shareholder of the company, who owned or controlled c. 25% of the outstanding stock and was also the company's chief executive officer and chairman, ibid 5.
[210] *Aronson v Lewis* (n 85) 813.
[211] ibid 814.
[212] *Levine v Smith*, 591 A.2d 194, 205 (Del. 1991).
[213] Pinto and Branson (n 39) §14.06[D]. For a more positive view on the behaviour of special litigation committees, see M Myers, 'The Decisions of the Corporate Special Litigation Committees: An Empirical Investigation' (2009) 84 Indiana Law Journal 1309.

to dismiss a lawsuit becomes vital. Again, state laws vary on the issue. The MBCA requires 'good faith' and a 'reasonable inquiry'.[214] The situation in Delaware is discussed in the following leading case.

***Zapata Corp v. Maldonado*, 430 A.2d 779 (Supreme Court of Delaware, 1981)**

Quillen, J:

In June, 1975, William Maldonado, a stockholder of Zapata, instituted a derivative action in the Court of Chancery on behalf of Zapata against ten officers and/or directors of Zapata, alleging, essentially, breaches of fiduciary duty. Maldonado did not first demand that the board bring this action, stating instead such demand's futility because all directors were named as defendants and allegedly participated in the acts specified ...

By June, 1979, four of the defendant-directors were no longer on the board, and the remaining directors appointed two new outside directors to the board. The board then created an 'Independent Investigation Committee' (Committee), composed solely of the two new directors, to investigate Maldonado's actions, as well as a similar derivative action then pending in Texas, and to determine whether the corporation should continue any or all of the litigation. The Committee's determination was stated to be 'final ... not ... subject to review by the Board of Directors and ... in all respects ... binding upon the Corporation'.

Following an investigation, the Committee concluded, in September, 1979, that each action should 'be dismissed forthwith as their continued maintenance is inimical to the Company's best interests ...' Consequently, Zapata moved for dismissal or summary judgment ... [Zapata's motion was denied by the Court of Chancery, and Zapata filed an appeal with the Supreme Court of Delaware.]

The question to be decided [is]: When, if at all, should an authorized board committee be permitted to cause litigation, properly initiated by a derivative stockholder in his own right, to be dismissed? As noted above, a board has the power to choose not to pursue litigation when demand is made upon it, so long as the decision is not wrongful. If the board determines that a suit would be detrimental to the company, the board's determination prevails. Even when demand is excusable, circumstances may arise when continuation of the litigation would not be in the corporation's best interests. Our inquiry is whether, under such circumstances, there is a permissible procedure under s 141(a) by which a corporation can rid itself of detrimental litigation. If there is not, a single stockholder in an extreme case might control the destiny of the entire corporation. This concern was bluntly expressed by the Ninth Circuit in Lewis v. Anderson ...: 'To allow one shareholder to incapacitate an entire board of directors merely by leveling charges against them gives too much leverage to dissident shareholders'. But, when examining the means, including the committee mechanism examined in this case, potentials for abuse must be recognized. This takes us to the second and third aspects of the issue on appeal.

Before we pass to equitable considerations as to the mechanism at issue here, it must be clear that an independent committee possesses the corporate power to seek the termination of a derivative suit. Section 141(c) allows a board to delegate all of its authority to a committee. Accordingly, a committee with properly delegated authority would have the power to move for dismissal or summary judgment if the entire board did.

Even though demand was not made in this case and the initial decision of whether to litigate was not placed before the board, Zapata's board, it seems to us, retained all of its corporate power concerning litigation decisions. If Maldonado had made demand on the board in this case, it could have refused to bring suit. Maldonado could then have asserted that the decision not to sue was wrongful and, if correct, would have been allowed to maintain the suit. The board, however, never would have lost its statutory managerial authority. The demand requirement itself evidences that the managerial power is retained by the board. When a derivative plaintiff is allowed to bring suit after a wrongful refusal, the board's authority to choose whether to pursue the litigation is not challenged although its conclusion reached through the exercise of that authority is not respected since it is wrongful. Similarly, Rule 23.1, by excusing demand in certain instances, does not strip the board of its corporate power. It merely saves the plaintiff the expense and delay of making a futile demand resulting in a probable tainted exercise of that

[214] MBCA, §7.44(a).

authority in a refusal by the board or in giving control of litigation to the opposing side. But the board entity remains empowered under s 141(a) to make decisions regarding corporate litigation. The problem is one of member disqualification, not the absence of power in the board.

The corporate power inquiry then focuses on whether the board, tainted by the self-interest of a majority of its members, can legally delegate its authority to a committee of two disinterested directors. We find our statute clearly requires an affirmative answer to this question. As has been noted, under an express provision of the statute, s 141(c), a committee can exercise all of the authority of the board to the extent provided in the resolution of the board. Moreover, at least by analogy to our statutory section on interested directors, 8 Del.C. s 141, it seems clear that the Delaware statute is designed to permit disinterested directors to act for the board ...

We do not think that the interest taint of the board majority is per se a legal bar to the delegation of the board's power to an independent committee composed of disinterested board members. The committee can properly act for the corporation to move to dismiss derivative litigation that is believed to be detrimental to the corporation's best interest.

Our focus now switches to the Court of Chancery which is faced with a stockholder assertion that a derivative suit, properly instituted, should continue for the benefit of the corporation and a corporate assertion, properly made by a board committee acting with board authority, that the same derivative suit should be dismissed as inimical to the best interests of the corporation.

At the risk of stating the obvious, the problem is relatively simple. If, on the one hand, corporations can consistently wrest bona fide derivative actions away from well-meaning derivative plaintiffs through the use of the committee mechanism, the derivative suit will lose much, if not all, of its generally-recognized effectiveness as an intra-corporate means of policing boards of directors ... If, on the other hand, corporations are unable to rid themselves of meritless or harmful litigation and strike suits, the derivative action, created to benefit the corporation, will produce the opposite, unintended result ... It thus appears desirable to us to find a balancing point where bona fide stockholder power to bring corporate causes of action cannot be unfairly trampled on by the board of directors, but the corporation can rid itself of detrimental litigation.

As we noted, the question has been treated by other courts as one of the 'business judgment' of the board committee. If a 'committee, composed of independent and disinterested directors, conducted a proper review of the matters before it, considered a variety of factors and reached, in good faith, a business judgment that (the) action was not in the best interest of (the corporation)', the action must be dismissed ... The issues become solely independence, good faith, and reasonable investigation. The ultimate conclusion of the committee, under that view, is not subject to judicial review.

We are not satisfied, however, that acceptance of the 'business judgment' rationale at this stage of derivative litigation is a proper balancing point. While we admit an analogy with a normal case respecting board judgment, it seems to us that there is sufficient risk in the realities of a situation like the one presented in this case to justify caution beyond adherence to the theory of business judgment.

The context here is a suit against directors where demand on the board is excused. We think some tribute must be paid to the fact that the lawsuit was properly initiated. It is not a board refusal case. Moreover, this complaint was filed in June of 1975 and, while the parties undoubtedly would take differing views on the degree of litigation activity, we have to be concerned about the creation of an 'Independent Investigation Committee' four years later, after the election of two new outside directors. Situations could develop where such motions could be filed after years of vigorous litigation for reasons unconnected with the merits of the lawsuit.

Moreover, notwithstanding our conviction that Delaware law entrusts the corporate power to a properly authorized committee, we must be mindful that directors are passing judgment on fellow directors in the same corporation and fellow directors, in this instance, who designated them to serve both as directors and committee members. The question naturally arises whether a 'there but for the grace of God go I' empathy might not play a role. And the further question arises whether inquiry as to independence, good faith and reasonable investigation is sufficient safeguard against abuse, perhaps subconscious abuse ...

Whether the Court of Chancery will be persuaded by the exercise of a committee power resulting in a summary motion for dismissal of a derivative action, where a demand has not been initially made, should rest, in our judgment, in the independent discretion of the Court of Chancery. We thus steer a middle course between those cases which yield to the independent business judgment of a board committee and this case as determined below which would yield to unbridled plaintiff stockholder control. In pursuit of the course, we recognize that '(t)he final substantive judgment whether a particular lawsuit should be maintained requires a balance of many factors ethical, commercial, promotional, public relations, employee relations, fiscal as well as legal'.... But we are content that such factors are not 'beyond the judicial reach' of the Court of Chancery which regularly and competently deals with fiduciary relationships, disposition of trust property, approval of settlements and scores of similar problems. We recognize the danger of judicial overreaching but the alternatives seem to us to be outweighed by the fresh view of a judicial outsider. Moreover, if we failed to balance all the interests involved, we would in the name of practicality and judicial economy foreclose a judicial decision on the merits. At this point, we are not convinced that is necessary or desirable.

After an objective and thorough investigation of a derivative suit, an independent committee may cause its corporation to file a pre-trial motion to dismiss in the Court of Chancery. The basis of the motion is the best interests of the corporation, as determined by the committee. The motion should include a thorough written record of the investigation and its findings and recommendations. Under appropriate Court supervision, akin to proceedings on summary judgment, each side should have an opportunity to make a record on the motion. As to the limited issues presented by the motion noted below, the moving party should be prepared to meet the normal burden under Rule 56 that there is no genuine issue as to any material fact and that the moving party is entitled to dismiss as a matter of law. The Court should apply a two-step test to the motion.

First, the Court should inquire into the independence and good faith of the committee and the bases supporting its conclusions. Limited discovery may be ordered to facilitate such inquiries. The corporation should have the burden of proving independence, good faith and a reasonable investigation, rather than presuming independence, good faith and reasonableness. If the Court determines either that the committee is not independent or has not shown reasonable bases for its conclusions, or, if the Court is not satisfied for other reasons relating to the process, including but not limited to the good faith of the committee, the Court shall deny the corporation's motion. If, however, the Court is satisfied under Rule 56 standards that the committee was independent and showed reasonable bases for good faith findings and recommendations, the Court may proceed, in its discretion, to the next step.

The second step provides, we believe, the essential key in striking the balance between legitimate corporate claims as expressed in a derivative stockholder suit and a corporation's best interests as expressed by an independent investigating committee. The Court should determine, applying its own independent business judgment, whether the motion should be granted. This means, of course, that instances could arise where a committee can establish its independence and sound bases for its good faith decisions and still have the corporation's motion denied. The second step is intended to thwart instances where corporate actions meet the criteria of step one, but the result does not appear to satisfy its spirit, or where corporate actions would simply prematurely terminate a stockholder grievance deserving of further consideration in the corporation's interest. The Court of Chancery of course must carefully consider and weigh how compelling the corporate interest in dismissal is when faced with a non-frivolous lawsuit. The Court of Chancery should, when appropriate, give special consideration to matters of law and public policy in addition to the corporation's best interests.

If the Court's independent business judgment is satisfied, the Court may proceed to grant the motion, subject, of course, to any equitable terms or conditions the Court finds necessary or desirable.

Questions and comments:

1. *Aronson v Lewis* and *Zapata Corp v Maldonado* establish three different standards of review, depending on the situation faced by a shareholder-plaintiff. First, if demand has been made on the board and refused, the directors' decision not to bring litigation is reviewed

under the business judgment rule. If the shareholder-plaintiff fails to rebut the presumptions of the business judgment rule, the shareholder's managerial power to continue a derivative action is terminated by the board's refusal.[215] Secondly, if the shareholder-plaintiff argues that demand is excused, the court will apply the two-pronged *Aronson* test and decide whether a reasonable doubt has been created that the directors were independent and disinterested at the time when the complaint was filed or the challenged transaction was the product of a valid exercise of business judgment.[216] Thirdly, even if demand has not been made *and* was excused, the board retains 'all of its corporate power concerning litigation decisions'.[217] The reason is, as the Supreme Court in *Zapata* explains, that demand futility as a consequence of board interestedness or lack of independence disqualifies individual members of the board, but does not change the allocation of statutory managerial authority.[218] Thus, the board can delegate its authority to a committee pursuant to section 141(c) Delaware General Corporation Law, and the committee has the power to move for dismissal of the derivative action if it determines that the action is not in the best interest of the company. The committee's decision is reviewed by the court in two steps. First, the court assesses the independence and good faith of the committee, and secondly, if the committee is independent, acts in good faith and has conducted a reasonable investigation, the court applies its own independent business judgment in order to determine whether the minority shareholder action is in the best interest of the corporation.[219] The *Zapata* test constitutes in two important respects a deviation from the traditional Delaware standard of review. First, the burden of proving the litigation committee's independence, good faith and reasonable investigation is on the corporation, not the shareholder-plaintiff. Secondly, the *Zapata* test is one of a few instances where the Delaware courts do not defer to the well-informed business judgment of independent directors, but exercise their own judgment to evaluate the substance of a business decision. The Supreme Court acknowledged that the *Zapata* second step required 'a balance of many factors ethical, commercial, promotional, public relations, employee relations, fiscal as well as legal', but it was of the opinion that 'such factors [were] not "beyond the judicial reach" of the Court of Chancery'.[220] Why was the Supreme Court willing to forgo the traditional restraint of the Delaware courts in this situation in favour of a more activist approach that, arguably, gives rise to the 'danger of judicial overreaching'?[221]

[215] *Aronson v Lewis* (n 85) 813. [216] ibid 814.

[217] *Zapata Corp v Maldonado*, 430 A.2d 779, 785. [218] ibid 786. [219] ibid 789.

[220] Ibid 788.

[221] ibid 788. Several states have adopted an alternative approach laid down in the MBCA, §7.44, which provides for business judgment rule review of the decision of a special litigation committee, rather than a substantive review of the committee's decision similar to the *Zapata* second step, provided the committee was appointed by a majority vote of the independent directors. For a similar approach, see *Auerbach v Bennett*, 393 N.E.2d 994 (N.Y. 1979) (no substantive review, but the burden of proving the preconditions of the business judgment rule is on the members of the special litigation committee). Other states have moved in the opposite direction and extended the *Zapata* second step by applying it to all derivative actions, irrespective of whether demand was refused or excused, *Alford v Shaw*, 320 N.C. 465 (N.C. 1987); *Houle v Low*, 556 N.E.2d 51 (Mass. 1990). Yet other courts have tried to limit the danger of judicial overreaching and unpredictable outcomes of litigation by establishing guidelines that narrow judicial discretion. In *Joy v North*, 692 F.2d 880, 892 (2d Cir. 1982), the Second Circuit held: 'Where the court determines that the likely recoverable damages discounted by the probability of a finding of liability are less than the costs to the corporation in continuing the action, it should dismiss the case. The costs which may properly be taken into account are attorney's fees and other out-of-pocket expenses related to the litigation and time spent by corporate personnel preparing for and participating in the trial. The court should also weigh indemnification which is mandatory under corporate by-laws, private contract or [state] law ... Where, having completed the above analysis, the court finds a likely net return to the corporation which is not substantial in relation to shareholder equity, it may take into account two other items as costs. First, it may consider the impact of distraction of key personnel by continued litigation. Second, it may take into account potential lost profits which may result from the publicity of a trial. Judicial scrutiny of special litigation committee recommendations should thus be limited to a comparison of the direct costs imposed upon the corporation by the litigation with the potential benefits. We are mindful that other less direct costs may be incurred, such as a negative impact on morale and upon the corporate image. Nevertheless, we believe that such factors, with the two exceptions noted, should not be taken into account. Quite apart from the elusiveness of attempting to predict such effects, they are quite likely to be directly related to the degree of wrongdoing'.

2. Will it ever be advisable for a shareholder-plaintiff to make a demand on the board, rather than arguing that demand is excused? Consider, first, the different standard of proof. Rebutting the business judgment rule requires that the plaintiff shows by a preponderance of evidence that a defendant director lacked independence, acted in bad faith, or disregarded relevant information.[222] In order to show that demand is excused, on the other hand, it is sufficient that the plaintiff pleads particularized facts (see Delaware Court of Chancery Rule 23.1(a)) that support the conclusion that the business judgment rule does not protect the directors.[223] Importantly, the plaintiff does not have to plead evidence.[224] Secondly, in *Spiegel v Buntrock*,[225] the Supreme Court of Delaware held that '[b]y making a demand, a stockholder tacitly acknowledges the absence of facts to support a finding of futility';[226] hence, the shareholder-plaintiff 'concedes the independence of a majority of the board to respond'.[227] The court, accordingly, examines only whether the board's decision to refuse demand was taken in good faith and after a reasonable investigation. This holding can be criticized for running counter to the goal of the demand rule to facilitate intra-corporate dispute resolution, since any pre-trial discussions with the company may be interpreted as having made a demand and hence having conceded the independence of the board.[228]

4. Germany

Until 2005, German stock corporation law did not provide for a derivative action. The predominant view, already expressed by commentators in the nineteenth century, was that shareholders did not have standing to claim damages from directors for breach of their duties, because there was no direct legal relationship between directors and shareholders on which such a claim could be based, and the directors' ability to manage the company efficiently would be compromised if they had to fear excessive litigation from shareholders.[229] As discussed, in recognition of the conflict of interest that might affect the supervisory board, the law allowed (and still allows[230]) the general meeting to request the supervisory board or management board (or a special representative) to bring litigation if the primarily authorized organ—in the case of a claim of the company against a member of the management board the supervisory board—failed to do so. In addition, minority shareholders representing at least 20 per cent of the legal capital could demand that the company instigate proceedings.[231] The high threshold was successively reduced to 10 per cent in 1937[232] and, under certain additional conditions, to 5 per cent in 1998.[233] However, these thresholds still made it impossible for minority shareholders in many large companies to initiate enforcement actions. Furthermore, minority shareholders had to compensate the company and the special representative for their costs if the action was dismissed, with the result that the minority right was rarely exercised, even if the share capital requirements were met.[234]

222 RF Balotti and JJ Hanks, Jr, 'Rejudging the Business Judgment Rule' (1992) 48 Business Lawyer 1337, 1347–9.
223 ibid 1350–2. See also n 276 below. 224 *Aronson v Lewis* (n 85) 816.
225 571 A.2d 767 (Del. 1990). 226 ibid 775. 227 ibid 777.
228 Pinto and Branson (n 39) §14.05[B].
229 A Renaud, *Das Recht der Actiengesellschaften* (2nd edn, Tauchnitz 1875) 611–14.
230 AktG, §147.
231 Allgemeines Deutsches Handelsgesetzbuch (ADHGB) [General German Commercial Code] of 1861, Art 223(1), as amended by Gesetz, betreffend die Kommanditgesellschaften auf Aktien und die Aktiengesellschaften [Act concerning limited partnerships by shares and joint stock corporations], RGBl 1884, 123.
232 Gesetz über Aktiengesellschaften und Kommanditgesellschaften auf Aktien [Act concerning stock corporations and limited partnerships by shares], RGBl I 1937, 107, §122(1). The threshold was 5% if a legally required audit opinion established facts that gave rise to a claim against the directors.
233 AktG, §147, as amended by Gesetz zur Kontrolle und Transparenz im Unternehmensbereich (KonTraG) [Control and Transparency in the Corporate Sector Act] of 1 May 1998, BGBl I, 786, Art 1, no 22. The general threshold of 10% was retained, and the lower threshold applied to the newly introduced right of shareholders to request the court to appoint a special representative if there were strong reasons to believe that the company had suffered a loss due to dishonesty or a gross breach of the law.
234 Cheffins and Black (n 101) 1425.

Legal reforms of 2005 replaced the right of the 5 per cent or 10 per cent minority to compel the company to bring litigation with a derivative action mechanism that resembles in some respects the statutory minority shareholder lawsuit in the UK.[235] The reforms seek to facilitate on the one hand the enforcement of the company's claims and strengthen minority shareholder protection, and on the other hand, prevent abusive and wasteful litigation by granting the right to instigate proceedings not to an individual shareholder, but a qualified minority, and requiring the plaintiffs to apply to the trial court for admission of the claim before the case can proceed to full trial.

The admission procedure can be initiated by shareholders representing together at least 1 per cent of the company's legal capital or €100,000. This threshold is comparatively low as far as small, non-listed public companies are concerned, but still often difficult to achieve in widely held corporations. The court will grant permission to continue the claim if four conditions are satisfied.[236] First, the petitioners must show that they had acquired their shares before they knew, or should have known, of the alleged breach of duty or the damage suffered by the company. This requirement tries to prevent the acquisition of shares for the sole purpose of bringing a (potentially abusive) lawsuit. Point of reference for what a shareholder should have known is the 'average private, that is, not institutional investor'.[237] If the facts that give rise to the claim have been reported widely in the media, for example in nationwide newspapers, broadcasts or online, investors can be presumed to be aware of the breach or damage. The provision is interpreted to bar litigation by any shareholder who reaches the relevant threshold (1 per cent or €100,000) after dissemination of the news. Thus, existing shareholders who acquire additional shares after the facts have become widely known, and because of this acquisition reach the quorum, are barred just as new shareholders.[238] However, it may be possible for the shareholder-plaintiffs to show that they could not be aware of the relevant facts owing to individual circumstances, for example because they were abroad during the relevant time.[239]

Secondly, a sufficient number of shareholders to constitute the required quorum must have requested the company to enforce the claim. Generally, the shareholders must set a reasonable time limit, for example two months, unless the competent organ (generally the supervisory board) has already made it clear that the claim will not be pursued.[240] This is an expression of the subsidiary nature of the derivative action, which is only admissible if the company fails to file a lawsuit within the time limit.

Thirdly, and most problematically, the derivative action is generally reserved for cases of dishonesty or a gross violation of the law or the articles of association. The plaintiffs bear the burden of presenting facts that disclose with sufficient probability such a case. However, if it emerges that the challenged conduct does not amount to dishonesty or a gross breach after the court has granted permission for the case to proceed to full trial, the shareholders will be allowed to continue the action.[241] Dishonesty refers to behaviour that goes beyond mismanagement and usually consists in breaches of the duty of loyalty bordering criminal

[235] AktG, §148, as amended by Gesetz zur Unternehmensintegrität und Modernisierung des Anfechtungsrechts [Act on Corporate Integrity and Modernisation of the Law of Avoidance] (UMAG) of 22 September 2005, BGBl I, 2802, Art 1, no 15. Minority shareholders representing at least 10% of the legal capital or EUR 1 million still have the right to apply to the court to appoint an alternative representative than the authorized organ or person, §147(2), sentence 2. The court must appoint one or more special representatives if it is convinced that the persons normally competent to pursue the claim do not have the neutrality and independence to guarantee that the action will be conducted in an orderly and efficient manner. The fact that the persons in question are inactive may indicate that this is the case. Whether the action is likely to be successful is irrelevant. The court is not bound to follow the suggestions of the minority as to the person to be appointed, but it will generally do so if the nominee has the necessary knowledge and skills.

[236] AktG, §148(1) sentence 2 nos 1–4.

[237] M Arnold in W Goette and M Habersack (eds), *Münchener Kommentar zum Aktiengesetz, vol 3* (4th edn, CH Beck 2018) §148 para 14.

[238] ibid para 19. [239] BT-Drs 15/5092, 21. [240] ibid 22. [241] ibid.

conduct.[242] Gross violations of the law or the articles require an evident and inexcusable breach. Breaches of the duty of care may reach this threshold if the breach is likely to have caused significant damage or has been committed intentionally or grossly negligently.[243] By restricting the derivative action to particularly severe types of misconduct, the legislator intended to strike a balance between respecting the views of the majority of shareholders, who, it is argued, at least implicitly decide against bringing an action by not exercising the enforcement right of the general meeting,[244] and penalizing breaches of duty and other misconduct. If the breach is comparatively minor, the views of the majority shareholders are given greater weight than if the breach is severe.[245] However, given what we said about rational apathy, especially of investors in widely held companies, and the transaction costs involved in procuring a resolution of the general meeting, it is questionable whether the views of the majority can be deduced from the mere fact that the general meeting remains inactive.[246] In addition, it might be argued that greater judicial discretion in deciding whether to grant permission would result in a more flexible and nuanced approach. Similar to a derivative action under the UK Companies Act 2006, the court could consider the severity of the breach as well as the views of the majority (and other factors), but the lack of a gross breach of the law would not constitute an absolute bar to a minority shareholder lawsuit.

The German derivative action mechanism contains a certain discretionary element, because, as a final condition of a minority shareholder lawsuit, the Stock Corporation Act requires that granting permission to continue the claim must not be contrary to overriding interests of the company. However, as it is formulated, the provision does not grant broad discretion to the court. Rather, if the three other conditions are satisfied, courts will admit the claim in all but exceptional cases.[247] We have examined some of the considerations that may exceptionally lead to a refusal to grant permission in Chapter 6, where we discussed the decision of the Bundesgerichtshof in ARAG/Garmenbeck.[248] The courts will assess, for example, whether litigation would have a detrimental effect on the reputation of the company or disrupt business operations. However, since the existence of a gross violation of the law or the articles militates strongly in favour of admission, these considerations will typically only outweigh the interests of the plaintiffs if the damage suffered by the company is minor or a lawsuit dealing with a related breach is already pending.[249]

If the claim is admitted, the shareholders who were parties to the admission procedure can pursue the claim in their own name by bringing an action within three months after the admission decision has become binding, provided the company is again requested to enforce the claim and again fails to do so.[250] In derogation from the 'loser pays' principle of general civil procedure law, the law seeks to apportion the litigation risk according to 'spheres of responsibility'. In order to deter shareholders from bringing test cases with little prospect of success, the plaintiffs generally bear the costs of the admission procedure if their petition is dismissed.[251] On the other hand, if the action proceeds to full trial and is dismissed then, the shareholder-plaintiffs can claim reimbursement of their costs from the company, unless the admission decision was based on deliberately or negligently incorrect submissions by the shareholders.[252] Finally, if the company is listed on a stock exchange, the admission of

[242] The explanatory memorandum points out that the provision is intended to capture cases where the failure to enforce a breach would be 'intolerable'; see ibid.

[243] Arnold (n 237) paras 36–41. [244] Text to n 93 above. [245] BT-Drs 15/5092, 22.

[246] See our discussion in Chapter 5C.I.3. [247] BT-Drs 15/5092, 22.

[248] BGHZ 135, 244; Chapter 6B.I.3. [249] Arnold (n 237) para 47.

[250] AktG, §148(4). Quorum requirements no longer apply, i.e. not all shareholders who were involved in the admission procedure need to continue the litigation. If the admission procedure was successful, it is likely that the action itself will also be successful. One can therefore expect that the company will take over the litigation, which renders the shareholder lawsuit inadmissible: ibid §148(3).

[251] ibid §148(6) sentence 1. On the legislative rationale, see BT-Drs 15/5092, 23.

[252] AktG, §148(6) sentence 5.

the derivative action and its conclusion, including any agreements in connection with the termination of the proceedings, must be published in the Federal Gazette.[253] By requiring transparency, the law seeks to prevent actions from being initiated for the sole purpose of extracting a settlement payment, including payments amounting to an unlawful distribution of the company's assets.[254]

5. *France*

French law offers ostensibly the most accommodating regime of our four jurisdictions for minority shareholder lawsuits. The *action sociale ut singuli*, the French version of the derivative action, is available to enforce claims of the company against a director or managing director.[255] It can be initiated by a group of shareholders representing not less than 5 per cent of the share capital.[256] If the legal capital of the company exceeds €750,000, the threshold is progressively reduced, and it is as low as 0.5 per cent for companies with a legal capital of more than €15 million.[257] Alternatively, the action may be brought by an individual shareholder irrespective of the number of shares held.[258] The plaintiff must be a shareholder when the action is launched and remain a shareholder throughout the proceedings. Finally, if the company's shares are listed on a regulated market, shareholders whose shares have been registered for at least two years and who hold at least 5 per cent of the voting rights (or a lower percentage of 1–4 per cent in companies exceeding certain size thresholds) may form a shareholder association to represent their rights and initiate the *action sociale ut singuli*.[259]

Apart from these standing requirements, the Commercial Code does not impose any conditions on shareholders who seek to bring a derivative action. Courts have held that the *action ut singuli* is of a subsidiary nature. It is inadmissible if the organ primarily authorized to act on behalf of the company, the board of directors, decides to initiate an *action sociale ut universi*.[260] However, the subsidiarity of the derivative action is not comparable to the demand requirement under Delaware law, and in contrast to Delaware corporations, the disinterested board does not act as a gatekeeper filtering out actions that are not in the interest of the company. Case law illustrates these differences. For example, in *Sté Testut*, the court of first instance had dismissed an action for damages brought by the new directors of Société Testut against the former managers.[261] When the board of directors of Société Testut decided not to appeal, one of the company's shareholders sought to pursue the company's claim with an *action ut singuli*. The court of appeal dismissed the action on the ground that the shareholder's claim was identical to the claim brought by the company. Importantly, it was argued that the company had not failed to enforce the claim, but it had brought an action and taken the decision not to appeal against a judgment dismissing the case. The Cour de Cassation overruled the decision. It held that 'the legal representatives of the company could not deprive the claimant of the right, vested in the shareholders, to bring a claim for the benefit of the company and appeal on behalf of the company'. Thus, the derivative action is only subsidiary if the company actively pursues the *action ut universi*, and it becomes available again when the company ceases to do so, even if this is attributable to a disinterested

[253] ibid §149. [254] BT-Drs 15/5092, 24.

[255] Com, Art L225-252. The right to bring an *action sociale ut singuli* cannot be restricted by the articles of association, waived in advance or made conditional on the authorization of the general meeting: Art L225-253. Furthermore, this provision has been interpreted as prohibiting any action by the board of directors or (in companies with a two-tier board) the supervisory board terminating the shareholder lawsuit; A Charveriat, A Couret, and B Zabala, *Mémento Pratique Sociétés Commerciales* (Francis Lefebvre 2017) para 14090.

[256] Com, Art L225-252. [257] ibid Art R225-169. [258] ibid Art L225-252.

[259] ibid Art L225-120.

[260] M Cozian, A Viandier, and F Deboissy, *Droit des sociétés* (31st edn, LexisNexis 2018) para 398.

[261] Cass crim, 12 December 2000 (*Sté Testut*), *Rev. sociétés* 2001, 323, discussed in Cozian, Viandier, and Deboissy (n 260) para 401.

decision of the directors who were not involved in the wrongdoing (or indeed members of the board at the time of the wrongdoing).[262]

Conversely, if the board initiates litigation, the court exercises only a limited oversight function. In principle, the mere fact of having brought the *action ut universi* bars shareholders from pursuing a derivative action. In some cases, courts have established an exception to this rule by equating litigating in a manner that renders the *action sociale ut universi* a 'sham' with inaction on the part of the board.[263] This has been held to be the case if the defendant continues to have influence over the board as either shareholder or director and the current directors do not substantiate the claim they pursue by alleging facts that would establish a breach of duty or a loss suffered by the company.[264] It is not entirely clear how far this exception can be taken. Commentators have argued that only the failure of the board to submit *any* proper grounds substantiating the company's claim renders the *action sociale ut singuli* admissible. If the current members of the board present a prima facie case, but do not advance particularly strong arguments for holding the defendant director liable, the *action ut singuli* presumably continues to be subsidiary.[265] It has been suggested that such a case should not be dealt with by calling the subsidiarity of the *action sociale ut singuli* into question, but holding the current directors responsible for mismanagement in the enforcement of the company's claim (if applicable, by allowing an *action ut singuli* against *these* directors).[266]

In spite of the relatively generous standing requirements, the derivative action is not common in France.[267] Arguably, unfavourable cost rules are the main deterrent.[268] Civil litigation is based on the 'loser pays' principle. As opposed to other countries that apply the same cost rule, such as Germany, French company law does not provide for a general exception to the 'loser pays' principle that would allow shareholder-plaintiffs to shift the litigation risk with some legal certainty to the company.[269] The costs, and hence the litigation risk, can be spread across several shareholders if these shareholders are able to bring litigation as a group or a shareholder association.[270] However, as mentioned, this is only possible if the shareholder litigants meet a threshold percentage of voting rights that ranges between 1 per cent and 5 per cent. This is not dissimilar to the standing requirements under German law and will often be difficult to achieve in large companies. In addition, it does not solve the

[262] See also Cass com, 27 September 2017, no 15-28835, *Revue des sociétés* 2018, 1211, note B Saintourens (holding that a shareholder who initiated a derivative action does not lose standing to pursue the claim if the company ultimately brings an *action ut universi*).

[263] Cass crim, 16 December 2009, *JCP E* 2010, 1993, no 1, note F Deboissy and G Wicker.

[264] ibid. In this case, the directors who acted on behalf of the company had largely abstained from criticizing the defendant director and had even embraced some of the latter's arguments.

[265] The Court of Appeal of Bordeaux in the above case had formulated the relevant test in an open-ended way, but the decision of the Cour de Cassation, arguably, has to be understood more restrictively. The court held that the *action sociale ut singuli* was admissible, because 'the company, acting through its legal representatives ... had not offered *any* criticism of [the defendant director], who was a shareholder and manager, and had not claimed the existence of *any* damage' on the part of the company (emphases by authors).

[266] Deboissy and Wicker (n 89) no 1.

[267] Comprehensive data does not exist, but several studies have examined different aspects of shareholder litigation in France, and the findings consistently show that minority shareholder lawsuits are rare, Cheffins and Black (n 101) 1453–4; PH Conac, L Enriques, and M Gelter, 'Constraining Dominant Shareholders' Self-Dealing: The Legal Framework in France, Germany, and Italy' (2007) 4 ECFR 491, 508–9; Gelter (n 101) 849.

[268] This argument has also been made by Cheffins and Black (n 101) 1453–4; Conac, Enriques, and Gelter (n 267) 508–9; L Enriques, 'The Comparative Anatomy of Corporate Law' (2004) 52 American Journal of Comparative Law 1011, 1023–4; Merle (n 88) para 463.

[269] As discussed, in Germany risk shifting has been achieved through the introduction of §148(6) AktG (see text to nn 251–252 above), which does not have a counterpart in French law. As mentioned (n 102 above), the French version of the 'loser pays' principle only requires the losing party to reimburse the winning party's court fees, but generally not lawyers' fees (unless the court provides for reimbursement under equitable considerations, Gelter (n 101) 863–4). Nevertheless, a mismatch exists between the judicial costs and litigation risk borne by the shareholder-plaintiff and the compensation received by the company and hence shared among all shareholders.

[270] Com, Art R225-169(1).

Table 1 Comparative effectiveness of the derivative action

	MBCA	Delaware	UK pre-2006	UK post-2006	Germany pre-2005	Germany post-2005	France
Size of share-holding	1 share	1 share	1 share	1 share	1884: 20% 1965: 10% 1998: 5%	1% or €100,000	1 share
Additional conditions	Demand rule; no dismissal by litigation committee	Demand refused or excused	Fraud on the minority	Claim admission procedure	1998: Bad faith or gross negligence	Claim admission procedure	Company refuses to take action
Cost rules	Court decides (corporation if lawsuit beneficial); contingency fee possible	Court decides (corporation if lawsuit beneficial); contingency fee possible	Indemnification order if good faith and reasonable grounds	Indemnification order if good faith and reasonable grounds	Shareholder bears litigation risk	Plaintiff can generally claim re-imbursement	Shareholder bears litigation risk

general misalignment of incentives, since a minority of shareholders continues to bear the litigation risk, while the lawsuit will benefit all shareholders if it is successful.[271]

6. *Comparative effectiveness of the minority shareholder lawsuit*

All legal systems analysed here provide for some form of derivative action mechanism to facilitate the enforcement of the company's claims against the directors. However, we have also identified considerable variation in the design of the mechanism between the four jurisdictions, and we have seen that the rules have changed significantly in some of them over time. Table 1 compares the jurisdictions along the three dimensions highlighted above: standing rules determining ownership thresholds, a 'screening mechanism' to filter out frivolous actions, and cost rules. Major legal reforms are also included: the replacement of the rule in *Foss v Harbottle* with the statutory derivative action in the UK and the successive reduction of ownership thresholds in Germany.

If it is correct, as claimed above, that the derivative action is only effective if a regulatory environment exists that is conducive to minority shareholder lawsuits along all three dimensions,[272] most legal systems at most points in time failed to provide for such an environment. In the UK, the 'fraud on the minority' requirement of the common law rendered minority shareholder lawsuits for most purposes impossible, at least in public companies. In Germany, the same was the case under the 10 per cent and 5 per cent standing thresholds, and even the new claim admission procedure has been called 'ineffective in practice', because the quorum of 1 per cent is still difficult to achieve for outside investors in many large companies. In addition, the requirement to show dishonesty or a gross violation of the law narrows the scope of the derivative action significantly.[273] In France, standing requirements are generous and the subsidiary nature of the *action sociale ut singuli* does not pose significant obstacles to bringing a minority shareholder lawsuit. However, the fact that the shareholders bear the costs of the proceedings acts as a disincentive to litigation. This leaves the

[271] The disincentives created by the French cost rules could be mitigate if a class action was available to enforce the company's claims. A legal reform of 2014 indeed introduced class actions into French law, Law no 2014-344 of 17 March 2014 (Loi relative à la consommation, so-called 'loi Hamon'), JORF no 65 of 18 March 2014, 5400. However, the law only applies to consumer and competition law disputes in relation to the sale of goods or provision of services and does not address the design problems of the derivative action in France.

[272] Text to nn 137–138 above.

[273] J Koch in U Hüffer and J Koch, *Aktiengesetz* (13th edn, CH Beck 2018) §148 para 3.

United States and the post-2006 statutory derivative action mechanism in the UK. In both countries, any shareholder can pursue the company's claims, provided they are able to create a reasonable doubt that the directors are independent or the challenged transaction was protected by the business judgment rule (Delaware law in the demand excused case),[274] or the court concludes that the action, on balance, is in the best interest of the company (UK).[275] It is difficult to argue that one of the two tests is inherently more difficult to satisfy than the other. Rather, the crucial question is how the courts interpret open-ended concepts such as 'reasonable doubt',[276] promoting 'the success of the company',[277] or 'views of members of the company'.[278] In both jurisdictions, the courts scrutinize minority shareholder actions carefully, but the hurdles are clearly not insurmountable if the claim is meritorious and the plaintiffs have access to relevant information to substantiate their allegations.[279] Finally, cost rules and the availability of contingency fees or comparable arrangements are favourable in the two countries and allow the litigation risk to be shifted to other parties.[280] Thus, UK and Delaware law (and the laws of other US states) are comparatively minority-shareholder friendly, whereas it is to be expected that derivative actions will remain rare in France and Germany.

What does this observation mean for the general effectiveness of duty-based constraints on managerial discretion in the four countries? We have seen that directors in Delaware corporations are well protected from liability for breaches of duty. Under the currently prevailing interpretation of the business judgment rule, courts are unlikely to second-guess business decisions made in good faith and without a conflict of interest.[281] In the other three countries, the duty of care is formulated more stringently. In the UK, an explicit business judgment rule does not exist and directors are held to an objective standard of accountability that is heightened if the director possesses particular skills or expertise.[282] Similarly, the French standard of care is defined as the care and diligence that can reasonably be expected from a person in the position of the director. The courts are prepared to hold directors liable for intentional acts and negligent mismanagement, as well as the failure to supervise the managers adequately.[283] German law now has its own version of the business judgment rule,[284] but with two important differences to its Delaware counterpart that render the protection of directors less comprehensive. The burden of proof is on the director to show that the threshold conditions of the business judgment rule are met,[285] and courts seem to interpret these conditions strictly, in particular the requirements that the director must have reasonably believed that the challenged act was in the best interest of the company and based on appropriate information.[286] Thus, in all three countries, the duty of care is formulated

[274] *Aronson v Lewis* (n 85) 808.

[275] As discussed, courts will consider all factors listed in Companies Act 2006, s 263(2)–(4).

[276] For an interpretation of the term, see *Starrels v First Nat. Bank of Chicago*, 870 F.2d 1168, 1175 (7th Cir. 1989) (questioning whether the term referred to the 'beyond reasonable doubt' standard under criminal law—'at least a 90% likelihood that the defendant is guilty'—which would mean that 'demand is excused whenever there is a 10% chance that the original transaction is not protected by the business judgment rule').

[277] Companies Act 2006, ss 263(2)(a), (3)(b).

[278] ibid s 263(4). For a discussion, see text to nn 175–182 above.

[279] In practice, this may be a serious obstacles for outside shareholders, see e.g. *Brehm v Eisner*, 746 A.2d 244, 266 (Del. 2000), where the plaintiffs complained 'that the system of requiring a stockholder to plead particularized facts in a derivative suit is basically unfair because the Court will not permit discovery ... to marshal the facts necessary to establish that pre-suit demand is excused'. The court did not accept this argument and referred the plaintiffs to their shareholder inspection rights under corporate law to obtain the relevant books and records of the company.

[280] In the UK, some uncertainty remains regarding the possibility to enter into damages-based agreements; see n 198 above.

[281] Chapter 6B.I.2. [282] Companies Act 2006, s 174(2).

[283] See the examples from the case law in Chapter 6B.I.4(a).

[284] AktG, §93(1) sentence 2. The provision is discussed in Chapter 6B.I.3.

[285] AktG, §93(2) sentence 2.

[286] A striking example of the stricter approach of the German courts (which, however, probably cannot be generalized in its entirety) is the *IKB* decision of the Higher Regional Court Düsseldorf, reproduced in Chapter 6B.I.3.

more stringently than under Delaware law.[287] At the same time, the enforcement of breaches is (or was) difficult in these countries (in the UK, until 2006). Could it be argued, then, that all four jurisdictions seek to achieve a certain equilibrium level of liability exposure of directors, and do so only with different means? Delaware courts are very much aware of the detrimental effects that excessive liability exposure may have on corporate activity, and they explicitly rely on this rationale to justify their broad interpretation of the business judgment rule.[288] Similarly, the restrictions built into derivative action mechanisms in the UK, Germany, and elsewhere are concerned with avoiding excessive litigation, even if this comes at the price of precluding certain meritorious lawsuits.[289] Of course, whether the equilibrium thus created is optimal depends on the details of the relevant rules: the applicable standard of care, threshold conditions of the business judgment rule, and the requirements that need to be satisfied in order to bring a derivative action (as well as the existence and effectiveness of any substitute enforcement mechanisms[290]). In any case, it is important to bear in mind that identifying, say, a lenient standard of care does not allow us to draw clear conclusions regarding the appropriateness of the standard if the analysis does not encompass enforcement questions.

D. Substitute Mechanisms

The lack of an effective minority shareholder lawsuit (or its complete absence, as for example in the Netherlands[291]) may not result in an inefficiently low level of investor protection if suitable substitute mechanisms are available in the legal system. This section gives a brief overview of the most relevant substitute mechanisms: administrative proceedings, in particular investigations conducted by a court or another public body that may lead to the disqualification of a director or an order regulating other aspects of a company's affairs, and criminal proceedings.[292] Both categories of enforcement mechanism are predominantly public in nature, but, as we will see, they also allow shareholders or the liquidator to exert some influence over the proceedings. Because of their public nature, they do

[287] As far as the duty of loyalty is concerned, we do not observe a similar relaxation of standards in Delaware. Conversely, for various reasons that we discussed in Chapter 6C.I, it can be argued that self-dealing transactions are regulated less effectively in France and Germany than in our two common law jurisdictions.

[288] See, for example, *In re Caremark Intern. Inc. Derivative Litigation*, 698 A.2d 959, 967 (Del. Ch. 1996): 'What should be understood, but may not widely be understood by courts or commentators who are not often required to face such questions, is that compliance with a director's duty of care can never appropriately be judicially determined by reference to the content of the board decision that leads to a corporate loss, apart from consideration of the good faith or rationality of the process employed. That is, whether a judge or jury considering the matter after the fact, believes a decision substantively wrong, or degrees of wrong extending through "stupid" to "egregious" or "irrational", provides no ground for director liability, so long as the court determines that the process employed was either rational or employed in a good faith effort to advance corporate interests. To employ a different rule—one that permitted an "objective" evaluation of the decision—would expose directors to substantive second guessing by ill-equipped judges or juries, which would, in the long-run, be injurious to investor interests'.

[289] See, e.g., BT-Drs 15/5092, 20–2, regarding the German minority shareholder lawsuit.

[290] We will turn to such substitute mechanisms in the next section.

[291] In the EU, only three countries, namely Estonia, Luxembourg, and the Netherlands, have no derivative action mechanism, and in one country, Malta, it is effectively not used in practice; see Gerner-Beuerle and Schuster (n 138) 216.

[292] Minority shareholders suits challenging decisions of the general meeting may also be regarded as substitutes of the derivative action, Gelter (n 101) 881. We said that such lawsuits are particularly important in countries where the general meeting has extensive decision-making powers and ownership structure is characterized by large block holdings, since the majority/minority shareholder problem is comparatively more pertinent in such economies than the managerial agency problem. Thus, we would expect lawsuits challenging resolutions of the general meeting to be more relevant in practice, and regulated in greater detail, in a country such as Germany than, for example, in the United States or UK. This is exactly what we found when we discussed the matter in Chapter 5C.III.

not pose the same problems that compromise the effectiveness of some private enforcement mechanisms. Importantly, the shareholders do not bear any litigation risk and may benefit from the investigative powers of the state official conducting the investigation. On the other hand, public enforcement, of course, comes with its own problems, in particular resource constraints of the relevant public body and a higher evidentiary burden in criminal proceedings.

Among our four legal systems, administrative proceedings that result in the disqualification of a director play the most important role in the UK. Annually, between 1,000 and 1,400 directors are disqualified and, as a consequence, prohibited from serving as a director of a company or participating directly or indirectly in the formation or management of a company for a specified period of no more than fifteen years.[293] The grounds for disqualification are laid down in the Company Directors Disqualification Act 1986. Most disqualification orders are made because directors are deemed 'unfit to be concerned in the management of a company'.[294] The concept of 'unfitness' is not defined in the act. It has been suggested that two main categories of unfitness can be derived from the case law: breach of commercial morality and incompetence.[295] The former refers to cases where the company's affairs are conducted in way that ignores the interests of the creditors. For example, directors may be disqualified for making loans to a director or transferring assets between group companies in violation of capital maintenance rules,[296] or for successively incorporating undercapitalized companies and allowing the companies to become insolvent, only to carry on the same business with another company (so-called Phoenix companies).[297] A good example of the latter category of unfitness, lack of competence, is the *Barings* case that we discussed in Chapter 6.[298] In this case, the court held that unfitness might consist in conduct 'completely lacking in judgment', even if the director was not guilty of misfeasance or breach of duty in relation to the company (although conduct 'completely lacking in judgment', such as the absence of a working internal control system and the disregard of warning signs in *Barings*, will generally also consist in a breach of duty).[299] Conversely, it is important to note that a disqualification order will not be issued in all instances of a breach of duty. Rather, the courts require a showing of recklessness or 'negligence in a very marked degree', for example where a director repeatedly fails to keep proper accounting records, fails to file annual returns, and causes loan transactions to be made between companies of a corporate group that were in severe financial difficulties.[300] Other grounds for disqualification include the commission of an indictable offence in relation with the promotion, formation, management or liquidation of a company, persistent breaches of reporting requirements under the Companies Acts and

[293] Data is published by Companies House, which manages the companies register in the UK; see Companies House, Management information tables 2017–18, Table 6.

[294] Company Directors Disqualification Act (CDDA) 1986, ss 6(1)(b), 8(2). A disqualification order for unfitness can be issued under either s 6 or s 8. Section 6 is narrower in scope than s 8, since it requires that the company has become insolvent (s 6(1)(a)). On the other hand, the minimum period of disqualification pursuant to s 6 is two years, whereas s 8 does not impose any minimum period (ss 6(4), 8(4)). Both provisions apply to directors as well as shadow directors (ss 6(3C), 8(1)). See Companies House, Management information tables 2017–18, Table 6. The table distinguishes between disqualification orders by the court and disqualifications 'by undertaking', which are out-of-court agreements between the director and the Secretary of State initiating the disqualification proceedings that have the same effect as a disqualification order. In 2017–18, 247 disqualification orders were issued because directors were convicted of an offence, 107 because directors were deemed unfit, and disqualification undertakings were given in 883 cases, which typically also relate to the unfitness of a director (see CDDA 1986, ss 1A, 7, 8). In prior years, the proportion of disqualifications for unfitness was similar.

[295] Davies and Worthington (n 34) para 10-9. From the case law, see, for example, *Re Barings plc and Others (No 5)* [1999] 1 BCLC 433, 483, holding that unfitness 'may be shown by conduct which is dishonest (including conduct showing a want of probity or integrity) or by conduct which is merely incompetent'.

[296] *Re Westminster Property Management Ltd (No 2)* [2004] BCC 581.

[297] *Re Travel Mondial (UK) Ltd* [1991] BCC 224.

[298] Chapter 6B.II.

[299] *Re Barings plc and Others (No 5)* (n 295) 486.

[300] *Re Sevenoaks Stationers (Retail) Ltd* [1991] Ch 164, 184.

the Insolvency Act 1986, or the finding that a director is liable to make a contribution to the company's assets because of wrongful or fraudulent trading.[301]

In the case of unfitness, an application for a disqualification order can be made by the relevant government minister (the Secretary of State) or upon delegation by the liquidator if the company is being wound up,[302] and in other cases also by any present or former member or creditor of the company.[303] If the director's company is insolvent and the conduct that has given rise to the disqualification order or disqualification undertaking has caused a loss to the company's creditors, the Secretary of State may seek compensation from the director for the benefit of the creditors.[304] The amount of compensation will usually not exceed the loss suffered by the company, but courts will also take into account the nature and seriousness of the director's misconduct.[305] Finally, any contravention of a disqualification order or undertaking constitutes a criminal offence[306] and entails personal liability of the disqualified director for the debts of the company incurred while the director was involved in the management of the company.[307]

Many legal systems are familiar with the concept of directors' disqualification, but commonly the disqualification regime is less wide-ranging than in the UK. The French Commercial Code enumerates a number of grounds on which courts may disqualify a director, including fraudulently operating a business in a situation that would necessarily lead to the company's insolvency, embezzling corporate assets, entering into transactions without consideration that are 'disproportionate', given the financial position of the company, making preferential payments after insolvency to the detriment of some creditors, or tampering with corporate books and accounts.[308] The administrator, liquidator, or public prosecutor, and under certain conditions a majority of creditors, can initiate disqualification proceedings.[309] The court can disqualify a director for up to fifteen years.[310] In addition, disqualified directors are deprived of their voting rights as shareholders and the court may order them to sell their shares and use the proceeds to pay the debts of the company.[311] While the French disqualification regime, therefore, provides for similar sanctions as the UK Company Directors Disqualification Act 1986, it is in two important respects more limited. First, disqualification requires that insolvency proceedings have been opened.[312] In the UK, disqualification orders are of course also frequently issued in the insolvency of a company, but, as we have seen, this is not a precondition for all categories of disqualification. Secondly, and more importantly, the grounds for disqualification under French law target specific cases of fraudulent or intentional misconduct, particularly misconduct that harms the creditors of a company. They generally do not extend to behaviour that falls short of fraud or intentional breach of law, in contrast to the UK concept of unfitness, which captures also recklessness and gross negligence. These differences may explain why the UK disqualification regime is of greater practical relevance as a mechanism to enforce directors' duties than the French regime.

US and German law do not provide for a separate disqualification regime, but certain circumstances that would disqualify a director under UK law, for example a conviction for a criminal offence, may become relevant in the context of determining whether someone is eligible to be appointed to the board of directors. Pursuant to the German Stock Corporation Act, persons who have been convicted of an insolvency offence, fraud or an offence concerning the disclosure of incorrect corporate information are prohibited from serving as members of the management board of a stock corporation for five years.[313] The company laws of the United States generally impose only minimal eligibility requirements

[301] CDDA 1986, ss 2–4, 10. [302] ibid s 7(1). [303] ibid s 16(2). [304] ibid ss 15A, 15B.

[305] ibid s 15B(3). For an interpretation of this provision, see Davies and Worthington (n 34) para 10-4 (suggesting that 'the loss suffered as a result of the director's conduct sets the outer boundary of the compensation to be awarded and, within that, the seriousness of the conduct will be crucial').

[306] CDDA 1986, ss 13, 14. [307] ibid s 15. [308] Com, Arts L653-4, L653-5.

[309] ibid Art L653-7. [310] ibid Art L653-11.

[311] ibid Art 653-9. For a more detailed discussion of the consequences of disqualification, see Charveriat, Couret, and Zabala (n 255) paras 91860–90.

[312] Com, Art L653-1(I). [313] AktG, §76(3).

on directors. For example, the Delaware General Corporation Law simply requires that directors are natural persons and leaves other qualifications to the certificate of incorporation or bylaws.[314] It is not common that the latter include grounds for disqualification comparable to those that can be found in UK or French law. Moreover, the relevant criminal offences do not provide for disqualification as a sanction.[315] Hence, neither US nor German law makes effective use of disqualification orders to strengthen enforcement or compensate for potential deficiencies of existing private enforcement mechanisms, and French law does not do so to the same extent as the UK. With regard to the United States, it may be argued that this is not necessary, since private enforcement is relatively efficient. In the two civil law countries, on the other hand, we have identified flaws in the design of the minority shareholder lawsuit, which explain the (probably inefficiently) low level of private enforcement activity in these countries. As we will see, criminal law functions as a backstop for misconduct of a severe nature, in particular in France, but it is questionable whether conduct not reaching that level is sufficiently stringently regulated. In addition, the absence of effective private or administrative enforcement mechanisms may result in the 'criminalization' of company law and the extensive reliance on provisions that are not well suited to address problems arising in the business world because of their criminal law nature.[316]

We will deal with other public or quasi-public enforcement mechanisms only briefly. Legal systems may permit minority shareholders to appoint a special auditor[317] who has the power to investigate the company's affairs and reports back to the shareholders and directors.[318] Importantly, pursuant to both German and French law, the court can decide that court fees and the remuneration of the special auditor must be borne by the company, thus alleviating one of the main shortcomings of the pre-2005 German and the French minority shareholder regimes.[319] A similar procedure, but with greater involvement of the court, is the Dutch inquiry proceeding, conducted by the Enterprise Chamber of the Amsterdam Court of Appeal.[320] This procedure has received considerable attention internationally, because it represents a largely public substitute of the minority shareholder lawsuit, which does not exist under Dutch law.[321] The inquiry proceeding is commonly regarded as effective, even though the threshold for shareholders to be able to request the opening of proceedings is high: 10 per cent of the issued share capital or shares with a nominal value of €225,000.[322] If shareholders can substantiate the claim that the company has not been managed properly,

[314] Del. Gen. Corp. Law, §141(b). For other states, see *Fletcher Cyclopedia of the Law of Corporations* (perm edn, Thomson Reuters 2018) §§297, 298.

[315] ibid §§1348–59.

[316] A widely discussed example is the application of the criminal offence of breach of trust to the payment of excessive management remuneration in the German case *Mannesmann*, BGHSt 50, 331. For an analysis of the decision in English and a comparison with US law, see FA Gevurtz, 'Disney in a Comparative Light' (2007) 55 American Journal of Comparative Law 453. See also Merle (n 88) para 469 (critically discussing the criminalization of French company law as a result of the increasingly broad interpretation of *abus de biens sociaux* by the courts).

[317] In Germany, shareholders representing at least 1% of the legal capital or €100,000 have the right to apply to the court to appoint a special auditor (AktG, §142(2)), and in France, 5% shareholders have a similar right (Com, Art L225-231(3)). However, according to German law, the court will only appoint a special auditor if the shareholders present facts indicating that the conduct complained of involved dishonesty or a gross violation of the law. For a discussion of these provisions, see Conac, Enriques, and Gelter (n 267) 512–13, and for further analysis of the special auditor under German law, see Chapter 6B.I.3.

[318] German AktG, §145; French Code de commerce, Art L225-231(5), (6).

[319] German AktG, §146; French Code de commerce, Art L225-231(5).

[320] Dutch Civil Code, Arts 2:344 to 2:359.

[321] Gelter (n 101) 889–91; JA McCahery and EPM Vermeulen, 'Role of Corporate Governance Reform and Enforcement in the Netherlands' in M Tison and others (eds), *Perspectives in Company Law and Financial Regulation* (Cambridge University Press 2009) 322, 337–41; L Timmerman, 'Application of the Dutch investigation procedure on two listed companies: the *Gucci* and *ABN AMRO* cases' in Tison and others, ibid 363; EPM Vermeulen and DA Zetzsche, 'The Use and Abuse of Investor Suits: An Inquiry into the Dark Side of Shareholder Activism' (2010) 7 ECFR 1, 13–23.

[322] Dutch Civil Code, Art 2:346(b). The request can also be made by the advocate general at the court, if this is in the public interest, Art 2:345(2), or by a workers' union, Art 2:347. For data regarding the number of proceedings, see Vermeulen and Zetzsche (n 321) 17.

the court will appoint an independent investigator, who is empowered to inspect the corporate books and records and request any other relevant information from the company's directors.[323] The Enterprise Chamber can adopt a range of measures to remedy problems identified in the investigator's report, including the annulment of resolutions, dismissal of directors, appointment of external auditors or independent directors, disapplication of specific provisions of the articles, and, as a last resort, winding up of the company.[324] It has been argued that this flexibility, combined with the power of the court to grant injunctive relief in a fast-track procedure, explains the success of the inquiry proceeding.[325] Furthermore, the procedure is cost-efficient for investors, provided they meet the filing threshold, since costs are imposed on the company and the court oversees the investigation.[326]

Finally, criminal offences for a violation of certain company law provisions exist in all legal systems. However, it is appropriate to focus on French law, because in France criminal investigations are seen as an important tool to enforce company law. In Chapter 6, we discussed the criminal offence of *abus de biens sociaux*, which complements the corporate law duties in cases where a director uses corporate assets in bad faith for private purposes.[327] As mentioned there, abuse of corporate assets will generally also give rise to civil liability.[328] This gives minority shareholders a possibility to enforce the company's claims without triggering the unfavourable cost rules of the derivative action and incurring court fees. They can file a criminal complaint and combine this complaint with a claim for damages on behalf of the company (*plainte avec constitution de partie civile*).[329] The judge will open criminal proceedings if the shareholders can show that 'the existence of a loss and the direct link between the loss and a criminal offence' (that is, the conditions for being able to act as *partie civile* in the criminal proceedings[330]) are 'possible'.[331] Thus, the evidentiary burden is relatively easy to satisfy, and if the necessary link has been shown, the judge is under a duty to investigate.[332] This enforcement mechanism is important in practice, with around 450–550 convictions for abuse of corporate assets per year.[333] Its function within the French enforcement architecture is somewhat comparable to the UK directors' disqualification regime, insofar as the latter allows creditors to obtain compensation for the loss suffered by the company as a result of the misconduct of a director.[334] In both cases, private parties can take advantage of a public enforcement mechanism to obtain damages. However, crucially, parties to the French *action civile* have control over the proceedings, whereas the creditors of companies falling within the scope of the UK Company Directors Disqualification Act 1986[335] have to rely on the Secretary of State to seek first a disqualification order and then compensation.

[323] Dutch Civil Code, Arts 2:350(1), (4), 2:351. [324] ibid Arts 2:355, 2:356.

[325] Vermeulen and Zetzsche (n 321) 18–19. Injunctive relief is set out in Art 2:349a(2) Dutch Civil Code.

[326] ibid Art 2:350(3).

[327] These conditions are interpreted broadly by the courts, see Chapter 6B.I.4(b). As a consequence, the offence covers situations that are primarily addressed by the duty of loyalty in other legal systems.

[328] Com, Art L225-251. [329] Code de procédure pénale [Code of Criminal Procedure], Arts 2, 3, 85.

[330] ibid Art 2. See also Chapter 6B.I.4(b), comments 2 and 3 after the excerpt from *Carignon*.

[331] Cass crim, 5 November 1991, no 90-82605 (*Société Industrielle et Financière Bertin*), *Revue des sociétés* 1992, 91, note B Bouloc. For a brief discussion of the decision in English, see Conac, Enriques, and Gelter (n 267) 518.

[332] Conac, Enriques, and Gelter (n 267) 518, with references.

[333] Annuaire statistique de la Justice, Edition 2011–2012, 191 (covering the years 2006–2010) www.justice.gouv.fr (follow hyperlinks 'Publications' and 'Statistiques').

[334] For the conditions under which compensation can be claimed for the benefit of the creditors, see text to n 304 above.

[335] These are not only companies incorporated in the UK, but also foreign-incorporated companies that may be wound up under the Insolvency Act 1986 (CDDA 1986, s 22(2)), which is the case if the company has a 'sufficient connection' with the UK; see L Collins and others, *Dicey, Morris & Collins on the Conflict of Laws* (15th edn, Sweet & Maxwell 2012) Rule 176(2). A 'sufficient connection' with the UK, which is the main requirement for a just and equitable winding-up pursuant to s 221(5)(c) of the Insolvency Act 1986, may result from the location of assets within the jurisdiction, the reasonable possibility that a winding-up order will benefit those who apply for the order, and the court's jurisdiction over persons interested in the distribution of the company's assets; see C Gerner-Beuerle and EP Schuster, 'The Costs of Separation: Friction between Company and Insolvency Law in the Single Market' (2014) 14 JCLS 287, 316–17.

PART 3

CREDITORS' PREFERENTIAL ACCESS TO CORPORATE PROPERTY

At the heart of corporate finance theory is the dichotomy of debt and equity. All financial claims issued by a corporation may be characterised as either debt- or equity-like, with hybrid instruments combining certain properties of debt and equity to a greater or lesser extent. Focussing on cash flow rights, debt signifies a fixed claim on the firm's income on a continuous basis, that is, a claim for a certain predetermined amount of interest and repayment of the principal.[1] The claim is fixed in the sense that payments have to be made when due; it is not necessarily fixed in terms of the amount payable, which may vary if based on a floating interest rate. By contrast, equity is the residual claim that entitles its holders to the firm's profit beyond the level of a predetermined amount of debt. However, only where debt has been paid in full may any payment be made to equity. Thus, equity is strictly subordinated to debt, or in other words, debt has a strictly preferential claim on the company's income and assets in priority to equity. As we have seen in Chapter 1, the principle of limited liability puts a cap on the downside risk of equity and thereby turns equity investment into a viable strategy with potentially unlimited up-side gains. This disparity in the risk-and-reward structure allows the shifting of (part of) the risk of a business venture from shareholders to creditors. To the extent that creditors can price their investments correctly, they will be compensated ex ante for the credit risk that they are taking on. Any such pricing will be based on the assumption that the creditors' preferential access to the corporation's assets will be ensured throughout the entire lifecycle of the company. In the remaining three chapters we will analyse the legal mechanism that seek to ensure this residuarity of equity.

Chapter 9 explores the doctrine of legal capital. In essence the doctrine requires that an amount of capital be fixed in the company's articles of association, which amount may only be changed by a formal capital reduction or increase. For the doctrine to have any credibility, mandatory provisions must seek to ensure that the stated capital is actually paid in, that the promised contributions have the stated value, and that the subscribers cannot be released from their commitments. Any amounts paid in may be used in trading, but must not be returned to the shareholders, except in liquidation after all creditors have been paid. Dividends may only be paid out of accumulated realized profits without reducing net asset value below the stated capital amount. The legal capital doctrine is enshrined at EU level and constitutes one of the cornerstones of the *acquis unionaire*. In US corporate law, despite a similar historical starting point, the doctrine has lost almost all significance although some remnants are still visible. This trajectory of trans-Atlantic divergence renders the doctrine particularly interesting from a comparative perspective. Brexit may provide new impetus for reform, at least in the UK, if not across the EU.

[1] J Tirole, *The Theory of Corporate Finance* (Princeton University Press 2006) 75–6.

Maintaining shareholder residuarity and creditor preference throughout the corporate existence is the price that corporate insiders have to pay for the privilege of limited liability. In Chapter 10 we analyse the principles and doctrines that our legal systems utilize for exceptionally disregarding limited liability and, thus, piercing the corporate veil, or going around it, with a view to allowing creditors to reach the assets of those who ultimately benefit from corporate activity. Comparative law methodology requires a broad functional approach not limited to corporate law doctrines in a strict sense, but taking into account also insolvency law, tort law and any other area of law that may provide relief. The legal mechanisms at play are diverse and show little coherence even within jurisdictions. Due to their gap-filling nature, they are often case law based or strongly determined by case law, resulting in open textured standards the application of which is very fact-sensitive with difficult to predict outcomes. A specific externalization problem arises where limited liability is used, as part of a certain business strategy, to pursue risky activities without making provisions for the expected externalized costs. All our legal systems have difficulties in tackling these situations. Tort law may potentially contribute to addressing the issue more satisfactorily.

The preferential access of creditors to corporate assets in priority to shareholders must also, and in particular, be maintained when the corporate existence comes to an end. This can have many reasons, only one of which being corporate failure. Chapter 11 looks first at the various grounds and processes for a solvent liquidation. Its key focus is, however, corporate insolvency as a game changer that significantly enhances the conflict of interest between shareholders and creditors and brings to the fore conflicts of interests between creditors or classes of creditors also. Both types of conflicts can be addressed by transitioning from the corporate governance system to the bankruptcy governance system. Corporate insolvency and restructuring law is, or should be, well equipped for channelling and resolving a multitude of stakeholder conflicts with a view to preserving any going concern surplus and fairly allocating it amongst different corporate constituencies. Where the company's business is not worth preserving, corporate insolvency law should ensure an orderly liquidation of corporate assets and the distribution of proceeds in accordance with a clearly defined order of priority. Overall, the rise of the 'rescue culture' has resulted in a considerable convergence of insolvency and restructuring law on both sides of the Atlantic with Chapter 11 of the United States Bankruptcy Code often serving as a source of inspiration. However, capital market developments are always ahead of the legislator and any reform efforts at national and EU level should be flexible so as to leave room for restructuring practice to adapt to market needs.

9

Legal Capital

In Chapter 1 we identified the principle of separate legal personality as one of the defining features of the modern business corporation. The law attributes assets and liabilities exclusively to the company or corporation. What ensues is an organized pool of assets reserved primarily for the legal entity's creditors and committed, exclusively, to discharging the obligations entered into in the entity's name as long as there are any such obligations outstanding. Stability and continuity of the asset pool is achieved by cutting off members' individual withdrawal and liquidation rights, and by insulating the corporate assets from members' individual creditors. However, without the credible threat of withdrawal of a member's contribution and partial liquidation, management and co-members have less incentive to contribute their fair share to the business enterprise and may be more inclined to shift wealth from one class of members to another.[1]

In order to guarantee the corporate creditors' preferential access—in priority to the shareholders and their personal creditors—to the corporation's assets, and in order to prevent shirking and inter-shareholder wealth transfers, legal systems developed, during the second half of the nineteenth century, the doctrine of 'legal capital', sometimes also referred to as 'stated capital' or 'fixed capital'. The core of the concept of 'legal capital' is that an amount of capital is fixed in the company's articles of association. This amount can be changed by formal reduction or increase only. Mandatory provisions on the payment for shares try to ensure that (part of) the stated capital is actually paid in, that the contributions actually have the stated value and that the subscribers cannot withdraw from their obligations.[2] The capital so contributed by shareholders may be used in trading, but, in principle, must not be returned to the shareholders, except in a liquidation after all creditors have been paid. Moreover, where capital has been reduced by trading, the amount of the original capital fund must first be restored before any payments may be made to the shareholders.[3] Thus, any dividends are restricted to the realized profits as stated on the balance sheet. The doctrine is inextricably linked with corporate accounting practice, and its efficacy for the protection of (minority) shareholders and corporate creditors cannot rise beyond the verity and consistence with which accounting principles are applied.[4]

The basic starting points for the development of the doctrine of legal capital were remarkably similar on both sides of the Atlantic. However, early in the twentieth century developments in the United States and Europe parted ways. In the United States the many loopholes in the doctrine's protective ambit led to its gradual demise, culminating in the Revised Model Business Corporation Act of 1984 doing away with the doctrine altogether.[5] By contrast, in Europe, and in particular in Germany, courts and legislatures tried to close any loopholes in, and ways around, the statutory framework by developing ever more complex legal concepts. In 1977, the Second Company Law Directive[6] imposed a concept of legal capital for public companies, heavily influenced by German law, on the Member States of the then European Economic Community, including France and the United Kingdom, who until then, had applied less rigorous versions of the doctrine. At the turn of the millennium, the Court of Justice's case law on freedom of establishment to some extent opened the door for regulatory competition in Europe.[7] At the same time, the Commission's SLIM initiative[8] and the Report of the High-level Group of Company Law Experts[9] proposed a number of amendments to the Second Company Law Directive, resulting in Directive 2006/68/EC.[10] Moreover, the IAS/IFRS Regulation[11] introduced 'fair value' accounting principles on a Europe-wide basis for

[1] cf Chapter 1B.

[2] W Bayer, 'Grundkapital, Kapitalaufbringung, Kapitalerhaltung' in W Bayer and M Habersack (eds), *Aktienrecht im Wandel Band II* (Mohr Siebeck 2007) 708, 711–12.

[3] J Rickford (ed), 'Reforming Capital' (2004) 15 European Business Law Review 919, 929.

[4] B Manning and J Hanks, *Legal Capital* (3rd edn, Foundation Press 1990) 37.

[5] ibid 179.

[6] Second Council Directive of 13 December 1976 on coordination of safeguards which, for the protection of the interests of members and others, are required by Member States of companies within the meaning of the second paragraph of Article 58 of the Treaty, in respect of the formation of public limited liability companies and the maintenance and alteration of their capital, with a view to making such safeguards equivalent (77/91/EEC), OJ 1977 L26/1.

[7] cf Chapter 2C.II.

[8] Commission of the European Communities: Report from the Commission to the European Parliament and the Council: Results of the Fourth Phase of SLIM, COM(2000) 56 final, 1–6.

[9] Report of the High-level Group of Company Law Experts on a Modern Regulatory Framework for Company Law in Europe of 4 November 2002, Chapter IV.

[10] Directive 2006/68/EC of the European Parliament and of the Council of 6 September 2006 amending Council Directive 77/91/EEC as regards the formation of public limited liability companies and the maintenance and alteration of their capital, OJ 2006 L264/32.

[11] Regulation (EC) No 1606/2002 of the European Parliament and of the Council of 19 July 2002 on the application of international accounting standards, OJ 11.9.2002 L243/1.

consolidated accounts of listed companies. In combination, these factors triggered a vigorous debate among academics, practitioners and law makers as to the efficacy and efficiency of the mandatory legal capital doctrine enshrined in the Second Company Law Directive, and whether it should be replaced by an alternative regime more akin to models prevalent in the United States or elsewhere. An external study on the feasibility of an alternative to the Second Directive's legal capital regime,[12] launched by the Commission as part of its 2003 Action Plan on Company Law and Corporate Governance,[13] found that, in comparison to alternative models, the Directive does not result in any excessive compliance costs and that the introduction of IFRS does not cause any major problems. Consequently, the Commission concluded that the current capital maintenance regime does not seem to cause significant operational problems for companies, and that, therefore, no further measures or changes to the Second Company Law Directive are necessary in the foreseeable future.[14] In the interest of clarity, the Directive was first recast[15] and has now been included as part of Directive (EU) 2017/1132.[16]

From a comparative law perspective, the concept of legal capital has much to offer. There are, first, the radically different trajectories on both sides of the Atlantic, despite very similar starting points. It is perhaps fair to say, that in respect of the issues that legal capital seeks to address—protection of shareholders against a dilution of their cash flow and control rights and safeguarding the creditors' preferential access to the company's assets—the differences in the regulatory strategies exhibited by European legal systems and in the United States are some of the most pronounced. Secondly, the area is of interest because with the Second Company Law Directive (now Directive (EU) 2017/1132) we have a detailed harmonization measure that allows us to assess the degree of harmonization that has been achieved within the three European jurisdictions under consideration here. Moreover, following Brexit, and subject to any new arrangement that may be in place, the United Kingdom will be free to derogate from the regime prescribed by the Directive. In the medium or long term, we may see perhaps a further liberalization of the restrictions on dividends, share repurchase, and financial assistance. The UK government has already hinted that it may review the current framework with a view to examining the case for a significant overhaul.[17] Any change that would go beyond a mere tinkering around the edges may reignite the policy debate regarding legal capital, at national if not at European level. Whether the doctrine and its underpinning regulatory framework will survive a second onslaught unscathed remains to be seen. However, in an era where tackling short-termism in equity markets has been identified as one of the main issues to be addressed by corporate law, the concept of legal capital, drawing on past experiences and abuses, may

[12] KPMG, Feasibility study on an alternative to the capital maintenance regime established by the Second Company Law Directive 77/91/EEC of 13 December 1976 and an examination of the impact on profit distribution of the new EU accounting regime, Main Report (2009).

[13] Communication from the Commission to the Council and the European Parliament—Modernising Company Law and Enhancing Corporate Governance in the European Union—A Plan to Move Forward, COM(2003) 284 final.

[14] Position of DG Internal Market and Services, Results of the external study on the feasibility of an alternative to the Capital Maintenance Regime of the Second Company Law Directive and the impact of the adoption of IFRS on profit distribution, 2 (http://ec.europa.eu/internal_market/company/docs/capital/feasbility/markt-position_en.pdf).

[15] Directive 2012/30/EU of the European Parliament and of the Council of 25 October 2012 on coordination of safeguards which, for the protection of the interests of members and others, are required by Member States of companies within the meaning of the second paragraph of Article 54 of the Treaty on the Functioning of the European Union, in respect of the formation of public limited liability companies and the maintenance and alteration of their capital, with a view to making such safeguards equivalent (Recast), OJ EU 14.11.2012 L315/74. References in the following text to articles of the Second Company Law Directive are references to the articles of Directive (EU) 2017/1132, unless specified otherwise.

[16] Directive (EU) 2017/1132 of the European Parliament and of the Council of 14 June 2017 relating to certain aspects of company law (codification) OJ EU 30.6.2017 L169/46.

[17] Department for Business, Energy & Industrial Strategy, Insolvency and Corporate Governance: Government response (26 August 2018) para 1.48.

have an important role to play in the future. On that basis, the doctrine of legal capital merits close scrutiny.

A. Basic Elements in Historic Perspective

The building blocks of the doctrine of legal capital require some clarification. The elements of legal capital at work today are the direct product of nineteenth and twentieth-century legal history. Legal capital provisions are comprehensible only in that context.[18] In this respect, it makes sense to distinguish between the American and the (continental) European experience.

I. The American experience

Foundations were laid[19] as early as 1824 by Justice Story's opinion in *Wood v Dummer*.[20] A chartered corporation conducting banking business became insolvent. The board of directors distributed most of the bank's liquid assets to the shareholders. Sued by certain creditors of the bank, some of the shareholders were ordered by the court to pay to the plaintiff creditors an amount of the debt owed by the bank in proportion to their shareholding. Justice Story held that 'upon general principles as well as the legislative intention … the capital stock of banks is to be deemed a pledge or trust fund for the payment of the debts contracted by the bank'. Consequently, 'creditors have the first claims upon it; and the stockholders have no rights until all the other creditors are satisfied. They have the full benefit of the profits made by the establishment, and cannot take any portion of the fund until all other claims on it are extinguished'. In Justice Story's view, this consideration explains why any capital stock is required by corporate charters at all, and why its amount is 'so studiously provided for and its payment by stockholders so diligently required'.

Upon formation of a corporate enterprise, the promoter would seek to convince 'capitalists' with spare money to invest in the business. This was done through 'subscription agreements' under which the subscriber agreed that, if sufficient subscribers signed up and the corporation was formed, he would, on call of the future board of directors, pay in a certain amount of money in consideration of a specified number of shares.[21] Thus, a fixed mathematical relationship was established between the amount of dollars to be invested and the number of shares the subscriber would receive. That relationship produced the concept of 'par value' of the shares to be issued: a fixed number of dollars, in early days typically US$100, stated on the share certificate, similar to paper currency or bank notes.[22] Over time, the par value of the shares and the number of shares that could be issued by the corporation was fixed in the corporate charter. This had a dual function. It was supposed to indicate to creditors what amount of funds the shareholders had contributed as 'security' for the corporation's debts, and as a substitute for the shareholders' personal liability.[23] There was an 'implied representation' that the company's capital, as stated in the charter, had in fact been paid in or subscribed.[24] This formed the basis for the shareholders' personal liability up to the amount of the par value of their shares vis-à-vis creditors where the corporation was unable to pay its debts and par value had not been contributed.[25] However, much more

[18] Manning and Hanks (n 4) 20. [19] ibid 31.
[20] *Wood v Dummer*, 30 F.Cas. 435 (no 17,944) (C.C.D. Me. 1824).
[21] Manning and Hanks (n 4) 22–3. [22] ibid 23.
[23] V Morawetz, *A Treatise on the Law of Private Corporations, Vol 2* (2nd edn, Little, Brown and Company 1886) 749.
[24] ibid 751.
[25] A Berle and G Means, *The Modern Corporation & Private Property* (2nd rev edn, Transaction Publishers 2009, originally published in 1932) 129–30.

important seems to have been the second function: to ensure the equal treatment of shareholders and to protect them against dilution of their shares through the issue of so-called 'watered stock':[26]

> Every shareholder in a corporation is entitled to insist that every other shareholder shall contribute his ratable part of the company's capital for the common benefit; ... It would be a plain violation of the equitable rights of those shareholders who have contributed, or who have incurred a liability to contribute, the amount of their shares in full, to allow any person to have the benefits of membership without adding the amount of their shares to the company's capital.[27]

'Capital' or 'capital stock' in this initial (economic) sense was synonymous with the actual assets put in by the shareholders (to be listed in the balance sheet under 'assets').[28] These assets were pledged as security for the creditors' claims and could, hence, not be returned to shareholders as dividends. The capital so contributed may be used in trading and is, therefore, constantly subject to change; not only in a physical sense: cash may be turned into real estate, chattels, debt receivables and vice versa; but also in terms of value: the 'capital stock' will decrease when the corporation incurs losses and will increase when it trades profitably. Over time courts and statutes combined the principle of *Wood v Dummer* and the par value notion in order to arrive at a legal concept of capital or 'legal capital' as a 'measuring rod' for the propriety of distributions and payment of dividends to shareholders.[29] 'Legal capital' is the product of par value multiplied by the number of shares outstanding. As such it is a number expressed in dollars. However, it no longer stands for a pool of assets and does not appear under 'assets' on a corporation's balance sheet. Rather, it is a constant number (subject to changes in the capital structure, possibly requiring charter amendment) and appears on the claimant's side of the balance sheet as a fixed and unchangeable entry under 'shareholders' equity'.[30] Dividends were payable 'out of surplus' only. 'Surplus', or in modern terminology positive earnings or profit, is what remains after liabilities and legal capital have been subtracted from assets.[31] Mediated through the 'profit and loss account', it is reflected under 'shareholders' equity' in the balance sheet and acts like a buffer that absorbs changes to assets and liabilities. It ensures that the balance sheet always balances (assets = liabilities + shareholders' equity). Surplus will be positive where the corporation has been trading profitably, and negative where the corporation has incurred losses. In the latter case, 'legal capital' is said to be impaired as 'shareholders' equity', the sum of 'legal capital' and 'surplus', falls below 'legal capital'.[32] A stylized balance sheet could look as in Table 1.

If we change this little example by increasing the outstanding liability on bonds say by 900,000, so that overall liabilities rise to 2,350,000, then surplus must be—50,000 in order for the balance sheet to balance when assets and capital remain constant. The corporation has traded at a loss and capital is impaired as 'shareholders' equity' is lower than capital (100,000 – 50,000).

The emergence of 'legal capital' in this sense was facilitated by inroads made into the par value concept. Par value causes problems where, possibly after years of trading, the market price of the shares is below par and the corporation wants to raise additional capital (in the economic sense) by issuing more shares. A rational investor will not be willing to pay more than the current market price for the shares, and will be deterred from paying even that by

[26] The term 'watered stock' derives from fraudulent practice used in the cattle business, where cattle drovers would feed salt to their cattle the night before they sold them at market by the pound. The thirsty cattle would drink gallons of water and would thus temporarily weigh more when they were sold the next day; see W Klein, J Coffee, and F Partnoy, *Business Organization and Finance* (Foundation Press 2010) 226–7; Manning and Hanks (n 4) 24.

[27] Morawetz (n 23) 269–70.

[28] Manning and Hanks (n 4) 33.

[29] ibid 34.

[30] ibid 39.

[31] Morawetz (n 23) 410–12.

[32] Manning and Hanks (n 4) 34–7.

Table 1 Balance Sheet*

Assets		Liabilities	
Cash	200,000	Payables	400,000
Receivables	500,000	Notes	300,000
Inventory	500,000	Bonds	750,000
Property, plant, and equipment	1,200,000		1,450,000
		Shareholders' equity	
		capital: US$100 par common, 1000 sh	100,000
		Surplus	850,000
		Shareholders' equity	950,000
	2,400,000		2,400,000

* G Mundstock, *A Finance Approach to Accounting for Lawyers* (2nd edn, Foundation Press 2006) 48; B Manning and J Hanks, *Legal Capital* (3rd edn, Foundation Press 1990) 36.

the prospect of being held liable for the difference to par.[33] This situation was addressed by the US Supreme Court in *Handley v Stutz*,[34] where it was held that if a company is in a state of financial emergency it may issue stock at the best price it can get, even if below par. In that case, new stock purchasers would not incur a risk of liability. Subsequently, the issue of low par value stock emerged as a more reliable strategy.[35] Par values as low as US$1 or even less became common.[36] This was possible because there was no minimum capital requirement to speak of; some corporation statutes retained a pro forma amount of US$1,000 or less.[37] Low par value virtually eliminated the risk of liability and greatly facilitated later issues of additional stock. It also meant that there was now often a marked difference between par value and issue price, say 1,000 US$1 par value shares issued for US$50 each. This required a new entry on the balance sheet. Under 'shareholders' equity', 'capital' would now stand at US$1,000, to which would be added the 'capital surplus' as the difference of issue price and 'capital', in our example US$49,000. The question, whether the 'capital surplus' could be used for distributions to shareholders was answered differently by state incorporation laws.[38]

From low par value it was only a small step to no par value shares. The issue of no par value shares was statutorily authorized in most states after 1912.[39] No par value shares have no designated par value and are issued for the price determined from time to time by the board of directors, usually the market price, which these shares constantly reflect when in circulation. Strangely enough, upon issue of no par value shares it was still necessary to designate some dollar amount as 'capital' in the corporation's balance sheet. Originally, this was to be the entire amount received by the issue,[40] later the board of director could designate some lesser amount with the difference entered as 'capital surplus'.[41] From here, the treatment was the same as with low par value shares. Mainly for tax reasons, no par value shares did not, and still have not, replaced (low) par value shares completely or even on a large scale. Rather, they exist side-by-side with par value, sometimes also within the same corporation as different classes of shares.[42]

The emergence of low par value and no par value significantly weakened the shareholder protection rationale. Where management could determine the issue price at will, dilution of existing shareholdings was a real possibility.[43] However, the par value notion was weakened even further. Originally shares had to be paid in cash; later, real and chattel property, but also services already performed by the subscriber, as well as commitments to future

[33] ibid 27. [34] *Handley v Stutz*, 139 U.S. 417 (1891). [35] Manning and Hanks (n 4) 28.
[36] Berle and Means (n 25) 145. [37] Manning and Hanks (n 4) 44. [38] ibid 28–9, 40–1.
[39] Berle and Means (n 25) 145.
[40] R Booth, 'Capital Requirements in United States Corporation Law' in M Lutter (ed), *Legal Capital in Europe* (de Gruyter Recht 2006) 620, 626.
[41] Manning and Hanks (n 4) 42. [42] ibid 30. [43] Berle and Means (n 25) 146.

performance by a third party (bonds or promissory notes issued by another company) became acceptable.[44] By contrast, future services or a commitment to future performance by the subscriber could not be used to pay for par value. However, the subscriber could exchange promissory notes with a third party and use the latter's note to pay for his shares in the company.[45] By allowing contributions to be made in assets other than cash the problem of valuation became pertinent. Older cases revolved around situations where it turned out in hindsight that the consideration paid in exchange for newly issued shares had been overvalued. Courts' approaches differed and oscillated between 'true value' requirements and mere 'reasonable prudence'. Eventually, state legislators awarded the board of directors the power to conclusively determine the value of property other than cash, subject only to fraud. These provisions virtually eliminated the valuation problem as a subject of litigation.[46] At the same time, they constituted a licence to dilute shares legally. Where a US$1 par value outstanding share has a market value of US$100 and a new share of the same class is issued for US$50, the value of the outstanding share is immediately reduced to some amount between US$50 and US$100, and the value of the new share appreciates accordingly.[47] The situation was exacerbated by the fact that the board of directors could, within the limits set by the corporate charter, issue new shares at will and thereby increase 'legal capital' by the product of the number of new shares times their par value, and 'capital surplus' by the number of shares times the difference of issue price and par. Initially, existing shareholders were protected by pre-emptive rights giving them the right to acquire new shares in proportion to their existing holdings.[48] This ensured that an existing shareholder's participation in current surplus and future earnings remained the same upon an issue of new shares. However, with capital structures becoming ever more complex through the introduction of several classes of common stock and preference shares with various properties pre-emptive rights were increasingly deemed to be impracticable and incorporation statutes began to allow corporations to exclude pre-emptive rights in their charters or even to make their existence dependent on a specific grant in the articles of association.[49]

Thus, gradually 'par value' and 'legal capital' lost their significance as investor protection mechanism. Since 1911, when the first 'blue sky law' was enacted by Kansas, this task was instead increasingly taken on by state and, subsequently, federal securities regulation. State 'blue sky laws' usually empowered the state securities commissioner to review the merits of an offering, and to prohibit an issue that was found not to be fair, just and equitable to investors.[50] However, owing to inadequate administration or coverage securities fraud was still widespread. After the Great Depression, Congress enacted the Securities Act 1933 and the Securities Exchange Act 1934. This federal framework is not based on merit regulation, but on a system of comprehensive disclosure. It also provides straightforward remedies for investors in case of misrepresentation and securities fraud. Effectively, under this system public offerings entail the sale of a fixed amount of stock at a fixed price per share.[51]

As we have seen, in order to preserve the corporation's creditors' prior claim on the corporate assets it was, and still is, 'a fundamental rule, that dividends can be paid only out of profits or the net increase of the capital of the corporation, and cannot be drawn upon the capital contributed by the shareholders'.[52] This is a balance sheet test that can still be found, in one form or another, in many of today's general incorporation laws. However, the rule that dividends can only be paid out of surplus was reasonably straightforward only as long as shares were issued at high par value. There was only one surplus, the 'earned surplus' or 'positive earnings'. With the emergence of low par value and no par value shares, however, 'capital surplus' or 'paid-in-surplus' appeared as a different type of surplus and entry on the balance sheet. Whether this surplus, stemming from the shareholders' contributions above

[44] ibid 144. [45] Manning and Hanks (n 4) 45–7. [46] ibid 47–8.
[47] Berle and Means (n 25) 144-5. [48] ibid 160–1. [49] ibid 162–3. [50] Booth (n 40) 625.
[51] ibid 626. [52] Morawetz (n 23) 410.

par, could be paid to shareholders as dividend was controversial and regulated differently in various state incorporation laws.[53] A further problem arose from the fact that a balance sheet test is ultimately based on accounting practice. In the United States, accounting rules and principles as such have never been cast into a statutory text subject to legal interpretation and application by courts of law. Accounting practice is based on 'generally accepted accounting principles' (GAAP) formulated by the Financial Accounting Standards Board (FASB) as a self-regulating body. GAAP do not contain clear rules for every possible transaction and a variety of different ways may be acceptable to account for a given item.[54] Hence, the presentation of a balance sheet involves a multitude of judgments as to how to account for and value assets and liabilities. This obviously has an impact on the available surplus. Where management believes that an asset has increased in value and they write up the figure with which the asset is carried (or write down a liability) there may appear a further '(appreciation) surplus' (as different from 'earned surplus' and 'capital surplus') that may or may not be available for distribution depending on the applicable state corporation law.[55] Yet another surplus may be created by a reduction of 'legal capital'. This may be done, for instance, by lowering the par value of the outstanding shares. Depending on the applicable state corporation law, it requires no more than a simple resolution by directors and shareholders in order to amend the certificate of incorporation. The corporation's creditors have no say in this. A reduction of 'legal capital' in this way creates, all else being equal, a 'reduction surplus' that may be distributed if state law so provides.[56] Another way to reduce 'legal capital' and to free up surplus for distributions is the reacquisition by the company of its own shares. This power, exercised by the board of directors or delegated to corporate officers, existed from early on. It is limited however to the amount of surplus funds.[57] The shares so acquired may be held 'in treasury'. In that case, they would still be 'outstanding' and not reduce 'legal capital', but restrict 'surplus' and reduce 'shareholder's equity'. They may also be retired to the status of authorized but unissued stock or cancelled. In these events, legal capital is reduced, and at the same time the available surplus may be increased: say, a company with assets of US$1,000 and liabilities of US$200 has two US$100 par value shares outstanding. The available surplus would be US$600. If the company buys back one share for US$100 and retires or cancels it, than assets would be reduced to US$900, and 'legal capital' to US$100. However, surplus would remain at US$600.[58] As a consequence, the company can distribute US$700 overall (US$600 on the remaining share and US$100 on the retired share) and effectively withdraw an amount of US$100 that is no longer available to creditors.

Whereas the reacquisition by the company of its own shares at least formally was still subject to 'legal capital' restrictions, this was not the case for say a bargain sale of corporate assets to shareholders, a waiver by the corporation of a debt owed by a shareholder or payment of assets to shareholders as compensation for services, or similar transactions.[59] Thus, overall the concept of 'legal capital' in this form appeared to offer at best very limited creditor protection. It has been said that, in the absence of insolvency, the experienced practitioner could devise more or less any distribution to shareholders in a way that would not infringe the legal capital regime.[60] Consequently, virtually no cases exist on statutorily imposed directors' or shareholders' liability in the context of unlawful dividends and distributions. Creditor protection is generally achieved by other means. Lenders and debt investors advance credit subject to complex debt covenants that may not only restrict the debtor company from taking on additional secured or prior unsecured debt; carefully crafted provisions will also limit the company's capacity to pay dividends, tailor-made on the basis of the debtor's financial parameters.[61] Another device available to creditors is fraudulent transfer

[53] G Mundstock, *A Finance Approach to Accounting for Lawyers* (2nd edn, Foundation Press 2006) 11.
[54] Mundstock (n 53) 11. [55] Manning and Hanks (n 4) 65–7. [56] ibid 72–4.
[57] Berle and Means (n 25) 158. [58] Manning and Hanks (n 4) 84–6.
[59] ibid 84. [60] ibid 90. [61] ibid 104–12.

law. As state law, it allows creditors to reverse certain transactions entered into by the debtor company to the detriment of its creditors at the time when the company was insolvent or became insolvent as a result of the transaction. The principal remedy is avoidance of the transaction and retransfer of the asset to the company to the extent necessary to satisfy the creditor's claim. Moreover, there is a rich case law on 'piercing the corporate veil', holding, under certain circumstances, shareholders liable for the corporation's debts, which we will be looking at in detail in Chapter 10.

II. The European experience prior to the Second Company Law Directive

All three European jurisdictions under consideration here had in place, by the end of the nineteenth century, a doctrine of a fixed 'legal capital' in one form or another. In France and England, the respective doctrines remained incomplete in respect of their creditor and shareholder protection objectives, without causing too much concern in law and business communities at the time. By contrast, German law developed a complex system in an attempt to fill any gaps within the framework. The Second Company Law Directive was significantly influenced by the German 'legal capital' doctrine,[62] although French and English law played a role as well.[63]

The *Code de Commerce* of 1807, which was also in force in parts of Germany west of the river Rhine, merely provided that a corporation must have a capital which is to be divided into shares of equal value. However, the amount of capital, the type of contribution and timing of payment was to be determined in the articles of association. As long as the *Code* followed the *octroi* system and incorporation was dependent on the grant of a state concession, public authorities had some control over the amount of capital and whether it had been adequately raised. Regardless, many contemporary charters did not contain a specified amount, and if they did, allowed for the issue of additional shares at will. Also, if the charter contained a specific amount of capital, this did not mean that all shares had to be subscribed before the corporation could come into existence. Rather, the remaining shares could be issued further down the line and often under more favourable terms.[64] Usually, and often owing to very high share prices, shares were not paid up instantly and shareholders could, on call of the management, pay in instalments. The *Code* did not prescribe a par value requirement.[65] The provisions on capital maintenance were also rather weak. Shareholders could expect, in addition to dividends paid out of profits, a fixed interest rate irrespective of whether the company was trading profitably or not. This situation was remedied in 1818 by a regulation prescribing that a fixed percentage of profits must be transferred to reserves in order to secure or restore the 'legal capital'. It was further provided that a dividend must not be paid if legal reserves and/or legal capital were impaired. Later, following the financial and banking crisis of 1825/1826 in England, payment of both dividend and interest were made dependent on the company having sufficient retained earnings.[66] It has often been emphasized in French company law that the notion of 'legal capital' is sacrosanct,[67] and that it is the price to pay in order to obtain limited liability;[68] that the company's capital constitutes a right of pledge over the company's assets in favour of its creditors.[69] Overall, however, the area

[62] S Grundmann, *European Company Law* (Intersentia 2012) 205.
[63] C Schmitthoff, 'The Second EEC Directive on Company Law' (1978) 15 Common Market Law Review 43, 54.
[64] Bayer (n 2) 714–15.
[65] A Deutsch, 'Die Aktiengesellschaft im Code de Commerce von 1807 und ihre Vorbildfunktion für die Entwicklung in Deutschland' in W Bayer and M Habersack (eds), *Aktienrecht im Wandel Band I* (Mohr Siebeck 2007) 46, 59.
[66] ibid 60–1.
[67] M Cozian, A Viandier, and F Deboissy, *Droit des sociétés* (31st edn, Lexis Nexis 2018) para 513.
[68] M Germain and V Magnier, *Les sociétés commerciales* (21st edn, LGDJ 2014) para 1925.
[69] Cozian, Viandier, and Deboissy (n 67) para 517.

received little attention from legal writers in the nineteenth and early twentieth centuries.[70] A general minimum capital requirement was introduced as late as 1966.[71] Interest in the topic increased significantly with implementation of the Second Company Law Directive.

In the United Kingdom the House of Lords, after several years of dispute, finally held in *Ooregum Gold Mining v Roper*[72] that shares may not be issued at a discount, that is, below their par value. This decision was informed by the dual rationale of creditor and shareholder protection. The latter—shareholder protection against dilution—was significantly weakened by the ruling in *Hilder v Dexter*,[73] where it was held that the company was not obliged to issue shares at a premium, that is, above par, even where the market conditions would allow it. Moreover, in *Re Wragg Ltd*[74] it was held that '[p]rovided a limited company does so honestly and not colourably ... agreements by limited companies to pay for property or services in paid-up shares are valid and binding on the companies and their creditors ... It is not law that persons cannot sell property to a limited company for fully paid-up shares and make a profit by the transaction. We must not allow ourselves to be misled by talking of value. The value paid to the company is measured by the price at which the company agrees to buy what it thinks it worth its while to acquire'. Thus, management could, subject to fraud, freely determine the price put on any contribution in kind. The dangers of dilution, discrimination and wealth transfers among shareholders were kept in check by fiduciary principles.[75] The restrictions on the payment of dividends were succinctly explained in *Re Exchange Banking Co, Flitcroft's case*:[76]

> [T]here is a statement that the capital shall be applied for the purposes of the business, and on the faith of that statement, which is sometimes said to be an implied contract with creditors, people dealing with the company give it credit. The creditor has no debtor but that impalpable thing the corporation, which has no property except the assets of the business. The creditor, therefore, I may say, gives credit to that capital, gives credit to the company on the faith of the representation that the capital shall be applied only for the purposes of the business, and he has therefore a right to say that the corporation shall keep its capital and not return it to the shareholders, though it may be a right which he cannot enforce otherwise than by a winding-up order.

Thus, the principle that the capital paid in by the shareholders may be reduced by trading, but may in no circumstances be returned to the shareholders was firmly established in British jurisprudence. It was further strengthened in *Trevor v Whitworth*,[77] by prohibiting the acquisition by the company of its own shares:

> When shares are purchased at par, and transferred to the company ... [t]he amount paid up on the shares is returned to the shareholder; and in the event of the company continuing to hold the shares (as in the present case) is permanently withdrawn from its trading capital. It appears to me that ... it is inconsistent with the essential nature of a company that it should become a member of itself.

These are the main building blocks of the legal capital system in Britain. As an investor protection device it remained incomplete. There was no minimum capital requirement, contributions in kind could be freely valued by the company's management, and existing shareholders had a right of pre-emption only where the articles of association provided for such a right.[78] Fiduciary principles were relied on in order to fill obvious gaps. The implementation of the Second Company Law Directive necessitated significant changes.

[70] I Urbain-Parléani, 'Working Group on the Share Capital in Europe: French Answers to the Questionnaire' in M Lutter (ed), *Legal Capital in Europe* (de Gruyter Recht 2006) 480, 481; J Simon, 'A Comparative Approach to Capital Maintenance: France' (2004) 15 European Business Law Review 1037.

[71] Germain and Magnier (n 68) para 1925; Urbain-Parléani (n 70) 481.

[72] [1892] AC 125 (HL).

[73] [1902] AC 474 (HL).

[74] [1897] 1 Ch 796 (CA) (Lindley LJ).

[75] *Lowry v Consolidated African Selection Trust Ltd* [1940] AC 648, 679.

[76] (1882) 21 Ch D 519 (CA) (Jessel MR).

[77] (1887) 12 App Cas 409 (HL) (Lord Watson).

[78] *Ving v Robinson and Woodcock Ltd* (1912) 56 SJ 412.

In Germany, the Prussian Stock Corporation Act 1843, following the earlier Prussian Railway Act of 1838, required that the amount of share capital and the par value of shares be fixed in the articles of association, without, however, prescribing a minimum capital requirement. Subscribers were unconditionally liable for 40 per cent of the par value of their shares; and shares to bearer could not be issued unless the amount of share capital had been fully paid. This was a reaction to widespread fraudulent speculation with partly paid up shares. The Act also contained the basics of the current capital maintenance regime. It made clear that shareholders had, absent liquidation, access only to the earned surplus on the basis of the annual balance sheet. Capital must not be returned to shareholders and fixed interest must not be promised or paid. The General German Commercial Code (ADHGB) of 1861, a model law to be implemented in the different German states, adopted this framework with minor modifications.[79]

The reform of 1870 replaced the concession system with a system of general incorporation. In order to protect investors, incorporation was subject to a number of normative conditions that had to be met prior to incorporation. However, whether and to what extent the organization and capital structure of a corporation should be regulated by mandatory provisions was hotly disputed during the legislative process. The City-states that were part of the Hanseatic League of trading cities argued for a system based on self-protection. However, Prussia prevailed and a system of legal capital was established as a central feature of the public company.[80] All shares making up 'legal capital' had to be subscribed prior to the company's registration. Management could not be authorized to issue new shares up to a certain ceiling, thus preventing the practice of an authorized capital, common in England. Rather, capital increase and reduction could only be effectuated by following specific procedures that, in principle, required shareholder approval.[81] The law distinguished between instant formation and successive formation. In the former case, the promoters would subscribe all shares instantly; whereas for the latter, the promoters would subscribe part of the shares only, publish a prospectus and offer the remaining shares to the public. In both cases, however, registration was subject to subscription of all shares and payment of at least 10 per cent on each share.[82] The Act installed a minimum par value of shares.[83] Issue below par was not explicitly prohibited, but shares to order could only be issued after payment of par. In general, the attitude towards contributions was not very strict. It was common that the payment of 10 per cent was merely pretended by showing the amount to the respective official without actually paying it.[84] For the first time, contributions in kind were explicitly regulated, although not in a very rigorous way. The articles of association had to stipulate the contributions in kind including the value attributed to them. In the event of successive formation, the contribution in kind had to be approved by general meeting upon formation.[85] In general, subscribers were unconditionally liable only up to 40 per cent of the par value of their shares. They could be released from up to 60 per cent of their nominal payment obligations, which was often done in practice. As a consequence, the amount of 'legal capital' stated in the articles and published in the register was seriously misleading. Speculation with these partly paid shares is often cited as one of the reasons for the boom and subsequent bust during the so-called Founders' Years in the 1870s.[86] Dividends were prohibited as long as 'legal capital' was

[79] Bayer (n 2) 717–21. [80] ibid 722.

[81] H Hirte, 'Kapitalmaßnahmen: Kapitalerhöhung und Kapitalherabsetzung' in W Bayer and M Habersack (eds), *Aktienrecht im Wandel Band II* (Mohr Siebeck 2007) 827, 842–3.

[82] Bayer (n 2) 723.

[83] 100 Thalers for shares to bearer (and for all shares in insurance companies); 50 Thalers for shares to order, respectively.

[84] Bayer (n 2) 724. [85] ibid 724–5.

[86] J Lieder, 'Die 1. Aktienrechtsnovelle vom 11. Juni 1870' in W Bayer and M Habersack (eds), *Aktienrecht im Wandel Band I* (Mohr Siebeck 2007) 318, 345–8.

impaired. They could be paid out of profits only, but impaired capital had to be restored first. The reacquisition by the company of its own shares was prohibited, presumably as a reaction to speculative and fraudulent trading with own shares at the Vienna Stock Exchange which may have caused the crash of May 1873. Where capital was impaired by 50 per cent or more, the management board had to call a general meeting to decide on whether to continue or liquidate.[87]

The introduction of general incorporation was followed by rampant abuse and speculation. The eminent German jurist Rudolf von Ihering characterized the stock corporations of the time as 'organised fraud and robbery institutions'.[88] As a result, a reform in 1884 was aimed at improving protection against abusive formations. Publicity requirements upon formation were significantly strengthened. Promoters became more visible as they had to approve the articles of association and their special rights had to be listed in the 'subscription agreement'. Contributions in cash had to be paid up to at least 25 per cent and they had to be 'in the possession of the management board'. Subscribers could no longer be released from their obligation to pay up; also subscribers had no right to set-off their liability against a claim owed to them by the company. In order to prevent speculation and dispersed ownership, the minimum par value was increased to 1,000 *Reichsmark*. Since at least five promoters were necessary to form a company, there was, thus, an—implicit—minimum capital requirement of 5,000 *Reichsmark*.[89] Details of contributions in kind had to be stipulated in the articles of association. The reform introduced the procedure of a formation-audit to be carried out by management board and supervisory board in order to certify that the pre-conditions on formation, and in particular as regards contributions in kind, had been complied with. An external auditor was required where promoters themselves had paid in contributions in kind. In order to prevent circumvention of the provisions on contributions in kind, the concept of subsequent-formation (*Nachgründung*) was introduced. Transactions concerning, in particular, real property transferred to the company within two years since registration whose value exceeded 10 per cent of 'legal capital' were valid only if approved by the general meeting. The general prohibition on acquisition by the company of its own shares was somewhat liberalized in cases where the shares were given as commission.[90] With the reform of 1884 the main features of the 'legal capital' system in its current form had been put in place, and, as we will see, many of these rules subsequently found their way into the Second Company Law Directive. Later amendments merely targeted specific shortcomings within this framework without questioning the soundness of its premise.[91]

The Commercial Code (HGB) of 1897 introduced rules on preference shares and shares with multiple voting rights. The acquisition of not fully paid up own shares was prohibited. Cash contributions could now also be made by cheque or by crediting a bank account; in any case the amount had to be at the free disposal of the management board. Statutory instruments of 1923/1924 introduced a minimum capital requirement of 50,000 *Reichsmark*. The minimum par value was reduced to 100 *Reichsmark*. The requirement of an external auditor conducting a formation audit was extended to cover all cases of contributions in kind (not just those of the promoters).[92] In the course of the comprehensive reform of 1937, the minimum capital requirement was increased to 500,000 *Reichsmark*, the minimum par was again set at 1,000 *Reichsmark*. The provisions on contributions in kind were strengthened. Their breach rendered both the respective contract and asset transfer invalid; the shareholder remained liable for the par value plus any *agio* (or premium: the difference between par and issue price). Disguised contributions in kind—asset transfers to the company in connection with a cash contribution that have the same economic result as a contribution in kind—could not be cured after registration by mere amendment of the articles, nor by going

[87] Bayer (n 2) 726–7.
[88] R von Jhering, *Der Zweck im Recht 1. Band* (Breitkopf & Härtel 1877) 222.
[89] Bayer (n 2) 728–9.
[90] ibid 729–31.
[91] ibid 732.
[92] ibid 732–4.

through the procedure of subsequent-formation. The latter was now subjected to the formation audit process.[93] The reform of 1965, leading to the Stock Corporation Act (AktG) 1965, did not contain any major changes to the system. Minimum capital and minimum par had in the meantime been reduced to 100,000 DM and 50 DM, respectively. However, subject to the articles of association, it was now possible to pay part of the profits as an interim dividend prior to a shareholders' resolution determining distributable profit. This amendment was introduced in order to encourage equity investments.[94] More significant changes became necessary with the implementation of the Second Company Law Directive.

III. The Second Company Law Directive

The harmonization of the concept of legal capital had been on the European agenda for a long time, even before the First Company Law Directive of 1968 was adopted. The accession of the UK, Ireland, and Denmark in 1973 required substantial amendments to the original proposals and the Second Company Law Directive was finally adopted in 1976.[95] It was the first directive with significant input from the common law jurisdictions, however the overall regulatory structure is predominantly German. In the Preamble to Directive (EU) 2017/1132 we still find the familiar dual rationale of creditor protection, by providing them with an equity 'cushion' as security for their claims,[96] and (minority) shareholders protection[97] against dilution of their control and economic rights.[98] The Second Company Law Directive has for a long time been subject to fundamental criticism and a number of reform initiatives have been undertaken at the European level. The streamlining of the First and Second Company Law Directives was part of the fourth phase of the Simpler Legislation for the Single Market (SLIM) initiative.[99] The recommendations made by the company law SLIM working group were taken up and extended by the High-level Group of Company Law Experts. Their Final Report[100] formed the basis for a Communication from the Commission on Modernising Company Law in the European Union.[101] Most of the reform proposals have been implemented as Directive 2006/68/EC of 6 September 2006.[102] In its Report, the High-level Group of Company Law Experts also floated a more radical reform proposal. The Group recommended the conducting of a review on the feasibility of an alternative regime that could be offered as an additional option for Member States. Further consideration was deemed to be necessary. Subsequently, the accounting firm KPMG conducted a comprehensive feasibility study,[103] finding that the compliance costs under the Directive were rather limited and did not significantly exceed the costs of alternative regimes. On that basis, the Commission concluded that no further reform was required in the immediate future.[104]

[93] ibid 734–5. [94] ibid 735–6.

[95] V Edwards, *EC Company Law* (OUP 1999) 51–2. [96] Recital (40). [97] Recital (46).

[98] In Case C-101/08 *Audiolux* ECLI:EU:C:2009:626, the Court of Justice held that the obligation, laid down in Art 85 Directive (EU) 2017/1132, to ensure equal treatment to all shareholders who are in the same position, only applies within the framework of the Second Directive, that is, in relation to the increase or reduction of capital. Thus, Art 85 cannot be considered as reflecting a general principle of Community law.

[99] Commission of the European Communities: Report from the Commission to the European Parliament and the Council: Results of the Fourth Phase of SLIM, COM(2000) 56 final, 1–6.

[100] Report of the High-level Group of Company Law Experts on a Modern Regulatory Framework for Company Law in Europe of 4 November 2002, Chapter IV.

[101] Communication from the Commission to the Council and the European Parliament—Modernising Company Law and Enhancing Corporate Governance in the European Union—A Plan to Move Forward, COM (2003) 284 final.

[102] Directive 2006/68/EC of the European Parliament and of the Council of 6 September 2006 amending Council Directive 77/91/EEC as regards the formation of public limited liability companies and the maintenance and alteration of their capital, OJ 2006 L264/32.

[103] KPMG (n 12).

[104] Position of DG Internal Market and Services, Results of the external study on the feasibility of an alternative to the Capital Maintenance Regime of the Second Company Law Directive and the impact of the adoption of IFRS on profit distribution, 2.

The legal capital regime of Directive (EU) 2017/1132 applies to public limited liability companies only,[105] according to recital (2), 'because their activities predominate in the economy of the Member States and frequently extend beyond their national boundaries'. The validity of this unsubstantiated claim is very doubtful. At least in the Member States under consideration here private companies by far outnumber their public counterparts; some private companies are of considerable size and are actively trading across borders. Also, given the high 'infant mortality' of private companies, securing their adequate capitalization seems to be the more pressing problem. Be that as it may, an extension of the scope of the Directive to private companies is no longer on the political agenda.[106] Prior to the Directive, the United Kingdom, under a unitary system, did not distinguish between private and public companies. Implementation introduced this distinction into UK law for the first time.[107] In terms of harmonization technique, the Directive follows a mixed approach: some provisions are minimum standard provisions, leaving room to be supplemented by Member States requiring stricter standards; other provisions leave no discretion.[108]

The legal capital regime can be broken down into three key elements. The raising of capital concerns primarily the payment for shares and the making of contributions. Capital maintenance rules seek to ensure that dividends are paid out of distributable profits only and that capital is not returned to shareholders, thus, enshrining the principle of creditor preference. Finally, the rules on an increase or a reduction of capital provide the mechanisms for a formal change in a company's legal capital as an important restructuring tool. There are, of course, various overlaps and interactions between these core elements: the rules on the payment for shares will be relevant where capital is increased through the issue of new shares; where a reduction of capital may result in a return of assets to the shareholders, the creditor preference may be implicated. These interactions have to be kept in mind.

In the following sections, we will first briefly lay out for each core element the regulatory framework provided by the Second Company Law Directive in the form of Directive (EU) 2017/1132.[109] On that basis, we can then delve into the national laws of our three European jurisdictions, and contrast our findings with the legal situation in the United States.

B. Raising of Capital

The legal issues in relation to the payment for shares, or raising of capital, are relevant both upon formation of a company and upon a subsequent issue of shares. The former will often be more relevant for private companies, as many firms are initially formed as such; the latter is more relevant in respect of public companies, possibly in the course of an initial or subsequent public offering. The legal capital regime of Directive (EU) 2017/1132 applies to public companies only[110] and treats payment for shares upon formation and upon subsequent issue in a similar way with only minor differences (in particular, that a cash premium must be paid in full only upon a subsequent issue).[111]

I. European jurisdictions

According to Article 45(1), Member States must provide for a minimum capital requirement of not less than €25,000 to be subscribed before a public company may be incorporated or obtain authorization to commence business. Shares may be issued for consideration in cash or for consideration other than cash.[112] The latter can take the form of any assets

[105] Article 44(1) with Annex I. [106] Grundmann (n 62) 207–8. [107] Schmitthoff (n 63) 43–6.

[108] Opinion of AG Tesauro in Case C-83/91 *Meilicke v ADV/ORGA* ECLI:EU:C:1992:178; Joined Cases C-19 and 20/90 *Karella and Karellas v Greek Minister of Industry, Energy and Technology* ECLI:EU:C:1991:229; Case C-338/06 *Commission v Spain* ECLI:EU:C:2008:740.

[109] These expositions draw on M Schillig, 'Chapter 2: General Company Law Provisions: Establishment and Functioning of Limited Liability Companies' in C Gerner-Beuerle (ed), *Gore-Browne on EU Company Law* (Jordan Publishing 2017).

[110] Article 44(1) with Annex I. [111] Articles 46–53, 69, 70. [112] Article 48(1) and (2).

of value, except an undertaking to perform work or to supply services.[113] Shares must not be issued at a price below par or accountable par, respectively.[114] 'Accountable par' denominates the value of a share by reference to the fraction of the aggregate of share capital contributed upon an issue, which the share represents (total consideration raised through the issue of shares divided by the number of shares in issue). The main difference compared to 'true' no par value shares of the US variety seems to be that with 'accountable par' there still is a fixed nominal value attributed to each share that does not reflect and does not change in accordance with the value of the company. Shares may be issued at a premium, that is, at a price higher than par or accountable par. Subject only to a reduction of the subscribed capital, the shareholders may not be released from the obligation to pay up their contributions.[115]

At the time the company is incorporated or authorized to commence business, shares issued for cash must be paid up at no less than 25 per cent of their nominal value or their accountable par, not including any premium.[116] If shares are issued for a contribution in kind the contribution must be transferred to the company in full within five years from the time of incorporation or authorization to commence business.[117] Member States are free to set the minimum amount of capital higher than the figure prescribed by the Directive. All the jurisdictions under consideration here have done so (Germany: €50,000; France: €37,000 in general and €225,000 for listed companies; United Kingdom: £50,000). Even these amounts are very low, considering the funding needs of most public companies.

In order to ensure adherence to the 'no issue below par rule', Article 49 installes a burdensome procedure for the valuation of contributions in kind. According to Advocate General Tesauro, the distinction of cash from non-cash consideration is a matter for determination at EU level, rather than Member State level,[118] although, as we will see, there is considerable deviation among the jurisdictions under consideration, in particular in respect of the contribution of a claim against the company. A consideration in kind has to be assessed by an independent expert, appointed or approved by an administrative or judicial authority. The expert must draw up a report containing a description of the assets which form the contribution, the methods of valuation and whether the value arrived at is at least equal to the par value or the accountable par and any premium of the shares issued. The report must then be published in accordance with the Directive's disclosure regime.[119] Initially, the Directive contained exemptions from the requirement of an expert report only for the group-restructuring context.[120] However, the regime has been relaxed further by Directive 2006/68/EC. Member States may derogate from the requirement of an expert report (i) if the consideration consists of securities traded on a regulated market, except where the price has been affected by 'exceptional circumstances'; (ii) if, under certain circumstances, the

[113] Article 46.

[114] Article 47. In Art 47 sentence 2, the Directive provides an exception: professional underwriters may be reimbursed for their services by paying less than the total price of the shares for which they subscribe in the course of the transaction. Moreover, in Case C-41/15 *Dowling and Others* ECLI:EU:C:2016:836 paras 48–53, the Court held that Art 47 cannot stand in the way of the recapitalization of a bank with a view to addressing a serious disturbance of the national economy and of the financial system of a Member State and the European Union.

[115] Article 53. [116] Article 48(1).

[117] Article 48(2). Article 84(1) derogations from these rules to the extent that this is necessary to encourage the participation of employees or other groups of persons in the capital of undertakings. In *Karella and Karellas* the Court of Justice held that a national rule may benefit from derogation only if its practical application helps to achieve the objective of (what is now) Art 84(1), that is, to encourage private individuals to hold shares. That condition will not be met where rules merely provide for the possibility of shares being transferred to employees or to individuals. The reference in Art 84(1) to other groups of persons refers to private individuals and is not concerned with the transfer of shares to credit institutions or to public-law bodies; Joined Cases C-19 and 20/90 *Karella and Karellas* (n 108) paras 32–5.

[118] Opinion of AG Tesauro in Case C-83/91 *Meilicke v ADV/ORGA* (n 108). [119] Article 16.

[120] Article 49(4) and (5).

contribution has already been subject to a fair value opinion; or (iii) if the fair value of the consideration is derived from the previous year's statutory accounts duly audited. If, however, exceptional circumstances would significantly change the value of the asset on its contribution, it is to be revalued in accordance with Article 49.[121]

Article 52 addresses the issue of attempts to circumvent the Article 49 regime. These may take the form of a subscription for cash and a subsequent purchase by the company from the subscribers of assets at an overvalue. Where the company acquires within a certain time limit any assets from one of its founders for a consideration of not less than one-tenth of the subscribed capital, the acquisition shall be subjected to the regime of Article 49 and must be approved by general meeting. The time limit is to be specified by Member States, but must not be less than two years from the time of incorporation. Member States may impose the same requirements if the assets belong to a (non-founding) shareholder or any other person. Article 52 raises the issue of whether Member States are allowed to maintain or introduce even stricter provisions, e.g. go below the 10 per cent requirement. In *Meilicke*[122] the Court of Justice refused to decide on the merits of the case, including this question. Today it is reasonably clear that the Second Directive allows Member States to introduce or maintain stricter standards in line with the Directive's rationale of creditor and/or minority shareholder protection as long as these standards are compatible with the freedom of establishment.[123]

Article 58 requires the company to hold a general meeting of its shareholders where there has been a 'serious loss' of capital, which must be set at a figure not higher than half the subscribed capital. The provision is widely seen as being pointless. It does not require any action to be taken or even proposed, and does not provide any remedies; all it seems to achieve is some negative publicity for the company as a result of the meeting.[124]

1. *Types of shares and issue process*

In Germany and France, shares in a public company (AG or SA, respectively) may be issued as either par value shares or as accountable par.[125] In both countries, the latter option was introduced only in 1998 in order to take account of international practice.[126] In Germany, the minimum nominal amount for par value shares is €1; as is the minimum proportion attributable to a single accountable par value share. A company may issue par value shares with different nominal values. However, a company cannot issue both

[121] Article 50. In cases (ii) and (iii) holders of at least 5 per cent of the company's capital may in any event demand an independent valuation. Where Art 50 applies, Art 51 requires publication of the necessary information in accordance with Art 16.

[122] Case C-83/91 *Meilicke v ADV/ORGA* ECLI:EU:C:1992:332.

[123] Case C-338/06 *Commission v Spain* (n 108).

[124] PL Davies and S Worthington, *Gower and Davies Principles of Modern Company Law* (10th edn, Sweet & Maxwell 2016) para 11-9. See also Case C-243/16 *Antonio Miravitlles Ciurana v Contimark SA, Jordi Socías Gispert*, ECLI:EU:C:2017:197 paras 31, 32: 'Neither Article [58] nor any of the other provisions of Directive [2017/1132] concern the liability of directors or impose particular requirements as to the jurisdiction of the courts in that regard. It is true that Article [58] lays down an obligation to convene a general meeting of the company in the case of a serious loss of the subscribed capital. However, that article merely sets forth the obligation but does not specify the other conditions necessary for its application, such as, for example, the organ of the company which is subject to the obligation. Above all, Article [58] does not make any provision as to the possible consequences of a failure to comply with that obligation.

Thus, Article [58] does not require there to be either (i) a right to compensation as against the director of a public limited liability company or (ii) a rule concerning the substantive and procedural conditions governing the liability of such a director, in the event of a failure to convene the general meeting despite a serious loss of the subscribed capital'.

[125] AktG, §8; Com Arts L225-1, L228-8.

[126] C Windbichler, *Gesellschaftsrecht* (24th edn, CH Beck 2017) 279 (§25 para 6); Germain and Magnier (n 68) para 1965.

par value shares and accountable par.[127] In France, there is no minimum par value (or accountable par) for shares. In the UK, shares in a limited company with a share capital, regardless of whether it is public or private, must each have a fixed nominal value.[128] Thus, the UK allows for the issue of par value shares only; accountable par and 'true' no par value shares are ruled out. In contrast with Germany, and similar to France, there is no minimum nominal amount.

Under all three jurisdictions, the rights conferred by a share may differ in respect of both the cash flow rights and control rights for different classes of shares. German law appears to be the most restrictive: preference shares without voting rights are possible;[129] however, shares with multiple voting rights are explicitly prohibited.[130] In France, the possibility to create a wide range of preference shares was introduced only in 2004, replacing and superseding previous forms of securities, and modified again in 2008.[131] Preference shares may confer all kinds of special cash flow and other rights on their holders, and may or may not carry voting rights.[132] In terms of cash flow rights, there is the fixed preference dividend in priority to ordinary shareholders, which may or may not be cumulative; a preferential right to repayment of capital upon liquidation or reduction of capital; in addition preference shares may also give a right to participate in profits and capital surplus. Special non-pecuniary rights include information rights, pre-emptive rights, and approval requirements on share issues and transfers.[133] The voting rights attached to these shares may be amended or suspended for a certain period or may be removed. They may be reserved for certain types of decisions, and may depend on certain economic parameters. The issue of non-voting preference shares is limited, however, to no more than half of the share capital; or ¼ of the share capital in companies whose shares are admitted to trading on a regulated market. As in Germany, shares with multiple voting rights are prohibited;[134] however, double voting rights are permissible under certain circumstances, in particular for a shareholder who has held the same shares for at least two years.[135] This obviously seeks to benefit long-term shareholders with a firm commitment to the company, in contradistinction to mere short-term speculators. For the simplified public company (SAS) there is no restriction on the creation of shares with multiple voting rights.[136] The UK provides the most flexibility: There are virtually no limits as to how the different rights as to dividends, return of surplus capital on liquidation, or voting, and different nominal values may be structured and allocated.[137] Preference shares may be 'participating' where they are entitled to a share in the profits and/or the surplus assets upon liquidation after the ordinary shares have received a specified return; or 'cumulative' where no dividend can be paid to ordinary shareholders until the preference shareholders have received a dividend for the current year plus previous years in which no dividend has been paid.[138] Often preference shares carry no voting rights, except on an amendment of class rights or if the company defaults on their preferential claims. A company with a share capital must have at least one class of ordinary shares,[139] with voting rights and rights to participate in profits and surplus assets. A public company will often have two or more classes of ordinary shares and preference shares, both with and without voting rights, or with multiple voting rights. Often, there will be a sliding scale from ordinary shares to preference shares to debt securities with no bright line separating the different types of securities, which may

[127] Windbichler (n 126) 279 (§25 para 6). [128] Companies Act 2006, s 542. [129] AktG, §139.
[130] ibid §12(2). [131] Cozian, Viandier, and Deboissy (n 67) paras 1337–1352.
[132] Com Art L228-11. [133] Germain and Magnier (n 68) para 2082. [134] Com Art L225-122.
[135] Com Art L225-123. [136] Germain and Magnier (n 68) para 2614.
[137] Davies and Worthington (n 124) para 23-6.
[138] ibid paras 23-7–23-8.
[139] Defined for Part 17, Chapter 3 of the Companies Act 2006 as 'shares other than shares that as respects dividends and capital carry a right to participate only up to a specified amount in a distribution'.

also be convertible from one type into the other.[140] The delineation of the different classes depends on the company's constitution and the drafting of its debentures. However, non-voting shares and shares with multiple voting rights are not very popular with institutional investors and occur less frequently in listed companies.[141]

Under German law, shares may be issued to bearer or to order.[142] However, as long as a share is not fully paid up it may only be issued to order, so as to make it easier for the company to identify the shareholder and call upon him to pay up.[143] Traditionally, share certificates were issued as negotiable instruments where the right incorporated in the document would follow the right on the document so that shares were transferable like chattels. Today, share certificates are usually issued in form of a global note that includes all shares of an issue. This allows the shares to be easily deposited with a central securities depository; share transfers are effectuated by mere book entries through a chain of intermediaries. French law follows a similar trajectory. The traditional system, under which shares were issued on the basis of share certificates as negotiable instruments that could be transferred by mere delivery of the document (bearer shares) or endorsement (order shares),[144] has been replaced by a dematerialized system as of 1981. Since then shares and other securities are represented by mere book entries in the issuer's share register or the registers of financial intermediaries.[145] The distinction of shares to bearer and shares to order (registered shares) is still significant. In the former case the shares are held via a qualifying financial intermediary who maintains an account with the central securities depository. The investor itself holds the shares through his account with the intermediary (or a chain of intermediaries).[146] Bearer shares are only relevant for listed companies and those companies the shares of which are held through a central securities depository. In respect of shares to order, the shares are held through entry in the register maintained by the issuer directly or a nominee appointed by the issuer.[147] For both types of shares a transfer is effectuated by mere book entry. For bearer shares the transfer instructions are given to the intermediary, for order shares to the issuer directly.[148] The transfer is complete when the shares are credited to the respective account of the buyer.[149] This may be contrasted with the UK where shares may be issued to order only: only a person who agrees to become a member of the company and whose name is registered on the register of members is a member of the company.[150] In respect of fully paid up shares it was possible, until 2015, to issue share-warrants to bearer.[151] However, share warrants were never popular in practice.[152] Under the Small Business, Enterprise and Employment Act 2015 new issues of share-warrants are prohibited, existing warrants had to be converted back into shares.[153] The main distinction in the UK is, thus, between registered shares issued in certificated form and in uncertificated form. In the former case, in addition to their name being entered in the members register maintained by the company, a shareholder will receive a share certificate in paper form.[154] This certificate is not a negotiable instrument and will be only 'prima facie evidence' of the shareholder's title.[155] In order to

[140] Davies and Worthington (n 124) para 23-4. [141] ibid. [142] AktG, §10.
[143] Windbichler (n 126) 280 (§25 para 8). [144] Germain and Magnier (n 68) para 2037.
[145] Com Art L228-1; C.mon.fin., art L211-4. [146] Germain and Magnier (n 68) para 2041.
[147] ibid. [148] ibid. [149] Com Art L228-1.
[150] Companies Act2006, s 112(2). The terms 'member' and 'shareholder' are not coterminous. A person may be a shareholder without being a member. This situation may occur where shares are transferred by operation of law. Upon death or bankruptcy of a member the personal representative of the deceased's estate or the trustee in bankruptcy will become a shareholder; but until registration will not be a member; Davies and Worthington (n 124) para 27-21. The main consequence is that without being a member a shareholder may have no right to attend and vote at general meeting; Model Articles Private Companies, reg 27(3); Model Article Public Companies, reg 66(2).
[151] Companies Act 2006, s 779. The share-warrant was a negotiable instrument, transferable by manual delivery, conferring upon its bearer the right to the shares specified in it. The bearer was entitled to have his name and shareholding reregistered if he surrenders the warrant to the company for cancellation.
[152] Davies and Worthington (n 124) para 24-22.
[153] Small Business, Enterprise and Employment Act 2015, s 84 and Sch 4, adding Companies Act 2006, s 779(4).
[154] Companies Act 2006, s 769. [155] ibid s 768.

transfer certificated shares, the seller completes and signs a transfer form which is then delivered together with the share certificate to the buyer, who in turn lodges the certificate with the company to have his name entered in the company's register of members.[156] This process is relevant for private companies and non-listed shares of public companies.[157] By contrast, all shares listed on the London Stock Exchange must be issued in uncertificated form[158] in order for them to be easily transferable through the CREST electronic transfer system. The register of members for uncertificated shares is not maintained by the company, but by the operator of the transfer system ('operator register of members') with the company merely keeping a record of its uncertificated shares.[159] Shares are transferred, upon transfer instructions, by corresponding changes to the seller's and buyer's account with CREST and in the operator register.[160] Investors may maintain an account with CREST themselves, through a broker in their own name, or through a broker as nominee. In the first two cases, the investor's name will appear on the operator register of members and the investor will hold legal title to the shares. In the latter case, the nominee's name will be registered and the nominee will hold legal title to the shares, whereas the end investor will have equitable title.[161] In any case, transfers are effectuated by electronically matching and settling instructions to the system through mere book entries.

Upon the formation of a public company all three legal systems require that the promoters subscribe all shares of the company.[162] In order to ensure that an issue is fully subscribed, large public offerings will usually be carried out through an investment bank subscribing for the whole issue and then making an offer for sale to the public. For smaller issues, instead of offering the shares to the general public, the advising investment bank may, in advance, obtain firm commitments to take up the issue from some of its institutional investor clients; such a so-called placement is substantially cheaper than a full-scale public offer. The same goes for a 'rights issue', where the shares are offered to the company's existing shareholders.[163] The technical details of the issue process differ. Under German law, the promoters, details of the subscribed shares, and the amount paid up at this stage are to be specified in the notarial deed necessary to incorporate the company.[164] Subscription entails the enforceable obligation to pay for the shares. The subscription agreement on formation must be in form of a notarial deed and is usually notarized together with the articles of association.[165] Upon a subsequent issue, usually following an increase of capital, the subscription agreement merely has to be in writing.[166] The future shareholder is bound to acquire the respective number of shares; the company is obliged to issue shares to the shareholder accordingly. However, there is no obligation on the part of the company to actually go through with the capital increase. Under French law, subscription in a public company is a legal act by which a person commits to acquire a share in the company in exchange for a contribution in cash or in kind of an amount equal to the nominal value of the shares.[167] The legal nature of the subscription is not entirely clear. The prevalent approach sees it as a synallagmatic contract with the company in formation being represented by its promoters. This view is not entirely persuasive because, in the context of formation, the company is not

[156] ibid ss 770–775.
[157] Davies and Worthington (n 124) para 27-3.
[158] Listing Rules 6.1.23, 6.1.24.
[159] Uncertificated Securities Regulation 2001 (SI 2001/3755), reg 20(1)(b); Sch 4 para 5.
[160] Uncertificated Securities Regulation 2001, reg 27.
[161] Davies and Worthington (n 124) para 27-12.
[162] AktG, §§2, 28; Companies Act 2006, s 578; Com Art L225-3; for a capital increase cf Com Art L225-134: if the subscriptions do not exhaust the entire issue, the increase will be limited to the amount subscribed as long as it reaches at least three quarters of the issue and the general meeting does not decide otherwise. The unsubscribed shares may be freely allotted or offered to the public.
[163] Davies and Worthington (n 124) paras 25-11–25-14.
[164] AktG, §23(2).
[165] ibid §23(2) no 2.
[166] ibid §185.
[167] Germain and Magnier (n 68) para 1942. In order for an SA to come into existence, at least seven persons must subscribe to at least one share each: Com Art L225-1.

yet in existence at the time of subscription; and it cannot be recharacterized as a contract with the promoters because they will not be able to issue the shares. Some have therefore argued that subscription is a unilateral promise of the subscriber to become a member of the company upon its coming into existence. This promise becomes binding and irrevocable when given by the subscriber.[168] The issue process is completed with the subscribers being entered in the respective register of the company or intermediary. In the UK, the process of issuance is carried out in a two-step procedure. Investors must first agree with the company to acquire the shares, and this 'contract of allotment' must then be implemented by making the investors members of the company. 'Allotment' is an enforceable contract for the issue of shares.[169] Shares are allotted at the time when a person acquires the unconditional right to be included in the register of members.[170] This contract may be consolidated in a letter of allotment, which may allow the allottee to assign, within a short period of time, his right to be registered to a third party.[171] Once the shares have been allotted, the company has to make a return of allotment of shares to the Registrar of Companies, providing details of the rights attached to the shares.[172] Issuance is completed when the investor's name is entered in the company's register of members.[173]

In Germany and France, private companies (GmbH and SARL) follow their own principles to a much greater extent than this is the case in the UK. GmbH promoters subscribe to the shares upon formation through the articles of association, which must be in notarial form.[174] The GmbHG allows for par value shares only, but the par value for individual shares may differ. Since the 2008 reforms,[175] there is a de facto minimum par value of €1 and a shareholder may subscribe to more than one share.[176] Thus, the 2008 reforms allow the formation of a GmbH with a number of shares greater than the number of members, and the shares may subsequently be transferred independently. This brings the GmbH much closer to a company type with a proper share capital. However, where the simplified formation procedure is used, each promoter can subscribe to one share only.[177] The subscription agreement upon a subsequent issue (following an increase in capital) requires a notarial deed.[178] This applies to both new shareholders and existing shareholders, with the latter having pre-emptive rights.[179] In the SARL the share capital is divided into shares of equal nominal value.[180] There is no longer a minimum nominal value. However, shares must have the same nominal value, but they do not have to confer the same rights. Thus, the creation of preference shares, with or without voting rights, or shares with multiple voting rights is possible.[181] Shares in a SARL cannot be negotiable instruments and, therefore, cannot be traded publicly.[182] They are transferable only by assignment; and to third parties only with the consent of a majority of the shareholders.[183]

[168] cf Germain and Magnier (n 68) paras 1950–5. In any case subscription is effectuated, where a cash contribution is promised, by signing a subscription form to be drawn up in accordance with statutory requirements; Com Art L225-4, R225-5. Contributions in kind must be determined in the articles of association without, however, the subscriber being required to sign them. Rather, the form of the subscription document will depend on the type of asset to be contributed; see Germain and Magnier (n 68) para 1947.

[169] *National Westminster Bank Plc v IRC* [1995] 1 AC 111, 126 (Lord Templeman).

[170] Companies Act 2006, s 558.

[171] This is particularly important for shareholders who want to cash in on their pre-emptive rights without wanting to take up new shares; see Davies and Worthington (n 124) para 24-19.

[172] Companies Act 2006, s 555.

[173] Registration shall be effectuated 'as soon as practicable' and not later than within two months of the date of allotment: Companies Act 2006, s 554.

[174] GmbHG, §§2, 3(1) no 4.

[175] Gesetz zur Modernisierung des GmbH-Rechts und zur Bekämpfung von Missbräuchen (MoMiG) vom 23. October 2008 BGBl 2008 Nr 48, 2026.

[176] GmbHG, §5(2). [177] ibid §2(1a).

[178] ibid §55(1). [179] Windbichler (n 126) 239 (§22 para 21). [180] Com Art L223-2.

[181] Germain and Magnier (n 68) para 1814. [182] Com Art L223-12.

[183] Com Art L223-14; cf Germain and Magnier (n 68) paras 1815–17.

2. Minimum capital requirements

The harmonized minimum capital requirement of Directive (EU) 2017/1132 applies to public companies only. There is some divergence in this respect, not just in terms of the minimum amount, but also as regards certain technicalities. In Germany and France, compliance with the statutory minimum is a condition for the valid formation of a public company (AG and SA, respectively). For the German AG the statutory minimum legal capital is €50,000.[184] For SAs it is €37,000; if listed the statutory minimum is €225,000.[185] Under both jurisdictions, a public company may be registered with contributed assets of less than the statutory minimum. For the AG, contributions in cash must be paid up only by 25 per cent of the par value (or accountable par) of the shares and any premium in full,[186] and contributions in kind consisting in the transfer of an asset to the company must be carried out within five years of registration.[187] Obviously, the shareholders' obligations to pay up the outstanding amounts and make the promised contributions remain. Under French law, shares subscribed for a contribution in cash must be paid up at least to 50 per cent of the nominal value; the rest at the discretion of the board within five years from the registration of the company. Contributions in kind must be made in full at the time of issue.[188] Under both jurisdictions, the share capital may be reduced below the statutory minimum only contingent on an increase of capital to at least the statutory minimum as part of a so-called *coup d'accordeon* in order to eradicate losses and to recapitalize the company.[189]

In the UK, the minimum capital requirement is not a condition for formation of a public company, but for doing business. A public company may commence trading only when the registrar has issued it with a trading certificate, which in turn depends on the registrar being satisfied that the nominal value of the company's allotted share capital is not less than the authorized minimum of £50,000 or the equivalent in euros.[190] Transactions entered into prior to a trading certificate being issued remain valid. However, if a company enters into a transaction under these circumstances and fails to comply with its obligations, the directors of the company may be liable jointly and severally to indemnify the other party to the transaction in respect of any loss or damage they sustained.[191] Similar to German law, shares issued for cash must not be allotted except as paid up to at least 25 per cent of their nominal value and the whole of any premium on them.[192] Where the consideration for shares consists in an undertaking to be performed in the future, this undertaking must be performed not later than five years after the date of the allotment. Otherwise, the share may be allotted as fully or partly paid up only for a consideration in cash.[193] In practice, the minimum capital requirement will be relevant mostly upon reregistration as public company of a company formed as private company limited by shares.

Following the CJEU's case law on freedom of establishment, the ensuing 'defensive' regulatory competition has resulted in a significant convergence across our three European jurisdictions in respect of the minimum capital requirements for private companies (which are outside the scope of the EU legal capital regime). The UK private company limited by shares has no explicit minimum capital requirement.[194] However, shares in any limited company having a share capital must each have a fixed nominal value denominated in any currency.[195] The Model Articles for Private Companies provide that shares cannot be issued if not fully paid. This does, however, not apply to shares taken on formation by the subscribers to the memorandum.[196] In the years following the CJEU's *Centros* line of cases, the English limited

[184] AktG §7.
[185] Com Art L224-2. [186] AktG, §36a(1). [187] ibid §36a(2). [188] Com Art L225-3.
[189] see Com Art L224-2. [190] Companies Act 2006, s 763. [191] ibid s 767(3).
[192] ibid s 586. [193] ibid s 587.
[194] However, the level of capitalization may be a relevant factor in deciding as to whether to lift the corporate veil: *FG Films* [1953] 1 WLR 483; in the context of wrongful trading: *Re Purpoint* [1991] BCC 121; and for a directors' disqualification: *Re Chartmore Ltd* [1990] BCLC 673.
[195] Companies Act 2006, s 542. [196] Model Articles Private Companies, reg 21.

proved to be an attractive vehicle for entrepreneurs from across Europe and a number of jurisdictions adjusted their law so as to become more attractive for domestic company promoters.[197] For the German GmbH, the statutory minimum remains at €25,000.[198] In practice, many GmbHs are formed with just the statutory minimum. Cash contributions must be paid up to at least 25 per cent each, contributions in kind must be made immediately and in full.[199] The company may be registered only when overall at least half of the statutory minimum (€12,500) has been contributed. However, since the 2008 reform (MoMiG), a so-called Entrepreneur Company (limited liability) may be formed with a minimum legal capital of €1.[200] This minimum capital requirement follows indirectly from the minimum nominal par value of €1. Legal capital must be paid up in full. Moreover, until legal capital has been increased up to at least €25,000, 25 per cent of the annual profits must be transferred to a statutory reserve, which may only be used to offset losses or to increase the statutory minimum. The previous statutory minimum for the French SARL of €7,500 has been abolished with a law of 1 August 2003. A SARL's amount of share capital can now be freely determined in its articles of association.[201] Because the share capital must be divided in shares of equal par value it is usually assumed that there must be at least one share with a denomination of at least 1 cent.[202] Cash contributions must be paid up to at least 20 per cent, with the remainder being payable within five years of registration. Contributions in kind must be paid in full.[203]

3. *Contributions in cash*

In accordance with Directive (EU) 2017/1132, our three European jurisdictions distinguish between contributions in cash and contributions in kind.[204] Shares for consideration in cash must be paid up, in Germany and the UK, to at least 25 per cent of their nominal value and the whole of any premium;[205] in France, to at least 50 per cent of their nominal value upon formation;[206] and 25 per cent of the nominal value upon an increase in capital, plus the entirety of the premium if any.[207] Shares must not be issued at a discount, that is, below par (or accountable par).[208] Where shares are allotted at a discount contrary to the statutory prohibition, the allottee will be liable to pay an amount equal to the discount plus interest.[209] Shares may be issued at a premium; however, a company is not strictly bound to issue its shares at a premium even where a price above par could be obtained.[210] As we have seen, this can be problematic in terms of the protection of existing shareholders against a dilution of their entitlements. Under UK law, company directors are under a duty to promote the success of the company.[211] This entails a duty owed to the company, not the individual shareholders, to obtain for its shares the full value, which they are able to get. They may issue for a price below market value (but not lower than par) only if there are good reasons for doing so,[212] as for instance in the context of share option schemes.[213] Where a company issues shares at a premium, whether for cash or otherwise, the premium must be credited to the 'share premium

[197] see Chapter 2C.II. [198] GmbHG, §5(1). [199] ibid §7(2) and (3). [200] ibid §5a.
[201] Com Art L223-2. [202] Urbain-Parléani (n 70) 484. [203] Com Art L223-7.
[204] AktG, §§27, 54; Companies Act 2006, s 582; Com Art L228-7.
[205] Companies Act 2006, s.586; AktG, §§36a(1), 9(1), 8(1). [206] Com Art L225-3.
[207] Com Art L225-144.
[208] Companies Act 2006, s 580; also *Ooregum Gold Mining Co of India Ltd v Roper* [1892] AC 125 (HL); AktG, §§36a(1), 9(1). In the UK, a company is explicitly prohibited from issuing any of its shares in payment of any commission, discount or allowance to any person in consideration for subscribing or agreeing to subscribe for its shares: Companies Act 2006, s 552. As an exception, professional underwriters may be compensated for their professional services by a discount of up to 10% of the issue price: Companies Act 2006, s 553. Under French law, case law does not seem to generally exempt a commission payment from the 'no issue below par' rule, but only in respect of financial institutions that facilitate the public placement of the shares. In that case, commission in the form of a discount appears as remuneration for services already provided: Germain and Magnier (n 68) para 1966.
[209] Companies Act 2006, s 580(2). [210] For the UK: *Hilder v Dexter* [1902] AC 474 (HL).
[211] Companies Act 2006, s 172.
[212] *Lowry v Consolidated African Selection Trust Ltd* [1940] AC 648, 679 (Lord Wright).
[213] Davies and Worthington (n 124) para 11-4.

account' and will be treated, by and large, as share capital[214] so that it cannot be used for the payment of dividends and distributions.[215]

Our legal systems deviate considerably when it comes to the definition of what counts as a contribution in cash. In the UK, 'cash consideration' is defined broadly in section 583 of the Companies Act 2006. Cash consideration does not just encompass cash or cheque received by the company (not a third party) or conferral upon the company of a present or future entitlement to a payment or credit equivalent to payment in cash, but also the release of a liability of the company for a liquidated sum and an undertaking to pay cash to the company in the future.[216] It appears that where the company is released from a debt it is the nominal value of the debt that matters in terms of the amount paid up, even if the market value is lower than nominal value because of the company's insolvency.[217] Under French law, cash contributions are defined in Com Article 228-7. They encompass payment in cash, but also shares issued on the basis of a capitalization of reserves, profits, or share premiums. Most importantly, set-off with a due and liquidated claim against the company or contribution of such a claim is, as in the United Kingdom, a contribution in cash.[218] There are, however, some differences. A contribution by way of set-off may be excluded by an extraordinary general meeting. Also, the claims against the company admitted for set-off must be stated in the company's accounts and verified by its auditors. Set-off as a contribution in cash seems to be permissible only where the company is solvent.[219] Treating the release of a liability of the company as contribution in cash stands in marked contrast to the German rules on set-off and waiver of a claim against the company as a contribution in kind. Under German law, a shareholder cannot be released from their obligation and cannot discharge their obligation to make a contribution in cash by way of set-off with a claim owed to them by the company.[220] By contrast, a set-off by the company or a set-off agreement is permissible to the extent that the shareholder's claim against the company is due, liquidated, and can be realized out of the company's assets.[221] A claim against the company may be contributed by the subscriber only by way of a contribution in kind.[222]

As the rationale for the German rules on set-off it is usually advanced that set-off is economically similar to the contribution of a claim and triggers, similar to a contribution in kind, complex valuation problems. In particular, where the company is insolvent on a balance sheet basis, the shareholder's claim against the company may have a market value significantly below its nominal value. Besides, set-off as well as the waiver of a claim do not contribute anything to the company's capitalization in terms of actual assets.[223] In

[214] Companies Act 2006, s 610. The share premium account may only be used to write off expenses of the issue and to pay up new shares to be allotted as fully paid bonus shares.

[215] This can have adverse consequences in case of group restructurings and mergers and takeovers; *Henry Head & Co Ltd v Ropner Holdings Ltd* [1952] 1 Ch 124. For instance, where the bidder company issues shares in itself to the shareholders of the target company, in exchange for shares in the target, undistributed profits of the target will be reflected in the market value of the target shares. Where this exceeds the par value of the bidder shares the bidder company will have to transfer the difference to the share premium account with the consequence that reserves that were distributable pre-acquisition become non-distributable after the takeover. This is because a dividend paid by the target after the takeover to the bidder will increase the bidder's cash account, but at the same time reduce the value of the target shares held by the bidder. Thus, despite the cash dividend, distributable surplus at bidder level does not increase and the bidder shareholders (including the former target shareholders) will receive nothing; see A Cahn and D Donald *Comparative Company Law* (CUP 2010) 176. For these and similar situations CA 2006, ss 611–615 provide relief. Where a wholly-owned subsidiary transfers assets at book value to the holding in exchange for the latter's shares, only the amount by which the book value of the transferred assets exceeds the nominal value of the shares must be transferred to the premium account: Companies Act 2006, s 611. Where, in a share exchange merger, the bidder has secured at least a 90% equity holding in the target, s 610 does not apply to the premiums on the shares issued by the bidder in consideration for the target shares: Companies Act 2006, s 612.

[216] There does not seem to be a time limit for the future payment as the five-year limit of s 587 only applies to non-cash contributions.

[217] Davies and Worthington (n 124) para 11-15.

[218] For a capital increase cf Com Art L225-128.

[219] Germain and Magnier (n 68) para 2528 n 82.

[220] AktG, §66(1).

[221] K Schmidt, *Gesellschaftsrecht* (4th edn, Heymann 2002) 882.

[222] ibid 883.

[223] ibid 882.

Meilicke, Advocate General Tesauro criticized this reasoning. From the point of view of the company, the value of the shareholder's claim, if liquidated and due, was always equal to its nominal value, even where the company is insolvent. Insolvency had an impact on the value as far as the contributor was concerned, but not on the value of the debt from the company's perspective. In the balance sheet, both the company's claims for payments still due from members and the debts of the company are shown at their nominal values. The economic assessment of a claim against the company was to be made from the company's perspective, and certainly not from the creditors' point of view.[224] This is not entirely convincing. Set-off, or the waiver of a claim against the company, removes a liability from the company's balance sheet, but also the company's outstanding claim against the shareholder. Both are shown with their nominal value. If, by contrast, the shareholder pays in cash there will be a mere exchange of *activa*: the cash account is increased and the company's claim against the shareholder removed accordingly. The essential difference lies in the fact that in the latter scenario the shareholder will participate as creditor in the value of his own contribution (and of other assets) only on a pro rata basis should the company go into insolvent liquidation. In the former case, the shareholder-creditor will be satisfied in full up to the amount that he owed the company. This asset, the company's claim against the shareholder-creditor, is withdrawn from the company for the preferential satisfaction of the shareholder-creditor and to the detriment of the other creditors. Moreover, the predominant rationale of the provisions on payment for shares is the protection of shareholders against dilution of their rights. Viewed in that light, it must be the creditor-shareholder's point of view that matters. If he can acquire a (higher) stake in the company at the nominal value of his claim where the actual value is lower, the existing shareholders' rights will be diluted, even if the company is insolvent at the time, because if the company's fortunes improve the creditor-shareholder will participate in any future profits pro rata on the basis of their higher stake.[225]

French and German law contain specific provisions on the payment of cash contributions. Under French law, the subscriber may pay in cash or by cheque or may use all available means to make a payment. The monies are to be held in an escrow account in the name of the company in formation maintained by either the *Caisses des depots et consignations*, a bank or financial intermediary, or a notary. In practice, the funds will often be held by the notary involved in the formation process of the company. It is doubtful whether payment is effective if it is made to an account maintained by a bank that is also acting as promoter or subscriber.[226] In order to ensure that funds obtained by the promoters are quickly deposited with the respective escrow account, Com Article L225-5 prescribes that no party, in particular the promoters, may hold funds for longer than one week. Subscription and payment are to be evidenced by a receipt to be issued by the depository upon deposit of the funds.[227] The funds may not be used or withdrawn from the account before the company is registered; only after it comes into existence may its first directors withdraw the funds. If the company is not registered within six months from the time the memorandum and articles have been lodged with the registry every subscriber may apply to the court to have the funds withdrawn and returned to the subscribers. If subsequently the formation process goes ahead, the funds must be raised anew.[228] Where shares remain unpaid it will be difficult for a company in formation to obtain payment.[229] This is because the company is not yet in existence and the promoters are not directly the creditors to whom the subscriber's obligation to contribute is owed. However, if the company is established, it may sue the subscriber for failing to pay up. In addition, it may, after giving formal notice, sell the shares, either

224 Opinion of AG Tesauro in Case C-83/91 *Meilicke* (n 108) paras 14–15.
225 cf BGHZ 110, 47 (IBH/Lemmertz) below. 226 Germain and Magnier (n 68) para 1971.
227 Com Art L225-6. 228 Com Art L225-11.
229 Germain and Magnier (n 68) para 1974. cf also Urbain-Parléani (n 70) 487.

through the stock market if listed, or otherwise by way of a public auction.[230] The company can chose between an action against the subscriber or the forced sale of the unpaid shares. A further remedy available to the company is the suspension of voting rights and dividends on unpaid shares.[231]

Under German law, the amount called before application for registration has to be paid in legal tender or by credit to a bank account of the company or of the management board.[232] The promoters may not file for registration until the amount agreed to be paid up before registration has been duly deposited and is at the free disposal of the management board.[233] In general, this is the case where the subscriber is no longer entitled to the use of the funds and management can dispose of them as it sees fit. The requirement obviously seeks to prevent fictitious payments such as the practice, common in the olden days, of showing the money to the notary, handing it over to the management who hand it back as soon as the parties leave the notary's office.[234] The same goes for circular payments where shareholders transfer the subscription price to the company's bank account and receive reimbursement from the company for the subscription.[235] Payment may be made, and in practice often is, by crediting a bank account of the company or of the management board.[236] Whether the contribution is at the management's free disposal may be in doubt where the account is in debit. In general, funds credited to an account that is overdrawn may still be at the free disposal of the company provided that the overdraft approved by the bank has not been exceeded, that is, the company may easily withdraw the funds. Hence, where the company has exhausted its line of credit and the payment is charged against the debit this will not amount to proper payment.[237] This is particularly relevant for contributions to a 'cash pool' in a group of companies where all subsidiaries are financed via a central account with a bank maintained by the holding company. According to the BGH, the following principles apply:[238] if the (subsidiary) company's account with the central cash management system is in debit at the time the contribution is credited to the central account, the contribution will not be a contribution in cash, but a (disguised) contribution in kind because what the company receives is release from a debt owed to the holding company through the cash pool. If the company's cash pool account is balanced or in credit there is a pure circular payment as the cash contribution is returned to the holding (or its controlling shareholders) as a loan through the cash pool. This would not satisfy the at-the-free-disposal requirement. The only exception is an agreement under which the company obtains a liquidated and fully realizable claim against the holding that is either due or can be rendered due by simply giving notice.[239] Such an arrangement must be disclosed in the application for registration. This exception was introduced precisely in order to cater for financially appropriate cash pooling.[240]

230 Com Art L228-27. 231 Com Art L228-29. 232 AktG, §54(3). 233 ibid §36(2).

234 For instance RGSt 24, 287. 235 BGHZ 122, 180 (coop). 236 AktG, §54(3).

237 S Hölters, *Aktiengesetz* (2nd edn, CH Beck 2014) §36 para 16. A related problem concerns the question of whether management can dispose of the funds prior to application for registration. In BGHZ 119, 177, it was held that the funds received in the course of an increase of capital do not have to remain untouched until application for registration. However, if management decides to invest the funds it has to ensure that the company receives adequate consideration. In other words, at the time of application (not at the time of registration) either the contributions themselves or assets of equivalent value have to be at the free disposal of the management. However, subsequently the BGH modified its case law. The court now differentiates between capital contributions that were made in the course of formation of a company and contributions after a capital increase. While in the former case the contributions served to raise the registered capital of an, until then, non-existent company, in the latter case they were made available to a company whose initial share capital had been paid up. Therefore, protection of creditors after a capital increase was not in the same way a concern of the law as during the stage of formation. Instead, by paying up the required amount and ensuring that it was at the free disposal of the management board, the process of raising capital was complete. From that time on—possibly before application for registration—the management board was entitled to make use of the funds for the management of the company; BGHZ 150, 197.

238 BGH, NJW 2009, 3091. 239 AktG, §27(4). 240 Hölters (n 237) §27 para 53.

4. *Contributions in kind*

Contributions in kind generally raise the issue of their (over)valuation. Traditionally, there has been considerable variation amongst legal systems. The English common law relied to a large extent on the business judgment and integrity of the directors, and courts would normally not interfere with a valuation made at the time of allotment unless its inadequacy was clearly obvious. In France, prior to 1967, an independent verification of the asset value of a contribution in kind was deemed to be unnecessary if all contributions consisted in contributions in kind.[241] Following the German tradition, the implementation of the Second Company Law Directive required the introduction of an elaborate statutory regime, which tries to ensure that contributions in kind do not result in shares being issued at a discount.

Contributions in kind may consist of any asset whose value may be determined in monetary terms and can be commercially exploited; also, it must be possible to transfer that asset so that it may be at the free disposal of the management board.[242] Contributions in kind may, thus, consist of real and personal property rights, intellectual property rights, a business or enterprise as a collection and combination of tangible and intangible assets, shares in companies and partnerships, claims against third parties and, in Germany, against the company itself.[243] Certain forms of consideration are banned altogether: the undertaking to do work for the company or to perform services.[244] Under French and German law, the fact of a contribution in kind, the asset it consist of, the respective (prospective) shareholder and the nominal value or number of shares it represents must be duly stipulated in the articles of association,[245] or the resolution to increase the share capital.[246] Where shares are issued for consideration other than payment in cash under UK law, the respective undertaking must be performed not more than five years after the date of allotment. In France, contributions in kind must be made in full immediately upon issue of the respective shares.[247] In Germany, contributions in kind must be contributed in full, except where the contributions consist of an obligation to transfer an asset to the company, in which case the asset must be made available to the company within five years from the time of incorporation.[248] In accordance with Directive (EU) 2017/1132, under all three jurisdictions, the value of a contribution in kind has to be independently verified by an external expert. Depending on the formation process, the technical details differ; there are also considerable differences in respect of the remedies for a breach of the statutory prerequisites.

Under German law, the promoters have to report on contributions in kind specifically in the formation report and must provide reasons that justify the valuation of the contribution.[249] This valuation has to be verified by a court-appointed external auditor.[250] External verification is unnecessary only in the case of securities with a readily ascertainable market price and in case of assets that have already been valued, and there are no reasons that suggest that market price or prior valuation may no longer be reliable.[251] The value of in-kind-contributions has to correspond to the lowest issue price (par value or accountable par) plus any premium. In case the contribution's value turns out to be lower than that, registration must be rejected. If the company/increase in capital has been registered nonetheless, the company may claim from the subscriber the difference in value as cash payment (in analogy to §9 GmbHG). This liability is strict; bad faith or negligence on the part of the subscriber is not required. Where the contribution consists of an enterprise and it turns out that the liabilities exceed the assets, the subscriber's liability may be for an amount that exceeds the issue price and that is necessary to balance the deficit.[252] Similar principles apply for private companies with the following exceptions: contributions in kind must in all cases be at the free

241 Germain and Magnier (n 68) para 1976.
242 Hölters (n 237) §27 para 7.
243 ibid §27 para 8; Germain and Magnier (n 68) para 1975.
244 Companies Act 2006, s 585; AktG, §27(2).
245 AktG, §27(1).
246 ibid §183(1).
247 Com Art L225-3.
248 AktG, §36a(2).
249 ibid §32(2).
250 ibid §§33–35.
251 ibid §33a.
252 Schmidt (n 221) 885.

disposal of the company's management prior to application for registration.[253] Upon formation, the shareholders must justify the valuation of the consideration in kind in a formation report,[254] but external verification is not required. Neither verification report nor external verification are statutory requirements upon an increase of capital. However, the Registrar may demand proof that the contribution actually reaches the stated value.[255]

In the UK, the valuation requirement is densely regulated in sections 593–609 of the Companies Act 2006. The valuation report must be made during the six months immediately preceding the allotment of shares.[256] It must describe the consideration, explain the method of valuation, and state to what extent the shares are to be treated as paid up by the consideration and in cash.[257] A copy must be sent to the proposed allottee[258] and one filed with the registrar of companies.[259] The valuer must be qualified to act as an auditor of the company.[260] Statutory tests of independence apply. Sections 594 and 595 of the Companies Act 2006 contain derogations from the valuation requirement for intra-group restructurings and mergers, respectively.[261] The sanctions for a failure to comply with the provisions on independent valuation are rather severe: the allottee is obliged to pay the company the nominal value of the shares and any premium, with interest, regardless of any benefit that the company may already have received.[262] This means that the allottee may in effect have to pay twice for the shares. Unless a bona fide purchaser for value without notice, a subsequent holder will be jointly and severally liable with the allottee for paying the same amount.[263] The only relief available to those who might be liable under these provisions is an application to the court to ask for exemption from the statutory liability.[264] Given the broad definition of 'cash contribution' and the history of the common law that did not feel the need for an independent valuation, it is not surprising that in the UK we do not find elaborate doctrines that try to prevent a circumvention of the statutory regime. In respect of transactions not covered by the statutory provisions the established common law principles still apply. Accordingly, the parties' valuation will be accepted, unless there is fraud, bad faith or its inadequacy is obvious.[265] The same generally applies for private companies.

For both SA and SARL, French law provides a procedure for the independent valuation of contributions in kind.[266] In respect of the SA, the subscriber must attribute a certain value to the asset, which, after verification, the shareholders in general meeting are asked to approve. The verification is to be carried out by verification auditors whose qualification and independence the law seeks to ensure. Where, after verification, the shareholders have approved the valuation, neither they nor the subscriber will be liable vis-à-vis third parties if the asset turns out to have been overvalued. However, in case of a fraudulent overvaluation the subscriber and the auditor involved may incur criminal liability.[267] One or more verification auditors will be appointed by the president of the commercial court on request of one or more promoters, or on request of the company in case of a capital increase. In the SARL, the verification auditors may be nominated by unanimous shareholder decision instead. In any

[253] GmbHG, §7(3). [254] ibid §5(4). [255] Schmidt (n 221) 1120–1.
[256] Companies Act 2006, s 593. [257] ibid s 596. [258] ibid s 593. [259] ibid s 597.
[260] ibid ss 596, 1150.
[261] They do not seem to be in full compliance with Art 49(4) and (5) of Directive (EU) 2017/1132. The derogations in Arts 50 and 51 have not been implemented in the UK.
[262] Companies Act 2006, s 593(3). [263] ibid ss 588, 605. [264] ibid ss 589, 606.
[265] Davies and Worthington (n 124) para 11-14. Pursuant to *Re Wragg Ltd* [1897] 1 Ch 796 (CA), courts may interfere with a valuation made at the time of allotment only if it can be shown that the company acted dishonestly or falsely or the contract for allotment itself can be set aside for fraud or duress or the like. Subsequently it was held that a transaction will be safe from court interference if the bargain was 'made by persons who were honestly acting in what they conceived to be the interests of the company'; *In re Innes & Co, Limited* [1903] 2 Ch 254 (Vaughan Williams LJ). This was qualified in *In Re White Star Line*, where it was held that even if the consideration the company receives is the best it can get in the circumstances and the directors are therefore acting in the best interest of the company, still the consideration must not be 'a mere blind or clearly colourable or illusory': *In re White Star Line Limited* [1938] Ch 458.
[266] Com Art L225-8; L223-9. [267] Germain and Magnier (n 68) para 1977.

case, the verification auditors must be selected from the list of company auditors, or a second list of experts maintained by the court. Strict requirements of independence apply.[268] The verification auditors have to draw up a report in which they state whether the value of the asset is at least equal to the nominal value of the shares (plus any premium upon capital increase). The auditors may incur professional liability for any wrongful valuation. The report must be deposited at least eight days before the constitutive general meeting of shareholders at the prospective seat of the company and with the local commercial court. The subscribers must have access to the report and can request a copy. On the basis of the report, the general meeting decides on the valuation of the contribution in kind. The subscriber to the contribution in kind does not have a vote.[269] If the general meeting approves the valuation the decision is final and cannot be challenged. With the decision of approval the contribution in kind is effectuated and the asset is transferred to the company.[270] If the general meeting refuses to accept the valuation, the company can come into existence, or the capital increase become effective, only if the capital is reduced accordingly. This requires a unanimous vote of all subscribers and express consent of the subscriber to the contribution in kind to be stated in the minutes of the meeting.[271] For private companies, similar principles apply. However, there is no approval of the valuation by shareholder meeting; rather, the valuation report is to be annexed to the articles of association.[272] Moreover, the future members may decide unanimously that no external verification is required if the contribution in kind has a value of not more than €7,500 and the overall value of all contributions in kind not independently valued is not more than half of the legal capital. If no verification takes place or if the stated value is different from that of the valuation report, the shareholders will be jointly and severally liable directly vis-à-vis third parties for the value attributed to the contribution in kind at the time of formation for up to five years thereafter.[273]

In implementation of Article 52 of Directive (EU) 2017/1132, the valuation requirement has been extended to certain transactions where the company acquires, within two years of the company having been issued with a trading certificate (UK) or registered (Germany and France), a non-cash asset from a subscriber to the memorandum on the company's formation or from a member on its conversion to a public company (UK), from a shareholder (France) or a promoter or shareholder holding more than 10 per cent of the share capital (Germany), and the consideration to be provided by the company is at least equal to one tenth of its issued share capital.[274] Unless carried out in the ordinary course of business or under court supervision, the transaction must be independently valued and is subject to approval by ordinary shareholder resolution.

[268] ibid paras 1978, 1979. [269] Com Art L225-10.

[270] Germain and Magnier (n 68) paras 1981, 1982. [271] Com Art L225-8.

[272] Com Art L223-9.

[273] Com Art L223-9(4). The legal nature of this liability is not entirely clear. Some commentators consider it to be contractual, others tortious; in the end, it is probably right to view it simply as a statutory guarantee obligation. This is relevant for the question as to who is a 'shareholder' for the purposes of the provision: only those who were involved in the formation of the company and could therefore have influenced the stated value or the decision not to have it externally verified, or also those who became shareholders later? It is in line with the statutory guarantee approach that all shareholders will be liable if they are shareholders at the time the action is initiated. Personal fault on the part of the shareholders does not matter. Similarly, although the shareholders only guarantee the value at the time of formation—not the value of the asset as constant over time—it has been argued that the shareholders would also be liable for all the consequences arising from the overvaluation. However, this is a delictual notion—liability for all the consequences of one's fault—and would require difficult considerations in terms of causality. The statutory guarantee concept is limited to the value on formation. The shareholders are liable jointly and severally. Internally they may take regress against the subscriber who contributed the asset. If he is insolvent the remaining shareholders will be liable in proportion to their shareholdings. To hold them liable internally in accordance with their contributory fault is again a delictual notion and would be unworkable in practice. cf Germain and Magnier (n 68) para 1802.

[274] Companies Act 2006, ss 598–604; AktG, §54; Com Art L225-101.

5. *The German doctrine of disguised contributions in kind*

Because the rules on contributions in kind are so rigid (stipulation in the articles of association; valuation by an external expert; liability of the shareholder for the difference in value) there is a strong incentive for the founders to circumvent these provisions. In order to prevent such circumvention, German courts have developed the concept of 'disguised contribution in kind'.[275] A disguised contribution in kind is a transaction under which a contribution in cash is linked with a business transaction in a way so that the economic result is similar to a contribution in kind. In a typical example, A may subscribe to 100,000 €1 shares in a company with a share capital of €5,000,000. A's main contribution to the business is a certain production process that he has invented and that both he and the promoters value at €100,000. However, neither A nor the promoters are sure whether the process is in fact worth €100,000. Moreover, they would like to spare the company the costs of an external auditor who would have to value the process if contributed as a contribution in kind. Therefore, A and the promoters agree that A will pay up €100,000 in cash, probably obtained as a loan. Following registration, the company buys A's process for €100,000. Such disguised contributions in kind occur both in respect of public companies and private companies and are treated in the same way. They are more relevant upon an increase in capital than upon formation.[276] The most common forms are circular payments of cash from the subscriber to the company and back in connection with the acquisition of an asset by the company from the subscriber; and further the set-off or discharge of existing claims of a shareholder/subscriber against the company with the amount obtained by the company from the same shareholder/subscriber in the course of an increase of capital.[277]

The following is one of the leading cases on the doctrine of disguised contributions in kind:

BGHZ 110, 47 (*IBH/Lemmertz*)

Lemmertz KGaA was a supplier of IBH. In December 1979, it provided a supplier's loan of DM 5m to IBH. IBH defaulted on the January 1982 instalment. The two parties met to discuss the termination of the loan and a possible continuation of business dealings. IBH suggested that Lemmertz subscribe to shares worth DM 5m to be issued pursuant to a capital increase and promised to pay back the loan with the funds thus raised. Lemmertz agreed, set up the defendant subsidiary and entered into a 'transfer of profits and control contract' and a trust agreement with it. Under these arrangements the defendant subsidiary would subscribe to the shares of IBH and would hold them as trustee for Lemmertz; in turn, Lemmertz would reimburse the defendant subsidiary for any costs and liabilities it may incur in the course of the transaction. Accordingly, the defendant subsidiary subscribed to the issue and paid DM 5m to IBH, which was credited to a bank account opened for the issue. IBH sent Lemmertz a cheque over DM 5m in discharge of the supplier's loan. The cheque was drawn against IBH's business account, which was balanced by using the proceeds from the capital increase. When subsequently IBH filed for insolvency, the liquidator alleged that the transaction amounted to a disguised contribution in kind, that, therefore, the subsidiary's payment of DM 5m was ineffective to discharge its obligation under the subscription, and that it was liable to pay DM 5m again.

...

Protection against circumvention [of the provisions on contributions in kind] is today more important than ever because a capital increase through contributions in kind has become an important and indispensible instrument of corporate finance ... This ex ante protection of legal capital is, under current economic conditions, not just an instrument to protect the shareholders, in particular minority shareholders; it also encompasses the protection of current and future creditors as well as the interests of economic life in general and of employees. The doctrine of 'disguised contribution in kind' constitutes, in light of the importance of the increase of capital in its different forms and their implementation in the course of European legal harmonization,

[275] Schmidt (n 221) 886–7. [276] ibid 887. [277] Hölters (n 237) §27 para 30.

not just a convenient but a necessary element of the law on public companies that seeks to prevent the circumvention of the provisions on the ex ante protection of the raising of legal capital.

...

If, pursuant to agreement with the management board, he who is able to make a contribution in kind was free, instead of following the prescribed procedure, to choose to subscribe for a contribution in cash and, in exchange for the paid in cash, could then transfer to the company an asset that could have been contributed as a contribution in kind, he would obtain the same economic result as in case of a contribution in kind, however without him or the company complying with the provisions on publicity and verification. If such a procedure was to be considered permissible there would be a real danger that the correct procedure of a contribution in kind would be followed less and less frequently, that the respective protective provisions would be circumvented and an effective protection of minority shareholders and creditors could, due to the disregrading of these provisions, no longer be guaranteed ...

The appellant has correctly pointed out that conclusion and settlement of a credit agreement is not covered by the wording of § 27(1) AktG because no 'assets' are being acquired. However, the wording of this provision cannot be decisive. Rather, what matters is that this provision is an emanation of the principle of effective raising of capital and serves its protection. In light of the provision's rationale it covers every transaction that as to its content seeks to avoid being recharacterized as a contribution in kind.

...

[The appellant argues that] the rationale of the provisions on contributions in kind does not require treating the contribution of a claim against the company arising from a loan agreement as a contribution in kind. Hence, the doctrine of disguised contribution in kind was inapplicable for that reason alone. This argument cannot succeed.

It is generally accepted that a claim arising from a loan contract of a shareholder against the AG may be contributed by way of a contribution in kind. Object matter of the contribution in kind is the claim. The contribution is carried out either by assigning the claim to the company upon which it expires due to the concept of 'Konfusion' [obligor and obligee are one and the same person] or the shareholder waives the claim ... Occasionally it has been argued in the legal literature that there is no need to re-characterize a contribution in cash and subsequent discharge of a debt out of the proceeds as a contribution in kind subject to the publicity and verification requirements ...

However, neither courts nor the majority of commentators have adopted this view ... In case of a conversion of liabilities into legal capital there is a change only on the liability-side [right-hand-side] of the balance sheet. However, this does not justify converting the liability with its nominal value. The shareholder can rely on a conversion only to the extent that the company can actually satisfy the claim; this is the measure for its value.

It has been argued that the rationale of the provisions on the raising of capital do not require adherence when a credit obligation is contributed because in case of the company's insolvency on a balance sheet basis the company's capital would have to be reduced in the course of the contribution so that the credit claim obtains its full value. However, there is no obligation to reduce the capital in that way. In practice this is often done, but not always. Also, the extent of the reduction does not have to be so as to completely restore the legal capital in a way that the claim obtains its full value. The argument that the conversion of company liabilities does not require adherence to the provisions on contributions in kind because current and future creditors are not prejudiced is also unpersuasive. This approach is based on the one-sided view of the transaction as a regrouping of persons on the liability-side of the balance sheet. It is alleged that shareholders would gain an advantage because the claim would no longer have priority and that this would balance out the disadvantage arising from the fact that the new shareholder would participate in future profits and a distribution upon liquidation on the basis of the nominal value of the claim. This is unpersuasive as the assessment is based on too many variables, making a general assessment impossible; each case would have to be assessed on its own merits.

It must not be overlooked that if shares were issued for the nominal value of the credit claim the other shareholders would immediately be prejudiced to the extent that the market value of the claim is lower than its nominal value. However, current creditors are not disadvantaged since the contribution of the claim does not reduce the company's liquidity. By contrast, future creditors will be disappointed in their expectation that the company has received new capital. Because by disclosing a capital increase in cash the fact of a mere regrouping of financial claims is not publicised, giving the impression that cash has been contributed. As a further consequence, the verification of the value of the claim at the moment of contribution through external auditor, general meeting and registrar will be omitted. Contrary to what the appellant believes, this is not an issue of the prohibition against a release of shareholders from their contributions (§ 66(1) AktG), rather it is a question of the ex ante protection of the raising of capital.

...

[The appellant further argued that the transaction at issue did not amount to a disguised contribution in kind because the parties had no intent to circumvent the provisions on contributions in kind.]

The intent to circumvent the provisions on contributions in kind is not a precondition for treating a contribution in cash and discharge of a debt of the AG as a unitary transaction subject to the provisions on ex ante protection of raising of capital and consequently as a 'disguised contribution in kind'. The circumvention of legal provisions is a question of the application of law on the basis of validity of the norm and the enforceability of its content in its own right... It cannot depend on subjectively culpable behaviour in the sense of intent.

The provisions on contributions in kind are an emanation of the principle of effective contribution of capital... Through disclosure and control mechanisms they seek to ensure the proper contribution of legal capital. This goal as well as the measures to its attainment are determined solely by the 'hidden' transaction. If enforceability of these norms were dependent upon the intent of the parties to circumvent them, realization of their rationale would, in the absence of such intent, depend on norm-extraneous circumstances. The law could not be enforced even if the parties were acting contrary to its rationale.

Whether, apart from that, it is sufficient for the application of the doctrine of disguised contribution in kind that exchange transactions between company and shareholder and contribution in cash are objectively closely linked in terms of chronology and subject matter... or whether, in addition to these objective criteria, there must be some agreement or understanding between the subscriber and the representative organ of the company envisaging the economic result of the circumvented provisions can remain undecided in the case at issue here. According to the findings of the trial court, the transaction at issue meets the requirements of a disguised contribution in kind under both approaches. The obligation to contribute cash was discharged on 2nd, the debt on 9th August 1982. On 13th August 1982 Lemmertz balanced the account of its subsidiary. The chronological and subject matter link between the payments is obvious. The trial court also found that between the managing director of IBH and the managing partner of Lemmertz there was an understanding, although not legally binding on IBH, to the effect that the debt should be discharged with the proceeds from the subsidiary's contribution in kind. This amounts to an understanding envisaging the economic result of the circumvented provision.

...

The appellant further argues that the creditor of the contributed claim and the subscriber of the shares were not identical. However, the fact that creditor and subscriber are not the same person is immaterial. It is generally recognized that the principles of disguised contributions in kind do not just apply if the proceeds of a contribution in cash are used to discharge a claim of the subscriber, but also where this is done for the benefit of an affiliated person ... Between the defendant and Lemmertz existed not just a 'transfer of profits and control' contract pursuant to § 291(1) AktG and consequently a group relationship (§ 18(1) AktG) under which, despite maintaining the separation of legal personalities, the principle of effective contribution of capital may be prejudiced in certain cases ... This question is here immaterial because the defendant and Lemmertz also concluded a trust agreement pursuant to which the defendant was obliged vis-à-vis Lemmertz to subscribe to 31,250 shares for a nominal value of 1,562,500 DM for a contribution in cash of DM 5m, to act according to the directions of Lemmertz and to transfer the shares to Lemmertz if called to do so. Lemmertz were obliged to reimburse the defendant for any expenses in connection with the trust agreement and to relieve it from any liability. On the basis of this agreement, with the proceeds of the defendants' cash contribution IBH did not just discharge Lemmertz's credit claim which would be sufficient to assume a disguised contribution in kind, rather, Lemmertz used these funds to reimburse the defendant for its expenses.

This circular payment within a three-partite relationship was accurately described by the trial court in the sense that the only contribution made by the defendant, and assisted by Lemmertz, to IBH was the credit claim. The reasons why the defendant was brought in at all are immaterial in this respect.

Questions and comments:

1. A statutory definition of 'disguised contribution in kind' can now be found in AktG, §27(3)1 and GmbHG, §19(4)1: a contribution in cash that, on the basis of a commercial assessment and pursuant to an agreement made in the context of the contribution in cash, amounts in economic terms to a contribution in kind. This requires (i) an obligation to make a contribution in cash upon formation or increase of capital; (ii) a business transaction between the company and the subscriber (or a third party acting in concert with the subscriber) pursuant to which an asset that may constitute a contribution in kind is transferred to the company in exchange for cash; and (iii) an agreement at the time of subscription between the subscriber and the promoters or the company that links (i) and (ii) to the effect that the economic result amounts to a contribution in kind.[278]
2. As we have seen in *IBH/Lemmertz*, the question as to how contribution in cash and business transaction ought to be connected was contentious. One approach required intent on the part of the shareholder and the company or its management to circumvent the statutory requirements. The second test was less strict, requiring that shareholder and company have an agreement that connects the promise of the company and the contribution of the shareholder (e.g. the understanding that the shareholder will subscribe to the shares because the company will perform a certain transaction). A third approach argued for doing away with any subjective elements and focussing on the objective connection between shareholder transaction and contribution. In IBH/Lemmertz, the BGH rejected the first option (intent to circumvent the statutory requirements) and did not decide between the remaining two because the requirements of both were satisfied in the case at issue. In later decisions the BGH has made it clear that some kind of—not necessarily legally binding—agreement between shareholder and company is required.[279] This solution has now been codified under the statutory definitions. Moreover, if objectively shareholder transaction and cash contribution occur in close chronological proximity (not more than six months) the required agreement or understanding is to be presumed and the burden of proof shifts to the defendant to show that there was no such agreement.[280]
3. A further question that was addressed by the court in this case was the compatibility of the doctrine of disguised contribution in kind with the Second Company Law Directive, in particular with what is now Article 52 of Directive (EU) 2017/1132. The BGH refused to refer the question to the Court of Justice on the premise that the answer was obvious and did not leave room for any reasonable doubt.[281] Since, according to Article 52, Member States are free to extend the scope of this provision to transactions with shareholders and other persons the BGH concluded that Article 52 and the provisions on contributions in kind provided only minimum standards, leaving room for the Member States to apply more protective rules under their national laws. Do you find these arguments persuasive or should the BGH have referred the question to the Court of Justice?
4. The question came finally before the Court in *Meilicke*.[282] Because the Court believed the question to be a purely hypothetical one it did not feel to have jurisdiction under what is now Article 267 of the TFEU. The case was brought be a German lawyer who, in a number of publications, had vehemently argued against the concept of 'disguised contributions in kind'. There were indications that he held his one share only in order to test his case before the Court. The

[278] Hölters (n 237) §27 para 30. [279] BGHZ 132, 133. [280] Hölters (n 237) §27 para 37.
[281] In line with the *acte clair* exemption under the CILFIT doctrine, Case 283/81 *CILFIT* ECLI:EU:C:1982:335 paras 13–15.
[282] Case C-83/91 *Meilicke* (n 108).

merits of the case were however discussed by Advocate General Tesauro who came to the conclusion that the concepts of contribution in cash and in kind must be applied uniformly in all Member States. 'The interpretation of the concepts in question may not be left to the discretion of the Member States but must be a Community definition: otherwise the Second Directive would be incapable of ensuring even a minimal degree of harmonization (in so far as it would vary from one State to another) and in any event even the 'minimum equivalent protection' referred to in the second recital to the directive would not be guaranteed'.[283] Further, the Advocate General believed that the rules on contributions in kind should not apply to the contribution of a claim against the company.[284] Due to the much broader definition of contribution in cash under French and English law, encompassing the contribution of a claim against the company, the issues tackled by the concept of disguised contribution in kind under German law do not seem to arise—at least not with the same pertinence—in these jurisdictions.

The consequences of a disguised contribution in kind were very harsh and, for that reason, were fiercely criticized in parts of the literature.[285] The legislature finally intervened.[286] A disguised contribution in kind is illegal and does not discharge the subscriber from his obligation to make a contribution in cash. The Registrar has to reject registration if he realizes that what is attempted amounts to a disguised contribution in kind.[287] However, the contract and conveyance that transfer the contribution in kind to the company are valid. The subscriber's continuing cash obligation will be discharged to the amount of the value of the asset so contributed. The burden of proof for the value of the contribution in kind is on the subscriber. He will be liable only for the difference between subscription price and value of the contribution in kind. If, however, the shareholder's transaction falls within the ambit of AktG, §52 (implementing Article 52 of Directive 2017/1132) the requirements of this provision must be complied with.[288] A disguised contribution in kind may be 'cured' if after registration the articles of association are amended accordingly and the contribution's value is duly verified externally. Since contract and transfer regarding the contribution in kind are valid no new transfer is required. The initial contribution in cash is simply requalified as a contribution in kind and the normal statutory requirements must be adhered to.[289]

[283] AG Tesauro, opinion in Case C-83/91 *Meilicke* (n 108) para 13. As we have seen, today the general perception seems to be that the Second Directive allows Member States to introduce or maintain stricter standards in line with the Directive's rationale of creditor or minority shareholder protection as long as these standards are compatible with freedom of establishment; Case C-338/06 *Commission v Spain* (n 108).

[284] AG Tesauro, opinion in Case C-83/91 *Meilicke* (n 108) para 15.

[285] Schmidt (n 221) 889. The shareholder's initial cash contribution was ineffective since it was recharacterized as a contribution in kind. The shareholder could claim repayment pursuant to the principles of unjust enrichment, but would be an ordinary creditor in the company's insolvency. The contribution in kind was invalid since it did not meet the statutory requirements. The shareholder was still liable to make a contribution in cash, but was not allowed to invoke as a defence that the contribution in kind was adequate consideration for the subscribed shares and, accordingly, that the company had not suffered any financial loss. The contract pursuant to which the shareholder made the contribution in kind and the transfer of property were both invalid; Pentz in *Münchner Kommentar zum Aktiengesetz* (4th edn, CH Beck 2016) §27 para 106. Accordingly, the shareholder could reclaim the assets that he transferred as contribution in kind relying on principles of unjust enrichment and property law. In return, the company could reclaim the benefit it conveyed to the shareholder (e.g. the purchase price it has paid for the shareholder's contribution in kind), in accordance with principles of unjust enrichment. As a consequence, the shareholder had to bear the risk of insolvency of the company and could end up paying the cash contribution a second time without being able to recover his initial (invalid) contributions.

[286] AktG, §27(3); GmbHG, §19(4). [287] Hölters (n 237) §27 para 29.

[288] Hölters (n 237) §27 para 41. Thus, a transaction, within two years of incorporation, involving a promoter or a shareholder representing more than 10 per cent of legal capital through which the company acquires assets for a consideration of more than 1/10 of the legal capital requires for its validity registration and a shareholder resolution. Moreover, a report by the management board and external verification of the value of the transferred asset are required similar to contributions in kind upon formation. Where these provisions are not complied with a disguised contribution in kind will not have any discharging effect for the subscriber's ongoing cash obligation.

[289] ibid para 42.

II. United States

Today, state general corporation laws vary widely on the issue of legal capital and consequently also on the issue of payment for shares.[290] The Model Business Corporation Act has eliminated completely any notion of legal capital and par value.[291] By contrast, important states such as New York[292] and Delaware[293] still retain stated capital concepts and par value. All the states, however, that still use the par value concept give corporations the option to issue 'true' no par value shares. These shares, first introduced in New York in 1912, do not have any nominal or par value attributed to them and they do not represent any fixed proportionate interest in the company's capital raised upon issue measured in Dollars (as is the case with the European concept of 'accountable par'); rather, they are simply a fraction of the whole number of shares issued.[294] As such their value is, at least theoretically, directly related to the value of the company and there is no arbitrarily fixed minimum price for which shares must be issued. By contrast, where par value shares are in use, they must not be issued below par.[295] In practice, the difference between par value and no par value shares in respect of the payment for shares and of dividends and distributions is not very significant. This is mainly because par value can be set at a nominal amount of US$1 or 1 cent. In that case it imposes virtually no restrictions on the power of the board or the shareholders to determine the price of the newly issued shares.[296] Where legal capital restrictions on dividends are still in place, a certain portion of the consideration received on an issue of no par value shares must be allocated to stated capital.[297] This amount can be very small. For par value shares, at least the aggregate of par value of the issued shares must be allocated to stated capital.[298] But again, if par value is nominal the difference may only be marginal.

State incorporation laws traditionally distinguish between common shares with full voting rights and an unlimited proportionate right to participate in the company's residual earnings, and preferred shares with preferential but limited rights to the company's cash flows and no voting rights.[299] Modern corporation statutes are extremely flexible and allow corporations to issue a wide variety of classes based on an authorization in their articles of incorporation.[300] Shares' defining features may relate to voting rights, including special, conditional or limited voting rights; dividend rights, including cumulative, non-cumulative and partially cumulative dividends; liquidation rights; redemption rights; and conversion rights.[301] The MBCA does not use the traditional 'common' and 'preferred' terminology anymore since nothing in modern statutes prevents the creation of common shares with preferential rights or preferred shares with voting rights so that the boundaries are inherently fluid.[302] Classes of shares may be further subdivided into different series of shares within a certain class. The various rights of every class and every series generally must be stipulated in the articles of incorporation.[303] Under Delaware law, the rights of a class may also depend on certain facts ascertainable outside the certificate of incorporation as long as the way in which these facts operate is properly set forth in the certificate of incorporation.[304] In general, shares of the same class or series must be treated equally.[305] The MBCA has abandoned this requirement and allows for differential treatment within a class or series as long as this is expressly stipulated in the articles.[306] This is particularly relevant in respect of defensive measures triggered by hostile takeovers.[307]

[290] WM Fletcher, *Cyclopedia of the Law of Corporations* (September 2018 update) §5080.
[291] American Bar Association, *Model Business Corporation Act Annotated* (2005) Official Comment §6.21.
[292] New York Business Corporation Law, §506.
[293] DGCL, §154.
[294] Fletcher (n 290) §5080.60.
[295] e.g. DGCL, §153(a).
[296] Fletcher (n 290) §5080.60.
[297] DGCL, §154.
[298] Fletcher (n 290) §5080.60.
[299] ibid §5086.
[300] e.g. DGCL, §151(a).
[301] Fletcher (n 290) §5086.
[302] American Bar Association (n 291) §6.01.
[303] Fletcher (n 290) §5086.
[304] e.g. DGCL, §151(a).
[305] DGCL, §151(f); Fletcher (n 290) §5086.
[306] MBCA, §6.01(e).
[307] Fletcher (n 290) §5086.

Registered shares may be issued in certificated from or in uncertificated form. In the former case a certificate is issued to the record holder bearing his name; no certificate is issued in the latter case and ownership is recorded merely on the corporate books.[308] Certificated shares are transferred by delivery and endorsement of the certificate.[309] Registration of the transfer on the books of the issuer is necessary to obtain recognition of the transfer by the company.[310] The issuer has a duty to register the transfer if the necessary documentation is duly presented. However, even before registration the transfer is binding between the parties with equitable title passing to the transferee. Prior to registration the transferor remains the nominal owner of the share vis-à-vis the corporation. However, he holds the share on trust for the transferee and is subject to his instructions.[311] Despite the inconvenience of share certificates when it comes to large volume trading, uncertificated shares have not obtained much relevance in practice.[312] What emerged for publicly traded companies is an indirect holding system where investors hold their shares indirectly through a broker or bank custodian, which in turn holds its customers' shares indirectly through a central depository, the Depository Trust Company (DTC), a subsidiary of the Depository Trust & Clearing Corporation (DTCC), which holds the shares in the name of Cede & Co, the name that is registered in the issuer's books as the shareholder of record.[313] Each of the custodians maintains an account with DTC where the respective custodian's shares are held in fungible bulk without any subdivision into separate accounts for the custodian's customers. Only the custodian's records indicate how many shares are held in which account and on behalf of which customer. Smaller banks and brokers that take custody of their customers' assets will deposit them with larger specialized custodians so that there can be three or four levels of intermediation from investor to issuer.[314] Article 8 UCC (and its implementation in the various states) provides a system of proprietary interests for this indirect holding system. The beneficial owner of the shares held in a custodial account with an intermediary is considered the holder of a 'securities entitlement' of a 'financial asset'. A customer becomes an entitlement holder as soon as the intermediary makes a book entry to the effect that the customer has bought shares.[315]

Subscription for the shares of a corporation is a contract by which a person, the subscriber, agrees to take a certain number of shares of a corporation and paying, or promising to pay, for them.[316] The MBCA distinguishes between pre-incorporation and post-incorporation subscriptions, with the former being a revocable offer rather than a binding contract, as the corporation is not yet in existence.[317] The latter is then simply a contract between the corporation and an investor by which the corporation agrees to issue shares for a stated consideration and the investor agrees to buy the shares for that consideration.[318] A subscription can only relate to an original issue of shares. Even in that case, however, the contract may be a purchase of shares (from the corporation) rather than a subscription. Whether it is one or the other depends on the interpretation of the respective document. This may have consequences in practice. For instance, as soon as a subscription is made it ordinarily confers the rights and liabilities of a shareholder (at least if the company is already in existence); whereas a purchaser will become a shareholder only upon the delivery of the share certificate and registration of the transfer in the books of the corporation.[319] Unless the applicable state corporation law provides otherwise, a subscription agreement does not have to be in any particular form.[320] Under Delaware law, the subscription agreement must be in writing

[308] ibid §5089; DGCL, §158. [309] Fletcher (n 290) §5482.
[310] ibid §5500. [311] ibid §5498. [312] ibid §5089. [313] ibid §5090.
[314] M Kahan and E Rock, 'The Hanging Chads of Corporate Voting' (2008) 96 Georgetown Law Journal 1227, 1237–40.
[315] ibid 1241–2.
[316] Fletcher (n 290) §1363.
[317] American Bar Association (n 291) §6.20. Under MBCA, §6.20, the offer is irrevocable for 6 months; cf also DGCL, §165.
[318] American Bar Association (n 291) §6.20. [319] Fletcher (n 290) §1372. [320] ibid §1465.

and signed by the subscriber.[321] The issue of shares is complete when share certificates have been issued and the subscriber is registered in the books of the corporation. However, the shares may be issued and outstanding even before then as soon as the corporation accepts the subscriber's consideration for the shares.[322]

Ordinarily, issuers will enlist the services of brokerage firms or investment banks to sell the shares to the public on behalf of the issuer. Whereas under a subscription agreement the subscriber's obligation is absolute, in an underwriting agreement the underwriter merely agrees to take on those shares that cannot be sold to the public.[323]

1. Consideration for shares

Under modern corporation statutes following MBCA and Delaware, shares may be issued for consideration 'consisting of cash, any tangible or intangible property or any benefit to the corporation, or any combination thereof'.[324] This includes services performed or services to be performed as well as promissory notes.[325] The underlying rationale here is that contracts for future services and promissory notes often have value that is as real as the value of tangible property. Moreover, a reduction of liability of the company or a release of a claim can constitute valid consideration. Only the business judgment of the directors determines what kind of property may be accepted as consideration for the issuance of shares.[326]

Par value shares may only be issued for a consideration of not less than par value.[327] Where par value is only nominal this requirement will be of very limited significance. Moreover, it only applies on an original issue. Where par value shares have been repurchased by the corporation and held as treasury shares they may be subsequently disposed of for such consideration as fixed by the board of directors from time to time. No-par value shares may be issued for such consideration as may be determined by the board of directors, unless this power is reserved to the shareholders.[328] A premium in excess of par is, of course, lawful and will constitute capital surplus, which may be available for the payment of dividends.[329]

The valuation of consideration to be received in exchange for shares is, in principle, a matter for the board of directors.[330] In case of par value shares the board must fix the value of non-cash considerations in dollars. In any case the board of directors determines the adequacy of consideration. This does not necessarily require an explicit and formal decision; rather adequacy may be inferred from the issue of shares for certain consideration.[331] In the absence of actual fraud or bad faith, the judgment of the board of directors will be conclusive in the sense that shares will be deemed to be fully paid and non-assessable upon receipt by the corporation of such consideration and the shares are deemed to be validly issued.[332] These rules protect both the directors, exercising their proper business judgment when determining the value of consideration, and the shareholders who receive the respective shares in exchange. In the absence of bad faith or fraud, the directors will not be liable for any overvaluation on their part, nor will the shareholders who contributed the overvalued asset.[333]

Moreover, in general, payment of consideration for shares issued at the time of incorporation, or within any particular time thereafter, is neither a necessary prerequisite for becoming a shareholder,[334] nor for corporate existence. A corporation may come into existence

[321] DGCL, §166. [322] Fletcher (n 290) §5126. [323] ibid §223.

[324] MBCA, §6.21(b); DGCL, §152.

[325] Older statutes may still prohibit payment for the issuance of shares in the form of future services or promissory notes. Fletcher (n 290) §5181.10.

[326] American Bar Association (n 291) §6.21. [327] DGCL, §153(a).

[328] Fletcher (n 290) §5181.11. [329] ibid §5183.

[330] MBCA, §6.21(c); DGCL, §152. [331] Fletcher (n 290) §5214.

[332] MBCA, §6.21(c); DGCL, §152. [333] Fletcher (n 290) §5214.

[334] The corporation may, however, be prevented from issuing and delivering share certificates for shares not fully paid: ibid §5182.

and start trading upon filing of the articles of incorporation or upon issuance of a certificate of incorporation, and thus without having received any consideration for shares at all. Moreover, shareholders may ratify the issuance of shares without consideration.[335]

2. *Protection mechanisms*

Creditor protection in the context of payment for shares is of little significance. Where the corporation issued par value shares in exchange for consideration less than par, the shareholder who received the shares may still be held liable for the difference between par value of the shares received and the value of the property contributed.[336] The basis for imposing liability is the notion of misrepresentation of the corporation's financial situation vis-à-vis its creditors. In case of par value shares, proof of reliance on an actual misrepresentation is not required.[337] However, liability will not be imposed if the valuation was made in good faith and without fraud. Shares may be issued without par value or with only nominal par value. In these cases, creditors may still have a common law action for fraud or deceit against directors and possibly also the contributing shareholder if the contribution was knowingly overvalued and appears with inflated value on the corporation's books. However, a creditor will not only have to prove actual fraud but also reliance on the corporation's inflated balance sheet. In practice creditors will be more interested in future cash flows of a company rather than the value with which certain assets appear on the balance sheet. Consequently, the reliance requirement will be very difficult to establish in court.[338]

As recognized by MBCA, the issue of payment for shares is primarily a matter of concern for shareholders whose interest may be diluted if shares are issued for overvalued assets.[339] Where consideration was overvalued, (dissenting) shareholders may bring a derivative action against the directors involved. However, such an action can be successful only if the overvaluation was fraudulent. In that case, an action in fraud may also lie against the contributing shareholder.[340] In the absence of fraud, however, contributing shareholder and directors will be protected by the statutory provisions on the conclusiveness of the directors' evaluation and the general business judgment rule.[341] Given the procedural hurdles of a derivative action, this seems a rather difficult remedy for a shareholder to pursue.

Therefore, the protection of (minority) shareholders against dilution of their interest is largely achieved through state and federal securities laws.[342] Offering securities to the public requires registration under the Securities Act 1933. 'Where common equity is being registered for which there is no established public trading market or where there is a material disparity between the offering price of the common equity being registered and the market price of outstanding shares of the same class' the various factors considered in determining the offering price must be disclosed in the registration statement.[343] Moreover, 'where common equity securities are being registered and there is substantial disparity between the public offering price and the effective cash cost to officers, directors, promoters and affiliated persons of common equity acquired by them in transactions during the past five years' a comparison of the public contribution under the proposed public offering and the effective cash contribution of such persons must be included in the registration statement.[344] These disclosure requirements allow investors to protect themselves. In addition, claims for securities fraud under Section 10(b) of the Securities Exchange Act of 1934 and Rule 10b-5 may be brought on the basis that securities have been sold for inadequate consideration.[345]

335 ibid. 336 ibid §5232. 337 Klein, Coffee, and Partnoy (n 25) 227–8. 338 ibid 228–9.
339 American Bar Association (n 291) §6.21. 340 Klein, Coffee, and Partnoy (n 25) 229.
341 ibid 227.
342 A Engert, 'Life without Legal Capital: Lessons from American Law' in M Lutter (ed), *Legal Capital in Europe* (de Gruyter Recht 2006) 646, 660; Fletcher (n 290) §5207.10.
343 Regulation S-K, 17 CFR §229.505. 344 Regulation S-K, 17 CFR §229.506.
345 Fletcher (n 290) §5207.10.

***Bailes v. Colonial Press, Inc.*, 444 F.2d 1241 C.A.Ala. 1971.**

Rives, Circuit Judge:

'...

The complaint seeks to recover damages under Section 10(b) of [the Securities Exchange Act of 1934], 15 U.S.C.A. 78j(b),[346] and S.E.C. Rule 10b-5, 17 C.F.R. 240, 10b-5.[347]

I. Sufficiency of Claim

According to the complaint as amended, the Bankrupt acquired by stock issue the assets and liabilities of Colonial Press, Inc., an Alabama corporation which published and sold books- principally textbooks to the State of Alabama. Its manager Twitty bought all of its stock in February 1963 for $6,000.00. A year later on February 6, 1964, Twitty and some of the other defendants caused American Southern, the bankrupt, to be incorporated in Alabama. The certificate of incorporation reflected that the total authorized stock of American Southern was $1,000,000.00, divided into a million shares of the par value of $1.00 each. It began business with $250,000.00 capital stock fully paid and nonassessable.[348] The certificate of incorporation represented Colonial Press, Inc., as having subscribed and paid for in cash or its equivalent 179,500 shares. On or about February 6, 1964, the date of American Southern's incorporation, the defendants caused it to issue to Colonial Press a total of 412,000 shares for a transfer to it of the assets and liabilities of Colonial Press represented to have a net worth of $412,000.00, 'when in truth and in fact the said Colonial Press was then insolvent and had an excess of liabilities over assets so transferred of $11,942.75'.

...

It is settled in this Circuit that, by the issuance of stock to Colonial Press, American Southern became a 'seller' of securities for purposes of the Securities Act ... and that, therefore, it has standing to seek redress for violations of those laws ...

There is sufficiently alleged a claim under Rule 10b-5(3), which prohibits 'any act, practice or course of business which operates or would operate as a fraud or deceit upon any person'. Fairly read, the amended complaint claims that American Southern's officers, directors and shareholders caused the corporation to engage in acts which would operate as a fraud or deceit upon others, even though at the time American Southern engaged in the proscribed acts all persons then interested in the corporation had knowledge. Paragraph 8 of the amended complaint may fairly be construed to allege a continuing scheme, of which the 1964 transaction was but the beginning, and which from its inception was intended to and in fact did operate in futuro to deceive and damage various persons who predictably would rely upon the bona fides of the issuance of stock to Colonial Press.

Paragraph 8 alleges that the scheme resulted in damage to, among others, 'persons contracting and dealing with AMERICAN SOUTHERN (including authors and other creditors)'. In dealing with American Southern after the 1964 transaction, such persons would be justified in believing that it began business with a net worth which included the $412,000.00 it was represented to have received from Colonial Press. It could be anticipated that, in reliance on these misrepresentations, some of these persons would extend credit in one form or another to American Southern which they might well have refrained from extending had they known the true state of the corporation's finances. The corporation was thereby exposed to the risk that it would

[346] 'It shall be unlawful for any person, directly or indirectly, by the use of any means or instrumentality of interstate commerce or of the mails, or of any facility of any national securities exchange- (b) To use or employ, in connection with the purchase or sale of any security registered on a national securities exchange or any security not so registered, any manipulative or deceptive device or contrivance in contravention of such rules and regulations as the Commission may prescribe as necessary or appropriate in the public interest or for the protection of investors' [fn in the original].

[347] 'It shall be unlawful for any person, directly or indirectly, by the use of any means or instrumentality of interstate commerce, or of the mails, or of any facility of any national securities exchange, (a) to employ any device, scheme, or artifice to defraud, (b) to make any untrue statement of a material fact or to omit to state a material fact necessary in order to make the statements made, in the light of the circumstances under which they were made, not misleading, or (c) to engage in any act, practice, or course of business which operates or would operate as a fraud or deceit upon any person, in connection with the purchase or sale of any security' [fn in the original].

[348] The statute required that at least twenty per cent of the stock be subscribed for before incorporation [fn in the original].

be caused to assume liabilities to creditors which, but for the misrepresentations, it would not have assumed, and which ultimately it would be unable to satisfy due to the absence of the $412,000.00 it was represented to, but did not, possess.

Paragraph 8 contains similar allegations with respect to subsequent shareholders, that is, that the corporation was caused to issue shares to the general public. Thus the corporation was thereby exposed to the risk that this class of persons, too, would assert claims against it.

American Southern cannot successfully maintain a 10b-5 action if proscribed acts it was caused to do did not operate as a fraud or deceit upon itself or upon others- subsequent creditors, subsequent public shareholders or subsequent holders of claims for taxes. The gravamen of a 10b-5 cause of action is deception, and if neither the corporation nor 'any (other) person', was deceived or defrauded, the corporation cannot proceed under this statutory federal remedy.

Mindful of the 'accepted rule that a complaint should not be dismissed for failure to state a claim unless it appears beyond doubt that the plaintiff can prove no set of facts in support of his claim which would entitle him to relief' ... we hold that the amended complaint stated a claim for relief under Section 10(b) of the Securities Exchange Act of 1934 and under S.E.A. Rule 10b-5.

...

Reversed and remanded'.

Questions and comments:

1. The action was brought by the trustee in bankruptcy of American Southern against the latter's promoters. According to the court, the corporation may have been damaged in at least two ways: '(1) by depriving it of the assets it would have possessed if it had received par value for the stock issued to Colonial Press; and (2) by exposing it to the risk of liability for taxes and of liabilities to persons extending credit to the corporation or purchasing stock of the corporation in reliance on misrepresentations flowing from the scheme to defraud'.
2. The court also recognized that other persons dealing with American Southern could have brought independent actions based on the Securities Exchange Act or other causes of action. However, this did not preclude American Southern or its trustee to sue in its own right. In fact, other constituencies may indirectly benefit therefrom, thus alleviating the fraud committed by the promoters.
3. The remedy under securities law protects both future creditors and future shareholders of the corporation; current shareholders only to the extent that they had no part in the scheme. What constituencies remain unprotected?
4. From a comparative perspective, Germany and the United States seem to occupy two opposite ends of a spectrum that ranges from extremely detailed substantive regulation of the payment for shares to extremely flexible regulation relying mainly on disclosure. Compare both systems. Would it be correct to say that Germany is mainly based on ex ante protection and US law on ex post remedies? Despite all the differences, are there any commonalities? What, do you think, accounts for the differences?

C. Capital Maintenance

One of the key functions of the legal capital concept from a corporate finance perspective is ensuring that the creditors have preferential access to the company's assets by limiting the company's power to pay dividends and make distributions to the shareholders. A multitude of legal issues arises in this context. There is, first, the question as to which company body has authority to decide whether a dividend is to be paid. Authority to declare a dividend is an important corporate governance tool. This question is not addressed by Directive (EU) 2017/1132 and is, therefore, to be determined by national law. Secondly, there are the statutory restrictions on the payment of dividends and distributions, and the consequences of unlawful distributions.

For public companies, the core concepts are prescribed by Directive (EU) 2017/1132. The repurchase by the company of its own shares is in economic terms similar to a distribution of assets to shareholders. And it could be argued that the same is true where the company's assets are used to enable a third party to acquire shares in the company (financial assistance). Financial assistance is particularly relevant in the context of leveraged buy-outs (LBOs), where the acquisition of control of a company is financed with the company's own assets as collateral. Directive (EU) 2017/1132 deals with both issues.

I. European jurisdictions

Article 56 of Directive (EU) 2017/1132 imposes statutory restrictions on distributions to the shareholders, including the payment of dividends. Article 56(1) delineates the amounts that may be distributed by reference to the company's balance sheet. Accordingly, distributions are unlawful if the net assets as set out in the company's annual accounts are, or due to the distribution would become, less than the amount of the subscribed capital plus those reserves that are mandatory under national law or the articles of association. By contrast, Article 56(3) defines the amount that can be distributed by reference to the profit and loss account: only the profits at the end of the financial year plus any profits brought forward and sums drawn from reserves available for that purpose, less any losses brought forward and sums placed to reserves in accordance with national law and the articles of association, can be lawfully are distributed. As a consequence, any premium (paid in surplus) cannot be used for making distributions to shareholders. Article 56(5) allows Member States to sanction the payment of interim dividends on the basis of interim accounts. The distributable amount follows from Article 56(3). According to Article 57, unlawful distributions must be returned by the shareholders who received them, provided the company can show that the respective shareholder knew that the distribution was made in breach of statutory restrictions or could not have been unaware thereof.

Whereas a company cannot subscribe for its own shares,[349] it may, subject to certain conditions, acquire its own shares, either directly or via an intermediary. Prior to Directive 2006/68/EC, Member States could allow a company to acquire its own shares subject to the following preconditions: (i) an authorization by the general meeting, setting out the terms and conditions of such acquisition, including the maximum number of shares, the duration of the period for which authorization has been given (maximum five years) and the maximum and minimum consideration; (ii) an absolute cap of shares that may be acquired of 10 per cent of the subscribed capital; (iii) adherence to the restrictions on distributions set out in Article 56(1); and (iv) the acquired shares being fully paid-up. Under the current regime the Member States have more leeway. Only requirements (i), (iii), and (iv) remain as mandatory restrictions. Member States are free to retain the 10 per cent limit.[350] Also, the Member States can impose further conditions: that terms and conditions of an acquisition of own shares must be set out in the articles of association; that the company must comply with reporting and notification requirements; that the acquired shares must be cancelled; and that creditors' claims must not be prejudiced. Member States may derogate from the requirement of authorization by general meeting where the acquisition is necessary to prevent serious and imminent harm to the company; or in order to distribute the shares to the company's employees. Article 61 allows Member States to introduce further exceptions in specific circumstances.[351] As long as the shares are held by the company, voting rights are suspended. The Directive's legal capital regime, including the restrictions on the company to own its own shares, concerns only the legal relationships established between the company and its

[349] Article 59. [350] Article 60.

[351] The most significant exceptions are contained in Art 61(1)(a) relating to an acquisition of own shares in the course of a reduction of capital, and, more importantly, in the case of redeemable shares. The latter exception was inserted into the Directive on the insistence of the UK. Article 82 allows Member States to authorize companies to issue redeemable shares subject to a number of preconditions.

shareholders, which derive from the memorandum and articles of association. These provisions are of relevance only to the internal relations within the company. Consequently, the Directive does not preclude a national liability regime according to which a company issuing shares in breach of capital markets law is obliged to repay to the purchaser a sum equivalent to the purchase price of the shares and to redeem the shares. In that case, the source of the liability is not the internal relationship on the basis of the memorandum and articles; rather it is the share purchase contract and the company's wrongful conduct. This is also the reason why the principle of equal treatment of shareholders does not apply.[352]

On insistence of the United Kingdom, the Second Company Law Directive as initially enacted contained a comprehensive prohibition of financial assistance granted by the company in the form of advancing funds, making loans or providing security to a third party for buying the company's shares. Financial assistance can be seen as in economic terms similar to a distribution to shareholders—out of its own pocket the company pays a third party to buy its shares from existing shareholders, thus indirectly distributing funds to shareholders, which is relevant from a capital maintenance perspective. Directive 2006/68/EC relaxed the initial prohibition and Article 64 contains a procedure whereby the management has to duly inform the general meeting, which in turn needs to give its prior consent to the transaction. The transaction takes place under the responsibility of the administrative or management board and is subject to being in accordance with 'fair market conditions'. The board draws up a report, containing a detailed analysis of the terms and conditions of the transaction, including its reasons and risks, the solvency of the company, and the price at which the third party is to acquire the shares. The report must be duly published in accordance with Article 16. On the basis of this report, the general meeting decides with a two-thirds majority of the capital represented at the meeting. Member States may provide for a simple majority when at least half the subscribed capital is represented. The granting of financial assistance is also subject to the restrictions of Article 56(1) and must not reduce the net assets of the company below the limit set out in this provision.[353]

1. *Declaring a dividend*

Under both French and German law, the balance sheet, the profit and loss account and an explanatory annex together form a unit that constitutes the annual accounts.[354] Parent companies are required to produce consolidated accounts.[355] For parent companies whose securities are admitted to trading on a regulated market the consolidated accounts must be in accordance with IFRS (international financial reporting standards).[356] Other parent companies can opt into IFRS, instead of using the accounting rules under the HGB[357] or the *Code de commerce*. However, other (than parent) companies are not allowed to prepare their accounts in accordance with IFRS, irrespective of whether their securities are traded on a regulated market or not.[358] On the basis of the IAS Regulation, in the UK consolidated accounts of parent companies whose shares are admitted to trading on a regulated market of any Member State must also be prepared in accordance with IFRS.[359] However, individual accounts of all companies and consolidated accounts of other parent companies

[352] Shareholders suffering loss as a result of the company's wrongful conduct are not in the same position as those shareholders who were not affected by the wrongful conduct; Case C-174/12 *Hirmann v Immofinanz AG* ECLI:EU:C:2013:856 paras 22–45.

[353] Transactions carried out by financial institutions in the normal course of business are exempt, as are transactions with a view to effectuating an employee share scheme, provided that the limits of Art 56(1) are adhered to.

[354] HGB, §264(1); Com Art L123-12.

[355] HGB, §290; Com Art L233-16.

[356] Regulation (EC) No 1606/2002 of the European Parliament and of the Council of 19 July 2002 on the application of international accounting standards, OJ 11.9.2002 L243/1, Art 4; HGB, §315a(1) and (2).

[357] HGB, §315a(3).

[358] Germain and Magnier (n 68) para 2449.

[359] Companies Act 2006, s 403(1); Regulation (EC) No 1606/2002 of the European Parliament and of the Council of 19 July 2002 on the application of international accounting standards, (OJ L243, 11.9.2002, 1) Art 4.

may be prepared as either 'Companies Act accounts' or 'IAS accounts'.[360] The former consist of balance sheet and profit-and-loss account;[361] the latter require in addition to the balance sheet the compilation of cash flow and income statements instead of profit and loss account.[362] Certain relaxations apply for small companies[363] and (to a lesser extent) for medium-sized companies.[364]

The annual accounts are compiled by the management board[365] or board of directors,[366] and are to be duly audited.[367] Thereafter, the governance arrangements differ. Under German law, the management board has to submit the annual accounts together with the annual report and the audit report, as well as a suggestion how the balance sheet profit may be applied, to the supervisory board for examination. They in turn have to report to the general meeting of shareholders.[368] Where the supervisory board accepts the annual accounts they are deemed verified and binding on the general meeting. Where the supervisory board does not accept the annual accounts, or management board and supervisory board have decided to refer the accounts to the general meeting it is upon the general meeting to verify the annual accounts.[369] Thus, unless management board and supervisory board disagree or leave it to the general meeting, the latter is normally not involved in the verification of the annual accounts.[370] By contrast, in France the annual accounts together with the directors' report are always subject to approval by the general meeting. Within the month following the general meeting the accounts must be registered with the commercial court, indicating whether the general meeting approved them or not.[371] Under English law, the accounts are filed with the Registrar of Companies[372] and circulated among members and debenture-holders.[373] In respect of public companies, the accounts must be laid before a general meeting of shareholders.[374] A shareholder resolution approving the accounts is, however, not required; shareholders shall merely have an opportunity to discuss them.[375]

Where, under French and German law, the annual accounts have been approved and the existence of a distributable profit verified, the general meeting of shareholders decides, by simple majority, on the application of the balance sheet profit.[376] Under French law, the terms of payment of the dividend are determined by the general meeting; if it fails to do so, the decision on the terms rests with the board of directors or management board, as the case may be. However, the dividend must be paid within nine months of the end of the financial year, subject to extension by court order.[377] Under German law, it is not necessarily the entire annual profit that is available for distribution. In addition to amounts that must be transferred to reserves,[378] management board and supervisory board may decide to transfer up to

[360] Companies Act 2006, ss 395(1), 403(2).
[361] Companies Act 2006, ss 396(1), 404(1).
[362] Davies and Worthington (n 124) para 21-18.
[363] Companies Act 2006, ss 381–385. A company is a small company if it satisfies at least two of the following conditions within a year: (i) turnover of not more than £10.2 million; (ii) balance sheet total of not more than £5.1 million; (iii) not more than 50 employees.
[364] ibid s 465(3). A company is of medium size if it satisfies at least two of the following conditions within a year: (i) turnover of not more than £36 million; (ii) balance sheet total of not more than £18 million; (iii) not more than 250 employees.
[365] AktG, §170(1). In France, depending on the company's board structure, the annual accounts are to be prepared by the management board or the board of directors and submitted to the auditors, and the supervisory board in case of a two-tier board structure; Com Arts L232-1, L232-3, L232-4.
[366] In the UK, the accounts are to be produced annually by the directors, approved by the board of directors and signed on behalf of the board by a director of the company; Companies Act 2006, ss 394, 399(2), 414.
[367] Small companies may be exempt from the audit requirement; Companies Act 2006, s 475.
[368] AktG, §§170, 171.
[369] ibid §§172, 173.
[370] The annual accounts may be void pursuant to AktG, §256 if they suffer from substantial defects. Where the annual accounts have been approved by the general meeting, they may be avoided pursuant to AktG, §257. In addition, there is the possibility of appointing special auditors pursuant to AktG, §§258–261a.
[371] Com Arts L232-22, L232-23.
[372] Companies Act 2006, s 441 and the provisions referred to therein.
[373] ibid s 423.
[374] ibid s 437.
[375] Davies and Worthington (n 124) para 21-42.
[376] AktG, §174; Com Art L232-12.
[377] Com Art L232-13.
[378] See below.

one half of the annual profits to reserve accounts in order to secure internal financing out of retained earnings.[379] This decision by management board and supervisory board is binding on the general meeting. The rule seeks to strengthen the interests of the company to have sufficient funds at its disposal as against the shareholders' interests in obtaining a cash return on their investment. The general meeting may decide to transfer further amounts to reserve accounts or to carry forward such amounts as profits.[380] Under English law, the authority to declare a dividend is usually determined in the articles of association. Where the articles are silent on this issue the decision would, in accordance with general principles, rest with the shareholders alone. However, exclusive authority to declare a dividend may be conferred on the directors in the articles; if done explicitly and unambiguously.[381] The Model Articles for both private and public companies limited by shares require both a recommendation by the directors and an ordinary resolution of shareholders declaring a dividend that must not exceed the amount recommended by the directors.[382] In general, shareholders do not have an enforceable right of a dividend being paid even if the company has accumulated sufficient distributable profits.

Under German law, subject to statute, the company's articles and the resolution of the general meeting on the application of the annual profit, the shareholders have a right to be paid a dividend in proportion to their shareholding.[383] In this respect, legal doctrine normally distinguishes the right inherent in the share to participate in the profits, and the enforceable claim to payment of a concrete dividend. The latter comes into existence only with the shareholders' resolution declaring a dividend. This claim can be transferred separately and independently of the share.[384] Similarly under French law: with the decision to pay a dividend by the general meeting and the determination of the amount to be paid, every shareholder acquires a corresponding claim against the company; every shareholder becomes a creditor in respect of the dividend payment. Prior to the decision to pay a dividend the shareholders as a group merely hold a global and unspecified claim against the company.[385]

2. *Restrictions on dividends and distributions*

For public companies, Article 56(1) and (3) of Directive (EU) 2017/1132 predetermine the restrictions on dividends and distributions. The regulatory techniques deployed in our three European jurisdictions to achieve the aim of these provisions differ.

French Commercial Code

Article L. 232-11[386]

The distributable profit consists of the profit for the financial period plus any retained earnings, less the losses brought forward and the sums to be placed in reserve pursuant to the law or the articles of association.

The general meeting may, moreover, decide to distribute sums taken from the reserves available for this purpose. In this case, the decision expressly indicates the reserve headings from

[379] The articles may provide that more than half of the profits can be retained in this way; however only as long as the reserve accounts do not exceed half of the legal capital; AktG, §58(2).

[380] AktG, §58(3). However, where the resulting dividend is less than 4% of legal capital and the transfer is not necessary in order to ensure the financial soundness of the company, the resolution may be challenged by shareholders whose shares amount to 5% of the legal capital or represent at least €500,000; AktG, §254.

[381] Davies and Worthington (n 124) para 12-1.

[382] Model Articles Private Companies, Art 30; Model Articles Public Companies, Art 70. The UK government has identified the practice of paying interim dividends that do not require a shareholder vote as a potential problem to be further investigated and if necessary tackled by new legislation; Department for Business, Energy & Industrial Strategy (n 17) para 1.53.

[383] AktG, §58(4).

[384] Windbichler (n 126) 397 (§30 para 19).

[385] Germain and Magnier (n 68) para 2488.

[386] https://www.legifrance.gouv.fr/Traductions/en-English/Legifrance-translations. The following translation from the German Stock Corporation Act is our own.

which the distribution is made. The dividends are nevertheless to be taken primarily from the distributable profit for the period.

Unless a capital reduction is taking place, no distribution can be made to the shareholders when the share capital is, or would thereby become, lower than the amount of the capital plus the reserves which the law or the articles of association require in order for a distribution to take place.

A surplus emanating from a reevaluation of assets is not distributable. It may be wholly or partly incorporated into the capital.

UK Companies Act 2006

Section 830: Distributions to be made only out of profits available for the purpose

(1) A company may only make a distribution out of profits available for the purpose.
(2) A company's profits available for distribution are its accumulated, realised profits, so far as not previously utilised by distribution or capitalisation, less its accumulated, realised losses, so far as not previously written off in a reduction or reorganisation of capital duly made.
(3) …

Section 831: Net asset restriction on distributions by public companies

(1) A public company may only make a distribution—
  (a) if the amount of its net assets is not less than the aggregate of its called-up share capital and undistributable reserves, and
  (b) if, and to the extent that, the distribution does not reduce the amount of those assets to less than that aggregate.
(2) For this purpose a company's "net assets" means the aggregate of the company's assets less the aggregate of its liabilities.
(3) …
(4) A company's undistributable reserves are—
  (a) its share premium account;
  (b) its capital redemption reserve;
  (c) the amount by which its accumulated, unrealised profits (so far as not previously utilised by capitalisation) exceed its accumulated, unrealised losses (so far as not previously written off in a reduction or reorganisation of capital duly made);
  (d) any other reserve that the company is prohibited from distributing—
    (i) by any enactment (other than one contained in this Part), or
    (ii) by its articles. The reference in paragraph (c) to capitalisation does not include a transfer of profits of the company to its capital redemption reserve.
(5) A public company must not include any uncalled share capital as an asset in any accounts relevant for purposes of this section.
(6) …

German Stock Corporation Act

§ 57 – No return of contributions, no interest payments

(1) Contributions must not be returned to the shareholders. The payment of the purchase price in the course of a permitted repurchase by the company of its own shares does not amount to a return of contributions. Sentence 1 does not apply for transfers in the course of a contract for control or transfer of profits (§ 291) or transfers which are covered by a claim against the shareholder for the full value or return of the asset. Sentence 1 further does not apply to the repayment of loans granted by a shareholder and payments on debts emanating from transactions that are economically equivalent to such shareholder loans.
(2) Interest payments to shareholders may not be promised nor actually paid.
(3) Prior to the liquidation of the company, only the balance sheet profit may be distributed to the shareholders.

French law closely tracks the Directive's structure. In accordance with Article 56(3), Com, article L232-11(1) provides that the distributable profit consists of the profits made during the financial year, less the losses carried forward, plus the sums placed into reserves pursuant to the law or the articles of association. The 'profits (or losses) made during the financial year' is the difference between the sum of the active side of the balance sheet and the sum of the passive side of the balance sheet.[387] Com, article L232-11(4) makes it clear that profits emanating from a revaluation of assets (unrealized profits) may not be utilized for dividend payments. Com, article L232-11(3) corresponds to Article 56(1). Subject to a capital reduction, no distribution may be made to the shareholders when the net equity (*capitaux propres*) is, or would thereby become, lower than the amount of the share capital plus those reserves that are non-distributable either pursuant to the law or to the articles of association. The only non-distributable reserve by law is the legal reserve pursuant to Com, article L232-10: 5 per cent of the annual profits, less any previous losses, must be allocated to the legal reserve until it reaches an amount equal to 10 per cent of the legal capital (or a higher amount if the articles of association so provide). By contrast, the share premium account is not a non-distributable reserve and a share premium, may, thus, be distributed to shareholders. This is a marked difference compared with German and UK law (below). The articles of association may prescribe further reserves that are unavailable for the purposes of distribution.[388] Moreover, by ordinary resolution the general meeting may decide not to use distributable profits for the payment of a dividend but to create so called free reserves in order to prepare the company for future risks or to expand the business or for other purposes. When free reserves are created it is not required that their purpose is specified in the respective shareholder resolution. Even under normal circumstances, prudent management of large French companies will often require the creation of free reserves.[389] The general meeting may decide to distribute profits accumulated over the years in free reserves. When doing so, it must be indicated from which reserves the respective amounts are to be taken. Moreover, dividends are primarily to be paid out of distributable profits of the financial year, only thereafter may the amounts stored in free reserves be used.[390]

In the UK, section 830 of the Companies Act 2006, applying to both public and private companies, provides that a company may only make a distribution out of profits available for that purpose, that is, out of accumulated, realized profits less its accumulated, realized losses. This reflects the requirements of Article 56(3) of Directive (EU) 2017/1132. Realized profits and losses are to be assessed over the years. In contrast with common law principles, the payment of 'nimble dividends' out of the profits of a single year that are insufficient to set off the losses incurred during previous years is not permitted.[391] Whether profits and losses are 'realised' is to be determined on the basis of applicable accounting principles. It is clear, however, that the appreciation of asset values on the balance sheet amounts to 'realised' profits only where the asset has been sold at market value to a third party; similar to the position under French law, the profit remains unrealized and unavailable for distribution if the asset is merely revalued on the balance sheet.[392] In respect of public companies, section

[387] Germain and Magnier (n 68) para 2461.

[388] The articles can prescribe the percentage to be allocated to these reserves and what they may be used for. When deciding on the payment of a dividend, the general meeting of shareholders has, in principle, no discretion and is bound by the provisions on reserves. However, by way of an extraordinary resolution it may derogate therefrom, thus freeing up amounts for dividend payments. This is because by extraordinary resolution the articles could be amended anyway; see Germain and Magnier (n 68) paras 2469–71.

[389] ibid para 2472. The general meeting is in principle free to transfer any amount of distributable profits to free reserves. There is however a risk that such a policy may interfere with the interests of certain minority shareholders who would prefer the immediate payment of a dividend or a higher dividend. The majority cannot exclude the minority indefinitely from any distribution. Although the general meeting may decide not to pay a dividend at all, such a decision must be justified in the interest of the company. The resolution not to pay a dividend and to allocate the distributable profits to free reserves may be challenged before the courts as an abuse of right (*abuse de droit*) on the part of the majority. However, for such a challenge to be successful it must be demonstrated to the court that the majority decisions was contrary to the interests of the company and designed to benefit the majority at the detriment of the minority; ibid para 2473.

[390] Com Art L232-11(2).

[391] Davies and Worthington (n 124) para 12-3.

[392] ibid.

831 further provides that distributions may only be made to the extent that the amount of the company's net assets are not reduced to less than the company's aggregated share capital and its non-distributable reserves. This corresponds to Article 56(1) of Directive (EU) 2017/1132. Non-distributable reserves are the 'share premium account', the 'capital redemption reserve', the amount by which accumulated unrealized profits exceed accumulated unrealized losses, and any other reserve that is non-distributable by virtue of law or the company's articles.[393] The 'share premium account' obviously contains any premium obtained on the issuance of shares, which, unlike under French law, is thus excluded from distribution. The 'capital redemption reserve' is created when a company repurchases or redeems its shares.[394] It operates to hold the legal capital constant by transferring the amount by which the share capital account (outstanding shares) is reduced to the 'capital redemption reserve'. In addition to incorporating legal capital into the restrictions on dividends, the difference between the general test for all companies (s 830) and the additional test for public companies (s 831) emanates from the third item on the list of non-distributable reserves: 'accumulated unrealised profits minus accumulated unrealised losses'. Since unrealized profits cannot justify payment of dividends in any case, the item becomes important where accumulated unrealized losses exceed the accumulated unrealized profits. Thus, unrealized losses reduce the maximum amount payable as a dividend in case of a public company. By contrast, a private company does not have to take into account its unrealized losses.[395] The UK government has identified the dividend regime as potentially problematic: its complexity and backward-looking approach which places little weight on current profitability and future prospects may provide only limited protection for creditors. Consequently, the government will further explore the case for a comprehensive review of the dividend regime, potentially also considering the merits of the introduction of a solvency based system,[396] which, following Brexit, would at least to some extent de-couple English law from the principles of the EU legal capital regime.

Under German law, AktG, §57(1) provides that in no event may the shareholders' contributions be returned to the shareholders; according to §57(3), dividends and distributions prior to liquidation may only be made out of the annual profits on the basis of the annual accounts. These provisions reinforce the principle that only profits as shown in the balance sheet as the positive difference of net assets and legal capital may be distributed. It follows that a share premium, to be accounted for in the capital surplus account, cannot be distributed as a dividend, similar to English law. However, not all profit is available for distributions (or transfer to reserve accounts by management board and supervisory board, and general meeting). Rather, similar to the situation in France, the company must build a legal reserve into which 5 per cent of the annual profit is to be transferred until the legal reserve and the capital surplus account[397] together amount to at least 10 per cent of the legal capital.[398] Prior to reaching this threshold legal reserve and capital surplus account may only be used to set-off losses if other reserve accounts are not available for that purpose; after reaching the threshold these accounts may also be used for a capital increase out of retained earnings.[399] For GmbHs, pursuant to GmbHG, §30(1), the assets needed to maintain a private company's subscribed capital must not be distributed to the shareholders. Consequently, distributions are not limited to realized profits, as is the case in respect of public companies. To the extent that the company's net assets exceed subscribed capital (as stated in the articles and on the

[393] Companies Act 2006, s 831(4). [394] ibid s 733.
[395] Davies and Worthington (n 124) para 12-4.
[396] Deparment for Business, Energy & Industrial Strategy (n 17) paras 1.46–1.48.
[397] HGB, §272(2). [398] AktG, §150. A higher amount may be stipulated in the articles.
[399] ibid §150(3) and (4).

right-hand-side of the balance sheet), surplus resulting from share premiums and any other sources may be distributed.

3. *Unlawful and disguised distributions*

Open dividends that do not comply with these restrictions and procedures are not very common in practice.[400] Much more relevant are hidden or disguised distributions, that is, transactions between the company and a shareholder that confer some economic benefit on the shareholder that he would not have obtained in a bargain at arm's length. These disguised distributions must be distinguished from normal exchange transactions between company and shareholder.[401] Unlawful disguised distributions out of capital may occur in various forms. In *Re Halt Garage* one of the two shareholder-directors continued to draw remuneration from the company, albeit at a reduced rate, even after she fell ill and ceased working. It was held that the moneys received were not 'genuinely remuneration', but in spite of the label, paid out of capital and thus *ultra vires*. Oliver J relied on the motive of the parties which was 'more important than the label' and also looked 'at the matter objectively' applying the standard of reasonableness.[402] In *Aveling Barford v Perion*, Aveling sold a plot of land to Perion for £350,000 at a time when Aveling was, although not insolvent, certainly not in a position to declare a dividend. Four months later Perion resold the same property for £1.52 million. Both Aveling and Perion were owned and controlled by the same person. Hoffmann J, 'looking at the matter objectively', found that the transaction 'was a sale at a gross undervalue for the purpose of enabling a profit to be realized by an entity controlled and put forward by its sole beneficial shareholder' amounting to a 'dressed-up distribution'. 'It was the fact that it was known and intended to be a sale at an undervalue which made it an unlawful distribution'.[403] Distinguishing disguised distributions out of capital to shareholders from other payments has proved to be difficult. A recurring issue in this respect is whether a transaction is to be assessed objectively, looking only at its effects in terms of a decrease of the company's assets to the detriment of its creditors; or whether subjective elements, knowledge and motives on the part of company and/or recipient shareholder, are to be taken into account.[404] German and English law differ in this respect:

[400] Under French law, the payment of dividends in violation of the restrictions mentioned above (*dividends fictifs*) constitutes a criminal offence on the part of the management involved (chairman of the board, managing director, other board members); Com Art L242-6-1. A dividend is unlawful, or fictitious, if it is not paid out of realized distributable profits. This will obviously be the case where the balance sheet does not report a profit. However, it also constitutes a fictitious dividend if the balance sheet reports a profit that does not actually exist. In its traditional form the offence requires the withdrawal of assets out of legal capital or legal reserves, contrary to the notion that these items are preferentially pledged to the company's creditors. In practice this is often achieved by hiding certain items on the passive side of the balance sheet, by not including compulsory depreciation, or by including items on the active side of the balance sheet representing unrealized profits. It also constitutes a fictitious dividend if the distribution is to be made out of profits that do not exist, and, as a consequence, is really made out of distributable free reserves. The protective ambit of the offence is thus extended so as to encompass shareholders as well (in addition to the creditors). In any case, the offence is committed only where a distribution is actually made. It is insufficient if the general meeting merely decides, on recommendation of the management, to pay a dividend. The latter is, however, covered by the separate offence of accounting fraud and falsification of accounts; Com Art L242-6-2. The offence requires further the establishment of bad faith on the part of the defendant or defendants. In this respect it is sufficient if the defendant knows about the inaccuracies on the balance sheet and the fictitious nature of the dividend; see Germain and Magnier (n 68) paras 2491, 2492. The offence may be punished by up to five years' imprisonment or a fine of up to €375,000. In addition, civil damages may be awarded.

[401] Hölters (n 237) §57 para 7.

[402] *Re Halt Garage* (1964) Ltd [1982] 3 All ER 1016.

[403] *Aveling Barford Ltd v Perion Ltd* [1989] BCLC 626.

[404] E Micheler, 'Disguised Returns of Capital: An Arm's Length Approach' [2010] CLJ 151, in particular 167–75.

Under German law, hidden (disguised) distributions may be characterized by the following two factors:[405] First, the distribution must be made to a shareholder.[406] Secondly, the benefit received by the shareholder and the consideration given to the company must be objectively disproportionate, that is, the company does not receive adequate consideration. Where there is a market price, it will be determinative. Any deviation therefrom must be objectively justified. If a market price cannot be easily ascertained there is to be a 'hypothetical market comparison' where the transaction is to be compared to similar transactions carried out with third parties.[407] The BGH and the prevalent opinion in the literature do not require intent or some other kind of subjective element on the part of the company's management. Thus, the claimant (e.g. the office holder in the company's insolvency) does not need to show that the management board has concluded the transaction because of the other party being a shareholder (*causa societatis*). The objectively determined inadequacy of the consideration received by the company is sufficient.[408] The typical examples are exchange transactions where the company acquires from, or sells to, a shareholder assets or services above, or below, market price.[409] This objective approach may be contrasted with the holistic approach adopted by the Supreme Court of the United Kingdom in *Progress Property Company Limited v Moorgarth Group Limited*:

***Progress Property Company Limited v Moorgarth Group Limited* [2010] UKSC 55**

The appellant company, Progress Property Company Ltd ('PPC'), sold the whole issued share capital of a wholly-owned subsidiary, YMS Properties (No. 1) Ltd ('YMS1') for the price of some £60.000 to another company, Moorgarth Group Ltd ('Moorgarth'). All these companies were indirectly controlled by the same investor, Dr Wiese. For the purposes of the appeal it was assumed that the net assets of YMS1 were worth as much as £4 million. However, Mr Moore, Dr Wiese's 'right hand man' and director of both PPC and Moorgarth, genuinely believed that the sale of the shares in YMS1 was at market value and a genuine arm's length

[405] In respect of private companies, the application of the dividend restriction of GmbHG, §30(1) has three prerequisites: (i) a benefit was granted by the company to a shareholder (or affiliated person) 'causa societatis', that is because of the membership in the company; (2) the result is a depletion of the company's assets; (3) causing or intensifying a state where the company's net assets are less than the subscribed capital; Schmidt (n 221) 1132. The provision also covers hidden/disguised distributions. The consequences of an unlawful distribution are regulated in GmbHG, §31. Unlawful distributions must be paid back to the company. Because GmbHG, §30 refers to the balance sheet, a retransfer in kind is not required; the shareholder may pay the (difference in) value of the received asset in cash. If the shareholder who received the unlawful distribution is incapable of restoring the company's assets to their former glory, the remaining shareholders will be liable pro rata in relation to their shareholdings. This liability for each and every shareholder is limited to the amount of the subscribed capital of the company. In addition, the directors may be liable for damages vis-à-vis the company and also vis-à-vis those shareholders who are liable under GmbHG, §31(3); GmbHG, §§31(6), 43.

[406] Distributions to third parties (non-shareholders) can be hidden distributions if they have been made in the light of the recipient having been or becoming a shareholder of the company; likewise, if the distribution has been made at the shareholder's instigation and has been received by somebody associated with the shareholder or close to him (e.g. a close relative).

[407] Hölters (n 237) §57 para 8.

[408] ibid §57 para 9.

[409] So called 'upstream loans'—where the company grants credit to a shareholder—used to be particularly problematic; Schmidt (n 221) 891. If the interest rate is less than the market rate or if the creditworthiness of the shareholder is questionable, the company would have made an unlawful distribution. However, where the shareholder is financially sound and the interest rate is adequate the transaction would not have diminished the company's assets on a balance sheet basis. Nevertheless, the BGH held that even in that case the exchange of liquid cash for a claim that will be due only later would put the company's creditors in jeopardy and that the transaction amounted to a hidden distribution; BGH NJW 2004, 1111. Since the 2008 reform legislation, an upstream loan is not a hidden distribution if the company obtains a claim that has full value; AktG, §57(1). This is the case if the claim is to be accounted for on the balance sheet with its nominal value and, under accounting rules, is not to be discounted due to financial unsoundness of the shareholder-debtor or a low interest rate; Hölters (n 237) §57 para 18. Similar principles apply for private companies: credit advanced by the company to a shareholder or similar transactions are not subject to the limitations on distributions as long as the claim that the company acquires is enforceable and realizable, that is, has real value, because the shareholder is financially healthy; GmbHG, §30(1). An advance of credit contrary to GmbHG, §30(1) to directors is however prohibited; GmbHG, §43a.

commercial transaction. This was because he erroneously believed that PPC was subject to indemnity liability to the sum of about £4 million from which it was to be released as part of the transaction. This indemnity liability did in fact not exist. PPC's action was dismissed at first instance, a decision upheld by the Court of Appeal. The issue on appeal before the Supreme Court was whether the transaction amounted to an unlawful distribution of capital. The appeal was dismissed.

Lord Walker:

'27 If there were a stark choice between a subjective and an objective approach, the least unsatisfactory choice would be to opt for the latter. But in cases of this sort the court's real task is to inquire into the true purpose and substance of the impugned transaction. That calls for an investigation of all the relevant facts, which sometimes include the state of mind of the human beings who are orchestrating the corporate activity.

28 Sometimes their states of mind are totally irrelevant. A distribution described as a dividend but actually paid out of capital is unlawful, however technical the error and however well-meaning the directors who paid it. The same is true of a payment which is on analysis the equivalent of a dividend, such as the unusual cases (mentioned by Dr Micheler) of In re Walters' Deed of Guarantee [1933] Ch 321 (claim by guarantor of preference dividends) and Barclays Bank plc v British & Commonwealth Holdings plc [1996] 1 BCLC 1 (claim for damages for contractual breach of scheme for redemption of shares). Where there is a challenge to the propriety of a director's remuneration the test is objective (Halt Garage), but probably subject in practice to what has been called, in a recent Scottish case, a 'margin of appreciation': Clydebank Football Club Ltd v Steedman 2002 SLT 109 , para 76 (discussed further below). If a controlling shareholder simply treats a company as his own property, as the domineering master-builder did in In re George Newman & Co Ltd [1895] 1 Ch 674 , his state of mind (and that of his fellow-directors) is irrelevant. It does not matter whether they were consciously in breach of duty, or just woefully ignorant of their duties. What they do is enough by itself to establish the unlawful character of the transaction.

29 The participants' subjective intentions are however sometimes relevant, and a distribution disguised as an arm's length commercial transaction is the paradigm example. If a company sells to a shareholder at a low value assets which are difficult to value precisely, but which are potentially very valuable, the transaction may call for close scrutiny, and the company's financial position, and the actual motives and intentions of the directors, will be highly relevant. There may be questions to be asked as to whether the company was under financial pressure compelling it to sell at an inopportune time, as to what advice was taken, how the market was tested, and how the terms of the deal were negotiated. If the conclusion is that it was a genuine arm's length transaction then it will stand, even if it may, with hindsight, appear to have been a bad bargain. If it was an improper attempt to extract value by the pretence of an arm's length sale, it will be held unlawful. But either conclusion will depend on a realistic assessment of all the relevant facts, not simply a retrospective valuation exercise in isolation from all other inquiries.

...

33 In this case there are concurrent findings that the sale of YMS1 to Moorgarth was a genuine commercial sale. The contrary was not pleaded or put to Mr Moore in cross-examination. I would dismiss this appeal'.

Lords Mance, Phillips, Collins and Clarke concurred with this analysis.

Questions and comments:

1. The case did not rely on sections 830 and 831 of the Companies Act 2006 but on the common law rule that a distribution out of capital other than in the course of a winding up or reduction of capital is unlawful.[410] The case is unusual in that the alleged undervaluation appears to be

[410] *Progress Property Company Limited v Moorgarth Group Limited* [2010] UKSC 55 para 13 (Lord Walker).

the result of a transaction negotiated between experienced businessmen advised by experienced surveyors, solicitors and accountants.[411]

2. The general principle that can be deduced is that a retrospective valuation establishing that the company sold at an undervalue will not necessarily be sufficient to render a transaction unlawful. The actual motives and intentions of the directors will be relevant. If, on the basis of a realistic assessment of all relevant facts, the transaction appears as an improper attempt to extract value from the company it may be held to be unlawful.
3. Compare this approach to the German concept of disguised distributions. In light of the rationale of the capital maintenance rules, which approach seems to be more appropriate?
4. The decision in *Aveling* that an undervalue transaction could amount to an unlawful distribution caused considerable concern in commercial circles. Intra-group transfers at book value, and below market value, were at risk of being struck down as unlawful distributions.[412] The problem was addressed by sections 845 and 846 of the Companies Act 2006. The amount of a distribution is set at zero if the consideration received by the company is not less than book value. Where book value exceeds the consideration received, the difference must be covered by profits available for distribution. In the reverse case of the consideration exceeding book value the company's distributable profits are increased accordingly.
5. Under French law, only openly gratuitous transfers of funds to shareholders in cash or in kind are considered to amount to the payment of a dividend or distribution. The concept of hidden or disguised dividends, that is, transfers of company assets carried out under the disguise of business transactions with the same economic effect as a dividend payment, is alien to French law. The problem does, however, exist, but is dealt with mainly through insolvency law. The payment of excessive remuneration or transactions at an undervalue may constitute a management fault or a misappropriation of company assets.[413] If the transaction has caused an excess of liabilities over assets and the company is in insolvent liquidation the managers involved may incur personal liability for damages;[414] and in addition they may be subject to criminal liability.[415]

In accordance with Article 57 of Directive (EU) 2017/1132, the recipient shareholders are liable to repay an unlawful dividend if they knew or ought to have known, at the time of payment, that the payment of a dividend was made in breach of the statutory restrictions.[416] The company is entitled to enforce the claim. Additionally, the company's creditors may assert the claim if they are unable to obtain satisfaction from the company.[417] Issues may arise from the interplay with the surrounding provisions of national law. Under German law, BGB, §134 provides that a transaction that violates a statutory prohibition is void, unless a contrary intention appears from the statute. AktG, §57 could be interpreted as constituting a statutory prohibition within the meaning of BGB, §134. The consequence would be the invalidity of the transaction effectuating the distribution. As a result, the company could, pursuant to the principles of unjust enrichment, reclaim the benefit transferred to the shareholder *in corpore*. AktG, §62(1), on the other hand, entitles the company only to the difference in value between the benefit granted and the consideration received.[418] The

[411] ibid para 5. [412] Davies and Worthington (n 124) para 12-11. [413] cf Chapter 10E.II.
[414] Com Art L651-2. [415] Com Art L241-3 (SARL), L242-6(3) (SA).
[416] AktG, §62(1); Com Art L232-17; Companies Act 2006, s 847. Under the later provision, a shareholder will be liable if he knew or ought to have known of the facts, which rendered the distribution unlawful under the Act. It is no defence that the shareholder did not know of the restrictions imposed by the Act; *It's a Wrap (UK) Ltd (in liquidation) v Gula* [2006] BCC 626 (CA).
[417] Germain and Magnier (n 68) para 2493.
[418] If a shareholder A of X AG has bought real estate worth €2 million from the company for €1.5 million, assuming that the manager of the company has not acted ultra vires when entering into the contract, the two possible interpretations of AktG, §§57, 62 lead to the following results: Under the first approach (BGB, §134 applies and the transaction is void), the company may reassert its property rights; A may reclaim his payment of €1.5 million. Alternatively, A retains title and possession. The company can claim payment of the difference in value of €0.5 million. The applicable limitation period may vary.

prevalent view[419] asserts that a transaction violating AktG, §57 is void pursuant to BGB, §134. However, AktG, §62 is considered *lex specialis* in relation to the principles of unjust enrichment. Therefore, the recipient shareholder is liable to the extent that the transaction has diminished the company's assets. Where the contract has not been executed the recipient of the benefit (the shareholder) may enforce the transaction. The company, on the other hand, may not require the shareholder to honour the contractual obligations, since this would have the consequence of imposing on the shareholder a more onerous obligation than initially agreed on in the contract (owing to the additional liability arising out of AktG, §62).[420]

Pursuant to section 847(2) of the Companies Act 2006, the common law principles on unlawful distributions remain applicable. A distribution of a company's assets to a shareholder, except in accordance with specific statutory procedures, such as a winding up or a reduction of capital, is an unlawful return of capital amounting to an *ultra vires* disposal of company property.[421] A recipient shareholder who knows or ought to have known the facts, which render the transaction *ultra vires*, is deemed to hold the received assets on constructive trust for the benefit of the company and is therefore liable to restore those assets to the company. It is not entirely clear whether the company's claim against the recipient is proprietary in nature, or, as in the case of section 847(1), merely personal. In the former case the company could retrieve its assets and any traceable proceeds in the recipient's bankruptcy without having to compete with ordinary creditors.[422] In addition, directors who authorized payments in breach of dividend restrictions may find themselves liable for breach of duty and liable to restore any loss to the company,[423] irrespective of whether the directors were recipients themselves. The basis for this liability may be the exercise of powers for improper purposes,[424] failure to promote the success of the company[425] or failure to exercise reasonable care, skill and diligence.[426] Overall, directors authorizing unlawful dividends seem to be more likely to be held liable to compensate the company than recipient shareholders.[427]

4. *Acquisition by the company of its own shares*

The repurchase by a company of its own shares may have significant implications for the company's creditors and shareholders. Where a company repurchases fully paid up shares it distributes assets to the shareholders, contrary to the idea of the creditors' preferential access to the company's assets. A repurchase of unpaid shares amounts to a release of the subscribers from their obligation to contribute to the company's capital.[428] Moreover, a regular dividend payment will be made easier in the future by reducing the company's legal capital account. From the shareholders' perspective, there is a clear danger of discrimination between various groups of shareholders: minority shareholders may be excluded from a lucrative deal. Moreover for listed companies, aggressively buying up a company's own shares increases demand and therefore may artificially increase the share price, which in turn has implications for the market for corporate control and may prevent potentially welfare enhancing takeover activity.[429] Consequently, all three European jurisdictions provide, as a starting point, for a general prohibition for a company

[419] BGHZ 136, 125.
[420] Schmidt (n 221) 893.
[421] *Progress Property Company Limited v Moorgarth Group Limited* (n 407) para 13 (Lord Walker).
[422] Davies and Worthington (n 124) para 12-12.
[423] *Bairstow v Queens Moat Houses plc* [2002] BCC 91 (CA).
[424] Companies Act 2006, s 171(a).
[425] ibid s 172.
[426] ibid s 174.
[427] Davies and Worthington (n 124) para 12-14. Directors may be granted relief by the court under s 1157 if they acted 'honestly and reasonably'.
[428] Under German law, the payment obligation would be extinguished under the doctrine of *Konfusion* (obligor and obligee are the same person), thus directly affecting the company's capital structure; Oechsler in *Münchner Kommentar zum Aktiengesetz* (4th edn, CH Beck 2016) §71 para 20.
[429] ibid §71 para 22-25.

to subscribe for its own shares and to repurchase its own shares.[430] However, in certain circumstances a repurchase of own shares makes good economic sense. The repurchase of shares can be a useful signalling device showing that the company is committed to capital discipline or that the market undervalues its shares. Also, the repurchase of shares is a way of increasing the leverage of the company, which can be beneficial for the remaining shareholders. Further, by reducing the company's cash reserves it may become less attractive for a hostile bidder. Moreover, by buying out disaffected shareholders it may be easier for the company to overcome a deadlock in decision-making.[431] Following the 2006 amendments, Directive (EU) 2017/1132 gives Member States significant leeway for allowing public companies to repurchase their own shares. The jurisdictions under consideration here have made use of these derogations to varying degrees.

Both AktG[432] and *Code de commerce*[433] contain a number of clearly defined exceptions to the general prohibition on the repurchase of shares (not however for the prohibition of subscription of own shares). Moreover, under both jurisdictions, the general meeting of shareholders may authorize the company for a period of no more than five years to acquire its own shares of up to 10 per cent of its legal capital.[434] The shares so acquired and held in treasury must, together with previously acquired own shares, not exceed at any time 10 per cent of the legal capital. The repurchase is to be financed out of distributable profits.[435] Shares held in treasury carry no voting rights, no rights to dividends and distributions, and no preemptive rights.[436] Shares held in contravention of the legal limitations must be sold within one year of the repurchase, failing which they must be cancelled;[437] under German law a three-year period applies if, and to the extent that, merely the 10 per cent holding threshold has been exceeded.[438] The reacquired own shares held in treasury should be neutralized on the company's balance sheet and not treated as an independent asset. This is because otherwise the company's finances would suffer a double whammy in case of a significant shock to its business. Not only would the company's value decrease because of the shock, it would decrease even further because of the simultaneous reduction of the value of its shares held in treasury.[439] The acquisition of shares of the company by a third party, but on behalf of the company is subject to similar restrictions.[440]

[430] AktG, §§56, 71(1); Com Art L225-206 I. and II.; Companies Act 2006, s 658. Under common law it is also illegal for a company to acquire its own shares; *Trevor v Whitworth* (1887) 12 App Cas 409 (HL).

[431] Oechsler (n 428) §71 para 1-10.

[432] Pursuant to AktG, §71(1) a public company may acquire its own shares: (i) to avoid severe and imminent damage to itself; (ii) for the purpose of an employee share scheme; (iii) in order to compensate minority shareholders in connection with the conclusion of a control agreement or an integration; (iv) if the acquisition is gratuitous or constitutes purchase commission for a bank; (v) where the company acquires the shares by way of universal succession in title; (vi) by way of a redemption in connection with a reduction of capital; (vii) where the company is a financial institution, on the basis of a shareholder resolution for the purpose of dealing in shares. A private company is prevented from acquiring own shares only to the extent that they are not fully paid. Fully paid up shares may be acquired to the extent that the shares can be paid for without reducing the company's net assets below the subscribed capital. As long as the shares are held in treasury their inherent membership rights cannot be exercised by the company; GmbHG, §33.

[433] A company may purchase its own shares in the course of a reduction of capital other than for setting off losses. The repurchased shares must be cancelled immediately; Com Art L225-207. Shares may be repurchased for the purpose of granting shares to the company's employees under a profit-sharing plan, a stock option plan or a plan to grant free shares. In these cases, the shares must be allotted or the option must be granted within one year of the repurchase; Com Art L225-208, L225-9-2. Further, shares may be repurchased in order to offer them as consideration in the context of a merger, demerger or contribution, in which case the shares must be allotted within two years of their repurchase; Com., Article L225-9-2. A private company may not purchase or subscribe its own shares. Only in the course of a reduction of capital other than for setting off losses may the managing director be authorized by the general meeting to buy a specified number of shares in order to cancel them; Com Art L225-34(4).

[434] Com Art L225-9-2. Under French law, a special regime applies for public companies whose shares are admitted to trading on a regulated market. The general meeting may authorize the board of directors or management board, as the case may be, to acquire up to 10% of the company's capital. The general meeting determines the purpose and the terms and conditions of the transaction. The authorization can be given for a maximum period of 18 months, and it may be delegated to the chairman, managing director or other board members Com Art L225-209. The relevant information must be notified to the Financial Markets Authority (AMF); Com Art L225-212.

[435] AktG, §71(2). [436] ibid §71b; Com Art L225-210. [437] Com Art L225-214.

[438] AktG, §71c. [439] Oechsler (n 428) §71 para 19. [440] AktG, §§71a(2), 71d.

Arguably, the UK provides the most liberal regime. In addition to the general exceptions pursuant to section 659,[441] sections 690–708 contain detailed procedures in accordance with which a company may purchase its own shares. The applicable procedure depends on whether the share purchase is an 'off-market' purchase or a 'market' purchase. A 'market purchase' is essentially one that relates to shares admitted to trading on a 'recognised investment exchange' and takes place on such an exchange;[442] that is, on the London Stock Exchange's Main Market or Alternative Investment Market. A 'market purchase' is less 'dangerous' for (minority) shareholders than an 'off-market purchase': there is likely to be an objectively ascertainable market price and the shareholders whose shares are to be repurchased are not identifiable in advance so that there is less scope for insider abuse.[443] In addition, the FCA's Listing Rules or the rules of the respective stock exchange will apply. A 'market purchase' requires prior authorization by ordinary shareholders' resolution, specifying the maximum number of shares to be acquired, maximum and minimum prices and the resolution's expiry date, which must not be later than five years from the passing of the resolution.[444] For companies with a premium listing on the London Stock Exchange's Main Market the FCA's Listing Rules apply and require a repurchase of more than 15 per cent of a class of a company's equity shares to be made by way of a tender offer to all shareholders of that class, or that the full terms of the repurchase have been specifically approved by the shareholders.[445] Thus, controlling shareholders are prevented from exploiting the repurchase by excluding the minority.[446] By contrast, in case of an 'off-market purchase' the company may be the only potential buyer and the value of the shares may be difficult to ascertain. Minority shareholders may be easily excluded from what is a good deal for insiders. Consequently, an 'off-market purchase' may be carried out only on the basis of a contract that has been approved in advance by an ordinary resolution of the shareholders.[447] Shareholders whose shares are to be repurchased under the resolution are excluded from voting.[448] In case of a public company, the resolution must determine its expiry date of not later than five years from the passing of the resolution.[449] In any case, only fully paid up shares may be purchased[450] and there may be no purchase if as a result no member of the company would be holding any shares other than redeemable shares.[451] A public company may purchase its own shares only out of distributable profits or out of the proceeds of a fresh issue specifically made for that purpose.[452] Where the repurchased shares are treated as cancelled[453] and the purchase was made out of distributable profits, the amount by which the company's issued share capital is diminished must be transferred to the non-distributable 'capital redemption reserve'.[454] This provision ensures that the company's legal capital (consisting of the aggregate of 'issued share capital account', 'share premium account', and 'capital redemption reserve') remains constant and that distributable profits are not increased.[455]

[441] Acquisition by way of gift; in the course of a reduction of capital duly made; purchase of shares in pursuance of a court order, for example as a result of unfairly prejudicial conduct.

[442] Complex definitions of 'off-market' and 'market purchase' are provided in Companies Act 2006, s 693(2)–(4).

[443] Davies and Worthington (n 124) para 13-19.

[444] Companies Act 2006, s 701.

[445] Listing Rules, 12.4.2.

[446] Davies and Worthington (n 124) para 13-22.

[447] Companies Act 2006, s 694.

[448] ibid s 695.

[449] ibid s 694(5).

[450] ibid s 691.

[451] ibid s 690(2).

[452] ibid s 692. A private company may purchase its own shares also out of capital: ibid ss 692(1), 709–723. The 'permissible capital payment' is whatever is required to effectuate the repurchase after applying for that purpose any distributable profits and proceeds of a fresh issue made in order to finance the repurchase: ibid s 710. Payment out of capital requires approval by special majority: ibid s 716. Creditors are protected by a directors' statement attesting that the company, following the repurchase, will be able to pay its debts as they fall due and will continue business as a going concern throughout the following year. The statement must be audited by the company's auditors: ibid s 714. Both directors' statement and auditors' report must be open for inspection and notice must be given to the public: ibid ss 718–720. Moreover, provided that it is authorized in the company's articles of association, a private company may spend in any financial year the lower of £15,000 or 5% of its share capital on repurchases without any further prerequisites: ibid s 692(1ZA).

[453] ibid s 706(b).

[454] ibid s 733.

[455] Where the repurchase is financed with the proceeds of a fresh issue the company's net asset position does not change and the reduction of the share capital account due to cancellation is balanced by the increase resulting from the fresh issue. The creation of a capital redemption reserve is therefore not required. The situation becomes more complex when shares are repurchased at a premium; Davies and Worthington (n 124) paras 13-11–13-13.

Prior to 2003, repurchased shares had to be treated as cancelled. Today, sections 724–732 of the Companies Act 2006 allow a company, under certain circumstances, to hold repurchased shares (but not redeemed shares) in treasury to be sold or transferred at some future date. This gives the company more flexibility and allows it to raise small amounts of capital whenever the market is favourably disposed towards its shares.[456] Only shares purchased out of distributable profits may be held in treasury.[457] Similar to German and French law, the company cannot exercise any voting rights in respect of treasury shares; nor can it receive any dividend or distribution on these shares.[458] When treasury shares are sold, existing shareholders' pre-emption rights apply.[459] Where the company sells the shares for a price up to the repurchase price, the resulting proceeds constitute a realized profit, which is available for distribution. However, where the shares are sold at a price above the repurchase price, the difference must be transferred to the share premium account, which cannot be used for distribution purposes.[460]

Whereas, a company may repurchase its own shares subject to the exceptions and procedures just explained, it has no obligation to repurchase its shares and shareholders have no obligation to sell. This will be different where the company has issued redeemable shares. These are shares that either will be redeemed at a certain point or that may be redeemed at the option of either the company or the respective shareholder.[461] Thus, redeemable shares come with the (possibly contingent) obligation on the part of the shareholder to sell and for the company to redeem its redeemable shares.[462] In this respect, our three European jurisdictions show significant diversity. Pursuant to sections 684–689 of the Companies Act 2006 a company may issue redeemable shares of any class. Redeemable shares may only be issued if the company has issued shares, which are not redeemable.[463] A public company may issue redeemable shares only if it is authorized to do so in its articles of association.[464] Thus, the power to issue redeemable shares must either be present from the start, or else can be introduced only by amendment of the articles requiring a special resolution.[465] The terms, conditions and manner of redemption of shares are determined by the directors, provided they are authorized to do so by the articles or by ordinary resolution of the company.[466] In that case, the terms, conditions and manner of redemption, must be defined before the shares are allotted and particulars must be included in the company's statement of capital.[467] Thus, shareholders are aware of these terms and conditions and do not require further protection. In terms of payment for, and financing of, redeemable shares, similar principles apply as for a repurchase of shares.[468] However, redeemed shares are treated as cancelled and cannot be held in treasury.

German law allows for the issuance of shares redeemable at the option of the company with a view to effectuating a reduction of capital.[469] Such redemption must be stipulated in the articles of association; an article amendment to this effect requires consent of the affected shareholders. The terms and conditions of the redemption are to be determined either in the articles or by resolution of the general meeting. Redemption may be compulsory on the occurrence of certain events, or may be at the company's option, in which case the principle of non-discrimination applies. If it isn't the entire class that is being redeemed, shareholders

456 Davies and Worthington (n 124) para 13-24.
457 Companies Act 2006, s 724(1)(b).
458 ibid s 726.
459 ibid s 560(2)(b).
460 Davies and Worthington (n 124) para 13-26: Since the shares have been repurchased out of distributable profits, the proceeds of sale should equally be available for distribution. Where the share price has increased between repurchase and sale by the company, the inherent increase in the value of the company should be treated as legal capital and booked to the share premium account.
461 Companies Act 2006, s 684(1).
462 Davies and Worthington (n 124) para 13-7.
463 Companies Act 2006, s 684(4).
464 ibid s 684(3).
465 For private companies such authorization is not required; however, the articles may restrict the issue of redeemable shares; ibid s 684(2).
466 ibid s 685(1).
467 ibid s 685(3).
468 ibid s 687.
469 AktG, §237(1).

will usually have to draw lots. Redeemed shares must be cancelled and capital will be reduced accordingly.[470] Conversely, under French law, where the articles of association or general meeting by extraordinary resolution so provide shares may be issued as redeemable shares and the entire class may be redeemed, without, however, resulting in a reduction of capital. Fully redeemed shares are known as *actions de jouissance*.[471] The shareholders receive back their initial contributions, but retain the status as shareholders. Fully redeemed shares forgo the right to a 'premier dividend' and to repayment of the nominal value upon liquidation, but retain all other rights, notably voting rights.[472] Since redemption must not result in a reduction of capital, it may be effectuated only out of distributable profits or distributable reserves. This type of share used to be very common in the nineteenth century and has regained popularity in recent years as a specific type of preference shares that allows recoupment of the initial contribution along the way.[473]

5. *Financial assistance*

Both France and Germany have implemented the prohibition on financial assistance as initially contained in Article 23 of the Second Company Law Directive, without the relaxations introduced by Directive 2006/68/EC. Thus, a public company may not advance funds, grant loans or security to enable a third party to subscribe or purchase the company's own shares. Under German law, the respective transaction will be void.[474] In France, the prohibition is backed by criminal liability of chairman, directors, or managing directors involved, punishable with a fine.[475] Overall, the provision does not seem to be of great practical significance. In France, it is interpreted narrowly and does for instance not apply where a dividend is paid which allows the recipient to acquire further shares. Where the assistance is granted some time after the subscription or acquisition took place, the prohibition would seem not to apply either.[476] The latter may, however, trigger the offence of an abuse of corporate assets or corporate powers.[477] In Germany, the provision is usually seen as filling certain gaps of the prohibition on the return of contributions to shareholders. Contrary to AktG, §57, it invalidates transactions that are balance sheet neutral, e.g. granting a loan to a liquid borrower, and also applies to transactions with persons other than shareholders.[478] The provision's main relevance is the takeover and LBO context, where the acquisition of control is financed with the company's own assets. The market for hostile takeovers and LBOs has traditionally been less developed in France and Germany than in the United Kingdom, where financial assistance as a legal issue has received significantly more attention.

In the UK, the prohibition on financial assistance did not emerge as a result of the nineteenth century common law developments regarding legal capital. As a statutory intervention, it first appeared in section 45 of the Companies Act 1929, in order to tackle abusive takeovers financed from the coffers of the target.[479] Section 678 of the Companies Act 2006 imposes on public companies a prohibition to grant financial assistance to a person, directly or indirectly, for the purpose of an acquisition of its own shares. Initially private companies were covered as well. However, they could avoid the consequences of financial assistance by

[470] Windbichler (n 126) 442–3 (§ 32 para 48). [471] Com Art L225-198.

[472] Com Art L225-199. [473] Cozian, Viandier, and Deboissy (n 67) para 1237.

[474] AktG, §71a. The prohibition of financial assistance does not apply in the context of a 'control and transfer of profits' agreement establishing a corporate group. A further exception is provided for transactions in the ordinary course of business of banks and financial institutions, and in the context of employee share schemes. In these cases, however, the financial assistance may only be granted out of distributable profits.

[475] Com Art L225-216 and L242-24(2). Transactions in the ordinary course of business of credit institutions or transactions carried out to enable employees to buy shares in the company, one of its subsidiaries or a company included in a group savings scheme are exempt.

[476] Germain and Magnier (n 68) para 2053. [477] Com Art L242-6-3, L242-6-4.

[478] Hölters (n 237) §71a para 1. [479] Davies and Worthington (n 124) para 13-44.

following a special 'whitewash' procedure.[480] Under the Companies Act 2006, private companies are no longer subject to the prohibition. According to section 678(1), it is unlawful for a public company (or its subsidiary)[481] to give financial assistance before or at the same time as the acquisition takes place directly or indirectly to a person for the purpose of that person acquiring shares in that public company ('pre-acquisition assistance'). Moreover, according to section 678(3): where a person has acquired shares in a public company and a liability has been incurred for the purpose of the acquisition, it is unlawful for that company or its subsidiary to give financial assistance directly or indirectly for the purpose of reducing or discharging the liability ('post-acquisition assistance'). Since the prohibition applies only where financial assistance is given by a public company, one easy way to finance a takeover with the target company's assets is to subsequently reregister it as a private company who may then discharge the bidder's liability incurred during the course of the transaction.[482] Section 677 provides a list of transactions that are prohibited, if they amount to financial assistance, irrespective of whether they cause any dicline in the company's net assets. These include financial assistance by way of gift, guarantee, loan, security, indemnity, release or waiver, and novation of a loan agreement or assignment. The residual category of 'any other financial assistance' requires for its application a reduction of the company's net assets to a 'material extent' or that the company has no net assets. 'Materiality' is to be determined on the basis of the relationship between the value of the assistance and the value of the net assets.[483] In the absence of a clear definition of what 'financial assistance' actually means it may be difficult to draw the line in any particular case. The question of whether financial assistance exists in any given case will depend on the 'commercial substance of the transaction'.[484] This is a fact-sensitive affair and cannot be answered simply by applying a legal definition: 'The question is whether from a commercial point of view the transaction impugned amounts to financial assistance'.[485] The application may thus be very wide and strike down transactions that appear to be unobjectionable. Thus, in *Chaston v SWP Group Ltd*[486] payment by the subsidiary for a due diligence carried out for the benefit of the bidder purporting to take over the group by acquiring the shares in the holding company was deemed to amount to financial assistance. In any case, the assistance given must be financial in nature. Thus, giving advice or providing financial information does not amount to financial assistance; also repayment of a debt that is due or the enforcement of security rights will normally not offend the prohibition.[487]

Financial assistance is a rather vague concept and its scope of application very wide. At the same time, in many contexts, granting financial assistance may make good commercial sense. To cate for these eventualities, the law recognizes a number of specific exceptions to the general prohibition.[488] Section 678(2) and (4) provide more general exceptions for both pre- and post-acquisition assistance. Accordingly, financial assistance is not unlawful where granting assistance is only an incidental part of some larger purpose of the company and assistance is given in good faith in the interest of the company. The delineation of the

[480] Companies Act 1985, ss 155–159. Financial assistance could be given where either no reduction of net assets was involved, or out of distributable profits, subject to a directors' solvency statement (to be audited) and a special resolution of the members.

[481] The holding company's giving of financial assistance to a third party for acquisition of a subsidiary's shares would not be caught by the prohibition. Foreign subsidiaries are not covered by the prohibition either.

[482] Davies and Worthington (n 124) para 13-55.

[483] ibid 13-48.

[484] *Charterhouse v Tempest Diesels* (1985) 1 BCC 99; *Barclays Bank plc v British & Commonwealth Holdings plc* [1995] BCC 1059.

[485] *Chaston v SWP Group Ltd* [2003] 1 BCLC 675 (CA).

[486] ibid.

[487] Davies and Worthington (n 124) para 13-49.

[488] Companies Act 2006 distinguishes between unconditional and conditional exceptions. The former relate to transactions where the company's assets are lawfully reduced, such as payment of a lawful dividend, distributions in the course of winding up, reduction of capital, redemption and repurchase of shares (s 681). Conditional exceptions apply where lending of money is part of the ordinary business of the company, or financial assistance is given as part of an employee share scheme (s 682). In all these cases financial assistance may be granted only out of distributable profits or to the extent that the company's net assets are not reduced.

'larger purpose' was clarified by the House of Lords in *Brady v Brady*.[489] Two brothers, Jack and Bob, were the controlling shareholders of a haulage and drinks business conducted by T Brady & Sons Ltd ('Brady'). The brothers fell out and the ensuing management deadlock put the company at risk of of being wound up. In order to save the business a scheme was devised under which Jack would take on the haulage side of the business, and Bob the drinks side. The latter was transferred to a new company controlled by Bob. Bob's shares in Brady were acquired by Jack through his company Motoreal. It was conceded that this transaction amounted to financial assistance: Motoreal's liability incurred in order to buy Bob's shares in Brady was discharged by Brady. In the proceedings brought by Jack against Bob for specific performance he argued that the prohibition of financial assistance did not apply since the transaction served a larger purpose: the removal of the deadlock between the two brothers in order to avoid liquidation. According to the House of Lords, per Lord Oliver, if the provision of financial assistance was to retain any useful application, it was important to distinguish between a purpose and the reason behind the prupose. The ultimate reason for forming the purpose of financing an acquisition may be more important to those making the decision than the immediate transaction itself. But 'larger' was not the same thing as 'more important' nor was 'reason' the same as 'purpose'. In *Brady* the reason for the transaction was to overcome management deadlock. However, a larger purpose could not be found in the benefits or the disadvantages considered to be likely to result from the acquisition to be facilitated by financial assistance. The acquisition was not merely incidental of the reorganisation devised to break the deadlock; rather, it was the very essence of the scheme itself and the object that the scheme set out to achieve. As a consequence of this decision, which is still good law, the 'larger purpose' exception appears to be very narrow and of limited use in protecting commercial reconstructions of businesses.[490]

Unlawful financial assistance constitutes a criminal offence on the part of the company and of every officer of the company who is in default.[491] A transaction providing unlawful financial assistance is illegal and unenforceable by either party. However, related transactions, in particular the acquisition of shares, remain, in principle, unaffected and enforceable. Only where financial assistance and acquisition of shares are combined in an integrated transaction and the terms of the latter cannot be severed from the former will the entire transaction be void. Financial assistance already given by the company may be recovered on the basis of a constructive trust. Directors will be liable for breach of fiduciary duty if they misapply assets of the company by giving unlawful financial assistance.[492] The recipients of company property will hold it on constructive trust for the company and will be liable as constructive trustees.

II. United States

State laws vary widely as regards the rules and restrictions on payment of dividends and distributions. The historical root of all these provisions is, as we have seen, the old 'trust fund doctrine' providing that a company's assets serve as a fund for the preferential satisfaction of its creditors.[493] Historically, a number of different tests have been in place. Under an 'earned surplus test', in principle, only the earned surplus (or positive earnings) may be distributed to shareholders by way of a dividend. Corporation statutes may then differ on the question

[489] *Brady v Brady* [1989] AC 755 (HL). [490] Davies and Worthington (n 124) para 13-54.

[491] Companies Act 2006, s 680. Davies aptly remarks that imposing a fine on the company, thus reducing the company's net assets further, does not sit well with the capital maintenance rationale; Davies and Worthington (n 124) para 13-56 fn 266.

[492] *Wallersteiner v Moir* [1974] 1 WLR 991; *Belmont Finance Corporation Ltd v Williams Furniture Ltd (No 2)* [1980] 1 All ER 393.

[493] Klein, Coffee, and Partnoy (n 25) 230; Manning and Hanks (n 4) 63.

of whether the appreciation of assets amounts to 'earned surplus' in that sense. 'Enhanced surplus statutes' or 'impairment of capital' statutes allow a dividend to be paid as long as, after payment, the company's assets are at least equal to the sum of its liabilities and its stated capital.[494] The source of the surplus here is immaterial. The question, however, whether asset appreciation and share premiums (capital surplus) can be distributed may again be answered differently under different statutes. Under a 'simple surplus test', 'balance sheet test', or 'net worth test', the question is whether following payment the company's assets still exceed the sum of its liabilities. Under these tests, 'stated capital' does not reduce the company's capacity to pay dividends.[495] These tests are usually combined with a 'solvency test' to the effect that a dividend may only be paid if the company remains able to pay its debts as they fall due (so-called 'equity insolvency').[496] The highly influential MBCA has adopted a 'balance sheet test' combined with a 'solvency test'. Delaware follows an 'impairment of capital test'. Because of low or no par value there may be little difference in practice.

In any case, all of these tests rely to a greater or lesser extent on a company's financial statements, in particular balance sheet, income statement (profit and loss account) and cash flow statement. Most state corporation laws require a company to maintain appropriate accounting records, without, however, prescribing their form and content or making the application of Generally Accepted Accounting Principles (US GAAP) compulsory.[497] Even if there is no statutory obligation, proper accounting is simply a practical necessity and also vital for tax purposes. In accordance with MBCA, §16.20, new state incorporation laws require all corporations—even smaller ones—to furnish their shareholders annual financial statements, including balance sheet, income statement and statement of changes in shareholders' equity for the year. Corporations whose shares are subject to registration under federal securities legislation are required to produce, and file with the SEC, annual financial statements on the basis of US GAAP duly audited by an independent auditor. Annual accounts are to be produced by corporate officers and directors; in corporations listed on one of the major national exchanges the financial reporting process, including auditing, will be overseen by the audit committee of the board of directors.[498] Shareholders have a right to inspect financial statements and accounting records. However, annual accounts are not subject to shareholder approval nor are they formally put before the general meeting.[499]

Subject to statutory restrictions and those contained in the articles of association, the payment of dividends is entirely in the discretion of the board of directors.[500] They may decide to pay a cash dividend, issue bonus shares to existing shareholders or repurchase outstanding shares, or not pay a dividend at all and reinvest the available funds. This great flexibility allows directors (or, rather, corporate officers) to use a certain dividend policy as signalling device for financial markets. The payment of a regular and increasing cash dividend may signal continuous profitability; bonus shares may be issued or shares repurchased in order to improve certain ratios or for tax purposes. Reinvestment of funds may signal the company's growth strategy or the management's ability to constantly find new investment opportunities.

In their decision whether and in what form to pay dividends, the directors are, however, not entirely free, rather, in line with general principles, they are subject to fiduciary duties, albeit

[494] Manning and Hanks (n 4) 68, 74–8.

[495] Manning and Hanks (n 4) 68–9. In the absence of 'legal capital' an 'adjusted net worth test' may take the form of a 'percentage test', that is, dividends may only be paid if, after payment, assets equal a certain percentage of liabilities, say 125% as pursuant to California Corporation Code, §500.

[496] Manning and Hanks (n 4) 64; Massachusetts used to rely on a pure 'solvency test' only; it now follows the MBCA, Massachusetts Business Corporation Act, §6.40.

[497] MBCA, §16.01(b); Fletcher (n 290) §2186.

[498] American Bar Association (n 291) §6.40 Official Comment; R Hamilton, J Macey, and D Moll *Cases and Materials on Corporations* (11th edn, West 2010) 1084.

[499] Fletcher (n 290) §2272-10.

[500] ibid §5325; Klein, Coffee, and Partnoy (n 25) 232.

protected by the business judgment rule. Under certain circumstances a company may be compelled to pay a dividend. In the iconic case *Dodge v Ford Motor Co.*[501] Ford, a corporation, had made massive profits. Instead of declaring extra dividends, that is, dividends in addition to the normal annual dividends, the management adopted a policy of reinvesting profits in order to increase wages, improve working conditions and expand the business. When minority shareholders demanded the payment of further dividends, the court held that, given the amount of available funds, much more than was needed in order to carry out the company's expansion strategy, it was the directors' 'duty to distribute ... a very large sum of money to stockholders'. By conducting the affairs of the corporation for the merely incidental benefit of shareholders and for the primary purpose of benefiting others, the board of directors were in breach of their duty to act within their lawful powers. The problem is most relevant for closely held corporations. The conditions under which minority shareholders may successfully demand the declaration of a dividend are further explained in *Gottfried v Gottfried*:[502]

> There is no essential dispute as to the principles of law involved. If an adequate corporate surplus is available for the purpose, directors may not withhold the declaration of dividends in bad faith. But the mere existence of an adequate corporate surplus is not sufficient to invoke court action to compel such a dividend. There must also be bad faith on the part of the directors ... The following facts are relevant to the issue of bad faith and are admissible in evidence: Intense hostility of the controlling faction against the minority; exclusion of the minority from employment by the corporation; high salaries, or bonuses or corporate loans made to the officers in control; the fact that the majority group may be subject to high personal income taxes if substantial dividends are paid; the existence of a desire by the controlling directors to acquire the minority stock interests as cheaply as possible. But if they are not motivating causes they do not constitute 'bad faith' as a matter of law. The essential test of bad faith is to determine whether the policy of the directors is dictated by their personal interests rather than the corporate welfare.

Further, on application of minority shareholders, the competent court may exercise its discretion to dissolve the corporation if it is established that the non-payment of dividends was 'illegal oppressive, or fraudulent'.[503] Alternatively, the court may order the minority shareholders to be bought out at a fair price.[504] The threshold for triggering the court's discretion is a high one and requires similar considerations as for the establishment of 'bad faith'.[505]

1. *Statutory restrictions on dividends*

The tests employed by state corporation laws constitute variations on a common structure with the modern trend being reflected by MBCA, §6.40(c). The provision introduces a two-pronged unitary test for all distributions consisting of an 'equity insolvency test' and a simple 'balance sheet test'. 'Distribution' is very broadly defined in MBCA, §1.40(6). The term includes all direct or indirect transfers of money or other property made by the corporation to any shareholder, in particular declaration or payment of a dividend, a purchase by a corporation of its own shares, a distribution of promissory notes of the corporation and a distribution in voluntary or involuntary liquidation. Moreover, the definition is intended to include any other transaction whose economic result is the same as a typical dividend or share repurchase, irrespective of its structure or label. Not included is, however, the issue of bonus shares (share dividends, share splits). The following prerequisites must be met, where payment of a cash dividend is authorized, at the time of authorization if payment occurs within 120 days following authorization, otherwise on the date of payment.[506]

[501] *Dodge v Ford Motor Co*, 240 Mich. 459 (Supreme Court of Michigan, 1919).
[502] *Gottfried v Gottfried* 73 N.Y.S.2d 692 (Supreme Court of New York, 1947).
[503] MBCA, §14.30(2)(ii).
[504] ibid §14.34(e).
[505] Fletcher (n 290) §8046.10; Klein, Coffee, and Partnoy (n 25) 232.
[506] MBCA, §6.40(e)(3).

Pursuant to MBCA, §6.40(c)(1), no distribution may be made if, after giving it effect the corporation would be unable to pay its debts as they become due in the ordinary course of business. This is the 'equity insolvency test'. Where the corporation operates as a going concern in the ordinary course of business with significant shareholders' equity this test appears to be of marginal importance as it will be quite clear on the information generally available from the balance sheet and the income statement that the test will be met. Only where circumstances indicate that the corporation encounters financial and/or economic difficulties must this issue be addressed. In that case, the directors or officers will have to ascertain whether the predicted demand for the corporation's products and services, its ability to borrow additional sums and to refinance existing indebtedness will generate cash flows over a period of time sufficient to meet its existing and anticipated obligations when due. A cash flow analysis, based on business forecast and budget may be useful in this respect.[507]

Further, pursuant to MBCA, §6.40(c)(2), no distribution may be made if, after giving it effect the corporation's total assets would be less than the sum of its total liabilities plus the dissolution preferences of senior equity securities (preference shares with a dissolution preference). This is a simple 'balance sheet test' or 'surplus test'. The innovation is the irrelevance of any 'stated capital' that may be impaired and thus limit the ability to pay a dividend. This is the conceptual difference, with limited significance in practice, with 'enhanced surplus' or 'capital impairment tests'. Assets and liabilities may be determined on the basis of either financial statements prepared in accordance with accounting practices and principles, or a fair valuation or other method that is reasonable in the circumstances. This leaves great leeway to the business judgment of the board of directors. In particular, the MBCA does not mandate the use of US GAAP, although directors may always rely on reasonably current financial statements prepared on the basis of US GAAP. Whereas publicly held corporations subject to federal securities laws are required to use US GAAP and many others do on a voluntary basis, many small and medium-sized corporations do not. The statutory standard of reasonableness is supposed to provide the necessary flexibility to accommodate the needs of different types of corporations. Although no particular method of valuation is prescribed and different methods may be appropriate in certain circumstances, corporations should not selectively revalue certain assets and liabilities in a manipulative way.[508]

By contrast, Delaware, retaining the traditional legal capital concept, prescribes an 'enhanced surplus' or 'impaired capital' test, and, alternatively, an 'earned surplus test'. Pursuant to DGCL, §170(a)(1), a dividend may be declared and paid, first out of the corporation's surplus. 'Surplus' is defined as the excess, if any, at a given time of net assets over the amount of capital. 'Net assets' is the amount by which total assets exceed total liabilities. 'Capital' is the sum of the aggregate par value of all issued shares with par value, plus any portion of the consideration received on the issue of shares designated by the directors as capital. Where (only) no-par value shares are issued, capital is the portion of consideration designated by the directors as capital and may be zero.[509] Thus, a dividend may be paid only if, following payment, assets still exceed liabilities plus capital, in other words, if capital is not impaired. However, because of low par value and no par value shares and the directors' discretion to designate amounts as capital, the latter may be very low or even zero. The sources of surplus are irrelevant; capital surplus may be distributed. Moreover, DGCL, §170(a)(2) allows payment of a dividend, even if there is no surplus, out of net profits for the fiscal year in which the dividend is declared and/or the preceding fiscal year ('nimble dividend'), as long as capital representing preference shares is not impaired. This 'earned surplus test' is extremely flexible as it does not rely on the accumulation of profits and losses over the years. Even if, overall, the corporation has traded at a loss, it may pay a dividend to the amount that profits

[507] American Bar Association (n 291) §6.40 Official Comment.
[508] ibid. [509] DGCL, §154.

exceed losses in a fiscal year (or the preceding fiscal year). The corporation may choose to apply either test.[510]

DGCL does not prescribe a specific accounting method. Many if not most Delaware corporations prepare US GAAP financial statements. The balance sheet net worth is however not controlling for purposes of determining compliance with the statutory tests. Rather, corporations may revalue assets and liabilities to reflect current realities, as long as the valuation method fully takes into account the assets and liabilities of the corporation.[511] In general, the board of directors has a wide discretion in respect of revaluation and accounting methods.[512] In the seminal case of *Klang v Smith's Food & Drug Centers, Inc.*[513] the Delaware Supreme Court held:

> In cases alleging impairment of capital ... the trial court may defer to the board's measurement of surplus unless a plaintiff can show that the directors 'failed to fulfill their duty to evaluate the assets on the basis of acceptable data and by standards which they are entitled to believe reasonably reflect present values'. In the absence of bad faith or fraud on the part of the board, courts will not 'substitute [our] concepts of wisdom for that of the directors'.

Under Delaware law, there is no formal 'equity insolvency test'.[514] However, in order to avoid a transaction being challenged under fraudulent transfer law, this test may be applied de facto as a practical matter.[515]

2. *Unlawful distributions*

In general, directors who are involved in authorizing distributions that are unlawful under the statutory standards will be personally liable, jointly and severally, to the company, and in case of dissolution or insolvency possibly also to its creditors, to the full amount unlawfully paid out.[516] This claim must be asserted within a certain period of time, e.g. under MBCA, two years from when the effect of the distribution was measured,[517] six years following payment under DGCL.[518] Usually, a plaintiff will have to show that the director acted 'wilfully or negligently' or contrary to good faith and to what he reasonably believed to be in the best interest of the corporation. In this respect, directors are protected by the business judgment rule. Moreover, directors will be protected if they relied in good faith upon the records of the corporation and upon such information, opinions, reports or statements presented to the corporation by any of its officers or employees, or board committees, or by other professionals or experts who have been selected with reasonable care.[519] A director found liable may claim compensation from his fellow directors if they were involved in the unlawful distribution.[520] A director may also recover from shareholders the amount they received if they had knowledge of the facts that made the distribution unlawful. MBCA, §8.33(b)(c) gives directors a direct claim against shareholders. Under DGCL, §174(c), directors are subrogated to the rights of the corporation against shareholders.

Thus, the liability of shareholders to repay unlawful dividends that they received is merely implicit in state corporation statutes. Such liability may however arise from general equitable principles such as 'knowing receipt' of misapplied assets of the corporation and on the

[510] A special test applies for so-called 'wasting assets corporations'—those exploiting non-replenishable assets such as natural resources, copyrights, patents or the like. These corporations may determine the net profits derived from the exploitation of such wasting assets without taking into consideration the depletion of such assets resulting from lapse of time, consumption, liquidation or exploitation, DGCL, §170(b); Booth (n 40) 639.

[511] *Klang v Smith's Food & Drug Centers, Inc.*, 702 A.2d 150 (Del. SC, 1997).

[512] Booth (n 40) 639.

[513] *Klang v Smith's Food & Drug Centers, Inc.* (n 511).

[514] Booth (n 40) 638.

[515] Manning and Hanks (n 4) 64–5.

[516] MBCA, §8.33; DGCL, §174.

[517] MBCA, §8.33(c).

[518] DGCL, §174(a).

[519] MBCA, §8.30(e)(f); DGCL, §172.

[520] MBCA, §8.33(b)(1); DGCL, §174(b).

basis of a constructive trust. Moreover, fraudulent transfer law plays an important role.[521] Fraudulent transfer law is state law largely based on the Uniform Fraudulent Transfer Act of 1984, which following minor amendments, is now the Uniform Voidable Transactions Act 2014. It allows creditors to reverse certain transactions entered into by the debtor company to the detriment of its creditors and applies to transactions where the company receives 'less than a reasonably equivalent value in exchange for such transfer'[522] or where the transfer was made with 'actual intent to hinder, delay or defraud creditors'.[523] Usually, at the time of the transaction the company must have been insolvent or must have become insolvent as a result of the transaction.[524] Occasionally, further preconditions apply such as knowledge, or reason to know, of the imminent insolvency of the debtor on the part of the transferee.[525] Fraudulent transfer law looks at the substance of a transaction which renders its scope of application very broad. It covers all transactions that have the same economic consequences as a dividend. For instance, where an (insolvent) corporation guarantees a bank loan of its principal shareholder, backed up with collateral, the difference in interest that the shareholder pays on the loan and what he would have paid on an unsecured loan is the economic equivalent of a dividend.[526] Fraudulent transfer law renders the guarantee and the security interest voidable so that the underlying assets remain with the debtor corporation and available to its creditors. Since shareholders, in particular in publicly held corporations, may be hard to track down, the preferred target in a fraudulent transfer action will often be the lender who financed a transaction and obtained collateral. The respective security interest will then be voided by the court. Lenders will be save only if they make sure that even after the transaction the corporation is and remains solvent.[527] This is particularly important in the Leveraged Buy Out (LBO) context where the target grants 'financial assistance'.[528]

3. *Contractual dividend restrictions*

Negotiated tailor-made restrictions on the corporation's ability to pay dividends as so-called debt covenants may be included in debenture indentures, used for public bond issues, in note purchase agreements for private placements of long-term debt securities, and in term loan agreements for long-term bank lending.[529]

These covenants typically restrict the transfer of corporate assets to shareholders, be it in the form of dividends or repurchase or redemption of outstanding shares.[530] The restrictions usually operate on the basis of the corporation's profitability and cash flows. Typically, the covenant will set a 'peg date', at or near the time of the loan. Dividends will be restricted to profits after the peg date, or a certain percentage thereof. A fixed sum, (typically one year's profits), the so-called 'dip' may be added, as may be the proceeds of a fresh issue of shares.[531] Frequently, the restrictions will be very elaborate in order to close any loopholes, thus specifying the maximum amounts for given periods, the frequency and recipients of payments, and conditioning the payments on certain measures of credit worthiness, such as credit

[521] D Baird, 'Legal Approaches to Restricting Distributions to Shareholders: The Role of Fraudulent Transfer Law' (2006) 7 European Business Organisation Law Review 199.

[522] Uniform Fraudulent Transfer Act 1984 (Uniform Voidable Transactions Act 2014), §§4(a)(2), 5(a).

[523] Uniform Fraudulent Transfer Act 1984 (Uniform Voidable Transactions Act 2014), §§4(a)(1), 5(b).

[524] Uniform Fraudulent Transfer Act 1984 (Uniform Voidable Transactions Act 2014), §§5(a) and (b), 4(b)(9).

[525] Uniform Fraudulent Transfer Act 1984 (Uniform Voidable Transactions Act 2014) §5(b).

[526] Baird (n 521) 206.

[527] ibid 208. [528] See below.

[529] W Bratton, 'Bond Covenants and Creditor protection: Economics and Law, Theory and Practice, Substance and Process' (2006) 7 European Business Organisation Law Review 39, 42.

[530] Committee on Trust Indentures and Indenture Trustees, ABA Section of Business Law 'Model Negotiated Covenants and Related Definitions' (2006) 61 Business Lawyer 1439, 1492.

[531] ibid 1509–13.

ratings and financial ratios.[532] Reliance on ratios often seeks to maintain an equity cushion, by, for instance, prohibiting a dividend if after payment debt would exceed some percentage of net tangible assets.[533] The following clause provides an example:

Section 4.05. Limitation on Restricted Payments[534]

The Company shall not ... make a Restricted Payment if at the time the Company ... makes such Restricted Payment:

(1) Default shall have occurred and be continuing (or would result therefrom);
(2) the Company is not entitled to incur an additional $1.00 of indebtedness under Section 4.04(a) [i.e the Consolidated Coverage Ratio does not exceed 2 to 1.0];
(3) the aggregate amount of such Restricted Payment and all other Restricted Payments since the Issue Date would exceed the sum of (without duplication):

(A) 50% of the Consolidated Net Income accrued during the period (treated as one accounting period) from the beginning of the fiscal quarter immediately following the fiscal quarter during which the Issue Date occurs to the end of the most recent fiscal quarter ending at least 45 days prior to the date of such Restricted Payment ...; plus
(B) 100% of the aggregate Net Cash Proceeds received by the Company from the issuance or sale of its Capital Stock (other than Disqualified Stock) subsequent to the Issue Date (other than an issuance or sale to a Subsidiary of the Company and other than an issuance or sale to an employee stock ownership plan or to a trust established by the Company or any of its Subsidiaries for the benefit of their employees) and 100% of any cash capital contribution subsequent to the Issue Date; plus
(C) the amount by which Indebtedness of the Company is reduced on the Company's balance sheet upon the conversion or exchange ... subsequent to the Issue Date of any Indebtedness of the Company convertible or exchangeable for Capital Stock (other than Disqualified Stock) of the Company (less the amount of any cash, or the fair market value of any other property, distributed by the Company upon such conversion or exchange).

Comments:

1. 'Restricted Payment' is defined as including the declaration or payment of any dividends or any other distributions of any sort in respect (including any payment in connection with any merger or consolidation) or similar payment to the direct or indirect holders of its shares.
2. Clause (2) refers to the 'Consolidated Coverage Ratio' of two to one as the benchmark for incurring further debt and the payment of dividends. 'Consolidated Coverage Ratio' as of any date of determination is the ratio of the aggregate amount of Consolidated EBITDA for the period of the most recent four consecutive fiscal quarters ending at least forty-five days prior to the date of such determination to Consolidated Interest Expense for such four fiscal quarters. EBITDA signifies Earnings before Interest, Taxes, Depreciation and Amortization. This is frequently perceived to be a better indicator of future cash flows since interest, taxes, depreciation and amortization do not relate to the day-to-day business and are not like cash.[535]
3. The 'peg date' in clause (3) is the issue date. Sub-clause (A) restricts dividends to 50 per cent of net income after the peg date. Sub-clause (B) makes the net proceeds of a fresh issue available for distribution.
4. Where debt is converted into equity, the company's indebtedness is reduced. The respective amount is available for distribution as well.

[532] M Bradley and M Roberts, 'The Structure and Pricing of Debt Covenants' (2004) 11 http://ssrn.com/abstract=466240.
[533] Klein, Coffee, and Partnoy (n 25) 256.
[534] Committee on Trust Indentures and Indenture Trustees (n 530) 1509-13.
[535] Mundstock (n 53) 132.

Where the debtor corporation is in breach of its debt covenants, the debt (principal and interest) will, at the lender's discretion, become immediately due and payable, and the lender may foreclose on any collateral he may have obtained.

4. Acquisition by the corporation of its own shares

Generally, a corporation, on decision of its board of directors, may repurchase or redeem or otherwise acquire its own shares and then resell, lend, transfer or otherwise dispose of the shares so acquired.[536] The acquisition of own shares is subject to the same restrictions as are imposed on the payment of dividends: The 'solvency test' and 'balance sheet test' under MBCA;[537] the 'capital impairment test' in Delaware.[538] Under Delaware law, a corporation may repurchase preferred shares or, if no preferred shares are outstanding, common shares even out of capital if these shares are then retired and the capital is reduced accordingly. Where shares are purchased out of surplus, they may be retired or retained as treasury shares. No specific maximum amount limits a corporation's acquisition of its own shares. In case of breach of the statutory restrictions, the remedies are the same as for payment of unlawful dividends.[539]

In closely held corporations, where there is no market for shares readily available, the repurchase of shares may further be restricted by fiduciary principles. Where the controlling majority initiate a repurchase by the corporation of (part of) their shares, they turn an illiquid investment into a liquid one and obtain corporate assets under exclusion of the minority. Consequently, the directors and controlling stockholders who caused the corporation to enter into the stock purchase agreement, must have acted with the utmost good faith and loyalty to the other shareholders. Where the shareholder whose shares were purchased was a member of the controlling group, the controlling shareholders must cause the corporation to offer each shareholder an equal opportunity to sell, on a pro rata basis, a number of his shares to the corporation at an identical price. Where these principles are not adhered to, the transaction may either be reversed or the corporation may be ordered to acquire an equivalent number of the plaintiff's shares at the same conditions.[540]

5. Financial assistance

Neither federal nor state law does directly address the problem of financial assistance or Leveraged Buy Outs. In addition to the usual remedies of breach of fiduciary duties and securities fraud, much of the problematic ground is covered by fraudulent transfer law[541] as can be seen in the following case:

***In re Bay Plastics Inc.* 187 B.R. 315 (Bankr. C.D. Cal. 1995)**

The defendant shareholders sold their interests in the debtor company, Bay Plastics, to Milhous Corporation for $3.5 million in cash and $1.8 million in deferred payments. The transaction was structured as follows: Milhous, through one of its subsidiaries, formed the acquisition vehicle 'BPI' to take ownership of the Bay Plastics shares. Milhous did not inject any funds of its own. Instead Bay Plastics borrowed $3.95 million from defendant bank 'BT' against a first priority interest on substantially all of Bay Plastics' assets. This was possible only because Bay Plastics'

536 MBCA, §6.31(a); DGCL, §160(a).

537 In respect of moment in time where the dividend restrictions must be met, MBCA, §6.40(e)(1) refers to the earlier of (i) the date money or other property is transferred or (ii) the date the shareholder ceases to be a shareholder with respect to the acquired shares.

538 DGCL, §160(a)(1).

539 MBCA, §8.33; DGCL, §174.

540 *Donahue v Rodd Electrotype Co.*, 367 Mass. 578 (Supreme Judicial Court of Massachusetts, 1975); Many courts have adopted a similar approach. Delaware, however, seems to have rejected *Donahue* in *Nixon v Blackwell*, 626 A.2d 1366 (Delaware Supreme Court, 1993); see Hamilton, Macey, and Moll (n 498) 366.

541 Baird (n 521) 207; E Warren and J Westbrook *The Law of Debtors and Creditors* (5th edn, Aspen Publishers 2006) 86–7.

main supplier, Shintech, could be convinced, on the basis of Milhous' good credit, to release its security interest on all of Bay Plastics' assets as well as the personal guarantees given by its shareholders. $3.5 million of the loan was disbursed directly to BPI, who in turn directed that that money be paid to the selling shareholders in payment for their stock. As a consequence of the transaction, the debtor's balance sheet showed $7 million in assets and $9 million in liabilities. Insolvency on a balance sheet basis was avoided merely by adding $2.26 million in goodwill, which had not appeared on previous balance sheets and for which no explanation was provided to the court. Prior to the transaction the debtor's balance sheet showed a net equity of $1.1 million. When the debtor was unable to service its debt and filed for bankruptcy, $4 million in secured debt was owed to BT, and $3.5 million in unsecured debt to Shintech.

Bufford, Bankruptcy Judge[542]

The basic structure of an LBO involves a transfer of corporate ownership financed primarily by the assets of the corporation itself. Typically the corporation borrows the funds, secured by the assets of the corporation, and advances them to the purchasers, who use the funds to pay the purchase price to the selling shareholders.

...

The Court finds it appropriate to apply fraudulent transfer law to an LBO. An LBO is different, not just in degree, but in character from the ordinary business and investment transactions engaged in by a corporation's management. An LBO is not a routine business transaction that should normally be given deference by the courts. It is not a corporate investment in a new venture, new equipment or property. Indeed, an LBO normally does not affect the business of the corporation at all: it only changes the ownership and adds a large layer of secured debt. Rather, an LBO is an investment of corporate assets, by borrowing against them, for the personal benefit of both old and new equity owners. Thus, the application of fraudulent transfer law to LBOs does not limit corporate entrepreneurial decisions.

Since an LBO reduces the availability of unencumbered assets, the buyout depletes estate assets available to pay creditors' claims. As the Ninth Circuit has stated:

Existing unsecured creditors are vulnerable in [an LBO]. From their perspective, a pledge of the company's assets as collateral to finance the purchase of the company reduces the assets to which they can look for repayment.

Kupetz, 845 F.2d at 846; accord, Moody v. Security Pacific Business Credit, Inc., 971 F.2d 1056, 1073 (3d Cir.1992). An LBO is attractive to the sellers, the buyers and the lender because it shifts most of the risk of loss to other creditors of the corporation. Mellon Bank v. Metro Communications, Inc., 945 F.2d 635 (3d Cir.1991). The acquired corporation receives little or nothing in exchange for the debt that it incurs.

From a creditor's point of view, an LBO is indistinguishable from a distribution or a gift to shareholders. The harm is quite like the harm imposed on creditors by donative transfers to third parties, which is one of the most traditional kinds of fraudulent transfers. If the value of the security interest given by the corporation does not exceed the shareholders' equity as shown on the balance sheet (after suitable revisions to mark the assets to market and to eliminate intangible assets of dubious value), there is usually no substantial harm to creditors. Indeed, typical corporate distribution statutes permit the payment of dividends in such circumstances, to the extent of the balance sheet equity. If the price paid to selling shareholders is higher, however, there may be insufficient assets remaining to satisfy creditors.

The vice of an LBO lies in the fact that the selling shareholders are paid indirectly with assets from the corporation itself, rather than by the purchasers. In effect, in an LBO the shareholders are paid with a corporate dividend or distribution. An LBO enables the selling shareholders to liquidate their equity interests, which are otherwise subordinate to general unsecured claims, without first paying creditors, which a normal liquidation would require....

The possible detriment to creditors is exacerbated if the corporation's cash flow is not sufficient to service the loan. The bank eventually proceeds to foreclose on the corporation's assets and sells them at foreclosure prices, and leaves nothing for other creditors. Such foreclosure is frequently interrupted by the filing of a bankruptcy case. So it happened in this case.

[542] The text has been rearranged.

Most courts that have considered the issue have decided that fraudulent transfer law should apply to LBOs. In fact, despite the reservations expressed in Kupetz, supra, and Credit Managers Ass'n of Southern California v. Federal Co., 629 F.Supp. 175 (C.D.Cal.1985), there appears to be no published opinion to the contrary.

...

We begin with the elements of the cause of action under the UFTA § 5, as adopted in California, for a constructive fraudulent transfer rendering the debtor insolvent. The elements of a cause of action under this statute are as follows: the debtor (1) made a transfer or incurred an obligation, (2) without receiving a reasonably equivalent value in exchange, (3) which rendered the debtor insolvent (or the debtor was already insolvent), and (4) which is attacked by a pre-transaction creditor.

1. Transfer or Obligation

The selling shareholders do not dispute that, in making the BT loan, the debtor made a transfer or incurred an obligation. In fact, the debtor did both. The debtor undertook the $3.95 million obligation to BT, it transferred a security interest in essentially all of its assets to BT, and it transferred $3.5 million ultimately to the selling shareholders. Thus the first element of the cause of action is satisfied.

2. Lack of Reasonably Equivalent Value

...

Nominally, BT's transaction was only with Bay Plastics. It lent the $3.95 million to the debtor, the debtor promised to repay the loan, and the debtor gave a first priority security interest in essentially all of its assets to secure the repayment. If this were the transaction, creditors likely would have no grounds for complaint, and it would not be vulnerable to fraudulent transfer attack.

However, the foregoing structure obscures the reality of the transaction. The selling shareholders' transaction was formally with Milhous, and eventually with BPI, the new owner of Bay Plastics. BPI purchased their stock, and arranged for their payment with funds that Bay Plastics borrowed from BT. Before Bay Plastics received the funds, it directed that $3.5 million be transferred to its incoming parent, BPI, and BPI in turn directed that the funds be paid out for the stock purchase. Thus in substance $3.5 million of the funds that Bay Plastics borrowed from BT went to pay for the stock of the selling shareholders, rather than to Bay Plastics.

This raises the question whether the Court should collapse the various transactions in this case into one integrated transaction. Under Lippi this turns on whether, from the perspective of the selling shareholders, the transaction appeared to be a straight sale without an LBO. Lippi, 955 F.2d at 612. If, in contrast, there is evidence that the parties knew or should have known that the transaction would deplete the assets of the company, the Court should look beyond the formal structure. Id. In Kupetz the Ninth Circuit found it improper to collapse the transactions where the selling shareholders had no knowledge of the LBO character of the transaction, and there were no pre-transaction creditors.

In this case, in contrast, the selling shareholders had full knowledge that this was an LBO ...

In addition, because Shintech qualifies as a pre-transaction creditor, the Court does not need to reach the issue of the knowledge of the LBO feature of the transaction by the selling shareholders: this is material to whether the transaction's various parts should be collapsed only when challenged by post-transaction creditors.

Thus, in this case the Court finds it appropriate to collapse the various pieces of this transaction into one integral transaction, in which the funds went to the selling shareholders, not to Bay Plastics or to its new parent BPI. The loan obligation, in contrast, was undertaken by Bay Plastics, which also provided the security for the loan.

...

From the debtor's perspective, it is apparent that the $450,000 that Bay Plastics presumably received (the $3.95 million loan less the $3.5 million paid to the selling shareholders) is not reasonably equivalent to the $3.95 million obligation that it undertook ... Thus Bay Plastics did not receive reasonably equivalent value for the loan obligation and security interest that it granted to BT.

3. Insolvency of the Debtor

...

The Court finds that the balance sheet must be adjusted by deleting the unamortized goodwill of $2.26 million. It was not carried on the balance sheet before the LBO, and in any case it could not be sold to satisfy a creditor's claim. Richmond Produce, 151 B.R. at 1019. This is a liquidation case, where goodwill has no other value. This downward adjustment left Bay Plastics with a negative net worth of approximately $2 million immediately after the LBO. For fraudulent transfer purposes, it was rendered insolvent by the transaction.

...

4. Attack by a Pre–Transaction Creditor

... This element is satisfied in this case ... Shintech, the principal unsecured creditor in this case, which holds more than 99% of the unsecured debt, is the pre-existing creditor.

Questions and comments:

1. The key issue in the case is the second element of the action under UFTA, §5: 'lack of reasonably equivalent value'. The difficulty arises from the fact that there are actually two transactions. The first one is the loan of US$3.95 million by BT to the debtor in exchange for a first priority security interest on all its assets. The payment of the loan principal constitutes equivalent value for the ensuing debt plus interest. The second transaction is the acquisition of shares by Milhous (through BPI) from the shareholders, paid for with the funds that the debtor obtained from BT.
2. The Court treated these transactions as one for two reasons: First, the shareholders had knowledge of the LBO character of the transaction, and that it would deplete the company's coffers. In this respect, 'reason to know' would have been sufficient. This is a subjective approach. Secondly, and independently, the transactions were collapsed into one because Shintech was a pre-transaction creditor whose claim against the debtor was jeopardized by the transactions. Normally, the mere existence of a pre-transaction creditor would be sufficient, however, only if this creditor could do nothing to prevent the LBO. In the present case, as a secured creditor, Shintech could have prevented the LBO. It was, therefore, necessary to establish that Shintech had agreed to give up its security only because the LBO nature of the transaction was hidden from it. Similar considerations (LBO remains hidden) would apply to creditors who appeared on the scene after the transaction went through. They also would have to argue that they were kept in the dark. Thus, what we see is a mixture of objective and subjective elements.
3. Compare the outcome in this case with the approach taken by the UK Supreme Court in *Progress Property v Moorgarth*. Can you see any similarities?
4. There are also striking similarities with the German doctrine of disguised (hidden) distributions. The approach taken under German law is, however, an objective one, relying purely on the inadequacy of the consideration received by the company.

D. Capital Measures

Capital increases and reductions are devices to amend a corporation's capital structure, that is, the combination of different financial assets—debt, equity and hybrid instruments—that the company has issued. Increasing or reducing legal capital changes a corporation's debt/equity ratio or leverage. Both increase and reduction may be 'effective' or 'nominal'. Where a capital increase is 'effective', new assets will be injected into the company and the stated capital entry will be increased accordingly. Where the increase is 'nominal', distributable retained earnings will be transformed into capital, thus increasing the equity cushion available for the company's creditors. In case of an 'effective' reduction, assets will be returned to shareholders with potentially detrimental effects for creditors. A 'nominal' reduction is used to offset losses in order to make it easier for a restructured company to pay dividends in the future. Overall, capital increases and reductions, often combined, are predominantly used in order to restructure a company in financial difficulties. As a general principle, since these measures have an impact on the allocation of control and cash flow rights of shareholders, the general meeting will be in the driving seat.

I. European jurisdictions

Article 68 of Directive (EU) 2017/1132 prescribes that the decision to increase the share capital must ultimately rest with the general meeting of shareholders. Article 68(1) and (2) reflect the historic difference between those Member States that traditionally did not distinguish between authorized and issued share capital (e.g. France and Germany) and those that did (e.g. the United Kingdom). According to Article 68(1), any increase in capital must be decided upon by the general meeting. This decision and the increase in subscribed capital must be duly disclosed in accordance with Article 16. The majority required for the decision to increase the capital is left to the Member States. Article 68(2) introduces the concept of authorized capital. In the memorandum or the articles of association or through its general meeting the company may be authorized to increase the subscribed capital up to a maximum amount. The decision to issue fresh shares out of the authorized capital subsequently rests with the company's management board. The general meeting may grant the power to issue fresh shares only for a maximum, albeit renewable, period of five years. Article 68(3) addresses the issue of class rights. Each class must approve separately any increase in capital and any authorization to increase. These provisions equally apply to the issue of securities that are convertible into shares. As for payment for the new shares, Articles 69 and 70 mirror the respective provisions on contributions in cash and in kind upon formation with minor modifications. In particular, in case of a consideration in cash, any premium must be paid in full.[543]

The scope and force of the principle enshrined in Article 68 was initially fleshed out in a number of cases referred to the Court of Justice from Greece. Greek legislation established a state-owned organization for the reorganization of companies (OAE) in financial distress. Subject to a decree by the competent secretary of state, the OAE would take over the management of the company with a power, in derogation from general principles, to increase its capital. Existing shareholders retained their pre-emptive rights. In *Karella and Karellas*,[544] one of the questions before the Court of Justice was whether Article 68(1) (in conjunction with Article 84(1)) was applicable in the extraordinary situation of an undertaking of particular national importance finding itself in serious financial distress. The Court ruled in the affirmative. Otherwise, the Directive's objective of providing a minimum level of shareholder protection would be seriously jeopardized. Whereas the Directive does not preclude placing a company under compulsory administration in the interests of its creditors, it continues to apply as long as the company's shareholders and normal bodies have not been divested of their powers.[545] In *Pafitis*[546] the same principle was extended to credit institutions in financial difficulties. Moreover, although a shareholder may be prevented from invoking his rights under Article 68 on the basis of national doctrines of abuse of right, merely exercising these rights in a situation where the shareholder benefited from the capital increase and did not exercise his pre-emptive rights cannot amount to an abuse of rights, even where

[543] Member States may decide not to apply the 'independent valuation' requirement of a contribution in kind if all shares (not just 90% of the nominal value as in Art 49(4)) are issued to one or more companies and the requirements of Art 49(4) are being met. Article 70(3) allows Member States to derogate from the 'independent valuation' requirement in the merger and division context, similar to Art 49(4), but extends this derogation to the situation of a public offer. Where an increase in capital is not fully subscribed, the capital will be increased by the amount of the subscription only if the conditions of the issue so provide; Art 71.

[544] Joined Cases C-19 and 20/90 *Keralla and Kerallas* (n 108), and Case C-381/89 *Ekklisias* ECLI:EU:C:1992:142.

[545] The Court arrived at similar conclusions in Case C-381/89 *Ekklisias* (n 544) and Joined Cases C-134/91 and 135/91 *Kerafina* ECLI:EU:C:1992:434.

[546] C-441/93 *Pafitis* ECLI:EU:C:1996:92.

the increase was essential to saving the company and was justified in the best interest of the national economy. Since an increase in capital is always designed to improve the economic situation of the company, the scope of Article 68 would be significantly reduced if a court were to decide otherwise. Only where the shareholder seeks to extract an improper advantage to the detriment of the company and manifestly contrary to the objective of Article 68 may a national court conclude that there has been an abuse of rights.[547] As a result of these decisions the principle according to which a decision to increase the capital must ultimately rest with the general meeting had obtained an almost invincible status in EU law.

However, in the wake of the global financial crisis of 2007–2009, the principle had to be relaxed somewhat. In two cases dealing with the recapitalization of, respectively, Slovenian and Irish banks, the Court of Justice has delineated possible exceptions. *Kotnik* concerned a challenge to the Commission's Banking Communication,[548] which requires adequate burden-sharing by existing investors before state aid may be granted. Accordingly, equity, hybrid capital holders and subordinated debt holders must have absorbed losses, by writing down or converting the respective instruments, with a view to restoring the minimum regulatory capital requirements. One of the questions referred to the Court was whether these requirements were compatible with what are now Articles 68, 73, 74, 79, and 81 of Directive (EU) 2017/1132, providing essentially that any increase or reduction in the capital of a public limited liability company must be subject to a decision by the general meeting. In *Dowling and Others* an Irish bank was recapitalized on the basis of a 'direction order', issued by the High Court, pursuant to which the Minister of Finance obtained new shares worth €2.7 billion at a share price significantly below par. This was part of an economic and financial readjustment programme under which Ireland obtained financial assistance from the European Union. According to the referring court, the 'direction order' was the only effective measure to prevent the bank's failure and was necessary to avert a serious threat to the financial stability of the European Union. Some shareholders challenged the 'direction order' on the basis that it was incompatible with what are now Articles 47 (no issue below par), 68 (capital increase decided on by general meeting), and 72 (pre-emptive rights) of Directive (EU) 2017/1132. In both cases, the Court held that the Directive's mechanisms for the protection of (minority) shareholders' interests relate to the 'normal operation of limited liability companies' only. However, the burden-sharing measures imposed by national authorities in the context of the granting of state aid as well as the 'direction order' constitute 'exceptional measures' taken by national authorities with an intention to prevent the company's failure in circumstances where there 'is a serious disturbance of the economy of a Member State and with the objective of preventing a systemic risk and ensuring the stability of the financial system'. The Second Company Law Directive (now Directive (EU) 2017/1132) does not stand in the way of capital measures under these circumstances. The court distinguished *Pafitis* on the basis that the latter concerned an 'ordinary reorganization measures' in respect of the insolvency of a single bank, whereas the measures at issue concerned extraordinary reorganizations, seeking to address a systemic financial crisis capable of adversely affecting the national financial system as a whole and the financial stability of the European Union.[549] The legal capital regime has now been amended so as to ensure that its protections do not stand in the way of the application of resolution tools and powers by national authorities in the course of a bank resolution procedure.[550]

[547] Case C-367/96 *Kefalas* ECLI:EU:C:1998:222; Case C-373/97 *Diamantis* ECLI:EU:C:2000:150.

[548] Communication from the Commission on the application, from 1 August 2013, of state aid rules to support measures in favour of banks in the context of the financial crisis, OJ 2013 C216/1.

[549] Case C-526/14 *Kotnik and Others* ECLI:EU:C:2016:570 paras 87–90; Case C-41/15 *Dowling and Others* (n 114) paras 48–53.

[550] Article 84 sub-paragraph 3; introduced by Art 123 of Directive 2014/59/EU of the European Parliament and of the Council of 15 May 2014 establishing a framework for the recovery and resolution of credit institutions and investment firms OJ 2014 L173/191.

(Minority) shareholder protection against dilution of their control and economic rights is further strengthened by Article 72: whenever the capital is increased by an issue for considerations in cash, the shares must be offered on a pre-emptive basis to the existing shareholders in proportion to the capital represented by their shares. Under the Directive, mandatory pre-emption rights are limited to issues for cash. The right of pre-emption may not be restricted or withdrawn in the articles of association; it may be restricted, however, by a decision of the general meeting on the basis of a written report submitted to the general meeting by the management board, indicating the reasons for the restriction and justifying the issue price. Shareholders can therefore block an under-priced issue, which would dilute the value of their shares. The decision to restrict or withdraw pre-emptive rights requires a qualified majority of two-thirds in general meeting; or, at the option of the Member States, a simple majority, provided that a quorum of at least half the subscribed capital is present at the meeting. In accordance with the notion of authorized capital, Article 72(5) allows Member States to provide that the authority to restrict or withdraw pre-emptive rights may be granted, either in the articles or by general meeting, to the management body, which has the power to decide on the issue of authorized shares. Pursuant to the Court's case law, Article 72 merely prescribes a minimum standard of shareholder protection. Thus, Member States may extend the scope of application of pre-emptive rights to issues for contributions in kind; and may impose more restrictive conditions on the withdrawal of the right of pre-emption by making such withdrawal dependent on certain substantive criteria or by setting a minimum issue price such as the 'net asset value' of the shares.[551] Article 72 also applies to the issue of convertible securities, but not to the actual conversion.[552]

Articles 73–81 deal with a reduction of capital. Any reduction in the subscribed capital must be subject to at least a decision by the general meeting, except a reduction pursuant to a court order. Article 73 refers to Article 83 which, in section (1), requires a two-thirds majority, but in section (2) allows Members States to let a simple majority suffice when at least half the subscribed capital is represented. Apparently, this reference means that a quorum of half the subscribed capital must always be present. Where a company has issued several classes of shares, each class must vote separately. Article 75 contains minimum requirements for the protection of creditors in situations where the reduction of capital is carried out with a view to return assets to shareholders ('effective' capital reduction). At least the creditors whose claims predate the disclosure of the decision to make the reduction shall be entitled to obtain security for claims, which have not fallen due by the date of disclosure. The Member States shall lay down the conditions for the exercise of that right. Member States are also allowed to maintain or introduce a regime under which creditors would need to consent to, or authorize, the reduction, or which gives creditors a right to challenge the reduction of capital. In any case, Member States must ensure that creditors are authorized to apply to the appropriate administrative or judicial authority for adequate safeguards provided that they can credibly demonstrate that owing to the reduction the satisfaction of their claims is in

[551] Case C-42/95 *Siemens AG v Nold* ECLI:EU:C:1996:444; Case C-338/06 *Commission v Spain* (n 108).

[552] Spanish law granted a right to pre-emption upon the issue of shares and of bonds convertible into shares not only to shareholders but also to the holders of bonds convertible into shares. According to the Court, what is now Art 72(1) and (6) do not provide that both the new shares and the bonds convertible into shares are to be offered exclusively to the shareholders. Consequently, these instruments can also be offered to holders of earlier issues of convertible bonds. However, the offer must not be made to both classes simultaneously, but 'on a pre-emptive basis' to the shareholders. Thus, only insofar as the shareholders have not exercised their right of pre-emption can those shares and bonds be offered to the holders of convertible bonds or other purchasers. Moreover, Spanish law provided that the right to pre-emption may be withdrawn under certain circumstances only upon the issue of new shares, not, however, on an issue of bonds convertible into shares. The Court held that although the Second Directive allowed Member States to adopt more restrictive conditions on withdrawal of the right of pre-emption, what is now Art 72(6) and (4) required that, in certain circumstances, the general meeting of shareholders should be able to decide to withdraw the right of pre-emption for all securities that are convertible into shares; Case C-338/06 *Commission v Spain* (n 108).

jeopardy and that no adequate safeguards have been obtained from the company. Article 76 deals with a 'nominal' reduction of capital, carried out to offset losses, and not intended to actually distribute company assets to the shareholders. In this case, the creditor protection regime of Article 75 does not apply. However, Member States must ensure that the reduction of subscribed capital may not be used for making payments or distributions to shareholders or discharging shareholders from the obligation to make their contributions. Article 77 caters for a so-called *coup d'accordéon*. In order to offset accumulated losses, the subscribed capital may be reduced below the minimum capital requirement, provided that the decision to reduce the subscribed capital takes effect only when the subscribed capital is simultaneously increased to an amount at least equal to the statutory minimum.

Articles 78-82 are owed to country-specific idiosyncrasies on redeemable shares. Article 78 caters for the French practice of redemption without reduction. Accordingly, Member States may authorize the total or partial redemption of the subscribed share capital without a reduction of the latter, subject to certain prerequisites, notably redemption only out of distributable profits. Article 79 concerns an analogous procedure for the German practice of redemption and compulsory withdrawal of shares.[553] And in accordance with the practice in the United Kingdom, Article 82 allows Member States to authorize companies to issue redeemable shares, which may be redeemed only out of distributable profits and subject to an amount equal to the par value of the redeemed shares being transferred to a non-distributable capital redemption reserve.

1. *'Effective' and 'nominal' increase*

An effective capital increase entails the issue of fresh shares for consideration in cash or in kind. Thus, the company's stated capital and share premium accounts will be increased by the aggregate of par value and share premium (if any), respectively, of the newly issued shares. At the same time, the company's assets will be increased by the aggregate amount of the consideration received. Looking across our three jurisdictions, we can perhaps distinguish three different forms of an effective capital increase. The most basic form is an 'orderly effective capital increase'.[554] A more flexible procedure that allows the management to quickly react to changing market conditions is provided by 'authorised capital'.[555] Finally, a simplified procedure applies in the context of the conversion of (debt) securities into shares.[556]

Under French and German law, an 'orderly effective capital increase' constitutes an amendment of the company's articles of association.[557] Consequently, the respective rules on article amendments apply. This requires a resolution of the general meeting of shareholders by which the stated capital figure is increased and new shares are created,[558] or, in France,

[553] Article 80 deals with the situation where the company compulsorily withdraws shares acquired by the company itself.

[554] AktG, §§182–191; Com Art L225-127 al. 1. [555] AktG, §§202–206. [556] ibid §§192–201.

[557] The law on private companies only recognizes the 'orderly effective capital increase'; 'authorised capital' is not available. Under German Law, an increase may be effectuated by an increase of the par value of shares or by formation of new shares; GmbHG, §55. In terms of procedure, similar principles as for public companies apply (n 555). In France, the necessary amendment to the articles of association requires a resolution by extraordinary general meeting of shareholders. The quorum and required majority are the same as in the case of a public company; Com Art 223-30 (n 556). For companies formed prior to 2 August 2005 a majority of ¾ of all shares (not just those represented at the meeting) is required; however these companies may opt into the new law. See also Germain and Magnier (n 68) para 1855.

[558] Under German law, a capital increase (and reduction) is subject to the general provisions of AktG, §§179–181. An amendment requires a resolution by the general meeting of shareholders with a qualified majority of 75% of the capital present or represented at the meeting. The articles may provide for a higher or lower majority requirement and further pre-conditions; AktG, §179(2). For certain transactions in the context of capital increase and reduction the 75% majority is the irreducible minimum so that only a higher majority may be stipulated. Where the amendment would affect the rights of certain classes of shares or the relationship between different classes, a separate resolution of classes that will be negatively affected is also required. The 75% majority applies for each and every class; AktG, §179(3). In order to be effective the amendment must be registered; AktG, §181.

the nominal value of existing shares is increased.[559] The decision must be duly disclosed.[560] The increase is executed by subscription of the new issue in its entirety.[561] The provisions on payment for shares apply.[562]

This procedure for an orderly effective capital increase is rather cumbersome and slow. This is remedied by the concept of 'authorised capital', on which our European jurisdictions slightly differ.[563] Under German law, the management board may be authorized, in the articles or by way of article amendment, to issue new shares.[564] The authorization may be granted for a period of up to five years only and up to a ceiling not exceeding 50 per cent of the share capital at the time of authorization. The management board can then decide when to issue fresh shares, how many and under what conditions, subject to approval by the supervisory board.[565] For the implementation of the increase the provisions on an 'orderly effective increase' apply accordingly.[566] Every time the management board decides to issue new shares, the implementation of the respective increase must be registered and it becomes effective only with registration. Only thereafter may shares be allotted and delivered to the new shareholders. The procedure is of great practical significance; virtually all listed companies have an 'authorised capital'.[567] Under French law, the extraordinary general meeting may delegate its competence to decide on an increase of capital to the board of directors or the executive board ('delegation of competence').[568] Alternatively, the extraordinary meeting may decide on the increase itself, but delegate the power to determine the terms and conditions of the issue to the board of directors or the executive board ('delegation of power').[569] In the former case, the board of directors or the executive board shall determine the period, not exceeding twenty-six months, during which the respective delegation may be exercised. Within these limits, the board then has the power to determine the conditions and terms of the issue, to declare the completion of the capital increases and to make the appropriate amendments to the articles of association.[570] Certain matters in this context require a separate resolution, in particular an issue without pre-emptive rights, an issue of convertible securities and of preference shares. In all other cases, the capital increase must be effectuated within five years of the extraordinary general meeting's decision or delegation of power.[571] In companies whose shares are admitted to trading on a regulated market the power to decide to proceed with the issue or to postpone it may be delegated further; by the board of directors to the managing director or with his approval to one or more other managers; by the executive board to its chairman or with his approval to one or more of its members.[572]

[559] Com Art L225-127 al. 1. In France, only an extraordinary general meeting is competent to decide on an increase in capital. An extraordinary general meeting, generally required for amendment of the company's articles of association (Com Art L225-96), requires the presence of at least a quorum of 25% of the voting shares when first convened, and 20% if reconvened. The general meeting decides with a majority of 2/3 of the votes present at the meeting and on the basis of a written report produced by the board of directors or management board as the case may be; Com Art L225-129.

[560] AktG, §184.

[561] Where the capital increase has not been subscribed in its entirety the board of directors or executive board has a number of options for retaining the benefits received; Germain and Magnier (n 68) para 2526: where at least 75% of the increase have been subscribed, the amount of the increase may be limited to the subscribed amount unless the general meeting decides otherwise; unsubscribed shares may be freely allotted unless the general meeting decides otherwise; and unsubscribed shares may be offered to the public if that was provided for by general meeting. The board may freely decide which ones of these options it wants to use and in what order. If thereafter the increase has not been subscribed by at least 75% it will be ineffective. In any case, however, the board may limit the increase to the amount received if the unsubscribed amount represents less than 3% of the capital increase; Com Art L225-134.

[562] AktG, §§183, 184, 188.

[563] In the UK, under the Companies Act 1985 the memorandum of association had to state the maximum total nominal value of shares that the company could issue. It was then up to the board of directors to decide on the issue of new shares within the ceiling imposed by the memorandum. The Companies Act 2006 has done away with this requirement; Davies and Worthington (n 124) para 11-12.

[564] Authorization by article amendment requires a resolution by general meeting with at least a 75% majority of the capital represented at the meeting; AktG, §202(2).

[565] AktG, §204. [566] ibid §203. [567] Windbichler (n 126) 436 (§32 para 29).

[568] Com Art L225-129 al. 1.

[569] Com Art L225-129-1. see also Germain and Magnier (n 68) para 2512.

[570] Com Art L225-129-2. [571] Com Art L225-129 al 2. [572] Com Art L225-129-4.

Under Companies Act 2006 the default rule is that the directors cannot exercise any power of the company to allot shares except in accordance with the prerequisites stipulated in the Companies Act.[573] In respect of both private companies and public companies,[574] the directors may allot shares only if authorized to do so by the company's articles or by ordinary resolution of the general meeting.[575] Authorization can be given for a particular project, or generally. It must specify the maximum amount of shares that may be allotted as well as its expiry date, which must not be more than five years from the time when authorization was granted. Authorization may be revoked, altered or renewed by ordinary resolution. Since the authorized share capital is no longer part of the memorandum a copy of any resolution granting, varying, revoking or renewing authority to allot must be sent to Companies House within fifteen days of being adopted.[576] Shares allotted in contravention of these provisions are not void; however, the directors involved who had knowledge of the contravention commit a criminal offence.[577]

An effective increase in capital may also result from an exercise of conversion rights embedded in debt and other securities (convertible securities).[578] The issuance of convertible securities is subject to the same principles.[579] However, no shareholder approval is required at the conversion stage.[580]

In the course of a nominal capital increase the company does not obtain any new assets. Rather, it is a purely numerical exercise in order to approximate the stated capital to an increased value of net assets. For that purpose, retained earnings are transformed into legal capital and, thus, subjected to the capital maintenance regime. Existing shareholders receive new 'bonus' shares in proportion to their existing holdings. A nominal capital increase may be effectuated for a number of different reasons. An increased equity cushion may increase the creditworthiness of the company and reduce the costs of debt finance. In contrast with a cash dividend, bonus shares will not be taxed at shareholder level because the aggregate value of a shareholder's interest remains the same. The greater number of shares outstanding reduces the dividend per share and the share price, which may render the shares more liquid and more attractive for small investors.[581] The procedures and prerequisites for the issue of bonus shares differ amongst our European jurisdictions. Under German law,[582] a nominal capital increase requires a resolution of the general meeting with a 75 per cent majority and

[573] Companies Act 2006, s 549.

[574] Except in private companies with only one class of shares, where directors may exercise the power of the company to allot shares of that class, unless the company's articles of association restrict this power to allot shares; ibid s 550.

[575] ibid s 551. [576] ibid ss 551(9), 30. [577] ibid s 549(6).

[578] Com Art L225-127 al. 2 and L225-149, L225-177. The AktG reserves the procedure for three situations: (i) the issue of convertible bonds which entitle the holder to either exchange them for shares or to acquire a certain number of shares; (ii) a merger where the target shareholders exchange their shares for shares in the bidder; and (iii) rights of share acquisition under an employee share scheme; AktG, §192(2). It requires a resolution of the general meeting with at least a 75% majority of the capital represented at the meeting; AktG, §193. The nominal value of the 'conditional capital' may not exceed 50% of legal capital at the time of the resolution (10% in case of employee share schemes); AktG, §192(3). The resolution becomes effective with registration in the commercial register; AktG, §200. The increase is implemented, step by step, if and when option holders exercise their options by written declaration; AktG, §198. Shares may be allotted only for the purpose stipulated in the resolution and only for full consideration; AktG, §199. Within one month following the end of each financial year, the management board must file with the commercial register a declaration as to the extent new shares were issued in accordance with 'conditional capital': AktG, §201. Registration is, however, not constitutive.

[579] Companies Act 2006, s 549(1)(b).

[580] ibid s 549(3). Moreover, shareholder approval is not required for the allotment of shares in pursuance of an employee share scheme, and the granting of a right to subscribe for, or to convert any security into, shares already allotted: ibid s 549(2). A bond convertible into existing, rather than new, shares is unusual; its issuance would however not require shareholder approval, presumably because such approval was required for the initial issue of the underlying shares; Davies and Worthington (n 124) para 24-5.

[581] F Kübler and H-D Assmann, Gesellschaftsrecht (6th edn, CF Müller Verlag 2006) 251.

[582] The law on private companies allows for a nominal capital increase by increasing the par value of existing shares or by formation of new shares to be attributed to existing shareholders in proportion to their existing shares; GmbHG, §§57c-57o.

subsequent registration.[583] Moreover, the amount of the increase must have been reported in the last annual balance sheet as 'capital reserve' or 'retained earnings'.[584] Thus, annual profits may not immediately be used for a nominal capital increase. To the extent that on the same balance sheet losses are reported or carried forward, 'capital reserve' and 'retained earnings' cannot be utilized for a nominal capital increase. The new shares can only be issued to the existing shareholders in proportion to the capital represented by their shares. This right of the existing shareholders cannot be restricted by resolution of the general meeting.[585] In case of accountable par, no new shares need to be issued because a share's participation in the company's capital increases automatically. In the UK, a nominal increase of capital can be effectuated by the 'capitalisation' of accumulated reserves (retained earnings) or the application of the share premium account to finance the issue of bonus shares.[586] Since the issue of bonus shares is not deemed to be a distribution,[587] non-distributable profits, that is, unrealized profits, may be used for the issue of bonus shares subject to the articles of association. The issue of bonus shares generally requires an ordinary resolution by the general meeting, unless the board of directors is authorized to issue bonus shares in the articles of association. In order to be able to issue bonus shares, the outstanding shares must be fully paid up.[588] Under French law, in addition to available reserves and annual profits, unrealized profits resulting from the revaluation of corporate assets and share premiums may also be used to effectuate a nominal capital increase.[589] The competence to decide on a nominal increase rests with the general meeting. However, it decides with a quorum of 20 per cent of the voting shares when first convened and no quorum when reconvened, and with a simple majority of the votes present or represented.[590] The available reserves are reduced by the amount of the increase and the capital account is increased accordingly. At the same time, the company may either increase the nominal amount of the outstanding shares in accordance with the increase or issue new and fully paid up shares (bonus shares) to the existing shareholders.[591]

2. *Pre-emptive rights*

Under German law, pre-emptive rights are deemed to be a cornerstone of minority shareholder protection. They were introduced as early as 1897 in order to prevent the management and supervisory board from diluting shareholdings. In France, prior to the introduction of statutory pre-emptive rights by decree law of 1935, they were already frequently provided for in the articles of association.[592] English law did not provide for statutory pre-emption rights before the implementation of the Second Company Law Directive in 1980; however, pre-emptive rights could be provided for in a company's articles.[593] In line with Directive (EU) 2017/1132, the default rule in all three jurisdictions currently is that upon an effective increase in capital (other than through a conversion of hybrid securities)[594] existing shareholders have pre-emptive rights and may subscribe freshly issued shares in proportion to their existing shareholdings.[595] For this purpose, and before any new shares may be allotted

[583] AktG, §§207, 212. [584] ibid §208. [585] ibid §212. [586] Companies Act 2006, s 610(3).
[587] ibid s 829(2)(a).
[588] *EIC Services Ltd v Phipps* [2005] 1 WLR 1377. [589] Germain and Magnier (n 68) para 2537.
[590] Com Art L225-130 and L225-98. [591] Germain and Magnier (n 68) para 2540.
[592] ibid para 2515. [593] See *Ving v Robinson and Woodcock Ltd* (1912) 56 SJ 412.
[594] Under German law, no pre-emptive rights apply in this case because such an increase takes place in pursuance of a specific and limited purpose only. Under French law, an issue of securities convertible into shares entails the waiving of pre-emptive rights to subscribe to shares resulting from the conversion Com Art L225-132 al 4 and 5.
[595] AktG, §§186, 203; Com Art L225-132. Pursuant to Companies Act 2006, s 561(1), a company may allot equity securities to any person only after it has made an offer to allot an equal proportion in nominal value on the same or more favourable terms to all persons holding ordinary shares in the company, and the period during which such an offer may be accepted has expired, or the company has received notice of acceptance or refusal of every offer so made.

to third parties, a proportionate amount of new shares must be offered to the existing shareholders, and the offer must remain open for a certain period of time.[596] The scopes of the respective pre-emptive rights schemes differ. Whereas, under German law pre-emptive rights apply regardless of whether the new shares are issued for a contribution in cash or in kind; under both English and French law an issue for contributions in kind is exempt.[597] This exemption greatly facilitates transactions in the takeover and merger context, which carry a considerable risk of dilution.[598] For example, where company A wishes to take over part of the business of company B, instead of issuing shares to the public in order to raise the necessary funds, A may issue shares directly to B in exchange for B's assets as a contribution in kind, thus avoiding the application of pre-emptive rights. Under a prearranged scheme, an investment bank may acquire the A shares from B at a fixed price and place them with interested investors, thus providing B with the cash it desired.[599] Minimum shareholder protection is provided by application of the provisions on contributions in kind, and in the UK under the Listing Rules.[600]

In addition to certain exceptions[601] and exclusions,[602] legal systems provide for a general procedure that allows for the removal of pre-emptive rights. In line with Directive (EU) 2017/1132, these procedures follow a similar trajectory, but differ in terms of certain additional substantive requirements. UK law is the most generous. Sections 570 and 571 of the Companies Act 2006 provide for the disapplication of pre-emptive rights either generally or in relation to a specific allotment. A general disapplication may be made if the directors are generally authorized to issue new shares.[603] In that case, the company's articles or the general meeting by special resolution may provide that the directors are authorized to issue shares as if section 561 would not apply or would only apply with certain modifications.[604] In respect of a specific allotment, the members may decide by special resolution that section 561 of the Companies Act 2006 will not apply or will apply only with modifications. Such a resolution is subject to a recommendation by the directors and the directors must provide a written report setting out the reasons for the recommendation, the amount to be paid for

596 In Germany: at least two weeks, AktG, §168(1); in the UK: at least 21 days, Companies Act 2006, s 562(5); France: five trading days, Com Art L225-141.

597 Companies Act 2006, s 565; Germain and Magnier (n 68) para 2515.

598 Davies and Worthington (n 124) para 24-8.

599 ibid.

600 see FCA Listing Rules, 9.5.10. Companies with a premium listing may issue shares, other than by way of a rights issue (to existing shareholders), with a discount only of no more than 10% to the mid-market price of the shares. Where a higher discount is intended, shareholder approval is required.

601 Under UK law, exceptions are: the issue of bonus shares: Companies Act 2006, s 564; and the issue to be held under an employee share scheme: Companies Act 2006, s 566. Under French law, an increase by way of incorporation of reserves into capital is also exempt; Germain and Magnier (n 68) para 2515.

602 Under UK Law, a private company may exclude pre-emptive rights, generally or in relation to allotments of a particular description, in its articles of association: Companies Act 2006, s 567. For public company's exclusion is available only where the statutory right of pre-emption is replaced, in the articles, with a pre-emption alternative that operates on a class basis; ibid s 568. Under French law, pre-emptive rights may be individually waived or renounced and may be separately transferable and are frequently actively traded. In fact the Paris stock exchange maintains a special listing for pre-emptive rights; Germain and Magnier (n 68) para 2520. Renunciation may be done for the benefit of a person specifically named, or generally without naming a beneficiary. In the former case, the effect is similar to a transfer of the right; ibid para 2517. Only the latter form is available for listed companies; Com Art R.225-122. In private companies, pre-emptive rights of existing shareholders are not provided for in the Code de commerce and may result only form a clause in the articles of association. However, where the new shares are subscribed by third parties their entry into the company must have been agreed by the existing shareholders, similar to entry on the basis of a transfer of shares; see Germain and Magnier (n 68) para 1857.

603 Directors may also be given power to disapply existing shareholders' right of pre-emption, in the articles or by special resolution, in a private company with only one class of shares: Companies Act 2006, s 569; and generally in respect of treasury shares: ibid s 573. In private companies, protection of minority shareholders is achieved through directors' fiduciary duties. Indeed, it was in connection with the allotment of shares by directors to the detriment of (certain) shareholders that the duty to act for proper purposes (now ibid s 171(b)) was developed; *Hogg v Cramphorn Ltd* [1967] Ch 254; *Howard Smith Ltd v Ampol Petroleum Ltd* [1974] AC 821 (PC), on appeal from the Supreme Court of New South Wales. Because of the leeway provided by the statutory provisions, this case law is still important as a protective device for minority shareholders.

604 Companies Act 2006, s 570.

the shares, and the justification for that amount.[605] Similarly, under French law, the extraordinary general meeting that decides or authorizes the capital increase may remove the pre-emptive rights for the total capital increase or one or more tranches thereof. The general meeting's decision will be based on a report drawn up by the board of directors or by the executive board and must take into account a report by the company's auditors when the increase is effectuated. Where the board of directors or the executive board decides on the increase on the basis of authorization granted by the general meeting, they may remove pre-emptive rights,[606] if so authorized by a separate resolution of the general meeting. Pursuant to these principles, pre-emptive rights may be removed only in three situations.[607] First, the general meeting may remove the pre-emptive rights in order to reserve the capital increase for one or more persons designated by name or certain persons who meet specific criteria. In the latter case, the board of directors or the executive board may be authorized to determine the persons who fall within the category and the number of securities to be allotted to them.[608] Secondly, removal of pre-emptive rights without naming specific beneficiaries or determining a certain category of potential beneficiaries is possible for public offerings in order to facilitate an issue to institutional investors or to the public in general.[609] Thirdly, for companies whose shares are admitted to trading on a regulated market, pre-emptive rights may be replaced by a priority subscription period of not less than three trading days for the benefit of existing shareholders.[610] However, German law is the most restrictive. AktG, §186(3) and (4) impose the following formal requirements:[611] The removal of pre-emptive rights must be stipulated in the shareholder resolution implementing the capital increase and requires at least a 75 per cent majority of the represented capital. The exclusion must be duly disclosed. The management board must prepare a written report for the general meeting outlining the reasons for the exclusion. In addition, case law has developed further substantive requirements.[612]

In BGHZ 71, 40 (*Kali + Salz*), the BGH held that the exclusion of pre-emptive rights had to be justified on objective grounds in the interest of the company. More precisely, the issue of the new shares and the exclusion of shareholders' pre-emptive rights must be in the interests of the company. Further, the exclusion has to be proportionate, that is, it must be necessary and the least restrictive means to achieve the objectives pursued. The interests of the company and of the shareholders have to be balanced. The more severely the interests of the shareholders are restricted, the more pressing have to be the operational needs of the company that weigh in favour of exclusion. The issue price of the new shares must not be inadequate in relation to the value of the securities. It is not necessary that the company would have collapsed but for the capital increase and exclusion of pre-emptive rights. However, the resolution will be unassailable only if the respective organs of the company have based their decision on objective grounds, have carefully balanced the conflicting interests, and have had reason to believe, at the time of decision-making, that the measures were necessary in order to safeguard the interests of the company. The application of these principles was very problematic in the case of 'authorised capital' where the management board decides also on the removal of pre-emptive rights. Thus, in BGHZ 83, 319 (*Phillip Holzmann*) it was held

[605] A resolution disapplying pre-emptive rights must be sent to Companies House within 15 days: ibid s 571.

[606] This decision must be based on an auditor's report drawn up for the respective board: Com Art L225-135.

[607] Germain and Magnier (n 68) para 2519.

[608] Com Art L225-138.

[609] Com Art L225-136.

[610] Com Art L225-135 al 2.

[611] The law on private companies does not contain a provision similar to AktG, §186. However, today it is generally accepted that the principle of equal treatment as well as the shareholders' interest in the maintenance of their undiluted influence is even stronger in private companies, justifying the analogous application of AktG, §186. The resolution excluding pre-emptive rights will be subject to similar formal and substantive requirements as in case of public companies.

[612] No further requirements apply if the amount of the increase is limited to 10% of the share capital and the issue price is close to the stock market price; AktG, §186(3).

that not only may pre-emptive rights be excluded only where necessary in the interest of the company (to be judged at the time of the decision of the management board), in addition, at the time of the authorizing resolution, specific facts had to be presented that indicated that in the future the exclusion of shareholders' pre-emptive rights might become necessary and would be justified. The objectives of the authorization had to be described precisely in the shareholders' resolution. A resolution that granted the management board a rubber-stamp authorization without being based on particular circumstances was voidable. In Case C-42/95 *Siemens AG v Nold* the conformity of this case-law with the Second Company Law Directive was challenged before the Court of Justice.[613] Although the Court did not have any objections, the BGH subsequently revised its case law.[614] In the interest of flexibility and the practical requirements of fast moving capital markets, the BGH deemed it sufficient that the shareholders' resolution delineates the objectives of the authorization in abstract form. The measures that the management board is authorized to adopt must be in the interest of the company. If pre-emptive rights are excluded in the resolution itself (as opposed to authorizing management to exclude pre-emptive rights), the general meeting shall apply the *Kali + Salz* test (balancing of the conflicting interests and analysis of the proportionality of the exclusion) as far as possible on the basis of the abstract description and facts at hand. The management board, on the other hand, has the obligation to ascertain whether in its opinion and in light of the more complete information available to it the shareholders' resolution is justified in the interest of the company. If this is not the case the management board must not make use of the authorization. If the shareholders' resolution authorizes the management to exclude the pre-emptive rights, management shall apply the *Kali + Salz* test in order to determine whether exclusion is permissible. Moreover, the management board may only exercise the authorization if the specific situation in which it intends to increase the capital (and possibly exclude shareholders' pre-emptive rights) is in conformity with the objectives of the authorization as set out in abstract form in the resolution; the measures to be adopted are in the interest of the company; and the supervisory board approves of the decision of the management board.[615]

Interestingly, at least for listed companies, the result under the restrictive German regime may not be so different from that under the very flexible UK regime. This is because in respect of listed companies, institutional investors are strongly opposed to dilution of their interests without their individual consent, and accordingly value pre-emptive rights very highly.[616] Consequently, the Pre-Emption Group, representing listed companies, institutional investors and intermediaries, has produced a Statement of Principles to be taken into account when considering the disapplication of pre-emptive rights in companies listed on the London Stock Exchange's Main Market. Under these Principles, which are of a non-binding nature, support of shareholders for a disapplication of pre-emptive rights is likely to be granted (only) where the company is seeking authority to issue non-pre-emptively no more than 5 per cent of ordinary share capital in any one year, and no more than an additional 5 per cent for a specific acquisition or capital investment ('routine disapplication'). Moreover, in any rolling three-year period, a company should issue no more than 7.5 per cent of cash equity securities on a 'routine disapplication' basis.[617] In other—non-routine—cases, however, shareholder support will depend on disapplication being justified on the basis of the purpose of the issue, the company's financing needs and alternative financing options, its track record of creating shareholder value, and the level of dilution.[618] In short, non-pre-emptive issues above the 5 per cent threshold require justification by objective

[613] Case C-42/95 *Siemens AG v Nold* ECLI:EU:C:1996:444.. [614] BGHZ 136, 133 (*Siemens/Nold*).
[615] AktG, §204(1). [616] Davies and Worthington (n 124) para 24-13.
[617] Pre-emption Group, *Disapplying Pre-Emption Rights: A Statement of Principles*, 2015, Pt 2A para 3; Part 2B para 1.
[618] ibid Pt 3.

business reasons. The result may be remarkably similar to German law, despite a completely different regulatory strategy.

3. *'Effective' and 'nominal' reduction*

In accordance with Directive (EU) 2017/1132, the European legal systems generally distinguish between an effective and a nominal reduction of capital. In the course of an effective capital reduction assets that the company no longer needs will be distributed to shareholders. This may be the case where the company downsizes for some reason, perhaps focussing on its core business, divesting from unprofitable lines of business, closing an unprofitable branch or subsidiary etc. A nominal reduction merely results in an approximation of legal capital to the net assets of the company that have been reduced by accumulating losses. This measure prepares the company for the payment of dividends in the future as soon as it starts to trade profitably again. Without the reduction, a dividend payment would be possible only after all accumulated losses have been offset by accumulated profits. This may take years and would render the injection of fresh capital very unattractive.[619] Thus, the nominal reduction is an indispensable tool for the restructuring of a company in financial distress. By contrast, the effective reduction of capital is of little practical significance.

Technically, a capital reduction may be effectuated in three different ways.[620] First, for par value shares, par value may be reduced equally for all shares in issue.[621] The aggregate of the new par value must then be equal to the reduced legal capital. The advantage is that all shareholders are affected in equal measure. In case of accountable par, the amount attributable to each share is reduced automatically with a reduction of share capital.[622] As a second technique,[623] the number of shares may be reduced by way of consolidation. Each shareholder delivers up his shares to the company and receives back a reduced number of shares in proportion to the reduction of share capital.[624] The third way to effectuate a capital reduction is the reacquisition by the company of its own shares and their subsequent cancellation. The company may acquire its own shares in pursuance of a resolution to reduce its capital.[625] In that case, the company acquires its shares for consideration from shareholders on a voluntary basis out of distributable profits. Alternatively, the company may redeem shares that were issued as redeemable at the option of the company on the basis of the articles or their subsequent amendment.[626]

The form of capital reduction is to be distinguished from the applicable procedure, which may vary depending on whether the reduction is effective or nominal.[627] An effective reduction that is aimed at allowing distributions out of capital is subject to much stricter

[619] Windbichler (n 126) 442 (§32 para 46); Kübler and Assmann (n 581) 251.

[620] Companies Act 2006, s 641(3): 'a company may reduce its share capital under this section in any way'.

[621] AktG, §222(4) sentence 1.

[622] Under German law, this type of reduction is unavailable where it would result in par values (or accountable par) below the statutory minimum of €1.

[623] AktG, §222(4) sentence 2.

[624] Germain and Magnier (n 68) para 2547. A problem arises where the result of this calculation is not a whole number of shares but a mere fraction. This is particularly likely in case of minority shareholders. Such a fraction may be raised to whole numbers in exchange for additional payment by the shareholder. Alternatively, shares of several shareholders may be consolidated and sold on behalf of these shareholders; Windbichler (n 126) 440–1 (§32 para 41).

[625] AktG, §71(1) no 6. [626] ibid §237; Com Art L225-207.

[627] In practice, a nominal reduction of capital is often combined with an effective increase of capital. In a first step, the share capital is reduced to offset accumulated losses, and may be reduced even below the statutory minimum capital requirement to zero. This ensures that losses are carried solely by the incumbent shareholders and facilitates the payment of dividends out of future profits. In a second step, the capital is increased at least up to the minimum capital with contributions by the new subscribers. The existing shares will be cancelled; the incumbent shareholders may exercise their right of pre-emption. If they waive their rights they will no longer be members of the company (a so-called '*coup d'accordéon*'); Windbichler (n 126) 444–5 (§32 para 52); Cozian, Viandier, and Deboissy (n 67) para 1234; Germain and Magnier (n 68) para 2548.

prerequisites in terms of creditor protection. Generally, a capital reduction, effective or nominal, requires a resolution of the general meeting with the necessary majorities and quora.[628] Legal systems differ in respect of the systems of creditor protection in place. Under German law, upon an effective reduction involving the distribution of company assets, creditors whose claims where in existence prior to the disclosure of the reduction and who come forward within six months following disclosure may demand security for their claims or payment if due. A distribution to shareholders may be made only after the six-month period has expired and if all creditors who came forward during that period have either been paid or have obtained security.[629] A simplified procedure is available for a nominal reduction in order to offset reduced asset values or other losses, or to transfer sums to the capital reserve.[630] It must not result in a distribution of corporate assets to shareholders.[631] Creditor protection is achieved by restricting the company's dividend paying capability.[632] Under French law, where the reduction is effective and aimed at allowing the distribution of assets among the shareholders, the representative of the body of bondholders and creditors whose debts predate the date on which the minutes of the decision to reduce the capital were filed with the register may raise an objection to the reduction within 30 days following that date. This objection can only be rejected by court order. The court may also order that the debts be repaid or that guarantees be provided if the company offers them and they are deemed to be sufficient. The capital reduction procedure is halted during the thirty-day time limit for raising an objection, and before a court decision has been given on any objection raised. If the judge grants the objection, the capital reduction procedure is immediately halted until sufficient guarantees are provided or until the debts are repaid. If the judge rejects the objection, the reduction procedure may recommence.[633] Under UK law, in respect of public companies, the special resolution to reduce the capital must be confirmed by the court,[634] irrespective of whether the reduction is carried out in order to return capital to its shareholders, extinguish or reduce the liability on shares not fully paid up, or, in preparation of a capital increase, as a write-off against share capital in order to approximate the share capital to the real value of the company's net assets.[635] If the reduction is an effective one, involving a payment to shareholders of any amount of paid up share capital or diminution of liability in respect of unpaid share capital, those creditors having a claim against the company at a date fixed by the court are entitled to object to the reduction, however, only if they can show 'that there is a real likelihood that the reduction would result in the company being unable to discharge his debt or claim when it fell due'.[636] This is a significant limitation of creditor

[628] In Germany, at least a 75% majority of the capital represented at the meeting. The resolution must specify the objective of the reduction and its form, and determine whether company assets are distributed to shareholders; AktG, §222 and §229(3) with AktG, §§222, 223, 227. An objective justification for the measure is not required. Both resolution and its execution are to be registered; AktG, §§223, 227. Under French law, an extraordinary general meeting decides on a reduction of capital (quorum of 25% of voting shares when first convened; 20% if reconvened; two-thirds majority of votes); Com Art L225-96, on the basis of an auditor's report assessing the causes and conditions of the transaction; Com Art L225-204. The general meeting may also delegate the decision to the board of directors or the executive board, as the case may be. In that case, the board must draw up and publish a report and make the appropriate amendments to the articles of association. The reduction of capital must not jeopardize equality among shareholders. Pursuant to Companies Act 2006, s 641, a company may reduce its share capital (including share premium account, capital redemption reserve and redenomination reserve), if it is a private company, by special resolution supported by a solvency statement of its directors; in all other cases, by special resolution to be confirmed by the court.

[629] AktG, §225. [630] ibid §229. [631] ibid §230.

[632] A dividend out of distributable profits may be paid only after statutory reserve and capital reserve together amount to at least 10% of the share capital. Moreover, a dividend of more than 4% may be paid only for a financial year that begins later than two years following the resolution, unless creditors have been paid in full or have obtained security; AktG, §233.

[633] Com Art L225-205. [634] Companies Act 2006, ss 641(1)(b), 645.

[635] ibid s 641(4). Subdivisions of shares into shares of smaller denomination or consolidation into shares of larger denomination is not a reduction of capital where the aggregate nominal value of the shares remains constant: ibid ss 617(3), 618.

[636] ibid s 646(1).

protection and makes a reduction of capital it easier for a company. The court may confirm the reduction only where it is satisfied with respect to any creditor entitled to object that either the creditor has consented to the reduction, or that their claim has been discharged or secured.[637] In general, the court may confirm a reduction of capital only:

> where the court is satisfied (a) that the proposed reduction affects all shareholders of equal standing in a similar manner, or that those treated in a different manner from their equals have consented to that different treatment, and (b) that the cause of the reduction (capital in excess of wants; capital lost; capital not represented by available assets, or as the case may be) was properly put to shareholders so that they could exercise an informed choice, and that the cause is proved by the evidence before the court.[638]

The court will refuse confirmation of the reduction if it is not fair and equitable as between the different classes of shareholders.[639]

Under French and German law, the procedures applicable for private companies are similar to those for the respective public company forms.[640] In the United Kingdom, pursuant to section 642 of the Companies Act 2006, private companies can reduce their share capital subject to the passing of a special resolution supported by a solvency statement. The solvency statement, to be made by the directors, must state that each of the directors has formed the opinion that there is no ground on which the company could be found to be unable to pay its debts and that the company will be able to pay its debts as they fall due during the year following the reduction (unless it is intended that the company be wound up within twelve months).[641] The solvency statement is backed by criminal liability of the directors involved if they had no reasonable grounds for the opinion expressed in it.[642] In addition, directors may be liable to the company for breach of their general duties; and directors and shareholders who received assets from the company in knowledge of the breach may be liable to restore them to the company. The principles on unlawful dividends apply.[643]

II. United States

In the United States, the increase and reduction of capital are straightforward affairs with a minimum of regulatory impediments. Generally, the board of directors are in the driving seat. Creditor and (minority) shareholder protection is achieved largely through fiduciary principles.

Irrespective of whether the legal capital and par value concepts apply, the articles of incorporation, or certificate of incorporation, must set forth any class of shares and series of shares within a class, and the number of each class and series, that the company is authorized to issue (authorized shares).[644] Within that limit, the board of directors is then free to decide whether and to what amount authorized shares may be issued and on what terms;[645] this power can be reserved for the shareholders in the articles of incorporation.[646] In contrast to our European legal systems, there is no limit on the amount of, or the maximum term of validity for, authorized capital. If all authorized shares are outstanding and the corporation wants to raise further equity capital, it must amend its articles of incorporation (or certificate of incorporation) so as to increase the number of shares authorized. The shareholders do not have a vested property right resulting from any provision in the articles. Consequently, the

637 ibid s 648.
638 *Re Jupiter House Investments (Cambridge) Ltd* [1985] 1 WLR 975.
639 *Poole v National Bank of China Ltd* [1907] AC 229.
640 GmbHG, §58; Com Art L223-34. see also Cozian, Viandier, and Deboissy (n 67) para 1502.
641 Companies Act 2006, s 643. The solvency statement together with the resolution confirming the reduction must be sent to Companies House within 15 days after the resolution: ibid s 644.
642 ibid s 643(4) and (5).
643 Davies and Worthington (n 124) para 13-41.
644 MBCA, §6.01(a); DGCL, §102(a)(4).
645 DGCL, §161.
646 MBCA, §6.21.

corporation may amend its articles at any time.[647] In principle, the proposed amendment must be adopted by the board of directors and must subsequently be approved by the general meeting with at least a majority of the votes entitled to be cast on the amendment.[648] Under the same principles, a corporation may issue a 'share dividend' or 'share split'[649] ('bonus shares' under UK terminology) out of retained profits to its existing shareholders on a pro rata basis.[650] Under MBCA, if the corporation has only one class of shares outstanding, the board of directors can, without shareholder approval, increase the number of authorized shares to the extent that is necessary to issue a 'share dividend'.[651]

Initially and in contrast to the situation in the UK, common law recognized pre-emptive rights entitling existing shareholders to acquire a proportionate amount of the new issue and to trade these rights.[652] Today state laws vary as to whether pre-emptive rights are granted. It is, however, generally accepted that pre-emptive rights are not an inherent aspect of the ownership of shares, but a right that may be granted or withheld by the articles of incorporation. If the state corporation law provides for pre-emptive rights the corporation will be able to 'opt out' of the respective provision. MBCA and DGCL adopt an 'opt in' solution instead. There will be no pre-emptive rights except to the extent that the articles of incorporation (or certificate of incorporation) so provide.[653] The MBCA further provides 'standard terms' for where the articles provide that 'the corporation elects to have pre-emptive rights'. In that case, the shareholders have a pre-emptive right to acquire proportional amounts of the unissued shares on uniform terms and conditions prescribed by the board of directors. There will be no pre-emptive rights in respect of shares issued as compensation to directors, officers or agents of the company, shares issued within six months of incorporation, and shares issued for non-cash consideration. Shares subject to pre-emptive rights not acquired by shareholders may be issued to the public for a period of one year for consideration not lower than the consideration set for the exercise of pre-emptive rights. If issued within one year for a lower consideration or after the expiration of one year the shareholders' pre-emptive rights will be triggered (again). This very flexible approach will hardly be enough to protect minority shareholders against dilution of their voting power. Indeed, since there will be no pre-emptive rights if shares are issued to directors and officers of the corporation pre-emptive rights seem to be somewhat futile. Today, it is generally thought that the law relating to fiduciary duties[654] will provide sufficient protection.[655]

Formal capital reductions are of no relevance in the United States. Effective capital reductions in order to distribute corporate assets to shareholders appear to be unnecessary given the very flexible restrictions on dividends and distributions. This is particularly true under a system that, following MBCA, has no concept of legal capital and applies a 'solvency test' and 'simple balance sheet test'. A nominal reduction is unnecessary because under a system of no par value shares, the shares always reflect the true value of the firm. Consequently, the MBCA does not contain any provisions on formal reductions of capital. The number of shares may be reduced, however, by the company acquiring its own shares and subsequently retiring (or cancelling) them.[656]

647 MBCA, §10.01; DGCL, §242(a)(3). 648 MBCA, §10.03; DGCL, §242(b).

649 'Share dividend' refers to a situation where the number of new shares in relation to outstanding shares is small; 'share split' is used when the number of new shares is high in relation to the number of outstanding shares, Klein, Coffee, and Partnoy (n 25) 291.

650 MBCA, §6.23. 651 MBCA, §10.05(4)(b).

652 *Stokes v Continental Trust Co. of City of New York*, 186 N.Y. 285 (N.Y. 1906).

653 MBCA, §6.30; DGCL, §102(b)(3).

654 e.g. *Lacos Land Company v Arden Group, Inc.*, 517 A.2d 271 (Del. Ch. 1986).

655 Klein, Coffee, and Partnoy (n 25) 234.

656 MBCA, §6.31. Delaware retains a formal provision on reduction of capital in DGCL, §244.

E. Comparative Analysis: Efficiency and Efficacy

Within the ambit of Directive (EU) 2017/1132's legal capital regime the national regulatory frameworks are structurally very similar. However, significant differences remain, in particular, but not exclusively, where the Directive provides only minimum standards and at the periphery of the Directive's scope. A prominent example is the German doctrine of 'disguised contributions in kind', which derives its inner reason from the treatment, under German law, of the contribution of a monetary claim against the company as a 'contribution in kind', contrary to the English and French approaches. Another issue where we see considerable deviation is the issue of disguised (hidden) distributions, where German law applies an objective approach, contrary to the UK Supreme Court's more holistic view, which takes subjective elements into account, and French law, which does not recognize the doctrine at all and relies instead on insolvency law to address the problem. A further issue worth mentioning is the disapplication of pre-emptive rights. German case law requires an objective justification for such disapplication in addition to the procedural requirements stipulated under the Directive. Interestingly, however, through soft law, English law may generate largely similar results for listed companies. None of these differences seem to cause significant problems for the functioning of the single market. This could mean that the scope and extent of minimum harmonization have been perfectly calibrated, or perhaps that the Directive's entire legal capital regime is difficult to justify on the basis of the single market rationale.

The European legal capital regimes are based on detailed technical rules, supplemented by broader fiduciary doctrines, such as disguised distributions, largely aimed at preventing the circumvention of the statutory regimes. In the United States, legal capital has lost almost all significance. However, the problems of dilution and creditor preference have to be addressed. With a reliance on securities regulation, fraudulent transfer law and fiduciary principles we see a similar mix of tight technical rules and broad flexible standards. Given the US economy's much greater reliance on capital market funding, as compared to Europe where traditional bank finance still prevails, the greater significance of securities regulation in the United States is perhaps not a big surprise. It will be interesting to see whether the current European push towards a Capital Markets Union and enhanced direct capital market access for European companies will, in the medium and long-term, result in greater convergence in this respect, which again raises the issue of efficiency and efficacy of Directive (EU) 2017/1132's legal capital regime. Brexit, and the UK government's intended review of the dividend regime, may also reinvigorate this debate.

Traditionally, the doctrine of legal capital is perceived as having a dual rationale: (i) the rules on the payment of shares, the raising and increase of capital, including pre-emptive rights, are predominantly aimed at protecting shareholders against a dilution of their control and cash flow rights; (ii) the rules restricting dividends and distributions to shareholders, including on reduction of capital, try to ensure the creditors' preferential claim on the company's assets. Legal capital rules are effective if they contribute to a considerable extent to the attainment of these goals. They are efficient if the benefits they generate are at least equal to the resulting costs (at the margin), and there are no less costly alternatives that are at least as effective. Over the last twenty years, the legal capital doctrine has come under severe attack. The criticism levelled against these rules is largely inspired by law and economics methodology. The direct focal point is the second objective; creditor protection; the shareholder protection rationale has been attacked to a much lesser extent.[657]

[657] Grundmann (n 62) 208–12.

I. Creditor protection

The critics' argument can be summarized as follows: legal capital rules do not significantly protect creditors; by contrast, the cost they impose on companies are substantial; and more efficient means of creditor protection are available.[658]

The minimum initial capital requirement provides no meaningful protection for creditors. The required amount of €25,000 is trivial even for a small business. It is also meaningless because it is unrelated to the debt that a company may incur and to the sorts of business activities that a company may pursue.[659] Its only real effect is merely to set an easily avoidable deterrent to incorporation as a public company.[660] Further, the fixed amount of a firm's legal capital as the aggregate nominal value of the shares actually issued is also arbitrary and bears no relation to a company's actual funding needs. Creditors are not at all concerned with the legal capital figure at the 'right hand side' of a company's balance sheet as it carries no useful information. This is because as soon as it starts trading, a firm may incur losses either in the normal course of business or through opportunistic transactions that the legal capital regime does not cover. This renders the legal capital figure meaningless. In order to get a proper picture of a firm's financial situation, creditors must examine its entire balance sheet. Moreover, creditors must consider the current value of the firm's assets, not merely the historical book value.[661] In any case, creditors are interested much more in a company's ability to pay its short term and long-term obligations out of its future cash flows.[662] Requiring an expert report on contributions in kind is also of little benefit to creditors. Not only do valuation techniques vary widely and give experts a significant range of discretion, experts will also never really be 'independent', even where appointed by a judge or other public authority. As a professional, the expert has to offer his services to the market. In order to attract and retain clients the expert has an incentive not to act too independently when valuing non-cash considerations. Rather, experts are likely to approve any contribution in kind that is not so outrageously overvalued that a non-expert could realize that the company had watered its stock.[663]

Legal capital rules generate significant costs in terms of both time and money. The minimum capital requirement may deter the formation of viable businesses, thus generating social cost.[664] The provisions on contributions in kind are likely to delay company formation and an increase of capital, and require a company to pay for an independent expert report. In order to go public and to tap into the capital markets, companies formed as private companies must first convert into a public company and must comply with, and bear the costs of, the procedures for contributions in kind. The prohibition against issuing stock in exchange for future services is problematic in an era where ideas are increasingly worth much more than physical assets. Companies are prevented from devising compensation packages to recruit and retain talented employees. High-tech start-up companies are affected most severely.[665] The no-issue-below-par-rule makes it difficult for companies to increase their capital when their shares are trading below par. A company will first have to reduce the par value of the shares by reducing their capital for losses, and only then proceed to the capital increase. This two-step procedure will entail higher administrative costs than

[658] L Enriques and J Macey, 'Creditors versus Capital Formation: The Case Against the European Legal Capital Rules' (2001) 86 Cornell Law Review 1165, 1185; J Armour, 'Share Capital and Creditor Protection: Efficient Rules for a Modern Company Law' (2000) 63 MLR 355, 370; 'Legal Capital: An Outdated Concept?' (2006) 7 European Business Organisation Law Review 5; P Mulbert and M Birke, 'Legal Capital: Is there a case against the European legal Capital Rules?' (2002) 3 European Business Organisation Law Review 695.

[659] Enriques and Macey (n 658) 1185–6.

[660] Rickford (n 3) 931.

[661] Enriques and Macey (n 658) 1186–7; Manning and Hanks (n 4) 92; Rickford (n 3) 931–2.

[662] Rickford (n 3) 932; Manning and Hanks (n 4) 113.

[663] Enriques and Macey (n 658) 1187.

[664] Armour (2000) (n 658) 372; (2006) (n 658) 16; F Easterbrook and D Fischel, *The Economic Structure of Corporate Law* (HUP 1991) 60.

[665] Enriques and Macey (n 658) 1195–6.

a system of true no par value shares.[666] The Article 56 balance-sheet test limits the ability to pay dividends and thus limits the potential of dividend policy as an effective signal to convey inside information about the firm's expected cash flows. This, in turn, prevents the market from processing information on dividend policy effectively, rendering the market less efficient and shares less liquid. An increase of the company's ability to pay dividends through a reduction of capital is no real alternative. The transaction costs of an effective reduction of capital are likely to be high because each creditor may effectively veto the transaction, allowing for strategic behaviour and hold up power on the part of creditors.[667] The limitations on share repurchases make equity investments less liquid and thus less attractive ex ante. Also, a company may be prevented from buying out the stock of dissenting shareholders, thus raising the costs of shareholder disputes and deadlock.[668] Moreover, where a company has greater bargaining power than its contractual counterparties, it may be able to pass on these costs imposed by the legal capital rules to its creditors. Thus, rather than protecting weak and vulnerable creditors, legal capital rules may end up hurting them the most.[669]

Some (groups of) creditors, as well as regulators, have a number of alternative options at their disposal in order to secure adequate creditor protection. These alternatives may provide the same or even a superior level of creditor protection at lower cost. Sophisticated long-term creditors can protect themselves by incorporating in their bond indentures or loan agreements so-called restrictive covenants that define what the debtor company is obliged to do or not to do. Any breach of these covenants constitutes an 'event of default'. Negative covenants may include limitations on the amount of dividends companies may pay, prohibitions or limitations on the issuance of additional secured debt, limitations on the issuance of additional unsecured debt, often contingent on certain ratios of assets and liabilities, prohibition of the sale or lease of major assets without approval of the lender, restrictions on mergers and other control transactions. Positive covenants may include the company's promise to maintain a specified minimum working capital, or the obligation to provide the lender with periodic financial statements or other information.[670] It cannot be argued that statutory dividend restrictions, as default rules, are beneficial for saving negotiation costs for covenants. This is because the negotiation costs in the default scenario are likely to be higher than in a purely contractual setting.[671] Restrictive covenants are designed to retain the debtor company's risk profile and to prevent the siphoning away of assets. In these respects they not only benefit the sophisticated creditors who negotiated them; rather, non-adjusting and involuntary creditors can free ride, however only as long as the debtor company is not in default. In case of default, the outstanding debt will typically be accelerated and/or the negotiating creditor may obtain collateral. Debt acceleration may accelerate the demise of the company with weaker creditors likely to lose out in the run on the company's assets (prior to insolvency). And the granting of collateral will reduce the fund of assets available to ordinary creditors.[672] However, non-adjusting and in particular involuntary creditors can be better protected by regulation and mandatory insurance for certain industries. Examples of the former are nuclear power and banking, of the latter transportation

[666] ibid 1198; Rickford (n 3) 934.

[667] Enriques and Macey (n 658) 1196–7. [668] ibid 1197. [669] ibid 1198–9.

[670] Mulbert and Birke (n 658) 723–4; Manning and Hanks (n 4) 103–13.

[671] The utility of dividend restrictions is likely to change over time triggering a need for renegotiation. The more difficult renegotiation will be the less strict will be the rules devised at the outset. Renegotiating statutory default rules would be difficult, as it would require input from all creditors including non-adjusting. Consequently, the default rules would likely be set at a level too low for adjusting creditors who would then have to insert a higher level in their debt covenants. This may result in a net increase of contracting costs as compared to a solution on the basis of complete private contracting. Armour (2006) (n 658) 19. The argument does not appear to be completely watertight.

[672] Mulbert and Birke (n 658) 724.

or legal or accounting services. These mechanisms are arguably superior to legal capital rules because they target particular hazardous activities irrespective of the legal form they are conducted under. Moreover, mandatory insurance completely shields creditors by providing them with an additional typically liquid creditor and companies will be forced to internalize higher risks via increased insurance premia.[673]

Given the apparent superiority of creditor self-protection and mandatory insurance it is somewhat surprising that alternative systems for restrictions on dividends have been suggested at all. Presumably, the alternative tests are relevant only in order to fill the gap in respect of non-adjusting creditors in industries where mandatory insurance may not be available. Borrowing heavily from the Revised Model Business Corporation Act, the universal starting point has been the creditors' main (only) concern for continued solvency of the company following a distribution.[674] The alternative tests consist, with differences in detail, of a two-pronged assessment.[675] In a first step, a distribution must satisfy a balance sheet or net asset test: following the distribution the assets must fully cover or exceed liabilities (excluding shareholders' equity) on the basis of an appropriate valuation method.[676] In addition, the distribution must satisfy a liquidity or current assets/current liability test: following the distribution the company must have sufficient liquid assets to pay its liabilities as they fall due over the next year[677] or the next two years.[678] These tests may then be backed by an audit of the relevant accounts[679] and a solvency certificate issued by the board of directors. The latter may, where misleading, form the basis for personal liability of the directors involved.[680]

II. Shareholder protection

It should be clear from our historic discussion earlier that the rules on the payment for shares including valuation of non-cash consideration and increase of capital are predominantly concerned with the protection of shareholders against a dilution of their cash flow and control rights. The shareholder protection element has not been the focus of criticism to a similar extent. Obviously, the costs associated with the rules on contributions in kind, the prohibitions of certain types of contributions, the no-issue-below-par-rule and the administrative costs associated with an increase in capital can be invoked against the shareholder protection rationale as well. Moreover, it has been argued that the respective rules are also ineffective in terms of shareholder protection (thus, not justifying the associated costs) and that more effective mechanisms exist.

The no-issue-at-a-discount rule will almost never protect shareholders effectively against dilution on an increase in capital. This is because the new shares will almost certainly be worth more or less than par value. In the latter case, a potentially beneficial increase in capital may not be carried out. In the former, the value of existing shares will be diluted if shares

[673] ibid 725–6. [674] Rickford (n 3) 967.

[675] Report of the High-level Group of Company Law Experts on a Modern Regulatory Framework for Company Law in Europe of 4 November 2002, 87--8 (High-level Group); Rickford (n 3) 986; M Lutter (ed), *Legal Capital in Europe*, 11, 392 (Lutter Group) (de Gruyter Recht 2006); HE Boschma, ML Lennarts, and JN Schutte-Veenstra, *Alternative Systems for Capital Protection, Final Report dated 18 August 2005*, 69 (Dutch Group).

[676] High-level Group (n 675) 87; Lutter Group (n 675) 11, 392; Dutch Group (n 675) 71. Under the Rickford Proposal, a company that does not meet the balance sheet test may still pay dividends. However, the company's financial statements as a whole must be taken into account and where the distribution is not covered by the balance sheet test that fact must be disclosed and justified. Rickford (n 3) 986.

[677] High-level Group (n 675) 88; Rickford (n 3) 980; Dutch Group (n 675) 72.

[678] Lutter Group (n 675) 11.

[679] Rickford (n 3) 981; Lutter Group (n 675) 11. Not required by the High-level Group and the Dutch Group.

[680] Rickford (n 3) 981; High-level Group (n 675) 88; Lutter Group (n 675) 392. Not provided for in the Dutch proposal.

are issued at any price above par, but below their fair or market value at the time of issue.[681] This practice would be possible under Directive (EU) 2017/1132. The only protection afforded is the shareholders' right of pre-emption. But this may not apply (consideration in kind) or may be withdrawn by majority vote. Also, the arguments as regards the inefficacy of the rules on non-cash contributions (wide discretion in terms of valuation; lack of independence)[682] equally apply in respect of shareholder protection and dilution of shares.

As a more effective mechanism it is suggested that the issue of new shares should be subject to a fiduciary standard that shares must be issued at a fair price, backed by personal liability of the company's directors.[683] Contributions in kind could be subject to a shareholder resolution and a directors' certificate that the issue was appropriate as to the value of the contribution,[684] presumably backed by personal liability of the directors.

III. Overall assessment and conclusion

What are we to make of this debate? First it should be realized that it arose from a particular intellectual and ideological mind-set prevalent at around the turn of the millennium. At that time the 'New Economy' was booming. Many people were convinced that corporate law would converge towards the 'Anglo-Saxon model', or more precisely the US-American model, which was widely seen as superior in terms of efficiency as compared to the less flexible and over-regulated continental-European model.[685] Capital market focus and deregulation were the order of the day. After the bursting of the 'Dot Com' bubble, the unprecedented corporate scandals of Enron, WorldCom, Global Crossing etc. and the financial crisis of 2007–2009, there is now dawning recognition that the market and in particular capital markets do not necessarily work efficiently and that mandatory regulation has an important role to play.[686] Whether this regulation concerns traditional core company law or focuses on securities markets is often largely a matter of legal tradition and immaterial as long as the respective interests are adequately protected. In light of these developments the arguments against the legal capital regime can be re-evaluated.

As we have seen, originally minimum capital was merely a reflex resulting from minimum par value and a minimum number of promoters. A statutory minimum capital requirement is, as such, not a necessary element of the legal capital doctrine[687] as should be clear from the UK experience prior to the implementation of the Second Company Law Directive. Where the corporate form is available without minimum capital requirements as it is on an EU-wide basis—prior to Brexit, through the UK private company, but also through the French €1 SARL and the German Entrepreneur-GmbH—minimum capital as a means of creditor protection seems to be redundant. The argument that it serves to prevent frivolous company formations[688] is not very persuasive for the same reason.

That creditors are not concerned with the fixed legal capital figure in the company's balance sheet may be true. It is also true that the assets obtained by the company in the course of an initial or subsequent issue of shares may be dissipated as soon as the company starts trading. However, the provisions on the raising of capital and payment for shares were never meant to prevent the insolvency of the company or to grant absolute protection to

681 Rickford (n 3) 934. 682 Enriques and Macey (n 658) 1187. 683 Rickford (n 3) 934.

684 High-level Group (n 675) 89.

685 H Hansmann and R Kraakman, 'The End of History for Corporate Law' (2001) 89 Georgetown Law Journal 439.

686 J Armour and others, 'Beyond the Anatomy' in R Kraakman and others, *The Anatomy of Corporate Law* (3rd edn, OUP 2017) 267, 271–2.

687 H Eidenmüller, B Grunewald, and U Noack, 'Minimum Capital in the System of Legal Capital' in M Lutter (ed), *Legal Capital in Europe* (de Gruyter Recht 2006) 17, 20.

688 High-level Group (n 675) 82; Stellungnahme der Arbeitsgruppe Europäisches Gesellschaftsrecht (Group of German Experts on Corporate Law) zum Report of the High-level Group of Company Law Experts on a Modern Regulatory Framework for Company Law in Europe, 43.

creditors.[689] The early common law-understanding that these provisions and the legal capital figure actually represent to creditors that the company has received the corresponding assets and that they will be maintained was unfortunate. On the continent they were never understood in that way, or at least not predominantly so. Their main focus has always been the protection of equity investors against speculation with partly paid up shares, dilution of their rights, and preferential treatment of certain groups or classes. No doubt, the Directive's legal capital regime contains significant gaps in this respect (subsequent issue below fair value; disguised contributions in kind outside Article 52). However, in accordance with the nature of the Directive as regulatory instrument, Member States are free to fill these gaps by, for instance, providing a fiduciary standard that shares may not be issued below fair value as in the UK,[690] or by subjecting 'disguised contributions in kind' more widely to the regime of the Directive as in Germany. The problem of a subsequent issue below par may be significantly alleviated by the issue of low par value shares and by the availability of a capital reduction to off-set losses. However, anyone ever involved in the formation, or increase of capital, through contributions in kind of a German company will likely have experienced the respective provisions on expert-valuation as extremely cumbersome and time consuming. The associated costs as well as those resulting from a reduction of capital for losses, where necessary to issue new shares, are perhaps the strongest arguments against the current regime. However, a true no par value regime without expert-valuation requirement would have to introduce equivalent safeguards in order to protect equity investors adequately.[691] This may be achieved through fiduciary standards and extensive disclosure requirements within the securities regulation framework; both backed by personal liability of the personnel in charge, likely the board or individual directors.[692] Whether these alternatives would be more cost efficient than the current regime is an empirical question and does not just depend on the applicable laws but also the wider legal environment, in particular procedural law and litigation culture. What works well in one jurisdiction may not necessarily work so well under a different legal system.

The core of the system's creditor protection arsenal is the restriction on dividends on the basis of the Article 56 enhanced balance sheet test. Its rationale is to secure the creditors' preference on the company's assets. As such, it is a defining feature of separate legal personality and the corporate form. It underpins the notion of residuarity as the defining feature of equity in delineation to debt and constitutes a cornerstone of corporate finance. Pegging the balance sheet test to accounting standards renders it vulnerable to the inherent weaknesses of accounting practice. Where accounting standards leave room for discretion the balance sheet test is open for manipulation.[693] Where accounting practice is switched from traditional to 'fair value' accounting unrealized profits may become available for distribution, or conversely the recognition of liabilities for, say, pension fund deficits may render a cash-rich company technically insolvent.[694] However, the problem here seems to lie rather with accounting practice then with the legal capital doctrine. In addition, creditor self-protection through restrictive covenants also frequently relies on accounting based benchmarks.[695] In order to secure the creditors' preferential claim on the company's assets a liquidity test would appear to be sufficient. After all, as long as the company is able to pay its debts as they fall due creditors will be paid in full. However, as Kershaw has demonstrated, the balance sheet test is likely to provide superior protection for non-adjusting, in particular involuntary

[689] M Lutter, 'Legal Capital of Public Companies in Europe' in M Lutter (ed), *Legal Capital in Europe* (de Gruyter Recht 2006) 1, 3.

[690] *Lowry v Consolidated African Selection Trust Ltd* [1940] AC 648, 679.

[691] Lutter (n 689) 1, 8.

[692] Manning and Hanks (n 4) 181; MBCA, §8.30.

[693] Manning and Hanks (n 4) 91.

[694] D Kershaw, 'Involuntary Creditors and the Case for Accounting Based Distribution Regulation' (2009) 2 Journal of Business Law 140, 159; Rickford (n 3) 964.

[695] Kershaw (n 694) 152.

creditors. These creditors are protected under a balance sheet test to the extent that, under accounting standards, potential and contingent liabilities arising, say, from future tort or product liability claims, have to be taken into account and reduce the amount that can legally be distributed to shareholders.[696] This makes it more likely (not certain) that sufficient funds will be available to satisfy the claims of (future) involuntary creditors also. The same could be achieved on the basis of a test based on a certificate of solvency for the reasonably foreseeable future.[697] However, whereas the balance sheet test provides a reasonably bright line restriction on dividends here and now, the liquidity test entails much more of a value judgment on the part of directors who will take into account not just the pressures coming from current shareholders keen on a dividend payment but also their potential liability for a mistaken solvency certificate, but discounted by the probability of insolvency and the probability that a plausible argument that the solvency statement was reasonable will be accepted by a court.[698] This appears to make it more likely that, under a (pure) liquidity test, a dividend will be more readily paid and fewer funds will be available for future involuntary creditors. In any case, with the exception of the Rickford Group, all past alternative proposals retained a balance sheet test in addition to a liquidity test, the same goes for the MBCA.[699] In this context, legal capital provides for an enhanced balance sheet test in the sense that, following a distribution, net assets must be equal to or exceed the fixed legal capital figure. This safety margin is not strictly necessary under the prior-creditor-claim rationale; it seems to provide, however, at least some additional protection for creditors in the sense that it makes it more likely that more funds will be retained. Moreover, given the centrality of the notion of residuarity and the creditor preference for corporate finance, on the one hand, and the difficulties inherent in the valuation of assets and liabilities, on the other, the safety margin of an enhanced balance sheet test seems to be justifiable. As regards the many forms of transaction—payment of excessive salaries, transfer of company assets below market value etc—that are not covered by the restrictions on dividends under the Directive, this does not provide a valid argument against the Directive's regime as it is again open to the Member States to close these loopholes through imposing fiduciary duties on directors, fraudulent transfer law, or a doctrine of disguised distributions.

As for the costliness of the legal capital regime in comparison to alternative regimes, the KPMG feasibility study has demonstrated that administrative costs generated by the European legal capital rules are not excessively burdensome and, thus, cannot be decisive in determining whether the transition to an alternative system would actually be beneficial for European business. By contrast, the implementation of an untested alternative regime in a certain jurisdiction can be very costly. Moreover, accompanying measures of shareholder and creditor protection would have to be considered.[700]

Overall, therefore, alternative regimes do not seem to be clearly superior to the legal capital doctrine embodied in Directive (EU) 2017/1132 and practiced in Europe. However, this does not necessarily mean that the Directive's regime should not be repealed, either as a whole or in parts. Its internal market rationale—to provide a minimum standard for the protection of shareholders and creditors so that they can freely invest cross-border without fear—does seem spurious. Creditors who invest cross border will usually be well equipped to protect themselves by acquiring the necessary information about the company's financial situation and by negotiating adequate protection. The Directive's regime will reduce transaction costs in this respect only marginally, if at all.[701] As for equity investors, protection against dilution of their rights is to a large extent left to the Member States anyway; the Directive's

[696] ibid 150. [697] See Rickford (n 3) 979.
[698] Kershaw (n 694) 163. [699] MBCA, §6.40(c)(2).
[700] KPMG (n 12) 314.
[701] P Mankowski, 'Does Contract Suffice to Protect the Creditors of a Company and Their Interests?' in M Lutter (ed), Legal Capital in Europe (de Gruyter Recht 2006) 394, 406.

provisions in this respect are so incomplete that they are hardly able to inspire much investor confidence. The restrictions on distributions on the basis of an enhanced balance sheet test are significant for the protection of non-adjusting, and in particular involuntary creditors.[702] It could be argued that consumers may be encouraged to shop cross-border, confident that their product liability claims are more likely to be met under the European legal capital regime. It is, however, illusory to assume that the seller's dividend policy can have any impact at all on a consumer's decision as to whether to shop at home or abroad. What remains is the dividend restrictions under the Directive as an expression of a particular European business culture that focuses on long-term and sustainable profitability of a company, rather than on a short term increase in share prices on the basis of an aggressive dividend policy, unconstrained by an enhanced balance sheet or net profits test. However, whether to adhere to such a more long-term perspective of doing business or to give companies and investors (also) the short-term option may be a decision best reserved for the Member States.

[702] From the point of view of a company trading on a Europe-wide basis, it makes sense to have to comply with only one creditor protection regime. However, this is the case anyway as under freedom of establishment a company will always be subject to the company law of the Member State of incorporation, and host state creditor protection rules may be applied only to the extent that home state law does not protect adequately.

10

Veil-piercing

In the preceding chapter we analysed legal capital as a strategy for preventing shirking and inter-shareholder wealth transfers as well as for guaranteeing corporate creditors' preferential access to the corporation's assets. In combination with disclosure requirements, legal capital has occasionally been characterized as the 'price' corporate shareholders and managers have to pay for trading under the shield of limited liability. These strategies aim to generate their impact ex ante, when the corporation is formed, when it changes its capital structure and on a continuous basis. The doctrine of legal capital is largely based on detailed and technical rules that invite circumvention. The current chapter focuses on strategies that, in a broad sense, set the principle of limited liability aside in order to reach (the assets of) the natural or legal persons that benefit from corporate activity. These concepts are complementary to the ex ante strategies. They are ex post in the sense that they will be triggered only if and when the former have failed for some reason. Their aim is to internalize as far as possible the social cost of corporate activity in order to set appropriate incentives for corporate decision-making. The legal concepts under consideration here are largely standard based with open textured norms whose application heavily depends on the factual settings in every individual case. Consequently, the challenge is to provide workable criteria and coherent guidance for courts in order to ensure predictability for entrepreneurs and their legal advisers.

A. Insider Opportunism and Veil-piercing

In Chapter 1 we discussed the economic rationale of limited liability. We said that limited liability decreases the costs of capital by reducing risks and monitoring costs for shareholders, facilitates specialization and the proper functioning of capital markets, and may have a disciplining effect on management decision-making via the market for corporate control. At the same time, limited liability makes the modern business corporation 'the perfect externalizing machine': shareholders as residual claimants reap all the benefits of a risk intense venture without having to pay for (part of) the costs imposed on others, and society as a whole, in terms of environmental damage or the losses inflicted on tort victims of corporate activity. This creates moral hazard and invites opportunistic behaviour on the part of corporate insiders. We also said that the financialization of corporate law and the rise of the new financial capitalism has made it more likely that negative externalities may exceed the benefits of corporate activity, creating the need for a recalibration of the system in order to tackle corporate opportunism and moral hazard effectively.

In respect of voluntary creditors, insider opportunism can take two forms: ex ante opportunism and ex post opportunism. Both forms rest on the notion that under normal circumstances externalities will not occur as long as voluntary creditors are able to correctly assess and predict the risk of default and obtain full ex ante compensation. There are, however, situations where creditors will be prevented from assessing the risk correctly and shareholders and managers are able to shift to creditors costs that they have not agreed to bear. Ex ante, the company's wealth may be misrepresented when the credit agreement is entered into.[1] This can take the form of outright fraud where the company enters into a contract in the knowledge that there is no reasonable prospect that the company will be able to meet its obligations when they fall due in the future. Ex ante opportunism can also be more subtle so where the company takes on additional debt, maybe to carry out a merger or acquisition, in disregard of the long-term business conditions and prospects. It may also be the case where financial reporting and disclosure rules have not been complied with or where the assets of shareholders, parent company, and subsidiaries or affiliates are indistinguishably mixed up.[2]

The risk of default may be increased ex post by transactions that reduce the company's assets or by engaging in new risk-intense activities.[3] Controlling shareholders may use their control power to siphon assets out of the company in the form of cash or non-cash dividends and disguised distributions. The company may also change its investment strategy and start to invest in highly risky projects with a negative net present value. In both cases the risk of default will increase and the claims of existing creditors will be worth less than what they have bargained for. Both scenarios are most likely to occur when insolvency is imminent and the firm no longer contemplates raising new finance on capital markets.[4]

As for involuntary creditors, limited liability allows for a deliberate externalization of costs and thereby encourages excessively risky activities. This is particularly relevant within corporate groups. A single business enterprise may be split into two (or more) legal entities, symbiotically linked by contract: the owning entity holds title to all the assets needed to conduct the enterprise and guarantees all contractual obligations; the operating entity, without owning any substantial assets, actually runs the business. The situation of the enterprise as

[1] R Posner, 'The Rights of Creditors of Affiliated Corporations' (1976) 43 University of Chicago Law Review 499, 507-9.

[2] R Posner, *Economic Analysis of Law* (9th edn, Aspen Publishers 2014) 559.

[3] Posner (n 1) 504 note 14; FH Easterbrook and DR Fischel, *The Economic Structure of Corporate Law* (HUP 1991) 51.

[4] Easterbrook and Fischel (n 3) 51; J Armour, G Hertig, and H Kanda, 'Transactions with Creditors' in R Kraakman and others (eds), *The Anatomy of Corporate Law* (3rd edn, OUP 2017) 111; H Hansmann and R Kraakman, 'The Essential Role of Organizational Law' (2000) 110 Yale Law Journal 387, 423.

a whole vis-à-vis contractual creditors is the same: because of the guarantee to be issued by the owning entity, the costs of credit would not increase; rather, they may decrease since voluntary creditors do not have to compete with involuntary creditors. Involuntary creditors will have access only to the assets of the operating enterprise which will be of zero value.[5] The enterprise is 'judgment-proof' in respect of tort creditors. There is no incentive to minimize the costs of accidents by taking cost-effective precautions or to abstain from profitable but hazardous activities. Moreover, undercapitalized subsidiaries may be sacrificed to the detriment of their creditors for the benefit of the group as a whole. Corporate opportunism occurs where the company engages in activities with a potential to harm third parties without providing for compensation out of the company's assets or the proceeds of an insurance policy.

In short, because they won't have to pay for it, managers and shareholders have an incentive to engage in excessive risk taking to gain personal benefits without taking into account the externalized costs imposed on creditors (and society as a whole) which may be far higher than the expected return for the company.[6] It is under these circumstances of opportunistic corporate behaviour[7] and in order to rebalance the costs and benefits of limited liability that legal systems sometimes disregard the principle and allow creditors to reach those who are ultimately responsible for the company's activities.

In accordance with the general methods of comparative law,[8] 'exceptions to limited liability' must be understood in a broad and functional sense. Exceptions in this respect are not just 'true' exceptions based on approaches which take as their starting point the principles of separate legal personality and/or limited liability and try to define their inherent teleological boundaries and limits in order to hold the shareholders directly or indirectly liable for the company's debts; rather it is every remedy resulting in the liability of shareholders and/or managers to contribute to the losses suffered by the company and/or its creditors that goes beyond what they agreed to invest when they became involved in the corporate enterprise. It is also immaterial whether this liability is conceptually based on company law, insolvency law, tort law, or any other branch of the law. For instance, ordinary tort law doctrines based on fraudulent or negligent misrepresentation cover some of the ex ante-opportunistic corporate behaviour. Provisions on fraudulent transfers and the avoidance of transactions allow those in charge of an insolvency proceeding to reverse transactions entered into by the debtor company to the detriment of its creditors ex post. These techniques form a patchwork of remedies rather than a single coherent doctrine. There are gaps, inconsistencies, and inefficiencies.

In the absence of clear statutory provisions, exceptions to the principle of limited liability have, in some jurisdictions to a large extent, been established by case law using 'a suggestive imagery to reinforce [the courts'] intuition that shareholders should pay the bill'.[9] In Anglophone systems the expressions 'lifting the corporate veil' or 'piercing the corporate veil' are widely used. Both expressions are, however, not synonymous. An explanation from the English point of view can be found in *Atlas Maritime Co SA v Avalon Maritime Ltd*:[10]

> Like all metaphors, this phrase [the corporate veil] can sometimes obscure reasoning rather than elucidate it. There are, I think, two senses in which it is used, which need to be distinguished. To *pierce* the corporate veil is an expression that I would reserve for treating the rights or liabilities or activities of a company as the rights or liabilities or activities of its shareholders. To *lift* the

[5] L LoPucki, 'The Essential Structure of Judgment Proofing' (1998–1999) 51 Stanford Law Review 147.
[6] ibid.
[7] D Millon, 'Piercing the Corporate Veil, Financial Responsibility, and the Limits of Limited Liability' (2007) 56 Emory Law Journal 1305, 1342–8.
[8] cf Chapter 1A. [9] AF Conard, *Corporations in Perspective* (Foundation Press 1976) 425.
[10] *Atlas Maritime Co SA v Avalon Maritime Ltd* [1991] 1 Lloyd's Rep 563, 571 (Staughton LJ).

corporate veil or *look behind* it, on the other hand, should mean to have regard to the shareholding in a company for some legal purpose.

More recently, in *Prest v Petrodel*, Lord Sumption adopted a very narrow understanding of piercing the corporate veil:

> But when we speak of piercing the corporate veil, we are not (or should not be) speaking of any of these situations [agency, equitable remedies etc.], but only of those cases which are true exceptions to the rule in Salomon v A Salomon and Co Ltd [1897] AC 22, i.e. where a person who owns and controls a company is said in certain circumstances to be identified with it in law by virtue of that ownership and control.[11]

'Piercing the corporate veil' in the United States has (largely) the meaning of imposing unlimited liability on (some of) the corporations' shareholders for the corporation's debts.[12] The German term *Durchgriffshaftung* is synonymous: 'liability that reaches through' to the shareholders. It is mainly this sense in which the expression will be used here. We can, however, not restrict our analysis to the cases and jurisdictions where unlimited liability is imposed on shareholders. Rather, in order to get a full picture, direct or indirect liability of managers for the company's debts will have to be taken into consideration as well. We will see that when it matters, shareholders will often participate directly or indirectly in the management of the company, either as de jure, de facto, or shadow managers.[13]

'Piercing the corporate veil' is often described as a rather messy, unprincipled, fact sensitive affair with a certain arbitrariness to it.[14] Also, as we will see, in some jurisdictions 'piercing the corporate veil' is not a single, coherent doctrine, but rather depends on a multitude of statutory provisions and case law. However, the economic rationale of limited liability, as discussed in Chapter 1, may enable us to discover behind these different rules and concepts a general maxim or policy which meaningfully connects these doctrines to a coherent body of law.

B. United States

Corporate law in the narrow sense of state general incorporation statutes is traditionally not concerned with the protection of creditors. There is today only a very rudimentary doctrine of legal capital with some limited restrictions on the payment of dividends and a very flexible attitude towards financial reporting (for closely held corporations). Rather, core corporate law is dominated by the relations of shareholders and management and focuses on the protection of equity investors against management opportunism or the insulation of management's discretionary powers from shareholder interference, in any case with a view to maximizing shareholder value. The reason for this lack of creditor concern may be that historically corporations have relied to a much greater extent on equity markets for their finance than European companies, where traditionally debt finance through bank loans has been more prevalent.[15]

Insider opportunism does, however, exist and legal systems had to come up with devices to tackle it. The torts of fraudulent or negligent misrepresentation cover some of the ground of ex ante opportunism, but leave significant gaps. Another important device is fraudulent transfer law that allows reversing transactions entered into by a debtor to the detriment of its creditors. In addition, courts have developed a number of company-specific doctrines.

[11] *Prest v Petrodel Resources Ltd* [2013] UKSC 34 para 16.

[12] Conard (n 9) 425; Millon (n 7) 1310.

[13] PL Davies and S Worthington, *Gower and Davies' Principles of Modern Company Law* (10th edn, Sweet & Maxwell 2016) paras 9-2, 9-7 (208, 214).

[14] WA Klein, JC Coffee, and F Partnoy, *Business Organization and Finance* (11th edn, Foundation Press 2010) 148; Easterbrook and Fischel (n 3) 55; K Schmidt, *Gesellschaftsrecht* (4th edn, Heymann 2002) 219 ff.

[15] K Vandekerckhove, *Piercing the Corporate Veil* (Kluwer Law International 2007) 163.

The academically most interesting and practically most important of these is the doctrine of 'piercing the corporate veil'.

I. Piercing the corporate veil

To impose personal liability for one of the corporation's debts on (one of) its shareholders is the single most litigated issue in corporate law.[16] Despite, or rather because, of this huge practical importance the law has, as yet, not developed any clear rules as to when the corporate veil may be pierced. It is not even clear whether veil piercing is a legal or equitable remedy.[17] Many commentators hold on to the remarks of Benjamin Cardozo who said in 1926 that the problem was 'still enveloped in the mists of metaphor'.[18] Indeed, when justifying veil piercing the courts rely on a multitude of metaphors when they find that the corporation was a 'mere instrumentality', the 'alter ego', an 'adjunct', 'agent', 'conduit', 'department', 'pocket', or 'puppet' of the shareholder or vice versa.[19] A threefold test, first formulated by Professor Powell[20] and subsequently restated and adopted by the Supreme Court of New York in *Lowendahl* has been relied on, often with certain modification, as a general guideline.[21]

> Restating the instrumentality rule, we may say that in any case except express agency, estoppel or direct tort, three elements must be proved:
>
> (1) Control, not mere majority or complete stock control, but complete domination, not only of finances but of policy and business practice in respect to the transaction attacked so that the corporate entity as to this transaction had at the time no separate mind, will or existence of its own; and
> (2) Such control must have been used by the defendant to commit fraud or wrong, to perpetrate the violation of a statutory or other positive legal duty, or a dishonest and unjust act in contravention of plaintiff's legal rights; and
> (3) The aforesaid control and breach of duty must proximately cause the injury or unjust loss complained of. (See Powell 'Parent and Subsidiary Corporations', chaps. I to VI, passim, and numerous cases cited.)[22]

Piercing the corporate veil doctrine varies among state legal systems and their courts mainly in respect of the degree of emphasis put on any one of the three criteria mentioned in *Lowendahl*.[23] The third criterion, causation of loss, is often neglected in decisions or is implicitly assumed since the need to pursue a shareholder will only arise where the corporation itself is judgment proof or insolvent. Whether a state adopts a strict approach, like Delaware, or a more lenient one, like California,[24] largely depends on the prerequisites that need to be met in terms of control of the company and the wrong committed by the controlling shareholder. In this respect courts often resort to so-called 'laundry lists',[25] which try to specify certain factors relevant to veil piercing.

[16] RB Thompson, 'Piercing the Corporate Veil: An Empirical Study' (1990-1991) 76 Cornell Law Review 1038. P Oh, 'Veil-Piercing' (2010) 89 Texas Law Review 81, 90 with n 59.

[17] SM Bainbridge, 'Abolishing Veil Piercing' (2001) 26 Journal of Corporation Law 479, 480 n 4. The Seventh Amendment to the United States Constitution requires that the right to a jury trial be preserved in federal court for suits at common law when the amount in controversy exceeds twenty dollars Hence, in respect of equitable remedies there is no right to trial by jury. Most commentators view veil piercing as an equitable remedy. DJ Morrissey, 'Piercing all the Veils: Applying an Established Doctrine to a New Business Order' (2007) 32 Journal of Corporation Law 529, 541; Millon (n 7) 1310.

[18] *Berkey v Third Ave. Ry. Co.*, 244 N.Y. 84 at p. 94 (Cardozo J).

[19] PI Blumberg, *The Law of Corporate Groups: Tort, Contract, and Other Common Law Problems in the Substantive Law of Parent and Subsidiary Corporations* (Little Brown 1987) 107.

[20] F Powell, *Parent and Subsidiary Corporations* (Callaghan 1931).

[21] Blumberg (n 19) 112.

[22] *Lowendahl v The Baltimore and Ohio Railroad Company*, 247 A.D. 144 (N.Y. 1936).

[23] Klein, Coffee, and Partnoy (n 14) 148; Conard (n 9) 431.

[24] Conard (n 9) 432.

[25] Bainbridge (n 17) 509.

Associated Vendors, Inc. v. Oakland Meat Co., 26 Cal. Rptr. 806 (District Court of Appeal 1962)

...

A review of the cases ... discloses the consideration of a variety of factors which were pertinent to the trial court's determination under the particular circumstances of each case. Among these are the following: [1] Commingling of funds and other assets, failure to segregate funds of the separate entities, and the unauthorized diversion of corporate funds or assets to other than corporate uses ...; [2] the treatment by an individual of the assets of the corporation as his own ...; [3] the failure to obtain authority to issue stock or to subscribe to or issue the same ...; [4] the holding out by an individual that he is personally liable for the debts of the corporation ...; [5] the failure to maintain minutes or adequate corporate records, and the confusion of the records of the separate entities ...; [6] the identical equitable ownership in the two entities; [7] the identification of the equitable owners thereof with the domination and control of the two entities; [8] identification of the directors and officers of the two entities in the responsible supervision and management; [9] sole ownership of all of the stock in a corporation by one individual or the members of a family ...; [10] the use of the same office or business location; [11] the employment of the same employees and/or attorney ...; [12] the failure to adequately capitalize a corporation; [13] the total absence of corporate assets, and undercapitalization ...; [14] the use of a corporation as a mere shell, instrumentality or conduit for a single venture or the business of an individual or another corporation ...; [15] the concealment and misrepresentation of the identity of the responsible ownership, management and financial interest, or concealment of personal business activities ...; [16] the disregard of legal formalities and the failure to maintain arm's length relationships among related entities ...; [17] the use of the corporate entity to procure labor, services or merchandise for another person or entity ...; [18] the diversion stockholder or other person or entity, to the detriment of creditors, or the manipulation of assets and liabilities between entities so as to concentrate the assets in one and the liabilities in another ...; [19] the contracting with another with intent to avoid performance by use of a corporate entity as a shield against personal liability, or the use of a corporation as a subterfuge of illegal transactions ...; [20] and the formation and use of a corporation to transfer to it the existing liability of another person or entity ... A perusal of these cases reveals that in all instances several of the factors mentioned were present. It is particularly significant that while it was held, in each instance, that the trial court was warranted in disregarding the corporate entity, the factors considered by it were not deemed to be conclusive upon the trier of fact but were found to be supported by substantial evidence.

...

Questions and comments:

1. The list provided by the court is non-exhaustive; some of the twenty different factors show considerable overlapping, some contain multiple sub-factors. The great weakness of this approach is the lack of any guidance as to the weight to be attributed to the different factors or as to how many of them must be present in order to pierce the corporate veil.[26]
2. Given the economic rationale for limited liability and its exceptions, which of the factors mentioned in the case seem relevant; which ones seem unrelated?

The courts' approach to veil piercing has often been criticized. Judicial decisions in this area have been described as 'irreconcilable and not entirely comprehensible',[27] as 'defy[ing] any

[26] Bainbridge (n 17) 510; Millon (n 7) 1327–30; R Thompson, 'Piercing the Veil: Is the Common Law the Problem' (2005) 37 Connecticut Law Review 619, 624.

[27] PI Blumberg, *The Law of Corporate Groups: Procedural Problems in the Law of Parent and Subsidiary Corporations* (Little Brown 1983) 8; 'The Transformation of Modern Corporation Law: The Law of Corporate Groups' (2005) 37 Connecticut Law Review 605, 611 ff.

attempt at rational explanation',[28] and as having a tendency 'to open with vague generalities and close with conclusory statements with little or no concrete analysis in between'.[29] Veil piercing is said 'to happen freakishly', to be 'rare severe and unprincipled'.[30] A further point of critique is the insensitivity of decisions to the different policies and objectives of the respective areas of law the cases arise from: '[I]n tort cases, for example, we frequently find courts citing cases involving issues in contracts, procedure, bankruptcy, and construction of statutes in support of a determination of tort law. This is unacceptable'.[31]

On the other hand, this critical attitude seems to focus mainly on the form of legal reasoning in these cases, rather than on the substance. As far as the outcome is concerned, the general sentiment seems to be that the courts 'are getting it right'.[32] Before we have a closer look at veil piercing in action, the results of the influential empirical study carried out by Robert Thompson are worth mentioning. Thompson examined all Westlaw cases until 1985, later extended until 1996, encompassing overall 3,800 cases concerning the issue of piercing the corporate veil.[33] He summarized his key findings as follows:

1. Courts pierced the corporate veil in approximately 40 per cent of all reported cases;
2. Piercing the veil is a doctrine directed exclusively at close corporations and corporate groups; piercing did not occur as to shareholders in public corporations or more precisely in corporations with more than nine shareholders;
3. Courts pierce the veil more often to get to an individual who is a shareholder than to reach another corporation who is a shareholder, [. . .]
4. Courts are less likely to pierce the veil in cases involving tort claims as opposed to those involving contractual or statutory claims; . . .
5. Undercapitalization and corporate informalities often lead to piercing, but appear in a relatively small percentage of all cases in which courts pierce and an even smaller number of the tort cases.[34]

Questions and comments:

1. Given the economic rationale of limited liability and of its exceptions, which of these findings could be expected; which ones come as a surprise?
2. One explanation for the courts' reluctance to pierce the corporate veil in tort cases is the idea that courts use the doctrine of limited liability 'as a brake on the application of tort principles' where the application of strict liability or other broad principles of tort law would lead to results which seem to be inappropriate in particular circumstances.[35] This would suggest that for the tort context the conflict between limited liability and creditor protection cannot be resolved by corporate law. Rather, the solution must come from tort law itself.[36]

[28] JM Launders, 'A Unified Approach to Parent, Subsidiary & Affiliate Questions in Bankruptcy' (1975) 42 University of Chicago Law Review 589, 620.

[29] Bainbridge (n 17) 513.

[30] FH Easterbrook and DR Fischel, 'Limited Liability and the Corporation' (1985) 52 University of Chicago Law Review. 89; also the Delaware Court of Chancery in *Allied Capital Corp v GC-Sun Holdings LP*, 910 A.2d (2006) 1020, 1042–3: 'legal doctrine in that area is rightfully criticized for ambiguity and randomness'; 'the tests used to determine whether a corporate veil should be pierced . . . yield few predictable results'.

[31] Blumberg (n 19) 108. [32] Thompson (n 16) 1037.

[33] ibid 1044; RB Thompson, 'Piercing the Veil Within Corporate Groups: Corporate Shareholders as Mere Investors' (1998–1999) 13 Connecticut Journal of International Law 379, 385.

[34] Thompson (n 33) 384. Another empirical study of a random sample of cases reported in Westlaw from 1 January 1986 to 31 December 1995 produced somewhat different results This study found, in particular, that courts were more likely to pierce in tort cases than in contract cases LC Hodge and AB Sachs, 'Piercing the Mist: Bringing the Thompson Study into the 1990s' (2008) 43 Wake Forest Law Review 341. The latest empirical study is Oh (n 16).

[35] Thompson (n 26) 632; Morrissey (n 17) 547. [36] Thompson (n 26) 635.

1. *Control*

Control exists in every parent-subsidiary relationship, as well as in any one-man company or close corporation with a dominant shareholder. If holding a majority or even a qualified majority of the voting power in general meeting would be sufficient to trigger veil piercing, the principle of limited liability would largely be redundant for a great number of closely held corporations. It is, therefore, generally accepted that something more is needed than holding a majority of the voting stock.[37] The approaches adopted by state legal systems and courts vary. Some require exclusive domination and control by the shareholder to the point that the company no longer has any significance of its own, or an intrusion by the parent company into the subsidiary's day-to-day decision-making process so severe as to destroy its separate existence. However, others let it suffice that decisions have been made for the company by the shareholder even though the company continues to function as a separate organization.[38] For instance in *Zaist v Olson*,[39] the plaintiffs brought an action against Martin Olson, The East Haven Homes, Inc., and Martin Olson, Inc. The allegations were that the plaintiffs rendered services, supplied materials and furnished equipment to The East Haven Homes, Inc., for work on properties owned or leased by Martin Olson and Martin Olson, Inc.; that the services, material and equipment were furnished at the instance and request of Martin Olson, and inured to the benefit of Martin Olson and Martin Olson, Inc. The majority of the court justified control in this case on the basis of the fact that Olson had created both Olson Inc. and East Haven; that he was the controlling shareholder as well as a director in both corporations; that the firms shared the same office; that it was Olson who profited from the work carried out and not East Haven; that corporate formalities had not been complied with and that East Haven did not have adequate funds at its disposal. Moreover, the majority pierced the corporate veil merely based on the exercise of control; the second limb of the *Lowendahl* test disappeared.[40] This may be contrasted with the following case.

***Fletcher v. Atex, Inc.*, 68 F.3d 1451 (United States Court of Appeals for the Second Circuit, 1995)**

Cabranes, Circuit Judge:

... The plaintiffs-appellants filed suit against Atex, Inc. ('Atex') and its parent, Eastman Kodak Company ('Kodak'), to recover for repetitive stress injuries that they claim were caused by their use of computer keyboards manufactured by Atex ... [A summary judgement was entered dismissing Kodak as a defendant and the plaintiffs appeal.]

From 1981 until December 1992, Atex was a wholly-owned subsidiary of Kodak ... In December 1992, Atex sold substantially all of its assets to an independent third party and again changed its name to 805 Middlesex Corp., which holds the proceeds from the sale. Kodak continues to be the sole shareholder of 805 Middlesex Corp.

...

The plaintiffs claim that the district court erred in granting Kodak's motion for summary judgment on their alter ego theory of liability ...

The district court correctly noted that '[u]nder New York choice of law principles, "[t]he law of the state of incorporation determines when the corporate form will be disregarded and liability

[37] Blumberg (n 19), 115; Conard (n 9) 428.

[38] Blumberg (n 19) 115.

[39] *Zaist v Olson*, 227 A.2d 552 (Conn., 1967).

[40] For this reason House, Associate Justice, dissented: 'I have no quarrel with the statement of legal principles expounded in the majority opinion, but I do not agree that the facts found by the referee support a conclusion that the control which the defendants Martin Olson and Martin Olson, Inc., undoubtedly did exercise over The East Haven Homes, Inc., was used by them or either of them 'to commit fraud or wrong, to perpetrate the violation of a statutory or other positive legal duty, or a dishonest and unjust act in contravention of' the plaintiffs' legal rights ... The referee who heard the evidence in this case did not find that this essential element had been proven, nor, in my opinion, do the facts found support a conclusion that it existed. Accordingly, I believe that there was error in the judgment and it should be reversed'.

will be imposed on shareholders"' ... Because Atex was a Delaware corporation, Delaware law determines whether the corporate veil can be pierced in this instance.

Delaware law permits a court to pierce the corporate veil of a company 'where there is fraud or where [it] is in fact a mere instrumentality or alter ego of its owner'. ... Although the Delaware Supreme Court has never explicitly adopted an alter ego theory of parent liability for its subsidiaries, lower Delaware courts have applied the doctrine on several occasions, as has the United States District Court for the District of Delaware. Thus, under an alter ego theory, there is no requirement of a showing of fraud. ... To prevail on an alter ego claim under Delaware law, a plaintiff must show (1) that the parent and the subsidiary 'operated as a single economic entity' and (2) that an 'overall element of injustice or unfairness ... [is] present'....

To prevail on an alter ego theory of liability, a plaintiff must show that the two corporations 'operated as a single economic entity such that it would be inequitable ... to uphold a legal distinction between them' ... Among the factors to be considered in determining whether a subsidiary and parent operate as a 'single economic entity' are:

[W]hether the corporation was adequately capitalized for the corporate undertaking; whether the corporation was solvent; whether dividends were paid, corporate records kept, officers and directors functioned properly, and other corporate formalities were observed; whether the dominant shareholder siphoned corporate funds; and whether, in general, the corporation simply functioned as a facade for the dominant shareholder.

... As noted above, a showing of fraud or wrongdoing is not necessary under an alter ego theory, but the plaintiff must demonstrate an overall element of injustice or unfairness ...

A plaintiff seeking to persuade a Delaware court to disregard the corporate structure faces 'a difficult task'. ... Courts have made it clear that '[t]he legal entity of a corporation will not be disturbed until sufficient reason appears' ...

Kodak has shown that Atex followed corporate formalities, and the plaintiffs have offered no evidence to the contrary. Significantly, the plaintiffs have not challenged Kodak's assertions that Atex's board of directors held regular meetings, that minutes from those meetings were routinely prepared and maintained in corporate minute books, that appropriate financial records and other files were maintained by Atex, that Atex filed its own tax returns and paid its own taxes, and that Atex had its own employees and management executives who were responsible for the corporation's day-to-day business ...

We find that the district court correctly held that, in light of the undisputed factors of independence cited by Kodak, 'the elements identified by the plaintiffs ... [were] insufficient as a matter of law to establish the degree of domination necessary to disregard Atex's corporate identity' ...

First, the district court correctly held that 'Atex's participation in Kodak's cash management system is consistent with sound business practice and does not show undue domination or control' ...

Courts have generally declined to find alter ego liability based on a parent corporation's use of a cash management system.... The plaintiffs offer no facts to support their speculation that Kodak's centralized cash management system was actually a 'complete commingling' of funds or a means by which Kodak sought to 'siphon [ ] all of Atex's revenues into its own account'.

Second, the district court correctly concluded that it could find no domination based on the plaintiffs' evidence that Kodak's approval was required for Atex's real estate leases, major capital expenditures, negotiations for a sale of minority stock ownership to IBM, or the fact that Kodak played a significant role in the ultimate sale of Atex's assets to a third party. Again, the parties do not dispute that Kodak required Atex to seek its approval and/or participation for the above transactions. However, this evidence, viewed in the light most favorable to the plaintiffs, does not raise an issue of material fact about whether the two corporations constituted 'a single economic entity'. Indeed, this type of conduct is typical of a majority shareholder or parent corporation ... Similarly, the district court in the instant case properly found that the presence of Kodak employees at periodic meetings with Atex's chief financial officer and comptroller to be 'entirely appropriate' ...

The plaintiffs' third argument, that Kodak dominated the Atex board of directors, also fails. Although a number of Kodak employees have sat on the Atex board, it is undisputed that between 1981 and 1988, only one director of Atex was also a director of Kodak. Between 1989 and

1992, Atex and Kodak had no directors in common. Parents and subsidiaries frequently have overlapping boards of directors while maintaining separate business operations … Since the overlap is negligible here, we find this evidence to be entirely insufficient to raise a question of fact on the issue of domination.

Fourth, the district court properly rejected the plaintiffs' argument that the descriptions of the relationship between Atex and Kodak and the presence of the Kodak logo in Atex's promotional literature justify piercing the corporate veil …

It is clear from the record that Atex never merged with Kodak or operated as a Kodak division. The plaintiffs offer no evidence to the contrary, apart from these statements in Atex and Kodak documents that they claim are indicative of the true relationship between the two companies. Viewed in the light most favorable to the plaintiffs, these statements and the use of the Kodak logo are not evidence that the two companies operated as a 'single economic entity' ….

Fifth, the plaintiffs contend that Atex's assignment of its former CEO's mortgage to Kodak in order to close the sale of Atex's assets to a third party is evidence of Kodak's domination of Atex. We reject this argument as well. The evidence is undisputed that Kodak paid Atex the book value of the note and entered into a formal repayment agreement with the former CEO. Formal contracts were executed, and the two companies observed all corporate formalities.

Finally … the plaintiffs offer no evidence on the second prong of the alter ego analysis. The plaintiffs have failed to present evidence of an 'overall element of injustice or unfairness' that would result from respecting the two companies' corporate separateness … In the instant case, the plaintiffs offer nothing more than the bare assertion that Kodak 'exploited' Atex 'to generate profits but not to safeguard safety'. There is no indication that Kodak sought to defraud creditors and consumers or to siphon funds from its subsidiary …

Questions and comments:

1. Note the emphasis put on the second limb of the 'instrumentality' test. Delaware law seems to be rather strict.[41] In his empirical study of 1991, Robert Thompson identifies only eleven Delaware cases and in none of them has the veil actually been pierced.[42] This is attributed to the fact that Delaware is home mainly to large publicly held companies.[43]
2. According to the case, what is the conflicts-of-law rule that governs veil-piercing cases in the United States? Given the rationale of that rule as well as that of the veil-piercing doctrine, does the conflicts rule seem to be appropriate?[44] What could be an alternative?

2. *Wrongful or unjust act*

Control must have been used to commit fraud or wrong so that upholding the principle of limited liability would result in an inequity or injustice. Again, courts and jurisdictions differ as to what they require in order for an act to be classified as a wrong.[45]

***DeWitt Truck Brokers, Inc. v. W. Ray Flemming Fruit Co.*, 540 F.2d 681 (US Court of Appeals for the Fourth Circuit, 1976)**

Russel, Circuit Judge:

In this action on debt, the plaintiff seeks, by piercing the corporate veil under the law of South Carolina, to impose individual liability on the president of the indebted corporation individually. The District Court, making findings of fact which may be overturned only if clearly

[41] See further *Harco National Insurance Co. v Green Farms, Inc.*, 1989 WL 110537 (Delaware Court of Chancery, 1989); *LaSalle National Bank v Perelman*, 82 F. Supp.2d 279 (United States District Court, Delaware, 2000).

[42] Thompson (n 16) 1051.

[43] ibid 1052.

[44] F Gevurtz, *Corporation Law* (2nd edn, West Academic Publishing 2010) 108–109.

[45] Blumberg (n 19), 115; Conard (n 9) 429–31.

erroneous, pierced the corporate veil and imposed individual liability. The individual defendant appeals. We affirm.

...

Certainly the [W. Ray Flemming Fruit Company] was, in practice at least, a close, one-man corporation from the very beginning. Its incorporators were the defendant Flemming, his wife and his attorney. It began in 1962 with a capitalization of 5,000 shares, issued for a consideration of one dollar each. In some manner which Flemming never made entirely clear, approximately 2,000 shares were retired. At the times involved here Flemming owned approximately 90% of the corporation's outstanding stock, according to his own testimony, though this was not verified by any stock records. Flemming was obscure on who the other stockholders were and how much stock these other stockholders owned, giving at different times conflicting statements as to who owned stock and how much. His testimony on who were the officers and directors was hardly more direct. He testified that the corporation did have one other director, Ed Bernstein, a resident of New York. It is significant, however, that, whether Bernstein was nominally a director or not, there were no corporate records of a real directors' meeting in all the years of the corporation's existence and Flemming conceded this to be true. Flemming countered this by testifying that Bernstein travelled a great deal and that his contacts with Bernstein were generally by telephone. The evidence indicates rather clearly that Bernstein was, like the directors in G. M. Leasing, 'nothing more than (a) figurehead(s),' who had 'attended no directors meeting,' and even more crucial, never received any fee or reimbursement of expenses or salary of any kind from the corporation.

The District Court found, also, that the corporation never had a stockholders' meeting ... It is thus clear that corporate formalities, even rudimentary formalities, were not observed by the defendant.

Beyond the absence of any observance of corporate formalities is the purely personal matter in which the corporation was operated. No stockholder or officer of the corporation other than Flemming ever received any salary, dividend, or fee from the corporation, or, for that matter, apparently exercised any voice in its operation or decisions. In all the years of the corporation's existence, Flemming was the sole beneficiary of its operations and its continued existence was for his exclusive benefit. During these years he was receiving from $15,000 to $25,000 each year from a corporation, which, during most of the time, was showing no profit and apparently had no working capital. Moreover, the payments to Flemming were authorized under no resolution of the board of directors of the corporation, as recorded in any minutes of a board meeting. Actually, it would seem that Flemming's withdrawals varied with what could be taken out of the corporation at the moment: If this amount were $15,000, that was Flemming's withdrawal; if it were $25,000, that was his withdrawal.

To summarize: The District Court found, and there was evidence to sustain the findings, that there was here a complete disregard of 'corporate formalities' in the operation of the corporation, which functioned, not for the benefit of all stockholders, but only for the financial advantage of Flemming, who was the sole stockholder to receive one penny of profit from the corporation in the decade or more that it operated, and who made during that period all the corporate decisions and dominated the corporation's operations.

That the corporation was undercapitalized, if indeed it were not without any real capital, seems obvious. Its original stated 'risk capital' had long since been reduced to approximately $3,000 by a reduction in the outstanding capital, or at least this would seem to be inferable from the record, and even this, it seems fair to conclude, had been seemingly exhausted by a long succession of years when the corporation operated at no profit. The inability of the corporation to pay a dividend is persuasive proof of this want of capital. In fact, the defendant Flemming makes no effort to refute the evidence of want of any capital reserves on the part of the corporation. It appears patent that the corporation was actually operating at all times involved here on someone else's capital. This conclusion follows from a consideration of the manner in which Flemming operated in the name of the corporation during the year when plaintiff's indebtedness was incurred.

The corporation was engaged in the business of a commission agent, selling fruit produce for the account of growers of farm products such as peaches and watermelons in the Edgefield, South Carolina, area. It never purported to own such products; to repeat, it (always acting through Flemming) sold the products as agent for the growers. Under the arrangement with the growers, it was to remit to the grower the full sale price, less any transportation costs incurred in transporting the products from the growers' farm or warehouse to the purchaser and its sales commission. An integral part of these collections was, as stated, represented by the plaintiff's transportation charges. Accordingly, during the period involved here, the corporation had as operating funds seemingly only its commissions and the amount of the plaintiff's transportation charges, for which the corporation had claimed credit in its settlement with its growers. At the time, however, Flemming was withdrawing funds from the corporation at the rate of at least $15,000 per year; and doing this, even though he must have known that the corporation could only do this by withholding payment of the transportation charges due the plaintiff, which in the accounting with the growers Flemming represented had been paid the plaintiff. And, it is of some interest that the amount due the plaintiff for transportation costs was approximately the same as the $15,000 minimum annual salary the defendant testified he was paid by the corporation. Were the opinion of the District Court herein to be reversed, Flemming would be permitted to retain substantial sums from the operations of the corporation without having any real capital in the undertaking, risking nothing of his own and using as operating capital what he had collected as due the plaintiff. Certainly, equity and fundamental justice support individual liability of Flemming for plaintiff's charges, payment for which he asserted in his accounting with the growers that he had paid and for which he took credit on such accounting. This case patently presents a blending of the very factors which courts have regarded as justifying a disregard of the corporate entity in furtherance of basic and fundamental fairness.

Finally, it should not be overlooked that at some point during the period when this indebtedness was being incurred whether at the beginning or at a short time later is not clear in the record the plaintiff became concerned about former delays in receipt of payment for its charges and, to allay that concern, Flemming stated to the plaintiff, according to the latter's testimony as credited by the District Court, that 'he (i. e., Flemming) would take care of (the charges) personally, if the corporation failed to do so * * *'. On this assurance, the plaintiff contended that it continued to haul for the defendant. The existence of this promise by Flemming is not disputed ... When one, who is the sole beneficiary of a corporation's operations and who dominates it, as did Flemming in this case, induces a creditor to extend credit to the corporation on such an assurance as given here, that fact has been considered by many authorities sufficient basis for piercing the corporate veil ... The only argument against this view is bottomed on the statute of frauds ... But reliance on such statute is often regarded as without merit in a case where the promise or assurance is given 'at the time or before the debt is created,' for in that case the promise is original and without the statute.

...

Questions and comments:

1. In this well-known and much cited case the court based its decision to affirm the veil-piercing of the District Court on the following considerations (in rearranged order): (i) There was a complete 'disregard of corporate formalities': no board or shareholders' meetings had been held, no salaries, fees or dividends had been paid to any person other than the defendant Flemming. (ii) Flemming promised the plaintiff that he would take care of the charges personally if the corporation failed to do so. (iii) Flemming misappropriated for himself the transportation charges the corporation had claimed credit for vis-à-vis the growers in order to pay the plaintiff. (iv) The corporation was 'undercapitalized'. It had no capital reserves and operated 'on someone else's capital'.
2. These four considerations are frequently cited in the literature and often relied on by courts in order to justify veil-piercing decisions.[46] All four criteria are somewhat puzzling. Or in the words of the Delaware Court of Chancery, '[m]any of the factors frequently employed in veil piercing analysis are irrelevant to the question of whether, in all fairness, a parent company should be forced to answer for the liability of its subsidiary'.[47] Try to relate the mentioned

[46] Oh (n 16) 133–9.

[47] *Allied Capital Corp. v GC-Sun Holdings LP*, 910 A.2d (2006) 1020, 1043.

criteria to the economic rationale of the piercing doctrine as discussed in paragraph A. above. In that light, which of the criteria make sense, which don't, and why?

The failure to observe corporate formalities, such as not holding board meetings or shareholders' meetings, failure to prepare minutes for such meetings, failure to issue stock or to pay dividends, has occasionally been relied on as sufficient reason to pierce the corporate veil.[48] Other courts have held that corporate informalities on their own are insufficient to justify veil piercing.[49] In any case, observance of corporate formalities seems to carry some weight and legal advisers are trained to warn their clients carefully about the consequences of non-observance.[50] In light of the economic rationale for veil-piercing, however, it is not clear why corporate formalities should have a bearing at all. The underlying idea seems to be that if a corporation fails to act like a corporation courts will not afford limited liability to the persons behind it.[51] However, only when creditors are misled by a business owner who gives them no reason to believe that he is operating in the corporate form, so that creditors cannot adjust their ex ante compensation accordingly, would it appear to be justified to pierce the corporate veil.[52] Otherwise, it is hard to see how corporate informalities, and in particular non-payment of dividends, salaries, and fees, may contribute to a potential loss suffered by corporate creditors.[53] Moreover, the modern trend seems to be to reduce corporate formalities and to grant greater flexibility to shareholders and management. In respect of LLCs, a number of statutes specifically exclude the failure to follow appropriate formalities as a ground for disregarding limited liability.[54] The same is true for close corporations under the revised MBCA.[55]

Outright fraud and fraudulent misrepresentation of the financial position of the company by its controlling shareholder is generally deemed to be a sufficient reason to pierce the corporate veil. Common law fraud covers not just intentionally false representations, but also misrepresentations of facts which, although not knowingly untrue, the person making the representation had no reasonable grounds for believing to be true.[56] If that is the case it may be asked why courts find it necessary to invoke veil-piercing at all. After all, if the controlling shareholder commits fraud he will be liable directly for his own tort for the amount unpaid on the creditor's claim against the company as damages. The result is the same as holding the shareholder liable for the company's debt.[57] The reason may be that fraud and fraudulent misrepresentation require a false statement of fact, albeit psychological, by the defendant. As long as the defendant believed at the moment the contract was entered into that he would be able to meet his obligations as and when they fall due, there can be no liability under these doctrines even if later the defendant acts in a way that frustrates his ability to pay. Piercing the corporate veil seems to be necessary in order to fill this gap. A comparable situation arises where the defendant gives the impression that someone else, he personally or a related corporation, will stand in for the corporation's debts.[58] This is what happened in *De Witt*. Where this promise is enforceable as a contract or personal guarantee there is no need to invoke veil-piercing. The defendant will simply be liable on his own contractual obligation. Enforceability may be uncertain, however, because of a lack of specificity of the respective promise. Moreover, the parole evidence rule may preclude naming the controlling shareholder as party to a written contract in addition or instead of the corporation; and an attempt to cast oral assurances as personal guarantees may fall foul of the statute of frauds[59] requiring certain contracts to be in writing.[60]

[48] *Victoria Elevator Co. v Meriden Grain Co.*, 283 N.W.2d 509, 512 (Minn. 1979).
[49] *Solomon v W. Hills Dev. Co.*, 312 N.W.2d 428, 432 (Mich. Ct. App. 1981).
[50] Gevurtz (n 44) 78.
[51] Morrissey (n 17) 544.
[52] Millon (n 7) 1335–6.
[53] Morrissey (n 17) 545.
[54] ibid 559.
[55] Close Corporation Supplement, §25.
[56] *Gagne v Bertran*, 43 Cal.2d 481 (Supreme Court of California, 1954) 487.
[57] Gevurtz (n 44) 82.
[58] ibid 84.
[59] eg California Civil Code, §1624(2).
[60] Gevurtz (n 44) 84.

Again, veil-piercing may be relied on in order to overcome these difficulties. The danger is, of course, that courts sympathetic to the plaintiff may disregard the policies behind the restrictions on contractual enforceability to get the result that they feel is right.[61] Reliance on piercing doctrine may, thus, prevent a careful analysis of the conflicting interests and efficiency trade-offs.

The withdrawal of the company's assets by corporate insiders to the detriment of its creditors is widely accepted as 'wrongful conduct' that satisfies the 'instrumentality test', occasionally even on its own.[62] This category does not just encompass outright transfers of assets from the debtor company to its shareholders, parent company or subsidiaries, but also loans advanced by the debtor company below the market rate of interest to the parent or other group companies; the pledging of the debtor company's assets as collateral for securing debts of parent or affiliate companies; repayment of debts owed by parent or other group companies to third parties.[63] Where the debtor company does not receive adequate consideration in exchange for such a transaction, the company's risk of default increases and there are fewer assets to be distributed among creditors upon liquidation. Where the company's remaining assets are insufficient to cover all its debts negative externalities are imposed on its creditors. Thus, asset stripping as a justification for veil-piercing is well in accordance with our economic rationale discussed above, both in respect of voluntary and involuntary creditors. However, the cases falling within this category are traditionally the domain of fraudulent transfer law. Fraudulent transfer law is state law with most states having adopted the Uniform Fraudulent Transfer Act of 1984, which, following minor amendments, is now the Uniform Voidable Transactions Act 2014. On that basis, creditors may reverse certain transactions entered into by the company to the detriment of its creditors where the company receives 'less than a reasonably equivalent value in exchange for such transfer'[64] or where the transfer was made with 'actual intent to hinder, delay or defraud creditors',[65] provided that at the time of the transaction the company was insolvent or became insolvent as a result of the transaction.[66] Sometimes knowledge, or reason to know, of the imminent insolvency of the debtor on the part of the transferee is also required.[67] The principal remedy is avoidance of the transaction and retransfer of the asset to the company to the extent necessary to satisfy the creditor's claim.[68] Thus, the remedy is capped at the value of the assets transferred. By contrast, veil-piercing results in unlimited liability of the responsible shareholder, irrespective of the value of the assets the company has been stripped of. There is, however, significant overlap as far as the preconditions for liability are concerned. Again, why the need for the piercing doctrine?[69] Fraudulent transfer law requires the plaintiff to identify precisely the relevant transactions and to prove that they were carried through without adequate consideration or with intent to defraud creditors, and at a time when the company was insolvent. This will often be difficult for an outside creditor, in particular where corporate transactions are not properly accounted for and do not appear in the company's documentation. By contrast, veil-piercing appears to focus on the overall situation of the debtor company. Where there are transactions with corporate insiders that left the company wanting for capital, the onus seems to shift to these insiders to show that the respective transactions were carried out at arm's length and/or for valid business reasons. The severe remedy of unlimited liability may be justified as a deterrent against asset stripping and an incentive to provide proper documentation.[70] Moreover, fraudulent transfer law would not cover an opportunistic investment strategy or a hazardous business activity that may cause harm to third parties without compensation.

61 ibid 85. 62 Vandekerckhove (n 15) 298. 63 ibid.
64 Uniform Fraudulent Transfer Act 1984 (Uniform Voidable Transactions Act 2014), §§4(a)(2), 5(a).
65 ibid §§4(a)(1), 5(b). 66 ibid §§5(a) and (b), 4(b)(9). 67 ibid §5(b). 68 ibid §7(a)(1).
69 Gevurtz (n 44) 88. 70 ibid.

One aspect often referred to, albeit usually unable to justify veil-piercing alone,[71] seems to be 'gross undercapitalization', usually defined as the company's assets being insufficient to satisfy its existing or foreseeable obligations.[72] The concept is problematic[73] and raises a number of questions. Given that most state incorporation statutes today do not require any minimum amount of legal capital, it may first be asked whether undercapitalization should be a valid reason for veil-piercing at all.[74] As far as voluntary creditors are concerned, it could be argued that, absent any misrepresentation, they can protect themselves by demanding personal guarantees or ex ante compensation for the additional risk arising from dealing with an undercapitalized company. In *Laya v Erin Homes, Inc.*[75] the court stated:

> In a breach of contract case many of the commentators and a few of the cases suggest that there may also be a [further] prong to the test for piercing the corporate veil which must be hurdled by certain types, and only certain types, of contract creditors of the corporation, specifically, those capable of protecting themselves. When, under the circumstances, it would be reasonable for that particular type of a party entering into the contract with the corporation, for example, a bank or other lending institution, to conduct an investigation of the credit of the corporation prior to entering into the contract, such party will be charged with the knowledge that a reasonable credit investigation would disclose. If such an investigation would disclose that the corporation is grossly undercapitalized, based upon the nature and the magnitude of the corporate undertaking, such party will be deemed to have assumed the risk of the gross undercapitalization and will not be permitted to pierce the corporate veil.

However, the court continued:

> Generally, the presumption is that the party dealing with the corporation did not assume the risk of grossly inadequate capitalization. '[I]n entering into such [contractual] relationships with corporate entities the parties are [generally] entitled to rely upon certain assumptions, one being that the corporation is more than a mere shell-that it has substance as well as form' ... In other words, the incorporators who actively participate in the operation of the business are not entitled to personal immunity when they fail to provide the quid pro quo for such immunity, specifically, a reasonably adequate capital fund to which creditors may resort.

Undercapitalization, thus, takes on a supporting role. Corporate insiders act fraudulently when they (implicitly) promise corporate performance knowing at the time that the corporation is unlikely to be able to perform. Undercapitalization in this context serves simply as evidence for fraudulent intent. Similarly, in the context of withdrawal of corporate assets undercapitalization of the company at the time, or as the result, of the transaction is a prerequisite to trigger liability. [76] The situation is different in respect of involuntary creditors, however. Inadequate capitalization externalizes the costs of accidents. Where corporate insiders fail to provide or retain adequate funds to cover the costs of potential and foreseeable accidents or to take out adequate insurance, these costs are not factored into the prices of products and services, and will be borne by the victims of accidents, thus subsidizing shareholders and customers. Moreover, corporate insiders have no incentives to adopt adequate accident prevention measures, contrary to the economic purposes of tort law. [77]

If undercapitalization is, or should be, a valid consideration for piercing, (at least) three further questions need to be addressed: (i) what is the relevant moment in time to measure capital; (ii) what constitutes capital; (iii) and how much capital is enough?[78] As for the

[71] Except maybe in California; see *Minton v Cavaney*, 56 Cal.2d 576 (Supreme Court of California, 1961): 'The equitable owners of a corporation, for example, are personally liable when they treat the assets of the corporation as their own and add or withdraw capital from the corporation at will ...; when they hold themselves out as being personally liable for the debts of the corporation ...; *or* when they provide inadequate capitalization and actively participate in the conduct of corporate affairs' (emphasis added).

[72] e.g. Keating J's dissenting opinion in *Walkovszky v Carlton*, 18 N.Y.2d 414 (New York Court of Appeals, 1966); Klein, Coffee, and Partnoy (n 14) 148.

[73] Bainbridge (n 17) 519–23. [74] Gevurtz (n 44) 90.

[75] *Laya v Erin Homes, Inc.*, 343, 352 SE2d 93, 100 (W.Va., 1986). [76] Gevurtz (n 44) 94–5.

[77] ibid 95. [78] ibid 96.

relevant time, courts often refer to the time of formation.[79] But this seems to make little sense. Even large initial amounts of equity may be used to cover operating expenses and therefore offer no protection to future creditors. What matters for a creditor entering into a contract with the corporation or a tort victim is the amount of capital available at the time of the contract or accident and whether the corporation will be able to pay when the respective claims fall due; or, respectively, whether a subsequent withdrawal of assets reduces the capital to insufficient amounts. There is no connection between the amount of shareholders' initial equity contribution and the corporation's ability to pay its debts as they fall due.[80] As for what counts as 'capital', the two principal modes of financing are equity and debt. The equity contributions of shareholders are easily characterized as capital for current purposes. However, for practical reasons—reduction of tax liability, lower risk of debt, limited funds available to founders of small businesses—responsible business owners will often fund part of their business with debt. And even highly leveraged businesses can be very valuable. The source of the underlying funds does not seem to matter as long as the corporation has sufficient working capital to pay its debts as they fall due. There seems to be no reason why the availability of short term and long term credit should not count as 'capital' for present purposes, as long as the respective obligations will be met in the future. In respect of tort creditors, liability insurance may be vital. A corporation will not be undercapitalized if it has sufficient liability coverage to meet all reasonably foreseeable damages from accidents, even if its insurance carrier becomes insolvent after the accident and before any claims can be made. 'The whole purpose of asking whether a subsidiary is 'properly capitalized', is precisely to determine its 'financial responsibility'. If the subsidiary is financially responsible, whether by means of insurance or otherwise, the policy [of preventing an abuse of the corporate form] is met. Insurance meets this policy just as well, perhaps even better, than a healthy balance sheet'.[81] In terms of the amount of capital, one would probably have to distinguish between the different types of lenders and tort creditors. Sophisticated long-term lenders stipulate capital requirements and financial ratios in their covenants with the debtor company. Absent fraud, there seems to be no need for courts to rewrite these contracts and to substitute their own perception of adequate capital for those of the professional lenders.[82] By contrast, trade creditors will usually be interested in the corporation's ability to pay its bills as they fall due as the appropriate measure of capitalization. And for tort creditors the adequate measure of capitalization is adequate insurance, maybe in the form of self-insurance, to cover all reasonably foreseeable damages payments.[83] A more general approach can be found in *Laya v Erin Homes, Inc.*:[84]

> With respect to determining the adequacy of the corporation's capital, in light of the nature and magnitude of the corporate undertaking, there are several tests and factors which can be utilized to analyze the financial data of the corporation. For example, comparison with the capitalization of other corporations in the same or a similar line of business may be made. The capitalization of the corporation in question could be compared with the average industry-wide ratios (current ratio, acid-test ratio, debt/equity ratio, etc.) obtained from published sources (Dunn & Bradstreet, Moody's Manual of Investments, Standard and Poor's Corporation Records, etc.). These average ratios could be buttressed by expert testimony from certified public accountants, securities analysts, investment counselors or other qualified financial analysts. See Barber, Piercing the Corporate Veil, 17 Willamette L.Rev. 371, 392-94 (1981). 'Grossly inadequate capitalization' for the purpose of piercing the corporate veil would generally be reflected by a substantial deficiency of capital compared with that level of capitalization deemed adequate in the case by the financial analyst experts.

[79] *Minton v Cavaney* 56 Cal.2d 576 (Supreme Court of California, 1961); *Slottow Fidelity Federal Bank v American Casualty Co.*, 10 F.3d 1355 (9th Cir. 1993).

[80] Millon (n 7) 1338.

[81] *Radaszewski v Telecom Corp.*, 981 F.2d 305 (8th Cir. 1992).

[82] Gevurtz (n 44) 98.

[83] ibid 99–101.

[84] *Laya v Erin Homes, Inc.* (n 75) 101.

In most cases, however, courts do not conduct a proper analysis of the issue of capitalization, in particular where the shareholders never contributed anything to the corporation.[85]

Questions and comments:

1. What are 'current ratio', 'acid-test ratio' and 'debt/equity ratio'? What do they tell us about a company's financial situation?
2. Critically evaluate the notion of 'gross undercapitalization' in light of the debate on legal capital as discussed in Chapter 9.
3. Professor Stephen Bainbridge has argued for the abolition of the veil piercing doctrine.[86] Where the creditor was misled by the shareholder and as a result forewent adequate ex ante compensation the tort claims of fraud and fraudulent misrepresentation will provide adequate remedies. Where the shareholder has subsequently increased the creditor's risk by siphoning away corporate assets the situation is adequately addressed by fraudulent transfer law. Given the economic rationale for limited liability and veil piercing, are there any situations not covered by fraudulent misrepresentation and fraudulent transfer law where veil piercing may still have a role to play?[87]
4. In *Castleberry v Branscum*, 721 S.W.2d 270 the Supreme Court of Texas had the following to say: 'We disregard the corporate fiction, even though corporate formalities have been observed and corporate and individual property have been kept separately, when the corporate form has been used as part of a basically unfair device to achieve an inequitable result'. Later on the court held that '[t]o prove there has been a sham to perpetrate a fraud, tort claimants and contract creditors must show only constructive fraud. We distinguished constructive from actual fraud in *Archer v. Griffith*: Actual fraud usually involves dishonesty of purpose or intent to deceive, whereas constructive fraud is the breach of some legal or equitable duty which, irrespective of moral guilt, the law declares fraudulent because of its tendency to deceive others, to violate confidence, or to injure public interests'. Under this standard it seemed no longer to be safe to conduct business in corporate form.[88] The Texas legislature reacted by providing in Article 2.21 of the Texas Business Corporation Act that a shareholder shall not be liable for 'any contractual obligation of the corporation' unless the obligee demonstrates that the shareholder 'did perpetrate an actual fraud on the obligee primarily for the direct personal benefit' of the shareholder. Please note that this restriction of veil piercing does only apply to contractual obligations and not torts.

II. Enterprise liability

In respect of corporate groups, sometimes the closely related concept of 'enterprise liability' is distinguished from 'piercing the corporate veil'. As adherents to this doctrine point out, the distinction is subtle: 'Properly understood, veil piercing is a vertical form of liability (i.e., it provides a mechanism for holding a shareholder personally liable for the corporation's obligations). Enterprise liability provides a horizontal form of liability (i.e., it offers a vehicle for holding the entire business enterprise liable)'.[89] There is considerable overlap when the enterprise is controlled by a holding company and the preconditions for liability seem to be

[85] *Kinney Shoe Corp. v Polan*, 939 F.2d 209 (4th Cir 1991): 'A stockholder's liability is limited to the amount he has invested in the corporation but Plan invested nothing in Industrial . . . When nothing is invested in the corporation, the corporation provides not protection to its owner; nothing in, nothing out, no protection'.

[86] Bainbridge (n 17) 517–23. According to Bainbridge, enterprise liability (see below) should, however, be retained. ibid 526–34.

[87] cf Millon (n 7) 1358–60.

[88] RW Hamilton, JR Macey, and DK Moll, *Cases and Materials on Corporations* (11th edn, Thomson-West 2010), 233–234.

[89] Bainbridge (n 17) 526; see also AA Berle, 'The Theory of Enterprise Entity' (1947) 47 Columbia Law Review 343, 348–350.

fairly similar. Enterprise liability requires (i) unity of interest and ownership so that the separateness of the corporations within the group has effectively ceased, and (ii) that upholding the principles of separate legal personality and limited liability would promote injustice or inequity. [90] The interplay between both doctrines can be observed in the following, well known and much discussed case:

***Walkovszky v. Carlton*, 18 N.Y.2d 414 (New York Court of Appeals, 1966)**

Fuld, Judge:

This case involves what appears to be a rather common practice in the taxicab industry of vesting the ownership of a taxi fleet in many corporations, each owning only one or two cabs.

The complaint alleges that the plaintiff was severely injured four years ago in New York City when he was run down by a taxicab owned by the defendant Seon Cab Corporation and negligently operated at the time by the defendant Marchese. The individual defendant, Carlton, is claimed to be a stockholder of 10 corporations, including Seon, each of which has but two cabs registered in its name, and it is implied that only the minimum automobile liability insurance required by law (in the amount of $10,000) is carried on any one cab. Although seemingly independent of one another, these corporations are alleged to be 'operated … as a single entity, unit and enterprise' with regard to financing, supplies, repairs, employees and garaging, and all are named as defendants. The plaintiff asserts that he is also entitled to hold their stockholders personally liable for the damages sought because the multiple corporate structure constitutes an unlawful attempt 'to defraud members of the general public' who might be injured by the cabs.

…

In the case before us, the plaintiff has explicitly alleged that none of the corporations 'had a separate existence of their own' and, as indicated above, all are named as defendants. However, it is one thing to assert that a corporation is a fragment of a larger corporate combine which actually conducts the business … It is quite another to claim that the corporation is a 'dummy' for its individual stockholders who are in reality carrying on the business in their personal capacities for purely personal rather than corporate ends … Either circumstance would justify treating the corporation as an agent and piercing the corporate veil to reach the principal but a different result would follow in each case. In the first, only a larger Corporate entity would be held financially responsible … while, in the other, the stockholder would be personally liable … Either the stockholder is conducting the business in his individual capacity or he is not. If he is, he will be liable; if he is not, then it does not matter-insofar as his personal liability is concerned-that the enterprise is actually being carried on by a larger 'enterprise entity' …

…

The individual defendant is charged with having 'organized, managed, dominated and controlled' a fragmented corporate entity but there are no allegations that he was conducting business in his individual capacity. Had the taxicab fleet been owned by a single corporation, it would be readily apparent that the plaintiff would face formidable barriers in attempting to establish personal liability on the part of the corporation's stockholders. The fact that the fleet ownership has been deliberately split up among many corporations does not ease the plaintiff's burden in that respect. The corporate form may not be disregarded merely because the assets of the corporation, together with the mandatory insurance coverage of the vehicle which struck the plaintiff, are insufficient to assure him the recovery sought. If Carlton were to be held individually liable on those facts alone, the decision would apply equally to the thousands of cabs which are owned by their individual drivers who conduct their businesses through corporations organized pursuant to section 401 of the Business Corporation Law, Consol.Laws, *c.* 4 and carry the minimum insurance required by subdivision 1 (par. (a)) of section 370 of the Vehicle and Traffic Law, Consol.Laws, *c.* 71. These taxi owner-operators are entitled to form such corporations … and we agree with the court at Special Term that, if the insurance coverage required by statute 'is inadequate for the protection of the public, the remedy lies not with the courts but with the Legislature'. It may very well be sound policy to require that certain corporations must

[90] *Las Palmas Assoc. v Las Palmas Centre Assoc.*, 235 Cal. App. 3d 1220, 1250; relying on *Pan Pacific Sash & Door Co v Greendale Park, Inc.*, 166 Cal. App. 2d 652 (1958).

take out liability insurance which will afford adequate compensation to their potential tort victims. However, the responsibility for imposing conditions on the privilege of incorporation has been committed by the Constitution to the Legislature (N.Y. Const., art. X, s 1) and it may not be fairly implied, from any statute, that the Legislature intended, without the slightest discussion or debate, to require of taxi corporations that they carry automobile liability insurance over and above that mandated by the Vehicle and Traffic Law.

This is not to say that it is impossible for the plaintiff to state a valid cause of action against the defendant Carlton. However, the simple fact is that the plaintiff has just not done so here. While the complaint alleges that the separate corporations were undercapitalized and that their assets have been intermingled, it is barren of any 'sufficiently particular(ized) statements' . . . that the defendant Carlton and his associates are actually doing business in their individual capacities, shuttling their personal funds in and out of the corporations 'without regard to formality and to suit their immediate convenience' . . . Such a 'perversion of the privilege to do business in a corporate form' . . . would justify imposing personal liability on the individual stockholders . . . Nothing of the sort has in fact been charged, and it cannot reasonably or logically be inferred from the happenstance that the business of Seon Cab Corporation may actually be carried on by a larger corporate entity composed of many corporations which, under general principles of agency, would be liable to each other's creditors in contract and in tort.

In point of fact, the principle relied upon in the complaint to sustain the imposition of personal liability is not agency but fraud. Such a cause of action cannot withstand analysis. If it is not fraudulent for the owner-operator of a single cab corporation to take out only the minimum required liability insurance, the enterprise does not become either illicit or fraudulent merely because it consists of many such corporations. The plaintiff's injuries are the same regardless of whether the cab which strikes him is owned by a single corporation or part of a fleet with ownership fragmented among many corporations. Whatever rights he may be able to assert against parties other than the registered owner of the vehicle come into being not because he has been defrauded but because, under the principle of Respondeat superior, he is entitled to hold the whole enterprise responsible for the acts of its agents.

In sum, then, the complaint falls short of adequately stating a cause of action against the defendant Carlton in his individual capacity.

The order of the Appellate Division should be reversed, with costs in this court and in the Appellate Division, the certified question answered in the negative and the order of the Supreme Court, Richmond County, reinstated, with leave to serve an amended complaint.

Keating, Judge (dissenting):

The defendant Carlton, the shareholder here sought to be held for the negligence of the driver of a taxicab, was a principal shareholder and organizer of the defendant corporation which owned the taxicab. The corporation was one of 10 organized by the defendant, each containing two cabs and each cab having the 'minimum liability' insurance coverage mandated by section 370 of the Vehicle and Traffic Law. The sole assets of these operating corporations are the vehicles themselves and they are apparently subject to mortgages.

From their inception these corporations were intentionally undercapitalized for the purpose of avoiding responsibility for acts which were bound to arise as a result of the operation of a large taxi fleet having cars out on the street 24 hours a day and engaged in public transportation. And during the course of the corporations' existence all income was continually drained out of the corporations for the same purpose.

The issue presented by this action is whether the policy of this State, which affords those desiring to engage in a business enterprise the privilege of limited liability through the use of the corporate device, is so strong that it will permit that privilege to continue no matter how much it is abused, no matter how irresponsibly the corporation is operated, no matter what the cost to the public. I do not believe that it is.

Under the circumstances of this case the shareholders should all be held individually liable to this plaintiff for the injuries he suffered . . . At least, the matter should not be disposed of on the pleadings by a dismissal of the complaint. 'If a corporation is organized and carries on business without substantial capital in such a way that the corporation is likely to have no sufficient assets available to meet its debts, it is inequitable that shareholders should set up such a flimsy organization to escape personal liability. The attempt to do corporate business without providing any sufficient basis of financial responsibility to creditors is an abuse of the separate entity and will be ineffectual to exempt the shareholders from corporate debts. It is coming to be recognized as the policy of law that shareholders should in good faith put at the risk of the business unincumbered capital reasonably adequate for its prospective liabilities. If capital is illusory or trifling compared with the business to be done and the risks of loss, this is a ground for denying the separate entity privilege'.

...

The defendant Carlton claims that, because the minimum amount of insurance required by the statute was obtained, the corporate veil cannot and should not be pierced despite the fact that the assets of the corporation which owned the cab were 'trifling compared with the business to be done and the risks of loss' which were certain to be encountered. I do not agree.

The Legislature in requiring minimum liability insurance of $10,000, no doubt, intended to provide at least some small fund for recovery against those individuals and corporations who just did not have and were not able to raise or accumulate assets sufficient to satisfy the claims of those who were injured as a result of their negligence. It certainly could not have intended to shield those individuals who organized corporations, with the specific intent of avoiding responsibility to the public, where the operation of the corporate enterprise yielded profits sufficient to purchase additional insurance. Moreover, it is reasonable to assume that the Legislature believed that those individuals and corporations having substantial assets would take out insurance far in excess of the minimum in order to protect those assets from depletion. Given the costs of hospital care and treatment and the nature of injuries sustained in auto collisions, it would be unreasonable to assume that the Legislature believed that the minimum provided in the statute would in and of itself be sufficient to recompense 'innocent victims of motor vehicle accidents ... for the injury and financial loss inflicted upon them'.

...

The defendant contends that a decision holding him personally liable would discourage people from engaging in corporate enterprise.

What I would merely hold is that a participating shareholder of a corporation vested with a public interest, organized with capital insufficient to meet liabilities which are certain to arise in the ordinary course of the corporation's business, may be held personally responsible for such liabilities. Where corporate income is not sufficient to cover the cost of insurance premiums above the statutory minimum or where initially adequate finances dwindle under the pressure of competition, bad times or extraordinary and unexpected liability, obviously the shareholder will not be held liable ...

The only types of corporate enterprises that will be discouraged as a result of a decision allowing the individual shareholder to be sued will be those such as the one in question, designed solely to abuse the corporate privilege at the expense of the public interest.

For these reasons I would vote to affirm the order of the Appellate Division.

DESMOND, C.J., and VAN VOORHIS, BURKE and SCILEPPI, JJ., concur with FULD, J.

KEATING, J., dissents and votes to affirm in an opinion in which BERGAN, J., concurs.

Questions and comments:

1. The defendant Carlton operated and controlled 10 corporations owning two cabs each and each carrying only the $10,000 minimum liability insurance. In order to reach the assets of the individual defendant Carlton, the plaintiff argued that 'none of the corporations had a separate existence of their own'. According to the court, if true, this could result only in enterprise liability so that the plaintiff would be able to reach the assets of all the corporations which are part of the group; not, however, the personal assets of the controlling individual shareholder. Carlton's corporate structure also did not amount to an unlawful fraud on the public. If the owner of a single cab corporation could take out only the minimum insurance, it was also not fraudulent to operate more than one such corporation under these conditions. The court itself, however, pointed the plaintiff in the direction as to how he may still reach Carlton's personal assets. If the plaintiff contended that Carlton was conducting the business via his corporations

in his personal capacity and for his own personal, rather than corporate ends, there might be a cause of action against Carlton based on the principles of agency if the corporation is a mere 'dummy' of the shareholder. The court granted the plaintiff leave to amend his complaint in this respect. The amended complaint was subsequently found to state a cause of action against Carlton personally.[91]

2. How does the statute which prescribes the mandatory minimum liability insurance influence the decision of the majority and the dissenting judge, respectively? What do these differing opinions tell you about the respective underlying approach to the principle of separation of powers and the roles attributed to legislature and courts in respect of corporate law?
3. Although such schemes that render a corporation 'judgment-proof' may result in above-optimal externalization of risk, LoPucki does not believe that 'enterprise liability' might be an effective cure because the search for the boundaries of the enterprise are condemned to failure: 'To hold the entity that commits the tort and all contractually related entities liable would be to hold the entire American economy liable'.[92] Do you agree with this rather pessimistic view?
4. Liability of a parent company for acts committed by its subsidiary may turn on the interpretation of a certain statutory provision. One example of increasing importance is the Comprehensive Environmental Response, Compensation, and Liability Act (CERCLA) passed by Congress in 1980. The Act provides a cause of action for the recovery of costs expended in response to the harm caused by the release of hazardous substances from a facility.[93] Inter alia, 'any person who at the time of disposal of any hazardous substance owned or operated any facility at which such hazardous substances were disposed of' shall be liable for the costs of removal etc incurred by the United States Government or a State or an Indian tribe, 42 U.S.C. §9607(a). 'Owner or operator' is 'any person owning or operating [a] facility', 42 U.S.C. §9601(20)(A)(ii). Consequently, a parent corporation may be liable for environmental harm caused by a subsidiary either directly as an operator or indirectly as an owner of the facility[94] (not of the subsidiary). In the landmark case of *United States v. Bestfoods*,[95] the United States Supreme Court acknowledged both the general principle of limited liability and the doctrine of piercing the corporate veil as an exception to it.[96] Accordingly, 'when (but only when) the corporate veil may be pierced, may a parent corporation [as an 'owner' of the facility] be charged with derivative CERCLA liability for its subsidiary's actions'.[97] However, absent the prerequisites for veil piercing, 'nothing in the statute's terms bars a parent corporation from direct liability for its own actions in operating a facility owned by its subsidiary'.[98] Remarking on the uselessness of the statutory definition the court defines parental operation as follows: '[U]nder CERCLA, an operator is simply someone who directs the workings of, manages, or conducts the affairs of a facility. To sharpen the definition for purposes of CERCLA's concern with environmental contamination, an operator must manage, direct, or conduct operations specifically related to pollution, that is, operations having to do with the leakage or disposal of hazardous waste, or decisions about compliance with environmental regulations'.[99] Parental operation goes beyond the normal relationship of parent and subsidiary: 'a parent can be held directly liable when the parent operates the facility in the stead of its subsidiary or alongside the subsidiary in some sort of a joint venture; ... when ... a dual officer or director might depart so far from the norms of parental influence exercised through dual officeholding as to serve the parent, even when ostensibly acting on behalf of the subsidiary in operating the facility; ... [or when] an agent of the parent with no hat to wear but the parent's hat might manage or direct activities at the facility'.[100] The case cleared up some long standing controversies among the lower courts as to what is required to assume parental operation.[101] However, the question whether veil piercing under CERCLA is to be determined based on the applicable state law or by a federal doctrine

[91] *Walkovszky v Carlton* (n 72) 546. [92] ibid 154.
[93] CA Hilbert, 'United States v Bestfoods: Parent Corporation Liability under CERCLA' (1999) 24 Delaware Journal of Corporate Law 919, 920.
[94] ibid 922. [95] 524 U.S. 51 (Supreme Court of the United States, 1998). [96] ibid 61–4.
[97] ibid 63. [98] ibid 64. [99] ibid 66. [100] ibid 71. [101] Hilbert (n 93) 924.

of veil piercing remains unresolved.[102] Can you think of any arguments that might support one or the other approach?

5. In addition to the 'piercing the corporate veil' and 'enterprise liability' doctrines, direct tort liability on the part of a parent corporation also plays a (limited) role.[103] A famous example is the silicone implants litigation.[104] Dow Chemical and Corning Enterprises each held 50 per cent of the shares of Dow Corning. The latter company produced silicone products to be used for several medical purposes, including breast implants. When it was established that silicone implants could cause damage to the immune system, Dow Corning faced a multitude of tort claims by injured people and filed for protection under Chapter 11 of the Bankruptcy Code in order to prevent new product liability claims. New claimants thereupon directed their claims at Dow Chemical as one of the shareholders of Dow Corning. Piercing the corporate veil failed because Dow Chemical's involvement did not go beyond the behaviour of an ordinary shareholder.[105] However, in *Dow Chemical Co. v. Mahlum*,[106] Dow Chemical was found liable on the basis of Restatement (Second) of Torts, section 324A, which provides:

> One who undertakes, gratuitously or for consideration, to render services to another which he should recognize as necessary for the protection of a third person or his things, is subject to liability to the third person for physical harm resulting from his failure to exercise reasonable care to perform his undertaking if (a) his failure to exercise reasonable care increases the risk of such harm or (b) he has undertaken to perform a duty owed by the other to the third person or (c) the harm is suffered because of reliance of the other or the third person upon the undertaking.
>
> The majority of the court held that, given Dow Chemical's 'knowledge about silicones in general and silicone gels in particular through its testing and advising on silicone fluids research over a thirty-year period, its involvement in and knowledge of breast implants through its controlled subsidiary Lepetit, its parent/subsidiary relationship with Dow Corning, including some control over Dow Corning's products and significant control of testing and protocol, one-third control of Dow Corning's board of directors, fifty percent control of Dow Corning's shares, and the control inferred from its various agreements with Dow Corning, Dow Chemical should have used its influence to halt the marketing of Dow Corning's silicone breast implants until the long-term effect of silicone breast implants on humans was understood and these products were determined to be safe ... Instead, it continued to market Dow Corning breast implants outside of the United States and to reap the financial benefits of Dow Corning's domestic sales'.

Thus, 'Dow Chemical negligently performed its undertaking with regard to the safety of the liquid silicone subsequently used in breast implants, as it failed to completely test the silicone liquid for safety and failed to protect the third-party implant recipients'.[107]

C. Germany

The German AktG of 1965 anticipated to some extent the opportunistic behaviour of controlling shareholders in the context of corporate groups. The statute contains detailed provisions on group law, which seek to protect minority shareholders and creditors of subsidiary companies against exploitation by the parent company in the interest of the group

102 Hamilton, Macey, and Moll (n 88) 251.

103 Vandekerckhove (n 15) 91. In *Amoco Cadiz* the parent company's liability for its own torts and for those of its subsidiaries under piercing doctrine are completely intertwined: *In re Oil Spill by Amoco Cadiz off Coast of France on March 16, 1978*, 1984 A.M.C. 2123, 2194 (ND Ill. 1984).

104 B Haar, 'Piercing the Corporate Veil and Shareholders' Product and Environmental Liability in American Law as Remedies for Capital Market Failures: New Developments and Implications for European and German law after "Centros"' (2000) 2 EBOR 334, 334–40.

105 *In re New York State Silicone Breast Implant Litigation*, 632 N.Y.S.2d 953 (Sup. Ct. 1995), aff'd, 642 N.Y.S.2d 681 (N.Y. App. Div. 1996); *In re Connecticut Breast Implant Litigation*, 1994 WL 668032 (Conn. Super Ct., Nov 21, 1994); *In re TMJ Implants Products Liability Litigation*, 880 F. Supp 1311 (D. Minn. 1995), aff'd, 113 F.3d 1484 (8th Cir. 1997).

106 *Dow Chemical Co. v Mahlum*, 970 P.2d 98 (Nev. 1998).

107 ibid 118–19.

as a whole.[108] Germany is the only legal system under consideration here that deals with corporate groups in any detail by legislation. The idea of statutorily regulating group structures has not caught on very widely. In Europe, only Portugal, Italy and, to a more limited extent, Slovenia, Croatia and Hungary have adopted comparable provisions.[109] Overall, German group law is largely seen as being not very effective. This is due mainly to its limited scope and, in parts, unclear structure. Thus, despite the statutory rules on group law, there still seems to be a need to occasionally disregard limited liability, within the group context and outside, and to impose liability for the company's debts on its controlling shareholders or managers on the basis of the doctrine of piercing the corporate veil (*Durchgrifsfhaftung*).

II. The law of corporate groups (*Konzernrecht*)

The statutory provisions on group law can be found in AktG, §§15–22 and §§291–338. The former contain definitions and apply to all enterprises irrespective of their legal form; the latter contain the substantive group law and apply where the dependent enterprise is organized in the form of an AG (or KGaA), or as a GmbH; in the latter case, the respective provisions apply by way of analogy and only in parts.

Central to the application of group law is the concept of 'affiliated enterprises'. The different forms of affiliations are listed in AktG, §15 and further defined in §§16–19. The statute distinguishes between 'majority participation', where one enterprise holds a majority of the voting shares in another enterprise;[110] a 'dependency relationship', where a dependent enterprise is subject to the direct or indirect control of another enterprise;[111] a 'concern relationship', where a dominant enterprise controls one or more dependent enterprises either vertically or horizontally;[112] and cross-participation, where participating corporations hold at least 25 per cent of each other's shares.[113] In any case, it is essential that the participating entities are legally autonomous and separate 'enterprises'. The term 'enterprise' is not defined and German law does not recognize a uniformly accepted concept of 'enterprise'. Any definition has to be in line with the underlying rationale of group law.

BGHZ 69, 334 (*Veba/Gelsenberg*)

The plaintiff was a shareholder of the defendant company G-AG. 96.1% of the defendant's shares were held by V-AG. The Federal Republic of Germany held about 43.7% of V-AG's shares. In June 1975 the shareholders of the defendant company were invited to a general meeting to vote on a 'Resolution regarding the integration[114] of G-AG into V-AG'. In an accompanying declaration V-AG offered the shareholders of G-AG compensation only in form of V-AG shares at a ratio of 2 V-AG shares for 3 G-AG shares. At general meeting G-AG's shareholders voted in favour of integration. The plaintiff objected to this resolution. Subsequently, the plaintiff asked for annulment of the resolution on the basis that V-AG did

[108] J Koch, *Hüffer and Koch, Aktiengesetz* (12th edn, Beck 2016) §15 para 3.

[109] M Andenas and F Wooldridge, *European Comparative Company Law* (CUP 2009) 451; K Vandekerckhove, *Piercing the Corporate Veil* (Kluwer Law International 2007) 46 n 86. Brazil and Taiwan also have regulated corporate groups. As part of recent reform efforts, the UK government contemplated the idea of introducing personal liability of the directors of a parent company if they sold a financially distressed subsidiary without taking into account the interests of the subsidiary's stakeholders. The liability proposal will not be taken forward; however, the UK government intends to introduce a new ground for directors' disqualification if, following the sale, the subsidiary enters insolvency proceedings within a certain period of time; Department of Business, Energy & Industrial Strategy, Insolvency and Corporate Governance: Government response (26 August 2018) paras 2.5–2.8.

[110] AktG, §16.

[111] ibid §17. In case of an enterprise of which a majority of shares is held by another enterprise, dependency is rebuttably presumed.

[112] ibid §18. [113] ibid §19.

[114] 'Integration' pursuant to ibid §§319, 320 is the comprehensive subordination of a company to the management of another, without, however losing its legal autonomy. In economic terms integration is similar to a merger in that the dependent company will be more like a branch or department of the controlling company.

not offer alternative compensation in cash contrary to what is now AktG, §320b(2).[115] The Regional Court decided in favour of the plaintiff. The defendant's leapfrog appeal was denied by the Federal Supreme Court.

...

II. Substantively, the success of the suit depends on whether V-AG is an enterprise dependent upon the Federal Republic of Germany as its 43.7% shareholder. The Regional Court answered the question in the affirmative. We agree.

1. Pursuant to AktG, §17(1), a dependent enterprise is a legally autonomous enterprise subject to the direct or indirect control of another enterprise (controlling enterprise). The question whether such a dependency relationship may arise from a substantial shareholding of the Federal Republic of Germany in an AG ... cannot be answered by simple recourse to wording and history of the statutory provisions; that much is more or less undisputed. In particular, there is no generally applicable definition of the term 'enterprise' on the basis of which it could be determined to what extent the Federal Republic as main shareholder can be a controlling enterprise or may be treated as such. In view of immense practical difficulties the legislature consciously refrained from stipulating a more precise definition ... Not only does the term have a different content depending on the area of law in which it is used ...; even for stock corporation law itself a different interpretation depending on each and every provision is argued for ... The history of the AktG also does not provide a clear indication as to how widely the net for possible bearers of controlling influence should be cast.

...

2. Under these circumstances the purpose of the respective set of provisions is of paramount importance. The decisive [AktG, §320b(2) sentence 3] belongs to the group of provisions that purport to protect mainly minority shareholders (and possibly creditors) from the perils which arise from outside control of their company. Its specific meaning is that the shareholders leaving the integrated company shall not be compelled to become again shareholders of a dependent company subject to the perils arising therefrom ...

Against this background it is explicable that the legislator distinguishes between entrepreneurial shareholders and other shareholders: of a major shareholder whose entrepreneurial activity is limited to this one enterprise it can be expected that his own interests and the interests of the enterprise will in principle be aligned, or at least that he will not pursue any specific interests that would conflict with the interests of the enterprise; in such a case the legislator could assume that the risk of the shareholder sacrificing the company's interests for his own would be insignificant and that the general devices for minority protection, in particular AktG, §117 [damages for unlawful interference with the company's management] and §243(2) [annulment of abusive shareholder resolutions] would be sufficient. By contrast, in case of a shareholder who pursues entrepreneurial activities outside and in addition to the company this risk is typically significant and creates a specific situation of conflict that requires specific statutory precautions ... This distinction, immanent in the statute, suggests that even a majority shareholding in itself does not transform the shareholder into a controlling enterprise. Rather, there must be an entrepreneurial commitment outside the company strong enough to justify the serious concern that the shareholder may, for its sake, exercise his influence to the detriment of the company. Only then will be triggered the statute's objective which is to protect minorities against the consequences of outside economic power.

This outside entrepreneurial commitment may relate to a commercial enterprise directly operated by the shareholder, as it is the case with a commercial partnership or a sole trader. However, under certain circumstances it may consist in an interdependence of commercial interests of a different kind. The legal form of the entity that may, as bearer of outside commitment, exercise its influence on the company is immaterial ... An association or foundation that according to their statutes can be expected to limit their interests in the company, like a private investor, to the generation of profit may be discounted as controlling enterprise. By contrast, natural persons who are not sole traders and legal persons that are not corporations may, due to

[115] Pursuant to ibid §320b(2) sentence 3, if in case of 'integration' the controlling company (parent) is itself dependent upon another company (grandparent), the compensation offered the minority shareholders of the subsidiary must include a cash alternative.

their other entrepreneurial interests, generate the conflict of interests that the statutory provisions try to protect the dependent company and its minority shareholders from, and may thus constitute a controlling enterprise.

3. Share owning legal persons of public law such as the Federal Republic of Germany are not excluded. In this respect it must be taken into account that the specific purposes and tasks of such legal persons may typically collide with the commercial interests of private investors in the prosperity of their company. Whether public law provides adequate safeguards in this situation or whether only the provisions on group law of the AktG are suitable and sufficient to prevent discrimination against the minority may depend on each and every case. However, the protective provisions of the AktG are at any rate an adequate and indispensable device for resolving the conflict where the *fiscus* engages in entrepreneurial activity to such an extent that private shareholders have to face the resulting peril that the interest of the company as well as their own interests may be sacrificed for an alien entrepreneurial objective.

...

Whether the entrepreneurial approach of a major shareholder is determined also or overwhelmingly by the public interest is immaterial from the point of view of the dependent enterprise, which is to be protected against alien entrepreneurial interference; the risk of becoming a victim of such interference is just as great.

...

At least in the industrial sector the Federal Republic of Germany exhibits, in respect of the companies in which it holds shares, all characteristics of a controlling enterprise.

In 1975, the year of the resolution at issue here, alone within the resort of the Ministry of Finance the Federation directly held shares to the value of 2.525 bn DM in 19 companies with a nominal capital of ca. 4.861 bn DM ...

In this case it is unnecessary to examine whether a substantial shareholding in another enterprise alone transforms a shareholder into an 'enterprise', or whether—as it is argued in respect of private investors—a certain degree of entrepreneurial planning activity is required ... The Federal Republic of Germany meets also this latter requirement. The mentioned shareholdings in their entirety guarantee the Federal Republic a very strong position of power within the industrial sector. This opens up the possibility and may even create a necessity to develop entrepreneurial initiative and to use one or the other subsidiary for alien or higher entrepreneurial objectives. That the Federal Republic views its shareholdings not just as investments, but actively participates in the running of these companies through its bureaucracies cannot be doubted and is moreover required by statute ...

...

III. At the time of the resolution the Federal Republic of Germany only held 43.74% of the shares in V-AG. Consequently the presumption of dependence pursuant to AktG, § 17(2) does not apply. The Regional Court nevertheless assumed a dependency relationship. This was based on the undisputed fact that in general meetings of V-AG usually no more than 80% of the share capital were represented. As a result the Federal Republic usually had a voting majority and could substantially influence the management of V-AG. In addition, it had a right to appoint members of the supervisory board. In this respect the judgment is also unobjectionable. A shareholding below 50% may in combination with other reliable circumstances of a legal or factual nature constitute controlling influence in the sense of AktG, § 17(1) ... The Regional Court without fault ascertained such circumstances. Consequently, its decision is overall correct.

Questions and comments:

1. Even within AktG, §17 different meanings of the term 'enterprise' must be distinguished: The 'dependent enterprise' must be a company controllable by holding a majority of its voting shares. In that case a majority shareholder can manipulate the company's capital structure in a way that may be detrimental to minority shareholders and creditors. It is more difficult, however, to decide when an entity in a dominant position amounts to an enterprise ('controlling enterprise'). If it were just the possibility to control the dependent corporation, then group law would be applicable to every private investor holding a majority. In *Velba/Gelsenberg* the BGH

based its definition on the potential conflict that can arise from the fact that the controlling entity pursues entrepreneurial activities in addition and separate from the dependent enterprise. Explain and summarize the rationale of group law according to the BGH.

2. A second issue addressed by the case is the question whether the state (*fiscus*) may act as a dominant enterprise in the group context. Again, the Court relies on the typical situation of conflict that group law seeks to address and that may equally obtain where public law entities are involved in a controlling position.
3. Finally, the case clarifies that a shareholding below 50 per cent in combination with other legal (e.g. appointment rights) or factual (e.g. dispersed share ownership) circumstances may suffice in order to establish control within the meaning of AktG, §17. This is particularly relevant for the application of the provisions on de facto groups in AktG, §§311–318. Can you think of any other legal or factual circumstances that may contribute to control in case of a shareholding below 50 per cent?

Tax law requires the formalization of the relationship between controlling and depended enterprise by way of a contract in order to be able to set-off the losses of one company against the profits generated by another within the group. This is the background for AktG, §§291–310 on 'enterprise agreements'. The statute envisaged that in case of a dependency relationship between an AG as dependent enterprise and another controlling enterprise an enterprise agreement pursuant to AktG, §§291, 292 should be concluded, or, respectively, the dependent company be 'integrated' into the controlling company pursuant to AktG, §§319–327.[116] 'Integration' comes close to an actual merger and has been regulated accordingly. In respect of enterprise agreements there are specific provisions for the protection of minority shareholders and creditors of the dependent company. Where the dependency relationship between parent and subsidiary is not formalized by contract, the provisions of AktG, §§311–318 on de facto groups apply. In the mind of the legislator, de facto groups were supposed to be the exception.[117] However, as their rules are less restrictive for the controlling company, in practice they dominate.

1. *Enterprise agreements*

The AktG distinguishes two types of enterprise agreements: (i) the 'contract for control' and the 'contract for a transfer of profits' pursuant to AktG, §291, and (ii) 'other enterprise agreements' pursuant to AktG, §292.[118] Only the 'contract for control' and the 'contract for a transfer of profits', usually combined for tax purposes, are 'organisational' contracts in the sense that they derogate from otherwise applicable mandatory company law and trigger the provisions on minority shareholder and creditor protection.

A 'contract for control' is a contract pursuant to which an AG (or KGaA) subjects its management to the control of another enterprise.[119] The ambit of the statutory provisions is limited to AG (or KGaA) as dependent company. The management powers of the dependent company are transferred to the controlling enterprise. The management board of the dependent company no longer conducts the business of the company in its own responsibility.[120] The 'self-interest' of the dependent company as guideline for its business strategy and conduct is replaced by the interest of the group as a whole. Its management board is no longer an independent organ; rather, primarily it must act in accordance with the instructions given by the controlling enterprise,[121] even if these directions are detrimental to the

[116] F Kübler and H-D Assmann, *Gesellschaftsrecht* (6th edn, CF Müller 2006) 427. [117] ibid.

[118] These are 'profit participation', 'contract on the partial transfer of profit', and 'business leasing agreement'. They are irrelevant for present purposes.

[119] AktG, §291(1).

[120] As would normally be the case pursuant to ibid §76(1). [121] ibid §308(1).

dependent company, as long as overall in line with the interests of the group.[122] The organs of the controlling enterprise as well as the members of the management board and supervisory board of the dependent AG are under a duty to act with due care and skill when issuing and implementing instructions. In case of breach they will be liable vis-à-vis the dependent AG for damages.[123] A 'contract for a transfer of profits' is a contract under which an AG (or KGaA) is obliged to transfer its entire profit to another enterprise.[124]

All 'enterprise agreements' must be concluded in writing.[125] The management boards of all participating AGs must submit a written report explaining the content of the agreement, and in particular the compensation to be paid to minority shareholders.[126] Unless the dependent company is wholly owned, the contract documents must be examined by auditors.[127] The general meeting of shareholders of all dependent AGs involved must approve the contract with a 75 per cent majority of the share capital present at the meeting. If the controlling enterprise is an AG, its shareholders must approve the contract as well, albeit with a simple majority.[128] To become effective, enterprise agreements must be registered in the register of the dependent AG.[129]

On the basis of its power to issue instructions, the controlling enterprise may, for instance, compel the dependent AG to disclose confidential information and know-how, to perform services, or to transfer assets without consideration, to surrender corporate opportunities in favour of another group entity, or to acquire assets from other group entities for a consideration above market price. Many of these transactions would normally amount to hidden dividends or distributions out of capital.[130] They are, however, lawful because the provisions on capital maintenance and restrictions on dividends are suspended.[131] These instructions and the transactions that follow may deplete the dependent company's assets. As a result, outside[132] minority shareholders can expect lower dividends and a reduced value of their shares. To protect their interests, the enterprise agreement must provide for appropriate compensation, either in the form of fixed annuity payments based on par value and expected return of the shares; or as variable payments on the basis of the dividends paid by the controlling company.[133] In addition, the enterprise agreement must provide for a right of outside minority shareholders to sell their shares in the dependent AG to the controlling enterprise for appropriate compensation in shares in the controlling enterprise if it is an AG or otherwise in cash. The amount and mode of compensation are to be stipulated in the agreement.[134]

From the point of view of creditors, the exercise of control and the transfer of profits may increase the risk of default on the part of the dependent company. Creditors are protected indirectly for the duration of the enterprise agreement by an obligation vis-à-vis the dependent AG of the controlling enterprise to compensate the dependent AG for its annual losses.[135] Where creditors cannot obtain payment from the dependent company, they may levy execution on this claim and then sue the controlling enterprise directly.[136] Moreover, on termination of the enterprise agreement the creditors of the dependent company have a claim against the controlling enterprise to provide security for the outstanding debts of the dependent AG.[137] More importantly, where it is clear that the dependent company will not be able to pay its debts as they fall due the claim to provide security is transformed into a direct claim for payment against the controlling enterprise. This is the case when insolvency proceedings in respect of the dependent company were not opened due to insufficient assets or were terminated for that reason.[138] The situation is less clear, however, where the

[122] The management board of the dependent company may object only where it is obvious that the direction is not in the interest of the group as a whole, ibid §308(2).
[123] ibid §§309, 310. [124] ibid §291(1). [125] ibid §293(3) [126] ibid §293a.
[127] ibid §293b. [128] ibid §293. [129] ibid §294. [130] Kübler and Assmann (n 116) 428.
[131] AktG, §291(3).
[132] These are shareholders of the dependent AG who do not hold shares in the controlling enterprise.
[133] AktG, §304. [134] ibid §305. [135] ibid §302.
[136] Kübler and Assmann (n 116) 433. [137] AktG, §303. [138] Koch (n 108); AktG, §303 para 7.

dependent company is subject to insolvency proceedings. Some argue that only the office holder can enforce the respective creditor claims against the controlling company, at least in so far as default remains uncertain.[139] Others want to grant the creditors a direct payment claim also in this case.[140] The direct payment claim is based on an analogy to AktG, §322. Pursuant to this provision, the controlling AG will be directly, and jointly and severally, liable for the dependent AG's debts in case of an 'integration'. 'Integration' is situated somewhere between a dependency relationship and an actual merger. The dependent company retains its legal autonomy, but is absorbed by the controlling company to such an extent that economically it is more like a branch or department within the controlling enterprise.[141] The latter has a complete and unrestricted power to direct and determine the management of the dependent company and to dispose of its assets and profits.[142] Integration is possible only where the controlling enterprise holds at least 95 per cent of the shares of the subsidiary. It requires approval by the general meeting of shareholders of both AGs, with a qualified majority on the part of the controlling AG,[143] and registration in the register of the dependent company.[144]

AktG, §§291–318 only apply if the dependent company is an AG, integration pursuant to AktG, §319 even requires AGs on both sides. In practice, however, subsidiaries and dependent companies are usually organized in the form of GmbHs. Neither AktG nor GmbHG contain a specific law on corporate groups for GmbHs as dependent enterprise. The question, thus, is to what extent the provisions on enterprise agreements may be applied, by way of analogy, to GmbHs. Contracts for control and transfer of profits are significant for GmbHs as well, and not just for tax purposes. Although pursuant to GmbHG, §37 the management is in any case subject to the instructions of the shareholders' meeting, a contract for control legalizes detrimental instructions and prevents the parent's liability for damages.[145] Thus, where a GmbH is subject to control and transfer of profit contracts, AktG, §§302, 303 apply by way of analogy with all the consequences discussed above.[146]

Questions:

Summarize the different ways in which the rules on enterprise agreements address the problems of insider opportunism. Do you think these rules are effective and efficient?

2. *De facto groups*

The formalized formation of corporate groups on the basis of enterprise agreements was supposed to be the rule. However, 'enterprise agreements' are not without transaction costs and will be entered into only where these are outweighed by tax advantages, that is, where one or more group companies generate significant losses that may reduce the profits of other group members. Thus, in practice, the majority of corporate groups and dependency relationships exist without a formalizing enterprise agreement simply on the basis of majority share ownership.

[139] J Hoffmann, 'Anmerkung zu OLG Frankfurt a.M., Urteil vom 16. 2. 2000–19 U 226/98' (2000) Neue Zeitschrift für Gesellschaftsrecht (NZG) 935, 936.

[140] Koch (n 108); AktG, §303 para 7.

[141] Kübler and Assmann (n 116) 437–8. The advantage of 'integration' as compared to a merger may be that the firm name and goodwill of the dependent company can be retained. Also, a subsequent separation of the two businesses is easier and hidden reserves do not have to be disclosed for tax purposes.

[142] AktG, §323.

[143] This is because the parent company will be liable for the debts of the subsidiary.

[144] AktG, §§319–320a.

[145] Kübler and Assmann (n 116) 435.

[146] ibid 436; Koch (n 108); AktG, §302 para 3.

For these 'de facto groups' AktG, §§311–318 contain provisions applicable only to the AG (and KGaA) as dependent company. They are triggered where an AG is subject to a dependency relationship (AktG, §17) without a 'contract for control' or 'integration'. In that case AktG, §311(1) allows the controlling enterprise to use its influence to cause the dependent AG to enter into detrimental transactions or take other measures, but only if the controlling enterprise compensates the dependent AG for any resulting losses. The compensation does not have to be instant; it is sufficient that the controlling enterprise promises to compensate at the end of the financial year. If, however, compensation does not come forward the dependent company and its shareholders have a claim for damages for which the following will be liable jointly and severally: (i) the controlling enterprise;[147] (ii) its organs who have caused the detrimental transaction or measure;[148] (iii) the members of the management board of the dependent AG if they did not mention the losses in the 'dependency report';[149] and (iv) the members of the supervisory board of the dependent company if they failed to properly examine the 'dependency report'.[150] These provisions are not very effective mainly because of difficulties of proof, in relation to both identifying particular disadvantageous transactions where the controlling enterprise interferes on a continuous basis, and the actual loss caused by the transaction.

It is now generally recognized that the statutory provisions on de facto groups not only sanction the formation of informal groups, but also legitimize detrimental interference by the controlling enterprise in the business of the dependent AG, subject only to compensation.[151] The formation of a de facto group is 'organizational' in nature in that it derogates from general capital maintenance and liability rules as long as the dependent AG is fully compensated.[152] However, the power to lawfully interfere in the management of the dependent company is not without limits. These will be overstepped where the interference causes the dependent company losses that can no longer be attributed to specific transactions or measures and cannot be fully compensated by individual adjustments.[153] For these situations, where the controlling enterprise systematically and on a continuous basis interferes with the business of the dependent AG in a way that affects the latter's entire range of activities so that the compensation mechanism of AktG, §§311-318 is no longer effective, doctrine has developed the concept of the 'qualified de facto group'.[154]

In a series of judgments since 1985,[155] the BGH established by way of analogy the application of AktG, §§302, 303 as a cause of action against the controlling shareholder/director of a GmbH. Thus, creditors of the company could demand from the shareholder-director not just security for their outstanding claims, but also payment where the company was ultimately unable to pay. This concept was subsequently extended to the AG as well.[156] In the meantime, however, the BGH has abandoned the concept of the 'qualified de facto group' for GmbHs and replaced it with the concept of 'liability for causing the company's insolvency'.[157] The question is, thus, whether the principles of the 'qualified de facto group' and the analogous application of AktG, §§302, 303 are still valid for dependent AGs. The BGH has not spoken yet. Lower courts and commentators disagree. It may be argued in favour of continued analogous application that, whereas GmbH-directors are generally subject to

147 AktG, §317(1).
148 ibid §317(3).
149 ibid §318(1). The purpose of the annual 'dependency report' is to ensure the proper functioning of the compensation regime. It is to be prepared and submitted by the management board of the dependent company, and to be examined by its auditors and supervisory board. It must contain detailed information on any transactions and measures that were carried out on instruction of the controlling enterprise, including any consideration, promised compensation and resulting losses ibid §§312–314.
150 ibid §318(2).
151 Koch (n 108); AktG, §311 para 4.
152 BGH, Urteil vom 1.12.2008–II ZR 102/07 (2009) NJW 850.
153 Koch (n 108); AktG, §311 para 7; Kübler and Assmann (n 116) 447.
154 Kübler and Assmann (n 116) 447.
155 BGHZ 95, 330 (*Autokran*); BGHZ 107, 7 (*Tiefbau*); BGHZ 115, 187 (*Video*).
156 L Fastrich in A Baumbach and A Hueck (eds), *GmbH-Gesetz* (21th edn, Beck 2017) GmbHG §13 para 48.
157 Text accompanying notes 175–8 below.

shareholders' instructions, a direct and comprehensive interference in the management of the AG is lawful only on the basis of a 'contract for control' that triggers the minority shareholder and creditor protection rules. Thus, the law for GmbHs and AGs is structurally different and it seems to be justified to install greater protection for an AG's creditors and minority shareholders in the case of qualified de facto groups.[158] Under this regime, the creditor protection rules are triggered in advance of the controlling enterprise causing the dependent AG's insolvency.

In any case, because of the limited scope and reach of statutory group law and the somewhat misplaced focus on 'enterprise agreements' instead of de facto groups, there always seemed to be a need for developing additional concepts that address the problems caused by limited liability more directly. This is what we turn to now.

II. Piercing the corporate veil

In line with the Imperial Court, from early on the BGH continuously emphasized that 'one should not disregard the concept of separate legal personality lightly', that, however, 'the reality of life and the power of factual circumstances and economic necessities' may demand, under certain circumstances, that the separateness and autonomy of a legal entity be pushed aside.[159] US law and legal scholarship have had a significant influence in this respect.[160]

Three main theories seem to dominate the legal landscape.[161] 'True piercing the corporate veil' theories are the *Mißbrauchslehre* ('abuse approach') and the *institutionelle Durchgriffslehre* ('institutional approach'). They are 'true piercing the corporate veil theories' because they take the concept of separate legal personality and limited liability as a starting point and try to define the inherent teleological limits and boundaries of these concepts. Under the 'abuse approach', separate legal personality and limited liability may be disregarded if the corporation is deliberately abused for unfair or dishonest purposes. The 'institutional approach' does away with subjective prerequisites and asks whether the separation of members and corporation is objectively in conflict with the legal order. The third approach sees 'piercing the corporate veil' not as a problem of the concept of legal personality and limited liability but as a problem of interpretation and application of the specific (non-corporate law) provision at issue, so-called *Normzwecklehren*. These are, therefore, not 'true piercing the corporate veil' doctrines. Their main field of application is the attribution of knowledge or causation in areas such as bona fide purchaser protection, insurance claims and brokerage.

The *Normzwecklehren* aside—which are of limited use in respect of limited liability anyway—these doctrines, owing to their vagueness, seem to be able to provide at best only modest assistance when deciding actual cases. Consequently, courts and legal advisers seek guidance mainly from previous case law nicely put together into different groups. Traditionally, three different groups of cases have been recognized: exercise of control, substantial undercapitalization, and amalgamation of assets.[162] The latter still stands largely unchanged; the former two seem to have been merged and modified in the new concept of *Existenzvernichtender Eingriff* (liability for causing the company's insolvency) which has dominated legal discourse in recent years.

[158] Koch (n 108); AktG, 11 para 29, §302 para 7.

[159] eg BGHZ 10, 205, 207.

[160] cf U Drobnig, *Haftungsdurchgriff bei Kapitalgesellschaften* (Metzner 1959); R Serick, *Rechtsform und Realität juristischer Personen* (de Gruyter 1955).

[161] Schmidt (n 14) 221; Fastrich (n 156) GmbHG §13 para 10.

[162] Schmidt (n 14) 233; H Wiedemann, *Gesellschaftsrecht: ein Lehrbuch des Unternehmens- und Verbandsrechts, Band I* (CH Beck 1980) 224.

1. *Liability for causing the company's insolvency—* Existenzvernichtender Eingriff

The GmbHG does not contain any provisions for the protection of subsidiaries and their creditors.[163] As we have seen, in respect of the so-called 'qualified de facto group' of GmbHs, the BGH used to apply by way of analogy AktG, §§302, 303 against the controlling shareholder-director.[164] This cause of action was available not just to the company itself but also to its creditors. The precondition for imposing unlimited liability was merely that the controlling director-shareholder exercised entrepreneurial activities in addition to, and apart from, those of the company.[165] The principle of limited liability as stipulated in GmbHG, §13(2) had de facto been reversed.

Following harsh criticism,[166] the Court in 1993 began to beg 'farewell to the qualified de facto group' with its decision in 'TBB'.[167] In 2001, the BGH finally introduced a new concept of liability in the decision *Bremer Vulkan*.[168] The protection of a dependent private company against interferences by its controlling shareholder was no longer based on an analogy to the law of public companies. According to the court, it was limited, rather, to the protection awarded by the provisions on capital maintenance and 'the guarantee of the company's right to continuity in the sense that the controlling shareholder has to have due regard to the company's own interests when he interferes with the company's assets and business opportunities'. This due regard would be lacking where, as a result of the shareholder's interferences, the company became unable to meet its obligations. Unlimited liability was, however, triggered only 'if the company's ability to meet its debts could not be regained by returning the assets it had been deprived of based on a claim under § 31 GmbHG'. In 'Bremer Vulkan' itself, this new concept of liability was not decisive in the end. Liability ensues only in the person of the controlling shareholder of the dependent company; not the shareholder's directors, which were the defendants in this case. In a decision of 25 February 2002, the BGH emphasized its departure from its earlier case law concerning the 'qualified de facto group' in favour of the new concept of 'liability for causing the company's insolvency'.[169] According to the Court, under this concept all those shareholders would incur unlimited liability who had a hand in the demise of the company by consenting to the transaction depriving the company of its assets. It was immaterial whether the respective shareholder had obtained any value for himself. In the case at hand was, liability did, however, not ensue; the reduction of the company's assets by only 22 per cent was held to be insignificant. Moreover, one of the defendants had actually increased the company's assets by more than DM 8.6 million.

In *KBV* the Court delivered the most comprehensive theoretical justification for the new concept of liability.[170] For the first time, based on the submitted facts, the Court accepted a claim for 'causing the company's insolvency'.

[163] According to GmbHG, §§30, 31, 43(3), distributions of assets that are needed to maintain the share capital are unlawful. The assets can be reclaimed from the recipients. The directors involved are liable to the company for damages. These claims can be pursued by a creditor directly against recipients and directors if insolvency proceedings, due to a lack of assets, are not opened, see BGHZ 134, 333, 341. However, according to the Court's case law, these provisions require single, identifiable transactions and cannot be of assistance if the company's loss was caused by a multitude of interferences so that single transactions which could be unwound are not identifiable or where the loss caused overall cannot be compensated in its entirety by merely unwinding these transactions, cf BGHZ 122, 123 (TBB), 127.

[164] BGHZ 95, 330 (*Autokran*); BGHZ 107, 7 (*Tiefbau*); BGHZ 115, 187 (*Video*).

[165] BGHZ 115, 187 (*Video*) 194.

[166] eg K Schmidt, 'Rechtsfortbildung im Unternehmens- und Gesellschaftsrecht durch die Rechtsprechung des BGH' (2000) Neue Juristische Wochenschrift (NJW) 2927, 2934.

[167] BGHZ 122, 123 (*TBB*). [168] BGHZ 149, 10 (*Bremer Vulkan*). [169] BGHZ 150, 61, 67 ff.

[170] BGHZ 151, 181 (*KBV*).

BGHZ 151, 181 (*KBV*)

K-GmbH with a legal capital of DM 100,000 was owned by B2, holding 40 per cent, and B3, holding 60 per cent of the company's shares. B3 was also managing director. In December 1995, B2 and B3 resolved to terminate the business of K-GmbH. All the company's assets with a value of DM 1,205,000 were transferred to a second GmbH (B1), also owned by B2 and B3. As consideration B1 took on the debts of K-GmbH up to an amount of only DM 823,000. Consequently, the company's estate was deprived of an amount of ca. DM 382,000. Plaintiff had a claim of ca. DM 80,000 against K-GmbH. An execution attempt against K-GmbH based on a default judgment failed. Subsequently, the application to open insolvency proceedings in respect of K-GmbH was rejected because of a lack of assets to cover the costs of the procedure. The same was the case in respect of B1.

...

2. In addition [to a claim based on § 826 BGB] the plaintiff may have a claim based on liability for causing the company's insolvency.

As the Senat has already held repeatedly, single members or shareholders acting in concert will be held liable for any loss caused to the company's creditors by depriving the company of the assets it needs to satisfy its liabilities ...

The system of liability limited to the company's assets is based on the implicit but for the law of legal persons indispensable precondition that the company's assets needed to satisfy the obligations entered into in the name of the company must remain with the company for the purpose of satisfying its creditors. In this respect the shareholders are deprived of the authority to dispose of the company's assets. The GmbH does not have a right vis-à-vis its members that guarantees its existence. On the contrary, the members can terminate the company's existence at any time, either by voluntary winding up or by winding up in insolvency proceedings. In any case, however, the termination must be achieved by an orderly procedure which guarantees that the company's assets are first and foremost used to satisfy its creditors. The members are not allowed to deprive the company of its assets without taking into consideration that these assets have the purpose to serve for the preferential satisfaction of the company's creditors, thereby wholly or partially depriving the company of the capability to discharge its obligations. The members are entitled only to the profits not needed to satisfy the company's obligations. The necessity to separate the assets of the company from those of its members and the strict preservation of the company's assets for the preferential satisfaction of the company's creditors remains during the entire existence of the company. Both are indispensible preconditions for the members to be able to rely on the principle of limited liability. The principle of limited liability pursuant to § 13(2) GmbHG can only be justified as long as the assets of company and members are kept separate and as long as the former's are reserved for its creditors. If, without having due consideration to this purpose, the shareholders deprive, to a significant extent, the company of its assets and thereby prejudice the company's ability to meet its obligations, the shareholders abuse the legal form of the private company. Thereby they lose the privilege of limited liability, but only so far as the loss suffered as a result of the interference cannot be adequately compensated under §§ 30, 31 GmbHG or adequate compensation is in fact not obtained. This applies a fortiori if the company shows a balance sheet deficit. If insolvency proceedings are not opened or have been terminated, creditors are entitled to directly pursue their claims against the shareholders to the extent that satisfaction could not be obtained from the company ...

According to the facts established by the Appeal Court these preconditions are satisfied in the persons of B2 and B3. By depriving K-GmbH of the assets it needed to satisfy its creditors B2 and B3 frustrated the orderly winding up of the company. B2 and B3 themselves rendered the privilege of limited liability inapplicable and are consequently jointly and severally liable for any amounts the plaintiff cannot retrieve from the company ...

In two subsequent decisions[171] the BGH further clarified the concept. The Court extended liability to an indirect shareholder who was able to exercise control over the company in the

[171] In the further decision, BGH (2004) ZIP 2138 (*Klinik*), the Court doubted whether a sister company could be liable under the new concept. However, it held the shareholder and the sister company liable, jointly and severely, under §826 BGB (deliberate cause of damage contrary to good morals). The justification the court gave

same way as a controlling shareholder would have been able to. According to the court, this was the case because the defendant owned 50 per cent in the mediating holding company and was sole director in the holding company as well as in the company itself.[172] At the same time the Court restricted liability in two respects: 'Liability for causing the company's insolvency' would only be triggered if the shareholder transferred the assets of the company to himself or to another company in which he was a shareholder, without giving full consideration on market terms to the company. The Court made it absolutely clear that the concept of 'liability for causing insolvency' is not based on mismanagement, but requires a deliberate deprivation of the company's assets for a non-operating purpose.[173] In addition, the Court held that the shareholder could reduce his liability by comparing the actual situation of the company with the hypothetical situation that would have ensued if the shareholder had acted properly, thereby demonstrating that the company suffered only a negligible loss which is then to be compensated.

Questions and comments:

1. According to this case law, 'liability for causing the company's insolvency' had three preconditions:[174] (i) the shareholders must deprive the company of its assets without full consideration; (ii) this deprivation must prejudice the company's ability to meet its debts, at least partially; and (iii) unlimited liability would only be incurred where the loss could not be fully compensated under GmbHG, §§30, 31, or, respectively, where the shareholder could not demonstrate that, had he acted lawfully, the company would have failed in any event, with the result that the shareholder would then be liable only to the extent that the actual loss of the creditors exceeds the hypothetical loss in case of lawful action. In respect of the burden of proof, the plaintiff had to coherently demonstrate a significant interference with the company's assets by the shareholder. Thereafter, the onus was on the shareholder to demonstrate and prove that the loss caused by his actions did not cause or contribute to the company's demise or that compensation through the unwinding of the respective transactions was appropriate and sufficient.
2. A successful claim for causing insolvency resulted in the unlimited liability of those shareholders who at least consented to the interference with the company's assets. During insolvency proceedings the claim could only be asserted by the liquidator. If insolvency proceedings (owing to a lack of assets) were not opened or had been terminated, every creditor could pursue his outstanding claims on the company directly against the shareholder if execution against the company proved to be unsuccessful.
3. Would the facts in *KBV* justify piercing the corporate veil under US laws?

In a ground-breaking judgment of 16 July 2007[175] the BGH revised its case law on the concept of 'liability for causing the company's insolvency'. Whilst retaining the familiar terminology, the Court transformed the independent concept of direct shareholder liability into tortious liability for damage caused intentionally and in violation of good morals under the broad umbrella of §826 of the Civil Code (BGB): .

for imposing liability under §826 BGB in this case closely resembles those for causing insolvency: Although the shareholders are not under any obligation to keep the company going and can terminate its business activities at any time, even by way of forming a new company which subsequently takes up the former's business, they must liquidate the company in the way provided for by law. In particular, they must not transfer the company's assets to the new company outside of the liquidation proceedings, thereby frustrating the creditors' access to the company's assets Such conduct would be contrary to good morals.

[172] BGH, II ZR 206/02 (*Autohändler*), (2005) ZIP 117.

[173] BGH, II ZR 256/02 (*Unterschlagung*) (2005) ZIP 250.

[174] cf M Schillig, 'The Development of a New Concept of Creditor Protection for German GmbHs' (2006) 27 Company Lawyer 348, 349.

[175] BGH, 16/07/2007–II ZR 3/04 (*Trihotel*) www.bundesgerichtshof.de.

BGH, 16/07/2007–II ZR 3/04 (*Trihotel*)

The office holder (*Insolvenzverwalter*) sued the defendant on behalf of creditors whose claims had been acknowledged in the insolvency proceeding. The defendant was, at first, sole managing director of the insolvent company (A-GmbH), later he became its authorised representative (*Prokurist*). The defendant was also lessor in respect of the property on which the company conducted its hotel business. The transactions in question were the following: (i) fiduciary transfer of ownership of the hotel inventory to the defendant's mother as security for a loan allegedly granted by the mother to the company; (ii) the premature termination of the lease regarding the hotel property; (iii) the conclusion of a management contract plus a later amendment thereto between the company and a second company (W-GmbH), both represented by the defendant. According to this management contract, the company was responsible for managing the hotel business in exchange for a 40 per cent share in turnover. The contract allowed for a reduction should the 40 per cent turn out to be too high. Subsequently it was reduced to 28 per cent.

Originally, the defendant held 52 per cent of the share capital of A-GmbH, with the remaining shares being held by his wife. At the time the transactions took place the defendant's 52 per cent shareholding had already been transferred to a J-GmbH which was owned by the defendant's mother. 10 per cent of the shares of W-GmbH were owned by the defendant's mother, the other 90 per cent were owned by J-GmbH. The defendant was sole managing director of both J-GmbH and W-GmbH, and was exempted from the prohibition on self-dealing, § 181 BGB. Furthermore, both his mother and his wife had granted the defendant general authority to represent them. After conclusion of the management contract but before reduction of the share in turnover to 28 per cent, the defendant acquired 100 per cent of the shares of J-GmbH based on the authority granted to him by his mother.[176]

...

The Senat abandons the model of 'liability for causing the company's insolvency' as an independent cause of action and considers the concept to be a specific case within the framework of the general tort liability under § 826 BGB resulting—in line with §§ 30, 31 GmbHG—in shareholder liability vis-à-vis the company.

Necessity and rationale for the concept of liability for causing the company's insolvency is provided by a lacuna in the provisions on capital maintenance. These provisions are ineffective in respect of those transactions which as such or as to their consequences are not adequately reflected on the balance sheet. Furthermore, the concept is necessary in respect of transactions which even if reversed in their entirety will still have caused the insolvency of the company ('collateral damage'). The reason for liability still is, as it originally was, a breach of the shareholders' duty to respect the principle of strict preservation of the company's assets for the preferential satisfaction of the company's creditors during the entire existence of the company. This duty is the system-immanent correlative to the employment of the GmbH as an instrument of limit liability.

...

There is, however no need to impose as a sanction for abuse of the corporate form unlimited direct liability vis-à-vis the creditors upon the shareholders. Such a concept of liability would, in many cases, go too far. Also, the factual settings here in question do not amount to an abuse of the corporate form; neither by definition nor functionally. This is due to the fact that the GmbH was, neither when it was formed nor later when in business, used as a mere sham or facade. Consequently, and in accordance with the capital maintenance rules, there is only room for liability vis-à-vis the company as the holder of the assets which have been depleted. In that sense the concept provides a supplement to the capital maintenance rules.

...

Allocating the concept a homestead within the framework of § 826 BGB is only natural since the factual circumstances that gave rise to the previous case law could already easily be subsumed under this provision. The application of § 826 BGB requires causation of damage intentional and in violation of good morals. This is the case if, contrary to their purpose to secure the preferential satisfaction of the creditors, the company's assets are systematically withdrawn resulting in the company's insolvency, in particular if the deprivation of assets directly

[176] M Schillig, 'Creditor Protection for German GmbHs: The Next Instalment' (2008) 29 Company Lawyer 251.

or indirectly benefits the shareholder or a third person. In terms of intention it is sufficient that the acting shareholder is aware of the fact that a transaction authorised or carried through by him or with his approval reduces the company's estate in violation of good morals. In this respect the shareholder must, at the time of the transaction, recognize the potential insolvency of the company as a foreseeable consequence of his acts. It is immaterial whether the shareholder believed that the company could still be rescued or that the transaction was in the best interest of the company (*dolus eventualis*).

...

This conceptual change will resolve the inconsistencies and contradictions caused by the previous concept of liability consisting of a multi-lane protection system with primary shareholder liability vis-à-vis the company pursuant to §§ 30, 31 GmbHG, subsequent direct and unlimited liability vis-à-vis the creditors, again subsequently partially transformed into liability limited to the actual collateral damage.

...

Liability for causing the company's insolvency pursuant to § 826 BGB operates purely internally. The proper claimant is exclusively the company as the entity who directly suffered a loss due to the shareholders' behaviour. A direct claim of the creditors against the shareholders cannot be reconciled with the principle, derived from the rules on capital maintenance, that creditor protection is mediated or 'channelled' through the company. If insolvency proceedings are being opened, only the office holder will have standing to bring the claim. If the opening of insolvency proceedings is rejected due to a lack of assets, creditors will first have to sue the company and, based on a title against the company, levy execution on the company's claim, based on § 826 BGB, against the shareholder. Only if the creditor has obtained this claim may he then pursue the shareholder.

...

The further requirement established by earlier case law that unlimited liability will only be incurred where the loss cannot be fully compensated under §§ 30, 31 GmbHG does no longer apply. Although the concept fills a lacuna in respect of the collateral damage not covered by §§ 30, 31 GmbHG, liability is not necessarily limited in this respect because its basis is formed by a unitary interference with the company's assets. Furthermore, the protective nature of the delictual provision of § 826 BGB precludes a limitation of recoverable damages in this respect. Consequently, both claims, liability for causing the company's insolvency and claims based on §§ 30, 31 GmbHG can be invoked in parallel.

In derogation from the principles developed in earlier case law, the burden of proof for all of these pre-conditions, including proof of causality, is now on the company as claimant in respect of the action in question.'

The Court considered first whether the defendant is at all a suitable addressee of liability. In the earlier case law the court had already extended liability to an indirect shareholder who was able to exercise control over the company. In this case, however, except when the share in turnover was reduced to 28 per cent, the defendant did not even have an indirect shareholding in the company when the transactions in question took place. According to the court, all that matters is the actual power to exert substantive influence on the management of the company. This was the case because as a 'direct de facto shareholder' the defendant was able to control the management of the company for as long as it was in business. The formal legal construction was immaterial.

The Court then rejected liability in respect of transactions (i) and (ii): The fiduciary transfer of ownership was either a sham transaction and void; or valid. In the latter case the transfer allowed for the continuation of using the inventory in the hotel business. A substantial interference with the company's credit worthiness was not ascertainable. In respect of (ii), the defendant was, due to outstanding leasing rates, entitled to terminate the lease immediately. The termination also meant that the company was no longer obliged to pay future instalments and the management contract allowed the company to maintain the hotel business and earn a share in turnover without having to pay the leasing rates.

However, the court considers transaction (iii), the management contract, as a transaction that might result in shareholder liability. This contract does not amount to a deprivation of the company's assets. On the contrary, it provides the basis for the company's remaining in business. Accordingly, it was essential whether the share in turnover as provided for by the management contract was manifestly inappropriate or unreasonable. Moreover, according to the court, liability will only ensue if the share in turnover under the contract was, to the knowledge of the defendant, so low that the insolvency of the company was practically inevitable. In this respect the appeal court had failed to sufficiently ascertain the facts by consulting experts as to whether contracts of this kind were habitually used in the trade in question and whether the 28 per cent were appropriate.

At first glance, it seems somewhat inconsistent that the court, on the one hand, requires awareness that insolvency might be a possible consequence, whereas in respect of the management contract insolvency must foreseeably be the inevitable consequence. What the court seems to have in mind is a distinction between (i) transactions amounting to direct and systematic deprivation of company assets and (ii) other managerial misconduct. In respect of (i) it suffices that the shareholder was aware that insolvency might be a possibility, whereas in respect of (ii) insolvency must, to the shareholder, appear as an inevitable consequence of the managerial decision at the time the decision is taken. Consequently, liability is not incurred by mere management fault. Only management decisions which are, ex ante, so outrageous that they inevitable will pave the way to insolvency may trigger personal liability.[177]

Questions and comments:

1. Certain passages in the judgment indicate that at least part of the reasons for the court's conceptual change was to secure the viability of the GmbH as a form of business organization in respect of international regulatory competition. Although the risk of actual liability was not as great under the original concept as was widely assumed—only in *KBV* did the BGH ever decide in favour of the claimant—there was a real risk to be dragged into interminable, expensive and unpredictable court proceedings. With the new decision, this risk has been reduced.
2. It is a very contentious question whether and to what extent liability for causing the company's insolvency can be applied to companies incorporated under the law of another Member State doing business exclusively in Germany. Can you explain the EU law background to this question? If not, please refer to Chapter 2.
3. In *Trihotel*, the court reserves for itself the option to allow a creditor to pursue a claim based on §826 BGB directly against the shareholder but only 'under exceptional circumstances'; for instance, if the company's remaining assets are misappropriated specifically to the detriment of a single creditor. Therefore, it seems fair to assume that, in extreme cases, creditors may still be able to pursue shareholders directly.[178]
4. The decision bears witness to a convergence of European company laws in respect of creditor protection. External shareholder liability is replaced by a concept of liability, in principle, only vis-à-vis the company. The same applies in France under Com Article L651-2 and in the UK under section 214 of the Insolvency Act 1986. Moreover, whereas under both jurisdictions imposing liability on managers and others who misappropriated or received misappropriated property of the company appears a relatively straightforward affair; it is much harder to incur liability for other managerial misconduct or management fault. Is this justified? Why is it immaterial that, in principle, under French and English law liability is primarily targeted at directors and managers; whereas the German concept is mainly concerned with shareholders?
5. So far all judgments dealt with GmbHs. The question is whether the liability for causing insolvency can also be applied in respect of AGs. This seems to be generally accepted, albeit unnecessary. AktG, §117 already establishes (tort) liability for damages of those who intentionally

[177] ibid 251, 252. [178] ibid.

interfere with the company's management in order to cause loss to the company or its shareholders. Members of the management board and supervisory board will be jointly and severally liable, in addition to the interfering third party, if they acted in breach of their fiduciary duties. The claim can be enforced by the company; its shareholders, provided they suffered a loss that goes beyond that of the company; and also creditors, if they cannot obtain satisfaction from the company. This does not seem to leave any gap that has to be filled by liability for causing insolvency on the basis of BGB, §826.[179]

In its follow-up decision in *Gamma*, the Court tried to clarify the relationship between the concept of liability for causing insolvency and 'undercapitalization'.[180] G-GmbH was formed as an 'Employment and Qualification Company' with a share capital of €25,000 to take on the employees of the financially struggling B-KG for two years, in order to avoid immediate redundancies. It had no other business than procuring employment or qualification opportunities for the transferred employees. A significant amount of the transferred employees' salaries and social security contributions was to be contributed by B-KG. G-GmbH had no other income than these payments and, when they stopped—because B-KG was insolvent—G-GmbH also filed for insolvency, leaving claims of employees and social security bodies of about €150,000 unpaid. G-GmbH's office holder sued the three shareholders of G-GmbH, one of them (B1) also being the only director of G-GmbH. The claim was based on the 'doctrine of liability for causing insolvency' and 'gross undercapitalization' because the defendants had failed to obtain security for B-KG's payment obligations, as was customary and good practice within the industry.

After confirming the principles established in *Trihotel*, the Court held that the claim could not be based on the doctrine of liability for causing insolvency. The failure to obtain security did not amount to an intrusion into the company's assets which serve as a fund for the preferential satisfaction of its creditors. Although the omission was causal for the company's insolvency, it could not be treated as an intrusion because it left the company's legal capital untouched. The doctrine could not be extended so as to cover cases such as the one at issue, because it only seeks to fill the gaps left by the provisions on capital maintenance and to prevent unlawful distributions. The issue here was not a withdrawal of company assets to the detriment of its creditors; rather, it was that the company had not received the funds necessary to carry out its assigned activity. This was mere 'undercapitalization' and as such did not fit the rationale of liability for causing insolvency. As we have seen, in *Trihotel* the Court in principle accepted that mere managerial misconduct (the management contract) may result in liability for causing insolvency, albeit only if insolvency appeared as the necessary and inevitable consequence. It is not clear whether the Court with its insistence on an 'intrusion' in *Gamma* intended to overrule this aspect of the doctrine. Probably not, as the Court's further deliberations suggest.

The Court then explicitly rejected 'undercapitalization' as a *separate and independent* ground for unlimited shareholder liability. The statute did not provide for a minimum capital to be set in accordance with the actual capital needs of each individual company and the legislator even reduced the minimum capital to €1 for the 'Entrepreneur GmbH'[181] without providing for any liability in case of undercapitalization. The Court goes on to say, that liability for undercapitalization as a corporate law concept cannot be established by case law. It would contradict the current regulatory system which is based exclusively on a minimum capital of €25,000 and its maintenance thereafter. By contrast, a general duty to keep the company adequately capitalized throughout its existence would endanger the character of the GmbH as such. The GmbHG does not aim to secure the continued existence of every company; rather, it seeks to provide only a minimum of creditor protection through its

[179] Koch (n 108); AktG §1 para 29, 30.
[180] BGH, 28/04/2008–II ZR 264/06 (2008) NZG 547.
[181] GmbHG, §§5a, 5(2).

rules on legal capital, supplemented by the concept of liability for causing insolvency on the basis of BGB, §826. Shareholders do not have an obligation to finance their company beyond these requirements; rather, they may liquidate the company at any time through the adequate statutory procedure, in particular when the company is in financial distress. Moreover, no concrete criteria or guidelines of any specificity which could determine the adequate capitalization of a company in each individual case were readily available as a basis for a general and far-reaching liability concept. This last argument seems misplaced in the case at issue here. The capital needs of G-GmbH were, right from the start, objectively ascertainable because the company's undertaking was of a fixed duration and dealt with a fixed number of employees and their salaries.[182] Overall, it does not seem to be very coherent to, on the one hand, address certain gaps in the capital maintenance regime on the basis of 'causing insolvency'; but to refuse doing so where the minimum capital is wholly inadequate right from the start so that it cannot even provide the envisaged minimum protection. This may have been the reason why the Court considered it possible, after all, to recognize 'liability for undercapitalization' as a special case of tort under the broad umbrella of BGB, §826, just like liability for causing insolvency. However, whether and under what circumstances such liability may arise was left open by the Court, because only creditors could enforce the respective claim directly, but not the company or its trustee in bankruptcy. All in all, the decision does not provide much clarity;[183] on the one hand, 'liability for undercapitalization' is rejected as contrary to the GmbH's system of legal capital; on the other, the Court may be willing to reactivate the notion under BGB, §826 in the future. This is unsatisfactory.

Tort law, in particular BGB, §826, can be utilized to impose direct liability on shareholders and directors for their own wrong doing, rather than for the debts of the company. Common grounds for liability are fraud or fraudulent misrepresentation, also in form of non-disclosure of material facts. In *Gamma*[184] the court considered possible tort claims of the employees against the shareholder-defendants for fraudulent misrepresentation on the basis of BGB, §826. When entering into the agreements with G-GmbH, it should have been disclosed to the employees that no security would be provided, or could be obtained, for guaranteeing B-KG's payment obligations. A possible disclosure duty rests primarily with the director who negotiated the contract on behalf of the company. Shareholders may be liable for aiding and abetting.[185] Creditors can claim damages in form of the reliance interest only. They are to be put in the same position they would have been in if the fraudulent misrepresentation or non-disclosure would not have occurred. In *Gamma* the employees likely would have concluded the contracts in the same way, because the alternative would have been immediate unemployment.

A further claim primarily against directors and managers may be found in the principles of *culpa in contrahendo* as quasi-contractual liability now codified in BGB, §311(2) and (3). Under this doctrine, the commencement of contractual negotiations or similar business contact may create a legal relationship between the parties according to which each party must have regard to the other's rights and interests. Where in that situation one party intentionally or negligently causes loss to the other, the former will be liable for damages in form of the reliance interest. Under the privity rule, the concept normally applies between the parties to the (envisaged) contract only. Under certain circumstances, however, third parties may find themselves liable. Two particular grounds are well established: First, the third party may hold itself out as particularly trustworthy and may significantly influence the negotiations between the parties. The requirements are strict: the third party must practically vouch vis-à-vis the creditor for the successful performance of the contract.

[182] C Schäfer and J Fischbach, 'Anmerkung zu BGH, Urteil vom 28.04.2008–II ZR 264/06 (OLG Düsseldorf), NZG 2008, 547' (2008) LMK 267714.

[183] ibid.

[184] BGH, 28/04/2008–II ZR 264/06 (2008) NZG 547.

[185] BGB, §830.

Liability of a third party may further arise where the third party has a substantial economic self-interest in the conclusion and/or performance of the contract. However, mere share ownership or the granting of security on the part of the negotiating director is normally insufficient. In *Gamma* the BGH considered briefly such a claim against the negotiating director of G-GmbH.[186]

2. *Amalgamation of assets*

According to German doctrine, limited liability is a result of the principle of separation (*Trennungsprinzip*) as provided for in AktG, §1(1) and GmbHG, §13(2). Consequently, if the members do not sufficiently separate their assets from those that belong to the company they will not be able to rely on the principle of limited liability. The pre-condition for assuming an amalgamation of assets is that, because of false or inadequate accounting, assets cannot be clearly attributed to either the shareholder or the company thereby rendering the provisions on capital maintenance completely ineffective.[187] The assumption of liability, therefore, requires that the defendant was somehow able to influence the accounting of the company.

The consequence of an amalgamation of assets is, based on an analogous application of §128 HGB, the unlimited liability for the company's debts of the shareholders involved. Preconditions and consequences of liability under this concept are further explained in the following example.

BGH, II ZR 178/03, 14 November 2005

The plaintiff is the office holder in respect of the insolvency proceeding concerning W.GmbH. The defendant was one of the founding members and since 1997 the only shareholder of W.GmbH. Between 1995 and 1998 the defendant was the single director of the company. The plaintiff asserts by way of 'piercing the corporate veil' (Durchgriffshaftung) claims filed by the company's creditors in the course of the insolvency proceeding. The alleged grounds for piercing the corporate veil are that the defendant did not maintain a system of orderly accounting and that there is an amalgamation of personal and company assets.

...

2. The Appeal Court correctly assumes that the plaintiff as office holder is, pursuant to analogous application of § 93 InsO, entitled to invoke the defendant's possible liability for the company's obligations (analogous application of § 128 HGB) by way of piercing the corporate veil. The respective basic question has been resolved by the decision of the Federal Labour Court of 14 December 2004 ... According to this decision, the personal liability of a shareholder who caused the company's insolvency and can therefore no longer rely on the liability privilege of § 13 (2) GmbHG can during insolvency proceedings, pursuant to § 93 InsO, only be invoked by the office holder. That is necessary in order to guarantee equal satisfaction of all creditors out of the personal assets of the personally liable shareholder. The Senat has decided in the same way in respect of cases that happened before the InsO entered into force ... In respect of liability because of amalgamation of assets at issue here the same principles apply, in particular because according to established case law §§ 128 et seq HGB are to be applied analogously which in itself is a sufficient reason for the application of § 93 InsO.

...

3. The appellant (defendant) is, however, correct in that the Appeal Court did not determine the pre-requisites for liability without legal and procedural mistakes.

a) According to the case law of the Senat, GmbH-shareholders will be personally liable vis-à-vis the creditors where the separation of company assets and personal assets has been obscured by intransparent accounting or by other means so that the provisions on capital

[186] BGH, 28/04/2008–II ZR 264/06 (2008) NZG 547.
[187] Fastrich (n 156); GmbHG, §13 paras 45–6.

maintenance, adherence to which is an indispensable precondition for limited liability, are no longer effective. In principle, piercing the corporate veil under these circumstances is not in dispute ... and is also not rendered obsolete by the Senat's new case law on the shareholder's liability for causing the company's insolvency. This is because in the cases here at issue control over the use of the company's assets is frustrated. This may be the case in particular if there is no accounting at all ...

b) Contrary to the view of the Appeal Court, however, lack of a 'double accounting system' pursuant to §§ 41 GmbHG, 238 HGB is insufficient to assume liability as long as the incoming and outgoing assets as well as the separation of personal and company assets can be ascertained by other means, in particular based on the existing documentation. The duty to keep the books in order is, pursuant to § 41 GmbHG, incumbent on the manager; breach of this duty may result in his liability for damages vis-à-vis the company pursuant to § 43 (2) GmbHG. It does, however, not without more result in external liability of a shareholder/manager vis-à-vis the company's creditors. The reason for imposing personal liability on the shareholder is not somehow defective accounting; rather it is disregard for the provisions on capital maintenance by an amalgamation of assets for which the shareholder is responsible. If, subject to these pre-conditions, there is uncontrollability of payments and as a consequence inseparability of company assets and personal assets of the shareholder the shareholder will be liable. The burden of proof for these pre-conditions is, in principle, on the office holder who may however rely on the principles of 'secondary burden of proof' because the shareholder, as the one who knows the company's situation better, cannot retreat to flatly denying the plaintiffs allegations.

As the appellant correctly points out, the Appeal Court considered the assertions of the defendant only selectively and in an incomplete manner ...

Questions and comments:

1. Amalgamation of assets under German law heavily relies on the lack of orderly accounting for which the shareholder in question is somehow responsible. Similar to the concept of liability for causing the company's insolvency the effectiveness of the capital maintenance rules seems to be at the heart of the matter. Can you explain the relationship between these different concepts? Is the distinction useful or necessary?
2. Compare the amalgamation of assets under German law and entity liability in the US. What are the conceptual differences? What are the differences in respect of preconditions and consequences?
3. Fraudulent transfer law is regulated in InsO, §§129-147. The relevance of these provisions in situations where corporate insiders withdraw corporate assets to the detriment of creditors is often neglected, despite the fact that these provisions are applicable alongside company law, in particular, the capital maintenance provisions.[188] Whereas part of the regime, in particular InsO, §§130, 131 purport to guarantee the principle of equal treatment of creditors prior to the opening of insolvency proceedings, provisions such as InsO, §§132-134 try to prevent and reverse transactions carried out prior to the company's insolvency to the detriment of its creditors. On application of the office holder, transactions at an undervalue may be reversed under the following conditions: (i) the consideration that the debtor company received was substantially lower than the consideration provided by the debtor company; (ii) the transaction was carried out within three months prior to the opening of insolvency proceedings; (iii) at a time when the debtor company was insolvent; and (iv) the transferee knew about the insolvency and that the transaction was detrimental to creditors.[189] If the transaction was an outright gift, it may be avoided if it was carried out within four years prior to the opening of insolvency proceedings, and there are no subjective requirements.[190] Similarly, intentionally

[188] U Haas, 'Kapitalerhaltung, Insolvenzanfechtung, Schadensersatz und Existenzvernichtung: wann wächst zusammen, was zusammen gehört' (2006) Zeitschrift für Wirtschaftsrecht—ZIP 1373, 1375.

[189] InsO, §132(1). [190] ibid §134.

detrimental transactions may be reversed (i) if carried out within 10 years prior to the opening of proceedings; (ii) the debtor acted with intent to disadvantage creditors; (iii) the transferee knew that the debtor acted with such intent.[191] Knowledge will be presumed if the transferee knew that the debtor was close to insolvency and that the transaction was prejudicial to the creditors. In any case, as a result of the transaction the general creditors must be disadvantaged by a reduction of the assets available for distribution.[192] It has been argued that these provisions leave little room for piercing doctrines such as the liability for causing insolvency.[193] However, owing to difficulties of proof, in particular in respect of the various subjective requirements, fraudulent transfer law does not seem to be very effective in practice.

D. England and Wales

The House of Lords' decision in *Salomon v A Salomon and Co Ltd*[194] has effectively secured the availability of the corporate form for all companies, even the smallest ones.[195] The gist of *Salomon* is that, as long as the promoter and single shareholder of a company complies with the formal requirements of the Companies Act, he will be able to rely on the principle of separate personality and also on the privilege of limited liability. In order to hold shareholders and managers personally liable for the company's debts or to compel them to contribute to the company's assets in order to satisfy its creditors, three main possibilities remain: 'piercing/lifting the corporate veil at common law'; statutory provisions targeted mainly at directors, in particular under the Insolvency Act 1986; and tortious liability of managers and controlling shareholders.

I. 'Piercing/lifting the corporate veil' at common law

A multitude of very different cases is usually discussed under the broad heading of 'lifting the corporate veil' or 'piercing the corporate veil'. Traditionally, these cases could be allocated to three different groups of arguments advanced in order to disregard the principles of separate personality and limited liability: the agency argument, the 'single economic unit' argument and the 'sham' or 'fraud' argument.[196]

Under the agency argument a (controlling) shareholder will, based on the principles of agency, be liable vis-à-vis a creditor, or will acquire rights against the counterparty, if the company acted as the shareholders' agent. The agency argument was accepted in *Smith, Stone and Knight Ltd v Birmingham Corporation*.[197] A holding company set up a subsidiary to run a business, of which the holding company retained ownership. When the business premises were compulsorily purchased, the holding company was held to be entitled to compensation. According to Kerr LJ, however, the circumstances in this case were so unusual that no general principle could be inferred from it.[198] Indeed, *Salomon* established that the fact that a person is a member of a company does not in itself make the company an agent of that person. Agency also cannot be inferred from the control exercisable by the members over the company or from the fact that one company is a subsidiary of another company. The shareholder will only be liable for the obligations entered into by the company if the company had authority, actual or ostensible, to bind the shareholder vis-à-vis third parties.[199]

Under the 'single economic unit' argument a group of companies may, under certain circumstances, be treated as one single undertaking. The classic example is *DHN Food*

[191] ibid §133(1). [192] ibid §129.
[193] Haas (n 188) 1381–2. [194] [1897] AC 22. [195] Davies and Worthington (n 13) para 8-2.
[196] ibid paras 8-7–8-13. [197] [1939] 4 All ER 116.
[198] *JH Rayner (Mincing Lane) Ltd v Department of Trade and Industry* [1989] Ch 72.
[199] L Sealy and S Worthington, *Cases and Materials in Company Law* (11th edn, OUP 2016) 76–8; D French, *Mayson, French & Ryan on Company Law* (35th edn, OUP 2018–2019) 112–114.

Distributors Ltd v Tower Hamlets London Borough Council.[200] In this case the parent company, DHN, conducted the business on the premises owned by a wholly-owned subsidiary, whereas the vehicles of the business were owned by a second wholly-owned subsidiary. When the business premises were compulsorily purchased, DHN was awarded compensation for disturbance of business, although it formally had no interest in the land. According to Lord Denning, '[t]he three companies should, for present purposes, be treated as one, and the parent company DHN should be treated as that one. So DHN are entitled to claim compensation accordingly'. This reasoning has, however, not been followed by the House of Lords in respect of a similar case two years later.[201] The circumstances under which a court may regard a group of companies as a single economic unit, therefore, remain somewhat uncertain.[202] It should be noted that in these cases the 'lifting of the corporate veil' is usually to the advantage of the shareholder and parent company.

The 'sham' or 'fraud' argument would apply in cases where shareholders use the company as the vehicle to circumvent or frustrate their own obligations vis-à-vis third parties. In *Jones v Lipman*[203] the defendant tried to frustrate his obligation to transfer title in real property to the plaintiff by contributing the land to a company formed for that purpose. Both defendant and company were held liable for specific performance. Similarly, in *Gilford Motor Co Ltd v Horne*[204] the defendant used a company to circumvent restrictions on trading activities he had agreed to with his former employer. An injunction was granted not only against the defendant but also against the company. In these cases, rather than holding the shareholders liable for the company's debts, it is obligations of shareholders that are extended and imposed on the company as well. Moreover, these cases can usually be explained without resort to the doctrines of separate personality and limited liability by adopting a wide interpretation of the obligation imposed on the shareholders or by assuming that the company has notice of any equity in the property the company receives from its shareholder.[205]

Prior to the Supreme Court's decisions in *VTB Capital plc v Nutritek International Corporation*[206] and *Prest v Petrodel Resources Ltd*,[207] the most thorough discussion by an English court of the problem of 'lifting the corporate veil' and the relevant case law could be found in the Court of Appeal's decision in *Adams v Cape*,[208] addressing all three traditional arguments mentioned above. The plaintiffs sought recognition and enforcement of judgments awarded in the US against the English parent company Cape. The awards were made in respect of claims for damages for personal injuries and consequential loss allegedly suffered by each plaintiff as a result of exposure to asbestos fibres. In order to minimize its presence in the US for tax and tort liability purposes Cape had, before the US court was seized with the claims, restructured its US business using a complicated group structure. Prerequisite for the recognition and enforcement of the US judgments in the UK was that Cape was, 'at the time the proceedings were instituted, resident (or, perhaps, present) in the foreign country'.[209] As regards the 'single economic unit' argument, the starting point was 'the fundamental principle' that 'each company in a group of companies (a relatively modern concept) is a separate legal entity possessed of separate legal rights and liabilities'. Thus,

> save in cases which turn on the wording of particular statutes or contracts, the court is not free to disregard the principle of Salomon v. A. Salomon & Co. Ltd. [1897] A.C. 22 merely because it considers that justice so requires. Our law, for better or worse, recognises the creation of subsidiary companies, which though in one sense the creatures of their parent companies, will

200 [1976] 1 WLR 852. 201 *Woolfson v Strathclyde Regional Council* 1978 SC 90 (HL).
202 Davies and Worthington (n 13) para 8-11. 203 [1962] 1 WLR 832. 204 [1933] Ch 935.
205 Sealy and Worthington (n 199) 64.
206 *VTB Capital plc v Nutritek International Cop* [2013] UKSC 5.
207 *Prest v Petrodel Resources Ltd* [2013] UKSC 34. 208 [1990] Ch 433.
209 *Adams v Cape Industries Plc* [1990] Ch 433 (Slade LJ), quoting from Dicey and Morris, *The Conflict of Laws, vol 1* (11th edn, Lawrence Collins 1987) 436–7.

> nevertheless under the general law fall to be treated as separate legal entities with all the rights and liabilities which would normally attach to separate legal entities.

Moreover, 'if a company chooses to arrange the affairs of its group in such a way that the business carried on in a particular foreign country is the business of its subsidiary and not its own, it is, in our judgment, entitled to do so'. In terms of the 'corporate veil' point, council for the plaintiffs submitted that the court would 'lift the corporate veil where a defendant by the device of a corporate structure attempts to evade (i) limitations imposed on his conduct by law; (ii) such rights of relief against him as third parties already possess; and (iii) such rights of relief as third parties may in the future acquire'. Whereas the Court seemed to accept (i) and (ii) as possible justification for 'lifting the corporate veil', neither of them were applicable in the present case. As for (iii), the Court did

> not accept as a matter of law that the court is entitled to lift the corporate veil as against a defendant company which is the member of a corporate group merely because the corporate structure has been used so as to ensure that the legal liability (if any) in respect of particular future activities of the group (and correspondingly the risk of enforcement of that liability) will fall on another member of the group rather than the defendant company. Whether or not this is desirable, the right to use a corporate structure in this manner is inherent in our corporate law.

Finally, in respect of the 'agency argument', according to the Court the relevant US subsidiary had no general authority to bind Cape to any contractual obligation, and there was no evidence that this subsidiary, whether with or without prior authority from Cape, ever effected any transaction in such manner that Cape thereby became subject to contractual obligations to any person. It has been said that *Adams v Cape* significantly limited the possibility to lift the corporate veil at common law.[210] In two recent decisions, the Supreme Court has further restricted the scope of 'corporate veil lifting' or 'veil piercing'.

In *VTB Capital plc v Nutritek International Corporation*,[211] the appellant bank, VTB, had entered into a facility agreement and interest rate swap agreement with a Russian company (RAP) under which VTB advanced a US$225m loan to RAP. The amount was meant to enable RAP to purchase certain companies from Nutritek, a British Virgin Island company. When RAP defaulted on the facility agreement, VTB wished to bring proceedings in England against Nutritek and the Russian businessman who ultimately owned and controlled both Nutritek and RAP (as well as a further affiliated company). VTB's case was based on fraudulent misrepresentation on the part of Nutritek for which the other respondents were jointly and severally liable. In order to bring proceedings in tort in England, VTB required permission to effect service on the respondents out of the jurisdiction, which was initially obtained. When the respondents applied to set service aside, VTB applied for leave to amend its particulars of claim to add a contractual claim, seeking to hold the respondents liable for breach of the facility and interest rate swap agreements on the basis of piercing RAP's veil.[212] Lord Neuberger, with whom their other Lordships agreed, addressed the 'piercing of the veil' point at length. According to Lord Neuberger, 'the precise nature, basis and meaning of the principle are all somewhat obscure, as are the circumstances in which the principle can apply'.[213] Whereas the finding of a 'façade' seems to have often been the trigger,

> words such as 'façade', and other expressions found in the cases, such as 'the true facts', 'sham', 'mask', 'cloak', 'device', or 'puppet' may be useful metaphors. However, such pejorative expressions are often dangerous, as they risk assisting moral indignation to triumph over legal principle, and,

[210] S Bainbridge and T Henderson, *Limited Liability: A Legal and Economic Analysis* (Edward Elgar Publishing 2016) 239–41.

[211] [2013] UKSC 5.

[212] This was deemed necessary because England may not be, and in fact was not, the appropriate forum for the resolution of VTB's tort claims.

[213] *VTB Capital plc v Nutritek International Corporation* (n 206) para 123 (Lord Neuberger).

while they may enable the court to arrive at a result which seems fair in the case in question, they can also risk causing confusion and uncertainty in the law.[214]

His Lordship remained unconvinced that all the cases where the courts have pierced the veil can be explained on the basis of agency, statutory interpretation or knowing receipt; and it may be right for the law to permit the veil to be pierced in certain circumstances in order to defeat injustice.[215] Moreover, in the present case it was unnecessary and inappropriate to decide whether, absent statutory authorization, the court cannot pierce the veil of incorporation at all.[216] This was because piercing the corporate veil could not succeed at all in the present case.[217] What the appellant asked the court to do was to hold the person controlling the company liable as if he had been a co-contracting party under the facility agreement and interest rate swap agreement. This would amount to an extension of the principle beyond the circumstances under which traditionally the veil could be pierced.[218] This did not mean in itself that in VTB's case veil piercing must necessarily fail, however a strong justification would be required to underpin such extension. However, there were overwhelming reasons against an extension.[219] A company should be treated like any natural persons; and one natural person controlling another does not result in the former being bound by contractual obligations incurred by the latter. Moreover, at the time the agreement was entered into neither of the contracting parties intended to contract with the controlling shareholder; and neither did the latter conduct himself subsequently as being bound by the agreement. Also, RAP was not used as a 'façade concealing the true facts'. Consequently, extending the circumstances in which the court may pierce to corporate veil to VTB's case would be contrary to authority and principle.[220]

In *Prest v Petrodel Resources Limited*,[221] Lord Sumption attempted to provide a more comprehensive and systematic assessment of the concept of 'piercing the corporate veil'.

***Prest v Petrodel Resources Limited* [2013] UKSC 34**

Following their divorce, the wife applied for ancillary relief on the basis of the Matrimonial Causes Act 1973 with a view to having seven London properties transferred to her. These properties were legally owned by various companies, which were wholly owned and controlled, directly or indirectly, by the husband. Under the Matrimonial Causes Act, the court may order that a party to a marriage shall transfer to the other party property to which the former is 'entitled, either in possession or reversion'. Given that the properties at issue were legally owned, not by the husband, but by various companies, a property transfer order could be justified only if either the husband was the beneficial owner of the relevant properties or if the corporate veil could be pierced. Whereas the Supreme Court unanimously accepted the former so that the transfer order could be made for the wife's benefit; a unanimous seven-member Supreme Court rejected the latter, although strictly speaking this was unnecessary for the outcome of the case.

Lord Sumption:

...

27. In my view, the principle that the court may be justified in piercing the corporate veil if a company's separate legal personality is being abused for the purpose of some relevant wrongdoing is well established in the authorities. It is true that most of the statements of principle in

[214] ibid para 124. [215] ibid para 127. [216] ibid para 130.

[217] Lord Neuberger considered piercing of the corporate veil on the basis of English law. His Lordship noted, however, that there might be choice of law issues to be addressed in cases which concern a foreign incorporated company such as RAP. Possible conflicts rules might be the *lex incorporationis*, the *lex fori*, the *lex contractus*, or there might not be room for a single conflicts rule to govern the issue: ibid para 131.

[218] ibid para 132. But see *Antonio Gramsci Shipping Corporation v Stepanovs* [2011] EWHC 333 (Comm), which Lord Neuberger believed to have been wrongly decided (paras 133, 147). Lord Clarke wished to reserve for future decision not just the question of the true scope of piercing the corporate veil, but also whether *Gramsci* was correctly decided or not (ibid para 238).

[219] ibid para 137 (Lord Neuberger). [220] ibid paras 138–45 (Lord Neuberger).

[221] [2013] UKSC 34.

the authorities are obiter, because the corporate veil was not pierced. It is also true that most cases in which the corporate veil was pierced could have been decided on other grounds. But the consensus that there are circumstances in which the court may pierce the corporate veil is impressive. I would not for my part be willing to explain that consensus out of existence. This is because I think that the recognition of a limited power to pierce the corporate veil in carefully defined circumstances is necessary if the law is not to be disarmed in the face of abuse. I also think that provided the limits are recognised and respected, it is consistent with the general approach of English law to the problems raised by the use of legal concepts to defeat mandatory rules of law.

28. The difficulty is to identify what is a relevant wrongdoing. References to a 'facade' or 'sham' beg too many questions to provide a satisfactory answer. It seems to me that two distinct principles lie behind these protean terms, and that much confusion has been caused by failing to distinguish between them. They can conveniently be called the concealment principle and the evasion principle. The concealment principle is legally banal and does not involve piercing the corporate veil at all. It is that the interposition of a company or perhaps several companies so as to conceal the identity of the real actors will not deter the courts from identifying them, assuming that their identity is legally relevant. In these cases the court is not disregarding the 'facade', but only looking behind it to discover the facts which the corporate structure is concealing. The evasion principle is different. It is that the court may disregard the corporate veil if there is a legal right against the person in control of it which exists independently of the company's involvement, and a company is interposed so that the separate legal personality of the company will defeat the right or frustrate its enforcement. Many cases will fall into both categories, but in some circumstances the difference between them may be critical. ...

...

34. These considerations reflect the broader principle that the corporate veil may be pierced only to prevent the abuse of corporate legal personality. It may be an abuse of the separate legal personality of a company to use it to evade the law or to frustrate its enforcement. It is not an abuse to cause a legal liability to be incurred by the company in the first place. It is not an abuse to rely upon the fact (if it is a fact) that a liability is not the controller's because it is the company's. On the contrary, that is what incorporation is all about. Thus in a case like VTB Capital, where the argument was that the corporate veil should be pierced so as to make the controllers of a company jointly and severally liable on the company's contract, the fundamental objection to the argument was that the principle was being invoked so as to create a new liability that would not otherwise exist. The objection to that argument is obvious in the case of a consensual liability under a contract, where the ostensible contracting parties never intended that anyone else should be party to it. But the objection would have been just as strong if the liability in question had not been consensual.

35. I conclude that there is a limited principle of English law which applies when a person is under an existing legal obligation or liability or subject to an existing legal restriction which he deliberately evades or whose enforcement he deliberately frustrates by interposing a company under his control. The court may then pierce the corporate veil for the purpose, and only for the purpose, of depriving the company or its controller of the advantage that they would otherwise have obtained by the company's separate legal personality. The principle is properly described as a limited one, because in almost every case where the test is satisfied, the facts will in practice disclose a legal relationship between the company and its controller which will make it unnecessary to pierce the corporate veil. Like Munby J in Ben Hashem, I consider that if it is not necessary to pierce the corporate veil, it is not appropriate to do so, because on that footing there is no public policy imperative which justifies that course. I therefore disagree with the Court of Appeal in VTB Capital who suggested otherwise at para 79. For all of these reasons, the principle has been recognised far more often than it has been applied. But the recognition of a small residual category of cases where the abuse of the corporate veil to evade or frustrate the law can be addressed only by disregarding the legal personality of the company is, I believe, consistent with authority and with long-standing principles of legal policy.

Lord Neuberger:

...

64. .... This is the second case in the space of a few months when the doctrine has been invoked before this court on what are, on any view, inappropriate grounds. It is also clear from the cases and academic articles that the law relating to the doctrine is unsatisfactory and confused. Those cases and articles appear to me to suggest that (i) there is not a single instance in this jurisdiction where the doctrine has been invoked properly and successfully, (ii) there is doubt as to whether the doctrine should exist, and (iii) it is impossible to discern any coherent approach, applicable principles, or defined limitations to the doctrine.

65. In these circumstances, there is obvious value in seeking to decide whether the doctrine exists, and if so, to identify some coherent, practical and principled basis for it, if we can do so in this case.

...

79 ... I was initially strongly attracted by the argument that we should decide that a supposed doctrine, which is controversial and uncertain, and which, on analysis, appears never to have been invoked successfully and appropriately in its 80 years of supposed existence, should be given its quietus. Such a decision would render the law much clearer than it is now, and in a number of cases it would reduce complications and costs: whenever the doctrine is really needed, it never seems to apply.

80. However, I have reached the conclusion that it would be wrong to discard a doctrine which, while it has been criticised by judges and academics, has been generally assumed to exist in all common law jurisdictions, and represents a potentially valuable judicial tool to undo wrongdoing in some cases, where no other principle is available. Accordingly, provided that it is possible to discern or identify an approach to piercing the corporate veil, which accords with normal legal principles, reflects previous judicial reasoning (so far as it can be discerned and reconciled), and represents a practical solution ... I believe that it would be right to adopt it as a definition of the doctrine.

81. Having read what Lord Sumption says in his judgment, especially in paras 17, 18, 27, 28, 34 and 35, I am persuaded by his formulation in para 35, namely that the doctrine should only be invoked where 'a person is under an existing legal obligation or liability or subject to an existing legal restriction which he deliberately evades or whose enforcement he deliberately frustrates by interposing a company under his control'.

...

Lady Hale:

...

92. I am not sure whether it is possible to classify all of the cases in which the courts have been or should be prepared to disregard the separate legal personality of a company neatly into cases of either concealment or evasion. They may simply be examples of the principle that the individuals who operate limited companies should not be allowed to take unconscionable advantage of the people with whom they do business. But what the cases do have in common is that the separate legal personality is being disregarded in order to obtain a remedy against someone other than the company in respect of a liability which would otherwise be that of the company alone (if it existed at all). In the converse case, where it is sought to convert the personal liability of the owner or controller into a liability of the company, it is usually more appropriate to rely upon the concepts of agency and of the 'directing mind'.

...

Following *VTB* and *Prest*, in respect of the agency argument and the 'single economic unit' argument, *Adams v Cape* is still good law. A shareholder or director will be personally liable as principal for the contracts entered into by a company they control only to the extent that the company had actual or apparent authority to bind the shareholder or director pursuant to an actual agency relationship. A group of companies may be treated as a 'single economic unit' only where a statutory provision—perhaps following its interpretation—so requires. The real innovation of *Prest* concerns the 'sham or fraud' argument, which has been replaced with the 'concealment principle' and the 'evasion principle'. The concealment principle does not involve 'veil piercing' at all; on this basis the court will merely seek to establish the facts of an arrangement hidden by the interposition of corporate entities with a view to applying general legal principles to the facts so discovered. The following case provides an example:

Trustor AB v Smallbone and Others **[2002] BCC 795**

The managing director of a Swedish company, Mr. Smallbone, misappropriated moneys which he transferred into the account of an English company, Introcom, controlled by him via a complicated trust structure. The issue was whether, in addition to Introcom, Smallbone himself was jointly liable for the misappropriated amounts based on the equitable concept of 'knowing receipt'

Sir Andrew Morritt V-C:

...

In my judgment the court is entitled to 'pierce the corporate veil' and recognise the receipt of the company as that of the individual(s) in control of it if the company was used as a device or facade to conceal the true facts thereby avoiding or concealing any liability of those individual(s) ...

Mr Smallbone is bound by the findings made by Rimer J and the Court of Appeal in relation to the issues before them. Thus it is established that Introcom was and is controlled by Mr Smallbone, the payments from the Trustor account with Barclays, Cheapside to the account of Introcom at Barclays, Cheapside were effected by Mr Smallbone or on his instructions and, in the words of Rimer J, Introcom was simply a vehicle Mr Smallbone used for receiving money from Trustor. Rimer J also concluded that the payments to Introcom were unauthorised and involved an inexcusable breach by Mr Smallbone of his duty as managing director of Trustor 'being payments to Mr Smallbone's own company which was then going to and did devote itself to further unauthorised and improper dissipations of the money'.

In my view these conclusions are such as to entitle the court to recognise the receipt of the money of Trustor by Introcom as the receipt by Mr Smallbone too. Introcom was a device or facade in that it was used as the vehicle for the receipt of the money of Trustor. Its use was improper as it was the means by which Mr Smallbone committed unauthorised and inexcusable breaches of his duty as a director of Trustor. Mr Smallbone has no real prospect of successfully defending this part of the claim because he is bound by the findings of Rimer J to which I have referred.

...

Given the 'veil piercing' language used in the judgment, at the time the case seemed to be a classic example of the 'fraud' or 'sham' exception to the principle of limited liability. However, even at the time it has been pointed out that, for knowing receipt, a company can be treated in the same way as any other person through whose hands the money passes. The key focus for personal liability is the ultimate beneficial receiver; consequently, 'Morritt V.-C.'s holding that the corporate veil could be pierced to allow Mr Smallbone's liability to be established appears ... in the context of establishing such knowing receipt liability, to have been conceptually unnecessary'.[222]

This leaves the 'evasion principle' as the only ground for 'piercing the corporate veil' according to Lord Sumption. Evasion involves an attempt to deliberately frustrate an existing legal relationship through the interposition of a company with a view to shielding its controller from any obligations arising from the pre-existing legal relationship. The prime examples hat would come under this heading, according to Lord Sumption, are cases such as *Gilford Motor Ltd v Horne* and *Jones and Lipman* where a company was used in order to, respectively, defeat restrictions on trading activities or an obligation to convey real estate. The evasion principle is based on the notion of an abuse of corporate legal personality,

[222] S Watson, 'Two Lessons From Trustor' (2003) 119 LQR 13, 14.

which itself is a manifestation of the broader principle that 'fraud unravels everything'.[223] One problem of the evasion principle is its indeterminacy. According to Lord Neuberger, neither *Gilford Motor Ltd v Horne* nor *Jones v Lipman* actually involved the doctrine at all; both cases could be decided on the basis of general legal principles (agency and specific performance, respectively) without the need to pierce the corporate veil.[224] Moreover, the evasion principle has a certain circularity about it: in order to establish whether the principle of separate legal personality should be disregarded we need to establish whether the corporate controller is the actual obligor under a pre-existing legal relationship, and in order to do that we need to look behind the corporate veil.[225] Overall, the Supreme Court's pronouncements in *VTB* and *Prest* seem to contribute at best only marginally to the clarification of the law in this area.[226]

Questions and comments:

1. In *Antonio Gramsci Shipping Corporation v Lembergs*,[227] Beatson LJ had the following to say about the future development of the law:

   > In *Prest*'s case Lord Sumption (at [28]) identified two underlying principles which he called 'the concealment principle' and 'the evasion principle'. But Lord Neuberger was of the view (at [75]) that there is a 'lack of any coherent principle' in the application of the doctrine of 'piercing the corporate veil', and Lord Walker's view (at [106]) was that it is not a doctrine in the sense of a coherent principle or rule of law but a label. Lady Hale (at [92]) was 'not sure whether it is possible to classify all of the cases in which the courts have been or should be prepared to disregard the separate legal personality of a company neatly into cases of either concealment or evasion'. Absent a principle, further development of the law will be difficult for the courts because development of common law and equity is incremental and often by analogical reasoning'.[228]

2. To sum up, 'piercing the corporate veil' at common law seems to be a rather uncertain remedy for creditors. Whether the corporate form has been abused and the evasion principle can be invoked largely seems to be in the eye of the beholder. Consequently, piercing the corporate veil is likely to remain of limited practical significance.[229]

3. Moreover, cases where the legal personality of the company has been disregarded for some reason and cases where the company's liabilities have been imposed on its shareholders or managers are to be distinguished. As Sealy has put it:

   > … many instances can be found in which for one reason or another, a court has decided that it was appropriate in the interests of justice for the separate corporate personality of the company to be disregarded; but one will search the reports in vain for a single English case where the principle of limited liability, as distinct from that of corporate personality, has not been respected—statute apart. This is true of cases brought against directors and dominant shareholders alike.[230]

[223] *Prest v Petrodel Resources Limited* [2013] UKSC 34 para 18 (Lord Sumption), citing Denning LJ in *Lazarus Estates Ltd v Beasley* [1956] 1 QB 702, 712.

[224] *VTB Capital plc v Nutritek International Corporation* (n 206) paras 70–3 (Lord Neuberger).

[225] T Cheng-Han, 'Veil piercing: a fresh start' (2015) Journal of Business Law 20, 28.

[226] C Hare, 'From *Salomon* to *Spiliada*: Orthodoxy and Uncertainty in the Supreme Court' (2013) 72(2) Cambridge Law Journal 280, 283; C Hare, 'Family Division, 0: Chancery Division, 1: Piercing The Corporate Veil in the Supreme Court (Again)' (2013) 72(3) Cambridge Law Journal 511, 513–14. for a different view, see Sealy and Worthington (n 199) 64: 'considerably more straightforward'.

[227] [2013] EWCA Civ 730.

[228] ibid para 66.

[229] Davies and Worthington (n 13) para 8-17.

[230] L Sealy, 'Personal Liability of Directors and Officers for Debts of Insolvent Corporations: A Jurisdictional Perspective (England)' in JS Ziegel (ed), *Current Developments in International and Comparative Corporate Insolvency Law* (Clarendon Press 1994) 485.

4. This has now been confirmed in *VTB*. The older case *Ord v Belhaven Pubs Ltd* is also instructive.[231] After the company had been sued all its assets were transferred to its parent company at net book value. The consideration paid by the parent company was sufficient to clear a balance sheet deficit of the company which, after the transactions, did not retain any substantial assets. The Court of Appeal rejected liability of the parent company for the company's debts because the transactions did not adversely affect the balance sheet of the company nor did they exacerbate its financial difficulties; no fraud or illegality was involved, and all transactions were properly disclosed. The case overruled the earlier decision in *Creasey v Breachwood Motors*[232] where an employee, left with a worthless judgment against a company, was allowed to pursue a second company to which the assets of the former had been transferred.
5. The concluding remarks of Sir John Balcombe in *Ord v Belhaven Pubs Ltd* are revealing: 'If there had been any substance in the allegations that there had been some impropriety in the handling of the group restructuring, insolvency law (and in particular I have in mind s. 423 of the Insolvency Act 1986) makes adequate provision for dealing with that eventuality'.
6. Compare the attitude of English courts to that of their US counterparts who apparently accept 'piercing of the corporate veil' arguments more readily. Given that both jurisdictions are rooted in the common law tradition, what may account for these differences in attitude?

II. Statutory liability under Insolvency Act 1986

The Insolvency Act 1986 contains several provisions, which allow the 'office holder', and sometimes creditors directly, to reach the personal assets of managers and controlling shareholders. From early on, English law contained provisions on fraudulent trading which impose both civil[233] and criminal liability[234] on anyone who knowingly participated in the carrying on of the business of the company with intent to defraud creditors or for any other fraudulent purpose. Civil liability pursuant to Insolvency Act 1986, ss. 213, 246ZA requires that the company is in the course of winding up or in administration.[235] On application of the office holder, a person found guilty of 'fraudulent trading' may be ordered to make such contributions to the company's assets as the court thinks proper. 'Intent to defraud' requires the office holder to show that there was 'actual dishonesty involving, according to current notions of fair trading among commercial men, real moral blame' on the part of the respondent.[236] Although not quite a dead letter, these strict standards of pleading and proof render the provision somewhat inconvenient as a tool of creditor protection. This led the Cork Committee to recommend the introduction of a 'civil remedy for those who have suffered foreseeable loss as a result, not only of fraudulent, but also of unreasonable behaviour'.[237] This resulted, in 1985, in the introduction of what is now section 214 of the Insolvency Act 1986; the liability for 'wrongful trading'.

A remedy pursuant to Insolvency Act 1986, ss. 214, 246ZB may be asserted only in the course of the winding up of a company when the company has gone into insolvent liquidation,[238] and, since the Small Business, Enterprise and Employment Act 2015, also when the company is in insolvent administration.[239] A company goes into insolvent liquidation or administration if, at the time the liquidation or administration commences, the company is

231 [1998] BCC 607. 232 [1992] BCC 638. 233 Insolvency Act 1986, s 213.

234 Companies Act 2006, s 993.

235 The possibility to bring a claim for fraudulent trading in administration was added by the Small Business, Enterprise and Employment Act 2015, s 117, introducing the new Insolvency Act 1986, s 246ZA.

236 *Re Patrick and Lyon Ltd* [1933] Ch 786, 790–1.

237 Sir Kenneth Cork, Report of the Review Committee on Insolvency Law and Practice (Cmnd 8558, 1982), 399 para 1777.

238 Insolvency Act 1986, s 214(2)(a); *Re MC Bacon Ltd* [1991] Ch 127, 138.

239 Small Business, Enterprise and Employment Act 2015, s 117, introducing Insolvency Act 1986, s 246ZB.

insolvent on a balance sheet basis.[240] The rationale for the balance sheet test in this context is that only in the event of balance sheet insolvency will creditors suffer a loss which necessitates a contribution to the company's assets.[241]

The wording of sections 214(1) and 246ZB(1) of the Insolvency Act 1986 makes it clear that only the office holder (liquidator or administrator) has standing. The rationale for this limitation is to prevent single creditors from exerting undue pressure on the company's directors just to get their particular claims paid.[242] The office holder has the burden for determining the 'material time' before the commencement of the proceedings at which the respondent 'knew or ought to have known that there was no reasonable prospect that the company would avoid going into insolvent liquidation/administration'.[243] The standard for what a director 'knew or ought to have known' is the general knowledge and skill that can reasonably be expected of a person in the same position as the director in question, taking into account the size and structure of the company; special knowledge and skill may be held against the director.[244] Overall, courts have adopted a robust approach. Directors are afforded a certain amount of discretion, they are allowed to be reasonably optimistic, and any doubts will usually work to their advantage.[245] They are, however, required to have at all times a reliable picture of the financial situation of their company.[246] Courts usually adhere to a two-pronged test. Liability will not be triggered before the company is insolvent on a cash flow basis. This cash flow test is applied on a 'commercial reality' basis, so that companies which have not in fact been paying their debts on time are not regarded as insolvent on a cash flow basis if they have been making payments within timescales acceptable to their creditors.[247] In addition to the company's inability to pay its debts as they fall due, courts will usually rely on a sufficiently clear event on the downward spiral of the company's fortunes, such as the withdrawal of a major supplier or customer, disastrous accounts, or warnings by legal and financial advisers.[248] A good illustration is the case of *Rubin v Gunner & Anor*.[249] The court found that the company was unable to pay its debts effectively from April 1998 onwards. However,

> the respondents had a genuine and reasonable belief, during the period prior to 15 October 1998 (albeit diminishing substantially in reasonableness from the end of September 1998), that Mr. Stables [an outside investor] would provide sufficient funding for RGO to avoid the company going into insolvent liquidation.[250]

Only after, by the end of September 1998, 'Mr. Stables had repeatedly failed to cause his promises and assurances of a substantial capital injection to materialise' ought the respondents have concluded that there was no reasonable prospect of the company to avoid going into insolvent liquidation.[251]

Wrongful trading liability applies only to a person who, at the 'material time', was a 'director' of the company.[252] Directors in that sense are those formally and lawfully appointed to the board (*de jure directors*);[253] de facto directors,[254] who, although not formally appointed

[240] Insolvency Act 1986, ss 214(6), 246ZB(6). Insolvency merely on a liquidity or cash flow basis would be insufficient. See R Goode, *Principles of Corporate Insolvency Law* (Sweet & Maxwell 2011) para 14-30 (666).

[241] ibid.

[242] A Hicks, 'Advising on Wrongful Trading: Part II' (1993) 14 Company Lawyer 55, 59.

[243] Insolvency Act 1986, ss 214(2)(b), 246ZB(2)(b).

[244] ibid ss 214(4), 246ZB(4), which introduce an objective minimum standard which may be tightened by subjective elements; cf Goode (n 237) para 14-44 (672–3).

[245] *Re Sherborne Associates Ltd* [1995] BCC 40, 49–56; *Re Brian D Pierson (Contractors) Ltd* [1999] BCC 26, 52.

[246] *Singla v Hedman* [2010] EWHC 902 para 102; *Re Bangha Television Ltd* [2010] BCC 143, 158.

[247] *Re Brian D Pearson (Contractors) Ltd* (n 245).

[248] A Hicks, 'Advising on Wrongful Trading: Part I' (1993) 14 *Company Lawyer* 16, 17; *Re Produce Marketing Consortium (No 2)* [1989] BCLC 520; *Re DKG Contractors Ltd* [1990] BCC 903; *Re Purpoint Ltd* [1991] BCLC 491; *Re Brian D Pierson (Contractors) Ltd* (n 242); *Official Receiver v Doshi* [2001] 2 BCLC 235.

[249] [2004] BCC 684.

[250] *Rubin v Gunner and Anor* [2004] BCC 684, 695.

[251] ibid 684, 697.

[252] Insolvency Act 1986, ss 214(2)(c), 246ZB(2)(c).

[253] Goode (n 237) para 14-32 (667).

[254] ibid.

to the board, openly and publicly act as if they were appointed;[255] and shadow directors 'in accordance with whose directions or instructions the directors of the company are accustomed to act';[256] persons giving advice in a 'professional capacity' being excluded.[257] A parent company may be a shadow director in respect of its subsidiary.[258]

If these preconditions are met, the respondent may escape liability only if he is able to prove,[259] that from the 'material time' onwards he took every step necessary in order to minimize the potential loss to the company's creditors.[260] The Act contains very little guidance[261] in this respect. Where directors have been held liable, they typically had closed their eyes to the reality of the company's position and had carried on trading as before, in the hope that the problem would go away.[262] Commentators have recommended a number of measures to escape liability: making sure that accounts are being properly kept and up-dated; that the board constantly receives an accurate and up-to-date picture of the company's trading, financial, and cash flow position; obtains competent outside advice; holds frequent board meetings; constantly informs and seeks the support of major secured as well as unsecured creditors.[263] A 'wholly responsible and conscientious attitude, both to [the company's] position and to their own responsibilities as directors' was demonstrated in *Re Continental Assurance Co of London Plc (No 4)*.[264] At a board meeting on 4 June 1991, major and unexpected losses were reported to the directors. At the adjourned continuation of that meeting on 14 June 1991, the managing director expressly raised the question of whether the company should continue to trade. The board did not ignore the question; rather they considered it 'directly, closely and frequently'. At regular and frequent board meetings from June to December 1991, the directors sought assurance from the finance director, the auditors and later from an external expert that the company was still solvent. As the financial position regularly looked bleaker through the later months of 1991, they reduced the scale of trading to minimal and cautious levels. On 20 December 1991, when the directors finally learned that newly reported losses meant that the company had become insolvent, they gave instructions that it should not do any more business, and took advice from insolvency practitioners. In order to keep open as long as possible the chance of selling the company, formal liquidation did not commence until 27 March 1992. This reaction to the financial crisis was considered by the court to be 'entirely appropriate'.[265]

Consequently, what attracts liability under section 214 of the Insolvency Act 1986 is not any form of negligent or reckless trading or mismanagement which brings the company to the brink of insolvency. Also, incurring new debt after the company has become insolvent is not in itself relevant. Indeed, putting an insolvent company into liquidation may itself constitute a breach of section 214 of the Insolvency Act 1986.[266] Liability may be triggered

[255] Decisive is whether the person appears to be, based on an overall appreciation of the circumstances, part of the management of the company. See *Re Kaytech International Plc* [1999] 2 BCLC 351, 423; following *Secretary of State for Trade and Industry v Tjolle* [1998] 1 BCLC 333, 341–2.

[256] The concept requires identification of those who exert 'real influence in the corporate affairs of the company'; although it is neither necessary that influence is exerted in all areas of the company's business activities, nor that board and alleged shadow director regard certain proposals as instructions rather than mere advice, nor that the board substantially limits its discretion. *Secretary of State for Trade and Industry v Deverell* [2001] Ch 340, 354–5.

[257] Insolvency Act 1986, s 251.

[258] *In Re Hydrom Ltd* [1994] 2 BCLC 180; *Re PFTZM Ltd* [1995] BCC 280.

[259] Hicks (n 239), 58; Goode (n 237) para 14-42 (671).

[260] Insolvency Act 1986, ss 214(3), 246ZB(3).

[261] ibid ss 214(4), 246ZB(4) also provides the standard of assessment for the steps to be taken.

[262] In *Re Produce Marketing Consortium Ltd* [1989] BCLC 520, 551–2, the company, after the 'material time', simply continued as before. Liability could possibly have been avoided by selling the goods in stock for the benefit of all parties involved and informing the respective supplier about the company's financial situation so that he could have made an informed decision as to how to proceed.

[263] Hicks (n 239) 55–9; Goode (n 237) para 14-46 (674–6) ('12 points of survival').

[264] *Re Continental Assurance Co of London Plc (No 4)*, (2001) WL 720239, paras 107–108.

[265] ibid para 292.

[266] ibid para 281 ('Ceasing to trade and liquidating too soon can be stigmatised as the cowards' way out').

simply by the failure to act properly in order to minimize the loss to the company's creditors when it has become apparent that the company is unlikely to survive.[267]

The court is given a wide discretion.[268] An order under ss. 214, 246ZB Insolvency Act 1986 is primarily of a compensatory nature and does not have a penal character.[269] In principle, therefore, the court will compel the respondent to compensate the company for any losses resulting from the fact that the necessary measures were not adopted in time.[270] The measure of compensation is the increase in net deficiency.[271] It seems, however, that the increase in net deficiency will be recoverable only if it can be specifically attributed to the wrongful decision to carry on trading; a mere *conditio sine qua non* connection will be insufficient.[272] Compensation paid pursuant to a court order will be held by the office holder on trust for the benefit of the unsecured creditors without being subject to a floating charge.[273] A court order stipulating that compensation payments may be used primarily for the benefit of a certain group of creditors will be unlawful.[274]

The following is one of the leading cases on section 214 of the Insolvency Act 1986.

***Re Produce Marketing Consortium (No 2)* [1989] 5 BCC 569**

Over a period of seven years the company had slowly drifted into insolvency. There was no suggestion of any wrongdoing on the part of the two directors involved; it was just that they did not put the company into liquidation in time.

Knox, J:

...

The first question is whether it appears that subsec. (2) applies to Mr. David and Mr. Murphy. There is no question but that they were directors at all material times and that PMC has gone into insolvent liquidation. The issue is whether at some time after 27 April 1986 and before 2 October 1987, when it went into insolvent liquidation, they knew or ought to have concluded that there was no reasonable prospect that PMC would avoid going into insolvent liquidation. It was inevitably conceded by Mr. Teverson, on their behalf, that this question has to be answered by the standards postulated by subsec. (4), so that the facts which Mr. David and Mr. Murphy ought to have known or ascertained and the conclusions that they ought to have reached are not limited to those which they themselves, showing reasonable diligence and having the general knowledge, skill and experience which they respectively had, would have known, ascertained or reached but also those that a person with the general knowledge, skill and experience of someone carrying out their functions would have known, ascertained or reached.

...

The Insolvency Act 1986 now has two separate provisions: sec. 213 dealing with fraudulent trading ... and sec. 214 which deals with what the side-note calls 'wrongful trading'. It is evident that Parliament intended to widen the scope of the legislation under which directors who trade on when the company is insolvent may, in appropriate circumstances, be required to make a contribution to the assets of the company which, in practical terms, means its creditors. Two

[267] Goode (n 237) para 14-31 (667).

[268] Pursuant to Insolvency Act 1986, ss 215, 246ZC, the court may order complementary measures in order to secure liability. For instance claims of the directors against the company may be declared to be subject to subordination.

[269] *Re Produce Marketing Consortium Ltd* [1989] BCLC 520, 553.

[270] ibid.

[271] *Re Continental Assurance Co of London Plc (No 4)* (n 261) para 297: 'The concept is that, if the directors had decided on 19 July 1991 that Continental was insolvent, and had caused it to be put in liquidation then or soon thereafter, there would have been a deficiency in the hypothetical 1991 liquidation of one amount, say £x. In the actual case Continental did not go into liquidation until 27 March 1992, and in the actual 1992 liquidation there was a deficiency of a different amount, say £y. If £y is greater than £x the excess is the increase in net deficiency'.

[272] ibid paras 376–80. One example for an increase in net deficiency not attributable to wrongful trading would be the worsening of the company's position due to bad weather in respect of a company engaged in the business of constructing and maintaining golf courses; see *Re Brian D Pierson (Contractors) Ltd* (n 242).

[273] *Re Oasis Merchandising Services Ltd* [1998] Ch 170, 181–7; see further Insolvency Act 1986, s 176ZB, introduced by the Small Business, Enterprise and Employment Act 2015, s 119.

[274] *Re Purpoint Ltd* [1991] BCLC 491, 499.

steps in particular were taken in the legislative enlargement of the court's jurisdiction. First, the requirement for an intent to defraud and fraudulent purpose was not retained as an essential, and with it goes the need for what Maugham J. called 'actual dishonesty involving real moral blame'. I pause here to observe that at no stage before me has it been suggested that either Mr. David or Mr. Murphy fell into this category.

The second enlargement is that the test to be applied by the court has become one under which the director in question is to be judged by the standards of what can be expected of a person fulfilling his functions, and showing reasonable diligence in doing so. I accept Mr. Teverson's submission in this connection, that the requirement to have regard to the functions to be carried out by the director in question, in relation to the company in question, involves having regard to the particular company and its business. It follows that the general knowledge, skill and experience postulated will be much less extensive in a small company in a modest way of business, with simple accounting procedures and equipment, than it will be in a large company with sophisticated procedures.

Nevertheless, certain minimum standards are to be assumed to be attained. Notably there is an obligation laid on companies to cause accounting records to be kept which are such as to disclose with reasonable accuracy at any time the financial position of the company at that time … In addition directors are required to prepare a profit and loss account for each financial year and a balance sheet as at the end of it … Directors are also required, in respect of each financial year, to lay before the company in general meeting copies of the accounts of the company for that year and to deliver to the registrar of companies a copy of those accounts, in the case of a private company, within ten months after the end of the relevant accounting reference period …

As I have already mentioned, Mr. Halls gave evidence that the accounting records of PMC were adequate for the purposes of its business. The preparation of accounts was woefully late, more especially in relation to those dealing with the year ending 30 September 1985, which should have been laid and delivered by the end of July 1986. The knowledge to be imputed in testing whether or not directors knew or ought to have concluded that there was no reasonable prospect of the company avoiding insolvent liquidation is not limited to the documentary material actually available at the given time. This appears from sec. 214(4) which includes a reference to facts which a director of a company ought not only to know but those which he ought to ascertain, a word which does not appear in sec. 214(2)(b). In my judgment this indicates that there is to be included by way of factual information not only what was actually there but what, given reasonable diligence and an appropriate level of general knowledge, skill and experience, was ascertainable. This leads me to the conclusion in this case that I should assume, for the purposes of applying the test in sec. 214(2), that the financial results for the year ending 30 September 1985 were known at the end of July 1986 at least to the extent of the size of the deficiency of assets over liabilities.

Mr. David and Mr. Murphy, although they did not have the accounts in their hands until January 1987, did, I find, know that the previous trading year had been a very bad one. They had a close and intimate knowledge of the business and they had a shrewd idea whether the turnover was up or down. In fact it was badly down in that year to £526,459 and although I have no doubt that they did not know in July 1986 that it was that precise figure, I have no doubt that they had a good rough idea of what it was and in particular that it was well down on the previous year. A major drop in turnover meant almost as night follows day that there was a substantial loss incurred, as indeed there was. That, in turn, meant again, as surely as night following day, a substantial increase in the deficit of assets over liabilities.

That deals with their actual knowledge but, in addition, I have to have regard to what they have to be treated as having known or ascertained, and that includes the actual deficit of assets over liabilities of £132,870. This was £80,000 over Mr. David's personal guarantee. It was a deficit that, for an indefinite period in the future, could not be made good, even if the optimistic prognostications of level of turnover entertained by Mr. David and Mr. Murphy were achieved. They later estimated, when they visited the bank on 16 February 1987, a turnover of £1.6m. If one assumes half as much again, at £2.4m, the gross income of the company would only have risen to £84,000 and the overheads were accepted as being not less than £65,000. That gives a notional profit of £19,000 per annum. If one takes the figure of £1.6m, overheads of £65,000 would not have been covered.

Mr. Teverson was not able to advance any particular calculation as constituting a basis for concluding that there was a prospect of insolvent liquidation being avoided. He is not to be criticised for that for, in my judgement, there was none available. Once the loss in the year ending 30 September 1985 was incurred PMC was in irreversible decline, assuming (as I must) that the directors had no plans for altering the company's business and proposed to go on drawing the level of reasonable remuneration that they were currently receiving.

It was stated by Mr. David that the persons and companies with whom PMC did business were in the main long established trading partners. In fact that could not be said of Ramona which was, by July 1986, a very important creditor. But even if one disregards that aspect, it would not be right to assume that even old established trading partners will wait indefinitely to have their debts paid. Nor, in my judgment, do the facts that the bank was throughout willing to continue its facilities and that Mr. Tough, although expressing the grave warnings that he did when the accounts for the years ending 30 September 1985 and 1986 were available to him, was willing to accompany Mr. David and Mr. Murphy to the bank in February 1987 to see if further facilities would be granted, detract from the conclusion I have reached that Mr. David and Mr. Murphy ought to have concluded at the end of July 1986 that there was no reasonable prospect that PMC would avoid going into insolvent liquidation. The bank was secured by Mr. David's guarantee, if not to any significant extent by the other securities which it took, and Mr. Tough's attitude was never more than one of doubt and caution.

The next question which arises is whether there is a case under sec. 214(3) for saying that after the end of July 1986 the respondents took every step with a view to minimising the potential loss to the creditors of PMC as, assuming them to have known that there was no reasonable prospect of PMC avoiding insolvent liquidation, they ought to have taken. This clearly has to be answered 'No', since they went on trading for another year.

...

I am therefore driven to the conclusion that the court's discretion arises under sec. 214(1).

...

In my judgment the jurisdiction under sec. 214 is primarily compensatory rather than penal. Prima facie the appropriate amount that a director is declared to be liable to contribute is the amount by which the company's assets can be discerned to have been depleted by the director's conduct which caused the discretion under sec. 214(1) to arise. But Parliament has indeed chosen very wide words of discretion and it would be undesirable to seek to spell out limits on that discretion, more especially since this is, so far as counsel were aware, the first case to come to judgment under this section. The fact that there was no fraudulent intent is not of itself a reason for fixing the amount at a nominal or low figure, for that would amount to frustrating what I discern as Parliament's intention in adding sec. 214 to sec. 213 in the Insolvency Act 1986, but I am not persuaded that it is right to ignore that fact totally.

...

Taking all these circumstances into account I propose to declare that Mr. David and Mr. Murphy are liable to make a contribution to the assets of PMC of £75,000.

As between the two of them it seems to me right that Mr. David should indemnify Mr. Murphy as to £50,000 and that above that figure they should be jointly liable. As against the liquidator they should be jointly and severally liable for the whole £75,000. I take this view regarding the indemnity to be given by Mr. David partly because Mr. David was Mr. Murphy's senior in every sense—age, standing in the company and personality—but principally because of the existence of Mr. David's guarantee to the bank.

...

Questions and comments:

1. When it was first introduced, section 214 of the Insolvency Act 1986 was greeted enthusiastically.[275] However, many believe that the provision has been unable to live up to these high expectations. This belief is nurtured by the relatively modest number of cases based on wrongful

[275] D Prentice, 'Creditor's Interests and Director's Duties' (1990) 10 OJLS 265, 277; F Oditah, 'Wrongful Trading' [1990] LMCLQ 205, 222.

trading that have been reported over the years.[276] This may be attributable to the difficulties of enforcing the provision. Originally, the liquidator did not have a preferential claim for reimbursement of his costs if a promising application under section 214 was ultimately rejected.[277] This particular disincentive for initiating litigation has been addressed as of 1 January 2003.[278] In addition, the Small Business, Enterprise and Employment Act 2015 introduced the power of the office holder to sell and assign the right of action (including the proceeds) under sections 214 and 246ZB of the Insolvency Act 1986. As a consequence, the office holder may obtain funds more quickly and the assignee, usually a specialized business, may be less risk averse in bringing a cause of action based on wrongful trading.[279]

2. One obstacle that remains is for the office holder to determine the 'material time'. This task will be straightforward only in the clearest of cases where, in the light of overwhelming evidence, the directors acted inappropriately.[280] Moreover, the office holder must select the relevant date in his pleadings and cannot change it if it becomes evident that the directors had the required knowledge only at a later date.[281] Conversely, directors may be unaware that they have reached the stage where liability is triggered. In that case the provision is hardly suitable to adjust director's incentives. Similarly, section 214(3) does not give any affirmative guidance as to what steps need to be taken in order for the director to be able to invoke the defence.[282] On the other hand it has been suggested that the low number of cases may not be an accurate pointer to the effectiveness of the provision. Wrongful trading may be operating behind the scenes in the minds of directors, who will have been warned by their legal and financial advisers about the dangers they face once the company becomes insolvent and different measures that they might consider will have been put to them.[283]

3. Following a recommendation by the High-level Group of Company Law Experts the introduction of a wrongful trading regime at European level was for a while on the agenda of the European legislator.[284] A provision that addresses similar issues has now appeared in the Commission's Proposal for a Directive on preventive restructuring frameworks. Article 18 provides for the duties of directors as follows:

   Member States shall lay down rules to ensure that, where there is a likelihood of insolvency, directors have the following obligations:

   (a) to take immediate steps to minimise the loss for creditors, workers, shareholders and other stakeholders;
   (b) to have due regard to the interests of creditors and other stakeholders;
   (c) to take reasonable steps to avoid insolvency;
   (d) to avoid deliberate or grossly negligent conduct that threatens the viability of the business.

   Critically evaluate this draft provision. Which elements are borrowed from section 214 of the Insolvency Act 1986? Do you think that wrongful trading is an adequate model for a European

[276] A Keay, 'Wrongful Trading and the Liability of Company Directors: a Theoretical Perspective' (2005) 25 Legal Studies 431, 434.

[277] *Re MC Bacon Ltd (No 2)* [1991] Ch 127.

[278] Insolvency (England and Wales) Rules 2016, rr 6.42, 7.108. Pursuant to Insolvency Act 1986, s 176ZA, as introduced by Companies Act 2006, s 1282, the liquidator's expenses have priority over both preferential claims and assets secured by a floating charge, thus overruling the result of *Buchler v Talbot* [2004] 2 WLR 582.

[279] Davies and Worthington (n 13) para 9-10.

[280] B Cheffins, *Company Law: Theory, Structure and Operation* (OUP 1997) 542.

[281] *Re Sherbourne Associates Ltd* [1995] BCC 40; *Re Continental Assurance Co of London Plc (No 4)* (n 261) para 99.

[282] Cheffins (n 280).

[283] A Reisberg and A Donovan, *Pettet, Lowry and Reisberg's Company Law* (5th edn, Pearson Longman 2018) 53–4.

[284] Report of the High-level Group of Company Law Experts on a Modern Regulatory Framework for Company Law in Europe (Brussels, 2002) ch III, 4.4; Communication from the Commission to the Council and the European Parliament, Modernising Company Law and Enhancing Corporate Governance in the European Union: A Plan to Move Forward, COM(2003) 284 final, 3.1.3. However, in the Commission's public consultation, launched in December 2005, on the future priorities for the Action Plan the proposal to introduce a pan-European rule against 'wrongful trading' was rejected by a vast majority of participants.

harmonization measure? What are the potential obstacles to the effectiveness of the draft provision across the EU?

4. Of some significance are the provisions on transaction avoidance that allow the liquidator or administrator to reverse transactions entered into by the company to the detriment of its creditors. Sections 238 to 241 of the Insolvency Act 1986—transactions at an undervalue and unlawful preferences—apply when the company is in liquidation or administration. At the time of the transaction at issue, the company must have been insolvent or must have become insolvent as a result of the transaction. Transactions can only be reversed if they were entered into within two years, or in respect of preferences given to a person not 'connected with the company',[285] six months before the onset of insolvency.[286] No such restrictions apply in respect of section 423 of the Insolvency Act 1986 regarding 'transactions defrauding creditors'. An application under this provision may even be made by any 'victim of the transaction',[287] including a single creditor. The applicant must, however, establish that the transaction had the purpose of putting the assets beyond the reach of creditors. Fraudulent or other dishonest motives are not required; the provision will apply even in cases where the transaction has been carried out in the best interest of the creditors as a whole.[288]

5. Interestingly, in a string of first instance decisions directors were held liable, when sued by the office holder, for making payments to certain creditors at a time when the respective company was insolvent, insolvency proceedings imminent and the payment entailed a personal benefit for the authorizing director.[289] Although the underlying transactions resembled (unlawful) preferences, the decisions were based on the doctrine, widely attributed to *West Mercia Safetywear v Dodd*,[290] that where the company is in (the vicinity of) insolvency its directors must have due regard to the interests of corporate creditors. Whereas a preference action pursuant to section 239 Insolvency Act 1986 would be aimed against the recipient of the payment, here the authorizing directors (in addition or alternatively) were ordered to restore the paid-out amounts to the company. Whether this additional remedy will stand the test of time and find wider acceptance remains to be seen.[291]

III. Liability based on tort law

When managers and controlling shareholders commit a tortious act in the course of the management of a company the latter will be vicariously liable; however, the manager or controlling shareholder who actually committed the act may also be liable as the primary tortfeasor.[292] This liability of managers and shareholders is not actually an exception to the principle of limited liability. It rather reinforces the separation of company and its shareholders. The latter will be liable not for the company's obligations but for their own tortious acts. These cases, therefore, do not concern a 'piercing of the corporate veil'; rather, a 'going around the corporate veil'. The main problem seems to be to define the cases in which managers and controlling shareholders owe a duty of care to third parties.

One of the main issues in recent years has been whether and under what circumstances a parent company may be held liable based on negligence for personal injuries and consequential loss suffered by the employees of its (foreign) subsidiaries.[293] The facts in *Connelly* and *Lubbe* were very similar. The plaintiffs were employed by Namibian or, respectively,

[285] Connected with a company are directors and shadow directors as well as their associates and the associates of the company: Insolvency Act 1986, s 249.

[286] ibid s 240(1) and (3).

[287] ibid ss 423(5), 424(1)(c).

[288] *Arbuthnot Leasing International Ltd v Havelet Leasing Ltd (No 2)* [1990] BCC 636, 644.

[289] *Re Cityspan Ltd* [2008] BCC 60; *Re HLC Environmental Projects Ltd* [2014] BCC 337; *Re Micra Contracts Ltd (in liquidation)* [2016] BCC 153; *Re Cosy Seal Insulation Ltd (in administration)* [2016] 2 BCLC 319.

[290] *West Marcia Safetywear Ltd (in liquidation) v Dodd and Another* [1988] BCLC 250; see further Chapter 11B.

[291] K van Zwieten, 'Director Liability in Insolvency and Its Vicinity' (2018) 38 OJLS 382-409.

[292] Reisberg and Donovan (n 283) 44.

[293] *Connelly v RTZ Corporation Plc* [1998] AC 854; *Lubbe v Cape Industries Plc* [2000] 1 WLR 1545.

South African companies mining uranium or asbestos. Years later, when they developed uranium or asbestos-related illnesses they sued the English holding companies based on negligence. Their claim was that the respective parent company itself was responsible for ensuring the observance of adequate standards of health and safety by its foreign subsidiaries and that the parent companies had failed to take adequate steps through their servants and agents to protect the plaintiffs from harm. The House of Lords decided only on the question of jurisdiction, holding that the respective cases could be tried in the UK. *Lubbe* was settled extra-judicially. However, the House of Lords seemed to accept at least in principle that there could be a duty of care on the parent company regarding health and safety of the employees of its subsidiaries. Lord Bingham held that

> resolution of this issue would be likely to involve an inquiry into what part the defendant played in controlling the operations of the group, what its directors and employees knew or ought to have known, what action was taken and not taken, whether the defendant owed a duty of care to employees of group companies overseas and whether, if so, that duty was broken.[294]

Connelly was subsequently dismissed by the High Court because the limitation period had expired. However, Wright J also accepted that under certain circumstances a parent company could owe a duty of care to its subsidiary's employees. That it is generally the employer who owes a duty of care to its employees does not preclude other persons from owing a duty of care as well. In particular, where 'an employer has entirely handed over responsibility for devising, installing and operating the various safety precautions required of an employer to an independent contractor, then that contractor may owe a duty of care to the individual employee which is virtually coterminous with that of the employer himself'.[295] According to the judge, this was what the plaintiff's statement of claim alleged, namely that the parent company had taken into its own hands the responsibility for devising an appropriate policy for health and safety to be operated at the subsidiary, and that the parent supervised the implementation of this policy through its own employees, who acted as supervisors at the subsidiary. If these allegations were true, the ensuing situation was likely to comprehend the three elements of proximity, foreseeability and reasonableness necessary to give rise to a duty of care. These considerations have been confirmed by the Court of Appeal in *Chandler v Cape*:

***Chandler v Cape plc* [2012] EWCA Civ 525**

Mr Chandler was an employee of Cape Products, a wholly owned subsidiary of Cape plc. Working outdoors, he was exposed to asbestos dust emanating from an asbestos factory with open sides operated by Cape Products at the site where Mr Chandler worked. More than 50 years later, Mr Chandler contracted asbestosis, at a time when Cape Products had already been dissolved; Cape Product's employer's liability insurance included an exception for asbestosis. Cape plc admitted that Cape Products were negligent in managing the site. However, Mr Chandler argued that Cape plc was in breach of a duty of care owed to him directly as an employee of Cape Products.

Lady Justice Arden:

62. The basis on which the judge found there was a duty of care on the part of Cape is on the basis of an assumption of responsibility. This falls within the second and third parts of the three-part Caparo test for determining whether there is a duty of care, namely proximity and the further requirement that it be fair, just and reasonable to impose liability. These two requirements are directed to the essentially same question. As Lord Oliver pointed out in Caparo:

> 'Proximity' is, no doubt a convenient expression so long as it is realised that it is no more than a label which embraces not a definable concept but merely a description of circumstances in which, pragmatically, the courts conclude that a duty of care exists'. (page 633)

294 *Lubbe v Cape Industries Plc* [2000] 1 WLR 1545, 1555 (Lord Bingham).
295 *Connelly v RTZ Corporation Plc* (n 293) 538.

63. The development of the law of negligence has to be incremental and the judge was in my judgment correct to hold that the analogous line of cases in negligence to the instant case is the line of authority on the duty of a person to intervene to prevent damage to another. As Lord Goff pointed out in Smith v Littlewoods Ltd [1987] AC 241 at 270, there is in general no duty to prevent third parties causing damage to another. But Lord Goff recognised that there were exceptions to this principle, for example where there was 'a relationship between the parties which gives rise to an imposition or assumption of responsibility' on the part of the defendant (page 272D).

64. Lord Goff speaks of the imposition or assumption of responsibility. Whether a party has assumed responsibility is a question of law. The court does not have to find that the relevant party has voluntarily assumed responsibility (see also on this point Customs and Excise Commissioners v Barclays Bank [2007] 1 AC 181, cited by Mr Weir). The word 'assumption' is therefore something of a misnomer. The phrase 'attachment' of responsibility might be more accurate.

...

69. I would emphatically reject any suggestion that this court is in any way concerned with what is usually referred to as piercing the corporate veil. A subsidiary and its company are separate entities. There is no imposition or assumption of responsibility by reason only that a company is the parent company of another company.

70. The question is simply whether what the parent company did amounted to taking on a direct duty to the subsidiary's employees.

...

73. In the present case, Cape was clearly in the practice of issuing instructions about the products of the company, for instance, about product mixes. We know that Cape Products could not incur capital expenditure without parent company approval. Cape's board minutes show that Cape approved the separate administration of Cape Products' operations 'in accordance with company policy' of Cape. There is nothing wrong in that but it suggests that the company policy of Cape on subsidiaries was that there were certain matters in respect of which they were subject to parent company direction. No doubt the illness of the employee of Cape Products which brought Dr Smither to Uxbridge had had to be reported to Cape under directions given by Cape.

74. I accept Mr Stuart-Smith's submission that Cape was not responsible for the actual implementation of health and safety measures at Cape Products. However, as Mr Weir points out, the problem in the present case was not due to non-compliance with recognised extraction procedures. It was due to dust in the atmosphere in the part of the Cowley Works in which Mr Chandler worked and which was not used for asbestos production. There is no evidence that what went wrong here was that Cape Products failed to maintain some dust extraction machines in the asbestos factory and in any event it is difficult to see how such machines could have avoided the escape of dust given the open sides of the factory. As the judge observed, the problem was systemic.

75. The configuration of the asbestos factory dated back to the time when Cape introduced its Pluto board manufacturing business into the Cowley Works. By installing its business there, it must have implicitly undertaken a duty of care to ensure that its business was carried on without risk to the employees in the other business of Cape Products carried on at the Cowley Works. In due course, it required Cape to purchase this business. Nonetheless, despite the sale, it maintained a certain level of control over the asbestos business carried on at Uxbridge. Products were for instance to be manufactured in accordance with its product specification. Product development, with a group chief chemist, was carried out in the Central Laboratory at Barking. Cape moreover had superior knowledge about the asbestos business. It was in a substantial way of business and its resources far exceeded those of Cape Products. Dr Smither was doing research into the link between asbestos dust and asbestosis and related diseases. He was also (if this label makes any difference) the group medical adviser of Cape.

76. Added to those factors was the role played by Dr Smither. Whether or not he was formally appointed group medical adviser in the relevant period, it is clear that he was engaged on research, based on empirical research done at Cape and its asbestos-producing subsidiaries, about the relationship between asbestos production and asbestosis ... Dr Smither must have known about the risks during some part or all of the relevant period. ... I do not see on what basis his

work could have been inspired by a personal research interest given that there is no evidence that he was carrying out this work privately and not for Cape's benefit. ...

77. Cape concedes that the system of work at Cape Products was defective. The judge inevitably found as a fact—and there is no appeal from this—that Cape was fully aware of the 'systemic failure' which resulted from the escape of dust from a factory with no sides. Cape therefore knew that the Uxbridge asbestos business was carried on in a way which risked the health and safety of others at Uxbridge, most particularly the employees engaged in the brick making business.

78. Given Cape's state of knowledge about the Cowley Works, and its superior knowledge about the nature and management of asbestos risks, I have no doubt that in this case it is appropriate to find that Cape assumed a duty of care either to advise Cape Products on what steps it had to take in the light of knowledge then available to provide those employees with a safe system of work or to ensure that those steps were taken. The scope of the duty can be defined in either way. Whichever way it is formulated, the injury to Mr Chandler was the result. As the judge held, working on past performance and viewing the matter realistically, Cape could, and did on other matters, give Cape Products instructions as to how it was to operate with which, so far as we know, it duly complied.

79. In these circumstances, there was, in my judgment, a direct duty of care owed by Cape to the employees of Cape Products. There was an omission to advise on precautionary measures even though it was doing research and that research had not established (nor could it establish) that the asbestosis and related diseases were not caused by asbestos dust. Moreover, while I have reached my conclusion in my own words and following my own route, it turns out that, in all essential respects, my reasoning follows the analysis of the judge in paragraphs 61 and 72 to 75 of his judgment.

80. In summary, this case demonstrates that in appropriate circumstances the law may impose on a parent company responsibility for the health and safety of its subsidiary's employees. Those circumstances include a situation where, as in the present case, (1) the businesses of the parent and subsidiary are in a relevant respect the same; (2) the parent has, or ought to have, superior knowledge on some relevant aspect of health and safety in the particular industry; (3) the subsidiary's system of work is unsafe as the parent company knew, or ought to have known; and (4) the parent knew or ought to have foreseen that the subsidiary or its employees would rely on its using that superior knowledge for the employees' protection. For the purposes of (4) it is not necessary to show that the parent is in the practice of intervening in the health and safety policies of the subsidiary. The court will look at the relationship between the companies more widely. The court may find that element (4) is established where the evidence shows that the parent has a practice of intervening in the trading operations of the subsidiary, for example production and funding issues.

Questions and comments:

1. *Chandler v Cape* is the first reported case in which a parent company was found to be in breach of a duty of care vis-à-vis the employees of one of its subsidiaries with damages being awarded.[296] The guidelines for ascertaining the existence of a duty of care, in respect of health and safety, owed by a parent company to the employees of its subsidiary spelled out by Lady Justice Arden have the potential of profoundly reshaping the principle of limited liability. Although 'emphatically' rejecting any suggestion that the case involves a piercing of the corporate veil, if rigorously applied these guidelines may significantly reduce the possibility to impose negative externalities through judgment-proof subsidiaries. It has been said that if these guidelines could be extended so as to cover situations where control is not established by equity holdings but by long-term supply contracts, multi-national corporations could potentially be liable for appalling working conditions at their suppliers' factories in developing countries around the world.[297] Do you agree?

[296] See also *Thompson v Renwick Group plc* [2014] EWCA Civ 635.

[297] A Sanger, 'Crossing the Corporate Veil: The Duty of Care Owed by a Parent Company to the Employees of its Subsidiary' (2012) 71 Cambridge Law Journal 478, 480–1.

2. In the context of a dispute concerning the jurisdiction of the English courts to try claims against a Zambian subsidiary together with claims against the English parent the *Chandler* test has been refined and extended beyond a subsidiary's employees to those 'affected by the operations of the subsidiary.' Through its Zambian subsidiary the English parent operated a copper mine in Zambia that polluted local waterways thereby causing damage to the communities reliant on clean water in the area.[298] Reviewing the case law, Simon LJ said:

> 83. It seems to me that certain propositions can be derived from these cases which may be material to the question of whether a duty is owed by a parent company to those affected by the operations of a subsidiary. (1) The starting point is the three-part test of foreseeability, proximity and reasonableness. (2) A duty may be owed by a parent company to the employee of a subsidiary, or a party directly affected by the operations of that subsidiary, in certain circumstances. (3) Those circumstances may arise where the parent company (a) has taken direct responsibility for devising a material health and safety policy the adequacy of which is the subject of the claim, or (b) controls the operations which give rise to the claim. (4) *Chandler v Cape Plc* and *Thompson v The Renwick Group Plc* describe some of the circumstances in which the three-part test may, or may not, be satisfied so as to impose on a parent company responsibility for the health and safety of a subsidiary's employee. (5) The first of the four indicia in *Chandler v Cape Plc* [80], requires not simply that the businesses of the parent and the subsidiary are in the relevant respect the same, but that the parent is well placed, because of its knowledge and expertise to protect the employees of the subsidiary. If both parent and subsidiary have similar knowledge and expertise and they jointly take decisions about mine safety, which the subsidiary implements, both companies may (depending on the circumstances) owe a duty of care to those affected by those decisions. (6) Such a duty may be owed in analogous situations, not only to employees of the subsidiary but to those affected by the operations of the subsidiary. (7) The evidence sufficient to establish the duty may not be available at the early stages of the case. Much will depend on whether, in the words of Wright J, the pleading represents the actuality.

Assessing whether there was 'a properly arguable case or serious question to be tried' between the claimants and the parent so as to establish jurisdiction also in respect of claims against the subsidiary, a unanimous Court of Appeal concluded that, on the basis of the facts as pleaded, there was a serious question to be tried.[299]

3. The question of tortious liability of directors also arose in the context of contractual negotiations in the name and on behalf of the company. If the tortious act in question is of a fraudulent nature the director will not be able to escape liability even if the tort can also be attributed to the company.[300] If mere negligent conduct is involved, the director's personal liability will depend on whether the claimant can rely on the principle set out in *Hedley Byrne v Heller & Partners Ltd.*[301] The House of Lords (Lord Steyn) held in *Williams v Natural Life Health Foods Ltd*[302] that in order to establish personal liability under the principle of *Hedley Byrne*, which requires the existence of a special relationship between plaintiff and tortfeasor, it is not sufficient that there should have been a special relationship with the principal. There must have been an assumption of responsibility such as to create a special relationship with the director or employee himself.

[298] *Lungowe and Others v Vedanta Resources Plc, Konkala Copper Mines Plc* [2017] EWCA Civ 1528.

[299] ibid para 90. An appeal is currently pending in the Supreme Court of the United Kingdom. In two other cases with similar factual backgrounds the Court for Appeal rejected the jurisdiction of the English courts on the basis of the pleaded facts, unanimously in *AAA and Others v Unilever Plc, Unilever Tea Kenya Ltd* [2018] EWCA Civ 1532, by a majority in *Okpabi and Others v Royal Dutch Shell Plc, Shell Petroleum Development Company of Nigeria Ltd* [2018] EWCA Civ 191.

[300] *Standard Chartered Bank v Pakistan National Shipping Corporation* [2003] AC 959.

[301] [1964] AC 465. [302] [1998] 2 All ER 577.

The test is an objective one:[303] 'whether the plaintiff could reasonably rely on the assumption of personal responsibility by the individual who performed the services on behalf of the company'.

E. France

Under French law, 'piercing the corporate veil' can be achieved on the basis of a number of different concepts. The Code de commerce contains several provisions that may impose civil liability on those in charge of the company. These provisions can be found in the law relating to private (SARL) and public companies (SA),[304] and, more importantly, in the law on corporate insolvency.[305] In this respect, case law has the conceptually limited, but practically very important, role of elucidating the often rather vague statutory terminology. Further concepts, entirely developed by case law, deal with situations where the company is essentially indistinguishable from its shareholder/parent company (*société fictive/confusion de patrimoines*).

I. Civil liability under company law legislation

Pursuant to Com Articles L223-22 and L225-251, respectively, those in charge of a SARL or a SA may personally or jointly and severally be liable vis-à-vis the company or third parties (*envers les tiers*) for any breach of company law and regulation, for any breach of a provision in the articles of association and, in particular, for any error committed in respect of the management of the company (*fautes commises dans leur gestion*). Com Article L223-22 applies to de jure directors of a SARL, but not to de facto directors.[306] As for the SA, Com Article L225-251 expressly covers the members of the management board (*administrateurs*) and the managing director or chief executive officer (*directeur général*). If the SA has a two-tier board structure, Com Article L225-251 only applies to the members of the board of directors (*directoire*).[307] The liability of the members of the supervisory board is determined by Com Article L225-257 and is severely restricted.

Both provisions allow 'third parties', in particular creditors, to pursue the company's managers directly for an actionable loss that the creditor may have suffered as a result of mismanagement of the company's affairs. Therefore, to the extent that the preconditions for liability vis-à-vis third parties are being met, the veil constituted by the company to protect the management from direct attacks by third parties is withdrawn.[308] The classical elements of liability are: (i) a fault on the part of the defendant, (ii) a loss suffered on the part of the claimant, and (iii) a causal link between fault and loss.[309]

As for (i), the Code de commerce enumerates three different types of fault: breach of statutory or regulatory provisions applicable to the SARL or the SA including rules on the functioning of the management board or the workings of the general meeting;[310] breach of the articles of association, in particular disregard for the limits of power provided for;[311] and, most importantly, fault in the management of the company (*faut de gestion*). The criteria for establishing a fault in management rest on the notion of the interest of the company (*intérêt social*).[312] A director commits a fault of management if he acts contrary to the interest of the company. Establishing a fault requires an assessment of the attitude of the respective director at the time and in the circumstances of the case as compared to what

303 Davies and Worthington (n 13) para 7-32.
304 Com Arts L223-22 and L225-251.
305 Com Art L641-2.
306 P Merle, *Droit commercial: Sociétés commerciales* (22nd edn, Dalloz 2018/2019) para 236 (n 3)..
307 Com Art L225-256.
308 M Cozian, A Viandier, and F Deboissy, *Droit des sociétés* (31st edn, LexisNexis 2018) para 405.
309 Merle (n 306) para 458.
310 ibid.
311 ibid.
312 Cozian, Viandier, and Deboissy (n 308) para 394.

a diligent director would have done. In general, a fault of management may be committed intentionally, negligently or by a mere oversight.[313] However, when it comes to the liability of management vis-à-vis third parties a far stricter standard is to be applied. Incompetence or negligence is no longer sufficient. Case law requires an act that is disconnected from the normal functions of management. A director will be liable only if he intentionally commits a fault of particular gravity incompatible with the normal office of a director,[314] although a criminal act is not necessarily required. The following is one of the leading cases on this issue:

Cour de cassation, Chambre commerciale, Appeal Nr. 99-17092, 20 May 2003

Whereas, according to the decision (Saint Denis de La Réunion, 4 May 1999), Mrs X, in her position as managing director for the firm SBTR, assigned to SATI two claims that she had assigned already to the Bank of La Réunion; SATI asked that Mrs X be held liable to repay the damages resulting from the lack of repayments in regards of the assigned claims;

On the first ground of appeal:

Whereas Mrs X disagrees with the judgment confirming her liability; according to the argument that the personal responsibility of a managing director can only be upheld if he has committed an error that can be separated from his functions and which is personally attributable to him; on the observations of the decision that SBTR, represented by their managing director Mrs X, assigned to SATI, as consideration for the delivery of materials, two independent claims against SEMADER and SHLMR after having assigned these claims to the Bank of La Réunion; that in holding Mrs X personally liable to repay the damage caused by the fact that SATI was not able to enforce the claims assigned to it; in holding that Mrs X had committed a fault that was separable from her duties without characterising the assignment of the two claims by her, both for and in the name of SBTR, as an act alien to the exercise of her duties as managing director, the Appeal Court decided in breach of [what is now Article L223-22 Code de commerce];

But although the personal liability of a managing director vis-à-vis third parties can only be upheld if he has made a mistake that can be separated from his duties; this will also be the case if the managing director intentionally commits a fault of particular severity that is incompatible with his fiduciary duties;

Given that Mrs X deliberately misled SATI about the solvency of the company she was managing, which allowed her to take advantage of deliveries which without such scheming she would not have been able to obtain, the Appeal Court correctly deduced that Mrs X had made an error that was detachable from her duties triggering her personal responsibility; the [appellant's] reasoning is not justified.

On the second and third grounds of appeal:

Given that Mrs X holds the decision to be incorrect also on the following reasons:

1. That Mrs X had assigned to the Bank of La Réunion only a fraction of the claim the company was owed by SEMADER . . . so that in respect of the remaining part of the claim the transfers to SATI was perfectly valid; by not considering this point in its verdict in order to establish the degree of fault and the amount of damage caused by the assignment, the Appeal Court decided in breach of Article 455 of the New Code on Civil Procedure [pursuant to which the judgment must consider all the points raised by the parties];
2. That in order to uphold the liability of Mrs X for the damages suffered by SATI resulting from the non-payment of claims assigned by SBTR, the Appeal Court only affirmed that in twice assigning the same claim, the appellant had deliberately misled SATI as to the solvency of SBTR; that, however, Mrs X relied on the fact that SATI and SBTR had concluded an agreement on 24 May 1995, before the transfers of the controversial claims, with the aim of determining the terms of repayment of SBTR's obligations vis-à-vis SATI; hence SATI was fully aware of the financial difficulties of SBTR and was at fault itself when accepting the controversial assignment, the Appeal Court has deprived its decision of the legal basis of

[313] Merle (n 306) para 458.

[314] Cozian, Viandier, and Deboissy (n 308) para 407–9.

Articles 1382 and 1383 of the Code civil [Articles 1240, 1241: tortious liability for damage caused intentionally or negligently].

But considering that the Appeal Court does neither have to reply to the unproven allegation of a partial transfer nor does it have to research automatically a possible imprudent mistake that was not invoked in front of it; these grounds of appeal are unjustified.

On these grounds: appeal rejected.

Questions and comments:

1. The reason for holding Mrs X liable was that by assigning a claim twice she deliberately (and fraudulently) misrepresented the financial situation of the company. This made it impossible for the creditor to appreciate the risk of default correctly. Without having to pay for it, Mrs X's company could carry on doing business with the materials delivered by the creditor and could generate a benefit for the company and its shareholders at the expense of the creditor. In this respect the decision is well in line with the economic rationale for disregarding the corporate veil.
2. As the case shows, liability vis-à-vis third parties is triggered only in cases of a 'deliberate fault of particular severity' that is separable from the regular office of director. This requirement restricts liability under Com Articles L223-22 and L225-251 effectively to cases of outright fraud and other criminal offences committed by the management. On the other hand, vis-à-vis the company and its shareholders any management fault suffices. This seems to be paradoxical: after all, the shareholders have the power to appoint and remove the directors from office, whereas third parties, in principle, have no influence on the management of the company. How can this difference in treatment be explained and justified?
3. The following are further examples of a fault disconnected from the normal office of director or manager:
   A director and majority shareholder changed the name, registered office, and objects of the company in order to disguise the fact that they were selling products similar to those of a client company.[315]
   A SARL had a mandate to sell a sports car on behalf of the owner. The owner of the car specifically instructed the director to use the car only for test drives. However, the company director allowed his relatives to use the car. They then had an accident and abandoned the car on the motorway.[316]
   Co-directors of a company operating a services station at a motorway hid the signs of the oil company from which they were leasing the station and sold petrol acquired on the free market on their own account.[317]
   The director of a company under whose name the company's vehicle was insured authorized an employee to use the vehicle at a time when the insurance contract had been terminated because the director had failed to pay the insurance premium.[318]
4. Given these examples, how should the liability under Articles L223-22 and L225-251 Code de commerce be conceptualized? Is it company law, contract law or tort law; piercing the corporate veil, or rather going around it?

If the strict requirements for liability can be established directors may be liable personally and individually or jointly and severally. A director will be liable individually if the management fault can be attributed to him individually and the other directors have had no part in the fault whatsoever. Otherwise, directors will be liable jointly and severally; if, for instance, the managing director has committed a fault and the other members of the board failed to

[315] CA Paris, 10 September 1999 (12/1999) *Revue de jurisprudence de droit des affairs* (RJDA) 1345.

[316] CA Paris, 22 March 2002 (8-9/2002) *Revue de jurisprudence de droit des affairs* (RJDA) 901.

[317] Cass com, 8 February 2005 (2005) *Bull. Joly* §193, 855.

[318] Cass com, 4 July 2006 (2006) Dalloz 1958.

supervise him effectively. In order to exonerate himself, a director will have to protest against a decision he objects to at a board meeting and make sure that this protest is duly recorded in the minutes. Simply voting against a decision at a board meeting may be insufficient to avoid liability. If a director frequently objects to the decisions taken by the board, he should probably resign.[319]

II. Civil liability based on insolvency legislation

Of great practical importance is an action provided for under the law of insolvency, originally developed by case law going back to the second half of the nineteenth century and first codified as *action en comblement du passif* in Article 99 of the Bankruptcy Code of 1967 and subsequently in Article 180 of the Bankruptcy Code of 1985. In 2000, the provision became part of the revised Code de commerce as Article L624-3 and can now be found, after further changes in 2005[320] and 2008,[321] in Com Article L651-2 as *action de la responsabilité pour insuffisance d'actif*. This action allows company directors to be held liable for management faults that have contributed to an excess of liabilities over assets where the company has entered insolvent liquidation.

Pursuant to Com Article L651-1, the action applies in respect of all entities established under French private law that have a separate legal personality, irrespective of whether they conduct a business activity or not (non-profit organizations). This includes not just public and private companies (SA, SAS, SARL), but also commercial partnerships, general and limited, as well as the civil law partnership pursuant to Civ., article 1832.[322] The action is usually classified as insolvency law and, pursuant to Article 7(1) of the 2015 European Insolvency Regulation may, therefore, be applied in respect of a company formed under the law of another EU Member State, but having its centre of main interest in France.[323] Since 19 February 2009 the action may only be initiated if the company has entered insolvent liquidation (*liquidation judiciaire*).[324]

Suitable defendants are de jure and de facto managers (*dirigeants de droit ou de fait*). De jure managers are those who have actually been appointed as managers in conformity with the statutory provisions and the articles of association. The notion encompasses in respect of a SARL its directors; in respect of the one-tier SA the members of the management board and the chief executive; in respect of the two-tier SA the members of the management board only, whereas the members of the supervisory board may be de facto directors if they have exercised an independent management activity.[325] In respect of a company incorporated in another EU member state the question as to who is a director is determined not by French law, but by the law of incorporation.[326] De facto managers are persons who, irrespective of their appointment, actually exercise the powers of management and effectively control the business of the company. A factual authority, which translates into positive acts of management, suffices. The mere holding of a controlling majority of shares and voting in the general meeting is, without further involvement in the running of the company, insufficient to classify a person as de facto manager. However, controlling shareholders, parent companies, and banks may be de facto directors if they exert their influence actively, regularly, and independently on the management of the company, where this translates into actual management decisions and transactions.[327]

[319] Merle (n 306) para 459. [320] Loi 2005-845 of 26 July 2005.

[321] Ordonnance No 2008-1345 of 18 December 2008, Art 131.

[322] M Jeantin and P Le Cannu, *Droit commercial: Entreprises en difficulté* (7th edn, Dalloz 2006) para 1249.

[323] ibid para 1250.

[324] Previously, it could also be initiated where a rescue plan (Articles L626-1 Code de commerce) or a reorganization plan (Article L631-19 Code de commerce) had been terminated by the court. The change was introduced by Ordonnance No 2008-1345 of 18 December 2008, Art 131.

[325] Jeantin and Le Cannu (n 322) paras 1251–60. [326] ibid para 1257.

[327] ibid paras 1261–5.

The action must be initiated at the court seized with the liquidation proceedings of the debtor company. Only the liquidator or the public prosecutor may initiate it.[328] Individual creditors do not have standing. However, the creditors' committee (*contrôleurs*) may initiate the action if this is in the best interest of the creditors collectively. Initiation by the creditors' committee is of strictly subsidiary nature.[329] It is only possible if the liquidator has failed to initiate the action and has left a default notice delivered to him unanswered for two months.[330]

Under Article 99 of the Bankruptcy Code of 1967 (*action en comblement du passif*), if the claimant could prove an excess of liability over assets it was presumed that the defendant had committed a management fault and that there was a causal link between fault and excess of liabilities.[331] Today, the *action en responsabilité pour insuffisance d'actif* resembles a traditional tort lawsuit whose specific objective is to compensate a loss suffered by the creditors collectively. Consequently, Com Article L.651-2 relies on the three basic prerequisites for a tort lawsuit: (management) fault, loss, and a causal link between the two, with the burden of proof being on the claimant.[332]

Management fault is any fault committed in the management of the enterprise. Typical examples are breach of fundamental rules of management such as (internally binding) limits of authority; accounting irregularities; payment of excessive remuneration; excessive borrowing that goes beyond the financial capabilities of the company; badly thought through contracts that produce a deficit that cannot be rectified by a company in financial difficulties; objectionable choice of general business policy; acquisition of stock too large to resell at a profit; pursuit of a loss making activity without any hope of restoring the company to profitable trading; formation and management of a company that is insufficiently capitalized; if the company is in a state of cessation of payment, failure to request the commencement of insolvency proceedings within forty-five days as required by Com Article L.631-4.[333] Moreover, a management fault may be committed by a mere forbearance: failure to supervise; complete passivity and carelessness; complete reliance on others; failure to make capital available if the company is in financial distress; failure of the members of the management board to meet and to discuss measures to remedy the difficulties of the company.[334] Where a management fault has been demonstrated, exoneration is not an easy task for the implicated director. He will have to show that when he acted (or refused to act) he did what a normal prudent and reasonable businessman would have done under similar circumstances. Even a management fault triggered by external causes does not automatically exclude liability.[335] 'Simple negligence' on the part of the defendant is, however, no longer sufficient.

The collective loss that has to be demonstrated by the claimant is an excess of liabilities over assets. It is somewhat unclear whether only liabilities in existence prior to the commencement of liquidation proceedings are to be taken into account or whether liabilities incurred after commencement may increase the excess of liabilities over assets. Given that creditors contracting with the company after commencement of insolvency proceedings are able to protect themselves, it is submitted that only prior liabilities count towards the excess of liabilities. The rescue procedure raises specific problems. A confirmed rescue plan replaces the debts and liabilities of the company with the obligations agreed in the plan. Hence, as long as the plan is in force, there can be no excess of liabilities over assets and an action based on Com Article L.651-2 cannot succeed. However, a management fault may

[328] Com Art L651-3. Previously the court nominee who was appointed to supervise the implementation of a rescue or reorganization plan also had standing to bring the action. With the changes introduced by Ordonnance No 2008-1345 of 18 December 2008 (Art 132), this possibility is now redundant.

[329] Jeantin and Le Cannu (n 322) para 1272.

[330] Com Art L651-3(2).

[331] Jeantin and Le Cannu (n 322) para 1292.

[332] ibid para 1316.

[333] ibid para 1293.

[334] Jeantin and Le Cannu (n 322) para 1293.

[335] ibid para 1294.

occur during the course of the procedure and the implementation of the rescue plan. If the rescue plan is later terminated and the company goes into insolvent liquidation, the excess of liabilities over assets may be the amount not covered by a sale of the business or realization of its assets pursuant to the rescue plan.[336] As for the causal link between fault and loss, it is sufficient that the management fault has contributed to the excess of liabilities over assets; it is not necessary that the *faut de gestion* was the exclusive reason or even the main reason for the loss.[337]

Com Article L651-2 confers a wide discretion to the court.[338] The court may decide which of the company's debts are to be paid, partially or in total, by the de jure or de facto directors who contributed to the management fault. Among these directors the court may impose individual liability in accordance with the respective degree of contribution to the management fault, or joint and several liability, or even a combination of both (e.g. individual liability of a director for some debts; joint and several liability of the same director together with others for other debts). The court also has the power to abstain from imposing any liability at all. However, the amount of excess of liabilities over assets constitutes an absolute limit on the amount that can be awarded under Com Article L.651-2. Although it allows taking into account the particular circumstances in each case, this wide discretion has been criticized for causing legal uncertainty and arbitrariness.[339] Sums recovered under Com Article L.651-2 are part of the assets of the company. They are to be distributed among the company's creditors, without regard to their order of priority or existing security interests.[340]

Cour de cassation, Chambre commerciale, Case 96-15827 of 29 February 2000

Whereas, according to the case (Douai, 28 March 1996) before the court, Mr B, president of the board of directors of the company Semade in liquidation, was found to be criminally liable for the abuse of corporate assets and for damages vis-à-vis Mr S, liquidator of the company; the latter sued in front of the tribunal for commerce seeking a declaration of personal bankruptcy of Mr B and an order against him to repay the debts of the company;

On the first grounds of appeal, based on three grounds

Whereas Mr B appeals against the decision that condemns him to pay, in order to contribute to the company's excess of liabilities over assets, the sum of 125,000 Francs; according to the appeal, when the liquidation of a legal entity reveals an excess of liabilities over assets, [what is now Com., article L.651-2] provides for a civil action for payment of the company's debts against the de jure or de facto managing director responsible for the administration of the company if a management error has contributed to the excess of liabilities over assets; that this action cannot be brought in addition to a lawsuit for liability under the general law; that in consequence, the liquidator, who has obtained in the criminal courts reparations for damages caused by a crime committed by the managing director, is inadmissible to bring an action for contribution to the excess of liabilities over assets based on the same management mistake; that in allowing that action by the liquidator against Mr B, although the liquidator had received reparations in criminal courts, the appeal court acted in breach of [what is now Com., article L.651-2 and article 1240] of the Civil Code; whilst, moreover, the existence and the total sum of the excess of liabilities over assets must be appreciated at the exact moment when the court was seized with the claim for the payment for all or part of the debts of the company, by holding Mr B liable for part of the company's debts based on a future excess of liabilities over assets, the Appeal Court acted in breach of [what is now Com., article L.651-2]; and whilst, finally, the existence of an excess of liabilities over assets must be certain; that it must be the actual result of the running of the business and that the liability must be the one that existed at the date of the opening of proceedings as determined by the creditors' verification procedure; that in establishing a minimal excess of liabilities over assets based on a simple evaluation

336 ibid para 1298.
337 ibid para 1299.
338 ibid para 1285.
339 ibid.
340 ibid para 1309.

of the company's real estate, the Appeal Court acted in breach of [what is now Com., article L.651-2];

But considering, firstly, that apart from the criminal liability for the abuse of corporate assets by lending them to a personal friend consented to by Mr B, as a result of the management fault the company suffered a loss in that it could take out credit only against increased fees; thus the Appeal Court was able to justify its decision;

Considering, secondly, that the Appeal Court, who evaluated the excess of liabilities over assets at the time when it ruled, in accordance with the best evaluation presented for the real estate which still formed part of the assets of the company and that there remained only a minimal sum of excess of liability over assets, the decision to hold Mr B liable to repay part of this sum, under deduction of the sum paid on the criminal conviction, is justified;

From which it follows that the appeal can be successful on none of the three grounds.

And on the second ground of appeal, based on the second and third grounds;

Whereas Mr B still reproaches the decision for having declared him personally bankrupt for a period of 5 years, according to the appeal, whilst entangling the responsibilities of managing director of a company and the function of the mayor does not constitute a case susceptible to justifying the pronouncement of personal bankruptcy of the said managing director; that in deciding to the contrary, the Appeal Court acted in breach of Articles 182, 188 and 189 of the law of the 25th January 1985; and whilst, on the other hand, the fact that a managing director responsible for the administration of a company in liquidation has been sentenced for abuse of corporate assets does not necessarily justify the pronouncement of his personal bankruptcy for having disposed of the assets of the legal entity as if they were his own; that in deciding to the contrary, the Appeal Court acted in breach of Articles 182 and 188 of the law of the 25th January 1985;

But considering that after having revealed that Mr B had been declared guilty of the crime of abuse of corporate assets, of which he was charged in accordance with [what is now Com., article L241-3], the Appeal Court has but only used the powers granted by Article 188 of the same law in pronouncing a measure of personal bankruptcy; that its decision is legally justified and that the appeal can be successful on neither of its two grounds;

On these grounds—Appeal rejected.

Questions and comments:

1. Misappropriation of the company's assets by the managing director without more amounts to a management fault in the sense of Com Article L651-2. Mr B had used the company's assets as if they were his own. This reveals an attitude incompatible with the tasks and responsibilities of a managing director. The issue in this case was, however, whether the liquidator could bring an action based on Com Article L651-2 in addition to compensation already received pursuant to a ruling by the criminal courts based on the same acts of Mr B. The court held that an action based on Com Article L651-2 was possible because the company had suffered a loss that went beyond the mere misappropriation of its assets. The creditworthiness of the company had been reduced. Consequently it could obtain credit only against higher cost. This justified the application of Com Article L651-2.
2. In order to obtain compensation for a loss suffered by a creditor personally, he needs to prove, pursuant to Com Articles L223-22 and L225-251, that the respective director committed a management fault of particular seriousness and severity separable from its regular functions as director. Conversely, compensation for a loss suffered by the creditors collectively under Com Article L651-2 merely requires the claimant to demonstrate any management fault.[341] How may this difference in treatment be justified?
3. As mentioned in the decision, courts have indicated that whenever an excess of liabilities over assets is invoked, the claimant must base his claim on Com Article L651-2 and cannot use

[341] Cozian, Viandier, and Deboissy (n 308) para 433.

general tort law or more specific (tort) provisions including Com Articles L.223-22 and 225-251. What might be the reason?

4. A liquidator who wishes to initiate an action under Com Article L651-2 may claim advances for the judicial costs from the Public Treasury pursuant to Com Article L663-1, 2 and can therefore bring an action without exposing his own resources. The members of the creditors' committee do not have this advantage. They have to advance the judicial costs themselves and will not be reimbursed if the claim fails. However, if the action is successful they will be able to claim repayment with priority.[342]
5. Criminal liability for the abuse of corporate assets pursuant to Com Articles L241-3 (SARL) and L242-6 (SA) is of utmost importance. Liability will be triggered by de jure or de facto directors using the company's property or credit, in bad faith, in a way which they know is contrary to the interests of the company, for personal purposes or for the benefit of another company or undertaking in which they are directly or indirectly involved. 'Use' of company property has a wide meaning and encompasses any act of disposition or administration of corporate assets, such as withdrawing of cash, paying excessive executive remuneration, using the company jet, yacht or car for personal purposes without compensation; also, within corporate groups, transfer of assets and rendering services between group companies at below market prices, or granting of loans or security at below market rates.[343] The 'use' of assets as such is insufficient to trigger liability. It must also be contrary to the interest of the company. This will be the case where the company's assets are reduced or the risk of such a reduction is being increased; moreover, where the director prevents the company from profiting by misappropriating a corporate opportunity; and finally, where corporate property is used for criminal purposes such as funding corruption or terrorist activity.[344] Liability further requires 'bad faith'. Negligence, passivity or ignorance is insufficient. The defendant must have known that he acted contrary to the company's interest. Finally, the corporate property must have been abused for some personal objective, in order to gain some personal benefit or to benefit an affiliated company. The benefit so obtained does not have to be of a monetary nature; reputational purposes or improved personal relationships with people in power are also sufficient.[345] If found guilty, the defendant may be sent to prison for up to five years or fined for up to €375,000. More importantly, the company, often through its liquidator, may claim within the criminal proceedings, compensation for any loss suffered as a result of the defendant's criminal acts. However, the company's creditors do not have standing to pursue this avenue for compensation.[346] The limitation period is three years, starting from the time of the criminal act.
6. Criminal liability for abuse of assets is one of the main devices to address the exploitation of one group company for the benefit of another. The transfer of assets within a group of companies may however be justified if carried out in the interest of the group as a whole. The use of corporate assets would then not be contrary to the interest of the company; in other words, the interest of the individual company is replaced by the group interest.[347] Pursuant to the *Rozenblum* doctrine,[348] the following criteria must be met in order to legitimately subordinate the interest of the company to that of the group as a whole: (i) there must be a common economic, social or financial interest shared by all the companies within the group resulting from and motivated by a coherent 'group policy'. This usually requires that the activities of the different companies are complementary to each other so that operating the different group companies together will increase the return for the group as a whole with group profits being larger than the sum of the profits of each company if they were operated separately. (ii) The advantages and disadvantages for the individual companies within the group must be appropriately balanced, and any transfers must not go beyond the financial capabilities of a disadvantaged company. Although developed in the context of criminal liability for abuse of assets, the *Rozenblum* doctrine may also be relied on in order to justify asset transfers within the framework of Com Article L651-2, or in the context of fraudulent transfer law.[349]

342 Jeantin and Le Cannu (n 322) paras 1282, 1283.
343 Cozian, Viandier, and Deboissy (n 308) para 926.
344 ibid para 848–50.
345 ibid paras 854–6.
346 ibid paras 860–61.
347 ibid para 1888.
348 Cass crim, 4 February 1985 (1985) *Recueil Dalloz Sirey* 478 (*Rozenblum*).
349 Vandekerckhove (n 15) 227.

7. The basis of fraudulent transfer law outside bankruptcy is Civ., article 1167. A creditor may challenge in its own name transactions performed by their debtor in order to defraud their rights. This is the so-called *action paulienne*.[350] It requires, on the part of the debtor, intent to harm the creditors or at least knowledge that harm will result; and actual harm, which may consist in the debtor's assets becoming less liquid or less easily available for attachment as a result of the transaction. The action is directed against the transferee and can be initiated by creditors directly, even where the company is in insolvency proceedings.[351] In this latter case, Com Article L632-1 and 632-2 also apply. Pursuant, to Com Article L631-8, the court determines the date of the cessation of payments, without going back more than eighteen months before the date of the commencement order. Pursuant to Com Article L632-1, certain acts which occurred during this period (after the date of cessation of payments) of suspicion will be void by law, in particular all gratuitous transfers of title in movable and immovable property, and all contracts under which the obligation of the debtor substantially exceeded the obligation of the other party. On application of the office holder, the court will merely declare the nullity of these acts which comes into effect by law. In case of facultative nullity pursuant to Com Article L632-2, the court will actively decide on the nullity of a transaction, in particular gratuitous transfers within six months prior to the date of cessation of payment. In any case, a successful action will have the effect of restoring the assets of the debtor. As mentioned above, transactions within corporate groups may be justified under the *Rozenblum* doctrine.
8. Compare *action de la responsabilité pour insuffisance d'actif* and liability for wrongful trading under section 214 Insolvency Act 1986. Do these provisions provide for adequate creditor protection? What are the advantages and disadvantages of these remedies as compared to the doctrine of piercing the corporate veil under US law?
9. In *Entreprise J Lefebvre*,[352] Lefebvre established a subsidiary in form of a SARL with the legally required minimum capital in order to subcontract certain tasks. The shares of the SARL seem to have been held by straw men for the parent company. The parent exercised strict control over the subsidiary and was responsible for almost all of the latter's orders. Moreover, the parent paid the subsidiary's suppliers directly, resulting in a large amount of debt owed by the subsidiary to the parent. When the parent realized the amount of debt owed by the subsidiary it suddenly refused to intervene any further, causing the subsidiary to file for bankruptcy. The plaintiff was an unpaid creditor of the subsidiary and claimed damages from the parent on the basis of general tort law, Civ., article 1240–1241. The Court held that the parent knew from the start that the company was not viable owing to a lack of assets. The parent should have taken the necessary steps to protect subsidiary's creditors, either by making sure that the SARL did not take on obligations it could not satisfy, or by satisfying those obligations itself. By failing to do so, the parent committed torts vis-à-vis the subsidiary's creditors. Consequently, it must stand in for the unpaid debts of the subsidiary. As the case involves an excess of liabilities over assets, today the application of general tort law would be excluded by the action under Com Article L651-2. The result on the basis of the latter provision may, however, be similar.[353]

III. Identity of company and shareholders: *société fictive* and *confusion de patrimoines*

The existence of a corporate group does not automatically result in disregarding the separate legal personalities (and limited liability) of the participating companies. The doctrines of *société fictive* and *confusion de patrimoine* are important exceptions. Under both doctrines, a parent company may be held liable for the debts of a subsidiary and insolvency proceedings in respect of one member of the group may be extended so as to cover the other group members and the parent company as well.[354] As a result, insolvency proceedings may cover

350 Jeantin and Le Cannu (n 322) para 625.
351 ibid 626.
352 Cour d'appel Aix-en-Provence, 18 June 1975 (1976) *Revue Trimestrielle Droit Commerciale* 370.
353 Vandekerckhove (n 15) 137, 138.
354 Jeantin and Le Cannu (n 322) para 231; Cozian, Viandier, and Deboissy (n 308) paras 263, 2100-2.

the group as a whole with the effect that assets of all entities and persons within the group are available for distribution among the group's creditors. This is of particular importance and poses a considerable risk for groups consisting of a company that carries out the business, a second company that owns the business premises and a third company that owns the inventory.[355] This form of organization is quite common and resembles LoPucki's model for making the business enterprise 'judgment proof' in respect of involuntary creditors.[356]

The notion of *fictivité*[357] rests on the idea that, for some reason, the company is a nullity. This may be attributable to a lack of intent to form a company, or where, in order to obtain certain legal effects, in particular limited liability, the participating entities create the mere outward appearance vis-à-vis third parties of the existence of a separate legal person. Declaration of nullity does not have retroactive effect. Since *société fictive* and *confusion de patrimoines* constitute exceptions to the principle of separate legal personality, reinforced by the availability of the single member company and the recognition of the general freedom to devise group structures, strict requirements apply.[358] The company must be used as mere façade vis-à-vis third parties, or respectively, there must be a complete commingling of assets.[359] The indicators are very similar for both concepts: identical directors and shareholders, similar objects, centralization of management of the participating companies at the same place, constant business transactions between the participating companies, or a common pool of clients. However, even in combination, these indicators will be insufficient, as long as the companies maintain independent activities, keep their assets and liabilities separate, and their books in order.[360] Thus, essential for both concepts seems to be the occurrence of abnormal or irregular financial flows of assets between the participating companies, which may manifest themselves in the transfer of substantially all the assets of one company to another within the group, or in the failure by one company to pay dividends to another company without any reaction by the latter,[361] accompanied by defective accounting. Under these circumstances, there may also be a *faut de gestion* that renders the parent company, as de facto director, liable pursuant to Com Article L651-2.[362]

It is not clear whether there is a difference between the two concepts. Some say that whereas in respect of *fictivité* the legal personality of the fictitious company is completely negated, in case of *confusion de patrimoines* the autonomy of the participating companies is, to some extent, still being maintained.[363] For instance, a participating company remains liable for any sums still unpaid on its shares in another participating company pursuant to Com Article 228-28. Also, a corporate group subject to a unitary insolvency proceeding will not be able to contract with a third party 'as a group'; only the single participating companies can enter into contracts with third parties. Moreover, the court order that commenced insolvency proceedings in respect of one company does not relate back to an earlier order commencing proceedings in respect of another company. Courts do not seem to clearly distinguish between both concepts and much remains unclear. Overall, however, the doctrines appear to be dangerous weapons in the hands of liquidators and administrators.[364] The following case is an example:

Cour de Cassation, Chambre commerciale, Case 97-12544 of 26 April 2000

Whereas, according to the affirmative decision (Basse-Terre, 4th November 1996) before the court and the pleading of the parties, an administration procedure was opened on 23 February 1994 concerning ... (SEAM); that, by the judgment of 23 September 1994, this procedure was extended to include the public companies ... (SOFILAG), ... (SAMATRA) and ... (SMD), Mrs R being designated as representative of the creditors and Mr L and Mr S being designated as

355 Jeantin and Le Cannu (n 322) para 233.
356 LoPucki (n 5).
357 Jeantin and Le Cannu (n 322) para 232.
358 ibid para 233.
359 Cozian, Viandier, and Deboissy (n 308) para 2102.
360 Jeantin and Le Cannu (n 322) para 233.
361 ibid.
362 ibid.
363 ibid 235.
364 Cozian, Viandier, and Deboissy (n 308) para 2100.

administrators; that, by a judgment of 15 March 1996, the Tribunal opened, as an extension of the preceding procedures, an administration procedure regarding .... (la SHAL), ... (la SHAM) and SCI Z;

...

On the second and third grounds of appeal;

Whereas SHAL and SHAM hold the decision to be incorrect for having ordered the extension of the proceedings that were opened in respect of SEAM to include them, whilst, according to the appeal ... the collective proceedings opened in respect of a company cannot be extended to include another non-fictive company unless there exists between them an amalgamation of assets, that is to say that there exists an overlap between their assets and liabilities with abnormal financial transactions taking place between them; in this particular case, the Appeal Court deduced the amalgamation of assets between, on the one hand, SMD, SAMATRA, SOFILAG and SEAM, and on the other hand SHAM and SHAL, from the identity of the shareholders, the identity of the objects of the companies, from the long-term contracts of lease and mandate linking SHAM and SHAL, respectively, to SEAM, from the fact that the acquisition of land in co-ownership by SHAL and SHAM was financed by the rents and indemnities of administration they owed to SEAM ... the existence of economic and financial links resulting in dependence, SEAM being a debtor in respect of various sums owed to SHAL and SHAM; that in finding the aforementioned amalgamation of assets based on these insufficient grounds, the Appeal Court acted in breach of [law], and, whilst, on the other hand, pursuant to Article 16 of the New Code of Civil Procedure the judge himself must respect the adversarial principle; that in this particular case, the Appeal Court relied on the longevity of the contracts as having an impact on the question of amalgamation of assets of the contracting parties as an argument it had raised spontaneously; that in deciding in this way, without reopening the debate and inviting the parties to submit on this point, the Appeal Court acted in breach of the aforementioned article;

But whereas, for appropriate and correct reasons, the judgment, using the only points considered in the arguments, maintains that the contracts between SHAL and SHAM and SEAM, for which the extension of the proceedings regarding SOFILAG, SAMATRA and SMD was granted, had an excessive duration and did not contain any possibility of revocation, and that there had been abnormal asset transfers as well as financial support revealing indivisible interests; under these circumstances the Appeal Court was able to assume the amalgamation of assets between SEAM, SOFILAG, SAMADRA and SMD, on the one hand, and Shal, Sham and SCI Z, on the other, thus the appeal can be successful on neither of the grounds;

On these grounds: appeal dismissed.

Questions and comments:

1. The assumption of a *confusion de patrimoines* in this case rested on the fact that all companies within the group had the same shareholders and identical purposes; that the companies were connected by contracts of unusually long duration without the possibility of termination and that unusual property transactions had taken place within the group. Do you think that these circumstances should be sufficient to assume a *confusion the patrimoines*? Does the court in this case not sacrifice the principles of separate legal personality and limited liability within a group of companies too lightly?
2. The possibility to extend insolvency proceedings regarding one company to another company of the same group under the doctrine of *confusion de patrimoines* causes considerable difficulties in the context of the 2015 EU Insolvency Regulation.[365] Can you explain why?
3. The concept of *société fictive* may also be problematic in respect of the First Company Law Directive, now Directive (EU) 2017/1132. Why?

[365] Jeantin and Le Cannu (n 322) 236.

F. Concluding Remarks

The concepts we have examined in the current Chapter are very diverse and have different doctrinal roots. Fraud and fraudulent misrepresentation are straightforward concepts in all jurisdictions, but they may be difficult to prove, in particular the knowledge at the time when obligations are incurred that they are unlikely to be satisfied. Negligent misrepresentation requires the establishment of some specific duty owed by the insider to the third party or a special relationship on the basis of an assumption of responsibility. These doctrines are not company-specific; the difficulties that they present are the same regardless of whether the contracting principal is a corporation or a natural person. The same is true for fraudulent transfer law. The claimant's difficulties of identifying specific transactions, insolvency, and certain mental states on the part of transferor and/or transferee are, in principle, the same in any creditor/debtor relationship. The specific externalization problem caused by limited liability arises where the corporate form is used to pursue risky activities, on the basis of a certain business strategy, without making provisions for the expected costs by either accumulating sufficient earnings or buying sufficient insurance. The typical example would be a company that in order to increase the profits of, say, drilling oil in the Gulf of Mexico, does not invest in the best available safety equipment and then pays huge dividends to its shareholders so that it has no reserves and is effectively judgment-proof when an oil spill occurs. Fraudulent or negligent misrepresentation have little to contribute in this situation, and fraudulent transfer law is also unhelpful. Sophisticated voluntary creditors may be able to protect themselves by stipulating certain financial ratios in their debt covenants, by restricting the payment of dividends or the transfer of assets, and generally by charging a higher interest rate or by obtaining security.[366] Less sophisticated contractors may not have the bargaining power to do so; and tort creditors never have a chance to negotiate their own protection. Moreover, small contract and tort creditors can free ride on the sophisticated creditors' efforts only as long as the company is solvent. However, when the corporation is in financial difficulties and protection is most relevant, sophisticated creditors' strong position may accelerate the company's demise to the detriment of its other creditors.[367] General tort law may provide some relief, but only to the extent that corporate insiders—controlling shareholders and/or managers—are liable for their own torts. This requires a breach of a duty of care owed on their part to the tort victims as third parties. This, in turn, requires the assumption of some kind of responsibility for conducting the injurious act in question. An externalizing business strategy will normally not satisfy this requirement.

It is in these circumstances that general exceptions to the principle of limited liability are most relevant. Conceptually there are stark differences between the United States and our three European legal systems. The doctrine of veil piercing in the US is construed as an exception to the principle of limited liability. Shareholders are being held directly liable vis-à-vis the company's creditors for the company's debts. The creditors themselves are the proper claimants. By contrast, in Germany (liability for causing insolvency), France (*action pour insuffisance d'actif*) and the UK (wrongful trading) liability is internal vis-à-vis the company; only the company itself through its liquidator or insolvency administrator can sue, creditors may benefit only indirectly from a greater pay-out in the company's insolvency. In the US and Germany proper defendants are primarily the shareholders in control of the company's management; these will often be formally involved as well. By contrast, in the UK and France directors and managers are the primary targets, extended to 'shadow (or de facto) directors' with a real and continuous influence on the management. Since more often

[366] P Mulbert and M Birke, 'Legal Capital: Is There a Case against the European Legal Capital Rules?' (2002) 3 EBOR 695, 723.

[367] ibid.

than not directors and shadow directors will at the same time be majority shareholders, the differences as regards the proper defendant may be conceptually more important than in practice. In terms of the substance of liability-triggering behaviour all four legal systems have in common a certain lack of clear guidelines for judges, legal advisers, and entrepreneurs. 'Piercing the corporate veil' requires some 'wrongful act' that causes loss to the plaintiff or the 'evasion' of an existing legal obligation; in Germany an interference with the company's assets is required that foreseeably caused the company's insolvency; France, in a similar vein, requires a management fault that contributed to the company's insolvency. By contrast, in the UK doing nothing when something should have been done triggers liability, without making clear what this something should have been. All these concepts are very fact sensitive, and it appears to be difficult to derive any coherent principle from the decided cases, arbitrariness and legal uncertainty result. The reason may be that limited liability—for shareholders, directors and management—is generally granted without exception. Where the law allows the free formation of companies without prescribing a duty of adequate capitalization for the envisaged activity, either in form of reserves that need to be built and maintained or adequate insurance, it becomes difficult to define the act or omission that can be the basis of liability-triggering wrongdoing. Limited liability and the possibility to externalize risk is one of the defining features of the corporate form. The uncertainty associated with the remedies currently available as well as the fact that they are successful only under rare circumstances renders them inadequate to set the right incentives for corporate insiders and to encourage them to conduct business in a financially responsible way.

A number of reform proposals have been devised. They include the general reintroduction of unlimited shareholder liability, pro rata shareholder liability or unlimited 'controlling shareholder liability' for corporate torts, enterprise liability or general liability of parent companies for debts of their subsidiaries. General shareholder liability in whatever form seems to be workable only in respect of closely held corporations or small private companies. Only in these will shareholders be easily identifiable and their number will be limited so that they can be held accountable.[368] By contrast, in large publicly traded firms shares will be held through several tiers of intermediaries on the basis of book entry systems. The company may not even know who the actual end-investors are.[369] Moreover, the shares of these companies are turned over so frequently and fast that it will be nigh impossible to identify who was a shareholder at any particular time when a corporate tort was committed. It may be easier to identify a 'controlling shareholder' holding a majority or a stake large enough to dominate the voting process and management. However, liability on that basis may be easily avoided. A multitude of techniques exist. Through financial contracts, vote-buying, derivatives and hedging techniques control-level benefits can be maintained without a formal shareholder relationship.[370] In order to be effective the scope of liability would have to be extended so as to cover anyone with actual control, however defined. The identification problem would re-emerge in a different guise. In any case, shareholder liability in whatever form would discourage equity investment and thus increase the costs of equity capital. Moreover, it would require statutory intervention in order to (re-)introduce shareholder liability in some form. This is unrealistic,[371] given the strong influence of corporate insiders on the political process through their lobbying power. The same goes for parent company liability for the debts of subsidiaries and to a lesser extent for enterprise liability. The latter may actually be detrimental to creditors, as they would have to compete with the creditors of the entire group and

[368] N Mendelson, 'A Control Based Approach to Shareholder Liability for Corporate Torts' (2002) 102 Columbia Law Review 1202, 1286; T Glynn, 'Beyond "Unlimiting" Shareholder Liability: Vicarious Tort Liability for Corporate Officers' (2004) 57 Vanderbilt Law Review 329, 380.

[369] M Kahan and E Rock, 'The Hanging Chads of Corporate Voting' (2008) 96 Georgetown Law Journal 1227, 1238–48.

[370] Glynn (n 368) 393.

[371] ibid 391.

not just those of their debtor subsidiary. The essential advantages and cost-reducing effects of separate legal personality would at least partly be sacrificed.

As an alternative, the highest-ranking corporate managers—essentially CEO or president of a corporation—may be held liable for corporate torts.[372] This proposal leaves untouched the efficiency gains of limited shareholder liability and imposes liability on a clearly identifiable group of persons who, arguably, are best placed to bear that risk. This is because highest-ranking managers are most directly in control of corporate operations. They have access to the best available information about the business, allowing them to appreciate the risks of tort liability correctly. They are in the best position to monitor corporate activity, to invest in risk reducing measures and to facilitate the build-up of capital reserves and to buy insurance. Moreover, they are in a strong bargaining position with shareholders in order to negotiate high remuneration for their additional risk taking, indemnification for any liability they may incur and/or payment by the company of personal liability insurance premiums.[373] The traditional counter arguments of risk aversion, over-deterrence to engage in risky projects, or overinvestment in risk reducing measures appear to be unpersuasive. Incentive based remuneration in stock options and the sheer size of remuneration of highest-ranking managers in publicly traded firms make them increasingly financially independent of their firm specific investments. Their incentives are aligned to that of shareholders. There is also some evidence that high-ranking officers can move quickly between firms. Over-deterrence is unlikely to be a problem as long as the company is adequately capitalized or insured. High-ranking management is in the best position to take care of that.[374] Thus, highest-ranking manager liability, in combination with executive compensation, indemnification and payment of personal insurance premiums, may internalize the costs of accidents and spread them among managers, shareholders, and costumers, through the risk of personal liability, reduced dividends, and higher prices. In every corporation, there will be at least one person in charge with an incentive to reduce corporate opportunism and to prevent negative externalities. Thus, holding highest-ranking managers, including 'shadow managers', liable for corporate torts seems to be a more efficient solution than shareholder liability in whatever form.[375] Moreover, in many small closely held firms, highest-ranking managers will be controlling shareholders at the same time, and even in large publicly traded companies managers often own major shareholdings in their company.

How may this liability be construed? One possibility is to hold highest-ranking managers liable for their own torts of negligence. This would generally require finding them in breach of a duty of care that they personally owe to third parties on the basis of an assumption of responsibility. As stated above, a financially irresponsible business strategy would generally not be sufficient. Alternatively, highest-ranking managers may be held liable on the basis of the doctrine of *respondeat superior*. Under this doctrine, a principal will be liable for the tortious acts of his agent, committed within the scope of the agency, where the principal has the capacity to control the conduct of the agent. Under the nexus-of-contract theory of the corporation, highest-ranking managers could be seen as principals with capacity to control the acts of other corporate employees.[376] The problem with this conception is that, in order to hold the principal liable, there must be some identifiable tortious act of a corporate

[372] ibid 396. [373] ibid 396–403. [374] ibid 403–16.

[375] A statutory example for imposing responsibility on high-ranking corporate officers is §302 of the US Sarbanes-Oxley Act. The 'principal executive officer or officers and the principal financial officer or officers, or persons performing similar functions' are required to certify that they have reviewed each quarterly or annual report filed with the SEC, that to their knowledge the report does not contain any untrue statements of material fact or omissions, and that it fairly presents the financial condition and results of the issuer. Moreover, the respective officers are responsible for establishing and maintaining internal controls and for monitoring their effectiveness. These responsibilities are backed by criminal liability.

[376] Glynn (n 368) 427–32.

employee. Where risks are externalized on the basis of a financially irresponsible business strategy, such an isolated act may not be easily identifiable.

An elegant solution, with the potential for wider application, was suggested in the *Stocznia* case. A parent company that refused to adequately capitalize its subsidiary was found liable under the (economic) tort of inducement of a breach of contract.[377] Similarly, it has been suggested to conceptualize the German concept of liability for causing insolvency as a form of liability for inducing breach of contract pursuant to BGB, §826 (*Verleitung zum Vertragsbruch*).[378] 'Inducement of breach'-language was also used in *Amfac Foods Inc. v International Systems & Controls Corp.*[379] in the piercing the corporate veil context.[380] Given that company law does not include any duty to adequately capitalize a company and that the company as such does not have a right to its existence, the concept of inducement of breach provides a proper focus for the defendant's misconduct: the creditor's claim against the company. The doctrine in its original conception under common law relates only to contractual claims, but there seems to be no good reason for not extending it to other claims, and tort claims in particular, as is the case already under German law.[381] The creditor's claim against the company, on whatever basis, is to be treated as a financial asset. This asset is interfered with where conducting business in a financially irresponsible manner renders it worthless. Thus, liability of the highest-ranking managers could be triggered where they conduct the company's business in a way that results in the company being unable to meet its obligations as they fall due, and this inability to pay is the reasonably foreseeable outcome of the defendant's business strategy. Moreover, and as a general safety valve, it should be required that the defendant's business strategy objectively appears to disregard the general standard of proper business conduct. This will be the case where risk is deliberately externalized and assigned to third parties, rather than borne by the corporation and its insiders. *Singla v Hedman*[382] may serve as an example for this requirement. The sole director and shareholder of a single purpose film production company with a paid-in share capital of £2 and no other assets entered into a production services agreement (PSA) under which the company was committed to payment of substantial sums. When the PSA was entered into the director knew or ought to have known that neither finance nor lead actor of the film project had been secured. The PSA was entered into merely in order to meet a deadline for the application for state funding. According to the court, 'the PSA was signed by [the company] when it had no means of honouring its obligations and no prospect of honouring them. It of course would not lose because all it had was £2 in assets. The loss and the bearing of the loss was born by [the creditor] and the losses and claims it sustained arising out of [the company's] failed obligations under the PSA. It was inevitable that [the company] would not fulfil its obligations and would not therefore be able to avoid going into insolvent liquidation'.[383] Further, it was not acceptable for the company 'to enter into arrangements with creditors which its director ought to have known could never be honoured on any reasonable prospect', thus driving the company into liquidation. It was inappropriate for the director 'to conduct the company's business on such a basis without regard to its impact on the creditors and the company's solvency'.[384]

[377] *Stocznia Gdanska SA v Latvian Shipping Co, Latreefer Inc. and Others* [2002] 2 Lloyd's Rep 436.

[378] M-P Weller, 'Die Existenzvernichtungshaftung im modernisierten GmbH-Recht - eine Außenhaftung für Forderungsvereitelung (§826 BGB)' (2007) Deutsches Steuerrecht 1166.

[379] 654 P.2d 1092 (1982).

[380] ibid 1101, 1102: 'The shareholder's alleged control over the corporation must not be only potential but must actually have been exercised in a manner either causing the corporation's default on the transaction or a resulting obligation. Similarly, the shareholder's conduct must have been improper either in relation to the plaintiff's entering the transaction or in preventing or interfering with the corporation's performance or ability to perform its obligations toward the plaintiff'.

[381] Weller (n 378) 1169. [382] [2010] BCC 684. [383] ibid para 100.

[384] ibid para 107. Consequently, the director was found liable under the wrongful trading provisions of the Insolvency Act 1986, s 214.

The proper claimant would be the creditor or creditors whose claims have been rendered worthless. This may upset the *pari passu* principle and result in a run on the assets of the defendant (or his insurer). Also, enforcing a single claim may not be worth the effort where the litigation costs are high. Both issues could be remedied to some extent by bundling the claims and concentrating the right to sue in the person of the office holder when the company is in formal insolvency proceedings. The actual damages caused by the defendant's actions may be hard to ascertain for an outsider and may be too low for setting an incentive for a single creditor to pursue his claim. On the other hand, simply relying on the nominal value of an outstanding claim would not be in line with general tort principles of causation. As a compromise, there could be a presumption that the outstanding nominal amount of the claim is the damage to be awarded, subject to the defendant proving that he caused only a smaller amount of loss.

Future research should focus on developing the elements of this new corporate tort so as to set the proper incentives for corporate insiders and to provide the most effective and efficient regime. One advantage of this solution (and others based on tort law) is that it could be achieved largely without statutory intervention by modification of tort law principles. Courts have demonstrated in the past their willingness to extend liability for corporate debts to other constituencies where doing so seemed to be justified. Moreover, judges are generally less vulnerable, than elected politicians, to the influence of strong economic interests and their lobbyists.

11

Corporate Insolvency

As market actors, business corporations are (or at least should be) subject to the correcting forces of markets and competition. Where a corporation is incapable of prevailing in a competitive market environment, corporate law should facilitate an orderly market exit. It is important to distinguish between the corporation as legal entity and the corporation's business as the combination of tangible and intangible assets, manpower, internal coordination and control systems, brand identities and other reputational capital, under the umbrella of a specific business concept. The corporation as a legal entity is merely a legal device that allows different investors to contribute capital to a common enterprise, whereby the corporation's capital structure determines the way the firm's earnings are divided among the investors. The corporation is not worth preserving for its own sake, and may be easily replaced with a new or off-the-shelf corporate structure. However, where the business is viable it may be worthy of being retained as a going concern with a view to preserving and creating jobs and investment opportunities.

Corporate failure—however defined—is only one possible reason for ending the corporate existence. At the other end of the spectrum may be spectacular corporate success: a company may attract the attention of a competitor and both companies may decide to join forces through a merger,[1] ending the existence of at least one of the participating companies.[2] There are many occurrences in-between: the corporate purpose may have been achieved so that the legal entity is no longer needed; the corporation may have been formed only for a limited period of time which has expired; or the shareholders may voluntarily decide to bring the corporation to an end for whatever reason. In all these incidences, corporate law has to provide a process that ensures that pre-existing contractual entitlements are respected in accordance with the idea of creditor preference and shareholder residuarity. From a corporate law perspective, it does not matter what happens to the corporation's business: the shareholders are free to end a viable business enterprise; as long as the creditors are being paid, they have no reason to complain.

The situation changes where the corporation's resources (cash flows and assets) are insufficient for paying its creditors in full, that is, where the corporation is insolvent.[3] The conflict of interest between shareholders and creditors intensifies: the former have a strong incentive to continue doing business at the expense of the latter; and a conflict of interest between different classes of creditors emerges. These conflicts of interest have to be addressed through a transition from corporate governance to bankruptcy governance. Corporate insolvency law (and restructuring law) and the bankruptcy governance system (should) seek to facilitate the determination of whether there is a potential going concern surplus—the added value resulting from keeping the business together as a functioning unit, and if so, preserve it, and facilitate its realization and allocation amongst different corporate constituencies, or else provide for the orderly liquidation of corporate assets and the payment of dividends in accordance with a clear order of priorities.

A. Ending the Corporate Existence

Corporate law utilizes a number of mechanisms in order to ensure corporate creditors' preferential access to the corporation's assets, in priority to the shareholders and their personal creditors. The doctrine of legal capital seeks to ensure that no assets are being returned to shareholders in a way that would leave creditors worse off.[4] Where the separation of corporation and its shareholders is disregarded and/or assets have been returned to corporate insiders contrary to the established creditor preference, the corporate veil may be pierced.[5] The rules and principles that deal with company liquidation and dissolution serve the same rationale: by providing a largely mandatory procedure for the orderly liquidation of corporate

[1] This is to be distinguished from a takeover, pursuant to which the target ends up as the subsidiary of the bidder company. The target's corporate existence is being retained; see P Davies and S Worthington, *Gower & Davies' Principles of Modern Company Law* (10th edn, Sweet & Maxwell 2016) 917 (para 28-1).

[2] Perhaps both of them if they consolidate into a new corporation. Assets are transferred to the receiving corporation by way of universal succession; C Windbichler, *Gesellschaftsrecht* (24th edn, CH Beck 2017) 319 (§26 para 38); W Fletcher, *Cyclopedia of the Law of Corporations* (2018 update) §7969.

[3] For different concepts of insolvency see section B below.

[4] Chapter 9.

[5] Chapter 10.

property and the distribution of proceeds in accordance with an established order of priorities, they seek to prevent the return of corporate assets to shareholders prior to the full satisfaction of all outstanding creditors' claims.

From a comparative point of view, the procedures and processes that lead up to and eventually bring the corporate existence to an end follow a fairly similar pattern in all the jurisdictions under consideration here. A certain ground or reason triggers the corporation to cease trading and to enter a liquidation process the completion of which results in the corporate existence coming to end, subject to a possible resurrection in certain circumstances. The terminology requires some clarification. French law, German law, and US legal systems distinguish between a corporation's/company's dissolution and its liquidation.[6] The former signifies an event upon which the corporation's object to conduct a business ceases and is replaced with a different object, the winding up of the corporation's affairs. Liquidation is the process through which this winding up occurs, notably the realization of corporate assets and the distribution of proceeds to corporate constituents. When liquidation is complete the corporate existence ends through some formal act, usually its removal from the companies register. In England, the term 'dissolution' is reserved for this very last step: the end of the corporate existence.[7] It makes sense to adopt the terminology that the majority of our legal systems adhere to. The dissolution stage is characterised by the grounds, which may trigger the transformation from a trading corporation into a corporation in liquidation. The liquidation process raises issues of control, value maximization, and orders of priority. Termination, finally, requires certain formalities and there is the issue of a potential resurrection.

I. Grounds for (solvent) dissolution

A first categorization of the various grounds for dissolving a company may be the distinction between the voluntary dissolution and the forced or compulsory dissolution, either judicially or administratively.[8] Each category encompasses various sub-groups in terms of substantive grounds and procedural triggers. The European legal systems must adhere to Articles 11 and 12 of Directive (EU) 2017/1132, restricting the circumstances under which a company may be declared a nullity.

Voluntary dissolution may occur where the articles of association of a company stipulate a fixed period of duration and this period expires. French law requires commercial companies, including private and public companies limited by shares, to stipulate in their articles of association the duration of the company, which must not exceed ninety-nine years.[9] Upon expiry of the initial period of duration the company is dissolved by operation of law. The shareholders by extraordinary resolution[10] may decide to continue the company for another term of up to ninety-nine years. In that case, no new legal person is being created and the continuing company is identical with the company as initially formed.[11] However, where the shareholders simply continue without a resolution to extend the life of the company, the initial company is dissolved and a new de facto company emerges.[12] Under German law this ground for dissolution[13] is of limited significance in practice.[14] An extension of the

[6] M Germain and V Magnier, *Les sociétés commerciales* (21st edn, LGDJ 2014) paras 1613–48; Windbichler (n 2) 317 (§26 para 32); Fletcher (n 2) §§7966, 7968.

[7] Davies and Worthington (n 1) 1173 (para 33-27).

[8] ibid 1152 (para 33-2); Germain and Magnier (n 6) para 1614; Fletcher (n 2) §7965.

[9] Com Art L210-2.

[10] This requires a quorum of one-quarter of voting shares (one-fifth if the meeting has to be reconvened) and a majority of two-thirds of the votes of shareholders being present in person or by proxy: Com Art L225-96.

[11] Germain and Magnier (n 6) para 1614.

[12] J-P Le Gall and C Ruellan, *Droit Commercial: Notions générales* (16th edn, Dalloz 2006) 63.

[13] AktG, §262(1) No 1; GmbHG, §60(1) No 1.

[14] Windbichler (n 2) 317 (§26 para 33).

company's lifespan requires a shareholders' resolution with a 75 per cent majority of the share capital represented at the meeting.[15] In the US, the corporate existence may expire on the basis of a term in the articles of association or the bylaws pursuant to which the corporation has a fixed duration. Upon expiration of the set period of time the corporation is dissolved, subject to an extension of the period of duration by amendment of the articles or bylaws.[16] Under English law, a members' voluntary winding up always requires the passing of a resolution in general meeting. Where the articles provide for a fixed period of duration for the company and the period has expired, or where the articles provide that the company be dissolved upon the occurrence of a specific event and this event has occurred, the resolution to wind up the company may be passed with a simple majority.[17] Otherwise, a special resolution[18] in general meeting is required.[19]

All legal systems under consideration here allow for dissolution on the basis of a shareholder vote. Under German law, the shareholders' meeting may, with a 75 per cent majority of the share capital represented at the meeting, vote for the dissolution of the corporation.[20] The articles of association may provide for a higher majority requirement, but may not exclude the possibility of dissolution on the basis of a shareholder resolution completely. The resolution to dissolve a corporation cannot be challenged on the basis that dissolution is not justified: shareholders are free to divest from a viable business and to bring it to an end through liquidation.[21] Under French law, prior to the expiration of the initial (or a subsequent) duration of the company, the shareholders may at any time decide to dissolve the company on the basis of an extraordinary resolution.[22] In the US, where a corporation has not issued shares or has not commenced business it may be dissolved by a majority of its incorporators or initial directors through the filing of articles of dissolution with the secretary of state.[23] More generally, a corporation may be dissolved on the basis of a shareholder vote. For that purpose, the board of directors may propose dissolution for submission to the shareholders. The board will normally be required to recommend dissolution to the shareholders, unless the board abstain from such recommendation on the basis of a conflict of interest. A shareholder vote approving dissolution requires normally a majority of the votes entitled to be cast on the proposal.[24] Voluntary dissolution by the board of directors and shareholders does not require any specific grounds: a solvent company may be dissolved as long as doing so does not injure third parties. This may, however, be the case where dissolution would be detrimental to creditors as where the corporation is insolvent but has a valuable claim against its officers or directors for breach of duty.[25] Under English law, a members' voluntary winding-up normally requires a special resolution[26] in general meeting.[27] A voluntary winding up will be a members' voluntary winding up only if the company is solvent. Thus, unless the directors make a statutory declaration that the company will be solvent for the next twelve months, it will be a creditors' voluntary winding up.[28] Even where such declaration has been made, the liquidator may subsequently find that the company will be unable to pay its debts during the period specified in the statement of solvency. In that case, the liquidator has to send a statement of affairs of the company to the creditors and the winding up will be converted into a creditors' voluntary winding up.[29]

[15] AktG, §274. [16] Fletcher (n 2) §7981. [17] Insolvency Act 1986, s 84(1)(a).
[18] Companies Act 2006, s 283(1): 75% majority. [19] Insolvency Act 1986, s 84 (1)(b).
[20] AktG, §262(1) No 2; GmbHG, §60(1) No 2. [21] Windbichler (n 2) 317 (§26 para 34).
[22] Germain and Magnier (n 6) para 2592. An extraordinary resolution requires a quorum of 25% of voting shares (20% if the meeting has to be reconvened) and a majority of two-thirds of the votes of shareholders being present in person or by proxy: Com Art L225-96.
[23] MBCA, §14.01; DGCL, §272; Fletcher (n 2) §8007.30.
[24] MBCA, §14.02; DGCL, §275; Fletcher (n 2) §8007.10. A corporation that has dissolved voluntarily may request to continue dissolution under court supervision: MBCA, §14.30(4).
[25] Fletcher (n 2) §8016. [26] Companies Act 2006, s 283(1): 75% majority.
[27] Insolvency Act 1986, s 84 (1)(b). [28] ibid ss 89, 90. [29] ibid ss 95, 96.

Our legal systems show much greater diversity when it comes to compulsory dissolution, which may be effectuated either judicially or administratively. There is still much common ground in respect of judicial liquidation for cause. Under French law, judicial dissolution for 'good reasons'[30] applies to both private limited companies and to public companies limited by shares.[31] Any shareholder can bring an action for dissolution on grounds of a disagreement between shareholders which paralyses the running of the company. Abuse of a voting majority may also justify dissolution. The court has a wide margin of discretion and takes into account all the relevant circumstances in the case, notably the gravity of the underlying reason for the petition. The judgment that orders dissolution is constitutive, not merely declaratory.[32] Under various corporation statutes in the US, judicial dissolution may be requested by the (secretary of) state, a shareholder, or a creditor, subject always to a sufficient ground for judicial dissolution having been shown.[33] The secretary of state may request the dissolution of a corporation, in particular, where the articles of incorporation have been obtained by fraud, for example on the basis of false statements concerning the number of shares, classes of shares or consideration paid for shares, and where the corporation exceeds or abuses its authority, as when the corporation is engaged in unlawful or fraudulent activities or in the unauthorized practice of certain professions.[34] On application of a shareholder, the court may order dissolution if it is established that directors or controlling shareholders have engaged in illegal, fraudulent, or oppressive conduct.[35] The latter may include the frustration of a minority shareholder's reasonable expectations, for example, to participate in the management. This ground should be limited to cases of actual abuse, rather than mere tactical behaviour in a power struggle for corporate control.[36] A shareholder may further request judicial dissolution where the directors are deadlocked in the management of corporate affairs, the shareholders are unable to break the deadlock, and this may cause irreparable injury to the corporation; or where the shareholders are deadlocked in voting power and have failed to elect successors to directors whose terms have expired.[37] Deadlock requires an inability to conduct the business of the corporation; mere disagreement is insufficient.[38] Misapplication or waste of corporate assets may also justify judicial dissolution upon a shareholder's request.[39] In all cases of judicial dissolution the court has a wide discretion and has to keep in mind that dissolution is an extreme remedy that should be used sparingly and only where the facts clearly merit it. In particular, a forced buy-out of the petitioning shareholder may be a milder and more proportionate remedy.[40] Under English law, a compulsory winding up is dependent upon a winding-up order by the court following a petition by either the company, the directors of the company or any creditor.[41] The petitioner must present a ground for making a winding-up order. One such ground is that it would be 'just and equitable' for the company to be wound up.[42] This ground provided an important minority shareholder remedy where the company was deadlocked. With the coming of age of the unfair prejudice remedy[43] it has lost some of its significance.[44] In any case, it is mainly relevant for small partnership-type companies. Accordingly, under German law, only the law on private companies provides for an action against the company with a view to obtain a court order for dissolution. The action can be brought by shareholders who either alone or together hold at least 10 per cent of the company's share capital. The court may order

30 Civ Art 1855-7 No 5.

31 Germain and Magnier (n 6) paras 1863, 2591.

32 ibid paras 1617–8.

33 MBCA, §14.30(1)–(3); Fletcher (n 2) §8034. The grounds for dissolution enumerated in corporation statutes or not exclusive and the court may issue an order to dissolve a corporation for any ground existing at common law: ibid §8045.

34 MBCA, §14.30(1); Fletcher (n 2) §§8046, 8047, 8056.

35 MBCA, §14.30(2)(ii).

36 Fletcher (n 2) §8046.10.

37 MBCA, §14.30(i) and (iii).

38 Fletcher (n 2) §8066.10.

39 MBCA, §14.30((2)(iv).

40 Fletcher (n 2) §§8035, 8043.

41 Insolvency Act 1986, s 124(1).

42 ibid s 122(1)(g).

43 Companies Act 2006, s 994.

44 Davies and Worthington (n 1) 682 (para 20-21).

dissolution where the company's objects can no longer be achieved, or where there are other significant grounds for dissolution emanating from the affairs of the company.[45] The practical significance of this action is limited, given that a shareholder may be able to exit or may be excluded if there is sufficient reason.[46]

Under French law,[47] a company is further dissolved when either its object has been achieved or has become futile.[48] These cases are very rare since a company's objects are usually formulated so widely that their complete achievement or futility cannot practically occur. The nationalization of certain industries may however fall under this heading.[49] Simply ceasing to do business and ceasing to carry on the company's previous activity does not amount to a statutory ground for dissolution.[50] Similarly, under German law, the ceasing to trade or to conduct a business, the disposal of the business as a whole, or of all the company's assets does not in itself result in dissolution; but neither does the impossibility or futility of its objects. Rather, these incidents may be an occasion for the shareholders' meeting to pass a resolution for the dissolution of the company; alternatively, the shareholders may amend the articles by providing the company with new objects, such as those of a holding company or a shelf company.[51]

Under German law, dissolution automatically occurs upon the opening of insolvency proceedings against a company.[52] In that case the corporation may be liquidated or restructured in accordance with the provisions of the InsO. Where the corporation is insolvent but its assets are insufficient to cover the costs of an insolvency proceeding,[53] it will be dissolved and liquidated in accordance with the liquidation process under corporate law.[54] Similarly, in France, a company will be dissolved upon a judgment ordering a judicial liquidation in accordance with insolvency law.[55] This necessitates that the company is insolvent, as defined.[56] Under US legal systems, a creditor may request judicial dissolution of an insolvent corporation where either the creditor's claim has been reduced to judgment and execution on the judgment has been returned unsatisfied, or the corporation has admitted in writing that the creditor's claim is due and owing.[57] This is an alternative to a proceeding under the Federal Bankruptcy Code.[58] In England, the most important ground for making a compulsory winding-up order is that the company is insolvent, that is, 'unable to pay its debts'.[59] In addition, the company may also be wound up if it has resolved by special resolution to be

[45] GmbHG, §61. [46] Windbichler (n 2) 260 (§24 para 3).

[47] Under French law, a number of provisions deal specifically with dissolution in the context of a reduction of a company's equity capital. Where, as a result of losses, equity falls below half of the amount of legal capital, the board of directors must call an extraordinary general meeting, at which the shareholders decide whether to prematurely dissolve the company. If no decision is taken to dissolve the company, the legal capital must be reduced to an amount equal to that of any losses not charged to reserves, unless equity has been restored to an amount equal to at least half the amount of legal capital. If no general meeting is held, or the meeting is inquorate, or where legal capital has not been reduced or equity restored, any interested party may petition the court for the dissolution of the company: Com Arts L223-42, L225-248. The same applies where the legal capital has been reduced to an amount below the minimum capital requirement of €37,000 subject to the condition precedent that there is an increase in legal capital to an amount at least equal to the minimum capital requirement. In the event of noncompliance with the condition precedent, any interested party may apply to the court for the dissolution of the company; Com Art L224-2. Moreover, on a petition filed by any interested party the court may order the dissolution of a public company that has had less than seven members for more than one year; the court may grant a six months grace period: Com Art L225-247. Conversely, a private limited company will be dissolved at the end of a one-year period at the beginning of which its membership had increased to more than one hundred members, unless during the one-year period the number of members have been lowered to the legally acceptable number or the company has been converted: Com Art L223-3.

[48] Civ Art 1844-7 No 2. [49] Germain and Magnier (n 6) paras 1615, 2591. [50] ibid para 1615.

[51] Windbichler (n 2) 319-20 (§26 para 40).

[52] AktG, §262(1) Nos 3 and 4; GmbHG, §60(1) Nos 4 and 5. [53] InsO, §25.

[54] Windbichler (n 2) 317-8 (§26 para 35). [55] Civ Art 1844-7 No 7. [56] Com Art L640-1.

[57] MBCA, §14.30(3).

[58] American Bar Association, *Model Business Corporation Act annotated* (2005) Official Comment §14.30 para 3.

[59] Insolvency Act 1986, s 122 (1)(f), 123.

wound up by the court;[60] where a public company has not been issued with a trading certificate[61] within one year of incorporation;[62] or the company does not commence business within a year from its incorporation or suspends its business for a whole year.[63]

Directive (EU) 2017/1132 restricts the circumstances under which a company may be declared a nullity. The grounds for nullity are listed in Article 11(b); any other grounds for nullity in national law are ruled out by the regime of the Directive. Pursuant to Article 11(a), nullity must be ordered by a decision of a court of law. With declaration of nullity the company goes into liquidation, which itself is regulated by national law. Nullity does not affect the validity of transactions entered into by or with the company before declaration of nullity. Hence, nullity has effect only *ex nunc*. Accordingly, under German law dissolution occurs where a shareholder, or a member of the management or supervisory board brings an action for nullity and the court determines that the articles of association are subject to defects that result in their nullity:[64] the articles do not show the total amount of legal capital or the objects of the company; or the objects of the company are unlawful.[65] Further defects—the articles do not show the name of the company; the amount of the individual subscriptions of capital, their number, par value, or class; the number of the members of the supervisory board; or the amount of legal capital specified in the articles is unlawful—require the register court to request the company to cure the defect by amending its articles within a certain period of time; failure to do so results in the register court's determination that the articles are defective and the company is dissolved.[66] The determination of the nullity (or defectiveness) of the articles of association does not have retroactive effect; rather the company is to be liquidated in accordance with the general liquidation procedure.[67] In France, the grounds for nullity of private limited companies and public companies limited by shares have been restricted to the incapacity of all founding members and to the illegality of the company's object.[68] These grounds have to be invoked through an action for nullity, which, if successful, results in the company's dissolution.[69] The Directive's provisions on nullity have not been specifically implemented in the UK. This is because the certificate of incorporation, issued by the registrar if he is satisfied that the requirements of the Act as to registration have been complied with, is conclusive evidence that the requirements of the Act have in fact been met. This makes English companies very robust and renders them virtually immune from any problems arising from defective incorporation.[70]

A related concept under US legal systems is the administrative dissolution which may be initiated by the secretary of state (or other relevant state official) on the following grounds: the corporation does not pay within a certain period of time any franchise taxes or penalties due; it does not deliver within a certain period of time its annual or semi-annual reports to the relevant official; it is without a registered agent or registered office in the state for a certain period of time or fails to notify the relevant state official within a certain period of time of any changes as regards its registered agent or registered office within the state.[71] Expiration of a corporations fixed period of duration may be a further ground for administrative dissolution. Where the secretary of state (or relevant state official) determines that a relevant ground for administrative dissolution exists it will give notice to the corporation

[60] ibid s 122(1)(a).

[61] A trading certificate will only be issued by the Registrar of Companies where he is satisfied that the nominal value of the company's allotted share capital is not less than the authorized minimum: Companies Act 2006, s 761.

[62] Insolvency Act 1986, s 122(1)(b).

[63] ibid s 122 (1)(d).

[64] AktG, §275; GmbHG, §75.

[65] AktG, §275; GmbHG, §75. Defects concerning the company's objects may be cured by amending its articles; Windbichler (n 1) 318 (§26 para 37).

[66] AktG, §262(1) No 5; GmbHG, §60(1) No 6; FamFG, §399.

[67] Windbichler (n 2) 318 (§26 para 37).

[68] Com Art L235-1.

[69] Germain and Magnier (n 6) para 1583.

[70] Davies and Worthington (n 1) 92-94 (paras 4-34–4-37).

[71] MBCA, §14.20; Fletcher (n 2) §§8048, 8049, 8052, 8053, 8054.

which may then remove the ground within a certain period of time, or else the secretary of state will dissolve the corporation administratively by issuing a certificate of dissolution.[72] Under German law, (only) a private limited company may be dissolved administratively where the company puts the public welfare at risk by its shareholders passing illegal resolutions or knowingly tolerating illegal actions of its directors.[73]

II. (Solvent) liquidation processes

The purpose of corporate law liquidation processes is twofold. Given the principle of limited liability, in the absence of a mandatory liquidation process the interests of creditors could be in jeopardy. Thus, corporate liquidation processes seek to ensure respect for the order of priority by preventing the return of corporate property to shareholders prior to the full satisfaction of creditors' claims. Value maximization of corporate property with a view to its realization and the distribution of proceeds to shareholders is (only) a secondary consideration.[74] In solvent companies, by definition, there are sufficient resources to satisfy at least all creditors. In principle, this makes it possible to leave the process largely in the hands of the parties with minimal outside supervision or interference. However, the potential for opportunistic behaviour on the part of the office holders necessitates mechanisms that allow for increasing the intensity of outside supervision and control if need be.

The liquidation process commences as soon as the company's dissolution takes effect.[75] In England, this is the passing of the shareholders' resolution to wind up the company.[76] Throughout the liquidation process the company retains its corporate existence. However, the company must cease to carry on business, except to the extent that the continuation of the business activity is necessary for an orderly winding up.[77] In France, the company's name is to be supplemented by the annex 'société en liquidation';[78] in Germany the annex 'in liquidation' is customary.[79] In principle, general corporate law continues to apply, subject to the mandatory provisions on liquidation.[80] Thus, the company in liquidation may sue and be sued under its name[81]—there is no moratorium or automatic stay; subject to the appointment of liquidators, the governance structure of the company remains unchanged, in particular the supervisory boards in Germany and France remain in office;[82] and the general meeting of shareholders may decide on an amendment of the articles of association, including an increase or decrease of legal capital; shares and other securities may continue to be transferred. English law is the odd one out in this respect. A transfer of shares that occurred after commencement of a voluntary winding up will be void if not made with the sanction of the liquidator; also, any alteration of the status of the company's members made after commencement will be void,[83] not however the disposal of company property as would be the case in a compulsory liquidation.[84]

Subject to the appointment of a receiver, trustee or custodian by the court, US legal systems generally entrust the liquidation to the directors. These have the general duty of causing the dissolved corporation to discharge or make reasonable provision for the payment of claims and make distributions of assets to shareholders after payment or provision for creditor's claims.[85] However, on application of a creditor, shareholder, director or other person in interest the court may appoint a trustee, custodian or receiver for good cause. Such appointment may occur in the proceeding leading up to judicial dissolution or in an independent proceeding following dissolution.[86] As a less intrusive remedy, the court will

[72] MBCA, §14.21. [73] GmbHG, §62. [74] Windbichler (n 2) 320 (§26 para 41).
[75] Com Art L.237-2; AktG, §264(1); Fletcher (n 2) §8113. [76] Insolvency Act 1986, s 86.
[77] ibid s 87. [78] Com Art L237-2(2). [79] Windbichler (n 2) 371 (§26 para 32).
[80] AktG, §263(3); GmbHG, §69. [81] AktG, §269(1); Com Art L237-2(3).
[82] AktG, §262(3); Com Art L237-16; Windbichler (n 2) 320–1 (§26 para 42).
[83] Insolvency Act 1986, s 88. [84] ibid s 127. [85] Fletcher (n 2) §§8157, 8158.
[86] ibid §§8174, 8196, 8197.

normally appoint one or more directors as trustees of the corporation. Trustees so appointed are not trustees of a trust in the ordinary sense of the word and are not officers of the court; they are merely 'statutory liquidators' who conduct the liquidation under the supervision of the court.[87] The court will interfere only where the directors as statutory trustees are neglecting their duties or abusing their powers.[88] The appointment of a liquidating receiver is a more intrusive remedy to be made as a last resort. The receiver is an agent of the court and has the task of selling off the corporation's assets and distributing the proceeds among the various creditors and shareholders.[89] Generally, appointment of a receiver is subject to it being necessary to preserve the assets of the corporation and to protect the rights of creditors and shareholders.[90] This may be the case where directors or trustees engage in misconduct or mismanagement of corporate affairs.[91] In an amicable[92] (or conventional[93]) liquidation under French law, the process for appointing the liquidators as well as its powers and duties are to be determined by the articles of association.[94] However, persons who have been disqualified from participating in any capacity in corporate management and governance cannot be appointed as liquidators.[95] In the absence of provisions in the articles of association, the provisions on judicial (or statutory) liquidation apply by way of default.[96] The powers of the board of directors or the executive board come to an end,[97] whereas the duties of the supervisory board and of the auditors continue.[98] Where the company is dissolved on the basis of a court order the court appoints one or more liquidators.[99] If the company is dissolved because the term of its duration has expired or because the members have decided to dissolve the corporation the members appoint one or more liquidators on the basis of an ordinary resolution.[100] Under German law, the members of the management board or the board of directors become statutory liquidators, provided the articles of association or a shareholder resolution does not provide otherwise.[101] The supervisory board or shareholders holding together at least 5 per cent of the share capital (or the amount of €500,000),[102] in private limited companies 10 per cent of the share capital,[103] may petition the court to appoint or remove the liquidators for sufficient cause. Lack of neutrality, gross breach of duty, or incompetence on the part of the directors or liquidators may amount to a sufficient cause for these purposes. In England, the company in general meeting appoints one or more liquidators for the purposes of winding up the company's affairs and distributing its assets.[104] Only a qualified insolvency practitioner may be appointed as liquidator; and, unlike in our other legal systems, not the company's directors.[105] With the appointment of the liquidators, all the powers of the directors cease, except so far as the company in general meeting or the liquidators sanction their continuance.[106]

The general responsibilities of liquidators are fairly similar across our jurisdictions. Liquidators have to bring to an end the company's business and its open transactions, collect any outstanding receivables against third parties, realize and turn into money the company's property, and satisfy creditors' claims and distribute any remaining amounts amongst the company's members pro rata in accordance with their participation in the share capital.[107]

[87] ibid §8175. [88] ibid §8177. [89] ibid §8196. [90] ibid. [91] ibid §8201.

[92] Germain and Magnier (n 6) para 1624. [93] Le Gall and Ruellan (n 12) 64.

[94] Com Art L237-1. [95] Com Art L237-4.

[96] Com Art L237-14(1); Germain and Magnier (n 6) para 1624. Moreover, an amicable liquidation may be converted into a statutory liquidation by court order on the request of shareholders who represent at least 5% of the company's capital or of the company's creditors: Com Art L237-14(2).

[97] Com Art L237-15. [98] Com Art L237-16. [99] Com Art L237-20.

[100] Com Art 237-18. If the members fail to appoint a liquidator, the court will make the appointment; Com Art 237-19.

[101] AktG, §265; GmbHG, §66.

[102] AktG, §265(3). Shareholders must have held their shares for at least three months prior to the petition.

[103] GmbHG, §66(2). [104] Insolvency Act 1986, s 91(1).

[105] Davies and Worthington (n 1) 1151 (para 33-1). [106] Insolvency Act 1986, s 91(2).

[107] AktG, §268(1); GmbHG, §70; Insolvency Act 1986, s 91; Com Art 237-24; Fletcher (n 2) §8158.

They may continue the business activity and contract for new business only to the extent that this is necessary for the orderly liquidation of the company; or under French law subject to the authorization by the members or the court.[108] The liquidators have the power to dispose of the company's property by public auction or by private contract;[109] the business may be sold on a going concern basis or piecemeal. The liquidators represent the company vis-à-vis third parties and may bring or defend any action or other legal proceeding in the name and on behalf of the company.[110] Vis-à-vis third parties the powers to dispose of the company's property and to represent the company cannot be restricted by the articles of association or by a shareholders' resolution.[111] In England, the payment in full of any class of creditors requires the sanction of a special resolution of the company.[112] Throughout the liquidation process, the company's members have to be kept informed. Consequently, under German law, at the beginning of the liquidation the liquidators have to prepare a commencement balance sheet and an explanatory report; and thereafter a balance sheet and explanatory report at the end of each year. The commencement balance sheet and each subsequent balance sheet is subject to a resolution by the shareholders in general meeting, who also decide on the discharge of the liquidators and the members of the supervisory board at the end of the liquidation on the basis of a final account.[113] Under French law, the liquidators' mandate is in principle limited to three years; it may be renewed by the members or the court.[114] Within an extendable period of six months of their appointment the liquidators have to convene a meeting of the members to which they report on the situation of the company's assets and liabilities, as well as the progress of the liquidation and give a time estimate for completion.[115] Within three months of the end of each financial year, the liquidators have to prepare the annual accounts and a written report explaining the liquidation operations during the last financial year. In principle, each year and within six months of the end of the financial year, a meeting of members is to be convened to decide on the annual accounts, giving the necessary authorizations and possibly extending the liquidators' mandate.[116] These decisions are to be made by ordinary resolution.[117] A final meeting of members is convened at the end of the liquidation in order to decide on the final accounts, the discharge of the liquidators and to record the end of the liquidation.[118] In England, provided the winding up continues for more than a year, the liquidator has to produce periodic progress reports and send a copy to the members of the company.[119] When the affairs of the company are fully wound up, the liquidator prepares an account of the winding up explaining how it has been conducted and how the company's property has been disposed of. A copy of the account is to be send to the members of the company within 14 days. Within the same period, the liquidator has to send a copy of the account to the Registrar of Companies.[120] US law is largely silent on these issues, reflecting the greater independence and insulation of the board of directors from shareholder interference.

Given that ensuring the payment of creditors in priority to the shareholders is the primary purpose of mandatory liquidation provisions, all our jurisdictions contain mechanisms that seek to safeguard this creditor preference. Under German law, the liquidators must request the creditors to submit proof of their claims by publishing the request three times in the Gazette, pointing out that the company is in liquidation.[121] Failure to submit a proof of claim does not exclude the respective creditor from distribution. All known claims and those that become known prior to the final account being taken have to be paid regardless of the submission of a proof of claim.[122] If a known creditor does not submit proof of claim

[108] Com Art L237-24(3).
[109] Com Art L237-24(1); Insolvency Act 1986, s 165, Sch 4 para 6.
[110] Insolvency Act 1986, s 165, Sch 4 para 4.
[111] AktG, §269(5); Com Art L237-24(1).
[112] Insolvency Act 1986, s 165, Sch 4 para 1.
[113] AktG, §§270, 273; GmbHG, §§71, 74.
[114] Com Art L237-21.
[115] Com Art L237-23.
[116] Com Art L237-25.
[117] Com Art L237-27.
[118] Com Art L237-9.
[119] Insolvency Act 1986, s 92A.
[120] ibid s 94.
[121] AktG, §267; GmbHG, §§65(2), 73.
[122] Windbichler (n 2) 320–1 (§26 para 42).

the respective amount must be deposited for safekeeping where possible.[123] When the request to the creditors for submitting proof of claim has been published in the Gazette for the third time, a year-long ban on distributions to shareholders begins to run.[124] Following the satisfaction of the creditors, a distribution to shareholders may only be made when this one-year period has expired.[125] Moreover, if a claim cannot be satisfied or is disputed, a distribution to shareholders may only be made if security is provided to the respective creditor.[126] Property remaining after the satisfaction of the creditors is to be distributed amongst the shareholders pro rata in accordance with their participation in the company's share capital, taking account of any class rights that may exist. Where not all shares are paid up to the same amount, the paid up contributions are to be redeemed first and any remaining surplus is then distributed on a pro rata basis. If the company's resources are insufficient to repay the contributions, any outstanding contributions are to be called upon and the shareholders have to bear any losses on a pro rata basis.[127] For distributions in breach of these provisions, the liquidators may be liable for breach of duty.[128] Moreover, the shareholders have to return any amounts that they received in excess of what was due to them in accordance with the statutory provisions. On that basis, creditors who did not obtain satisfaction from the company may enforce a claim directly against the respective shareholders.[129] Under French law, the disposal of all or part of the company's assets to a member of the management team requires unanimous consent of the members or authorization by the court.[130] A disposal of company property to the liquidator or affiliated persons is prohibited.[131] Property remaining after the satisfaction of creditors has to be distributed, first, to the holders of preference shares and then the holders of ordinary shares, pro rata in accordance with their participation in the share capital.[132] Subject to a three-year limitation period, the liquidators are liable vis-à-vis both the company and third parties, including creditors, for a negligent breach of their duties.[133] In England, a certain measure of creditor protection is achieved by the mere fact that the liquidation is conducted by an external (neutral) expert who is a qualified insolvency practitioner. In a voluntary winding up, the liquidator is likely to adopt a procedure that follows closely that which applies in a compulsory winding up.[134] The liquidator will require creditors to submit written proof of their claims. All claims by creditors are provable, regardless of whether they are present or future, certain or contingent, ascertained or sounding only in damages, as long as the company was subject to the respective claim at the time when liquidation commenced.[135] The liquidator examines the proofs and decides whether to admit all or part of the claim or to reject it; he may estimate the value of contingent or uncertain claims, and where necessary, apply to the court for assistance. The liquidator's decisions are subject to review by the court.[136] The liquidator owes fiduciary duties and a duty of care to the company; not to individual creditors or members. In misfeasance proceedings the liquidator may be held personally liable for the misapplication of corporate property, negligence or breach of duty.[137] In the latter case, a constructive trust arises with proceeds being held by the liquidator on constructive trust for the beneficiaries (creditors and/or shareholders); subject to their traceability, transferred assets may be retrieved from third party recipients for the benefit of the company. Under many US legal

[123] AktG, §272(2); GmbHG, §73(2). [124] AktG, §272(1); GmbHG, §73(1).

[125] AktG, §271(1); GmbHG, §72. Where a corporation has been dissolved on the basis of a shareholders' resolution (or due to expiry of the period of its duration) the shareholders may decide to continue the corporation with a 75% majority of the share capital present and voting, provided the liquidators have not yet started to distribute corporate assets amongst the shareholders; AktG, §274(1).

[126] AktG, §272(3); GmbHG, §73(2). [127] AktG, §271; GmbHG, §72.

[128] AktG, §§268(2), 93; GmbHG, §§73(3), 43(3) and (4).

[129] AktG, §62; GmbHG, §31 by way of analogy. [130] Com Art L237-6. [131] Com Art L237-7.

[132] Com Art L237-29, L237-30. [133] Com Art 237-12.

[134] Davies and Worthington (n 1) 1168 (para 33-22).

[135] Insolvency (England and Wales) Rules 2016, rr 14.1, 14.2. [136] ibid rr 1.2, 14.3, 14.7, 14.8, 14.9.

[137] Davies and Worthington (n 1) 1163 (para 33-22).

systems, the company in dissolution may set a cut-off date for the registration of claims. The corporation may give notice of the dissolution to any person with a claim against the corporation requiring that person to present their claims in writing and with sufficient information to inform the corporation of the identity of the claimant and the substance of the claim. In the notice, the corporation sets the date by which the claim must be received by the corporation; otherwise, the claim will be barred.[138] The minimum time period for setting the 'bar date' varies.[139] A claim that has been received in time, but rejected by the corporation will be barred if the claimant does not commence an action in respect of the claim within a certain period of time after receiving the rejection notice.[140] A bar date may also be set for future and contingent claims; moreover, the corporation may offer to such claimants security sufficient to provide compensation if the claim matures.[141] Known claimants are to be given actual notice. In order to reach unknown claimants, the notice is to be published in a local newspaper at the corporation's principal place of business, and depending on the corporation's size, also has to be published in a national newspaper.[142] In order to provide for unknown claims or claims that have not arisen but that are likely to arise or become known within a certain number of years since dissolution, the corporation may petition the court to determine the amount and form of security that is likely to be sufficient to provide compensation for such claims.[143] Such claims will not be barred and can rely on the security provided as long as they are brought within the relevant period of years.[144] Corporate property is to be applied first to the payment of accepted claims and as security for future, contingent, and unknown claims. Any remaining assets are to be distributed to the shareholders of the corporation on a pro rata basis, taking into account any preferential rights that may attach to certain classes of shares.[145] Distributions to shareholder may be subject to a temporary ban and may only be possible after expiration of a certain period of time—in Delaware 150 days since the last notice of rejection given to a claim holder.[146] As an alternative to the statutory procedures, a corporation may adopt a plan of distribution under which known claims are satisfied, and reasonably sufficient provision is made for future, contingent, and unknown claims.[147] Moreover, the plan must not discriminate between claims and must be adequately funded.[148] Directors will be jointly and severally liable to corporate creditors for wrongful distributions to shareholders.[149] According to the trust fund doctrine, corporate officers and directors hold corporate assets on trust for pro rata distribution to creditors. A breach of duty may result in personal liability of officers and directors. In respect of the wrongfully distributed corporate assets a constructive trust arises, and, traceability provided, the recipient shareholders will be liable as constructive trustees.[150] Their liability may be capped at the amount received.[151] The trust fund doctrine only applies to claims accrued at the time of dissolution.

III. Termination and resurrection

Under German law, at the end of the liquidation when the liquidators have provided the final accounts they will apply to the register court to have the liquidation registered. The corporate existence comes to an end with the company's removal from the register. Where it transpires, retrospectively, that further liquidation action is necessary, for example corporate property is discovered after termination, any party in interest may apply to the court

[138] MBCA, §14.06; DGCL, §280. [139] MBCA: 120 days; Delaware: 60 days.
[140] MBCA, §1406(c)(2); DGCL, §280(a)(3). [141] DGCL, §280(b).
[142] MBCA, §14.07; DGCL, §280(a)(1). [143] MBCA, §14.08; DGCL, §280(c)(3).
[144] Fletcher (n 2) §8158.50. [145] DGCL, §281(a); Fletcher (n 2) §§8219, 8224–6.
[146] DGCL, §281(a). [147] DGCL, §281(b). [148] Fletcher (n 2) §8219.
[149] ibid; MBCA, §14.09. [150] Fletcher (n 2) §8219. [151] DGCL, §282(c).

to have the liquidators reappointed.[152] Where a corporation does not have any assets it may be removed from the register, either on the register court's own motion or on an application of the tax authorities.[153] Removal from the register results in dissolution, and owing to a lack of distributable assets, immediately in the corporation's termination, subject to a potential resurrection should assets appear later.[154] French law works in a very similar way. Following approval of the final accounts by the general meeting, which may be substituted by a decision of the president of the commercial court, the liquidators submit the final accounts to the office of the commercial court as an annex to the commercial register.[155] Notice of the closure of the liquidation is to be published in the journal nominated by the company for its legal announcements as well as in the Bulletin for obligatory legal announcements (BALO).[156] Upon compliance with these formalities, the company is removed from the register.[157] Interestingly, it is the date on which the shareholder's meeting or the court decided that the liquidation is closed (and the final accounts approved) when the corporate existence comes to an end. However, this fact may be invoked against third parties only with the company being removed from the register.[158] In the US, corporate existence normally comes to an end when the winding up process is complete and the state issues a certificate of voluntary dissolution or a court enters a decree of involuntary or court supervised dissolution.[159]

Under English law, the liquidator sends to the Registrar of Companies his final account.[160] Upon the expiration of a three-month period from registration, the corporate existence is deemed to have come to an end ('dissolved'), unless on application of the liquidator or any other person in interest, the court defers the date of 'dissolution'.[161] Where the Registrar of Companies believes that a company is not carrying on any business, in particular, where it is in arrears with submitting its annual returns and accounts,[162] the Registrar may initiate a process that will result in the striking off of the company from the register.[163] A similar procedure is available where liquidation proceedings have been started but resources are insufficient to complete them.[164] Moreover, a company may apply to the Registrar of Companies for a voluntary striking off. Upon receipt of such application, the Registrar may publish a notice in the *Gazette* and, if no person has shown cause to the contrary within a three-month period, the registrar may strike off the company from the register and publish a notice in the *Gazette* upon which the company is 'dissolved'.[165] On application of a former director or member, a creditor at the time of 'dissolution', or any person with a potential claim against the company and others, the court may restore a 'dissolved' company if it was struck off as defunct but was carrying on business at the time; in case of a voluntary striking off, if the preconditions for it had not been met; and in all other cases if the court thinks it just to restore the company.[166]

[152] AktG, §273; GmbHG, §74.
[153] FamFG, §394. [154] Windbichler (n 2) 318 (§26 para 36). [155] Com Art R237-7.
[156] Com Art R237-8. [157] Com Art R237-9. [158] Germain and Magnier (n 6) para 1636.
[159] Fletcher (n 2) §8113. [160] Insolvency Act 1986, s 94. [161] ibid s 201.
[162] Davies and Worthington (n 1) 1157 (para 33-29).
[163] If a first letter to the company inquiring whether the company is in operation remains unanswered for a month, the Registrar must send a (registered) letter stating that if no answer is received within one month notice will be published in the *Gazette* with a view to striking the company's name off the register. If this second letter goes unanswered for a month, the Registrar may publish a notice in the *Gazette* and mail a notice to the company to the effect that the company will be struck off and dissolved after the expiry of a three-months period starting from the date of notice, unless cause is shown to the contrary. If no cause is shown to the contrary within said period, the company is to be struck off from the register, notice of which is to be published in the *Gazette*, upon which the corporate existence comes to an end: Companies Act 2006, s 1000. Where the striking off was unjustified because the company was carrying on business at the time, former directors or members of the company may apply for administrative restoration: ibid ss 1024, 1025.
[164] Companies Act 2006, s 1001. [165] ibid s 1003. [166] ibid ss 1029–1031.

B. The Special Case of Insolvency

Insolvency is usually perceived as a game changer. Provisionally (and un-technically), insolvency may be defined as a state of affairs where a corporation's resources are insufficient to satisfy all the claims of its creditors. Arguably, this has consequences for the relationship between debt and equity, as well as for the relationship between the various debt holders. First, consider the relationship between equity and debt. Owing to the principle of limited liability, a shift in residual risk bearing occurs as soon as the equity holders are out of the money; or in other words, firm value is lower than the nominal value of the aggregate of all creditor claims.[167] At this point, equity holders will be immune to any further reduction in firm value; whereas they may still benefit from any increase that goes beyond the difference between current firm value and the amount of debt. Creditors, on the other hand, may suffer an immediate reduction of the value of their entitlement as firm value declines, and will immediately benefit from any increase in firm value. Management controlled by shareholders and acting in their best interest have, thus, an incentive to take excessive risks:[168] they may exclusively focus on the upside of potential projects, no matter how remote the possibility of success may be. The potential losses will be borne entirely by the corporation's (unsecured) creditors.[169] Owing to this asymmetric distribution of gains and losses,[170] managers and shareholders may even be inclined to pursue projects with a negative net present value.

Let us assume that our company, financed by equity and debt, has assets with an aggregate value of 1,000; the nominal aggregate value of its claims is 1,500. The firm is insolvent (on a balance sheet basis). Let us further assume that company management has the choice of investing in either project A or project B. Project A requires an investment of 1,000 and has a 10 per cent probability of returning 2,500 in one year's time and a 90 per cent chance of failing, in which case it will return nothing at all. Project B also costs 1,000 today; with a probability of 50 per cent it will return 1,500 in a year's time, the probability of failure is also 50 per cent in which case the project will return only 600. If the management invest in project A, there is a 10 per cent chance that firm value will increase to 2,500 in a year's time.[171] Not only could the company pay back its creditors in full, the value of equity would have increased by 1,000 as well. If the project fails, equity will have lost nothing (or so the argument goes); however, the market value of the aggregate of the creditors' claims will have declined to 0 (from 1,000 previously). By contrast, in the best case scenario of project B the company may just break even; it will be able to pay its creditors in full, leaving nothing for the equity holders. If project B fails, the aggregate value of creditors' claims will be reduced to 600. The net present value of project A is negative (–750);[172] whereas the net present value of project B is positive (+50).[173] Management should invest in positive net present value projects because this creates value immediately. Investment in project B would increase firm value by +50 and would benefit claim holders by the same amount. It would do nothing for equity holders. Management acting in the interest of equity holders would invest in project A. Such investment would reduce firm value and the value of creditors' claims immediately to 250;

[167] S Schwarcz, 'Rethinking a Corporation's Obligation to Creditors' (1996) 17 Cardozo Law Review 647, 667.

[168] R de R Barondes, 'Fiduciary Duties of Officers and Directors of Distressed Corporations' (1998) 7 George Mason Law Review 45, 48–9; J Armour, G Hertig, and H Kanda, 'Transactions with Creditors' in R Kraakman and others, *The Anatomy of Corporate Law* (3rd edn, OUP 2017) 109, 111.

[169] F Easterbrook and D Fischel, *The Economic Structure of Corporate Law* (HUP 1991) 69; CW Adams, 'An Economic Justification for Corporate Reorganizations' (1991) 20 HOFSTRA Law Review 117, 125; LM LoPucki, 'A General Theory of the State Remedies/Bankruptcy System' (1982) Wisconsin Law Review 311, 328.

[170] H Fleischer, 'Erweiterte Außenhaftung der Organmitglieder im Europäischen Gesellschafts- und Kapitalmarktrecht' (2004) ZGR 437, 446.

[171] Current firm value of 1,000 is invested, and generates 2,500 at the end of the year.

[172] (10% x 2,500 + 90% x 0) – 1,000.

[173] (50% x 1,500 + 50% x 600) – 1,000.

whereas the value of equity will immediately increase by an amount of 100 (10% x 1,000) at creditors' expense. The risk of failure is paid for entirely by the creditors.

The problem seems to be most relevant for small partnership-like companies where the owner-managers are likely either to simply carry on with a loss-making activity in the hope that things might get better or actively dissipate the company's assets to the detriment of its creditors. One strategy to prevent suboptimal and inefficient management decisions consists in shifting corporate management's fiduciary and common law duties from shareholders to creditors when the company is in financial distress. Across the common law world, duty-shifting doctrines in the vicinity of insolvency are widely recognized. With the onset of insolvency, the assets of the company are in economic terms no longer attributable to the shareholders; rather, these assets are the creditors', mediated through the company pending liquidation or return to solvency.[174] Consequently, when a company approaches insolvency a 'duty is owed by the directors to the company and to the creditors of the company to ensure that the affairs of the company are properly administered and that its property is not dissipated or exploited for the benefit of the directors themselves to the prejudice of the creditors'.[175] This is not a fiduciary duty directly owed towards an individual creditor, nor is an individual creditor entitled to sue for breach of the fiduciary duty owed by the director to the company.[176] Rather, in (the vicinity of) insolvency the interests of the creditors have to be taken into account.[177] The relevance of the principles of directors' duties vis-à-vis creditors as a self-standing ground for directors' liability remains doubtful.[178] It seems that the duty to take the creditors' interests into consideration is more significant as a ground for invalidating the ratification through a shareholders' resolution of a director's breach of (non-creditor) duties, and for rendering invalid a board resolution that would disregard the creditors' interests.[179] Duty shifting doctrines are also recognized in US law.[180] Here, it is also unclear what the effect of duty shifting is. In the past it was used to protect directors against shareholders who demanded excessive risk taking.[181] And although it may provide creditors with standing to bring a derivative claim on behalf of the corporation against its directors,[182] the content of the duty and what it requires of management remains opaque.[183]

[174] *West Marcia Safetywear Ltd (in liquidation) v Dodd and Another* [1988] BCLC 250, 252–3, citing the Australian decision *Kinsela v Russel Kinsela Pty Ltd (in liquidation)* (1986) 4 NSWLR 722, 730.

[175] *Winkworth v Edward Baron Development Co Ltd* [1986] 1 WLR 1512, 1516.

[176] *Yukong Line Ltd of Korea v Rendsburg Investments Corp of Liberia and Others* [1998] 2 BCLC 485, 503.

[177] To be taken into account are the creditors' interests as a group, that is, where a transaction accords with the interests of creditors as a group there will not be a breach of duty even though the transaction may disadvantage individual creditors. See *Re Pantone 485 Ltd* [2002] 1 BCLC 266, 286.

[178] L Sealy, 'Directors' Duties: An Unnecessary Gloss' (1988) 47 Cambridge Law Journal 175, 177. In a string of first instance decisions directors were held liable, when sued by the office holder, for making payments to certain creditors at a time when the respective company was insolvent, insolvency proceedings imminent and the payment generated a personal benefit for the authorizing director; *Re Cityspan Ltd* [2008] BCC 60; *Re HLC Environmental Projects Ltd* [2014] BCC 337; *Re Micra Contracts Ltd (in liquidation)* [2016] BCC 153; *Re Cosy Seal Insulation Ltd (in administration)* [2016] 2 BCLC 319. Whether this line of reasoning will find wider acceptance remains doubtful; see K van Zwieten 'Director Liability in Insolvency and Its Vicinity' (2018) 38 OJLS 382-409.

[179] *Colin Gwyer & Associates Ltd v London Wharf (Limehouse) Ltd* [2003] BCC 885.

[180] *Credit Lyonnais Bank Nederland NV v. Pathe Communications Corporation*, 1991 WL 277613 (Del. Ch.); *Geyer v. Ingersoll Publications Company*, 621 A.2d 784 (Del. Ch. 1992); *Production Resources Group LLC v. NCT Group Inc.*, 863 A.2d 772 (Del. Ch. 2004). For Delaware law, the point which triggers duty shifting has recently been clarified as being actual insolvency, rather than some vaguely defined 'vicinity of insolvency'; see *North American Catholic Educational Programming Foundation, Inc. v. Gheewalla* 930 A.2d 92, 101. See further *Berg & Berg Enterprises, LLC, v. Boyle*, 2009 Cal. App. LEXIS 1740 (Oct. 29, 2009), holding that 'the scope of any extra-contractual duty owed by corporate directors to the insolvent corporation's creditors is limited in California, consistently with the trust-fund doctrine, *to the avoidance of actions that divert, dissipate, or unduly risk corporate assets that might otherwise be used to pay creditors claims*' (italics in the original).

[181] *Credit Lyonnais Bank Nederland NV v. Pathe Communications Corporation* (n 180).

[182] *Production Resources Group LLC v. NCT Group Inc.* (n 180) 790–6; *North American Catholic Educational Programming Foundation, Inc. v. Gheewalla*, 930 A.2d 92, 101.

[183] For a review of the literature see HTC Hu and JL Westbrook, 'Abolition of the Corporate Duty to Creditors' (2007) 107 Columbia Law Review 1321, 1340–3.

For large publicly traded companies the issue of management pursuing a strategy that benefits shareholders at the cost of creditors appears to be somewhat overstated and its impact may be reduced by a number of mitigating factors. The more insulated management are from shareholder control and the less aligned management and shareholder interests are, the less likely that management will pursue actions that benefit shareholders at the expense of creditors. Owing to their firm specific investment and lack of diversification, management are likely to be more risk averse than shareholders and would perhaps prefer project B over project A, as this would enhance their chances of staying in the job.[184] Moreover, it is not necessarily correct to say that at a state of (balance sheet) insolvency shares have lost all their value and that shareholders will not suffer any further loss. The share still carries voting rights which may be valuable in themselves, and inherent in the share is the option value of a potential upturn of the firm's fortunes which shareholders may be reluctant to forgo, although for highly diversified shareholders this option value may matter little. On the other hand, creditors may be hedged in a way that skews their incentives. A creditor that has bought credit protection will be insensitive to either project A or project B; where the same creditor has bought a call option on the company's shares he may even prefer project A despite the fact that this project reduces firm value.

Turning to the impact of insolvency on inter-creditor relationships, as a baseline, creditors are free to negotiate the conditions for their withdrawal from the firm. Withdrawal will normally require default, resulting in a right to termination and acceleration of the outstanding debt and enforceability of security interests. Thus, provided the freely negotiated trigger conditions have been met, the creditor can retrieve his contribution and walk away. In a situation where the pool of assets pledged to the creditors for their preferential satisfaction is insufficient to satisfy all the creditors' claims, free individual withdrawal rights may result in the destruction of firm specific investment and a potential going concern surplus. Even where there is no going concern surplus, individual withdrawal may directly interfere with other creditors' entitlements by rendering them less valuable. Thus (at least to the extent that they are unable to sell their claim in the distressed debt market), each creditor has an incentive to enforce their individual property rights as soon as possible.[185] Where, owing to prohibitively high transaction costs, creditors cannot reach prior agreement and plausibly commit to co-operation, the situation they find themselves in may be characterized as a 'classic example' of a 'prisoners' dilemma'. Each creditor, unless assured of the others' cooperation, has an incentive to take advantage of individual enforcement rights, and to do so before the other creditors act. Assume that our debtor company has assets with a break-up value of 1,000; however, if these assets would remain together as a functioning unit, the going concern value would be 1,600. The firm has two creditors A and B, ranking pari passu, each with a nominal claim of 900. The respective pay-off bimatrix could be depicted as in Figure 1.[186]

		Creditor B	
		Enforce (don't cooperate)	Don't enforce (cooperate)
Creditor A	Enforce (don't cooperate)	500; 500	900; 100
	Don't enforce (cooperate)	100; 900	800; 800

Figure 1: Tragedy of the commons

[184] Armour, Hertig, and Kanda (n 168) 109, 112.
[185] T Jackson, *The Logic and Limits of Bankruptcy Law* (HUP 1986) 12.
[186] The following draws on M Schillig, 'Corporate Insolvency Law in the 21st Century: State-imposed or Market-based?' (2014) 14 Journal of Corporate Law Studies 1, 8.

The socially optimal outcome would be the realization of the going concern surplus (see Figure 1) through cooperation (non-enforcement of individual rights). The creditors as a whole would be better off and the amount of 1,600 could be split equally (bottom right). If transaction costs are high, it may not be possible for either creditor to credibly commit to cooperation. In that case, each creditor will always be better off by enforcing (not cooperating) regardless of what the other creditor does. Under the assumption that each creditor's chance of coming first in the race on the debtor's assets is equal, the pay-off for each creditor would be 500 (50% x 900 + 50% x 100). Each creditor will have a pay-off of only 100 when he cooperates and the other enforces. Therefore, the dominant strategy for each creditor is to enforce (not cooperate).

On the basis of 'nexus of contract' theories, corporate insolvency law requires a contractarian explanation. This can be found in Thomas Jackson's 'creditors' bargain theory'. The 'creditors' bargain' is a hypothetical model which seeks to replicate the agreement one would expect self-interested rational creditors to conclude among themselves were they able to negotiate ex ante.[187] These creditors would prefer the existence of a government-imposed system of collective debt enforcement because this would reduce or eliminate the costs associated with a race of the creditors on the company's assets.[188] According to Jackson, this race creates (monitoring) costs for the individual creditor, and is also likely to result in a premature termination of the debtor's business since each creditor will consider only their own advantage, not the disadvantages imposed on other creditors individually and collectively. To the extent that there is a going concern surplus, maintaining the debtor's business as a going concern is likely to increase the aggregate pool of assets and imposing a collective enforcement regime is advantageous to the creditors as a group.[189]

On the basis of proprietary theories of corporate law, corporate insolvency law is a logical extension of the asset partitioning/legal entity concept.[190] Separate legal personality protects a firm's going concern surplus by preventing shareholders and their personal creditors from withdrawing their contributions at will, thus creating a stable pool of assets pledged for the preferential satisfaction of creditors. Outside insolvency, creditors have access to this resource on the basis of their individual enforcement (withdrawal) rights. However, when the debtor is insolvent, the creditors' incentives are misaligned: the exercise of any one creditor's individual enforcement right (in priority to others) may result in a fully internalized benefit—full satisfaction—whereas the costs emanating from the destruction of the going concern value are externalized and borne by all the other creditors as a group. Where there is no going concern value, individual enforcement action may still result in negative externalities in the form that the other creditors may receive a reduced dividend.[191] The misalignment of incentives is a result of the combination of individual enforcement rights with a common pool of assets. Individual rights can be used to extract private benefits, whilst at the same time imposing costs on the common pool.[192] This 'tragedy of the commons' can be remedied by reducing the degree of incongruity between the individual rights and the common pool through decoupling individual rights from the right of access to the common pool by either concentrating individual rights in the hands of a single rights holder ('privatisation')[193] or in the hands of a collectivity that can act as one

[187] T Jackson, 'Bankruptcy, Non-Bankruptcy Entitlements, and the Creditors' Bargain' (1982) 91 Yale Law Journal 857, 858.

[188] ibid 861.

[189] ibid 865. For a critical assessment see RJ Mokal, 'The Authentic Consent Model: Contractarianism, Creditors' Bargain, and Corporate Liquidation' (2001) 21 Legal Studies 400.

[190] See Schillig (n 186) 4–14.

[191] LA Fennell, 'Commons, Anticommons, Semicommons' in K Ayotte and H Smith (eds), *Research Handbook on the Economics of Property Law* (Edward Elgar Publishing 2011) 35–9.

[192] ibid 37.

[193] From a comparative perspective, solutions based on 'privatization' are rare. An example is the English law concept of administrative receivership: A single creditor with a security over all or substantially all of the debtor's

('collectivisation').[194] Corporate insolvency law as a form of organizational law largely follows the latter approach by imposing a comprehensive moratorium on individual enforcement rights and by locking all creditors into a collective procedure. In continuation of the asset partitioning/legal entity concept, creditors as residual claimants can no longer withdraw their contributions. Rather, withdrawal (enforcement) rights are transformed into participation rights in form of voting rights and access to information. However, collectivization does not eliminate the mismatch between individual rights and common pool completely. When locked into a collective procedure, parties still need to decide how to realize and distribute a potential going concern surplus. During these negotiations each party has an incentive to extract as much as possible of the surplus for itself. By pushing too far, a deal may collapse and the going concern surplus may be lost. Thus, collectivization may result in a 'tragedy of the anti-commons' that corporate insolvency law needs to address.

Thus, in order to prevent shareholders and management from exploiting creditors when the latter have taken the place of the shareholders as residual risk bearers and to prevent a creditors' race on the company's assets the corporate governance regime must at some point transition into the corporate insolvency law (bankruptcy) governance regime, which, in turn, must address and seek to alleviate the ensuing 'tragedy of the anti-commons' problem. We will consider both issues below. At this point it is necessary to get a better idea of the different concepts of 'insolvency' that are prevalent in our jurisdictions.

I. Overview

In accordance with the idea of residuarity, a concept of insolvency frequently referred to in insolvency statutes is balance sheet insolvency, defined as a financial situation where the value of the company's assets is insufficient to discharge all its obligations.[195] The amount of the company's debts (on the right hand side of the balance sheet) exceeds the value of the company's assets (on the left hand side of the balance sheet). If the company were liquidated at this moment in time, the value of the company's assets would be insufficient to discharge all its obligations in full. Its (unsecured) creditors would be paid only pro rata and would receive only a certain percentage on their respective claims (rate = nominal value of the claim x value of the company's assets/nominal value of all claims against the debtor). As residual claimants, shareholders are entitled only to what is left after all creditors have been paid, that is, nothing in the state of insolvency. The concept is essentially an accounting exercise and not without complexity. Despite huge amounts of debt on the right-hand side of the balance sheet, owing to its profitability or (perceived) potential, the market value of the company's assets on a going concern basis may be so high that it still exceeds the amount of debt. Thus, valuation of both assets and liabilities, either on a going concern or break up basis, becomes essential, and in practice may often be more an art than a science.

Perhaps, a more straightforward concept is insolvency on a cash flow basis. According to this test, a company is insolvent if it is unable to pay its debts as they fall due.[196] This state is comparatively easy to ascertain if supplemented by a test of cessation of payments: the

assets can appoint a receiver to control the common pool for the benefit of the appointing creditor; R Goode, *Principles of Corporate Insolvency Law* (4th edn, Sweet & Maxwell 2011) paras 10-06–10-24. Junior creditors are prevented from exercising their individual enforcement rights against the debtor's assets in the possession of the receiver; *Evans v Rival Granite Quarries Ltd* [1910] 2 KB 979; see also Insolvency Act 1986, s 43.

[194] 'Collectivisation' is the most common strategy and can be observed with English administration procedure where an administrator is appointed—by the court or out-of-court—with far-reaching powers over the debtor's assets and a duty to act in the best interest of all creditors. Individual enforcement rights are transformed, subjected to a comprehensive moratorium and reduced to a right to participate in the process by voting on the administrator's proposals.

[195] Insolvency Act 1986, s 123(2); 11 U.S.C., §101(32); InsO, §19.

[196] Insolvency Act 1986, s 123(1)(e); InsO, §17; Com Art L631-1, L640-1.

company does not pay (a substantial amount of) its due debts. The danger is however, that companies with a healthy financial basis are pushed into formal proceedings merely because of a temporary illiquidity. It is important to realize that a company which is insolvent on a balance sheet basis may still be able to pay its debts and, conversely, that a company with sufficient assets to cover all its obligations may be short of liquidity and unable to pay all its debts as they fall due. In the light of the so-called rescue culture, some legal systems have introduced a further concept which arguably facilitates the early initiation of reorganization proceedings at a time when there is still a good prospect for business recovery. This concept can be termed prospective cash flow insolvency: although currently still able to pay, the company will, in the foreseeable future, be unable to pay its debts when they fall due.[197] The concept has a strong prognostic element.

The state of (in)solvency is relevant for a number of issues in the course of insolvency proceedings. Under some legal systems, insolvency in one form or another is a precondition for commencing formal insolvency proceedings. This is the case under German and French law, but also for English law in respect of a winding up by the court or an administration order (provided the petition has not been filed by the holder of a qualifying floating charge). In the US an involuntary petition by creditors requires the showing of cash flow insolvency if the filing is controverted. A determination that the company was insolvent at the relevant time may further be essential for the setting aside of fraudulent transactions, transactions at an undervalue, and unlawful preferences, and further for any potential management liability for breach of a duty to file for bankruptcy, for wrongful trading or for directors' disqualification. Within the same legal system, different concepts of insolvency may be relevant for different purposes.

II. England and Wales

Insolvency Act 1986

Section 123 Definition of inability to pay debts

(1) A company is deemed unable to pay its debts—
   (a) if a creditor (by assignment or otherwise) to whom the company is indebted in a sum exceeding £750 then due has served on the company, by leaving it at the company's registered office, a written demand (in the prescribed form) requiring the company to pay the sum so due and the company has for 3 weeks thereafter neglected to pay the sum or to secure or compound for it to the reasonable satisfaction of the creditor, or
   (b) if, in England and Wales, execution or other process issued on a judgment, decree or order of any court in favour of a creditor of the company is returned unsatisfied in whole or in part, or
   (c) …
   (d) …, or
   (e) if it is proved to the satisfaction of the court that the company is unable to pay its debts as they fall due.

(2) A company is also deemed unable to pay its debts if it is proved to the satisfaction of the court that the value of the company's assets is less than the amount of its liabilities, taking into account its contingent and prospective liabilities.

(3) …

Pursuant to section 123(1)(e) of the Insolvency Act 1986, a company is deemed to be unable to pay its debts if it is proved to the satisfaction of the court that the company is unable to pay its debts as they fall due.[198] A company is also deemed unable to pay its debts if it is proved to

[197] InsO, §18; Com Art L620-1.

[198] Insolvency Act 1986, s 123(1)(a) and (b) prescribe two very straightforward means of showing that a company is unable to pay its debts.

the satisfaction of the court that the value of the company's assets is less than the amount of its liabilities, taking into account its contingent and prospective liabilities. Thus, the concept of 'inability to pay' encompasses both, cash flow insolvency (commercial insolvency) and insolvency on a balance sheet basis.

1. *Cash flow test or commercial insolvency test*

A company is insolvent on a cash flow basis if it is unable to pay its debts as they fall due. For this test it is immaterial whether the company's assets exceed its liabilities. For example, where a company holds a valuable but illiquid asset, creditors do not have to wait until the company is able to realize the asset's value at some point in the future.[199] The essential question is whether the company's financial situation allows it to continue in business; and whether any liquidity problems are only temporary and can be cured in the reasonably near future.[200] The test is relatively straightforward: what matters is whether the company is actually paying its debts as they fall due, if not it is deemed to be insolvent.[201] Generally, courts will adopt a commercial view taking into account the fact that it is quite normal for debtors to make and for creditors to accept late payment as long as payment can be made within the period that a creditor would consider acceptable.[202] In principle, only due debts are to be taken into account, that is, debts which are both existing and immediately payable.[203] The issue of whether and to what extent debts may be considered that will be due only at some point in the future has been discussed extensively by Mr Justice Briggs (as he then was) in *Cheyne*.

In the matter of Cheyne Finance Plc (in Receivership) **[2007] EWHC 2401 (Ch)**

Cheyne concerned a special investment vehicle in a 'run-off situation'. Following a major loss of capital caused by a reduction of asset prices due to the US subprime crisis, the security trustee had to appoint receivers which had to pay senior creditors on a 'pay as you go' basis, that is, incoming monies had to be used to pay in full senior obligations (only) as and when they became due, which was in accordance with a maturity schedule on the basis of a series of rolling dates over a two year period. By continuing with the 'pay as you go' approach, the receivers would have been able to pay all maturing debts in full up until a certain date; but unable to pay debts maturing after this date. By contrast, by selling the issuer's entire investment portfolio as a whole in exchange for an underwritten note, the receivers would be able to pay all senior creditors in full but not on time. The latter modus operandi was available only in the case of an 'Insolvency Event'. This was defined in the Trust Deed as a determination by the receiver that the issuer 'is, or is about to become, unable to pay its debts as they fall due to Senior Creditors ... as contemplated by Section 123(1) of the United Kingdom Insolvency Act 1986'. The receivers asked the court for instructions on the interpretation of the term 'Insolvency Event'.

Mr Justice Briggs (as he then was):

36 In the Insolvency Act 1985, repeated in s.123 of the 1986 Act, commercial and balance sheet insolvency are for the first time split apart. In place of the mandatory requirement to take account of contingent and prospective liabilities there has been added in s.123(1)(e) the phrase 'as they fall due' after 'debts'. The mandatory requirement to consider contingent and prospective liabilities now only appears in s.123(2). There is no English authority on the question whether, as Mr. Trower submitted, those changes prevent reference to prospective, i.e. future, debts under s.123(1)(e).

37 To the limited extent that academic writers have addressed this point, they are divided ...

41 There is a wealth of Australian authority on the question of whether a cashflow or commercial insolvency test permits references to debts which will fall due in the future, i.e. in English

199 Goode (n 193) 114 (para 4-05). 200 ibid 123 (para 4-15).

201 ibid 114 (para 4-05). Only debts are to be taken into account, that is, 'liquidated claims' for an amount that is ascertained or can be readily ascertained: ibid 124 (para 4-17).

202 ibid 126–7 (para 4-19). 203 ibid 124–6 (para 4-18).

terminology 'prospective debts', rather than 'prospective or contingent liabilities'. The reason why this question has, unlike in England, been analysed in such detail in Australia is probably that neither the Australian courts nor legislature have developed a balance sheet test of the type found in s.123(2).

...

51 It is clear from that brief review of the Australian decisions that in an environment shorn of any balance sheet test for insolvency, cash flow or commercial insolvency is not to be ascertained by a slavish focus only on debts due as at the relevant date. Such a blinkered review will, in some cases, fail to see that a momentary inability to pay is only the result of a temporary lack of liquidity soon to be remedied, and in other cases fail to see that due to an endemic shortage of working capital a company is on any commercial view insolvent, even though it may continue to pay its debts for the next few days, weeks or even months before an inevitable failure.

52 Furthermore, the common sense requirement not to ignore the relevant future was found to be implicit in the Australian cases in the simple phrase 'as they become due'.

53 Returning to the English legislation, it is, in my view, critical to note that when separating out balance sheet insolvency from commercial insolvency in 1985 the legislature did not merely remove the requirement to include contingent and prospective liabilities in framing s.123(1)(e) out of its predecessor, but added what in Australia have always been regarded as the key words of futurity, namely the phrase 'as they fall due'. In that context 'fall due' is, in my judgment, synonymous with "become due".

54 Mr. Trower submitted that the existence of the balance sheet test in s.123(2) makes an Australian type of approach to the commercial insolvency test unnecessary, because a company will always be balance sheet insolvent in circumstances where a review of future debts shows that it is commercially insolvent. I disagree. First, I can see no good reason why the developed understanding in Australia of the nature of the exercise required by the phrase 'unable to pay debts as they become (or fall) due' should not be recognised when the same phrase is, for the first time, deliberately inserted into the English insolvency test. The Australian approach makes commercial sense, whereas the blinkered approach of ignoring the future does not.

55 Secondly, a company may not always be balance sheet insolvent where an Australian style test for commercial insolvency is satisfied, as in this example: The company has £1,000 ready cash and a very valuable but very illiquid asset worth £250,000 which cannot be sold for two years. It has present debts of £500, but a future debt of £100,000 due in six months. On any commercial view the company clearly cannot pay its debts as they fall due, but it is, or would be, balance sheet solvent.

56 In my judgment, the effect of the alterations to the insolvency test made in 1985 and now found in s.123 of the 1986 Act was to replace in the commercial solvency test now in s.123(1)(e), one futurity requirement, namely to include contingent and prospective liabilities, with another more flexible and fact sensitive requirement encapsulated in the new phrase 'as they fall due'.

57 In the case of a company which is still trading, and where there is therefore a high degree of uncertainty as to the profile of its future cash flow, an appreciation that s.123(1)(e) permits a review of the future will often make little difference. In many, if not most, cases the alternative balance sheet test will afford a petitioner for winding up a convenient alternative means of proof of a deemed insolvency.

58 The irony of the present case is that the Insolvency Event test, when applied by the Receivers appointed under the Trust Deed, will be in relation to a company in run-off, closed to future business, when its future cash flow profile is abnormally clear and when no balance sheet alternative test is available.

59 This leads me to my second main reason for rejecting Party A's case on the future debts issue. In my judgment, the presumed common intention to be derived from the parties' choice to define inability to pay debts by reference to s.123(1) rather than s.123(2) is simply that they wished Cheyne's solvency to be adjudicated on a commercial rather than balance sheet basis, and nothing more than that. The definition incorporates the whole of s.123(1), not just s.123(1)(e). The common feature of the lettered sub-sub-sections of s.123(1) is that they are indiciae of commercial rather than balance sheet insolvency. Companies which fail to pay their judgment

debts or, without good reason, to respond to statutory demands, are usually unable to pay their debts as they fall due regardless of the state of their balance sheets.

60 Even if my view as to the meaning and effect of s.123(1)(e) were wrong and a higher court concluded that it was to be interpreted as imposing the blinkers for which Mr. Trower contends, it would, in my judgment, be perverse to conclude that the parties to the Common Terms Agreement and Trust Deed intended that consequence, because of its potentially bizarre and uncommercial effects in the context of the affairs of Cheyne. In my last judgment I questioned whether, if the Receivers had sold all Cheyne's assets for cash, and knew for sure that it would default in the distant rather than near future, it could not be determined to be insolvent until that distant event of default was about to occur. The Receivers would be obliged to go on paying early maturing Senior Debts in full, knowing that a failure to pay anything in respect of later maturing debts of identical seniority was a racing certainty. I cannot envisage any reason why the parties to the Common Terms Agreement and Trust Deed should have intended thereby to confer an absolute priority on the holders of early maturing Senior Debt. The manner in which that priority would impact on Senior Creditors would depend, not upon anything to be found in the Payment Priority, but upon the unpredictable outcome of a run-off which, at the time both of the framing of the contractual documents and the making of any investment in Cheyne pursuant to them, must have been regarded by the participants as an unpleasant but hopefully remote future risk.

Questions and comments:

1. Note that in *Cheyne* section 123 of the Insolvency Act 1986 did not apply directly, but only by virtue of reference in the relevant contractual documentation. To what extent do you think has this influenced the outcome in this case?
2. Most English cases on the interpretation of the concepts of insolvency concern contractual references to the statutory provisions, rather than a direct application of the statute. Why do you think this is the case?
3. It is often said that English judges apply a 'commercial reality approach' in corporate and commercial law cases. Can you see this approach reflected in *Cheyne*?

2. Balance sheet insolvency

In its current form, the definition of balance sheet insolvency first appeared in 1985 as a result of the Cork Report and the White Paper which followed. In contrast to the cash flow test, the balance sheet test takes into account liabilities, including contingent and prospective liabilities. The term 'liabilities' encompasses not only debts but also non-liquidated claims.[204] A contingent liability is a liability which arises out of an existing legal obligation or state of affairs which is dependent on the occurrence of an event which may or may not occur in the future.[205] Prospective liability is a debt which will certainly become due in the future, either on some date which has already been determined or on some date determinable by reference to future events.[206] On the asset side of the balance sheet, only current assets of the company may be included; the prospect of receiving further injections of cash or other assets in the future (contingent assets) cannot be taken into account.[207] The valuation of assets and (contingent) liabilities is vital for the effective functioning of this test. However, it is not an exact science; rather a matter of judgment as to the amount a willing buyer would pay in the market when dealing with a willing seller.[208] Valuation on a going concern basis may result in significantly higher value than valuation on a break-up basis. Whether going concern value or break-up value should prevail should turn on whether, at the relevant time, the

204 Goode (n 193) 130 (para 4-23).
205 ibid 134 (para 4-26).
206 ibid 136 (para 4-27).
207 ibid 142 (para 4-34).
208 ibid 115 (para 4-06).

business is more likely to be continued as a going concern, than not.[209] The Supreme Court had an opportunity to consider the concept of balance sheet insolvency in *Eurosail*:

BNY Corporate Trustee Services Limited et al v Eurosail-UK 2007-3BL plc **[2013] UKSC 28**

Eurosail concerned structured finance transactions under the documentation of which balance sheet insolvency was used as a trigger for a switch in priorities. A typical structure for collateralised loan obligations or asset-backed securities involves the issue of notes in different tranches with each tranche offering a different maturity and a different interest rate. Prior to an Event of Default, the different tranches will be redeemed in accordance with a pre-established order of maturity. However, following an Event of Default, different tranches may rank pari passu in order to avoid 'time subordination': although investors subscribing for a class with a longer term maturity are happy to put up their money for an extended period of time, they may not want to bear any more of the credit risk than the other classes with shorter maturities. In Eurosail, the definition for Event of Default referred to Insolvency Act sec.123(2) (excluding the words 'it is proved to the satisfaction of the court').

Lord Walker (with whom Lord Mance, Lord Sumption and Lord Carnwath, and also Lord Hope agreed)

37 … [T]he 'cash-flow' test is concerned, not simply with the petitioner's own presently-due debt, nor only with other presently-due debt owed by the company, but also with debts falling due from time to time in the reasonably near future. What is the reasonably near future, for this purpose, will depend on all the circumstances, but especially on the nature of the company's business … The express reference to assets and liabilities is in my view a practical recognition that once the court has to move beyond the reasonably near future (the length of which depends, again, on all the circumstances) any attempt to apply a cash-flow test will become completely speculative, and a comparison of present assets with present and future liabilities (discounted for contingencies and deferment) becomes the only sensible test. But it is still very far from an exact test, and the burden of proof must be on the party which asserts balance-sheet insolvency. The omission from Condition 9(a)(iii) of the reference to proof 'to the satisfaction of the court' cannot alter that.

38 Whether or not the test of balance-sheet insolvency is satisfied must depend on the available evidence as to the circumstances of the particular case. The circumstances of Eurosail's business, so far as it can be said to have a business at all, are quite unlike those of a company engaged in normal trading activities. There are no decisions to be made about choice of suppliers, stock levels, pricing policy, the raising of new capital, or other matters such as would constantly engage the attention of a trading company's board of directors. Instead Eurosail is (in Mr Moss's phrase) in a 'closed system' with some resemblance to a life office which is no longer accepting new business. The only important management decision that could possibly be made would be to attempt to arrange new hedging cover in place of that which was lost when Lehman Brothers collapsed. To that extent Eurosail's present assets should be a better guide to its ability to meet its long-term liabilities than would be the case with a company actively engaged in trading. But against that, the three imponderable factors …—currency movements, interest rates and the United Kingdom economy and housing market—are and always have been outside its control. Over the period of more than 30 years until the final redemption date in 2045, they are a matter of speculation rather than calculation and prediction on any scientific basis.

39 At first instance the Chancellor started with three propositions derived from the case law (paras 29 to 32): that the assets to be valued are the present assets of the company; that 'contingent and prospective liabilities' are not to be taken at their full face value; and that:

'"Taking account of" must be recognised in the context of the overall question posed by the subsection, namely whether the company is to be deemed to be insolvent because the amount of its liabilities exceeds the value of its assets. This will involve consideration of the relevant facts of the case, including when the prospective liability falls due, whether it is payable in sterling or some other currency, what assets will be available to meet it and what if any provision is made for the allocation of losses in relation to those assets.' (para 32)

[209] ibid 142–4 (para 4-35).

He then set out four reasons (paras 34 to 37) for concluding (para 38) that the value of Eurosail's assets exceeded its liabilities, 'having taken account of its contingent and prospective liabilities to such extent as appears to be necessary at this stage'.

40 In the Court of Appeal Lord Neuberger MR did not disagree with anything in the Chancellor's judgment so far as it related to statutory construction. He did however go further in his detailed discussion of section 123(2). He observed (para 44):

'In practical terms, it would be rather extraordinary if section 123(2) was satisfied every time a company's liabilities exceeded the value of its assets. Many companies which are solvent and successful, and many companies early on in their lives, would be deemed unable to pay their debts if this was the meaning of section 123(2). Indeed, the issuer is a good example of this: its assets only just exceeded its liabilities when it was formed, and it was more than possible that, even if things went well, it would fall from time to time within the ambit of section 123(2) if the appellants are right as to the meaning of that provision'.

41 Lord Neuberger MR developed this at paras 47 to 49 of his judgment:

'47. More generally, I find it hard to discern any conceivable policy reason why a company should be at risk of being wound up simply because the aggregate value (however calculated) of its liabilities exceeds that of its assets. Many companies in that position are successful and creditworthy, and cannot in any way be characterised as 'unable to pay [their] debts'. Such a mechanistic, even artificial, reason for permitting a creditor to present a petition to wind up a company could, in my view, only be justified if the words of section 123(2) compelled that conclusion, and in my opinion they do not.

48. In my view, the purpose of section 123(2) has been accurately characterised by Professor Sir Roy Goode in Principles of Corporate Insolvency Law, 3rd ed (2005). Having referred to section 123(1)(e) as being the 'cash flow test' and to section 123(2) as being the 'balance sheet test', he said this, at para 4-06:

'If the cash flow test were the only relevant test [for insolvency] then current and short-term creditors would in effect be paid at the expense of creditors to whom liabilities were incurred after the company had reached the point of no return because of an incurable deficiency in its assets.'

49. In my judgment, both the purpose and the applicable test of section 123(2) are accurately encapsulated in that brief passage'.

42 Toulson LJ agreed with Lord Neuberger MR but expressed himself in a more guarded way. He agreed that Professor Sir Roy Goode had 'rightly discerned the underlying policy' (para 115) but added (para 119) that Professor Goode's reference to a company having 'reached the point of no return because of an incurable deficiency in its assets' illuminates the purpose of the subsection but does not purport to be a paraphrase of it. He continued:

'Essentially, section 123(2) requires the court to make a judgment whether it has been established that, looking at the company's assets and making proper allowance for its prospective and contingent liabilities, it cannot reasonably be expected to be able to meet those liabilities. If so, it will be deemed insolvent although it is currently able to pay its debts as they fall due. The more distant the liabilities, the harder this will be to establish'.

I agree with what Toulson LJ said here, and with great respect to Lord Neuberger MR I consider that 'the point of no return' should not pass into common usage as a paraphrase of the effect of section 123(2). But in the case of a company's liabilities that can as matters now stand be deferred for over 30 years, and where the company is (without any permanent increase in its borrowings) paying its debts as they fall due, the court should proceed with the greatest caution in deciding that the company is in a state of balance-sheet insolvency under section 123(2).

...

48 The crucial issue, to my mind, is how far the Court of Appeal's conclusion depended on the 'point of no return' test. For reasons already mentioned, I consider that that is not the correct test, if and in so far as it goes beyond the need for a petitioner to satisfy the court, on the balance of probabilities, that a company has insufficient assets to be able to meet all its liabilities,

including prospective and contingent liabilities. If it means no more than that, it is unhelpful, except as illuminating (as Toulson LJ put it) the purpose of section 123(2).

49 In my view the Court of Appeal would have reached the same conclusion without reference to any 'point of no return' test; and I would myself reach the same conclusion. Eurosail's ability or inability to pay all its debts, present or future, may not be finally determined until much closer to 2045, that is more than 30 years from now. The complex documentation under which the loan notes were issued contains several mechanisms ... for ensuring that liabilities in respect of principal are, if necessary, deferred until the final redemption date, unless the post-enforcement regime comes into operation. The movements of currencies and interest rates in the meantime, if not entirely speculative, are incapable of prediction with any confidence. The court cannot be satisfied that there will eventually be a deficiency.

50 I would therefore dismiss the appeal ...

Questions and comments:

1. On the basis of *Cheyne* and *Eurosail*, both the cash flow test and the balance sheet test are forward-looking tests. The cash flow test concerns the 'reasonably near future'; the balance sheet test deals with situations that go beyond the 'reasonably near future'. In combination with the burden of proof being on the party asserting balance sheet insolvency, *Eurosail* seems to suggest that there comes a second point beyond the 'reasonably near future' beyond which even balance sheet insolvency is no longer a workable concept. The future is simply too unpredictable. This benefits the debtor. Unless it cannot be reasonably expected that the debtor will meet its future liabilities, the debtor may continue to trade.
2. Do you agree that the 'point of no return' should not be the correct test? Wouldn't that test have made the concept of balance sheet insolvency more workable and predictable?
3. By rejecting the 'point of no return', the Supreme Court has adopted a concept of balance sheet insolvency that is more akin to that prevalent in the United States, rather than the more restrictive German approach. What are the consequences for the balance sheet concept in England?

III. Germany

Increased corporate mobility in Europe and the global financial crisis of 2007–2009 have inspired significant changes to German insolvency law, some directly affecting the concepts of insolvency.[210] A related factor is a renewed and enhanced emphasis on corporate reorganization and rescue.[211] The InsO contains, and defines, three different concepts of insolvency as grounds for opening insolvency proceedings: cash flow insolvency, prospective cash flow insolvency and balance sheet insolvency.[212]

German Insolvency Act (InsO)

§17 Cash flow insolvency

(1) A general ground for opening proceedings is cash flow insolvency.
(2) The debtor is cash flow insolvent if he is unable to pay his due debts. In principle, cash flow insolvency is to be presumed if the debtor has ceased to pay his debts.

[210] Gesetz zur Modernisierung des GmbH-Rechts und zur Bekämpfung von Mißbräuchen (MoMiG); Finanz marktstabilisierungsgesetz (FMStG).

[211] Restrukturierungsgesetz (RestG); Gesetz zur weiteren Erleichterung der Sanierung von Unternehmen (ESUG).

[212] The following is based on M Schillig and R Parsons, 'Balance Sheet Insolvency: Controversy in Different Jurisdictions, Part 2' (2012) Journal of International Banking and Financial Law 551–6. Translations of extracts from the German Insolvency Act are our own.

§ 18 Prospective cash flow insolvency

(1) If the debtor applies for the opening of proceedings, prospective cash flow insolvency constitutes a ground for opening proceedings.
(2) The debtor is prospectively cash flow insolvent if foreseeably he will be unable to pay his debts when they become due.
(3) In case of a legal person or company without legal personality, if the application to open proceedings is not made by all members of the organ of representation, all personally liable members or all liquidators, paragraph 1 only applies if the person or persons making the application are authorized to represent the legal person or company.

§ 19 Balance sheet insolvency

(1) For a legal person balance sheet insolvency is also a ground for opening proceedings.
(2) Balance sheet insolvency occurs, if the debtor's assets no longer cover his existing liabilities, unless the continuation of the business is, given the circumstances, predominantly likely. Liabilities concerning the repayment of shareholder loans or commercially equivalent transactions, which are subordinated by agreement between creditor and debtor pursuant to § 39(2) to the liabilities listed in §39(1) No 1 to 5, are not to be taken into account as liabilities for sentence 1.
(3) Where in a company without legal personality no personally liable member is a natural person, paragraphs 1 and 2 apply by way of analogy. This does not apply if among the personally liable members there is a company in which one personally liable member is a natural person.

1. *Cash flow insolvency and prospective cash flow insolvency*

Cash flow insolvency is a general ground for opening proceedings and applies to all debtors, regardless of their legal form. It triggers a duty to file for insolvency on the part of the management organ of corporate debtors,[213] backed by civil and criminal liability.[214] Cash flow insolvency is defined as the company's inability to pay its debts as they fall due.[215] The relevant debts and liquid funds are to be juxtaposed in a liquidity statement for the relevant time (when the court decides as to whether to open proceedings). Relevant debts are those that are due at the relevant time, and also those that will fall due within the next three weeks; liquid funds are cash and cash-like instruments available at the relevant time and assets that can be turned into cash within the next three weeks.[216] Cash flow insolvency is to be distinguished from a mere delay in payments. The latter is a short-term illiquidity which can be rectified within a period that does not go beyond what a creditworthy person needs in order to obtain the necessary funds.[217] In order to make this standard workable in practice, courts usually regard a period of three weeks as necessary but also sufficient.[218] In cases of considerable complexity courts may be willing to accept a period exceeding three weeks.[219] Even if the company is unable to obtain, within the three-week period, the funds required to pay all its debts, defaults that are 'insignificant' may not result in cash flow insolvency.[220] Again, for practical reasons the courts have stipulated a rebuttable presumption according to which cash flow insolvency is to be presumed only if the debtor is unable to pay more than 10 per cent of its obligations.[221] If the illiquidity exceeds 10 per cent a director may rebut the presumption of cash flow insolvency by pleading and proving facts which support the assumption that the illiquidity will be rectified in its entirety within a reasonable period of

[213] InsO, §15a.
[214] M Schillig, 'The Transition from Corporate Governance to Bankruptcy Governance: Convergence of German and US Law?' (2010) 7 ECFR 116, 126.
[215] InsO, §17(2)(1). [216] BGH, II ZR 88/16, 19 December 2017, paras 31–4.
[217] G Fischer, 'Krisenbewältigung durch Insolvenzrecht' (2006) Zeitschrift für Gesellschaftsrecht (ZGR) 403, 405.
[218] ibid. [219] ibid 406. [220] ibid. [221] ibid 408.

time.[222] Conversely, if the illiquidity does not reach 10 per cent a creditor may still be able to invoke circumstances that suggest that the company will not be able to recover. The work of courts and trustees is further alleviated by a statutory presumption stipulating that cash flow insolvency is, in principle, to be presumed in case of cessation of payments.[223] It is sufficient that the company, by and large, does not satisfy its monetary obligations; even non-payment of one of its obligations will be sufficient as long as this obligation is not insignificant.[224] Cessation of payments is, in practical terms, the most important reason for determining that the company is insolvent on a cash flow basis.

Prospective cash flow insolvency constitutes a ground for opening proceedings only in the case of a voluntary filing.[225] The debtor, and only the debtor, may initiate proceedings on the ground that the debtor will prospectively be unable to pay its debts when they become due in the future. The relevant period has not been specified in the statute. An assessment of the next twelve to twenty-four months is common. Prospective cash flow insolvency may be determined on the basis of a cash flow plan for the relevant time span. This includes cash and cash like instruments currently available and those that will become available within the relevant period. In addition to debts currently due and falling due within the next three weeks,[226] the cash flow plan also includes existing debts that will mature within the relevant period. Prospective cash flow insolvency was included as a means to encourage the debtor to petition for the commencement of proceedings early, at a time when significant assets are still available for either corporate rescue or the payment of a higher dividend to the creditors.

Questions and comments:

1. It is perhaps fair to say that the English forward-looking concept of cash flow insolvency as the functional equivalent encompasses both the German cash flow insolvency and prospective cash flow insolvency. The former is a static concept, taking into account only debts due at the material time (and falling due within the next three weeks) and liquid assets available at (and during) that time. Prospective cash flow insolvency is forward looking and prognostic, with the 'reasonably foreseeable future' being determined as twelve to twenty-four months.
2. In public policy terms, how can the differences in approach to the English cash flow insolvency concept on the one hand, and the German concepts of cash flow insolvency and prospective cash flow insolvency be accounted for?

2. *Balance sheet insolvency*

Balance sheet insolvency is a ground for opening insolvency proceedings only for debtors organized as legal persons (limited liability company, corporation, co-operative society, association, foundation) or as partnerships where the personally liable managing partner is not a natural person (GmbH & Co KG). It is likely to trigger the filing duty in advance of the company's inability to pay its debts as they fall due. Balance sheet insolvency is generally defined as a situation where the company's assets are insufficient to cover its debts[227] and is to be determined on the basis of a specific balance sheet to be compiled for the sole purpose of

[222] ibid. [223] InsO, §17(2). [224] Fischer (n 217) 409. [225] InsO §18(1).

[226] Given that under recent case law, cash flow insolvency takes into account due debts and those maturing within the next three weeks, there is an issue of delineation. According to the BGH, cash flow insolvency ensues where on the relevant date the debtor is unable to pay 10 per cent or more of its debts currently due and maturing within the next three weeks and will not be able to mobilize sufficient liquid funds within the three week period to reduce the liquidity gap below 10 per cent. By contrast, (only) prospective cash flow insolvency may persist where no such liquidity gap exists on the relevant date, but may ensue later (beyond the three-week period); BGH, II ZR 88/16, 17 December 2017, paras 45–6.

[227] InsO, §19(2).

determining the solvency status of the company.[228] Under the old *Konkursordung*, applicable until 31 December 1998, balance sheet insolvency rested on a two pronged test: a company was insolvent on a balance sheet basis only if (i) in case of instant liquidation the company's assets, valued on a liquidation basis, would be insufficient to cover its debts; and (ii) there was no 'positive going concern prognosis', that is, the continuation of the business was not predominantly likely. Consequently, a 'positive going concern prognosis' was sufficient reason to assume that the company was not insolvent. The reform legislator of the InsO rejected this approach. It was feared that under the two-pronged test a company could continue in business with insufficient assets to cover its debts. This could cause substantial damage to the creditors if the 'positive prognosis' turned out to be wrong.[229] Hence, a valuation approach was established under InsO. Pursuant to this approach, the insolvency balance sheet was to be compiled on the basis of the liquidation value of the company's assets.[230] However, where the continuation of the business was predominantly likely, a going concern valuation could form the basis of the insolvency balance sheet. If, based on going concern value, the liabilities still exceeded the assets, the company was insolvent on a balance sheet basis, irrespective of a 'positive going concern prognosis'.[231] In the light of the global financial crisis the law has been changed as of 18 October 2008.[232] According to the legislature, the global financial crisis resulted in a substantial devaluation of assets, in particular of investment securities and real property. Under the valuation approach, even viable businesses would be compelled to file for insolvency proceedings if they were affected by the financial crises and could not off-set their losses with sufficient assets valued on a going concern basis. In order to avoid the economically undesirable result of forcing viable businesses into (unnecessary) insolvency proceedings, emergency legislation reinstated the two-pronged test as it was applied before the InsO entered into force,[233] at first only temporarily until 31 December 2013, but now permanently. Accordingly, the mere fact that the business has a 'positive going concern prognosis' (currently) precludes the company from being insolvent on a balance sheet basis.

In order to give a reliable picture as to whether the company's assets are sufficient to satisfy all its debts, the insolvency balance sheet follows its own rules in regard of inclusion and valuation. The asset side of the insolvency balance sheet will include only those assets that in the case of liquidation are realizable and likely to increase the debtor's estate for the benefit of its creditors.[234] Future assets may not be included as they would not be realizable if the company was liquidated on the relevant accounting date. Unrealized gains and hidden reserves have to be disclosed. Goodwill and know how may be included only if a concrete and binding offer to buy the business or part of it is on the table and the owners are willing to sell. Under the applicable two-pronged test, assets are valued on a liquidation basis only, regardless of whether the going concern prognosis is positive or not. The liabilities side of the insolvency balance sheet shows all the company's obligations that, in the case of the opening of proceedings, are to be paid out of the estate.[235] If the liability is current and undisputed, it is to be included at its nominal amount. Liabilities not yet due at the relevant accounting date will automatically fall due with the opening of proceedings.[236] They are to be included at their discounted present value. Liabilities that are either in respect of their existence or their

[228] BGHZ 164, 264, 268 (2001). The company will, however, be insolvent on a balance sheet basis, regardless of whether an insolvency balance sheet has in fact been compiled.

[229] Bericht und Beschlussempfehlung des Rechtsausschusses zur InsO, BT-Drucks 12/7302 at 157.

[230] InsO, §19(2), as it was in force until 18 October 2008.

[231] BGH, II ZR 51/06, [2007] Neue Juristische Wochenschrift: Rechtsprechungsreport (NJW-RR), 1490, 1491; BGHZ 171, 46, 54 (2007).

[232] FMStG, Art 5, amending InsO, §19(2).

[233] Amtl Begründung BT-Drucks 16/10600, 20–1.

[234] On this and the following see C Nickert and U Lamberti, *Überschuldungs- und Zahlungsunfähigkeitsprüfung im Insolvenzrecht* (2nd edn, CH Beck 2011) paras *366–869*.

[235] ibid paras 870–1.

[236] InsO, §41(1). 'Liability' is generally defined as an obligation, owed to a third party, that is enforceable and determinate, or at least determinable, in respect of its content and amount.

amount uncertain (contingent, prospective liabilities, unliquidated claims) are included by way of provisions on the liabilities side of the insolvency balance sheet. Shareholder loans are to be included on the liabilities side of the insolvency balance sheet, except loans that have been subordinated to the claims of deferred creditors.[237]

Generally, the 'going concern prognosis' will be positive where the continuation of the business, even in reduced or amended form, is predominantly likely, that is more likely than liquidation. A positive going concern prognosis requires, first, the intention and willingness on the part of the owners—shareholders and management—to continue the business.[238] Secondly, continuation of the business must be objectively feasible. The standard of assessment is the ex ante perspective of a reasonable business manager: on the basis of a conscientious and competent assessment taking into account all material facts available at the relevant accounting date, a reasonable business manager would decide to continue the business.[239] This test obviously has a strong prognostic element. The prognosis must have a basis in ascertainable facts such as the characteristics of the relevant markets or the company's relations with its customers and suppliers.[240] Based on these facts, the directors must provide a coherent, reliable and realistic business plan that constitutes the basis for a profit forecast and financial plan which demonstrate that the company is more likely than not to survive at least until the end of the current and the following financial year.[241]

Questions and comments:

1. The reasons given for the change in the law from a 'positive going concern prognosis' being relevant only for valuation purposes to the two pronged test where a 'positive going concern prognosis' prevents balance sheet insolvency altogether echoes to some extent the reasoning of Lord Neuberger MR in *Eurosail* (reproduced in the extract above): it prevents the pushing into formal proceedings of companies that, although liabilities temporarily exceed assets, are not in financial distress. The concept of the 'point of no return,' mentioned and rejected in *Eurosail* as a paraphrase of section 123, may still serve as a valuable metaphor with a similar purpose to the 'positive going concern prognosis'.
2. But there seems to be a difference in emphasis. Under English law, the 'point of no return' would seem to be the exception and the burden of proof for the supporting facts is on the party that invokes balance sheet insolvency. In Germany, the 'positive going concern prognosis' is the exception with the burden of proof being on the company director defending against an action for breach of the duty to file for insolvency brought by the insolvency administrator. Despite the return to the two-pronged balance sheet insolvency test, German law remains more restrictive: balance sheet insolvency seems to be more easily established and sooner than under English law.
3. What are the policy implications of these differences in approach?

IV. United States

In the United States, (in)solvency analysis is relevant mainly in the context of avoidance actions (fraudulent transfers and preferences) under both federal and state law, in connection with breach of fiduciary duty cases for the benefit of creditors, and as a test for the payment of dividends and distributions.[242] Depending on the context, the concepts of insolvency may

[237] InsO, §§19(2) sentence 2; 39(1)(2).
[238] BGH, 9/10/2006–II ZR 303/05 para 3; BGH, 18/10/2010–IIZR 151/09 para 13.
[239] M Dahl, 'Die Änderung des Überschuldungsbegriffs durch Art. 5 des Finanzmarktstabilisierungsgesetzes (FMStG)' (2008) Neue Zeitschrift für Insolvenzrecht 719, 720.
[240] Nickert and Lamberti (n 234) para 280.
[241] BGH, 9-10-2006–II ZR 303/05 para 3; BGH, 18/10/2010 - II ZR 151/09 para 13.
[242] See Chapter 9C.II.

have divergent meanings also in accordance with whether the respective test is derived from federal or state law, statute, or case law.[243]

1. *'Equitable (in)solvency' (cash flow insolvency) and 'unreasonably small capital'*

In order to file for bankruptcy protection under the federal Bankruptcy Code (11 USC), the debtor does not have to be insolvent, nor have any debts at all. However, where the debtor controverts an involuntary filing initiated by creditors,[244] the court will take on the case only under the further condition that the debtor generally does not pay its debts as they fall due.[245] The 'inability to pay debts as they fall due' is generally referred to as the 'equitable (in)solvency' or 'cash flow insolvency' test,[246] which is also relevant, at state and federal level, in the context of fraudulent transfers laws;[247] and under state corporate law in the context of distributions to shareholders.[248] Moreover, upon a corporation's cash flow insolvency, its creditors may gain standing to bring derivative actions for breach of fiduciary duty, and in addition the focus of fiduciary duties may shift from shareholders to creditors.[249] Generally, the concept is forward looking: the debtor must be able to match its cash resources to its maturing obligations, including future obligations.[250] This forward-looking nature seems to be inherent in the subjective nature of the test in the context of fraudulent transfers. What matters is the debtor's intent or belief, at the time of the transaction, 'that it would incur debts that would go beyond its ability to pay as such debts matured'.[251]

The concept of 'unreasonably small capital' is also relevant in the context of fraudulent transfer law.[252] The term is not defined in the Bankruptcy Code or the Uniform Voidable Transactions Act 2014. It is generally perceived as the corporation's 'inability to generate sufficient profits to sustain operations'[253] and refers to a situation where the corporation is in financial distress short of insolvency but with insolvency (in either the cash flow or balance sheet sense) being reasonably foreseeable.[254]

2. *'Legal insolvency' (balance sheet insolvency)*

Within the realm of the Bankruptcy Code, 'legal insolvency' is defined in 11 U.S.C. §101(32) on a balance sheet basis as a 'financial condition such that the sum of such entity's debts is greater than all of such entity's property, at a fair valuation'. Balance sheet insolvency is relevant in the context of fraudulent transfers and unlawful preferences under both the Bankruptcy Code[255] and state fraudulent transfer law.[256] Balance sheet insolvency is also a trigger for a creditor's standing in a derivative action for the enforcement of fiduciary duties and the potential refocusing of duties towards the interest of creditors.[257] Moreover, in the

[243] The following is based on M Schillig and R Parsons, 'Balance Sheet Insolvency: Controversy in Different Jurisdictions, Parts 3' (2012) Journal of International Banking and Financial Law 627, 627–33.

[244] 11 U.S.C., §303(b). [245] ibid §303(h).

[246] JB Heaton, 'Solvency Tests' (2007) 62 Business Lawyer 983.

[247] 11 U.S.C. §548(a)(1)(B)(ii)(III); Uniform Voidable Transactions Act 2014, §4(a)(2)(ii).

[248] (Revised) Model Business Corporation Act (MBCA) §6.40(c)(1). In addition, pursuant to MBCA §6.40(c)(2) distributions must also meet a balance sheet test in order to be lawful.

[249] *Geyer v. Ingersoll Publications Company* (n 180); *Production Resources Group LLC v. NCT Group Inc.* (n 180); *North American Catholic Educational Programming Foundation Inc. v. Gheewalla* (n 180) 101.

[250] Heaton (n 246) 983, 989.

[251] 11 U.S.C., §548(a)(B)(III); Uniform Voidable Transactions Act 2014, §4(a)(2)(ii). RJ Stearn, 'Proving Solvency: Defending Preference and Fraudulent Transfer Litigation' (2007) 62 Business Lawyer 359, 391.

[252] "Gross undercapitalization" may be one of the factors to be taken into account when deciding whether to pierce the corporate veil: *Minton v Cavaney*, 56 Cal.2d 576 (Supreme Court of California, 1961).

[253] *Moody v. Security Pacific Business Credit, Inc.*, 971 F.2d 1056, 1070 (C.A.3 (Pa.), 1992).

[254] Heaton (n 246) 983, 995. [255] 11 U.S.C. §548(a)(B)(ii)(I), §547(b)(3).

[256] Uniform Voidable Transactions Act 2014, §5(a) and (b).

[257] *Geyer v. Ingersoll Publications Company* (n 180); *Production Resources Group LLC v. NCT Group Inc.* (n 180); *North American Catholic Educational Programming Foundation Inc. v. Gheewalla* (n 180).

context of dividends and distributions, pursuant to MBCA, §6.40(c)(2), no distribution may be made if, after giving it effect, the corporation's total assets would be less than the sum of its total liabilities (plus the dissolution preferences of senior equity securities).

The application of the balance sheet test generally involves a two-step process.[258] First, the court determines whether the debtor was a 'going concern' or was 'on its deathbed'. Secondly, the court values the debtor's assets, depending on the status determined in the first part of the inquiry, and applies a simple balance sheet test to determine whether the debtor was solvent.[259] The going concern valuation standard contemplates a realization of the value of assets within a reasonable period of time. It is the fair value that a willing buyer would pay to a willing seller at arm's length where the seller is not in a hurry and can take a reasonable time to wait for a better offer and a higher price.[260] It is assumed that the assets are sold as an income-producing unit that includes the value of the synergistic relationship that connects all tangible and intangible assets. Conversely, the liquidation premise of value contemplates a forced piecemeal sale of the debtor's assets without a normal level of exposure to the market.[261] These 'fire sale' prices will be significantly lower than fair market value. Thus, much may turn on the appropriate premise of valuation. Courts generally presume that the proper standard of valuation is the fair market value of the firm as a going concern.[262] Liquidation value will only be applied in exceptional circumstances where the 'business is wholly inoperative, defunct, or dead on its feet',[263] where liquidation is 'clearly imminent',[264] or where the entity is 'on its deathbed'[265] or only 'nominally in existence'.[266] 'A debtor lies on its deathbed where the debtor is 'in a precarious financial condition' so that 'liquidation was imminent when the petition was filed'.[267] Overall, therefore, the balance sheet test relies on a simple comparison of assets and liabilities at the relevant date. The going concern status of the business matters only for the method of valuation (valuation approach), with a presumption for going concern valuation in all but exceptional cases.

In determining the going concern value of a business, courts generally accept any recognized method of valuation such as the income approach (discounted cash flow analysis), the market approach (comparable company or transaction analysis) or the asset approach (purchase offers or replacement costs).[268] In any case, the assets are valued on a debt-free basis without having regard to the capital structure.[269] Courts seem to prefer the discounted cash flow method as the most reliable approach.[270] The insolvency of a firm is determined on the basis of its discounted future earnings[271] which must be sufficient to cover its expenditure on a continuous basis. As a consequence, balance sheet insolvency does not look so different from the 'equitable insolvency' test and it has been pointed out that under both tests solvency is measured by the ability to pay debts: in the case of equitable insolvency promptly, in

[258] Stearn (n 251) 369; Heaton (n 246) 983, 992.

[259] *Union Bank of Switzerland v. Deutsche Financial Services Corp.*, 2000 WL 178278, *9 (S.D.N.Y., 2000); *In re Heilig-Meyers Co.*, 319 B.R. 447, 457 (Bkrtcy. E.D.Va., 2004), aff'd, 328 B.R. 471 (E.D.Va., 2005).

[260] *In re Heilig-Meyers Co.*, 328 B.R. 471, 470 (E.D.Va., 2005) (citing *Lawson v. Ford Motor Co. (In re Roblin Indus.)*, 78 F.3d 30, 36 (2d Cir. 1996)).

[261] Stearn (n 251) 369. [262] ibid 371.

[263] *In re Bellanca Aircraft Corp.*, 56 B.R. 339, 387 (Bkrtcy. D. Minn., 1985).

[264] *In re American Classic Voyages Co.*, 367 B.R. 500, 508 (Bkrtcy. D. Del., 2007).

[265] *In re Heilig-Meyers Co.* (n 260).

[266] *In re Joy Recovery Technology Corp.*, 286 B.R. 54, 77 (Bkrtcy. N. D. Ill., 2002).

[267] *In re Heilig-Meyers Co.* (n 260).

[268] *In re Nellson Nutraceutical, Inc.*, 356 B.R. 364, 370 (Bkrtcy. D. Del., 2006); *In re Winstar Communications, Inc.*, 348 B.R. 234, 274 (Bkrtcy.D.Del.,2005).

[269] Stearn (n 251) 379.

[270] *In re Med Diversified, Inc.*, 334 B.R. 89, 98 (Bkrtcy.E.D.N.Y.,2005); *Lippe v. Bairnco Corp.*, 288 B.R. 678, 689 (S.D.N.Y.,2003), aff'd., 99 Fed. Appx 274 (2d Cir. 2004); *In Re American Classic Voyages Co* 367 B.R. 500, 509 note 13 (Bkrtcy. D. Del., 2007).

[271] *In re Winstar Communications, Inc.* (n 268) 278.

the case of legal insolvency, over time.[272] This similarity may account for the fact that courts frequently do not properly distinguish between both tests.[273]

Financial statements prepared in accordance with US GAAP record assets at their historical cost and not at fair market value. As a consequence, they can only provide a starting point.[274] In order to determine the solvency status of a company, all assets that would have value for a creditor attempting to satisfy his claim are included at fair valuation. The firm's goodwill may be included as an independent asset only where it can be shown that it has an independent market value and could be sold to satisfy a creditor's claim.[275] Contingent assets may be taken into consideration as well,[276] reduced to their present, or expected value, on the basis of probability that the conditions will be met.[277] Whereas the debtor's assets are valued on the basis of the present value of its future cash flows, its debts are valued at face value regardless of whether the valuation premise is going concern or liquidation.[278]

Questions and comments:

1. Whether a corporation 'is on its deathbed' only matters for valuation purposes. However, the absence of a deathbed situation does not automatically mean that the company is not insolvent on a balance sheet basis where a going concern valuation reveals an excess of liabilities over assets. Similar to the 'point of no return' metaphor, a corporation being 'on its deathbed' remains the exception.
2. There are similarities with German law when it comes to the financial statements on the basis of which balance sheet insolvency is to be determined. Overall, however, US law is much closer to the English law approach: cash flow and balance sheet insolvency are forward-looking concepts with the latter being merely the extension of the former.
3. It is worth keeping in mind the contexts in which US courts consider insolvency concepts. It is often the trustee in bankruptcy or the debtor in possession suing (former) officers, directors, shareholders or lenders on the basis of fraudulent transfer law in order to recover corporate assets for the estate that have been siphoned away. This is different from English law, where insolvency concepts are considered almost exclusively in the course of the interpretation of contractual documentation referring to the relevant provisions of the Insolvency Act 1986. In Germany, the issue comes up in the course of the opening of proceedings and where corporate management are sued by the insolvency administrator for a breach of the duty to timely file for insolvency.
4. On that basis, what are the policy implications of adopting a 'lenient' approach or a 'strict' approach in any of these three legal systems?

V. France

France deviates from our other legal systems in that it primarily relies on a single concept of cash flow insolvency: cessation of payment. This concept is relevant as a precondition for the opening of judicial reorganization and liquidation proceedings,[279] and for excluding or limiting the availability of court-assisted (pre-insolvency) restructuring proceedings.[280] It triggers the debtor's duty to apply to the court for the opening of insolvency proceedings

[272] RM Cieri and others, 'An Introduction to Legal and Practical Considerations in the Restructuring of Troubled Leveraged Buyouts' (1989) 45 Business Lawyer 333, 359.

[273] Paradigmatic in this respect *Geyer v Ingersoll Publications Ltd* (n 180).

[274] *In re Trans World Airlines, Inc.*, 180 B.R. 389, 405 (Bkrtcy. D. Del., 1994).

[275] *In re Richmond Produce Co., Inc.*, 151 B.R. 1012, 1019 (Bkrtcy. N.D. Cal., 1993), aff'd 195 B.R. 455 (N.D.Cal., 1996).

[276] *In re R.M.L., Inc.*, 92 F.3d 139, 156 (C.A.3 (Pa.), 1996).

[277] *In re Xonics Photochemical, Inc.*, 841 F.2d 198, 200 (C.A.7 (Ill.), 1988).

[278] Heaton (n 246) 994.

[279] Com Arts L631-1, 640-1.

[280] Com Art L620-1.

within forty-five days of the onset of cash flow insolvency.[281] Moreover, cash flow insolvency sets in motion the so-called period of suspicion: certain transaction carried out during this period may be subsequently reversed by the office holder.[282] In order to protect the creditors, the court may retrospectively adjust the period of suspicion and, in its discretion, push it back to up to eighteen months prior to commencement of insolvency proceedings.

1. *Cash flow insolvency*

Cash flow insolvency is defined as a financial position where the debtor's liquid and easily liquefiable assets are insufficient to pay its due debts.[283] The latter encompass all monetary claims that are undisputed and due at the time of commencement. The debtor's unsubstantiated challenging of a due debt is insufficient to exclude that debt from being taken into account. It is not necessary that a creditor actually has demanded payment; the objective fact of maturity at the relevant time is sufficient. The number of unpaid debts or their importance is irrelevant, as is their nature. The debtor may avert cash flow insolvency by demonstrating his ability to obtain further credit or a deferral of payment in agreement with his creditors. The liquid and liquefiable assets encompass the available cash, bank accounts in credit, and other assets that can be easily converted into cash within a short period of time, such as securities and negotiable instruments that may be sold at any time, debt receivables currently due or becoming due in the near future provided the liquidity of the third party debtor is not in doubt. Inventory and stock in trade that has already been sold may also count as liquid assets; not however real property even if the sale is imminent; nor other fixed assets and inventory that cannot be disposed of within a short period of time. In respect of the balance between liquid assets and due debts, the deficiency of assets over liabilities has to be significant in the sense that it must be of a nature that appears to be permanent and not remediable within a short period of time.[284]

Cash flow insolvency triggers, on the part of the debtor, the duty to file for insolvency proceedings within forty-five days, unless the debtor voluntarily initiates a conciliation procedure as a court-assisted extra-judicial settlement procedure prior to the expiry of the forty-five days period.[285] In addition to the debtor, upon the onset of cash flow insolvency, its creditors, the public prosecutor, and the competent court on its own motion may petition for the opening of insolvency proceedings.[286] Whether the court should order the judicial reorganization or the judicial liquidation of the debtor company depends on whether the debtor's continuation prognosis is positive or negative, respectively. A petition may result in judicial liquidation only where the continuation of the business activity is obviously and manifestly impossible.[287] This is a factual question and may be answered in the affirmative where the debtor no longer has any assets or no longer conducts any business activity at all. It is interesting to see that the notion of 'point of no return' or 'positive going concern prognosis' reappears in a different function by guiding the determination of the applicable procedure.

2. *Pre-insolvency procedures*

At the debtor's request, the competent court may appoint a special crisis adviser with a view to assisting incumbent management in turning the debtor's fortunes around.[288] The special crisis adviser may be appointed where the company faces or anticipates any difficulties of

[281] Com Arts L631-4, L640-4. [282] Com Arts L632-1–L632-4. [283] Com Art L631-1.
[284] A Jacquemont and R Vabres, *Droit des entreprises en difficulté* (9th edn, LexisNexis 2015) 142–50 (paras 212–23).
[285] Com Arts L631-4, L640-4. [286] Com Arts L631-5, L640-4. [287] Com Art 640-1.
[288] Com Art L611-3.

a legal, economic or financial nature that can be rectified through an improvement of the internal business organization and/or through negotiations with individual particularly important creditors and counterparties. The appointment requires that the company is not cash flow insolvent at the time.

Where the company's difficulties have become so serious that they can only be addressed through a comprehensive recovery effort, on application of the debtor, the competent court may commence a conciliation procedure and appoint a conciliator.[289] The conciliation procedure is a court-supervised rescue procedure under which the conciliator facilitates the negotiation of a settlement or compromise between the debtor and its main creditors. Upon court approval, the settlement will be binding on all creditors and those creditors that have advanced new funds as part of the restructuring attempt will obtain super-priority should the company subsequently enter insolvency proceedings.[290] Conciliation may be initiated even though the company is cash flow insolvent, provided insolvency has lasted less than forty-five days. Regardless, conciliation may also be commenced where the company encounters an actual or foreseeable legal, economic, or financial difficulty that is so serious that it cannot be averted by the appointment of a mere special crisis adviser.

The safeguard procedure, with its two recent modifications (accelerated financial safeguard procedure/accelerated safeguard procedure), forms the heart of the French insolvency law. It is a judicial pre-insolvency reorganization procedure that has the aim of implementing a comprehensive reorganization plan that, upon court approval, binds all parties involved. The safeguard procedure is only available to a debtor that is not (yet) cash flow insolvent, but faces difficulties that it is unable to overcome by itself.[291] The relevant time for the presence of these insurmountable difficulties is the time of commencement, not the time of the petition. Whether the difficulties are actually insurmountable depends on the concrete circumstances of the case. Only the actual financial situation of the debtor company may be taken into account; the overall position of the group of companies to which the debtor belongs is immaterial. Where, following commencement, it transpires that the debtor is actually cash flow insolvent, the procedure must be converted into a judicial reorganization procedure.

Concluding comments:

1. After our survey of the prevalent insolvency concepts in the jurisdictions under consideration here there are a few points worthy of note: on the surface the concepts look very similar with cash flow insolvency and balance sheet insolvency as more or less well established tests in England, the US, and Germany, and France relying on cash flow insolvency only. There are, however, significant differences in approach. In France and Germany, the tests are static (Germany's prospective cash flow insolvency aside), determining the (in)solvency status of a company at a particular moment, the tests seem, in tendency, more mechanistic than the approaches in England and the US. The latter rely on forward-looking dynamic concepts that seem to allow more room for discretion. One reason for this discrepancy may be the strict liability-backed filing duties in Germany and France that require a minimum in terms of predictability as regards their triggers. Filing duties, at least in such strict form, are absent in the common law systems.
2. The contexts in which disputes or controversies concerning the interpretation of insolvency concepts arise and reach the courts are very different. In England these controversies arise almost exclusively in the context of the interpretation of the contractual documentation of debt instruments that refer to the statutory provisions. The conflict inherent in these controversies is between different classes of creditors. In this respect, a strict or lenient approach to insolvency has little bearing on the insolvency law system's attitude towards corporate rescue

[289] Com Art L611-4. [290] Com Art L611-11. [291] Com Art L620-1.

and management incentives. By contrast, in the US, most disputes concerning the insolvency concepts arise in fraudulent transfer actions where the office holder (trustee in bankruptcy or debtor in possession) seeks to retrieve corporate property from former managers, shareholders, and/or lenders. The more difficult to establish insolvency, the easier for the defendant to get off the hook. Similarly, in Germany, it will usually be corporate managers that have to defend against actions brought by office holders for breach of the filing duty or for unlawful payments made when the company was insolvent. In these instances, a strict or more lenient approach may have a direct impact on the incentive structures of corporate actors. It is perhaps fair to assume that the different contexts in which insolvency disputes arise have shaped the content of these concepts, at least to some extent.

C. Transition Regimes

The interests of shareholders are relatively homogenous, with their entitlements being standardized through the articles of association and bylaws. The corporate governance system (in its various manifestations) allows the shareholders to participate in the running of the firm through appointed representatives (or more directly) and is (largely) geared towards benefiting the shareholders in amounts proportionate to their stakes. By contrast, every creditor's relationship with the corporation may be governed by its own individual regime of rights and obligations arising from contract or other causes such as tort law or public law.[292] The corporate governance system is ill-equipped to deal with the widely divergent interests of different creditor constituencies.[293] However, corporate insolvency and restructuring law anticipates a highly complex set of stakeholder conflicts and contains a number of mechanisms and doctrines for channelling and resolving them. An automatic stay or moratorium on individual enforcement action will prevent a run on the company's assets for the benefit of the creditors collectively by preventing the destruction of a potential going concern value. Where the management remains in control its powers will be curtailed by external supervision through a creditors' committee, external experts, and/or the courts. Incumbent management may even be replaced completely by an external expert. Those in control of the proceedings will owe fiduciary duties to all stakeholders involved. All stakeholders collectively may decide upon the future of the business and the resolution of the insolvency case.[294] Thus, corporate insolvency law provides a governance regime that includes shareholder and creditor representation, negotiation and rules regarding the allocation of value in a reorganization or liquidation, as well as judicial oversight over the most important issues.[295] The transition from the corporate governance system to the bankruptcy governance system requires an effective transition mechanism.

The transition regime needs to address at least the following three crucial questions: (i) at what point in time should the corporate governance system be replaced with the bankruptcy governance system; (ii) who is best placed to make the transition decision; and (iii) how can it be ensured that the optimal decision is being taken at the right time.[296] As for (i), the right time for transitioning should be determined in accordance with the underlying rationales for the transition: to prevent shareholders and managers from exploiting creditors when the latter have become the residual risk bearers; and to prevent a creditors' race on the company's assets so as to safeguard a potential 'going concern surplus'. Generally, creditors will be able to withdraw their investment only where the debtor is in default. Consequently, a race on the company's assets is likely to ensue as soon as

[292] Hu and Westbrook, 'Abolition of the Corporate Duty to Creditors' (n 183) 1352.
[293] ibid 1367–9. [294] ibid 1372.
[295] RB Campbell and CW Frost, 'Managers' Fiduciary Duties in Financially Distressed Corporations: Chaos in Delaware (and Elsewhere)' (2007) 32 Journal of Corporation Law 491, 509.
[296] Hu and Westbrook (n 183) 1399.

the company is unable to pay (a significant amount of) its debts when they fall due. If a multitude of debts is affected the race will be on. Conceptually, creditors would need protection against shareholder/management opportunism as soon as the creditors have taken the shareholders' place as residual risk bearers, that is, where the value of the firm's assets is less than its liabilities, or even before that in the so-called vicinity of insolvency. This 'twilight zone' is notoriously difficult to determine and, on the basis of fair market valuation, a debtor may seamlessly cross the threshold of balance sheet insolvency back and forth. It could also be argued that as long as the creditors are being paid in full they get exactly what they have bargained for, even though liabilities exceed assets. However, this leaves the problem of 'time subordination' where long term creditors lose out against short term creditors. Thus, the question that should be asked is whether the business (possibly after an informal workout) will be able to generate future cash flows sufficient to service its debts as and when they fall due. This is essentially a question of probabilities and necessitates the prediction of future developments. Consequently, the corporate governance system should be replaced with the bankruptcy governance system as soon as the financial situation of the company has reached a state where it is more likely than not that the company will be unable to generate sufficient cash flows to pay its debts as they fall due in the foreseeable future. This accords with a dynamic concept of balance sheet insolvency as developed by the UK Supreme Court in *Eurosail*.

Transition may be initiated by three principal (groups of) actors: the state, the creditors, or the (management of the) debtor company itself. Highly regulated (and supervised) industries such as banking aside, state officials and authorities are unlikely to be in possession of the necessary information regarding the company's financial situation and decisions may be tainted by political considerations, rather than determined on the basis of financial viability. The creditors either do not have the right incentives to initiate transition, or do not have the necessary information to initiate transition at the right time.[297] The sophisticated lenders that are capable of effectively monitoring the company will usually be better off by enforcing their claims ahead of other creditors. Those creditors who are likely to benefit from a collective insolvency law regime are unlikely to have the necessary information gathering and processing capacities. Moreover, the fragmentation of debt and property rights may skew creditor incentives, preventing them from making an optimal decision. The debtor company through its management is in the perfect position to monitor the company's business and ascertain its financial situation.[298] However, corporate management are subject to strong disincentives for initiating transition. Their personal costs resulting from transition will generally be high[299] owing to the potential loss of firm specific investment, job losses, reputational losses, and more concrete financial losses arising from personal liability or disqualification. Behavioural biases (overconfidence and unrealistic optimism) may also have an impact. This leads us to the question as to how these disincentives to initiate transition may be addressed. There are two principal strategies: corporate management will be more likely to initiate transition where their personal costs of doing so are lower than their costs in case of a delayed (or no) transition. Consequently, the law may either (i) reduce management's personal costs in case of transition (affirmative incentives) or (ii) increase management's personal costs in case of a delayed (or no) transition (liability incentives). Most legal systems combine both strategies to a greater or lesser extent.

[297] DG Baird, 'The Initiation Problem in Bankruptcy' (1991) 11 International Review of Law & Economics 223, 224.

[298] ibid 228; E Warren and JL Westbrook, *The Law of Debtors and Creditors* (5th edn, Aspen Publishers 2006) 375.

[299] ibid 374.

I. Affirmative incentives

The US Federal Bankruptcy Code traditionally relies predominantly on affirmative incentives that sweeten corporate management's decision to file for bankruptcy and render the Bankruptcy Code particularly debtor friendly.[300] Anyone who may be a debtor under Chapter 7 or Chapter 11 can commence a case simply by filing under the relevant chapter.[301] The case will be administered by the court subject only to a proper voluntary petition. The debtor does not have to be insolvent nor have any debts at all.[302] This approach avoids the difficult and expensive determination of insolvency and allows for early initiation of bankruptcy.[303] In principle, incumbent management will remain in control of the debtor company as debtor in possession (DIP).[304] The DIP has the exclusive right to propose a plan for reorganization within the first 120 days following filing[305] and has another sixty days to obtain the acceptance of the creditors.[306] The automatic stay which comes into existence with filing will stop any efforts by creditors, even those with a security interest in the company's property, to tear the company apart.[307] In order to allow the firm to keep going, the Code is designed to encourage post-petition lending. The plan process may result in substantial renegotiation of pre-petition entitlements in favour of the debtor.[308] Even old equity may get a chunk out of the company emerging from Chapter 11, at least as long as they contribute new value in satisfaction of a market test.[309] Moreover, in the United States bankruptcy is often perceived not as a stigma of failure but as a sign of courageous and vibrant risk-taking, positive attributes in a capitalist society.

Germany traditionally put her faith into liability incentives. However, a number of reforms have strengthened the debtor's affirmative incentives to file. Only the debtor may initiate proceedings on the ground of prospective cash flow insolvency.[310] This allows the debtor to file for formal insolvency protection in advance of actual insolvency. The debtor can freely decide when to file, which, in turn, may induce recalcitrant creditors to be more cooperative. It was the explicit objective of the InsO reform legislator to make formal insolvency proceedings more attractive to the debtor.[311] Consequently, the debtor was granted the right to propose a plan for reorganization within formal proceedings[312] and to apply to the court for an order to be left in control, albeit subject to supervision by a court appointed supervisor (self-administration).[313] The reform legislation of 2012 resulted in a further strengthening of the concept of self-administration. The debtor's management may remain in control even whilst the petition for opening proceedings is pending. Previously, the court would appoint a provisional insolvency administrator, replacing the incumbent management 'for all to see,' thus significantly reducing the attraction of self-administration. During preliminary self-administration, corporate management remains capable of disposing of the debtor's property generally, and without the need for approval by a preliminary liquidator, subject, however, to the supervision of a preliminary supervisor. In order to facilitate

300 JR Franks and WN Torous, 'Lessons from a Comparison of US and UK Insolvency Codes' (1992) 8(3) Oxford Review of Economic Policy 70.

301 11 U.S.C., §301.

302 However, pursuant to 11 U.S.C. 1112(b), on motion of 'a party in interest' a case may be converted to a case under chapter 7 or may be dismissed for 'cause'. A case will be subject to dismissal unless filed in 'good faith'. See *In re SGL Carbon Corporation*, 200 F.3d 154, 160, 166 (3d Cir. 1999).

303 *In re SGL Carbon Corporation*, 200 F.3d 154, 163 (3d Cir. 1999).

304 11 U.S.C., §1102(a).

305 ibid §1121(b).

306 ibid §1121(c)(3).

307 ibid §362(a).

308 JR Franks, KG Nyborg, and WN Torus, 'A Comparison of US, UK, and German Insolvency Codes' (1996) 25(3) Financial Management 86, 94.

309 *Bank of America National Trust & Savings Assn. v 203 North Lasalle Street Partnership*, 526 U.S. 434 (U.S. Ill., 1999).

310 InsO, §18(1).

311 Gesetzentwurf der Bundesregierung, Entwurf einer Insolvenzordnung (InsO), BT-Drs 12/2443, 86 (self-administration as a strong incentive for timely filing).

312 InsO, §§217–269.

313 ibid §§270–285.

corporate rescue, the so-called 'protective shield procedure' goes even further. Where the debtor files for insolvency on the basis of prospective cash flow insolvency or balance sheet insolvency and applies for self-administration with a view to effectuating a corporate restructuring, the court may, without opening proceedings, set a period of time for the presentation of a plan of reorganization. On application of the debtor the court must impose a stay on any attempts by creditors to enforce a claim against the debtor's movable property, and the debtor may be empowered to incur obligations which in subsequent proceedings obtain administrative expense priority. Overall, however, affirmative incentives under German law are less strong than under US law. The office holder may propose a concurrent plan of reorganization in addition to the debtor,[314] and creditors may vote on both plans separately. There is no exclusivity period. The automatic stay[315] is far less comprehensive than under US law. Creditors holding a security interest based on ownership and a right to repossess the collateral do not take part in the formal proceedings and may still enforce their rights based on non-bankruptcy enforcement mechanisms.[316]

In the UK, significant affirmative incentives have been incorporated into the transition regime by the Enterprise Act 2002, mainly in respect of the administration procedure. Introduced first through the Insolvency Act 1986, administration is not in itself a reorganization procedure; rather it provides a framework for carrying out a restructuring or reorganization via a Company Voluntary Arrangement (CVA)[317] or a scheme of arrangement[318] by imposing a moratorium on the enforcement of creditors' rights.[319] In addition to administration by court order,[320] administration may be initiated out of court,[321] through the appointment of an administrator, by the company,[322] its directors[323] or the holder of a qualifying floating charge.[324] An appointment by the company or its directors will be subject to the condition that the company is or is likely to become unable to pay its debts.[325] The holder of a qualifying floating charge may appoint an administrator even if the company is not insolvent or facing insolvency. This allows it to place the company in administration before its financial position has become critical.[326] In turn, where directors wish to propose a CVA or scheme of arrangement incorporating proposals that will continue to leave the day-to-day management in their hands, there is every incentive for them to take steps early before any holder of a qualifying floating charge has become entitled to enforce the charge.[327] However, in many respects administration remains less debtor friendly than Chapter 11[328] and, on a scale from debtor friendly to creditor friendly regimes, seems to be situated somewhere in the middle between the US and Germany. Administration of a company will be placed in the hands of an external manager, a qualified insolvency practitioner,[329] sometimes working in close co-operation with a creditor's committee;[330] although the administrator may leave the day-to-day business of the company in the hands of the existing management ('light touch' administration).[331] Administration imposes a statutory moratorium on the

[314] ibid §218. [315] ibid §89.

[316] ibid §47; L Häsemeyer, *Insolvenzrecht* (4th edn, Carl Heymanns Verlag 2007) 295–8.

[317] Insolvency Act 1986, ss 1–8. A Company Voluntary Arrangement, although an insolvency proceeding, is contractual in nature; see Goode (n 193) 495 (para 12-26).

[318] Companies Act 2006, ss 895–9. [319] Goode (n 193) 394 (para 11-18).

[320] Insolvency Act 1986, Sch B1, paras 10–13. [321] ibid paras 14–39. [322] ibid para 22(1).

[323] ibid para 22(2).

[324] ibid para 14. A floating charge qualifies if created by an instrument which states that para 14 applies and which purports to empower the holder to appoint an administrator; para 14(2). A person is the holder of such a charge if in respect of the company's property he holds one or more debentures secured by a qualifying floating charge, a number of qualifying floating charges or a qualifying floating charge and other security, which together relate to the whole or substantially the whole of the company's property: ibid para 14(3).

[325] This follows from the statutory declaration the company or its directors must make if they intend to appoint an administrator, ibid para 27(2)(a).

[326] Goode (n 193) 420 (para 11-45). [327] ibid.

[328] For a very succinct comparison of Chapter 11 and administration see ibid 394–5 (para 11-18).

[329] Insolvency Act 1986, Sch B1, paras 5 and 6. [330] Goode (n 193) 394 (para 11-18).

[331] ibid 397 (para 11-22).

enforcement of the rights of creditors, including secured creditors and sellers under retention of title or a hire-purchase agreements and financial lessors.[332] However, the effectiveness of the moratorium seems to be somewhat reduced by the courts' readiness to exercise their discretion so as to allow enforcement actions by secured creditors against the company during the moratorium.[333] Under current reform proposals affirmative incentives will be further enhanced: companies of any size will be able to file for a restructuring moratorium on the basis of prospective insolvency. During the moratorium corporate management will remain in control, supervised only by a monitor that ensures the integrity of the moratorium process. This seeks to give the company and its managers a chance to negotiate an informal restructuring with its creditors.[334]

The French safeguard procedure, first introduced in the course of the 1995 reforms and extended in 2014, forms the core of the modern French insolvency law. It is meant to be a preventive rescue procedure. As a voluntary procedure, it may be initiated only prior to the debtor company becoming insolvent on a cash flow basis.[335] In the conceptualization of the procedure, the French legislature was inspired by Chapter 11 of the US Bankruptcy Code. The objective of the procedure is two-fold: (i) the continuation of the economic activity of the business, protection of jobs and a reduction of debt; and (ii) the facilitation of reorganization and restructuring of the business. Given its voluntary nature, the procedure exhibits a number of features that are meant to render it particularly attractive for corporate management. Incumbent management retains the power to manage the business and to dispose of its assets during the observation phase of the proceedings,[336] and, depending on the content of the restructuring plan, possibly also during the implementation phase. The court appointed administrator merely supervises and where necessary supports corporate management. Commencement has no impact on executive remuneration and directors and officers retain the power to trade in the shares of their company. During a safeguard proceeding, management are immune from the imposition of disqualification measures as well as from insolvency related criminal liability. Civil liability in accordance with the provisions on the *action de la responsabilité pour insuffisance d'actif*[337] is limited to a situation where the restructuring plan confirmed by the court is subsequently invalidated. Natural persons who act as sureties or guarantors for the debtor company—usually corporate managers or their close relatives—are privileged in a number of ways. The automatic stay is extended so as to also protect these third parties. Upon commencement, statutory or contractual interest no longer accrues vis-à-vis these sureties and guarantors.[338] A restructuring plan confirmed by the court also benefits them and they can invoke vis-à-vis creditors any of the provisions in the restructuring plan that reduce the burden of the debtor company.

II. Liability incentives

European legal systems traditionally and almost exclusively relied on a strategy based on liability incentives. In particular, Germany imposes on directors of entities that afford limited liability to their members a duty to file for insolvency proceedings without culpable delay and within three weeks of the materialization of either cash flow insolvency or balance sheet insolvency.[339] This duty is backed by criminal and civil liability; the latter is tort based and is usually referred to as the liability for delaying insolvency proceedings. The constitutive elements of liability are, objectively, a breach of the duty to file and a loss suffered by the

332 Insolvency Act 1986, Sch B1, para 43.
333 V Finch and D Milman, *Corporate Insolvency Law* (3rd edn, CUP 2017) 308.
334 Department for Business, Energy & Industrial Strategy, Insolvency and Corporate Governance: Government response (26 August 2018) paras 5.5–5.87.
335 Com Art L620-1. 336 Com Art L622-1. 337 see Chapter 10E.II.
338 Com Art L622-28. 339 See Schillig (n 214) 126–37.

creditors; and subjectively, fault on the part of the respective director(s). The three-week period begins to run as soon as the company is objectively insolvent on either a cash flow or balance sheet basis. This short period will enable the management to consider the chances of an informal workout. If it becomes clear before the end of the three-week period that any efforts to reorganize the company outside formal proceedings are likely to be unsuccessful, the management must file immediately and cannot exhaust the three-week period. Liability ensues where the director is in breach of the filing duty which requires fault on the part of the respective director at least in the form of negligence, which is to be rebuttably presumed. The standard of care is that of a conscientious director. This subjective element in combination with the concept of the 'positive going concern prognosis' seems to introduce a certain amount of flexibility into the regime. Management is afforded a 'certain margin of discretion'.[340] In respect of the content of the claim and its enforcement, creditors whose claims came into existence before the duty to file arose (pre-duty creditors) and creditors whose claims came into existence after the duty arose, but before formal proceedings were opened, (post-duty creditors) are to be distinguished. Pre-duty creditors may recover their losses (only) to the extent that the rate they receive on their claim was reduced as a consequence of the breach of the filing duty (so-called *Quotenschaden*, or 'rate reduction loss').[341] By contrast, post-duty creditors may recover their full individual losses (reliance interest), that is, the loss they suffered because they entered into a contract with an insolvent company which should have been put into formal insolvency proceedings.[342] Only contractual creditors will be protected in this way.[343] During formal insolvency proceedings only the office holder has standing to sue the directors for the aggregate of the rate reduction damages suffered by all pre-duty creditors collectively.[344] Irrespective of whether insolvency proceedings are opened or not, post-duty creditors have standing and must pursue their claims individually.[345]

Similarly, under French law, the debtor has a statutory duty to petition the court for the opening of judicial restructuring proceedings or liquidation proceedings within forty-five days of the onset of cash flow insolvency. The filing duty may be averted by initiating conciliation proceedings prior to the expiry of the forty-five day period.[346] Breach of this duty may result in criminal and/or civil liability of the respective director, the latter on the basis of the *action de la responsabilité pour insuffisance d'actif*:[347] failure to request the commencement of insolvency proceedings within forty-five days if the company is in a state of cessation of payment may amount to a management fault that triggers liability.[348]

The English concept of liability for 'wrongful trading'[349] may be asserted where the company has gone into insolvent liquidation or insolvent administration. Only the liquidator or administrator has standing and has the burden of determining the 'material time' before the commencement of the winding up at which the respondent director 'knew or ought to have known that there was no reasonable prospect that the company would avoid going into insolvent liquidation' or insolvent administration.[350] It is then up to the respondent to prove, that from the 'material time' onwards he took every step necessary in order to minimize the potential loss to the company's creditors.[351] There is no strict filing duty; liability is triggered by the failure to act properly in order to minimize the losses to the company's creditors when it has become apparent that the company is unlikely to survive.[352]

Even US law has been flirting with the development of liability based incentives, complementing the traditional affirmative approach. 'Deepening insolvency' emerged as a

[340] BGHZ 126, 181, 199 (1994). [341] ibid 190. [342] ibid 192, 193. [343] ibid 191.
[344] InsO, §92. [345] BGHZ 126, 181, 201 (1994). [346] Com Arts L631-4, L640-4.
[347] see Chapter 10E.II.
[348] M Jeantin and P Le Cannu, *Droit commercial: Entreprises en difficulté* (7th edn, Dalloz 2006) para 1293.
[349] see Chapter 10D.II. [350] Insolvency Act 1986, ss 214(2)(b); 246ZB(2)(b).
[351] Insolvency Act 1986, ss 214(3); 246ZB(3). [352] Goode (n 193) 667 (para 14-32).

doctrine that could be used for a multitude of purposes.[353] It was first developed in the federal courts[354] and largely in the context of a motion to dismiss.[355] Trustees in bankruptcies acting on behalf of corporate debtors sought to hold not just directors and officers but also outsiders such as legal and financial advisers, auditors, underwriters, and lenders liable for prolonging the life of the company by taking on additional debt, thereby increasing the company's net deficiency.[356] By predicting state tort law,[357] federal courts developed 'deepening insolvency' as an independent cause of action and as a theory to measure the harm done to the corporation. In the leading case *Official Committee of Unsecured Creditors v Lafferty*[358] the Court of Appeals, Third Circuit held that even in the event of insolvency when 'a corporation's debts exceed the fair market value of its assets', corporate property may still have value and that '[t]he fraudulent and concealed incurrence of debt can damage that value in several ways'.[359] '[W]here "deepening insolvency" causes damage to corporate property', the court believed, 'the Pennsylvania Supreme Court would provide a remedy by recognizing a cause of action for that injury'.[360] Thus, 'deepening insolvency' was established as a cause of action under Pennsylvania tort law. However, much remained unclear in respect of both the preconditions for liability and the categories of damages that could be recovered, and the doctrine was subject to severe criticism. In *Trenwick*[361] the Delaware Court of Chancery and the Delaware Supreme Court rejected 'deepening insolvency' as a cause of action under Delaware law.[362] These decisions have resulted in an ever declining significance of 'deepening insolvency', at least as an independent cause of action.

Questions and comments:

1. Following this short survey we can perhaps detect a convergence towards greater emphasis on affirmative incentive in line with the US model. This is also reflected in EU harmonization attempts. In its 2002 Final Report, the High Level Group of Company Law Experts argued that the introduction of a European 'framework rule' on management liability in times of crisis would enhance creditors' confidence and encourage their cross-border business activity in order to facilitate the establishment of the internal market, creating a level playing field for creditor protection across the EU.[363] Liability for 'wrongful trading' was envisaged as the source of inspiration for such a rule at EU level. The 2014 Commission Recommendation exclusively relies on affirmative incentives: the debtor should be able to restructure at an early stage, should remain in control of the day-to-day operation of the business and should be able to obtain a temporary stay.[364] The Commission's Proposal for a Directive on preventive

[353] L Colasacco, 'Where Were the Accountants? Deepening Insolvency as a Means of Ensuring Accountants' Presence when Corporate Turmoil Materializes' (2009) 78 Fordham Law Review 793.

[354] Pursuant to 28 U.S.C. §1334 (b) the district courts have 'original but not exclusive jurisdiction of all civil proceedings arising under title 11 or arising in or related to a case under title 11'. The reach of this jurisdiction is very broad and may encompass any proceeding the outcome of which can have an impact on the estate. BE Adler, DG Baird, and TH Jackson, *Bankruptcy: Cases, Problems, and Materials* (4th edn, Foundation Press 2007) 47.

[355] Federal Rule of Bankruptcy Procedure 7012(b), Federal Rule of Civil Procedure 12(b)(6). The purpose of a motion to dismiss is to test the legal sufficiency of the claim based on the allegations made in the complaint which the court is required to accept as true. *In re Exide Technologies, Inc.*, 299 B.R. 732 (Bkrtcy, D.Del. 2003) 739.

[356] A comprehensive list of cases with potential plaintiffs and defendants can be found in T Bateman Farrell, '"Deepening Insolvency" as a Cause of Action in Tort' (2007) 23 ALR 6th 457.

[357] If a federal court faces an issue governed by state law and the highest tribunal of that state has not yet decided the question, the federal court must predict how the highest state court would act if it were presented with the question. See *Official Committee of Unsecured Creditors v Lafferty & Co., Inc.*, 267 F.3d 340, 349 (C.A. 3rd, 2001).

[358] ibid. [359] ibid 349. [360] ibid 351.

[361] *Trenwick America Litigation Trust v Ernst & Young, LLP*, 902 A.2d 168 (Del. Ch., 2006), affirmed in *Trenwick America Litigation Trust v. Billett*, 931 A.2d 438 (Del. Supr., 2007).

[362] *Trenwick America Litigation Trust v Ernst & Young, LLP*, 902 A.2d 168, 174 (Del. Ch., 2006).

[363] Report of the High Level Group of Company Law Experts on A Modern Regulatory Framework for Company Law in Europe (Brussels, 2002) Chapter III, para 4.4.

[364] Commission Recommendation of 12.3.2014 on a New Approach to Business Failure and Insolvency, C(2014) 1500 final, Art 6(a)–(c).

restructuring frameworks, second chance and measures to increase the efficiency of restructuring, insolvency and discharge procedures[365] focuses primarily on affirmative incentives: a moratorium, debtor-in possession governance, an optional DIP financing facility. It also contains a provision that mandates the installation of directors' duties to minimize losses for creditors, to have due regard to their interests, to take reasonable steps to avoid insolvency, and to avoid grossly negligent conduct that threatens the viability of the business. The Proposal thus follows a dual approach.

2. Strict filing duties, as in Germany and France, are often perceived as being counterproductive when it comes to facilitating corporate rescue. In particular when combined with a static balance sheet test, viable businesses may be forced into formal proceedings prematurely with all the ensuing costs in form of negative publicity and the loss of trust from customers and suppliers. Also, the grace periods of three weeks or forty-five days may be too short to mount a credible rescue attempt for any decent size business. At the same time, enforcement of the filing duty on the basis of civil liability appears to be rather ineffective and does not seem to encourage management to take steps early in order to address a deteriorating financial situation.[366]
3. Affirmative incentives do not seem to be much better. As Professor Lynn LoPucki writes: 'In all but a few cases, the meaningful stages of financial decay, recovery or liquidation occur outside the bankruptcy court. The bankruptcy court deals not with businesses in financial difficulty, but with their skeletons, already picked clean by workouts, state court proceedings, informal liquidations, or merely the ravages of time and poor management'.[367]
4. Given that neither affirmative incentives nor liability incentives seem to be very effective in incentivizing corporate management to do the right thing at the right time, is it likely that a combination of both strategies can be more successful?

D. From a Tragedy of the Commons to a Tragedy of the Anti-commons

The tragedy of the commons resulting from the combination of individual enforcement rights and an insufficient common pool of assets may be addressed by delinking individual rights from the right of access to the common pool. Most insolvency law systems pursue a 'collectivization' strategy: individual enforcement (withdrawal) rights are subjected to a comprehensive moratorium or stay; the power to manage the common pool is temporarily assigned to, or put under the supervision of, an external expert who is neutral and under a duty to act in the best interest of all constituencies; creditors' individual enforcement rights are transformed into participation rights in a collective procedure, essentially consisting of information rights and voting rights with a view to reaching a collective decision on the treatment of the common pool of assets. This is the bankruptcy governance regime. The transition from corporate governance to bankruptcy governance may avert the 'tragedy of the commons' by overriding individual enforcement rights and preserving the potential going concern value inherent in the common pool. However, in this situation a 'tragedy of the anti-commons' may ensue. When locked into a collective procedure and deciding how to realize and distribute a potential going concern surplus, each party has an incentive to extract as much value for itself as possible. By misreading the other parties' intentions, misjudging their incentives or by being in error of the amount of surplus, a party may push too far thus preventing agreement and the surplus may be lost. In particular, a party

[365] European Commission, Proposal for a Directive of the European Parliament and of the Council on preventive restructuring frameworks, second chance and measures to increase the efficiency of restructuring, insolvency and discharge procedures and amending Directive 2012/30/EU COM(2016) 723 final.

[366] Schillig (n 214) 135–7.

[367] LM LoPucki, 'A General Theory of the Dynamics of the State Remedies/Bankruptcy System' (1982) Wisconsin Law Review 311, 312.

		Creditor B	
		Won't cooperate	Cooperate
Creditor A	Won't cooperate	500; 500	900; 700
	Cooperate	700; 900	800; 800

Figure 2: Tragedy of the anti-commons

whose contribution would significantly increase any surplus has a great incentive to engage in hold out behaviour with a view to extracting a higher than proportionate price for its cooperation.[368]

Whereas the commons problem may be said to derive from too many private access rights or 'use privileges' resulting in 'over-use' of a common resource, the anti-commons problem is often characterized by private exclusion or veto rights resulting in 'under-use' of a common resource.[369] In the insolvency context this distinction is not very helpful.[370] More illuminating are the different strategic behaviour patterns of commons and anti-commons. As we have seen, the commons problem resembles a typical Prisoners' Dilemma with one dominant strategy. Regardless of whether the focus is on individual access rights or exclusion rights, every creditor is always better off by enforcing his individual rights (or vetoing a workout). By contrast, the anti-commons problem resembles a 'game of chicken' with no dominant strategy where the best strategy for each individual player depends on what the other does.[371] Modifying our example above,[372] the creditors are now locked in a collective corporate insolvency process, preventing them from exercising their individual enforcement rights and temporarily preserving the common pool of assets. Channelled through the bankruptcy governance system, the creditors need to reach a decision on the realization and distribution of the going concern surplus, which will be lost if they do not reach an agreement. The pay-off bimatrix could look as in Figure 2.

From a social welfare point of view, any outcome that realizes the going concern surplus is equally desirable (bottom row and right column). However, each creditor has an incentive to hold out in order to extract a share of the surplus that exceeds what would be due to them on a pro rata basis. Thus, where creditor B holds out and creditor A is willing to forgo some of the surplus in order to reach agreement, the pay-offs may look like in the bottom left corner with creditor B receiving a pay-off of 900 and creditor A of 700 (or vice versa: top right). Creditor A may be willing to cooperate because his pay-off in that case still exceeds his pay-off were the agreement to fail and both creditors would share equally in the break-up value (top left corner). In this game, each creditor's optimal strategy depends on what the other does. The risk is that strategic behaviour may prevent creditors from reaching agreement that would

[368] This and the following is based on Schillig (n 186).

[369] M Heller, 'The Tragedy of the Anticommons: Property in the Transition from Marx to Markets' (1998) 111 Harvard Law Review 621, 677.

[370] The pre-bankruptcy situation of creditors may be analysed as a commons problem (see above): too many individual enforcement rights resulting in a premature liquidation of the debtor company and over-use of the common pool. However, since, in the absence of a general moratorium, every creditor's consent would be required to effectuate a workout, and every creditor would have to credibly commit to not enforcing his individual rights, by vetoing a workout for strategic reasons a possible going concern value may be lost, thus under-using the common pool due to the exercise of veto rights. Commons and anti-commons would thus appear as merely the two sides of the same coin.

[371] Fennell (n 191) 35, 43–5; DG Baird, RH Gertner, and RC Picker, *Game Theory and the Law* (HUP 1994) 44–5. See also R de Weijs, 'Too Big to Fail as a Game of Chicken with the State: What Insolvency Law Theory Has to Say about TBTF and Vice Versa' (2013) 14 EBOR 201.

[372] Debtor company with assets of a break-up value of 1,000 and going concern value of 1,600; two creditors A and B, ranking pari passu, each with a nominal claim of 900.

maximize firm value. This may easily happen where parties overestimate asset values and/or other parties' willingness to cooperate.[373] The bankruptcy governance system addresses these issues through information rights, possibly channelled through a creditors' committee, majority voting requirements instead of unanimity (veto rights) and possibly 'cram-down' mechanisms so as to prevent hold outs and preserve the ability to impose a value enhancing solution on individual dissenting creditors or even on an entire class of similarly situated creditors.

The bankruptcy governance regime is premised on the general assumption that on the whole (unsecured) creditors have an economic interest in the maximization of the value of the debtor company's assets, that the participants are easily identifiable and their property rights sufficiently well defined.[374] However, this general assumption seems to have lost some of its plausibility. The 'derivatives revolution' and technological and financial innovation have resulted in a much enhanced ability of equity and debt investors—as well as directors and executives—to rearrange and modify their property rights and to decouple and reassemble economic interests and control rights, resulting in more complex and fragmented proprietary interests and increased complexity of capital structures.[375] For example, a creditor may hedge its exposure to the default risk of the debtor by holding a 'credit default swap' (CDS). Although fully hedged, the protection buyer retains all contractual rights under the credit instrument and may exercise, dispose of, waive, or renegotiate these rights and vote in a collective insolvency procedure.[376] Through securitization, via 'collateralised debt obligations' (CDOs), a pool of debt contracts or instruments may be repackaged into separate tranches with different risk profiles, parcelled out and sold to a multitude of investors around the world which in turn will hold only a small portion of the economic interest in the underlying portfolio. Moreover, these investors may be fully or partially hedged and actively trade in their positions which renders the identification of the ultimate holder of the economic interest very difficult. Hedge funds and other investment funds are lightly regulated and their investment strategies are often opaque; these funds may not be repeat players and may be largely unconcerned by adverse publicity. The same is true for distressed debt investors who are often interested in realizing a short-term profit, rather than participating in a lengthy reorganization. These developments amplify the significance of the 'tragedy of the anti-commons'. The heightened complexity through debt fragmentation, the resulting realignment of incentive structures as well as the appearance of new and opaque players make it more difficult to correctly identify and assess the incentives of the other players and calculate their behaviour in a scenario where there is no dominant strategy.[377]

[373] Let us assume that our going concern value is only 1,300 (instead of 1,600). However, the non-cooperating creditor overestimates the going concern value, whereas the other creditor is aware of the actual value.

		Creditor B	
		Won't cooperate	Cooperate
Creditor A	Won't cooperate	500; 500	900; 400
	Cooperate	400; 900	650; 650

If creditor A is non-cooperating and holding out by demanding 900, the cooperating creditor B has no incentive to agree to the proposed deal (and vice versa) as he would be worse off than in the break up scenario. The outcome is the same where both creditors are aware of the actual going concern value of 1300, but the non-cooperating creditor (A) believes the other creditor (B) to be more of a 'push over' than they actually are. In either scenario, the socially optimal outcome—realization of the going concern value—will not be achieved.

[374] DG Baird and RK Rasmussen, 'Anti-Bankruptcy' (2010) 120 Yale Law Journal 648, 654.

[375] HTC Hu and B Black, 'The New Vote Buying: Empty Voting and Hidden Ownership' (2006) 79 Southern California Law Review 811; 'Equity and Debt Decoupling and Empty Voting II: Importance and Extensions' (2008) 156 University of Pennsylvania Law Review 635; 'Debt, Equity, and Hybrid Decoupling: Governance and Systemic Risk Implications' (2008a) 14 European Financial Management 663.

[376] Hu and Black (2008a) (n 375) 679–80; F Partnoy and D Skeel, 'The Promise and Perils of Credit Derivatives' (2007) 75 University of Cincinnati Law Review 1019, 1021–2.

[377] Fennell (n 191) 35, 45.

		Creditor B	
		Won't cooperate	Cooperate
Creditor A	Won't cooperate	250; 250	450; 700
	Cooperate	700; 450	800; 800

Figure 3: Repricing of property rights with 50 per cent tax

One way of addressing the problem may be the redefining the parties' property rights and thereby repricing the choice between cooperation and defection. For example, creditors' rights could be redefined in the sense that the non-cooperating creditor will always be subject to a 50 per cent tax or penalty on any dividend he receives on his claim. The pay-off bimatrix now looks as set out in Figure 3.

Cooperation becomes the dominant strategy for each creditor and coincides with the outcome represented by the bottom right corner. Practically, however, such a tax-based solution will be difficult to implement.[378] More promising is a solution based on giving the parties the choice of selecting a bankruptcy governance regime that best fits their individual incentive structures from a menu of different options. For example, if it is expected that the debtor company's capital structure will be highly fragmented with many difficult to identify and to reach debt investors, a bankruptcy governance regime that relies on (relatively) low quora and voting thresholds may be best suited to overcome the anti-commons problem. Similarly, where it is anticipated that numerous investors will be hedged or may even have a negative economic interest in the debtor company, a bankruptcy governance system that allows for the discounting of the votes of creditors whose control rights have been de-coupled from their economic interest in the debtor company may be most suitable. Repricing of property rights through the selection of a certain bankruptcy governance regime from a menu of different options may occur either ex ante when the debtor company is formed and/or prior to it being financially distressed, or ex post when financial distress is already manifesting itself. Ex post repricing would appear to be more problematic as it may interfere with established property rights and legitimate investor expectations.

An extreme form of ex post repricing is the switch from 'collectivisation' to 'privatisation' in order to overcome the anti-commons situation caused by forcing creditors into a collective procedure.[379] Creditors' collective decision-making rights and procedural participation rights are bundled together and concentrated in the hands of a single rights holder or lead creditor (or leading class of creditors). The lead creditor in conjunction with the office holder or the DIP drives the procedure forward and determines its outcome. The other creditors retain their substantive rights, but have little or no say in how the common pool of assets is to be administered, thus avoiding potential holdouts and the deadlock scenario. However, where a piecemeal sale of the debtor's assets generates sufficient proceeds to satisfy the lead creditors claim, the latter has no incentive to expand any effort in order to continue

[378] It will be difficult to decide ex ante whether there is a going concern surplus inherent in the common pool. If not, cooperation (through prolonged negotiation) would itself be a waste of time and resources. It may also be difficult to decide whether any one creditor is a non-cooperating creditor liable to pay the 50% tax. This is to a large extent due to the valuation problem: it will be difficult to determine the value of the common pool and a potential going concern surplus. This makes it difficult to decide whether a particular creditor is holding out and demands more than would be due to him on a *pro rata* basis.

[379] See also D Skeel, 'Competing Narratives in Corporate Bankruptcy: Debtor in Control vs. No Time to Spare' (2009) 4 Michigan State Law Review 1187, 1203: '[T]he coexistence of several possible narratives could assure a closer correspondence between the narrative and the underlying facts in any given case'. Skeel's 'No Time to Spare' narrative is roughly equivalent to 'privatisation', whereas 'Debtor in Control' represents the collectivization alternative.

trading and selling the business as a going concern. The mismatch of procedural power and substantive entitlement may result in a (partial) destruction of going concern value. These concerns call for certain mandatory safeguards.

E. Menu of Insolvency Options

According to Rasmussen's 'menu approach', corporate insolvency law and the bankruptcy governance system is simply an implied term in the contract between a firm and those who extend credit to it.[380] The applicable bankruptcy law and governance regime determine the pricing of the lender's property rights when the firm is in general default. The lender will factor this into its lending decision. The interest rate will depend on the quality of the applicable bankruptcy governance regime. In order to reduce transaction costs, a certain amount of standardization is necessary and can be achieved by making available a 'menu of bankruptcy options'. Upon formation, the firm would be required to select one option from the menu (or devise its own bankruptcy contract) in its corporate charter. The firm's creditors would, thus, be on notice of the applicable bankruptcy governance regime.[381] The problem of strategic manipulation requires that the firm's ability of changing its initial selection after it has incurred debt must be restricted in order to prevent unjustified wealth transfers. Moreover, non-consensual creditors require protection through mandatory provisions unalterable by contract.[382] Menu choice may be provided domestically, where different procedures are available within a certain jurisdiction, including options that are based on a 'privatisation' model; as well as internationally, where firms are able to select the bankruptcy governance regime of a foreign jurisdiction.[383]

The latter is particularly relevant within the European Union, but also in relation to the United States, which make it easy for foreign firms to use the restructuring options under the Federal Bankruptcy Code. Within the European Union, substantive corporate insolvency law is a matter for individual Member States and remains fragmented. So far only a non-binding Recommendation on a new approach to business failure and insolvency has been issued by the Commission, encouraging Member States to put in place a framework that enables the efficient restructuring of viable enterprises in financial difficulties.[384] Drawing on the experience with the Recommendation and on national regimes that work well,[385] the Commission has published a Proposal for a Directive on preventive restructuring frameworks, second chance and measures to increase the efficiency of restructuring, insolvency and discharge procedures.[386] The Proposal contains substantive 'minimum standards' at EU level and requires Member States to provide for a restructuring procedure with a moratorium, debtor-in possession governance, a cram-down across classes, and, optionally, a DIP financing facility. This Proposal aside, the order of priority of claims in respect of banks and

[380] R Rasmussen, 'Debtor's Choice: A Menu Approach to Corporate Bankruptcy' (1992) 71 Texas Law Review 51, 56.

[381] ibid 66. [382] ibid 67, with n 52.

[383] R Rasmussen, 'A New Approach to Transnational Insolvencies' (1997) 19 Michigan Journal of International Law 1.

[384] Commission Recommendation of 12.3.2014 on a new approach to business failure and insolvency, C(2014) 1500 final.

[385] Communication from the Commission to the European Parliament, Council, European Economic and Social Committee and the Committee of the Regions: Action plan on building a capital markets union COM(2015) 468 final 25; Communication from the Commission to the European Parliament, the Council, the European Central Bank, the European Economic and Social Committee and the Committee of the Regions: Towards the Completion of the Banking Union, COM(2015) 587 final 10.

[386] European Commission, Proposal for a Directive of the European Parliament and of the Council on preventive restructuring frameworks, second chance and measures to increase the efficiency of restructuring, insolvency and discharge procedures and amending Directive 2012/30/EU, COM(2016) 723 final.

investment firms has been harmonized to some extent.[387] In the past, the practical feasibility of large-scale harmonization in this area found a formidable obstacle in the disparity in common law and civil law countries of (personal) property law, which insolvency law is inherently linked to, and intertwined with. Moreover, the United Kingdom enjoyed a comparative advantage as the corporate insolvency and restructuring destination in Europe and therefore had little incentive to facilitate the introduction of an effective pan-European insolvency framework. With the UK's departure from the EU and the resultant weakening of common law influences, it remains to be seen whether the EU will be able to forge ahead with insolvency law harmonization, or whether substantive corporate insolvency law will remain predominantly domestic.

The EU Insolvency Regulation (EUIR)[388] which has been reformed and recast in 2015 (2015 EUIR)[389] is a conflict of laws instrument containing mainly[390] rules on jurisdiction, the applicable law and the recognition and enforcement of foreign decisions. The 2015 EUIR follows the principle of 'modified universalism':[391] it distinguishes between main proceedings with universal scope opened in the Member State where the debtor has its Centre of Main Interests (COMI) and territorial proceedings in Member States where the debtor has an establishment.[392] Albeit entity based, the 2015 EUIR contains extensive provisions on cooperation and communication between insolvency practitioners and courts involved in the proceedings concerning different entities within a group of companies.[393] It also introduces a framework for group coordination proceedings that allows for the bundling and joint administration of the various proceedings of different group members on the basis of a group coordination plan.[394] Through the concept of COMI, the 2015 EUIR allows to a certain extent the ex ante and ex post repricing of property rights in accordance with the menu approach.[395]

I. Menu choice

Under the 2015 EUIR, main insolvency proceedings with a universal scope[396] may be opened exclusively by the courts of the Member State in the territory of which the debtor's

[387] The Bank Recovery and Resolution Directive (2014/59/EU) has harmonized the ranking of depositors and deposit guarantee schemes to some extent (Art 108). In order to enhance the effectiveness of the bail-in tool, the new Art 108(2) has introduced the asset class of non-preferred senior debt, which has a ranking below ordinary unsecured claims and above capital instruments; Directive (EU) 2017/2399 of the European Parliament and of the Council of 12 December 2017 amending Directive 2014/59/EU as regards the ranking of unsecured debt instruments in insolvency hierarchy, OJ EU 27.12.2017 L345/96..

[388] Council Regulation (EC) No 1346/2000 of 29 May 2000 on insolvency proceedings OJ 30.06.2000 L160/1.

[389] Regulation (EU) 2015/848 of the European Parliament and of the Council of 20 May 2015 on insolvency proceedings (recast) OJ EU 5.6.2015 L141/19. Most of the provisions of the 2015 EUIR apply since 26 June 2017: 2015 EUIR, Art 92.

[390] It also contains certain provisions of a substantive nature, in particular: ibid Art 10.

[391] 'Universalism' as one approach to cross-border insolvency signifies that jurisdiction over all the debtor's assets and affairs is vested exclusively in the courts of a single state with which the debtor has the closest connection ('principle of unity'), and the jurisdiction of the insolvency court covers all the debtor's assets worldwide ('principle of universality'). The alternative approach, 'territorialism', refers to a state of affairs where a number of concurrent and parallel proceedings may be conducted in different countries subject to some connecting factor ('principle of plurality') with each proceeding being confined to local assets and those portions of the company that lie within the territory of the respective state ('principle of territoriality'). Intermediate approaches, 'modified universalism' or 'qualified territorialism' are generally more feasible in practice; Goode (n 193) 782–4 (para 16-04).

[392] 2015 EUIR, Art 3.

[393] ibid Arts 56–60; drawing to some extent on UNCITRAL's efforts on the treatment of enterprise groups in insolvency; see United Nations, UNCITRAL Legislative Guide on Insolvency Law (Pts 1 and 2 2004; Pt 3 2010; Pt 4 2013).

[394] 2015 EUIR, Arts 61–77.

[395] See further Schillig (n 186) 1–38.

[396] Subject, however, to the opening of secondary (territorial) proceedings in a Member State where the debtor has an establishment which proceeding will be governed by the law of that Member State with a territorial reach only; 2015 EUIR, Art 3(2)–(4).

COMI is situated. The applicable substantive corporate insolvency law,[397] including commencement of proceedings, the treatment of assets forming part of the estate and of executory contracts, the powers of the office holder, the claims procedure and ranking of creditors, the closure of proceedings, and transaction avoidance, is tied to the jurisdiction for opening main proceedings and, thus, to COMI.[398] Consequently, by establishing COMI in a certain jurisdiction a debtor company can effectively select ex ante the insolvency law of that jurisdiction as the applicable bankruptcy governance regime from the menu of options across all EU Member States. COMI is defined as the place where the debtor conducts the administration of its interests on a regular basis and which is ascertainable by third parties; for corporate type entities, COMI is the place of the registered office unless there is proof to the contrary.[399] The concept has generated a significant amount of case law by the Court of Justice over the years, the main principles of which have now been codified in the 2015 EUIR.[400]

Case C-341/04 *Eurofood IFSC* ECLI:EU:C:2006:281

The case concerned the strength of the presumption in favour of the registered office for a subsidiary controlled by a foreign parent:

29 Article 3(1) of the Regulation provides that, in the case of a company, the place of the registered office shall be presumed to be the centre of its main interests in the absence of proof to the contrary.

30 It follows that, in the system established by the Regulation for determining the competence of the courts of the Member States, each debtor constituting a distinct legal entity is subject to its own court jurisdiction.

31 The concept of the centre of main interests is peculiar to the Regulation. Therefore, it has an autonomous meaning and must therefore be interpreted in a uniform way, independently of national legislation.

32 The scope of that concept is highlighted by the 13th recital of the Regulation, which states that 'the 'centre of main interests' should correspond to the place where the debtor conducts the administration of his interests on a regular basis and is therefore ascertainable by third parties'.

33 That definition shows that the centre of main interests must be identified by reference to criteria that are both objective and ascertainable by third parties. That objectivity and that possibility of ascertainment by third parties are necessary in order to ensure legal certainty and foreseeability concerning the determination of the court with jurisdiction to open main insolvency proceedings. That legal certainty and that foreseeability are all the more important in that, in accordance with Article 4(1) of the Regulation, determination of the court with jurisdiction entails determination of the law which is to apply.

34 It follows that, in determining the centre of the main interests of a debtor company, the simple presumption laid down by the Community legislature in favour of the registered office of that company can be rebutted only if factors which are both objective and ascertainable by third parties enable it to be established that an actual situation exists which is different from that which locating it at that registered office is deemed to reflect.

[397] This includes a claim pursuant to GmbHG, §64(2) against the managing director of an English private company limited by shares with COMI in Germany to reimburse the company for any payments made after the company became insolvent; see Case C-594/14 *Kornhaas v Dithmar* ECLI:EU:C:2015:806. Such a claim is directly derived from and closely linked to the insolvency proceedings so that the courts of the Member State within the territory of which insolvency proceedings have been opened have jurisdiction to hear and determine the respective action; Case C-295/13 *H v HK* ECLI:EU:C:2014:2410.

[398] In order to protect the legitimate expectations of certain parties, 'choice of law carve-outs' exempt from the application of the *lex fori concursus*, the following arrangements: third parties' rights in rem, creditors' rights under reservation of title clauses, contracts relating to immovable property, and employment contracts.

[399] EUIR, Art 3(1) and recital (13); 2015 EUIR, Art 3(1).

[400] 2015 EUIR, recitals (28) and (30).

35 That could be so in particular in the case of a 'letterbox' company not carrying out any business in the territory of the Member State in which its registered office is situated.

36 By contrast, where a company carries on its business in the territory of the Member State where its registered office is situated, the mere fact that its economic choices are or can be controlled by a parent company in another Member State is not enough to rebut the presumption laid down by the Regulation.

Case C-396/09 *Interedil Srl* ECLI:EU:C:2011:671

The case concerned an Italian company that had transferred its registered office from Italy to the United Kingdom (*ex post* re-pricing) where it was subsequently, and prior to the lodging of a request to open proceedings in Italy, removed from the register following a transfer of its assets to other group companies. The Court of Justice addressed both the issue of the relevant criteria for establishing COMI, as well as the relevant time for determining the debtor's COMI.

The relevant criteria for determining the centre of the debtor's main interests

47 While the Regulation does not provide a definition of the term 'centre of a debtor's main interests', guidance as to the scope of that term is, nevertheless, as the Court stated at paragraph 32 of Eurofood IFSC, to be found in recital 13 in the preamble to the Regulation, which states that 'the 'centre of main interests' should correspond to the place where the debtor conducts the administration of his interests on a regular basis and [which] is therefore ascertainable by third parties'.

48 As the Advocate General observed at point 69 of her Opinion, the presumption in the second sentence of Article 3(1) of the Regulation that the place of the company's registered office is the centre of its main interests and the reference in recital 13 in the preamble to the Regulation to the place where the debtor conducts the administration of his interests reflect the European Union legislature's intention to attach greater importance to the place in which the company has its central administration as the criterion for jurisdiction.

49 With reference to that recital, the Court also stated, at paragraph 33 of Eurofood IFSC, that the centre of a debtor's main interests must be identified by reference to criteria that are both objective and ascertainable by third parties, in order to ensure legal certainty and foreseeability concerning the determination of the court with jurisdiction to open the main insolvency proceedings. That requirement for objectivity and that possibility of ascertainment by third parties may be considered to be met where the material factors taken into account for the purpose of establishing the place in which the debtor company conducts the administration of its interests on a regular basis have been made public or, at the very least, made sufficiently accessible to enable third parties, that is to say in particular the company's creditors, to be aware of them.

50 It follows that, where the bodies responsible for the management and supervision of a company are in the same place as its registered office and the management decisions of the company are taken, in a manner that is ascertainable by third parties, in that place, the presumption in the second sentence of Article 3(1) of the Regulation that the centre of the company's main interests is located in that place is wholly applicable. In such a case, as the Advocate General observed at point 69 of her Opinion, it is not possible that the centre of the debtor company's main interests is located elsewhere.

51 The presumption in the second sentence of Article 3(1) of the Regulation may be rebutted, however, where, from the viewpoint of third parties, the place in which a company's central administration is located is not the same as that of its registered office. As the Court held at paragraph 34 of Eurofood IFSC, the simple presumption laid down by the European Union legislature in favour of the registered office of that company can be rebutted if factors which are both objective and ascertainable by third parties enable it to be established that an actual situation exists which is different from that which locating it at that registered office is deemed to reflect.

52 The factors to be taken into account include, in particular, all the places in which the debtor company pursues economic activities and all those in which it holds assets, in so far as those places are ascertainable by third parties. As the Advocate General observed at point 70 of her

Opinion, those factors must be assessed in a comprehensive manner, account being taken of the individual circumstances of each particular case.

53 In that context, the location, in a Member State other than that in which the registered office is situated, of immovable property owned by the debtor company, in respect of which the company has concluded lease agreements, and the existence in that Member State of a contract concluded with a financial institution—circumstances referred to by the referring court—may be regarded as objective factors and, in the light of the fact that they are likely to be matters in the public domain, as factors that are ascertainable by third parties. The fact nevertheless remains that the presence of company assets and the existence of contracts for the financial exploitation of those assets in a Member State other than that in which the registered office is situated cannot be regarded as sufficient factors to rebut the presumption laid down by the European Union legislature unless a comprehensive assessment of all the relevant factors makes it possible to establish, in a manner that is ascertainable by third parties, that the company's actual centre of management and supervision and of the management of its interests is located in that other Member State.

The relevant date for the purpose of locating the centre of the debtor's main interests

54 First, it should be noted that the Regulation does not contain any express provisions concerning the specific case involving the transfer of a debtor's centre of interests. In the light of the general terms in which Article 3(1) of the Regulation is worded, the last place in which that centre was located must therefore be regarded as the relevant place for the purpose of determining the court having jurisdiction to open the main insolvency proceedings.

55 That interpretation finds support in the Court's case-law. The Court has held that, where the centre of a debtor's main interests is transferred after the lodging of a request to open insolvency proceedings, but before the proceedings are opened, the courts of the Member State within the territory of which the centre of main interests was situated at the time when the request was lodged retain jurisdiction to rule on those proceedings (Case C-1/04 Staubitz-Schreiber [2006] ECR I-701, paragraph 29). It must be inferred from this that, in principle, it is the location of the debtor's main centre of interests at the date on which the request to open insolvency proceedings was lodged that is relevant for the purpose of determining the court having jurisdiction.

56 In a case such as that in the main proceedings in which the registered office is transferred before a request to open insolvency proceedings is lodged, the centre of the debtor's main interests is therefore presumed, in accordance with the second sentence of Article 3(1) of the Regulation, to be located at the place of the new registered office and, accordingly, it is the courts of the Member State within the territory of which the new registered office is located which, in principle, have jurisdiction to open the main insolvency proceedings, unless the presumption in Article 3(1) of the Regulation is rebutted by evidence that the centre of main interests has not followed the change of registered office.

57 The same rules must apply where, at the date on which the request to open insolvency proceedings is lodged, the debtor company has been removed from the register of companies and where, as submitted by Interedil in its observations, it has ceased all activity.

58 As is apparent from paragraphs 47 to 51 above, the term 'centre of main interests' meets the need to establish a connection with the place with which, from an objective viewpoint and in a manner that is ascertainable by third parties, the company has the closest links. It is therefore logical in such a situation to attach greater importance to the location of the last centre of main interests at the time when the debtor company was removed from the register of companies and ceased all activities.

It is clear from these cases, and recitals (28) to (31) of the 2015 EUIR, that the COMI concept is a fact sensitive affair, to be determined by taking into account a multitude of different factors: the location of the debtor's internal accounting and human resources functions, as well as of its treasury management and IT systems, the law governing the debtor's main contracts, the location of its main lenders and of its employees, the location from where purchasing control is exercised and where its business relations with clients have been established, and further the domicile of its directors, and where board meetings and restructuring negations with creditors take place. In accordance with the 'objective and ascertainable by third parties' criterion, the perception of creditors is vital in this respect.

It is also clear from *Interedil* and the earlier case of *Staubitz-Schreiber*[401] that a debtor company may transfer its COMI to a different Member State prior to the lodging of an application to open insolvency proceedings. Consequently, the 2015 EUIR allows, in principle, for the ex post repricing of property rights, or 'forum shopping' in the parlance of the 2015 EUIR. In recent years, a number of large European corporate groups have availed themselves of this possibility by transferring their COMI to the United Kingdom in order to benefit from the available restructuring options. This can be achieved through the accretion method (*Anwachsung*), where a corporate-type entity is first converted into a partnership-type entity; then a newly incorporated company with its headquarters and principal place of business in the Member State of destination enters as managing partner, all other remaining partners withdraw. By operation of law, all assets of the partnership will vest automatically in the newly formed company with its COMI in the Member State of destination, provided it actually operates from its new address, notifies the creditors of the change, and carries out its negotiations from there.[402] Alternatively, the debtor company may establish its head office and independent management in the Member State of destination, recruit legal and financial advisers there, transfer its books to and open bank accounts in the new location, conduct all business activities from there whilst at the same time terminating existing contracts under the law of the previous location, carry out board meetings and restructuring negotiations in the new location, register as a foreign company and for tax purposes in the new location and duly notify the creditors of the transfer. This was the technique used in the second *Wind Hellas* restructuring.[403] Under the 2015 EUIR, menu choice is greatly facilitated by the automatic recognition of the judgment opening insolvency proceedings, whether main, secondary or territorial, as well as ancillary judgments of the opening court concerning the course or closure of insolvency proceedings, in all other EU Member States, subject only to public policy considerations.[404] Following Brexit, and subject to any new arrangement, a company can no longer be certain that, following a transfer of its COMI to the UK for restructuring purposes, an administration order obtained in the English courts will automatically be recognized and enforced in other Member States. In the absence of the 2015 EUIR, English courts will have jurisdiction to make an administration order against any company incorporated in an EEA State other than the United Kingdom, and regardless of where that company's COMI is situated. Moreover, a company not incorporated in an EEA State but with its COMI in a Member

[401] In this case, the debtor—a natural person—relocated from Germany to Spain after filing a bankruptcy request in Germany but before proceedings had been opened in Germany. It was held that the COMI cannot be shifted between the date on which a bankruptcy request is filed and the date on which bankruptcy proceedings are opened; Case C-1/04 *Staubitz-Schreiber* ECLI:EU:C:2006:39. The implication is that COMI may be shifted before the request to open proceedings has been lodged.

[402] This technique was used for example in the cases of *Deutsche Nickel*, *Schefenacker*, *Hans Brochier*, and the first restructuring of *Wind Hellas: Hans Brochier Ltd v Exner* [2006] EWHC 2594; *Re Hellas Telecommunications (Luxembourg) II SCA* [2009] EWHC 3199 (Ch).

[403] B Davies and M Glengarry, 'WIND Hellas' in K Asimacopoulos and J Bickle (eds), *European Debt Restructuring Handbook* (Globe Law and Business 2013) 163–74.

[404] 2015 EUIR, Arts 19, 32, 33.

State (other than Denmark) may be the subject of an administration order.[405] However, the recognition of this administration order in the company's home Member State will depend on the applicable private international insolvency law of that Member State, which may subject recognition and enforcement of a then third country administration order to certain formalities and substantive conditions.[406]

The potential for opportunistic ex post repricing resulting in unjustified and inefficient wealth transfers from one constituency to another requires a balanced approach. The freedom of establishment[407] allows a debtor, in principle, to transfer its registered office and head office freely within the European Union, even if done with a view to benefit from a more favourable corporate insolvency law. Moreover, ex post repricing with a view to maximizing asset values for the benefit of creditors and other constituencies by taking advantage of a more appropriate bankruptcy governance system in a particular jurisdiction is socially desirable. On the other hand, a transfer in order to make it more difficult for certain constituencies to reach the debtor's assets or to shield those in charge from potential liability is undesirable under the menu approach. The 2015 EUIR contains a number of mechanisms that seek to prevent 'abusive' forum shopping. A court seised of a request to open insolvency proceedings will assess *ex officio* whether it has jurisdiction, and has to specify the grounds on which the jurisdiction of the court is based should it decide to open proceedings.[408] Also, the debtor or any creditor may challenge the decision opening main proceedings on grounds of international jurisdiction.[409] In this context, the presumption in favour of the debtor company's registered office may be rebutted where it can be established that the principle reason for the transfer was to file for insolvency proceedings in the new jurisdiction and where such filing would materially impair the interests of pre-existing creditors.[410] Moreover, where the circumstances cast doubt on the debtor company's assertions for a particular COMI, the court should require the debtor to provide additional evidence in support, and give the creditors an opportunity to present their views on the question of jurisdiction where national procedure allows for this.[411] Generally, the presumption in favour of the registered office does not apply where the registered office has been moved to another Member State within a three-month period prior to the request for the opening of insolvency proceedings,[412] although COMI may still be established in the new location on the basis of the usual factors. Overall, it remains doubtful whether these provisions are sufficient to combat opportunistic ex post repricing.[413]

Outside the framework of the 2015 EUIR, the English scheme of arrangement procedure[414] has emerged as the mechanism of choice for balance sheet restructurings of groups of companies from across Europe and from around the world. A scheme can be used for a multitude of purposes, including takeovers, mergers and debt restructurings. As a restructuring mechanism, schemes are extremely flexible. Insolvency is not a prerequisite,

405 Insolvency Act 1986, Sch B1, para 111(1A).

406 M Schillig, 'Corporate Law after Brexit' (2016) 27 King's Law Journal 431, 439. The UNCITRAL Model Law on Cross-Border Insolvency, adopted by the UK through the Cross-Border Insolvency Regulations 2006, SI 2006/1013, will be of very limited assistance in this respect. It is an inward-looking instrument that for the EU has only been adopted by Greece, Poland, Romania and Slovenia. Moreover, it does not produce automatic effects but requires the recognition of foreign proceedings by a national court. The applicable insolvency law remains outside the remit of the Model Law; M Penades-Fons and M Schillig, 'The Impact of Brexit on Debt Restructuring and Insolvency Practice' in A Biondi, P Birkinshaw, and M Kendrick (eds), *Brexit: The Legal Implications* (Wolters Kluwer 2019) 121, 130-1.

407 See Chapter 2C.II.

408 2015 EUIR, Art 4(1).

409 ibid Art 5(1).

410 ibid recital (30).

411 ibid recital (32).

412 ibid Art 3(1) and recital (31).

413 G McCormack, 'Something Old, Something New: Recasting the European Insolvency Regulation' (2016) 79 Modern Law Review 121, 131–2.

414 Having its origin in the Companies Act 1862, the scheme of arrangement is regulated as part of company law (Companies Act 2006, Pt 26), rather than insolvency law.

the incumbent directors may initiate a scheme and remain in control of the company, and the scheme may concern only certain classes of shareholders and/or creditors; provided that the scheme is fair to the class as a whole, there are no restrictions on the possible content of a scheme. As a multi-stage process with extensive court involvement at the convening and sanctioning stages the scheme process is rather lengthy and costly,[415] and therefore attractive mainly for companies of a certain size and with a certain complexity of capital structure. Generally, English courts have jurisdiction to sanction a creditor scheme where the scheme company is a company 'liable to be wound up under the Insolvency Act 1986';[416] in addition, and in order to prevent the *carte blanche* exercise of exorbitant jurisdiction, judge-made constraints require that the company has a sufficiently close connection with England.[417] Under the Insolvency Act 1986, the court has jurisdiction to wind up companies registered under the Companies Act 2006,[418] but also unregistered companies.[419] The latter include companies incorporated under the law of a foreign country.[420] As regards this first prerequisite, this is the end of the matter for companies incorporated and headquartered in countries other than EU Member States.[421] Prior to Brexit taking effect, for companies incorporated and with their COMI in the EU, matters are complicated by the 2015 EUIR and by the Brussels I Regulation.[422] A literal application of the directly effective 2015 EUIR would seem to override the English courts' jurisdiction to wind up a (foreign) company that has neither its COMI nor an establishment in England. As a consequence, the option of restructuring debt through a scheme of arrangement would not be available for foreign companies without transferring their COMI (or setting up an establishment) in England.[423] However, so far English courts have not gone down that route and have generally held that the EUIR has no impact on their scheme jurisdiction.[424] Where launched outside of administration, a scheme of arrangement is not a 'collective insolvency proceeding, which entails the partial or total divestment of a debtor and the appointment of a liquidator'. Moreover, the scheme of arrangement is not listed in Annex A of the 2015 EUIR and is thus outside the respective scope of application. On that basis it is persuasive to say that the 2015 EUIR was never intended to have an impact on the scheme jurisdiction of English courts.[425] The Brussels I Regulation[426] poses similar problems in the form of its Article 24(2), conferring exclusive jurisdiction to wind up a solvent company on the courts of the Member State where the company has its seat; and Article 4, referring for jurisdictional purposes to the domicile of the 'defendant'. Even if the Brussels I Regulation were to apply to schemes in general,[427] which is by no means certain,[428] it is perhaps fair to assume that Article 24(2) would not apply because a scheme is not meant to result in the (solvent) dissolution of the scheme company, neither would Article 4 because it is difficult to see how the

415 J Payne, 'Cross-border Schemes of Arrangement and Forum Shopping' (2013) 14 EBOR 563, 567.

416 Companies Act 2006, s 895(2)(b).

417 *Re Rodenstock GmbH* [2011] EWHC 1104 (Ch) para [20]; *Real Estate Development Co* [1991] BCLC 210, 217.

418 Insolvency Act 1986, s 117(1).

419 ibid ss 220, 221.

420 *Re Rodenstock GmbH* [2011] EWHC 1104 (Ch) para [19].

421 See eg *Bluecrest v Vietnam Shipbuilding Industry Group* [2013] EWHC 1146 (Comm), involving a Vietnamese company.

422 For a detailed account see J Payne, *Schemes of Arrangement* (CUP 2014) 286–324.

423 ibid 295.

424 *Re Drax Holdings Ltd* [2003] EWHC 2743 (Ch); *Re DAP Holdings NV* [2005] EWHC 20192 (Ch); *Re La Seda de Barcelona SA* [2010] EWHC 1364 (Ch); *Re Rodenstock GmbH* [2011] EWHC 1104 (Ch); *Re Primacom Holding GmbH* [2012] EWHC 164 (Ch); *Re Sovereign Marine & General Insurance Co Ltd* [2006] EWHC 1335; *Re APCOA Parking Ltd* [2014] EWHC 997 (Ch); *Re APCOA Parking Holdings GmbH* [2014] EWHC 1867 (Ch); *Re APCOA Holdings GmbH* [2014] EWHC 3849 (Ch).

425 Payne (n 422) 296–9.

426 Regulation (EU) No 1215/2012 of the European Parliament and of the Council of 12 December 2012 on jurisdiction and the recognition and enforcement of judgments in civil and commercial matters (recast) OJ 20.12.2012. L351/1.

427 *Re Rodenstock GmbH* [2011] EWHC 1104 (Ch) para [51].

428 Payne (n 422) 304. The arguments on both sides are summarized in *Re Van Gansewinkel Groep BV & Others* [2015] EWHC 2151 (Ch) paras 42–4; *Re Lehman Brothers International (Europe) (in administration)* [2018]

scheme creditors could be deemed to be 'defendants'. In any case, Article 8 of the Brussels I Regulation may be relied on to safely confer jurisdiction on the English courts, provided at least one scheme creditor is domiciled in England. Moreover, where the facility agreement that is subject to the scheme contains a jurisdiction clause pointing to England and/or creditors enter an appearance in England (without contesting jurisdiction) Articles 25 and 26 of the Brussels I Regulation may be relied on to safely confer jurisdiction on English courts.[429] Following the UK's exit from the EU, these jurisdictional concerns will no longer be relevant, subject of course to any new arrangements that would leave the 2015 EUIR and the Brussels I Regulation in place.

In any case, the second prerequisite mentioned above requires a sufficiently close connection of the scheme company with England. This is undoubtedly the case where the scheme company carries on business or has assets in England.[430] In *Rodenstock*, concerning a German company, the scheme jurisdiction of English courts has been extended:

***Re Rodenstock GmbH* [2011] EWHC 1104 (Ch)**

Mr Justice Briggs

...

Sufficient Connection

64 Although Mr Snowden placed some reliance upon the Company's modest English customer base, and upon the fact that a majority in value of the Scheme Creditors were based in England, he readily acknowledged that, in reality, the case for a sufficient connection with this jurisdiction essentially depended upon the combination of the Senior Lenders' choice of English law and (for their benefit) English jurisdiction as governing their lending relationship with the Company. This case therefore raises in stark form, although not for the first time, the question whether an English law legal relationship (including a choice of English jurisdiction) is, on its own, sufficient to establish a sufficient connection with this jurisdiction to justify its application to the affairs of a foreign company as being less than exorbitant ...

66 It would not in my view be right to treat the Senior Lenders' choice of English jurisdiction for the purposes of resolving disputes under or in connection with the Existing Senior Facilities Agreement as involving a deliberate decision voluntarily to subject themselves to the English court's scheme jurisdiction. The Existing Senior Facilities Agreement contained its own limited provisions for the resolution of certain matters by majority, but it is acknowledged that those provisions are insufficient to achieve the variation in the Senior Lenders' rights contemplated by the Scheme.

67 Nonetheless the Senior Lenders' choice of English law clearly did have the consequence that their rights as lenders were liable to be altered by any scheme sanctioned by a court (whether or not the English court) to the extent that English law recognises the jurisdiction of that court to do so. The alteration of the English law contractual rights of the dissentient majority achieved by a scheme of arrangement sanctioned under Part 26 of the Companies Act 2006 occurs because Parliament has legislated precisely to that effect by conferring upon the English court jurisdiction to do so.

EWHC 1980 (Ch) paras 167–86: schemes might be excluded pursuant to Art 1(2)(b) referring to the winding up of insolvent companies and related proceedings, including 'judicial arrangements and compositions'; the 'being sued' terminology does not seem to fit at all; on the other hand, the European Insolvency Regulation and the Brussels I Regulation are meant to dovetail into one another with no overlap or gap so that schemes involving solvent companies (or even insolvent companies unless in formal insolvency proceedings) would fall within the scope of Brussels I.

429 *Re Primacom Holding GmbH* [2012] EWHC 164 (Ch) paras [10]–[17]; *Van Gansewinkel Groep BV & Ors, Re* [2015] EWHC 2151 (Ch) para 51; *Re Lehman Brothers International (Europe) (in administration)* [2018] EWHC 1980 (Ch) para 179–188.

430 Payne (n 422) 290.

68 I have, on a fairly narrow balance, come to the conclusion that the connection with this jurisdiction constituted by the choice of English law and, for the benefit of the Senior Lenders, exclusive English jurisdiction is on its own a sufficient connection for the purposes of permitting the exercise by this court of its scheme jurisdiction in relation to the Company. This is not a case where, merely by happenstance, a majority or even all of the Scheme Creditors have separately chosen English law and/or jurisdiction to govern their individual lending relationships with the Company. Rather, it is a case where they have collectively done so by a single agreement, governing what is in substance a single facility or set of facilities to which they have all contributed. The single agreement therefore regulates not merely a series of individual creditor/debtor relationships between each lender and the Company, but the relationship between each of the Senior Lenders inter se, and between them as a body and the Company.

In APCOA the scheme jurisdiction of English courts was further extended to a situation where the facility agreement, initially governed by German law (and with a jurisdiction clause pointing to Germany), was subsequently amended on the basis of majority creditor consent to be governed by English law (and conferring jurisdiction for disputes arising to English courts). Given that the facility agreement did not prohibit, neither explicitly nor impliedly, a change in the applicable law and that it required unanimity for its amendment only in certain defined circumstances but not in others and not in respect of a change in the applicable law, the evidence on German law suggested that the change of the governing law was valid under German law and in line with the Rome I Regulation.[431] The choice of law pursuant to a change of the governing law took effect from the validity of the amendment and did not have any lesser force than an original choice of law.[432] A further consideration to be taken into account by the English courts is whether the scheme, if sanctioned, has any chance of being recognized and enforced in the foreign jurisdiction. Given that schemes are outside the scope of the 2015 EUIR, this instrument cannot be relied on for enforcement purposes.[433] If one takes the view that the Brussels I Regulation applies to schemes, the question arises whether the decision to sanction a scheme must be automatically recognized in other Member States as a 'judgment' in accordance with Article 36. This may be answered in the affirmative only if one adopts a broad understanding of 'judgment' in accordance with Articles 2(a) and 35, as not being limited to a decision that concludes adversarial proceedings.[434] National courts may disagree on this issue, which may ultimately be settled only by the Court of Justice.[435] In any case, the Rome I Regulation seems to ensure that a creditor who seeks to enforce their claims in another EU Member State would be bound by the amendment of their contractual rights under the applicable law,[436] rendering the scheme effective abroad.[437] This will not change following Brexit. The provisions of the Rome I Regulation constitute the autonomous private international law of the Member States and also apply vis-à-vis third countries.[438]

The United States Bankruptcy Code (11 USC) offers a further option on the menu for bankruptcy governance systems. A person, whether natural or legal, comes under the jurisdiction of the Bankruptcy Code if that person has its residence or domicile, a place of business or property in the United States. In particular, the latter requirement has been

[431] Regulation (EC) No 593/2008 of the European Parliament and of the Council of 17 June 2008 on the law applicable to contractual obligations (Rome I) OJ 4.7.2008 L177/6.

[432] *Re APCOA Holdings GmbH* [2014] EWHC 3849 (Ch) paras [227]–[245].

[433] Payne (n 422) 307–308.

[434] BGH, IV ZR 194/09, 15 February 2012, para 26.

[435] Payne (n 422) 311.

[436] Rome I Regulation, Arts 3, 12. Although an argument could be made that schemes are excluded from the scope of the Rome I Regulation pursuant to its Art 1(2)(f): certain questions 'governed by the law of companies'. However, in the restructuring context schemes are concerned with the rearrangement of the company's contractual obligations vis-à-vis its creditors, rather than affecting the status of the company per se; see Payne (n 422) 312–13.

[437] *Re Rodenstock GmbH* [2011] EWHC 1104 (Ch) para [76].

[438] Rome I Regulation, Art 2.

interpreted very widely. The quantity of property is irrelevant: 'a dollar, dime or peppercorn located in the United States'[439] would be sufficient:

***In re Global Ocean Carriers Limited*, 251 BR 31 (Bkrtcy. D. Del. 2000)**

Global Ocean Carriers Limited, the ultimate parent, and fifteen of its direct or indirect subsidiaries (the debtors) sought a restructuring under Chapter 11 of the US Bankruptcy Code. Most of the debtors were headquartered in Athens and incorporated in Liberia, Cyprus or Singapore; except for one group company which was a Delaware entity. The parent's stock had been listed on the American Stock Exchange, but had been delisted shortly before the filing for bankruptcy. Some of the group's creditors were situated in the US. The issue was whether the debtors could file for bankruptcy under Chapter 11, which required that each debtor individually had property in the US.

Mary F Walrath, Bankruptcy Judge

...

The Debtors did have property in the United States on the petition date, however, namely funds in various bank accounts. See, e.g., In re McTague, 198 B.R. 428, 429 (Bankr.W.D.N.Y.1996)($194 in bank account was sufficient property for bankruptcy eligibility). One account was at The Bank of New York in New York City (an account in use since 1989) and another was at Chase Manhattan Bank in Delaware (opened shortly before the bankruptcy filing). Both these bank accounts are in the name of Global Ocean. The Debtors' deputy financial officer, Mr. Panagopoulis, testified that the funds in the bank accounts represent the revenues from the operations of all the vessels. Those revenues belong to the vessel owning subsidiaries and, through their ownership of the subsidiaries, the various other Debtors. Mr. Panagopoulis also testified that the funds of the various Debtors have always been commingled and deposited into the Global Ocean account and that none of the other Debtors even have bank accounts ...

[7] It is not relevant, as Arabella [a small noteholder and minority shareholder that asked for the case to be dismissed] suggests, that there is only a relatively small amount in the Debtors' bank accounts in the United States (less than $100,000 in both). As the Court in McTague concluded:

Nonetheless, $194 in a bank account is clearly "property," and at least two courts have held that such an account is property "in" the district in which the deposit account is located, even though bank deposits may be viewed as being "in" the place of residence of the depositor for certain other purposes.

Consequently, as applied to the case at bar, the statute does not appear to be vague or ambiguous, and it seems to have such a plain meaning as to leave the Court no discretion to consider whether it was the intent of Congress to permit someone to obtain a bankruptcy discharge solely on the basis of having a dollar, a dime or a peppercorn located in the United States. The Court will so rule.

Therefore, the Court concludes that the language of § 109(a) is clear, and the Court does not have discretion to look behind the language and declare that the quantity of property in the United States will be decisive of eligibility to be a debtor under the Code.

198 B.R. at 431–32.

Thus, we conclude that the bank accounts constitute property in the United States for purposes of eligibility under section 109 of the Bankruptcy Code, regardless of how much money was actually in them on the petition date.

However, Arabella asserts that the Debtors' argument that the funds in the account represent property of all the Debtors is incorrect ... The Debtors rely heavily on the World of English decision which held that claims by subsidiaries to funds in their parent's bank account located in the United States constituted sufficient property in the United States for eligibility purposes under section 109. 23 B.R. at 1023.

The Debtors also point to the existence of retainers paid by the Debtors to their bankruptcy counsel as evidence of the requisite property in the United States. Before the petitions were filed,

[439] *In re McTague*, 198 BR 428, 429 (Bankr. W.D.N.Y. 1996).

> retainers totalling $400,000 were paid to bankruptcy counsel, which still hold those funds. The Debtors assert that such retainers held in escrow by counsel for a debtor are property of the estate ... The Debtors assert that they all have an interest in the escrow funds which were paid to counsel on all their behalf. We agree. The retainers were paid on behalf of all the Debtors and, therefore, all the Debtors have an interest in those funds. It is not relevant who paid the retainer, so long as the retainer is meant to cover the fees of the attorneys for all the Debtors, as it clearly was in these cases ... Thus, we conclude that the Debtors do have sufficient property in the United States to make them eligible to file bankruptcy petitions under section 109 of the Bankruptcy Code.

Professor LoPucki has pointed out that this decision makes it virtually impossible for any corporation to fail to meet the jurisdictional requirements for filing under the US Bankruptcy Code. As soon as any corporation pays a US lawyer to file the corporation's bankruptcy the corporation has property in the US. With the filing in the US, the corporation benefits from the automatic stay with its assets on a worldwide basis, even though its (other) links to the US may be virtually non-existent.[440] The restructuring of the Truvo group is an example of a European based concern availing itself of the restructuring options under US Bankruptcy law. Truvo did not rely on having property in the US, but on the fact that some of its holding and financing companies were incorporated in Delaware and, thus, domiciled in the US. Whereas the Delaware entities filed for Chapter 11, the court extended the automatic stay through a temporary restraining order to the European subsidiaries which had guaranteed some of the debt issued by the financing companies.[441]

Questions and comments:

1. Menu choice/forum shopping and regulatory competition are two sides of the same coin. Menu choice and forum shopping create the demand for different regulatory options supplied by competing jurisdictions. The extension of domestic restructuring options to foreign debtor companies, as in case of the English scheme jurisdiction and under the US Bankruptcy Code, increases the revenue and prestige of local lawyers who will inevitably be necessary to administer a case. Indirectly the jurisdiction's tax base is being increased as well.
2. Menu choice/forum shopping and regulatory competition raise the issue of whether they result in a 'race to the bottom' or a 'race to the top'. The former signifies the lowering of standards, in particular, in terms of the protection of constituencies that are somehow disadvantaged. The latter is based on the idea of an increase in efficacy and/or efficiency of the available regulatory regimes. Whether, in any given scenario, one or the other view is correct is not primarily an empirical question. The selection of the relevant standard of assessment as the basis for any empirical analysis is essentially a political consideration. Moreover, empirical analysis often has a tendency of being inconclusive.
3. In the context of the mechanism for menu choice discussed in this section, what are the arguments that would support a 'race to the bottom' analysis, what are those in favor of a 'race to the top'? For each alternative, what should be the relevant standard of assessment?
4. The possible implications of Brexit have corporate restructuring practitioners in London worried. On the back of the EUIR and the English courts' extensive scheme jurisdiction, London has emerged as the restructuring capital of Europe. By transferring its COMI to England, a company can restructure through a fast pre-pack administration, combined with a scheme of

[440] L LoPucki, *Courting Failure* (University of Michigan Press 2005) 186–7.

[441] K McMaster and Y Ng, 'Truvo' in K Asimacopoulos and J Bickle (eds), *European Debt Restructuring Handbook* (Globe Law and Business 2013) 61–74.

arrangement, provided its facility agreements are governed by English law. Although Brexit will leave schemes largely unscathed, a (pre-pack) administration will no longer be recognized automatically across the other EU Member States. This may significantly reduce the attraction of the United Kingdom as a restructuring destination, also for firms from outside the EU.[442]

II. Collective restructuring procedures and 'privatization' options

Since about the 1990s, corporate insolvency law reform in many countries in Europe and around the world has focused on enhancing and implementing a so-called 'rescue culture' seeking to preserve floundering businesses as functioning units.[443] The global financial crisis of 2007–2009 added new impetus and triggered further reform efforts at national level,[444] culminating in the EU Commission's Recommendation on a new approach to business failure of 2014[445] and its ongoing work on a legislative initiative with the same focus.[446] Two distinctions are vital for the understanding of the concept of 'rescue culture'. First, the business enterprise is to be distinguished from the entity that holds it.[447] The former is a pool of assets, human resources, institutional knowledge and knowledge management systems with the potential of generating (future) cash flows. The latter is a legal structure that determines the contributions to be made in order to set up the business and the way any cash flows generated by it may be distributed. In particular, corporate type entities provide a mechanism for the pooling of resources from different participants—equity investors, debt investors, employees, and the capital structure of the respective corporate entity determines how incoming cash flows are to be allocated to and distributed amongst the different constituencies.[448] The corporate holding entity is not worth preserving for its own sake; it is only facilitative in nature and may be easily replaced with a more suitable structure.[449] However, the business enterprise, or parts thereof, may be worth preserving and this is what the 'rescue culture' relates to. The question is then how to identify those businesses that

[442] The UK government is keen to explore a new bilateral agreement with the EU which would include insolvency matters and largely replicate the framework of the EUIR. This agreement is to be negotiated during the transition period following an orderly exit on the basis of a Withdrawal Agreement; HM Government, The Future Relationship between the United Kingdom and the European Union (Cm 9593, July 2018) para 148. In case of a no-deal Brexit, the UK government intends to repeal the majority of the domesticated provisions of the EUIR with the exception of the COMI test for jurisdiction, which would apply in addition to other tests under national law. Thus, having COMI elsewhere in Europe would no longer restrict the opening of proceedings in England. However, recognition of UK proceedings in other EU countries would have to be sought under the respective country's domestic law; Department for Business, Energy & Industrial Strategy and Ministry of Justice, Guidance: Handling civil cases that involve EU countries if there's no Brexit deal (13 September 2018), https://www.gov.uk/government/publications/handling-civil-legal-cases-that-involve-eu-countries-if-theres-no-brexit-deal/handling-civil-legal-cases-that-involve-eu-countries-if-theres-no-brexit-deal#cross-border-insolvency-cooperation.

[443] Finch and Milman (n 333) 209.

[444] R Bork, *Rescuing Companies in England and Germany* (OUP 2012) 5–13 (paras 1.10–1.26).

[445] Commission Recommendation of 12.3.2014 on a new approach to business failure and insolvency, C(2014) 1500 final.

[446] Communication from the Commission to the European Parliament, the Council, the European Economic and Social Committee and the Committee of the Regions: Action plan on building a capital markets union COM(2015) 468 final 25; Communication from the Commission to the European Parliament, the Council, the European Central Bank, the European Economic and Social Committee and the Committee of the Regions: Towards the Completion of the Banking Union, COM(2015) 587 final 10; Proposal for a Directive of the European Parliament and of the Council on preventive restructuring frameworks, second chance and measures to increase the efficiency of restructuring, insolvency and discharge procedures and amending Directive 2012/30/EU COM(2016) 723 final.

[447] Bork (n 444) 13 (para 1.28); Finch and Milman (n 333) 198.

[448] Adler, Baird, and Jackson (n 354) 26. [449] ibid 29.

are worth preserving and to distinguish them from those that are not.[450] This leads to our second distinction, which is theoretically easy, but practically extremely difficult: the distinction between economic distress and financial distress. Economic distress refers to a situation where a business is not viable regardless of the capital structure of its holding entity. A business held by a sole owner with no debt at all may not be able to generate sufficient cash flows to cover the fixed costs of the business;[451] the net present value[452] of the business would be negative and value destroying. It should be dismantled and its assets and resources put to better use.[453] By contrast, financial distress is caused by an unsustainable capital structure of the holding entity. The business is fundamentally sound, that is, its net present value would be positive were it held by a sole owner with no debt; it is the debt obligations issued by the corporate holding entity that have to be serviced out of insufficient cash flows that causes distress.[454] In practice, the larger and more complex a business is the more difficult it will be to determine precisely whether it is economically or financially distressed. Moreover, both types of distress may exist simultaneously and may reinforce each other.[455]

The law has limited capacity for addressing economic distress; successful interventions will be managerial: new and better products, divesting from unprofitable and investing in more profitable lines of business, decreasing the fixed costs of the business by shedding parts of the workforce or relocating abroad etc. However, corporate insolvency law with a business rescue aim can provide a framework that allows the parties to determine the extent to which the business is economically and/or financially distressed and, in respect of the latter, enable the firm to acquire a new capital structure with a reduced and more manageable debt load.[456] This can be achieved through a negotiated debt reduction or conversion of debt to equity; alternatively, the viable parts of the business may be transferred to a new entity, leaving some (junior) creditors behind so that the new entity emerges with a more sustainable capital structure. Today, most reorganizations or restructurings are effectuated through a sale of the business, or parts thereof; often to previous management and/or previous owners and investors.[457] This is in accordance with the concept of 'privatization' as a reaction to an ensuing and aggravated anti-commons problem.[458] It is perhaps no coincidence that the rise of the rescue culture and the emphasis on corporate restructuring and reorganization correlated with the extensive leveraged buyout activities during the 1980s and 1990s and up until the global financial crises.[459] By financing the transfer of corporate ownership with funds borrowed by the corporation and secured against its assets, which funds are then advanced to the purchasers and used to pay off the selling shareholders,[460] leveraged buyouts have a propensity to create financial distress for fundamentally sound businesses. This is the case, in particular, where refinancing cannot be easily obtained owing to capital markets drying up, as happened in the course of the global financial crisis.[461] The new restructuring practice

[450] Jackson (n 185) 2; S Paterson, 'Rethinking Corporate Bankruptcy Theory in the Twenty-First Century' (2016) 36 OJLS 697, 710–11, 721, suggesting that identifying a 'restructuring surplus' should be left to the (distressed debt) market, although its efficiency in this respect remains doubtful.

[451] Adler, Baird, and Jackson (n 354) 26–8.

[452] As the value of all future cash flows discounted to present value minus all present and future costs (the latter discounted to present value); I Welch, *Corporate Finance* (4th edn, Printing Source Inc 2017) 26.

[453] This statement is not necessarily decisive for the question as to whether corporate insolvency law should pursue 'creditor wealth maximization' as its exclusive goal or whether there is room also for social and distributional goals; DG Baird, 'Bankruptcy's Uncontested Axioms' (1998) 108 Yale Law Journal 573, 573–99; Finch and Milman (n 333) 201. This is because the costs resulting from a negative effect of the dismantling of the firm on the local community or society etc could, at least conceptually, be factored into the net present value formula.

[454] Adler, Baird, and Jackson (n 354) 26–8. [455] ibid 28. [456] ibid.

[457] K Asimacopoulos and J Bickle (eds), *European Debt Restructuring Handbook* (Global Law and Business 2013).

[458] Schillig (n 186).

[459] L Gullifer and J Payne, *Corporate Finance Law: Principles and Policy* (2nd edn, Hart Publishing 2015) 765–7.

[460] *In re Bay Plastics Inc.*, 187 BR 315, 323 (Bkrtcy. C.D. Cal 1995).

[461] Bork (n 444) 10 (para 1.18).

that has emerged since the global financial crisis primarily relates to businesses that had previously been subject to leveraged buyouts.[462]

Chapter 11 of the US Bankruptcy Code has its roots in the equity receiverships that were used to restructure the great railroads at the turn of the 18th and 19th centuries. As there was no other sensible use for the railroads' assets—steel rails and roadbed—the restructuring of these businesses was the most efficient option.[463] Chapter 11 is the ultimate debt-restructuring device and has inspired law reforms around the world; including repeated reforms in Germany and France over the last few years. Its impact on English law has to date been much more limited. The Enterprise Act 2002 significantly improved the administration procedure with a view to strengthening its rescue aspects. Its success in this respect was, however, limited.[464] It was the development of new and innovative techniques combined with traditional mechanisms, like the old scheme of arrangement under the Companies Act 2006, by a bourgeoning restructuring practice that has made the United Kingdom the prime restructuring location in the European Union, although this may change as a result of Brexit. In an attempt to strengthen the insolvency law framework further and enhance its reputation, the UK government has embarked on an ambitious reform agenda that draws much more heavily on Chapter 11.[465]

1. *United States: Chapter 11 and §363 sales*

Chapter 11 provides a mechanism for the reorganization of the capital structure of a financially distressed business with a view to ensuring its continuous operation for the benefit of employees, creditors and stockholders alike.[466] Generally, Chapter 11 has proved to be a very effective mechanism for restructuring large publicly traded companies successfully.[467] Over the years, capital structures have become more complex, with higher leverage and several layers of secured debt; claims trading and the derivatives revolution have changed the composition of classes and the incentive structures of claim holders. As a consequence, there has been a shift towards rapid going-concern sales of the debtor's business as a way to realize any going concern value, largely for the benefit of senior secured lenders. Because of these developments, the American Bankruptcy Institute has undertaken a comprehensive three-year study on the reorganization of financially distressed businesses under Chapter 11.[468] The recommendations for reform do not seek to radically change the structure of the Chapter 11 process, but seek to adapt it to the ever-changing business and financial environment. It remains to be seen whether any of these recommendations will become law.

It is relatively difficult for creditors to subject a debtor to an involuntary bankruptcy proceeding.[469] As a consequence, involuntary cases are rare.[470] By contrast, anyone who may be

[462] See the case studies discussed in Asimacopoulos and Bickle (n 457).

[463] D Baird, *Elements of Bankruptcy* (6th edn, Foundation Press 2014) 59–70.

[464] Goode (n 193) 31–2 (para 1-32).

[465] Department for Business, Energy & Industrial Strategy, Insolvency and Corporate Governance: Government response (26 August 2018).

[466] American Bankruptcy Institute (ABI), Commission to Study the Reform of Chapter 11, 2012–2014 Final Report and Recommendations (American Bankruptcy Institute 2014) [ABI Study] 8–11.

[467] This section draws on M Schillig, *The Resolution and Insolvency of Banks and Financial Institutions* (OUP 2016) 418–34 (paras 14.53–14.79).

[468] ABI Study (n 466) 12.

[469] If the debtor has fewer than 12 creditors, an involuntary case may be initiated only by one or more creditors who together hold unsecured, non-contingent and undisputed claims of at least US$10,000 (adjusted for inflation); if the debtor has 12 or more creditors, at least three of them must act together with their unsecured claims reaching the same amount: 11 U.S.C., §303(b). If the debtor controverts the filing, the court will take on the case only under the further condition that the debtor generally does not pay its debts as they fall due: ibid §303(h).

[470] One example is the bankruptcy of Zais Investment Grade Limited VII, a special purpose vehicle serving as a so-called 'CDO Squared' that was incorporated in the Cayman Islands. A group of senior note holders filed an

a 'debtor' under Chapter 11 can commence a case simply by filing a proper voluntary petition.[471] With filing a petition, an automatic stay comes into force, comprehensively blocking any pre-petition creditors from enforcing their claims and rights against the property of the estate.[472] The estate constitutes a new legal entity, established by operation of law upon filing, and is controlled by the DIP, that is, the incumbent management (subject to the potential appointment of a trustee[473] or replacement of certain officers on insistence of major lenders). Trading may continue in the ordinary course of business under the supervision of the bankruptcy court.[474] The automatic stay comes into effect automatically and instantly by operation of law. It prevents pre-petition creditors from enforcing their rights against the debtor or against property of the estate, including secured creditors and creditors with a right to set-off. Any attempts to perfect or create liens against property of the estate also violate the automatic stay.[475] The automatic stay has nationwide as well as extra-territorial (worldwide) effect. In principle, it only blocks enforcement action 'against the debtor'. Creditors remain free to pursue claims against third parties such as guarantors or co-defendants.[476] However, the automatic stay may be extended so as to protect non-debtors where 'there is such an identity between the debtor and the third-party defendant that the debtor may be said to be the real defendant and that a judgment against the third-party defendant will in effect be a judgment or finding against the debtor'.[477] In the course of the restructuring of the Truvo Group, the automatic stay was extended by way of injunction so as to cover, in addition to the holding companies incorporated in Delaware as debtors in Chapter 11, the European operating companies that had guaranteed some of the outstanding debt. Otherwise, the chances of a successful reorganization would have been jeopardized.[478] Upon request of a party in interest and after notice and a hearing, the court may grant relief from the stay by terminating, annulling, modifying or conditioning it.[479] Stay-lift motions are particularly relevant for secured creditors. Under the automatic stay, secured creditors are prevented from exercising their non-bankruptcy remedies.[480] A secured creditor (and any other creditor) may request the court to lift the stay for cause.[481] Given that the secured creditor is entitled to the value of its secured interest in property, there will be sufficient cause if the collateral is at risk of a decrease in value over the course of the bankruptcy case.[482] The DIP must ensure that the value of the secured creditor's rights is adequately protected.[483] In the

involuntary petition with a view to amending the trust indenture through a Chapter 11 restructuring so as to be able to manage the collateral securities properly (instead of merely collecting proceeds) and to achieve a better return for the senior note holders whilst the junior tranches were out of the money. Since the debtor did not contest the petition, the order of relief was entered by default and could not be contested by junior note holders. See *In re Zais Investment Grade Limited VII*, Case No 11-20243 (RTL) Bktcy NJ 26/08/2011.

[471] 11 U.S.C., §301(a). [472] ibid §362(a). [473] ibid §1104.

[474] Warren and Westbrook (n 298) 403–404.

[475] 11 U.S.C., §362(a). The pursuit of post-petition claims is not stayed; however, such creditors cannot actually enforce any title they obtain against the property of the estate: Baird (n 463) 198.

[476] Baird (n 463) 198.

[477] This was found to be the case where a judgment against the third-party defendant would in effect be a judgment or finding against the debtor triggering the debtor's indemnification obligation vis-à-vis the third party defendant. The indemnity obligation would impair a successful reorganization by depleting assets currently available: *In re Grace & Co*, 2004 WL 954772 (Bkrtcy. D. Del.).

[478] *In re Truvo USA LLC* Case No 10-13513 (AJG) 7/14/2010.

[479] 11 U.S.C., §362(d). Within 30 days after the request to have the stay lifted, the court must decide whether to lift the stay for cause in respect of the requesting party or, in the absence of cause, order the stay to continue, either temporarily until a final hearing or permanently. Otherwise, the stay will be lifted automatically; ibid §362(e).

[480] Baird (n 463) 203. [481] 11 U.S.C., §362(d)(1). [482] Baird (n 463) 203.

[483] Adequate protection may be provided in the form of periodic cash payments or an additional or replacement lien to the extent that the stay results in a decrease in the value of the secured creditor's interest in the property; or some other relief as will result in the realization of the 'indubitable equivalent': 11 U.S.C., §361. If subsequently it turns out that the protection offered was in fact inadequate, to the extent of the shortfall the secured creditor obtains an administrative expense priority, ranking higher than the costs and expenses of the DIP's financial and legal advisers: ibid §507(b).

absence of cause, a secured creditor may have the stay lifted only if the debtor does not have equity in the collateral (i.e. the creditor is under-secured) and the collateral is not necessary for an effective reorganization.[484] The automatic stay is subject to a long list of exceptions.[485] In particular, the automatic stay does not protect against governmental or regulatory intervention on public policy grounds. Moreover, the stay has no effect on qualified financial contracts:[486] derivative and repo counterparties can seize collateral, and exercise their set-off and netting rights undisturbed. This is particularly relevant for the resolution and insolvency of (non-bank) financial institutions.[487]

The DIP, essentially the debtor's incumbent management, has all the rights and powers and performs all the functions and duties of a Trustee in Bankruptcy (TIP).[488] Unless the court otherwise orders, the DIP continues to operate the debtor's business.[489] In the ordinary course of business, the DIP may enter into transactions, including the sale or lease of property of the estate, or may use property of the estate, without the need for notice and a hearing and court approval.[490] Transactions outside the ordinary course of business and dispositions of assets subject to security interests require court approval.[491] A party in interest may request the court to appoint a TIB for cause, such as fraud, dishonesty, incompetence or gross mismanagement of the affairs of the debtor by current management.[492] These prerequisites are stringent and appointments rare, even in cases where fraudulent misconduct would seemingly be obvious.[493] In addition to court supervision and oversight, the DIP is further constrained in the running of the business by the extensive power that major creditors may be able to exert over the bankruptcy process. New finance will be essential for the business to continue as a going concern. The Bankruptcy Code provides a framework that encourages post-petition lending, so-called 'DIP financing'. The possibility to grant a first ranking lien on already encumbered property in order to secure pre-petition credit through 'priming' is the culmination of an ascending order of incentives for old and new creditors to fund the reorganization.[494] Senior lenders may subtly force a replacement at the helm of the debtor, and DIP financing may come with strict covenants giving the DIP lender almost complete control of the bankruptcy process, including of the debtor's exclusive right to propose a plan of reorganization for the (extendable) period of 120 days since commencement.[495] Other than through voting on the plan, unsecured creditors and shareholders may influence the bankruptcy process through one or more creditor's committees or equity security holder's committees. These may consult with the DIP concerning the administration of the case, investigate the affairs of the debtor, and may participate in the formulation of a plan, advise

[484] ibid §362(d)(2). [485] ibid §362(b). [486] ibid §362(b)(6), (7), (17).
[487] Schillig (n 467) 379–88 (paras 13.50–13.65). [488] 11 U.S.C., §1107(1). [489] ibid §1108.
[490] ibid §363(c). [491] ibid §363(b). [492] ibid §1104(a)(1).
[493] LoPucki (n 440) 145–51. Alternatively, on request the court may appoint an examiner. Whilst leaving the operation of the business with the DIP, the examiner is tasked with comprehensively investigating the debtor's affairs and monitoring its past and present activities: 11 U.S.C., §1104(c).
[494] 11 U.S.C., §364. Since the DIP is by default authorized to operate the debtor's business, it may obtain unsecured credit in the ordinary course of business. Such credit will have administrative expense priority. Outside the ordinary course of business, the DIP may obtain unsecured credit with administrative expense priority status subject to authorization by the court, after notice and a hearing. Where the DIP is unable to obtain unsecured credit in this way, creditors may be incentivized to come forward by four alternative packages, all of which are subject to authorization by the court. First, the DIP may offer credit with priority over other administrative expenses, thus creating a 'super senior administrative expense priority'. Secondly, new credit may be secured by a lien on property of the estate that is unencumbered. The existence of unencumbered property of the estate is facilitated by removing from the scope of any pre-commencement security interest property acquired by the estate after commencement of the case. Thus, after-acquired property clauses in a security agreement are ineffective in bankruptcy. Thirdly, new credit may be secured by a junior lien on property of the estate that is already encumbered. If all else fails and the DIP is unable to obtain credit otherwise, the court may authorize, after notice and a hearing, the obtaining of credit secured by a first ranking or equally ranking security on property of the estate that is subject to a pre-existing security interest, provided the holder of the pre-existing security obtains adequate protection.
[495] D Baird and R Rasmussen, 'Private Debt and the Missing Lever of Corporate Governance' (2006) 154 University of Pennsylvania Law Review 1209, 1236–42.

the creditors they represent on the plan, and collect and file with the court acceptances or rejections of a plan.[496]

The core of Chapter 11 is an elaborate plan procedure for the negotiation, acceptance and implementation of a plan of reorganization that provides the ailing business with a new and more sustainable capital structure. Initially, the debtor has the exclusive right to file a plan within 120 days since commencement of the case and creditors and shareholders must accept the plan within 180 days of commencement.[497] Following expiry of the exclusivity period, or rejection of the plan by the creditors and shareholders, any party in interest, notably creditors and shareholders, may file their own, alternative plan.[498] In order to allow creditors and shareholders to make a fully informed decision, the debtor (and any other plan proponent) may solicit acceptance of a plan after commencement only on the basis of a disclosure statement that is transmitted to the claim holders or equity holders together with a copy or a summary of the plan.[499] The disclosure statement must have been approved by the court, after notice and a hearing, as containing 'adequate information.[500] A court approved disclosure statement as a precondition for soliciting acceptance or rejection of the plan is only required if solicitation takes place after commencement of the case.[501] A pre-packaged plan has been negotiated and acceptance has been solicited and obtained prior to filing for Chapter 11.[502] Thus, no court approved disclosure statement is required. However, solicitation has to comply with potentially more stringent applicable non-bankruptcy law,[503] in particular securities law.[504] In respect of plan acceptance and confirmation requirements, pre-packaged plans follow the standard procedure.[505]

The plan of reorganization must allocate the claims of creditors and the interests of shareholders to different classes, and set out the treatment that each class receives under the plan.[506] Only claims or interests that are 'substantially similar' may be put in the same class. What matters are the legal attributes of a claim or interest. Claims with different legal rights must be allocated to separate classes.[507] By contrast, substantially similar claims may not be separately classified in order to gerrymander an affirmative vote on a reorganization plan; however, separate classification is permitted for good business reasons, as in a case where a continuing relationship with an unsecured creditor is essential for the continued operations of the debtor.[508] Within each class, each claim or interest must be treated equally, unless the claim or interest holder has consented to a less favorable treatment.[509] Generally, the greater the number of classes, the more likely that one will dissent, but also that one will accept the plan. Both incidents are relevant for the substantive plan requirements and plan confirmation. Plan acceptance requires that within a class of claim holders, creditors holding at least two-thirds in amount and more than one-half in number of the allowed claims of the class

[496] 11 U.S.C., §1103.

[497] Either period may be extended for cause by court order for up to 18 months or 20 months, respectively, since commencement.

[498] 11 U.S.C., §1121(a)–(d).

[499] ibid §1125(b).

[500] That is, 'information of a kind, and in sufficient detail, as far as is reasonably practical in light of the nature and history of the debtor ... that would enable [a hypothetical investor typical of the holders of claims or interests] of the relevant class to make an informed judgment about the plan': ibid §1125(a)(1).

[501] ibid §1125(g).

[502] R Olivares-Caminal and others, *Debt Restructuring* (2nd edn, OUP 2016) 182 (para 3.143).

[503] 11 U.S.C., §§1125(g), 1126(b)(1).

[504] Olivares-Caminal and others (n 502) 183 (para 3.146). By contrast, a pre-arranged plan has been negotiated prior to filing, but solicitation and acceptance (or rejection) take place after commencement. As a consequence, the standard 'in-bankruptcy' disclosure and solicitation rules apply: ibid 182 (para 3.101).

[505] This is a major difference compared to the pre-pack administration under English law.

[506] 11 U.S.C., §1123.

[507] ibid §1122.

[508] *In re Bernhard Steiner Pianos USA, Inc.*, 292 BR 109 (Bankr. N.D. Tex 2002); citing *In re Briscoe Enterprises Ltd II*, 994 F.2d 1160 (5th Cir. 1993).

[509] 11 U.S.C., §1123(a)(4).

accept the plan.[510] A class of interests has accepted the plan if shareholders holding at least two-thirds in amount of the shares within that class have accepted the plan.[511] A class that is unimpaired under the plan is conclusively presumed to have accepted the plan.[512] A class that receives nothing under the plan is deemed to have rejected it.[513]

In order to become binding, the plan requires confirmation by the court, on the basis of a confirmation hearing following solicitation of acceptance.[514] The plan proponent has the burden of demonstrating that all the confirmation requirements[515] have been satisfied.[516] In particular, the plan itself must comply with the provisions on plan content and designation of classes of claims and interests.[517] The plan proponent must have complied with the disclosure and solicitation rules,[518] and must have filed the plan in 'good faith', that is, for a purpose that is in accordance with the objectives of the Bankruptcy Code.[519] Under the 'feasibility test' the court must be satisfied that the plan is not likely to be followed by liquidation or the need for further reorganization, in other words, the plan must have a reasonably chance of resulting in a successful reorganization. One indicator is the leverage of the corporation emerging from Chapter 11. If too highly leveraged compared to other corporations within the same line of business, plan feasibility is likely to be in doubt.[520] In addition, the plan must have been accepted by the holders of claims and interests. Confirmation requirements differ depending on the degree of acceptance within a class and across different classes. Where not all holders of claims or interests within a class have accepted the plan, the court may confirm the plan, and cram it down on dissenters within that class, subject to the 'best interest test'. This test requires that each member of the class receives at least the liquidation value of its claim or interest under the plan.[521] It necessitates a hypothetical liquidation analysis on the basis of expert evidence submitted by the plan proponent.[522] Where not every class of impaired claims and interests has accepted the plan, the plan may still be confirmed and crammed down on dissenting classes, provided that at least one class of impaired claims has accepted the plan, not including acceptance by any insider.[523] A cram-down of an entire class or classes requires that the plan meets the 'fair and equitable test'[524] which introduces the absolute priority rule as a substantive plan confirmation requirement.[525] It seeks to ensure that the plan respects the order of priority established outside of bankruptcy under non-bankruptcy law.[526] Accordingly, and subject to the 'new value' exception, a class junior to the dissenting class may obtain any value under the plan only to the extent that the dissenting (senior) class has been paid in accordance with their entitlements.[527]

[510] ibid §1126(c). [511] ibid §1126(d).

[512] ibid §1126(f). A claim or interest is unimpaired if the plan does not alter the legal, equitable or contractual rights to which the claim or interest holder is entitled. Any defaults that occurred in the past must be cured, any initial maturities reinstated, and any losses suffered must be compensated: 11 U.S.C., §1124.

[513] 11 U.S.C., §1126(g). [514] ibid §§1141(a), 1128.

[515] ibid, §1129(a)(1)–(13), and (b), provided (a)(8) has not been met (cram-down of the plan on dissenting classes).

[516] Olivares-Caminal and others (n 502) 168 (para 3.107). [517] 11 U.S.C., §§1122, 1123.

[518] ibid §§1125, 1126.

[519] *In re Sentinel Management Group, Inc.*, 398 B.R. 281, 315 (Bkrtcy N.D. Ill. 2008).

[520] Baird (n 463) 243. [521] 11 U.S.C., §1129(7).

[522] Olivares-Caminal and others (n 502) 170 (para 3.111). [523] 11 U.S.C., §1129(a)(10).

[524] ibid §1129(b).

[525] *Case v Los Angeles Lumber Products Co.*, 308 U.S. 106, 117 (1939): 'rule of full or absolute priority'.

[526] Baird (n 463) 70. The ABI recommended a significant amendment to the absolute priority rule. In order to cram down the plan on an immediately junior class, this junior class must receive at least the 'redemption option value', that is, the value of a hypothetical option to purchase the entire firm for an amount equal to the face value of the senior debt for a period of three years. A plan may be crammed down on a dissenting senior class, if the senior creditors are not paid in full only because the redemption option value is conferred on the immediately junior class. Giving junior creditors the possibility to participate in any increase in value in the future seeks to prevent potentially very costly litigation: ABI (n 466) 207–11.

[527] 11 U.S.C., §1129(b)(2).

Upon confirmation, the plan binds the debtor and any creditor or shareholder, as well as any entity issuing securities or acquiring property under the plan. The property of the estate vests in the debtor or any entity provided for under the plan.[528] All debts that arose prior to confirmation of the plan are discharged except to the extent that they are dealt with in the plan.[529] Where the plan does not meet the plan confirmation requirements and the court cannot, therefore, confirm the plan, the court may order a conversion of the case into a Chapter 7 liquidation. Alternatively, the court may dismiss the case, which will result in the restoration of the prepetition financial status quo, unless the court deviates therefrom for 'cause'. Such a 'structured dismissal' may be justified where a reinstatement of the prepetition status quo is not easily possible and may entail certain distributions to creditors, releases and other substantive amendments to property rights. However, a 'structured dismissal' 'cannot, without the consent of the affected parties, deviate from the basic priority rules that apply under the primary mechanisms the Code establishes for final distributions of estate value in business bankruptcies'. In particular, the bankruptcy court cannot order a 'structured dismissal' that allocates money to certain high-priority secured creditors and certain low-priority unsecured creditor, whilst skipping certain mid-priority dissenting creditors, notably employee wage claims.[530]

More complex capital structures, fragmented proprietary interests and shifting incentives have made plan negotiation, acceptance and confirmation more lengthy and difficult.[531] A move from the collective Chapter 11 plan process towards a 'privatization' solution may take the form of a going concern sale pursuant to 11 USC §363(b). To the extent that quick going concern sales become more and more attractive, senior secured lenders may be interested in using the Chapter 11 process primarily in order to realize the value of their collateral through a sale free and clear;[532] distressed debt investors buying up senior debt may initiate a going concern sale as part of a 'loan to own' strategy similar to a take-over outside of bankruptcy and 'credit bid' – in consideration for release of their debt claims – for the business themselves.[533] After notice and a hearing and subject to an authorization by the bankruptcy court, the DIP may dispose of property of the estate other than in the ordinary course of business,[534] prior to acceptance and outside of a plan of reorganization. However, the court may authorize a going-concern sale only where, on the basis of the evidence presented at the hearing, there is a good business reason for the sale. Taking all the relevant circumstances into account, the sale must advance the diverse interests of the debtor, creditors, and equity holders alike. Relevant factors in determining the business justification may be the proportionate value to the estate of the assets sold, the amount of time elapsed since the filing, the likelihood of acceptance and confirmation of a viable plan in the near future, and whether the assets at issue are increasing or decreasing in value.[535] In addition to the sound business purpose for the sale, the debtor has to show that the proposed sale price is fair on the basis of adequate marketing with a view to maximizing value for creditors; the debtor has given adequate and reasonable notice to all parties in interest; and the buyer has acted in good faith without collusion or taking unfair advantage of other bidders.[536] The further the proposed transaction moves away from a proper sale, by providing for non-cash consideration in the form of assumption of certain liabilities and the issue of notes and participation rights, the closer it is in substance to a plan of reorganization.[537] In order to prevent a circumvention of the plan confirmation requirements, such '*sub rosa* plans' may not be authorized by

[528] ibid §1141. [529] Baird (n 463) 243.

[530] *Czyzewski et al. v. Jevic Holding Corp.*, 580 U.S. ____ (2017). [531] Baird (n 463) 223–8.

[532] ibid 230–1. [533] ibid 217. [534] 11 U.S.C., §363(b).

[535] *In re Lionel Corp.*, 722 F.2d 1063, 1071 (2d Cir. 1983).

[536] *In re Exaeris, Inc.*, 380 B.R. 741, 744 (Bkrtcy. D. Del., 2008); Olivares-Caminal and others (n 502) 194–5 (paras 3.180–3.183).

[537] Baird (n 463) 237.

the court.[538] The §363 sale procedure has been used successfully in the reorganizations of both Chrysler[539] and General Motors.[540] In both cases, substantially all of the assets of the respective business were transferred to newly established entities sponsored primarily by the US government. The restructured enterprises emerged from Chapter 11 within 42 and 40 days, respectively.[541]

2. *England and Wales: (Pre-pack) administration, CVA, scheme of arrangement, reform proposals*

Administration[542] provides a temporary holding mechanism that allows a business to continue trading under external management until a decision has been made about the best way forward.[543] The statutory hierarchy of administration purposes is, in descending order, 'rescuing the company as a going concern'; if this is not reasonably practicable, to achieve a better result for the creditors as a whole; or to make at least a distribution to secured or preferential creditors.[544] The business may be rescued through a going concern sale; and occasionally through a balance sheet restructuring where administration is combined with a CVA[545] or scheme of arrangement.[546]

Administration may be initiated, and an administrator appointed, either by court order,[547] or out-of-court.[548] The company, its directors or one or more of its creditors[549] may apply for an administration order. The court may make an administration order only if it is satisfied that the company is or is likely to become[550] unable to pay its debts and that it is reasonably likely that the purpose of administration will be achieved.[551] The first condition is dispensed with where the application is made by the holder of a qualifying floating charge who could have made an appointment out-of-court.[552] An administrator may further be appointed out-of-court by the company,[553] its directors,[554] or the holder of a qualifying floating charge.[555] Prior written notice of intention to appoint must be given to any holder of a qualifying floating charge,[556] or, respectively, the holder of any prior qualifying floating charge,[557] and must be filed with the court so as to trigger the interim moratorium.[558] The actual appointment takes effect when the notice of appointment and the prescribed documentation is filed with the court.[559] An out-of-court appointment by the company or its directors will be subject to the condition that the company is or is likely to become unable to pay its debts.[560]

538 *In re Braniff Airways, Inc.*, 700 F.2d 935, 940 (C.A. Tex., 1983). The ABI recommended the introduction of a statutory provision pursuant to which a going concern sale would be subject to certain plan confirmation requirements; see ABI (n 466) 201.

539 *In re Chrysler L.L.C.*, 576 F.3d 108 (C.A.2 (N.Y.), 2009); vacated as moot, 130 S. Ct. 1015 (2009).

540 *In re General Motors Corp.*, 407 B.R. 463 (Bkrtcy. S.D.N.Y., 2009).

541 Olivares-Caminal and others (n 502) 197–8 (para 3.189–3.191).

542 This section draws on Schillig (n 467) 391–402 (paras 14.04–14.22).

543 Goode (n 193) 394 (para 11-18).

544 Insolvency Act 1986, Sch B1, para 3.

545 ibid s 1-7B.

546 Companies Act 2006, s 895–901.

547 Insolvency Act 1986, Sch B1, paras 10–13.

548 ibid paras 14–39.

549 ibid para 12 (1)(a)–(c).

550 That is, insolvency must be more likely than not; *Re AA Mutual International Insurance Co Ltd* [2004] EWHC 2430 (Ch).

551 Insolvency Act 1986, Sch B1, para 11(a), (b).

552 ibid para 35(2)(a).

553 ibid para 22(1).

554 ibid para 22(2).

555 ibid para 14(1)–(3).

556 ibid, paras 26, 27; the notice period is five business days.

557 Unless the holder of the prior charge has consented to the appointment in writing: Insolvency Act 1986, Sch B1, para 15; the notice period is two business days.

558 ibid para 44(2) and (3).

559 ibid paras 18, 19; provided the floating charge is enforceable, no provisional liquidator has been appointed, and no administrative receiver is in office: ibid paras 16, 17; or, respectively, ibid paras 29, 31; provided the company is not in winding up, no petition for a winding up or administration application is pending, no administrative receiver is in office, and the five-business day notice period has expired, or any addressee of such notice has consented in writing to the appointment: ibid paras 8, 25, 28(1).

560 see ibid para 27(2)(a).

Administration imposes a comprehensive statutory moratorium on individual debt enforcement mechanisms and other creditor rights.[561] In principle, the moratorium stays resolutions, petitions and orders for the winding up of the company.[562] No steps may be taken to enforce security over the company's property,[563] or to repossess goods in the company's possession under any hire-purchase agreement, except with the consent of the administrator or the permission of the court.[564] Rights holders are prevented from instituting or continuing any legal process against the company or property of the company except with the consent of the administrator, or with the permission of the court.[565] However, the moratoria do not prevent the exercise of a right to terminate a contract, either on the basis of a contractually stipulated right or by accepting the administrator's repudiation of the contract.[566] In principle, rights holders can enforce their rights only with the permission of the court (or with the consent of the administrator). In deciding whether to grant permission, the court will normally attribute great importance to the proprietary interests of a creditor asking for leave.[567]

Upon appointment of the administrator—out-of-court or by court order—the powers conferred on the company or its officers are exercisable only with the administrator's consent so far as they could be exercised in such a way as to interfere with the exercise of the administrator's powers.[568] Consequently, the directors are almost completely divested of their powers;[569] but the administrator may leave the day-to-day business in the hands of the existing management ('light touch' administration).[570] In practice, the company and its major creditors[571] will likely agree on who should be appointed, and the appointment of more than one administrator is common. Often a team of accountants will take over the day-to-day running of the business. The administrator is an officer of the court,[572] and is deemed to act as agent of the company in exercising his powers.[573] The administrator is responsible for taking control of the company's property and for managing its affairs, business and property in the interests of the company's creditors.[574] Subject to general fiduciary duties and a duty of care owed to the company's creditors as a whole,[575] the administrator has extensive powers, which cannot, however, exceed those conferred on the company by its articles of

561 An interim moratorium comes into effect at the time an administration application is made and lasts until the application is dismissed or the appointment of an administrator takes effect and the company is in administration, upon which the 'full' moratorium becomes effective. In out-of-court administrations, the interim moratorium begins when a copy of the notice of intention to appoint is filed with the court, and ends when either the appointment takes effect, or with the expiry of a 5 or 10-day period (depending on whether notice of intention has been filed by the holder of a qualifying floating charge, or the company or its directors) during which no appointment has been made: ibid para 44(2) and (4). The scope of both interim moratorium and moratorium are nearly congruent; see Schillig (n 467) 393 (para 14.07 n 35).

562 Insolvency Act 1986, Sch B1, paras 40(1), 42(1). Also, with the taking effect of the administration order, an administrative receiver has to vacate office; any other receiver has to vacate office if the administrator requires him to do so: ibid para 41.

563 ibid para 43(2).

564 ibid para 43(3). Hire-purchase agreement is defined so as to include a conditional sale agreement, a chattel leasing agreement and retention of title agreement: ibid para 111(1).

565 ibid para 43(6).

566 Goode (n 193) 437–8 (para 11-69). As part of its reform agenda, the government intends to prohibit the enforcement of ipso facto clauses by a supplier in contracts for the supply of goods and services; Department for Business, Energy & Industrial Strategy (n 334) para 5.97.

567 *Re Atlantic Computer Systems Plc* [1992] Ch 505, 542–4 (Nicholls LJ).

568 Insolvency Act 1986, Sch B1, para 64.

569 Goode (n 193) 452–3 (para 11-87).

570 V Dennis, *Insolvency Law Handbook* (3rd edn, The Law Society 2013) 348.

571 In particular, the holder of a qualifying floating charge, who may prevent appointment by the company by appointing his own administrator.

572 Insolvency Act 1986, Sch B1, para 5.

573 ibid para 69. As a consequence, he will not be personally liable for debts incurred under any new contracts entered into post-commencement. However, as expenses properly incurred by the administrator, such debts will rank in priority to the administrator's fees and remuneration: ibid para 99(4).

574 ibid paras 3, 67, 68.

575 Not, however, individual creditors; see *Kyrris v Oldham* [2004] BCC 111.

association. The administrator has the power to do anything that is necessary or expedient for the management of the affairs, business, and property of the company,[576] in particular take possession and dispose of the company's property,[577] including property subject to a floating charge, with the proceeds taking the place of the initial collateral.[578] Distributions may be made to secured and preferential creditors and, with the permission of the court, also to unsecured creditors.[579] Throughout the process, the administrator may apply to the court for directions in connection with his functions.[580] The conduct of the administrator will only be scrutinized by the court if challenged ex post on the basis that the interests of a creditor or member have been harmed unfairly[581] or that the administrator has breached his fiduciary or other duties.[582] The courts will normally not interfere with the administrators' commercial judgments provided that they were made in good faith and will normally allow a considerable margin of discretion.[583] In administration, a creditors' committee assists the administrator in discharging his functions.[584] It may require the administrator to attend on the committee and to provide it with information about the exercise of his functions.[585] Creditors' committees are often used to sanction sales processes and they can fix the administrators' remuneration[586] and discharge the administrator from personal liability.[587]

As soon as is reasonably practicable after the company has entered administration,[588] the administrator must prepare a statement setting out proposals for achieving the purpose of administration. The administrator must then seek a decision from the company's creditors as to whether they approve the proposals set out in the statement; the initial decision date must be within ten weeks from the time the company entered administration.[589] The statement of proposals sets out the administrators' overall intended strategy.[590] Approval of these proposals by the creditors does not itself effectuate a substantive modification of the parties' rights and obligations. It merely determines the way ahead during the administration. Often the administrator will dispose of the company's business, or parts thereof, prior to any creditors' decision by way of a pre-pack administration. A pre-pack administration is an 'arrangement under which the sale of all or part of a company's business or assets is negotiated with a purchaser prior to the appointment of an administrator, and the administrator effects the sale immediately on, or shortly after, his appointment'.[591] The business survives relatively intact, having shed some or all of its unsecured debt. The courts have confirmed that an administrator can dispose of the assets of the company without the leave of the court and prior

[576] Insolvency Act 1986, Sch B1, para 59. He may remove and appoint directors of the company, and call a meeting of its members or seek a decision from its creditors: ibid paras 61, 62.

[577] ibid para 60 and Sch 1.

[578] ibid para 70. With the permission of the court, the administrator may dispose of any property subject to a fixed charge or a hire-purchase agreement, provided that the disposal would likely promote the purpose of the administration. The net proceeds must be applied to the discharge of the secured obligation: ibid paras 71, 72.

[579] ibid para 65.

[580] ibid para 63.

[581] ibid para 74.

[582] ibid para 75.

[583] *Re Kayley Vending Ltd* [2009] EWHC 904 (Ch).

[584] Insolvency (England and Wales) Rules 2016, r 17.2.

[585] Insolvency Act 1986, Sch B1, para 57.

[586] Insolvency (England and Wales) Rules 2016, r 18.18.

[587] Insolvency Act 1986, Sch B1, para 98(2)(b).

[588] With a maximum time limit of 8 weeks: ibid para 49.

[589] ibid para 51. Both time limits may be varied by the court on an application of the administrator or by up to 28 days with the consent of the creditors. The seeking of a decision from the creditors on the proposals is unnecessary where the administrator thinks that the company has sufficient assets to pay all creditors, or insufficient assets to make a distribution to unsecured creditors, or where the rescue of the business as a going concern or a better result for creditors as a whole cannot be achieved: ibid para 52. A decision from the company's creditors must also be sought upon request of creditors holding at least 10% of the company's total debt, and also where the court so requires: ibid para 56.

[590] In substantive terms, a proposal may not include any action which affects the right of a secured creditor of the company to enforce his security; would result in a preferential debt of the company being paid otherwise than in priority to its non-preferential debts, or would result in one preferential creditor of the company being paid a smaller proportion of his debt than another; except with the relevant creditor's consent: ibid para 73.

[591] Statement of Insolvency Practice (SIP) 16, para 1.

to the approval of his proposals by the company's creditors.[592] Even a majority (unsecured) creditor does not have a veto on the implementation of the administrator's proposals.[593] The consent of the holders of fixed security is required, however, as seeking court permission for disposal[594] would unacceptably delay the process. And the holder of a qualifying floating charge may either appoint an administrator himself or prevent the company from making the appointment. The practice of pre-pack administration has been repeatedly under scrutiny:[595] a pre-packaged business often has not been exposed to the competitive forces of the market and may be sold for a consideration below market value. There seems to be no incentive to negotiate a consideration that goes beyond the amount necessary to discharge the secured indebtedness and the insolvency practitioners' fees and expenses. The rights of stakeholders to participate in the decision making process are marginal at best and the practice lacks transparency. The general creditors will not be asked to approve the proposal,[596] and court oversight in a pre-pack administration is minimal.[597] The latest instalment was the Graham Report of June 2014.[598] The report highlighted a lack of transparency of pre-packs. Whereas the secrecy surrounding negotiations is necessary in order to retain the confidence of customers, suppliers and employees, unsecured creditors will often be surprised by a 'done deal' without any input. The marketing of pre-pack companies is often insufficient, resulting in diminished returns for creditors. Moreover, no consideration is given to the future viability of the business emerging from the pre-pack sale. The recommendations of the Graham Report for remedying these shortcomings are very mild. On a voluntary basis, connected parties should disclose details of the proposed sale to a panel of experts ('pre-pack pool') to opine on it. Also, on a voluntary basis, connected parties should complete a 'viability review'. Marketing of the pre-packed business should be subject to principles of 'good marketing' and valuations should be carried out by an independent valuer who holds professional indemnity insurance. The statements of administrators involved in pre-packs (SIP16 statements) should be monitored by the Recognized Professional Bodies (instead of by the Insolvency Service). These recommendations have been taken up in the revised SIP 16 and work on the basis of a 'comply or explain' approach. According to the Graham report, only if the proposed measures do not result in an improvement of current practice should a legislative intervention be considered.

Another option is the combination of administration with a CVA, consisting of an agreement between the company and its creditors effectuating a composition in satisfaction of the company's debts or a scheme of arrangement of its affairs. A CVA is essentially contractual in nature, although with a statutory overlay in order to provide a mechanism for making an approved CVA binding on dissenting minority creditors. The small company moratorium aside, a CVA does not provide for an automatic statutory moratorium of creditors' entitlements. It also does not allow for a cram-down of the rights of secured and preferential creditors. It may, however, be combined with, and provide an exit route from, administration. Since the Court of Appeal's decision in *Thomas v Ken Thomas Ltd*,[599] CVAs have gained some popularity for the (balance sheet) restructuring of businesses with large long-term leasehold property portfolios, such as retail outlets. Accrued rent may be consumed by a CVA; thus, modifying the landlord's remedies and preventing him from exercising his right

[592] Pre-Enterprise Act 2002: *Re T&D Industries plc* [2000] 1 WLR 646; post-Enterprise Act 2002: *Transbus International Ltd (in liquidation)* [2004] 2 BCLC 550.

[593] *DKLL Solicitors v Revenue and Customs Commissioners* [2007] BCC 908.

[594] Pursuant to Insolvency Act 1986, Sch B1, paras 71, 72.

[595] S Frisby, 'A preliminary analysis of pre-packaged administrations' Report to the Association of Business Recovery Professionals (R3, 2007) 8–9; Graham Review into Pre-Pack Administration: Report to the Rt Hon Vince Cable MP (June 2014).

[596] L Qi, 'The Rise of Pre-Packaged Corporate Rescue on Both Sides of the Atlantic' (2007) Insolvency Intelligence 129, 133.

[597] ibid 133.

[598] Graham Review (n 595).

[599] [2006] EWHC Civ 504.

of forfeiture. By compromising the claims of landlords and thus reducing the overall debt burden, the retail business may be helped to recover.[600] If launched in administration, the CVA may be proposed only by the administrator who will likely act as 'nominee' to become the CVA's supervisor upon approval. Where the administrator proposes a CVA with himself acting as nominee, he must proceed to summon the meeting of the company and seek a decision from the company's creditors, unless the court otherwise orders.[601] The meeting of the company, normally chaired by the nominee, and the creditors through a 'qualifying decision procedure'[602] must then decide whether to approve the proposed arrangement, with or without modification.[603] Every creditor, secured or unsecured, who has notice of the decision procedure is entitled to vote.[604] A decision approving a proposed CVA or a modification is passed when a majority of three-quarters or more (in value) of those voting have voted in favour of it.[605] At the company meeting a resolution is regarded as passed if voted for by more than one-half in value of the members present in person or by proxy, with value being determined by the number of votes conferred on each member by the company's articles.[606] The rights of secured and preferential creditors may not be interfered with, except with the relevant creditors' consent.[607] The decision has effect if it has been taken by the creditors and the company meeting; or by the creditors alone, subject to an order of the court made on an application of a member of the company.[608] Once the decision to approve the CVA has become effective it binds every person who was entitled to vote at the meeting or would have been entitled to vote if they had had notice of it.[609]

Administration may further be combined with a scheme of arrangement,[610] which has become very popular, not just for English companies, but also for companies from abroad.[611] There is no automatic stay or moratorium for a self-standing scheme, although the courts may impose a stay on the basis of the rules of civil procedure on application of the debtor.[612] If launched in administration, a scheme benefits form the statutory moratorium in administration. The scheme proponent must apply to the court for it to summon meetings of the classes of creditors or classes of shareholders included in the proposal.[613] During the convening or summons hearing the court, in its discretion, decides whether to summon the meetings of the classes of creditors and/or shareholders. The classes are composed of different types of shareholders (preference shares, ordinary shares), and different types of creditors (preferential, secured, ordinary). Incorrect identification of classes may invalidate the scheme.[614] The second stage consists of the class meetings during which the respective classes of creditors and shareholders vote on the scheme. Entitled to vote are only those creditors or classes of creditors (or members or classes of members) summoned by the court

[600] Dennis (n 570) 631. [601] Insolvency Act 1986, s 3.

[602] The requirement to hold meetings in company insolvencies has been abolished by the Small Business, Enterprise and Employment Act 2015, s 122. Pursuant to Insolvency Act 1986, s 246ZE, whenever the office-holder in an administration, administrative receivership, Company Voluntary Arrangement, or a voluntary or compulsory winding-up seeks a decision about any matter from the company's creditors, he may rely on any of the 'qualifying decision procedures' as he sees fit, with the exception of a creditors' meeting. The latter will be available only where at least 10% in value, or 10% in number, or 10 creditors so request in writing. The 'qualifying decision procedures,' in addition to a physical meeting, are correspondence, electronic voting through an electronic voting system, a virtual meeting on the telephone or online, or any other decision-making procedure which enables all creditors who are entitled to participate in the decision-making process to participate on an equal basis; Insolvency (England and Wales) Rules 2016, r 15.3.

[603] Insolvency Act 1986, s 4. [604] Insolvency (England and Wales) Rules 2016, r 15.7.

[605] Votes are calculated according to the amount of the creditor's debt as at the date of commencement of administration: ibid r 15.7(2). For other resolutions a majority in value of those voting in person or by proxy voting in favour of it is sufficient. A resolution is invalid if those voting against it include more than half in value of the creditors to whom notice of the meeting was sent and who are not persons connected with the company: ibid r 15.31.

[606] ibid r 2.36. [607] Insolvency Act 1986, s 4(4). [608] ibid s 4A. [609] ibid s 5.

[610] Pursuant to Companies Act 2006, Pt 26. [611] Payne (n 415) 567–8.

[612] *Bluecrest Mercantile BV v Vietnam Shipbuilding Industry Group and Others* [2013] EWHC 1146 (Comm).

[613] Companies Act 2006, s 896. [614] *Re Hawk Insurance Co Limited* [2002] BCC 300.

as a result of the summons hearing. For approval, a scheme requires a majority in number representing 75 per cent in value of the creditors or class of creditors or (members or class of members) present at the meeting summoned by the court and voting either in person or by proxy. If the class meetings approve the scheme, the court conducts a sanctioning hearing as the final stage,[615] during which it will assess whether each class was properly constituted, each class meeting duly held, each resolution duly passed, and each class fairly represented at the meeting, and finally whether the scheme is fair to creditors generally.[616] Upon the sanctioning of the scheme and delivery of a copy of the respective court order to the Registrar of Companies, the scheme becomes effective and binding on the company and all creditors and shareholders included in the scheme.[617] Although a cram-down of the minority within a class is possible, a scheme does not allow for the cram-down of an entire class of creditors or shareholders.[618] However, the functional equivalent of a cram-down of an entire class can be achieved by combining a scheme of arrangement with a pre-packed administration. Such a combination seems to be used more frequently than a self-standing scheme (for debt restructuring purposes) and results in a combination of a balance sheet restructuring with a going concern sale. Typically, the senior 'in the money' creditors will partake in the scheme under which they will exchange their debt for equity and/or new debt in a new holding company structure. The previous holding company will be put through a pre-pack administration with the administrator transferring the assets—essentially the shares in the operating companies—to the new group immediately upon his appointment. Junior 'out of the money' creditors will be left behind with the old holding company as an empty shell. It is this combination of pre-pack administration and scheme of arrangement that has emerged as an internationally very attractive restructuring mechanism for larger companies with a complex capital structure. What we see here is a clear example of a move from 'collectivization' to 'privatization:' The restructuring deal is struck between the debtor company and its senior (in the money) creditors who, as a class, emerge as the lead creditors in control of the process. Junior (unsecured) creditors retain their substantive entitlements; however, their procedural involvement is severly curtailed.

In administration, there is no equivalent to the DIP financing regime.[619] Any debt or liability incurred by the administrator in his role as the agent of the company will be payable in priority to the administrator's fees and expenses and also in priority to floating charges.[620] It is not possible however to grant the provider of new finance a first ranking security on assets subject to a fixed charge, without the existing charge holder's consent. As a consequence, new finance that allows the company to keep trading for the benefit of mainly unsecured creditors may only be forthcoming where the company has significant unencumbered assets.[621] This makes it somewhat difficult to fund trading administrations, and more often than not the administrator will sell the business as a going concern shortly after his appointment under a pre-pack administration.

Where the purpose of administration has been achieved, either by way of a CVA, a scheme or otherwise, an administration by court order comes to an end by court order on application of the administrator.[622] In an out-of-court administration, the administrator simply gives notice to the court that the purpose of administration has been achieved.[623] Other than

[615] Companies Act 2006, s 899.

[616] *Re Bluebrook Limited* [2010] BCC 209; *Re Lehman Brothers International (Europe) (in administration)* [2018] EWHC 1980 (Ch) para 61 – 166.

[617] Companies Act 2006, s 899(3). [618] Payne (n 415) 566.

[619] Reform proposals aimed at allowing rescue finance providers to be granted security in priority to existing chargeholders will not currently be pursued any further; Department for Business, Energy & Industrial Strategy (n 334) para 5.186.

[620] Insolvency Act 1986, Sch B1, para 99(4).

[621] Olivares-Caminal and others (n 502) 210 (para 3.232).

[622] Insolvency Act 1986, Sch B1, para 79(3) [623] ibid para 80.

that, an administration comes to an end automatically after one year since commencement, subject to the possibility of repeated extensions by court order.[624] Administration may further end in a creditors' voluntary winding up,[625] or, where the company has no property, in dissolution.[626]

As part of its ambitious reform agenda, the UK government intends to introduce two further procedures, each of which could be applied on either a stand-alone basis or in combination with other options. A restructuring moratorium, similar in scope to the moratorium in administration, would be available to companies of all sizes, provided that the company has not been subject to insolvency or restructuring proceedings in the previous twelve months (eligibility); is currently solvent, but prospectively insolvent if no action is taken; on the balance of probabilities its rescue is more likely than not; and it will be able to meet current obligations during the moratorium (qualifying conditions). The moratorium will be triggered by filing the necessary papers at court, and will last for an initial period of 28 days, which may be extended up to 56 days, and even beyond with the approval of a majority of creditors. A proposed monitor will need to file their consent to act and confirmation that they have assessed the eligibility criteria and qualifying conditions and are satisfied that these have been met. Only an insolvency practitioner may act as monitor, who will be responsible for supporting the integrity of the moratorium process and ensuring that creditors' interests are protected. Incumbent management will remain in charge of running the company's business. Typically, the moratorium will result in an informal restructuring agreement between the company and its creditors, or alternatively in an insolvency procedure. If the latter, any unpaid costs incurred during the moratorium will enjoy super-priority over any costs or claims in a subsequent administration or liquidation.[627]

In addition, the government intends to introduce a new restructuring plan process that will allow the cross-class cram-down of both secured and unsecured creditors. Without making any changes to the existing law of schemes of arrangement, the new process will closely resemble that for schemes, which will ensure that the well-established body of case law for schemes can be drawn upon in the context of the new restructuring plan. Consequently, a plan proposal instigated by the company will be subject to a first court hearing on class formation, following which a vote may be conducted on the proposal with majorities similar to those for schemes, followed by a second hearing at which the court will consider whether the statutory requirements have been met and, if so, whether to exercise its discretion to confirm the restructuring plan and make it binding on affected creditors and shareholders. The key innovation is the possibility of a cross-class cram-down. Provided that at least one class of impaired creditors has voted in favour of the plan, the court may confirm the plan and impose it on a dissenting class of creditors. This is subject to an absolute priority rule: the dissenting class must be satisfied in full before a more junior class may receive anything under the plan. Importantly, this absolute priority rule will be less strict than its Chapter 11 counterpart: the court may confirm a plan even though the absolute priority rule has not been complied with where this is necessary to achieve the aims of the restructuring and is just and equitable given the circumstances. As an additional safeguard in the cram-down scenario, under the plan creditors should receive at least as much value as they would receive under the next best alternative, which is likely to be administration rather than liquidation.[628]

[624] On application of the administrator, the court may terminate the administration where its purpose cannot be achieved, where the company should not have entered administration in the first place, or where the creditors' meeting has required the administrator to apply for a termination order: ibid para 79(2). A creditor may apply to the court for a termination order on the basis of an improper motive of the person who either appointed the administrator or who applied for an administration order: ibid para 81.

[625] ibid para 83. [626] ibid para 84.

[627] Department for Business, Energy & Industrial Strategy (n 334) para 5.5–5.87.

[628] Department for Business, Energy & Industrial Strategy (n 334) paras 5.114–5.176.

3. *France: court-assisted and in-court recovery and reorganization proceedings*

Over the last ten years, the French legislature has reformed French insolvency and restructuring law three times. The reform of 2005 introduced the safeguard procedure as a pre-insolvency rescue procedure modelled on Chapter 11 of the US Bankruptcy Code. The reforms of 2008/2009 were aimed at increasing the appeal of the safeguard procedure and at simplifying and enhancing the clarity of French insolvency law. The latest reform of 2014 introduced the accelerated safeguard procedure and a right for creditors' committees to present a restructuring plan.[629] Under the Loi PACTE (Project de loi relative à la croissance et la transformation des entrepries) further amendments are already in the pipeline, also with a view to implementing the expected EU Directive on preventive restructuring frameworks. On the basis of the current law, a multitude of procedures for corporate rescue and restructuring are available to companies in distress: the *mandat ad hoc* and the conciliation procedure are court-assisted proceedings, with limited court involvement and geared towards amicable contractual solutions; the safeguard procedure with its two modifications: accelerated financial safeguard procedure and accelerated safeguard procedure, and the judicial reorganization procedure are in-court reorganization procedures; we may add the judicial liquidation procedure where it entails a going concern sale of the business.[630] Although these procedures present a menu of restructuring options, the parties are restricted in their menu choice by the different prerequisites for individual procedures, which largely depend on the financial (solvency) status of the debtor company.

Usually in the course, or following the completion, of an early warning procedure (*procedure d'alert*),[631] the president of the competent commercial court may appoint a crisis manager (*mandataire ad hoc*).[632] A crisis manager may only be appointed on application of the debtor company's representative, and only where the company is solvent, but faces or anticipates legal, economic or financial difficulties. The procedure is most suitable if these difficulties relate to the organizational structure of the business and can be addressed through internal reconfigurations. Although the debtor company may propose a person for the role of crisis manager, the presiding judge of the court has discretion in selecting the crisis manager and in defining his duties. Despite the presence of a court appointed *mandataire ad hoc*, incumbent management retains full powers to manage the business and to dispose of its assets. There is no automatic stay or moratorium and the creditors are free to enforce their claims against the debtor. The *mandat ad hoc* is not subject to any time limits. The crisis manager's duties, as determined by the court, may generally consist in supporting corporate management in analysing the company's financial situation and in developing strategic plans for remedying its difficulties.[633] Typically, a *mandataire ad hoc* may provide support in carrying out capital measures, in negotiating with the general meeting and with key suppliers and creditors with a view to obtaining moratoria or a deferral of payment, and may seek to obtain new lines of credit with new or existing lenders; he may further prepare a going concern sale of the business.[634] Any agreements reached in this way are purely contractual in nature and only bind those parties who consented to it. Non-consenting creditors remain free to pursue their individual enforcement rights. Throughout the process, the crisis manager keeps the court informed; other than that the procedure remains confidential.[635]

Where it becomes clear that the company's difficulties cannot be remedied through purely internal measures or a selective negotiation with a few main lenders and suppliers, but

[629] For an overview see Jacquemont and Vabres (n 284) 9–24 (paras 13–35); P Omar, 'A Reform in Search of a Purpose: French Insolvency Law Changes (Again!)' (2014) 23 International Insolvency Review 201.

[630] Jacquemont and Vabres (n 284) 22–4 (para 35).

[631] Where the auditors come to the conclusion that the continuation of the business is in jeopardy, they have to inform the debtor company's management and, if the financial difficulties are not sufficiently addressed, the president of the competent commercial court. If the financial difficulties continue, an extraordinary general meeting must be called and the president of the commercial court may summon the management and further investigate the financial situation of the company: Com Art L234-1–L234-2.

[632] Com Art L611-3; Jacquemont and Vabres (n 284) 53 (para 83).

[633] ibid 55 (para 87).

[634] ibid.

[635] ibid 57–8 (paras 90–1).

requires a more comprehensive restructuring solution, the debtor company may apply to the court for the opening of conciliation proceedings, either following a *mandat ad hoc* or independent of it. The court may open conciliation proceedings and appoint a conciliator where the debtor company faces, or is likely to face in the near future, legal, economic or financial difficulties and has not been in a state of cessation of payments for more than forty-five days.[636] Only the debtor company can apply for the opening of conciliation proceedings.[637] It may suggest a person to be appointed as conciliator and reject the conciliator appointed by the court; other than that the court has discretion as to who to appoint as conciliator. Similar to the *mandate ad hoc*, the conciliation procedure does not impose a stay or moratorium on creditors' enforcement rights, although the court may grant the debtor a grace period of up to two years.[638] The duration of conciliation proceedings is limited to four months, extendable by one month.[639] Whereas incumbent management retains full management powers, the conciliator's duty is to promote an amicable agreement between the debtor and its main creditors and counter-parties with a view to addressing and remedying the difficulties the company faces and to ensuring continuation of its business activity and employment.[640] This may entail an agreement under which debts are rescheduled or (partly) waived, possibly changes to the company's capital structure and by-laws, or a disposal of assets. Any agreement so reached is purely contractual in nature and only binds consenting parties. Through conciliation, it is not possible to impose a restructuring solution on dissenting creditors.[641] Where agreement has been reached amongst the participating creditors, on a joint application of all participants the court may formally acknowledge the agreement,[642] or, on application of the debtor, the court may formally approve it.[643] Acknowledgement confers on the agreement the enforceability of a judgment, whilst at the same time keeping it confidential. Formal approval requires publication of the agreement and removes confidentiality, but confers certain important privileges on the participating creditors. The court may formally approve a conciliation agreement only where the court is satisfied that the company is not (or as a result of the agreement is no longer) insolvent; the agreement appears to ensure the solvent continuation of the company's business; and the agreement does not prejudice the interests of those creditors who are not parties to it. Creditors who have advanced new funds or other assets to the debtor in order to ensure the long-term viability of its business will benefit from a 'new money priority' in subsequent in-court insolvency proceedings. Although ranking behind the employees' super-priority and procedural costs, these creditors take priority over other pre-petition creditors, even secured creditors.[644] Deferrals of payment on the basis of a subsequent plan of reorganization approved in an in-court procedure may not be imposed on 'new money' creditors.[645] Moreover, in a subsequent in-court insolvency proceeding, the court is prevented from setting the time at which the company became insolvent prior to the date of approval of the conciliation agreement.[646] Consequently, creditor initiatives during conciliation are no longer vulnerable to transaction avoidance as they will fall outside the 'period of suspicion'. During the implementation phase of an acknowledged or approved conciliation agreement, participating creditors are prevented from enforcing their individual rights.[647] Moreover, guarantors or sureties for the debtor's obligations fully benefit from the provisions of an acknowledged or approved conciliation agreement.[648]

The safeguard procedure is an in-court pre-insolvency recovery procedure. Only the debtor may petition the court for the opening of safeguard proceedings. A successful petition requires the debtor company to demonstrate that, without being insolvent on a cash flow basis, it faces difficulties to such an extent that it cannot overcome them on its own.[649]

[636] Com Art L611-4. [637] Com Art L611-6(1). [638] Civ Art L1244-1–L1244-3.
[639] Com Art L611-6(2). [640] Com Art 611-7.
[641] Jacquemont and Vabres (n 284) 74–5 (paras 111–13). [642] Com Art L611-8(I).
[643] Com Art L611-8(II). [644] Com Art L611-11. [645] Com Art L626-20.
[646] Com Art L631-8. [647] Com Art L611-10-1. [648] Com Art L611-10-2.
[649] Com Art L620-1.

Where it transpires at the time of the opening decision, or subsequently, that the debtor company is insolvent, the court may only commence a judicial reorganization or liquidation procedure, as the case may be; a previously opened safeguard procedure must be converted accordingly.[650] However, accelerated safeguard proceedings and accelerated financial safeguard proceedings may also be opened where the debtor company has not been in a state of insolvency for longer than forty-five days.[651] In its opening decision, the court appoints the supervising judge, the insolvency administrator and the creditors' representative.[652] The supervising judge oversees the proceedings with a view to ensuring their speedy progress and the protection of the parties' interests;[653] certain transactions including the disposal of assets outside the ordinary course of business and by way of granting security and the obtaining of credit during the observation phase require the judge's prior approval.[654] The insolvency administrator supervises and supports the debtor company's management in their effort to ensure the continuation of the company's business activities.[655] During the six months observation period that the opening decision sets in motion the incumbent management remain in office and retain full management powers, except for making payments on any pre-commencement debts or granting any further security over the company's property;[656] on the assumption or rejection of executory contracts the insolvency administrator decides.[657] The creditors' representative collects the creditors' proofs of claim, verifies the debtor's liabilities and collates a table of liabilities to be submitted to the supervising judge.[658] The observation period of six months may, on application of the administrator, be extended once for another six months, and exceptionally up to eighteen months.[659] During the observation period a moratorium is in place that prevents secured and unsecured creditors from enforcing their rights as far as they relate to the payment of a sum of money or the rescission of a contract on grounds of non-payment of a sum of money. Secured creditors are prevented from foreclosing.[660] Proceedings pending at commencement will be stayed and may only be resumed, following submission of a proof of claim, for the determination of the amount owed.[661] The only proceedings that may be commenced during the observation period are those concerning the payment of a sum of money incurred during the observation period for the purpose of the proceedings or in exchange for goods or services provided to the debtor during the observation period.[662] The observation period provides the company with a breathing space during which it can negotiate with its creditors with a view to obtaining a waiver or rescheduling of debt and/or implementing capital measures within the framework of a recovery plan. Supported by the debtor's management and possibly by specifically appointed insolvency experts, the insolvency administrator investigates the affairs of the debtor on which basis he will make restructuring proposals and support the management in preparing the restructuring plan.[663] Accelerated financial safeguard proceedings and accelerated safeguard proceedings are only available for companies whose accounts are either regularly audited, or produced by a certified public accountant and the company exceeds the threshold of twenty employees, €3 million turnover or €1.5 million balance sheet total.[664] For both types of accelerated safeguard proceedings, the debtor must have made a previous attempt at conciliation, and a restructuring plan which is likely to obtain the necessary creditor support must have been prepared prior to filing. The observation period and the accompanying moratorium in accelerated financial safeguard proceedings is only one month (extendable up to two months) and in accelerated safeguard proceedings only three

[650] Com Art L621-12; Jacquemont and Vabres (n 284) 188 (para 279). [651] Com Art L628-1.
[652] Com Art L621-4. [653] Com Art L621-9. [654] Com Art L622-7(II).
[655] Com Art L622-1. [656] Com Art L622-7. [657] Com Art L622-13(II).
[658] Com Art L620-20, L620-24, L624-1. [659] Com Art L621-3. [660] Com Art L622-21.
[661] Com Art L622-22. [662] Com Art L622-17(I). [663] Com Art L626-2.
[664] Com Art 628-1.

months. In accelerated financial safeguard proceedings the moratorium does not affect trade creditors; it only relates to the financial creditors who are involved in the plan process.[665]

If the debtor company is insolvent, its management must apply for the opening of insolvency proceedings in form of judicial reorganization or liquidation within forty-five days of the onset of insolvency, unless the appointment of a conciliator has been requested.[666] Where the court determines that the company is insolvent, but considers that the continuation of the company's business is possible it will order the opening of judicial reorganization proceedings and appoint a supervising judge, insolvency administrator and creditors' representative.[667] The commencement of proceedings sets in motion a six months observation period and moratorium, which is extendable up to eighteen months, but must be reviewed by the court within two months with a view to establishing whether the debtor has sufficient financial resources to continue.[668] During the observation period, the insolvency administrator supports the incumbent management in the continuation of the debtor's business activities, either comprehensively or in respect of specific lines of business and transactions. In principle, incumbent management remain in charge; in exceptional circumstance the insolvency administrator may take over the management of the company wholly or in parts.[669] Again, the insolvency administrator examines the debtor's affairs and makes proposals for its reorganization in support of the management with a view to drawing up a reorganization plan.[670] Where the court considers that the debtor is insolvent and the continuation of its business is obviously and manifestly impossible it must order the opening of judicial liquidation proceedings instead.[671]

Both, safeguard proceedings (including its modifications) and judicial reorganization proceedings are geared towards the confirmation of a restructuring or reorganization plan at the end of the observation period.[672] The plan is to be prepared by the debtor with the support of the insolvency administrator.[673] Since the 2014 reforms, the members of a creditors' committee may propose an alternative recovery or reorganization plan. The establishment of creditors' committees is mandatory for companies with more than 150 employees or with an annual turnover of €20 million.[674] The creditors' representative has to organize two creditors' committees. The 'credit institutions committee' consists of all financial institutions, and creditors who acquired their claim from a financial institution or from a supplier of goods and services. The 'main suppliers committee' consists of the suppliers of goods and services holding at least 3 per cent of the outstanding amount of trade liabilities.[675] Bondholders do not form their own creditors' committee, and can therefore not propose an alternative recovery or reorganization plan. However, they do take part in plan negotiation and confirmation through the bondholders' general meeting.[676] The recovery or reorganization plan should contain an assessment of the prospects for the continuation of the business considering its operational capabilities, market conditions and available financial resources; the terms and conditions as regards the reduction of debt through waivers or rescheduling or a debt-for-equity swap; an assessment of the prospects for retaining jobs and possible redundancies; a list and assessment of takeover offers by third parties for the business or certain lines of business; and an assessment of possible further investment in, or divestment from, certain lines of business.[677] It may further provide for a change of control and/or the sale of certain business units. The plan's duration may not exceed ten years. The creditors' representative asks each creditor who has submitted a proof of claim whether they approve

[665] Com Art L628-6. [666] Com Art L631-4; L640-4. [667] Com Art L631-1; L631-7.
[668] Com Art L631-15. [669] Com Art L631-12. [670] Com Art L631-19.
[671] Com Art L640-1.
[672] The provisions on judicial reorganization proceedings refer for the plan process to the provisions on safeguard proceedings; Com Art L631-19.
[673] Com Art L626-2. [674] Com Art L626-29. [675] Com Art L.626-30.
[676] Com Art L626-32. [677] Com Art L626-2.

of the waivers and rescheduling proposed in the plan and collates and summarizes the responses.[678] The plan proposal will be negotiated between the debtor, the insolvency administrator and the creditors' committees. Following statements on the plan from the creditors' representative and the employees' representative, the creditors' committees decide on the plan within thirty days of having received the plan proposal. Plan approval requires approval by each creditors' committee, and where applicable by the bondholders' general meeting. A committee, and the bondholders' general meeting, will have approved the plan if members representing at least two-thirds of the aggregate amount of claims of those voting have voted in favour of the plan.[679] Whether the claims are secured, unsecured, or subordinated is irrelevant; no separate classes are formed within the creditors' committees. Where the plan contains capital measures such as a debt-for-equity swap, plan approval requires the shareholders' consent with a two-thirds majority.[680] In accelerated safeguard proceedings, creditors' committees are formed regardless of whether the usual threshold has been met. In accelerated financial safeguard proceedings only the financial institutions committee and the bondholders' general meeting vote on the plan and only their claims may be compromised under the plan,[681] which may bee seen as a form of partial 'privatization.' Where the plan has been approved by the creditors' committees and the bondholders' general meeting, the court may confirm the plan provided it is satisfied that the plan is in accordance with the statutory provisions, adequately protects the interests of creditors and that there is a real prospect that plan implementation may result in a sustainable continuation of the debtor's business.[682] Plan confirmation brings the observation period to an end and makes the plan binding on all creditors including those who did not vote in favour of the plan proposal.[683] Where no creditors' committees have been formed or where the creditors' committees have not approved a plan proposal within six months of the commencement of proceedings, or the court has rejected a plan approved by the creditors' committees, creditors will be consulted on an individual basis. Even where the creditors so consulted reject the plan proposal, the court may still impose a uniform rescheduling of debt over a ten-year period.[684] In order to implement an approved and confirmed plan, the court will appoint a plan examiner with the task of ensuring plan compliance and a duty to report annually to the court.[685] Provided the debtor satisfies its obligations under the plan, its management retains full management powers and upon full implementation of the plan the court will order the closure of proceedings.[686] Conversely, where the debtor does not comply with its plan obligations the court may, on application of the creditors, the public prosecutor or the plan examiner or on its own motion, dissolve the plan upon which creditors may again enforce their individual rights against the debtor.[687]

Conceptually, French insolvency law envisages a going concern sale of the business to take place in a judicial liquidation procedure.[688] However, since the 2005 reforms it is possible for the court, on application of the insolvency administrator, to order a going concern transfer at the end of a judicial reorganization procedure, provided the court considers the debtor no longer capable of ensuring the continuation of its business and purchase offers have been received during the observation period.[689] The sale plan process in judicial reorganization is

[678] Com Art L626-5. A creditor who fails to respond within 30 days of the request is deemed to have approved the plan.

[679] Com Art L626-30. [680] Com Art L626-3. [681] Com Art L628-4.

[682] Com Art L626-31. [683] Com Art L626-11.

[684] Com Art L626-18. Such a rescheduling may not be imposed on creditors who benefit from a 'new money' priority resulting from funds provided under a court approved conciliation agreement; Com Art L626-20.

[685] Com Art L626-25. [686] Com Art L626-28. [687] Com Art L626-27.

[688] Com L642-1–642-24.

[689] Com Art L631-22. Moreover, since the 2014 reforms a sale of the business, or parts thereof, may be arranged by the conciliator, upon request of the debtor and after consultation with the creditors. The sale may be subsequently implemented through judicial reorganization or liquidation proceedings.

the same as in judicial liquidation. It is an open bidding process; however, the debtor, its de jure or de facto management, and their relatives are excluded from bidding.[690] The debtor's shareholders are not explicitly excluded, however controlling shareholders may be classified as de facto management and may be excluded on that basis. In order to ensure their legitimacy, purchase offers must comply with strict formalities in order to be considered.[691] Each purchase offer must seek to achieve three objectives: the continuation of the transferred business, the preservation of jobs, and the repayment of creditors.[692] The insolvency administrator sets a certain period of time during which all offers have to be submitted to him. He will examine the offers and will present them to the court with a recommendation as to which offer to approve. After having consulted the debtor and the employees' representative, the court will approve the offer that it considers to be most suitable to ensure the continuation of the business, the preservation of jobs and the satisfaction of creditors.[693] Following approval, the sale plan is implemented through an asset deal where the insolvency administrator transfers individual assets and rights to the purchaser;[694] liabilities do not transfer and remain with the debtor, except debts secured on assets to be transferred which debts will automatically be transferred together with the asset that serves as collateral. Once the transfer is complete, the creditors' representative distributes the proceeds to the creditors in accordance with the statutory order of priority and the debtor company will be liquidated.

4. *Germany: standard procedure, self-administration, and insolvency plan*

The general insolvency procedure under the InsO has as its objective the collective satisfaction of the creditors either through a realization of the debtor's assets and distribution of the proceeds or by rescuing the business as a going concern, possibly on the basis of an insolvency plan.[695] Traditionally, the procedure has been firmly in the hands of the insolvency court and the court-appointed insolvency administrator. The 2012 reforms have somewhat loosened their grip, however. Through a strengthening of the powers of creditors' committees, the introduction of the 'protective shield procedure', and the extension of self-administration, the roles of creditors and of the debtor's management have been significantly enhanced. Insolvency proceedings are initiated through a petition to the competent insolvency court.[696] A petition can be filed either by the debtor or by a creditor who has a 'legal interest' in filing.[697] If the debtor is a corporate entity, every member of the management board, irrespective of how authority is allocated among several directors, may file a petition on their own.[698] The court will order the opening of proceedings only if: (i) the petition is admissible; if the court is satisfied that (ii) there is a 'ground for opening proceedings';[699] and (iii) that the company's assets are sufficient to cover the expenses of the proceedings.[700] The grounds for opening proceedings are the debtor's inability to pay its debts as they fall due,[701] and, where the debtor is a corporate entity, insolvency on a balance sheet basis.[702] On

690 Com Art L642-3.

691 Any purchase offer must contain a detailed description of the assets, rights and contracts to which the offer relates; an explanation of the envisaged on-going business activity and the way it will be financed; the purchase price and the terms and conditions of payment; the envisaged date of completion of the purchase; a prognosis in terms of the jobs to be transferred and the employment prospects; any guarantees provided for completion of the purchase; any plans for anticipated sales of assets during the two years following the transfer; and the duration of the offeror's commitments; Com Art L642-2.

692 Com Art L642-1. 693 Com Art L642-5. 694 Com Art L642-8.

695 InsO, §1. The following partially draws on Schillig (n 467) 448–52 (paras 15.17–15.21).

696 InsO, §13.

697 ibid §14. In principle, every creditor has a 'legal interest' in filing. An interest may, however, be lacking if the creditor is secured.

698 ibid §15(1). 699 ibid §16.

700 ibid §26. If not, the petition to open insolvency proceedings will be rejected and the company will be dissolved and liquidated under company law.

701 ibid §17(1). 702 ibid §19(1).

application of the debtor, prospective cash flow insolvency constitutes a further ground for opening proceedings.[703]

Prior to the opening of proceedings, the court may impose preliminary measures in order to preserve the status quo in the interest of creditors. In particular, the court may appoint a preliminary insolvency administrator and/or a preliminary creditors' committee, and further may impose a ban on disposals of the debtors' assets or subject such disposals to the preliminary administrator's consent; the court may also stay any enforcement attempts against the debtor's movable property, and may prevent secured creditors from enforcing their security.[704] A preliminary creditors' committee may exert significant influence during the subsequent course of the procedure.[705] Where the court orders the opening of proceedings it appoints a person as insolvency administrator.[706] If the preliminary creditors' committee unanimously suggests a person as insolvency administrator, the court is bound to appoint that person unless that person is unsuitable for office.[707] In its order, the court further determines a date for an initial creditors' meeting during which creditors will resolve, on the basis of the administrator's report, how the proceedings should progress; and a date for a further creditors' meeting for an assessment of the submitted proofs of claim.[708] During the initial creditors' meeting the creditors may vote to appoint a different person as administrator, in which case the court will be bound unless the person is unsuitable for office.[709] Prior to the initial creditors' meeting, the court may appoint a creditors' committee (if no preliminary creditors' committee has been appointed) representing the secured creditors, as well as unsecured creditors with the largest and smallest claims.[710] The creditor's committee is tasked with assisting and monitoring the administrator in discharging his responsibilities.[711]

Generally, upon the opening of insolvency proceedings, the debtor's management can no longer dispose of the debtor's property.[712] Any disposal carried out in contravention is invalid, unless approved by the administrator.[713] With his appointment, the administrator obtains comprehensive management powers and may henceforth dispose of the debtor's assets. The administrator is not the debtor's agent but acts on his own account by virtue of his office. He is subject to the supervision of the insolvency court.[714] The administrator's main responsibility is to take possession of the debtor's property,[715] realize its assets[716] and distribute the proceeds to the creditors in accordance with the statutory order of priority.[717] For the duration of the insolvency proceeding, an automatic stay prevents ordinary creditors from enforcing their claims against the debtor.[718] However, creditors with a right to separation based on ownership do not take part in the formal proceedings and may still

[703] ibid §18(1). [704] ibid §§21–25.

[705] U Foerste, *Insolvenzrecht* (7th edn, CH Beck 2018) 60 (§11 para 105b). Where the debtor company meets at least two of the following thresholds: a balance sheet total of at least €4,840,000, an annual turnover of at least €9,680,000, or at least 50 employees as an annual average, the court must appoint a preliminary creditors' committee; the court shall appoint a preliminary creditors' committee where the debtor, a creditor, or the preliminary insolvency administrator apply for it and nominate potential members who have agreed to serve; these cases aside, the appointment is in the discretion of the court: InsO, §22a. A preliminary creditors' committee must not be appointed where the debtor's business activity has ceased, or where the costs of the appointment would be disproportionate in relation to the prospective value of the debtor's assets, or where the ensuing delay would detrimentally affect the debtor's financial situation. Only creditors may be members of the preliminary creditors' committee, nominated by the debtor or a preliminary insolvency administrator. The selection should reflect a fair representation of the creditors as a whole: ibid §67.

[706] ibid §27(1). [707] ibid §56a. [708] ibid §29. Both meetings may be set for the same date.

[709] ibid §57.

[710] ibid §67. Alternatively, the creditors' meeting may decide to appoint a creditors' committee, to retain the court appointed one, or to replace its members: ibid §68.

[711] ibid §69.

[712] ibid §80. This is subject to a successful application of the debtor for self-administration under which the debtor in possession retains management powers albeit monitored and supervised by a court appointed supervisor: ibid §270.

[713] ibid §81. [714] ibid §58. [715] ibid §148. [716] ibid §159. [717] ibid §§187–206.

[718] ibid §89.

enforce their rights based on non-bankruptcy enforcement mechanisms.[719] Depending on the type of collateral, the liquidator may realize the value of assets subject to a security interest proper, thus preventing secured creditors from relying on their individual enforcement rights.[720] On the basis of the insolvency administrator's comprehensive management powers including the power to dispose of the debtor's property, the debtor's business may be restructured through a going concern sale. By way of an asset deal, the administrator may sell and transfer the debtor's business or parts thereof to a willing purchaser on a going concern basis and distribute the proceeds to the creditors through the standard insolvency procedure. The asset deal may have been negotiated by a preliminary administrator to be immediately executed upon the opening of proceedings.[721] Creditors remain closely involved: If the transfer takes place after the initial creditors' meeting the insolvency administrator will be bound by any instructions decided upon during the meeting.[722] A transfer prior to the initial creditors' meeting requires approval by the creditors' committee,[723] which will be necessary throughout the process for all transactions that are particularly significant for the insolvency proceeding.[724] In the absence of a creditors' committee the creditors' meeting decides. On application of the debtor or any participant holding more than 20 per cent of the debt the court may subject the transfer to approval by the creditors' meeting.[725]

As a modification on the standard insolvency procedure, self-administration allows the debtor to retain its management powers, including the power to dispose of property, albeit under the supervision of a court-appointed supervisor.[726] In its order to open insolvency proceedings, the court may order self-administration if the debtor has applied for it and if there are no known facts suggesting that self-administration would be detrimental to creditors by, for example, delaying the process or endangering the debtor's assets available for distribution.[727] Where a preliminary creditors' committee has been appointed and unanimously supports the application, self-administration is deemed not to be detrimental to the creditors in which case the court has to order self-administration even though the court itself may have concerns.[728] Prior to the 2012 reforms, even a successful application for self-administration meant that the debtor would forgo its management powers during the period between filing the petition for opening proceedings and the court's decision. For this period of time which may last as long as three months, the debtor was publicly replaced by a preliminary insolvency administrator, thus greatly diminishing the affirmative incentive that a subsequent self-administration was meant to provide.[729] Now preliminary self-administration is possible, provided the application for self-administration is not obviously futile. The debtor will retain its management powers and powers of disposal where a petition for opening proceedings is pending. Only a preliminary supervisor will be appointed who oversees the conduct of business and whose approval will be required for certain transactions outside the ordinary course of business.[730] The possibility of preliminary self-administration seems to have greatly increased the popularity of self-administration in particular for large insolvency cases.[731] Where the debtor does not apply for self-administration initially or where the court rejects an application for self-administration in its opening decision, self-administration must be ordered subsequently at the request of the creditors' meeting provided the vote found the support of a majority of creditors by amount and heads, and the debtor consents.[732] In self-administration, the debtor's management retains the power to manage the

[719] ibid §47. [720] ibid §§165, 166. [721] Bork (n 444) 48 (para 5.09).
[722] InsO, §159; Foerste (n 705) 236 (§28 para 434). [723] InsO, §158. [724] ibid §160.
[725] ibid §161. Approval of the creditors' meeting is mandatory if the purchaser is closely connected to the debtor, through a shareholding of 20% or more and either is part of corporate management (or a close relative of a member of the management) or, as a general creditor or secured creditor, holds more than 20% of the overall debt: ibid §162.
[726] ibid §270. [727] Foerste (n 705) 308 (§37 para 606). [728] InsO, §270(3).
[729] Foerste (n 705) 314 (§37 para 626). [730] InsO, §270a.
[731] Foerste (n 705) 314 (§37 para 626). [732] InsO, §271.

business and to dispose of the debtor's property. However, this is subject to the powers of the supervisor who has to examine the economic and financial situation of the debtor and to supervise its management in the conduct of business.[733] Where there is reason to suggest that the continuation of self-administration would be detrimental to the creditors the supervisor has to give notice to the court and to the creditors' committee or, in the absence of such, to the creditors' meeting.[734] The debtor's management may enter into obligations in the ordinary course of business, unless the supervisor objects. In order to enter into obligations outside the ordinary course of business, the debtor requires the supervisor's consent.[735] Moreover, at the request of the creditors' meeting the court must order that certain transactions are only valid if the supervisor consents.[736] Transactions that are of particular relevance for the procedure require the consent of the creditors' committee, or, in the absence thereof, of the creditors' meeting. Such transactions of particular significance include the transfer of the business as a whole or of parts thereof, the obtaining of a loan that constitutes a significant burden on the debtor's assets, or the commencement or settlement of court proceedings concerning claims of significant value.[737] The power to reject or accept executory contracts remains with the debtor, but should be exercised in agreement with the supervisor.[738] The supervisor receives submissions for proofs of claim and may challenge avoidable transactions.[739]

The 'protective shield procedure' constitutes a further enhancement of preliminary self-administration. Provided the debtor has applied for the opening of proceedings on the basis of prospective cash flow insolvency or balance sheet insolvency and has asked for self-administration, the court may, on application of the debtor, determine a period of not more than three months within which the debtor may submit an insolvency plan. This is subject to the condition that a successful restructuring of the business is not obviously futile. These prerequisites are to be determined on the basis of a statement issued by an experienced insolvency practitioner who may be a tax adviser, certified public accountant, or solicitor.[740] During the period set by the court the debtor will not be subject to the appointment of a preliminary insolvency administrator. The debtor may propose a person for the office of the preliminary supervisor who the court has to appoint unless that person is obviously unsuitable for office. On application of the debtor, the court must impose a moratorium or automatic stay that prevents creditors from seizing any of the debtor's property. Consequently, the debtor can carry on with its business activities free from any creditor interference. Moreover, on application of the debtor the court must empower the debtor to enter into obligations which in case of a subsequent opening of proceedings will obtain administrative expense priority, thus potentially enhancing the debtor's liquidity during the protective shield procedure.[741]

The standard insolvency procedure is tightly regulated and dominated by the court and the insolvency administrator. The insolvency plan procedure, as a further modification that may be combined with self-administration, allows the creditors and the debtor and its shareholders to agree on a solution that deviates from the provisions of the insolvency statute, in particular with a view to corporate rescue.[742] The insolvency plan provides a flexible framework and may take the form of a 'recovery or reorganization plan', changing the debtor's capital structure, or a 'going concern transfer plan', providing for the transfer of the business or parts thereof to a purchaser, or a 'liquidation' plan that deviates from the statutory liquidation regime.[743] An insolvency plan proposal may be submitted to the court by either the debtor or the insolvency administrator. The latter may act on his own motion or on a request of the creditors' meeting.[744] The debtor may combine a petition to open insolvency

733 ibid §274(2). 734 ibid §274(3). 735 ibid §275. 736 ibid §277(1).
737 ibid §276 with §§160–162. 738 ibid §279. 739 ibid §§270c, 280. 740 ibid §270b.
741 Foerste (n 705) 315-6 (§37 para 629). 742 ibid 237–9 (paras 469–74).
743 ibid 239–240 (paras 475–7). 744 InsO, §218.

proceedings with the submission of a 'pre-packaged' insolvency plan, in particular following the 'protective shield procedure'. There is no exclusivity period for the benefit of the debtor and the creditors may be asked to approve two conflicting plans, which at least theoretically may both find the necessary majorities. In that situation it remains unclear whether the court should confirm the plan that received the most votes or reject both plans.[745] An insolvency plan consists of two parts: a declaratory part and a regulatory part.[746] The declaratory part contains comprehensive information on the plan's underlying assumptions and potential effects in order to allow the plan participants and the court to make an informed decision when approving or, respectively, confirming the plan.[747] This information should include, in particular the previous development of the business, its organization and legal structures, its financial situation, its characteristics in terms of supply, production and sales, the causes for its demise, its current situation and in particular the objectives of the plan.[748] The regulatory part contains the provisions that modify the legal position of the different plan participants.[749] These are the debtor, its shareholders, the general (unsecured) creditors, and secured creditors with a right to preferential satisfaction. By contrast, the rights of secured creditors with a right to separation and creditors with a claim that enjoys administrative expense priority cannot be affected by the insolvency plan; they may however voluntarily waive their rights or consent to their modification.[750] The plan participants have to be allocated to different classes to the extent that their legal positions differ. Thus, general (unsecured) creditors form a single class that may remain the only one. Where the rights of secured creditors with a right to preferential satisfaction are affected, they form a separate class, as do shareholders if the plan interferes with their entitlements.[751] Employees may form a class if they hold claims as general creditors that are not insignificant. Statutorily subordinated creditors only form separate classes to the extent that their claims are not deemed to be waived. In addition, classes may be subdivided in accordance with the economic interests that participants share,[752] such as financial institutions and suppliers, corporate management and other employees, shareholder-creditors, or secured creditors with valuable collateral and worthless collateral etc. The plan proponent has some flexibility in devising the different classes, subject to a test of appropriateness in order to prevent class manipulation.[753] Within each class, creditors must be treated equally unless they individually consent to unequal treatment.[754] Moreover, opposing creditors must not be worse off under the plan than they would have been on the basis of a liquidation under the standard insolvency procedure.[755] The same applies for the debtor.[756] It follows that secured creditors with a right to preferential satisfaction cannot be forced to endure an infringement of their rights under the plan.[757] They may however consent to a total or partial waiver of their security interests in order to facilitate corporate rescue. General creditors may be subject, in particular, to a partial waiver of their claims and/or a deferral of payment possibly in exchange for security.[758] Since the 2012 reforms, the insolvency plan may provide for a debt-to-equity swap.[759] This may be effectuated through a so-called 'capital cut': legal capital is reduced in order to neutralize accumulated loses, typically to zero, followed by a capital increase to which the creditors subscribe.[760] Their contributions in kind consist of their claims which are assigned to the debtor upon which they come to an end by way of '*Konfusion*'.[761] The plan may further provide for an amendment of the articles of association, a squeeze out of shareholders, a merger or transformation or the replacement of the management.

[745] Foerste (n 705) 260 (§33 para 496). [746] InsO, §219. [747] ibid §220.
[748] Foerste (n 705) 252 (§32 para 478). [749] InsO, §221.
[750] Foerste (n 705) 253 (§32 para 479). [751] InsO, §222(1). [752] ibid §222(2).
[753] Foerste (n 705) 254 (§32 para 483). [754] InsO, §226. [755] ibid §251(1).
[756] ibid §247(2). [757] ibid §223. [758] ibid §224. [759] ibid §225a.
[760] see Chapter 9D.I.
[761] Foerste (n 705) 258-9 (§32 paras 493a–493b). '*Konfusion*' denotes the situation where, in relation to a claim, the same person is simultaneously creditor and debtor; as a result the claim will be extinguished.

Upon plan submission, the court will carry out a preliminary assessment and reject the plan (proposal) if it does not comply with the statutory provisions on plan submission and plan content and the defect cannot be cured within a reasonable period of time; a plan proposal submitted by the debtor is further to be rejected where it is obvious that it will not receive the necessary majorities amongst plan participants, will not be confirmed by the court, or the obligations created under the plan will not be satisfied. A plan proposal of the debtor who has been unsuccessful with an earlier plan proposal is to be rejected if the insolvency administrator so requests.[762] If the plan proposal passes muster at this stage, the court will convene an assessment and voting hearing during which participants' individual rights to vote will be ascertained[763] and the individual classes will vote separately on the plan proposal.[764] For the plan proposal to be approved, within each class a majority of the voting members representing more than 50 per cent of the aggregate amount of all claims/shares of voting members must vote in favour of the plan proposal.[765] This seeks to ensure that a few holders of large claims cannot easily impose their will on a number of small claim holders.[766] The insolvency plan process allows for the cram-down of the plan on opposing classes. This is subject to the following prerequisites: (i) the members of the opposing class must not be worse off under the plan than they would have been in a liquidation through the standard insolvency procedure; (ii) a majority of classes has voted in favour of the plan; (iii) under the plan, the opposing class adequately participates in the economic value of the debtor's assets.[767] This latter requirement installs some form of absolute priority: no other creditor may receive more than the nominal value of his claim and no creditor junior to the opposing class, including shareholders, may receive anything under the plan; further no creditor of equal ranking with the opposing class may obtain better treatment than that class.[768] Generally, debtor consent is required which will be deemed to have been obtained where the debtor does not explicitly oppose the plan. The debtor's explicit opposition will be disregarded if, under the plan, the debtor is unlikely to be worse off than in liquidation and no creditor receives more than the nominal value of their claim.[769] Following plan approval and having obtained statements from the insolvency administrator, the debtor, and the creditors' committee, the court decides as to whether to confirm the plan.[770] The court ascertains whether the plan has been approved by each class, and, if not, whether a cram-down is possible. Plan confirmation must be rejected by the court of its own motion if the plan fails to comply with the provisions on plan content and the plan procedure in a significant point and the defect cannot be cured, or plan approval has been obtained fraudulently.[771] On application of a creditor, plan confirmation must be rejected if the applicant would be worse off under the plan than in liquidation.[772] The plan enters into force as soon as the decision on plan confirmation is no longer subject to appeal.[773] It binds all plan participants, including those classes or creditors that have objected to it.[774] Following the payment of claims that have administrative expense priority by the insolvency administrator, the court will lift the insolvency proceeding in order to implement the plan.[775] The insolvency administrator may remain in office in order to oversee plan implementation.[776]

Questions and comments:

1. In the past, Chapter 11 of the US Bankruptcy Code and the English pre-pack administration in combination with schemes of arrangement have attracted large international restructurings. Traditionally, French and German law have been much more rigid, relying on court centered

[762] InsO, §231. [763] ibid §§237–238a. [764] ibid §235. [765] ibid §244.
[766] Foerste (n 705) 263 (§33 para 503). [767] InsO, §245(1).
[768] ibid §245(2); similar principles apply for the shareholders as opposing class: ibid §245(3).
[769] ibid §247. [770] ibid §248. [771] ibid §250. [772] ibid §251. [773] ibid §254.
[774] ibid §254b. [775] ibid §258. [776] ibid §§260, 261.

procedures that left much less room for party autonomy in the restructuring context. Both systems have tried to catch up by implementing reforms largely inspired by the Chapter 11 plan process. The Commission's Proposal for a Directive on preventive restructuring frameworks, second chance and measures to increase the efficiency of restructuring, insolvency and discharge procedures[777]follows a similar approach. However, this may come too late as international financing and restructuring practices have moved on and with the prevalence of fast going concern sales even Chapter 11 may be perceived as being outdated. Although the Commission Proposal pays lip service to the practice of going concern sales, it contains very little that would facilitate it.

2. The modern restructuring practice has developed in respect of businesses that previously had emerged from private equity transactions. Typically, the target group's holding company will be acquired by a Bidco held through a string of special purpose vehicles leading up to the private equity investors as ultimate equity holders. Senior debt will be issued by BidCo, granting maximum security over all its assets, essentially the shares in the target holding company. Mezzanine debt and other junior debt may be issued by financing companies further up the chain, and may thus be structurally subordinated. This structure allows the senior lenders to sell the group as a whole, if it becomes financially distressed, without interference from junior lenders and shareholders.[778] This is reinforced where security is held and administered by a collective security trustee, as an impartial intermediary, holding the security interests for the benefit of a multitude of lenders. The underlying documentation usually contains extensive provisions on the enforcement and release of security. This is crucial for a successful restructuring. Notably, a majority of senior debt, subject to certain conditions, will be able to instruct the trustee to enforce the security and release group companies from indebtedness, thus facilitating a going concern sale of the group as a whole free and clear. The ranking between creditors will be determined by inter-creditor agreements with enforcement 'waterfalls'. By recognizing and enforcing these structures, contract law, property law, and corporate insolvency law may effectively facilitate contractual restructuring solutions. Perhaps this should be the focus of any harmonization efforts in this area at EU level.
3. How do you rate the political feasibility of an EU harmonization attempt that, instead of proposing a plan procedure along the lines of the 2014 Recommendation and the Commission Proposal, would focus on enabling contractual restructuring options? What could such a harmonization measure look like?

III. Group restructuring

Insolvency law is entity-based. In principle, the preconditions for opening proceedings have to be met by, and the effects of commencement, in particular an automatic stay or moratorium, pertain to individual corporate entities separately. However, most businesses, except perhaps the very smallest ones, are run through groups of companies or 'enterprise groups'.[779] These consist of two or more legal entities that are linked by some form of direct or indirect ownership and/or control. The organizational patterns of corporate groups vary widely, ranging from simple hierarchical structures to multi-layered and highly complex systems with numerous holding and sub-holding companies, financing vehicles, operating subsidiaries and service companies. Groups may be vertically integrated with descending layers of parent and controlled subsidiaries, or horizontally integrated with a number of sibling companies operating at the same level underneath a unit of common control. Decision-making and

[777] Proposal for a Directive of the European Parliament and of the Council on preventive restructuring frameworks, second chance and measures to increase the efficiency of restructuring, insolvency and discharge procedures and amending Directive 2012/30/EU, COM(2016) 723 final.

[778] Penades-Fons and Schillig (n 406) 122.

[779] I Mevorach, 'Appropriate Treatment of Corporate Groups in Insolvency: A Universal View' (2007) 8 European Business Organization Law Review 179, 180; UNCITRAL Legislative Guide on Insolvency Law, Part 3: Treatment of enterprise groups in insolvency (United Nations 2010) 5–6.

governance patterns are just as diverse: at one end of the spectrum is the group run from a single 'nerve centre' as a single enterprise and economic unit; at the other end is the conglomerate where individual companies or sub-groups determine their own business goals and policies. Management and decision-making may be organized divisionally along product lines, or geographically or regionally. Ownership and control may be based on direct or indirect equity ownership, contractual or partnership-type arrangements such as joint ventures, or specific governance arrangement in the form of appointment rights to the boards of various group members and/or overlapping personnel in management positions.[780]

Corporate groups pose particular difficulties in insolvency at both domestic and international levels. Financial distress may affect only one or a few subsidiaries or subgroups or the entire group; it may be located at the level of the parent company, of finance vehicles or may affect, or even emanate from, the operating companies. Depending on the organizational structures, it may be possible and sufficient to cut an ailing subsidiary loose and let it sink in order to rescue the rest of the group; or a comprehensive restructuring of various group members may be necessary in order to save the business as a functioning unit. Generally, the more integrated the group, that is, the more it is managed as a single economic unit, the more likely that a successful rescue attempt requires an integrated solution encompassing the entire group.[781] At the same time, the principles of separate legal personality and limited liability have to be respected as far as possible; otherwise the economic rationale of the business corporation as a legal concept would be redundant when it matters most—in insolvency.[782] Given the enormous diversity of group structures, it is perhaps not surprising that an easy and fully functional solution to these issues has remained elusive. Domestic mechanisms for dealing with group insolvencies remain underdeveloped.[783] Problems are amplified at the international level, where different group entities may be subject to different insolvency laws in a multitude of jurisdictions, making a coordinated approach to a group restructuring exceedingly difficult. UNCITRAL's Legislative Guide on Insolvency Law provides for an approach based on cross-border cooperation and coordination between courts and office holders.[784] In its chapter on 'group coordination proceedings' the 2015 EUIR tries to be somewhat more ambitious.

1. *Domestic solutions*

Domestically, legal systems may tackle the problem of group insolvency on the basis of two principal strategies: procedural consolidation and substantive consolidation. Procedural consolidation entails the joint administration of multiple insolvency proceedings commenced in respect of two or more group members. The degree of procedural consolidation may vary; ideally the individual proceedings would be concentrated at a single court and the same person or persons would be appointed as office holders in all the proceedings involved. This has clear cost-saving advantages: a duplication of efforts may be minimized, comprehensive information gathering and valuation of the group as a whole is more easily possible, and a holistic restructuring attempt can be more easily implemented. Importantly, the assets and liabilities attributable to each affected group member remain separate and distinct. Procedural consolidation has no effect on the substantive entitlements of the individual group members and their respective claimants.[785] All our legal systems under consideration here allow for the procedural consolidation of proceedings. Under German law, the insolvency court may combine different proceedings and administer them jointly, provided it has jurisdiction for each of them.[786] Jurisdiction of the insolvency court is determined by

[780] UNCITRAL (n 779) 6–11.
[781] Mevorach (n 779) 185–6.
[782] See Chapter 1B and C.
[783] Mevorach (n 779) 181.
[784] UNCITRAL (n 779) 83–108.
[785] ibid 27.
[786] InsO, §4 with ZPO, §147.

an individual company's seat, which is normally the place from where it is managed.[787] This seems to allow for the joint administration of the insolvency proceedings of companies that are part of an integrated group with centralized management. The same is true for France, where courts tend to use the concept of COMI in order to centralize proceedings concerning group companies before the same court. The 2014 reforms allow for the appointment of the same persons as insolvency administrator and, respectively, creditors' representative in respect of insolvency proceedings concerning companies within the same group. In the US, group companies frequently file petitions at the same time and the cases are administered jointly.[788] In England, the law does not formally provide for procedural consolidation. However, it is common for the company or the holder of a qualifying floating charge to appoint the same administrator (or administrators) in all the separate administrations over affected group companies. Also, all parallel proceedings are concentrated at the High Court, which has comprehensive (albeit concurrent) jurisdiction. The management of separate but related proceedings by the same insolvency practitioners and in the same court significantly enhances the possibility to efficiently coordinate a group-wide restructuring attempt.[789]

Substantive consolidation entails the pooling of the assets and liabilities of different group entities and to treat them as a single entity. In doing so, the separate legal personality of the group companies involved is being disregarded. This may be problematic from the creditors' perspective. The assets of the entity they contracted with suddenly have to be shared with the creditors of other group entities, contrary to expectations. For other creditors, this may be an unexpected windfall. There will be winners and losers. Against this background, substantive consolidation can only be justified in exceptional circumstances. In the US, substantive consolidation as an equitable remedy has been recognized (implicitly) since the 1940s.[790] It 'treats separate legal entities as if they were merged into a single survivor left with all the cumulative assets and liabilities (save for inter-entity liabilities, which are erased). The result is that claims of creditors against separate debtors morph to claims against the consolidated survivor'.[791] As a last resort remedy, it is closely related to other concepts which have to be exhausted first: piercing the corporate veil imposes liability on shareholders; controlling shareholder-creditors may be equitably subordinated to other creditors; and improperly transferred assets may be retrieved on the basis of fraudulent transfer law.[792] Substantive consolidation goes further than any of these remedies and may have a significant effect on the entitlements of 'innocent creditors'.[793] Consequently, it may only be considered where it is proven to the satisfaction of the court by the proponents of substantive consolidation that (i) pre-petition the respective entities 'disregarded separateness so significantly [that] their creditors relied on the breakdown of entity borders and treated them as one legal entity, or (ii) post-petition their assets and liabilities are so scrambled that separating them is prohibitive and hurts all creditors'.[794] Under French law, on the basis of the doctrines of *société fictive* and *confusion de patrimoine*[795] a parent company may be held liable for the debts of a subsidiary and insolvency proceedings in respect of one member of the group may be extended so as to cover the other group members and the parent company as well.[796] Consequently, insolvency proceedings may cover the group as a whole with the effect that assets of all entities and persons within the group are available for distribution among the group's creditors. Germany does not recognize the concept of substantive consolidation. However, where

[787] InsO, §§3, 4 with ZPO, §17. [788] Bankruptcy Rule 1015(b).
[789] Bork (n 444) 287 (para 20.11).
[790] *Sampsell v Impartial Paper & Color Corp.*, 313 US 215 (1941).
[791] *Genesis Health Ventures, Inc. v Stapleton (In re Genesis Health Ventures, Inc)* 402 F.3d 416, 423 (3d Cir. 2005).
[792] for details see Chapter 10B.I.
[793] *In re Owens Corning Corp.*, 419 F.3d 195, 205–206 (3d Cir. 2005). [794] ibid 211–12.
[795] for details see Chapter 10E.III.
[796] Jeantin and Le Cannu (n 348) para 231; M Cozian, A Viandier, and F Deboissy, *Droit des sociétés* (31st edn, LexisNexis 2018) paras 263, 2100–2.

the members do not sufficiently separate their assets from those that belong to the company they will not be able to rely on the principle of limited liability. An amalgamation of assets obtains where, owing to false or inadequate accounting, assets cannot be clearly attributed to either the shareholder/parent or the company/subsidiary. As a consequence, the shareholders/parent involved will be liable for the company's/subsidiary's debts.[797] In the subsidiary's insolvency, only the insolvency administrator may bring a claim against the shareholders/parent.[798] Where both companies are insolvent and subject to procedural consolidation, the practical outcome may be very similar to substantive consolidation. Since the House of Lords' decision in *Salomon v A Salomon and Co Ltd*[799] the principle of separate personality and the privilege of limited liability enjoy great force in English common law. Substantive consolidation of assets and liabilities of different group companies may only be considered where their affairs 'are so hopelessly intertwined that a pooling of their assets, with a distribution enabling the like dividend to be paid to both companies' creditors, is the only sensible way to proceed' and where it 'would make no sense to spend vast sums of money and much time in trying to disentangle and unravel'.[800]

It is possible, however, to devise schemes of arrangement for an entire group of companies, or a part of the group. *Re Bluebrook Ltd*,[801] for example, concerned three schemes of arrangement each of which between a group company and its senior creditors. Although tied together economically, each scheme takes effect separately and only for the company included in it. Each scheme has to be approved separately by the required majority of scheme creditors of the respective company. The process may be coordinated by filing joint applications for all companies involved, and by holding creditors' meetings on the same day. This allows for a coordinated restructuring solution for the group as a whole.[802]

2. *International solutions, in particular under the 2015 EUIR*

The solutions propagated by the UNCITRAL Legislative Guide on Insolvency Law for the treatment of cross-border insolvencies of multinational corporations essentially consist in a framework for the cooperation between courts and office holders in the different jurisdictions involved.[803] The 2015 EUIR provides similar rules on cooperation and communication between office holders and courts,[804] which also draw on the interaction between officials involved in main and secondary proceedings.[805] Accordingly, the office holders appointed in the insolvency proceedings relating to the different members of a group of companies[806] are under an obligation to cooperate with each other, to the extent that this facilitates the effective administration of the proceedings and is not incompatible with applicable insolvency law. Cooperation includes, in particular, the exchange of information and working towards the proposal and negotiation of a coordinated restructuring plan.[807] The courts having opened proceedings concerning different group members, or before which a request for opening proceedings is pending, are under a similar cooperation duty and may communicate directly with each other. Courts may cooperate in particular with a view to the appointment of office holders, the exchange of information, the conduct of hearings and

[797] see Chapter 10. [798] InsO, §92. [799] [1897] AC 22.

[800] *Re Bank of Credit and Commerce International SA (No 3)* [1993] WL 96496 (Dillon LJ), quoting and affirming the decision of Sir Donald Nicholls V-C at first instance.

[801] [2009] EWHC 2114 (Ch). For an overall restructuring arrangement involving CVAs for 14 group companies: *Re Olympia & York Canary Wharf Holdings Ltd and Ors* [1993] BCC 866.

[802] Bork (n 444) 286–7 (para 20.10). [803] UNCITRAL Legislative Guide (n 779) 83–108.

[804] 2015 EUIR, Arts 56–60. [805] ibid recital (52).

[806] 'Group of companies' is defined as 'a parent undertaking and all its subsidiary undertakings'; with 'parent undertaking' being defined as 'an undertaking which controls, either directly or indirectly, one or more subsidiary undertakings': ibid Art 2(13) and (14).

[807] ibid Art 56.

the approval of protocols.[808] Moreover, office holders will cooperate and communicate with any of the courts concerned with the proceedings relating to any group member, and may request the necessary information and assistance.[809] The office holder in an insolvency proceeding concerning a group member may be heard in proceedings concerning other members of the same group, and may request a stay, for a period not exceeding three months, of any measure related to the realization of assets in the proceedings concerning any other member of the group, provided a coordinated restructuring plan has been proposed and has a reasonable chance of being successful; the stay must further be necessary for plan implementation and would benefit the creditors in the proceedings for which the stay is requested. This only applies where neither the insolvency proceedings in which the requesting office holder has been appointed nor those for which the stay is requested, are subject to group coordination proceedings.[810]

The office holder appointed in insolvency proceedings concerning a group member may request before any court having jurisdiction for the insolvency proceedings of any member of the group the opening of group coordination proceedings[811] that would run alongside the separate insolvency proceedings opened in respect of individual group companies.[812] In its request, the office holder must nominate a person to be appointed as group coordinator, provide an outline of the proposed group coordination and a list of the office holders appointed in relation to group members, as well as of the courts and competent authorities involved, and provide an estimate of the costs of group coordination and how these should be allocated amongst the group members. If the courts seised with the request is satisfied that (i) the opening of group coordination proceedings is appropriate to facilitate the effective administration of the proceedings relating to the different group members, that (ii) no creditor of any group member is likely to be disadvantaged by the inclusion of this group member in the coordination proceedings, and that (iii) the person nominated as coordinator meets the professional requirements for acting as an insolvency practitioner, has no conflict of interest and has not been appointed as the office holder in proceedings relating to a group member,[813] the court will notify the office holders appointed in proceedings concerning the different group members and give them an opportunity to be heard.[814] Any of these office holders may object to the inclusion of the insolvency proceedings in which they have been appointed.[815] Such objection is subject to approval in accordance with the applicable insolvency law and may only be lodged within thirty days following the receipt of notice. As a result of an objection, the respective proceeding will not be included in eventual group coordination proceedings.[816] Following the expiry of the thirty-day period, the court may decide to open group coordination proceedings provided it is satisfied that the preconditions (i)–(iii) above are met. In that case, the court appoints the coordinator, decides on the outline of the coordination and on the estimation and allocation of its costs.[817] The coordinator is tasked with identifying and outlining recommendations for the coordinated conduct of the proceedings. Moreover, the coordinator must propose a group coordination

[808] ibid Art 57. [809] ibid Art 58. [810] ibid Art 60.

[811] ibid Art 61. The court of the member state first seized with a request for the opening of group coordination proceedings shall have jurisdiction; ibid Art 62. However, by a two-thirds majority the office holders involved may decide that the court of another Member State may be a more appropriate venue in which case that court will have exclusive jurisdiction; ibid Art 66.

[812] McCormack (n 413) 143. [813] 2015 EUIR, Art 71. [814] ibid Art 63. [815] ibid Art 64.

[816] ibid Art 65. An office holder may also object to the person of the proposed coordinator, in which case the court may refrain from appointing that person and invite the objecting office holder to submit a new request to open group coordination proceedings: ibid Art 67.

[817] ibid Art 68. Office holders who either objected to inclusion or have been appointed in proceedings opened after the commencement of group coordination proceedings may request inclusion, and the coordinator may grant such request, having consulted the office holders involved, provided that he is satisfied that the above prerequisites (i) and (ii) are met, taking into account the stage of proceedings at the time of the request; alternatively, all office holders involved may agree to the inclusion: ibid Art 69.

plan with a view to adopting an integrated approach to the resolution of the group members' insolvencies. The plan should be based on a comprehensive set of measures, and may provide, in particular, for the restoration of the economic performance and financial soundness of the group or any of its parts, for the settlement of intra-group disputes, and agreements between the office holders involved. However, the plan may not include recommendations for procedural or substantive consolidation. Further, the coordinator may participate in any of the included proceedings, mediate disputes between participating office holders, request information from participating office holders, and request a stay for up to six months of any included proceedings where the stay is necessary for proper plan implementation and would benefit the creditors in the proceeding concerned.[818] The participating office holders and the coordinator are subject to mutual cooperation duties.[819] However, the office holders are merely required to take the coordinator's recommendations and the group coordination plan into consideration. They are not obliged to follow any recommendations or the plan; however, in that case they must give reasons for their deviation (the comply-or-explain approach).[820]

Questions and comments:

1. Added to the initial Commission Proposal by the European Parliament, the possibility of group coordination proceedings constitutes one of the major innovations of the 2015 EUIR. However, the practical significance remains doubtful. This is largely attributable to the non-binding nature of group coordination. Any relevant office holder may opt out, and even if they do not opt out, they are not obliged to follow any of the coordinator's recommendations or the plan. Moreover, the possibility of a stay of individual proceedings may cause considerable delay and may incentivize the affected office holders to opt out. In the words of Gerry McCormack:

   > Group coordination proceedings are noble in intention. Nobody is obliged to participate and a would-be participant can even effectively opt out at a later stage. Moreover, before opening such proceedings a court needs to be satisfied that the proceedings are appropriate and that none of the creditors of the participating companies are financially disadvantaged. The voluntary nature of the regime however, may mean that they are unlikely to be much used in practice but they may have a use in the 'big ticket' cases where there is a high degree of coordination among IPs at the outset.[821]

2. In what other contexts have you encountered a 'comply or explain' approach? How would you generally rate the efficacy of this approach?

IV. Insolvent liquidation

Locked into a collective procedure, creditors have an opportunity to negotiate a solution that maximizes firm value for the benefit of all constituencies. These negotiations take place in the shadow of the alternative to a successful corporate restructuring (in whatever form) which is a liquidation of the company's business on a piecemeal basis. Thus, the participants' incentives during negotiations are determined by their respective positions in case of liquidation, notable by the place they would occupy within the statutory order of priorities. Liquidation analysis is, thus, vital for determining the strength of the position a party may take in restructuring negotiations. It is also vital for assessing whether a plan or arrangement meets the safeguards that are in place for the protection of outvoted creditors, be it in the form of the 'best interest' test, a 'no-worse-off' principle or a more fluid 'fairness' test. Thus, any successful corporate rescue attempt must be grounded in a robust liquidation analysis.

[818] ibid Art 72. [819] ibid Art 74. [820] ibid Art 70. [821] McCormack (n 413) 144.

1. *Insolvent liquidation processes*

Insolvent liquidation processes have in common that upon a certain trigger event a liquidator will be appointed with extensive powers to sell off the debtor company's property and to distribute any proceeds to the creditors and shareholders in accordance with a statutory order of priority.[822] There are subtle differences in respect of the initiation, effects and control of the respective procedure. However, the most significant differences concern the statutory order of priorities. In England and Wales, in addition to liquidation through administration, a company may be liquidated either voluntarily[823] or by court order. In Germany, the standard insolvency procedure is in essence a liquidation procedure. Although it may be utilized to rescue the company's business through a going concern sale, most standard insolvency proceedings will eventually result in the liquidation of the company and of its business. In France, since the 2005 reforms, judicial liquidation is a procedure in its own right. Chapter 7 of the United States Bankruptcy Code is the liquidation chapter.

In England, the company, its directors, and any of its creditors or shareholders[824] may present a petition to the court for the making of a winding up order in respect of the company. Most compulsory winding-up proceedings are initiated by creditors. The court may grant a winding-up order if it is satisfied that the company is unable to pay its debts or where the court is of the opinion that winding up of the company is just and equitable.[825] Upon the court making a winding up order, the official receiver automatically becomes the liquidator by virtue of his office, until another person is appointed.[826] The official receiver may seek nominations from the company's creditors and shareholders for the purpose of appointing another person as liquidator and/or establish a liquidation committee.[827] The nomination of the creditors (if any) will prevail, unless the court orders otherwise.[828] Upon making a winding up order or the appointment of a provisional liquidator, a statutory moratorium comes into effect, blocking the commencement or continuation of any action or proceeding against the company or its property, except with the leave of the court.[829] Secured creditors and holders of quasi security will usually be able to obtain leave, since to the extent of the security an asset is not the property of the company.[830] For the time between presenting the petition and making the winding up order any proceedings pending against the company may be stayed on application of the company, or any creditor or shareholder.[831] The making of a winding-up order and the official receiver taking office as liquidator terminates the powers of the company's directors and removes them from office. The power to dispose of company property vests in the liquidator.[832] In France, the court may order the opening of judicial liquidation proceedings only where the company is in cessation of payment and the

[822] This draws on Schillig (n 467) 378–9, 440–4, 452–3 (paras 13.46–13.49, 15.05–15.09, 15.22–15.23).

[823] This normally requires a special resolution (75% majority) of the company's members: Insolvency Act 1986, s 84(1)(b); Companies Act 2006, s 283. It will be a creditors' voluntary winding up if the company is insolvent: Insolvency Act 1986, ss 89, 90, 94A, 96. This procedure closely follows the trajectory of a (solvent) members' voluntary winding up, however, with enhanced creditor input. It is the creditors who may decide on the person of the liquidator, unless the court orders otherwise (ibid s 100) and who may exercise significant control over the process through a liquidation committee: ibid s 101.

[824] ibid s 124. Further, a petition may be made by the office holder in a foreign main proceeding, by the official receiver if the company is in a voluntary winding up proceeding, as well as by the Secretary of State on public interest grounds. On behalf of the company a petition may be made by the administrative receiver, the administrator, or the supervisor of a CVA, if the company is subject to the respective procedure.

[825] Insolvency Act 1986, s 122(1)(f) and (g).

[826] ibid s 136(2).

[827] ibid ss 136(5), 141. The official receiver has 12 weeks in which to decide whether to seek nominations: ibid s 136(5).

[828] ibid s 139.

[829] ibid s 130(2).

[830] Goode (n 193) 269–70 (para 8-47).

[831] Insolvency Act 1986, s 126(1).

[832] Goode (n 193) 158, 174 (paras 5-08, 5-24). Moreover, any disposal of the company's property and any transfer of shares or alteration in the status of shareholders made after the commencement of the winding up is void, unless the court orders otherwise: Insolvency Act 1986, s 127. In principle, commencement of the winding

continuation of the business is obviously unfeasible.[833] Where this is the case, the court may order the opening of judicial liquidation proceedings immediately (without a prior judicial reorganization attempt); an ongoing safeguard procedure or judicial reorganization has to be converted into a judicial liquidation.[834] In its commencing order, the court appoints a person as liquidator which may be the same person as the creditors' representative if the case is converted from a safeguard or judicial reorganization procedure. In this latter case, the observation period comes to an end immediately. The insolvency administrator may remain in office to the extent that the court orders the continuation of the business with a view to facilitating a potential going concern sale. In any case, however, the debtor's management immediately forgoes any management powers including the power to dispose of company property.[835] A case under Chapter 7 of the US Bankruptcy Code commences in the same way as a case under Chapter 11[836] and triggers an automatic stay of similar scope and effect.[837] Following commencement, the United States trustee appoints a disinterested person from a pre-established panel of private trustees as interim trustee.[838] At the initial meeting of creditors, the creditors may select a different person to serve as trustee[839] and may appoint a creditors' committee to consult with the trustee in connection with the administration of the case.[840] The German standard insolvency procedure as a liquidation procedure has the same triggers and effects as where it is used for restructuring purposes.

The liquidator in an English compulsory winding-up by the court must be a qualified insolvency practitioner and has the main function of getting in the assets of the company, realizing their value and distributing the proceeds in accordance with the statutory order of priority.[841] For that purpose, the liquidator takes into his custody and brings under his control all the tangible and intangible property to which the company appears to be entitled.[842] The liquidator has the general power to do whatever is necessary for winding up the company's affairs and distributing its assets. He may, in particular, sell any of the company's property by public auction or private contract and may borrow on the security of the company's assets.[843] The purpose of the judicial liquidation procedure in France is to end the business activity and to sell the debtor's business or parts thereof on either a going concern or piecemeal basis

up is the presentation of the petition for winding up, not the making of the winding up order: ibid s 129(2), unless prior to the presentation of a petition a resolution has been passed for the voluntary winding up of the company in which case the winding up is deemed to have commenced at the time of the resolution; where the court makes a winding up order on an administration application, the winding up commences with the order. Disposals made in contravention of this provision are void and the property disposed of may be reclaimed by the liquidator. The situation is complex and depends on the nature of the property disposed of. The court may make a validation order where the disposal concerns a transaction in the ordinary course of business for the benefit of the company, such as the payment of employees or suppliers whose services are necessary for an orderly liquidation; Goode (n 193) 610–12, 619–21 (paras 13-127, 13-134, 13-135).

[833] Com Art L640-1.

[834] Com Art L641-1(III). A simplified liquidation procedure is available for companies that do not own immovable property, have an annual turnover of not more than €750,000 and not more than five employees during the six months preceding commencement. The liquidator can sell any asset freely within a three months period following commencement; thereafter a public auction is necessary. Only the claims of those classes of creditors need to be verified that in accordance with their ranking have any prospect of receiving a dividend: Com Art L644-1--L644-6.

[835] Com Art L641-9. [836] 11 U.S.C., §§301, 303. [837] ibid §362. [838] ibid §701.

[839] ibid §702. [840] ibid §705. [841] Insolvency Act 1986, s 143(1).

[842] ibid s 144. On application of the liquidator, the court may make a vesting order pursuant to which the company's property will automatically vest in the person of the liquidator: ibid s 145.

[843] ibid s 167 and Sch 4 paras 13, 6, and 10. Prior to the Small Business, Enterprise and Employment Act 2015, certain powers of the liquidator could only be exercised with the sanction of the liquidation committee (or the court, or where no committee has been established, with the consent of the creditors' meeting). These were the power to pay any class of creditors in full (except preferential creditors), the power to make any compromise or arrangement with creditors, the power to bring legal proceedings for fraudulent or wrongful trading, transactions at an undervalue, unlawful preferences, and transactions defrauding creditors, the power to bring or defend any action or other legal proceeding in the name and on behalf of the company, and the power to carry on the business of the company so far as may be necessary for its beneficial winding up: Insolvency Act 1986, Sch 4 Pts I and II. All these powers are now exercisable without sanction: Small Business, Enterprise and Employment Act 2015, s 120, amending Insolvency Act 1986, ss 165, 167.

and distribute the proceeds in accordance with the statutory order of priorities. Where a going concern sale of the debtor's business, or parts thereof, appears to be feasible, the court may allow the liquidator to continue the business activity for a certain period of time within which potential purchase offers may be submitted.[844] To the extent that the business or parts thereof are not transferred on the basis of the sale plan process, the liquidator may transfer them piecemeal. Having verified the claims in respect of which proofs have been duly submitted, the liquidator distributes the proceeds in accordance with the statutory order of priority. Similarly, under the US Bankruptcy Code: the trustee's main responsibility is to collect the property of the estate to reduce it to money and to close the estate as soon as possible in accordance with the best interest of all stakeholders.[845] The trustee is accountable for all property received and is tasked with investigating the financial affairs of the debtor. He may be authorized by the court to operate the debtor's business for a limited period of time if such operation is in the best interest of the estate and consistent with its orderly liquidation.[846] Assets subject to a security interest will be released to the secured creditors,[847] and the trustee will sell the remaining assets piecemeal or in units. He may negotiate with buyers and, subject to court approval, select the best method of disposal. Any proceeds will be distributed according to the statutory order of priority following non-bankruptcy law.[848] In a German standard insolvency procedure, the insolvency administrator's main responsibility is to take possession of the debtor's property,[849] realize the assets[850] and distribute the proceeds to the creditors in accordance with the statutory order of priority.[851]

2. *Statutory orders of priority*

The statutory orders of priority of our jurisdictions under consideration here vary significantly. The ranking of creditors has significant (re)distributive effects. For example, a high ranking of employee wage claims benefits labour as non-adjusting creditors at the expense of other investors; carve-outs from a security interest for the benefit of unsecured creditors may work to the advantage of customers and suppliers at the expense of financial institutions as secured creditors. In this respect, a certain order of priority may reflect the fundamental value judgements inherent in an insolvency law regime and pertain in the classification of a legal system as a particular variety of capitalism. On the other hand, the assigning of preferential status to a certain class of creditors may indicate nothing more than the lobbying power of a certain social group at a particular moment in time. Whether the status of a class of creditors within the creditor hierarchy is reflective of the former or the latter is not necessarily obvious and requires careful historical research. Despite all the differences, we can perhaps discern a basic common structure of classes that we find in all our jurisdictions: secured credit normally takes priority over administrative expenses, which rank ahead of general unsecured creditors, and equity.[852] Depending on the legal system, further classes may be added: creditors with a super-priority, preferential creditors, subordinated creditors. Given the great variety of the available security interests across our jurisdictions, it is perhaps not surprising that the treatment of secured creditors is not without complexity. On that basis and looking across our legal systems we can see the following (descending) order of priority:

[844] Com Art L641-10. [845] 11 U.S.C., §704(a). [846] ibid §721. [847] ibid §§724, 725.
[848] ibid §726. [849] InsO, §148. [850] ibid §159. [851] ibid §§187–206.
[852] See also *Czyzewski et al. v. Jevic Holding Corp.*, 580 U.S. ___ (2017), at 4: 'The Code also sets forth a basic system of priority, which ordinarily determines the order in which the bankruptcy court will distribute assets of the estate. Secured creditors are highest on the priority list, for they must receive the proceeds of the collateral that secures their debts. 11 U. S. C. §725. Special classes of creditors, such as those who hold certain claims for taxes or wages, come next in a listed order. §§507, 726(a)(1). Then come low- priority creditors, including general unsecured creditors. §726(a)(2). The Code places equity holders at the bottom of the priority list. They receive nothing until all previously listed creditors have been paid in full. §726(a)(6)'.

Under French law, employee claims for wages and reimbursement for accrued holidays incurred within sixty days prior to the commencement of proceedings enjoy a first-ranking so-called super-priority. The super-priority claim is capped, however, at an amount equal to twice the maximum base for the calculation of contributions to the French national insurance system. These claims are to be paid ideally within 10 days of the announcement of the opening decision.[853] They take priority over administrative expenses and secured credit (as well as general unsecured creditors).

In other legal systems, it is normally secured credit, which takes the top spot in the creditor hierarchy. However, there is great variation. Under the US Bankruptcy Code, as a general rule, if a particular right is fully effective outside of bankruptcy, the claimant holding the right will be able to assert it in bankruptcy, subject only to any overriding Federal interests.[854] Consequently, the holder of a perfected and unvoidable security interest or other interest in property is entitled to have that claim satisfied first, up to an amount equal to the value of the collateral. The TIB must 'dispose of any property in which an entity other than the estate has an interest'[855] and distribute the proceeds to the holder of the security interest. Under English law, the holders of fixed security interests (mortgage, fixed charge, lien) or quasi-security (seller under retention of title, conditional sale, hire-purchase, lessor under a finance lease) are first in line to have their claims satisfied out of the collateral, including prior to the expenses of the liquidation/administration. To the extent of the security/quasi-security, the asset is not part of the debtor's estate and is not available for distribution to unsecured creditors. Similarly, assets held on trust by the debtor for a third party belong in equity to that third party and are not available for distribution. Secured creditors do not compete with preferential and general (unsecured) creditors.[856] However the holder of a floating charge occupies a place further down within the hierarchy: So far as the assets of the debtor company available for payment of general creditors are insufficient to meet expenses, these take priority over any claims to property subject to a floating charge and are to be paid out of any such property.[857] Further, to the extent that the assets of the company available for payment of general creditors are insufficient to meet the claims of preferential creditors, these also have priority over the claims of floating charge creditors.[858] And for floating charges created on or after 15 September 2003, the liquidator, administrator or receiver, as the case may be, has to make available for the satisfaction of unsecured debts a 'prescribed part' of the company's net property.[859] German law distinguishes between secured creditors with a right to separation and secured creditors with a right to preferential satisfaction. Creditors with a right to separation are those who can reclaim an asset that does not belong to the debtor company's estate, either on the basis of a personal or a proprietary right.[860] The key is that the substance of the asset belongs to the creditor, rather than the debtor. Prime example is the creditor's right of ownership where he has delivered possession of an asset to the debtor on the basis of a financial leasing agreement or under (simple) reservation of

[853] Trav Arts L3253-3, L3253-4. [854] *Butner v United States*, 440 U.S. 48, 55 (1979).

[855] 11 U.S.C., §725. [856] Goode (n 193) 247–8, 271–2 (paras 8-16, 8-49).

[857] Insolvency Act 1986, s 176ZA, reversing *Buchler v Talbot* [2004] 2 AC 298. However, litigation expenses incurred by the liquidator may have priority only subject to the approval of the amount of the litigation expenses by the creditors holding floating charges, and by preferential creditors. Insolvency (England and Wales) Rules 2016, rr 6.44–6.48; 7.111–7.116.

[858] Insolvency Act 1986, s 175(2)(b).

[859] ibid s 176A(2). 'Net property' is the property that would be available for the satisfaction of floating charge holders in the absence of the provisions on the prescribed part. Currently, the prescribed part is for a net property of up to £10,000: 50%; for £10,000 and above: 50% of the first £10,000 and 20% of the excess; but not more than £600,000 overall; Insolvency Act 1986 (Prescribed Part) Order 2003, SI 2003/2097. Parties may agree in a CVA or Scheme of Arrangement to derogate from the requirement. The government intends to increase the cap to £800,000 in line with inflation; Department for Business, Energy & Industrial Strategy (n 334) para 1.84.

[860] InsO, §47.

title. Creditors with a right to separation are unaffected by the insolvency proceeding and can enforce their rights on the basis of non-bankruptcy individual enforcement mechanisms. Creditors holding a security interest proper have a right to preferential satisfaction out of the proceeds of sale of collateral.[861] Here, the substance of the asset belongs to the debtor and the creditor has an interest only in the value of the asset to be applied in satisfaction of its debt. Realization of collateral is largely integrated into the insolvency process and can be effectuated by the liquidator, depending on the nature of the collateral (movable or immovable property).[862] Typical examples are extended reservation of title arrangements (manufacturing clause, proceeds clause), security transfers of ownership and land charges and mortgages. Under French law, the claims of secured creditors with either a security interest on immovable property (hypothec) or with a fixed security interest in movable property take priority over all other claims, except the employee super-priority and further the costs of the proceeding and the new money priority. The costs and fees duly incurred after the commencement order has been made come second under French law (after the employee super-priority), and include in particular the court fees as well as the remuneration for the court appointed office holders: insolvency administrator, creditors' representative, and liquidator. Those who under a court approved conciliation agreement have made a contribution of fresh funds to the debtor or have supplied new assets or services to the debtor in order to ensure the continuation and long-term future of the debtor's business activity enjoy the new money priority if subsequently safeguard or judicial reorganization or liquidation proceedings have been opened.[863]

Under English law, the expenses properly incurred in the liquidation/administration are payable out of the debtor's assets in priority to all other claims (except those mentioned in the previous paragraph). This includes all fees, costs, charges and other expenses incurred in the course of winding up or administration proceedings,[864] including the office holder's remuneration, claims of post-commencement contractual creditors, and any future payments that become due post-commencement under an executory contract assumed for the purposes of the liquidation/administration (the *Lundy Granite* principle).[865] Similarly, under German law, administrative expenses and obligations incurred by the estate are to be paid in full, not on a pro rata basis, ahead of general unsecured creditors.[866] Administrative expenses consist of the court fees incurred in the course of the insolvency proceedings; and the fees and expenses incurred by the insolvency administrator, the preliminary administrator and the members of the creditors' committee.[867] The obligations of the estate include the obligations incurred by the administrator after commencement of the case, which are necessary for the administration of the estate and the distribution of its assets (post-petition creditors); as well as obligations arising from executory contracts assumed by the administrator.[868] In France, claims that have been duly incurred following the issuance of the order commencing the judicial liquidation (post-commencement) must be paid as they fall due and in priority to the general (pre-commencement) creditors, provided these claims were necessary for the conduct of the proceedings or for the provisional continuation of the debtor's business activity or as consideration for goods or services provided to the debtor in

[861] ibid §§49, 50. [862] Häsemeyer (n 316) 445. [863] Com Art L611-11.
[864] Insolvency (England and Wales) Rules 2016, rr 3.50, 6.42, 7.108.
[865] *Re Lundy Granite Co Ex p. Heavan* (1871) 6 Ch App 462; *In re Oak Pits Colliery Co* (1882) 21 Ch D 322, 330 (Lindley LJ); *Re Atlantic Computer Systems Plc* [1992] Ch 505, 527 (Nicholls LJ).
[866] InsO, §53. [867] ibid §54.
[868] ibid §55. If the debtor's assets are insufficient to cover the administrative expenses and the other obligations of the estate, the liquidator has to inform the court which has to make it public and the creditors in this category are to be satisfied in the following order: the costs of the proceedings; the obligations of the estate that arose after the court gave notice of the estate being insufficient; the remaining obligations of the estate. Within these different categories, creditors are to be satisfied on a pro rata basis: ibid §§208, 209.

order to allow the continuation of its business activity.[869] Under the US Bankruptcy Code, among creditors who do not hold property interests,[870] administrative expenses, including the actual necessary costs and expenses of preserving the estate (in particular wages, salaries and commissions for services rendered after commencement of the case); any tax incurred post-petition; the actual necessary expenses of creditors other than attorney's fees, and reasonable compensation for fees of attorneys or accountants of the creditors,[871] rank ahead of other preferential creditors.

In the US, this latter category includes certain employee claims for wages, salaries, or commissions up to US$10,000 earned within 180 days prior to the date of filing; and thereafter tax liabilities incurred pre-petition.[872] Under English law, with the exception of fixed charge creditors and expenses, preferential claims are to be paid in priority to all other debts. Preferential claims are to be paid in full, unless the assets are insufficient to meet them, in which case individual claims participate on a pro rata basis.[873] To the extent that the assets of the debtor company available for payment of general creditors are insufficient to meet the claims of preferential creditors, they have priority over the claims of the holders of any floating charge and must be paid out of any property subject to such charge.[874] Since the abolition of Crown preference through the Enterprise Act 2002, the only remaining preferential debts for most (non-bank)[875] companies are certain claims of employees.[876]

Following the payment of the classes that take priority, any remaining proceeds will be distributed to the general (unsecured) pre-commencement creditors in proportion to their admitted claims.[877] Under English law, in principle, all claims of creditors are provable as debts against the company, whether present or future, certain or contingent, ascertained or unascertained, provided the company was subject to the debt or liability at the date it entered the respective insolvency procedure (the cut-off date), or became subject to the debt or liability subsequently on the basis of an obligation that had been incurred prior to the cut-off date.[878] Parties cannot contract out of the insolvency legislation,[879] which is embodied by the *pari passu* principle and the anti-deprivation principle.[880] The former concerns the distribution of the debtor's assets in accordance with the statutory order of priority. It seeks to ensure that all creditors within the same class are treated equally on the basis of their pre-insolvency entitlements and that no creditor (or class of creditors) obtains preferential treatment.[881] It is particularly relevant for general unsecured creditors. In *British Eagle*, the House of Lords

[869] Com Art L641-13. [870] 11 U.S.C., §§726, 507, 502, 503. [871] ibid §503.
[872] ibid §507. [873] Insolvency Act 1986, s 175. [874] ibid s 176(2)(b).
[875] Pursuant to the Banks and Building Societies (Depositor Preference and Priorities) Order 2014 (SI 2014/3486), preferential claims of employees and the claims of eligible depositors for amounts of up to £85,000 form the class of 'ordinary preferred creditors' as a special class of preferred creditors. Deposits from individuals and micro, small, and medium-sized enterprises that exceed the maximum amount of coverage of £85,000 form the class of 'secondary preferential creditors'. These claims are preferred to other senior unsecured liabilities but not super-preferred.
[876] Any sums owed by the insolvent employer in respect of unpaid employer's or employees' contributions to an occupational pension scheme, provided Schedule 4 of the Pension Schemes Act 1993 applies; the claims of employees and former employees of the debtor for remuneration (including wages, salary, and related employment rights such as sickness pay and maternity pay) in respect of the whole or any part of the period of four months next before the relevant date, up to the amount of £800; and claims to accrued holiday remuneration, in respect of any period of employment before the relevant date (without limitation), of a person whose employment by the debtor has been terminated either before, on, or after the relevant date: Insolvency Act 1986, s 386, Sch 6 paras 8, 9, 10, 13. The relevant date is defined in Insolvency Act 1986, s 387, with reference to the different proceedings.
[877] Com Art L643-8; In the US: claims allowed pursuant to 11 U.S.C., 502; InsO, §38.
[878] Insolvency (England and Wales) Rules 2016, rr 14.1, 14.2. [879] see further Schillig (n 186) 32–7.
[880] *Belmont Park Investments PTY Ltd v BNY Corporate Trustee Services Ltd and Lehman Brothers Special Financing Inc* [2011] UKSC 38 paras [1]–[15] (Lord Collins); Goode (n 193) 217–18 (paras 7-01–7-03); S Worthington, 'Good Faith, Flawed Assets and the Emasculation of the UK Anti-Deprivation Rule' (2012) 75 Modern Law Review 112, 112–13.
[881] *British Eagle International Airlines Ltd v Compagnie Air France* [1975] 1 WLR 758, 780G–H (Lord Cross).

made clear that a contractual arrangement that would allow certain (unsecured) creditors to opt out of *pari passu* distribution to their advantage would be contrary to public policy and ineffective, whether or not the contractual provision was expressed to take effect only on insolvency.[882] By contrast, a contractual subordination between creditors to the effect that one creditor (junior) cannot collect from the debtor until another creditor (senior) has been paid in full is valid and enforceable in the debtor's insolvency; as is an agreement between the junior and the debtor that the senior is entitled to be paid in full before any payments may be made to the junior. This is because subordination does not (adversely) affect the rights of the remaining creditors.[883] Pursuant to the anti-deprivation principle the debtor may not contract at any time, either before or after the commencement of insolvency proceedings, for its property to be removed or disposed of or dealt with otherwise than in accordance with the statute.[884] In principle, the rule seeks to prevent a decrease in the debtor company's net assets by removing assets that otherwise would have been available for distribution. The exact boundaries of the anti-deprivation principle are not easily defined. Traditionally, a distinction was made between interests that were granted as limited so as to come to an end, automatically or by way of termination, when the company goes into winding up; and absolute interests where a party is given the right to recapture the asset upon the debtor's insolvency. Only the latter was considered to offend against the anti-deprivation rule; in the former type of cases the interest never was the outright property of the company.[885] In the aftermath of the financial crisis, the scope and ambit of the anti-deprivation principle came under scrutiny in the context of complex financial arrangements.[886] In *Belmont*[887] the Supreme Court held that the anti-deprivation principle has to be applied in a commercially sensitive manner, upholding proper commercial bargains. What is essential is whether 'a complex commercial transaction' was 'entered into in good faith', and whether the provisions were intended to evade insolvency law, or not.[888] Each transaction has to be assessed on its own merits in order to distinguish between a commercial rearrangement of rights to reflect the economic consequences of insolvency and an attempt to pre-empt the distribution of assets in a bankrupt estate.[889]

Subordinated creditors will receive a dividend only after the general creditors have been satisfied in full. Under the US Bankruptcy Code, these are claims for the payment of interest on unsecured claims.[890] Similarly, under English law, any surplus remaining after the general unsecured creditors have been paid in full must be applied to paying interest accrued on pre-commencement unsecured debts since commencement of the insolvency proceedings.[891]

[882] *British Eagle International Airlines Ltd v Compagnie Air France* [1975] 1 WLR 758; also *National Westminster Bank Ltd v Halesowen Presswork & Assemblies Ltd* [1972] AC 785.

[883] *Re Maxwell Communications Corp (No 2)* [1993] BCC 369, 377 (Vinelott J); *Re SSSL Realisations (2002) Ltd* [2005] [2004] EWHC 1760 (Ch) [45] (Lloyd J); *Re Kaupthing Singer & Friedlander Ltd* [2010] EWCH 316 (Ch) [10] (Blair J).

[884] *Ex parte Jay* (1880) LR 14, 25 (Ch D) (James LJ): '[A] simple stipulation that upon a man's becoming bankrupt, that which was his property up to the date of bankruptcy should go over to somebody else and be taken away from his creditors, is void as being a violation of the policy of the bankruptcy law'; *ex parte Mackay* (1873) LR 8 Ch App 643, 647 (James LJ): 'A man is not allowed by stipulation with a creditor, to provide for a different distribution of his effects in the event of bankruptcy from that which the law provides'.

[885] Goode (n 193) 220–1 (para 7-05); R Calnan, *Proprietary Rights and Insolvency* (OUP 2010) paras 1-20–1.22: 'distinction without a difference'.

[886] See also *Lomas v Rixson* [2012] EWCA Civ 419; *Folgate London Market Ltd (formerly Towergate Stafford Knight Co Ltd) v Chaucer Insurance Plc* [2011] EWCA Civ 328; *Lehman Brothers Special Financing Inc v Carlton Communications Ltd* [2011] EWHC 718 (Ch).

[887] *Belmont Park Investments PTY Ltd v BNY Corporate Trustee Services Ltd and Lehman Brothers Special Financing Inc* (n 880); see also *Perpetual Trustee Company Ltd v BNY Corporate Trustee Services Ltd* [2009] EWHC 1912 (Ch); *Butters and Others v BBC Worldwide Ltd and Others* [2009] EWHC 1954 (Ch); *Perpetual Trustee Company Ltd v BNY Corporate Trustee Services Ltd* [2009] EWCA Civ 1160.

[888] *Belmont Park Investments PTY Ltd v BNY Corporate Trustee Services Ltd and Lehman Brothers Special Financing Inc* (n 880) paras [102]–[108] (Lord Collins).

[889] *Lomas v Rixson* (n 886) paras [86], [91].

[890] 11 U.S.C., §726.

[891] Insolvency Act 1986, ss 189(2), 328(4).

The applicable interest rate is determined by statute.[892] All statutory interest claims rank *pari passu*, the priority of the underlying debt is immaterial.[893] Any surplus still remaining is to be applied for the satisfaction of non-provable liabilities. These are liabilities incurred after the cut-off date that do not amount to expenses of the insolvency procedure. A typical example would be claims concerning injuries of third parties caused by the negligence of an employee of the debtor company during the course of an administration (if not a necessary disbursement), or claims of victims of an air crash which occurred after the debtor company's entry into liquidation and which was caused by faulty engines manufactured by the insolvent company.[894] Any remaining surplus is to be paid to creditors whose claims are deeply subordinated by contract[895] or otherwise.[896] Under German law, deferred creditors are to be paid in the following order: interest accrued since commencement; expenses of creditors for taking part in the proceedings (including attorneys' fees); fines and penalties; obligations arising out of gratuitous promises of the debtor; loans advanced by a shareholder to the debtor company, except where the shares were acquired in the context of a corporate rescue attempt or the shareholder-creditor holds less than 10 per cent of the share capital.[897] Within the individual classes of deferred creditors, pro rata sharing applies. As a mere rule of interpretation, contractually subordinated claims rank below deferred creditors. However, the parties to a subordination agreement may agree otherwise, ie to a ranking of their claims just below senior unsecured bonds and ahead of deferred creditors.

As residual claimants, shareholders[898] in the order of preference shares and ordinary shares, form the end of the line.

Questions:

The order of priority of claims is likely to be a key focus of any future insolvency law harmonization attempt. Having looked at the orders of priority in England, Germany and France is it possible to identify a 'common denominator'? Which features of individual orders of priority are likely to be most controversial in any future negotiations?

F. Conclusion

Following this survey of corporate insolvency law systems it is perhaps fair to say that the rise of the 'rescue culture' has resulted in a remarkable convergence on both sides of the Atlantic. Chapter 11 has been transplanted with modifications in both France and Germany. The English system has until now predominantly relied on 'home-grown' solutions, with the outcomes of restructuring cases being fairly comparable. The UK government's current reform agenda also shows a dominant influence of Chapter 11. On the surface, our systems show remarkable similarities as regards the basic structural features: automatic stay or

[892] ibid ss 189(4), 328(5). [893] ibid ss 189(3), 328(4).

[894] *Re Lehman Brothers International Europe (in administration)—Waterfall I* [2015] EWCA Civ 485 para [26] (Lewison LJ); this was not an issue on appeal: *The Joint Administrators of LB Holdings Intermediate 2 Limited (Appellant) v The Joint Administrators of Lehman Brothers International (Europe) and others (Respondents)* [2017] UKSC 38.

[895] ibid paras [28]–[62] (Lewison LJ).

[896] Where the court makes a declaration that a director is liable to make a contribution to the company's assets for fraudulent or wrongful trading, and the director is a creditor of the company, the court may direct that the whole or any part of any debt owed by the company to the director and any interest thereon shall be subordinated to all other debts owed by the company including statutory interest: Insolvency Act 1986, s 215(4).

[897] InsO, §39.

[898] Under English law, sums due to any member of the company in his capacity as a member by way of dividends, profits, or otherwise are not deemed to be a debt in relation to other (non-member) creditors; Insolvency Act 1986, s.74(2)(f). The provision is confined to claims arising purely from membership; it does not apply to claims emanating from independent contracts between the member and the company.

moratorium, reliance on external expertise even under a debtor in possession system, creditor participation in a plan process and a possible cram-down, and overall a move towards fast and easy going concern sales. Cultural differences remain. Our civil law jurisdictions seem to rely much more on a top-down approach, with courts and office holders still mostly in the driving seat and with less room for party autonomy. This makes these systems less attractive as restructuring destinations. Moreover, with creditors and investors dispersed around the world, our English-speaking jurisdiction will always retain a competitive advantage. Being confronted with more large-scale international restructurings, these systems have a greater incentive to cater for the needs of these firms. As the numerous reforms in France and Germany demonstrate, financial innovation and business practices will always be ahead of statutory restructuring regimes. An attempt to catch up by borrowing from systems that are perceived as being more attractive seems to be an almost impossible task. A flexible framework that leaves room for market-based solutions and that can easily adapt to changing financing and business practices would seem to be any jurisdiction's best bet. This is perhaps something to keep in mind for the European Union's harmonization projects in this area.

Competences and Decision-Making of the General Meeting

I. Competences of the General Meeting

Competences	US	UK	Germany	France
Amendment of articles	§10.03 MBCA: (a) adopted by the board (b) approval by shareholders Quorum: majority of the votes entitled to be cast Majority: simple (c) no exception pursuant to §§10.05, 10.07, 10.08[1]	Special resolution, s 21(1) Quorum: 2 members, s 318(2) Majority: 75%, s 283	Special resolution, §179 Quorum: none Majority: 75%; articles may provide for a higher but not lower majority	Extraordinary general meeting,[2] Art L225-96 Quorum: 25% Majority: 33.3%
Fundamental changes (merger/ sale of assets/ voluntary winding up)	(1) Merger, §11.04 (a) plan of merger adopted by board (b) shareholder approval Quorum: majority of the votes entitled to be cast Majority: simple[3]	(1) Scheme of arrangement: 75% in value of the creditors or members present and voting, s 899(1) (2) Merger (a) terms of merger drawn up and adopted by the directors of the merging companies, s 905(1)	(1) Merger, §65 Transformation Act Quorum: none Majority: 75%; articles may provide for a higher but not lower majority (2) Sale of assets, §179a(1) Quorum: none Majority: 75%; articles may provide for a higher but not lower majority	(1) Merger: extraordinary general meeting, Art L236-9 Quorum: ⅓ Majority: 33.3% (2) Voluntary winding up: extraordinary general meeting, Art L225-246

[1] Similar in Delaware: s 242(b) Del. Gen. Corp. Law.

[2] To be distinguished from a special meeting pursuant to Art L225-99:

The holders of shares in a given category attend special meetings.

A decision to vary the rights relating to a share category taken at a general meeting is not final until it has been approved by that category's special meeting of shareholders.

Special meetings may only validly deliberate when first convened if the shareholders present or represented hold at least one third of the voting shares whose rights are to be varied and, if reconvened, one fifth of those shares. Failing this, the second meeting may be postponed to a date not later than two months after the date originally scheduled. In companies which do not make public offerings, the memorandum and articles of association may require higher quorums.

They rule as stipulated in the third paragraph of article L225-96 [majority of two thirds of the votes held by the shareholders present or represented]'.

[3] ibid s 251(b).

Competences	US	UK	Germany	France
	(2) Sale of assets: shareholder approval required if the disposition would leave the corporation without a significant continuing business activity, §12.02[4] (a) initiated by a resolution of the board (b) shareholder approval (quorum and majority see (a)) (3) Voluntary winding up, §14.02 (a) proposal by board (b) shareholder approval (quorum and majority see (a))	(b) approved by majority in number, representing 75% in value, of each class of members of each of the merging companies, present and voting, s 907(1) (c) directors' explanatory report and expert's report, ss. 908, 909 (3) Sale of assets: no special requirements if not sale to directors; but listed companies: significant transactions (25% of the company's value) require shareholder approval[5] (4) Voluntary winding up: special resolution, s 84 Insolvency Act	(3) Voluntary winding up, §262(1) no 2 Quorum: none Majority: 75%; articles may provide for a higher but not lower majority (4) Other matters that constitute a substantial interference with shareholders' rights: Holzmüller (generally shareholder approval by qualified majority)	
Appointment and removal of directors	(1) Appointment: shareholders elect directors, §8.03(c) Cumulative voting: possible if provided for in the articles; default rule is election by a plurality of the votes cast, §7.28 (2) Removal: by ordinary shareholder resolution with or without cause, unless the articles provide that removal is only possible with cause, §8.08(a)[6] Problem of entrenchment: *Carmody v. Toll Bros.*, 723 A.2d 1180 (Del. Ch. 1998)	(1) Appointment: by ordinary resolution or by a decision of the directors, Art 20 Model Articles for Public Companies (2) Removal: ordinary resolution, s 168; cannot be excluded in the articles, but problem of entrenchment: *Bushell v Faith* [1970] AC 1099 (House of Lords)	(1) Appointment: members of the management board appointed by resolution of the supervisory board, §84(1); members of the supervisory board appointed by the general meeting, §101 (unless co-determination) (2) Removal of members of the MB: resolution of SB *and* serious cause (gross breach of duty, inability to manage, withdrawal of confidence by general meeting), §84(3); SB: general meeting with 75% majority, §103(1)	(1) Appointment: ordinary general meeting, Art L225-18 Quorum: one fifth Majority: simple majority of the votes present (2) Removal: at any time with or without cause by the ordinary general meeting, Art L225-18

[4] ibid s 271: approval required if the transaction amounts to all or substantially all of the assets of the company. *Gimbel v. Signal Companies*, 316 A.2d 599 (Del. Ch. 1974): 'If the sale is of assets quantitatively vital to the operation of the corporation and is out of the ordinary and substantially affects the existence and purpose of the corporation, then it is beyond the power of the Board of Directors'. Typically, this requires the sale of assets worth in excess of 50% of the value of the company.

[5] UKLA LR 10.5: A listed company must, in relation to a class 1 transaction (LR 10.2.2: a transaction where any percentage ratio [size of the transaction relative to that of the listed company] is 25% or more): (1) comply with the requirements of LR 10.4 (Class 2 requirements) for the transaction; (2) send an explanatory circular to its shareholders and obtain their prior approval in a general meeting for the transaction; and (3) ensure that any agreement effecting the transaction is conditional on that approval being obtained.

[6] Delaware: s 141(k): 'Any director or the entire board of directors may be removed, with or without cause, by the holders of a majority of the shares then entitled to vote at an election of directors, except as follows:

(1) Unless the certificate of incorporation otherwise provides, in the case of a corporation whose board is classified as provided in subsection (d) of this section, stockholders may effect such removal only for cause; or

(2) In the case of a corporation having cumulative voting, if less than the entire board is to be removed, no director may be removed without cause if the votes cast against such director's removal would be sufficient to elect such director if then cumulatively voted at an election of the entire board of directors, or, if there be classes of directors, at an election of the class of directors of which such director is a part.

Competences	US	UK	Germany	France
Approval of directors' compensation	(1) Board decides on compensation, §8.11 (2) Shareholder approval not required, but see NYSE Listing Manual, s 303A.08: Shareholders must be given the opportunity to vote on all equity-compensation plans. (3) a 14A Sec. Ex. Act 1934: Approval of the compensation of executives by shareholder resolution at least every 3 years (advisory vote, s 14A(c)).	Approval of directors' remuneration report by ordinary resolution (advisory vote), s 439	(1) Compensation of members of the management board: determined by supervisory board, §§87, 112 (2) Compensation of members of the supervisory board: determined in the articles or by shareholders with simple majority, §113	Determined by resolution of the general meeting, Art L225-45
Approval of interested transactions	§8.61(b)[7] An interested transaction is valid if: (1) approval by a majority of the fully informed disinterested directors; *Or*: (2) approval by fully informed shareholders Quorum: majority of the votes entitled to be cast by the holders of qualified shares (i.e. not held by the interested director or related persons) Majority: simple *Or*: (3) the transaction is fair to the corporation	By ordinary resolution for: (1) service contracts of directors for more than two years, s 188(2) (2) substantial property transactions with a director (more than 10% of the company's asset value or more than £100,000, s 190(1) (2) loans, quasi-loans or credit transactions with a directors, ss. 197(1), 198(2), 201(2) (3) payment to the director for loss of office, s 217(1) (4) Listed companies: UKLA LR 11 (related party transactions)[8]	(1) The supervisory board represents the company in dealings with members of the management board, §112. (2) Contracts with or loans made by the company to members of the supervisory board require approval by the supervisory board, §§114, 115.	(1) Agreements between the company and the general manager, an assistant general manager, a director, or shareholder holding more than 10% of the voting shares, are subject to the prior consent of the board of directors, Art L225-38. The interested party must not participate in the vote, Art L225-40. (2) The chairman of the board of directors must advise the auditors of all agreements authorised and submit them to the general meeting for approval.

[7] Delaware: s 144 Del. Gen. Corp. Law is similar.

[8] LR 11.1. Related party: (1) a person who is a substantial shareholder (holding at least 10 percent of the voting rights); or (2) a director or shadow director (3) a person exercising significant influence; or (4) an associate of a related party (defined similar to 'connected person' in s 252).

LR 11.1.7: If a listed company enters into a related party transaction, the listed company must: (1) make a notification (containing the name of the related party and details of the nature and extent of the related party's interest); (2) send a circular to its shareholders containing the information required by LR 13.3 and LR 13.6 (in particular, the circular must state that the transaction is fair and reasonable and that the company has been so advised by an independent advisor); (3) obtain the approval of its shareholders for the transaction or arrangement; and (4) ensure that the related party: (a) does not vote on the relevant resolution; and (b) takes all reasonable steps to ensure that the related party's associates do not vote on the relevant resolution.

Note that the requirement in LR 11.1.7 does not apply to 'small transactions' as defined in LR 11 Annex 1.1: transactions that do not exceed 0.25% of the value of the company.

Competences	US	UK	Germany	France
				(3) Special report by the auditors to the general meeting, including reasons why the agreement is in the interest of the company. (4) Approval by general meeting. The interested party must not participate in the vote, Art L225-40.[9]
Authority to issue and allot shares	(1) The board issues shares, §6.21(b) (2) Approval by shareholders if: (a) shares are issued for consideration other than cash; and (b) comprise more than 20% of the shares outstanding, §6.21(f)[10]	The directors have power to allot shares if: (1) authorised by the articles; or (2) by ordinary resolution, s 551(1)	(1) Capital increase: (a) shareholders by 75% majority §182(1)[11] (b) management board if authorised by shareholders with 75% majority, §202(2)[12] (2) Allotment: by management board	(1) Extraordinary general meeting by 33.3% majority, Art L225-129; or (2) board of directors if delegated competence from extraordinary general meeting, Art L225-129-2
Disapplication of pre-emption rights	Default rule: no pre-emption rights	The directors can disapply pre-emption rights if: (1) they have general authority to allot shares and are given power by the articles or special resolution to disapply pre-emption rights, s 570 (2)(a) recommendation by the directors; (b) statement setting out reasons for the recommendation; (c) special resolution, s 571	(1) shareholders by 75% majority, §186(3); articles may provide for a higher but not lower majority (2) management board if authorised by shareholders with 75% majority, §203(2); articles may provide for a higher but not lower majority	Pre-emption rights if shares are issued for cash, Art L225-132; may be removed by the meeting that decides on or authorises the capital increase (33.3% majority), Art L225-135

[9] The refusal of the general meeting to grant approval does not invalidate the agreement with respect to third parties, unless it is fraudulent and, accordingly, cancelled. Even in the absence of fraud, the prejudicial consequences to the company of refused agreements may be charged to the interested party and, potentially, to the other members of the board of directors: Art L225-41.

[10] Delaware: The directors issue stock; no requirement of approval by shareholders, ss. 151, 152, 161 Del. Gen. Corp. Law.

[11] The articles may provide for a higher *or* lower majority.

[12] The articles may provide for a higher, but not a lower majority.

Competences	US	UK	Germany	France
Appointment of company's auditors	No requirements in corporate law. Companies subject to the Securities Exchange Act[13] must ensure that: (1) the audit committee is responsible for the appointment, compensation, and oversight of the auditor (2) all members of the audit committee are independent directors,[14] §10A(m)	Ordinary resolution, s 489(4)	Resolution by simple majority, §§119(1) no 4 Stock Corporation Act, 318(1) Commercial Code	Ordinary general meeting, Art L225-228
Distribution of company's profits	The board may authorise distributions, §6.40	Ordinary resolution, Art 70(1) Model Articles for Public Companies	Resolution by simple majority, §119(1) no 2, §174(1)	Ordinary resolution of the general meeting, Art L232-12

[13] Section 10A applies to any issuer, which is defined as 'any person who issues or proposes to issue any security'; see §3(a)(8).

[14] Definition of independence: The director 'may not, other than in his or her capacity as a member of the audit committee, the board of directors, or any other board committee—(i) accept any consulting, advisory, or other compensatory fee from the issuer; or (ii) be an affiliated person of the issuer or any subsidiary thereof': §10A(m)(3)(B).

II. Procedure

Procedure	US	UK	Germany	France
Requirement to hold general meeting	Annual general meeting at a time fixed in the bylaws, §7.01(a)	Annual general meeting: Public companies within six months after the accounting reference date, s 336(1)	Ordinary general meeting held annually during the first eight months of the financial year, §175(1)	Ordinary general meeting held at least once each year within six months of the close of the financial year, Art L225-100
Who can call the general meeting?	MBCA: board of directors or shareholders holding at least 10% of voting shares, §7.02(a) Del.: Special meetings called by the board of directors; by the shareholders only if the constitutional documents provide for this, §211(d) Del. Gen. Corp. Law	(1) Directors, s 302 (2) Shareholders holding at least 5% of voting shares, s 303	(1) Management board, §121(1) (2) Supervisory board, §111(3) (3) Shareholders: 5% or less if so stipulated in the articles, §122(2)	(1) Board of directors or management (2) Representative appointed by the court upon application by shareholders holding at least 5% of the share capital, Art L225-103
Who can table resolutions?	(1) Corporate law: directors or shareholders; for special meetings notice of the business to be conducted must be given, §§7.02(d), 7.05(c)[15] (2) Proxy regulation: Eligibility to submit a proposal for inclusion in the company's proxy statement: the shareholder(s) must have held continuously at least $2,000 in market value, or 1% of the company's securities for at least one year, Exchange Act Rule 14a-8(b)(1)	(1) Directors (2) Shareholders: (a) power to require the company to circulate statements, for example in order to oppose a resolution proposed by the directors (5% of the voting rights or 100 members), s 314 (b) power to place items on the agenda (5% of the voting rights or 100 members), ss. 303(4), 338[16]	(1) Directors (2) Shareholders: 5%, §122(2)	The convenor or shareholders representing at least 5% of the capital, Art L225-105

[15] The company's bylaws may contain advance notice provisions also for the annual general meeting, requiring that shareholder nominations for election to the board of directors or resolutions intended to be voted on at the meeting must be made in writing and received by the company a prescribed number of days in advance of the meeting. These requirements are permitted provided that there is reasonable opportunity for shareholders to comply with them and they are reasonable in relation to the company's needs. See MBCA, §7.08(c): 'Any rules adopted for, and the conduct of, the meeting shall be fair to shareholders.'

[16] Note: applies to meetings called by the members (s 303(4)) and to the annual general meeting of public companies (s 338).

Procedure	US	UK	Germany	France
Who pays for proxies?	Shareholders unless they can require the company to include their proposal in its proxy statement, Exchange Act Rule 14a-8; grounds for exclusion are listed in Rule 14a-8(i)[17]	(1) Circulation of statements according to s 314: the company has to bear the expenses if the request relates to an annual general meeting and is received before the end of the financial year preceding the meeting, s 316 (2) Shareholder resolutions for AGMs, s 338: company if the request is received before the end of the financial year preceding the meeting. (3) If the directors are required under s 303 to call a meeting but fail to do so, the shareholders may themselves call the meeting and have a claim against the company to be reimbursed for reasonable expenses, s 305	Company, §122(4)	Draft shareholder resolutions are included in the agenda and brought to the knowledge of the shareholders by the company, Art L225-105
Quorum/voting	MBCA: (1) Quorum: majority of the votes entitled to be cast (2) Majority: affirmative vote of the majority of shares present, for example §10.03(e) (amendment of articles)[18]	(1) Quorum: two persons, s 318 (2) Majority: (a) Ordinary resolution: simple majority, s 282 (b) Special resolution: majority of not less than 75%, s 283	(1) Quorum: none (2) Majority: (a) Ordinary resolution: simple majority, §133(1) (b) Qualified majority of 75% for particular transactions, e.g. fundamental changes	(1) Ordinary general meeting, Art L225-98 Quorum: one fifth Majority: simple majority of the votes present (2) Extraordinary general meeting, Art L225-96 Quorum: 25% Majority: 33.3% (3) Special shareholders' meeting, Art L225-99 Quorum: ⅓ Majority: 33.3%

[17] The most important grounds for exclusion are:

(5) Relevance: If the proposal relates to operations which account for less than 5 percent of the company's total assets at the end of its most recent fiscal year, and for less than 5 percent of its net earnings and gross sales for its most recent fiscal year, and is not otherwise significantly related to the company's business;
(6) Absence of power/authority: If the company would lack the power or authority to implement the proposal;
(7) Management functions: If the proposal deals with a matter relating to the company's ordinary business operations;
(8) Relates to election: If the proposal relates to a nomination or an election for membership on the company's board of directors or analogous governing body or a procedure for such nomination or election …

Problems:
Rule 14a-8(i)(5): when is a proposal 'otherwise significantly related to the company's business'? See *Lovenheim v. Iroquois Brands, Ltd.*, 618 F. Supp. 554 (D.D.C. 1985).
Rule 14a-8(i)(7): what is part of 'the company's ordinary business operations'? See SEC Rel. No. 34-12999, 41 Fed. Reg. 52,994, 52,998 (1976); *Cracker Barrel Old Country Store, Inc.*, Fed. Sec. L. Rep. P 76,418 (1991); Exchange Act Rel. No. 40018 (21 May 1998).

[18] Same in Delaware: s 216 Del. Gen. Corp. Law.

Index